WISDEN

CRICKETERS' ALMANACK

2011

EDITED BY SCYLD BERRY

WISDEN

CRICKETERS' ALMANACK

2011

148th EDITION

John Wisden & Co

JOHN WISDEN & CO
An imprint of Bloomsbury Publishing Plc
36 Soho Square, London W1D 3QY

Reader feedback: almanack@wisden.com

www.wisden.com

Follow Wisden on Twitter @WisdenAlmanack

WISDEN CRICKETERS' ALMANACK
Editor **Scyld Berry**
Deputy editors **Hugh Chevallier**, **Steven Lynch** and **Harriet Monkhouse**
Publishing assistant **James Coyne**
Consultant editor **Matthew Engel**
Production co-ordinator **Peter Bather**
Chief statistician **Philip Bailey**
Proofreader **Charles Barr**
Database and typesetting **Stephen Cubitt**
Publisher **Charlotte Atyeo**
Consultant publisher **Christopher Lane**

Typeset in Times New Roman and Univers by David Lewis XML Associates, Bungay NR35 1JB
Printed in the UK by CPI William Clowes Ltd, Beccles NR34 7TL

A CIP catalogue record for this book is available from the British Library

"Wisden" and its woodcut device are registered trademarks of John Wisden & Co

© John Wisden & Co 2011
Published by John Wisden & Co, an imprint of Bloomsbury Publishing Plc, 2011

EDITIONS

Cased ISBN 978-1-408131-30-5 £45
Soft cover ISBN 978-1-408138-93-9 £45
Large format ISBN 978-1-408138-92-2 £55
Leatherbound ISBN 978-1-408154-84-7 £260

A Taste of Wisden 2011

"If you start a chocolate factory, you cannot compete with
Cadbury in the first ten years."
Tamim Iqbal, Cricketers of the Year, page 104

* * *

"His fellow-selector Doug Insole once translated Bedserese at a
pre-Test dinner: 'If he says you're not bad, you're one of the best
three in the world.'"
Sir Alec Bedser, page 181

* * *

"At Taunton, they managed to coax spite from the most genteel of
squares, rather as if persuading Jane Austen to venture rap lyrics."
County Championship review, page 367

* * *

"Jimmy Anderson made the Kookaburra talk... sing... and even
do a little jig."
Why Australia Lost, by Kerry O'Keeffe, page 249

* * *

"The island of Skellig Michael loomed up; there hadn't been a
larger, less mobile presence in the slips since the retirement of
Inzamam-ul-Haq."
Following the Ashes from Afar, page 60

* * *

"The aerial route is popular, especially among the Solomon
Islanders, most of whom believe a straight bat is an unhappy bat."
Cricket Round the World, page 1187

* * *

"He was a Marylebone vet who treated an astonishing variety of
animals in Central London, ranging from the Queen's horses to
circus animals, and once had to rescue a Soho stripper who was
being strangled by a boa constrictor."
Obituaries, page 199

6

LIST OF CONTRIBUTORS

Tanya Aldred
David Rayvern Allen
Chris Aspin
James Astill
Philip August
Charlie Austin
Charles Barr
Colin Bateman
Edward Bevan
Ian Bishop
Paul Bolton
Lawrence Booth
Ken Borland
Stephen Brenkley
Daniel Brettig
Simon Briggs
Gideon Brooks
Colin Bryden
Ian Callender
Don Cameron
Ian Chappell
Simon Cleaves
David Clough
Patrick Collins
Patrick Compton
Charlie Connelly
Craig Cozier
Tony Cozier
Robert Craddock
Rob Crilly
John Curtis
Geoffrey Dean
Tim de Lisle
Ralph Dellor
Norman de Mesquita
William Dick
Ben Dorries
Philip Eden

Paul Edwards
Mark Eklid
Peter English
John Etheridge
Stephen Fay
David Foot
Angus Fraser
Haydn Gill
Nagraj Gollapudi
Ramachandra Guha
Julian Guyer
Gideon Haigh
David Hardy
Norman Harris
Douglas Henderson
Paul Hiscock
David Hopps
Nasser Hussain
Steve James
Paul Jones
Abid Ali Kazi
Paul Kelso
Prashant Kidambi
Patrick Kidd
Jarrod Kimber
Josh Knappett
Stephen Lamb
Richard Latham
Lynn McConnell
Sir John Major
Neil Manthorp
Vic Marks
Christopher Martin-Jenkins
R. Mohan
Benj Moorehead
Tony Munro
Mark Nicholas
Kerry O'Keeffe

Mark Pennell
Sarah Potter
Derek Pringle
Qamar Ahmed
Andrew Radd
Ramiz Raja
Charles Randall
Andrew Renshaw
Graham Russell
Osman Samiuddin
Faraz Sarwat
Neville Scott
Mike Selvey
Shahid Hashmi
Utpal Shuvro
Mehluli Sibanda
Ed Smith
Richard Spiller
Fraser Stewart
Alec Swann
Will Swanton
Pat Symes
Bruce Talbot
Ivo Tennant
Sa'adi Thawfeeq
Anand Vasu
Michael Vaughan
Sriram Veera
Michael Vockins
Mark Wallace
John Ward
David Warner
Tim Wellock
Simon Wilde
Marcus Williams
Martin Williamson
Andy Wilson
John Woodcock

Photographers are credited as appropriate. Special thanks to Patrick Eagar, Graham Morris and Philip Brown.

Cartoons by Nick Newman.

Cricket Round the World Contributors to this section are listed after their articles.

The editor also acknowledges with gratitude assistance from the following: Robin Abrahams, Andy Arlidge, Ali Bacher, Derek Barnard, Mark Bawden, Trevor Bedells, Benedict Bermange, Keith Booth, John Clay, Howard Clayton, Brian Croudy, Prakash Dahatonde, Nigel Davies, Peter Della Penna, Ted Dexter, George Dobell, Frank Duckworth, Gulu Ezekiel, M. L. Fernando, Ric Finlay, David Frith, Ghulam Mustafa Khan, Richard Gillard, Tony Greig, Mike Griffith, Michael Hatt, Brian Hunt, David Kendix, Rajesh Kumar, Jeremy Lloyds, Nirav Malavi, Mahendra Mapagunaratne, Ian Marshall, Gerald Mortimer, Francis Payne, Bryce Payton, Elaine Pickering, Neil Priscott, Carolyn Prosser, Andrew Samson, Derek Scott, Mike Smedley, Peter Trego, Charlie Wat, Alan West, Alan Williams and Graeme Wright.

The production of *Wisden* would not be possible without the support and co-operation of many other cricket officials, county scorers, writers and lovers of the game. To them all, many thanks.

PREFACE

This year, for the first time, *Wisden* has four Cricketers of the Year. Originally I selected five, in accordance with custom. Serious allegations of corruption were then made against one of them, and subsequent events rendered his selection in my opinion unsustainable.

Since 1890, five has always been the number of the Cricketers of the Year, except when a player has been so colossal as to be honoured on his own, such as W. G. Grace in 1896. It is sad to break this tradition, but I considered that an exception was unavoidable this year, and it points up the realities that confront the modern game.

The decision by the Crown Prosecution Service, announced in early February, that three of Pakistan's best cricketers should face criminal charges, imposed legal restrictions which have influenced the reporting of what might be called "the Pakistan case". Never has *Wisden* been so constrained by legal dictates – and I hope it never will again – when it should have been focused on England's magnificent retention of the Ashes.

Alan Williams, *Wisden's* lawyer, deserves extra gratitude for all his work. In addition, I wish to record my thanks to all colleagues who have been loyal and have helped me maintain traditional standards, while implementing more desirable changes.

The amount of work as the deadline approaches is superhuman – no day is so brief as 12 working hours. The heroic example is set by the three deputy editors: Hugh Chevallier, Harriet Monkhouse and Steven Lynch. Peter Bather is the master of proof production, Philip Bailey of statistics, and Christopher Lane of everything else. This year we have also welcomed an able addition to the team, James Coyne.

Since 2008, the first of my four years as editor, readers have been able to find Grace's Test record in *Wisden* – and that of every Test cricketer. Each of the Test-playing countries now has its own separate section containing its international and domestic cricket. To accommodate the proliferation of 20-over cricket, a different kind of scorecard has been introduced, giving more information – sixes, fours and balls faced by each batsman – in less space. The Wisden Test XI, meanwhile, reinforces the importance of Test cricket as the sport's ultimate form, a fight to the finish usually unaffected by time. And the precedent has been established that women, too, are eligible to be Cricketers of the Year.

In this edition, some of the regular sections have been reordered. The Review, which includes the obituaries, now follows Part One (Comment), putting all articles at the front. Records and Registers moves to the back, between the other largely reference sections of Law and Administration and The Almanack. In short, the book now has a logical structure: articles, then reportage, then reference.

I hope readers of recent *Wisdens* have enjoyed the longer articles, such as the one on page 74 celebrating the centenary of the All-India tour of Britain in 1911, the strangest of tours. Whoever captains India in England this summer, he will do well if he is so colourful as the Maharajah of Patiala – and badly if he is so absent.

The game is still the thing, and it goes on, and long may *Wisden* too.

SCYLD BERRY   Bristol, March 2011

CONTENTS

Part One – Comment

Part Two – The Wisden Review

Part Three – The Ashes

Part Four – English and European Cricket

STATISTICS

INTERNATIONAL CRICKET IN ENGLAND

LV= COUNTY CHAMPIONSHIP

ONE-DAY COUNTY COMPETITIONS

OTHER ENGLISH CRICKET

EUROPEAN CRICKET

Part Five – Overseas Cricket

CRICKET IN AUSTRALIA

CRICKET IN BANGLADESH

CRICKET IN INDIA

CRICKET IN NEW ZEALAND

CRICKET IN PAKISTAN

CRICKET IN SOUTH AFRICA

Part Six – Law and Administration

Part Seven – Records and Registers

Part Eight – The Almanack

SYMBOLS AND ABBREVIATIONS

*	In full scorecards and lists of tour parties signifies the captain. In short scores, averages and records signifies not out.
†	In full scorecards signifies the designated wicketkeeper. In averages signifies a left-handed batsman.
‡	In short scores signifies the team who won the toss.
MoM	In short scores signifies the Man of the Match.
D/L	Signifies where a result has been decided under the Duckworth/Lewis method for weather-affected matches.

Other uses of symbols are explained in notes where they appear.

FIRST-CLASS MATCHES

Men's matches of three or more days' duration are first-class, unless otherwise stated. All other matches are not first-class, including one-day and Twenty20 internationals. Records for these – and List A limited-overs matches between senior teams – can be found in the appropriate section.

SCORECARDS

Where full scorecards are not provided in this book, they can be found at Cricinfo (www.cricinfo.com) or Cricket Archive (www.cricketarchive.co.uk). Full scorecards from matches played overseas can also be found in the *ACS Overseas First-Class Annual* for 2010 and 2011.

RECORDS

Further information on certain tournament winners can be found at *Wisden's* website (www.wisden.com/almanacklinks).

PART ONE

Comment

Wisden Honours

THE LEADING CRICKETER IN THE WORLD

Sachin Tendulkar (page 97)

The Leading Cricketer in the World is chosen by the editor of *Wisden* in consultation with some of the world's most experienced cricket writers and commentators. The selection is based on a player's class and form shown in all cricket during the calendar year, and is guided by statistics rather than governed by them. There is no limit to how many times a player may be chosen. A list of past winners can be found on page 97; a notional list, backdated to 1900, appeared on page 35 of *Wisden 2007*.

CRICKETERS OF THE YEAR

Eoin Morgan (page 99) Chris Read (page 101)
Tamim Iqbal (page 104) Jonathan Trott (page 106)

The Cricketers of the Year are chosen by the editor of *Wisden*, and represent a tradition that dates back to 1889, making this the oldest individual award in cricket. Excellence in and/or influence on the previous English summer are the major criteria for inclusion as a Cricketer of the Year. No one can be chosen more than once. A list of past winners can be found on page 1590.

THE WISDEN TEST XI

The Wisden Test XI, based solely on performances in Test cricket during the previous calendar year, is selected by a panel of three experienced cricket writers and commentators – all former Test cricketers – from around the world; the editor of *Wisden* has the deciding vote where necessary. The Wisden Test XI (page 94) was first introduced in *Wisden 2009*.

YOUNG WISDEN SCHOOLS CRICKETER OF THE YEAR

Will Vanderspar (page 726)

The Schools Cricketer of the Year, based on first-team performances during the previous English summer, is chosen by *Wisden's* schools correspondent in consultation with the editor of *Wisden* and other experienced observers of schools cricket. The winner's school must be in the UK, play cricket to a standard approved by *Wisden's* schools correspondent and provide reports to this Almanack. A list of past winners can be found on page 762.

WISDEN BOOK OF THE YEAR

The Cricketer's Progress: Meadowland to Mumbai by Eric Midwinter (page 135)

The *Wisden* Book of the Year is selected by *Wisden's* guest book reviewer; all cricket books published in the previous calendar year and submitted to *Wisden* for possible review are eligible. A list of past winners can be found on page 139.

WISDEN–MCC CRICKET PHOTOGRAPH OF THE YEAR

was won by Scott Barbour

The Wisden–MCC Cricket Photograph of the Year (page 96) is chosen by a panel of independent experts; all images on a cricket theme photographed in the previous calendar year are eligible.

Full details of past winners of all these honours can be found at www.wisden.com.

NOTES BY THE EDITOR

It would be hard to think of a sizeable human organisation that has come closer to perfection for a couple of months than England's cricket team during the Ashes series in Australia. For those of us who have had to watch, for decades, the failure to translate the many resources of English cricket into achievement by the national side, England's performance over the last year – culminating in their retention of the Ashes – was especially satisfying.

A few England teams have triumphed in Australia by a greater numerical margin in distant days. But this side won as emphatically as any, for all three of their victories were achieved by an innings – and very likely they would have won the Brisbane Test if it had been played to a finish (as Tests in Australia used to be before the Second World War), after declaring their second innings with 1000 on the board. The success flowed from the thorough and considerate – not over-analytical and paralysing – planning of what I call the Andocracy, led by Andrew Strauss and Andy Flower. It would be wrong to say they conducted England's tour with military precision, because there was nothing regimented about it. The squad conveyed their enjoyment, whether doing their Sprinkler dance – a nice touch – or cavorting in Graeme Swann's video diaries or, most significantly, when playing.

A feature of the Andocracy – although Strauss began it before Flower became head coach – has been the attempt to win every tour game from the outset. This might seem an obvious objective, but treating warm-up games as little more than middle-practice was one of the manifestations of England's old failure to maximise resources. The impact of playing excellent cricket in the three first-class matches before the opening Test in Brisbane should never be underestimated. During this build-up a self-doubt emerged in Australia's cricket that I had not seen before on eight previous England tours there; and, by creating an aura of invincibility, the tourists increased it. The Australian public, even their media, seemed to some extent prepared for their team's failure.

The Andocracy not only chose the right personnel but brought them in, and sent them away, at the right time: the number of coaches and support staff was never so numerous as to overwhelm and diminish the players. Among them one should mention Richard Halsall, the fielding coach originally appointed – to Sussex then England – by Flower's predecessor Peter Moores. The first two hours of the second day at Sydney formed the finest exhibition of England fielding I have ever seen in some 400 Tests: they smothered the Australian batsmen just as Australia's fielders had suffocated England's four years before, not so much through natural athleticism as the maximisation of collective effort. England's co-ordination and unity in the field reflected the spirit of the whole touring party. It is worth noting that England took more catches (66) than they had taken wickets by all forms of dismissal in either of their two previous series in Australia; and a total of four run-outs to nil illustrated the difference in fielding and in teamwork.

One Cook was enough

It was a temptation to change the parameters for the Five Cricketers of the Year so Alastair Cook could be included on the strength of his batting in Australia – his aggregate of 766 runs was the second-highest for England in an Ashes series – and in Bangladesh, where he also captained promisingly. Yet Cook's achievement in Australia was all the more admirable for the very fact that he had been through a most difficult summer, when opening batsmen on both sides in the England–Pakistan series were troubled by the ball swinging under the cloud that prevailed. His mental strength in persevering until he had sorted out his footwork was astonishing – the opposite of Australia's self-doubt. The chief criterion for being selected as a Wisden Cricketer of the Year has to remain "influence on the English season". But Cook deserves to be enshrined on this year's cover, and continued good form – one hopes – will soon make him a Cricketer of the Year. With Jonathan Trott selected in this almanack, it is worth noting that nine of England's 13 players in the Ashes have won this accolade.

Of the man of the series award that Cook won in Australia, I am inclined to think James Anderson deserved a half-share. He took 24 wickets in the five Tests, which were all the more demanding for being crammed into seven weeks. A mark of England's organisation was that Anderson and Cook shared the responsibility for polishing the ball, whereas Australia had nobody in that specialist role; and even when a pitch was dead, England still found reverse swing. By the end of the series, such was the versatility of Anderson and his fellow pace bowlers that they were just as threatening with an old ball as a new one: and never, surely, has that been the case in the history of England's cricket.

Huge totals, including large individual centuries, and usually in the first innings; superlative fielding, so that England dropped only a couple of regulation chances; pace bowlers who could swing the ball both ways, whatever its age; and a spinner who could be relied on to threaten throughout and wrap up Australia's second innings provided the pace bowlers did not feast first. The joys for England's followers knew no bounds. Even the weather favoured the tourists, making conditions – pitches starting damp, cloud overhead – as near to English as traditional Australian: it was the wettest period ever recorded in some parts of eastern Australia, leading to horrifying floods. So nature made it easier for England to defy precedent and get away with four specialist bowlers and no all-rounder to speak of, and aided their seam-and-swing rather than the bang-it-in bowlers that Australia had; and it was luck they had earned.

Where we come from…

Another ingredient of England's success was their travelling supporters, who grew to number some 15,000 by the Melbourne and Sydney Tests. Not all of them belonged to the Barmy Army, but the majority did, and they contributed both to the atmosphere in the grounds and to England's morale: Paul Collingwood said England's slip fielders had goosepimples during the final rounds of singing in Sydney. My opinion of the Barmy Army was not favourable when it began, because the songs contained foul language which should not have been imposed on children watching. But last winter their songs were no worse than bawdy, ridiculed senior Australian players rather than the juniors, and were surprisingly tuneful; and their focus was on the cricket rather than themselves. Strauss was not entirely joking when he said the Barmy Army had prepared for the tour better than his players. I urge the ECB to help it parade at home matches – in designated areas – by enabling ticket-buyers to book more than a few seats in a row, as well as by lowering prices.

Hoist with their own fixture list

Australian and English commentators alike, by the end of the series, observed that England had all the ingredients to become the leading cricket country. India's pace bowling was over-reliant on Zaheer Khan; South Africa, as usual, lacked an attacking spinner, and Sri Lanka tall fast bowlers; while Australia had not only lost their great cricketers but damaged their own domestic structure by exactly the sort of tinkering in which England's administrators have specialised. The sort that does not attract new supporters but does alienate existing ones.

Andrew Hilditch, Australia's chairman of selectors, referred last winter to their game having "three formats": no wonder he could not keep up. Australia not only had a 20-over tournament, 50-over internationals, and first-class (including Test) cricket: the states also played games of 45 overs a side, split into two innings each. But the essence of any cricket match is whether a batsman can dominate the bowling in the time available, and whether the bowlers and fielders can thwart him. If there is a break of a couple of hours in a batsman's innings, everyone loses the thread. In addition, such tinkering turns players into jacks of all formats and masters of none.

All too soon, however, the obstacle to stop England becoming No. 1 was apparent. The day after winning the Ashes series in Sydney, England's cricketers had to get on to a bus to Canberra and play four games in the next eight days. Their reward for winning the most famous prize in cricket was to play two Twenty20 internationals and seven one-day internationals, then return home for four nights before going to the World Cup. Unsurprisingly the players, especially the bowlers, fell like flies. We are not talking about a large reduction: five one-day internationals, instead of seven, would have allowed the players ten days at home, to clear their heads of their Australian tour and visualise the World Cup.

England, I fear, will never be No. 1 for a sustained period until the ECB obey the two key recommendations of the Schofield Review that they themselves commissioned after the disastrous 2006-07 tour of Australia: to reduce the amount of England fixtures and of domestic fixtures. If this is not done, I foresee that Strauss will retire prematurely, Flower will abandon the England job for one that allows him to spend more than the odd night at home, and we will relapse into the square-one position of failing to maximise our national resources. From Andocracy back to mediocrity.

Don't trash the Ashes

While the Ashes were being contested, South Africa played India in a fine example of how *not* to organise a Test series. It was as if the object of this contest between the two top-ranked countries was to demean Test cricket and reduce its popularity. The Indians turned up for the opening Test without a single day of match-practice, let alone at altitude (Centurion is at 5,000 feet), and were swept aside. The charge of bringing the game into disrepute, under the ICC Code of Conduct, should be levelled at administrators as well. Instead of staging mini-Test series every five minutes, it is their duty to promote Test cricket properly – and also the concept of the five-Test series, which captures everything that is best in the sport and allows for dramatic fluctuations. Then there would be no need for the experiment of the ICC Test Championship play-offs in the summer of 2013, when England can expect to be involved, in addition to staging home Test series against both New Zealand and Australia; and when luck with the toss on a damp morning at Edgbaston or Headingley could decide who the Test champions will be, at least nominally, for the next four years.

Nothing should be allowed to diminish the popularity of Ashes cricket, which appeals to millions of people who otherwise have no interest in the sport. Yet the administrators of England and Australia have decided to violate traditions built up over more than a century by staging a series in England in 2013 *and* 2015 *and* one in Australia in between. It is desirable that Ashes series in Australia should not be staged in the same winters as the World Cup, as the last three have been, but nothing whatever can justify this overkill of three series in three years, including back-to-back Ashes. Long-winded World Cups have jeopardised the popularity of 50-over cricket; cheapening the Ashes will do the same to Test cricket and the one surviving five-Test series. It would only be a gesture, but MCC – as owners of the urn – should withhold their seal of approval from any future Test series between England and Australia that violate the traditional timetable without justification and are conceived entirely out of greed.

The case of the three no-balls

English cricket had largely been able to get away with thinking of match-fixing as a foreign concern, but last season this illusion was shattered. In mid-May two Essex players, Mervyn Westfield and Danish Kaneria, were charged with "match irregularities" arising from the county's 40-over game against Durham in September 2009. While charges against Kaneria were dropped, the case against Westfield – which he denies – continues at the time of going to press. Then, last August, the *News of the World* published a scoop by their reporter Mazher Mahmood who, a decade earlier, had tried to entrap the former Pakistan captain, Salim Malik, by engaging him in an illegal betting scam. This time the current Pakistan captain, Salman Butt, and his two best pace bowlers, Mohammad Aamer and Mohammad Asif, were alleged to have been drawn into a plan by their agent, Mazhar Majeed, to bowl three no-balls at specific moments in the Fourth Test at Lord's against England. The newspaper said it gave the agent £150,000 in cash.

Cricket has not been alone in facing allegations of large-scale corruption. Other professional sports have been embroiled simultaneously – even the International Olympic Committee. After the IOC had been involved in corruption when Salt Lake City successfully bid for the 2002 Winter Olympics, several august figures like Henry Kissinger and Lord Coe helped to reform it. Last year Coe, now head of the London Olympics in 2012, made a pertinent comment: "If any organisation is looking at similarities [to the Olympic scandal], then they have to ensure they absolutely grab control of it [i.e. corruption] as quickly as they can. It can't be death by a thousand cuts."

Cricket suffered innumerable cuts to its reputation as a result of the allegations about the three Pakistanis conspiring to bowl deliberate no-balls at Lord's. Bad blood arose between England's players and Pakistan's in the rest of that Test and the limited-over series which followed; the lack of enjoyment for England's players, when the validity of what they were doing was in doubt, naturally communicated itself to those watching. If there is an exception to the rule about there being no such thing as bad publicity, it is when match-fixing or spot-fixing is involved. I regretfully concluded that never has the end of the professional season been more welcomed than in 2010.

The three Pakistanis were questioned by a three-man independent tribunal, sitting in Qatar, and most of the ICC Code of Conduct charges against them were found proven. At the same time, the Crown Prosecution Service announced that the players, and their agent, would face criminal charges in London – as a result of which *Wisden's* reporting of this whole affair has been circumscribed to avoid contempt of court. But it can be said that the sanctions handed out to the three players by the tribunal were generally considered, outside Pakistan, to be lenient. I would observe that the punishments probably fitted the charges that were found proved, but this was the ICC's first corruption case and a newspaper was necessary to bring it about. Even though the Anti-Corruption and Security Unit could hardly be seen to entrap in the same way, they could have done more in the decade of their existence than wring their hands, and plead that having insufficient evidence is the fault of players failing to come forward rather than their own.

It would be comfortable to conclude that the episode was just an isolated incident – but wiser to observe how almost *all* inquiries lift the lid only so far as to find a transgressor or two, then close the lid again. It is, alas, not in officialdom's interest to probe more deeply, because "stakeholders" – especially sponsors and broadcasters – will be scared away. It is up to those of us who follow the game without vested interests to be eternally vigilant, and it would appear that we have not been sufficiently so.

Flower's wise words

The season of 2010 had begun so promisingly. Even though the start was the earliest on record – MCC had to play the Champion County in March in Abu Dhabi – the spring weather allowed two fine rounds of Championship matches.

Definite results were reached partly because the heavy roller was not to be used after the start of a Championship game: dents which the ball made in the surface could not be ironed out completely so, whether it was the Dukes brand of ball in the first division or Tiflex in the second, it seamed around and made life unusually difficult for top-order batsmen. Nottinghamshire, who went on to win the title, did not have an opening stand of more than 75 all season.

Into these smoothly operating works came the spanner of 40-over games. The value of them is dubious, at best, as no international cricket of this length has ever been scheduled. The ECB advertised the Clydesdale Bank 40 competition as "what Sunday afternoons were made for", referring to the 1970s when Sunday League games often made for a jolly afternoon, especially at an outground; but now 40-over matches were staged on every day of the week, seemingly at every hour of day and night, and the schedule for the 2010 season was soon reviled as the biggest hotch-potch that English cricket had ever devised. Without doubt it was the most ill-conceived fixture list since 1919, when scarce national resources were a justification for making Championship matches last only two days.

Every county had to play a minimum of 44 matches (92 scheduled match days). This rose to 49 matches if the county reached the finals of the 40-over and 20-over competitions, as Somerset did, and they also played the Pakistanis and Cardiff MCCU: 51 first-team fixtures in all, in five months. Professional football teams play a similar number of games in a season of nine months; their games last only 90 minutes; and even then there are widespread calls for a mid-season winter break.

The expansion in the number of 20-over games from ten to 16 in the qualifying stage outweighed the abolition of the fourth competition of 50 overs. The result was saturation: once the golden goose, Twenty20 became junk food. When it had been a novelty and rarity, Twenty20 had attracted newcomers to the game, like women and youngsters, as it was designed to do. Last season the average attendance for Twenty20 matches dropped, and crowds seemed to be the traditional hard-core county faithful with a few extra walk-ups on the day.

I commend to the ECB the words of Andy Flower, the coach they so sapiently appointed: "Scheduling is tricky, but to have a situation whereby you have a Twenty20 game the day before or the day after a four-day game cannot be right. You cannot allocate the right amount of energy, concentration, planning, skill, preparation, review or recovery. You can't create consistently high standards with those schedules."

Success at last

While the season was in full flow, or indeed overflowing, England were winning their first global trophy, the World Twenty20. After 17 failed attempts, England finally made it, the last of the eight main Test-playing countries to do so. It was another result that stemmed from the thorough organisation which the Andocracy had introduced into England's cricket, even though Strauss had given up Twenty20. One might add a third left-handed batsman to this honourable list of reformers: Hugh Morris, England's managing director.

What was also notable, however, was the reaction which the winners underwent as soon as they returned to England in mid-May. The batsmen could hardly make a run, and the top four fell by the wayside one by one: Michael Lumb was dropped from the Hampshire team, Craig Kieswetter from England's 50-over side, and Kevin Pietersen from England's 50-over and 20-over sides – while Paul Collingwood, the captain, nominally rested for the Tests against Bangladesh owing to an injured shoulder, laboured until he retired from Test cricket after the Ashes. The system, which Flower and Strauss had adapted so that players could peak and win, is still not designed to allow them to rest after their efforts. Instead, they are forced to keep on playing, and playing.

Systematic rotation was in effect introduced last summer, although no official announcement was made. Collingwood, Pietersen, Swann and Stuart Broad were rested and made unavailable for England selection when in less hectic times they would have played. This did nothing for the game's popularity. It was a pragmatic necessity to get through the overwhelming demands of the schedule – at the expense of the spectator, television viewer and broadcaster. The benefits for the England team were not unqualified either: they lost their unbeaten record against Bangladesh when the tourists won the one-day international at Bristol. Strauss conceded afterwards that if the rested Swann had played, it "would have made a difference". And England would have been better served if they had gone into the 2011 World Cup with an unbeaten record against one of the hosts, Bangladesh, who were in the same qualifying group.

Obviously there have always been cases when a pace bowler has needed a winter off. As a rule, though, a country should be represented by the best 11 players in the best possible condition. Anything less is a con trick.

More beauty, less speed

The signal given by a captain after the toss at any level of the sport, to tell his players that they are batting first, has become an anachronism. A forward defensive push with the left hand in no way conveys the action of batting as it has become. While it would be safe to generalise that before the 1970s the average good-length ball, at whatever level, was not scored off, it will probably be hit for runs now. Scoring-rates have rocketed: Don Bradman sped along at 61 runs per 100 balls in Tests. In some 20-over tournaments, batsmen – Kieron Pollard, for example, in the Champions League – have scored at more than 200. Teams too have been recalibrated to score at ten runs per over for a whole innings: Surrey clouted 386 off 38 overs against Glamorgan at The Oval last season. In the IPL, teams have scored at 12 an over. And last November in a Hong Kong final, admittedly of a six-a-side tournament, Australia needed 46 off the last eight-ball over – and won with a ball to spare.

This is, on the surface, exciting stuff. But we have reached the stage of too much of a good thing. The scoring of a boundary should be a moment for spectators to applaud rather than barely notice; it is dramatic when a period of scorelessness is broken by a stroke, especially a well-made one. Now, a ball disappearing out of a ground is routine. Limited-overs batting is increasingly like baseball-hitting and leg-sided, so the off-side strokes that are the game's beauty – relying more on technique and timing than force – are being rapidly eroded.

Aussie Rules rules

The game has other ills, from bottom to top. Groundsmen are not recognised and rewarded sufficiently: everything stems from the strip of 22 yards of turf they produce, and most international pitches are plain dull. In the West Indies, specifically, if their governments want to revive cricket as they profess, they would do well to employ groundsmen to care for club grounds and their pitches.

At the highest level of administration, politicians are taking over, which cannot be healthy. There may be something to be said for a former politician, such as John Howard, becoming an administrator, as he tried to do in the election for the ICC presidency; but precious little for active politicians. They have too little time for the game and too many vested interests.

While in Australia I was impressed, and a little disheartened, by the way that Australian Rules football is taking over from cricket as the national team sport. The game was invented by the Melbourne Cricket Club as a way to keep its cricketers fit in winter, using the acreage of the MCG, but by the 1980s it was moribund and mostly confined to Melbourne. This crisis forced a change in the constitution of its governing body: instead of the clubs electing a lot of diehard committeemen from their own number, as in cricket, a much smaller board of great-and-good was appointed. They had specifically required skills, including a former leader of Australia's trade unions to deal with strained player relations.

Now the Victorian Football League is the Australian Football League, thriving nationwide and attracting young elite athletes with its average salary of $A230,000 (about £150,000), twice that of the state cricketer, and with 800 jobs available – eight times as many as in professional cricket. The offspring has taken over the parent, because the constitution of Cricket Australia is the same as in the 19th century. In the same way the constitutions of most Test-playing countries, as well as the ICC's, are unfit for modern purpose.

Play!

But nobody – no politician, administrator or cricketer, corrupt or not – can destroy the essential pleasure of bat and ball. You may choose to believe the pronouncement of the ICC's chief executive Haroon Lorgat, after three of Pakistan's finest cricketers were banned, that the international game is clean; or the statement by Pakistan's wicketkeeper Zulqarnain Haider, later retracted, that this incident was only "the tip of the iceberg". If you read our article on Asia's illicit gambling dens following these Notes, you will probably incline more to Haider's initial view. But the game's vitality will be reaffirmed by a look at our Cricket Round The World section. From Afghanistan – especially Afghanistan – to Ukraine to Timbuktu, cricket is spreading ever more widely.

And, as it spreads, cricket shows itself to be an excellent vehicle for racial integration. True, in the past and still in the present, cricket teams have been composed on racial and religious lines: one need only think of the Bombay Pentangular Tournament, which Gandhi came to preach against, or apartheid South Africa. But cricket teams should be assembled without racial or religious distinctions, and it scores every time over other team sports like rugby and football by being non-contact. There is so much less risk of friction, misunderstanding or violence. You can be as physical as you like, bowling fast or standing at slip, but physical contact is never allowed.

More than any other first-class county I know, Nottinghamshire has been active in promoting cricket in deprived areas; and the statistics seem unequivocal in showing how crime has been reduced in the poorer areas of Nottingham where cricket has been promoted. In an ever more polarised world, cricket becomes more – not less – relevant.

Even if you are in your fifth decade of playing cricket, as I am, the pleasures at the start of a new season continue – at least until the first misfield. Taking the kit out of the cupboard, to find socks from last autumn and boots lacking studs; removing the rope from around the square, allowing access to the sanctum of the 22 yards of grass; the first outdoor net and the first ball that comes blessedly off the bat's middle; then the day itself of the opening game, and the most reassuring of sounds, that of the mower, for it means rain has relented enough to allow cricket; leaves on the trees as the earth springs into life again; then the palpitating moment when, after seven dark months, the umpire calls "Play" and everything is right with the world – until that first misfield or mistake. Very much like hope, the joy of cricket springs eternal.

THE PAKISTAN CASE (1)

Asia's illicit gambling dens

ROB CRILLY

Business is good for Goshi and his small band of bookmakers, tucked away in a smoky front room overlooking the slums of Lahore. And it's about to get better.

"I'm going to buy a Prado after the World Cup – you know, one of the big 4×4s with the alloys and the fancy stuff," he says, throwing back his head and laughing.

It is not an idle boast. His makeshift gambling operation rakes in millions of rupees with every one-day international – even in a conservative Muslim country where betting is illegal.

The den was in full swing barely a day after Salman Butt, Mohammad Aamer and Mohammad Asif had received lengthy bans for their role in the spot-fixing scandal. Yet nobody thought the punishments would help clean up Pakistani cricket. "The bans aren't as heavy as they could have been. No one has been banned for life," says Goshi. "So when you look at how much players can earn from working with bookies – and many of these players come from very poor homes – I don't think this will put people off getting involved in fixing."

A flat-screen television on one wall shows the action as James Anderson fires a delivery at Brad Haddin in the seventh one-day international between Australia and England. Five bookies keep one eye on the TV as they answer phones, shout odds and note down wagers in neat Urdu script. It does not matter to them that, in Doha, three of Pakistan's leading players have just been sanctioned for corruption.

A scattering of cushions on the floor is the only concession to comfort. The bookies sit cross-legged as they concentrate on their calculators, pausing only for a drag on marijuana-laced cigarettes. Illicit dens just like this are thriving across Pakistan, and in India, where bookmakers run tiny businesses from bedrooms, empty offices and half-built houses – almost anywhere with a television and a mobile phone signal.

One of the eight wireless phones spread in a semi-circle on the floor suddenly belts out a lively Bollywood tune. Even at 8.30 a.m. there are punters ready to place bets on a match taking place on the other side of the world.

"This is nothing," says Goshi, who asks that his full name is not used. "It's early. Everyone spent yesterday watching the Pakistan match [a one-day international in New Zealand]. They are only getting up now. It will get busier."

He notes down a bet of 20,000 rupees (£160) on an England win. The minimum stake is set at Rs5,000, a considerable amount of money in a country where one third of the population survives on less than a pound a day. "Our clients are businessmen. No one else can really afford it," says Goshi in Urdu, as he sits leaning against the wall.

The phones – each connected to a tape recorder to avoid any disagreements over who paid what – ring incessantly when punters dial in to bet on the match outcome, or a complicated series of "figure" bets, gambling on the score after 10- or 20-over periods. Goshi's crew shun fancy bets, where gamblers lay wagers on the outcome of individual balls, as too complex and too easy to fix.

One telephone is left permanently on speakerphone to receive odds from a bookmaking mastermind in Karachi; another so that the figures can be passed on to some 20 smaller outfits near by that pay Goshi for a slice of the action.

The business relies in part on trust. Cash will not change hands until tomorrow, when Goshi's runners will fan out through the richer suburbs to collect payments and deliver winnings.

Another day at the office: Lahore, February 2011.

The figures soon mount up. A day earlier Goshi's small team took Rs2m (£16,000) during the match between Pakistan and New Zealand. During the World Cup, he reckons they will earn Rs10m (£80,000) in profit alone. And with as many as 1,000 illegal dens operating in Lahore – according to police estimates – millions of pounds change hands each match.

But with that comes the darker side of Pakistan's illegal industry. Allegations of match-fixing and spot-fixing have dogged the national team for years. "It stands to reason. You see how big this is," says Goshi. "If Australia are the favourites and loads of money is being put on them, then people could make a lot of money by getting them to lose."

On another afternoon, in another den – this one set up in a squalid bedroom, a temporary home while police raided properties close to the normal office – another bookie, PK, said he had no doubt fixing was rife during the England–Pakistan series of 2010.

"When we set our own odds we always lose. But when we take the odds from bookmakers in Karachi then we stay in profit. So we think they must have inside information on what is going on," he says. "We knew Pakistan would win last week. The odds we were given didn't make sense."

He has little in the way of evidence, other than a hunch and some painful losses. At the same time, though, these Lahore bookmakers say their operation sits at the bottom of a web connected by telephone to Karachi, the teeming, chaotic commercial capital of Pakistan, and from there on to Mumbai. The money, they say, ends up in Dubai and England.

Many believe Dawood Ibrahim, the notorious Indian crime lord, sits at the top. As well as suspecting him of racketeering and drug-running, the US believes he has links to al-Qaeda and has funded terrorist attacks in India. "Nothing this big, and crossing so many borders, could run without his say-so," according to a police officer speaking on condition of anonymity.

The phones ring all morning, as the narrow room gradually fills with smoke, dimming the sunshine flooding through a single window. Only when England's fifth wicket falls for 64 in the early afternoon, and Australia look certain to end up winning the series 6–1, does the betting stop.

"It's difficult to judge when Australia are batting because you never know what they might do," says Goshi. "But I think it's obvious the match is over. The book is closed." Not for long.

Rob Crilly is Pakistan correspondent of the Daily Telegraph *and previously reported from Africa. His book* Saving Darfur: Everyone's Favourite African War *was published in 2010.*

THE PAKISTAN CASE (2)

The power of denial

OSMAN SAMIUDDIN

Hours after three wise men found that he had bowled deliberate, pre-planned no-balls in a Test at Lord's and banned him for five years, Mohammad Aamer gave an instructive interview to the most popular, mood-controlling TV channel in Pakistan, Geo.

To the nation at midnight, he said it felt as if his life had come to an end. He couldn't understand, he said, how you can get five years for two no-balls. He had spoken to his mother and told her to stay strong like he had. Expertly, the camera drew close into the 19-year-old's eyes to reveal tears trickling down.

Hanging around Aamer in his Doha hotel were the regular punters of Pakistan cricket, the fans who on foreign tours seem to have such dangerous and easy access to players, plying them with food, entertainment, companionship, sometimes business contracts, sometimes something more. Mostly they offer a home away from home.

As the interview came to an end – an exclusive first reaction by any of the three banned players – the reporter gave an instruction rather than asked a question. "Aamer *aaya*, Aamer *chaaya* [roughly, Aamer came, Aamer conquered]… Aamer, I want you to look into the camera, to all of Pakistan, and tell them you will be back, you WILL BE BACK!" Of course, Aamer did.

It was quite a journalistic feat, for in an interview lasting more than nine minutes Aamer wasn't asked whether he had done it or why he had done it. There was not even any acknowledgment that he had been found guilty by the ICC's independent tribunal of a grave breach of the ICC Code of Conduct. They could have been talking about an injury that would keep him out of the game for a few years. Only the pom-poms and ra-ra skirt were missing on the reporter, who had long ago confessed that saving Aamer was a campaign he would run.

In Pakistan, never underestimate the power of denial and the vividness of delusion which stems from it.

The days immediately following the *News of the World* video were strange, disturbing ones in Pakistan, the kind endured after a particularly seismic suicide attack, which leaves you simultaneously full and empty of emotion. Foremost, the affair was a triumph for the former Test fast bowler Sarfraz Nawaz.

For over 20 years, Sarfraz had come to embody Pakistan's attitude to corruption in cricket: it must be happening because, well, corruption is everywhere and it must all be a conspiracy against Pakistan. At first, when he made allegations after the 1987 World Cup semi-final which Pakistan lost to Australia in Lahore, no one took him seriously. But, over the next decade, his voice took on an unnerving loudness.

Pop star or war hero? Mohammad Aamer is mobbed as he leaves the ICC independent tribunal in Doha, February 2011.

By the time of the first real wave of match-fixing, in the early and mid-1990s, he had become a key freelance crusader in the fight against corruption. He was the first person to appear before the Qayyum commission, which began in September 1998. But after cricket officially declared a victory in the war in 2000, Sarfraz simply continued. Through the 2000s, every loss, collapse, each dropped catch, unsuccessful slog, any feather that carried on it the lightest trace of a rumour, was grasped by Sarfraz as proof that fixing was rife.

Little of what he said ever came with any evidence. I met him in 2008 and asked him why he thought every match was fixed. The response was not necessarily built on full sentences, but how magnificently provocative – and possibly deranged – was its range of reference: Musharraf/Blair cover-ups, Benazir's assassination, verbal testimonies of the greatest players, Scotland Yard goof-ups, Sharjah, Mumbai dons.

"If I see a match I can see things are fishy. Children say misfield has happened, I don't. Sharjah, why has it been banned? ICL, IPL, what is this? All fixing. Toss, declaring early, you can tell from these things, what are you talking about, *yaar* [mate]?" But the chamber in which Sarfraz shrieked was particularly febrile, increasingly unable to distinguish fact from fiction, proof from allegation. Over the decades, people have come to accept the corruption of public figures in Pakistan – politicians, big businessmen mostly, but anyone and everyone really – as a fact of life, like death (but not taxes). If cricketers were found to be doing it, or were under constant suspicion thereafter… well, there was really no reason for it to be otherwise. And as Pakistan began to lose itself in a growing isolation through the 2000s, to slowly unplug itself from the world, conspiracy theories surged. Mossad, RAW (India's secret service), the CIA, fixing syndicates: they all merged into one narrative, a galaxy of evil out to undo Pakistan.

Nothing, however, juiced up the environment quite like the findings of the Qayyum Report. What was he saying? That some are guilty and banished, and many others are guilty but not enough, so are fine to stay on? The perception grew thereafter not only that corruption never stopped because tainted players stayed on, but – more damagingly – that it wasn't perhaps so bad.

So when that video came out, the most resounding piece of evidence of its kind ever seen – more so than Hansie Cronje's confession and more than the same newspaper's 2000 sting operation on Salim Malik – Sarfraz won. Everyone else lost.

The absoluteness of the video and the statistical starkness of the question it posed – the no-balls, as the tribunal later asked, were simply either fluke or fix – were stunning. Some decided India was behind it, even men of position such as the country's High Commissioner to the UK, Wajid Shamsul Hasan. Wasn't the wife of Mazhar Majeed, the agent at the centre of the fix, of Indian origin, after all?

Others looked suspiciously at Mazher Mahmood, the *News of the World* man behind the story, and decided he was a long-time Pakistan-hater. A story ran in an Urdu newspaper that he was equally hated by the Pakistani community in London because of damaging stories he had written in the past. In any case, wasn't the *NOTW* an entirely dodgy tabloid, and isn't this what dodgy tabloids did? Stitch people up and then do business off their misfortune? They had done it before, hadn't they?

Some sought refuge, and deflection, in fantasy. Spot-fixing is rampant around the world. Everyone is doing it. The IPL and ICL are dens of gambling. When Suresh Raina was allegedly videoed in Sri Lanka with alleged associates of an alleged bookie and nothing came of a tape and subsequent report that may or may not have existed, Pakistanis jumped on it twice over: here was proof that others – Indians at that – were involved, and proof also that the ICC were targeting them alone.

Many asked, and still ask, whether anybody checked when the video was shot, and whether or not it could have been doctored. The best were those who, in the same sentence, cursed the players for being corrupt *and* cursed the Indians for hatching such conspiracies.

This being the land of a new, loud electronic media still unable to contain the excitement at its very own existence, controversies and scandals come and pass, as do captains. Bombs, corruption, political intrigue, secular–religious divides: new days brought new issues to shout about. Terrorists soon struck, and the discordant beat to which life moves resumed.

Perhaps things became too normal. Of the three, Butt and Aamer were particularly public in their defence. Regularly the pair appeared on current-affairs shows and prime-time news bulletins to protest their innocence. When the pair's appeals (Asif, quiet all along, chose not to appeal) for provisional suspensions were dismissed, they became louder. Butt's lawyers at the time cranked up the volume, spewing about conspiracies and how we would all shake when the iceberg was unsheathed. Locals bought into the bluster the same way people buy into miracle hair-growing creams.

If ill-advised, the platforms made some sense. What made no sense was a series of appearances by the three on lighter TV fare. Butt and Kamran Akmal – not charged anywhere but the suspicions do not go away – appeared on a show celebrating Eid, laughing about the joy of festive occasions. Asif appeared with his new spouse on a breakfast show chatting about marriage and weddings and in-laws, a TV version of the obligatory post-wedding *Hello!* spread.

Aamer, by now the most popular of the three because of his youth and extraordinary talent, turned up on the most-watched breakfast show shortly before the hearings, the host and he revelling in their rags-to-riches stories. No sense existed that these players might be facing the end of their careers or had done anything wrong.

That this all confirmed Pakistan's evolution into the modern world – in which exists man as controversy as celebrity – was to be taken either as consolation or grief.

Aamer was mobbed as he came out of the Qatar Financial Centre in Doha on February 5 with nothing to do for five years. A group of 50 or so expatriate Pakistani fans, rounded up by Geo, greeted him as a pop star, or a returning war hero, or even an arriving World Cup winner. In some photographs he is smiling as grown men grapple to hold, kiss and touch him.

Butt and Asif drew more mixed reactions, but even those who booed them tried to get autographs and photos. Justice Albie Sachs, one of the members of the tribunal, came out a little later. Sachs, a renowned anti-apartheid activist and eminent judge, is a man of great reason and no little compassion. It is his spirit that runs behind the sanctions and the hope they offer all three for redemption and rehabilitation as human beings, if not cricketers.

He was roundly jeered, sign of a wider disconnect.

Osman Samiuddin is the Pakistan editor of ESPNcricinfo. His history of Pakistan cricket will be published by HarperCollins India later in 2011.

THE PAKISTAN CASE (3)

Say it ain't so, Salman

PAUL KELSO

The summer of 2010 will be remembered, not for the quality of the cricket played by England and Pakistan, but for the infamous events in the final Test at Lord's that plunged the game into its most serious corruption crisis in a decade.

The myth that the cancer of match-fixing and manipulation was in remission was exploded by events that passed almost unnoticed on the opening two days. In the first 20 overs of England's first innings – split over two days by rain – Mohammad Aamer delivered two no-balls and Mohammad Asif one. With Aamer almost bowling England out of the game before lunch on the second day, they were initially the most minor of footnotes. By the evening of the third day, however, following allegations in the *News of the World*, they had became the most notorious extras in the game's history: the principal exhibits in an affair that left the reputations of Pakistan cricket and the ICC metaphorically on trial, and three of its leading players literally so.

The newspaper, still the most muscular and unceremonious British tabloid, alleged that Pakistan's captain Salman Butt, Aamer and Asif had colluded with Butt's agent Mazhar Majeed to deliver the three no-balls to order in exchange for £150,000. The allegation was not of match-fixing, but its insidious variant "spot-fixing", in which discrete elements of games are distorted for the benefit of gamblers or bookmakers, largely based in the subcontinent, focusing on event-specific markets known as "brackets".

The allegations were backed by video and audio evidence, including a notorious passage in which Majeed counted out £140,000 in cash while discussing the fix. The footage was filmed during a series of meetings in the fortnight before the Lord's Test between Majeed and the newspaper's notorious investigations editor Mazher Mahmood who, acting on a tip-off from a former member of the Pakistan team management, posed as the front man for an Asian betting syndicate.

According to the *News of the World*, Majeed claimed to represent Indian bookmakers specialising in offering odds on ten-over brackets that lent themselves to manipulation. Deliberate low scoring, for example, could lead to a profit on a market for the number of runs that would be scored. He claimed to represent at least six of the touring squad, and to have huge influence over them, thanks in part to Butt's leadership. Majeed appeared to brag of his influence and claimed involvement in numerous "fixed matches", including the Sydney Test the previous winter, which Pakistan lost from a position of apparent impregnability.

In the week of the Oval Test, which preceded the final Test at Lord's, Majeed promised the reporters he would "give" them two no-balls as a show

The accused: Mohammad Aamer, Salman Butt and Mohammad Asif, during the Lord's Test.

of good faith. He also promised that Butt would play out a maiden over in Pakistan's second innings at The Oval. Majeed said that the signal for the maiden would be conveyed via the ubiquitous practice of "gardening". A prod of the pitch by Butt after the second dot-ball in his first complete over at the crease would be the signal to the reporters and their supposed backers to bet on a maiden. Majeed proved his access to the captain by calling Butt and playing the conversation on speaker-phone, so the reporters could hear his voice.

In the event, neither the no-balls nor the maiden were delivered at The Oval. Majeed explained that Pakistan's unexpected dominance in the game, and a lecture from coach Waqar Younis on the need to reduce extras, meant the deal had been cancelled. He promised to make good the bargain in the Lord's Test, however, in exchange for a "deposit" of £150,000.

In a pivotal meeting at the Copthorne Tara Hotel the night before the Fourth Test, the reporters handed over £140,000 in used £50 notes. The *News of the World* footage showed Majeed stacking the money into piles as he counted it, and explaining precisely how events would be manipulated in the match.

Majeed said the first ball of Aamer's second over and the last delivery of Asif's fifth would be no-balls. The third no-ball was to be the final delivery of the first over in which Aamer went round the wicket to a right-handed batsman (England's openers Strauss and Cook both being left-handed). The first two no-balls were delivered precisely as promised in the hour of play possible on the first day, but the third had to be delayed as the first wicket did not fall in time. That evening, the newspaper alleged, Majeed told them he had arranged that the third delivery of Aamer's third over next morning would be the no-ball. It was delivered precisely as predicted.

The impact of the newspaper's story justified its billing as "sensational". Earlier in 2010 the same newspaper had entrapped snooker player John Higgins in a similar undercover operation that subsequently saw him banned from his sport for six months. Football was to face an entrapment scandal of its own in the autumn, when members of FIFA's executive committee appeared to discuss improper payments with undercover reporters from the *Sunday Times*. But in sport's year of the sting, cricket was cut the deepest. The revelation of such specific allegations, published while the match was still in progress, coupled with Majeed's apparently direct line into the Pakistan dressing-room, was both unprecedented and seismic for cricket's reputation.

Clarke handed Aamer an oversized cheque

The Metropolitan Police took immediate action, arriving at the Pakistan team hotel in Swiss Cottage on Saturday night before the paper was on the news-stands. They briefly questioned the players and searched their rooms, finding money in the rooms of Butt and Aamer that bore serial numbers matching those on the banknotes given to Majeed by the newspaper.

Despite suggestions that the Test might be abandoned, the teams arrived at Lord's on Sunday morning, and it concluded in a surreal atmosphere, Pakistan collapsing to a dismal innings defeat. In a bizarre compromise, the end-of-series ceremonials were conducted in the Long Room rather than on the field. The presentation concluded with ECB chairman Giles Clarke handing Aamer an oversize cheque for his award as Pakistan's Man of the Series.

Proceedings took a vastly more serious turn thereafter. The police stepped up their investigation, while the Pakistan government, through the offices of their voluble and media-friendly High Commissioner in London, heightened the diplomatic tension, claiming the players had been framed and the evidence against them fabricated.

Majeed, his wife and another man were detained and questioned on that Sunday afternoon by officials from Her Majesty's Revenue and Customs, in connection with a money-laundering investigation understood to relate to Majeed's ownership of Croydon Athletic, a football club in the Ryman League. All three were bailed pending further inquiries.

In a febrile atmosphere, and with a now-unwelcome limited-overs programme to fulfil, the Pakistan team travelled to Taunton the following day for a warm-up match. Butt, Aamer and Asif travelled with them, but returned to London two days later to discuss their position with lawyers and the High Commissioner. The ECB, meanwhile, began negotiating with the Pakistan board to ensure that the players were not selected for the remaining games. After a stand-off in which the PCB chairman Ijaz Butt appeared to be countenancing the players appearing, they were announced as "unavailable for selection".

THE SPOT-FIXING TIMELINE

Aug 21　Oval Test, day four: Salman Butt does not play out a maiden over, but is later sanctioned by the ICC's independent tribunal for failing to report an approach to do so. Pakistan win by four wickets.

Aug 26　Lord's Test, day one, first ball of third over: Mohammad Aamer, bowling to Alastair Cook, no-balls by approximately one foot; last ball of tenth over: Mohammad Asif, bowling to Andrew Strauss, oversteps by two inches.

Aug 27　Lord's Test, day two, third ball of 19th over: Aamer, in his third complete over of the day, no-balls by approximately one foot bowling to Jonathan Trott.

Aug 28　On Saturday evening, the *News of the World* breaks "the most sensational sporting scandal ever". Video footage shows a man, believed to be Mazhar Majeed, receiving £140,000 from undercover reporter Mazher Mahmood, in return for information concerning three no-balls by Aamer and Asif. *NOTW* claims the meeting took place three days earlier, in the Copthorne Tara Hotel, Kensington. At 7.30 p.m., Metropolitan Police arrive at Pakistan team hotel in Swiss Cottage, to question Aamer, Asif and Butt. Mazhar Majeed arrested.

Aug 29　"These are just allegations," says Butt. "Anybody can stand up and say things about you – it doesn't make them true." Police confiscate the three players' mobile phones. Customs officials make three arrests in a separate money-laundering investigation involving Croydon Athletic FC.

Aug 30　Mazhar Majeed released on bail without charge. PCB chairman Ijaz Butt refuses to suspend the three players ahead of the one-day series. ICC confirm the ACSU are investigating the no-balls.

Sep 2　Pakistan team manager Yawar Saeed confirms that Aamer, Asif and Butt have been replaced in the squad for the one-day series. PCB say the three have "voluntarily withdrawn". ICC suspend the three players and charge them with "various offences under Article 2 of the ICC anti-corruption code".

Sep 3　The three players are questioned by police at Kilburn Police Station.

Sep 4　Shahid Afridi, captain for the limited-overs series, says, "On behalf of these boys I want to say sorry to all cricket lovers and all the cricketing nations." *NOTW* publishes claims by Pakistan batsman Yasir Hameed, videoed in a Nottingham hotel five days earlier. "They were [fixing] in almost every match," says Hameed. "It makes me angry because I'm playing my best and they are trying to lose."

Sep 5　Hameed claims he was merely repeating hearsay, and that he thought his interviewer a prospective sponsor.

Sep 6　Pakistan's Federal Bureau of Revenue announce investigation of personal finances of past and present players.

Sep 9　Ijaz Butt acknowledges that Salman Butt and Kamran Akmal had been sent notices by the ACSU asking for information about their activities during the World Twenty20.

Sep 10　Aamer, Asif and Butt board flight to Lahore. PCB issue instructions to all players that agents must be registered with and approved by the board before September 30.

Sep 14　Police question a fourth player, Wahab Riaz. Aamer and Asif file official replies to the ICC.

Sep 16　Umpire Tony Hill tells New Zealand's *Dominion Post* he immediately suspected the third no-ball was deliberate, as a tactic to intimidate the batsman, Jonathan Trott.

Sep 17　Police pass a file to the Crown Prosecution Service, to investigate if there has been a conspiracy to defraud bookmakers.

Sep 18　ICC announce investigation of "certain scoring patterns" in Pakistan's innings in the previous day's ODI at The Oval, following a tip-off by *The Sun*.

Sep 19	Ijaz Butt says of the Oval ODI: "There is loud and clear talk in the bookies circle that some English players were paid enormous amounts of money to lose the match."
Sep 20	ECB "completely reject" Ijaz Butt's claims, but vow to continue with the one-day series. Andrew Strauss reveals his team had "strong misgivings" about playing the final two matches. Trott and Riaz involved in fracas before play in fourth ODI, at Lord's.
Sep 23	In a letter also signed by the ECB and PCA, England team threaten legal proceedings against Ijaz Butt unless a "full and unreserved apology" is forthcoming.
Sep 29	Ijaz Butt apologises for his statement, but says he was misunderstood. Salman Butt is the first to file an official appeal against his provisional suspension. Aamer and Asif soon follow suit.
Oct 13	ICC give the Oval ODI the all-clear: "No compelling evidence to suspect individual players or support staff" of irregularities.
Oct 22	Asif withdraws his appeal against provisional suspension.
Oct 31	ICC tribunal in Doha upholds the provisional suspension of Aamer and Butt from international cricket.
Nov 3	PCB suspend the three players' central contracts.
Nov 12	ICC set the hearing into the spot-fixing allegations for January 6–11 in Doha, Qatar, and appoint a three-man tribunal.
Nov 14	It is reported that the PCB will send a list of probable World Cup players to the ACSU for clearance before selecting their final squad, an unprecedented move.
Nov 30	Additional video footage from the *NOTW* sting appears on Geo. Mazhar Majeed says, "We've got Umar Akmal, Kamran Akmal, Mohammad Aamer, Mohammad Asif, Salman Butt, Wahab Riaz and Imran Farhat… that's seven out of 11 players. Saeed Ajmal is too religious."
Dec 13	Salman Butt is reported as claiming the £29,000 found in his London hotel room consisted of tour and entertainment allowances, advance payment for bat sponsorship, and £2,500 for opening Afters, an ice-cream parlour in Tooting.
Dec 22	Michael Beloff, QC, chairman of the Anti-Corruption Tribunal, refuses an application from Salman Butt's new legal team to adjourn the Doha hearings.
Dec 28	Waqar Younis, the Pakistan coach, reveals he questioned Aamer about his no-ball to Trott. Butt stepped in and explained it was a tactic to disrupt the batsman.
Jan 11	Tribunal defers its verdict until February 5, to allow time to "give the issues careful consideration and provide written reasons".
Feb 4	CPS announce the three players, plus Mazhar Majeed, will face charges at Westminster Magistrates Court on March 17.
Feb 5	ICC tribunal announces its sanctions. Salman Butt is banned from all cricket for ten years (five suspended), Asif for seven years (two suspended), and Aamer for five years.
Feb 8	Yasir Hameed lodges formal complaint with Press Complaints Commission against *NOTW*.
Feb 24	Yasir Hameed suspended from domestic cricket in Pakistan.
Feb 26	Butt, Aamer an Asif meet the 21-day deadline for appealing to the Court of Arbitration for Sport against their verdicts and suspensions.

Compiled by James Coyne

On September 2 the ICC, acting with uncharacteristic speed, removed any doubt over their participation. The trio were provisionally suspended from all cricket, and charged with an array of offences under the ICC's anti-corruption code. The following day they were questioned for five hours by the Metropolitan Police before being released without being charged. A week later they flew back to Lahore, having agreed to return if requested.

The ICC's charges included: being a party to an effort to fix the conduct of any international match; accepting a bribe to fix the conduct of any international match; and failing for reward to perform to one's abilities in any international match. If convicted, they would face bans of between five years and life.

As the wheels of ICC and criminal justice turned, England and the residue of the Pakistan squad were condemned to play out a one-day series robbed of credibility and relevance. The tension was clear before the fourth match at Lord's, when Jonathan Trott and Wahab Riaz squared up during net practice. The administrators were hardly less confrontational, with Ijaz Butt claiming that England's defeat in the Oval one-day international might have been suspicious. "There is loud and clear talk in bookies circle that some English players were paid enormous amounts of money to lose the match," he said. "No wonder there was total collapse of the English side."

Clarke, chairman of the ICC's Pakistan Task Team, had spent much of the summer discussing the rehabilitation of the domestic game with Ijaz Butt, and was almost as horrified as Andrew Strauss and his players at the outburst. An apology was eventually extracted under threat of legal action, but the tensions of a long summer were unmistakable.

With the police investigating and the Crown Prosecution Service considering charges, the ICC began an unprecedented disciplinary process of their own in the autumn. For the first time the governing body were to pursue their own prosecution of a corruption case. All previous suspensions for fixing – including the life bans handed down to Salim Malik, Mohammad Azharuddin and Hansie Cronje – were the work of domestic boards. In this case, unprecedentedly, the ICC would be prosecuting players using a new, revised Code of Conduct.

Against a background hum of cynicism and conspiracy theories in Pakistan, the case wound on into the winter. Aamer and Butt appealed unsuccessfully against their provisional sentences, and then asked for the ICC case to be adjourned until the CPS had made a decision on whether they would face criminal charges.

The independent tribunal that was convened to hear the case, chaired by British QC Michael Beloff, declined all appeals, and the case was scheduled to be heard in the second week of January in Doha, Qatar. The ICC's home in Dubai was the first choice, but Asif had been detained on suspicion of possessing a small amount of opium on a previous visit to the UAE, meaning an alternative location was required. (He was detained for 19 days in Dubai in June 2008 and released without charge.)

Asif was represented at the hearing by Alexander Cameron, QC, the brother of the British prime minister. Butt, on his third set of lawyers, also had British

The independent tribunal: Sharad Rao, Albie Sachs and Michael Beloff arrive at the Doha Financial Centre.

counsel in Yasin Patel. Aamer was represented by a Pakistani lawyer, Shahid Karim.

The ICC's case, led by their legal director David Becker and Jonathan Taylor of London solicitors Bird and Bird, was based closely on the *News of the World's* evidence. It was augmented by transcripts of police interviews with the players, and telephone records of calls and texts between the trio and Majeed that, according to the tribunal, painted a "vivid narrative" of what occurred.

They also provided evidence from a statistician, who testified that the chances of Majeed accurately predicting the timing of three no-balls without prior knowledge at 1.5 million to one.

All three players pursued different defences, but consistently denied any involvement in fixing. While Aamer and Butt offered no explanation for Majeed's ability to predict the no-balls accurately, Asif said there appeared to be a conspiracy but he had no knowledge of it at the time.

After six days of evidence in the unlovely Doha Financial Centre Tower, the case was adjourned for three weeks to allow Beloff and his colleagues, Sharad Rao of Kenya and the South African Albie Sachs, to consider their verdicts.

They were scheduled to reconvene to announce their verdicts on February 5, 2011, and all parties had already gathered in Doha when, on February 4, the CPS announced that the players and Majeed were to face criminal charges. The four were all charged with conspiracy to obtain and accept corrupt payments, and conspiracy to cheat. The charges, denied by the players, are punishable by maximum prison sentences of seven and two years respectively.

The following day the tribunal dismissed the charge that Salman Butt agreed to bat out a maiden over in the Oval Test, but found the charge proved that he failed to disclose to the ICC's Anti-Corruption and Security Unit the approach by Majeed. It also found that Asif agreed to bowl, and did bowl, a deliberate no-ball in the Lord's Test; that Aamer agreed to bowl, and did bowl, two deliberate no-balls; and that Butt was party to the bowling of these deliberate no-balls.

As captain, Butt was given "a sanction of ten years ineligibility, five years of which are suspended on condition that he commits no further breach of the code and that he participates under the auspices of the PCB in a programme of Anti-Corruption education". Asif was given a sanction of seven years ineligibility, with two years suspended on the same conditions. Aamer was given a sanction of five years ineligibility. The bans were backdated to September 2, 2010, and the players were given 21 days to appeal. No orders were made as to costs.

The criminal charges provided a complication for the ICC and the tribunal. Both were keen to publish the judgment in full in order to bolster the credibility of their process, but feared that making the document public in the UK risked prejudicing the impending criminal trial and placing the ICC in contempt of court.

The solution required a final contortion by the governing body. A read-only version of the judgment with some passages redacted was published on the ICC website, but users were required to certify that they were not in England or Wales to gain access. This did not prevent elements of the judgment being published in the UK media.

The final, uncontroversial passage captured the regret felt by all involved in cricket's darkest episode in many years. "We cannot leave this case without exercising our regret at the events that led to it," the tribunal wrote. "In the Black Sox Scandal of 1919, sometimes described as the Sporting Scandal of the Century, the famous American baseball player 'Shoeless' Joe Jackson was found to have thrown a match. A distraught fan uttered the memorable words 'Say it ain't so, Joe'. We too wish in this case that it was not so."

No one who was at Lord's that dismal August Bank Holiday weekend would argue.

Paul Kelso is the Daily Telegraph's *chief sports reporter.*

SIR ALEC BEDSER, 1918–2010

A nod of satisfaction

JOHN WOODCOCK

Alec Bedser was one of the great bowlers, and someone to whom commitment was the first commandment. That he remained wedded to cricket until his dying day, and got out and about until into his nineties, made him a national treasure, chunter though he would at an open-chested bowling action, the absence of a third man or for want of a pint of bitter.

Through having served six years in the Second World War, by the time his career started in earnest he already had something of the veteran about him. His bowling was essentially a product of the English game as it was played for the first two-thirds of the last century. Still being uncovered, the pitches encouraged lateral movement at medium-pace to an extent seldom found elsewhere, and that was Bedser's stock-in-trade.

He followed in the correspondingly imposing footsteps of Maurice Tate, of whom R. C. Robertson-Glasgow wrote, as he might have done of Bedser, that "he had many imitators but no equals". They were both supreme in their day, and, as if to quell all argument, each had his triumphs in Australia as well as England, Bedser's 30 wickets there in 1950-51 being heroic in the same way as Tate's 38 had been in 1924-25, also in a losing cause.

Such is the emphasis placed now on fitness, agility and bowling speed that it is perfectly possible they would both be left on the rack today. More with regret than rancour, Bedser would say so himself. But to his contemporaries he was the champion, and you can ask no more than that. One could but marvel and despair at the frequency with which he beat the bat on the first morning of the Second Test at Melbourne on that tour of 1950-51, a spell of bowling which prompted those who had seen or played against the legendary Sydney Barnes to compare the two. Neil Harvey, already a very fine player, was as utterly confounded as Warren Bardsley, Clem Hill and Victor Trumper must have been by Barnes on the same ground 39 years earlier.

Bedser's chief pride and joy was his bowling action, the culmination of a methodical yet rhythmical run-up of no more than six full strides. On average he took two and a half minutes to bowl an over. He had the frame for the job, the heart to go with it, and big hands. The ball with which he bowled Don Bradman for nought in the Fourth Test at Adelaide in February 1947, a fillip like no other, had a lot to do with the size of his hands.

Often referred to as the perfect leg-cutter, and by Bradman as being as good a ball as ever got him out, Bedser always insisted that he didn't *cut* it but that he *spun* it, which he was able to do because his hands were so large. His natural movement in the air was into the right-handed batsman, and that, when followed by what amounted to a fast leg-break, was some combination. He spurned the outswinger, mainly in the interests of accuracy.

John Woodcock

At the races: Ken Barrington, another Surrey stalwart, and Bhausaheb Nimbalkar, who once scored 443 not out, with Alec Bedser at Bombay Racecourse in 1979-80.

Bowling was Bedser's abiding interest, the theory of it as much as the practice. No one ever went to him without coming away the wiser. This was particularly so during his days on the county circuit, and the younger players loved him for it. He enjoyed playing the part of the guru. When James Anderson was starting to make a name for himself, Bedser, by then in his mid-eighties, wrote him a long letter in his own hand with what he hoped would be helpful suggestions.

When he was managing the England side in Australia in 1974-75, I can see him now laying out a page of Melbourne's *Age*, then a broadsheet, on a net pitch as he set about drilling Mike Hendrick in the adjustment he would need to make to his English length on Australia's faster, bouncier pitches. And when I said to him one day that I had a great nephew who was showing a bit of form as a right-arm spinner, his message was typically brief and to the point: "Tell him to bowl over his left shoulder," as Bedser himself had done so inveterately and for so long.

Bedser finished playing in 1961, the end of his Test career precipitated, unhappily, by a bout of shingles on the 1954-55 tour to Australia, barely a year after his having taken a record 39 wickets in the Ashes series of 1953 in England. As a manager and selector of England teams for 23 years after his retirement, he cared almost to a fault. Nothing was too much trouble to him, other than coming to terms with all the changing proprieties of a sportsman's life.

Once, when paying his customary visit to the England dressing-room after a day's play at The Oval, either as chairman of selectors or manager of the side, he heard a strange whirring noise. "What's that?" he asked Tony Greig, the

England captain. "Bob Woolmer's hair-dryer," came the reply. *"Hair-dryer,"* said Alec, "what's wrong with a bloody towel?" As Woolmer had just made a hundred and England were playing Australia, Bedser needed to be careful not to seem to be ridiculing him – but, to the old-timer, hair-dryers were for women and always would be. Just as "strength and conditioning courses for bowlers", to use the current term, were best spent not in the gymnasium but out in the middle, bowling, or even digging the garden.

Not even Sir Pelham Warner and Lord Hawke between them can have helped to pick more Test sides than Bedser, and he had a remarkable memory for all the whys and wherefores of the different eras. More than anything, selectors need genuine all-rounders to help them out, and for his last few years Bedser was fortunate in having Ian Botham round whom to build a side. The successful decisions to bring back Mike Brearley as captain in 1981 in place of Botham, and to plump for Ray Illingworth ahead of Colin Cowdrey to lead the side in Australia in 1970-71, were not quite as straightforward as they may seem now. Bedser was not, I think, given to agonising over things, but he always wanted to see justice done. The irony was certainly not lost on him when, 36 years after the selectors, under Bedser's chairmanship, had felt obliged to suspend Tom Graveney for three Test matches for "a serious breach of discipline", the villain became president of MCC!

From the days when, as a member of the groundstaff at The Oval, he had to do what he was told by Mr Holmes and Mr Garland-Wells, until he was assured of a right royal reception at Lord's and knighted by the Queen, Bedser's career has nothing in cricket quite to match it. It would make a good film if twins of the right shape could be found to play Alec and his identical and inseparable brother, Eric, who predeceased him by four years. They would be seen getting away together from Dunkirk, and their mother would be heard to say "But that's what he's paid for, isn't it?" when asked what she thought of Alec taking 11 wickets in his first Test match.

Alec must have taken after his mother. I wasn't there to see him bowl Bradman at Adelaide in 1947, the most famous of his 236 Test wickets, but I saw most of the others and each one brought no more than a nod of satisfaction. The hugging and mauling which go on today, and that he would have so detested, had yet to come in. There was a native dignity about Alec, besides a becoming unselfconsciousness and gentle homespun humour, a candour, an incumbent melancholy and a liking for the old ways, which all went towards making him the institution he was – along with his indomitable bowling.

John Woodcock edited Wisden *for six years from 1981 to 1986 and was for 34 years the cricket correspondent of* The Times; *he retired in 1988.*

The indefatigable giant

Sir John Major

Alec and Eric Bedser were indivisible: even God made them complementary. One bowled medium-fast. One was a spinner. One was a batsman. One wasn't. Both fielded – in a stately fashion.

And both would have been surprised – and enormously touched – that thousands of years of friendship and admiration are gathered here today to say farewell to Alec.

Arthur Morris and Micky Stewart are from cricket's high table, and have spoken with affection of the Alec they knew. Alec would have liked that: he didn't approve of everyone but he did approve of Micky. And he loved Arthur Morris like a brother and – in Alec's world – nothing meant more than that.

As a boy, I idolised Alec Bedser from the cheap seats: later, I came to know him as a friend. There was nothing false or puffed-up about Alec. His values and opinions didn't change with fashion. What you saw was what you got: a big man – with an even bigger heart.

And – as St Peter will surely have learned by now (at least from Eric) – Alec was a cricketer. An *English* cricketer. In Alec's lexicon, only Australia came close to England as a nation. "And they" – as he explained his affection for Australians – "were English once." Two hundred years of nationhood had not changed Alec's mind about Australian origins.

Such men as the Bedser brothers are rare. In times long gone, their forebears fought at Agincourt and Waterloo. Alec – and Eric – served their country too, in the Royal Air Force during the Second World War. Alec fought on after the war: at Lord's, The Oval, Brisbane and Sydney. For years he was the English pace attack: an indefatigable giant in the direct line of Sydney Barnes and Maurice Tate, untiring and often unplayable: but not always, so I am told, uncomplaining.

Alec's views on cricket were trenchant – often generous, sometimes not, but always backed by his love – and knowledge – of the game. However, he wasn't a lover of every aspect of modern cricket. I sat with him when an English fast bowler hurled himself full-length to save a run. "Wonderful," breathed an eminent fellow guest, "…and he'll have to bowl after tea."

Alec didn't agree. His view was different: "Bloody fool – if he'd hurt himself he couldn't bowl, could he?"

To watch cricket with Alec was an education. To listen to him was a masterclass. He and Eric had prodigious memories. "Brother had him caught at second slip," Eric would say of some obscure game played 50 years ago. "Yeah," Alec would add, "low down, left hand. Old Laurie Fishlock nearly dropped it."

When Alec was knighted for services to cricket, the brothers were delighted. Eric said: "He's the first bowler to be knighted since Sir Francis Drake."

At home at The Oval: in 1997, John Major celebrates his birthday while prime minister, with Alec Bedser, who was knighted the same year.

Those of us privileged to know Alec could offer a thousand vignettes.

He came to No. 10 one summer's evening, clutching a bag of his home-grown runner beans. These were promptly removed and searched for explosive devices. However – as I learned later on – the only explosive device present had been Alec: "Beans!" he said to me. "Beans! If I was going to blow you up I'd have put it in me cauliflower."

Alec was a good friend to have. His support – in all circumstances – was total. He lived life like he played cricket – for the team, never for himself. And always – of course – for Eric. In life, they were inseparable. Now, they're reunited, and will never be apart again.

I like to think they've rejoined old friends, formed a celestial cricket team, and now discuss tactics over their usual midday pint. I can picture Alec on some green field: bowling again to Bradman, perhaps, and testing himself against Grace and Trumper. A little cloud cover would help his swing and, with luck, the heavenly turf will allow the leg-cutter to grip. If so, the batsmen had better be on their mettle: they are facing the greatest medium-fast bowler of his time – perhaps any time.

Alec played cricket like a poet: his length and line were perfect. The finest poem cricket has known, written of a much earlier great bowler, ended with the plea that "the turf may lay softly upon him".

And on you, dear Alec. And on you.

This address was given at the thanksgiving service for the life of Sir Alec Bedser at Southwark Cathedral on July 12. The Rt Hon. Sir John Major, KG, CH, prime minister from 1990 until 1997, is a lifelong supporter of Surrey.

TREVOR BAILEY, 1923–2011

The man for every crisis

CHRISTOPHER MARTIN-JENKINS

Environment, talent, unshakable self-confidence and an astute, pragmatic mind combined to make Trevor Bailey one of England's greatest all-rounders. Happy to face any challenge, he took the new ball, held brilliant close catches, shored up the middle order, and even opened the batting in 14 of his 61 Tests for his country, doing everything but captain them. Traces of cynicism and iconoclasm prevented that happening, but he was at the right hand of both Len Hutton and Peter May.

He was a pillar of Essex cricket from the late 1940s to his last year as captain in 1966. As a swift and incisive soccer forward, despite having played only rugby at school, he won an FA Amateur Cup winner's medal in 1952. As a writer and broadcaster, his analytical mind got to the heart of things, maintaining his popularity through a second period of fame as a pundit on BBC's *Test Match Special*. As a husband and father, he was as steadfast as his famous forward defensive.

With other household names of the early 1950s like Alec Bedser, Bailey first helped the national team's post-war recovery and then joined emerging talents such as Cowdrey, May, Trueman, Tyson and Statham to become the resolute pivot of the best side in the world. His death at 87 in sad circumstances on February 10, 2011, after a fire in his retirement flat, left alive only Tom Graveney, Reg Simpson and Roy Tattersall of the England players who had shared in the series victory over Australia in the Coronation Year of 1953.

That the Ashes were regained amid national rejoicing after 19 years owed much to Bailey's verve, intelligence and bottomless determination. At Lord's, he shared with Willie Watson the fifth-wicket stand on the last day that lasted from 12.42 until 5.50 p.m., saving England from defeat. At Headingley, Australia needed only 66 runs in 45 minutes with seven wickets left when he persuaded Len Hutton to change tactics, taking the initiative and bowling outside the leg stump to a heavily protected on-side field. Graeme Hole, who had put on 57 with Neil Harvey in half an hour, was caught on the boundary, Bailey conceded only nine runs from six overs, and England survived again. At The Oval, his solid 64 ensured the first-innings lead that paved the way for Jim Laker and Tony Lock to spin through Australia.

Over the next three years Bailey took a leading part in two more winning series against Australia. His impassable forward-defensive stroke, played well ahead of his front pad, had become a symbol of British defiance. It made him a folk hero and earned him his soubriquet "Barnacle".

He was a familiar voice on radio from 1966 to 1999, combining his role as a summariser with writing on cricket and football for a number of newspapers, notably the *Financial Times*. His penchant at the microphone was the succinct

Breaking free for once: Trevor Bailey reaches his fifty in the decisive 1953 Oval Test.

summary of a player or an incident, the pithier the better. He was a likeable companion off the air, always cheerful, and a most sympathetic colleague to work with, understanding the need for the commentator to set the scene, give the score and bring new listeners up to date.

Fond of a glass – be it a half of bitter or, better still, a glass of champagne ("the medicine", as he called it with a yelp of delight whenever the cork was popped late on a hot day) – he tended to be sharper in the mornings than after a good lunch. But he did nothing to excess (except when defending an apparently lost cause), and his analysis was always shrewd and perfectly timed. No one assessed players better. It was Trevor who immediately spotted, on the first Test appearance in England of the tearaway Richard Hadlee, the seeds of a great bowler.

Perceptive as he was, he could be vague about names – a "Sadiq" was liable to become a "Shafiq", and the West Indian left-arm spinner Raphick Jumadeen was always "Jumbadeen" – and in his life generally. He took his wife Greta to the spa town of Harrogate on the rest day of his first Test in Leeds, under the firm impression that they were about to enjoy a day on the beach. In 1993, conducting England supporters around India, he arrived at Bombay airport with a party of 30 but no tickets. They had been thrown away in the hotel waste-paper basket. But Trevor's charm, and his calmness, averted every crisis.

Christopher Martin-Jenkins was for three decades a colleague of Trevor Bailey on Test Match Special. *A full obituary of Bailey will appear in* Wisden 2012.

ENGLAND'S FIRST GLOBAL TROPHY

When everything just clicked

NASSER HUSSAIN

For winning England's first global trophy, the credit must go firstly to Andrew Strauss and Andy Flower for setting the wheels in motion. England would not have won the third ICC World Twenty20 if they hadn't started to improve their limited-overs cricket before then. You do not go into a tournament well down the list and win it from nowhere except, perhaps, if you are Pakistan.

The first time I noticed a turnaround in England's limited-overs cricket was after their 6–1 drubbing by Australia in the one-day series of September 2009. When England went to the Champions Trophy in South Africa straight afterwards, there was a definite change of plan in the batting. The attitude became "If you're going down, then play some shots in the process": a no-fear approach that gave batsmen licence to swing from the hip from the first ball.

It was one thing of course for the management to say this; another for the players to put it into practice. I reckon Paul Collingwood led the way in that Champions Trophy, along with Eoin Morgan. When they knocked out South Africa at Centurion, England hit 12 sixes, their most ever in a limited-overs match. On that occasion Collingwood and Morgan were supported by Owais Shah, but he soon paid the price for his fielding.

So here was an approach to England's batting that had never been seen before. Even in the days when England had been successful, like Graham Gooch's side in the 1992 World Cup, they had not played this brand of cricket. By the 2007 World Cup in the West Indies, England were still batting in their old-fashioned way – starting slowly and keeping wickets in hand.

Clearly England also needed to change their personnel to make this approach work. In the past, the Test players had been given every chance to come good in the shorter format: as recently as England's tour of South Africa in 2009-10, the T20 opening batsman (and stand-in captain) was Alastair Cook. But when England went to Abu Dhabi in February 2010 to play the Lions and Pakistan, Flower saw something in the Lions' openers Michael Lumb and Craig Kieswetter. England's selectors quickly brought them in, not minding about any backlash over their South African origins. So credit to the selectors as well for making the policy change.

Another good piece of selection came when three spinners were chosen in the squad. England must have had good feedback about the West Indian pitches, and they themselves had toured there a year before. In one-day cricket of any kind England had never really played two spinners before, except occasionally in Asia. Graeme Swann and Mike Yardy made a fine combination: Swann's guile and drift on the strong tropical breeze blowing across most grounds, and Yardy sneaking up on the batsman, darting in and angling it without much subtle variation.

Some fortune was involved too, as it always is in winning a world trophy. The "IPL balance" was just right, enabling England to peak for once at a global tournament. Traditionally, we have played 50-over World Cups straight after the Ashes at our lowest ebb – straight after being blown away by Australia, when everything has been in turmoil and the last thing you need is a World Cup.

This time the schedule worked in England's favour. All their batsmen except Kieswetter played in some part of the IPL, while the bowlers were resting in England, and Duncan Fletcher always said it was better to be under- than overcooked. Collingwood also had the chance to pick up on Twenty20 skills when he was at IPL3, and he saw that the most successful bowlers were fast left-armers like Doug Bollinger, Ashish Nehra and Dirk Nannes. For him, the selection of Ryan Sidebottom was non-negotiable.

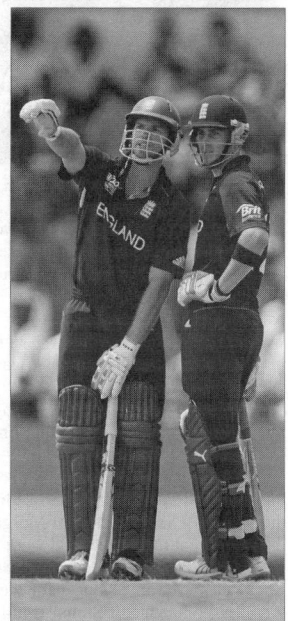

Several other countries had many more players in IPL3, and they arrived looking tired and overweight. In the IPL, it seems to me, you play and travel, and don't spend time in the gym. To India, the IPL was the Lord Mayor's Show – and the World Twenty20 was just another event. To England, it was the main event, and their mentality was spot-on. They had energy, and they and Australia were the two fittest sides.

The one point that concerned me was the one-paced nature of England's seam attack. I remember them winning a 50-over tournament in Sharjah under Adam Hollioake with lots of military-medium, then going to the West Indies and getting whacked everywhere. Now, before the first game in Guyana, I saw England's bowlers having a long meeting beside the pool one afternoon with new bowling coach David Saker; Flower joined them halfway through.

Planning the assault (1): Michael Lumb (*left*) and Craig Kieswetter, England's explosive openers.

After that, I sensed England were going to use the short ball a lot. The default setting in the past had been for England to bowl yorkers to contain batsmen, but the IPL had shown they no longer worked against big heavy bats. When England toured India in late 2008, Andrew Flintoff had bowled his yorker at Yuvraj Singh and disappeared out of the ground. There is so much weight at the bottom of the modern bat that a yorker that is not absolutely spot-on will get whacked.

Planning the assault (2): David Saker (*left*) and Andy Flower.

Where England's pace bowlers were so good was in mixing their deliveries up intelligently. They almost never bowled two deliveries the same – cutters, yorkers, bouncers and the slower-ball bouncer that is so difficult to hit – and always kept the batsman guessing. No country scored 150 against them; no batsman reached 60. The backroom staff deserve credit as well for coming up with the right plans for certain batsmen – lots of short balls for David Hussey in the final for example – but it was the bowlers who had the gut feeling of what to bowl when.

England got through the qualifying round in Guyana thanks to their net run-rate, and to Morgan. Historically, England had always been poor on very slow pitches against the likes of Daniel Vettori and Harbhajan Singh. We either had nudgers and nurdlers, like me, who couldn't get off strike and built up pressure on the non-striker, or the likes of Flintoff, who would try to hit the ball out of the ground – and get caught. Morgan added so much by being able to play three different roles. He could work the ball around, or hit sixes to any part of the ground, or do the unorthodox reverse-sweeps and switch-hits. When England arrived in St Lucia for the Super Eights and played New Zealand, their TV commentator Simon Doull said England were now better than New Zealand at working the ball around in the middle overs: a change from the old days, thanks mainly to Morgan.

Another instance of how roles had been reversed came when England played South Africa. In the 2007 World Cup match between them, on the same ground in Barbados, England had been 28 for one after ten overs and South Africa 85 for one. This time England were 65 for one after six overs – and they attacked Dale Steyn and Morne Morkel so much that their eight overs cost 90. Then South Africa were 34 for one after six, as Graeme Smith and Jacques Kallis prodded and pushed the asking-rate up to ten an over. It was the way England beat South Africa that made me think they could go all the way.

Everything flowed from their good starts, whether England bowled or batted. In every game unaffected by the weather they were ahead at the six-over stage, and they kept going from there. They were never playing catch-up, because their top-order batting was so powerful and their bowling up-front – led by Sidebottom and Tim Bresnan – was phenomenal in getting top players out early. England's confidence was never knocked because they were always ahead of the game.

The final ingredient was the range-hitting which England practised before every game. From Kevin Pietersen to James Anderson, the only thing the batsman had to do was hit the ball for six as Richard Halsall, the fielding coach, fed them a mix of cutters, bouncers and slower balls. It was a great way to train the brain. I remember a session in St Lucia when Pietersen came first by a country mile: he pretty much hit every ball for six, followed by Morgan who nailed about 70%. Bresnan and Luke Wright were pretty good too, while Kieswetter hit the ball highest. The ones who hit the ball best in practice were the ones who hit the most sixes next day. The local security guards loved it, doing the fielding and collecting the balls. When David Lloyd was England's coach, we would be worried about injuring spectators, and if Bumble lost a lot of balls the ECB would be on his case…

It was a massive advantage for England to play the final in Barbados. It is Little England, and they always enjoy playing there with so many supporters flying in. Even though England were playing Australia, they still had no fear: they had beaten them in two of the last three Ashes series. And if Nannes and Shaun Tait bowled a few tight overs, they knew they were going to whack Shane Watson when he came on.

One other feature was the strength of England's squad. India had neither Virender Sehwag nor Sachin Tendulkar, and there was a big drop in standard between them and their replacements. England's one-day team used to struggle if Flintoff or Marcus Trescothink was unavailable, but you have got a pretty good pool if you can leave out Anderson or Ravi Bopara. And as England have now assembled a fine squad in all three formats, the future is bright.

Nasser Hussain captained England in 45 Tests (winning 17, losing 15 and drawing 13) and in 56 one-day internationals (28 wins, 27 defeats and one no-result); he is a regular commentator for Sky Sports.

THE ACADEMY'S FIRST TEN YEARS

From boot camp to think tank

MARK WALLACE

"So you're the Pommie lads who've been sent over here to learn how to play cricket then, are you?"

The passing comment of an elderly female dog-walker on the warm sands of Adelaide's Henley Beach was less a question of curiosity than an accusatory statement of fact. The first intake of the ECB's newly established National Cricket Academy had been on Australian soil for a matter of hours and it seemed the promised "toughening-up" process had already begun.

That was in October 2001. England had just lost their seventh successive Ashes series by four Tests to one on home soil, and the powers-that-be had decided on a new direction to nurture the next generation of England players. The traditional A-team tour was shelved for the time being, and the brainchild of Hugh Morris, in his former role as performance director at the ECB, was being put into place. It was his vision that there should be a National Academy facility and squad to better develop the nation's international players. The facility would have to wait, but the squad was chosen and dispatched Down Under.

Morris had believed in a National Academy since developing the ECB's age-group and coaching programmes in 1997. Previously, money had been a stumbling block for such a venture and had stopped the then Test and County Cricket Board from following Australia's lead soon after they launched their academy programme back in 1987-88. But by the time Morris arrived, Lottery funding was available and, after a feasibility study, £4m was released to help fund the project.

I was part of the first Academy intake (and the second, a year later) that set up camp in Adelaide while the ECB's state-of-the art facilities were being built at Loughborough University. Homeless and unwelcome is perhaps an apt description of that squad and, in fairness to the lady with the labrador, there was at least some logic behind her thinking.

For a start, our base for five months was at Australia's highly regarded Institute of Sport in Adelaide, where the likes of Ricky Ponting, Glenn McGrath and Brett Lee were groomed for the baggy green cap. That we were treading an Australian path was plain from the outset, and much of our programme followed the tried and tested methods they had in place. So we had their facilities, their methods and – in Rod Marsh – their man.

Marsh's appointment as director of the National Academy was a coup for the ECB. He had held the equivalent post in Australia for some time and been credited with much of its success. He was also an iconic figure whose reputation as a tough and uncompromising character preceded him. And an appointment from outside the English game was in keeping with the fresh wind of change.

Which Academy did you say? Members of the ECB Academy's first intake toughen up at Sandhurst Royal Military Academy in October 2001. The author is far left, behind Chris Tremlett; Andrew Strauss in the middle, behind Steve Harmison.

Marsh's modus operandi was hard work, and tales of the brutal training sessions and gruelling schedules during his time at the helm are legendary. Early-morning sweat sessions were the norm, often to gut-wrenching extremes, and there was very little let-up in intensity when it came to cricket either.

To term the experience a boot camp would probably be to understate the importance and reasoning of the approach. Marsh believed that physical exertion, while increasing fitness levels and decreasing injury rates, would mould attitudes as well as having a cultural impact. Hard work, he argued, would be rewarded on the field, and the sweat and sacrifices made elsewhere would breed the mental toughness and steely resolve needed to succeed at the highest level. There was no hollow praise: when he gave you a pat on the back, you knew you had earned it.

Marsh was apoplectic on hearing that we were paid handsomely by the ECB while under his command. Indeed, £15,000 for the winter was considerably more than my salary as a young pro at Glamorgan. Not averse to occasional Anglo-Saxon, Marsh would often call us "overpaid Pommie bastards". So a significant reduction in the next winter's wage packet came as no surprise.

It's no real secret that some players weren't enamoured of Marsh's autocratic methods – but that was part of the process. He wasn't going to lose any sleep over a few young noses being put out of joint. I can vividly remember my state of shock when he gave us the hair-dryer treatment after a game against our Australian counterparts in Sydney. We had won, but the result wasn't going to mask a stuttering performance, and he gave us both barrels. I'm not sure any of us had experienced anything like it before, and we were left in no doubt that under-par performances would not be tolerated. The processes of victory and the habits of not simply winning, but winning well, were essential.

Marsh's tenure lasted four more winters, two in Australia and two in Loughborough, where the £4.5m National Academy building was opened by the Queen in November 2003. As a recent alumnus, I was present; after we met Her Majesty, the Duke of Edinburgh sidled up and remarked: "So this is where we're going to learn how to give the Aussies a thrashing." The Academy programme may have found a new home, but the shadow of Australia still loomed large.

Graham Morris

A study in concentration: Rod Marsh peruses Kyle Hogg's technique, Adelaide 2002.

That home – as the price tag suggests – was, and still is, an all-singing, all-dancing facility at the cutting edge of the modern game. Loughborough's reputation as a centre of excellence for other sports chimed with the ECB's vision of a culture of high achievement, and had helped them get the nod to host the site, which the ECB have on a 25-year lease. It was crucial that they quickly moved away from the Australian model by setting up their own camp, and the evolution of the building has been significant for English cricket. The intakes have varied down the years from genuine second-string players to promising youngsters – sometimes a mixture of the two. Playing experience overseas has remained a constant feature, either through training camps or tours under the guise of the National Academy side, England A or, more recently, the England Lions.

Peter Moores replaced Marsh in 2005, and his enthusiastic and forward-thinking approach was a real success. He moved away from players spending large periods of time on site, preferring shorter periods of high-intensity work and longer spells of rest. Moores's tenure was greeted with widespread approval; he is still highly regarded by those he worked with during his time at Loughborough. I was there in early 2009 on a wicketkeeping course when news of Moores's demise as England coach filtered through – and the place went into something akin to a state of mourning.

When David Parsons took over from Moores – the role is now called national performance director – his arrival completed an intriguing evolution, so far as the men at the helm are concerned: from Marsh, veteran of 96 Tests, via Moores, a long-serving county player without higher honours, to Parsons, who has no first-class experience.

But while it is easy to see why there has been some scepticism towards Parsons holding his current position, the role, depth and number of his support staff have grown significantly, making the impact of any shortcomings in experience negligible. There are now national lead coaches based at Loughborough for each of the game's technical disciplines. Bruce French (wicketkeeping), Graham Thorpe (batting), Kevin Shine (fast bowling), Richard Halsall (fielding) and Peter Such (spin bowling) direct their respective crafts; they are supplemented by other coaches from around the country, not to mention a host of experts operating under the umbrella of the ECB's sports science and medicine team.

The facility itself has undergone several changes of identity, and since the Schofield Report in 2007 it has been known as the National Cricket Performance Centre. According to the ECB, this better reflects the scope of activities at the centre which, while being a home for the full side when in the country, also houses a range of other national squads: male, female, disability and various age-group sides. Similarly, the Performance Programme Squad has replaced the Academy squad, and a greater range of players now falls under its umbrella as part of the overall Performance Programme.

I spent a night alone on a snow-topped mountain

Select parties of players continue to go on overseas training camps, be they batsmen working on technical skills on the subcontinent or fast bowlers improving their conditioning in Florida.

Morris highlights the broadening range of the Performance Programme: "Now we don't just focus on the best 12 or so England cricketers, but the best players in the country from 16 onwards. Therefore we can instil the right values about representing your country from an early age."

It is now a place where ideas are fostered, and forward thinking encouraged. High-tech equipment such as Hawk-Eye and the spin-bowling machine, Merlyn, have been there for several years, while the latest innovations – Trackman, for measuring the revolutions a spinner is putting on the ball, and the cutting-edge virtual-reality bowling machine ProBatter (see Cricket Equipment, page 164) – have each been developed and installed at the centre.

While these may grab press coverage, quirkier ideas are also tested, assessed, and then kept or discarded. Bruce French, for example, is trying to grow sections of turf on large wooden pallets. The aim is to replicate conditions found overseas – such as keeping wicket on the subcontinent with the ball bouncing out of five-day-old footmarks. "We'll bring India to Loughborough," he enthused, as some young spinners got the ball spitting out of the dusty slab of grass he had dragged on to a length. In another experiment, fielders, in so much padding that they resemble Michelin men, stand as close as they can to a bowling machine while balls whizz at them at high speed.

When I turned up for a course a few years back, I was surprised to see Jonny Wilkinson's place-kicking guru Dave Alred in the nets, working with some of the country's best young batsmen. And I was even more surprised to spend a night alone, wandering around a snow-topped mountain in the Peak District, as a means of improving my glovework. Some things work, some don't, but there's no harm in trying: after all, genius and madness are often the closest of neighbours.

But after myriad changes, tweaks and innovations, as well as a fair amount of money over the last ten years, the question remains: how successful has the National Academy/Performance Programme set-up been in making England a better international side? It is hard to answer.

Take that first squad, of which I was a part. Twelve of the 18 played for England: Simon Jones, Andrew Strauss, Ian Bell, Andrew Flintoff, Steve Harmison, Graeme Swann, Ryan Sidebottom, Owais Shah, Alex Tudor, Rob Key, Chris Tremlett and Chris Schofield. That's no surprise: when you select a group of the best young players and place them unequivocally on the selection radar, you would expect many to progress to higher honours. But the success of these players on joining the international ranks is telling: seven are now Ashes winners, while ten have made what can be considered a match-winning contribution (a century or five wickets) for the national side.

That's a fair success rate and, though it's impossible to gauge what impact, if any, the time spent at the Academy had on their achievements, it cannot be ignored. Wouldn't they have come through and played anyway? Possibly; in some cases certainly, but as the ECB mantra says it is about producing "England cricketers, rather than cricketers who play for England" – i.e. players who are successful for England and forge international careers rather than those who simply appear and disappear within a few games.

Nowadays players do seem more prepared and less daunted when stepping up to international cricket. If you include wicketkeeper Matt Prior, six of the eight batsmen on the 2010-11 Ashes tour made at least one score of over fifty on Test debut; four made centuries.

Of course the easing of that step up could be attributed to other factors that have influenced English cricket over the last ten years. Two-division first-class cricket has raised the intensity and standard of the domestic game, while the influx of Kolpak and EU-qualified players has also had a positive effect, reducing a large player pool and creating greater competition for places among home-grown talent. All are viable arguments, and all have helped develop the successful England sides of the past decade. The Performance Programme will always have its sceptics, and cricket has always been resistant to change, especially its old pros and former stars, who are often the most critical of new ideas.

It's true there are some cricketers who regressed during a spell at Loughborough. I have a good mate who spent a winter at the Academy after a stellar county season, only to return with a barely recognisable bowling action. He lost much of the next season trying to get back to what he had done before, and never sniffed higher honours again, though he has remained a force at domestic level. So was the gamble of changing his action worth it? You bet it was: it might have created a successful international bowler.

Leicestershire batsman Will Jefferson doesn't recall any extra pressure after a winter at the Academy, but highlights the difficulties in refocusing on county cricket after having your name associated with the international team: "It's difficult when you know you have been that close to selection [for England];

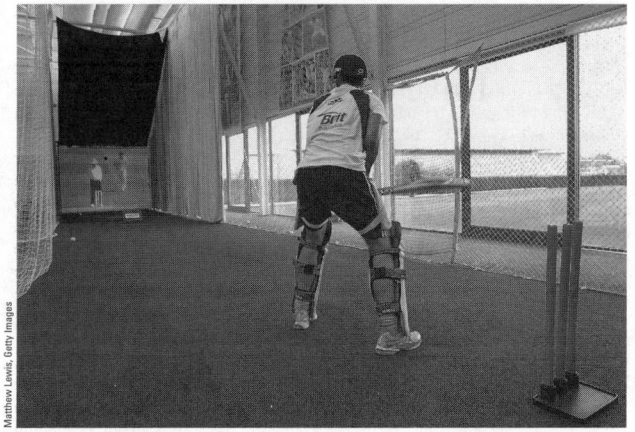

Matthew Lewis, Getty Images

Know thine enemy… Jade Dernbach faces Pro Batter at Loughborough in November 2010.

you have to learn to move on and redirect your focus back to the day job of scoring runs, which I haven't done, apart from one big season, due to injury and dips in form."

The winters I spent at the Academy were among the most enjoyable and rewarding periods of my career. I haven't played for England, and it's highly unlikely now that I will, but from the time I spent under Marsh's tutelage I believe the Academy has had a positive effect on the English game. Today's young players are the senior pros of tomorrow, and the core values of hard work and dedication instilled in me during those two years have stuck. Now, as a senior player, I believe those values will be passed through me to our next generation of cricketers. I'm sure this is the case round the counties, and also that the long-term impact of cultural change is an unseen benefit of the system.

Whichever way you view it, it's hard to escape the conclusion that the Performance Centre is a world-leading institution for the development and nurturing of cricketers. The resources and facilities are the best available, and as a result performance levels can only be enhanced. We may have started out by gleaning a thing or two from the Aussies, but now the rest of the world looks on in envy and realises that they have to do the catching up.

Mark Wallace became Glamorgan's youngest-ever wicketkeeper in the Championship when he made his debut, aged 17, in 1999. He was Glamorgan's vice-captain in 2010.

FOLLOWING THE ASHES FROM AFAR

Drive west, young man

CHARLIE CONNELLY

I knew immediately that I was out. It was a horrible delivery to receive first ball, landing on a perfect length and going straight on with the arm. My footwork had deserted me; I'd played all around it and felt the ball brush against my front leg before thudding into my back leg just below the knee. If the certainty of my internal cricketing GPS wasn't damning enough, the ball had then dropped to the ground and come to a gentle halt nestling against the base of my middle stump. I clamped my eyes shut, winced and waited for the appeal.

On the other side of the world England were on the point of clinching one of the greatest Ashes triumphs of all time, but here an attempt at my own piece of cricket history was falling apart. What had seemed a veritable monolith of a fabulous idea at home a few weeks earlier was now crumbling all around me in the unforgiving reality of the middle.

What made it even worse was that my girlfriend had never bowled a ball in her life before that one.

When the last wicket fell at the Sydney Test a few hours later to clinch England's thumping Ashes series victory, above the tumult and hullaballoo you may have heard a faint but audible metallic clang. It was the sound of two iron horses of British broadcasting, *Test Match Special* and the shipping forecast, coming together in a conflict that belied the gentle poetic dignity of their reputations. For the third time in the series England had clinched victory while the *TMS* Long Wave broadcast had paused for the shipping forecast. Once is unfortunate, twice unlucky, but three times is extraordinary.

The thing is I can't help feeling faintly responsible: for that day I was at one of the coastal weather stations mentioned in the broadcast – who knows, maybe the very coastal station being announced just as the wicket fell. Not only that, I'd been playing cricket there. Badly.

There had to be a connection. And I'm sorry.

Since moving to Ireland from England three years ago I've learned that inside the expat, no matter how happy he may be in his new land, there burns an unquenchable hankering for certain aspects of home. London to Dublin is not a massive displacement as these things go, but still I found the relative absence of cricket tugging far more imploringly at my subconscious than I'd expected. Having also once written a book about my lifelong love affair with the shipping forecast, I was missing that too.

Luckily I can still catch the latter via the internet, and for the former the Irish national team obligingly plays many of its matches at the end of my road in north Dublin, meaning I can get a relatively easy and thoroughly enjoyable live cricket fix.

As a result I have lost a significant portion of my cricketing heart to Ireland and its wonderful national team. However, years of immersion in English cricket and childhood summer memories of a windswept Peter West looking grimly into a rain-speckled camera while heavy grey clouds scudded over a covered Edgbaston behind him, are not usurped that easily. So with the winter Ashes series approaching, my first in Ireland and arguably the most important in decades, I was determined to follow it as closely as possible. But without access to Sky Sports at home, I faced a winter of long nights in front of the computer listening to *TMS*.

As midnight approached on the first day of the series I brewed a pot of coffee, sat in front of the computer, called up the BBC Five Live Sports Extra website, and thought back to childhood nights with a radio under my pillow listening to muffled crackly news of distant Test matches accompanied by curious whines, hisses, pops and the occasional intrusion of a burst of French.

I remember the foetal-position tension as Allan Border and Jeff Thomson added 70 for the last wicket in the Melbourne Ashes Test of 1982-83 before a bit of pat-a-cake in the slips between Chris Tavaré and Geoff Miller won the match for England by three runs. For all its faults, this low-fi quality somehow helped to underline just how far away the match really was and, if anything, enhanced the suspense and excitement. A cricket ball dropping towards the ground in Melbourne causing a 12-year-old to all but swallow an entire pillow on the other side of the world, well, it's exactly what Lord Reith had in mind when he talked about nation speaking peace unto nation.

It's different today, of course, with satellites whizzing around the upper atmosphere and crystal-clear streaming internet making it seem as though the game is taking place right outside the window (before long entire Test matches will be played via Skype with each team remaining in its own country, you mark my words). Hence, as the umpires walked out in Brisbane, my Dublin internet connection pulled on to the information superhighway and there, clear as day without so much as a crackle, the broadcast eased out of my computer's speakers.

"Sorry, but due to rights issues this transmission is not available in your territory."

Ah.

There were barely five minutes to go before the first ball and, where four years ago I'd been sitting in a London flat preparing to watch Steve Harmison ping the ball straight to second slip in pin-sharp colour and surround sound, here I was listening to someone talking repeatedly about rights issues and territories like some Victorian colonial diamond-mine magnate.

I acted quickly and, indeed, irresponsibly, digging out an email from a friend containing details of a dodgy-sounding piece of software, possibly of questionable legality, that could fool broadcasters into thinking that I was actually in their territory after all. I typed in my card details, mentally kissing goodbye to the entire contents of my bank account and bracing myself for a police helicopter appearing at my window with a loudhailer telling me to move slowly away from the internet keeping my hands where they could see them.

No one was more surprised than me when it worked, and within a couple of minutes the softly reassuring voices of the *TMS* team were drifting into a room dark save for the pool of light cast by my desk lamp. It turned out that I'd missed only a couple of deliveries, too. I pressed the plunger on the coffee pot, settled back into my chair and heard, "Hilfenhaus in, bowls to Strauss… and he's caught!"

It was going to be a long night.

So began a winter that settled into a reassuring nocturnal pattern of hearing the first five or six overs, then waking with a start a few hours later still sitting in my chair with dribble down my shirtfront and the first milky hint of dawn seeping around the curtains.

The reassuring rhythms of a Test series, especially such an engrossing one as this, provided much needed relief through the year's darkest months as Ireland fell further into economic ruin (I could barely get to my computer for all the nylons and chewing-gum I was stockpiling) and was brought to a complete standstill by snow and ice. Notwithstanding the fact I'd never expected to be roused from slumber by Jonathan Agnew talking softly into my ear, the night-time voices from the sun on the other side of the world provided glorious escape, and for once the England team didn't let me down.

As I drifted in and out of sleep, scores like 517 for one and 620 for five made it hard to tell if I was awake or dreaming. While being chased naked across the MCG by a warthog definitely *was* a dream (it was, wasn't it? Maybe I should check YouTube just in case), the news filtering back from Australia enriched beyond measure an Irish winter steeped in parsimony and gloom. Perth gave me a small dose of the horrors, fearing an Australian stampede through the rest of the series, but it took merely the first day at Melbourne when Australia were skittled out for 98 to convince me that this was indeed a momentous tour.

It was then that I thought there must be a better way of marking the events in Australia than these lonely nocturnal shifts feeling like the only cricket fan in Ireland. Which is when my other haven of expat nostalgia popped into my head: the shipping forecast.

I realised that for the duration of the Sydney Test I would be on Valentia Island at the very western fringe of Europe, just off the Atlantic-battered coast of County Kerry. I'd be visiting the Valentia weather station, permanent fixture in the late-night shipping forecast and a place about as far removed from the brouhaha of the Sydney Test as one can imagine. I'd been fretting about keeping up with the cricket in such a remote place: indeed, there was even a

chance that I'd have access to the exact barometric pressure reading over the SCG but not to the score.

Faced with the prospect of missing the climax of the series altogether, I had to come up with something cricket-related to occupy me out there, about as far west in Europe as one can be without making eye contact with the Statue of Liberty. And it was that very geographical realisation that gave me a solid gold winner of an idea.

I would mark England's retention of the Ashes by playing the westernmost cover-drive in the history of the European continent.

I checked the map. There was only a sliver of the Dingle peninsula protruding further west than Valentia; that and the remote Blasket Islands, whose hardy Irish-speaking population had been evacuated in the 1950s. I was pretty sure no cover-drives would have been played in either location. I found a cheap cricket set in a Dublin sports shop, threw it into the boot of the car and headed for the sunset.

Kerry has more of a cricketing heritage than you might think. Its county cricket club thrives today in Tralee, a club whose first recorded match was against a Valentia side in 1872. For a small, rocky, hilly island in the far south-west of Ireland it's remarkable that Valentia itself once boasted two clubs. The first transatlantic communications cable came ashore at this point in the mid-19th century, and a large number of workers were posted there, many from England. Valentia CC and the Anglo-American CC (named after the cable company) both played regularly through the 1860s and 1870s.

Not only that, there is a remarkable Kerry link to the Ashes themselves, as local cricket buff Gordon Revington told me. "Florence Morphy, the lady who presented the urn to the Hon. Ivo Bligh during the 1882-83 tour, was one of the girls believed to have actually burnt the bail or whatever it is that's in the urn," he said. "Her father was a John Morphy – who had emigrated to Australia from Killarney."

So with a Kerrywoman having apparently created the actual Ashes, not only was I marking England's retention of them by playing the continent's westernmost cover-drive, I was reinforcing the link between the county of Kerry and the little urn itself. Sort of. Either way, I felt very important.

It was a chilly, sunny, blustery morning when I struck out with my girlfriend for the western tip of Valentia. The winter sun stayed low in the sky and turned the choppy surface of the Atlantic to quicksilver. We were heading for an old abandoned signal tower a good two-mile uphill walk through the remotest part of the island at the end of its westernmost peninsula and, having given Jude a brief outline of the basics of the game over breakfast, I demonstrated my cricketing faith in her by allowing her to carry the gear all the way there.

The signal tower made the best possible location for this epoch-defining sporting encounter. It had been built on the flattest – or rather least undulating – part of the west end of Valentia, and best of all had a boundary wall, meaning that when I creamed Jude's bowling effortlessly through the covers the ball wouldn't end up bobbing about in the Atlantic breakers far below.

I found the flattest part of the courtyard, pushed the stumps into the ground, positioned the bails, handed the ball to Jude and gave her a brief and basic lesson in bowling. She nodded, pursed her lips in concentration and retreated to the far end of the makeshift pitch while I walked to the wicket.

It was years since I'd held a bat, more years than I cared to remember. I'd been a passably unspectacular player – in my early teens I'd once been caught by a young Alec Stewart, or "Micky Stewart's boy" as he was then – but a badly broken arm had put paid to my cricket some years ago. Yet as I stood there with the bat in my hand it was like I'd never stopped playing. Long-forgotten habits returned: squinting at the sky to adjust to the light and examining the pitch, with its rocks in the crease, three-foot slope falling away outside the corridor of uncertainty and pile of sheep droppings just back of a length.

> A sheep retreated
> from short leg to
> deeper midwicket

I surveyed the field. A sheep retreated from short leg to a deeper midwicket position. Behind me, out at sea, the island of Skellig Michael loomed up in the haze; there hadn't been a larger, less mobile presence in the slips since the retirement of Inzamam-ul-Haq.

I tapped the toe of the bat behind my right foot and looked up ready. All those years of summer weekends given over to playing for schools and clubs, all the net practices and coaching, the Test and county matches I'd followed, the books and magazines I'd devoured; now, at last, by playing Europe's westernmost cover-drive I was finally making my indelible mark on the game.

I bounced lightly on the balls of my feet in a way that belied the weight of history resting on my shoulders. It would be the first ball I'd faced in years. It would certainly be the first ball I'd faced from a bowler wearing a fur-trapper's hat and sunglasses. Jude windmilled her arms, released the ball and, well, you know what happened next.

I opened my eyes. There'd been no appeal. Jude stood there looking at me hopefully from the far end of the pitch. "Was that OK?" she asked.

She didn't know about lbw.

For a fleeting moment I considered keeping mum, or saying, "not bad for a first go," and throwing the ball back to her and urging her to pitch it up a bit. But for the honour of the game, the Ashes, the shipping forecast and Kerry cricket, I confessed that I was out. Palpably, irrefutably out.

That night, on the other side of the world, England won the Ashes right in the middle of the shipping forecast. The final wicket could have fallen just as the announcer said, "Valentia, east-north-east four, 24 miles, 999, now falling." It might even have been my fault somehow for bringing the game and the forecast together there on the western edge of Europe at such a pivotal moment Down Under.

One thing is certain, however. For as long as I live, no one will ever take away from me the honour of achieving the westernmost golden duck in the history of the European continent.

Charlie Connelly is the author of Attention All Shipping: A Journey Round the Shipping Forecast.

THE BIRTH OF THE COUNTY CHAMPIONSHIP

Adding some Glos?

DAVID FOOT

Abject frustration arrived for Somerset in triplicate last summer. They came agonisingly close to three titles, but in the end their aspirations were just too fragile. Their supporters were painfully reminded that this once pastoral and portly team cruelly finished as runners-up in all three competitions. As the final day's events emerged, the ashen, disbelieving inhabitants from the Quantock, Mendip and Blackdown terrains were left to gaze at the unseeing scoreboard. It had not been enough for Somerset to compile the same number of points as Nottinghamshire, who, crucially, had won one game more.

Most accept, of course, that the County Championship is the unchallenged pinnacle of our annual domestic cricketing achievement. Yet in earlier days, its status was disparaged by those who fiddled almost comically with juvenile attempts to give it overdue shape and a proper structure. Even at this distance, we cringe at the succession of proposals to invest the Championship with the importance and arithmetical logic that the public were beginning to expect.

Somerset, despite erstwhile rallying calls from their tetchy skipper Herbert "The Colonel" Hewett, and the more recent endeavours of Justin Langer and Marcus Trescothick, have never won the Championship. Nor have Northamptonshire. Nor, in the strictest sense, have Gloucestershire. It is an absurd omission. W. G. Grace was a mighty talent, feared by opponents who dared to question his autocracy and cowed by his intimidating hirsute presence. He was rightly dubbed "The Champion", but he was never quite seen officially at the summit of the Championship.

The absence of Gloucestershire from this hallowed roll of willowed honour is, it could be argued, a bureaucratic outrage. There was simply no formally established county competition to occupy W. G. and incorporate his all-powerful batting and bowling skills (not to mention his hypnotic human ones). For a long time he supplemented his finest seasons with little more than a pretence at full county rivalry, and played instead for MCC or the Gentlemen.

It is true that for some years county matches were recorded with an unreliable pen, and patently do not warrant retrospective recognition. Names were misspelt; statistics wavered. Victorian newspaper reports probably stood a better chance of publication if the wing-collared editor got invited to one of the cricket-orientated country-house parties.

W. G. and his fiery older brother, E. M., strongly disapproved – as they did about many aspects of cricket administration, not to mention the contentious matters of match and travel expenses – of how some of the leading counties found themselves challenging each other with minimal purpose or sense of genuine competitiveness. W. G. believed in proper games – and proper organisation to ensure players caught the right trains. He was angry when a

Gloucestershire in 1877. *Back row:* William Moberly, Walter Fairbanks, G. F. Grace, Francis Monkland, Walter Gilbert, Billy Midwinter, C. K. Pullin (*umpire*). *Front row:* Henry Kingscote, Frank Townsend, Robert Miles, W. G. Grace, E. M. Grace. Pullin was Gloucestershire's umpire, who stood in every game.

fixture needed a late change of venue or when the estate gardener hadn't made a decent job of mowing the lawn before the match. They never quite knew whom to blame. "Let's get this notion of a County Championship sorted out" was a recurrent theme.

After many false starts and a surfeit of petty squabbles, as administrators went through the motions of devising how best to distribute the points or determine the order of respective merits, "Championship cricket" was finally given some degree of rational operation. For a start, the teams needed to play the same number of games.

Take the measured words of the Rev. R. S. Holmes who, in 1897, in his book *The County Cricket Championship*, did his best – no straightforward job – to evaluate what was happening. He wrote with fervour that the Championship should be rigidly structured year by year: "The counties have hitherto given forth no pronouncement on this important matter. And the result is that the supremacy has been decided by the representatives of the press… Thus, from 1873 to 1886, the smallest number of lost matches decided the order of merit. An absurd and sometimes wholly unfair test."

He cited what happened in 1883. Nottinghamshire had four wins, one defeat and seven draws. By comparison, Yorkshire had nine wins, two defeats and five draws. "Yet, as Notts lost one match less than Yorkshire, they were placed first. In 1887, 1888 and 1889, another rule prevailed – a win counted one point, a draw half a point. From 1894, losses were deducted from wins. Drawn games were ignored altogether. At the end of 1894, MCC took the matter in hand and came up with a scheme for the better regulation of the county championship, of which the county clubs approved."

The biographer Ronald Mason, contributing to *Barclays World of Cricket*, confirmed 1873 as the year when the formerly haphazard method of inter-county matches was superseded by a competition "in recognisable form". Inevitably, some anomalies persisted. In 1874, for example, Derbyshire's case for top spot was ruled out because of their uncertain first-class status. Gloucestershire, generally accepted as the eventual leaders, had shared the symbolic title the previous year with Nottinghamshire, and they went on imperiously to illustrate their supremacy, or at least W. G.'s, in 1876 and 1877. This was the Age of Grace, and his monumental sense of monopoly has been endlessly and justifiably documented.

As long as a county game of sorts had been arranged, and a decent crowd had come to watch him mesmerise the sporting landscape, the game's politics didn't much bother the Champion. He rattled the score along, at times in spite of the most taxing of tracks, with his unrivalled technique. But he was well aware (and much in favour) of the privately convened meeting in December 1889, attended by representatives from eight counties, including Gloucestershire. Ironically, it was held on the day various county secretaries were sitting down at Lord's to juggle with the fixture list for the following season. The private meeting had a more pressing agenda: to put an end to the complacency, as some saw it, of how the counties' indeterminate programme was run. They agreed, with welcome signs of enthusiasm, to reject some of the more fanciful options. In future, they decided, they wanted to see one point for a win and one deducted for a defeat. There was nothing for a draw.

Here, it seemed, was positive progress and a real Championship on the way. Surrey were the first champions. County cricket had taken on much-needed purpose. Since then, Gloucestershire should have walked off with the title. They were, after all, runners-up in 1930, 1931, 1947, 1959, 1969 and 1986. Had there been any justice, they would have monopolised the title in those golden, unrecognised years of the 1870s. There just wasn't a trophy in sight.

THE AGE OF GRACE

1876	P	W	L	D	1877	P	W	L	D
Gloucestershire	8	5	0	3	Gloucestershire	8	7	0	1
Yorkshire	10	5	2	3	Kent	12	7	4	1
Lancashire	10	5	5	0	Surrey	12	6	3	3
Nottinghamshire	10	4	3	3	Lancashire	10	6	4	0
Kent	10	4	6	0	Derbyshire	8	5	2	1
Hampshire	4	3	1	0	Nottinghamshire	12	5	5	2
Sussex	8	3	4	1	Yorkshire	12	2	5	5
Derbyshire	6	2	4	0	Middlesex	6	0	4	2
Surrey	12	2	8	2*	Hampshire	4	0	4	0
Middlesex	6	1	1	4*	Sussex	8	0	7	1

* = includes one tie.

These unofficial tables are based on most wins.

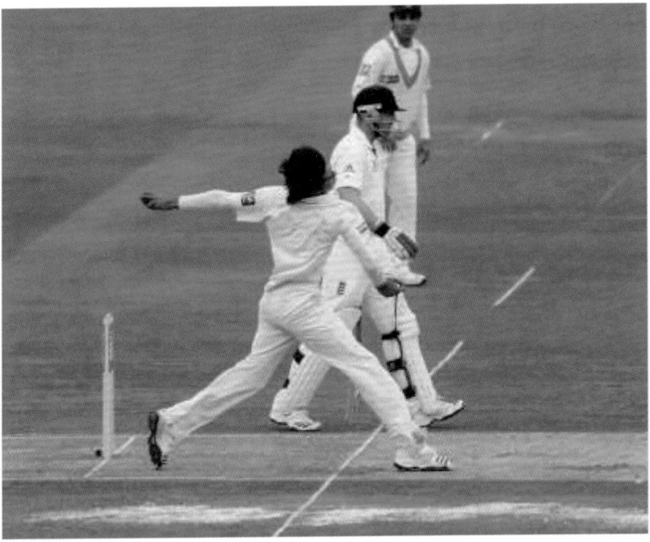

Kerry Davies, News of the World

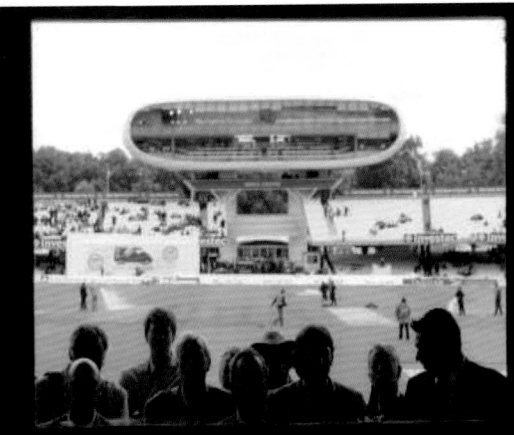

SINISTER PACE? In the Lord's Test against Pakistan, Salman Butt watches Mohammad Aamer bowl a no-ball, later alleged by the *News of the World* to have been deliberate. The end-of-series presentations were moved inside the Pavilion, but some MCC members were keen to get a glimpse.

Philip Brown

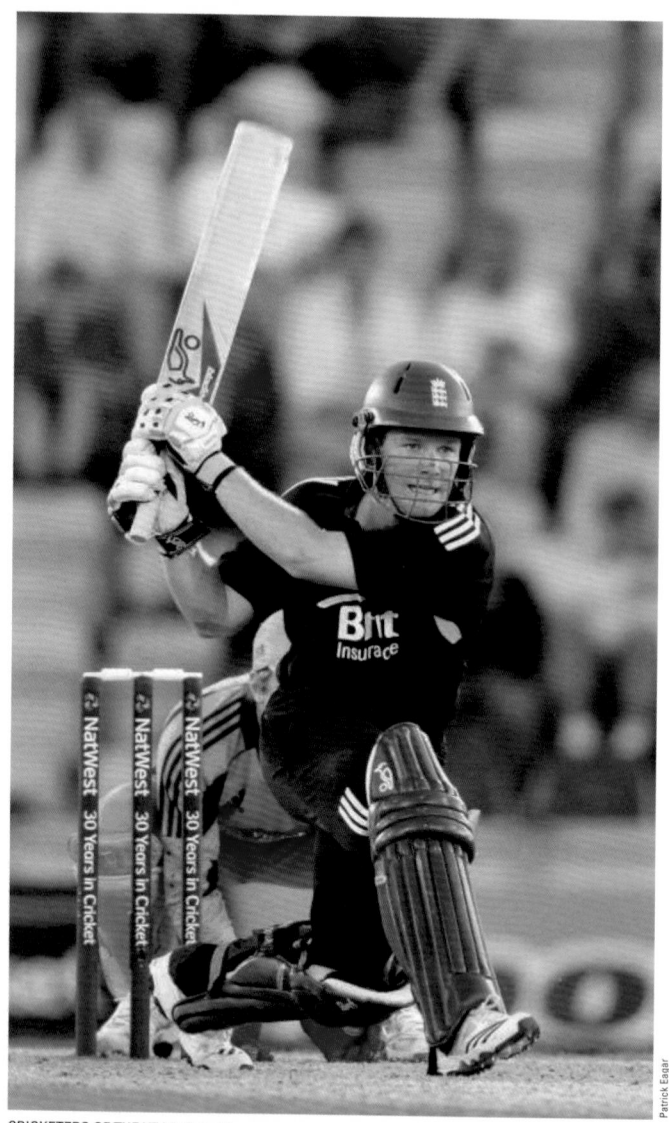

CRICKETERS OF THE YEAR: Eoin Morgan.

Patrick Eagar

CRICKETERS OF THE YEAR: Tamim Iqbal.

CRICKETERS OF THE YEAR: Chris Read.

Graham Morris

CRICKETERS OF THE YEAR: Jonathan Trott.

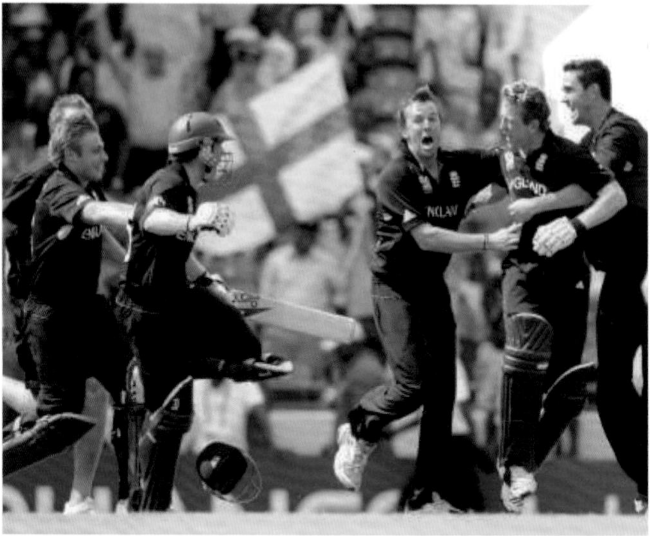

Philip Brown

BREAKING THEIR DUCK… Paul Collingwood is mobbed after hitting the winning runs in the final of the World Twenty20, to give England their first global trophy.

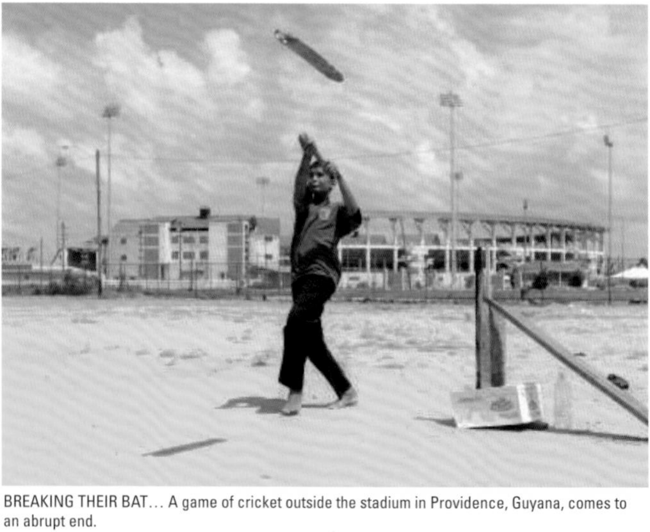

Philip Brown

BREAKING THEIR BAT… A game of cricket outside the stadium in Providence, Guyana, comes to an abrupt end.

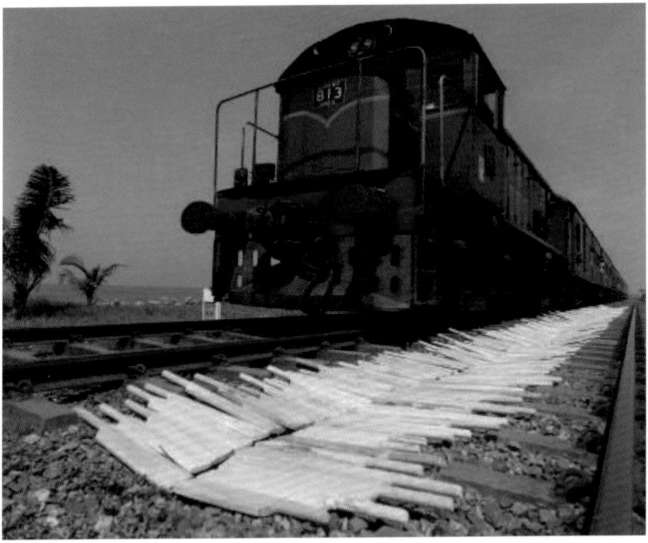

Andrew Caballero-Reynolds, Reuters

CRICKET MAD! The Indian subcontinent gears up for the tenth World Cup in early 2011… Batting displays in Sri Lanka included a railway line near Colombo and an elephant practising its technique. Meanwhile, Andrew Strauss takes part in the opening ceremony in Dhaka, Bangladesh.

Andrew Caballero-Reynolds, Reuters

Prakash Singh, AFP/Getty Images

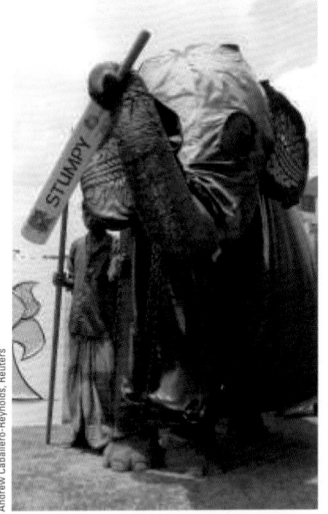

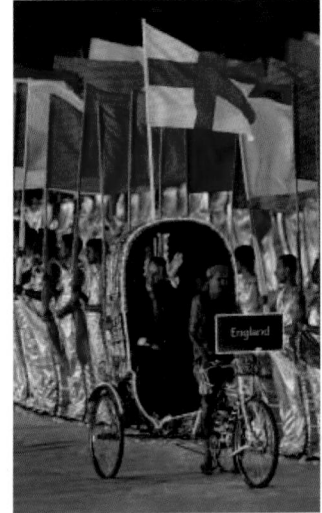

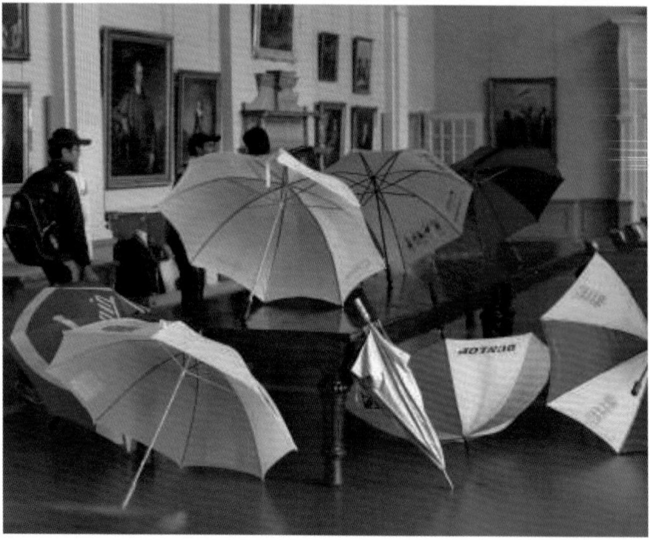

Graham Morris

FOR THE RAIN IT RAINETH EVERY DAY – from Lord's, the traditional home of cricket, to Pallekele outside Kandy in Sri Lanka.

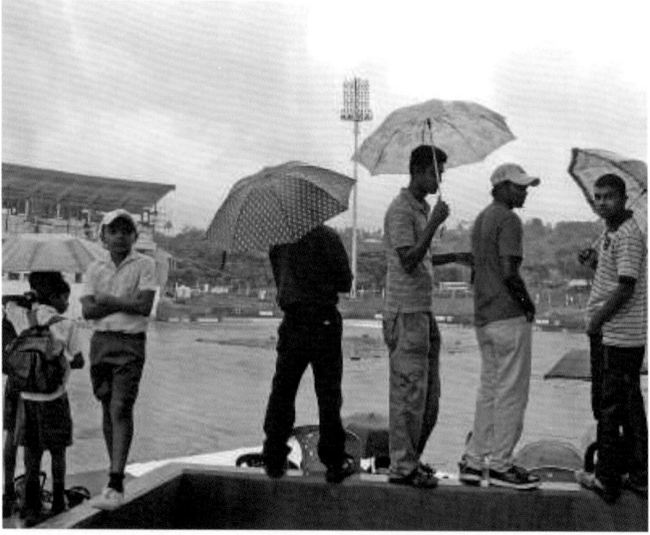

Lakruwan Wanniarachchi, AFP/Getty Images

THE NEW TWENTY20 SEASON

A midsummer night's cricket

TANYA ALDRED

The wind sprints across the dusty outfield at Grace Road. In front of the Fox Bar, dark-pink petunias, marigolds and roses grow in the dry earth while the ice-cream van and the sound system tussle for attention. Children try to deconstruct the dugouts, while upstairs in The Meet, home-made coffee-and-walnut cake with chunky icing sits alluringly. On the first floor of the pavilion, in the away dressing-room where the ceiling is splotched with yellowing patches of damp, Mick Newell, the Nottinghamshire manager, tap-tap-taps away on his computer.

Newell has been in charge of Notts since 2002, with some success. But they have never got their hands on the Twenty20 Cup. So during the winter of 2009-10 Newell worked on it – improving fielding, and drafting T20 specialists into the squad.

The competition has grown fat for 2010, from ten group games to 16 over a five-and-a-half week marathon, including three days in a row in mid-June. With 11 games gone, and eight won, Notts are happy. But they have never won a Twenty20 game at Grace Road.

Newell, disarmingly scruffy, is a combination of easy smiles, and frank: "We don't like Leicester, they don't like us – it's a Test match ground thing. They've got a number of ex-Notts players, and they use the small-club mentality to good effect. And they really went for Twenty20 from the start in a way that perhaps we didn't.

"The shortest form of the game is easier to win; it's like if I was playing Phil Taylor, I might beat him over one dart but no more than that. You don't have to be the most talented team to win, and it can still be taken away from you by the performance of one person."

The players start to arrive from the other side of the East Midlands. They have a quick team meeting and then it is out to warm up. They're not allowed phones, telly or computers in the dressing-room: concentration mustn't lapse.

On the outfield, cones and bibs and balls and the players' blue water bottles, individually identified with sticky labels, pile up. The warm-ups are fast and fun – a quick game of football, catching, stretches, quick-fire sprints around cones. The idea, says the physio Ross Hollinworth, is to prepare the body to be explosive and to prepare the mind for a fast game of cricket. Players are expected to think faster and throw harder.

Wayne Noon, who signed as a wicketkeeper in 1994 and became Newell's assistant in 2003, watches from the balcony, cradling a cup of tea. "The skills are sky-high compared to the first year, when I played. Then the players thought of Twenty20 as a beer match, but now for the younger guys it's the first thing. The bowlers used to bowl yorkers but the batters adapted, so slower

Before the flood: Alex Hales en route to 83; Gareth Cross keeps wicket for Lancashire.

Martin Rickett, PA Photos

balls, bouncers and slow long-hops are coming into it. But 16 games is too many. Our job is to do something pre-match to help mental fatigue."

Tiredness doesn't seem a problem today. A brilliant century from Leicester's Brad Hodge is not enough. Fifties from Matthew Wood and Ali Brown and a 60-yard direct-hit run-out from debutant Scott Elstone together bring victory with nine balls to spare. The team are delighted. They are also delighted with the food that arrives at the end of the game – pizza, samosas, sausage rolls, chicken and beer. Fitness coach Kevin Paxton rolls his eyes.

"It's not ideal," he says. "During the Twenty20 period last year we found that the lads were putting weight on. They were thinking they were doing a normal day's cricket and eating like that. This year we've made them do more strength and conditioning." Stomachs full, they jump into their cars for a two-and-a-half-hour drive to Essex, where an incongruous Championship match, slotted in between the 20-over fiesta, starts in the morning. Nottinghamshire lose, in three days.

Paul Franks, the old-hand all-rounder, is blunt. "We were underdone. In Twenty20 not many guys leave the ball, whereas in the first session of a Championship game, on a wicket which had a bit in it… with hindsight we should have left the ball more, and I think Essex would probably say the same. There is no excuse, but you're asking a lot of players to squeeze such a lot of games into a ridiculously short period of time and to play four-day Championship cricket as well.

"I think I've been quoted saying I'd play cricket every day if I could, and I've felt like that since I was a young boy, but there comes a time when the quality starts to suffer, and ours did at the back end of the Twenty20. You want to win every game, of course, but with one eye on qualifying there are times when you think 'Does it really matter if we lose today – we've got two home games next week.' And that's with us being successful. And I'm an enthusiast."

The dynamics of the Twenty20 mean that for almost six weeks, lifestyles can change. At Notts, players train between 10 and 12 in the morning and are then free, and for a home game they can come back just an hour and a half before the match. Suddenly there's some breathing space. For Newell that might be going out for coffee before the game and taking the kids to school; for Steven Mullaney a couple of leisurely sleeps in the afternoon; and for Ali Brown a chance to look at the day a bit differently, do a bit of range-hitting, have a swim, chill.

It can also give everyone a small escape – from each other. Franks sums it up: "When you live in everybody's pockets for the best part of seven months you can get cabin fever. As well as we all get on – and we do as well as any group I've ever played with – it's nice to get a break, to get back to reality. And for me it's a chance to do the everyday dad things."

By mid-July the team are travelling up to Old Trafford. The coach mooches at Trent Bridge while a couple of the players do a last minute Co-op run for some snacks, and leaves just before one. It is humid and gloomy on the M1. The bus resonates to crisps, rustling newspapers, laughing and chat. Some sleep; some listen to their iPods. An unofficial seating plan emerges. From the front: the scorer and his wife; then the support staff; the batsmen; young bowlers; and towards the back the older, louder, huger fast bowlers; David Hussey, the Twenty20 captain; and wicketkeeper and Championship captain, Chris Read. It's a happy club.

> You can squeeze T20 around your wife and kids

The young players love Twenty20. Luke Fletcher, a 21-year-old medium-fast BFG, enjoys the challenge. "In four-day cricket you bowl to your field, and the ball goes to your field; in Twenty20 it can go anywhere." For Graeme White, a left-arm spinner and chocoholic, 23, it is the excitement. "You never know what's going to happen. So many people come to watch it, it feels more like a football game. And it's a first foot in the door."

Dirk Nannes, the Australian fast bowler, is older, blunter and more ruthlessly practical. At 34, he has chosen to be a Twenty20 specialist. "If you play for three hours you can squeeze cricket in around your wife and kids. In the current financial climate – plus time, wear and tear on the body, and money – it's the way forward for me."

At Old Trafford, Andrew Flintoff, still recovering from injury and still hoping to resume his career, greets the Nottinghamshire players off the bus, shaking every hand.

They warm up by the looming building of the scarlet Point. The ground has barely a quorum of people. Lancashire make plenty of noise jogging around the ground, but Newell in his green Outlaws hoodie and hidden behind his sunglasses is confident – Lancashire are without Flintoff and Glen Chapple, while Ryan Sidebottom is back for Notts.

They have already qualified, but want a home quarter-final. The toss is won, and in the dressing-room, Newell's team talk is short and sweet: work the

It never rains but pours: David Hussey (*right*) and Kieron Pollard as Nottinghamshire's Twenty20 season is washed away.

angles in the middle of the innings, field as well as they did against Lancs at Trent Bridge. "Let's give this lot a second bashing – it would be a really good feeling for us." And out they go.

In the dugout, the atmosphere is relaxed. There is banter with the Lancashire players – Kyle Hogg, who had a loan spell with Notts a couple of summers ago, is getting married in October, and is ribbed gently for his haircut. They nobble the Chewits dragon who patrols the ground for more sweets. Alex Hales plays beautifully for 83, but after 20 overs biblical rain falls. In the dressing-room the rugby league comes on the telly. There is lots of pacing around. Noon entertains the troops by jumping on the physio's table and asking for a massage, Newell practises some shots, Sidebottom reads the programme. A couple of the players who have just come along for the experience sit quietly.

Then the umpires come in – they're back on at eight o'clock with a revised target of 81 off ten overs. Suddenly Newell, Sidebottom and Hussey talk tactics, jumpers are put on, flip-flops are removed, cups of tea are put down, the bell rings, and studs crunch down the pavilion steps.

The second ball is hit for six, and Lancashire are on top from then on, winning with ten balls to spare. Newell is phlegmatic. "We're lucky – it's the first rain-affected game of the year. Rain ruins the atmosphere. I really can't see the attraction of playing Twenty20 all season: it's a midsummer game." A couple of players have a pint in the members' bar and then it's back on the coach, and a late night home.

Nottinghamshire still get their home quarter-final, and beat Sussex. "It was amazing," says Mullaney, whose tight bowling and running catch won him the match award. "Such a buzz playing in front of that electric crowd."

Finals day at the Rose Bowl in mid-August isn't quite so successful. David Hussey and Samit Patel bat wonderfully in the second semi, until Somerset's Kieron Pollard takes a sensational catch on the boundary to dismiss Patel, and put Notts behind on Duckworth/Lewis. Then the rain falls. "The dressing-room afterwards was pretty quiet," says Brown. "But I went and found my children – you just can't be depressed then."

On the last Monday of the season, Newell is back at Old Trafford. The Championship race has gone down to the wire – with Notts, Yorkshire and Somerset all in with a chance. He looks dishevelled, and there is lots of head scratching as he reflects on the season.

"Although on balance 16 Twenty20 games is too many, and the crowds were down this year, it does act like a mid-season break. Because of where Nottingham is geographically, we only get one night away, in Durham, during the Twenty20, whereas during a season we'll have maybe 60. So the midseason has a different feel.

"It's very easy to enjoy Twenty20 when you're winning; then it seems like the best game in the world. But it's an instant thrill. It's not like a Championship game. Today I will be living it for all 14 hours till I go to bed and a win stays with you until the next game."

This game, it turns out, will live longer still. Late on the final afternoon, despite almost three days lost to the rain, Nottinghamshire reach 400 and then take the three Lancashire wickets they need. In autumnal sunshine, they win the Championship.

Read is ecstatic. He has got the one he wanted. For him, there is just no comparison. "From a player's point of view, Twenty20 can be an unfulfilling business – you can quite feasibly hit 20 runs off five balls and have done a job. For me, there's not the same satisfaction. You can go through a game and just take half a dozen takes and no dismissals. Four-day cricket makes cricketers what they are."

CANTERBURY WEEK

Fascinating! It's Ladies' Day

P ATRICK C OLLINS

This is an extract from the essay on a visit to Canterbury Week in Patrick Collins's new book Among the Fans, *due to be published in September 2011 by Wisden's new all-sports publishing imprint, Wisden Sports Writing. The aim of the imprint is to extend our long-standing commitment to the best cricket writing to a wider range of subjects: "Books I want to read," says the series editor, Matthew Engel.*

Canterbury divides cricketing opinion. Some see it as a place for people who are still coming to terms with the death of King Edward VII: a theme park for vaguely distracted gentlefolk, who find the sport engaging but would really rather be pacifying the North-West Frontier or civilising the dusty outback. Others are seduced by the understated grandeur of the setting: the quaintly decorous pavilion, the lush, encircling trees, the low, staid stands named after Kentish heroes – Woolley, Ames, Cowdrey. And, in Canterbury Week, the marquees, jostling shoulder to billowing shoulder about the sightscreen, gurgling with strong drink and humming with gossip and goodwill. And never more than on Ladies' Day.

It is best to arrive early, not merely to watch the watchers, but to test the validity of Tom Cartwright's theory. Cartwright dealt in swing and seam, but the late England bowler was also a wonderfully perceptive observer of the rhythms and rituals of the game he loved so well. He was a shy man with the soul of a poet, and this was how he approached the day: "If I go on to a ground in the morning, an hour before a game, it's the loveliest times… There may be a mower still ticking and the groundsman marking the ends, but there's a silence as well. You can stand and think and listen. You've got the birds singing, the craftsman working, the mower ticking, the smell of everything. That's something that makes cricket different from all the other games."

This, the second of the match, is a morning that Tom would have recognised, with sombre cloud to promote swing, and brief, flickering shafts of sunshine to encourage spectating. The cars begin to occupy the space beyond the boundary, moderate of pace and bumping gently across the grass. They ought to be Hillmans and Humbers, but are mostly Toyotas and Hondas, of exceptionally low mileage and carefully driven by considerate owners. One such owner unwinds himself from his vehicle, clutching his back and staring hopefully at the sky. He has been dressed by Central Casting, in blazer and regimental tie, Viyella shirt, stout brogues and trousers of that shade of red which only men of a certain age and rank can carry off. A panama hat might complete the picture. He reaches into the back seat, and pulls out a panama hat.

Kent CCC

Cricket and the shires: Ladies' Day at Canterbury.

As he salutes chums and passing acquaintances, his wife excavates the car boot. She brings out a small trestle table, two fold-up chairs, a flask of tea, two cups, two paper plates, a packet of shortbread biscuits, a carton of milk and copies of the *Daily Telegraph* and the *Daily Mail*. She pours the tea, adds the milk, distributes the biscuits and hands her husband the *Telegraph* while she retains the *Mail*. They sit in their chairs, sipping tea, and she smoothes down her sensible skirt, kicks off her sensible shoes and primps the collar of her sensibly cut jacket. It is only then that I notice the object on her head. It is small and feathery and its colour may well be cerise. It is, I am informed, a "fascinator", loosely defined as "a stylish, hand-crafted cocktail hat". By now, she too is nodding to friends, many of whom are wearing similar confections: bright, wispy, verging on the exotic. Just the thing for Ladies' Day.

The marquee guests are arriving. There are suited men, purposefully striding, and women tottering on precipitous heels, with hands clutching improbable hats. Tickets are offered, credentials examined. There are manly handshakes and fluttering air-kisses. Trays of drinks appear and bashful banter is exchanged.

"Swift sharpener?"

"Ooooh! Too early for me."

"Come on, just the one."

"Go on, then. Twist my arm."

Outside, a few yards away, the cricketers of Kent and Somerset are sprinting and stretching, darting and drilling in preparation for the day ahead. Their efforts go largely unnoticed in the marquees.

On the two "popular" sides of the ground, square of the wicket, Ladies' Day makes a more marginal impact. Here the audience is both overwhelmingly male and nearer 60 than 50. Many are tanned from countless days spent in the glare of the Kentish sun. They appear thoroughly knowledgeable about the game and the people who play it. A raffish few wear singlets, exposing patriotic tattoos. Some wear football shirts: Charlton Athletic, Gillingham, and one which puzzles me but turns out to be Real Zaragoza. The talk is of the old-timers, of Underwood, Denness, Leary, Woolmer. Every conversation touches on the nonpareil, Cowdrey. They do not forget the great ones in this corner of England. On the opening day of every Canterbury festival, a large and respectful group lays a wreath at the memorial to Colin Blythe, a left-arm spin bowler for Kent and England, who died at Passchendaele in November 1917. He was 38 years old, played in 19 Tests and took 100 wickets at a remarkable 18.63. His first-class career spanned 15 years, during which he took 2,503 wickets. He once took 17 in a single day at Northampton, and they say that he did it all with style and grace and rare humility. There is something curiously affecting in remembering such a man.

Meanwhile, the moderns are being analysed. A small, slightly nerdish, clique sits by the scoreboard, swapping anecdotes about the Kent team. Articulate men in late middle-age, they use the players' first names, coyly, self-consciously: "As Joe was saying… you know what Geraint's like… typical Rob, eh? Typical bloody Rob!" They make plans for next week, when they intend to watch a Kent Second Eleven match against the Universities at Cambridge. In the course of their conversation, one man is asked: "Coming on Saturday?" He shakes his head, regretfully. "I was hoping to," he says, "but we have a family wedding and the wife's put her foot down." I sense that the wedding in question might well be his daughter's.

"Bless you!" calls a Somerset fielder

The visitors, enjoying a vibrant season, have brought a fair smattering of followers. One young couple, part of a group down at deep extra cover, drove up from Taunton at six o'clock this morning. They covered the 200 miles in something over four hours, and they will make the return journey this evening. By motorcycle. The Somerset supporters mingle easily with the home fans, swapping details of decent pubs and reasonable restaurants. "It's nice and friendly, just the way football used to be," one of them tells me. I'm not sure that English football was ever so nice or so friendly.

After a prosperous first day, Somerset's innings ends this morning at 380. Kent then dwindle to a worrying 47 for three just before lunch, when Geraint Jones and Martin van Jaarsveld come together to confront the crisis. The ground falls quiet, an almost resigned silence. More than 30 years have passed since Kent last won the County Championship, and the tide shows no obvious signs of turning. Somebody sneezes loudly at the long-on boundary. "Bless you!" calls a Somerset fielder. Such is the silence that everybody hears the remark, and some giggle. A small number desert the Woolley Stand and make an early run for refreshment, hurrying across to the Bat & Ball pub on the Old Dover Road. There they stand and stare incuriously into their pints to the background blather of Sky Sports News. One man, with hands like hams, delicately picks out the lettuce and tomato from his cheese sandwich. They shrug off their disappointing morning, and speak of football.

Back at the ground, the announcer is urging us to welcome the band of the Parachute Regiment. They drift to and fro across the outfield, pumping out standards like "Soldiers of the Queen", "The Minstrel Boy" and, as a concession to modernity, "Puttin' on the Ritz", by Mr Irving Berlin. Toes are tapped, memories are jogged and there is spasmodic applause. As they troop away, the field is recolonised by a babble of small children with bats and balls. The announcer is ready for them: "We remind those on the outfield that you're very welcome to be out there, but NO hard balls are allowed," he barks. The words "health" and "safety" come spitting from every stand...

Patrick Collins is chief sports writer of the Mail on Sunday. *Among the Fans is a collection of sporting vignettes in which Collins captures the mood at events ranging from Crayford greyhound track to the Adelaide Oval.*

ALL-INDIA'S VISIT TO BRITAIN IN 1911

The most extraordinary cricket tour

PRASHANT KIDAMBI

On the morning of Saturday, May 6, 1911, a large crowd gathered at Bombay's Ballard Pier to see off a motley group of Indian men who were about to undertake a historic voyage. The people the crowd were cheering lustily that warm and sultry morning were members of the first Indian cricket team to tour the British Isles, and they made for an improbable cast of characters. The captain of the team was Maharajah Bhupindar Singh of Patiala, a flamboyant 19-year-old Sikh prince with an apparently insatiable appetite for the high life (his harem came to number more than 300). Accompanying him were cricketers from different regions and religions of the Indian subcontinent. Astonishingly, two of them – Palwankar Baloo and Palwankar Shivram – were from the lowly *chamaar* caste, deemed "untouchable" by upper-caste Hindus. Over the course of a momentous summer, in which they travelled to all parts of the British Isles, these men participated in what can justifiably claim to be the most extraordinary of all cricket tours.

The All-India tour of 1911 was not the first time that a group of Indians had travelled to Britain to test their cricketing mettle. That distinction goes to the Parsis of Bombay, who were the first Indian community to embrace the game. By 1877, cricket among the Parsis had made such rapid strides that even Bombay Gymkhana, the bastion of European social exclusivity, condescended to play a match against the Parsi Cricket Club. In the same year, Ardeshir Patel, a founding member of the club, tried to put together a team of Parsis to tour England the following summer. Patel's attempt failed, not least because of internal divisions within the Parsi CC regarding the venture. Famously, the matter ended up in court with a libel case involving Patel and his principal antagonist, K. N. Kabraji, the irascible editor of *Rast Goftar*, a local Gujarati newspaper, who also happened to be the president of the Parsi CC.

Undeterred by this setback, the promoters of the aborted scheme redoubled their efforts to send a Parsi team to England, and finally succeeded nine years later. The pioneering Parsi tour of 1886 was a failure, both in sporting and in financial terms. Two years later, a second Parsi team made the journey to England, under the captaincy of P. D. Kanga, and was somewhat more successful.

Nor was the 1911 tour the first attempt to send a representative Indian team to England. Eight years earlier, cricket enthusiasts in Bombay had embarked on precisely such a venture, following the visit of the Oxford University Authentics, a team of amateur cricketers who travelled all over the subcontinent playing both European and Indian teams. According to J. M. Framji Patel, an influential figure in Bombay cricket and author of the first history of Indian cricket, "The vivifying effect produced on the Indian cricket world by the visit

In Ranji's footsteps: Homi Kanga leads out the Indian team for the first day's play v Sussex at Hove.

of the Authentics and the easy victory of the Parsi team over the visitors, resulted in a revival of the idea of sending an Indian Team to England." It was Patel himself who led the way, organising a meeting of prominent Parsi, Hindu and Muslim members of Bombay's cricketing fraternity in February 1903. But although matters initially appeared to progress well, the organising committee eventually called off the tour on the grounds that it was financially unviable and that they had been unable to put together a squad that was "perfectly representative of Indian cricket". The decision was strongly criticised in the local press, with some newspapers accusing Patel and his Parsi associates of deliberately scuppering the scheme.

It is therefore ironic that when the idea of sending an Indian team to England was seriously pursued six years later, it was Framji Patel who was once again the prime mover. In the autumn of 1909, Patel sounded out prominent patrons of the game in colonial India about the possibility of resuscitating the project. Encouraged by their positive response, he quickly set about forming a tour committee, whose membership reflected Bombay's famed cosmopolitanism.

At the first meeting of the committee, held at the offices of Ratan Tata, one of India's wealthiest merchant princes, Framji Patel outlined the political rationale that lay behind this initiative:

> Gentlemen – I am a firm believer in the educational and political advantages of such a tour because cricket has an Imperial side to it… Cricket, in the end, will kill racial antagonism. Let us try our best to send the friendly cricketing mission to the old country which is the chosen home of the king of games, and thus strengthen at the present juncture the bonds of union that always ought to exist between England and India. There are many links that bind us together as citizens of the greatest Empire the world has ever seen, and among those the Imperial game of cricket is not the least.

In dwelling on the imperial bond, Framji Patel was echoing the opinion of those supporters of the Indo-British relationship who viewed with concern the deepening antagonism between the Raj and the representatives of Indian nationalism. It is not surprising, therefore, that Patel's scheme received the wholehearted support of the Governor of Bombay, Sir George Clarke, who believed that the proposed Indian tour to England "would be most beneficial" when the previously "happy relations" between Indians and Englishmen were "in danger of being overlooked". At the same time, the idea also elicited the support of those who believed that cricket could serve as a unifying force among the various communities of India. "In an eleven consisting of Hindus, Parsis and Moslems," noted "A Native Thinker", "each one will instinctively feel that he is an Indian first, and a member of his own race afterwards".

The Indian Cricket Team for England Committee launched a vigorous fund-raising campaign to secure financial support for the tour. Their efforts met with immediate success and, by the summer of 1910, more than 53,000 rupees had been collected. Among the principal donors were the ruling princes of Patiala, Baroda, Mysore, Natore, Cooch Behar, and Bikaner, as well as the Aga Khan and Bombay's biggest merchant princes, most notably Sir Dorab Tata. Contributions to the guarantee fund were also forthcoming from some European officials, including the Governor of Bombay.

The fate of the tour also depended crucially on the attitude of MCC. In November 1909, the MCC committee wrote to Patel offering their support for the proposed tour and guaranteed the Indian tourists £200 for their match at Lord's. But they also asked the tour organisers to consider sending the Indian team in the summer of 1911 rather than 1912, since the triangular series between England, Australia and South Africa had already been scheduled for then. Framji Patel and the organising committee quickly accepted the suggestion. In a subsequent letter to Patel, Francis Lacey, the MCC secretary, declared the visit would "do much to remove prejudices and promote friendship" and assured him that "everyone with Imperial views… will cordially welcome the All India team in England".

Apart from the financial requirements of the tour, the other major issue facing its Indian organisers was team selection. To carry out the delicate task of picking a representative team, the organisers constituted a seven-member selection committee. It was entirely in keeping with the political culture of colonial India that this committee was presided over by a European: Major John Glennie ("Jungly") Greig, a fine Hampshire batsman who in his heyday was the most prolific European run-scorer in the subcontinent. The other six members of the committee were nominated with a view to balancing the interests of the different Indian communities: J. M. Framji Patel and Dr M. E. Pavri (Parsis); C. V. Mehta and V. J. Naik (Hindus); and Ibrahim Rahimtulla and Ameeruddin Tyabji (Muslims).

At the outset, the selection committee wrote to 30 prominent Indian cricketers to ask if they would be willing to tour. Framji Patel also approached Ranjitsinhji – by now the Jam Saheb of Nawanagar – in the hope that he would agree to lead the team. But notwithstanding rumours to the contrary, it soon became apparent that Ranji had no intention of participating in the tour. Nor should this have come as a surprise: the elusive Ranji had made it amply clear in his pronouncements that he did not regard himself as an *Indian* cricketer.

The organisers also decided to hire a coach to help identify the best players and train those who were finally chosen for the tour. The job was entrusted to John Alexander Cuffe, an Australian-born professional cricketer who played for Worcestershire. Cuffe arrived in Bombay in November 1910 and stayed on until shortly before the team's departure for England. Under his watchful eye, a series of trial matches was organised in order to evaluate the form of the players under consideration.

The final selection meeting took place in Bombay on March 1, 1911. Easily the most colourful character in the team was its captain: the sturdy, dark-eyed Farzand-i-Khas-i-Daulat-i-Inglishia, Mansur-i-Zaman, Amir-ul-Umara, Maharajadhiraja Rajeshwar, Sri Maharaja-i-Rajgan Bhupindar Singh, Mahindar Bahadur of Patiala. The rulers of Patiala, a state the size of Yorkshire, had been loyal allies of the British in India ever since they had helped quell the great uprising of 1857. But their personal conduct had often been a source of anxiety and irritation for the colonial government. In the 1890s, British officials in the Punjab were particularly vexed by the antics of Maharajah Rajender Singh – Bhupindar's father – who became notorious for his unbridled pursuit of wine and (European) women. Rajender's excesses resulted in his untimely demise in November 1900, and thrust his nine-year-old heir into the political limelight.

In October 1909, shortly after his 18th birthday, Bhupindar was granted full ruling powers by the colonial

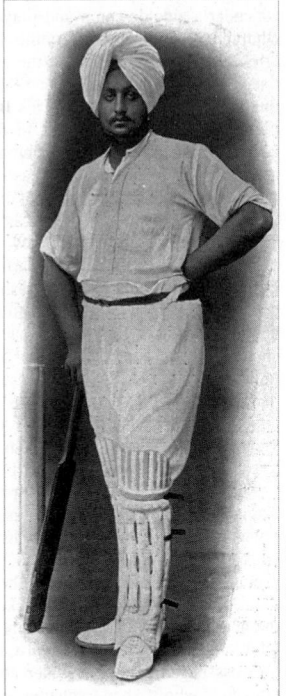

Bhupindar Singh, Maharajah of Patiala.

Bob Thomas, Popperfoto/Getty Images

government. But he got off to a rocky start with the British political establishment stationed at his court. A steady stream of reports from the British officials at Patiala repeatedly warned that the new ruler, egged on by undesirable companions, was going the way of his father in adopting an increasingly bibulous and debauched lifestyle. Official concerns about Bhupindar's reckless escapades became so acute that the colonial authorities even considered cancelling his formal investiture ceremony, which was scheduled to take place in Patiala in November 1910. In the event, the ceremony went ahead only because the Viceroy, Lord Minto, had a soft spot for the young prince.

But Bhupindar also shared one, rather more commendable, trait with his father. Rajendar Singh had been a major patron of sport, especially cricket. During his rule Patiala possessed one of the finest cricket teams in colonial India, which included in its ranks well-known English professionals such as William Brockwell and Jack Hearne. Indeed, even Ranji had served briefly as Rajendar's aide-de-camp and played for his cricket team in the late 1890s. Bhupindar continued this tradition of patronage and was himself a keen cricketer. His enthusiasm for the game has even led some writers to assume that he was the moving spirit behind the 1911 tour. However, Bhupindar's ongoing power struggle with his British minders precluded him from taking more than a cursory interest in the venture. And while he was quick to contribute financially, his participation in the tour was by no means certain until very late in the day. The reason is that the colonial authorities were rather unenthusiastic about the prospect of the Maharajah travelling to England at the time of the coronation of King George V, due to take place in the summer of 1911, to which only a select few Indian princes were being invited. Some officials regarded Bhupindar's participation in the cricket tour as a clever ruse, designed to enable him to gatecrash the event.

Bhupindar Singh's elevation to the captaincy was symptomatic of an era when it was taken for granted that the Indian princes were natural leaders of society. But in another way the composition of the Indian team was quite radical for its time. For, in choosing Baloo and Shivram, the selectors had included in the team two players from an untouchable caste that had long experienced the most degrading forms of social exclusion. The singularity of their selection can be gauged from the fact that more than half a century was to pass before an untouchable, or Dalit, cricketer next played for India.

The story of Baloo – the "first great Indian cricketer" as the historian Ramachandra Guha has argued – is quite remarkable. Born in July 1875, in the town of Dharwad (in present-day Karnataka), Baloo learnt his cricket in Poona, where his father was employed in the army. Hired as a member of the groundstaff at the Poona Club, the principal European watering hole in the town, Baloo commenced his cricketing career by bowling to its members in the nets. It was in this manner that he came to the attention of Jungly Greig, who spent hours batting against his left-arm spin. Soon, though, Baloo's prowess began to attract wider attention, not least that of the local Hindu cricketers who wished to challenge the Poona Club. But at first Baloo's low-caste status was a deterrent, with the Poona Brahmins being especially averse to his inclusion in the team. The ensuing controversy was fuelled by Greig, who publicly questioned the judgment of those who wished to exclude Baloo on account of his caste.

In the late 1890s, Baloo moved from Poona to Bombay, where he played for two teams, the Bombay Berar and Central Indian Railway Company, who offered him employment, and the P. J. Hindu Gymkhana, the most prominent Hindu club. He was a prolific wicket-taker who reserved his best for when he was up against European sides. As the premier slow bowler of his day, Baloo was thus an automatic choice for the 1911 tour. However, his younger brother Shivram, a talented batsman, joined the team only the day before the Indian cricketers were due to depart for England, when Noor Elahi and Manek Chand, both in the service of the Maharajah of Kashmir, pulled out, apparently because their whimsical employer declared that he "could not spare them". The desperate selectors turned to Shivram, their first-choice reserve, who thus made the voyage along with his brother, and went on to become one of the success stories of the tour.

While Bhupindar and the Palwankar brothers came from opposite ends of the traditional social hierarchy, the other team members belonged to the emergent urban middle class. Here, it was the Parsis, with seven players in the squad, who were preponderant. Of the Parsi cricketers, the most accomplished was Major Kekhashru ("Keki") Manekshaw Mistry, an aggressive left-handed batsman, dubbed "the Clem Hill of India". Mistry, who first shot to prominence in the Parsi–Presidency matches of the 1890s, had been enticed to Patiala by Rajendar Singh. After Rajendar's death, he was appointed as Bhupindar's guardian and soon came to earn the boy's trust. When Bhupindar finally took charge of his state, Mistry became his private secretary, and was one of the few members of the prince's inner circle of whom the British political establishment approved. Another Parsi player with a connection to a princely state was Manekji Pallonji Bajana, who was employed by the Maharajah of Cooch Behar and travelled to England as part of his entourage in the spring of 1911. After the conclusion of the Indian tour, Bajana was recruited by Somerset, against whom he had scored a century. "Pyjamas", as he came to be known at Taunton, was a square-shouldered figure who looked more like a *pailwan* (wrestler) than a typical Parsi.

Most of the other Parsi players who were selected for the tour made a living in Bombay: Homi Kanga, who had returned to India in 1910 after completing his medical studies in England, was a doctor; Hormusji Mulla, an articled clerk in a prominent firm of solicitors; and Jehangir Warden, a teacher of French at one of its elite schools. We do not know Rustom Meherhomji's occupation, but he too was a Bombay man, who played for the city's famous Baronet CC and was popularly known as "the Lionel Palairet of the Parsis". The exception here was the 34-year-old Maneksha Bulsara – supposedly the only "swerve bowler" in India at this time – who had been born in Daman, a Portuguese-controlled territory, and was a resident of Delhi.

Of the three Hindu middle-class men in the team, the 39-year-old "Bangalore" Jayaram was the most experienced. In 1891, while a student at the city's Central College, Jayaram had played an innings of 185 against the Yorkshire Regiment and soon acquired the reputation of being about the best batsman in Southern India, who never played any bowler from behind the batting crease. But by 1911, the ageing Bangalore man was not the formidable player he had once been.

The other South Indian Brahmin in the side, 34-year-old Kilvidi Seshachari from Madras, was easily the best stumper in India. "He is both quick and neat at the same time," remarked one contemporary, "and what he does he does with pluck, determination and skill." Mukundrao Pai, the youngest of the Hindu players, was also a Brahmin, but from Bombay, where he was employed as a manager in the offices of E. D. Sassoon and Co.

Kent v All-India, July 3–4, 1911. *Standing:* H. G. Day (*umpire*), Kilvidi Seshachari, Colin Blythe, Syed Hassan, Arthur Snowden, Maneksha Bulsara, Frank Woolley, Rustom Meherhomji, Palwankar Shivram, Walter Hearne, Salamuddin Khan, Arthur Fielder, Bill Fairservice, Manekji Bajana, Mukundrao Pai, J. B. Murrin (*umpire*). *Seated:* Tom Pawley, Fred Huish, Palwankar Baloo, W. G. Grace, Homi Kanga, Lord Harris, Edward Dillon, J. M. Divecha (*manager*), Lionel Troughton, Jehangir Warden. *On the ground:* Wally Hardinge, Shafqat Hussein, Henry Preston, Edward Humphreys, Hormusji Mulla.

Interestingly, none of these Hindu players appears to have been deterred by the stricture of travelling across the sea without losing caste. Indeed, two of them had previously been to England. Jayaram went to London for higher studies in the early 1900s and, apparently at the invitation of W. G. Grace, had even played for London County; Seshachari was an alumnus of Dulwich College. In the absence of evidence, one can only speculate about the extent to which the three Brahmins, who had a high regard for Baloo the cricketer, interacted with him off the field during the 1911 tour.

Unlike their Hindu team-mates, the Muslim players – Salamuddin Khan (a Pathan from the Jalandhar district in the Punjab), Syed Hassan (from Moradabad) and the one-eyed Shafqat Hussein (from Meerut) – were all students at the Muhammadan Anglo-Oriental College in Aligarh, which had been founded in 1875 by Sir Syed Ahmed Khan, a modernist Muslim reformer. One observer noted of the Aligarh trio that they were "the youngest members of the party, learned and cultured, with an astounding knowledge of British politics... They are new to travel, but are keen on seeing and knowing everything so that they may be of use when they return."

After a trying two-week voyage, the Indian cricketers disembarked at Marseilles and covered the last leg of their journey to London by train. They arrived in an imperial metropolis gearing up for the coronation and swarming with awe-struck visitors from all corners of the globe. Yet even amid the immense bustle, the Indian cricketers did not go unnoticed. Attention centred, in particular, on the 19-year-old captain of the team, who stepped off his de luxe train at Charing Cross, accompanied by his private suite. "His Highness's gorgeous costume of rich flowered silk of bright hue," reported the *Daily Express*, "attracted much attention as he strode down the platform wearing about his neck a garland of roses." While the Maharajah and his entourage proceeded to a fine house on Addison Road that had been rented for his use, the rest of the team made their way from Victoria Station – they had arrived on an ordinary train – to the Imperial Hotel in Russell Square.

The Indians got down to business straightaway with a net session at Lord's, watched by an interested crowd of journalists, photographers and groundstaff. "From what little I have seen of the Indians at practice at Lord's," reported "Old Shako" in the *Daily News*, "I should say they will interest the British public better than any of our county sides – win or lose." But there were two notable absentees at the nets: Bhupindar Singh and his secretary, Keki Mistry. Both also missed the first practice match of the tour against Hampstead (for whom Homi Kanga had played during his time in London). "Clearly cricket is not His Highness's sole objective on this trip," remarked E. H. D. Sewell, "or something would have been done ere this to try to get used to the light and strange surroundings."

This set the tone for the rest of Bhupindar's time in England. After a fortnight in which he played three matches – against Oxford, Cambridge and MCC – the Maharajah took no further part in the tour. Handing over to Homi Kanga, Bhupindar spent his time attending the various coronation-related events and parties that were such a conspicuous feature of elite London life that sizzling summer. The splendidly attired prince was "everywhere given a prominent position", his dazzling jewellery the subject of much comment.

The young Maharajah's constant socialising during this tour has commonly been attributed to an innately princely penchant for partying. But this simplistic interpretation glosses over the political considerations that drove him. Arguably, Bhupindar attended these soirées, which brought together the crème de la crème of British high society, to cultivate powerful new friends and supporters.

This was a pressing imperative at a time when he was being harried in India by colonial officials keen to clip his wings. Bhupindar was also quick to use his position as captain of the Indian cricket team in forging personal connections at the highest levels. He was granted a private audience with the new King-Emperor himself, who "showed great interest in the team and the tour" and invited him to lunch in the royal pavilion at Ascot.

For their part, the colonial establishment kept a close watch on the Patiala prince. As soon as Bhupindar arrived in England, he was met by Sir James Dunlop-Smith, Political Aide-de-Camp to the Secretary of State for India, and an old Punjab hand. Dunlop-Smith, who as the first political agent at Patiala had known Bhupindar since he was born, told him with perfect frankness

Palwankar Baloo.

about the gravity of his situation and "how anxious the authorities were regarding himself and his future". He also informed Bhupindar that a special political officer had been appointed for the duration of his visit, to act "not as a spy… but as a friend and helper". But it soon became quite clear to Bhupindar that he was being kept under strict surveillance. This had the intended effect, and Dunlop-Smith later reported with satisfaction that Bhupindar's general conduct during his stay in England was excellent.

There was, however, one moment of high drama involving the Maharajah. In early July, as the dust began to settle over the coronation celebrations, Bhupindar proceeded to have a long-delayed operation on his troublesome adenoids. The doctor who attended on him noted that "it was as bad an operation of the kind as he had ever done". Shortly thereafter the prince suffered a violent, life-threatening haemorrhage. Miraculously, Bhupindar survived and proceeded to Harrogate to recuperate.

His team could also have been said to be haemorrhaging. The Indian cricketers' tour had got off to a miserable start with 11 successive losses. Admittedly, most of these defeats were against the strongest first-class teams in England. One failure, against Minor County Staffordshire at Stoke in late June, was due to running into the great Sydney Barnes, who skittled the Indians for 74 and 57, taking 14 wickets for 29 runs. It did not help that Mistry's duties as Bhupindar's private secretary resulted in his withdrawal from the tour, thereby depriving the Indian team of their best batsman.

As the defeats piled up, the critics became increasingly uncharitable. "The plain truth must now be told that the rupees spent on giving these estimable Indian gentlemen a sight of the Coronation, and of the pavilions of the United Kingdom, would have been much better spent in having a good English team out to India," declared one cricket reporter. Some even questioned the wisdom of bestowing first-class status on some matches involving the Indians, asserting that "our visitors… would scarcely hold their own against the Minor Counties".

Rumours also began to circulate about dissensions within the team. One report alleged the Parsi bowlers had refused to bowl to a Hindu batsman in the nets. Another claimed that catches had been deliberately floored because of sectarian friction within the team. E. H. D. Sewell's reports to the *Times of India* lent further credence to these rumours. Sewell hinted darkly about the presence of a Parsi clique biased against the Hindu players, citing as clinching proof the frequent exclusion of Jayaram and Pai from key matches.

However, in mid-July, just when their supporters had all but given up, the tourists confounded expectations by successively beating Leicestershire and Somerset, both first-class teams. From this point on, there was a marked improvement in their collective performance. Significantly, it was the Palwankar brothers who spearheaded the Indian resurgence – Shivram hit a hundred against Somerset – backed up by important contributions from Salamuddin, Kanga, Meherhomji and Bajana.

The Indians went on to play three matches in Scotland. "They all seem dead sick of cricket," reported one Scottish cricketer who played against them at Galashiels. Socially, however, this leg of the Indians' tour was an unqualified success, and they were feted wherever they went. The Inverness town council hosted a dinner in the team's honour, while A. T. Bell, the whisky magnate, "spared no pains to make the visitors feel at home and to show the beauties of Loch Rannoch where he took some of them in his car".

From Scotland, the Indians crossed the Irish Sea to beat the Northern Cricket Union in Belfast by an innings and 233 runs. The game was notable for two individual achievements: Meherhomji completed 1,000 runs in all matches, while Baloo claimed his 100th wicket of the summer. Incredibly, Baloo, who often had to open the bowling, had accomplished this feat despite a painful shoulder injury that had progressively worsened. In first-class matches he eventually finished with 75 wickets at 20 runs apiece, a fine record in a dry summer, and was 25th in the national averages.

In late August, the Indian cricketers returned to England and played the final two fixtures of the tour: a defeat by Sussex – Ranji's old team – at Brighton, and a draw against Gloucestershire at Bristol. Once again, the Indian bowlers

---

ALL-INDIA TOUR RESULTS

	Played	Won	Lost	Drawn
First-class matches	14	2	10	2
Total matches	23	6	15	2

The leading first-class run-scorers for the tourists were R. P. Meherhomji (684 at 24.42), B. P. Shivram (631 at 28.68) and H. D. Kanga (617 at 28.04). The leading first-class wicket-takers were B. P. Baloo (75 at 20.12), J. S. Warden (44 at 25.59) and Salamuddin Khan (32 at 32.81)

acquitted themselves creditably, but the batting and fielding let the side down. An interesting feature of these matches was the reappearance in the Indian team of Prince Sivaji Rao, the Oxford-educated scion of the Gaekwad dynasty of Baroda, who had played both for and against them earlier in the summer.

Soon thereafter the Indians were homeward bound. Prior to their departure Homi Kanga and Jijibhai Divecha wrote to *The Times*, thanking all those who had hosted them "for the warm welcome and cordial treatment they uniformly extended to us" and reiterating that their tour was not motivated by "any spirit of rivalry or competition on equal terms".

The cricketers arrived back in Bombay to a sympathetic reception in the local press. "Our national cricket team has returned from England with the confession that it had to learn much and teach little," admitted the *Indian Spectator*, but advised its readers to forget the early defeats, and congratulate the team on its later triumphs. "They have, moreover," added the *Hindi Punch*, "established good fellowship all round. They have been on freedom's soil where caste is powerless."

The tour had indeed shown that Indians of different communities could play alongside each other, and thereby inaugurated a new idea of India on the sporting field. As Pelham Warner was quick to recognise, the "travelling and living together of natives of various castes and creeds will have far-reaching effect in India". The splendid performance of the Palwankar brothers was no less politically significant. Baloo, in particular, became a hero and inspiration to countless untouchables. It was in recognition of this fact that the Depressed Classes Mission felicitated the bowler at a public function in Bombay; notably, the welcome address in Baloo's honour was presented by the young Bhimrao Ambedkar, who went on to become the greatest of all lower-caste politicians and reformers.

The summer of 2011, when an Indian cricket team will once again be seen on the playing fields of England, marks the centenary of this long-forgotten All-India tour. In the intervening century, England has yielded its place to India as the centre of world cricket. With power has come a new self-assertiveness, and it is hard to imagine the players of today's Team India being deferential, like the All-India cricketers, towards their opponents. Equally, one doubts whether the members of Team India would even contemplate going on a tour that brought them no pecuniary benefits, as was the case with the All-India side. Yet for all that, there are significant continuities between 1911 and 2011. In mirroring the country's social diversity, the All-India tour started a tradition that endures: now, as then, the national cricket team comprises players from different communities and regions, even if the middle classes remain the core constituency of Indian cricket, providing the bulk of the game's players and followers. Finally, even though sporting tours have changed beyond recognition since the imperial high noon of 1911, such visits continue both to affirm and strain the bonds between nations in the post-colonial commonwealth of cricket.

Prashant Kidambi is senior lecturer in historical studies at the University of Leicester. The Leverhulme Trust awarded a fellowship to research this article.

LALIT MODI AND THE INDIAN PREMIER LEAGUE

Cricket à la Modi

JAMES ASTILL

Lalit Modi had thought a whiff of scandal would add to the IPL's vast appeal. But the allegations of skulduggery, outcry and the havoc of legal accusation and leaked counter-claim that engulfed the contest in 2010 amounted to far more than its brilliant and divisive creator could ever have wanted.

By the time the third IPL season concluded on April 25 in victory for M. S. Dhoni's Chennai Super Kings over Sachin Tendulkar's Mumbai Indians, Modi had been toppled. To an emptying stadium in Mumbai, he declared: "I reassure millions of passionate fans of the league and the game across the globe that IPL is clean and transparent." Minutes later, the BCCI suspended him for what it called "alleged acts of individual misdemeanour". He was alleged to have presided over widespread tax evasion and other financial misdeeds.

Protesting his innocence, Modi withdrew to a splendid flat in London's Cadogan Square; and there he remained, amid reports that, should he go home, the Indian government intended to impound his passport. Only a week or two before his fall, this outcome would have seemed scarcely imaginable.

The IPL's commercial success has been staggering: the third tournament drew 143m television viewers in India, 20m more than in 2009. The IPL's television advertising revenues were up 60%. And in March 2010 two additional IPL teams were sold for over $700m – more than the existing eight had together fetched in 2008. For all this Modi rightly took much of the credit.

The controversial son of a north Indian business family, he had brought a new entrepreneurism to India's cricket board since his induction, as an acolyte of Sharad Pawar, into its senior ranks in 2005. Indeed, long before this, he had talked of setting up a new domestic Indian cricket tournament – a slick and highly commercialised production, more English Premier League or National Basketball Association than Ranji Trophy. The board was reluctant. But, faced with an unprecedented challenge to its monopoly in 2007 when Subhash Chandra, a media mogul, launched his Indian Cricket League, the BCCI's wary denizens gave Modi his head.

In a mere three months, he and his contacts at International Management Group designed the IPL tournament, flogged off its television rights and teams to an A-list of Indian tycoons, and thereby made the BCCI $1.7bn richer. Leaving aside the vexed question of what the IPL will do to Indian and world cricket, this was a remarkable achievement.

And Modi trumpeted it. As the contest's self-styled "CEO and commissioner", a title that went well with his hint of an American drawl, he used the IPL to launch himself as a celebrity. Jetting between the eight city bases, he seemed to be at every IPL game. A dedicated camera – "Modicam" his retinue called it – awaited him at the stadiums. He was said to make every

Rajansh Kakade, AP/PA

In his element: Lalit Modi with Bollywood actresses Shilpa Shetty and Preity Zinta, and Gayatri Reddy, owner of the Deccan Chargers.

important decision on the tournament, and most of the minor ones. With his love of Twitter, he was ubiquitous in India's cricket-obsessed media. He was on the cover of every major Indian newspaper and business weekly, dressed in his trademark bespoke suit with a silk handkerchief cascading from its breast pocket, sometimes lounging dandily on a cricket bat.

His rise was stratospheric, and perhaps kidded him into thinking himself invincible. Modi certainly offended many brittle colleagues on the Indian board. You want IPL tickets? Go buy them, he is said to have told one of India's foremost politicians-in-cricket. He was a road-crash waiting to happen.

The smash-up started with a tweet. A few hours after signing off on one of the new IPL teams, to be based in the Keralan city of Kochi, Modi invited his many followers on Twitter to reflect on its ownership structure. He wrote that 25% of the Kochi team's equity was owned by an entity called Rendezvous Sports, then he listed its stakeholders. One was a marketing professional from Dubai, Sunanda Pushkar, better known as the girlfriend (now wife) of Shashi Tharoor, a Keralite and government minister who had lobbied for the Kochi bid. What ensued was as compelling, or at least as closely followed in India, as the IPL's on-field events.

Tharoor, an urbane former UN diplomat who had stood for Secretary-General when Ban Ki-moon was elected, had been reckoned a rare incorruptible Indian politician – and so an excellent target for the government's opponents. Parliament was in uproar, as MPs accused Tharoor of trying to enrich himself, which he denied, demanded his head and also an inquiry into the IPL. The government delivered both, but not before more damaging allegations had been aired. An investor in the Kochi franchise claimed Modi had offered him and his fellows $50m to withdraw their winning bid.

Tax and other inspectors descended on the BCCI headquarters, on those of three IPL teams, based in Jaipur, Mohali and Kolkata, and on World Sports Group, a company that had bought the IPL's broadcast rights and then sold them on to Sony. The three teams were linked to Modi: his brother-in-law held a stake in the Rajasthan Royals; a more distant in-law owned part of Kings XI Punjab; a close friend owned part of the Kolkata Knight Riders. India's finance minister, Pranab Mukherjee, said all aspects of the contest were under investigation. The BCCI meanwhile began scrutinising the broadcasting contract, renegotiated by Modi in 2009 for $1.6bn over nine years.

The Commissioner wriggled hard. But his opponents in the board – all those jealous of, offended by or justly worried by the excesses of the braggart Modi – knew that this was their hour. After suspending him, board members accused Modi of responsibility for multiple financial irregularities, including in the team auctions, sale of mid-over advertising and concerning an $85m facilitation fee paid by Sony to WSG. He was further accused of colluding to set up a rebel Twenty20 contest in England. There were, separately, dark whispers of match-fixing in the IPL. Thankfully, no credible allegation, let alone proof, has followed, to date. Yet revelations from the Mumbai police that a gangster had sent two assassins to kill Modi did nothing to dampen suspicions of something rotten in the league. This also justified Modi in claiming his exile in London was motivated by fear for his safety. As the IPL tsar's halo dimmed, plans for a Bollywood biopic (working title: *The Commissioner*) were shelved.

Modi's enemies on the board were not sated, however. In October they expelled the Rajasthan and Punjab IPL teams, citing irregularities in their ownership. Most assumed this was an effort to rid the league of all traces of Modi. The board also promised a less brash, more modest IPL. There would be no more IPL Nights – a series of spin-off parties featuring yawning cricketers and pretty models cavorting for the benefit of MTV's cameras. Rather, the board's members insisted, the IPL would henceforth be all about the cricket, not Bollywood glamour and other Modi-inspired frippery. There was even some rash talk of dropping the IPL's scantily clad cheerleaders, but that soon died. India's mostly male crowds love them.

By order of the courts, the expelled teams were also reprieved, in time to participate in the January 2011 auction of players, for the fourth IPL season. During two days of bidding – watched live on television by 20m people – the auction raised $62m. The Pathan brothers, Yusuf and Irfan, were awarded contracts together worth $4m per six-week season. (But no one bid for Brian Lara or Sourav Ganguly, and only seven England players – Paul Collingwood, Kevin Pietersen, Stuart Broad, Eoin Morgan, Michael Lumb, Dimitri Mascarenhas and Owais Shah – were picked up.)

The board's proceedings against Modi dragged on: he launched a legal challenge to the composition of its disciplinary committee, providing yet more work for the BCCI's lawyers. But the scandal, which had dominated India's airwaves for much of 2010, was by now starting to dissipate. The official investigations into the IPL seemed to have run into the sand. Perhaps the

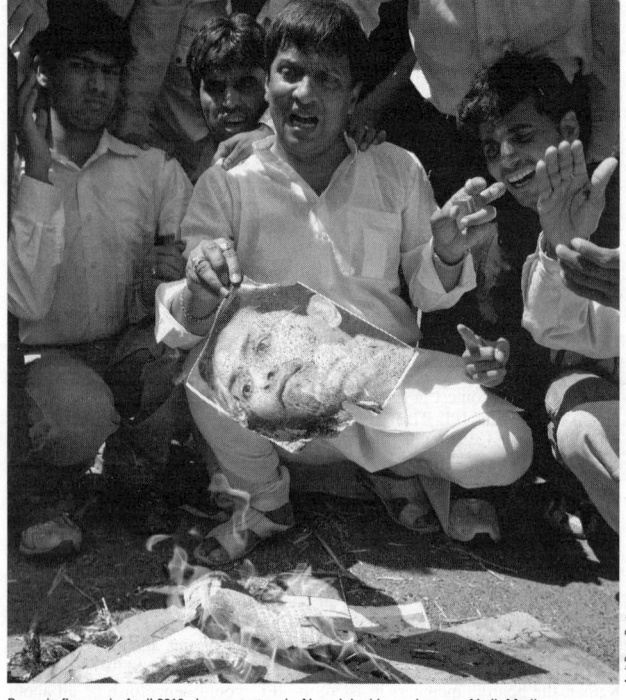

Down in flames: in April 2010, demonstrators in Ahmedabad burn pictures of Lalit Modi.

government, a coalition led by the Congress Party, which was riven by corruption scandals of its own, considered the IPL too popular to frown on. And Modi, who denies all allegations of wrongdoing, also has his fans. Many Indians shrug over the claims that he feathered his nest and say at least he put on a great show. No one else, for that matter, looks likely to face prosecution over the IPL's troubles. In India, powerful miscreants rarely do.

Whether the league had been damaged by all these scandals remained to be seen. The biggest risk must be whether the BCCI, shorn of Modi, can run it competently. But at least India's appetite for the IPL brand of overhyped, crash-bash cricket appeared undiminished. As the fourth IPL season approached, Sony predicted its IPL advertising revenues would be up 20%.

James Astill is the South Asia bureau chief of The Economist. *His book,* The Great Tamasha: Cricket, Corruption and India's Unstoppable Rise, *is due to be published in early 2012.*

CRICKET AND TELEVISION

The box of tricks

LAWRENCE BOOTH

When ESPN Star Sports, the ICC's global broadcast and production partner, announced that the 2011 World Cup would be watched by one billion viewers in every corner of the globe bar the Latin swathes of South America, it was a reminder that televised cricket is a rather different beast from the sport first screened by the BBC from Lord's and The Oval in 1938.

Back then, the public had Len Hutton's 364, a camera at one end and commentary of the kind that later provided fame for Mr Cholmondley-Warner, Harry Enfield's comic embodiment of Empire and the King's English. Now, the armchair viewers expect their cricket on a plate, with side helpings of Hawk-Eye, Hot-Spot and High Definition – all served up by accents ranging from Bumble's Accrington burr to Michael Holding's Jamaican lilt.

With its discrete vignettes – 540 of them in a day of 90 overs – cricket lends itself more comfortably to the microscope than any sport. And if a trip to the game promises mood, colour and a rewarding sense of the sport beyond the cut strip, then a stumble to the sofa may provide a more detailed insight.

In one sense, this is a matter of pure numbers. The 2011 World Cup was touted in advance as television's grandest cricket project yet. The pre-tournament publicity made an unabashed virtue of the sheer size of it all: 550 production-crew members at six outside-broadcast units (four in India, one each in Bangladesh and Sri Lanka) were expected to generate a total of 2,350 international and domestic flights, as well as 13,000 "room nights". There would be 27 cameras at each venue, not including the six required for Hawk-Eye. "The permutations," said Aarti Dabas, the ICC's media rights and broadcast manager, "are amazing." Presumably the expenses claims would hardly bear thinking about either.

When you consider that England's trip to West Indies in 1989-90, the first overseas tour broadcast live in the UK, was covered by seven cameras and a small crew including – in the words of the producer, Gary Franses – "only one guy, a freelance cameraman, who had ever done cricket before", the sense of an industry shedding its skin is palpable.

Cricket broadcasting's Rubicon was crossed that winter after the West Indies board – impecunious then as now – approached the sports agency IMG to sound out methods of cashing in on the world's most successful team. The answer, IMG suggested, was to display the talents of Viv Richards, Malcolm Marshall and Co on TV. This was less Baldrickian than it sounded, since Caribbean cricket had no tradition of regular or centralised coverage. (The footage of Colin Cowdrey's England taking advantage of Garry Sobers's declaration to win in Trinidad in 1967-68, for example, exists only because the local TV station had its act together at the time.) But the region as a whole lacked a broadcasting legacy. Coverage, therefore, was placed in the hands of Trans World International, IMG's TV arm, and – to the horror of MPs who swore by the sanctity of the BBC – the British rights were sold to Sky, then in its embryonic phase.

And while the BBC, whose coverage of the game had grown increasingly tired during its half-a-century monopoly, believed the Caribbean posed too many logistical pitfalls for a successful outside broadcast, Franses and his team picked up the gauntlet. When Graham Gooch's unfancied team pulled off a

Tony Harris, PA Photos

A new opening partnership: Rupert Murdoch of Sky and IMG's Mark McCormack (*right*) announced the first television coverage of an England tour, to the West Indies, in 1989-90.

shock win in the First Test at Sabina Park, Sky – unaccustomed back then to covering major sporting events – did not have enough satellite dishes to go around. Without that first foray, the TV revolution may have taken a less precipitous course.

But the task of transmitting events in the Caribbean to fans back in the UK was not a straightforward one. For all the slickness of contemporary coverage, there was a needs-must air to proceedings. One of the commentators, the Middlesex and England left-arm spinner Phil Edmonds, was employed because he was on holiday in Jamaica at the time. Equipment was transported around the Caribbean in an ancient aeroplane by Carry Cargo, a West Indian company based in Miami, while facilities at the venues ranged from the non-existent to the rudimentary.

"The whole experience was terrifying," says Franses. "We didn't know what we were doing from one day to the next. We forever needed help designing commentary boxes. At the old Bourda ground in Georgetown, Guyana, there was a ditch around the perimeter and we had to place the camera on top of a moat. We had visions of it floating away."

The image captured the precariousness of the whole shebang. But progress was being made in other areas. By now, for example, viewers could watch the action from both ends – a gift from Kerry Packer, who was aghast that half the coverage had, until his World Series came along in 1977-78, been obscured by the batsman's backside. The BBC took a while to fall into line, arguing that one-ended coverage replicated the experience of the turnstiles customer, and it took another piece of Australian strong-arming to change their minds. When

Channel 9 sent its own commentators to cover the 1985 Ashes in England, they told a reluctant BBC that unless they installed cameras at both ends, Channel 9 would do the job for them. Not wishing to be upstaged on home turf, the BBC took the hint. And if the physics of positioning a cameraman on scaffolding at the Nursery End at Lord's were occasionally challenged by the wind, a template had been set.

As British TV coverage of the sport entered a new competitive era that felt an age away from Peter West's avuncular summaries and fuzzy black-and-white scorecards, the international game was going through a revolution of its own. Andrew Wildblood, now a vice-president at IMG and a central figure in the rise of the Indian Premier League, remembers the change of emphasis in the early 1990s. "When Gatting played that reverse-sweep in the 1987 World Cup final," he says, "it was broadcast by Doordarshan, the Indian state network. It looked as if the stroke had been played in snow.

> Negotiations continued while the crew's plane was impounded

"Then, in 1992, we signed the Indian board for $200,000. I remember sitting with Henry Blofeld, my travelling companion on that tour, and we were arguing with Jagmohan Dalmiya and I. S. Bindra over $25,000. That would barely buy you an over these days. But we got three Tests and five ODIs for the money, despite Doordarshan having a court case with the BCCI about coverage going to a foreign company."

The impasse – in an age when cricket was still coming to grips with globalisation – continued into the one-day Hero Cup, in November 1993, when the TWI production crew was informed by Indian police that, despite its purchase of the international rights for the tournament, it was breaking the law by treading on Doordarshan's toes. Negotiations continued while the crew's plane was sealed and impounded at Bombay airport; the competition's opening fixtures went untelevised until a deal was brokered.

Back in England, a bunfight was developing for slices of an increasingly mouth-watering pie. The summer after Sky's ground-breaking Caribbean broadcast had shaken a nation out of its belief that televised cricket meant perforce the BBC, the Benson & Hedges Cup final was televised by British Satellite Broadcasting – before it merged with Sky in November 1990 to form BSkyB. It was the first time a major county match had escaped the clutches of the terrestrial channels. Four years later, BSkyB bought the rights for England's home one-day internationals, and in 1999 Channel 4 entered the fray. BSkyB's share of the deal gave them one home Test a summer. The BBC were left with nothing. It was as if a member of royalty had been debagged.

It was around this time that cricket cottoned on to a truism that had previously been neglected. Gary Franses, by now at Sunset + Vine, who produced Channel 4's award-winning coverage, explains: "It's what you do in the 20 seconds between deliveries that makes the coverage, using the toys you have." If the BBC's toys had been largely limited to slow-motion replays, which in any case had been around since the 1960s, Channel 4 characteristically brought its outsider's eye to bear. "It was a wonderful contract to win," says Franses. "I'd been doing cricket for about ten years, so I

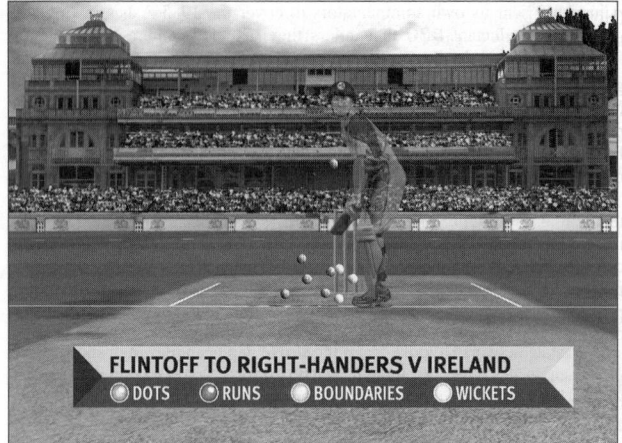

FLINTOFF TO RIGHT-HANDERS V IRELAND
○ DOTS   ◉ RUNS   ○ BOUNDARIES   ○ WICKETS

Hawk-Eye Innovations

Causing a buzz: Hawk-Eye's Beehive illustrates Andrew Flintoff's accuracy.

knew who to get. The Channel 4 years were a World XI of TV cameramen and videotape experts. It wasn't hard. We just had to throw a bit more at it. The ECB, who by the late 1990s were fed up with the BBC, wanted innovation."

Rabbits had already been pulled from the hat. In 1995 TWI came up with Spin-Vision following Australia's tour of the Caribbean. Shane Warne would bequeath many legacies to the game, but here was his first televisual gift, a long lens that in effect shortened the length of the pitch and allowed viewers a close-up of his wristy repertoire. Gloriously, leggies and flippers were no longer dry abstractions. "Even Channel 9 agreed it was a good idea," says Franses in a nod to the industry's highly competitive nature.

But it was Channel 4 who introduced the British audience to the kind of wizardry we now take for granted. If the BBC's coverage had slipped into a clubhouse comfort in which a nudge or a wink could convey the necessary to a clique of well-informed viewers, Channel 4 went back to basics with their newcomer's zeal. And, crucially, they did so with Richie Benaud on board – cricket broadcasting's papal seal of approval.

The Snickometer, the brainchild of Alan Plaskett, a computer scientist, was unveiled in 1999 and went some way – but not all of it – to settling debates about caught-behind decisions. Hawk-Eye, an ingenious computer system designed to track the path of the ball, was developed in time for the 2001 Lord's Test against Pakistan. It, along with its New Zealand cousin Virtual Eye, is now a fundamental, if occasionally controversial, part of the Decision Review System, and the generator of such team analysts' delights as the Beehive, which superimposes a bowler's grouping against an upright batsman.

(Hot Spot, the infra-red imaging system used to capture points of impact, was first rolled out by Channel 9, and not until the 2006-07 Ashes.)

Other innovations were simpler, and perhaps more effective at spreading the gospel: if viewers were baffled by the concept of the doosra, the former Middlesex and Durham seamer Simon Hughes was on hand in a dark production van to explain all. As both The Analyst and begetter of Jargon-Busting, Hughes held the casual fan's hand in a manner that might have been regarded as a bit too touchy-feely by the BBC. Cricket was being democratised.

The process continues, and it is necessarily imperfect. If the straight lines of tennis make the application of Hawk-Eye a relatively simple one, and the interaction between rugby's on-field referee and TV official has become clear-cut, then cricket's many angles, perspectives and scenarios preclude complete precision. The issue of low catches, a perennial victim of foreshortening – the process by which a three-dimensional occurrence is rendered on a two-dimensional screen – is a case in point.

But for the sheer breadth of possibilities, cricket remains a technician's dream. Plans for the 2011 World Cup included a movable "slips" camera, the better to capture the split-second reaction times required to field there, and a camera low down at 45 degrees from the batsman. The ESPN brainwave of crunching the screen to show the view from side-on as batsmen run between the wickets was set to continue.

Perhaps no gizmo has taken us closer to the game, however, than High Definition – or "HD" – television. Superior, for the time being, to the 3D experiment that received a lukewarm reception when it was trialled during a one-day international at Trent Bridge in 2010, HD has celebrated the little details we previously missed: the twist of the bat in the hand, the bend of the blade itself, the explosion of ball through turf and the beads of sweat on the forehead of the perspiring batsman. Where a regular camera offers 24 frames a second and the super slo-mo about 200–300, the 4-Sight camera used for HD coverage boasts 1,000.

Franses says TV has become the supreme arbiter. But if that is to the regret of some, then the sight of a batsman's eyes closing and lips pursing as he prepares to pull a bouncer heading for his grille has added the kind of drama Peter West and chums might only have dreamed about.

Lawrence Booth writes on cricket for the Daily Mail, *and is the author of the weekly e-newsletter,* The Top Spin.

THE WISDEN TEST XI

Giving in to temptation

SCYLD BERRY

The temptation was irresistible. It was like a wide long-hop.

The most sensible option would be to open the innings of the 2010 Wisden Test XI with **Virender Sehwag** and Graeme Smith, which is what one of the three selectors, Ian Chappell, proposed. Or with Sehwag and Andrew Strauss, as Ramiz Raja voted. But the third selector, Ian Bishop, opted – slightly mischievously? – for Sehwag and his young left-handed heir apparent from Bangladesh, **Tamim Iqbal**.

Sehwag and Tamim could effectively win a Test match in the opening session. Sehwag has scored a Test hundred in a session before; Tamim, against England at Mirpur in March 2010, was well on course to becoming only the fifth batsman to hit a century before lunch on the first day of a Test – on his 21st birthday. Pair them together and by tea on day one, if they are still batting for the World XI, the Martians will be saying to themselves: "Start the spaceship!" As convenor of *Wisden's* three-man selection panel – this year Ramiz, the former Pakistan captain, joined Bishop and Chappell – I had to decide between their three nominations to be Sehwag's opening partner: Smith, Tamim and Strauss, all left-handers for contrast. And the temptation of opening with Sehwag and Tamim was irresistible.

It could, of course, go wrong. The wide long-hop could be cut to the sweeper on the cover boundary. But then sobriety follows the headiness: **Kumar Sangakkara** comes in at No. 3, followed by **Sachin Tendulkar** and **Jacques Kallis**. Sangakkara faced competition from Hashim Amla, nominated by Chappell as "a run-machine who improved his scoring-rate", but the Sri Lankan edged out the emerging South African by the convenor's casting vote. Not without reason was Sangakkara briefly top of the ICC's world rankings for Test batsmen in 2010. As Bishop summarised him: "Good against fast bowling, great against spin, a perfect No. 3."

Tendulkar and Kallis are two of the eight unanimous selections by the panel, in addition to Sehwag. Let Chappell's encomium of Tendulkar suffice: "He defied the advancing years and enjoyed an amazing resurgence. He even rediscovered the art of dominating bowlers." Kallis remains the one top-class batsman who can bowl quickly. Of several cricketers it has been said: "We shall not see his like again," and of Kallis it is almost certainly true, because of the ever-increasing demands of an ever-increasing number of formats. Shane Watson is the only other top-order Test batsman who even tries to bowl pace.

For the No. 6 position, two selectors went for **V. V. S. Laxman**. Bishop's citation was: "VVS over A. B. de Villiers for me because of the ability of Laxman to get those match-saving or match-winning runs." Laxman's 73 not out in the fourth innings at Mohali to achieve India's one-wicket victory over

Australia was a prime example; so too his 96 at Durban. Ramiz said of Laxman: "The best player on the circuit against spin, he gets runs in make-or-break situations."

As in the two previous years of the Wisden Test XI, **Mahendra Singh Dhoni** was the unanimous choice as wicketkeeper. But this year, for the first time, he was not the unanimous choice as captain. Bishop and Chappell went for Dhoni, but Ramiz chose Strauss as captain as well as opening batsman, not least because Strauss is "good with DRS technology" – now one of a captain's prime responsibilities.

It is convenient that all three selectors are agreed on their choice of the bowling attack for the Wisden Test XI of 2010. But is it healthy? The four bowlers are led by **Dale Steyn**, and supplemented by Kallis. As Bishop noted: "Dale continues to be the best fast bowler around. He offers cutting-edge with his pace, he swings the ball and is adding to his repertoire all the time."

James Anderson is Steyn's opening partner. "He swings the ball both ways at respectable pace," said Chappell. "He seems to me to be a bowler at the peak of his powers," said Bishop of the leader of England's attack in the Ashes.

Zaheer Khan knows every trick, with new ball and old, and can be relied upon to create some rough for **Graeme Swann** to bowl into. "One of the most skilful and clever seamers even at reduced pace and across varied conditions," Bishop said. Ramiz was even more lavish in his praise: "Fantastic with the old ball and a wicket-taker; his left-arm angle will provide variety for the attack."

Swann again has no challenger as the specialist spinner, although Daniel Vettori was economical as ever and Harbhajan Singh found his flight again during India's tour of South Africa. "Swann has the ability to probe while bowling accurately," according to Chappell. "The best spinner since Shane Warne's retirement, he brings freshness to the art of off-spin," says Ramiz.

But where are the young rivals? While new Test batsmen appear – like Amla, Tamim and Alastair Cook – young bowlers are in short supply. Has this always been the case? Or does an elite sportsman now look at the IPL and other 20-over competitions around the world, and decide that batting, or rather hitting, along with a few overs of something not too physically demanding, is the most lucrative way?

V. Sehwag (*India*)
Tamim Iqbal (*Bangladesh*)
K. C. Sangakkara (*Sri Lanka*)
S. R. Tendulkar (*India*)
J. H. Kallis (*South Africa*)
V. V. S. Laxman (*India*)
*†M. S. Dhoni (*India*)
G. P. Swann (*England*)
D. W. Steyn (*South Africa*)
Zaheer Khan (*India*)
J. M. Anderson (*England*)

The 2010 team shows four changes from the Wisden Test XI of 2009 (see *Wisden 2010*, page 93), which included G. Gambhir, A. J. Strauss, M. G. Johnson and P. M. Siddle instead of Tamim Iqbal, Laxman, Steyn and Zaheer Khan.

THE WISDEN–MCC CRICKET PHOTOGRAPH OF 2010

Distilling the spirit of cricket

HUGH CHEVALLIER

So often during the Ashes, England's bowling attack was sharp and penetrative. A writer, feeling for an image, might have been tempted to describe it as an arrow homing in on its target. But how much better to illustrate that theme with a real image – of the England team transformed into an arrowhead? Opposite is Scott Barbour's photograph from the last day of the Adelaide Test, where miraculously that metamorphosis has happened.

It takes immense skill – plus a bit of luck – to see the moment amid the action, and capture it. For his picture of a skein of England fielders, flying in James Anderson's wake, Barbour, of Getty Images, is the winner of the first Wisden–MCC Cricket Photograph of the Year, in association with Park Cameras, the leading Canon professional dealer (www.parkcameras.com).

The competition, announced in *Wisden 2010*, attracted over 250 entries from amateur and professional photographers around the world. Essentially, the stipulations were that each photograph must have been taken in the calendar year 2010, and that it illustrated the game of cricket, in its broadest sense.

Chris Smith, 25 years the chief sports photographer of the *Sunday Times*, chaired the selection panel. Its other members were Nigel Davies, art director of *The Wisden Cricketer*, Bob Martin, photo manager for the London 2012 Olympics, Claire Taylor, an England cricketer for more than a decade and a keen amateur photographer, and Graham Wood, director of photography for the *Times* magazine.

Smith and Davies spent hours whittling the number for consideration down to 100, then 55, and then 27. This was when the remainder of the judges joined the discussion. The next number they were aiming for was 11. (This first team will have their works displayed around Lord's during 2011.) From now on the panel were working from hard copies, and the job became harder still.

Some were rejected, only to be reinstated. Smith was particularly impressed by a picture of beach cricket in the Chennai rain. The mountainous seas contrasted with the calm waters in another shot of beach cricket, this time silhouettes from Perth in Western Australia, championed by Taylor. In the end, though, neither made it into the top three and so into these pages.

Third place went to Supriya Biswas from Kolkata, for an image brimming with *joie de vivre*, if not technical excellence on the batsman's part. Runner-up was Gareth Copley from the Press Association, whose composition of four South African fielders appealing (unsuccessfully) is sculptural – "almost cricket's version of Canova's *The Three Graces*" said Smith, tongue in cheek.

The entry requirements are the same for 2011: any image taken in the calendar year on the theme of cricket is eligible. Go to www.lords.org/photooftheyear for details.

THE WISDEN–MCC CRICKET PHOTOGRAPH OF 2010: Scott Barbour won the inaugural award for his image of James Anderson and his England team-mates celebrating the wicket of Brad Haddin during the Adelaide Test in December.

THE WISDEN–MCC CRICKET PHOTOGRAPH OF 2010: Gareth Copley was runner-up for his image of South African fielders Jacques Kallis, Ashwell Prince, Paul Harris and Dale Steyn going up as one to claim (unsuccessfully) the wicket of Stuart Broad, at Cape Town in January.

Gareth Copley, PA Photos

THE WISDEN–MCC CRICKET PHOTOGRAPH OF 2010: Supriya Biswas won third prize for this image of cricket in Kolkata, India, in December.

Supriya Biswas

GULLY FIELDSMEN: The cricket team of the Ship Inn at Elie, Fife, play their home games on the beach. This image from August 2010 is taken from the forthcoming *From the Boundary's Edge*, (Atlantic Publishing).

Laurence Griffiths

Eranga Jayawardena, AP/PA

A TERRIFYING PROSPECT FOR BATSMEN... A giant figure of Muttiah Muralitharan looks down from the Galle fort as he nears his 800th Test wicket.

Deshakalyan Chowdhury, AFP/Getty Images

...AND FOR FIELDERS – or at least for India's Suresh Raina, who cowers from a stray dog behind the better-protected Grant Elliott of New Zealand, Guwahati, November 2010.

Graham Morris

LINE AND LENGTH: MCC members queue for the best seats for the Test against Bangladesh, while in Dhaka cricket fans spend the night waiting to buy World Cup tickets, January 2011.

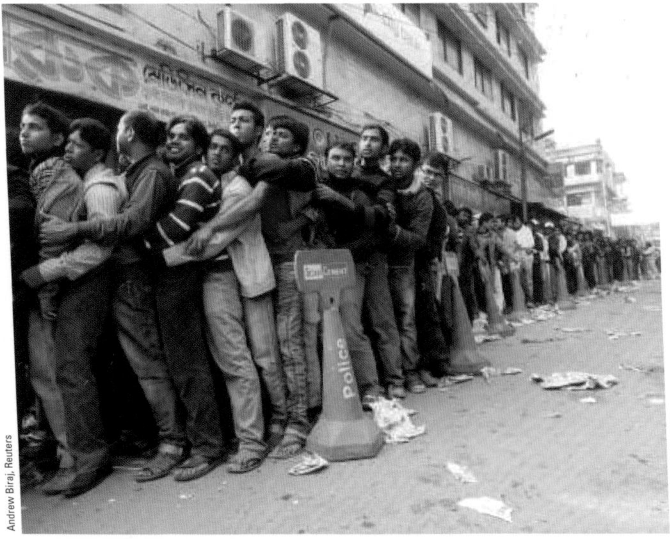

Andrew Biraj, Reuters

THE LEADING CRICKETER IN THE WORLD: Sachin Tendulkar.

THE LEADING CRICKETER IN THE WORLD, 2010

The Leading Cricketer in the World was instituted in Wisden 2004. *The six previous winners were* **Ricky Ponting, Shane Warne, Andrew Flintoff, Muttiah Muralitharan, Jacques Kallis** *and* **Virender Sehwag.** *A full list of past notional winners, backdated to 1900, appears on page 35 of* Wisden 2007. *Players can be chosen more than once for this award, as Sehwag was in 2009 and 2010. Tendulkar was also the notional winner in 1998.*

Sachin Tendulkar

RAMACHANDRA GUHA

From the middle of October to the middle of December 2010, the Republic of India was beset by a series of corruption scandals – money illegally made on contracts for the Commonwealth Games, on housing projects in Mumbai and mining schemes in Karnataka, on the allocation of scarce airwaves for mobile-phone companies. The amount stolen by politicians (of all parties) ran into hundreds of billions of rupees. The scandals dominated the headlines for weeks until they were temporarily set aside to make way for Sachin Tendulkar's 50th Test hundred. This was met with relief, but also with wonder and admiration – indeed, it revived calls for the batsman to be awarded the Bharat Ratna, India's highest honour, previously reserved for politicians, scientists and musicians.

For Tendulkar to be viewed as a balm for the nation's (mostly self-inflicted) wounds was not new. As long ago as 1998, the Bombay poet C. P. Surendran wrote: "Batsmen walk out into the middle alone. Not Tendulkar. Every time Tendulkar walks to the crease, a whole nation, tatters and all, marches with him to the battle arena. A pauper people pleading for relief, remission from the lifelong anxiety of being Indian, by joining in spirit their visored saviour."

Over the next decade, the social anxieties of Indians abated. Economic liberalisation created a class of successful entrepreneurs, who in turn generated a growing middle class. Hindu–Muslim riots became less frequent. Meanwhile, Rahul Dravid, Sourav Ganguly, V. V. S. Laxman and Virender Sehwag arrived to take some of the burden of making runs (and relieving fans) off Tendulkar. It became possible once more to appreciate him in purely cricketing terms, rather than as the Saviour of the Nation.

Viewed thus, there appear to have been three distinct stages in Tendulkar's career as an international cricketer. For a full decade following his debut as a 16-year-old in 1989, he was a purely *attacking* batsman. Coming in at (say) ten for two, he would seek not to stabilise an innings but to wrest the game away from the opposition. This he did frequently, and in dazzling fashion, through slashing square cuts and pulls, and drives past the bowler and wide of mid-on. There was no shot he would not play, no form of bowling that in any way intimidated or even contained him.

Then Tendulkar began to slow down. He now ducked the short ball (previously he would have hooked it), and played spin bowlers from the crease.

The back-foot force through cover that was his trademark became scarce. He still scored runs regularly, but mostly through the on side, via dabs, sweeps, drives and the occasional pull.

We now know that this transformation in Tendulkar's game was due to a sore elbow. But while it lasted it appeared to be permanent; I even wrote at the time that "the genius has become a grafter". (My embarrassment at recalling this is tempered by the fact that some other writers were even more dismissive.) On the advice of a Mumbai doctor, he rested his left hand completely – he would not even, I am told, lift a coffee mug with it. The treatment worked, for as his elbow healed he recovered his fluency. The hook shot and the lofted drive were used sparingly, but his mastery of the off side was once more revealed in all its splendour.

It is commonplace to juxtapose Tendulkar with Don Bradman, but a more relevant comparison might be with the great Surrey and England opening batsman Jack Hobbs. There was a pre-war and a post-war Hobbs, and there has been a pre-tennis elbow and post-tennis elbow Tendulkar. Like Hobbs, in his late thirties he no longer so wholly dominates the bowling, but he is still pleasing to watch, and remains the batsman whose wicket (Sehwag, Dravid, Laxman notwithstanding) the opposition prizes most highly.

Young Sachin enjoyed several truly fabulous years, but 2010 was the *annus mirabilis* of the Late Tendulkar. Last year he scored more Test runs (1,562, at an average of 78) than anybody else. In February he scored the first double-century in one-day internationals; in December, he became the first man to score 50 Test hundreds, both landmarks achieved against the best pace attack in world cricket, South Africa. I was privileged to watch, live, a magnificent double-hundred he made against Australia at Bangalore, marked by cuts, drives, pulls, hooks and even two colossal sixes into the stands.

As he has grown older, Tendulkar has taken several measures to prolong his career. He does not play any Twenty20 internationals, bowls rarely, and fields mostly at mid-on, a position Sir Robert Menzies once called "the last refuge of mankind", but in this case a measure intended to preserve his fingers from damage (when younger he fielded very effectively in the slips).

Hanif Mohammad once said of Garfield Sobers that he "had been sent by God to Earth to play cricket". It is not only Indians who think that way about Tendulkar. Like Hobbs, he is equally admired by fans and players, by team-mate and adversary alike. His off-field conduct has been exemplary (with one trifling exception – when he asked for a tariff waiver on the import of a fancy foreign car). Australians venerate him; they do not even sledge him.

What might mean even more to him is the frank adoration and love of his team-mates. Indian cricket was long marked by personal rivalries and parochial jealousies; if that seems now to be behind us, this is the handiwork of a generation of gifted and selfless cricketers, among them Dravid, Laxman, Ganguly and Anil Kumble, but perhaps Tendulkar most. One image captures it all. A cake was being cut to mark victory in a hard-fought one-day series in Pakistan several years ago. The first piece was offered to the player of the tournament, Yuvraj Singh, who immediately turned the plate towards his hero and said, *"Pehlé Sachin bhai ko"*: the first one is for our elder brother, Sachin.

CRICKETERS OF THE YEAR

The Five Cricketers of the Year represent a tradition that dates back in Wisden *to 1889, making this the oldest individual award in cricket. The Five are picked by the editor, and the selection is based, primarily but not exclusively, on the players' influence on the previous English season. No one can be chosen more than once. A list of past Cricketers of the Year appears on page 1590.*

> The editor of *Wisden 2011* originally chose five Cricketers of the Year, as normal. However, the findings, shortly before this book went to press, of the ICC's independent tribunal made the selection of one of the five unsustainable. As a result, only four players have been instated.

Eoin Morgan

ANGUS FRASER

High-quality cricketers have emerged from the unlikeliest of places but very few people, if any, would have predicted that a housing estate in north County Dublin would give birth to one. But it was here, within hitting distance of the Irish Sea, that Eoin Morgan took his first steps to becoming England's finest limited-overs batsman and, arguably, the most versatile in world cricket. Without him to keep their batting afloat in the early stages, it is safe to say that England would not have won their first global trophy, the World Twenty20 in 2010.

Morgan had shown immense promise since joining Middlesex as a teenager, but it was at Canterbury on May 11, 2009, that he confirmed his exceptional talent. Morgan scored 161 off just 136 balls in a 50-over game against Kent, one of the most awesome displays of limited-overs batting you are ever likely to see. What stood out was the composed and controlled way in which he constructed his innings. There was no slogging, just wonderfully crafted shots that allowed him to score all around the ground. Wherever the Kent captain Robert Key moved a fielder from, the ball duly went.

One of the highlights of his display was the array of reverse sweeps. There was a rhythm and cleanness of hitting to this innovative shot that few had seen before, and nobody can currently match. Morgan's quality was not missed by the selectors, who handed him his England one-day international debut 13 days later against West Indies at Bristol.

Morgan is not the first young Irishman to have made the journey from humble Dublin club cricketer to England star via the Ireland national side and Middlesex. Ed Joyce had paved the way several years earlier. But where Joyce hesitated, Morgan stormed through like a juggernaut.

Morgan had sported the green of Ireland in 23 one-day internationals before wearing the blue of England, and it did not take him long to feel at home in his new surroundings. On his sixth appearance for England he struck 58 off just 41 balls against Australia at Trent Bridge. That performance was backed up with 62 not out against Sri Lanka and 67 against hosts South Africa in the Champions Trophy in September 2009.

A maiden hundred for England soon followed, against Bangladesh at Mirpur, and again it was a memorable performance. Most modern batsmen celebrate hugely when they reach three figures for the first time (although he had scored 115 for Ireland in a one-day international against Canada in 2007), but Morgan showed little emotion, as England were yet to complete victory. It was only when he won the close game with a six that he celebrated. Further undefeated hundreds, each at more than a run a ball, followed against Australia and Pakistan. The message was becoming clear: when Morgan gets in, he scores heavily and quickly, and more often than not wins his side the game.

The manner in which he had been able to adapt to match situations encouraged the England selectors to give him a Test debut against Bangladesh at Lord's. Morgan scored 44, and quickly topped that with a majestic 130 against Pakistan in just his third innings, as he dominated a stand of 219 with Paul Collingwood at Trent Bridge.

EOIN JOSEPH GERARD MORGAN was born in Dublin on September 10, 1986. In a city where football, rugby, Gaelic football and hurling tend to catch the eye of young sports enthusiasts, Morgan, surprisingly, was born into a family of cricket fanatics. The passion came from Jack Morgan, Eoin's great-grandfather, who fell in love with the game when he lived in England. The affection was passed through generations via Eoin's grandfather Sonny and his father Jody. As a youngster Eoin was never short of bodies to play cricket with: older brothers Gareth and Gavin, who played for Leinster, were cricket-mad, as were sisters Laura and Gwen, who have both played for Irish representative sides.

Morgan's early cricketing experiences were either at Rush Cricket Club in Dublin or on a concrete path in the St Catherine's housing estate. Stories of his hitting and performances against men as a 15-year-old have become legend in the area.

Middlesex became aware of him in 2001 when Jason Pooley, the Second Eleven coach, received a phone call from an Irish contact who said he should go and watch a young lad playing for Ireland's Under-15s against England Under-13s at Eton College. Morgan only scored around 20, but made an instant impression on Pooley: "He was small, but you could see straight away that he had real natural talent," he said. "It was hard to put your finger on what he had, but during my playing career I spent many hours at the other end watching Mark Ramprakash bat so I knew what a good player looks like, and Eoin had something special.

"There was a calmness about his batting. He made it look so easy, and he struck the ball beautifully. It wasn't strength that got the ball to the boundary, it was timing. He was wristy and wasn't afraid to hit the ball over the top. I met his father, and we arranged for him to come over to spend time with Middlesex during the summer and stay with an Irish lady in Finchley. He was very mature at a young age. At the age of 14 or 15 he would think nothing of flying over from Ireland on his own. I would meet him at the airport; he would pick his bag up, jump in the car and just get on with it. From an early age he knew what he wanted to do, and that was to play cricket."

Many believe it was the fact that Morgan played hurling when young which allowed him to develop the dexterity for such a wide array of strokes. But he knocks down that idea, saying it was the wide variety of sports that helped him. "I played pretty much every sport when I was young – football, Gaelic football, rugby and hurling," said Morgan. "I was not particularly academic at school, in fact if I hadn't played sport I would have left when I was 16. Hurling obviously contributed to my hand–eye co-ordination, but it was not a major thing. I just always played sport, and playing lots of sports, not specialising in one, was I believe the biggest influence on having an eye for a ball."

The reverse sweep has become the shot Morgan is most famous for, but it is not a stroke he worked on before representing Middlesex. "Up until I was 18 or 19 I didn't reverse-sweep," he said. "I only started when I began playing Twenty20 for Middlesex at Lord's. I couldn't hit the ball over the straight boundaries so I had to learn to score in different areas, so I began practising shots that opened up these areas. I found playing the sweeps and reverse sweeps quite easy, but I also worked very hard at it."

Morgan's change of allegiance was, understandably, not greeted with universal approval at home. Irish cricket had recently lost the services of Joyce, and now the English were pinching another one of their brightest prospects. The move to England, however, did not have a huge effect on Morgan himself. "It has been an easy transformation," he said. "I was 15 when I first came over to play properly, and 16 when I was offered a summer contract. I played for the South of England when I was 17. I still follow the Ireland results closely and Will Porterfield, the Ireland captain, is one of my closest friends.

"The last year has been brilliant. I have outdone myself in all areas and being rewarded with a couple of Tests was unbelievable." The Eoin Morgan story is still in its infancy, but the early signs are that it will be a fast-moving, page-turning best-seller.

Chris Read

VIC MARKS

In the end it was a bit of a heist. Nottinghamshire may have been leading the County Championship for much of the summer, but by the penultimate day of the season their hopes appeared to be sinking amid the Old Trafford drizzle. Chris Read, the captain of Nottinghamshire, recalls the mood on the third evening of the last round of matches, which would produce one of the Championship's most riveting finales: "There was a resigned air after two and a half days watching the rain fall in Manchester. Two weeks before we had a 20-point lead. Then we played some poor cricket. We lost two matches and it all seemed to be slipping away."

On that Wednesday night there was a team dinner, at which all of Nottinghamshire's options were discussed. Should they try to negotiate a game with Lancashire? Or should they go for the maximum number of bonus points? Read, unlike his senior advisers, always favoured the second course. "It was odd," he recalls. "The game was on TV and the commentators – with more than enough time for discussion – did not even consider the possibility of us winning the Championship without winning that game at Old Trafford. Of course I had a chat with Mark Chilton [Lancashire's acting-captain] and Glen Chapple [their club captain], but they were driving such a hard bargain that I thought we would be simply handing the game to them."

So on that final day of the season – despite the loss of an hour's play at the start – Read decided upon a headlong pursuit of bonus points in the hope that neither Yorkshire nor Somerset would win elsewhere. As it turned out, neither of them could achieve victory, but still Nottinghamshire, 89 for two overnight, had to race to 400 and then take three Lancastrian wickets to overtake Somerset at the top of the table. "Getting 400 was much the hardest part of that equation," recalls Read. "Once we had achieved that I was very confident that we would get those three wickets. All season Andre Adams and Darren Pattinson had been so potent with the new ball, and Lancashire had nothing to play for."

Nottinghamshire had 18 overs to take those three wickets – but it took them only 28 balls. And so, after two seasons as runners-up, Nottinghamshire clinched the Championship by the narrowest of margins – they had the same number of points as Somerset but had won one game more, the first tie-breaker. It was a triumph for one of the country's more stable clubs, and for one of the more stable captains, who has endured his fair share of disappointments – though usually as a consequence of his experiences at international rather than county level.

CHRISTOPHER MARK WELLS READ was born on August 10, 1978, in Paignton in Devon, for whom he made his Minor County debut at 16. His flair for keeping first became apparent in a fundraising fixture in Torquay between Somerset and a scratch side, which included the diminutive teenager Read and the recently retired Malcolm Marshall. In the first over Marshall bowled, he found a thick outside edge: Read took off like one of the curious seagulls nearby and pouched the ball in the tip of his outstretched right hand. It was a wonderful moment and a wonderful catch, not least for the way in which Marshall beamed and celebrated a vignette of brilliance from a precocious young cricketer.

Read was precocious. After selection for England Under-19s, he went on the England A tour of Kenya and Sri Lanka in 1997-98 after he had made his single appearance for Gloucestershire. At home it then became apparent that Gloucestershire, with Jack Russell no longer required by England, had become a cul-de-sac, so in 1998 Read moved to Trent Bridge.

It was only a matter of time before he was selected for England's Test team, although maybe that honour came too soon in an international career that has amounted to just 15 Test matches, in three phases. In 1999 he played three Tests against New Zealand, keeping competently, scoring few runs and being memorably bamboozled by Chris Cairns's slower ball at Lord's (he ducked it and was bowled).

Four years later he played eight matches in a row before being dropped for the final Test of the 2003-04 West Indies tour, in Antigua, which was a surprising decision. England held a 3–0 lead; Read had kept immaculately throughout the tour, but had contributed modestly with the bat.

However, Read says he was most disappointed by his omission at the start of the 2006-07 Ashes tour. He had kept in the last two Tests of the English summer against Pakistan, and this time he had contributed with the bat. He assumed as he boarded the plane that he was the man in possession, but when Geraint Jones was preferred for the warm-up games in Australia it was obvious Read had been rejected again. He was recalled at the end of the series, but by then his confidence was badly dented. He kept well, but was way out of form with the bat.

For the purists, it seems a travesty that Read, often regarded as the best gloveman in the country, did not play more for England (although there were also 37 limited-overs appearances). "In a way I never felt like an England player," says Read now. "I never felt comfortable. It wasn't that I did not feel good enough. But I was never there long enough and never had a central contract."

For many, Read came to epitomise the strains behind the England team of that era. Rod Marsh was his great advocate, and before long the Australian's forthright support may not have been that helpful as the relationship between Marsh, at the head of the Academy, and Duncan Fletcher, as England coach, grew ever more hostile. Read himself always maintains a diplomatic silence when asked about his treatment by Fletcher.

Nottinghamshire, however, would benefit from Read's England exile. Read knew in 2007 that he was likely to captain the county in 2008, so paid special attention to what Stephen Fleming, his predecessor, was up to when he stood next to him at first slip. "That was a fantastic education," says Read, who tries to follow the same simple principles of captaincy as evinced by Fleming. Neither is the sort of captain eager to pluck a magical rabbit out of the proverbial hat.

The captaincy seemed to enhance Read's output with the bat. In his first three seasons in charge at Trent Bridge he averaged 42, 75 and 45 in the Championship, often rescuing the innings along the way (his 75 was the highest average by a regular keeper in any Championship season). In 2010 he stood down from leading in the Twenty20 competition, partly because he was concerned that the frenetic captain's role was affecting his wicketkeeping in that format. "I love the glovework," he explains. "I take a real pride in that. If I have a bad session or game I get down on myself far more than if I fail a couple of times with the bat." There goes the purist, in an age when runs from a wicketkeeper are regarded as more important than silky-smooth glovework.

Tamim Iqbal

Utpal Shuvro

In his first Test innings at Lord's Tamim Iqbal was run out for 55. Stepping into the dressing-room, he asked the attendant, "Why is the honours board reserved for centurions? There should be one for fifties as well." "You will need a century to get your name on this," the attendant replied. And Tamim said, "OK, I'm not leaving here without a century," even though he was only 21 years old and on his first tour of England – in early season at that.

In the second innings Tamim made 103, the first century by a Bangladeshi at Lord's, with 15 fours and two sixes. The hundred came up from just 94 balls, the fastest on the hallowed turf since Mohammad Azharuddin's in 88 balls in 1990. And in no way was Tamim's celebration less spectacular than his strokeful innings. After hitting Tim Bresnan for four, four, two and four from successive balls to race from 87 to a century, he ran towards the dressing-room and leapt up. Pointing to the imagined name on his shirt, he gesticulated as if to say "now put down my name".

Old Trafford was next to be lit up by the glory of Tamim's bat. He scored another hundred, which took six balls longer, but Tamim rates it higher: "The Lord's century was far more emotional... it was Lord's, after all. But I batted much better at Old Trafford – the challenge was bigger. After getting out trying to pull a bouncer at Lord's, I realised that they would unleash a flurry of bouncers in the next two innings – and that's exactly what happened. But I've never batted with as much determination as I did that day. I told myself, I'm not leaving here even if I die. I forced them to change their bowling plans. That was also a big victory."

Through that innings, and especially after it, there was one person on Tamim's mind – Kevin Pietersen, who was present on the field. "When I was hitting the ball all over the park during the Chittagong Test, KP told me 'It's easy to hit here, but come to Old Trafford and see the fun.' I didn't realise what he was saying. I knew there was a Test at Lord's, but didn't know there was one at Old Trafford too. Later, only after I asked my team-mates, I came to know that Old Trafford is the fastest wicket in England and the ball really swings there."

English cricket – or rather an English cricketer – played a role in Tamim's batting during the Lord's Test, too. He saw Geoffrey Boycott on TV discussing Bangladesh's right, or lack of it, to Test status, and his words stung Tamim. "Boycott was a great player – it's people like him who should be encouraging us to perform better. I was sitting alone in my room, watching TV, and I can't tell you how bad I felt. Honestly, I had a very troubled sleep that night. If you start a chocolate company, you can't compete with Cadbury in the first ten years. The next day, after scoring the century, I thought to myself, 'Thank goodness, at least I didn't have to say it out in words.'"

It wasn't only the words of Boycott that made the Lord's century memorable for Tamim, it was the connection with his late father. "The Lord's century was special because of my father – he was mad about cricket, in fact he was a keen student of cricket history. Whenever they showed Lord's on TV, he would always tell us, 'Look, this is where the game began.' That's why I really missed him after that Lord's century."

Tamim's father died in 2000, but his favourite son believes his father watches his every deed on the cricket field from the world beyond. That is his constant inspiration. "I love cricket, but however much I want to succeed for myself, I want to succeed much, much more for my father's sake. You can say I play the game to fulfil his dreams."

TAMIM IQBAL KHAN was born in Chittagong on March 20, 1989, into a family obsessed with cricket, and grew up with it. So organic is cricket to his life that he cannot remember the first time he picked up a bat. His father was a football coach by trade but a cricketer by passion. So was the rest of his sprawling extended family – especially his uncles, one of whom, Akram Khan, captained Bangladesh and played a large role in leading his country to victory in the 1997 ICC Trophy and securing a place in cricket's top tier.

The joy of qualifying for the World Cup, as a result of that ICC Trophy win, spread right across the country. In Chittagong, the epicentre of the celebrations was Akram Khan's – and Tamim's – home. "I'll never forget that time. Thousands of people visited our house day and night, there was colour and festivity everywhere. You may not believe me but our rooms were under two feet of coloured water. My dreams took wings then – I would also be a major cricketer one day, people would sing and dance in my honour as well."

More than the pursuit of that dream, it was the sheer joy of playing cricket that took over Tamim's life. The long narrow lane leading to his house was the venue of cricket matches morning and evening; it was here, in an arena where hitting high meant the risk of losing the ball and getting out, that he learned to hit straight. Almost unknowingly he had mastered the first art of batting.

A stone's throw from Tamim's house lies the M. A. Aziz Stadium, Chittagong's first Test ground. The graduation from the lane near his house to the Outer Stadium – as the periphery was known – took a matter of days. "I would wake up early in the morning to grab the best pitch and set up stumps. I used to be so excited I couldn't sleep at night – I would wonder, what if it rains? From two or three in the morning I would look out at the sky – someone had told me that if I could see the stars there'd be no rain." Matches were played on the roof of the house as well, even at night. Recognising the boy's obsession with cricket, Tamim's father rigged up nets and lights. The son still recalls the intensity of the competition with the neighbours over their imagined "Ashes".

His brother Nafis Iqbal – four years older, and also a Bangladesh opener – is inextricably linked to Tamim's earliest cricket memories. The World Cup on the subcontinent in 1996 obviously affected Bangladesh – and none more so than the Khan family of Chittagong. "My father and uncles would watch all the matches on TV together. One day, before a match, *bhaiyya* [Nafis] told me, 'Sri Lanka are playing today, they have a player who hits really hard.' That was the first time I watched a match with full concentration, and I became a diehard fan of Sanath Jayasuriya."

The realisation that international cricket was no walk in the park also came via Sri Lanka. After destroying India in the 2007 World Cup in the West Indies – his first match on the biggest stage – Tamim forgot all his strokeplay while touring Sri Lanka. "Because I did OK in the World Cup all the teams researched my game. There were a lot of flaws in my batting at the time, and Sri Lanka spotted those weaknesses and directed the ball at my ribs. I had no leg-side game at that time, so I just couldn't hit the ball."

The feeling of helplessness did Tamim a major service. He understood there was no alternative to hard work. "It has happened that the national team training session starts at 2 o'clock, and I've been practising indoors on my own from 9 a.m. The entire right side of my body has got bruised black and blue because of balls from the bowling machine. That's why my weakest point is now my strongest point."

The performances bear him out. He passed 50 in nine of his 14 Test innings in 2010. His maiden Test century, on the West Indies tour in 2009, played a major role in winning Bangladesh their first Test abroad. His second – against India, at Mirpur – is his highest Test score, 151 off 183 balls. But Tamim holds his two consecutive hundreds in England above them all: "From the self-confidence perspective, I would consider those two centuries the turning point in my career. Playing in England, that too in May… the biggest gain from those centuries was the belief that if I could do it once I can do it again."

Cricket is now his religion, a dream that transcends barriers. "I imagine weird stuff – what if I hit 100 centuries, or what if I make 400 or 500 in an innings? I dream of Bangladesh needing 60 runs in two overs and I win them the match." These are mere dreams to Tamim Iqbal. To anyone who has seen his spectacular batting, they are possibilities.

Jonathan Trott

Paul Bolton

The sight of Jonathan Trott painstakingly marking his crease as if he were digging a trench drove opponents to distraction during 2010, but it was a reassuring one for England. Trott batted for over 33 hours in six home Tests, including a marathon nine and a quarter hours for his 184 against Pakistan at Lord's. He spent a further 20 hours at the crease in Australia last winter, when his 445 runs in just seven innings were crucial to England's Ashes defence, then batted his way into England's World Cup team.

Trott does not worry too much about complaints from opponents about his exaggerated crease-marking, nor the teasing of his England team-mates at the amount of time he spends in the nets. "I am trying to bat for six hours every day and I don't see how you can do that by batting for 15 minutes in the nets," he says. "I like to bat for 30–40 minutes. Even the coaches have gone when I have finished. It's a bit of a running joke in the England dressing-room, but it's the way I like to prepare."

Trott's methods certainly produce results. He completed 1,000 runs in Test cricket one year and one week after he made his debut. Just as he had on his Second Eleven and County Championship debuts for Warwickshire, Trott marked his first Test appearance with a century – in this case a match-shaping second innings of 119 in the Ashes decider at The Oval in August 2009. Clearly he is a man who believes that first impressions count.

IAN JONATHAN LEONARD TROTT was born in Cape Town on April 22, 1981, into a sporting family. His parents, Ian and Donna, were both talented hockey players. Donna also represented South Africa at softball, and a son from her first marriage, Kenny Jackson, played for Western Province as a middle-order batsman. Trott knew from an early stage that he also wanted to be a professional cricketer. Though he excelled at hockey and rugby at Rondebosch Boys' HS, the school was close enough to Newlands for Trott to gaze out from the classrooms and dream of batting for Western Province and South Africa.

After school Trott would spend hours at his father's sports shop knocking in or sanding cricket bats, while weekends were spent at the private coaching sessions run by his father or watching Jackson play for Western Province. His potential was first identified by the South Africa age-group selectors, who took him to the Under-15 Challenge in England in 1995. By the time he went to the Under-19 World Cup in Sri Lanka in early 2000, Trott was on a cricket scholarship at Stellenbosch University, but he completed only one year of a four-year degree in Human Movement Science. "I was always away playing cricket, so had to cram a whole year's biology syllabus into two days," Trott said. "When it came to the psychology exams I had to look at the board to see how to spell it."

By that stage Trott had already made his senior debut for Boland, playing alongside and outscoring Jackson, in a one-day match against Eastern Province. Trott joined Western Province in 2001 before he took the momentous decision to emigrate. His father, now a cricket coach at St John's School in Leatherhead, was born in England, and was reputedly a distant relative of the Australian Test players Harry and Albert Trott. Jonathan decided to use his British passport to qualify to play for England.

"I had benefited from the South African system. I had played for South Africa Under-15s and Under-19s, I was in their development system so it wasn't as if I wasn't in the selectors' plans," he said. "I just felt that I had not kicked on as I would have liked at Western Province. When I said that I was going to play in England, Eric Simons, the Western Province coach, said that if he was talking to me as my coach he would tell me not to go, but if he was my father he would tell me to go and play in England."

Warwickshire, who had close links with South Africa through Bob Woolmer and Allan Donald, was the obvious choice, and it was Woolmer, in his second spell as director of cricket at Edgbaston, who fixed him up with a trial. Trott was playing club cricket for HBS in Holland when he travelled to a second-team match against Somerset at the Knowle & Dorridge club near Solihull in July 2002. Dropped when he had five, he needed only one innings, 245, the highest score by a debutant in the Second Eleven Championship, to persuade

Warwickshire to sign him. When the contract arrived in Cape Town, Jackson told Trott: "Your life has changed." Prescient words indeed.

Trott followed up his second-team double-century with an imperious maiden first-class hundred on his Championship debut against Sussex at Edgbaston in May 2003, failing by only three runs to reach three figures before lunch. He spent four years qualifying for England, but his form dipped in 2007, the first year he became eligible – although he did have his first taste of full international cricket, in two unsuccessful Twenty20 matches against West Indies. Trott's form suffered as Warwickshire endured double relegation in the depressing reign of coach Mark Greatbatch, and he managed only two Championship fifties that season.

Trott's career was transformed by two decisions made within a month in the autumn of 2007. First Warwickshire replaced Greatbatch with Ashley Giles, the recently retired former England spinner; then Trott was a rather surprise selection for an England Performance Programme tour of India, which suggested he had not been forgotten by the selectors. Giles, soon to become a part-time selector himself, encouraged Trott to be less intense in the dressing-room and more focused in his practice, suggesting that hitting 1,000 balls rather than 100 in the nets would not necessarily make him a better player. "Ash's motto is train hard, play easy," says Trott, "whereas mine was train harder, play hard."

Trott has played his best cricket under Giles, who admires his single-mindedness, though they have been known to row like a married couple. Trott's actual marriage, to Abi Dollery, Warwickshire's press officer and granddaughter of the county's former captain Tom, has proved less tempestuous. "Abi has made me a more rounded person, not one that eats, sleeps and drinks cricket," says Trott. "She can also tell when I walk out to bat whether or not I am going to get runs. Don't ask me how, but I can count on one hand the number of times she has been wrong."

There can have been few occasions in 2010 when Mrs Trott knew her husband was likely to fail, as he rattled up 1,084 runs in first-class cricket, 940 in one-day matches and 306 in Twenty20 games. "I just love batting," Trott said. "I would rather be out there than sitting in the dressing-room having a laugh and joke. I prefer to find out over dinner what the jokes have been in the dressing-room during the day."

THE YIPS

Why's it gone there?

Alec Swann

As sporting enigmas go, the yips are one of the most unfathomable. How can a skill that has been delivered countless times, in a wide variety of situations, suddenly become a complete mystery? What triggers the breakdown in ability – not simply a loss of form – to the extent it is, in many cases, irretrievable?

This phenomenon is not unique to cricket, as many sporting disciplines have had sufferers, but cricket has seen more than its share down the years. The first well-known post-war instance was Fred Swarbrook, the Derbyshire left-arm spinner, who gave up playing and emigrated to South Africa, where he became a highly respected coach. A more recent case was Michael Davies, a similar type of bowler, who rose rapidly through Northamptonshire's ranks to the England A tour of Bangladesh and New Zealand in 1999-2000, before falling victim to the yips.

One year Davies was one half of a potent partnership with Graeme Swann. The next he was struggling, not only to achieve the same standards, but to land the ball consistently – and the ultimate outcome, following a brief stint at Essex, was the end of his professional career. But while the majority of recorded cases affect left-arm bowlers, they are not alone.

Scott Boswell was a right-arm seamer whose steady career, divided between Northamptonshire and Leicestershire, came to a shuddering end in the 2001 Cheltenham & Gloucester Trophy final between the Foxes and Somerset. It was far from being a decline: Boswell's problems surfaced suddenly on the domestic game's biggest occasion, when he bowled eight wides – five of them in a row – in his second (and last) over.

Looking back a decade later, the two victims have gained some perspective on their life-changing misfortunes. Davies remembers: "I bowled a ball that pitched halfway down the wicket and on the leg side that got hit away, and the first thought was 'Why has it gone there? I don't usually do that.' It continued to the stage where I was scared to bowl and looked for any reason not to, even in the nets. I was embarrassed by it, and you find that people behave differently towards you – and it didn't help that I was continually being picked when I needed to be taken out of it.

"It's on your mind all the time. You can't sleep because you're continually thinking about it, and the question of how something so natural can suddenly become so difficult keeps coming back. I don't really know any more about it now than I did when I was going through it, and no one really understands it. Just to say it's a concentration issue or a confidence thing is not giving it the attention it deserves."

Boswell is now a teacher and coach at Nottingham High School. "My problems were a bit different in that it was just one occasion. I had no idea that

Yip, yip – not hooray: Scott Boswell struggles to complete his second over in the 2001 C&G final at Lord's; George Sharp stretches his arms.

it was going to happen. I hadn't been bowling at my best in the lead-up to the game, but the odd wide happens – and my performance hadn't really deteriorated.

"The first over on the day felt fine, but when I bowled the first wide the noise of the crowd was something I hadn't expected. Then I bowled the second and it got louder, then the third and it got louder still. It was like the roof was coming off and I just froze. The moment knocked me off balance completely. What should have been the biggest day of my cricketing life became the worst, and it affected me afterwards for a long time.

"Playing club cricket the next year, if it was my turn to bowl, I felt sick and had a fear about completing an over. I couldn't let go of the ball, it felt solid in my hand and I would just freeze. I could bowl a good spell one week but the next it would be back to not knowing where it was going to go."

Surrey's Keith Medlycott, another left-arm spinner, made it as far as the England team that toured the West Indies in 1989-90, and the A-side that went to Pakistan and Sri Lanka the following winter, but he was forced to retire not long afterwards, aged only 26. "People have related my problems to the England tour I went on, but that had nothing to do with it. The last seven or eight games of the 1990 season I put myself under far too much pressure to do well and get on the Australian tour, and every time I had a bad day or bowled a bad delivery it just got worse. Your team-mates don't know how to react, which affects how you go about your business. You think you're going to do badly and you end up becoming isolated."

Any personal testimony from sportsmen or women – be they golfers, baseball pitchers, darts players or goal-kicking fly-halves – alludes to the problem being in the mind. Of the high-profile golfers to have suffered, Bernhard Langer and Ian Baker-Finch have both spoken about the depths to which they sank when their skills – in Langer's case with the putter and in Baker-Finch's with his all-round game – deserted them. Baker-Finch, who won The Open in 1991, has referred to playing well on a practice day but being unable to bring that performance to the theatre of competition. Langer has specified his putting problem as one of focusing on what could go wrong.

The parallels between golf and bowling are striking: both disciplines depend heavily on visualisation for their successful delivery. A golf coach will tell a pupil, when faced with a tee-shot that needs to avoid a hazard, to concentrate on the fairway and not on the hazard – a successful outcome as opposed to a negative one. When coaching bowling, a basic principle is to get the bowler to imagine where he wants to pitch the ball: to think about dismissing the batsman, not about what could go amiss. When the latter overtakes the former, then it often leads to difficulties, and the opposite of positive thought occurs. What was a natural action is second-guessed, and delivering the ball becomes a cluttered chain of events. The thought of "How do I land it?" – in stark contrast to "Where am I going to land it?" – becomes dominant.

Davies thinks that his attack of the yips started as a technical fault and became more and more of a psychological problem as it went on. "Everyone has bad trots and that is how it started with me, but the problem was that I couldn't find any way out of it. I've read that extroverted people are less likely to suffer from this kind of problem – those who can disconnect themselves from what they do and simply put a bad day to one side and not let it worry them. But I wasn't like this at all, and that added to the problem.

"I didn't feel my legs or the ball in my hands like I was used to. It just didn't feel the same. And this affects your confidence, which is spiralling away quickly to the point where bowling is the last thing you want to do. There's a snowball effect about it all. You put more pressure on yourself, which leads to a feeling of tenseness, which means you can't do what you need to and so on, like a vicious circle."

In retrospect, Boswell says: "For me it was a mental thing, I would say at least 85–90%. It started in the Lord's final, but it was after that when it came to a head. I could bowl in the nets and in a practice situation, but as soon as it became competitive then I would be gone and wouldn't be able to let the ball go. I couldn't feel my action, and I would be that stiff that I simply couldn't get through the act of bowling. My thought process was entirely negative, not just with cricket, and I would turn everything round to its negative side – and that was never going to allow the problem to be solved."

Medlycott, now the coach at Reed's School in Surrey, reflects: "It's a mental issue, no question about it. I had a mental frailty which meant that when the problems started I was unable to get myself out of them. I so desperately wanted to play at the highest level, and when it started to go wrong I didn't know where to turn. It's described as a vicious circle and that's exactly what it is. I'd spend hours every day bowling, but that natural feel that you need had gone. And then you end up telling yourself that it isn't right, and the problem keeps repeating itself because your confidence isn't there.

"When coaching, my approach has always been to stay as positive as possible, to have a 'What's the worst that can happen?' mentality. I'd have loved to have had the mentality of my coaching when I played, to not get caught up in the external stuff and just approach it without any fear."

On the physical side, the complexity of bowling plays a part. Like the golf swing, the bowling action has a number of movements that can potentially go wrong. The ideal may be a robust, repetitive action; the reality, however, is often far from it. If the brain is telling the body there is something wrong, and the body refuses to play ball, then the outcome will inevitably fall short of expectation.

Michael Davies, bowling for Northants in 1999.

According to Boswell: "My arm was low and that was definitely a technical thing, but I don't think that was a problem. My action wasn't different to before the final when I was able to bowl where I wanted, but the outcome of the mental block is the ball going everywhere, so technique has to come into it somewhere. The only way I found to stop it was to bowl round the wicket and try to bowl bouncers. Just hitting the pitch would make a difference, but as soon as I came back over the wicket then the problem would come back."

External factors also contribute significantly. Professional sport carries its own unique pressures, and it would be naive to think that these don't contribute. There is competition from other players; in the game itself there is the pressure of playing for your livelihood; and there is also the pressure of expectation. These may have nothing to do with any breakdown in skills, or they may contribute to such a degree that they cannot be isolated from the problem.

"There was pressure on me to do well because of the season I had had the year before," says Davies, "and that pressure was from outside to win games and from myself to keep performing to a previous level. My contract was up at the end of the year and that did play on my mind. Whereas in the past my only thought would've been 'How do I get this batsman out?', it became 'Where is this going?', and the external factors certainly added to it."

Yet the yips aren't terminal. Langer – the golfer – battled through his by practising religiously, and to watch Davies bowl in league cricket now, you would be hard pushed to believe that anything untoward had ever occurred. Batsmen often talk of form returning with a single shot or during an innings, and for no immediately obvious reason, so there is the possibility that the yips could disappear as readily as they appear.

According to Mark Bawden, England's team psychologist, the yips are an emotional disorder, sometimes caused by factors completely unrelated to sport. "They are usually caused by an individual experiencing some form of emotional trauma which they have not fully dealt with. The yips are the physical manifestation of the emotional problem. The irony is that often the person does not consider the causing event to be traumatic, and that in itself is the problem. The emotional event can be anything that the person holds as important at a less conscious level."

In neurological terms, Bawden says, the yips cause what psychologists call an "amygdala hijack". The amygdala is the part of the brain that detects threat and throws our body into a "fight/flight/freeze" response. If the individual feels he is unable to get out of the situation, then this part of the brain codes the experience as threatening. Thus, whenever a bowler is in a similar situation, the amygdala recognises the cues and automatically triggers a fight/flight/freeze response. Many players report that they are able to bowl in nets, practice games and even in some matches without any problem. It all depends on what the amygdala coded in the original experience. One of the factors that intensifies the experience of the yips is the fact that if you bowl a no-ball or wide – as Boswell did – you have to repeat the delivery. Then you can feel like you are "trapped inside a burning building", as one bowler put it.

There are many different types of interventions that can cure or "cheat" the yips, according to Bawden. "The right solution is very individual-specific. It is definitely not a 'one size fits all'. The basic principle of cheating the yips is that you have to convince your brain that bowling is not threatening, or that you are performing a different skill by changing your technique. Many fast bowlers with the yips have no problem bowling spin or even medium-pace – if they change their action – because the messages to the brain are different.

"However, to truly get rid of the yips you need to become emotionally free from the original experience that is blocked within you and caused the problem. Once you have identified the trigger event – which is often outside sport – you can work with a skilled practitioner to use methods such as EFT (emotional freedom technique) or hypnosis to recode the initial experience, so that the brain doesn't interpret bowling as threatening any more. When you have done that, the brain can be allowed to remember the old cues and you can get back to enjoying playing cricket again!"

Alec Swann, elder brother of England off-spinner Graeme, played county cricket for Northamptonshire and Lancashire.

CRICKET'S LOVE OF NUMBERS

A dance to the music of stats

TIM DE LISLE

Of all the memorable quotes that have lodged in cricket folklore, possibly only one is to do with breaking records. It was uttered by Fred Trueman in 1964, after he became the first to take 300 Test wickets. He was asked if anyone would ever break his record. "Aye," said Fred, "but whoever does will be bloody tired."

It was a good line, if only partly prescient. The man who overhauled Trueman's final tally of 307 was Lance Gibbs, who had to bowl 27,000 balls to do it – about 12,000 more than Trueman. So he may well have been exhausted, and, if actions speak louder than words, he definitely was: after beating the record, he took only one more wicket. But by the end of 2010, both had been overtaken by 22 other bowlers, and a couple of them – Daniel Vettori on 339, Harbhajan Singh on 386 – were young enough to take many more. Some already had. The record for a fast bowler stands at 563, set by Glenn McGrath. And the record for all bowlers is not 600 wickets, or 700, but 800, set by Muttiah Muralitharan last July. What on earth is goin' off out there?

Nor was it just the bowlers. Another mountain was scaled in October 2010 when Sachin Tendulkar made his 50th Test century. Fifty! Even Don Bradman managed only 29. Bradman, of course, played far less Test cricket: just 52 matches, 125 fewer than Tendulkar. If Bradman had played 177 Tests in the style to which he was accustomed, he would have finished with 98 hundreds – though, being Bradman, he would have surely wanted to kick on to 99.94.

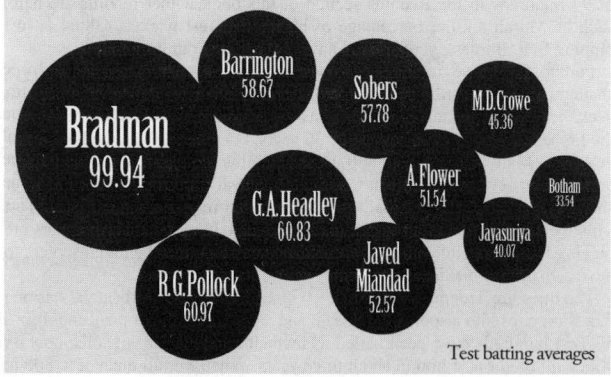

Test batting averages

Ben Ashworth

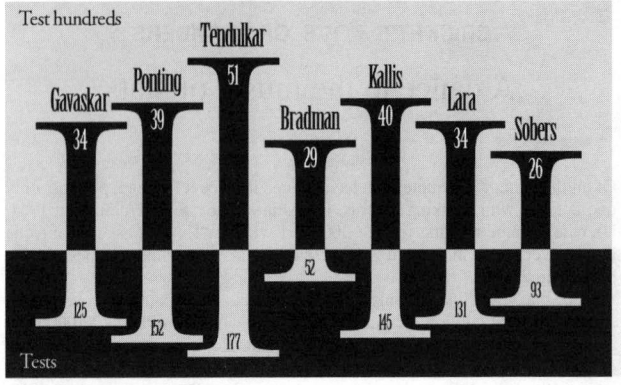

Ben Ashworth

Not that the length of his career diminishes Tendulkar's feat. He has had to start a Test series and face a new set of questions 67 times, to Bradman's 11, never mind playing 450 one-day internationals to the highest standards. His 50 Test centuries are a staggering achievement. Yet, outside India, there was little fanfare – less, for instance, than there was in 1977 when Geoff Boycott made his 100th (first-class) hundred in an Ashes Test. That could change when Tendulkar reaches 100 hundreds in all international cricket; he went into the 2011 World Cup on 97, another astonishing figure – the batsmen fourth and fifth on this list, Brian Lara and Rahul Dravid, have 96 between them. But will it really change? Record-lovers are conservative, even by cricket standards: they deal in stone. They tend to give more weight to records they have seen broken before, and to records in single disciplines: you won't find that figure of 97 hundreds in the Records section of this book. Other records are here, such as Murali's killer percentage of his team's Test wickets (38.64%, just pipping S. F. Barnes), yet they still haven't lodged in our heads.

Perhaps we have just become too used to seeing international records shattered. Even records are susceptible to fashion, and the last 20 years have been the age of the international record breaker. Garry Sobers's 365 reigned as the highest individual Test score for 36 years, but Lara's 375 lasted only nine years and Matthew Hayden's 380 just six months. Lara's 400 has been on its pedestal for seven years, but it too is under threat. Only four men have ever shown the compound of appetite and aggression required to make two Test triple-centuries, and while Lara and Bradman are two of them, the others are playing today: Virender Sehwag and Chris Gayle, both fast enough scorers to have a chance of making 401.

The question Trueman was asked – will the record ever be beaten? – is one that soon pops into a sports fan's head, and we tend to answer no. Tendulkar's 50 Test hundreds have been hailed as invincible, yet Jacques Kallis, now on 40, could motor past him in about three years. When Murali made it to 800 in

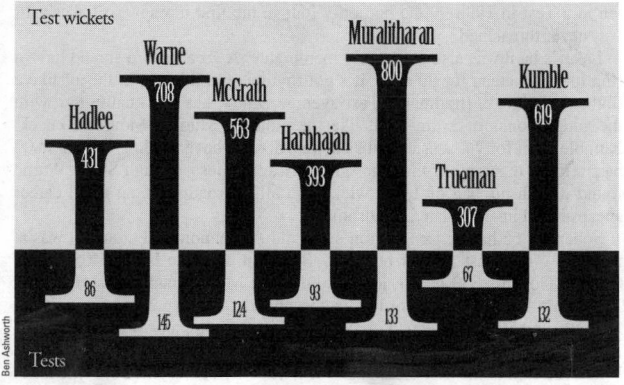

Test wickets

Hadlee 431
Warne 708
McGrath 563
Harbhajan 393
Muralitharan 800
Trueman 307
Kumble 619

86
145
124
93
133
67
132

Ben Ashworth
Tests

his final Test, with delicious drama, many observers said his feat would never be surpassed. But the same would have been said of Bradman's 29 hundreds, and eventually, 33 years on, Sunil Gavaskar's 30. If Murali can do it, maybe someone else can: bowling still awaits its Bradman. Whoever he is, he really will be bloody tired.

Statistics are like currencies, prone to sudden devaluation. A Test triple-hundred, which used to have immense rarity value, now comes along about once every two years. Australia's record of 721 first-class runs in a day (1948) has gained lustre as over-rates have slowed – although it has its modern counterparts in two Australian co-productions: 872 in a day (Johannesburg, 2006) and 428 in an evening (Christchurch, 2010).

Most of the big Test records have changed hands in recent years, but there is one that looks today, as it looked to Neville Cardus in *Wisden 1968*, unbeatable: Jim Laker's 19 for 90. "The most wonderful of all happenings," Cardus wrote: "…here, for certain, is a record which will remain unbeaten." Fate, so far, remains untempted. Laker's feat has towered over its landscape for 54 years and 1,560 Tests. (The sheer volume of modern Test cricket still takes some grasping. The first 800 Tests took 100 years; the last 800 have taken 19.)

Laker's 19 may have been achieved with undue help from the pitch: Old Trafford in 1956 was so sticky that it had already glued itself into the record books two weeks earlier, when Lancashire beat Leicestershire without losing a wicket. But then every batsman from Bradman down will have had help from a few shirtfronts. And Laker's 19 has two qualities to make it stand out even among records.

First, it is way out in front. Before Laker, nobody had taken 18 wickets in a Test; since him, nobody has taken 17. Instances of all ten in first-class cricket are not that rare, coming at about four a decade, but what is almost unheard of is for the same bowler to shine in both innings. When Anil Kumble took all ten in a Test in 1998-99, he had only four in the first innings, so Laker's 19 was never threatened.

Laker's haul was also supremely memorable. A great record should have a ring to it. Nineteen for 90 does: it's got rhythm, and it hangs in the air like a flighted off-break. Bradman's Test average, 99.94, has this quality too, with the added bonus of a tiny blot, like the mole on Marilyn Monroe's cheek. Kumble's ten for 74, sensational as it was, doesn't have rhythm. Murali's 800 has it, more than any of the other great wicket tallies – though Shane Warne found it with his bag of 1,001 wickets in all internationals, an artful career encapsulated in an elegant palindrome.

Sobers's 365 had it; Len Hutton's 364 didn't, phenomenal though it was at the time – not least for not being by Bradman. Graeme Hick's 405 had it, Graham Gooch's 333 had it, and so did Hanif Mohammad's 499. Hayden's 380 didn't. Lara, a born record collector, understood the power of resonance: 375, 400 and 501 all have it. You could name a bat after any of them.

As international cricket has multiplied, so first-class cricket has shrivelled. When you turn to the first-class pages of *Wisden's* Records, the bold type fades away and today's stars, even one as renewable as Mark Ramprakash, bow to the golden oldies – Hobbs, Compton, Bradman, Freeman, Rhodes. Freeman, a colossus named Tich, has now topped the table for most wickets in a season for 83 years, and his nearest rival is himself. George Hirst has clocked up a century as the only man to do the "double" double. And the award for the longest-lasting major record in *Wisden* goes to… John Wisden himself, the only man to take all ten wickets in an innings without the help of either a fielder or an umpire – all ten bowled, for the North v the South at Lord's in 1850. Ten for how many, you wonder? History, alas, doesn't relate. No wonder he launched an almanack.

Tim de Lisle edits Intelligent Life *magazine and is a past editor of* Wisden Cricket Monthly *and* Wisden Cricketers' Almanack. *His book* Young Wisden: A New Fan's Guide to Cricket, *revised and updated by Lawrence Booth, is now available.*

PART TWO

The Wisden Review

CRICKET BOOKS, 2010

A kind of pagan worship

GIDEON HAIGH

Cricket is mutating rapidly, experimenting with new varieties. So is cricket literature. Revived in 2010 was the old sub-genre of the travelogue, in the spirit of Geoffrey Moorhouse's *The Best-Loved Game*, itself one of cricket's best-loved books. With his superfine biographies of Brian Clough and Harold Larwood, Duncan Hamilton created a hard act for himself to follow in **A Last English Summer**, a meditative journey through the 2009 season, from county match to village match to league match, from Ridge Meadow to Riverside. Thanks to a lifetime's thoughtful contemplation and a darting, quicksilver eye, he furnishes such delectable descriptions as this of Sulieman Benn:

> His body is shaped like a bone-handled knife: slightly stooped, long frame, long legs and long sensitive fingers, which he wraps around the seam as tightly as twine. His spinning finger is already callused, and the knuckles are as prominent as knurls on a tree… He doesn't so much bowl as gradually uncoil himself, like a line of stiff rope, in the five sure steps he takes from mark to crease. He holds the ball tight to his chest, his sharp elbows extended, as though rocking a baby between his arms… He entices the batsmen forward like a beckoning finger.

Hamilton also exhibits a Brysonesque sense of the absurd, noting that the British government's current Sports Visitor application form asks whether the budding league pro has "ever been involved in… war crimes, crimes against humanity or genocide", while his reverie in Ramsbottom's annual 1940s war weekend is disturbed "when a gangling man in the tailored grey of a Nazi uniform takes a call on his mobile phone". My sole reservation about an otherwise delicious reading experience is whether it amounts to more than the sum of its parts, whether the vignettes form enough of a progression, whether the evidence is directed to sufficient of a conclusion. Hamilton, while capable of astringent analytical commentary on the state of the game, settles for a broadly affirming ending: "It [cricket] will survive whatever else happens to it; I'm convinced of that, and comforted by it too." Yet if survival is the best that can be hoped for, then a note of despondency would surely be more apposite: Hamilton leaves himself open to the charge of reversing Pope's couplet, of being "willing to strike but afraid to wound". The pointlessness of the ballast of scores, statistics and postscript, meanwhile, is even more annoying than the appearances of Daniel Vittori, Frank Worrall, Chris Gale and Mark Waugh (when it should be Wagh). That said, *A Last English Summer* maintains Hamilton's reputation – and that is no little matter.

When the Jamaican Brenton Parchment signed to pro for Ramsbottom in the Lancashire League in 2009, he would hardly have foreseen his chronicling by two top-class English writers in the season. But not only was he watched failing against Accrington by Hamilton, but failing against Bacup by Harry

Pearson, performing his own smaller circuit of cricket in the north. Readers of *The Far Corner* will already be aware that Pearson is an extremely funny writer who turns a phrase like a doosra, and **Slipless in Settle** finds him in his element, criss-crossing the invisible boundaries separating the Ribblesdale and Bradford Leagues from the North-East Premier and Craven and District Leagues, taking in pros like Parchment and humble strivers alike, while coming over as a mixture of a vagrant Nick Hornby, capable of describing Yorkshire in the 1880s as "the Lynyrd Skynyrd of cricket", and an over-educated Fred

Trueman, disgruntled by modern phenomena like on-field chatter: "A cricket match has come to resemble that moment at a children's party when all the 11-year-old boys, hyper with sugar and E-numbers, start shrieking out their favourite catchphrases from *Little Britain*." Likewise is Pearson vexed by the fitness of international cricketers: "The result is that England players' muscles have been gradually ratcheted tighter and tighter until all it takes is one ab crunch too many and in a glissando of twangs the body explodes like an over-wound clock. Many doctors believe that it is only a matter of time before a cricketer becomes so taut he actually turns himself inside out." It's premium banter, and Pearson coins a put-down which, if it is original, deserves the widest possible circulation: "If he'd bought a bat with four middles he'd never have found any of them." But *Slipless in Settle* peters out somewhat, because Pearson doesn't dwell anywhere quite long enough to form other than superficial impressions, and because the only recurrent sentiment is put in the mouths of spectators – that cricket in the northern leagues is "not what it were". Surely nothing ever is. That said, it's hard to dislike a book containing the sentence: "A Manchester tart is basically a Bakewell tart with meringue on the top, because everything from Manchester is a bit showy."

On a decidedly arduous journey last year embarked the *Express's* veteran cricket correspondent Colin Bateman, two of his sons and a nephew, and press-box colleagues David Lloyd and Ian Todd: a 16-day, 1,100-mile cycle through the first-class cricket counties. The party appear on the back cover of **String Fellows** aboard their velocipedes like The Magnificent Seven astride their steeds, although their purpose was philanthropic, raising money for the Laurie Engel Fund, named for the son of former *Wisden* editor Matthew Engel's 13-year-old son, victim of cancer in September 2005. Good heart and good fellowship shine through all the pain and punctures: if not unputdownable, the result is assuredly pickupable. Nor was a cricket book published last year to a nobler end.

Stephen Chalke's peregrinations in quest of the eyewitness testimony of county cricketers of the 1950s and 1960s have provided some of the most memorable cricket writing of the last 15 years, recreating a lost artisanal milieu in our midst. In **A Long Half-Hour**, he shares the background to half a dozen of his most intriguing encounters, with Ken Biddulph, Arthur Milton, Geoff Edrich, Eric Hill, Dickie Dodds and Bomber Wells – no world-beaters here, but a variety of life experience to which the modern cricketer has become a total stranger, some moving moments, and a few timeless mots, including this from Northamptonshire's Freddie Jakeman: "Out of every hundred cricketers there's probably two shits. And if the 98 of us can't look after those two, we're a poor bunch." Chalke himself comes into firmer focus in a fictionalised memoir of an ageing captain's season in Division Nine of the Wiltshire League, although the personal reminiscences of **Now I'm 62** rather overshadow the more conventional cricket narrative.

David Tossell sets off on an updated version of Chalke's missions in **Following On**, choosing to trace the members of the England team that won the Under-19 World Cup in 1998-99, three of whom have played Test cricket, while several of the rest have drifted from the game altogether. But an idea does not a book make. After a pedestrian retelling of that win, Tossell settles into rather repetitive retellings of the various careers, buttressed with too many bland direct quotes. Graeme Swann, who features on the cover as though leaping out of a cupboard to frighten a player of hide-and-seek, provides typically good copy; otherwise one learns little more than that some make it and most don't. It was ever thus.

Cricket life stories also took a new, raunchy turn. Herschelle Gibbs's **To The Point** walked off shelves in South Africa, thanks to its breaching the "what-happens-on-tour-stays-on-tour" dressing-room *omertà* with tales of Mötley Crüe-esque excess. Yet he succeeds only in appearing a braggart, not so much stormy petrel as horny teenager, soliciting sponsorship for his heavily notched bedpost. It's like being cornered in a bar by the biggest, dumbest, most self-fascinated arsehole in the universe. There's this: "'Live life to the max' has pretty much been my mantra. With this default setting and an outgoing personality, I've had a lot of fun in my life. I'm also a pretty generous guy, both with my money and my time." And this: "I have the gift of the gab, which I get from my dad, and clearly women love it. My open demeanour often comes across as flirting, but that's just the way I am. I guess you could say I am charming and, as I said, chicks dig it." And, of course, this: "As I've said, people can seldom tell when I'm drunk, unless – obviously – I'm properly slaughtered. Or maybe I should say: I don't think people notice when I'm drunk, but I can't really tell when I'm the one who's pissed, can I?" By Gibbs's standards, this qualifies as a shaft of personal insight. Perhaps the most repellent passages concern his year-long marriage, which ended when he texted his wife seeking a divorce: "Apart from one occasion during our engagement, I wasn't unfaithful during the marriage. Well, not technically,

anyway." Actually, on second thoughts, it's worse than a drunken ear-bashing: at least in a bar, you'd be able to excuse yourself by adjourning to the Gents.

In a profile of Robert Maxwell, Francis Wheen once noted the fondness of his biographers for the expression "man of contradictions". This was, said Wheen, "another way of saying he is a colossal hypocrite". Matthew Hayden tries on the "man of contradictions" mantle for **Standing My Ground**, which he does, arguing that God-fearing Catholics with old-fashioned family values can be gobby, overbearing boors if it helps them win games of cricket: "My role became one of intimidator. And just as a good actor completely gives himself to a part, I went all the way." Further, even. That said, his zealous and well-informed amanuensis Robert Craddock has done the best possible job, in a book generous to opponents such as Muttiah Muralitharan, Rahul Dravid, Brian Lara and Andrew Flintoff, and frank about feuds with Mark Taylor, Rod Marsh, Matthew Elliott, Harbhajan Singh, Shoaib Akhtar and even Glenn McGrath (for a while). Best of all is the way in which *Standing My Ground* brings to life the mano-a-mano combat of beating back top-class bowling. The accounts of tackling Shoaib, Harbhajan and Shaun Pollock are edge-of-the-seat stuff; likewise Hayden's being haunted by Allan Donald, Andrew Flintoff and Curtly Ambrose. Sprinkled throughout are the sorts of insight that can come only from the centre of the action, such as: "Unlike Australian umpires, who mark centre through the middle of the bat, English umpires mark centre through the edge, which can put you a centimetre away from where you think you are." There is finally an appreciative glimpse of the IPL, including a vignette of Hayden giving an up-and-at-'em address to his polyglot Chennai Super Kings dressing-room. "I could understand the F-words," responded a Sri Lankan team-mate, "but apart from that… nothing." You may reach the end still wondering if you like Hayden, but you will have learned a few things along the way.

Move along, there's nothing much to see in **Slow Death**, the memoirs of Rudi Koertzen. Koertzen explains that his motif originated in a habit of gripping his left wrist with his right hand because it helped to "stop me from shooting up my left hand without thinking about my decision", but not why his hand seemed to rise so often at the wrong moment regardless. He wasn't much of an umpire and this isn't much of a book: pedestrian, repetitive, and, where the fiasco at the end of the 2007 World Cup final is concerned, frankly evasive. Koertzen's attitude to referrals, too, that the ICC elite panel "were the so-called best umpires in the world and therefore should never be guilty of taking the easy option of referring every decision to the TV umpire", has the merit of being honest and the demerit of being entirely wrong-headed. If certainty in decision-making makes it necessary, pride should play no part.

Henry Olonga is more modest in **Blood, Sweat and Treason**: "Make no mistake, I was no world-beater anyway and I had an average career… I was never going to be that good." It sets the tone for a disarmingly candid autobiography with more than its share of event: Olonga suffers depression, gets kidnapped and beaten up, writes a hit song, has his life threatened and his phone tapped by his country's secret police, and even has a prostitute tell him she "doesn't do black guys". Most valuable of all is the skinny on his famous protest with Andy Flower against Zimbabwe's iniquitous regime during the 2003 World Cup, which splashes some grey around a hitherto black and white tale. There *was* a racial divide in the Zimbabwe team of his career, mirroring that in his own country, which some white players were loath to acknowledge. A meeting at the Harare Sports Club, intended to ventilate the issue, worsened animosities: "It was like being in a Ku Klux Klan meeting." Olonga was mortified, however, when his concerns were used as a pretext for the Zimbabwe Cricket Union's strongarm tactics, as ZANU–PF led the country to rack and ruin. Flower and Olonga originally fantasised about a team boycott; they settled for their black-tape armbands rather than jeopardise the careers of others.

Olonga gives belated praise to England for declining to play in Harare: "I thought it was fantastic that they should ask us if we felt it was morally right

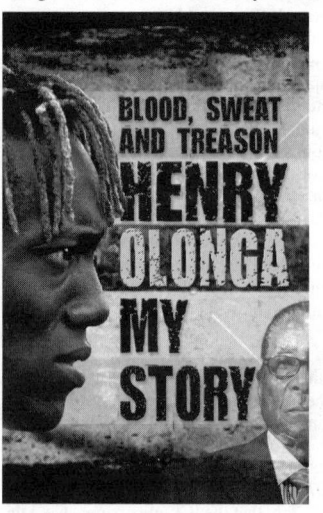

to play. Most of the other countries didn't care two hoots about the moral issue." Ironically, the most racist fans he encountered were in Pakistan, who pelted him and a black team-mate with banana skins, coins and small pieces of concrete, and the worst umpiring was in Sri Lanka, whose home-town official cheated Zimbabwe of what looked like an inevitable Test victory in Colombo in 1998. This is a bigger book than perhaps the man himself; its lapses into the standard patois of autobiography ("We bowled them out for 133 in 29 overs. I took six wickets for just 28 runs. It was one of those days when everything you try comes off.") are jarring. But it is as close as most autobiographies come to required reading.

Having penned *Whispering Death* in 1993, Michael Holding is back for a second innings at the autobiographical crease, although in **No Holding Back** he's mainly off his short run. "How do I look back on the career I had?" he asks. "I have never really thought about it very much. I'm not one who sits at home and pours (*sic*) over old scorecards, reminiscing how I got so-and-so out, I haven't even got a cricket picture on any wall at home and I don't look up old footage on YouTube." An admirable attitude in a man, it can hardly have been helpful to co-author Edward Hawkins. Holding is an excellent commentator and brooks no nonsense, parting ways with Allen Stanford when people still asked why, and quitting the ICC when others involved in overturning the result of the 2006 Oval Test asked why not. "They did it for political gain, without a thought of the damage they were doing to the game itself," says Holding. "It was all about people doing favours for each other. It was about as cheap a shot as you could get." Otherwise, you'll have more fun searching for clips of Holding on YouTube.

Having mastered the dark arts of Twitter, meanwhile, both Jonathan Agnew and David Lloyd have set out to prove they can still write longer than 140 characters. Agnew's **Thanks, Johnners** is described as an "affectionate tribute" to Brian Johnston, although it unfolds as what Alan Ross might have called a Bob Cunis of a book – neither one thing nor the other. There's a bit of Johnners, rather a lot of Aggers, some jolly japes, some cricket issues, and 17 entire pages about the 20-year-old "Botham didn't quite get his leg over" double entendre, which when it comes down to it isn't exactly "The Fleet's lit up!" or "Oh, the humanity!" Agnew writes fluently and sometimes engagingly, but his ostensible subject rather fades into the background, to be recalled in occasional abrupt asides like: "Johnners would have loved Twenty20, of that I am certain."

David Lloyd oozes out of **Start the Car** from the first page, falling over himself in enthusiasm for all things Sky, and providing a seeming excess of information about some of its stars: "There is nothing that Beefy can neck that four Red Bulls, three black coffees, two enormous belches and a huge fart won't fix the next morning." Thanks for sharing, Bumble. On the other hand, my regard for Bumble was quite unreasonably enhanced by his effusions about The Fall: "In pop music, if you're introduced to The Fall, you either get them or you don't. I did and feel richer for it." I could hardly have been more surprised had Johnners turned up in a 1977 photo pogoing to the Buzzcocks at the 100 Club.

There are some cheerful selections from Lloyd's (very funny) after-dinner repertoire, and also a few well-formed opinions, including a keen semantic observation about the county game: "The most damning word we can possibly use in relation to our domestic cricket is *circuit*. Players pound round and round it until their bodies blow up… Forget this convenient excuse of serving county members for a second and ask whether anybody has questioned why we are prepared to short-change them. Why should they field players operating at well below their optimum capacity?" Plus a homage to Mark E. Smith – which may not mean much to you but it does to me…

By far the year's handsomest life story was **Hugh Trumble: A Cricketer's Life**: two hardback volumes, heavily footnoted and sumptuously illustrated. Nor could Trumble's career have been more assiduously tracked than by Alf Batchelder, a former teacher who has written a fine two-volume history of the Melbourne Cricket Club in whose library he is now an industrious volunteer. Trouble is that Trumble was a great and consistent cricketer who lived a blameless life and left a legacy of undiluted goodwill – his life was a gift to the game, but not to biography.

Batchelder has unearthed a good deal of charming detail, such as the 1896 Australians having their luggage plundered by a ring of shipboard thieves. The perishability of opinion is also to be savoured in a book like this, so we encounter Lord Harris's deploring the "cheeky" Australian habit of declaring in "a tone of disgust", Tom Horan's damnation of the soon-to-be-all-conquering

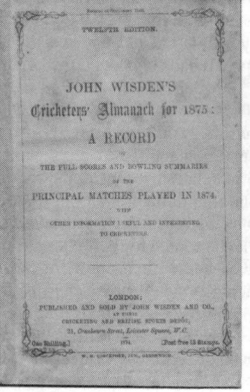

1902 Australian team as "a surprising manifestation of fatuous ineptitude on the part of the selection committee", and Trumble's denunciation of the googly as "the most unpleasant ball I have ever known" and a "nasty, deceitful, tricky packet of trouble". But this being about as trenchant as Trumble became, there's not quite enough colour or insight to leaven the rigidly chronological recitation of contemporary match reports.

Anthologies were thick on the shelf in 2009. Editor John Stern harvested a popular *Wisden Cricketer* series for **My Favourite Cricketer** – a disclaimer being necessary here that my own rhapsody of Chris Tavaré is among them. It is a happy collection long on youthful veneration, though with some touching variations, none so moving as the contribution of the *Daily Telegraph's* revered obituaries editor, Hugh Massingberd, who was sustained through a final illness by his adoration of Ali Brown: "I am now just living in hope of one more season of The Lord."

It appears a mixed blessing to have actually met the favourite in question. Simon Hattenstone's obsession with Graeme Hick was somehow completed by interviewing him, while all Simon Wilde got for his troubles on shaking Geoff Boycott's hand was a terse: "I don't know why I'm shaking your hand, son, because you never write anything nice about me…" Brooding on his hopeless infatuation with Graeme Wood, Christian Ryan recalls fretting: "Why couldn't the world see what I saw?" Such is the nature of adulation. Some of the profiles are like the stuff of benefit brochures, but most contain a line, a reflection, a sentiment worth reading, and a few could have been longer – I would happily volunteer to go on and on and on about Chris Tavaré.

Erstwhile producer Peter Baxter sifted 30 years of *Test Match Special's* lunchtime interviews, in which celebrities of various descriptions are revealed as closet cricket fans, for **The Best Views from the Boundary**. Like anything involving "celebrity", it could be rubbish, but thanks to judicious choice of guests and the hearty good humour of the interlocutors, the results are surprisingly informative and personally disclosing. The breadth of cricket's appeal is hearteningly confirmed: the game must be doing something right if it can captivate actors like Stephen Fry, Daniel Radcliffe, John Cleese and Peter O'Toole, and musos as diverse as Elton John, Lily Allen, Bill Wyman and Hugh Cornwell. Administrators take note: there are ways to love cricket other than buying replica kit and roaring for Freddie.

Put together by freelance journalist Andrew Collomosse, **Magnificent Seven** contains long interviews with 15 surviving members of the Yorkshire team that owned the County Championship through the 1960s, including Brian Close and Ray Illingworth (although not Geoff Boycott, perhaps because of the involvement of the other two). It's well done, even if the idea of using a different player or combination of players to tell each season doesn't quite come off, and the concept of introducing each year by its popular culture ("The Shadows were top of the UK charts with 'Wonderful Land' when Yorkshire took the field for their opening match of the season against MCC") soon loses novelty and point. In fact, the period flavour emerges quite naturally, as in Mick Cowan's reminiscence of appearing on *Beat the Clock* on his honeymoon and winning a washer and spin dryer, then bumping into a Yorkshire committeeman in the same hotel with a woman other than his wife. "I know I've got at least one vote on the selection committee now," said Cowan.

Magnificent Seven is invaluable as a survey of professional attitudes from the era, with Gordon Barker telling Brian Bolus that he should aim for 1,500 rather than 2,000 runs a season "otherwise they'll expect that every year", and

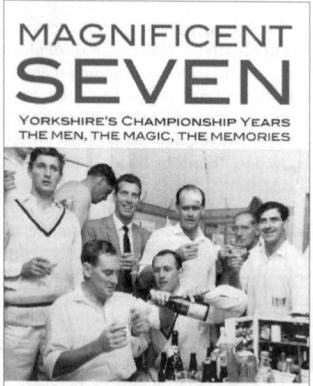

MAGNIFICENT
SEVEN
YORKSHIRE'S CHAMPIONSHIP YEARS
THE MEN, THE MAGIC, THE MEMORIES

THE PLAYERS' OWN STORY
WITH ANDREW COLLOMOSSE
FOREWORD BY RAY ILLINGWORTH
AFTERWORD BY BRIAN CLOSE

Mel Ryan recoiling from one-day cricket: "I honestly thought people were joking when they said we could only bowl 15 overs and that it didn't matter if we didn't get anybody out." Professionalism was, however, no match for a hidebound amateur administration, which purged most of Boycott's great contemporaries – something that the autocratic chairman Brian Sellers did not realise until it was too late. "Don," he told Don Wilson, "I buggered Yorkshire cricket up, not you."

The title of the year's outstanding anthology, **Frith on Cricket**, is almost tautologous: David Frith *is* cricket, to an almost indivisible degree. The book assembles "Half a Century of Cricket Writing", mainly in *The Cricketer*, which he edited, and *Wisden Cricket Monthly*, which he founded, although also beneath less predictable mastheads, such as the *Esher News and Advertiser* and *New Zealand Woman's Day*. The sample shows Frith in the round, as painstaking historian, passionate collector, trenchant editorialist, striving player and adoring fan, in the act always of looking back, even on himself. A choice early essay from the *Journal of the Cricket Society* recounts listening to the 1961 Old Trafford Test on radio in Australia: "Now for a look in on the boys, both sleeping so peacefully. One day I'll tell them all about this, and they can stay up and listen to the Test with me." *Frith on Cricket* proves the author to have been forward-looking as well, in June 1976 foreseeing helmets ("Crash hats with visors are a repugnant prospect, but if some batsmen decide to wear them, for the sake of their wives and children, no-one will have the power to stop them") and in June 1979 *l'affaire Chappell* ("I have been waiting with trepidation for the moment when, with six runs needed off the final ball and a lot of money at stake, the bowler informs the umpire of a change of action and rolls the ball along the ground").

The structure of *Frith on Cricket* is rigidly chronological, and being jerked back and forth from the obituary of a childhood hero to a contemporary Test report to a personal reminiscence to a book review asks something of a reader's attention. But the writing is also infused with droll observations, like a glimpse of John Edrich and Ray Illingworth having "hardly more flamboyance and affability than a pair of Russian field marshals" and Henry Blofeld sounding always "as if he is calling down a dubious line from Ootacamund". When Frith slashes, too, he follows the old adage of slashing hard. "Nothing can save him from going down in history as a challenging, brave, aggressive cricketer… who are respected little off the field," he writes of Ian Botham. His review of Devon Malcolm's autobiography zeroes in like an unplayable yorker.

Such unvarnished views have made Frith a controversial figure. "Cricket's welfare was then and is now the central consideration," is his personal apologia. That can be problematical, because there *is* more to life. Sympathy for the lot of exiled South African cricketers in the 1970s and 1980s made Frith rather rheumy-eyed where that country was concerned; a distaste for aggression and brutality had persuaded him by the early 1990s that life under the Caribbean cosh was cricket's ruin. Unapologetically included is the *Wisden Cricket Monthly* editorial branding the West Indies team the "most unpopular in the world", their ethos "founded on vengeance and violence" and "fringed by arrogance". Frith explained subsequently that he had "vengeance and violence" in mind in cricket terms, Clive Lloyd and Viv Richards having been radicalised by their hellish tour of Australia in 1975-76, and following in a sequence of express-pace retribution. Yet it's arguable that such misunderstanding was too easily reached, and cricket terms were not the only material ones: after all, a bouncer from Fred Trueman to Colin McDonald has a context quite different to one from Michael Holding at Tony Greig. But cricket would be a better game if more writers, and many more administrators, cared half as much as David Frith, and were prepared to think as independently. In a touching evocation of his long friendship with Sir Donald Bradman, Frith gives a glimpse of himself. Bradman, he explains, had a love for "debate and argument on the economy, politics, cricket – with him preferably having the final word. Just like my own dad. Just like me."

Frith's book appeared in a year in which the historical pickings were thin. One welcome exception was Mark Rowe's **The Victory Tests**, few cricket summers being as overdue historical inquiry as the season of 1945. The well-qualified author, with a first-class degree in history, has combed the written record diligently, has interviewed the last handful of survivors, and understands the period well. The book is full of historical curios, plus some trappings of modernity, like the scorer for the Australian Services team using a typewriter rather than a conventional scorebook, and a player in an RAF v RAAF game wearing the new-fangled contact lenses. There are priceless glimpses too of the chief protagonists, of Keith Miller losing £150 at Epsom then winning £250 at two-up, and Wally Hammond ordering his young amateurs to place bets on the greyhounds at White City.

My hesitation in recommending *The Victory Tests* is that the author exhibits some of what E. P. Thompson once called "the overwhelming condescension of posterity". Over the last of the foregoing cameos, for instance, he dwells laboriously, trying to draw possible inferences about class; it hardly seems worth it. The book obtained some publicity on release by revealing Miller's wartime flying record to be less extensive than mythology suggested, and

Rowe seems to think that Miller was disingenuous in failing to counteract the impression: "A man could hardly have done less; and Miller knew it. For a man who put so much of his life into public print as Miller, it's suspicious that he never aired this. That would imply that it ate away at him; because it would have been there, on his conscience, guilt that he did not do as much as others." Yet the embroidery of Miller's war record, the image of the debonair fighter pilot turned devil-may-care cricketer, says much less about Miller than it does about modern mores, like the increasingly martial edge to Australian patriotism, with its tendency to see every returned serviceman in the Anzac Day Parade as a forgotten hero. In person – and I write here as someone who *did* discuss the war with him – Miller was supremely self-effacing about his active duty, and the sentiment that a man who spent three years in uniform abroad "could hardly have done less" actually borders on contemptible. Elsewhere, Rowe envisions Miller as a kind of rebel in a conformist's body: "Here lay Miller's unresolved, and unresolvable, sadnesses. The great athlete could not stop thinking." That seems to be Rowe's problem, not Miller's.

Rowe draws some interesting lessons from the Victory Tests, and makes some thoughtful conjectures about the state of English cricket at the time, postulating, not unconvincingly, that league cricket in 1945 might have been stronger than county cricket, even though "a Lord's selector would no more watch a northern league game than a lord would visit a fish and chip shop". He also argues that the success of the series provided an argument for the status quo, and tended to head off possible innovations such as one-day cricket, multiple divisions and bigger stadiums: "The authorities saw the Victory summer as proof that they did not have to change things – indeed, ought not to." Yet did these "authorities" have the kind of scope for action with which Rowe credits them? English cricket in 1945 was, like the rest of the country, dirt poor; innovation came a long way second to survival. It's the easiest thing in the world to

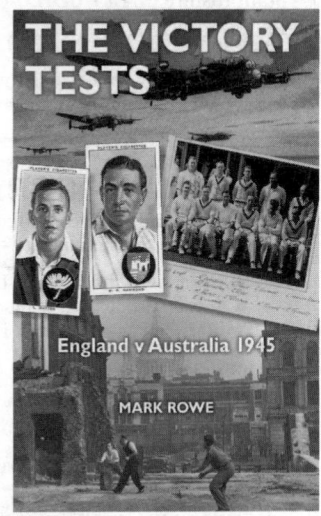

deplore the short-sightedness of "authorities"; more challenging, but the responsibility of historians, is to examine exactly of what they were capable and why.

Beth Hise has an appealing task in **Swinging Away**, the catalogue to an exhibition exploring the parallels and contrasts between cricket and baseball curated under the aegis of the Marylebone Cricket Club and the National

Baseball Hall of Fame. The games have, she reliably informs us, "no direct evolutionary relationship", but their paths have intersected often and fruitfully enough to provide grist for a historian's mill.

Contra the nativist myths concocted in the US, both games look to have English origins: Hise shows us a 1760 English children's volume called the *Little Pretty Pocket Book, Intended for the Instruction and Amusement of Little Master Tommy and Pretty Polly* delineating both games in verse. She then surveys the respective social histories, set-ups, folklores, founding clubs (Marylebone, Knickerbocker) and *lares et penates* (the Ashes, the Doubleday Ball). Egos too: both W. G. Grace and Babe Ruth thought they would have excelled at each other's sports.

Perhaps the most instructive complementarities are technical. Baseball, for example, originally involved an appeal, and catchers, like keepers, went back and forward in baseball according to the pitching until 1902; and the first catcher to wear shinguards five years later, Roger Bresnahan, first used cricket pads. Bart King, meanwhile, whom Plum Warner thought in the world's best XI in 1912, brought from baseball an approach in which he held both hands behind his head, a legacy of his pitching career. Overlooked areas of overlap include the question of ball-tampering, baseball having abolished the spitter but cricket having condoned with some equivocation reverse swing, and the slide on to base which may well have influenced the grass surfing now popular in cricket outfields. The book sets the cogs ticking, nonetheless, and the illustrations are handsome indeed.

The cheeriest take on history came in a tiny yellow package. Not everyone responds with an amused snicker to names like Arbuthnot, Frobisher, Catchpole and W. G. Denholm-Elliott. Some remain stony-faced at the idea of P. C. R. Tufnellton's exploits in *An Hilarious Collection of Cricketing Mishaps and Anecdotal Tomfooleries* and in *I'm a Notable Personage… Please Assist me in Extricating Myself from this Present Complicatedness*. There are even those who remain entirely unmoved by the Assam Untouchables and the Baluchistan Opium Exporters competing in the final of The Indian Territories Pre-Eminent League, the boisterous Ebenezer Catchweasel and The Barmington Army Marching Band, and C. B. Fry's invention of the iPad, apparently "a type of slate useful for striking a recalcitrant domestic servant". These folk should ignore at all costs **W. G. Grace Ate My Pedalo**, a compendium of the comic writing of Alan Tyers, whose speciality is refracting cricket events of today through a Victorian prism, lest they encounter the musings of that eminent muscular Christian, the Rev M. L. Hayden, and be scandalised by Mr D. C. Boon's consumption of 1,452 bottles of port wine on the steamship from Sydney to Southampton. This leaves more for the rest of us, including the complementary illustrations by Beach.

The best of 2010, however, revived a small and very select cricket genre: the synoptic history, proceeding in the footsteps of Altham and Swanton, Bowen, Green, Wynne-Thomas and a few others. Eric Midwinter's **The Cricketer's Progress** comes in an unprepossessing package, produced to the quality of your average cricket club history, while a cricket-minded proofreader would have ensured against such gaffes as Syd Barnes touring Australia in

1903-04, Kerry Packer's Australians touring the Caribbean in 1978 and Sri Lanka drawing their first Test; likewise should it be "mental disintegration" not "mental deterioration" and "doosra" not "doostra". Yet looks are deceiving. Midwinter, a historian of entertainment and leisure, has brought a perceptive and panoramic outlook to the challenge of placing cricket in a social and cultural perspective; the result is limpid, accessible and often provocative.

Midwinter begins by evaluating each of cricket's various foundation myths, propagated because they "reflect some human whim that prefers the immediacy of a Genesis to the muddle of a Darwinian solution." He cleverly finds a validity in each, and arrives at a view of cricket as the convergence of broadly similar regional pursuits, using the metaphor of playing cards: "There was a universally used pack of cards but a hundred ways of playing with them." He also finds an enchanting means of integrating cricket with England's gambling heritage: "Does not legend have it that John Montague, Fourth Earl of Sandwich, patron saint of the English cricket tea, had his cut of ham stuffed between bread in eponymous fashion, in order that he might continue playing cards for heavy stakes, while not greasing a possible winning hand as he replenished his energy?"

Author of at least two underestimated but indispensable works on cricket, *The Lost Seasons* and *Quill on Willow*, Midwinter seems to have just the right perspective. He is fond without sentimentality, thorough without pedantry, and wears his learning lightly. He sees beyond and behind the "urbanised diversion with rural yearnings" that cricket became, identifying such salient factors in its development as the 1830 invention of the cylinder mower and the role of the railway boom not just in cricket's diffusion, but also in its failure to penetrate those parts of England denied it: "Paddington plays as important a part in the Grace saga as does Lord's." He writes particularly well of the Victorian regard for cricket as a kind of pagan worship: "If the Church of England was, in the old phrase, the Conservative Party at prayer, cricket was the Church of England at play… Not for nothing did *Wisden*, first published in 1864, become known as 'the Cricketer's Bible'."

A sceptical assessor of cricket's character-building potentialities, Midwinter notes what a hard sell it is at school level: "Given, say, an hour or so for a games period, cricket… is difficult to organise, while… it engages few intensely at any one juncture. Nine are sitting waiting to bat, while several fielders may also be fairly unchallenged. Once one clears one's head of the

outmoded hogwash about character-building and concentrates on cricket as a companionable and wholesome recreation, it takes its place, an honourable place, amid a series of other possibilities." He takes pleasure, nonetheless, in imparting his finding that "more people, especially young people, are playing organised cricket than at any other time in English history".

Midwinter is perhaps slightly less sure-footed in the present, but the book is stunningly contemporary, the most recent event described being Muralitharan's 800th Test wicket. He brings value, too, by being the author three years ago of a similarly discursive history of football, *Parish to Planet*, neatly condensing the differences in their parallel spreads: "No former British colony has ever won the football World Cup, and England has only managed it once; only former British colonies, and not even England, have won the world cricket cup." The casual browser might pass by this unassuming volume, sans glossy cover, embossed lettering or celebrity name; it may be the dowdiest title to be *Wisden* Book of the Year, but there will be few more deserving.

WISDEN BOOK OF THE YEAR

Since 2003, *Wisden's* reviewer has selected a Book of the Year. The winners have been:

2003 *Bodyline Autopsy* by David Frith
2004 *No Coward Soul* by Stephen Chalke and Derek Hodgson
2005 *On and Off the Field* by Ed Smith
2006 *Ashes 2005* by Gideon Haigh
2007 *Brim Full of Passion* by Wasim Khan
2008 *Tom Cartwright: The Flame Still Burns* by Stephen Chalke
2009 *Sweet Summers: The Classic Cricket Writing of JM Kilburn* edited by Duncan Hamilton
2010 *Harold Larwood: The authorized biography of the world's fastest bowler* by Duncan Hamilton
2011 *The Cricketer's Progress: Meadowland to Mumbai* by Eric Midwinter

THE CRICKET SOCIETY AND MCC BOOK OF THE YEAR AWARD

The Cricket Society Literary Award has been presented since 1970 to the author of the cricket book judged best of the year. The 2010 award, the first to be made by the Cricket Society in association with MCC, was won by Anthony Gibson for *Of Didcot and the Demon* The Cricketing Times of Alan Gibson (Fairfield Books); he received £3,000.

BOOKS RECEIVED IN 2010

GENERAL

Balfour, Sandy **What I love about cricket** (Ebury, paperback, £7.99)
Baloch, K. H. **K. H. Baloch's Journey through the Bibliography of Pakistan Cricket (1947–2009)** (Christopher Saunders, paperback, £30 plus £3 p&p from the publisher, Kingston House, High Street, Newnham-on-Severn, Gloucestershire GL14 1BB)
Bateman, Colin **String Fellows** A Cycling Odyssey into Cricket's Heartland Foreword by Angus Fraser (Matador, paperback, £12)
Baxter, Peter comp. **The Best Views from the Boundary** Test Match Special's Greatest Interviews (Corinthian Books, £14.99)
Blackshaw, Bill **100 Not Out** Chronicles of the Cryptics Cricket Club (privately published; paperback, available for £15, inc p&p, from the author, Squash Court, Rottingdean, East Sussex BN2 7HA)
Chalke, Stephen **A Long Half Hour** Six Cricketers Remembered (Fairfield Books, paperback, £10)
Chalke, Stephen **Now I'm 62** The Diary of an Ageing Cricketer (Fairfield Books, paperback, £12)

Collomosse, Andrew ed. **Magnificent Seven** Yorkshire's Championship Years: The Men, The Magic, The Memories – The Players' Own Story   Foreword by Ray Illingworth, Afterword by Brian Close (Great Northern Books, £16.99)

Ellis, Clive and Pennell, Mark **Trophies and Tribulations** Forty Years of Kent Cricket (Greenwich Publishing, £16.99)

Haigh, Gideon **Sphere of Influence** Writings on cricket and its discontents (Victory Books, paperback, \$A34.99)

Hamilton, Duncan **A Last English Summer** (Quercus, £20)

Harris, Norman **What Are You Doing Out Here** Heroism and Distress at a Cricket Test (Last Side Publishing, paperback, £9.99 from www.cricketbooks.co.uk)

Haselhurst, Alan **Unusually Cricket** (The Professional and Higher Partnership Ltd, £18.99)

Hise, Beth **Swinging Away** How Cricket and Baseball Connect   Introduction by Matthew Engel, Foreword by Andrew Flintoff (Scala Publishers, paperback, £20)

Lloyd, David **Start the Car** The World According to Bumble (HarperSport, £18.99)

Midwinter, Eric **The Cricketer's Progress** Meadowland to Mumbai (Third Age Press, paperback, £14.50)

Pearson, Harry **Slipless in Settle** A Slow Turn around Northern Cricket (Little, Brown, paperback, £12.99)

Piesse, Ken **Great Australian Cricket Stories** (The Five Mile Press, \$A35)

Rowe, Mark **The Victory Tests** England v Australia 1945 (SportsBooks, £17.99)

Shawcroft, John **Golden Mondays** The Story of Cricket's Bank Holiday Matches (ACS, paperback, £20)

Smith, Andrew **125 Not Out** The Story of Illingworth St Mary's Cricket Club (privately published; paperback, available for £10, plus £2 p&p from psmith67@sky.com)

Smyth, Rob **The Spirit of Cricket** What Makes Cricket the Greatest Game on Earth (Elliott & Thompson, £12.99)

Stern, John ed. **My Favourite Cricketer** (A&C Black, £14.99)

Telfer, Kevin **Peter Pan's First XI** The Extraordinary Story of J. M. Barrie's Cricket Team (Sceptre, £16.99)

Tossell, David **Following On** A year with English cricket's golden boys (Know the Score, £14.99)

Turbervill, Huw **The Toughest Tour** The Ashes away series since the war Foreword by Scyld Berry (Aurum, £16.99)

Tyers & Beach **W. G. Grace Ate My Pedalo** (John Wisden & Co, £9.99)

Valentine, Ian **Out for a Duck** A Celebration of Cricketing Calamities   Foreword by Henry Blofeld, Illustrations by Oliver Preston (Quiller, £18.95)

Wilson, Martin **First Cricket in...** (Christopher Saunders, paperback, limited edition of 150, £25 plus £2 p&p from the publisher, Kingston House, High Street, Newnham-on-Severn, Gloucestershire GL14 1BB)

BIOGRAPHY

Agnew, Jonathan **Thanks, Johnners** An affectionate tribute to a broadcasting legend (Blue Door, £20)

Batchelder, Alf **Hugh Trumble** A Cricketer's Life (Melbourne Cricket Club, two-volume limited edition, \$A220)

Brooke, Robert **F. R. Foster** The Fields Were Sudden Bare (ACS, paperback, £12)

Ezekiel, Gulu **Sachin** The Story of the World's Greatest Batsman, revised and updated (Penguin Books, paperback, Rs450)

Miller, Douglas **Jack Bond** Lancashire Lad, Lancashire Leader (ACS, paperback, £12)

Moulton, Roger **Joe Hardstaff** Supreme Stylist (ACS, paperback, £12)

Musk, Stephen **Michael Falcon** Norfolk's Gentleman Cricketer (ACS, paperback, £12)

Piesse, Ken **Brad Hodge** The Little Master (cricketbooks.com.au, paperback, \$A20)

Rendell, Brian **Fuller Pilch** A Straightforward Man (ACS, paperback, £12)

Stevens, Dr Phil **Sporting Heroes of Essex and East London 1960–2000** Bobby Moore and Graham Gooch   Foreword by Tony Cottee (Apex Publishing, £15.99)

AUTOBIOGRAPHY

Benaud, Richie **Over But Not Out** My Life So Far (Hodder & Stoughton, £19.99)

Foot, David **Footsteps from East Coker** (Fairfield Books, £15)
An engaging memoir by Wisden's former Somerset correspondent – from the lost feudal world of his childhood in pre-war East Coker to his years in journalism in the West Country. He writes of his love of theatre, his fascination with scandal and his lifelong enchantment with cricket.

Gibbs, Herschelle, with Smith, Steve **To The Point** The No-Holds-Barred Autobiography (Zebra Press, paperback, R200)

Hayden, Matthew, with Craddock, Robert **Standing My Ground** (Michael Joseph, $A49.95/Aurum, £18.99)

Holding, Michael **No Holding Back** The Autobiography (Weidenfeld & Nicolson, £18.99)

Koertzen, Rudi **Slow Death** Memoirs of a Cricket Umpire (Zebra Press, R200, available from www.kalahari.net or www.exclus1ves.co.za)

Olonga, Henry **Blood, Sweat and Treason** My Story (Vision Sports Publishing, £18.99)

Scovell, Brian **Thank You, Hermann Goering** The Life of a Sports Writer (Amberley, £20)

Smith, Graeme with Manthorp, Neil **A Captain's Diary 2007–2009** (Jonathan Ball Publishers, paperback, R147)

ANTHOLOGIES

Craig, Edward **Cricket 2010** The story of the year as told by *The Wisden Cricketer* (Wisden Cricketer Publishing, paperback, £7.99)

Frith, David **Frith on Cricket** (Great Northern Books, £18)

ILLUSTRATED

Anderson, Duncan **Echoes from a Golden Age** Postcard Photographs of Cricketers by Foster and Hawkins (Boundary Books, limited edition of 100, £100 plus £7 p&p from the publisher, The Haven, West Street, Childrey, Oxfordshire OX12 9UL)

Whimpress, Bernard **The Official MCC Ashes Treasures** (Carlton, £30)
Thirty facsimile reproductions of rare Ashes memorabilia from scorecards and cigarette cards to tickets and souvenir brochures complement the tale of sport's greatest rivalry in this attractive, high-quality production.

FICTION

Heller, Richard **The Network** (Bearmondsey Publishing, paperback, £9 inc p&p, from richardkheller @hotmail.com)

TECHNICAL

Boycott, Geoff **Play Cricket the Right Way** (Great Northern Books, £9.99)

Dellor, Ralph **Cricket** Steps to Success (Human Kinetics, paperback, £14.99)

Pont, Ian **Coaching Youth Cricket** Foreword by Andy Flower (Human Kinetics, paperback, £13.99)

Pyke, Frank and Davis, Ken **Cutting Edge Cricket** Skills, Strategies and Practices for Today's Game Foreword by James Sutherland (Human Kinetics, paperback, £14.99)

STATISTICAL

Bailey, Philip comp. **First-Class Cricket Matches 1922** and **1923** (ACS Sales, Blue Bell House, 2–4 Main Street, Scredington, Sleaford, Lincolnshire NG34 0AE, email: sales@acscricket.com, £20 and £22)

Bryant, John ed. **Great Cricket Matches 1772–1800** (ACS, £20)
Full scorecards for 237 eighteenth-century "great" matches.

Bryant, John ed. **Overseas Matches 2007/08** (ACS, £32)

McCarron, Tony comp. **New Zealand Cricketers 1863/64–2010** (ACS, £22)

Percival, Tony comp. **Northumberland Cricketers** (ACS, £8)
Webb, Tony ed. **The Minor Counties Championship 1904** and **1905** (ACS, £12 and £13)

HANDBOOKS AND ANNUALS

Agnew, Jonathan **Jonathan Agnew's Cricket Year 2010** (TME Publishing, £24.99)
Bailey, Philip ed. **ACS International Cricket Year Book 2010** (ACS Sales, Blue Bell House, 2–4 Main Street, Scredington, Sleaford, Lincolnshire NG34 0AE, email: sales@acscricket.com, £20)
Bryant, John ed. **ACS Overseas First-Class Annual 2010** (ACS, £35)
   Full scorecards for first-class matches outside England.
Bryden, Colin ed. **Mutual & Federal SA Cricket Annual 2010** (CSA, from cricket@mf.co.za, R180 plus p&p)
Gerrish, Keith ed. **First-Class Counties Second Eleven Annual 2010** (ACS, £8)
Heatley, Michael ed. **The Cricketers' Who's Who 2010** (Green Umbrella, £18.99)
Irish Cricket Annual 2010 (from Cricket Ireland, Sport HQ, 13 Joyce Way, Parkwest, Dublin 12, £5/Euros 5.94)
Lynch, Steven ed. **The Wisden Guide to International Cricket 2011** (John Wisden, paperback, £8.99)
Marshall, Ian ed. **Playfair Cricket Annual 2010** (Headline, £6.99, paperback)
Payne, Francis and Smith, Ian ed. **2010 New Zealand Cricket Almanack** (Hodder Moa, $NZ49.99)
Vikram Singh, Indra **The Little Big Book of World Cup Cricket** (Media Eight, Rs 295)
All first-class counties produce handbooks of varying quality. Details available from each club.

REPRINTS AND UPDATES

John Wisden's Cricketers' Almanack for 1896, **1897**, **1898** and **1899** (facsimile editions, Willows Publishing, 17 The Willows, Stone, Staffordshire ST15 0DE, tel: 01785 814700, email: jenkins.willows@ntlworld.com. £65 each (tan binding), £68 (original hardcloth cover); all editions plus £4 p&p, or £7 p&p overseas)
John Wisden's Cricketers' Almanack for 1934, **1935** and **1936** (facsimile editions, Willows Publishing, as above. £63 each (tan binding), £67 (original hardcloth cover); all editions plus £4 p&p, or £7 p&p overseas)
Kynaston, David **WG's Birthday Party** (Bloomsbury, £9.99)
Ramprakash, Mark **Strictly Me** My Life Under the Spotlight (Mainstream, paperback, £7.99)
Steen, Rob and McLellan, Alastair **500–1** The Miracle of Headingley '81 Forewords by Mike Brearley and Gideon Haigh (John Wisden, paperback, £9.99)
Vaughan, Michael **Time to Declare** My Autobiography (Hodder, paperback, £8.99)

CATALOGUE

Saunders, Christopher **Twenty10** Cricket books and memorabilia (paperback, free from Orchard Books, Kingston House, High Street, Newnham-on-Severn, Gloucestershire GL14 1BB)

PERIODICALS

All Out Cricket ed. Andy Afford (PCA Management/TriNorth, £4.25. Subscriptions: www.allout-cricket.co.uk)
The Cricket Statistician (quarterly) ed. Simon Sweetman (ACS, £3 to non-members)
The Journal of the Cricket Society (twice yearly) ed. Andrew Hignell (from D. Seymour, 13 Ewhurst Road, Crofton Park, London, SE4 1AG, £5 to non-members)
SPIN ed. Duncan Steer (WW Magazines, £3.95. Subscriptions: www.spincricket.com/)
The Wisden Cricketer (monthly) ed. John Stern (Wisden Cricketer Publishing, £3.95. Subscriptions: Dovetail Services, 800 Guillat Avenue, Kent Science Park, Sittingbourne, Kent ME9 8GU, 0844 815 0864, email: twc@servicehelpline.co.uk)

CRICKET IN THE MEDIA, 2010

Beer out, champagne in

MARCUS WILLIAMS

Cricket appeared on front pages and at the top of news bulletins far more than for many years. It began with England's victorious Caribbean crusade in the World Twenty20 and climaxed with the euphoria of the Ashes success; in between came the spot-fixing allegations (dealt with at length elsewhere) that provided as wide an exposure in the world's media as the game can ever have had. On successive Sundays the *News of the World* devoted 30 pages, including a supplement titled "The Fix", to the exclusive it billed as "the most sensational sporting scandal ever". Perhaps it was: the episode prompted a letter-writer in *The Times* to suggest deleting "not" from "it's not cricket" as a mark of disapproval. However, by the end of the Ashes, Player of the Series Alastair Cook was appearing in the news and feature pages, jokes about Australian cricket – once unthinkable – were abounding, and English newspapers were producing happier souvenir supplements.

As England completed their 3–1 victory shortly before 1 a.m. GMT on January 7, many thousands – perhaps millions – of established and new fans back home stayed awake to witness the triumph on radio, television or internet. Nasser Hussain on Sky captured the moment most eloquently as Australia's last man Michael Beer edged the ball into his stumps: "Bowled him... Tremlett's the man. Put the Beer away; put the champagne on ice. Twenty-four years of pain in Australia – finally they are beaten at home by England." It was heartfelt, too: Hussain knew a fair bit of that pain as a 4–1 losing captain Down Under, as did a fellow commentator, Mike Atherton, who reminded readers in *The Times* that "Those of us who have worn the England cap can be thankful because they have restored faith in the English game in a part of the world that had come to look upon it with scorn."

Those fans reliant upon analogue radios, however, were listening not to grown men waxing emotional about the end of Australian domination, but to the shipping forecast. At odds estimated at almost 6,000-1, those three England wins all came while Long Wave abandoned *Test Match Special* in favour of reports from coastal stations. It put Sandettie Light Vessel Automatic irrevocably on the sporting map – and perhaps gave digital radios a sales boost.

On firmer ground, the English press were for once in the position of being able to report a tour of almost unbroken success. "I've been waiting a long time to write this story; but I didn't expect it to be like this," Simon Barnes wrote on the front page of *The Times*. Unlike other Ashes victories of recent memory, this time there had been "an overwhelming sense of certainty". For Martin Samuel in the *Daily Mail* it was "not just the margin of the eventual victory, but the style in which it has been achieved that is so impressive. Huge winning totals – an innings and this, an innings and that, an innings and the

OUR WORST XI

Today, England should become the first team in history to inflict three innings
defeats on Australia in a single series. Commence the post-mortem.
FULL COVERAGE PAGES 34–40

The Sydney Morning Herald, January 7.

other – have been established, records lasting the best part of centuries have
been shattered and the myth and aura of the baggy green cap exploded." Their
Australian counterparts, who had been sharpening their knives throughout the
series, vented their spleen. *The Sydney Morning Herald* branded the losers
"The worst Australian team ever fielded for an Ashes series", and cricket
Down Under was "in its deepest crisis since the Packer revolution".

The Ashes attracted a huge travelling corps, with the regular cricket
correspondents and writers supported at various points by the chief sports
writers. The *Telegraph* group fielded the largest team in Australia, mustering
a full by-lined XI of journalists and current or former player columnists;
they even squeezed a pre-series article out of Lord (Sebastian) Coe, who
observed that there was no longer in Australia "quite the same strut in the
national walk". For quality writing throughout the series it was hard to beat
The Times's team, led by Atherton, a deserved recipient of two major sports
journalism awards in 2010, and Gideon Haigh, Australia's most respected
cricket scribe and historian, who focused the long lens of perspective on
the unfolding events. It was with feeling that he could lament that there
was "a good deal more [Australian] talent in the commentary box than on
the field".

How did the English observers explain their team's success? Mike Selvey
in *The Guardian* said the seeds had been sown in Jamaica two years previously
by the humiliating 51 all out against West Indies, when Andrew Strauss and
Andy Flower were first in charge. "If it was ignominious, then it can be seen
as perhaps the pivotal moment when England began the slow climb back up to
the position in which they now find themselves." In the same paper, former
England coach Duncan Fletcher, whose teams twice lost heavily in Australia,
attributed the success to the "strength of character" of the players. Simon
Hughes in the *Telegraph* analysed it thus: "Man for man, there is not a massive
difference in talent between the teams. But the difference in the application of
their skills is vast. It is scientists versus labourers."

The England captain drew wide praise, and batsman-turned-*Times*-leader-
writer Ed Smith offered a fascinating assessment of his former Middlesex
contemporary: "Able but not intimidating, assured but not overbearing,
analytical but not fretful, amenable but not compliant, Strauss is a master of
moderation." Smith also recalled an England schools trial: "He was not the kid
in the county tracksuit earmarked for professional greatness. He just clipped
the ball deftly off the back foot, a rare skill for a schoolboy, and let others big-
note about county contracts and bat deals."

Strauss's opening partner attracted much attention, and Cook's days as a choirboy and part-time farmer were a boon to reporters, who latched on to an English sporting hero in the mould of Coe, David Gower and Tim Henman. As Kevin McKenna noted in *The Observer*: "They are great English sportsmen all, but possessed of those sovereign and gentlemanly qualities that elevate them above mere excellence," although McKenna and his fellow Celts "seem to prefer our sporting heroes to be cast from a rougher mould".

A cricketer who fits that bill, Shane Warne, was also a member of Sky's Ashes team and, when not commentating for them or Australia's Channel 9, he was hosting his own (short-lived) chat show, featuring in fast-food commercials at the Test grounds, offering outspoken columns in the *Telegraph* as well as in the Australian press and, according to another *News of the World* exclusive, having an affair with the actress Liz Hurley.

The Hurley episode was of dubious substance, as were a couple of stories between the Perth and Melbourne Tests. First we were told that the Aussies

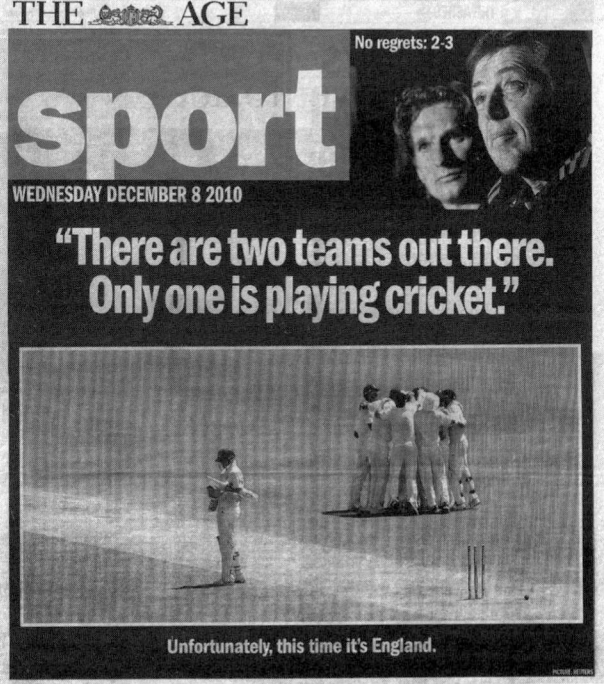

were underhandedly going to switch the pitch to favour their fast bowlers (in fact, England would bowl them out for 98 and win by an innings); then came the attempts to talk up an Australian recovery after their win in Perth. It was, it transpired, more of a "dead-cat bounce" as Richard Hobson put it in *The Times*, or like "the cheap Chinese gift that never made it to Boxing Day" of Peter Lalor in *The Australian*. (Warne, incidentally, provided television with a Johnners–Aggers "leg over" moment during the English summer when he and Ramiz Raja collapsed in hysterics over the slapstick run-out of Danish Kaneria in the Pakistan–Australia Test at Headingley.)

How the media landscape has changed since England's previous win in Australia. In 1986, much as had been the case for the previous half-century, those back in England could ruin their sleep patterns and follow play on the radio during the night, and read about it in the evening or (a day in arrears) the morning papers. From the 1970s, they could also watch highlights on TV – but that was it. No live ball-by-ball television coverage from overseas; no world wide web; no Cricinfo; no Twitter; and no podcasts.

In 2010, BBC radio's decision to issue the highlights of each day's play, together with an excellent summary by Jonathan Agnew and Geoffrey Boycott, as a podcast just as the UK was waking up, was a godsend; so too were Sky's regular highlights programmes. But it was ITV – on its out-of-the-way fourth, though nonetheless free, channel – that stepped into the breach to show the Australian TV highlights after the BBC confirmed it regarded cricket as a radio sport. The absence of live coverage from free-to-air television did mean England's triumph was not the shared national experience of the Ashes victory of 2005, but those who complained should remember that their argument in this case lay with the rights-holder, Cricket Australia, and the free-to-air broadcasters who declined to bid.

On the domestic front, county cricket continued to struggle for column inches in the printed press, but for the first time it was possible to view short daily highlights – if only from a fixed camera – of each match on the ECB website. There was regular ball-by-ball commentary on local radio, though often accessible only online. When overall space was tight, there were occasions when *The Times*, alone among the nationals in having a reporter at every Championship game, carried no words in its pages apart from a cross-reference to reports on its (now paid-for) website – and sometimes even omitted full scorecards.

County coverage seems to be migrating more and more to the online world. *The Guardian's* county blog, a couple of years old now, has become home to exactly what you'd expect from a lively group of writers liberated from the restraints of print. Near the end of the season, it was attracting daily feedback of 300 or more comments, as readers responded to the wide-ranging posts, some of which had the power to jolt you from your established view of the universe. One was David Hopps's revelation that cricketers – even international ones – are not always the most worldly of creatures. "It's the first time I've been to London," Ajmal Shahzad, who was in town for the 10 Downing Street reception given to England's triumphant World Twenty20 squad, told Hopps in May. "This sounds really sad, but I used to play Monopoly when I was

Filming frenzy: the England party at Sydney.

younger. I met Ravi Bopara, and he drove me down Pall Mall, and I thought, 'I remember this place. I used to put a hotel on here.' I saw Harrods, Big Ben, Buckingham Palace. It was amazing."

Perhaps Andrew Flintoff was as ingenuous once. It was, though, symptomatic that Flintoff, formerly of Lancashire, should announce his retirement on the gripping final day of the Championship and steal some of the limelight from Nottinghamshire's success. The timing, as Selvey put it in *The Guardian*, was "abject and thoughtless". At least the final round of matches received comprehensive coverage on BBC digital radio and on Sky, whose live coverage included the most drama-laden moment of the county summer: the final ball of the Twenty20 final at the Rose Bowl, when an injury, a runner, a painting of new creases, Somerset's ignorance of the Laws and failure to run out Hampshire's Dan Christian conspired to deny them victory. Sky also scored a first by showing a one-day international against Bangladesh in 3D, even if it was hard to find anyone who had actually watched it.

On radio *TMS* remains a treasure, especially for those dependent upon it for live cricket. If it can occasionally be faulted for leaving the listener waiting too long for the score, or for some of its newer members talking at too many tangents or over the live action, the programme nonetheless throws up little gems: Christopher Martin-Jenkins being persuaded by Phil Tufnell to give a reading of the football results, or Mark Butcher singing one of his own compositions during an interval chat.

Marcus Williams was a senior member of The Times *sports department for more than 30 years. He also edited* The Way to Lord's *and* Double Century: 200 Years of Cricket in The Times.

CRICKET AND FILM, 2010

Caught up in the romance

CHARLES BARR

On the day England rounded off their Ashes campaign with an innings win at Sydney, the British Film Institute sent out an email message on the subject of "England's Glorious Victory". It gave a link to a short item newly placed on the YouTube website: clicking on it revealed footage not from Sydney but from The Oval in 1926, silent newsreel of the victory of Percy Chapman's team in the final Test. Anyone who types "1926 cricket" into the YouTube search box can watch these amazingly evocative images: the 48-year-old Wilfred Rhodes bowling in his cap, Hobbs and Sutcliffe serenely running short singles, a cluster of Australian short legs that anticipate Bodyline fields by six years, a scramble for ball and stumps as the last wicket falls – and then the invasion of the field by decorously jubilant hat-wearing spectators.

To see this kind of precious film material, you used to have to go to the vaults of the BFI itself, or buy tickets for the annual film evenings presented by David Frith and Clyde Jeavons at the BFI's Southbank cinema. When the press made a big story, in December 2010, of the rediscovery of "Cricket", a short British Council film of 1948, Jeavons pointed out that it was a regular feature of their archival shows. Now, however, it too can be seen in full on YouTube. Type in "Lord's Cricket 1948" and you are directed to 20 minutes of glorious material from the summer's Second Ashes Test, both on the field and behind the scenes. Bradman and Lindwall, Compton and Hutton... and John Arlott.

In 2010, around 60% of UK adults were accessing the internet every day. For cricket enthusiasts, this is becoming as rich a source of audio-visual material as it has long been, via sites such as Cricinfo, of scores, news and comment. Another story from late 2010 was the discovery – the word this time is accurate – of film shot by Percy Fender during the England tour to Australia in 1928-29, which he was covering as a journalist; it too has generously been made available online*. Along with fragments of Test match action, the highlight is a series of off-field shots of the players. It was wonderfully prescient, or just lucky, of Fender to capture, in close-up, a rising star of the home team, giving to posterity what is the first surviving film footage of Donald Bradman.

MCC now offer for sale three DVDs based on home movies. The first, from the 1930s, has one-Test wonder "Hopper" Read behind the camera. The other two record England tours of the mid-1950s: to West Indies and Australia (*England's Finest: On Tour with Hutton's Men*); and to South Africa (*Cape Summer*). The tour DVDs, compiled from footage shot by several participants, contain unmissable material, such as Frank Tyson at his lethal peak in Australia, and Johnny Wardle bowling his equally lethal chinamen. Both have a wealth of background extras, including Peter Richardson's tribute to the formidable drinking capacity of England's tour manager in South Africa, Freddie Brown.

For years, feature films offered, at best, marginal attention to cricket, ranging from the notoriously clumsy and parochial *The Final Test* (1953) to more convincing but brief episodes in films like *The Go-Between* (1971), scripted by the cricket-mad Harold Pinter. But if the rules and culture of baseball have been no barrier to the international success of such films as *Pride of the Yankees* and *Field of Dreams*, why not cricket? More recent films like *Playing Away* (1987) and *Wondrous Oblivion* (2003), both available on DVD, have accepted the challenge, with partial success. The Indian feature *Lagaan* has much more cricket than either, and stands as a genuine crossover in appealing to non-expert audiences: it was nominated for an Oscar as best foreign film in 2001. President Obama's enthusiasm for Joseph O'Neill's novel *Netherland*, with its New York cricket subplot, can do no harm to its prospects of film adaptation. Meanwhile, from Sri Lanka, we can look forward to *Sinhawalokanaya: The Cricket Film 2011*, featuring Tillekeratne Dilshan.

Its director, Suneth Malinga Lokuhewa, claims that "even for non Sri Lankans the underdog coming back to defeat the colonial masters will inspire". This is the theme common to most recent cricket films, including two spectacular new feature documentaries, both due for DVD release in 2011. *Fire in Babylon* celebrates the dominance of West Indies in the 1980s under Clive Lloyd, characterised as underdogs taking brutal revenge on Australian and English arrogance. It takes outrageous liberties with history, suggesting, in unstated defiance of C. L. R. James, that the entire pre-Lloyd story was one of subservience, of teams content to go on losing entertainingly – what of players like Worrell and Sobers and Hall and Griffith, and of series like 1950, 1963 and 1966? – but the combination of talking heads plus archival footage of flying stumps and wounded batsmen builds up an undeniably compulsive momentum. *Out of the Ashes* is altogether gentler, tracing the steady rise of the Afghan team, classic underdogs, to one-day international status and participation in the World Twenty20. While the treatment of particular matches is impressionistic rather than lucid, we get to know a good range of players and coaches, and are caught up, with them, in the romance of the team's rise, and its meaning for the nation.

Although Lokuhewa's theme of defying the "colonial masters" cannot be as central here as it is to *Fire in Babylon* or to *Lagaan*, the film achieves a coup, at the start, in finding a gentleman from the British Embassy in Kabul who is happy to pass supercilious comment on the crudity of the players' technique. When they come up against a decent team "they're going to be stuffed!" How wrong he was.

Charles Barr, emeritus professor of Film Studies at the University of East Anglia, currently teaches in Ireland.

* www.guardian.co.uk/sport/video/2010/dec/26/percy-fender-archive-cricket-match

CRICKET AND TWITTER, 2010

140 characters in search of some sense

JARROD KIMBER

Time was when blogs were all the rage in the cricket world. From 2005 to 2009 they were what the kids were doing. Then Twitter took over. Why spend an hour writing a carefully crafted attack on Scott Styris's thighs when you can slate them in 140 characters or fewer? Cricket blogs still exist, and they contain some of the best (and worst) writing. But they aren't the force of independent commentary they once were. Nor are they so easy to find.

The cricket world first woke up to Twitter during the 2009 Ashes series when Phillip Hughes let slip that he had been dropped from the Australian side. Since then it has become the major online source of cricket information, misinformation, rumour and humour. At the start of 2010 Lalit Modi alleged on Twitter that the former New Zealand all-rounder Chris Cairns had a history of match-fixing. Cairns took offence, and the dispute is headed to court. Later, Modi used Twitter to attack Indian politicians and, after much public discourse, prefixed "chairman of the IPL" with "suspended". Shortly after, he was forced to remove both elements, and called himself "founder and architect of the Indian Premier League and Champions League T20".

Throughout the year international cricketers took to Twitter, none apparently worried by Tim Bresnan's faux pas in 2009 (see *Wisden 2010*, page 1628). They just jumped in, with mixed results. Paul Collingwood seemed ill at ease and ran for the door, Stuart Broad hung around, as did Steve Finn, who contemplated making a run for it for different reasons: "…staying in a haunted hotel. I have a single room and I'm heading to my room now. Genuinely scared!" Kevin Pietersen joined in, though probably wished he hadn't. "Done for rest of summer!" he tweeted. "Man of the World Cup T20 and dropped from the T20 side too. Its a fuck up!" Pietersen later said he thought he was addressing one friend. The ECB has yet to appoint a Twitter coach to prevent such errors happening again.

Also in trouble was Dimi Mascarenhas. After what he claimed was a few drinks he tweeted early one Sunday morning: "chairman of selectors came to Liverpool and didn't even come and say hi. What a prick. Doesn't take much to come and say hello does it?" Just in case the first post was missed, he followed it up with a second and more abusive tweet about Geoff Miller. This came eight hours later, so it was either quite some bender – or Mascarenhas knew exactly what he was doing.

The lesser-known Azeem Rafiq was another to get his fingers publicly burned after messing around on Twitter – quite some going for someone with only 17 followers. Over two days he put up a series of unashamedly foul-mouthed rants about John Abrahams, his England Under-19 coach. Rafiq had just been dropped for breaching a team curfew, and in his defence he claimed he didn't know Twitter was public. Of course: 19-year-olds are *always* the slowest to understand new technology. On the plus side, he now has more than 17 followers.

Someone else happy to court controversy joined Twitter during the year and gave lazy editors the world over a free headline or two. Australia were losing a Test in India when Shane Warne tweeted "How the hell can hauritz bowl to this field?" Then: "Feeling for hauritz, terrible! What are these tactics? Sorry Ricky but what are you doing?" Ponting replied, in a different medium, that Hauritz set his own field.

It wasn't merely controversy Warne was busy courting on Twitter. After tabloids tucked in to his moans about first-class travel on British Airways, they gorged themselves on his public flirting with actress-cum-model-cum-socialite Liz Hurley. Her tweets about Warne in his underwear were irresistible to the red-tops, especially when put together with a picture of them kissing.

There is no bigger property in cricket than Sachin Tendulkar, and his arrival on Twitter was a huge event for the Indian and worldwide media. To confirm he was real, and not one of the fake Sachin Tendulkar profiles, he published a photo of himself in bed – perhaps the most revealing public statement he has made. He picked up followers at a prodigious rate, racing past six figures and comfortably becoming the most popular cricket tweeter, though he is still waiting for his 1,000,000th fan. Not holding the all-time Twitter record is perhaps the only one to elude him.

Not that it was all glamour and excitement. Some players never got the hang of Twitter, using it to give updates on their golf game or their prowess at Guitar Hero. Others preferred to plug their sponsors, while Johan Botha quoted verses from the Bible. Alviro Petersen did announce some real news, though revealed more than he intended: "Yes its true, I have signed with Glamourgan as their captain for 2011 english county season." He later clarified: "Everyone, its Glamorgan and not Glamourgan."

The online social networking story of the year, however, spanned Twitter, Facebook and the forum PakPassion.net. It concerned Zulqarnain Haider. He first crossed my radar back in March 2010 when he "friended" – the word has become second nature on the site – me on Facebook; he also friended 5,000 others. That number is significant: it's the level at which a normal Facebook profile becomes a fan page, which he saw as a useful staging-post in his campaign to oust Kamran Akmal as Pakistan's first-choice wicketkeeper. Trouble is, when a profile gains friends at such a rapid rate, Facebook investigate. If they discover it's because the individual is being friended by others, that's fine; but when it's the individual doing the friending, that person is banned for spamming. And Haider was banned. Later in the year, however, he was back, though not behaving in a way that alerted Facebook. Soon afterwards, he had his own fan page.

When this page was struggling to gain followers, Haider switched attention to Twitter. Far from using it like Graeme Swann (to abuse his team-mates) or Virender Sehwag (to thank those who praise him), Haider used Twitter to direct traffic to his Facebook fan page. Sometimes adding up to 15 tweets in 20 minutes – all essentially urging readers to check out his Facebook page –

he was trying to build a community of online support in his campaign to step out of Akmal's shadow. By November, he had done just that and, when he left Dubai in a hurry after claiming his life ha been threatened, he used Facebook to announce his hasty departure.

Haider also canvassed support on PakPassion.net, one of the world's most important cricket fan sites. For years online forums were the wild west of the internet; combine that with the passion of Pakistan fans, and PakPassion.net can be an interesting place to drop by. Unfortunately for Haider, the forum was busy with another player. It had adopted Mohammad Irfan, a bowler reckoned at anything from 6ft 9in to 12ft 10in tall, and it had a significant role in getting him into the Pakistan team. A shame, then, that Irfan's international debut was ropey at best.

CRICKET AND BLOGS

Swann, Gul and other flights of fancy

Where people are free to create content unfettered by rules or lawyers, they usually do. Cricket, it seems, generates more words than any other sport. You can read a cricket book a week and still not get through them all. And some of the best writing, hidden behind a weird domain name or Twitter account, never makes it to the mainstream. Whether it's a perfectly constructed 140 characters on Twitter about Umar Gul's sideburns, an 800-word epic on why New Zealand's batting order starts at No. 7, a Facebook group devoted to Graeme Swann's chin or a forum that is equal parts madness and genius, cricket fans just want to talk about their sport online. More than a few do it very well. It's worth finding a couple of them.

Some of the newer blogs include the award-winning paddlesweep.net, written mostly by Ant Sims, a South African (and proud of it) who seems to dislike the Proteas much of the time. Wes from playforcountrynotforself.blogspot.com is a German woman who believes Tasmania's Mark Cosgrove found her, and who is obsessed by the volatile state of Zimbabwe cricket. Also worth a read is thoughtsfromthedustbin.blogspot.com which, aside from its Nathan Hauritz bias, is a fun read from an Australian in the UK.

One of the best new blogs is fantasybob.blogspot.com. This quite often produces a completely random piece of genius: "The format for *I'm (Not) a Cricketer Get Me Out of Here* – simple: 11 randomly selected Australians are placed together in a hostile environment and have to go through various tests of strength and character – sometimes referred to as bowling, batting and catching – specially designed to humiliate them. The prize – being allowed to stay at home for the Adelaide round."

Other blogs worth digging out include the following. All are free, apart from Patrick Kidd's Cricket Central (formerly known as Line & Length), which deserves better than being shoved behind *The Times's* paywall:

Kingcricket.co.uk
boredcricketcrazyindians.com
lastofthesummerwhine.com
nightwatchgirl.com
sacricketblog.com
cricket.mailliw.com

shortofalength.wordpress.com
tcwj.blogspot.com
theoldbatsman.blogspot.com
cricketactionart.com
duckingbeamers.wordpress.com
thetimes.co.uk/tto/sport/cricket/cricket-central

Jarrod Kimber

RETIREMENTS

It would have broken lesser men

STEVE JAMES

Good teams possess solid senior players: consistent and reliable performers who are role models and guardians of a team ethos that can endure. And Sussex have not possessed two greater modern examples than **Robin Martin-Jenkins** and **James Kirtley**. Little wonder that the county has been so successful in recent times. Both played their parts in the three Championship triumphs of 2003, 2006 and 2007.

Martin-Jenkins was the most solid of all-rounders, an uncomplaining worker, a bustling seamer and a clean striker of the ball always striving hard to overcome the tall man's problem of the short ball. He may not have been quite good enough at either discipline to warrant England recognition – although in other times of names-in-a-hat selection, plenty of lesser cricketers were chosen – but his value to Sussex was always high. Indeed, in his final season he had a Championship batting average of 62.90 and took 30 wickets at less than 20.

But it was also an indication of his well-rounded character that he should choose his time of leaving so astutely. It was time for the youngsters to shine, he said. At 34 years old, and only halfway through the 2010 season, he announced he was off.

His family had known as much since the season's start, but it was not a story that a certain Christopher Martin-Jenkins could break. Paternal pressure does indeed come in many different guises, and RMJ's was to be the son of his generation's doyen of cricket writers. But both men handled any potentially difficult scenarios – and CMJ was often there covering Sussex matches! – with common sense and humour. Robin can write too, as he has demonstrated ably in these pages, but has decided instead to embark on a different career path, teaching geography and religious studies at Hurstpierpoint College.

Kirtley faced a very different pressure throughout his career: the whispers about the legality of his bowling action. He could bowl quickly and swing the ball late, but there was a jerk in his delivery that always aroused suspicion. As an opposing batsman there were times, I will admit, when inexplicably I lost sight of balls bowled by Kirtley, always a sign to invite scepticism.

An ECB panel had cleared Kirtley's action before his one-day international debut in Zimbabwe late in 2001, but the match referee, Pakistan's Colonel Naushad Ali, immediately declared it suspect. Then, during the 2005 county season, Kirtley was twice reported mid-match. At the end of the season he was suspended, and it was indeed found that his elbow exceeded the permitted 15 degrees of flexion. He was ordered to undertake remedial work: surely the longest of dark winters. It would have broken lesser men, but Kirtley is a man of deep strength and resolve. He satisfied the authorities with his adjustments and, sweetness of sweetness, in 2006 received the match award for his five for

27 in a tense C&G Trophy final victory over Lancashire. His skill and determination surely merited more than four Test caps.

Ben Smith never did play for England, but in 1999 his then-Leicestershire team-mate Aftab Habib did, even though Smith was batting at No. 4 and Habib at No. 5. Specialist international batsmen should not be plucked from so low a spot. And Smith was a better back-foot player, staying deep in his crease to be a rapacious cutter. He moved to Worcestershire, where he became captain, but resigned mid-match in 2004 after apparent disagreements with coach Tom Moody. His later years proved fallow in terms of runs, but his overall record remained fine. Always a brilliant fielder and swift runner between the wickets, he is now an assistant coach at New Road.

Shaun Udal retired once before, in 2007, after nearly 20 seasons of service at Hampshire. He was due to play at Minor County level for Berkshire when the call came from Middlesex. Before the 2008 season was out, he was captain too, having taken over the reins in the later stages of a surprising, yet stirring, Twenty20 Cup success. He then led the side – unprofitably as it happened – in the doomed Stanford Super Series in Antigua, and would later have taken Middlesex to the Champions League but for the Mumbai terrorist atrocities.

Udal's career was an advertisement for persistence. Selected prematurely for England's one-day side in 1994, he had to wait a further 11 years for a Test debut at the grand old age of 36! He played four Tests, and will always be remembered for

Shaun Udal in December 2005.

his four for 14 on the final day of the Mumbai Test in 2006, helping England to a series-levelling victory against India. He was a wily off-spinner, able to extract turn and bounce – I would like to think that is why he was the only spinner to have me caught at leg slip in first-class cricket! – and later, under the guidance of Shane Warne at Hampshire, considerable drift.

Two quicker bowlers have also taken their leave from the first-class arena, although Durham's **Neil Killeen** will remain in the game as a coach. A seamer from the old school, both in terms of nagging accuracy and a more relaxed form of match preparation, he almost had a "loop" on his deliveries. That is no mocking criticism – Surrey's ultra-skilful Martin Bicknell was the same – because his medium-pacers then garnered surprising kick from the pitch.

While Killeen was a one-county man, **Andrew Harris** (or "AJ" as he liked to be called) was the first to play first-class cricket for five counties, three permanently – Derbyshire, Nottinghamshire and Leicestershire, where he finished – and two on loan, Gloucestershire and Worcestershire. But it was still a career spanning 18 seasons, and he was always an energetic, bustling away-swing bowler. And in 2009 he was the last man to dismiss Michael Vaughan in first-team cricket. It might only have been a Twenty20 match, but it is something to tell the grandchildren.

ANDREW FLINTOFF

We all owe you one, Fred

Ed Smith

When Andrew Flintoff walked out to the middle in a Test match he took with him the good wishes of the nation. Cheeky grin, natural stride, helmet off: Flintoff never liked the anonymity of hiding behind a grille. He revelled in making a human connection, with team-mates, with friends, with the crowd. People thrilled to the fact he was a little bit like them – only much, much better at cricket.

In his early days in an England shirt, that popularity rankled with some older pros. "Why the huge cheer? What's he ever actually done on a cricket field?"

Andrew Flintoff, most human of personalities.

one England player asked me before Flintoff really hit his straps. That misjudges why people watch sport. It wasn't what Flintoff had done that raised people's spirits. It was what he might do next. Crowds did not invest their faith in Flintoff after a shrewd calculation of the odds. They bet on him with their hearts.

For a long time, it looked as though they were on the wrong end of the gamble. Would he ever come good? The Flintoff debate seemed to go on for ever. Picked for England as a lad in 1998, there was obviously some magic there. But would he stay fit and disciplined enough to deliver?

He bowled some seriously quick deliveries on Duncan Fletcher's first tour as coach, in South Africa in 1999-2000. Was this the real beginning? No, we had some more waiting to do. So why did the selectors persist?

Because Flintoff was different, in every way. He could hit harder than anyone and bowl just as fast. He caught in the slips as though he never considered dropping them, and threw the ball as hard and flat as Andrew Symonds. He could turn games, stun crowds and destroy opponents. Playing for Kent against Lancashire on a freezing day in 2000, I remember him hitting fours at will, mostly off good balls. It was unavoidable: he was Botham's heir.

From 2003 to 2006, at the peak of his powers, he was that much and more. Flintoff was incredible. He grabbed games and changed their course, he stayed fit and defined series. I'll never forget the 98 he hit off South Africa in 2003. One blow, no more than a checked drive, looked like it would just clear mid-off. It did more than that. It broke the Oval dressing-room window, just by my left knee, a hundred yards from the middle.

He was even better in the 2005 Ashes. For all the brilliance of his cricket, it was, though, a human gesture that defined the series. When England finally won at Edgbaston, Flintoff's first thought was to console Brett Lee. It was the finest moment of a great summer.

Flintoff could be a generous colleague, too. On my debut, when England took the last South African wicket, the England players joyously grabbed the stumps and ran off the field. Flintoff walked slowly towards me in the pandemonium, and handed me one of the stumps. I have kept virtually no cricket memorabilia. But that stump I'll have for the rest of my life.

The timing of his retirement was unsatisfactory, more a case of bowing to the inevitable than going out on a high. We had all lost track of his injuries. But cricket will miss him.

Just before Christmas 2010, his first as a non-cricketer, he gave out the prizes at the BBC Sports Personality of the Year. Again, Flintoff raised the biggest cheer. At the reception afterwards, other sports stars were mostly left alone. Lee Westwood, David Ginola, Graeme McDowell: they were all admired, but not mobbed. Flintoff, in contrast, could scarcely finish a sentence without another fan begging to have his photo taken with him.

People want to meet him, to shake his hand, to buy him a beer – for the same reason they cheered loudest for him when he walked out to bat. In Flintoff's naturalness, they see a reflection of their own humanity and vulnerability. Many champion sportsmen have cold, wary eyes. Flintoff doesn't. For all his brutal hitting and fierce bowling, you sense an enduring softness. That juxtaposition of the heroic and the ordinary does not come along very often. In fact, I cannot think of anyone else who has it.

Flintoff will always have the look of someone who could be your mate. That's why he'll need some good ones, now more than ever. It is cruelly ironic that fame latches on to the most human personalities. It is vulnerability that people love in celebrities; but being loved by so many people tends to exacerbate that vulnerability. It is the cycle of celebrity. Whatever he does with the rest of his life, Flintoff will always raise the biggest cheer of the night. That popularity will keep him famous and make him rich. There is always a danger in that.

Perhaps he has thought more than enough about the pitfalls of fame. And anyway maybe this is not the time. Either way I can hear his voice in my head as I write this. "Enough of the long words, Ed, buy me a beer." I will indeed. We all owe you one, Fred.

CAREER FIGURES

Players not expected to appear in county cricket in 2011

(minimum 40 first-class appearances)

BATTING

	M	I	NO	R	HS	100s	Avge	1,000r/ season
U. Afzaal	235	406	47	14,055	204*	32	39.15	7
Kadeer Ali	99	180	10	4,906	161	6	28.85	–
C. C. Benham	48	80	3	2,103	111	2	27.31	–
J. G. E. Benning	42	67	7	1,938	128	4	32.30	–
J. W. M. Dalrymple	123	192	16	6,013	244	10	34.16	1
A. Flintoff	183	290	23	9,027	167	15	33.80	–
G. W. Flower	188	318	25	10,898	243*	23	37.19	–
A. J. Harris	147	197	50	1,253	41*	0	8.52	–
C. B. Keegan	47	57	6	607	44	0	11.90	–
N. Killeen	102	145	31	1,302	48	0	11.42	–
R. J. Kirtley	170	231	76	2,040	59	0	13.16	–
T. Lungley	55	77	16	885	50	0	14.50	–
R. S. C. Martin-Jenkins	184	276	41	7,448	205*	5	31.69	1
J. K. Maunders	90	159	3	4,689	180	8	30.05	–
J. L. Sadler	66	111	15	3,047	145	3	31.73	1
B. M. Shafayat	119	201	7	5,828	161	9	30.04	1
B. F. Smith	334	529	58	18,777	204	40	39.86	8
S. D. Snell	41	69	7	1,679	127	1	27.08	–
S. D. Udal	301	430	79	7,931	117*	1	22.59	–
D. H. Wigley	50	62	22	532	70	0	13.30	–
M. J. Wood†	101	170	8	5332	297	9	32.91	1

BOWLING AND FIELDING

	R	W	BB	Avge	5W/i	10W/m	Ct/St
U. Afzaal	5,078	98	4-101	51.81	–	–	104
Kadeer Ali	304	3	1-4	101.33	–	–	54
C. C. Benham	37	0	–	–	–	–	51
J. G. E. Benning	1,433	24	3-43	59.70	–	–	17
J. W. M. Dalrymple	6,893	160	5-49	43.08	1	–	82
A. Flintoff	11,059	350	5-24	31.59	4	–	185
G. W. Flower	5,605	166	7-31	33.76	3	–	174
A. J. Harris	14,733	451	7-54	32.66	17	3	38
C. B. Keegan	4,887	140	6-114	34.90	6	–	14
N. Killeen	8,215	262	7-70	31.35	9	–	26
R. J. Kirtley	16,607	614	7-21	27.04	29	4	60
T. Lungley	4,784	149	5-20	32.10	3	–	25
R. S. C. Martin-Jenkins	12,253	384	7-51	31.90	8	–	55
J. K. Maunders	928	24	4-15	38.66	–	–	56
J. L. Sadler	250	3	1-5	83.33	–	–	46
B. M. Shafayat	642	8	2-25	80.25	–	–	107/9
B. F. Smith	488	4	1-5	122.00	–	–	214
S. D. Snell	15	0	–	–	–	–	96/3
S. D. Udal	26,695	822	8-50	32.47	37	5	127
D. H. Wigley	4,932	136	6-72	36.26	4	–	22
M. J. Wood†	79	0	–	–	–	–	31

† *M. J. Wood is the former Somerset and Nottinghamshire batsman (b. Exeter, 1980).*

CRICKETANA IN 2010

Deposits, disposals, duplicates and deaccessions…

DAVID RAYVERN ALLEN

The world, we are told, divides into depositors and disposers, collectors and chuckers-out. Without such a division, the auction houses and bookdealers would struggle for business.

Not so very long ago, the then operations manager at The Oval made a remarkable discovery. He came across a splendid marble bust of W. G. Grace that had been dumped in a skip. Quite who was responsible is unclear, though it must have been a disposer on a grand scale – and one with distinct philistine tendencies. Once the Doctor had been saved from such ignominy, his rescuer presented him to a young lady of his acquaintance. Every December, spurred on by the famous forked beard, she would unearth a red hood and dress the bust as Father Christmas. Now, however, W. G. is – if the reader will excuse the choice of verb – gracing a new home.

At Tim Knight's last sale of the season, the extremely rare figure, sculpted by William Henry Tyler in 1888 and one of only three known, fetched a hammer price of £15,000. To think that for someone, it had meant so little.

June saw the culmination of a not dissimilar story; in this case the tale began with either an act of wonderful philanthropy or complete ignorance. As reported a year ago in *Wisden 2010*, editions of the first four Almanacks, from 1864 to 1867, bound as one, had been dropped off in a 99p pile in an Oxfam shop in Hertford. Alert staff realised the gift's potential and, after the four editions were rebound into separate volumes, they raised a total of £8,520 at Bonhams in Oxford. At a specialist sporting sale, they might have fetched considerably more.

Nevertheless, there has been a wide range of desirable items coming up for sale in the past year – and numerous happy collectors as a result. At Knight's February sale in Leicester there was a most attractive early-Victorian silver christening mug with cricketing scenes; at Trevor Vennett-Smith's auction at Gotham in March several of Herbert Sutcliffe's possessions were sold, including an unusual 9ct-gold waistcoat fob; and in November at Graham Budd's auction at Sotheby's, London, a gold medal presented to English cricketer Harry Charlwood at the first official Test at Melbourne in 1877 changed hands. All went for competitive prices, with the medal just reaching its lower estimate at £10,000. In his last few catalogues, bookdealer Christopher Saunders has included some delightful examples of early 19th-century juvenilia containing cricket illustrations, which in recent years has strangely been a rather neglected area of cricketana.

A somewhat surprising auction took place at Dreweatts, Bloomsbury, in June. Glamorgan were offering a substantial quantity of books, letters and

memorabilia from their archives; the aim was to develop the Museum of Welsh Cricket at Cardiff's revamped stadium. Archivist Dr Andrew Hignell declared that "although we were selling items that told the story of Welsh cricket, these originals would never be on display, as the story is being displayed digitally". Apparently, there had been viewings in Cardiff, and some items were sold in Bristol before the auction in London. Autograph letters from Ivo Bligh, of Ashes fame, and documents relating to the formation of Monmouthshire CCC in 1859 attracted interest, though many lots associated with less familiar names remained unsold. A 1916 *Wisden*, which features a tribute to W. G. from Lord Harris, was sold for £4,200, indicating the enduring demand for wartime editions. Most of the other Almanacks sold well, even if many were rather dilapidated.

In December, with snow paralysing much of the country, the residue of cricketing items from Sir Alec Bedser's estate went on sale at Send, in Surrey. An antique opal ring belonging to his mother (£210), two of Plum Warner's weighty limited-edition tomes (£1,600) and Bedser's engraved Cornhill Insurance Test Series medals (£280) attracted most interest.

However, the undoubted high point of the cricketana year was the November sale at Christie's South Kensington branch. This came about after the MCC library went through its collection, rooting out duplicates and earmarking the inferior copy for sale. This disposal – "deaccessioning" in the jargon – produced intense excitement in the packed saleroom, never more than when auctioneer Rupert Neelands presided over bidding for William Epps's *A Collection of all the Grand Matches of Cricket Played in England from 1771 to 1791,* published in Troy Town, Rochester, in 1799. Described in the catalogue as "the black tulip of cricket collecting", it is an assemblage of early scorecards so remarkably rare that the British Library does not have a copy (though MCC, until November, had two).

The initial estimate for the *Epps* of £50,000–70,000 was left far behind as two phone bidders jousted for supremacy on the way to an astonishing £125,000, a record for a single cricket book. With buyer's premium and VAT, the bookseller J. W. McKenzie, who purchased it for a customer, was £151,250 worse off after acquiring 104 pages. "Now, back to reality," commented Neelands drily after bringing down the gavel.

In his preface, Epps acknowledged the MCC scorer Samuel Britcher, whose series of annual scores, running from 1790–1805, allowed Epps to end the scope of his publication in 1791. Three of Britcher's *A Complete List of All the Grand Matches of Cricket that have been played in the year…* (for 1792, 1793 and 1796) were also in the sale. Once again internet and phone bidding – perhaps 50% of all bidding now happens this way – dominated proceedings, and the three volumes made a total of £99,000 before premium and tax. Once again, the purchaser was McKenzie.

Other treasures enticed a core of wealthy collectors to raid their offshore accounts: *The Trip to Australia: Scraps from the Diary of One of the Twelve* (1864) by E. M. Grace (W. G.'s brother) far exceeded its estimate of £3,000– 5,000 to sell for £18,000; a bound volume of three separate verse works – *Surry* (sic) *Triumphant, The Kentish Cricketers* and *Cricket, An Heroic*

Poem – reached £24,000; while a Gujarati translation of *The Laws of Cricket* rocketed past its £250–300 estimate to make £3,500 (all hammer prices).

There were, however, a couple of sought-after booklets that, relatively speaking, fell into the bargain basement. Boxall's *Rules and Instructions for playing at the Game of Cricket* (*c.* 1802) changed hands for £2,600, while Fuller Pilch's *The Whole Art of Cricket* (*c.* 1875) sold for £480. Given the heady heights reached by a handful of books, it was not surprising that a few fared distinctly less well.

The sale also included one or two non-print items, such as *The Young Cricketer: Portrait of Lewis Cage,* an oil painting (1950) by Katharine Lloyd, after Francis Cotes's 1768 original. It was commissioned by MCC to mark the opening of the Lord's museum. For many years the portrait hung in the Pavilion, but in 2008 MCC bought the Cotes original, now in the Long Room – hence the sale of the copy. It quadrupled its estimate and sold for £23,000, plus premium and VAT. All told, MCC's duplicates cleared nearly £550,000.

Before the sale, some expressed concern that specific gifts to the library were being offloaded without consulting donors or their families, and that the money raised would be spent outside the library. Adam Chadwick, the curator of collections, was quick to allay anxiety. "MCC acquired most of the books a very long time ago… and much care and research has been undertaken in order to contact any living relatives of those who bequeathed some of the items. Any new purchase will retain a dedication recording the fund which enabled it to be bought. We are delighted with the results of the sale… The considerable amount realised will be ring-fenced and dedicated to future acquisitions as the Club seeks to broaden and strengthen what is the world's finest museum, library and archive devoted to cricket."

CRICKET EQUIPMENT, 2010

More than a sideline

Norman Harris

Inventors of cricket equipment come in different guises, though a background in engineering or science is often a common theme. Frank Thorogood, on the other hand, is an Essex farmer whose connection with engineering lay in driving his father's combine harvester, and with science in selling horse feed.

An interest in cricket is a given, and Frank had shown enterprise with his use of an old barn as an indoor nets facility for local players. But nothing hinted at the remarkable adventure that started after he saw dog-walkers propelling balls into the air with a device resembling a long-handled soup ladle.

The ball nestled in the spoon end and, with a swift over-the-shoulder movement, was launched far and high – rather like casting with a fishing rod. The ball shot up because it rested only loosely in the spoon, but Frank saw a way of delivering it with force and with a much flatter trajectory – such as could be used for throw-downs in cricket practice.

He worked hard on the prototypes of his Sidearm cricket ball thrower, and applied for a patent. He also entered it in an entrepreneurs' competition run by Barclays, who offered regional prizes of £50,000; in the meantime he spent £43,000 of his own money on development. Bravely, he didn't go to an established sports goods firm, but set up his own company, Thorogoods Ball Thrower Ltd.

His courage was rewarded when news came that he had won the Barclays money for East Anglia. Soon he was in China telling a factory in Guangdong province the specifications: the ball must be held firmly enough by the spoon's small "wings" to prevent it being dislodged prematurely when the device was swung above the shoulder, yet loosely enough to allow it to fly out at the right moment with precisely the right angle and velocity.

In late summer 2010, Frank took delivery of 2,000 Sidearms, which he would sell at £19.99 (for the basic model) and £24.99 (for the "pro" version). Happily, the England coaching hierarchy was preparing for the Ashes, and no one was more enthusiastic about the Sidearm than chief batting coach Graham Gooch. He, after all, is the king of throw-downs. Indeed, many thought the Sidearm a Gooch invention; Frank Thorogood wasn't complaining about that.

Bowling machines have a longer and more complex story. First, in the 19th century, there was Felix's Catapulta. Then Bola introduced some more advanced models, before Merlyn and ProBatter arrived. Merlyn, which the ECB gave to every county and is carried around by England teams, can produce almost every known type of spin – and with variable pace and bounce. Whatever it has done for England's batsmen, it has done in spades for batsmen from counties without a high-class spinner and who were once all at sea playing sides with a Shane Warne, Mushtaq Ahmed or Muttiah Muralitharan. One such side was Durham, whose batting coach Jon Lewis now tells how "batsmen can spend hours and hours against it; they've learnt to be less rigid mentally, more flexible and imaginative and to expand their game by finding out how their footwork can take them into different areas".

The device can run through any number of different balls in a sequence with, say, a googly thrown in among a series of leg-breaks. For the batsman, unaware of what delivery is coming next and with no hand action to give clues, that can make life especially awkward. Unless, of course, he or she can read spin through the air…

So, is a device that can propel the ball like the proverbial bolt from the blue "fair" on the batsman? Possibly not. True, the coach feeding the machine could raise a hand to give a one-second warning, but the routine is still far removed from the reality of a bowler running in. Mike Brearley once wrote that there were times when he felt so much in tune with the bowler that it almost seemed they were performing *together*. Central to that feeling would have been the batsman's ability to synchronise mentally with the bowler's delivery action.

ProBatter was developed to give baseball batters virtual practice against particular pitchers. It shows front-on video of the pitcher at the point of delivery, at which moment a ball is fired from the machine. Adapted to cricket, England batsmen have now "faced" Mitchell Johnson, and others. There is a weakness: Johnson is a left-armer and so bowls from the other side of the stumps from, say, Peter Siddle. But the ProBatter incarnation of both delivers the ball from a fixed, central aperture.

ECB coaches acknowledge this is not ideal, and point out that there are lots of cues to be identified (especially in super slow-motion) during the bowler's run-up and at a point just before release. Whether it is helpful to try to combine this with playing a real ball coming from a slightly unfaithful angle is a moot point. Maybe simply watching the video and playing an imaginary stroke might be as helpful.

Australia's batsmen might perhaps have been better off doing just that when, at Brisbane in November, they had their first try against ProBatter. Unfortunately for them, there was no special video of the England bowlers. Every bowler must be recorded delivering a ball to be programmed into the system. Australia's players had obliged; England's had not. So Australia practised against video of James Pattinson of Victoria, only to find the equipment malfunctioning.

As Ricky Ponting was facing, the screen suddenly went blank; a moment later a ball almost decapitated him. Shane Watson lasted two balls – bowled by the first and thin-edging the second – before quitting, muttering darkly "I'll try anything once."

CRICKET AND THE WEATHER, 2010

Somerset second yet again

PHILIP EDEN

After a winter of severe frosts and frequent heavy snow – the coldest quarter in most parts of the UK since 1978-79 – one might have wondered what sort of meteorological extremes the summer would bring. In the event, the weather took something of a back seat during the 2010 season. A trawl through the records reveals that summers following severe winters are rarely long and hot. Of the 20 coldest winters during the last century the subsequent summer turned out to be generally cool on eight occasions, average on 11, and significantly warmer than average just once. That was 1947, the legendary golden summer of Compton and Edrich.

Unlike 2009, there were no large geographical contrasts during summer 2010. Instead, the contrasts were temporal, with much the best weather during the first half of the season, in April, May, June, and early-July, followed by a shortage of sunshine and frequent rain during the middle and latter parts of July, and most of August. September brought a slight improvement.

The university matches began in cold showery weather during the first week of April, and snow lay across parts of northern England after a major storm – the last of the winter – at the very end of March. But by the time the Championship started on April 9 high pressure had settled across the country, bringing a fortnight of sunny and often warm weather. The last week of April saw a few showers, though it was still warm, but May 1 was a very wet day across the South, and the remainder of the first half of May was quite cold with well-scattered showers. After mid-month all parts of the country became mostly sunny, and very warm at times too.

A spell of rather cool, changeable weather between May 29 and June 9 encompassed the two Bangladesh Tests, but it was warm and sunny again for the rest of June and, in eastern, central and southern England, for the first ten days of July. In western districts, though, the weather had already turned, and from then until the last week of August conditions were rather disturbed with frequent rain, subdued temperatures and little sunshine.

The first three Pakistan Tests unfolded against cloudy skies and in humid conditions, so it was no surprise that the ball swung. High pressure returned for the final Test at Lord's and, apart from a wet interlude around September 6–9, the month brought long spells of settled weather. Autumnal rains swept the country on the 24th – two days after the season ended – and the rest of the month was very wet.

The meteorological statistics, averaged over England and Wales, for the 2010 season, were:

	Average max temperature (°C)	Difference from normal (1971–2000) (°C)	Total rainfall (mm)	% of normal	Total sunshine (hours)	% of normal
April	8.8	+0.7	31	50	222	142
May	11.0	–0.3	40	65	219	108
June	15.1	+1.5	41	60	260	137
July	17.4	+0.9	123	155	165	82
August	15.3	–0.9	106	147	153	78
September	13.8	+0.1	82	99	143	99
2010 season	**13.6**	**+0.3**	**423**	**96**	**1162**	**108**

Each summer has slightly different regional variations, though in most years northern and western counties are cooler, cloudier and damper than those in the east and south. The Wisden Summer Index (see page 1597 of *Wisden 2004* for the precise formula) compares the season county by county. In essence, an index over 650 indicates a good summer; one below 500 a poor one. Values for the summer of 2010 against the average for the standard reference period of 1971–2000 were:

	2010	Normal	Difference		2010	Normal	Difference
Derbyshire	581	580	+1	Middlesex	655	670	–15
Durham	534	525	+9	Northamptonshire . .	594	615	–21
Essex	637	640	–3	Nottinghamshire . .	588	590	–2
Glamorgan	577	555	+22	Somerset	667	620	+47
Gloucestershire . . .	616	595	+21	Surrey	659	675	–16
Hampshire	666	645	+21	Sussex	673	665	+8
Kent	637	655	–18	Warwickshire	573	555	+18
Lancashire	525	530	–5	Worcestershire	615	615	0
Leicestershire	586	585	+1	Yorkshire	595	560	+35

Broadly speaking the counties blessed with the best of the weather in 2010 were towards the south-west, including Glamorgan, Gloucestershire, Hampshire and Somerset. Almost inevitably, Somerset, who enjoyed a much better-than-average season in both meteorological and cricketing terms, came second (behind Sussex), just as they did all summer long. Yorkshire, sheltered by the Pennines from the westerly winds that prevailed for most of July and August, also fared well, but county champions Nottinghamshire were not especially favoured. Some eastern counties were down on 2009, notably Kent and Essex, but all western and northern parts enjoyed their best summer since 2006.

Nationally, last season's index of 610 was 42 higher than the year before, some 20 above the long-term average and the first above-average summer for four years. It must be said, though, that it was a very small excess, and in no way was 2010 comparable with the great summers such as 1911, 1976, 1989 and 1995. Indeed the index for 2010 was more than 200 points below 1976.

1999	637		2002	506	2005	623	2008	525
2000	559		2003	647	2006	633	2009	568
2001	632		2004	541	2007	503	**2010**	**610**

Highest: 812 in 1976   Lowest: 309 in 1879

CRICKET GROUNDS IN 2010

Watching the debts grow

IVO TENNANT

Alas for them, the first-class counties were never likely to be immune from the recession. Several, not just the smaller ones, returned worrying losses in 2010, and in a period of substantial wage bills were to some extent unsure how to return to profitability. This was in spite of the ECB allocating £1.6–2m to each of the 18 clubs, depending on performance-related payments, and making loans available if a county were in serious trouble.

A confidential report by Deloitte into the finances of county cricket revealed last summer that the clubs with Test grounds had invested £156m in facilities since 2000, with a further £56m committed over the next four years. Since much of that had been borrowed, their debt stood at £91m, raising concerns of potential bankruptcy if interest rates were to shoot up. These counties, after bidding against each other to stage England matches, urged this practice to be discontinued. In 2011, the ECB are expected to make £17.5m from the bidding process, compared with £5.4m in 2006.

Hampshire were largely indebted to their chairman, Rod Bransgrove. His personal injection of capital over a decade has amounted to more than £5m, and this summer will see the dividend of the Rose Bowl's first Test.

The question was whether the first-class counties in general should have embarked on extensive and expensive redevelopment, or whether in some cases they would have been better off merging with one another. "Every Test match ground has a Test match built into its business plan, and I understand why they do it – but that is not too clever," said Nigel Hilliard, chairman of Essex and a director of the ECB. "Lord's and The Oval are not going to have a problem, but at the extremities, is a Test at Chester-le-Street in May going to work? I don't see clubs going out of business, but possibly some will go into administration. Football clubs do, but how many go bust? There is a lot of talk about counties joining forces, but it won't happen.

"Leicestershire are the most critical club," Hilliard said. "They clearly got it wrong. Their crowds are atrocious and their wage bill too high. Too much was spent on signing Matthew Hoggard, whose best days are behind him. But a club can be run on £1.5m a year. Players' salaries will have to come down and there won't be as much movement around the counties as in the past."

"There is no end in sight to the recession," said Jim Cumbes, Lancashire's chief executive. "We have lost £2m. The issue for clubs with big grounds such as ours is that we are forced to develop the facilities to meet ICC standards. The crowds for our T20 matches last year were no bigger, and the public showed a weariness towards the end of the programme.

"This is going to be another critical year. Some members will not be renewing their subscriptions until we play our Championship matches at Old

Trafford again, and we are affected by not staging a Test match. We didn't expect the dip to be as big as it was last year, and have to feed debts while decisions are made over which of the Category A grounds stage the seven Tests a year. And I don't want to have to make employees redundant."

The "Vision" at Lord's was stalled by the concerns of the chairman of MCC, Oliver Stocken, and the treasurer, Justin Dowley, over the scale of the proposed redevelopment. The plans, which included the rebuilding of five stands and creating an underground village at the Nursery End, were supposed to have been put before the membership and Westminster City Council for planning approval in 2010, but Stocken favoured an alternative proposal: building on the site of the existing indoor school and ECB offices. MCC lost £3m last year.

The extent to which provincial clubs are dependent on owning their own grounds was illustrated by Kent selling off land in the Bat & Ball car park and an area used for net practice behind the Cowdrey Stand. Hence on paper, Kent were able to turn a loss of more than £500,000 into a profit in excess of £4m. Even so, George Kennedy, the chairman, still had to lend the club an interest-free six-figure sum. Leicestershire, by contrast, are constrained by covenant in not being able to sell any land for more than £24,000; not surprisingly, the club are attempting to alter this stipulation.

"Something radical needs to happen within the game – there almost needs to be legislation passed stating that no club can invest more than a certain percentage of their turnover in players' salaries," said Jamie Clifford, Kent's new chief executive. "But then that would not constrain the Surreys of this world. We keep looking for benefactors, but most people want to have a stake in their investment."

Mike Siddall, Leicestershire's new chief executive, has the unenviable task of coping with the fallout from the acrimonious departures of his predecessor, David Smith, and Neil Davidson, the chairman, to say nothing of a horrendous loss of more than £400,000. He dismisses speculation that the easiest way for the club to overcome their difficulties would be to merge with Nottinghamshire. "I like going to Trent Bridge, but it's an hour away and I wouldn't want us to become their second eleven," he said.

Still, there is doubtless room for a more innovative approach. Somerset make more money from subscriptions to their new Long Room in the pavilion – which has the best view at the County Ground – than some counties do from their entire membership. "I don't understand why clubs in big cities do not attract crowds," said Richard Gould, their chief executive. "Their T20 attendances are lower than for Conference football. I would like to see more efforts made by the ECB to drive income schemes."

CRICKET PEOPLE

Not a freaking cricket match

LAWRENCE BOOTH

The sleepy town of Westfield, Massachusetts, unexpectedly found itself on the cricket map in late November when one of its inhabitants – a 22-year-old babysitter called **Ashley Kerekes** – became an instant internet sensation. Rejoicing in the Twitter handle @theashes, given to her by her boyfriend, Kerekes was awoken one night in late November by a flurry of messages from fellow users on the social networking site who mistakenly assumed she was involved with events almost 10,000 miles away at the Gabba in Brisbane. "I am not a freaking cricket match," wrote a despairing Kerekes. "Stop mentioning me and check profiles before you send messages. Its [sic] really annoying."

But her irritation merely fanned the flames of cyberspace, and a campaign to "#gettheashestotheashes" – the addendum (known as a "hash-tag") that accompanied relevant posts on the website – developed unstoppable momentum. From a Twitter following of a few hundred, Kerekes quickly moved into the thousands. As Qantas prepared to jump on the bandwagon and fly her to the Sydney Test, she told Sky News: "At first I thought it was a couple of people making a simple mistake and it would be over and done with. But I have so many fans now, they would be upset if I changed my name."

Once in Sydney, Kerekes was treated like royalty, enjoying a guided tour of the SCG from Steve Waugh, glad-handing Julia Gillard, Australia's prime minister – and even earning a lunchtime interview on *Test Match Special*. By now, about 14,000 followers were hanging on her every word. "The score for those in Australia 9/636," she tweeted as England racked up the runs. "And for those in England, it is 636/9."

Kerekes's rise to fame placed Westfield – estimated population: 40,000 – on the map in a manner not seen since the local-born Frederick H. Gillett became the 42nd speaker of the House of Representatives in 1919. But did Kerekes intend to continue following cricket once the series whose name changed her life was over? "Yes!" she told her loyal tweeters. "Pls tell me when and where to find it." She was not expected to be short of offers.

John Howard found himself on the wrong end of a different kind of campaign. The former prime minister of Australia, a self-professed "cricket tragic", had been nominated by Australia and New Zealand for the vice-presidency of the ICC, a two-year term of office due to start in 2012. But his appointment was torpedoed when the boards of six Full Members – Bangladesh, India, Pakistan, South Africa, Sri Lanka and West Indies – signed a letter rejecting his nomination. With a seventh, Zimbabwe, indicating it would abstain, Howard was left with the support of only England and the two countries who had put him forward in the first place. His candidature was withdrawn without a vote.

Howard described himself as "furious, at the very least", adding: "I'm personally disappointed because everyone in Australia knows how much I love cricket." Conscious they had been outmanoeuvred, the Australia–New Zealand axis later nominated a second candidate, the chairman of New Zealand Cricket, Alan Isaac. And while Isaac's nomination was greeted favourably, it remained unclear precisely why Howard had fallen foul of the Asian bloc and its allies.

Some cited his anti-Robert Mugabe stance during an 11-year reign in which he banned Zimbabwe from touring Australia in 2007 – a decision he later insisted he wore as a "badge of honour". But he may also have upset the Asian nations by claiming, in 2004, that the Sri Lanka off-spinner Muttiah Muralitharan was a chucker, arguing "they proved it in Perth with that thing" – a reference to the biomechanical laboratory tests Murali had undergone at the University of Western Australia. Murali pulled out of Sri Lanka's tour to Australia later that year.

In the week following the rejection of his candidature, Howard called Muralitharan a "very good bowler". But by then the often unaccountable nature of global cricket politics had begun to assert itself. The damage had been done.

For 13-year-old **Hugo Blogg**, the game is still played very much on the field. Blogg, a pupil at Chigwell School in Essex, was – at the age of 12 – thought to have become the youngest person to attain the ECB's Level 1 umpiring qualification, and now stands in judgment over his peers in the Essex County Boys and Girls Leagues and the Metropolitan Essex Board Indoor League. "They quite like it," he jokes. "If they see an older umpire, they might feel as if they're going to get a few poor decisions. My eyesight is in good order."

Blogg still plays the game, and last summer captained Chigwell Under-14s to a second successive unbeaten season, but the thrill of split-second decision-making may determine his future plans. "I like the sense of anticipation you get when you have to make a big decision," he says. "Those moments where you realise you have the power to change the course of a game but have to make the right decision are moments I love."

Blogg's array of distinctive signals are, he says, his own, and he sums up the appeal of umpiring with the kind of level-headed analysis that presumably helped him on to the first rung of officialdom's ladder: "When you're playing, you can be too involved with the game to appreciate it properly. If you're in the crowd, you can feel too far away. So being an umpire is the best of both worlds."

In between doing his homework and representing his school, Blogg now hopes to tick off Level 2 – beyond which, who knows? "I want to go as far as I can," he says. "The older umpires I've stood with have all been very supportive and I really enjoy it." Batsmen, though, beware: if it's hitting leg stump, Blogg says he'll have no problem giving you out. The benefit of the doubt, he insists, is a figment of the cricket-lover's imagination.

CRICKET AND THE LAW, 2010

WESTFIELD AT OLD BAILEY ON CONSPIRACY CHARGE

The 22-year-old former Essex bowler Mervyn Westfield appeared at the Old Bailey on October 28 accused of conspiracy to defraud over an allegation of spot-fixing. The case was said to involve Westfield's bowling in the televised Durham v Essex NatWest Pro40 match at Chester-le-Street on September 5, 2009. In Durham's total of 276 for six, Westfield had figures of 7–0–60–0 with four wides and two no-balls. Essex scored 279 for three and won by seven wickets.

Westfield was charged with attempting to defraud "members of Essex County Cricket Club, his team-mates and spectators and supporters watching the match". The case was adjourned until 2011. Westfield had been arrested on May 15, 2010, along with his team-mate Danish Kaneria, but charges against Kaneria were dropped.

THE STRANGE CASE OF SWANN, CAT AND CAR

When police officers stopped a white Porsche at 3 a.m. in an area of Nottingham known for its burglaries, they were surprised to find that the driver was (a) quite famous (b) had slightly slurred speech (c) was in possession of two screwdrivers that might have been used for burglary and (d) had a very original explanation.

Nottingham magistrates heard the story on August 16 when England cricketer Graeme Swann appeared on a drink-drive charge, having been tested at 83mg of alcohol per 100ml of blood, just over the limit of 80.

Swann told the police that he arrived home (by taxi) from a night out to discover that one of his cats, Max, had become trapped under the floorboards. He had gone out in his car to the 24-hour supermarket to buy the screwdrivers and release the cat. PC Caroline Voce told the court that Swann had climbed out of the car with something glinting in his hand. "As he approached us, I thought we had a burglar or a stolen vehicle," she said.

Swann denied the charge and his lawyer said police had not followed the correct procedure for blood samples with a borderline reading. The case was adjourned until February 16, 2011 when Swann was briefly at home for the birth of his child. District judge Julia Newton ruled in his favour on the matter of procedure, and he was cleared.

CRICKET BALLS WITH UNEXPECTED CONTENTS

Liaqat Ali, 28, was jailed for eight years for his part in a plot to smuggle heroin hidden in cricket balls. Bradford Crown Court heard that around 200g of pure heroin was contained in a consignment of balls sent from Pakistan to Liaqat's home in the city. After a similar parcel was intercepted by Customs, police raided another house he owned and found cut-up balls and packages of heroin. Liaqat pleaded guilty and was sentenced on March 25.

AIRLINE PRICES "FIXED" AT CRICKET MATCH

Executives of British Airways and Virgin Atlantic agreed to fix the prices of fuel surcharges in a conversation held at a cricket match played at the Oxfordshire home of Virgin's president, Sir Richard Branson, claimed Richard Latham, QC, prosecuting, at the trial at Southwark Crown Court of four BA employees charged with illegal price-fixing. Virgin executives had been granted immunity for whistle-blowing. However, the case collapsed on May 10. Defence counsel Ben Emmerson, QC called the evidence "ludicrous".

MOTHER ARRESTED FOR REFUSING TO RETURN BALL

A Hampshire mother of four was arrested and detained for five hours after she refused to return a cricket ball belonging to neighbouring children. Lorretta Cole, 47, said the ball had repeatedly landed on her property and finally damaged her car. She was visited three times by police and told she could face prosecution for theft. Finally, she was forced to attend Lyndhurst police station, where her fingerprints and a DNA swab were taken. "I couldn't believe it," Mrs Cole said. She said she asked the police if they could speak to the parents but they refused. A police spokeswoman said she was "obstructive".

OBITUARIES

AAMER BASHIR, who died of cancer on December 20, 2010, aged 38, was often spoken of as a possible Pakistan player. However, he came close only once: when he made the squad, but not the team, for a one-dayer against India at Kolkata in November 2004. Bashir made more than 9,000 first-class runs, his 16 centuries including two doubles, both in 2004. "He was a stylish batsman, not unlike Mark Waugh," said the former Pakistan Test player Basit Ali. "He was unlucky not to have played at international level, but could not fit into Inzamam-ul-Haq's team because there were too many good batsmen around at the time." Bashir complained of stomach pains during a match in 2008, and a tumour was eventually diagnosed. Former team-mates helped raise funds for his treatment, and after his death there were calls for a proper Pakistan players' association which could assist in similar cases. His father, Bashir Malik, also played for Multan.

ABLACK, ROBERT KENNETH, died on December 15, 2010, aged 91. The Trinidadian Ken Ablack was the Caribbean voice on the BBC radio commentary team during the West Indian tours of England in 1950 and 1957, the second of which represented the first summer of virtually continuous ball-by-ball commentary on *Test Match Special*. Ablack was working as a producer in the BBC's Caribbean Section at the time; earlier he had played three matches for Northamptonshire as a slow left-armer, taking six wickets, five of them in the match against Glamorgan at Rushden in 1946. He returned home in 1962, eventually becoming chairman of Trinidad and Tobago's National Broadcasting Service, and an influential member of the Queen's Club, which owns the Test ground in Port-of-Spain. "His commentary style was rather slow and precise," recalled his eventual successor Tony Cozier, "along the lines, say, of Don Mosey, although with a melodic Trinidadian, rather than Yorkshire, accent."

ANDREW, KEITH VINCENT, who died on December 27, 2010, aged 81, was recognised for most of his career as the best wicketkeeper in England. This was stated so often in the 1950s and 1960s by small boys and distant newspaper readers that it came to seem more like a proven fact than a matter of opinion. Nonetheless, it was believed by the best judges

Bob Thomas, Popperfoto/Getty Images

Chaired and cheered: Keith Andrew (*left*) and Frank Tyson are hailed by their Northamptonshire colleagues after being chosen for the 1954-55 tour of Australasia.

too. "Keith was my schoolboy hero," said Bob Taylor, before pausing. "No, that's not right. Godfrey Evans was my schoolboy hero. When I became a pro, I changed my allegiances." However, Andrew played two Tests to Evans's 91. Beyond question, Evans was a far better batsman (first-class career average 21 v 13), but the undemonstrative style that made Andrew so much admired was a drawback in catching selectors' eyes. He also suffered from the unfortunate circumstances of his Test debut and, perhaps, because he played for put-upon Northamptonshire. But he had a remarkable career as keeper, captain and pioneering coach and, throughout, was one of the most admired and best-loved men in cricket.

An only child, abandoned by his father, Andrew was spotted in a school playground in Oldham and began keeping wicket for Oldham Boys when the previous incumbent was injured. He played in the Central Lancashire League for Werneth, and in 1949 made a brilliant stumping off the Australian George Tribe, then pro-ing for Milnrow, to dismiss Winston Place in a League representative match against Lancashire. This was to prove highly significant four years later, after Andrew had completed National Service, when Northamptonshire were looking for someone to keep to Tribe, their almost unreadable new signing. He was to make another important stumping, Ian Craig off Freddie Brown, in his first major appearance for the county, against the Australians in 1953. More characteristic was his ball-by-ball competence and, when he qualified and became the county's regular No. 1 the following year, he won immediate admiration.

Brown had just retired both as Northamptonshire captain and chairman of the Test selectors, but still had influence at Lord's, which may explain why both Andrew and his team-mate Frank Tyson became shock selections for the 1954-55 Ashes tour before they had even completed their first full season. Tyson came back from Australia a star. For Andrew, chosen as reserve to Godfrey Evans, it was a different story. He got married in the short gap between the end of the season and setting sail, leaving his bride for six months. The captain, Len Hutton, was obviously baffled by his presence, which would not have mattered had not Evans fallen ill on the eve of the First Test at the Gabba. Hutton put Australia in, and in the third over Arthur Morris offered a hard chance off the inside edge – no more than a quarter-chance, according to many observers – which Andrew failed to take. Morris scored 153, Australia passed 600, the England fielding became woefully ragged, they lost by an innings, and Hutton needed a scapegoat. Most accounts suggest Andrew kept well, but the nervous novice did not have Evans's cheerleading qualities, and his moment in the sun was over. "Neat and efficient in an ordinary way," sniffed *Wisden* as he returned to the county circuit.

But as the years passed, his reputation grew for being neat and efficient in an extraordinary way. "He made it look so easy, just used to catch the ball and send it back," said Bob Taylor, who quickly acquired a pair of Andrew's comfy Australian gloves, with no webbing. "I remember Keith standing up to Brian Crump, who was a nippy little skidder, and he would take it with no trouble at all time after time. That's the hard part, standing up, and he was the master." "I can't ever remember Keith diving," said his county colleague Jim Watts. "He didn't dive. He anticipated." But over the next nine years half the keepers in England got a turn as Evans's deputy or successor before Andrew returned to the Test team. He was chosen at Old Trafford in 1963, a reaction to the scrappiness in the field that had cost England the Ashes the previous winter. England were outmatched by West Indies and, though Andrew was his usual unruffled self, with nine years' more experience, and also proved a sturdy nightwatchman, England rapidly returned to the comfort of Jim Parks at No. 7 rather than Andrew at 10, and to hell with the purists.

So Andrew went back to Northampton, where no one had to be impressed. In 1962, he had become county captain, leading a team on the way up again, and he did an outstanding, if idiosyncratic, job. The young players thought he was dotty, forgetting their names, making bizarre bowling changes. Batsmen were often bewildered as he muttered from behind the stumps: "You don't want to play this fella from the crease," David Lloyd recalled him saying, "you need to get down the wicket." Another stumping, thank you. He could indeed be a bit vague, but it was mostly an act. Instinctively he was a touch defensive

(Watts credits him with inventing short third man as a run-saving position). And he thought of everything, including probability theory when related to the toss – and the players' feelings. In 1965 he took the county agonisingly close to the Championship. And all the while his keeping never wavered: he had an eight-match spell that summer when opponents scored more than 2,000 runs without a bye. He retired a year later and moved into coaching. Freddie Brown pushed him to take charge of the north in the embryonic national coaching set-up, and Andrew then became a key figure at Lord's for 15 years, first as national director of coaching and then as chief executive of the National Cricket Association until 1994. He was a devoted, beloved figure in coaching; less predictably, he was also an incisive administrator. His marriage, after its unpromising start, was long and loving, and Keith and Joyce's son Neale became a successful sculptor. And always he believed – article of faith No. 1 – that England should pick the best wicketkeeper without thinking of his batting.

BANTON, DENNIS, who died on June 23, 2010, aged 80, was connected with Oxfordshire cricket for almost 50 years as a player and administrator. "Joe" Banton made 168 consecutive appearances in the Minor Counties Championship – the run ended when he finally took a holiday – and was one of the most-admired all-rounders (mixing off-spin with inswing) on the minors' circuit throughout the 1950s and 1960s, much of the time sharing a feared bowling partnership with David Laitt for both club (Cowley St John) and county. He was captain for six years, and a schoolteacher.

BEDSER, Sir ALEC VICTOR, CBE, died on April 4, 2010, aged 91. In his playing days, Alec Bedser was the epitome of the English seam bowler, the role that represents the nation's often underestimated cricketing virtues more than anything else. In the half-century of retirement that followed – almost all of it devoted to the game he loved – he became something more: the epitome of the spirit of English cricket itself, its values, its history and its perpetual sense of decay.

Hitler's war meant that Bedser did not make his Test debut until he was nearly 28. But he made up for lost time, taking 11 wickets in each of England's first two Tests after the war. For the next decade, he was the engine-room of the team: unflagging in the defeats that came all too often in the 1940s, before emerging triumphant at Melbourne in 1950-51 when England beat Australia for the first time in 15 post-war Tests. And he remained a crucial figure in the Surrey team throughout their triumphant sequence of seven Championships in the 1950s. Later, he spent an unprecedented 24 seasons as an England selector, 13 of them as chairman.

His celebrity went far beyond cricket, because he was not just Alec but one of a pair. His identical twin Eric, not quite an England player himself, was a Surrey stalwart and, by default, a national figure too. In the 1950s, just about everyone in Britain could identify "Alec and Eric" without benefit of their surnames; everyone in cricket had a story about the mystical connections and coincidences that seemed to attend them. Both were bachelors, though the word does their situation no justice: they were virtually inseparable until Eric died in 2006, a relationship that would be hard for even the most devoted spouse to imagine. Modern doctors now urge mothers to let monozygotic twins (the preferred term) develop their own separate personalities. Alec and Eric – peas in a pod from birth to old age – knew no other way and wanted nothing else: they had each other. (For more on this aspect of Alec's life, see Eric's obituary in *Wisden 2007*, page 1541). They also had cricket.

The boys grew up in difficult circumstances near Woking: their father, a fine non-league footballer, was a £4-a-week bricklayer who – in the phrase later made famous by the politician Norman Tebbit – really did have to get on his bike looking for work. Alec was a Test cricketer before the family had a bathroom. After leaving school, both got jobs as clerks in the same solicitors' office. But in 1938 they tossed aside the security for a place on the Oval groundstaff. Alec was the leading Second Eleven bowler in both 1938 and 1939, when he played, without taking a wicket, in the first-class fixtures against the two universities. He might have become a first-team regular in 1940; instead the twins found themselves under bombardment at Merville and being evacuated from Dunkirk.

Already they had enough celebrity to ease the passage: during the retreat the unmistakable pair were spotted by a van driver who happened to be a Surrey member, and given a lift to the French coast. And they managed to keep together – Alec forewent promotion so he could stay with Eric. Yet their war was not a soft one, and they both got jaundice during the invasion of Italy. When he was in England, however, Alec began to be a favourite choice for wartime matches, and was selected for a powerful England XI against a West Indies XI in front of a huge crowd at Lord's in 1943. He took six for 27, including a hat-trick. So he was not a wholly unknown quantity when cricket resumed. Just in case, though, he wasted no time: in Surrey's first post-war match he took six for 14 at Lord's, bowling out a formidable MCC team for 78. Through the sodden early summer of 1946, he kept taking wickets, even bowling 37 overs (and dismissing Hutton and Hammond) in the Test trial while suffering from a pulled thigh muscle which he had bound up with Elastoplast.

Barely a week later, he took the train, tube and bus to Lord's to make his Test debut. It is true that there was not much competition: his first two England opening partners were Bill Bowes and Bill Voce, both nearly 38. But before the day was done he had bowled India out for 200, taking seven for 49. "Through half-closed eyes it might have been a

Surrey boys: the Bedser twins in their element, 1946.

Popperfoto/Getty Images

Maurice Tate out there, hurling them down," wrote Harold Dale in the *Daily Express*. For once *Wisden* was more fulsome than the press: "Probably the finest performance ever recorded by a bowler in his first Test," was Hubert Preston's verdict.

When he followed with seven for 52 at Old Trafford, Alec's course was set. It was already clear that in English conditions he was a superb bowler, able to generate exceptional lateral movement off damp uncovered pitches. But the other half of him was to be revealed a few months later in Australia: he was a lionheart. Leading a hopelessly overmatched England attack, he bowled 246.3 eight-ball overs in the Ashes alone without a hint of injury. The Australian spearheads, Lindwall and Miller, bowled less between them. Bedser did get ill in ferocious heat in both Brisbane and Adelaide, where he went to the dressing-room to be sick and walked straight back out again. But that was also the Test when he produced his master-ball: the fast, dipping leg-break that bowled Don Bradman for nought in the final over of the second day.

That ball cemented a lasting friendship with Bradman, and a love of Australia. And his equilibrium on tour was undoubtedly helped by the presence of Eric, shipped out to keep him company through sponsorship from the pools magnate Alfie Cope. The stamina that kept Alec going in Australia would be needed at home in the summers ahead, both for England and Surrey. Year after year, he would bowl more than 1,000 overs (1,253 in 1953, when he was 35) and pass 100 wickets. There was little support, even at Surrey, in the early days.

After two Tests in 1947, England decided they were in danger of running him into the ground and rested him until the following year's Ashes. Again he bowled and bowled,

dismissing Bradman four times in the first two Tests (and making 79 as nightwatchman at Headingley). But this was a near-impossible series for England, and Bedser was fighting an uphill battle until the last Test of the 1950-51 series. He took ten for 105 at Melbourne, was hailed as "the best bowler in the world" by the *Express*, given a civic reception in Woking and had his waxwork placed in Madame Tussauds. The Australian writer Ray Robinson said it should be in the Chamber of Horrors.

By now all the elements of Bedser's bowling were in place. Essentially his method was based on inswing, bowled into a consistent area back of a length and assisted by an absence of restriction on the number of fielders backward of square on the leg side. On wet wickets he could become unplayable. He could also bowl outswing, never stopped thinking and never stopped trying, which was possible well into cricketing old age thanks to his economy of action. He had height, strength, huge hands and ferociously strong wrists. There was also what was most often

Stamina: Bedser in 1953, when he sent down 1,253 overs in first-class cricket.

called his leg-cutter, though those who faced it insist this was an inadequate description. "It was swerve, not swing," says Jack Bannister, who as a tailender came out to face him on a wet wicket for MCC against the Champions in 1955. "I got one that was coming in towards leg stump. The ball ended up going past my right ear and a clod of earth past my left. He was bowling probably around 78, 79 miles an hour. I don't believe anyone has ever moved the ball that much at that pace."

By then Bedser was the linchpin of a Surrey team that were turning into champions in perpetuity, and for England he had partners of the calibre of Bailey, Statham and Trueman.

At Trent Bridge in 1953 – a potential thriller wrecked by rain – Bedser had match figures of 14 for 99, and took a record 39 wickets as England recovered the Ashes at last. But soon the young men would eclipse him. On the boat out to Australia in 1954-55 he had shingles, which went undiagnosed. He still bowled 296 balls in an innings in the Brisbane Test and had already changed for the Sydney Test when he saw the team-sheet posted on the door. The captain, Len Hutton, had failed to tell him he had been dropped in favour of Frank Tyson. Bedser played only once more for England, at Old Trafford the following summer: in 51 Tests he had taken a then-world record 236 wickets.

He played on for Surrey until 1960, and took another five-for in his final match, against Glamorgan. By then he was 42, yet he was to remain at the heart of the game. In 1962-63 he went to Australia as assistant manager to the Duke of Norfolk, in charge of both the cricket and the money – he was canny about both. By then he was already an England selector, and was to prove even more undroppable than he had been as a player. He was a conscientious traveller, a shrewd observer and a collegiate chairman, staunchly defending even those selections he had opposed in private (such as the recall of the aged Brian Close in 1976). But his greatest plus, as far as Lord's was concerned, was that he came cheap. As a successful but not overworked businessman (he and Eric owned an office equipment business) with frugal tastes and no family to support, he was happy to devote his summers to the job without pay.

But as the years went by, he had less and less empathy for the younger generation in general, and grew increasingly dyspeptic about England players in particular. Habitually, he would measure them against his benchmark of professionalism – Eric, as his own alter ego – and find them wanting. His fellow-selector Doug Insole once translated Bedserese at a pre-Test dinner: "If he says you're not bad, you're one of the best three in the world." And thus, in time, Alec's greatest virtues, his standards and cricketing integrity, became millstones: his fatalism turned into defeatism and seemed to enter the team's soul. He was always affable, and there was always a certain bleak, even surreal, humour in his grumbling. When he complained about Chris Old carrying his child's teddy bear into the team hotel in Australia, one suspects he was half-teasing himself, just as he had been when

One last accolade: Micky Stewart presents Bedser with a leatherbound *Wisden* in 2007, on the 60th anniversary of his selection as a Cricketer of the Year.

he lost a game of deck quoits to John Woodcock on the voyage to Australia in 1954. "You and your effing Oxford University!" he groaned.

When Alec was finally elbowed aside as a selector, he and Eric continued to enjoy the cricketing social scene, their golf and their grumbles. Their friend John Major engineered Alec's knighthood as prime minister in 1997. Their 80th birthday in 1998 was celebrated with a huge dinner at a London hotel, and they kept in fine fettle until Eric's death in 2006. Conventional wisdom had been that, whichever died first, the other would quickly pine away. But perhaps, in his deepest subconscious, Alec felt a sense of release, and for a while he seemed to enjoy a new lease of life without always having to ensure that his less famous brother was included. In 2007, *Wisden* made a unique presentation to him to mark the 60th anniversary of his selection as a Cricketer of the Year. Alec wept, and soon the whole room joined in. Two years later, his health began to decline but, even in 2009, watching Australia v Pakistan on TV, he was explaining how he would have got Ricky Ponting out.

BHATTI, GUL HAMEED, who died on February 4, 2010, aged 61, was a prominent sports journalist and statistician in Pakistan. He edited the Pakistani *Cricketer* magazine and later became sports editor – and briefly editor – of the Karachi-based daily *The News*. "He succeeded in changing the trend of sports journalism in the country by making it investigative, colourful and informative," wrote Waheed Khan, one of his many protégés. He was also a fount of cricketing information. "If anyone wanted to find out details of some obscure record or details of a particular domestic match," Waheed added, "*Bhatti Sahib* was the final word."

BRODERICK, VINCENT, died on November 14, 2010, aged 90. Vince Broderick was a tall slow left-arm bowler and not-quite-middle-order batsman who came down from Bacup to be at the heart of the improving post-war Northamptonshire team. His best years actually came in 1947 and 1948, when the county were still rooted to the bottom: in 1948 he did

This way, lads: Vince Broderick coaches at Lord's, 1957.

the double, reaching his 1,000 runs in a dead match at Clacton, perhaps with a nod and a wink from the Essex boys. In other respects "Brod" seemed unlucky: he made his first-class debut a fortnight before war broke out, and in 1948 he was picked for the pre-Ashes Test trial at Edgbaston, making a good impression. But he was to be the only player from that match never to get a Test, and his role at Northamptonshire diminished in the years ahead when his gentle spin was overshadowed by the more expansive skills of the Australians, George Tribe and Jack Manning. Nonetheless, Broderick remained a regular member of the side until 1955. "The Aussies on the staff could not understand why the selectors persevered with Brod," wrote his team-mate Frank Tyson. "There was little fluency in his dogged left-handed batting; he evinced only negligible turn… They believed that success belonged to natural talents. They could not comprehend the virtues of industry and character: qualities which Vince possessed in abundance." Those were precisely the qualities that Broderick worked hard to instil in his charges at Winchester College after he moved there as coach in 1959. He remained for 28 years – ramrod-straight in his bearing and urging always the importance of a straight bat – and even after retirement he maintained a kindly interest in each new Wykehamist generation from his home at Colden Common, where he drove the community bus, and his perch at the Wykeham Arms.

BUSH, LUKE, was killed in a road accident in Goulburn, New South Wales, on April 10, 2010. He was 18, and the previous evening had been named the Queanbeyan Cricket Club's most promising junior at the annual presentation night. He had been about to travel to Ireland to play for Dublin University during the northern summer. A promising left-arm fast bowler, Bush had played for the Australian Capital Territory's age-group teams.

BUXTON, IAN RAY, who died of cancer on October 1, 2010, aged 72, was as Derbyshire as his name, and the last of the long line of sporting all-rounders who played cricket for the county and football for Derby County. As a centre-forward Buxton was a steady goal-scorer (43 in 158 games for Derby) but not quite strong or skilful enough – and too committed to cricket – to maintain a place in the ambitious team Brian Clough was planning at the Baseball Ground. But as an adaptable player and a solid team man, he fitted perfectly into the ethos of Derbyshire cricket. A capable if unspectacular batsman and gifted fielder, he also bowled banana inswingers that often troubled batsmen of unexpected quality and sometimes enabled Bob Taylor to pick up improbable leg-side stumpings when batsmen overbalanced. Buxton once took 11 for 33 in an innings defeat of Worcestershire. In 1970 he took over the captaincy, a job he did thoughtfully and with considerable initial success – Derbyshire led both the Championship and the Sunday League for a while in his first season.

"As Derbyshire as his name": Ian Buxton pads up in 1961.

Unusually for them, however, their seam bowling was not robust enough; these challenges faded and in the following two years Derbyshire took the Championship wooden spoon. Buxton paid the price. He played on for another season, out of a characteristic sense of loyalty, before retiring to run a sports shop, initially in partnership with his team-mate Peter Gibbs. He finished his 15-year county career with 11,803 runs at 23.94 and 483 wickets at 26.38. His football career also included spells at Luton, Notts County and Port Vale. "He was a lovely, placid, intelligent bloke," said Taylor.

CHISHTI, KARIM, who died on May 13, 2010, aged 74, was a wicketkeeper-batsman for Uttar Pradesh. He played 25 Ranji Trophy matches over a dozen seasons from 1963-64, latterly as captain. Firmly retired, and two days before his 42nd birthday, he was managing Central Zone in the one-day Deodhar Trophy in 1977-78 when a shortage of players forced him to turn out in the quarter-final against East Zone, though he did not have to bat.

COLLINS, AUDREY TOLL, OBE, who died on February 14, 2010, aged 94, was one of the longest-serving administrators in women's cricket. Born in India, she was brought to Britain by her Australian mother after her father was killed in the Great War. She took up cricket at 12, and after showing promise as a teenage fast-medium bowler was considered unlucky to miss the 1934-35 tour of Australasia on which the first women's Tests were contested. She did play, aged 22, for England against Australia at The Oval in 1937, scoring 27 in an important partnership of 55 in half an hour with Betty Archdale. Collins was selected for the next tour of Australia, in 1939-40, but that was cancelled when war broke out. When cricket resumed she continued playing, although further international recognition proved elusive, and increasingly she moved into administration. Collins founded the Vagabonds women's cricket club, which later joined forces with Radlett CC, near St Albans where she worked as a teacher for 35 years. She was successively secretary, chairman and then president (1983–1994) of the Women's Cricket Association, and was later among the first batch of ten women given MCC membership in 1999. Despite all that, she is probably best remembered in women's cricket circles for her tireless fund-raising efforts, which usually involved circling the boundary inveigling spectators to buy chocolate bars obtained cheaply from Nestlé. The England leg-spinner Kathryn Leng recalled "fond memories of my mum scrabbling around in her purse for money whenever she saw her, even though none of us really ate the chocolate". Others remember her driving to games – for which, in later years, she usually did the scoring – in a battered old car she only gave up as she approached 90. Not long before that Collins had appeared on a Nike advertisement hoarding – typically, she donated her fee to the WCA – in a campaign which aimed to confront stereotypes in female sport.

The trail-blazers: Rachael Heyhoe-Flint, Netta Rheinberg, Carole Cornthwaite, Sheila Hill, Audrey Collins, Diana Rait Kerr, Jackie Court and Norma Izard – eight of MCC's first women members, on their election in 1999.

CRAVEN, HIRAM NICHOLAS, MBE, died on April 16, 2010, aged 84. Nico Craven ("Nico rhyming with Psycho," as he sometimes explained) was perhaps the last representative of the tradition of the great county cricket spectator, as much part of the show at the Cheltenham festival as Loppylugs at Worcester or The Linnet at Northampton. But Craven was no raucous barracker. A gentle, Harrow-educated vicar's son, he was best known for his "effusions": 34 self-published books that recorded his annual ramblings round the country's more picturesque grounds, including the likes of Adlestrop and Sheepscombe. They always climaxed with his beloved festival, where he knew *everyone*. "It took him three hours to stroll round the boundary," wrote David Foot. The books were a sort of private joke, for Nico's benefit more than anyone else's, but they were charmingly written, illustrated and even priced (by the late 1990s they reached £6.66), and will be much cherished when the happy but threatened world they record is finally lost. Few of Nico's Cheltenham friends knew anything about his other life: he lived far from the Cotswolds, at Seascale on the Cumberland coast, and was a local character there too, for his charity work. Having gone north to work as a housemaster in an approved school, he became secretary of the Cumbria Association of Boys Clubs and was also honorary president of the Howgill Family Centre, where he had been involved since its foundation in 1977.

DAS, BIBHUTI BHUSAN, who died on February 10, 2010, aged 85, was the secretary of the Orissa Cricket Association from 1976 to 2000, and a former vice-president of the Indian board (1990–92). He was the driving force behind the decision to install floodlights at the Barabati Stadium in Cuttack, which has now staged 15 one-day internationals, in addition to two Tests during Das's tenure as secretary.

DE CAILA, ANTHONY MARIE HENRY, died on May 19, 2009, aged 70. Tony de Caila was a polished wicketkeeper from Bulawayo who played 34 matches for Rhodesia (now Zimbabwe) between 1961-62 and 1973-74. He was a fine keeper, but weakness with the bat – he never reached 50 in 44 attempts – meant his place was rarely secure.

DE CLERMONT, STEPHEN GEOFFREY, who died on December 8, 2010, aged 68, was the founding chairman of the Sussex Cricket Museum and Educational Trust, which aims to develop a museum in the pavilion at Hove. A passionate Sussex supporter since the 1950s, he was one of Britain's foremost coin-collectors, and also built up an impressive library of cricket books.

DETTMER, COLIN PETER, shot himself on January 12, 2010, aged 51, to the baffled consternation of friends and colleagues. Dettmer was a solid batsman, who usually opened, for Boland and Western Transvaal in the early 1990s, scoring one first-class century. He had been a lieutenant-commander in the South African navy, during which time he played for Cape Town CC. On leaving the navy he turned to coaching, latterly at the University of Pretoria ("Tuks"). Hein Raath, the former chairman of the Tuks Cricket Club, said he would remember Dettmer's "precision, detail, pride, dedication and passion". Dettmer also acted as liaison man for international teams in South Africa, and the Australians wore black armbands in his memory during their Test against Pakistan at Hobart, confusing spectators who thought they must be connected with the Haiti earthquake.

DHAGAMWAR, SUDHIR MARUTIRAO, who died on April 10, 2010, aged 59, was a batsman who played 11 Ranji Trophy matches for Vidarbha in the 1970s, scoring 77 on debut against Madhya Pradesh in 1972-73.

FAIRBAIRN, CLIVE LINDSAY, OAM, who died on May 12, 2010, aged 90, played once for Victoria in 1948-49. During his opening over with the new ball he tore a rib muscle, but struggled on for nine wicketless overs. The injury, however, was so severe that he missed the last two days of the match and was never recalled to the side. Yet Fairbairn became integral to cricket in Victoria: a stalwart of the Melbourne Cricket Club for over 70 years, he captained their first-grade team, for which he took 374 wickets, coached their junior players, selected the sides, represented the club on state committees, and helped to choose Victoria's teams for many years. For over 30 years he dispensed encouragement, advice and gossip – and generosity to struggling young cricketers – at his Melbourne sports store. He was awarded the Medal of the Order of Australia in 1990 for his services to cricket. During the Second World War Fairbairn had served as a bombardier in the Australian army and was a "Desert Rat". Of modern batsmen, he noted: "We never wore helmets at Tobruk."

FARID MALIK, GHULAM, who died of a heart attack on July 1, 2010, aged 59, was a well-known umpire in the United Arab Emirates. Born in Lahore, he was the TV umpire in four matches at the 1995-96 World Cup, and regularly officiated in the UAE until his death.

FERNANDO, PALLIYA MADINAGE SUMITH MARLON, died of lung cancer on July 9, 2010, aged 22. Marlon Fernando was a promising wicketkeeper-batsman who opened for Sri Lanka Schools. He played for the Air Force, making an unbeaten 100 for them in a one-day game against Saracens on New Year's Eve 2008; his highest first-class score was 94, against the Police in Colombo in November 2009.

GILES, RONALD JAMES, died on January 30, 2010, aged 90. Ron Giles made an impact for Nottinghamshire in his second match. Playing as a tailender and slow left-armer, he was given the ball for the last possible over at Bournemouth in 1938. With the final two balls, he claimed the last two wickets to bowl Hampshire out for 75 and complete an improbable victory with an analysis of 5–4–1–3. Other than that, his bowling proved innocuous (in 1939 his eight wickets cost 111.75 apiece), but he did better as a batsman. After the war, he was a consistent scorer in the Second Eleven and finally blossomed as a forceful front-foot player in 1951. Given a chance to open, he made 137 against Oxford and finished the season with 788 runs at 32. With 46-year-old Walter Keeton finally

Happy at the top: Ron Giles (*right*) and Reg Simpson open for Nottinghamshire at Lord's, 1952.

calling it a day, Giles became Reg Simpson's regular opening partner, offering the bonus of brilliant outfielding. "He had the best arm I've ever seen, flat to the keeper from anywhere," said his team-mate John Clay. By 1955 Giles had lost his form and his place; but, restored to the top order when Simpson was injured, he hit back with three sizable centuries – two against Lancashire, one against Yorkshire – in 18 days. He continued to make runs regularly in 1956 before drifting again until, after a two-year absence, he was restored to the team in 1959 for his own benefit match, scoring 75 not out. Rising 40, he was then released, but took umbrage, vowing never to return to Trent Bridge: despite living only a few miles away in Long Eaton, he is thought to have broken his promise only once, for an old players' reunion. He became a builder and a successful breeder of racing pigeons. "A down-to-earth bloke," said Clay.

GOLDIE, THOMAS HUGH EVELYN, DFC and bar, died on December 23, 2010, aged 91. An RAF pilot twice decorated for his work on anti-submarine patrols, Hugh Goldie became a theatre director after the war. For much of the time he was resident director at the Theatre Royal, Windsor, but he also took several plays to the West End, including Richard Harris's thriller *The Business of Murder*, which ran for most of the 1980s. He batted in the middle order for Oxfordshire several times in the 1950s and was a stalwart of Richmond CC, where as chairman he was instrumental in the signing of a promising 17-year-old Australian, Adam Gilchrist, in 1989. His son, Chris Goldie, kept wicket for Cambridge University and Hampshire.

GUNASEKERA, CONROY IEVERS, died on July 29, 2010, aged 90. "C. I." Gunasekera was one of Sri Lanka's finest all-rounders in the days before they acquired Test status, remaining a tall, lean fixture in the national side into his mid-forties. In February 1952, playing for a Commonwealth XI in Colombo against the England touring team which had just finished a five-Test series in India, Gunasekera scored 135, reaching his hundred with a six and outscoring Keith Miller in a stand of 207. Seven years later he made 212 for Ceylon in the Gopalan Trophy match against the Indian domestic champions, Madras, and in April 1961 hit 24 off an over from Lindsay Kline's chinamen against Richie Benaud's Australians, making a stopover en route to England. The following October, when England called on their way south, Gunasekera, now 42, struck the first five balls he received from Ray Illingworth for fours on the way to 76. Also an accomplished leg-spinner, Gunasekera took eight for 69 on New Year's Day 1954 against the touring Pakistan Combined Services, his first five victims all being Test players.

HALE, IVOR EDWARD, who died on October 6, 2010, his 88th birthday, played three matches for Sussex in 1946 before moving to Gloucestershire. He made a solitary appearance in 1947 and a dozen more the following year, with modest results, though he scored a determined unbeaten 43 in a low-scoring contest against Derbyshire (billed as the W. G. Grace centenary) to keep Gloucestershire in the game.

HAMENCE, RONALD ARTHUR, who died on March 24, 2010, aged 94, might have been the forgotten "Invincible" of 1948, but the confident power of his batting remained bright in the memories of those who saw him. He was small and compact, and his assured footwork allowed him to drive exuberantly through the off side. A precocious schoolboy cricketer, he made his debut as the youngest-ever player in the Adelaide A-grade at the age of 15 years 67 days in January 1931. Five years later he was selected for South Australia, and pummelled the Tasmanian attack for 121 in a three-hour partnership of 356 for the third wicket with Don Bradman, who made 369. Hamence's next four seasons, however, produced little of note, although he did score a century in each innings against Victoria at Melbourne in 1940-41.

When cricket resumed after the war, there was a new sense of maturity about his batting, and he won a place on the tour of New Zealand in 1945-46. Next season, he again hit a hundred in each innings, this time against New South Wales. His 145 against the MCC tourists caused Bill O'Reilly to assure his readers that "Hamence's off-side play was

PA Photos

Involved in something big: Ron Hamence (*left*) and Ron Saggers at Southend in May 1948. The touring Australians made 721 in a day against Essex, a first-class record; Hamence hit 46.

executed with all the grace and vigour of Walter Hammond at his best." That innings gained him selection for the Fifth Test of the series, in which he made 30 not out as the first innings crumbled around him. Despite a quiet year, he played two more Tests against the Indians in 1947-48. In the first of those, at Sydney, he kept his composure on a treacherous wet pitch to top-score with 25 in a total of 107.

This helped Hamence to be picked out of the ruck of competing middle-order batsmen for the 1948 tour, on which his pleasant tenor voice made more impact than his batting. He reached the nineties twice, with 99 against Somerset at Taunton, but little allowance was made for him to play substantial innings in meaningful situations. Even after the final Test, he had to come in against the South of England with the score at 412 for four, after Bradman, Lindsay Hassett and Neil Harvey had all hit hundreds. His medium-pace bowling, however, did have the occasional outing and produced seven of his eight first-class wickets. Bradman described him as "an extremely useful reserve who could have played in the Tests with confidence", and "a great tourist who did wonders for the morale of the side". In 1950-51, he ended his first-class career with 114 against Freddie Brown's MCC tourists, his batting as satisfying as ever and his fleetness of foot in the covers undiminished.

Hamence spent his entire working life in the service of the South Australian Government Printer, his trade skills being utilised in his service with the Royal Australian Air Force. Courteous and self-effacing, he was a much-admired presence during the 1998 anniversary celebrations of the Bradman tour. His later years were much afflicted with arthritis, which he bore with stoic dignity, concentrating his efforts on nursing his wife, Nora, until her death in 2006. Following the death of Bill Brown in 2008, Hamence had been Australia's oldest Test cricketer, a position now occupied by Sam Loxton – one of the three surviving Invincibles (the others being Harvey and Arthur Morris) at the end of 2010. Hamence was a cousin of Charlie Walker, who toured England as the reserve wicketkeeper in 1930 and 1938.

HARGREAVES, PETER SANFORD, who died on September 3, 2010, aged 82, lived in Denmark for more than half his life and was perhaps the staunchest supporter of Danish cricket. Hargreaves arrived there in 1965 via New Zealand and England; thereafter, he managed Denmark's national team, encouraged the introduction of indoor and women's cricket, supplied details of Danish and other European cricket to *Wisden* for many years, and compiled more than 30 books. The most important of them was probably *The Story of Continental Cricket*, a history of the game in Europe, co-written with Thomas Provis and Piet Labouchere: one of its claims was that cricket developed from the ancient Viking sport of *knattleikr*. *Wisden* editors who were less convinced of Danish cricket's vital global importance than he was, or who rendered Danish orthography incorrectly, were rewarded by long, closely typed letters of complaint. His later years were troubled by illness, and he lost the use of his legs. His end was sad: he was being driven to hospital for a check-up when the ambulance was forced to brake suddenly to avoid an accident. Hargreaves's chair shifted; he injured his neck, and died a few days later.

HARTMAN, RODNEY JOHN, who died of cancer on May 18, 2010, aged 61, was a leading figure in South African sports journalism for 30 years. In a country where cricket was often caught in the middle of contending political forces, he cut a gentle, emollient figure. Hartman's instinctive response to any situation was a kindly one, both as a sports editor – a job he fulfilled on both the South Africa *Sunday Times* and *Sunday Independent* – and as a writer. Having spent much of his career in the depths of South Africa's isolation, he revelled in its return to world cricket in the 1990s, and wrote two well-received books: *Ali*, an authorised biography of Ali Bacher, and *Hansie and the Boys*, an enthusiastic account of the team's international comeback written before Cronje's downfall. Without enemies, he was a good choice to act as communications director of the 2003 World Cup.

HAWKINS, DEREK GRAHAM, who died on November 27, 2010, aged 75, played over 130 matches for Gloucestershire in ten years from 1952, without ever quite doing justice to his talent. He had captained England Schools in 1950, and signed for Gloucestershire at 16 – but he lost two years to National Service and struggled to find a niche. "He was a useful batter," remembered Tom Graveney, "but we had a lot of young blokes all coming through at the same time." Hawkins was also a handy off-spinner – but Gloucestershire were overstocked with those too. England calls and injuries gave him opportunities: he was capped after making a century at Hove in 1957 and passed 1,000 runs in 1961. But he retired after that, aged only 26, to concentrate on the family car dealership, although he was persuaded to play a couple of matches in 1962. He became a force in club cricket for Thornbury.

HILL, ERIC, DFC, DFM, who died on July 27, 2010, aged 87, was close to the heartbeat of Somerset cricket for more than half a century. After a dramatic war, he returned to Taunton, his home town, and joined the Somerset staff. He made his debut in 1947 and played 72 matches over five seasons, mainly as an opener, but he never made a century nor averaged more than 20. "He was a tall, upright opening batsman of undisputed correctness and style," wrote David Foot. "He had injuries and little luck, when one remembers the succession of agile catches that dismissed him." Hill went into journalism, working for the *Somerset County Gazette*. Yet he was quickly to move nearer the centre of events than ever before. With Somerset rooted to the foot of the table, he was one of the ringleaders – with two other journalists, Ron Roberts and Bob Moore – of a campaign to oust a sleepy committee and revitalise the club. They narrowly lost the battle, but hindsight suggests they won the war: Hill became captain of the Second Eleven; the other two were voted on to the committee, and Somerset slowly grew more competitive and professional. Hill became sports editor of the *Gazette*, south-western cricket and rugby correspondent for the *Daily Telegraph*, and covered England overseas tours as a freelance. He then

Struggling to find a niche: Derek Hawkins steers the ball past Denis Compton at slip during Gloucestershire's match against Middlesex at Lord's in 1957.

settled into his perch in the Taunton press-box, complete with old inkwells, where he spread out his phones and lunch, and ruled the roost for three decades, as the correspondent for the press agencies and *Wisden*. He was a most unusual freelance. Far from relishing calls from national papers to chase potentially lucrative stories, he kept his number ex-directory to deter them, especially during the Botham years when Fleet Street wanted to phone regularly. He had high cricketing standards and disapproved of much of the behaviour of modern cricketers, and also of press-box colleagues who he felt knew nothing of the game. For a young journalist, the moment Eric decided you were worthy of his attention was an important rite of passage: he was not just knowledgable but a fount of cricketing wisdom. He was also very brave. He had volunteered for the RAF and trained as a navigator, before teaming up with Frank Dodd, later an air vice-marshal, flying 53 reconnaissance missions in unarmed Mosquitos. In the latter stages of the war, they flew a series of dangerous sorties to photograph German defences and warships, suffering both a hit from anti-aircraft fire and intense cold. Hill's navigation in often dreadful conditions was described as "brilliant". "I think he must have been exceptionally brave," said John Woodcock, "but he never, ever let on."

HILTON, CHRISTOPHER, died on November 28, 2010, aged 66. Chris Hilton was a sports writer for the *Daily Express* who also produced more than 60 books. Many of them were about motor racing, but three featured cricket, including a reconstruction of Don Bradman's triumphant first tour of England in 1930. "There was nothing clichéd or routine

In his perch: Eric Hill in the early-1980s Taunton press-box.

about his copy," remembered his *Express* colleague Colin Bateman. "He wrote in short, dramatic sentences. And he was an original."

HOOPER, JOHN MICHAEL MACKENZIE, died of cancer on April 2, 2010, aged 62. Mike Hooper was a talented batsman, mainly for the Surrey club Esher, who never quite found a niche for himself in first-class cricket. One of his early matches for Surrey was against the 1968 Australian tourists: he was called up on the back of a rapid 168 for the Second Eleven at East Molesey. But at The Oval Hooper was reduced to strokelessness, playing out several maidens before his batting partner Micky Stewart had a word: "I went up and told him to just relax. The advice must have worked as the very next over he got off the mark when he smashed Ashley Mallett straight back over his head for six into the pavilion." Hooper made 25 that day, but his highest score in 20 other first-class games was only 41. He retired after 1971 and went to work in the City: he remained a considerable club batsman, helping Charterhouse Friars win the Cricketer Cup for old boys' sides three times. Hooper's son, Harry, played for Oxford UCCE.

HORNE, FREDERIC THOMAS, who died on January 24, 2010, aged 92, was an enthusiastic club cricketer who made an improbable debut for MCC, aged 56. He happened to be on the Isle of Man in 1973 when the team had an injury crisis before a fixture against the island team. Fred Horne was also Chief Taxing Master of the Supreme Court: the 1992 Horne Report established principles for assessing court costs.

HOWELL, JOHN HOLLIS, who died on November 10, 2010, aged 67, became New Zealand's national coaching director in 1984, and continued to work with the board until 2003, when he retired and set up his own cricket academy in Tauranga. Before turning to coaching he had been an enthusiastic fast-medium bowler for Central Districts, who won the Plunket Shield three times during his career. His son Llorne won 12 one-day caps for New Zealand, while his other son, Glynn, also played first-class cricket.

HOWLAND, CHRISTOPHER BURFIELD, died on May 14, 2010, aged 74. Chris Howland was a tidy wicketkeeper and handy batsman who captained Cambridge University in 1960, the last of his three years there. Howland also played occasionally for Sussex and Kent, and represented the Players against the Gentlemen at Lord's in 1959, scoring 36 "boldly" (*Wisden*) in a first innings of just 194. His first Cambridge captain was Ted Dexter. "He was the ideal shape for keeping wicket," said Dexter, "naturally low to the ground with gloves that looked rather large. He had a smile for everyone, friend and foe alike." In 1961 Howland returned to Fenner's with the Free Foresters and hit 124, his only first-class century. The demands of a City job curtailed his first-class cricket soon after that, although he remained an enthusiastic club player and served on several committees at Lord's. Howland was an active member of the Lord's Taverners, becoming their chairman in 1978-79. His brother Peter also played for Cambridge.

HUDSON, ROBERT CECIL, who died on June 3, 2010, aged 90, was a BBC commentator who worked on events ranging from royal weddings to rugby internationals, and covered Test matches for 20 years. Bob Hudson was also a senior BBC executive – a quiet and effective administrator who rose to become head of radio outside broadcasts between 1969 and 1974. However, his most important achievement may have come much earlier, when – after being cut off from a county radio commentary at Scarborough in 1955 just as Fred Trueman completed a hat-trick – he persuaded his superiors that this should at least never happen in a Test match. Two years later *Test Match Special* was born, using the slogan "don't miss a ball – we broadcast them all". Hudson's first Test commentary was for television, in 1949, but he was primarily a radio man, and appeared regularly on the programme he conceived. His *TMS* career reached a climax with England's dramatic win against Australia at The Oval in 1968, before he was promoted out of the job. He was perhaps the least distinctive of all *TMS* commentators, with a neutral, newsreader's kind of voice. But he never sounded stuffy, and was highly professional and conscientious, making notes in advance, and basing himself at the back of the box when off-air to avoid repeating what another commentator had said. Peter Baxter, a Hudson protégé, recalled: "The lightness of touch in his delivery rather belied his meticulous preparation."

HUNT, ROBERT GEOFFREY, who died on January 10, 2010, aged 94, was an amateur batsman who was asked to become Sussex's captain in 1950. But he never led the side, as his appointment infuriated members, who shouted down the president, the Duke of Norfolk, and successfully proposed a vote of no confidence in the committee. The Duke, according to the *Sussex Daily News*, "picked up his hat and gloves and walked out". The impasse, which arose out of the committee's determination to replace Hugh Bartlett, was resolved when the professional James Langridge agreed to take over until Hubert Doggart came down from Cambridge in mid-season. Hunt had played 11 matches for Sussex before this, scoring 66 at Worcester in 1946, and won a Blue himself at Cambridge in 1937, not long after scoring what turned out to be his only first-class hundred, 117 against the Army. He also enjoyed some success with his off-spin that year, taking five for 51 against MCC.

ISAACS, EBRAHIM, died on June 13, 2010, aged 65. Braima Isaacs played more than 50 games for various South African non-white sides in the 1970s and 1980s, in matches later accorded first-class status. A wicketkeeper who had 43 stumpings to go with 125 catches, he also often opened, and made a century for Western Province against Natal in 1979-80. Isaacs later became a member of the Western Cape provincial parliament.

JAJBHAY, MAHOMED, who died of pancreatitis on May 5, 2010, aged 51, was a senior judge in the Johannesburg High Court. He had been a fine schoolboy cricketer, being named vice-captain of the (non-white) South African Schools team in 1974. He played 33 matches subsequently given first-class status for Transvaal's non-white side, scoring 67 against Western Province in January 1991. Jajbhay also became chairman of the Gauteng Cricket Board and a member of Cricket South Africa's general council.

JALALUDEEN, NABEEL, died on May 19, 2010, aged 19. The Colombo *Sunday Leader* reported that his death was due to complications suffered after he sustained a cut jumping over the boundary fence to congratulate a team member at the big schools match between his alma mater, Royal College, and Thomians. Jalaludeen had played for the Royal rugby team and the cricket Second Eleven. The family said it was considering legal action because he was given the wrong drugs in hospital.

JONES, ROBERT EDWARD OWEN, died on May 9, 2010, aged 67. Bob Jones joined Lancashire from the Lord's groundstaff as a batsman in 1962, but never appeared in first-class cricket. He began coaching, returning to Lord's as Len Muncer's assistant in the 1970s, and later becoming the national coach of first Bermuda, then Nigeria. Jones coached at various schools in England – and in South Africa, where one of those who came under his eye was the future Test batsman Daryll Cullinan. Jones and Cullinan would meet up each year at the Cape Town Test and talk technique – and Cullinan scored centuries in four successive Tests there between 1998 and 2001. He flew to England when he heard of Jones's final illness.

KAMAT, PRABHAKAR KRISHNA, died on June 7, 2010, aged 80. "Joe" Kamat was a batsman who played 18 first-class matches in the 1950s, mostly as an opener for Bombay. His only two centuries – 158 and 102 – both came against Maharashtra, and both during big stands with Polly Umrigar. Kamat was often one of the few non-Test players in the star-studded Bombay side of the time. He was known for his brave fielding, and his hooking. "He believed in going for the bowling right from the first ball," wrote Sunil Gavaskar. "I think this adventurous spirit cost him a lot because he did not stay in the Bombay team for long." Later, he coached Ajit Wadekar.

KING-HAMILTON, MYER ALAN BARRY, died on March 23, 2010, aged 105. Judge Alan King-Hamilton was an outspoken and idiosyncratic Old Bailey judge who presided over some of the highest-profile trials of the mid-20th century, including those of the fraudster Emil Savundra and the editor of *Gay News*, who had been charged with blasphemy. Though unbendingly stern towards criminals, King-Hamilton was happy to interrupt trials to relay the Test score.

KNIGHT, NORMAN OAKLEY, died of a heart attack on April 22, 2010, aged 63, while on holiday in Mauritius. Knight played 36 matches for Border from 1966-67, several of them as captain. His highest score was 75 in 1972-73, but his best-remembered innings had come two years previously, in Rhodesia, when he arrived at the crease with the scoreboard reading one for five. The first five batsmen had departed for ducks, Mike Procter was steaming in at his fastest – he finished with five for eight from ten overs – but Knight put his head down and made 21, the only double-figure score in a total of 57. He top-scored in the second innings, too, with 54.

LANCE, HERBERT ROY, died on November 10, 2010, aged 70, of complications after a car accident. "Tiger" Lance was, as his nickname implied, a combative all-rounder for Transvaal, and in 13 Tests for South Africa between 1962 and 1970. He was tall, and hit the ball hard: "His best shot was off the back foot through the covers, which was a pretty unique stroke in our day – he was one of the first to play it with excellence," remembered Ali Bacher, his captain in the famous series in 1969-70 when South Africa crushed Australia in all four Tests. Lance, whose father and brother also played first-class cricket, made his debut at 18 in December 1958, and the following season hit his first two centuries. When New Zealand toured in 1961-62 he played in the last two Tests, but did little of

Team man: Tiger Lance in 1965.

PA Photos

note and was ignored by the selectors until Tony Pithey withdrew from the 1965 England tour. In England, Lance obligingly moved up to open with Eddie Barlow in the first two Tests, but failed, then made 69 and 53 when restored to the middle order at The Oval. "He looked a different man," said John Woodcock in *The Times*, "a fine strong driver… and possessor of a good defensive method." South Africa played only nine more Tests before they ran out of opponents because of their government's apartheid policies – and Lance appeared in eight of them. His highest score was 70, though at domestic level he could be a prodigious run-getter in important games. He was also a fine slip fielder, and a medium-pacer who had the knack of taking timely wickets, once going round the wicket to Graeme Pollock in a vital Currie Cup match and knocking out his middle stump. Always a popular team man, he attracted (and cultivated) anecdotes, about himself and others. "No one could tell a story like Tiger Lance," said Bacher. "I heard some of his stories 50 times and I laughed hardest the 50th time."

LAWRENCE, EDWARD, died on March 16, 2010, aged 81. Eddie Lawrence was a familiar face around the County Ground at Taunton, latterly as honorary librarian and custodian of the club museum. He was also Somerset's acting chief executive for a time in the 1980s, and acted as chairman (and later president) of the Former Players' Association.

LE CLUSE, DAVID, was found dead from gunshot wounds on October 2, 2010, aged 44. He is thought to have committed suicide. Le Cluse was chairman of Croydon Athletic Football Club, owned by the alleged cricket match-fixer Mazhar Majeed. In the *News of the World* story, Majeed was quoted as saying he had laundered millions of pounds through the club, and that was his sole reason for buying it.

LETTS, RICHARD FRANCIS BONNER, died on December 28, 2010, aged 82. Dick Letts took over Oakley Hall prep school in Cirencester from his father in 1962, and ran it for 30 years in idiosyncratic style, "cherishing cricket, classics and the cane" according to the *Daily Telegraph*. His bowling action was equally idiosyncratic – "like a crouching crab" said his journalist son Quentin – and his reputation for eccentricity was enhanced by him driving a 1931 Morris Minor, and later a Sinclair C5 electric cart. As a schoolboy at Haileybury in 1947 Letts took 13 wickets – five for 39 and eight for 62 – with his leg-breaks in the annual match against Cheltenham at Lord's; the previous year he had scored 110 in the same fixture. He played occasionally for Gloucestershire's Second Eleven, and in 1949 returned to Lord's and made 73 opening for Combined Services against the Public Schools, resisting the leg-spin of 16-year-old Colin Cowdrey and easily outshining his team-mate P. B. H. May. Quentin added: "He loved gadgets, double cream, the *Book of Common Prayer* and my mother, though not necessarily in that order."

LONG, ROBERT INDER, died on February 11, 2010, aged 77. Bob Long played 15 first-class matches for Otago, his career spanning a decade, although his second match came more than six years after his first, against the 1953-54 Fijians. Usually an opener, Long made several decent scores, including 71 against a strong MCC touring side at Dunedin in 1960-61, but he faded out after six innings in 1963 produced only 24 runs.

LYON, JOHN, who died after a short illness on January 1, 2010, aged 58, was a St Helens boy who succeeded Farokh Engineer as Lancashire's regular wicketkeeper in 1977. He was a tidy keeper, but a weak link as a batsman, which was very noticeable after the county had been spoiled by Engineer's talents. Lyon was a stubborn tailender and a frequent nightwatchman, and did hit one unlikely century: at Old Trafford in 1979 Lancashire had to follow on against Warwickshire, and were in sight of defeat at 230 for seven when Lyon was joined by Bob Ratcliffe. They saved the match with a stand of 158 – still the Lancashire record for the eighth wicket – and both made their only first-class hundreds. That proved to be Lyon's last season: he was supplanted in 1980 by Chris Scott, who was viewed as a better batting prospect. Lyon spent some time playing and coaching in Ireland before moving to South Africa. There he combined running a sports bar in

"He always played with a smile on his face." John Lyon keeping wicket for MCC against the Australians in 1977. The batsman is David Hookes (c Lyon b Hendrick in both innings).

Johannesburg with coaching, organising development programmes in the nearby town of Klerksdorp. "He always played the game with a smile on his face," remembered his former team-mate John Abrahams, "grateful to be doing something he loved for the county he loved."

MacGIBBON, ANTHONY ROY, died on April 6, 2010, aged 85. A tall (6ft 5$\frac{1}{2}$in) fast-medium swing bowler from Christchurch, Tony MacGibbon was a whole-hearted performer who often carried the New Zealand attack during the 1950s. He made his reputation in South Africa in 1953-54, taking 22 wickets in the series after reducing his run-up by five paces: "I always had been troubled with no-balling. I once bowled a 14-ball over," he said. "But by reducing my run-up I was more controlled, and could think about what I was doing." MacGibbon also played a big part in New Zealand's historic first Test victory, after 26 years of trying, against West Indies at Auckland in 1955-56: he followed four first-innings wickets with an important 35, from the unaccustomed heights of No. 3, to help swell the lead to 267, which proved more than enough. John Reid, his captain, remembered: "Tony was a hell of a good team man and he had some good figures. I can't say we won too many Tests with him, but we did win one and that was the first." MacGibbon had taken seven for 56 to bowl Canterbury to victory over Auckland in January 1955, but shortly after that he was one of the unfortunates who failed to score as New Zealand slumped to 26 all out – still the lowest Test total – against England at Auckland. Three years later MacGibbon was one of the few to emerge from the wretched 1958 tour of England with any credit. As his side slumped to a 4–0 defeat, he took 20 wickets at 19.45, including five for 64 on the opening day of the series at Edgbaston. He also hit 66 at Old Trafford, New Zealand's highest score of a series in which they were bowled out for less than 100 five times. Sometimes MacGibbon was not quite so accurate. There were days when his action didn't quite gel, his front foot pointed towards midwicket on delivery, and he could send down wides which, according to wicketkeeper Sammy

PA Photos

At the start of a difficult tour: Tony MacGibbon (*left*) and Trevor Meale in May 1958.

Guillen, "were not in my parish". That 1958 tour marked the end of MacGibbon's Test cricket: he stayed in England to study at Durham University and, although he later returned to play for Canterbury, the selectors looked elsewhere. He finished with 70 Test wickets, a New Zealand record at the time.

McNAMARA, LISLE ANTHONY, who died on May 19, 2010, aged 67, was a batsman who played 35 matches without making a century for the South African province Griqualand West over a decade from 1962-63. His father, whose first name was also Lisle, played exactly 35 matches, most of them for Griquas too.

MADSEN, Flight Lieutenant HAYDEN PETER, was killed on April 25, 2010, aged 33. He was piloting an elderly New Zealand Air Force Iroquois helicopter on its way to Anzac Day celebrations when it crashed into a hillside near Wellington. As a cricketer, Madsen was an all-rounder who had played for Manawatu, alongside Jamie How and Ross Taylor, in the Hawke Cup Challenge Matches of 2001-02 and 2002-03. He also captained the NZ Defence Force team.

MANSELL, ALAN WILLIAM, died on April 22, 2010, aged 58. He had been suffering from multiple sclerosis. Mansell had two full seasons as Sussex's wicketkeeper after Jim Parks left to join Somerset in 1973. The floppy-haired Mansell was a fine keeper, but a modest batsman with a career average of 15. "Alan was neat and tidy and had great hands," remembered Parks. "He would stand up when Tony Greig was firing in his off-cutters, and he kept immaculately." Greig said: "He was one of those genuinely nice young men who worked very hard at his own game while never forgetting the importance of being a team player." But Arnold Long arrived at Hove from Surrey in 1976, and Mansell returned to club cricket and coaching: he worked with Border in South Africa for eight years, helping Mark Boucher and Makhaya Ntini, among others, into the national side.

MEALE, TREVOR, died on May 21, 2010, aged 81. Few players have been chosen for a tour of England on more flimsy evidence than Meale had offered before New Zealand's 1958 visit. A tall left-hander, he had played a dozen matches for Wellington in the early

1950s, scoring centuries against both the 1951-52 West Indian tourists and the 1953-54 Fijians. After that, Meale tried his luck in England, where he played for Ealing and attempted, unsuccessfully, to qualify for Kent. He returned to first-class cricket in New Zealand by playing one match before the 1958 touring team was selected – and a score of 48, remarkably, was enough to win him a place, presumably because the selectors wanted to include someone with experience of English conditions, however limited. Meale started the tour proper with 89 at Worcester (including, uncharacteristically, six sixes), but never exceeded that and finished a sorry trip – New Zealand avoided a 5–0 whitewash only because of rain at The Oval – with 502 runs at 21.82. Meale played in the first and last Tests, scoring 21 runs in four innings, and never played first-class cricket again after the tour. Although he later became involved in cricket administration in the Hutt Valley, and did some umpiring, he may have been soured by his experiences in England: he was the only former player to decline to be interviewed for a recent television series on New Zealand's international cricket.

MEHRA, RAJAN, who died on October 4, 2010, aged 76, played 14 Ranji Trophy matches for Delhi in the 1950s and 1960s, occasionally captaining them. Originally a leg-spinner, he made himself into a useful batsman and was also a fine slip fielder. Later he turned to umpiring, and stood in two Tests and three one-day internationals in the 1980s.

MERRICK, GILBERT HAROLD, died on February 3, 2010, aged 88. Gil Merrick was England's goalkeeper during the 1954 football World Cup, and won 23 international caps in all. A one-club man who made a record 551 senior appearances for Birmingham City, he was also a good cricketer, playing for Olton & West Warwickshire CC and occasionally for Warwickshire's Second Eleven.

MOORE, HARRY IAN, died on February 16, 2010, aged 68. Ian Moore was a tenacious batsman who emerged from Minor Counties cricket with his native Lincolnshire to have eight seasons with Nottinghamshire in the 1960s. He made only seven hundreds, but they included an unbeaten five-hour century against the 1964 Australian tourists, and 206 not out against the 1967 Indians. He was strong off the back foot and a fine player of spin, according to his team-mate Mike Smedley, as illustrated by his treatment of the Indian attack. He was, however, a bit accident-prone. "He once smashed the ball straight back down the pitch," said Smedley. "The umpire couldn't get out of the way and it hit him, then bounced away and he was caught at mid-on." Released in 1969, Moore returned to Lincolnshire, captaining them to a famous victory over Glamorgan at Swansea in the 1974 Gillette Cup. Ten years later he was persuaded to turn out for Macclesfield CC after buying a house opposite the ground, and promptly topped the Cheshire League batting averages. Moore originally wore glasses, but was one of the first professional cricketers to try contact lenses, leading to the interruption of one net practice when the whole team went down on their hands and knees to hunt for a missing lens.

MOTHERSDALE, DANIEL, was found hanged in Bawtry, near Doncaster, on September 18, 2010. Police said foul play was not suspected. Dan Mothersdale was 21, was working as a trainee surveyor, and had just topped Bawtry CC's batting averages with 709 runs at 32.22. "He was a fine cricketer and a fine young man who spent a lot of his time helping coach the junior players," said club treasurer Paul Warren.

MULLINS, DAMIEN, who died of cancer on September 19, 2010, aged 49, had been chairman of Queensland Cricket for ten years, and a director for 20. In 1993, he had become the youngest director of what was then called the Australian Cricket Board: he stood down in 2007. A well-respected barrister, Mullins was also a useful batsman, once scoring a century for a touring Queensland University side against a Somerset Second Eleven containing Andy Caddick.

MUSLEHUDDIN BUTT, MUHAMMAD, collapsed and died while fielding during a semi-final of Pakistan's National Veterans Twenty20 Cup in Lahore on December 4, 2010. He was 49. Muslehuddin was a fast-medium bowler for Railways who took 92 wickets, including six for 23 when Rawalpindi were bowled out for 56 in the 1982-83 Quaid-e-Azam Trophy, and a handy batsman. In 1980-81, he played for a strong Pakistan Combined XI against the touring West Indians, and dismissed Viv Richards for a duck.

NILANTHA, AKMEEMANA ACHARIGE DON HARSHA, drowned while swimming in a river at Padukka, near Colombo, on June 27, 2010. He was 28. Harsha Nilantha was a well-regarded fast-medium bowler who took 45 wickets in 16 matches for Ragama in Sri Lanka's first-class competition. Against the Sinhalese Sports Club in February 2004 he took seven for 92 on the first day, and finished with ten wickets in the match, including Marvan Atapattu – soon to be Sri Lanka's Test captain – in both innings.

NURUDDIN KHAWAJA, Lt.-Col., who died of liver failure on January 29, 2010, aged 57, had been the regional security manager for Pakistan and Bangladesh in the ICC's Anti-Corruption and Security Unit since it was set up in 2002. Before that Colonel Nur, as he was widely known, worked for the Pakistan board as their domestic cricket manager, following a 28-year army career. He played his part in the aftermath of the terrorist attack on the Sri Lankan team bus in Lahore in March 2009: "He took charge of the situation and personally spoke to all the players, and arranged immediate security around the dressing-rooms to avoid the chaos that often follows such deadly and shocking attacks, when the entire administration goes numb," said Ravi Sawani, the ACSU's general manager. "His presence and personal interaction with the players and match officials gave them a lot of confidence." The Pakistani journalist Qamar Ahmed said: "He was a very friendly and warm man, heartbroken because his 25-year-old son had died a year before he did."

PATEL, MAHENDRA, who died on April 29, 2010, aged 66, was one of the main driving forces behind uniting the various leagues in Scotland and forming the Scottish National Cricket League in 1998. He subsequently served as president of Cricket Scotland between 2006 and 2008. An opening bowler for Clackmannanshire who played on into his fifties, Patel was born in Uganda but came to Britain to study, and later worked for BP in Scotland.

PATRICKS, MICHAEL ANTHONY, who died on May 14, 2010, aged 66, played 21 matches later given first-class status for Natal's non-white sides in South Africa in the 1970s, scoring 90 against Transvaal in 1972-73. "He could hit the ball a mile and was an excellent bowler as well," said his contemporary "Sweetie" Naidoo.

PAWLE, JOHN HANBURY, who died on January 20, 2010, aged 94, was a good schoolboy batsman who never quite fulfilled his talent in first-class cricket. While at Harrow, Pawle passed 90 at Lord's three times without reaching three figures: 96 and 93 not out against Eton in 1933 and 1934, and then 92 for a Lord's Schools XI the following month. At Cambridge he missed out on a Blue in 1935, but received one in each of the next two seasons, and also played a few games for Essex. His best year was 1937, when he scored two centuries inside a week at Fenner's, against Northamptonshire and the Free Foresters – but he bagged a pair in the Varsity Match. After the war Pawle won the British amateur rackets title four years running from 1947, and twice unsuccessfully contested the world championship. After retiring from the Stock Exchange he devoted himself to painting, and had several exhibitions at London galleries.

PETHER, STEWART, who died on January 17, 2010, aged 93, was a fast-medium swing bowler who played ten matches for Oxford University in 1939, taking five for seven as Derbyshire were shot out for 72 on a helpful pitch in the Parks. (Oxford made only 47 and lost inside two days.) Pether, who had previously played for Oxfordshire, also won Blues for golf and rugby, but was badly injured towards the end of the Second World War in

1945. He had earlier had a miraculous escape when a bullet hit a brandy flask in his breast pocket. He became a schoolmaster, running the cricket and rugby at St Edward's, Oxford, for many years.

PLUMBLY, GERALD PERCIVAL, who died on January 26, 2010, aged 95, was life president of the midweek wandering club, Stoics CC, founded by A. E. Stoddart. Plumbly was a Marylebone vet who treated an astonishing variety of animals in Central London, ranging from the Queen's horses to circus animals, and once had to rescue a Soho stripper who was being strangled by a boa constrictor. However, his appointments had to fit in with his cricket, and he would often play several times a week. Though a modest performer, he was thrilled to hit a six on his favourite ground, the Saffrons at Eastbourne. In any case, his zest and sociability and devotion to the club made him a revered figure among his fellow Stoics. After he stopped playing, he kept the score – immaculately – until he was 92. And when he was too frail to travel with them on tour to Sri Lanka in 2008, they took a large picture of him instead and displayed it at every match.

POLE, Professor JACK RICHON, who died on January 31, 2010, aged 87, was one of Britain's leading experts in US history, and from 1979 to 1989 was professor of American history at Oxford. He was also a cricket obsessive, and founder of the Trojan Wanderers team. His batting average was said to have surpassed his age until late in life. Godfrey Hodgson wrote in *The Guardian* that his style in intellectual argument and in cricket resembled each other: "He would defend, if necessary, for hours, with infinite tenacity, then abruptly deliver the most elegant of off-drives or a blatant slog over the bowler's head."

RAIJI, MADAN NAISADRAI, who died on March 29, 2010, aged 87, was a useful all-rounder for Bombay in the 1940s. His finest hour probably came at the Brabourne Stadium in March 1948, when he scored 170 against Hyderabad and put on 360 for the fifth wicket with Uday Merchant (brother of the more famous Vijay). Raiji also took five for 103 with his leg-spin for West Zone against the West Indian tourists in December 1948, his victims including Clyde Walcott for one and Everton Weekes for a duck. His older brother Vasant Raiji, who also played for Bombay, became a noted cricket historian.

RANGARAJ, SRINIVAS VENKATACHAR, who died on February 2, 2010, aged 77, was a batsman who usually opened for Mysore in the 1950s. Shortly after making 135, his only century, against Hyderabad in 1958-59, Rangaraj opened for South Zone against the touring West Indians, but was cleaned up in both innings by the fearsome Roy Gilchrist, and rapidly faded from first-class cricket.

ROBERTSON, WILLIAM DUNCAN, CBE, died on September 24, 2010, aged 88. "Robbie" Robertson was a long-serving RAF officer – rising to the rank of Air Commodore – who flew several sorties over India and Malaya during turbulent times there in the 1940s and '50s. He was also a good cricketer, who was once replaced on a mission against a terrorist jungle base at short notice after being selected for a Far East services team to play their Australian counterparts in a match in Hong Kong. The plane he should have been flying crashed in fog, and there were no survivors; ever after, Robertson said he owed his life to cricket.

ROXBY, ROBERT CHARLES, died on February 7, 2010, aged 83. Born in the New South Wales city of Newcastle, Bob Roxby took eight for 109 there with his leg-spinners for NSW Country against the South African tourists of 1952-53. His performance earned him four matches for NSW the following season, and he took five for 84 on debut against South Australia at Adelaide. He then moved to South Australia, but took only 11 expensive wickets over five seasons. As a lamp-maker in Newcastle, Roxby habitually worked the night shift; he claimed that playing first-class cricket was a way of ensuring he could sleep when he had a night off.

SCHREIBER, EDWIN FREDERICK, who died on October 7, 2010, aged 74, was a parsimonious off-spinner who played 40 first-class matches, starting as an 18-year-old in 1954-55, when he took five for 49 in 39 overs for Border against North Eastern Transvaal. Schreiber was soon being mentioned as a Test prospect, but had no chance of displacing South Africa's resident off-spinner, Hugh Tayfield. His domestic figures were highly respectable – 155 wickets at 24.34 – and some days he was irresistible: against Eastern Province in 1957-58 he took eight for 67, and the following season collected 11 for 103 in 72.4 overs against North Eastern Transvaal. Schreiber's career seemed to have ended in 1961-62, but he made one last appearance five years later, returning the startling figures of 45–24–46–0 against Griqualand West, then batting stubbornly at No. 10 in the follow-on to force the draw.

SHAHZAD HUMAYUN, who died of cancer on November 3, 2010, aged 65, was a long-serving English-language cricket commentator on Pakistan television and radio, and was on the air during the 2006 Oval Test when Pakistan forfeited the game after being accused of ball-tampering. "He had a beautiful, soft and expressive voice with complete command over the language and technical aspects of the game," said his sometime colleague Hasan Jalil.

SHARMA, PARTHASARATHY HARISHCHANDRA, died of cancer on October 20, 2010, aged 62. Parath Sharma was a battling right-hander, particularly fluent against spin, who made 54 and 49 in his first Test for India, defying the West Indian pace attack led by Andy Roberts at Delhi in December 1974. Already a consistent domestic run-scorer for Rajasthan and Central Zone, Sharma seemed set for a run in the national side but played only four more Tests, in which he failed to reach 30, not helped by being pushed up the order. He was short and stocky – Bishan Bedi, while allowing that "in the domestic arena he was an outstanding batsman", felt that Sharma could have worked harder on his fitness. Sharma's 18 first-class centuries included 206 while captaining the Rest of India in the annual Irani Trophy match against the Ranji Trophy winners, Bombay, in January 1978, and he made more than 8,000 runs in all: he also took almost 200 wickets with his skiddy medium-pacers, including six for 26 for Rajasthan against Vidarbha in November 1974. Once his first-class career was over he switched to coaching, and helped turn round Gautam Gambhir's career after he had been dropped by India. "He changed me completely as a player," said Gambhir. "My stance, my grip, my falling across, and the way we discussed how to go about things."

SHEPHERD, WILLIAM HERBERT, died on January 19, 2010, aged 70, less than three months after his brother David, the famous umpire, had also succumbed to cancer. Bill was a fine cricketer himself – David used to say he was the better batsman – but never quite made the grade in the first-class game. He had a spell on the MCC groundstaff and scored 100 for the Young Professionals against the London Federation of Boys' Clubs at Lord's in 1959: in the previous year's fixture he had taken six for 29 with his off-spin. Also in 1959 he played for the Young Professionals against an England Schools side containing his brother. After that, though, while David started a long county career with Gloucestershire, Bill contented himself with league cricket and occasional appearances for Devon's Minor Counties side. He returned to the village of Instow, to help his mother Dolly run the post office: in later years David would himself lend a hand there when not umpiring.

SLICER, ROBERT, died on June 4, 2010, aged 85. Bob Slicer was one of the prime movers behind the Yorkshire Reform Group, which campaigned successfully for the reinstatement of Geoff Boycott after he was sacked by Yorkshire in October 1983. Slicer enlivened one of the campaigners' early meetings by asking "What sort of theatre is it that sacks the top of the bill because the supporting acts are rubbish?" For a time he was chairman of the protest group, which successfully overthrew the county committee and had the decision reversed: Boycott played on for Yorkshire until 1986. A successful businessman who eventually retired to Australia, Slicer was one of the three co-founders in 1970 of the National Breakdown Recovery Club, now Green Flag.

SRINIVASAN, THIRUMALAI ECHAMBADI, who died of a brain tumour on December 6, 2010, aged 60, was a dashing batsman from Tamil Nadu, strong off the back foot, who won one Test cap for India in New Zealand in 1980-81. He also played two one-day internationals, the first in Australia earlier in the tour, which he started, legend has it, by instructing a reporter who greeted the team at Perth airport to "tell Dennis Lillee that T. E. has arrived". Lillee was not unduly bothered: in their only meeting, in a one-day international at Melbourne, he had Srinivasan caught at slip for six. Srinivasan was a stylish performer at home, popular with the crowds, many of whom would leave when he was out. He scored only five centuries, but they were made in style. "He walked to the wicket with a swagger, collar up in the manner of his hero M. L. Jaisimha, looked around the field with the air of a man who understood it belonged to him, and struck the ball with startling power for a man his size," remembered the Indian writer Suresh Menon.

STACKPOOLE, JOHN, died on October 24, 2010, aged 93. Jack Stackpoole played only three matches for Queensland, but made a sensational start, dismissing Don Bradman first ball on his debut at the Gabba in January 1940. Bradman was surprised by a delivery that stood up slightly, causing him to push a sharp catch to silly mid-on. Stackpoole's response was typical both of the man and his times: "I don't want to be made a hero at Don Bradman's expense… but I am definitely pleased for Queensland's sake." His daughter was in her late teens before she learned of her father's feat from a man who complained that Jack had ruined his day by dismissing The Don. The story behind Stackpoole's selection for the game in the first place added to its magical quality: he was on holiday in Adelaide when called on, and had to trek to Brisbane across Australia by train and plane, arriving just in time. He finished with match figures of nine for 138.

SUNDERAM, GUNDIBAIL RAMA, who died on June 20, 2010, aged 80, played two Tests for India against New Zealand in 1955-56. He opened the bowling in both matches and took three wickets, including the touring captain John Reid for 120 at Calcutta. Sunderam had first caught the eye by taking four top-order wickets for Indian Universities against the touring Pakistanis in 1952-53 in only his second first-class game. But he was to have an unusual career: he had played just ten matches before his Test debut, and, after helping Bombay win the Ranji Trophy that season, did not play another first-class match for more than five years, reappearing for Rajasthan in 1961-62. His son Pradeep also played for Rajasthan, taking all ten wickets in an innings against Vidarbha in 1985-86.

SURESH, KITTU GUNDAPPA, who died on January 6, 2010, aged 64, played 23 matches for Mysore between 1966-67 and 1971-72. As a batsman he never bettered the 92 he made on debut against Andhra at Bangalore in October 1966, but he was also a handy medium-pacer who took seven for 61 against Kerala two seasons later.

THEWLIS, JOSEPH, died on November 24, 2010, aged 71. Joe Thewlis was a regular in the Northumberland side for almost two decades, scoring 4,225 runs in more than 150 matches between 1963 and 1981.

THOMAS, FRANK GILBERT, OBE, died on November 20, 2010, aged 86. Frankie Thomas, a contemporary of Frank Worrell's at Combermere School, played one match for his native Barbados in March 1945. He scored 21 and took one wicket, then joined the civil service in St Vincent, rising to be cabinet secretary and chief personnel officer. He captained his adopted island in the annual Windwards Islands Cork Cup tournament for several years, and led the Windwards against Len Hutton's touring MCC side in 1953-54. Thomas's most enduring legacy is as an administrator while the smaller islands were assuming greater importance in West Indian cricket. A stand at the Arnos Vale Sports

Complex carries his name, a tribute to his role in its development as an international venue. He was West Indies' assistant manager on the triumphant 1976 tour of England, and manager in the home series against Pakistan early the following year.

THOMPSON, JOHN ROSS, who died on June 15, 2010, aged 92, was an outstanding amateur batsman who, some felt, might have played for England had war not interrupted his career after two highly successful seasons for Cambridge University. In 1938 his 858 runs at 50.47 included 191 against the Free Foresters: *Wisden* praised a man who "in very correct style, indicated the makings of a brilliant batsman". The following year Thompson was less fluent, but he still made centuries against Middlesex and Leicestershire – cutting and driving "with effortless ease" during an opening partnership of 262 with George Mann. After the war, however, he concentrated on teaching mathematics and physics at Marlborough College, although he played occasionally for Warwickshire in the school holidays. In 1949 he scored two centuries in half a dozen matches for them on his way to 609 runs at 60.90, which put him sixth in the national averages, a record helped somewhat by 97 and 102 not out against the Combined Services. Thompson's first-class career ended in 1954, although he continued to play for Wiltshire and MCC. In 1959 he was the British Open rackets champion: he won the amateur title five times and the doubles on 11 occasions. Thompson also played squash for England, and later took up golf. Mike Griffith, the Marlborough boy who later captained Sussex, said: "He had tremendous focus, which was a bit unfashionable at the time. Some coaches were content just to let natural talent get on with it – but he believed in technique and coaching, and he was meticulous in working out the angles. You had to buckle down."

TINDILL, ERIC WILLIAM THOMAS, died on August 1, 2010, four months short of becoming the first Test cricketer to celebrate his 100th birthday. He was a legend in New Zealand, as he was the only man to play international rugby for the All Blacks and Test

Nearing his century: on his 99th birthday Eric Tindill is given a signed bat by Alan Isaac, then chairman of New Zealand Cricket.

cricket as well. He later refereed rugby internationals – including two Tests of the British Lions' tour in 1950 – and umpired a cricket Test (against England at Christchurch in 1958-59). Either leg of this double double would seem inconceivable nowadays. Just how crowded Tindill's sporting life was can be gauged from his wedding day, Monday, March 27, 1937: a civil servant, he started by tidying his office desk; he got married at 9 a.m.; by 11 he was at the Basin Reserve for the final day of New Zealand's unofficial Test against Gubby Allen's England tourists (he finished the day with 24 not out, helping his side salvage a draw); and at 8 p.m. he joined the rest of the New Zealand cricket team on board ship for the voyage to England. His new bride followed in a different vessel.

"Snowy" Tindill first made a mark as a rugby half-back, skilled at the opportunistic drop-goal. He toured England with the All Blacks in 1935-36, and won his only cap in the match at Twickenham which has gone down in history for the Russian prince Alex Obolensky's two stunning solo tries for England, who won 13–0.

Tindill returned in 1937, this time with New Zealand's cricket team: he played in all three Tests, *Wisden* observing that he "did nothing out of the common with the bat, but as a wicketkeeper he was always worth his place". He finished the tour with 47 dismissals, 18 of them stumpings, in 23 matches. On the way home the tourists played against South Australia at Adelaide, and Tindill caught Don Bradman for 11: it was the only time The Don played against any team from New Zealand. After the war, he played two more Tests, and began to acquire a reputation as an exceptional rugby referee. The 1950 Lions were so pleased with his performance in the first two Tests of their tour (though they won neither) that they asked if he could do the whole series, but were told it had to be shared around. His life was not entirely serene: he lost his wife and one of his four sons in accidents. But he continued to live at home, tended by his daughter Molly. And when a great-nephew came by and said he wanted to be a wicketkeeper, Tindill – well into his nineties – got down on his haunches to demonstrate technique. He scored six first-class centuries, including one on his first-class debut, but he just missed the most coveted century of all. The mantle of the oldest surviving Test player – and the last to have played before the Second World War – passed to the South African fast bowler Norman Gordon, who was 99 in August 2010.

TURNER, BRUCE ALEXANDER, who died on March 30, 2010, aged 79, played 15 times for Central Districts in the 1950s. He made fifties in his opening two matches in 1951-52, but his form fell away. In the Manawatu region, however, he was a legend, mainly for his hockey prowess. He represented New Zealand aged 19, played in the 1956 and 1960 Olympics (the second time as captain), and selected the team that won gold at Montreal in 1976. He was considered in India to be the best right-half in the world. The pavilion at Fitzherbert Park in Palmerston North was named after him.

WALSH, ALBERT COSTAYNE HAYDEN, was found dead in a swimming pool on January 9, 2010, while on a family outing in his native Antigua. He was 46, and drowned after suffering a stroke. Hayden Walsh played 18 first-class games for the Leeward Islands from 1987-88, scoring 92 and 59 against Barbados in Nevis in 1992-93. But he was better known as a coach, who opened his own academy in Antigua in 1999, and a prominent administrator. "You have to consider Hayden one of the cricket soldiers," said Leon Rodney, a fellow member of the local board.

WARD, SYDNEY WILLIAM, who died on December 31, 2010, aged 103, was born near Sydney, but when he was ten his family moved to New Zealand, where he played ten matches for Wellington in the 1930s. His highest score was 61, at Auckland in January 1935, and later that year he was part of the side which defeated the MCC touring team captained by Errol Holmes. Syd Ward was also a good rugby player, and played indoor bowls until he was 101. He ascribed his longevity to a diet of porridge,

OLDEST KNOWN FIRST-CLASS CRICKETERS

Years	Days		First match	Last match
103	344	J. M. Hutchinson (Derbyshire)....................	1920	1931
103	**148**	**S. W. Ward (Wellington)**........................	**1929-30**	**1937-38**
102	253	R. de Smidt (Western Province)...................	1912-13	1912-13
102	247	E. A. English (Hampshire).......................	1898	1901
102	101	J. Wheatley (Canterbury)........................	1882-83	1903-04
101	253	E. J. Martin (Western Australia).................	1932-33	1932-33
101	222	D. B. Deodhar (Hindus, Maharashtra).............	1911-12	1947-48
101	191	G. R. U. Harman (Dublin University).............	1895	1895
101	57	A. G. Finlayson (Eastern Province)...............	1921-22	1921-22
100	214	H. H. Forsyth (Dublin University)................	1926	1926
100	77	G. O. Deane (Hampshire)........................	1848	1848

The oldest-known Test cricketer, E. W. T. Tindill of New Zealand, was 99 years 226 days old when he died in 2010 (see above).

---

onions and garlic. Of first-class cricketers, only Derbyshire's Jim Hutchinson, who died 22 days short of his 104th birthday in 2000, is known to have survived to a greater age.

WICKREMASINGHE, WICKREMA ARACHCHIGE UDAYA, died on April 12, 2010, aged 70. Udaya Wickremasinghe was a Sri Lankan umpire who stood in three Tests and 13 one-day internationals between 1987 and 1998. In the Wills Trophy final at Sharjah in October 1991 "Wicky" despatched three successive Indian batsmen lbw, giving Aqib Javed of Pakistan a hat-trick.

WILSON, ELIZABETH REBECCA, died on January 22, 2010, aged 88. Betty Wilson was one of the outstanding all-rounders in women's cricket, indispensable to the Australian side from the beginning to the end of her career. Her Australian team-mate Norma Whiteman (now Johnston) said Wilson was "by the length of the field, the best woman cricketer in either department I have ever seen. Everything she did on and off the field was class." Her batting was stylish and powerful, with skilful footwork that made her an expansive off-driver. From a beautifully balanced delivery, she bowled accurate off-breaks at a pace which pinned batters to the crease. She came from a supportive working-class background in Melbourne, where the skills of her bootmaker father meant she habitually appeared in handsomely crafted cricket shoes.

The cricket of her childhood had an archetypically Australian quality to it: matches in the street, precocious natural skill and confidence which were fostered without being stifled by coaching, and dedication to self-improvement through relentless practice. She often spent hours hitting a ball in a stocking attached to the family clothes line. When she was struck by a ball during one of her first district matches as a young teenager, there were mutterings about her suitability for an "adult" game, but her father's response was "She's been hit once… she won't be hit again." And she wasn't.

Wilson began her Test career – against New Zealand at Wellington in 1947-48 – as she continued it, by stamping her presence with both bat and ball. A lively 90, during which she added 163 with Una Paisley, was followed by four for 37 and six for 28 from 40 overs in all. Playing for a Combined Australian XI, she greeted the 1948-49 England tourists with an unbeaten 100 in just over two hours, followed by 111 in the First Test at Adelaide, which saw another century stand with Paisley, together with figures of six for 23 and three for 39.

Wilson was one of the successes of the 1951 tour of England, hitting 100 not out in 71 minutes and taking five for 14 against Yorkshire at Headingley, while her steadiness with both bat and ball in the Second Test, at Worcester, allowed Australia to register only their second Test victory in England. Until that point, her performances had been outstanding;

A beautifully balanced delivery: Betty Wilson bowling against England at Worcester, June 1951.

in her final series, against England in Australia in 1957-58, they reached their zenith. The opening day of the Second Test, at the Junction Oval at St Kilda in Melbourne, was rained off, and play began next day on a treacherous pitch on which Australia could only scramble to 38. "England were killing themselves laughing," remembered Wilson. But not for long: she exploited the conditions so artfully that her seven for seven from 10.3 overs, which included the first hat-trick in women's Test cricket — "bowled by an off-break, stumped from a wrong'un and lbw to a straight one," she recited over half a century later – allowed England to register only 35. In Australia's second innings, Wilson hit 100 out of 157 made while she was at the crease, and then took a further four for nine from 19 overs. She was the first cricketer of either sex to score over a hundred runs and take ten wickets in a Test, nearly three years before Alan Davidson matched the feat in the Tied Test at Brisbane. Then, on a shirtfront Adelaide pitch, Wilson made 127 and took a further six for 71.

It was during this summer that the future Test player Patricia Thomson played her first interstate match against Victoria, where Wilson was in her last season. Thomson said she exuded such an air of confident mastery that it became a form of psychological intimidation.

Of necessity, Wilson left school at 14 and worked in a variety of clerical and secretarial positions. She never married, postponing two engagements because there were Tests to be played; when she was picked to go to England, her fiancé finally got fed up and called the whole thing off. She was married to cricket, she would say later. A month before her death, she was a guest in the Melbourne Cricket Club's committee-room on Boxing Day where, at long last, she was honoured and acclaimed as an equal in the ranks of former Test players there.

WOODBRIDGE, CLIVE EDWARD, who died on November 7, 2009, aged 72, was a long-time supporter of cricket in Spain, where a ground in Alicante was named after him. Formerly a good club batsman for Chesham in Buckinghamshire, Woodbridge moved to Spain in the late 1980s and helped set up the Sporting Alfas Cricket Club, which has hosted many touring sides. He occasionally contributed details of Spanish cricket to *Wisden*, and in 2009 received an ICC award for services to cricket in Spain.

Off again: Jim Yardley bats for Worcestershire against Leicestershire in the 1973 Gillette Cup.

YARDLEY, THOMAS JAMES, died of cancer on November 20, 2010, aged 64. Jim Yardley was a unique county cricketer who, with a limited left-hand game and indifferent record, managed to eke out a career with Worcestershire and Northamptonshire that lasted 15 years. "Squirter Jim" really only had one shot, the squirt to third man, but he employed it to extraordinary effect. "His whole game was a roundabout route through the off side. How he got the ball there sometimes I do not know," recalled the former Northamptonshire captain Jim Watts. "You could post nine gullies and he'd still find a way through," said one exasperated opponent, Mike Selvey. Even more galling was the fact that he kept smiling the whole time. The Australian fast bowler Rodney Hogg endured a classic display of the Yardley technique when he was trying to win the tour match at Northampton the weekend before the 1981 Headingley Test. "Christ," he shouted finally, "do you play for the first team regular?" "If I said I didn't," said a timid voice from the other end, "would you bowl a little slower?" Yardley saved the game with an unbeaten 38. And this was how he earned his place: by making runs when they mattered, and being a good sort – plus, perhaps above all, catching beautifully at slip. Yardley, born in Worcestershire, made his debut for his home county in 1967. He passed 1,000 runs just once (1971) and made only five centuries in his 16 seasons. But by 1974 he was an important member of the team that, rather flukily, won the Championship and was the leading fielder in the country (jointly with Clive Radley), taking 34 catches. However, a year later Worcestershire slumped and Yardley was victim of a clear-out. Northamptonshire snapped him up, mainly to act as deputy-dogsbody for David Steele, who was then in the Test team. Though Steele's Test career was soon over, Yardley lasted until 1982. "He was very supportive," said Watts. "He didn't worry about his own performance, he worried about his side." Yardley later emigrated to Canada, where he died.

The obituaries section comprises those who died, or whose deaths were notified, in 2010. Wisden always welcomes information about those who might be included. Please send details to almanack@wisden.com, or to John Wisden & Co, 13 Old Aylesfield, Golden Pot, Alton, Hampshire, GU34 4BY.

BRIEFLY NOTED

The following, whose deaths were noted during 2010, played in ten or fewer first-class (fc) matches. Further details can be found on www.cricinfo.com (enter the player's name in the search box on the home page) or at www.cricketarchive.co.uk.

	Died	*Age*	*Main team*
Birtle, Thomas William	1.1.2010	83	Nottinghamshire

Fast bowler: seven fc matches in 1952, taking three wickets on debut but only five more.

Burton, John Edward Ledgard — 11.5.2010 — 85 — Ceylon
New Zealand-born batsman who played three matches for Ceylon, and one for Wellington.

Calder, John Wilson — 29.9.2010 — 59 — Canterbury
Off-spinner whose only fc match was for a New Zealand Under-23 side in 1971-72.

Chatterjee, Chaplakanta "Champi" — 20.8.2010 — 51 — Bengal
Medium-pacer who played one match in 1983-84; once took all ten wickets in a club game.

Cullinan, Thomas David — 24.1.2010 — 63 — North Eastern Transvaal
Batsman who played four Currie Cup matches in 1968-69, scoring 40 v Griqualand West.

Dalpathado, Fairlie George — 6.1.2010 — 85 — Ceylon
All-rounder who played three unofficial Tests, v West Indies in 1949 and Pakistan in 1950.

Dowell, Alastair McQueen — 9.4.2010 — 89 — Scotland
Fast bowler from Clackmannan who played three fc matches in the 1950s.

Fismer, Kenneth Gerard — 24.4.2010 — 95 — Western Province
Scored 54 in his only fc match, v Transvaal in 1941-42.

Forrest, James Edward — 4.7.2010 — 88 — Transvaal
Played once v Natal in 1952-53; for his native Suffolk, made 164 v Lincolnshire in 1939.

Fraser, Neville Graham — 17.5.2010 — 79 — Queensland
Slow left-armer who played two Sheffield Shield matches in 1950-51.

Ganapathy Rao, K. — 4.8.2010 — 80 — Madras/Mysore
Wicketkeeper-batsman who scored 125 against Kerala in 1957-58.

Gay, Major David William Maurice, MC — 10.7.2010 — 90 — Sussex
Seam bowler who played twice for Sussex in 1949.

Goodson, Donald — 13.9.2010 — 77 — Leicestershire
Amateur fast bowler; seven wickets in nine county games, plus 5-39 for Army v Navy, 1957.

Gopal Pai, Sringeri — 9.12.2010 — 88 — Madras/Mysore
Eight fc matches: never improved on debut 72 for Madras v Madhya Pradesh in 1951-52.

Hemming, Leonard Ernest Gerald — 10.7.2010 — 93 — Minor Counties
Oxfordshire all-rounder who played one fc match, against Kent in 1951.

Henderson, Henry James ("Harry") — 13.9.2010 — 77 — Umpire
Stood in several of Ireland's international matches, including fc game v Scotland in 1993.

Howe, Bennett Frederick — 22.4.2010 — 77 — Border
Two fc matches in 1955-56; played two rugby internationals for South Africa in 1956.

Howell, Neville Vivian — 10.1.2010 — 92 — Umpire
Stood in 14 fc matches in South Africa, and a women's Test at Cape Town in 1960-61.

Itaat Hussain — 25.9.2010 — 73 — Sind
Fast bowler: 19 wickets in seven fc games, including 5-82 v Karachi Greens in 1956-57.

	Died	Age	
			Main team

Mackle, John McGregor   27.6.2010   56   Canterbury
Wicketkeeper who played ten fc matches in the early 1980s.

Manley, Kevin Charles   29.12.2010   60   Umpire
Auckland umpire who stood in five fc matches and was reserve official for two Tests.

Morse, Eric George Arnold   2.3.2010   91   Tasmania
Seamer who dismissed Lindsay Hassett and Keith Miller in the first of his three fc matches.

Nicholls, Derek George   14.7.2010   62   Minor Counties
Staffordshire stalwart who took 6-43 v Worcestershire in 1982 Benson and Hedges Cup.

Nolan, Geoffrey John   30.6.2010   72   Essex
One fc match in 1968, against Derbyshire at Colchester, his home town.

Padmanabhan, Ananthakrishnaiyer   13.10.2010   70   Kerala
All-rounder: five Ranji Trophy matches between 1959 and 1962, with little success.

Pariwal, Subhash   11.10.2010   62   Rajasthan
Spinner who played two Ranji Trophy matches in the 1970s without taking a wicket.

Robinson, Gladstone Adolph   8.1.2010   66   Jamaica
Made 53 in the last of his three matches, against the 1964-65 Australian tourists.

Tomlinson, John Derek Williams   1.4.2010   84   Derbyshire
One Championship match in 1946, scoring two against Somerset.

Townshend, Trevor John   1.7.2010   58   Rhodesia
Batsman who played three fc matches; also represented Leicestershire II.

Wankhede, A.   9.4.2010   59   Vidarbha
Off-spinner: 5-111 on debut, v Rajasthan (1979-80) but only one wicket in four other games.

Webb, John Kingdon Guy, OBE   17.8.2010   91   Oxford University
Essex-born batsman (one match in 1938) who became a missionary doctor in India.

Woods, Basil Joseph Pontifex   3.3.2010   87   Cambridge University
South African-born leg-spinner who took three wickets in two fc matches in 1951.

Woolley, Kenneth McDowell   19.5.2010   85   Cambridge University
South African opening bowler who failed to take a wicket in his only fc match, in 1947.

CAREER FIGURES OF TEST CRICKETERS

	Tests				First-class		
	Runs	Avge	Wkts	Avge	Runs	Avge	Wkts	Avge
K. V. Andrew	29	9.66	–	–	4,230	13.38	2	15.50
A. V. Bedser	714	12.75	236	24.89	5,735	14.51	1,924	20.41
R. A. Hamence	81	27.00	–	–	5,285	37.75	8	29.87
H. R. Lance	591	28.14	12	39.91	5,336	34.87	167	25.65
A. R. MacGibbon	814	19.85	70	30.85	3,699	19.88	356	26.12
T. Meale	21	5.25	–	–	1,352	27.59	0	–
P. H. Sharma	187	18.70	0	–	8,614	39.15	191	24.51
T. E. Srinivasan	48	24.00	–	–	3,487	34.18	3	48.66
G. R. Sunderam	3	–	3	55.33	558	14.68	127	26.10
E. W. T. Tindill	73	9.12	–	–	3,127	30.35	–	–

Andrew took 723 catches and 181 stumpings in first-class cricket, including one catch in two Tests.
Tindill took 96 catches and 33 stumpings in first-class cricket, including six catches and one stumping in five Tests.

FOR CHARITY!

LONDON TO BRISBANE

www.cyclingtothegashes.com

PART THREE

The
Ashes

AUSTRALIA v ENGLAND, 2010-11

ASHES SERIES REVIEW BY MARK NICHOLAS

Test matches (5): Australia 1, England 3

In Barack Obama-speak, the Ashes of 2010-11 was a shellacking. Indeed, the 3–1 scoreline barely did justice to England's superiority and certainly flattered Australia. In each discipline of the game Andrew Strauss's team were stronger, more consistent, just better than their opponents. Never before in a celebrated history had the Australians suffered three innings defeats in a series. Unlikely as it might seem, the question now was how long might it be before Australia were a superpower again?

In those three matches out of five – Adelaide, Melbourne and Sydney – England appeared to be playing on a different pitch. Alastair Cook and Jonathan Trott batted their team into impregnable positions before Kevin Pietersen and Ian Bell led the crushing of Australian minds. Pietersen's double-hundred at Adelaide was an innings of spectacular enterprise. Bell's first hundred against Australia came at Sydney, and confirmed the image of a complete batsman.

On all three occasions England passed 500 with extraordinary ease before the bowlers took on the role of executioner. Suddenly these flat tracks spat venom at batsmen whose footwork was found wanting, and whose "previous" counted for nothing. Ricky Ponting, the greatest Australian batsman of the modern era and, some say, the second-greatest of all Australians, averaged 16 in the series – and that with a stress-free 51 not out at the Gabba after England declared unnecessarily. Michael Clarke, his pretender, averaged 21. Only Mike Hussey showed the qualities for which Australian batting is famous: sound technique, unwavering application and the spirit to counter-attack.

Strauss led his team into the history books and joined an illustrious group of men who have won Ashes series away from home. Among them, Ray Illingworth may have been a smarter tactician, Len Hutton a finer batsman and Douglas Jardine a more ruthless autocrat, but the sum of this captain's parts was greater than the whole, and it was right that Strauss now joined such rarefied company.

Alongside him was a steely Zimbabwean, a man raised in a beautiful but now so wretched land. Eight years previously he had taken a stand against its leader, Robert Mugabe, and in so doing had to start afresh elsewhere with a young family. Andy Flower's part in England's success cannot be under-estimated. He cut the waffle, the whingeing and the excuses, and with a narrow eye told a talented group of players where they were at, and what could be achieved with clear thinking.

The campaign was planned with a realistic grasp of their own capabilities and a forensic study of their opponents. Attention to detail was its theme, while the basic skills of the game were rehearsed as though the series depended upon them. Of the 90 wickets taken by England, 66 fell to catches – an unusually

Philip Brown

A nightmare start… Andrew Strauss departs to the third ball of the Brisbane Test.

high number – many of them worthy of a slot in Channel 9's famous "Classic Catches" segment, which Tony Greig and Bill Lawry continued to drool over, 30 years after they first burst into broadcasting life.

Such riches! This was English cricket's kingdom of days, enjoyed by huge crowds, thousands having made the pilgrimage from Britain in the hope of witnessing revenge for the humiliation of four years earlier when Australia romped to a clean sweep. Much of Strauss's determination to win this time, and win in style, had come from that despair and from what he learned about how *not* to conduct a tour of Australia. Certainly the path had been cleared for him after the messy divorce between Pietersen and the former coach, Peter Moores, for which Pietersen must take some credit. Strauss will also reflect on Duncan Fletcher's decision not to appoint him captain on that previous tour: "Some day you will thank me," Fletcher told him.

Amid a near-unhealthy frenzy of anticipation at the Gabba in Brisbane on November 25, Strauss won an important toss, made the correct decision to

THREE INNINGS VICTORIES IN A TEST SERIES

England v West Indies (3 Tests in series)	1928	England v New Zealand (5 Tests)...	1958
Australia v West Indies (5 Tests)	1930-31	England v India (5 Tests)	1959
Australia v South Africa (5 Tests)	1931-32	India v Sri Lanka (3 Tests)	1993-94
Australia in South Africa (5 Tests)....	1935-36	Sri Lanka v Bangladesh (3 Tests) ...	2007
Australia v India (5 Tests)	1947-48	**England in Australia (5 Tests)**	**2010-11**
England v West Indies (5 Tests)......	1957		

Notes: Only Australia in 1935-36 and England in 2010-11 achieved the feat away from home. The series in 1928 comprised West Indies' first three Test matches.

bat – and promptly slapped the third ball of the match to gully, where Hussey held on to the catch. If there had been an earlier loss of a wicket in an Ashes series, no one could immediately recall it (1936-37 was the eventual answer). Strauss's left hand clasped his helmet in shock, and Ben Hilfenhaus's right fist jabbed feverishly in delight while his colleagues mobbed him.

Strauss had been in wicked form during England's impressive run into the Test, making back-to-back hundreds against Western Australia and South Australia, and thus was considered England's banker for the series. The same consideration suggested that Cook's technique would not withstand an Australian examination, but the tall, slim left-hander delights in defying such opinion. Cook continued along his stubborn path until the gladiatorial Peter Siddle unleashed hell with the fifth hat-trick by an Australian against England. The calm of 197 for four became the relative carnage of 260 all out.

Hussey then played one of the great Test innings, clawing his way back from anonymity after a desperately lean patch to the front page of every newspaper in the Great Southern Land. Ten days earlier he was all but dropped after a duck for Western Australia in the Sheffield Shield game billed as his last-chance saloon, but in the second innings he saved the selectors with a sparkling hundred, while his Australia A challengers subsided against England in Hobart.

On the third day at the Gabba, Hussey extended to 307 his partnership with Brad Haddin. Australia made 481, and England faced a deficit of 221. It was from that unpromising moment on – with the exception of an incomprehensible couple of days at Perth – that England took command of the series. Strauss made a thrilling hundred before Trott took his place at the crease and, when the declaration came, about half an hour before tea on the final afternoon, they were an unbelievable 517 for one. Match saved, tone set, the value of a draw never more evident. In more than ten hours, Australia had taken just one wicket. Not only was Cook's 235 the highest Test score ever at the Gabba, it was a portent of things to come.

When Trott is by the fire, slippers on and pipe lit, his long Australian vigils will be cause for immense satisfaction. None of them, however, will remain so vivid as the electric moment that kick-started and then defined the Second Test at Adelaide: the first-over run-out of Simon Katich.

Trott is no Paul Collingwood, but his swoop from midwicket was a thing of unlikely beauty, the throw of perfect technique and deadly effect. It was also the benefit of hours of practice, and contrasted with a similar opportunity that

Patrick Eagar

... becomes a dream ending: Chris Tremlett bowls Michael Beer at the SCG, and England win the Ashes 3–1.

later came the way of Xavier Doherty to run out Trott himself, which he bungled. It is worth pointing out that England completed four run-outs in the series to Australia's none. This tells us something about the batsmen as well as the fielders.

Katich had not faced a ball, and was to limp out of the series by the end of the Test after tearing an Achilles in the field. His talented opening partner, Shane Watson, was involved in too many run-outs, an indication of growing insularity as he strained to become the cricketer he knew he could be.

Next ball, James Anderson found a perfect outswinger for Ponting and, in his second over, another for Clarke. Australia were two for three – and, in hindsight, match over. This is an appropriate time to dwell on these three protagonists. Anderson may now be the best fast bowler in the world, though Dale Steyn will take issue. Steyn has greater impact but Anderson has more variation. He has learned to defend as easily as to attack, and clearly relishes the way in which the captain turns to him. It was an oddity that Andrew Flintoff's presence in the side had diminished Anderson, for it made him feel less wanted and therefore less worthy. They were friends but not compadres. At times – specifically in Brisbane, Melbourne and Sydney – even hard-bitten Australians marvelled at the younger Lancastrian's ability to move the old ball as if it were new and to sustain this brilliance. It is a moot point whether Anderson or Cook was truly the Man of the Series.

There were times when England's ability to reverse-swing the ball seemed to surprise their opponents, as if it were the work of some supernatural force. During the second innings at Melbourne, for instance, this happened after just

FOUR TOTALS OF 500-PLUS IN THE SAME TEST SERIES

Australia in West Indies	1954-55	South Africa v West Indies	2003-04
Australia v West Indies	1968-69	**England in Australia**	**2010-11**

Note: All five-Test series. There are 11 further instances of a team reaching 500 on three occasions in a Test series.

---

21 overs, and clearly changed the dynamic of the play. Rarely did Australia move the ball at all, yet England invariably found something for the conditions or surface.

It was in Adelaide that Ponting saw his own technique most exposed. There is an area, no more than six inches outside his off stump on a full length, where he has always been uneasy. At his best, an eagle eye and the fastest hands combine to save the day – but when he is out of form, the right shoulder dominates the forward move, balance is lost, and bat and body become disconnected. This happened in both innings, first to Anderson's outswing and then to Graeme Swann's over-spin. England had not needed to challenge the Australian captain with the short ball; they simply outplayed him in the orthodox way.

In general, Clarke appeared a shadow of his naturally effervescent self. Newspapers rage against him for the bling, and he feels their anger. He is the

Rubbish: a discarded paper at the MCG considers Australia's performance – and Ponting's future.

Philip Brown

right man to lead Australia next, but he must make runs again. He admitted that neither he, nor the team at large, had prepared adequately for the steepling bounce the tall England bowlers used to such good effect. That is inexcusable, and raises questions about the Australian coaching staff. Clarke, such a nimble fellow at his best, no longer moves back into his crease. It is forward only these days, which leads him to push hard at balls wide of the stumps and/or back of a length. His hands are a mile from his body, and from there control is lost. It was sad to see the brightness of his youth fade to introspection.

By sucking the life from this pair, England put fear into the others. It was much as Shane Warne and Glenn McGrath had done to key Englishmen for years. Knowing the value of big totals, Strauss and Flower had resolved to play with six specialist batsmen the minute Flintoff's career was over. This meant a four-man bowling attack, and huge dependence on Swann, who did not let his side down. There is no mystery to Swann, just high standards and a skill honed at the coalface of county cricket. He has both spirit and a sense of humour, traits needed in a harsh land for finger-tweakers. He had no great bounty to show for his consistency, but the others played off him with relish. With the quality spinner now on the other side, the Australians went into an Adelaide freefall.

The story was not so different at Perth, except that Mitchell Johnson, dropped for Adelaide but now recalled, played a miracle match alongside Hussey, who had one last defiant hour left in him. For sure England were complacent, if subconsciously, and some observers blamed distraction by the wives and children who had arrived for the Christmas holidays. But it wasn't any such thing. It was Johnson's heroic 62 on the first day, after Strauss had chosen to bowl first on a grassy pitch, and then his all-time great spell of fast inswing on the second – for an hour he might have been Wasim Akram – that won it. England were caught napping and well beaten, but Strauss stayed calm and told the world his team would continue on the path that had served them well up to that point.

MOST RUNS FOR ENGLAND IN A TEST SERIES IN AUSTRALIA

Runs	Avge			Runs	Avge		
905	113.12	W. R. Hammond	1928-29	633	63.30	M. P. Vaughan	2002-03
766	**127.66**	**A. N. Cook**	**2010-11**	582	72.75	K. F. Barrington	1962-63
734	81.55	H. Sutcliffe	1924-25	573	63.66	J. B. Hobbs	1924-25
662	82.75	J. B. Hobbs	1911-12	533	88.83	L. Hutton	1950-51
657	93.85	G. Boycott	1970-71	505	50.50	J. B. Hobbs	1920-21
648	72.00	J. H. Edrich	1970-71				

Note: All played five Tests except for Edrich, who played six.

How right he was. The toss was won again on Boxing Day in Melbourne as almost 85,000 people settled nervously into their seats, the series locked at 1–1. Again England bowled, but this time without a hint of complacency. That accusation could be levelled against the Australians, who were blown away inside 43 overs for just 98. There was liberal movement off the seam – Ponting was on the wrong end of a fine ball from a resurgent Chris Tremlett, and another sharp catch was held by England's impressive slip cordon – but there were culpable batsmen too.

Tremlett had replaced the injured Stuart Broad in Perth, and so beautifully did he bowl for the remainder of the series that no difference was noticed. Outrageously tall and strong, he was the find of the tour, a finished product at last with the ability to swing the ball through long accurate high-bounce spells that made the Australians play at more deliveries than was good for them. By 5 p.m. most Melburnians had left the building. By the close of the first day, England led by 59 with all their wickets intact. It beggared belief.

From that position of strength, the Ashes were easily retained. Too easily, in fact, and so the Australian post-mortems began. Fingers were pointed in all directions, when the truth lay in the talent at Australia's disposal. It is the hardest thing to admit that the players are not up to it. Mind you, the selectors

The only time England lacked co-ordination? Graeme Swann leads the Sprinkler dance at the MCG.

had plenty to answer for, such confusion did they create over their choice of spinner and so daft was their reluctance to invest in fresh faces at the start of the series. Greg Chappell had been appointed Australia's first full-time "National Talent Manager", and a selector to boot, but Andrew Hilditch was retained as the part-time chairman. They were clearly at odds, and even the home press corps could not fathom which way to turn for a quote.

Cricket Australia must take some of the blame for this, and for its overzealous attention to the commercial peripherals. For many reasons, it was unwise to play four limited-overs matches against Sri Lanka in the lead-up to the Ashes, not least for their undermining of the once-proud Sheffield Shield. The production line is not working as it used to. Youngsters are no longer put through their paces; many of them look as green as the Poms once did. The fall has been quick. No cricketing body searching for leaders, opening batsmen, athletic fielders and, most of all, spinners can afford to waste a moment in appraisal and action.

Almost a week after the massacre of Melbourne, the captains tossed on a Sydney pitch with more grass than usual. Clarke led Australia for the first time in a Test after Ponting withdrew with a finger injury sustained at Perth (should he really have played at Melbourne?), and looked a throwback in his striped blazer and baggier-than-baggy green. He bravely chose to bat, but was unable to change the storyline. Australia failed to score enough runs, though Usman Khawaja made a decent first impression, and after England had scored 644 of them the bowlers completed another rout. "Are you Bangladesh in disguise?" came the refrain from the glittering new Trumper Stand, where the Barmy Army had taken up residence.

It was there that Strauss took his men first for their curtain call. New-age, twittering, Facebook cricketers in chorus with the modern fan – the people

TALE OF THE TAPE

	England		Australia		
	Runs per wicket	Runs per over	Runs per wicket	Runs per over	Result
2001	26.44	3.50	49.11	4.26	Aus 4–1
2002-03	29.30	3.02	46.81	4.09	Aus 4–1
2005	31.84	3.87	31.57	3.72	Eng 2–1
2006-07	26.35	2.84	52.77	3.90	Aus 5–0
2009	34.15	3.77	40.64	3.63	Eng 2–1
2010-11	**51.14**	**3.50**	**29.23**	**3.09**	**Eng 3–1**

Research: Benedict Bermange

who had braved the strong dollar to sing from the rooftops about their heroes. First among equals in their affection was Matt Prior, whose all-round performance at Sydney capped a splendid tour. Not far behind was Tim Bresnan, the bluff Yorkshireman who was best proof of England's depth of talent, and who replaced Steve Finn beautifully. Revenge was sweet. This was a good day to be an Englishman in the midday Australian sun.

Cook received the Compton–Miller Medal awarded to the Man of the Series. He had spent nearly 36 hours at the crease in just seven innings, scoring 766 runs at an average of 127.66. The figures speak for themselves, and put him second on the list of English batsmen in Australia behind Walter Hammond (905 in 1928-29) but ahead of Herbert Sutcliffe, Jack Hobbs and Geoffrey Boycott. The previous August, Cook was not much of a bet even to make the tour, but a dashing hundred in the penultimate Test of the summer, against Pakistan at The Oval, bought him the ticket and the rest, as they say, is history. As with most of England's players, improvement was there for all to see: notably, in Cook's case, when he played well forward around off stump and both defended and drove to a straighter arc.

It was not so long ago (1994-95) that Australia featured both the national team and their A-team in a one-day tournament alongside an embarrassed England, who failed to make the finals. That depth of quality has long gone, but the delusion that all was well remained. Hard-earned home series wins against weak West Indian and Pakistan teams in 2009-10 were considered satisfactory, but were misleading. When Ashes fortunes swing so violently, it is usually in favour of the home side, or there are mitigating circumstances such as retirements or rebel tours. This time Australia had no alibi.

If this writer had had the privilege of reviewing the previous Ashes series Down Under, the praise heaped upon a Warne- and Ponting-inspired Australia would have endorsed their status as one of the exceptional teams of all time, while the criticism of England would have been stratospheric. Such is the circle of life.

After years of neglect, the game in England plugged into the facts and did something about itself. That alone is cause for celebration, though the margins of victory in this Ashes series and the excellence of the cricket which brought them will for ever be treasured.

HOW THEY MEASURED UP

England		Australia
England		**Australia**
3	Tosses won	2
2,864	Runs scored	2,631
56	Wickets lost	90
51.14	Runs per wicket	29.23
3.50	Runs per over	3.09
9	100s	3
32 / 24	10–99s / 0–9s	54 / 44

Partnership averages

78.42	1st	36.90
95.50	2nd	30.66
71.16	3rd	17.66
30.33	4th	45.55
40.33	5th	30.88
87.80	6th	60.33
33.20	7th	10.55
36.80	8th	24.11
11.20	9th	21.44
9.20	10th	11.37
68.88 / 31.11	% runs by wkts 1–5 / 6–10	56.70 / 43.29

Average by batting position

43.85	No. 1	48.33
127.66	No. 2	19.40
89.00	No. 3	19.00
60.00	No. 4	21.44
12.83	No. 5	63.33
42.80	No. 6	19.11
51.00	No. 7	56.57
28.60	No. 8	13.55
15.60	No. 9	15.75
17.33	No. 10	13.75
5.33	No. 11	8.33
445	Average first-innings total	274

70 at 27.64 / 16 at 38.31	Wickets taken by seam / spin	51 at 40.96 / 5 at 135.80
14.09	Over-rate per hour	13.85
3	Five-wicket hauls	4
59.37	Bowling strike-rate (excl. run-outs)	87.57
30 / 48 / 21 / 13 / 5 / 117	B / l-b / w / n-b / pen / total extras	46 / 50 / 34 / 21 / 0 / 151
4.45	% total runs scored in extras	5.27
47.55	% runs off bat in boundaries	49.80
312 / 7	Fours / sixes	292 / 14

How each side took their wickets

14	Bowled	13
23 / 43	Caught behind / elsewhere	8 / 25
6	lbw	9
4 / 0	Run out / stumped	0 / 1

8 / 13	Successful / unsuccessful reviews	7 / 12

Research: Benedict Bermange

ENGLAND TOURING PARTY

*A. J. Strauss (Middlesex), J. M. Anderson (Lancashire), I. R. Bell (Warwickshire), T. T. Bresnan (Yorkshire), S. C. J. Broad (Nottinghamshire), P. D. Collingwood (Durham), A. N. Cook (Essex), S. M. Davies (Surrey), S. T. Finn (Middlesex), E. J. G. Morgan (Middlesex), M. S. Panesar (Sussex), K. P. Pietersen (Surrey), M. J. Prior (Sussex), A. Shahzad (Yorkshire), G. P. Swann (Nottinghamshire), C. T. Tremlett (Surrey), I. J. L. Trott (Warwickshire).

Shahzad was not originally named in the squad but accompanied it throughout after originally being added as cover for Anderson, who broke a rib during a pre-tour bonding exercise. Broad left the tour after injuring his side during the Second Test at Adelaide, but was not replaced.

Coach: A. Flower. *Assistant coach:* R. G. Halsall. *Bowling coach:* D. J. Saker. *Additional coaches:* G. A. Gooch, Mushtaq Ahmed. *Team operations manager:* P. A. Neale. *Team analyst:* N. A. Leamon. *Physiotherapist:* K. A. Russell. *Strength and conditioning:* H. R. Bevan. *Team doctor:* Dr N. Peirce. *Team psychologist:* Dr M. A. K. Bawden. *Massage therapist:* M. E. S. Saxby. *Security manager:* R. C. Dickason. *Security assistant:* S. Dickason. *Media relations manager:* J. D. Avery.

TEST MATCH AVERAGES

AUSTRALIA – BATTING AND FIELDING

	T	I	NO	R	HS	100s	50s	Avge	Ct/St
†M. E. K. Hussey	5	9	0	570	195	2	3	63.33	5
S. R. Watson	5	10	1	435	95	0	4	48.33	5
B. J. Haddin	5	9	0	360	136	1	3	45.00	8/1
S. P. D. Smith	3	6	1	159	54*	0	1	31.80	2
†S. M. Katich	2	4	0	97	50	0	1	24.25	1
M. J. Clarke	5	9	0	193	80	0	1	21.44	3
P. M. Siddle	5	9	1	154	43	0	0	19.25	2
†M. G. Johnson	4	7	0	122	62	0	2	17.42	0
†M. J. North	2	3	0	49	26	0	0	16.33	1
†P. J. Hughes	3	6	0	97	31	0	0	16.16	0
R. T. Ponting	4	8	1	113	51*	0	1	16.14	4
B. W. Hilfenhaus	4	7	2	55	34	0	0	11.00	1
†X. J. Doherty	2	3	0	27	16	0	0	9.00	0
R. J. Harris	3	5	1	14	10*	0	0	3.50	0

Played in one Test: M. A. Beer 2*, 2 (1 ct); †D. E. Bollinger 0*, 7*; †U. T. Khawaja 37, 21.

BOWLING

	Style	O	M	R	W	BB	5W/i	Avge
R. J. Harris	RF	83.4	19	281	11	6-47	1	25.54
P. M. Siddle	RFM	147.1	28	484	14	6-54	2	34.57
M. G. Johnson	LF	136.3	22	554	15	6-38	1	36.93
B. W. Hilfenhaus	RFM	157.5	42	415	7	3-121	0	59.28
S. R. Watson	RFM	76	19	223	3	1-30	0	74.33
X. J. Doherty	SLA	75.5	11	306	3	2-41	0	102.00

Also bowled: M. A. Beer (SLA) 38–3–112–1; D. E. Bollinger (LFM) 29–1–130–1; M. J. Clarke (SLA) 3.2–0–13–0; M. E. K. Hussey (RM) 1–0–2–0; M. J. North (OB) 38–3–110–1; S. P. D. Smith (LBG) 31–3–138–0.

ENGLAND – BATTING AND FIELDING

	T	I	NO	R	HS	100s	50s	Avge	Ct
†A. N. Cook	5	7	1	766	235*	3	2	127.66	5
I. J. L. Trott	5	7	2	445	168*	2	1	89.00	1
I. R. Bell	5	6	1	329	115	1	3	65.80	3
K. P. Pietersen	5	6	0	360	227	1	1	60.00	5
M. J. Prior	5	6	1	252	118	1	1	50.40	23
†A. J. Strauss	5	7	0	307	110	1	3	43.85	8
G. P. Swann	5	5	1	88	36*	0	0	22.00	6
P. D. Collingwood	5	6	0	83	42	0	0	13.83	9
C. T. Tremlett	3	4	1	19	12	0	0	6.33	0
†J. M. Anderson	5	5	0	22	11	0	0	4.40	4
S. T. Finn	3	3	2	3	2	0	0	3.00	2

Played in two Tests: T. T. Bresnan 4, 35; †S. C. J. Broad 0.

BOWLING

	Style	O	M	R	W	BB	5W/i	Avge
T. T. Bresnan	RFM	82.4	25	215	11	4-50	0	19.54
C. T. Tremlett	RF	122.3	28	397	17	5-87	1	23.35
J. M. Anderson	RFM	213.1	50	625	24	4-44	0	26.04
S. T. Finn	RFM	107.4	9	464	14	6-125	1	33.14
G. P. Swann	OB	219.1	43	597	15	5-91	1	39.80

Also bowled: S. C. J. Broad (RFM) 69.5–17–161–2; P. D. Collingwood (RM) 31–6–73–2; K. P. Pietersen (OB) 5–0–16–1.

WESTERN AUSTRALIA v ENGLAND XI

At Perth, November 5–7, 2010. England XI won by six wickets. Toss: Western Australia.

On the first two days England showed the effects of their six-week lay-off. Only Broad bowled well, taking two wickets in his first over and dismissing North in a second spell stocked with variations. Finn struggled with his footholds on the shiny pitch, and Anderson was at less than full pace after his rib injury. England's batsmen were too loose in their shot selection before Broad hit three sixes and Swann 37 off 25 balls, allowing Strauss to make an astute declaration: if England had not bowled Western Australia out, the onus would have been on North to set a target. On the third morning Finn, from the Swan River End, found his length, as did Broad, which freed Swann from focusing on containment. England's fielding clicked too – Morgan ran out North while briefly subbing for Strauss – so they chased only 243 off 52 overs, and Western Australia had already lost their attack leader, Magoffin, to a knee injury. Strauss scored his first hundred in Australia since his Academy days – his unbeaten 120 came off 141 balls – while Pietersen, after a controlled first innings, drove three consecutive fours off Hogan before missing a reverse sweep against Beer, who did not suggest he was near Test selection. It was the first time England had won their opening first-class game in Australia since M. J. K. Smith's side in 1965-66, also against Western Australia.

Close of play: First day, England XI 10-1 (Strauss 5, Anderson 0); Second day, Western Australia 109-1 (Robinson 46, Swart 16).

Western Australia

W. M. Robinson c and b Collingwood	62	– (2) st Prior b Swann	54
L. M. Davis c Swann b Broad	0	– (1) lbw b Finn	43
M. R. Swart c Collingwood b Broad	0	– lbw b Finn	30
*M. J. North b Broad	19	– run out	1
A. C. Voges run out	72	– c Prior b Broad	1
L. A. Pomersbach c Prior b Anderson	21	– c Collingwood b Swann	21
†L. Ronchi c Anderson b Finn	32	– c and b Swann	27
S. J. Magoffin not out	17	– (10) not out	13
R. Duffield c Prior b Swann	3	– (8) c Prior b Broad	0
M. A. Beer not out	2	– (9) c Cook b Swann	5
M. G. Hogan (did not bat)		– run out	21
L-b 12, n-b 2	14	L-b 5, n-b 2	7

1/0 (2) 2/0 (3) 3/42 (4)   (8 wkts dec, 82 overs) 242   1/77 (1) 2/130 (3)   (69.5 overs) 223
4/129 (1) 5/183 (6)   3/134 (2) 4/135 (4)
6/187 (5) 7/225 (7) 8/230 (9)   5/142 (5) 6/164 (6) 7/177 (8)
                                                         8/185 (7) 9/194 (9) 10/223 (11)

Anderson 22–6–48–1; Broad 18–5–47–3; Finn 19–3–65–1; Swann 20–4–60–1; Collingwood 3–0–10–1. *Second Innings*—Anderson 11–3–37–0; Broad 12–2–26–2; Swann 28.5–4–101–4; Finn 15–3–50–2; Collingwood 3–2–4–0.

England XI

*A. J. Strauss c Ronchi b Magoffin	14	– not out	120
A. N. Cook b Magoffin	5	– b Hogan	9
J. M. Anderson c Pomersbach b Duffield	4		
I. J. L. Trott c Ronchi b Beer	24	– (3) c Ronchi b Pomersbach	23
K. P. Pietersen b North b Hogan	58	– (4) lbw b Beer	35
P. D. Collingwood c North b Hogan	4	– (5) c and b Beer	26
I. R. Bell c Pomersbach b Beer	21	– (6) not out	22
†M. J. Prior c Voges b Beer	0		
S. C. J. Broad not out	53		
G. P. Swann not out	37		
W 2, n-b 1	3	B 4, l-b 2, w 2	8

1/8 (2) 2/19 (1) 3/27 (3)   (8 wkts dec, 62 overs) 223   1/11 (2)   (4 wkts, 47.4 overs) 243
4/88 (4) 5/101 (6) 6/116 (5)   2/76 (3) 3/142 (4)
7/117 (8) 8/159 (7)   4/196 (5)

S. T. Finn did not bat.

Duffield 17–3–57–1; Magoffin 5.4–2–12–2; Hogan 13.2–6–36–2; Beer 24–4–108–3; Pomersbach 2–0–10–0. *Second Innings*—Hogan 12–3–37–1; Duffield 10–0–52–0; Beer 16.4–0–99–2; Pomersbach 4–1–15–1; Swart 5–0–34–0.

Umpires: I. H. Lock and J. D. Ward.   Referee: R. J. Evans.

SOUTH AUSTRALIA v ENGLAND XI

At Adelaide, November 11–13, 2010. Drawn. Toss: England XI. First-class debut: T. E. Lang.

The value of this warm-up was reduced by it being contested almost throughout under floodlights and cloud, which turned to drizzle and wiped out the penultimate session after the state had been set 308 from 65 overs; and by the home side again losing one of their pace bowlers, this time Haberfield. The only other unsatisfactory note for England was that they did not compile a big first innings, Trott and Pietersen both bounced out on the sluggish surface. Thereafter England played excellently: first through Collingwood, on his return to the scene of his 2006-07 double-century, and Bell. Then Anderson swung the ball under the cloud, and Swann pitched a fuller length than at Perth, though again without any favours from the umpires. While making his second hundred of the tour, with four sixes, Strauss rather knocked the stuffing out of George, who had made his Test debut in India the previous month. Cook found his feet and some fluency, before accelerating to his hundred against sloggable spin and the medium-pace of a 29-year-old debutant, Tim Lang.

Close of play: First day, South Australia 26-0 (Smith 16, Harris 10); Second day, England XI 94-0 (Strauss 56, Cook 37).

England XI

*A. J. Strauss c Manou b George	4	– b O'Brien	102	
A. N. Cook c Manou b George	32	– not out	111	
I. J. L. Trott c and b George	12	– not out	20	
K. P. Pietersen c Blizzard b Edmondson	33			
P. D. Collingwood c Ferguson b Haberfield	94			
I. R. Bell b Edmondson	61			
†M. J. Prior not out	22			
S. C. J. Broad c Smith b O'Brien	1			
G. P. Swann c Edmondson b O'Brien	25			
L-b 4	4	L-b 1, w 1, n-b 5	7	

1/12 (1) 2/30 (3)   (8 wkts dec, 78.3 overs)   288   1/181 (1)   (1 wkt dec, 52 overs)   240
3/63 (2) 4/95 (4) 5/226 (5)
6/255 (6) 7/256 (8) 8/288 (9)

J. M. Anderson and S. T. Finn did not bat.

George 17–4–65–3; Edmondson 21–4–73–2; Lang 14–5–39–0; Haberfield 15–0–67–1; O'Brien 11.3–3–40–2. *Second Innings*—George 12–1–50–0; Edmondson 12–2–34–0; Haberfield 0.4–0–4–0; Lang 13.2–0–78–0; O'Brien 13–1–72–1; Harris 1–0–1–0.

South Australia

J. D. Smith c Prior b Broad	23	– (2) c Collingwood b Anderson	9	
D. J. Harris c Trott b Anderson	10	– (1) not out	18	
*M. Klinger c Pietersen b Anderson	38	– c Trott b Anderson	8	
C. J. Ferguson c Broad b Finn	35	– not out	11	
A. C. Blizzard c Anderson b Swann	49			
†G. A. Manou c Strauss b Anderson	0			
A. W. O'Brien not out	43			
T. E. Lang c Pietersen b Swann	8			
J. A. Haberfield b Finn	0			
B. M. Edmondson lbw b Swann	4			
P. R. George st Prior b Swann	4			
L-b 3, w 1, n-b 3	7	W 1, n-b 1	2	

1/34 (1) 2/34 (2) 3/79 (4)   (67.4 overs)   221   1/19 (2)   (2 wkts, 20.5 overs)   48
4/136 (3) 5/140 (6) 6/164 (5)   2/28 (3)
7/176 (8) 8/176 (9) 9/205 (10) 10/221 (11)

Anderson 17–3–62–3; Broad 13–2–41–1; Finn 15–4–47–2; Swann 22.4–4–68–4. *Second Innings*—Anderson 8–2–23–2; Broad 6–1–13–0; Finn 4–1–11–0; Collingwood 2.5–2–1–0.

Umpires: S. D. Fry and B. N. J. Oxenford.   Referee: R. W. Stratford.

AUSTRALIA A v ENGLAND XI

At Hobart, November 17–20, 2010. England XI won by ten wickets. Toss: England XI.

"Flawless display for Poms" was the local newspaper's summary of England's performance in a fixture which used to be a contest between well-matched sides. After the Adelaide warm-up, Strauss had called on his players to "ramp up" another level, and they did – even their reserve attack, on their first tour outing, while the first-choice bowlers flew to Brisbane on the opening day of this game to acclimatise. The only real blemishes were a dropped slip catch by Collingwood off a top-edged cut by Hughes at Panesar, and Tremlett's seven no-balls: none of the other bowlers delivered a wide or no-ball. England had the fortune to bowl first when the rye-grassed pitch was damp and lively: Khawaja and Ferguson had been named in Australia's 17-man squad for the First Test, but did nothing to overtake Mike Hussey, who was making a century against Victoria. After Trott had been bounced out and Pietersen had missed a straight ball from O'Keefe, a left-arm spinner, Bell and Collingwood put on 240 in even time. Bell, after an early dab past gully, was superlative in strokeplay and placement. Smith's first six-over spell cost 41, but he did make the cut from Australia's 17 to 13. England's disciplined attack dismissed Australia A by tea on the last day in spite of a rugged hundred by White. Panesar persevered into the wind while the three pace bowlers were all impressive downwind.

Close of play: First day, England XI 22-1 (Cook 10, Panesar 2); Second day, England XI 335-5 (Collingwood 74, Bell 121); Third day, Australia A 128-3 (Hughes 58, White 22).

Australia A

P. J. Hughes c Strauss b Tremlett	2	– (2) c Strauss b Tremlett 81
E. J. M. Cowan c Panesar b Bresnan	31	– (1) b Bresnan 33
U. T. Khawaja c Prior b Shahzad	13	– c Prior b Bresnan 0
C. J. Ferguson c Prior b Bresnan	7	– b Bresnan 10
*C. L. White b Tremlett	5	– c Prior b Panesar 111
†T. D. Paine c Prior b Tremlett	27	– lbw b Tremlett 2
S. P. D. Smith b Shahzad	59	– b Tremlett......................... 0
S. N. J. O'Keefe c Prior b Tremlett	66	– c Pietersen b Panesar 27
C. J. McKay c Cook b Shahzad	0	– not out 19
M. A. Cameron c Collingwood	9	– lbw b Panesar...................... 0
P. R. George not out	0	– c Tremlett b Bresnan 4
B 3, l-b 1, n-b 7	11	B 1, l-b 12, n-b 1 14

1/4 (1) 2/41 (3) 3/48 (4) 4/58 (2) (80.1 overs) 230
5/66 (5) 6/118 (6) 7/177 (7)
8/179 (9) 9/224 (10) 10/230 (8)

1/66 (1) 2/66 (3) (97 overs) 301
3/84 (4) 4/185 (2)
5/191 (6) 6/191 (7) 7/269 (8)
8/276 (5) 9/276 (10) 10/301 (11)

Tremlett 17.1–3–54–4; Shahzad 21–6–57–3; Bresnan 19–3–65–2; Collingwood 3–1–2–1; Panesar 20–3–48–0. *Second Innings*—Tremlett 24–5–67–3; Shahzad 19–2–69–0; Panesar 28–4–63–3; Bresnan 22–3–86–4; Collingwood 4–1–3–0.

England XI

*A. J. Strauss c O'Keefe b Cameron	10	– not out 9
A. N. Cook c McKay b O'Keefe	60	– not out 2
M. S. Panesar c Cameron b McKay	13	
I. J. L. Trott c Khawaja b Cameron	41	
K. P. Pietersen b O'Keefe	5	
P. D. Collingwood c Paine b McKay	89	
I. R. Bell c Cowan b Smith	192	
†M. J. Prior c Hughes b Smith	27	
T. T. Bresnan lbw b O'Keefe	36	
A. Shahzad not out	18	
C. T. Tremlett c McKay b O'Keefe	16	
L-b 1, w 7, n-b 8	16	

1/20 (1) 2/37 (3) 3/124 (2) (141 overs) 523
4/127 (4) 5/137 (5) 6/377 (6)
7/407 (8) 8/487 (7) 9/493 (9) 10/523 (11)

(no wkt, 1.3 overs) 11

Cameron 28–3–108–2; George 33–6–135–0; McKay 29–8–73–2; O'Keefe 24–3–88–4; Smith 27–3–118–2. *Second Innings*—Cameron 1–0–6–0; George 0.3–0–5–0.

Umpires: S. D. Fry and P. R. Reiffel.   Third umpire: G. C. Joshua.
Referee: R. W. Stratford.

AUSTRALIA v ENGLAND

First Test Match

ROBERT CRADDOCK

At Brisbane, November 25–29, 2010. Drawn. Toss: England. Test debut: X. J. Doherty.

Visiting teams arrive at the famous Gabba ground via the provocatively titled Vulture Street entrance – but, for once, the vultures never landed. Australia's proud record of not being beaten at Brisbane since 1988-89 remained unbroken, but a draw felt like a loss considering their position of absolute superiority after a Peter Siddle hat-trick and a first-innings lead of 221.

The match will always be remembered for the starkness of England's history-defying second innings: 517 for one, including Alastair Cook's epic 235 not out – which completely mocked the ground's reputation as a fast bowler's haven, symbolised by its nickname the Gabbatoir. In that extraordinary run-feast, Strauss and Trott also made centuries, with Cook and Trott adding 329 to complete an innings of utter humiliation for Australia, whose pacemen bowled 98 wicketless overs between them.

With Brisbane receiving near-record rainfall in the month preceding the Test, the pitch lacked hardness and was one of the slowest seen at the Gabba for decades. Both teams played the game conservatively. The headline writer who called it a chess match not a bullfight got it right. The match was like the first round of one of those boxing bouts where both opponents throw occasional jabs but the big priority is avoiding the knockout punch.

England were aware that visiting teams had often contributed to their demise on bouncy Australian pitches, so they resolved to let as many balls go outside off as they could. Some bowlers suffered more than others, with Johnson finding the baited hooks he angled across the right-handers' bodies could not get a bite. To compound Australia's embarrassment, the only wicket in England's second innings went to a part-timer, North.

Cook's innings was the highest Test score by any batsman at the Gabba – beating Sir Donald Bradman's 226 against South Africa in the first match played there, in 1931-32 – and the first double-century by a visiting Test batsman. Cook's effort was the highlight of England's performance, and summed up the professionalism of a side which bowled just one no-ball in the match. He batted for over 15 hours in all, the equivalent of two and a half days' play, including more than ten hours in his masterful second innings.

"I'm not great on cricketing history, but you'd be hard pressed to think of a better innings in Australia," said Strauss of Cook's performance. "It must be a long time ago that a player batted as well as Cooky did, with the concentration to see it through for such a long time. It's one of the really special innings from an England player."

On the previous Ashes tour in 2006-07, Australia's wicketkeeper Adam Gilchrist caught Cook six times, as he had more nibbles than a greedy man at an all-you-can-eat buffet. Not this time, though. His front foot was firm and well forward, his bat straight and his judgment almost perfect.

It was a match of records, run-harvests and, for Australia, revealing insights into their shortcomings, after they surged forward with rattling sabres on the third day only to end the match feeling exhausted and exposed. There were all sorts of quirky landmarks. It was only the sixth time in Test history that a team had gone past the 500 mark for the loss of only one wicket; the first time five centuries had been scored in a match at the Gabba; and the average runs per wicket of 62.04 was – by more than 14 runs – the highest in any of the 53 Tests there. Fittingly, Cook and Strauss, during their second-innings stand of 188, eclipsed Jack Hobbs and Herbert Sutcliffe (3,249 runs opening together) as England's most productive first-wicket pair.

Ashes history is littered with extraordinary opening days which shaped the series, and several times the pivotal moment came as early as the first ball, as was the case four years previously, with Steve Harmison's infamous shocker to Andrew Flintoff at second slip.

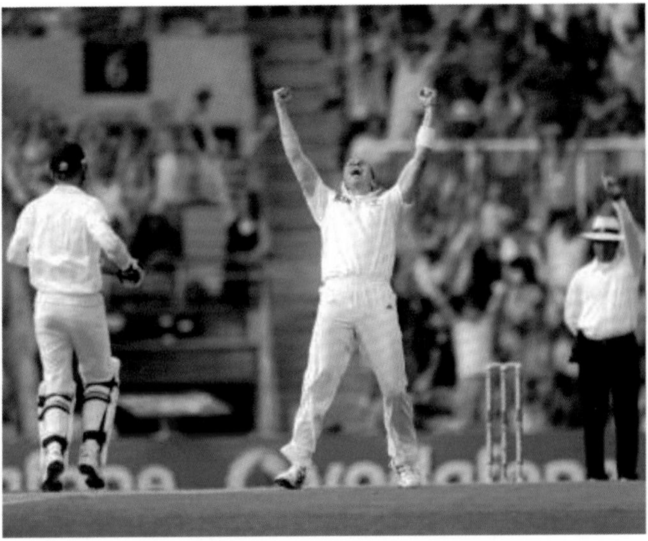

Graham Morris

RUNNING THEM RAGGED: Peter Siddle savours his first-day hat-trick as Australia seize the initiative at Brisbane. But Alastair Cook and Jonathan Trott wrest back control for England.

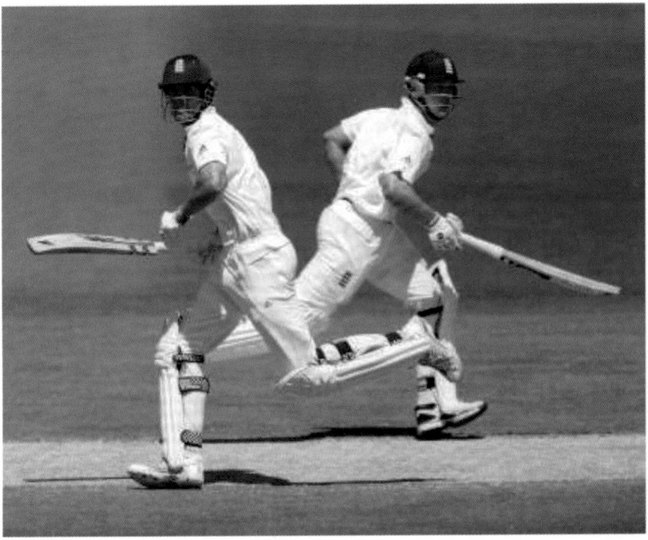

Graham Morris

DANCING TO HIS TUNE: At Adelaide, Kevin Pietersen discomfits Ricky Ponting with the bat, and then removes Michael Clarke with the last ball of the fourth day – thanks to a smart catch by Alastair Cook.

Gareth Copley, PA Photos

Philip Brown

Philip Brown

DARK DAYS FOR AUSTRALIAN CRICKET: A couple of hours after England win the Second Test, the Adelaide skies show their anger.

Hamish Blair, Getty Images

FLIGHT OR FIGHT? Paul Collingwood pulls off an outrageous catch to dismiss Ricky Ponting in the Third Test, at Perth, but Mitchell Johnson tore through England to level the series.

Patrick Eagar

Hamish Blair, Getty Images

Graham Morris

THE POINT OF NO RETURN: Ben Hilfenhaus lies prone while Alastair Cook jogs another during the Fourth Test. And when Hilfenhaus edges behind to Prior, England have retained the Ashes.

Gareth Copley, PA Photos

THE HALLMARK OF THE SERIES (1): Alastair Cook on the offensive.

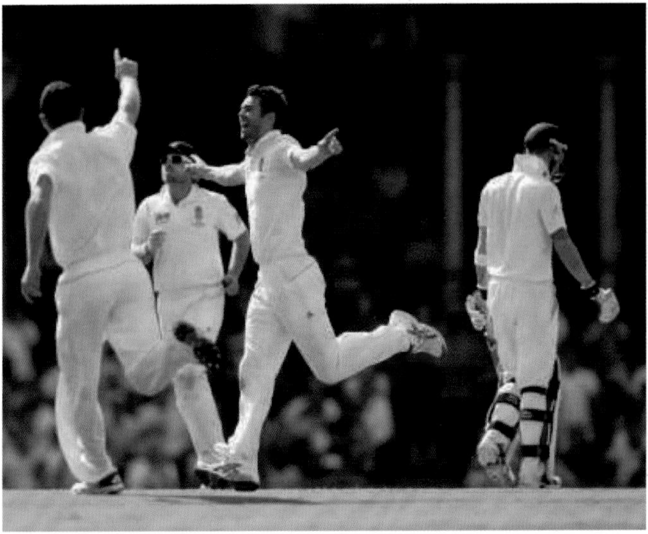

Graham Morris

THE HALLMARK OF THE SERIES (2 AND 3): James Anderson celebrates the dismissal of another Australian batsman – this time stand-in captain Michael Clarke at Sydney, before England achieve a third innings victory to take the series 3–1.

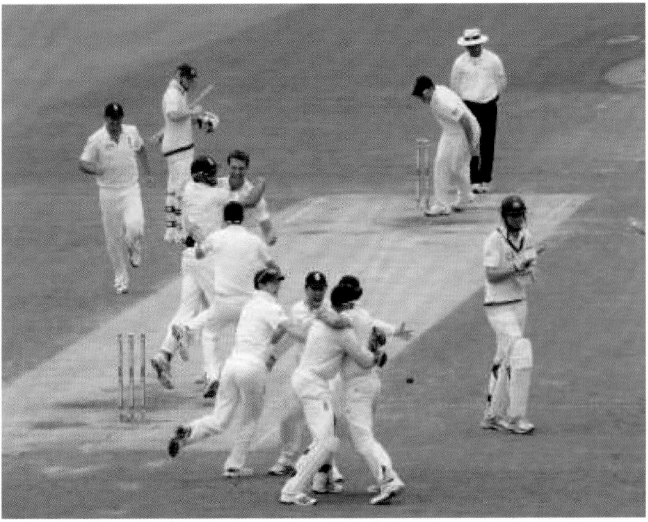

Philip Brown

MISSION ACCOMPLISHED... The victorious England squad after the Fifth Test. Standing: Steve Finn, Chris Tremlett, Kevin Pietersen, Monty Panesar, Eoin Morgan, Ajmal Shahzad, Steve Davies. Crouching: Graeme Swann, Tim Bresnan, Matt Prior, Paul Collingwood, Andrew Strauss, Jonathan Trott, Ian Bell, Alastair Cook, James Anderson.

Patrick Eagar

Australia sensed their fist-through-the-wall moment might have arrived with the third ball of the match when Strauss – his mind perhaps cluttered after all the opening ceremonies – cut too close to his body and was caught by Hussey in the gully. It was the earliest dismissal in any Ashes series since 1936-37, when England's Stan Worthington fell to Ernie McCormick's first ball at Brisbane.

The Australians smelt blood again later on the first day when, after England had been nursed by Cook to 197, Siddle, who comes from a family of axemen, chopped through the middle order and captured a hat-trick. Cook edged to slip, Prior airily missed a full-pitched ball and was bowled, and Broad – who seemed not to have been fully dressed and ready to bat – was hit on the boot and palpably lbw even though he appealed against the decision.

Siddle – something of a surprise inclusion ahead of Doug Bollinger – was the ninth Australian to register a Test hat-trick (Hugh Trumble and Jimmy Matthews managed two each), and his achievement electrified the Gabba after a slow middle session on the first day. England were mowed down for 260, despite the wicketless Johnson sliding deeper into a form slump that would cost him his place for the next Test. Bell managed to ignore the mayhem at the other end to make a serene 76, which confirmed the strong body of opinion that the relatively timid youngster who first confronted Australia in 2005 had grown up as a man and a player.

When Australia were 143 for five, including a brilliant, low caught-and-bowled by Finn, England had visions of a first-innings lead – but Hussey and Haddin provided the nerve-settler, becoming only the fifth pair in Test history to share a sixth-wicket stand of more than 300. Hussey had been thought to be one failure away from losing his place before a century against Victoria just before the team was selected saved his hide. From being the man who looked likely not to get in the side, he soon became the man England could not get out. His early gift to Australia was to rock his former Northamptonshire team-mate Swann with a blistering early assault which looked premeditated, though Hussey denied it. Even so, Swann's first four overs of the series – spread over three spells – cost 34 confidence-denting runs.

BRISBANE NOTES AND QUOTES

Graeme Swann's Ashes video diary for the ECB website, in its third instalment before the Test, unveiled England's "Sprinkler" celebration dance. There was no immediate call for it at the Gabba, but plenty afterwards.

A chastening explanation emerged for Andy Flower's absence on the second and third days. The England coach heeded advice from the team's security adviser Reg Dickason to have a growth on his cheek looked at, and surgery swiftly followed on a cancerous melanoma. Flower returned for the end of the Test, with a reassuring prognosis.

"SID VICIOUS SMASHES POMS" – The *Herald Sun* in Melbourne wasted little time delivering some early triumphalism, after the first-day hat-trick by Victoria's Peter Siddle.

Movember – a charity in aid of prostate cancer research – was responsible for a clutch of unsightly moustaches at the Gabba, notably on the upper lips of Mitchell Johnson and Kevin Pietersen. Johnson was probably delighted to shave his off, after his miserable Test with ball and bat. Pietersen's was gone, too, by the time the teams arrived in Adelaide.

The "Earl of Twirl" made his series debut. Channel 9 viewers had to guess the identity of the first masked "mystery" spinner in the Gabba nets: either (a) Greg Matthews (b) Tim May or (c) Michael Vaughan. Given the Earl's build, several inches taller than Matthews and even more pounds lighter than May, Vaughan was a pretty safe bet.

When Kevin Pietersen came in to bat, a home-made banner proclaimed "Just another Kevin to get rid of". It referred to Australia's former prime minister Kevin Rudd, who was forced to stand down earlier in the year, and whose constituency included the Gabba ground. When KP got out, his name was replaced on the banner by "Cook".

All Notes and Quotes compiled by David Clough

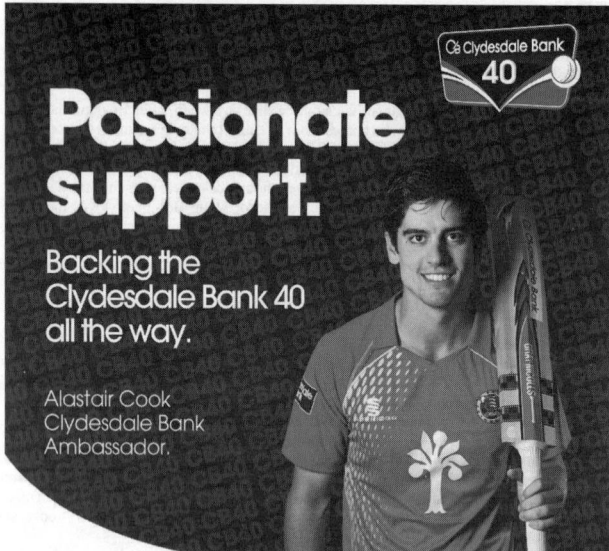

We're totally committed to cricket and proud to be sponsoring the Clydesdale Bank 40. Having already established itself as one of the highlights of domestic cricket, 2011's competition promises even more thrilling action.

We're delighted to play our part in developing UK cricket, and look forward to another incredible season. We hope you'll join us.

www.cbonline.co.uk www.ybonline.co.uk

Clydesdale Bank | always thinking | Yorkshire Bank

Philip Brown

In no mood to go quietly: Mike Hussey, written off by some, scores his third Ashes hundred.

When Haddin was on 77, Richie Benaud declared it the greatest innings he had played for his country, and he bounded from 94 to 100 with a straight six off Swann. Anderson bowled arguably the best spell of his career on the third morning – surely the best wicketless one – but Hussey and Haddin somehow absorbed it. England's best card seemed to have been slapped on the table. The game looked gone.

But the docile pitch beat everyone in the end. It yielded ten wickets on the first day then five, five, one and one over the next four. After Strauss had declared on the fifth afternoon, Australia's 107 for one off 26 overs was a spirit-lifter for a side who were given enough time to conclude that the track was indeed as flat as they thought it was when they were bowling. Nevertheless, Australia knew when they left the Gabba that the British bulldog had come to fight.

Man of the Match: A. N. Cook.   *Attendance:* 132,858.

Close of play: First day, Australia 25-0 (Watson 9, Katich 15); Second day, Australia 220-5 (Hussey 81, Haddin 22); Third day, England 19-0 (Strauss 11, Cook 6); Fourth day, England 309-1 (Cook 132, Trott 54).

England

*A. J. Strauss c Hussey b Hilfenhaus	0	– st Haddin b North ... 110
A. N. Cook c Watson b Siddle	67	– not out ... 235
I. J. L. Trott b Watson	29	– not out ... 135
K. P. Pietersen c Ponting b Siddle	43	
P. D. Collingwood c North b Siddle	4	
I. R. Bell c Watson b Doherty	76	
†M. J. Prior b Siddle	0	
S. C. J. Broad lbw b Siddle	0	
G. P. Swann lbw b Siddle	10	
J. M. Anderson b Doherty	11	
S. T. Finn not out	0	
L-b 8, w 7, n-b 5	20	B 17, l-b 4, w 10, n-b 6 ... 37
	260	**517**

1/0 (1) 2/41 (3) 3/117 (4)   (76.5 overs) 260   1/188 (1)   (1 wkt dec, 152 overs) 517
4/125 (5) 5/197 (2) 6/197 (7) 7/197 (8)
8/228 (9) 9/254 (6) 10/260 (10)

Hilfenhaus 19–4–60–1; Siddle 16–3–54–6; Johnson 15–2–66–0; Watson 12–2–30–1; Doherty 13.5–3–41–2; North 1–0–1–0. *Second Innings*—Hilfenhaus 32–8–82–0; Siddle 24–4–90–0; North 19–3–47–1; Johnson 27–5–104–0; Doherty 35–5–107–0; Watson 15–2–66–0.

Australia

S. R. Watson c Strauss b Anderson	36	– not out		41
S. M. Katich c and b Finn	50	– c Strauss b Broad		4
*R. T. Ponting c Prior b Anderson	10	– not out		51
M. J. Clarke c Prior b Finn	9			
M. E. K. Hussey c Cook b Finn	195			
M. J. North c Collingwood b Swann	1			
†B. J. Haddin c Collingwood b Swann	136			
M. G. Johnson b Finn	0			
X. J. Doherty c Cook b Finn	16			
P. M. Siddle c Swann b Finn	6			
B. W. Hilfenhaus not out	1			
B 4, l-b 12, w 4, n-b 1	21	B 4, l-b 1, w 1, p 5		11

1/78 (1) 2/96 (3) 3/100 (2)   (158.4 overs) 481   1/5 (2)   (1 wkt, 26 overs) 107
4/140 (4) 5/143 (6) 6/450 (7)
7/458 (5) 8/462 (8) 9/472 (10) 10/481 (9)

Anderson 37–13–99–2; Broad 33–7–72–0; Swann 43–5–128–2; Finn 33.4–1–125–6; Collingwood 12–1–41–0. *Second Innings*—Anderson 5–2–15–0; Broad 7–1–18–1; Swann 8–0–33–0; Finn 4–0–25–0; Pietersen 2–0–6–0.

Umpires: Aleem Dar and B. R. Doctrove.   Third umpire: A. L. Hill.
Referee: J. J. Crowe.

AUSTRALIA v ENGLAND

Second Test Match

MATTHEW ENGEL

At Adelaide, December 3–7, 2010. England won by an innings and 71 runs. Toss: Australia.

No follower of English cricket, inured to dismal news from Australia by many years' experience, would have been surprised by the revelation that the final day of the Adelaide Test – which began with England in a commanding position – turned out to be the city's wettest December day on record. The surprise was that the rain did not start until two hours after England had wrapped up the match and taken a 1–0 lead in the series. By the time it began raining – not just cats and dogs but kangaroos, possums, wombats and all – Andrew Strauss and his team were in full celebratory mode.

If the gods smiled on them on this occasion, then they may consider that a reward for a display of all the cricketing virtues. As the vanquished captain, Ricky Ponting, admitted: "They outbowled us, they outbatted us, they outfielded us the entire game." In terms of the big picture, England seized control in the first over and never relinquished it – Australia were nought for two after five balls and two for three after 13, and never discovered any equilibrium. This was even more one-sided than the massacre they had themselves inflicted at Headingley in 2009.

England were the masters in every aspect of the game, from planning to execution of the smaller details. Australia's fallibility showed even in their running between the wickets

One amazing thing… Jonathan Trott's deft pick-up-and-throw runs out Simon Katich for a duck.

(there were two needless run-outs). In the field, where England were near-flawless, there was a moment when Ponting and North let a catch offered by Prior fall harmlessly to earth between them – precisely the sort of incompetence Australian crowds associate with England teams of the past two decades. And this was merely the most extreme example.

The upshot was England's first innings win over Australia since the Ashes-clinching victory at Melbourne in December 1986; their first win in any Test in Australia since then with the Ashes still at stake; and Australia's first innings defeat against any team in 101 home Tests since February 1993.

In the 17 Adelaide Tests before this one, Australia's first-innings score had never fallen below 350, with an average total of 476. The first Test pitch prepared by the Adelaide Oval's new curator, Damian Hough, was very much in the tradition established by his long-serving predecessor Les Burdett, offering nothing but blood, toil, tears and sweat to the team forced to field first – especially as the temperature on the first two days was also in the Adelaide tradition: above 35°C. Australia were bowled out for 245. There was an overwhelming sense of an era ending.

England came into the match unchanged, their morale sky-high after their match-saving effort at Brisbane. Australia reshuffled their disheartened attack, recalling Bollinger and Harris for Johnson and Hilfenhaus. Nonetheless, this was a toss Strauss was displeased to lose – but only for a moment. Off the fourth ball of the game, Watson called (or, as he admitted later, mumbled) for a quick single; Trott brilliantly hit the stumps from square-on; and Katich was out for what some Australians call a diamond duck – without facing. Next ball Anderson induced the edge, Swann took a terrific low slip catch, and Ponting – in his 150th Test – was gone for what everyone knows as a golden duck. Then Clarke drove loosely at the first ball of Anderson's second over, Swann again took the catch, and the English contingent was close to delirium.

Hussey and a repentant Watson calmed things down until after lunch. But another good low catch did for Watson; and North, having got himself in, played a strange late flick of a shot against Finn. It was in keeping with Australia's day that Hussey fell seven runs short of his third successive Ashes century. Swann, getting a little first-day turn, took out Harris next ball, and Australia's underpowered tail duly folded. The first-day crowd, 38,615, was the biggest on any day's Test cricket on this ground since 1954-55, a statistic made possible by the huge new stand. It would be tempting to say most spectators watched in horror. But the Adelaide Test is a great local social occasion and, as the day wore on, a lot of them opted for socialising out the back instead of spectating.

Strauss gave them some encouragement to watch next morning when he was bowled, not offering, to the third ball. It was only a tease. As a pairing, Trott and Cook may not sound as obviously euphonious as Compton and Edrich or Fortnum and Mason. But Australia feared they might be bracketed together for ever: they just carried on where they left off in Brisbane. Trott, once again, was implacably determined. Cook was sublime, not in the way a great strokeplayer is sublime (although one square cut off Siddle would have

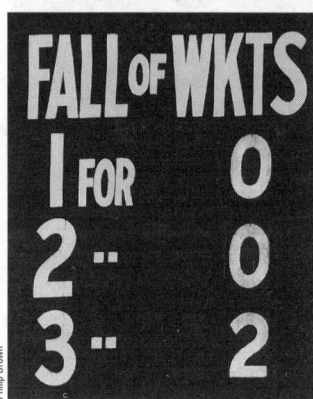

Philip Brown

… leads to another: after 13 balls, Australia are three down for two runs.

done credit to David Gower), but in the utter certainty of his method. Batsmanship is meant to be a tightrope walk, in which one small error means a plunge into the abyss. He turned it into a stroll into the park. Australia's attack hurled themselves unavailingly against these immovable objects. Harris finally had Trott (almost run out when six, and dropped on ten and 76) caught at mid-wicket for a mere 78. Their stand – combining the two Tests – had yielded 502 runs. But that only brought Pietersen to the crease.

His strut to the wicket had an unmistakable purpose: Ponting would probably have bought him out for 100 then and there, and it would have been a bargain. After 21 months without a Test century, Pietersen was awesome: he never compromised his instinct for aggression, but his judgment lost its fallibility. There was a moment on the second afternoon when the situation was summed up by the expression on the face of poor Xavier Doherty, his limitations as Shane Warne's latest successor now brutally exposed. "I've spent my life dreaming about playing for Australia," he seemed to be saying. "What on earth?"

Cook went next day for 148, having taken his average for the series to 50… if he made seven consecutive noughts from then on. Pietersen went on and on. Until this tour, only one England batsman had made an Ashes double-century in Australia since the war. Now England had hit two in a week. But tauntingly the first rain of the match came just when the total reached 551, precisely the score at which Flintoff made his ill-starred declaration after the one previous post-war visit 200: by Collingwood on this ground four years earlier.

The score stayed that way overnight, tempting Strauss to accept fate and declare. Instead, he batted on next morning (with Bell now looking in exquisite form) until the total reached 620 and the lead 375. Now, however, Australia's batsmen dug in. Katich – battling the Achilles injury that would knock him out of the series – and Watson on 84 this time. And, though Ponting failed again, Hussey and Clarke, showing more of his usual elan, steered Australia through another rain-interrupted afternoon to see them into the final over of the day. England's attack was also starting to look ragged – Broad went off the field with the abdominal injury which would see him pulled out of the tour next day – and Strauss was forced to bowl the part-timer Pietersen. But when you're hot, you're hot. Pietersen's bounce surprised Clarke into offering a catch to short leg and, after a referral, he was gone for 80.

That transformed the fifth-morning mood. Australia seemed fatalistic, proving the point when the staunch Hussey got out to a crazed hoick to mid-on. The rest went quietly to

ADELAIDE NOTES AND QUOTES

"PATHETIC!!!!!!!!!!!!" – Kevin Pietersen was a little touchy too, venting his frustration on Twitter at groundstaff he thought too slow to cover the nets before a downpour (they had, not unreasonably, covered the main square first). He missed his outdoor practice two days before the Test, but showed no ill effects when it mattered.

Ryan Harris was out first ball in both innings, becoming only the second man known to have bagged a king pair in an Ashes Test, after Dick Attewell of England at Sydney in 1891-92. Harris unsuccessfully called for a review both times: Gideon Haigh observed that he "thereby completed the surely unique experience of being given out four times in two deliveries". By the end of this Test, neither side's No. 8s had scored a run in the series.

"Within two or three balls of my spell, I knew I was in big trouble… I got through a few overs, but it felt like someone stabbing me in the stomach. I put a couple of bouncers in and I could hardly breathe. I knew my tour was over." Even as England were closing in on their innings victory, Stuart Broad was coming to terms with his injury.

James Anderson had to keep his post-match celebrations low-key, in preparation for a flight back to England. He was granted permission to return home for the birth of his second daughter, and had just enough time to complete the trip before the Third Test.

Relations between former Test captains Ian Botham and Ian Chappell had been sour for more than 30 years, but they apparently hit a new low on the fourth day in the Adelaide Oval car park. The pair denied reports claiming punches were landed before they had to be pulled apart. That did not stop another ex-Australian batsman, Damien Martyn, calling mischievously for a charity boxing match between the heavyweight pair.

The Age in Melbourne plastered a black-bordered cricket picture over its front page after the match and, reprising a famous quote from Bill Woodfull, Australia's captain during the Adelaide Test in the 1932-33 Bodyline series, captioned it "There are two teams out there. Only one of them is playing cricket." Underneath, in smaller print, they added "Unfortunately this time it's England."

Anderson and Swann, bowling beautifully. The Barmy Army were not quiet in the least. Nor was the afternoon's storm. But by then Australia were beyond even divine help.

Man of the Match: K. P. Pietersen.   *Attendance:* 134,658.

Close of play: First day, England 1-0 (Strauss 0, Cook 0); Second day, England 317-2 (Cook 136, Pietersen 85); Third day, England 551-4 (Pietersen 213, Bell 41); Fourth day, Australia 238-4 (Hussey 44).

Australia

S. R. Watson c Pietersen b Anderson	51	– c Strauss b Finn	57
S. M. Katich run out	0	– c Prior b Swann	43
*R. T. Ponting c Swann b Anderson	0	– c Collingwood b Swann	9
M. J. Clarke c Swann b Anderson	2	– c Cook b Pietersen	80
M. E. K. Hussey c Collingwood b Swann	93	– c Anderson b Finn	52
M. J. North c Prior b Finn	26	– lbw b Swann	22
†B. J. Haddin c Finn b Broad	56	– c Prior b Anderson	12
R. J. Harris lbw b Swann	0	– lbw b Anderson	0
X. J. Doherty run out	6	– b Swann	5
P. M. Siddle c Cook b Anderson	3	– b Swann	6
D. E. Bollinger not out	0	– not out	7
L-b 6, w 1, n-b 1	8	B 5, l-b 1, w 5	11

1/0 (2)   2/0 (3)   3/2 (4)   4/96 (1)   (85.5 overs) 245
5/156 (6)   6/207 (5)   7/207 (8)
8/226 (9)   9/243 (10)   10/245 (7)

1/84 (2)   2/98 (3)   (99.1 overs) 304
3/134 (1)   4/238 (4)
5/261 (5)   6/286 (7)   7/286 (8)
8/286 (6)   9/295 (9)   10/304 (10)

Anderson 19–4–51–4; Broad 18.5–6–39–1; Finn 16–1–71–1; Swann 29–2–70–2; Collingwood 3–0–8–0. *Second Innings*—Anderson 22–4–92–2; Broad 11–3–32–0; Swann 41.1–12–91–5; Finn 18–2–60–2; Collingwood 4–0–13–0; Pietersen 3–0–10–1.

England

*A. J. Strauss b Bollinger	1	†M. J. Prior not out	27
A. N. Cook c Haddin b Harris	148	B 8, l-b 13, w 8	29
I. J. L. Trott c Clarke b Harris	78		—
K. P. Pietersen c Katich b Doherty	227	1/3 (1) 2/176 (3) (5 wkts dec, 152 overs)	620
P. D. Collingwood lbw b Watson	42	3/351 (2) 4/452 (5)	
I. R. Bell not out	68	5/568 (4)	

S. C. J. Broad, G. P. Swann, J. M. Anderson and S. T. Finn did not bat.

Harris 29–5–84–2; Bollinger 29–1–130–1; Siddle 30–3–121–0; Watson 19–7–44–1; Doherty 27–3–158–1; North 18–0–62–0.

Umpires: M. Erasmus and A. L. Hill.   Third umpire: B. R. Doctrove.
Referee: J. J. Crowe.

VICTORIA v ENGLAND XI

At Melbourne, December 10–12, 2010. Drawn. Toss: Victoria. First-class debuts: R. G. L. Carters, A. R. Keath.

A fixture dating back to January 1, 1862, ended in a draw, partly because it was not a four-day game as the inaugural fixture had been against XVIII of Victoria. Most of England's Test batsmen played – although not Pietersen, who had got himself a \$A239 speeding fine the day before this game, or Trott – along with their reserve bowling attack. Nobody could make a conclusive case for replacing the homebound Broad, but Tremlett stayed just ahead of the field by generating the little bounce that was to be had from a pudding of a pitch and bowling accurately. After sporting declarations by both sides by lunch on the second day, Victoria's batsmen had to be fed joke bowling – 81 runs from 32 balls, some donated by Morgan, who had his first bowl of the tour before his first innings – to set up a declaration target of 311 on the third day. Rain interrupted several times, and only Prior, who had kept wicket in Victoria's second innings after dropping two outfield catches in their first, made the most of his chance, reaching his hundred off 138 balls. Jayde Herrick, a well-built fast bowler making his debut for Victoria, was banned from bowling after two high full tosses at Prior. In the first innings Cook had asked the shaven-headed Herrick to remove a "distracting" black headband.

Close of play: First day, England XI 50-1 (Strauss 17, Bell 6); Second day, Victoria 278-6 (McKay 58, Herrick 40).

Victoria

R. G. L. Carters c Davies b Bresnan	16	– b Collingwood	68
M. W. Hill not out	105	– (7) lbw b Strauss	4
*C. L. White c Shahzad b Panesar	23		
D. J. Hussey not out	67		
A. J. Finch (did not bat)		– (2) c Bell b Panesar	45
A. R. Keath (did not bat)		– (3) c Prior b Collingwood	46
†M. S. Wade (did not bat)		– (4) c Cook b Collingwood	1
J. W. Hastings (did not bat)		– (5) c Collingwood b Panesar	7
C. J. McKay (did not bat)		– (6) not out	58
J. M. Herrick (did not bat)		– (8) not out	40
L-b 4, w 1	5	L-b 4, w 1, n-b 4	9

1/19 (1) 2/69 (3)	(2 wkts dec, 74 overs) 216	1/72 (2) (6 wkts dec, 60 overs) 278
		2/147 (1) 3/163 (4)
		4/174 (5) 5/176 (3) 6/197 (7)

J. M. Holland did not bat.

Tremlett 15–5–29–0; Shahzad 19–6–47–0; Bresnan 18–4–56–1; Panesar 15–1–53–1; Collingwood 7–3–27–0. *Second Innings*—Tremlett 9–1–28–0; Bresnan 10–2–28–0; Panesar 21–4–83–2; Shahzad 7–0–28–0; Collingwood 6–1–19–3; Strauss 4–0–51–1; Morgan 3–0–37–0.

England XI

*A. J. Strauss c Carters b Holland	66	– (8) not out	22
A. N. Cook c Wade b Holland	27	– b McKay	10
I. R. Bell not out	60	– (7) c Keath b McKay	17
P. D. Collingwood not out	29	– (3) lbw b Herrick	8
†S. M. Davies (did not bat)		– (1) c White b McKay	18
M. J. Prior (did not bat)		– (4) not out	102
E. J. G. Morgan (did not bat)		– (5) c Wade b Herrick	6
T. T. Bresnan (did not bat)		– (6) c Wade b McKay	19
W 1, n-b 1	2	B 1, l-b 5, w 1, n-b 2	9

1/39 (2) 2/131 (1)	(2 wkts dec, 45 overs)	184	1/15 (2)	(6 wkts, 54 overs) 211
			2/36 (3) 3/36 (1)	
			4/55 (5) 5/100 (6) 6/149 (7)	

A. Shahzad, C. T. Tremlett and M. S. Panesar did not bat.

McKay 10–4–24–0; Herrick 12–2–51–0; Holland 12–2–53–2; Hastings 8–0–42–0; White 3–0–14–0. *Second Innings*—McKay 17–4–68–4; Herrick 11.4–0–74–2; Hastings 8.2–3–26–0; Holland 10–2–22–0; White 6–0–14–0; Finch 1–0–1–0.

Umpires: G. C. Joshua and P. Wilson.   Referee: R. W. Stratford.

AUSTRALIA v ENGLAND

Third Test Match

Scyld Berry

At Perth, December 16–19, 2010. Australia won by 267 runs. Toss: England.

For the first, and only, time England departed from the game plan that otherwise served them so well on this tour. In their attempt to wrap up the Ashes before Christmas, as never before, they gave up their strategy of patience, discipline and plenty of spin, and tried to bomb out Australia with short balls and verbals. It was an outright failure. Australia went for all-out attack with a barrage of words and four fast bowlers, levelled the series at 1–1, and maintained the tradition of the WACA being England's least successful ground (they have won only one of 12 Tests there, and that in 1978-79, when Australia's best players were otherwise engaged in Kerry Packer's World Series Cricket).

England also ran into Mitchell Johnson at his best, as Australia's fast left-armer momentarily rediscovered his conventional swing and the tourists failed to react. Ponting was justified in claiming that, when Johnson turned the game on its head, it was "probably one of the great all-time Ashes spells".

Patrick Eagar

Back on track: Mitchell Johnson comes good – very good – at Perth, here castling Chris Tremlett.

On the second morning England had cruised untroubled to 78 without loss, and looked set for a total way beyond 200, a barrier which had often been insuperable for them at Perth. The ball was 24 overs old. The Australians, at Ponting's insistence, had left out their latest specialist spinner (the novice from nowhere, Michael Beer) and had hoped to bowl first, but instead they had been sent in and dismissed for a modest 268. England, as their opening partnership grew, could have been forgiven for entertaining the notion that they might avoid their sixth consecutive defeat at the WACA.

Then came Johnson, from the Gloucester Park End. He had not swung the ball in the First Test at Brisbane – indeed he had not swung more than the odd ball since the Durban Test almost two years before – and had been dropped for the Second in Adelaide. But in that interim he had worked on getting closer to the stumps, shortening his delivery stride, reaching higher with his front arm and keeping his left wrist behind the ball. In any event, his action clicked. He was also helped by a wind that blew from the east across the ground – and Johnson bowled not only with it but like it.

England's players admitted afterwards to being surprised when Johnson rediscovered his conventional swing. First, he moved one away from Cook just enough for him to thick-edge a drive to gully, then – much as Mohammed Aamer had done in the Lord's Test – he swung the ball into England's three right-handers for three lbws. Trott, driving, and Pietersen, whipping to leg, played shots that were inappropriate when England had to avoid losing wickets in a fatal cluster. Collingwood was, forgivably, startled when a ball swung back a long way from outside off stump; he was originally given not out, but had to go after Ponting asked for a review.

Johnson had taken four wickets for seven runs. As Harris – half as much of a bowler again with Johnson firing at the other end – had Strauss edging a ball angled across him, England collapsed to 98 for five. Australia's players and supporters were inflated with renewed belief; England, in less than an hour, went from buoyant to broken. But they had not given their 1–0 lead away. Johnson, principally, had seized it from them.

As normal with Johnson, his runs and wickets came together. After Australia had been justifiably sent in on a very grassy surface, and some hostile bowling from Tremlett for Broad's replacement, they had been reduced to 69 for five. Two of their form batsmen – Hussey, who with his local knowledge left the ball immaculately, and Haddin – resurrected Australia, before Johnson clubbed 62 from 93 balls and did not allow Swann to settle as he had in Adelaide. Australia, from 201 for eight, wriggled out of England's grasp. The Fremantle Doctor was conspicuously absent for most of the game, but it did blow after tea on the first day and England were slow to harness Swann with it as they had in the state game. They tried to blast out Australia's tailenders, and Hussey was right to claim their total was little short of par.

Johnson and Harris, on the second day, proceeded to show England exactly how to bowl at Perth: bouncers or full length, not in between. The bouncers ruffled most of England's batsmen, and made them reluctant to get forward when the follow-up ball was full. Bell had the technique to cope, but not enough scope to employ it with tailenders for company.

Watson and, for the second time, Hussey then showed England how to bat at the WACA. Both were masterly at leaving the ball or, if they played it, pulling or driving. Indeed, with their full strides, the right-hander and left-hander played some off-drives of perfection. They used vertical or horizontal bats, nothing in between, as several England batsmen and Clarke had done; and again Swann was not allowed to settle by Hussey's footwork. Still, Tremlett maintained his control – whereas Anderson had lost his Adelaide rhythm on the flight home to see his new baby – and England bowled out Australia twice for only the third time at Perth.

UNHAPPY HUNTING GROUNDS

Grounds where England have played at least five Tests and won no more than one of them:

		Tests	Won	Lost	Drawn
St John's	1981–2009	7	0	3	4
Perth	**1970–2010**	**12**	**1**	**8**	**3**
Georgetown	1930–1998	9	1	4	4
Calcutta	1934–1993	9	1	3	5
Lahore	1961–2005	8	1	2	5
Karachi	1962–2000	7	1	1	5
Kanpur	1952–1985	6	1	0	5

An unusual feature of this match, a consequence of the pitch regaining some of its famous bounce, was that one bowler from each side tried an over of Bodyline – short balls rather than outright bouncers – from round the wicket. After Siddle had done it to Prior, who was particularly uncomfortable against the short ball, Tremlett responded by doing the same to Smith – and getting him caught gloving down the leg side. Neither umpire – Erasmus, who had an excellent game, and Doctrove, most of whose decisions had to be reviewed – appeared to intervene.

As the pitch was a bit uneven, after the ball had dented the relatively thick grass on the first morning, England's target of 391 was fairly notional. Even so, their batting was poor – on a par with their collapses at Headingley in 2009 and Johannesburg earlier in the year – as Johnson barely swung the ball this time. Pietersen was angry when he waved with a bat at 45°, following his 227 with nought and three; as was Collingwood when he edged the last ball of the third day to third slip, after the nightwatchman Anderson, the non-striker, had misjudged the previous ball and turned down a single.

Five down overnight, England were ripped apart in less than an hour on the fourth day with the same combination of bouncer then full-length follow-up. Harris finished with six for 47, his Test-best. Of all their collapses at Perth – this was England's seventh total below 200 in their last six Tests there – it was the most startling, because they had been ahead in this series in every respect, until Johnson bounded in and routed them.

Ponting was unable to field on the fourth day, his 36th birthday, as he had broken the little finger of his left hand when palming a catch from Trott to the wicketkeeper. He also

PERTH NOTES AND QUOTES

After Michael Beer's shock inclusion in the squad for Perth, inventive Australian sub-editors decided the four-man selection panel deserved to have fried eggs superimposed on their faces. There was no such treatment for Shane Warne, who had played club cricket with the slow left-armer in Melbourne, even though he suggested that "Jason" Beer might be the answer for Australia at the WACA.

Beer's two immediate predecessors in the Test squad, Xavier Doherty and Nathan Hauritz, were also outspoken. "It looks to be a little bit of trial and error," said Doherty. Hauritz gave away some of his Test kit at an impromptu garage sale. "I don't play for them any more," he said.

The Australian firm Sportsbet.com.au paid out on all bets on an England series victory – a total of around $400,000 – just before England's first-innings collapse. "The writing is on the wall and we can't see the Aussies coming back from here," said a spokesman, who had an uncomfortable few days – until the Melbourne Test.

"I didn't offer to take him into the car park or fight him after the game. If I saw him right now I would go over and talk about cricket and have a beer with him." Matt Prior used his *Independent* column to set the record straight over reports about his demonstrative reaction after Peter Siddle dismissed him during a consistently fractious match at the WACA.

"How embarrassing. All those kids going through the ranks not being taught cricket's most fundamental skill, how to sledge Aussie-style… clearly the Test side has slipped to fourth on the world rankings below England and lost four Tests out of five without a victory for the first time in 26 years because the players haven't been noisy enough." *The Australian's* Malcolm Conn had an alternative take on the suggestion that a return to sledging powered the home side to their series-levelling win.

There was further disappointment for England's Graeme Swann after the match: he failed to win the BBC's Sports Personality of the Year award, for which he had been on the shortlist of ten. Jockey Tony McCoy won, ahead of darts player Phil Taylor and athlete Jessica Ennis.

---

failed in both innings, as at Adelaide, after being superlatively caught one-handed at third slip then getting the faintest touch with his glove down the leg side. But he had sold his formula – four pace bowlers hunting as a pack, while Watson concentrated on his batting – to his selectors, and had got Australia back into the series.

   Man of the Match: M. G. Johnson.   *Attendance:* 78,823.

   Close of play: First day, England 29-0 (Strauss 12, Cook 17); Second day, Australia 119-3 (Watson 61, Hussey 24); Third day, England 81-5 (Anderson 0).

Australia

S. R. Watson lbw b Finn	13	– lbw b Tremlett	95
P. J. Hughes b Tremlett	2	– c Collingwood b Finn	12
*R. T. Ponting c Collingwood b Anderson	12	– c Prior b Finn	1
M. J. Clarke c Prior b Tremlett	4	– b Tremlett	20
M. E. K. Hussey c Prior b Swann	61	– c Swann b Tremlett	116
S. P. D. Smith c Strauss b Tremlett	7	– c Prior b Tremlett	36
†B. J. Haddin c Swann b Anderson	53	– b Tremlett	7
M. G. Johnson c Anderson b Finn	62	– c Bell b Collingwood	1
R. J. Harris b Anderson	3	– c Bell b Finn	1
P. M. Siddle not out	35	– c Collingwood b Anderson	8
B. W. Hilfenhaus c Cook b Swann	13	– not out	0
L-b 3	3	L-b 6, w 4, n-b 2	12

1/2 (2) 2/17 (3) 3/28 (4) 4/36 (1)   (76 overs) 268
5/69 (6) 6/137 (5) 7/189 (7) 8/201 (9)
9/233 (8) 10/268 (11)

1/31 (2) 2/34 (3)   (86 overs) 309
3/64 (4) 4/177 (1)
5/252 (6) 6/271 (7) 7/276 (8)
8/284 (9) 9/308 (10) 10/309 (5)

Anderson 20–3–61–3; Tremlett 23–3–63–3; Finn 15–1–86–2; Collingwood 2–0–3–0; Swann 16–0–52–2. *Second Innings*—Anderson 26–7–65–1; Tremlett 24–4–87–5; Finn 21–4–97–3; Swann 9–0–51–0; Collingwood 6–3–3–1.

England

*A. J. Strauss c Haddin b Harris	52	– c Ponting b Johnson	15
A. N. Cook c Hussey b Johnson	32	– lbw b Harris	13
I. J. L. Trott lbw b Johnson	4	– c Haddin b Johnson	31
K. P. Pietersen lbw b Johnson	0	– c Watson b Hilfenhaus	3
P. D. Collingwood lbw b Johnson	5	– c Smith b Harris	11
I. R. Bell c Ponting b Harris	53	– (7) lbw b Harris	16
†M. J. Prior b Siddle	12	– (8) c Hussey b Harris	10
G. P. Swann c Haddin b Harris	11	– (9) b Johnson	9
C. T. Tremlett b Johnson	2	– (10) not out	1
J. M. Anderson c Watson b Johnson	0	– (6) b Harris	3
S. T. Finn not out	1	– c Smith b Harris	2
B 8, l-b 4, w 1, n-b 2	15	L-b 8, n-b 1	9

1/78 (2) 2/82 (3) 3/82 (4) 4/94 (1)   (62.3 overs) 187   1/23 (2) 2/37 (1)   (37 overs) 123
5/98 (5) 6/145 (7) 7/181 (8)   3/55 (4) 4/81 (3) 5/81 (5)
8/186 (6) 9/186 (9) 10/187 (10)   6/94 (6) 7/111 (7) 8/114 (8)
                                       9/120 (9) 10/123 (11)

Hilfenhaus 21–6–53–0; Harris 15–4–59–3; Siddle 9–2–25–1; Johnson 17.3–5–38–6. *Second Innings*—Hilfenhaus 10–4–16–1; Harris 11–1–47–6; Johnson 12–3–44–3; Siddle 4–1–8–0.

Umpires: B. R. Doctrove and M. Erasmus.   Third umpire: Aleem Dar.
Referee: J. J. Crowe.

AUSTRALIA v ENGLAND

Fourth Test Match

Gideon Haigh

At Melbourne, December 26–29, 2010. England won by an innings and 157 runs. Toss: England.

Having played what their coach called a "perfect" game at Adelaide, England went close to improving on perfection in the Boxing Day Test, rebounding from their setback at the WACA to lead all the way, ensuring the retention of the Ashes just before noon on the fourth day. It was a victory for preparation, discipline but also fun: the players celebrated in front of their fans in the Great Southern Stand by performing the Sprinkler dance popularised through the video diaries posted on the ECB website by their incurably game off-spinner Graeme Swann. Victory, of course, begets enjoyment; here, one fancied, was a case of enjoyment begetting victory.

Observing a pitch with an unusual carpet of grass, Australia stuck with an unchanged side from Perth, Ponting having come through tests on his fractured left little finger during the preliminaries to Christmas. For their part, England replaced the tiring Finn with Bresnan, who had swung the new ball and reverse-swung the old in the tour game against

Try to see it my way: Ricky Ponting, seconded by Peter Siddle, gets his point across to Aleem Dar.

Victoria. Both probably read the conditions correctly: Siddle, least of the home pacemen in the previous Test, claimed six for 75 in one innings; Bresnan, despite bowling only 69 first-class overs in almost two months, claimed six for 75 in two innings. The first difference was that England's pace attack enjoyed initial use of the pitch and overhead conditions; the second was that they were clearly superior, taking only two sessions to demoralise their hosts on the first day for Australia's lowest score in an MCG Ashes Test.

The only interruption to England's progress was a rain-break which banished the players from the field in the middle of the day for an hour and a half. It gave England the chance to savour the dismissal of their stalwart rival, Hussey, who nicked the penultimate ball of the session to provide Prior with the first of his eventual six catches. All ten batsmen eventually offered chances behind the wicket; all were accepted. Clarke eked out 20 in 89 minutes; nobody else lasted an hour. Ponting received an excellent delivery from Tremlett that lifted and left him; otherwise a succession of batsmen fell going hard at the ball, as though they had never seen swing so wicked. On only 17 occasions in the previous century had Australia been dismissed for double figures in Test cricket; not since falling for 78 at Lord's in 1968 had they collapsed for fewer against England.

Harris and Hilfenhaus belted off the ground as the Australian innings concluded, as though in a hurry to take advantage of the conditions. They were too late. Over the tea-break, the clouds parted, and the ground was bathed in sunshine. The opening bowlers found no swing, Johnson and Siddle little pace or lift: Australia's Perth match-winner sprayed two early long-hops, nailed for four each, and four byes well wide of Haddin. Strauss and Cook held their bats from any semblance of harm, and overhauled Australia's total in the 31st over with their tenth century partnership in their 86th opening stand. At 46, Strauss also passed 6,000 runs in Tests. The dire opening day for the home team was a disappointment to the Melbourne Cricket Club too. They had been confident of challenging the ground's 50-year-old attendance record of 90,800, but the number of their members disdaining Boxing Day kept the total to 84,345.

On a cooler, darker second morning, Siddle gave his home crowd something to salute, dismissing both openers, and testing Trott and Pietersen by attacking the stumps with speed and aggression. The pair applied themselves painstakingly, which for Trott is a natural state, for Pietersen perhaps less so. Only when Smith came into the attack just before lunch did Pietersen indulge himself by hitting in the air, and he reverted to steady accumulation immediately Ponting went on the defensive. Australia's captain, sequestered at mid-off and mid-on for the sake of the little finger he had broken at Perth, looked isolated and embattled – until the fourth over with the second new ball, when he became apoplectic.

The cause was a delivery from Harris which cut Pietersen (49) in half and elicited a ragged appeal from the Australians, although there was no interest from the bowler and a quizzical look from Haddin after he took the ball. Although the enquiry was rejected by Aleem Dar, and the review by Marais Erasmus, Australia's interest was reawakened by Siddle's observation of a small white dot at the bottom of Pietersen's bat on the big-screen replay of the Hot Spot analysis, even if other technologies suggested that the ball had been nowhere in that vicinity. Ponting remonstrated with Dar, hands on hips when he wasn't gesticulating, then exchanged words with both Pietersen and the other umpire, Tony Hill. Dar handled the contretemps with the utmost calm, and called "over" to end it, amid booing from the crowd and bemusement in the media area, where lip-reading skills were at a premium.

At close of play, Siddle gave a press conference in which he gave up little more than name, rank and serial number. Ponting was meantime consenting to plead guilty before referee Ranjan Madugalle to a charge of breaching article 2.1.3(h) of the ICC Code of Conduct, which relates to "arguing or entering into a prolonged discussion with the umpire about his decision". In return, his offence was reduced to Level 1, resulting in a fine of 40% of his match fee ($5,400), even if his subsequent comments hardly suggested profound contrition: "I still, in my heart and in my mind, believe that he inside-edged that ball," he told ABC Radio. "I think if you look at the replay properly, in the way that it needs to be looked at, I think everyone will understand that Hot Spot mark wasn't a long way away from where the ball passed the bat."

There's a chance that we might fall apart before too long… Ponting, bowled by Tim Bresnan, muses on defeat.

MELBOURNE NOTES AND QUOTES

A capacity crowd of 96,500 was confidently expected for Boxing Day at the MCG. In the event, though, much of the members' area was empty – and the final attendance was a mere 84,345. After Australia were bowled out for only 98, much of the home support voted with their feet, and a conservative assessment was that 30,000 or more had left early after tea. Michael Vaughan tweeted: "Lovely ground, the MCG… even when it's half full… must have all gone home to watch *Neighbours*."

The Age in Melbourne conducted a readers' poll to discover where the hapless first-innings total stood among the "most embarrassing events in recent Australian sporting history": 78% put it first.

"To use the Australian vernacular, we're stuffed. This was a dark day for Australian cricket. Large chunks of the crowd went home early because Boxing Day had become such a debacle. This was the day the urn was lost. Fat ladies in the Barmy Army are already singing their lungs out." – Will Swanton in the Sydney *Telegraph*.

The Barmy Army mocking of Mitchell Johnson took full root in Melbourne. With trumpeter Billy Cooper in place – he was controversially denied entry to some Test venues on the previous Ashes tour – and a song "dedicated" to Australia's mercurial fast bowler, there was no mercy here or at the SCG. Barmy Army member Paul Hanslow said of the near-the-knuckle lyrics: "We have rules on decency, and these definitely push the barriers. But if they [Australia's players] continue to wind us up then no doubt we will use them."

Former New Zealand seamer Iain O'Brien, meanwhile, had become a Sprinkler convert. With the Ashes retained, he tweeted: "Congrats to England. Respect. Have they also found their Haka reply? Better than Morris dancing, I guess."

Actor Sam Troughton (brother of Warwickshire captain Jim), who was starring as Romeo at Stratford, revealed the RSC cast had performed the Sprinkler dance at the Capulets' ball on New Year's Day.

In terms of the Test, the decision's impact was minimal. Reintroduced to the attack after a probably overlong break, Siddle, tail up, trapped Pietersen and then at fine leg he caught Collingwood and Bell, who played nearly identical hooks at Johnson. Johnson also had Prior, when five, caught at the wicket, only for Dar to double-check the delivery's fairness with Erasmus, who detected a no-ball. England would have been mildly embarrassed had Trott, returning for a third to wide mid-on from Siddle to go to 49, not just made his ground, thanks to a well-timed and well-rehearsed dive. Hilfenhaus's crouching behind the stumps to take Ponting's fast, flat return also cost a crucial nanosecond or two. As it was, the partnership blossomed, extending 20 minutes into the third morning, Trott enjoying the opportunity to squirrel runs away at his natural pace, Prior enjoying the venue where he had made 102 not out against Victoria a fortnight earlier. Trott came to his third century in five Ashes Tests, Prior nearly a fourth Test century. The biggest partnership of the match was among the swiftest: 173 in 274 balls.

If they could not shift Trott, who outlasted everyone in an innings of 486 minutes and would spend all but three and a half hours of the Test on the field, Australia made short work of England's tail, leaving themselves 415 in arrears on first innings. This they set about tackling at a merry clip, Watson and Hughes surging to 50 in 40 minutes, whereupon the Trott–Prior partnership added a new dimension. While there was never a single in Watson's off-side push, a lesser fieldsman and a slower keeper might not have punished the error: intercepting Trott's side-arm flick and steering it on to the stumps, Prior sent a tremor through Australia's frail batting.

At tea, Australia were still just alive at 95 for one, but accurate and creative spells of reverse swing from Bresnan and Anderson prised their fingers from the window ledge. Watson squandered another fifty by padding up; shape into the right-handed Ponting and a drive by Hussey to short extra cover roused the Barmy Army to a crescendo of noise.

Swann, reunited with his trademark drift, seemed to hypnotise the out-of-form Clarke, who looked almost relieved when his 81-minute stay was ended by a smart catch at second slip off Swann, bowling round the wicket. The precocious Smith played a hare-brained pull in sight of stumps, leaving little for the morrow but tidying.

In the shadow of defeat, Haddin and Siddle compiled the best Australian partnership of the match, a lusty 86 in 99 deliveries, each hitting four fours and a six. England's fielding grew a little demob-happy, but they could be forgiven, having maintained such a high standard for so long. They also had only nine Australian wickets to take, the hapless Harris having sustained a stress fracture of the left ankle necessitating surgery and a lengthy lay-off. There were more X-rays for Australia's captain during the last morning too, which revealed that the fracture in his left finger had moved slightly, necessitating more intensive treatment, and his standing down from the Sydney Test. "It was a tough decision, and as you would expect with Ricky, he did not take it all that well," said Australia's physiotherapist Alex Kountouris. One pictured him, hands on hips, remonstrating angrily with the specialist over the X-ray, and sledging the nursing staff, complaining about "piss-weak orthopaedics". It was a last fight at Melbourne he was not destined to win.

Man of the Match: I. J. L. Trott. *Attendance:* 239,120.

Close of play: First day, England 157-0 (Strauss 64, Cook 80); Second day, England 444-5 (Trott 141, Prior 75); Third day, Australia 169-6 (Haddin 11, Johnson 6).

Australia

S. R. Watson c Pietersen b Tremlett	5	– lbw b Bresnan	54
P. J. Hughes c Pietersen b Bresnan	16	– run out	23
*R. T. Ponting c Swann b Tremlett	10	– b Bresnan	20
M. J. Clarke c Prior b Anderson	20	– c Strauss b Swann	13
M. E. K. Hussey c Prior b Anderson	8	– c Bell b Bresnan	0
S. P. D. Smith c Prior b Anderson	6	– b Anderson	38
†B. J. Haddin c Strauss b Bresnan	5	– not out	55
M. G. Johnson c Prior b Anderson	0	– b Tremlett	6
R. J. Harris not out	10	– absent hurt	
P. M. Siddle c Prior b Tremlett	11	– (9) c Pietersen b Swann	40
B. W. Hilfenhaus c Prior b Tremlett	0	– (10) c Prior b Bresnan	0
L-b 2, n-b 5	7	B 1, l-b 6, w 2	9

1/15 (1) 2/37 (2) 3/37 (3) 4/58 (5)   (42.5 overs) 98
5/66 (6) 6/77 (4) 7/77 (7) 8/77 (8)
9/92 (10) 10/98 (11)

1/53 (2) 2/99 (1)   (85.4 overs) 258
3/102 (3) 4/104 (5)
5/134 (4) 6/158 (6) 7/172 (8)
8/258 (9) 9/258 (10)

Anderson 16–4–44–4; Tremlett 11.5–5–26–4; Bresnan 13–6–25–2; Swann 2–1–1–0. *Second Innings*—Anderson 20–1–71–1; Tremlett 17–3–71–1; Swann 27–11–59–2; Bresnan 21.4–8–50–4.

England

*A. J. Strauss c Hussey b Siddle	69	C. T. Tremlett b Hilfenhaus	4
A. N. Cook c Watson b Siddle	82	J. M. Anderson b Siddle	1
I. J. L. Trott not out	168		
K. P. Pietersen lbw b Siddle	51	B 10, l-b 2, w 3, n-b 3	18
P. D. Collingwood c Siddle b Johnson	8		
I. R. Bell c Siddle b Johnson	1	1/159 (2) 2/170 (1) (159.1 overs) 513
†M. J. Prior c Ponting b Siddle	85	3/262 (4) 4/281 (5)
T. T. Bresnan c Haddin b Siddle	4	5/286 (6) 6/459 (7) 7/465 (8)
G. P. Swann c Haddin b Hilfenhaus	22	8/508 (9) 9/512 (10) 10/513 (11)

Hilfenhaus 37–13–83–2; Harris 28.4–9–91–0; Johnson 29–2–134–2; Siddle 33.1–10–75–6; Watson 10–1–34–0; Smith 18–3–71–0; Clarke 3.2–0–13–0.

Umpires: Aleem Dar and A. L. Hill.   Third umpire: M. Erasmus.
Referee: R. S. Madugalle.

AUSTRALIA v ENGLAND

Fifth Test Match

MIKE SELVEY

At Sydney, January 3–7, 2011. England won by an innings and 83 runs. Toss: Australia. Test debuts: M. A. Beer, U. T. Khawaja.

The ground was empty now. It was late as Andrew Strauss led his team, most of them in their cups and deservedly so, to the middle of the Sydney Cricket Ground one last time in order to toast one another and contemplate the immensity of what this band of brothers had achieved. Many hours earlier the side of the ground opposite the pavilion had been heaving with the fervour of thousands of England supporters assembled to witness the completion of another crushing Australian defeat. Then minutes before midday, it fell strangely silent as Billy Cooper, the Barmy Army trumpeter, sounded a ringing Last Post. As he did so, right on cue, the man-mountain Tremlett splattered the stumps of Australia's debutant Michael Beer, to complete victory in the final Test and spark the celebrations: three Australian innings defeats in four matches, an unprecedented humiliation for them on home soil.

This final match was one England simply had to win for total endorsement of the way in which Australia had been outplayed, out-thought, out-selected and out-planned from the day the touring party arrived at the end of October. A draw here would have secured the series although, in the fullness of time, the margin would have hinted at closeness. A loss on the other hand would have been unthinkable, blowing asunder the idea of dominance, and leaving the retention of the Ashes as a technical footnote. Following their Melbourne win, England remained unchanged while the wind of necessity blew through Australia, with the young left-hander Usman Khawaja replacing the injured Ponting, and left-armer Beer a spin substitute for the damaged pace bowler Harris.

England might reflect that, with the exception of a potential blip midway through their own first innings, they had the match under control from the moment that Strauss called

"Shouldn't you be...?" Shane Watson and Phillip Hughes meet at the bowler's end.

Patrick Eagar

SYDNEY NOTES AND QUOTES

As England's New Year celebrations approached in Sydney, *Warnie* bit the dust. Channel 9 ditched Shane Warne's chat show early – its audience had fallen from 850,000 to 500,000. The broadcasters were quick to say that there was no slight on the host, but the resolution of the Ashes before the final Test meant there was no appropriate vehicle for the programme's scheduled concluding episode.

Warne still grabbed a share of centre-stage, though. Even as Alastair Cook was cementing England's position on the second day, the crowd was captivated by the sight of the world's greatest leg-spinner bowling, in front of the Bradman Stand, to *Baywatch* star – and Swann diary contributor – David Hasselhoff. "The Hoff" was in town to promote an ice-cream company, and did not look a natural with bat in hand.

"POWER URN THE GLORY" – The Ashes took on religious connotations in *The Sun's* moment-of-victory headline.

"The joy after Australia's 24-year monopoly on their home turf was there for all to see as the team went into a huddle and danced on the grave of Australian dominance." Derek Pringle, *Daily Telegraph*.

"The Sydney Cricket Ground, that most famous of all Australian sporting stages, stood as a monument to English excellence as this humbled, chastened and – yes – humiliated nation came to terms with the reality that their era of greatness has finally come to a crushing end while another takes hold. The era of English dominance." Paul Newman, *Daily Mail*.

"In 1948 we sent the Invincibles, now we have the Unwatchables." *The Courier-Mail*, Brisbane.

"The Australian bobsleigh team have asked the Australian cricket team for advice. They want to learn how to go downhill so fast." One of the jokes doing the rounds after the Sydney Test.

incorrectly at the toss. Whatever induced Clarke, Australia's 43rd Test captain, to bat first is unknown. Perhaps it was the residue of the paranoia existing in Ponting since his 2005 Edgbaston blunder – there had been not one single insertion by Australia since – or maybe a fear of what Swann might do on a fifth-day Sydney pitch. Certainly England looked up and saw overcast skies, looked down and saw dampness and patchiness in the pitch that might make early strokeplay difficult, and were overjoyed to be bowling first. They were right. The first morning was a struggle for survival. If Paul Simon identified 50 ways to leave your lover, then Watson, with great skill and fortitude, found as many to leave the parsimonious England seam bowlers, while Hughes battled against his attacking instincts, surviving to the very stroke of lunch before relapsing when the initial job was all but done and poking a gentle catch to slip.

"Bowling dry" – attritional cricket – had been England's catchphrase throughout the series, and here they were arid. There was a brief flurry from Khawaja to set the Australian crowd aflutter, swivelling as if on castors to pull his second ball to the boundary and racing to 15 from eight deliveries before the reality of international cricket took hold: a further 87 deliveries brought no more than 22 runs, the pressure applied by England bringing his downfall as he tried to sweep Swann and was caught backward of the umpire. The ovation as he returned to the pavilion was disproportionate to the achievement. By then Watson's vigil had ended at slip, and the captain had sliced to gully.

From 134 for four after a day restricted to 59 overs, Australia were able to extend their first innings into the second afternoon thanks to a robust 53 from Johnson – allowed space by generous, ill-conceived field settings – and a ninth-wicket stand of 76 that helped them to 280. England's response was robust against impoverished bowling, Strauss leading the way by flaying dross for 60 from only 58 balls, and Cook digging in once again, to play the innings that was both to seal the series and to establish him as an Ashes phenomenon. Good fortune followed him. When 46, keen not to let Beer settle, he attempted a leg-side hit, only for the ball to skew to mid-on. But as he walked off, Billy Bowden, suspecting a tight no-ball, called for a replay which confirmed as much. England finished the second day at 167 for three, 113 adrift.

The following morning, looking for the single to take him to his third century of the series, Cook turned Beer low and straight to short leg, where the fielder Hughes at first appeared to claim the catch before indicating he was uncertain whether it had carried. Once more the replay reprieved Cook. By then, the nightwatchman Anderson had gone and, shortly after reaching his hundred, Cook lost Collingwood as well, Brigadier Block attempting one last uncharacteristic grand hurrah in what was to prove his last Test innings but falling foul of mid-on instead (he announced his retirement on the fourth morning). At 226 for five, the game was in the balance. These were the situations where once England might have buckled.

"We did it." Andrew Strauss and Alastair Cook after the Test – and before the celebrations.

Graham Morris

Instead, the breach was filled by Cook, whose 189 gave him 766 runs in the series, second only to Wally Hammond (905 in the 1928-29 Ashes) for England; by Bell with 115, his first Ashes hundred, an innings of great significance in terms of his development and one that in the easy richness and variety of strokeplay surely confirmed him as the most naturally gifted English batsman since David Gower; and by Prior, whose 118 came from 130 balls, England's fastest Ashes hundred since Ian Botham's 1981 Old Trafford epic. With help from Bresnan they produced stands of 154 for the sixth wicket, 107 for the seventh, and 102 for the eighth, an unprecedented sequence of century stands for those wickets in Tests. Bell had made 67 when he was given out after an appeal from an inside edge against Watson: the snickometer, by no means infallible, later appeared to confirm it; but the equally temperamental Hot Spot, used for the England referral, detected no contact, so the batsman was reprieved. By the time Hilfenhaus finished the England innings after lunch on the fourth day, it was their highest ever in Australia, beating 636 on the same ground in 1928-29.

But for an unlikely eighth-wicket partnership of 86 between Smith and Siddle, which saw Australia through the extra half-hour claimed by England, the game would have been done inside four days. Australia had subsided to 171 for seven, a decline sparked by the farcical run-out of Watson, the third of the series in which he had been involved but the first where he was the victim. It was then rammed home by the wicked reverse swing – a skill largely beyond the Australian bowlers – of the brilliant Anderson (too soft for the Ashes contest in 2009, according to Justin Langer's notes), Tremlett and Bresnan, and the

ENGLAND'S HIGHEST TEST TOTALS AGAINST AUSTRALIA

903-7 dec	The Oval	1938	620-5 dec	Adelaide	2010-11
658-8 dec	Nottingham	1938	611	Manchester	1964
644	**Sydney**	**2010-11**	595-5 dec	Birmingham	1985
636	Sydney	1928-29	592-8 dec	Perth	1986-87
627-9 dec	Manchester	1934	589	Melbourne	1911-12

wicketkeeping of Prior, who equalled the England record of 23 catches in an Ashes series. This was a record series for records.

Man of the Match: A. N. Cook.   *Attendance:* 179,004.

Man of the Series (Compton–Miller Medal): A. N. Cook.

Close of play: First day, Australia 134-4 (Hussey 12); Second day, England 167-3 (Cook 61, Anderson 1); Third day, England 488-7 (Prior 54, Bresnan 0); Fourth day, Australia 213-7 (Smith 24, Siddle 17).

Australia

S. R. Watson c Strauss b Bresnan	45	– run out	38
P. J. Hughes c Collingwood b Tremlett	31	– c Prior b Bresnan	13
U. T. Khawaja c Trott b Swann	37	– c Prior b Anderson	21
*M. J. Clarke c Anderson b Bresnan	4	– c Prior b Anderson	41
M. E. K. Hussey b Collingwood	33	– c Pietersen b Bresnan	12
†B. J. Haddin c Prior b Anderson	6	– c Prior b Tremlett	30
S. P. D. Smith c Collingwood b Anderson	18	– not out	54
M. G. Johnson b Bresnan	53	– b Tremlett	0
P. M. Siddle c Strauss b Anderson	2	– c Anderson b Swann	43
B. W. Hilfenhaus c Prior b Anderson	34	– c Prior b Anderson	7
M. A. Beer not out	2	– b Tremlett	2
B 5, l-b 7, w 1, n-b 2	15	B 11, l-b 4, w 3, n-b 2	20

1/55 (2) 2/105 (1) 3/113 (4)   (106.1 overs) 280
4/134 (3) 5/143 (6) 6/171 (5)
7/187 (7) 8/189 (9) 9/265 (8) 10/280 (10)

1/46 (1) 2/52 (2)   (84.4 overs) 281
3/117 (3) 4/124 (4)
5/161 (5) 6/171 (6) 7/171 (8)
8/257 (9) 9/267 (10) 10/281 (11)

Anderson 30.1–7–66–4; Tremlett 26–9–71–1; Bresnan 30–5–89–3; Swann 16–4–37–1; Collingwood 4–2–5–1. *Second Innings*—Anderson 18–5–61–3; Tremlett 20.4–4–79–3; Swann 28–8–75–1; Bresnan 18–6–51–2.

England

*A. J. Strauss b Hilfenhaus	60	G. P. Swann not out	36
A. N. Cook c Hussey b Watson	189	C. T. Tremlett c Haddin b Hilfenhaus	12
I. J. L. Trott b Johnson	0		
K. P. Pietersen b Beer b Johnson	36	B 3, l-b 11, w 5, n-b 4	23
J. M. Anderson b Siddle	7		
P. D. Collingwood c Hilfenhaus b Beer	13	1/98 (1) 2/99 (3) (177.5 overs) 644
I. R. Bell c Clarke b Johnson	115	3/165 (4) 4/181 (5) 5/226 (6)
†M. J. Prior c Haddin b Hilfenhaus	118	6/380 (2) 7/487 (7) 8/589 (9)
T. T. Bresnan c Clarke b Johnson	35	9/609 (8) 10/644 (11)

Hilfenhaus 38.5–7–121–3; Johnson 36–5–168–4; Siddle 31–5–111–1; Watson 20–7–49–1; Beer 38–3–112–1; Smith 13–0–67–0; Hussey 1–0–2–0.

Umpires: Aleem Dar and B. F. Bowden.   Third umpire: A. L. Hill.
Referee: R. S. Madugalle.

Details of England's limited-overs matches in Australia, including two Twenty20 internationals and seven one-day internationals, can be found in The Commonwealth Bank Series (page 859).

WHY ENGLAND WON

Better in every department

Michael Vaughan

It was not a surprise that England won the Ashes series in Australia 3–1. They were better selected, better prepared, better captained and better managed. What was unexpected was the manner and margin of their victory, as they ground Australia into the dirt three times by an innings.

As always, the key difference between the two teams lay in their spine. England had an excellent pair of opening batsmen and opening bowlers, a very good wicketkeeper in Matt Prior, and a captain who led by example. The innings of the series was Andrew Strauss's hundred in the second innings at Brisbane. The pitch had flattened and deadened, but with a deficit of over 200 Strauss still had to counter-attack and make a statement, and he did it brilliantly.

Australia's opening bowlers throughout pitched both sides of the wicket and too short. I was amazed they did not come round the wicket to Strauss and Alastair Cook from the start. You have to ask questions of batsmen that they least like having to answer when they come in, not when they reach 30. Even in my time, the Australian team was not full of great thinkers, apart from Shane Warne: when I had my 633-run series in 2002-03 they never worked out the right place to bowl at me, and always pitched too short. That was when I first thought that, if we could get them into a contest in 2005, we could out-think them, and the same still applied last winter.

The Australian attack had no X-factor bowler – except Mitchell Johnson in Perth when he swung it – who could bowl a batsman out once he had got in. There was no Warne or Murali or Shoaib Akhtar who could bowl a ball that the batsman, even if he was on 120, couldn't prepare for. There was no fear for England's batsmen, no sleepless nights. So on batting pitches Cook and Jonathan Trott just had to play to their strengths and concentrate, which they did brilliantly.

For their opening pair of bowlers, England had James Anderson, first with Stuart Broad then with Chris Tremlett. It comes to a stage when a player knows his time has come to deliver, and that was the case with Anderson. After the 2009 Ashes series he had realised he could not bowl big booming swingers all the time, and mostly had to hit the right lengths as all the great bowlers have done. He threatened with the new and old ball because, like Shaun Pollock, or Chaminda Vaas at a slower pace, he had also worked on wobbling the seam of the old ball so it would nip either way.

And the Australians did not attack Anderson, as Hayden and Langer and Ponting had done in previous series. This time the mindset of Australia's openers was survival, and they let Anderson get into the series. I thought Shane Watson should have been more attacking – more like Hayden – but that would have been easier for him if Simon Katich had lasted the series as his partner.

The Australians seemed a bit like a league team: they turned up and waited to see what would happen without preparing for every eventuality. Tremlett caught them by surprise. He had bowled beautifully against India in 2007 when I was still captain: he troubled Sachin Tendulkar, Sourav Ganguly and Rahul Dravid before picking up a serious injury. He had all the attributes: and as he and Anderson, Steve Finn or Tim Bresnan, along with Graeme Swann, kept dismissing Australia in 80 or 90 overs, England only needed four bowlers. It was the first Ashes series since 1956 in which none of Australia's top four made a hundred.

Xavier Doherty has to go down as one of the most bizarre selections in the history of the Ashes, picked from nowhere when the Australians had had a year and a half to prepare after the 2009 series. Nathan Hauritz had better figures than Swann in that series before the Oval Test, but that seemed to have been forgotten. Last winter Australia should have played to their strength, picking two left-armers in Johnson and Doug Bollinger – Cook and Strauss don't like left-armers any more than right-armers bowling round the wicket – and Hauritz bowling into that rough.

Australia can carry on doing what they are doing, or take stock and prepare for the 2013 Ashes in England by building a side that is tough to beat. A side that has Hauritz batting at No. 8 and Johnson at 9, and perhaps Peter Siddle at 10, would be tough to beat. When they batted Ryan Harris at No. 8 in the Adelaide Test, it was a throwback to England in the 1990s when we had someone like Andy Caddick or Dean Headley in that position.

Every member of England's management team did a wonderful job, enjoying each other's success, sensing that it was a special time for English cricket. Whatever you do in the game, you have to be passionate about it: the type who spends a day at the ground then goes back home or to the hotel and switches on the TV and watches cricket. Graham Gooch, David Saker and Richard Halsall, the batting, bowling and fielding coaches, are all like that. Saker doesn't take himself too seriously, has a sense of humour, and doesn't think of himself as a magician. England reaped the reward from the years of hard work that Halsall has put in: everything the players do in practice is now measured and analysed, like joining the 50 Club for taking 50 catches in a row.

Andy Flower and Duncan Fletcher are very similar. Both had visions of England becoming No. 1. But when Fletcher was coach, England did not have such a pool of reserves breathing down the players' necks as they do now. Flower and Strauss have dropped almost every player at some time, but Fletcher and I couldn't do that as we didn't have the same depth. Australia were also standing in our way, just as West Indies had stood in the way in the 1980s. But England now have a great chance to become the world No. 1, in every format.

Michael Vaughan captained England in 51 of his 82 Tests, including the 2005 Ashes series in England. In Australia in 2002-03 he scored 633 runs, with three centuries.

WHY AUSTRALIA LOST

Outflanked by the master of strategy

KERRY O'KEEFFE

If Australia is a desert then Andy Flower could well be Rommel. The strategic precision of the English campaign must be down to the former Zim wicky. The Australians, on the other hand, had been in the unfamiliar conditions of India, then returned home to play Sri Lanka in 50-over and Twenty20 "friendlies"... a little like swimming the English Channel to tune up for the London Marathon. England sent their chosen bowling quartet on an acclimatising mission to Brisbane five days before the Ashes opener, while Australia named such a bulky squad, of 17 players, that the producers of *Gladiator* were thought to have used fewer extras.

At the Gabba, Australia led on the first innings by 221, yet finished the drawn match with all the problems. However, as significant as the performances of Alastair Cook and Steve Finn was the dominant way in which Mike Hussey played Graeme Swann. The English off-spinner – as cool and gregarious as he may appear – can occasionally pull down deliveries under pressure. Hussey pulled or cut any Swann offering not centimetre-perfect, and sent a message to the tweaker – curve the Kookaburra through the air, or a modest series return awaits! Given that Swann's over-the-top release point disallows any change of flight unless the prevailing wind is kind, his card was marked.

Another Australian plus was that Peter Siddle pitched the ball up and snared a hat-trick – he could be Jason Gillespie using this method. Sadly, Ricky Ponting always seems to cast him in the bully-boy role, and the great team man toes the line.

At Adelaide, England had Australia three down in a quarter of an hour, and they never recovered. Jimmy Anderson made the Kookaburra talk... sing... and even do a little jig. Kevin Pietersen's thunderous on-driving made Ponting's same shot in his pomp look like a nervous push past the bowler. Swann did the job with five wickets in the second innings: Doug Bollinger – or should I say "Big Foot" – had created crevasses on a good length that Sir Edmund Hillary would have thought twice about abseiling into. A confident Swann ploughed his off-breaks into that rough, and won the Test by lunch on the fifth day. On surfaces likely to scuff up, Bollinger should bowl in ballet shoes. Nonetheless, the Australian batsmen are technically poor when the ball turns: their alternative to smashing one on the up to the rope on good non-spinning surfaces is to get caught on the crease with low hands when it's going. I'll have a bit of that, cried Swanny.

At Perth, the Barmy Army hardly sang "he bowls to the left... he bowls to the right" because Mitchell Johnson didn't bowl "shite". Johnson himself doesn't know day to day when he is going to be good – that is his challenge over the next few years. His nine wickets put England away: left-arm-over inswingers to right-handers at pace was the Alan Davidson way in the '60s, and it still works. In-form Hussey let the ball go, punished Swann when he dropped short, cut out risk and scored an "English" century. Ryan Harris demonstrated how to bowl perfectly to Paul Collingwood – keep the ball outside his eyeline for sustained periods and hesitancy enters the room.

The pitch on Boxing Day made it a good toss for Andrew Strauss to win and bowl, of course. All Australians love the bowling machine for batting practice – it is said that Michael Clarke and Ponting are addicted. But given the way they play the moving ball, I would ban it… so many of the shots played looked a direct result of bowling-machine cricket. Anderson, Chris Tremlett and Tim Bresnan moved the ball hour after hour, and all the Australians were out to catches behind the wicket. Then Jonathan Trott hit 80 of his first 100 runs through the leg side – like Mark Waugh before him, Trott's off stump is his leg stump. The Ashes were gone, but would a dead-rubber game at Sydney lead to English complacency? Not with "Rommel" Flower at the helm.

Hughes, Clarke and Steve Smith were all out of form by Sydney – two of the three had serious technical deficiencies – and that was half the top order. Batting first Australia only managed 280: defeat was a fait accompli. The English pacemen were a force: Tremlett's bounce worried everybody. Batting coach Justin Langer declared that Australia had to find this sort of giant. Centuries from Cook, Ian Bell and Matt Prior put Australia away. Debutant spinner Michael Beer has a nice action… and bowls nice deliveries. Nothing hurtful – just nice. Like Xavier Doherty before him, Australia keep producing finger-spinners with no straightening of the elbow and no doosra. We really must get with the programme!

Overall:
- England counted their batting in hours (and days). Australians looked at minutes.
- David Saker taught the English bowlers "to do a McGrath" – to nag away, be patient and create pressure by denying batsmen the four-ball.
- England were happy to let balls go – Australia had a "hit it" mentality.
- Kevin Pietersen's Lamborghini speeding fine was the only English "scandal" – the Australians faced constant criticism from the media and the public.
- When England got on top, they stayed on top – there was a Steve Waugh mentality to the team approach.
- Australia had no strike bowler. Your main man (Johnson) shouldn't be afraid of the new ball: imagine Dennis Lillee saying "No, I'd like to bowl after Thommo and Tangles have roughed it up." Australia have to find a new-ball strike bowler – not three or four containing bowlers. International teams now know that if you sit on Australia and grind them, big totals result.

Kerry O'Keeffe played 24 Tests for Australia in the 1970s, as a leg-spinning all-rounder. He also took part in World Series Cricket, and is now a radio commentator.

PART FOUR

English and
European Cricket

THE ENGLAND TEAM IN 2010

Stable? Stupendous!

Vic Marks

Stability was the watchword for 2010. But somehow when England go to Australia and retain the Ashes there for the first time in 24 years, "stable" does not seem quite adequate. There were times after England had defeated Australia by an innings – at Adelaide, at Melbourne and, at the start of 2011, at Sydney – when "sensational" or "stupendous" felt a more fitting way to describe the Test team.

But Andrew Strauss and Andy Flower would probably settle for "stable". Once the euphoria of the Ashes victory had settled, they could point out that

ENGLAND IN 2010

	Played	Won	Lost	Drawn/No result
Tests	14	9	3	2
One-day internationals	17	12	5	–
Twenty20 internationals	11	8	2	1

NOVEMBER		
DECEMBER	4 Tests, 5 ODIs and 2 T20Is (a) v South Africa	(see *Wisden* 2010, page 1269)
JANUARY		
FEBRUARY	2 T20Is (a) (in UAE) v Pakistan	(page 1004)
MARCH	2 Tests and 3 ODIs (a) v Bangladesh	(page 890)
APRIL		
MAY	World Twenty20 (in West Indies)	(page 797)
	2 Tests (h) v Bangladesh	(page 283)
JUNE	1 ODI (a) v Scotland	(page 772)
	5 ODIs (h) v Australia	(page 303)
JULY	3 ODIs (h) v Bangladesh	(page 283)
AUGUST	4 Tests, 5 ODIs and 2 T20Is (h) v Pakistan	(page 322)
SEPTEMBER		
OCTOBER		
NOVEMBER		
DECEMBER	5 Tests, 7 ODIs and 2 T20Is (a) v Australia	(page 210)
JANUARY		
FEBRUARY		

England were still only the third-best side in the world, according to the ICC's rankings. The journey had only just begun.

Both Flower and Strauss can be ostriches; though they never stick their heads in the sand, their feet remain planted firmly on the ground. Both were too polite to add that the Australian side that England had just defeated was, quite properly, ranked fifth in the world. Ricky Ponting may still have been around (for four of the Tests, anyway), but the giants of the past had moved on to lesser things: coaching positions, the IPL, commentary-boxes, poker tables.

For a second year Strauss and Flower were not only singing from the same hymn sheet, but from the same hymn; more than that, they were singing from the same line of the same hymn from the aforesaid sheet. By December 2010 their authority within the England team was beyond question, and neither showed any sign of getting carried away by what had been achieved. If ever they were at variance, we never knew.

However, both were prepared to concede that this England team had something special within their grasp. There was talent but, much better than that, there was a true unity of purpose and a genuine delight in each other's success, two qualities that can be very elusive at this level. Everyone, it seemed, was buying into the regime, which may not have been the case even when England were at their most powerful in recent times, in 2004 and 2005.

The stability was reflected by the teamsheets at the start and end of the year. In January, England experienced one of their three Test defeats in 2010 at Johannesburg, where they were walloped by an innings and 74 runs. Twelve months later at Melbourne and Sydney nine of the Johannesburg XI were still in the team (and no doubt Stuart Broad would still have been there as well but for the side strain he acquired at Adelaide).

Often the defeats can be more illuminating. Apart from that setback at the Wanderers, England also lost to Pakistan at The Oval, and to Australia at Perth. One theory was that they were peculiarly vulnerable after a resounding victory: before the matches at The Oval and the WACA they had thrashed their opponents. A more likely explanation of their defeats – one routinely rejected by the England camp – was that the batting unit was vulnerable against pace bowlers on the sort of bouncy surfaces that can be found at Johannesburg and Perth. But in the modern game the coincidence of fast bowlers and a fast pitch is rare indeed.

Against Pakistan the batsmen were undermined not so much by pace but by a couple of the capricious Dukes balls from the devilish 2010 batch, expertly propelled by Mohammad Asif and Mohammad Aamer. For some reason, in the English summer of 2010 the ball just kept moving around in the air and off the pitch.

The three defeats were more than counterbalanced by nine victories, although four of those were against Bangladesh. For the Tests at Dhaka and Chittagong, where it is slightly more difficult to beat Bangladesh, Strauss and James Anderson were rested and Alastair Cook captained the team. Strauss's absence aroused some criticism, not least from former England captains, which was surprising at the time and which seemed utterly misplaced when Strauss triumphantly held up a replica of the Ashes urn in Australia nine months later.

The schedule for international cricketers is currently so crowded that everyone needs a rest at some point – and that includes the captain.

Of the victories before the Ashes campaign, the most remarkable was in the final Test at Lord's, when England beat Pakistan by an innings and 225 runs after being 47 for five in their first innings. Broad and Jonathan Trott combined to add a staggering 332 for the eighth wicket, a Test record. Yet that match will be remembered for something else: three no-balls, which are discussed at length elsewhere.

Once in Australia there were three wins that bordered upon cricketing perfection, regardless of the limitations of their opponents. England's fielding was routinely superior to Australia's. (How often have we been able to say *that* when watching English fielders patrol the vast expanses of Antipodean cricket grounds?) Whichever four bowlers were selected – yes, four were quite sufficient – the attack was far more disciplined than their opponents', and capable of finding greater movement.

Moreover, once the English batsmen spied pitches containing runs, their concentration never wavered. Cook (three times), Trott (twice) and Kevin Pietersen (once) delivered "daddy" hundreds, an expression coined by the new batting coach, Graham Gooch, to indicate big ones.

Gooch was one of a substantial band of backroom staff, but no one queried the size of the support group in Australia. The players, in particular, seldom left a microphone without singing the praises of those helping them behind the scenes. And they must have had a point.

Alongside Gooch, Flower had at his disposal the fielding coach Richard Halsall, whose reputation burgeoned every time England took to the field.

David Saker, a no-nonsense Victorian, soon won the confidence of his pace bowlers, and insisted on a straightforward policy of "bowling dry" (building pressure through accuracy); Bruce French enhanced the wicketkeepers; Mushtaq Ahmed may have helped Graeme Swann, who was present throughout the year and was joined just once by a second spinner (James Tredwell, who, along with Michael Carberry, may have the dubious honour of being a one-Test wonder after their appearance in Bangladesh). No England touring side can ever have been fitter, thanks in part to the physio, Kirk Russell, who stood down after nine years by the couch, and the conditioning coach, Huw Bevan.

Saker insisted on a policy of "bowling dry"

But, as Flower was always quick to point out, it was the players who deserved the plaudits: "They are the ones who have to make the split-second decisions under pressure out on the pitch."

Strauss – who must surely be played by Colin Firth when they make the biopic – led without fuss and scored his quota of runs. As a captain, he is more a strategist than a tactician; as a batsman, he has become more fluent if, perhaps, less consistent. He never used to play breathtaking shots; he does occasionally now.

The artisans did most of the run-scoring throughout the year. Neither Trott nor Cook necessarily quicken the walk of any latecomers to the ground, but

Andrew Biraj, Reuters

Preparation is key: Richard Halsall (fielding coach), Alastair Cook (captain) and Andy Flower (coach) in Chittagong, March 2010.

Trott – for most of the year – and Cook, in Australia, just kept batting, trusting their own techniques and relying upon phenomenal powers of concentration and fitness. Curiously Cook, who faced 1,438 deliveries in 2,151 minutes at the crease in the Ashes series, never sweats, which is why he is one of those detailed to look after the ball in the field (perspiration can undermine the pursuit of reverse swing).

The artists, Pietersen and Ian Bell, also contributed, if less prolifically. Pietersen endured the indignity of being dropped from the one-day side in September with reasonable equanimity, though he could not avoid a grumpy tweet. Bell's status in the side, if not his place in the batting order, advanced despite a foot injury, which kept him out of the series against Pakistan. Often he looked England's best batsman, even if he was not their most productive one.

No one thought about querying Matt Prior's place in the team, nor Swann's. England's off-spinner proved that his 2009 success was no flash in the pan. By the end of 2010 Swann was regarded by most judges – as well as the ICC rankings – as the best spinner in the world, despite the absence of a doosra, zooter or carrom ball in his armoury. In 2010 he was probably England's most indispensable cricketer.

However, the greatest advance came from the rest of the bowling attack. By the end of the year England could genuinely boast of strength in depth. Indeed, no one could be absolutely certain which quartet constituted their best bowling line-up. For certain, Anderson was in it (alongside Swann). He enjoyed his best year in international cricket, quietly revelling in the responsibility of leading the attack. He swung the new ball conventionally; he swung the old one via reverse swing, and on the rare occasions when the damn thing would not swing at all he was no longer flummoxed. If anything, Anderson became a more conservative bowler, prepared to bide his time in the knowledge that the wickets would come in the end. And so they did.

For most of the year Anderson was accompanied by Broad and Steven Finn, but by the end of the Ashes tour when Broad was injured and Finn a little jaded, Chris Tremlett and Tim Bresnan were alongside Anderson – and the attack looked none the worse for the change.

Just one player laboured at Test level, and that was Paul Collingwood. Throughout 2010 he scored 514 Test runs at an average of 28.55, and he knew that was not enough, whatever else he brought to the team. Thus he announced his retirement from the five-day game during the Sydney Test. His likeliest replacement seems to be Eoin Morgan, who played six Tests in the 2010 summer, during which he hit a maiden century against Pakistan without establishing his Test credentials beyond doubt.

Yet Collingwood can remember 2010 with much pleasure. Leaving aside the Ashes, England had never won a major limited-overs competition until Collingwood led them to victory in the World Twenty20 in the Caribbean in May. He oversaw a spirited campaign, which began with a Duckworth/Lewis defeat by West Indies and a squeaky no-result against Ireland, but which ended with memorable victories against Sri Lanka in the semi-final and Australia in the final.

Collingwood's England were daring in their selection, picking two rookie openers, Craig Kieswetter and Michael Lumb, and they were innovative, as evidenced by their bowlers' mastering of the slow bouncer. Moreover they were as good as any team in the field. Pietersen scored the most runs for England, and Swann and Ryan Sidebottom took the most wickets, but it was a magnificent team effort. And a very stable team it was: England used the same 11 players in all their fixtures except the one against New Zealand, when Ravi Bopara replaced the absent Pietersen.

In the longer form of limited-overs cricket there was a more modest advance. England beat Bangladesh in two series, but they did suffer their first-ever loss to them at Bristol. They beat Australia 3–2 at home, and they prevailed in a highly charged series against Pakistan, also 3–2, at the end of a season when tempers on all sides were getting frayed.

By then Strauss had dispelled any doubts about his ability to bat at the top of the order, even though it was far from clear who was his best partner, and Morgan had cemented his reputation as the side's ice-cool finisher. England could at least head off to the World Cup with some confidence and a reasonably settled side – aside from an alarming number of injuries – which has rarely been the case in recent times.

But in another year of progress for Team England it was their Test side which had been the greatest source of delight. This was appropriate for a nation that seems to cherish Test cricket more than any other. Those victories forged at Adelaide and Melbourne cheered a lot of people suffering a freezing winter back home. Winning an Ashes series in Australia may only be a step along the way for Flower and Strauss, but the rest of us got rather more excited about it.

ENGLAND PLAYERS IN 2010

LAWRENCE BOOTH

The following 27 players (30 in 2009, and 25 in 2008) appeared for England in the calendar year 2010, when the team played 14 Tests, 17 one-day internationals and 11 Twenty20 internationals. All statistics refer to the full year, not the 2010 season.

JAMES ANDERSON   Lancashire

The final piece in Anderson's personal jigsaw was triumphantly added in Australia, where any doubts over his ability to thrive outside England were finally dispelled. No longer merely a swing bowler, but a formidable exploiter of seam movement too, he capped a superb year in which only Swann and Dale Steyn claimed more Test wickets, and he was, at times, unplayable. In England, Anderson averaged under 17, repeatedly making Pakistan look like novices (figures of 15–8–17–6 at Trent Bridge were a swing bowler's dream) and producing an old-ball spell during the defeat at The Oval that promised much for the winter ahead. In Australia, armed with the supposedly dreaded Kookaburra, the promise bore fruit. His penetration with the new ball was matched by his skill at reversing the old, and a series haul of 24 wickets was England's best there since John Snow, 40 years earlier. He was accurate too: an economy-rate of 2.82 was his best in a calendar year, as were his wicket haul and average. His batting, though, fell away. After only one Test duck in his first 60 innings, he made five in 16 in 2010 and failed to pass 13. But when he was bowling as well as this – all the while making up for the disappointment of being dropped from the Twenty20 side – no one much cared.

2010   12 Tests: 65 runs @ 5.00; 57 wickets @ 22.96.
      13 ODI: 12 runs @ 6.00; 18 wickets @ 33.83.

IAN BELL   Warwickshire

Few players in the world batted with such lip-smacking elegance as Bell in 2010, but there was frustration in the aftertaste too. A broken ankle cost him four Tests against Pakistan, and his Ashes slot of No. 6 – even lower when Anderson was nightwatchman – frequently left him with the tail. When he finally converted the 12th of his Ashes fifties into his first hundred against Australia, at Sydney, it was from No. 7. Yet the suspicion that his graduation from boy to man at Cape Town a year earlier was for life – and not just for after Christmas – proved correct. Bell continued his love affair with Bangladesh, at one point taking his average against them to 488 prior to his dismissal in Dhaka, where he finally scored a Test hundred without being beaten to three figures by a team-mate in the same innings. A punishing fitness regime, including exercises borrowed from cage-fighting, contributed to his new-found resilience without eroding the aesthetics, and only circumstance got in the way of a larger haul in Australia, where he averaged 65 and looked the classiest player on either side. A promotion up the order was inevitable.

2010   10 Tests: 786 runs @ 65.50.
       4 ODI: 139 runs @ 69.50.

RAVI BOPARA   Essex

The trauma of the 2009 Ashes may have gone but it had not quite been forgotten: first he had to regain the trust of the selectors. Chances were limited, but Bopara did his bit, scoring 103 one-day runs off 71 balls, seven of them hit for six, and winning the match award at Edgbaston after cleaning up Bangladesh's lower order. But a sole appearance at the World Twenty20 summed up his new home on the sidelines – which felt harsh, given his capacity for late-order rope-clearing, especially against the spinners – and the subsequent glimpses of talent paradoxically provoked regret over what had gone before. Two winter months with the Dolphins in South Africa produced a handful of fifties, but not the big hundred he needed to catch Flower's eye.

2010   4 ODI: 103 runs @ 51.50; 4 wickets @ 9.50.
       3 T20I: 32 runs @ 10.66.

TIM BRESNAN   Yorkshire

To compare and contrast his tours to Bangladesh and Australia was to understand the progress Bresnan made as an international bowler. On the first, he earned praise for plugging away on thankless strips of mud; on the second, where he was called up to replace Finn in Melbourne, he produced a high-class

Tim Hales, AP/PA

spell of accurate reverse-swing to wind Australia's top order, before claiming the wicket that retained the Ashes. Previously regarded as the final prong in any five-man attack, Bresnan – no longer sending down one boundary-ball per over – was now trusted to be first change in a group of four. A wasteful spell with the new ball against Bangladesh at Lord's, where he reverted to limited-overs mode – going wide of the crease and angling the ball in – had been forgiven. His batting had its moments too, from a gritty Test 91 in Dhaka, via a nerveless unbeaten 23 off 11 balls to see off New Zealand in the World Twenty20, to a cool-headed 14 not out to seal a one-wicket win over Australia at Old Trafford and with it the one-day NatWest Series. Bresnan was not yet the No. 7 England craved for post-Flintoff balance, but he wasn't too far away either.

2010   4 Tests: 120 runs @ 40.00; 17 wickets @ 27.64.
       15 ODI: 155 runs @ 19.37; 19 wickets @ 36.84.
       11 T20I: 41 runs @ 13.66; 9 wickets @ 26.77.

STUART BROAD Nottinghamshire

Life was always going to feel anticlimactic after the zenith of The Oval 2009, and Broad's high point this year came with bat rather than ball: a ground-breaking 169 from No. 9 against Pakistan at Lord's after being demoted beneath Swann – even if the no-ball scandal subsequently removed the gloss. But his bowling produced mixed returns. England's leading wicket-taker in 50-over cricket, Broad failed to take a Test five-for, despite being handed the new ball from the tour of Bangladesh onwards. Perhaps aided by a strength and conditioning programme that ruled him out of the home series against the Bangladeshis, Broad's accuracy improved in Tests as the year went on – a one-day economy-rate of 5.21 reflected his licence to attack – and his miserliness in the first two Ashes Tests played an underrated part in England's early series lead. But a freak tear of an abdominal muscle in Adelaide brought his winter to a premature close, leaving Broad to reflect on an emotional year in which he lost his stepmother to motor neurone disease, and was fined for throwing the ball at the Pakistan wicketkeeper, Zulqarnain Haider, during the Edgbaston Test.

2010   10 Tests: 292 runs @ 24.33; 26 wickets @ 37.69.
16 ODI: 34 runs @ 5.66; 30 wickets @ 24.86.
11 T20I: no runs without being dismissed; 13 wickets @ 18.23.

MICHAEL CARBERRY Hampshire

A pair of gritty thirties on Test debut at Chittagong felt like a missed opportunity, not least when Trott was promoted to open in the next game at Dhaka to accommodate an extra bowler. But neither had he failed, and another run-laden county season did nothing to ease the pre-Ashes pressure on Cook.

2010   1 Test: 64 runs @ 32.00.

PAUL COLLINGWOOD Durham

His batting waned, but Collingwood will always be known as the first Englishman to lift a global one-day trophy, courtesy of the Twenty20 triumph in the Caribbean. A perennial willingness to buy into the team ethic took priority over an instinctive dislike of the captaincy, and Collingwood remained a team man, even while he was scratching around for his runs all summer and then in Australia. His first five innings – in South Africa and Bangladesh – yielded 322 of his Test runs for the year, after which he passed 50 only once in 13 attempts, a sequence including nine single-figure scores. A tendency to become trapped on the crease became more pronounced: he was lbw in Tests seven times. And only a handful of enterprising 50-over knocks – of a piece with his free-spirited performances in the IPL with Delhi Daredevils – countered the jibe that he was in the team for his fielding alone. In that, he remained England's heartbeat. But when he announced during the Ashes finale at Sydney that he would be quitting Tests, it was possible to offer thanks while praising the timing too.

2010   12 Tests: 514 runs @ 28.55; 1 wicket @ 122.00.
16 ODI: 500 runs @ 35.71; 5 wickets @ 54.20.
11 T20I: 97 runs @ 10.77; no wicket for 47.

ALASTAIR COOK   Essex

A year that began and ended triumphantly sagged so dispiritingly in the middle that Cook's Ashes run-glut might never have happened. His century against Pakistan at The Oval was the definitive career-saver after he had failed to reach 30 in his previous eight innings amid suffocating analyses of a complex technique. Some discerned a more flexible front knee at The Oval and beyond, but just as important was a return to the refusal to flirt outside off stump that had brought him a dozen previous Test hundreds, including two as a stand-in captain on the tour of Bangladesh. Even so, the Ashes went beyond mere redemption. A match-saving 235 at Brisbane was followed by 148 at Adelaide, then 189 in the win at Sydney, and Cook finished the series with 766 runs at 127 to expel the memories of 2006-07, earn the respect of the Australian players and public, and enter folklore. By the time the series was over, the 26-year-old Cook had 16 Test centuries to his name – and was back on track to take over from Strauss when the day came.
2010   14 Tests: 1,287 runs @ 58.50.
            3 ODI: 156 runs @ 52.00.

STEVEN DAVIES   Surrey

Kieswetter's demise was Davies's gain. Drafted in as an opener for the one-dayers against Pakistan at the end of the summer, left-hander Davies freed his arms outside off stump to such good effect that he cracked 87 off 67 balls in the first match at Chester-le-Street. The straighter ball caused him more problems, but his series strike-rate of 105 was justification enough, and he leapfrogged Kieswetter in the Test squad too to earn a tour of Australia, albeit an unproductive one. Once again, England's one-day wicketkeeping hierarchy was in flux.
2010   5 ODI: 197 runs @ 39.40; 7 catches.
            2 T20I: 42 runs @ 21.00; 2 catches, 1 stumping.

JOE DENLY   Kent

The brief trip to Dubai in February was, for the time being, as far as Denly would travel in England colours. Already ditched from the one-day side during the tour of South Africa, he failed twice in the Twenty20 games against Pakistan amid concern over shot selection, then made way for the more dynamic Kieswetter. With Davies emerging later in the year as a one-day opener, it was hard to see an immediate route back.
2010   2 T20I: 6 runs @ 3.00.

STEVE FINN   Middlesex

A heady first year in international cricket ended in anticlimax when Finn was dropped for Melbourne after taking more wickets in the first three Ashes Tests – 14 – than anyone on either side. His Australian experience, where he combined a strike-rate of 46 with an economy-rate of 4.3, summed up a year that appeared to play itself out in fast-forward, so it was no surprise when the selectors applied the brakes. But they had already seen enough. After replacing the injured Onions in Bangladesh, Finn proved a quiet but industrious fourth seamer, then cashed in on juicier pitches back home to collect successive second-innings five-fors against the Bangladeshis. His ability to find the splice off a good length unsettled Pakistan, and by the time England arrived in Australia, he was undisputed first change. The runs flowed off his bowling, mainly when he dropped too short at Perth, but he kept chipping in: six wickets to start the fightback at Brisbane, and the

Philip Brown

crucial scalp of Hussey on the final morning in Adelaide. If 36 overs for 183 at the WACA sealed his fate, then the 21-year-old Finn – strikingly adept at fielding off his own bowling – could be excused his youthful excesses. Here, plainly, was a bowler for the future.

2010   11 Tests: 16 runs @ 5.33; 46 wickets @ 26.23.

CRAIG KIESWETTER **Somerset**

For a while, Kieswetter could do no wrong (other than offend those who believed the England team already contained enough players born in South Africa). Fast-tracked into the limited-overs sides after smashing a 66-ball 81 for the Lions against the senior side in a Twenty20 game in Dubai, he made 107 in his third one-day international, at Dhaka, then won the match award in the World Twenty20 final. Despite his occasionally fallible keeping, England appeared to have found, in advance, a World Cup opener capable of clearing the infield on the slow pitches of the subcontinent. But home conditions proved less welcoming, and eight one-day internationals against Australia and Bangladesh brought a best of 38 and tut-tutting over stiff wrists and a sizeable gate. By the end of the summer he had lost the Twenty20 gloves and his 50-over place altogether – both to Davies. Rarely had the Flower regime felt so ruthless.

2010   12 ODI: 320 runs @ 26.66; 11 catches, 2 stumpings.
        9 T20I: 244 runs @ 27.11; 4 catches, 1 stumping.

MICHAEL LUMB **Hampshire**

At 30, Lumb may have imagined his best chance had come and gone, but his surprise inclusion in the World Twenty20 team turned into a feather in the selectors' cap. If his opening partner Kieswetter stole the headlines, Lumb was arguably the more selfless, sacrificing his average for a strike-rate of 141 – better than any of his team-mates. It was with cruel irony, then, that his foot was broken by a Kieswetter drive during a county game in August: an injury that put on hold any immediate prospect of maintaining his energetic start and summed up a poor summer with Hampshire.

2010   7 T20I: 137 runs @ 19.57.

EOIN MORGAN   Middlesex

Three unbeaten 50-over hundreds, each at better than a run a ball, confirmed Morgan's status as the one-day wicket most craved by the opposition – more so, even, than Pietersen. If his occasionally fortunate 110 at Dhaka reflected an impish brilliance against spin and near-mastery of the reverse-sweep, then his century against Australia at the Rose Bowl – where he would later repeat the deed against Pakistan – possessed genuine star quality, an impression not lost on Ricky Ponting. Morgan also grew into England's Twenty20 deal-clincher, but Test cricket proved a tougher nut to crack. Innings of 44 and 37 at home to Bangladesh merely served to highlight the dangers of flirting outside off in five-day cricket, but when Bell broke a foot prior to the Pakistan Tests, Morgan rode his luck to make a stylish match-winning 130 at Trent Bridge. Yet no sooner had the cries for an Ashes spot gone up, than they began to die down: his remaining five innings in the series yielded 45 runs, and when Bell returned for Brisbane, Morgan made way. The suspicion, though, was that his chance would come again sooner rather than later.

2010   6 Tests: 256 runs @ 32.00.
            17 ODI: 691 runs @ 53.15.
            11 T20I: 315 runs @ 52.50.

GRAHAM ONIONS   Durham

Onions's chance to build on his *Boy's Own* displays of batting defiance in South Africa – where he was unfortunate to miss out on helpful conditions at Johannesburg after toiling in tougher circumstances elsewhere – was ruined by a back injury which curtailed his trip to Bangladesh almost before it had begun. At first he targeted a return in time for the Ashes, but an operation in September – expected to rule him out of all cricket for nine months – underlined the severity of the stress fracture, leaving England's other seamers to forge their own bond without him.

2010   1 Test: 4 runs without being dismissed; 3 wickets @ 52.00.

KEVIN PIETERSEN   Hampshire/Surrey

Catharsis came late, but it came in style. A career-best 227 at Adelaide – plus the crucial wicket late on the fourth evening of Michael Clarke – bookended a page-turner of a year in which Pietersen managed to be named player of the tournament at the World Twenty20 and get dropped four months later from England's limited-overs sides. A tour of Bangladesh, in which he knuckled down in an unnoticed Test series but looked shaky against left-arm spin before opting to stay leg-side of the ball, was followed by a high-profile summer of struggles, prompting him to declare he was "not the man I used to be". The source of his angst became evident in the post-Melbourne glow when Pietersen claimed England would not have retained the Ashes had he not helped oust Peter Moores as coach two years earlier. That unstinting sense of drama had already been obvious when he was fined for inadvertently tweeting his displeasure at being dropped. But after turning the World Twenty20 into a personal tour de force, Pietersen became a frenetic presence at the crease, seeking to impose himself before he had settled in. Obliged to join Surrey after leaving Hampshire, his 50-over form ebbed too. But the thrill of an Ashes battle refocused the mind – and softened other blows.

2010 14 Tests: 831 runs @ 41.55; 1 wicket @ 59.00.
      9 ODI: 153 runs @ 17.00; 1 wicket @ 45.00.
      8 T20I: 353 runs @ 70.60.

LIAM PLUNKETT   Durham

Try as they might, England could not quite bring themselves to add Plunkett to their increasingly competitive squad of seamers. At times this felt cruel, and in Bangladesh his only international appearance yielded two wicketless overs in the Chittagong one-dayer: more a slap in the face than a spell of bowling. But others were progressing more quickly, and talk of advances made since his previous crack at the highest level in 2007 remained just that.

2010 1 ODI: did not bat; no wicket for 12.

MATT PRIOR   Sussex

If the loss of the gloves at 50-over and Twenty20 level had one silver lining, it was that Prior could concentrate on establishing his unrivalled class in five-day cricket. On both sides of the stumps, Prior was untouchable in Tests, even if his relative lack of explosiveness and dexterity meant England preferred the balance Kieswetter or Davies provided at the top of the order in the limited-over formats. But neither man offered Prior's combative reliability, and his stock was rarely higher than when making an unbeaten 102 in the second innings against Pakistan at Trent Bridge, or 118 at Sydney, where he hit England's fastest Ashes century since Ian Botham in 1981. His keeping went unnoticed, which was the highest compliment. And when he unfussily collected six catches in the first innings at Melbourne, part of a series haul of 23 – more catches than any England player in any Ashes in Australia – it felt a world away from his occasionally clumsy beginnings as a Test keeper. The reward was a World Cup place.

2010 14 Tests: 640 runs @ 40.00; 54 catches, 2 stumpings.
      3 ODI: 72 runs @ 72.00; 3 catches.
      2 T20I: 1 run without being dismissed; 2 catches, 1 stumping.

AJMAL SHAHZAD   Yorkshire

From the moment Shahzad collected two wickets in his first international over – in a Twenty20 game against Pakistan in Dubai – it was clear England had unearthed a seamer with the chutzpah to be more than an obliging tourist. His single Test, at Old Trafford, showcased weaknesses, then strengths: pummelled at first by Tamim Iqbal, he produced a second spell (4–2–10–3) full of nip and reverse-swing, a skill he had honed in the nets in Bangladesh. The management took note,

Gareth Copley, PA Photos

elevating him to the new ball for the Bristol one-day international. And although Bresnan's superior batting initially edged him out of the Ashes squad, Shahzad was drafted in as the 17th man when Anderson broke a rib during the bonding trip to Bavaria.

2010 1 Test: 5 runs @ 5.00; 4 wickets @ 15.75.
        4 ODI: 5 runs @ 5.00; 8 wickets @ 18.87.
        1 T20I: did not bat; 2 wickets @ 19.00.

RYAN SIDEBOTTOM   Nottinghamshire

Sidebottom's retirement from international cricket in September came as no great shock to those who had long sensed his tendency towards Twenty20 specialism. A solitary Test appearance, at Johannesburg at the start of the year, was wholehearted and luckless as well as controversial: many believed Onions should have played instead. But he was about to be pigeonholed for good. The World Twenty20, where a clever display in a practice match against South Africa reduced Anderson to a bench-warmer for the tournament's duration, allowed one last hurrah, and two wickets in his first two overs in the final set England on their way. But when it became clear that Sidebottom, his pace on the wane, would not be part of the Ashes plans – despite Flower's love of his left-arm angles – he pre-empted the squad announcement and called it a day.

2010 1 Test: 15 runs @ 7.50; 2 wickets @ 49.00.
        1 ODI: did not bat; 1 wicket @ 46.00.
        10 T20I: did not bat; 12 wickets @ 19.58.

ANDREW STRAUSS   Middlesex

Strauss's below-par batting return in Tests – the second-worst of his seven-year career – was easily forgiven when he became the first man to lead England to a series win in Australia for 24 years. If more than one commentator questioned his conservative instincts in the field, there was no doubting his rise to sporting statesmanship, nor the esteem in which his peers held him: this was Strauss's side and he was quietly proud of it. So it was typical that his one Test hundred of the year was arguably the most important of the 17 compiled by England batsmen in 2010, an initiative-grabbing 110 at Brisbane to underpin the second-innings resistance and engender Australian doubt. That alone turned his summer struggles against Pakistan's seamers into a distant memory – to say nothing of his third-ball dismissal in the first innings at the Gabba three days earlier. His one-day batting, though, was a revelation – proof, after all, that an old dog can learn new tricks. Building on a game that had previously revolved around back-foot ferocity and front-foot husbandry, Strauss now drove powerfully down the ground too, outscoring all his colleagues, galloping along at 96 runs per 100 balls and more than doubling his career tally of sixes from 10 to 22. But it was all an appetite-whetter to the Ashes *pièce de résistance*.

2010 12 Tests: 657 runs @ 34.57.
        14 ODI: 806 runs @ 57.57.

GRAEME SWANN   Nottinghamshire

By the end of 2010 it no longer felt odd to hear a player who nearly quit cricket a few years earlier being described as the "world's best spinner". Swann rose to No. 2 in the Test rankings after a ten-wicket haul at Chittagong in March – and stayed there. No one came within 30 wickets of his year's tally of 111 in all formats, and if he bowled more overs – 736 – than anyone, then one comparison told the tale: India's off-spinner Harbhajan Singh bowled almost as many (685) for fewer than half the wickets (52). Quite simply, Swann was irrepressible. He was also the player who justified England's preference for a four-man attack, employed both as a wicket-taker and – as a Twenty20 economy-rate of 5.86 confirmed – a run-stemmer. His batting fell away when he inched to No. 8 ahead of Broad, but his bowling was remorseless, and there was outrage in England when he was omitted from the ICC's player of the year shortlist, an oversight corrected almost immediately. In Australia, he attacked when necessary – sealing the win at Adelaide – and defended impeccably, conceding 23 runs in 22 overs on the third day at Melbourne. A minor celebrity thanks to his cult-status video diaries, he was also the progenitor and public face of the "Sprinkler", the team dance which embodied England's happy state of mind. It was a wonder the dressing-room ever managed without him.

2010   14 Tests: 242 runs @ 14.23; 64 wickets @ 25.96.
         14 ODI: 68 runs @ 11.33; 28 wickets @ 18.67.
         11 T20I: 9 runs without being dismissed; 19 wickets @ 11.42.

JAMES TREDWELL   Kent

After narrowly missing out on a Test debut at Chittagong, Tredwell toiled tirelessly at Dhaka, chipping in with useful runs from No. 10 and taking the burden off Swann in the second innings with four hard-earned wickets. Lacking Swann's guile, however, he was never likely to be more than a second spinner picked exclusively for trips to south Asia, and Monty Panesar ousted him in the Ashes party.

2010   1 Test: 37 runs @ 37.00; 6 wickets @ 30.16.
         2 ODI: 2 runs without being dismissed; no wicket for 70.

CHRIS TREMLETT   Surrey

Tremlett's successful return to the Test team more than three years after he had been discarded was a credit both to his own determination to start afresh and to the England fast-bowling coach David Saker's insistence that here was a bowler to persist with. A change of county signalled a desire to put the past – and the myth that he lacked sufficient drive – behind him, and when the injured Broad was ruled out of the last three Ashes Tests, Tremlett immediately set to work. He took a wicket in his first

Philip Brown

over, seven more in the same game at Perth, then helped Anderson dismantle Australia on the first day at Melbourne before taking the final wicket of the series at Sydney. Crucially, a refusal to camouflage his natural diffidence with manufactured snarl ensured he was comfortable in his own skin. The same could not be said for Australian batsmen trying to negotiate the bounce he produced from a good length, and England suddenly had another, potentially lethal, string to their bow.

2010   2 Tests: 7 runs @ 3.50; 13 wickets @ 19.00.

JONATHAN TROTT   Warwickshire

If few batsmen work as hard for their runs, no England player worked harder to win over the sceptics, who cited in evidence a fading tour to South Africa, where the locals were said to have got under Trott's skin, and a curiously becalmed innings in Dubai, which cost him his Twenty20 place. A mixed tour of Bangladesh did little to silence the carping, but the summer signalled a sequence that would eventually settle the matter. An insatiable 226 against Bangladesh at Lord's could be partly ascribed to the quality of the opposition, but his 184 there against Pakistan was an all-time great demonstration of skill against the swinging ball and stamina. Two more epics followed: 135 not out to help save the Brisbane Test, then an unbeaten 168 to lay the foundations for the Ashes-retaining win at the MCG – and leave Trott with a Test average of 64, second only to Don Bradman among those to have batted in 20 innings. His second-gear calmness may have felt old-fashioned, but – in an era of faddish cricket – no one provided more reassurance. For the first time in years, England's No. 3 position in Tests no longer felt like a poisoned chalice, an he booked that place in the 50-over side too.

2010   14 Tests: 1,325 runs @ 66.25; 1 wicket @ 58.00.
       7 ODI: 335 runs @ 47.85; no wicket for 18.
       2 T20I: 43 runs @ 21.50.

LUKE WRIGHT   Sussex

There was no getting away from the ongoing sense of identity crisis. No one doubted Wright's team ethic or his professionalism: his single over in the World Twenty20 final – five runs and the wicket of the rampaging Cameron White – punched well above its weight. But contributions from No. 6 or 7 felt like a bonus rather than an expectation, and a run of seven one-day internationals without a wicket was ended only by a dubious leg-before shout against Pakistan at the Rose Bowl. An economy-rate of 4.85 was respectable, but too often Wright's limitations exposed the discrepancy between the cricketer he was and the cricketer England wanted him to be. Neither did one Championship hundred and a single five-for further his cause.

2010   14 ODI: 172 runs @ 19.11; 5 wickets @ 60.20.
       11 T20I: 103 runs @ 20.60; 2 wickets @ 26.50.

MICHAEL YARDY   Sussex

Until Cameron White hit him out of the attack in the final at Bridgetown, Yardy was one of the quieter successes of England's World Twenty20 campaign. His mean left-arm darts were yin to Swann's off-spinning yang, and the tactic worked in 50-over cricket too – at least until the Pakistanis milked him for a run a ball in September. England's only problem was where he should bat. Five one-day innings at No. 6 produced an average of 22 and a strike-rate of 71, and his presence could leave the side feeling a batsman light. Overall, though, this was a triumph for pragmatism, and his World Twenty20 economy-rate of 6.80 was a heroic effort for someone who, at first-class level, did not bowl a single over all summer for his county.

2010   13 ODI: 121 runs @ 20.16; 10 wickets @ 48.00.
         9 T20I: 49 runs @ 24.50; 5 wickets @ 33.40.

ENGLAND TEST AVERAGES IN CALENDAR YEAR 2010

BATTING AND FIELDING

	T	I	NO	R	HS	100s	Avge	SR	Ct/St
I. J. L. Trott	14	24	4	1,325	226	4	66.25	49.44	7
I. R. Bell............	10	14	2	786	138	2	65.50	52.26	6
†A. N. Cook.........	14	24	2	1,287	235*	5	58.50	54.76	10
K. P. Pietersen	14	22	2	831	227	1	41.55	62.20	11
M. J. Prior	14	20	4	640	102*	1	40.00	61.47	54/2
T. T. Bresnan	4	3	0	120	91	0	40.00	34.98	1
†J. C. Tredwell......	1	1	0	37	37	0	37.00	58.73	1
†A. J. Strauss	12	20	1	657	110	1	34.57	52.06	17
†E. J. G. Morgan	6	8	0	256	130	1	32.00	52.56	4
†M. A. Carberry.....	1	2	0	64	34	0	32.00	45.71	1
P. D. Collingwood ...	12	18	0	514	145	1	28.55	50.94	22
†S. C. J. Broad	10	12	0	292	169	1	24.33	55.93	3
G. P. Swann	14	18	1	242	32	0	14.23	77.81	17
†R. J. Sidebottom.....	1	2	0	15	15	0	7.50	65.21	0
S. T. Finn	11	12	9	16	9*	0	5.33	16.66	3
†J. M. Anderson	12	16	3	65	13	0	5.00	28.88	6
A. Shahzad.........	1	1	0	5	5	0	5.00	41.66	2
C. T. Tremlett......	2	3	1	7	4	0	3.50	29.16	0
G. Onions..........	1	2	2	4	4*	0	–	20.00	0

BOWLING

	Style	O	M	R	W	BB	5W/i	Avge	SR
A. Shahzad	RFM	17	4	63	4	3-45	0	15.75	25.50
C. T. Tremlett.......	RF	75.5	15	247	13	5-87	1	19.00	35.00
J. M. Anderson	RFM	463	120	1,309	57	6-17	3	22.96	48.73
G. P. Swann	OB	576	121	1,662	64	6-65	6	25.96	54.00
S. T. Finn	RFM	304.4	64	1,207	46	6-125	3	26.23	39.73
T. T. Bresnan	RFM	168	54	470	17	4-50	0	27.64	59.29
J. C. Tredwell.......	OB	65	13	181	6	4-82	0	30.16	65.00
S. C. J. Broad	RFM	332.4	79	980	26	4-38	0	37.69	76.76
R. J. Sidebottom.....	LFM	31	6	98	2	2-98	0	49.00	93.00
G. Onions..........	RFM	42	8	156	3	2-69	0	52.00	84.00
I. J. L. Trott	RM	13	0	58	1	1-16	0	58.00	78.00
K. P. Pietersen	OB	21	1	59	1	1-10	0	59.00	126.00
P. D. Collingwood ...	RM	45	7	122	1	1-3	0	122.00	270.00

> " The only first division side to gain a positive result on general election day, Yorkshire were such clear winners that, had this been politics, their opponents would have lost their deposit."
> Yorkshire v Essex, page 617.

ENGLAND ONE-DAY INTERNATIONAL AVERAGES IN CALENDAR YEAR 2010

BATTING AND FIELDING

	M	I	NO	R	HS	100s	Avge	SR	Ct/St
M. J. Prior	3	2	1	72	42	0	72.00	75.78	3
I. R. Bell.	4	4	2	139	84*	0	69.50	71.64	1
†A. J. Strauss	14	14	0	806	154	2	57.57	95.95	11
†E. J. G. Morgan	17	17	4	691	110*	3	53.15	93.88	8
†A. N. Cook	3	3	0	156	64	0	52.00	90.69	3
R. S. Bopara	4	4	2	103	45*	0	51.50	145.07	1
I. J. L. Trott	7	7	0	335	110	1	47.85	77.54	1
†S. M. Davies.	5	5	0	197	87	0	39.40	105.91	7
P. D. Collingwood . . .	16	16	2	500	95	0	35.71	70.52	6
C. Kieswetter	12	12	0	320	107	1	26.66	85.79	11/2
†M. H. Yardy	13	11	5	121	57	0	20.16	77.56	2
T. T. Bresnan	15	13	5	155	34	0	19.37	98.10	5
L. J. Wright	14	11	2	172	48*	0	19.11	75.43	6
K. P. Pietersen	9	9	0	153	33	0	17.00	74.27	0
G. P. Swann	14	7	1	68	33	0	11.33	101.49	6
†J. M. Anderson	13	6	4	12	5*	0	6.00	46.15	6
†S. C. J. Broad	16	6	0	34	21	0	5.66	58.62	4
A. Shahzad	4	1	0	5	5	0	5.00	55.55	1
†J. C. Tredwell	2	1	1	2	2*	0	–	28.57	0
L. E. Plunkett	1	–	–	–	–	–	–	–	0
†R. J. Sidebottom.	1	–	–	–	–	–	–	–	0

BOWLING

	Style	O	M	R	W	BB	4W/i	Avge	SR	ER
R. S. Bopara	RM	10	1	38	4	4-38	1	9.50	15.00	3.80
G. P. Swann	OB	123	1	523	28	4-37	2	18.67	26.35	4.25
A. Shahzad	RFM	32.5	3	151	8	3-41	0	18.87	24.62	4.59
S. C. J. Broad	RFM	143	6	746	30	4-44	3	24.86	28.60	5.21
J. M. Anderson	RFM	120	9	609	18	3-22	0	33.83	40.00	5.07
T. T. Bresnan	RFM	130.4	5	700	19	4-28	1	36.84	41.26	5.35
K. P. Pietersen	OB	10	0	45	1	1-36	0	45.00	60.00	4.50
R. J. Sidebottom	LFM	7.4	0	46	1	1-46	0	46.00	46.00	6.00
M. H. Yardy	SLA	100	2	480	10	3-41	0	48.00	60.00	4.80
P. D. Collingwood	RM	57	2	271	5	1-8	0	54.20	68.40	4.75
L. J. Wright	RFM	62	1	301	5	2-34	0	60.20	74.40	4.85
J. C. Tredwell	OB	13	0	70	0	–	–	–	–	5.38
I. J. L. Trott	RM	3	0	18	0	–	–	–	–	6.00
L. E. Plunkett	RFM	2	0	12	0	–	–	–	–	6.00

ENGLAND TWENTY20 INTERNATIONAL AVERAGES IN CALENDAR YEAR 2010

BATTING AND FIELDING

	M	I	NO	R	HS	50s	Avge	SR	4	6	Ct/St
K. P. Pietersen	8	8	3	353	73*	3	70.60	134.22	31	10	3
†E. J. G. Morgan	11	11	5	315	67*	2	52.50	132.91	32	8	7
C. Kieswetter	9	9	0	244	63	1	27.11	117.87	23	12	4/1
†M. H. Yardy	9	5	3	49	35*	0	24.50	125.64	5	0	6
I. J. L. Trott	2	2	0	43	39	0	21.50	70.49	3	0	0
†S. M. Davies........	2	2	0	42	33	0	21.00	127.27	4	0	2/1
L. J. Wright	11	7	2	103	45*	0	20.60	124.09	4	6	2
†M. J. Lumb.........	7	7	0	137	33	0	19.57	141.23	18	3	3
T. T. Bresnan	11	5	2	41	23*	0	13.66	132.25	5	0	4
P. D. Collingwood ...	11	11	2	97	21	0	10.77	101.04	2	5	5
R. S. Bopara	3	3	0	32	12	0	10.66	68.08	3	0	2
J. L. Denly	2	2	0	6	5	0	3.00	46.15	0	0	1
G. P. Swann	11	3	3	9	7*	0	–	112.50	0	0	2
M. J. Prior	2	1	1	1	1*	0	–	100.00	0	0	2/1
†S. C. J. Broad	11	1	1	0	0*	0	–	–	0	0	7
†R. J. Sidebottom.....	10	–	–	–	–	–	–	–	–	–	2
A. Shahzad.........	1	–	–	–	–	–	–	–	–	–	0

BOWLING

	Style	O	M	R	W	BB	4W/i	Avge	SR	ER
G. P. Swann	OB	37	1	217	19	3-14	0	11.42	11.68	5.86
S. C. J. Broad.......	RFM	36.5	0	237	13	2-18	0	18.23	17.00	6.43
A. Shahzad.........	RFM	4	0	38	2	2-38	0	19.00	12.00	9.50
R. J. Sidebottom.....	LFM	32.3	0	235	12	3-23	0	19.58	16.25	7.23
L. J. Wright	RFM	7	0	53	2	1-5	0	26.50	21.00	7.57
T. T. Bresnan	RFM	35.4	0	241	9	3-10	0	26.77	23.77	6.75
M. H. Yardy........	SLA	28	0	167	5	2-19	0	33.40	33.60	5.96
P. D. Collingwood ...	RM	5	0	47	0	0-8	–	–	–	9.40

FIRST-CLASS AVERAGES, 2010

BATTING AND FIELDING

(Qualification: 10 innings)

Note: These averages include MCC v Durham in Abu Dhabi.

		M	I	NO	R	HS	100s	50s	Avge	Ct/St
1	G. P. Smith (*Durham MCCU & Leics*) .	7	12	5	652	158*	3	3	93.14	6
2	J. C. Hildreth (*Somerset*)	16	23	1	1,440	151	7	5	65.45	7
3	R. S. C. Martin-Jenkins (*Sussex*)	9	13	3	629	130	2	5	62.90	4
4	M. R. Ramprakash (*Surrey*)	16	28	2	1,595	248	5	5	61.34	5
5	†M. E. Trescothick (*Somerset*)	16	28	4	1,397	228*	4	6	58.20	26
6	†S. M. Davies (*Surrey & England Lions*)	14	22	3	1,090	137	2	9	57.36	38
7	I. J. L. Trott (*Warwicks & England*) . .	12	21	2	1,084	226	3	5	57.05	14
8	†S. Chanderpaul (*Lancs*)	8	14	1	698	120	2	5	53.69	2
9	†C. J. L. Rogers (*Derbys*)	15	27	3	1,285	200	4	5	53.54	19
10	†E. C. Joyce (*Sussex*)	10	17	3	738	154	2	3	52.71	17
11	M. W. Goodwin (*Sussex*)	16	26	3	1,201	142	4	5	52.21	5
12	†A. Lyth (*Yorks*)	16	29	0	1,509	142	3	9	52.03	9
13	†M. A. Carberry (*Hants*)	16	28	1	1,385	164	6	4	51.29	9
14	†J. A. Rudolph (*Yorks*)	16	29	2	1,375	228*	4	6	50.92	20
15	†M. J. Cosgrove (*Glam*)	15	26	2	1,187	142	5	4	49.45	10
16	†M. J. Di Venuto (*Durham*)	17	28	3	1,223	131	4	7	48.92	30
17	†J. H. K. Adams (*Hants*)	16	29	1	1,351	196	3	8	48.25	16
18	N. J. Dexter (*Middx*)	12	21	2	907	118	2	5	47.73	10
19	†A. W. Gale (*Yorks & England Lions*) . .	14	24	4	950	151*	3	4	47.50	2
20	J. du Toit (*Leics*)	13	20	1	899	154	2	6	47.31	16
21	S. D. Peters (*Northants*)	16	30	2	1,320	199	3	7	47.14	16
22	N. D. McKenzie (*Hants*)	15	25	5	942	141*	3	4	47.10	21
23	†M. M. Ali (*Worcs & England Lions*) . . .	16	30	3	1,270	126	3	9	47.03	12
24	A. U. Rashid (*Yorks*)	16	24	8	732	76	0	6	45.75	14
25	C. M. W. Read (*Notts*)	17	26	5	945	124*	2	5	45.00	60/4
26	J. Allenby (*Glam*)	16	25	4	933	105	1	10	44.42	16
27	†B. A. Stokes (*Durham*)	14	21	3	798	161*	2	3	44.33	8
28	A. B. McDonald (*Leics*)	6	11	1	442	176*	2	1	44.20	2
29	A. N. Kervezee (*Worcs*)	16	30	3	1,190	155	3	6	44.07	14
30	M. van Jaarsveld (*Kent*)	17	29	2	1,188	110*	3	6	44.00	36
31	I. R. Bell (*Warwicks & England*)	8	13	1	526	128	2	2	43.83	11
32	A. McGrath (*Yorks*)	16	29	1	1,219	124*	3	9	43.53	9
33	B. C. Brown (*Sussex*)	9	14	2	515	112	2	2	42.91	9/2
34	D. I. Stevens (*Kent*)	15	26	3	979	197	4	2	42.56	6
35	†S. M. Ervine (*Hants*)	17	27	4	976	237*	1	5	42.43	7
36	L. J. Wright (*Sussex*)	9	12	1	465	134	1	3	42.27	3
37	D. K. H. Mitchell (*Worcs*)	16	31	3	1,180	165*	4	4	42.14	32
38	J. W. A. Taylor (*MCC, Leics & Eng. Lions*)	19	31	4	1,134	206*	3	4	42.00	16
39	J. M. Bairstow (*Yorks*)	16	29	7	918	81	0	8	41.72	29/5
40	M. A. Wagh (*Notts*)	16	24	1	953	139	3	3	41.43	8
41	†E. J. G. Morgan (*Middx & England*) . . .	7	10	1	372	130	1	2	41.33	4
42	†C. F. Hughes (*Derbys*)	12	21	2	784	156	2	4	41.26	12
43	†A. G. Prince (*Lancs*)	7	13	2	450	115	1	4	40.90	7
44	†P. Mustard (*Durham*)	17	26	6	815	120	2	5	40.75	43/2
45	K. J. Coetzer (*Durham*)	8	15	2	526	172	1	3	40.46	3
46	M. J. Prior (*Sussex & England*)	13	19	3	639	123*	2	2	39.93	41/1
47	S. J. Mullaney (*Notts*)	11	17	4	512	100*	1	3	39.38	6
48	R. S. Bopara (*England Lions & Essex*) .	9	17	2	590	142	2	3	39.33	4
49	C. D. Nash (*Sussex*)	17	29	2	1,051	184	3	1	38.92	12
50	Z. de Bruyn (*Somerset*)	14	21	0	814	95	0	5	38.76	10

		M	I	NO	R	HS	100s	50s	Avge	Ct/St
51	J. M. Vince (*Hants*)	16	27	4	891	180	1	4	38.73	11
52	S. J. Croft (*Lancs*)	16	26	3	883	93	0	8	38.39	13
53	D. Murphy (*Lough. MCCU & Northants*)	11	18	7	421	76	0	4	38.27	30
54	†M. J. Walker (*Essex*)	12	24	2	838	105	1	4	38.09	8
55	W. I. Jefferson (*Leics*)	11	20	1	722	135	2	4	38.00	14
56	†W. T. S. Porterfield (*Glos*)	7	14	0	531	175	2	1	37.92	6
57	†D. J. Malan (*MCC & Middx*)	17	31	3	1,055	115	3	5	37.67	21
58	A. D. Brown (*Notts*)	17	26	3	863	134	1	6	37.52	12
59	G. J. Muchall (*Durham*)	10	15	1	520	140*	2	1	37.14	3
60	O. A. Shah (*Middx*)	13	23	1	804	156	2	3	36.54	10
61	†P. J. Franks (*Notts*)	16	22	1	765	114	1	6	36.42	1
62	†N. M. Carter (*Warwicks*)	11	20	3	617	99*	0	4	36.29	0
63	G. K. Berg (*Middx*)	15	26	5	761	125	1	3	36.23	7
64	†J. G. Cameron (*Worcs*)	10	17	1	576	105	1	3	36.00	7
65	W. A. White (*Leics*)	9	13	2	394	101*	1	1	35.81	4
66	Umar Akmal (*Pakistanis*)	7	13	2	393	153	1	1	35.72	5
67	A. D. Hales (*Notts*)	12	20	1	677	136	1	4	35.63	12
68	N. Pothas (*Hants*)	9	15	0	531	87	0	4	35.40	33
69	H. J. H. Marshall (*Glos*)	15	27	2	884	89*	0	7	35.36	15
70	†G. P. Rees (*Glam*)	17	30	4	918	106*	2	5	35.30	6
71	†P. A. Nixon (*Leics*)	16	27	1	915	106	1	7	35.19	4
72	†I. D. Blackwell (*Durham*)	16	26	2	833	86	0	8	34.70	2
73	S. D. Robson (*Middx*)	8	15	0	513	204	1	2	34.20	8
74	†U. Afzaal (*Surrey*)	13	22	2	682	159*	1	4	34.10	4
75	R. N. ten Doeschate (*Essex*)	11	19	2	577	85	0	5	33.94	9
76	†N. Boje (*Northants*)	9	15	1	471	98	0	4	33.64	3
77	†A. N. Cook (*Essex, Eng. Lions & England*)	14	24	1	773	110	2	3	33.60	12
78	W. L. Madsen (*Derbys*)	16	29	1	940	179	4	2	33.57	11
79	A. V. Suppiah (*Somerset*)	16	26	3	771	125	1	4	33.52	5
80	J. C. Buttler (*Somerset*)	13	20	3	569	144	1	2	33.47	23
81	J. K. H. Naik (*Leics*)	8	12	3	301	72	0	1	33.44	5
81	†K. W. Hogg (*Lancs*)	9	13	4	301	88	0	2	33.44	3
83	†A. J. Strauss (*Middx & England*)	14	25	1	801	92	0	6	33.37	25
84	N. R. D. Compton (*Somerset*)	11	17	3	465	72	0	2	33.21	5
85	†J. E. C. Franklin (*Glos*)	16	29	3	862	108	1	4	33.15	7
86	P. D. Trego (*Somerset*)	16	23	2	693	108	1	5	33.00	12
87	†M. D. Stoneman (*Durham*)	11	17	1	525	118	1	4	32.81	5
88	†S. A. Newman (*MCC & Middx*)	16	29	0	950	126	2	6	32.75	10
89	†G. M. Andrew (*Worcs*)	9	14	1	425	79	0	4	32.69	2
90	B. J. Wright (*Glam*)	17	27	1	847	172	2	4	32.57	7
91	R. I. Newton (*Northants*)	6	11	0	357	102	1	2	32.45	1
92	†T. J. New (*Leics*)	17	27	4	746	91	0	6	32.43	46/1
93	G. O. Jones (*Kent*)	17	31	0	1,003	178	3	2	32.35	49/6
94	C. G. Taylor (*Glos*)	15	27	2	803	89	0	6	32.12	11
95	O. P. Rayner (*Sussex*)	7	10	2	256	67*	0	2	32.00	10
96	†T. J. Lancefield (*Surrey*)	8	13	1	381	74	0	2	31.75	3
97	†M. A. G. Boyce (*Leics*)	15	27	3	761	90	0	6	31.70	19
98	†M. H. Yardy (*Sussex*)	9	13	2	345	100*	1	1	31.36	12
99	S. I. Mahmood (*Lancs*)	15	20	2	564	72	0	5	31.33	2
100	R. W. T. Key (*Kent*)	16	28	2	814	261	2	1	31.30	1
101	B. J. M. Scott (*Worcs*)	7	12	2	313	98	0	3	31.30	30/1
102	D. M. Benkenstein (*Durham*)	17	28	1	840	114	1	5	31.11	14
103	J. S. Foster (*MCC & Essex*)	17	29	1	871	169	1	4	31.10	49/6
104	†P. A. Jaques (*Worcs*)	8	15	0	465	94	0	3	31.00	9
105	P. S. Jones (*Derbys*)	12	18	4	427	86	0	1	30.50	4
106	R. J. Hamilton-Brown (*Surrey*)	17	29	1	844	125	2	3	30.14	11
107	†M. N. W. Spriegel (*Surrey*)	10	14	1	391	108*	2	0	30.07	10
108	M. J. Chilton (*Lancs*)	16	29	4	750	69	0	4	30.00	6
109	G. L. Brophy (*Yorks*)	9	17	1	472	103	1	1	29.50	20

		M	I	NO	R	HS	100s	50s	Avge	Ct/St
110	R. Clarke (*Warwicks*)	15	28	5	673	127*	0	3	29.26	23
111	A. J. Hall (*Northants*)	15	27	3	696	133	1	3	29.00	21
	L. A. Dawson (*Hants*)	8	13	1	348	86	0	3	29.00	4
	G. D. Cross (*Lancs*)	7	11	1	290	100*	1	0	29.00	12
114	S. R. Patel (*Notts*)	17	28	2	750	104	1	4	28.84	9
115	†B. W. Harmison (*Durham*)	6	10	0	286	96	0	2	28.60	0
116	A. G. Wakely (*Northants*)	13	22	0	627	108	1	4	28.50	6
117	†M. Kartik (*Somerset*)	11	12	5	199	52*	0	2	28.42	9
118	J. C. Mickleburgh (*Essex*)	16	30	0	852	174	1	3	28.40	11
119	†J. J. Sayers (*Yorks*)	9	14	0	395	63	0	5	28.21	3
120	L. D. Sutton (*Lancs*)	13	21	2	530	118	1	2	27.89	37/5
121	G. M. Smith (*Derbys*)	16	27	1	721	165*	1	4	27.73	4
122	T. L. Maynard (*Glam*)	11	18	0	495	98	0	4	27.50	11
123	C. Kieswetter (*Somerset*)	12	18	1	467	84	0	4	27.47	29
124	†M. A. Wallace (*Glam*)	16	24	1	626	113	1	4	27.21	43/4
125	†J. C. Tredwell (*Kent*)	12	20	2	489	115	1	1	27.16	21
126	D. G. Cork (*Hants*)	13	17	3	380	55	0	2	27.14	8
127	†Salman Butt (*Pakistanis*)	7	14	0	376	92	0	2	26.85	1
128	V. S. Solanki (*Worcs*)	15	28	1	717	114	1	4	26.55	18
129	†B. H. N. Howgego (*Northants*)	7	13	2	292	80	0	1	26.54	3
130	Azhar Ali (*Pakistanis*)	6	12	1	291	92*	0	2	26.45	3
131	†J. A. Simpson (*Middx*)	16	27	2	657	101*	1	2	26.28	42/2
132	†C. P. Schofield (*Surrey*)	8	13	0	341	90	0	2	26.23	5
133	†T. C. Smith (*Lancs*)	14	25	3	576	128	2	2	26.18	14
134	†I. J. Westwood (*Warwicks*)	16	32	4	726	86*	0	5	25.92	6
135	†C. D. J. Dent (*Glos*)	16	31	3	725	98	0	4	25.89	24
136	T. Westley (*Durham MCCU & Essex*)	10	18	1	440	132	1	2	25.88	1
137	†A. Harinath (*Surrey*)	14	25	1	621	63	0	4	25.87	3
138	†B. A. Godleman (*Essex*)	12	22	0	569	106	1	2	25.86	12
139	J. L. Denly (*Kent*)	18	33	0	848	106	1	5	25.69	10
140	†J. K. Maunders (*Essex*)	7	12	0	307	126	1	1	25.58	6
141	G. T. Park (*Derbys*)	11	19	2	431	124*	1	1	25.35	6
142	T. T. Bresnan (*Yorks & England*)	7	10	1	228	70	0	2	25.33	3
143	J. D. Middlebrook (*MCC & Northants*)	13	23	4	479	84	0	3	25.21	6
144	G. Chapple (*Lancs*)	14	22	6	403	54*	0	2	25.18	4
145	J. W. M. Dalrymple (*Glam*)	15	22	0	554	105	1	2	25.18	19
	B. M. Shafayat (*Notts*)	7	11	0	277	159	1	0	25.18	7
147	S. C. Moore (*Lancs*)	9	17	0	426	61	0	2	25.05	6
148	G. J. Batty (*Surrey*)	15	24	2	550	67	0	2	25.00	12
	M. J. Powell (*Glam*)	7	12	1	275	55	0	1	25.00	1
150	M. L. Pettini (*Essex*)	15	27	3	599	96	0	2	24.95	7
151	K. P. Pietersen (*England & Surrey*)	8	12	1	273	80	0	2	24.81	6
152	M. B. Loye (*Northants*)	10	18	1	420	164	1	1	24.70	0
153	A. J. Hodd (*Sussex*)	10	14	1	319	109	1	1	24.53	29/1
154	A. Shahzad (*Yorks & England*)	10	13	3	243	45	0	0	24.30	3
155	S. J. Walters (*Surrey*)	6	10	0	242	53	0	1	24.20	8
156	V. Chopra (*Warwicks*)	9	18	1	409	54	0	3	24.05	9
157	C. R. Woakes (*Warwicks & Eng. Lions*)	14	22	3	457	136*	1	1	24.05	7
158	S. A. Northeast (*Kent*)	17	30	0	719	71	0	4	23.96	6
159	†D. J. Redfern (*Derbys*)	9	15	1	331	85	0	1	23.64	3
160	B. F. Smith (*Worcs*)	8	14	2	282	80	0	2	23.50	9
161	A. P. R. Gidman (*MCC & Glos*)	17	31	0	725	99	0	3	23.38	17
162	M. A. Thornely (*Sussex*)	12	21	1	467	89	0	4	23.35	8
163	†N. J. Edwards (*Notts*)	7	11	0	255	85	0	1	23.18	17
164	†Shakib Al Hasan (*Bangladeshis & Worcs*)	11	20	2	415	90	0	3	23.05	4
165	†R. J. Peterson (*Derbys*)	15	24	3	484	58	0	2	23.04	9
166	D. J. Sales (*MCC & Northants*)	16	30	0	687	127	1	2	22.90	22
167	P. J. Horton (*Lancs*)	16	30	2	634	123	1	3	22.64	19
	Azhar Mahmood (*Kent*)	8	14	0	317	64	0	2	22.64	1
	†T. J. Murtagh (*MCC & Middx*)	16	25	11	317	55*	0	2	22.64	4

		M	I	NO	R	HS	100s	50s	Avge	Ct/St
170	†S. G. Borthwick (*Durham*)	12	17	3	315	68	0	2	22.50	9
171	†A. J. Blake (*Kent*)	9	17	1	359	105*	1	0	22.43	5
172	†M. T. Coles (*Kent*)	14	23	6	378	51	0	1	22.23	4
173	R. D. B. Croft (*Glam*)	9	14	3	244	63	0	2	22.18	0
174	A. Nel (*Surrey*)	7	10	0	219	96	0	1	21.90	4
175	W. J. Durston (*Derbys*)	6	11	0	240	69	0	1	21.81	9
	Kadeer Ali (*Glos*)	6	12	1	240	74	0	1	21.81	5
177	T. D. Groenewald (*Derbys*)	13	19	9	216	35*	0	0	21.60	3
178	C. C. Benham (*Hants*)	7	13	0	278	45	0	1	21.38	11
179	†Imran Farhat (*Pakistanis*)	6	12	0	256	67	0	1	21.33	5
180	D. S. Lucas (*Northants*)	11	17	2	316	40*	0	0	21.06	1
181	E. Chigumbura (*Northants*)	6	10	1	189	44	0	0	21.00	0
182	C. T. Tremlett (*Surrey*)	12	17	6	230	53*	0	1	20.90	1
183	D. A. Wheeldon (*Worcs*)	7	14	1	269	65	0	2	20.69	2
184	A. C. Thomas (*Somerset*)	15	20	4	328	44	0	0	20.50	1
	P. M. Borrington (*Derbys*)	7	13	1	246	79*	0	1	20.50	4
186	†J. O. Troughton (*Warwicks*)	16	30	1	585	78	0	5	20.17	5
187	R. A. White (*Northants*)	10	19	1	363	95	0	2	20.16	3
188	W. R. Smith (*Durham*)	6	10	0	195	57	0	1	19.50	3
189	D. L. Maddy (*Warwicks*)	14	27	1	499	61	0	2	19.19	16
190	J. J. Cobb (*Leics*)	5	10	2	153	55*	0	1	19.12	3
191	L. M. Daggett (*Northants*)	12	17	8	167	48	0	0	18.55	3
192	†T. J. Phillips (*Essex*)	10	16	3	240	46*	0	1	18.46	8
193	O. B. Cox (*Worcs*)	9	16	4	218	59	0	1	18.16	18/1
194	S. D. Snell (*Glos*)	10	19	1	322	71	0	2	17.88	18
195	†A. G. Botha (*Warwicks*)	8	14	0	248	76	0	1	17.71	7
196	D. A. Cosker (*MCC & Glam*)	17	26	10	283	49*	0	0	17.68	7
197	†Umar Amin (*Pakistanis*)	5	10	0	174	73	0	1	17.40	1
198	D. D. Masters (*Essex*)	14	22	1	356	50	0	1	16.95	8
199	Imran Tahir (*Warwicks*)	16	27	4	384	69*	0	1	16.69	4
200	L. J. Goddard (*Derbys*)	8	11	1	165	67	0	1	16.50	24
201	J. Lewis (*MCC & Glos*)	17	30	2	451	50	0	1	16.10	7
202	J. N. Batty (*Glos*)	15	30	2	450	61	0	1	16.07	53/3
203	A. R. Adams (*Notts*)	14	20	5	240	37	0	0	16.00	13
204	†M. E. Claydon (*Durham*)	13	16	4	185	38*	0	0	15.41	2
205	H. M. C. M. Bandara (*Kent*)	6	10	3	105	29	0	0	15.00	5
206	B. J. Phillips (*Somerset*)	11	15	3	179	55	0	1	14.91	5
207	J. A. R. Harris (*Glam & England Lions*)	14	20	2	267	49	0	0	14.83	3
208	S. A. Patterson (*Yorks*)	14	17	4	184	39*	0	0	14.15	3
209	J. B. Hockley (*Kent*)	6	11	1	141	82	0	1	14.10	7
210	J. S. Gatting (*Sussex*)	8	11	0	155	31	0	0	14.09	4
211	D. S. Harrison (*Glam*)	12	18	0	253	35	0	0	14.05	2
212	J. W. Dernbach (*Surrey*)	15	20	9	154	56*	0	1	14.00	1
213	†Mohammad Aamer (*Pakistanis*)	7	14	3	151	44*	0	0	13.72	0
214	M. S. Mason (*Worcs*)	8	12	2	137	51*	0	1	13.70	6
215	S. C. Meaker (*Surrey*)	11	14	1	175	94	0	1	13.46	3
216	C. J. C. Wright (*Essex*)	11	17	5	161	28*	0	0	13.41	2
217	T. R. Ambrose (*Warwicks*)	11	20	0	267	54	0	1	13.35	33/3
218	C. W. Henderson (*Leics*)	16	21	1	265	33	0	0	13.25	6
219	L. E. Plunkett (*Durham & England Lions*)	15	18	0	238	51	0	1	13.22	10
220	†J. A. Tomlinson (*Hants*)	15	21	5	198	42	0	0	12.37	3
221	S. J. Cook (*Kent*)	14	24	7	205	26*	0	0	12.05	2
222	S. D. Udal (*Middx*)	13	19	1	216	55	0	1	12.00	6
223	†J. E. Anyon (*Sussex*)	11	15	0	174	34	0	0	11.60	3
224	A. M. Bates (*Hants*)	8	11	3	92	31	0	0	11.50	28
225	T. S. Roland-Jones (*Middx*)	8	12	1	124	26	0	0	11.27	3
226	†M. S. Panesar (*Sussex & England Lions*)	16	20	5	163	46*	0	0	10.86	2
227	Kamran Akmal (*Pakistanis*)	6	12	0	128	46	0	0	10.66	27/1
228	C. Rushworth (*Durham*)	9	14	2	127	28	0	0	10.58	1

		M	I	NO	R	HS	100s	50s	Avge	Ct/St
229	D. R. Briggs (*Hants*)	13	14	3	116	28	0	0	10.54	2
230	J. A. Brooks (*Northants*)	14	20	3	177	53	0	1	10.41	2
231	A. Richardson (*Worcs*)	14	18	11	71	11	0	0	10.14	1
232	D. J. Pattinson (*Notts*)	13	14	4	101	27	0	0	10.10	0
233	†V. Banerjee (*Glos*)	7	14	3	108	35	0	0	9.81	1
234	S. P. Kirby (*MCC, Glos & England Lions*)	12	20	6	135	22*	0	0	9.64	2
235	G. M. Hussain (*Glos*)	15	26	10	153	28*	0	0	9.56	1
236	†T. Lungley (*Derbys*)	7	10	1	85	21	0	0	9.44	6
237	A. S. Miller (*Warwicks*)	7	12	5	65	35	0	0	9.28	4
238	T. E. Linley (*Surrey*)	7	10	4	55	16	0	0	9.16	4
239	A. Khan (*Kent*)	12	18	5	115	24	0	0	8.84	4
240	C. D. Collymore (*Sussex*)	14	17	8	78	19*	0	0	8.66	3
241	M. H. A. Footitt (*Derbys*)	9	12	3	69	30	0	0	7.66	3
242	H. T. Waters (*Glam*)	11	13	4	67	16	0	0	7.44	1
243	†C. M. Willoughby (*Somerset*)	16	18	6	85	16	0	0	7.08	1
244	†W. B. Rankin (*Warwicks*)	9	16	7	63	13	0	0	7.00	2
245	Danish Kaneria (*Essex & Pakistanis*)	9	14	2	82	16*	0	0	6.83	1
246	†J. M. Anderson (*Lancs & England*)	10	13	2	69	25*	0	0	6.27	3
247	N. L. Buck (*Leics*)	15	20	5	93	26	0	0	6.20	4
248	S. J. Harmison (*Durham*)	9	12	6	36	11*	0	0	6.00	2
249	R. A. Jones (*Worcs*)	11	19	2	100	21*	0	0	5.88	7
250	†J. D. Shantry (*Worcs*)	11	15	5	55	13*	0	0	5.50	3
251	†Mohammad Asif (*Pakistanis*)	6	10	3	37	14	0	0	5.28	1
252	M. A. Chambers (*Essex*)	11	16	5	53	14	0	0	4.81	5
253	S. T. Finn (*Middx & England*)	13	19	9	47	18	0	0	4.70	1
254	†S. C. Kerrigan (*Lancs*)	13	15	5	45	16*	0	0	4.50	3
255	P. T. Collins (*Middx*)	10	13	4	36	13	0	0	4.00	0
256	†O. J. Hannon-Dalby (*Yorks*)	17	15	7	29	11*	0	0	3.62	1
257	M. J. Hoggard (*Leics*)	15	17	6	31	6	0	0	2.81	5
258	A. J. Ireland (*Glos*)	8	12	2	21	11	0	0	2.10	0

BOWLING

(Qualification: 10 wickets in 5 innings)

		Style	O	M	R	W	BB	5Wi	Avge
1	R. S. Bopara (*Eng. Lions & Essex*)	RM	35.1	5	122	11	4-14	0	11.09
2	J. K. H. Naik (*Leics*)	OB	205	40	619	35	7-96	1	17.68
3	J. M. Anderson (*Lancs & England*)	RFM	355.2	115	884	48	6-17	3	18.41
4	C. P. Wood (*Hants*)	LFM	71.1	17	240	13	5-54	1	18.46
5	Mohammad Aamer (*Pakistanis*)	LFM	224.5	47	656	35	6-84	3	18.74
6	G. P. Swann (*Notts & England*)	OB	200.1	58	567	30	6-65	3	18.90
7	S. C. J. Broad (*Notts & England*)	RFM	179.5	37	626	33	8-52	2	18.96
8	M. A. Ashraf (*Yorks*)	RFM	75	20	212	11	5-32	1	19.27
9	M. Kartik (*Somerset*)	SLA	383.2	107	882	45	6-42	5	19.60
10	T. S. Roland-Jones (*Middx*)	RFM	230.2	34	745	38	5-41	2	19.60
11	G. Chapple (*Lancs*)	RFM	372.4	89	1,027	52	5-27	2	19.75
11	M. Ntini (*Kent*)	RFM	164	44	474	24	6-51	2	19.75
13	R. S. C. Martin-Jenkins (*Sussex*)	RFM	201.1	35	593	30	5-45	1	19.76
14	C. D. Collymore (*Sussex*)	RFM	414	115	1,133	57	6-48	2	19.87
15	C. T. Tremlett (*Surrey*)	RF	361.5	88	969	48	4-29	0	20.18
16	R. J. Sidebottom (*Notts*)	LFM	236	62	630	30	5-35	1	21.00
17	C. W. Henderson (*Leics*)	SLA	489.3	136	1,179	56	6-21	3	21.05
18	L. J. Hatchett (*Sussex*)	LFM	66.4	15	256	12	5-47	1	21.33
19	C. R. Woakes (*Warwicks & Eng. Lions*)	RFM	424.2	107	1,246	58	6-52	3	21.48
20	J. A. R. Harris (*Glam & Eng. Lions*)	RFM	463.4	117	1,356	63	5-56	2	21.52

		Style	O	M	R	W	BB	5W/i	Avge
21	J. Allenby (*Glam*)	RM	330.1	81	885	41	5-59	1	21.58
22	A. J. Ireland (*Glos*)	RFM	222.5	33	784	36	5-25	2	21.77
23	S. T. Finn (*Middx & England*)	RFM	407.1	92	1,410	64	9-37	4	22.03
24	N. M. Carter (*Warwicks*)	LFM	356.2	70	1,129	51	5-60	4	22.13
25	A. R. Adams (*Notts*)	RFM	455.5	101	1,508	68	6-79	4	22.17
26	G. Keedy (*Lancs*)	SLA	246.5	43	688	31	7-68	2	22.19
27	G. M. Hussain (*Glos*)	RFM	417.4	86	1,497	67	5-36	2	22.34
28	B. J. Phillips (*Somerset*)	RFM	277.3	79	661	29	5-72	1	22.79
29	O. P. Rayner (*Sussex*)	OB	148.2	38	412	18	4-62	0	22.88
30	T. Westley (*Essex & Durham MCCU*)	OB	88.3	15	229	10	4-55	0	22.90
31	D. D. Masters (*Essex*)	RFM	487	138	1,223	53	5-43	1	23.07
32	D. A. Cosker (*MCC & Glam*)	SLA	470	109	1,224	53	5-93	1	23.09
33	D. G. Cork (*Hants*)	RFM	407.2	102	1,042	45	5-50	2	23.15
34	J. Lewis (*MCC & Glos*)	RFM	435.3	106	1,275	55	4-25	0	23.18
35	R. Clarke (*Warwicks*)	RFM	212.5	31	743	32	6-63	1	23.21
36	J. E. C. Franklin (*Glos*)	LFM	334.2	69	1,083	46	7-14	1	23.54
37	M. A. Chambers (*Essex*)	RFM	269.3	51	909	38	6-68	2	23.92
38	A. Carter (*Essex*)	RFM	100.5	15	311	13	5-40	1	23.92
39	E. Chigumbura (*Northants*)	RFM	114	17	482	20	5-92	1	24.10
40	A. Richardson (*Worcs*)	RFM	524	153	1,342	55	5-44	2	24.40
41	M. J. Hoggard (*Leics*)	RFM	416.4	105	1,222	50	6-63	3	24.44
42	A. C. Thomas (*Somerset*)	RFM	377.5	85	1,202	49	5-40	2	24.53
43	Imran Tahir (*Warwicks*)	LBG	430.4	58	1,376	56	8-114	3	24.57
44	G. G. Wagg (*Derbys*)	LM/SLA	77	13	246	10	3-31	0	24.60
45	Yasir Arafat (*Sussex*)	RFM	256	43	896	36	5-74	2	24.88
46	D. L. Maddy (*Warwicks*)	RM	206.5	62	523	21	4-37	0	24.90
47	L. J. Wright (*Sussex*)	RFM	154.5	22	573	23	5-65	1	24.91
48	Shakib Al Hasan (*Bangladeshis & Worcs*)	SLA	345.3	56	1,088	43	7-32	4	25.30
49	Kabir Ali (*Hants*)	RFM	137.2	27	488	19	5-33	2	25.68
50	M. S. Panesar (*Sussex & Eng. Lions*)	SLA	518.2	135	1,336	52	5-44	2	25.69
51	A. P. R. Gidman (*MCC & Glos*)	RM	68	11	257	10	2-10	0	25.70
52	S. J. Harmison (*Durham*)	RF	265.4	55	895	34	7-29	1	26.32
53	J. E. Anyon (*Sussex*)	RFM	227.2	41	767	29	3-23	0	26.44
54	R. N. ten Doeschate (*Essex*)	RM	191.3	16	716	27	5-13	1	26.51
55	Naved-ul-Hasan (*Sussex*)	RFM	162.4	44	532	20	4-28	0	26.60
56	A. B. McDonald (*Leics*)	RM	103	21	320	12	5-40	1	26.66
57	S. A. Patterson (*Yorks*)	RFM	392.5	96	1,201	45	5-50	1	26.68
58	P. J. Franks (*Notts*)	RFM	410.2	106	1,129	42	3-15	0	26.88
59	D. G. Wright (*Somerset*)	RFM	154.1	41	377	14	5-41	1	26.92
60	S. P. Kirby (*MCC, Glos & Eng. Lions*)	RFM	306.4	72	970	36	4-50	0	26.94
61	W. B. Rankin (*Warwicks*)	RFM	145.3	19	594	22	5-16	1	27.00
62	J. W. Dernbach (*Surrey*)	RFM	447	98	1,390	51	5-68	2	27.25
63	C. M. Willoughby (*Somerset*)	LFM	512.1	118	1,582	58	6-101	1	27.27
64	I. E. O'Brien (*Middx*)	RFM	205.1	36	628	23	7-48	1	27.30
65	N. L. Buck (*Leics*)	RFM	381.5	85	1,340	49	4-44	0	27.34
66	M. S. Mason (*Worcs*)	RFM	278	72	849	31	4-87	0	27.38
67	D. I. Stevens (*Kent*)	RM	280.1	74	768	28	4-38	0	27.42
68	I. D. Blackwell (*Durham*)	SLA	488.3	139	1,291	47	5-78	2	27.46
69	A. P. Palladino (*Essex*)	RFM	142	30	499	18	4-57	0	27.72
70	P. T. Collins (*Middx*)	LFM	284.4	51	999	36	4-46	0	27.75
71	Umar Gul (*Pakistanis*)	RFM	119.4	21	391	14	4-61	0	27.92
72	Azhar Mahmood (*Kent*)	RFM	279.3	55	847	30	5-62	2	28.23
73	C. D. Thorp (*Durham*)	RFM	158.3	46	452	16	4-54	0	28.25
74	A. Shahzad (*Yorks & England*)	RFM	309.2	51	1,076	38	5-51	1	28.31
75	G. M. Andrew (*Worcs*)	RFM	196.4	32	656	23	4-45	0	28.52
76	M. N. Malik (*Leics*)	RFM	193.2	45	599	21	4-32	0	28.52
77	T. C. Smith (*Lancs*)	RFM	279.5	58	913	32	6-94	1	28.53

		Style	O	M	R	W	BB	5W/i	Avge
78	Mohammad Asif (*Pakistanis*)	RFM	211.1	46	657	23	5-77	1	28.56
79	B. W. Harmison (*Durham*)........	RFM	86.4	14	402	14	4-70	0	28.71
80	N. J. Dexter (*Middx*)............	RM	120	25	378	13	3-50	0	29.07
81	J. L. Clare (*Derbys*)	RFM	69.3	8	324	11	4-42	0	29.45
82	D. J. Balcombe (*Hants*)	RFM	246.1	52	812	27	3-69	0	30.07
83	T. E. Linley (*Surrey*)	RFM	170	46	483	16	5-105	1	30.18
84	J. C. Tredwell (*Kent*)	OB	377	71	1,151	38	7-22	2	30.28
85	A. S. Miller (*Warwicks*)	RFM	154.4	42	488	16	5-58	2	30.50
86	S. G. Borthwick (*Durham*)......	LBG	173.4	20	702	23	4-27	0	30.52
87	S. J. Cook (*Kent*)	RFM	331.3	68	1,132	37	4-62	0	30.59
88	R. J. Peterson (*Derbys*).........	SLA	553.3	129	1,566	51	4-10	0	30.70
89	P. S. Jones (*Derbys*)	RFM	313.5	68	959	31	4-26	0	30.93
90	R. D. B. Croft (*Glam*)	OB	323.4	67	805	26	4-20	0	30.96
91	D. S. Harrison (*Glam*)	RFM	323.3	44	1,156	37	7-45	2	31.24
92	A. U. Rashid (*Yorks*)	LBG	504.4	67	1,784	57	5-87	3	31.29
93	A. J. Hall (*Northants*)..........	RFM	318	57	1,047	33	4-44	0	31.72
94	A. Nel (*Surrey*).................	RFM	227	67	671	21	4-68	0	31.95
95	Shahadat Hossain (*Bangladeshis*) ..	RFM	108.3	12	416	13	5-98	1	32.00
96	C. E. Shreck (*Notts*)	RFM	199	50	577	18	4-81	0	32.05
97	Z. de Bruyn (*Somerset*)	RM	94.2	10	386	12	4-23	0	32.16
98	S. C. Kerrigan (*Lancs*)	SLA	319	46	967	30	6-74	3	32.23
99	D. S. Lucas (*Northants*)	LFM	300.4	59	1,038	32	5-64	1	32.43
100	K. W. Hogg (*Lancs*).............	RFM	202.2	48	650	20	4-53	0	32.50
101 {	M. E. Claydon (*Durham*)........	RFM	303.1	53	1,140	35	3-17	0	32.57
	G. M. Smith (*Derbys*)..........	RFM/OB	414.3	77	1,368	42	5-54	1	32.57
103	A. Khan (*Kent*).................	RFM	372.2	82	1,258	38	5-43	1	33.10
104	P. D. Trego (*Somerset*)..........	RFM	227.1	50	729	22	4-26	0	33.13
105	T. Lungley (*Derbys*).............	RFM	165	25	630	19	3-39	0	33.15
106	H. F. Gurney (*Leics*)	LFM	96	12	332	10	3-82	0	33.20
107	T. T. Bresnan (*Yorks & England*) ..	RFM	238.4	56	707	21	5-52	1	33.66
108	R. A. Jones (*Worcs*).............	RFM	298.2	48	1,281	38	7-115	2	33.71
109	S. D. Udal (*Middx*).............	OB	284.3	38	917	27	5-128	1	33.96
110	D. A. Griffiths (*Hants*)	RFM	152	18	646	19	5-85	1	34.00
111	J. A. Brooks (*Northants*)	RFM	373.3	86	1,260	37	4-88	0	34.05
112	T. D. Groenewald (*Derbys*)	RFM	413.5	105	1,295	38	5-86	1	34.07
113	M. H. A. Footitt (*Derbys*).......	LFM	239.2	48	786	23	4-78	0	34.17
114	S. C. Meaker (*Surrey*)	RF	269.5	48	998	29	5-48	2	34.41
115	V. Banerjee (*Glos*)	SLA	222	28	793	23	5-74	2	34.47
116	H. T. Waters (*Glam*)............	RFM	297.4	79	898	26	4-39	0	34.53
117	J. D. Shantry (*Worcs*)...........	LM	308	73	945	27	5-49	1	35.00
118	L. M. Daggett (*Northants*)	RFM	321.4	65	1,058	30	4-25	0	35.26
119	J. A. Tomlinson (*Hants*)	LFM	559.1	149	1,624	46	7-85	2	35.30
120	J. W. M. Dalrymple (*Glam*)	OB	127	13	391	11	4-71	0	35.54
121	D. J. Pattinson (*Notts*)	RFM	310.2	54	1,180	33	5-95	1	35.75
122	Robiul Islam (*Bangladeshis*)	RFM	104	10	432	12	4-77	0	36.00
123	D. Evans (*Middx*)...............	RFM	102.3	19	397	11	5-87	1	36.09
124	G. K. Berg (*Middx*).............	RFM	235	32	877	24	4-72	0	36.54
125	P. T. Turnbull (*Cambridge MCCU*) .	RFM	108.2	22	366	10	5-92	1	36.60
126	M. M. Ali (*Worcs & Eng. Lions*) ..	OB	179.4	29	626	17	5-36	1	36.82
127	C. J. C. Wright (*Essex*)..........	RFM	301.5	55	1,156	31	5-70	1	37.29
128	L. E. Plunkett (*Durham & England Lions*)...................	RFM	415.4	64	1,499	40	4-107	0	37.47
129	T. J. Phillips (*Essex*)...........	SLA	246.2	45	752	20	4-94	0	37.60
130	Danish Kaneria (*Essex & Pakistanis*)	LBG	316.4	56	1,130	30	4-51	0	37.66
131	D. R. Briggs (*Hants*)	SLA	377.2	59	1,294	34	4-93	0	38.05
132	S. I. Mahmood (*Lancs*)...........	RFM	348	54	1,263	33	5-55	1	38.27
133	M. T. Coles (*Kent*).............	RFM	280	47	1,040	27	4-55	0	38.51
134	C. Rushworth (*Durham*).........	RFM	214.4	43	821	21	4-90	0	39.09
135	T. J. Murtagh (*MCC & Middx*)	RFM	486.2	130	1,524	38	5-52	2	40.10

		Style	O	M	R	W	BB	5W/i	Avge
136	S. R. Patel (*Notts*)	SLA	345.3	73	1,044	26	4-55	0	40.15
137	O. J. Hannon-Dalby (*Yorks*)	RFM	382.4	61	1,372	34	5-68	2	40.35
138	G. J. Batty (*Surrey*)	OB	488.5	70	1,696	42	5-76	1	40.38
139	H. M. C. M. Bandara (*Kent*)	LBG	210.4	31	745	18	4-42	0	41.38
140	D. J. Malan (*MCC & Middx*)	LBG	92.1	3	427	10	4-20	0	42.70
141	C. P. Schofield (*Surrey*)	LBG	184	34	606	14	4-63	0	43.28
142	T. L. Best (*Yorks*)	RF	198	20	793	18	4-86	0	44.05
143	J. D. Middlebrook (*MCC & Northants*)	OB	294.2	46	1,003	22	3-23	0	45.59
144	H. M. R. K. B. Herath (*Hants*)	SLA	175.3	42	463	10	4-98	0	46.30
145	L. J. Fletcher (*Notts*)	RFM	169.2	40	563	12	3-39	0	46.91
146	D. J. Wainwright (*Yorks*)	SLA	184.2	27	716	14	3-48	0	51.14
147	N. Boje (*Northants*)	SLA	230.3	42	796	15	2-47	0	53.06
148	S. M. Ervine (*Hants*)	RFM	362.5	77	1,073	20	4-31	0	53.65

The following bowlers took ten wickets in fewer than five innings:

	Style	O	M	R	W	BB	5W/i	Avge
S. R. Watson (*Australians*)	RFM	29.5	5	117	11	6-33	2	10.63
J. D. Unadkat (*India A*)	LFM	83.3	24	203	16	7-41	2	12.68
A. D. Russell (*West Indies A*)	RF	68	18	207	11	5-68	2	18.81
J. D. Nel (*Kent*)	RFM	54	12	190	10	6-62	1	19.00
D. C. Pascoe (*Oxford MCCU/Univ.*)	SLA	107	37	245	12	6-68	2	20.41
Iqbal Abdulla (*India A*)	SLA	97.2	26	232	10	4-42	0	23.20
B. E. McGain (*Essex*)	LBG	64.3	4	260	10	5-151	1	26.00
Saeed Ajmal (*Pakistanis*)	OB	125.1	19	353	12	5-82	1	29.41

BOWLING STYLES

LBG	Leg-breaks and googlies (8)	**RF**	Right-arm fast (6)
LFM	Left-arm fast medium (13)	**RFM**	Right-arm fast medium (88)
LM	Left-arm medium (2)	**RM**	Right-arm medium (9)
OB	Off-breaks (13)	**SLA**	Slow left-arm (19)

Note: The total comes to 158 because G. G. Wagg and G. M. Smith have two styles of bowling.

INDIVIDUAL SCORES OF 100 AND OVER

There were **232** three-figure innings in 172 first-class matches in 2010, 60 fewer than in 2009 when 171 first-class matches were played. Of these, 12 were double-hundreds, compared with 19 in 2009. The list includes 189 hundreds hit in the County Championship, compared with 253 in 2009.

J. C. Hildreth (7)
106   Somerset v Hants, Southampton
102* Somerset v Yorks, Taunton
131   Somerset v Warwicks, Taunton
142   Somerset v Notts, Taunton
151   Somerset v Kent, Canterbury
130   Somerset v Hants, Taunton
105   Somerset v Durham, Chester-le-Street

M. A. Carberry (6)
164   Hants v Oxford MCCU, Oxford
113   Hants v Durham, Chester-le-Street
132   Hants v Notts, Southampton
158   Hants v Kent, Southampton
162 }
107 } Hants v Durham, Basingstoke

M. J. Cosgrove (5)
113* Glam v Leics, Leicester
115   Glam v Northants, Northampton
117   Glam v Leics, Swansea
123   Glam v Glos, Cheltenham
142   Glam v Sussex, Hove

M. R. Ramprakash (5)
102   Surrey v Derbys, The Oval
223 }
103* } Surrey v Middx, The Oval
248   Surrey v Northants, The Oval
179   Surrey v Leics, Leicester

M. J. Di Venuto (4)
131   Durham v MCC, Abu Dhabi
108* Durham v Yorks, Leeds
117* Durham v Yorks, Chester-le-Street
129   Durham v Somerset, Chester-le-Street

M. W. Goodwin (4)
142   Sussex v Leics, Hove
111   Sussex v Worcs, Hove
121   Sussex v Derbys, Derby
100* Sussex v Derbys, Horsham

W. L. Madsen (4)
109   Derbys v Leics, Derby
179   Derbys v Northants, Northampton
109 }
105 } Derbys v Surrey, Chesterfield

D. K. H. Mitchell (4)
148   Worcs v Derbys, Worcester
104 }
134* } Worcs v Glos, Cheltenham
165* Worcs v Glam, Colwyn Bay

C. J. L. Rogers (4)
200 }
140* } Derbys v Surrey, The Oval
141   Derbys v Northants, Northampton
115   Derbys v Glos, Derby

J. A. Rudolph (4)
228* Yorks v Durham, Leeds
106   Yorks v Essex, Chelmsford
141   Yorks v Notts, Leeds
100   Yorks v Durham, Chester-le-Street

D. I. Stevens (4)
101* Kent v Lancs, Manchester
100   Kent v Essex, Chelmsford
102   Kent v Durham, Chester-le-Street
197   Kent v Notts, Tunbridge Wells

M. E. Trescothick (4)
117   Somerset v Yorks, Leeds
188* Somerset v Kent, Canterbury
228* Somerset v Essex, Colchester
128   Somerset v Durham, Taunton

J. H. K. Adams (3)
169   Hants v Essex, Chelmsford
196   Hants v Yorks, Scarborough
194   Hants v Lancs, Liverpool

M. M. Ali (3)
126   Worcs v Surrey, Whitgift School, Croydon
106   Worcs v Glos, Worcester
115   Worcs v Sussex, Worcester

A. W. Gale (3)
101   Yorks v Somerset, Leeds
135   Yorks v Essex, Scarborough
151* Yorks v Notts, Nottingham

G. O. Jones (3)
112   Kent v Loughborough MCCU, Canterbury
135   Kent v Essex, Chelmsford
178   Kent v Somerset, Canterbury

A. N. Kervezee (3)
130   Worcs v Derbys, Worcester
155   Worcs v Derbys, Derby
144   Worcs v Surrey, Worcester

A. Lyth (3)
142   Yorks v Somerset, Taunton
133   Yorks v Hants, Southampton
100   Yorks v Lancs, Manchester

A. McGrath (3)
105   Yorks v Durham, Leeds
112   Yorks v Essex, Scarborough
124* Yorks v Durham, Chester-le-Street

N. D. McKenzie (3)
141* Hants v Oxford MCCU, Oxford
115* Hants v Notts, Nottingham
113   Hants v Kent, Southampton

D. J. Malan (3)
115   Middx v Glam, Lord's
100* Middx v Sussex, Hove
107   Middx v Surrey, Lord's

C. D. Nash (3)
184   Sussex v Leics, Leicester
156   Sussex v Derbys, Horsham
169   Sussex v Northants, Hove

S. D. Peters (3)
183* Northants v Middx, Northampton
136   Northants v Sussex, Northampton
199   Northants v Middx, Lord's

G. P. Smith (3)
114   Durham MCCU v Notts, Durham
158* Leics v Glos, Leicester
104   Leics v Northants, Northampton

J. W. A. Taylor (3)
206* Leics v Middx, Leicester
106* Leics v Middx, Lord's
156   Leics v Northants, Northampton

I. J. L. Trott (3)
150   Warwicks v Lancs, Birmingham
226   England v Bangladesh, Lord's
184   England v Pakistan, Lord's

M. van Jaarsveld (3)
106   Kent v Loughborough MCCU,
      Canterbury
106   Kent v Essex, Canterbury
110* Kent v Warwicks, Birmingham

M. A. Wagh (3)
100   Notts v Durham MCCU, Durham
131* Notts v Hants, Southampton
139   Notts v Warwicks, Birmingham

I. R. Bell (2)
128   England v Bangladesh, Manchester
104   Warwicks v Hants, Southampton

R. S. Bopara (2)
142   ⎫ Essex v Yorks, Chelmsford
102   ⎭

B. C. Brown (2)
110* Sussex v Cambridge MCCU,
      Cambridge
112   Sussex v Derbys, Horsham

S. Chanderpaul (2)
118   Lancs v Hants, Southampton
120   Lancs v Kent, Canterbury

A. N. Cook (2)
102   Essex v Yorks, Chelmsford
110   England v Pakistan, The Oval

S. M. Davies (2)
122* Surrey v Cambridge MCCU, Cambridge
137   Surrey v Worcs, Whitgift School,
      Croydon

N. J. Dexter (2)
112   Middx v Derbys, Lord's
118   Middx v Leics, Leicester

J. du Toit (2)
154   Leics v Cambridge MCCU, Cambridge
122   Leics v Surrey, Leicester

R. J. Hamilton-Brown (2)
125   Surrey v Worcs, Whitgift School,
      Croydon
103   Surrey v Northants, The Oval

C. F. Hughes (2)
118   Derbys v Glos, Derby
156   Derbys v Northants, Chesterfield

W. I. Jefferson (2)
101* Leics v Cambridge MCCU, Cambridge
135   Leics v Surrey, The Oval

E. C. Joyce (2)
135* Sussex v Cambridge MCCU,
      Cambridge
164   Sussex v Derbys, Horsham

R. W. T. Key (2)
140   Kent v Loughborough MCCU,
      Canterbury
261   Kent v Durham, Canterbury

A. B. McDonald (2)
113   Leics v Glam, Leicester
176* Leics v Middx, Leicester

R. S. C. Martin-Jenkins (2)
102   Sussex v Glos, Bristol
130   Sussex v Derbys, Derby

G. J. Muchall (2)
140* Durham v Hants, Basingstoke
111   Durham v Notts, Chester-le-Street

P. Mustard (2)
100   Durham v Warwicks, Birmingham
120   Durham v Notts, Chester-le-Street

S. A. Newman (2)
112   Middx v Northants, Northampton
126   Middx v Derbys, Derby

W. T. S. Porterfield (2)
175   Glos v Worcs, Cheltenham
150   Glos v Northants, Northampton

M. J. Prior (2)
123* Sussex v Middx, Hove
102* England v Pakistan, Nottingham

C. M. W. Read (2)
124* Notts v Durham, Nottingham
112* Notts v Kent, Tunbridge Wells

G. P. Rees (2)
102 Glam v Derbys, Derby
106* Glam v Derbys, Cardiff

O. A. Shah (2)
156 Middx v Leics, Leicester
117 Middx v Worcs, Lord's

T. C. Smith (2)
108* Lancs v Yorks, Leeds
128 Lancs v Hants, Southampton

M. N. W. Spriegel (2)
108* Surrey v Bangladeshis, The Oval
103 Surrey v Northants, The Oval

B. A. Stokes (2)
106 Durham v Notts, Nottingham
161* Durham v Kent, Canterbury

L. D. Sutton (2)
118 Lancs v Somerset, Manchester
101* Lancs v Durham, Chester-le-Street

Tamim Iqbal (2)
103 Bangladesh v England, Lord's
108 Bangladesh v England, Manchester

B. J. Wright (2)
172 Glam v Glos, Cardiff
121* Glam v Worcs, Colwyn Bay

The following each played one three-figure innings:

U. Afzaal, 159*, Surrey v Bangladeshis, The Oval; S. S. Agarwal, 117, Oxford U. v Cambridge U., Oxford; J. Allenby, 105, Glam v Glos, Cardiff; H. M. Amla, 129, Notts v Kent, Nottingham.
D. M. Benkenstein, 114, Durham v Kent, Canterbury; G. K. Berg, 125, Middx v Derbys, Lord's; A. J. Blake, 105*, Kent v Yorks, Leeds; S. C. J. Broad, 169, England v Pakistan, Lord's; G. L. Brophy, 103, Yorks v Warwicks, Leeds; A. D. Brown, 134, Notts v Durham, Nottingham; J. C. Buttler, 144, Somerset v Hants, Southampton.
J. G. Cameron, 105, Worcs v Sussex, Worcester; R. Clarke, 127*, Warwicks v Yorks, Leeds; K. J. Coetzer, 172, Durham v MCC, Abu Dhabi; G. D. Cross, 100*, Lancs v Hants, Southampton.
J. W. M. Dalrymple, 105, Glam v Northants, Cardiff; J. L. Denly, 106, Kent v Loughborough MCCU, Canterbury; S. Dhawan, 179, India A v Yorks, Leeds.
S. M. Ervine, 237*, Hants v Somerset, Southampton.
A. D. S. Fletcher, 123, West Indies A v India A, Whitgift School, Croydon; J. S. Foster, 169, Essex v Durham, Chester-le-Street; J. E. C. Franklin, 108, Glos v Worcs, Cheltenham; P. J. Franks, 114, Notts v Durham MCCU, Durham.
B. A. Godleman, 106, Essex v Somerset, Taunton.
A. D. Hales, 136, Notts v Hants, Nottingham; A. J. Hall, 133, Northants v Middx, Lord's; A. J. Hodd, 109, Sussex v Middx, Hove; P. J. Horton, 123, Lancs v Essex, Chelmsford; D. M. Housego, 102*, Middx v Oxford MCCU, Oxford; D. J. Hussey, 251*, Notts v Yorks, Leeds.
Jahurul Islam, 158, Bangladeshis v Surrey, The Oval.
D. A. King, 189, Oxford U. v Cambridge U., Oxford.
M. B. Loye, 164, Northants v Surrey, Northampton; M. J. Lumb, 158, Hants v Durham, Basingstoke.
J. K. Maunders, 126, Essex v Bangladeshis, Chelmsford; J. C. Mickleburgh, 174, Essex v Durham, Chester-le-Street; E. J. G. Morgan, 130, England v Pakistan, Nottingham; S. J. Mullaney, 100*, Notts v Hants, Southampton.
Naved-ul-Hasan, 101, Sussex v Leics, Hove; R. I. Newton, 102, Northants v Leics, Northampton; P. A. Nixon, 106, Leics v Surrey, Leicester.
G. T. Park, 124*, Derbys v Worcs, Worcester; S. R. Patel, 104, Notts v Somerset, Taunton; A. G. Prince, 115, Lancs v Kent, Manchester; C. A. Pujara, 208*, India A v West Indies A, Whitgift School, Croydon; R. M. Pyrah, 134*, Yorks v Loughborough MCCU, Leeds.
A. M. Rahane, 118, India A v Yorks, Leeds; S. D. Robson, 204, Middx v Oxford MCCU, Oxford.
D. J. Sales, 127, Northants v Glam, Northampton; B. M. Shafayat, 159, Notts v Durham MCCU, Durham; A. S. Sharma, 185*, Oxford U. v Cambridge U., Oxford; J. A. Simpson, 101*, Middx v Northants, Northampton; D. S. Smith, 170, West Indies A v India A, Whitgift School, Croydon; G. M. Smith, 165*, Derbys v Glam, Derby; V. S. Solanki, 114, Worcs v Surrey, Whitgift School, Croydon; M. D. Stoneman, 118, Durham v Durham MCCU, Durham; A. V. Suppiah, 125, Somerset v Kent, Canterbury.
J. C. Tredwell, 115, Kent v Notts, Tunbridge Wells; P. D. Trego, 108, Somerset v Lancs, Manchester.
Umar Akmal, 153, Pakistanis v Kent, Canterbury.
J. M. Vince, 180, Hants v Yorks, Scarborough; A. C. Voges, 126, Notts v Lancs, Manchester.
A. G. Wakely, 108, Northants v Middx, Lord's; M. J. Walker, 105, Essex v Durham, Chelmsford; M. A. Wallace, 113, Glam v Glos, Cheltenham; T. Westley, 132, Essex v Kent, Chelmsford;

W. A. White, 101*, Leics v Derbys, Derby; G. C. Wilson, 125, Surrey v Leics, Leicester; C. R. Woakes, 136*, Warwicks v Hants, Birmingham; L. J. Wright, 134, Sussex v Middx, Uxbridge. M. H. Yardy, 100*, Sussex v Surrey, Guildford.

FASTEST HUNDREDS BY BALLS...

Balls	Mins		
68	89	J. C. Hildreth...............	Somerset v Yorks, Taunton.
79	76	A. M. Rahane................	India A v Yorks, Leeds.
83	89	M. W. Goodwin.............	Sussex v Derbys, Horsham.
83	113	P. D. Trego.................	Somerset v Lancs, Manchester.
89	127	P. J. Franks.................	Notts v Durham MCCU, Durham.
94	138	Tamim Iqbal................	Bangladesh v England, Lord's.
96	114	W. I. Jefferson..............	Leics v Cambridge MCCU, Cambridge.
96	119	R. J. Hamilton-Brown........	Surrey v Worcs, Whitgift School, Croydon.
96	152	L. J. Wright.................	Sussex v Middx, Uxbridge.
100	114	R. J. Hamilton-Brown........	Surrey v Northants, The Oval.
100	131	N. J. Dexter.................	Middx v Derbys, Lord's.
100	132	Tamim Iqbal................	Bangladesh v England, Manchester.

The fastest hundred in terms of minutes not in the above list was by M. A. Wagh (106 minutes, 115 balls) for Notts v Durham MCCU, Durham.

...AND THE SLOWEST

Balls	Mins		
273	379	J. H. K. Adams......................	Hants v Lancs, Liverpool.
251	310	M. E. Trescothick.....................	Somerset v Kent, Canterbury.
250	335	G. T. Park...........................	Derbys v Worcs, Worcester.
242	309	D. K. H. Mitchell.....................	Worcs v Glos, Cheltenham.
241	291	A. McGrath..........................	Yorks v Durham, Leeds.

TEN WICKETS IN A MATCH

There were **ten** instances of bowlers taking ten or more wickets in a first-class match in 2010, two fewer than in 2009. All but two were in the County Championship.

M. Kartik (2)

11-72, Somerset v Warwicks, Birmingham; 10-107, Somerset v Kent, Taunton.

The following each took ten wickets in a match on one occasion:

J. M. Anderson, 11-71, England v Pakistan, Nottingham.
S. C. J. Broad, 11-131, Notts v Warwicks, Birmingham.
M. A. Chambers, 10-123, Essex v Notts, Chelmsford.
S. T. Finn, 14-106, Middx v Worcs, Worcester.
G. Keedy, 10-128, Lancs v Durham, Manchester.
M. Ntini, 10-104, Kent v Durham, Chester-le-Street.
J. D. Unadkat, 13-103, India A v West Indies A, Leicester.
C. R. Woakes, 11-97, Warwicks v Kent, Birmingham.

ENGLAND v BANGLADESH, 2010

Review by Derek Pringle

Test matches (2): England 2, Bangladesh 0
One-day internationals (3): England 2, Bangladesh 1

Bangladesh's second full tour of England marked their tenth year as a Test-playing country. Not that a decade's experience at the top table was evident, as they were easily defeated in both Tests – the second, at Old Trafford, inside three days. Twice in that match they lost ten wickets in a session. Except for Tamim Iqbal, their swashbuckling opener whose successive hundreds at least elevated the contest to men against man and boys, their cricket struggled for the legitimacy to compete at this level.

The one-sided nature of England's fourth clean sweep against them – the kind of 100% record not held by an England Test team since they won their first eight Tests against South Africa in the late 19th century – inevitably drew criticism that the visitors were not worthy opponents. They did manage to dilute that view with their first-ever victory over England when they won the second one-day international, at Bristol, under the captaincy of Mashrafe bin Mortaza, who was much less defensive than Shakib Al Hasan had been in the Test series.

Test cricket's increasing struggle to justify itself, in the face of Twenty20's global march, was not well served by Bangladesh's capitulation. Having handed them Test status in 2000, the International Cricket Council now suggested they should play Tests against the leading teams only at home. This seemed to be a sop to countries with valuable broadcasting deals to protect; to improve, Bangladesh needed more experience of foreign conditions, not less.

There were few mitigating circumstances for the tourists' dire cricket, save the expected callowness in England's early-season conditions. Even the volcanic ash from Iceland's Eyjafjallajökull, which in the end produced less fire and brimstone than Jamie Siddons, Bangladesh's Australian coach, failed to provide an excuse for their failings. Eruptions from the volcano managed to disrupt the travel plans of thousands coming to Europe, but a brief change in the wind allowed Bangladesh to arrive on time for their three scheduled warm-up games, so they did not lack acclimatisation.

Pitches in England during May test the techniques and temperaments even of batsmen born and bred on them. But the Bangladeshis, with Tamim's glorious exception, appeared resigned to failure against the moving ball. Two of their three warm-up matches, at Chelmsford against virtually an Essex second team and against England Lions at Derby, ended in defeat, the need for adjustments with bat and ball – respectively to play late and straight, and to pitch it up – going unheeded.

A brawny left-hander, Tamim batted with destructive abandon. His refusal to limit his ambition or adjust his strokes was born of the confidence that only an exceptional eye for the ball can bring. Nobody else, on either side, managed

Four, five, six: at Lord's, Steve Finn took four wickets in the Bangladesh first innings and five in the second, including Tamim Iqbal, here striking Graeme Swann for six.

to treat the bowling with such splendid disdain, and his hundreds in both Tests meant he could stand shoulder to shoulder with Chris Gayle and Matthew Hayden, those other left-handed bully boys of recent times.

When Tamim was at the crease, England's bowlers, like a football side 3–0 down in a relegation battle, lurched between attack and defence, often in successive balls. It was the batting equivalent of Graham Gooch's quip about his 183 against New Zealand and Richard Hadlee at Lord's in 1986: "Like facing the World XI one end and Ilford Seconds the other." That jibe had inspired New Zealand, however, who produced T-shirts emblazoned with both names as they won the next Test, and the series.

There was no such humble pie for England in these Tests, though Tamim did produce some royal entertainment for those spectators who turned up. He followed a fifty in his first innings at Lord's – where the ground was at least half full for each of the first three days – with 103, at more than a run a ball, in the second. Ever the showman, he celebrated with a Houdini-like contortion as he pointed at his name, printed on the back of his shirt, instructing team-mates on the dressing-room balcony to put it up on the Lord's honours board.

Tamim's hundred was not a lone effort; his fellow left-handers Imrul Kayes and Junaid Siddique both passed 50, Siddique for the second time in the match. The sluggish nature of the Lord's pitch prevented them from being overwhelmed by England's pace attack after they had overcome the new ball. It was a different matter at Old Trafford, where a combination of good carry and James Anderson's snaking swingers illustrated the gulf between Tamim, who struck a defiant 108, and the rest.

Having assessed Bangladesh on the winter tour, team director Andy Flower decided he could do without Paul Collingwood and Stuart Broad and withdrew them from front-line duties, part of his plan to manage the workloads of key players. Although England refused to call it rest, that is essentially what it was – though Broad may have begged to differ. He was sent on a month's strength and conditioning course overseen by fitness trainer Huw Bevan.

Collingwood's absence created a vacancy which allowed Jonathan Trott to settle again, after disappointing winter tours of South Africa and Bangladesh. Similarly, with Broad absent, Middlesex's promising fast bowler Steve Finn was afforded a chance to express himself in more sympathetic conditions than the lifeless pitches in Chittagong and Mirpur.

Trott, who had looked mentally shot on tour, needed to impress and did so, with a monumental double-hundred in England's first innings at Lord's after Bangladesh had put them in. He was always strong off his legs, with a calm control of his cut shots; Bangladesh's bowlers simply weren't consistent enough to deny him these comfort strokes and put him under pressure. Shahadat Hossain ended with five wickets, but his rally came too late to prevent England running the show.

Could he be England's missing link?

A habit of repeatedly scratching his mark in long scars at the crease (which prompted Siddons to accuse Trott of bringing the game into disrepute, because it kept bowlers waiting) suggested a man of superstition or excessive nervous energy. But while South Africa managed to prey upon the quirk and distract him, Trott had come into this match in good form, having recently made a century for Warwickshire.

The role of county cricket, something which also benefited Ian Bell before his hundred in the Second Test, is sometimes underestimated in this era of coaches. Yet, as Kevin Pietersen's struggles for form revealed later in the summer, when Hampshire refused to disrupt team dynamics by giving him a game, there is no better preparation for batting than runs in the middle.

Finn was impressive at Lord's, with nine wickets in the match. His habit of falling over in his follow-through, which he did often, was disconcerting, though it did not dampen his rhythm or his aggression. Once the one-day series against Australia began, however, he was frogmarched into the same boot camp Broad had attended, to strengthen his beanpole frame.

Having recorded his first five-wicket Test haul on his home ground, Finn took another five in Bangladesh's second innings at Old Trafford, though Anderson deserved the lion's share there for an exhibition of swing bowling that left the batsmen wishing they had taken BlackBerries to the crease, in order that they might Google a solution. In the first innings it was Ajmal Shahzad, on his Test debut, who had induced similar panic among the visitors, this time with reverse swing. Indeed, the manner of his three for 45 suggested he could be the missing link in England's pace attack between the conventional swing of Anderson and the hit-the-pitch aggression of Finn and Broad.

A series that had looked tediously predictable before the start proved more interesting in the discoveries it had thrown up by the end.

BANGLADESHI TOURING PARTY

*Shakib Al Hasan, Abdur Razzak, Imrul Kayes, Jahurul Islam, Junaid Siddique, Mahbubul Alam, Mahmudullah, Mohammad Ashraful, Mushfiqur Rahim, Naeem Islam, Robiul Islam, Rubel Hossain, Shafiul Islam, Shahadat Hossain, Shamsur Rahman, Tamim Iqbal.

Coach: J. D. Siddons. *Head of delegation:* Jalal Yunus. *Manager:* Tanjeeb Ahsan Saad. *Assistant coach:* Khaled Mahmud. *Analyst:* Nasir Ahmed. *Physiotherapist:* M. L. Henry. *Strength and conditioning coach:* G. T. Luden.

After the Tests, Bangladesh travelled to Sri Lanka to play in the Asia Cup; they returned in July for the one-day internationals, when Mashrafe bin Mortaza joined the party as captain, while Faisal Hossain, Nazmul Hossain, Raqibul Hasan and Syed Rasel replaced Mahbubul Alam, Mohammad Ashraful, Naeem Islam, Robiul Islam, Shahadat Hossain and Shamsur Rahman. After Mushfiqur Rahim and Raqibul Hasan were injured in the first one-day international, Mohammad Ashraful and Naeem Islam were recalled and Saghir Hossain added as cover.

SURREY v BANGLADESHIS

At The Oval, May 9–11. Drawn. Toss: Surrey. First-class debuts: M. P. Dunn, T. J. Lancefield.

A plunge of 30°C from Barbados, where their World Twenty20 campaign ended on May 5, did not prevent Bangladesh gaining useful practice against some county youngsters. The uncapped Robiul Islam was chiefly responsible for Surrey listing at 135 for six before Spriegel and Meaker added 183, both scoring career-bests. In bitter cold next day, Mohammad Ashraful and Jahurul Islam responded with a stand of 194. A foot taller than Ashraful, but just as stylish, Jahurul reached his century with a six over long-on and rattled along to his own best score. England Under-19 seamer Matt Dunn – a product of Surrey's academy, like fellow debutant Tom Lancefield – made the most of sloppy batting late on, but the tourists declared overnight, 54 ahead. While helicopters circled above Downing Street, which David Cameron finally occupied on the third evening, Evans made his case for a premier post in a right–left coalition with Afzaal worth 225, but was deprived of a century when Mahmudullah tipped a drive on to the non-striker's stumps. Afzaal remained to bat out the match.

Close of play: First day, Bangladeshis 12-0 (Imrul Kayes 6, Jahurul Islam 1); Second day, Bangladeshis 372-6 (Shakib Al Hasan 5).

Surrey

L. J. Evans b Robiul Islam	22	– (2) run out ... 98
A. Harinath c Mahmudullah b Mahbubul Alam	19	– (1) c Mushfiqur Rahim b Mahbubul Alam . 20
T. J. Lancefield c Jahurul Islam b Robiul Islam	47	– c sub (Shafiul Islam) b Shahadat Hossain . 11
U. Afzaal c Shakib Al Hasan b Rubel Hossain	6	– not out ... 159
M. N. W. Spriegel not out	108	
†G. C. Wilson lbw b Robiul Islam	0	– (5) not out ... 10
*C. P. Schofield c Mahmudullah b Rubel Hossain	5	
S. C. Meaker lbw b Shahadat Hossain	94	
B 4, l-b 1, n-b 12	17	B 1, l-b 9, n-b 5 ... 15

1/35 (1) 2/72 (2) (7 wkts dec, 82.2 overs) 318 1/32 (1) (3 wkts dec, 72.2 overs) 313
3/84 (4) 4/121 (3) 2/61 (3) 3/286 (2)
5/123 (6) 6/135 (7) 7/318 (8)

M. P. Dunn, S. J. King and T. M. Jewell did not bat.

Mahbubul Alam 12–0–50–1; Shahadat Hossain 11.2–0–43–1; Robiul Islam 14–0–67–3; Rubel Hossain 12.3–2–30–2; Naeem Islam 14–1–56–0; Mahmudullah 5.3–0–16–0; Shakib Al Hasan 6–0–27–0; Mohammad Ashraful 7–0–24–0. *Second Innings*—Mahbubul Alam 12–2–38–1; Shahadat Hossain 16–0–73–1; Robiul Islam 14–3–47–0; Naeem Islam 17–2–77–0; Mahmudullah 9–1–35–0; Mohammad Ashraful 4.2–0–33–0.

Bangladeshis

Imrul Kayes b Evans	16	*Shakib Al Hasan not out	5
Jahurul Islam c Schofield b King	158	B 9, l-b 6, w 2, n-b 8	25
Mohammad Ashraful b Jewell	89		
†Mushfiqur Rahim c Spriegel b Dunn	52	1/49 (1) (6 wkts dec, 102.5 overs)	372
Mahmudullah c sub (J. J. Roy) b Dunn	27	2/243 (3) 3/310 (2)	
Naeem Islam b Dunn	0	4/361 (4) 5/367 (5) 6/372 (6)	

Rubel Hossain, Shahadat Hossain, Mahbubul Alam and Robiul Islam did not bat.

Meaker 6–3–15–0; Jewell 16–7–22–1; Dunn 14.5–5–7–48–3; Evans 6–0–30–1; King 28–1–134–1; Schofield 21–1–65–0; Spriegel 8–0–32–0; Afzaal 3–0–11–0.

Umpires: M. R. Benson and I. Dawood.

ESSEX v BANGLADESHIS

At Chelmsford, May 14–16. Essex won by five wickets. Toss: Essex. First-class debuts: M. A. Comber, M. Osborne.

On the opening day, Essex players Danish Kaneria and Mervyn Westfield (not included in this second-choice eleven) were arrested, interviewed by police about "match irregularities", and released on bail. Meanwhile, in front of sparse crowds and on a green pitch offering seam movement, the tourists struggled, missing captain Shakib Al Hasan (chicken-pox) and Tamim Iqbal (left wrist). Although they batted entertainingly, watchfulness and defensive technique did not feature in their repertoire. Mohammad Ashraful scored two run-a-ball fifties, and the tail wagged to offer some substance after the upper order's loose shots. The bowling, too, was inconsistent and often erratic. Maunders hit three sixes and 16 fours in his 126, the defining contribution for Essex. When the county's four-man seam attack – two of them debutants – dismissed Bangladesh cheaply again, the target was 130. Then five wickets fell for 78, and Bangladesh sensed a morale-boosting victory, until acting-captain Grant Flower put the run-chase back on track. The captains agreed to forgo the final tea interval, and Essex won by the time the sandwiches would have been consumed.

Close of play: First day, Essex 83-2 (Maunders 54, Walker 5); Second day, Bangladeshis 148-6 (Shahadat Hossain 13, Shafiul Islam 8).

Bangladeshis

Imrul Kayes b Palladino	12	– c Godleman b Chambers	4
Jahurul Islam b Chambers	0	– lbw b Palladino	4
Junaid Siddique b Palladino	20	– c Phillips b Osborne	34
Mohammad Ashraful c Wheater b Osborne	58	– lbw b Comber	61
*†Mushfiqur Rahim c Wheater b Comber	14	– c Mickleburgh b Osborne	6
Mahmudullah c Comber b Palladino	25	– c Wheater b Osborne	5
Naeem Islam c Flower b Osborne	8	– (9) c Wheater b Chambers	5
Shafiul Islam c Wheater b Chambers	24	– c Wheater b Palladino	8
Abdur Razzak c Wheater b Chambers	22	– (10) c Godleman b Comber	23
Shahadat Hossain b Chambers	33	– (7) c Godleman b Palladino	23
Robiul Islam not out	3	– not out	17
L-b 4, w 6, n-b 2	12	B 8, l-b 8, n-b 5	21

1/5 (2) 2/31 (3) 3/40 (1) 4/85 (5) (60.4 overs) 231
5/136 (4) 6/140 (6) 7/152 (7)
8/190 (8) 9/196 (9) 10/231 (10)

1/8 (2) 2/12 (1) (45.2 overs) 211
3/102 (3) 4/114 (5)
5/124 (6) 6/124 (4) 7/149 (8)
8/157 (9) 9/165 (7) 10/211 (10)

Chambers 15.4–3–32–4; Palladino 23–3–91–3; Osborne 14–2–60–2; Comber 7–0–44–1; Phillips 1–1–0–0. *Second Innings*—Chambers 17–5–51–2; Palladino 15–2–75–3; Osborne 6–1–35–3; Comber 7.2–1–34–2.

Essex

B. A. Godleman c Jahurul Islam b Robiul Islam . . .	17	– lbw b Robiul Islam. 20
J. K. Maunders c Shafiul Islam b Robiul Islam	126	– b Robiul Islam 2
J. C. Mickleburgh c Mushfiqur Rahim		
b Robiul Islam.	2	– c Imrul Kayes b Shafiul Islam 11
M. J. Walker c Jahurul Islam b Shahadat Hossain . .	45	– b Shahadat Hossain 11
T. J. Phillips c Robiul Islam b Mahmudullah.	11	– c Jahurul Islam b Abdur Razzak 21
*G. W. Flower b Shahadat Hossain	46	– not out 34
†A. J. Wheater c Mushfiqur Rahim b Mahmudullah . .	22	– not out 19
M. A. Comber b Shahadat Hossain	19	
A. P. Palladino c Junaid Siddique b Robiul Islam . .	0	
M. A. Chambers c Mahmudullah		
b Shahadat Hossain .	0	
M. Osborne not out	0	
L-b 7, w 6, n-b 12.	25	B 5, l-b 3, w 1, n-b 3 12

1/60 (1) 2/66 (3) 3/176 (4)   (87.1 overs) 313   1/6 (2)   (5 wkts, 43.2 overs) 130
4/220 (5) 5/237 (2) 6/269 (7)   2/35 (1) 3/37 (3)
7/309 (8) 8/311 (6) 9/313 (9) 10/313 (10)   4/71 (4) 5/78 (5)

Shafiul Islam 20–5–56–0; Shahadat Hossain 21.1–5–72–4; Robiul Islam 21–2–77–4; Abdur Razzak 9–2–26–0; Mahmudullah 15–1–70–2; Mohammad Ashraful 1–0–5–0. *Second Innings*—Shahadat Hossain 9–1–27–1; Robiul Islam 11–2–33–2; Shafiul Islam 6.2–4–5–1; Mohammad Ashraful 0.4–0–4–0; Abdur Razzak 8.2–2–22–1; Mahmudullah 8–0–31–0.

Umpires: P. K. Baldwin and R. A. Kettleborough.

ENGLAND LIONS v BANGLADESHIS

At Derby, May 19–21. England Lions won by nine wickets. Toss: England Lions.

Cook, who had recently led England's seniors to a clean sweep in Bangladesh, guided the second string to victory with almost five sessions to spare, even if his own form fell short of his standards on that tour. Nobody else quite earned a Test place. In his first first-class match of 2010 (after one World Twenty20 outing) Bopara wound up the tail twice to finish with seven wickets, but failed with the bat on the opening day and was bowled seeking ten to win from the last over before lunch on the third. Moeen Ali completed the job in three balls after the interval. On the first afternoon, the Bangladeshis had collapsed from 136 for two to 220 all out, with Kirby dismissing three in 18 balls before Mahmudullah briefly fought back, hooking consecutive sixes off Plunkett. In a convincing all-round performance, Davies followed 81 in 88 balls – the match's highest score – with six second-innings catches, three of them off Plunkett as the tourists stumbled to 86 for six. Jahurul Islam batted over three hours and last man Rubel Hossain 66 minutes, pushing the game into the third morning. A disappointed Panesar bowled two overs in the match.

Close of play: First day, England Lions 124-3 (Gale 63, Taylor 8); Second day, Bangladeshis 139-9 (Jahurul Islam 44, Rubel Hossain 3).

Bangladeshis

Tamim Iqbal c Harris b Plunkett	36	– c Davies b Kirby	19
Imrul Kayes c Davies b Woakes	42	– c Ali b Woakes	5
Junaid Siddique c Ali b Kirby	30	– c Davies b Woakes	0
Jahurul Islam c Woakes b Plunkett	21	– not out	58
Mohammad Ashraful c Davies b Kirby	1	– c Davies b Plunkett	1
*†Mushfiqur Rahim c Ali b Kirby	1	– c Davies b Plunkett	4
Mahmudullah c Panesar b Bopara	40	– c Davies b Plunkett	21
Abdur Razzak c Cook b Woakes	5	– c Cook b Bopara	30
Shafiul Islam not out	16	– c Plunkett b Bopara	0
Robiul Islam c Plunkett b Bopara	0	– lbw b Bopara	0
Rubel Hossain b Bopara	5	– c Davies b Bopara	5
B 4, l-b 7, w 2, n-b 10	23	B 4, l-b 1, w 8, n-b 5	18

1/68 (1) 2/109 (2) 3/136 (3)   (57.2 overs) 220   1/20 (1) 2/20 (3)   (52.5 overs) 161
4/144 (5) 5/146 (6) 6/153 (4)   3/29 (2) 4/38 (5)
7/158 (8) 8/205 (7) 9/205 (10) 10/220 (11)   5/43 (6) 6/86 (7) 7/121 (8)
                                                     8/121 (9) 9/121 (10) 10/161 (11)

Woakes 15–3–53–2; Kirby 11–1–49–3; Harris 13–1–38–0; Plunkett 15–4–60–2; Bopara 3.2–2–9–3. *Second Innings*—Woakes 13–4–28–2; Kirby 8–3–28–1; Plunkett 16–3–53–3; Harris 7–1–25–0; Bopara 6.5–1–14–4; Panesar 2–0–8–0.

England Lions

*A. N. Cook c Tamim Iqbal b Rubel Hossain	31 – not out	42
R. S. Bopara c Imrul Kayes b Robiul Islam	12 – b Abdur Razzak	28
M. M. Ali c Imrul Kayes b Robiul Islam	0 – not out	10
A. W. Gale c Tamim Iqbal b Shafiul Islam	74
J. W. A. Taylor c Mushfiqur Rahim b Shafiul Islam	12
†S. M. Davies c Tamim Iqbal b Mahmudullah	81
C. R. Woakes c Rubel Hossain b Robiul Islam	26
L. E. Plunkett b Abdur Razzak	0
J. A. R. Harris lbw b Abdur Razzak	10
M. S. Panesar c Tamim Iqbal b Rubel Hossain	9
S. P. Kirby not out	6
B 20, l-b 4, w 1, n-b 10	35 B 1, n-b 5	6

1/16 (2) 2/16 (3) 3/75 (1)   (77.4 overs) 296   1/76 (2)   (1 wkt, 16.4 overs) 86
4/147 (5) 5/148 (4) 6/232 (7)
7/238 (8) 8/281 (9) 9/281 (6) 10/296 (10)

Shafiul Islam 14–3–44–2; Robiul Islam 18–1–72–3; Rubel Hossain 16.4–3–71–2; Mahmudullah 6–0–16–1; Abdur Razzak 22–3–67–2; Mohammad Ashraful 1–0–2–0. *Second Innings*—Shafiul Islam 5–0–19–0; Robiul Islam 3–0–17–0; Rubel Hossain 5–0–32–0; Abdur Razzak 3.4–0–17–1.

Umpires: R. J. Bailey and R. T. Robinson.

ENGLAND v BANGLADESH

First npower Test

Hugh Chevallier

At Lord's, May 27–31. England won by eight wickets. Toss: Bangladesh. Test debuts: E. J. G. Morgan; Robiul Islam.

Last time Bangladesh visited Lord's, England sauntered home with indecent ease in little more than two days. Five years on, the getting of this victory was rather different. True, the weather pilfered around two sessions on the third day, but this Test intrigued

In the groove: Jonathan Trott checks his mark, seemingly oblivious that the Test is over.

until tea on the fifth. In 2005, Bangladesh lost all 20 wickets inside 80 overs; now they frustrated England for more than 200. There were perhaps five sessions, on the Friday and Sunday, when the visitors competed on equal terms; and in Tamim Iqbal's coruscating second-innings hundred, they provided the most joyous and entertaining moments of a genuine scrap, a Test in reality, not just name.

Yet Bangladesh's negativity, stemming from 57 defeats in 66 Tests, meant they never posed a potent threat. They were either too defensive in the field or recklessly attacking at the crease. Yes, the electrifying Tamim had a licence to thrill at the top of the order, but the others should have knuckled down to save the match. The defeatist mentality seeped into Shakib Al Hasan's field placings for all but the first hour: even as Eoin Morgan faced his first ball in Tests at an uncertain 258 for four, Shakib preferred to people the boundary rather than apply pressure through close catchers. A dab to leg and Morgan was away. And in both innings, the Bangladeshis suffered the failure of what might be called their "muddle" order: Mahmudullah, for example, was either all caution – distrusting the seemingly sound Rubel Hossain and spurning single after single – or all attack, smearing across the line to bring the second innings to a crass end moments before lunch on the last day. Bangladesh's one hope of gaining a draw lay in denying England time for their run-chase; losing the two-over break between innings could yet have been crucial. As it was, England had two full sessions to make 160.

Defeat was hard on the top four, who contributed 75% of the runs from Bangladeshi bats. Twice they engineered a position from which a draw was possible, reaching 179 for two in the first innings and 289 for two in the second. On a blameless pitch against a largely ordinary attack, those foundations should have produced substantial totals. But 282 could not prevent the follow-on, nor could 382 set an adequate target.

When Cook fell lbw in the game's fifth over, he scowled as darkly as the skies that prompted Shakib to field. Hawk-Eye suggested the ball was high (just as it did when umpire de Silva again gave Cook lbw in the second innings), but without the umpires'

Decision Review System – BSkyB and the ICC each said the other should foot the bill – there could be no reprieve. Within an hour the clouds lifted, the ball lost all lateral movement, Shakib adopted defensive mode, and England made hay. Strauss, in his first Test for four months, eased into the runs before gloving a ball from Mahmudullah. Umpire Bowden missed the contact but, concentration broken, Strauss chopped on next ball.

Concentration was not an issue for Trott. After a lean winter, he dug in, almost literally: his focusing routine involved taking guard so frequently and scoring his boot down the line of leg stump so vigorously that a canyon opened up in front of him. However infuriating his method, it worked. Characteristically strong on the leg, Trott now scored more heavily on the off, unleashing a flurry of drives through extra cover, some of exquisite timing; his 226 from 349 balls included 20 fours.

The other England batsmen hardly shone. Pietersen looked as if, mentally, he was still in the Caribbean, where 11 days earlier he had powered England to the World Twenty20 title. The decision to rest England's triumphant captain Paul Collingwood (nominally to nurse a sore right shoulder) allowed Morgan, Dublin-born but four years a Middlesex player, to make his Test debut at his adopted home. Just as he appeared to have made the considerable readjustment – from a Twenty20 against Australia to a Test against Bangladesh – he fell to a one-day open-faced push, giving the persevering Shahadat Hossain the second of five wickets. England were eventually dismissed for 505: useful, though on this generous pitch far from dominant. Without Trott, they would have been embarrassed.

TEST DOUBLE-HUNDREDS AT LORD'S

Runs	Balls	Mins	4s	6s			
333	485	628	43	3	G. A. Gooch	England v India	1990
259	370	574	34	0	G. C. Smith	South Africa v England	2003
254	376	341	25	0	D. G. Bradman	Australia v England	1930
240	394	367	32	0	W. R. Hammond	England v Australia	1938
226	**349**	**490**	**20**	**0**	**I. J. L. Trott**	**England v Bangladesh**	**2010**
221	288	426	31	0	R. W. T. Key	England v West Indies	2004
214*	242	302	29	2	C. G. Greenidge	West Indies v England	1984
211	–	280	15	0	J. B. Hobbs	England v South Africa	1924
208	–	352	20	0	D. C. S. Compton	England v South Africa	1947
206*	370	369	22	0	W. A. Brown	Australia v England	1938
206	–	355	26	0	M. P. Donnelly	New Zealand v England	1949
205*	–	318	16	0	J. Hardstaff, jun.	England v India	1946
202	330	468	26	1	Mohammad Yousuf	Pakistan v England	2006
200	386	495	23	0	Mohsin Khan	Pakistan v England	1982

Tamim took a shine to Bresnan, walloping him for seven of his eight fours, before Pietersen's fluid pick-up-and-throw from point silenced the artillery. Bresnan was still in one-day mode, angling the ball in from wide of the crease. Anderson, a paid spectator in the West Indies, was anodyne; so was the 6ft 7in Steve Finn, playing on his home ground instead of the rested Stuart Broad, until he switched to his preferred Pavilion End and wrested life from the wicket. Even so, Bangladesh ended the second day on 172 for two.

When play belatedly started on the Saturday, at 3.20, conditions were heaven-sent for swing. Anderson regained his misplaced inswinger to the left-hander, while Bresnan, despite a sore left foot, found some rhythm. The light, though, was crepuscular, stopping play three times in successive overs as clouds scudded across St John's Wood. Maximising play was laudable, but Mushfiqur Rahim, cleaned up in conditions wholly unsuitable for batting, was the loser. In tacit admission of their error, the umpires promptly marched the players off.

Bank holiday stroll: a large fifth-day crowd promenade on the Lord's turf.

Philip Brown

On television that evening Geoffrey Boycott denounced the Bangladeshi attack as unfit for Test cricket, though Tamim believed the slight levelled at the whole team. Next morning, with the tourists' tail polished off, Strauss enforced the follow-on – and Tamim set about putting the record straight. He reached a ferocious peak against Swann, whom he slog-swept for two sixes in three balls; in between he cracked a four through cover. It was not an infallible innings – acts of such aggression never are – but few ripostes are so eloquent.

Tamim archly said he had formed no opinion of the English bowlers as he was too busy punishing the bad balls. Perhaps, but he punished a few good ones, too, betraying few nerves in tearing through the nineties in four balls, all from Bresnan. He disdainfully hit a length delivery on off stump over mid-on to reach his hundred from 94 balls, Bangladesh's fastest Test century (and the quickest at Lord's since India's Mohammad Azharuddin needed just 88 in 1990). In celebration, Tamim ebulliently gestured for the sign-writer to start work on the honours board.

Imrul Kayes, his opening partner, could also smile. No Test opener had gone longer without reaching 50, but now, in his 24th innings, he made it; their 185 was Bangladesh's best for the first wicket. With determined support from Junaid Siddique and Jahurul Islam (Trott's first Test victim), Bangladesh reached 328 for five by the fourth evening. Without Finn, whose bounce, accuracy and hostility lifted him head and shoulders above his colleagues, taking him to a maiden Test five-for and nine in the match, the draw might have been inescapable.

The fight, though, was draining from Bangladesh. They battled next morning against tighter bowling, but once the breach was made the end was quick and, in Mahmudullah's mow, ugly. A bank holiday crowd of almost 10,000 had queued patiently, partly to see the denouement, and partly to perambulate on the Lord's outfield, which for the first time in more than a generation became *terra legitima* during a Test-match lunch interval. MCC chief executive Keith Bradshaw rightly basked in widespread approbation.

There was another piece of eminent good sense before the finish. A target of 160 in two sessions left no doubt about an England victory, though there was doubt about when it would arrive – especially once Pietersen, scores level, dead-batted the last scheduled over before tea. Would the umpires really lead the players off for 20 minutes? Mercifully, pragmatism won the day – and Trott, next ball, the Test.

Man of the Match: S. T. Finn.   *Attendance:* 79,568.

Close of play: First day, England 362-4 (Trott 175, Morgan 40); Second day, Bangladesh 172-2 (Junaid Siddique 53, Jahurul Islam 16); Third day, Bangladesh 237-7 (Mahmudullah 7, Shahadat Hossain 3); Fourth day, Bangladesh 328-5 (Junaid Siddique 66, Shakib Al Hasan 2).

England

*A. J. Strauss b Mahmudullah	83	– c Mushfiqur Rahim b Shakib Al Hasan	82
A. N. Cook lbw b Shahadat Hossain	7	– lbw b Mahmudullah	23
I. J. L. Trott c Imrul Kayes b Shahadat Hossain	226	– not out	36
K. P. Pietersen b Shakib Al Hasan	18	– not out	10
I. R. Bell b Rubel Hossain	17		
E. J. G. Morgan c Mushfiqur Rahim b Shahadat Hossain	44		
†M. J. Prior run out	16		
T. T. Bresnan c Junaid Siddique b Shahadat Hossain	25		
G. P. Swann c Rubel Hossain b Shakib Al Hasan	22		
J. M. Anderson b Shahadat Hossain	13		
S. T. Finn not out	3		
L-b 10, w 8, n-b 13	31	L-b 5, w 1, n-b 6	12

1/7 (2) 2/188 (1) 3/227 (4)   (125 overs) 505   1/67 (2)   (2 wkts, 35.1 overs) 163
4/258 (5) 5/370 (6) 6/400 (7)   2/147 (1)
7/463 (8) 8/478 (3) 9/498 (9) 10/505 (10)

Shahadat Hossain 28–3–98–5; Robiul Islam 22–2–107–0; Shakib Al Hasan 27–3–109–2; Rubel Hossain 23–0–109–1; Mahmudullah 23–3–59–1; Mohammad Ashraful 2–0–13–0. *Second Innings*—Shahadat Hossain 2–0–19–0; Robiul Islam 1–0–12–0; Shakib Al Hasan 16–1–48–1; Rubel Hossain 1–0–8–0; Mahmudullah 15.1–1–71–1.

Bangladesh

Tamim Iqbal run out	55	– c Trott b Finn	103
Imrul Kayes c Strauss b Finn	43	– c Bell b Finn	75
Junaid Siddique c Prior b Finn	58	– c Bresnan b Finn	74
Jahurul Islam c Prior b Anderson	20	– c and b Trott	46
Mohammad Ashraful lbw b Finn	4	– c Prior b Anderson	21
*Shakib Al Hasan c Strauss b Anderson	25	– (7) c Morgan b Finn	16
†Mushfiqur Rahim b Finn	16	– (8) c Prior b Finn	0
Mahmudullah b Anderson	17	– (9) c Prior b Bresnan	19
Shahadat Hossain b Anderson	20	– (6) b Bresnan	0
Rubel Hossain c Cook b Bresnan	9	– c Strauss b Bresnan	4
Robiul Islam not out	9	– not out	0
L-b 2, w 3, n-b 1	6	B 7, l-b 14, w 2, n-b 1	24

1/88 (1) 2/134 (2) 3/179 (3)   (93 overs) 282   1/185 (1) 2/189 (2)   (110.2 overs) 382
4/185 (5) 5/191 (4) 6/221 (6)   3/289 (4) 4/321 (5)
7/234 (7) 8/255 (9) 9/266 (8) 10/282 (10)   5/322 (6) 6/347 (7) 7/354 (3)
                                                        8/361 (9) 9/381 (10) 10/382 (9)

Anderson 31–6–78–4; Bresnan 24–5–76–1; Finn 25–5–100–4; Swann 11–6–19–0; Trott 2–0–7–0. *Second Innings*—Anderson 29–8–84–1; Bresnan 26.2–9–93–3; Finn 24–6–87–5; Swann 27–5–81–0; Trott 4–0–16–1.

Umpires: B. F. Bowden and E. A. R. de Silva.   Third umpire: R. K. Illingworth.

ENGLAND v BANGLADESH

Second npower Test

Paul Edwards

At Manchester, June 4–6. England won by an innings and 80 runs. Toss: England. Test debut: A. Shahzad.

At 4.24 p.m. on the second day of this curious Test, Bangladesh's players could look back with pride on over five sessions of hard-fought cricket in which they had shared the spoils equally with England. After they restricted the home batsmen to a first-innings total of 419, Tamim Iqbal and Imrul Kayes picked up where they had left off at Lord's, opening with 126 in 23.5 overs of uninhibited strokeplay. Taking the game into a fifth day seemed eminently possible; embarrassing their hosts was not out of the question. Yet less than 24 hours later, England's players were spraying each other with champagne, and Bangladesh coach Jamie Siddons was reflecting on the fact that his side had lost all 20 wickets in scoring 213 further runs in 64.3 overs. Ten fell in Saturday's prolonged evening session, chiefly to a rejuvenated Swann and the impressive debutant Ajmal Shahzad; then, on a cloudy Sunday afternoon, all ten were swept aside, again in a single extended session – 34.1 overs of cricketing carnage when they were, indeed, easy meat for England's

Philip Brown

Middle order, high class: Ian Bell nears a polished hundred.

three seamers. Many neutrals, and even some local supporters, thought that this was rather a sad end to a series in which Shakib Al Hasan's players had contributed much.

Bangladesh's second collapse was easier to explain than their first. Drizzle had prevented any play on the third morning and, by the time conditions were fit, a combination of heavy skies and the warm atmosphere, not to mention a poor weather forecast, made Strauss's decision regarding the follow-on very straightforward. (Even here, though, Bangladesh were a shade unlucky: had the England captain been forced to decide late on Saturday evening, indications were that he would have batted again.) As it was, the top order suffered a grievous blow as early as the second ball of the innings, when Tamim edged a nasty, lifting delivery from Anderson to Prior and thus collected only his second score below 52 in eight Test innings against England. Once they lost their young champion – the man who had flayed Strauss's bowlers in scoring 108 the previous afternoon – the technique of the Bangladesh batsmen was mercilessly exposed, in conditions beloved of English seamers but almost never seen in Chittagong. Finn claimed Kayes's wicket with a short ball for the fourth time in the series, when the opener hooked him to Shahzad at deep backward square leg; Anderson, swinging the ball both ways and obtaining plenty of movement off a pitch offering a modicum of variable bounce, added Junaid Siddique and Mohammad Ashraful to his bag. At 39 for six in the 14th over, Bangladesh's plight had statisticians checking the country's lowest score in Test cricket. It was 62 against Sri Lanka, but Mahmudullah's resistance averted similar indignity. Finn's five for 42, which gave him 15 wickets in the series, included some very easy dismissals and prompted Mike Atherton's observation that Bangladesh lacked stomach for the fight. Perhaps so, but one wondered how often they had faced an international attack in such custom-made conditions.

The previous afternoon, it was the quartet of England bowlers who had attracted sympathy as they vainly attempted to cope with Tamim's glittering talent. He became the first Bangladeshi to score hundreds in successive Test innings when he cut Swann for four; he reached the landmark off exactly 100 balls, 11 of which he smacked to the boundary. Some of the sun-soaked 11,226 spectators – only a thousand or so below the capacity at an Old Trafford stadium in the middle of a major redevelopment – may later have recalled Tamim's one six, which disappeared deep into the crowd beyond the long-on boundary to bring up his fifty. But a square drive off Anderson, hit on the up and off the back foot, had a claim to be the best shot of the international summer. After the match, Tamim was asked why he had coped with the England attack better than his colleagues: "I work harder," he replied simply, as if to remind everyone of the effortful sweat that so often lies behind seemingly effortless style.

Once Tamim was dismissed, caught behind off a tired cut at Anderson, the Bangladesh batting looked fragile indeed. Swann got plenty of turn in a 15-over spell from the Stretford End, and collected his seventh five-wicket haul in only his 20th Test, but too many of the tourists – Shakib was a good example – played his off-spin naively, relying on firm-footed crease-bound drives instead of a more mobile approach. At the Brian Statham End, Yorkshire's Shahzad, whose first six overs had gone for 35, settled into Test cricket in fine style, taking three wickets in 16 deliveries. His first success owed something to luck, when Ashraful's slash went straight to Morgan at backward point, but the scalps of Mahmudullah and Shafiul Islam were claimed by Shahzad's ability to swing the ball and obtain movement off the pitch at around 90mph. His use of reverse swing made comparisons with Simon Jones understandable, and not in any way fanciful.

However, while it was the England bowlers who roused the crowd in a final session described by Swann as "crazy", the foundation for the victory had been laid by their middle-order batsmen, in particular Bell, whose 128 was full of understated class. Coming to the wicket a quarter of an hour before lunch on the first day, a Friday, he would probably have departed immediately had Shakib put a forward short leg in for his first ball. Instead, Bell survived to play one of his most composed innings, unfussy in defence and polished in attack.

Bell's 70-run partnerships with Pietersen and Morgan repaired the damage done to England's innings by Shafiul, who was overbowled on the first morning – when he had the admirable figures of 9–2–18–2 – and was too tired to continue in this vein. By the close Bell and Prior had guided England to 275 for five, and they were to take their partnership to 153 on Saturday before Bell was bowled, by a sublime ball from Shakib which pitched middle and leg and hit the top of off stump. Shakib also claimed the wicket of Prior, whose reverse swat prevented him from reaching the century which would have conclusively answered Craig Kieswetter's challenge to his place.

This match was originally scheduled for Leeds, but it was transferred to Old Trafford, which had been told it would not stage another Test before 2012, because Headingley was assigned one of the two neutral Tests between Pakistan and Australia in July.

Man of the Match: I. R. Bell.   *Attendance:* 22,175.

Men of the Series: England – S. T. Finn; Bangladesh – Tamim Iqbal.

Close of play: First day, England 275-5 (Bell 87, Prior 21); Second day, Bangladesh 216.

England

*A. J. Strauss c Imrul Kayes b Shafiul Islam	21		G. P. Swann lbw b Abdur Razzak	20
A. N. Cook c Junaid Siddique			A. Shahzad c Abdur Razzak	
b Abdur Razzak	29		b Shakib Al Hasan	5
I. J. L. Trott b Shafiul Islam	3		J. M. Anderson not out	2
K. P. Pietersen st Mushfiqur Rahim			S. T. Finn lbw b Shakib Al Hasan	0
b Shakib Al Hasan	64		B 6, l-b 5, w 4, n-b 2	17
I. R. Bell b Shakib Al Hasan	128			
E. J. G. Morgan c Jahurul Islam			1/44 (1) 2/48 (3) 3/83 (2) (121.3 overs)	419
b Shahadat Hossain	37		4/153 (4) 5/223 (6)	
†M. J. Prior c Jahurul Islam			6/376 (5) 7/399 (8)	
b Shakib Al Hasan	93		8/414 (6) 9/419 (7) 10/419 (11)	

Shahadat Hossain 21–3–84–1; Shafiul Islam 21–2–63–2; Mahmudullah 12–1–31–0; Shakib Al Hasan 37.3–4–121–5; Abdur Razzak 30–3–109–2.

Bangladesh

Tamim Iqbal c Prior b Anderson	108	– c Prior b Anderson	2
Imrul Kayes c Shahzad b Finn	36	– c Shahzad b Finn	9
Junaid Siddique c Prior b Swann	1	– c Pietersen b Anderson	6
Jahurul Islam b Swann	5	– (5) c Prior b Finn	0
Mohammad Ashraful c Morgan b Shahzad	11	– (4) c Trott b Anderson	14
*Shakib Al Hasan c Anderson b Swann	10	– b Shahzad	1
†Mushfiqur Rahim c Anderson b Swann	11	– c sub (K. R. Brown) b Finn	13
Mahmudullah b Shahzad	8	– c Prior b Finn	38
Shafiul Islam b Shahzad	4	– (10) c Strauss b Finn	4
Abdur Razzak not out	0	– (9) c Morgan b Swann	19
Shahadat Hossain lbw b Swann	0	– not out	4
B 4, l-b 7, w 8, n-b 3	22	B 13	13

1/126 (2) 2/153 (3) 3/169 (1)   (54.1 overs) 216
4/169 (4) 5/185 (6) 6/200 (5)
7/210 (8) 8/214 (9) 9/216 (7) 10/216 (11)

1/2 (1) 2/14 (2)   (34.1 overs) 123
3/18 (3) 4/21 (5)
5/37 (4) 6/39 (6) 7/76 (7)
8/97 (8) 9/119 (10) 10/123 (9)

Anderson 14–4–45–1; Finn 8–1–39–1; Swann 22.1–4–76–5; Shahzad 10.2–2–45–3. *Second Innings*—Anderson 10.3–3–16–3; Finn 10.2–2–42–5; Shahzad 7–2–18–1; Swann 7.1–0–34–1.

Umpires: B. F. Bowden and E. A. R. de Silva. Third umpire: R. A. Kettleborough.
Series referee: A. G. Hurst.

At Hove, July 3. **Sussex won by 149 runs.** ‡Sussex 253 (47.5 overs) (M. A. Thornely 56, B. C. Brown 58, W. A. Adkin 30); **Bangladeshis 104** (28.4 overs) (J. E. Anyon 3-29, M. S. Panesar 3-21). *County debuts:* W. A. Adkin, J. A. Thorpe, L. W. P. Wells. *Returning to England after a trip to Sri Lanka for the Asia Cup, with Mashrafe bin Mortaza restored to the captaincy after Shakib Al Hasan was deposed, the Bangladeshis collapsed ignominiously against a young Sussex side; only Raqibul Hasan, at No. 7, reached 20.*

At Lord's, July 5. **Bangladeshis won by 141 runs.** ‡Bangladeshis 301-7 (50 overs) (Imrul Kayes 77, Jahurul Islam 88, Shakib Al Hasan 38; D. Evans 3-51); **Middlesex 160** (39.3 overs) (O. A. Shah 61, D. J. Malan 32; Shafiul Islam 3-31). *County debut:* T. E. Scollay. *The tourists played far more convincingly than at Hove, plundering an inexperienced attack, as Imrul Kayes (who hit three sixes) and Jahurul Islam (who made 88 in 93 balls) added 143 in 25 overs, and then running through the Middlesex batting, whose only partnership over 18 was 87 from Owais Shah and Dawid Malan.*

ONE-DAY INTERNATIONAL REPORTS BY JULIAN GUYER

ENGLAND v BANGLADESH

First One-Day International

At Nottingham, July 8 (floodlit). England won by six wickets. Toss: Bangladesh.
In his first one-day international since November 2008, Bell seized the opportunity created by Pietersen's thigh injury to score a well-paced 84 that saw England to a comfortable, if unspectacular, victory. Bangladesh's latest defeat was compounded by injuries which deprived them of two players for the rest of the series. Raqibul Hasan marked his return to duty (he had "retired" after being omitted from the World Twenty20 squad) by compiling 76 before an Anderson yorker broke his toe; a runner arrived, but was run out in the next over. The blow was arguably Anderson's most telling contribution, and Bresnan was also too often short and wide in the opening overs. Tamim Iqbal eagerly accepted the presents on offer. Bangladesh's other injury came when wicketkeeper Mushfiqur Rahim, not wearing a helmet, was struck in the face by a ball from spinner Faisal Hossain. Mushfiqur

fell to the turf in sickening fashion; after several minutes of on-field treatment, he was carried off on a stretcher. It was a rare graphic moment for those watching in 3D, an event much hyped by the host broadcaster, but the technology was ill-matched to a one-dimensional contest.

Man of the Match: I. R. Bell.   *Attendance:* 8,618.

Bangladesh

Tamim Iqbal lbw b Broad	28	*Mashrafe bin Mortaza c Bell b Anderson	5
Imrul Kayes c Morgan b Anderson	14	Abdur Razzak b Bresnan	3
Junaid Siddique lbw b Yardy	51	B 1, l-b 7, w 11	19
Raqibul Hasan run out	76		
Shakib Al Hasan c Anderson b Broad	20	1/40 (1) 2/70 (2) (9 wkts, 50 overs)	250
†Mushfiqur Rahim c Wright b Bresnan	22	3/136 (3) 4/186 (5)	
Mahmudullah lbw b Anderson	4	5/222 (6) 6/234 (7) 7/236 (4)	
Faisal Hossain not out	8	8/243 (9) 9/250 (10) 10 overs: 47-1	

Shafiul Islam did not bat.

Anderson 10–0–74–3; Bresnan 10–0–40–2; Broad 10–1–43–2; Tredwell 3–0–18–0; Wright 3–0–20–0; Collingwood 9–1–32–0; Yardy 5–0–15–1.

England

*A. J. Strauss run out	50	M. H. Yardy not out	10
†C. Kieswetter c Faisal Hossain b Shakib Al Hasan	32		
I. R. Bell not out	84		
P. D. Collingwood c Junaid Siddique b Shakib Al Hasan	33	B 5, l-b 4, w 10	19
E. J. G. Morgan c Shafiul Islam b Abdur Razzak	23	1/75 (1) 2/93 (2) (4 wkts, 45.1 overs)	251
		3/173 (4) 4/213 (5) 10 overs: 66-0	

L. J. Wright, T. T. Bresnan, J. C. Tredwell, S. C. J. Broad and J. M. Anderson did not bat.

Mashrafe bin Mortaza 6–0–30–0; Shafiul Islam 5–0–46–0; Abdur Razzak 10–0–64–1; Shakib Al Hasan 10–0–35–2; Mahmudullah 8–0–41–0; Faisal Hossain 6.1–0–26–0.

Umpires: Asad Rauf and N. J. Llong.   Third umpire: R. K. Illingworth.

ENGLAND v BANGLADESH

Second One-Day International

At Bristol, July 10. Bangladesh won by five runs. Toss: England.

As Strauss pointed out later, it was inevitable that Bangladesh would one day defeat England. But, after Nottingham, few would have foreseen a victory that ended a run of 24 losses in all formats since they beat Zimbabwe in November. And when Tamim Iqbal went early, caught behind off Shahzad, who had replaced fellow-Yorkshireman Bresnan, they appeared on course for their 21st defeat in all matches against England. But Imrul Kayes, missed twice in the field by Shahzad, grafted 76 in 111 balls. That gave what was for once a well-disciplined attack – ably marshalled by Mashrafe bin Mortaza – just enough runs to play with. Bell was unable to bat at No. 3 after breaking his left foot in a forlorn attempt at a leaping catch. But England had picked an extra batsman in Trott, and a target of 237 should not have been difficult. This time, though, they not only lost early wickets but continued to lose them as the ball did not quite come on to the bat. Strauss, having spoken of the dangers of getting too "funky", was caught behind trying to upper-cut Rubel Hossain, who also accounted for Kieswetter. Only Trott held firm, but he seemed unable to change gear against accurate bowling. Most of the impetus in the final powerplay came from Broad, until he was caught

David Jones, PA Photos

The wait is over: Shafiul Islam (*centre*) celebrates Bangladesh's first victory over England.

by a leaping Shakib Al Hasan off Mortaza, who then caught and bowled Anderson. Some Bangladesh players began celebrating but had to be calmed down; Bell, wearing a surgical boot and with Morgan as his runner, limped out with England needing ten off the last over and Trott on strike. Two twos followed before Trott, whose 94 took 130 balls, was caught behind off Shafiul Islam, sparking scenes of unspoilt joy in a Bangladesh side well worth this win.

Man of the Match: Mashrafe bin Mortaza.   *Attendance:* 9,509.

BANGLADESH COMPLETE THE SET

Bangladesh had now beaten all the other nine Test sides in one-day internationals. They made their debut in 1985-86, but had won only two games – against fellow Associates Kenya and Scotland – in 34 one-day internationals before beating Pakistan in the 1999 World Cup.

	First ODI win	Attempt		First ODI win	Attempt
Pakistan	1999	7th	South Africa	2006-07	8th
Zimbabwe	2003-04	11th	New Zealand	2008-09	12th
India	2004-05	13th	West Indies*	2009	14th
Australia	2005	7th	**England**	**2010**	**13th**
Sri Lanka	2005-06	16th			

* *Bangladesh had already beaten West Indies in a Twenty20 international in 2007-08 and two Tests in 2009 before their first one-day international victory.*

Bangladesh

Tamim Iqbal c Kieswetter b Shahzad	18	
Imrul Kayes c Collingwood b Shahzad	76	
Junaid Siddique c Kieswetter b Broad	21	
†Jahurul Islam c Kieswetter b Shahzad	40	
Shakib Al Hasan b Collingwood	1	
Mohammad Ashraful run out	14	
Mahmudullah not out	24	

*Mashrafe bin Mortaza run out	22
Abdur Razzak not out	1
L-b 4, w 12, n-b 3	19

1/19 (1) 2/65 (3)   (7 wkts, 50 overs) 236
3/148 (4) 4/149 (5)
5/174 (6) 6/196 (2) 7/233 (8)   10 overs: 50-1

Rubel Hossain and Shafiul Islam did not bat.

Anderson 9–0–46–0; Shahzad 10–0–41–3; Broad 10–0–60–1; Wright 6–0–30–0; Yardy 10–0–39–0; Collingwood 5–0–16–1.

England

*A. J. Strauss c Jahurul Islam b Rubel Hossain	33	J. M. Anderson	
†C. Kieswetter c Jahurul Islam		c and b Mashrafe bin Mortaza .	2
b Rubel Hossain .	20	I. R. Bell not out	0
I. J. L. Trott c Jahurul Islam b Shafiul Islam	94		
P. D. Collingwood lbw b Abdur Razzak . . .	10		
E. J. G. Morgan lbw b Abdur Razzak	1		
M. H. Yardy b Shakib Al Hasan	10	L-b 7, w 13	20
L. J. Wright c Junaid Siddique			
b Shafiul Islam .	15	1/49 (1) 2/58 (2) 3/86 (4) (49.3 overs)	231
A. Shahzad b Shakib Al Hasan	5	4/90 (5) 5/115 (6) 6/146 (7)	
S. C. J. Broad c Shakib Al Hasan		7/166 (8) 8/209 (9)	
b Mashrafe bin Mortaza .	21	9/227 (10) 10/231 (3) 10 overs: 61-2	

Mashrafe bin Mortaza 10–0–42–2; Abdur Razzak 10–0–43–2; Shafiul Islam 9.3–3–38–2; Rubel Hossain 9–0–52–2; Shakib Al Hasan 10–0–40–2; Mohammad Ashraful 1–0–9–0.

Umpires: Asad Rauf and R. K. Illingworth.   Third umpire: R. A. Kettleborough.

ENGLAND v BANGLADESH

Third One-Day International

At Birmingham, July 12. England won by 144 runs. Toss: Bangladesh.

Any hope that Bangladesh might build on their success in Bristol was demolished as England swept to a huge victory. Strauss's utterly dominating 154, with five sixes and 16 fours in 140 balls, called into question his decision to retire from Twenty20 internationals, containing an array of shots that contradicted his self-deprecating remarks about his batting. Before this game, England had produced fewer one-day innings of 150-plus than any other Test-playing country except Pakistan and Bangladesh, but Strauss supplied his second – both against Bangladesh – to take their total to four. His stand of 250 with Trott, who on his home ground reached the hundred that had eluded him two days earlier, was England's all-wicket record; it came after the admirable Mashrafe bin Mortaza had bowled Kieswetter for a duck. Just when it seemed England might fall short of a total befitting the pair's efforts, Bopara, in for the stricken Bell, hit an unbeaten 45 off 16 balls with almost disdainful ease. Shafiul Islam conceded 97 runs, a record for nine overs at this level. Bangladesh were obliged to come out swinging. But when Tamim Iqbal was deceived by an excellent slower ball from Shahzad – held seam-up but in the tips of his fingers – the game was up. It was as if Saturday's events had been an illusion.

Man of the Match: A. J. Strauss.   *Attendance:* 9,576.

Man of the Series: A. J. Strauss.

England

*A. J. Strauss c Shakib Al Hasan		R. S. Bopara not out	45
b Rubel Hossain .	154	T. T. Bresnan c Tamim Iqbal b Shafiul Islam	10
†C. Kieswetter b Mashrafe bin Mortaza	0	M. H. Yardy not out	8
I. J. L. Trott c Shakib Al Hasan			
b Mashrafe bin Mortaza .	110		
L. J. Wright c Jahurul Islam		B 1, l-b 4, w 4, n-b 2	11
b Mashrafe bin Mortaza .	0		
P. D. Collingwood c Mohammad Ashraful		1/1 (2) 2/251 (3) (7 wkts, 50 overs)	347
b Rubel Hossain .	8	3/251 (4) 4/272 (5)	
E. J. G. Morgan c Tamim Iqbal		5/280 (6) 6/283 (1)	
b Shafiul Islam .	1	7/297 (8) 10 overs: 45-1	

A. Shahzad and S. C. J. Broad did not bat.

Mashrafe bin Mortaza 10–2–31–3; Shafiul Islam 9–0–97–2; Rubel Hossain 9–0–61–2; Abdur Razzak 9–0–63–0; Shakib Al Hasan 10–0–75–0; Mahmudullah 3–0–15–0.

Bangladesh

Tamim Iqbal c Wright b Shahzad	16	Shafiul Islam b Bopara		16
Imrul Kayes c Kieswetter b Shahzad	4	Rubel Hossain not out		1
Junaid Siddique c Wright b Bresnan	25			
†Jahurul Islam c Strauss b Broad	27	L-b 3, w 5, n-b 4		12
Shakib Al Hasan run out	6			
Mohammad Ashraful lbw b Bopara	13	1/20 (1) 2/24 (2) 3/64 (3)	(45 overs)	203
Mahmudullah lbw b Yardy	42	4/77 (4) 5/86 (5) 6/102 (6)		
*Mashrafe bin Mortaza c Kieswetter b Bopara	14	7/124 (8) 8/180 (7)		
Abdur Razzak c Bresnan b Bopara	27	9/190 (9) 10/203 (10)	10 overs: 59-2	

Shahzad 4–1–24–2; Bresnan 7–0–39–1; Broad 10–1–27–1; Wright 7–0–27–0; Bopara 10–1–38–4; Trott 3–0–18–0; Yardy 4–0–27–1.

Umpires: Asad Rauf and R. A. Kettleborough. Third umpire: N. J. Llong.
Series referee: J. Srinath.

Details of Bangladesh's matches against Ireland, Scotland and Netherlands in July can be found from pages 770–773.

ENGLAND v AUSTRALIA NATWEST SERIES, 2010

John Etheridge

One-day internationals (5): England 3, Australia 2

England won a home one-day series against Australia for the first time since 1997. It meant they could claim domination over Australia in all three formats: England held the Ashes and the 50-over NatWest Series trophy, and the memory of their victory over Australia in the World Twenty20 final little more than a month beforehand was still glowing warmly.

Domination might be stretching things, however, as a description of England's win in this series. They won the first two matches comfortably enough, almost tossed away victory in the third, then were comprehensively beaten in the last two after Australia added hostility to their attack in the shape of the big, bustling, slinging fast bowler Shaun Tait.

Tait's spectacular opening spell at Lord's, when he bowled Andrew Strauss and Mike Yardy in the same over, after being clocked at 100.1mph, was one of the highlights of the series. But even that was not as good as Eoin Morgan's dazzling century in the first game at the Rose Bowl, one of the finest limited-overs innings played for England. Morgan scored runs in the next three matches and was Man of the Series, although his effectiveness diminished once the bowlers began testing him with bouncers.

England played the same eleven in all five matches and bowled first each time. Maybe not a case of Groundhog Day, but the reality was England won

Head of steam: Shaun Tait beats Paul Collingwood for pace in the fifth one-day international.

Matthew Lewis, Getty Images

both the first two games by four wickets, while Australia's margin in the final two was 78 runs and 42 runs. Only in the third match at Old Trafford did it get close. Neither side could claim any psychological superiority four and a half months ahead of the First Test at Brisbane: England won the series, but Australia finished the stronger. It was at least closer than the post-Ashes afterthought of the previous autumn, which Australia won 6–1.

Shane Watson and Tim Paine produced half-century opening partnerships in the first three games, but wicketkeeper Paine's slow strike-rate was a problem for Australia, as was Watson reaching 30 four times but never going beyond 61. In the first three matches, England's bowlers were able to suffocate Australia's batting in the middle overs and take wickets as well. Mike Yardy was frugal with his left-arm uglies, and Graeme Swann showed the guile and capacity to take wickets that England had come to take almost for granted. Stuart Broad collected four wickets in Cardiff and 12 in the series, but on the other hand Tim Bresnan had series figures of one for 236 and went for 5.61 an over, as the new ball would not swing for him or James Anderson.

Australia handed Josh Hazlewood a debut in the opening match – he was the youngest to play a one-day international for Australia – and Clint McKay appeared in the second. Their attack looked toothless. But then Tait was summoned from the domestic Twenty20 competition with Glamorgan, ostensibly as the replacement for injured spinner Nathan Hauritz, and Australia were transformed. They now had three genuinely fast bowlers: Doug Bollinger was a threat throughout the series, Ryan Harris returned after missing the second match through injury, and Tait was the intimidating spearhead. Craig Kieswetter was usually blown away at the start of England's innings and made just 69 runs in five attempts, while Kevin Pietersen extended his sequence without a half-century in 50-over internationals to 16 innings. Steve Smith showed promise and exuberance for Australia, as much with his inventive batting as with his wrist-spin.

Bollinger and Tait obliterated England's middle and lower order at Old Trafford with speed and reverse swing. It meant that the last-wicket pair, Bresnan and Anderson, needed ten to clinch England's win, which they just managed – but the momentum of the series had already shifted in those few overs.

At The Oval and Lord's, Australia's three most experienced batsmen – Ricky Ponting, Michael Clarke and Michael Hussey – made significant contributions, and the three fast men were formidable. Whereas the Australian fast bowlers had most success when they pitched the ball up, England's tried a lot of short ones. Clarke was bounced out in Cardiff, Ponting twice perished to short deliveries, and Watson and Cameron White showed discomfort at times when the ball was dug in.

AUSTRALIAN TOURING PARTY

*R. T. Ponting, D. E. Bollinger, M. J. Clarke, R. J. Harris, N. M. Hauritz, J. R. Hazlewood, J. R. Hopes, M. E. K. Hussey, C. J. McKay, S. E. Marsh, S. N. J. O'Keefe, T. D. Paine, S. P. D. Smith, S. R. Watson, C. L. White. *Coach:* T. J. Nielsen.

B. J. Haddin and M. G. Johnson were originally selected but pulled out beforehand with elbow problems, to be replaced by Paine and Hazlewood. Hauritz injured his left foot during the series, and was replaced by S. W. Tait.

At Dublin (Clontarf), June 17. AUSTRALIA beat IRELAND by 39 runs (see Cricket in Ireland, page 770).

At Lord's, June 19. **Australians won by five wickets.** ‡**Middlesex 273-5** (50 overs) (A. C. Gilchrist 38, O. A. Shah 92, N. J. Dexter 45, S. A. Newman 55*; D. E. Bollinger 3-24); **Australians 277-5** (47.5 overs) (C. L. White 106, M. E. K. Hussey 72*; T. J. Murtagh 3-43). *After Middlesex's captain Adam Gilchrist gave his former team-mates a reminder of his talents, hitting two sixes in 38 from 43 balls, Owais Shah shepherded the county to a decent total. When Tim Murtagh trapped both Michael Clarke (0) and Ricky Ponting (17) lbw the Australians looked in trouble at 64-4, but Hussey and White added 176 in 33 overs to reclaim the upper hand.*

ENGLAND v AUSTRALIA

First One-Day International

At Southampton, June 22 (day/night). England won by four wickets. Toss: Australia. One-day international debut: J. R. Hazlewood.

In the 3,000th official one-day international, Morgan produced an innings that had rarely been bettered in the previous 2,999. He hauled England from the perils of 97 for four with a dazzling 103 not out from 85 balls, which included 16 fours, the last of which – a sizzling straight-drive – won the match. He displayed some of his trademark unorthodoxy – a reverse lap and a flick over the wicketkeeper's head – but this was an innings based mainly on rasping cover drives and a calm head. Morgan put on 95 with Wright, then 71 with Bresnan at better than a run a ball. Australia were struggling themselves at 98 for four but Clarke, out for ducks in the previous two tour games, skilfully marshalled the innings with 87 not out, although he was not able to accelerate enough to worry England. After the straightforward Test wins over Bangladesh, the intensity of the cricket was notched up several levels, and the two new stands at the sold-out Rose Bowl added to the sense of occasion. The tall New South Wales fast bowler Josh Hazlewood became the youngest Australian to play a one-day international, at 19 years 165 days, knocking more than three months off the previous record, set by the left-arm spinner Ray Bright in 1973-74.

Man of the Match: E. J. G. Morgan. *Attendance*: 17,895.

Australia

S. R. Watson c and b Broad	32	N. M. Hauritz c Strauss b Broad		22
†T. D. Paine b Wright	26	R. J. Harris not out		0
*R. T. Ponting c Broad b Wright	21	L-b 2, w 4, n-b 1		7
M. J. Clarke not out	87			
C. L. White b Anderson	10	1/52 (1) 2/66 (2)	(7 wkts, 50 overs)	267
M. E. K. Hussey c Kieswetter b Yardy	28	3/86 (3) 4/98 (5)		
J. R. Hopes c Bresnan b Anderson	34	5/168 (6) 6/225 (7) 7/266 (8) 10 overs: 58-1		

J. R. Hazlewood and D. E. Bollinger did not bat.

Anderson 9–1–43–2; Bresnan 8–1–49–0; Broad 8–0–54–2; Wright 7–1–34–2; Yardy 10–2–41–1; Swann 8–0–44–0.

England

*A. J. Strauss c Paine b Harris	10	M. H. Yardy not out		1
†C. Kieswetter b Hazlewood	38			
K. P. Pietersen c Ponting b Watson	29	L-b 8, w 4, n-b 1		13
P. D. Collingwood c Hopes b Watson	11			
E. J. G. Morgan not out	103	1/16 (1) 2/75 (3)	(6 wkts, 46 overs)	268
L. J. Wright lbw b Harris	36	3/81 (2) 4/97 (4)		
T. T. Bresnan b Harris	27	5/192 (6) 6/263 (7)	10 overs: 50-1	

G. P. Swann, S. C. J. Broad and J. M. Anderson did not bat.

Bollinger 9–0–48–0; Harris 9–2–42–3; Hazlewood 7–0–41–1; Watson 8–1–55–2; Hopes 5–0–30–0; Hauritz 8–0–44–0.

Umpires: Aleem Dar and I. J. Gould. Third umpire: R. K. Illingworth.

ENGLAND v AUSTRALIA

Second One-Day International

At Cardiff, June 24 (day/night). England won by four wickets. Toss: Australia.

Broad was the star turn in another disciplined England bowling performance. He took four for 44 – including his 100th wicket in one-day internationals – on his 24th birthday, and provided early vindication for the strength and conditioning programme he undertook while England were beating Bangladesh. His slim physique looked strong and stable in the delivery stride, and Broad himself acknowledged the work was having short-term as well as the hoped-for long-term benefits. White made 86 not out from 98 balls, but Australia's total never looked sufficient on a slowish pitch. Clarke failed to keep down a bouncer three balls after Strauss positioned Swann at short leg. Later, while still fielding at short leg, Swann was sent off the field for one ball by Strauss to avoid the risk of injury as White lined up a free hit against Wright – captains cannot change the field unless the batsmen have crossed. Half-centuries by Strauss, which included a straight six and a four from free hits off McKay, and Morgan allowed England to reach their target with few alarms; Collingwood overhauled Alec Stewart's England record of 4,677 runs in one-day internationals during his innings of 48.

Man of the Match: S. C. J. Broad. Attendance: 15,124.

Australia

S. R. Watson c Kieswetter b Wright	57	J. R. Hopes run out	8
†T. D. Paine c Kieswetter b Broad	16	N. M. Hauritz not out	0
*R. T. Ponting c Kieswetter b Broad	13	W 2, n-b 1	3
M. J. Clarke c Swann b Broad	1		
C. L. White not out	86	1/51 (2) 2/67 (3) (7 wkts, 50 overs) 239	
M. E. K. Hussey b Anderson	14	3/77 (4) 4/94 (1)	
S. P. D. Smith c Collingwood b Broad	41	5/118 (6) 6/202 (7) 7/238 (8) 10 overs: 51-0	

C. J. McKay and D. E. Bollinger did not bat.

Anderson 10–1–63–1; Bresnan 9–0–44–0; Broad 10–0–44–4; Wright 9–0–38–1; Yardy 8–0–31–0; Swann 4–0–19–0.

England

*A. J. Strauss c and b Hauritz	51	G. P. Swann not out	19
†C. Kieswetter c Paine b Bollinger	8		
K. P. Pietersen c Ponting b Smith	33	L-b 2, w 3, n-b 5	10
P. D. Collingwood b Bollinger	48		
E. J. G. Morgan c Paine b Bollinger	52	1/23 (2) 2/91 (3) (6 wkts, 45.2 overs) 243	
L. J. Wright b Hopes	10	3/109 (1) 4/192 (4)	
T. T. Bresnan not out	12	5/211 (6) 6/211 (5) 10 overs: 63-1	

M. H. Yardy, S. C. J. Broad and J. M. Anderson did not bat.

Bollinger 10–2–46–3; McKay 9.2–0–60–0; Hopes 5–0–30–1; Hauritz 10–0–56–1; Smith 8–0–40–1; Watson 3–0–9–0.

Umpires: Aleem Dar and N. J. Llong. Third umpire: I. J. Gould.

ENGLAND v AUSTRALIA

Third One-Day International

At Manchester, June 27. England won by one wicket. Toss: England.

England survived a late collapse and a thrilling finish to clinch the series with two matches still to play. It meant they had beaten Australia in their most recent contests in all three formats: the 2009 Ashes, the 2010 World Twenty20 final and now this series. Strauss led the way with 87 from 121 balls as England strode to 185 for three in the 42nd over, apparently cruising in pursuit of 213. But a devastating burst by Tait and Bollinger, combining pace and reverse swing, swept away the middle and lower order. Six wickets tumbled for 18 runs in 38 balls, and suddenly England were nine down,

---

ENGLAND'S ONE-WICKET ONE-DAY VICTORIES

v West Indies at Leeds	1973		v Zimbabwe at Bulawayo	1999-2000
v Pakistan at Birmingham	1987		v West Indies at Bridgetown	2006-07
v West Indies at Birmingham	1991		**v Australia at Manchester**	**2010**

---

still ten short of their target with two overs left – but Bresnan saved the day with a couple of slightly streaky boundaries off Harris and Hopes. England's eighth successive win (equalling their record run) was set up by Swann, who removed four of Australia's top five with another beautiful demonstration of flight, guile and turn: they were too orthodox-minded to sweep him fine or reverse-sweep. From 75 for none, Australia lost all ten wickets for 137. A few thousand of the sell-out crowd disappeared when the World Cup football match between England and Germany started – Lancashire said they could not show it on the giant screen because of safety concerns – but most returned to watch the tense conclusion of the cricket. This match featured the first use of The Point, Old Trafford's new £12m conference centre overlooking the ground, for hospitality purposes.

Man of the Match: G. P. Swann. *Attendance:* 21,332.

Australia

S. R. Watson c Strauss b Swann	61		D. E. Bollinger b Anderson	3
†T. D. Paine lbw b Yardy	44		S. W. Tait not out	1
*R. T. Ponting st Kieswetter b Swann	3			
M. J. Clarke c sub (I. R. Bell) b Swann	33		W 6	6
C. L. White c Strauss b Swann	12			
M. E. K. Hussey b Collingwood	21		1/75 (2) 2/93 (3) 3/130 (1) (46 overs) 212	
S. P. D. Smith lbw b Anderson	20		4/154 (5) 5/169 (4) 6/183 (6)	
J. R. Hopes b Anderson	7		7/202 (8) 8/207 (9) 9/211 (7)	
R. J. Harris c Strauss b Broad	1		10/212 (10) 10 overs: 54-0	

Anderson 8–1–22–3; Bresnan 6–0–43–0; Broad 6–1–30–1; Wright 1–0–14–0; Yardy 10–1–45–1; Swann 10–1–37–4; Collingwood 5–0–21–1.

England

*A. J. Strauss c Paine b Harris	87		S. C. J. Broad b Bollinger	0
†C. Kieswetter b Tait	0		J. M. Anderson not out	0
K. P. Pietersen c and b Tait	25			
P. D. Collingwood b Bollinger	40		B 1, l-b 3, w 6, n-b 2	12
E. J. G. Morgan c Ponting b Smith	27			
M. H. Yardy c Paine b Tait	8		1/1 (2) 2/52 (3) (9 wkts, 49.1 overs) 214	
L. J. Wright c Hopes b Smith	0		3/128 (4) 4/185 (5)	
T. T. Bresnan not out	14		5/189 (1) 6/190 (7) 7/197 (6)	
G. P. Swann b Bollinger	1		8/203 (9) 9/203 (10) 10 overs: 37-1	

Tait 10–1–28–3; Bollinger 10–3–20–3; Harris 10–0–59–1; Hopes 6.1–0–44–0; Clarke 4–0–25–0; Smith 9–0–34–2.

Umpires: Aleem Dar and I. J. Gould. Third umpire: R. A. Kettleborough.

ENGLAND v AUSTRALIA

Fourth One-Day International

At The Oval, June 30 (day/night). Australia won by 78 runs. Toss: England.

There would be no whitewash for England, who made the questionable decision to bowl on a flat pitch when the game began at 1 p.m.: in fact they were outplayed as the Australians functioned properly for the first time in the series. Ponting made 92, with ten fours, while Clarke was stranded on 99 after not facing any of the last five balls. They put on 155 in 26 overs, largely with traditional strokes, although Ponting did unveil one reverse sweep for four on his way to becoming only the

---

99 NOT OUT IN A ONE-DAY INTERNATIONAL

B. A. Edgar	New Zealand v India at Auckland	1980-81
D. M. Jones	Australia v Sri Lanka at Adelaide	1984-85
R. B. Richardson	West Indies v Pakistan at Sharjah	1985-86
A. Flower	Zimbabwe v Australia at Harare	1999-2000
A. D. R. Campbell	Zimbabwe v New Zealand at Bulawayo	2000-01
R. R. Sarwan	West Indies v India at Ahmedabad	2002-03
B. J. Hodge	Australia v New Zealand at Melbourne	2006-07
Mohammad Yousuf	Pakistan v India at Gwalior	2007-08
M. J. Clarke	**Australia v England at The Oval**	**2010**
V. Sehwag	**India v Sri Lanka at Dambulla**	**2010**

Richardson, Campbell, Hodge and Sehwag were batting when the match was won; all the others remained unbeaten at the end of their side's allotted overs.

---

third man, after Sachin Tendulkar and Sanath Jayasuriya, to pass 13,000 runs in one-day internationals. Australia's total proved more than enough as Tait and Bollinger again rocked England's batting. This time they were well supported by Harris, who claimed five wickets. Despite resilience by Morgan, who deposited three sixes into the crowd off Hopes, and Yardy, who made his first international half-century, England never got close.

Man of the Match: R. J. Harris. *Attendance:* 22,326.

Australia

S. R. Watson c Morgan b Swann........	41	S. P. D. Smith not out	18	
†T. D. Paine c Morgan b Bresnan	8	B 3, l-b 2, w 9	14	
*R. T. Ponting c Strauss b Anderson......	92			
M. J. Clarke not out................	99	1/33 (2) 2/73 (1)	(5 wkts, 50 overs)	290
C. L. White c Anderson b Broad........	17	3/228 (3) 4/263 (5)		
M. E. K. Hussey run out	1	5/266 (6)	10 overs: 38-1	

J. R. Hopes, R. J. Harris, D. E. Bollinger and S. W. Tait did not bat.

Anderson 10–1–66–1; Bresnan 9–1–52–1; Broad 10–0–46–1; Yardy 9–0–49–0; Swann 6–0–31–1; Wright 3–0–14–0; Collingwood 3–0–27–0.

England

*A. J. Strauss c Paine b Tait	37	S. C. J. Broad c Hussey b Harris	4	
†C. Kieswetter b Harris	12	J. M. Anderson not out	0	
K. P. Pietersen lbw b Harris	8			
P. D. Collingwood lbw b Smith	15	B 1, l-b 3, w 3	7	
E. J. G. Morgan c Paine b Harris........	47			
M. H. Yardy c White b Bollinger	57	1/37 (2) 2/53 (3) 3/61 (1)	(42.4 overs)	212
L. J. Wright b Smith	2	4/90 (4) 5/140 (5) 6/151 (7)		
T. T. Bresnan c Watson b Harris........	22	7/199 (8) 8/207 (9) 9/208 (6)		
G. P. Swann c Paine b Bollinger	1	10/212 (10)	10 overs: 52-1	

Tait 7–2–23–1; Bollinger 8–0–38–2; Harris 8.4–1–32–5; Hopes 10–0–56–0; Smith 9–0–59–2.

Umpires: Aleem Dar and R. A. Kettleborough. Third umpire: R. K. Illingworth.

ENGLAND v AUSTRALIA

Fifth One-Day International

At Lord's, July 3. Australia won by 42 runs. Toss: Australia.

Tait, the Australian fast bowler who had retired from first-class cricket, was clocked at 100.1mph on the speed gun used by host broadcasters Sky. In the inexact science of recording the velocity of bowlers (the technology quoted by the Cricinfo website had Tait's ball at 97mph), it is thought he became the third man officially to register 100mph after Shoaib Akhtar and Brett Lee. The "ton-up" ball – the fifth legal delivery of the first over of the innings – was played off his hip by Kieswetter towards midwicket. Far more devastating were the two full-length swinging balls that shattered the stumps of Strauss and Yardy in the fifth over. Yardy had been promoted to No. 3 because Pietersen had been off the field with a thigh injury and had to wait 44 minutes before he could bat. When he finally came in, with Kieswetter as his runner, England were four down – which soon became five when Pietersen was out for a duck. England, fielding first for the fifth time in the series, had earlier restricted Australia to 147 for four in 39 overs - Paine's 54 occupied 90 balls – but an early powerplay, called by Hussey and Marsh (playing only because Clarke had a sore back), prompted a blitz that brought 63 from those five overs and 130 runs from the final 11: the switch from accuracy and a little seam movement to a full length on one side of the wicket or the other proved fatal. Collingwood made 95 from 121 balls but England lost too many wickets too early for it to be anything more than a gesture of defiance.

Man of the Match: S. W. Tait. *Attendance:* 27,425.

Man of the Series: E. J. G. Morgan.

Australia

S. R. Watson c Anderson b Broad	14	J. R. Hopes not out	12
†T. D. Paine b Swann	54	R. J. Harris not out	0
*R. T. Ponting c Kieswetter b Broad	15	L-b 3, w 6	9
C. L. White c Yardy b Swann	20		
S. E. Marsh c Morgan b Swann	59	(7 wkts, 50 overs)	277
M. E. K. Hussey c Anderson b Broad	79	1/27 (1) 2/55 (3)	
S. P. D. Smith c Anderson b Broad	15	3/104 (4) 4/106 (2)	
		5/213 (5) 6/263 (7) 7/265 (6) 10 overs: 31-1	

D. E. Bollinger and S. W. Tait did not bat.

Anderson 10–0–75–0; Bresnan 10–1–48–0; Broad 10–0–64–4; Wright 6–0–32–0; Yardy 5–0–19–0; Swann 8–0–32–3; Collingwood 1–0–4–0.

England

*A. J. Strauss b Tait	6	S. C. J. Broad c and b Bollinger	3
†C. Kieswetter c Hussey b Harris	11	J. M. Anderson not out	5
M. H. Yardy b Tait	0		
P. D. Collingwood b Tait	95	B 4, l-b 6, w 8	18
E. J. G. Morgan c Marsh b Hopes	9		
K. P. Pietersen b Smith	0	1/14 (1) 2/19 (3) 3/44 (2) (46.3 overs)	235
L. J. Wright c Marsh b Smith	21	4/72 (5) 5/73 (6) 6/129 (7)	
T. T. Bresnan run out	34	7/194 (8) 8/194 (4) 9/229 (10)	
G. P. Swann c Harris b Tait	33	10/235 (9) 10 overs: 50-3	

Tait 8.3–0–48–4; Bollinger 8–0–26–1; Harris 8–1–38–1; Hopes 10–1–42–1; Smith 10–0–49–2; Hussey 2–0–22–0.

Umpires: Aleem Dar and N. J. Llong.   Third umpire: R. A. Kettleborough.
Series referee: J. Srinath.

For Australia's Twenty20 and Test matches against Pakistan in England (and their tour game against Derbyshire), see Pakistan v Australia section on page 310.

PAKISTAN v AUSTRALIA, 2010

Review by Ian Chappell

Test matches (2): Pakistan 1, Australia 1
Twenty20 internationals (2): Pakistan 2, Australia 0

In general the Pakistan Cricket Board is a dysfunctional body, prone to poor and erratic decision-making, but they deserve credit for experimenting with a "home" series against Australia in England. These were the first neutral Tests staged in England since Australia v South Africa in the Triangular Tournament of 1912 and, although the attendances were poor for the Second Test at Headingley – an adult ticket price of £30, while pitched right for Lord's, was too much for Leeds – the MCC Spirit of Cricket series turned out to be a minor success. Indeed it seemed to be enough of a coup to be worth building on in future – until the allegations of spot-fixing and subsequent suspensions kicked in during the England v Pakistan series that followed, and the ECB's attitude towards staging home games for Pakistan cooled.

The lead-up to the experimental tour saw the Pakistan administration in a more normal guise. As if handing out a series of fines and bans to various players for a range of misdemeanours wasn't a big enough distraction, the highly eccentric Shahid Afridi decided to bail out of the Test captaincy after a devastating loss at Lord's. The only question was why? Not why did Afridi bail out, but why was he ever appointed Test captain in the first place?

Surely his eccentric past – a pirouette to scuff up the pitch and a bite at a cricket ball, along with other strange incidents – was enough evidence. If not, then his batting (never a model of common sense) had recently been so lacking in rationality that not even his place in the eleven could be justified.

Afridi's decision to quit apparently did Pakistan a favour: it enabled them to pick a superior batsman and also appoint a level-headed captain in Salman Butt for the Second Test, which Pakistan won to share the series 1–1. However, all was not what it seemed. By the end of August, Pakistan had lost another captain, in sensational circumstances, after a *News of the World* sting claimed Butt had been involved in spot-fixing during the Test series against England that followed. The ICC suspended him – as well as his pace bowlers Mohammad Aamer and Mohammad Asif – and in February 2011 all three were banned, Butt for ten years with five years suspended.

Despite the illogical appointment of Afridi, Pakistan had gone into the Test series with a bit of confidence after beating Australia in two Twenty20 matches. At Lord's, however, Afridi's illusory leadership qualities were quickly dispelled when he resorted to ultra-defensive field placings in Australia's second innings, despite still having an outside chance of victory. But what really made a nonsense of his appointment was his lacklustre bowling and nonsensical batting, particularly on the fourth day.

In the first innings, Afridi's immediate onslaught with the bat could be described as tactically well-timed. Australia had control of what was then a

Hunting scalps: Mohammad Aamer bowls at Lord's, watched by umpire Rudi Koertzen, standing in his last Test series.

low-scoring affair, and Pakistan needed to break the spell: Afridi did so with some calculated hitting – 31 in 15 balls – but his lack of self-control got the better of him just when his team were regaining traction. He became Shane Watson's third victim in successive overs but, more importantly, by playing an ill-advised shot, he was divested of the respect he might have had in the dressing-room. Any team-mates still allowing him the benefit of the doubt would have joined the majority when his second-innings demise was bereft of any cricketing sense, tactical or otherwise.

Afridi's main contribution at Lord's was to win the toss and ask Australia to bat. The overcast conditions were ideal for his premier pace bowlers, Aamer and Asif, and the talented Aamer quickly had two huge scalps in Watson and Ricky Ponting. Left-arm youngster Aamer had been impressive right from his international debut as a 17-year-old in the 2009 World Twenty20, and everything he had done since had served to confirm his enormous talent and active cricket brain. He swung the ball late, bowled a good length at a reasonable pace, and had a plan when he ran to the wicket. These are all traits of a champion bowler, but not always evident in one so green. He was the best of a talented young group that Pakistan played in this series – blooding youngsters being one of the few things their abysmal administration does actually get right.

Aamer was fortunate to have one of the best medium-fast bowlers as his opening partner. Given even slightly favourable conditions, Asif could be damn near unplayable, with only England's James Anderson matching him for late swing. If complemented by a half-decent batting line-up, and if not suspended or banned, these two and Umar Gul could provide Pakistan with many victory opportunities.

As well as the pair bowled, they found an obstinate opponent in Simon Katich, Australia's ungainly left-hander, who epitomised the saying "It's not how you look but the number that goes next to your name." He provided a solid foundation at Lord's, leading Australia to control the game. Another left-handed opener, Butt, was the building block in both Pakistan innings, playing thoughtfully and picking off any generous offerings. Left-handers are indeed taking over the cricket world.

From Australia's point of view it was a good win, but the worrying sign was their heavy reliance on two part-time bowlers in Watson and Marcus North to achieve victory. Both Doug Bollinger and Mitchell Johnson were disappointing and, given Johnson's problems during the previous Ashes series, it could be that he needed extra bounce in the pitch to be really successful. Nevertheless, a debut haul of three wickets for leg-spinning all-rounder Steve Smith was encouraging; Australia headed to Leeds buoyed by victory and Pakistan's captaincy turmoil.

The fact that Pakistan were immediately able to level the series against a comparatively settled Australian side was a tribute to Butt's unflustered approach, the resilience of his players, and the skill of Aamer and Asif.

Butt got a break in his first Test as captain when Ponting decided to bat after winning the toss on an overcast day. It was a tough decision, but not an unreasonable one for a bat-first captain; the pitch was dry and the sun had not long disappeared. However, it did not reappear until late afternoon, and neither did any semblance of Australia's batting form. Aamer and Asif bowled beautifully, making the ball swing late and often, but four of the first five were lbw and the other bowled, not sound technique from top-order batsmen.

Ponting copped a lot of flak for his decision but, when a captain says "We'll bat", there's no subliminal message adding the word "badly". The skipper could also point to the fact that, at stumps, Pakistan were 60 ahead with only three wickets down in not dissimilar conditions from those in which Australia had slumped to 88 all out.

Once again Australia depended heavily on Watson's medium-pace swingers, which he bowled accurately and thoughtfully. By stumps on the second day

Philip Brown

Up and away: Shahid Afridi's brief return to the Test fold ends with an intemperate heave at Lord's.

they were well on the way to erasing the deficit with Ponting and Clarke in control. However, the admirable Aamer held his nerve to dismiss Ponting, Hussey and a struggling North quickly. Australia then had to rely on tyros Tim Paine and Smith to provide an awkward 180-run chase. Smith's sensible, aggressive batting declared his readiness for the upcoming Ashes series.

In the end, the steady Imran Farhat and resourceful Azhar Ali supplied enough of a cushion for the later batsmen to scrape home. Nevertheless, it was a close-run thing: on the last morning Bollinger rediscovered his best form, Hilfenhaus got the ball to swing and Umar Akmal gave the impression he had either learned his batting from Afridi or pined for his return.

The win was a wonderful morale boost for Pakistan, a team in the wilderness. They had garnered support from their fans as the match wore on, but their batting was still such that it couldn't fill those supporters with much confidence. Nevertheless, the solid technique and sound temperament of newcomers Azhar and Umar Amin were something to build on.

From the Australian point of view, they could be thankful the Ashes would be played at home, well away from overcast skies and the Dukes ball.

Details of Australia's and Pakistan's touring parties and their matches against the counties may be found in England v Australia (pages 303–309) and England v Pakistan (pages 322–354).

> **❝**The last ten days coincided with the annual World Buskers Festival for circus acts in the city. Night-time rain and a cruel Antarctic south wind made conditions unpleasant for players, umpires, coaches and clowns alike."
> The Under-19 World Cup, page 835.

TWENTY20 INTERNATIONAL REPORTS BY BEN DORRIES

PAKISTAN v AUSTRALIA

First Twenty20 International

At Birmingham, July 5. Pakistan won by 23 runs. Toss: Pakistan.

Many of Birmingham's large Pakistani population turned up, horns blaring, to make this a home game in more ways than the technical one. They watched their side ambush Australia, despite being on the back foot when they fell to 47 for four. Some big hitting from Umar Akmal produced a 21-ball fifty – the fastest by a Pakistan batsman in this format – and got them to a handy 167 for eight. Australian opener Warner created some early carnage, plundering Shoaib Akhtar for fours off his first five deliveries. But when the captain Clarke succumbed to another Twenty20 failure, holing out in the covers, it slowed the scoring. Mohammad Aamer bowled with fire and older hand Umar Gul with superb late swing to skittle the middle order, while off-spinner Saeed Ajmal produced a cocktail of doosras to knock over the tail. The victory was Pakistan's first over Australia in 13 matches in all cricket since May 2009, and offered some revenge for their semi-final defeat in the recent World Twenty20.

Man of the Match: Umar Akmal. *Attendance:* 9,682.

Pakistan		B	4	6
Salman Butt *c 1 b 4*	13	21	1	0
Shahzaib Hasan *c 4 b 10*	0	1	0	0
†Kamran Akmal *run out*	23	19	2	1
Shoaib Malik *c 8 b 10*	21	18	3	0
*Shahid Afridi *lbw b 7*	0	1	0	0
Umar Akmal *b 11*	64	31	7	3
Abdul Razzaq *b 11*	7	11	0	0
Mohammad Aamer *not out*	11	13	0	0
Umar Gul *run out*	10	6	0	1
L-b 1, w 16, n-b 1	18			
6 overs: 43-1 (20 overs)	167-8			

1/2 2/45 3/45 4/47 5/98 6/137 7/153 8/167

Shoaib Akhtar and Saeed Ajmal did not bat.

Nannes 4–0–41–2; Tait 4–0–25–2; Johnson 4–0–33–0; D. J. Hussey 4–0–33–1; Smith 4–0–34–1.

Australia		B	4	6
D. A. Warner *b 11*	41	31	6	0
S. R. Watson *lbw b 8*	0	2	0	0
*M. J. Clarke *c 5 b 7*	5	6	0	0
D. J. Hussey *c 4 b 5*	34	28	4	1
C. L. White *c 5 b 8*	17	13	1	1
M. E. K. Hussey *b 9*	18	15	3	0
S. P. D. Smith *b 8*	12	8	2	0
†T. D. Paine *b 9*	1	4	0	0
M. G. Johnson *st 3 b 11*	3	3	0	0
D. P. Nannes *not out*	0	0	0	0
S. W. Tait *st 3 b 11*	6	3	0	1
L-b 3, w 3, n-b 1	7			
6 overs: 56-2 (18.4 overs)	144			

1/2 2/29 3/81 4/85 5/109 6/132 7/134 8/137 9/138

Mohammad Aamer 4–0–27–3; Shoaib Akhtar 2–0–34–0; Abdul Razzaq 2–0–15–1; Shahid Afridi 4–0–26–1; Umar Gul 3–0–13–2; Saeed Ajmal 3.4–0–26–3.

Umpires: Aleem Dar and Asad Rauf.   Third umpire: Ahsan Raza.

PAKISTAN v AUSTRALIA

Second Twenty20 International

At Birmingham, July 6. Pakistan won by 11 runs. Toss: Pakistan. Twenty20 international debut: S. N. J. O'Keefe.

The script for the second Twenty20 game read much the same as for the previous day. Pakistan chose to bat, got into trouble – off-spinner David Hussey, an unexpected new-ball bowler, opened with a wicket maiden – but managed to compile a tidy if not altogether imposing total. Australia rested Watson and Steve Smith, and their main bowling ace turned out to be another spinner, left-armer Steve O'Keefe, who hadn't even played Twenty20 for New South Wales for 18 months but took three wickets on his international debut. Promoting himself to open, Clarke provided some overdue top-order batting fireworks, but it was mostly downhill for Australia after that. Their old problems against quality swing bowling resurfaced, with Mohammad Aamer claiming three victims. The Hussey brothers took turns to threaten a resurgence, but the mountain was too tall to climb. Pakistan won the series 2–0 to take some momentum into the Tests.

Man of the Match: Mohammad Aamer. *Attendance:* 9,298.

Pakistan

		B	4	6
Shahzaib Hasan lbw b 5	0	4	0	0
Salman Butt c 6 b 8	31	21	6	0
†Kamran Akmal c 2 b 9	33	25	4	1
Shoaib Malik c 8 b 10	12	16	0	0
Umar Akmal c and b 10	25	21	4	0
*Shahid Afridi c 3 b 10	18	13	2	1
Abdul Razzaq run out	3	3	0	0
Mohammad Aamer not out	21	11	1	2
Umar Gul b 8	0	1	0	0
Shoaib Akhtar b 8	0	2	0	0
Saeed Ajmal not out	6	4	1	0
B 2, l-b 1, w 9, n-b 1	13			

6 overs: 50-1   (20 overs) 162-9

1/0 2/61 3/78 4/100 5/130 6/130 7/140 8/146 9/154

D. J. Hussey 3–1–16–1; Tait 4–0–37–0; Nannes 4–0–30–3; Johnson 4–0–39–1; O'Keefe 4–0–29–3; Hopes 1–0–8–0.

Australia

		B	4	6
D. A. Warner lbw b 8	1	3	0	0
*M. J. Clarke b 8	30	17	6	0
†T. D. Paine c 9 b 10	0	2	0	0
J. R. Hopes st 3 b 6	30	28	3	0
D. J. Hussey c and b 11	33	27	3	0
C. L. White c 4 b 6	7	8	1	0
M. E. K. Hussey lbw b 9	25	14	4	0
S. N. J. O'Keefe run out	5	8	1	0
M. G. Johnson lbw b 8	0	1	0	0
D. P. Nannes not out	12	7	1	1
S. W. Tait run out	2	4	0	0
L-b 3, w 2, n-b 1	6			

6 overs: 47-3   (19.4 overs) 151

1/17 2/22 3/33 4/83 5/104 6/113 7/127 8/136 9/139

Shoaib Akhtar 4–0–29–1; Mohammad Aamer 4–0–27–3; Saeed Ajmal 4–0–26–1; Umar Gul 3.4–0–36–1; Shahid Afridi 4–0–30–2.

Umpires: Asad Rauf and Zameer Haider.   Third umpire: Ahsan Raza.   Series referee: J. Srinath.

At Derby, July 8–9 (not first-class), **Drawn.** ‡Australians 436 (R. T. Ponting 116, M. E. K. Hussey 132, T. D. Paine 52*, S. P. D. Smith 48; M. H. A. Footitt 3-68, J. Needham 3-124); **Derbyshire 235-5** (C. J. L. Rogers 93, W. L. Madsen 58, G. T. Park 43). *County debut:* M. Higginbottom. *Each side fielded 12 players, of whom 11 could bat and 11 field. Ponting and Hussey, who hit 29 fours and seven sixes between them, rescued the tourists with a stand of 210 after they had dipped to 48-3. Next day Chris Rogers made most of the running in an opening stand of 147 with Wayne Madsen, but missed out on a century against his compatriots.*

At Leicester, July 8–9 (not first-class). **Drawn.** ‡Leicestershire 296-7 dec (G. P. Smith 87, W. A. White 79); **Pakistanis 280-7** (Salman Butt 57, Azhar Ali 41, Yasir Hameed 58, Umar Amin 51). *First-team debut:* W. S. Jones. *All four Pakistani batsmen passing 40 retired out in this warm-up for their Test series with Australia.*

PAKISTAN v AUSTRALIA

First Test Match

Christopher Martin-Jenkins

At Lord's, July 13, 14, 15, 16. Australia won by 150 runs. Toss: Pakistan. Test debuts: Azhar Ali, Umar Amin; T. D. Paine, S. P. D. Smith.

That cricket can never be played in isolation from its social and political context was proved long ago. Pakistan, out of bounds to touring teams since the murderous attack by terrorists on the Sri Lankans in Lahore in March 2009, had to play international cricket elsewhere for the foreseeable future, bound to follow John of Gaunt's advice to the newly outlawed Henry Bolingbroke in Shakespeare's *Richard II*: "All places that the eye of heaven visits / Are to a wise man ports and happy havens."

Graham Morris

Elementary: Shane Watson makes light work of catching Umar Gul at first slip.

Sixteen months after the atrocity, Lord's provided Pakistan with a home from home, staging the first of two Tests against Australia in a series sponsored by MCC, who saw the encounter as an opportunity to promote both their Spirit of Cricket message and their role as the game's conscience. One consequence was a ground with fewer advertising placards and an outfield blessedly free of those garish outsized logos that these days seem to yell to the onlooker Money Matters Most.

The match may have remained intriguing only for as long as it took Australia's relatively modest bowling attack to expose the naivety of much of Pakistan's batting, but the first neutral Test in England since the triangular tournament of 1912 attracted more than 50,000 spectators over four days. A significant minority were London-based Pakistanis; the majority, however, appeared to be neutral themselves, to some extent reflecting the magnetic attraction that any Australian touring team continue to have for British cricket followers. Others, perhaps, saw the game as a refreshingly traditional alternative to the inordinately lengthy domestic Twenty20 tournament that was reaching the end of its league stage. A few, no doubt, wondered how quickly Pakistan would confirm their reputation for unpredictability.

It did not take long. Since their 3–0 defeat in Australia six months before – a result that had prompted the usual gossip, a PCB inquiry and disciplinary action against seven players, including then captain Mohammad Yousuf – the board had put another of the seven, Shahid Afridi, in charge. Afridi, surely the wildest spirit ever to lead his country, had been suspended by the ICC for two Twenty20 matches after biting the ball during a tense one-day international in Perth, but had led Pakistan through the World Twenty20 in the Caribbean. Now he found himself recalled to the Test team after four years playing only limited-overs cricket at international level. The ninth Pakistan Test captain in ten years, and the 27th in all, was also the shortest-lived. Having set an irresponsible example with the bat in both innings, Afridi resigned his post immediately after Australia's 150-run victory had taken their winning sequence against Pakistan to 13 Tests, a record for one nation against another.

Even so, the impression that Australia's hegemony had ended after the retirements of Warne, McGrath, Gilchrist and Hayden was reinforced on the first day at Lord's. The combination of the experienced wrist-spinner Danish Kaneria and three fresh, talented and complementary fast bowlers limited them to 229 for nine in the 70 overs possible on a cloudy day, despite a dogged, vigilant 80 from Katich. The lissom Mohammad Asif, the tall and committed Umar Gul, and the slim, slippery and skilful Mohammad Aamer – all made good use of the swing and seam movement available.

The cricket was properly combative, but not to excess. Aamer, however, was ticked off by the referee, Chris Broad – a friendly warning for over-exuberance – after brushing the arm of Ponting as he followed through to celebrate a quick reaction catch by Umar Amin at short leg. Some, not least Aamer's team-mates, thought that, by lifting an elbow towards the jubilant bowler, Australia's captain was as much to blame.

The Dukes ball, chosen by Pakistan as the "home" authority, moved no less on the second day, in similar weather, despite the customary trueness of a hard Lord's pitch. A flawless 56 not out by Hussey, 24 of them scored in a last-wicket partnership with Bollinger, gave Australia's bowlers a par total. Hilfenhaus, resuming his Test career after a knee injury, immediately reminded everyone of virtues that include reliable outswing at a lively pace and an inclination to get back to bowl the next ball quickly. He took the first two wickets, both caught behind by his fellow-Tasmanian, the accomplished young wicketkeeper-batsman Tim Paine, who made his Test debut as Brad Haddin was recovering from an elbow strain.

Salman Butt, stroking wide balls through the off side with crisp timing off either foot to gather 12 fours, defended with sound judgment as wickets fell swiftly around him, until he was ninth out. His apparent intelligence, education and calm bearing suggested that he might be the right man to lead Pakistan. Watson pitched the ball up and swung it at around 80mph to take five wickets, thereby joining Warren Bardsley and Charlie Kelleway, Lord's centurions for Australia against South Africa in 1912, on a new honours board for performances in neutral Tests.

MOST SUCCESSIVE TEST VICTORIES AGAINST ONE TEAM

13	Australia v Pakistan	**November 1999–July 2010**
12	Sri Lanka v Bangladesh	September 2001–January 2009*
10	West Indies v England	June 1984–April 1986
9	Australia v West Indies	April 1999–May 2003
8	England v South Africa	March 1889–April 1899†
8	Australia v England	December 1920–July 1921
8	South Africa v Bangladesh	October 2002–November 2008*
8	**England v Bangladesh**	**October 2003–June 2010***

Complete head-to-head record to date.   † First eight Tests between these teams.

Australia were soon in trouble again, reduced to 100 for four, a lead of 205, by the close of the second day after Gul removed Clarke and Hussey with successive balls. When North, his Test place looking precarious, was seventh out at 188 just after lunch on the third day, the game was still in the balance. But sunnier weather and typical Australian resolution combined to leave Pakistan in need of a record winning fourth-innings total of 440. Paine confirmed himself ready to replace Haddin when the time was ripe, while the last two men, Hilfenhaus and Bollinger, made career-bests.

Australia's other debutant, the boyish but vibrant all-rounder Steve Smith, broke the left-handed opening partnership of 50 when Imran Farhat pulled a short ball to midwicket, and might have been expected to be a match-winner on the fourth day. Instead, just as Pakistan were beginning to dream at 186 for two, with another pair of left-handers at the wicket, it was North, called on in a moment of intuition by Ponting, who provided the second unlikely name on the honours board. He dismissed Butt first ball, with a delivery that drifted down the slope outside the left-hander's legs to enable Paine to make an accomplished stumping, and went on to a career-best six for 55, which owed something to sensibly flighted off-breaks, but more to heedless and over-optimistic hitting.

Men of the Match: S. M. Katich and Salman Butt. *Attendance:* 53,268.
Close of play: First day, Australia 229-9 (Hussey 39, Bollinger 0); Second day, Australia 100-4 (Katich 49, Johnson 2); Third day, Pakistan 114-1 (Salman Butt 58, Azhar Ali 28).

Australia

S. R. Watson b Mohammad Aamer	4	– c Imran Farhat b Mohammad Asif	31
S. M. Katich c Kamran Akmal b Mohammad Asif	80	– c Kamran Akmal b Umar Gul	83
*R. T. Ponting c Umar Amin b Mohammad Aamer	26	– lbw b Mohammad Asif	0
M. J. Clarke lbw b Mohammad Asif	47	– b Umar Gul	12
M. E. K. Hussey not out	56	– c Imran Farhat b Umar Gul	0
M. J. North b Mohammad Asif	0	– (7) c Kamran Akmal b Mohammad Asif	20
†T. D. Paine c Kamran Akmal b Umar Gul	7	– (8) b Shahid Afridi	47
S. P. D. Smith lbw b Danish Kaneria	1	– (9) lbw b Danish Kaneria	12
M. G. Johnson b Danish Kaneria	3	– (6) b Umar Gul	30
B. W. Hilfenhaus b Mohammad Aamer	1	– not out	56
D. E. Bollinger b Mohammad Aamer	4	– b Danish Kaneria	21
B 10, l-b 2, w 2, n-b 10	24	B 6, l-b 5, w 2, n-b 9	22

1/8 (1) 2/51 (3) 3/171 (4)   (76.5 overs) 253
4/174 (2) 5/174 (6) 6/206 (7)
7/208 (8) 8/213 (9) 9/222 (10) 10/253 (11)

1/61 (1) 2/73 (3)   (91 overs) 334
3/97 (4) 4/97 (5)
5/149 (6) 6/188 (2) 7/188 (7)
8/208 (9) 9/282 (8) 10/334 (11)

Mohammad Aamer 19.5–2–72–4; Mohammad Asif 19–5–63–3; Umar Gul 17–3–32–1; Shahid Afridi 3–0–25–0; Danish Kaneria 18–7–49–2. *Second Innings*—Mohammad Aamer 18–3–67–0; Mohammad Asif 21–3–77–3; Umar Gul 21–5–61–4; Danish Kaneria 17–2–74–2; Shahid Afridi 14–0–44–1.

Pakistan

Imran Farhat c Paine b Hilfenhaus	4	– c Watson b Smith	24
Salman Butt b Watson	63	– st Paine b North	92
Azhar Ali c Paine b Hilfenhaus	16	– c Paine b Hilfenhaus	42
Umar Amin c Paine b Johnson	1	– c Katich b North	33
Umar Akmal lbw b Watson	5	– c Clarke b North	22
†Kamran Akmal lbw b Watson	0	– b Smith	46
*Shahid Afridi c Johnson b Watson	31	– c Hussey b North	2
Mohammad Aamer c Paine b Bollinger	0	– c Hussey b North	19
Umar Gul c Watson b Bollinger	7	– c Ponting b Smith	1
Danish Kaneria c Smith b Watson	14	– c Ponting b North	2
Mohammad Asif not out	4	– not out	1
L-b 2, n-b 1	3	B 2, l-b 1, n-b 2	5

1/11 (1) 2/45 (3) 3/54 (4) 4/75 (5)   (40.5 overs) 148
5/83 (6) 6/117 (7) 7/117 (8)
8/129 (9) 9/133 (2) 10/148 (10)

1/50 (1) 2/152 (3)   (91.1 overs) 289
3/186 (2) 4/216 (5)
5/227 (4) 6/229 (7) 7/283 (6)
8/285 (8) 9/287 (9) 10/289 (10)

Bollinger 11–3–38–2; Hilfenhaus 12–2–37–2; Johnson 10–2–31–1; Watson 7.5–1–40–5. *Second Innings*—Bollinger 12–4–43–0; Hilfenhaus 16–8–37–1; Johnson 18–5–74–0; Smith 21–5–51–3; Watson 6–0–26–0; North 18.1–1–55–6.

Umpires: I. J. Gould and R. E. Koertzen.   Third umpire: Ahsan Raza.

> **❝** Even the American Secretary of State Hillary Clinton hailed the growth of cricket in Afghanistan: 'I might suggest that if we are searching for a model of how to meet tough international challenges with skill, dedication and teamwork, we need only look to the Afghan national team."
> Cricket in Afghanistan 2010, page 1174

PAKISTAN v AUSTRALIA

Second Test Match

SCYLD BERRY

At Leeds, July 21, 22, 23, 24. Pakistan won by three wickets. Toss: Australia.

It was the most startling result of the season. Pakistan had lost every competitive match on their tour of Australia. They had lost all of their 13 previous Tests against Australia, and had not won one for 15 years. But in spite of a second-innings collapse which betrayed their lack of a senior batsman, and all those memories, they edged home in front of a couple of thousand or so of their supporters – and some English ones – waving green flags. The one ingredient missing from a knife-edged Test was a sizeable crowd: ticket prices that had been reasonable for London kept numbers down to a few thousand on each of the four remarkable days, in spite of Yorkshire's promotional campaign in their Asian community. Chief executive Stewart Regan said the club was £500,000 to £750,000 short of what they had expected to take from the match.

Fight though the Australians did, they could never recover from being bowled out for 88 – their lowest total for more than 25 years, and their worst against Pakistan since they first met in 1956-57 – despite winning the toss. After Edgbaston in 2005 ended in disaster, Ponting had never sent opponents in to bat, and he was not going to do so again on an essentially dry pitch which he expected to crack and become uneven. But according to local opinion the low cloud on the first morning – after a night of heavy rain – dictated: field first. And Pakistan's attack, which out-bowled Australia's until the excellent Hilfenhaus was joined by Bollinger in finding the right length on the last morning, wasted not a moment.

At the start of the Lord's Test, Katich had not been given lbw for two when all the evidence suggested he would have been if the review system had been in place. Here, he was not so lucky and Australia, without their anchor, were cast adrift. Katich and Mike Hussey were the two specialist batsmen who played the ball late, whereas the others reached for it. Mohammad Asif swung the ball both ways in his superlative opening spell

Bull's eye: Umar Gul hits the top of middle to send Michael Clarke back for three in Australia's calamitous first innings.

from the end of the new Carnegie pavilion, which was opened by the Duke of Gloucester at lunch: Asif kept drawing Ponting across his crease with outswingers until pinning him so decisively the batsman walked as Ian Gould raised his finger. The second of Mohammad Aamer's deliveries after lunch – the first having burst through Steve Smith's stiff-legged defence – was a candidate for Ball of the Season. It pitched on Johnson's middle-and-leg stump and swung away to hit the top of off. None of the Australians had the skill of wrist and fingers which Aamer and Asif had to make the Dukes ball swing so late: it was thrilling craftsmanship that exploited ideal conditions to the full.

AUSTRALIA'S LOWEST TEST TOTALS SINCE 1945

75	v South Africa at Durban	1949-50
76	v West Indies at Perth	1984-85
78†	v England at Lord's	1968
80	v Pakistan at Karachi	1956-57
82	v West Indies at Adelaide	1951-52
83	v India at Melbourne	1980-81
84	v England at Manchester	1956
88	**v Pakistan at Leeds**	**2010**
90	v West Indies at Port-of-Spain	1977-78

† *One man retired hurt.*

Salman Butt's first day as a Test captain had already included a successful hunch, bringing on the occasional inswing of Umar Amin which North reached to nibble; it continued with an opening stand of 80 that had almost taken Pakistan into the lead by the time he was out, soon after tea on day one. Without an experienced player to bat around, however, they could not build a clearly decisive advantage against Watson, who failed in his principal job as opening bat but bowled the right length, unlike most of Australia's main bowlers. Pakistan's first innings was petering out until a rousing last-wicket stand of 24 at a run a ball showed how hittable the Australian bowling was: Ponting put five men on the boundary for Danish Kaneria, who pulled one four off Johnson like Ponting himself.

Throughout the second day, which was colder, and indeed for the rest of the match, the ball would not swing so much as on day one. But Aamer had the skill to keep on making decisive interventions. Katich was bowled behind his legs by a ball which did not swing. Ponting might have gone first ball, padding up to one from Aamer that did, then dragged his team back into the game in a fighting partnership with Clarke, becoming the second man after Tendulkar to reach 12,000 Test runs when he was 40. In the first hour of the third day Aamer bowled another brilliant spell: Ponting threw his bat at a ball going wider, Hussey gloved a cutter which bounced off the slow turf, and North chopped on. Thereafter Pakistan were in charge so long as they maintained their self-control.

This they did while bowling, even though Umar Gul pitched far too short and Smith played swashbuckling strokes – two consecutive straight sixes off Kaneria – as well as nursing the tailenders: in his second Test, Smith hit 77 from 100 balls, even though like Watson he did not contribute in his main capacity, as a leg-spinner. When Pakistan pursued 180, it was after a calm and calculated century stand between Azhar Ali and Imran Farhat, dropped by Watson at first slip off Bollinger when four, that the nerves set in. Spread over the third evening and fourth morning, Pakistan lost six wickets for 42 runs and nearly gave the game away, which they had done in the Sydney Test six months earlier after another big lead. If Clarke had not dropped Shoaib Malik off Bollinger to his right at second slip, Pakistan would have been 154 for six. At 175, Hussey at gully appealed for a very low catch given by Kamran Akmal off Johnson that was not clearly supported by the replays. Even though it was the MCC Spirit of Cricket series, the batsman did not walk – not that anyone except the fielders expected him to.

Kamran fell to the same combination of Hussey and Johnson when the scores were level, and Umar Gul was almost caught by extra cover next ball but ran a single. It was thanks in no small part to the calmness under pressure of umpire Rudi Koertzen, in his 108th and final Test, that Pakistan lurched over the line. The Australians applauded him on to the field at the start of day four, and the Pakistanis off it at the close, before Butt dedicated this victory to people back home who had not been able to watch it in person because of the team's current exile. The value of neutral umpiring was not in doubt, even if that of a neutral venue was; and Ponting still had not won a Test series in England in three tours as captain.

Men of the Match: Mohammad Aamer and S. R. Watson. *Attendance:* 18,396.

Close of play: First day, Pakistan 148-3 (Umar Amin 1, Umar Akmal 8); Second day, Australia 136-2 (Ponting 61, Clarke 32); Third day, Pakistan 140-3 (Azhar Ali 47, Umar Akmal 2).

Australia

S. R. Watson lbw b Mohammad Asif	5	– b Umar Amin	24
S. M. Katich lbw b Mohammad Aamer	13	– b Mohammad Aamer	11
*R. T. Ponting lbw b Mohammad Asif	6	– c Kamran Akmal b Mohammad Aamer	66
M. J. Clarke b Umar Gul	3	– c Kamran Akmal b Mohammad Asif	77
M. E. K. Hussey lbw b Umar Gul	5	– c Umar Akmal b Mohammad Aamer	8
M. J. North c Kamran Akmal b Umar Amin	16	– b Mohammad Asif	0
†T. D. Paine c Kamran Akmal b Mohammad Asif	17	– c Azhar Ali b Danish Kaneria	33
S. P. D. Smith b Mohammad Aamer	10	– b Umar Gul	77
M. G. Johnson b Mohammad Aamer	0	– lbw b Mohammad Asif	12
B. W. Hilfenhaus run out	3	– c Umar Akmal b Danish Kaneria	17
D. E. Bollinger not out	2	– not out	0
L-b 6, n-b 2	8	B 4, 1-b 10, w 2, n-b 8	24

1/20 (2) 2/20 (1) 3/27 (4) 4/29 (3) (33.1 overs) 88
5/41 (5) 6/60 (6) 7/73 (8) 8/73 (9)
9/86 (10) 10/88 (7)

1/15 (2) 2/55 (1) (95.3 overs) 349
3/144 (3) 4/158 (5)
5/164 (6) 6/217 (4) 7/246 (7)
8/283 (9) 9/320 (10) 10/349 (8)

Mohammad Aamer 11–4–20–3; Mohammad Asif 10.1–1–30–3; Umar Gul 9–3–16–2; Umar Amin 2–0–7–1; Danish Kaneria 1–0–9–0. *Second Innings*—Mohammad Aamer 27–6–86–4; Mohammad Asif 26–4–83–2; Umar Gul 15.3–1–80–1; Umar Amin 6–1–12–1; Danish Kaneria 21–2–74–2.

Pakistan

Imran Farhat lbw b Watson	43	– b Bollinger	67
*Salman Butt b Hilfenhaus	45	– c Clarke b Hilfenhaus	13
Azhar Ali c Paine b Watson	30	– c Paine b Bollinger	51
Umar Amin c North b Hilfenhaus	25	– c Paine b Bollinger	0
Umar Akmal c Paine b Johnson	21	– c Paine b Hilfenhaus	8
Shoaib Malik c Paine b Watson	26	– c North b Hilfenhaus	10
†Kamran Akmal c North b Watson	15	– c Hussey b Johnson	13
Mohammad Aamer lbw b Watson	0	– not out	5
Umar Gul b Watson	0	– not out	1
Danish Kaneria run out	15		
Mohammad Asif not out	9		
B 11, 1-b 9, n-b 9	29	L-b 7, n-b 5	12

1/80 (2) 2/133 (1) 3/140 (3) (64.5 overs) 258
4/171 (5) 5/195 (4) 6/222 (7)
7/222 (8) 8/224 (9) 9/234 (6) 10/258 (10)

1/27 (2) (7 wkts, 50.4 overs) 180
2/137 (1) 3/137 (4)
4/146 (3) 5/150 (5) 6/161 (6) 7/179 (7)

Bollinger 17–4–50–0; Hilfenhaus 20.5–3–77–2; Watson 11–3–33–6; Johnson 15–0–71–1; Smith 1–0–7–0. *Second Innings*—Bollinger 13–2–51–3; Hilfenhaus 13–2–39–3; Johnson 10.4–1–41–1; Watson 5–1–18–0; Smith 9–2–24–0.

Umpires: I. J. Gould and R. E. Koertzen. Third umpire: Nadeem Ghauri.
Series referee: B. C. Broad.

ENGLAND v PAKISTAN

REVIEW BY STEPHEN BRENKLEY

Test matches (4): England 3, Pakistan 1
One-day internationals (5): England 3, Pakistan 2
Twenty20 internationals (2): England 2, Pakistan 0

The storm broke on the eve of the fourth day of the Fourth Test. It was never to recede. Until that moment, it had been going so well – or as well as could have been expected, considering the deeply unpromising beginnings: not plain sailing, but not choppy waters either.

After assuming the Pakistan captaincy upon Shahid Afridi's sudden resignation in July, Salman Butt had helped to engineer a Test win against Australia at the first time of asking in July. Following two heavy defeats by England in the next couple of weeks, he had overseen another unexpected victory to make it 2–1 with one Test remaining.

So there was all to play for at Lord's in the final match. It began wonderfully for Pakistan, with their 18-year-old fast bowler Mohammad Aamer initially irresistible, putting the seal on a summer he had illuminated and which augured a golden future. But the contest then lurched away from them, irretrievably. A Test-record eighth-wicket partnership for England preceded the sort of batting collapse that had become a motif of Pakistan's tour. Disappointing as this was, the feeling still persisted that honour might be satisfied on both sides.

England could be proud of an eventually emphatic series victory, achieved on the back of astute swing and spin bowling, brittle opposition batting and eventually the epic stand of 332 between Jonathan Trott and Stuart Broad; both played extraordinary innings which did not deserve to be eclipsed by the events that followed. Pakistan's callow team could point to progress. Butt, disarmingly impressive since taking charge, would make his usual plea for his inexperienced but gifted charges to be given time.

All that changed overnight. The rest of the season – and indeed what had gone before – was overshadowed by a startling report in the *News of the World* which emerged on Saturday night accusing Pakistan of bowling no-balls to order during England's first innings. The newspaper named Aamer and his new-ball colleague Mohammad Asif, and claimed they had acted with the collusion of their captain, Butt. It alleged that undercover reporters, posing as businessmen who wished to be involved in a purported scam taking advantage of illegal Asian betting markets, paid a middleman £150,000 to ensure that the deliveries were bowled at pre-arranged moments.

The allegations provoked a furore. There were immediate fears that the match itself would be unfinished and the tour cancelled there and then. Both went ahead. In an eerie, sepulchral atmosphere on Sunday morning, England duly completed an innings victory to win the series 3–1. Celebrations were muted and the mood sombre.

The presentation ceremony was transferred from the Lord's outfield to the privacy of the Long Room. It supplied an enduring image which embodied the turn of events. Giles Clarke, the ECB chairman handing out the gongs, could not bring himself to shake the hand of Aamer, who had entranced audiences throughout the summer, as he stepped forward to receive his Man of the Series award.

Such a calculated snub was a measure not only of Clarke's response to the newspaper allegations but also of deep personal hurt. Clarke had long championed Pakistan's cause and had been instrumental in their being invited to England to play their series against Australia, which could not be staged at home because of fears of terrorism. As head of the ICC task force established to help cricket in Pakistan, he took his duties seriously.

The tour limped on, though nobody's heart was in it. In the days that followed, open season was declared on the game in general and Pakistan in particular. The issue of corruption, always lurking on the undercard, was back at the top of the bill. Speculation, most of it without the small matter of compelling evidence, mounted that it was rife. Both Ijaz Butt, the chairman of the Pakistan Cricket Board, and Wajid Shamsul Hasan, the country's High Commissioner in London, attempted to defend their players.

Later in the week Salman Butt, Asif and Aamer withdrew from the squad, citing mental torture. They made their decision just in time; it was clear that England were reluctant to continue with

The storm breaks.

them present. All three were then provisionally suspended by the ICC pending the outcome of both the criminal investigation by the Metropolitan Police, to which the *News of the World* had handed its dossier, and the ICC's own inquiry. The trio were charged with various breaches of its anti-corruption code and warned that, if found guilty, life bans could ensue. (In the event, on February 5, 2011, the three were given five-year bans, while Butt was given another five years suspended, and Asif two years suspended.) No matter the outcome of the eventual hearings, it seemed to be an example of the governing body wishing to be seen governing.

The combined effect of these actions ensured that the tour went on its wretched way, the cricket somehow contriving to rise above it all. But before it tottered over the line there was yet another stumble in the finishing straight.

Before the third of the five one-day internationals at The Oval, *The Sun*, sister paper of the *News of the World*, told the ICC that it had evidence of pre-ordained scoring patterns. ICC chief executive Haroon Lorgat telephoned Clarke to stop the match going ahead, but Clarke said no, as it was about to start. Instead, when the scoring-rate in certain parts of Pakistan's innings appeared to be close to the forecast, the ICC announced an immediate investigation of this international (which Pakistan had won).

By now, Pakistan were feeling aggrieved, outraged and persecuted. Ijaz Butt, confronted by reporters as he returned to Lahore, tried to divert attention and suggested that, far from Pakistan being embroiled in nefarious activities during the Oval match, it was England. He said he had heard that England had thrown the match for "enormous amounts of money". To say this claim emerged from left field is to give it credence. It came from nowhere, and it was England's turn to be angry. They came within an ace of refusing to play the remaining two games, while the ECB threatened legal action, but diplomacy persuaded the players not to withdraw their labour. In the event, the ICC inquiry into the Oval game found insufficient evidence that the scoring patterns handed to the newspaper matched those in the middle.

If the ECB were anxious not to pull the plug for many reasons, some of which would have involved paying compensation to grounds, ticket-holders and broadcasters all deprived of the scheduled action, the decisive intervention probably came from the government. The sports minister, Hugh Robertson, warned that relations with Pakistan could be severely harmed if the matches were cancelled.

England's players were barely appeased. Relations between the teams, already strained, reached breaking point. In the nets before the fourth match, at Lord's, Trott and the Pakistan bowler, Wahab Riaz, were involved in an altercation witnessed by scores of supporters in the hospitality area around the Nursery Ground. Pakistan won that match as well to level the series at 2–2, and England were more than usually jubilant to win the decisive fifth encounter. Clearly they felt it was their just deserts.

A few days after the cricket was all done, Ijaz Butt flew back to London to meet Clarke. There followed an abject retraction in which Butt withdrew all his previous allegations unreservedly and apologised to England's players. The joint statement by the boards talked of lines being drawn under the issue, but everyone concerned knew that would not be possible until the original allegations had been dealt with.

There was to be a further bizarre twist to an already arcane plot when Pakistan pitched up in the United Arab Emirates a few weeks later to play South Africa. No sooner had they levelled a tight one-day series at 2–2, with a one-wicket victory in Dubai, than their wicketkeeper, Zulqarnain Haider, jumped ship for England, alleging that he had been approached by men representing bookmakers who threatened him and his family.

Zulqarnain had made a mark in England with an engaging rearguard innings in the Edgbaston Test, his debut, before injury ended his tour. His story was that in Dubai, where he made 19 not out as Pakistan levelled the series, he had been told to help to lose the fourth and fifth one-day internationals, and he had fled out of fear. His account was not always consistent but, long before then,

The eyes have it: Giles Clarke and Mohammad Aamer at the post-series presentations, held in the Long Room at Lord's.

with police and ICC inquiries running, it had become impossible to tell who had what agenda, and what the truth was.

Against this contentious backdrop, any assessment of Pakistan's 13th Test tour of England is probably compromised. The tourists, who had done valiantly to share a two-match series against Australia – the first neutral Tests staged in England for 98 years – were well beaten. Confronted by sporting conditions in a damp English summer, which suited swing and seam bowling, their batting was simply not up to it, raw as well as technically and temperamentally unsuited.

Yet Salman Butt was at least partially justified in his regular pleas for sympathy for his team. Some of their bowling, at least that delivered by the dazzling Aamer and the controlled Asif, was of the highest calibre. With work – plenty of it – the batting had the potential to prosper on blander pitches.

England's batsmen struggled too, but there were enough individual performances, at least one in each match, to see them through some torrid times. At various stages worries were expressed about the entire top order; its most illustrious member, Kevin Pietersen, never fully found his form. In his one innings of note, at Edgbaston, he was dropped three times before reaching 40. By the end of the summer there was a suspicion that Pietersen was neither as prolific nor as indispensable as he had been.

The bowlers, however, did most of what could have been expected of them. There was a largely unspoken feeling that it was about time bowlers had matters in their favour. When the ball swung, as it often did, James Anderson could be unplayable; his control on these occasions bore comparison with the masters of yore. Despite the conditions seemingly favouring quicker bowling, England's off-spinner, Graeme Swann, could not be kept out of the picture for long. His irrepressible nature, allied to a keen intelligence and skill, brought him only one wicket fewer (22 to 23) than Anderson.

Pakistan came into the Test series nicely cooked. They had beaten Australia in a Test for the first time in 15 years, and in Salman Butt they seemed to have found, almost by accident, a captain of charm and calm. Shahid Afridi had resigned after only one Test, a defeat by Australia at Lord's, and Butt seemed an ideal contrast in character.

But the tourists were outflanked in the opening game against England at Trent Bridge, where they had the worse of the conditions – inevitably the fate of teams up against it. England overcame the early incursions made into their first innings thanks to Eoin Morgan's maiden Test century. Morgan had already excited spectators in the one-day arena, but at Nottingham he demonstrated that he was also at home with the self-denial sometimes demanded in the longer form.

Pakistan's fielding was as dreadful as the bowling, especially of Aamer and Asif, was splendid. It was epitomised in the clumsy wicketkeeping of Kamran Akmal, who could be both ridiculous and sublime, but usually the former. England never surrendered the advantage given them by Morgan and, when they were again in trouble in their second innings, the admirable Matt Prior came to the rescue with his third Test hundred. Anderson did the rest, and his second-innings figures of six for 17 gave him his best match analysis in Tests, 11 for 71.

The tourists collapsed for 80 on the fourth day, then their lowest total in England, though it was to be only the first of three occasions when they were dismissed in double figures in this series. If it said something about the bowler-friendly circumstances and the quality of England's attack, it also bespoke Pakistan's fragility. Including Australia's 88 all out at Headingley, there were four double-figure Test totals in England in 2010, more than in any year since 1958, when the hapless New Zealanders were all out for under 100 five times. There were also five instances in 1912, the last year of neutral Tests in England, though the record remains six in the 1888 Ashes.

When Salman Butt opted to bat in the Second Test at Edgbaston, the writing was immediately on the wall for his team. The skies were slate-grey, the ball again moved alarmingly, and Pakistan folded again, lowering their worst total in England to 72. At the toss Butt had invoked a poetic analogy. Pointing to the building site at the Pavilion End (given the number of international venues in England, there never was a satisfactory explanation for playing a Test at

All's well that ends well: Graeme Swann hangs on to a chance from Mohammad Asif, and England win the Trent Bridge Test.

Edgbaston while it was being redeveloped), he said that what was now ugly and barely formed would one day be beautiful, as would his team.

That claim was hardly buttressed by his batsmen in the next few hours, and there was no way back. England also found conditions difficult, but Pietersen's atypically misfiring 80 gave them a substantial lead. Eventually, however, Pakistan exhibited considerable pluck through the debutant wicket-keeper Zulqarnain, who survived a king pair thanks to the Decision Review System and went on to make a diligent 88. This rearguard action did not bring out the best in England, whose tetchiness suggested they had come to expect to have things their way. But a home win was merely delayed, not prevented.

What followed at The Oval exemplified Pakistan's unpredictability. They won by four wickets, and it was England's turn to crumple. In the first innings, they were 94 for seven; in their second, they lost their last seven wickets for 28. Their improbable nemesis on the first morning was the debutant seam bowler Riaz and, although Alastair Cook's second-innings hundred repelled the circling vultures, England were undone by Aamer's swing and Saeed Ajmal's doosra.

Not even a side as permanently mercurial as Pakistan could mess up a run-chase of 148, though they lost six wickets on the way. Their batting order was bolstered by the introduction of former captain Mohammad Yousuf, summoned from Pakistan; though the results were not spectacular, he added indubitable and telling class in this match.

It was all set up so well for Lord's. Until this point, the most contentious element of the tour had been the staging of the matches. Crowds had been well short of capacity, and no wonder, since the ECB had decided to schedule Tests in successive weeks in the Midlands followed by two in succession in London. But if early attendances at The Oval had suffered, Lord's performed its habitual magic, despite a heavily curtailed first day.

The ground was in splendid late-summer order, and it was to witness some cricket to match. England were in desperate trouble early on, and Aamer was magnificent on the second morning – when, it was later alleged, he bowled the second of two deliberate no-balls. England had no worthwhile response to his pace and brutal late movement, and they were 47 for five, then 102 for seven. Never before had England's Nos 4, 5 and 6 in the order all made ducks in the same Test innings. Pakistan, it seemed, really could level the series.

Trott and Broad, however, were astonishing. Trott is no stylist, but he was nerveless and determined in everything he did, measuring precisely what it was he had to do. Broad was perhaps the more assertive, though equally vigilant. Their partnership was the highest for the eighth wicket in all Tests, and Broad's 169 was the second-highest score by a No. 9.

The stuffing was knocked out of Pakistan. Seventeen wickets fell on the third day – England's last three, plus 14 of their opponents', Anderson was compelling, Broad barely less so, though Swann and Steve Finn took a bigger share of the spoils. England could and should have gone to bed that night feeling chuffed with the world. It lasted until the late-evening news, by when the early editions of the newspapers were out, one of which contained the startling allegations that were to dominate the next month.

No mutual invitations to Sunday tea

Over nine pages the *News of the World* made a number of claims under the heading "Cricket in the Dock". Nobody could disagree that it was. England duly won on Sunday morning, Swann running through the tourists, though it was difficult to care.

At first, Pakistan were in no shape whatever for limited-overs matches. England won both Twenty20s at a deserted Cardiff and were easily in the ascendancy in the first two one-day internationals. In the second, Andrew Strauss, England's captain, made his fifth one-day hundred. Given what he had to deal with as the team's leader and chief spokesman, it was a tour de force.

The wholly sorry position meant Strauss had to act as statesman, negotiator and public-relations expert while continuing to lead the team on the field. In no area was he found wanting. It was also to Pakistan's credit that they pulled themselves back into the series, with Umar Gul at last finding the reverse-swinging abilities which had made him so potent in the short game.

By now, both sides had had enough. If they were not quite at each other's throats – though Trott and Riaz were not far off – they were unlikely to issue mutual invitations to Sunday tea. The controversies lent the series its own sense of theatre, and the final match at the Rose Bowl, for which ticket sales had been sluggish, attracted a near-capacity attendance whose support was more or less evenly divided.

England's batting was again in some disarray – and this against a side without their two most incisive bowlers – but Morgan played a mature,

Slipping away: Yasir Hameed drops Graeme Swann off Saeed Ajmal at Edgbaston.

composed and conclusive hand. At the end, England seemed to be celebrating much more than victory in a one-day match and series. For everybody else there could only be relief – not just that this wretched tour had ended but that the game had somehow survived. (Until, the sad but overwhelming feeling was, the next time.)

PAKISTANI TOURING PARTIES

*Shahid Afridi, Azhar Ali, Danish Kaneria, Imran Farhat, Kamran Akmal, Mohammad Aamer, Mohammad Asif, Saeed Ajmal, Salman Butt, Shoaib Malik, Tanvir Ahmed, Umar Akmal, Umar Amin, Umar Gul, Wahab Riaz, Yasir Hameed, Zulqarnain Haider.

For the Twenty20 series against Australia preceding their Test series, Abdul Razzaq, Abdur Rehman, Fawad Alam, Shahzaib Hasan and Shoaib Akhtar replaced Azhar Ali, Danish Kaneria, Imran Farhat, Mohammad Asif, Tanvir Ahmed, Umar Amin, Yasir Hameed and Zulqarnain Haider. Salman Butt replaced Shahid Afridi as captain, when he resigned after the First Test against Australia.

Mohammad Yousuf and Raza Hasan joined the party after the Second Test against England, when Danish Kaneria was released; shortly afterwards, Zulqarnain Haider's tour was ended by a finger injury. Salman Butt, Mohammad Aamer and Mohammad Asif withdrew after the Test series because of the spot-fixing allegations.

Shahid Afridi resumed the captaincy for the limited-overs internationals against England. This time, Abdul Razzaq, Fawad Alam, Mohammad Hafeez, Shahzaib Hasan and Shoaib Akhtar replaced Imran Farhat, Shoaib Malik, Tanvir Ahmed, Umar Amin and Yasir Hameed. Asad Shafiq and Mohammad Irfan further reinforced the squad for the one-day series which concluded the tour.

Coach: Waqar Younis. *Manager:* Yawar Saeed. *Associate coach:* Ijaz Ahmed. *Assistant coach:* Aqib Javed. *Associate manager:* Shafqat Rana. *Physiotherapist:* Faisal Hayat. *Trainer:* D. Dwyer. *Analyst:* Umer Farooq. *Security manager:* Khawaja Najam.

TEST MATCH AVERAGES

ENGLAND – BATTING AND FIELDING

	T	I	NO	R	HS	100s	50s	Avge	Ct/St
I. J. L. Trott	4	7	1	404	184	1	2	67.33	1
M. J. Prior	4	6	2	234	102*	1	1	58.50	12/1
†S. C. J. Broad	4	6	0	250	169	1	0	41.66	0
†E. J. G. Morgan	4	6	0	175	130	1	0	29.16	1
†A. J. Strauss	4	7	1	155	53*	0	1	25.83	5
†A. N. Cook	4	7	0	167	110	1	0	23.85	3
K. P. Pietersen	4	6	0	140	80	0	1	23.33	5
P. D. Collingwood	4	6	0	119	82	0	1	19.83	8
S. T. Finn	4	6	5	10	9*	0	0	10.00	0
G. P. Swann	4	6	0	48	28	0	0	8.00	9
†J. M. Anderson	4	6	0	19	11	0	0	3.16	1

BOWLING

	Style	O	M	R	W	BB	5W/i	Avge
G. P. Swann	OB	106.5	38	269	22	6-65	2	12.22
J. M. Anderson	RFM	140.3	55	316	23	6-17	2	13.73
S. T. Finn	RFM	79	24	298	13	3-38	0	22.92
S. C. J. Broad	RFM	113.5	30	327	14	4-38	0	23.35

Also bowled: P. D. Collingwood (RM) 11–2–25–0; K. P. Pietersen (OB) 1–0–2–0.

PAKISTAN – BATTING AND FIELDING

	T	I	NO	R	HS	100s	50s	Avge	Ct
Umar Gul	2	4	2	87	65*	0	1	43.50	0
Umar Akmal	4	8	2	184	79*	0	1	30.66	2
Mohammad Yousuf	2	4	0	99	56	0	1	24.75	0
Saeed Ajmal	3	5	2	67	50	0	1	22.33	2
Azhar Ali	4	8	1	152	92*	0	1	21.71	2
†Salman Butt	4	8	0	128	48	0	0	16.00	0
†Imran Farhat	4	8	0	118	33	0	0	14.75	3
Shoaib Malik	2	4	0	53	38	0	0	13.25	0
Yasir Hameed	2	4	0	41	36	0	0	10.25	4
†Umar Amin	2	4	0	40	23	0	0	10.00	0
Wahab Riaz	2	3	0	29	27	0	0	9.66	0
†Mohammad Aamer	4	8	1	67	25	0	0	9.57	0
Kamran Akmal	3	6	0	24	13	0	0	4.00	17
Mohammad Asif	4	7	0	23	14	0	0	3.28	1

Played in one Test: Danish Kaneria 7, 16*; Zulqarnain Haider 0, 88 (2 ct).

BOWLING

	Style	O	M	R	W	BB	5W/i	Avge
Mohammad Aamer	LFM	133	30	349	19	6-84	2	18.36
Wahab Riaz	LFM	53.2	11	195	7	5-63	1	27.85
Saeed Ajmal	OB	125.1	19	353	12	5-82	1	29.41
Umar Gul	RFM	42.1	8	126	4	3-41	0	31.50
Mohammad Asif	RFM	135	33	404	12	5-77	1	33.66

Also bowled: Azhar Ali (LB) 1–0–9–0; Danish Kaneria (LBG) 33–0–171–1; Imran Farhat (LB) 14–1–40–0; Shoaib Malik (OB) 26.3–2–90–2; Umar Amin (RM) 14–3–44–1; Yasir Hameed (OB) 1–1–0–0.

At Lord's, June 27 (not first-class). **Pakistanis won by six runs.** ‡Pakistanis 165-5 (20 overs) (Shahzaib Hasan 34, Umar Akmal 51*; C. Z. Harris 3-26); MCC 159-5 (20 overs) (A. C. Blizzard 73, B. C. Lara 37). *Umar Akmal's 30-ball 51* led the tourists to 165, and a stand of 94 between Aiden Blizzard, an Australian celebrating his 26th birthday, and 41-year-old Brian Lara was not enough for MCC (who were captained by Sourav Ganguly) to catch up.*

KENT v PAKISTANIS

At Canterbury, June 28–30. Drawn. Toss: Pakistanis. First-class debuts: J. E. Goodman, C. D. Piesley. County debut: M. A. K. Lawson.

Kent's first meeting with the Pakistanis in nine years ended in stalemate, just as their last had in 2001. An experimental county side, led by former Pakistan all-rounder Azhar Mahmood, featured two debutants and a triallist leg-spinner in Mark Lawson, who had previously played for Yorkshire, Middlesex and Derbyshire. Predictably, Pakistan used their opening first-class fixture of a near three-month tour for batting practice, only to be undone by swing and seam movement on a humid first morning. From 53 for three and the loss of their talismanic skipper Shahid Afridi for a six-ball duck, and then a side strain, the tourists recovered to reach 360, with the centrepiece 153 off 188 balls from Umar Akmal, who hit 17 fours and five sixes. Lawson recovered from a hiding to take four for 93, and six in the match, and contributed a feisty 31 to Kent's 259, which also included fifties for Denly and the first-class debutant James Goodman. Mohammad Aamer, like Umar Akmal making his first-class debut in England, delivered express pace with consummate control to earn five wickets and, as if to prove his all-round talents, hit an unbeaten 44 to enliven the final afternoon.

Close of play: First day, Kent 2-0 (Coles 2, Denly 0); Second day, Pakistanis 86-1 (Umar Amin 42, Fawad Alam 29).

Pakistanis

Salman Butt lbw b Azhar Mahmood	26	– lbw b Azhar Mahmood	9
Umar Amin lbw b Coles	2	– c Denly b Lawson	73
Fawad Alam lbw b Nel	20	– retired out	68
Shoaib Malik c Blake b Lawson	27	– not out	48
Umar Akmal st Dixey b Lawson	153		
†Kamran Akmal c Coles b Blake	28	– (5) c Azhar Mahmood b Lawson	2
*Shahid Afridi c Nel b Blake	0		
Abdur Rehman st Dixey b Goodman	30		
Mohammad Aamer st Dixey b Lawson	16	– (6) not out	44
Umar Gul not out	30		
Wahab Riaz lbw b Lawson	6		
B 7, l-b 7, w 1, n-b 7	22	B 8, l-b 6, n-b 6	20

1/10 (2) 2/53 (3) 3/53 (1) 4/112 (4) (87 overs) 360
5/180 (6) 6/180 (7) 7/291 (8)
8/313 (5) 9/330 (9) 10/360 (11)

1/14 (1) (4 wkts dec, 65 overs) 264
2/155 (2) 3/173 (3)
4/179 (5)

Joseph 16–2–51–0; Coles 13–1–61–1; Azhar Mahmood 11–2–33–1; Nel 12–1–54–1; Lawson 16–0–93–4; Blake 5–1–9–2; Hockley 7–1–27–0; Goodman 6–0–16–1; Denly 1–0–2–0. *Second Innings*—Azhar Mahmood 11–2–40–1; Coles 9–1–40–0; Hockley 12–1–60–0; Joseph 9–3–22–0; Lawson 18–2–71–2; Nel 6–1–17–0.

Kent

M. T. Coles b Mohammad Aamer	12			
J. L. Denly b Mohammad Aamer	63	– (1) lbw b Abdur Rehman	69	
C. D. Piesley c Salman Butt b Mohammad Aamer	0	– (2) c Kamran Akmal b Shoaib Malik	43	
A. J. Blake b Umar Gul	0	– (3) st Kamran Akmal b Shoaib Malik	28	
J. B. Hockley b Mohammad Aamer	0	– (4) not out	2	
J. E. Goodman b Wahab Riaz	59	– (5) not out	0	
*Azhar Mahmood c Wahab Riaz b Umar Gul	28			
†P. G. Dixey c Umar Akmal b Mohammad Aamer	22			
R. H. Joseph not out	18			
M. A. K. Lawson c Wahab Riaz b Shoaib Malik	31			
J. D. Nel c Kamran Akmal b Shoaib Malik	4			
B 6, l-b 4, n-b 7, p 5	22	B 6, l-b 1, w 1	8	

1/31 (1) 2/31 (3) 3/32 (4) 4/33 (5)   (69 overs) 259   1/100 (1)   (3 wkts, 28 overs) 150
5/122 (2) 6/160 (7) 7/198 (6)   2/132 (2) 3/145 (3)
8/201 (8) 9/252 (10) 10/259 (11)

Umar Gul 11–1–47–2; Mohammad Aamer 13–2–54–5; Abdur Rehman 15–3–45–0; Wahab Riaz 13–0–63–1; Shoaib Malik 13–4–27–2; Fawad Alam 4–1–8–0. *Second Innings*—Umar Gul 4–0–29–0; Mohammad Aamer 3–0–8–0; Abdur Rehman 10–1–54–1; Shoaib Malik 5–0–17–2; Wahab Riaz 5–0–25–0; Umar Akmal 1–0–10–0.

Umpires: M. A. Eggleston and J. F. Steele.

At Chelmsford, July 2. **Pakistanis won by 66 runs.** ‡Pakistanis **204-4** (20 overs) (Salman Butt 41, Shahzaib Hasan 49, Shoaib Malik 38*, Umar Akmal 38); **Essex 138-9** (20 overs) (T. J. Phillips 57*; Abdul Razzaq 3-19). *A packed house saw powerful and positive batting by the tourists, whose compatriot, leg-spinner Danish Kaneria, received heavy punishment, conceding 46 in three overs. Abdul Razzaq then wrecked the county's reply with the first three wickets in his opening two overs.*

At Northampton, July 3 (not first-class). **Pakistanis won by six wickets. Northamptonshire 133-3** (20 overs) (A. G. Wakely 55, E Chigumbura 58*); ‡Pakistanis **137-4** (15.3 overs) (Shahzaib Hasan 64, Shahid Afridi 42). *Captain Shahid Afridi hit 42 in 14 balls, with six fours and a six, before retiring out.*

Details of Pakistan's two Twenty20 internationals and two Test matches against Australia in July can be found in Pakistan v Australia (see pages 310–321), along with their game against Leicestershire.

ENGLAND v PAKISTAN

First npower Test

RAMIZ RAJA

At Nottingham, July 29–August 1, 2010. England won by 354 runs. Toss: England.

Pakistan were on a high when they met England at Trent Bridge. The win against Australia, fashioned by their swing bowlers, had made the world take notice of their talent again. England had to deal with a team that had found some direction, while the tourists had to reassure their fans that the victory at Headingley was not an aberration. The result was Pakistan's second-biggest defeat in terms of runs.

After Strauss chose to bat, on a dry pitch and under the leaden skies which prevailed almost throughout the game, Kamran Akmal helped him settle in by dropping a dolly.

While Strauss recovered to bat fluently, Akmal regressed behind the stumps, grappling with the ball like a baby with his first toy. Nevertheless, Mohammad Aamer's magic with the ball was complemented by Mohammad Asif's sleight of hand: they reduced England to 118 for four before the afternoon skies cleared and permitted the best batting conditions of the match.

Then Collingwood, with his calmness, and Morgan, with his maturity, began a marathon that would soon tire Pakistan. A natural improviser, Morgan balanced his one-day energy with the classical tone of Test batting to produce an enchanting innings of grace and poise. His stand of 219 with Collingwood, which beat England's previous fifth-wicket best against Pakistan (192 between Denis Compton and Trevor Bailey on the same ground in 1954), had a stroke of luck and drama. Collingwood, when 48, had graciously offered a free hand to Akmal to stump him off Danish Kaneria at his leisure. The keeper's fumble would prove fatal: it allowed England control from there on. Morgan reached his maiden Test century in style with a straight six off Shoaib Malik. In fact, such was his class that Collingwood's dogged innings almost went unnoticed. Some colourless bowling from Kaneria and Umar Gul limited Pakistan's ability to cage England, their colleagues' dullness stretching Aamer and Asif to the full.

Aerial assault: Eoin Morgan strikes Shoaib Malik for six to move to his maiden Test hundred.

Earlier, history had been made when the Decision Review System was used for the first time in a Test in England. Trott's lbw decision came up for review after Asoka de Silva had upheld Kaneria's appeal. Trott straight away made the T-signal with his arms, and won the case when Hot Spot showed an edge. On the evidence of this match, the DRS had a future. Its strongest selling point was that it removed much of the uncertainty from a decision, and cricket became less exposed to the whims of luck and human error. Importantly the umpires, the party most affected, by and large welcomed it; and so did the crowd, which previously had not been allowed to watch the evidence replayed on big screens in slow motion. Critics, however, argued that it tampered with the flow of the game, and the element of luck which makes cricket intriguing: to turn decision-making into an exact science would be changing its structure. They also questioned the technology's reliability. The debate between the romantic and the realist regarding human against machine was bound to continue unless the ICC invested not only in more foolproof kit but enough to make them available in all contests.

The second morning held a lot of promise for England as the rested pair of Morgan and Collingwood swaggered out to boss Pakistan again. But Asif produced a great spell to break England's stride. In conditions that were still overcast, he turned into an artist with the ball, varying his swing and length ever so subtly. His figures in a seven-over spell that derailed England stood at four for 12, giving him a five-wicket haul and equality with his coach Waqar Younis as the quickest Pakistanis to 100 wickets, in only 20 Tests. England lost their last six wickets for 17 runs.

But the tourists soon realised that, when it came to swing, Anderson was the undisputed sultan. On his 28th birthday he combined with Finn's bounce to shred Pakistan to 47 for six. Anderson's side-on arched body with bolt-upright wrist made a perfect set-up for swing bowling. The delivery that bowled Imran Farhat – a round-the-wicket, wide-of-the-crease outswinger which hit the top of his off stump – was a spectacular example. Seven of Pakistan's batsmen were caught behind or in the slips, thanks to what Anderson later said was the best catching display by England that he could remember. The only chance that went begging was an edge from Shoaib Malik that Swann got his right fingertips to at second slip. At the close of play Pakistan, at 147 for nine, still required another eight runs to force England to bat again.

Gul took England by surprise when, having wiped off that deficit, he went on to an unbeaten 65 with four pulled sixes, three of them when Finn dropped short, off only 46 balls. His knock was the ideal tonic to re-energise Pakistan, but Strauss, with the pitch so

Philip Brown

Airborne attack: James Anderson celebrates another wicket.

dry and increasingly uneven, had not intended to enforce the follow-on anyway. England led by 172, which looked enough to guarantee victory, but started their second innings in a surprisingly ungainly fashion, losing their first six wickets for just 98, including Strauss in the first over. Cook's batting had been under the scanner, and his uncertain footwork turned out to be his biggest foe in both innings. Pietersen looked rusty with the bat – he had been denied the chance to play a 40-over game for Hampshire after announcing his intention to leave the county, and his unusual technique, tailored to his requirements, meant he took longer to get back into the groove.

The innings finally took shape when Prior got in on the act with the tail. He did not go for the knockout punch, milking the bowlers and cashing in on loose stuff after adjusting his off-driving to the slow pitch. The last four wickets piled up 164 runs, to put the game well and truly beyond Pakistan's reach. Prior was on 63 when last man Finn joined him, but remained calm and did not try to farm the bowling, taking a single off the first ball of an over seven times. Finn drew strength from this, handling

pressure balls with intelligence, including a couple when his partner was on 99. Prior's third Test century was a complete performance, for he was responsible and explosive at the same time. Before the day was out, Pakistan were in deep trouble, three of their top four out for just 15.

As expected, on the fourth morning England moved in for the kill. Pakistan were shot out before lunch for a miserable 80, their lowest total against England at the time, again obliterated by Anderson's swing. He preyed on a batting line-up that had given up in the mind, and for the first time in his Test career picked up 11 wickets. He was helped once again by the slip catching, led by Collingwood who was world-class with his hands, picking up one high and one very low chance. Pakistan's batsmen had seemingly learned nothing from their first-innings mess; six perished behind the wicket this time. Their batting lasted for just 83 overs in the game, putting unbearable pressure on the bowlers, whose workload was made harder by lapses in the field. Such a performance – prompting the recall of Mohammad Yousuf, even though he had been banned and was completely out of practice – was bound to scar Pakistan mentally for the rest of the series.

Man of the Match: J. M. Anderson. *Attendance:* 51,601.

Close of play: First day, England 331-4 (Collingwood 81, Morgan 125); Second day, Pakistan 147-9 (Umar Gul 30, Mohammad Asif 0); Third day, Pakistan 15-3 (Imran Farhat 6, Mohammad Aamer 0).

England

*A. J. Strauss c Kamran Akmal b Mohammad Aamer	45	– c Kamran Akmal
		b Mohammad Aamer. 0
A. N. Cook c Imran Farhat b Mohammad Aamer ..	8	– c Kamran Akmal b Mohammad Asif. 12
I. J. L. Trott lbw b Mohammad Aamer	38	– b Umar Gul 26
K. P. Pietersen b Mohammad Asif.............	9	– c Kamran Akmal b Umar Gul 22
P. D. Collingwood lbw b Mohammad Asif.......	82	– lbw b Umar Gul 1
E. J. G. Morgan lbw b Mohammad Asif	130	– run out 17
†M. J. Prior run out	6	– not out 102
G. P. Swann lbw b Mohammad Asif............	2	– lbw b Danish Kaneria............ 28
S. C. J. Broad b Umar Gul	3	– c Imran Farhat b Shoaib Malik...... 24
J. M. Anderson lbw b Mohammad Asif.........	0	– c Kamran Akmal b Shoaib Malik.... 2
S. T. Finn not out	0	– not out 9
B 5, l-b 14, w 5, n-b 7	31	B 4, l-b 11, w 1, n-b 3 19

1/42 (2) 2/93 (1) 3/116 (4)   (104.1 overs) 354   1/2 (1)   (9 wkts dec, 75.3 overs) 262
4/118 (3) 5/337 (5) 6/344 (6)   2/18 (2) 3/65 (4)
7/351 (7) 8/354 (8) 9/354 (10) 10/354 (9)   4/66 (3) 5/72 (5) 6/98 (6)
                                                            7/147 (8) 8/203 (9) 9/213 (10)

Mohammad Aamer 24–7–41–3; Mohammad Asif 27–9–77–5; Umar Gul 18.1–5–61–1; Danish Kaneria 21–0–100–0; Shoaib Malik 11–2–39–0; Azhar Ali 1–0–9–0; Umar Amin 1–0–3–0; Imran Farhat 1–0–5–0. *Second Innings*—Mohammad Aamer 16–3–35–1; Mohammad Asif 17–1–56–1; Umar Gul 15–2–41–3; Umar Amin 5–1–13–0; Danish Kaneria 12–0–71–1; Shoaib Malik 10.3–0–31–2.

Pakistan

Imran Farhat b Anderson	19	– c Strauss b Anderson 15
*Salman Butt c Prior b Anderson.............	1	– c Collingwood b Broad 8
Azhar Ali c Prior b Anderson..............	14	– lbw b Broad 0
Umar Amin c Swann b Finn.................	2	– lbw b Anderson 1
Umar Akmal c Swann b Finn...............	4	– (6) lbw b Anderson 4
Shoaib Malik c Strauss b Anderson.........	38	– (7) c Collingwood b Anderson...... 9
†Kamran Akmal c Collingwood b Finn........	0	– (8) lbw b Finn............ 0
Mohammad Aamer c Swann b Anderson......	25	– (5) c Pietersen b Finn 4
Umar Gul not out	65	– c Collingwood b Anderson 9
Danish Kaneria b Broad.................	7	– not out 16
Mohammad Asif run out	0	– c Swann b Anderson 0
B 5, l-b 2	7	B 4, l-b 8, w 1, n-b 1 14

1/5 (2) 2/32 (1) 3/35 (4) 4/41 (3)   (54 overs) 182   1/10 (2) 2/10 (3)   (29 overs) 80
5/45 (5) 6/47 (7) 7/105 (6) 8/108 (8)   3/11 (4) 4/31 (1) 5/37 (6)
9/147 (10) 10/182 (11)   6/41 (5) 7/41 (8) 8/50 (9)
                                                             9/65 (7) 10/80 (11)

Anderson 22–7–54–5; Broad 17–4–59–1; Finn 13–5–50–3; Swann 2–1–12–0. *Second Innings*—Anderson 15–8–17–6; Broad 8–2–23–2; Finn 6–3–28–2.

Umpires: E. A. R. de Silva and A. L. Hill. Third umpire: M. Erasmus.

ENGLAND v PAKISTAN

Second npower Test

JOHN ETHERIDGE

At Birmingham, August 6–9. England won by nine wickets. Toss: Pakistan. Test debut: Zulqarnain Haider.

England's crushing victory was all but guaranteed less than an hour after lunch on the first day, by which time Pakistan had been bowled out for less than 100 for the second time in six days. There were pockets of resistance in the subsequent three days, but Swann made sure they came to nothing. His first six-wicket haul in Test cricket included a contender for the best delivery sent down in England since Shane Warne's fabled Ball of the Century at Old Trafford in 1993.

Pakistan's problems were exacerbated by dropping ten catches in the match, at least two of them almost comically easy. Their captain, Salman Butt, said he counted a total of 14 missed full or half-chances, but that figure seemed a tad harsh even for a team with so many butter-fingered players. The fielding fumbles summed up their struggles, and the series was in danger of becoming embarrassingly one-sided.

PAKISTAN'S LOWEST TEST TOTALS

53†	v Australia at Sharjah (2nd inns) . .	2002-03	**72**	**v England at Birmingham** . .	**2010**
59	v Australia at Sharjah (1st inns) . . .	2002-03	**74**	**v England at Lord's**	**2010**
62	v Australia at Perth	1981-82	77†	v West Indies at Lahore	1986-87
72	v Australia at Perth	2004-05	**80**	**v England at Nottingham** . . .	**2010**

† *One man absent.*

The swinging and seaming conditions on the first day would have tested any team. Pakistan's batting, short of experience and confidence, was wiped out by Anderson and Broad, who took four wickets each. The techniques and temperaments of the batsmen were tormented. Butt had tried to be positive by choosing to bat – and the increasing spin and uneven bounce as the match progressed lent legitimacy to his decision – but he exposed his team to a trio of rampant quick bowlers in helpful conditions.

Pakistan dropped Kamran Akmal and also left out Mohammad Yousuf, who had been summoned following the poor batting display at Trent Bridge. He arrived in Birmingham at lunchtime the day before the match, but decided he was too jet-lagged and short of practice to play. Yousuf, who had received an indefinite ban from the PCB in March after Pakistan's calamitous tour of Australia and then announced his retirement from international cricket, was pencilled in for the Third Test.

The rest of Pakistan's batsmen responded to criticism of loose strokeplay in the previous Test by hardly playing a shot in anger. They scored nine runs in the first 13 overs, and there was a spell of 49 balls without a run off the bat between the third and 11th overs. England's bowlers were allowed to dominate, with nothing coming back by way of aggressive intent. Imran Farhat made a 24-ball duck, then Azhar Ali beat that by occupying 32 deliveries before succumbing for nought. Pakistan's demise meant Test totals of 88, 80 and 72 had been recorded in England in the space of little more than two weeks.

If Pakistan had held their catches, England would have struggled to reach half the 251 they eventually managed in their first innings. Trott and Pietersen, the main scorers, were both put down in single figures, and Pietersen went on to be reprieved at least three times. There was also the curious incident of Pietersen, apparently disturbed by Trott shooing some flies at the non-striker's end, backing away just as Mohammad Asif released the ball. Umpire Marais Erasmus said he called dead ball as it left Asif's hand but, instead of allowing the ball to pass as is the custom, Pietersen could not help himself and patted it to mid-off where, amazingly, it was caught. Pietersen, who had 41 at the time, survived through a mixture of the Laws (which some believed a touch ambiguous) and common sense.

England's middle and lower order fell away sharply following the third-wicket stand of 133 between Trott and Pietersen. The last seven wickets fell for 46, following a similar collapse at Trent Bridge, where they lost six for 17: an area of concern for England in their otherwise dominant performance. Saeed Ajmal took his first five-for in a Test, three with his doosra.

After Anderson removed Butt on the second evening, Swann bowled Farhat with a fizzing, spitting delivery that pitched outside leg stump and turned so sharply that it struck the top of the left-hander's off stump. It was a brilliant delivery, virtually unplayable.

Swann then made further inroads into the top order and, at one stage, bowled no fewer than 67 dot-balls in a row.

When Pakistan were 101 for six in their second innings, still 78 behind, the match looked as if it might be over before tea on the third day – but a few hours later people were frantically ringing hotels to reclaim their rooms. The final four Pakistan wickets put on 195: Zulqarnain Haider scored 88, with 15 fours, after being given out lbw to Swann for a king pair on his Test debut… but reprieved by the review system because the ball was missing leg stump by a whisker.

Ajmal made his best Test score – which was not difficult, considering his previous highest was ten – and helped Zulqarnain put on 115 for the eighth wicket. Ajmal took a number of blows on his body from legitimate balls, while Zulqarnain was struck on the finger as he protected his chest when Broad threw the ball towards him in anger. Whether it was intended to strike Zulqarnain or reach wicketkeeper Prior was open to debate, but Broad, who had been simmering

Effort ball: Graeme Swann en route to six second-innings wickets.

like a saucepan for much of the day, was fined 50% of his match fee. Zulqarnain's eccentric mannerisms and permanent smile appeared to get under the skins of England's players, but Broad's actions were so frowned upon that the ECB emailed all 18 counties two days later to request that fielders and bowlers did not throw the ball close to batsmen.

Cook failed again – bringing his total in seven Test innings in the summer of 2010 to just 100 runs – but Strauss, dropped three times, and Trott made half-centuries as England knocked off their target with no further mishap.

Man of the Match: G. P. Swann. *Attendance:* 28,504.

Close of play: First day, England 112-2 (Trott 31, Pietersen 36); Second day, Pakistan 19-1 (Imran Farhat 10, Azhar Ali 5); Third day, Pakistan 291-9 (Umar Gul 9, Mohammad Asif 13).

Pakistan

Imran Farhat c Prior b Broad	0	– b Swann	29
*Salman Butt c Swann b Finn	7	– c Strauss b Anderson	0
Azhar Ali lbw b Broad	0	– b Swann	19
Shoaib Malik c Prior b Anderson	3	– c Prior b Finn	3
Umar Akmal lbw b Finn	17	– lbw b Swann	20
Umar Amin c Collingwood b Broad	23	– st Prior b Swann	14
†Zulqarnain Haider c Prior b Broad	0	– c Strauss b Swann	88
Mohammad Aamer c Cook b Anderson	12	– c Strauss b Broad	16
Umar Gul c Pietersen b Anderson	0	– (10) not out	13
Saeed Ajmal not out	5	– (9) c Collingwood b Swann	50
Mohammad Asif c Pietersen b Anderson	0	– c Pietersen b Broad	14
L-b 4, n-b 1	5	B 16, l-b 14	30

1/8 (1) 2/9 (2) 3/12 (4) 4/29 (3)   (39.3 overs)   72   1/1 (2) 2/53 (1)   (117.5 overs) 296
5/33 (5) 6/36 (7) 7/63 (6) 8/64 (9)   3/54 (3) 4/76 (4)
9/67 (8) 10/72 (11)   5/82 (5) 6/101 (6) 7/153 (8)
                                             8/268 (9) 9/269 (7) 10/296 (11)

Anderson 14.3–6–20–4; Broad 17–7–38–4; Finn 8–3–10–2. *Second Innings*—Anderson 28–13–62–1; Broad 28.5–8–66–2; Finn 16–5–57–1; Swann 37–20–65–6; Collingwood 7–2–14–0; Pietersen 1–0–2–0.

England

*A. J. Strauss c Zulqarnain Haider b Mohammad Aamer	25	– not out	53
A. N. Cook c Umar Akmal b Mohammad Asif	17	– b Mohammad Aamer	4
I. J. L. Trott c sub (Yasir Hameed) b Umar Amin	55	– not out	53
K. P. Pietersen c and b Saeed Ajmal	80		
P. D. Collingwood c Imran Farhat b Saeed Ajmal	28		
E. J. G. Morgan c Zulqarnain Haider b Mohammad Asif	6		
†M. J. Prior lbw b Saeed Ajmal	15		
G. P. Swann c and b Saeed Ajmal	4		
S. C. J. Broad c sub (Yasir Hameed) b Saeed Ajmal	0		
J. M. Anderson lbw b Mohammad Aamer	0		
S. T. Finn not out	0		
B 10, l-b 9, w 1, n-b 1	21	B 5, n-b 3	8

1/44 (2) 2/44 (1) 3/177 (3)   (83.1 overs) 251   1/7 (2)   (1 wkt, 36.3 overs) 118
4/205 (4) 5/220 (6) 6/243 (7)
7/248 (5) 8/248 (9) 9/251 (10) 10/251 (8)

Mohammad Aamer 20–4–57–2; Mohammad Asif 20–5–41–2; Umar Gul 9–1–24–0; Saeed Ajmal 26.1–5–82–5; Umar Amin 8–2–28–1. *Second Innings*—Mohammad Aamer 11–1–31–1; Mohammad Asif 6–0–20–0; Saeed Ajmal 14.3–1–42–0; Shoaib Malik 5–0–20–0.

Umpires: S. J. Davis and M. Erasmus. Third umpire: A. L. Hill.

At Worcester, August 13–14 (not first-class). **Drawn. ‡Pakistanis 112-2** (Mohammad Yousuf 40*) **v Worcestershire.** *First-team debuts: A. Kapil, C. J. Russell. Only 28.1 overs were possible on the first day, and none on the second.*

ENGLAND v PAKISTAN

Third npower Test

STEPHEN FAY

At The Oval, August 18–21. Pakistan won by four wickets. Toss: England. Test debut: Wahab Riaz.

England arrived at The Oval believing in their own publicity. After winning six straight Tests, optimistic noises were already to be heard about the forthcoming tour of Australia; and their boosters in the media were joining in. No matter that four of the wins had been against Bangladesh and two against a severely demoralised Pakistan, two more would equal England's record winning streak.

But England were ignominiously undone at The Oval, principally by the 18-year-old prodigy Mohammad Aamer, a debutant named Wahab Riaz, and Mohammad Yousuf, a recently discredited old hand resuming his Test career. Pakistan beat England in only three and a half days, not easily but conclusively. England's support team could usefully have checked the dictionary definition of hubris. They would have discovered that it applied; and, in the distraction of the post-mortem, the first hint of Pakistan cricket's summer of scandal was overlooked.

The Oval is accustomed to selling out the first three days of an August Test many months earlier, but this was not so in 2010. Before the start – on a Wednesday rather than the traditional Thursday – many hands were wrung about unsold seats. Various reasons were on offer: a surfeit of cricket; or Pakistan's supine performances at Trent Bridge and Edgbaston; even disenchantment with Test cricket itself starting to set in. When Strauss won the toss and chose to bat, there were large gaps in the stands and terraces. The absentees missed the best cricket of the series so far.

At lunch, five wickets were down for 70; after 31 overs, England were 94 for seven. Their out-of-form batsmen, Cook and Pietersen, scored six runs apiece, and the little-known Riaz, a rangy 25-year-old left-arm pace bowler from Lahore, had taken four wickets, three of them caught by the unpredictable Kamran Akmal, who had been restored behind the stumps because his replacement, Zulqarnain Haider, had broken a finger. Zulqarnain had played the Edgbaston Test with this injury and had wanted to play here too, but was instead sent home.

Prior, at No. 7, began the resistance, and it grew stronger when he was joined by Broad at No. 9. Broad had had a very thin summer, scoring only 27 runs in three innings in his previous two Tests. Now he took risks, and they came off. Prior performed like an established veteran, playing his natural attacking game, and together they scored at more than four an over, putting on 119 for the eighth wicket. Their stand was the difference between humiliation and survival.

Riaz, who took five for 63 in 18 overs, appeared alone at the evening press conference, charming, pleased with himself, and provocative; he claimed that he got more pleasure from the dismissal of Morgan than that of Pietersen. However, Pakistani journalists were happy to inform their English colleagues that the president of the Islamabad Cricket Association had accused Riaz's father of paying a bribe of Rs1.5m (about £11,000) to the selector, Shafqat Rana, to pick his son for the 2008 Asia Cup. Shafqat, now Pakistan's associate manager, and the father had both denied the accusation, and threatened to sue.

Pakistan had lost the first two Tests because of the frailty of their batting against swing bowling. The return of Yousuf was intended to restore the backbone. The previous day, he had dropped what might have been the simplest catch of the summer, perhaps of the decade (his blushes were spared when Saeed Ajmal's next ball ended the innings), and in the first few overs he faced, he was clearly out of touch. His technique allowed him to survive long enough to restore timing and serenity. He and Swann brought out the best in

Left in shreds: Wahab Riaz, another left-armer, runs through England with five wickets on debut.

each other, until Swann, having bowled three pushed-through deliveries, cleverly gave the ball more air, causing Yousuf to play fractionally early and offer a return catch. It was Swann's 100th wicket in his 23rd Test, the same rate as Shane Warne.

Yousuf talked Azhar Ali through the early stages of his innings – guidance which he had lacked in his previous Tests of the summer – and Azhar grew visibly until he was fully in control of a last-wicket stand of 38 (Pakistan's tenth wicket was their most productive in this series). A dropped catch at first slip by Strauss off Mohammad Asif when the score was 278 helped Pakistan extend their lead to 75.

Strauss's poor match deteriorated: he edged the fourth ball of the second innings to second slip. Cook, his place in jeopardy after only 106 runs in his previous eight Test innings, decided that desperation was the better part of valour and took risks. When he was 23, an edge flew between first and second slip, but otherwise the tactic worked. Once he realised that, Cook played some uncharacteristically handsome cover-drives. Instead of looking back at his bat as the bowler ran in, to start a complicated series of trigger movements, he watched the ball and hit it. Cook was caught behind for 110, including 17 fours, but by tea on the third day England were 194 for three and the match seemed well balanced.

By 5.15 p.m., though, it was all over, bar another Pakistan batting catastrophe. Aamer's whippy left arm reminded his admirers of Wasim Akram, and Ajmal's doosra embarrassed England's increasingly fragile middle order. Aamer's reverse-swing – from round and over the wicket – defeated Collingwood, Prior and Broad, and he also winkled out the patient and defiant Trott, whose 36 took only seven minutes fewer than Cook's 110, and invited the criticism that he had not cashed in before the ball began to reverse-swing.

Pietersen's loss of form had become a serious matter, while Morgan had failed again, and Collingwood had fallen into another slump. Of England's top seven, none was averaging over 50 in the year 2010, and only Trott and Prior had batted with any consistency. This was a withering augury before Brisbane in November.

England lost seven wickets for 28 in 16 overs after tea. Aamer's five for 52 made him the youngest bowler ever to take five wickets in a Test innings in England, by around 20 months from Ramakant "Tiny" Desai of India in 1959. Ajmal again played a significant supporting role, the fielders held their catches for once, and England's collapse left Pakistan just 148 to win.

They made a meal of it. Salman Butt scored 48 from 64 balls, but was later charged under Article 2.1.1 of the ICC's Code of Conduct. The allegation was that he had agreed to bat out a maiden over during this innings, but the charge was dismissed. The charge of failing to disclose the approach made to him to bat out a maiden over was found proved, however, and Butt was given a one-year ban, to run concurrently with the rest of his suspension.

At 131 Yousuf was dismissed by a stunning yorker from Anderson, who previewed his winter with a spell of unerring old-ball accuracy from the Pavilion End in partnership with Swann. When the sixth wicket fell one run later, 16 more were required.

Umar Akmal and Aamer, the two youngest members of the Pakistan team, spent 33 agonising minutes compiling the winning runs. Both had good reason to kneel and kiss the pitch at the end.

After the match Butt praised his youthful team, saying he had never seen such a young talent as Aamer, who had also batted coolly in the crisis. Asked about England's prospects in Australia, he replied that their bowlers would find it hard and that, at home, Australia were always favourites. It was a confident, composed performance, and a number of the journalists present concluded that, while Pakistan cricket might have problems, the captaincy was no longer one of them. Ah well.

Man of the Match: Mohammad Aamer. *Attendance:* 72,246.

Close of play: First day, Pakistan 48-1 (Yasir Hameed 36, Wahab Riaz 0); Second day, England 6-1 (Cook 0, Anderson 2); Third day, England 221-9 (Broad 6, Finn 0).

England

*A. J. Strauss c Kamran Akmal b Wahab Riaz	15	– c Yasir Hameed b Mohammad Aamer	4
A. N. Cook c Kamran Akmal b Mohammad Asif	6	– c Kamran Akmal b Wahab Riaz	110
I. J. L. Trott c Yasir Hameed b Wahab Riaz	12	– (4) c Azhar Ali b Mohammad Aamer	36
K. P. Pietersen c Kamran Akmal b Wahab Riaz	6	– (5) b Saeed Ajmal	23
P. D. Collingwood b Mohammad Aamer	5	– (6) c Kamran Akmal b Mohammad Aamer	3
E. J. G. Morgan c Kamran Akmal b Wahab Riaz	17	– (7) b Saeed Ajmal	5
†M. J. Prior not out	84	– (8) c Kamran Akmal b Mohammad Aamer	5
G. P. Swann c Umar Akmal b Mohammad Asif	8	– (9) b Saeed Ajmal	6
S. C. J. Broad lbw b Wahab Riaz	48	– (10) c Mohammad Asif b Mohammad Aamer	6
J. M. Anderson lbw b Mohammad Asif	0	– (3) c Kamran Akmal b Saeed Ajmal	11
S. T. Finn lbw b Saeed Ajmal	0	– not out	1
B 10, l-b 11, w 6, n-b 5	32	L-b 5, w 2, n-b 5	12

1/9 (2) 2/35 (1) 3/40 (3) 4/47 (5) (62.3 overs) 233 1/4 (1) 2/40 (3) (77 overs) 222
5/67 (4) 6/74 (6) 7/94 (8) 8/213 (9) 3/156 (2) 4/194 (5)
9/214 (10) 10/233 (11) 5/195 (4) 6/202 (6) 7/206 (7)
8/210 (8) 9/220 (9) 10/222 (10)

Mohammad Aamer 15–4–49–1; Mohammad Asif 20–5–68–3; Wahab Riaz 18–6–63–5; Saeed Ajmal 9.3–1–32–1. *Second Innings*—Mohammad Aamer 19–5–52–5; Mohammad Asif 16–7–45–0; Wahab Riaz 8–1–40–1; Saeed Ajmal 31–7–71–4; Imran Farhat 3–0–9–0.

Pakistan

Imran Farhat b Anderson	11	– lbw b Swann	33
Yasir Hameed c Prior b Finn	36	– c Swann b Anderson	0
Wahab Riaz lbw b Swann	27		
*Salman Butt c Prior b Swann	17	– (3) c Collingwood b Swann	48
Mohammad Yousuf c and b Swann	56	– (4) b Anderson	33
Azhar Ali not out	92	– (5) run out	5
Umar Akmal run out	38	– (6) not out	16
†Kamran Akmal c Morgan b Broad	10	– (7) lbw b Swann	0
Mohammad Aamer c Prior b Broad	6	– (8) not out	4
Saeed Ajmal b Anderson	0		
Mohammad Asif c Anderson b Swann	8		
L-b 4, w 1, n-b 2	7	B 4, l-b 2, w 2, n-b 1	9

1/48 (1) 2/48 (2) 3/76 (4)   (100.2 overs) 308   1/5 (2)   (6 wkts, 41.4 overs) 148
4/110 (3) 5/179 (5) 6/236 (7)   2/57 (1) 3/103 (3)
7/251 (8) 8/269 (9) 9/270 (10) 10/308 (11)   4/124 (5) 5/131 (4) 6/132 (7)

Anderson 24–6–79–2; Broad 25–4–72–2; Finn 20–4–74–1; Swann 27.2–9–68–4; Collingwood 4–0–11–0. *Second Innings*—Anderson 14–5–39–2; Broad 6–0–35–0; Swann 18.4–4–50–3; Finn 3–0–18–0.

Umpires: S. J. Davis and A. L. Hill.   Third umpire: B. F. Bowden.

ICC TRIBUNAL FINDINGS, FEBRUARY 2011

The ICC's Independent Anti-Corruption Tribunal heard the ICC's case against the three Pakistan players, and found unproved the allegation that Salman Butt agreed to bat out a maiden over in the Oval Test. But it found that the following charges had been proved:

- that Salman Butt had failed to disclose to the ICC's Anti-Corruption and Security Unit the approach by Mazhar Majeed that Butt should bat out a maiden over in the Oval Test;
- that Mohammad Asif agreed to bowl, and did bowl, a deliberate no-ball in the Lord's Test;
- that Mohammad Aamer agreed to bowl, and did bowl, two deliberate no-balls in the same Test;
- and that Salman Butt was party to the bowling of those deliberate no-balls.

All three have vigorously denied the charges. Sanctions have been applied by the ICC. All three players have appealed to the Court of Arbitration for Sport against the verdicts and sanctions.

Separately, all three players and their agent Mazhar Majeed face charges in the UK of conspiracy to obtain and accept corrupt payments and conspiracy to cheat.

ENGLAND v PAKISTAN

Fourth npower Test

Scyld Berry

At Lord's, August 26–29. England won by an innings and 225 runs. Toss: Pakistan.

The last Test of England's previous home series against Pakistan had ended in the first forfeiture in the history of Test cricket. The last Test of this England series against Pakistan was even more controversial.

On the third evening of the game, a Saturday, news came out of an alleged conspiracy involving some of Pakistan's leading players. Reporters from the *News of the World* said they had paid a middleman or agent, Mazhar Majeed, £150,000 to arrange "spot-fixing": specifically for Pakistan's two opening bowlers, Mohammad Aamer and Mohammad Asif, to deliver three no-balls at pre-arranged moments. The bowlers did so – and, although match-fixing had been a dominant theme in Asia over the previous two decades, cricket in England would not be quite the same again.

The first two alleged transgressions, later to be proven in the eyes of the ICC's independent tribunal, occurred on the rain-interrupted opening day when play was limited to 12.3 overs in the afternoon. At 1.56 p.m. Aamer delivered a no-ball as the first ball of his second over from the Pavilion End – the third over of England's innings – as predicted. The left-armer was a foot beyond the line of the popping crease, a remarkable distance. Moreover, the fact that he no-balled at all was unusual: in the three previous Tests of the series Aamer had bowled only three no-balls in total.

Aamer spent time examining the spikes of his right boot, and scraping some mud off them, but the amount was minimal: the fine Lord's drainage system had done its work. His captain Salman Butt brought some sawdust in his cupped hands from the pile near the start of Aamer's run-up. But the ground did not appear to have been slippery, and Aamer's front foot had landed firmly.

From the Nursery End, Asif delivered a no-ball for what would have been the last ball of his fifth over, although only by a small margin later to be measured as two inches. After Strauss had pushed the ball to point for a single, Butt again brought up sawdust for the bowler to spread around the crease. Asif was later reported to have said he was making an extra effort: the illegal delivery was timed at 80.2mph, 0.8mph faster than his average speed in this opening spell.

Shortly afterwards Strauss was bowled by one that swung sharply into him, and next over play was abandoned for the day, without any further no-balls. The large crowd was disappointed at having seen so little, but they were to hear much more about this brief passage.

On the second morning, dry and cloudy, Aamer began with a superlative spell of swing bowling in which, for the first time in England's history, their Nos 4, 5 and 6 all made nought. However, after Butt had walked up to Aamer at the start of his run and talked, without any change being made in the field, Aamer's third ball of his third full over of the day – the 19th of England's innings – was a no-ball. Again he was about a foot past the popping crease, and prompted the Sky TV commentator Michael Holding to say: "How far over was that? Wow!"

Aamer's second no-ball was a bouncer at Trott – and all the more threatening for being delivered well over the line and that much closer to the batsman. Trott only just managed to fend it away for a single. He could have been injured. Part of Butt's subsequent defence was that he and Aamer wanted to stop Trott pushing forward to reduce the swing.

These controversial no-balls overshadowed some of the finest cricket played at Lord's in recent times. From Pakistan came Aamer's new-ball spell that mixed inswingers and the ball going across the right-hander at a speed in the mid-80s. After Cook had edged a stiff-legged push to be caught behind, Aamer dismissed Pietersen and Collingwood in his next over, then Morgan in the one after that, to give him four wickets for no runs in only eight balls: an omen of the very similar spell that Mitchell Johnson was to bowl in the Perth Test.

Pietersen, who had admitted before the game that his confidence was low after not scoring a century since March 2009, played a wild drive at his first ball, the one angled across the right-hander. Collingwood was beaten by an inswinger – umpire Bowden's not-out decision was overturned on review – while Morgan had to play a ball swinging away from him on the line of off stump and was caught low down at second slip.

This second no-ball by Aamer came in the over after he had dismissed Morgan, and he took no further wickets in this superlative spell, which had given Pakistan a chance to square the series. If every ball of a Test match is regarded as a battle, those three no-balls played a small but significant part in the outcome of this war. Three runs to England, or three free bricks in the imposing structure they were going to build.

After lunch, Aamer returned to dismiss Prior and Swann (second ball) when they outside-edged loose drives, but Trott – 45 when Swann was out at 102 for seven – had not been troubled as his team-mates had been. Following some criticism of his being too

Graham Morris

On and on... and on: Jonathan Trott and Stuart Broad at one of many landmarks during their record eighth-wicket stand.

passive at The Oval, he was more assertive from the start here, standing well outside his crease to Asif and moving further forward to him (at around 80mph, his bouncer was much less threatening than Aamer's); and eventually Trott found a partner in Broad, who joined him in what became a Test-record partnership of 332 for the eighth wicket.

By the close of the second day, the stand between Trott and Broad was only two short of England's previous record of 246, by Les Ames and Gubby Allen against New Zealand in 1931, and Lord's was almost intoxicated with delight at this fighting spirit being shown in the last Test before the Ashes. Broad had also joined two Middlesex players, Allen and John Murray, in becoming only the third No. 9 to score a Test century for England. It was batting, too, not hitting, as he blocked the good balls and stroked the loose ones along the ground, with a touch of Woolley-like grace in his off-drive. Such was his calmness, there was no guessing that Broad's hundred was his first in Test or county cricket, and only the second of his life. While Broad often swept Saeed Ajmal, Trott played him off the back foot – appreciative that the pitch was that much slower than The Oval had been – and worked singles square of the wicket to either side.

The third day was one of the very few sunny ones of this series, ahead of the gloom that was to descend in the evening. Pakistan in the field tried every obvious avenue, but Trott and Broad carried their stand to new heights, past the previous Test record of 313 by Wasim Akram and Saqlain Mushtaq for Pakistan against Zimbabwe at Sheikhupura in 1996-97. By the time Broad eventually missed a sweep and Pakistan's review had been upheld, their eighth-wicket stand had not been exceeded in first-class cricket except by Arthur Sims and Victor Trumper, who added 433 for the Australians in New Zealand in 1913-14 (Trumper went in unusually low at No. 9, and scored 293). Broad moved past his father's highest Test innings of 162 – they had become the first father and son to make a Test hundred for England. He finished with the second-highest Test score by a No. 9, behind only Ian Smith's 173 for New Zealand against India in 1989-90. It was a worthy achievement, devalued only by some village-like fumbles in the field by Pakistan's fielders towards the end, but that was consistent with their fielding through the series.

If Pakistan's bowling backed up Strauss's subsequent assertion – "There was no way Pakistan were not trying to win" – their batting was poor even by the standard of their previous collapses in the series. They fell to 74 all out and 41 for four before the end of the third day. Still, it was England's best bowling performance of the summer.

Excellent use of the new ball reduced Pakistan's first innings to 44 for three from 18 overs before Swann came on (one loose over by Finn from the Pavilion End had cost 16). Broad, even though he had just batted for seven hours, took the new ball and the first wicket, Yasir Hameed edging to second slip. Anderson, continuing his resourceful development into a bowler for all conditions, bowled his first ten overs for ten runs. As usual, he tried a yorker first ball against Mohammad Yousuf, and almost succeeded; soon afterwards Broad did.

Swann found far more turn than Lord's had provided in its early-season Tests. He had to wait until his third over of the match before taking a wicket by bowling Butt, and then a while longer as Butt refused to believe that the ball had clipped his off stump. When Finn switched to the Nursery End, Umar Akmal found the bowler's arm was coming over the sightscreen, and he could not sight his yorker. It was the third time in the series that Pakistan had been bowled out for well under 100.

Similarly tight new-ball bowling reduced Pakistan to 30 for two in their follow-on before Swann came on to take his first five-for in a Lord's Test. Tony Hill, who had an almost perfect match and series, gave Butt lbw – a decision that was queried but upheld on review. And Yousuf pulled Finn to deep square leg off the final ball before bad light and rain halted play.

It was just before the close that the tourists heard of the *News of the World* story and the police's arrival at Lord's. No Pakistani player turned up for the press conference after the close, a departure from custom; and later that evening the police interviewed Butt, Aamer and Asif at the team hotel.

In a sombre atmosphere Pakistan were wrapped up before lunch on the fourth day for their heaviest Test defeat. They made little attempt at a fight, arriving late at the ground and doing no warming up or practising before the resumption: paying spectators had every right to feel robbed. In his first innings of any substance on the tour Umar Akmal played some swashbuckling shots in a last-wicket stand with Asif. Like Aamer, Asif was greeted with silence, then by a shout of "No-ball!" from a spectator when he batted.

In the presentations afterwards, conducted in the discreet environment of the Pavilion rather than outside, the ECB chairman Giles Clarke refused to shake Aamer's hand after he had been made Pakistan's Man of the Series. The police then resumed their inquiries.

Man of the Match: S. C. J. Broad.   *Attendance:* 94,619.

Men of the Series: England – I. J. L. Trott; Pakistan – Mohammad Aamer.

Close of play: First day, England 39-1 (Cook 10, Trott 8); Second day, England 346-7 (Trott 149, Broad 125); Third day, Pakistan 41-4 (Azhar Ali 0, Umar Akmal 0).

England

*A. J. Strauss b Mohammad Asif 13	G. P. Swann c Azhar Ali
A. N. Cook c Kamran Akmal	b Mohammad Aamer . 0
b Mohammad Aamer . 10	S. C. J. Broad lbw b Saeed Ajmal 169
I. J. L. Trott c Kamran Akmal b Wahab Riaz 184	J. M. Anderson c Yasir Hameed
K. P. Pietersen c Kamran Akmal	b Saeed Ajmal . 6
b Mohammad Aamer . 0	S. T. Finn not out 0
P. D. Collingwood	
lbw b Mohammad Aamer . 0	B 4, l-b 17, w 7, n-b 14 42
E. J. G. Morgan c Yasir Hameed	
b Mohammad Aamer . 0	1/31 (1) 2/39 (2) 3/39 (4) (139.2 overs) 446
†M. J. Prior c Kamran Akmal	4/39 (5) 5/47 (6) 6/102 (7)
b Mohammad Aamer . 22	7/102 (8) 8/434 (9) 9/446 (10) 10/446 (3)

Mohammad Aamer 28–6–84–6; Mohammad Asif 29–6–97–1; Wahab Riaz 27.2–4–92–1; Saeed Ajmal 44–5–126–2; Yasir Hameed 1–1–0–0; Imran Farhat 10–1–26–0.

Pakistan

Imran Farhat c Prior b Anderson	6	– c Cook b Broad	5
Yasir Hameed c Swann b Broad	2	– lbw b Anderson	3
*Salman Butt b Swann	26	– lbw b Swann	21
Mohammad Yousuf b Broad	0	– c Trott b Finn	10
Azhar Ali c Cook b Swann	10	– b Swann	12
Umar Akmal b Finn	6	– not out	79
†Kamran Akmal c Prior b Finn	13	– c Prior b Anderson	1
Mohammad Aamer lbw b Finn	0	– b Swann	0
Wahab Riaz lbw b Swann	2	– c Pietersen b Swann	0
Saeed Ajmal not out	4	– run out	8
Mohammad Asif c and b Swann	0	– c Collingwood b Swann	1
L-b 4, n-b 1	5	B 1, l-b 2, w 3, n-b 1	7

1/9 (2) 2/9 (1) 3/10 (4) 4/46 (3)   (33 overs) 74   1/7 (1) 2/9 (2)   (36.5 overs) 147
5/53 (5) 6/57 (6) 7/57 (8) 8/70 (7)   3/41 (3) 4/41 (4) 5/63 (5)
9/74 (9) 10/74 (11)   6/64 (7) 7/65 (8) 8/73 (9)
                                                             9/97 (10) 10/147 (11)

Anderson 10–6–10–1; Broad 6–4–10–2; Finn 9–4–38–3; Swann 8–3–12–4. *Second Innings*—Anderson 13–4–35–2; Broad 6–1–24–1; Finn 4–0–23–1; Swann 13.5–1–62–5.

Umpires: B. F. Bowden and A. L. Hill.   Third umpire: S. J. Davis.
Series referee: R. S. Madugalle.

At Taunton, September 2. **Pakistanis won by eight runs. Pakistanis 264** (47.3 overs) (Shahzaib Hasan 105, Fawad Alam 97; M. L. Turner 3-52, L. Gregory 4-49); ‡**Somerset 256-9** (50 overs) (N. R. D. Compton 50, Z. de Bruyn 122*, J. C. Hildreth 31; Umar Gul 3-66, Saeed Ajmal 3-40). *First-team debut:* L. Gregory. *Shahzaib Hasan (ten fours and two sixes in 120 balls) and Fawad Alam added 169 for the tourists' fourth wicket, but seven of their team-mates made eight runs between them. Zander de Bruyn hit a one-day best 122* in 142 balls, but Somerset lost six wickets in the last seven overs.*

LIMITED-OVERS INTERNATIONAL REPORTS BY COLIN BATEMAN AND GIDEON BROOKS

ENGLAND v PAKISTAN

First Twenty20 International

At Cardiff, September 5. England won by five wickets. Toss: England.

What should have been a prime attraction – the meeting of the two most recent World Twenty20 champions – was overshadowed by the storm clouds of the latest accusations of corruption. This was England's first 20-over game since their victory in the Caribbean in May, and the trophy was on display at Cardiff, but the week leading up to this series had been consumed by the fallout from the newspaper spot-fixing allegations. England's players and the ECB made it clear that they would not be happy meeting a Pakistan side containing the three men under suspicion – Salman Butt, Mohammad Aamer and Mohammad Asif – and there were doubts about whether the limited-overs matches would take place at all, until the ICC suspended the trio pending investigations by the police and the ICC's own Anti-Corruption and Security Unit. On the eve of the series, Pakistan's one-day captain Shahid Afridi apologised on behalf of the three suspended players: "I want to say sorry to all cricket lovers and all cricket nations." On the morning of this game came further allegations in the *News of the World*, in an interview with the Pakistan Test batsman Yasir Hameed. He was reported as saying he had turned down "up to £150,000" to fix a Test, and that his team-mates were involved in fixing "nearly" every match, but later claimed he had been misquoted. The cricket was far less interesting. England, well-drilled and efficient, restricted Pakistan to a modest 126, Swann proving almost unplayable. England's batting suffered an early wobble, and Pakistan sensed a chance at 62 for five at halfway, but Morgan, fast earning a reputation as the team's expert finisher, and Yardy took them home with a stand of 67 in 7.1 overs.

Man of the Match: M. H. Yardy.   *Attendance:* 10,339.

Pakistan

		B	4	6
†Kamran Akmal *c 7 b 8*	6	4	0	0
Shahzaib Hasan *st 2 b 9*	21	25	2	0
Mohammad Yousuf *c 5 b 9*	26	18	3	0
Fawad Alam *c and b 7*	20	29	0	0
Umar Akmal *not out*	35	30	2	0
*Shahid Afridi *not out*	16	14	1	0
L-b 1, w 1	2			

6 overs: 49-1   (20 overs) 126-4

1/13 2/50 3/56 4/88

Abdul Razzaq, Umar Gul, Wahab Riaz, Shoaib Akhtar and Saeed Ajmal did not bat.

Sidebottom 4–0–32–0; Bresnan 3–0–18–1; Broad 4–0–32–0; Swann 4–0–14–2; Yardy 4–0–21–1; Collingwood 1–0–8–0.

England

		B	4	6
C. Kieswetter *c 1 b 10.*	6	7	1	0
†S. M. Davies *c 9 b 8*	33	27	3	0
R. S. Bopara *c 3 b 10*	11	13	1	0
*P. D. Collingwood *b 6*	4	4	0	0
E. J. G. Morgan *not out*	38	24	6	0
L. J. Wright *b 6*	0	2	0	0
M. H. Yardy *not out*	35	26	4	0
L-b 1, w 1	2			

6 overs: 42-2   (17.1 overs) 129-5

1/9 2/42 3/55 4/57 5/62

T. T. Bresnan, G. P. Swann, S. C. J. Broad and R. J. Sidebottom did not bat.

Abdul Razzaq 2–0–20–0; Shoaib Akhtar 4–1–23–2; Wahab Riaz 2–0–11–0; Shahid Afridi 4–0–27–2; Umar Gul 2.1–0–17–1; Saeed Ajmal 3–0–30–0.

Umpires: R. A. Kettleborough and N. J. Llong.   Third umpire: R. K. Illingworth.

ENGLAND v PAKISTAN

Second Twenty20 International

At Cardiff, September 7 (floodlit). England won by six wickets. Toss: Pakistan.

The most telling aspect of the second international in Cardiff in three days was the crowd – or lack of it. Fewer than 6,000 spectators witnessed England's second victory, sparking concern about overkill and overpricing of the 20-over game. It also brought into question the wisdom of staging two matches at the same venue so close together. Glamorgan claimed the attendance had been affected by rumours that the fixture might not go ahead because of the match-fixing controversy, and the ECB subsequently refunded them 50% of the staging fee. For those who did turn up there was precious little entertainment on a gloomy Tuesday evening. Pakistan, weakened by suspensions and showing a distinct lack of collective will in the field, were hapless and helpless. England, on the other hand, were again ruthless, bowling their opponents out for 89, their lowest 20-over total. Yardy conceded only ten runs off his four overs, the most economical completed spell by an England bowler in a Twenty20 game. A home win arrived with six overs to spare.

Man of the Match: T. T. Bresnan.   *Attendance:* 5,691.

Pakistan

	B	4	6
†Kamran Akmal *c 9 b 8*	11	10	2	0
Shahzaib Hasan *c 2 b 10*.......	3	8	0	0
Mohammad Yousuf *c 3 b 8*	4	6	0	0
Umar Akmal *b 9*.............	17	13	0	2
*Shahid Afridi *c 5 b 10*........	2	4	0	0
Mohammad Hafeez *run out* ...	14	32	1	0
Abdul Razzaq *c 6 b 11*	11	20	1	0
Fawad Alam *c 2 b 9*	0	1	0	0
Umar Gul *c 3 b 11*...........	16	13	1	1
Shoaib Akhtar *b 8*...........	4	4	1	0
Saeed Ajmal *not out*	0	1	0	0
L-b 2, w 5	7			

6 overs: 23-4   (18.4 overs)   89

1/11 2/18 3/20 4/22 5/44 6/55 7/56 8/85 9/85

Sidebottom 3–0–22–2; Bresnan 3.4–0–10–3; Broad 4–0–18–2; Yardy 4–0–10–0; Swann 4–0–27–2.

England

	B	4	6
C. Kieswetter *run out*	16	10	2	1
†S. M. Davies *c 4 b 10*........	9	6	1	0
R. S. Bopara *lbw b 5*........	12	24	1	0
*P. D. Collingwood *c 6 b 11*....	21	25	0	1
E. J. G. Morgan *not out*	18	14	3	0
M. H. Yardy *not out*	6	6	0	0
B 4, l-b 2, w 1, n-b 1........	8			

6 overs: 35-2   (14 overs)   90-4

1/26 2/26 3/57 4/63

L. J. Wright, T. T. Bresnan, G. P. Swann, S. C. J. Broad and R. J. Sidebottom did not bat.

Shoaib Akhtar 4–1–18–1; Umar Gul 2–0–23–0; Saeed Ajmal 3–0–13–1; Shahid Afridi 3–0–15–1; Mohammad Hafeez 2–0–15–0.

Umpires: I. J. Gould and R. K. Illingworth.   Third umpire: R. A. Kettleborough.
Series referee: J. J. Crowe.

ENGLAND v PAKISTAN

First One-Day International

At Chester-le-Street, September 10. England won by 24 runs. Toss: Pakistan. One-day international debut: Mohammad Irfan.

Although England made the first breakthrough in this five-match NatWest Series, there was to be no escape from the shadows cast by the spot-fixing scandal. A few days earlier it had emerged that Kamran Akmal and the suspended Salman Butt had been officially notified before the Lord's Test that they were under investigation by the ACSU, having failed to satisfactorily explain their off-field activities during the World Twenty20 earlier in the year. Kamran was later assured by the ICC that he remained eligible for international selection. The PCB also let it be known they were unhappy with the ICC's decision to suspend Butt, Mohammad Aamer and Mohammad Asif. Then, on the eve of the game, it was revealed that a fourth player, fast bowler Wahab Riaz, was to be questioned by police (he was, on September 14, but released without charge). In spite of such swirling negativity – and similarly bad weather that saw the match reduced to 41 overs apiece – the crowd was treated to a comfortable England win featuring a classy knock of 87 from 67 balls from Davies, an innings beautifully timed in every sense: it underpinned a good total of 274 for six and sealed his position as back-up wicketkeeper for the Ashes tour. Trott weighed in with a solid 69, and Bopara added a late thrash which included three hefty sixes. Pakistan produced some muscular cameos of their own in reply, but were unable to string together a convincing narrative, a 62-run stand for the first wicket between Kamran and Mohammad Hafeez their only partnership of note. Umar Akmal briefly looked capable of lifting his side close but, disappointingly, the tail hung limply, their all-round vulnerability shown by the fact England's bowlers shared the wickets around. Mohammad Irfan's debut was less remarkable than his height – estimated at between 6ft 10in and 7ft 1in – and he was believed to be the tallest to have played international cricket.

Man of the Match: S. M. Davies.   Attendance: 11,911.

England

*A. J. Strauss b Saeed Ajmal	41	R. S. Bopara not out	35
†S. M. Davies c Kamran Akmal b Saeed Ajmal	87	T. T. Bresnan run out	1
		M. H. Yardy not out	1
I. J. L. Trott b Saeed Ajmal	69	B 2, l-b 2, w 9	13
P. D. Collingwood c Fawad Alam b Saeed Ajmal	14		

1/78 (1) 2/153 (2) (6 wkts, 41 overs) 274
E. J. G. Morgan c Kamran Akmal b Shahid Afridi. 13 | 3/179 (4) 4/205 (5)
5/253 (3) 6/255 (7) 8 overs: 51-0

G. P. Swann, S. C. J. Broad and J. M. Anderson did not bat.

Shoaib Akhtar 8–1–28–0; Mohammad Irfan 5.3–0–37–0; Umar Gul 6–0–67–0; Mohammad Hafeez 5–0–28–0; Saeed Ajmal 9–0–58–4; Shahid Afridi 7.3–0–52–1.

Pakistan

†Kamran Akmal c Broad b Swann	53	Saeed Ajmal not out	9
Mohammad Hafeez c Bresnan b Swann	30	Mohammad Irfan not out	3
Mohammad Yousuf lbw b Yardy	8		
Fawad Alam c sub (L. J. Wright) b Bresnan	39	L-b 1, w 5, n-b 3	9
Umar Akmal c Davies b Broad	43		
*Shahid Afridi c Swann b Anderson	19	1/62 (2) 2/82 (3) (9 wkts, 41 overs) 250
Asad Shafiq b Yardy	19	3/123 (1) 4/158 (4)
Umar Gul c Morgan b Anderson	18	5/191 (5) 6/218 (7) 7/233 (6)
Shoaib Akhtar b Bresnan	0	8/238 (9) 9/244 (8) 8 overs: 41-0

Anderson 9–0–35–2; Bresnan 8–0–61–2; Broad 8–0–54–1; Swann 8–0–50–2; Yardy 8–0–49–2.

Umpires: B. R. Doctrove and I. J. Gould.   Third umpire: R. A. Kettleborough.

ENGLAND v PAKISTAN

Second One-Day International

At Leeds, September 12. England won by four wickets. Toss: Pakistan.

A full and vibrant house, a beautiful late-summer day and a thrillingly tight contest seemed just what the doctor ordered, and there was icing for home fans, too, as England scrambled over the line to extend their series lead to 2–0. Strauss produced an innings that, while tipping its hat to good fortune on more than one occasion, allowed him to answer those who had questioned his one-day credentials. Pakistan's decision to bat looked a good one as they racked up a formidable total, although Shahid Afridi thought it some 30 runs short. A belligerent 74 from Kamran Akmal, a maiden international fifty from Asad Shafiq and an assured 46 from Mohammad Yousuf certainly put wind in the sails of the large Pakistani contingent in the stands. It said something that the most successful of England's bowlers was Broad, who returned the most expensive four-wicket haul in one-day international history. England replied confidently: Strauss's defiant 126 from 134 balls contained ten fours, one six over long-on (to bring up his 50), and two strokes of good luck. Dropped on 23, he then looked to glove a chance off Umar Gul to a diving Kamran when 38, only to be reprieved by umpire Doctrove. Trott hit his fifth consecutive one-day international half-century as England built a platform that should have made victory comfortable. But Strauss's departure in the 45th over prompted a late wobble, and it was left to Yardy and Bresnan to inch them over the line with a scrambled single and three balls to spare.

Man of the Match: A. J. Strauss.   *Attendance:* 16,912.

Pakistan

†Kamran Akmal lbw b Collingwood	74	Saeed Ajmal c Strauss b Broad	4
Mohammad Hafeez b Swann	43	Shoaib Akhtar not out	0
Mohammad Yousuf c Davies b Broad	46	L-b 12, w 5	17
Asad Shafiq c Bopara b Broad	50		
Umar Akmal c Davies b Broad	28	1/122 (1) 2/137 (2) (8 wkts, 50 overs)	294
*Shahid Afridi c Strauss b Anderson	9	3/211 (3) 4/246 (4)	
Fawad Alam not out	20	5/258 (5) 6/278 (6)	
Umar Gul b Bresnan	3	7/284 (8) 8/289 (9) 10 overs: 55-0	

Mohammad Irfan did not bat.

Bresnan 9–0–53–1; Anderson 10–1–36–1; Broad 10–0–81–4; Yardy 6–0–43–0; Swann 10–0–43–1; Collingwood 5–0–26–1.

England

*A. J. Strauss lbw b Saeed Ajmal	126	M. H. Yardy not out	13
†S. M. Davies c Kamran Akmal b Shoaib Akhtar	26	T. T. Bresnan not out	10
I. J. L. Trott run out	53		
P. D. Collingwood c sub (Azhar Ali) b Shahid Afridi	19	L-b 3, w 13	16
E. J. G. Morgan c Mohammad Hafeez b Umar Gul	16	1/43 (2) 2/189 (3) (6 wkts, 49.3 overs)	295
R. S. Bopara c Mohammad Hafeez b Saeed Ajmal	16	3/220 (4) 4/248 (1)	
		5/265 (5) 6/282 (6) 10 overs: 54-1	

G. P. Swann, S. C. J. Broad and J. M. Anderson did not bat.

Shoaib Akhtar 8–0–49–1; Mohammad Irfan 7–0–40–0; Umar Gul 9.3–0–59–1; Saeed Ajmal 10–0–52–2; Shahid Afridi 9–0–59–1; Mohammad Hafeez 6–0–33–0.

Umpires: B. R. Doctrove and N. J. Llong.   Third umpire: I. J. Gould.

ENGLAND v PAKISTAN

Third One-Day International

At The Oval, September 17 (day/night). Pakistan won by 23 runs. Toss: Pakistan.

Pakistan's emotional celebrations after the first one-day victory of their tour had barely subsided before they were confronted by further newspaper allegations of match-fixing. A few hours after Umar Gul's stunning six-wicket performance had dragged his side back into the NatWest Series, the early editions of *The Sun* hit the streets with claims that scoring patterns during Pakistan's innings had been fixed, and the details had been passed on to the ICC for investigation. The cricket, by now, seemed an irrelevance. The insinuations, doubts and bad blood between the teams overshadowed the sport, although Pakistan's delight at finally defeating England was unconfined, and Gul's career-best figures were a magnificent display of late-swing bowling under the lights in front of a packed crowd. Pakistan had made a piecemeal 241, their batting never getting out of third gear after another poor start. Fawad Alam made a solid 64, but the acceleration did not come. Anderson continued his impressive summer with his own demonstration of swing bowling that ensured the batsmen never flourished. The task appeared straightforward enough for England, but their batting was casual and clumsy. Strauss held the innings together after an early slump, and then Morgan and Wright (playing instead of the unwell Collingwood), seemed to have set up another win with a stand of 98. England should have cruised to victory from there, but Gul was a man inspired as the last five wickets tumbled for 17. Wright had one fortunate escape on 26 when Umar Akmal, standing in as wicketkeeper for his injured brother Kamran, appeared to have stumped him, but Doctrove at square leg infuriated the Pakistanis by not asking for a replay. A month later, after their investigation into *The Sun's* story, the ICC announced there was "no compelling evidence" of wrongdoing during the match, which was given a clean bill of health.

Man of the Match: Umar Gul.   *Attendance:* 19,504.

Pakistan

†Kamran Akmal b Bresnan	5	Saeed Ajmal lbw b Anderson	2	
Mohammad Hafeez c Davies b Anderson	1	Shoaib Akhtar not out	6	
Asad Shafiq c Morgan b Swann	40			
Mohammad Yousuf lbw b Anderson	16	L-b 6, w 8	14	
Fawad Alam c Strauss b Yardy	64			
Umar Akmal c Swann b Bresnan	14	1/8 (2) 2/8 (1) 3/31 (4) (49.4 overs)	241	
*Shahid Afridi run out	34	4/95 (3) 5/121 (6) 6/181 (5)		
Abdul Razzaq c Anderson b Broad	31	7/185 (7) 8/227 (8) 9/234 (10)		
Umar Gul b Bresnan	14	10/241 (9) 10 overs: 31-3		

Bresnan 9.4–1–51–3; Anderson 10–2–26–3; Broad 10–0–45–1; Swann 10–0–53–1; Wright 2–0–18–0; Yardy 8–0–42–1.

England

*A. J. Strauss b Umar Gul	57	S. C. J. Broad b Umar Gul	4	
†S. M. Davies b Abdul Razzaq	18	G. P. Swann c Shahid Afridi b Umar Gul	0	
I. J. L. Trott b Shoaib Akhtar	2	J. M. Anderson b Abdul Razzaq	3	
R. S. Bopara c Kamran Akmal b Saeed Ajmal	7	L-b 6, w 8	14	
E. J. G. Morgan c sub (Wahab Riaz) b Umar Gul	61	1/35 (2) 2/42 (3) 3/77 (4) (45.4 overs)	218	
M. H. Yardy lbw b Umar Gul	4	4/95 (1) 5/103 (6) 6/201 (5)		
L. J. Wright not out	48	7/201 (8) 8/207 (9) 9/211 (10)		
T. T. Bresnan b Umar Gul	0	10/218 (11) 10 overs: 51-2		

Shoaib Akhtar 10–0–43–1; Abdul Razzaq 7.4–0–38–2; Umar Gul 10–0–42–6; Saeed Ajmal 9–0–42–1; Shahid Afridi 9–0–47–0.

Umpires: B. R. Doctrove and R. K. Illingworth. Third umpire: N. J. Llong.

ENGLAND v PAKISTAN

Fourth One-Day International

At Lord's, September 20 (day/night). Pakistan won by 38 runs. Toss: Pakistan.

Pakistan may have levelled the series at 2–2 with a brutal display with both bat and ball, but such hostility on the pitch was nothing compared to the growing tension off it, as relations between the teams and their respective boards hit a new low. With the ICC admitting on the eve of the match that they were launching a full investigation into suspicious scoring patterns in the previous one-day international, and Pakistan captain Shahid Afridi dismissing such claims as "rubbish", what was needed was calm diplomacy. Instead, the PCB chairman Ijaz Butt promptly poured fuel on smouldering embers. In a strident defence of Pakistan's reputation, Butt claimed, among other things, that several of England's players had taken money to throw the previous match at The Oval. Referring to accusations of spot-fixing levelled at the tourists, he said: "This is not a conspiracy to defraud bookies but a conspiracy to defraud Pakistan and Pakistan cricket." He added: "There is loud and clear talk in the bookies circle that some English players have taken enormous amounts of money to lose the match. No wonder there was such a collapse."

Butt's comments prompted a furious and indignant response from both England's dressing-room and the ECB, who in addition to seeking "a full and unreserved apology", under threat of legal action, also promptly withdrew the offer to provide a neutral venue for Pakistan's cricket the following summer. Further threats came from the players who, firmly led by Strauss, issued a strongly worded statement: "We would like to express our surprise, dismay and outrage at the comments. We are deeply concerned that our integrity as cricketers has been brought into question. We refute these allegations completely and will be working closely with the ECB to explore all legal options open to us. Under the circumstances, we have strong misgivings about continuing to play in the last two games of the current series and urge the Pakistani team and management to distance themselves from Mr Butt's allegations."

Simmering tensions also boiled over in the nets before the match, when Trott and Wahab Riaz became involved in a physical confrontation in which the England player reportedly grabbed his opponent by the throat. England's batting coach Graham Gooch had to step in to split the pair up, and the referee Jeff Crowe talked to both captains before the game.

Though several players on both sides were reluctant to play, the match went ahead. There were solid contributions from Pakistan's batsmen. Mohammad Hafeez top-scored with 64, then a clearly pumped-up Afridi hit 37 from 22 balls, before a power-packed finish from Abdul Razzaq, who stole the show with a blistering 40 off his last ten deliveries. His explosion took Pakistan from 223 for seven at the end of the 48th over to 265, and wrested control of the game from English hands; Anderson and Bresnan each conceded 21 from his final over. Strauss and Davies again set the pace of the chase beautifully – reaching 50 in 50 balls and 100 in 101 – and put on 113 before they were separated. But their exits prompted a wobble as Umar Gul and Shoaib Akhtar once again took a shine to bowling under lights. Bell, making his England return after a broken foot, and fresh from a match-winning century for Warwickshire two days earlier in the CB40 final, contributed 27 and Morgan 28, but the rest fell away as Gul and Akhtar got the ball reversing in the final overs, and ripped through England's tail.

Man of the Match: Abdul Razzaq.   *Attendance:* 21,193.

Pakistan

†Kamran Akmal c Strauss b Broad	28	Abdul Razzaq not out	44
Mohammad Hafeez c Trott b Swann	64	Umar Gul not out	5
Asad Shafiq b Swann	11	L-b 19, w 4	23
Mohammad Yousuf c Davies b Swann	3		
Fawad Alam b Swann	29	1/62 (1) 2/86 (3) (7 wkts, 50 overs) 265	
Umar Akmal c Davies b Broad	21	3/94 (4) 4/137 (2)	
*Shahid Afridi c Strauss b Bresnan	37	5/155 (5) 6/209 (7) 7/210 (6) 10 overs: 44-0	

Saeed Ajmal and Shoaib Akhtar did not bat.

Bresnan 10–0–62–1; Anderson 10–1–54–0; Broad 10–0–44–2; Yardy 7–0–39–0; Swann 10–0–37–4; Collingwood 3–0–10–0.

England

*A. J. Strauss c Fawad Alam b Shoaib Akhtar	68	G. P. Swann b Umar Gul	12
†S. M. Davies b Saeed Ajmal	49	S. C. J. Broad b Umar Gul	2
I. J. L. Trott b Shahid Afridi	4	J. M. Anderson not out	2
I. R. Bell c sub (Azhar Ali) b Saeed Ajmal	27	B 4, l-b 1, w 14, n-b 2	21
P. D. Collingwood b Umar Gul	4		
E. J. G. Morgan c Mohammad Yousuf		1/113 (2) 2/125 (3) (46.1 overs) 227	
b Shoaib Akhtar	28	3/127 (1) 4/149 (5) 5/171 (4)	
M. H. Yardy b Shoaib Akhtar	9	6/197 (7) 7/205 (8) 8/211 (6)	
T. T. Bresnan b Umar Gul	1	9/224 (9) 10/227 (10) 10 overs: 73-0	

Shoaib Akhtar 10–0–59–3; Abdul Razzaq 7–0–42–0; Umar Gul 8.1–0–32–4; Mohammad Hafeez 7–0–27–0; Saeed Ajmal 7–0–31–2; Shahid Afridi 7–0–31–1.

Umpires: B. R. Doctrove and R. A. Kettleborough.   Third umpire: R. K. Illingworth.

ENGLAND v PAKISTAN

Fifth One-Day International

At Southampton, September 22 (day/night). England won by 121 runs. Toss: England.

The last act of this strained summer saw England emerge with a 3–2 victory, and their ninth straight series win in all formats of the game (excluding a one-off match against Scotland). Just as importantly, it allowed them to occupy the moral high ground, a position from where Strauss observed it would have been unpalatable for them to have to watch Pakistan celebrate a series win. Calling on the ICC to take a "strong lead" to clear cricket of malign influences, Strauss added: "This summer has clearly demonstrated that when there's a sniff of something in the air it devalues the game, and no one wants to play cricket in those circumstances." Such happy closure seemed unlikely for England at one stage. They slumped to 59 for three after 15 overs, at which point Collingwood returned to the pavilion suffering with a migraine, but Morgan again gave notice that the only thing

Time to say farewell? At the end of a long and fractious series, Stuart Broad and Mohammad Hafeez seem to have had enough of each other.

he likes better than a scrap is one that starts off in a corner. His unbeaten 107 turned out to be the match-winner. It was his fourth one-day international century, and his second at the Rose Bowl following 103 against Australia in June. More importantly in the context of this match, it allowed England to set a total that had looked beyond them earlier. Collingwood returned pain-free to score 47, but Morgan's innings shone brightest. He offered just one clear-cut chance: Mohammad Yousuf caught him at long-on, but had to offload the ball as his momentum took him over the boundary. Morgan's finish was impressive, too, with 54 coming from his last 43 balls, including 16 off a final over from Saeed Ajmal that brought up his century. His excellent work was backed up by the spin of Swann and the bounce and pace of Broad. They both set up – and narrowly failed to convert – hat-trick balls, but still cut through a Pakistan line-up that collapsed after a good start. Kamran Akmal and Mohammad Hafeez had rattled along to 57 in the compulsory powerplay. However, Pakistan found the boundary ropes increasing strangers as the match wore on, failing to hit a four in a block of 23 barren overs from the tenth to the 32nd. By that stage they were teetering at 117 for six, with the match, series and summer as good as done.

Man of the Match: E. J. G. Morgan. *Attendance:* 12,762.

Man of the Series: A. J. Strauss.

England

*A. J. Strauss c Kamran Akmal b Shoaib Akhtar.	25	L. J. Wright b Shoaib Akhtar	1
†S. M. Davies st Kamran Akmal b Mohammad Hafeez.	17	T. T. Bresnan not out.	18
I. J. L. Trott b Shoaib Akhtar	3	L-b 5, w 5	10
I. R. Bell b Shahid Afridi.	28		
P. D. Collingwood b Umar Gul.	47	1/31 (2) 2/46 (3) (6 wkts, 50 overs)	256
E. J. G. Morgan not out	107	3/47 (1) 4/106 (4)	
		5/199 (5) 6/202 (7) 10 overs: 46-2	

G. P. Swann, S. C. J. Broad and J. M. Anderson did not bat.

Collingwood, when 5, retired ill at 59 and resumed at 106.

Shoaib Akhtar 10–0–40–3; Abdul Razzaq 3–0–26–0; Mohammad Hafeez 9–1–40–1; Umar Gul 10–1–55–1; Saeed Ajmal 8–0–50–0; Shahid Afridi 10–0–40–1.

Pakistan

†Kamran Akmal lbw b Wright	41	Saeed Ajmal run out		2
Mohammad Hafeez c Collingwood b Broad	29	Shoaib Akhtar c Morgan b Broad		0
Asad Shafiq c Davies b Broad	0			
Mohammad Yousuf b Swann	20	L-b 3, w 2, n-b 1		6
Fawad Alam b Swann	1			
Umar Akmal c and b Collingwood	19	1/63 (2) 2/63 (3) 3/80 (1)	(37 overs)	135
*Shahid Afridi b Swann	0	4/83 (5) 5/104 (4) 6/104 (7)		
Abdul Razzaq not out	11	7/121 (6) 8/130 (9) 9/135 (10)		
Umar Gul run out	6	10/135 (11)	10 overs: 57-0	

Bresnan 7–0–31–0; Anderson 6–1–26–0; Broad 8–1–25–3; Wright 6–0–16–1; Swann 9–0–26–3; Collingwood 1–0–8–1.

Umpires: B. R. Doctrove and I. J. Gould.   Third umpire: N. J. Llong.
Series referee: J. J. Crowe.

INDIA A AND WEST INDIES A IN ENGLAND, 2010

James Coyne

The triangular format, which had not been used since 2005, was reintroduced in 2010 when the ECB invited two international A-teams to tour simultaneously, presenting the opportunity for a three-way one-day series also involving England Lions. And by pitting the two visitors against each other in unofficial Tests – instead of weakened county opposition – the ECB hoped the longer games would carry more substance. Crowd numbers were not a concern: barely a soul watches A-side matches, no matter where they are. Or so we thought. But more than 1,000 tickets were sold for the second match between India A and West Indies A at Whitgift School, where observers noted a healthy gaggle of Afro-Caribbean supporters.

The West Indies Cricket Board had been keen to send a team, and stepped in when New Zealand asked to postpone their visit for financial reasons. But unlike in 2009, when West Indies' distracted IPL players and youngsters were jetted in to fulfil two unwanted Tests in early May, it was England's turn to accommodate. The WICB requested the first-class games be moved from late July to early June (before the triangular series), so their players could be home in time for the domestic Caribbean T20 competition. As a result, the neutral A-Tests had to be moved from Old Trafford and the Rose Bowl.

The West Indians were captained by Devon Smith, now 28 and making his seventh trip to England with a West Indies team in ten seasons. He batted for almost eight hours on a Croydon shirtfront, and scored two one-day hundreds, taking his tally of centuries in the British Isles to nine but, infuriatingly, none in a proper international. The success story was 22-year-old Andre Russell, a tall, genuinely quick bowler who had scored a hundred in his eighth first-class game for Jamaica. He was lethal with the wearing ball, especially against the previously unflustered Indians at Leicester. Russell thought it no accident; he had spent six weeks playing in the Worcestershire League as preparation. His progress excited West Indies coach Ottis Gibson, and won him a Test debut at Galle in November.

India provided the artistry. They tested the patience of umpires and opposition with deplorable over-rates, but there was no doubting their ability. The top four, all aged under 24 – Abhinav Mukund, Shikhar Dhawan, Ajinkya Rahane and captain Cheteshwar Pujara – landed with 40 first-class centuries between them, and departed with three more. Every member of the squad had played in the IPL. On flat pitches in the Midlands, this made for an astonishingly high-scoring triangular series, where the average first-innings score in seven games was 310 (and not always enough to win).

Pujara, a methodical, classical off-side player, scored 776 runs in 11 innings on tour, and failed only twice. He batted at his own pace, sometimes to the detriment of his team, as in the triangular final at Worcester. "I kept running in, and he kept gently patting the ball back, which was quite pleasing," said Lions bowler Peter Trego.

Jaydev Unadkat was only 18, but had the finest of tutors, the left-arm fast bowler nonpareil, Wasim Akram, his bowling coach at Kolkata Knight Riders. Unadkat too could move the ball both ways, from an upright, front-on action. He took 13 of his 20 wickets in one showing, on first-class debut at Leicester. The other bowlers, Dhawal Kulkarni aside, often went missing, particularly in the first match at Glasgow, when Scotland made one of the great comebacks.

The England management used the tournament to the full. They shuffled fringe players to and from the senior side, who were competing concurrently in one-day series against Australia and Bangladesh. Alastair Cook, the Lions captain, sustained a back problem in the opening game, but recovered in time for the final. Three other batsmen – Jonathan Trott, Ravi Bopara and Ian Bell – scored dominant centuries before returning, with success, to one-day international cricket. For Bopara, his 168 from 140 balls at New Road – 12 months on from his Ashes baptism – was almost cathartic. "I try not to think too much these days," said Bopara. "Nasser Hussain told me to go out and enjoy my cricket. He said, 'take it from someone who tried too hard'." Bell made an assertive 158, and two days later he was under lights at Trent Bridge, beating Bangladesh with 84 not out in his first one-day international since November 2008.

INDIA A TOURING PARTY

*C. A. Pujara, S. Dhawan, C. Ganapathy, Iqbal Abdulla, K. M. Jadhav, Jaskaran Singh, D. S. Kulkarni, A. Mithun, A. Mukund, M. K. Pandey, A. M. Rahane, W. P. Saha, B. Sharma, M. K. Tiwary, S. S. Tiwary, S. Tyagi, J. D. Unadkat. *Coach:* P. K. Amre. *Manager:* S. Dixit.

Ganapathy was added to the party before departure, when Mithun was called up to the senior India squad in Zimbabwe. Mithun joined the A squad ahead of the triangular series. S. S. Tiwary left on June 7, when named in the India squad for the Asia Cup.

WEST INDIES A TOURING PARTY

*D. S. Smith, L. S. Baker, D. E. Bernard, K. C. Brathwaite, D. M. Bravo, O. V. Brown, K. A. Edwards, A. D. S. Fletcher, A. B. Fudadin, J. C. Guillen, I. Khan, O. J. Phillips, A. D. Russell, G. C. Tonge, C. A. K. Walton. *Coach:* H. W. D. Springer.

Bravo and N. T. Pascal were originally selected, but called up to the senior West Indies squad for the home one-day series against South Africa, and replaced by Fudadin and Russell. N. O. Miller and K. A. Pollard were due to join for the triangular series, but Miller was withdrawn, while Pollard played for the senior West Indies team, and then Somerset. For the one-day leg, A. Martin and K. A. Stoute replaced Brathwaite, Brown and Guillen. Bravo joined midway through the triangular series.

GLAMORGAN v WEST INDIES A

At Cardiff, June 5–7. Drawn. Toss: Glamorgan.

Rain aborted a challenging run-chase for the West Indians in their tour opener. After a fine start, the visiting bowlers lost their way on the first afternoon, allowing David Brown and Shantry to cheerily add 98 for the ninth wicket. Brown struck his namesake, the Jamaican leg-spinner Odean, for four sixes, but after No. 11 Ashling survived an over from Gavin Tonge, Brown picked up mid-off one shy of a maiden hundred on first-class debut for Glamorgan. The West Indians went on to concede four wickets to Croft and a 110-run deficit. In the short time available on the last day, Nick James completed a patient half-century in his second first-class match, while Croft raced to his in 57 balls by upper-cutting Tonge for six. Maynard (at 21 years and 72 days, the youngest man to captain Glamorgan) declared with a lead of 286 and 66 overs remaining, but rain arrived at 3.05 p.m. to kill the game. Croft was left stranded on 997 first-class wickets for Glamorgan, through six weeks of Twenty20 cricket and his omission at Northampton, until Leicestershire visited Swansea.

Close of play: First day, West Indies A 11-2 (Phillips 6, Fletcher 1); Second day, Glamorgan 126-6 (James 36, Croft 33).

Glamorgan

G. P. Rees b Brown	55	– lbw b Tonge		0
†W. D. Bragg b Baker	0	– run out		0
*T. L. Maynard b Baker	0	– lbw b Baker		21
B. J. Wright lbw b Tonge	17	– lbw b Tonge		9
M. J. Powell c Walton b Brown	25	– lbw b Baker		0
N. A. James c Baker b Brown	15	– not out		60
D. O. Brown c Khan b Brown	99	– c Phillips b Khan		15
R. D. B. Croft c Fletcher b Tonge	4	– not out		56
W. T. Owen b Brown	0			
A. J. Shantry c Smith b Tonge	22			
C. P. Ashling not out	8			
B 5, l-b 5, n-b 6	16	B 5, l-b 1, w 4, n-b 5		15

1/4 (2) 2/8 (3) 3/31 (4) 4/84 (5) (82.2 overs) 261 1/5 (1) (6 wkts dec, 52 overs) 176
5/105 (1) 6/122 (6) 7/132 (8) 2/7 (2) 3/27 (3)
8/137 (9) 9/235 (10) 10/261 (7) 4/27 (5) 5/46 (4) 6/76 (7)

Tonge 20–5–53–3; Baker 19–7–49–2; Fudadin 9–1–27–0; Brown 25.2–4–92–5; Khan 9–2–30–0. *Second Innings*—Tonge 16–4–53–2; Baker 16–6–53–2; Khan 8–2–18–1; Fudadin 5–0–15–0; Brown 7–0–31–0.

West Indies A

*D. S. Smith b Owen	0	– not out		34
J. C. Guillen c Maynard b Owen	3	– c Bragg b Shantry		0
O. J. Phillips c Powell b Ashling	9	– not out		19
A. D. S. Fletcher lbw b Ashling	26			
K. A. Edwards lbw b Ashling	8			
A. B. Fudadin c Maynard b Croft	3			
†C. A. K. Walton c Brown b Croft	34			
I. Khan c Bragg b Owen	33			
L. S. Baker b Croft	6			
G. C. Tonge st Bragg b Croft	19			
O. V. Brown not out	0			
B 2, l-b 6, w 2	10	L-b 5		5

1/0 (1) 2/5 (2) 3/28 (3) 4/40 (5) (45.3 overs) 151 1/6 (2) (1 wkt, 10 overs) 58
5/53 (6) 6/53 (4) 7/121 (8) 8/121 (7)
9/132 (9) 10/151 (10)

Owen 14–2–65–3; Shantry 10–3–20–0; Ashling 10–2–18–3; Croft 10.3–2–39–4; James 1–0–1–0. *Second Innings*—Owen 4–0–28–0; Shantry 4–1–21–1; Ashling 1.1–0–4–0; Croft 1–1–0–0.

Umpires: P. K. Baldwin and R. T. Robinson.

YORKSHIRE v INDIA A

At Leeds, June 5–7. Drawn. Toss: India A. First-class debuts: A. Z. Lees, J. R. Lowe, C. G. Roebuck; Jaskaran Singh.

Yorkshire retained none of the eleven that played a Friends Provident T20 match at Worcester the previous evening, and neither their replacements, nor unfamiliar conditions, could faze the next generation of Indian batsmen. Charlie Roebuck, one of seven Yorkshire players aged under 21, dropped Shikhar Dhawan on ten; the left-handed opening pair forged on to 204. Dhawan was particularly ruthless off his legs in his first century outside India. On the eve of his 22nd birthday, Ajinkya Rahane underlined his fondness for English bowlers – he hit 172 for West Zone against England Lions in Vadodara in early 2008 – and it took Best, a Barbadian armed with the second new ball, to unseat him. With 473 runs conceded by the close, Yorkshire were relieved when Cheteshwar Pujara declared before play could resume on a rain-ruined second day. The home batsmen found scoring tough, allowing Dhawal Kulkarni and Iqbal Abdulla 18 maidens to go with their nine wickets. Sayers captained Yorkshire in what proved his last first-team game before suffering post-viral fatigue syndrome.

Close of play: First day, India A 473-3 (Pujara 55, Pandey 11); Second day, Yorkshire 20-2 (Sayers 4, Roebuck 3).

India A

A. Mukund c Hodgson b Ashraf	91
S. Dhawan c Ballance b Hodgson	179
A. M. Rahane c Root b Best	118
*C. A. Pujara not out	55
M. K. Pandey not out	11
B 12, l-b 4, n-b 3	19

1/204 (1) 2/345 (2) 3/452 (3) (3 wkts dec, 95 overs) 473

M. K. Tiwary, †W. P. Saha, D. S. Kulkarni, Iqbal Abdulla, Jaskaran Singh and S. Tyagi did not bat.

Best 14–1–66–1; Hannon-Dalby 17–3–73–0; Hodgson 16–2–86–1; Ashraf 16–1–71–1; Wainwright 25–1–134–0; Root 7–0–27–0.

Yorkshire

J. E. Root c Saha b Kulkarni	4	†J. R. Lowe run out	5
*J. J. Sayers c Iqbal Abdulla b Kulkarni	19	O. J. Hannon-Dalby not out	8
G. S. Ballance b Kulkarni	0	M. A. Ashraf lbw b Iqbal Abdulla	5
C. G. Roebuck c Iqbal Abdulla b Kulkarni	23		
A. Z. Lees c Pujara b Kulkarni	38	L-b 16, w 1, n-b 7	24
D. J. Wainwright lbw b Iqbal Abdulla	19		
L. J. Hodgson c sub (S. S. Tiwary) b Iqbal Abdulla	34	1/4 (1) 2/6 (3) 3/54 (4) (91.2 overs) 219
T. L. Best b Iqbal Abdulla	40	4/57 (5) 5/93 (6) 6/151 (5)

1/4 (1) 2/6 (3) 3/54 (4) (91.2 overs) 219
4/57 (5) 5/93 (6) 6/151 (5)
7/165 (7) 8/186 (9) 9/204 (8) 10/219 (11)

Kulkarni 20–6–31–5; Tyagi 5–2–4–0; Jaskaran Singh 22–3–77–0; Pandey 2–0–12–0; Iqbal Abdulla 27.2–12–42–4; Dhawan 4–1–15–0; Tiwary 5–1–14–0; Mukund 3–1–3–0; Rahane 3–1–5–0.

Umpires: R. J. Bailey and A. Hicks.

INDIA A v WEST INDIES A

At Leicester, June 10–13. India A won by six wickets. Toss: India A. First-class debut: J. D. Unadkat.

The 50 or so spectators who witnessed Jaydev Unadkat's debut will never forget it: he took 13 for 103 with high-class, unpredictable left-arm swing, and at a pace comparable to James Anderson, in the estimation of umpire Jeremy Lloyds. His figures were the finest by a first-class debutant in 36 years. Following a first-day washout, Unadkat, unafraid to change his line of attack, tore through the incapable West Indians inside two sessions. India fared better, although from 202 for three on the third morning, their serenity was rocked by Andre Russell, who took four wickets in 19 deliveries with the old ball. Abdulla's wicket gave Russell career-best figures, but Kulkarni survived the next ball to deny him a hat-trick. Unadkat returned, darting the ball back into the right-handers to win four lbw verdicts in the innings. Only when he tired did the ninth-wicket pair lend the score some respectability. India almost botched their chase of 111: they meandered to 71 for three in 21 overs going into the last session but, perturbed by dark clouds, Rahane hastily knocked off the rest. Minutes later, the ground was drenched. Lloyds called India's over-rate "dreadful", but as this was a non-competition match, the umpires could issue no punishment.

BEST MATCH FIGURES ON FIRST-CLASS DEBUT SINCE 1945

15-102 (8-58, 7-44)	Nadeem Malik	Lahore Reds v Sargodha at Lahore	1973-74
14-100 (7-56, 7-44)	F. Fee	Ireland v MCC at Dublin (College Park)	1956
13-71 (9-35, 4-36)	V. B. Ranjane	Maharashtra v Saurashtra at Khadakvasla	1956-57
13-103 (7-41, 6-62)	**J. D. Unadkat**	**India A v West Indies A at Leicester**	**2010**
13-107 (7-53, 6-54)	G. V. Kumar	Karnataka v Tamil Nadu at Bangalore	1977-78
13-146 (4-24, 9-122)	G. G. Hall	South African Universities v Western Province at Cape Town	1960-61

Close of play: First day, No play; Second day, India A 183-2 (Rahane 66, Pujara 34); Third day, West Indies A 125-5 (Edwards 7, Bernard 0).

West Indies A

*D. S. Smith c Pandey b Unadkat	5	– b Ganapathy	37
K. C. Brathwaite c Tiwary b Unadkat	13	– lbw b Unadkat	1
O. J. Phillips lbw b Unadkat	6	– b Unadkat	35
A. D. S. Fletcher c Mukund b Kulkarni	20	– run out	14
K. A. Edwards lbw b Unadkat	1	– c Pujara b Iqbal Abdulla	18
†C. A. K. Walton b Unadkat	0	– lbw b Unadkat	13
D. E. Bernard lbw b Iqbal Abdulla	22	– b Unadkat	0
I. Khan c Tiwary b Unadkat	28	– lbw b Unadkat	62
A. D. Russell c Pujara b Kulkarni	19	– lbw b Iqbal Abdulla	1
L. S. Baker b Unadkat	3	– (11) not out	1
G. C. Tonge not out	9	– (10) b Unadkat	46
B 5, l-b 11, w 1, n-b 1	18	B 8, l-b 17, w 2, n-b 2	29

1/5 (1) 2/17 (3) 3/26 (2) 4/63 (5) (43.3 overs) 144
5/63 (4) 6/63 (6) 7/113 (8) 8/113 (7)
9/116 (10) 10/144 (9)

1/16 (2) 2/75 (1) (81.5 overs) 257
3/102 (3) 4/106 (4)
5/125 (6) 6/125 (7) 7/164 (5)
8/176 (9) 9/256 (8) 10/257 (10)

Kulkarni 13.3–6–41–2; Unadkat 18–6–41–7; Ganapathy 7–2–24–0; Iqbal Abdulla 5–1–22–1. *Second Innings*—Kulkarni 24–6–70–0; Unadkat 27.5–9–62–6; Ganapathy 12–3–53–1; Iqbal Abdulla 15–4–40–2; Tiwary 3–1–7–0.

India A

A. Mukund lbw b Khan	54	– run out	17
S. Dhawan c Smith b Tonge	17	– b Russell	21
A. M. Rahane c sub (J. C. Guillen) b Russell	69	– not out	33
*C. A. Pujara c Smith b Tonge	44	– lbw b Baker	15
M. K. Pandey c Smith b Russell	6	– (6) not out	1
M. K. Tiwary b Russell	2	– (5) c Walton b Baker	19
†W. P. Saha lbw b Baker	50		
C. Ganapathy c Walton b Russell	1		
Iqbal Abdulla b Russell	0		
D. S. Kulkarni c Walton b Baker	13		
J. D. Unadkat not out	12		
L-b 8, w 12, n-b 3	23	L-b 4, w 4	8

1/48 (2) 2/130 (1) 3/188 (3) (91.5 overs) 291
4/202 (5) 5/206 (6) 6/206 (4)
7/207 (8) 8/207 (9) 9/230 (10) 10/291 (7)

1/40 (2) (4 wkts, 26.4 overs) 114
2/40 (1) 3/67 (4)
4/109 (5)

Tonge 26–3–86–2; Baker 16.5–3–55–2; Russell 27–9–68–5; Bernard 13–2–36–0; Khan 8–0–33–1; Smith 1–0–5–0. *Second Innings*—Bernard 6–0–22–0; Tonge 3–0–15–0; Russell 10–1–42–1; Baker 7.4–0–31–2.

Umpires: R. J. Bailey and J. W. Lloyds.

INDIA A v WEST INDIES A

At Whitgift School, Croydon, June 17–20. Drawn. Toss: India A.

After a deserted Leicester, more than 1,000 flocked to Whitgift School's international debut, complete with three hospitality tents and curry provided by local chefs. If only the cricket, played by underpowered attacks on a dry wicket and short boundaries, had been half as spicy. The exception was Russell, who persevered to take four of the last five wickets, but could not shift the Indian captain. Pujara, driving straight and precisely, had the perfect environment to satisfy his appetite for runs; he passed 150 for the seventh time out of 14 hundreds, and pressed on to a third double before declaring on 543, coincidentally the same score South Africa made in the St Kitts Test the next day. Smith dropped down to No. 4 and, with maiden centurion Andre Fletcher, dug in for most of the third day to add 225. Smith grew fatigued approaching his eighth hour in the middle, but Bernard and Tonge swung lustily, clearing the ropes six times and prompting the biggest cheer of all when they took their side into the lead.

Close of play: First day, India A 329-5 (Pujara 111, Saha 32); Second day, West Indies A 12-1 (Phillips 9, Fletcher 0); Third day, West Indies A 332-3 (Smith 131, Edwards 19).

India A

A. Mukund c Brathwaite b Russell	39	Jaskaran Singh c Walton b Bernard	58
S. Dhawan c Walton b Tonge	43	D. S. Kulkarni not out	2
A. M. Rahane c Smith b Russell	13		
*C. A. Pujara not out	208	B 16, l-b 2, w 7, n-b 9	34
M. K. Pandey c Khan b Russell	36		
M. K. Tiwary c Smith b Tonge	36	(8 wkts dec, 149 overs)	543
†W. P. Saha c Walton b Russell	62		
Iqbal Abdulla c Khan b Russell	12		

J. D. Unadkat did not bat.

1/69 (1) 2/100 (2) 3/102 (3) 4/191 (5) 5/237 (6) 6/373 (7) 7/385 (8) 8/522 (9)

Tonge 30–8–114–2; Baker 21–2–57–0; Russell 31–8–97–5; Bernard 35–5–102–1; Khan 27–1–136–0; Fletcher 5–0–19–0.

West Indies A

K. C. Brathwaite lbw b Unadkat	3	G. C. Tonge c Dhawan b Unadkat	54
O. J. Phillips b Jaskaran Singh	22	L. S. Baker not out	2
A. D. S. Fletcher c Pandey b Unadkat	123		
*D. S. Smith lbw b Dhawan	170	B 26, l-b 11, w 1, n-b 20	58
K. A. Edwards c Saha b Iqbal Abdulla	40		
†C. A. K. Walton st Saha b Iqbal Abdulla	4	(169.4 overs)	563
D. E. Bernard c and b Tiwary	70		
I. Khan c Mukund b Iqbal Abdulla	0		
A. D. Russell c Pujara b Tiwary	17		

1/11 (1) 2/54 (2) 3/279 (5) 4/402 (5) 5/402 (4) 6/411 (6) 7/413 (8) 8/477 (9) 9/528 (7) 10/563 (10)

Kulkarni 30–6–111–0; Unadkat 37.4–9–100–3; Jaskaran Singh 23–3–97–1; Iqbal Abdulla 50–9–128–3; Tiwary 24–1–72–2; Dhawan 5–1–18–1.

Umpires: M. J. D. Bodenham and R. K. Illingworth.

At Belfast, June 23, 2010. **West Indies A won by 50 runs.** ‡**West Indies A 251** (49.5 overs) (A. B. Fudadin 50, K. A. Stoute 61, A. D. Russell 64; P. S. Eaglestone 3-48, K. J. O'Brien 3-43); **Ireland 201** (48.1 overs) (A. R. White 75, Extras 31; A. D. Russell 6-42). *Andre Russell produced a stunning all-round display, the best of his one-day career, deciding the result almost single-handedly. Arriving in the 39th over with West Indies 150-7, he blasted six fours and four sixes, accounting for 64 of the last 101 runs. He then removed Ireland's top three, and forced Andrew White to chop on after his highest List A score. White badly missed a hitter in the middle order to accompany him.*

At Glasgow, June 23, 2010. **Scotland won by one wicket. India A 276-9** (50 overs) (A. M. Rahane 108, M. K. Pandey 32, M. K. Tiwary 71; G. Goudie 4-46, R. D. Berrington 3-45); ‡**Scotland 277-9** (49.3 overs) (R. D. Berrington 106, M. M. Iqbal 67, Extras 31; S. Tyagi 3-45, D. S. Kulkarni 3-50). *From 64-7, Richie Berrington and Moneeb Iqbal scripted one of the great comebacks in one-day cricket. With the field up and India's over-excited bowlers dropping short, Berrington hooked* superbly and Iqbal drove eagerly; they amassed 174 in 26 overs (just 13 runs short of Scotland's eighth-wicket record in all cricket, by James Henderson and William Edward against Ireland at Paisley in 1954). With four needed from the last over, Iqbal was run out backing up, but Gordon Goudie cut for the winning runs. Even in victory, Scotland were unhappy with India's go-slow tactics: they took four hours and ten minutes to bowl their overs. "If a captain had resorted to this in an official ODI he would have been looking at a ban of at least one game," said assistant coach Tony Judd.

At Belfast, June 25, 2010. **West Indies A won by eight wickets.** ‡Ireland 217 (46 overs) (K. J. O'Brien 37, A. D. Poynter 64, A. R. White 57; D. E. Bernard 3-24, I. Khan 3-44); **West Indies A 220-2** (38.2 overs) (D. S. Smith 114, A. D. S. Fletcher 81*). *Andrew Poynter scored a maiden half-century and added 88 with fifth-wicket partner Andrew White, but Ireland lost their last six in 13.2 overs. Devon Smith sauntered to a century in 88 balls, and shared 130 for the second wicket with Andre Fletcher.*

At Glasgow, June 25, 2010. **India A won by 152 runs.** ‡India A 281-7 (50 overs) (A. Mukund 50, C. A. Pujara 122*; M. K. Tiwary 41; R. D. Berrington 3-70); **Scotland 129** (35.3 overs) (M. M. Iqbal 33; D. S. Kulkarni 5-29, Iqbal Abdulla 3-21). *After their humiliation two days earlier, India brutally re-established their supremacy. Pujara batted 40 overs for his highest one-day score, and his stand of 83 with Abhinav Mukund was only ended by a questionable run-out decision. Moneeb Iqbal was promoted to No. 5, but could not reprise his heroics.*

A-TEAM TRIANGULAR SERIES

1. England Lions   2. India A   3. West Indies A

ENGLAND LIONS SQUAD

*A. N. Cook, R. S. Bopara, S. M. Davies, A. W. Gale, S. I. Mahmood, L. E. Plunkett, D. I. Stevens, J. W. A. Taylor, J. C. Tredwell, P. D. Trego, I. J. L. Trott, C. R. Woakes. Coach: D. Parsons.

I. R. Bell and A. Shahzad were temporarily released from the England squad for the one-day series against Australia, and made available to the Lions on June 28. Bell, Shahzad, Tredwell and Trott returned to the England one-day squad to face Bangladesh on July 6. Tredwell was replaced in the Lions squad by S. D. Parry.

At Northampton, June 28, 2010. **West Indies A won by 166 runs. West Indies A 329-6** (50 overs) (D. S. Smith 104, A. D. S. Fletcher 88, K. A. Stoute 52*, A. D. Russell 42); ‡India A 163 (33.2 overs) (C. A. Pujara 31, Jaskaran Singh 51; A. Martin 3-47). *West Indies A 5pts. Openers Devon Smith and Andre Fletcher blazed 193 in the first 30.3 overs, until Smith was run out after 98 balls, having scored his fourth one-day century. West Indies never looked back, and earned a bonus point.*

At Northampton, June 29, 2010. **England Lions won by five wickets.** ‡West Indies A 279-6 (50 overs) (K. A. Edwards 147, A. B. Fudadin 51); **England Lions 281-5** (48.4 overs) (A. N. Cook 71, I. J. L. Trott 118, I. R. Bell 44; G. C. Tonge 3-55). *England Lions 4pts. Smith bumped back down to earth, out to the first delivery of the match from Ajmal Shahzad (10–2–25–2), whose first five overs cost just six runs. Kirk Edwards's memorable and destructive maiden hundred included three sixes, one of which hit the roof of the Lynn Wilson Indoor School. Cook and Trott scored freely in a stand of 113, and Trott, keeping the powerplay in reserve, waltzed to his second one-day hundred of the season.*

At Leicester, July 1, 2010. **England Lions won by five wickets. India A 254** (49.3 overs) (A. Mukund 39, C. A. Pujara 73, W. P. Saha 35; A. Shahzad 3-56, R. S. Bopara 3-32); ‡**England Lions 255-5** (45.3 overs) (I. R. Bell 31, R. S. Bopara 41, D. I. Stevens 58*, P. D. Trego 48*). *England Lions 4pts. Cook sat out the match with a back problem, passing the captaincy to Gale. Bopara bowled superbly on a wicket offering little assistance, taking three wickets in five overs to slow India mid-innings. All the Lions batsmen contributed to a methodical chase. Trego dealt two huge blows at Iqbal Abdulla in the same over, and wrapped up the match alongside Stevens, a former Leicestershire batsman, in their stand of 90*.*

At Leicester, July 2, 2010. **India A won by 53 runs. India A 340-6** (50 overs) (A. Mukund 36, S. Dhawan 59, A. M. Rahane 90, C. A. Pujara 114); ‡**West Indies A 287-7** (50 overs) (A. D. S. Fletcher 38, D. M. Bravo 83, A. D. Russell 49, K. A. Stoute 30*, D. E. Bernard 33; A. Mithun 3-49). *India A 4pts. India were hauled back into the series by their vaunted top order, chiefly Pujara, who* *gracefully compiled 114 from 90 balls, his third century of the tour. Darren Bravo, playing his first competitive match in England, offered West Indies' only hope until he was fifth out.*

At Worcester, July 4, 2010. **England Lions won by 124 runs.** ‡England Lions 345 (49.1 overs) (S. M. Davies 34, R. S. Bopara 168, D. I. Stevens 43, P. D. Trego 73; G. C. Tonge 4-69, A. D. Russell 3-75); **West Indies A 221** (40 overs) (D. M. Bravo 62, K. A. Stoute 64; P. D. Trego 5-40, R. S. Bopara 4-43). *England Lions 5pts. Bopara and Trego's finest all-round performances in one-day cricket swept the Lions into the final with a bonus-point victory. They lost Gale to a snorter from Gavin Tonge first ball, and were 14-3, before Bopara started tearing into ill-conceived bowling. "There were some bizarre tactics," said Trego, batting at the other end. "Their right-armers were coming around the wicket and planting it on Ravi's pads, and he's not bad off his legs." Bopara contemplated the second one-day double-century of his career, but picked out midwicket needing 32 with 28 balls to go. Trego's blows ensured the highest total of the series. West Indies were teetering even before Bopara removed Stoute and Russell within three balls; he was beaten to a five-for by Trego, just his second in 96 List A matches.*

At Worcester, July 6, 2010. **Tied.** ‡England Lions 343-8 (50 overs) (S. M. Davies 54, I. R. Bell 158, D. I. Stevens 64); **India A 343-8** (50 overs) (A. Mukund 114, S. Dhawan 46, M. K. Tiwary 46, W. P. Saha 36*; L. E. Plunkett 4-58). *England Lions 2pts, India A 2pts. Abdulla was run out attempting a second run, which left India needing two to win off the last ball. Bopara slipped a yorker under Abhimanyu Mithun's flailing bat, but wicketkeeper Davies could not gather, and India scrambled a bye to tie the game and score the two points necessary to pip West Indies to the final. Bell, captain for the day, constructed his sixth and highest one-day century, setting a seemingly insurmountable benchmark. Mukund matched him for skilful accumulation, scoring only 48 in boundaries.*

England Lions 15pts, India A 6pts, West Indies A 5pts.

At Manchester, July 8, 2010. **Lancashire won by 53 runs.** ‡Lancashire 271 (50 overs) (L. A. Procter 97, K. R. Brown 56, G. D. Cross 30; K. A. Stoute 8-52); **West Indies A 218** (43.4 overs) (A. D. S. Fletcher 30, I. Khan 74; G. Keedy 3-34). *West Indies' consolation prize for missing out on the final was a trip to Old Trafford. Luke Procter holed out at deep square leg three shy of a maiden hundred, and his vanquisher, Kevin Stoute, took the next seven wickets, finishing with a return catch off Keedy. His figures were the ninth-best in one-day history, and the second eight-for against Lancashire, after another Barbadian quick bowler, Keith Boyce, who took 8-26 for Essex in a John Player League match here in May 1971. Stoute finished on the losing side because of Keedy, who took three wickets in 11 balls in his first appearance since breaking his collarbone in a pre-season match.*

FINAL

At Worcester, July 8, 2010. **England Lions won by five wickets. India A 278-7** (50 overs) (A. Mukund 62, S. Dhawan 39, C. A. Pujara 87*; S. D. Parry 3-48); ‡England Lions 279-5 (48.4 overs) (S. M. Davies 55, A. W. Gale 90, R. S. Bopara 30, D. I. Stevens 68). *No score below 329 batting first had been enough to win all series, and India's comparatively subdued innings on a new wicket did not seriously threaten the Lions' march to the trophy. Pujara was unable to manipulate the strike: he faced only 89 balls in 35 overs, and watched two partners waste deliveries before they fell to Parry. With Trott and Bell missing, and Cook out cheaply, Gale expertly underpinned the run-chase. After he was caught behind with 60 needed, Stevens hit four fours and a six.*

LV= COUNTY CHAMPIONSHIP, 2010

NEVILLE SCOTT

The first six months of 2010 were the driest in England since 1929, when Nottinghamshire won their sole title in a span of 74 years. That success was followed, weeks later, by the Wall Street crash, before a decade of economic despair and a world war. Nottinghamshire were presumably not to blame.

But they were responsible, last season, for shredding supporters' nerves in the most nail-biting finish to a Championship since the crown was last shared in 1977. In an age of winners, no fewer than five tie-breakers now ensure that hung titles are impossible. With points equal, **Nottinghamshire** prevailed over **Somerset** only by virtue of having claimed one more win.

The dry start was critical. By mid-May when, astonishingly, 30% of the overall race was already run, Nottinghamshire had won all four of their opening games – three at home – and led Somerset by 54 points with a match in hand. Their ultimate rivals were not even seen as nuisances then. Somerset had begun with away defeats by Yorkshire and Nottinghamshire, and no victory in their first five games. By the time they got going, it was fractionally too late. Rain would crucially affect three second-half matches at Taunton.

COUNTY CHAMPIONSHIP TABLE

					Bonus points			
Division One	Matches	Won	Lost	Drawn	Batting	Bowling	Penalty	Points
1 – Nottinghamshire (**2**)...	16	7	5	4	47	43	0	214
2 – Somerset (**3**).........	16	6	2	8	53	41	0	214
3 – Yorkshire (**7**)........	16	6	2	8	41	42	0	203
4 – Lancashire (**4**).......	16	5	3	8	35	43	0	182
5 – Durham (**1**)...........	16	5	3	8	30	39	0	173
6 – Warwickshire (**5**).....	16	6	9	1	20	47	0	166
7 – Hampshire (**6**).......	16	3	6	7	47	41	0	157
8 – Kent (*1*).............	16	3	7	6	42	44	1	151
9 – Essex (*2*).............	16	2	6	8	29	43	2	126

					Bonus points			
Division Two	Matches	Won	Lost	Drawn	Batting	Bowling	Penalty	Points
1 – Sussex (**8**)...........	16	8	3	5	45	47	0	235
2 – Worcestershire (**9**)	16	7	4	5	39	42	0	208
3 – Glamorgan (*5*)	16	7	4	5	33	43	0	203
4 – Leicestershire (*9*)	16	7	5	4	31	44	0	199
5 – Gloucestershire (*4*) ..	16	6	9	1	28	47	2	172
6 – Northamptonshire (*3*)..	16	6	7	3	28	34	0	167
7 – Surrey (*7*)...........	16	4	6	6	43	36	2	159
8 – Middlesex (*8*)	16	4	7	5	37	41	2	155
9 – Derbyshire (*6*)	16	3	7	6	30	42	0	138

2009 positions are shown in brackets: Division One in bold, Division Two in italic.

* Includes one match abandoned.

Win = 16pts; draw = 3pts. Penalties were deducted for slow over-rates.

Richard Heathcote, Getty Images

The very point of victory: Andre Adams is mobbed after taking Lancashire's third wicket, the moment Nottinghamshire gained the bonus point that won the Championship.

And more rain seemed set to reduce the final round to farce. Avidly awaited, it began with Nottinghamshire two points clear of Somerset, seven ahead of **Yorkshire**. But, with satellite television recording every drop, the elements granted only 28 overs in three days at Old Trafford, where Nottinghamshire were attempting to play Lancashire. At Chester-le-Street, anxiety was marginally less acute. Somerset had managed maximum bonus points during play extended to permit an early finish on day four, when they were booked to fly south for the 40-over final at Lord's. It meant that 84 overs remained when Durham resumed, 31 ahead, with eight second-innings wickets in hand.

"At that time, we thought Yorkshire were the bigger threat," said Marcus Trescothick, the Somerset captain. He was undoubtedly right. In the wild excitement that ensued six hours later, it was widely missed that Yorkshire had in fact blown the clearest chance of the title. In Leeds, they added 42 rapid runs to reach 93 for one against a **Kent** side that had played without conviction all summer and were effectively already condemned. Yorkshire's admirably young, largely home-grown team had never been bowled out twice in the same match all season. Yet, with a lead of 52, and pressing too desperately for triumph, they now lost nine wickets in 55 balls, three to a James Tredwell hat-trick. Youth had finally succumbed to panic. The very fact that Kent, on a dodgy pitch, surrendered six wickets making the 90 they needed to win emphasised how great a chance had slipped.

So part of Nottinghamshire's gamble had paid off. At dinner the night before, they had discussed manufacturing a run-chase in their own match. But they resolved, instead, to bank on Yorkshire and Somerset not winning. This assumption, though brave, was the easy bit. They now had to find six bonus points on the field, with yet another hour lost to Manchester's damp at the start.

From 89 for two, they needed 400 runs and three wickets. Or 350 and six. At 172 for four before lunch, their bid stood in the balance. But Adam Voges and Samit Patel (who was having a poor season, with only ten runs in his four previous innings) hammered 153 at 5.5 per over to put full batting points in tantalising reach.

At Chester-le-Street, in contrast, strokeplay had ceased. Events were 100 miles distant, but 50 years in the past. Determined not to yield the title on their own ground, Durham made 32 runs in the afternoon session but lost only one wicket, their sixth. The honour of cricket north of Charnwood Forest had been preserved and, when eventually dug out, they left Somerset to make 181 from 17 overs. Even as Trescothick led a chase that was never really on, Nottinghamshire were faltering in Manchester.

From 325 for four they fell to 390 for nine, each man going to the left-arm spin of 21-year-old Simon Kerrigan, a product, like Andrew Flintoff, of a Preston comprehensive school. He thus claimed the third five-wicket bag of his maiden Championship season. If this were not redolent enough of a ripping yarn, Nottinghamshire's last two batsmen, Ryan Sidebottom and Darren Pattinson, were now required to make ten runs to complete the 400. And they got 'em in singles.

As Somerset called off their chase to concede the draw, Nottinghamshire had 18 overs in which to grasp three wickets and take one more point. After light rain, a low sun now shone at Old Trafford. For once, it was an intruder. With the east–west pitch set to be realigned in the winter, the glare had already halted play early the previous evening. Good light might mock them yet. But, wicketless for 3.2 overs, Nottinghamshire peremptorily whipped out three men in eight balls and, 38 minutes from the close of a five-month campaign, they seized their second Championship title in six summers. It merited a *Times* editorial next morning.

At Worcester, they still waited. For one final issue remained. Sussex, their promotion confirmed eight days before on the same afternoon that Essex were relegated, had set **Worcestershire** 301 to win in 70 overs, a target stiffer than it looked. But, disregarding a poor pitch, the home side romped in with more than an hour to spare. They now hung on for news from Cardiff. There, **Glamorgan** needed five Derbyshire wickets in the last 55 minutes if they, not Worcestershire, were to come up. To cheers from the throng at New Road, it was announced that they had failed. So, like manic bungee jumpers, Worcestershire continued their five-season bounce between the divisions: up in even years, down in odd. In fact, both counties relegated at the end of 2009 were promoted – and vice versa.

All of which was deeply, even romantically, compelling. The dear old Championship had held its own in a world where the ECB, prostrate before Twenty20, had courted Allen Stanford, a corrupt Texan banker, and Lalit Modi, an IPL power broker now scrutinised for alleged financial misconduct. Cricket à la Modi the Championship was not. But it had its problems, and they lurked still behind the cheers.

Prime here were the old suspects: pitches and Kolpaks. Ungracious though it may be to point it out, Somerset came close to taking the pennant with an essentially franchise attack. Replete with classic West Country names like Kieswetter, de Bruyn and Kartik, they relied upon foreign bowlers for a staggering three-quarters of their Championship wickets. It is true that Andre Adams, a 35-year-old Kiwi of West Indian parentage, was the key man in the summer, becoming the tournament's leading wicket-taker when he secured those two final scalps for Nottinghamshire. But less than 40% of his county's wickets came from imported players, and they also gave three bowlers to England. In addition to Murali Kartik and Damien Wright, the official overseas signings, Somerset had three South African Kolpak bowlers, who remained eligible despite tighter ECB rules because they had British wives, though Zander de Bruyn decamped in the crucial final fortnight for Champions League cricket at home and then left for Surrey.

Other counties found foreign numbers trimmed: the proportion of appearances by players whose formative cricket was outside Britain fell from 32% to 27%, the lowest since the influx (mainly of South Africans) in 2004. Moreover, new financial incentives meant almost a third (31%) of appearances were made by those aged 25 or under who had learned the game in Britain. A lot struggled. But their increased opportunity had to be to the good.

The pitch inspectors stayed mute (again)

Less beneficial were many pitches. After berating dead pitches in 2009, it seems captious to quibble over their new-found life. But the ECB's laudable amendment of the points regime undoubtedly swung too far. Two points were added for the win, now worth 16; one was taken from the draw, down to three; and batting points were (quite rightly) restricted to 110 overs, a move that reduced their aggregate by nearly a fifth, though the bowling aggregate was almost unchanged. A victory, once 3.5 times more rewarding, suddenly became 5.33 times more valuable than the draw.

Result pitches were the outcome, threatening a return to those blighted days when batsmen settled for quick sixties and honest seamers prospered as they never might in Tests. Once it became clear that pitch inspectors would stay mute (again), an arms race developed. The Championship's overall average runs per wicket, excluding "joke" bowling, fell to 30, the lowest for ten years. The strike-rate in the second division, where cricket could become a lottery, was the lowest (one wicket per 53 balls) since purely four-day play began in 1993. And, even ignoring matches where rain brought contrivance, 51 out of 144 fixtures ended in the equivalent of three days or less.

Some pointed to the heavy roller, or its banning, as culprit. But the first division saw a higher percentage of wins by sides opting to field than in all the 17 previous seasons of four-day play. Batting second remained a major advantage. And winning the toss brought its highest premium since the top flight's inception in 2000. Excessive grass, early on, was clearly more relevant than wear.

The points system made a playing record of W7 L5 D4 better than W6 L2 D8, with 124 points to 120 before the application of bonus points. That is how the Championship was won. Greater anomalies were conceivable: W8 L8 (128) would trump W6 L0 (126); W7 L8 (115) would best W5 L0 (113). Both are now feasible. If inspectors are not going to prevent a slide back to lottery pitches, one point should perhaps be cut from the win. And bowling points could be rescinded in all home defeats. The pitch debate is the most difficult in English cricket. At Taunton, they managed to coax spite from the most genteel of squares, rather as if persuading Jane Austen to venture rap lyrics. Edgbaston, a nightmare of numbing stalemate in recent years, now offered six finishes in the equivalent of three days or under. There is no doubt that such results were preferable to earlier tedium. But the best balance is still not there.

It was Yorkshire's mistake, for the second time in ten months (neither under Andrew Gale), to set a target and lose at Taunton on one of the old bland surfaces. It gave Somerset their first win in their sixth match, and arguably cost Yorkshire the title. And Yorkshire also squandered at least six batting points by cautious cricket when perfectly poised to secure them. Both they and **Lancashire** won three of their first five games, but Lancashire, with endemic weak batting, did not win again for another seven, a hiatus from which they never recovered. **Durham's** bid for a third successive crown was overwhelmed by injuries to fast bowlers, and Will Smith became the first of six county captains to resign. Leaders fell last year as if inspired by first-century Rome; a couple more went post-season.

Of the rest in the top tier, **Warwickshire** lost nine times yet beat all three sides below them twice, **Hampshire** showed character after injuries to evade the drop, Kent showed none at all. **Essex** were cruelly hit by rain in a spirited first half, but expired in the second. All four were permanently threatened; only two found steel when it mattered.

Sussex, by no means outstanding on paper, went up because they had the will to do so, with Worcestershire joining them after four wins in their last six games. Glamorgan, with none from their last four, undid a fine season and were then convulsed by internal conflict that managed to make the Borgias seem like the Waltons. **Leicestershire's** young side showed heartening promise despite an insurgency provoked by their chairman, Neil Davidson, the would-be grandee of Grace Road. **Gloucestershire's** pitch policy was a disgrace, and they contrived to lose three games that were easier to win. **Northamptonshire** were mercurial, **Surrey** and **Middlesex** struggled again to realise talent. **Derbyshire** were both South African and supine: a novel combination in a remarkable summer.

Pre-season betting (best available prices): *Division One* – 15-8 Durham; 11-2 Hampshire; 7-1 NOTTINGHAMSHIRE; 9-1 Kent and Lancashire; 10-1 Somerset; 14-1 Warwickshire; 22-1 Yorkshire; 25-1 Essex. *Division Two* – 5-2 SUSSEX; 11-4 Surrey; 7-1 Middlesex; 14-1 Leicestershire; 16-1 Glamorgan, Gloucestershire, Northamptonshire and Worcestershire; 18-1 Derbyshire.

Prize money

Division One
£550,000 for winners: NOTTINGHAMSHIRE.
£235,000 for runners-up: SOMERSET.
£115,000 for third: YORKSHIRE.
£35,000 for fourth: LANCASHIRE.

Division Two
£135,000 for winners: SUSSEX.
£70,000 for runners-up: WORCESTERSHIRE.

(These prizes are divided between players' prize money and a county performance payment. For the winners, players receive £400,000 and the county £150,000; for runners-up, the split is £185,000/£50,000; for third, £100,000/£15,000; for fourth, £30,000/£5,000. In the second division, the split for the winners is £100,000/£35,000, and for the runners-up £60,000/£10,000.)

Winners of each match (both divisions): £1,350.

Leaders: *Division One* – from April 12 Essex and Yorkshire; April 18 Yorkshire; May 13 Nottinghamshire; May 27 Yorkshire; June 1 Nottinghamshire; July 1 Yorkshire; August 6 Nottinghamshire. Nottinghamshire became champions on September 16.
Division Two – from April 12 Derbyshire; April 18 Sussex; May 20 Glamorgan; July 9 Sussex; August 12 Glamorgan; August 20 Sussex. Sussex became champions on September 10.

Bottom place: *Division One* – from April 18 Kent and Somerset; from April 24, Somerset and Warwickshire; April 30 Hampshire; May 20 Kent; May 27 Warwickshire; June 1 Hampshire; July 8 Warwickshire; August 28 Essex.
Division Two – from April 18 Gloucestershire; April 30 Middlesex; May 8 Surrey; July 1 Middlesex; July 31 Derbyshire.

Scoring of Points

(*a*) For a win, 16 points plus any points scored in the first innings.

(*b*) In a tie, each side scores eight points, plus any points scored in the first innings.

(*c*) In a drawn match, each side scores three points, plus any points scored in the first innings.

(*d*) If the scores are equal in a drawn match, the side batting in the fourth innings scores eight points, plus any points scored in the first innings, and the opposing side scores three points plus any points scored in the first innings.

(*e*) First-innings points (awarded only for performances in the first 110 overs of each first innings and retained whatever the result of the match).

   (i) A maximum of five batting points to be available: 200 to 249 runs – 1 point; 250 to 299 runs – 2 points; 300 to 349 runs – 3 points; 350 to 399 runs – 4 points; 400 runs or over – 5 points. Penalty runs awarded within the first 110 overs of each first innings count towards the award of bonus points.

   (ii) A maximum of three bowling points to be available: 3 to 5 wickets taken – 1 point; 6 to 8 wickets taken – 2 points; 9 to 10 wickets taken – 3 points.

(*f*) If a match is abandoned without a ball being bowled, each side scores three points.

(*g*) The side which has the highest aggregate of points shall be the Champion County of their respective division. Should any sides in the Championship table be equal on points, the following tie-breakers will be applied in the order stated: most wins, fewest losses, team achieving most points in head-to-head contests between teams level on points, most wickets taken, most runs scored. At the end of the season, the top two teams from the second division will be promoted and the bottom two teams from the first division will be relegated.

(*h*) The minimum over-rate to be achieved by counties will be 16 overs per hour. Overs will be calculated at the end of the match and penalties applied on a match-by-match basis. For each over (ignoring fractions) that a side is bowled short of the target number, one point will be deducted from their Championship total.

(*i*) A county which is adjudged to have prepared a pitch unfit for four-day first-class cricket will have 24 points deducted. A county adjudged to have prepared a poor pitch will have eight points deducted. This penalty will rise to 12 points if the county has prepared a poor or unfit pitch within the previous 12 months. A county adjudged to have provided a playing area in a condition substantially reducing the possibility of play (subsequent to actions within that county's control) will have eight points deducted.

Under ECB playing conditions, two extras were scored for every no-ball bowled whether scored off or not, and one for every wide. Any runs scored off the bat were credited to the batsman, while byes and leg-byes were counted as no-balls or wides, as appropriate, in accordance with Law 24.13, in addition to the initial penalty.

CONSTITUTION OF COUNTY CHAMPIONSHIP

At least four possible dates have been given for the start of county cricket in England. The first, patchy, references began in 1825. The earliest mention in any cricket publication is in 1864 and eight counties have come to be regarded as first-class from that date, including Cambridgeshire, who dropped out after 1871. For many years, the County Championship was considered to have started in 1873, when regulations governing qualification first applied; indeed, a special commemorative stamp was issued by the Post Office in 1973. However, the Championship was not formally organised until 1890 and before then champions were proclaimed by the press; sometimes publications differed in their views and no definitive list of champions can start before that date. Eight teams contested the 1890 competition – Gloucestershire, Kent, Lancashire, Middlesex, Nottinghamshire, Surrey, Sussex and Yorkshire. Somerset joined in the following year, and in 1895 the Championship began to acquire something of its modern shape when Derbyshire, Essex, Hampshire, Leicestershire and Warwickshire were added. At that point MCC officially recognised the competition's existence. Worcestershire, Northamptonshire and Glamorgan were admitted to the Championship in 1899, 1905 and 1921 respectively and are regarded as first-class from these dates. An invitation in 1921 to Buckinghamshire to enter the Championship was declined, owing to the lack of necessary playing facilities, and an application by Devon in 1948 was unsuccessful. Durham were admitted to the Championship in 1992 and were granted first-class status prior to their pre-season tour of Zimbabwe. In 2000, the Championship was split for the first time into two divisions, on the basis of counties' standings in the 1999 competition. From 2000 onwards, the bottom three teams in Division One were relegated at the end of the season, and the top three teams in Division Two promoted. From 2006, this was changed to two teams relegated and two promoted.

COUNTY CHAMPIONS

The title of champion county is unreliable before 1890. In 1963, *Wisden* formally accepted the list of champions "most generally selected" by contemporaries, as researched by the late Rowland Bowen (see *Wisden 1959*, pp 91–98). This appears to be the most accurate available list but has no official status. The county champions from 1864 to 1889 were, according to Bowen: 1864 Surrey; 1865 Nottinghamshire; 1866 Middlesex; 1867 Yorkshire; 1868 Nottinghamshire; 1869 Nottinghamshire and Yorkshire; 1870 Yorkshire; 1871 Nottinghamshire; 1872 Nottinghamshire; 1873 Gloucestershire and Nottinghamshire; 1874 Gloucestershire; 1875 Nottinghamshire; 1876 Gloucestershire; 1877 Gloucestershire; 1878 undecided; 1879 Lancashire and Nottinghamshire; 1880 Nottinghamshire; 1881 Lancashire; 1882 Lancashire and Nottinghamshire; 1883 Nottinghamshire; 1884 Nottinghamshire; 1885 Nottinghamshire; 1886 Nottinghamshire; 1887 Surrey; 1888 Surrey; 1889 Lancashire, Nottinghamshire and Surrey.

Official champions

1890	Surrey	1911	Warwickshire	1936	Derbyshire
1891	Surrey	1912	Yorkshire	1937	Yorkshire
1892	Surrey	1913	Kent	1938	Yorkshire
1893	Yorkshire	1914	Surrey	1939	Yorkshire
1894	Surrey	1919	Yorkshire	1946	Yorkshire
1895	Surrey	1920	Middlesex	1947	Middlesex
1896	Yorkshire	1921	Middlesex	1948	Glamorgan
1897	Lancashire	1922	Yorkshire	1949	{ Middlesex / Yorkshire
1898	Yorkshire	1923	Yorkshire		
1899	Surrey	1924	Yorkshire	1950	{ Lancashire / Surrey
1900	Yorkshire	1925	Yorkshire		
1901	Yorkshire	1926	Lancashire	1951	Warwickshire
1902	Yorkshire	1927	Lancashire	1952	Surrey
1903	Middlesex	1928	Lancashire	1953	Surrey
1904	Lancashire	1929	Nottinghamshire	1954	Surrey
1905	Yorkshire	1930	Lancashire	1955	Surrey
1906	Kent	1931	Yorkshire	1956	Surrey
1907	Nottinghamshire	1932	Yorkshire	1957	Surrey
1908	Yorkshire	1933	Yorkshire	1958	Surrey
1909	Kent	1934	Lancashire	1959	Yorkshire
1910	Kent	1935	Yorkshire	1960	Yorkshire

Official champions

1961	Hampshire	
1962	Yorkshire	
1963	Yorkshire	
1964	Worcestershire	
1965	Worcestershire	
1966	Yorkshire	
1967	Yorkshire	
1968	Yorkshire	
1969	Glamorgan	
1970	Kent	
1971	Surrey	
1972	Warwickshire	
1973	Hampshire	
1974	Worcestershire	
1975	Leicestershire	
1976	Middlesex	

1977	{ Middlesex / Kent
1978	Kent
1979	Essex
1980	Middlesex
1981	Nottinghamshire
1982	Middlesex
1983	Essex
1984	Essex
1985	Middlesex
1986	Essex
1987	Nottinghamshire
1988	Worcestershire
1989	Worcestershire
1990	Middlesex
1991	Essex
1992	Essex
1993	Middlesex

1994	Warwickshire
1995	Warwickshire
1996	Leicestershire
1997	Glamorgan
1998	Leicestershire
1999	Surrey
2000	Surrey
2001	Yorkshire
2002	Surrey
2003	Sussex
2004	Warwickshire
2005	Nottinghamshire
2006	Sussex
2007	Sussex
2008	Durham
2009	Durham
2010	Nottinghamshire

Notes: Since the Championship was constituted in 1890 it has been won outright as follows: Yorkshire 30 times, Surrey 18, Middlesex 10, Lancashire 7, Essex, Kent, Nottinghamshire and Warwickshire 6, Worcestershire 5, Glamorgan, Leicestershire and Sussex 3, Durham and Hampshire 2, Derbyshire 1. Gloucestershire, Northamptonshire and Somerset have never won.

The title has been shared three times since 1890, involving Middlesex twice, Kent, Lancashire, Surrey and Yorkshire.

Wooden Spoons: Since the major expansion of the Championship from nine teams to 14 in 1895, the counties have finished outright bottom as follows: Derbyshire 15; Somerset 12; Northamptonshire 11; Glamorgan 10; Gloucestershire, Leicestershire, Nottinghamshire and Sussex 8; Worcestershire 6; Durham and Hampshire 5; Warwickshire 3; Essex and Kent 2; Yorkshire 1. Lancashire, Middlesex and Surrey have never finished bottom. Leicestershire have also shared bottom place twice, once with Hampshire and once with Somerset.

From 1977 to 1983 the Championship was sponsored by Schweppes, from 1984 to 1998 by Britannic Assurance, from 1999 to 2000 by PPP healthcare, in 2001 by Cricinfo, from 2002 to 2005 by Frizzell and from 2006 by Liverpool Victoria (LV).

COUNTY CHAMPIONSHIP – FINAL POSITIONS, 1890–2010

	Derbyshire	Durham	Essex	Glamorgan	Gloucestershire	Hampshire	Kent	Lancashire	Leicestershire	Middlesex	Northamptonshire	Nottinghamshire	Somerset	Surrey	Sussex	Warwickshire	Worcestershire	Yorkshire
1890	–	–	–	–	6	–	3	2	–	7	–	5	–	1	8	–	–	3
1891	–	–	–	–	9	–	5	2	–	3	–	4	5	1	7	–	–	8
1892	–	–	–	–	7	–	7	4	–	5	–	2	3	1	9	–	–	6
1893	–	–	–	–	9	–	4	2	–	3	–	6	8	5	7	–	–	1
1894	–	–	–	–	9	–	4	4	–	3	–	7	6	1	8	–	–	2
1895	5	–	9	–	4	10	14	2	12	6	–	12	8	1	11	6	–	3
1896	7	–	5	–	10	8	9	2	13	3	–	6	11	4	14	12	–	1
1897	14	–	3	–	5	9	12	1	13	8	–	10	11	2	6	7	–	4
1898	9	–	5	–	3	12	7	6	13	2	–	8	13	4	9	9	–	1
1899	15	–	6	–	9	10	8	4	13	2	–	10	13	1	5	7	12	3
1900	13	–	10	–	7	15	3	2	14	7	–	5	11	7	3	6	12	1
1901	15	–	10	–	14	7	7	3	12	2	–	9	12	6	4	5	11	1
1902	10	–	13	–	14	15	7	5	11	12	–	3	7	4	2	6	9	1
1903	12	–	8	–	13	14	8	4	14	1	–	5	10	11	2	7	6	3

	Derbyshire	Durham	Essex	Glamorgan	Gloucestershire	Hampshire	Kent	Lancashire	Leicestershire	Middlesex	Northamptonshire	Nottinghamshire	Somerset	Surrey	Sussex	Warwickshire	Worcestershire	Yorkshire
1904	10	–	14	–	9	15	3	1	7	4	–	5	12	11	6	7	13	2
1905	14	–	12	–	8	16	6	2	5	11	13	10	15	4	3	7	8	1
1906	16	–	7	–	9	8	1	4	15	11	11	5	11	3	10	6	14	2
1907	16	–	7	–	10	12	8	6	11	5	15	1	14	4	13	9	2	2
1908	14	–	11	–	10	9	2	7	13	4	15	8	16	3	5	12	6	1
1909	15	–	14	–	16	8	1	2	13	6	7	10	11	5	4	12	8	3
1910	15	–	11	–	12	6	1	4	10	3	9	5	16	2	7	14	13	8
1911	14	–	6	–	12	11	2	4	15	3	10	8	16	5	13	1	9	7
1912	12	–	15	–	11	6	3	4	13	5	2	8	14	7	10	9	16	1
1913	13	–	15	–	9	10	1	8	14	6	4	5	16	3	7	11	12	2
1914	12	–	8	–	16	5	3	11	13	2	9	10	15	1	6	7	14	4
1919	9	–	14	–	8	7	2	5	9	13	12	3	5	4	11	15	–	1
1920	16	–	9	–	8	11	5	2	13	1	14	7	10	3	6	12	15	4
1921	12	–	15	17	7	6	4	5	11	1	13	8	10	2	9	16	14	3
1922	11	–	8	16	13	6	4	5	14	7	15	2	10	3	9	12	17	1
1923	10	–	13	16	11	7	5	3	14	8	17	2	9	4	6	12	15	1
1924	17	–	15	13	6	12	5	4	11	2	16	6	8	3	10	9	14	1
1925	14	–	7	17	10	9	5	3	12	6	11	4	15	2	13	8	16	1
1926	11	–	9	8	15	7	3	1	13	6	16	4	14	5	10	12	17	2
1927	5	–	8	15	12	13	4	1	7	9	16	2	14	6	10	11	17	3
1928	10	–	16	15	5	12	2	1	9	8	13	3	14	6	7	11	17	4
1929	7	–	12	17	4	11	8	2	9	6	13	1	15	10	4	14	16	2
1930	9	–	6	11	2	13	5	1	12	16	17	4	13	8	7	15	10	3
1931	7	–	10	15	2	12	3	6	16	11	17	5	13	8	4	9	14	1
1932	10	–	14	15	13	8	3	6	12	10	16	4	7	5	2	9	17	1
1933	6	–	4	16	10	14	3	5	17	12	13	8	11	9	2	7	15	1
1934	3	–	8	13	7	14	5	1	12	10	17	9	15	11	2	4	16	5
1935	2	–	9	13	15	16	10	4	6	3	17	5	14	11	7	8	12	1
1936	1	–	9	16	4	10	8	11	15	2	17	5	7	6	14	13	12	3
1937	3	–	6	7	4	14	12	9	16	2	17	10	13	8	5	11	15	1
1938	5	–	6	16	10	14	9	4	15	2	17	12	7	3	8	13	11	1
1939	9	–	4	13	3	15	5	6	17	2	16	12	14	8	10	11	7	1
1946	15	–	8	6	5	10	6	3	11	2	16	13	4	11	17	14	8	1
1947	5	–	11	9	2	16	4	3	14	1	17	11	11	6	9	15	7	7
1948	6	–	13	1	8	9	15	5	11	3	17	14	12	2	16	7	10	4
1949	15	–	9	8	7	16	13	11	17	1	6	11	9	5	13	4	3	1
1950	5	–	17	11	7	12	9	1	16	14	10	15	7	1	13	4	6	3
1951	11	–	8	5	12	9	16	3	15	7	13	17	14	6	10	1	4	2
1952	4	–	10	7	9	12	15	3	6	5	8	16	17	1	13	10	14	2
1953	6	–	12	10	6	14	16	3	3	5	11	8	17	1	2	9	15	12
1954	3	–	15	4	13	14	11	10	16	7	7	5	17	1	9	6	11	2
1955	8	–	14	16	12	3	13	9	6	5	7	11	17	1	4	9	15	2
1956	12	–	11	13	3	6	16	2	17	5	4	8	15	1	9	14	9	7
1957	4	–	5	9	12	13	14	6	17	7	2	15	8	1	9	11	16	3
1958	5	–	6	15	14	2	8	7	12	10	4	17	3	1	13	16	9	11
1959	7	–	9	6	2	8	13	5	16	10	11	17	12	3	15	4	14	1
1960	5	–	6	11	8	12	10	2	17	3	9	16	14	7	4	15	13	1
1961	7	–	6	14	5	1	11	13	9	3	16	17	10	15	8	12	4	2
1962	7	–	9	14	4	10	11	16	17	13	8	15	6	5	12	3	2	1
1963	17	–	12	2	8	10	13	15	16	6	7	9	3	11	4	4	14	1
1964	12	–	10	11	17	12	7	14	16	6	3	15	8	4	9	2	1	5
1965	9	–	15	3	10	12	5	13	14	6	2	17	7	8	16	11	1	4
1966	9	–	16	14	15	11	4	12	8	12	5	17	3	7	10	6	2	1
1967	6	–	15	14	17	12	2	11	2	7	9	15	8	4	13	10	5	1

	Derbyshire	Durham	Essex	Glamorgan	Gloucestershire	Hampshire	Kent	Lancashire	Leicestershire	Middlesex	Northamptonshire	Nottinghamshire	Somerset	Surrey	Sussex	Warwickshire	Worcestershire	Yorkshire
1968	8	–	14	3	16	5	2	6	9	10	13	4	12	15	17	11	7	1
1969	16	–	6	1	2	5	10	15	14	11	9	8	17	3	7	4	12	13
1970	7	–	12	2	17	10	1	3	15	16	14	11	13	5	9	7	6	4
1971	17	–	10	16	8	9	4	3	5	6	14	12	7	1	11	2	15	13
1972	17	–	5	13	3	9	2	15	6	8	4	14	11	12	16	1	7	10
1973	16	–	8	11	5	1	4	12	9	13	3	17	10	2	15	7	6	14
1974	17	–	12	16	14	2	10	8	4	6	3	15	5	7	13	9	1	11
1975	15	–	7	9	16	3	5	4	1	11	8	13	12	6	17	14	10	2
1976	15	–	6	17	3	12	14	16	4	1	2	13	7	9	10	5	11	8
1977	7	–	6	14	3	11	1	16	5	1	9	17	4	14	8	10	13	12
1978	14	–	2	13	10	8	1	12	6	3	17	7	5	16	9	11	15	4
1979	16	–	1	17	10	12	5	13	6	14	11	9	8	3	4	15	2	7
1980	9	–	8	13	7	17	16	15	10	1	12	3	5	2	4	14	11	6
1981	12	–	5	14	13	7	9	16	8	4	15	1	3	6	2	17	11	10
1982	11	–	7	16	15	3	13	12	2	1	9	4	6	5	8	17	14	10
1983	9	–	1	15	2	3	7	12	4	2	6	14	10	8	11	5	16	17
1984	12	–	1	13	17	15	5	16	4	3	11	2	7	8	6	9	10	14
1985	13	–	4	12	3	2	9	14	16	1	10	8	17	6	7	15	5	11
1986	11	–	1	17	2	6	8	15	7	12	9	4	16	3	14	12	5	10
1987	6	–	12	13	10	5	14	2	3	16	7	1	11	4	17	15	9	8
1988	14	–	3	17	10	15	2	9	8	7	12	5	11	4	16	6	1	13
1989	6	–	2	17	9	6	15	4	13	3	5	11	14	12	10	8	1	16
1990	12	–	2	8	13	3	16	6	7	1	11	13	15	9	17	5	4	10
1991	3	–	1	12	13	9	6	8	16	15	10	4	17	5	11	2	6	14
1992	5	18	1	14	10	15	2	8	11	3	4	9	13	7	6	17	16	12
1993	15	18	11	3	17	13	8	13	9	1	4	7	5	6	10	16	2	12
1994	17	16	6	18	12	13	9	10	2	4	5	3	11	7	8	1	15	13
1995	14	17	5	16	6	13	18	4	7	2	3	11	9	12	15	1	10	8
1996	2	18	5	10	13	14	4	15	1	9	16	17	11	3	12	8	7	6
1997	16	17	18	1	7	14	2	11	10	4	15	13	12	8	18	4	3	6
1998	10	14	18	12	4	6	11	2	1	17	15	16	9	5	7	8	13	3
1999	9	8	12	14	18	7	5	2	3	16	13	17	4	1	11	10	15	6
2000	**9**	**8**	**2**	*3*	*4*	**7**	**6**	**2**	*4*	*8*	*1*	**7**	**5**	**1**	*9*	**6**	*5*	**3**
2001	*9*	*8*	**9**	**8**	*4*	**2**	**3**	*6*	*5*	*5*	**7**	**7**	**2**	**4**	*1*	*3*	*6*	**1**
2002	*6*	*9*	*1*	**5**	*8*	**7**	**3**	**4**	**5**	*2*	*7*	*3*	**8**	**1**	*6*	**2**	**4**	*9*
2003	*9*	*6*	**7**	**5**	*3*	*8*	**4**	**2**	*9*	*6*	**2**	**8**	*7*	**3**	**1**	*5*	*1*	**4**
2004	*8*	*9*	**5**	*3*	**6**	**2**	**2**	*8*	*6*	*4*	*9*	**1**	**4**	**3**	**5**	*1*	*7*	**7**
2005	*9*	**2**	**5**	*9*	*8*	**2**	**5**	*1*	*7*	*6*	*4*	**1**	*8*	**7**	**3**	**4**	*6*	**3**
2006	*5*	**7**	**3**	*8*	*7*	**3**	**5**	**2**	*4*	*9*	*6*	*8*	*9*	**1**	**1**	**4**	*2*	**6**
2007	*6*	**2**	*4*	*9*	**7**	**5**	**7**	**3**	*8*	*3*	*5*	**2**	*1*	**4**	**1**	*8*	*9*	**6**
2008	*6*	**1**	**5**	*8*	*9*	**3**	**8**	**5**	*7*	*3*	*4*	**2**	**4**	*9*	**6**	*1*	*2*	**7**
2009	*6*	**1**	**2**	*5*	*4*	**6**	*1*	**4**	*9*	**8**	*3*	**2**	**3**	*7*	**8**	**5**	*9*	**7**
2010	*9*	**5**	*9*	*3*	*5*	**7**	**8**	**4**	*4*	**8**	*6*	**1**	**2**	*7*	*1*	**6**	*2*	**3**

Note: For the 2000–2010 Championships, Division One placings are shown in bold, Division Two in italic.

MATCH RESULTS, 1864–2010

County	Years of Play	Played	Won	Lost	Drawn	Tied	% Won
Derbyshire	1871–87; 1895–2010	2,451	599	902	949	1	24.43
Durham	1992–2010	315	72	141	102	0	22.85
Essex	1895–2010	2,413	700	706	1,001	6	29.00
Glamorgan	1921–2010	1,945	431	665	849	0	22.15
Gloucestershire	1870–2010	2,687	785	994	906	2	29.21
Hampshire	1864–85; 1895–2010	2,522	665	853	1,000	4	26.36
Kent	1864–2010	2,810	1,009	840	956	5	35.90
Lancashire	1865–2010	2,884	1,066	596	1,219	3	36.96
Leicestershire	1895–2009	2,379	543	856	979	1	22.82
Middlesex.	1864–2010	2,590	941	664	980	5	36.33
Northamptonshire ...	1905–2010	2,148	537	737	871	3	25.00
Nottinghamshire....	1864–2010	2,719	827	735	1,156	1	30.41
Somerset.	1882–85; 1891–2010	2,421	580	947	891	3	23.95
Surrey	1864–2010	2,965	1,165	657	1,139	4	39.29
Sussex	1864–2010	2,859	811	973	1,069	6	28.36
Warwickshire......	1895–2010	2,393	660	685	1,046	2	27.58
Worcestershire	1899–2010	2,332	597	803	930	2	25.60
Yorkshire	1864–2010	2,988	1,296	530	1,160	2	43.37
Cambridgeshire	1864–69; 1871	19	8	8	3	0	42.10
		21,920	13,292	13,292	8,603	25	

Notes: Matches abandoned without a ball bowled are wholly excluded.

Counties participated in the years shown, except that there were no matches in the years 1915–1918 and 1940–1945; Hampshire did not play inter-county matches in 1868–1869, 1871–1874 and 1879; Worcestershire did not take part in the Championship in 1919.

COUNTY CHAMPIONSHIP STATISTICS FOR 2010

County	For			Runs scored per 100 balls	Against		
	Runs	Wickets	Avge		Runs	Wickets	Avge
Derbyshire (9).	7,329	254	28.85	53.62	8,358	253	33.03
Durham (5).	7,217	228	31.65	57.73	7,941	227	34.98
Essex (9).	7,429	273	27.21	50.20	7,473	248	30.13
Glamorgan (3)	7,321	240	30.50	60.14	7,230	262	27.59
Gloucestershire (5)	6,860	286	23.98	53.81	7,317	272	26.90
Hampshire (7).	8,349	242	34.50	53.29	8,189	235	34.85
Kent (8).	7,401	272	27.20	58.46	8,539	259	32.96
Lancashire (7).	7,346	243	30.23	52.07	6,629	228	29.07
Leicestershire (4)	7,370	229	32.18	52.34	6,761	245	27.59
Middlesex (8)	7,544	255	29.58	56.26	8,132	258	31.51
Northamptonshire (6) ..	7,802	273	28.57	53.78	7,493	208	36.02
Nottinghamshire (1) ...	7,577	222	34.13	62.19	7,591	253	30.00
Somerset (2)	8,137	217	37.49	63.81	7,082	245	28.90
Surrey (7)	7,902	250	31.60	57.82	7,965	236	33.75
Sussex (1).	7,569	222	34.09	60.87	7,021	282	24.89
Warwickshire (6)	6,551	282	23.23	52.29	7,096	271	26.18
Worcestershire (2)	8,222	262	31.38	58.69	7,642	255	29.96
Yorkshire (3).	9,029	228	39.60	56.91	8,496	241	35.25
	136,955	4,478	30.58	56.18	136,955	4,478	30.58

2010 Championship positions are shown in brackets; Division One in bold, Division Two in italic.

ECB PITCHES TABLE OF MERIT, 2010

	First-class	One-day		First-class	One-day
Derbyshire	4.70	4.93	Sussex	4.81	5.73
Durham	4.75	5.06	Warwickshire	4.22	5.56
Essex	4.55	5.12	Worcestershire	4.30	5.29
Glamorgan	4.45	4.31	Yorkshire	4.82	5.69
Gloucestershire	4.56	5.40	Netherlands		4.17
Hampshire	4.25	5.30	Scotland		4.67
Kent	4.70	4.69	Unicorns		4.83
Lancashire	4.89	5.00	Cambridge MCCU	5.00	
Leicestershire	4.60	5.20	Cardiff MCCU	5.00	
Middlesex	5.45	5.32	Durham MCCU	4.50	
Northamptonshire	5.11	5.44	Leeds/Bradford MCCU	4.33	
Nottinghamshire	4.67	5.20	Loughborough MCCU	4.67	
Somerset	4.89	5.32	Oxford MCCU	4.57	
Surrey	5.36	5.47			

Each umpire in a match marks the pitch on the following scale: 6 – Very good; 5 – Good; 4 – above average; 3 – Below average; 2 – Poor; 1 – Unfit.

The tables, provided by the ECB, cover major matches, including Tests, Under-19 internationals, women's internationals and MCCU games, played on grounds under the county or MCCU's jurisdiction. Middlesex pitches at Lord's are the responsibility of MCC. The "First-class" column includes Under-19 and women's Tests, and inter-MCCU games.

Middlesex had the highest marks for first-class cricket and Sussex for one-day cricket, though the ECB points out that the tables of merit are not a direct assessment of the groundsmen's ability. Marks may be affected by many factors including weather, soil conditions and the resources available.

COUNTY CAPS AWARDED IN 2010

Derbyshire	P. S. Jones.
Essex	M. J. Walker.
Glamorgan*	J. Allenby, J. A. R. Harris.
Gloucestershire*	J. N. Batty, C. D. J. Dent, J. M. R. Taylor, E. G. C. Young.
Hampshire	N. D. McKenzie.
Lancashire	S. Chanderpaul, S. J. Croft, K. W. Hogg, T. C. Smith.
Leicestershire	M. J. Hoggard.
Middlesex	G. K. Berg, N. J. Dexter, A. C. Gilchrist, D. J. Malan.
Nottinghamshire	H. M. Amla.
Sussex	M. S. Panesar.
Warwickshire	Imran Tahir.
Worcestershire*	J. G. Cameron, S. H. Choudhry, A. Richardson, B. J. M. Scott, Shakib Al Hasan.
Yorkshire	A. Lyth, R. M. Pyrah, A. Shahzad, D. J. Wainwright.

* *Glamorgan's capping system is now based on a player's number of appearances; Gloucestershire now award caps to all first-class players; Worcestershire have replaced caps with colours awarded to all Championship players. Durham abolished their capping system after 2005.*

No caps were awarded by Kent, Northamptonshire, Somerset or Surrey.

COUNTY BENEFITS AWARDED FOR 2011

Essex	J. S. Foster.	Leicestershire	C. W. Henderson.
Glamorgan	M. J. Powell.	Sussex	M. J. G. Davis
Hampshire	N. Pothas.		(Testimonial).
Kent	R. W. T. Key.	Warwickshire	I. R. Bell.
Lancashire	M. J. Chilton.	Yorkshire	G. L. Brophy.

No benefit was awarded by Derbyshire, Durham, Gloucestershire, Middlesex, Northamptonshire, Nottinghamshire, Somerset, Surrey or Worcestershire.

DERBYSHIRE

Back to the basement

MARK EKLID

A season that opened with such bright hope closed with Derbyshire bottom of the Championship for the fourth time since it was split in two ten years before. The wooden spoon has had a regular place in an otherwise bare trophy cabinet at Derby, but they had looked capable of challenging at the top of the table when the opening round of matches brought a resounding victory over Surrey, Derbyshire's first win at The Oval since 1966.

After beating Glamorgan to make it two wins out of three, the peak came as Derbyshire's batsmen dominated and demoralised the home side on the second day at Northampton. But then it all went horribly wrong. Six defeats and no victories in the next nine Championship matches culminated in the nadir of Sussex's top four all plundering centuries off feeble bowling at Horsham in mid-August – a stark and painful contrast to that promising day in the April sun at Wantage Road.

It is easier to plot the path of decline than to explain it. Unquestionably, a lack of seam-bowling options because of injuries, adding to the burden that placed on the few who remained, was a factor. Derbyshire especially felt the absence of Graham Wagg, their vivacious all-rounder. A torn calf muscle kept him out for four months and, by the time he was fit to return, he had announced he was to leave at the end of the summer to join Glamorgan.

Derbyshire also had to cope for almost the whole of the season without Ian Hunter and Jon Clare, while Tom Lungley's campaign – and, it later transpired, his 11-season career with his home county – came to an end when his arm was broken by his batting partner Steffan Jones as they tried to win the match against Surrey at Chesterfield at the beginning of July.

Derbyshire did not have the resources to cover such losses, although Jones, Tim Groenewald, Greg Smith and Mark Footitt shouldered the extra workload with unfailing spirit. So too did the South African left-arm spinner Robin Peterson, a Kolpak signing for the summer, who bowled more first-class overs than anyone in the division and was rewarded with a haul of 51 wickets. Visa restrictions meant Peterson would not be eligible to return in 2011, and the loss of another experienced presence in the dressing-room, as well as on the field, may be difficult to overcome.

It would be wrong to attribute all Derbyshire's problems to the injuries that restricted their bowling options, because their batting was often far too fragile as well. The form of Wayne Madsen, the South African-born opener in his first full year of county cricket, served as a good illustration of this: he scored four centuries, including a career-best 179 at Northampton and two in the home match against Surrey, but bagged a pair in the final game at Cardiff and fell 60 runs short of 1,000 for the season.

Chesney Hughes

Madsen, though, was one of the few batsmen to produce close to his expected quota of runs, another being his opening partner, the Australian Chris Rogers. After hitting Surrey for 340 for once out in the first match, 1,000 runs before the end of May seemed a modest prediction; although in the end it was August before he reached four figures, a final return of 1,285 runs at 53.54 was another invaluable effort.

Rogers gave up the captaincy later in August when doubts arose over his willingness to return to Derbyshire – Smith took over until the end of the season – and later it was confirmed that Rogers would join Middlesex for 2011. The man who led the batting with distinction for three years and proved a fine captain for two of them will leave very large shoes to fill.

The return of wicketkeeper-batsman Luke Sutton, five years after he left for Lancashire, will help strengthen a brittle middle order and gives the club another proven leader. In January, the club announced the signings of two international overseas batsmen – the new Australian Test player Usman Khawaja, and New Zealander Martin Guptill.

The biggest single source of optimism from 2010 was the emergence of Chesney Hughes, a 19-year-old left-hander from the small Caribbean island of Anguilla. Not only was he physically mature beyond his years, the temperamental maturity he showed, from the moment he made his first-class debut at Lord's in May, was immensely impressive; two centuries, plus an unforgettable unbeaten 96 in an astonishing five-session Championship victory at Bristol in September, encouraged the belief that Hughes had the ability to play at the highest level. It was his stated intention to play Test cricket for England, if selected.

Three Championship victories were actually one more than Derbyshire had managed in a far more heartening 2009 (when they finished sixth in their division); they were also more effective in the Friends Provident Twenty20, in which they would have qualified for the quarter-finals had they beaten Northamptonshire in their penultimate game. In the Clydesdale Bank 40, four defeats in the first five matches, including a humbling loss at home to the Netherlands (their only win over a first-class county), left too much ground to make up.

Overall, the disappointment of their Championship and limited-overs form was inescapable and, with all trace of the progress made over the previous two years having disappeared, Derbyshire had to start from the bottom again.

DERBYSHIRE RESULTS

All first-class matches – Played 16: Won 3, Lost 7, Drawn 6. Abandoned 1.
County Championship matches – Played 16: Won 3, Lost 7, Drawn 6.

LV= County Championship, 9th in Division 2;
Friends Provident T20, 5th in North Division; Clydesdale Bank 40, 4th in Group B.

COUNTY CHAMPIONSHIP AVERAGES, BATTING AND FIELDING

Cap		M	I	NO	R	HS	100s	50s	Avge	Ct
2008	C. J. L. Rogers§	15	27	3	1,285	200	4	5	53.54	19
	C. F. Hughes.	12	21	2	784	156	2	4	41.26	12
	W. L. Madsen¶	16	29	1	940	179	4	2	33.57	11
2010	P. S. Jones.	12	18	4	427	86	0	1	30.50	4
2009	G. M. Smith¶	16	27	1	721	165*	1	4	27.73	4
	G. T. Park	11	19	2	431	124*	1	2	25.35	6
	S. J. Adshead.	4	7	2	125	49	0	0	25.00	13
	D. J. Redfern.	9	15	1	331	85	0	1	23.64	3
	R. J. Peterson¶	15	24	3	484	58	0	2	23.04	9
	W. J. Durston	6	11	0	240	69	0	1	21.81	9
	T. D. Groenewald¶	13	19	9	216	35*	0	0	21.60	3
	P. M. Borrington.	7	13	1	246	79*	0	1	20.50	4
	L. J. Goddard.	8	11	1	165	67	0	1	16.50	24
	T. Poynton.	4	6	0	88	25	0	0	14.66	5
2007	G. G. Wagg.	4	7	0	82	37	0	0	11.71	1
	J. L. Sadler	3	4	0	45	16	0	0	11.25	3
2007	T. Lungley†.	7	10	1	85	21	0	0	9.44	6
	M. H. A. Footitt	9	12	3	69	30	0	0	7.66	3
	J. L. Clare	4	6	0	45	24	0	0	7.50	4

Also batted: A. Sheikh (1 match) 6, 0 (1 ct).

† *Born in Derbyshire.* § *Official overseas player.* ¶ *Other non-England-qualified player.*

BOWLING

	O	M	R	W	BB	5W/i	Avge
G. G. Wagg	77	13	246	10	3-31	0	24.60
J. L. Clare	69.3	8	324	11	4-42	0	29.45
R. J. Peterson	553.3	129	1,566	51	4-10	0	30.70
P. S. Jones	313.5	68	959	31	4-26	0	30.93
G. M. Smith	414.3	77	1,368	42	5-54	1	32.57
T. Lungley	165	25	630	19	3-39	0	33.15
T. D. Groenewald.	413.5	105	1,295	38	5-86	1	34.07
M. H. A. Footitt	239.2	48	786	23	4-78	0	34.17

Also bowled: W. J. Durston 16–0–76–1; C. F. Hughes 11–0–81–1; W. L. Madsen 8.2–0–68–1;
G. T. Park 83.3–9–327–9; T. Poynton 8–0–96–2; D. J. Redfern 3–0–14–0; C. J. L. Rogers
1–0–5–0; A. Sheikh 25–1–152–5.

LEADING CB40 AVERAGES (100 runs/4 wickets)

Batting

	Runs	HS	Avge	S-R	Ct
G. G. Wagg	137	48*	68.50	106.20	2
W. L. Madsen . . .	404	71*	50.50	95.28	8
C. J. L. Rogers . . .	336	73	37.33	79.80	3
C. F. Hughes	422	72	35.16	86.47	5
J. L. Sadler	135	41	33.75	103.05	0
W. J. Durston	189	72*	31.50	81.11	3

Bowling

	W	BB	Avge	E-R
G. G. Wagg	9	3-22	17.77	5.13
J. Needham	9	3-36	25.00	4.59
M. H. A. Footitt	10	3-20	27.30	5.57
T. Lungley	7	3-41	30.57	5.78
T. D. Groenewald . . .	10	2-42	34.50	5.47
P. S. Jones	4	3-27	35.50	5.46

LEADING FPT20 AVERAGES (100 runs/18 overs)

Batting	Runs	HS	Avge	S-R	Ct	Bowling	W	BB	Avge	E-R
P. S. Jones	103	40	34.33	174.57	1	C. K. Langeveldt	13	3-36	23.76	7.35
J. L. Sadler	157	39	31.40	146.72	4	R. J. Peterson	8	2-38	47.50	7.42
L. E. Bosman	368	94	26.28	134.79	1	T. D. Groenewald	16	3-18	23.43	7.45
W. J. Durston	445	111	37.08	129.36	6	W. J. Durston	6	2-18	23.16	7.72
R. J. Peterson	252	35*	19.38	123.52	2	G. M. Smith	13	3-19	23.61	7.83
G. M. Smith	225	38	16.07	105.14	11	G. T. Park	8	3-11	28.25	8.07

FIRST-CLASS COUNTY RECORDS

Highest score for	274	G. A. Davidson v Lancashire at Manchester	1896
Highest score against	343*	P. A. Perrin (Essex) at Chesterfield	1904
Leading run-scorer	23,854	K. J. Barnett (avge 41.12)	1979–1998
Best bowling for	10-40	W. Bestwick v Glamorgan at Cardiff	1921
Best bowling against	10-45	R. L. Johnson (Middlesex) at Derby	1994
Leading wicket-taker	1,670	H. L. Jackson (avge 17.11)	1947–1963
Highest total for	801-8 dec	v Somerset at Taunton	2007
Highest total against	662	by Yorkshire at Chesterfield	1898
Lowest total for	16	v Nottinghamshire at Nottingham	1879
Lowest total against	23	by Hampshire at Burton upon Trent	1958

LIST A COUNTY RECORDS

Highest score for	173*	M. J. Di Venuto v Derbyshire CB at Derby	2000
Highest score against	158	R. K. Rao (Sussex) at Derby	1997
Leading run-scorer	12,358	K. J. Barnett (avge 36.67)	1979–1998
Best bowling for	8-21	M. A. Holding v Sussex at Hove	1988
Best bowling against	8-66	S. R. G. Francis (Somerset) at Derby	2004
Leading wicket-taker	246	A. E. Warner (avge 27.13)	1985–1995
Highest total for	366-4	v Combined Universities at Oxford	1991
Highest total against	369-6	by New Zealanders at Derby	1999
Lowest total for	60	v Kent at Canterbury	2008
Lowest total against	42	by Glamorgan at Swansea	1979

TWENTY20 RECORDS

Highest score for	111	W. J. Durston v Nottinghamshire at Nottingham	2010
Highest score against	109	I. J. Harvey (Yorks) at Leeds	2005
Leading run-scorer	883	G. M. Smith (avge 23.86)	2007–2010
Best bowling for	5-27	T. Lungley v Leicestershire at Leicester	2009
Best bowling against	5-14	P. D. Collingwood (Durham) at Chester-le-Street	2008
Leading wicket-taker	30	T. Lungley (avge 21.46)	2003–2010
Highest total for	222-5	v Yorkshire at Leeds	2010
Highest total against	220-5	by Lancashire at Derby	2009
Lowest total for	98	v Lancashire at Manchester	2005
Lowest total against	84	by West Indians at Derby	2007

ADDRESS

County Ground, Grandstand Road, Derby DE21 6AF (01332 388101; **email** info@ derbyshireccc.com). **Website** www.derbyshireccc.com

OFFICIALS

Captain 2010 – C. J. L. Rogers	**Chairman** D. K. Amott
2011 – L. D. Sutton	**Chief executive** K. A. Loring
Head of cricket J. E. Morris	**Head groundsman** N. Godrich
Director of academy K. M. Krikken	**Scorer** J. M. Brown
President to be announced	

DERBYSHIRE v LOUGHBOROUGH MCCU

At Derby, April 3–5. Abandoned.

A sodden outfield meant that Derbyshire's opening first-class match of a new season was abandoned without a ball bowled for the first time in their history. It also meant there was a little longer to wait for the sight of first-class cricket being played on a north–south facing pitch at the County Ground for the first time since 1963.

At The Oval, April 9–12. DERBYSHIRE beat SURREY by 208 runs. *Chris Rogers becomes the first to score a double and single century in the same match for Derbyshire.*

DERBYSHIRE v LEICESTERSHIRE

At Derby, April 15–18. Leicestershire won by 203 runs. Leicestershire 21pts, Derbyshire 4pts. Toss: Derbyshire.

In a low-scoring match, runs from the only two Derby-born players on view proved crucial. Sadly for the home side, though, both men were playing for Leicestershire: Jefferson, who hit 14 fours and a six, helped his side to a first-innings lead of 72, then a maiden first-class century from the former Derbyshire player White, out of 136 scored after he went in at No. 7, set up a position of unassailable strength. Derbyshire did not remotely threaten their target of 403, although Madsen's battling century kept hopes of a draw alive into the final hour. He was finally eighth out in the 87th over, one of seven victims in the match for the impressive 18-year-old fast bowler Nathan Buck. The one comfort for Derbyshire was that their newly aligned wicket met with the approval of pitch liaison officer Tony Pigott after a first day on which 12 wickets went down.

Close of play: First day, Derbyshire 40-2 (Madsen 26, Park 6); Second day, Leicestershire 83-2 (Boyce 40, Taylor 21); Third day, Derbyshire 13-1 (Madsen 6, Borrington 2).

Leicestershire

W. I. Jefferson c Goddard b Smith	94	– lbw b Jones	6
M. A. G. Boyce c Goddard b Groenewald	0	– c Borrington b Peterson	90
P. A. Nixon c Redfern b Groenewald	37	– lbw b Groenewald	12
J. W. A. Taylor c Goddard b Jones	6	– lbw b Footitt	25
J. J. Cobb lbw b Park	13	– c Park b Peterson	25
†T. J. New run out	61	– c Groenewald b Peterson	20
W. A. White c Goddard b Groenewald	4	– not out	101
C. W. Henderson b Peterson	25	– c Rogers b Peterson	1
N. L. Buck lbw b Peterson	0	– b Park	14
A. J. Harris not out	5	– not out	1
*M. J. Hoggard b Smith	0		
B 9, l-b 17, w 4, n-b 4	34	B 18, l-b 7, w 8, n-b 2	35

1/9 (2) 2/113 (3) 3/126 (4)   (77.2 overs) 279
4/162 (5) 5/180 (1) 6/204 (7)
7/250 (8) 8/250 (9) 9/278 (6) 10/279 (11)

1/11 (1)   (8 wkts dec, 129 overs) 330
2/42 (3) 3/94 (4)
4/158 (5) 5/194 (2)
6/206 (6) 7/214 (8) 8/309 (9)

Groenewald 16–5–44–3; Footitt 13–0–51–0; Jones 17–3–64–1; Smith 15.2–2–45–2; Peterson 10–2–24–2; Park 6–0–25–1. *Second Innings*—Groenewald 20–8–46–1; Jones 17–4–38–1; Smith 27–4–76–0; Footitt 19–4–43–1; Peterson 42–11–91–4; Park 3–1–6–1; Redfern 1–0–5–0.

Derbyshire

*C. J. L. Rogers c New b Hoggard	3	– c New b Buck	0
W. L. Madsen c Jefferson b Buck	26	– c Taylor b Buck	109
P. M. Borrington c Jefferson b Buck	0	– lbw b Hoggard	25
G. T. Park b Buck	8	– c Jefferson b Hoggard	5
G. M. Smith c Taylor b Henderson	54	– b Harris	28
D. J. Redfern c New b Hoggard	6	– c New b Harris	0
R. J. Peterson c New b Henderson	54	– c Cobb b Henderson	1
†L. J. Goddard b Buck	5	– b Henderson	0
T. D. Groenewald lbw b Henderson	2	– c White b Harris	12
P. S. Jones not out	20	– c Boyce b Buck	0
M. H. A. Footitt b Hoggard	12	– not out	2
B 4, l-b 10, w 1, n-b 2	17	B 1, l-b 14, n-b 2	17

1/8 (1) 2/9 (3) 3/40 (2) 4/59 (4) (68 overs) 207
5/72 (6) 6/166 (7) 7/167 (5) 8/173 (8)
9/173 (9) 10/206 (11)

1/0 (1) 2/105 (3) (91.4 overs) 199
3/125 (4) 4/163 (5)
5/163 (6) 6/164 (7) 7/170 (8)
8/187 (2) 9/187 (10) 10/199 (9)

Hoggard 18–4–43–3; Buck 15–4–44–4; Harris 11–1–49–0; White 6–1–27–0; Henderson 18–6–30–3. *Second Innings*—Buck 20.9–9–35–3; Hoggard 21–8–45–2; Henderson 28–17–32–2; Harris 12.4–4–43–3; White 8–3–26–0; Cobb 2–0–3–0.

Umpires: B. Dudleston and T. E. Jesty.

DERBYSHIRE v GLAMORGAN

At Derby, April 21–24. Derbyshire won by eight wickets. Derbyshire 22pts, Glamorgan 5pts. Toss: Glamorgan.

Greg Smith's century, in his 100th first-class innings, helped Derbyshire recover from a poor start to their reply to a modest 272. They were nine down and only 13 ahead by the end of the second day, but next morning Smith advanced to a career-best 165 not out, taking his tenth-wicket stand with Jones to 78 from 86 balls. Arguably, though, the real damage to Glamorgan's chances came before the start: the decision to leave out Robert Croft, who had taken more than 100 first-class wickets against Derbyshire, was greeted with relief in the home changing-room. The omission looked stranger as the match wore on, as Croft's guile was badly missed. Glamorgan batted recklessly in their first innings and were also poor in their second, except for a noble effort from Rees, who made 102 before trying one reverse sweep too many. Wagg was unable to bowl in the second innings, after suffering a leg injury which would keep him out for four months, but Glamorgan succumbed to the spin of Smith and Peterson, leaving Derbyshire to complete victory before lunch on the fourth day.

Close of play: First day, Derbyshire 7-0 (Lungley 1, Madsen 0); Second day, Derbyshire 285-9 (Smith 121); Third day, Derbyshire 26-1 (Rogers 9, Borrington 0).

Glamorgan

G. P. Rees c Goddard b Jones	15	– lbw b Smith	102
M. J. Cosgrove lbw b Jones	4	– c Jones b Lungley	11
M. J. Powell c Lungley b Jones	10	– c Sadler b Peterson	4
B. J. Wright b Peterson	60	– c Goddard b Jones	13
*J. W. M. Dalrymple c Madsen b Smith	21	– lbw b Park	3
J. Allenby lbw b Peterson	57	– lbw b Peterson	12
†M. A. Wallace c Goddard b Lungley	58	– b Smith	11
D. A. Cosker lbw b Park	11	– c Lungley b Smith	7
D. S. Harrison c Lungley b Peterson	5	– b Smith	2
H. T. Waters c Goddard b Jones	5	– not out	13
C. P. Ashling not out	7	– c Sadler b Park	20
L-b 10, w 5, n-b 4	19	L-b 7, w 1, n-b 5	13

1/6 (2) 2/26 (3) 3/43 (1) 4/80 (5) (89.4 overs) 272
5/153 (4) 6/202 (6) 7/237 (8)
8/254 (9) 9/260 (7) 10/272 (10)

1/21 (2) 2/50 (3) (69.3 overs) 211
3/101 (4) 4/106 (5)
5/127 (6) 6/156 (7) 7/170 (8)
8/175 (1) 9/182 (9) 10/211 (11)

Lungley 15–5–30–1; Jones 17.4–2–60–4; Wagg 12–1–25–0; Smith 10–1–39–1; Park 10–0–31–1; Peterson 25–7–77–3. *Second Innings*—Lungley 9–1–31–1; Jones 11–3–36–1; Peterson 22–4–51–2; Smith 20–1–66–4; Park 7.3–2–20–2.

Derbyshire

T. Lungley c Wallace b Harrison	1			
W. L. Madsen c Wallace b Waters	3	– lbw b Cosker	17	
*C. J. L. Rogers lbw b Allenby	28	– (1) not out	51	
P. M. Borrington c Cosker b Ashling	27	– (3) lbw b Cosker	8	
G. T. Park b Cosgrove	61	– (4) not out	43	
G. M. Smith not out	165			
J. L. Sadler c Wallace b Cosker	10			
R. J. Peterson lbw b Harrison	19			
†L. J. Goddard lbw b Harrison	0			
G. G. Wagg c Wright b Waters	0			
P. S. Jones c Wallace b Harrison	33			
B 4, l-b 9, w 1, n-b 2	16	L-b 2	2	

1/10 (1) 2/10 (2) 3/65 (4) 4/65 (3) (115.5 overs) 363 1/22 (2) (2 wkts, 35.5 overs) 121
5/221 (5) 6/244 (7) 7/274 (8) 2/40 (3)
8/274 (9) 9/285 (10) 10/363 (11) 110 overs: 332-9

Harrison 20.5–4–53–4; Waters 22–5–71–2; Ashling 17–1–74–1; Allenby 6–1–17–1; Cosker 30–7–76–1; Dalrymple 14–2–35–0; Wright 2–0–7–0; Cosgrove 4–1–17–1. *Second Innings*—Harrison 2–0–16–0; Cosker 17–3–53–2; Dalrymple 13.5–1–42–0; Ashling 3–0–8–0.

Umpires: V. A. Holder and R. K. Illingworth.

At Northampton, April 27–30. DERBYSHIRE drew with NORTHAMPTONSHIRE.

At Lord's, May 10–12. DERBYSHIRE lost to MIDDLESEX by an innings and 35 runs.

At Worcester, May 17–20. DERBYSHIRE lost to WORCESTERSHIRE by eight wickets.

DERBYSHIRE v GLOUCESTERSHIRE

At Derby, May 24–27. Gloucestershire won by 134 runs. Gloucestershire 20pts, Derbyshire 6pts. Toss: Gloucestershire. First-class debut: A. Sheikh.

Chesney Hughes became the youngest to score a first-class century for Derbyshire, at 19 years 125 days, beating Ian Hall's record from 1959. Hughes, a muscular Anguillan left-hander in only his third Championship match, drove powerfully with an immaculately straight bat, and left with good judgment – but that was in stark contrast to many of his colleagues as Gloucestershire's more disciplined bowling brought them victory in the end. Derbyshire donated an astonishing 76 extras to their opponents' first innings of 242 – the proportion of 31.4% had been exceeded only four times in a completed Championship innings – but Hughes's century, which followed another from Rogers,

---

DERBYSHIRE'S YOUNGEST CENTURIONS

Years	Days			
19	125	**C. F. Hughes (118)**	**v Gloucestershire at Derby**	**2010**
19	226	I. W. Hall (113)	v Hampshire at Derby	1959
19	348	C. J. Adams (111*)	v Cambridge University at Cambridge	1990
20	76	J. E. Morris (116)	v Yorkshire at Harrogate	1984
20	267	L. C. Docker (107)	v Kent at Maidstone	1881

Hughes, Adams and Morris all scored more than one hundred before their 21st birthday.

forged a handy lead. Gloucestershire exploited some uninspiring bowling to set a target of 301 on the final day: Chris Dent, born on the same day as Hughes, pulled his 85th ball to deep midwicket two short of a deserved maiden century, after hitting 14 fours and two sixes. Derbyshire's response was quickly in disarray at 15 for four as Kirby and Lewis got stuck in, and only another promising innings from Hughes avoided a heftier beating as Gloucestershire completed their fourth victory of the season. The match featured five wicketkeepers: after Batty dislocated a finger, Snell replaced him for the last 19 overs of Derbyshire's first innings, and caught the debutant Atif Sheikh. In Gloucestershire's second innings, Tom Poynton was unable to take the field on the third day because of flu: Jamie Pipe, the former Derbyshire keeper who is now their physio, deputised for eight overs before Lee Goddard arrived from a Second Eleven match in Cardiff.

Close of play: First day, Derbyshire 71-3 (Rogers 49, Hughes 8); Second day, Gloucestershire 47-1 (Kadeer Ali 21, Kirby 4); Third day, Derbyshire 5-0 (Madsen 0, Rogers 5).

Gloucestershire

†J. N. Batty c Hughes b Lungley	61	– (4) c Lungley b Smith 18
S. D. Snell c Hughes b Smith	9	– (1) b Smith 21
C. D. J. Dent c Poynton b Sheikh	0	– (5) c Peterson b Sheikh 98
H. J. H. Marshall c Poynton b Smith	5	– (6) c Madsen b Sheikh 40
*A. P. R. Gidman c Hughes b Sheikh	37	– (7) b Peterson 42
J. E. C. Franklin lbw b Smith	29	– (8) lbw b Lungley 37
Kadeer Ali b Lungley	5	– (2) c Park b Groenewald 74
J. Lewis c Hughes b Groenewald	14	– (9) c Rogers b Lungley 34
V. Banerjee not out	3	– (10) c and b Smith 2
G. M. Hussain c Sheikh b Peterson	3	– (11) not out 2
S. P. Kirby lbw b Peterson	0	– (3) c sub (L. J. Goddard) ....
		b Groenewald . 13
B 6, l-b 19, w 13, n-b 38	76	B 7, l-b 2, w 1, n-b 12 22

1/48 (2) 2/56 (3) 3/97 (4) 4/169 (1)   (72 overs) 242
5/169 (5) 6/192 (7) 7/220 (8) 8/234 (6)
9/242 (10) 10/242 (11)

1/38 (1) 2/102 (3)   (86.3 overs) 403
3/125 (4) 4/185 (4)
5/252 (6) 6/281 (5) 7/355 (7)
8/398 (8) 9/399 (9) 10/403 (10)

Lungley 11–1–45–2; Sheikh 12–1–78–3; Groenewald 16–5–45–1; Smith 13–4–28–2; Peterson 16–5–19–2; Park 4–2–2–0. *Second Innings*—Groenewald 12–3–53–2; Sheikh 13–0–74–2; Smith 12.3–1–54–3; Peterson 28–3–124–1; Lungley 15–3–59–2; Hughes 2–0–16–0; Park 4–0–14–0.

Derbyshire

*C. J. L. Rogers c Batty b Hussain	115	– (2) c Gidman b Kirby 7
W. L. Madsen lbw b Lewis	0	– (1) c Kadeer Ali b Kirby 4
G. T. Park lbw b Hussain	4	– c Batty b Lewis 0
G. M. Smith c Dent b Hussain	4	– c Batty b Lewis 0
C. F. Hughes run out	118	– lbw b Lewis 75
D. J. Redfern c Batty b Banerjee	12	– c Batty b Franklin......... 27
R. J. Peterson b Banerjee	8	– c Snell b Banerjee 3
†T. Poynton c Batty b Banerjee	22	– c Marshall b Hussain 12
T. Lungley c and b Banerjee	1	– c Franklin b Lewis 11
T. D. Groenewald not out	34	– not out 4
A. Sheikh c Snell b Lewis	6	– b Lewis 0
B 5, l-b 13, w 1, n-b 2	21	B 14, l-b 1, n-b 8 23

1/7 (2) 2/32 (3) 3/50 (4)   (105.4 overs) 345
4/184 (1) 5/205 (6) 6/225 (7)
7/269 (8) 8/273 (9) 9/316 (5) 10/345 (11)

1/10 (2) 2/11 (3)   (57.5 overs) 166
3/11 (2) 4/15 (4)
5/62 (6) 6/84 (7) 7/121 (8)
8/160 (9) 9/166 (5) 10/166 (11)

Lewis 20.4–3–73–2; Kirby 25–11–54–0; Hussain 18–2–65–3; Banerjee 27–6–62–4; Franklin 5–1–24–0; Gidman 3–0–24–0. *Second Innings*—Kirby 13–5–22–2; Lewis 12.5–3–25–4; Franklin 5–2–20–1; Hussain 11–1–46–1; Banerjee 16–2–38–2.

Umpires: J. F. Steele and P. Willey.

DERBYSHIRE v SUSSEX

At Derby, June 5–8. Drawn. Derbyshire 8pts, Sussex 11pts. Toss: Sussex.

Robin Martin-Jenkins left another venue on his farewell tour with applause ringing in his ears, but rain stymied a potentially exciting finale, preventing any play on the final day. Derbyshire's bowlers had the better of the early exchanges until Martin-Jenkins, playing his last away game in the Championship before taking up a teaching post, joined Goodwin, who had been dropped on 15. Both reached centuries: their partnership of 225 was a Sussex record for any wicket against Derbyshire (openers Ed Joyce and Chris Nash were to improve on it later in the summer at Horsham), and the highest for the seventh wicket against Derbyshire by any county. The home side recovered well, but the loss of Hughes and Redfern late on the second day following a break for bad light was costly. Wright mopped up the tail to finish with a five-for, but a burst of four wickets – including three for one in 15 balls – from Peterson tipped the balance again late on the third day. Sussex, who lost five for nine in the last hour, ended the day only 163 in front, but the weather had the last word.

Close of play: First day, Sussex 371-8 (Yasir Arafat 13, Anyon 4); Second day, Derbyshire 244-6 (Peterson 4, Poynton 4); Third day, Sussex 71-7 (Brown 2).

Sussex

*M. H. Yardy c Smith b Lungley	8	– lbw b Footitt		8
C. D. Nash b Lungley	5	– c sub (J. L. Clare) b Peterson		18
E. C. Joyce c Hughes b Lungley	9	– c sub (J. L. Clare) b Peterson		20
M. W. Goodwin b Jones	121	– c Poynton b Smith		6
M. A. Thornely c Poynton b Footitt	8	– lbw b Peterson		4
L. J. Wright b Peterson	20	– c sub (J. L. Clare) b Peterson		0
†B. C. Brown b Footitt	5	– (8) not out		2
R. S. C. Martin-Jenkins c Park b Jones	130			
Yasir Arafat not out	34			
J. E. Anyon c sub (T. D. Groenewald) b Peterson	34	– (7) lbw b Smith		1
M. S. Panesar run out	0			
B 27, l-b 11, w 1, n-b 16	55	B 5, w 1, n-b 6		12

1/14 (1) 2/27 (2) 3/30 (3)　　　　　(116.5 overs) 429　　1/9 (1) 2/44 (3) (7 wkts, 33 overs) 71
4/64 (5) 5/117 (6) 6/126 (7) 7/351 (4)　　　　　　　　3/62 (4) 4/64 (2)
8/362 (8) 9/426 (10) 10/429 (11)　110 overs: 417-8　　5/68 (6) 6/69 (5) 7/71 (7)

Lungley 15–1–71–3; Jones 24–6–62–2; Smith 16–2–70–0; Footitt 17.5–3–48–2; Park 7–0–46–0; Peterson 37–7–94–2. *Second Innings*—Jones 6–2–17–0; Footitt 7–1–15–1; Peterson 11–5–10–4; Smith 9–3–24–2.

Derbyshire

*C. J. L. Rogers c Thornely b Panesar	79	T. Lungley lbw b Wright		5
W. L. Madsen lbw b Yasir Arafat	0	M. H. A. Footitt c Brown b Wright		0
G. T. Park c Joyce b Martin-Jenkins	24			
G. M. Smith c and b Panesar	2	B 18, l-b 15, w 1, n-b 4		38
C. F. Hughes lbw b Wright	62			
D. J. Redfern b Wright	44	1/7 (2) 2/103 (3)	(101.5 overs)	337
R. J. Peterson c Joyce b Anyon	31	3/114 (4) 4/127 (1) 5/225 (5)		
†T. Poynton b Wright	14	6/234 (6) 7/272 (8) 8/299 (7)		
P. S. Jones not out	38	9/337 (10) 10/337 (11)		

Yasir Arafat 17–3–54–1; Anyon 21–3–74–1; Martin-Jenkins 11–1–38–1; Wright 20.5–2–65–5; Panesar 30–6–71–2; Nash 2–0–2–0.

Umpires: M. A. Gough and D. J. Millns.

DERBYSHIRE v SURREY

At Chesterfield, June 28–July 1. Surrey won by 42 runs. Surrey 23pts, Derbyshire 4pts. Toss: Surrey.

The drama in an incident-packed match began on the first day, when a scoreboard error gave Ramprakash a century too soon and he was out shortly afterwards for 99. Surrey still achieved a commanding position, although Groenewald claimed Derbyshire's first five-for of 2010. Seamer Tim

Linley then tore through the home side with four for 13 before breaking down with a foot injury in his 11th over, leaving Madsen to salvage the innings with the first of his two centuries in the match (he was the 15th to do this for Derbyshire – and the second of the season after Rogers, also against Surrey). The visitors extended their lead with some solid batting throughout the order, in which the top score was Nel's 35. Derbyshire were left needing a higher total – 408 – than they had ever made in the fourth innings. With Linley absent, Nel hobbling in off a short run with hamstring trouble, and off-spinner Batty nursing a broken finger, Surrey relied heavily on Tremlett – and he took the final wicket, bowling Lungley, who had bravely returned despite his right arm having been broken when he was unable to get out of the way of a firm drive from Jones when the score was 341. He survived 21 balls until he was out with just 9.1 overs remaining.

Close of play: First day, Surrey 364-9 (Tremlett 15, Linley 2); Second day, Surrey 50-1 (Harinath 20, Ramprakash 24); Third day, Derbyshire 136-1 (Madsen 55, Park 30).

Surrey

A. Harinath lbw b Groenewald	16	– c Rogers b Groenewald	25
*R. J. Hamilton-Brown c Rogers b Jones	24	– c Goddard b Groenewald	4
M. R. Ramprakash b Groenewald	99	– c Rogers b Lungley	30
Younis Khan c Goddard b Jones	45	– lbw b Smith	30
U. Afzaal c Hughes b Groenewald	73	– c Rogers b Peterson	26
S. J. Walters c Hughes b Groenewald	53	– c Rogers b Peterson	15
†G. C. Wilson c Rogers b Peterson	6	– c Park b Smith	28
G. J. Batty b Jones	4	– c Goddard b Lungley	26
A. Nel b Groenewald	0	– c Goddard b Groenewald	35
C. T. Tremlett not out	29	– not out	10
T. E. Linley c Hughes b Jones	15	– c Groenewald b Peterson	7
B 6, l-b 11, n-b 10	27	B 1, l-b 10, w 2, n-b 4	17

1/38 (2) 2/48 (1) 3/135 (4) (100 overs) 391 1/8 (2) 2/67 (3) (78.2 overs) 253
4/276 (5) 5/285 (3) 6/300 (7) 3/69 (1) 4/123 (5)
7/340 (8) 8/341 (9) 9/360 (6) 10/391 (11) 5/127 (4) 6/149 (6) 7/187 (7)
8/201 (8) 9/242 (9) 10/253 (11)

Lungley 14–2–67–0; Jones 22–4–65–4; Smith 11–0–52–0; Groenewald 27–8–86–5; Park 4–0–25–0; Peterson 20–5–65–1; Durston 2–0–14–0. *Second Innings*—Jones 13–3–37–0; Groenewald 19–1–63–3; Lungley 15–2–60–2; Smith 13–2–36–2; Peterson 18.2–3–46–3.

Derbyshire

*C. J. L. Rogers c Walters b Nel	14	– (2) c Hamilton-Brown b Batty	33
W. L. Madsen b Batty	109	– (1) c Wilson b Afzaal	105
G. T. Park c Wilson b Linley	6	– c Wilson b Tremlett	54
G. M. Smith b Linley	2	– c sub (M. N. W. Spriegel) b Nel	34
C. F. Hughes c Wilson b Linley	2	– c Hamilton-Brown b Afzaal	0
W. J. Durston b Linley	8	– lbw b Tremlett	16
R. J. Peterson c Younis Khan b Tremlett	5	– c Harinath b Nel	40
†L. J. Goddard c Hamilton-Brown b Batty	67	– lbw b Nel	0
T. Lungley lbw b Batty	0	– b Tremlett	21
P. S. Jones lbw b Tremlett	4	– not out	20
T. D. Groenewald not out	4	– c Younis Khan b Tremlett	3
B 5, l-b 5, n-b 6	16	B 22, l-b 2, w 5, n-b 10	39

1/18 (1) 2/25 (3) 3/29 (4) 4/33 (5) (69.1 overs) 237 1/45 (2) 2/205 (3) (117.5 overs) 365
5/59 (6) 6/81 (7) 7/218 (2) 8/226 (9) 3/227 (1) 4/227 (5)
9/231 (10) 10/237 (8) 5/270 (6) 6/270 (4) 7/284 (8)
8/337 (9) 9/353 (11) 10/365 (9)

In the second innings Lungley, when 20, retired hurt at 341 and resumed at 353.

Nel 19–3–63–1; Tremlett 18.4–5–64–2; Linley 10.2–4–13–4; Younis Khan 5–0–22–0; Batty 13.1–1–50–3; Walters 3–0–15–0. *Second Innings*—Nel 25–6–74–3; Tremlett 32.5–7–94–4; Batty 38–9–99–1; Younis Khan 6–0–25–0; Afzaal 10–1–33–2; Hamilton-Brown 6–0–16–0.

Umpires: M. R. Benson and N. G. C. Cowley.

At Derby, July 8-9 (not first-class). DERBYSHIRE drew with AUSTRALIANS (see Pakistan v Australia section, pages 310–321).

DERBYSHIRE v WORCESTERSHIRE

At Derby, July 21–24. Drawn. Derbyshire 9pts, Worcestershire 7pts. Toss: Worcestershire. County debut: Shakib Al Hasan.

Worcestershire were in a precarious position at the end of the third day, but Kervezee, the 20-year-old Dutch international, showed great maturity to steer his side to safety. Forceful, clean hitting all around the wicket brought him a career-best 155, and underlined his liking for Derbyshire's bowling: his only previous first-class century had come against them at New Road in May. Worcestershire survived countless near misses on the first morning, but Wheeldon batted for more than three hours before Shakib Al Hasan, the first Bangladeshi to play in the Championship, and the Zimbabwean James Cameron – whose 89 in his third first-class match included eight fours and four sixes, three of them in succession off Peterson – frustrated the home attack further. Madsen missed out on a third consecutive Championship century, but Smith helped build a lead of 126, which appeared even more useful when Worcestershire dipped to 70 for three by the end of the third day. Then Kervezee was dropped by Rogers at slip off Smith when 39; he and Mitchell made the match safe, batting through more than 53 overs and adding 181 for the fourth wicket.

Close of play: First day, Derbyshire 43-0 (Rogers 22, Madsen 15); Second day, Derbyshire 183-4 (Smith 18, Redfern 5); Third day, Worcestershire 70-3 (Mitchell 21).

Worcestershire

D. K. H. Mitchell b Groenewald	14	– c Rogers b Footitt	71
D. A. Wheeldon c Footitt b Park	20	– c Goddard b Jones	14
*V. S. Solanki c Redfern b Jones	22	– c Rogers b Groenewald	3
M. M. Ali c Goddard b Groenewald	2	– c Jones b Peterson	29
A. N. Kervezee lbw b Groenewald	8	– c Footitt b Hughes	155
Shakib Al Hasan c Goddard b Smith	90	– c Goddard b Park	21
J. G. Cameron c Hughes b Peterson	89	– not out	9
†O. B. Cox lbw b Peterson	17	– not out	6
R. A. Jones c Rogers b Smith	3		
M. S. Mason run out	1		
A. Richardson not out	0		
B 3, l-b 3, w 1, n-b 6	13	L-b 12, w 2, n-b 6	20

1/18 (1) 2/45 (3) 3/56 (4) 4/66 (5)   (82.2 overs) 279   1/28 (2)   (6 wkts dec, 104 overs) 328
5/106 (2) 6/207 (6) 7/247 (8)   2/31 (3) 3/70 (4)
8/260 (9) 9/279 (10) 10/279 (7)   4/251 (1) 5/309 (6) 6/314 (5)

Groenewald 15–3–65–3; Footitt 17–6–39–0; Smith 18–4–33–2; Jones 16–3–57–1; Park 4–1–13–1; Peterson 12.2–1–66–2. *Second Innings*—Groenewald 20–6–49–0; Footitt 19–6–39–2; Smith 20–4–60–0; Jones 9–2–22–1; Peterson 22–4–81–1; Redfern 2–0–9–0; Park 9–2–42–1; Hughes 2–0–9–1; Rogers 1–0–5–0.

Derbyshire

*C. J. L. Rogers c Cox b Richardson	22	T. D. Groenewald not out	3
W. L. Madsen c Wheeldon b Jones	75	M. H. A. Footitt c Mason b Shakib Al Hasan	2
G. T. Park lbw b Mason	1	
C. F. Hughes c Cox b Jones	44	B 9, l-b 32, w 3	44
G. M. Smith c Shakib Al Hasan b Ali	91	
D. J. Redfern c Mitchell b Mason	19	1/43 (1) 2/44 (3) (135.5 overs) 405
R. J. Peterson c Kervezee b Shakib Al Hasan	26	3/157 (2) 4/158 (4) 5/237 (6)
†L. J. Goddard c Shakib Al Hasan b Jones	38	6/308 (5) 7/324 (7) 8/391 (9)
P. S. Jones c Cameron b Shakib Al Hasan	40	9/402 (8) 10/405 (11) 110 overs: 308-6

Mason 29–8–80–2; Jones 23–4–83–3; Shakib Al Hasan 37.5–9–94–3; Richardson 30–7–64–1; Ali 16–3–43–1.

Umpires: R. A. Kettleborough and J. F. Steele.

At Leicester, August 3–6. DERBYSHIRE lost to LEICESTERSHIRE by ten wickets.

DERBYSHIRE v NORTHAMPTONSHIRE

At Chesterfield, August 9–12. Drawn. Derbyshire 9pts, Northamptonshire 7pts. Toss: Derbyshire. County debut: G. C. Baker.

Hughes, already Derbyshire's youngest century-maker after his 118 against Gloucestershire in May, now added a second hundred – and this one was even more spectacularly accomplished, as he dominated a low-scoring first innings with a masterful 156 full of muscular front-foot shots. Hughes faced 183 balls, and hit 27 fours and a huge six off Middlebrook into the trees over long-on: "He's the best 19-year-old I've seen for a long time," said John Morris, Derbyshire's head of cricket. Clare marked his first Championship appearance of the season with four wickets, and Greg Smith claimed his only five-for of the summer, but Northamptonshire provided sterner resistance in the second innings as the pitch flattened out and the outfield quickened up. Four batsmen reached 80: Rob Newton made an impressive 82 in only his second Championship appearance after a first-ball duck on the opening day, while Middlebrook's 84 was his first half-century for his new county. The last three wickets added 167, which left Derbyshire 352 to win – but rain, which allowed only 17.1 overs on the fourth day, played spoilsport again.

Close of play: First day, Derbyshire 124-5 (Hughes 61, Peterson 18); Second day, Northamptonshire 181-2 (Howgego 74, Sales 84); Third day, Derbyshire 30-0 (Madsen 11, Rogers 14).

Northamptonshire

M. B. Loye c Rogers b Groenewald	3	– c Rogers b Jones	4
B. H. N. Howgego b Smith	35	– b Jones	80
A. G. Wakely c Durston b Clare	13	– run out	10
D. J. Sales c Rogers b Clare	36	– lbw b Jones	92
R. I. Newton c Durston b Clare	0	– c Madsen b Smith	82
*A. J. Hall c Durston b Smith	29	– c Redfern b Clare	7
E. Chigumbura c Clare b Smith	26	– b Jones	33
†D. Murphy b Smith	0	– c Adshead b Groenewald	7
J. D. Middlebrook c Madsen b Smith	16	– c Clare b Peterson	84
G. C. Baker c Adshead b Clare	14	– c Durston b Peterson	35
L. M. Daggett not out	9	– not out	14
L-b 2, w 6, n-b 12	20	B 6, l-b 5, w 2, n-b 8	21

1/17 (1) 2/59 (2) 3/59 (3) 4/59 (5) (64 overs) 201
5/127 (4) 6/127 (6) 7/127 (8)
8/166 (9) 9/175 (7) 10/201 (10)

1/4 (1) 2/25 (3) (136.1 overs) 469
3/197 (4) 4/198 (2)
5/221 (6) 6/281 (7) 7/302 (8)
8/371 (5) 9/445 (9) 10/469 (10)

Jones 15–4–42–0; Groenewald 18–4–57–1; Smith 19–6–54–5; Clare 11–3–42–4; Peterson 1–0–4–0. *Second Innings*—Jones 29–7–96–4; Groenewald 37–3–136–1; Clare 16–3–54–1; Smith 20–2–81–1; Peterson 34.1–5–91–2.

Derbyshire

*C. J. L. Rogers run out	9	– (2) not out	42
W. L. Madsen lbw b Chigumbura	0	– (1) not out	25
C. F. Hughes b Hall	156		
W. J. Durston c Hall b Chigumbura	3		
G. M. Smith b Chigumbura	4		
D. J. Redfern c Murphy b Chigumbura	21		
R. J. Peterson c Wakely b Daggett	58		
J. L. Clare b Daggett	9		
†S. J. Adshead c Howgego b Hall	13		
P. S. Jones b Chigumbura	6		
T. D. Groenewald not out	13		
B 5, l-b 3, w 5, n-b 14	27	L-b 5, w 2, n-b 2	9

1/10 (1) 2/10 (2) 3/36 (4) 4/40 (5) (64.5 overs) 319
5/98 (6) 6/196 (7) 7/218 (8)
8/257 (9) 9/274 (10) 10/319 (3)

(no wkt, 33.1 overs) 76

Daggett 20–3–70–2; Chigumbura 15–0–92–5; Baker 10–1–52–0; Hall 16.5–1–78–2; Middlebrook 3–0–19–0. *Second Innings*—Daggett 15.5–5–35–0; Chigumbura 9–3–17–0; Baker 3–2–2–0; Middlebrook 2–0–4–0; Hall 4.1–0–13–0.

Umpires: J. H. Evans and R. K. Illingworth.

At Horsham, August 18–20. DERBYSHIRE lost to SUSSEX by an innings and 109 runs.

DERBYSHIRE v MIDDLESEX

At Derby, August 25–28. Drawn. Derbyshire 6pts, Middlesex 8pts. Toss: Middlesex.

When the third day featured such reckless shots that 21 wickets clattered, thoughts of a rain-affected draw were briefly suspended. In the end neither side had the firepower to force a positive outcome. Four sessions were washed out, including the whole of the second day, but the lost time was partially negated by batting which went a long way to explaining why these teams finished at the bottom of the table. Newman, who was marooned on 119 for 44 hours, was the first man out early on the third day, and suffered the indignity of being dismissed a second time before the close. Middlesex's last seven first-innings wickets fell for 22 in 13.4 overs, but Derbyshire still conceded a deficit of 81 after another indifferent batting performance in which Hughes picked up the first half of a pair. Fears of a second Middlesex collapse were averted by their captain, Dexter, whose doughty unbeaten 92 allowed him to declare 302 ahead with 53 overs remaining. Rogers, playing his last home Championship match for Derbyshire, added 96 to his first-innings 75 against the county he was to join in 2011, but the target was only briefly threatened.

Close of play: First day, Middlesex 228-3 (Newman 119, Dexter 15); Second day, No play; Third day, Middlesex 71-4 (Dexter 9, Berg 5).

Middlesex

S. A. Newman c Footitt b Peterson	126	– lbw b Groenewald	7
†J. A. Simpson c Adshead b Jones	21	– lbw b Wagg	8
O. A. Shah c Durston b Wagg	12	– c Adshead b Footitt	29
D. J. Malan b Durston	41	– c Madsen b Footitt	10
*N. J. Dexter c Durston b Footitt	20	– not out	92
G. K. Berg lbw b Peterson	4	– c Adshead b Jones	9
T. M. J. Smith not out	2	– b Peterson	33
S. D. Udal lbw b Footitt	0	– c Adshead b Wagg	6
T. J. Murtagh c Adshead b Footitt	6	– not out	11
T. S. Roland-Jones c Adshead b Groenewald	3		
P. T. Collins c Jones b Groenewald	0		
B 8, l-b 5, w 11, n-b 4	28	B 2, l-b 6, w 6, n-b 2	16

1/36 (2) 2/55 (3) 3/194 (4) (79.4 overs) 263
4/241 (1) 5/245 (6) 6/245 (5)
7/245 (8) 8/259 (9) 9/263 (10) 10/263 (11)

1/7 (1) (7 wkts dec, 61.2 overs) 221
2/27 (2) 3/51 (4)
4/56 (3) 5/98 (6) 6/177 (7) 7/188 (8)

Wagg 14–3–35–1; Groenewald 16.4–8–30–2; Jones 10–1–45–1; Footitt 13–4–50–3; Smith 5–0–33–0; Peterson 19–7–48–2; Durston 2–0–9–1. *Second Innings*—Wagg 10–1–41–2; Groenewald 11–3–36–1; Footitt 9.2–2–28–2; Peterson 15–2–45–1; Smith 7–2–25–0; Jones 5–2–18–1; Durston 4–0–20–0.

Derbyshire

C. J. L. Rogers b Udal	75	– (2) c Simpson b Roland-Jones	96
W. L. Madsen c Newman b Murtagh	10	– (1) c Shah b Udal	41
C. F. Hughes b Collins	0	– (6) lbw b Udal	0
W. J. Durston c Simpson b Collins	17	– c Simpson b Roland-Jones	1
*G. M. Smith c Simpson b Collins	5	– lbw b Udal	15
R. J. Peterson c Dexter b Udal	15	– (7) not out	9
†S. J. Adshead c Simpson b Roland-Jones	7	– (8) not out	11
G. G. Wagg c Shah b Udal	3	– (3) b Roland-Jones	4
P. S. Jones st Simpson b Udal	30		
T. D. Groenewald not out	9		
M. H. A. Footitt c Simpson b Collins	4		
B 1, l-b 6	7	B 8, l-b 4	12

1/37 (2) 2/38 (3) 3/68 (4) 4/82 (5) (51.3 overs) 182   1/131 (1)   (6 wkts, 52 overs) 189
5/122 (6) 6/133 (1) 7/135 (7)   2/139 (3) 3/143 (4)
8/139 (8) 9/177 (9) 10/182 (11)   4/156 (5) 5/157 (6) 6/166 (5)

Murtagh 9–1–41–1; Collins 17.3–3–46–4; Dexter 5–2–16–0; Udal 12–2–37–4; Roland-Jones 6–0–27–1; Smith 2–0–8–0. *Second Innings*—Murtagh 4–0–22–0; Collins 4–2–7–0; Roland-Jones 14–1–42–3; Udal 20–3–61–3; Smith 8–2–40–0; Shah 2–0–5–0.

Umpires: S. C. Gale and N. A. Mallender.

At Bristol, August 31–September 1. DERBYSHIRE beat GLOUCESTERSHIRE by 54 runs. *Derbyshire are bowled out for 44 on the first morning – yet go on to win.*

At Cardiff, September 13–16. DERBYSHIRE drew with GLAMORGAN. *Derbyshire finish bottom of Division Two for the first time since 2005.*

DURHAM

Third time unlucky

Tim Wellock

Such was Durham's domination of the 2009 County Championship that they were tipped to become the first team since Yorkshire in 1968 to complete a hat-trick of titles. But a rapid decline set in once they had easily triumphed in the MCC v Champions curtain-raiser in Abu Dhabi.

Barely a month into the season, 13 players had been injured – which raised a question about the fitness regime – and, a day after their first Championship defeat in 24 games, Will Smith was replaced as captain by Phil Mustard. There were occasional signs of improvement but, as the casualties continued, so did the comedown. Durham finished fifth in the Championship, fifth out of seven in their group in the 40-over league, and eighth out of nine in the Friends Provident T20 North Division.

Graham Onions's back injury ruled him out altogether; Steve Harmison, Mark Davies and Callum Thorp made 18 Championship appearances between them. Liam Plunkett missed only two matches, but his batting average declined from 44 in 2009 to 14, and his 35 wickets cost nearly 40 apiece: spending much of the winter with the England squad clearly hadn't helped. The elder Harmison had put on weight and was troubled by a foot problem; he admitted he should not have played in the Championship defeat by Kent, when his 11 overs cost 83 runs.

The number of foot and ankle injuries defied belief. The final casualty was Ben Stokes, described by Kent captain Robert Key as the best young batsman he had ever seen after an unbeaten 161 at Canterbury, shortly before his 19th birthday. From an athletic 15-stone frame, Stokes struck the ball with phenomenal power for one so young. He topped the averages with 740 runs at 46. Durham stressed that Stokes would not have played had they engaged an overseas player for the Championship.

In 2009, four bowlers passed 40 wickets, and Onions reached that landmark in his first five games. This time, Ian Blackwell matched his 43 wickets of the previous year, but the next best were Plunkett and Mitch Claydon with 35 each. Sunderland seamer Chris Rushworth, released from the academy several years earlier, was engaged and called upon far more than had seemed likely. Energetic young leg-spinner Scott Borthwick played ten games, making all-round progress.

Claydon remained inconsistent and was left out of the final match to give an opportunity to West Indian triallist Ruel Brathwaite, a 25-year-old paceman who had been to Dulwich College, Loughborough and Cambridge. He was offered a two-year contract, filling one of the gaps left by the retirement of Neil Killeen and Will Gidman's decision to join his brother Alex at Gloucestershire from 2011.

Ben Stokes

Mustard was the only ever-present in all three competitions, although Michael Di Venuto and Dale Benkenstein played in all the Championship games. Benkenstein battled on after tearing a patella tendon in his knee, but was barely able to walk by September, when he needed a hernia operation. His form suffered and, at 36, this seemed unlikely to be reversed. Di Venuto, six months older, saw his average drop from 80 to 45, but had reached 1,000 Championship runs in the final match.

No other batsman passed 800. Gordon Muchall stepped into Smith's No. 3 slot and scored two centuries. Mark Stoneman still failed to average 30 after regaining the opening spot from Kyle Coetzer, who scored 172 against MCC in Abu Dhabi, but had the misfortune to have his shortcomings exposed by Makhaya Ntini for Kent.

The greater misfortune, however, belonged to Smith. He began the season determined to rediscover his 2008 form. But a lack of runs, which hadn't mattered during his first season at the helm, suddenly became a problem. Immediately after the innings defeat at Trent Bridge, by Durham's eventual successors as champions, he told the media he was determined to fight on; less than 24 hours later, it was announced that he had stood down by mutual agreement. He later said he wished it to be known that he wasn't a quitter, and claimed to be unaware that he had lost the backing of some senior players. Back in the ranks, Smith appeared in the Twenty20 and the odd one-day game, batting down the order, but mostly played second-team cricket.

After stressing how hard he had worked to get fit for his first season with Durham in 2009, Blackwell appeared a little more rotund, and his one-day form was disappointing. But he remained the four-day side's most valuable member in terms of runs and wickets. In a season of five wins and three defeats, he was a match-winner against Hampshire and Lancashire.

When handed the captaincy, Mustard was told to remain his bubbly self, the priority being to restore morale. He took to the task surprisingly well, and it brought the best out of his batting: he scored two Championship centuries, four years after his first two. But his one-day form suffered and, without his bright starts, the team rarely fired. In November, it was announced that Mustard would continue to lead the Championship side but Benkenstein would resume the captaincy in 40-over and Twenty20 cricket.

Ross Taylor and Albie Morkel, the overseas men recruited for Twenty20 purposes, headed those batting averages with impressive strike-rates. But after Durham twice raised their highest Twenty20 total, at Edgbaston and against Leicestershire, then followed up with an easy home victory over Yorkshire, they managed only one more win. It questioned the wisdom of chasing Twenty20 glory when the elusive Championship hat-trick was the real goal.

DURHAM RESULTS

All first-class matches – Played 18: Won 6, Lost 3, Drawn 9.
County Championship matches – Played 16: Won 5, Lost 3, Drawn 8.

LV= County Championship, 5th in Division 1;
Friends Provident T20, 8th in North Division; Clydesdale Bank 40, 5th in Group C.

COUNTY CHAMPIONSHIP AVERAGES, BATTING AND FIELDING

Cap		M	I	NO	R	HS	100s	50s	Avge	Ct/St
	B. A. Stokes	13	19	3	740	161*	2	2	46.25	8
	M. J. Di Venuto¶	16	27	3	1,092	129	3	7	45.50	29
2005	G. J. Muchall	9	14	1	508	140*	2	1	39.07	3
	P. Mustard†	16	24	5	742	120	2	4	39.05	40/2
	I. D. Blackwell	15	24	2	794	86	0	8	36.09	2
2005	D. M. Benkenstein¶	16	26	1	799	114	1	5	31.96	13
	B. W. Harmison	5	9	0	265	96	0	2	29.44	0
	M. D. Stoneman	10	16	1	407	78	0	4	27.13	5
	K. J. Coetzer	6	12	1	280	72	0	2	25.45	2
	S. G. Borthwick†	10	14	3	269	68	0	2	24.45	8
	M. E. Claydon	12	15	4	185	38*	0	0	16.81	2
	W. R. Smith	4	7	0	114	44	0	0	16.28	2
2005	M. Davies†	5	4	2	32	27	0	0	16.00	0
	L. E. Plunkett	14	17	0	238	51	0	1	14.00	8
	C. D. Thorp¶	5	6	1	64	29	0	0	12.80	2
	C. Rushworth†	9	14	2	127	28	0	0	10.58	1
1999	S. J. Harmison	8	11	6	29	11*	0	0	5.80	2

Also batted: R. M. R. Brathwaite (1 match) 2, 0*; G. R. Breese¶ (cap 2005) (1 match) 8, 5 (1 ct);
P. D. Collingwood†‡ (cap 1998) (1 match) 12.

† *Born in Durham.*   ‡ *ECB contract.*   ¶ *Non-England-qualified player.*
Durham ceased to award caps after 2005.

BOWLING

	O	M	R	W	BB	5W/i	Avge
S. J. Harmison	240.4	50	801	30	7-29	1	26.70
I. D. Blackwell	455.3	129	1,205	43	5-78	2	28.02
B. W. Harmison	86.4	10	402	14	4-70	0	28.71
M. E. Claydon	287.1	49	1,087	35	3-17	0	31.05
C. D. Thorp	148.3	39	427	13	4-54	0	32.84
C. Rushworth	214.4	43	821	21	4-90	0	39.09
L. E. Plunkett	384.4	57	1,386	35	4-107	0	39.60
S. G. Borthwick	153.5	18	615	15	2-22	0	41.00

Also bowled: D. M. Benkenstein 81–43–143–4; R. M. R. Brathwaite 30.1–2–118–4; K. J. Coetzer
7–0–33–0; P. D. Collingwood 7–3–11–1; M. Davies 128–45–273–2; G. J. Muchall 1–0–2–0; W. R.
Smith 4–0–27–0; B. A. Stokes 66.3–6–328–5.

LEADING CB40 AVERAGES (100 runs/4 wickets)

Batting	Runs	HS	Avge	S-R	Ct/St
G. J. Muchall	318	77	35.33	76.25	9
M. J. Di Venuto ...	134	63	33.50	105.51	3
B. W. Harmison ...	323	52	32.30	70.67	3
P. Mustard	304	90	27.63	84.44	9/6
G. R. Breese	171	42	24.42	104.26	6
D. M. Benkenstein .	110	34	22.00	83.33	3

Bowling	W	BB	Avge	E-R
W. R. S. Gidman ...	6	4-36	9.00	5.06
C. Rushworth	15	3-6	15.06	4.34
I. D. Blackwell	10	3-22	27.50	4.88
M. E. Claydon	6	3-51	31.50	5.13
G. R. Breese	9	2-13	36.33	5.39
L. E. Plunkett	5	2-46	38.40	6.22

LEADING FPT20 AVERAGES (100 runs/18 overs)

Batting	Runs	HS	Avge	S-R	Ct/St
L. R. P. L. Taylor ..	315	80*	39.37	**173.07**	4
L. E. Plunkett	102	31	25.50	**141.66**	2
J. A. Morkel	272	48	34.00	**128.90**	1
D. M. Benkenstein .	249	57*	24.90	**125.75**	5
I. D. Blackwell	198	79	19.80	**125.31**	2
P. Mustard.........	284	70*	23.66	**124.56**	11/3

Bowling	W	BB	Avge	E-R
G. R. Breese	11	3-14	22.00	**6.75**
I. D. Blackwell ...	8	2-14	26.62	**7.34**
B. W. Harmison ...	8	2-22	28.50	**8.44**
S. J. Harmison.....	14	5-41	20.21	**8.57**
J. A. Morkel	7	2-25	42.42	**8.91**
M. E. Claydon.....	4	1-17	52.25	**9.08**

FIRST-CLASS COUNTY RECORDS

Highest score for	273	M. L. Love v Hampshire at Chester-le-Street	2003
Highest score against	501*	B. C. Lara (Warwickshire) at Birmingham.......	1994
Leading run-scorer	7,854	J. J. B. Lewis (avge 31.41)	1997–2006
Best bowling for	10-47	O. D. Gibson v Hampshire at Chester-le-Street	2007
Best bowling against	9-36	M. S. Kasprowicz (Glamorgan) at Cardiff	2003
Leading wicket-taker	518	S. J. E. Brown (avge 28.30)	1992–2002
Highest total for	648-5 dec	v Nottinghamshire at Chester-le-Street	2009
Highest total against	810-4 dec	by Warwickshire at Birmingham	1994
Lowest total for	67	v Middlesex at Lord's.......................	1996
Lowest total against	56	by Somerset at Chester-le-Street...............	2003

LIST A COUNTY RECORDS

Highest score for	145	J. E. Morris v Leicestershire at Leicester.........	1996
Highest score against	151*	M. P. Maynard (Glamorgan) at Darlington	1991
Leading run-scorer	4,350	P. D. Collingwood (avge 31.52)	1995–2008
Best bowling for	7-32	S. P. Davis v Lancashire at Chester-le-Street......	1983
Best bowling against	6-22	A. Dale (Glamorgan) at Colwyn Bay...........	1993
Leading wicket-taker	298	**N. Killeen (avge 23.96).**	**1995–2010**
Highest total for	332-5	v Worcestershire at Chester-le-Street...........	2007
Highest total against	361-7	by Essex at Chelmsford	1996
Lowest total for	72	v Warwickshire at Birmingham................	2002
Lowest total against	63	by Hertfordshire at Darlington................	1964

TWENTY20 RECORDS

Highest score for	80*	**L. R. P. L. Taylor v Leicestershire at Chester-le-St**	**2010**
Highest score against	100	M. B. Loye (Lancashire) at Manchester..........	2005
Leading run-scorer	**1,371**	**P. Mustard (avge 22.85).**....................	**2003–2010**
Best bowling for	5-14	P. D. Collingwood v Derbyshire at Chester-le-Street	2008
Best bowling against	4-12	A. Flintoff (Lancashire) at Chester-le-Street	2008
Leading wicket-taker	54	**G. R. Breese (avge 21.40).**	**2004–2010**
Highest total for	225-2	**v Leicestershire at Chester-le-Street.**	**2010**
Highest total against	208-4	by Lancashire at Manchester	2005
Lowest total for	93	v Kent at Canterbury	2009
Lowest total against	90-9	by Yorkshire at Chester-le-Street...............	2009

ADDRESS

County Ground, Riverside, Chester-le-Street, County Durham DH3 3QR (0191 387 1717; **email** reception@durhamccc.co.uk). **Website** www.durhamccc.co.uk

OFFICIALS

Captain 2010 – W. R. Smith
    2011 – P. Mustard
Head coach G. Cook
President I. D. Mills

Chairman C. W. Leach
Chief executive D. Harker
Head groundsman D. Measor
Scorer B. Hunt

At Abu Dhabi, March 29–April 1. DURHAM beat MCC by 311 runs (see MCC section).

DURHAM v ESSEX

At Chester-le-Street, April 15–18. Drawn. Durham 4pts, Essex 9pts. Toss: Durham. Championship debut: B. A. Stokes.

Put in on a cold, cloudy morning, Essex recovered from 102 for four through a county fifth-wicket record of 339 between Mickleburgh and Foster – also the highest stand at Riverside. Compiling a maiden century, Mickleburgh scored 121 of his 174 through the leg side, and was particularly strong through mid-on. Missing Harmison and Onions because of back injuries, Durham lacked an enforcer on a flat pitch. Although runs came at only three an over, they went nearly seven hours without a wicket before four arrived in 14 balls. Mickleburgh played on and Foster slapped a short ball to point as Essex lost their last six for 43; Plunkett, initially erratic, collected four. The clusters of wickets continued as Durham went from 124 for one to 198 all out, and four for two when they followed on for the first time since September 2006. Then Benkenstein and Di Venuto added 212, before both fell just short of hundreds, swiftly followed by Ben Stokes, whose 11 runs on a disappointing Championship debut carried little hint of what was to come. Durham were 66 ahead with three wickets left when rain ended play.

Close of play: First day, Essex 263-4 (Mickleburgh 103, Foster 66); Second day, Durham 83-1 (Coetzer 34, Smith 24); Third day, Durham 147-2 (Di Venuto 75, Benkenstein 62).

Essex

B. A. Godleman lbw b Thorp	0	D. D. Masters c Smith b Blackwell	9
A. N. Cook c Di Venuto b Claydon	44	C. J. C. Wright not out	5
J. K. Maunders lbw b Thorp	11		
J. C. Mickleburgh b Plunkett	174	B 14, l-b 8, w 5, n-b 16	43
*M. L. Pettini c Di Venuto b Thorp	4		
†J. S. Foster c Benkenstein b Thorp	169	1/1 (1) 2/29 (3) 3/89 (2) (162.3 overs) 484
R. N. ten Doeschate lbw b Plunkett	3	4/102 (5) 5/441 (4)
G. R. Napier c Benkenstein b Plunkett	0	6/445 (7) 7/447 (6) 8/447 (8)
T. J. Phillips c Coetzer b Plunkett	22	9/458 (10) 10/484 (9) 110 overs: 310-4

Claydon 27–6–83–1; Thorp 36–12–79–4; Davies 29–9–54–0; Stokes 10–0–34–0; Plunkett 31.3–3–112–4; Blackwell 25–4–85–1; Coetzer 4–0–15–0.

Durham

M. J. Di Venuto c Cook b Wright	21	– (2) c Cook b Phillips	99
K. J. Coetzer lbw b ten Doeschate	55	– (1) b Masters	0
*W. R. Smith c Foster b Wright	44	– c Foster b Masters	0
D. M. Benkenstein c Foster b Masters	18	– c Maunders b Phillips	98
I. D. Blackwell b Wright	17	– b Phillips	52
B. A. Stokes c Foster b Phillips	7	– c Godleman b ten Doeschate	4
†P. Mustard lbw b ten Doeschate	2	– not out	60
L. E. Plunkett b ten Doeschate	14	– lbw b Phillips	0
C. D. Thorp b Phillips	0	– not out	10
M. E. Claydon b Phillips	4		
M. Davies not out	–		
B 5, l-b 5, n-b 6	16	B 12, l-b 12, w 1, n-b 4	29

1/33 (1) 2/124 (2) 3/130 (3) (79.2 overs) 198
4/165 (5) 5/165 (4) 6/174 (7)
7/178 (6) 8/178 (9) 9/198 (10) 10/198 (8)

1/0 (1) 2/4 (3) (7 wkts, 105 overs) 352
3/216 (4) 4/225 (2)
5/233 (6) 6/315 (5) 7/317 (8)

Masters 20–9–48–1; Wright 19–8–42–3; Napier 18–4–37–0; ten Doeschate 17.2–3–53–3; Phillips 5–0–8–3. *Second Innings*—Masters 21–4–57–2; Wright 18–2–76–0; Napier 12–2–32–0; Phillips 36–5–113–4; ten Doeschate 17–1–44–1; Mickleburgh 1–0–6–0.

Umpires: M. J. D. Bodenham and R. A. Kettleborough.

DURHAM v HAMPSHIRE

At Chester-le-Street, April 21–24. Durham won by five wickets. Durham 23pts, Hampshire 5pts. Toss: Hampshire.

On another dry, docile pitch, Blackwell scored 83 and 62 and also took five wickets. His blistering assaults gave impetus to a match which might have meandered to a draw. Hampshire allowed him an easy start when he first went in, at 146 for three in reply to 345, and cracked 36 off his first 21 balls. On the final day, Durham required 260 in 57 overs, which was 139 from 27 when Blackwell arrived; once he had stroked 20 off six balls, the pressure was off. Hampshire had opened the match with a stand of 183, Carberry playing some glorious strokes as he scored his second fifty in only 53 balls. But he became a little carefree and cracked Stokes's first delivery to backward point to give him a maiden Championship wicket. Again, Plunkett was expensive early on but improved in his third spell, when his hostility undermined Hampshire. In cold conditions, there was little swing for the visiting new-ball pair, Kabir Ali and Tomlinson. Kabir found some movement to complete a five-wicket haul on the third day, but Tomlinson was underused in the second innings. Durham's injury list lengthened when Claydon suffered an abdominal strain.

Close of play: First day, Hampshire 298-8 (Kabir Ali 9, Briggs 5); Second day, Durham 284-5 (Stokes 28, Davies 8); Third day, Hampshire 174-5 (Pothas 30, Tomlinson 2).

Hampshire

M. A. Carberry c Plunkett b Stokes	113	– lbw b Claydon		18
J. H. K. Adams c Mustard b Plunkett	68	– c Stokes b Blackwell		25
C. C. Benham lbw b Blackwell	30	– lbw b Blackwell		43
N. D. McKenzie c Di Venuto b Blackwell	30	– c and b Thorp		5
J. M. Vince b Plunkett	13	– b Stokes		46
*†N. Pothas lbw b Claydon	14	– c Mustard b Plunkett		76
S. M. Ervine c Mustard b Plunkett	3	– (8) c Thorp b Stokes		46
Kabir Ali c Mustard b Claydon	18	– (9) lbw b Blackwell		9
J. A. Tomlinson lbw b Claydon	0	– (7) run out		9
D. R. Briggs c Mustard b Plunkett	28	– lbw b Plunkett		0
D. A. Griffiths not out	7	– not out		1
L-b 3, n-b 18	21	B 3, l-b 5, n-b 12		20

1/183 (1) 2/189 (2) 3/244 (4)   (104.2 overs) 345   1/22 (1) 2/66 (2)   (98.3 overs) 298
4/265 (5) 5/265 (3) 6/284 (7)   3/83 (4) 4/117 (3)
7/284 (6) 8/284 (9) 9/309 (8) 10/345 (10)   5/170 (5) 6/202 (7) 7/247 (6)
                                              8/267 (9) 9/268 (10) 10/298 (8)

Claydon 23-3-84-3; Thorp 14-3-54-0; Plunkett 28.2-3-107-4; Davies 19-5-49-0; Blackwell 15-5-33-2; Stokes 5-0-15-1. *Second Innings*—Claydon 3.4-0-8-1; Thorp 14-1-71-1; Plunkett 32.2-7-86-2; Davies 10-5-15-0; Blackwell 30-7-78-3; Stokes 8.3-1-32-2.

Durham

M. J. Di Venuto lbw b Briggs	71	– (2) c McKenzie b Tomlinson		18
K. J. Coetzer b Briggs	47	– (1) c Kabir Ali b Briggs		72
*W. R. Smith lbw b Ervine	28	– c Ervine b Briggs		20
D. M. Benkenstein b Griffiths	10	– lbw b Tomlinson		10
I. D. Blackwell c Ervine b Kabir Ali	83	– c Adams b Briggs		62
B. A. Stokes b Kabir Ali	41	– not out		27
M. Davies lbw b Carberry	27			
†P. Mustard b Kabir Ali	0	– (7) not out		32
L. E. Plunkett c Pothas b Kabir Ali	41			
C. D. Thorp b Kabir Ali	11			
M. E. Claydon not out	6			
B 5, l-b 8, n-b 6	19	B 1, l-b 11, w 1, n-b 8		21

1/108 (2) 2/129 (1) 3/146 (4)   (117 overs) 384   1/28 (2)   (5 wkts, 53.1 overs) 262
4/205 (5) 5/272 (5) 6/303 (6)   2/78 (3) 3/121 (4)
7/307 (8) 8/364 (7) 9/377 (9)   4/188 (1) 5/216 (5)
10/384 (10)   110 overs: 363-7

Kabir Ali 24–4–98–5; Tomlinson 24–7–55–0; Griffiths 19–2–79–1; Ervine 18–2–39–1; Briggs 29–5–89–2; McKenzie 1–0–6–0; Carberry 2–0–5–1. *Second Innings*—Kabir Ali 11–0–67–0; Tomlinson 10–4–20–2; Griffiths 10–0–54–0; Ervine 8–1–34–0; Briggs 14.1–1–75–3.

Umpires: S. C. Gale and N. A. Mallender.

At Leeds, April 27–30. DURHAM drew with YORKSHIRE.

At Durham, May 5–7. DURHAM drew with DURHAM MCCU.

At Nottingham, May 10–13. DURHAM lost to NOTTINGHAMSHIRE by an innings and 62 runs.

At Canterbury, May 17–20. DURHAM beat KENT by six wickets.

DURHAM v KENT

At Chester-le-Street, May 24–25. Kent won by an innings and four runs. Kent 22pts, Durham 3pts. Toss: Durham.

Durham suffered their first home defeat for nearly two years, succumbing inside five sessions. It was an emphatic revenge for Kent, who had lost to them the previous week and entered the match bottom of the table without a win. After the flat tracks of April, Durham wanted a pitch with more life, but their own depleted attack could not exploit it; Harmison started unfit and conceded 83 in 11 overs, whereas Ntini bowled superbly for ten wickets in his final Championship game. In warm, sunny conditions, he and Khan swung the ball, and Durham never recovered from losing their top three at 24. Batting as though they didn't trust the pitch (though there was little wrong with it), Kent raced to 71 without loss before reckless strokes saw them slip to 152 for six. Stevens ended the day on 99, and next morning completed a 107-ball century before chopping on to his stumps, all in the opening over. Following two successive hundreds away from home, Stokes top-scored with 27 in Durham's first innings, then thrashed 53 in 40 balls in the second, batting with a runner after he sprained his ankle in the field.

Close of play: First day, Kent 305-8 (Stevens 99, Khan 12).

Durham

M. J. Di Venuto c van Jaarsveld b Ntini	9	– (2) c Tredwell b Ntini	86
K. J. Coetzer lbw b Khan	10	– (1) lbw b Ntini	4
S. G. Borthwick c Jones b Ntini	0	– c Jones b Khan	1
D. M. Benkenstein c Blake b Khan	1	– c Jones b Cook	7
G. R. Breese c Denly b Khan	8	– c and b Khan	5
B. A. Stokes c Blake b Ntini	27	– (7) b Ntini	53
*†P. Mustard lbw b Khan	2	– (6) c Jones b Cook	16
L. E. Plunkett c van Jaarsveld b Coles	9	– b Ntini	0
M. E. Claydon not out	22	– not out	11
C. Rushworth b Ntini	16	– c Jones b Ntini	0
S. J. Harmison lbw b Khan	4	– lbw b Ntini	0
B 1, l-b 4, w 2, n-b 6	13	B 1, l-b 7, w 2, n-b 2	12

1/24 (1) 2/24 (3) 3/24 (2) 4/27 (4) (34.5 overs) 121 1/10 (1) 2/27 (3) (54.3 overs) 195
5/48 (5) 6/50 (7) 7/78 (6) 8/78 (8) 3/50 (4) 4/59 (5)
9/101 (10) 10/121 (11) 5/91 (6) 6/172 (7) 7/172 (8)
  8/187 (2) 9/187 (10) 10/195 (11)

Ntini 17–6–53–4; Khan 11.5–1–43–5; Coles 6–1–20–1. *Second Innings*—Ntini 17.3–3–51–6; Khan 13–3–29–2; Cook 9–0–43–2; Coles 7–0–31–0; Tredwell 5–1–20–0; Stevens 3–0–13–0.

Kent

J. L. Denly c Di Venuto b Plunkett	24	S. J. Cook c Di Venuto b Rushworth	0
*R. W. T. Key c Benkenstein b Plunkett	40	A. Khan not out	16
†G. O. Jones c Coetzer b Claydon	21	M. Ntini c Breese b Plunkett	7
M. van Jaarsveld c Borthwick b Harmison	36	B 1, l-b 12, w 7, n-b 10	30
S. A. Northeast lbw b Claydon	8		
D. I. Stevens b Claydon	102	1/71 (2) 2/78 (1) 3/124 (3) (63 overs) 320
A. J. Blake c Plunkett b Harmison	2	4/140 (5) 5/146 (4) 6/152 (7)
M. T. Coles b Rushworth	34	7/246 (8) 8/246 (9) 9/309 (6) 10/320 (11)

J. C. Tredwell replaced Blake after returning from England's reception at Downing Street.

Harmison 11–0–83–2; Rushworth 16–3–72–2; Plunkett 18–1–94–3; Claydon 15–2–50–3; Borthwick 3–0–8–0.

Umpires: N. L. Bainton and R. A. Kettleborough.

At Birmingham, May 29–June 1. DURHAM drew with WARWICKSHIRE.

DURHAM v WARWICKSHIRE

At Chester-le-Street, June 28–July 1. Durham won by 219 runs. Durham 21pts, Warwickshire 4pts. Toss: Warwickshire.

When the final day began Warwickshire needed a further 243, with seven wickets left, but they were all out in the 11th over, Harmison claiming six. As he had dismissed Westwood with the third ball of the innings, he finished with his first seven-wicket haul for Durham, including his 700th in first-class cricket. With good bounce available, Harmison hit the right length: most of his victims were caught at the wicket or in the slips, though his first of the day was 18-year-old Ateeq Javid, lbw without addition after making a confident 30 in his second Championship game. Blackwell led a charmed life during his first-day 86 and contributed a useful 36 to delay Durham's second-innings slide from 158 without loss to 289 all out. Despite being a bowler light once Miller suffered a foot injury, Warwickshire persisted with seam as Di Venuto scored 61 in 55 balls on the third morning. Then Imran Tahir came on and swiftly removed both openers, taking most of his six wickets with googlies. A final stand of 55 between Clarke and Rankin had earned Warwickshire their first batting point in five games, despite the absence of Trott and Bell on England Lions duty.

Close of play: First day, Warwickshire 7-0 (Westwood 1, Maddy 2); Second day, Durham 78-0 (Stoneman 42, Di Venuto 31); Third day, Warwickshire 111-3 (Troughton 38, Javid 30).

Durham

M. J. Di Venuto c Ambrose b Carter	6	– (2) c Javid b Imran Tahir	92
M. D. Stoneman c Clarke b Carter	12	– (1) lbw b Imran Tahir	60
G. J. Muchall c Rankin b Clarke	27	– c Maddy b Rankin	18
D. M. Benkenstein c Ambrose b Maddy	14	– b Clarke	1
I. D. Blackwell b Clarke	86	– b Imran Tahir	36
B. A. Stokes c Miller b Rankin	16	– c Imran Tahir b Rankin	4
*†P. Mustard c Clarke b Imran Tahir	35	– b Imran Tahir	25
C. D. Thorp st Ambrose b Imran Tahir	29	– c Maddy b Carter	6
M. E. Claydon b Miller	18	– c Botha b Imran Tahir	20
C. Rushworth c Ambrose b Carter	26	– lbw b Imran Tahir	1
S. J. Harmison not out	0	– not out	1
B 5, l-b 5, w 1, n-b 8	19	B 9, l-b 7, n-b 10	26

1/8 (1) 2/19 (2) 3/58 (3) 4/71 (4) (83.4 overs) 288   1/158 (1) 2/163 (2) (78.1 overs) 289
5/112 (6) 6/203 (7) 7/221 (5) 3/166 (4) 4/201 (3)
8/245 (8) 9/284 (10) 10/288 (9) 5/215 (6) 6/227 (5) 7/242 (8)
8/280 (7) 9/280 (10) 10/289 (9)

Carter 15–1–36–3; Miller 14.4–0–55–1; Maddy 13–3–35–1; Clarke 12–0–51–2; Imran Tahir 19–3–57–2; Rankin 10–2–44–1. *Second Innings*—Carter 18–3–62–1; Miller 4–2–18–0; Clarke 10–0–43–1; Rankin 19–2–58–2; Imran Tahir 24.1–1–69–6; Maddy 3–0–23–0.

Warwickshire

*I. J. Westwood b Harmison	11	– c Benkenstein b Harmison	0
D. L. Maddy c Mustard b Harmison	8	– lbw b Claydon	6
A. G. Botha c Di Venuto b Claydon	19	– c Mustard b Claydon	33
J. O. Troughton c Mustard b Rushworth	44	– b Claydon	43
A. Javid c Stokes b Thorp	6	– lbw b Harmison	30
†T. R. Ambrose lbw b Rushworth	31	– c Di Venuto b Harmison	0
R. Clarke c Stokes b Rushworth	68	– not out	8
N. M. Carter c Harmison b Thorp	2	– c Mustard b Harmison	3
A. S. Miller c Di Venuto b Thorp	2	– (11) c Stokes b Harmison	4
Imran Tahir c Claydon b Thorp	10	– c Mustard b Harmison	0
W. B. Rankin not out	10	– (9) c Stoneman b Harmison	0
B 1, l-b 12	13	L-b 2, w 3, n-b 2	7

1/22 (2) 2/35 (1) 3/56 (3) 4/67 (5) (74.5 overs) 224
5/115 (4) 6/140 (6) 7/147 (8)
8/157 (9) 9/169 (10) 10/224 (7)

1/0 (1) 2/39 (3) (48.2 overs) 134
3/46 (2) 4/114 (5)
5/116 (4) 6/116 (6) 7/120 (8)
8/120 (9) 9/120 (10) 10/134 (11)

Harmison 19–6–45–2; Thorp 20–4–54–4; Rushworth 16.5–3–46–3; Claydon 13–1–42–1; Blackwell 4–1–12–0; Stokes 2–0–12–0. *Second Innings*—Harmison 15.2–6–29–7; Thorp 8–3–23–0; Claydon 14–2–47–3; Rushworth 4–1–19–0; Blackwell 5–1–10–0; Stokes 2–1–4–0.

Umpires: B. Dudleston and S. A. Garratt.

DURHAM v LANCASHIRE

At Chester-le-Street, July 20–23. Drawn. Durham 7pts, Lancashire 9pts. Toss: Durham. County debut: S. Chanderpaul.

Rain ruined a contest which saw Collingwood's first Championship appearance for two years, Chanderpaul's Lancashire debut against his former team-mates, and Anderson forming a powerful new-ball pairing with Chapple. In conditions generally favouring seam, Chapple had Collingwood caught at second slip for 12 and collected a richly deserved five for 65, while Anderson bowled unchanged for 26 overs, though his spell spanned three days. Chanderpaul enjoyed several moments of fortune – he was dropped at slip early in both innings – but rescued Lancashire from their first-day stumble to 110 for five, adding 135 with Sutton, who took advantage of better conditions on the second day in a chanceless century. Play ended at 3 p.m. on the first day, resumed at 1.55 on the second and was restricted to 21 overs on the third. Durham began an uninterrupted final day needing 99 to avoid the follow-on with five wickets standing; once Mustard took them to safety with two wickets intact, an afternoon of tedium was inevitable.

Close of play: First day, Lancashire 136-5 (Chanderpaul 30, Sutton 14); Second day, Durham 27-1 (Di Venuto 11); Third day, Durham 96-5 (Stokes 13, Mustard 7).

Lancashire

P. J. Horton c Di Venuto b Claydon	29	– run out	9
S. C. Moore c Mustard b Claydon	27	– c Di Venuto b Claydon	26
M. J. Chilton c Benkenstein b Thorp	1	– b Blackwell	25
S. Chanderpaul c Mustard b Plunkett	92	– not out	23
S. J. Croft lbw b Collingwood	4	– b Plunkett	1
T. C. Smith c Mustard b Thorp	23	– not out	2
†L. D. Sutton not out	101		
*G. Chapple c Mustard b Plunkett	4		
S. I. Mahmood b Harmison	42		
J. M. Anderson c Stoneman b Harmison	0		
S. C. Kerrigan c Mustard b Claydon	1		
B 4, l-b 8, w 4, n-b 4	20	B 1, n-b 4	5

1/52 (2) 2/59 (3) 3/59 (1) (101.3 overs) 344
4/74 (5) 5/110 (6) 6/245 (4) 7/253 (8)
8/328 (9) 9/332 (10) 10/344 (11)

1/25 (1) (4 wkts dec, 40 overs) 91
2/41 (2) 3/73 (3)
4/78 (5)

Plunkett 17–1–75–2; Harmison 25–3–93–2; Thorp 28–7–60–2; Claydon 15.3–3–65–3; Collingwood 7–3–11–1; Blackwell 9–1–28–0. *Second Innings*—Harmison 9–4–14–0; Thorp 7–2–14–0; Claydon 6–1–25–1; Plunkett 8–0–22–1; Blackwell 9–6–5–1; Stokes 1–0–10–0.

Durham

M. J. Di Venuto c Sutton b Anderson	12		C. D. Thorp b Chapple		8
M. D. Stoneman c Sutton b Anderson	11		M. E. Claydon run out		5
P. D. Collingwood c Smith b Chapple	12		S. J. Harmison b Chapple		0
D. M. Benkenstein lbw b Smith	21		B 4, l-b 9, w 4, n-b 14		31
I. D. Blackwell b Chapple	3				—
B. A. Stokes c Croft b Anderson	37		1/27 (2) 2/48 (3) 3/48 (1) (64.2 overs)		216
*†P. Mustard not out	71		4/53 (5) 5/85 (4) 6/146 (6)		
L. E. Plunkett c Sutton b Chapple	5		7/166 (8) 8/184 (9) 9/216 (10) 10/216 (11)		

Anderson 27–8–74–3; Chapple 23.2–4–65–5; Smith 9–1–39–1; Mahmood 5–0–25–0.

Umpires: R. J. Bailey and J. W. Lloyds.

At Basingstoke, August 3–6. DURHAM drew with HAMPSHIRE.

At Manchester, August 9–12. DURHAM beat LANCASHIRE by six wickets.

DURHAM v YORKSHIRE

At Chester-le-Street, August 16–19. Yorkshire won by four wickets. Yorkshire 21pts, Durham 4pts. Toss: Yorkshire.

Yorkshire had no hesitation in bowling on a damp pitch under heavy cloud, and 17 wickets fell on the first day. Bresnan then left to join England's squad at The Oval; though he returned on the third afternoon, by then Yorkshire were chasing 299 on a pitch which eased throughout. On the opening day, Di Venuto carried his bat for the third time for Durham, while Shahzad, bowling full and straight, outshone Bresnan with his first five-wicket haul: three bowled and two lbw. At 116 for seven, Yorkshire were 97 adrift, but McGrath battled bravely to reach 28 off 85 balls on the first evening (passing 1,000 for the season). In sunny conditions next morning, he scored another 96 off 108 balls; often driving on the up, he had rarely batted better. Durham quickly wiped out a 42-run deficit, as Stoneman played fluently for his best Championship score in almost three years, but then collapsed from 134 for one to 177 for six. Although the tail helped Benkenstein raise the target, it was not enough. Rudolph put on 113 with Lyth, cruising to a flawless century, before Gale attacked vigorously to complete victory 50 minutes into the final day.

Close of play: First day, Yorkshire 125-7 (McGrath 28, Pyrah 4); Second day, Durham 207-6 (Benkenstein 35, Plunkett 8); Third day, Yorkshire 245-4 (Gale 36, Patterson 3).

Durham

M. J. Di Venuto not out	117	– (2) lbw b Hannon-Dalby	18
M. D. Stoneman c Brophy b Patterson	1	– (1) c Brophy b Patterson	78
G. J. Muchall lbw b Shahzad	12	– b Shahzad	31
D. M. Benkenstein b Shahzad	0	– c Brophy b Patterson	74
I. D. Blackwell c Bairstow b Bresnan	6	– c Bairstow b Hannon-Dalby	13
B. A. Stokes lbw b Shahzad	0	– c Bairstow b Patterson	8
*†P. Mustard c Brophy b Pyrah	53	– c Rudolph b Hannon-Dalby	2
L. E. Plunkett b Shahzad	0	– c Pyrah b Hannon-Dalby	30
M. E. Claydon b Shahzad	4	– lbw b Shahzad	29
C. Rushworth c Bairstow b Pyrah	0	– b Patterson	28
S. J. Harmison run out	4	– not out	11
B 2, l-b 13, w 1	16	B 4, l-b 14	18
	—		—
1/11 (2) 2/32 (3) 3/32 (4) 4/53 (5) (57.2 overs)	213	1/50 (2) 2/134 (3) (92.3 overs)	340
5/54 (6) 6/169 (7) 7/172 (8)		3/134 (1) 4/157 (5)	
8/176 (9) 9/183 (10) 10/213 (11)		5/174 (6) 6/177 (7) 7/255 (8)	
		8/298 (9) 9/304 (4) 10/340 (10)	

Bresnan 16–4–58–1; Patterson 13.2–5–44–1; Shahzad 16–2–51–5; Pyrah 11–2–40–2; McGrath 1–0–5–0. *Second Innings*—Shahzad 26–6–81–2; Patterson 25.3–4–87–4; Pyrah 11–2–53–0; Hannon-Dalby 21–3–73–4; Rashid 9–2–28–0.

Yorkshire

A. Lyth c Plunkett b Claydon	6	– c Di Venuto b Stokes 48
J. A. Rudolph b Claydon	7	– b Claydon 100
T. T. Bresnan c Plunkett b Harmison	25	
A. McGrath not out	124	– (3) c Stokes b Claydon 29
A. W. Gale lbw b Harmison	0	– (4) not out 70
J. M. Bairstow lbw b Plunkett	18	– (5) c Mustard b Claydon 13
G. L. Brophy b Blackwell	4	– c Stokes b Harmison 0
A. U. Rashid c Mustard b Harmison	17	– not out 15
R. M. Pyrah lbw b Plunkett	8	
A. Shahzad c Mustard b Rushworth	15	
S. A. Patterson c Benkenstein b Plunkett	7	– (6) lbw b Harmison 3
B 4, l-b 10, n-b 10	24	B 1, l-b 10, w 2, n-b 8 21

1/17 (1) 2/26 (2) 3/52 (3) 4/52 (5) (72 overs) 255
5/79 (6) 6/84 (7) 7/116 (8) 8/143 (9)
9/209 (10) 10/255 (11)

1/113 (1) (6 wkts, 72.5 overs) 299
2/181 (2) 3/204 (3)
4/228 (5) 5/273 (6) 6/275 (7)

O. J. Hannon-Dalby briefly replaced Bresnan, who was called up by England but then released.

Harmison 23–3–81–3; Claydon 8–0–37–2; Rushworth 11–4–50–1; Blackwell 13–5–17–1; Plunkett 17–4–56–3. *Second Innings*—Harmison 18–3–56–2; Claydon 18–5–74–3; Blackwell 5–0–24–0; Plunkett 11–1–57–0; Rushworth 13.5–2–51–0; Stokes 7–0–26–1.

Umpires: N. G. C. Cowley and B. Dudleston.

At Taunton, August 24–27. DURHAM drew with SOMERSET.

DURHAM v NOTTINGHAMSHIRE

At Chester-le-Street, August 31–September 3. Durham won by 210 runs. Durham 23pts, Nottinghamshire 6pts. Toss: Durham.

Sixteen points clear with a game in hand, Nottinghamshire would have settled for the draw that seemed likely early on the fourth afternoon: they were 52 for one after being set 391 in 78 overs. Then Ben Harmison took three wickets in four balls. Recalled because of injuries, he came on when Plunkett limped off and, after a wayward start, finished with four for 70 as the leaders crumbled. Nottinghamshire had Sidebottom for the first two days before he joined England's Twenty20 squad; departing as an unbeaten nightwatchman, he had to be marked down as retired not out. His replacement, Pattinson, suffered an ankle injury delivering his first ball, but later returned to bowl two overs for 26, setting Muchall on his way to a fluent century. On the first day Durham had recovered from 76 for four through Mustard's hundred; his second fifty came off 34 balls, and he added 174 with Borthwick, who contributed a career-best 68. Blackwell made two half-centuries and had figures of 19–13–23–3 on the final day. Nottinghamshire's best moments came from Adams, swinging the ball into Durham's seven left-handers to earn his five for 92.

Close of play: First day, Durham 347-6 (Mustard 117, Borthwick 54); Second day, Nottinghamshire 257-6 (Mullaney 23, Sidebottom 5); Third day, Durham 279-5 (Blackwell 50, Mustard 13).

Durham

M. J. Di Venuto lbw b Sidebottom	0	– (2) lbw b Adams	15
M. D. Stoneman lbw b Adams	67	– (1) lbw b Adams	13
G. J. Muchall c Patel b Fletcher	13	– lbw b Patel	111
D. M. Benkenstein c Read b Adams	13	– st Read b Patel	58
B. W. Harmison c Read b Franks	2	– b Patel	11
I. D. Blackwell b Adams	59	– c Read b Fletcher	50
*†P. Mustard c Read b Sidebottom	120	– not out	51
S. G. Borthwick c Mullaney b Adams	68	– not out	43
L. E. Plunkett c Read b Sidebottom	0		
M. E. Claydon c Read b Adams	1		
M. Davies not out	5		
L-b 15, w 1, n-b 8	24	L-b 5, w 2, n-b 2	9

1/4 (1) 2/29 (3) 3/53 (4) 4/76 (5)   (103.5 overs) 372
5/163 (2) 6/188 (6) 7/362 (7)
8/362 (9) 9/363 (10) 10/372 (8)

1/20 (2)   (6 wkts dec, 86 overs) 361
2/35 (1) 3/179 (4)
4/191 (5) 5/242 (3) 6/282 (6)

Sidebottom 27–3–100–3; Fletcher 22–4–85–1; Adams 27.5–6–92–5; Franks 18–4–48–1; Patel 7–1–15–0; Mullaney 2–0–17–0. *Second Innings*—Fletcher 20–3–67–1; Pattinson 2.1–0–26–0; Adams 15.5–1–76–2; Franks 13–1–51–0; Patel 30–3–113–3; Voges 1–0–2–0; Mullaney 4–0–21–0.

Nottinghamshire

A. D. Hales c Mustard b Davies	13	– c Di Venuto b Harmison	36
S. R. Patel c Borthwick b Claydon	4	– (5) lbw b Harmison	2
M. A. Wagh b Plunkett	30	– c Mustard b Blackwell	18
A. C. Voges lbw b Davies	48	– c Mustard b Harmison	0
A. D. Brown c sub (M. A. Wood) b Borthwick	52	– (6) lbw b Blackwell	29
*†C. M. W. Read c Mustard b Plunkett	56	– (7) c sub (G. R. Breese) b Harmison	0
S. J. Mullaney c Benkenstein b Plunkett	25	– (8) c Mustard b Borthwick	64
R. J. Sidebottom retired not out	5		
D. J. Pattinson c sub (G. R. Breese) b Claydon	19	– (11) not out	0
P. J. Franks c Mustard b Harmison	26	– (2) lbw b Claydon	8
A. R. Adams c Di Venuto b Harmison	10	– (9) c Blackwell b Claydon	5
L. J. Fletcher not out	23	– (10) c Muchall b Blackwell	5
B 4, l-b 15, w 5, n-b 8	32	B 5, l-b 2, w 2	9

1/5 (2) 2/23 (1) 3/71 (3) 4/146 (4)   (113 overs) 343
5/196 (5) 6/252 (6) 7/259 (7)
8/296 (10) 9/306 (11) 10/343 (9)
110 overs: 338-9

1/31 (2) 2/52 (1)   (54.1 overs) 180
3/52 (4) 4/54 (5)
5/84 (3) 6/97 (7) 7/103 (6)
8/128 (9) 9/170 (10) 10/180 (8)

In the first innings Sidebottom retired not out at 257 after being called up by England, and was replaced by Pattinson.

Claydon 21–2–78–2; Davies 15–11–10–2; Benkenstein 7–2–31–0; Plunkett 25–5–66–3; Blackwell 21–8–33–0; Borthwick 20–2–78–1. *Second Innings*—Plunkett 2–0–8–0; Harmison 4–0–28–2; Claydon 15–4–61–2; Harmison 15–2–70–4; Blackwell 19–13–23–3; Borthwick 3.1–0–11–1.

Umpires: T. E. Jesty and N. A. Mallender.

At Chelmsford, September 7–10. DURHAM drew with ESSEX.

DURHAM v SOMERSET

At Chester-le-Street, September 13–16. Drawn. Durham 8pts, Somerset 11pts. Toss: Durham. County debut: R. M. R. Brathwaite.

Somerset arrived only two points adrift of leaders Nottinghamshire, and hoping to overtake them to win their first Championship. By the third day they had forged six points ahead; despite not starting until 3.25 p.m. on the opening day, they became the only team to gain full bonus points on this ground in 2010, while Nottinghamshire were frustrated by the weather at Old Trafford. But after struggling to dismiss Durham a second time on an easing pitch, Somerset needed 181 in 17 overs to guarantee the title. With their old team-mate Blackwell bowling into the fourth-day rough, that proved impossible; after losing three wickets, they settled for the draw. Along with around 300 supporters who had travelled north to see them crowned, they had to suffer as Nottinghamshire captured three Lancashire wickets and a title-clinching bowling point. Trescothick said Somerset were distraught, and it was no surprise. Durham handed a county debut to triallist Ruel Brathwaite, a Barbadian pace bowler who had emerged from Loughborough and Cambridge Universities. He took Somerset's last three wickets when they hoped to press on, starting with Hildreth, whose seventh century of the season provided solid ballast for the strokemakers. Their lead of 140 was wiped out with only one wicket down as Di Venuto reached 1,000 Championship runs and went on to 129. Somerset's bowling was probing rather than penetrating, a large factor in their ultimate failure.

Close of play: First day, Durham 132-2 (Muchall 23, Benkenstein 71); Second day, Somerset 226-4 (Hildreth 31, Trego 33); Third day, Durham 171-2 (Di Venuto 84, Harmison 2).

Durham

M. J. Di Venuto lbw b Phillips	18	– (2) c Kieswetter b Trego	129
M. D. Stoneman c Kieswetter b Willoughby	15	– (1) lbw b Phillips	16
G. J. Muchall c Kieswetter b Phillips	37	– b Trego	33
D. M. Benkenstein c Trescothick b Thomas	72	– (7) c Trescothick b Willoughby	25
B. W. Harmison c Suppiah b Trego	35	– (4) c Kieswetter b Thomas	15
I. D. Blackwell lbw b Trego	23	– (5) c Buttler b Kartik	23
†P. Mustard b Willoughby	42	– (6) lbw b Thomas	12
S. G. Borthwick c Trescothick b Phillips	9	– b Trego	5
L. E. Plunkett c Kartik b Willoughby	11	– lbw b Willoughby	2
R. M. R. Brathwaite lbw b Phillips	2	– (11) not out	0
C. Rushworth not out	0	– (10) c Kieswetter b Trego	16
B 7, l-b 4, n-b 6, p 5	22	B 18, l-b 14, n-b 12	44

1/25 (2) 2/33 (1) 3/140 (4) (89.5 overs) 286   1/33 (1) 2/146 (3) (110.4 overs) 320
4/160 (3) 5/217 (6) 6/222 (5)   3/214 (4) 4/255 (2)
7/256 (8) 8/277 (9) 9/284 (7) 10/286 (10)   5/255 (5) 6/275 (6) 7/289 (8)
8/294 (9) 9/315 (10) 10/320 (7)

Willoughby 20–5–81–3; Phillips 23.5–5–60–4; Kartik 11–2–28–0; Trego 19–3–60–2; Thomas 13–3–32–1; Suppiah 3–1–9–0. *Second Innings*—Willoughby 22.4–5–51–2; Phillips 22–3–67–1; Thomas 17–4–52–2; Trego 17–2–61–4; Kartik 32–11–57–1.

Somerset

*M. E. Trescothick c Mustard b Harmison	75	– c Borthwick b Brathwaite	21
A. V. Suppiah c and b Plunkett	18		
N. R. D. Compton lbw b Harmison	46	– (5) not out	12
J. C. Hildreth b Brathwaite	105		
*C. Kieswetter b Rushworth	10	– (2) b Blackwell	3
P. D. Trego b Plunkett	69	– (3) st Mustard b Blackwell	2
J. C. Buttler lbw b Harmison	39	– (4) not out	6
B. J. Phillips lbw b Harmison	0		
A. C. Thomas b Brathwaite	26		
M. Kartik c Blackwell b Brathwaite	11		
C. M. Willoughby not out	1		
B 8, l-b 7, w 1, n-b 10	26	B 3, l-b 1	4

1/48 (2) 2/132 (1) 3/153 (3) (100.1 overs) 426   1/20 (2) (3 wkts, 12 overs) 48
4/180 (5) 5/284 (6) 6/348 (7)   2/28 (1) 3/32 (3)
7/348 (8) 8/406 (4) 9/423 (9) 10/426 (10)

Rushworth 14–1–70–1; Plunkett 29–3–105–2; Blackwell 14–3–47–0; Brathwaite 24.1–2–93–3; Harmison 18–1–94–4; Muchall 1–0–2–0. *Second Innings*—Brathwaite 6–0–25–1; Blackwell 6–1–19–2.

Umpires: R. J. Bailey and R. T. Robinson.

ESSEX

Wanted: more runs

PAUL HISCOCK

By finishing bottom of Division One in the County Championship, Essex merely confirmed what many supporters feared from the outset: that they were simply not good enough to survive in the top echelon. Admittedly they proved formidable foes in one-day cricket, reaching the semi-finals in both the 40- and 20-over competitions, but in the four-day game it was soon obvious that they would soon go straight down again.

The major weakness lay in the strength – or rather lack of it – of the batting. Essex failed to achieve maximum batting bonus points in any of their 16 matches, and on five occasions were unable to muster even one. A change of captaincy in mid-season, after the out-of-form Mark Pettini handed over to James Foster, failed to halt a decline which reached its nadir in the final month of the season, when Essex lost four of their last five matches. Two of those defeats were to Warwickshire, propping up the table at the time, while another came away to Kent, who were also involved in the relegation dogfight.

In three matches during that wretched spell, Essex failed to claim any batting points, which underlined the major problem of a season in which they passed 400 only once and not one batsman managed to reach 1,000 runs. The nearest were Foster and 20-year-old Jaik Mickleburgh, who both made 839 in the Championship. Mickleburgh's came in his first full season, and he was one of the two undoubted successes, the other being fast bowler Maurice Chambers, whose summer was curtailed by injury just as he seemed finally to have turned potential into performance.

Alastair Cook made seven appearances in between England calls, but scored only one century, while Ravi Bopara was another who was expected to score freely and substantially but failed to do so on a regular basis. He did make two hundreds, both in the same match against Yorkshire, but after that – feeling spurned by England until his World Cup call-up – managed only 122 runs in his next eight innings.

Thirty-nine-year-old Grant Flower, in what proved to be his final season with Essex, was as effective as ever in the one-day games, scoring 527 runs in the CB40 alone, a number exceeded by only three others around the country. He returned to Zimbabwe, where he made a brief international comeback before retiring to concentrate on coaching.

With the ball, David Masters proved as reliable and effective as ever. He ended up as their leading Championship wicket-taker with 53, just reward for his determination and professionalism, but there was little back-up. Unusually, Essex were found wanting in the spin department. It had been expected that the departure of James Middlebrook to Northampton would allow Tim Phillips to blossom, but he proved inconsistent, leaving Essex bereft of true menace.

Their cause was not helped by the situation of their leg-spinner, Danish Kaneria, who was involved in police investigations into alleged spot-fixing in a match against Durham the previous season, which rumbled on through the summer until the charges against Kaneria were finally dropped early in September. He was ditched by Pakistan halfway through their Test series against England, and returned to Chelmsford, but managed only 23 wickets in six matches, his least productive season in county cricket. Fast bowler Mervyn Westfield, however, was charged: by then,

David Masters

Graham Morris

Essex had decided not to renew his contract, although they insisted it had nothing to do with the criminal case.

Five overseas players appeared during the season. The Australian Bryce McGain proved a more than adequate leg-spin stand-in for Kaneria in the Championship – he claimed a five-for in his first match, at the age of 38 – while Scott Styris, drafted in exclusively for the Friends Provident T20, proved a massive hit and was one of the reasons Essex reached the semi-finals. His unbeaten 106 in a successful run-chase against Surrey thrilled the crowd and showed the value of quality all-rounders: Essex were unfortunate to lose both Graham Napier, whose back problems allowed him only four one-day games, and Ryan ten Doeschate, out for two months with a leg injury.

However, the two other overseas signings made no impact whatsoever. The New Zealander Chris Martin captured only two wickets in three matches, two of them one-day games, while the West Indian all-rounder Dwayne Bravo, drafted in solely for Twenty20 finals day, was a major disappointment. He made five and then took one for 46 in his four overs, further infuriating many supporters who had been unhappy at his call-up – at a reputed cost of £10,000 – in the first place.

The season had begun promisingly with victory over Hampshire, when Essex grabbed all ten wickets in the final session, followed by the better of a draw with Durham, where Mickleburgh scored a magnificent 174 in a stand of 339 with Foster. But it proved a false dawn: Essex won only one more match – ironically against the eventual champions Nottinghamshire, who were beaten inside three days at Chelmsford.

Crowd levels remained encouraging, particularly for floodlit Twenty20 matches at Chelmsford, where full houses generated income of approximately £90,000 per game. They made a fun evening out for commuters returning by train from the city – and helped finance the acquisition of experienced batsman Owais Shah from Middlesex.

Looking to the future, Mickleburgh and Chambers are expected to make further progress, while Tom Westley and Adam Wheater are bright prospects who could help Essex make an immediate return to the top flight.

ESSEX RESULTS

All first-class matches – Played 17: Won 3, Lost 6, Drawn 8.
County Championship matches – Played 16: Won 2, Lost 6, Drawn 8.

LV= County Championship, 9th in Division 1;
Friends Provident T20, s-f; Clydesdale Bank 40, s-f.

COUNTY CHAMPIONSHIP AVERAGES, BATTING AND FIELDING

Cap		M	I	NO	R	HS	100s	50s	Avge	Ct/St
2005	R. S. Bopara‡	8	15	2	550	142	2	3	42.30	4
2005	A. N. Cook‡	7	12	0	474	102	1	3	39.50	6
2010	M. J. Walker	11	22	2	782	105	1	4	39.10	8
2006	R. N. ten Doeschate¶	11	19	2	577	85	0	5	33.94	9
2001	J. S. Foster†	16	27	1	839	169	1	4	32.26	48/5
	J. C. Mickleburgh	15	28	0	839	174	1	3	29.96	10
	B. A. Godleman	11	20	0	532	106	1	2	26.60	9
	T. Westley	9	18	1	440	132	1	2	25.88	1
2006	M. L. Pettini	15	27	3	599	96	0	2	24.95	7
	B. E. McGain§	2	4	2	46	24	0	0	23.00	
2006	T. J. Phillips	9	14	3	208	46*	0	0	18.90	7
	A. P. Palladino	4	8	1	130	66	0	1	18.57	1
	J. K. Maunders	6	10	0	179	70	0	1	17.90	4
2008	D. D. Masters	14	22	1	356	50	0	1	16.95	8
	C. J. C. Wright	11	17	5	161	28*	0	0	13.41	2
2003	G. R. Napier†	4	6	1	67	35	0	0	13.40	1
	A. Carter	3	5	1	45	16*	0	0	11.25	2
	M. A. Chambers	10	15	5	53	14	0	0	5.30	5
2004	Danish Kaneria§	6	9	1	28	9	0	0	3.50	1

Also batted: M. J. Comber† (1 match) 0, 0; G. W. Flower (2 matches) 36*, 5, 2 (2 ct); C. S. Martin§ (1 match) 0*, 11; M. Osborne† (1 match) 5, 0*.

† *Born in Essex.*   ‡ *ECB contract.*   § *Official overseas player.*   ¶ *Other non-England-qualified player.*

BOWLING

	O	M	R	W	BB	5W/i	Avge
D. D. Masters	487	138	1,223	53	5-43	1	23.07
A. Carter	100.5	15	311	13	5-40	1	23.92
M. A. Chambers	236.5	43	826	32	6-68	2	25.81
B. E. McGain	64.3	4	260	10	5-151	1	26.00
R. N. ten Doeschate	191.3	16	716	27	5-13	1	26.51
A. P. Palladino	104	25	333	12	4-57	0	27.75
Danish Kaneria	226.4	45	753	23	4-51	0	32.73
C. J. C. Wright	301.5	55	1,156	31	5-70	1	37.29
T. J. Phillips	245.2	44	752	20	4-94	0	37.60

Also bowled: R. S. Bopara 25-2-99-4; M. A. Comber 8-1-16-1; A. N. Cook 8-1-36-1; G. W. Flower 9-0-32-1; C. S. Martin 25-10-84-1; J. C. Mickleburgh 1.1-0-11-0; G. R. Napier 95-18-280-3; M. Osborne 16-2-56-1; M. J. Walker 18-2-71-3; T. Westley 68-10-174-6.

LEADING CB40 AVERAGES (100 runs/4 wickets)

Batting	Runs	HS	Avge	S-R	Ct		**Bowling**	W	BB	Avge	E-R
R. S. Bopara	308	88*	77.00	95.35	1		G. R. Napier	7	3-54	20.42	5.95
G. W. Flower	527	116	65.87	95.64	6		D. D. Masters	15	4-41	26.13	4.61
R. N. ten Doeschate	272	109*	45.33	134.65	1		C. J. C. Wright	13	3-43	34.00	6.06
M. J. Walker	232	71	38.66	93.92	2		T. J. Phillips	6	4-37	34.83	5.88
A. N. Cook	167	101*	33.40	83.08	3		R. N. ten Doeschate	10	2-30	39.10	6.62
M. L. Pettini	342	82	28.50	87.91	8		Danish Kaneria	5	2-41	42.60	5.19

LEADING FPT20 AVERAGES (100 runs/18 overs)

Batting	Runs	HS	Avge	S-R	Ct/St
R. N. ten Doeschate	296	102	59.20	177.24	2
S. B. Styris	392	106*	35.63	161.98	2
J. S. Foster	172	54*	19.11	147.00	4/9
A. N. Cook	388	73	38.80	132.42	5
M. L. Pettini	332	81	30.18	129.18	5
R. S. Bopara	473	105*	33.78	128.88	5

Bowling	W	BB	Avge	E-R
Danish Kaneria	17	3-32	17.11	6.84
R. S. Bopara	16	3-13	24.81	7.35
D. D. Masters	12	2-18	34.83	7.86
S. B. Styris	13	2-28	31.38	8.32
T. J. Phillips	8	1-7	36.37	8.55
C. J. C. Wright	21	4-25	29.00	9.22

FIRST-CLASS COUNTY RECORDS

Highest score for	343*	P. A. Perrin v Derbyshire at Chesterfield	1904
Highest score against	332	W. H. Ashdown (Kent) at Brentwood	1934
Leading run-scorer	30,701	G. A. Gooch (avge 51.77)	1973–1997
Best bowling for	10-32	H. Pickett v Leicestershire at Leyton	1895
Best bowling against	10-40	E. G. Dennett (Gloucestershire) at Bristol	1906
Leading wicket-taker	1,610	T. P. B. Smith (avge 26.68)	1929–1951
Highest total for	761-6 dec	v Leicestershire at Chelmsford	1990
Highest total against	803-4 dec	by Kent at Brentwood	1934
Lowest total for	30	v Yorkshire at Leyton	1901
Lowest total against	14	by Surrey at Chelmsford	1983

LIST A COUNTY RECORDS

Highest score for	201*	R. S. Bopara v Leicestershire at Leicester	2008
Highest score against	158*	M. W. Goodwin (Sussex) at Chelmsford	2006
Leading run-scorer	16,536	G. A. Gooch (avge 40.93)	1973–1997
Best bowling for	8-26	K. D. Boyce v Lancashire at Manchester	1971
Best bowling against	7-29	D. A. Payne (Gloucestershire) at Chelmsford	2010
Leading wicket-taker	616	J. K. Lever (avge 19.04)	1968–1989
Highest total for	391-5	v Surrey at The Oval	2008
Highest total against	318-8	by Lancashire at Chelmsford	1992
Lowest total for	57	v Lancashire at Lord's	1996
Lowest total against	{ 41	by Middlesex at Westcliff-on-Sea	1972
	{ 41	by Shropshire at Wellington	1974

TWENTY20 RECORDS

Highest score for	152*	G. R. Napier v Sussex at Chelmsford	2008
Highest score against	124*	M. J. Lumb (Hampshire) at Southampton	2009
Leading run-scorer	1,444	M. L. Pettini (avge 26.74)	2003–2010
Best bowling for	4-10	G. R. Napier v Northamptonshire at Chelmsford	2008
Best bowling against	5-11	Mushtaq Ahmed (Sussex) at Hove	2005
Leading wicket-taker	60	Danish Kaneria (avge 20.18)	2005–2010
Highest total for	242-3	v Sussex at Chelmsford	2008
Highest total against	219-2	by Hampshire at Southampton	2009
Lowest total for	99	v Kent at Chelmsford	2007
Lowest total against	94	by Surrey at Chelmsford	2008

ADDRESS

County Ground, New Writtle Street, Chelmsford CM2 0PG (01245 252420; **email** administration@
essexcricket.org.uk). **Website** www.essexcricket.org.uk

OFFICIALS

Captain 2010 – M. L. Pettini
2011 – J. S. Foster
Head coach A. P. Grayson
Batting coach G. A. Gooch
Bowling coach C. E. W. Silverwood
President D. J. Insole

Chairman N. R. A. Hilliard
Chief executive D. E. East
Chairman, cricket committee G. J. Saville
Head groundsman S. Kerrison
Scorer A. E. Choat

At Chelmsford, April 3–5 (not first-class). **Drawn. Essex 318-8 dec** (J. K. Maunders 51, R. N. ten Doeschate 106*, D. D. Masters 31, C. J. C. Wright 46*; R. A. L. Moore 3-49) **and 312-9 dec** (B. A. Godleman 61, J. K. Maunders 51, M. J. Walker 30, T. J. Phillips 42, R. N. ten Doeschate 81; A. J. Blake 4-47); ‡**Leeds/Bradford MCCU 139** (A. J. Blake 43; D. D. Masters 4-20, C. J. C. Wright 3-40, R. N. ten Doeschate 3-28) **and 160-6** (A. J. Blake 73, R. A. L. Moore 38*). *County debut*: B. A. Godleman. *Essex stumbled to 124-7 on the first day before ten Doeschate, who added 65 with Masters for the eighth wicket and 129* with Wright for the ninth, led a recovery. Alex Blake then fulfilled much the same role for the students, steering them from deep water at 25-5. Mark Pettini declined to enforce the follow-on, whereupon Blake, on Kent's books, demonstrated his all-round potential with four wickets for his medium-pace. Pettini declared a second time, setting the students a notional 492. Once again Blake held firm amid the rubble of 6-3; another young all-rounder, Rick Moore, helped ensure the draw.*

ESSEX v HAMPSHIRE

At Chelmsford, April 9–12. Essex won by 62 runs. Essex 21pts, Hampshire 6pts. Toss: Hampshire. County debuts: K. Ali, N. D. McKenzie. This match exploded into life in the very last session: Hampshire, needing 248 from 48 overs, had reached tea at 34 for none from 13. Adams, who had earlier made a steadfast eight-hour 169, was first to go, at 71, and by the 32nd over the score was 124 for four. With ten overs left, Hampshire needed 78 with six wickets in hand. But ten Doeschate had Benham caught behind, and in a flash it was Essex glimpsing victory. In just five balls 180 for five became 180 for eight, and as the last over began, Essex were one wicket from success. Griffiths kept out four balls, but from the fifth Masters took the catch at leg slip that brought Essex victory and ten Doeschate his best return in the Championship. On the first day Godleman had made 92 to give them a decent total. Hampshire then edged into the lead thanks to Adams's patient hundred. Essex began the final day effectively 122 for four, and it wasn't until the last few minutes that a home win seemed feasible. During the game it emerged that two Essex players (later identified as Danish Kaneria and Mervyn Westfield, neither of whom was playing) were being investigated for irregularities in a Pro40 match against Durham the previous September

Close of play: First day, Essex 325-7 (Napier 2, Masters 4); Second day, Hampshire 234-5 (Adams 113, Tomlinson 0); Third day, Essex 131-4 (Westley 69).

Essex

B. A. Godleman b Briggs	92	– c Adams b Tomlinson ... 4
J. K. Maunders run out	33	– lbw b Kabir Ali ... 1
T. Westley c Pothas b Griffiths	1	– c Pothas b Tomlinson ... 69
M. J. Walker c Pothas b Briggs	57	– (7) lbw b Carberry ... 25
*M. L. Pettini c Pothas b Briggs	10	– (4) c Carberry b Griffiths ... 23
†J. S. Foster c McKenzie b Griffiths	88	– (5) c Benham b Griffiths ... 27
R. N. ten Doeschate c Adams b Griffiths	23	– (6) not out ... 66
G. R. Napier c McKenzie b Kabir Ali	13	– c Benham b Kabir Ali ... 7
D. D. Masters lbw b Griffiths	4	– lbw b Kabir Ali ... 0
C. J. C. Wright c McKenzie b Griffiths	9	– c McKenzie b Kabir Ali ... 9
M. A. Chambers not out	0	– b Kabir Ali ... 2
B 1, l-b 8, n-b 6	15	B 5, l-b 8, n-b 10 ... 23

1/68 (2) 2/79 (3) 3/165 (1) (107.4 overs) 345
4/177 (5) 5/252 (4) 6/300 (6)
7/319 (7) 8/325 (9) 9/343 (10) 10/345 (8)

1/4 (1) 2/6 (2) (96.4 overs) 256
3/86 (4) 4/131 (5) 5/135 (3)
6/195 (7) 7/220 (8) 8/220 (9)
9/242 (10) 10/256 (11)

Kabir Ali 25.4–5–71–1; Tomlinson 24–7–75–0; Ervine 15–5–44–0; Griffiths 22–5–85–5; Briggs 21–7–61–3. *Second Innings*—Tomlinson 25–8–72–2; Kabir Ali 22.4–9–33–5; Griffiths 18–3–75–2; Ervine 14–5–33–0; Briggs 9–2–22–0; McKenzie 5–1–8–0; Carberry 3–3–0–1.

Hampshire

M. A. Carberry c ten Doeschate b Masters	3	b Chambers	47
J. H. K. Adams b Masters	169	c Foster b Wright	45
L. A. Dawson c Maunders b Napier	9	c Wright b Napier	7
N. D. McKenzie c Masters b Westley	39	c Maunders b Masters	8
C. C. Benham c Foster b Chambers	21	c Foster b ten Doeschate	24
†N. Pothas c sub (T. J. Phillips) b ten Doeschate	9	c Foster b ten Doeschate	39
J. A. Tomlinson c Foster b Chambers	7	(9) not out	4
S. M. Ervine c Maunders b Masters	8	(7) c Foster b Masters	3
Kabir Ali run out	10	(8) c Foster b ten Doeschate	0
D. R. Briggs c Pettini b Masters	21	lbw b ten Doeschate	1
D. A. Griffiths not out	9	c Masters b ten Doeschate	0
L-b 24, w 1, n-b 24	49	L-b 5, w 2	7

1/34 (1) 2/55 (3) 3/160 (4)   (124.4 overs) 354   1/71 (2) 2/85 (3)   (47.5 overs) 185
4/206 (5) 5/232 (6) 6/265 (7)   3/98 (4) 4/124 (1)
7/294 (8) 8/310 (9) 9/331 (2)   5/170 (5) 6/180 (6) 7/180 (8)
10/354 (10)   110 overs: 314-8   8/180 (7) 9/185 (10) 10/185 (11)

Masters 36.4–9–67–4; Wright 25–6–66–0; Napier 30–7–68–1; Chambers 19–2–76–2; ten Doeschate 10–1–46–1; Westley 4–0–7–1. *Second Innings*—Masters 13–4–24–2; Wright 11–0–55–1; Napier 12–1–61–1; Westley 1–0–6–0; Chambers 5–0–21–1; ten Doeschate 5.5–2–13–5.

Umpires: R. K. Illingworth and N. J. Llong.

At Chester-le-Street, April 15–18. ESSEX drew with DURHAM. *Jaik Mickleburgh and James Foster add 339, an Essex record for the fifth wicket.*

ESSEX v LANCASHIRE

At Chelmsford, April 21–23. Lancashire won by eight wickets. Lancashire 22pts, Essex 3pts. Toss: Lancashire.

Lancashire totally outplayed Essex to coast home with four sessions to spare and make it two wins out of two. In helpful conditions for swing on the opening day, Anderson topped and tailed the Essex innings to claim six for 44, his best Championship figures since 2002. Essex floundered to 16 for four in the 14th over, and were six down by lunch. Ten Doeschate oversaw the fightback in the afternoon, but Lancashire's ability to find the edge and cling on to the chance – seven catches were held behind the wicket, to go with three lbws – ensured Essex failed to bank any batting points. The feature of the match was Horton's patience: he batted six hours before being last out for 123. Masters, who beat the bat time and again, might easily have picked up more than four wickets. There was a half-century second time around for Cook, but little other resistance. Anderson missed out on a ten-for after Mickleburgh was recalled: umpire Willey initially gave him out but, after consultation with his colleague, they ruled the ball had hit helmet and nothing more.

Close of play: First day, Lancashire 83-3 (Horton 11, Prince 0); Second day, Essex 46-2 (Cook 29, Mickleburgh 7).

Essex

B. A. Godleman c Horton b Anderson	4	– lbw b Anderson	7
A. N. Cook c Moore b Anderson	3	– c Sutton b Chapple	50
J. K. Maunders lbw b Chapple	0	– lbw b Anderson	1
J. C. Mickleburgh lbw b Chapple	9	– c Sutton b Mahmood	27
*M. L. Pettini c Moore b Anderson	28	– b Anderson	22
†J. S. Foster c Croft b Mahmood	27	– c Sutton b Smith	14
R. N. ten Doeschate not out	55	– c Sutton b Mahmood	0
T. J. Phillips c Moore b Anderson	5	– lbw b Mahmood	0
D. D. Masters c Smith b Chapple	2	– c Prince b Chapple	17
C. J. C. Wright lbw b Anderson	21	– st Sutton b Kerrigan	15
M. A. Chambers c Sutton b Anderson	0	– not out	11
B 15, l-b 5, w 2	22	L-b 9	9

1/6 (1) 2/7 (2) 3/7 (3) 4/16 (4) (70.5 overs) 176
5/78 (6) 6/78 (5) 7/91 (8) 8/102 (9)
9/172 (10) 10/176 (11)

1/18 (1) 2/30 (3) (65.4 overs) 173
3/86 (2) 4/90 (4)
5/111 (6) 6/112 (7) 7/112 (8)
8/143 (9) 9/143 (5) 10/173 (10)

Anderson 20.5–5–44–6; Chapple 16–6–30–3; Mahmood 16–1–38–1; Smith 13–0–40–0; Kerrigan 5–2–4–0. *Second Innings*—Anderson 22–7–53–3; Chapple 20–6–60–2; Kerrigan 4.4–1–13–1; Mahmood 11–3–18–3; Smith 8–2–20–1.

Lancashire

T. C. Smith lbw b Masters	7	– c Foster b Chambers	1
S. C. Moore lbw b Chambers	61	– c Masters b Phillips	17
P. J. Horton c Foster b Wright	123	– not out	12
J. M. Anderson c ten Doeschate b Masters	0		
A. G. Prince c Pettini b Masters	16	– (4) not out	1
M. J. Chilton c Foster b Wright	1		
S. J. Croft b ten Doeschate	56		
†L. D. Sutton c Phillips b Masters	11		
*G. Chapple c ten Doeschate b Chambers	1		
S. I. Mahmood b Wright	14		
S. C. Kerrigan not out	0		
B 6, l-b 5, w 1, n-b 10	22	B 5, n-b 2	7

1/38 (1) 2/82 (2) 3/83 (4) (97.2 overs) 312
4/125 (5) 5/134 (6) 6/264 (7) 7/281 (8)
8/288 (9) 9/306 (10) 10/312 (3)

1/3 (1) (2 wkts, 12.3 overs) 38
2/36 (2)

Masters 29–6–81–4; Wright 16.2–3–76–3; ten Doeschate 15–1–62–1; Chambers 23–4–58–2; Phillips 14–6–24–0. *Second Innings*—Wright 6.3–1–16–0; Chambers 3–1–13–1; Phillips 3–1–4–1.

Umpires: N. J. Llong and P. Willey.

At Taunton, April 27–30. ESSEX drew with SOMERSET.

At Scarborough, May 4–6. ESSEX lost to YORKSHIRE by an innings and 96 runs.

ESSEX v KENT

At Chelmsford, May 10–13. Drawn. Essex 8pts, Kent 11pts. Toss: Kent.

On a wicket offering slow turn, the promoted teams from 2009 eventually reached stalemate. Responsible batting and unexacting bowling saw Kent to a useful total: Jones laid the foundations with a brisk 135 from 177 balls before Stevens maintained the momentum. With Jones feeling unwell on the second day, Hockley kept wicket until Paul Dixey arrived from a Second Eleven game at Beckenham; Jones returned to action next morning. Careful shot selection allowed Westley to glue Essex's innings together; his 132 equalled his one previous first-class hundred. Even so, Kent led by 133, but let control slip as Northeast, with his second fifty of the match, alone sustained the innings against Danish Kaneria, in his first appearance of the season. Essex were convinced he was out on 41 when Phillips claimed a return catch, but Northeast stood his ground, the umpires were unsure of the carry, and the batsman survived. His fifty received scant acknowledgment from the fielding side. Set 338 from a minimum 78 overs, Essex reduced that to 188 from 28 with seven wickets intact. The loss of ten Doeschate soon after persuaded them to shut up shop.

Close of play: First day, Kent 355-6 (Stevens 57, Azhar Mahmood 15); Second day, Essex 172-4 (Westley 84, Foster 17); Third day, Kent 150-5 (Northeast 49, Coles 2).

Kent

J. L. Denly c Foster b Wright	1	– run out	17
*R. W. T. Key c ten Doeschate b Masters	7	– c Masters b Wright	25
†G. O. Jones c Cook b Westley	135	– c Godleman b ten Doeschate	36
M. van Jaarsveld c Foster b ten Doeschate	51	– c Cook b Wright	7
S. A. Northeast st Foster b Phillips	65	– c Phillips b Danish Kaneria	71
D. I. Stevens c Phillips b Danish Kaneria	100	– lbw b Danish Kaneria	9
J. B. Hockley b Danish Kaneria	2	– (8) b Masters	3
Azhar Mahmood b ten Doeschate	64	– (9) c Foster b Danish Kaneria	6
M. T. Coles c Foster b ten Doeschate	0	– (7) c Mickleburgh b Masters	6
S. J. Cook b ten Doeschate	19	– not out	19
M. Ntini not out	0	– lbw b Danish Kaneria	0
B 13, l-b 9, n-b 8	30	L-b 1, n-b 4	5

1/1 (1) 2/53 (2) 3/190 (3)   (119.2 overs) 474
4/244 (3) 5/299 (5) 6/306 (7)
7/440 (8) 8/440 (9) 9/470 (6)
10/474 (10) 110 overs: 416-6

1/38 (1) 2/42 (2) (63 overs) 204
3/60 (4) 4/110 (3)
5/141 (6) 6/154 (7) 7/164 (8)
8/171 (9) 9/204 (5) 10/204 (11)

Masters 29–10–67–1; Wright 24–3–118–1; ten Doeschate 17.2–1–77–4; Danish Kaneria 33–3–124–2; Phillips 14–1–57–1; Westley 2–0–9–1. *Second Innings*—Masters 16–5–41–2; Wright 9–1–37–2; Danish Kaneria 24–5–68–4; ten Doeschate 10–0–51–1; Phillips 4–1–6–0.

Essex

B. A. Godleman b Azhar Mahmood	45	– c van Jaarsveld b Hockley	31
A. N. Cook c Hockley b Ntini	0	– b Denly	72
J. C. Mickleburgh lbw b Azhar Mahmood	2	– lbw b Denly	25
T. Westley c Denly b Cook	132	– not out	58
*M. L. Pettini c van Jaarsveld b Ntini	13	– (6) not out	40
†J. S. Foster c van Jaarsveld b Azhar Mahmood	21		
R. N. ten Doeschate lbw b Ntini	66	– (5) lbw b Azhar Mahmood	13
T. J. Phillips c Jones b Ntini	0		
D. D. Masters not out	36		
C. J. C. Wright c van Jaarsveld b Azhar Mahmood	6		
Danish Kaneria lbw b Azhar Mahmood	1		
B 10, l-b 5, w 2, n-b 2	19	B 7, l-b 3, n-b 5	15

1/4 (2) 2/13 (3) 3/89 (1) (108.2 overs) 341
4/115 (5) 5/176 (6) 6/291 (7) 7/297 (8)
8/303 (4) 9/335 (10) 10/341 (11)

1/52 (1) (4 wkts, 81.4 overs) 254
2/116 (3) 3/150 (2)
4/169 (5)

Azhar Mahmood 25.2–4–63–5; Ntini 23–7–68–3; Coles 19–4–72–0; Cook 22–5–60–2; van Jaarsveld 8–0–22–0; Denly 9–0–38–0; Stevens 2–1–3–0. *Second Innings*—Azhar Mahmood 16–4–54–1; Ntini 6–2–20–0; van Jaarsveld 19–3–48–0; Denly 27–1–100–2; Hockley 5–1–8–1; Cook 3–0–9–0; Coles 5.4–3–5–0.

Umpires: N. G. C. Cowley and D. J. Millns.

At Chelmsford, May 14–16. ESSEX beat BANGLADESHIS by five wickets (see Bangladeshi tour section).

At Manchester, May 24–27. ESSEX drew with LANCASHIRE.

At Nottingham, May 29–June 1. ESSEX drew with NOTTINGHAMSHIRE.

At Southampton, June 4–7. ESSEX drew with HAMPSHIRE.

At Chelmsford, July 2. ESSEX lost to PAKISTANIS by 66 runs (see Pakistani tour section).

ESSEX v NOTTINGHAMSHIRE

At Chelmsford, July 5–7. Essex won by 143 runs. Essex 19pts, Nottinghamshire 3pts. Toss: Essex.

Nottinghamshire's second and least expected defeat of the season was inflicted by Chambers, who angled the ball in at the batsmen's toes to claim ten wickets in the match – the first Essex fast bowler to do so since Andy Bichel at Derby in 2007. Foster, captain now that Pettini had stood down, bucked his predecessor's trend by winning Essex's first Championship toss of the season, though probably wished he hadn't when he lost half his side before lunch. However, Chambers helped Phillips scramble 34 from the last wicket, and would not leave Nottinghamshire's sight. His burst of three for eight in 18 balls on the second morning was sharp enough to have Adams backing away towards square leg. Driving straight and with conviction, Mickleburgh shared the only two century partnerships of the match, though his assurance had waned by the time Patel had him lbw within sight of a second first-class hundred. Essex mustered just 103 from the last seven wickets, handing Nottinghamshire almost five sessions to chase 303. They had little chance once Hales, Patel and Mullaney were all beaten for pace by Chambers inside 12 overs. Brown patiently compiled his second fifty of the match, but received little help.

Close of play: First day, Nottinghamshire 126-5 (Brown 30, Read 31); Second day, Essex 265-4 (Westley 19, Chambers 0).

Essex

J. K. Maunders run out	2	– c Read b Shreck	70
B. A. Godleman c Read b Adams	15	– c Mullaney b Shreck	3
J. C. Mickleburgh b Shreck	2	– lbw b Patel	91
M. J. Walker c Read b Adams	13	– c Hales b Franks	70
T. Westley c Read b Franks	4	– c Read b Adams	32
*†J. S. Foster c Read b Shreck	22	– (7) c and b Shreck	8
M. L. Pettini c Read b Shreck	10	– (8) b Adams	11
T. J. Phillips not out	46	– (9) not out	12
D. D. Masters lbw b Franks	20	– (10) c Patel b Adams	0
Danish Kaneria c Read b Franks	2	– (11) c Patel b Adams	9
M. A. Chambers c Adams b Mullaney	14	– (6) b Shreck	8
L-b 4	4	L-b 11, w 1, n-b 2	14

1/7 (1) 2/11 (3) 3/36 (2) 4/37 (4) (61.5 overs) 154
5/45 (5) 6/69 (7) 7/84 (6) 8/114 (9)
9/120 (10) 10/154 (11)

1/15 (2) 2/119 (1) (112.1 overs) 328
3/225 (3) 4/263 (4)
5/276 (6) 6/294 (5) 7/296 (7)
8/316 (8) 9/316 (10) 10/328 (11)

Shreck 16–5–40–3; Fletcher 16–1–50–0; Franks 12–7–20–3; Adams 14–4–26–2; Patel 3–0–13–0; Mullaney 0.5–0–1–1. *Second Innings*—Shreck 23–4–81–4; Fletcher 19–7–57–0; Adams 25.1–4–57–4; Franks 17–5–37–1; Mullaney 4–1–14–0; Patel 24–7–71–1.

Nottinghamshire

A. D. Hales b Chambers	9	– b Chambers	7
B. M. Shafayat lbw b Chambers	1	– c Foster b Masters	5
M. A. Wagh lbw b Phillips	20	– b Chambers	26
S. R. Patel c Godleman b Phillips	25	– c Maunders b Chambers	4
S. J. Mullaney lbw b Chambers	1	– b Danish Kaneria	12
A. D. Brown not out	50	– c Phillips b Masters	62
†C. M. W. Read c Foster b Chambers	32	– c Mickleburgh b Danish Kaneria	20
P. J. Franks c Foster b Chambers	4	– c Walker b Danish Kaneria	0
A. R. Adams b Chambers	10	– b Danish Kaneria	0
L. J. Fletcher st Foster b Danish Kaneria	12	– c Chambers b Danish Kaneria	9
C. E. Shreck lbw b Danish Kaneria	0	– not out	7
B 5, l-b 1, n-b 10	16	L-b 1, n-b 6	7

1/4 (2) 2/13 (1) 3/61 (3) 4/62 (5)   (47 overs) 180
5/72 (4) 6/127 (7) 7/131 (8) 8/151 (9)
9/180 (10) 10/180 (11)

1/11 (1) 2/17 (2)   (44.3 overs) 159
3/22 (4) 4/42 (5)
5/95 (3) 6/126 (7) 7/134 (8)
8/142 (9) 9/144 (6) 10/159 (10)

Masters 16–4–47–0; Chambers 15–2–68–6; Danish Kaneria 10–1–42–2; Phillips 6–0–17–2. *Second Innings*—Masters 13–2–48–2; Chambers 13–2–55–4; Danish Kaneria 15.3–2–51–4; Phillips 3–1–4–0.

Umpires: I. J. Gould and G. Sharp.

ESSEX v YORKSHIRE

At Chelmsford, July 20–23. Drawn. Essex 10pts, Yorkshire 8pts. Toss: Essex.

Frantically chasing a win to open breathing space at the top, Yorkshire ran out of steam when Wright took two wickets in three balls, compelling them to batten down the hatches. Bopara struck centuries in both innings, showing imperious form and brilliant timing, but England still preferred Eoin Morgan for the First Test against Pakistan. Yorkshire's persistent attack denied Essex maximum batting points when it seemed a formality: they conceded just five runs in nine overs as the 110-over cut-off point loomed. Rashid wrapped up the innings, and later might have wiped out Essex's lead had partners not abandoned him. Cook, without a century for Essex in 35 first-class innings, ended his wait with a necessarily gritty effort. Far more pleasing on the eye was Bopara's second hundred, confirmed when he hoisted Rashid over the Tom Pearce Stand for his third six. Both were given let-offs by McGrath. Their partnership of 199 allowed Foster to set Yorkshire 369 in 83 overs. Anything looked possible while the superb Rudolph was at the crease; when Phillips bowled him at 218 for four, his successors still had 24 overs at their disposal. Bairstow and Brophy added a quick 92, but when Walker dived full-length at cover to catch Brophy, Yorkshire's priorities changed.

Close of play: First day, Essex 353-6 (Flower 5, Phillips 11); Second day, Yorkshire 227-5 (Brophy 25, Bresnan 3); Third day, Essex 229-3 (Cook 90, Walker 13).

Essex

J. C. Mickleburgh b Rashid	38	– b Bresnan	0
A. N. Cook c Brophy b Patterson	44	– c Bairstow b Bresnan	102
T. Westley lbw b Patterson	6	– b Patterson	7
R. S. Bopara c Rashid b Best	142	– b Rashid	102
M. J. Walker c Bairstow b Rashid	26	– b Rashid	38
†J. S. Foster c Patterson b Hannon-Dalby	61	– not out	22
G. W. Flower c McGrath b Rashid	5	– c Best b Patterson	2
T. J. Phillips b Rashid	30		
C. J. C. Wright not out	13		
M. A. Chambers b Best	0		
A. Carter c Hannon-Dalby b Rashid	8		
B 10, l-b 6, w 8, n-b 2	26	B 6, l-b 10, n-b 4	20

1/97 (1) 2/97 (2) 3/120 (3)   (116.5 overs) 399
4/200 (5) 5/324 (6) 6/336 (4)
7/368 (7) 8/381 (8) 9/386 (10)
10/399 (11)

1/0 (1)   (6 wkts dec, 67.5 overs) 293
2/15 (3) 3/214 (4)
4/264 (2) 5/282 (5) 6/293 (7)

110 overs: 368-6

Bresnan 28–8–73–0; Best 16–1–63–2; Patterson 23–5–89–2; Rashid 25.5–7–87–5; Hannon-Dalby 14–3–54–1; McGrath 10–4–17–0. *Second Innings*—Bresnan 18–2–44–2; Patterson 7.5–2–30–2; Rashid 16–2–76–2; Best 9–0–45–0; Rudolph 5–1–26–0; Hannon-Dalby 6–0–35–0; McGrath 6–0–21–0.

Yorkshire

A. Lyth b Wright	75	– st Foster b Phillips	42
J. A. Rudolph c Cook b Carter	32	– b Phillips	106
A. McGrath c Mickleburgh b Phillips	11	– c and b Carter	16
*A. W. Gale c Foster b Westley	47	– b Westley	41
J. M. Bairstow b Phillips	18	– c Flower b Wright	62
†G. L. Brophy b Carter	33	– c Walker b Wright	28
T. T. Bresnan c and b Phillips	5	– (8) st Foster b Flower	1
A. U. Rashid not out	52	– (7) not out	19
S. A. Patterson c Flower b Phillips	16	– not out	0
T. L. Best b Carter	0		
O. J. Hannon-Dalby run out	1		
B 4, l-b 8, n-b 22	34	B 1, l-b 11, w 2, n-b 4	18

1/81 (2) 2/104 (3) 3/146 (1)   (112.1 overs) 324   1/79 (1)   (7 wkts, 82.4 overs) 333
4/177 (5) 5/215 (4) 6/236 (6)   2/106 (3) 3/199 (4)
7/254 (7) 8/304 (9) 9/304 (10)   4/218 (2) 5/310 (6) 6/315 (5) 7/319 (8)
10/324 (11)   110 overs: 323-9

Chambers 17–6–39–0; Wright 15–3–64–1; Phillips 44–15–94–4; Westley 10–2–25–1; Carter 24.1–3–77–3; Flower 2–0–13–0. *Second Innings*—Chambers 13–1–59–0; Wright 7–1–42–2; Phillips 28.4–3–116–2; Carter 15–1–55–1; Westley 12–1–30–1; Flower 7–0–19–1.

Umpires: M. R. Benson and N. J. Llong.

At Canterbury, July 29–August 1. ESSEX lost to KENT by 99 runs.

ESSEX v WARWICKSHIRE

At Southend, August 4–6. Warwickshire won by seven wickets. Warwickshire 19pts, Essex 3pts. Toss: Essex. Championship debut: J. E. Ord.

Warwickshire's great escape began here. They emerged from a largely unedifying three-day scrap – in which only nine runs separated all four innings – with their first Championship win since May. Essex turned in a dismal performance to lose at their newest festival ground for the fourth successive season. Buffeted by the sea breeze and befuddled by swing, they were almost bowled out by the time a thunderstorm arrived in mid-afternoon on the first day. Warwickshire replied with 95 for the 41st over, when Bryce McGain – knowing he was likely to be jettisoned now Pakistan had dropped Danish Kaneria – delivered the game's first ball of spin; with it he had Ambrose caught behind, the sixth of 17 wickets on day two. Terrible shot selection denied Essex a route back into the game; for them, Walker's 111-ball essay in how to cope with lateral movement came too late. Imran Tahir swept him and the last two tailenders up in 22 balls. Warwickshire reached 155 again, this time with less agitation; Westwood knuckled down for the game's only fifty, sharing 82 with Maddy, the solitary half-century partnership. On the first day, Warwickshire issued a statement denying reports they had approached Essex about signing Bopara; he scored only seven runs in the match.

Close of play: First day, Essex 149-9 (Palladino 31, Carter 2); Second day, Essex 78-6 (Walker 9).

Essex

M. L. Pettini lbw b Woakes	1	– c Ambrose b Rankin	16
J. C. Mickleburgh b Carter	10	– lbw b Carter	30
T. Westley c Maddy b Carter	12	– c Westwood b Clarke	1
R. S. Bopara lbw b Carter	1	– c Ambrose b Carter	6
M. J. Walker lbw b Woakes	29	– c Clarke b Imran Tahir	39
†J. S. Foster lbw b Clarke	3	– c Maddy b Woakes	12
T. J. Phillips c Woakes b Clarke	9	– (8) c Ord b Rankin	1
D. D. Masters c Ambrose b Rankin	5	– (9) lbw b Imran Tahir	34
B. E. McGain lbw b Clarke	24	– (10) not out	0
A. P. Palladino not out	32	– (7) st Ambrose b Imran Tahir	0
A. Carter c Rankin b Clarke	2	– lbw b Imran Tahir	8
B 5, l-b 9, n-b 8	22	B 3, l-b 4, w 1, n-b 4	12

1/4 (1) 2/29 (3) 3/30 (2) 4/31 (4)   (44.3 overs) 150
5/34 (6) 6/52 (7) 7/67 (8) 8/91 (5)
9/134 (9) 10/150 (11)

1/33 (1) 2/36 (3)   (65.4 overs) 159
3/55 (4) 4/56 (2)
5/77 (6) 6/78 (7) 7/98 (8)
8/144 (9) 9/151 (9) 10/159 (11)

Woakes 13–2–39–2; Carter 15–3–48–3; Clarke 9.3–2–27–4; Rankin 7–0–22–1. *Second Innings—* Woakes 15–5–36–1; Carter 10.2–4–18–2; Clarke 12–2–27–1; Rankin 7–1–32–2; Barker 6.4–1–10–0; Imran Tahir 8.4–3–20–4; Maddy 6–2–9–0.

Warwickshire

†I. J. Westwood c Westley b Carter	7	– lbw b McGain	61
J. E. Ord b Carter	1	– c Pettini b Masters	6
D. L. Maddy lbw b Masters	39	– c Phillips b Masters	39
J. O. Troughton b Palladino	10	– not out	18
R. Clarke lbw b Masters	36	– not out	22
†T. R. Ambrose c Foster b McGain	6		
K. H. D. Barker lbw b McGain	22		
C. R. Woakes c Mickleburgh b Masters	1		
N. M. Carter c Foster b McGain	13		
Imran Tahir c Foster b McGain	13		
W. B. Rankin not out	1		
N-b 6	6	L-b 7, w 2	9

1/8 (2) 2/11 (1) 3/35 (4) 4/84 (3)   (59 overs) 155
5/95 (6) 6/115 (5) 7/117 (8) 8/129 (7)
9/150 (9) 10/155 (10)

1/20 (2)   (3 wkts, 49.1 overs) 155
2/102 (3) 3/118 (1)

Masters 19.4–8–51–3; Carter 12.2–1–41–2; Palladino 17–8–30–1; McGain 10–2–33–4. *Second Innings—* Masters 16.2–3–36–2; Carter 5.4–1–17–0; Palladino 9–4–18–0; McGain 15–1–57–1; Phillips 3–0–15–0; Mickleburgh 0.1–0–5–0.

Umpires: N. G. C. Cowley and I. Dawood.

ESSEX v SOMERSET

At Colchester, August 18–20. Somerset won by 219 runs. Somerset 20pts, Essex 1pt (after 2pt penalty). Toss: Somerset.

Somerset's two finest batsmen conjured masterful knocks when they were needed; Essex could not match such resilience. Sixteen batsmen fell on the opening day on an uneven surface, although ECB pitch inspector Jack Birkenshaw declared it satisfactory. Masters had Trescothick caught at slip third ball in his first five-wicket haul of the summer, but Hildreth responded with supreme judgment amid general strife, striking 12 fours. Somerset benefited from umpire Willey overturning his own decision in a Championship match for the third time in 11 months. Having initially given de Bruyn out lbw, Willey concluded there had been an inside edge; de Bruyn and Hildreth added a further 49.

Essex then capitulated against the movement of Willoughby and Thomas, and Somerset were batting again an hour into the second day. Though Trescothick was dropped on 85 and 178, his third double-century was outstanding. Essex's frustration was reflected in Palladino, who kicked out at the stumps after fluffing a run-out chance, so allowing Kartik to score a demoralising half-century. Palladino was given a club fine, which was donated to charity, and later three penalty points from the ECB. Somerset's straightforward victory was completed with four sessions remaining, as de Bruyn collected his best figures in England. Essex were deducted two points for a slow over-rate, dropping them further behind Hampshire and Kent.

Close of play: First day, Essex 126-6 (ten Doeschate 36); Second day, Essex 38-1 (Godleman 20, Palladino 3).

Somerset

*M. E. Trescothick c Walker b Masters	0	– not out	228
A. V. Suppiah c Godleman b Masters	4	– c Walker b Palladino	0
Z. de Bruyn c Pettini b Danish Kaneria	34	– lbw b Palladino	10
†C. Kieswetter b Wright	10	– b Masters	0
J. C. Hildreth c Godleman b Masters	84	– c Bopara b Danish Kaneria	59
J. C. Buttler lbw b Masters	21	– lbw b Wright	6
P. D. Trego b Palladino	27	– c Danish Kaneria b Wright	2
B. J. Phillips lbw b Palladino	10	– lbw b Masters	0
A. C. Thomas b Masters	12	– lbw b Masters	0
M. Kartik c Foster b Wright	0	– not out	52
C. M. Willoughby not out	0		
L-b 4, w 1, n-b 8	13	L-b 8, n-b 2	10

1/0 (1) 2/21 (2) 3/32 (4) 4/92 (3) (58.1 overs) 215
5/116 (6) 6/167 (5) 7/181 (8)
8/209 (5) 9/215 (10) 10/215 (9)

1/0 (2) (8 wkts dec, 74 overs) 367
2/24 (3) 3/41 (4)
4/198 (5) 5/225 (6) 6/233 (7)
7/240 (8) 8/240 (9)

Masters 21.1–6–43–5; Palladino 13–2–61–2; Wright 13–1–56–2; Danish Kaneria 11–0–51–1. *Second Innings*—Masters 18–4–53–3; Palladino 12–1–67–2; Wright 15–1–83–2; Danish Kaneria 20–1–120–1; Walker 9–0–36–0.

Essex

B. A. Godleman lbw b Thomas	32	– c Kieswetter b Trego	53
J. C. Mickleburgh c Kieswetter b Phillips	2	– c Kieswetter b Willoughby	15
R. S. Bopara lbw b Willoughby	1	– (4) b Trego	15
M. J. Walker c Buttler b Phillips	3	– (5) c de Bruyn b Kartik	13
M. L. Pettini c Kieswetter b Thomas	34	– (6) c and b Trego	6
*†J. S. Foster c Trego b Willoughby	16	– (7) c Kieswetter b de Bruyn	10
R. N. ten Doeschate lbw b Thomas	40	– (8) b de Bruyn	41
D. D. Masters b Willoughby	4	– (9) c Phillips b Phillips	14
C. J. C. Wright lbw b Willoughby	10	– (10) not out	7
A. P. Palladino c Trego b Thomas	6	– (3) c Buttler b Phillips	16
Danish Kaneria not out	0	– c Willoughby b de Bruyn	0
L-b 1, n-b 2	3	B 15, w 1, n-b 6	22

1/14 (2) 2/19 (3) 3/30 (4) 4/58 (1) (45 overs) 151
5/79 (5) 6/126 (6) 7/130 (7) 8/134 (8)
9/149 (10) 10/151 (9)

1/31 (2) 2/64 (3) (67.2 overs) 212
3/94 (4) 4/115 (1)
5/127 (5) 6/127 (6) 7/175 (7)
8/205 (9) 9/212 (8) 10/212 (11)

Willoughby 15–1–67–4; Phillips 7–2–13–2; Trego 7–3–20–0; Thomas 13–3–44–4; Kartik 3–1–6–0. *Second Innings*—Willoughby 11–0–38–1; Phillips 17–4–51–1; Thomas 13–2–37–0; Trego 11–3–27–3; Kartik 8–1–21–1; de Bruyn 7.2–1–23–4.

Umpires: J. F. Steele and P. Willey.

At Birmingham, August 25–28. ESSEX lost to WARWICKSHIRE by seven wickets.

ESSEX v DURHAM

At Chelmsford, September 7–10. Drawn. Essex 8pts, Durham 6pts. Toss: Essex. Championship debuts: M. A. Comber, M. Osborne.

With relegation almost inevitable, Essex rested Masters and ten Doeschate ahead of their CB40 semi-final in Somerset the next day, and Foster surprisingly shook hands with 23 overs still available. A well-organised innings from Mickleburgh helped Essex to their first batting point in four matches. By bowling straight, Palladino and Wright had Durham five for four in the fourth over; it took Ben Harmison to restore a semblance of normality. Having fought hard for a strong lead, Essex almost blew it: four quick wickets went down on the third morning, and they might have lost Walker several times – nearly run out on 32, and dropped twice. He survived to score his first century of the summer, the day after winning a new one-year contract aged 36. Harmison was denied a hundred by, of all things, Cook's non-turning off-spin.

Close of play: First day, Essex 248-9 (Wright 14, Osborne 0); Second day, Essex 103-1 (Cook 61, Mickleburgh 31); Third day, Durham 31-1 (Di Venuto 21, Muchall 0).

Essex

B. A. Godleman lbw b Claydon	9	– c Muchall b Rushworth	9
A. N. Cook c Claydon b Plunkett	33	– lbw b Blackwell	68
J. C. Mickleburgh c Benkenstein b Borthwick	72	– b Rushworth	34
M. J. Walker c Stoneman b Blackwell	32	– c Benkenstein b Blackwell	105
M. L. Pettini c Plunkett b Borthwick	10	– b Rushworth	2
T. Westley run out	16	– lbw b Rushworth	0
*†J. S. Foster lbw b Plunkett	42	– c Di Venuto b Borthwick	64
M. A. Comber b Blackwell	0	– c Di Venuto b Borthwick	0
A. P. Palladino b Rushworth	10	– c Di Venuto b Blackwell	66
C. J. C. Wright not out	28	– c Benkenstein b Blackwell	12
M. Osborne c Mustard b Plunkett	5	– not out	0
B 1, l-b 3, w 1, n-b 6	11	L-b 3, w 2, n-b 2	7

1/11 (1) 2/53 (2) 3/127 (4) (93.2 overs) 268
4/151 (5) 5/174 (3) 6/197 (6)
7/213 (8) 8/234 (9) 9/236 (7) 10/268 (11)

1/29 (1) 2/113 (3) (111.1 overs) 367
3/113 (2) 4/120 (5)
5/120 (6) 6/253 (7) 7/257 (8)
8/323 (4) 9/359 (10) 10/367 (9)

Rushworth 22–8–69–1; Claydon 12–1–60–1; Harmison 8–2–20–0; Blackwell 16–3–30–2; Plunkett 14.2–4–33–3; Benkenstein 7–4–11–0; Borthwick 14–5–41–2. *Second Innings*—Claydon 9–1–32–0; Rushworth 20–4–90–4; Benkenstein 18–10–26–0; Plunkett 15–1–54–0; Borthwick 19–4–75–2; Blackwell 23.1–4–70–4; Harmison 7–2–17–0.

Durham

M. J. Di Venuto lbw b Palladino	0	– (2) b Wright	58
M. D. Stoneman lbw b Palladino	0	– (1) b Palladino	5
G. J. Muchall c Mickleburgh b Wright	3	– c Mickleburgh b Osborne	6
D. M. Benkenstein b Wright	0	– b Westley	2
B. W. Harmison c Wright b Comber	66	– c Palladino b Cook	96
I. D. Blackwell b Palladino	24	– lbw b Westley	22
*†P. Mustard lbw b Palladino	31	– not out	24
S. G. Borthwick lbw b Wright	3		
L. E. Plunkett c Godleman b Wright	0		
M. E. Claydon not out	38		
C. Rushworth c Mickleburgh b Wright	0		
B 2, l-b 3, w 1, n-b 6	12	L-b 7, w 2, n-b 12	21

1/0 (1) 2/3 (3) 3/3 (2) 4/5 (4) (55.5 overs) 177
5/58 (6) 6/103 (7) 7/106 (8)
8/108 (9) 9/170 (5) 10/177 (11)

1/23 (1) (6 wkts, 83 overs) 234
2/56 (3) 3/60 (4) 4/95 (2)
5/143 (6) 6/234 (5)

Palladino 21–3–57–4; Wright 17.5–2–70–5; Osborne 7–1–31–0; Westley 7–2–10–0; Walker 1–1–0–0; Comber 2–0–4–1. *Second Innings*—Palladino 15–2–41–1; Wright 17–4–48–1; Osborne 9–1–25–1; Westley 29–5–68–2; Comber 6–1–12–0; Cook 7–1–33–1.

Umpires: M. R. Benson and N. J. Llong.

GLAMORGAN

Times of trouble

EDWARD BEVAN

When Glamorgan failed to win promotion on the final day of the Championship season – they missed out by just five points – there followed a period of turmoil and unrest which lasted throughout the winter. As Matthew Maynard, the director of cricket, and captain Jamie Dalrymple were blanked by a committee member as they climbed the Cardiff pavilion steps on that last day, it became clear that Dalrymple was likely to be removed following a review of the season conducted by the county's former wicketkeeper Colin Metson – who, it transpired, was soon to be appointed managing director of cricket.

Maynard had earlier warned that if Dalrymple was replaced he would leave too. And when Metson, chairman Paul Russell and chief executive Alan Hamer travelled to Dubai in November to sign the South African batsman Alviro Petersen as captain without Maynard's knowledge, he did, claiming his position was now untenable – although he was later offered the role of first-team coach.

Dalrymple also went and, when the president Peter Walker resigned shortly afterwards, saying he had "serious concerns" about the likely impact of the changes, three prominent officers had left within 48 hours. During the following weeks, a protest group attempted unsuccessfully to gather the 300 signatures required to force an extraordinary general meeting. Glamorgan's vice-chairman Nigel Roberts resigned and threatened to withdraw his company's sponsorship, but then returned a few days later after a summit meeting instigated by David Morgan, a former chairman of Glamorgan and the ECB, and also a one-time president of the ICC. Early in the new year, Petersen flew from Cape Town to spend a weekend with the players, and the following week Matthew Mott, who had been in charge of New South Wales for four years, agreed to move to old south Wales instead and was appointed first-team coach.

On the field in 2010 Glamorgan did show a marked improvement in four-day cricket, with seven wins compared to two the previous year, but they failed abysmally in the one-day game: bottom of their CB40 group, and next to bottom in the Friends Provident T20. Three successive wins at the start of the Twenty20 gave a misleading impression, as they lost the next four games and rarely threatened thereafter.

There seemed to be no plan or pattern to the one-day strategy, and the bowlers set several records for the wrong reasons. Surrey and Somerset both made their highest 40-over totals, while David Harrison's nought for 100 at Taunton was the most expensive analysis in domestic 40-over cricket. Shaun Tait was signed for the T20, but missed six games after being called up into Australia's one-day squad. Another Australian, Mark Cosgrove, was the country's third-highest T20 run-scorer with 562, while 40-year-old Robert Croft had the best economy-rate (5.93) of regular bowlers.

Cosgrove stood out as Glamorgan's leading batsman in all forms. Four of his five first-class hundreds were scored away from home, and an aggregate of 2,146 in all cricket was testament to his value to the team. Surprisingly, and to the consternation of many, he was not offered a full contract for 2011 but will return as the second overseas player for the T20.

Jamie Dalrymple

Even in a low-scoring summer, 33 batting points compared unfavourably to 56 the previous year, while 12 Championship centuries were four fewer than in 2009. Dalrymple and Gareth Rees endured frustrating seasons, while Michael Powell failed to regain his place after playing the first six Championship matches and never featured in one-day cricket. He was overtaken by Tom Maynard, who played some thrilling one-day innings and was beginning to adapt to Championship cricket before he followed his father out of the club, and joined Surrey. "I resent how me and my father have been treated in the last couple of months," he said, "and have been shocked by what has happened."

Ben Wright, another of the younger brigade, needs to add consistency to his undoubted talent, while Mark Wallace underachieved again. His keeping was faultless, but his batting returns were disappointing – only 626 runs in the Championship, despite 72 and 113 in the defeat of Gloucestershire at Cheltenham.

Only two bowlers nationwide took more Championship wickets than James Harris, whose 63 at little more than 20 apiece was a wonderful achievement for a 20-year-old destined for higher honours. His new-ball partners, Harrison and Huw Waters, were steady, but Harris was astonishingly accurate, and especially menacing on seaming pitches. The consistent Jim Allenby, with 41 wickets and 933 runs in his first full Championship season after joining from Leicestershire in August 2009, proved to be one of Glamorgan's best signings of recent years.

Eyebrows were raised at the start of the season when Matthew Maynard said that Dean Cosker, not Croft, would be the club's leading spinner. Cosker revelled in the challenge, taking 51 wickets at 22.11, the first time he had reached 50 in a season. Croft, who captured his 1,000th first-class wicket for Glamorgan, to go with more than 10,000 runs, also took the first hat-trick of his career, in that Cheltenham victory.

Towards the end of the season, Glamorgan signed the all-rounder Graham Wagg from Derbyshire on a three-year contract. When asked "Why Glamorgan?" Wagg replied that he wanted to play first division cricket. He will have to wait for another season, at least.

GLAMORGAN RESULTS

All first-class matches – Played 17: Won 7, Lost 4, Drawn 6.
County Championship matches – Played 16: Won 7, Lost 4, Drawn 5.

LV= County Championship, 3rd in Division 2;
Friends Provident T20, 8th in South Division; Clydesdale Bank 40, 7th in Group A.

COUNTY CHAMPIONSHIP AVERAGES, BATTING AND FIELDING

Cap		M	I	NO	R	HS	100s	50s	Avge	Ct/St
	M. J. Cosgrove§	15	26	2	1,187	142	5	4	49.45	10
2010	J. Allenby	16	25	4	933	105	1	10	44.42	16
2009	G. P. Rees†	16	28	4	863	106*	2	4	35.95	6
	B. J. Wright	16	25	1	821	172	2	4	34.20	6
	T. L. Maynard†	10	16	0	474	98	0	4	29.62	9
2000	M. J. Powell†	6	10	1	250	55	0	1	27.77	0
2003	M. A. Wallace†,	16	24	1	626	113	1	4	27.21	43/4
	J. W. M. Dalrymple	15	22	0	554	105	1	2	25.18	19
2000	D. A. Cosker	16	24	10	268	49*	0	0	19.14	7
1992	R. D. B. Croft†	8	12	2	184	63	0	1	18.40	5
2010	J. A. R. Harris†	13	19	2	257	49	0	0	15.11	2
2006	D. S. Harrison†	12	18	0	253	35	0	0	14.05	2
	W. D. Bragg†	2	4	0	56	44	0	0	14.00	1
	C. P. Ashling	2	4	1	29	20	0	0	9.66	0
	H. T. Waters†	11	13	4	67	16	0	0	7.44	1

Also batted: W. T. Owen† (2 matches) 0*, 38, 0.

† *Born in Wales.* § *Official overseas player.* ¶ *Other non-England-qualified player.*

BOWLING

	O	M	R	W	BB	5W/i	Avge
J. A. R. Harris	443.4	115	1,293	63	5-56	2	20.52
J. Allenby	330.1	81	885	41	5-59	1	21.58
D. A. Cosker	432	101	1,128	51	5-93	1	22.11
D. S. Harrison	323.3	44	1,156	37	7-45	2	31.24
H. T. Waters	297.4	79	898	26	4-39	0	34.53
R. D. B. Croft	312.1	64	766	22	4-20	0	34.81
J. W. M. Dalrymple	127	13	391	11	4-71	0	35.54

Also bowled: C. P. Ashling 44–3–178–3; M. J. Cosgrove 35–5–140–3; T. L. Maynard 3–0–20–0;
W. T. Owen 36–6–139–0; G. P. Rees 1–0–3–0; M. A. Wallace 1–0–3–0; B. J. Wright 2–0–7–0.

LEADING CB40 AVERAGES (100 runs/3 wickets)

Batting	Runs	HS	Avge	S-R	Ct/St
M. J. Cosgrove	397	88	49.62	120.30	4
T. L. Maynard	285	103*	31.66	102.51	5
B. J. Wright	217	79	27.12	78.33	2
J. W. M. Dalrymple	142	54*	23.66	80.22	5
J. Allenby	182	61	22.75	81.25	1
M. A. Wallace	140	38	20.00	78.21	4/2

Bowling	W	BB	Avge	E-R
W. T. Owen	13	5-49	24.61	6.53
J. A. R. Harris	4	2-41	35.25	6.71
D. A. Cosker	11	4-33	37.72	5.68
M. J. Cosgrove	3	2-21	40.00	7.50
J. W. M. Dalrymple	3	2-55	54.33	6.51
H. T. Waters	3	1-30	62.33	7.19

LEADING FPT20 AVERAGES (100 runs/18 overs)

Batting	Runs	HS	Avge	S-R	Ct/St
T. L. Maynard	380	78*	29.23	**150.19**	5
M. J. Cosgrove....	562	89	35.12	**132.23**	2
M. A. Wallace	130	42*	16.25	**120.37**	8/6
J. Allenby	317	54	22.64	**105.66**	4
G. P. Rees........	183	35	18.30	**104.57**	5
J. W. M. Dalrymple	281	46*	23.41	**100.35**	4

Bowling	W	BB	Avge	E-R
R. D. B. Croft.....	22	3-19	15.59	**5.93**
D. A. Cosker	9	2-23	30.88	**7.51**
J. W. M. Dalrymple	8	3-25	30.75	**7.68**
S. W. Tait........	7	2-28	40.71	**7.91**
J. Allenby........	9	3-23	40.88	**8.14**
J. A. R. Harris	7	2-23	40.71	**9.50**

FIRST-CLASS COUNTY RECORDS

Highest score for	309*	S. P. James v Sussex at Colwyn Bay............	2000
Highest score against	322*	M. B. Loye (Northamptonshire) at Northampton ..	1998
Leading run-scorer	34,056	A. Jones (avge 33.03)	1957–1983
Best bowling for	10-51	J. Mercer v Worcestershire at Worcester.........	1936
Best bowling against	10-18	G. Geary (Leicestershire) at Pontypridd	1929
Leading wicket-taker	2,174	D. J. Shepherd (avge 20.95)...................	1950–1972
Highest total for	718-3 dec	v Sussex at Colwyn Bay	2000
Highest total against	712	by Northamptonshire at Northampton	1998
Lowest total for	22	v Lancashire at Liverpool	1924
Lowest total against	33	by Leicestershire at Ebbw Vale................	1965

LIST A COUNTY RECORDS

Highest score for	162*	I. V. A. Richards v Oxfordshire at Swansea	1993
Highest score against	268	A. D. Brown (Surrey) at The Oval..............	2002
Leading run-scorer	12,278	M. P. Maynard (avge 37.66)	1985–2005
Best bowling for	7-16	S. D. Thomas v Surrey at Swansea	1998
Best bowling against	7-30	M. P. Bicknell (Surrey) at The Oval	1999
Leading wicket-taker	354	**R. D. B. Croft (avge 31.75)**	**1989–2010**
Highest total for	429	v Surrey at The Oval	2002
Highest total against	438-5	by Surrey at The Oval	2002
Lowest total for	42	v Derbyshire at Swansea	1979
Lowest total against	59	by Combined Universities at Cambridge..........	1983
	59	by Sussex at Hove	1996

TWENTY20 RECORDS

Highest score for	116*	I. J. Thomas v Somerset at Taunton.............	2004
Highest score against	117	**M. J. Prior (Sussex) at Hove**	**2010**
Leading run-scorer	862	D. L. Hemp (avge 27.80).....................	2003–2008
Best bowling for	5-16	R. E. Watkins v Gloucestershire at Cardiff	2009
Best bowling against	5-24	C. O. Obuya (Warwickshire) at Birmingham	2003
Leading wicket-taker	68	**R. D. B. Croft (avge 24.22)**	**2003–2010**
Highest total for	206-6	v Somerset at Taunton	2006
Highest total against	239-5	**by Sussex at Hove.**.........................	**2010**
Lowest total for	**94-9**	**v Essex at Cardiff.**.........................	**2010**
Lowest total against	113-6	by Somerset at Cardiff.......................	2009

ADDRESS

Swalec Stadium, Sophia Gardens, Cardiff CF11 9XR (029 2040 9380; **email** info@glamorgancricket.co.uk). **Website** www.glamorgancricket.com

OFFICIALS

Captain 2010 – J. W. M. Dalrymple
2011 – A. N. Petersen
Director of cricket 2010 – M. P. Maynard
Managing director of cricket 2011 – C. P. Metson
First-team coach 2011 – M. P. Mott

President to be announced
Chairman R. P. Russell
Chief executive A. Hamer
Head groundsman K. Exton
Scorer/archivist Dr A. K. Hignell

GLAMORGAN v SUSSEX

At Cardiff, April 9–12. Sussex won by 201 runs. Sussex 21pts, Glamorgan 3pts. Toss: Glamorgan. County debuts: J. E. Anyon; M. S. Panesar.

Sussex, playing their first game in Division Two since 2001, won comprehensively. Despite missing front-line seamers David Harrison and Adam Shantry, Glamorgan opted to field, leaving the 21-year-old Chris Ashling, with just one first-class match to his name, to share the new ball with Harris – even younger, if more experienced. Thanks to a last-wicket stand of 47, Sussex reached 284; once Martin-Jenkins had dismantled the top order and Panesar, on debut for his new county, had sliced through the tail, that brought a lead of 93. Goodwin's half-century allowed Yardy to set a target of 405. Glamorgan soon subsided to 65 for five, before Ben Wright and Allenby fought back in a partnership worth 113. However, Nash's first ball broke the stand; his little-seen off-spin claimed another two balls later, and he ended with a career-best four for 12, rather eclipsing his more famous slow-bowling partner. It was Sussex's first-ever win at Sophia Gardens, as their last in Cardiff, in 1961, had come at the Arms Park.

Close of play: First day, Sussex 284; Second day, Sussex 65-1 (Nash 28, Anyon 1); Third day, Glamorgan 51-3 (Powell 17, Cosker 7).

Sussex

*M. H. Yardy c Allenby b Harris	43	– lbw b Croft	34
C. D. Nash lbw b Harris	8	– c Dalrymple b Croft	36
J. S. Gatting lbw b Harris	15	– (4) lbw b Harris	21
M. W. Goodwin b Allenby	30	– (5) b Ashling	83
L. J. Wright c Cosker b Allenby	34	– (6) c Allenby b Harris	0
M. A. Thornely c and b Harris	3	– (7) lbw b Cosker	46
†A. J. Hodd lbw b Ashling	37	– (8) c Cosker b Harris	18
R. S. C. Martin-Jenkins c Dalrymple b Cosker	65	– (9) not out	33
J. E. Anyon b Cosker	13	– (3) b Cosker	11
M. S. Panesar c Allenby b Cosker	0	– c Bragg b Harris	4
C. D. Collymore not out	19	– not out	6
B 7, l-b 8, n-b 2	17	B 6, l-b 10, w 1, n-b 2	19

1/27 (2) 2/73 (1) 3/74 (3)   (96.3 overs)   284
4/135 (4) 5/144 (5) 6/153 (6) 7/215 (7)
8/237 (6) 9/237 (10) 10/284 (8)

1/60 (1)   (9 wkts dec, 92 overs)   311
2/81 (2) 3/85 (3)
4/126 (4) 5/126 (6) 6/232 (5)
7/254 (7) 8/265 (8) 9/296 (10)

Harris 23–6–68–4; Ashling 15–2–61–1; Allenby 18–4–53–2; Croft 14–0–33–0; Cosker 20.3–4–43–3; Dalrymple 6–2–11–0. *Second Innings*—Harris 16–2–46–4; Ashling 9–0–35–1; Cosker 32–4–90–2; Allenby 11–2–33–0; Croft 20–2–75–2; Dalrymple 4–0–16–0.

Glamorgan

G. P. Rees c Yardy b Anyon	9	– c Hodd b Martin-Jenkins	15
W. D. Bragg c Hodd b Collymore	6	– lbw b Collymore	1
M. J. Powell lbw b Martin-Jenkins	48	– lbw b Collymore	24
*J. W. M. Dalrymple lbw b Wright	31	– c Yardy b Martin-Jenkins	4
B. J. Wright lbw b Martin-Jenkins	10	– (6) c Gatting b Nash	57
J. Allenby b Martin-Jenkins	0	– (7) c Thornely b Panesar	62
†M. A. Wallace c Hodd b Wright	21	– (8) b Nash	0
J. A. R. Harris lbw b Panesar	19	– (9) c Hodd b Nash	7
R. D. B. Croft not out	9	– (10) not out	7
D. A. Cosker lbw b Panesar	11	– (5) lbw b Wright	2
C. P. Ashling c Hodd b Panesar	2	– c Hodd b Nash	0
B 1, l-b 10, n-b 14	25	B 6, l-b 4, n-b 4	14

1/15 (1) 2/19 (1) 3/83 (4)   (69.5 overs)   191
4/109 (5) 5/109 (6) 6/130 (3) 7/160 (8)
8/164 (7) 9/185 (10) 10/191 (11)

1/7 (2) 2/30 (1)   (83.3 overs)   203
3/34 (4) 4/61 (3)
5/65 (5) 6/178 (6) 7/178 (8)
8/194 (9) 9/200 (7) 10/203 (11)

Collymore 12–3–42–1; Anyon 12–2–32–1; Wright 15–3–52–2; Martin-Jenkins 16–3–34–3; Panesar 13.5–5–20–3; Nash 1–1–0–0. *Second Innings*—Collymore 17–6–25–2; Anyon 12–4–37–0; Wright 12–3–41–1; Martin-Jenkins 11–1–32–2; Panesar 22–5–46–1; Nash 9.3–3–12–4.

Umpires: N. G. C. Cowley and J. F. Steele.

At Lord's, April 15–18. GLAMORGAN beat MIDDLESEX by 78 runs.

At Derby, April 21–24. GLAMORGAN lost to DERBYSHIRE by eight wickets.

At Worcester, April 27–28. GLAMORGAN beat WORCESTERSHIRE by nine wickets.

At Cardiff, May 5–7 (not first-class). **Glamorgan won by 215 runs. ‡Glamorgan 362** (T. L. Maynard 112, N. A. James 80, M. J. Powell 56*, M. P. Maynard 46, W. T. Owen 30; M. J. Leach 4-101, T. M. J. Warner 3-75) **and 185-9 dec** (B. J. Wright 108; T. M. J. Warner 3-41, S. M. Moore 3-48); **Cardiff MCCU 168** (R. J. Burns 51, J. N. K. Shannon 32; W. T. Owen 3-35) **and 164** (R. J. Burns 42; R. D. B. Croft 3-49). *County debut:* A. J. Jones. *Matthew Maynard, Glamorgan's director of cricket, played his first county game since 2005. He kept wicket (taking three catches) and made 46 from 32 balls at No. 7. He was captained by his son Tom, who hit his second hundred in four days, but they did not bat together. Top score in all four innings came from the No. 1: Tom Maynard and Ben Wright for Glamorgan; wicketkeeper Rory Burns (twice) for the students.*

GLAMORGAN v NORTHAMPTONSHIRE

At Cardiff, May 10–13. Glamorgan won by an innings and four runs. Glamorgan 23pts, Northamptonshire 3pts. Toss: Glamorgan.

Glamorgan's third Championship win of the season – one more than they managed throughout 2009 – was their first innings victory over Northamptonshire in 32 years. Consistency was the hallmark of Glamorgan's batting, with the top three all passing 60 and seven batsmen reaching 25. Dalrymple struck his first hundred of the season, and Allenby his fifth half-century in seven innings. In one respect, though, Glamorgan were careless: Allenby and Wallace needed just two from the 110th over to gain full batting points, but failed by a single. The batsmen later admitted forgetting that the qualifying period for bonus points was ten overs shorter than the previous season's 120. Northamptonshire, who in seamer-friendly conditions on the first day had plummeted from a reasonable 213 for five to 253 all out, batted again 197 behind. Rain swallowed 21 overs on the third afternoon, but Glamorgan still had a day and a half to seal the game. On the final morning Northamptonshire lost six wickets for 67, with Harris taking his second five-for in successive games. Glamorgan moved into second place in the table, behind Sussex.

Close of play: First day, Northamptonshire 253; Second day, Glamorgan 348-5 (Allenby 39); Third day, Northamptonshire 126-4 (Sales 18, Lucas 4).

Northamptonshire

S. D. Peters c Rees b Cosker	72	– c Harrison b Cosker	48
†N. J. O'Brien c Rees b Waters	49	– c Wallace b Harris	33
M. B. Loye lbw b Waters	0	– c Wright b Harris	9
D. J. Sales c Cosgrove b Allenby	25	– b Harrison	27
R. A. White c Allenby b Harris	5	– lbw b Harris	14
A. J. Hall c Allenby b Cosgrove	56	– (7) lbw b Harris	1
*N. Boje b Allenby	11	– (8) lbw b Allenby	6
J. D. Middlebrook c Cosgrove b Harris	10	– (9) not out	8
D. S. Lucas b Harris	13	– (6) lbw b Allenby	32
L. M. Daggett b Waters	7	– c Dalrymple b Allenby	0
J. A. Brooks not out	0	– c Wallace b Harris	7
L-b 3, w 2	5	L-b 8	8

1/66 (2) 2/66 (3) 3/113 (4)　　　(94.1 overs) 253
4/124 (5) 5/173 (1) 6/213 (7)
7/223 (6) 8/239 (8) 9/253 (10) 10/253 (9)

1/43 (2) 2/90 (1)　　　(66.5 overs) 193
3/91 (3) 4/117 (5)
5/147 (4) 6/158 (7) 7/170 (8)
8/171 (6) 9/171 (10) 10/193 (11)

Harris 20.1–4–77–3; Harrison 19–3–74–0; Waters 25–8–55–3; Allenby 20–10–29–2; Cosker 3–2–1–1; Dalrymple 1–0–1–0; Cosgrove 6–1–13–1. *Second Innings*—Harris 22.5–3–62–5; Harrison 12–2–54–1; Waters 19–7–54–0; Allenby 10–5–12–3; Cosker 3–2–3–1.

Glamorgan

G. P. Rees c O'Brien b Hall	64		D. S. Harrison b Lucas	27
M. J. Cosgrove c Sales b Daggett	85		H. T. Waters not out	0
*J. W. M. Dalrymple c Hall b Boje	105			
B. J. Wright c Hall b Daggett	25		B 4, l-b 17, w 5, n-b 4	30
M. J. Powell lbw b Hall	10			
J. Allenby c Sales b Brooks	72		1/147 (2) 2/174 (1) (125.1 overs)	450
†M. A. Wallace lbw b Hall	27		3/231 (4) 4/269 (5) 5/348 (3)	
J. A. R. Harris lbw b Hall	2		6/402 (7) 7/418 (8) 8/420 (6)	
D. A. Cosker lbw b Lucas	3		9/445 (9) 10/450 (10) 110 overs: 399-5	

Brooks 24.1–5–86–1; Lucas 22.1–3–72–2; Daggett 28.5–7–80–2; Hall 24–2–93–4; Middlebrook 8–1–36–0; Boje 18–1–62–1.

Umpires: N. L. Bainton and J. W. Lloyds.

GLAMORGAN v GLOUCESTERSHIRE

At Cardiff, May 17–20. Glamorgan won by an innings and four runs. Glamorgan 23pts, Gloucestershire 6pts. Toss: Gloucestershire.

For the first time since 2004, Glamorgan won three Championship games in a row. And for the first time since 1948, when they first became champions, they won successive innings victories. Coincidentally, they won this and the game against Northamptonshire a week before by identical margins, leapfrogging Sussex to the top of Division Two. Gloucestershire began poorly, losing the top three for single figures, before recovering through a string of five fifties. There were a record-equalling eight lbws in the innings, but none in Glamorgan's positive reply, scored at four an over,

---

MOST LBWS IN A FIRST-CLASS INNINGS

8	Oxford University v Warwickshire at Oxford	1980
8	Sussex v Essex at Hove	1992
8	Bengal v Hyderabad at Secunderabad	1997-98
8	Rajasthan v Uttar Pradesh at Jaipur	2000-01
8	Kerala v Goa at Palakkad	2008-09
8	**Gloucestershire v Glamorgan at Cardiff**	**2010**

---

which earned them a substantial lead. Wright hit the second and higher hundred of his career, while Allenby's consistency saw him pass 50 for the eighth Championship match in a row, a sequence extending back to September 2009. Needing 166 to avoid an innings defeat, Gloucestershire were undone by the spinners Croft and Cosker. When Croft, playing only his second game of the season, dismissed Franklin, he moved past Malcolm Nash's total of 991 first-class wickets for Glamorgan; only Don Shepherd, Jack Mercer and Johnnie Clay had taken more. (Just a fortnight earlier, Gloucestershire's request to take Croft on loan had been turned down.) Glamorgan barely seemed to notice the loss of their strike bowler, James Harris, who was playing for the England Lions.

Close of play: First day, Gloucestershire 303-5 (Taylor 45, Snell 43); Second day, Glamorgan 257-3 (Wright 77, Powell 20); Third day, Gloucestershire 12-1 (Batty 9).

Gloucestershire

†J. N. Batty lbw b Waters	6	– c Allenby b Waters	11
C. D. J. Dent lbw b Harrison	6	– b Cosker	3
H. J. H. Marshall lbw b Waters	1	– lbw b Allenby	22
*A. P. R. Gidman lbw b Allenby	97	– lbw b Cosker	34
J. E. C. Franklin c Wallace b Cosker	95	– lbw b Croft	28
C. G. Taylor lbw b Allenby	65	– c Rees b Cosker	10
S. D. Snell c Wallace b Allenby	71	– run out	4
J. Lewis lbw b Cosker	50	– not out	37
V. Banerjee lbw b Croft	8	– lbw b Croft	0
G. M. Hussain not out	5	– c Wright b Dalrymple	7
A. J. Ireland lbw b Croft	2	– run out	0
L-b 11	11	B 1, l-b 5	6

1/11 (1) 2/17 (2) 3/27 (3)   (129.1 overs) 417
4/182 (4) 5/224 (5) 6/344 (6)
7/373 (7) 8/407 (8) 9/415 (9)
10/417 (11)   110 overs: 353-6

1/12 (2) 2/25 (1)   (78.1 overs) 162
3/65 (3) 4/77 (4)
5/99 (6) 6/112 (7) 7/119 (5)
8/123 (9) 9/150 (10) 10/161 (11)

Harrison 29–1–105–1; Waters 27.3–6–92–2; Allenby 21–6–71–3; Cosker 29–8–66–2; Dalrymple 3.3–1–18–0; Croft 15.1–3–45–2; Cosgrove 4–1–9–0. *Second Innings*—Waters 8–1–29–1; Cosker 25–13–32–3; Croft 28.1–7–51–2; Harrison 6–0–22–0; Allenby 6–3–8–1; Dalrymple 5–2–14–1.

Glamorgan

G. P. Rees b Ireland	48	D. S. Harrison c Dent b Ireland	10
M. J. Cosgrove b Ireland	34		
*J. W. M. Dalrymple st Batty b Banerjee	58	B 23, l-b 15, w 1, n-b 6	45
B. J. Wright c Batty b Lewis	172		
M. J. Powell b Franklin	37	1/50 (2) (9 wkts dec, 145.5 overs) 583
J. Allenby c Franklin b Ireland	105	2/125 (1) 3/203 (3)
†M. A. Wallace c Dent b Ireland	0	4/360 (5) 5/390 (4) 6/392 (7)
R. D. B. Croft st Batty b Banerjee	63	7/545 (8) 8/564 (6)
D. A. Cosker not out	11	9/583 (10) 110 overs: 443-6

H. T. Waters did not bat.

Lewis 25–4–85–1; Franklin 15–2–63–1; Ireland 29.5–2–114–5; Hussain 24–3–107–0; Banerjee 38–5–132–2; Marshall 14–2–44–0.

Umpires: S. C. Gale and G. Sharp.

At Leicester, May 24–26. GLAMORGAN beat LEICESTERSHIRE by ten wickets. *Glamorgan led Division Two by 23 points after recording their fourth successive win.*

GLAMORGAN v SURREY

At Cardiff, May 29–June 1. Drawn. Glamorgan 10pts, Surrey 9pts. Toss: Surrey. County debut: Younis Khan.

The rain, which had largely been absent from Glamorgan's first seven Championship games, finally arrived, allowing just eight overs on the first day and none on the last, scuppering any hopes of a fifth successive win, something Glamorgan have never managed. Century partnerships from the openers – for the second game in succession – and, after a mid-innings wobble, from Wallace and Harris steered Glamorgan to four batting points. Surrey replied in positive fashion and, once Harinath fell in Dalrymple's only over, Ramprakash held centre-stage, passing 34,000 first-class runs on the way. Another century beckoned until he was dismissed by a lifter from Harris, who twice took two wickets in an over. Younis Khan, on his Surrey debut, lasted only five balls. Surrey declared late on the third day, but the weather had the last laugh. Glamorgan remained on top of the division halfway through the season, and Surrey bottom.

Close of play: First day, Glamorgan 19-0 (Rees 9, Cosgrove 5); Second day, Glamorgan 363-8 (Cosker 4); Third day, Glamorgan 7-0 (Rees 2, Cosgrove 5).

Glamorgan

G. P. Rees c Davies b Tremlett	86	– not out	2
M. J. Cosgrove b Meaker	82	– not out	5
*J. W. M. Dalrymple b Meaker	11		
B. J. Wright c Batty b Dernbach	23		
T. L. Maynard c Davies b Dernbach	3		
J. Allenby c Davies b Meaker	15		
†M. A. Wallace c Davies b Dernbach	58		
J. A. R. Harris c Davies b Dernbach	49		
D. A. Cosker not out	6		
D. S. Harrison c Linley b Tremlett	1		
H. T. Waters b Tremlett	2		
B 5, l-b 21, n-b 10	36		

1/135 (2) 2/153 (3) 3/204 (4)   (109 overs) 372   (no wkt, 3 overs) 7
4/218 (5) 5/242 (1) 6/247 (6)
7/354 (8) 8/363 (7) 9/364 (10) 10/372 (11)

Tremlett 24–8–55–3; Linley 22–2–71–0; Dernbach 24–7–78–4; Meaker 23–2–83–3; Batty 13–2–51–0; Hamilton-Brown 3–0–8–0. *Second Innings*—Dernbach 2–0–5–0; Tremlett 1–0–2–0.

Surrey

†S. M. Davies c Wallace b Harris	83	J. W. Dernbach b Waters	2
A. Harinath lbw b Dalrymple	31	T. E. Linley not out	6
M. R. Ramprakash c Wallace b Harris	73		
Younis Khan b Harris	0	B 4, l-b 12	16
U. Afzaal c Dalrymple b Allenby	49		
*R. J. Hamilton-Brown lbw b Harris	0	1/83 (2) 2/157 (1) (9 wkts dec, 84 overs) 303
G. J. Batty b Cosker	32	3/157 (4) 4/222 (3)
S. C. Meaker lbw b Cosker	4	5/222 (6) 6/280 (5) 7/282 (7)
C. T. Tremlett not out	7	8/287 (8) 9/290 (10)

Harris 20–2–82–4; Harrison 17–1–73–0; Waters 16–4–43–1; Allenby 15–2–44–1; Cosker 15–4–40–2; Dalrymple 1–0–5–1.

Umpires: M. A. Gough and D. J. Millns.

At Cardiff, June 5–7. GLAMORGAN drew with WEST INDIES A (see A-team tours of the British Isles).

At Northampton, July 5–7. GLAMORGAN lost to NORTHAMPTONSHIRE by ten wickets.

GLAMORGAN v LEICESTERSHIRE

At Swansea, July 21–24. Drawn. Glamorgan 7pts, Leicestershire 7pts. Toss: Leicestershire.

On the day Muttiah Muralitharan broke the 800-wicket barrier in Tests, a more conventional off-spinner carved his own slice of history. Robert Croft took his 1,000th first-class wicket for Glamorgan when he had White caught down the leg side by Wallace in Leicestershire's first innings. The fourth bowler to reach four figures for Glamorgan, Croft also became the first player since 1972 to complete the double of 1,000 wickets and 10,000 runs for a single first-class team. Glamorgan's leading wicket-taker Don Shepherd (still 1,174 ahead of Croft) and president Peter Walker came on to the field with a glass of champagne for Croft, who received a standing ovation on the ground where he started as a schoolboy. "It will be challenging for anyone to do this double again," Croft predicted, with understatement. Leicestershire made little attempt to play positive cricket. They averaged

MAKE MINE A DOUBLE!

10,000 runs and 1,000 wickets in first-class cricket for a single county since 1945.

	Career	Matches	Runs	Wkts	Matches for double
T. E. Bailey (Essex)	1946–1967	482	21,460	1,593	286
F. J. Titmus (Middlesex).	1949–1982	642	17,320	2,361	307
R. Illingworth (Yorkshire)	1951–1983	496	14,986	1,431	353
J. B. Mortimore (Gloucestershire) . .	1950–1975	594	14,918	1,696	347
D. C. Morgan (Derbyshire).	1950–1969	540	17,842	1,216	436
T. W. Cartwright (Warwickshire). . .	1952–1969	353	10,781	1,058	343
A. S. Brown (Gloucestershire)	1953–1976	489	12,684	1,223	389
P. J. Sainsbury (Hampshire)	1954–1976	593	19,576	1,245	499
R. D. B. Croft (Glamorgan)	**1989–2010**	**348**	**11,756**	**1,013**	**343**

Note: A. W. Wellard (1927–1950) completed the double for Somerset in 1947.

around two runs an over in both innings and, had they shown more adventure, could have set a target on the last day. By contrast, Cosgrove attacked with relish to reach his century before Glamorgan had made 150.

Close of play: First day, Leicestershire 225-5 (New 7, White 0); Second day, Glamorgan 45-0 (Rees 15, Cosgrove 27); Third day, Leicestershire 41-2 (du Toit 26, Naik 1).

Leicestershire

W. I. Jefferson c Cosgrove b Allenby	27	– lbw b Cosker	10
M. A. G. Boyce c Wallace b Croft.	38	– c Dalrymple b Harris	0
J. du Toit c Wallace b Croft.	75	– b Harris.	26
J. W. A. Taylor lbw b Cosker	70	– (5) c Rees b Croft.	43
P. A. Nixon c Dalrymple b Harris	0	– (6) not out	57
†T. J. New c Wallace b Harris	7	– (7) c Wallace b Harris	18
W. A. White c Wallace b Croft	8	– (8) not out.	24
J. K. H. Naik not out	12	– (4) b Dalrymple	35
C. W. Henderson c Dalrymple b Harrison	1		
M. N. Malik c Allenby b Cosker	0		
*M. J. Hoggard lbw b Cosker	0		
B 1, l-b 6, n-b 2	9	B 1, l-b 3, n-b 4	8

1/57 (1) 2/92 (2) 3/201 (3)   (116.2 overs) 247   1/1 (2)   (6 wkts dec, 107 overs) 221
4/206 (5) 5/225 (4) 6/226 (6)   2/36 (1) 3/41 (3)
7/242 (7) 8/244 (9) 9/245 (10)   4/104 (5) 5/146 (4) 6/176 (7)
10/247 (11)   110 overs: 244-7

Harris 29–11–45–2; Harrison 15–2–39–1; Allenby 14–1–45–1; Cosgrove 3–1–10–0; Cosker 19.2–7–35–3; Croft 33–11–54–3; Dalrymple 3–0–12–0. *Second Innings*—Harris 18–6–40–3; Croft 40–8–77–1; Cosker 26–13–33–1; Harrison 2–0–8–0; Dalrymple 20–3–56–1; Wallace 1–0–3–0.

Glamorgan

G. P. Rees c Boyce b Malik.	15	R. D. B. Croft lbw b Naik	6
M. J. Cosgrove st New b Henderson	117	D. A. Cosker c Taylor b Naik	0
T. L. Maynard b Naik	19	D. S. Harrison c Hoggard b Henderson	19
B. J. Wright lbw b Henderson	3	L-b 5, w 2, n-b 2	9
*J. W. M. Dalrymple c Taylor b Naik	48		
J. Allenby c Nixon b Henderson	30	1/74 (1) 2/138 (3) (81.5 overs) 290
†M. A. Wallace c Taylor b Henderson	9	3/153 (4) 4/176 (2) 5/230 (5) 6/249 (7)
J. A. R. Harris not out	15	7/254 (6) 8/263 (9) 9/263 (10) 10/290 (11)

Hoggard 13–1–50–0; Malik 11–2–44–1; White 2–0–9–0; Naik 31–3–110–4; Henderson 24.5–3–72–5.

Umpires: R. K. Illingworth and G. Sharp.

At Cheltenham, July 30–August 1. GLAMORGAN beat GLOUCESTERSHIRE by 176 runs.

GLAMORGAN v WORCESTERSHIRE

At Colwyn Bay, August 9–12. Glamorgan won by 241 runs. Glamorgan 22pts, Worcestershire 7pts. Toss: Glamorgan.

The fortunes of these two sides were so divergent that Nostradamus would have struggled to predict the turnaround to come over the next four games. Chasing 417 in 87 overs, Worcestershire were never in contention and lost their last seven wickets for 47 runs, the final four to Cosker. Glamorgan's seventh victory sent them top of Division Two; not since their Championship-winning season of 1997 had they won as many. Defeat left Worcestershire sixth, 37 points behind. Solanki resigned the captaincy, followed the next day by chief executive Mark Newton after ten years in the role. On an easy-paced pitch, Mitchell, soon to be announced as Solanki's successor, prepared for his coronation by scoring his third hundred in a week. He had batted for 14 hours and 13 minutes without being dismissed until he was brilliantly caught by Dalrymple at extra cover in Worcestershire's second innings. Glamorgan sped along in search of a target, mindful that Worcestershire had chased down 339 at Cheltenham. Maynard unleashed an astonishing barrage, striking Shakib Al Hasan for four sixes, only to edge Mason to slip two runs short of a maiden hundred. Wright, 97 not out going into the last day, pulled Shakib Al Hasan to complete his century before the declaration.

Close of play: First day, Glamorgan 319-9 (Cosker 7, Waters 0); Second day, Worcestershire 281-6 (Mitchell 136, Cox 2); Third day, Glamorgan 355-6 (Wright 97, Croft 4).

Glamorgan

G. P. Rees c Cox b Jones	25	– c Cox b Mason	65
M. J. Cosgrove st Cox b Shakib Al Hasan	84	– b Mason	0
T. L. Maynard c Cox b Richardson	21	– c Mitchell b Mason	98
B. J. Wright c Mitchell b Cameron	72	– not out	121
*J. W. M. Dalrymple c Jones b Shakib Al Hasan	56	– c Jones b Shakib Al Hasan	6
J. Allenby c Kervezee b Mason	14	– c Wheeldon b Shakib Al Hasan	62
†M. A. Wallace c Solanki b Jones	0	– c Mason b Ali	12
R. D. B. Croft c Kervezee b Shakib Al Hasan	9	– c Ali b Mason	4
D. A. Cosker not out	41	– (10) not out	14
D. S. Harrison c Kervezee b Richardson	11	– (9) b Shakib Al Hasan	3
H. T. Waters b Shakib Al Hasan	10		
B 12, l-b 10, w 2, n-b 2	26	L-b 6, n-b 6	12

1/100 (1) 2/127 (2) 3/145 (3) (109.4 overs) 369
4/242 (4) 5/275 (6) 6/280 (7)
7/289 (8) 8/302 (5) 9/318 (10) 10/369 (11)

1/21 (2) (8 wkts dec, 83 overs) 397
2/171 (3) 3/176 (1) 4/187 (5)
5/322 (6) 6/346 (7) 7/355 (8) 8/366 (9)

Mason 29–9–82–2; Richardson 27–12–59–2; Jones 18–1–105–2; Ali 7–1–36–0; Shakib Al Hasan 23.4–9–38–3; Cameron 5–1–27–1. *Second Innings*—Mason 20–4–87–4; Richardson 4–0–17–0; Shakib Al Hasan 31–3–147–3; Jones 3–0–20–0; Cameron 11–1–50–0; Mitchell 7–1–28–0; Ali 7–0–42–1.

Worcestershire

D. K. H. Mitchell not out	165	– c Dalrymple b Harrison	45
D. A. Wheeldon c Dalrymple b Croft	0	– run out	26
*V. S. Solanki lbw b Cosker	9	– lbw b Allenby	10
M. M. Ali lbw b Harrison	10	– c Wallace b Allenby	0
A. N. Kervezee c Maynard b Allenby	72	– c Wallace b Harrison	45
Shakib Al Hasan c Maynard b Waters	47	– b Cosker	25
J. G. Cameron lbw b Croft	0	– lbw b Harrison	12
†O. B. Cox b Waters	2	– c Dalrymple b Cosker	1
R. A. Jones c Cosgrove b Harrison	12	– lbw b Cosker	0
M. S. Mason not out	25	– lbw b Cosker	3
A. Richardson (did not bat)		– not out	1
L-b 6, n-b 2	8	L-b 2, n-b 5	7

1/7 (2) 2/27 (3) (8 wkts dec, 92.1 overs) 350
3/38 (4) 4/183 (5) 5/275 (6)
6/278 (7) 7/285 (8) 8/302 (9)

1/49 (2) 2/73 (3) (59.5 overs) 175
3/73 (4) 4/128 (1)
5/135 (5) 6/149 (7) 7/154 (8)
8/154 (9) 9/160 (10) 10/175 (6)

Harrison 18–3–64–2; Waters 20–3–92–2; Croft 23.1–4–63–2; Allenby 15–0–71–1; Cosker 15–3–51–1; Cosgrove 1–0–3–0. *Second Innings*—Harrison 14.1–1–48–3; Waters 14–4–31–0; Croft 7–5–11–0; Allenby 11–2–36–2; Cosgrove 3–0–20–0; Cosker 10.5–5–27–4.

Umpires: P. J. Hartley and N. J. Llong.

GLAMORGAN v MIDDLESEX

At Cardiff, August 16–19. Middlesex won by six wickets. Middlesex 19pts, Glamorgan 3pts. Toss: Glamorgan.

It wasn't just Glamorgan's promotion hopes wounded by this dispiriting defeat. Dalrymple, a Middlesex player for eight years, was dismissed in the first innings by a lifter from Collins which struck his right glove, flew to second slip and left him nursing a broken thumb. Glamorgan, who reached a modest total only thanks to Cosker and Harrison's last-wicket stand of 62, went on to establish a first-innings lead of 17, but it could have been more had Croft, at fine leg, not dropped Newman on 12. Murtagh then sliced through a brittle top order and, with Glamorgan ahead by a featherweight 137, Dalrymple was obliged to come out at No. 10 approaching stumps on day two. He held firm for 64 balls, adding 76 with Allenby, who stayed put for three and a half hours to set Middlesex 250. But the pitch had lost much of its venom, and they coped quite easily. Malan and Berg reconvened on the final morning to knock off the remaining 50 in 38 minutes, shortly before heavy rain swirled in.

Close of play: First day, Middlesex 68-2 (Newman 40, Malan 13); Second day, Glamorgan 156-8 (Allenby 58, Dalrymple 17); Third day, Middlesex 200-4 (Malan 52, Berg 11).

Glamorgan

G. P. Rees c Newman b Murtagh	6	– lbw b Murtagh		0
M. J. Cosgrove c Simpson b Collins	0	– b Collins		11
*J. W. M. Dalrymple c Dexter b Collins	37	– (10) lbw b Roland-Jones		27
B. J. Wright c Malan b Murtagh	0	– b Murtagh		17
T. L. Maynard lbw b Roland-Jones	37	– c Malan b Dexter		40
J. Allenby c Simpson b Collins	20	– not out		91
†M. A. Wallace c Murtagh b Collins	10	– c Shah b Roland-Jones		1
J. A. R. Harris c Simpson b Dexter	7	– c Malan b Dexter		3
R. D. B. Croft c Shah b Dexter	12	– (3) lbw b Murtagh		0
D. A. Cosker not out	28	– (9) c Malan b Roland-Jones		1
D. S. Harrison c Smith b Murtagh	35	– c Simpson b Roland-Jones		26
L-b 5, w 1	6	L-b 4, n-b 11		15

1/0 (2) 2/8 (1) 3/8 (4) 4/58 (5) (72.1 overs) 198
5/90 (6) 6/114 (7) 7/117 (3)
8/131 (8) 9/136 (9) 10/198 (11)

1/0 (1) 2/4 (3) (65.2 overs) 232
3/16 (4) 4/34 (5) 5/99 (5)
6/102 (7) 7/111 (8) 8/120 (9)
9/196 (10) 10/232 (11)

Murtagh 17.1–7–34–3; Collins 19–5–55–4; Roland-Jones 14–4–43–1; Dexter 16–5–40–2; Smith 4–0–14–0; Udal 2–0–7–0. *Second Innings*—Murtagh 17–2–64–3; Collins 19–2–51–1; Dexter 12–3–31–2; Roland-Jones 12.2–0–54–4; Smith 5–0–28–0.

Middlesex

S. A. Newman c Cosker b Allenby	99	– st Wallace b Croft	64
†J. A. Simpson lbw b Allenby	11	– c Maynard b Harrison	14
O. A. Shah c Wallace b Harris	1	– c Harris b Cosker	47
D. J. Malan b Harris	31	– not out	84
*N. J. Dexter c Allenby b Harris	4	– c Rees b Croft	11
G. K. Berg run out	0	– not out	30
T. M. J. Smith lbw b Cosker	18		
S. D. Udal c Maynard b Allenby	3		
T. J. Murtagh c Allenby b Croft	1		
T. S. Roland-Jones not out	0		
P. T. Collins lbw b Cosker	0		
L-b 11, n-b 2	13	B 1, l-b 1, w 1	3

1/36 (2) 2/39 (3) 3/109 (4)   (60.3 overs) 181
4/113 (5) 5/124 (6) 6/174 (1)
7/180 (8) 8/181 (9) 9/181 (7) 10/181 (11)

1/31 (2)   (4 wkts, 81.4 overs) 253
2/102 (1) 3/150 (3) 4/173 (5)

Harris 19–4–63–3; Harrison 18–1–60–0; Allenby 18–6–43–3; Croft 5–3–4–1; Cosker
0.3–0–0–2. *Second Innings*—Harris 16–3–53–0; Harrison 12.4–2–56–1; Allenby 7–3–15–0; Croft
29–5–66–2; Cosker 17–2–61–1.

Umpires: N. G. B. Cook and T. E. Jesty.

At Hove, August 27–30. GLAMORGAN drew with SUSSEX.

At The Oval, September 7–10. GLAMORGAN drew with SURREY. *Second-placed Glamorgan
lead Worcestershire by nine points following the penultimate round of matches.*

GLAMORGAN v DERBYSHIRE

At Cardiff, September 13–16. Drawn. Glamorgan 6pts, Derbyshire 8pts. Toss: Glamorgan.
    When it became clear on the final afternoon that Worcestershire were going to beat Sussex,
Dalrymple realised only a win would do for Glamorgan to be promoted. He swiftly brokered an
agreement with Greg Smith, but time was not on his side. Madsen and wicketkeeper Poynton
dutifully sent down 17 overs of declaration bowling, and Rees hardly acknowledged his hundred.
Dalrymple declared at 2.30 p.m., leaving Glamorgan with a minimum of 37 overs to take ten wickets;
Derbyshire needed 160. Harris soon dismissed both openers and, when Rogers, in an incongruous
end to his Derbyshire career, was bowled trying to leave Allenby, Glamorgan were galvanised. It
was a false dawn: from 63 for five, Redfern and Peterson – another on his way out of Derbyshire –
safely batted out 20 overs until stumps. Glamorgan trooped dejectedly from the field, consigned to a
sixth consecutive season in the second division. "To be in this position now is horrific," said
Dalrymple. "I think we deserved to go up." Glamorgan faltered by playing loosely outside off stump
in the first innings and failing to score a batting point, though rain deprived them of 56 overs on the
first day and all of the second. They then allowed Derbyshire to turn 142 for six into a 110-run first-
innings lead. Confirmation of Graham Wagg's move from Derby to Cardiff did not lift the gloom;
indeed, it would only darken for Glamorgan in a turbulent winter.
    Close of play: First day, Glamorgan 120-6 (Allenby 34, Harris 25); Second day, No play; Third
day, Derbyshire 234-8 (Poynton 12, Jones 29).

Glamorgan

G. P. Rees b Clare	7	– not out	106
M. J. Cosgrove b Smith	32	– c Hughes b Poynton	75
*J. W. M. Dalrymple c Durston b Clare	1		
B. J. Wright c Hughes b Smith	0	– (3) c Peterson b Madsen	24
T. L. Maynard c and b Groenewald	4	– (4) c Smith b Poynton	25
J. Allenby b Clare	57	– (5) not out	35
†M. A. Wallace c Peterson b Jones	3		
J. A. R. Harris lbw b Groenewald	36		
R. D. B. Croft b Peterson	5		
D. A. Cosker not out	4		
H. T. Waters c Rogers b Peterson	3		
B 4, l-b 6, w 2, n-b 2	14	B 4	4

1/31 (1) 2/43 (3) 3/43 (4) 4/48 (5)   (57.2 overs) 166   1/122 (2)   (3 wkts dec, 33.2 overs) 269
5/56 (2) 6/66 (7) 7/154 (6)   2/148 (3) 3/183 (4)
8/159 (9) 9/159 (8) 10/166 (11)

Groenewald 19–7–43–2; Clare 19–2–75–3; Smith 7–3–19–2; Jones 7–1–19–1; Peterson 5.2–5–0–2. *Second Innings*—Clare 4–0–16–0; Groenewald 4–1–31–0; Peterson 4–0–31–0; Smith 5–0–23–0; Madsen 8.2–0–68–1; Poynton 8–0–96–2.

Derbyshire

W. L. Madsen lbw b Harris	0	– c Wallace b Harris	0
C. J. L. Rogers lbw b Croft	33	– (4) b Allenby	9
C. F. Hughes b Dalrymple	29	– (2) lbw b Harris	1
W. J. Durston c Wallace b Harris	46	– (3) lbw b Cosker	38
*G. M. Smith c Wright b Harris	42	– lbw b Cosker	12
D. J. Redfern c Wallace b Cosker	7	– not out	29
R. J. Peterson c Allenby b Cosker	5	– not out	34
J. L. Clare b Cosker	24		
†T. Poynton lbw b Cosker	25		
P. S. Jones lbw b Cosker	45		
T. D. Groenewald not out	13		
B 3, l-b 2, n-b 2	7		

1/0 (1) 2/42 (3) 3/98 (2)   (103.2 overs) 276   1/1 (2)   (5 wkts, 41.5 overs) 123
4/116 (4) 5/126 (6) 6/142 (7)   2/8 (1) 3/33 (4)
7/187 (5) 8/189 (8) 9/259 (10) 10/276 (9)   4/48 (3) 5/63 (5)

Harris 22–5–46–3; Waters 8–3–16–0; Croft 38–8–100–1; Dalrymple 5–0–16–1; Cosker 30.2–4–93–5. *Second Innings*—Harris 10–2–15–2; Croft 9.5–1–30–0; Waters 2–0–12–0; Allenby 5–1–23–1; Cosker 12–1–34–2; Dalrymple 3–0–9–0.

Umpires: S. A. Garratt and D. J. Millns.

GLOUCESTERSHIRE

Losing money – and players

GRAHAM RUSSELL

According to the old saying, money is the root of all evil – but Gloucestershire discovered that the shortage of it brings its own crop of problems. With a predicted six-figure loss for the second year running, they had to put prudence before ambition, and embarked on the biggest cull in their peacetime history.

Eight players left after the season, the cruellest loss being the pace bowlers Steve Kirby and Gemaal Hussain to neighbours Somerset. Kirby still had two years left on his contract, while the 26-year-old Hussain completed his first full summer as the second-highest wicket-taker in the country with 67.

Hampshire and Nottinghamshire also made approaches about Hussain: there was a half-hearted attempt to keep him, but Somerset were able to offer more, both in pay and prospects. In the six seasons since he moved from Yorkshire, Kirby had built himself into a top front-line bowler, but even so Hussain was the bigger loss. Gloucestershire's former wicketkeeper Jack Russell came across him during a scouting mission and, impressed by his physique and the way he could swing the ball or hit the deck hard, persuaded the county to offer him a contract. Hussain responded to a winter of intense coaching by taking wickets from the start in 2010.

Their departures raised a question the cricket authorities have so far ducked: how much were they worth? If Gloucestershire had been able to demand transfer fees – it could perhaps be called compensation – other players might not have been forced to leave.

As it was, the mass exodus saw Ireland's captain Will Porterfield, another opener in Kadeer Ali, wicketkeeper Steve Snell and the Zimbabwean fast-medium bowler Anthony Ireland all reluctantly moving on.

The New Zealander James Franklin, who had another fine all-round season, spoke openly of his desire to stay on as Gloucestershire's overseas player if they made him a decent offer. But that was never likely to come at the level he was entitled to expect, and four counties lined up to talk to him.

It was all very sad, as new chairman Rex Body and chief executive Tom Richardson acknowledged. Money would be found to continue upgrading Bristol as a one-day international venue, and the coaching staff was strengthened with the signing of Richard Dawson – but director of cricket John Bracewell was left with a small core of senior players and a brief to discover and develop younger (and cheaper) recruits.

There was another unanswered question: what would have happened if Gloucestershire had won promotion? In a bizarre season which brought some startling results, that was on the cards for much of the summer.

In fact, if they could have played Middlesex more often, promotion would probably have been achieved. In all they met six times in various competitions in 2010, and Gloucestershire won all six games. Such delights were rare, though: starker in the memory was the way a 202-run lead over Worcestershire in another ill-fated Cheltenham festival evaporated into a six-wicket defeat. And against Derbyshire at Bristol there was an even more unbelievable result – defeat inside two days after the visitors had been bowled out for 44 on the first morning.

Gemaal Hussain

The seam attack, led by Kirby, Hussain and Jon Lewis, was as good as any in either division; pitches were often prepared for them, a tactic which rebounded when the opening two matches at Bristol were lost, as was that Derbyshire debacle near the end. Each time the pitch inspectors cleared the groundsman of blame, and found the batsmen guilty of poor technique and bad shot selection.

The attack was light on spin: a cheeky attempt to borrow Robert Croft from Glamorgan came to nothing but, while the seamers constantly put the team into a strong position, the batting failed too often. "Unacceptable" was the word often on the lips of captain Alex Gidman, especially after they had been shot out by Hampshire in a Twenty20 game for 68, their lowest 20-over total. Failure in the shorter forms, at which Gloucestershire had excelled a few years earlier, contributed to the financial plight.

No one made 1,000 runs, and the first Championship hundred had to wait until August, when both Porterfield and Franklin reached three figures in the same innings at Cheltenham. Porterfield topped the averages, just ahead of Hamish Marshall, who was consistent without producing a three-figure score. Most of the others will have been disappointed with their figures, among them Jon Batty, signed from Surrey at 36 to open the batting as well as keep wicket. He averaged only 16 in the Championship, although his total of 56 dismissals was exceeded only by Chris Read.

In a season of batting underachievement there was one shining exception, the 19-year-old left-hander Chris Dent, from the Thornbury club, who caught Bracewell's eye with a hundred against Cardiff MCCU in April. He was picked for all 16 Championship games, remained positive while others dithered, and produced three scores in the nineties, which earned him a three-year deal.

David Payne, like Dent an England Under-19 player, was given a similar contract after his seven for 29 in a CB40 match against Essex. A left-arm swing bowler from Poole, he is described as an exciting prospect. Adding to the springtime impression of green shoots, Muttiah Muralitharan was signed for the T20.

GLOUCESTERSHIRE RESULTS

All first-class matches – Played 16: Won 6, Lost 9, Drawn 1.
County Championship matches – Played 16: Won 6, Lost 9, Drawn 1.

LV= County Championship, 5th in Division 2;
Friends Provident T20, 9th in South Division; Clydesdale Bank 40, 3rd in Group B.

COUNTY CHAMPIONSHIP AVERAGES, BATTING AND FIELDING

Cap		M	I	NO	R	HS	100s	50s	Avge	Ct/St
2008	W. T. S. Porterfield¶	7	14	0	531	175	2	1	37.92	6
2006	H. J. H. Marshall¶	15	27	2	884	89*	0	7	35.36	15
2004	J. E. C. Franklin§	16	29	3	862	108	1	4	33.15	7
2001	C. G. Taylor†	15	27	2	803	89	0	6	32.12	11
2010	C. D. J. Dent†	16	31	3	725	98	0	4	25.89	24
2004	A. P. R. Gidman	16	29	0	679	99	0	3	23.41	16
2005	Kadeer Ali	6	12	1	240	74	0	2	21.81	5
2005	S. D. Snell	10	19	1	322	71	0	2	17.88	18
1998	J. Lewis	16	28	2	419	50	0	1	16.11	7
2010	J. N. Batty	15	30	2	450	61	0	1	16.07	53/3
2006	V. Banerjee	7	14	3	108	35	0	0	9.81	1
2009	G. M. Hussain	15	26	10	153	28*	0	0	9.56	1
2005	S. P. Kirby	10	17	5	100	22*	0	0	8.33	2
2010	J. M. R. Taylor	2	4	0	11	6	0	0	2.75	2
2007	A. J. Ireland¶	8	12	2	21	11	0	0	2.10	0

Also batted: E. G. C. Young (cap 2010) (2 matches) 1, 19, 38 (3 ct).

† *Born in Gloucestershire.* § *Official overseas player.* ¶ *Other non-England-qualified player.*
Since 2004, Gloucestershire have awarded caps to all players making their first-class debut.

BOWLING

	O	M	R	W	BB	5W/i	Avge
A. J. Ireland	222.5	33	784	36	5-25	2	21.77
G. M. Hussain	417.4	86	1,497	67	5-36	3	22.34
J. Lewis	419.3	103	1,222	54	4-25	0	22.62
J. E. C. Franklin	334.2	69	1,083	46	7-14	1	23.54
S. P. Kirby	261.4	59	835	29	4-50	0	28.79
V. Banerjee	222	28	793	23	5-74	2	34.47

Also bowled: C. D. J. Dent 11–0–43–0; A. P. R. Gidman 53–7–203–9; H. J. H. Marshall 61–19–153–0; W. T. S. Porterfield 5–0–49–0; C. G. Taylor 52.2–5–172–3; J. M. R. Taylor 5–2–13–1; E. J. C. Young 38–1–154–1.

LEADING CB40 AVERAGES (100 runs/4 wickets)

Batting	Runs	HS	Avge	S-R	Ct/St
J. E. C. Franklin . . .	511	133*	73.00	91.74	3
C. G. Taylor	385	105	42.77	108.75	5
A. P. R. Gidman . . .	452	104*	41.09	87.42	7
S. D. Snell	267	95	38.14	118.66	13/1
H. J. H. Marshall . .	333	85	33.30	103.41	5
W. T. S. Porterfield	303	65	27.54	93.80	7

Bowling	W	BB	Avge	E-R
D. A. Payne	16	7-29	11.18	4.85
V. Banerjee	4	2-20	12.75	3.92
J. Lewis	16	3-3	21.87	5.22
S. P. Kirby	17	3-41	23.52	5.47
R. K. J. Dawson . . .	10	3-41	27.10	5.58
A. J. Ireland	12	3-36	29.75	7.59

LEADING FPT20 AVERAGES (100 runs/18 overs)

Batting	Runs	HS	Avge	S-R	Ct/St
W. T. S. Porterfield . .	331	65	27.58	**151.83**	7
C. G. Taylor	257	67	19.76	**146.02**	1
S. D. Snell	166	50	18.44	**143.10**	8/3
J. E. C. Franklin . .	470	90	39.16	**130.19**	3
H. J. H. Marshall . .	283	52*	28.30	**125.22**	7
C. D. J. Dent	162	63	27.00	**122.72**	0

Bowling	W	BB	Avge	E-R
S. P. Kirby	13	3-17	20.69	**7.72**
V. Banerjee	7	2-30	37.42	**8.18**
J. Lewis	8	2-26	46.50	**8.26**
R. K. J. Dawson . . .	10	2-20	21.70	**8.34**
J. E. C. Franklin . . .	8	2-33	39.75	**8.83**
A. J. Ireland	12	3-35	32.41	**9.84**

FIRST-CLASS COUNTY RECORDS

Highest score for	341	C. M. Spearman v Middlesex at Gloucester	2004
Highest score against	319	C. J. L. Rogers (Northamptonshire) at Northampton	2006
Leading run-scorer	33,664	W. R. Hammond (avge 57.05)	1920–1951
Best bowling for	10-40	E. G. Dennett v Essex at Bristol	1906
Best bowling against	{10-66	A. A. Mailey (Australians) at Cheltenham	1921
	{10-66	K. Smales (Nottinghamshire) at Stroud	1956
Leading wicket-taker	3,170	C. W. L. Parker (avge 19.43)	1903–1935
Highest total for	695-9 dec	v Middlesex at Gloucester	2004
Highest total against	774-7 dec	by Australians at Bristol	1948
Lowest total for	17	v Australians at Cheltenham	1896
Lowest total against	12	by Northamptonshire at Gloucester	1907

LIST A COUNTY RECORDS

Highest score for	177	A. J. Wright v Scotland at Bristol	1997
Highest score against	189*	J. G. E. Benning (Surrey) at Bristol	2006
Leading run-scorer	7,825	M. W. Alleyne (avge 26.89)	1986–2005
Best bowling for	**7-29**	**D. A. Payne v Essex at Chelmsford**	**2010**
Best bowling against	6-16	Shoaib Akhtar (Worcestershire) at Worcester	2005
Leading wicket-taker	393	M. W. Alleyne (avge 29.88)	1986–2005
Highest total for	401-7	v Buckinghamshire at Wing	2003
Highest total against	496-4	by Surrey at The Oval	2007
Lowest total for	49	v Middlesex at Bristol	1978
Lowest total against	48	by Middlesex at Lydney	1973

TWENTY20 RECORDS

Highest score for	100*	I. J. Harvey v Warwickshire at Birmingham	2003
Highest score against	116*	C. L. White (Somerset) at Taunton	2006
Leading run-scorer	1,180	C. G. Taylor (avge 24.08)	**2003–2010**
Best bowling for	4-22	I. D. Fisher v Somerset at Bristol	2004
Best bowling against	5-16	R. E. Watkins (Glamorgan) at Cardiff	2009
Leading wicket-taker	**44**	**J. Lewis (avge 29.88)**	**2003–2010**
Highest total for	227-4	v Somerset at Bristol	2006
Highest total against	250-3	by Somerset at Taunton	2006
Lowest total for	**68**	**v Hampshire at Bristol**	**2010**
Lowest total against	**97**	**by Surrey at The Oval**	**2010**

ADDRESS

County Ground, Nevil Road, Bristol BS7 9EJ (0117 910 8000; **email** info@glosccc.co.uk). **Website**
www.glosccc.co.uk

OFFICIALS

Captain A. P. R. Gidman	**Chief executive** T. E. M. Richardson
Director of cricket J. G. Bracewell	**Chairman, cricket committee** R. C. Russell
Academy director O. A. Dawkins	**Head groundsman** S. Williams
President A. S. Brown	**Scorer** K. T. Gerrish
Chairman R. Body	

At Bristol, April 3–5 (not first-class). **Drawn. ‡Gloucestershire 316** (C. D. J. Dent 135, S. D. Snell 46, R. K. J. Dawson 46; M. T. Reed 3-53, T. M. J. Warner 3-65); **Cardiff MCCU 158** (J. N. K. Shannon 33, S. M. Moore 44; A. J. Ireland 4-29) **and 159-5** (J. N. K. Shannon 33, A. M. J. Barber 51). *After the weather allowed just ten overs on the first day, Chris Dent, a 19-year-old from Bristol, batted almost four hours on the second for his 135, which came from 198 balls and included 13 fours and four sixes. For the students, the pace and economy of Michael Reed drew respect. James Shannon, from Northern Ireland, twice made 33, battling hard on a green surface for more than three and a half hours in all. Michael Barber hit ten fours in his fifty.*

GLOUCESTERSHIRE v NORTHAMPTONSHIRE

At Bristol, April 15–17. Northamptonshire won by 94 runs. Northamptonshire 19pts, Gloucestershire 3pts. Toss: Gloucestershire. First-class debut: C. D. J. Dent. County debuts: J. N. Batty; L. Evans.

ECB pitch inspector Jack Birkenshaw was soon on the case once 23 wickets had fallen on the first day. "I give it the benefit of the doubt, but they could have taken a bit more off the top," was his verdict. After seeing his side put out for 86 in just 25 overs – and conceding a 100-run deficit – Gidman was less forgiving. There were no excuses, he said, for a three-day defeat: his batsmen had been indecisive and played badly. Lewis and Hussain, who ended with nine wickets in only his second first-class match, kept Gloucestershire in touch, but twice the game swung away from them. Northamptonshire had been in deep trouble at 77 for six on the green first-day pitch before a dynamic 95 from White containing five sixes and ten fours rescued them. He and wicketkeeper Harrison put on 71 in 13 overs. And in the second innings Harrison was again instrumental in steering them from an awkward 134 for eight: Brooks, with a maiden first-class fifty, helped him add 82. Gloucestershire needed 344, but had neither the skill nor the resolve.

Close of play: First day, Northamptonshire 34-3 (Sales 6, Lucas 4); Second day, Gloucestershire 85-2 (Kadeer Ali 29, Marshall 12).

Northamptonshire

S. D. Peters c Gidman b Hussain	23	– c Batty b Franklin	1
V. Tripathi lbw b Franklin	2	– lbw b Hussain	19
M. B. Loye c Snell b Hussain	4	– c Snell b Lewis	0
D. J. Sales b Hussain	2	– c Snell b Lewis	39
R. A. White c Kadeer Ali b Hussain	95	– (6) c Taylor b Hussain	10
A. J. Hall c Batty b Lewis	14	– (7) c Batty b Lewis	19
*N. Boje c Batty b Kirby	11	– (8) c Batty b Gidman	4
†P. W. Harrison lbw b Gidman	20	– (9) b Franklin	44
D. S. Lucas lbw b Gidman	3	– (5) c Kirby b Hussain	31
J. A. Brooks c Taylor b Hussain	0	– c Snell b Hussain	53
L. Evans not out	0	– not out	8
B 4, l-b 5, w 1, n-b 2	12	B 4, l-b 7, w 4	15

1/8 (2) 2/25 (3) 3/29 (4) 4/34 (1) (54.5 overs) 186
5/57 (6) 6/77 (7) 7/148 (8) 8/182 (9)
9/185 (10) 10/186 (5)

1/1 (1) 2/8 (3) (75.2 overs) 243
3/22 (2) 4/75 (5)
5/87 (6) 6/127 (7) 7/134 (8)
8/134 (4) 9/216 (9) 10/243 (10)

Lewis 15-3-58-1; Franklin 12-4-36-1; Kirby 10-2-37-1; Hussain 11.5-3-36-5; Gidman 6-2-10-2. *Second Innings*—Lewis 15-3-56-3; Franklin 16-4-35-2; Kirby 17-4-41-0; Hussain 17.2-4-62-4; Gidman 7-0-34-1; Taylor 3-0-4-0.

Gloucestershire

Kadeer Ali b Lucas	8	– (2) b Lucas	29
†J. N. Batty c Hall b Lucas	14	– (1) c Harrison b Lucas	6
C. D. J. Dent c Sales b Brooks	1	– c Tripathi b Boje	23
H. J. H. Marshall not out	28	– c Hall b Brooks	27
*A. P. R. Gidman c Sales b Hall	9	– c Hall b Evans	21
C. G. Taylor lbw b Hall	4	– c Peters b Evans	31
J. E. C. Franklin lbw b Hall	0	– b Hall	1
S. D. Snell run out	0	– lbw b Brooks	52
G. M. Hussain c Hall b Evans	1	– c Harrison b Evans	4
J. Lewis c Tripathi b Lucas	16	– c Harrison b Brooks	4
S. P. Kirby c White b Lucas	0	– not out	22
L-b 3, n-b 2	5	B 2, l-b 13, n-b 14	29

1/14 (1) 2/21 (3) 3/27 (2)   (24.5 overs)   86
4/55 (5) 5/59 (6) 6/59 (7) 7/67 (8)
8/69 (9) 9/86 (10) 10/86 (11)

1/8 (1) 2/52 (3)   (70.2 overs)   249
3/89 (2) 4/113 (4)
5/136 (5) 6/147 (7) 7/171 (6)
8/179 (9) 9/190 (10) 10/249 (8)

Lucas 7.5–3–21–4; Brooks 6–1–21–1; Evans 6–1–24–1; Hall 5–0–17–3. *Second Innings*—Lucas 19–4–68–2; Brooks 18.2–4–55–3; Evans 15–5–53–3; Boje 7–1–12–1; Hall 11–1–46–1.

Umpires: M. A. Gough and D. J. Millns.

GLOUCESTERSHIRE v SUSSEX

At Bristol, April 21–23. Sussex won by 207 runs. Sussex 19pts, Gloucestershire 3pts. Toss: Sussex.
   Once again pitch inspector Jack Birkenshaw was on hand to judge a grassy spring surface; this time 20 wickets tumbled on the first day, including 11 lbws. Birkenshaw blamed poor shot selection rather than the pitch. With the Tiflex ball swinging throughout, the cricket was as green as the wicket, but Sussex, chasing a third successive win, were always the more disciplined and determined as they turned a lead of 24 into a commanding victory by 207 runs. On the first day, Nash proved runs were

MOST LBWS IN A FIRST-CLASS MATCH

19	Patiala v Delhi at Patiala	1953-54
18	Services v Himachal Pradesh at Delhi	1990-91
18	Rajasthan v Uttar Pradesh at Jaipur	2000-01
18	Sebastianites v Army at Colombo	2006-07
18	**Gloucestershire v Sussex at Bristol**	**2010**
18	**Sussex v Middlesex at Hove**	**2010**
18	**Gloucestershire v Glamorgan at Cheltenham**	**2010**

Research: Philip Bailey

gettable, reaching 47 at a run a ball, while on the second Martin-Jenkins made his first century since 2003. Dropped on ten, he went on to 102 from 132 balls: a considerable effort on a wicket prepared to help the battery of home seamers. Thornely, who has come up through the Sussex ranks, offered confident support en route to a career-best 64.
Close of play: First day, Gloucestershire 128; Second day, Gloucestershire 12-1 (Kadeer Ali 5).

Sussex

C. D. Nash lbw b Kirby	47	– c Batty b Kirby	35
M. A. Thornely c Batty b Hussain	25	– lbw b Gidman	64
J. S. Gatting c Batty b Gidman	14	– lbw b Kirby	0
*M. W. Goodwin lbw b Franklin	24	– lbw b Franklin	14
M. J. Prior lbw b Franklin	2	– c Batty b Hussain	20
†A. J. Hodd c Batty b Hussain	1	– c Snell b Hussain	2
R. S. C. Martin-Jenkins c Gidman b Franklin	2	– c Gidman b Kirby	102
Naved-ul-Hasan b Franklin	10	– (9) c Lewis b Franklin	13
J. E. Anyon b Lewis	8	– (8) lbw b Hussain	25
M. S. Panesar not out	7	– not out	0
C. D. Collymore lbw b Kirby	0	– lbw b Lewis	1
B 6, l-b 6	12	B 12, l-b 10, n-b 4	26

1/61 (2) 2/76 (1) 3/100 (3) (46.3 overs) 152
4/102 (5) 5/111 (6) 6/118 (7)
7/127 (4) 8/132 (8) 9/147 (9) 10/152 (11)

1/53 (1) 2/53 (3) (88.1 overs) 302
3/77 (4) 4/117 (5)
5/119 (6) 6/171 (2) 7/244 (8)
8/281 (9) 9/297 (11) 10/302 (11)

Lewis 9–1–32–1; Franklin 15–2–27–4; Hussain 10–1–42–2; Kirby 9.3–3–25–2; Gidman 3–0–14–1. *Second Innings*—Kirby 18–3–54–3; Franklin 19–4–56–2; Hussain 18–5–66–3; Lewis 14.1–1–55–1; Marshall 14–4–28–0; Gidman 3–0–14–1; Taylor 2–0–7–0.

Gloucestershire

Kadeer Ali c Hodd b Collymore	13	– (2) b Naved-ul-Hasan	6
†J. N. Batty lbw b Collymore	1	– (1) c Prior b Naved-ul-Hasan	4
S. D. Snell b Martin-Jenkins	9	– (8) c and b Anyon	25
H. J. H. Marshall lbw b Anyon	14	– c Prior b Collymore	7
*A. P. R. Gidman lbw b Martin-Jenkins	11	– c Goodwin b Martin-Jenkins	13
C. G. Taylor lbw b Martin-Jenkins	37	– c Gatting b Collymore	3
C. D. J. Dent lbw b Naved-ul-Hasan	0	– (3) lbw b Collymore	10
J. E. C. Franklin c Prior b Naved-ul-Hasan	2	– (7) lbw b Anyon	29
J. Lewis c Prior b Naved-ul-Hasan	23	– c Hodd b Martin-Jenkins	3
G. M. Hussain lbw b Collymore	10	– c Prior b Anyon	11
S. P. Kirby not out	0	– not out	0
L-b 4, n-b 4	8	L-b 2, n-b 6	8

1/14 (2) 2/15 (1) 3/35 (3) 4/47 (5) (44.4 overs) 128
5/75 (4) 6/76 (7) 7/84 (8) 8/99 (6)
9/128 (10) 10/128 (9)

1/12 (1) 2/21 (2) (39.1 overs) 119
3/29 (3) 4/34 (4)
5/40 (6) 6/80 (7) 7/80 (5)
8/92 (9) 9/116 (8) 10/119 (10)

Naved-ul-Hasan 15.4–2–49–4; Collymore 11–6–15–3; Anyon 11–2–44–1; Martin-Jenkins 7–0–16–2. *Second Innings*—Naved-ul-Hasan 10–4–24–2; Collymore 12–1–30–3; Martin-Jenkins 10–1–34–2; Anyon 7.1–1–29–3.

Umpires: B. Dudleston and R. T. Robinson.

At Lord's, April 27–30. GLOUCESTERSHIRE beat MIDDLESEX by 103 runs. *Gloucestershire score their first batting point, three matches into the season.*

At The Oval, May 4–6. GLOUCESTERSHIRE beat SURREY by 77 runs.

GLOUCESTERSHIRE v LEICESTERSHIRE

At Bristol, May 10–13. Gloucestershire won by nine wickets. Gloucestershire 23pts, Leicestershire 3pts. Toss: Leicestershire.

A hefty defeat brought little joy for Leicestershire, though there was one moment when they celebrated like lottery winners. On the last morning, with Gloucestershire set just 12 for their third win on the trot, Hoggard opened the bowling with Nixon, now a specialist batsman after handing on the wicketkeeping gloves. His rarely aired medium-pace trapped Porterfield lbw to give him his first senior wicket in a career that spanned 22 seasons and 804 first-team games. Nixon had already made a dogged 63 from 205 balls, putting on 125 with Boyce for the first wicket after Leicestershire followed on 274 in arrears. There was little fight from the other batsmen, though; without weather interruptions the game might not have spilled into a fourth day. Earlier, Hoggard's optimism in asking Gloucestershire to bat on a greenish Bristol wicket with history had backfired: substantial fifties from the middle order took them to 300 for the first time in the season. The richest partnership was the 138 added for the fourth wicket by Marshall and Gidman, dismissed for his eighth score in the nineties. Leicestershire were then bundled out for 102 in 35 overs by the home seamers.

Close of play: First day, Gloucestershire 314-6 (Franklin 12, Snell 2); Second day, Leicestershire 122-0 (Nixon 50, Boyce 59); Third day, Leicestershire 282-9 (du Toit 32, Hoggard 4).

Gloucestershire

†J. N. Batty lbw b Hoggard	6	– not out	7
W. T. S. Porterfield c Jefferson b Hoggard	0	– lbw b Nixon	1
C. D. J. Dent lbw b Henderson	34	– not out	5
H. J. H. Marshall lbw b Harris	86		
*A. P. R. Gidman c Harris b Hoggard	99		
C. G. Taylor c New b Buck	62		
J. E. C. Franklin c New b Hoggard	15		
S. D. Snell c Boyce b Harris	28		
J. Lewis c Jefferson b Buck	0		
G. M. Hussain c and b Henderson	28		
A. J. Ireland not out	0		
B 6, l-b 12	18	L-b 2	2

1/7 (2) 2/8 (1) 3/74 (3) 4/212 (4) (111.2 overs) 376   1/9 (2)   (1 wkt, 4.1 overs) 15
5/271 (5) 6/312 (6) 7/317 (7)
8/322 (9) 9/370 (8) 10/376 (10)   110 overs: 376-9

Hoggard 25-6-67-4; Buck 24-5-91-2; Harris 20-5-90-2; McDonald 17-1-60-0; Henderson 25.2-6-50-2. *Second Innings*—Nixon 2.1-1-7-1; du Toit 1-0-4-0; Boyce 1-0-2-0.

Leicestershire

W. I. Jefferson b Ireland	51	– (5) lbw b Lewis	9
M. A. G. Boyce c Batty b Franklin	6	– c Gidman b Hussain	62
P. A. Nixon c Dent b Franklin	0	– (1) c Porterfield b Ireland	63
J. W. A. Taylor c Batty b Hussain	4	– (3) b Franklin	39
A. B. McDonald b Ireland	4	– (4) c Franklin b Gidman	12
J. du Toit c Gidman b Lewis	5	– not out	33
†T. J. New c Batty b Ireland	0	– c Dent b Franklin	9
C. W. Henderson c Batty b Franklin	28	– c Taylor b Ireland	29
N. L. Buck c Batty b Hussain	1	– lbw b Ireland	0
A. J. Harris b Hussain	0	– c Batty b Lewis	0
*M. J. Hoggard not out	0	– c Batty b Ireland	6
L-b 1, n-b 6	7	B 10, l-b 7, n-b 6	23

1/28 (2) 2/28 (3) 3/67 (4) 4/68 (5)   (34.3 overs) 102   1/125 (2) 2/167 (1)   (127 overs) 285
5/73 (1) 6/73 (7) 7/73 (6) 8/92 (9)   3/188 (4) 4/205 (5)
9/98 (10) 10/102 (8)   5/205 (3) 6/219 (7) 7/273 (8)
                              8/273 (9) 9/274 (10) 10/285 (11)

Lewis 9-2-33-1; Franklin 7.3-1-21-3; Hussain 11-4-26-3; Ireland 7-1-21-3. *Second Innings*—Ireland 30-6-85-4; Franklin 25-9-44-2; Lewis 26-9-44-2; Hussain 26-8-57-1; Marshall 9-4-17-0; Gidman 8-2-13-1; Taylor 3-0-8-0.

Umpires: R. J. Bailey and M. J. D. Bodenham.

At Cardiff, May 17–20. GLOUCESTERSHIRE lost to GLAMORGAN by an innings and four runs.

At Derby, May 24–27. GLOUCESTERSHIRE beat DERBYSHIRE by 134 runs.

At Worcester, May 29–June 1. GLOUCESTERSHIRE drew with WORCESTERSHIRE.

GLOUCESTERSHIRE v MIDDLESEX

At Bristol, June 28–30. Gloucestershire won by ten wickets. Gloucestershire 23pts, Middlesex 3pts. Toss: Gloucestershire. Championship debuts: J. H. Davey, T. S. Roland-Jones.

On yet another green pitch Gloucestershire played five seamers, while Middlesex had to cope without Steve Finn; he was at the ground but required by England to work on his strength and conditioning. James Franklin, searching for Gloucestershire's first hundred of the season, fell one short (after being left on 92 not out v Surrey and dismissed for 95 v Glamorgan) when his top-edged pull carried to Tom Smith at deep square leg. However, Franklin's innings did see Gloucestershire past 400, for the first time on the Bristol square, in 2010. Dent, with the second fifty of his career, and Marshall added 126 for the third wicket before Franklin ensured Gloucestershire's start was not wasted. Middlesex had 19-year-old Josh Davey to thank for rescuing their first innings from a precarious 97 for five; he hit a half-century on Championship debut as Ireland cut a swathe through the batting. Trailing by 184, the visitors could find no way back in to the match as Lewis claimed four wickets. This was Middlesex's fourth defeat of the season by Gloucestershire, a double in the Championship and two in the shorter games, one of which only began at 5.30 the evening before this fixture.

Close of play: First day, Gloucestershire 81-2 (Dent 13, Marshall 21); Second day, Gloucestershire 404-8 (Hussain 23, Kirby 0).

Middlesex

S. D. Robson lbw b Ireland	39	– (2) c Batty b Lewis 12
S. A. Newman c Gidman b Hussain	25	– (1) lbw b Lewis 5
O. A. Shah c Gidman b Lewis	4	– c Batty b Lewis 32
D. J. Malan c Taylor b Franklin	29	– c Dent b Franklin 13
*N. J. Dexter c Batty b Ireland	0	– c Dent b Hussain 54
†J. A. Simpson c Marshall b Ireland	9	– lbw b Taylor.................... 23
J. H. Davey c Franklin b Lewis	61	– c Batty b Hussain 9
T. M. J. Smith c Kadeer Ali b Ireland	7	– c Taylor b Hussain 18
T. J. Murtagh c Batty b Hussain	17	– c Marshall b Ireland 8
T. S. Roland-Jones c Kirby b Ireland	19	– b Lewis........................ 21
P. T. Collins not out	1	– not out 7
B 4, l-b 11, n-b 10	25	B 12, l-b 2, n-b 12 26

1/63 (2) 2/77 (3) 3/77 (1) 4/83 (5)   (67 overs) 236
5/97 (6) 6/134 (4) 7/156 (8) 8/181 (9)
9/234 (10) 10/236 (7)

1/5 (1) 2/40 (2)   (67.2 overs) 228
3/67 (3) 4/79 (4)
5/139 (5) 6/168 (6) 7/181 (7)
8/194 (8) 9/216 (9) 10/228 (10)

Lewis 13–4–29–2; Franklin 9–1–37–1; Hussain 15–2–70–2; Kirby 13–3–43–0; Ireland 11–2–25–5; Marshall 6–3–17–0. *Second Innings*—Kirby 14–3–29–0; Lewis 14.2–5–45–4; Ireland 12–2–38–1; Hussain 15–3–61–3; Franklin 5–1–22–1; Taylor 7–1–19–1.

Gloucestershire

†J. N. Batty lbw b Collins	20	– (2) not out	18
Kadeer Ali b Collins	13	– (1) not out	26
C. D. J. Dent c Newman b Roland-Jones	53		
H. J. H. Marshall b Dexter	68		
*A. P. R. Gidman lbw b Malan	61		
C. G. Taylor b Dexter	1		
J. E. C. Franklin c Smith b Dexter	99		
J. Lewis run out	30		
G. M. Hussain not out	28		
S. P. Kirby c Newman b Smith	9		
A. J. Ireland c Malan b Roland-Jones	0		
B 4, l-b 13, w 7, n-b 14	38	W 1	1

1/30 (2) 2/41 (1) 3/167 (3)   (129.3 overs) 420   (no wkt, 13.1 overs) 45
4/193 (4) 5/199 (6) 6/275 (5)
7/324 (8) 8/399 (7) 9/419 (10)
10/420 (11)   110 overs: 382-7

Murtagh 22–6–85–0; Collins 21–6–55–2; Davey 8–2–20–0; Roland-Jones 26.3–4–88–2; Smith 29–7–84–1; Dexter 19–3–64–3; Malan 4–1–7–1. *Second Innings*—Davey 2–0–7–0; Roland-Jones 4–0–18–0; Smith 5–1–13–0; Malan 2.1–0–7–0.

Umpires: V. A. Holder and G. Sharp.

At Arundel, July 7–9. GLOUCESTERSHIRE lost to SUSSEX by eight wickets.

GLOUCESTERSHIRE v GLAMORGAN

At Cheltenham, July 30–August 1. Glamorgan won by 176 runs. Glamorgan 20pts, Gloucestershire 4pts. Toss: Gloucestershire.

In May, Gloucestershire made an unsuccessful request to borrow Glamorgan's veteran spinner Croft. Now 40 and playing his 387th first-class match, he justified that interest in a valuable partnership of 105 with Wallace, and his first career hat-trick, confirming victory for a side containing just two front-line seamers. That outcome looked unlikely when Glamorgan were put in and cut down to 104 for seven. As the ball aged, Croft and Wallace removed the sting from a four-man pace attack through an eighth-wicket record for Glamorgan against Gloucestershire. Fifteen wickets fell on the first day, but ECB pitch inspector David Hughes deemed no action necessary. Dent, unaccustomed to batting down the order, worked hard to earn a lead – it proved nominal. Cosgrove hit his fourth hundred in five games, before Wallace broke Gloucestershire's resolve with an outstanding 113 from 124 balls, his ninth first-class century, stretching the target to 345. Gloucestershire's heart wasn't in it, with the exception of Chris Taylor. Stranded on 63, Taylor watched Croft send back the last three in successive balls 16 overs after tea on the third day, No. 11 Kirby plumb leg-before. This was the second Championship match involving Gloucestershire in 2010 (their defeat to Sussex in April was the other) in which 18 wickets fell lbw (see page 435).

Close of play: First day, Gloucestershire 145-5 (Franklin 22, Kirby 4); Second day, Glamorgan 283-7 (Wallace 51, Croft 17).

Glamorgan

G. P. Rees c Gidman b Franklin	9	– lbw b Franklin	2
M. J. Cosgrove c Lewis b Hussain	41	– b Hussain	123
T. L. Maynard lbw b Franklin	0	– b Franklin	6
B. J. Wright lbw b Lewis	17	– lbw b Lewis	16
*J. W. M. Dalrymple lbw b Kirby	11	– b Hussain	36
J. Allenby b Kirby	3	– c Dent b Kirby	15
†M. A. Wallace c Dent b Hussain	72	– lbw b Hussain	113
J. A. R. Harris c Gidman b Hussain	0	– lbw b Kirby	11
R. D. B. Croft c Gidman b Hussain	44	– c Batty b Lewis	17
D. A. Cosker lbw b Lewis	1	– lbw b Lewis	10
H. T. Waters not out	0	– not out	8
B 4, l-b 8, n-b 6	18	B 4, l-b 8, n-b 2	14

1/35 (1) 2/39 (3) 3/74 (2) 4/74 (4)   (51.3 overs) 216
5/84 (6) 6/89 (5) 7/104 (8) 8/209 (7)
9/210 (10) 10/216 (9)

1/11 (1) 2/23 (3)   (89.3 overs) 371
3/84 (4) 4/183 (2)
5/184 (5) 6/219 (6)
7/241 (8) 8/283 (9)
9/333 (10) 10/371 (7)

Kirby 12–0–68–2; Franklin 8–1–26–2; Lewis 13–5–19–2; Hussain 13.3–3–57–4; Banerjee 5–1–34–0. *Second Innings*—Lewis 22–5–72–3; Franklin 18.2–2–79–2; Hussain 13.3–1–60–3; Kirby 17–3–68–2; Banerjee 18–1–80–0; Marshall 1–1–0–0.

Gloucestershire

†J. N. Batty lbw b Allenby	18	– b Harris	10
W. T. S. Porterfield c Wallace b Waters	41	– c Allenby b Harris	41
H. J. H. Marshall c Allenby b Cosker	34	– c Wallace b Waters	1
*A. P. R. Gidman lbw b Allenby	17	– lbw b Harris	4
J. E. C. Franklin c Maynard b Croft	59	– lbw b Waters	2
C. G. Taylor b Waters	8	– not out	63
S. P. Kirby lbw b Cosker	5	– (11) lbw b Croft	0
C. D. J. Dent not out	45	– (7) st Wallace b Croft	12
J. Lewis c Wallace b Allenby	8	– (8) c Dalrymple b Waters	24
V. Banerjee lbw b Allenby	1	– (9) lbw b Croft	8
G. M. Hussain lbw b Allenby	1	– (10) b Croft	0
L-b 6	6	L-b 3	3

1/55 (1) 2/63 (2) 3/90 (4) 4/121 (3)   (70 overs) 243
5/140 (6) 6/175 (7) 7/201 (5) 8/209 (9)
9/219 (10) 10/243 (11)

1/51 (1) 2/52 (1)   (55.3 overs) 168
3/56 (3) 4/58 (4) 5/60 (5)
6/94 (7) 7/126 (8) 8/168 (9)
9/168 (10) 10/168 (11)

Harris 5.4–0–30–0; Waters 19–6–64–2; Allenby 23–6–59–5; Croft 12.2–1–42–1; Cosker 10–1–42–2. *Second Innings*—Harris 17–1–73–3; Waters 17–9–29–3; Croft 6.3–0–20–4; Allenby 5–2–11–0; Dalrymple 4–0–16–0; Cosker 6–1–16–0.

Umpires: A. Hicks and N. A. Mallender.

GLOUCESTERSHIRE v WORCESTERSHIRE

At Cheltenham, August 4–7. Worcestershire won by six wickets. Worcestershire 19pts, Gloucestershire 7pts. Toss: Gloucestershire.

Gidman's calamitous decision not to enforce the follow-on saw Gloucestershire throw away a lead of 202 and slump to a defeat which left them without a Championship win at this crown-jewel festival since 2001, a miserable run of 17 matches. Gidman thought his bowlers were tired, so preferred to bat Worcestershire out of the game. But after running up a season's-highest of 480, Gloucestershire were dismissed for 136, a score more in keeping with their summer. With a day left to bowl on a wicket beginning to spin, Gidman remained confident. He hadn't reckoned on Mitchell. Fresh from 104 in the first innings, and now backed by Moeen Ali and a vigorous Solanki – from whom he would soon inherit the captaincy – Mitchell took Worcestershire home with 14 overs to spare, finishing unbeaten on 134. It overshadowed Porterfield's 175 – the first Championship century of the summer by a Gloucestershire batsman after six scores in the nineties. Porterfield broke the hoodoo with a six over midwicket off Shakib Al Hasan, then a cover-driven four. A second innings, from Franklin, followed the next day. Both Shakib and Richardson received a pummelling, but they came back in the second innings to share nine wickets.

Close of play: First day, Gloucestershire 324-4 (Franklin 50, Taylor 19); Second day, Worcestershire 126-2 (Mitchell 50, Ali 36); Third day, Worcestershire 8-0 (Mitchell 6, Wheeldon 2).

Gloucestershire

†J. N. Batty lbw b Mason	1	– b Mason	3
W. T. S. Porterfield c Mason b Shantry	175	– c Cox b Richardson	33
H. J. H. Marshall c Solanki b Mason	14	– c Kervezee b Richardson	20
*A. P. R. Gidman c Solanki b Mason	40	– b Shakib Al Hasan	1
J. E. C. Franklin run out	108	– c Mitchell b Shakib Al Hasan	9
C. G. Taylor c Cox b Mason	39	– c Cox b Richardson	45
C. D. J. Dent c Cameron b Shakib Al Hasan	38	– c Solanki b Shakib Al Hasan	6
J. Lewis c Mitchell b Shakib Al Hasan	19	– b Shakib Al Hasan	10
V. Banerjee run out	4	– (10) not out	0
G. M. Hussain not out	6	– (9) lbw b Richardson	0
A. J. Ireland b Ali	2	– c Richardson b Shakib Al Hasan	0
B 6, l-b 23, w 1, n-b 4	34	B 5, l-b 4	9

1/4 (1) 2/52 (3) 3/172 (4)   (133.1 overs) 480   1/7 (1) 2/54 (3)   (39.4 overs) 136
4/287 (2) 5/368 (6) 6/435 (5)   3/60 (4) 4/60 (2)
7/462 (7) 8/467 (8) 9/473 (9)   5/88 (5) 6/102 (7)
10/480 (11)   110 overs: 399-5   7/136 (6) 8/136 (9)
                                            9/136 (8) 10/136 (11)

Mason 32–3–92–4; Richardson 29–6–89–0; Shantry 13–1–65–1; Cameron 8–0–37–0; Shakib Al Hasan 25–2–85–2; Ali 26.1–5–83–1. *Second Innings*—Richardson 15–0–57–4; Mason 5–1–12–1; Shantry 2–0–13–0; Shakib Al Hasan 12.4–3–23–5; Ali 5–0–22–0.

Worcestershire

D. K. H. Mitchell c Dent b Hussain	104	– not out	134
D. A. Wheeldon c Porterfield b Hussain	16	– c Batty b Hussain	2
*V. S. Solanki lbw b Ireland	9	– c Taylor b Lewis	64
M. M. Ali c Taylor b Ireland	59	– (5) c and b Franklin	94
A. N. Kervezee c Marshall b Banerjee	8	– (6) not out	17
Shakib Al Hasan c Porterfield b Ireland	19	– (4) c Porterfield b Banerjee	10
J. G. Cameron b Franklin	26		
†O. B. Cox c Dent b Hussain	4		
M. S. Mason c Porterfield b Franklin	1		
J. D. Shantry lbw b Hussain	6		
A. Richardson not out	4		
L-b 14, n-b 8	22	B 4, l-b 5, w 7, n-b 2	18

1/55 (2) 2/64 (3) 3/163 (4)   (92.4 overs) 278   1/9 (2)   (4 wkts, 87.4 overs) 339
4/191 (5) 5/218 (6) 6/258 (1)   2/105 (3) 3/122 (4)
7/258 (8) 8/262 (8) 9/270 (9) 10/278 (10)   4/303 (5)

Lewis 15–5–45–0; Franklin 14–3–43–2; Ireland 22–5–76–3; Hussain 15.4–6–30–4; Marshall 2–0–5–0; Banerjee 21–2–51–1; Taylor 3–0–14–0. *Second Innings*—Hussain 16–4–53–1; Franklin 16–3–49–1; Ireland 13–1–53–0; Lewis 9–2–27–1; Banerjee 27.4–1–124–1; Taylor 6–0–24–0.

Umpires: M. A. Gough and T. E. Jesty.

At Northampton, August 16–18. GLOUCESTERSHIRE beat NORTHAMPTONSHIRE by seven wickets.

GLOUCESTERSHIRE v DERBYSHIRE

At Bristol, August 31–September 1. Derbyshire won by 54 runs. Derbyshire 19pts, Gloucestershire 3pts. Toss: Gloucestershire. First-class debut: J. M. R. Taylor.

There were a number of strange results in a summer of swinging balls and green surfaces, but this one out-quirked the lot. Despite skittling Derbyshire for 44 in the 17th over, Gloucestershire had lost by the second afternoon. "We've blown our chance of promotion and I don't know where to start the apology," said a crestfallen Gidman. ECB pitch inspector John Jameson arrived at tea on the first day, by which point 20 of 24 wickets had already fallen. "Nothing wrong with the pitch, plenty wrong with the technique," was the gist of Jameson's forthright verdict. On a well-grassed wicket there was swing, accuracy and a touch of seam, but that hardly explained Derbyshire's 77-minute

---

BEGINNINGS AREN'T EVERYTHING

Teams that scored under 50 in the first innings of a Championship match and still won:

Glos (31 and 294-9 dec) beat Middx (74 and 190) by 61 runs at Bristol (Greenbank)	1924
Yorks (42 and 228) beat Sussex (95 and 83) by 92 runs at Hove	1922
Derbys (44 and 236) beat Glos (156 and 70) by 54 runs at Bristol (Nevil Road)	**2010**
Notts (47 and 128) beat Kent (110 and 52) by 13 runs at Maidstone	1894
Lancs (49 and 208-8 dec) beat Glam (22 and 107) by 128 runs at Liverpool	1924

---

miscarriage of an innings, their lowest total since June 1975, when Lancashire ran through them for 42 on a Buxton pitch thawing from an inch of snow. At nine for six, their all-time low of 16 (at Trent Bridge in 1879) was in danger. Franklin moved the ball around with subtlety, though several batsmen obliged him in a career-best seven for 14. From such depths, Derbyshire's recovery was remarkable. Steffan Jones took the last four Gloucestershire wickets in five balls, and then came Chesney Hughes. At the earlier meeting in Derby he scored his maiden hundred; now he finished unbeaten on 96, driving more confidently than anyone, as a deficit of 112 was turned into a 124-run lead. While Marshall was comfortable in passing 40 for a second time, no one else apart from last man Ireland made more than three; 70 was Gloucestershire's lowest Championship score for 21 years. The match was over in a day and a half.

Close of play: First day, Derbyshire 127-4 (Hughes 47, Adshead 2).

Derbyshire

C. J. L. Rogers c Snell b Franklin	1	– (2) run out		31
W. L. Madsen c Snell b Lewis	0	– (1) c Snell b Hussain		39
C. F. Hughes lbw b Franklin	5	– not out		96
W. J. Durston c C. G. Taylor b Franklin	2	– b Hussain		7
*G. M. Smith lbw b Franklin	0	– (7) b Lewis		4
R. J. Peterson c Lewis b Ireland	15	– (8) c J. M. R. Taylor b Ireland		12
J. L. Clare lbw b Franklin	0	– (9) c sub (J. N. Batty) b Ireland		0
†S. J. Adshead c Gidman b Franklin	4	– (6) b Ireland		10
G. G. Wagg b Franklin	6	– (10) c Snell b Hussain		16
P. S. Jones c J. M. R. Taylor b Lewis	7	– (11) c Gidman b Hussain		10
T. D. Groenewald not out	2	– (5) c Snell b Ireland		0
N-b 2	2	B 4, l-b 3, w 2, n-b 2		11

1/1 (2) 2/1 (1) 3/6 (3) 4/6 (5)	(16.1 overs) 44	1/58 (2) 2/106 (1)	(73 overs) 236
5/9 (4) 6/9 (7) 7/19 (8) 8/31 (9)		3/124 (4) 4/125 (5)	
9/38 (6) 10/44 (10)		5/144 (6) 6/158 (7) 7/175 (8)	
		8/175 (9) 9/211 (10) 10/236 (11)	

Lewis 4.1–0–13–2; Franklin 6–3–14–7; Hussain 4–0–15–0; Ireland 2–1–2–1. *Second Innings*—Lewis 15–1–50–1; Franklin 17–2–67–1; Hussain 21–7–53–3; Ireland 20–2–59–4.

Gloucestershire

W. T. S. Porterfield c Adshead b Groenewald	0	– lbw b Wagg	0
C. D. J. Dent b Wagg	4	– b Groenewald	2
H. J. H. Marshall lbw b Wagg	45	– c Adshead b Clare	44
*A. P. R. Gidman c Rogers b Wagg	13	– b Groenewald	0
J. E. C. Franklin c Clare b Smith	5	– c Peterson b Groenewald	1
C. G. Taylor c Adshead b Clare	37	– c Peterson b Wagg	0
†S. D. Snell c Durston b Jones	31	– c Durston b Wagg	1
J. M. R. Taylor b Jones	6	– (9) c and b Jones	3
J. Lewis c Adshead b Jones	0	– (8) lbw b Groenewald	2
G. M. Hussain lbw b Jones	0	– not out	1
A. J. Ireland not out	0	– b Clare	11
L-b 9, n-b 6	15	L-b 1, n-b 4	5

1/3 (1) 2/7 (2) 3/25 (4) 4/30 (5)   (35.1 overs) 156
5/99 (6) 6/132 (3) 7/149 (8)
8/149 (9) 9/149 (10) 10/156 (7)

1/0 (1) 2/12 (2)   (24.3 overs) 70
3/16 (4) 4/18 (5)
5/25 (6) 6/31 (7) 7/46 (8)
8/58 (9) 9/58 (10) 10/70 (11)

Wagg 13–2–54–3; Groenewald 4–0–16–1; Smith 6–0–28–1; Clare 5–0–23–1; Jones 7.1–1–26–4. *Second Innings*—Wagg 10–3–31–3; Groenewald 10–5–22–4; Clare 2.3–0–7–2; Jones 2–0–9–1.

Umpires: N. L. Bainton and N. G. C. Cowley.

At Leicester, September 7–10. GLOUCESTERSHIRE lost to LEICESTERSHIRE by 329 runs.

GLOUCESTERSHIRE v SURREY

At Bristol, September 13–16. Surrey won by ten runs. Surrey 17pts, Gloucestershire 3pts. Toss: Surrey.

Gloucestershire's season ended in misery and confusion. With several players afflicted by a stomach bug, they attempted to contrive a result, only to suffer another batting collapse which led to their sixth defeat in seven Championship matches. The game was also disappointing for Pietersen, left out of England's one-day squad and on loan to Surrey to get runs under his belt. They were 37 for two when he came in on a first day restricted by rain and bad light. Pietersen drove his first ball through extra cover for three and moved to 40 by the close. The next day was washed out, and when play resumed he nicked his second ball, an unremarkable outswinger from Hussain, to second slip. He declined another opportunity to bat, not that it would have been of much consequence as Gloucestershire served up declaration overs. They had closed their first innings 80 behind (Gidman and Marshall were among the most unwell and did not bat) before Surrey eventually set a target of 261 in 74 overs. From 216 for four, Gloucestershire's last six wickets went down for 34. Marshall managed a fifty despite his ailments, while Dent ended his first full season with his third score in the nineties, dismissed sweeping at Schofield.

Close of play: First day, Surrey 112-3 (Pietersen 40, Hamilton-Brown 28); Second day, No play; Third day, Surrey 55-2 (Lancefield 15, Linley 0).

Surrey

T. J. Lancefield c Marshall b Ireland	11	–	not out	67
J. J. Roy c Dent b Lewis	11	–	c Franklin b Lewis	6
M. R. Ramprakash c Batty b Hussain	15	–	b Ireland	33
K. P. Pietersen c Dent b Hussain	40			
*R. J. Hamilton-Brown c Lewis b Ireland	40	–	not out	50
†G. C. Wilson c c C. G. Taylor b Franklin	34			
C. P. Schofield c Dent b Lewis	3			
C. T. Tremlett b J. M. R. Taylor	5			
S. C. Meaker lbw b Lewis	4			
J. W. Dernbach c Batty b Ireland	5			
T. E. Linley not out	0	–	(4) st sub (S. D. Snell) b C. G. Taylor	16
L-b 6, w 8, n-b 4	18		B 4, l-b 2, n-b 2	8

1/15 (2) 2/37 (1) 3/45 (3)   (57.2 overs) 186   1/10 (2)   (3 wkts dec, 38.2 overs) 180
4/115 (4) 5/152 (5) 6/159 (7)   2/55 (3) 3/99 (4)
7/176 (8) 8/176 (6) 9/186 (10) 10/186 (9)

Lewis 15.2–6–25–3; Franklin 11–0–49–1; Ireland 16–4–50–3; Hussain 11–2–48–2; J. M. R. Taylor 4–2–8–1. *Second Innings*—Hussain 10–2–30–0; Lewis 6–1–22–1; Ireland 9–2–25–1; Franklin 3–1–5–0; J. M. R. Taylor 1–0–5–0; Porterfield 5–0–49–0; C. G. Taylor 4.2–0–38–1.

Gloucestershire

†J. N. Batty c Linley b Tremlett	10	–	(7) lbw b Schofield	1
W. T. S. Porterfield c Wilson b Tremlett	54	–	(1) b Tremlett	7
C. D. J. Dent lbw b Tremlett	0	–	(2) b Schofield	94
C. G. Taylor lbw b Meaker	33	–	(8) b Dernbach	28
J. E. C. Franklin not out	1	–	(4) lbw b Schofield	40
J. M. R. Taylor lbw b Tremlett	0	–	(5) c Tremlett b Schofield	2
*A. P. R. Gidman (did not bat)		–	(3) lbw b Meaker	3
H. J. H. Marshall (did not bat)		–	(6) c Wilson b Dernbach	51
J. Lewis (did not bat)		–	b Dernbach	0
G. M. Hussain (did not bat)		–	not out	1
A. J. Ireland (did not bat)		–	b Dernbach	0
B 1, l-b 6, w 1	8		B 15, l-b 3, w 1, n-b 4	23

1/26 (1) 2/26 (3)   (5 wkts dec, 36.5 overs) 106   1/8 (1) 2/33 (3)   (69.2 overs) 250
3/101 (4) 4/104 (2)   3/121 (4) 4/127 (5)
5/106 (6)   5/216 (6) 6/219 (7) 7/238 (2)
                                                        8/239 (4) 9/250 (8) 10/250 (11)

Tremlett 9.5–3–29–4; Dernbach 9–4–24–0; Linley 7–1–20–0; Meaker 9–2–18–1; Schofield 2–0–8–0. *Second Innings*—Tremlett 13–3–37–1; Dernbach 16.2–5–55–4; Meaker 14–2–46–1; Linley 5–1–20–0; Hamilton-Brown 5–0–11–0; Schofield 16–1–63–4.

Umpires: S. C. Gale and M. A. Gough.

HAMPSHIRE

Homing in on success

Pat Symes

By the narrowest of margins at a packed, passionate and raucous Rose Bowl, Hampshire realised their pre-season ambition of winning the Friends Provident T20 on home soil. They also set great store by retaining their place in Division One of the Championship – their coach, Giles White, said it was as vital as the Twenty20 triumph – and in this too they were successful, overcoming a disastrous start in which they lost their first four games and having to cope without several key players.

Hampshire were plagued by injuries: the captain, Dimitri Mascarenhas, damaged an ankle during the IPL in March and played just one game; Michael Lumb, another IPL participant, returned from the World Twenty20 in May an England winner but his form initially in tatters, and later broke his foot; while Kabir Ali and Nic Pothas were injured for much of the season. There was also the case of Simon Jones, the former England fast bowler, who spent most of the summer rehabilitating from long-standing injuries; he played in only the final Championship fixture and a handful of limited-overs matches.

The county's overseas signings swelled the total number of players to 26. There might have been more, but the announced recruitment of Ajantha Mendis, Shahid Afridi and Brett Lee never materialised. Among those who did arrive, Rangana Herath and Phil Hughes endured modest returns.

The personal successes were, in the main, home-grown. None surpassed the opening batsman, Jimmy Adams, who came of age at 29: he contributed 20 scores over 50 in the three competitions, batting more than ten and a half hours in compiling 194 in a losing cause at Liverpool, and hitting two Twenty20 centuries. Even without Lumb, Hampshire could often rely on sound starts given them by Adams and the consistent Michael Carberry; their reward was inclusion in England's winter Performance Programme in Australia, but Carberry dropped out due to illness.

They were joined by the left-arm spinner and academy product Danny Briggs, whose rise to prominence in his first full season, aged 19, was spectacular. He allied accuracy and bounce with an unruffled temperament in taking 67 wickets in all competitions, including a crucial 31 in the Twenty20. Chris Wood, a left-arm pace bowler who turned 20 mid-season, also shone in the shortest form, while James Vince, given a whole season to confirm high expectations, responded with a mature 180 against Yorkshire. Eight of the academy players nurtured by director Tony Middleton appeared in a CB40 victory against Leicestershire.

While Adams was indisputably Player of the Year, Dominic Cork was a serious contender. Entrusted with the captaincy after injuries to Mascarenhas and Pothas, he rose to the challenge with the enthusiasm and commitment of a

Philip Brown

Jimmy Adams

man half his 39 years. He led by example, his force of personality instrumental in turning Hampshire's shaky start into Twenty20 silver. Cork took 73 wickets over the season as well as contributing useful runs; Hampshire were delighted he agreed to return for his 21st full season as a professional.

Hampshire's 20-over success was the more surprising since they had struggled to qualify for the knockouts, slipping through by dint of a better run-rate than Surrey and Middlesex. The quarter-final win at Edgbaston ensured their first appearance at finals day – and home advantage. Few of the 22,000-plus at the Rose Bowl for the floodlit final against Somerset will forget the tension of that last over – that last ball – as Hampshire scraped home with scores level. A clash with the Championship run-in denied them entry to the Champions League, but they were invited to the Caribbean T20, where they lost the January final to a strong Trinidad & Tobago side.

With two new stands built during the previous winter and the promise of further development now that plans for a hotel at the motorway end are unopposed, the Rose Bowl promises to take full advantage of becoming a Test venue in June.

Hampshire can claim to be one of the more progressive counties, and their pre-season link with the IPL's Rajasthan Royals was an example of independent thinking. The team transform into the Royals for one-day purposes, and Hampshire were ready to provide Lumb and Mascarenhas to their new partners. Kevin Pietersen also played in the IPL while on Hampshire's books, but after one Championship appearance in the past five seasons (and complaints about the commute from Chelsea) he was released from his contract by mutual consent – and played a few late-season games for Surrey.

The CB40 campaign was hamstrung by Hampshire losing their first four matches, and though six wins raised hopes of an unexpected semi-final they lost their last two. In the Championship, they were candidates for relegation after also losing their first four games (and winning just one of their first eight). But an unbeaten run of nine matches saw them out of the drop zone, and safety came thanks to victory over Kent in the penultimate fixture.

With prolific leg-spinner Imran Tahir returning from Warwickshire as an overseas player, Sean Ervine preferring to stay after agreeing to return to Zimbabwe, and batsman Johann Myburgh and seamer Friedel de Wet arriving as South African Kolpaks, White believes his young team – if they can stay fit – have matured enough to compete for the Championship.

They will have to start without Mascarenhas, however: he showed a distinct lack of maturity by railing against national selector Geoff Miller on Twitter, and was banned by the ECB for 14 days.

HAMPSHIRE RESULTS

All first-class matches – Played 17: Won 3, Lost 6, Drawn 8.
County Championship matches – Played 16: Won 3, Lost 6, Drawn 7.

LV= County Championship, 7th in Division 1;
Friends Provident T20, winners; Clydesdale Bank 40, 4th in Group C.

COUNTY CHAMPIONSHIP AVERAGES, BATTING AND FIELDING

Cap		M	I	NO	R	HS	100s	50s	Avge	Ct
2008	M. J. Lumb.............	5	7	0	381	158	1	1	54.42	4
2006	J. H. K. Adams†.........	16	29	1	1,351	196	3	8	48.25	16
2006	M. A. Carberry.........	15	27	1	1,221	162	5	4	46.96	9
2005	S. M. Ervine¶.........	16	26	4	944	237*	1	5	42.90	7
2010	N. D. McKenzie¶........	14	24	4	801	115*	2	4	40.05	21
2003	N. Pothas............	9	15	0	531	87	0	4	35.40	33
	J. M. Vince..........	15	25	2	795	180	1	3	34.56	11
2009	D. G. Cork...........	13	17	3	380	55	0	2	27.14	8
	C. C. Benham.........	6	11	0	268	45	0	2	24.36	8
	L. A. Dawson.........	7	11	1	230	74	0	2	23.00	3
	H. M. R. K. B. Herath§	4	6	3	59	17*	0	0	19.66	1
	C. P. Wood†..........	2	4	0	68	35	0	0	17.00	0
	P. J. Hughes§.........	3	6	0	85	38	0	0	14.16	0
2008	J. A. Tomlinson†........	15	21	5	198	42	0	0	12.37	3
	A. M. Bates†.........	7	10	2	92	31	0	0	11.50	23
	D. A. Griffiths.......	5	9	6	34	9*	0	0	11.33	1
	D. J. Balcombe........	7	6	1	56	30	0	0	11.20	2
	D. R. Briggs.........	12	14	3	116	28	0	0	10.54	2
	Kabir Ali...........	4	8	0	64	18	0	0	8.00	2

Also batted: D. T. Christian§ (1 match) 28, 36; S. P. Jones (1 match) 0*, 0*.

† *Born in Hampshire.* § *Official overseas player.* ¶ *Other non-England-qualified player.*

BOWLING

	O	M	R	W	BB	5W/i	Avge
D. G. Cork	407.2	102	1,042	45	5-50	2	23.15
Kabir Ali	137.2	27	488	19	5-33	2	25.68
D. J. Balcombe.................	214.1	42	721	24	3-69	0	30.04
D. A. Griffiths	152	18	646	19	5-85	1	34.00
J. A. Tomlinson	559.1	149	1,624	46	7-85	2	35.30
D. R. Briggs	358.2	53	1,262	32	4-93	0	39.43
H. M. R. K. B. Herath	175.3	42	463	10	4-98	0	46.30
S. M. Ervine..................	345.5	74	1,023	18	4-31	0	56.83

Also bowled: J. H. K. Adams 2–1–5–0; M. A. Carberry 37–9–100–4; D. T. Christian 22.1–1–115–2; L. A. Dawson 18–1–61–1; S. P. Jones 22.5–5–60–4; N. D. McKenzie 2–0–3–95–2; J. M. Vince 4.2–0–24–0; C. P. Wood 41–9–156–6.

LEADING CB40 AVERAGES (100 runs/4 wickets)

Batting	Runs	HS	Avge	S-R	Ct
J. H. K. Adams ...	496	131	49.60	95.56	3
N. D. McKenzie...	319	62*	39.87	79.75	3
S. M. Ervine......	359	96	35.90	114.33	2
M. A. Carberry ...	346	103	34.60	113.81	4
M. J. Lumb	130	75	32.50	86.09	3
J. M. Vince	263	62	23.90	88.25	5

Bowling	W	BB	Avge	E-R
C. P. Wood	18	4-33	20.44	5.17
J. A. Tomlinson	9	3-33	21.66	5.79
S. M. Ervine	14	4-39	29.92	6.13
H. M. R. K. B. Herath.	5	2-28	34.00	5.48
D. G. Cork.........	13	3-30	34.23	6.44
D. R. Briggs	4	1-26	65.50	4.85

LEADING FPT20 AVERAGES (100 runs/18 overs)

Batting	Runs	HS	Avge	S-R	Ct/St
S. M. Ervine....	470	74*	36.15	**146.41**	4
J. M. Vince....	353	77	27.15	**144.08**	10
J. H. K. Adams....	668	101*	39.29	**132.27**	6
Abdul Razzaq	183	44	20.33	**127.97**	1
N. D. McKenzie...	440	73	40.00	**123.94**	7
N. Pothas	165	59	23.57	**120.43**	8/1

Bowling	W	BB	Avge	E-R
D. G. Cork.......	15	2-9	30.33	**6.61**
D. R. Briggs....	31	3-5	14.35	**6.64**
Abdul Razzaq	7	2-16	35.00	**7.81**
D. T. Christian...	9	2-37	31.55	**7.81**
C. P. Wood.......	20	3-27	27.55	**8.45**
S. P. Jones	8	3-20	24.37	**8.47**

FIRST-CLASS COUNTY RECORDS

Highest score for	316	R. H. Moore v Warwickshire at Bournemouth	1937
Highest score against	303*	G. A. Hick (Worcestershire) at Southampton	1997
Leading run-scorer	48,892	C. P. Mead (avge 48.84)	1905–1936
Best bowling for	9-25	R. M. H. Cottam v Lancashire at Manchester	1965
Best bowling against	10-46	W. Hickton (Lancashire) at Manchester	1870
Leading wicket-taker	2,669	D. Shackleton (avge 18.23)	1948–1969
Highest total for	714-5 dec	v Nottinghamshire at Southampton	2005
Highest total against	742	by Surrey at The Oval	1909
Lowest total for	15	v Warwickshire at Birmingham................	1922
Lowest total against	23	by Yorkshire at Middlesbrough	1965

LIST A COUNTY RECORDS

Highest score for	177	C. G. Greenidge v Glamorgan at Southampton....	1975
Highest score against	203	A. D. Brown (Surrey) at Guildford'1997.........	1997
Leading run-scorer	12,034	R. A. Smith (avge 42.97)	1983–2003
Best bowling for	7-30	P. J. Sainsbury v Norfolk at Southampton.......	1965
Best bowling against	7-22	J. R. Thomson (Middlesex) at Lord's	1981
Leading wicket-taker	411	C. A. Connor (avge 25.07).....................	1984–1998
Highest total for	371-4	v Glamorgan at Southampton	1975
Highest total against	358-6	by Surrey at The Oval	2005
Lowest total for	43	v Essex at Basingstoke.......................	1972
Lowest total against	{ 61	by Somerset at Bath.........................	1973
	61	by Derbyshire at Portsmouth	1990

TWENTY20 RECORDS

Highest score for	124*	M. J. Lumb v Essex v Southampton	2009
Highest score against	98	L. J. Wright (Sussex) at Hove	2007
Leading run-scorer	**1,161**	**S. M. Ervine (avge 27.64)**.....................	**2005–2010**
Best bowling for	5-14	A. D. Mascarenhas v Sussex at Hove...........	2004
Best bowling against	5-21	A. J. Hollioake (Surrey) at Southampton........	2003
Leading wicket-taker	**46**	**A. D. Mascarenhas (avge 17.17)**	**2003–2010**
Highest total for	225-2	v Middlesex at Southampton	2006
Highest total against	**220-4**	**by Somerset at Taunton.....................**	**2010**
Lowest total for	85	v Sussex at Southampton	2008
Lowest total against	67	by Sussex at Hove	2004

ADDRESS

The Rose Bowl, Botley Road, West End, Southampton SO30 3XH (023 8047 2002; **email** enquiries@rosebowlplc.com). **Website** www.rosebowlplc.com

OFFICIALS

Captain A. D. Mascarenhas
Director of cricket T. M. Tremlett
Team manager G. W. White
President N. E. J. Pocock
Chairman/chief executive R. G. Bransgrove

Group managing director G. D. W. Delve
Chairman, members committee T. Crump
Head groundsman N. Gray
Scorer A. E. Weld

At Chelmsford, April 9–12. HAMPSHIRE lost to ESSEX by 62 runs.

At Oxford, April 15–17. HAMPSHIRE drew with OXFORD MCCU.

At Chester-le-Street, April 21–24. HAMPSHIRE lost to DURHAM by five wickets.

At Birmingham, April 27–30. HAMPSHIRE lost to WARWICKSHIRE by eight wickets.

HAMPSHIRE v NOTTINGHAMSHIRE

At Southampton, May 4–7. Nottinghamshire won by five wickets. Nottinghamshire 22pts, Hampshire 6pts. Toss: Hampshire.

The Boer War had been over for just four years when Hampshire last endured as dreadful a start to a Championship season. In 1906 they lost their first four matches, and this defeat by Nottinghamshire meant they did so again; they had also lost both games in the CB40. Carberry, showing the form that had earned a winter elevation to the Test team, hit his third first-class century of the summer, but received little support against a pace attack who derived encouraging movement. Nottinghamshire found batting no easier against Kabir Ali and Cork, and stumbled to 122 for six before Brown and Mullaney put on 111 for the seventh wicket. Mullaney just had time to reach his first Championship century before the Nottinghamshire innings ended, 28 ahead. Carberry went early second time round, and Patel found turn for his left-arm spin, prompting the hope that Hampshire's own slow left-armer, Herath, would be a key figure as Nottinghamshire chased 246 in just under two sessions. However, Kabir limped out of the attack after only two overs, and Herath proved expensive as Wagh and Amla all but made sure of victory in a stand worth 118. Cork briefly kept wicket after Pothas fell awkwardly.

Close of play: First day, Nottinghamshire 3-0 (Edwards 3, Shafayat 0); Second day, Nottinghamshire 273-7 (Mullaney 72, Franks 26); Third day, Hampshire 177-4 (Vince 29, Pothas 29).

Hampshire

M. A. Carberry c Wagh b Franks	132	– c Read b Pattinson	14
J. H. K. Adams c Read b Franks	15	– c Shafayat b Patel	60
C. C. Benham c Brown b Shreck	9	– lbw b Patel	18
N. D. McKenzie lbw b Shreck	2	– c Read b Shreck	12
J. M. Vince c Wagh b Pattinson	39	– lbw b Franks	46
*†N. Pothas c Read b Pattinson	6	– lbw b Pattinson	30
S. M. Ervine c Brown b Patel	25	– c Shafayat b Patel	45
D. G. Cork lbw b Patel	21	– lbw b Patel	28
Kabir Ali c Shreck b Mullaney	10	– b Shreck	0
H. M. R. K. B. Herath not out	16	– c Read b Shreck	0
D. A. Griffiths b Pattinson	3	– not out	5
B 4, l-b 9, w 1, n-b 8	22	L-b 2, n-b 8, p 5	15

1/40 (2) 2/59 (3) 3/77 (4)　　　(92.1 overs) 300　　1/34 (1) 2/73 (3)　　(109.2 overs) 273
4/133 (5) 5/139 (6) 6/177 (7)　　　　　　　　3/109 (4) 4/121 (2)
7/229 (8) 8/276 (1) 9/289 (9) 10/300 (11)　　5/190 (6) 6/200 (5) 7/248 (8)
　　　　　　　　　　　　　　　　　　　　　8/249 (9) 9/249 (10) 10/273 (7)

Pattinson 20.1–1–85–3; Shreck 24–4–74–2; Franks 21–4–58–2; Mullaney 12–1–30–1; Patel 15–3–40–2. *Second Innings*—Pattinson 21–5–66–2; Shreck 23–6–70–3; Patel 36.2–14–55–4; Franks 22–4–63–1; Mullaney 7–1–12–0.

Nottinghamshire

N. J. Edwards c Vince b Kabir Ali..............	3	– c Carberry b Griffiths.............	8
B. M. Shafayat c Pothas b Kabir Ali	2	– c Benham b Herath...............	12
M. A. Wagh b Kabir Ali	11	– not out	131
H. M. Amla c Pothas b Ervine................	5	– c sub (B. A. C. Howell) b Griffiths ..	54
S. R. Patel c Cork b Herath	41	– c Benham b Griffiths.............	1
A. D. Brown c Cork b Herath	81	– c Griffiths b Herath..............	14
*†C. M. W. Read b Cork	9	– not out	7
S. J. Mullaney not out	100		
P. J. Franks lbw b Cork	48		
D. J. Pattinson c McKenzie b Cork	1		
C. E. Shreck c McKenzie b Cork..............	0		
B 6, l-b 10, w 2, n-b 9	27	B 5, l-b 3, w 5, n-b 6	19

1/5 (2) 2/16 (1) 3/17 (3) 4/33 (4)   (102.3 overs) 328
5/102 (5) 6/122 (7) 7/233 (6)
8/312 (9) 9/324 (10) 10/328 (11)

1/12 (1)   (5 wkts, 56 overs) 246
2/86 (2) 3/204 (4)
4/209 (5) 5/229 (6)

Kabir Ali 24–2–92–3; Cork 16.3–7–34–4; Ervine 13–0–48–1; Griffiths 14–1–70–0; Herath 34–7–68–2; Carberry 1–1–0–0. *Second Innings*—Kabir Ali 2–0–11–0; Cork 7–2–16–0; Griffiths 16–4–59–3; Herath 23–2–111–2; Ervine 8–1–41–0.

Umpires: R. J. Bailey and J. W. Lloyds.

HAMPSHIRE v SOMERSET

At Southampton, May 10–13. Drawn. Hampshire 7pts, Somerset 8pts. Toss: Hampshire.

This was an old-style Rose Bowl wicket: lively in the first session – when Willoughby exploited it to reduce Hampshire to 18 for two – before flattening out. Both sides passed 500, preventing a positive result but at least ending Hampshire's run of four defeats. They had stumbled to 123 for five before Pothas and Ervine – with the highest score by a Hampshire No. 7 – oversaw the recovery; Ervine added 130 for the ninth wicket with Tomlinson. But without the injured Kabir Ali, Hampshire

---

HIGHEST FIRST-CLASS SCORES AT THE ROSE BOWL

311*	J. P. Crawley	Hampshire v Nottinghamshire	2005
243	P. A. Jaques	Yorkshire v Hampshire	2004
237*	**S. M. Ervine**	**Hampshire v Somerset**	**2010**
222	W. I. Jefferson	Essex v Hampshire	2004
204	M. A. Carberry	Hampshire v Warwickshire..............................	2009
203*	S. R. Watson	Hampshire v Warwickshire..............................	2005
202*	Younis Khan	Yorkshire v Hampshire	2007

---

found the task of bowling out Somerset twice in two days beyond them, and failed to capitalise on a substantial first innings. Hildreth and Buttler, who was standing in for Craig Kieswetter, each scored centuries to help Somerset gain a slight lead on the final day. Buttler, aged 19 and especially strong on the off side, hit an impeccable 144 in only his fourth first-class innings. As the match drifted to a draw, Pothas used ten bowlers. Hampshire remained bottom of the first division.

Close of play: First day, Hampshire 281-7 (Ervine 75); Second day, Somerset 104-2 (Compton 17, de Bruyn 11); Third day, Somerset 441-6 (Buttler 105, Wright 17).

Hampshire

M. A. Carberry c Buttler b Willoughby	8	– c Buttler b Willoughby	2
J. H. K. Adams lbw b Willoughby	1	– c Trescothick b Willoughby	0
L. A. Dawson lbw b Munday	28	– not out	13
N. D. McKenzie b Trego	48	– not out	20
J. M. Vince c Buttler b Willoughby	26		
*†N. Pothas c Munday b Phillips	87		
S. M. Ervine not out	237		
D. G. Cork c Trescothick b Phillips	0		
H. M. R. K. B. Herath c Buttler b Phillips	15		
J. A. Tomlinson c Buttler b Phillips	42		
D. A. Griffiths c Trescothick b Compton	5		
B 7, 1-b 6, w 2	15	N-b 2	2

1/1 (1) 2/18 (1) 3/64 (3)   (156.2 overs) 512   1/1 (2) 2/2 (1)   (2 wkts, 17 overs) 37
4/113 (5) 5/123 (4) 6/281 (6)
7/281 (8) 8/329 (9) 9/459 (10)
10/512 (11)   110 overs: 321-7

Willoughby 43–18–83–3; Wright 26–1–81–0; Phillips 33–10–75–4; Trego 17–0–69–1; Munday 12–1–78–1; de Bruyn 14–0–70–0; Suppiah 11–2–42–0; Compton 0.2–0–1–1. *Second Innings*— Willoughby 7–3–7–2; Wright 6–1–9–0; Trego 2–0–7–0; de Bruyn 2–0–14–0.

Somerset

*M. E. Trescothick lbw b Griffiths	41	M. K. Munday not out	0
A. V. Suppiah c Cork b Herath	27	C. M. Willoughby b Herath	0
N. R. D. Compton run out	49		
Z. de Bruyn b Griffiths	21	B 10, 1-b 10, w 10, n-b 10	40
J. C. Hildreth c Tomlinson b Griffiths	106		
†J. C. Buttler c Dawson b Herath	144	1/60 (1) 2/77 (2) (164.3 overs) 524
P. D. Trego c Pothas b Griffiths	35	3/122 (4) 4/212 (3) 5/317 (5)
D. G. Wright c Ervine b Dawson	51	6/396 (7) 7/499 (8) 8/517 (9)
B. J. Phillips b Herath	10	9/524 (6) 10/524 (11) 110 overs: 332-5

Cork 20–7–50–0; Tomlinson 35–6–107–0; Griffiths 31–2–121–4; Ervine 15–5–33–0; Herath 38.3–10–98–4; Dawson 18–1–61–1; Carberry 3–0–19–0; Vince 1–0–9–0; McKenzie 1–0–1–0; Adams 2–1–5–0.

Umpires: R. T. Robinson and P. Willey.

At Nottingham, May 17–20. HAMPSHIRE beat NOTTINGHAMSHIRE by two wickets.

HAMPSHIRE v YORKSHIRE

At Southampton, May 24–27. Drawn. Hampshire 9pts, Yorkshire 9pts. Toss: Hampshire.

Adam Lyth came within two runs of a century in each innings as an otherwise featureless draw briefly took Yorkshire back to the top of the table. Profiting from Hampshire's decision to field first, Lyth made 133 of an opening partnership of 195 with Sayers; in the second innings, he was well caught in the slips for 98. Adams and McKenzie led a positive response to Yorkshire's imposing total before Pothas, attempting to retrieve his error at the toss, declared 64 behind. However, Gale was not interested in agreeing a challenge and, with an hour lost to rain on the last morning, did not call a halt until the game was dead. Michael Lumb, making his first Championship appearance of the season, missed the opening day to attend a Downing Street reception for England's World Twenty20 winners. Playing against his old employers, Lumb contributed little to the game after falling for a fourth-ball duck.

Close of play: First day, Yorkshire 300-3 (McGrath 55, Gale 38); Second day, Hampshire 162-3 (McKenzie 48, Vince 8); Third day, Yorkshire 152-1 (Lyth 64, McGrath 60).

Yorkshire

A. Lyth c Ervine b Tomlinson	133	– c McKenzie b Balcombe	98
J. J. Sayers c McKenzie b Cork	49	– c Carberry b Balcombe	13
A. McGrath c Pothas b Tomlinson	64	– c Adams b Cork	64
J. A. Rudolph c Pothas b Cork	3	– c Pothas b Herath	28
*A. W. Gale c Pothas b Cork	56	– c McKenzie b Carberry	12
†J. M. Bairstow c Pothas b Tomlinson	4	– not out	36
A. U. Rashid c Pothas b Balcombe	51	– not out	11
R. M. Pyrah c Vince b Balcombe	8		
T. L. Best lbw b Herath	6		
S. A. Patterson not out	3		
O. J. Hannon-Dalby b Balcombe	0		
B 8, l-b 6, w 4, n-b 20	38	B 13, l-b 6, w 1, n-b 10	30

1/195 (1) 2/209 (2) 3/215 (4)   (136.1 overs) 415   1/36 (2)   (5 wkts dec, 100 overs) 292
4/327 (3) 5/333 (5) 6/337 (6) 7/393 (8)   2/158 (3) 3/231 (4)
8/408 (7) 9/410 (9) 10/415 (11)   110 overs: 339-6   4/233 (1) 5/262 (5)

Tomlinson 33–2–115–3; Cork 34–11–78–3; Balcombe 24.1–6–69–3; Ervine 24–1–88–0; Herath 21–5–51–1. *Second Innings*—Cork 14–4–30–1; Tomlinson 18–5–53–0; Herath 31–10–78–1; Balcombe 17–2–48–2; Ervine 4–1–15–0; Carberry 9–3–16–1; Vince 2–0–9–0; McKenzie 5–1–24–0.

Hampshire

M. A. Carberry c and b Rashid	19	– not out	6
J. H. K. Adams c Rudolph b Hannon-Dalby	82	– not out	6
M. J. Lumb c Rudolph b Rashid	0		
N. D. McKenzie c Rudolph b Pyrah	91		
J. M. Vince run out	24		
S. M. Ervine c Rudolph b Best	20		
*†N. Pothas c and b Rashid	23		
D. G. Cork lbw b Best	26		
D. J. Balcombe b Rashid	30		
H. M. R. K. B. Herath not out	17		
J. A. Tomlinson not out	0		
B 5, l-b 11, w 1, n-b 2	19		

1/49 (1) 2/49 (3)   (9 wkts dec, 97.4 overs) 351   (no wkt, 14 overs) 12
3/143 (2) 4/200 (5) 5/226 (6)
6/262 (7) 7/270 (4) 8/325 (8) 9/341 (9)

Lumb replaced L. A. Dawson after returning from England's reception at Downing Street.

Best 21–4–91–2; Hannon-Dalby 21–3–70–1; Patterson 22–7–60–0; Rashid 18.4–3–62–4; Pyrah 14–1–50–1; Sayers 1–0–2–0. *Second Innings*—Rashid 6–3–3–0; Sayers 6–1–6–0; Lyth 1–0–3–0; Rudolph 1–1–0–0.

Umpires: J. H. Evans and G. Sharp.

HAMPSHIRE v ESSEX

At Southampton, June 4–7. Drawn. Hampshire 8pts, Essex 8pts. Toss: Hampshire.

Bottom-placed Hampshire and Essex, just ten points better off, reached the break in the Championship programme with one win each. Hampshire came closer to making it two after reducing Essex to 99 for six when rain intervened with 24 overs remaining. Chambers had claimed his maiden five-for in Hampshire's first innings, grabbing the last three wickets (without assistance) in five balls on the second morning. Walker held the Essex reply together before slicing to backward point, where the catch was held at the second attempt: it was his first 99 in 341 first-class innings. Pothas then helped set up the second-innings declaration, sharing a seventh-wicket stand of 97 with Cork. Left 75 overs to score 328, Essex were in immediate trouble as threatening clouds gathered. Westley went in the second over, Mickleburgh in the third; Balcombe then seized two more wickets in the 14th to leave Essex reeling at 16 for four. Bopara and Foster survived 25 overs, though both had gone when the rain arrived.

Close of play: First day, Hampshire 298-7 (Cork 54, Balcombe 6); Second day, Essex 209-7 (Walker 60, Napier 9); Third day, Hampshire 235-6 (Pothas 28, Cork 14).

Hampshire

M. A. Carberry c Mickleburgh b Masters	50	– c Walker b Bopara	35
J. H. K. Adams c Foster b Chambers	3	– lbw b ten Doeschate	56
M. J. Lumb b Danish Kaneria	31	– c Pettini b Danish Kaneria	38
N. D. McKenzie b Bopara	83	– c Foster b Masters	8
J. M. Vince c and b Chambers	44	– c Foster b Chambers	16
S. M. Ervine c Pettini b Danish Kaneria	15	– c Mickleburgh b Bopara	19
*†N. Pothas lbw b Bopara	1	– c Foster b Chambers	59
D. G. Cork b Chambers	55	– not out	41
D. J. Balcombe c and b Chambers	6	– not out	10
D. R. Briggs b Chambers	0		
J. A. Tomlinson not out	1		
L-b 3, w 6, n-b 2	11	B 13, l-b 5, n-b 11	29

1/9 (2) 2/84 (3) 3/102 (1) 4/168 (5)   (98 overs) 300
5/187 (6) 6/190 (7) 7/290 (4) 8/299 (8)
9/299 (10) 10/300 (9)

1/62 (1)   (7 wkts dec, 87.5 overs) 311
2/115 (2) 3/133 (4) 4/163 (5)
5/163 (3) 6/189 (6) 7/286 (7)

Masters 19-6-46-1; Chambers 19-5-49-5; Napier 9-1-35-0; Danish Kaneria 27-7-71-2; ten Doeschate 14-1-63-0; Bopara 10-2-33-2. *Second Innings*—Chambers 19-5-50-2; Masters 16.5-3-61-1; Bopara 11-0-49-2; ten Doeschate 11-2-33-1; Danish Kaneria 30-7-100-1.

Essex

T. Westley c and b Cork	36	– b Tomlinson	1
J. C. Mickleburgh c Pothas b Cork	21	– b Cork	2
R. S. Bopara c Pothas b Tomlinson	39	– lbw b Briggs	61
M. J. Walker c Carberry b Balcombe	99	– c McKenzie b Balcombe	3
R. N. ten Doeschate lbw b Tomlinson	6	– lbw b Briggs	0
†J. S. Foster b Briggs	14	– c Adams b Ervine	18
*M. L. Pettini c McKenzie b Briggs	0	– not out	12
D. D. Masters c McKenzie b Tomlinson	15		
G. R. Napier c Vince b Balcombe	35	– (8) not out	0
Danish Kaneria b Ervine	8		
M. A. Chambers not out	0		
B 1, l-b 6, n-b 4	11	L-b 2	2

1/48 (2) 2/65 (1) 3/127 (3)   (116.4 overs) 284
4/133 (5) 5/166 (6) 6/166 (7) 7/189 (8)
8/265 (9) 9/280 (10) 10/284 (4)   110 overs: 252-7

1/3 (1)   (6 wkts, 51.2 overs) 99
2/7 (2) 3/16 (4) 4/16 (5)
5/81 (3) 6/99 (6)

Cork 30-8-60-2; Tomlinson 28-4-66-3; Balcombe 21.4-9-47-2; Ervine 22-5-62-1; Briggs 15-4-42-2. *Second Innings*—Cork 12-4-12-1; Tomlinson 12.2-5-37-1; Balcombe 8-3-14-2; Ervine 12-5-16-1; Briggs 7-3-18-1.

Umpires: T. E. Jesty and P. Willey.

HAMPSHIRE v KENT

At Southampton, July 5–7. Hampshire won by an innings and 111 runs. Hampshire 24pts, Kent 3pts. Toss: Kent.

Hampshire's second win of the season – the biggest of their five innings victories over Kent stretching back to 1792 – lifted them from the foot of Division One. They outplayed Kent from the moment Key chose to bat on a lively wicket, which offered plenty of bounce and movement on the first day, but not afterwards. Cork, captaining Hampshire in the Championship for the first time just a month short of his 39th birthday, exploited the conditions to take five first-innings wickets. His batsmen, helped by a hamstring injury that limited Khan to just eight overs, found life altogether easier: Carberry, with 23 fours, and McKenzie, who hit 13 plus a straight six off Bandara, shared 254, a county record for any wicket at home to Kent. Cork declared 302 ahead, and promptly broke Key's finger, as Kent crumbled. Van Jaarsveld's stubborn 82 not out merely delayed the inevitable; victory came on the third evening just after Hampshire claimed the extra half-hour.

Close of play: First day, Hampshire 51-2 (Carberry 22, Tomlinson 2); Second day, Hampshire 404-5 (Vince 26, Pothas 36).

Kent

J. L. Denly c Pothas b Balcombe	67	– c Dawson b Cork	9
*R. W. T. Key c and b Cork	17	– retired hurt	4
†G. O. Jones c Pothas b Ervine	11	– c McKenzie b Tomlinson	1
M. van Jaarsveld c and b Briggs	17	– not out	82
S. A. Northeast c McKenzie b Balcombe	50	– c Pothas b Balcombe	32
J. B. Hockley b Cork	0	– c Carberry b Cork	8
A. J. Blake c Cork b Briggs	31	– c Pothas b Tomlinson	13
H. M. C. M. Bandara c Pothas b Cork	0	– lbw b Briggs	12
S. J. Cook b Cork	2	– c Pothas b Ervine	16
A. Khan c Balcombe b Cork	21	– (11) b Balcombe	0
R. H. Joseph not out	7	– (10) b Ervine	5
B 10, l-b 8, n-b 10	28	B 2, l-b 5, n-b 2	9

1/31 (2) 2/62 (3) 3/98 (4)   (80.2 overs) 251
4/172 (1) 5/177 (5) 6/181 (6) 7/189 (8)
8/191 (9) 9/227 (7) 10/251 (10)

1/14 (1) 2/14 (3)   (60.2 overs) 191
3/59 (5) 4/78 (6)
5/114 (7) 6/145 (8) 7/172 (9)
8/182 (10) 9/191 (11)

In the second innings Key retired hurt at 5.

Cork 22.2–6–50–5; Tomlinson 20–5–47–0; Balcombe 12–1–67–2; Ervine 15–4–43–1; Briggs 11–3–26–2. *Second Innings*—Cork 12–3–16–2; Tomlinson 12–4–28–2; Ervine 11–1–36–2; Balcombe 13.2–2–48–2; Briggs 12–0–56–1.

Hampshire

M. A. Carberry c Jones b Joseph	158	*D. G. Cork not out	15
J. H. K. Adams c Northeast b Khan	0		
L. A. Dawson c van Jaarsveld b Joseph	6	B 17, w 7, n-b 35	59
J. A. Tomlinson c Jones b Cook	11		
N. D. McKenzie c Hockley b Cook	113	1/7 (2)	(7 wkts dec, 145 overs) 553
J. M. Vince lbw b Blake	57	2/26 (3) 3/76 (4)	
†N. Pothas lbw b Bandara	78	4/330 (5) 5/348 (1)	
S. M. Ervine not out	56	6/449 (6) 7/520 (7)	110 overs: 409-5

D. J. Balcombe and D. R. Briggs did not bat.

Khan 8–0–28–1; Joseph 27–3–112–2; Bandara 47–10–167–1; Hockley 6–1–27–0; Cook 29–6–95–2; Blake 14–1–60–1; van Jaarsveld 14–2–47–0.

Umpires: J. H. Evans and D. J. Millns.

HAMPSHIRE v LANCASHIRE

At Southampton, July 29–August 1. Drawn. Hampshire 10pts, Lancashire 7pts. Toss: Lancashire. Championship debut: A. M. Bates.

Lancashire remained the only unbeaten side in either division despite determined efforts by their ex-team-mate Cork. Chapple decided they should bat first under heavy skies, but only Chanderpaul could master the conditions, scoring a 54th first-class century. The match was just his second for Lancashire, but as wickets tumbled around the West Indian it must have felt like business as usual. An undaunted Cork eventually claimed him and three others. Lumb, without a meaningful score all season and surplus to requirements in the Friends Provident T20 quarter-final win at Edgbaston four days earlier, contributed 48 to Hampshire's battle for a first-innings lead, which came to 86. But as the wicket flattened, Lancashire dug in, avoiding defeat their only realistic ambition. As Tom Smith and Chilton laboured over a match-saving stand of 134 in 62 overs for the second wicket, Hampshire ran out of ideas. Smith's 128 in six hours and 41 minutes was a career-best, as was 100 not out for Cross, a 26-year-old wicketkeeper playing here as a specialist batsman. His century hastened the end of Sutton's Lancashire career, and allowed the captains to shake hands with the visitors 265 ahead.

Close of play: First day, Lancashire 262-8 (Mahmood 9, Kerrigan 3); Second day, Hampshire 287-6 (Bates 5, Cork 8); Third day, Lancashire 106-1 (Smith 60, Chilton 32).

Lancashire

P. J. Horton c McKenzie b Balcombe	21	– (2) b Tomlinson	5
T. C. Smith c Bates b Tomlinson	2	– (1) c Adams b Briggs	128
M. J. Chilton c Bates b Ervine	17	– c Bates b Balcombe	47
S. Chanderpaul c Bates b Cork	118	– c Lumb b Briggs	11
S. J. Croft b Briggs	41	– c Lumb b Briggs	23
G. D. Cross c Bates b Briggs	4	– not out	100
†L. D. Sutton c Vince b Balcombe	29	– c Balcombe b Carberry	2
*G. Chapple c Vince b Cork	9	– not out	11
S. I. Mahmood not out	21		
S. C. Kerrigan c Adams b Cork	4		
G. Keedy b Cork	8		
L-b 2, w 1, n-b 6	9	B 3, l-b 6, w 3, n-b 12	24

1/4 (2)   2/35 (1)   3/41 (3)   4/119 (5)   (101 overs) 283   1/8 (2)   (6 wkts dec, 127 overs) 351
5/127 (6)   6/204 (7)   7/246 (8)   2/142 (3)   3/181 (4)
8/249 (4)   9/267 (10)   10/283 (11)   4/212 (5)   5/277 (1)   6/312 (7)

Cork 24–5–57–4; Tomlinson 21–5–51–1; Balcombe 22–3–75–2; Ervine 14–5–33–1; Briggs 18–4–54–2; Carberry 2–0–11–0. *Second Innings*—Cork 17–4–45–0; Tomlinson 17–7–40–1; Ervine 17–4–43–0; Briggs 47–6–142–3; Balcombe 21–6–41–1; Carberry 8–1–31–1.

Hampshire

M. A. Carberry b Chapple	0	J. A. Tomlinson c Horton b Keedy	19
J. H. K. Adams b Sutton b Keedy	72	D. R. Briggs c Chapple b Keedy	1
M. J. Lumb c Kerrigan b Mahmood	48		
N. D. McKenzie c Chilton b Keedy	33	B 17, l-b 14, w 1, n-b 14	46
J. M. Vince lbw b Croft	33		
S. M. Ervine c Smith b Chapple	56	1/0 (1) 2/117 (3) (112.2 overs) 369
†A. M. Bates b Chapple	7	3/160 (2) 4/179 (4) 5/255 (5)
*D. G. Cork not out	54	6/271 (6) 7/307 (7) 8/317 (9)
D. J. Balcombe b Chapple	0	9/365 (10) 10/369 (11) 110 overs: 365-8

Chapple 25–5–68–4; Mahmood 18–0–69–1; Kerrigan 31–6–90–0; Smith 10–3–38–0; Keedy 25.2–3–56–4; Croft 3–0–17–1.

Umpires: R. K. Illingworth and R. A. Kettleborough.

HAMPSHIRE v DURHAM

At Basingstoke, August 3–6. Drawn. Hampshire 10pts, Durham 7pts. Toss: Hampshire.

Carberry scored a century in each innings for Hampshire, but rain deprived the match of 129 overs and the chance of a positive outcome. With short boundaries aiding them, Carberry and Lumb hit 56 fours on the opening day (but only one six, by Lumb) in a monumental partnership of 314. It was comfortably the highest at May's Bounty, and by Hampshire against Durham, and just seven runs short of the county's 90-year second-wicket record. Lumb sailed 110 beyond his previous highest score of the Championship season. A thunderstorm washed out all but 11 overs of the second day, and prompted Steve Harmison to question the wisdom of playing at club grounds. "Considering the fortunes the ECB are spending on drainage at most county grounds you have to ask whether we should be coming to places like this," he said. His words were quite a kick in the teeth for Basingstoke

Sports and Social Club, who had been desperate for Harmison to play and boost their gate. On a freshened wicket, Durham lurched to 40 for four until Muchall put together 176 with Stokes, who was caught at long-on one short of a third first-class century in his first full season. Mustard declared 101 behind, yet the same left-handed pair frustrated Durham, sharing 150 before rain intruded for a final time.

Close of play: First day, Hampshire 373-5 (Vince 4, Tomlinson 8); Second day, Hampshire 421-5 (Vince 27, Tomlinson 31); Third day, Hampshire 41-2 (Carberry 22).

Hampshire

M. A. Carberry c Borthwick b Benkenstein	162	– st Mustard b Blackwell	107
J. H. K. Adams c Mustard b Harmison	18	– b Blackwell	5
M. J. Lumb lbw b Thorp	158	– (4) c Harmison b Blackwell	64
N. D. McKenzie b Blackwell	1	– (5) not out	3
J. M. Vince not out	27	– (6) c Di Venuto b Blackwell	0
S. M. Ervine lbw b Thorp	8	– (7) not out	3
J. A. Tomlinson not out	31	– (3) c Plunkett b Blackwell	2
B 1, l-b 3, w 6, n-b 6	16	B 4, l-b 12, w 1, n-b 2	19

1/31 (2) 2/345 (1)   (5 wkts dec, 109 overs) 421   1/19 (2)   (5 wkts, 62.2 overs) 203
3/346 (4) 4/348 (3) 5/365 (6)   2/41 (3) 3/191 (4)
                                                               4/200 (1) 5/200 (6)

*D. G. Cork, †A. M. Bates, D. J. Balcombe and D. R. Briggs did not bat.

Harmison 28–4–106–1; Thorp 19–6–66–2; Stokes 9–2–41–0; Plunkett 14–0–72–0; Blackwell 17–2–61–1; Borthwick 8–0–52–0; Benkenstein 14–6–19–1. *Second Innings*—Harmison 6.3–0–34–0; Thorp 2.3–1–6–0; Blackwell 25–7–79–5; Borthwick 8–1–41–0; Benkenstein 13–11–5–0; Stokes 3–1–8–0; Plunkett 4.2–0–14–0.

Durham

M. J. Di Venuto lbw b Cork	4	S. G. Borthwick c Lumb b Cork	54
M. D. Stoneman lbw b Tomlinson	9		
G. J. Muchall not out	140	L-b 4, n-b 4	8
D. M. Benkenstein c Bates b Balcombe	5		
I. D. Blackwell lbw b Tomlinson	1	1/4 (1) 2/30 (2) (7 wkts dec, 82.4 overs) 320
B. A. Stokes c Ervine b Briggs	99	3/39 (4) 4/40 (5)
*†P. Mustard c McKenzie b Balcombe	0	5/216 (6) 6/218 (7) 7/320 (8)

L. E. Plunkett, C. D. Thorp and S. J. Harmison did not bat.

Cork 19.4–2–73–2; Tomlinson 16–4–43–2; Balcombe 15–2–67–2; Briggs 21–1–68–1; Ervine 11–0–65–0.

Umpires: N. L. Bainton and M. R. Benson.

At Taunton, August 9–12. HAMPSHIRE drew with SOMERSET.

At Scarborough, August 23–26. HAMPSHIRE drew with YORKSHIRE.

At Liverpool, August 31–September 3. HAMPSHIRE lost to LANCASHIRE by three wickets.

At Canterbury, September 7–10. HAMPSHIRE beat KENT by 130 runs.

HAMPSHIRE v WARWICKSHIRE

At Southampton, September 13–16. Warwickshire won by ten wickets. Warwickshire 22pts, Hampshire 4pts. Toss: Warwickshire.

Warwickshire ensured their first division status with a third successive victory and sixth in all competitions leading to the CB40 final, which they also won. Quite simply, they were steelier than their rivals when it mattered, securing Championship doubles over Essex, Kent and now Hampshire.

They seized upon early movement and sloppy Hampshire batting, and it was down to Dawson, plus the tail, to provide respectability. Bell's solitary Championship hundred of the season was far more accomplished than anything else on show, and crucial in establishing a first-innings lead of 85. For Hampshire, there was solace to be found in Simon Jones, now 31, and playing his first Championship match for more than two years. He began with a long-hop, which Westwood duly pulled to the boundary, but recovered to take four wickets while sometimes approaching the pace of his England prime. When Hampshire batted a second time, Woakes devastated the top order. With their opponents 44 for six – still 41 behind – Warwickshire eyed a short cut to victory, but Ervine made them wait with a bold 62. What proved Westwood's last act as Warwickshire captain was to knock off the winning runs with Chopra before tea.

Close of play: First day, Hampshire 147-6 (Dawson 40, Cork 41); Second day, Warwickshire 29-0 (Westwood 9, Chopra 17); Third day, Warwickshire 303.

Hampshire

M. A. Carberry c Clarke b Woakes	7	– c Johnson b Miller	1
J. H. K. Adams lbw b Maddy	13	– c Johnson b Woakes	8
P. J. Hughes b Maddy	11	– lbw b Woakes	4
L. A. Dawson c Johnson b Barker	74	– c Johnson b Woakes	9
J. M. Vince c Bell b Maddy	0	– lbw b Maddy	6
S. M. Ervine c Maddy b Clarke	15	– (7) c and b Woakes	62
†A. M. Bates b Barker	2	– (6) c Johnson b Woakes	6
*D. G. Cork c Clarke b Maddy	41	– c Clarke b Maddy	9
J. A. Tomlinson c Bell b Clarke	1	– c Clarke b Imran Tahir	7
D. R. Briggs lbw b Imran Tahir	27	– lbw b Imran Tahir	11
S. P. Jones not out	0	– not out	0
B 4, l-b 12, w 1, n-b 10	27	L-b 5, w 2, n-b 2	9

1/29 (1) 2/31 (2) 3/42 (3)   (73.3 overs) 218   1/13 (2) 2/13 (1)   (38.1 overs) 132
4/42 (5) 5/71 (6) 6/85 (7) 7/149 (8)   3/23 (3) 4/30 (4)
8/156 (9) 9/216 (10) 10/218 (4)   5/40 (6) 6/44 (5) 7/54 (8)
                                                            8/76 (9) 9/132 (10) 10/132 (7)

Woakes 20–3–60–1; Miller 9–3–21–0; Maddy 18–8–37–4; Clarke 15–2–47–2; Barker 7.3–0–22–2; Imran Tahir 4–0–15–1. *Second Innings*—Woakes 15.1–5–34–5; Miller 6–0–20–1; Maddy 7–2–16–2; Clarke 4–0–36–0; Imran Tahir 6–1–21–2.

Warwickshire

*I. J. Westwood lbw b Tomlinson	9	– not out	27
V. Chopra lbw b Jones	27	– not out	18
I. R. Bell c Bates b Jones	104		
D. L. Maddy b Briggs	40		
J. O. Troughton c Carberry b Jones	2		
R. Clarke c Bates b Tomlinson	52		
†R. M. Johnson c Bates b Jones	0		
K. H. D. Barker c Cork b Briggs	21		
C. R. Woakes not out	14		
Imran Tahir lbw b Briggs	20		
A. S. Miller c Dawson b Tomlinson	5		
B 1, l-b 4, n-b 4	9	B 4, n-b 2	6

1/39 (2) 2/39 (1) 3/135 (4)   (100.5 overs) 303   (no wkt, 16.2 overs) 51
4/140 (5) 5/223 (3) 6/227 (7)
7/264 (6) 8/264 (8) 9/294 (10) 10/303 (11)

Cork 16–1–40–0; Tomlinson 31.5–12–83–3; Jones 22–5–60–4; Ervine 7–1–15–0; Briggs 24–2–100–3. *Second Innings*—Tomlinson 7–1–23–0; Briggs 8–2–18–0; Vince 1.2–0–6–0.

Umpires: M. R. Benson and B. Dudleston.

KENT

Digging for victory?

MARK PENNELL

On a dewy October morning, mechanical diggers skimmed away the topsoil from Kent's impeccably tended practice area backing on to St Lawrence Forstal. This was no routine close-season pitch resurfacing by groundstaff, however. It marked the start, if a belated one, of the county's multimillion-pound redevelopment of their Canterbury headquarters.

Losing those pristine practice pitches, used by generations of Kentish legends, was the trade-off for a county whose coffers were nigh empty before the land was sold for housing. There was no fanfare to commemorate the digging, but it is hoped that the scheme – including refurbished stands, pavilion, dressing-rooms, club shop and offices, as well as permanent retractable floodlights – will lead to new and improved income streams and a healthier financial future.

There was no doubt that reduced budgets played some part in Kent's immediate return to the second tier of the Championship. Rob Key's cut-price squad battled manfully to the end, scuppering Yorkshire's title challenge with a rare victory at Headingley on the final day of the summer. But three wins, only one on home soil, could not stave off relegation.

"I'm disappointed," said head coach Paul Farbrace after a painful first full season in charge. "You take knock-backs like this personally. I've never been one who's quick to blame others. I always look at my own contribution first, and I have areas where I obviously need to do better as a coach… We didn't score enough runs consistently, we dropped vital catches in many matches, and we didn't have enough bowling depth. They are the three basic reasons we went down."

Kent's cause was damaged further by injuries that forced seam bowlers Dewald Nel and Robbie Joseph to miss most of the season. This heaped pressure on the likes of Amjad Khan, Simon Cook, the experienced Azhar Mahmood and the greener Matt Coles. All four played through minor ailments during the summer. Coles caught the eye with gusty all-round performances; Mahmood and Cook played far more cricket than planned and ran out of steam; while Khan, the county's leading wicket-taker in the Championship, became a victim of austerity.

Despite his nine years of loyal service, Kent felt unable to make 30-year-old Danish firebrand Khan a contract offer for 2011, and allowed him to leave for Sussex. The squad became so threadbare like this personally. I've never been in for ad hoc appearances, while Tony Palladino joined on loan from Essex, though – such was the mystery surrounding selection – he never made an appearance. Come the end of the season, Key was giving Darren Stevens the new ball.

South Africa's Makhaya Ntini arrived for a short stint before the Twenty20 break, and enlivened proceedings, taking 24 wickets in five Championship starts. Without him, Kent struggled to bowl sides out twice. A less financially draining – though less successful – recruit was Sri Lankan wrist-spinner Malinga Bandara who, according to Farbrace, was taken on for the equivalent of a second-team salary. He tried his utmost, particularly in limited-overs games, but 18 Championship scalps cost over 41 apiece.

Mike Egerton, PA Photos

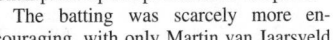
Darren Stevens

The batting was scarcely more en-couraging, with only Martin van Jaarsveld and Geraint Jones reaching the 1,000-run mark in first-class games. Jones managed it by the skin of his teeth, while van Jaarsveld hit four figures for a sixth successive season. Van Jaarsveld entered into talks to join Lancashire, though it seemed likely he would begin his seventh season with Kent in April. The remainder of Kent's top order all suffered disappointing patches or, in some cases, more prolonged loss of form.

Despite hitting 261 – the highest score of the 2010 season – in a losing cause against Durham, Key endured his worst summer in a decade. His opening partner Joe Denly made just 610 in the Championship, and even Player of the Season Stevens tailed off to finish just short of 1,000. The weight of expectation heaped on Harrow School batting prodigy Sam Northeast proved too much. Having failed at No. 5 and No. 3, he ended the campaign opening with Denly (and Key at first drop). Northeast's average of 24 told a story.

A late flurry of wickets from off-spinner James Tredwell, including a maiden hat-trick in the win over Yorkshire, meant he ended with 37 Championship wickets, yet it proved a difficult season. Tredwell, who was in England's triumphant World Twenty20 squad but not used, appeared distracted and unsettled; his selection at a critical time (together with Stevens's absence on England Lions duty) undoubtedly hindered Kent's hopes of a fourth successive Twenty20 finals day.

Stevens and Mahmood occasionally inspired CB40 success but, when they failed, the rest followed suit. Seven wins from 12 games saw Kent finish second in their group, behind Warwickshire, but with insufficient points to make the semi-finals.

In 2011, Kent will have a new, larger dressing-room, but even fewer players to fill it. Farbrace expects to operate with a skeleton staff of 16 to 18, up to half a dozen of whom will remain in full-time education at college or university. He doubts whether the salary budget will stretch to an overseas signing, though Ntini was reportedly keen to return.

Financial adversity, however, brings the chance to blood local talent. So Kentish fledglings such as Coles, Alex Blake, Adam Ball, James Goodman and 17-year-old Daniel Bell-Drummond – the sole addition to the playing staff after signing a three-year contract – should not be lacking opportunity.

KENT RESULTS

All first-class matches – Played 18: Won 3, Lost 7, Drawn 8.
County Championship matches – Played 16: Won 3, Lost 7, Drawn 6.

LV= County Championship, 8th in Division 1;
Friends Provident T20, 7th in South Division; Clydesdale Bank 40, 2nd in Group C.

COUNTY CHAMPIONSHIP AVERAGES, BATTING AND FIELDING

Cap		M	I	NO	R	HS	100s	50s	Avge	Ct/St
2005	D. I. Stevens	14	24	3	935	197	4	2	44.52	6
2005	M. van Jaarsveld¶	16	28	2	1,082	110*	2	6	41.61	35
2003	G. O. Jones	16	29	0	865	178	2	2	29.82	48/5
2007	J. C. Tredwell†	11	18	2	472	115	1	1	29.50	20
2001	R. W. T. Key	15	27	2	674	261	1	1	26.96	1
	S. A. Northeast†	16	28	0	688	71	0	4	24.57	6
	A. J. Blake†	8	15	1	331	105*	1	0	23.64	4
2008	Azhar Mahmood¶	7	13	0	289	64	0	2	22.23	0
2008	J. L. Denly†	16	29	0	610	95	0	3	21.03	9
	M. T. Coles†	12	20	4	322	51	0	1	20.12	3
	J. B. Hockley†	5	9	0	139	82	0	1	15.44	7
	H. M. C. M. Bandara§	6	10	3	105	29	0	0	15.00	5
2007	S. J. Cook	14	22	6	161	26*	0	0	10.06	1
	A. Khan	12	18	5	115	24	0	0	8.84	4
	M. Ntini§	5	8	3	25	13	0	0	5.00	0

Also batted: P. D. Edwards† (1 match) 6*, 13; R. S. Ferley (1 match) 19, 1; R. H. Joseph (1 match) 7*, 5; J. D. Nel (1 match) 2 (1 ct).

† *Born in Kent.*   § *Official overseas player.*   ¶ *Other non-England-qualified player.*

BOWLING

	O	M	R	W	BB	5W/i	Avge
M. Ntini	164	44	474	24	6-51	2	19.75
D. I. Stevens	267.1	71	725	27	4-38	0	26.85
Azhar Mahmood	257.3	51	774	28	5-62	2	27.64
J. C. Tredwell	348.1	61	1,098	37	7-22	2	29.67
S. J. Cook	310.3	58	1,108	34	4-62	0	32.58
A. Khan	372.2	82	1,258	38	5-43	1	33.10
M. T. Coles	234	32	881	24	4-55	0	36.70
H. M. C. M. Bandara	210.4	31	745	18	4-42	0	41.38

Also bowled: A. J. Blake 14–1–60–1; J. L. Denly 47–2–205–2; P. D. Edwards 14–3–77–1; R. S. Ferley 26–2–142–2; J. B. Hockley 24–3–88–2; G. O. Jones 1–0–8–0; R. H. Joseph 27–3–112–2; R. W. T. Key 11.2–3–31–2; J. D. Nel 36–10–119–9; S. A. Northeast 3–1–2–0; M. van Jaarsveld 110–14–299–3.

LEADING CB40 AVERAGES (100 runs/4 wickets)

Batting	Runs	HS	Avge	S-R	Ct
A. J. Blake	128	81*	128.00	126.73	1
M. van Jaarsveld . . .	388	104*	55.42	101.04	5
J. L. Denly	467	102*	46.70	79.42	3
R. W. T. Key	352	87	39.11	94.87	1
Azhar Mahmood . . .	109	44	36.33	126.74	2
D. I. Stevens	212	55	35.33	99.06	2

Bowling	W	BB	Avge	E-R
M. T. Coles	14	4-45	10.57	6.16
H. M. C. M. Bandara	13	5-35	11.00	4.33
M. van Jaarsveld . . .	5	3-23	13.00	4.75
J. C. Tredwell	11	4-20	18.81	3.76
S. J. Cook	10	3-39	25.10	4.62
Azhar Mahmood . . .	6	2-7	37.16	5.43

LEADING FPT20 AVERAGES (100 runs/18 overs)

Batting	Runs	HS	Avge	S-R	Ct/St	Bowling	W	BB	Avge	E-R
D. I. Stevens	369	52*	41.00	**149.39**	5	Azhar Mahmood	15	2-18	26.26	**6.91**
R. W. T. Key	277	98*	25.18	**137.81**	4	S. J. Cook	21	3-13	19.66	**7.24**
M. van Jaarsveld	421	82	28.06	**128.35**	5	D. I. Stevens	12	3-17	23.91	**7.35**
A. J. Blake	122	33	12.20	**127.08**	9	H. M. C. M. Bandara	17	3-14	22.58	**8.00**
G. O. Jones	240	54	17.14	**118.22**	8/2	J. C. Tredwell	11	3-13	24.36	**8.64**
J. L. Denly	382	65	31.83	**115.75**	6	M. T. Coles	15	3-30	21.60	**8.67**

FIRST-CLASS COUNTY RECORDS

Highest score for	332	W. H. Ashdown v Essex at Brentwood	1934
Highest score against	344	W. G. Grace (MCC) at Canterbury	1876
Leading run-scorer	47,868	F. E. Woolley (avge 41.77)	1906–1938
Best bowling for	10-30	C. Blythe v Northamptonshire at Northampton	1907
Best bowling against	10-48	C. H. G. Bland (Sussex) at Tonbridge	1899
Leading wicket-taker	3,340	A. P. Freeman (avge 17.64)	1914–1936
Highest total for	803-4 dec	v Essex at Brentwood	1934
Highest total against	676	by Australians at Canterbury	1921
Lowest total for	18	v Sussex at Gravesend	1867
Lowest total against	16	by Warwickshire at Tonbridge	1913

LIST A COUNTY RECORDS

Highest score for	146	A. Symonds v Lancashire at Tunbridge Wells	2004
Highest score against	167*	P. Johnson (Nottinghamshire) at Nottingham	1993
Leading run-scorer	7,814	M. R. Benson (avge 31.89)	1980–1995
Best bowling for	8-31	D. L. Underwood v Scotland at Edinburgh	1987
Best bowling against	6-5	A. G. Wharf (Glamorgan) at Cardiff	2004
Leading wicket-taker	530	D. L. Underwood (avge 18.93)	1963–1987
Highest total for	384-6	v Berkshire at Finchampstead	1994
Highest total against	344-5	by Somerset at Taunton	2002
Lowest total for	60	v Somerset at Taunton	1979
Lowest total against	60	by Derbyshire at Canterbury	2008

TWENTY20 RECORDS

Highest score for	112	A. Symonds v Middlesex at Maidstone	2004
Highest score against	**106**	**A. C. Gilchrist (Middlesex) at Canterbury**	**2010**
Leading run-scorer	**1,400**	**D. I. Stevens (avge 31.81)**	**2005–2010**
Best bowling for	4-14	D. I. Stevens v Essex at Chelmsford	2007
Best bowling against	5-18	A. Symonds (Surrey) at Beckenham	2006
Leading wicket-taker	**68**	**J. C. Tredwell (avge 23.30)**	**2003–2010**
Highest total for	**217**	**v Gloucestershire at Gloucester**	**2010**
Highest total against	217-4	by Surrey at Canterbury	2006
Lowest total for	91	v Surrey at The Oval	2006
Lowest total against	**82**	**by Somerset at Taunton**	**2010**

ADDRESS

St Lawrence Ground, Old Dover Road, Canterbury CT1 3NZ (01227 456886; **email** kent@ecb.co.uk).
Website www.kentccc.com

OFFICIALS

Captain R. W. T. Key
Team director P. Farbrace
High-performance director S. C. Willis
President J. N. Shepherd
Chairman G. M. Kennedy

Chief executive J. A. Clifford
Chairman, cricket committee G. W. Johnson
Grounds co-ordinator A. Peirson
Scorer J. C. Foley

KENT v LOUGHBOROUGH MCCU

At Canterbury, April 10–12. Drawn. Toss: Kent. First-class debuts: H. S. Gandam, S. A. L. Rose, W. A. Tavaré, R. M. L. Taylor, A. S. Welsh, T. S. Winslade. County debut: J. D. Nel.

A slow, early-season pitch gave batsmen the opportunity for practice in what became a relatively high-scoring draw. Key and Jones shared a second-wicket stand of 272, the best for any Kent wicket against University opposition; van Jaarsveld also reached three figures, as did Denly in the second innings, making him – at the age of 24 – the first Kent player to score a duck and a hundred in the same game on four occasions. David Murphy's 76 ensured some respectability for the students, though Key had the option to make them follow on. The luckless Dewald Nel, a close-season recruit from Scotland, ricked his back coming down the dressing-room steps and played no part in his Kent debut. For the first time in almost 18 years, there was a Tavaré playing first-class cricket at Canterbury: Will, nephew of the dependable Chris, was one of six debutants. On the first day, Key arguably became the first to retire out in a Kent innings, though some claim it had happened at Hove in 1891 when Charles Fox, nought not out at lunch, dined with friends and returned too late to resume his innings.

Close of play: First day, Kent 504-7 (Cook 25, Coles 40); Second day, Kent 10-0 (Northeast 8, Stevens 0).

Kent

J. L. Denly lbw b Groves	0	– (3) lbw b Baker	106
*R. W. T. Key retired out	140		
†G. O. Jones c Evans b Taylor	112	– (4) lbw b Welsh	26
M. van Jaarsveld c Welsh b Rose	106		
S. A. Northeast lbw b Welsh	10	– (1) b Baker	21
D. I. Stevens lbw b Evans	25	– (2) c and b Taylor	19
J. C. Tredwell c Murphy b Taylor	11	– (5) lbw b Taylor	6
S. J. Cook not out	25	– (6) c Taylor b Welsh	19
M. T. Coles not out	40	– (7) not out	4
P. D. Edwards (did not bat)		– (8) lbw b Welsh	1
B 3, l-b 12, w 8, n-b 12	35	B 1, l-b 5, n-b 4	10

1/0 (1)　2/272 (3)　　　　(7 wkts dec, 103 overs)　504
3/286 (2)　4/342 (5)
5/403 (6)　6/438 (4)　7/438 (7)

1/42 (1)　　　(7 wkts dec, 57.4 overs)　212
2/56 (2)　3/117 (4)
4/136 (5)　5/195 (6)　6/211 (3)　7/212 (8)

J. D. Nel did not bat.

Groves 14–0–87–1; Baker 19–3–77–0; Rose 21–5–72–1; Taylor 19–1–105–2; Welsh 17–1–91–1; Evans 13–0–57–1. *Second Innings*—Baker 9–1–35–2; Taylor 14–2–60–2; Rose 12–0–53–0; Evans 6–0–16–0; Welsh 14.4–1–32–3; Cope 2–0–10–0.

Loughborough MCCU

W. A. Tavaré b Cook	0	– run out	11
T. S. Winslade lbw b Cook	1	– lbw b Denly	17
H. S. Gandam lbw b Coles	11		
*A. C. Cope c van Jaarsveld b Edwards	18	– (3) st Jones b van Jaarsveld	7
†D. Murphy b Coles	76	– (4) not out	15
A. S. Welsh c Jones b Edwards	21	– (5) not out	8
R. M. L. Taylor c Tredwell b van Jaarsveld	17		
R. F. Evans c Cook b Tredwell	44		
G. C. Baker b Cook	4		
P. R. Groves lbw b Stevens	43		
S. A. L. Rose not out	0		
B 4, l-b 6, w 6, n-b 8	24	L-b 2	2

1/0 (1)　2/1 (2)　3/36 (4)　4/38 (3)　　　(103.5 overs)　259
5/77 (6)　6/131 (7)　7/186 (5)
8/193 (9)　9/257 (10)　10/259 (8)

1/25 (1)　　　(3 wkts, 28 overs)　60
2/37 (3)　3/37 (2)

Cook 21–10–24–3; Coles 22–8–50–2; Edwards 18–6–60–2; Tredwell 24.5–8–50–1; van Jaarsveld 10–1–29–1; Key 1–0–7–0; Stevens 7–1–29–1. *Second Innings*—Coles 2–0–8–0; Edwards 2–1–8–0; Stevens 6–2–14–0; Tredwell 4–2–3–0; Denly 5–0–8–1; van Jaarsveld 3–2–4–1; Northeast 3–2–6–0; Key 3–0–7–0.

Umpires: R. J. Bailey and G. Sharp.

At Nottingham, April 15–17. KENT lost to NOTTINGHAMSHIRE by an innings and 32 runs.

KENT v YORKSHIRE

At Canterbury, April 21–24. Drawn. Kent 9pts, Yorkshire 8pts. Toss: Kent.

With no overseas support and three front-line seamers injured, Kent fought hard to earn parity in the 200th first-class meeting between the counties. Bresnan's fourth five-for, his first for two seasons, restricted Kent to three batting points after Stevens – whose 92 from 125 balls was the highest of the game's 11 half-centuries – had steered them from trouble at 131 for five. Yorkshire stumbled in reply, and at 120 for six seemed set for a substantial deficit; at 246 for six, however, with Bairstow and Rashid each hitting a patient fifty, they looked likely to gain a lead. But four wickets fell for 37 to give Kent the edge. A first-class best from Hockley enabled Key to declare four overs into the final day. With the promoted Bresnan leading the charge, Yorkshire appeared on course to overhaul a target of 392 in 90 overs and make it three wins out of three. Surprisingly, they opted for the draw.

Close of play: First day, Kent 313-9 (Coles 3); Second day, Yorkshire 280-8 (Shahzad 12, Wainwright 16); Third day, Kent 327-7 (Tredwell 65, Azhar Mahmood 1).

Kent

J. L. Denly c Sayers b Wainwright	32	– c Bairstow b Bresnan	2
*R. W. T. Key c Bairstow b Shahzad	5	– lbw b Hannon-Dalby	9
†G. O. Jones b Bresnan	28	– lbw b Wainwright	53
M. van Jaarsveld c Bairstow b Bresnan	20	– lbw b Rashid	78
S. A. Northeast lbw b Wainwright	27	– lbw b Bresnan	1
D. I. Stevens c McGrath b Shahzad	92	– c Rashid b Wainwright	5
J. B. Hockley c Bresnan b Shahzad	14	– c Bairstow b Rashid	82
J. C. Tredwell b Bresnan	32	– not out	72
Azhar Mahmood c Rudolph b Bresnan	21	– b Shahzad	18
M. T. Coles not out	6		
A. Khan lbw b Bresnan	1		
B 18, l-b 16, w 1, n-b 4	39	B 14, l-b 12, w 9, n-b 2	37

1/28 (2) 2/74 (1) 3/78 (3)　　　　　(97.2 overs) **317**　　1/4 (1)　　(8 wkts dec, 92 overs) **357**
4/131 (5) 5/131 (4) 6/195 (7) 7/284 (6)　　　　2/39 (2) 3/98 (3)
8/292 (8) 9/313 (9) 10/317 (11)　　　　　　　4/99 (5) 5/116 (6) 6/207 (4)
　　　　　　　　　　　　　　　　　　　　　　7/320 (7) 8/357 (9)

Bresnan 24.2–7–52–5; Shahzad 26–3–65–3; Hannon-Dalby 18–3–59–0; Wainwright 14–4–49–2; McGrath 3–0–18–0; Rashid 11–1–39–0; Rudolph 1–0–1–0. *Second Innings*—Bresnan 18–5–33–2; Shahzad 15–2–55–1; Hannon-Dalby 9–1–37–1; McGrath 4–1–14–0; Rashid 20–2–80–2; Wainwright 26–1–112–2.

Yorkshire

A. Lyth c Jones b Khan	8	– c Jones b Hockley 84
J. J. Sayers lbw b Azhar Mahmood	0	– c van Jaarsveld b Tredwell........ 61
A. McGrath lbw b Stevens	40	– (4) c Denly b Tredwell......... 55
*A. W. Gale c van Jaarsveld b Azhar Mahmood	13	– (6) not out 2
J. A. Rudolph c Jones b Tredwell	38	– c Denly b Tredwell............ 3
†J. M. Bairstow c Hockley b Khan	70	– (7) not out 6
T. T. Bresnan c van Jaarsveld b Tredwell	0	– (3) run out 70
A. U. Rashid lbw b Azhar Mahmood	59	
A. Shahzad lbw b Khan	14	
D. J. Wainwright not out	16	
O. J. Hannon-Dalby lbw b Azhar Mahmood	0	
B 5, l-b 12, n-b 8	25	B 3, l-b 5, w 1, n-b 10 19

1/8 (1) 2/10 (2) 3/44 (4) 4/84 (3)   (97.3 overs) 283
5/120 (5) 6/120 (7) 7/246 (6)
8/248 (8) 9/282 (9) 10/283 (11)

1/155 (1)   (5 wkts, 84 overs) 300
2/155 (2) 3/278 (4)
4/289 (5) 5/294 (3)

Khan 25–9–60–3; Azhar Mahmood 21.3–5–58–4; Coles 11–0–40–0; Tredwell 18–3–53–2; Stevens 17–3–43–1; van Jaarsveld 5–0–12–0. *Second Innings*—Khan 19.1–95–0; Azhar Mahmood 21–2–75–0; Tredwell 29–5–69–3; Stevens 3–0–11–0; Hockley 5–1–13–1; Denly 6–1–29–0; Coles 1–1–0–0.

Umpires: N. G. B. Cook and D. J. Millns.

At Manchester, April 27–30. KENT drew with LANCASHIRE.

KENT v WARWICKSHIRE

At Canterbury, May 4–7. Warwickshire won by 44 runs. Warwickshire 21pts, Kent 7pts. Toss: Kent.

A game containing no hundreds but 17 lbws – a record for Kent matches – ended in Warwickshire's first win in Kent since 1995. With Ntini going wicketless on home debut, it was the introduction of the bustling 19-year-old seamer Matt Coles that altered the course of the first day. The fifth Kent bowler to be used, he shared eight wickets with Cook to dismiss Warwickshire for 250. Though never fluent, Denly hit 95 in almost four hours; supported by useful cameos from nightwatchman Coles and most of the middle order, he eased Kent into a comfortable 127-run lead, despite Clarke's maiden five-wicket return, in his ninth season. The absence of James Tredwell – in the Caribbean with England's World Twenty20 squad – meant Key called on van Jaarsveld's occasional off-spin for 30 overs as Warwickshire, who began the final day 131 ahead with six wickets left, eventually set a target of 201 in 68 overs. Seemingly in control at 51 for two and 114 for three, Kent lost their last seven wickets for 42 in 21 overs; Imran Tahir, giving his leg-breaks plenty of air, picked up four as Warwickshire won with eight overs to spare.

Close of play: First day, Kent 43-1 (Denly 15, Coles 1); Second day, Kent 374-9 (Stevens 57, Ntini 0); Third day, Warwickshire 258-4 (Trott 65).

Warwickshire

*I. J. Westwood c Northeast b Khan	18	– lbw b van Jaarsveld	68
D. L. Maddy c Jones b Cook	39	– lbw b Khan	3
I. R. Bell c Khan b Cook	10	– lbw b Khan	94
I. J. L. Trott b Coles	67	– lbw b Coles	66
J. O. Troughton lbw b Khan	1	– c Jones b Stevens	24
R. Clarke lbw b Coles	8	– lbw b Cook	4
†T. R. Ambrose lbw b Coles	14	– lbw b Cook	14
C. R. Woakes c Jones b Cook	11	– c Hockley b Khan	11
N. M. Carter c Jones b Cook	43	– not out	37
N. S. Tahir c Hockley b Coles	8	– c Stevens b van Jaarsveld	0
Imran Tahir not out	17	– b Cook	0
B 6, l-b 5, w 3	14	B 1, l-b 4, w 1	6

1/51 (1) 2/70 (3) 3/78 (2) 4/91 (5) (80.4 overs) 250
5/113 (6) 6/137 (7) 7/168 (8)
8/203 (4) 9/211 (10) 10/250 (9)

1/3 (2) 2/160 (1) (118.5 overs) 327
3/170 (3) 4/258 (5)
5/259 (4) 6/263 (6) 7/278 (8)
8/325 (7) 9/326 (10) 10/327 (11)

Khan 20–6–48–2; Ntini 9–2–30–0; Cook 14.4–0–66–4; Stevens 21–6–34–0; Coles 14–0–55–4; van Jaarsveld 2–1–6–0. *Second Innings*—Khan 20–6–63–3; Ntini 16–2–47–0; Stevens 6–1–30–1; Coles 19–5–47–1; Cook 25.5–4–75–3; van Jaarsveld 30–6–50–2; Hockley 2–0–10–0.

Kent

J. L. Denly c Clarke b Maddy	95	– b Woakes	0
*R. W. T. Key c Ambrose b Woakes	18	– lbw b Clarke	22
M. T. Coles c Ambrose b Clarke	41	– (8) c N. S. Tahir b Imran Tahir	1
†G. O. Jones c Woakes b Clarke	10	– (3) c Ambrose b Woakes	12
M. van Jaarsveld c Trott b Imran Tahir	47	– (4) lbw b Maddy	59
S. A. Northeast c Ambrose b Clarke	40	– (5) lbw b Imran Tahir	26
D. I. Stevens lbw b Clarke	57	– (6) c Woakes b Imran Tahir	18
J. B. Hockley lbw b Clarke	20	– (7) b Maddy	1
S. J. Cook lbw b Clarke	1	– lbw b Imran Tahir	7
A. Khan lbw b Imran Tahir	0	– not out	4
M. Ntini not out	3	– b Woakes	0
B 6, l-b 28, w 1, n-b 10	45	B 5, w 1	6

1/36 (2) 2/125 (3) 3/143 (4) (109.3 overs) 377
4/211 (1) 5/251 (5) 6/336 (6)
7/362 (8) 8/366 (9) 9/367 (10) 10/377 (7)

1/0 (1) 2/33 (3) (59.3 overs) 156
3/51 (2) 4/114 (5)
5/126 (4) 6/128 (7) 7/137 (8)
8/145 (9) 9/156 (6) 10/156 (11)

Woakes 25–4–82–1; Carter 20–2–76–0; N. S. Tahir 17–2–45–0; Imran Tahir 19–3–55–2; Maddy 13–5–22–1; Clarke 15.3–1–63–6. *Second Innings*—Woakes 18.3–3–43–3; Carter 7–1–22–0; Clarke 9–0–28–1; N. S. Tahir 3–0–11–0; Imran Tahir 16.5–27–4; Maddy 6–1–20–2.

Umpires: B. Dudleston and N. A. Mallender.

At Chelmsford, May 10–13. KENT drew with ESSEX.

KENT v DURHAM

At Canterbury, May 17–20. Durham won by six wickets. Durham 23pts, Kent 7pts. Toss: Kent.

Rob Key made a commanding 261, but he was eclipsed by a stunning, unbeaten 161 from 18-year-old Ben Stokes that inspired Durham to their fifth successive win over Kent. Cannily, Key avoided the strike during Steve Harmison's six-over burst on the opening morning that accounted for Denly and Jones, and became the first batsman to hit a double-hundred for Kent against Durham.

Last man out from the final delivery of the day, he faced 270 balls, hitting 38 fours and three sixes in just over six hours. Durham trailed by just six on first innings after Benkenstein and England Under-19 powerhouse Stokes added 143, a fifth-wicket county record against Kent. Benkenstein was steady, reaching three figures from 158 balls, while the muscular flame-haired left-hander Stokes drove and pulled with exceptional confidence; in all he faced 202 balls and hit 19 fours and two sixes in his glorious four-and-a-half-hour innings. Seemingly shell-shocked by Stokes and without a win all season, Kent capitulated inside 50 overs. The champions had more than 100 overs to make 169. Thanks to the belligerence of the middle order in general – and of Stokes, whose undefeated 42 flashed from 22 balls, in particular – they needed a fraction of that.

Close of play: First day, Kent 424; Second day, Durham 347-6 (Stokes 122, B. W. Harmison 0); Third day, Durham 67-3 (Benkenstein 24, Blackwell 18).

Kent

J. L. Denly c Mustard b S. J. Harmison	0	– lbw b Rushworth	14
*R. W. T. Key b B. W. Harmison	261	– c Borthwick b Claydon	20
†G. O. Jones c Di Venuto b S. J. Harmison	9	– b Rushworth	17
M. van Jaarsveld c Benkenstein b S. J. Harmison	30	– c Di Venuto b S. J. Harmison	44
S. A. Northeast c Mustard b S. J. Harmison	4	– b Blackwell	9
Azhar Mahmood c Di Venuto b Benkenstein	43	– lbw b Blackwell	11
A. J. Blake c Mustard b B. W. Harmison	31	– b Blackwell	7
R. S. Ferley c Di Venuto b Rushworth	19	– b Borthwick	1
S. J. Cook b Rushworth	0	– c Di Venuto b Borthwick	5
A. Khan c Borthwick b B. W. Harmison	10	– not out	12
M. Ntini not out	2	– c Mustard b S. J. Harmison	13
L-b 7, w 4, n-b 4	15	L-b 7, n-b 2	9

1/0 (1) 2/10 (3) 3/127 (4) (93.4 overs) 424
4/141 (5) 5/247 (6) 6/289 (7) 7/354 (8)
8/354 (9) 9/410 (10) 10/424 (2)

1/34 (2) 2/34 (1) (49.5 overs) 162
3/71 (3) 4/97 (5)
5/121 (4) 6/124 (6) 7/127 (8)
8/135 (7) 9/137 (9) 10/162 (11)

S. J. Harmison 18–5–52–4; Rushworth 15–2–66–2; Claydon 21–1–106–0; B. W. Harmison 15.4–2–87–3; Blackwell 13–2–62–0; Stokes 1–0–11–0; Benkenstein 6–3–13–1; Borthwick 4–0–20–0. *Second Innings*—S. J. Harmison 11.5–2–39–2; Rushworth 10–1–36–2; Claydon 8–3–23–1; Blackwell 11–4–35–3; Borthwick 9–1–22–2.

Durham

M. J. Di Venuto b Ferley	67	– (2) c Khan b Azhar Mahmood	10
K. J. Coetzer lbw b Ntini	12	– (1) b Ntini	1
S. G. Borthwick c van Jaarsveld b Ntini	1	– b Khan	14
D. M. Benkenstein b Khan	114	– c van Jaarsveld b Ferley	49
I. D. Blackwell b Khan	17	– not out	53
B. A. Stokes not out	161	– not out	42
*†P. Mustard c Jones b Ntini	10		
B. W. Harmison c van Jaarsveld b Ntini	8		
M. E. Claydon c van Jaarsveld b Ntini	3		
C. Rushworth c Northeast b Khan	18		
S. J. Harmison c Jones b Azhar Mahmood	0		
L-b 5, w 2	7	L-b 1, n-b 2	3

1/22 (2) 2/26 (3) 3/144 (1) (119.4 overs) 418
4/165 (5) 5/308 (4) 6/327 (7)
7/356 (8) 8/374 (9) 9/417 (10)
10/418 (11)

1/7 (1) 2/19 (2) (4 wkts, 34 overs) 172
3/37 (3) 4/117 (4)

110 overs: 374-8

Khan 28–7–81–3; Ntini 29–8–84–5; Azhar Mahmood 24.4–3–66–1; Cook 14–2–64–0; Ferley 18–2–88–1; van Jaarsveld 5–0–27–0; Denly 1–0–3–0. *Second Innings*—Azhar Mahmood 9–0–35–1; Ntini 12–3–44–1; Khan 3–1–6–1; Ferley 8–0–54–1; van Jaarsveld 1–0–6–0; Denly 1–0–26–0.

Umpires: P. J. Hartley and T. E. Jesty.

At Chester-le-Street, May 24–25. KENT beat DURHAM by an innings and four runs.

KENT v NOTTINGHAMSHIRE

At Tunbridge Wells, June 4–7. Drawn. Kent 10pts, Nottinghamshire 9pts. Toss: Nottinghamshire.

A docile pitch and shortcomings in both bowling line-ups guaranteed a high-scoring draw. Kent's already weakened attack lost Khan, its spearhead, with a strained hamstring during his 20th over and, to ensure dominance of bat over ball, Swann, Sidebottom and Broad were all absent through various England commitments. The highly promising Hales fell within five runs of a second Championship hundred in three weeks, while Hussey, in his first match since his wedding in May, delighted a 2,500 crowd with a brisk fifty. An unbeaten century from Read kept Kent in the field almost until lunch on day two, whereupon Denly suffered a third successive first-innings duck at The Nevill (two were first-ballers). Kent struggled to produce a convincing innings until Stevens and Tredwell shared a ground-record sixth-wicket stand of 270. Playing straighter and more wisely than hitherto, Stevens cantered to his fourth century of the summer, missing a double by three. Then, as the game meandered towards a draw, Tredwell, on the ground where in 2007 he made his first century, dug in for his third. Almost forgotten amid the runs were five wickets for Adams.

Close of play: First day, Nottinghamshire 393-8 (Read 72, White 6); Second day, Kent 274-5 (Stevens 80, Tredwell 35); Third day, Kent 478-6 (Stevens 181, Coles 11).

Nottinghamshire

A. D. Hales c and b Bandara	95	– c sub (W. W. Lee) b Coles	13
S. R. Patel c Jones b Cook	10	– not out	76
M. A. Wagh b Jones b Cook	44	– b Tredwell	34
D. J. Hussey b Bandara	52	– b Bandara	22
S. J. Mullaney c Jones b Cook	1	– not out	48
A. D. Brown c Jones b Tredwell	39		
*†C. M. W. Read not out	112		
P. J. Franks lbw b Tredwell	17		
A. R. Adams b Cook	35		
G. G. White c Tredwell b Coles	29		
D. J. Pattinson c Denly b Bandara	5		
B 4, l-b 14, w 1, n-b 4	23	B 5, l-b 10, n-b 2	17

1/43 (2) 2/154 (3) 3/172 (1)   (124 overs) 462   1/16 (1)   (3 wkts dec, 62 overs) 210
4/173 (5) 5/242 (6) 6/266 (4)   2/121 (3) 3/150 (4)
7/317 (8) 8/386 (9) 9/444 (10)
10/462 (11)   110 overs: 406-8

Khan 19.5–3–77–0; Coles 6–0–37–1; Cook 22–2–85–4; Bandara 40.1–5–125–3; Tredwell 36–4–120–2. *Second Innings*—Coles 8–1–35–1; Cook 7–4–9–0; Bandara 25–7–63–1; Tredwell 22–1–88–1.

Kent

J. L. Denly c Hussey b Pattinson	0	S. J. Cook not out	26
*R. W. T. Key c Brown b Patel	56	A. Khan b Franks	5
†G. O. Jones c Hussey b Adams	37		
M. van Jaarsveld c Read b Adams	44	B 3, l-b 12, w 6, n-b 6	27
S. A. Northeast b Adams	12		
D. I. Stevens c Read b Adams	197	1/0 (1) 2/53 (3) 3/128 (4) (148.1 overs) 570
J. C. Tredwell c and b White	115	4/142 (5) 5/176 (2)
M. T. Coles b Adams	22	6/446 (7) 7/504 (8) 8/511 (6)
H. M. C. M. Bandara c Hales b Franks	29	9/564 (9) 10/570 (11) 110 overs: 412-5

Pattinson 21–5–89–1; Adams 31–2–106–5; White 23–3–104–1; Franks 28.1–6–75–2; Mullaney 5–0–33–0; Patel 37–6–129–1; Hussey 3–0–19–0.

Umpires: J. H. Evans and N. J. Llong.

At Canterbury, June 28–30. KENT drew with PAKISTANIS (see Pakistani tour section).

At Southampton, July 5–7. KENT lost to HAMPSHIRE by an innings and 111 runs.

At Taunton, July 20–23. KENT drew with SOMERSET.

KENT v ESSEX

At Canterbury, July 29–August 1. Kent won by 99 runs. Kent 24pts, Essex 4pts. Toss: Kent. County debut: B. E. McGain.

The game turned Kent's way on a flash of wicketkeeping brilliance by Geraint Jones on the fourth morning. With Essex 120 for three in pursuit of 277, he stood up to Cook to create pressure on Bopara. Cook got one to lift and leave and, as Bopara shifted his balance, Jones completed a sharp stumping, sparking a collapse of seven wickets for 57. Jones also contributed brightly with the bat, dismissed for 99 for the first time, adding 176 for the fourth wicket with van Jaarsveld, whose first Championship hundred of the season was unusually late in arriving. Bryce McGain, the 38-year-old Australian leg-spinner whose only Test appearance brought figures of none for 149, took five expensive wickets as he began his spell standing in for Danish Kaneria. Few expected Essex to challenge from 141 behind. But with Chambers off the field with a side strain, Andy Carter, on loan from Nottinghamshire, took the new ball and returned a maiden five-for. Kent had to rely on Azhar Mahmood, reluctant to play four-day cricket in the twilight of his career, but who thrived on a wearing pitch to confirm their only maximum-point win of the season.

Close of play: First day, Kent 360-6 (Tredwell 18, Khan 1); Second day, Essex 194-6 (Pettini 80, Masters 6); Third day, Essex 48-1 (Mickleburgh 19, Westley 20).

Kent

J. L. Denly c Foster b McGain	40	– c Foster b Carter	6
*R. W. T. Key c Mickleburgh b Chambers	13	– c Foster b Carter	0
S. A. Northeast c sub (G. W. Flower) b McGain	25	– c Foster b Masters	7
M. van Jaarsveld c Masters b McGain	106	– lbw b Walker	18
†G. O. Jones c Carter b McGain	99	– c Foster b Carter	4
D. I. Stevens c Phillips b Masters	34	– lbw b Carter	0
J. C. Tredwell c Foster b Carter	19	– c Bopara b Walker	40
A. Khan lbw b Masters	1	– (11) c Masters b Carter	0
Azhar Mahmood c sub (C. J. C. Wright) b Carter	28	– (8) lbw b Masters	19
H. M. C. M. Bandara not out	19	– b Walker	23
S. J. Cook c Foster b McGain	7	– (10) not out	7
B 1, l-b 17, w 3, n-b 8	29	B 4, l-b 3, n-b 4	11

1/26 (2) 2/82 (3) 3/106 (1)   (115.3 overs) 420
4/282 (4) 5/330 (5) 6/359 (6)
7/361 (7) 8/361 (8) 9/413 (9)
10/420 (11)   110 overs: 403-8

1/4 (2) 2/13 (1)   (47.4 overs) 135
3/25 (3) 4/36 (5)
5/36 (4) 6/40 (6) 7/68 (8)
8/114 (9) 9/133 (7) 10/135 (11)

Masters 29–7–62–2; Chambers 8–1–24–1; Carter 26–4–81–2; McGain 33.3–1–151–5; Phillips 16–1–65–0; Westley 3–0–19–0. *Second Innings*—Masters 16–6–34–2; Carter 17.4–5–40–5; Walker 8–1–35–3; McGain 6–0–19–0.

Essex

M. L. Pettini c Tredwell b Khan	88	– c Tredwell b Azhar Mahmood	4
J. C. Mickleburgh c Stevens b Khan	20	– b Azhar Mahmood	24
T. Westley c Tredwell b Cook	0	– c van Jaarsveld b Khan	25
M. J. Walker c Jones b Azhar Mahmood	10	– (5) lbw b Azhar Mahmood	35
*†J. S. Foster b Azhar Mahmood	41	– (6) run out	12
T. J. Phillips c Denly b Bandara	11	– (7) c van Jaarsveld b Tredwell	12
R. S. Bopara c Jones b Khan	2	– (4) st Jones b Cook	31
D. D. Masters lbw b Bandara	42	– b Azhar Mahmood	1
B. E. McGain c Jones b Tredwell	14	– not out	8
A. Carter not out	16	– (11) c Cook b Tredwell	11
M. A. Chambers c Tredwell b Bandara	6	– (10) b Azhar Mahmood	0
B 9, l-b 14, n-b 6	29	B 2, l-b 8, n-b 4	14

1/49 (2) 2/50 (3) 3/68 (4)   (102.2 overs) 279
4/141 (5) 5/176 (6) 6/183 (7)
7/226 (1) 8/257 (9) 9/257 (8) 10/279 (11)

1/12 (1) 2/58 (3)   (59.5 overs) 177
3/64 (2) 4/120 (4)
5/145 (5) 6/146 (6) 7/151 (8)
8/161 (7) 9/162 (10) 10/177 (11)

Khan 22–7–47–3; Azhar Mahmood 22–6–54–2; Stevens 10–5–13–0; Cook 16–7–35–1; Bandara 12.2–2–44–3; Tredwell 20–5–63–1. *Second Innings*—Azhar Mahmood 21–5–62–5; Khan 10–2–33–1; Cook 8–2–26–1; Stevens 1–1–0–0; Tredwell 17.5–3–40–2; Bandara 2–0–6–0.

Umpires: B. Dudleston and I. J. Gould.

KENT v SOMERSET

At Canterbury, August 3–6. Drawn. Kent 10pts, Somerset 10pts. Toss: Somerset.

Canterbury Week began with a match of fluctuating moods and fortunes, and one constant: the bat's domination. The last of five major innings, by Trescothick, led to a turgid conclusion. Somerset gained early impetus in a fourth-wicket stand of 253 between Suppiah (who received confirmation of permanent UK residency the previous day) and Hildreth, who moved to 997 first-class runs with his fifth century of the season. After wobbling against former colleague Phillips, Kent regrouped through Jones and van Jaarsveld. Jones's storming, career-best 178 featured three sixes in back-to-back overs from Kartik and Thomas. Somerset began the final day 146 ahead with seven wickets intact, but no agreement could be reached for an improvised run-chase. Trescothick contentedly batted through the last three sessions for his highest score since May 2007, angering Kent supporters into slow hand-claps and heckles. Once Tredwell had completed his five-for, Key showed his disapproval by bowling everyone except Cook, who had a finger injury. Key took his second and third first-class wickets, and the penultimate over had Denly keeping wicket to Jones's medium-pace. There was no lasting animosity: Jones later presented Trescothick, his former England teammate and lover of bangers, with a pack of sausages produced from hand-reared pigs at his smallholding in nearby Ash.

Close of play: First day, Somerset 363-7 (Kieswetter 26, Thomas 0); Second day, Kent 175-3 (van Jaarsveld 70, Jones 49); Third day, Somerset 138-3 (Trescothick 61, Hildreth 27).

Somerset

*M. E. Trescothick c Stevens b Azhar Mahmood	5	– not out	188
A. V. Suppiah c Stevens b Tredwell	125	– lbw b Tredwell	28
Z. de Bruyn c Jones b Cook	23	– c Bandara b Tredwell	14
J. C. Butler b Khan	0	– c Denly b Tredwell	0
J. C. Hildreth c Key b Tredwell	151	– b Tredwell	32
†C. Kieswetter b Jones b Azhar Mahmood	26	– c and b Tredwell	58
P. D. Trego run out	8	– c Tredwell b Key	37
B. J. Phillips c Tredwell b Azhar Mahmood	14	– c Tredwell b Key	14
A. C. Thomas c van Jaarsveld b Khan	11	– not out	0
M. Kartik not out	2		
C. M. Willoughby c Bandara b Khan	4		
B 7, l-b 2, n-b 2	11	B 2, l-b 4, w 1, n-b 4, p 5	16

1/6 (1) 2/50 (3) 3/59 (4)   (103.4 overs) 380
4/312 (2) 5/317 (5) 6/333 (7) 7/363 (8)
8/366 (6) 9/376 (9) 10/380 (11)

1/78 (2)   (7 wkts dec, 127.2 overs) 387
2/94 (3) 3/94 (4) 4/147 (5)
5/247 (6) 6/334 (7) 7/374 (8)

Azhar Mahmood 22–7–65–3; Khan 26.4–4–89–3; Cook 8.5–3–25–1; Stevens 18.1–5–64–0; Bandara 16–2–72–0; Tredwell 12–3–56–2. *Second Innings*—Azhar Mahmood 21–2–60–0; Khan 23–5–74–0; Tredwell 42–9–95–5; Bandara 13–0–60–0; Stevens 7–2–16–0; Key 11.2–3–31–2; Denly 2–0–5–0; van Jaarsveld 4–0–25–0; Northeast 3–1–2–0; Jones 1–0–8–0.

Kent

J. L. Denly c Kieswetter b Phillips	8	H. M. C. M. Bandara c Trego b Phillips	0	
*R. W. T. Key lbw b Phillips	17	A. Khan lbw b Kartik	11	
S. A. Northeast lbw b Phillips	18	S. J. Cook not out	0	
M. van Jaarsveld lbw b Phillips	71	B 9, l-b 16, n-b 4	29	
†G. O. Jones lbw b Thomas	178			
D. I. Stevens c and b Trego	33	1/9 (1) 2/46 (2) 3/47 (3)	(98.2 overs)	372
J. C. Tredwell c Butler b Kartik	7	4/176 (4) 5/231 (6) 6/254 (7)		
Azhar Mahmood lbw b Willoughby	0	7/259 (8) 8/260 (9) 9/350 (10) 10/372 (5)		

Willoughby 27–2–93–1; Phillips 28–8–72–5; Thomas 13.2–2–72–1; Trego 11–1–58–1; Kartik 18–4–50–2; de Bruyn 1–0–2–0.

Umpires: M. J. D. Bodenham and R. A. Kettleborough.

KENT v LANCASHIRE

At Canterbury, August 18–21. Lancashire won by 121 runs. Lancashire 21pts, Kent 4pts. Toss: Lancashire.

Chapple and Keedy shared 15 wickets as Lancashire won at Canterbury for only the second time since 1936. Kent dropped their overseas spinner Malinga Bandara, recalled Alex Blake, and included Amjad Khan for what proved his final game for the club; they also became the latest attack to discover that Sajid Mahmood had worked on his batting. Once an unpretentious tailender, he struck three sixes in a robust fifth Championship half-century of the summer, swelling Lancashire's score. Denly, clearly out of form, grafted for 69, but the tail crumbled to Keedy, causing Kent to miss a second batting point by one run. Key's bowling resources may not have been Test-class – he opened with Stevens's little outswingers following his three successive wicket-maidens in the first innings – but Chanderpaul still delighted in the match's only century, chipping Tredwell nonchalantly over the infield. Kent never promised to chase 339, even in four sessions: seven batsmen were out on the last morning and then, nine balls after lunch, Cook swept to midwicket to give Keedy his eighth victim.

Close of play: First day, Kent 53-2 (Denly 32, van Jaarsveld 3); Second day, Lancashire 103-3 (Chanderpaul 23, Croft 38); Third day, Kent 84-2 (Northeast 14, van Jaarsveld 21).

Lancashire

P. J. Horton c Jones b Stevens	16	– (2) lbw b Stevens	29
T. C. Smith c Coles b Stevens	32	– (1) lbw b Stevens	5
M. J. Chilton c van Jaarsveld b Khan	0	– lbw b Cook	7
S. Chanderpaul c Jones b Stevens	0	– lbw b Cook	120
S. J. Croft c Blake b Cook	65	– c Jones b Cook	43
G. D. Cross lbw b Cook	30	– b Coles	50
†L. D. Sutton c sub (P. D. Edwards) b Coles	13	– c Stevens b Coles	9
*G. Chapple c van Jaarsveld b Tredwell	1	– st Jones b Tredwell	5
S. I. Mahmood c Tredwell b Khan	60	– not out	41
K. W. Hogg not out	20	– b Cook	0
G. Keedy c Tredwell b Coles	5	– c Coles b Tredwell	0
L-b 16, n-b 8	24	B 5, l-b 5, n-b 2	12

1/55 (2) 2/56 (1) 3/56 (4) 4/56 (3)   (76 overs) 266
5/115 (6) 6/152 (7) 7/157 (8)
8/219 (5) 9/242 (9) 10/266 (11)

1/19 (1) 2/36 (2)   (98.2 overs) 321
3/52 (3) 4/130 (5)
5/219 (6) 6/233 (7) 7/246 (8)
8/294 (4) 9/294 (10) 10/321 (11)

Khan 19–6–61–2; Cook 15–2–65–2; Stevens 14–5–33–3; Coles 12–1–35–2; Tredwell 16–2–56–1. *Second Innings*—Khan 20–4–59–0; Stevens 20–6–55–2; Cook 20–5–62–4; Tredwell 25.2–2–99–2; van Jaarsveld 2–1–1–0; Coles 11–1–35–2.

Kent

J. L. Denly b Chapple	69	– b Chapple	12
*R. W. T. Key c Smith b Chapple	8	– st Sutton b Keedy	30
S. A. Northeast lbw b Chapple	0	– lbw b Smith	18
M. van Jaarsveld c Cross b Hogg	34	– c Horton b Chapple	30
†G. O. Jones b Chapple	10	– c Sutton b Smith	0
D. I. Stevens b Keedy	28	– c Sutton b Chapple	3
A. J. Blake lbw b Keedy	28	– b Smith	10
J. C. Tredwell b Mahmood	20	– st Sutton b Keedy	36
M. T. Coles c Chilton b Keedy	24	– c Mahmood b Keedy	51
S. J. Cook c Chanderpaul b Keedy	8	– c Cross b Keedy	10
A. Khan not out	1	– not out	0
B 3, l-b 8, n-b 8	19	B 7, l-b 6, n-b 4	17

1/29 (2) 2/35 (3) 3/111 (4)   (81.5 overs) 249
4/137 (5) 5/142 (1) 6/181 (7)
7/212 (8) 8/218 (6) 9/230 (10) 10/249 (9)

1/28 (1) 2/56 (2)   (57.3 overs) 217
3/97 (4) 4/97 (3)
5/100 (5) 6/100 (6) 7/118 (7)
8/190 (9) 9/214 (8) 10/217 (10)

Chapple 23–6–45–4; Mahmood 22–3–90–1; Smith 8–2–22–0; Hogg 9–2–32–1; Keedy 19.5–9–49–4. *Second Innings*—Chapple 17–5–39–3; Mahmood 12–2–48–0; Smith 12–2–44–3; Hogg 5–1–15–0; Keedy 10.3–3–53–4; Croft 1–0–5–0.

Umpires: R. K. Illingworth and R. T. Robinson.

At Birmingham, August 31–September 2. KENT lost to WARWICKSHIRE by 95 runs.

KENT v HAMPSHIRE

At Canterbury, September 7–10. Hampshire won by 130 runs. Hampshire 20pts, Kent 3pts. Toss: Hampshire.

Five minutes decided the fates of these two counties. Hampshire, seven points ahead of Kent going into the match, knew victory would confirm their place in Division One, and leave Kent and Warwickshire to scramble over the second relegation spot in the final round of fixtures. With the top five all contributing in their second innings, Hampshire built their lead to an impregnable 377 by the time Cork declared an hour into the fourth day. He could scarcely have cut it finer. With Kent 229 for six in the final hour, a draw, inconclusive to both sides' futures, was favourite. But Hampshire would not give up and, at 5.25 p.m., with the allocated overs already bowled and the close just five minutes away, Tomlinson had last man Cook held at short leg. A third successive defeat left Kent, who had now lost seven matches in a season for the first time since 1995, reliant upon others to escape. Yet their start was encouraging. Owing to Bandara's best figures of the season, Hampshire scored just a single batting point, and Kent's openers were taking guard before the first day was out. Rain delayed the resumption until after lunch the following day but, on a decent pitch, Cork and Tomlinson needed less than two sessions to rout their opponents. Hampshire then set about ensuring their safety against an impoverished, spin-heavy attack; for the fifth innings in a row, Stevens took the new ball.

Close of play: First day, Kent 15-1 (Denly 2, Key 7); Second day, Hampshire 16-0 (Carberry 7, Adams 9); Third day, Hampshire 272-6 (Vince 38, Cork 0).

Hampshire

M. A. Carberry c Jones b Stevens	15	– lbw b Bandara	56
J. H. K. Adams c Jones b Tredwell	84	– c Bates b Tredwell	52
P. J. Hughes c van Jaarsveld b Tredwell	1	– lbw b Tredwell	38
L. A. Dawson c van Jaarsveld b Bandara	9	– c Tredwell b Stevens	50
J. M. Vince c van Jaarsveld b Coles	36	– not out	68
S. M. Ervine c Northeast b Cook	11	– c Tredwell b Stevens	0
†A. M. Bates b Cook	1	– c Jones b Stevens	26
*D. G. Cork lbw b Bandara	20	– lbw b Bandara	14
C. P. Wood c van Jaarsveld b Bandara	8	– c and b Tredwell	24
J. A. Tomlinson not out	2	– c Northeast b Bandara	12
D. R. Briggs lbw b Bandara	8		
L-b 8, w 1	9	B 4, l-b 9, w 2	15

1/37 (1) 2/44 (3) 3/68 (4)   (81.5 overs) 204   1/92 (2)   (9 wkts dec, 103.2 overs) 355
4/116 (5) 5/134 (6) 6/136 (7)   2/137 (1) 3/181 (3)
7/180 (8) 8/192 (2) 9/194 (9) 10/204 (11)   4/225 (4) 5/225 (6) 6/271 (7)
                                          7/307 (8) 8/342 (9) 9/355 (10)

Stevens 19–8–31–1; Coles 9–1–28–1; Cook 13–3–46–2; Tredwell 24–8–49–2; Bandara 16.5–3–42–4. *Second Innings*—Stevens 15–3–51–3; Coles 19–3–78–0; Bandara 28.2–2–99–4; Tredwell 30–10–84–2; Cook 6–1–20–0; van Jaarsveld 5–0–10–0.

Kent

S. A. Northeast b Cork	0	– lbw b Tomlinson	71
J. L. Denly b Ervine	42	– c Bates b Cork	10
*R. W. T. Key lbw b Cork	19	– lbw b Briggs	1
M. van Jaarsveld b Cork	41	– c Vince b Briggs	5
†G. O. Jones lbw b Briggs	8	– lbw b Cork	21
D. I. Stevens c Bates b Tomlinson	13	– b Cork	45
A. J. Blake b Tomlinson	0	– c Vince b Briggs	46
J. C. Tredwell c Carberry b Ervine	18	– c Bates b Briggs	14
H. M. C. M. Bandara lbw b Tomlinson	4	– (10) not out	9
M. T. Coles c Bates b Tomlinson	9	– c Briggs b Cork	1
S. J. Cook not out	11	– c Adams b Tomlinson	2
B 8, l-b 2, w 1, n-b 6	17	B 8, l-b 8, n-b 6	22

1/1 (1) 2/41 (3) 3/90 (2) 4/107 (5)   (68.4 overs) 182   1/15 (2) 2/31 (3)   (86 overs) 247
5/135 (6) 6/135 (7) 7/139 (4)   3/39 (4) 4/78 (5)
8/150 (9) 9/160 (10) 10/182 (8)   5/159 (6) 6/191 (1) 7/229 (7)
                                          8/235 (8) 9/244 (9) 10/247 (11)

Cork 22–8–44–3; Tomlinson 21–4–59–4; Briggs 8–2–23–1; Wood 5–1–11–0; Ervine 12.4–4–35–2. *Second Innings*—Cork 18–4–43–4; Tomlinson 23–9–41–2; Briggs 28–3–93–4; Wood 5–0–28–0; Ervine 5–1–13–0; Carberry 7–1–13–0.

Umpires: R. J. Bailey and N. G. C. Cowley.

At Leeds, September 13–16. KENT beat YORKSHIRE by four wickets. *Despite victory, Kent are relegated by Warwickshire's win at Hampshire.*

LANCASHIRE

A glimpse of what might have been

ANDY WILSON

It was quite a climax to a season that might otherwise have been best remembered for the arrival of The Point, the huge red hospitality building that dwarfed Old Trafford's old pavilion. The last first-class match at the ground in its familiar orientation, with the pitches running west–east from the Stretford End towards the tram station, ended with the newly crowned county champions spraying champagne on the outfield on a sunny September afternoon.

But after three days of frustration – kept in the pavilion briefly by the glare of the evening sun, which should no longer be a problem when the square is turned, but mostly by the persistent Mancunian rain that unfortunately will – it was Nottinghamshire's players who celebrated their fourth Championship since 1981, while Lancashire's wait for an outright title entered its 77th year.

A second consecutive fourth place, with one more win and seven more points, represented a solid achievement, considering the withdrawal of Sri Lankan captain Kumar Sangakkara before the season's start, serious injuries to Gary Keedy and Stephen Moore, plus confirmation of the end of Andrew Flintoff's career. But the usual cluster of if-onlys convinced Lancashire's coach Peter Moores and captain Glen Chapple that they might have been in contention with Nottinghamshire.

They could argue that rain denied them good chances of three more wins, at home to Kent and away to Yorkshire and Durham. In addition, two of the three defeats – the most Lancashire had suffered in five Championship seasons – were in tight games that hung in the balance for long periods. But Moores and Chapple were honest enough to concede that, at home to Durham on a dusty Old Trafford turner, and at Trent Bridge, when a combination of rain and the title situation forced Lancashire to dangle a tasty carrot, a youthful team's limitations were exposed.

As so often in recent years, the problems began with the top order. Paul Horton played in all 16 Championship games but managed only 634 runs from 30 innings. Moore, recruited from Worcestershire, fared no better, averaging 25 with only two fifties in the first nine matches, before he seriously dislocated his shoulder diving in the outfield in a draining T20 quarter-final loss to Essex.

Mark Chilton grafted hard for a few handy half-centuries but was unable to reach three figures and, although Tom Smith continued to open when required, he looked much happier scoring a fine unbeaten hundred at Headingley from No. 6. Luke Sutton was also thrust up the order, against Somerset at Old Trafford in May, and responded with an excellent century, but he too returned to more familiar territory when he made another at Riverside. At the end of the year he re-signed for Derbyshire as captain, giving Gareth Cross the opportunity to become the permanent wicketkeeper.

Graham Morris

Steven Croft

Lancashire had hoped to build their team around Sangakkara for most of the season but, when Sri Lanka accepted additional commitments, they were forced into a hasty rethink on their overseas players. Ashwell Prince gave good value until the end of May. But Simon Katich struggled in the Twenty20 qualifiers, and Lancashire were relieved when the predictably excellent Shivnarine Chanderpaul replaced him in July. Nathan McCullum made useful but unspectacular Twenty20 contributions, and Daren Powell, the Jamaican seamer signed as a Kolpak to add depth and experience, was a disaster. He took seven wickets in four Championship matches, and his embarrassingly bad fielding in a floodlit CB40 game against Sussex compelled the club to cut short his stay.

By that stage, Lancashire were using the 40-over tournament to bring on their younger players, their hopes having disappeared with four defeats in their first six matches. The small step forward in the Championship was undermined by deterioration in both one-day competitions; the Twenty20 defeat at Chelmsford followed a less convincing qualification than in 2009.

Bizarrely, Lancashire chose to go into that quarter-final with three left-arm spinners, a decision that backfired on the night but reflected a real strength. Stephen Parry's consistent one-day excellence was recognised by a call-up for England Lions, and Simon Kerrigan seized his opportunity when Keedy fractured his collarbone pre-season, making significant contributions in three of his 13 Championship games.

Perhaps inspired by the extra competition, Keedy bowled as well as ever when he returned for the last seven matches. But his 31 wickets at 22 were eclipsed by his captain's 52 at less than 20. It was another outstanding season for Chapple, now 36; he finished it 17th on the list of the county's all-time wicket-takers, with 743, and needing only 55 runs to complete 7,000, a double achieved by four previous Lancashire all-rounders.

With continuing uncertainty over the cost of ground redevelopment – chief executive Jim Cumbes predicted the club's financial losses for 2010 would be "the biggest in county cricket" – Lancashire must depend more on home-grown players. Steven Croft made good progress in all formats, and was the leading Championship run-scorer with 883; Kyle Hogg finally earned his cap, nine seasons after his debut; and there was a significant transformation in Sajid Mahmood, from gifted but erratic youngster to a senior pro who could be relied on to lead the attack with Chapple and to score handy runs. He put it down to a simple change in approach: "I've started to watch the ball."

With the new square settling in during 2011, five of Lancashire's home Championship matches were scheduled for Liverpool, with visits to Southport and Blackpool before returning to Old Trafford in September. One-day games were to continue as normal at headquarters.

LANCASHIRE RESULTS

All first-class matches – Played 16: Won 5, Lost 3, Drawn 8. Abandoned 1.
County Championship matches – Played 16: Won 5, Lost 3, Drawn 8.

LV= County Championship, 4th in Division 1;
Friends Provident T20, q-f; Clydesdale Bank 40, 4th in Group A.

COUNTY CHAMPIONSHIP AVERAGES, BATTING AND FIELDING

Cap		M	I	NO	R	HS	100s	50s	Avge	Ct/St
2010	S. Chanderpaul§	8	14	1	698	120	2	5	53.69	2
	A. G. Prince§	7	13	2	450	115	1	4	40.90	7
2010	S. J. Croft†	16	26	3	883	93	0	8	38.39	13
2010	K. W. Hogg...........	9	13	4	301	88	0	2	33.44	3
2007	S. I. Mahmood†	15	20	2	564	72	0	5	31.33	2
2002	M. J. Chilton........	16	29	4	750	69	0	4	30.00	6
	G. D. Cross	7	11	1	290	100*	1	1	29.00	12
2007	L. D. Sutton	13	21	2	530	118	2	0	27.89	37/5
2010	T. C. Smith†	14	25	3	576	128	2	2	26.18	14
1994	G. Chapple	14	22	6	403	54*	0	2	25.18	4
	S. C. Moore..........	9	17	0	426	61	0	2	25.05	6
2007	P. J. Horton........	16	30	2	634	123	1	3	22.64	19
2000	G. Keedy............	7	9	2	89	34	0	0	12.71	0
	D. B. Powell¶........	4	4	1	29	16*	0	0	9.66	0
2003	J. M. Anderson†‡	4	5	1	35	25*	0	0	8.75	0
	S. C. Kerrigan	13	15	5	45	16*	0	0	4.50	3

Also batted: K. R. Brown† (2 matches) 21, 0, 4; S. M. Katich§ (1 match) 32, 8 (1 ct); L. J. Procter† (2 matches) 13, 19, 32.

† *Born in Lancashire.*   ‡ *ECB contract.*   § *Official overseas player.*   ¶ *Other non-England-qualified player.*

BOWLING

	O	M	R	W	BB	5W/i	Avge
G. Chapple................	372.4	89	1,027	52	5-27	2	19.75
J. M. Anderson.............	130.5	39	345	16	6-44	1	21.56
G. Keedy.................	246.5	43	688	31	7-68	2	22.19
T. C. Smith..............	279.5	58	913	32	6-94	1	28.53
S. C. Kerrigan	319	66	967	30	6-74	3	32.23
K. W. Hogg	202.2	48	650	20	4-53	0	32.50
S. I. Mahmood	348	54	1,263	33	5-55	1	38.27

Also bowled: S. J. Croft 14–2–51–1; D. B. Powell 99–16–343–7; L. J. Procter 7.3–0–47–1.

LEADING CB40 AVERAGES (100 runs/4 wickets)

Batting	Runs	HS	Avge	S-R	Ct/St	Bowling	W	BB	Avge	E-R
S. C. Moore....	335	118	55.83	107.71	1	S. I. Mahmood...	11	4-40	23.18	5.54
S. J. Croft	425	93*	53.12	96.81	4	L. A. Procter	7	3-29	24.14	6.03
A. G. Prince ...	207	102*	51.75	97.18	1	G. Keedy	9	4-41	24.77	4.95
K. R. Brown ...	230	65*	46.00	84.24	2	T. C. Smith	13	3-49	26.07	6.16
P. J. Horton ...	371	78*	41.22	81.18	5	K. W. Hogg	12	2-27	30.25	5.82
L. D. Sutton....	119	47	29.75	68.39	7/3	S. D. Parry	11	2-18	42.81	5.36

LEADING FPT20 AVERAGES (100 runs/18 overs)

Batting	Runs	HS	Avge	S-R	Ct/St	Bowling	W	BB	Avge	E-R
S. C. Moore....	331	83*	25.46	**152.53**	9	N. L. McCullum .	11	3-31	29.54	**6.50**
G. D. Cross....	184	65*	20.44	**138.34**	7/2	S. C. Kerrigan ...	11	3-17	24.00	**6.60**
S. J. Croft	394	88	26.26	**127.92**	13	S. D. Parry......	26	4-28	16.42	**7.11**
N. L. McCullum	155	32*	17.22	**124.00**	5	T. C. Smith	13	3-12	23.53	**7.34**
T. C. Smith	543	92*	36.20	**119.60**	9	S. I. Mahmood...	23	4-21	18.69	**8.11**
S. M. Katich ...	185	41*	26.42	**117.83**	5	G. Chapple......	13	3-36	30.53	**8.66**

FIRST-CLASS COUNTY RECORDS

Highest score for	424	A. C. MacLaren v Somerset at Taunton	1895
Highest score against	315*	T. W. Hayward (Surrey) at The Oval............	1898
Leading run-scorer	34,222	E. Tyldesley (avge 45.20)	1909–1936
Best bowling for	10-46	W. Hickton v Hampshire at Manchester	1870
Best bowling against	10-40	G. O. B. Allen (Middlesex) at Lord's	1929
Leading wicket-taker	1,816	J. B. Statham (avge 15.12)...................	1950–1968
Highest total for	863	v Surrey at The Oval	1990
Highest total against	707-9 dec	by Surrey at The Oval	1990
Lowest total for	25	v Derbyshire at Manchester..................	1871
Lowest total against	22	by Glamorgan at Liverpool	1924

LIST A COUNTY RECORDS

Highest score for	162*	A. R. Crook v Buckinghamshire at Wormsley	2005
Highest score against	186*	C. G. Greenidge (West Indians) at Liverpool	1984
Leading run-scorer	11,969	N. H. Fairbrother (avge 41.84).	1982–2002
Best bowling for	6-10	C. E. H. Croft v Scotland at Manchester	1982
Best bowling against	8-26	K. D. Boyce (Essex) at Manchester	1971
Leading wicket-taker	480	J. Simmons (avge 25.75)....................	1969–1989
Highest total for	381-3	v Hertfordshire at Radlett....................	1999
Highest total against	343-6	by Surrey at The Oval	1994
Lowest total for	59	v Worcestershire at Worcester................	1963
Lowest total against	52	by Minor Counties at Lakenham	1998

TWENTY20 RECORDS

Highest score for	102*	L. Vincent v Derbyshire at Manchester..........	2008
Highest score against	108*	I. J. Harvey (Yorkshire) at Leeds...............	2004
Leading run-scorer	1,131	M. B. Loye (avge 33.26)	2003–2009
Best bowling for	4-12	A. Flintoff v Durham at Chester-le-Street	2008
Best bowling against	5-21	J. Allenby (Leicestershire) at Manchester	2008
Leading wicket-taker	**51**	**S. I. Mahmood** (avge 22.23)...................	**2003–2010**
Highest total for	220-5	v Derbyshire at Derby	2009
Highest total against	198-5	by Nottinghamshire at Nottingham	2005
Lowest total for	91	v Derbyshire at Manchester..................	2003
Lowest total against	**88**	**by Northamptonshire at Manchester**	**2010**

ADDRESS

County Cricket Ground, Old Trafford, Manchester M16 0PX (0161 282 4000; **email** enquiries@lccc.co.uk). **Website** www.lccc.co.uk

OFFICIALS

Captain G. Chapple
Director of cricket M. Watkinson
Head coach P. Moores
President J. Livingstone
Chairman M. A. Cairns

Chief executive J. Cumbes
Chairman, cricket committee G. Ogden
Head groundsman M. Merchant
Scorer A. West; D. M. White

At Durham, April 3–5. DURHAM MCCU v LANCASHIRE. Abandoned.

LANCASHIRE v WARWICKSHIRE

At Manchester, April 15–18. Lancashire won by 121 runs. Lancashire 21 pts, Warwickshire 5 pts. Toss: Warwickshire. First-class debut: S. C. Kerrigan. County debut: S. C. Moore.

Simon Kerrigan returned the best figures by a Championship debutant for Lancashire since Australian Mick Malone's seven for 88 in 1979 to condemn Warwickshire to defeat. A 20-year-old left-arm spinner from Preston, Kerrigan took five of the six wickets that fell in the space of 16 overs on the final morning, before a stand between last man Imran Tahir and Westwood, who carried his bat (only the second Warwickshire captain to do so since 1907, after Nick Knight – deputising for Brian Lara – in 1998). Kerrigan bowled strikingly well but was helped by some brainless batting. Lancashire had been in trouble at 14 for four on the first morning, and again at 113 for six in their second innings – every morning saw a rush of wickets, usually to swing – but were twice rescued by middle and lower-order resistance led by Croft and Chapple. Mahmood's 52 in 41 balls played a crucial role as he and Chapple shared a last-wicket stand of 77 that extended Warwickshire's target from 242 to 319.

Close of play: First day, Warwickshire 13-1 (Westwood 9, N. S. Tahir 0); Second day, Lancashire 84-2 (Moore 43, Anderson 4); Third day, Warwickshire 52-3 (Westwood 24, Troughton 6).

Lancashire

T. C. Smith c Bell b Woakes	0	– c Ambrose b Carter	7
S. C. Moore c Bell b Woakes	6	– lbw b Carter	43
P. J. Horton c Trott b Woakes	2	– c Clarke b Woakes	26
A. G. Prince c N. S. Tahir b Carter	82	– (5) c Bell b Carter	0
M. J. Chilton c Bell b Carter	3	– (6) c Ambrose b Woakes	0
S. J. Croft c Chopra b N. S. Tahir	64	– (7) c Trott b Carter	56
†L. D. Sutton c Troughton b Trott	33	– (8) c Trott b N. S. Tahir	33
*G. Chapple not out	54	– (9) not out	53
J. M. Anderson b Trott	0	– (4) b Carter	10
S. C. Kerrigan c Chopra b Imran Tahir	3	– lbw b Imran Tahir	2
S. I. Mahmood c Clarke b Carter	0	– c Chopra b Imran Tahir	52
B 1, l-b 1, n-b 4	6	B 9, l-b 12, w 4, n-b 12	37

1/0 (1) 2/8 (3) 3/9 (2) 4/14 (5)   (85.4 overs) 253   1/16 (1) 2/70 (3)   (91.5 overs) 319
5/147 (6) 6/168 (4) 7/227 (7)   3/88 (2) 4/98 (5)
8/227 (9) 9/232 (10) 10/253 (11)   5/103 (6) 6/113 (4) 7/197 (7)
8/215 (8) 9/242 (10) 10/319 (11)

Woakes 20–7–44–3; N. S. Tahir 16–4–57–1; Carter 19.4–2–64–3; Imran Tahir 23–4–66–1; Trott 7–2–20–2. *Second Innings*—Carter 26–10–79–5; Woakes 25.7–7–73–2; N. S. Tahir 14–2–45–1; Imran Tahir 25.5–2–95–2; Trott 1–0–6–0.

Warwickshire

*I. J. Westwood b Chapple	15	– not out	82
V. Chopra b Anderson	1	– lbw b Chapple	6
N. S. Tahir b Chapple	4	– (10) lbw b Kerrigan	0
I. R. Bell c Chilton b Kerrigan	47	– (3) lbw b Mahmood	9
I. J. L. Trott c Sutton b Anderson	0	– (4) lbw b Smith	6
J. O. Troughton c Horton b Smith	44	– (5) c Prince b Kerrigan	39
R. Clarke b Mahmood	43	– (6) st Sutton b Kerrigan	7
†T. R. Ambrose c Sutton b Kerrigan	9	– (7) lbw b Kerrigan	0
C. R. Woakes c Moore b Smith	29	– (8) c Horton b Kerrigan	0
N. M. Carter run out	19	– (9) c Prince b Smith	0
Imran Tahir not out	8	– c Prince b Mahmood	36
B 8, l-b 18, w 1, n-b 8	35	B 10, l-b 2	12

1/8 (2) 2/26 (1) 3/27 (3) 4/28 (5)   (77 overs) 254   1/8 (2) 2/24 (3)   (69.5 overs) 197
5/138 (4) 6/162 (8) 7/202 (7)   3/34 (4) 4/99 (5) 5/122 (6)
8/239 (10) 9/239 (6) 10/254 (9)   6/122 (7) 7/128 (8) 8/129 (9)
9/134 (10) 10/197 (11)

In the first innings Troughton, when 44, retired ill at 132 and resumed at 239–8.

Anderson 20–5–62–2; Chapple 15–1–50–2; Mahmood 16–2–48–1; Smith 8–1–24–2; Kerrigan 18–4–44–2. *Second Innings*—Anderson 15–7–27–0; Chapple 3–1–7–1; Mahmood 18.5–3–65–2; Smith 14–6–27–2; Kerrigan 17–2–43–5; Croft 2–0–16–0.

Umpires: R. T. Robinson and G. Sharp.

At Chelmsford, April 21–23. LANCASHIRE beat ESSEX by eight wickets.

LANCASHIRE v KENT

At Manchester, April 27–30. Drawn. Lancashire 9pts, Kent 6pts (after 1pt penalty). Toss: Kent. County debut: M. Ntini.

Rain ended Lancashire's hopes of a third consecutive win after Stevens and Coles staved off a rout on the second afternoon. Kent had sunk to 97 for seven, still 74 short of avoiding the follow-on, after a lively pitch was skilfully exploited by the home seamers; Chapple reached 700 first-class wickets for Lancashire when opposing captain Key was caught behind. But Stevens, who had already eclipsed a wholehearted performance by Ntini to record the best return in Lancashire's innings, added a resilient 92 with Coles, and batted with intelligent aggression for his 18th first-class century. Only 38.5 overs were possible on the last two days. Ntini bowled 21 overs on the first day, less than 24 hours after his arrival in England to join Kent, but he was frustrated by a high-class century from his Warriors team-mate Prince and a near miss from the consistent Croft. He made a less welcome contribution to Kent's slow over-rate, which cost them a point.

Close of play: First day, Lancashire 317-9 (Kerrigan 1, Powell 5,); Second day, Lancashire 68-3 (Prince 8, Chilton 6); Third day, Lancashire 177-3 (Prince 71, Chilton 52).

Lancashire

T. C. Smith b Ntini	7	– c Khan b Khan	2
S. C. Moore b Khan	0	– b Ntini	38
P. J. Horton b Stevens	15	– c Stevens b Ntini	10
A. G. Prince run out	115	– not out	71
M. J. Chilton c van Jaarsveld b Ntini	11	– not out	52
S. J. Croft c Hockley b Stevens	93		
†L. D. Sutton c Jones b van Jaarsveld	14		
*G. Chapple c Khan b Stevens	27		
S. I. Mahmood c van Jaarsveld b Stevens	4		
S. C. Kerrigan not out	3		
D. B. Powell c Denly b Ntini	5		
B 8, l-b 10, w 2, n-b 6	26	B 4	4

1/12 (1) 2/12 (2) 3/53 (3) 4/86 (5) (97.3 overs) 320   1/9 (1) (3 wkts dec, 43 overs) 177
5/230 (4) 6/255 (7) 7/303 (8)   2/42 (3) 3/54 (2)
8/307 (9) 9/310 (6) 10/320 (11)

Khan 17–2–67–1; Ntini 21.3–5–46–3; Cook 13–5–44–0; Stevens 20–4–44–4; Coles 10–0–49–0; van Jaarsveld 12–1–38–1; Hockley 4–0–14–0. *Second Innings*—Ntini 13–6–31–2; Khan 11–2–67–1; Stevens 7–3–23–0; Cook 6–0–23–0; Coles 2–1–10–0; van Jaarsveld 2–0–3–0; Hockley 2–0–16–0.

Kent

J. L. Denly c Sutton b Mahmood	14	– b Mahmood	10
*R. W. T. Key c Sutton b Chapple	5	– not out	19
†G. O. Jones c Sutton b Chapple	25	– c Horton b Mahmood	1
M. van Jaarsveld c Kerrigan b Chapple	1		
S. A. Northeast c Prince b Smith	13		
D. I. Stevens not out	101		
J. B. Hockley c Sutton b Smith	9		
S. J. Cook c Croft b Chapple	0		
M. T. Coles c Croft b Mahmood	33	– (4) not out	10
A. Khan lbw b Mahmood	0		
M. Ntini c Chilton b Mahmood	0		
B 12	12	P 5	5

1/19 (2) 2/23 (1) 3/26 (4) 4/53 (5) (60.5 overs) 213
5/64 (3) 6/96 (7) 7/97 (8) 8/189 (9)
9/205 (10) 10/213 (11)

1/22 (1) (2 wkts, 11.5 overs) 45
2/28 (3)

Chapple 16–4–45–3; Mahmood 18.5–4–55–5; Smith 13–2–49–2; Powell 12–3–51–0; Kerrigan 1–0–1–0. *Second Innings*—Chapple 6–0–19–0; Mahmood 5.5–1–21–2.

Umpires: N. L. Bainton and N. J. Llong.

LANCASHIRE v SOMERSET

At Manchester, May 4–7. Drawn. Lancashire 8pts, Somerset 10pts. Toss: Lancashire.

Notable centuries for Sutton and Trego were the highlights of a match that Somerset could have won without lengthy interruptions on two days out of four. Lancashire chose to bat, but Wright reduced them to 27 for three before Sutton, relishing his promotion to open, grafted his first century in three seasons, ending a run of 35 Championship innings without even a fifty. Somerset slipped to 157 for five although the Lancashire attack was missing Mahmood, who had damaged his calf hitting 64 from 76 balls. Then Trego joined Hildreth and struck 108 out of a stand of 186. His eighth century, but first outside Somerset, came off 83 balls – the most rapid of the summer so far, after he scored the fastest of 2009 in 54. Trego was dropped on 22 and 40, and Lancashire were in danger of paying for those misses when Thomas had them at 100 for four one ball after lunch on the last day. But Croft's sixth half-century in seven first-class innings steered them to safety.

Close of play: First day, Somerset 14-1 (Trescothick 4); Second day, Somerset 155-4 (Hildreth 13, Buttler 18); Third day, Lancashire 32-0 (Sutton 25, Moore 7).

Lancashire

†L. D. Sutton c Buttler b de Bruyn	118	– b Thomas	38
S. C. Moore c Trego b Wright	4	– b Thomas	31
P. J. Horton c Buttler b Wright	2	– b Thomas	25
A. G. Prince lbw b Wright	2	– c Buttler b Thomas	3
M. J. Chilton lbw b Thomas	41	– c Trescothick b Munday	16
S. J. Croft c de Bruyn b Thomas	18	– not out	66
K. W. Hogg c Buttler b Thomas	4	– c Compton b Wright	6
*G. Chapple run out	10	– not out	30
S. I. Mahmood b Wright	64		
S. C. Kerrigan not out	0		
D. B. Powell c Compton b Wright	6		
B 8, l-b 5, w 4, n-b 6	23	B 2, l-b 3, w 1	6

1/4 (2) 2/25 (3) 3/27 (4) 4/131 (5) (85.1 overs) 292
5/151 (6) 6/165 (7) 7/175 (8)
8/283 (1) 9/286 (9) 10/292 (11)

1/53 (1) (6 wkts, 90 overs) 221
2/94 (3) 3/97 (2)
4/100 (4) 5/126 (5) 6/145 (7)

Willoughby 14–6–30–0; Wright 18.1–5–41–5; Thomas 23–5–84–3; Trego 13–4–41–0; Munday 4–0–27–0; de Bruyn 10–0–40–1; Suppiah 3–0–16–0. *Second Innings*—Willoughby 20–3–70–0; Wright 26–8–48–1; Thomas 19–7–33–4; Trego 12–5–18–0; Munday 6–2–28–1; Suppiah 5–1–6–0; de Bruyn 2–0–13–0.

Somerset

*M. E. Trescothick c Sutton b Hogg	56	M. K. Munday c sub (L. A. Procter) b Powell	0
A. V. Suppiah b Hogg	10	C. M. Willoughby not out	0
N. R. D. Compton c Sutton b Hogg	0		
Z. de Bruyn lbw b Kerrigan	48	B 6, l-b 4, w 5	15
J. C. Hildreth c Sutton b Chapple	99		
†J. C. Buttler b Chapple	20	1/14 (2) 2/14 (3) (102.2 overs)	383
P. D. Trego c Chapple b Powell	108	3/115 (1) 4/129 (4) 5/157 (6)	
D. G. Wright c Croft b Chapple	18	6/343 (7) 7/367 (5) 8/376 (8)	
A. C. Thomas c Chapple b Hogg	9	9/379 (10) 10/383 (9)	

Chapple 33–5–146–3; Hogg 30.2–11–96–4; Powell 24–5–81–2; Kerrigan 12–5–41–1; Croft 3–0–9–0.

Umpires: M. R. Benson and R. A. Kettleborough.

At Birmingham, May 17–20. LANCASHIRE beat WARWICKSHIRE by 65 runs.

LANCASHIRE v ESSEX

At Manchester, May 24–27. Drawn. Lancashire 6pts, Essex 8pts. Toss: Lancashire.
   For the second successive home game, Lancashire were happy to escape with a draw. Chapple admitted that he misread a lurid green pitch in inserting Essex; ten Doeschate batted especially well, though four quick wickets on the second morning gave left-arm spinner Kerrigan the second significant haul of his young career. He took two in the 110th over, the deadline for bonus points: Essex started it on 299 for seven yet ended up conceding a point rather than gaining one. The home batting then flopped miserably, only Mahmood's fourth half-century of the season averting the follow-on. That proved vital. A lengthy rain stoppage on the third afternoon ate into the time available for Essex to press for victory on a pitch now devoid of life. Lancashire also bowled tightly, with Bopara – who replaced Grant Flower after attending a Downing Street reception for England's Twenty20 champions – restricted to five singles from 53 balls. Though Pettini declared, Lancashire showed no interest in chasing 336 in 85 overs.
   Close of play: First day, Essex 251-6 (Flower 12, Masters 6); Second day, Essex 26-1 (Mickleburgh 16, Wright 4); Third day, Essex 155-4 (Walker 36, ten Doeschate 31).

Essex

B. A. Godleman c Moore b Kerrigan	39	– c Sutton b Hogg	6
J. C. Mickleburgh lbw b Kerrigan	39	– run out	64
M. J. Walker b Mahmood	42	– (5) not out	53
*M. L. Pettini c Chilton b Hogg	12	– (7) not out	14
R. N. ten Doeschate lbw b Chapple	85	– (6) c Croft b Kerrigan	56
†J. S. Foster lbw b Chapple	6		
G. W. Flower not out	36		
D. D. Masters lbw b Kerrigan	33		
C. J. C. Wright lbw b Kerrigan	1	– (3) c Sutton b Hogg	8
Danish Kaneria b Kerrigan	0		
M. A. Chambers c Chilton b Kerrigan	1		
R. S. Bopara (did not bat)		– (4) c Horton b Powell	5
B 3, l-b 3, w 1, n-b 6	13	B 5, l-b 1	6

1/73 (1) 2/86 (2) 3/130 (4)   (115.3 overs) 307   1/20 (1)   (5 wkts dec, 72 overs) 212
4/196 (3) 5/226 (6) 6/239 (5) 7/297 (8)   2/42 (3) 3/61 (4)
8/299 (9) 9/299 (10) 10/307 (11)   110 overs: 299-9   4/106 (2) 5/197 (6)

Bopara replaced Flower after returning from England's reception at Downing Street.

Chapple 22–7–47–2; Mahmood 23–3–89–1; Powell 11–2–40–0; Kerrigan 38.3–10–74–6; Hogg 21–6–51–1. *Second Innings*—Chapple 10–5–20–0; Mahmood 17–5–37–0; Hogg 16–4–45–2; Powell 14–5–38–1; Kerrigan 15–1–66–1.

Lancashire

P. J. Horton c Bopara b ten Doeschate	19	– (3) c Foster b Wright 64
†L. D. Sutton b Chambers	4	– (1) c Foster b ten Doeschate....... 26
A. G. Prince b Chambers	2	– (4) c Godleman b Danish Kaneria .. 29
M. J. Chilton lbw b Danish Kaneria	49	– (5) not out................... 12
S. J. Croft lbw b Wright	4	– (6) c Foster b Wright 0
S. C. Moore c Foster b ten Doeschate	3	– (2) c Foster b Masters............. 5
*G. Chapple c Foster b Masters	10	– not out 21
K. W. Hogg run out	7	
S. I. Mahmood c Walker b Danish Kaneria	58	
S. C. Kerrigan c Bopara b Danish Kaneria	4	
D. B. Powell not out	16	
L-b 6, n-b 2	8	B 4, l-b 6, n-b 10 20

1/10 (2) 2/18 (3) 3/48 (1) 4/53 (5)   (58.1 overs) 184   1/7 (2)   (5 wkts, 83.4 overs) 177
5/68 (6) 6/89 (7) 7/101 (4) 8/123 (8)   2/100 (1) 3/144 (4)
9/151 (10) 10/184 (9)   4/144 (3) 5/144 (6)

Masters 13–7–15–1; Chambers 15–4–52–2; ten Doeschate 6–0–30–2; Wright 8–1–23–1; Danish Kaneria 13.1–3–42–3; Bopara 3–0–16–0. *Second Innings*—Masters 11.4–4–25–1; Chambers 15–5–36–0; Wright 13–4–30–2; Danish Kaneria 33–16–49–1; ten Doeschate 10–2–26–1; Bopara 1–0–1–0.

Umpires: M. J. D. Bodenham and M. A. Gough.

At Leeds, May 29–June 1. LANCASHIRE drew with YORKSHIRE.

LANCASHIRE v YORKSHIRE

At Manchester, June 28–July 1. Drawn. Lancashire 8pts, Yorkshire 10pts. Toss: Yorkshire.

The tensest climax to a Roses match in years ended in frustration for Yorkshire, even though they regained the top of the table: Lancashire's eighth-wicket pair, Croft and Hogg, survived half an hour with seven fielders crowded round the bat to salvage a draw. They had come together in the 52nd over after Rashid took his eighth wicket of a match in which he and his teenage off-spin partner, Azeem Rafiq, underlined their promise. But Hogg, who had scored a career-best 88 to save the follow-on, again showed a more effective combination of technique and temperament than Lancashire's established batsmen. This time Croft was a notable exception. He arrived in the ninth over, when Best claimed his third victim of an exuberant opening spell, and ended with an unbeaten three-hour 85 – drawing nods of approval from the few hundred souls scattered around the ground on a gloomy evening. Yorkshire had been dominant from the start. Lyth struck ten fours in the first hour on his way to a 122-ball century, and shared a first-wicket stand of 166 with Rudolph, promoted to open when Joe Sayers was ruled out by asthma. Rudolph had already taken over the captaincy from Andrew Gale, who was away with England Lions; the draw ended his record of losing each of his seven previous games in charge of Yorkshire.

Close of play: First day, Yorkshire 379-8 (Pyrah 8, Patterson 2); Second day, Lancashire 187-6 (Smith 15, Sutton 1); Third day, Yorkshire 111-3 (McGrath 50, Brophy 6).

Yorkshire

A. Lyth c Sutton b Smith	100	– c Moore b Hogg	29
*J. A. Rudolph c Smith b Powell	83	– c Sutton b Powell	4
A. McGrath b Powell	61	– lbw b Kerrigan	57
J. M. Bairstow c Katich b Smith	47	– c Smith b Kerrigan	11
†G. L. Brophy lbw b Chapple	35	– c Smith b Powell	23
A. U. Rashid c Croft b Chapple	13	– not out	42
R. M. Pyrah run out	32	– b Kerrigan	16
Azeem Rafiq c Sutton b Chapple	4	– (9) not out	13
T. L. Best c and b Chapple	1	– (8) st Sutton b Kerrigan	6
S. A. Patterson c Kerrigan b Hogg	27		
O. J. Hannon-Dalby not out	11		
B 7, l-b 18, n-b 8	33	B 4, l-b 2, n-b 8	14

1/166 (1) 2/220 (2) 3/299 (4) (127.3 overs) 447 1/10 (2) (7 wkts dec, 69 overs) 215
4/338 (3) 5/350 (5) 6/367 (6) 2/56 (1) 3/97 (4)
7/371 (8) 8/373 (9) 9/418 (7) 4/118 (3) 5/170 (5)
10/447 (10) 110 overs: 411-8 6/193 (7) 7/199 (8)

Chapple 31–7–75–4; Powell 20–0–88–2; Hogg 21.3–4–78–1; Kerrigan 27–4–101–0; Smith 28–7–80–2. *Second Innings*—Chapple 10–3–24–0; Powell 18–1–45–2; Hogg 11–0–47–1; Smith 5–0–14–0; Kerrigan 24–8–77–4; Croft 1–0–2–0.

Lancashire

P. J. Horton lbw b Rashid	63	– lbw b Best	19
S. C. Moore c and b Rashid	40	– b Best	8
S. M. Katich c Lyth b Azeem Rafiq	32	– c Rashid b Best	8
M. J. Chilton c Rudolph b Rashid	7	– lbw b Patterson	23
S. J. Croft c Rudolph b Azeem Rafiq	16	– not out	85
T. C. Smith c and b Best	16	– c Brophy b Rashid	11
S. C. Kerrigan b Azeem Rafiq	0		
†L. D. Sutton not out	47	– (7) c Bairstow b Rashid	0
*G. Chapple c Patterson b Azeem Rafiq	21	– (8) c Best b Rashid	23
K. W. Hogg c Pyrah b Rashid	88	– (9) not out	4
D. B. Powell c Lyth b Rashid	2		
B 11, l-b 11, w 2, n-b 2	26	B 6, l-b 5	11

1/94 (2) 2/131 (1) 3/143 (4) (121.5 overs) 358 1/9 (2) (7 wkts, 63.4 overs) 192
4/169 (5) 5/176 (3) 6/182 (7) 2/33 (3) 3/42 (1) 4/91 (4)
7/194 (6) 8/235 (9) 9/356 (10) 5/124 (6) 6/124 (7) 7/158 (8)
10/358 (11) 110 overs: 320-8

Best 15–2–45–1; Patterson 9–0–31–0; Hannon-Dalby 15–4–52–0; Pyrah 6–2–15–0; Rashid 38.5–6–90–5; Azeem Rafiq 35–9–92–4; Rudolph 3–0–11–0. *Second Innings*—Best 10–0–40–3; Hannon-Dalby 4–1–15–0; Azeem Rafiq 20–3–66–0; Patterson 9–4–14–1; Rashid 20.4–8–46–3.

Umpires: N. J. Llong and D. J. Millns.

At Manchester, July 8. LANCASHIRE beat WEST INDIES A by 53 runs (see A-team tours of England section).

At Chester-le-Street, July 20–23. LANCASHIRE drew with DURHAM.

At Southampton, July 29–August 1. LANCASHIRE drew with HAMPSHIRE.

LANCASHIRE v DURHAM

At Manchester, August 9–12. Durham won by six wickets. Durham 20pts, Lancashire 3pts. Toss: Lancashire.

Durham ended the last remaining unbeaten Championship record in the country – they were the first team to beat Lancashire in 21 first-class matches stretching back 13 months – and leapt from eighth to fourth in the first division. Blackwell was the key figure, taking nine wickets on a pitch that started very dry but did not deteriorate as much as Lancashire hoped when they chose to bat first. He also hit 65 from 81 balls in the first innings, Durham's top score of the match. But the pivotal moment was Blackwell's second dismissal of Chanderpaul, a 2009 team-mate who grafted to 67 on the third day then fell to an extravagant shot off the last ball before tea. Steve Harmison, though increasingly impeded by an ankle injury, had bowled a significant spell of three for 17 in nine overs on the second morning. For Lancashire, Keedy's seven for 68 was the best return of his long career, and he ended with ten in a match for the sixth time.

Close of play: First day, Lancashire 131-4 (Chilton 68, Cross 17); Second day, Lancashire 22-2 (Chilton 4, Keedy 7); Third day, Durham 58-2 (Di Venuto 34, Claydon 1).

Lancashire

P. J. Horton c Stokes b Claydon	9	– (2) c Mustard b Claydon	8
T. C. Smith c Mustard b Claydon	0	– (1) c Di Venuto b Harmison	2
M. J. Chilton lbw b Blackwell	69	– lbw b Blackwell	50
S. Chanderpaul b Blackwell	10	– (5) b Blackwell	67
S. J. Croft c Di Venuto b Blackwell	17	– (6) c Di Venuto b Borthwick	28
G. D. Cross lbw b Blackwell	17	– (7) lbw b Blackwell	13
†L. D. Sutton c Benkenstein b Blackwell	12	– (8) lbw b Plunkett	6
*G. Chapple c Di Venuto b Harmison	5	– (9) run out	19
S. I. Mahmood lbw b Harmison	20	– (10) c Mustard b Blackwell	0
S. C. Kerrigan lbw b Harmison	4	– (11) not out	0
G. Keedy not out	2	– (4) lbw b Borthwick	24
B 2, l-b 10, n-b 4	16	B 2, l-b 2, w 1, n-b 4	9

1/0 (2) 2/17 (1) 3/59 (4) 4/95 (5)   (69.2 overs) 181
5/131 (6) 6/132 (3) 7/137 (8)
8/167 (9) 9/177 (10) 10/181 (7)

1/10 (2) 2/10 (1)   (84.5 overs) 226
3/66 (4) 4/107 (3)
5/164 (6) 6/194 (5) 7/201 (7)
8/211 (8) 9/222 (10) 10/226 (9)

Harmison 18–8–27–3; Claydon 9–3–29–2; Plunkett 16.5–5–29–0; Blackwell 23.2–6–78–5; Borthwick 3–0–6–0. *Second Innings*—Harmison 10–2–19–1; Claydon 11–4–28–1; Blackwell 33–8–102–4; Plunkett 18.5–6–41–1; Borthwick 11–4–32–2; Benkenstein 1–1–0–0.

Durham

M. J. Di Venuto lbw b Mahmood	13	– (2) c Croft b Keedy	63
M. D. Stoneman lbw b Keedy	7	– (1) b Keedy	14
G. J. Muchall c Sutton b Keedy	14	– c Horton b Keedy	3
D. M. Benkenstein lbw b Chapple	32	– (5) not out	41
I. D. Blackwell b Keedy	65	– (3) not out	20
B. A. Stokes c Sutton b Kerrigan	32		
*†P. Mustard c Horton b Keedy	0		
S. G. Borthwick c Horton b Keedy	30		
L. E. Plunkett b Keedy	28		
M. E. Claydon c Chanderpaul b Keedy	2	– (4) b Kerrigan	8
S. J. Harmison not out	1		
B 4, l-b 3, n-b 6	13	B 9, l-b 13, n-b 2	24

1/21 (1) 2/38 (3) 3/41 (2)   (61.2 overs) 237
4/124 (4) 5/169 (5) 6/169 (7)
7/175 (6) 8/226 (8) 9/230 (10) 10/237 (9)

1/27 (1)   (4 wkts, 68.5 overs) 173
2/43 (3) 3/80 (4)
4/132 (2)

Chapple 14–0–45–1; Mahmood 3–0–24–1; Kerrigan 16–3–60–1; Keedy 21.2–2–68–7; Smith 7–2–33–0. *Second Innings*—Chapple 9–3–16–0; Smith 2–0–11–0; Keedy 32–8–60–3; Kerrigan 25.5–5–64–1.

Umpires: N. G. B. Cook and T. E. Jesty.

At Canterbury, August 18–21. LANCASHIRE beat KENT by 121 runs.

At Nottingham, August 24–27. LANCASHIRE lost to NOTTINGHAMSHIRE by three wickets.

LANCASHIRE v HAMPSHIRE

At Liverpool, August 31–September 3. Lancashire won by three wickets. Lancashire 22pts, Hampshire 2pts. Toss: Lancashire. Championship debut: C. P. Wood.

Lancashire's coach Peter Moores described this match as "one of the best I've ever been involved with". It was finally settled when Chilton drove Cork through backward point for the winning boundary with two balls to spare. But it also featured the season's longest Championship innings, from Adams, who came in late on the second day with Hampshire 238 behind and was last out just before tea on the fourth. He batted for 635 minutes, facing 508 balls. Lancashire, who had been especially frustrated by his last-wicket stand of 88 in 43 overs with Briggs, needed 168 from 33, and made hard work of it. All this after Hampshire had lost five wickets in 16 balls while the pitch was damp on the first morning, slumping to 63 for six. Lancashire almost ground to a halt next morning, managing 40 runs for three wickets before lunch as Tomlinson bowled eight maidens in ten overs. The 173 later added by their last three wickets turned out to be crucial; Mahmood passed 500 runs for the season, and Hogg enjoyed a fine all-round match.

Close of play: First day, Lancashire 124-2 (Chilton 47, Chanderpaul 26); Second day, Hampshire 15-0 (Carberry 3, Adams 11); Third day, Hampshire 275-5 (Adams 110, Bates 27).

Hampshire

M. A. Carberry c Cross b Hogg	30	– c Cross b Hogg 17
J. H. K. Adams b Chapple	5	– c Cross b Hogg 194
P. J. Hughes c Horton b Smith	20	– c Horton b Keedy 11
N. D. McKenzie lbw b Hogg	0	– c Cross b Smith 31
J. M. Vince b Smith	21	– b Smith 0
S. M. Ervine lbw b Smith	0	– c Horton b Smith 48
†A. M. Bates c Smith b Hogg	0	– b Smith 31
*D. G. Cork c Horton b Chapple	24	– b Smith 8
C. P. Wood c Horton b Hogg	35	– b Smith 1
J. A. Tomlinson lbw b Mahmood	12	– c and b Mahmood. 3
D. R. Briggs not out	2	– not out 15
B 4, l-b 7	11	B 15, l-b 10, w 1, n-b 20 46

1/19 (2) 2/62 (1) 3/62 (4) 4/62 (5)   (47.4 overs) 160
5/62 (6) 6/63 (7) 7/85 (5) 8/115 (8)
9/158 (9) 10/160 (10)

1/45 (1) 2/67 (3)   (165.3 overs) 405
3/141 (4) 4/141 (5)
5/219 (6) 6/279 (7) 7/295 (8)
8/299 (9) 9/317 (10) 10/405 (2)

Chapple 10–4–16–2; Mahmood 11.4–1–40–1; Hogg 14–2–53–4; Smith 12–1–40–3. *Second Innings*—Mahmood 31–4–129–1; Hogg 31.3–12–50–2; Smith 41–10–94–6; Keedy 58–13–105–1; Croft 4–2–2–0.

Lancashire

P. J. Horton lbw b Cork	0	– (2) b Tomlinson	5
K. R. Brown c Bates b Ervine	21	– (3) lbw b Tomlinson	0
M. J. Chilton c Bates b Tomlinson	48	– (9) not out	18
S. Chanderpaul run out	38	– c Bates b Wood	51
S. J. Croft c Bates b Wood	3	– c Bates b Cork	10
T. C. Smith lbw b Wood	31	– (1) c Bates b Tomlinson	9
†G. D. Cross c Adams b Wood	44	– (6) c Cork b Wood	26
S. I. Mahmood lbw b McKenzie	47	– (7) c Adams b Wood	24
K. W. Hogg c Vince b Briggs	81	– (8) not out	17
*G. Chapple c Adams b McKenzie	19		
G. Keedy not out	12		
B 8, l-b 13, w 1, n-b 32	54	B 5, l-b 3, w 1, n-b 2	11

1/4 (1) 2/49 (2) 3/135 (3) 4/143 (5) (134 overs) 398   1/10 (2) (7 wkts, 32.4 overs) 171
5/144 (4) 6/219 (7) 7/225 (6) 8/314 (8)   2/10 (3) 3/17 (1)
9/344 (10) 10/398 (9)   110 overs: 312-7   4/44 (5) 5/84 (6) 6/130 (7) 7/140 (4)

Cork 33–13–77–1; Tomlinson 30–11–60–1; Ervine 28–5–89–1; Wood 26–8–85–3; Briggs
8–0–36–1; McKenzie 9–0–30–2. *Second Innings*—Cork 11.4–0–55–1; Tomlinson 9–2–27–3;
Briggs 7–0–49–0; Wood 5–0–32–3.

Umpires: N. G. B. Cook and D. J. Millns.

At Taunton, September 7–9. LANCASHIRE lost to SOMERSET by nine wickets.

LANCASHIRE v NOTTINGHAMSHIRE

At Manchester, September 13–16. Drawn. Lancashire 6pts, Nottinghamshire 9pts. Toss: Nottinghamshire.

For Nottinghamshire, three days of frustration and helplessness ended in the exhilaration of a Championship title that had looked wholly improbable during a further delay on the final morning. Only 28 overs had been possible on the previous days – a single over on day one, and on the second, when conditions were dry enough to resume after tea, the glare of the sun off the commentary boxes' roof at the Stretford End forced another halt. It was not the first time sun had stopped play at Old Trafford, but it should be the last, as the pitches were to be reorientated to run from north to south. Meanwhile, rival contenders Somerset and Yorkshire were making progress against Durham and Kent, forcing Read to consider contrivance to salvage his side's bid. They decided instead to gamble that a draw plus bonus points would be enough and, in that unwanted extra hour in the pavilion on the last morning, Durham and Kent offered fresh reasons for optimism. Nottinghamshire resumed on 89 for two, needing another 311 from 82, but it was only when Patel joined Voges that the strategy became clear. Patel hit 96 from 91 balls, his best performance of a lean first-class season, and Voges's century was a fine effort considering the pressure he had felt after replacing David Hussey. They added 153 in 28 overs but, after Patel holed out to long-off, Nottinghamshire lost four more wickets. They were still ten short of the magic 400 when last man Pattinson joined Sidebottom. While their team-mates sweated in a silent dressing-room, the tailenders held their nerve, eking out the runs from 31 balls. Provided there were no further sun delays – a live possibility on what had become a glorious Manchester evening – that left 18 overs to take three Lancashire wickets for a sixth bonus point, which would put them level on points with Somerset but ahead on matches won. After a single over from the Statham End, Sidebottom switched and had Karl Brown caught low down by Hales at first slip. Adams then had Chilton caught behind off the first ball of the next over and, three deliveries later, Chanderpaul at third slip – a fittingly high-calibre victim for his 68th and most crucial of the season.

Close of play: First day, Nottinghamshire 8-0 (Hales 7, Franks 1); Second day, Nottinghamshire 89-2 (Wagh 3, Voges 8); Third day, No play.

Nottinghamshire

A. D. Hales c Cross b Keedy	36	R. J. Sidebottom not out		7
P. J. Franks c Cross b Smith	40	D. J. Pattinson not out		4
M. A. Wagh b Mahmood	32			
A. C. Voges c Croft b Kerrigan	126	B 1, l-b 13, w 4, n-b 4		22
A. D. Brown lbw b Mahmood	10			
*C. M. W. Read c Hogg b Kerrigan	12	1/75 (1) (9 wkts dec, 89.4 overs)		400
S. J. Mullaney c Cross b Kerrigan	0	2/79 (2) 3/144 (3)		
A. R. Adams b Kerrigan	15	4/172 (5) 5/325 (6) 6/353 (7)		
		7/365 (8) 8/386 (4) 9/390 (9)		

Mahmood 12–0–69–2; Hogg 10–0–47–0; Keedy 34.4–3–140–1; Smith 13–3–50–1; Kerrigan 20–3–80–5.

Lancashire

P. J. Horton not out	6
K. R. Brown c Hales b Sidebottom	4
*M. J. Chilton c Read b Adams	1
S. Chanderpaul c Patel b Adams	0
1/6 (2) 2/11 (3) (3 wkts, 4.4 overs)	11
3/11 (4)	

T. C. Smith, S. J. Croft, †G. D. Cross, S. I. Mahmood, K. W. Hogg, G. Keedy and S. C. Kerrigan did not bat.

Sidebottom 2–0–6–1; Pattinson 1–0–2–0; Adams 1.4–0–3–2.

Umpires: N. L. Bainton and P. J. Hartley.

LEICESTERSHIRE

The summer of discontent

PAUL JONES

Leicestershire was a club in danger of tearing itself apart in 2010. A backdrop of bitter internal unrest diverted attention from a substantial improvement in the Championship, where a young team, under the leadership of Matthew Hoggard for the first time, won seven matches and finished fourth in their division. Leicestershire's limited-overs form was wretched by comparison: they managed just two home wins, both in the CB40, four and a half months apart. It was their poor results in the Friends Provident T20 which sparked the irrevocable split that led to chief executive David Smith, chairman Neil Davidson and senior coach Tim Boon all leaving the club.

On June 27, Leicestershire won a Twenty20 match at Headingley. But back at Grace Road, the club was heading for turmoil. Smith resigned next morning, citing interference in team selection by the board, an accusation which Davidson strenuously denied. Two club members, Anna Stead and Stewart Walker, attempted to call a special general meeting to hear Smith's reasons and hold a vote of no confidence in Davidson and the board, but their petition did not comply with club rules.

The crisis came to a head in late August. Boon and Hoggard put their names to a letter calling for Davidson to stand down, and were believed to have the support of all players, groundstaff, and several administrators. Davidson refused to go; he admitted intervening in cricketing matters, but not interfering in selection. "I'm elected by members," he said. "Our finances are under pressure because of poor performances on the pitch, so I see it as part of my fiduciary duty to intervene." He added that the relationship between him and Boon had become "unsustainable". Boon invoked a clause in his contract which allowed him to leave for a development role with the ECB. In October, Davidson did resign, declaring that Hoggard's refusal to withdraw his name from the August letter had made his own position "untenable".

Davidson's departure persuaded the petitioners and directors to reach a compromise and call off an SGM set for November (a second petition had succeeded). Three local businessmen were co-opted on to a revamped board, which pledged to put the club's finances back in order. But the true extent of the mess was laid bare in January 2011, when Leicestershire announced a record annual loss of £404,862. "In almost every area, costs are either over budget or income targets have not been achieved," said Mike Siddall, the new chief executive. Leicestershire faced the prospect of legal proceedings with Smith, pursuing constructive dismissal, and Davidson, seeking to recoup money he had lent the club.

The off-field squabbling seemed to galvanise the players, such was Leicestershire's strong finish to the season. They beat Derbyshire, fell just

David Rogers, Getty Images

Nathan Buck

short in draws against Middlesex and Surrey, and closed with emphatic wins over Gloucestershire and Northamptonshire.

Hoggard was at the heart of it all. His arrival gave a huge lift to a club which finished bottom of the Championship in 2009, and had never looked like being promoted in six years in Division Two. He relished the challenges of captaincy and, most importantly, took wickets, finishing with 50 in first-class cricket for the first time since 2005.

The slow bowlers also caught the eye: Claude Henderson, the left-arm spinner, enjoyed the most productive of his seven seasons with Leicestershire, playing all 16 Championship matches and taking 56 wickets. He was voted Player of the Year. Henderson's partnership with off-spinner Jigar Naik, who took 31 wickets in seven, blossomed after they shared 16 in an innings victory at The Oval. When the pair played, Leicestershire were a well-balanced side who could apply pressure for long periods.

The revelation, though, was Nathan Buck. Still 18 when the season began, he was always likely to figure in the first team. The question was, how much? More than anybody had anticipated. He bowled with lively pace, aggression and control, and his 49 Championship wickets, and call-up to the Lions tour of the Caribbean, were another triumph for Leicestershire's academy.

For batsmen, life was more of a struggle. Leicestershire were not helped by losing Andrew McDonald to Australia A duty, and later a shoulder injury. He was due to rejoin in 2011 after the IPL, and is likely to be Leicestershire's only overseas player.

James Taylor defied the doomsayers who predicted that bowlers would work him out after a prodigious first full year. He had lean spells, like any batsman, but emphasised how quickly he learns, scoring a second double-century and passing 1,000 runs for a second successive season, before the age of 21. Paul Nixon was typically resolute and, approaching 40, turned down the opportunity to be Kenya's batting and wicketkeeping coach for the 2011 World Cup, preferring a new one-year contract. Of great encouragement were the 509 runs made by Greg Smith in five games after his return from Durham University. But his colleagues must be more consistent, as 31 batting points attest.

Leicestershire did not advertise Boon's position, instead promoting Phil Whitticase to a role combining first-team and academy duties. After 12 years at Leicester as a player and nine as a coach, he ought to make the change as seamless as possible. Stability is imperative throughout the club. Hoggard, with the dressing-room behind him, has the chance to mould a very good side from a mix of youngsters and experienced professionals. It would be a sporting tragedy if they were to be undermined by politics.

LEICESTERSHIRE RESULTS

All first-class matches – Played 17: Won 7, Lost 5, Drawn 5.
County Championship matches – Played 16: Won 7, Lost 5, Drawn 4.

LV= County Championship, 4th in Division 2;
Friends Provident T20, 7th in North Division; Clydesdale Bank 40, 6th in Group C.

COUNTY CHAMPIONSHIP AVERAGES, BATTING AND FIELDING

Cap		M	I	NO	R	HS	100s	50s	Avge	Ct/St
	G. P. Smith†	5	10	4	509	158*	2	3	84.83	6
2009	J. W. A. Taylor.	16	27	4	1,027	206*	3	3	44.65	15
	A. B. McDonald§	6	11	1	442	176*	2	1	44.20	2
	J. du Toit¶	12	18	1	745	122	1	6	43.82	14
1994	P. A. Nixon.	16	27	1	915	106	1	7	35.19	4
	W. A. White.	8	12	2	346	101*	1	1	34.60	3
	W. I. Jefferson	10	18	0	598	135	1	4	33.22	14
	M. A. G. Boyce	14	26	3	750	90	0	6	32.60	19
2009	T. J. New	16	25	3	690	91	0	6	31.36	42/1
	J. K. H. Naik†	7	10	2	181	36	0	0	22.62	4
	J. J. Cobb†	4	8	1	97	27	0	0	13.85	2
2004	C. W. Henderson¶	16	21	1	265	33	0	0	13.25	6
	A. J. Harris	4	7	4	27	20*	0	0	9.00	2
	M. N. Malik	7	8	2	53	34	0	0	8.83	0
	N. L. Buck†	15	20	5	93	26	0	0	6.20	4
2010	M. J. Hoggard.	15	17	6	31	6	0	0	2.81	5
	H. F. Gurney.	4	4	1	6	4	0	0	2.00	0

Also batted: J. G. E. Benning (1 match) 29, 26* (1 ct).

† *Born in Leicestershire.* § *Official overseas player.* ¶ *Other non-England-qualified player.*

BOWLING

	O	M	R	W	BB	5W/i	Avge
J. K. H. Naik	186	32	586	31	7-96	1	18.90
C. W. Henderson	489.3	136	1,179	56	6-21	3	21.05
M. J. Hoggard	416.4	105	1,222	50	6-63	3	24.44
A. B. McDonald.	103	21	320	12	5-40	1	26.66
N. L. Buck	381.5	88	1,340	49	4-44	0	27.34
M. N. Malik	167	41	521	19	4-32	0	27.42

Also bowled: J. G. E. Benning 19–2–59–3; M. A. G. Boyce 1–0–2–0; J. J. Cobb 6–1–31–0; J. du
Toit 2–0–20–0; H. F. Gurney 76–15–276–8; A. J. Harris 96.4–23–385–9; P. A. Nixon 2.1–1–7–1;
J. W. A. Taylor 4–0–15–0; W. A. White 116.2–18–464–6.

LEADING CB40 AVERAGES (100 runs/4 wickets)

Batting	Runs	HS	Avge	S-R	Ct	**Bowling**	W	BB	Avge	E-R
J. W. A. Taylor.	407	103*	45.22	89.64	3	S. J. Cliff	4	3-27	17.75	3.73
P. A. Nixon.	166	40	41.50	88.29	2	C. W. Henderson . .	12	4-25	18.25	5.21
W. I. Jefferson	123	55	41.00	119.41	2	J. W. A. Taylor.	5	4-61	19.60	8.90
J. du Toit	485	141	40.41	89.64	6	H. F. Gurney.	9	5-24	20.33	4.46
J. G. E. Benning	228	62	32.57	106.04	2	M. N. Malik	7	4-40	22.00	5.73
M. A. G. Boyce	176	60	29.33	79.27	3	W. A. White.	8	6-29	23.62	7.56

LEADING FPT20 AVERAGES (100 runs/18 overs)

Batting	Runs	HS	Avge	S-R	Ct/St
W. I. Jefferson	289	83	22.23	138.94	4
J. W. A. Taylor . . .	407	62*	37.00	136.12	5
A. B. McDonald. . .	174	67	87.00	134.88	1
P. A. Nixon	214	44*	19.45	127.38	7/6
B. J. Hodge	431	103	28.73	124.20	5
J. du Toit	273	69	19.50	119.21	12

Bowling	W	BB	Avge	E-R
C. W. Henderson . .	14	3-33	28.28	6.94
B. J. Hodge	10	3-26	18.70	7.48
M. N. Malik	13	4-25	28.53	8.03
N. L. Buck	10	3-20	25.10	8.36
J. G. E. Benning. . .	5	1-10	31.00	8.37
M. J. Hoggard	18	3-19	25.83	8.48

FIRST-CLASS COUNTY RECORDS

Highest score for	309*	H. D. Ackerman v Glamorgan at Cardiff.	2006
Highest score against	341	G. H. Hirst (Yorkshire) at Leicester.	1905
Leading run-scorer	30,143	L. G. Berry (avge 30.32)	1924–1951
Best bowling for	10-18	G. Geary v Glamorgan at Pontypridd	1929
Best bowling against	10-32	H. Pickett (Essex) at Leyton	1895
Leading wicket-taker	2,131	W. E. Astill (avge 23.18).	1906–1939
Highest total for	701-4 dec	v Worcestershire at Worcester.	1906
Highest total against	761-6 dec	by Essex at Chelmsford	1990
Lowest total for	25	v Kent at Leicester.	1912
Lowest total against {	24	by Glamorgan at Leicester	1971
	24	by Oxford University at Oxford.	1985

LIST A COUNTY RECORDS

Highest score for	201	V. J. Wells v Berkshire at Leicester.	1996
Highest score against	201*	R. S. Bopara (Essex) at Leicester.	2008
Leading run-scorer	8,216	N. E. Briers (avge 27.66)	1975–1995
Best bowling for	6-16	C. M. Willoughby v Somerset at Leicester	2005
Best bowling against	6-21	S. M. Pollock (Warwickshire) at Birmingham.	1996
Leading wicket-taker	308	K. Higgs (avge 18.80)	1972–1986
Highest total for	406-5	v Berkshire at Leicester.	1996
Highest total against	350-5	by Essex at Leicester	2008
Lowest total for	36	v Sussex at Leicester	1973
Lowest total against {	62	by Northamptonshire at Leicester	1974
	62	by Middlesex at Leicester	1998

TWENTY20 RECORDS

Highest score for	111	D. L. Maddy v Yorkshire at Leeds.	2004
Highest score against	92*	S. G. Law (Lancashire) at Manchester.	2005
Leading run-scorer	1,278	P. A. Nixon (avge 22.82)	2003–2010
Best bowling for	5-13	A. B. McDonald v Nottinghamshire at Nottingham	2010
Best bowling against	5-27	T. Lungley (Derbyshire) at Leicester.	2009
Leading wicket-taker	49	C. W. Henderson (avge 24.46).	2004–2010
Highest total for	221-3	v Yorkshire at Leeds	2004
Highest total against	225-2	by Durham at Chester-le-Street	2010
Lowest total for	97-9	v Durham at Leicester	2004
Lowest total against	104-8	by Durham at Chester-le-Street	2006

ADDRESS

County Ground, Grace Road, Leicester LE2 8AD (0116 283 2128; **email** enquiries@ leicestershireccc.co.uk). **Website** www.leicestershireccc.co.uk

OFFICIALS

Captain M. J. Hoggard
Senior coach 2010 – T. J. Boon
Head coach/academy director P. Whitticase
President D. Wilson
Chairman P. R. Haywood

Chief executive M. J. Siddall
Operations director P. Atkinson
Head groundsman A. Ward
Scorer G. A. York

LEICESTERSHIRE v NORTHAMPTONSHIRE

At Leicester, April 9–12. Leicestershire won by six wickets. Leicestershire 22pts, Northamptonshire 2pts. Toss: Northamptonshire. County debuts: M. J. Hoggard, W. I. Jefferson. Championship debut: V. Tripathi.

Hoggard's tenure as Leicestershire captain could hardly have had a more invigorating start. He took over a side that managed just two wins in 2009 and inspired them to a morale-boosting victory. Leicestershire dominated from the outset in fresh spring conditions. Solid batting – rarely in evidence the previous season – earned them a third bonus point and coaxed a career-best score out of the unheralded Wayne White. Seam was expected to be decisive, but Leicestershire took control through left-arm spinner Henderson, their only player born outside England. He took a brilliant low return catch to dismiss Sales with his third ball and went on to claim six for 21 in 20 overs of unstinting accuracy. Faced with such feeble batting, Hoggard had no hesitation in enforcing the follow-on. The tenacious Buck, two weeks short of his 19th birthday, prevented Northamptonshire building any meaningful partnerships until Lucas and Daggett scrambled 75 from the last two wickets to make Leicestershire bat again. Lucas and Brooks came out firing on the final morning, but Leicestershire crept over the line through an overthrow. "We were at 80% efficiency," said a demanding Hoggard.

Close of play: First day, Leicestershire 303-5 (New 59, White 52); Second day, Northamptonshire 179-9 (Hall 22, Daggett 3); Third day, Leicestershire 14-1 (Jefferson 10, Nixon 0).

Leicestershire

W. I. Jefferson c Harrison b Brooks	7	– lbw b Lucas	10
M. A. G. Boyce c Harrison b Daggett	47	– c Boje b Lucas	3
P. A. Nixon c Sales b Brooks	5	– lbw b Brooks	8
J. W. A. Taylor b Daggett	88	– lbw b Brooks	1
J. J. Cobb b Lucas	27	– not out	20
†T. J. New b Lucas	82	– not out	14
W. A. White c Sales b Hall	89		
C. W. Henderson b Lucas	6		
N. L. Buck lbw b Lucas	0		
*M. J. Hoggard c Sales b Lucas	2		
A. J. Harris not out	20		
B 7, l-b 7, w 6, n-b 2	22	L-b 4, w 1, n-b 4	9

1/15 (1) 2/25 (3) 3/108 (2) (125.1 overs) 395   1/14 (2) (4 wkts, 19.5 overs) 65
4/173 (5) 5/198 (4) 6/337 (6)   2/19 (1) 3/24 (4)
7/349 (8) 8/349 (9) 9/363 (10)   4/29 (3)
10/395 (7) 110 overs: 349-6

Lucas 28–7–64–5; Brooks 30–5–103–2; Daggett 25–3–107–2; Hall 26.1–7–66–1; Boje 16–3–41–0. *Second Innings*—Lucas 10–2–33–2; Brooks 9.5–3–28–2.

Northamptonshire

S. D. Peters c Jefferson b Harris	9	– b Buck	28
†P. W. Harrison c Boyce b Harris	0	– b White	16
M. B. Loye c Taylor b Henderson	44	– lbw b White	8
D. J. Sales c and b Henderson	39	– c Jefferson b Harris	24
R. A. White c New b Hoggard	4	– c Harris b White	68
V. Tripathi lbw b Henderson	8	– lbw b Henderson	28
A. J. Hall not out	26	– lbw b Buck	4
*N. Boje c Buck b Henderson	20	– b White	8
D. S. Lucas lbw b Henderson	13	– not out	40
J. A. Brooks c Taylor b Henderson	2	– b Henderson	2
L. M. Daggett c New b Hoggard	7	– c Boyce b Buck	28
B 1, l-b 11, w 6	18	B 3, l-b 12	15

1/0 (2) 2/13 (1) 3/96 (4) 4/101 (5) (70.4 overs) 190   1/37 (2) 2/55 (3) (81.4 overs) 269
5/105 (3) 6/110 (6) 7/146 (8)   3/59 (1) 4/118 (4)
8/168 (9) 9/172 (10) 10/190 (11)   5/164 (5) 6/182 (7) 7/194 (6)
8/194 (8) 9/217 (10) 10/269 (11)

Hoggard 14.4–3–35–2; Harris 15–5–55–2; Buck 13–5–32–0; White 8–0–35–0; Henderson 20–9–21–6. *Second Innings*—Hoggard 13–2–67–0; Harris 14–3–46–1; White 16–3–58–4; Buck 12.4–4–36–3; Henderson 25–9–47–2; Cobb 1–1–0–0.

Umpires: R. A. Kettleborough and S. J. Malone.

At Derby, April 15–18. LEICESTERSHIRE beat DERBYSHIRE by 203 runs.

At Cambridge, April 21–23. LEICESTERSHIRE drew with CAMBRIDGE MCCU (see Universities section).

At Hove, April 27–29. LEICESTERSHIRE lost to SUSSEX by ten wickets.

LEICESTERSHIRE v WORCESTERSHIRE

At Leicester, May 4–7. Worcestershire won by 173 runs. Worcestershire 22pts, Leicestershire 3pts. Toss: Worcestershire.

Leicestershire were a pale shadow of the side which won their first two games so convincingly. Moeen Ali's high-class 80, which included 18 off a Henderson over and was harsh on anything loose, launched Worcestershire towards a respectable first-innings score. Nixon apart, the Leicestershire batsmen could not cope with Jack Shantry's movement through the air and off the seam, and he claimed a maiden five-wicket haul in his seventh first-class match. Kervezee, still searching for a first Championship century in his 22nd innings, missed out by a solitary run when he was lbw to Buck, but Leicestershire were still obliged to make an unlikely 405. An unrelenting display from Richardson, the day after his 35th birthday, ensured they did not get close. Going for less than two runs an over, he shot through the heart of the batting and returned with the old ball to break the stubborn resistance of du Toit and New. White was unable to bat after breaking his finger in Leicestershire's first innings.

Close of play: First day, Leicestershire 9-0 (Jefferson 9, Boyce 0); Second day, Worcestershire 62-2 (Mitchell 23, Ali 21); Third day, Leicestershire 107-1 (Jefferson 60, Nixon 36).

Worcestershire

D. K. H. Mitchell lbw b Hoggard	56	– lbw b Buck	23
P. A. Jaques b Buck	0	– lbw b Buck	0
*V. S. Solanki c Henderson b Hoggard	9	– c Taylor b Buck	5
M. M. Ali lbw b Hoggard	80	– lbw b McDonald	42
A. N. Kervezee c Jefferson b McDonald	32	– lbw b Buck	99
B. F. Smith lbw b Henderson	8	– not out	51
†B. J. M. Scott c New b McDonald	5	– b McDonald	16
G. M. Andrew c White b Buck	53	– c New b McDonald	1
R. A. Jones not out	21	– b McDonald	0
A. Richardson c New b Buck	6	– (11) not out	10
J. D. Shantry lbw b White	7	– (10) lbw b McDonald	8
B 18, l-b 12, w 1	31	B 1, l-b 14, w 7	22
	308		**277**

1/0 (2) 2/15 (3) 3/160 (4) 4/177 (1) (92 overs) 308
5/186 (6) 6/199 (7) 7/250 (5) 8/286 (8)
9/292 (10) 10/308 (11)

1/5 (2) (9 wkts dec, 75 overs) 277
2/10 (3) 3/62 (1)
4/131 (4) 5/230 (5) 6/249 (7)
7/252 (8) 8/252 (9) 9/264 (10)

Hoggard 26–7–69–3; Buck 19–2–64–3; White 13–5–31–1; McDonald 20–3–54–2; Henderson 14–3–60–1. *Second Innings*—Hoggard 22–4–70–1; Buck 20–2–72–3; McDonald 17–4–40–5; White 12–1–63–0; Henderson 4–0–17–0.

Leicestershire

W. I. Jefferson lbw b Jones	9	– c Scott b Richardson	60
M. A. G. Boyce c Scott b Jones	19	– c Scott b Richardson	4
P. A. Nixon b Jones	74	– lbw b Jones	45
J. W. A. Taylor c Scott b Shantry	5	– c Scott b Richardson	3
A. B. McDonald c Mitchell b Shantry	15	– c Ali b Jones	0
J. du Toit lbw b Shantry	0	– c Solanki b Richardson	52
†T. J. New c Jaques b Richardson	22	– lbw b Richardson	42
W. A. White c Scott b Shantry	7	– absent hurt	
C. W. Henderson c Jaques b Richardson	23	– (8) b Andrew	0
N. L. Buck c Scott b Shantry	1	– (9) not out	4
*M. J. Hoggard not out	0	– (10) b Shantry	3
B 4, l-b 2	6	B 1, l-b 15, w 2	18

1/13 (1) 2/38 (2) 3/47 (4) 4/81 (5) (70.1 overs) 181
5/85 (6) 6/124 (7) 7/135 (8)
8/166 (9) 9/181 (3) 10/181 (10)

1/23 (2) 2/108 (1) (79 overs) 231
3/120 (3) 4/120 (5)
5/124 (4) 6/212 (7) 7/213 (8)
8/225 (6) 9/231 (10)

Richardson 21–10–45–2; Jones 18–3–49–3; Shantry 22.1–9–49–5; Andrew 9–0–32–0. *Second Innings*—Richardson 25–9–44–5; Jones 18–4–70–2; Shantry 17–3–62–1; Andrew 16–6–35–1; Ali 2–1–1–0; Mitchell 1–0–3–0.

Umpires: S. A. Garratt and J. F. Steele.

At Bristol, May 10–13. LEICESTERSHIRE lost to GLOUCESTERSHIRE by nine wickets.

LEICESTERSHIRE v GLAMORGAN

At Leicester, May 24–26. Glamorgan won by ten wickets. Glamorgan 19pts, Leicestershire 5pts. Toss: Leicestershire.

Glamorgan trailed by 125 runs on first innings, yet cantered home by ten wickets on the third afternoon in a game that demonstrated many of the second division's shortcomings. An excellent first Championship century by McDonald, countering considerable aerial movement, was accompanied by the unwelcome news that he would be needed by Australia A for five weeks in June and July, ruling him out of much of the Friends Provident T20. Hoggard took advantage of the conditions to race through Glamorgan for a mere 166 in reply. However, by the close of the second day the swinging ball had reduced Leicestershire to 45 for five. The fall of 17 wickets in 91 overs prompted an ECB pitch panel, though most observers agreed the deficiencies were the batsmen's. The panel concurred, rating the surface "above average", a verdict vindicated by the third day. Leicestershire may have sunk to a paltry 71 (their lowest total since folding for 69 at Worcester in 1997), but Glamorgan's openers encountered no problems in polishing off a target of 197 inside 34 overs. Cosgrove put bat to ball with devastating effect in his first century of the season, including 19 fours. It was Leicestershire's fourth defeat in a row.

Close of play: First day, Leicestershire 263-8 (McDonald 86, Hoggard 2); Second day, Leicestershire 45-5 (Taylor 19, Naik 6).

Leicestershire

P. A. Nixon c Dalrymple b Cosker	90	– c Wallace b Harrison	9
M. A. G. Boyce c Wallace b Harrison	45	– lbw b Harrison	1
†T. J. New lbw b Harris	1	– c Maynard b Harris	5
J. W. A. Taylor lbw b Harris	0	– not out	34
A. B. McDonald c Wallace b Harrison	113	– lbw b Harris	2
J. J. Cobb c Wallace b Harris	3	– lbw b Allenby	2
J. K. H. Naik lbw b Allenby	15	– lbw b Harris	6
C. W. Henderson lbw b Cosker	0	– c Maynard b Harrison	6
N. L. Buck c Dalrymple b Harrison	10	– c Allenby b Harrison	0
*M. J. Hoggard not out	3	– run out	0
H. F. Gurney c Dalrymple b Harrison	0	– c Harrison b Harris	4
B 4, l-b 3, w 2, n-b 2	11	B 1, l-b 1	2

1/94 (2) 2/95 (3) 3/104 (4) (103 overs) 291 1/8 (2) 2/11 (1) (36.4 overs) 71
4/161 (1) 5/177 (6) 6/200 (7) 7/205 (8) 3/15 (3) 4/17 (5)
8/242 (9) 9/291 (5) 10/291 (11) 5/36 (6) 6/45 (7) 7/54 (8)
8/59 (9) 9/67 (10) 10/71 (11)

Harris 27–7–74–3; Harrison 18–0–71–4; Owen 20–5–65–0; Cosker 18–4–44–2; Allenby 19–6–29–1; Dalrymple 1–0–1–0. *Second Innings*—Harris 14.4–7–34–4; Harrison 12–4–17–4; Allenby 6–2–10–1; Owen 4–1–8–0.

Glamorgan

G. P. Rees c McDonald b Gurney	14	– not out	73
M. J. Cosgrove lbw b Hoggard	25	– not out	113
*J. W. M. Dalrymple c Boyce b McDonald	17		
B. J. Wright lbw b Gurney	1		
T. L. Maynard c Naik b Hoggard	2		
J. Allenby c New b Hoggard	8		
†M. A. Wallace b Naik	36		
J. A. R. Harris lbw b Hoggard	23		
D. A. Cosker lbw b Henderson	8		
D. S. Harrison lbw b Henderson	17		
W. T. Owen not out	0		
B 12, l-b 3	15	B 8, l-b 2, n-b 2	12

1/41 (1) 2/45 (2) 3/46 (4) 4/53 (5) (56.1 overs) 166 (no wkt, 33.5 overs) 198
5/67 (6) 6/89 (3) 7/125 (7) 8/148 (9)
9/166 (10) 10/166 (8)

Hoggard 14.1–2–32–4; Buck 8–1–31–0; Gurney 12–6–33–2; McDonald 7–4–14–1; Naik 9–0–33–1; Henderson 6–5–8–2. *Second Innings*—Hoggard 8–1–48–0; Gurney 4–0–24–0; Buck 5.5–0–34–0; McDonald 5–1–21–0; Henderson 7–1–45–0; Naik 4–0–16–0.

Umpires: K. Coburn and B. Dudleston.

LEICESTERSHIRE v MIDDLESEX

At Leicester, May 29–June 1. Drawn. Leicestershire 9pts, Middlesex 8pts. Toss: Middlesex.

Rain washed out 86 overs of the first day and all of the fourth, so a draw – Leicestershire's first of the Championship season – was likely enough without four batsmen scoring centuries. Taylor and McDonald wrote themselves into the Leicestershire record books by adding an unbroken 360 in 73 overs. Coach Tim Boon watched while the pair took away the fourth-wicket record he had held with Peter Willey since 1984. For Taylor, still only 20 years old, it was his second double-hundred, while McDonald finished on a career-best 176 not out, guiding Leicestershire to maximum batting points for the first time in 11 months. Middlesex replied in kind, though Leicestershire's bowlers showed a little more gusto. They had Middlesex 35 for three, and missed a further opportunity when Shah was dropped on 39 by Jefferson, diving to his right at second slip. Thereafter, Shah and Dexter played with sense and application in stringing together 266, also for the fourth wicket. Adam Gilchrist,

Middlesex's marquee Twenty20 signing, dropped by and saw his new team-mates reach their hundreds.

Close of play: First day, Leicestershire 23-2 (Boyce 18, Taylor 0); Second day, Middlesex 19-0 (Robson 3, Newman 14); Third day, Middlesex 356-5 (Simpson 34, Berg 7).

Leicestershire

W. I. Jefferson run out	0	
M. A. G. Boyce b Berg	42	
P. A. Nixon c Simpson b O'Brien	4	
J. W. A. Taylor not out	206	
A. B. McDonald not out	176	
B 3, l-b 7, w 6, n-b 20	36	

1/0 (1)   2/16 (3)   (3 wkts dec, 97 overs) 464
3/104 (2)

J. du Toit, †T. J. New, C. W. Henderson, *M. J. Hoggard, N. L. Buck and H. F. Gurney did not bat.

Murtagh 23–8–82–0; O'Brien 10–0–51–1; Collins 15–1–86–0; Berg 15–1–78–1; Dexter 11–0–43–0; Udal 13–0–60–0; Malan 9–0–48–0; Robson 1–0–6–0.

Middlesex

S. D. Robson c Boyce b Gurney	7	G. K. Berg not out	7
S. A. Newman c New b Gurney	14	L-b 11, n-b 4	15
O. A. Shah c and b McDonald	156		
D. J. Malan lbw b Hoggard	5	1/23 (1) 2/28 (2) (5 wkts, 103 overs)	356
N. J. Dexter c Taylor b Gurney	118	3/35 (4) 4/301 (5)	
†J. A. Simpson not out	34	5/348 (3)	

*S. D. Udal, T. J. Murtagh, I. E. O'Brien and P. T. Collins did not bat.

Hoggard 24–9–46–1; Gurney 24–3–82–3; McDonald 16–4–52–1; Buck 18–4–71–0; Henderson 20–2–78–0; du Toit 1–0–16–0.

Umpires: M. R. Benson and N. G. B. Cook.

At The Oval, June 4–6. LEICESTERSHIRE beat SURREY by an innings and 60 runs.

At Worcester, June 28–30. LEICESTERSHIRE beat WORCESTERSHIRE by seven wickets.

At Leicester, July 8–9. LEICESTERSHIRE drew with PAKISTANIS (see Pakistani tour section).

At Swansea, July 21–24. LEICESTERSHIRE drew with GLAMORGAN.

LEICESTERSHIRE v SUSSEX

At Leicester, July 29–31. Sussex won by an innings and 19 runs. Sussex 23pts, Leicestershire 4pts. Toss: Sussex.

Nash, who had previously converted just six of his 30 fifties into centuries, expertly laid the platform for Sussex to complete an innings victory with a day to spare. Without his determined 246-ball 184, the highest score of his career, the result might have been considerably closer. After 40 overs of their first innings Sussex were stuttering on 144 for five with Hoggard causing real problems. But Nash began to treat the Leicestershire attack with disdain, striking Buck for three fours and a six in the first over of the second new ball. He chiselled out a lead of 175, and Leicestershire wilted in response. Undone by Lewis Hatchett's maiden five-wicket return in their first innings, they succumbed to a more seasoned campaigner in Collymore, who bustled in with six for 48, his best figures for Sussex. Only du Toit mastered the balance between attack and defence, striking 13 fours before edging Collymore to slip.

Close of play: First day, Sussex 128-4 (Nash 52, Hatchett 0); Second day, Leicestershire 59-4 (du Toit 31, New 2).

Leicestershire

W. I. Jefferson lbw b Hatchett	7	– lbw b Collymore	6
P. A. Nixon c Joyce b Collymore	22	– lbw b Collymore	0
J. du Toit b Collymore	19	– c Yardy b Collymore	81
J. W. A. Taylor lbw b Yasir Arafat	19	– c Brown b Yasir Arafat	5
A. B. McDonald lbw b Panesar	63	– b Yasir Arafat	10
†T. J. New run out	9	– b Hatchett	2
W. A. White b Hatchett	21	– st Brown b Panesar	23
C. W. Henderson b Hatchett	11	– c Yardy b Collymore	0
M. N. Malik c Brown b Hatchett	0	– lbw b Collymore	6
N. L. Buck not out	4	– not out	8
*M. J. Hoggard b Hatchett	2	– c Yardy b Collymore	1
B 6, l-b 11, w 5, n-b 6	28	B 4, l-b 2, n-b 8	14

1/27 (1) 2/49 (2) 3/58 (3)   (61.1 overs) 204
4/110 (5) 5/133 (6) 6/172 (5) 7/193 (8)
8/193 (9) 9/202 (7) 10/204 (11)

1/0 (2) 2/13 (1)   (43.1 overs) 156
3/18 (4) 4/54 (5)
5/59 (6) 6/138 (3) 7/138 (8)
8/146 (7) 9/150 (9) 10/156 (11)

Yasir Arafat 13–2–47–1; Collymore 18–8–42–2; Hatchett 14.1–2–47–5; Aga 7–1–38–0; Panesar 9–4–13–1. *Second Innings*—Yasir Arafat 11–1–42–2; Collymore 13.1–5–48–6; Hatchett 8–0–45–1; Panesar 11–4–15–1.

Sussex

*M. H. Yardy lbw b Hoggard	2	R. G. Aga c New b Buck	0
C. D. Nash c Buck b Hoggard	184	M. S. Panesar b Buck	0
E. C. Joyce c Taylor b Hoggard	14	C. D. Collymore not out	12
M. W. Goodwin lbw b Buck	19	B 2, l-b 10, w 2, n-b 2	16
L. J. Wright b Hoggard	36		
L. J. Hatchett b Hoggard	0	1/2 (1) 2/40 (3) 3/70 (4) (98.5 overs) 379
†B. C. Brown c White b Henderson	38	4/127 (5) 5/144 (6) 6/253 (7)
Yasir Arafat b Henderson	58	7/321 (2) 8/327 (9) 9/328 (10) 10/379 (8)

Hoggard 25–4–81–5; Buck 20–0–110–3; Malik 20–4–53–0; White 14–2–48–0; Henderson 19.5–3–75–2.

Umpires: N. L. Bainton and N. G. B. Cook.

LEICESTERSHIRE v DERBYSHIRE

At Leicester, August 3–6. Leicestershire won by ten wickets. Leicestershire 21pts, Derbyshire 3pts. Toss: Derbyshire.

Few at Grace Road could have anticipated an emphatic ten-wicket win for Leicestershire as the final day dawned. They held the upper hand, but Derbyshire's lead of 144 with five wickets intact was beginning to look useful in a match hitherto controlled by bowlers. The bottom side's self-belief swiftly unravelled as they were routed for a further 24 runs, the rot setting in after Hoggard struck two early blows, including the wicket of Hughes, his 700th first-class victim. With Buck producing a venomous spell at the other end, Leicestershire were left to chase 169. That seemed far from straightforward with the ball swinging appreciably under heavy cloud cover, especially without the reassuring McDonald, out for the season with a shoulder injury. But openers Boyce and Greg Smith, playing his first Championship match of the summer after completing his second year at Durham University, made light of the task, helped by wayward fielding and bowling that contributed 32 extras. Derbyshire also fielded a Greg Smith, and each was instrumental in the other's downfall during the match. It was Leicestershire's first victory at home in any competition since April 25. A group of disgruntled members were collecting signatures to secure a vote of no confidence in club chairman Neil Davidson.

Close of play: First day, Leicestershire 117-1 (Boyce 51, du Toit 30); Second day, Leicestershire 260-6 (New 45, Henderson 24); Third day, Derbyshire 238-5 (Hughes 30, Peterson 1).

Derbyshire

*C. J. L. Rogers lbw b Hoggard	8	– (2) c Boyce b Malik	47
W. L. Madsen c New b Hoggard	14	– (1) c Nixon b Henderson	66
G. T. Park c du Toit b Hoggard	9	– c New b Henderson	29
C. F. Hughes lbw b Hoggard	0	– lbw b Hoggard	32
G. M. Smith lbw b Malik	4	– c Smith b Buck	27
D. J. Redfern c Boyce b Henderson	85	– c Taylor b Henderson	17
R. J. Peterson c Smith b Malik	6	– b Hoggard	1
†L. J. Goddard c New b Malik	0	– c New b Buck	6
P. S. Jones c du Toit b Malik	14	– b Buck	1
T. D. Groenewald b Buck	21	– c New b Buck	11
M. H. A. Footitt not out	2	– not out	0
B 4, l-b 11, w 2, n-b 2	19	B 6, l-b 17, w 2	25

1/18 (1) 2/23 (2) 3/32 (3) 4/37 (5)   (56.2 overs) 182   1/86 (2) 2/144 (3)   (86 overs) 262
5/37 (4) 6/46 (7) 7/46 (8) 8/67 (9)   3/153 (1) 4/196 (5)
9/156 (10) 10/182 (6)   5/237 (6) 6/240 (7) 7/245 (4)
                                                                8/250 (9) 9/253 (8) 10/262 (10)

Hoggard 24–6–77–4; Buck 14–4–38–1; Malik 14–6–32–4; White 2–0–8–0; Henderson 2.2–0–12–1. *Second Innings*—Hoggard 14.1–1–59–2; Buck 20–6–60–4; Henderson 25–7–46–3; Malik 15.3–3–37–1; White 12–1–37–0.

Leicestershire

G. P. Smith b Smith	21	– not out	52
M. A. G. Boyce c Rogers b Groenewald	60	– not out	86
J. du Toit c Peterson b Jones	44		
J. W. A. Taylor c Goddard b Footitt	18		
P. A. Nixon b Smith	18		
†T. J. New run out	54		
W. A. White c Hughes b Footitt	4		
C. W. Henderson b Jones	24		
M. N. Malik lbw b Smith	0		
N. L. Buck lbw b Jones	5		
*M. J. Hoggard not out	1		
B 5, l-b 8, w 4, n-b 10	27	B 13, l-b 14, w 1, n-b 4	32

1/54 (1) 2/139 (3) 3/140 (2)   (103.1 overs) 276   (no wkt, 40.4 overs) 170
4/163 (4) 5/181 (5) 6/196 (7)
7/262 (8) 8/263 (9) 9/274 (10) 10/276 (6)

Groenewald 22–6–65–1; Footitt 19.1–6–67–2; Jones 27–7–67–3; Smith 23–4–40–3; Peterson 11–4–22–0; Park 1–0–2–0. *Second Innings*—Jones 5–1–13–0; Groenewald 10–1–34–0; Footitt 8–2–41–0; Smith 9.4–2–30–0; Peterson 5–0–17–0; Park 3–0–8–0.

Umpires: P. J. Hartley and R. K. Illingworth.

At Lord's, August 9–12. LEICESTERSHIRE drew with MIDDLESEX.

LEICESTERSHIRE v SURREY

At Leicester, August 24–27. Drawn. Leicestershire 4pts, Surrey 8pts. Toss: Leicestershire. First-class debut: J. J. Roy. Championship debut: S. P. Cheetham.

Cricket played out against a backdrop of mutiny at Grace Road, following calls from players and staff for chairman Neil Davidson to stand down. Hoggard and Boon had written to the board alleging he had interfered in selection; Davidson came out fighting when he addressed the media on the boundary edge as the match began. He maintained any interventions were justified by Leicestershire's "dreadful" form. The players contemplated an on-field protest, but eventually decided against it. Surrey dominated the first two days through 179 from Ramprakash, a maiden first-class century for Ireland wicketkeeper Gary Wilson (playing as a specialist batsman), and 76 in 65 balls from debutant

Jason Roy, who hit three sixes. Rain wiped out much of day two and all of the third, prompting the captains to concoct a formula that ultimately required Leicestershire to chase 361 in a minimum of 76 overs. They made a good fist of it, too, and a stand of 183 for the fourth wicket between du Toit and Nixon had them on course for victory. But when du Toit fell for an excellent century 69 runs short of the target, Leicestershire lost momentum – and five wickets for 42 runs. Nixon was unable to lift the scoring-rate against excellent bowling, notably from Tremlett, who hit yorker length with unerring accuracy in the closing overs to leave them 23 runs adrift.

Close of play: First day, Surrey 353-4 (Ramprakash 179, Wilson 94); Second day, Leicestershire 32-0 (Smith 9, Boyce 16); Third day, No play.

Surrey

T. J. Lancefield lbw b Hoggard	5	J. W. Dernbach c du Toit b Malik 0
A. Harinath lbw b Hoggard	4	S. P. Cheetham not out 0
M. R. Ramprakash b Hoggard	179	
*R. J. Hamilton-Brown c Taylor b Henderson	36	L-b 20, w 3, n-b 2 25
†S. M. Davies c du Toit b Henderson	19	
G. C. Wilson c Boyce b Malik	125	1/10 (2) 2/11 (1) 3/66 (4) (121.1 overs) 483
J. J. Roy c Buck b Henderson	76	4/136 (5) 5/354 (3) 6/425 (6)
G. J. Batty c Hoggard b Henderson	13	7/476 (8) 8/483 (9)
C. T. Tremlett c New b Malik	1	9/483 (10) 10/483 (7) 110 overs: 414-5

Hoggard 27–5–68–3; Buck 23–5–105–0; White 11–1–75–0; Malik 24–4–83–3; Henderson 33.1–3–119–4; Taylor 3–0–13–0.

Surrey forfeited their second innings.

Leicestershire

G. P. Smith not out.	58	– lbw b Cheetham 23
M. A. G. Boyce not out	57	– b Batty 44
J. du Toit (did not bat)		– c Batty b Cheetham 122
J. W. A. Taylor (did not bat)		– lbw b Batty 0
P. A. Nixon (did not bat)		– b Dernbach 106
†T. J. New (did not bat)		– c Wilson b Batty 2
W. A. White (did not bat)		– b Tremlett 7
C. W. Henderson (did not bat)		– b Tremlett 3
M. N. Malik (did not bat)		– not out 0
N. L. Buck (did not bat)		– not out 4
L-b 3, w 1, n-b 4	8	L-b 20, w 3, n-b 4 27

(no wkt dec, 30.4 overs)	123	1/38 (1) (8 wkts dec, 75.5 overs) 338
		2/109 (2) 3/109 (4)
		4/292 (3) 5/298 (6) 6/322 (7)
		7/334 (5) 8/334 (10)

*M. J. Hoggard did not bat.

Tremlett 7–1–18–0; Dernbach 6–1–12–0; Wilson 9–0–44–0; Ramprakash 1–0–6–0; Harinath 2–0–12–0; Hamilton-Brown 5.4–0–28–0. *Second Innings*—Tremlett 21–0–87–2; Dernbach 14.5–5–64–1; Cheetham 16–1–71–2; Roy 1–0–6–0; Batty 22–3–78–3; Hamilton-Brown 1–0–12–0.

Umpires: N. L. Bainton and V. A. Holder.

LEICESTERSHIRE v GLOUCESTERSHIRE

At Leicester, September 7–10. Leicestershire won by 329 runs. Leicestershire 21pts, Gloucestershire 3pts. Toss: Leicestershire.

Gloucestershire were the side with promotion on their minds ahead of the match, but it was Leicestershire who emerged with a faint chance of going up. After their tail wagged them towards 300, Buck ensured a first-innings lead of 136. Greg Smith then batted Gloucestershire out of the contest on day three through an unflustered, career-best unbeaten 158. It was a marathon effort: he hit only ten fours but always looked secure as he established an unassailable advantage of 487. Gloucestershire's attack badly missed the energetic Steve Kirby, whose move to Somerset was confirmed a few days later. Leicestershire's principal concern on the last day was the weather, which delayed the start for 45 minutes and caused an early lunch. They needn't have worried: Buck had already dismantled the top order, and spinners Henderson and Naik exploited a wearing pitch to claim six of the last seven wickets. The total number of first-class runs conceded by Leicestershire went past the one million mark on the first day.

Close of play: First day, Gloucestershire 54-2 (Batty 24, Marshall 19); Second day, Leicestershire 147-1 (Smith 70, du Toit 34); Third day, Gloucestershire 78-5 (Gidman 23).

Leicestershire

G. P. Smith c Taylor b Lewis	28	– not out	158
M. A. G. Boyce c Batty b Hussain	1	– c Young b Franklin	36
J. du Toit c Marshall b Ireland	46	– c Hussain b Lewis	70
J. W. A. Taylor lbw b Lewis	0	– lbw b Taylor	36
P. A. Nixon lbw b Franklin	43	– c Dent b Ireland	23
†T. J. New c Dent b Ireland	63	– not out	10
J. K. H. Naik c Dent b Gidman	0		
C. W. Henderson c Marshall b Young	33		
N. L. Buck c Batty b Lewis	26		
M. N. Malik c Batty b Lewis	34		
*M. J. Hoggard not out	2		
B 7, l-b 3, w 1, n-b 8	19	B 5, l-b 7, n-b 6	18
	——		——

1/30 (2) 2/30 (1) 3/36 (4) 4/91 (3)   (78.1 overs) 295   1/69 (2)   (4 wkts dec, 100 overs) 351
5/167 (5) 6/167 (7) 7/223 (8)   2/197 (3) 3/288 (4)
8/226 (6) 9/288 (10) 10/295 (9)   4/326 (5)

Lewis 16.1–9–42–4; Hussain 16–4–54–1; Ireland 13–0–71–2; Franklin 11–5–17–1; Young 18–0–75–1; Gidman 4–0–26–1. *Second Innings*—Hussain 16–3–58–0; Lewis 13–4–28–1; Ireland 18–3–73–1; Franklin 10–2–38–1; Young 11–0–50–0; Taylor 21–4–49–1; Dent 11–0–43–0.

Gloucestershire

†J. N. Batty c New b Hoggard	29	– c Naik b Buck	1
W. T. S. Porterfield lbw b Buck	5	– c Hoggard b Buck	1
C. D. J. Dent lbw b Buck	0	– lbw b Hoggard	0
H. J. H. Marshall c Boyce b Malik	61	– c New b Henderson	45
*A. P. R. Gidman c New b Buck	8	– b Henderson	29
C. G. Taylor lbw b Malik	5	– c Boyce b Naik	4
J. E. C. Franklin c and b Henderson	23	– c Boyce b Henderson	31
E. G. C. Young c du Toit b Naik	19	– b Naik	38
J. Lewis lbw b Henderson	0	– lbw b Naik	0
G. M. Hussain not out	0	– not out	1
A. J. Ireland c Hoggard b Naik	0	– c Smith b Buck	0
B 4, l-b 3, w 2	9	B 2, l-b 5, w 1	8
	——		——

1/10 (2) 2/10 (3) 3/81 (1) 4/96 (5)   (59.5 overs) 159   1/2 (1) 2/5 (2)   (87.2 overs) 158
5/116 (4) 6/117 (6) 7/155 (7)   3/5 (3) 4/71 (4) 5/78 (6)
8/155 (9) 9/159 (8) 10/159 (11)   6/88 (5) 7/151 (7) 8/152 (9)
      9/157 (8) 10/158 (11)

Buck 12–2–47–3; Hoggard 15–4–47–1; Malik 11–2–32–2; Henderson 18–9–17–2; Naik 3.5–0–9–2. *Second Innings*—Buck 10.2–5–25–3; Hoggard 12–6–15–1; Henderson 34–12–62–3; Malik 6–2–14–0; Naik 25–13–35–3.

Umpires: N. L. Bainton and B. Dudleston.

At Northampton, September 13–16. LEICESTERSHIRE beat NORTHAMPTONSHIRE by ten wickets.

MIDDLESEX

Too many captains, too few starts

Norman de Mesquita

A stranger attending the Middlesex end-of-season dinner could have been excused for thinking the county had just enjoyed a highly successful year, as more than a dozen players received awards. In fact, 2010 was yet another disappointing season, ending in a regrettable controversy surrounding the release of Owais Shah, a Middlesex player since his teens. Shah was upset to hear of it through a friend, after a local news agency broke a pre-arranged embargo with the club. Managing director of cricket Angus Fraser apologised to Shah for the bungled announcement, but reiterated his belief that the squad needed "freshening up".

Members were divided. Some were adamant that, too often, Shah would reach a half-century, and then, with the match on the line and a big innings required, would get himself out to a bizarre shot. Just as many felt that Middlesex's batting lacked genuine class, and Shah was one of the few in possession of it. Either way, he commanded a high salary. Shah described 2010 as "one poor season in a 16-year career". He scored a fifty in his last one-day match, and a Championship century – only his second of the season – in his farewell at Lord's. He made it clear where his sympathies lay, raising his bat to the crowd, but not the dressing- or committee-rooms. So Shah leaves with 13,377 runs and 38 hundreds from 200 first-class matches for Middlesex, and no doubt will take great delight in scoring many more for Essex against his former county, just as Mark Ramprakash has done with Surrey.

There was simply no coming back from four consecutive defeats, the worst start to a Championship season in Middlesex's history. The early absence of Neil Dexter through injury, and of Shah and Eoin Morgan, in the IPL and World Twenty20, did not help. Neither did Scott Newman's inability to find any form: of his first 11 Championship innings, seven ended in single figures. He recovered to score 945 runs, second only to Dawid Malan, who hit three centuries and was the sole batsman to pass 1,000. Imposing early-season scores from Newman, or indeed Andrew Strauss in the seven matches he played before resuming the England captaincy, would have made a world of difference.

Shaun Udal, a proud man, took the defeats personally and decided that the cares of captaincy were affecting his bowling, so he stood down during the Friends Provident T20, soon after Northamptonshire had completed a Championship double. His retirement from all first-class cricket followed in October. Adam Gilchrist, a box-office Twenty20 signing, took over as captain for his last six games, until handing over to Dexter. So, as in 2008, Middlesex had three different captains in one season. Such inconsistency in leadership is not likely to help a struggling side. Encouragingly, Dexter still finished top of the county's first-class averages and was named Player of the Year.

As MCC helped to sign him, Gilchrist was originally contracted to play only at Lord's. But his two memorable innings came elsewhere: 51 on his return to Richmond (where he played as a 17-year-old in the Middlesex League), and a 47-ball hundred at Canterbury, which won him the Walter Lawrence Trophy. He left midway through the tournament, and Middlesex failed to make the quarter-finals on run-rate alone. A miserable CB40 campaign featured six consecutive defeats.

Toby Roland-Jones

The advances made by Adam London, Dan Housego and Kabir Toor were cited as reasons for optimism in last year's review. But there was no way of knowing if their promise could be fulfilled because, in 2010, London appeared in only four matches, Housego two and Toor one. London scored 77 against Northamptonshire and was sent back to the second team; Housego made three centuries and two fifties in the Second Eleven Championship.

Two who did come to the fore were John Simpson and Toby Roland-Jones, both 22. Simpson's wicketkeeping improved steadily, justifying the decision to promote him above Ben Scott, who spent the first half of the season on loan at Worcestershire. Simpson possessed a good, basic batting method, although asking him to combine opening with keeping wicket (as he did from July onwards) seemed unfair. Roland-Jones played only seven Championship matches, but his bustling fast-medium brought him 36 wickets – more than any of his team-mates. He does need to work on his fielding.

With Steve Finn now an England regular and Pedro Collins moving on after one season, Middlesex's new-ball resources look stretched. The club had hoped to sign Makhaya Ntini as a Kolpak player, but Ntini believed he could still win his place back with South Africa, so he spent a few weeks as an official overseas player at Kent instead.

Unfortunately, injuries restricted Middlesex's overseas seamer Iain O'Brien to seven matches and, while he blossomed in the commentary box, that was hardly what he was signed for. By the winter, O'Brien's future was in doubt: Middlesex lost their appeal to have him registered as a home-qualified player.

The excessive work shouldered by Tim Murtagh, who looked somewhat jaded, was another worry. Two bowlers have been signed to support him, Corey Collymore, from Sussex, and Anthony Ireland, from Gloucestershire. A third newcomer will be Chris Rogers, who was persuaded to leave Derbyshire and become lead overseas player. In 15 Championship matches in 2010, he scored 1,285 runs, and he scored them quickly. Rogers should give Middlesex the starts they so desperately need.

MIDDLESEX RESULTS

All first-class matches – Played 17: Won 5, Lost 7, Drawn 5.
County Championship matches – Played 16: Won 4, Lost 7, Drawn 5.

LV= County Championship, 8th in Division 2;
Friends Provident T20, 6th in South Division; Clydesdale Bank 40, 6th in Group B.

COUNTY CHAMPIONSHIP AVERAGES, BATTING AND FIELDING

Cap		M	I	NO	R	HS	100s	50s	Avge	Ct/St
2010	N. J. Dexter¶	12	21	2	907	118	2	5	47.73	10
2010	D. J. Malan	16	29	3	1,001	115	3	5	38.50	19
2000	O. A. Shah‡	13	23	1	804	156	2	3	36.54	10
2010	G. K. Berg¶	15	26	5	761	125	1	3	36.23	7
	S. A. Newman	15	27	0	945	126	2	6	35.00	8
2001	A. J. Strauss‡	8	15	0	460	92	0	3	30.66	16
	J. A. Simpson	16	27	2	657	101*	1	2	26.28	42/3
	A. B. London†	3	5	0	120	77	0	1	24.00	3
	S. D. Robson¶	7	13	0	291	59	0	2	22.38	6
	J. H. Davey	3	5	0	94	61	0	1	18.80	2
2008	T. J. Murtagh	15	23	10	241	50*	0	1	18.53	4
	T. M. J. Smith	4	7	1	110	33	0	0	18.33	3
2008	S. D. Udal	13	19	1	216	55	0	1	12.00	6
	D. Evans	3	4	2	23	19*	0	0	11.50	1
	T. S. Roland-Jones†	7	11	1	109	26	0	0	10.90	2
	I. E. O'Brien§	7	9	1	39	14*	0	0	4.87	1
2009	S. T. Finn‡	7	11	3	34	18	0	0	4.25	1
	P. T. Collins¶	10	13	4	36	13	0	0	4.00	0

Also batted: D. M. Housego (1 match) 32, 4 (1 ct); E. J. G. Morgan‡ (cap 2008) (1 match) 58, 58*.

† *Born in Middlesex.* ‡ *ECB contract.* § *Official overseas player.* ¶ *Other non-England-qualified player.*

BOWLING

	O	M	R	W	BB	5W/i	Avge
T. S. Roland-Jones	206.2	27	688	36	5-41	2	19.11
S. T. Finn	261.1	54	844	36	9-37	2	23.44
I. E. O'Brien	205.1	36	628	23	7-48	1	27.30
P. T. Collins	284.4	51	999	36	4-46	0	27.75
N. J. Dexter	120	25	378	13	3-50	0	29.07
S. D. Udal	284.3	38	917	27	5-128	1	33.96
G. K. Berg	235	32	877	24	4-72	0	36.54
T. J. Murtagh	459.2	127	1,405	38	5-52	2	36.97

Also bowled: J. H. Davey 13–2–42–0; D. Evans 81.4–14–324–9; D. J. Malan 74.1–2–339–6; S. D. Robson 2–0–17–0; O. A. Shah 43.5–5–133–4; T. M. J. Smith 72–12–262–2.

LEADING CB40 AVERAGES (100 runs/4 wickets)

Batting	Runs	HS	Avge	S-R	Ct/St
O. A. Shah	337	111	42.12	76.94	4
N. J. Dexter	242	56*	40.33	92.01	3
G. K. Berg	306	53	34.00	95.92	5
S. A. Newman	357	122	32.45	94.94	3
J. A. Simpson	219	82	31.28	79.34	8/3
D. J. Malan	231	42	23.10	69.57	5

Bowling	W	BB	Avge	E-R
I. E. O'Brien	4	4-41	10.25	6.15
S. T. Finn	4	2-31	17.75	4.43
P. T. Collins	13	4-25	18.76	5.34
T. M. J. Smith	7	3-26	21.28	5.13
T. J. Murtagh	14	3-35	30.78	5.57
T. S. Roland-Jones .	10	3-55	31.60	5.96

LEADING FPT20 AVERAGES (100 runs/18 overs)

Batting	Runs	HS	Avge	S-R	Ct/St
E. J. G. Morgan	148	79*	74.00	189.74	1
G. K. Berg	160	41	26.66	170.21	7
A. C. Gilchrist	212	106	30.28	153.62	4/5
D. J. Malan	364	86	33.09	130.00	2
D. A. Warner	268	43	20.61	126.41	4
N. J. Dexter	349	62*	26.84	114.05	6

Bowling	W	BB	Avge	E-R
N. J. Dexter	14	2-8	22.64	6.91
S. D. Udal	5	3-24	29.20	6.95
T. Henderson	9	3-25	28.66	7.37
T. M. J. Smith	18	5-24	17.27	7.80
P. T. Collins	16	3-27	26.37	7.81
G. K. Berg	6	2-45	48.66	7.89

FIRST-CLASS COUNTY RECORDS

Highest score for	331*	J. D. Robertson v Worcestershire at Worcester	1949
Highest score against	341	C. M. Spearman (Gloucestershire) at Gloucester	2004
Leading run-scorer	40,302	E. H. Hendren (avge 48.81)	1907–1937
Best bowling for	10-40	G. O. B. Allen v Lancashire at Lord's	1929
Best bowling against	9-38	R. C. Robertson-Glasgow (Somerset) at Lord's	1924
Leading wicket-taker	2,361	F. J. Titmus (avge 21.27)	1949–1982
Highest total for	642-3 dec	v Hampshire at Southampton	1923
Highest total against	850-7 dec	by Somerset at Taunton	2007
Lowest total for	20	v MCC at Lord's	1864
Lowest total against	{ 31	by Gloucestershire at Bristol	1924
	31	by Glamorgan at Cardiff	1997

LIST A COUNTY RECORDS

Highest score for	163	A. J. Strauss v Surrey at The Oval	2008
Highest score against	163	C. J. Adams (Sussex) at Arundel	1999
Leading run-scorer	12,029	M. W. Gatting (avge 34.96)	1975–1998
Best bowling for	7-12	W. W. Daniel v Minor Counties East at Ipswich	1978
Best bowling against	6-27	J. C. Tredwell (Kent) at Southgate	2009
Leading wicket-taker	491	J. E. Emburey (avge 24.68)	1975–1995
Highest total for	341-7	v Somerset at Lord's	2009
Highest total against	353-8	by Hampshire at Lord's	2005
Lowest total for	23	v Yorkshire at Leeds	1974
Lowest total against	41	by Northamptonshire at Northampton	1972

TWENTY20 RECORDS

Highest score for	106	A. C. Gilchrist v Kent at Canterbury	2010
Highest score against	112	A. Symonds (Kent) at Maidstone	2004
Leading run-scorer	1,376	O. A. Shah (avge 34.40)	2003–2010
Best bowling for	5-13	M. Kartik v Essex at Lord's	2007
Best bowling against	6-24	T. J. Murtagh (Surrey) at Lord's	2005
Leading wicket-taker	46	T. Henderson (avge 23.69)	2007–2010
Highest total for	213-4	v Glamorgan at Richmond	2010
Highest total against	225-2	by Hampshire at Southampton	2006
Lowest total for	104-6	v Kent at Canterbury	2009
Lowest total against	99	by Hampshire at Southampton	2010

ADDRESS

Lord's Cricket Ground, London NW8 8QN (020 7289 1300; **email** enquiries@middlesexccc.com).
Website www.middlesexccc.com

OFFICIALS

Captain 2010 – S. D. Udal
2011 – N. J. Dexter
Managing director of cricket A. R. C. Fraser
First-team coach R. J. Scott
President to be announced

Chairman I. N. Lovett
Secretary/chief executive V. J. Codrington
Head groundsman M. J. Hunt
Scorer D. K. Shelley

At Worcester, April 9–11. MIDDLESEX lost to WORCESTERSHIRE by 111 runs. *Steve Finn takes 14-106 in a losing cause, the best match figures of the 2010 season.*

MIDDLESEX v GLAMORGAN

At Lord's, April 15–18. Glamorgan won by 78 runs. Glamorgan 22pts, Middlesex 3pts. Toss: Glamorgan.

Glamorgan won a Championship match at Lord's for the first time since 1954. In the 55 seasons since Wilf Wooller took nine wickets in a 22-run victory, they had lost 15 and drawn 17, though they did triumph in Middlesex once, at Southgate in 2000. The reason for the sequence ending was not hard to fathom. Missing Shah (in the IPL), Morgan (between the IPL and the World Twenty20) and Dexter (who cracked a vertebra when he slipped putting the rubbish out), Middlesex's batting was callow and flimsy. Glamorgan fought back from two tough exposures to the new ball and, though the absence of the heavy roller aided the bowlers, Middlesex largely self-destructed as Harrison claimed his first five-for in four years. Only Strauss and Simpson passed 17. Dalrymple declined to enforce the follow-on, and Glamorgan were almost caught napping. Cosgrove ducked into a Finn bouncer and retired hurt; six others followed him to the pavilion before the second day – which yielded 17 wickets – was out. Gritty tail-end resistance set Middlesex 375 and, despite crunching strokes from Strauss and a determined century by Malan – his first since his debut in 2008 – the chase was never really on.

Close of play: First day, Glamorgan 309-9 (Wallace 73, Waters 5); Second day, Glamorgan 119-6 (Wallace 12, Cosker 0); Third day, Middlesex 187-4 (Malan 94, O'Brien 2).

Glamorgan

G. P. Rees c London b O'Brien	38	– c Malan b Berg	20
M. J. Cosgrove b Finn	0	– c London b Berg	17
M. J. Powell c Simpson b Murtagh	55	– b Murtagh	47
B. J. Wright b Berg	11	– lbw b O'Brien	4
*J. W. M. Dalrymple lbw b Berg	24	– c Malan b Berg	0
J. Allenby lbw b Malan	57	– lbw b Finn	15
†M. A. Wallace not out	79	– c Simpson b Berg	37
J. A. R. Harris c Strauss b Murtagh	7	– lbw b Murtagh	2
D. A. Cosker lbw b O'Brien	10	– not out	49
D. S. Harrison c Udal b Berg	9	– c London b Udal	24
H. T. Waters c Robson b Finn	5	– c and b Murtagh	1
L-b 13, w 1, n-b 6	20	L-b 3	3

1/0 (2) 2/84 (3) 3/105 (1) (97.2 overs) 315   1/57 (1) 2/72 (4) (73 overs) 219
4/131 (4) 5/147 (5) 6/258 (6) 7/274 (8)   3/73 (5) 4/101 (6)
8/291 (9) 9/300 (10) 10/315 (11)   5/107 (3) 6/117 (8) 7/153 (7)
                                      8/153 (2) 9/207 (10) 10/219 (11)

In the second innings Cosgrove, when 17, retired hurt at 23 and resumed at 153-7.

Murtagh 24–7–57–2; Finn 22.2–5–69–2; O'Brien 20–2–59–2; Berg 17–4–59–3; Udal 10–2–33–0; Malan 4–0–25–1. *Second Innings*—Murtagh 19–3–53–3; Finn 18–4–45–1; O'Brien 14–2–40–1; Berg 18–1–72–4; Udal 4–1–6–1.

Middlesex

S. A. Newman c Cosgrove b Harrison	7	– lbw b Harris	0
A. J. Strauss b Allenby	44	– b Dalrymple	69
S. D. Robson lbw b Harrison	0	– c Dalrymple b Harrison	0
D. J. Malan b Allenby	17	– c Wallace b Dalrymple	115
A. B. London b Harrison	6	– c Allenby b Cosker	13
†J. A. Simpson lbw b Cosker	32	– (7) c Dalrymple b Cosker	12
G. K. Berg lbw b Harrison	14	– (8) c Wallace b Waters	28
*S. D. Udal lbw b Allenby	15	– (9) c Cosker b Waters	23
T. J. Murtagh c Cosgrove b Allenby	13	– (10) not out	9
I. E. O'Brien c Wallace b Harrison	0	– (6) c Cosgrove b Waters	13
S. T. Finn not out	0	– c Dalrymple b Waters	0
L-b 12	12	B 8, l-b 6	14
	—		—
	160		296

1/11 (1) 2/21 (3) 3/71 (4) 4/72 (2) (51.2 overs) 160
5/80 (5) 6/103 (7) 7/141 (6)
8/153 (8) 9/160 (10) 10/160 (9)

1/0 (1) 2/1 (3) (95.1 overs) 296
3/144 (2) 4/184 (5)
5/208 (6) 6/236 (4) 7/240 (7)
8/285 (8) 9/290 (9) 10/296 (11)

Harris 7–1–21–0; Harrison 18–2–62–5; Waters 10–1–28–0; Allenby 13.2–3–29–4; Cosker 3–1–8–1. *Second Innings*—Harris 27–10–66–1; Harrison 14–2–64–1; Allenby 7–0–31–0; Waters 21.1–7–39–4; Cosker 10–2–37–2; Cosgrove 2–0–14–0; Dalrymple 14–1–31–2.

Umpires: R. J. Bailey and S. A. Garratt.

At Northampton, April 21–24. MIDDLESEX lost to NORTHAMPTONSHIRE by six wickets.

MIDDLESEX v GLOUCESTERSHIRE

At Lord's, April 27–30. Gloucestershire won by 103 runs. Gloucestershire 21pts, Middlesex 4pts. Toss: Gloucestershire.

Middlesex's fourth consecutive defeat completed their worst start to a Championship season. Gidman's most illustrious predecessor as Gloucestershire captain, W. G. Grace, inflicted the final defeat when Middlesex last suffered a similar sequence, in 1885 – before the Championship was officially constituted. Defeat came in spite of O'Brien's best figures in England (Finn had been rested at the ECB's request), and the return of Shah for his first domestic match of the season. After some eye-catching drives, he contributed just 36 and, with Newman making his eighth single-figure score in his last ten first-class innings, the batting remained brittle. Fourteen wickets fell on the first day, another 13 on the second, and from there on the match was Gloucestershire's. Taylor survived 17 overs into the third morning in adding 83 with the tail, and Middlesex were set 289 to win, comfortably the highest score of the match. Instead they recorded the lowest, with Hussain (born ten miles away in Leytonstone) curtailing starts by Newman and Malan in another lethal display. After a frank dressing-room post-mortem, Udal – blameless having scored 55 and 12 not out – immediately despatched his batsmen to the nets.

Close of play: First day, Middlesex 71-4 (Malan 10, Robson 16); Second day, Gloucestershire 139-7 (Taylor 18, Lewis 12); Third day, Middlesex 166-7 (Udal 4, Murtagh 1).

Gloucestershire

Kadeer Ali b O'Brien	7	– (2) b O'Brien	1
†J. N. Batty b Evans	49	– (1) c Strauss b Evans	22
C. D. J. Dent c Simpson b Evans	19	– c Simpson b Evans	42
H. J. H. Marshall c Robson b O'Brien	72	– c Malan b Berg	9
*A. P. R. Gidman c O'Brien b Udal	16	– lbw b Murtagh	23
C. G. Taylor c sub (T. S. Roland-Jones) b O'Brien	32	– c sub (K. S. Toor) b Berg	61
J. E. C. Franklin not out	44	– lbw b Murtagh	11
S. D. Snell c Robson b O'Brien	0	– c Robson b Berg	0
J. Lewis lbw b O'Brien	11	– b Berg	43
G. M. Hussain c Udal b O'Brien	1	– not out	3
S. P. Kirby c Murtagh b O'Brien	0	– c sub (K. S. Toor) b Udal	1
B 7, l-b 9, w 1	17	B 4, l-b 3	7

1/7 (1) 2/46 (3) 3/145 (4)   (71.2 overs) 268
4/177 (5) 5/177 (2) 6/226 (6) 7/226 (8)
8/250 (9) 9/254 (10) 10/268 (11)

1/16 (2) 2/31 (1)   (70.4 overs) 223
3/58 (4) 4/96 (3)
5/100 (5) 6/118 (7) 7/123 (8)
8/193 (9) 9/222 (6) 10/223 (11)

Murtagh 20–3–81–0; O'Brien 21.2–6–48–7; Berg 7–1–47–0; Evans 12–3–45–2; Udal 10–1–24–1; Malan 1–0–7–0. *Second Innings*—Murtagh 19–6–53–2; O'Brien 15–3–57–1; Evans 10–4–22–2; Berg 20–3–74–4; Udal 6.4–1–10–1.

Middlesex

S. A. Newman b Batty b Franklin	1	– c Gidman b Hussain	42
A. J. Strauss c Dent b Kirby	18	– b Lewis	9
O. A. Shah lbw b Kirby	20	– c Gidman b Hussain	16
D. J. Malan c Batty b Lewis	25	– c Batty b Hussain	60
I. E. O'Brien c Batty b Kirby	0	– (10) c Snell b Kirby	2
S. D. Robson c Dent b Hussain	17	– (5) c Dent b Gidman	4
†J. A. Simpson c Snell b Franklin	43	– (6) b Kirby	0
G. K. Berg c Snell b Hussain	4	– (7) c Batty b Hussain	24
*S. D. Udal c Kadeer Ali b Kirby	55	– (8) not out	12
T. J. Murtagh not out	10	– (9) c sub (A. J. Ireland) b Hussain	9
D. Evans c Batty b Hussain	1	– c sub (A. J. Ireland) b Kirby	0
L-b 6, w 1, n-b 2	9	L-b 3, n-b 4	7

1/7 (1) 2/37 (3) 3/49 (2) 4/49 (5)   (64.5 overs) 203
5/76 (6) 6/111 (4) 7/124 (8)
8/157 (7) 9/202 (9) 10/203 (11)

1/27 (1) 2/53 (3)   (54.4 overs) 185
3/80 (1) 4/110 (5)
5/117 (6) 6/157 (7) 7/166 (4)
8/180 (9) 9/183 (10) 10/185 (11)

Lewis 16–4–47–1; Franklin 15–5–42–2; Kirby 14–2–50–4; Hussain 13.5–2–50–3; Marshall 6–3–8–0. *Second Innings*—Lewis 14–6–31–1; Franklin 7–0–34–0; Hussain 15–0–46–5; Kirby 11.4–1–36–3; Gidman 4–0–24–1; Taylor 1–0–2–0.

Umpires: R. A. Kettleborough and J. F. Steele.

At Hove, May 5–8. MIDDLESEX beat SUSSEX by three wickets.

MIDDLESEX v DERBYSHIRE

At Lord's, May 10–12. Middlesex won by an innings and 35 runs. Middlesex 23pts, Derbyshire 3pts. Toss: Derbyshire. First-class debut: C. F. Hughes.

Rogers won a toss he would rather have lost, and thought long and hard before opting to bat. With 563 first-class runs already to his name in seven innings, his choice was understandable. But Rogers's lack of decisiveness was contagious, and Derbyshire batted without conviction. They were not helped by travelling down from Leeds late the previous evening after a similarly comprehensive CB40 defeat, nor by the return of Finn, who made run-scoring difficult. But surely not so difficult that Derbyshire could bat through the first day without scoring a bonus point, even if bad light trimmed

13 overs from the end. Middlesex, buoyed by their win at Hove, were infinitely more positive. Berg was the star with his maiden century, 125 from as many balls, and, with Dexter in tow, put on 202 for the sixth wicket, a Middlesex record against Derbyshire. Chesney Hughes, a 19-year-old left-hander and only the third Anguillan to play in the Championship after Hampshire's Cardigan Connor and Omari Banks of Somerset, went to 100 in the match with a brazen 59 not out, which featured a towering six off Udal into the MCC members. Finn, though, had bounded through the top order, striking Rogers high on the elbow for his pains, and Middlesex did not need to bat again.

Close of play: First day, Derbyshire 190-9 (Lungley 19, Footitt 2); Second day, Middlesex 366-9 (Murtagh 10, Finn 2).

Derbyshire

*C. J. L. Rogers c Strauss b Finn	9	– c Newman b Murtagh	10
W. L. Madsen lbw b Murtagh	29	– c Shah b Finn	2
P. M. Borrington c Simpson b O'Brien	46	– lbw b Finn	0
G. T. Park lbw b Murtagh	1	– b Berg	19
G. M. Smith lbw b Finn	1	– c Strauss b Finn	8
J. L. Sadler c Simpson b Berg	16	– c Simpson b Berg	5
C. F. Hughes c Strauss b O'Brien	41	– not out	59
†L. J. Goddard lbw b Dexter	15	– lbw b O'Brien	1
T. Lungley not out	20	– c Simpson b Finn	4
T. D. Groenewald c Simpson b Finn	4	– c sub (T. E. Scollay) b Udal	27
M. H. A. Footitt c Udal b O'Brien	7	– b Murtagh	0
B 1, l-b 3, w 1, n-b 2	7	B 4, l-b 4	8

1/9 (1) 2/64 (2) 3/78 (4) 4/79 (5) (87 overs) 196
5/105 (6) 6/105 (3) 7/131 (8) 8/182 (7)
9/187 (10) 10/196 (11)

1/10 (2) 2/14 (3) (40.4 overs) 143
3/20 (1) 4/37 (5)
5/48 (4) 6/61 (6) 7/66 (8)
8/71 (9) 9/143 (10) 10/143 (11)

Murtagh 18–7–36–2; Finn 21–6–45–3; O'Brien 23–6–47–3; Berg 18–4–47–1; Udal 5–0–14–0; Dexter 2–1–3–1. *Second Innings*—Murtagh 10.4–2–35–2; Finn 9–4–19–4; Berg 10–2–49–2; O'Brien 10–5–25–1; Udal 1–0–7–1.

Middlesex

S. A. Newman lbw b Groenewald	0	T. J. Murtagh not out	14
A. J. Strauss c Madsen b Groenewald	13	I. E. O'Brien run out	0
O. A. Shah c Goddard b Lungley	21	S. T. Finn lbw b Groenewald	6
D. J. Malan c Park b Footitt	37	L-b 8, w 7, n-b 6	21
N. J. Dexter c Madsen b Park	112		
†J. A. Simpson lbw b Footitt	11	1/0 (1) 2/23 (2) 3/56 (3) (93.1 overs) 374
G. K. Berg lbw b Lungley	125	4/105 (4) 5/126 (6) 6/328 (5)
*S. D. Udal lbw b Groenewald	14	7/353 (7) 8/355 (8) 9/356 (10) 10/374 (11)

Groenewald 22.1–6–62–4; Lungley 21–4–67–2; Smith 18–5–91–0; Footitt 15–0–54–2; Park 10–0–36–1; Hughes 7–0–56–0.

Umpires: M. A. Gough and P. J. Hartley.

At The Oval, May 17–20. MIDDLESEX drew with SURREY.

At Oxford, May 25–27. MIDDLESEX beat OXFORD MCCU by 101 runs (see Universities section).

At Leicester, May 29–June 1. MIDDLESEX drew with LEICESTERSHIRE.

MIDDLESEX v NORTHAMPTONSHIRE

At Lord's, June 4–7. Northamptonshire won by nine wickets. Northamptonshire 23pts, Middlesex 4pts. Toss: Middlesex.

Middlesex had seen more than enough of Peters and Wakely six weeks earlier, when their long partnership spurred Northamptonshire on to a record run-chase. Now the same stubborn accumulators held them up for almost two sessions at Lord's. On a ground where he previously averaged 9.28, Peters surpassed his career-best score for the second time this season against Middlesex. He had batted for nine hours and moved to within one run of a double-century when he chipped a return catch to Udal, whose left hand was strapped after he split the webbing between his fingers. Wakely's contribution to their stand of 182 was an overdue second Championship hundred. Hall foraged on to the third century of the innings before his dismissal at 581 for seven – Northamptonshire's biggest total against Middlesex – prompted the declaration. Holding out on the final day should have been well within Middlesex's compass. But their muddled thinking was epitomised by the dismissal of Shah, caught on the long-on boundary when survival was required. Udal resigned the captaincy four days later.

Close of play: First day, Middlesex 341-9 (Evans 3, Collins 5); Second day, Northamptonshire 280-4 (Peters 115, Boje 12); Third day, Middlesex 48-1 (Robson 24, Shah 22).

Middlesex

S. D. Robson c Murphy b Vaas	59	– c Peters b Daggett 42
S. A. Newman c Peters b Brooks	11	– c Hall b Brooks 0
O. A. Shah lbw b Brooks	5	– c Daggett b Boje 77
D. J. Malan lbw b Vaas	28	– b Hall 44
N. J. Dexter c Murphy b Daggett	61	– c Murphy b Boje 37
†J. A. Simpson c Peters b Wakely	65	– c Hall b Daggett 32
G. K. Berg c Howgego b Daggett	83	– c Boje b Hall 11
*S. D. Udal c Murphy b Vaas	3	– lbw b Hall 4
T. J. Murtagh c Daggett b Hall	9	– lbw b Daggett 8
D. Evans not out	3	– not out 19
P. T. Collins c Murphy b Vaas	10	– c Peters b Hall 2
L-b 4, n-b 6	10	L-b 5, n-b 4 9

1/36 (2) 2/52 (3) 3/103 (4)   (100.2 overs) 347   1/4 (2) 2/79 (1)   (90.1 overs) 285
4/108 (1) 5/207 (5) 6/270 (6)   3/142 (4) 4/196 (3)
7/282 (8) 8/332 (9) 9/334 (7) 10/347 (11)   5/212 (5) 6/229 (7) 7/237 (8)
    8/258 (6) 9/280 (9) 10/285 (11)

Vaas 21.2–6–49–4; Brooks 21–5–74–2; Hall 20–6–57–1; Daggett 20–2–87–2; Boje 17–2–72–0; Wakely 1–0–4–1. *Second Innings*—Vaas 23–7–47–0; Brooks 18–4–78–1; Daggett 14–2–49–3; Hall 13.1–3–44–4; Boje 22–5–62–2.

Northamptonshire

S. D. Peters c and b Udal	199	– lbw b Collins 2
B. H. N. Howgego lbw b Collins	23	– not out 13
M. B. Loye c Malan b Berg	0	
A. G. Wakely c Berg b Udal	108	
R. A. White c Evans b Udal	12	– (3) not out 31
N. Boje c Shah b Collins	37	
*A. J. Hall b Collins	133	
†D. Murphy not out	50	
B 1, l-b 10, n-b 8	19	L-b 1, n-b 6 7

1/44 (2) 2/58 (3)   (7 wkts dec, 167.1 overs) 581   1/3 (1)   (1 wkt, 7.3 overs) 53
3/240 (4) 4/260 (5)
5/330 (6) 6/474 (1) 7/581 (7)   110 overs: 361-5

W. P. U. J. C. Vaas, L. M. Daggett and J. A. Brooks did not bat.

Murtagh 27–7–86–0; Collins 33.1–5–122–3; Evans 28–7–99–0; Berg 14–3–35–1; Udal 36.1–3–112–3; Malan 20–0–87–0; Shah 5.5–2–9–0; Dexter 2–0–9–0; Robson 1–0–11–0. *Second Innings*—Murtagh 3–1–16–0; Collins 3.3–0–28–1; Evans 1–0–8–0.

Umpires: N. L. Bainton and J. W. Lloyds.

At Lord's, June 19. MIDDLESEX lost to AUSTRALIANS by five wickets (see Australian tour section).

At Bristol, June 28–30. MIDDLESEX lost to GLOUCESTERSHIRE by ten wickets.

At Lord's, July 5. MIDDLESEX lost to BANGLADESHIS by 141 runs (see Bangladeshi tour section).

MIDDLESEX v SUSSEX

At Uxbridge, July 21–24. Drawn. Middlesex 10pts, Sussex 11pts. Toss: Middlesex. Championship debut: L. J. Hatchett.

Morgan, playing his only Championship match of the season, offered compelling evidence to win over sceptics who questioned his capacity for graft. Twice he made 58, on the second occasion staying for 137 balls to deny Sussex victory. Encouraged by a green pitch, Dexter chose to bowl, but his decision raised eyebrows on a high-scoring ground. Sussex took advantage and earned full batting points by stumps, which Wright reached in thunderous fashion. He pillaged 36 from the closing four overs, smashing Finn for six to bring up a 96-ball century from the day's final delivery. Rain swept in, and it was not until 55 overs into the third day that Middlesex ended their first innings. Yardy was over-cautious in his declaration, setting Middlesex an impossible target of 343 in less than two sessions. Yet they were sufficiently flaky to collapse to a rampaging Panesar, who saw a catch and a stumping missed before bowling Strauss with a quicker ball. But Morgan found allies in Dexter, for 23 overs, and the arch-blocker Finn, who safely negotiated 35 balls for an invaluable nought. On the first day a spectator, Jan Marszal, saw an object fall from the sky and land metres inside the ropes. It split in half, with one piece hitting him on the chest. Astronomers hoped it might be the UK's first recorded meteorite since 1992, but tests revealed otherwise. "I'm afraid it's nothing more than a piece of Portland cement with flecks of brick dust and flint in it," said Dave Harris of the British and Irish Meteorite Society. "It most probably fell off the undercarriage of a plane."

Close of play: First day, Sussex 413-9 (Wright 105, Collymore 3); Second day, Middlesex 127-2 (Simpson 58, Malan 8); Third day, Sussex 109-5 (Thornely 19, Hatchett 2).

Sussex

*M. H. Yardy lbw b O'Brien	5	– b Roland-Jones	21
C. D. Nash c Berg b Roland-Jones	46	– c Simpson b Finn	14
E. C. Joyce c Shah b O'Brien	85	– lbw b Finn	7
M. W. Goodwin c Roland-Jones b Finn	80	– lbw b Dexter	35
†M. J. Prior b Roland-Jones	30	– c Simpson b Roland-Jones	4
M. A. Thornely c Strauss b Roland-Jones	10	– b Dexter	53
L. J. Wright c Simpson b Finn	134	– (8) lbw b Udal	62
O. P. Rayner b Roland-Jones	0	– (9) c Shah b Udal	18
M. S. Panesar c and b Udal	9	– (10) not out	9
L. J. Hatchett c Strauss b Finn	20	– (7) c Simpson b Finn	6
C. D. Collymore not out	12		
B 2, l-b 8, w 1, n-b 10	21	B 1, l-b 10	11

1/6 (1) 2/81 (2) 3/194 (3) 4/259 (4) (103 overs) 452
5/259 (5) 6/276 (6) 7/276 (8)
8/321 (9) 9/374 (10) 10/452 (7)

1/37 (1)　(9 wkts dec, 74.2 overs) 240
2/37 (2) 3/54 (3)
4/65 (5) 5/105 (4) 6/121 (7)
7/207 (6) 8/229 (8) 9/240 (9)

Finn 30–3–134–3; O'Brien 20–2–104–2; Roland-Jones 28–3–100–4; Berg 7–0–43–0; Udal 15–1–45–1; Dexter 3–0–16–0. *Second Innings*—Finn 23.1–1–83–3; O'Brien 2.5–0–8–0; Roland-Jones 21.1–3–54–2; Dexter 20–4–48–2; Udal 6.2–1–28–2; Malan 1–0–8–0.

Middlesex

A. J. Strauss lbw b Collymore	8	– b Panesar	37
†J. A. Simpson c Rayner b Collymore	58	– lbw b Panesar	14
O. A. Shah c Prior b Wright	38	– c Prior b Thornely	14
D. J. Malan b Panesar	51	– c Thornely b Panesar	5
E. J. G. Morgan b Rayner	58	– not out	58
*N. J. Dexter c Rayner b Collymore	43	– b Rayner	46
G. K. Berg b Thornely	26	– b Nash b Rayner	0
S. D. Udal c Prior b Hatchett	8	– c Thornely b Panesar	2
T. S. Roland-Jones b Collymore	15	– c Joyce b Panesar	1
I. E. O'Brien not out	14		
S. T. Finn b Hatchett	3	– (10) not out	0
B 5, l-b 7, n-b 16	28	B 17, l-b 2, n-b 8	27

1/36 (1) 2/118 (3) 3/133 (2)   (93.1 overs) 350
4/236 (4) 5/248 (5) 6/298 (7)
7/314 (8) 8/328 (6) 9/339 (9) 10/350 (11)

1/42 (2)   (8 wkts, 66 overs) 204
2/57 (3) 3/62 (4) 4/89 (1) 5/160 (6)
6/160 (7) 7/173 (8) 8/175 (9)

Collymore 19–6–66–4; Hatchett 16.1–5–62–2; Wright 15–3–47–1; Thornely 6–1–19–1; Rayner 18–2–84–1; Panesar 19–6–60–1. *Second Innings*—Collymore 16–4–42–0; Hatchett 2–1–13–0; Panesar 30–11–89–5; Thornely 2–0–11–1; Rayner 16–6–30–2.

Umpires: J. H. Evans and D. J. Millns.

MIDDLESEX v SURREY

At Lord's, July 29–31. Middlesex won by an innings and 44 runs. Middlesex 24pts, Surrey 1pt (after 2pt penalty). Toss: Surrey.

Middlesex beat their neighbours by an innings for the first time in 15 years. Their 1995 win, also at Lord's, was built upon a double-hundred from Ramprakash. Now with Surrey, he gave another masterclass against the moving ball, withstanding Murtagh and Collins – both former Surrey bowlers – for 70 balls until seeing his stumps rearranged by an inswinger from Collins, who had earlier dismissed Lancefield and Hamilton-Brown to successive deliveries. Traipsing off for a golden duck, Hamilton-Brown must have questioned his decision to bat. Conditions relaxed sufficiently for Middlesex to end a run of 24 matches without maximum batting points, and Malan's third century of a productive season established a lead of 256. But the game belonged to Roland-Jones, playing his third Championship match. He followed his highest score – which began by surviving Tremlett's hat-trick ball – with his maiden five-for, which knocked over four of Surrey's top five in just 26 balls.

Close of play: First day, Middlesex 179-2 (Shah 44, Malan 35); Second day, Surrey 110-6 (Walters 12, Batty 9).

Surrey

T. J. Lancefield lbw b Collins	15	– c Dexter b Udal	24
†S. M. Davies b Murtagh	24	– c Simpson b Roland-Jones	43
M. R. Ramprakash b Collins	44	– c Simpson b Roland-Jones	6
*R. J. Hamilton-Brown lbw b Collins	0	– c Dexter b Roland-Jones	1
U. Afzaal lbw b Roland-Jones	11	– c Dexter b Roland-Jones	6
S. J. Walters b Murtagh	14	– c Simpson b Collins	43
M. N. W. Spriegel c Simpson b Murtagh	25	– c Malan b Roland-Jones	0
G. J. Batty c Davey b Murtagh	15	– c Davey b Murtagh	12
C. T. Tremlett c Dexter b Murtagh	2	– not out	53
J. W. Dernbach c Berg b Collins	12	– c Shah b Udal	15
T. E. Linley not out	0	– c Newman b Collins	0
B 1, l-b 4	5	B 4, l-b 2, w 1, n-b 2	9

1/39 (2) 2/43 (1) 3/43 (4) 4/69 (5)   (46.3 overs) 167
5/108 (3) 6/116 (6) 7/142 (8)
8/144 (9) 9/167 (10) 10/167 (7)

1/75 (2) 2/75 (1)   (50.4 overs) 212
3/76 (4) 4/82 (5)
5/91 (3) 6/91 (7) 7/116 (8)
8/183 (6) 9/212 (10) 10/212 (11)

Murtagh 14.3–5–52–5; Collins 18–4–68–4; Roland-Jones 5–1–19–1; Dexter 9–3–23–0. *Second Innings*—Murtagh 14–4–55–1; Collins 13.4–3–63–2; Roland-Jones 11–2–41–5; Udal 12–1–47–2.

Middlesex

S. A. Newman lbw b Batty	54	T. J. Murtagh not out		25
†J. A. Simpson b Dernbach	36	P. T. Collins c Afzaal b Tremlett		1
O. A. Shah c Davies b Dernbach	63			
D. J. Malan b Tremlett	107	B 4, l-b 18, w 1, n-b 6		29
*N. J. Dexter c Linley b Spriegel	24			
G. K. Berg b Tremlett	45	1/82 (2) 2/112 (1)	(108.2 overs)	423
J. H. Davey lbw b Linley	13	3/212 (3) 4/271 (5)		
S. D. Udal b Tremlett	0	5/343 (4) 6/348 (6) 7/348 (8)		
T. S. Roland-Jones b Linley	26	8/383 (9) 9/412 (7) 10/423 (11)		

Tremlett 29.2–6–90–4; Linley 25–9–96–2; Dernbach 21–4–87–2; Batty 22–3–87–1; Afzaal 1–0–7–0; Spriegel 8–0–23–1; Hamilton-Brown 2–0–11–0.

Umpires: N. J. Llong and S. J. O'Shaughnessy.

MIDDLESEX v LEICESTERSHIRE

At Lord's, August 9–12. Drawn. Middlesex 7pts, Leicestershire 8pts. Toss: Middlesex.

Leicestershire were poised to win a Championship match at Lord's for just the fourth time until the arrival of rain and bad light. New had repaired their teatime position of 85 for four, chasing 193, but almost 20 overs disappeared during four interruptions, leaving Leicestershire 54 runs adrift when the umpires led them off for the last time. The hard work was done by Hoggard, who claimed season-best figures on the first day, helped by several ill-conceived wafts outside off stump. Then, in a triumph of concentration, Taylor stood firm for 93 overs – from shortly after tea, through a truncated second day to the third afternoon – for his third unbeaten hundred against Middlesex. Newman and Simpson showed rare defiance in erasing a deficit of 63 and ploughing on to 119 without loss, only for Middlesex to surrender their position by losing all ten wickets for 136. Murtagh was irresistible when Leicestershire began their pursuit, but the home side were still the more relieved to see the skies open.

Close of play: First day, Leicestershire 105-2 (Smith 64, Taylor 32); Second day, Leicestershire 186-5 (Taylor 65, Naik 21); Third day, Middlesex 168-4 (Shah 25, Roland-Jones 1).

Middlesex

S. A. Newman c New b Hoggard	13	– c du Toit b Henderson		70
†J. A. Simpson c New b Malik	13	– lbw b Henderson		44
O. A. Shah lbw b Hoggard	1	– c du Toit b Naik		55
D. J. Malan b Smith b Hoggard	0	– c du Toit b Naik		4
*N. J. Dexter c du Toit b Hoggard	47	– lbw b Malik		18
G. K. Berg lbw b Henderson	53	– (7) c New b Buck		21
J. H. Davey c Smith b Hoggard	11	– (8) c New b Buck		0
S. D. Udal c Nixon b Hoggard	0	– (9) c New b Buck		9
T. S. Roland-Jones c Naik b Malik	8	– (6) c Boyce b Henderson		13
T. J. Murtagh not out	50	– not out		8
P. T. Collins b Naik	13	– c Boyce b Hoggard		1
B 1, l-b 8, w 1	10	B 4, l-b 5, w 1, n-b 2		12

1/14 (1) 2/22 (3) 3/22 (4) 4/32 (2)	(65.4 overs)	219	1/119 (1) 2/120 (2)	(88.5 overs) 255
5/130 (5) 6/142 (6) 7/143 (8)			3/125 (4) 4/165 (5)	
8/152 (7) 9/161 (6) 10/219 (11)			5/186 (6) 6/226 (3) 7/228 (8)	
			8/241 (7) 9/250 (9) 10/255 (11)	

Hoggard 20–5–63–6; Buck 7–1–23–0; Malik 18–5–77–2; Henderson 18–6–40–1; Naik 2.4–0–7–1. *Second Innings*—Hoggard 12.5–3–54–1; Buck 9–2–37–3; Malik 11–3–26–1; Naik 27–4–78–2; Henderson 28–5–49–3; Taylor 1–0–2–0.

Leicestershire

G. P. Smith c Newman b Murtagh	65	– b Murtagh	0
M. A. G. Boyce lbw b Collins	5	– b Udal	52
J. du Toit lbw b Collins	0	– c Malan b Murtagh	10
J. W. A. Taylor not out	106	– lbw b Collins	0
P. A. Nixon c Malan b Collins	10	– c Newman b Shah	24
†T. J. New b Roland-Jones	14	– not out	41
J. K. H. Naik lbw b Malan	36	– not out	6
C. W. Henderson c Simpson b Roland-Jones	31		
M. N. Malik b Collins	0		
N. L. Buck lbw b Roland-Jones	1		
*M. J. Hoggard c Udal b Roland-Jones	4		
B 4, l-b 6	10	B 4, l-b 2	6

1/16 (2) 2/22 (3) 3/106 (1) (100.5 overs) 282 1/0 (1) (5 wkts, 47.3 overs) 139
4/117 (5) 5/145 (6) 6/215 (7) 2/28 (3) 3/29 (4)
7/272 (8) 8/275 (9) 9/276 (10) 10/282 (11) 4/84 (5) 5/92 (2)

Murtagh 22–4–59–1; Collins 28–5–76–4; Roland-Jones 22.5–5–52–4; Dexter 5–0–28–0; Udal 19–7–37–0; Davey 3–0–15–0; Malan 1–0–5–1. *Second Innings*—Murtagh 8–6–7–2; Collins 10.3–1–56–1; Roland-Jones 6–1–16–0; Udal 15.2–2–37–1; Shah 8–1–17–1.

Umpires: N. G. C. Cowley and P. Willey.

At Cardiff, August 16–19. MIDDLESEX beat GLAMORGAN by six wickets.

At Derby, August 25–28. MIDDLESEX drew with DERBYSHIRE.

MIDDLESEX v WORCESTERSHIRE

At Lord's, September 7–10. Worcestershire won by 111 runs. Worcestershire 21pts, Middlesex 5pts (after 2pt penalty). Toss: Worcestershire.

Middlesex saved their worst for last, somehow losing a match they had dominated for the best part of three days. They batted so abjectly that they were crushed by 111 runs, precisely the margin of their defeat at Worcester five months earlier. Middlesex left out Udal, their only specialist spinner, in order to play an extra batsman, and then witnessed Worcestershire's slow bowlers deliver career-best performances: Moeen Ali took five wickets with his occasional off-breaks, before Shakib Al Hasan's seven routed Middlesex for 66, their second-lowest total this century (after 49 at Trent Bridge in 2006). Roland-Jones missed the first 40 minutes after being held up in traffic caused by strikes on the London Underground, but shrugged off the delay to take nine wickets in the match. Somewhat predictably, Shah scored a century on his final Championship appearance for Middlesex, but acknowledged neither the committee-room nor the home dressing-room when he raised his bat. In the second innings, he showed his infuriating side, getting out to a dreadful shot, though he was far from alone. To make matters worse, Middlesex were docked two points for a slow over-rate.

Close of play: First day, Middlesex 0-0 (Finn 0, Newman 0); Second day, Middlesex 244-5 (Shah 70, Dexter 26); Third day, Worcestershire 195-7 (Ali 71, Andrew 34).

Worcestershire

*D. K. H. Mitchell b Finn	47	– b Collins	19
D. A. Wheeldon c Simpson b Roland-Jones	14	– run out	22
V. S. Solanki c Malan b Dexter	39	– lbw b Shah	2
M. M. Ali c Shah b Dexter	66	– lbw b Roland-Jones	81
A. N. Kervezee c Dexter b Roland-Jones	5	– lbw b Collins	0
Shakib Al Hasan c Malan b Shah	34	– c Malan b Roland-Jones	10
J. G. Cameron lbw b Collins	28	– c Malan b Roland-Jones	17
†O. B. Cox c Housego b Dexter	4	– c Dexter b Roland-Jones	0
G. M. Andrew b Roland-Jones	36	– c and b Roland-Jones	73
J. D. Shantry not out	10	– c Simpson b Collins	0
A. Richardson c Simpson b Roland-Jones	11	– not out	10
B 4, l-b 4, w 1, n-b 10	19	B 5, l-b 14, w 1, n-b 2	22

1/41 (2) 2/101 (1) 3/120 (3)   (92.2 overs) 313
4/126 (5) 5/204 (6) 6/236 (4)
7/248 (8) 8/261 (7) 9/293 (9) 10/313 (11)

1/47 (2) 2/49 (3)   (59.1 overs) 256
3/62 (1) 4/62 (5)
5/102 (6) 6/148 (7) 7/148 (8)
8/211 (4) 9/222 (10) 10/256 (9)

Murtagh 17–4–47–0; Collins 14–4–50–1; Finn 17–5–40–1; Roland-Jones 16.2–2–51–4; Dexter 13–3–50–3; Shah 13–1–51–1; Malan 2–0–16–0. *Second Innings*—Finn 9–2–45–0; Murtagh 8–3–26–0; Shah 8–1–18–1; Collins 13–2–63–3; Roland-Jones 19.1–1–83–5; Dexter 2–1–2–0.

Middlesex

S. T. Finn run out	3	– (10) c Cox b Shakib Al Hasan	1
S. A. Newman c Shakib Al Hasan b Cameron	78	– (1) c Mitchell b Richardson	12
†J. A. Simpson c Ali b Shantry	9	– (2) lbw b Richardson	0
O. A. Shah c Mitchell b Ali	117	– (3) c Shantry b Shakib Al Hasan	25
D. J. Malan c Cox b Shakib Al Hasan	9	– (4) b Shakib Al Hasan	2
D. M. Housego c Solanki b Ali	32	– (5) lbw b Shakib Al Hasan	4
*N. J. Dexter c and b Ali	97	– (6) c Solanki b Ali	21
G. K. Berg run out	10	– (7) c Mitchell b Shakib Al Hasan	0
T. J. Murtagh c Cameron b Ali	8	– (8) c Richardson b Shakib Al Hasan	0
T. S. Roland-Jones b Ali	2	– (9) lbw b Shakib Al Hasan	1
P. T. Collins not out	0	– not out	0
B 9, l-b 17, w 1	27		

1/17 (1) 2/38 (3) 3/114 (2)   (114.3 overs) 392
4/131 (5) 5/198 (6) 6/356 (4)
7/377 (7) 8/390 (8) 9/390 (9)
10/392 (10)   110 overs: 385-7

1/3 (2) 2/22 (1)   (31.1 overs) 66
3/33 (4) 4/37 (5)
5/54 (3) 6/54 (7) 7/54 (8)
8/58 (9) 9/66 (6) 10/66 (10)

Richardson 19–3–68–0; Shantry 25–7–58–1; Andrew 14–0–63–0; Cameron 10–3–29–1; Shakib Al Hasan 35–2–112–1; Ali 10.3–0–36–5; Mitchell 1–1–0–0. *Second Innings*—Richardson 13–3–20–2; Shantry 4–1–11–0; Shakib Al Hasan 11.1–3–32–7; Ali 3–1–3–1.

Umpires: S. A. Garratt and P. Willey.

NORTHAMPTONSHIRE

Do the maths

ANDREW RADD

Statistics can sometimes mislead, but in the case of Northamptonshire's 2010 season they tell a major part of the story. A total of 23 players used in the Championship – no county used more – highlighted the serious problems faced by head coach David Capel through injuries to key personnel at crucial times. Only one batsman passed 1,000 first-class runs, and no bowler took 40 wickets, which exposed a lack of consistency from those who did play regularly. And for the first season since 2000, not a single century was scored in limited-overs competition, indicating either unwillingness or inability on the part of those players to take personal responsibility for the destiny of an innings or match.

Results fell short of expectations on all fronts. After their heartbreaking near miss in 2009, Northamptonshire spent much of the summer on the fringes of the Championship promotion race, but heavy defeats in three of the last four matches, plus the untimely arrival of rain at home to Worcestershire, condemned them to a seventh successive season in Division Two. Little went right in the CB40, and hopes of an immediate return to Twenty20 finals day were dashed by three run-outs in the quarter-final at Taunton.

In a year of mediocrity, Stephen Peters stood head and shoulders above the rest. Diligent and committed to the cause, he scored 1,296 Championship runs – 600 more than anyone else – including two big, career-best hundreds (183 not out at Northampton, and then 199 at Lord's) to secure a Championship double over Middlesex. He thoroughly deserved the Player of the Year award, and supporters were greatly relieved when he signed a new contract to stay at Northamptonshire until at least 2012.

Much was expected of both Mal Loye, back with his native county aged 37 after seven years with Lancashire, and the fit-again David Sales, who missed all of 2009 following knee surgery. Loye produced only one substantial innings in the Championship, and was sidelined for much of the Twenty20 – almost his cricketing "specialist subject" – through injury. Sales fared little better, enduring a couple of serious troughs, and the season became deeply frustrating for a batsman of his undoubted class. Alex Wakely scored a fine century at Lord's, and led successful run-chases against Sussex and Worcestershire, only to fade sharply. Rob White – like Loye and Sales – had a year to forget.

Northamptonshire needed a fit David Lucas to give themselves the best chance of bowling sides out in the longer game, and his absence from six matches was keenly felt. Jack Brooks, from Oxfordshire, led the way with 34 wickets and – almost as importantly – showed himself to be a cricketer of character and enthusiasm, who injected much-needed "buzz" into the side. Sporting a trademark headband, he became a crowd favourite, and the Supporters Club donated £1,000 to help fund his winter trip to Dennis Lillee's academy in Chennai. Brooks and the veteran Sri Lankan Chaminda Vaas, an outstanding short-term signing due to return in 2011, were both superb in the Friends Provident T20. Vaas's 396 runs in 14 innings as an opener – a surprise move by Capel – turned around the group campaign. Lee Daggett was another to enhance his reputation, and Zimbabwe captain Elton Chigumbura often looked the part during his ten-week stay.

Stephen Peters

By mid-May, Nicky Boje had relinquished the captaincy after two seasons in charge, and was replaced by his fellow-South African, Andrew Hall. The club's clumsy handling of Boje's resignation – announcing the "news" only after it had featured extensively in the local media – fuelled speculation of a breakdown in relationship between captain and coach. But Capel paid a warm tribute to Boje, who left altogether in August: "Nicky is a first-rate guy and a very impressive individual."

The ever-tenacious Hall shouldered the responsibility manfully, and took a hat-trick in July's thumping win over Glamorgan, when Northamptonshire's prospects of promotion were probably healthiest.

Although a less than vintage summer, it is possible that 2010 will go down in Northamptonshire's history as a year of significant new beginnings. Rob Newton, 20, in his sixth season at the academy, took to first-class cricket with a refreshing air of purpose. Short in stature and aggressive in intent, he illuminated the second half of the year with sparkling strokeplay, culminating in a maiden Championship century against Leicestershire.

Niall O'Brien required finger surgery in July (he was also briefly suspended and stripped of the vice-captaincy after arriving late for a Twenty20 match following international duty), so wicketkeeping duties passed to David Murphy, an academy product and Loughborough University student. He was reassuringly neat behind the stumps and chipped in with handy runs.

Other youngsters came to the fore, too. In a CB40 match at Southend in August, all-rounder Christian Davis became the first 17-year-old since Sales to make a competitive first-team appearance for Northamptonshire; he toured Sri Lanka with England Under-19 in January. Left-arm spinner Tom Brett and batsman Rob Keogh also made first-team appearances. David Willey suffered fitness problems in his second season, but will surely come again.

This crop of promising home-produced cricketers reflects credit on the development team of David Ripley, Kevin Innes and Phil Rowe. In the final Championship match, at home to Leicestershire, Northamptonshire fielded an all English-born eleven for the first time since 1999 – an encouraging signpost to the future. Often guilty of starting slowly, Northamptonshire decided to make their first pre-season trip overseas for nine years, to Port Elizabeth in March 2011.

NORTHAMPTONSHIRE RESULTS

All first-class matches – Played 17: Won 6, Lost 7, Drawn 4.
County Championship matches – Played 16: Won 6, Lost 7, Drawn 3.

LV= County Championship, 6th in Division 2;
Friends Provident T20, q-f; Clydesdale Bank 40, 5th in Group B.

COUNTY CHAMPIONSHIP AVERAGES, BATTING AND FIELDING

Cap		M	I	NO	R	HS	100s	50s	Avge	Ct/St
2007	S. D. Peters	15	29	2	1,296	199	3	7	48.00	16
	N. J. O'Brien.	3	6	0	216	49	0	0	36.00	7/1
2008	N. Boje¶.	9	15	1	471	98	0	4	33.64	3
	R. I. Newton	6	11	0	357	102	1	2	32.45	1
	D. Murphy	9	15	6	276	55	0	2	30.66	26
	A. G. Wakely	12	21	0	614	108	1	4	29.23	5
2009	A. J. Hall¶.	15	27	3	696	133	1	3	29.00	21
	B. H. N. Howgego	7	13	2	292	80	0	1	26.54	3
	J. D. Middlebrook	12	21	3	459	84	0	3	25.50	6
1999	D. J. Sales	15	28	0	680	127	1	2	24.28	20
	V. Tripathi	3	6	0	141	71	0	1	23.50	3
1994	M. B. Loye†	9	17	0	378	164	1	1	22.23	0
2008	R. A. White	9	18	1	361	95	0	2	21.23	2
2009	D. S. Lucas	10	17	2	316	40*	0	0	21.06	1
	E. Chigumbara§	6	10	1	189	44	0	0	21.00	0
	P. W. Harrison	4	7	1	126	44	0	0	21.00	7/2
	D. J. Willey†	2	4	2	41	18*	0	0	20.50	1
	L. M. Daggett	11	17	8	167	48	0	0	18.55	3
	J. A. Brooks	13	20	3	177	53	0	1	10.41	2

Also batted: G. C. Baker (1 match) 14, 35; D. A. Burton (1 match) 0, 2* (1 ct); L. Evans (2 matches) 0*, 8*, 8 (1 ct); W. P. U. J. C. Vaas§ (2 matches) 0, 17 (1 ct).

† *Born in Northamptonshire.* § *Official overseas player.* ¶ *Other non-England-qualified player.*

BOWLING

	O	M	R	W	BB	5W/i	Avge
E. Chigumbara	114	17	482	20	5-92	1	24.10
A. J. Hall	318	57	1,047	33	4-44	0	31.72
D. S. Lucas	282.4	54	993	31	5-64	1	32.03
L. M. Daggett	303.4	64	1,009	30	4-25	0	33.63
J. A. Brooks	351.3	79	1,227	34	4-88	0	36.08
J. D. Middlebrook	251.2	40	863	18	3-23	0	47.94
N. Boje	230.3	42	796	15	2-47	0	53.06

Also bowled: G. C. Baker 13–3–54–0; D. A. Burton 20–4–75–5; L. Evans 57–10–201–5; B. H. N. Howgego 2–0–16–0; R. I. Newton 2.1–0–19–0; D. J. Sales 1–0–10–0; V. Tripathi 2–0–11–0; W. P. U. J. C. Vaas 73.2–20–161–6; A. G. Wakely 9.1–0–57–1; R. A. White 1–0–7–0; D. J. Willey 41.5–3–171–5.

LEADING CB40 AVERAGES (100 runs/4 wickets)

Batting	Runs	HS	Avge	S-R	Ct	**Bowling**	W	BB	Avge	E-R
D. J. Sales	408	84	37.09	86.99	5	L. M. Daggett	20	4-17	16.50	4.64
R. A. White	248	69	35.42	92.53	0	N. Boje	5	3-10	23.80	3.92
J. D. Middlebrook . . .	150	57*	30.00	99.33	4	A. J. Hall	15	4-39	27.86	6.22
S. D. Peters.	231	56	28.87	81.05	2	J. A. Brooks	6	3-41	33.83	4.95
M. B. Loye	223	66	27.87	70.34	0	J. D. Middlebrook . .	10	3-34	36.60	4.94
R. I. Newton	194	66	27.71	83.62	1	D. S. Lucas	5	1-23	40.20	6.09

LEADING FPT20 AVERAGES (100 runs/18 overs)

Batting	Runs	HS	Avge	S-R	Ct/St
N. Boje	114	54*	14.25	**134.11**	4
W. P. U. J. C. Vaas	412	73	25.75	**122.98**	3
E. Chigumbura	160	39*	22.85	**119.40**	7
D. J. Sales	128	49	16.00	**117.43**	3
N. J. O'Brien	215	37	21.50	**115.59**	9/4
A. J. Hall	252	40*	42.00	**111.50**	3

Bowling	W	BB	Avge	E-R
J. A. Brooks	12	3-24	22.41	**6.25**
W. P. U. J. C. Vaas	23	3-16	15.82	**6.33**
J. D. Middlebrook	12	2-12	27.00	**6.35**
N. Boje	11	3-20	20.63	**7.24**
E. Chigumbura	10	4-14	21.00	**7.24**
A. J. Hall	16	2-8	26.43	**8.66**

FIRST-CLASS COUNTY RECORDS

Highest score for	331*	M. E. K. Hussey v Somerset at Taunton	2003
Highest score against	333	K. S. Duleepsinhji (Sussex) at Hove	1930
Leading run-scorer	28,980	D. Brookes (avge 36.13)	1934–1959
Best bowling for	10-127	V. W. C. Jupp v Kent at Tunbridge Wells	1932
Best bowling against	10-30	C. Blythe (Kent) at Northampton	1907
Leading wicket-taker	1,102	E. W. Clark (avge 21.26)	1922–1947
Highest total for	781-7 dec	v Nottinghamshire at Northampton	1995
Highest total against	673-8 dec	by Yorkshire at Leeds	2003
Lowest total for	12	v Gloucestershire at Gloucester	1907
Lowest total against	33	by Lancashire at Northampton	1977

LIST A COUNTY RECORDS

Highest score for	172*	W. Larkins v Warwickshire at Luton	1983
Highest score against	175*	I. T. Botham (Somerset) at Wellingborough	1986
Leading run-scorer	11,010	R. J. Bailey (avge 39.46)	1983–1999
Best bowling for	7-10	C. Pietersen v Denmark at Brøndby	2005
Best bowling against	7-35	D. E. Malcolm (Derbyshire) at Derby	1997
Leading wicket-taker	251	A. L. Penberthy (avge 30.45)	1989–2003
Highest total for	360-2	v Staffordshire at Northampton	1990
Highest total against	344-6	by Gloucestershire at Cheltenham	2001
Lowest total for	41	v Middlesex at Northampton	1972
Lowest total against	56	by Leicestershire at Leicester	1964
	56	by Denmark at Brøndby	2005

TWENTY20 RECORDS

Highest score for	111*	L. Klusener v Worcestershire at Kidderminster	2007
Highest score against	116*	G. A. Hick (Worcestershire) at Luton	2004
Leading run-scorer	1,202	**D. J. Sales** (avge 30.05)	**2003–2010**
Best bowling for	6-21	A. J. Hall v Worcestershire at Northampton	2008
Best bowling against	4-10	G. R. Napier (Essex) at Chelmsford	2008
Leading wicket-taker	50	**A. J. Hall** (avge 19.22)	**2008–2010**
Highest total for	224-5	v Gloucestershire at Milton Keynes	2005
Highest total against	227-6	by Worcestershire at Kidderminster	2007
Lowest total for	88	**v Lancashire at Manchester**	**2010**
Lowest total against	86	by Worcestershire at Worcester	2006

ADDRESS

County Ground, Wantage Road, Northampton NN1 4TJ (01604 514455; **email** reception@nccc.co.uk). **Website** www.northantscricket.com

OFFICIALS

Captain 2010 – N. Boje
2011 – A. J. Hall
First-team coach D. J. Capel
Director of academy D. Ripley
President Lord Naseby

Chairman M. P. Lawrence
Chief executive M. J. Tagg
Head groundsman P. Marshall
Scorer A. C. Kingston

At Oxford, April 3–5. NORTHAMPTONSHIRE drew with OXFORD MCCU (see Universities section).

At Leicester, April 9–12. NORTHAMPTONSHIRE lost to LEICESTERSHIRE by six wickets.

At Bristol, April 15–17. NORTHAMPTONSHIRE beat GLOUCESTERSHIRE by 94 runs.

NORTHAMPTONSHIRE v MIDDLESEX

At Northampton, April 21–24. Northamptonshire won by six wickets. Northamptonshire 20pts, Middlesex 6pts. Toss: Middlesex.

Outplayed for three days, Northamptonshire produced an exceptional batting performance on the fourth to steal an unlikely victory. They were inspired by Peters, who shouldered the responsibility – and took full advantage of two missed chances by Newman at leg slip off Udal's bowling – to set about executing the county's highest successful run-chase. Defeat came out of a clear blue sky for Middlesex. Robson and London – aged 20 and 21 – added 127 on the first day before Simpson, also 21, took over, completing a well-organised maiden first-class century in four and a half hours.

HIGHEST FOURTH-INNINGS TOTALS BY NORTHAMPTONSHIRE

411	(*set 416 to win*) v Gloucestershire at Gloucester	2007
395-4	(**won**) **v Middlesex at Northampton**	**2010**
387	(*set 582 to win*) v Kent at Canterbury	2004
384-8	(*won*) v Worcestershire at Northampton	1961
367	(*set 461 to win*) v Middlesex at Northampton	2008
353-9	(*won*) v Durham at Northampton	2002

Northamptonshire's first innings was declared at 0-0 and Durham's second innings forfeited.

Northamptonshire were in a generous mood, giving away 69 in extras, only seven short of their record (against Warwickshire on this ground in 2000). Boje and last man Luke Evans, who was reprieved ten short of the follow-on target, kept the deficit to 135, but Newman's aggressive first hundred for Middlesex dealt out further punishment. With Malan and Berg quickly into their stride, 191 runs came in 26 overs after tea on the third day, enabling Udal to declare shortly before the close. Peters then dropped anchor in a career-best 183; he was well supported initially by Wakely in a second-wicket stand worth 179, then more aggressively by Sales and White. Victory came with ten overs to spare.

Close of play: First day, Middlesex 281-5 (Simpson 28, Berg 4); Second day, Northamptonshire 178-4 (Sales 35, Hall 31); Third day, Northamptonshire 29-0 (Peters 14, Loye 15).

Middlesex

S. A. Newman b Lucas	44	– st Harrison b Boje		112
A. J. Strauss b Hall	25	– c Evans b Boje		32
S. D. Robson c Hall b Boje	52	– c Hall b Lucas		10
D. J. Malan lbw b Brooks	1	– not out		56
A. B. London st Harrison b Boje	77			
†J. A. Simpson not out	101			
G. K. Berg c Hall b Evans	41	– (5) not out		37
*S. D. Udal c Harrison b Brooks	25			
T. J. Murtagh c Harrison b Brooks	5			
S. T. Finn not out	2			
B 20, l-b 26, w 15, n-b 8	69	B 1, l-b 2, w 4, n-b 4		11

1/72 (2) 2/80 (1)	(8 wkts dec, 142.4 overs)	442
3/90 (4) 4/217 (3) 5/268 (5)		
6/354 (7) 7/417 (8) 8/430 (9)	110 overs: 329-5	

1/94 (2)	(3 wkts dec, 51 overs)	258
2/134 (3) 3/188 (1)		

D. Evans did not bat.

Lucas 28–3–86–1; Brooks 30–7–89–3; Evans 25–4–73–1; Hall 28.4–8–76–1; Boje 31–8–72–2. *Second Innings*—Lucas 10–1–54–1; Brooks 12–2–49–0; Evans 11–0–51–0; Hall 5–0–14–0; Boje 13–1–87–2.

Northamptonshire

S. D. Peters b Evans	62	– not out	183
M. B. Loye c Malan b Finn	13	– c Strauss b Murtagh	19
A. G. Wakely b Murtagh	24	– b Finn	87
D. J. Sales c Strauss b Finn	55	– lbw b Malan	30
R. A. White lbw b Evans	0	– b Finn	40
A. J. Hall c Malan b Berg	39	– not out	15
*N. Boje not out	61		
†P. W. Harrison lbw b Evans	8		
D. S. Lucas c Robson b Udal	16		
J. A. Brooks c Finn b Evans	1		
L. Evans c Robson b Evans	8		
B 1, l-b 8, w 1, n-b 10	20	B 16, l-b 3, n-b 2	21

1/44 (2) 2/94 (3) 3/108 (1)   (83.4 overs) 307
4/108 (5) 5/194 (6) 6/228 (4)
7/245 (8) 8/278 (9) 9/281 (10) 10/307 (11)

1/43 (2)   (4 wkts, 89.1 overs) 395
2/222 (3) 3/269 (4)
4/354 (2)

Murtagh 16–4–52–1; Finn 18–3–75–2; Berg 17–1–54–1; Evans 20.4–0–87–5; Udal 12–2–30–1. *Second Innings*—Murtagh 23–4–63–1; Finn 18.1–1–81–2; Berg 14–0–60–0; Evans 10–0–63–0; Udal 16–1–80–0; Malan 8–0–29–1.

Umpires: N. G. C. Cowley and J. H. Evans.

NORTHAMPTONSHIRE v DERBYSHIRE

At Northampton, April 27–30. Drawn. Northamptonshire 4pts, Derbyshire 10pts. Toss: Northamptonshire.

Northamptonshire avoided a withering defeat through the stubborn efforts of their tailenders in the final session. Tripathi and Wakely appeared to be saving the game comfortably until both departed shortly before lunch, precipitating a middle-order collapse. When Middlebrook became Greg Smith's third victim they were 194 for eight, still trailing by 66, but Harrison and Lucas used up 24 overs in adding 36 for the ninth wicket, and Brooks managed to keep Harrison company for the last 79 deliveries. The loss of 57 overs to rain on the third day and 11 on the fourth cost Derbyshire their chance of victory, and knowing they were the better side throughout was scant consolation. Their varied attack bowled tidily to dismiss Northamptonshire cheaply first time around, aided by poor shot selection. Rogers and Madsen took them into the lead without being parted, and their stand of 273 in 74 overs was a Derbyshire first-wicket record against Northamptonshire. Madsen hit 17 fours and a six in his career-best score, made from 344 balls.

Close of play: First day, Derbyshire 57-0 (Rogers 31, Madsen 17); Second day, Derbyshire 377-2 (Madsen 163, Borrington 41); Third day, Northamptonshire 17-0 (Peters 10, Tripathi 5).

Northamptonshire

S. D. Peters c Rogers b Footitt	32	– lbw b Peterson	14
V. Tripathi lbw b Lungley	13	– c Park b Smith	71
A. G. Wakely b Lungley	0	– run out	39
D. J. Sales c Madsen b Peterson	33	– c Lungley b Peterson	2
R. A. White b Footitt	0	– c Goddard b Footitt	5
A. J. Hall c Goddard b Footitt	33	– b Smith	27
*N. Boje c Madsen b Footitt	54	– b Park	12
†P. W. Harrison c Goddard b Lungley	6	– not out	32
J. D. Middlebrook not out	26	– b Smith	4
D. S. Lucas b Peterson	13	– lbw b Smith	16
J. A. Brooks c Sadler b Peterson	0	– not out	5
B 2, l-b 4, n-b 4	10	B 2, l-b 2, n-b 6	10

1/25 (2) 2/25 (3) 3/66 (1) 4/70 (5) (78.2 overs) 220
5/118 (6) 6/118 (4) 7/149 (8)
8/196 (7) 9/220 (10) 10/220 (11)

1/27 (1)   (9 wkts, 107 overs) 237
2/132 (2) 3/132 (3)
4/137 (5) 5/145 (4) 6/174 (7)
7/188 (6) 8/194 (9) 9/230 (10)

Lungley 13–2–39–3; Groenewald 12–5–32–0; Footitt 17–1–78–4; Smith 8–2–20–0; Peterson 24.2–8–33–3; Park 4–0–12–0. *Second Innings*—Lungley 13–3–42–0; Groenewald 11–3–26–0; Peterson 40–14–62–2; Smith 27–9–47–4; Footitt 12–1–42–1; Park 4–1–14–1.

Derbyshire

*C. J. L. Rogers lbw b Middlebrook	141	R. J. Peterson not out	22
W. L. Madsen c Hall b Brooks	179	B 17, l-b 6, n-b 14	37
G. T. Park c Hall b Boje	0		
P. M. Borrington not out	79	1/273 (1) (7 wkts dec, 138.1 overs) 480
G. M. Smith c Tripathi b Middlebrook	8	2/274 (3) 3/397 (2)
J. L. Sadler b Boje	14	4/406 (5) 5/441 (6) 110 overs: 373-2

†L. J. Goddard, T. Lungley, T. D. Groenewald and M. H. A. Footitt did not bat.

Lucas 24.1–0–77–0; Brooks 29–8–83–1; Middlebrook 38–4–126–2; Boje 27–2–111–2; Hall 18–1–49–0; Tripathi 2–0–11–0.

Umpires: N. G. B. Cook and R. T. Robinson.

At Cardiff, May 10–13. NORTHAMPTONSHIRE lost to GLAMORGAN by an innings and four runs.

NORTHAMPTONSHIRE v SUSSEX

At Northampton, May 18–20. Northamptonshire won by three wickets. Northamptonshire 21pts, Sussex 3pts. Toss: Sussex.

In an engrossing seesaw contest dominated by bowlers, Peters's obdurate century proved the decisive performance that allowed Hall to celebrate his first match as Northamptonshire's official captain with a win (he had been announced as Boje's replacement the day before). Not long after Willey, a late replacement for the injured Lucas, had swung one in to have the free-flowing Prior lbw, Sussex collapsed in spectacular fashion against full bowling from Hall and Daggett, losing their last six wickets for nine runs in 45 balls. Only Nash, whose dismissal sparked the slump, had appeared confident for long. The resilient Peters also played a lone hand for nearly five and a quarter hours, no one else passing 25, and his efforts secured a priceless lead of 99. It took a 64-run partnership for the seventh wicket between Martin-Jenkins and Rayner (with a collective height approaching 13 feet) to give Sussex a realistic chance of putting Northamptonshire under pressure. At 88 for five, chasing 171, the result was still in the balance, but Wakely dug in after surviving a vehement appeal for caught behind, and Boje played with positive abandon to hasten victory for his successor.

Close of play: First day, Northamptonshire 118-5 (Peters 55); Second day, Sussex 137-2 (Thornely 45, Goodwin 21).

Sussex

C. D. Nash c O'Brien b Daggett	78	– c Sales b Daggett	32
M. A. Thornely c Brooks b Willey	6	– c O'Brien b Daggett	51
E. C. Joyce c Hall b Daggett	14	– c Wakely b Middlebrook	30
*M. W. Goodwin b Middlebrook	30	– c Sales b Daggett	39
†M. J. Prior lbw b Willey	23	– lbw b Brooks	0
A. J. Hodd b Hall	7	– c Wakely b Brooks	5
R. S. C. Martin-Jenkins run out	2	– not out	55
O. P. Rayner c Sales b Daggett	3	– b Middlebrook	27
Naved-ul-Hasan not out	2	– c Sales b Willey	7
J. E. Anyon lbw b Hall	0	– b Brooks	1
C. D. Collymore lbw b Hall	0	– lbw b Willey	5
B 8, l-b 2	10	B 10, l-b 7	17

1/16 (2) 2/45 (3) 3/105 (4)   (52 overs) 175
4/142 (5) 5/166 (1) 6/168 (6) 7/173 (8)
8/175 (7) 9/175 (10) 10/175 (11)

1/46 (1) 2/110 (3)   (85.5 overs) 269
3/155 (2) 4/164 (5)
5/170 (4) 6/170 (6) 7/234 (8)
8/245 (9) 9/256 (10) 10/269 (11)

Brooks 8–0–31–0; Willey 12–2–47–2; Daggett 15–3–38–3; Hall 7–2–19–3; Boje 7–2–14–0; Middlebrook 3–1–16–1. *Second Innings*—Brooks 19–3–45–3; Willey 14.5–0–57–2; Daggett 20–5–50–3; Boje 9–4–28–0; Hall 14–3–35–0; Middlebrook 9–2–37–2.

Northamptonshire

S. D. Peters c Prior b Collymore	136	– lbw b Naved-ul-Hasan	4
†N. J. O'Brien c Prior b Collymore	22	– c Anyon b Collymore	24
A. G. Wakely lbw b Martin-Jenkins	17	– c Prior b Nash	51
D. J. Sales c Thornely b Martin-Jenkins	1	– b Anyon	12
R. A. White c Joyce b Rayner	15	– c and b Rayner	9
*A. J. Hall b Anyon	2	– lbw b Rayner	0
N. Boje c Martin-Jenkins b Anyon	1	– c Collymore b Nash	42
J. D. Middlebrook c Joyce b Rayner	25	– not out	3
D. J. Willey lbw b Rayner	11	– not out	9
L. M. Daggett not out	13		
J. A. Brooks b Collymore	4		
B 2, l-b 13, n-b 12	27	B 2, l-b 9, n-b 6	17

1/38 (2) 2/77 (3) 3/79 (4)   (88.5 overs) 274
4/113 (5) 5/118 (6) 6/132 (7) 7/202 (8)
8/246 (9) 9/254 (1) 10/274 (11)

1/12 (1)   (7 wkts, 48.3 overs) 171
2/40 (2) 3/57 (4)
4/86 (5) 5/88 (6) 6/157 (7) 7/161 (3)

Naved-ul-Hasan 19–5–62–0; Collymore 22.5–6–56–3; Martin-Jenkins 14–2–36–2; Anyon 14–2–53–2; Rayner 15–2–45–3; Nash 4–1–7–0. *Second Innings*—Naved-ul-Hasan 7–2–19–1; Collymore 7–1–24–1; Anyon 10–1–37–1; Martin-Jenkins 6–0–30–0; Rayner 14–3–34–2; Nash 4.3–0–16–2.

Umpires: V. A. Holder and N. A. Mallender.

NORTHAMPTONSHIRE v SURREY

At Northampton, May 24–27. Surrey won by seven wickets. Surrey 22pts, Northamptonshire 7pts. Toss: Surrey. County debut: W. P. U. J. C. Vaas. Championship debut: T. M. Jewell.

Surrey won a Championship match for only the second time since September 2007; both victories had been at Wantage Road. The result hinged on a remarkable last-wicket stand of 118 between Nel and Dernbach, which restricted Surrey's deficit to just 11 and so wrested the psychological advantage from Northamptonshire that their own batting fell away alarmingly. Hamilton-Brown's decision to bowl first seemed to have backfired as Loye hit 21 fours and two sixes in his first century since returning from Lancashire; he was playing only because Wakely had a groin injury. Loye and Boje added 193 for the sixth wicket but the lower order were swept aside by Dernbach and Linley. Surrey's batsmen struggled before the last pair came together early on the third day. Staying for 129 balls, Nel looked destined for the first hundred of his 14-year career until Boje had him lbw four short. Nel and Dernbach went on to share seven second-innings wickets, and Surrey, with Ramprakash at the helm, comfortably reached their target of 241 with seven overs to spare on what remained a good pitch. Nel may have been roused by another brush with the law on the first day. When Davies spilled a chance off his bowling, Nel hurled the ball in fury towards the stumps, hitting batsman O'Brien on the pads. Nel apologised to umpire Llong, but Surrey took the unusual step of independently suspending him for two matches and fining him £5,000.

Close of play: First day, Northamptonshire 330-5 (Loye 121, Boje 77); Second day, Surrey 210-7 (Spriegel 25, Nel 0); Third day, Northamptonshire 154-4 (Boje 18, Hall 8).

Northamptonshire

S. D. Peters c Schofield b Linley	61	– b Nel	9
†N. J. O'Brien c Davies b Linley	44	– c Davies b Dernbach	44
M. B. Loye b Linley	164	– lbw b Schofield	20
D. J. Sales b Nel	0	– (7) run out	0
R. A. White c Davies b Dernbach	8	– (4) c Linley b Nel	29
*A. J. Hall c Davies b Jewell	5	– c Davies b Nel	32
N. Boje run out	88	– (5) c Spriegel b Linley	18
J. D. Middlebrook lbw b Dernbach	1	– lbw b Nel	5
W. P. U. J. C. Vaas b Linley	0	– lbw b Dernbach	17
D. J. Willey b Afzaal b Linley	3	– not out	18
L. M. Daggett not out	4	– b Dernbach	2
B 5, l-b 7, n-b 7	19	B 13, l-b 5, w 1, n-b 16	35

1/90 (2) 2/127 (1) 3/134 (4)   (115.4 overs) 397
4/162 (5) 5/169 (6) 6/362 (7) 7/365 (8)
8/370 (9) 9/378 (10) 10/397 (3)   110 overs: 370-8

1/36 (1) 2/86 (2)   (74.5 overs) 229
3/86 (3) 4/136 (4)
5/154 (5) 6/159 (7) 7/179 (6)
8/188 (8) 9/219 (9) 10/229 (11)

Nel 26–7–79–1; Dernbach 24–5–84–2; Linley 34.4–11–105–5; Jewell 11–0–56–1; Schofield 6–0–27–0; Spriegel 8–0–19–0; Hamilton-Brown 4–0–11–0; Afzaal 2–0–4–0. *Second Innings—* Nel 17–4–68–4; Linley 12–3–31–1; Dernbach 17.5–7–42–3; Jewell 3–1–18–0; Schofield 21–9–43–1; Hamilton-Brown 3–0–5–0; Afzaal 1–0–4–0.

Surrey

†S. M. Davies c O'Brien b Daggett	33	– c Willey b Boje	25
A. Harinath c Middlebrook b Vaas	0	– c White b Willey	48
M. R. Ramprakash c Vaas b Middlebrook	70	– not out	79
*R. J. Hamilton-Brown c O'Brien b Boje	30	– st O'Brien b Middlebrook	45
U. Afzaal b Daggett	12	– not out	33
M. N. W. Spriegel c O'Brien b Vaas	43		
C. P. Schofield b Hall	29		
T. M. Jewell lbw b Hall	1		
A. Nel lbw b Boje	96		
T. E. Linley c O'Brien b Daggett	0		
J. W. Dernbach not out	56		
B 9, l-b 5, n-b 2	16	B 2, l-b 7, n-b 2	11

1/1 (2) 2/50 (1) 3/115 (4)   (115.3 overs) 386
4/136 (5) 5/159 (3) 6/208 (7) 7/210 (8)
8/255 (6) 9/268 (10) 10/386 (9)   110 overs: 366-9

1/37 (1)   (3 wkts, 58.4 overs) 241
2/99 (2) 3/153 (4)

Vaas 22–5–37–2; Willey 11–1–53–0; Daggett 25–5–119–3; Hall 15–1–65–2; Boje 23.3–8–47–2; Middlebrook 16–3–51–1. *Second Innings—* Vaas 7–2–28–0; Boje 18–4–88–1; Daggett 11–1–45–0; Hall 4–0–10–0; Willey 4–0–14–1; Middlebrook 13.4–3–40–1; White 1–0–7–0.

Umpires: S. A. Garratt and N. J. Llong.

At Lord's, June 4–7. NORTHAMPTONSHIRE beat MIDDLESEX by nine wickets.

At Northampton, July 3. NORTHAMPTONSHIRE lost to PAKISTANIS by six wickets (see Pakistani tour section).

NORTHAMPTONSHIRE v GLAMORGAN

At Northampton, July 5–7. Northamptonshire won by ten wickets. Northamptonshire 24pts, Glamorgan 2pts. Toss: Northamptonshire. Championship debut: E. Chigumbura.

Division Two leaders Glamorgan slipped to their first defeat in six matches, after Hall became the first bowler to claim a first-class hat-trick for Northamptonshire since Richard Williams against Gloucestershire on this ground in 1980. At 232 for two in their second innings, Glamorgan were making a good fist of saving the game until Hall threw them violently off course. Wright skied to point, and Dalrymple and Allenby both edged behind to Murphy, the composed 21-year-old wicketkeeper who took nine catches in the match, one short of Laurie Johnson's club record set at Worthing in 1963. Northamptonshire's big total owed a great deal to Sales, whose only century of the summer was his first for nearly two years – he had missed the entire 2009 season through injury. He took 28 balls to get off the mark, but went on to add 175 with Boje, before Hall and Elton Chigumbura – the first non-white Zimbabwean to play in the Championship – pressed home the advantage. Glamorgan never truly recovered from a disastrous start to their reply which saw Lucas and Brooks scatter the top order. They followed on 287 adrift and, despite Cosgrove's robust effort, failed to take the match into a fourth day.

Close of play: First day, Northamptonshire 355-5 (Chigumbura 5, Hall 6); Second day, Glamorgan 207.

Northamptonshire

S. D. Peters c Wallace b Cosker	76	– not out	17
B. H. N. Howgego c Cosgrove b Harris	18	– not out	23
A. G. Wakely c Dalrymple b Harrison	16		
D. J. Sales b Harrison	127		
N. Boje lbw b Harris	98		
E. Chigumbura b Dalrymple	44		
*A. J. Hall not out	84		
†D. Murphy c Wallace b Dalrymple	0		
J. D. Middlebrook lbw b Cosker	11		
D. S. Lucas c Allenby b Dalrymple	8		
J. A. Brooks c Wallace b Dalrymple	0		
L-b 12	12		

1/47 (2) 2/75 (3) 3/169 (1)   (142.4 overs) 494   (no wkt, 13.1 overs) 40
4/344 (5) 5/344 (4) 6/452 (6)
7/454 (8) 8/481 (9) 9/492 (10)
10/494 (11)   110 overs: 400-5

Harris 27–7–75–2; Harrison 28–4–96–2; Owen 12–0–66–0; Allenby 21–3–54–0; Cosker 33–3–96–2; Dalrymple 18.4–1–71–4; Cosgrove 3–0–24–0. *Second Innings*—Harris 4–1–10–0; Harrison 6.1–2–24–0; Cosker 3–1–6–0.

Glamorgan

G. P. Rees lbw b Brooks	29	– c Middlebrook b Brooks	14
M. J. Cosgrove c Murphy b Lucas	0	– c Murphy b Hall	115
T. L. Maynard c Murphy b Brooks	6	– c Hall b Boje	64
B. J. Wright c Murphy b Lucas	5	– c Sales b Hall	33
*J. W. M. Dalrymple c Peters b Lucas	8	– c Murphy b Hall	0
J. Allenby not out	59	– c Murphy b Hall	0
†M. A. Wallace c Boje b Chigumbura	21	– c Murphy b Lucas	20
J. A. R. Harris lbw b Chigumbura	8	– c Murphy b Middlebrook	39
D. A. Cosker b Chigumbura	0	– not out	7
D. S. Harrison b Chigumbura	18	– c Hall b Chigumbura	15
W. T. Owen c Murphy b Boje	38	– run out	0
B 6, l-b 1, n-b 8	15	B 5, l-b 3, n-b 10	18

1/1 (2) 2/16 (3) 3/29 (4) 4/55 (5)   (50 overs) 207
5/55 (1) 6/108 (7) 7/122 (8) 8/122 (9)
9/152 (10) 10/207 (11)

1/58 (1) 2/167 (3)   (77.2 overs) 325
3/232 (4) 4/232 (5)
5/232 (6) 6/243 (2) 7/275 (7)
8/308 (8) 9/325 (10) 10/325 (11)

Lucas 13–3–48–3; Brooks 11–5–32–2; Hall 9–2–22–0; Boje 9–1–31–1; Chigumbura 8–0–67–4. *Second Innings*—Lucas 13–5–54–1; Brooks 12–3–43–1; Hall 16–4–49–4; Boje 13–0–69–1; Chigumbura 7–0–45–1; Middlebrook 16.2–3–57–1.

Umpires: N. G. B. Cook and J. F. Steele.

At The Oval, July 20–22. NORTHAMPTONSHIRE lost to SURREY by an innings and 175 runs.

At Worcester, July 29–31. NORTHAMPTONSHIRE beat WORCESTERSHIRE by four wickets.

At Chesterfield, August 9–12. NORTHAMPTONSHIRE drew with DERBYSHIRE.

NORTHAMPTONSHIRE v GLOUCESTERSHIRE

At Northampton, August 16–18. Gloucestershire won by seven wickets. Gloucestershire 22pts, Northamptonshire 3pts. Toss: Northamptonshire. Championship debut: E. G. C. Young.

Brave resistance from Middlebrook and Murphy – whose 141-run partnership was a record for Northamptonshire's eighth wicket against Gloucestershire – only delayed the inevitable as the visitors were able to clinch victory at 4.07 p.m. on day three. Coming together at 108 for seven in the follow-on, still 70 behind, the pair kept their opponents in the field throughout the third morning before Lewis broke through again, and Gloucestershire closed out the match despite a couple of early strikes by the effervescent Brooks. Porterfield, assured and impressive throughout, laid the first-innings foundations with Dent; the ease with which they added 219 on a pitch of variable bounce could be largely explained by wayward bowling. The wickets later tumbled: Gloucestershire lost their last nine for 60 before Northamptonshire's agitated batsmen crumbled against Hussain, Franklin and Kirby with a flurry of loose drives. A total of 15 home wickets fell on a second day cut short by rain and bad light, placing Hall's side in danger of total humiliation until Middlebrook and Murphy demonstrated some mettle. The *Times* correspondent estimated that only 50 spectators came to watch the third day.

Close of play: First day, Northamptonshire 4-2 (Howgego 0); Second day, Northamptonshire 128-7 (Middlebrook 20, Murphy 1).

Gloucestershire

†J. N. Batty lbw b Brooks	2	– c Murphy b Brooks	5
W. T. S. Porterfield c Sales b Brooks	150	– c Wakely b Brooks	23
C. D. J. Dent b Middlebrook	92	– not out	28
*A. P. R. Gidman b Chigumbura	1	– b Chigumbura	9
J. E. C. Franklin b Daggett	7		
C. G. Taylor not out	21		
S. D. Snell c Sales b Daggett	0	– (5) not out	10
E. G. C. Young c Howgego b Brooks	1		
J. Lewis c Murphy b Daggett	11		
G. M. Hussain c Murphy b Hall	0		
S. P. Kirby c and b Daggett	1		
B 5, l-b 10, w 1	16	B 1	1

1/23 (1) 2/242 (3) 3/243 (4) (91.5 overs) 302
4/268 (2) 5/268 (5) 6/274 (7)
7/275 (8) 8/298 (9) 9/299 (10) 10/302 (11)

1/28 (2) (3 wkts, 17 overs) 76
2/33 (1) 3/52 (4)

Daggett 19.5–4–57–4; Brooks 21–10–63–3; Chigumbura 18–5–63–1; Hall 12–2–42–1; Middlebrook 21–2–62–1. *Second Innings*—Daggett 6–2–17–0; Brooks 8–3–45–2; Chigumbura 3–0–13–1.

Northamptonshire

S. D. Peters c Dent b Hussain	1	– b Hussain	25
B. H. N. Howgego lbw b Hussain	17	– c Batty b Hussain	11
J. D. Middlebrook c Porterfield b Lewis	1	– (8) lbw b Lewis	81
A. G. Wakely b Franklin	21	– (3) c Young b Hussain	8
D. J. Sales c Batty b Hussain	25	– (4) b Kirby	19
*A. J. Hall c Young b Kirby	23	– c Batty b Franklin	13
R. I. Newton b Kirby	10	– (5) c Dent b Lewis	6
E. Chigumbura b Kirby	8	– (7) c Lewis b Hussain	14
†D. Murphy not out	8	– lbw b Lewis	55
J. A. Brooks c Lewis b Franklin	4	– lbw b Franklin	1
L. M. Daggett c Batty b Franklin	0	– not out	0
B 2, l-b 4	6	L-b 13, n-b 6	19

1/3 (1) 2/4 (3) 3/42 (2) 4/42 (4) (36.5 overs) 124
5/76 (6) 6/92 (7) 7/104 (5) 8/112 (8)
9/124 (10) 10/124 (11)

1/34 (1) 2/39 (2) (84.2 overs) 252
3/62 (4) 4/77 (5)
5/90 (3) 6/100 (6) 7/108 (7)
8/249 (8) 9/250 (10) 10/252 (9)

Lewis 10–1–25–1; Hussain 12–5–39–3; Franklin 5.5–1–22–3; Kirby 9–2–32–3. *Second Innings*—Lewis 19.2–5–45–3; Franklin 16–2–54–2; Hussain 17–6–46–4; Kirby 21–7–62–1; Gidman 2–1–3–0; Young 9–1–29–0.

Umpires: S. A. Garratt and N. J. Llong.

NORTHAMPTONSHIRE v WORCESTERSHIRE

At Northampton, August 25–28. Drawn. Northamptonshire 6pts, Worcestershire 5pts. Toss: Northamptonshire.

Rain, which permitted only 34.5 overs on the first day and none at all on the second, proved intensely frustrating for two teams eyeing the second promotion place. When conditions improved, Northamptonshire opted to bat through the third day to amass bonus points and achieved three thanks to a strong collective effort, rounded off by a breezy stand between Murphy and Brooks. Rob Newton, just 20 years old, holed out at deep square leg shortly after completing a fifty rich with promise. The captains agreed a formula for keeping the match alive on the final day and, following a mercifully brief episode of joke bowling, Worcestershire set out in search of 341 from a minimum of 88 overs. Northamptonshire were firmly on top at 46 for three when Solanki misread a straight ball from Chigumbura and, although Moeen and Kervezee steadied the innings, Worcestershire were struggling when more wet weather forced an early tea and nothing more could be done.

Close of play: First day, Northamptonshire 96-3 (Peters 38, Newton 0); Second day, No play; Third day, Northamptonshire 385-9 (Murphy 36, Daggett 6).

Northamptonshire

S. D. Peters lbw b Shakib Al Hasan	75	J. A. Brooks b Richardson		34
B. H. N. Howgego c Andrew b Richardson	4	L. M. Daggett not out		6
A. G. Wakely c Solanki b Richardson	48			
D. J. Sales c Solanki b Shantry	4	B 4, l-b 4		8
R. I. Newton c Richardson b Andrew	56			
*A. J. Hall c Cox b Shakib Al Hasan	65	1/21 (2) 2/91 (3) (9 wkts dec, 132 overs)	385
E. Chigumbura c Cox b Richardson	3	3/96 (4) 4/176 (5)	
J. D. Middlebrook b Shakib Al Hasan	40	5/210 (1) 6/240 (7) 7/293 (6)	
†D. Murphy not out	36	8/308 (8) 9/370 (10)	110 overs: 306-7

Richardson 29–7–83–4; Shantry 26–7–61–1; Andrew 16–3–57–1; Shakib Al Hasan 29–9–75–3; Cameron 14–2–58–0; Ali 14–3–38–0; Solanki 4–1–5–0.

Northamptonshire forfeited their second innings.

Worcestershire

*D. K. H. Mitchell not out	31	– c Peters b Brooks		3
D. A. Wheeldon not out	12	– c Hall b Daggett		7
V. S. Solanki (did not bat)		– b Chigumbura		27
M. M. Ali (did not bat)		– c Murphy b Hall		62
A. N. Kervezee (did not bat)		– c Peters b Middlebrook		52
Shakib Al Hasan (did not bat)		– not out		9
J. G. Cameron (did not bat)		– lbw b Hall		0
†O. B. Cox (did not bat)		– not out		10
W 2	2	B 8, n-b 4		12
(no wkt dec, 5.1 overs)	45	1/5 (1) 2/21 (2) (6 wkts, 52 overs)	182
		3/46 (3) 4/163 (5)	
		5/163 (4) 6/165 (7)	

G. M. Andrew, A. Richardson and J. D. Shantry did not bat.

Sales 1–0–10–0; Newton 2.1–0–19–0; Howgego 2–0–16–0. *Second Innings*—Daggett 11–5–20–1; Brooks 11–3–30–1; Chigumbura 6–0–32–1; Hall 12–2–47–2; Middlebrook 12–1–45–1.

Umpires: M. R. Benson and N. G. B. Cook.

At Hove, September 7–9. NORTHAMPTONSHIRE lost to SUSSEX by an innings and 19 runs.

NORTHAMPTONSHIRE v LEICESTERSHIRE

At Northampton, September 13–16. Leicestershire won by ten wickets. Leicestershire 23pts, Northamptonshire 3pts. Toss: Northamptonshire. County debut: D. A. Burton.

The Championship season ended as it had begun for the two counties back in April – Leicestershire winning all too convincingly over their old rivals. Leicestershire's internal upheaval continued with rumours of Tim Boon's departure to head the England Development Programme; on this evidence he looked well qualified. Greg Smith (educated at Oundle School, in Northamptonshire) struck his second consecutive Championship century, while Taylor passed 1,000 first-class runs for the season in the course of his 156. For their part, Northamptonshire could derive some comfort from Newton's maiden first-class century, full of lusty pulls and easily the highlight of an otherwise stuttering first-innings display. It was clear to see how Northamptonshire had failed to claim maximum batting points since their meeting with Glamorgan in July. Leicestershire built a huge lead, though Burton, appearing for his third county after spurning the chance to play for the Unicorns, plugged away manfully; he was rewarded with four wickets in 14 balls amid the search for quick runs. Facing a deficit of 198, Northamptonshire (fielding their first all English-born eleven in a Championship match since August 1999, at home to Somerset) displayed little stomach for the fight until Middlebrook and Daggett hit cheerfully to help avoid the embarrassment of an innings defeat – by a single run.

Close of play: First day, Northamptonshire 186-6 (Murphy 5, Lucas 3); Second day, Leicestershire 159-2 (Smith 102, Taylor 32); Third day, Northamptonshire 10-1 (Loye 4, Wakely 2).

Northamptonshire

*S. D. Peters c du Toit b Hoggard	55	– lbw b Buck	4
M. B. Loye c New b Hoggard	0	– c Boyce b Gurney	15
A. G. Wakely c Taylor b Buck	9	– c New b Buck	6
D. J. Sales c Smith b Hoggard	5	– b Hoggard	9
R. I. Newton c Taylor b Henderson	102	– b Gurney	18
J. D. Middlebrook lbw b Naik	3	– c Hoggard b Naik	62
†D. Murphy lbw b Hoggard	5	– c du Toit b Naik	6
D. S. Lucas b Naik	31	– lbw b Naik	11
J. A. Brooks b Hoggard	9	– c New b Buck	7
L. M. Daggett not out	22	– b Naik	48
D. A. Burton lbw b Naik	0	– not out	2
B 1, l-b 8	9	B 4, l-b 4, n-b 2	10

1/1 (2) 2/12 (3) 3/23 (4) 4/122 (1) (77.4 overs) 250
5/147 (6) 6/183 (5) 7/186 (7)
8/204 (9) 9/250 (8) 10/250 (11)

1/7 (1) 2/21 (3) (53.4 overs) 198
3/30 (4) 4/39 (2)
5/62 (5) 6/83 (7) 7/105 (8)
8/120 (9) 9/194 (6) 10/198 (10)

Hoggard 21–7–48–5; Buck 19–5–74–1; Gurney 10–0–50–0; Henderson 9–0–18–1; Naik 18.4–2–51–3. *Second Innings*—Hoggard 8–4–14–1; Buck 20–2–89–3; Gurney 6–2–24–2; Naik 14.4–1–58–4; Henderson 5–3–5–0.

Leicestershire

G. P. Smith b Burton	104	– (2) not out	0
M. A. G. Boyce c Burton b Lucas	2	– (1) not out	4
J. du Toit c and b Middlebrook	14		
J. W. A. Taylor c Sales b Burton	156		
P. A. Nixon c Murphy b Brooks	65		
†T. J. New c Lucas b Middlebrook	43		
J. K. H. Naik c Sales b Burton	27		
C. W. Henderson not out	23		
N. L. Buck b Burton	2		
*M. J. Hoggard b Burton	0		
H. F. Gurney not out	0		
L-b 2, w 2, n-b 8	12		

1/27 (2) 2/58 (3) (9 wkts dec, 134 overs) 448
3/165 (1) 4/297 (5)
5/367 (6) 6/423 (4) 7/423 (7)
8/439 (9) 9/439 (10)

(no wkt, 0.1 overs) 4

110 overs: 357-4

Lucas 28–4–108–1; Brooks 24–7–68–1; Middlebrook 38–8–117–2; Daggett 18–3–57–0; Burton 20–4–75–5; Wakely 6–0–21–0. *Second Innings*—Wakely 0.1–0–4–0.

Umpires: M. J. D. Bodenham and J. F. Steele.

NOTTINGHAMSHIRE

Chokers no more

SIMON CLEAVES

Nottinghamshire's Championship triumph saw them gain full reward for finally casting off the nerves that had gripped them in pressure situations in recent seasons. A recurrent theme since they finished top of the pile in 2005, those worries reared up again in September 2010 – but this time, with the cards seemingly stacked against them more than in previous years, Nottinghamshire rose to the occasion.

After leading the table for much of the season, they had established a 16-point lead over Somerset with three matches to go. The wheels promptly wobbled alarmingly, with a fourth-day collapse at Chester-le-Street followed by the ignominy of being bowled out for 59 by Yorkshire at home. That meant the lead over Somerset had been reduced to just two points, with Yorkshire a further five behind. With rain allowing only 28 overs on the first three days of the final game at Old Trafford, and Somerset gaining the upper hand over Durham, affairs appeared to be conspiring against Nottinghamshire before the incredible events of the decisive day.

That morning, captain Chris Read was in a quandary: should he try to arrange a fourth-innings run-chase with Lancashire, or claim as many bonus points as possible and hope that Durham could hold off Somerset? After much dressing-room debate, Nottinghamshire chose the second option and threw off the straitjacket. While Durham did their bit by battling to a draw, Adam Voges demonstrated his worth in a dazzling partnership with Samit Patel, Ryan Sidebottom and Darren Pattinson eked out the most important ten runs of their lives to claim the last batting point. When Andre Adams claimed the wickets that brought the crucial bowling point, the Championship pennant was on its way back to Trent Bridge.

That had seemed likely after Nottinghamshire won their first four matches, three of them at home. It was their best start to a season since 1922, when they won their first six (but ended up second behind Yorkshire), and they maintained their momentum with further victories at crucial times, victories based around a pedigree bowling attack and long batting line-up. Adams was the country's leading wicket-taker with 68 and a deserving choice as Player of the Season; he proved Read's "go-to" man, with extravagant sideways movement off the seam and a slippery quicker ball. Around him, the seamers chipped in with the occasional match-winning display – Stuart Broad picked up 19 wickets in his two appearances – and nine different batsmen made Championship hundreds.

Read was once again the most consistent player, while overseas batsmen Hashim Amla, David Hussey and Voges were exceptional. Paul Franks claimed 41 wickets, hit six half-centuries and volunteered for the thankless task of facing the new ball with Alex Hales in the final three matches. Opening had

proved too much for Neil Edwards, Bilal
Shafayat and Matt Wood, the last two being
released at the end of the season.

While the Championship trophy was the
highlight, director of cricket Mick Newell
took almost as much pleasure from the way
his side improved in limited-overs cricket.
After some dismal performances in 2009,
Newell set out to generate more dynamism
in the side, favouring younger and more
athletic players and promoting a more
aggressive mindset. That paid particular
dividends in the Friends Provident T20,
where Hussey was a brutal match-winner

Andre Adams

and effervescent captain, as Read concentrated on his keeping. Hales
demonstrated his exciting potential at the top of the order, while Sidebottom,
Pattinson and Dirk Nannes bullied opposition batsmen with their pace and
accuracy. With new signings Steven Mullaney and Graeme White throwing
themselves around in the field – and making crucial contributions with bat and
ball – Nottinghamshire were favourites with many pundits come finals day
and, had it not been for the outstretched hand of Kieron Pollard, and an ill-
timed rain shower, might well have added a second trophy to the cabinet.

They also did enough in the CB40 to keep their semi-final hopes alive into
the final group game, but an underpowered side, missing senior bowlers to
injury, were defeated by a Warwickshire team boasting both Ian Bell and
Jonathan Trott.

Winning the Championship may represent the high-water mark for many of
this generation of players. Sidebottom's return to Yorkshire, after turning
down a conditional three-year contract, leaves a massive hole in the bowling
attack. Adams, at 35, enjoyed the finest season of his career but will surely not
pick up so many wickets again, Pattinson was dangerous in bursts but proved
expensive, and Charlie Shreck has increasingly been dogged by injury. With
the bat, the stabilising influence of Mark Wagh will be missing from August
when he retires to begin a legal career, while Ali Brown, 41 in February 2011,
cannot defy his age for ever.

The weight of responsibility will fall even more heavily on skipper Read
and the overseas batsman, and the likes of Hales, Mullaney and Samit Patel
will need to step up. All three illustrated their talent at times during 2010: the
only lean thing about Patel, in the last two seasons, has been his batting
aggregate in the Championship. Supporters will also be hoping to see more of
young, local talent: Luke Fletcher and Andrew Carter can expect a greater
workload, while the likes of Akhil Patel, Jake Ball and Scott Elstone should
continue to be given a chance in the 40-over competition. Consistency will
therefore become the key question for 2011, when it may be that the one-day
format offers a greater chance of further silverware than the Championship.

NOTTINGHAMSHIRE RESULTS

All first-class matches – Played 17: Won 7, Lost 5, Drawn 5.
County Championship matches – Played 16: Won 7, Lost 5, Drawn 4.

LV= County Championship, winners in Division 1;
Friends Provident T20, s-f; Clydesdale Bank 40, 3rd in Group C.

COUNTY CHAMPIONSHIP AVERAGES, BATTING AND FIELDING

Cap		M	I	NO	R	HS	100s	50s	Avge	Ct/St
2010	H. M. Amla§	4	6	1	377	129	1	4	75.40	1
2004	D. J. Hussey§	5	7	1	399	251*	1	1	66.50	7
2008	A. C. Voges§	3	5	0	254	126	1	1	50.80	1
1999	C. M. W. Read	16	24	4	916	124*	2	5	45.80	59/4
	S. J. Mullaney	11	17	4	512	100*	1	3	39.38	6
2007	M. A. Wagh	15	23	1	853	139	2	3	38.77	8
	A. D. Hales	12	20	1	677	136	1	4	35.63	12
	A. D. Brown	16	24	1	805	134	1	6	35.00	11
1999	P. J. Franks†	15	21	1	651	79	0	6	32.55	1
2008	S. R. Patel	16	26	2	641	104	1	3	26.70	5
	M. J. Wood	4	6	0	148	72	0	2	24.66	1
	N. J. Edwards	6	9	0	189	85	0	1	21.00	5
	L. J. Fletcher†	5	8	3	81	23*	0	0	16.20	2
2007	A. R. Adams¶	14	20	5	240	37	0	0	16.00	13
	B. M. Shafayat†	6	10	0	118	49	0	0	11.80	4
2008	D. J. Pattinson	12	13	4	93	27	0	0	10.33	0
2006	C. E. Shreck	5	7	1	10	7*	0	0	1.66	4
2004	R. J. Sidebottom‡	8	6	6	44	18*	0	0	–	3

Also batted: S. C. J. Broad†‡ (2 matches) 1, 6, 0; G. P. Swann‡ (cap 2005) (1 match) 1; G. G. White (1 match) 29 (1 ct).

† *Born in Nottinghamshire.* ‡ *ECB contract.* § *Official overseas player.* ¶ *Other non-England-qualified player.*

BOWLING

	O	M	R	W	BB	5W/i	Avge
S. C. J. Broad	66	7	299	19	8-52	2	15.73
R. J. Sidebottom	218	58	582	27	5-35	1	21.55
A. R. Adams	455.5	101	1,508	68	6-79	4	22.17
P. J. Franks	386.2	102	1,046	41	3-15	0	25.51
C. E. Shreck	199	50	577	18	4-81	0	32.05
D. J. Pattinson	294.2	49	1,128	31	5-95	1	36.38
S. R. Patel	311.3	64	954	24	4-55	0	39.75

Also bowled: A. D. Brown 7-0-53-0; L. J. Fletcher 144.2-31-508-9; A. D. Hales 5.5-1-26-0; D. J. Hussey 18-1-82-0; S. J. Mullaney 93.3-19-321-9; G. P. Swann 26-5-88-2; A. C. Voges 1-0-2-0; G. G. White 23-3-104-1; M. J. Wood 1-0-11-0.

LEADING CB40 AVERAGES (100 runs/4 wickets)

Batting	Runs	HS	Avge	S-R	Ct/St
A. C. Voges	127	71*	63.50	79.87	1
D. J. Hussey	114	80	57.00	137.34	3
S. R. Patel	467	108*	46.70	95.50	3
C. M. W. Read . . .	263	69*	43.83	109.12	8/3
A. D. Hales	370	96*	37.00	104.22	6
M. J. Wood	110	60	22.00	75.86	0

Bowling	W	BB	Avge	E-R
S. J. Mullaney . . .	13	3-24	21.53	5.28
R. J. Sidebottom . . .	6	3-45	27.00	5.22
G. G. White	11	5-35	27.81	5.61
P. J. Franks	11	3-22	31.90	6.38
D. J. Pattinson . . .	6	3-70	33.33	4.63
S. R. Patel	11	2-19	33.45	5.23

LEADING FPT20 AVERAGES (100 runs/18 overs)

Batting	Runs	HS	Avge	S-R	Ct
D. J. Hussey	524	81*	43.66	**142.00**	9
A. D. Hales	466	83	29.12	**135.86**	8
S. R. Patel	459	63	28.68	**133.04**	3
A. D. Brown	337	73*	19.82	**132.15**	5
S. J. Mullaney	145	53	18.12	**122.88**	7
M. J. Wood	328	61	21.86	**111.56**	1

Bowling	W	BB	Avge	E-R
S. R. Patel	17	3-26	22.17	**6.50**
D. J. Pattinson	20	4-19	17.65	**7.06**
S. J. Mullaney	14	3-12	28.07	**7.27**
G. G. White	12	3-22	22.50	**7.46**
R. J. Sidebottom	7	2-19	45.00	**7.68**
D. P. Nannes	17	2-20	27.41	**7.92**

FIRST-CLASS COUNTY RECORDS

Highest score for	312*	W. W. Keeton v Middlesex at The Oval	1939
Highest score against	345	C. G. Macartney (Australians) at Nottingham	1921
Leading run-scorer	31,592	G. Gunn (avge 35.69)	1902–1932
Best bowling for	10-66	K. Smales v Gloucestershire at Stroud	1956
Best bowling against	10-10	H. Verity (Yorkshire) at Leeds	1932
Leading wicket-taker	1,653	T. G. Wass (avge 20.34)	1896–1920
Highest total for	791	v Essex at Chelmsford	2007
Highest total against	781-7 dec	by Northamptonshire at Northampton	1995
Lowest total for	13	v Yorkshire at Nottingham	1901
Lowest total against {	16	by Derbyshire at Nottingham	1879
	16	by Surrey at The Oval	1880

LIST A COUNTY RECORDS

Highest score for	167*	P. Johnson v Kent at Nottingham	1993
Highest score against	191	D. S. Lehmann (Yorkshire) at Scarborough	2001
Leading run-scorer	11,237	R. T. Robinson (avge 35.33)	1978–1999
Best bowling for	6-10	K. P. Evans v Northumberland at Jesmond	1994
Best bowling against	7-41	A. N. Jones (Sussex) at Nottingham	1986
Leading wicket-taker	291	C. E. B. Rice (avge 22.60)	1975–1987
Highest total for	346-9	v Ireland at Nottingham	2009
Highest total against	361-8	by Surrey at The Oval	2001
Lowest total for	57	v Gloucestershire at Nottingham	2009
Lowest total against	43	by Northamptonshire at Northampton	1977

TWENTY20 RECORDS

Highest score for	91	M. A. Ealham v Yorkshire at Nottingham	2004
Highest score against	**111**	**W. J. Durston (Derbyshire) at Nottingham**	**2010**
Leading run-scorer	**1,359**	**S. R. Patel (avge 25.64)**	**2003–2010**
Best bowling for	5-26	R. J. Logan v Lancashire at Nottingham	2003
Best bowling against	**5-13**	**A. B. McDonald (Leicestershire) at Nottingham**	**2010**
Leading wicket-taker	**54**	**S. R. Patel (avge 23.31)**	**2003–2010**
Highest total for	213-6	v Northamptonshire at Nottingham	2006
Highest total against	207-7	by Yorkshire at Nottingham	2004
Lowest total for	91	v Lancashire at Manchester	2006
Lowest total against	106	by Lancashire at Nottingham	2005

ADDRESS

County Cricket Ground, Trent Bridge, Nottingham NG2 6AG (0115 982 3000; **email** administration@nottsccc.co.uk). **Website** www.nottsccc.co.uk

OFFICIALS

Captain C. M. W. Read
Director of cricket M. Newell
President M. J. Smedley
Chairman P. G. Wright

Chief executive D. M. Brewer
Chairman, cricket committee P. G. Wright
Head groundsman S. Birks
Scorer L. B. Hewes

At Durham, April 10–12. NOTTINGHAMSHIRE drew with DURHAM MCCU.

NOTTINGHAMSHIRE v KENT

At Nottingham, April 15–17. Nottinghamshire won by an innings and 32 runs. Nottinghamshire 24pts, Kent 4pts. Toss: Kent.

Nottinghamshire started their Championship campaign with a thumping victory over the previous year's second division champions, who were made to look underpowered with bat and ball. After Kent decided to bowl first under heavy skies and captured two early wickets, Amla marked his home debut with a century as assured as it was elegant, and shared a 103-run stand with Edwards, who had been signed from Somerset to shore up Nottinghamshire's leaky opening partnership. Amla's application – he batted for just over five hours, and hit 19 fours – was complemented by half-centuries from Read and Franks, who helped secure maximum batting points. Kent were unable to show the same discipline, with easy pickings from the home attack. Sidebottom started the slide by gating Denly for a 13-ball duck, then trapped Key in front in his next over. Edwards showed a safe pair of hands to take five catches at second slip, the most in an innings by a Nottinghamshire fielder since Derek Randall in 1987, and two more wickets fell before the end of the second day when Kent followed on. Victory was wrapped up before tea on the third.

Close of play: First day, Nottinghamshire 396-8 (Franks 35); Second day, Kent 51-2 (Edwards 5, Jones 5).

Nottinghamshire

N. J. Edwards lbw b Tredwell	85	L. J. Fletcher c van Jaarsveld b Coles	13
B. M. Shafayat c Tredwell b Khan	4	R. J. Sidebottom not out	8
M. A. Wagh c Tredwell b Khan	0		
H. M. Amla st Jones b Stevens	129	B 9, l-b 7, w 4, n-b 10	30
S. R. Patel c Jones b Azhar Mahmood	15		
A. D. Brown lbw b Khan	18	1/41 (2) 2/43 (3)	(111.4 overs) 456
*†C. M. W. Read run out	62	3/146 (1) 4/165 (5) 5/203 (6)	
P. J. Franks b Coles	73	6/328 (7) 7/367 (4) 8/396 (9)	
A. R. Adams c Jones b Edwards	19	9/429 (10) 10/456 (8)	110 overs: 451-9

Khan 25–5–108–3; Azhar Mahmood 26–5–75–1; Edwards 14–3–77–1; Coles 15.4–2–65–2; Tredwell 18–2–68–1; Denly 1–0–4–0; Stevens 12–1–43–1.

Kent

J. L. Denly b Sidebottom	0	(7) lbw b Adams	37
*R. W. T. Key lbw b Sidebottom	4	b Fletcher	15
†G. O. Jones b Adams	28	(4) c Adams b Fletcher	11
M. van Jaarsveld c Read b Adams	7	(5) lbw b Fletcher	1
S. A. Northeast c Edwards b Fletcher	38	(6) st Read b Patel	18
D. I. Stevens c Edwards b Adams	7	(8) not out	42
J. C. Tredwell c Edwards b Adams	19	(1) b Adams	20
Azhar Mahmood c Brown b Franks	52	(9) c Read b Adams	19
M. T. Coles c Edwards b Sidebottom	6	(10) b Patel	28
A. Khan c Edwards b Franks	24	(11) b Patel	9
P. D. Edwards not out	6	(3) c Wagh b Sidebottom	13
B 1, l-b 6, n-b 2	9	B 2, l-b 9	11

1/4 (1) 2/13 (2) 3/33 (3) 4/44 (4)	(62 overs) 200	1/41 (2) 2/45 (1)	(65.4 overs) 224
5/58 (6) 6/100 (5) 7/140 (7) 8/151 (9)		3/66 (4) 4/70 (5)	
9/168 (8) 10/200 (10)		5/72 (3) 6/125 (6) 7/125 (7)	
		8/163 (8) 9/194 (10) 10/224 (11)	

Sidebottom 16–6–31–3; Fletcher 13–2–47–1; Adams 18–3–63–4; Franks 11–2–35–2; Patel 4–1–17–0. *Second Innings*—Sidebottom 14–6–35–1; Fletcher 15.2–8–43–3; Adams 18–1–78–3; Franks 11.4–4–33–0; Patel 6.4–1–24–3.

Umpires: R. K. Illingworth and P. Willey.

NOTTINGHAMSHIRE v SOMERSET

At Nottingham, April 21–23. Nottinghamshire won by two wickets. Nottinghamshire 21pts, Somerset 5pts. Toss: Nottinghamshire.

A fast-moving game on a pitch that ensured a good contest between bat and ball came to a thrilling climax inside three days, with two of Nottinghamshire's Test stars Amla and Broad proving the difference between the sides. Broad, making a rare county appearance after practice match practice ahead of the World Twenty20, was wayward on the first morning but on fire on the second day, when he grabbed five wickets in 27 balls to leave Somerset reeling at 43 for six in their second innings. Trescothick alone survived the Broadside, but perished two short of a hundred when he edged to first slip: he was helped in a partnership of 136 by Wright as Somerset's last five wickets easily outscored the top five for the second time in the match. Chasing a potentially tricky 250, Shafayat and Wagh shared an important stand of 125 before both fell at the same score. Unperturbed by regular wickets at the other end, Amla stayed put and, with the close approaching, upped the run-rate and sealed victory with a pull to the square-leg boundary in the extra half-hour. It was Amla's second diligent innings of a match in which Franks made an important all-round contribution.

Close of play: First day, Nottinghamshire 26-2 (Wagh 12, Amla 4); Second day, Somerset 120-6 (Trescothick 63, Wright 37).

Somerset

*M. E. Trescothick c Amla b Broad	22	– c Brown b Franks	98
A. V. Suppiah c Brown b Adams	10	– c Adams b Broad	11
N. R. D. Compton c Wagh b Fletcher	42	– c Read b Adams	1
J. C. Hildreth lbw b Fletcher	14	– lbw b Broad	0
Z. de Bruyn c Edwards b Franks	1	– c Adams b Broad	0
†C. Kieswetter c Read b Franks	1	– c Read b Broad	0
P. D. Trego c Read b Franks	66	– c Patel b Broad	3
D. G. Wright c Edwards b Broad	43	– b Fletcher	78
A. C. Thomas not out	40	– c Edwards b Franks	12
D. A. Stiff c Fletcher b Broad	14	– not out	5
C. M. Willoughby c Wagh b Adams	8	– b Franks	4
L-b 7, n-b 4	11	L-b 5, n-b 10	15

1/23 (2) 2/35 (1) 3/65 (4) 4/66 (5)   (76.1 overs) 272
5/78 (6) 6/142 (3) 7/199 (7)
8/220 (8) 9/254 (10) 10/272 (11)

1/25 (2) 2/26 (3)   (48.5 overs) 227
3/33 (4) 4/33 (5)
5/33 (6) 6/43 (7) 7/179 (8)
8/216 (1) 9/223 (9) 10/227 (11)

Broad 19–1–79–3; Fletcher 16–5–48–2; Adams 19.1–4–68–2; Franks 16–6–45–3; Patel 6–0–25–0. *Second Innings*—Broad 15–2–89–5; Fletcher 10–1–49–1; Adams 14.5–5–59–1; Franks 6.5–0–22–3; Patel 3–1–3–0.

Nottinghamshire

N. J. Edwards lbw b Willoughby	2	– c Trescothick b Willoughby	1
B. M. Shafayat c Trescothick b Thomas	1	– lbw b Wright	49
M. A. Wagh b Stiff	16	– c Wright b Trego	70
H. M. Amla c Kieswetter b Wright	58	– not out	64
S. R. Patel c Wright b Willoughby	33	– lbw b Thomas	10
A. D. Brown lbw b Thomas	2	– lbw b de Bruyn	16
*†C. M. W. Read lbw b Trego	29	– c Trescothick b Willoughby	0
P. J. Franks lbw b Willoughby	61	– c Kieswetter b Thomas	12
S. C. J. Broad c Hildreth b Willoughby	1	– c Suppiah b Willoughby	6
A. R. Adams b Wright	10	– not out	0
L. J. Fletcher not out	5		
B 4, l-b 14, w 2, n-b 12	32	L-b 6, w 4, n-b 12	22

1/2 (1) 2/4 (2) 3/56 (3) 4/121 (5)   (87 overs) 250
5/124 (6) 6/129 (4) 7/231 (7)
8/235 (9) 9/236 (8) 10/250 (10)

1/2 (1)   (8 wkts, 71.5 overs) 250
2/127 (2) 3/127 (3)
4/171 (5) 5/195 (6) 6/198 (7)
7/233 (8) 8/246 (9)

Willoughby 23–8–40–4; Wright 19–10–41–2; Thomas 17–7–34–2; Stiff 12–1–52–1; Trego 7–2–22–1; de Bruyn 6–1–31–0; Suppiah 3–0–12–0. *Second Innings*—Willoughby 22–5–83–3; Thomas 15.5–3–54–2; Wright 10–1–30–1; Stiff 5–0–36–0; Trego 13–4–30–1; Suppiah 4–2–3–0; de Bruyn 2–0–8–1.

Umpires: T. E. Jesty and G. Sharp.

At Southampton, May 4–7. NOTTINGHAMSHIRE beat HAMPSHIRE by five wickets.

NOTTINGHAMSHIRE v DURHAM

At Nottingham, May 10–13. Nottinghamshire won by an innings and 62 runs. Nottinghamshire 24pts, Durham 3pts. Toss: Nottinghamshire.

Remembering Durham's crushing victory in this fixture in 2009, locals were delighted to see the tables turned as the champions of the previous two years were put to the sword. It was their first Championship defeat in 24 games since August 2008, but Nottinghamshire's fourth straight win, their best start to a season since 1922. Durham were under pressure from the start. The top three departed inside 12 overs of a rain-interrupted first day, then three wickets in 16 balls just before lunch next day exposed the tail. Durham's bowling was less impressive: Steve Harmison looked laboured in his first Championship appearance of the season following a back strain. After Amla and Wagh blunted what little threat was posed by the bowling, Brown and Read put on 237, Nottinghamshire's second-highest seventh-wicket partnership as Durham – hit for 610 by Yorkshire in their previous match – conceded more than 500 for the second match running. Needing 341 to avoid the innings defeat, Durham slumped again: although left-hander Ben Stokes, three weeks short of his 19th birthday, became their second-youngest Championship centurion (behind Nicky Peng in 2001) with a swashbuckling maiden hundred – he shot from 82 to 102 with four, six, six and four from successive balls from Patel – even he could not prevent a chastening defeat. It was a memorable match for Read: his catch to remove Ben Harmison was his 700th first-class dismissal, then his unbeaten century took him past 10,000 runs.

Close of play: First day, Durham 79-3 (Benkenstein 20, Blackwell 24); Second day, Nottinghamshire 191-3 (Wagh 44, Mullaney 4); Third day, Durham 88-4 (Rushworth 0, Blackwell 2).

Durham

M. J. Di Venuto c Patel b Pattinson	15	– (2) c Edwards b Pattinson	29
K. J. Coetzer c Franks b Shreck	3	– (1) lbw b Shreck	45
*W. R. Smith c Read b Shreck	10	– c Read b Mullaney	4
D. M. Benkenstein b Shreck	36	– c Edwards b Franks	8
I. D. Blackwell c Shafayat b Pattinson	43	– (6) c Shreck b Pattinson	15
B. A. Stokes st Read b Patel	32	– (7) c Mullaney b Franks	106
†P. Mustard c Read b Franks	31	– (8) st Read b Mullaney	23
B. W. Harmison c Read b Franks	14	– (9) b Pattinson	18
L. E. Plunkett c Shafayat b Patel	3	– (10) c Edwards b Franks	3
C. Rushworth c Edwards b Franks	9	– (5) c Read b Pattinson	6
S. J. Harmison not out	4	– not out	4
B 4, l-b 2, w 6, n-b 6	18	B 1, l-b 4, w 3, n-b 10	18

1/16 (2) 2/32 (1) 3/36 (3) (67.4 overs) 218
4/117 (5) 5/129 (4) 6/188 (6)
7/188 (7) 8/191 (9) 9/205 (8) 10/218 (10)

1/49 (2) 2/69 (3) (85 overs) 279
3/84 (4) 4/86 (1)
5/104 (6) 6/109 (5) 7/179 (8)
8/266 (7) 9/269 (10) 10/279 (9)

Pattinson 17–2–63–2; Shreck 23–6–73–3; Franks 15.4–4–38–3; Mullaney 5–1–21–0; Patel 7–3–17–2. *Second Innings*—Pattinson 21–3–95–4; Shreck 19–5–30–1; Franks 21–8–58–3; Mullaney 12–6–35–2; Patel 12–3–56–0.

Nottinghamshire

N. J. Edwards b Plunkett................ 33	P. J. Franks c Mustard b S. J. Harmison ... 64
B. M. Shafayat lbw b Plunkett.......... 16	
M. A. Wagh c Di Venuto b Rushworth.... 44	B 2, l-b 22, w 11, n-b 14......... 49
H. M. Amla c Mustard b B. W. Harmison . 67	
S. J. Mullaney c Di Venuto b Rushworth .. 24	1/34 (2) 2/91 (1) (8 wkts dec, 118 overs) 559
S. R. Patel lbw b Rushworth.......... 4	3/179 (4) 4/191 (3)
A. D. Brown c Mustard b Plunkett....... 134	5/199 (6) 6/226 (5)
*†C. M. W. Read not out............... 124	7/463 (7) 8/559 (9) 110 overs: 492-7

D. J. Pattinson and C. E. Shreck did not bat.

S. J. Harmison 28–4–123–1; Rushworth 28–4–113–3; Plunkett 21–1–115–3; B. W. Harmison 19–1–86–1; Blackwell 16–5–39–0; Stokes 6–0–59–0.

Umpires: J. H. Evans and G. Sharp.

NOTTINGHAMSHIRE v HAMPSHIRE

At Nottingham, May 17–20. Hampshire won by two wickets. Hampshire 22pts, Nottinghamshire 5pts. Toss: Hampshire.

An exciting match saw fortunes sway to and fro before Hampshire finally clinched their first win of the season in any form of cricket, although all four results seemed possible late in the final session. On a pitch tinged with green, Nottinghamshire – without Amla (on tour with South Africa) and Wagh (sitting law exams) – were in deep trouble after losing four wickets in the first hour, before a recovery ensured a par total. Mullaney fell three short of a century, two weeks after his maiden Championship hundred against the same opposition at Southampton, while Franks passed 50 for the sixth time in eight first-class innings. Hampshire enjoyed similarly up-and-down fortunes on their way to a 35-run lead, with Jimmy Adams showing particular application for more than four hours. Hales, still only 21, finally replicated his one-day form with a superbly constructed maiden first-class hundred, reached with a six off Herath, which helped set a target of 281. With two down at lunch and four at tea, Hampshire looked marginal favourites, for only four more wickets to fall, three of them to the new ball. But there were still two Test players at the crease, in McKenzie and Herath, and the South African ended the match in fine style with seven balls to spare, three leg-side pick-ups off Andre Adams proving decisive.

Close of play: First day, Hampshire 23-1 (Adams 16, Tomlinson 1); Second day, Hampshire 305; Third day, Hampshire 7-0 (Adams 2, Dawson 5).

Nottinghamshire

N. J. Edwards c Pothas b Cork..............	4	– c Pothas b Ervine...............	23
B. M. Shafayat c Adams b Tomlinson..........	14	– c and b Tomlinson.............	14
A. D. Hales lbw b Tomlinson...............	0	– c Benham b Cork...............	136
S. R. Patel c Pothas b Cork...............	11	– c Pothas b Ervine.............	0
S. J. Mullaney c Pothas b Balcombe	97	– lbw b Cork.................	7
A. D. Brown lbw b Ervine...............	42	– lbw b Cork.................	15
*†C. M. W. Read c Pothas b Tomlinson.........	22	– b Balcombe.................	27
P. J. Franks not out.................	57	– c Pothas b Cork.............	45
A. R. Adams c Herath b Balcombe	8	– not out.................	26
D. J. Pattinson lbw b Tomlinson.............	8	– b Ervine.................	7
C. E. Shreck c Pothas b Tomlinson	0	– c Vince b Ervine.............	0
B 1, l-b 2, n-b 4.........	7	L-b 11, w 2, n-b 2.........	15

1/5 (1) 2/6 (3) 3/19 (4) 4/29 (2)   (85 overs) 270   1/25 (2) 2/55 (1)   (92 overs) 315
5/107 (6) 6/147 (7) 7/226 (5) 8/238 (9)   3/59 (4) 4/79 (5)
9/270 (10) 10/270 (11)   5/125 (6) 6/220 (7) 7/264 (3)
   8/293 (8) 9/315 (10) 10/315 (11)

Tomlinson 25–7–66–5; Cork 13–2–43–2; Balcombe 17–1–92–2; Ervine 15–4–47–1; Herath 15–5–19–0. *Second Innings*—Tomlinson 23–6–90–1; Cork 23–2–85–4; Ervine 15–2–31–4; Balcombe 18–1–60–1; Herath 13–3–38–0.

Hampshire

J. H. K. Adams c Read b Franks	96	– c Read b Adams	21
L. A. Dawson c Read b Pattinson	4	– c Brown b Franks	21
J. A. Tomlinson c Read b Pattinson	5		
C. C. Benham b Shreck	38	– (3) b Adams	45
N. D. McKenzie lbw b Pattinson	55	– (4) not out	115
J. M. Vince c Mullaney b Franks	0	– (5) c Read b Franks	8
*†N. Pothas lbw b Adams	22	– c Edwards b Pattinson	17
S. M. Ervine not out	31	– (6) lbw b Patel	26
D. G. Cork c Read b Adams	11	– (8) c Hales b Adams	1
D. J. Balcombe b Adams	4	– (9) lbw b Pattinson	6
H. M. R. K. B. Herath c Brown b Adams	1	– (10) not out	10
B 13, l-b 14, w 1, n-b 10	38	B 4, l-b 6, w 1	11

1/21 (2) 2/39 (3) 3/154 (4)   (104.5 overs) 305   1/42 (1)   (8 wkts, 97.5 overs) 281
4/168 (1) 5/168 (6) 6/242 (5)   2/52 (2) 3/127 (3)
7/249 (7) 8/277 (9) 9/293 (10) 10/305 (11)   4/138 (5) 5/182 (6)
                                    6/213 (7) 7/214 (8) 8/225 (9)

Pattinson 24–7–58–3; Shreck 26–9–70–1; Adams 25.5–8–56–4; Franks 20–5–57–2; Mullaney 5–1–15–0; Patel 4–1–22–0. *Second Innings*—Pattinson 21–4–51–2; Shreck 16–6–38–0; Adams 29.5–5–118–3; Franks 16–3–41–2; Patel 15–7–23–1.

Umpires: B. Dudleston and J. F. Steele.

NOTTINGHAMSHIRE v ESSEX

At Nottingham, May 29–June 1. Drawn. Nottinghamshire 7pts, Essex 9pts. Toss: Nottinghamshire.

For the first time all season in the Championship, Nottinghamshire found themselves on the back foot throughout as Essex – who had previously been struggling – produced a disciplined performance with bat and ball, only to be left frustrated by persistent rain on the final day. Just 17 overs were possible on day one and, with conditions assisting the seamers, Essex had every reason to be pleased with their first-innings total. While the top order struggled, skipper Pettini, who dropped himself to No. 7, added 103 with Foster for the sixth wicket and 80 for the eighth with Masters but, with the last man in, he perished just short of his first Championship hundred for almost a year, trying for a second straight six off Mullaney. Nottinghamshire were in some disarray at 88 for six before Mullaney followed his career-best bowling figures with a century partnership alongside Read as the bowlers pitched too short, but the constant menace of Masters eventually earned Essex a lead of 112. Bopara's half-century further strengthened their position, but the weather had the final say.

Close of play: First day, Essex 61-2 (Bopara 13, Walker 2); Second day, Nottinghamshire 33-2 (Edwards 9, Wagh 0); Third day, Essex 152-2 (Bopara 57, Walker 46).

Essex

T. Westley c Read b Pattinson	17	– c Edwards b Adams	23
J. C. Mickleburgh lbw b Adams	10	– lbw b Franks	25
R. S. Bopara lbw b Sidebottom	22	– not out	57
M. J. Walker lbw b Pattinson	6	– not out	46
R. N. ten Doeschate lbw b Franks	26		
†J. S. Foster c Edwards b Adams	59		
*M. L. Pettini c Read b Mullaney	96		
G. R. Napier lbw b Mullaney	12		
D. D. Masters c Patel b Mullaney	32		
C. J. C. Wright c Read b Mullaney	0		
M. A. Chambers not out	1		
B 4, l-b 32, n-b 12	48	L-b 1	1

1/27 (1) 2/57 (2) 3/74 (4)   (102.5 overs) 329   1/36 (1)   (2 wkts, 43 overs) 152
4/76 (3) 5/118 (5) 6/221 (6) 7/240 (8)   2/70 (2)
8/320 (9) 9/322 (10) 10/329 (7)

Sidebottom 22–4–49–1; Pattinson 22–2–60–2; Adams 24–6–82–2; Franks 17–6–45–1; Patel 4–0–26–0; Mullaney 13.5–5–31–4. *Second Innings*—Sidebottom 5–1–24–0; Pattinson 10–1–33–0; Adams 9–2–34–1; Franks 8–1–13–1; Patel 8–0–30–0; Mullaney 3–0–17–0.

Nottinghamshire

A. D. Hales c and b Masters	6	P. J. Franks c ten Doeschate b Masters	23
N. J. Edwards c and b Chambers	30	A. R. Adams c and b Napier	1
D. J. Pattinson c Walker b Masters	2	R. J. Sidebottom not out	0
M. A. Wagh b Chambers	10	B 4, l-b 6, n-b 18	28
S. R. Patel c Walker b Wright	12		
S. J. Mullaney c Pettini b Chambers	53	1/14 (1) 2/32 (3) 3/65 (4) (58.4 overs)	217
A. D. Brown lbw b ten Doeschate	0	4/84 (5) 5/84 (2) 6/88 (7)	
†C. M. W. Read c Foster b Masters	52	7/189 (6) 8/193 (8) 9/202 (10) 10/217 (9)	

Masters 16.4–6–48–4; Chambers 15–3–63–3; Napier 14–3–47–1; Wright 12–1–44–1; ten Doeschate 1–0–5–1.

Umpires: P. J. Hartley and V. A. Holder.

At Tunbridge Wells, June 4–7. NOTTINGHAMSHIRE drew with KENT.

At Chelmsford, July 5–7. NOTTINGHAMSHIRE lost to ESSEX by 143 runs.

At Birmingham, July 20–22. NOTTINGHAMSHIRE beat WARWICKSHIRE by ten wickets. *Stuart Broad takes the first seven wickets as Warwickshire slip to 33 for seven in their second innings.*

At Taunton, July 29–31. NOTTINGHAMSHIRE lost to SOMERSET by ten wickets.

At Leeds, August 3–6. NOTTINGHAMSHIRE drew with YORKSHIRE. *David Hussey scores 251 not out.*

NOTTINGHAMSHIRE v WARWICKSHIRE

At Nottingham, August 16–17. Nottinghamshire won by an innings and 55 runs. Nottinghamshire 22pts, Warwickshire 3pts. Toss: Nottinghamshire.

If the idea of two-division cricket was to improve standards, this fixture suggested it was failing. Nottinghamshire's total in their first home Championship match for 11 weeks was little more than solid – and helped by four dropped catches – but Warwickshire's batting on the second day, when they lost all 20 wickets, was simply shambolic. In the face of accurate seam bowling, their batsmen didn't know whether to defend and wait for the storm to pass, or counter-attack and put the pressure back on the bowlers. Adams bowled 52 deliveries and took three wickets before conceding a run from the bat, finishing with four for 14, while Franks also sent down six consecutive maidens. Asked to follow on before tea, Warwickshire made a better start, reaching 48 in 17 overs before Westwood was bowled by the irrepressible Adams. But the last nine wickets then tumbled for 65, with Sidebottom collecting his best county figures for four years. A thoroughly bad day was worst of all for Javid, twice bowled playing no shot, and Ambrose, whose nightmare season reached its nadir with a pair inside two sessions as Nottinghamshire won inside the extra half-hour.

Close of play: First day, Warwickshire 13-0 (Westwood 10, Chopra 3).

Nottinghamshire

A. D. Hales c Ambrose b Rankin	9	A. R. Adams b Clarke	6
M. J. Wood c Ambrose b Woakes	15	R. J. Sidebottom not out	18
M. A. Wagh c Maddy b Woakes	54	D. J. Pattinson c Maddy b Rankin	6
S. R. Patel c Javid b Maddy	34	L-b 8, n-b 8	16
D. J. Hussey b Woakes	32		
A. D. Brown c Chopra b Rankin	76	1/19 (1) 2/45 (2) 3/105 (4) (87.5 overs)	328
*†C. M. W. Read b Maddy	45	4/146 (5) 5/165 (3) 6/248 (7)	
P. J. Franks lbw b Imran Tahir	17	7/279 (8) 8/292 (9) 9/322 (6) 10/328 (11)	

Woakes 18–4–59–3; Rankin 14.5–0–66–3; Barker 9–1–35–0; Clarke 11–1–53–1; Maddy 17–3–52–2; Imran Tahir 18–1–55–1.

Warwickshire

*I. J. Westwood c Read b Sidebottom	19	– b Adams	14
V. Chopra lbw b Adams	15	– b Sidebottom	54
D. L. Maddy c Hales b Adams	8	– c Wood b Adams	11
J. O. Troughton lbw b Adams	0	– c Read b Sidebottom	13
R. Clarke c Read b Franks	15	– b Sidebottom	1
A. Javid b Franks	5	– b Adams	1
†T. R. Ambrose c Adams b Sidebottom	0	– lbw b Sidebottom	0
K. H. D. Barker c Hussey b Sidebottom	4	– c Read b Sidebottom	10
C. R. Woakes not out	19	– c Hussey b Franks	20
Imran Tahir c Adams b Franks	1	– b Franks	11
W. B. Rankin c Sidebottom b Adams	13	– not out	0
B 13, l-b 7, n-b 2	22	L-b 10, n-b 4	14

1/32 (1) 2/53 (3) 3/53 (4) 4/58 (2) (54.1 overs) 121
5/83 (5) 6/84 (6) 7/86 (7) 8/97 (8)
9/98 (10) 10/121 (11)

1/48 (1) 2/87 (3) (52 overs) 152
3/91 (2) 4/95 (5)
5/108 (4) 6/108 (7) 7/118 (6)
8/122 (8) 9/151 (10) 10/152 (9)

Sidebottom 18–5–37–3; Pattinson 12–3–35–0; Adams 13.1–9–14–4; Franks 11–6–15–3. *Second Innings*—Sidebottom 16–4–35–5; Pattinson 5–1–34–0; Adams 16–7–37–3; Patel 4–2–16–0; Franks 11–3–20–2.

Umpires: N. L. Bainton and R. A. Kettleborough.

NOTTINGHAMSHIRE v LANCASHIRE

At Nottingham, August 24–27. Nottinghamshire won by three wickets. Nottinghamshire 20pts, Lancashire 4pts. Toss: Lancashire.

A match which seemed destined for a draw after rain washed out four sessions ended up as an unexpected Nottinghamshire victory, to provide crucial impetus as the title race entered the home straight. Given the situation late on the first day, it was all the more unlikely: Lancashire's top four had all scored half-centuries, but Chanderpaul's dismissal precipitated a collapse, the last eight wickets falling for the addition of 39 runs in 16 overs, with Adams claiming his best county figures. Nottinghamshire were then in trouble themselves at 37 for three, but the back-up bowlers failed to maintain the pressure before rain arrived at tea. The third day was washed out completely, and a sleepy accumulation of bonus points seemed inevitable. Instead Chapple, keen to stay in the title hunt himself, offered generous terms for a run-chase: two declarations and some part-time bowling set up a target of 260 in 64 overs. Nottinghamshire wobbled again early on, but Patel and Brown counter-attacked while Hales produced another well-judged innings. He fell just short of three figures for the second time that day, and later Brown and Franks departed to successive balls, but Mullaney and Adams completed the job with almost nine overs to spare as Nottinghamshire stretched their Championship lead to 16 points.

Close of play: First day, Lancashire 303-6 (Chilton 61, Sutton 5); Second day, Nottinghamshire 178-4 (Hales 87, Read 35); Third day, No play.

Lancashire

P. J. Horton lbw b Adams	51	– (2) b Mullaney	4
T. C. Smith c Hales b Sidebottom	61	– (1) not out	76
M. J. Chilton lbw b Sidebottom	67	– not out	49
S. Chanderpaul lbw b Sidebottom	92		
S. J. Croft c Adams b Sidebottom	9		
G. Keedy lbw b Adams	4		
G. D. Cross c Hales b Adams	0		
†L. D. Sutton c Patel b Adams	11		
S. I. Mahmood lbw b Adams	4		
*G. Chapple not out	0		
K. W. Hogg c Read b Adams	0		
B 4, l-b 7, w 3, n-b 6	20	L-b 2, w 10, n-b 2	14

1/87 (1) 2/129 (2) 3/280 (4)   (100 overs) 319   1/4 (2)   (1 wkt dec, 24 overs) 143
4/292 (5) 5/297 (6) 6/297 (7)
7/311 (8) 8/319 (3) 9/319 (9) 10/319 (11)

Sidebottom 26–7–79–4; Pattinson 15–3–61–0; Adams 26–6–79–6; Franks 17–4–40–0; Mullaney 8–2–16–0; Patel 8–1–33–0. *Second Innings*—Pattinson 3–1–11–0; Mullaney 8–0–45–1; Hales 5–1–21–0; Brown 7–0–53–0; Wood 1–0–11–0.

Nottinghamshire

A. D. Hales c Sutton b Hogg	98	– c Sutton b Keedy	93
M. J. Wood c Sutton b Chapple	0	– c Cross b Mahmood	2
M. A. Wagh c Smith b Mahmood	6	– c Smith b Chapple	3
S. R. Patel c Sutton b Hogg	10	– b Mahmood	37
A. D. Brown lbw b Mahmood	28	– c Smith b Hogg	65
*†C. M. W. Read not out	49	– c Croft b Keedy	2
S. J. Mullaney not out	0	– not out	34
P. J. Franks (did not bat)		– c Horton b Hogg	0
A. R. Adams (did not bat)		– not out	8
B 1, l-b 3, n-b 8	12	B 4, l-b 5, w 2, n-b 6	17

1/1 (2) 2/14 (3)   (5 wkts dec, 58.1 overs) 203   1/20 (2)   (7 wkts, 55.2 overs) 261
3/37 (4) 4/94 (5) 5/199 (1)   2/23 (3) 3/109 (4) 4/193 (1)
                                                 5/199 (6) 6/252 (5) 7/252 (8)

R. J. Sidebottom and D. J. Pattinson did not bat.

Chapple 13–3–41–1; Mahmood 15–4–43–2; Hogg 12–2–47–2; Smith 13–1–49–0; Keedy 5.1–1–19–0. *Second Innings*—Chapple 17.2–4–67–1; Mahmood 16–1–77–2; Smith 5–0–31–0; Hogg 3–0–20–2; Keedy 14–0–57–2.

Umpires: M. J. D. Bodenham and M. A. Gough.

At Chester-le-Street, August 31–September 3. NOTTINGHAMSHIRE lost to DURHAM by 210 runs.

NOTTINGHAMSHIRE v YORKSHIRE

At Nottingham, September 7–9. Yorkshire won by five wickets. Yorkshire 21pts, Nottinghamshire 3pts. Toss: Yorkshire. Championship debut: M. A. Ashraf.

Not for the first time in recent years, Nottinghamshire appeared to choke with a major trophy almost in their grasp. Conditions were extremely helpful to seam bowling on the first day, but to be bowled out for 59 – their lowest total for 22 years – left them with too big a mountain to climb. The highlight for Yorkshire was their Academy graduate Moin Ashraf, making his Championship debut at 18, who produced two perfect away-swingers to knock back Voges's off stump and have Patel caught behind. Gale then batted superbly for his third century of the season, but the rest of the batsmen were unable to cope with Adams, who claimed his third five-for in consecutive matches. Still, Yorkshire were 201 ahead by the end of the first day, and Gale admitted: "It wasn't a great pitch in the morning, it went around a bit. But it did get a bit better as the day went on." Next day the promoted Franks combined with Hales for Nottinghamshire's highest opening stand of the summer so far, and some handy contributions down the order left Yorkshire chasing 209 on the third day. Lyth and Rudolph hit 65 off the first 12 overs, and although Pattinson took three wickets in three fiery overs after a shower, the ice-cool Bairstow – whose 51-ball innings featured 12 fours – helped Yorkshire close the gap at the top of the table to just seven points.

Close of play: First day, Yorkshire 260-8 (Gale 147, Hannon-Dalby 0); Second day, Nottinghamshire 357-6 (Read 24, Pattinson 20).

Nottinghamshire

A. D. Hales c Rashid b Shahzad	3	–	c Brophy b Ashraf		24
P. J. Franks c Bairstow b Shahzad	0	–	c Rudolph b Rashid		79
M. A. Wagh c Rudolph b Shahzad	22	–	c sub (R. M. Pyrah) b Rashid		90
A. C. Voges b Ashraf	8	–	c Brophy b Hannon-Dalby		72
S. R. Patel c Brophy b Ashraf	0	–	c Bairstow b Shahzad		4
A. D. Brown lbw b Hannon-Dalby	16	–	c Brophy b Shahzad		4
*†C. M. W. Read lbw b Hannon-Dalby	0	–	b Shahzad		47
S. J. Mullaney lbw b Hannon-Dalby	0	–	(9) b Patterson		15
A. R. Adams c Lyth b Shahzad	3	–	(10) not out		0
L. J. Fletcher not out	6	–	(11) b Shahzad		8
D. J. Pattinson c Brophy b Hannon-Dalby	0	–	(8) lbw b Patterson		27
L-b 1	1		B 16, l-b 27		43
1/1 (2) 2/4 (1) 3/18 (4) 4/18 (5) (33.2 overs)	59		1/56 (1) 2/187 (2) (102 overs)		413
5/41 (6) 6/47 (7) 7/47 (8) 8/49 (3)			3/278 (3) 4/283 (5)		
9/52 (9) 10/59 (11)			5/291 (6) 6/329 (4) 7/373 (6)		
			8/405 (9) 9/405 (7) 10/405 (11)		

Shahzad 11–4–21–4; Patterson 7–2–8–0; Ashraf 6–4–11–2; Hannon-Dalby 9.2–4–18–4. *Second Innings*—Shahzad 29–6–100–4; Patterson 21–2–83–2; Hannon-Dalby 18–2–71–1; Ashraf 14–1–50–1; Rashid 17–4–48–2; McGrath 3–0–18–0.

Yorkshire

A. Lyth c Voges b Adams	19	–	c Hales b Pattinson		45
J. A. Rudolph c Brown b Adams	10	–	c Brown b Pattinson		29
A. McGrath c Adams b Franks	10	–	c Read b Pattinson		4
*A. W. Gale not out	151	–	b Adams		5
J. M. Bairstow lbw b Adams	36	–	not out		63
†G. L. Brophy b Adams	5	–	c Hales b Adams		41
A. U. Rashid c Fletcher b Patel	11	–	not out		9
A. Shahzad c Read b Franks	7				
S. A. Patterson c Read b Franks	0				
O. J. Hannon-Dalby lbw b Adams	0				
M. A. Ashraf b Patel b Adams	0				
L-b 8, w 1, n-b 6	15		B 1, l-b 10, n-b 2		13
1/30 (2) 2/31 (1) 3/60 (3) (62.1 overs)	264		1/70 (2) (5 wkts, 42.3 overs)		209
4/171 (5) 5/195 (6) 6/228 (7) 7/251 (8)			2/78 (3) 3/91 (1)		
8/251 (9) 9/260 (10) 10/264 (11)			4/95 (4) 5/192 (6)		

Fletcher 8–0–39–0; Pattinson 10–2–58–0; Adams 20.1–3–82–6; Franks 15–3–58–3; Patel 9–1–19–1. *Second Innings*—Fletcher 5–0–23–0; Pattinson 13–2–67–3; Adams 16–0–77–2; Franks 3–0–23–0; Patel 5.3–2–8–0.

Umpires: M. A. Gough and R. T. Robinson.

At Manchester, September 13–16. NOTTINGHAMSHIRE drew with LANCASHIRE. *Nottinghamshire clinch the Championship title at the last gasp after a rain-affected finale.*

SOMERSET

The eternal second

RICHARD LATHAM

Few would dispute that Somerset were the outstanding county side in England during 2010. Led for the first time by Marcus Trescothick, they won more matches than any of their rivals and achieved that without abandoning a free spirit and, at times, a cavalier approach to the game which had been a trademark of less successful eras. Yet they lifted not a single trophy, and finished runners-up in all three competitions through a mixture of misfortune, human error, and mental and physical fatigue at the end of a long season.

Trescothick took on the captaincy knowing the extra responsibility might provoke the stress problems which ended his international career. After the first two Championship games at Headingley and Trent Bridge ended in defeats, he appeared tense and later admitted to having had second thoughts about becoming captain. Director of cricket Brian Rose provided support and advice based on his own successful period as skipper.

Although his batting never scaled the heights of 2009, Trescothick still scored 1,397 first-class runs, including 228 not out at Colchester, the second-highest score of his career. He also proved immensely popular, encouraging his team after every one-day home game to sign autographs and pose for photographs with supporters. It was known long before Twenty20 finals day that a return to the Champions League was out of the question because it clashed with the Championship finale. When Somerset and Hampshire were compensated with a place in the Caribbean T20 in January 2011, Trescothick, as expected, did not travel, and Alfonso Thomas captained instead.

James Hildreth finished top of Somerset's batting averages in all competitions, having matured as a cricketer at the age of 25. The previous season had seen Hildreth fail to reach 1,000 first-class runs despite a triple-century in the opening game. Now, having worked on simplifying his technique, this multitalented sportsman added consistency to his many qualities, scoring seven Championship centuries and missing out by one run on an eighth at Old Trafford. Importantly, three of Hildreth's hundreds came at the Rose Bowl, Canterbury and Chester-le-Street. No longer could he be accused of only scoring big runs at Taunton.

The most exciting individual prospect – arguably in the country – was 19-year-old Jos Buttler, who grabbed the early-season opportunity afforded by Craig Kieswetter's absence in the World Twenty20 to demonstrate a burgeoning batting talent and no little wicketkeeping skill. A maiden Championship century, away to Hampshire, was followed by a sequence of one-day innings characterised by deceptive power and audacious shot selection. Two of those spectacular innings were televised, spreading word about a new boy wonder in the West Country.

Philip Brown

Alfonso Thomas

Kieswetter, who returned bearing medals from the Caribbean, struggled to match his billing. His time will come again. Zander de Bruyn was reliable at No. 4, before departing early for the Champions League, and then to Surrey for 2011.

Arul Suppiah proved an efficient opening partner for Trescothick, without converting enough promising starts, and Nick Compton suggested that he could emerge stronger from a testing first year at the club. Peter Trego performed capably with bat and ball, almost doubling his career-best one-day score when bludgeoning 147 against Glamorgan at Taunton.

Thomas enhanced his reputation as the canniest one-day bowler in the country: his deceptive changes of pace, slow bouncers and arrowed-in yorkers earned him 33 Twenty20 victims, and 109 in all competitions. Charl Willoughby passed 50 wickets in first-class cricket for the fifth time in as many seasons with Somerset, and Ben Phillips benefited from a rare summer without injury, before moving on to Nottinghamshire, his fourth county. The signing of Steve Kirby and Gemaal Hussain from Gloucestershire should more than offset that loss.

Ultimately, it was the arrival of Indian left-arm spinner Murali Kartik, combined with a change in the nature of the Taunton pitches – overseen for the first time by Rose, after the departure of long-serving groundsman Phil Frost – which at last enabled Somerset to feel confident of bowling opponents out twice at home. Despite missing the first five matches because of IPL commitments Kartik took 45 Championship wickets at an average below 20, with masterly control of flight and pace. Frost, meanwhile, decided against taking the club to an industrial tribunal for wrongful dismissal, and accepted a role at Portsmouth FC.

Kieron Pollard proved an explosive and popular overseas signing for the T20, but suffered a nasty eye injury when a bouncer from Dominic Cork penetrated his grille in the final, preventing him from fielding or bowling. Somerset were beaten by Hampshire on wickets lost, with the scores tied.

The final day of the Championship was equally heartstopping – and heartbreaking. Somerset called off their run-chase at Chester-le-Street, and finished level on points with Nottinghamshire, the first time two counties had been tied at the top since 1977. Somerset lost out, having won one match fewer. After a seamless run to Lord's, the CB40 final was a more straightforward defeat: Somerset's late batting collapse handed Warwickshire the initiative, ruthlessly rammed home by Ian Bell. A season which promised so much had ended in frustration and bitter disappointment.

SOMERSET RESULTS

All first-class matches – Played 16: Won 6, Lost 2, Drawn 8.
County Championship matches – Played 16: Won 6, Lost 2, Drawn 8.

LV= County Championship, 2nd in Division 1;
Friends Provident T20, finalists; Clydesdale Bank 40, finalists.

COUNTY CHAMPIONSHIP AVERAGES, BATTING AND FIELDING

Cap		M	I	NO	R	HS	100s	50s	Avge	Ct
2007	J. C. Hildreth	16	23	1	1,440	151	7	5	65.45	7
1999	M. E. Trescothick†	16	28	4	1,397	228*	4	6	58.20	26
2008	Z. de Bruyn¶	14	21	0	814	95	0	5	38.76	10
	D. A. Stiff	2	4	2	71	40	0	0	35.50	0
	D. G. Wright§	5	7	0	236	78	0	2	33.71	4
2009	A. V. Suppiah¶	16	26	3	771	125	1	4	33.52	5
	J. C. Buttler†	13	20	3	569	144	1	2	33.47	23
	N. R. D. Compton	11	17	3	465	72	0	2	33.21	5
2007	P. D. Trego†	16	23	2	693	108	1	5	33.00	12
	M. Kartik§	11	12	5	199	52*	0	2	28.42	9
2009	C. Kieswetter¶	12	18	1	467	84	0	4	27.47	29
2008	A. C. Thomas¶	15	20	4	328	44	0	0	20.50	1
	B. J. Phillips	11	15	3	179	55	0	1	14.91	5
2007	C. M. Willoughby¶	6	8	6	85	16	0	0	7.08	1

Also batted: M. K. Munday (3 matches) 0, 0, 0* (1 ct). C. R. Jones (1 match) did not bat.

† *Born in Somerset.*   § *Official overseas player.*   ¶ *Other non-England-qualified player.*

BOWLING

	O	M	R	W	BB	5W/i	Avge
M. Kartik	383.2	107	882	45	6-42	5	19.60
B. J. Phillips	277.3	79	661	29	5-72	1	22.79
A. C. Thomas	377.5	85	1,202	49	5-40	2	24.53
D. G. Wright	154.1	41	377	14	5-41	1	26.92
C. M. Willoughby	512.1	118	1,582	58	6-101	1	27.27
Z. de Bruyn	94.2	10	386	12	4-23	0	32.16
P. D. Trego	227.1	50	729	22	4-26	0	33.13

Also bowled: N. R. D. Compton 14.2–0–87–2; J. C. Hildreth 13–0–95–1; M. K. Munday 52.1–9–238–6; D. A. Stiff 40.5–3–207–2; A. V. Suppiah 99–18–300–3.

LEADING CB40 AVERAGES (100 runs/4 wickets)

Batting	Runs	HS	Avge	S-R	Ct/St		**Bowling**	W	BB	Avge	E-R
J. C. Hildreth	627	100*	69.66	110.19	8		A. C. Thomas	27	4-34	15.92	5.29
J. C. Buttler	440	90*	55.00	153.84	9/1		M. Kartik	20	4-30	16.05	4.61
C. Kieswetter	391	107	43.44	101.03	9/2		D. G. Wright	6	3-43	18.16	7.26
P. D. Trego	396	147	39.60	119.63	5		Z. de Bruyn	15	3-27	19.40	6.14
Z. de Bruyn	433	106*	39.36	93.72	2		B. J. Phillips	19	4-31	24.52	5.55
A. V. Suppiah	160	80	32.00	91.95	4		M. L. Turner	9	4-36	26.00	7.35

LEADING FPT20 AVERAGES (100 runs/18 overs)

Batting	Runs	HS	Avge	S-R	Ct/St
K. A. Pollard	354	89*	32.18	**175.24**	8
J. C. Buttler	240	55*	30.00	**160.00**	19/2
M. E. Trescothick	572	83	31.77	**157.14**	4
P. D. Trego	294	72*	22.61	**135.48**	6
Z. de Bruyn	303	95*	30.30	**124.18**	8
N. R. D. Compton	165	74	20.62	**117.85**	2

Bowling	W	BB	Avge	E-R
A. C. Thomas	33	3-11	13.93	**6.31**
M. Kartik	13	3-18	30.92	**6.59**
K. A. Pollard	29	4-15	15.10	**7.50**
B. J. Phillips	19	3-33	24.52	**7.76**
Z. de Bruyn	7	2-21	35.42	**8.85**
M. L. Turner	14	3-25	26.57	**8.85**

FIRST-CLASS COUNTY RECORDS

Highest score for	342	J. L. Langer v Surrey at Guildford	2006
Highest score against	424	A. C. MacLaren (Lancashire) at Taunton	1895
Leading run-scorer	21,142	H. Gimblett (avge 36.96)	1935–1954
Best bowling for	10-49	E. J. Tyler v Surrey at Taunton	1895
Best bowling against	10-35	A. Drake (Yorkshire) at Weston-super-Mare	1914
Leading wicket-taker	2,165	J. C. White (avge 18.03)	1909–1937
Highest total for	850-7 dec	v Middlesex at Taunton	2007
Highest total against	811	by Surrey at The Oval	1899
Lowest total for	25	v Gloucestershire at Bristol	1947
Lowest total against	22	by Gloucestershire at Bristol	1920

LIST A COUNTY RECORDS

Highest score for	184	M. E. Trescothick v Gloucestershire at Taunton	2008
Highest score against	167*	A. J. Stewart (Surrey) at The Oval	1994
Leading run-scorer	7,349	I. V. A. Richards (avge 39.94)	1974–1986
Best bowling for	8-66	S. R. G. Francis v Derbyshire at Derby	2004
Best bowling against	7-39	A. Hodgson (Northamptonshire) at Northampton	1976
Leading wicket-taker	309	H. R. Moseley (avge 20.03)	1971–1982
Highest total for	413-4	v Devon at Torquay	1990
Highest total against	357-3	by Warwickshire at Birmingham	1995
Lowest total for	{ 58	v Essex at Chelmsford	1977
	{ 58	v Middlesex at Southgate	2000
Lowest total against	60	by Kent at Taunton	1979

TWENTY20 RECORDS

Highest score for	141*	C. L. White v Worcestershire at Worcester	2006
Highest score against	116*	I. J. Thomas (Glamorgan) at Taunton	2004
Leading run-scorer	**1,447**	**M. E. Trescothick (avge 32.15)**	**2004–2010**
Best bowling for	{ 4-15	A. W. Laraman v Worcestershire at Taunton	2004
	{ **4-15**	**K. A. Pollard v Kent at Beckenham**	**2010**
Best bowling against	5-27	J. F. Brown (Northamptonshire) at Northampton	2003
Leading wicket-taker	**73**	**A. C. Thomas (avge 14.67)**	**2008–2010**
Highest total for	250-3	v Gloucestershire at Taunton	2006
Highest total against	227-4	by Gloucestershire at Bristol	2006
Lowest total for	**82**	**v Kent at Taunton**	**2010**
Lowest total against	**97**	**by Hampshire at Southampton**	**2010**

ADDRESS

County Ground, St James's Street, Taunton TA1 1JT (0845 337 1875; **email** info@somersetcountycc.co.uk). **Website** www.somersetcricketclub.co.uk

OFFICIALS

Captain M. E. Trescothick
Director of cricket B. C. Rose
Head coach A. Hurry
Development director J. I. D. Kerr
President R. C. Kerslake

Chairman A. J. Nash
Chief executive R. A. Gould
Chairman, cricket committee V. J. Marks
Scorer G. A. Stickley

At Taunton Vale, April 10–12 (not first-class). **Somerset won by 385 runs. Somerset 246** (N. R. D. Compton 92, C. Kieswetter 32, D. A. Stiff 54; M. T. Reed 4-32, A. J. Jones 3-67) **and 417-6 dec** (M. E. Trescothick 134, N. R. D. Compton 77, J. C. Hildreth 75, P. D. Trego 50*); ‡**Cardiff MCCU 160** (R. Bishop 66, R. J. Burns 46; D. A. Stiff 5-38) **and 118** (M. A. Jones 37, D. S. Bendon 44; D. A. Stiff 4-26, M. L. Turner 3-30). *County debut:* N. R. D. Compton. *As he did in 2009, David Stiff took nine wickets against Cardiff MCCU at Taunton Vale, only to flop later against county opposition. He began the students' decline with five for four in 4.1 overs, after Ryan Bishop and Rory Burns had opened with 116. A full-strength Somerset batting line-up hit their stride second time round: Trescothick bludgeoned a 104-ball hundred, and Nick Compton carefully constructed his second half-century on debut. None of Cardiff's bottom five scored a run in the second innings.*

At Leeds, April 15–18. SOMERSET lost to YORKSHIRE by six wickets.

At Nottingham, April 21–23. SOMERSET lost to NOTTINGHAMSHIRE by two wickets.

SOMERSET v ESSEX

At Taunton, April 27–30. Drawn. Somerset 10pts, Essex 10pts. Toss: Somerset.
    The perils of playing touch rugby as a warm-up landed Hildreth in Musgrove Park Hospital for five stitches in his left knee, following a collision with Willoughby's studs. Chris Jones, a 19-year-old batsman, pulled into a motorway service station on standby but, when Hildreth was given the all-clear, he drove on to a second team game at The Oval and scored 48 not out. Hildreth felt "a bit stiff", but shook off the discomfort, dropped one place down the order, and made 73 from 110 deliveries until shouldering arms to the second new ball; he was one of four Somerset batsmen unable to kick on from the early seventies. Trescothick disagreed with his director of cricket about the wisdom of competitive warm-ups: "Brian Rose will have to tackle me before imposing a ban on touch rugby." Rose's dry pitch was light years away from the greentops being produced elsewhere, and leg-spinner Munday exploited slow turn to remove three of the top four, including Godleman, bowled by a rank long-hop after a fluent first century for Essex. A third-day washout killed the game, with the captains never likely to concoct a run-chase in April. Masters hit 11 fours, earning Essex a fourth batting point, and after more rain, Trescothick and Suppiah enjoyed a glorified net session.
    Close of play: First day, Somerset 328-7 (Trego 30, Thomas 1); Second day, Essex 262-5 (Foster 29, ten Doeschate 18); Third day, No play.

Somerset

*M. E. Trescothick c ten Doeschate b Chambers....	19	– not out	....	42
A. V. Suppiah lbw b Masters..................	7	– not out	....	47
N. R. D. Compton c Masters b Phillips..........	72			
Z. de Bruyn b ten Doeschate..................	73			
J. C. Hildreth b Masters.....................	73			
†J. C. Buttler c Maunders b Masters.............	36			
P. D. Trego not out........................	71			
D. G. Wright run out.......................	0			
A. C. Thomas c Foster b Wright..............	8			
M. K. Munday lbw b Masters.................	0			
C. M. Willoughby run out...................	9			
B 8, l-b 3, n-b 8	19	L-b 1, n-b 10		11

1/15 (2) 2/52 (1) 3/142 (3)   (108.4 overs) 387   (no wkt dec, 24.3 overs) 100
4/229 (4) 5/286 (5) 6/305 (6)
7/305 (8) 8/339 (9) 9/348 (10) 10/387 (11)

Masters 27–5–83–4; Wright 23–8–84–1; ten Doeschate 20–1–69–1; Chambers 8–1–30–1; Phillips 29.4–6–107–1; Cook 1–0–3–0. *Second Innings*—Masters 3–0–13–0; Wright 7–1–29–0; Chambers 9.3–0–47–0; Phillips 5–1–10–0.

Essex

B. A. Godleman b Munday	106	C. J. C. Wright not out	9
A. N. Cook c Trescothick b Wright	41	M. A. Chambers lbw b Munday	1
J. K. Maunders c Trego b Munday	22		
J. C. Mickleburgh c Trescothick b Munday	23	B 2, l-b 1, n-b 6	9
*M. L. Pettini c Buttler b Suppiah	14		
†J. S. Foster lbw b Trego	35	1/89 (2) 2/156 (3) (105.1 overs) 353
R. N. ten Doeschate lbw b Willoughby	21	3/200 (4) 4/203 (1)
T. J. Phillips c Compton b Willoughby	22	5/231 (5) 6/265 (7) 7/271 (6)
D. D. Masters c de Bruyn b Trego	50	8/321 (8) 9/344 (9) 10/353 (11)

Willoughby 24–7–87–2; Wright 17–6–41–2; Thomas 11–2–35–0; Munday 30.1–6–105–4; Suppiah 9–1–29–1; Trego 14–3–53–1.

Umpires: B. Dudleston and J. H. Evans.

At Manchester, May 4–7. SOMERSET drew with LANCASHIRE.

At Southampton, May 10–13. SOMERSET drew with HAMPSHIRE.

SOMERSET v YORKSHIRE

At Taunton, May 17–20. Somerset won by six wickets. Somerset 21pts, Yorkshire 6pts. Toss: Yorkshire. County champion: M. Kartik.

For the second successive season, Yorkshire's captain rued setting Somerset a last-day target at Taunton. Eleven months earlier, they ran down McGrath's challenge of 476; this time, after a compact between the captains led to a morning of tossed-up bowling from Somerset, Rudolph (standing in for Gale, absent with England Lions) offered them 68 overs for a shot at 362. Best was restricted to two overs by fitness problems, and Bresnan and Shahzad were on their way back from the World Twenty20 but, so supremely did Hildreth bat, they might have made no difference. His sweeping was touch-perfect, his running between the wickets enterprising; he brought up the quickest first-class hundred of the season – from 68 balls – just before the finish. Victory was sewn up in the passage after tea, when Hildreth and de Bruyn traded strokes in a partnership of 149. Rudolph had now lost all seven matches captaining Yorkshire, but maintained his declaration was consistent with the attacking cricket they had pledged to play. Batsmen dominated all four days, none more than Lyth, whose 235 runs installed him as the first division's leading scorer.

Close of play: First day, Yorkshire 296-4 (McGrath 73, Patterson 1); Second day, Somerset 226-4 (Suppiah 78, Buttler 13); Third day, Yorkshire 154-2 (McGrath 38).

Yorkshire

A. Lyth c Phillips b de Bruyn	142	– lbw b Kartik	93
J. J. Sayers c Kartik b Phillips	50	– lbw b Thomas	12
A. McGrath c Trego b Phillips	73	– c Compton b Hildreth	83
*J. A. Rudolph c de Bruyn b Phillips	11	– c de Bruyn b Compton	66
G. S. Ballance c Buttler b Phillips	4	– not out	31
S. A. Patterson c Kartik b Thomas	25		
†J. M. Bairstow c Compton b Kartik	17	– (6) not out	29
A. U. Rashid b Thomas	1		
D. J. Wainwright c Phillips b Kartik	39		
T. L. Best lbw b Kartik	15		
O. J. Hannon-Dalby not out	2		
B 9, l-b 5, w 2, n-b 10	26	B 8, w 1, n-b 10	19

1/115 (2) 2/251 (1) 3/280 (6) (131.5 overs) 405   1/39 (2) (4 wkts dec, 74 overs) 333
4/286 (5) 5/297 (3) 6/339 (4) 7/343 (8)   2/154 (1) 3/269 (4)
8/343 (7) 9/359 (10) 10/405 (9)   4/273 (4)
110 overs: 322-5

Willoughby 29–8–95–0; Phillips 36–13–76–4; Thomas 18–6–60–2; Trego 7–0–40–0; Kartik 35.5–8–106–3; Compton 1–0–2–0; Suppiah 3–1–3–0; de Bruyn 2–1–9–1. *Second Innings*— Willoughby 10–1–35–0; Phillips 6–1–14–0; Thomas 8–1–20–1; Kartik 18–2–48–1; de Bruyn 6–0–29–0; Compton 13–0–84–1; Hildreth 13–0–95–1.

Somerset

*M. E. Trescothick lbw b Hannon-Dalby	39	– c Wainwright b Rashid	53
A. V. Suppiah c Rudolph b Wainwright	99	– b Patterson	16
N. R. D. Compton c Bairstow b Patterson	5	– c Lyth b Rashid	65
Z. de Bruyn b Rashid	47	– c McGrath b Wainwright	93
J. C. Hildreth c McGrath b Rashid	31	– not out	102
†J. C. Buttler c Lyth b Wainwright	52	– not out	31
P. D. Trego lbw b Hannon-Dalby	22		
B. J. Phillips lbw b Rashid	16		
A. C. Thomas c Bairstow b Rashid	14		
M. Kartik not out	15		
C. M. Willoughby b Wainwright	10		
B 4, l-b 16, w 7	27	B 1, l-b 3	4

1/51 (1) 2/60 (3) 3/160 (4)   (104.4 overs) 377   1/37 (2)   (4 wkts, 65.4 overs) 364
4/204 (5) 5/285 (2) 6/296 (6)   2/116 (1) 3/165 (3)
7/324 (8) 8/350 (9) 9/360 (7) 10/377 (11)   4/314 (4)

Best 19–2–95–0; Patterson 22–7–54–1; Hannon-Dalby 20–3–50–2; McGrath 9–2–25–0; Wainwright 15.4–3–48–3; Rashid 19–0–85–4. *Second Innings*—Patterson 19–2–96–1; Hannon-Dalby 12–2–47–0; Best 2–0–16–0; Wainwright 12–1–78–1; Rashid 20.4–0–123–2.

Umpires: N. L. Bainton and M. A. Gough.

RUNS PER WICKET IN THE CHAMPIONSHIP AT TAUNTON, 2000–2010

	Matches	Total runs	Total wickets	Runs/wicket	National runs/wicket
2000	7	5,643	141	40.02	28.98
2001	7	7,542	204	36.97	33.55
2002	7	8,408	209	40.22	33.40
2003	7	8,082	202	40.00	33.50
2004	7	6,994	183	38.21	35.54
2005	7	7,676	177	43.36	34.62
2006	7	7,628	183	41.68	36.38
2007	8	9,596	217	44.22	34.23
2008	8	7,851	222	35.36	32.49
2009	8	10,067	175	57.52	35.90
2010	**8**	**7,132**	**204**	**34.96**	**30.58**

SOMERSET v WARWICKSHIRE

At Taunton, May 24–26. Somerset won by nine wickets. Somerset 21pts, Warwickshire 3pts. Toss: Somerset.

Warwickshire received an unusual greeting upon arrival at Taunton: a thick covering of grass on the wicket. Somerset, 38 points behind Nottinghamshire, were clearly desperate to avoid a repeat of the previous year's fixture, when just 15 wickets fell and 1,280 runs flowed, 303 of them scored by Hildreth. His serene batting was about the only constant. With Bell and Trott preparing for the First Test against Bangladesh, the eyes of Somerset's long-suffering seamers lit up when Trescothick won the toss. Thomas seized his best first-class figures outside South Africa, as Warwickshire recorded the lowest score by a Championship team visiting Taunton since September 1999, when Glamorgan made 113. Hildreth's technique held up superbly on a challenging pitch, shutting Warwickshire out of the match in a confident, four-hour 131. The sight of Kartik finding bounce and turn on the third morning was a rare delight for Somerset; he hastened victory with five for 19 in seven overs. Buttler kept wicket on the first day when Kieswetter – Man of the Match in the World Twenty20 final – attended a Downing Street reception with his England team-mates.

Close of play: First day, Somerset 145-3 (Suppiah 61, Hildreth 35); Second day, Warwickshire 111-3 (Troughton 2, Clarke 10).

Warwickshire

*I. J. Westwood c Buttler b Phillips	4	– c Phillips b Willoughby	1
D. L. Maddy c Kartik b Thomas	13	– lbw b Kartik	61
V. Chopra c Hildreth b Thomas	45	– c Kieswetter b Phillips	31
J. O. Troughton b Willoughby	22	– lbw b Kartik	6
R. Clarke lbw b Thomas	7	– lbw b Kartik	17
†T. R. Ambrose b Thomas	0	– c de Bruyn b Kartik	8
A. G. Botha b Phillips	4	– b Kartik	10
C. R. Woakes b Willoughby	28	– c Kieswetter b Kartik	10
Imran Tahir b Willoughby	0	– c Suppiah b Thomas	28
W. B. Rankin b Thomas	1	– b Willoughby	12
A. S. Miller not out	1	– not out	2
L-b 1, w 1	2	B 15, l-b 3, n-b 4	22

1/6 (1) 2/63 (3) 3/64 (2) 4/78 (5) (47.3 overs) 127
5/78 (6) 6/85 (7) 7/110 (4) 8/112 (9)
9/113 (10) 10/127 (8)

1/4 (1) 2/99 (2) (82 overs) 207
3/99 (3) 4/123 (4) 5/124 (5)
6/141 (6) 7/163 (8) 8/174 (7)
9/194 (9) 10/207 (10)

Willoughby 15.3–3–51–3; Phillips 11–1–25–2; Trego 6–3–9–0; Thomas 13–1–41–5; Kartik 2–2–0–0. *Second Innings*—Willoughby 14–6–41–2; Phillips 11–2–23–1; Thomas 19–3–51–1; Kartik 29–7–61–6; de Bruyn 4–1–5–0; Trego 2–1–4–0; Suppiah 3–1–4–0.

Somerset

*M. E. Trescothick c and b Miller	3	– b Imran Tahir	30
A. V. Suppiah c Ambrose b Miller	64	– not out	15
N. R. D. Compton c Ambrose b Miller	4		
Z. de Bruyn c Chopra b Imran Tahir	34		
J. C. Hildreth c Miller b Rankin	131		
†J. C. Buttler c Ambrose b Maddy	24	– (3) not out	0
P. D. Trego c Clarke b Maddy	1		
B. J. Phillips c Ambrose b Clarke	0		
A. C. Thomas not out	15		
M. Kartik c Ambrose b Miller	0		
C. M. Willoughby b Miller	0		
B 3, l-b 7, n-b 4	14		

1/15 (1) 2/29 (3) 3/78 (4) 4/164 (2) (94 overs) 290
5/229 (6) 6/233 (7) 7/240 (8) 8/290 (5)
9/290 (10) 10/290 (11)

1/43 (1) (1 wkt, 10.4 overs) 45

C. Kieswetter replaced Compton after returning from England's reception at Downing Street.

Woakes 22–3–63–0; Miller 22–8–72–5; Rankin 9–1–27–1; Clarke 9–2–22–1; Imran Tahir 16–0–70–1; Maddy 14–3–24–2; Botha 2–1–2–0. *Second Innings*—Miller 4–3–8–0; Imran Tahir 5–0–27–1; Botha 1.4–0–10–0.

Umpires: M. R. Benson and T. E. Jesty.

At Birmingham, June 4–6. SOMERSET beat WARWICKSHIRE by 181 runs.

SOMERSET v KENT

At Taunton, July 20–23. Drawn. Somerset 7pts, Kent 6pts. Toss: Kent.

A third-day washout cost Somerset dearly. Their batsmen sought to make up for lost time – 158 overs all told – by galloping along at seven and a half an over on the final morning in search of a target. Trescothick blasted eight fours and three sixes in his 80; unusually for Taunton, it was the game's only half-century. He eventually declared 23 minutes before lunch with a lead of 334, leaving his bowlers at least 71 overs. Given the meekness of Kent's batting (Key was absent with a broken finger), and that Kartik was enjoying the purplest of patches, Trescothick may have been a tad cautious in his calculations. Geraint Jones saved the match for Kent in a dogged three-hour stay, until his downfall in the penultimate over gave Kartik his fifth five-for in successive innings, and the fifth ten-match haul of his career. The first-day success of Stevens's unexceptional medium-pace, which accounted for Buttler, Hildreth and Kieswetter in a sequence of six wickets in 11 overs, exposed the danger of producing grassy pitches.

Close of play: First day, Somerset 122-7 (de Bruyn 7, Thomas 4); Second day, Somerset 128-2 (Trescothick 59, Thomas 0); Third day, No play.

Somerset

*M. E. Trescothick lbw b Stevens	27	– c Tredwell b Khan	80
A. V. Suppiah c Denly b Cook	34	– c Jones b Coles	24
J. C. Buttler c van Jaarsveld b Stevens	20	– lbw b Bandara	42
Z. de Bruyn c Jones b Cook	44	– (5) c Jones b Coles	43
J. C. Hildreth c Jones b Stevens	0	– (6) c Jones b Tredwell	48
†C. Kieswetter c Bandara b Stevens	6	– (7) not out	9
P. D. Trego c van Jaarsveld b Khan	3	– (8) c Bandara b Coles	4
B. J. Phillips c Jones b Khan	0	– (9) not out	2
A. C. Thomas c van Jaarsveld b Khan	17	– (4) b Bandara	30
M. Kartik c Jones b Tredwell	15		
C. M. Willoughby not out	11		
B 3, l-b 7, w 12, n-b 6	28	B 12, l-b 2, w 3, n-b 2	19

1/64 (1) 2/101 (2) 3/101 (3)   (49.4 overs) 205   1/45 (2)   (7 wkts dec, 54 overs) 301
4/101 (5) 5/111 (6) 6/116 (7)   2/124 (3) 3/190 (1)
7/118 (8) 8/154 (9) 9/192 (4) 10/205 (10)   4/194 (5) 5/285 (6) 6/285 (5) 7/289 (8)

Khan 18–4–63–3; Cook 14–1–65–2; Coles 4–0–28–0; Stevens 13–4–38–4; Tredwell 0.4–0–1–1. *Second Innings*—Khan 13–4–60–1; Cook 7–0–23–0; Coles 13–1–73–3; Tredwell 11–1–64–1; Bandara 10–1–67–2.

Kent

S. A. Northeast c Kartik b Willoughby	24	– c Suppiah b Kartik	40
J. L. Denly lbw b Kartik	34	– c and b Thomas	36
†G. O. Jones c and b Kartik	16	– lbw b Kartik	47
*M. van Jaarsveld lbw b Thomas	4	– c Buttler b Willoughby	6
A. J. Blake c Buttler b Kartik	15	– lbw b Kartik	10
D. I. Stevens c Trego b Willoughby	22	– c Trescothick b Kartik	9
J. C. Tredwell c Buttler b Kartik	14	– lbw b Kartik	15
M. T. Coles b Kartik	23	– not out	1
H. M. C. M. Bandara c Kieswetter b Thomas	5	– not out	4
S. J. Cook not out	7		
A. Khan c Trescothick b Thomas	0		
B 5, l-b 1, w 2	8	B 14, l-b 9	23

1/35 (1) 2/76 (3) 3/81 (4) 4/87 (2)   (45 overs) 172   1/67 (2)   (7 wkts, 74.4 overs) 191
5/114 (5) 6/126 (6) 7/159 (8) 8/164 (7)   2/77 (1) 3/94 (4)
9/172 (9) 10/172 (11)   4/116 (5) 5/134 (6) 6/166 (7) 7/187 (3)

Willoughby 12–1–46–2; Phillips 9–2–33–0; Trego 2–0–16–0; Thomas 8–3–21–3; Kartik 14–4–50–5. *Second Innings*—Willoughby 13–3–22–1; Thomas 16–2–53–1; Phillips 8–1–21–0; Kartik 31–13–57–5; Trego 2–1–1–0; Suppiah 4.4–1–14–0.

Umpires: N. L. Bainton and M. A. Gough.

SOMERSET v NOTTINGHAMSHIRE

At Taunton, July 29–31. Somerset won by ten wickets. Somerset 24pts, Nottinghamshire 5pts. Toss: Somerset.

Even though Nottinghamshire had not won at Taunton for 25 years, Somerset could scarcely have expected the title favourites to prove such pushovers. Sidebottom injured himself in a game of football before the start, further compromising an attack which had lost Broad and Swann to England. Pattinson delivered the opening over instead, and bowled Trescothick behind his legs first ball. In a hat-trick of sorts, he removed Compton immediately after lunch, and then Hildreth with the first delivery of the second new ball. In between, Hildreth played delightful sweeps and drives in an exuberant partnership of 210 with Buttler, as a dry but well-grassed pitch began to flatten out. More punishment came from Trego and Kieswetter, whose half-century was only his second in 15 innings for Somerset after the World Twenty20. When Nottinghamshire responded, Hussey and Brown were out loosely to Willoughby within three balls, and, although Read and Patel embarked upon a brave stand of 157, they followed on 178 behind on the third morning. They buckled again to Thomas, who improved on his county-best. Nottinghamshire coach Mick Newell was furious: "We should have made this an exercise in points gathering," he said. Instead, they allowed Somerset to cut the gap from 31 points to 12.

Close of play: First day, Somerset 423-6 (Kieswetter 43, Trego 36); Second day, Nottinghamshire 278-5 (Patel 92, Read 75).

Somerset

*M. E. Trescothick b Pattinson	0	– not out	4
A. V. Suppiah c Hales b Adams	30		
N. R. D. Compton c Hussey b Pattinson	17	– (2) not out	5
Z. de Bruyn lbw b Pattinson	44		
J. C. Hildreth c Wagh b Pattinson	142		
J. C. Buttler b Patel	88		
†C. Kieswetter b Patel	73		
P. D. Trego c Wagh b Pattinson	54		
A. C. Thomas not out	30		
M. Kartik lbw b Shreck	7		
C. M. Willoughby c Shreck b Patel	5		
B 8, l-b 5, n-b 14	27	N-b 4	4

1/0 (1) 2/44 (3) 3/77 (2)   (118.3 overs) 517   (no wkt, 1.5 overs) 13
4/126 (4) 5/336 (6) 6/347 (5) 7/460 (8)
8/489 (7) 9/504 (10) 10/517 (11)   110 overs: 477-7

Pattinson 20-3-95-5; Shreck 29-5-101-1; Adams 26-4-121-1; Franks 15-2-50-0; Patel 18.3-0-93-3; Hussey 10-1-44-0. *Second Innings*—Hussey 1-0-8-0; Hales 0.5-0-5-0.

Nottinghamshire

A. D. Hales c Trescothick b Kartik	6	– c Kieswetter b Kartik	28
M. J. Wood c Trescothick b Suppiah	72	– lbw b Willoughby	0
M. A. Wagh c de Bruyn b Trego	4	– lbw b de Bruyn	45
S. R. Patel lbw b Thomas	104	– c Trescothick b Thomas	1
D. J. Hussey c Trescothick b Willoughby	4	– b de Bruyn	30
A. D. Brown c de Bruyn b Willoughby	2	– lbw b Thomas	47
*†C. M. W. Read c Kieswetter b Willoughby	80	– c de Bruyn b Thomas	4
P. J. Franks lbw b Willoughby	15	– c Hildreth b Thomas	4
A. R. Adams c Kieswetter b Willoughby	20	– lbw b Kartik	10
D. J. Pattinson not out	7	– not out	7
C. E. Shreck b Willoughby	0	– b Thomas	3
B 12, l-b 1, w 6, n-b 6	25	B 1, l-b 9, n-b 4	14

1/41 (1) 2/48 (3) 3/119 (2)   (92.3 overs) 339   1/1 (2) 2/41 (1)   (58.4 overs) 190
4/128 (5) 5/130 (6) 6/287 (7)   3/42 (4) 4/93 (3)
7/297 (4) 8/332 (9) 9/339 (8) 10/339 (11)   5/134 (6) 6/162 (7) 7/168 (8)
                                                     8/175 (6) 9/179 (9) 10/190 (11)

Willoughby 22.3–3–101–6; Thomas 13–3–68–1; Kartik 33–15–59–1; Trego 6–1–17–1; Suppiah 11–2–48–1; de Bruyn 7–1–33–0. *Second Innings*—Willoughby 13–1–52–1; Thomas 14.4–4–40–5; Kartik 26–3–64–2; de Bruyn 5–1–24–2.

Umpires: M. A. Gough and J. W. Lloyds.

At Canterbury, August 3–6. SOMERSET drew with KENT.

SOMERSET v HAMPSHIRE

At Taunton, August 9–12. Drawn. Somerset 11pts, Hampshire 8pts. Toss: Somerset. Championship debut: D. T. Christian.

Both counties were involved in Twenty20 finals day less than 48 hours after this match, which, although a draw, kept Hampshire's medical staff disconcertingly busy. Ervine and Cork were already nursing back problems when Lumb was struck on the ankle trying to stop a forceful drive from Kieswetter, his opening partner in the World Twenty20, on the third day. Lumb carried on fielding, but X-rays later revealed a fracture. As Hampshire scrapped to save the match, Dan Christian was cut and bruised by a de Bruyn bouncer which slipped through his grille on to his nose. While groundstaff sprinkled sawdust on the bloodied wicket, Cork waved a mock white flag of surrender. But his side did no such thing: McKenzie batted out the last 47 overs unscathed. On the first day, Lumb's wicket sparked Hampshire's collapse from 180 for two on a surface offering less to bowlers than of late. Somerset were about to take the lead when de Bruyn was bowled reverse-sweeping five short of a century; the stroke was more profitable for his fifth-wicket ally, Hildreth, who survived a missed stumping, also on 95, to score a third century in consecutive matches. He was the sixth of seven wickets for Tomlinson, a bowler unworried by Taunton's reputation: in 2008 he had claimed career-best figures of eight for 46.

Close of play: First day, Hampshire 217-5 (Ervine 18, Christian 11); Second day, Somerset 16-1 (Suppiah 7, Thomas 0); Third day, Somerset 392-7 (Hildreth 128, Phillips 0).

Hampshire

M. A. Carberry c Kieswetter b Kartik	71	– b Willoughby	22
J. H. K. Adams c Kieswetter b Trego	34	– c de Bruyn b Kartik	19
M. J. Lumb c and b Kartik	42		
N. D. McKenzie lbw b Willoughby	23	– (3) not out	60
J. M. Vince lbw b Kartik	4	– (4) c Trescothick b de Bruyn	43
S. M. Ervine c Buttler b Thomas	48		
D. T. Christian b Willoughby	28	– (5) b Suppiah	36
†A. M. Bates b Willoughby	2	– (6) not out	16
*D. G. Cork c Hildreth b Willoughby	12		
J. A. Tomlinson lbw b Thomas	0		
D. R. Briggs not out	0		
B 10, l-b 6, n-b 4	20	B 14, l-b 3, w 1, n-b 10	28

1/62 (2) 2/130 (1) 3/180 (3)   (92.3 overs) 284   1/47 (2)   (4 wkts, 67 overs) 224
4/186 (5) 5/186 (4) 6/252 (7)   2/55 (1) 3/140 (4) 4/195 (5)
7/254 (8) 8/284 (6) 9/284 (10) 10/284 (9)

Willoughby 23.3–4–80–4; Phillips 13–7–33–0; Thomas 21–4–69–2; Trego 9–3–27–1; Kartik 23–7–51–3; de Bruyn 3–0–8–0. *Second Innings*—Willoughby 12–2–44–1; Phillips 6.4–1–12–0; Kartik 20–5–50–1; Suppiah 7.2–2–21–1; Thomas 5–0–28–0; Trego 10–1–35–0; de Bruyn 6–2–17–1.

Somerset

*M. E. Trescothick c and b Tomlinson	7	M. Kartik c Adams b Tomlinson	2
A. V. Suppiah c McKenzie b Tomlinson	37	C. M. Willoughby b Christian	5
A. C. Thomas c Adams b Tomlinson	5		
Z. de Bruyn b Briggs	95	B 3, l-b 2, w 10, n-b 10	25
†C. Kieswetter c Lumb b Tomlinson	43		
J. C. Hildreth c Vince b Tomlinson	130	1/11 (1) 2/49 (3) 3/60 (2) (109.1 overs) 412
J. C. Buttler lbw b Christian	20	4/128 (5) 5/283 (4)
P. D. Trego b Tomlinson	32	6/338 (7) 7/386 (8) 8/399 (6)
B. J. Phillips not out	11	9/403 (10) 10/412 (11)

Cork 10.1–2–22–0; Tomlinson 32–10–85–7; Ervine 6–1–21–0; Christian 22.1–1–115–2; Briggs 27.5–0–139–1; McKenzie 10–1–24–0; Carberry 1–0–1–0.

Umpires: M. A. Gough and N. A. Mallender.

At Colchester, August 18–20. SOMERSET beat ESSEX by 219 runs. *Trescothick hits 228* in Somerset's second-innings 367 for eight declared.*

SOMERSET v DURHAM

At Taunton, August 24–27. Drawn. Somerset 8pts, Durham 5pts. Toss: Somerset.

Trescothick's masterly century took him to 551 runs in five Championship innings, but his success probably dissuaded Durham from participating in a contrived run-chase. Somerset were 287 for four before torrential rain swept in, washing out days two and three. Trescothick and Mustard did meet to discuss terms, but could not agree, despite there being 61 overs available when play resumed at 2 p.m. Instead, Somerset ploughed on until they had achieved maximum batting points; the declaration came too late for Durham to gain any of their own, so hands were shaken at 4.50 p.m. When Nottinghamshire beat Lancashire in an improvised finish at Trent Bridge on the same evening, Somerset slipped 16 points behind, having played one more game.

Close of play: First day, Somerset 287-4 (de Bruyn 18, Kieswetter 27); Second day, No play; Third day, No play.

Somerset

*M. E. Trescothick c Stoneman		P. D. Trego not out	18
b Benkenstein	128	B. J. Phillips not out	8
A. V. Suppiah lbw b Blackwell	54		
N. R. D. Compton c Borthwick		L-b 7, n-b 4	11
b Benkenstein	45		
Z. de Bruyn c Borthwick b Plunkett	54	1/119 (2) (6 wkts dec, 104.4 overs) 400
J. C. Hildreth b Claydon	7	2/232 (3) 3/235 (1)
†C. Kieswetter lbw b Borthwick	75	4/249 (5) 5/358 (4) 6/381 (6)

A. C. Thomas, M. Kartik and C. M. Willoughby did not bat.

Davies 27–5–85–0; Claydon 20–3–86–1; Plunkett 16–2–64–1; Stokes 3–1–24–0; Blackwell 28–7–79–1; Benkenstein 3–0–17–2; Borthwick 7.4–0–38–1.

Durham

M. J. Di Venuto not out	10
M. D. Stoneman not out	22
B 4, l-b 1	5

(no wkt dec, 15 overs)   37

G. J. Muchall, D. M. Benkenstein, I. D. Blackwell, B. A. Stokes, *†P. Mustard, S. G. Borthwick, L. E. Plunkett, M. E. Claydon and M. Davies did not bat.

Willoughby 8–1–26–0; Phillips 4–3–2–0; Kartik 3–0–4–0.

Umpires: R. K. Illingworth and J. W. Lloyds.

At Taunton, September 2. SOMERSET lost to PAKISTANIS by eight runs (see Pakistani tour section).

SOMERSET v LANCASHIRE

At Taunton, September 7–9. Somerset won by nine wickets. Somerset 23pts, Lancashire 5pts. Toss: Somerset. First-class debut: C. R. Jones.

Somerset's all-round determination carried their fight for a maiden Championship title into the last game at Chester-le-Street – and eliminated Lancashire's own nominal challenge. Thriving on a strip barely distinguishable from the surrounding square, Willoughby led the attack with late swing, taking seven for 97 in all, and passing 50 first-class wickets for Somerset for the fifth consecutive season. It was mostly aerial movement and, in Chanderpaul's case, uncharacteristically poor shot selection, which undid Lancashire's uncertain batsmen. ECB inspector Jack Birkenshaw reported no problem with the pitch. Kieswetter returned from international duty, ending a brief debut for Chris Jones, and smashed his highest Championship score of the season. Though Keedy restored some balance with three wickets in four balls, Kartik's fifty squeezed 106 out of the last two wickets, and extended Somerset's first-innings lead to 123. For once, Kartik wasn't needed with the ball: the seamers shared all ten second-innings wickets, with help from a scuttler to dismiss Chanderpaul and a generous bat-pad decision against a furious Croft. Somerset promptly raced to their fourth win at Taunton; they had never won so many at home in a Division One season.

Close of play: First day, Somerset 54-1 (Suppiah 13, Thomas 1); Second day, Somerset 350-8 (Phillips 29, Kartik 37).

Lancashire

P. J. Horton b Willoughby	7	– (2) lbw b Phillips 2
T. C. Smith lbw b Willoughby	23	– (1) c Trego b Willoughby 16
*M. J. Chilton lbw b Thomas	12	– lbw b Thomas 0
S. Chanderpaul c Trescothick b Kartik	56	– lbw b Thomas 20
S. J. Croft run out	31	– c Buttler b Trego 46
L. A. Procter lbw b Kartik	19	– c Kieswetter b Willoughby 32
†G. D. Cross lbw b Willoughby	6	– c Kartik b Trego 0
S. I. Mahmood c Suppiah b Kartik	29	– lbw b Phillips 0
K. W. Hogg lbw b Willoughby	0	– not out 37
G. Keedy b Phillips	34	– b Willoughby 0
S. C. Kerrigan not out	16	– lbw b Thomas 0
B 4, l-b 10, n-b 12	26	B 8, l-b 2, w 1, n-b 6 17

1/29 (2) 2/32 (1) 3/77 (3) 4/126 (5) (83 overs) 259
5/153 (4) 6/164 (7) 7/164 (6) 8/169 (9)
9/203 (8) 10/259 (10)

1/22 (2) 2/22 (1) (59.5 overs) 170
3/32 (3) 4/54 (4)
5/109 (6) 6/109 (7) 7/116 (8)
8/157 (6) 9/159 (10) 10/170 (11)

Willoughby 20–3–60–4; Phillips 13–5–21–1; Trego 10–3–30–0; Thomas 16–3–69–1; Kartik 24–8–65–3. *Second Innings*—Willoughby 14–4–37–3; Phillips 8–3–17–2; Thomas 15.5–4–53–3; Kartik 14–3–33–0; Trego 8–3–20–2.

Somerset

*M. E. Trescothick c Smith b Keedy	33	– c Croft b Mahmood	8
A. V. Suppiah c Cross b Smith	13	– not out	12
A. C. Thomas b Mahmood	8		
N. R. D. Compton lbw b Procter	49	– (3) not out	26
J. C. Hildreth lbw b Keedy	26		
†C. Kieswetter c Cross b Keedy	84		
P. D. Trego lbw b Keedy	51		
J. C. Buttler lbw b Keedy	0		
B. J. Phillips lbw b Smith	30		
M. Kartik not out	52		
C. M. Willoughby run out	16		
B 13, l-b 3, n-b 4	20	N-b 2	2

1/42 (1) 2/57 (2) 3/71 (3) (96.5 overs) 382   1/8 (1)   (1 wkt, 8.3 overs) 48
4/128 (5) 5/160 (4) 6/271 (7) 7/271 (8)
8/276 (6) 9/351 (9) 10/382 (11)

Kieswetter replaced C. R. Jones after returning from England duty.

Hogg 7–1–33–0; Mahmood 26–7–77–1; Keedy 26–1–81–5; Smith 16.5–5–67–2; Kerrigan 16–2–82–0; Procter 5–0–26–1. *Second Innings*—Mahmood 3–0–21–1; Smith 3–1–11–0; Procter 1.3–0–13–0; Kerrigan 1–0–3–0.

Umpires: P. J. Hartley and N. A. Mallender.

At Chester-le-Street, September 13–16. SOMERSET drew with DURHAM. *Somerset finish level on points with Nottinghamshire at the top of the table, but are runners-up after winning one match fewer.*

SURREY

Round and round at The Oval

RICHARD SPILLER

When Surrey complete their next major building project at The Oval, might they replace the Hobbs Gates with a revolving door? A season which started under the shadow of Sir Alec Bedser's death ended with 19 office staff being made redundant. The economic recession, reflected in poor sales for the Pakistan Test and Surrey's Twenty20 matches, finally reached Kennington. The most senior casualty was managing director of cricket Gus Mackay, who had arrived from Sussex two years earlier with an abrasive reputation, and lived up to it.

The much-delayed £35m hotel project should be finished by 2013, but whether reconstruction of the team is completed by then is another matter. Surrey won more matches than they had done in the previous two seasons put together – no great achievement given that those were among the worst years in the county's history – yet made few tangible gains.

They failed to reach the knockout stages of either one-day competition, and although four Championship victories was four times as many as in 2009, it took a ten-run victory in the dying moments of the summer to avoid eighth place in the second division, which would have been their lowest-ever finish. Retaining the Second Eleven Championship was encouraging, though.

Impatience among Surrey's committee and members increased, given that manager Chris Adams had spent £3.3m radically reshaping his squad after taking over for 2009, which he described as "Year Zero". For all the promises of a better tomorrow, his second summer barely got beyond Year 0.5.

What progress there was under new captain Rory Hamilton-Brown was offset by several dire displays. Surrey achieved a world-record score in 40-over cricket (386 for three against Glamorgan), while the innings victory over Northamptonshire in July was their first Championship win at The Oval since 2007. Yet such days were overshadowed by disasters like the innings defeat at Lord's, being booed off The Oval after losing the opening Twenty20 game to Gloucestershire by ten wickets, and surrender on the last morning at Worcester, where six wickets went down for 18 in 27 balls to leave one player lamenting: "We're the laughing stock of English cricket."

Pre-season promotion ambitions received a major setback when leg-spinner Piyush Chawla was refused permission to join by the Indian board. The short-term replacements Iftikhar Anjum and Younis Khan were largely ineffective, like most of Surrey's recent overseas signings, while Twenty20 specialist Andrew Symonds featured in two victories over Kent but did little else, and was hit for 22 in the final over as Essex stole the match at Chelmsford.

There were some individual successes, two from Adams's expensive new signings: Steven Davies scored 887 runs in the Championship and 874 in

Nigel French, PA Photos

Jason Roy

one-day competitions at a high tempo, and kept wicket tidily throughout to earn selection as reserve keeper for the Ashes tour. Chris Tremlett, a controversial signing originally but one which paid dividends once he shook off a groin strain, extracted lift at good pace from all surfaces – including Bill Gordon's excellent ones at The Oval – to claim 48 Championship wickets at 20, and 80 overall. He also made the Ashes tour, and proved a major success in the later Tests. Tremlett's progress camouflaged Andre Nel appearing in only seven Championship matches: he was suspended twice for disciplinary reasons, then suffered a serious leg injury.

Jade Dernbach, despite a mid-season side strain, also earned an England Performance Programme place, while Stuart Meaker's high pace was increasingly augmented by improved control and late swing. Without Chawla, though, Surrey often failed to build on breakthroughs: off-spinner Gareth Batty – returning after eight seasons at Worcestershire – bowled better than his figures suggest, but managed only one five-for. Fast bowler Chris Jordan missed the whole season with a back injury.

Once more Mark Ramprakash's enduring quality shone through, even if he was 41 in September. His 1,595 first-class runs were again the most in the country, but support was often in short supply. Usman Afzaal faded out of the side after July and was eventually released, while Hamilton-Brown, like his team, could be spectacularly good – if he got through the early overs – or woefully bad. His captaincy was positive, but he looked tired by the time he turned 23 in September.

Nowhere was a scattergun approach to selection more apparent than at the top of the order. An elbow injury kept Michael Brown out, and nine different opening combinations were tried in the Championship. Arun Harinath battled hard, but having seven different partners hardly helped, and he was also jettisoned in late summer. The muscular Jason Roy (who scored a Twenty20 century against Kent and could prove a special talent), reserve wicketkeeper Gary Wilson and Tom Lancefield all offered hope for the future, but will need more patient and consistent treatment than that handed out to Stewart Walters (who left the county at the end of 2010) and Matthew Spriegel. Laurie Evans's reward for making 98 against Bangladesh was a third Championship appearance in two seasons, but then he was dropped again and snapped up by Warwickshire.

Kevin Pietersen arrived on loan after he fell out with Hampshire in mid-season: his one significant contribution was a CB40 century. He signed a one-year deal for 2011. Zander de Bruyn, Tom Maynard and Yasir Arafat, three other new signings, should be available more often than Pietersen.

Adams was under growing pressure as he entered the final year of his contract. When he told members that he wanted to build a side for the next decade, they hoped he did not mean the 2020s.

SURREY RESULTS

All first-class matches – Played 18: Won 4, Lost 6, Drawn 8.
County Championship matches – Played 16: Won 4, Lost 6, Drawn 6.

LV= County Championship, 7th in Division 2;
Friends Provident T20, 5th in South Division; Clydesdale Bank 40, 3rd in Group A.

COUNTY CHAMPIONSHIP AVERAGES, BATTING AND FIELDING

Cap		M	I	NO	R	HS	100s	50s	Avge	Ct
2002	M. R. Ramprakash.............	16	28	2	1,595	248	5	5	61.34	5
	S. M. Davies.................	12	20	2	887	137	1	8	49.27	29
	G. C. Wilson.................	5	7	0	339	125	1	1	48.42	14
	Younis Khan§................	3	5	1	155	77*	0	1	38.75	2
	J. J. Roy....................	3	5	0	170	76	0	2	34.00	0
	T. J. Lancefield†.............	7	11	1	323	74	0	2	32.30	3
	R. J. Hamilton-Brown.........	16	28	1	808	125	2	3	29.92	11
	C. P. Schofield..............	7	12	0	336	90	0	2	28.00	4
	A. Harinath†................	12	21	0	529	63	0	3	25.19	3
2009	U. Afzaal...................	11	19	1	451	87	0	3	25.05	4
	S. J. Walters¶...............	6	10	0	242	53	0	1	24.20	8
	G. J. Batty..................	14	23	2	483	65	0	1	23.00	11
	A. Nel¶....................	7	10	0	219	96	0	1	21.90	4
	C. T. Tremlett...............	12	17	6	230	53*	0	1	20.90	1
	M. N. W. Spriegel†...........	8	12	0	248	103	1	0	20.66	9
	Iftikhar Anjum§..............	3	5	1	61	29	0	0	15.25	0
	J. W. Dernbach¶.............	14	20	9	154	56*	0	0	14.00	1
	T. E. Linley.................	6	10	4	55	16	0	0	9.16	4
	S. C. Meaker................	9	12	1	63	21	0	0	5.72	3

Also batted: S. P. Cheetham (1 match) 0*; L. J. Evans (1 match) 10, 7 (1 ct); T. M. Jewell (1 match) 1; K. P. Pietersen‡ (2 matches) 0, 1, 40.

† *Born in Surrey.* ‡ *ECB contract.* § *Official overseas player.* ¶ *Other non-England-qualified player.*

BOWLING

	O	M	R	W	BB	5W/i	Avge
C. T. Tremlett..................	361.5	88	969	48	4-29	0	20.18
J. W. Dernbach.................	421	89	1,344	46	5-68	2	29.21
T. E. Linley...................	142	34	437	14	5-105	1	31.21
A. Nel........................	227	67	671	21	4-68	0	31.95
S. C. Meaker..................	241.5	41	896	28	5-48	2	32.00
C. P. Schofield................	163	33	541	14	4-63	0	38.64
G. J. Batty....................	470.3	66	1,638	41	5-76	1	39.95

Also bowled: U. Afzaal 71.3–9–201–8; S. P. Cheetham 16–1–71–2; R. J. Hamilton-Brown 42.3–1–167–0; A. Harinath 2–0–12–0; Iftikhar Anjum 65–8–240–6; T. M. Jewell 14–1–74–1; T. J. Lancefield 1–0–9–0; M. R. Ramprakash 1–0–6–0; J. J. Roy 3–0–18–0; M. N. W. Spriegel 57.3–3–175–5; S. J. Walters 3–0–15–0; G. C. Wilson 9–0–44–0; Younis Khan 18–0–64–0.

LEADING CB40 AVERAGES (100 runs/4 wickets)

Batting	Runs	HS	Avge	S-R	Ct/St
K. P. Pietersen....	154	116	77.00	111.59	0
U. Afzaal........	124	51*	62.00	83.78	4
S. M. Davies.....	485	101	60.62	128.98	8/2
M. R. Ramprakash.	326	85*	46.57	99.08	5
R.J.Hamilton-Brown	478	115	43.45	150.78	2
S. J. Walters......	271	88	38.71	95.75	0

Bowling	W	BB	Avge	E-R
A. Nel	7	3-29	20.00	5.83
Iftikhar Anjum....	4	3-39	22.00	5.86
G. J. Batty	12	3-44	28.25	5.94
R.J.Hamilton-Brown	4	2-50	33.50	6.38
S. P. Cheetham ...	5	4-32	39.20	7.84
C. P. Schofield....	8	2-40	41.37	5.91

LEADING FPT20 AVERAGES (100 runs/18 overs)

Batting	Runs	HS	Avge	S-R	Ct/St
S. M. Davies	389	89	29.92	161.41	14/2
A. Symonds	263	63	20.23	151.14	5
J. J. Roy	242	101*	30.25	148.46	2
R. J. Hamilton-Brown	397	87*	28.35	125.23	5
M. R. Ramprakash	331	63*	36.77	116.96	3
S. J. Walters	184	53*	46.00	113.58	9

Bowling	W	BB	Avge	E-R
C. T. Tremlett	24	3-17	17.12	6.85
M. N. W. Spriegel	7	2-23	29.71	7.17
C. P. Schofield	14	2-15	28.64	7.31
A. Nel	7	2-30	54.42	7.32
G. J. Batty	7	4-23	22.57	7.97
R. J. Hamilton-Brown	7	2-23	23.57	9.16

FIRST-CLASS COUNTY RECORDS

Highest score for	357*	R. Abel v Somerset at The Oval	1899
Highest score against	366	N. H. Fairbrother (Lancashire) at The Oval	1990
Leading run-scorer	43,554	J. B. Hobbs (avge 49.72)	1905–1934
Best bowling for	10-43	T. Rushby v Somerset at Taunton	1921
Best bowling against	10-28	W. P. Howell (Australians) at The Oval	1899
Leading wicket-taker	1,775	T. Richardson (avge 17.87)	1892–1904
Highest total for	811	v Somerset at The Oval	1899
Highest total against	863	by Lancashire at The Oval	1990
Lowest total for	14	v Essex at Chelmsford	1983
Lowest total against	16	by MCC at Lord's	1872

LIST A COUNTY RECORDS

Highest score for	268	A. D. Brown v Glamorgan at The Oval	2002
Highest score against	180*	T. M. Moody (Worcestershire) at The Oval	1994
Leading run-scorer	10,358	A. D. Brown (avge 32.16)	1990–2008
Best bowling for	7-30	M. P. Bicknell v Glamorgan at The Oval	1999
Best bowling against	7-15	A. L. Dixon (Kent) at The Oval	1967
Leading wicket-taker	409	M. P. Bicknell (avge 25.21)	1986–2005
Highest total for	496-4	v Gloucestershire at The Oval	2007
Highest total against	429	by Glamorgan at The Oval	2002
Lowest total for	64	v Worcestershire at Worcester	1978
Lowest total against	44	by Glamorgan at The Oval	1999

TWENTY20 RECORDS

Highest score for	101*	J. J. Roy v Kent at Beckenham	2010
Highest score against	106*	S. B. Styris (Essex) at Chelmsford	2010
Leading run-scorer	1,719	M. R. Ramprakash (avge 32.43)	2003–2010
Best bowling for	6-24	T. J. Murtagh v Middlesex at Lord's	2005
Best bowling against	4-21	Yasir Arafat (Sussex) at Hove	2006
Leading wicket-taker	53	N. D. Doshi (avge 14.66)	2004–2007
Highest total for	224-5	v Gloucestershire at Bristol	2006
Highest total against	217-4	by Lancashire at The Oval	2005
Lowest total for	94	v Essex at Chelmsford	2008
Lowest total against	68	by Sussex at Hove	2007

ADDRESS

The Oval, Kennington, London SE11 5SS (0871 246 1100; **email** enquiries@surreycricket.com).
Website www.surreycricket.com

OFFICIALS

Captain R. J. Hamilton-Brown	**President** R. Harman
Professional cricket manager C. J. Adams	**Chairman** R. W. Thompson
Batting coach G. P. Thorpe	**Chief executive** P. C. J. Sheldon
Bowling coach M. P. Bicknell	**Chairman of cricket** A. J. Murphy
Coach/consultant A. J. Stewart	**Head groundsman** S. A. Patterson
Managing director 2010 – A. J. Mackay	**Scorer** K. R. Booth

At Cambridge, April 3–5. SURREY drew with CAMBRIDGE MCCU.

SURREY v DERBYSHIRE

At The Oval, April 9–12. Derbyshire won by 208 runs. Derbyshire 23pts, Surrey 6pts. Toss: Derbyshire. County debuts: M. H. A. Footitt, R. J. Peterson.

Hamilton-Brown had admitted he might not know what to do in his first Championship match as Surrey's captain if Rogers made 300 – and actually he made 340 runs in all, leaving his opposite number looking helpless at times. Rogers was the first Derbyshire player to make a double-century and century in the same match, as his side achieved their first victory at The Oval since 1966. By the end of the first day his 178 had established an unassailable position: he enjoyed some early fortune, but proved merciless on anything overpitched or on his legs. He was dropped at 46 and 182 on the way to a third double-century in four matches for Derbyshire: only Eddie Barlow had made a higher score for them against Surrey (217 at Ilkeston in 1976). Although Ramprakash's 109th first-class hundred restricted the lead, he was soon back watching Rogers bat before collecting a duck as Surrey, set an unlikely 374 in what became 77 overs, crumbled to defeat with 35 balls remaining. Left-arm spinner Robin Peterson, Derbyshire's Kolpak signing from South Africa, marked his debut by sweeping away the tail – starting with Meaker after a 77-ball rearguard – despite Davies's impressive resistance.

Close of play: First day, Derbyshire 306-5 (Rogers 178, Peterson 7); Second day, Surrey 185-5 (Ramprakash 63, Batty 0); Third day, Derbyshire 161-3 (Rogers 99, Smith 12).

Derbyshire

*C. J. L. Rogers lbw b Batty	200	– not out 140
W. L. Madsen c Batty b Linley	5	– lbw b Linley 15
P. M. Borrington c Davies b Batty	21	– c Hamilton-Brown b Batty 12
G. T. Park c Nel b Batty	10	– lbw b Dernbach 19
G. M. Smith c Dernbach b Afzaal	66	– c and b Spiegel 20
D. J. Redfern c Meaker b Afzaal	1	– c Spiegel b Afzaal 44
R. J. Peterson lbw b Meaker	23	
G. G. Wagg b Nel	37	– (7) c Ramprakash b Batty 16
†L. J. Goddard not out	33	
T. D. Groenewald c Davies b Nel	5	
M. H. A. Footitt b Meaker	30	
B 2, 1-b 13, w 3, n-b 2	20	B 1, 1-b 5, n-b 2 8

1/36 (2) 2/90 (3) 3/133 (4)   (131.5 overs) 451   1/50 (2)   (6 wkts dec, 60.5 overs) 274
4/261 (5) 5/265 (6) 6/337 (7) 7/358 (1)   2/79 (3) 3/141 (4)
8/394 (8) 9/400 (10) 10/451 (11)   110 overs: 358-7   4/172 (5) 5/256 (6) 6/274 (7)

Nel 29–8–94–2; Dernbach 24–4–82–0; Linley 20–3–53–1; Meaker 14.5–4–58–2; Batty 34–3–115–3; Hamilton-Brown 2–0–8–0; Afzaal 8–0–26–2. *Second Innings*—Nel 6–1–21–0; Dernbach 9–1–48–1; Meaker 3–1–15–0; Batty 16.5–2–82–2; Linley 6–0–28–1; Hamilton-Brown 4–1–20–0; Spiegel 12–1–35–1; Afzaal 4–0–19–1.

Surrey

M. N. W. Spriegel c Goddard b Smith	27	– (2) b Smith	28
A. Harinath c Borrington b Smith	16	– (1) b Footitt	5
M. R. Ramprakash c Goddard b Footitt	102	– b Groenewald	0
U. Afzaal c Peterson b Smith	4	– b Smith	3
*R. J. Hamilton-Brown lbw b Groenewald	9	– c Goddard b Wagg	8
†S. M. Davies c Madsen b Peterson	55	– b Footitt	56
G. J. Batty c Rogers b Smith	65	– lbw b Groenewald	12
S. C. Meaker c Borrington b Peterson	6	– b Peterson	21
A. Nel run out	37	– lbw b Peterson	15
T. E. Linley lbw b Peterson	10	– not out	1
J. W. Dernbach not out	0	– c Wagg b Peterson	1
B 3, l-b 5, w 1, n-b 12	21	B 5, l-b 8, n-b 2	15

1/44 (1) 2/47 (2) 3/53 (4)   (109.2 overs) 352
4/74 (5) 5/183 (6) 6/264 (3) 7/290 (8)
8/326 (7) 9/349 (9) 10/352 (10)

1/9 (1) 2/10 (3)   (71.1 overs) 165
3/16 (4) 4/33 (5) 5/67 (2)
6/105 (7) 7/126 (6) 8/152 (8)
9/159 (9) 10/165 (11)

Groenewald 26–6–90–1; Footitt 20–6–62–1; Wagg 13–1–47–0; Smith 20–5–58–4; Peterson 30.2–8–87–3. *Second Innings*—Groenewald 20–6–47–2; Footitt 13–5–25–2; Smith 13–5–35–2; Wagg 5–2–13–1; Peterson 20.1–10–32–3.

Umpires: M. J. D. Bodenham and N. G. B. Cook.

At Hove, April 15–18. SURREY lost to SUSSEX by ten wickets.

SURREY v WORCESTERSHIRE

At Whitgift School, Croydon, April 21–24. Drawn. Surrey 9pts, Worcestershire 9pts. Toss: Surrey.

Having limped away from heavy defeat at Hove on crutches after being hit on the foot, Hamilton-Brown now turned from lame duck to golden goose. He was dropped by Mitchell at second slip off Jones when one, but his first century for Surrey came up in only 96 balls, his off-side shots particularly imperious. Davies reminded his former county of his batting prowess in helping his captain add 177 for the fifth wicket in only 33 overs. After losing both openers without scoring, Worcestershire had their own captain to thank for an aggressive response: Solanki attacked the spinners fiercely, although he was lucky to escape on 94 when he gave a return catch to Schofield off a no-ball. Solanki's third-wicket stand of 223 with Moeen Ali was a county record against Surrey, then Kervezee and Smith threatened a sizeable lead until the last five wickets tumbled for only six runs. Ramprakash, who passed 1,000 first-class runs on this ground in just eight matches, and another good innings from Davies enabled Hamilton-Brown to set 268 from what became 58 overs. But although Batty – another former Worcestershire player – and Schofield worked through the batting, Moeen's resistance for 52 overs ensured Surrey paid heavily for dropping him at 16.

Close of play: First day, Surrey 415-6 (Davies 119, Schofield 23); Second day, Worcestershire 262-3 (Ali 122, Kervezee 16); Third day, Surrey 57-2 (Ramprakash 22, Afzaal 7).

Surrey

S. J. Walters c Smith b Richardson	0	– (2) c Smith b Shantry 19
A. Harinath c Scott b Shantry	45	– (1) c Scott b Richardson 1
M. R. Ramprakash lbw b Imran Arif	40	– c Scott b Imran Arif 82
U. Afzaal c Jaques b Imran Arif	0	– run out 9
*R. J. Hamilton-Brown c Kervezee b Shantry	125	– st Scott b Ali 9
†S. M. Davies c Richardson b Ali	137	– not out 69
G. J. Batty c Mitchell b Jones	47	– c Solanki b Ali 0
C. P. Schofield c Ali b Jones	23	– c Kervezee b Solanki 21
A. Nel run out	28	– c Solanki b Shantry 4
Iftikhar Anjum c Shantry b Ali	12	
J. W. Dernbach not out	8	
B 8, l-b 16, n-b 4	28	B 11, l-b 12, w 2 25

1/0 (1) 2/82 (3) 3/82 (4) 4/108 (2)	(117 overs) 493	1/3 (1) (8 wkts dec, 68.3 overs) 239
5/285 (5) 6/363 (7) 7/415 (8)		2/33 (2) 3/66 (4)
8/459 (6) 9/468 (9) 10/493 (10)	110 overs: 461-8	4/83 (5) 5/173 (3) 6/174 (7)
		7/234 (8) 8/239 (9)

Richardson 27–9–69–1; Jones 22–5–119–2; Shantry 27–2–98–2; Imran Arif 14–2–63–2; Ali 24–3–107–2; Mitchell 3–1–13–0. *Second Innings*—Richardson 13–2–48–1; Jones 3–1–18–0; Shantry 20.3–7–52–2; Ali 24–5–59–2; Solanki 5–0–22–1; Imran Arif 3–0–17–1.

Worcestershire

D. K. H. Mitchell lbw b Nel	0	– (2) b Dernbach 5
P. A. Jaques c Davies b Iftikhar Anjum	0	– (1) c Hamilton-Brown b Nel 0
*V. S. Solanki b Nel	114	– lbw b Batty 44
M. M. Ali c Batty b Nel	126	– not out 70
A. N. Kervezee lbw b Schofield	68	– b Batty 14
B. F. Smith c Davies b Dernbach	80	– lbw b Batty 10
†B. J. M. Scott c Walters b Dernbach	55	– lbw b Schofield 19
R. A. Jones not out	3	– c Davies b Afzaal 0
J. D. Shantry c Davies b Dernbach	0	– lbw b Schofield 0
A. Richardson c and b Schofield	2	– not out 0
Imran Arif c Ramprakash b Batty	0	
B 4, l-b 5, n-b 8	17	B 1, l-b 2, w 1, n-b 4 8

1/0 (1) 2/0 (2) 3/223 (3)	(143.4 overs) 465	1/0 (1) (8 wkts, 57.5 overs) 170
4/279 (4) 5/344 (5) 6/459 (6) 7/460 (7)		2/13 (2) 3/67 (3) 4/95 (5)
8/460 (9) 9/464 (10) 10/465 (11)	110 overs: 363-5	5/109 (6) 6/161 (7) 7/162 (8) 8/168 (9)

Nel 22–8–41–3; Iftikhar Anjum 18–4–57–1; Dernbach 24–3–85–3; Batty 33.4–4–121–1; Schofield 33–6–120–2; Hamilton-Brown 1–0–6–0; Afzaal 12–2–26–0. *Second Innings*—Nel 5–1–17–1; Dernbach 5.5–0–16–1; Batty 23–3–75–3; Schofield 18–9–42–2; Afzaal 5–4–4–1; Hamilton-Brown 1–0–13–0.

Umpires: R. J. Bailey and N. L. Bainton.

SURREY v GLOUCESTERSHIRE

At The Oval, May 4–6. Gloucestershire won by 77 runs. Gloucestershire 20pts, Surrey 3pts. Toss: Gloucestershire. County debut: C. T. Tremlett.

Capturing wickets had been Surrey's biggest problem, but having solved that they now looked short of runs. Tremlett's impressive first appearance after a groin strain – his new county had invited ridicule by claiming he was being rested to "manage his workload" – undermined opponents suffering a famine of their own. The former Surrey captain Batty fell to the fourth ball of the match after collecting two fours off Iftikhar Anjum, but Gloucestershire's modest total of 229 soon looked more impressive, as Surrey lost seven for 42 on a frenetic second morning as Lewis and Kirby, bowling a fuller length than the home attack. A valuable lead of 51 was stretched by the aggressive Franklin, and 73 vital runs were gleaned from the final two wickets, despite the speedy Meaker's best first-class figures. The first Surrey fast bowler to take a five-for at The Oval since 2006, he rated the surface as "spicy". Surrey never looked likely to get close to their target of 300 despite the best efforts of Davies. Their main destroyer, the slow left-armer Banerjee, picked up a maiden five-for; he had once played a few miles down the road for Dulwich.

Close of play: First day, Surrey 56-1 (Harinath 19, Tremlett 1); Second day, Gloucestershire 139-7 (Franklin 34, Banerjee 0).

Gloucestershire

†J. N. Batty c Davies b Iftikhar Anjum	8	– lbw b Tremlett	31
C. D. J. Dent lbw b Batty	32	– lbw b Meaker	17
H. J. H. Marshall c Hamilton-Brown b Tremlett	1	– c Davies b Dernbach	4
*A. P. R. Gidman c Afzaal b Tremlett	1	– lbw b Iftikhar Anjum	24
J. E. C. Franklin lbw b Iftikhar Anjum	35	– not out	92
C. G. Taylor lbw b Tremlett	13	– lbw b Meaker	10
S. D. Snell c Davies b Meaker	48	– c Batty b Meaker	0
J. Lewis c Harinath b Schofield	17	– c Davies b Meaker	1
V. Banerjee lbw b Schofield	35	– c Meaker b Dernbach	16
G. M. Hussain lbw b Tremlett	5	– lbw b Meaker	22
S. P. Kirby not out	20	– c Ramprakash b Dernbach	0
B 1, l-b 7, n-b 6	14	B 13, l-b 13, w 3, n-b 2	31

1/8 (1) 2/9 (3) 3/15 (4) 4/63 (2)	(80 overs) 229	1/37 (2) 2/49 (3) (75.2 overs) 248
5/93 (6) 6/102 (5) 7/127 (8) 8/179 (7)		3/86 (4) 4/86 (1)
9/187 (10) 10/229 (9)		5/122 (6) 6/122 (7) 7/133 (8)
		8/175 (9) 9/245 (10) 10/248 (11)

Iftikhar Anjum 14–0–53–2; Tremlett 18–7–35–4; Meaker 12–4–33–1; Dernbach 16–2–45–0; Batty 10–3–17–1; Schofield 10–1–38–2. *Second Innings*—Iftikhar Anjum 9–0–43–1; Tremlett 14–4–36–1; Dernbach 18.2–3–61–3; Meaker 20–2–48–5; Schofield 9–1–23–0; Batty 5–1–11–0.

Surrey

G. J. Batty b Hussain	31	– c Batty b Kirby	8
A. Harinath c Batty b Franklin	51	– c Snell b Banerjee	38
C. T. Tremlett b Hussain	1	– (9) c Lewis b Hussain	31
M. R. Ramprakash b Lewis	12	– (3) c Batty b Franklin	7
U. Afzaal b Kirby	19	– (4) b Banerjee	16
*R. J. Hamilton-Brown b Kirby	0	– (5) c Marshall b Lewis	13
†S. M. Davies not out	23	– (6) c Franklin b Banerjee	54
C. P. Schofield c Batty b Lewis	6	– (7) c Batty b Hussain	6
S. C. Meaker c Batty b Lewis	2	– (8) c Marshall b Banerjee	0
Iftikhar Anjum run out	4	– c Marshall b Banerjee	29
J. W. Dernbach b Kirby	16	– not out	13
L-b 3, w 1, n-b 9	13	L-b 3, n-b 4	7

1/52 (1) 2/56 (3) 3/99 (4)	(46.4 overs) 178	1/15 (1) 2/43 (3) (57.2 overs) 222
4/109 (2) 5/116 (6) 6/125 (5) 7/132 (8)		3/64 (2) 4/87 (5)
8/136 (9) 9/141 (10) 10/178 (11)		5/87 (4) 6/108 (7) 7/109 (8)
		8/152 (6) 9/201 (9) 10/222 (10)

Lewis 12–2–46–3; Franklin 9–1–32–1; Kirby 10.4–0–42–3; Hussain 13–2–53–2; Banerjee 2–1–2–0. *Second Innings*—Lewis 8–4–32–1; Kirby 13–4–30–1; Hussain 12–2–74–2; Franklin 5–1–9–1; Banerjee 19.2–4–74–5.

Umpires: R. K. Illingworth and D. J. Millns.

At The Oval, May 9–11. SURREY drew with BANGLADESHIS (see Bangladeshi tour section).

SURREY v MIDDLESEX

At The Oval, May 17–20. Drawn. Surrey 9pts, Middlesex 7pts. Toss: Surrey. Championship debut: G. C. Wilson.

Ramprakash spent 12 hours at the crease – and even that could not bring victory. It was the first time he had scored a double and single century in the same match, although it was the seventh time he had managed twin hundreds – one more than Jack Hobbs and Glenn Turner, level with Wally Hammond, and just one behind Ricky Ponting and Zaheer Abbas in the first-class list. On a slow, dry, true pitch, Ramprakash's early mastery gained consistent support – Irish wicketkeeper Gary Wilson ensured that Davies was not too badly missed while playing for England Lions – while Udal's marathon efforts were rewarded with five wickets. Middlesex's reply bustled along while Strauss and Newman, released by Surrey the previous season, were together. But the rest fell apart against Dernbach's sustained and intelligent assault, which included a burst of three for 11 in 21 balls. The follow-on was not enforced, and Ramprakash took over again: his second, more imperious, innings was his sixth century for his new county against his old one, beating the five he made for Middlesex v Surrey. Finally, Strauss and Newman again tempered home ambitions with their second century stand, as both pitch and match became increasingly moribund.

Close of play: First day, Surrey 286-4 (Ramprakash 125); Second day, Middlesex 148-0 (Strauss 54, Newman 79); Third day, Surrey 165-2 (Ramprakash 86, Hamilton-Brown 5).

Surrey

L. J. Evans b Murtagh	10	– (2) b Finn 7
A. Harinath c Simpson b Udal	39	– (1) b Shah 63
M. R. Ramprakash c Dexter b Malan	223	– not out 103
*R. J. Hamilton-Brown c Berg b Udal	55	– c Strauss b Collins 29
U. Afzaal c Berg b Udal	42	
M. N. W. Spriegel c Simpson b Berg	12	
G. J. Batty c Simpson b Collins	13	
†G. C. Wilson st Simpson b Malan	62	
A. Nel c Simpson b Udal	3	
C. T. Tremlett c Berg b Udal	13	
J. W. Dernbach not out	2	
L-b 6, n-b 10	16	L-b 2, w 1, n-b 2 5

1/12 (1) 2/101 (2) 3/187 (4)   (157.2 overs) 490   1/20 (2)   (3 wkts dec, 50.3 overs) 207
4/286 (5) 5/321 (6) 6/355 (7) 7/443 (8)   2/150 (1) 3/207 (4)
8/458 (9) 9/480 (3) 10/490 (10)   110 overs: 321-4

Murtagh 32–13–97–1; Finn 28–9–62–0; Berg 21–6–62–1; Collins 22–3–67–1; Udal 39.2–7–128–5; Malan 12–0–51–2; Shah 3–0–17–0. *Second Innings*—Murtagh 8–2–25–0; Finn 10–2–40–1; Udal 15–2–59–0; Collins 5.3–0–17–1; Malan 6–0–28–0; Berg 2–0–20–0; Shah 4–0–16–1.

Middlesex

A. J. Strauss c Spriegel b Dernbach	92	– c Hamilton-Brown b Dernbach 61
S. A. Newman c Wilson b Tremlett	91	– c Wilson b Batty 43
O. A. Shah c Wilson b Nel	3	– not out 40
D. J. Malan c Hamilton-Brown b Batty	27	– c Evans b Afzaal 30
N. J. Dexter c Wilson b Dernbach	9	– not out 5
†J. A. Simpson c Hamilton-Brown b Dernbach	2	
G. K. Berg not out	45	
*S. D. Udal lbw b Dernbach	13	
T. J. Murtagh c Wilson b Nel	0	
P. T. Collins lbw b Dernbach	1	
S. T. Finn c Wilson b Batty	18	
B 3, l-b 10, n-b 10	23	B 5, l-b 3, n-b 2 10

1/163 (2) 2/177 (3) 3/220 (1)   (89.4 overs) 324   1/103 (2)   (3 wkts, 65 overs) 189
4/230 (5) 5/236 (6) 6/248 (4)   2/130 (1) 3/183 (4)
7/292 (8) 8/295 (9) 9/296 (10) 10/324 (11)

Nel 17–3–71–2; Tremlett 15–1–36–1; Dernbach 17–3–68–5; Batty 34.4–5–113–2; Spriegel 4–0–18–0; Afzaal 2–0–5–0. *Second Innings*—Tremlett 9–2–28–0; Dernbach 12–2–33–1; Batty 22–4–65–1; Nel 5–4–5–0; Afzaal 14–0–42–1; Spriegel 3–0–8–0.

Umpires: M. J. D. Bodenham and R. A. Kettleborough.

At Northampton, May 24–27. SURREY beat NORTHAMPTONSHIRE by seven wickets. *Andre Nel and Jade Dernbach put on 118 for Surrey's tenth wicket in the first innings.*

At Cardiff, May 29–June 1. SURREY drew with GLAMORGAN.

SURREY v LEICESTERSHIRE

At The Oval, June 4–6. Leicestershire won by an innings and 60 runs. Leicestershire 23pts, Surrey 2pts. Toss: Leicestershire.

When Leicestershire had last beaten Surrey, 12 years previously at The Oval, it had sealed their second Championship title in three seasons: this time the two teams were propping up the second division table. Jefferson's commanding century, on a ground where his father Richard played with distinction more than four decades earlier, ensured that Leicestershire profited from winning the toss. He used his height to make finding the right length all but impossible for the bowlers, and reached his first Championship century since 2005 by sweeping Batty for six over square leg. Du Toit and New then cemented Leicestershire's position, despite the perseverance of Dernbach and Batty. When Surrey batted, only Afzaal had much answer to the bounce and increasing turn of Henderson once Davies and Ramprakash were parted. Following on 243 adrift, Surrey were undone by off-spinner Naik, who had never previously taken more than four wickets in an innings but now claimed seven: his mentor Henderson supported in miserly manner at the other end, and only cultured resistance from Younis Khan pushed the match much beyond tea on the third day. Leicestershire's victory appeared a delight to the ever-present fox at the Vauxhall End: his landlords, meanwhile, wondered if it could get any worse.

Close of play: First day, Leicestershire 337-4 (du Toit 72, New 15); Second day, Surrey 160-6 (Afzaal 25, Schofield 3).

Leicestershire

W. I. Jefferson c Batty b Schofield	135	*M. J. Hoggard not out	1
M. A. G. Boyce lbw b Dernbach	0	H. F. Gurney c and b Batty	2
P. A. Nixon b Tremlett	41		
J. W. A. Taylor b Batty	63	B 4, l-b 9, w 1, n-b 8	22
J. du Toit c Davies b Dernbach	81		
†T. J. New c Davies b Dernbach	91	1/6 (2) 2/111 (3) (142.2 overs)	479
J. K. H. Naik b Dernbach	34	3/229 (1) 4/269 (4) 5/359 (5)	
C. W. Henderson b Dernbach	9	6/457 (7) 7/471 (6) 8/476 (9)	
N. L. Buck c Hamilton-Brown b Batty	0	9/476 (8) 10/479 (11) 110 overs: 376-5	

Tremlett 28–6–69–1; Dernbach 32–7–87–5; Batty 35.2–4–122–3; Meaker 16–1–87–0; Schofield 19–2–69–1; Younis Khan 7–0–17–0; Hamilton-Brown 1–0–3–0; Afzaal 4–0–12–0.

Surrey

†S. M. Davies c Naik b Henderson	69	– lbw b Buck	5
A. Harinath c Jefferson b Gurney	4	– c Jefferson b Naik	15
M. R. Ramprakash c Jefferson b Henderson	30	– b Naik	20
Younis Khan c and b Buck	3	– not out	77
U. Afzaal c New b Henderson	54	– lbw b Naik	0
*R. J. Hamilton-Brown c and b Henderson	13	– b Henderson	8
G. J. Batty c Taylor b Naik	0	– lbw b Naik	4
C. P. Schofield c New b Henderson	29	– c Boyce b Henderson	7
S. C. Meaker run out	13	– c Boyce b Naik	1
C. T. Tremlett not out	7	– b Naik	12
J. W. Dernbach c New b Henderson	0	– b Naik	16
B 5, l-b 5, n-b 4	14	B 4, l-b 13, w 1	18

1/6 (2) 2/110 (1) 3/111 (3)   (76.5 overs) 236   1/7 (1) 2/48 (2)   (69 overs) 183
4/125 (4) 5/156 (6) 6/157 (7)   3/57 (3) 4/59 (5) 5/74 (6)
7/202 (8) 8/219 (5) 9/236 (9) 10/236 (11)   6/93 (7) 7/100 (8) 8/111 (9)
                                          9/137 (10) 10/183 (11)

Hoggard 5–1–27–0; Gurney 15–3–42–1; Buck 11–5–36–1; Naik 15–3–37–1; Henderson 30.5–8–84–6. *Second Innings*—Gurney 5–1–21–0; Buck 6–4–3–1; Hoggard 7–6–1–0; Henderson 28–10–45–2; Naik 23–3–96–7.

Umpires: P. J. Hartley and J. F. Steele.

At Chesterfield, June 28–July 1. SURREY beat DERBYSHIRE by 42 runs.

SURREY v NORTHAMPTONSHIRE

At The Oval, July 20–22. Surrey won by an innings and 175 runs. Surrey 24pts, Northamptonshire 3pts. Toss: Surrey. Championship debut: T. J. Lancefield.

Surrey's first Championship victory at The Oval for almost three years came in emphatic manner. Ramprakash again supplied the backbone, driving deliciously on the way to his 17th double-century – his 12th for Surrey, one behind Jack Hobbs's record – seemingly unperturbed at being abused outside the ground after the first day in a road-rage incident. Northamptonshire's bowlers gave him fewer problems, Chigumbura apart. Hamilton-Brown, in cavalier mood, dominated as 100 runs were piled on in the hour after lunch on the first day. He had an early escape, as did Spriegel, before settling in for the sixth-wicket stand of 182 with Ramprakash which surpassed Alan Peach and Percy Fender's unbroken alliance of 171 at Northampton 90 years earlier, when Fender hammered first-class cricket's fastest-ever century in 35 minutes. Wakely alone looked comfortable in the reply, as Batty's first five-for of the season built on the speed and hostility of Surrey's pacemen. Northamptonshire's follow-on started smoothly, but they lost four wickets at 96 – including Sales for his third duck in four Championship innings against his native county in 2010 – as Tremlett, finding lift from a good length, grabbed three in nine balls: not a run was scored for 35 minutes. Meaker helped finish off insipid opponents, with remarkable catches by Nel and Afzaal capping an overwhelming victory.

Close of play: First day, Surrey 430-5 (Ramprakash 137, Spriegel 85); Second day, Northamptonshire 174-8 (Murphy 5, Lucas 0).

Surrey

T. J. Lancefield c Murphy b Chigumbura	31	G. J. Batty not out	48
†S. M. Davies c Middlebrook b Lucas	5		
M. R. Ramprakash c Peters b Hall	248	B 4, l-b 13, w 3, n-b 24	44
*R. J. Hamilton-Brown c Hall b Chigumbura	103		
U. Afzaal c and b Brooks	7	1/13 (2) (7 wkts dec, 134 overs) 620	
S. J. Walters c Murphy b Chigumbura	31	2/61 (1) 3/225 (4) 4/239 (5)	
M. N. W. Spriegel c Murphy b Chigumbura	103	5/284 (6) 6/466 (7) 7/620 (3) 110 overs: 482-6	

A. Nel, C. T. Tremlett and S. C. Meaker did not bat.

Lucas 30–5–146–1; Brooks 20–1–116–1; Chigumbura 29–4–100–4; Hall 21–1–81–1; Middlebrook 32–3–132–0; Wakely 2–0–28–0.

Northamptonshire

S. D. Peters c Davies b Batty	41	– c Spriegel b Nel	50
B. H. N. Howgego c Davies b Nel	12	– b Tremlett	45
A. G. Wakely c Davies b Batty	50	– c Nel b Meaker	7
D. J. Sales c Davies b Meaker	7	– c Nel b Tremlett	0
R. A. White c Walters b Nel	16	– b Tremlett	0
E. Chigumbura b Tremlett	23	– c Walters b Meaker	25
*A. J. Hall lbw b Tremlett	0	– c Lancefield b Meaker	2
†D. Murphy not out	18	– b Meaker	8
J. D. Middlebrook lbw b Batty	13	– c Ramprakash b Afzaal	36
D. S. Lucas lbw b Batty	13	– c Afzaal b Batty	14
J. A. Brooks c Meaker b Batty	36	– not out	6
L-b 8, w 1, n-b 2	11	B 4, l-b 6, w 2	12

1/15 (2) 2/94 (3) 3/113 (4) (68.5 overs) 240
4/115 (1) 5/154 (6) 6/154 (7)
7/158 (5) 8/174 (9) 9/198 (10) 10/240 (11)

1/96 (1) 2/96 (2) (67.3 overs) 205
3/96 (4) 4/96 (5) 5/113 (3)
6/117 (7) 7/140 (6) 8/151 (8)
9/186 (10) 10/205 (9)

Nel 11–6–23–2; Tremlett 15–3–38–2; Meaker 21–6–95–1; Batty 20.5–4–76–5; Afzaal 1–1–0–0.
Second Innings—Nel 17–7–36–1; Tremlett 17–6–34–3; Meaker 13–2–59–4; Batty 13–3–47–1; Afzaal 7.3–1–19–1.

Umpires: N. G. C. Cowley and B. Dudleston.

At Lord's, July 29–31. SURREY lost to MIDDLESEX by an innings and 44 runs.

SURREY v SUSSEX

At Guildford, August 9–12. Drawn. Surrey 8pts, Sussex 7pts. Toss: Surrey. First-class debut: W. A. Adkin.

Yardy's only century of the season finally shut the door on Surrey. Sussex had been under pressure since Tremlett had taken advantage of a grassy pitch, extracting considerable lift and claiming three for four in 11 balls on the first morning. The addition of 116 for the final three wickets owed much to Sussex's debutant Will Adkin, a 6ft 9in Surrey-born academy all-rounder given his chance by injuries: he supported Rayner's initial fightback then grew in stature, batting more than two hours for his 45. The loss of the second day made Surrey's task much harder, and they handicapped themselves further with some careless shots, which restricted their lead to 75 after they had pulled ahead with only four wickets down: Panesar removed Davies and Walters, then Yasir Arafat made excellent use of the second new ball. Two wickets by Meaker on the third evening gave Surrey fresh hope and, when Goodwin played on to him shortly before lunch, Sussex were only 19 ahead with five wickets left. Yardy was dropped once, but in typically unfussy style constructed the highest stand of the match, 108 with Ben Brown, to ensure safety.

Close of play: First day, Surrey 47-0 (Lancefield 20, Harinath 19); Second day, No play; Third day, Sussex 39-2 (Joyce 16, Thornely 0).

Sussex

E. C. Joyce c Hamilton-Brown b Tremlett	0	– b Batty	40
C. D. Nash c Lancefield b Batty	21	– lbw b Meaker	22
M. A. Thornely b Tremlett	1	– (4) c Ramprakash b Tremlett	0
M. W. Goodwin lbw b Tremlett	0	– (5) b Meaker	23
*M. H. Yardy c Walters b Batty	18	– (6) not out	100
†B. C. Brown lbw b Dernbach	18	– (7) c Davies b Meaker	52
Yasir Arafat c Harinath b Batty	23	– (8) not out	23
O. P. Rayner c Batty b Spriegel	47		
W. A. Adkin c Walters b Tremlett	45		
M. S. Panesar not out	20	– (3) lbw b Meaker	0
C. D. Collymore b Dernbach	2		
B 6, l-b 4, w 2, n-b 10	22	B 5, l-b 8, n-b 2	15

1/0 (1) 2/12 (3) 3/12 (4) 4/44 (2)   (76.1 overs) 217
5/47 (5) 6/87 (6) 7/101 (7) 8/160 (8)
9/201 (9) 10/217 (11)

1/38 (2)   (6 wkts dec, 88 overs) 275
2/38 (3) 3/39 (4)
4/82 (1) 5/94 (5) 6/202 (7)

Tremlett 18–5–32–4; Dernbach 12.1–2–34–2; Meaker 17–3–42–0; Batty 22–2–81–3; Spriegel 7–0–18–1. *Second Innings*—Tremlett 16–5–45–1; Dernbach 19.1–4–49–0; Meaker 26–5–86–4; Hamilton-Brown 2.5–0–8–0; Batty 16–3–42–1; Spriegel 7–0–23–0; Lancefield 1–0–9–0.

Surrey

T. J. Lancefield c Joyce b Adkin	37	
A. Harinath c Joyce b Collymore	20	
M. R. Ramprakash b Yasir Arafat	21	
*R. J. Hamilton-Brown c Goodwin b Yasir Arafat	22	
†S. M. Davies lbw b Panesar	62	
S. J. Walters c Rayner b Panesar	45	
M. N. W. Spriegel lbw b Rayner	1	
G. J. Batty c Thornely b Yasir Arafat	19	
C. T. Tremlett c Rayner b Yasir Arafat	28
S. C. Meaker not out	9
J. W. Dernbach c Rayner b Yasir Arafat	0
B 4, l-b 9, w 1, n-b 14	28

1/64 (2) 2/90 (1) 3/115 (3)   (98.1 overs) 292
4/130 (4) 5/219 (5) 6/228 (7)
7/232 (6) 8/283 (8) 9/284 (9) 10/292 (11)

Yasir Arafat 21.1–3–81–5; Collymore 25–8–54–1; Adkin 11–2–38–1; Panesar 24–8–50–2; Thornely 3–0–15–0; Rayner 13–2–33–1; Nash 1–0–8–0.

Umpires: S. A. Garratt and J. F. Steele.

At Worcester, August 16–19. SURREY lost to WORCESTERSHIRE by 238 runs.

At Leicester, August 24–27. SURREY drew with LEICESTERSHIRE.

SURREY v GLAMORGAN

At The Oval, September 7–10. Drawn. Surrey 10pts, Glamorgan 8pts. Toss: Surrey.

Stiff resistance on the final afternoon ultimately cost Glamorgan promotion. When Surrey lurched to 21 for five in their second innings on a blameless pitch, following Harris's blast of four for 18 in ten overs and some careless batting, Glamorgan looked almost certain winners. The culprits included Pietersen, who walked across a straight delivery to finish with one run on his Championship debut for his third county – he lasted two balls in the first innings and 23 in the second. But a stand of 124 between Schofield and Wilson ended any prospect of a victory which would have all but guaranteed Glamorgan the runners-up spot with a match to spare. Rain filleted 100 overs from the first three days, although Surrey's batting on the first shone brilliantly in the form of Jason Roy, whose second Championship appearance confirmed the excellent impression left by his first at Leicester, and some scintillating off-side strokes from Hamilton-Brown, who hit six fours and six sixes from 84 balls. The guileful Cosker was the only bowler to keep them quiet. Glamorgan were in danger of following on as Tremlett's bounce was matched by Meaker allying pace and away movement for his second Oval five-for of the season, until Allenby shepherded the tail intelligently.

Close of play: First day, Surrey 324-6 (Schofield 32, Batty 29); Second day, Glamorgan 72-2 (Dalrymple 15, Wright 16); Third day, Glamorgan 273-9 (Allenby 65, Waters 16).

Surrey

T. J. Lancefield c Maynard b Harris	18	– c Wright b Harris	6
J. J. Roy b Cosker	69	– c Cosker b Waters	8
M. R. Ramprakash b Cosker	40	– c Maynard b Harris	0
K. P. Pietersen lbw b Cosker	0	– lbw b Harris	1
*R. J. Hamilton-Brown st Wallace b Cosker	96	– b Harris	6
†G. C. Wilson b Cosgrove	39	– c Wright b Croft	45
C. P. Schofield b Harris	63	– st Wallace b Dalrymple	90
G. J. Batty b Allenby	34	– not out	32
C. T. Tremlett c Wallace b Harris	15	– not out	0
S. C. Meaker c Wallace b Allenby	1		
J. W. Dernbach not out	2		
L-b 3	3	B 5, l-b 9, w 2, n-b 2	18

1/40 (1) 2/119 (2) 3/119 (4)   (95.5 overs) 380
4/136 (3) 5/263 (6) 6/263 (5)
7/340 (8) 8/369 (9) 9/378 (7) 10/380 (10)

1/14 (1)   (7 wkts dec, 75 overs) 206
2/14 (2) 3/14 (3) 4/20 (5)
5/21 (4) 6/145 (6) 7/199 (7)

Harris 27–6–120–3; Waters 17–2–74–0; Allenby 17.5–1–70–2; Cosker 17–4–48–4; Croft 10–2–41–0; Cosgrove 4–1–12–1; Dalrymple 3–0–12–0. *Second Innings*—Harris 14–5–36–4; Waters 9–3–16–1; Allenby 10–4–14–0; Croft 21–4–54–1; Cosker 9–1–27–0; Cosgrove 4–0–17–0; Dalrymple 7–0–25–1; Rees 1–0–3–0.

Glamorgan

G. P. Rees lbw b Tremlett	4	R. D. B. Croft c Wilson b Meaker	8
M. J. Cosgrove b Meaker	26	D. A. Cosker c Batty b Tremlett	21
*J. W. M. Dalrymple c Batty b Meaker	25	H. T. Waters lbw b Dernbach	16
B. J. Wright c Schofield b Tremlett	17	B 4, l-b 11, n-b 6	21
T. L. Maynard c Batty b Meaker	61		
J. Allenby not out	68	1/20 (1) 2/38 (2) 3/73 (4) (82 overs) 276
†M. A. Wallace b Schofield	0	4/97 (3) 5/184 (5) 6/185 (7)
J. A. R. Harris lbw b Meaker	9	7/194 (8) 8/204 (9) 9/237 (10) 10/276 (11)

Tremlett 17–4–53–3; Dernbach 20–7–46–1; Meaker 24–1–97–5; Batty 9–2–23–0; Roy 2–0–12–0; Schofield 10–1–30–1.

Umpires: M. J. D. Bodenham and N. G. B. Cook.

At Bristol, September 13–16. SURREY beat GLOUCESTERSHIRE by ten runs.

SUSSEX

Hungry return to the top table

Bruce Talbot

The hallmark of a good team is surely one which can maintain success even in a period of transition. Sussex won their 11th trophy in 12 years in 2010 and, although the second division title was their minimum requirement, it was achieved with a significantly different team from that which had won most of the other ten.

When Sussex won their third Championship in five seasons in 2007, they did so using 17 players. Three years later, only nine of those survived in the squad of 22 that clinched their return to Division One at the first attempt, including one who had retired mid-season.

Acting-captain Murray Goodwin's reluctance to spray champagne around when he received the trophy was understandable. Tenth out of 18, in effect, represented their joint lowest finish since they were bottom in 2000. But, while cricket manager Mark Robinson insisted that Sussex had no right to be a top-flight county on their meagre resources, this was their first season in the second tier since 2001. It felt right when they returned to Division One.

Sussex won their first four games, then lost the next two, before regrouping in the second half of the season with four more victories; the title was secured with a match to spare. It was a commendable performance, given the sparing contributions of four key players. Captain Mike Yardy, Luke Wright and Ed Joyce each missed seven of the 16 games, and Matt Prior nine. While Wright's and Prior's England calls were expected, few had foreseen that Yardy would resurrect his international career, or that Joyce's summer would be badly curtailed by injury and illness.

For the second season running, just two players passed 1,000 runs – Murray Goodwin and Chris Nash, who made three scores of 150-plus in the second half of the summer. Goodwin rediscovered his form after a disappointing 2009 and captained intelligently in Yardy's absence, while Nash came good after struggling on seamer-friendly surfaces early on. Michael Thornely, who was released, and Joe Gatting failed to make the most of their opportunities. But Ben Brown, who scored his maiden Championship hundred in the massacre of Derbyshire at Horsham, took his chance at No. 3, although he still regarded himself predominantly as a wicketkeeper-batsman.

When the top order was exposed, Sussex's lower end consistently dug them out of trouble. The division's highest partnerships for each of the seventh, eighth and ninth wickets all came from a combination of Murray Goodwin, Naved-ul-Hasan and Robin Martin-Jenkins, whose demob-happy form before he bowed out in July was the most consistent of his 15-year career. James Kirtley, another cornerstone of a decade of success, also retired in September. He played only limited-overs cricket in 2010, but had the immense satisfaction

Graham Morris

Robin Martin-Jenkins

of bowling Kevin Pietersen with a trademark in-swinging yorker for his final wicket.

Sussex rediscovered how to bowl teams out twice, something that had been a problem in the immediate post-Mushtaq Ahmed era. In 30 Championship innings, the opposition were dismissed 23 times, on 15 occasions for under 250, while Sussex conceded 350 or more only twice. Compare that to 2009, when their opponents reached 350 ten times.

Former West Indian international Corey Collymore's consistency brought him 57 wickets, and he would have had a few more had Sussex's slip catching been less fallible. His departure to Middlesex – he wanted to be in London for family reasons – left a gaping hole in the attack although Amjad Khan, recruited from Kent, looked an ideal replacement.

The emergence of left-armer Lewis Hatchett was an unexpected bonus. Hatchett was not considered good enough for second-team cricket two years ago, but he worked prodigiously, took his maiden five-for in his second Championship game and was rewarded with a three-year contract.

In his first season at Hove, Monty Panesar rediscovered his mojo with 52 wickets, the second-most by an English-qualified spinner, and earned himself a recall to the Ashes squad. Panesar's fielding and batting also improved, although his rehabilitation seemed to remain a work in progress.

If Championship promotion was the priority, it was still disappointing that Sussex failed to defend either of their one-day trophies. They started their Twenty20 defence with eight wins out of nine before key personnel dropped out of the team for a variety of reasons. Only two of the side that had won the 2009 final were absent for the quarter-final, but by then Sussex had run out of steam and their exit was no surprise. Crowds and revenue increased, so they were among those counties keen to retain eight home games in 2011. The absence of a quarter-final round left little room for error in the Clydesdale Bank 40. Sussex finished second in their group, but that was not enough; they were always struggling to reach the semis after being embarrassed by the part-time Unicorns.

Sussex were matching progress on the field beyond the boundary. The second phase of the redevelopment of the County Ground began in the autumn. The £5m scheme was to see the Sea End transformed, with new stands and facilities, while a refurbishment of the pavilion and improvements to the players' dressing-rooms were all due to be completed in time for the start of the 2011 season. "We will have a ground fit for purpose," declared chairman Jim May. The same could be said of a team whose hunger for trophies shows no sign of weakening.

SUSSEX RESULTS

All first-class matches – Played 17: Won 9, Lost 3, Drawn 5.
County Championship matches – Played 16: Won 8, Lost 3, Drawn 5.

LV= County Championship, winners in Division 2;
Friends Provident T20, q-f; Clydesdale Bank 40, 2nd in Group A.

COUNTY CHAMPIONSHIP AVERAGES, BATTING AND FIELDING

Cap		M	I	NO	R	HS	100s	50s	Avge	Ct/St
2000	R. S. C. Martin-Jenkins......	9	13	3	629	130	2	5	62.90	4
2001	M. W. Goodwin¶...........	16	26	3	1,201	142	4	5	52.21	5
2009	E. C. Joyce	9	15	2	590	164	1	3	45.38	15
2007	L. J. Wright‡...............	9	12	1	465	134	1	3	42.27	3
2008	C. D. Nash†	16	27	2	1,029	184	3	1	41.16	10
	B. C. Brown†	8	12	1	404	112	1	2	36.72	6/1
	Yasir Arafat	9	9	2	255	58	0	2	36.42	1
	Naved-ul-Hasan§	5	8	2	208	101	1	1	34.66	0
2005	M. H. Yardy‡	9	13	2	345	100*	1	1	31.36	12
2003	M. J. Prior‡..............	7	11	1	296	123*	1	0	29.60	19
	A. J. Hodd†...............	10	14	1	319	109	1	1	24.53	29/1
	M. A. Thornely	12	21	1	467	89	0	4	23.35	8
	O. P. Rayner	6	8	1	135	47	0	0	19.28	3
	J. S. Gatting†	7	9	0	124	24	0	0	13.77	3
	J. E. Anyon	10	15	0	174	34	0	0	11.60	3
2010	M. S. Panesar	15	19	5	154	46*	0	0	11.00	1
	C. D. Collymore¶.........	14	17	8	78	19*	0	0	8.66	3
	L. J. Hatchett†...........	3	4	0	30	20	0	0	7.50	1

Also batted: W. A. Adkin (1 match) 45; R. G. Aga¶ (1 match) 0; W. A. T. Beer† (1 match) 37* (1 ct); L. W. P. Wells† (1 match) 62, 8.

† *Born in Sussex.* ‡ *ECB contract.* § *Official overseas player.* ¶ *Other non-England-qualified player.*

BOWLING

	O	M	R	W	BB	5W/i	Avge
R. S. C. Martin-Jenkins	201.1	35	593	30	5-45	1	19.76
C. D. Collymore	414	115	1,133	57	6-48	2	19.87
Yasir Arafat	256	43	896	36	5-74	2	24.88
L. J. Wright......................	154.5	22	573	23	5-65	1	24.91
M. S. Panesar	516.2	135	1,328	52	5-44	2	25.53
Naved-ul-Hasan	162.4	44	532	20	4-28	0	26.60
J. E. Anyon	192.2	29	696	26	3-23	0	26.76
O. P. Rayner	118.3	32	334	12	3-24	0	27.83

Also bowled: W. A. Adkin 11–2–38–1; R. G. Aga 7–1–38–0; W. A. T. Beer 14.4–3–61–3; L. J. Hatchett 52.2–11–207–8; C. D. Nash 49–8–115–7; M. A. Thornely 21–2–75–4; L. W. P. Wells 2–0–16–0.

LEADING CB40 AVERAGES (100 runs/4 wickets)

Batting	Runs	HS	Avge	S-R	Ct/St
M. H. Yardy.......	216	66*	72.00	127.81	3
L. J. Wright	149	95	49.66	133.03	2
E. C. Joyce.......	299	117	42.71	107.55	1
C. D. Nash	457	85	41.54	105.29	3
M. W. Goodwin....	402	92*	40.20	113.23	1
A. J. Hodd	225	91	37.50	107.65	7/6

Bowling	W	BB	Avge	E-R
R. J. Kirtley	24	4-30	19.83	6.55
Naved-ul-Hasan ...	7	3-37	21.71	5.24
L. J. Wright	4	3-41	24.25	9.23
C. J. Liddle	5	4-49	25.20	7.00
C. B. Keegan	9	2-23	27.33	6.50
M. S. Panesar.....	11	2-11	35.00	4.93

LEADING FPT20 AVERAGES (100 runs/18 overs)

Batting	Runs	HS	Avge	S-R	Ct/St	Bowling	W	BB	Avge	E-R
M. J. Prior	443	117	34.07	169.08	6	M. H. Yardy	8	2-14	19.87	**5.48**
L. J. Wright	155	39	19.37	146.22	1	C. D. Nash	13	2-17	17.38	**6.84**
B. B. McCullum. . .	200	59*	33.33	145.98	4	W. A. T. Beer. . . .	10	3-19	26.80	**7.24**
D. R. Smith	215	49	19.54	139.61	4	C. B. Keegan	12	3-11	26.58	**7.87**
J. S. Gatting	157	30*	15.70	134.18	6	R. J. Kirtley	13	3-3	32.53	**8.10**
A. J. Hodd	131	26	18.71	128.43	1/3	D. R. Smith	8	2-19	34.50	**8.19**

FIRST-CLASS COUNTY RECORDS

Highest score for	344*	M. W. Goodwin v Somerset at Taunton	2009
Highest score against	322	E. Paynter (Lancashire) at Hove	1937
Leading run-scorer	34,150	J. G. Langridge (avge 37.69)	1928–1955
Best bowling for	10-48	C. H. G. Bland v Kent at Tonbridge	1899
Best bowling against	9-11	A. P. Freeman (Kent) at Hove	1922
Leading wicket-taker	2,211	M. W. Tate (avge 17.41)	1912–1937
Highest total for	742-5 dec	v Somerset at Taunton	2009
Highest total against	726	by Nottinghamshire at Nottingham	1895
Lowest total for {	19	v Surrey at Godalming	1830
{	19	v Nottinghamshire at Hove	1873
Lowest total against	18	by Kent at Gravesend	1867

LIST A COUNTY RECORDS

Highest score for	163	C. J. Adams v Middlesex at Arundel	1999
Highest score against	198*	G. A. Gooch (Essex) at Hove	1982
Leading run-scorer	7,969	A. P. Wells (avge 31.62)	1981–1996
Best bowling for	7-41	A. N. Jones v Nottinghamshire at Nottingham	1986
Best bowling against	8-21	M. A. Holding (Derbyshire) at Hove	1988
Leading wicket-taker	370	R. J. Kirtley (avge 22.35)	1995–2010
Highest total for	384-9	v Ireland at Belfast	1996
Highest total against	377-9	by Somerset at Hove	2003
Lowest total for	49	v Derbyshire at Chesterfield	1969
Lowest total against	36	by Leicestershire at Leicester	1973

TWENTY20 RECORDS

Highest score for	117	M. J. Prior v Glamorgan at Hove	**2010**
Highest score against	152*	G. R. Napier (Essex) at Chelmsford	2008
Leading run-scorer	1,606	M. W. Goodwin (avge 28.67)	2003–2010
Best bowling for	5-11	Mushtaq Ahmed v Essex at Hove	2005
Best bowling against	5-14	A. D. Mascarenhas (Hampshire) at Hove.	2004
Leading wicket-taker	64	R. J. Kirtley (avge 25.89)	2003–2010
Highest total for	239-5	v Glamorgan at Hove.	**2010**
Highest total against	242-3	by Essex at Chelmsford	2008
Lowest total for	67	v Hampshire at Hove	2004
Lowest total against	85	by Hampshire at Southampton	2008

ADDRESS

County Ground, Eaton Road, Hove BN3 3AN (01273 827100; **email** info@sussexcricket.co.uk).
Website www.sussexcricket.co.uk

OFFICIALS

Captain M. H. Yardy   **Chief executive** D. G. Brooks
Professional cricket manager M. A. Robinson   **Chairman, cricket committee** J. R. T. Barclay
Academy director K. Greenfield   **Head groundsman** A. Mackay
President B. Bedson   **Scorer** M. J. Charman
Chairman J. R. May

At Cardiff, April 9–12. SUSSEX beat GLAMORGAN by 201 runs.

SUSSEX v SURREY

At Hove, April 15–18. Sussex won by ten wickets. Sussex 23pts, Surrey 3pts. Toss: Sussex. County debut: Iftikhar Anjum.

Hamilton-Brown's return to Hove could barely have gone much worse. Not only were his side roundly beaten but he trooped off after scoring 36 and 11 to choruses of "Cheerio, cheerio" from Sussex supporters, not in a forgiving mood following his winter move back to The Oval. In a final ignominy, he departed on crutches, having been struck on the foot by a yorker from Wright during Surrey's second-innings collapse. The decisive periods came at either end of the third day. Sussex led by 86 with two wickets standing when Naved-ul-Hasan, beginning another spell with the county, joined Martin-Jenkins for the day's seventh over. When they were parted 21 overs later, the advantage was a distant 210. Naved then joined Wright in wrecking Surrey's middle order with high-class pace and swing. Five wickets went down for 30, Sussex claimed the extra half-hour, but they had to wait until 35 minutes into Sunday morning to celebrate victory. A handful of protesters gathered outside the Tate Gates on the opening day, angry at the club hiring a marksman to shoot a fox that had been gnawing at the covers. There was scratching around of a different kind by Harinath, who laboured over the slowest recorded half-century in Championship history, from 233 balls, eight more than Sussex's Jamie Hall at The Oval 16 years earlier. Even Ramprakash, who had scored ten centuries against Sussex, was subdued, perhaps distracted by the announcement during the match that he and his wife were to divorce.

Close of play: First day, Surrey 199-7 (Schofield 44, Nel 1); Second day, Sussex 278-7 (Panesar 0); Third day, Surrey 243-9 (Iftikhar Anjum 16, Dernbach 1).

Surrey

M. N. W. Spriegel c Hodd b Naved-ul-Hasan	4	– (2) lbw b Collymore	0
A. Harinath c Wright b Martin-Jenkins	62	– (1) b Collymore	17
M. R. Ramprakash lbw b Martin-Jenkins	5	– lbw b Wright	14
U. Afzaal b Martin-Jenkins	0	– c Goodwin b Wright	87
*R. J. Hamilton-Brown c Yardy b Naved-ul-Hasan	36	– (6) b Naved-ul-Hasan	11
†S. M. Davies c Yardy b Panesar	1	– (5) c Yardy b Wright	37
G. J. Batty c Hodd b Martin-Jenkins	23	– b Naved-ul-Hasan	9
C. P. Schofield lbw b Martin-Jenkins	46	– lbw b Panesar	13
A. Nel b Naved-ul-Hasan	1	– c Thornely b Naved-ul-Hasan	0
Iftikhar Anjum lbw b Naved-ul-Hasan	0	– not out	16
J. W. Dernbach not out	1	– c Yardy b Panesar	1
B 1, l-b 10, n-b 15	26	B 6, l-b 3, n-b 29	38

1/6 (1) 2/15 (3) 3/15 (4) 4/80 (5) (99.1 overs) 205
5/81 (6) 6/136 (7) 7/198 (2)
8/199 (9) 9/199 (10) 10/205 (8)

1/0 (2) 2/35 (1) (77.4 overs) 243
3/35 (3) 4/173 (5)
5/178 (4) 6/196 (7) 7/203 (6)
8/203 (9) 9/233 (8) 10/243 (11)

Naved-ul-Hasan 20–8–28–4; Collymore 19–7–27–0; Martin-Jenkins 19.1–4–45–5; Wright 16–4–48–0; Panesar 23–8–44–1; Nash 2–1–2–0. *Second Innings*—Naved-ul-Hasan 18–3–89–3; Collymore 10–4–16–2; Wright 15–1–44–3; Panesar 25.4–7–54–2; Martin-Jenkins 5–1–18–0; Nash 4–0–13–0.

Sussex

*M. H. Yardy lbw b Schofield	68	– not out	17
C. D. Nash lbw b Nel	1	– not out	12
J. S. Gatting c Spriegel b Iftikhar Anjum	15		
M. W. Goodwin b Batty	74		
L. J. Wright c Schofield b Iftikhar Anjum	63		
M. A. Thornely b Dernbach	32		
†A. J. Hodd b Dernbach	7		
M. S. Panesar lbw b Dernbach	0		
R. S. C. Martin-Jenkins c Spriegel b Dernbach	64		
Naved-ul-Hasan not out	68		
C. D. Collymore c Nel b Spriegel	0		
B 6, l-b 6, n-b 12	24	B 4	4

1/1 (2) 2/26 (3) 3/143 (4)   (117.3 overs) 416   (no wkt, 6.4 overs) 33
4/191 (1) 5/241 (5) 6/271 (6) 7/278 (6)
8/291 (8) 9/415 (9) 10/416 (11)   110 overs: 358–8

Nel 28–9–79–1; Iftikhar Anjum 24–4–87–2; Dernbach 29–11–65–4; Batty 16–0–90–1; Schofield 19–3–78–1; Spriegel 1.3–0–5–1. *Second Innings*—Dernbach 3.4–0–20–0; Batty 3–1–9–0.

Umpires: M. R. Benson and J. H. Evans.

At Bristol, April 21–23. SUSSEX beat GLOUCESTERSHIRE by 207 runs.

SUSSEX v LEICESTERSHIRE

At Hove, April 27–29. Sussex won by ten wickets. Sussex 23pts, Leicestershire 3pts. Toss: Sussex. Championship debut: A. B. McDonald.

Little went Leicestershire's way from the moment Hoggard was sick on the outfield before play and withdrew; Australian all-rounder Andrew McDonald captained on his county debut. Battling against surface moisture, Leicestershire lost ten wickets in 27 overs and then allowed Goodwin, with his 60th first-class hundred, and Naved, with his fifth, to bat them out of contention on the second morning, when an attack that badly missed Hoggard leaked 166 runs. Naved beat Goodwin to his hundred by two balls despite giving him a head start of 22 overs. Leicestershire, 278 behind, made a better fist of their second innings. Nixon relished the battle more than most, particularly against Panesar, with whom he enjoyed an intriguing duel until he reverse-swept once too often. Panesar bowled beautifully, while Goodwin's hunches invariably paid off. Three bowling changes on the last day promptly produced wickets; he was, though, reprimanded for excessive appealing.

Close of play: First day, Sussex 213-7 (Goodwin 59, Naved-ul-Hasan 35); Second day, Leicestershire 226-3 (Nixon 68, McDonald 36).

Leicestershire

W. I. Jefferson b Naved-ul-Hasan	27	– c Nash b Anyon	44
M. A. G. Boyce lbw b Martin-Jenkins	18	– c Prior b Anyon	28
P. A. Nixon c Hodd b Naved-ul-Hasan	0	– lbw b Panesar	93
J. W. A. Taylor c Hodd b Martin-Jenkins	6	– lbw b Anyon	24
*A. B. McDonald lbw b Anyon	4	– c Nash b Panesar	47
J. J. Cobb c Nash b Anyon	2	– c and b Nash	47
†T. J. New c Martin-Jenkins b Collymore	18	– lbw b Panesar	1
W. A. White lbw b Naved-ul-Hasan	11	– lbw b Collymore	47
C. W. Henderson b Collymore	3	– b Naved-ul-Hasan	1
N. L. Buck lbw b Naved-ul-Hasan	1	– not out	8
A. J. Harris not out	0	– b Collymore	1
L-b 2, n-b 22	24	B 1, l-b 17, n-b 18	36

1/38 (1) 2/44 (3) 3/54 (2) 4/61 (5)   (35.3 overs) 114   1/76 (1) 2/91 (2)   (111.1 overs) 338
5/67 (6) 6/67 (4) 7/86 (8) 8/91 (9)   3/156 (4) 4/251 (5)
9/100 (10) 10/114 (7)   5/266 (6) 6/271 (7) 7/291 (3)
                                                                 8/310 (9) 9/336 (8) 10/338 (11)

Naved-ul-Hasan 11–2–49–4; Collymore 9.3–2–32–2; Martin-Jenkins 8–4–15–2; Anyon 7–2–16–2. *Second Innings*—Naved-ul-Hasan 24–6–95–1; Collymore 19.1–3–37–2; Anyon 17–3–63–3; Martin-Jenkins 17–5–35–0; Panesar 29–6–77–3; Nash 5–0–13–1.

Sussex

M. A. Thornely c Jefferson b Harris	9	– (2) not out	29
J. E. Anyon c New b Buck	32		
J. S. Gatting c New b Henderson	21		
C. D. Nash lbw b McDonald	4	– (1) not out	27
*M. W. Goodwin lbw b McDonald	142		
M. J. Prior c Cobb b Buck	8		
†A. J. Hodd lbw b Buck	0		
R. S. C. Martin-Jenkins c Boyce b Henderson	15		
Naved-ul-Hasan c Nixon b McDonald	101		
M. S. Panesar c New b White	14		
C. D. Collymore not out	7		
B 6, l-b 5, w 8, n-b 20	39	B 2, l-b 5, w 1	8
	392	(no wkt, 13.3 overs)	**64**
(93.5 overs)			

1/19 (1) 2/61 (3) 3/68 (4) 4/82 (2)
5/92 (6) 6/112 (7) 7/161 (8)
8/325 (9) 9/372 (5) 10/392 (10)

Buck 22–6–70–3; Harris 19.5–5–77–1; McDonald 21–4–79–3; White 10.5–1–38–1; Henderson 18–2–89–2; Cobb 3–0–28–0. *Second Innings*—Buck 4–1–19–0; Harris 5–0–25–0; Henderson 3–1–4–0; White 1.3–0–9–0.

Umpires: G. D. Lloyd and G. Sharp.

SUSSEX v MIDDLESEX

At Hove, May 5–8. Middlesex won by three wickets. Middlesex 21pts, Sussex 4pts. Toss: Sussex. County debut: P. T. Collins.

Sussex strutted into this match with four Championship wins from four; despondent Middlesex had lost all theirs. But Strauss resumed the captaincy for this one match, Murtagh bowled superbly, and an elegant hundred by Malan took Middlesex to their target of 243 after they had been reduced to 78 for five. Sussex, tired and lackadaisical, seldom played like pacesetters. In choosing to bat, Goodwin underestimated how much assistance swinging conditions would provide the bowlers, and was fortunate to have Prior, cutting and pulling with murderous power, on hand after he was passed over for the World Twenty20. Prior was responsible for almost two-thirds of the runs scored by batsmen in Sussex's first innings. Middlesex chalked up a 79-run lead and, when Prior was fifth out, early on the third day, Sussex were only 39 ahead. The recovery was stoked by Hodd, who struck an aggressive hundred 364 days on from his last, and Panesar, who ran out of partners when a maiden fifty was in sight, then hammered home by Martin-Jenkins in a surge of three wickets in 14 balls. However, Sussex bowled poorly on the final day, dropped two catches – and Malan made them pay. Eighteen lbws were given in the match, one short of the first-class record (see Gloucestershire, page 435).

Close of play: First day, Middlesex 46-3 (Shah 9, Dexter 6); Second day, Sussex 113-4 (Prior 48, Hodd 6); Third day, Middlesex 122-5 (Malan 56, Berg 10).

Sussex

C. D. Nash lbw b Murtagh	0	– lbw b Collins	42
M. A. Thornely c Simpson b Murtagh	5	– lbw b Murtagh	15
J. S. Gatting b Berg	14	– c Strauss b Murtagh	0
*M. W. Goodwin c Strauss b Murtagh	17	– b O'Brien	0
†M. J. Prior not out	123	– c Smith b O'Brien	49
A. J. Hodd b Smith	9	– lbw b O'Brien	109
R. S. C. Martin-Jenkins lbw b Collins	0	– lbw b Murtagh	17
J. E. Anyon run out	6	– c Malan b Murtagh	19
Naved-ul-Hasan b Collins	6	– lbw b Murtagh	1
M. S. Panesar c Dexter b Berg	7	– not out	46
C. D. Collymore lbw b Berg	0	– lbw b Collins	13
B 10, l-b 6, w 8, n-b 6	30	B 1, l-b 9	10

1/0 (1) 2/11 (2) 3/28 (3) 4/80 (4)   (69.3 overs) 217
5/135 (6) 6/136 (7) 7/159 (8)
8/166 (9) 9/215 (10) 10/217 (11)

1/33 (2) 2/39 (3)   (92.5 overs) 321
3/44 (4) 4/84 (1)
5/118 (5) 6/154 (7) 7/219 (8)
8/223 (9) 9/288 (6) 10/321 (11)

Murtagh 19–7–32–3; O'Brien 17–2–50–0; Collins 12–2–39–2; Berg 13.3–1–45–3; Dexter 1–0–5–0; Smith 7–1–30–1. *Second Innings*—Murtagh 21–5–91–5; O'Brien 24–3–65–3; Collins 15.5–3–50–2; Berg 18–1–49–0; Smith 12–1–45–0; Malan 2–1–11–0.

Middlesex

S. A. Newman c Prior b Collymore	13	– lbw b Collymore	5
*A. J. Strauss c Prior b Naved-ul-Hasan	13	– lbw b Martin-Jenkins	23
O. A. Shah b Collymore	24	– b Collymore	4
D. J. Malan lbw b Collymore	0	– not out	100
N. J. Dexter lbw b Martin-Jenkins	80	– b Martin-Jenkins	8
†J. A. Simpson c Prior b Martin-Jenkins	45	– c Prior b Martin-Jenkins	0
G. K. Berg lbw b Panesar	60	– lbw b Martin-Jenkins	49
T. M. J. Smith lbw b Panesar	24	– c Prior b Anyon	8
T. J. Murtagh not out	13	– not out	9
I. E. O'Brien lbw b Collymore	0		
P. T. Collins lbw b Collymore	0		
B 7, l-b 10, w 1, n-b 6	24	B 6, l-b 5, w 2, n-b 19, p 5	37

1/30 (2) 2/40 (1) 3/40 (4) 4/89 (3)   (83.2 overs) 296
5/197 (5) 6/198 (6) 7/244 (8)
8/287 (7) 9/294 (10) 10/296 (11)

1/16 (1)   (7 wkts, 61.2 overs) 243
2/22 (3) 3/52 (2)
4/74 (5) 5/78 (6) 6/205 (7) 7/222 (8)

Naved-ul-Hasan 18–6–68–1; Collymore 15.2–1–67–5; Martin-Jenkins 14–3–31–2; Anyon 7–0–41–0; Panesar 25–7–65–2; Nash 4–2–7–0. *Second Innings*—Naved-ul-Hasan 20–6–49–0; Collymore 15–0–68–2; Martin-Jenkins 9–1–46–4; Panesar 13.2–2–52–0; Anyon 4–0–12–1.

Umpires: S. C. Gale and P. Willey.

At Cambridge, May 12–14. SUSSEX beat CAMBRIDGE MCCU by 84 runs (see Universities section).

At Northampton, May 18–20. SUSSEX lost to NORTHAMPTONSHIRE by three wickets.

SUSSEX v WORCESTERSHIRE

At Hove, May 24–27. Drawn. Sussex 8pts, Worcestershire 10pts. Toss: Worcestershire. County debut: S. H. Choudhry. Championship debut: B. C. Brown.

The loss of 65 overs to rain, including the entire fourth morning, rendered the last day an exercise in futility, but an outclassed Sussex were simply glad for respite after successive Championship defeats and a humbling in the Unicorns in the CB40 the day before this match began. The pitch lacked pace and bounce, and Worcestershire applied themselves diligently to set up a strong position, although Scott was denied his first hundred for nearly two years when he was beaten by a direct hit from Nash with only the last man Richardson for company. Richard Jones then bowled superbly in front of national selector Geoff Miller to claim career-best figures. He shifted Goodwin, but only after he had moved into joint seventh place on the list of Sussex century-makers (level with Jim and Harry Parks) with a sublime 42nd for them. On the day he announced his imminent retirement to become a schoolteacher, Martin-Jenkins counter-attacked impressively to save the follow-on with Yasir Arafat. The final day did not begin until 1.20, and a soporific conclusion was inevitable once Solanki declined to entertain a contrived run-chase.

Close of play: First day, Worcestershire 302-6 (Scott 24, Choudhry 11); Second day, Sussex 188-4 (Goodwin 109, Yardy 3); Third day, Worcestershire 76-2 (Solanki 12, Jones 3).

Worcestershire

D. K. H. Mitchell c Joyce b Collymore	9	– c Nash b Panesar	15
P. A. Jaques lbw b Collymore	80	– b Martin-Jenkins	40
*V. S. Solanki b Yasir Arafat	70	– b Thornely	61
M. M. Ali lbw b Martin-Jenkins	22	– (5) c Yardy b Thornely	21
A. N. Kervezee c Brown b Panesar	50	– (6) c Martin-Jenkins b Panesar	15
B. F. Smith c Joyce b Anyon	17	– (7) not out	7
†B. J. M. Scott run out	98	– (8) not out	4
S. H. Choudhry lbw b Panesar	63		
G. M. Andrew lbw b Martin-Jenkins	21		
R. A. Jones lbw b Yasir Arafat	5	– (4) c and b Collymore	11
A. Richardson not out	0		
B 6, l-b 9, n-b 14	29	B 21, l-b 3, w 1, n-b 6	31

1/31 (1) 2/168 (2) 3/191 (3)   (143.3 overs) 464   1/57 (1)   (6 wkts dec, 66 overs) 205
4/204 (4) 5/263 (5) 6/269 (6) 7/412 (8)   2/69 (2) 3/104 (4)
8/439 (9) 9/451 (10) 10/464 (7)   110 overs: 357-6   4/164 (5) 5/185 (3) 6/197 (6)

Yasir Arafat 24–3–112–2; Collymore 23–7–66–2; Martin-Jenkins 21–5–59–2; Anyon 18–2–62–1; Panesar 44.3–14–98–2; Wright 9–0–31–0; Nash 4–0–21–0. *Second Innings*—Yasir Arafat 9–1–31–0; Collymore 12.5–5–29–1; Martin-Jenkins 12–2–40–1; Panesar 16–4–47–2; Wright 6–0–12–0; Thornely 7–1–14–2; Nash 4–0–8–0.

Sussex

C. D. Nash c and b Jones	4	R. S. C. Martin-Jenkins not out	66
M. A. Thornely c Scott b Jones	4	Yasir Arafat c Jaques b Andrew	40
E. C. Joyce c Mitchell b Choudhry	67	C. D. Collymore c Scott b Jones	0
M. W. Goodwin c Scott b Jones	111	B 8, l-b 11	19
M. S. Panesar c and b Jones	0		
*M. H. Yardy c Richardson b Jones	3	1/8 (2) 2/13 (1) 3/182 (3) (82 overs) 328
L. J. Wright c Choudhry b Richardson	14	4/183 (5) 5/188 (6) 6/191 (4)
†B. C. Brown c Scott b Jones	0	7/193 (8) 8/217 (7) 9/327 (10) 10/328 (11)

Yardy and Wright replaced J. S. Gatting and J. E. Anyon after returning from England's reception at Downing Street.

Richardson 22–5–80–1; Jones 26–3–115–7; Choudhry 10–3–32–1; M. M. Ali 8–0–40–0; Andrew 16–1–42–1.

Umpires: N. G. B. Cook and N. G. C. Cowley.

At Derby, June 5–8. SUSSEX drew with DERBYSHIRE.

At Hove, July 3. SUSSEX beat BANGLADESHIS by 149 runs (see Bangladeshi tour section).

SUSSEX v GLOUCESTERSHIRE

At Arundel, July 7–9. Sussex won by eight wickets. Sussex 23pts, Gloucestershire 6pts. Toss: Gloucestershire.

Consigned to the second team and club cricket with Bexhill during Sussex's Twenty20 campaign, Panesar reappeared on a slow turner and produced his most devastating county performance for three years. Sussex's circumspect reply to 307 was buttressed by Martin-Jenkins who, having ground out an unbeaten 73 on day two, should have marked his final Championship appearance with a sixth career century; he promptly nicked Hussain to second slip next morning. Still, with help from Yasir Arafat's ebullient cameo, he carved out a lead of 82. Banerjee exploited the surface, but he was outperformed by fellow-left-arm spinner Panesar, who claimed his maiden Sussex five-for and his best match analysis since taking nine for 112, also against Gloucestershire, at Northampton in July 2007. Panesar looked an England bowler again as he and Rayner swept up the last seven wickets in 16 overs; the game was won on the third evening. Martin-Jenkins departed red-eyed to a standing ovation, and aggregate crowds of nearly 8,000 demonstrated the enduring appeal of the Arundel Festival.

Close of play: First day, Gloucestershire 286-9 (Hussain 3, Kirby 4); Second day, Sussex 314-6 (Martin-Jenkins 73, Yasir Arafat 18).

Gloucestershire

†J. N. Batty lbw b Yasir Arafat	4	– lbw b Panesar	3
Kadeer Ali c Martin-Jenkins b Panesar	58	– lbw b Yasir Arafat	0
C. D. J. Dent c Joyce b Panesar	35	– c Nash b Collymore	0
H. J. H. Marshall b Yasir Arafat	9	– not out	89
*A. P. R. Gidman lbw b Collymore	20	– c Thornely b Rayner	18
C. G. Taylor c Prior b Martin-Jenkins	89	– lbw b Panesar	0
J. E. C. Franklin lbw b Collymore	0	– c Nash b Panesar	4
J. Lewis b Panesar	32	– c Joyce b Panesar	2
V. Banerjee c Joyce b Martin-Jenkins	12	– lbw b Panesar	2
G. M. Hussain not out	13	– c Yasir Arafat b Rayner	0
S. P. Kirby c Prior b Yasir Arafat	14	– c Gatting b Rayner	0
B 3, l-b 12, n-b 6	21	B 7, l-b 5, n-b 2	14

1/10 (1) 2/82 (3) 3/98 (4)   (102.5 overs) 307
4/132 (2) 5/142 (5) 6/142 (7)
7/215 (8) 8/263 (9) 9/282 (6) 10/307 (11)

1/3 (2) 2/3 (1)   (40.3 overs) 131
3/16 (4) 4/79 (5)
5/88 (6) 6/98 (7) 7/102 (8)
8/118 (9) 9/119 (10)
10/131 (11)

Yasir Arafat 21.5–6–55–3; Collymore 18–4–58–2; Martin-Jenkins 18–2–66–2; Thornely 2–0–10–0; Panesar 31–8–70–3; Rayner 12–4–33–0. *Second Innings*—Yasir Arafat 7–2–24–1; Collymore 5–2–9–1; Panesar 15–3–44–5; Martin-Jenkins 3–0–18–0; Rayner 10.3–3–24–3.

Sussex

C. D. Nash c Marshall b Banerjee	49	– lbw b Kirby	0
M. A. Thornely c Dent b Hussain	7	– c Marshall b Banerjee	6
E. C. Joyce c Kadeer Ali b Banerjee	43	– not out	17
*M. W. Goodwin lbw b Hussain	44	– not out	26
†M. J. Prior c Taylor b Banerjee	37		
J. S. Gatting lbw b Banerjee	24		
R. S. C. Martin-Jenkins c Gidman b Hussain	78		
Yasir Arafat c Batty b Franklin	58		
O. P. Rayner lbw b Kirby	20		
M. S. Panesar b Banerjee	5		
C. D. Collymore not out	1		
L-b 8, w 11, n-b 4	23	L-b 3	3

1/34 (2) 2/83 (1) 3/124 (3)   (111.1 overs) 389
4/179 (4) 5/202 (5) 6/257 (6)
7/337 (7) 8/375 (8) 9/382 (10)
10/389 (9)   110 overs: 389-9

1/0 (1) 2/20 (2)   (2 wkts, 11 overs) 52

Lewis 17–1–63–0; Kirby 20.1–4–75–1; Hussain 19–1–78–3; Franklin 21–5–57–1; Banerjee 30–5–94–5; Gidman 2–0–7–0; Taylor 2–0–7–0. *Second Innings*—Kirby 4–1–11–1; Banerjee 5–0–23–1; Hussain 2–0–15–0.

Umpires: S. A. Garratt and T. E. Jesty.

At Uxbridge, July 21–24. SUSSEX drew with MIDDLESEX.

At Leicester, July 29–31. SUSSEX beat LEICESTERSHIRE by an innings and 19 runs.

At Guildford, August 9–12. SUSSEX drew with SURREY.

SUSSEX v DERBYSHIRE

At Horsham, August 18–20. Sussex won by an innings and 109 runs. Sussex 24pts, Derbyshire 1pt. Toss: Derbyshire.

Even when Mushtaq Ahmed was inspiring them to three titles in five years, Sussex rarely won as easily as this. Derbyshire looked rudderless without Rogers; two days earlier he had resigned the captaincy, and now he was laid low with tonsillitis. Borrington was plucked out of a second-team game at Old Trafford and hastily flown down to Gatwick to replace him, but scored just two from No. 9. Nash and Joyce blossomed on a placid pitch, and on the second day they, plus Brown and Goodwin, dipped their bread as the top four all scored hundreds in a Sussex innings for the first time. Only Middlesex (against Sussex at Lord's in 1920 and at Southampton in 1923) and Somerset in 2007 against Leicestershire at Taunton) had done this before in the Championship. For Nash, on his home ground, and Brown, making his maiden Championship century, there was particular pleasure. Although Derbyshire batted with marginally greater conviction in the second innings, Sussex won with more than four sessions to spare. "Like men versus boys," was the frank assessment of Rogers's replacement as captain, Greg Smith.

Close of play: First day, Sussex 170-0 (Joyce 69, Nash 81); Second day, Derbyshire 27-2 (Madsen 9, Durston 12).

Derbyshire

W. L. Madsen lbw b Collymore	2	– c Brown b Collymore	23
C. F. Hughes lbw b Collymore	22	– (3) b Collymore	4
W. J. Durston b Yasir Arafat	69	– (4) lbw b Wright	33
*G. M. Smith c Hodd b Wright	9	– (5) lbw b Panesar	49
D. J. Redfern c Hodd b Wright	0	– (6) c Joyce b Panesar	19
R. J. Peterson c Rayner b Panesar	20	– (7) c Goodwin b Collymore	6
J. L. Clare c Hodd b Panesar	0	– (8) lbw b Panesar	12
†S. J. Adshead lbw b Yasir Arafat	49	– (9) not out	31
P. M. Borrington c Joyce b Panesar	2	– (2) c Rayner b Collymore	1
P. S. Jones not out	35	– st Hodd b Panesar	17
M. H. A. Footitt b Yasir Arafat	6	– b Yasir Arafat	4
L-b 14, n-b 14	28	B 4, l-b 8, n-b 14	26

1/9 (1) 2/42 (2) 3/61 (4) 4/69 (5)   (61 overs) 242
5/94 (6) 6/96 (7) 7/198 (3) 8/199 (8)
9/219 (9) 10/242 (11)

1/8 (2) 2/12 (3)   (73 overs) 225
3/53 (1) 4/77 (4) 5/130 (6)
6/147 (7) 7/155 (5) 8/178 (8)
9/212 (10) 10/225 (11)

Yasir Arafat 18–5–57–3; Collymore 14–4–37–2; Wright 9–1–60–2; Panesar 13–2–55–3; Rayner 7–3–19–0. *Second Innings*—Yasir Arafat 18–0–66–1; Collymore 23–7–50–4; Panesar 24–5–67–4; Rayner 2–2–0–0; Wright 6–1–30–1.

Sussex

E. C. Joyce c Adshead b Smith	164
C. D. Nash c Clare b Peterson	156
†B. C. Brown c Peterson b Smith	112
M. W. Goodwin not out	100
O. P. Rayner not out	4
B 6, l-b 6, w 12, n-b 16	40

1/294 (2)   (3 wkts dec, 111.4 overs) 576
2/421 (1) 3/566 (3)   110 overs: 564-2

A. J. Hodd, *M. H. Yardy, L. J. Wright, Yasir Arafat, M. S. Panesar and C. D. Collymore did not bat.

Jones 23–4–82–0; Footitt 20–1–104–0; Clare 12–0–107–0; Smith 21–2–108–2; Peterson 27.4–2–130–1; Durston 8–0–33–0.

Umpires: J. W. Lloyds and N. A. Mallender.

SUSSEX v GLAMORGAN

At Hove, August 27–30. Drawn. Sussex 8pts, Glamorgan 9pts. Toss: Sussex.

The meeting of the top two produced some intriguing cricket, but a positive result was always unlikely after the opening day was washed out. A pattern emerged over the next two of batsmen dominating before lunch and wickets clattering afterwards. Cosgrove played with characterful aggression for his fifth Championship hundred of the season, yet he was one of seven Glamorgan wickets to go down for 82. Sussex were going well, reaching 166 for two until complacency set in. Goodwin fell to the first delivery of the third afternoon, when Harris and Waters had the ball jagging about disconcertingly. Nash took a sensational one-handed boundary catch to remove Cosgrove when Glamorgan batted again, and without him they could not score quickly enough to declare. Twenty points in front of their closest rivals before the match, Sussex had little incentive to attempt a target of 261 in 45 overs after losing Nash and Brown inside the first six.

Close of play: First day, No play; Second day, Sussex 30-0 (Joyce 14, Nash 16); Third day, Glamorgan 37-1 (Rees 20, Bragg 1).

Glamorgan

G. P. Rees c Wright b Panesar	12	– c Hodd b Yasir Arafat		20
M. J. Cosgrove b Yasir Arafat	142	– c Nash b Yasir Arafat		9
W. D. Bragg lbw b Wright	44	– lbw b Yasir Arafat		5
B. J. Wright b Yasir Arafat	16	– c Goodwin b Collymore		25
T. L. Maynard c Yardy b Collymore	12	– lbw b Wright		76
J. Allenby c Hodd b Anyon	13	– c Hodd b Anyon		8
*†M. A. Wallace lbw b Collymore	8	– c Hodd b Wright		16
J. A. R. Harris b Anyon	0	– not out		14
D. A. Cosker not out	9	– b Wright		2
D. S. Harrison c Yardy b Anyon	25	– b Wright		5
H. T. Waters (did not bat)		– c Hodd b Anyon		4
L-b 7, w 2, n-b 10	19	B 5, l-b 8, w 7, n-b 6		26

1/44 (1) 2/164 (3)   (9 wkts dec, 80.2 overs) 300   1/29 (2) 2/38 (1)   (64.5 overs) 210
3/218 (4) 4/239 (5) 5/239 (2)   3/43 (3) 4/112 (4)
6/256 (7) 7/259 (8) 8/266 (6) 9/300 (10)   5/127 (6) 6/174 (7) 7/191 (5)
                                         8/193 (9) 9/199 (10) 10/210 (11)

Yasir Arafat 15–0–67–2; Collymore 18–4–57–2; Panesar 22–3–70–1; Anyon 15.2–3–52–3; Nash 4–0–6–0; Wright 6–0–41–1. *Second Innings*—Yasir Arafat 21–6–64–3; Collymore 13–2–52–1; Panesar 13–3–38–0; Anyon 10.5–2–19–2; Wright 7–2–24–4.

Sussex

E. C. Joyce lbw b Harris	56	– not out		24
C. D. Nash lbw b Harris	19	– c Wallace b Waters		0
B. C. Brown b Allenby	59	– c Wallace b Waters		10
M. W. Goodwin c Allenby b Harris	28	– not out		58
*M. H. Yardy lbw b Waters	18			
L. J. Wright b Waters	8			
†A. J. Hodd lbw b Cosker	26			
Yasir Arafat c Wallace b Waters	0			
J. E. Anyon lbw b Cosker	8			
M. S. Panesar lbw b Allenby	17			
C. D. Collymore not out	0			
B 4, l-b 5, n-b 2	11	L-b 1		1

1/39 (2) 2/111 (3) 3/166 (4)   (67.3 overs) 250   1/4 (2) 2/14 (3)   (2 wkts, 27 overs) 93
4/179 (1) 5/192 (6) 6/203 (5)
7/211 (8) 8/229 (7) 9/250 (10) 10/250 (9)

Harris 16–6–37–3; Waters 20–7–71–3; Allenby 8–0–33–2; Harrison 12–2–61–0; Cosker 10.3–0–38–2; Cosgrove 1–0–1–0. *Second Innings*—Harris 9–4–14–0; Waters 9–1–35–2; Cosker 5–1–21–0; Allenby 1–0–2–0; Maynard 3–0–20–0.

Umpires: B. Dudleston and P. Willey.

SUSSEX v NORTHAMPTONSHIRE

At Hove, September 7–9. Sussex won by an innings and 19 runs. Sussex 23pts, Northamptonshire 3pts. Toss: Northamptonshire.

Sussex achieved everything they set out to in their penultimate match, and a meek Northamptonshire were simply elbowed aside. An immediate return to Division One was confirmed when Rayner pushed a single to mid-off, with the help of Brooks's misfield, taking Sussex's first innings to 350 and a seventh bonus point. Twenty-three points also secured the second division title once Glamorgan managed only eight from their draw with Surrey. Northamptonshire folded pitifully on a pitch which was certainly no minefield; they had no answer to an energised Yasir Arafat, bowling as quickly as at any time during the summer. Sussex soon put conditions into perspective, with Nash passing 150 for the third time in five matches. He also completed 1,000 Championship runs for the second successive season. He and Thornely established a first-wicket record for Sussex against Northamptonshire, and the lead was a mighty 198 by the time Lucas took three wickets in four balls. Loye alone offered lasting second-innings resistance, though Newton made a startling impression upon the attending journalists when he shattered the window of the Jack Arlidge press box with a hooked six. It was not a costly blow; the building was about to be knocked down as part of Hove's redevelopment.

Close of play: First day, Sussex 236-2 (Nash 122, Brown 4); Second day, Northamptonshire 48-2 (Loye 16).

Leaving his mark: Rob Newton gave the demolition team a helping hand at Hove.

Northamptonshire

S. D. Peters b Yasir Arafat	10	– b Yasir Arafat	22
M. B. Loye c Hodd b Collymore	2	– b Panesar	73
A. G. Wakely b Yasir Arafat	4	– lbw b Yasir Arafat	8
D. J. Sales lbw b Panesar	15	– c Hodd b Collymore	6
R. I. Newton c Hodd b Anyon	8	– lbw b Collymore	19
*A. J. Hall c Rayner b Anyon	10	– lbw b Anyon	20
J. D. Middlebrook c Hodd b Anyon	2	– b Yasir Arafat	26
†D. Murphy not out	47	– lbw b Yasir Arafat	0
D. S. Lucas b Yasir Arafat	10	– not out	28
J. A. Brooks c Hodd b Yasir Arafat	1	– c Anyon b Yasir Arafat	5
L. M. Daggett c Nash b Panesar	0	– c Collymore b Panesar	7
N-b 16	16	B 10, l-b 5, n-b 8	23

1/14 (2) 2/18 (1) 3/23 (3) 4/43 (5)   (46 overs) 125   1/32 (1) 2/48 (3)   (71.5 overs) 237
5/51 (4) 6/57 (6) 7/64 (7) 8/120 (9)   3/63 (4) 4/95 (5)
9/124 (10) 10/125 (11)   5/133 (6) 6/188 (7) 7/188 (2)
                                                            8/188 (8) 9/208 (10) 10/237 (11)

Yasir Arafat 15–4–43–4; Collymore 12–5–39–1; Thornely 1–0–6–0; Anyon 8–1–23–3; Panesar 10–4–14–2. *Second Innings*—Yasir Arafat 21–1–74–5; Collymore 15–4–45–2; Anyon 7–1–35–1; Panesar 17.5–5–36–2; Rayner 11–5–32–0.

Sussex

C. D. Nash c Peters b Lucas	169	M. S. Panesar c Sales b Daggett	16
M. A. Thornely b Brooks	89	C. D. Collymore not out	0
J. E. Anyon c Sales b Brooks	0		
B. C. Brown c Sales b Middlebrook	39	B 2, l-b 7, n-b 18	27
*M. W. Goodwin c Newton b Lucas	0		
M. J. Prior c Sales b Lucas	0	1/228 (1) 2/232 (3) (89.1 overs) 381
†A. J. Hodd b Hall b Middlebrook	7	3/323 (1) 4/323 (5) 5/323 (6)
Yasir Arafat lbw b Brooks	18	6/325 (4) 7/334 (7) 8/358 (5)
O. P. Rayner c Peters b Brooks	16	9/381 (10) 10/381 (9)

Lucas 16–2–74–3; Brooks 19.1–1–88–4; Daggett 23–4–87–1; Hall 10–0–61–0; Middlebrook 21–4–62–2.

Umpires: T. E. Jesty and D. J. Millns.

At Worcester, September 13–16. SUSSEX lost to WORCESTERSHIRE by four wickets.

WARWICKSHIRE

Survival of the fittest

PAUL BOLTON

It all came right for Warwickshire, when they ended a season that frequently tested patience by winning the CB40 and retaining first division status in the Championship. The celebrations that greeted Warwickshire's first major trophy in six years were unimaginable a month earlier, when they were routed in two days by Nottinghamshire. Warwickshire were favourites for relegation at that stage, and Ashley Giles, whose future as director of cricket seemed uncertain, was afraid that his shell-shocked side might disintegrate. But defeat at Trent Bridge galvanised Warwickshire: they won their last seven games – three in the Championship, four in the CB40 – to convert a depressing season into a success, if a qualified one.

"Trent Bridge was the lowest point of the season without a doubt. I wasn't sure how we would come back from that," said Giles. "But the players showed a lot of character in the final month. I think we wanted to win those three Championship games more than the opposition. In the CB40, we slipped under the radar a bit. Our one-day form was good all season, but people tended to overlook that because we were struggling in the Championship."

Though Warwickshire doubled their number of Championship wins from 2009, all six were achieved against the sides which finished below them in the table – relegated Essex and Kent, plus Hampshire. They were intimidated by a higher class of opposition. No team had stayed up before with nine defeats since the two-division structure was introduced in 2000. Warwickshire's record was easily explained by regular batting collapses and a meagre 20 batting points, by far the lowest in the country. More resilient in limited-overs cricket, Warwickshire topped a strong group in the Friends Provident T20, but missed out on finals day when they stumbled against a youthful Hampshire side in the quarter-finals.

As an England selector, Giles knew that Ian Bell and Jonathan Trott, his two best batsmen, would often be on international duty. Giles hoped that the remaining senior batsmen could compensate for their runs, but such optimism proved wholly misplaced. Darren Maddy, Jim Troughton and Tim Ambrose lost form so wretchedly that they mustered just four half-centuries between them in 77 Championship innings. Maddy, who missed most of the 2009 season with a knee problem, sustained a serious eye injury on the pre-season tour to South Africa and, despite scoring a double-century on his comeback for the Second Eleven, struggled to rediscover his best form.

Troughton's only first-class fifty came in his second innings, but he stayed in the side simply because the understudies, who reached the Second Eleven Championship final, were also short of runs. Ambrose was not so lucky. The former England wicketkeeper twice lost his place to the talented Richard

Neil Carter

Johnson, but persuaded Warwickshire to give him another chance and a new contract, having cleared his dressing-room locker before the end of the season.

Ian Westwood rarely batted with fluency, but played some gritty innings, and was alone in topping 700 runs. Westwood captained in all Championship matches, but was replaced by Troughton early in the T20 campaign, and by Bell for the last three CB40 matches. Troughton was appointed Warwickshire's tenth captain since 1996 when Westwood stepped down at the end of the season to concentrate on his batting.

It was a difficult environment for Varun Chopra, a winter recruit from Essex, to establish himself, and his season was disrupted further by a broken hand. The signings of Younis Khan, the former Pakistan captain, and William Porterfield and Laurie Evans, from Gloucestershire and Surrey, should address some of the deficiencies. Warwickshire were a different proposition when Bell and Trott were available. Bell scored his two centuries after returning from a broken foot, and when they were sorely needed: in the CB40 final, and to help secure safety in the last Championship game.

Too often it was left to Neil Carter, Chris Woakes and Imran Tahir, three bowlers who took 50 wickets, to bail Warwickshire out with the bat. Carter, who reported back fitter than ever after a winter of mountain biking in his native South Africa, enjoyed his most productive season, aged 35. Often undervalued, he returned 617 runs and 51 wickets in the Championship, and aggressive all-round contributions in the other competitions. Woakes found seamer-friendly conditions to his liking, and took a career-best 11-wicket haul against Kent. Giles admitted that, in easier circumstances, he would have sought to manage the 21-year-old's workload. During the winter Woakes's work on his physical strength was rewarded by selection for England's one-day team in Australia. The appointment of Graeme Welch as bowling coach, following the departure of Allan Donald, also benefited Andy Miller, Boyd Rankin and Rikki Clarke, who took his maiden five-for in his ninth season in county cricket.

Imran Tahir proved a popular overseas player, despite it being known from the outset that he would return to Hampshire in 2011. Used, turning pitches were prepared to help his leg-spin, but its effectiveness was compromised by frequent first-innings batting failures. Tahir signed off with five wickets in the Lord's final.

The CB40 success helped Neil Houghton celebrate his retirement as a low-profile chairman. Norman Gascoigne, a former banker, must now ensure that Warwickshire pay off the £20m loan required to fund Edgbaston's new pavilion. An irritating accompaniment of drilling, angle-grinding and pile-driving continued throughout the season.

WARWICKSHIRE RESULTS

All first-class matches – Played 16: Won 5, Lost 9, Drawn 1.
County Championship matches – Played 16: Won 5, Lost 9, Drawn 1.

LV= County Championship, 6th in Division 1;
Friends Provident T20, q-f; Clydesdale Bank 40, winners.

COUNTY CHAMPIONSHIP AVERAGES, BATTING AND FIELDING

Cap		M	I	NO	R	HS	100s	50s	Avge	Ct/St
2001	I. R. Bell†‡	6	11	1	381	104	1	2	38.10	10
2005	I. J. L. Trott‡	6	11	0	415	150	1	3	37.72	10
2005	N. M. Carter	11	20	3	617	99*	0	4	36.29	0
	R. Clarke	15	28	5	673	127*	1	3	29.26	23
2008	I. J. Westwood†	16	32	4	726	86*	0	5	25.92	6
	V. Chopra	9	18	0	409	54	0	1	24.05	9
2009	C. R. Woakes†	13	21	3	431	136*	1	1	23.94	6
2002	J. O. Troughton	16	30	1	585	78	0	1	20.17	5
2007	D. L. Maddy	14	27	1	499	61	0	2	19.19	16
	A. G. Botha¶	8	14	0	248	76	0	1	17.71	7
	R. M. Johnson†	5	8	1	118	39	0	0	16.85	12/2
2010	Imran Tahir§	16	27	4	384	69*	0	1	16.69	4
	K. H. D. Barker	4	5	1	57	22	0	0	14.25	1
2007	T. R. Ambrose	11	20	0	267	54	0	1	13.35	33/3
	A. Javid†	4	7	0	91	48	0	0	13.00	3
	N. S. Tahir†	3	6	0	69	34	0	0	11.50	2
	A. S. Miller	7	12	5	65	35	0	0	9.28	4
	W. B. Rankin¶	9	16	7	63	13	0	0	7.00	3

Also batted: L. J. Evans (1 match) 15, 3 (1 ct); J. E. Ord† (1 match) 1, 6 (1 ct); S. A. Piolet (1 match) 6, 4 (2 ct).

† *Born in Warwickshire.* ‡ *ECB contract.* § *Official overseas player.* ¶ *Other non-England-qualified player.*

BOWLING

	O	M	R	W	BB	5W/i	Avge
C. R. Woakes	396.2	100	1,165	54	6-52	3	21.57
N. M. Carter	356.2	70	1,129	51	5-60	4	22.13
R. Clarke	212.5	31	743	32	6-63	1	23.21
Imran Tahir	430.4	58	1,376	56	8-114	3	24.57
D. L. Maddy	206.5	62	523	21	4-37	0	24.90
W. B. Rankin	145.3	19	594	22	5-16	1	27.00
A. S. Miller	154.4	42	488	16	5-58	2	30.50

Also bowled: K. H. D. Barker 36.1-4-135-2; A. G. Botha 50.4-11-175-4; S. A. Piolet 17-3-80-1; N. S. Tahir 83-15-238-5; I. J. L. Trott 19-4-71-4.

LEADING CB40 AVERAGES (100 runs/4 wickets)

Batting	Runs	HS	Avge	S-R	Ct
I. J. L. Trott	460	103	76.66	83.18	6
I. R. Bell	554	107	61.55	106.53	4
V. Chopra	156	76	39.00	81.67	0
D. L. Maddy	283	74	35.37	96.58	5
I. J. Westwood	167	47	33.40	93.82	2
J. O. Troughton	325	66*	32.50	83.54	5

Bowling	W	BB	Avge	E-R
W. B. Rankin	15	4-34	16.26	5.85
Imran Tahir	22	5-41	19.59	5.32
K. H. D. Barker	14	4-33	26.50	6.11
C. R. Woakes	15	3-16	31.26	5.59
D. L. Maddy	10	3-25	36.10	6.11
A. G. Botha	5	2-27	41.00	5.00

LEADING FPT20 AVERAGES (100 runs/18 overs)

Batting	Runs	HS	Avge	S-R	Ct	Bowling	W	BB	Avge	E-R
I. R. Bell	166	85	41.50	137.19	0	S. A. Piolet	7	2-9	21.71	6.33
D. L. Maddy	456	88	32.57	132.55	8	N. M. Carter	16	3-28	23.93	6.38
N. M. Carter	231	39	13.58	128.33	2	Imran Tahir	20	3-14	20.05	6.57
R. Clarke	200	39	25.00	121.95	9	A. G. Botha	12	3-16	21.08	6.83
K. H. D. Barker	177	46	22.12	121.23	2	K. H. D. Barker	21	4-19	16.66	7.21
J. O. Troughton	365	66	26.07	119.67	7	C. R. Woakes	15	3-21	20.66	7.38

FIRST-CLASS COUNTY RECORDS

Highest score for	501*	B. C. Lara v Durham at Birmingham	1994
Highest score against	322	I. V. A. Richards (Somerset) at Taunton	1985
Leading run-scorer	35,146	D. L. Amiss (avge 41.64)	1960–1987
Best bowling for	10-41	J. D. Bannister v Combined Services at Birmingham	1959
Best bowling against	10-36	H. Verity (Yorkshire) at Leeds	1931
Leading wicket-taker	2,201	W. E. Hollies (avge 20.45)	1932–1957
Highest total for	810-4 dec	v Durham at Birmingham	1994
Highest total against	887	by Yorkshire at Birmingham	1896
Lowest total for	16	v Kent at Tonbridge	1913
Lowest total against	15	by Hampshire at Birmingham	1922

LIST A COUNTY RECORDS

Highest score for	206	A. I. Kallicharran v Oxfordshire at Birmingham	1984
Highest score against	172*	W. Larkins (Northamptonshire) at Luton	1983
Leading run-scorer	11,254	D. L. Amiss (avge 33.79)	1963–1987
Best bowling for	7-32	R. G. D. Willis v Yorkshire at Birmingham	1981
Best bowling against	6-27	M. H. Yardy (Sussex) at Birmingham	2005
Leading wicket-taker	396	G. C. Small (avge 25.48)	1980–1999
Highest total for	392-5	v Oxfordshire at Birmingham	1984
Highest total against	341-6	by Hampshire at Birmingham	2010
Lowest total for	59	v Yorkshire at Leeds	2001
Lowest total against	56	by Yorkshire at Birmingham	1995

TWENTY20 RECORDS

Highest score for	89	N. V. Knight v Worcestershire at Worcester	2003
Highest score against	100*	I. J. Harvey (Gloucestershire) at Birmingham	2003
Leading run-scorer	1,870	I. J. L. Trott (avge 41.55)	2003–2010
Best bowling for	5-19	N. M. Carter v Worcestershire at Birmingham	2005
Best bowling against	4-11	J. Ormond (Surrey) at Nottingham	2003
Leading wicket-taker	75	N. M. Carter (avge 24.26)	2003–2010
Highest total for	205-2	v Northamptonshire at Birmingham	2005
	205-7	v Glamorgan at Swansea	2005
Highest total against	215-6	by Durham at Birmingham	2010
Lowest total for	114	v Sussex at Hove	2009
Lowest total against	102-9	by Northamptonshire at Milton Keynes	2008

ADDRESS

County Ground, Edgbaston, Birmingham B5 7QU (0121 446 4422; **email** info@edgbaston.com).
Website www.edgbaston.com

OFFICIALS

Captain 2010 – I. J. Westwood
2011 – J. O. Troughton
Director of cricket A. F. Giles
Bowling coach G. Welch
President Earl of Aylesford

Chairman N. Gascoigne
Chief executive C. Povey
Head groundsman S. J. Rouse
Scorer D. E. Wainwright

WARWICKSHIRE v YORKSHIRE

At Birmingham, April 9–12. Yorkshire won by four wickets. Yorkshire 21pts, Warwickshire 4pts. Toss: Yorkshire. County debuts: V. Chopra, Imran Tahir.

A perfectly calculated assault on the final afternoon from Bairstow and Rudolph allowed Gale to begin his reign as Yorkshire captain with an unexpected win. Pursuing 291, Yorkshire spent the morning scratching around for 73 runs, but the sixth-wicket pair presided over a change of approach that Warwickshire's bowlers failed to handle. Yorkshire took care of the last 161 in 30 overs, Bairstow hitting 14 fours from 104 balls. Gale admitted they had attacked to unsettle Warwickshire debutant Imran Tahir, who had gone wicketless on his solitary appearance for Yorkshire, in 2007, but here claimed his 100th Championship victim in 24 matches. Gale deployed his bowlers intelligently: five times in the first innings they struck in the first over of a spell. The youngest and tallest of them, Hannon-Dalby, found life in an untypical Edgbaston surface, disrupting Warwickshire's second innings with four wickets in 29 balls. Bell and Trott, who both opted to play in this match two weeks after returning from England's tour of Bangladesh, batted fluently but fell when well set. Edgbaston provided an unappealing backdrop, with the old pavilion and three stands flattened ahead of redevelopment.

Close of play: First day, Yorkshire 128-3 (Rudolph 43, Gale 9); Second day, Warwickshire 84-1 (Chopra 33, Bell 41); Third day, Yorkshire 57-1 (Lyth 34, Shahzad 4).

Warwickshire

*I. J. Westwood lbw b Hannon-Dalby	39	– c Bairstow b Shahzad	0
V. Chopra lbw b Shahzad	4	– c Rudolph b Bresnan	45
I. R. Bell c Bairstow b Bresnan	31	– c Lyth b Shahzad	54
I. J. L. Trott c Bairstow b Patterson	7	– c McGrath b Hannon-Dalby	88
J. O. Troughton c McGrath b Shahzad	39	– b Patterson	78
†T. R. Ambrose c Rudolph b Patterson	5	– lbw b Hannon-Dalby	0
C. R. Woakes b Patterson	9	– b Hannon-Dalby	2
N. M. Carter lbw b Rashid	41	– c Gale b Hannon-Dalby	9
N. S. Tahir c Patterson b Bresnan	23	– lbw b Hannon-Dalby	34
Imran Tahir c Rudolph b Shahzad	12	– c Bairstow b Patterson	3
A. S. Miller not out	0	– not out	11
B 5, l-b 2	7	L-b 22, w 1	23

1/6 (2) 2/59 (3) 3/68 (4) 4/99 (1)   (59.2 overs) 217
5/132 (6) 6/134 (5) 7/156 (7)
8/203 (9) 9/215 (8) 10/217 (10)

1/9 (1) 2/105 (2)   (98 overs) 347
3/126 (3) 4/231 (4)
5/231 (6) 6/239 (7) 7/261 (8)
8/325 (5) 9/329 (10) 10/347 (9)

Bresnan 19–3–71–2; Shahzad 13.2–3–40–3; Hannon-Dalby 8–2–35–1; Patterson 14–1–51–3; McGrath 1–0–2–0; Rashid 4–1–11–1. *Second innings*—Bresnan 23.5–5–74–1; Shahzad 19–1–72–2; Hannon-Dalby 17–1–68–5; Patterson 20–5–69–2; Rashid 10–1–24–0; McGrath 9–1–18–0.

Yorkshire

A. Lyth c Westwood b Woakes	6	– c Ambrose b Carter	67
J. J. Sayers st Ambrose b Imran Tahir	50	– c Ambrose b N. S. Tahir	12
A. McGrath c Ambrose b N. S. Tahir	13	– (4) lbw b Imran Tahir	16
J. A. Rudolph b Imran Tahir	75	– (5) not out	69
*A. W. Gale lbw b Carter	23	– (6) c Trott b Imran Tahir	0
†J. M. Bairstow c Woakes b Carter	2	– (7) c Woakes b Carter	81
T. T. Bresnan c Ambrose b N. S. Tahir	10	– (8) not out	11
A. U. Rashid c Bell b Trott	44		
A. Shahzad not out	30	– (3) lbw b Carter	11
S. A. Patterson c Ambrose b Woakes	0		
O. J. Hannon-Dalby c Ambrose b Imran Tahir	1		
B 4, l-b 13, w 1, n-b 2	20	L-b 12, n-b 12	24

1/20 (1) 2/45 (3) 3/107 (2)   (108.2 overs) 274
4/176 (5) 5/176 (4) 6/180 (6)
7/197 (7) 8/260 (8) 9/273 (10) 10/274 (11)

1/48 (2)   (6 wkts, 79.5 overs) 291
2/82 (3) 3/111 (1)
4/119 (4) 5/123 (6) 6/276 (7)

Woakes 22–10–43–2; N. S. Tahir 19–5–49–2; Carter 18–9–37–2; Miller 19–6–57–0; Imran Tahir 28.2–6–67–3; Trott 2–1–4–1. *Second Innings*—Woakes 15–5–57–0; Miller 10–1–48–0; N. S. Tahir 14–2–31–1; Imran Tahir 26–1–81–2; Carter 13.5–3–50–3; Trott 1–0–12–0.

Umpires: N. L. Bainton and T. E. Jesty.

At Manchester, April 15–18. WARWICKSHIRE lost to LANCASHIRE by 121 runs.

WARWICKSHIRE v HAMPSHIRE

At Birmingham, April 27–30. Warwickshire won by eight wickets. Warwickshire 23pts, Hampshire 5pts. Toss: Hampshire.

Woakes's second first-class century (his first came at Southampton in July 2009) transformed Hampshire's promising position into their third successive defeat. Warwickshire were 98 for seven, and struggling to avoid the follow-on, when Woakes came to the crease on the second morning. With audacious contributions from Carter and Imran Tahir, the last three wickets conjured 284 and a lead of 99. Woakes, strong off his legs, was on 77 when last man Tahir joined him and drove his former team-mates to distraction in a stand of 103. When Tahir was eventually out, Woakes had hit 17 fours and two sixes from 200 balls. Tahir bowled only 15 overs on a pitch that had been raked at the ends for him. Instead it was Carter's swing which unsettled Hampshire, after Carberry had taken his aggregate against Warwickshire to 612 in five innings. Maddy (playing his first Championship match for 12 months), Trott and Bell were out without adding a run, and Warwickshire needed Ambrose to start the phenomenal fightback. Persistent bad weather cleared in time for Carter to return career-best match figures of nine for 130, then lead the run-chase as a pinch-hitter.

Close of play: First day, Warwickshire 45-1 (Maddy 21, Bell 17); Second day, Hampshire 3-0 (Carberry 3, Adams 0); Third day, Hampshire 104-5 (Pothas 21).

Hampshire

M. A. Carberry c Westwood b Woakes	74	– c Maddy b Carter	14
J. H. K. Adams c Ambrose b Carter	4	– c Ambrose b Carter	0
C. C. Benham lbw b Carter	8	– lbw b Carter	6
N. D. McKenzie c Trott b Maddy	13	– c Clarke b Carter	8
J. M. Vince lbw b Carter	6	– lbw b Imran Tahir	52
*†N. Pothas c Clarke b Trott	47	– c Ambrose b Woakes	23
S. M. Ervine c Clarke b Imran Tahir	70	– lbw b Carter	59
Kabir Ali c Ambrose b Carter	16	– c Bell b Carter	1
J. A. Tomlinson c Imran Tahir b Woakes	29	– c Trott b Woakes	1
D. R. Briggs b Imran Tahir	0	– c Maddy b Woakes	2
D. A. Griffiths not out	0	– not out	4
B 4, l-b 10, n-b 2	16	L-b 2, w 2, n-b 2	6

1/6 (2) 2/18 (3) 3/61 (4) 4/84 (5)   (80.5 overs) 283
5/120 (1) 6/203 (6) 7/238 (8)
8/273 (7) 9/273 (10) 10/283 (9)

1/17 (2) 2/23 (1)   (60.3 overs) 176
3/31 (4) 4/32 (3)
5/104 (5) 6/111 (6) 7/120 (8)
8/129 (9) 9/147 (10) 10/176 (7)

Woakes 16.5–4–60–2; Carter 23–6–59–4; Maddy 17–3–53–1; Clarke 6–0–32–0; Trott 8–1–29–1; Imran Tahir 8–0–23–2; Botha 2–0–13–0. *Second Innings*—Carter 23.3–2–71–5; Woakes 26–7–75–4; Maddy 4–1–20–0; Imran Tahir 7–1–8–1.

Warwickshire

I. J. Westwood lbw b Kabir Ali	0	– (3) not out	21
D. L. Maddy c Adams b Kabir Ali	22	– c Ervine b Kabir Ali	24
I. R. Bell c Pothas b Griffiths	17	– (4) not out	10
I. J. L. Trott c McKenzie b Kabir Ali	0		
J. O. Troughton lbw b Kabir Ali	13		
R. Clarke c Benham b Griffiths	1		
T. R. Ambrose c Carberry b Griffiths	54		
A. G. Botha c Pothas b Tomlinson	13		
C. R. Woakes not out	136		
N. M. Carter c Kabir Ali b Griffiths	62	– (1) c Vince b Tomlinson	24
Imran Tahir c Pothas b Ervine	40		
B 10, l-b 9, w 1, n-b 4	24	W 1	1

1/2 (1) 2/46 (2) 3/46 (4) 4/46 (3) (95.1 overs) 382 1/48 (2) (2 wkts, 12.2 overs) 80
5/50 (6) 6/68 (5) 7/98 (8) 8/175 (7) 2/49 (1)
9/279 (10) 10/382 (11)

Kabir Ali 24–7–89–4; Tomlinson 24–3–97–1; Ervine 14.1–4–38–1; Griffiths 20–1–96–4; McKenzie 1–0–2–0; Briggs 12–4–41–0. *Second Innings*—Kabir Ali 4–0–27–1; Tomlinson 6–1–42–1; Griffiths 2–0–7–0; Briggs 0.2–0–4–0.

Umpires: M. R. Benson and P. J. Hartley.

At Canterbury, May 4–7. WARWICKSHIRE beat KENT by 44 runs.

At Weetwood, Leeds, May 10–12. WARWICKSHIRE drew with LEEDS/BRADFORD MCCU (see Universities section).

WARWICKSHIRE v LANCASHIRE

At Birmingham, May 17–20. Lancashire won by 65 runs. Lancashire 23pts, Warwickshire 3pts. Toss: Lancashire. First-class debut: L. A. Procter.

Trott's assiduous seven-hour 150 carried Warwickshire closer to a target of 441 than they deserved, on a pitch which held up adequately to a fifth day's cricket (after a CB40 match on May 16). A seventh-wicket stand of 102 was a last-day irritant for Chapple, forced into posting a long-stop when Carter twice top-edged pulls off Mahmood. Lancashire could not breathe easily until Carter was out for 73, giving him 308 runs in six innings. Twenty wickets fell on an extraordinary second day, though not Croft, who batted for almost four hours and nursed Lancashire to four batting points. Ten fell between lunch and tea, largely due to indeterminate batting against the swinging ball. Chapple claimed five of the ten Warwickshire batsmen out for single figures. The freak exception was Carter, who required 15 stitches in his left ear after being struck by a Mahmood lifter, but still accounted for 61% of Warwickshire's first-innings runs. Chapple declined the follow-on, and watched Miller (Preston-born and nurtured in Lancashire's academy) knock over five of the top seven, before Mahmood's 72 put the result beyond reasonable doubt. On the second day, Anderson was whisked from Gatwick Airport, direct from the World Twenty20 (where he played just one warm-up match). He made useful runs, but his bowling was understandably rusty.

Close of play: First day, Lancashire 323-8 (Croft 75, Mahmood 4); Second day, Lancashire 152-8 (Mahmood 55, Anderson 1); Third day, Warwickshire 263-6 (Trott 102, Carter 17).

Lancashire

†L. D. Sutton lbw b Rankin	3	– c Bell b Miller	0
S. C. Moore c Troughton b Imran Tahir	61	– b Miller	13
P. J. Horton c Ambrose b Maddy	24	– lbw b Maddy	5
A. G. Prince b Imran Tahir	51	– c Clarke b Miller	0
M. J. Chilton c Ambrose b Miller	39	– c Trott b Clarke	43
S. J. Croft not out	89	– lbw b Miller	0
T. C. Smith c Trott b Miller	7	– c Ambrose b Miller	0
L. A. Procter c Miller b Rankin	13		
*G. Chapple lbw b Miller	29	– (8) c Clarke b Maddy	22
S. I. Mahmood lbw b Imran Tahir	9	– (9) b Carter	72
S. C. Kerrigan c Ambrose b Carter	6	– c Bell b Clarke	2
J. M. Anderson (did not bat)		– (10) not out	25
B 14, l-b 7, n-b 2	23	B 9, l-b 6, n-b 2	17

1/3 (1) 2/45 (3) 3/139 (4)   (102.5 overs) 354
4/149 (2) 5/227 (5) 6/241 (7)
7/264 (8) 8/318 (9) 9/331 (10) 10/354 (11)

1/1 (1) 2/16 (2)   (53.2 overs) 199
3/16 (4) 4/20 (3)
5/21 (6) 6/33 (7) 7/68 (8)
8/122 (5) 9/184 (9) 10/199 (11)

Anderson replaced Procter after returning from England's World Twenty20 campaign.

Carter 20.5–5–60–1; Rankin 18–1–90–2; Maddy 7–3–19–1; Miller 16–5–45–3; Clarke 8–0–26–0; Imran Tahir 33–7–93–3. *Second Innings*—Rankin 5–1–28–0; Miller 14–2–58–5; Maddy 13–5–25–2; Clarke 9.2–0–28–2; Imran Tahir 4–0–25–0; Carter 8–0–20–1.

Warwickshire

*I. J. Westwood lbw b Chapple	1	– c Sutton b Chapple	13
D. L. Maddy c Horton b Mahmood	5	– lbw b Chapple	11
I. R. Bell c Prince b Chapple	5	– c Sutton b Chapple	0
I. J. L. Trott c Sutton b Mahmood	6	– c Croft b Mahmood	150
J. O. Troughton c Horton b Mahmood	4	– c Horton b Chapple	41
R. Clarke b Chapple	0	– lbw b Kerrigan	42
†T. R. Ambrose b Smith	2	– c and b Smith	22
N. M. Carter not out	69	– b Mahmood	73
Imran Tahir c Croft b Smith	9	– c Sutton b Anderson	4
A. S. Miller b Chapple	0	– c Sutton b Anderson	0
W. B. Rankin b Chapple	5	– not out	0
L-b 5, n-b 2	7	B 8, l-b 9, w 2	19

1/2 (1) 2/10 (2) 3/16 (4) 4/22 (3)   (34 overs) 113
5/22 (6) 6/22 (5) 7/56 (7) 8/96 (9)
9/99 (10) 10/113 (11)

1/22 (2) 2/22 (3)   (112.5 overs) 375
3/30 (1) 4/119 (5)
5/205 (6) 6/244 (7) 7/346 (8)
8/353 (9) 9/355 (10) 10/375 (4)

Chapple 12–4–27–5; Mahmood 13–5–44–3; Procter 1–0–8–0; Smith 8–2–29–2. *Second Innings*—Anderson 26–7–85–2; Chapple 21–3–69–4; Mahmood 21.5–3–83–2; Smith 16–2–55–1; Kerrigan 28–7–66–1.

Umpires: S. A. Garratt and J. W. Lloyds.

At Taunton, May 24–26. WARWICKSHIRE lost to SOMERSET by nine wickets.

WARWICKSHIRE v DURHAM

At Birmingham, May 29–June 1. Drawn. Warwickshire 6pts, Durham 10pts. Toss: Durham. Championship debut: R. M. Johnson.

Warwickshire crumpled for their lowest score since making 86 at Chelmsford in April 1999, and escaped with their only draw of the season because of rain, which wiped out the last day and all but 21 overs of the first. Their policy of preparing a dry, used pitch met with limited success. Imran Tahir delivered the best figures for Warwickshire in eight years, and their finest by a leg-spinner save Eric

Hollies, but Durham still prospered. Stoneman and Muchall made patient fifties on their first Championship appearances of the season before falling to Tahir, who took three wickets in 15 balls without conceding a run. Mustard counter-attacked with his first century in almost four years, including a belligerent 38-ball second fifty as he lost partners. Warwickshire could only scrape together Mustard's score between them in a supine display. Thanks to Westwood's grit and Clarke's brazen strokeplay, they showed more bottle following on. Tim Ambrose, who had scored just 128 runs in 11 Championship innings, was given time off to clear his head, and made way for 21-year-old Richard Johnson.

Close of play: First day, Durham 65-1 (Stoneman 31, Muchall 21); Second day, Warwickshire 18-1 (Westwood 16, Miller 0); Third day, Warwickshire 229-4 (Westwood 86, Johnson 20).

Durham

M. J. Di Venuto lbw b Woakes	4	M. E. Claydon lbw b Botha		14
M. D. Stoneman st Johnson b Imran Tahir	77	C. Rushworth not out		3
G. J. Muchall lbw b Imran Tahir	60			
D. M. Benkenstein lbw b Imran Tahir	26	B 13, l-b 18, w 1, n-b 6		38
I. D. Blackwell c Maddy b Imran Tahir	0			
B. A. Stokes c Troughton b Imran Tahir	16	1/4 (1) 2/157 (3)	(110.2 overs)	379
†P. Mustard c Westwood b Imran Tahir	100	3/170 (2) 4/172 (5) 5/190 (6)		
S. G. Borthwick c Barker b Imran Tahir	0	6/235 (4) 7/235 (8) 8/330 (9)		
L. E. Plunkett b Imran Tahir	41	9/353 (10) 10/379 (7)	110 overs: 373-9	

Woakes 20–5–39–1; Miller 17–7–39–0; Barker 13–2–68–0; Maddy 2.5–1–8–0; Clarke 8–2–31–0; Imran Tahir 30.3–5–114–8; Botha 19–4–49–1.

Warwickshire

*I. J. Westwood c Benkenstein b Claydon	16	– not out		86
D. L. Maddy c Rushworth b Claydon	0	– lbw b Claydon		16
A. S. Miller b Blackwell	35			
V. Chopra lbw b Rushworth	1	– (3) c Mustard b Borthwick		6
J. O. Troughton c Mustard b Claydon	1	– (4) lbw b Borthwick		9
R. Clarke c Muchall b Rushworth	5	– (5) lbw b Blackwell		66
†R. M. Johnson c Stokes b Blackwell	9	– (6) not out		20
A. G. Botha c Stoneman b Plunkett	20			
C. R. Woakes c Mustard b Plunkett	5			
K. H. D. Barker not out	0			
Imran Tahir b Plunkett	0			
B 4, n-b 4	8	B 10, l-b 7, w 1, n-b 8		26
1/1 (2) 2/22 (1) 3/23 (4) 4/28 (5)	(35 overs) 100	1/25 (2)	(4 wkts, 72 overs)	229
5/39 (6) 6/59 (7) 7/86 (3) 8/95 (9)		2/48 (3) 3/62 (4)		
9/100 (8) 10/100 (11)		4/176 (5)		

Claydon 9–3–17–3; Rushworth 9–1–38–2; Plunkett 9–3–16–3; Blackwell 8–0–25–2. *Second Innings*—Plunkett 14–4–50–0; Rushworth 8–2–15–0; Claydon 9–1–52–1; Borthwick 17–1–69–2; Blackwell 24–11–26–1.

Umpires: R. J. Bailey and P. Willey.

WARWICKSHIRE v SOMERSET

At Birmingham, June 4–6. Somerset won by 181 runs. Somerset 21pts, Warwickshire 3pts. Toss: Somerset.

With Imran Tahir in mind, groundsman Steve Rouse produced another bone-dry, turning surface, used the previous evening for a Friends Provident T20 match. Unfortunately for Warwickshire, it was equally suited to Somerset slow left-armer Kartik, whose 11 for 72 was his best performance in England. The toss, lost by Westwood for the seventh match in eight, proved significant. On a sweltering day, the pitch immediately offered bounce and turn (but passed muster with the umpires), and Hildreth, who had plundered 531 in four innings against Warwickshire on surfaces far removed from this, was surprised by Botha's fifth ball, which spat and flicked his glove on the way to slip. Warwickshire were dismissed for under 150 in their first innings for the fourth consecutive match, their lack of confidence evident against Kartik. Tahir led the fightback, helping reduce Somerset to 90 for seven, but Kartik lent Phillips valuable support in a ninth-wicket partnership of 56 which left Warwickshire needing 312, the highest total of the match. Predictably, they collapsed to Kartik again, losing their last four wickets in 24 balls after rain, which delayed play for two hours and 20 minutes on the third day.

Close of play: First day, Warwickshire 2-1 (Maddy 0); Second day, Somerset 151-8 (Phillips 44, Kartik 11).

Somerset

*M. E. Trescothick c Botha b Clarke	53	– lbw b Woakes	4
A. V. Suppiah c Johnson b Clarke	2	– b Miller	8
J. C. Buttler c Westwood b Clarke	1	– lbw b Woakes	19
Z. de Bruyn lbw b Woakes	25	– c and b Imran Tahir	24
J. C. Hildreth c Clarke b Botha	52	– lbw b Imran Tahir	14
†C. Kieswetter c Chopra b Botha	40	– c Johnson b Imran Tahir	5
P. D. Trego c Botha b Imran Tahir	25	– b Clarke	0
B. J. Phillips c Chopra b Botha	9	– st Johnson b Imran Tahir	55
A. C. Thomas c Johnson b Woakes	27	– c Clarke b Imran Tahir	12
M. Kartik not out	11	– c Maddy b Imran Tahir	32
C. M. Willoughby b Woakes	4	– not out	0
B 2, l-b 14, w 1, n-b 2	19	B 8, n-b 2	10

1/53 (2) 2/61 (3) 3/66 (1)   (90.5 overs) 268
4/134 (4) 5/161 (5) 6/208 (7) 7/220 (6)
8/235 (8) 9/264 (9) 10/268 (11)

1/4 (1) 2/28 (3)   (46.4 overs) 183
3/40 (2) 4/65 (5)
5/71 (6) 6/72 (7) 7/90 (4)
8/120 (9) 9/176 (10) 10/183 (8)

Woakes 15.5–5–44–3; Miller 12–5–24–0; Rankin 9–3–33–0; Maddy 10–5–12–0; Clarke 12–4–53–3; Imran Tahir 19.2–4–54–1; Botha 13–5–50–3. *Second Innings*—Woakes 10.2–2–37–2; Miller 7–0–23–1; Imran Tahir 17.4–2–58–6; Clarke 7–1–28–1; Rankin 2–0–15–0; Botha 3–0–14–0.

Warwickshire

*I. J. Westwood c Hildreth b Willoughby	2	– c Kieswetter b Phillips	22
D. L. Maddy c Buttler b Thomas	3	– c Trescothick b Willoughby	3
V. Chopra c Kieswetter b Willoughby	27	– lbw b Thomas	46
J. O. Troughton c Hildreth b Kartik	27	– c Hildreth b Kartik	7
R. Clarke c Kartik b Phillips	17	– lbw b Kartik	1
†R. M. Johnson c Trescothick b Kartik	12	– c Trescothick b Willoughby	10
A. G. Botha b Kartik	19	– c Buttler b Kartik	0
C. R. Woakes c Trescothick b Kartik	21	– lbw b Kartik	21
A. S. Miller not out	2	– c Phillips b Kartik	3
Imran Tahir c Kieswetter b Kartik	0	– c Trego b Kartik	2
W. B. Rankin c Trescothick b Thomas	1	– not out	0
B 6, l-b 3	9	B 1, l-b 12, n-b 2	15

1/2 (1) 2/15 (2) 3/55 (3) 4/79 (5)   (61.1 overs) 140
5/79 (4) 6/108 (7) 7/114 (6)
8/139 (8) 9/139 (10) 10/140 (11)

1/3 (2) 2/60 (1)   (49.3 overs) 130
3/81 (4) 4/89 (3)
5/91 (6) 6/91 (7) 7/125 (8)
8/125 (6) 9/130 (10) 10/130 (9)

Willoughby 11–4–20–2; Phillips 14–4–32–1; Thomas 13.1–3–37–2; Kartik 20–8–30–5; Trego 1–0–3–0; Suppiah 2–1–9–0. *Second Innings*—Willoughby 10–3–20–2; Thomas 12–3–36–1; Kartik 18.3–3–42–6; Phillips 7–4–14–1; Suppiah 2–1–5–0.

Umpires: M. J. D. Bodenham and R. K. Illingworth.

At Chester-le-Street, June 28–July 1. WARWICKSHIRE lost to DURHAM by 219 runs.

At Leeds, July 5–8. WARWICKSHIRE lost to YORKSHIRE by six wickets.

WARWICKSHIRE v NOTTINGHAMSHIRE

At Birmingham, July 20–22. Nottinghamshire won by ten wickets. Nottinghamshire 23pts, Warwickshire 6pts. Toss: Nottinghamshire.

Warwickshire's crushing defeat, their sixth in seven matches, was confirmed ruthlessly by Broad, whose career-best eight for 52 was unsurpassed by anyone in Division One all season. While the accurate Sidebottom built the pressure, Warwickshire rashly sacrificed themselves to Broad, who bowled well within himself a week before the opening Test against Pakistan. The only batsman who could plead mitigation was Maddy, caught hooking as a rope from the Pavilion End building site dangled in front of the sightscreen. Broad, Sidebottom and Swann appeared together in the Championship for the first time since April 2008, but came in for rough treatment in the first innings. Carter took all five of his sixes off the England seamers: he pulled, upper-cut and cleared extra cover in a single Broad over. He became the fifth Warwickshire batsman (and from No. 9, the lowest in the order) to be stranded unbeaten on 99 when Rankin, backing up too far, was run out from midwicket by Swann. Carter made early inroads with the ball, until Wagh rescued Nottinghamshire with his second hundred at Edgbaston since leaving Warwickshire in 2006. He was beaten to his half-century by Read, despite a 36-over start.

Close of play: First day, Nottinghamshire 18-0 (Patel 1, Hales 16); Second day, Nottinghamshire 373-9 (Wagh 127, Sidebottom 6).

Warwickshire

*I. J. Westwood c Hussey b Adams	17	– c Hales b Broad	0
A. G. Botha c Read b Sidebottom	1	– c Brown b Broad	4
I. J. L. Trott c Read b Broad	21	– c Hales b Broad	4
J. O. Troughton c Read b Swann	25	– b Broad	9
D. L. Maddy c Sidebottom b Broad	21	– c Mullaney b Broad	8
R. Clarke c Hussey b Adams	27	– lbw b Broad	0
†T. R. Ambrose c Read b Broad	34	– c Adams b Broad	22
C. R. Woakes b Adams	13	– c Adams b Broad	0
N. M. Carter not out	99	– c Mullaney b Adams	27
Imran Tahir lbw b Swann	29	– run out	17
W. B. Rankin run out	5	– not out	8
B 8, l-b 9, n-b 4	21	L-b 1	1

1/1 (2) 2/28 (3) 3/54 (1) 4/92 (4) (86.4 overs) 313 1/0 (1) 2/4 (3) (25.3 overs) 100
5/98 (5) 6/135 (6) 7/157 (8)   3/9 (2) 4/18 (4) 5/18 (6)
8/200 (7) 9/266 (10) 10/312 (11)   6/29 (5) 7/33 (8) 8/74 (9)
                                                  9/75 (7) 10/100 (10)

Sidebottom 20–3–81–1; Broad 19–1–79–3; Adams 17.4–7–35–3; Swann 26–5–88–2; Mullaney 4–1–13–0. *Second Innings*—Broad 13–3–52–8; Sidebottom 8–4–14–0; Adams 4.3–0–33–1.

Nottinghamshire

S. R. Patel b Carter	1	– not out	10
A. D. Hales c Clarke b Carter	53	– not out	10
M. A. Wagh c Troughton b Carter	139		
D. J. Hussey c Maddy b Carter	8		
S. J. Mullaney c Ambrose b Rankin	31		
A. D. Brown b Rankin	1		
*†C. M. W. Read c Clarke b Carter	83		
G. P. Swann c Trott b Woakes	1		
S. C. J. Broad c Rankin b Woakes	0		
A. R. Adams b Imran Tahir	37		
R. J. Sidebottom not out	6		
B 8, l-b 16, w 1, n-b 4	29	W 5	5

1/25 (1) 2/61 (2) 3/69 (4) (105.4 overs) 389 (no wkt, 3 overs) 25
4/127 (5) 5/131 (6) 6/287 (7)
7/288 (8) 8/298 (9) 9/347 (10) 10/389 (3)

Woakes 18–5–59–2; Carter 27.4–3–116–5; Maddy 12–4–22–0; Rankin 10–2–49–2; Imran Tahir 26–5–79–1; Clarke 7–0–25–0; Botha 5–1–15–0. *Second Innings*—Woakes 2–0–15–0; Carter 1–0–10–0.

Umpires: P. J. Hartley and P. Willey.

At Southend, August 4–6. WARWICKSHIRE beat ESSEX by seven wickets.

At Nottingham, August 16–17. WARWICKSHIRE lost to NOTTINGHAMSHIRE by an innings and 55 runs.

WARWICKSHIRE v ESSEX

At Birmingham, August 25–28. Warwickshire won by seven wickets. Warwickshire 19pts, Essex 3pts. Toss: Warwickshire.

The importance of this match – billed as a relegation decider – was clear from both teams' jittery batting. The game bore a remarkable resemblance to their dogfight at Southend three weeks earlier: the margin of victory and points taken were identical; Warwickshire scored 155 in all four innings; and Essex's even flimsier batsmen again failed to construct a fifty partnership. Bopara scored a half-century, but only after Woakes had undermined the innings with three wickets in 12 balls. Rankin polished off the tail to claim career-best figures, split by five washed-out sessions, consigning Essex to their lowest total in two years. However, Rankin's season ended later on the third day when he suffered a recurrence of a foot injury. Warwickshire owed their lead of 41 to Johnson, who knuckled down for two hours on his recall after Tim Ambrose's pair against Nottinghamshire. Walker and Pettini battled gamely for Essex, until three wickets in five Clarke overs left Warwickshire needing just 153. Maddy's second fifty of a trying season left Essex as good as relegated: five points adrift at the bottom with only one game remaining.

Close of play: First day, Essex 90-7 (Bopara 42); Second day, No play; Third day, Essex 99-3 (Walker 33, Pettini 5).

Essex

B. A. Godleman c Johnson b Woakes	22	– lbw b Maddy	39
J. C. Mickleburgh lbw b Woakes	14	– b Woakes	0
R. S. Bopara not out	53	– lbw b Woakes	13
M. J. Walker lbw b Woakes	0	– run out	38
M. L. Pettini b Clarke	3	– b Clarke	35
*†J. S. Foster c Javid b Maddy	0	– lbw b Woakes	8
R. N. ten Doeschate c Johnson b Rankin	7	– b Clarke	10
D. D. Masters lbw b Rankin	0	– c Maddy b Clarke	18
A. P. Palladino lbw b Rankin	0	– b Maddy	0
M. A. Chambers c Troughton b Rankin	0	– not out	9
Danish Kaneria c Imran Tahir b Rankin	0	– b Carter	8
B 2, l-b 3, w 8, n-b 2	15	B 5, l-b 6, n-b 4	15

1/36 (1) 2/41 (2) 3/41 (4) 4/60 (5) (35.4 overs) 114
5/61 (6) 6/90 (7) 7/90 (8) 8/96 (9)
9/114 (10) 10/114 (11)

1/1 (2) 2/39 (3) (57.2 overs) 193
3/83 (1) 4/108 (4)
5/120 (6) 6/156 (7) 7/163 (5)
8/170 (9) 9/178 (8) 10/193 (11)

Woakes 14–6–37–3; Carter 7–2–25–0; Clarke 5–1–24–1; Maddy 4–2–7–1; Rankin 5.4–1–16–5. *Second Innings*—Woakes 16–2–69–3; Carter 16.2–2–54–1; Rankin 1–0–8–0; Clarke 13–5–20–3; Maddy 10–4–24–2; Imran Tahir 1–0–7–0.

Warwickshire

*I. J. Westwood b Masters	4	– lbw b Danish Kaneria	40
V. Chopra b Masters	14	– c Godleman b Masters	36
D. L. Maddy b Palladino	7	– not out	50
J. O. Troughton lbw b Palladino	5	– lbw b Masters	4
R. Clarke c and b ten Doeschate	24	– not out	16
A. Javid b Masters	0		
†R. M. Johnson c Foster b Chambers	39		
C. R. Woakes c Foster b ten Doeschate	0		
N. M. Carter lbw b Danish Kaneria	28		
Imran Tahir c and b Chambers	4		
W. B. Rankin not out	7		
L-b 10, w 3, n-b 10	23	B 5, l-b 4	9

1/4 (1) 2/30 (2) 3/43 (3) 4/44 (4)   (51.3 overs) 155
5/45 (6) 6/78 (5) 7/78 (8) 8/132 (9)
9/150 (10) 10/155 (7)

1/62 (1)   (3 wkts, 38.5 overs) 155
2/90 (2) 3/108 (4)

Masters 19–5–39–3; Chambers 14.3–1–55–2; Palladino 10–4–17–2; ten Doeschate 6–0–27–2; Danish Kaneria 2–0–7–1. *Second Innings*—Masters 18–6–45–2; Palladino 7–1–42–0; Chambers 5.5–0–31–0; Danish Kaneria 8–0–28–1.

Umpires: R. J. Bailey and J. H. Evans.

WARWICKSHIRE v KENT

At Birmingham, August 31–September 2. Warwickshire won by 95 runs. Warwickshire 21pts, Kent 3pts. Toss: Warwickshire. County debut: L. J. Evans.

Carter and Woakes hauled Warwickshire away from the relegation zone for the first time since late May. The new-ball pair shared 19 wickets in the match and, when Carter had Blake caught behind he became the first Warwickshire seamer since Dougie Brown, in 2002, to take 50 wickets in a Championship season. Woakes, who claimed a career-best 11 for 97, reached the landmark in the final round. Warwickshire were in familiar disarray until Botha, circumspectly, and Imran Tahir, boisterously and with some fortune, compiled their highest scores for the county in a last-wicket stand of 118. It was the turning point: Denly shouldered arms to the first ball of the reply, one of five ducks in Kent's lowest total for two years. Westwood batted again, only for Warwickshire to nosedive to 54 for eight on a day that claimed 22 batsmen. Carter and Woakes showed what could be done, smacking 72 for the ninth wicket and helping set Kent a distant 324. Van Jaarsveld's imperious hundred, his 26th for Kent, showed judgment lacking in his colleagues, who surrendered inside 24 overs of the third day.

Close of play: First day, Kent 37-3 (Northeast 19, Tredwell 8); Second day, Kent 131-5 (van Jaarsveld 44).

Warwickshire

*I. J. Westwood c van Jaarsveld b Stevens	14	– b Azhar Mahmood	7
V. Chopra lbw b Stevens	24	– c Jones b Stevens	9
D. L. Maddy c Jones b Stevens	11	– lbw b Stevens	0
J. O. Troughton lbw b Cook	9	– lbw b Azhar Mahmood	9
R. Clarke c and b Coles	10	– b Azhar Mahmood	0
L. J. Evans b Cook	15	– lbw b Azhar Mahmood	3
†R. M. Johnson lbw b Azhar Mahmood	18	– lbw b Stevens	10
A. G. Botha c Jones b Coles	76	– c van Jaarsveld b Stevens	7
C. R. Woakes b Tredwell	30	– b Cook	51
N. M. Carter c Blake b Coles	6	– c Tredwell b Coles	26
Imran Tahir not out	69	– not out	9
L-b 6, w 2, n-b 4	12	B 8, l-b 1	9

1/31 (2) 2/40 (1) 3/55 (4) 4/65 (3)   (84.4 overs) 294
5/74 (5) 6/99 (7) 7/107 (6) 8/167 (9)
9/176 (10) 10/294 (8)

1/11 (1) 2/11 (3)   (33.1 overs) 140
3/17 (1) 4/17 (5)
5/28 (4) 6/33 (6) 7/49 (7)
8/54 (8) 9/126 (10) 10/140 (9)

Azhar Mahmood 15–5–56–1; Stevens 21–4–63–3; Cook 16–4–65–2; Coles 17.4–3–49–3; Tredwell 14–1–51–1; van Jaarsveld 1–0–4–0. *Second Innings*—Stevens 13–4–38–4; Azhar Mahmood 13–3–51–4; Coles 4–0–21–1; Cook 3.1–0–21–1.

Kent

J. L. Denly b Woakes	0	– b Woakes	4
*R. W. T. Key b Woakes	0	– c Johnson b Woakes	7
S. A. Northeast c Botha b Woakes	32	– (4) c Chopra b Carter	14
S. J. Cook b Woakes	9	– (10) lbw b Woakes	0
J. C. Tredwell c Clarke b Carter	12	– (3) c Maddy b Carter	7
M. van Jaarsveld c Evans b Woakes	0	– (5) not out	110
†G. O. Jones lbw b Woakes	0	– (6) lbw b Woakes	41
D. I. Stevens c Botha b Carter	0	– (7) c Chopra b Carter	14
A. J. Blake b Clarke	33	– (8) c Johnson b Carter	0
Azhar Mahmood lbw b Carter	8	– (9) c Maddy b Woakes	0
M. T. Coles not out	13	– c Botha b Carter	13
L-b 4	4	B 8, l-b 5, w 1, n-b 4	18

1/0 (1) 2/3 (2) 3/21 (4) 4/50 (3) (31.3 overs) 111 1/4 (1) 2/13 (2) (60.1 overs) 228
5/50 (6) 6/54 (5) 7/54 (7) 8/58 (8) 3/29 (3) 4/36 (4)
9/72 (10) 10/111 (9) 5/131 (6) 6/152 (7) 7/152 (8)
8/161 (9) 9/161 (10) 10/228 (11)

Woakes 14–3–52–6; Carter 15–3–46–3; Imran Tahir 2–1–5–0; Clarke 0.3–0–4–1. *Second Innings*—Woakes 15–3–45–5; Carter 16.1–2–60–5; Clarke 6–0–30–0; Maddy 13–3–39–0; Imran Tahir 10–0–41–0.

Umpires: J. W. Lloyds and J. F. Steele.

At Southampton, September 13–16. WARWICKSHIRE beat HAMPSHIRE by ten wickets. *Warwickshire confirm their safety with their sixth win, all against the three sides that finished below them in Division One.*

WORCESTERSHIRE

Yo-yoing Young Turks

JOHN CURTIS

Worcestershire were one of the success stories of 2010 – and one of the least expected. Steven Davies, Stephen Moore, Kabir Ali and Gareth Batty had all left of their own accord by January, while the injury-prone Simon Jones was not offered a new contract; it seemed an irreplaceable drain of experience. Contrary to their recent up-and-down history, Worcestershire appeared resigned to a long absence from the top flight.

But a combination of astute signings, the success of younger players and the shortcomings of rival counties allowed Worcestershire to embark on a stunning turnaround over the last month of the season, to accompany Sussex out of Division Two at the very last. After negotiations, they succeeded in chasing down 301 against the team already assured of the title, with Alexei Kervezee striking the winning six. When Glamorgan failed to overcome Derbyshire, Worcestershire's third promotion in five seasons was assured.

Such a triumphant ending seemed unthinkable on August 12. A crushing defeat at Colwyn Bay left Worcestershire 37 points adrift of leaders Glamorgan, and 36 behind Sussex, with four matches to go. Immediately after the game, Vikram Solanki announced the end of his five-year tenure as captain, identifying his modest return with the bat as the principal reason. The reins were handed to 26-year-old opener Daryl Mitchell, and Worcestershire responded immediately, winning three of their remaining matches.

A greater task awaits Mitchell, who must succeed where his predecessor failed if Worcestershire are to avoid being steamrollered in Division One. For a club which has yo-yoed between divisions with indecent haste for the past eight years, 2011 promises to be every bit as tough as 2007 and 2009. The champagne was still bubbling when chairman Martyn Price declared that no new money would be available. Worcestershire will have to rely on the same group of players, and hope their overseas signings, Damien Wright and Saeed Ajmal, prove as potent as Shakib Al Hasan. "The players may not get as many single hotel rooms and nice coach travel, but we can employ some decent cricketers," said director of cricket Steve Rhodes.

Worcestershire must also address their continued limited-overs struggle. Six of the first eight Twenty20 matches were lost, and Sanath Jayasuriya and Steve Smith underwhelmed in their short spells. A worse fate loomed in the CB40, where Worcestershire lost their first seven games, culminating in defeat by the Unicorns, until Mitchell's appointment sparked a mini-revival. The high point was Solanki and Gareth Andrew hitting hundreds in a mammoth 376 for six at The Oval, overshadowing Kevin Pietersen's Surrey debut.

The bowling cupboard had looked empty, but the recruitment of Alan Richardson was an inspired move by Rhodes. Turning 35, Richardson had

Alexei Kervezee

been restricted by injuries during the previous two seasons at Middlesex, but his return of 55 wickets was decisive in their promotion. Worcestershire fielded the oldest new-ball pair in county cricket when 36-year-old Matt Mason was fit, but they were unerringly accurate. They compensated for Richard Jones, who faded after a promising start, and Andrew, whose most significant contributions were with the bat. He attracted interest from Sussex, but signed a new one-year deal. Jack Shantry took 36 wickets in the shorter formats.

Worcestershire were perhaps fortunate that the heavy roller was banned and green pitches prevailed, for they lacked a front-line spinner until Shakib arrived in July. The first Bangladeshi to play county cricket, he was inconsistent with the bat, but his left-arm spin was pivotal in three victories: most notably against Gloucestershire, after Alex Gidman had waived the follow-on, and then in routing Middlesex for 66 when defending a modest target. Spin remains a concern. International commitments are expected to restrict Shakib to a seven-week return for the T20 in 2011, so the emphasis falls on Moeen Ali to continue developing his off-spin.

Ben Smith lost his place midway through the season and announced his retirement, aged 38, after two decades of fine service at Leicestershire and then Worcestershire, to take up a role as assistant coach. The batting was held together by Mitchell, Moeen and Kervezee, who all passed 1,000 first-class runs. Kervezee took major strides in his third season, producing masterful strokeplay and four hundreds, including his first in the Championship and one-day competitions, before committing until 2015. Moeen's talent had never been in question, but he was more disciplined and possessed the stomach for a battle – especially when plundering 377 runs in a week in late April.

Mitchell's appetite for centuries at outgrounds continued at Cheltenham and Colwyn Bay in August, as he ascended towards the captaincy. His consistency helped compensate for Phil Jaques's mixed three-month stay; the Australian made six ducks in 15 Championship innings. David Wheeldon and James Cameron, whose hundred was crucial to the last-day run-chase, will vie to open alongside Mitchell in 2011. Ben Scott, on loan from Middlesex, performed reliably behind the stumps until Ben Cox finished school. Cox's batting will need to improve in Division One.

The most significant change came at the top, where Mark Newton stood down after a decade as chief executive. He will be remembered for overseeing the recovery from the severe floods of 2007 which placed a strain on finances. David Leatherdale, a popular former player, was promoted from commercial director, and one of his priorities was to press ahead to secure a hotel development on the New Road side of the ground, to bring in desperately needed revenue.

WORCESTERSHIRE RESULTS

All first-class matches – Played 16: Won 7, Lost 4, Drawn 5.
County Championship matches – Played 16: Won 7, Lost 4, Drawn 5.

LV= County Championship, 2nd in Division 2;
Friends Provident T20, 9th in North Division; Clydesdale Bank 40, 5th in Group A.

COUNTY CHAMPIONSHIP AVERAGES, BATTING AND FIELDING

Cap/Colours		M	I	NO	R	HS	100s	50s	Avge	Ct/St
2007	M. M. Ali	15	28	2	1,260	126	3	9	48.46	9
2009	A. N. Kervezee¶	16	30	3	1,190	155	3	6	44.07	14
2005	D. K. H. Mitchell†	16	31	3	1,180	165*	4	4	42.14	32
2010	J. G. Cameron	10	17	1	576	105	1	3	36.00	7
2008	G. M. Andrew	9	14	1	425	79	0	4	32.69	2
2010	B. J. M. Scott	7	12	2	313	98	0	3	31.30	30/1
2006	P. A. Jaques§	8	15	0	465	94	0	3	31.00	9
1998	V. S. Solanki	15	28	1	717	114	1	4	26.55	18
2010	Shakib Al Hasan§	8	15	1	358	90	0	1	25.57	3
2002	B. F. Smith	8	14	2	282	80	0	2	23.50	9
2009	D. A. Wheeldon	7	14	1	269	65	0	2	20.69	2
2009	O. B. Cox†	9	16	4	218	59	0	1	18.16	18/1
2002	M. S. Mason	8	12	2	137	51*	0	1	13.70	6
2010	A. Richardson	14	18	11	71	11	0	0	10.14	5
2007	R. A. Jones†	11	19	2	100	21*	0	0	5.88	7
2009	J. D. Shantry	11	15	5	55	13*	0	0	5.50	3

Also batted: S. H. Choudhry (colours 2010) (1 match) 63 (1 ct); Imran Arif§ (colours 2008) (2 matches) 0, 4, 4* (1 ct); C. D. Whelan (colours 2008) (1 match) 5, 0 (0 ct).

† *Born in Worcestershire.* § *Official overseas player.* ¶ *Other non-England-qualified player.* In 2002, Worcestershire replaced caps with colours awarded to all players making their Championship debut.

BOWLING

	O	M	R	W	BB	5W/i	Avge
Shakib Al Hasan	259	48	783	35	7-32	3	22.37
A. Richardson	524	153	1,342	55	5-44	2	24.40
M. S. Mason	278	72	849	31	4-87	0	27.38
G. M. Andrew	196.4	32	656	23	4-45	0	28.52
R. A. Jones	298.2	48	1,281	38	7-115	2	33.71
J. D. Shantry	308	73	945	27	5-49	1	35.00
M. M. Ali	179.4	29	626	17	5-36	1	36.82

Also bowled: J. G. Cameron 93.5–17–332–8; S. H. Choudhry 10–3–32–1; Imran Arif 33–2–141–4; A. N. Kervezee 4.3–0–63–0; D. K. H. Mitchell 15–3–64–0; V. S. Solanki 29–4–96–1; C. D. Whelan 9–1–34–1.

LEADING CB40 AVERAGES (100 runs/4 wickets)

Batting	Runs	HS	Avge	S-R	Ct
S. H. Choudhry	115	39	57.50	98.29	3
P. A. Jaques	249	110	49.80	98.03	3
Shakib Al Hasan	187	91	37.40	119.10	1
V. S. Solanki	436	129	36.33	92.76	8
M. M. Ali	383	121	31.91	98.20	5
D. K. H. Mitchell....	283	70	31.44	81.55	6

Bowling	W	BB	Avge	E-R
Shakib Al Hasan	9	4-32	17.77	5.48
A. Richardson	4	2-22	19.50	5.20
C. D. Whelan.......	4	3-34	21.00	7.63
J. D. Shantry	18	3-33	27.05	5.96
S. H. Choudhry	6	4-54	35.50	6.45
J. G. Cameron	7	4-44	41.71	6.61

LEADING FPT20 AVERAGES (100 runs/18 overs)

Batting	Runs	HS	Avge	S-R	Ct		Bowling	W	BB	Avge	E-R
S. T. Jayasuriya	267	87	26.70	158.92	2		J. D. Shantry	18	3-23	19.16	7.04
P. A. Jaques	330	78*	33.00	131.47	6		S. T. Jayasuriya	5	1-20	55.60	7.12
M. M. Ali	385	72	27.50	129.19	7		M. M. Ali	13	3-19	21.92	7.27
V. S. Solanki	121	51	20.16	114.15	2		J. G. Cameron	8	3-22	29.87	8.01
D. K. H. Mitchell	215	39	19.54	112.56	6		D. K. H. Mitchell	5	1-15	42.00	8.28
J. G. Cameron	158	51*	15.80	107.48	2		Imran Arif	2	1-30	99.00	9.00

FIRST-CLASS COUNTY RECORDS

Highest score for	405*	G. A. Hick v Somerset at Taunton	1988
Highest score against	331*	J. D. Robertson (Middlesex) at Worcester	1949
Leading run-scorer	34,490	D. Kenyon (avge 34.18)	1946–1967
Best bowling for	9-23	C. F. Root v Lancashire at Worcester	1931
Best bowling against	10-51	J. Mercer (Glamorgan) at Worcester	1936
Leading wicket-taker	2,143	R. T. D. Perks (avge 23.73)	1930–1955
Highest total for	701-6 dec	v Surrey at Worcester	2007
Highest total against	701-4 dec	by Leicestershire at Worcester	1906
Lowest total for	24	v Yorkshire at Huddersfield	1903
Lowest total against	30	by Hampshire at Worcester	1903

LIST A COUNTY RECORDS

Highest score for	180*	T. M. Moody v Surrey at The Oval	1994
Highest score against	158	W. Larkins (Northamptonshire) at Luton	1982
	158	R. A. Smith (Hampshire) at Worcester	1996
Leading run-scorer	16,416	G. A. Hick (avge 44.60)	1985–2008
Best bowling for	7-19	N. V. Radford v Bedfordshire at Bedford	1991
Best bowling against	7-15	R. A. Hutton (Yorkshire) at Leeds	1969
Leading wicket-taker	370	S. R. Lampitt (avge 24.52)	1987–2002
Highest total for	404-3	v Devon at Worcester	1987
Highest total against	358-8	by New Zealanders at Worcester	2008
Lowest total for	58	v Ireland v Worcester	2009
Lowest total against	45	by Hampshire at Worcester	1988

TWENTY20 RECORDS

Highest score for	116*	G. A. Hick v Northamptonshire at Luton	2004
Highest score against	141*	C. L. White (Somerset) at Worcester	2006
Leading run-scorer	1,201	G. A. Hick (avge 36.39)	2004–2008
Best bowling for	4-11	D. K. H. Mitchell v Gloucestershire at Bristol	2008
Best bowling against	6-21	A. J. Hall (Northamptonshire) at Northampton	2008
Leading wicket-taker	41	G. J. Batty (avge 28.19)	2003–2009
Highest total for	227-6	v Northamptonshire at Kidderminster	2007
Highest total against	222-3	by Northamptonshire at Kidderminster	2007
Lowest total for	86	v Northamptonshire at Worcester	2006
Lowest total against	93	by Gloucestershire at Bristol	2008

ADDRESS

County Ground, New Road, Worcester WR2 4QQ (01905 748474; **email** info@wccc.co.uk).
Website www.wccc.co.uk

OFFICIALS

Captain 2010 – V. S. Solanki
2011 – D. K. H. Mitchell
Director of cricket S. J. Rhodes
Academy director D. B. D'Oliveira
President C. D. Fearnley

Chairman J. M. Price
Chief executive D. A. Leatherdale
Head groundsman T. R. Packwood
Scorers N. D. Smith; D. Pugh

WORCESTERSHIRE v MIDDLESEX

At Worcester, April 9–11. Worcestershire won by 111 runs. Worcestershire 21pts, Middlesex 3pts. Toss: Middlesex. County debuts: A. Richardson, B. J. M. Scott; S. A. Newman, I. E. O'Brien.

Finn had bottled up enough frustration from a winter bowling on lifeless tracks in Asia to prove unplayable at a lush, capricious New Road. His nine for 37 and match haul of 14 for 106 were the best analyses of the first-class summer, yet from lunch on the second day he must have suspected his team would lose. There was a short boundary towards the cathedral, but only on the first morning did batsmen take advantage of it, when Worcestershire's openers shared 105. Finn returned to claim Mitchell in a surge of four for one, giving Strauss just enough time to edge behind in his first innings since the Johannesburg Test of mid-January. Middlesex began – and ended – the busy second day on

BEST BOWLING IN AN INNINGS FOR MIDDLESEX

10-40	G. O. B. Allen	v Lancashire at Lord's	1929
10-42	A. E. Trott	v Somerset at Taunton	1900
10-45	R. L. Johnson	v Derbyshire at Derby	1994
10-59	G. Burton	v Surrey at The Oval	1888
10-104	V. E. Walker	v Lancashire at Manchester	1865
9-32	J. T. Hearne	v Nottinghamshire at Nottingham	1891
9-37	**S. T. Finn**	**v Worcestershire at Worcester**	**2010**
9-41	F. A. Tarrant	v Gloucestershire at Bristol	1907

There have been 14 further instances of a bowler taking nine wickets in an innings for Middlesex. F. A. Tarrant did so another four times; J. T. Hearne, J. W. Hearne and F. J. Titmus twice each; W. W. Daniel, J. M. Sims, V. E. Walker and J. J. Warr once.

12 for one. With indentations sitting in the surface, 20 wickets tumbled, five to Richard Jones in a superb 70-minute opening spell and a more abrupt burst after lunch. Handed a lead of 161, Solanki decided to bat again, and he almost came to regret it. Finn charged in for nine wickets, all but two bowled or lbw. He would have taken all ten wickets had Strauss not dropped Jaques at slip. It was a happier occasion for Richardson, who joined from Middlesex over the winter, and bowled his new county to their first victory in 20 Championship matches, with a day to spare.

Close of play: First day, Middlesex 12-1 (Newman 5, O'Brien 5); Second day, Middlesex 12-1 (Strauss 10, O'Brien 1).

Worcestershire

D. K. H. Mitchell c Strauss b Finn	85	– c Strauss b Finn	1
P. A. Jaques lbw b O'Brien	47	– c Strauss b O'Brien	41
*V. S. Solanki c Simpson b Berg	8	– b Finn	5
M. M. Ali c Simpson b Berg	7	– b Finn	0
A. N. Kervezee b Finn	44	– b Finn	43
B. F. Smith c Strauss b Finn	46	– lbw b Finn	2
†B. J. M. Scott c Simpson b Finn	0	– b Finn	3
G. M. Andrew c Simpson b Finn	0	– c Berg b Finn	12
R. A. Jones c sub (T. S. Roland-Jones) b Udal	16	– lbw b Finn	3
C. D. Whelan c Simpson b Berg	5	– lbw b Finn	0
A. Richardson not out	1	– not out	4
B 5, l-b 15, w 4, n-b 4	28	L-b 4, w 1	5

1/105 (2) 2/125 (3) 3/143 (4)	(87.3 overs) 287	
4/208 (5) 5/211 (1) 6/214 (7)		
7/214 (8) 8/271 (9) 9/285 (6) 10/287 (10)		

1/8 (1) 2/26 (3)	(42.4 overs) 119	
3/26 (4) 4/81 (2)		
5/96 (6) 6/97 (5) 7/104 (7)		
8/112 (9) 9/112 (10) 10/119 (8)		

Murtagh 17–5–34–0; Finn 22–4–69–5; O'Brien 18–4–47–1; Berg 17.3–3–62–3; Udal 11–1–45–1; Malan 2–0–10–0. *Second Innings*—Finn 15.4–5–37–9; O'Brien 10–1–27–1; Murtagh 7–1–20–0; Udal 4–0–10–0; Berg 6–1–21–0.

Middlesex

S. A. Newman c Mitchell b Richardson	8	– c Mitchell b Richardson	1
A. J. Strauss c Scott b Jones	1	– lbw b Richardson	15
I. E. O'Brien b Jones	5	– c Mitchell b Jones	5
S. D. Robson c and b Whelan	32	– c Scott b Andrew	17
D. J. Malan b Jones	1	– c Smith b Andrew	69
A. B. London run out	9	– run out	15
†J. A. Simpson lbw b Jones	20	– c Scott b Jones	0
G. K. Berg not out	13	– lbw b Richardson	22
*S. D. Udal c Kervezee b Richardson	11	– c Kervezee b Richardson	13
T. J. Murtagh b Jones	8	– not out	0
S. T. Finn c Smith b Jones	0	– c Jones b Andrew	1
B 1, l-b 5, w 12	18	B 4, l-b 2, w 5	11

1/6 (2) 2/13 (3) 3/24 (1) 4/29 (5) (49.2 overs) 126
5/47 (6) 6/86 (4) 7/92 (7) 8/113 (9)
9/122 (10) 10/126 (11)

1/2 (1) 2/19 (2) (54.3 overs) 169
3/28 (3) 4/70 (4)
5/107 (6) 6/110 (7) 7/149 (8)
8/168 (5) 9/168 (9) 10/169 (11)

Richardson 20–7–41–2; Jones 17.2–5–37–6; Andrew 8–2–21–0; Whelan 4–0–21–1. *Second Innings*—Richardson 19–9–35–4; Jones 15–1–68–2; Andrew 13.3–1–40–3; Whelan 5–1–13–0; Mitchell 2–0–7–0.

Umpires: V. A. Holder and D. J. Millns.

At Kidderminster, April 15–17 (not first-class). **Worcestershire won by 250 runs. Worcestershire 358-8 dec** (V. S. Solanki 30, G. M. Andrew 75, O. B. Cox 110*, Extras 42; R. A. Whiteley 4-64, R. A. L. Moore 3-84) **and 131-6 dec** (J. G. Cameron 41, V. S. Solanki 62*; R. A. L. Moore 4-16); ‡**Leeds/Bradford MCCU 142** (A. J. Blake 43, B. P. Kruger 34; Imran Arif 4-32, J. D. Shantry 5-18) **and 97** (J. D. Shantry 7-47, M. M. Ali 3-27). *County debuts*: J. G. Cameron, J. K. Manuel. *Leeds/ Bradford were overwhelmed by Jack Shantry's late left-arm swing; he delivered ten maidens in 15.3 overs in the first innings, and finished with match figures of 12-65. Worcestershire limped to 140-6 after being put in, losing Wheeldon and Moeen Ali in the same Ross Whiteley over, until Ben Cox, playing his second first-team match, turned the tables with Andrew in a demoralising stand of 164. Later, Andrew's price for holding a slip catch was a cut finger; George Rhodes, the 16-year-old son of Worcestershire director of cricket Steve, replaced him and took two catches.*

At Whitgift School, Croydon, April 21–24. WORCESTERSHIRE drew with SURREY.

WORCESTERSHIRE v GLAMORGAN

At Worcester, April 27–28. Glamorgan won by nine wickets. Glamorgan 21pts, Worcestershire 3pts. Toss: Worcestershire.

Worcestershire's surrender inside two days validated widely held concerns about their brittle batting. The shining exception was Moeen Ali, who carried on as if still batting at Croydon by striking 13 fours in 135 balls. His defiance was cut short by the surrounding mayhem, as Harrison, gaining steep bounce from just short of a length, knocked over the tail to claim his first seven-wicket haul. By stumps, Glamorgan's lead was already 94 and, though Wright and Allenby were out early on the second day as six wickets went down for 31, Worcestershire never truly recovered. Harris, at 19 years and 347 days, became the youngest Glamorgan player to reach 100 first-class wickets when he had Jaques caught by Wright at square leg. Moeen and Kervezee – whose 27 was the next highest score by a home batsman – at least wiped out the deficit, but Worcestershire could go little further. Having passed 50 for the fourth consecutive time, Moeen was strangled down the leg side, and the rest waved the white flag: from 160 for four, Worcestershire were all out for 171.

Close of play: First day, Glamorgan 228-4 (Wright 71, Allenby 49).

Worcestershire

P. A. Jaques c Wallace b Harris	0	– (2) c Wright b Harris	25
D. K. H. Mitchell c Waters b Harrison	5	– (1) c Wallace b Harris	19
*V. S. Solanki c Dalrymple b Harrison	1	– b Allenby	18
M. M. Ali not out	85	– c Wallace b Harrison	58
A. N. Kervezee c Wallace b Harris	6	– c Cosker b Harris	27
B. F. Smith lbw b Allenby	15	– b Allenby	6
†B. J. M. Scott c Rees b Harrison	5	– lbw b Harris	1
R. A. Jones lbw b Harrison	3	– b Allenby	3
A. Richardson lbw b Harrison	2	– lbw b Allenby	0
J. D. Shantry lbw b Harrison	0	– c Cosgrove b Harris	0
Imran Arif c Cosgrove b Harrison	4	– not out	4
B 1, l-b 4, w 1, n-b 2	8	B 5, l-b 3, n-b 2	10

1/0 (1) 2/10 (2) 3/19 (3) 4/36 (5)   (47.5 overs) 134
5/62 (6) 6/88 (7) 7/97 (8) 8/123 (9)
9/123 (10) 10/134 (11)

1/26 (1) 2/47 (2)   (52.2 overs) 171
3/105 (3) 4/142 (4)
5/160 (5) 6/162 (6) 7/166 (8)
8/166 (9) 9/166 (7) 10/171 (10)

Harris 15–5–50–2; Harrison 16.5–5–45–7; Waters 7–2–14–0; Allenby 9–2–20–1. *Second Innings—* Harris 17.2–7–56–5; Harrison 13–3–44–1; Waters 7–0–33–0; Allenby 13–6–23–4; Cosker 2–0–7–0.

Glamorgan

G. P. Rees c Ali b Shantry	42	– not out	21
M. J. Cosgrove c Jones b Imran Arif	26	– b Shantry	10
M. J. Powell b Richardson	5	– not out	10
B. J. Wright c Scott b Jones	79		
*J. W. M. Dalrymple c Ali b Shantry	25		
J. Allenby c Scott b Richardson	55		
†M. A. Wallace c Imran Arif b Shantry	14		
J. A. R. Harris c Jones b Richardson	6		
D. A. Cosker not out	2		
D. S. Harrison c Solanki b Richardson	1		
H. T. Waters c Jaques b Richardson	0		
L-b 7, w 1, n-b 4	12		

1/42 (2) 2/51 (3) 3/110 (1)   (67.2 overs) 267   1/12 (2)   (1 wkt, 7.4 overs) 41
4/140 (5) 5/236 (4) 6/250 (6)
7/262 (8) 8/264 (7) 9/265 (10) 10/267 (11)

Richardson 26.2–10–86–5; Jones 17–2–82–1; Imran Arif 12–0–44–1; Shantry 12–2–48–3. *Second Innings—* Imran Arif 4–0–17–0; Shantry 3.4–0–24–1.

Umpires: M. J. D. Bodenham and M. A. Gough.

At Leicester, May 4–7. WORCESTERSHIRE beat LEICESTERSHIRE by 173 runs.

WORCESTERSHIRE v DERBYSHIRE

At Worcester, May 17–20. Worcestershire won by eight wickets. Worcestershire 24pts, Derbyshire 3pts. Toss: Worcestershire. First-class debut: J. G. Cameron.

Jaques entered this match in the roughest trot imaginable, with five ducks in six Championship innings. By the end, his indiscriminate hitting had Derbyshire's bowlers cowering. There were signs of Jaques regaining his touch in the first innings, as the home batsmen exacted sweet revenge upon New Road; 71 wickets had fallen in four and a half days of Championship cricket here before this orgy. Mitchell accumulated calmly, and Kervezee ended his wait for a maiden Worcestershire hundred, in front of his parents, visiting from Rotterdam. Derbyshire slumped to 172 for nine before Steffan Jones pummelled 15 fours and a six in his 86, the highest score by a No. 11 in the county's history. But Derbyshire still followed on, and trailed by 81 at the close. Last-day spectators were admitted free, and watched Park – whose unbeaten century spanned six and a half hours – resist bravely with the lower order until a delayed tea, in the face of superb bowling by Richardson. Thanks to Jaques, who hit 80 runs in boundaries and was caught at deep midwicket attempting a 57-ball hundred, Worcestershire needed barely half their 30 overs.

Close of play: First day, Worcestershire 376-3 (Kervezee 66, Cameron 2); Second day, Derbyshire 138-6 (Peterson 34, Poynton 6); Third day, Derbyshire 183-3 (Park 34, Smith 54).

Worcestershire

D. K. H. Mitchell b Peterson	148	– c Borrington b Lungley ... 5
P. A. Jaques b Lungley	92	– c Madsen b Peterson ... 94
*V. S. Solanki run out	42	– not out ... 18
A. N. Kervezee c Peterson b Lungley	130	– not out ... 4
J. G. Cameron c Poynton b Jones	25	
B. F. Smith lbw b Peterson	14	
†B. J. M. Scott not out	40	
G. M. Andrew c Smith b Peterson	33	
R. A. Jones c Lungley b Peterson	0	
B 9, l-b 15, w 3, n-b 8	35	L-b 1, n-b 4 ... 5

1/167 (2) 2/243 (3)   (8 wkts dec, 142 overs) 559   1/32 (1)   (2 wkts, 15.5 overs) 126
3/357 (1) 4/442 (5) 5/471 (4)   2/122 (2)
6/491 (6) 7/558 (8) 8/559 (9)   110 overs: 439-3

J. D. Shantry and A. Richardson did not bat.

Jones 28–6–79–1; Groenewald 24–2–96–0; Smith 21–2–93–0; Lungley 21–1–90–2; Peterson 47–7–170–4; Park 1–0–7–0. *Second Innings*—Jones 3–2–5–0; Groenewald 2–0–21–0; Peterson 5.5–0–46–1; Lungley 3–0–29–1; Park 2–0–24–0.

Derbyshire

*C. J. L. Rogers c Mitchell b Richardson	50	– (2) c Jaques b Shantry ... 32
W. L. Madsen c Mitchell b Jones	8	– (1) c Smith b Andrew ... 34
P. M. Borrington c Scott b Jones	0	– c Jaques b Andrew ... 25
G. T. Park c Solanki b Shantry	14	– not out ... 124
G. M. Smith c Scott b Richardson	3	– c Scott b Jones ... 64
C. F. Hughes b Jones	18	– c Kervezee b Shantry ... 20
R. J. Peterson c Mitchell b Richardson	46	– c Scott b Richardson ... 25
†T. Poynton c Smith b Richardson	13	– c Solanki b Jones ... 2
T. Lungley c Scott b Andrew	8	– lbw b Andrew ... 14
T. D. Groenewald not out	35	– c Jaques b Jones ... 14
P. S. Jones c Cameron b Andrew	86	– c Scott b Richardson ... 21
B 8, l-b 4, w 2	14	B 6, l-b 6, w 2 ... 14

1/26 (2) 2/26 (3) 3/75 (4) 4/75 (1)   (86.3 overs) 295   1/51 (2) 2/85 (1)   (121 overs) 389
5/80 (5) 6/108 (6) 7/158 (7)   3/104 (3) 4/197 (5)
8/165 (8) 9/172 (9) 10/295 (11)   5/234 (6) 6/276 (7) 7/279 (8)
                                           8/300 (9) 9/343 (10) 10/389 (11)

Richardson 27–6–72–4; Jones 28–9–93–3; Shantry 14–4–51–1; Andrew 12.3–1–57–2; Solanki 1–0–10–0. *Second Innings*—Richardson 31–9–82–2; Jones 22–2–108–3; Shantry 19–4–57–2; Andrew 19–0–61–3; Cameron 12–1–29–0; Solanki 18–3–40–0.

Umpires: N. J. Llong and D. J. Millns.

At Hove, May 24–27. WORCESTERSHIRE drew with SUSSEX.

WORCESTERSHIRE v GLOUCESTERSHIRE

At Worcester, May 29–June 1. Drawn. Worcestershire 10pts, Gloucestershire 5pts (after 2pt penalty). Toss: Gloucestershire.

It was rain, rather than any hindrance by Gloucestershire, which prevented Worcestershire from occupying a promotion place heading towards the Twenty20 break. Play did not start until 3.15 p.m. on the first day, or 3.45 on the fourth and, after a final aimless passage, Solanki shook hands with

Gloucestershire 100 runs ahead and seven wickets down. Worcestershire's last chance passed when Banerjee was dropped at fourth slip by Solanki, denying Richardson a fifth wicket in the innings. Mason, making his first Championship appearance of the season following a prolonged back injury, was one of five bowlers to take two wickets as Gloucestershire underperformed in their first innings. The increasingly dependable Moeen Ali constructed Worcestershire's lead, scoring at nearly six an over alongside Kervezee and adding a further 96 with Scott, playing his last Championship innings before the end of his loan period from Middlesex. Kirby was out of the attack on the third day with back spasms, and it showed. Gloucestershire would have claimed second position outright had they not been docked two points for a slow over-rate.

Close of play: First day, Gloucestershire 78-3 (Marshall 23, Gidman 0); Second day, Worcestershire 229-6 (Ali 70, Scott 0); Third day, Gloucestershire 189-5 (Taylor 18, Franklin 21).

Gloucestershire

†J. N. Batty c Kervezee b Richardson	38	– c Mitchell b Richardson	43
S. D. Snell c Mitchell b Jones	6	– c Smith b Mason	7
C. D. J. Dent c Mason b Jones	5	– c Scott b Shantry	21
H. J. H. Marshall c Scott b Mason	37	– c Smith b Richardson	50
*A. P. R. Gidman c Scott b Mason	10	– c Scott b Shantry	18
C. G. Taylor b Richardson	71	– b Richardson	30
J. E. C. Franklin c Mitchell b Ali	32	– c Kervezee b Richardson	23
J. Lewis c Scott b Shantry	14	– not out	16
V. Banerjee c Mitchell b Ali	0	– not out	17
S. P. Kirby not out	15		
A. J. Ireland c Jones b Shantry	6		
B 2, l-b 6, w 1, n-b 2	11	B 4, l-b 14	18

1/14 (2) 2/24 (3) 3/78 (1) 4/97 (5) (77.4 overs) 245 1/19 (2) (7 wkts dec, 83 overs) 243
5/106 (4) 6/173 (7) 7/190 (8) 2/61 (3) 3/100 (1)
8/201 (9) 9/234 (6) 10/245 (11) 4/138 (4) 5/154 (5) 6/195 (7) 7/218 (6)

Mason 17–7–42–2; Jones 17–3–69–2; Richardson 21–3–58–2; Shantry 14.4–4–48–2; Ali 8–2–20–2. *Second Innings*—Mason 19–4–53–1; Jones 11–1–54–0; Shantry 20–7–39–2; Richardson 28–8–68–4; Ali 5–1–11–0.

Worcestershire

D. K. H. Mitchell c Marshall b Ireland	29	J. D. Shantry not out	13
P. A. Jaques c Snell b Ireland	38	A. Richardson st Batty b Banerjee	5
*V. S. Solanki c Marshall b Lewis	27	M. S. Mason c Marshall b Lewis	27
M. M. Ali c Dent b Banerjee	106	B 7, l-b 4, n-b 4	15
A. N. Kervezee lbw b Lewis	57		
B. F. Smith c Snell b Lewis	3	1/53 (1) 2/70 (2) 3/107 (3) (82.1 overs) 388
R. A. Jones b Gidman	1	4/214 (5) 5/218 (6) 6/221 (7)
†B. J. M. Scott b Ireland	67	7/317 (4) 8/345 (8) 9/352 (10) 10/388 (11)

Lewis 20.3–4–55–4; Kirby 9.4–1–56–0; Ireland 20–2–92–3; Franklin 8–1–61–0; Banerjee 13–0–79–2; Gidman 11–2–34–1.

Umpires: I. Dawood and R. T. Robinson.

WORCESTERSHIRE v LEICESTERSHIRE

At Worcester, June 28–30. Leicestershire won by seven wickets. Leicestershire 22pts, Worcestershire 3pts. Toss: Worcestershire.

The internal conflict at Grace Road began to unravel when chief executive David Smith resigned during a meeting on the first morning. Sixty miles south-west, Leicestershire's bowlers were taking strides towards a fourth victory of the season. They had Worcestershire 77 for six, and a worse plight was prevented by stubborn knocks from Andrew and Cox, six days after completing his A-levels at

Bromsgrove School. With Jefferson and du Toit sharing a century partnership, Leicestershire suffered few problems in comparison and led by 134 on first innings. Briefly, a two-day conclusion looked possible: Worcestershire were 59 for four when Ben Smith was out to Malik, ending a distinguished but fading 21 seasons in service for both counties (he had not scored a hundred since July 2006). Against the odds, Worcestershire made a game of it: acting-captain Mitchell was dropped three times before reaching his fifty, and gritty seventies from Cameron and Andrew set Leicestershire a potentially hazardous 182. But wayward new-ball bowling and more slapdash fielding – Nixon was missed on five and 12 – assured them comfortable passage.

Close of play: First day, Leicestershire 163-3 (Taylor 13, Buck 4); Second day, Worcestershire 168-4 (Mitchell 63, Cameron 62).

Worcestershire

*D. K. H. Mitchell b Hoggard	0	– lbw b Malik	77
P. A. Jaques c Henderson b Malik	8	– c du Toit b Buck	0
M. M. Ali lbw b Benning	33	– c New b Buck	24
A. N. Kervezee b Malik	1	– b Buck	8
B. F. Smith c New b Buck	14	– c New b Malik	9
J. G. Cameron c du Toit b Buck	15	– c New b Malik	75
†O. B. Cox c New b Naik	42	– lbw b Benning	22
G. M. Andrew not out	53	– b Naik	79
R. A. Jones lbw b Henderson	0	– b Benning	4
M. S. Mason c Jefferson b Naik	1	– c Benning b Henderson	3
J. D. Shantry c Jefferson b Henderson	1	– not out	5
B 4, l-b 1, w 2	7	L-b 3, w 4, n-b 2	9

1/0 (1) 2/24 (2) 3/29 (4) 4/60 (3)   (59.1 overs) 175
5/66 (5) 6/77 (6) 7/148 (7) 8/149 (9)
9/154 (10) 10/175 (11)

1/4 (2) 2/32 (3)   (90.1 overs) 315
3/40 (4) 4/59 (5)
5/197 (1) 6/209 (6) 7/238 (7)
8/246 (9) 9/284 (10) 10/315 (8)

Hoggard 13–5–34–1; Buck 12–3–29–2; Malik 12–4–50–2; Benning 9–2–21–1; Henderson 8.1–1–21–2; Naik 5–2–15–2. *Second Innings*—Hoggard 14–1–62–0; Buck 17–1–65–3; Malik 25–6–73–3; Henderson 17–5–33–1; Naik 7.1–1–41–1; Benning 10–0–38–2.

Leicestershire

W. I. Jefferson lbw b Jones	64	– c Jaques b Andrew	32
P. A. Nixon c Cox b Mason	11	– c Cox b Shantry	55
J. du Toit c Cox b Ali	57	– lbw b Andrew	11
J. W. A. Taylor c Smith b Mason	27	– not out	43
N. L. Buck lbw b Mason	4		
J. G. E. Benning c Smith b Shantry	29	– (5) not out	26
†T. J. New b Jones	58		
J. K. H. Naik c Mitchell b Andrew	10		
C. W. Henderson b Andrew	8		
M. N. Malik not out	13		
*M. J. Hoggard b Andrew	6		
B 12, l-b 10	22	B 8, l-b 7	15

1/23 (2) 2/130 (3) 3/150 (1)   (79.2 overs) 309
4/167 (5) 5/202 (6) 6/222 (4)
7/258 (8) 8/280 (9) 9/294 (7) 10/309 (11)

1/61 (1)   (3 wkts, 45.5 overs) 182
2/73 (3) 3/139 (2)

Mason 25–9–56–3; Jones 19–0–96–2; Andrew 19.2–4–68–3; Shantry 11–0–42–1; Ali 5–1–25–1. *Second Innings*—Mason 14–4–52–0; Jones 4–1–26–0; Shantry 10.3–3–35–1; Andrew 10–3–24–2; Ali 6–2–20–0; Cameron 1.5–0–10–0.

Umpires: J. H. Evans and N. A. Mallender.

At Derby, July 21–24. WORCESTERSHIRE drew with DERBYSHIRE.

WORCESTERSHIRE v NORTHAMPTONSHIRE

At Worcester, July 29–31. Northamptonshire won by four wickets. Northamptonshire 19pts, Worcestershire 5pts. Toss: Worcestershire. First-class debut: R. I. Newton.

There was little mistaking the importance of Richard Jones's erratic tenth over. Northamptonshire were 113 for eight in their first innings before Jones conceded three sets of four leg-byes and a four; Murphy and Lucas gratefully knocked off the remaining nine runs needed to avoid the follow-on. Northamptonshire conceded a first-innings deficit of 129, but their bowlers had next use of a springy, unpredictable pitch, and Daggett raced through the top four with the new ball. Seventeen wickets fell in the day and, when the last two Worcestershire tailenders were brushed aside on the third morning, Northamptonshire had salvaged an achievable target of 223. The decisive hand came from Wakely, who batted from the sixth to the 49th over in resisting Richardson and Mason, who had shared six wickets (and 21 maidens) in dismantling Northamptonshire's first innings. Howgego and Hall were both run out for the second day in a row, but Murphy (one of the guilty parties) took care of the winning runs. On the opening day, Bangladesh High Commissioner Sayeedur Rahman Khan came to watch Shakib Al Hasan's home Championship debut; in the event, Shakib was upstaged by Cox and Mason, who blasted his first fifty in six years, from just 30 balls.

Close of play: First day, Northamptonshire 3-1 (Howgego 0, Middlebrook 2); Second day, Worcestershire 72-8 (Jones 1, Mason 0).

Worcestershire

D. K. H. Mitchell c Middlebrook b Chigumbura	23	– c Middlebrook b Daggett	7
D. A. Wheeldon b Chigumbura	50	– lbw b Daggett	14
*V. S. Solanki c Peters b Lucas	17	– c Peters b Daggett	0
M. M. Ali c Wakely b Lucas	0	– c Hall b Daggett	9
A. N. Kervezee b Middlebrook	28	– c Murphy b Hall	24
Shakib Al Hasan c Peters b Chigumbura	9	– b Lucas	0
J. G. Cameron c Murphy b Lucas	7	– b Middlebrook	7
†O. B. Cox c Peters b Hall	59	– c Peters b Middlebrook	0
R. A. Jones run out	8	– lbw b Middlebrook	7
M. S. Mason not out	51	– c Murphy b Hall	8
A. Richardson lbw b Lucas	11	– not out	0
B 2, l-b 9, w 1, n-b 12	24	B 8, l-b 7, n-b 2	17

1/45 (1) 2/84 (3) 3/84 (4)   (87.3 overs) 287
4/128 (5) 5/130 (2) 6/145 (6) 7/158 (7)
8/195 (9) 9/233 (8) 10/287 (11)

1/8 (1) 2/14 (3)   (38.2 overs) 93
3/23 (2) 4/42 (4)
5/43 (6) 6/70 (5) 7/71 (8)
8/72 (7) 9/89 (10) 10/93 (9)

Daggett 19–6–66–0; Lucas 23.3–9–84–4; Chigumbura 19–5–53–3; Hall 17–5–53–1; Middlebrook 9–2–36–1. *Second Innings*—Daggett 10–4–25–4; Lucas 10–3–20–1; Middlebrook 9.2–3–23–3; Hall 9–6–10–2.

Northamptonshire

S. D. Peters c Mitchell b Mason	0	– c Mitchell b Richardson	37
B. H. N. Howgego run out	8	– run out	3
J. D. Middlebrook c Cox b Richardson	2		
A. G. Wakely c Solanki b Cameron	20	– (3) c Kervezee b Ali	68
D. J. Sales c Mitchell b Mason	0	– (4) lbw b Mason	46
R. I. Newton c Solanki b Cameron	23	– (5) c Cox b Cameron	33
*A. J. Hall run out	28	– (6) run out	9
E. Chigumbura c Cox b Mason	0	– (7) not out	7
†D. Murphy c Ali b Richardson	26	– (8) not out	10
D. S. Lucas b Richardson	24		
L. M. Daggett not out	0		
B 6, l-b 21	27	B 3, l-b 6, n-b 4	13

1/0 (1) 2/7 (3) 3/16 (2) 4/16 (5)   (60.4 overs) 158
5/56 (4) 6/73 (6) 7/74 (8) 8/98 (7)
9/141 (9) 10/158 (10)

1/9 (2) 2/54 (1)   (6 wkts, 58 overs) 226
3/127 (4) 4/196 (3)
5/206 (6) 6/208 (5)

Mason 20–9–34–3; Richardson 20.4–12–28–3; Cameron 6–1–18–2; Jones 11–2–36–0; Shakib Al Hasan 3–0–15–0. *Second Innings*—Mason 15–4–62–1; Richardson 17–3–50–1; Jones 6–1–33–0; Shakib Al Hasan 10–2–35–0; Cameron 7–0–25–1; Ali 3–0–12–1.

Umpires: M. J. D. Bodenham and R. T. Robinson.

At Cheltenham, August 4–7. WORCESTERSHIRE beat GLOUCESTERSHIRE by six wickets.

At Colwyn Bay, August 9–12. WORCESTERSHIRE lost to GLAMORGAN by 241 runs. *Vikram Solanki resigns as captain, with Worcestershire 36 points adrift of the promotion places.*

At Worcester, August 13–14. WORCESTERSHIRE drew with PAKISTANIS (see Pakistani tour section).

WORCESTERSHIRE v SURREY

At Worcester, August 16–19. Worcestershire won by 238 runs. Worcestershire 22pts, Surrey 5pts. Toss: Worcestershire.

Worcestershire's emphatic win was overshadowed by a confrontation between their former spinner Gareth Batty and a home spectator. Batty had been heckled throughout and, after driving to point on the final day, stopped several times on his way off the pitch to exchange comments with members of the crowd. Having briefly returned to the changing-room, he sat down next to one individual, and asked him, "What have I done to offend you?" Batty was led away by Surrey assistant coach Ian Salisbury, and later seen in tears, being comforted by team-mates. His mother was also subjected to abuse. Worcestershire apologised to Batty and spoke to some of those involved, but took no further action. "We don't want to be known for this sort of thing," said chairman Martyn Price. "All our former players are welcome back and Gareth, who always gave his best, is a fine chap." Though Davies, afforded a warmer reception on his return, passed 1,000 first-class runs for the season in his 68, Surrey were always playing catch-up. Tremlett and Batty gave them brief hope, but came a cropper against a fearless counter-attacking century by Kervezee, who plundered 98 on the third afternoon alone. Ramprakash was bowled second ball by a beauty from Shakib Al Hasan as Surrey limped to 66 for four by the close, then folded spinelessly in 48 minutes on the last morning.

Close of play: First day, Surrey 12-0 (Lancefield 7, Harinath 1); Second day, Worcestershire 13-0 (Mitchell 4, Wheeldon 7); Third day, Surrey 66-4 (Hamilton-Brown 3, Davies 4).

Worcestershire

*D. K. H. Mitchell c Walters b Tremlett	5	– b Batty	16
D. A. Wheeldon lbw b Dernbach	65	– lbw b Batty	7
V. S. Solanki b Batty	37	– c Spiegel b Tremlett	0
M. M. Ali lbw b Batty	13	– c Spiegel b Batty	22
A. N. Kervezee b Dernbach	0	– b Tremlett	144
Shakib Al Hasan b Tremlett	18	– c Davies b Tremlett	34
J. G. Cameron c Walters b Tremlett	95	– b Meaker	17
†O. B. Cox lbw b Batty	18	– b Spiegel	13
G. M. Andrew b Dernbach	24	– b Batty	34
M. S. Mason c Lancefield b Tremlett	4	– b Dernbach	8
J. D. Shantry not out	4	– not out	1
B 14, l-b 9, w 2	25	B 5, l-b 12, w 4, n-b 2	23

1/10 (1) 2/55 (3) 3/83 (4) 4/84 (5) (90.1 overs) 308
5/106 (6) 6/211 (2) 7/254 (8)
8/296 (7) 9/300 (9) 10/308 (10)

1/13 (2) 2/16 (3) (76.5 overs) 319
3/50 (1) 4/63 (4)
5/125 (6) 6/181 (7) 7/218 (8)
8/292 (9) 9/313 (5) 10/319 (10)

Tremlett 19.1–5–45–4; Meaker 18–5–76–0; Dernbach 25–4–78–3; Batty 23–3–68–3; Spiegel 4–2–11–0; Hamilton-Brown 1–0–7–0. *Second Innings*—Dernbach 18.5–3–76–1; Tremlett 19–7–42–4; Batty 25–1–116–3; Meaker 11–1–53–1; Spiegel 3–0–15–1.

Surrey

T. J. Lancefield b Shakib Al Hasan	74	– c Cameron b Shakib Al Hasan	35
A. Harinath c Mitchell b Mason	8	– lbw b Andrew	21
M. R. Ramprakash run out	20	– (4) b Shakib Al Hasan	0
*R. J. Hamilton-Brown c Mitchell b Andrew	1	– (5) c Cameron b Shakib Al Hasan	34
†S. M. Davies lbw b Cameron	68	– (6) c Shantry b Shakib Al Hasan	19
S. J. Walters c Cameron b Shakib Al Hasan	21	– (7) lbw b Mason	1
M. N. W. Spriegel lbw b Cameron	4	– (8) b Mason	1
G. J. Batty b Mason	30	– (9) c Kervezee b Mason	6
C. T. Tremlett lbw b Mason	10	– (10) lbw b Shakib Al Hasan	6
S. C. Meaker c Mitchell b Shantry	1	– (3) lbw b Shakib Al Hasan	1
J. W. Dernbach not out	0	– not out	4
B 4, l-b 6, w 10, n-b 2	22	B 1, l-b 1	2

1/29 (2) 2/71 (3) 3/73 (4) 4/161 (1)   (90 overs) 259
5/213 (5) 6/213 (6) 7/224 (7) 8/258 (8)
9/259 (9) 10/259 (10)

1/57 (1) 2/59 (3)   (33.4 overs) 130
3/59 (4) 4/61 (2)
5/112 (6) 6/112 (5) 7/113 (8)
8/119 (9) 9/122 (7) 10/130 (10)

Mason 23–5–60–3; Andrew 11–4–38–1; Shantry 20–7–57–1; Cameron 14–6–30–2; Ali 2–1–4–0; Shakib Al Hasan 20–4–60–2. *Second Innings*—Mason 12–0–60–3; Shantry 5–1–16–0; Shakib Al Hasan 11.4–0–42–6; Andrew 5–1–10–1.

Umpires: S. C. Gale and M. A. Gough.

At Northampton, August 25–28. WORCESTERSHIRE drew with NORTHAMPTONSHIRE.

At Lord's, September 7–10. WORCESTERSHIRE beat MIDDLESEX by 111 runs.

WORCESTERSHIRE v SUSSEX

At Worcester, September 13–16. Worcestershire won by four wickets. Worcestershire 20pts, Sussex 4pts. Toss: Sussex. First-class debut: L. W. P. Wells.

Worcestershire performed superbly under new captain Mitchell to claw back a deficit of 36 points over four matches and steal promotion on the final day of the season. They needed ten more points than Glamorgan from the last round, but there seemed little room for manoeuvre with only 81 overs bowled on the first two days; Luke Wells, son of former captain Alan batted for 46 of them. Then Goodwin, perhaps in a compliant mood after Sussex were presented with the Division Two trophy on the third evening, agreed to a contrived run-chase. Wright and Hodd were gifted 106 runs in 51 balls, allowing Sussex to stretch their lead to 300. It left Worcestershire 70 overs to pursue a distant target on a two-paced pitch, against an attack missing Collymore and Yardy. At 44 for two they were up against it, until a remarkably assured third-wicket partnership of 215 in 35.4 overs between Cameron, who scored a maiden century in his first match as opener, and Moeen Ali, with his third hundred of the season. Worcestershire succeeded with 15 overs to spare, and could afford some over-zealous swipes with the line approaching. Players and supporters waited anxiously for more than an hour before it was confirmed that Glamorgan had failed to beat Derbyshire at Cardiff, prompting jubilation in front of the pavilion. It was Worcestershire's third promotion in five seasons.

Close of play: First day, Sussex 191-7 (Hodd 31, Beer 22); Second day, Sussex 225-7 (Hodd 51, Beer 35); Third day, Sussex 102-2 (Brown 37, Goodwin 34).

Sussex

L. W. P. Wells c Andrew b Richardson	62	– c Solanki b Richardson 8
C. D. Nash lbw b Mason	0	
B. C. Brown lbw b Andrew	32	– c Mitchell b Richardson 37
*M. W. Goodwin c Solanki b Richardson	34	– run out 63
L. J. Wright c Mitchell b Mason	0	– not out 94
†A. J. Hodd b Andrew	52	– not out 39
Yasir Arafat lbw b Cameron	1	
J. E. Anyon c Mitchell b Richardson	0	– (2) c Ali b Andrew 16
W. A. T. Beer not out	37	
L. J. Hatchett c Mason b Andrew	4	
M. S. Panesar c Mason b Andrew	0	
B 10, l-b 4, w 1	15	L-b 1, n-b 6 7

1/3 (2) 2/77 (3) 3/131 (4)   (83.2 overs) 237   1/25 (1)   (4 wkts dec, 44.3 overs) 264
4/132 (5) 5/136 (1) 6/145 (7)   2/29 (2) 3/119 (3) 4/149 (4)
7/148 (8) 8/227 (6) 9/237 (10) 10/237 (11)

Mason 17–5–63–2; Richardson 27–7–47–3; Shantry 14–4–37–0; Andrew 16.2–4–45–4; Shakib Al Hasan 5–2–13–0; Cameron 4–2–18–1. *Second Innings*—Andrew 11–2–63–1; Richardson 13–6–32–2; Mason 1–0–14–0; Shantry 4–0–22–0; Shakib Al Hasan 4–0–12–0; Ali 4–0–24–0; Kervezee 4.3–0–63–0; Solanki 1–0–19–0; Mitchell 1–0–13–0; Cameron 1–0–1–0.

Worcestershire

*D. K. H. Mitchell c Hodd b Yasir Arafat	3	– lbw b Panesar 16
J. G. Cameron run out	49	– b Panesar 105
V. S. Solanki lbw b Beer	52	– c Wright b Yasir Arafat 4
M. M. Ali b Wright	24	– c Brown b Yasir Arafat 115
A. N. Kervezee lbw b Wright	10	– not out 24
Shakib Al Hasan c Hodd b Beer	18	– b Panesar 14
G. M. Andrew c Hodd b Wright	5	– c Hatchett b Anyon 1
†O. B. Cox not out	18	– not out 2
M. S. Mason c Beer b Panesar	5	
J. D. Shantry c Hodd b Beer	0	
A. Richardson not out	4	
B 3, l-b 6, n-b 4	13	B 13, l-b 11, w 1 25

1/4 (1) 2/81 (2)   (9 wkts dec, 61.4 overs) 201   1/37 (1)   (6 wkts, 55.1 overs) 306
3/132 (4) 4/138 (3) 5/146 (5)   2/44 (3) 3/259 (2)
6/160 (7) 7/180 (6) 8/185 (9) 9/190 (10)   4/261 (4) 5/291 (6) 6/298 (7)

Yasir Arafat 12–4–29–1; Hatchett 9–3–25–0; Wright 15–2–48–3; Anyon 3–0–11–0; Panesar 14–2–48–1; Beer 8.4–2–31–3. *Second Innings*—Yasir Arafat 12–2–50–2; Hatchett 3–0–15–0; Panesar 21.1–3–85–3; Wright 3–0–30–0; Beer 6–1–30–0; Anyon 8–0–56–1; Wells 2–0–16–0.

Umpires: R. A. Kettleborough and J. W. Lloyds.

YORKSHIRE

New fire burns in Broad Acres

David Warner

Yorkshire were given a standing ovation as they trooped off the field on the final day of the season despite the Championship having just slipped through their grasp: in the circumstances, a unique tribute in the county's history.

A calamitous 44 minutes that morning, when they lost nine wickets in nine overs, led to sudden defeat by Kent at the very time events taking shape elsewhere would have seen the Championship pennant fluttering above Headingley's new pavilion had Yorkshire been victorious. Instead, they finished third behind Nottinghamshire and Somerset. Players and fans were momentarily stunned. But appreciation for what had been achieved, during a season in which the team had been written off even before the action started, soon had the crowd on their feet.

After Yorkshire's recent struggles to survive in the first division, the general feeling was that they would falter again without Michael Vaughan and Matthew Hoggard. In fact, their absence freed up places for others, who responded magnificently to the demands of new captain Andrew Gale.

Not once did Yorkshire drop out of the top three in the Championship, while in the Clydesdale Bank 40 they won ten of their 12 group matches, before a below-par bowling performance in the semi-final against Warwickshire denied them a visit to Lord's. Only in the Friends Provident T20 did Yorkshire underperform, leaving them still to compete in a Twenty20 finals day.

When Gale's appointment as captain was confirmed, one wondered whether the 26-year-old – the county's youngest captain since Brian Sellers in 1933 – would have the resolve to bind the team together without his own batting form being adversely affected. Wins from the first two Championship matches, plus his own scores of 101 and 64 not out in the second game, against Somerset, quickly confirmed that he was the right man for the job.

Few players failed, and some positively sparkled: none more so than 22-year-old left-hander Adam Lyth who, with Vaughan's retirement, was able to claim a place from the start. He never looked back. Opening the batting, Lyth was straight out of the traps and showed remarkable consistency. He was the first in the country to complete 1,000 first-class runs, in early July, and remained the leading scorer in the first division with 1,509 at 52. Only Mark Ramprakash, with 1,595, scored more. But though Lyth made his runs rapidly, Yorkshire's progress was so slow overall that, even with wickets in hand, they picked up maximum batting points only once.

The worst-kept secret of the season was that Jacques Rudolph would not return in 2011 to complete his contract. He was granted his release in late September so that he could return full-time to South Africa, where his wife was anxious to develop her career as a doctor. There was much sorrow at

Graham Morris

Andrew Gale

Rudolph's departure. As well as being liked by all, he had been outstanding in each of his four seasons at Yorkshire and, next to the incomparable Darren Lehmann, was their best acquisition from abroad. He signed off with a personal best of 1,375 Championship runs – he never made fewer than a thousand – and hit 17 centuries in all. Even so, he expressed some disappointment in his final year that he did not convert more fifties into hundreds. If his batting in the Championship was excellent, it was on an even higher plane in the CB40: no other batsman in the country could get close to his 861 runs at 95, including four centuries.

Freed of the captaincy, Anthony McGrath also found sufficiently good form to top 1,000 runs, making it the first time since 1995 that three batsmen had reached the mark for Yorkshire. Jonathan Bairstow enjoyed a marvellous first full season; his batting was particularly impressive under intense pressure in the second innings of several matches. Adil Rashid, with 732 valuable middle-order runs, could not be faulted, and the only batsman to suffer misfortune was Joe Sayers, who carefully constructed five fifties in the first six matches but missed the second half of the season with an energy-sapping virus.

The most satisfying aspect for Martyn Moxon, the director of professional cricket, was that the quick bowling showed an overall improvement, despite Tim Bresnan and Ajmal Shahzad missing several matches through England duties and West Indian Tino Best proving disappointing, not through any lack of effort or enthusiasm, but because he was too erratic. All this was offset by Steven Patterson finally establishing himself as a reliable front-line bowler, Oliver Hannon-Dalby deservedly holding his Championship place after hauls of five for 68 in each of the first two matches, and Rashid's leg-breaks leading the way with 57 wickets, the most by any spinner in 2010. But the more rounded a cricketer Rashid becomes, the less interest England seem to show in him. After seven seasons with Nottinghamshire, Ryan Sidebottom returns in 2011 to add further strength to the bowling.

Off the field at Headingley, Yorkshire unveiled their £21m pavilion. Its design was felt to be better suited to students of Leeds Metropolitan University, which owns most of the building, than to cricket. The club managed to defer payments on its bank debts, but this could not prevent office redundancies as the financial belt was tightened. Soon after the season ended, Stewart Regan, Yorkshire's energetic chief executive for the past five seasons, left to fill a similar role with the Scottish FA. Chairman Colin Graves took over on a temporary basis. He blamed half of the club's £2m losses on the inability to attract a significant crowd to the neutral Pakistan–Australia Test at Headingley. As a result, Yorkshire will not bid to host an Ashes Test in 2013 or 2015.

YORKSHIRE RESULTS

All first-class matches – Played 18: Won 6, Lost 2, Drawn 10.
County Championship matches – Played 16: Won 6, Lost 2, Drawn 8.

LV= County Championship, 3rd in Division 1;
Friends Provident T20, 6th in North Division; Clydesdale Bank 40, s-f.

COUNTY CHAMPIONSHIP AVERAGES, BATTING AND FIELDING

Cap		M	I	NO	R	HS	100s	50s	Avge	Ct/St
2010	A. Lyth†	16	29	0	1,509	142	3	9	52.03	9
2007	J. A. Rudolph¶	16	29	2	1,375	228*	4	6	50.92	20
2008	A. W. Gale†	13	23	4	876	151*	3	3	46.10	2
2008	A. U. Rashid†‡	16	24	8	732	76	0	6	45.75	14
2010	D. J. Wainwright†	5	5	3	89	39	0	0	44.50	1
1999	A. McGrath†	16	29	1	1,219	124*	3	9	43.53	9
	J. M. Bairstow†	16	29	7	918	81	0	8	41.72	29/5
2010	R. M. Pyrah†	6	6	1	170	61	0	1	34.00	4
2007	J. J. Sayers†	8	13	0	376	63	0	5	28.92	3
2010	A. Shahzad†	9	12	3	238	45	0	0	26.44	1
2008	G. L. Brophy	8	16	1	383	103	1	0	25.53	17
2006	T. T. Bresnan†‡	6	9	1	203	70	0	2	25.37	2
	S. A. Patterson†	14	17	4	184	39*	0	0	14.15	3
	T. L. Best§	8	8	0	46	15	0	0	5.75	4
	O. J. Hannon-Dalby†	16	14	6	21	11*	0	0	2.62	1

Also batted: M. A. Ashraf† (2 matches) 0, 10, 0 (1 ct); Azeem Rafiq (2 matches) 4, 13*, 12; G. S. Ballance (1 match) 4, 31*.

† *Born in Yorkshire.* ‡ *ECB contract.* § *Official overseas player.* ¶ *Other non-England-qualified player.*

BOWLING

	O	M	R	W	BB	5W/i	Avge
S. A. Patterson	392.5	96	1,201	45	5-50	1	26.68
A. Shahzad	292.2	47	1,013	34	5-51	1	29.79
A. U. Rashid	504.4	67	1,784	57	5-87	3	31.29
T. T. Bresnan	188.2	42	538	17	5-52	1	31.64
O. J. Hannon-Dalby	365.4	58	1,299	34	5-68	2	38.20
T. L. Best	184	19	727	17	4-86	0	42.76
D. J. Wainwright	138.2	20	535	12	3-48	0	44.58

Also bowled: M. A. Ashraf 42–12–106–9; Azeem Rafiq 76–12–222–4; A. Lyth 2–0–16–0; A. McGrath 74–13–226–0; R. M. Pyrah 84.4–16–326–7; J. A. Rudolph 11–2–43–0; J. J. Sayers 24–3–61–0.

LEADING CB40 AVERAGES (100 runs/4 wickets)

Batting	Runs	HS	Avge	S-R	Ct/St
J. A. Rudolph	861	124*	95.66	91.79	4
A. McGrath	414	77*	51.75	89.41	7
G. L. Brophy	315	93*	39.37	96.62	8/3
A. W. Gale	458	125*	38.16	93.27	4
J. M. Bairstow	153	46*	30.60	130.76	7
A. Lyth	348	91	29.00	91.09	5

Bowling	W	BB	Avge	E-R
T. L. Best	10	4-46	16.60	6.30
S. A. Patterson	21	6-32	22.38	5.10
B. W. Sanderson . .	7	2-17	23.85	5.75
R. M. Pyrah	20	4-24	24.20	5.97
T. T. Bresnan	12	3-40	25.75	5.61
A. McGrath	5	2-24	27.40	6.00

LEADING FPT20 AVERAGES (100 runs/18 overs)

Batting	Runs	HS	Avge	S-R	Ct/St
A. Lyth.........	227	59	22.70	**156.55**	4
H. H. Gibbs......	443	101*	36.91	**148.16**	8
A. W. Gale......	382	65*	31.83	**128.61**	7
J. M. Bairstow....	219	49*	21.90	**125.14**	4/1
A. U. Rashid.....	128	34	14.22	**117.43**	4
A. McGrath......	251	73*	41.83	**110.57**	7

Bowling	W	BB	Avge	E-R
A. U. Rashid......	26	4-20	16.46	**7.01**
R. M. Pyrah......	21	3-12	19.42	**7.03**
T. L. Best........	7	2-26	34.71	**8.28**
C. J. McKay......	10	4-33	25.80	**8.32**
S. A. Patterson....	15	4-30	30.00	**8.88**
Azeem Rafiq.....	7	3-23	38.71	**9.62**

FIRST-CLASS COUNTY RECORDS

Highest score for	341	G. H. Hirst v Leicestershire at Leicester.........	1905
Highest score against	318*	W. G. Grace (Gloucestershire) at Cheltenham.....	1876
Leading run-scorer	38,558	H. Sutcliffe (avge 50.20).....................	1919–1945
Best bowling for	10-10	H. Verity v Nottinghamshire at Leeds.........	1932
Best bowling against	10-37	C. V. Grimmett (Australians) at Sheffield.......	1930
Leading wicket-taker	3,597	W. Rhodes (avge 16.02)......................	1898–1930
Highest total for	887	v Warwickshire at Birmingham................	1896
Highest total against	681-7 dec	by Leicestershire at Bradford................	1996
Lowest total for	23	v Hampshire at Middlesbrough................	1965
Lowest total against	13	by Nottinghamshire at Nottingham.............	1901

LIST A COUNTY RECORDS

Highest score for	191	D. S. Lehmann v Nottinghamshire at Scarborough...	2001
Highest score against	177	S. A. Newman (Surrey) at The Oval...........	2009
Leading run-scorer	8,699	G. Boycott (avge 40.08)......................	1963–1986
Best bowling for	7-15	R. A. Hutton v Worcestershire at Leeds........	1969
Best bowling against	7-32	R. G. D. Willis (Warwickshire) at Birmingham...	1981
Leading wicket-taker	308	C. M. Old (avge 18.96)......................	1967–1982
Highest total for	411-6	v Devon at Exmouth.........................	2004
Highest total against	375-4	by Surrey at Scarborough....................	1994
Lowest total for	54	v Essex at Leeds............................	2003
Lowest total against	23	by Middlesex at Leeds.......................	1974

TWENTY20 RECORDS

Highest score for	109	I. J. Harvey v Derbyshire at Leeds...........	2005
Highest score against	111	D. L. Maddy (Leicestershire) at Leeds..........	2004
Leading run-scorer	**1,311**	**A. McGrath** (avge 31.21)..................	**2004–2010**
Best bowling for	{4-20	R. M. Pyrah v Derbyshire at Leeds............	2008
	4-20	**A. U. Rashid v Leicestershire at Leeds**.......	**2010**
Best bowling against	4-9	C. K. Langeveldt (Derbyshire) at Leeds........	2008
Leading wicket-taker	47	**T. T. Bresnan** (avge 23.02).................	**2003–2010**
Highest total for	213-7	v Worcestershire at Leeds....................	**2010**
Highest total against	222-5	by Derbyshire at Leeds......................	**2010**
Lowest total for	90-9	v Durham at Chester-le-Street................	2009
Lowest total against	98	by Durham at Chester-le-Street................	2006

ADDRESS

Headingley Cricket Ground, Leeds LS6 3BU (0113 278 7394; **email** cricket@yorkshireccc.com).
Website www.yorkshireccc.com

OFFICIALS

Captain A. W. Gale
Director of cricket M. D. Moxon
Assistant director of cricket C. White
Batting coach K. Sharp
Bowling coach S. Oldham

President R. Illingworth
Chairman/acting-chief executive C. Graves
Director of cricket operations I. Dews
Head groundsman A. W. Fogarty
Scorer J. T. Potter

At Birmingham, April 9–12. YORKSHIRE beat WARWICKSHIRE by four wickets.

YORKSHIRE v SOMERSET

At Leeds, April 15–18. Yorkshire won by six wickets. Yorkshire 22pts, Somerset 4pts. Toss: Somerset. County debut: D. G. Wright.

Any fears that the captaincy would have an adverse effect on Gale's batting were quickly dispelled as his century first tilted the scales Yorkshire's way, and then a calm second-innings 64 not out eased the path to a hard-earned victory. It was their first Championship win at home in close to two years. Trescothick, also new to the captaincy, struck a masterly 117 which allowed his side to compete but never dominate. With Yorkshire 142 for five, Somerset looked set to claim a lead, but Gale and Bresnan's judicious stand of 149 changed that. The turning point came when Trescothick took the second new ball, and watched the pair determinedly add 47 from seven overs. Yorkshire would surely have won more easily had Suppiah not been dropped twice; they were kept in the field by resolute batting right down the order, despite Hannon-Dalby equalling career-best figures set the previous week. Chasing 198, Yorkshire looked uncomfortable when Rudolph fell at 61 for three, but Lyth and Gale's positive 107-run partnership quickly relieved the pressure. A total of 14 lbw dismissals – one short of the record in a Yorkshire match – was evidence of the variable bounce.

Close of play: First day, Yorkshire 16-1 (Sayers 7, McGrath 6); Second day, Yorkshire 320-7 (Rashid 12, Shahzad 7); Third day, Somerset 201-6 (de Bruyn 49, Wright 7).

Somerset

*M. E. Trescothick lbw b Rashid	117	– lbw b Bresnan	16
A. V. Suppiah c Bairstow b Shahzad	5	– lbw b Hannon-Dalby	71
N. R. D. Compton lbw b Hannon-Dalby	6	– b Wainwright	21
J. C. Hildreth lbw b Bresnan	30	– run out	4
Z. de Bruyn c Sayers b Bresnan	4	– c Bresnan b Hannon-Dalby	83
†C. Kieswetter lbw b Bresnan	7	– lbw b Shahzad	17
P. D. Trego b Hannon-Dalby	45	– c Bairstow b Shahzad	10
D. G. Wright c Shahzad b Rashid	21	– lbw b Hannon-Dalby	25
A. C. Thomas lbw b Wainwright	8	– c Bairstow b Hannon-Dalby	44
D. A. Stiff not out	12	– c Rudolph b Hannon-Dalby	40
C. M. Willoughby c Rudolph b Wainwright	4	– not out	4
L-b 11, n-b 2	13	B 2, l-b 7	9

1/12 (2) 2/35 (3) 3/121 (4)   (75.4 overs) 272   1/30 (1) 2/69 (3)   (93.2 overs) 344
4/127 (5) 5/139 (6) 6/206 (1)   3/88 (4) 4/140 (2)
7/244 (7) 8/252 (8) 9/264 (9) 10/272 (11)   5/177 (6) 6/193 (7) 7/244 (8)
                                                               8/259 (5) 9/333 (9) 10/344 (10)

Bresnan 17–3–48–3; Shahzad 14–3–54–1; Hannon-Dalby 17–3–54–2; McGrath 5–1–22–0; Wainwright 13.4–0–42–2; Rashid 9–1–41–2. *Second Innings*—Bresnan 23–5–78–1; Shahzad 16–2–63–2; Wainwright 27–4–99–1; Hannon-Dalby 18.2–1–68–5; Rashid 9–2–27–0.

Yorkshire

A. Lyth lbw b Willoughby	0	– c Kieswetter b Stiff	90
J. J. Sayers lbw b Wright	51	– c Kieswetter b Wright	0
A. McGrath lbw b Willoughby	21	– c Trescothick b Thomas	4
J. A. Rudolph c Kieswetter b Thomas	33	– c Trego b de Bruyn	27
*A. W. Gale c Wright b de Bruyn	101	– not out	64
†J. M. Bairstow lbw b Trego	11	– not out	6
T. T. Bresnan lbw b Wright	61		
A. U. Rashid c Wright b Trego	63		
A. Shahzad c Kieswetter b Trego	45		
D. J. Wainwright b Trego	0		
O. J. Hannon-Dalby not out	1		
B 3, l-b 8, w 3, n-b 18	32	B 1, w 1, n-b 6	8

1/0 (1) 2/45 (3) 3/110 (2)   (142.1 overs) 419   1/2 (2)   (4 wkts, 45.5 overs) 199
4/122 (4) 5/142 (6) 6/291 (5) 7/304 (7)   2/17 (3) 3/61 (4)
8/415 (9) 9/417 (10) 10/419 (8)   110 overs: 339-7   4/168 (1)

Willoughby 29–6–105–2; Wright 26–8–63–2; Thomas 22–5–52–1; Stiff 18–2–77–0; Suppiah 23–2–55–0; Trego 14.1–4–26–4; de Bruyn 10–1–30–1. *Second Innings*—Willoughby 7–2–17–0; Wright 6–1–23–1; Thomas 8–2–27–1; Trego 7–0–35–0; de Bruyn 7–1–30–1; Suppiah 5–0–24–0; Stiff 5.5–0–42–1.

Umpires: N. J. Llong and N. A. Mallender.

At Canterbury, April 21–24. YORKSHIRE drew with KENT.

YORKSHIRE v DURHAM

At Leeds, April 27–30. Drawn. Yorkshire 9pts, Durham 6pts. Toss: Yorkshire. First-class debut: C. Rushworth. Championship debut: T. L. Best.

Rudolph took full advantage of a bland pitch and an injury-ravaged Durham attack to spend seven and three-quarter hours patiently assembling his third and highest double-century. The hardest part of the process, he said, was making sure he went from 50 to 100, at which point he knew he was in for a big one. McGrath hit his first century since the previous May in a stand of 206 with Rudolph. Earlier, Lyth and Sayers shared 146, meaning that Yorkshire's openers had both scored a fifty in each of the first four matches. Despite such dominance, Yorkshire progressed so slowly that they managed only three batting points, and their new West Indian fast bowler, Tino Best, had to wait until the last day to enjoy any success. Durham were handicapped when Di Venuto could not resume his unbeaten 108 on the fourth morning because of a side strain. Bad luck was catching: Benkenstein twisted his knee in the field, and the sight of Steve Harmison (one of five pace bowlers absent through injury or loan) jogging around the boundary was another frustration. Even without rain on the third afternoon and again on the last, a draw would have been likely.

Close of play: First day, Yorkshire 304-2 (McGrath 73, Rudolph 68); Second day, Durham 54-3 (Di Venuto 30, Benkenstein 4); Third day, Durham 215-4 (Di Venuto 108, Blackwell 12).

Yorkshire

A. Lyth c Di Venuto b Blackwell	85	D. J. Wainwright not out 14
J. J. Sayers c Smith b Blackwell	63	
A. McGrath run out	105	L-b 9, w 3, n-b 10 22
J. A. Rudolph not out	228	
*A. W. Gale c Plunkett b Stokes	41	1/146 (1)　(6 wkts dec, 176 overs) 610
†J. M. Bairstow b Borthwick	9	2/173 (2)　3/379 (3)
A. U. Rashid c sub (B. W. Harmison)		4/490 (5)　5/503 (6)
b Borthwick	43	6/586 (7)　110 overs: 329-2

T. L. Best, S. A. Patterson and O. J. Hannon-Dalby did not bat.

Davies 28–10–60–0; Rushworth 27–7–86–0; Plunkett 23–3–110–0; Stokes 9–0–52–1; Benkenstein 12–6–21–0; Blackwell 43–15–105–2; Borthwick 27–0–122–2; Coetzer 3–0–18–0; Smith 4–0–27–0.

Durham

M. J. Di Venuto retired hurt 108		
K. J. Coetzer c Rudolph b Patterson	8	– (1) not out 23
*W. R. Smith b Rashid	8	
M. Davies b Rashid	0	
D. M. Benkenstein st Bairstow b Wainwright	64	
I. D. Blackwell b Best	21	
B. A. Stokes c Bairstow b Best	28	
†P. Mustard c Bairstow b Best	0	
L. E. Plunkett b Patterson	51	
S. G. Borthwick not out	20	– (2) not out 21
C. Rushworth b Best	5	
B 5, l-b 12	17	B 1, w 1 2

1/17 (2)　2/49 (3)　3/49 (4)　4/194 (5)　(98 overs)　330
5/228 (6)　6/228 (8)　7/287 (7)
8/320 (9)　9/330 (11)

(no wkt, 22 overs)　46

In the first innings Di Venuto retired hurt at 215.

Best 22–2–86–4; Hannon-Dalby 17–4–50–0; Patterson 15–6–41–2; Rashid 27–4–83–2; Wainwright 16–3–50–1; Sayers 1–0–3–0. *Second Innings—*Best 3–2–6–0; Hannon-Dalby 4–0–13–0; Patterson 5–2–6–0; Rashid 7–0–20–0; Wainwright 3–3–0–0.

Umpires: R. K. Illingworth and D. J. Millns.

YORKSHIRE v ESSEX

At Scarborough, May 4–6. Yorkshire won by innings and 96 runs. Yorkshire 23pts, Essex 2pts. Toss: Yorkshire.

The only first division side to gain a positive result on general election day, Yorkshire were such clear winners that had this been politics their opponents would have lost their deposit. Performing for Gale with an all-round confidence not seen since their high-water mark in the 1960s, Yorkshire were able to enforce the follow-on for the second consecutive match – the first time since May 1960, when Vic Wilson did so three times in eight days. Centuries for Gale and McGrath, his liberated predecessor as captain, enabled Yorkshire to reach their highest home score against Essex, even if they missed another golden opportunity to bank maximum batting points. Essex twice crumbled in the face of spirited bowling. Best, if occasionally overenthusiastic, extracted every ounce of pace from the pitch, but it was the steadier Patterson whose unwavering accuracy brought him career-best figures. Pettini twice knuckled down before falling to Best, but no visiting batsman could manage a half-century.

Close of play: First day, Yorkshire 313-3 (McGrath 112, Gale 89); Second day, Essex 159-5 (Foster 35, ten Doeschate 16).

Yorkshire

A. Lyth b ten Doeschate	47	
J. J. Sayers c Cook b Martin	5	
A. McGrath lbw b Masters	112	
J. A. Rudolph c and b ten Doeschate	45	
*A. W. Gale st Foster b Phillips	135	
†J. M. Bairstow c Foster b Wright	62	
A. U. Rashid c Godleman b ten Doeschate	16	
R. M. Pyrah c ten Doeschate b Wright	61	
T. L. Best b Phillips	4	

S. A. Patterson b Wright 5
O. J. Hannon-Dalby not out. 1

B 8, l-b 9, w 2, n-b 4 23

1/32 (2) 2/72 (1) (144.1 overs) 516
3/150 (4) 4/316 (3) 5/392 (5)
6/419 (7) 7/475 (6) 8/480 (9)
9/489 (10) 10/516 (8) 110 overs: 370-4

Masters 29–9–89–1; Martin 25–10–84–1; Wright 25.1–4–97–3; ten Doeschate 31–1–117–3; Phillips 34–3–112–2.

Essex

B. A. Godleman lbw b Rashid	15	– c Rashid b Hannon-Dalby	1
A. N. Cook lbw b Patterson	7	– c Bairstow b Hannon-Dalby	10
J. K. Maunders c Pyrah b Best	6	– c Bairstow b Patterson	33
J. C. Mickleburgh lbw b Hannon-Dalby	33	– lbw b Pyrah	33
*M. L. Pettini b Best	44	– lbw b Best	47
†J. S. Foster lbw b Patterson	35	– c Bairstow b Pyrah	5
R. N. ten Doeschate lbw b Best	24	– c Lyth b Patterson	35
T. J. Phillips c Rashid b Patterson	19	– not out	19
D. D. Masters c Sayers b Patterson	11	– st Bairstow b Rashid	9
C. J. C. Wright b Patterson	4	– st Bairstow b Rashid	4
C. S. Martin not out	0	– lbw b Rashid	11
L-b 1, w 1, n-b 6.	8	B 5, l-b 2	7

1/23 (2) 2/27 (1) 3/32 (3) 4/74 (4) (57.5 overs) 206
5/135 (5) 6/159 (6) 7/167 (7)
8/192 (9) 9/204 (10) 10/206 (8)

1/1 (1) (67.5 overs) 214
2/28 (2) 3/57 (3)
4/97 (4) 5/105 (6) 6/158 (5) 7/179 (7)
8/196 (9) 9/200 (10) 10/214 (11)

Best 15–2–54–3; Hannon-Dalby 11–1–38–1; Patterson 19.5–7–50–5; Rashid 9–0–42–1; Pyrah 3–1–21–0. *Second Innings*—Best 13–0–51–1; Hannon-Dalby 10–3–26–2; Rashid 25.5–2–98–3; Patterson 10–6–19–2; Sayers 3–1–5–0; Pyrah 6–2–8–2.

Umpires: P. J. Hartley and R. T. Robinson.

YORKSHIRE v LOUGHBOROUGH MCCU

At Leeds, May 10–12. Drawn. Toss: Yorkshire. First-class debuts: M. A. Ashraf, C. J. Geldart, J. E. Root.

Pyrah's century was his second for Yorkshire, the only other coming against the same opponents three years earlier. Brophy, in his first first-class game of the season, also batted confidently in their fourth-wicket stand. Time lost to rain ruled out a positive result but the students' innings was not without flair, particularly when David Murphy and Will Tavaré were at the crease. Ben Sanderson became Yorkshire's third uncapped seamer (after Hannon-Dalby and Patterson) to take a first-class five-wicket haul in the opening five weeks of the season.

Close of play: First day, Yorkshire 218-3 (Brophy 62, Pyrah 65); Second day, Loughborough MCCU 53-1 (Tavare 24, Murphy 11).

Yorkshire

J. E. Root lbw b Baker	14	– not out	20
G. S. Ballance c Murphy b Groves	43	– not out	6
C. J. Geldart c Murphy b Groves	17		
†G. L. Brophy c Gandam b Malan	89		
R. M. Pyrah not out	134		
L. J. Hodgson c Murphy b Taylor	33		
L-b 5, w 7, n-b 6	18	L-b 1, w 2	3

1/23 (1) 2/68 (2) (5 wkts dec, 91 overs) 348 (no wkt dec, 7.1 overs) 29
3/98 (3) 4/262 (4) 5/348 (6)

D. J. Wainwright, Azeem Rafiq, B. W. Sanderson, *J. A. R. Blain and M. A. Ashraf did not bat.

Rose 16–3–71–0; Baker 19–4–82–1; Taylor 13–3–37–1; Groves 15–2–55–2; Malan 10–1–28–1; Evans 5–0–27–0; Cope 2–0–14–0; Welsh 11–0–29–0. *Second Innings*—Rose 4–0–20–0; Baker 3.1–0–8–0.

Loughborough MCCU

W. A. Tavaré lbw b Wainwright	49	C. C. Malan lbw b Sanderson	11
R. F. Evans c Brophy b Sanderson	11	P. R. Groves not out	37
†D. Murphy lbw b Wainwright	54	S. A. L. Rose c Brophy b Hodgson	14
*A. C. Cope lbw b Sanderson	8	L-b 13	13
H. S. Gandam lbw b Ashraf	33		
A. S. Welsh b Azeem Rafiq	1	1/36 (2) 2/92 (1) 3/127 (4) (96.5 overs) 253
R. M. L. Taylor lbw b Sanderson	22	4/131 (3) 5/136 (6) 6/189 (7)
G. C. Baker c Brophy b Sanderson	0	7/189 (8) 8/201 (5) 9/201 (9) 10/253 (11)

Blain 14–7–20–0; Ashraf 17–7–35–1; Sanderson 18–3–50–5; Hodgson 14.5–4–42–1; Wainwright 21–6–47–2; Azeem Rafiq 12–1–46–1.

Umpires: S. A. Garratt and J. S. Wilson.

At Taunton, May 17–20. YORKSHIRE lost to SOMERSET by six wickets.

At Southampton, May 24–27. YORKSHIRE drew with HAMPSHIRE.

YORKSHIRE v LANCASHIRE

At Leeds, May 29–June 1. Drawn. Yorkshire 5pts, Lancashire 8pts. Toss: Lancashire.

The loss of the first and fourth days to bad weather made a draw inevitable, but Lancashire so dominated the match that they might have forced victory had the final day been dry. Although too sluggish to collect the last two batting points, they were scarcely troubled by mediocre bowling, allowing Tom Smith, back in the safe haven of No. 6 following a fraught spell as opener, to discover his form with a maiden Championship century. He then picked up four wickets as Yorkshire made only a partial recovery from 55 for five. Lyth arrived at the crease immediately after lunch on day three, needing 147 in two sessions to become the first man since Graeme Hick, in 1988, to complete 1,000 runs before the end of May. Those hopes vanished when he chopped the second ball of the innings from Chapple on to his stumps. Had just one ball been bowled on the last day either side could have picked up another bonus point, but the chance never came.

Close of play: First day, No play; Second day, Lancashire 272-5 (Smith 46, Sutton 16); Third day, Yorkshire 199-8 (Shahzad 38, Patterson 0).

Lancashire

P. J. Horton c Rashid b Hannon-Dalby	24	S. I. Mahmood lbw b Shahzad			3
S. C. Moore b Shahzad	43	K. W. Hogg st Bairstow b Rashid			37
A. G. Prince c Rashid b Patterson	78	B 5, l-b 9, w 1, n-b 2			17
M. J. Chilton c Rudolph b Rashid	42				
S. J. Croft c Gale b Rashid	15	1/53 (1)	(9 wkts dec, 128.2 overs)		416
T. C. Smith not out	108	2/104 (2) 3/185 (4) 4/198 (3)			
†L. D. Sutton lbw b Patterson	20	5/225 (5) 6/276 (7) 7/324 (8)			
*G. Chapple st Bairstow b Rashid	29	8/337 (9) 9/416 (10)	110 overs: 337-8		

S. C. Kerrigan did not bat.

Shahzad 29–3–87–2; Best 14–1–49–0; Hannon-Dalby 16–1–52–1; Rashid 36.2–6–121–4; Patterson 20–8–48–2; Sayers 13–1–45–0.

Yorkshire

A. Lyth b Chapple	0	T. L. Best c Hogg b Kerrigan			12
J. J. Sayers lbw b Smith	10	S. A. Patterson not out			0
A. McGrath lbw b Chapple	4				
J. A. Rudolph c Sutton b Smith	30	N-b 2			2
*A. W. Gale c Prince b Smith	9				
†J. M. Bairstow c Smith b Kerrigan	29	1/0 (1) 2/4 (3)	(8 wkts, 63 overs)		199
A. U. Rashid lbw b Smith	65	3/40 (2) 4/54 (5) 5/55 (4)			
A. Shahzad not out	38	6/123 (6) 7/170 (7) 8/191 (9)			

O. J. Hannon-Dalby did not bat.

Chapple 6–3–6–2; Mahmood 12–2–53–0; Smith 15–5–46–4; Hogg 11–3–36–0; Kerrigan 19–3–58–2.

Umpires: N. G. C. Cowley and B. Dudleston.

At Leeds, June 5–7. YORKSHIRE drew with INDIA A (see A-team tours of England section).

At Manchester, June 28–July 1. YORKSHIRE drew with LANCASHIRE.

YORKSHIRE v WARWICKSHIRE

At Leeds, July 5–8. Yorkshire won by six wickets. Yorkshire 23pts, Warwickshire 4pts. Toss: Yorkshire. Championship debut: S. A. Piolet.

A match which fleetingly slipped from Yorkshire's grasp was won vigorously with 14 balls remaining, taking them 21 points clear at the top. The uncapped Lyth became the first batsman in the country to score 1,000 first-class runs when he reached 18, and Brophy weighed in with his second century for Yorkshire. But the game's outstanding batting came from Clarke, whose defences were never breached. He occupied the crease for more than eight hours in all, and his century in the follow-on appeared to have done its job in saving the match for Warwickshire. But by seeking to retain the strike, he was culpable in the run-out of Rankin. Troughton, forced to retire hurt earlier in the innings when Best struck him above the right eye, came in last but did not hold out for long; the final three wickets had collapsed in 15 balls. Suitably energised, Yorkshire responded positively to a chase of 200 in 37 overs. When acting-captain Rudolph was run out for 80, they needed 73 from ten; Bairstow exhibited exemplary calmness under pressure, as well as a deft touch against Imran Tahir, to see them home. He was ably supported by Rashid, who had bowled splendidly to take nine wickets on a surface offering only slow turn.

Close of play: First day, Yorkshire 325-4 (Brophy 92, Rashid 29); Second day, Warwickshire 221-7 (Clarke 19, Carter 12); Third day, Warwickshire 193-3 (Clarke 51, Javid 37).

Yorkshire

A. Lyth lbw b Carter	84	– c Clarke b Rankin	1
*J. A. Rudolph c Clarke b Carter	0	– run out	80
A. McGrath c Maddy b Carter	57	– lbw b Rankin	15
J. M. Bairstow lbw b Piolet	44	– not out	64
†G. L. Brophy c Botha b Clarke	103	– b Imran Tahir	14
A. U. Rashid lbw b Carter	29	– not out	16
R. M. Pyrah not out	45		
Azeem Rafiq c Piolet b Clarke	12		
S. A. Patterson run out	14		
T. L. Best c Piolet b Rankin	2		
O. J. Hannon-Dalby c Westwood b Imran Tahir	0		
B 13, l-b 16, n-b 6	35	B 4, l-b 5, w 1	10

1/5 (2) 2/153 (3) 3/156 (1)   (124.5 overs) 425
4/256 (4) 5/325 (6) 6/345 (5)
7/369 (8) 8/414 (9) 9/424 (10)
10/425 (11)   110 overs: 386-7

1/5 (1)   (4 wkts, 34.4 overs) 200
2/47 (3) 3/127 (2)
4/161 (5)

Carter 30–7–87–4; Rankin 20–4–73–1; Clarke 24–8–63–2; Piolet 15–3–67–1; Imran Tahir 21.5–5–73–1; Maddy 10–4–18–0; Botha 4–0–15–0. *Second Innings*—Carter 5–0–29–0; Rankin 8–1–33–2; Imran Tahir 11.4–2–71–1; Maddy 7–0–38–0; Piolet 2–0–13–0; Botha 1–0–7–0.

Warwickshire

*I. J. Westwood lbw b Rashid	66	– lbw b Rashid	42
D. L. Maddy lbw b Hannon-Dalby	35	– b Rashid	16
A. G. Botha c Lyth b Rashid	19	– c Brophy b Rashid	24
J. O. Troughton c Lyth b Rashid	22	– (5) c Rashid b Patterson	17
A. Javid lbw b Patterson	1	– (6) c Brophy b Rashid	48
†T. R. Ambrose b Best	30	– (7) b Pyrah	16
R. Clarke not out	46	– (4) not out	127
S. A. Piolet lbw b Rashid	6	– lbw b Patterson	4
N. M. Carter c Best b Patterson	15	– lbw b Rashid	21
Imran Tahir c Pyrah b Patterson	1	– c McGrath b Patterson	41
W. B. Rankin lbw b Patterson	0	– run out	0
B 5, l-b 7	12	B 8, l-b 6, w 1	15

1/102 (2) 2/104 (1) 3/148 (4)   (82 overs) 253
4/153 (5) 5/153 (3) 6/200 (6) 7/208 (8)
8/237 (9) 9/243 (10) 10/253 (11)

1/26 (2) 2/82 (3)   (125.3 overs) 371
3/83 (1) 4/210 (6)
5/231 (5) 6/244 (8) 7/285 (9)
8/360 (10) 9/361 (11) 10/371 (5)

In the second innings Troughton, when 17, retired hurt at 129 and resumed at 361.

Best 7–0–32–1; Patterson 22–6–57–4; Hannon-Dalby 13–5–42–1; Pyrah 6–1–24–0; Rashid 29–5–71–4; Azeem Rafiq 5–0–15–0. *Second Innings*—Hannon-Dalby 18–3–54–0; Patterson 15.3–4–25–3; Rashid 39–3–137–5; Pyrah 14–5–35–1; Best 18–3–54–0; McGrath 5–3–3–0.

Umpires: M. J. D. Bodenham and J. W. Lloyds.

At Chelmsford, July 20–23. YORKSHIRE drew with ESSEX.

YORKSHIRE v NOTTINGHAMSHIRE

At Leeds, August 3–6. Drawn. Yorkshire 5pts, Nottinghamshire 11pts. Toss: Yorkshire.

As Australia discovered to their cost against Pakistan in July, winning the toss and batting first at Headingley is not always an easy option. It was a decision which Gale soon came to regret as Yorkshire were bundled out for their lowest total in two years. Yorkshire's own attack was innocuous as Hussey hit a superb unbeaten 251, the highest Championship score by a visiting batsman on this ground. Only Bradman, with his Ashes triple-hundreds here in 1930 and 1934, had scored more for an opposing side. Hussey's 184-run partnership with Patel was a fourth-wicket record for Nottinghamshire against Yorkshire, and their total was also their highest. It was Hussey's fourth century in five Championship matches against Yorkshire. Unfazed by having to make 367 to avoid an innings defeat, Yorkshire batted with much greater determination the second time. When Rudolph and McGrath's second-wicket alliance ended at 211, Patterson came in as nightwatchman and stayed on duty until early on the fourth afternoon. Two quick wickets for Sidebottom, the second ushering in tea, left Yorkshire effectively 39 for eight when rain set in. The only consolation for Nottinghamshire was that they replaced their opponents at the top of the table, with a lead of five points.

Close of play: First day, Nottinghamshire 147-3 (Patel 37, Hussey 35); Second day, Nottinghamshire 497-6 (Hussey 222, Franks 57); Third day, Yorkshire 272-2 (McGrath 78, Patterson 3).

Yorkshire

A. Lyth c Read b Sidebottom	0	– c Adams b Franks	37
J. A. Rudolph run out	1	– c Adams b Pattinson	141
A. McGrath c Read b Adams	29	– c Read b Pattinson	80
*A. W. Gale lbw b Franks	24	– (5) c and b Sidebottom	14
J. M. Bairstow b Sidebottom	45	– (6) b Pattinson	7
†G. L. Brophy b Adams	5	– (7) c Read b Sidebottom	37
A. U. Rashid lbw b Pattinson	13	– (8) not out	34
A. Shahzad c Read b Franks	17	– (9) c Adams b Sidebottom	3
D. J. Wainwright not out	20		
S. A. Patterson lbw b Patel	10	– (4) c Wagh b Patel	26
O. J. Hannon-Dalby lbw b Patel	2		
B 3, l-b 3, w 2, n-b 4	12	B 6, l-b 12, w 1, n-b 8	27

1/0 (1) 2/5 (2) 3/36 (4) 4/82 (3)   (58.3 overs) 178
5/89 (6) 6/104 (7) 7/136 (5)
8/144 (8) 9/176 (10) 10/178 (11)

1/58 (1)   (8 wkts, 153 overs) 406
2/269 (2) 3/276 (3)
4/322 (5) 5/326 (4) 6/336 (6)
7/398 (7) 8/406 (9)

Sidebottom 15–6–25–2; Pattinson 12–1–61–1; Franks 14–3–40–2; Adams 14–3–44–2; Patel 3.3–1–2–2. *Second Innings*—Sidebottom 29–9–66–3; Pattinson 24–3–78–3; Franks 26–11–61–1; Adams 29–11–68–0; Patel 41–6–104–1; Hussey 4–0–11–0.

Nottinghamshire

A. D. Hales c Brophy b Patterson	2	P. J. Franks c Bairstow b Shahzad	61
M. J. Wood lbw b Patterson	59	A. R. Adams not out	13
M. A. Wagh b Hannon-Dalby	4	B 5, l-b 5, w 3, n-b 2	15
S. R. Patel c Rudolph b Rashid	96		
D. J. Hussey not out	251	1/22 (1) 2/52 (3) (7 wkts dec, 117 overs) 545	
*†C. M. W. Read c Rashid b Shahzad	42	3/97 (2) 4/281 (4) 5/395 (6)	
A. D. Brown b Patterson	0	6/400 (7) 7/511 (8) 110 overs: 471-6	

R. J. Sidebottom and D. J. Pattinson did not bat.

Shahzad 21–1–115–2; Patterson 29–3–110–3; Hannon-Dalby 22–1–104–1; Rashid 23–0–104–1; Wainwright 11–1–57–0; McGrath 10–1–32–0; Lyth 1–0–13–0.

Umpires: R. J. Bailey and N. J. Llong.

At Chester-le-Street, August 16–19. YORKSHIRE beat DURHAM by four wickets.

YORKSHIRE v HAMPSHIRE

At Scarborough, August 23–26. Drawn. Yorkshire 7pts, Hampshire 11pts. Toss: Hampshire.

Yorkshire signed an agreement with Scarborough CC to play ten days a year at North Marine Road for the next decade; a chilly and wet 124th Scarborough Festival was no adequate way to mark it. After the first day was lost, a good batting pitch got even better, but Yorkshire still encountered one or two anxious moments in the final session. Had Brophy been held by Vince at first slip before he had scored, Yorkshire would have been 15 runs ahead with five wickets left and 27 overs remaining. Bairstow's fluent half-century soon allayed concerns. Cork bowled splendidly on the second day, yet it was Adams and the 19-year-old Vince who broke records with their 278-run partnership, in front of a healthy crowd of 4,500. It was Hampshire's highest for the fourth wicket, surpassing the 263 Roy Marshall and Danny Livingstone shared at Lord's in 1970; it eased them to their biggest total in Yorkshire. Vince was upright and certain in his maiden century, while 196 for the dependable Adams gave him two hundreds and five fifties against Yorkshire since 2006. Bresnan scored 20 and bowled two wicketless overs before leaving at the halfway point to join up with England for the Lord's Test against Pakistan, even though he was always likely to be twelfth man.

Close of play: First day, No play; Second day, Hampshire 8-0 (Carberry 1, Adams 7); Third day, Hampshire 367-3 (Adams 162, Vince 122).

Yorkshire

A. Lyth c Bates b Cork	63	– c Adams b Cork	44
J. A. Rudolph c Bates b Balcombe	34	– c Carberry b Balcombe	54
A. McGrath c Bates b Cork	21	– c McKenzie b Briggs	20
*A. W. Gale c McKenzie b Tomlinson	3	– c Benham b Briggs	24
J. M. Bairstow lbw b Cork	5	– not out	50
†G. L. Brophy c Benham b Cork	44	– not out	10
A. U. Rashid lbw b Ervine	76		
T. T. Bresnan c Bates b Cork	20		
A. Shahzad not out	21		
S. A. Patterson c Ervine b Balcombe	7		
O. J. Hannon-Dalby not out	1		
B 12, l-b 5, n-b 10	27	B 12, n-b 11	23

1/61 (2) 2/126 (1)   (9 wkts dec, 91 overs) 322   1/87 (1)   (4 wkts dec, 52 overs) 225
3/129 (3) 4/133 (4) 5/141 (5)   2/129 (2) 3/147 (3)
6/252 (6) 7/287 (7) 8/292 (8) 9/310 (10)   4/190 (4)

R. M. Pyrah replaced Bresnan, who was called up by England.

Cork 23–6–64–5; Tomlinson 22–6–96–1; Balcombe 16–4–58–2; Ervine 14–5–41–1; Briggs 16–2–46–0. *Second Innings*—Cork 9–1–48–1; Tomlinson 10–2–46–0; Briggs 15–2–60–2; Balcombe 9–2–35–1; Carberry 1–0–4–0; Ervine 8–2–20–0.

Hampshire

M. A. Carberry c McGrath b Pyrah	40	†A. M. Bates not out	1
J. H. K. Adams b Patterson	196	B 12, l-b 8, w 1, n-b 4	25
C. C. Benham b Shahzad	26		
N. D. McKenzie b Patterson	0	1/105 (1) (6 wkts dec, 121.4 overs) 498
J. M. Vince c Bairstow b Rashid	180	2/135 (3) 3/152 (4) 4/430 (2)
S. M. Ervine run out	30	5/493 (5) 6/498 (6) 110 overs: 418-3

D. G. Cork, D. J. Balcombe, J. A. Tomlinson and D. R. Briggs did not bat.

Bresnan 2–0–7–0; Shahzad 26–5–90–1; Patterson 27–6–77–2; Hannon-Dalby 20–4–78–0; Rashid 25–1–114–1; Pyrah 13.4–0–80–1; McGrath 7–0–27–0; Rudolph 1–0–5–0.

Umpires: T. E. Jesty and R. A. Kettleborough.

At Nottingham, September 7–9. YORKSHIRE beat NOTTINGHAMSHIRE by five wickets.

YORKSHIRE v KENT

At Leeds, September 13–16. Kent won by four wickets. Kent 22pts, Yorkshire 5pts. Toss: Kent.

It took just 44 minutes for Yorkshire to plunge from the heights of optimism to the depths of despair as all hope of clinching the title for the first time since 2001 evaporated. "We threw away the game, no doubt about it," said a rueful Gale. In that brief period on the final morning Yorkshire collapsed from 93 for one to 130 all out, their lowest of the season, leaving Kent to make only 90, albeit nervously. Victory could not prevent Kent's slide into the second division: Warwickshire's win at the Rose Bowl put paid to that. The destroyer-in-chief was Tredwell, with seven for 22, including the first hat-trick against Yorkshire by a spinner since Intikhab Alam's at The Oval in 1972. Tredwell's last six wickets came in 19 balls at a cost of 15 runs, from two sixes and a three. Yorkshire's demise was due to over-excitement more than anything else. Put in on a green pitch, they were glad to reach 261, and then keep Kent within their sights despite a maiden century from Alex Blake, a student at Leeds Metropolitan University. Moin Ashraf, aged 18, and not permitted to bowl spells longer than seven overs, speared a terrific yorker through Jones's defences in the course of taking five wickets on his second Championship appearance. Shahzad was less impressive, however. More salt was rubbed into Yorkshire's wounds when results elsewhere revealed they would have been champions had they sent Kent packing.

Close of play: First day, Yorkshire 205-7 (Bairstow 62, Patterson 0); Second day, Kent 216-6 (Blake 40, Tredwell 0); Third day, Yorkshire 51-1 (Lyth 26, McGrath 4).

Yorkshire

A. Lyth c Tredwell b Cook	17	– b Tredwell	46
J. A. Rudolph b Nel	25	– lbw b Tredwell	13
A. McGrath c van Jaarsveld b Coles	1	– c Jones b Nel	30
*A. W. Gale lbw b Nel	39	– b Nel	2
J. M. Bairstow c van Jaarsveld b Nel	64	– c Nel b Tredwell	9
†G. L. Brophy b Coles	1	– st Jones b Tredwell	0
A. U. Rashid c Jones b Nel	29	– c van Jaarsveld b Nel	4
A. Shahzad lbw b Nel	21	– st Jones b Tredwell	16
S. A. Patterson not out	39	– c Northeast b Tredwell	2
O. J. Hannon-Dalby lbw b Nel	1	– not out	0
M. A. Ashraf c Jones b Tredwell	10	– c van Jaarsveld b Tredwell	0
B 4, l-b 9, w 1	14	B 4, l-b 4	8

1/30 (1) 2/31 (3) 3/81 (4) 4/92 (2) (76.3 overs) 261
5/93 (6) 6/158 (7) 7/200 (8)
8/207 (5) 9/209 (10) 10/261 (11)

1/40 (2) 2/93 (3) (29.5 overs) 130
3/95 (4) 4/99 (1)
5/99 (6) 6/108 (5) 7/118 (7)
8/123 (9) 9/130 (8) 10/130 (11)

Stevens 17–4–51–0; Coles 19–3–68–2; Cook 15–2–67–1; Nel 25–9–62–6; Tredwell 0.3–0–0–1.
Second Innings—Nel 11–1–57–3; Stevens 8–1–28–0; Cook 3–0–15–0; Tredwell 6.5–1–22–7; Coles 1–1–0–0.

Kent

S. A. Northeast c Brophy b Shahzad	20	– lbw b Shahzad		5
J. L. Denly c Rashid b Hannon-Dalby	26	– lbw b Ashraf		1
*R. W. T. Key lbw b Rashid	25	– c McGrath b Patterson		27
M. van Jaarsveld c Brophy b Ashraf	89	– c Rudolph b Rashid		44
D. I. Stevens lbw b Ashraf	0	– (6) not out		4
†G. O. Jones b Ashraf	6	– (5) c Ashraf b Patterson		0
A. J. Blake not out	105	– b Rashid		0
J. C. Tredwell c Brophy b Ashraf	8	– not out		4
M. T. Coles b Ashraf	0			
S. J. Cook lbw b Rashid	5			
J. D. Nel lbw b Patterson	2			
L-b 7, w 3, n-b 6	16	L-b 5		5

1/44 (2) 2/46 (1) 3/129 (3) (81.5 overs) 302
4/132 (5) 5/142 (6) 6/210 (4)
7/240 (8) 8/240 (9) 9/261 (10) 10/302 (11)

1/6 (2) (6 wkts, 24.5 overs) 90
2/6 (1) 3/68 (3)
4/70 (5) 5/82 (4) 6/82 (7)

Shahzad 25–4–102–1; Patterson 10.5–1–42–1; Hannon-Dalby 7–0–36–1; Ashraf 18–7–32–5; Rashid 21–2–83–2. *Second Innings*—Shahzad 6–2–17–1; Ashraf 4–0–13–1; Rashid 7.5–1–41–2; McGrath 1–0–4–0; Patterson 6–1–10–2.

Umpires: J. H. Evans and N. A. Mallender.

FRIENDS PROVIDENT T20, 2010

STEVE JAMES

FINALS DAY REPORTS BY HUGH CHEVALLIER

Marathons rarely have photo finishes. So the 2010 Friends Provident T20, a grisly and spectacularly ill-conceived endurance test whose group stage squeezed 144 matches into 48 days, scarcely deserved a dead-heat final.

But that's what happened, and Hampshire won only by dint of losing fewer wickets against Somerset at the Rose Bowl on August 14. For once, Twenty20 had a tale to linger long in the memory: the story of a batsman injured in taking two from the penultimate ball, a runner summoned, a scampered leg-bye to tie the scores and then Somerset's glaring ignorance of the laws in not running out the supposedly lame striker who had absent-mindedly advanced to the wrong end. Talk about drama. All that was missing was a place in the lucrative Champions League. That clashed with the climax of the English season and, after much debate, it was deemed imprudent that English teams should devalue their own domestic cricket by departing early to seek prize money abroad.

Hampshire were popular victors, not just because they became the first finals-day hosts to lift the cup. On paper they looked the weakest of the semi-finalists, shorn of club captain Dimitri Mascarenhas, wicketkeeper Nic Pothas, ICC World Twenty20 winner Michael Lumb, strike bowler Kabir Ali (all injured) and also Kevin Pietersen, whom they controversially chose not to select despite his availability. In their absence, they backed James Vince, Danny Briggs, Chris Wood and Michael Bates, all under 21. And, after Pothas had declined the Twenty20 reins, they shrewdly nominated Dominic Cork, who turned 39 a week before the finals, as babysitter. They were handsomely rewarded. In defeating a side that had beaten them twice in the group stage (in the home match they lost their last six wickets for four runs on a poor pitch that incurred a two-point penalty for next year's competition) they may even have surprised themselves.

But the very fact they lost eight group games tells you everything about the horrendous length of this competition. They just sneaked into the quarter-finals, finishing level with Surrey and Middlesex, who also won eight and lost eight. But their net run-rate proved marginally superior.

Tellingly, Hampshire possessed the competition's leading run-scorer. Jimmy Adams, a left-handed opener previously known for stodge and a Twenty20 average of 17, now boasted an exaggerated backlift and a liberated mind. He made 668 runs with two centuries.

They also unearthed a rare talent in the 19-year-old Briggs, a left-arm spinner with an action and temperament reminiscent of Daniel Vettori. Not

Home rule: Hampshire whoop it up after winning the Twenty20 on their own ground.

once in 19 games did he concede more than 32 runs, and he finished with 31 wickets, second only to Alfonso Thomas's 33 for Somerset. Against Hampshire at Southampton, Thomas, the wily South African seamer, recorded the most economical four-over return (4–2–5–2) in the competition's history. Three weeks later, Briggs trumped that with 4–0–5–3 against Kent at Canterbury.

Hampshire had to beat Sussex convincingly at home in their final group match. And they did so rather controversially. They brought in the boundaries – only just within legal limits – and made a formidable 195. They then strangled the life out of Sussex, such that their usually mild-mannered skipper, Mike Yardy, run out for a duck, was reduced to screaming and swearing at team-mate Murray Goodwin.

Yardy's ire was understandable. Barely anybody had a good word to say about the group stages, except the bean-counters at Essex, Sussex and Somerset, who reported increased crowds and healthy profits. Somerset attracted 49,282 spectators to their eight home games (27,680 in five home games in 2009); Essex increased from 27,752 to 36,421 (with gate receipts up from £382,398 to £549,000), and that doesn't include a rafters-packed quarter-final. When it was mooted that the home quota might be cut back to five in 2011 (ten games, rather than 16, per county), chief executive Richard Gould reckoned it would lead to a budget shortfall for Somerset of around £250,000. Small grounds, good sides: it was a potent mix for the few.

Mostly, however, crowds were down. Despite three more home games, Yorkshire, Kent, Derbyshire and Hampshire took less in gate receipts than in 2009. And Derbyshire (14,059) and Hampshire (33,637) had fewer spectators for eight home games than for five in 2008 (15,245 and 40,578). Most dispiriting was the 4,020 – a fifth of capacity – that attended Warwickshire's quarter-final against Hampshire at Edgbaston. Absentees missed a brilliant match-winning 66 not out from 19-year-old Vince. It was in sharp contrast to the 8,558 at a raucous Trent Bridge where Nottinghamshire defeated Sussex, the 2009 winners.

MOST EXPENSIVE BOWLING FIGURES IN TWENTY20 MATCHES

4–0–67–0	R. J. Kirtley	Sussex v Essex at Chelmsford	2008
4–0–67–1	**P. K. K. K. Naidu**	**Hyderabad v Mumbai at Indore**	**2009-10**
4–0–66–1	Riaz Afridi	Peshawar Panthers v Lahore Eagles at Karachi	2005-06
4–0–65–2	M. J. Hoggard	Yorkshire v Lancashire at Leeds	2005
4–0–64–1	J. M. Anderson	England v Australia at Sydney	2006-07
4–0–64–0	S. T. Jayasuriya	Sri Lanka v Pakistan at Johannesburg	2007-08
4–0–64–0	T. S. Chisoro	Centrals v Easterns at Bulawayo	2008-09
4–0–64–0	**Abdul Razzaq**	**Hampshire v Somerset at Taunton**	**2010**
4–0–63–1	R. J. Kirtley	Sussex v Surrey at Hove......................	2004

MOST ECONOMICAL BOWLING FIGURES IN TWENTY20 MATCHES

4–1–4–3	Shantanu Pitre	Madhya Pradesh v Uttar Pradesh at Jaipur	2006-07
4–1–4–2	S. J. Benn	Barbados v Grenada at St John's, Coolidge	2007-08
4–1–5–3	Mohammad Hafeez	Faisalabad Wolves v Quetta Bears at Lahore	2009
4–0–5–3	**D. R. Briggs**	**Hampshire v Kent at Canterbury**	**2010**
4–0–5–2	P. Kumar	Uttar Pradesh v Madhya Pradesh at Jaipur	2006-07
4–2–5–2	**A. C. Thomas**	**Somerset v Hampshire at Southampton**	**2010**

Note: Yasir Arafat had figures of 3.3–0–5–3 for Rawalpindi Rams v Quetta Bears at Lahore, 2008-09.

Less successful sides offered grumbles aplenty. The switch from three groups to two, North and South, meant that some heavily attended local derbies were lost. Worcestershire were worst affected, forfeiting games against Gloucestershire, Glamorgan and Somerset, and having to travel to Durham – where the match was washed out.

Amid the group stages there were also three rogue rounds of Championship matches. Madness then hit new heights: in the week between the end of the preliminaries and the quarter-finals, seven of the qualifiers played a Championship and a 40-over game. Hampshire alone could rest – aside from a CB40 – and prepare.

No wonder captains dropped like flies. Essex's Mark Pettini, Warwickshire's Ian Westwood and Middlesex's Shaun Udal all stepped down mid-tournament. Others, such as Nottinghamshire's Chris Read and Derbyshire's Chris Rogers, handed over to Twenty20 deputies in advance.

Injuries were inevitable. Ryan ten Doeschate had been magnificent for Essex, but when he flew into Bristol airport from duty with the Netherlands to play at Taunton he was asking for trouble. He duly snapped a calf muscle when batting, departing the competition in his fifth game with 295 runs at an average of 73.75 and a strike rate of 181. (He was just about fit for finals day, but could make little impact.) And in a highly charged quarter-final at

Chelmsford that concluded at 11.16 p.m. – surely the latest finish to a game in Britain – Lancashire's Stephen Moore dislocated a shoulder. For Hampshire's Lumb, injury (in a Championship game, this time) was added to insult: just months after collecting his World Twenty20 medal, he was dropped from his county side then, immediately before finals day, had his foot broken in the field off a drive from Somerset's Craig Kieswetter, his England opening partner in the Caribbean.

Most England players were occupied by one-day internationals. Graeme Swann did not play a single Twenty20 game for Nottinghamshire until the semi-final, and Stuart Broad played only two. Pietersen did manage one (unsuccessful) outing for Hampshire before observing: "Geographically, it just doesn't work. I live in Chelsea." This did not go down well in Southampton.

Meanwhile, assorted overseas players proved that freelancing, too, can be difficult. Dwayne Bravo's calamitous one-off performance for Essex at finals day was the most glaring example. For a fee of somewhere between £8,000 and £10,000, he completed an 8,600-mile round trip to make five runs and concede 46 from four overs. His lone wicket was little recompense for Essex, who lost their semi to Hampshire.

Elsewhere, David Warner did not make a fifty in 13 innings for Middlesex. At the same county, Adam Gilchrist hardly set the tournament on fire, either. He recorded the fastest century of the season, at Canterbury, but so poor was the Kent bowling that one home player admitted: "It was the easiest hundred I've ever seen." Andrew Symonds flopped for Surrey, who ended up dropping Younis Khan. Even Shaun Tait, so stunningly fast and hostile when summoned by Australia for the one-day series against England, was generally ineffective for Glamorgan. But it was instructive to see how various domestic players dealt with Tait's raw speed: the old stager, Marcus Trescothick, was quite imperious (and also made the competition's fastest-ever fifty, in just 13 balls, against Hampshire at Taunton); impressive, too, were Sussex's Chris Nash and Middlesex's Dawid Malan; not so, Somerset's James Hildreth at Cardiff.

One exception among the overseas stars was Somerset's Kieron Pollard, with 29 wickets at 15 and 354 runs at a strike-rate of 175, unsurprising given that he hit 29 sixes, the competition's best. His premature departure in the final to his seventh ball – struck a nasty blow in the eye by a Cork bouncer after making 22 – was crucial, not least because he could not then bowl or field.

Northamptonshire's Sri Lankan left-armer, Chaminda Vaas, was another success. Surprisingly, but very effectively, promoted to open the batting, he ended the campaign as the Professional Cricketers' Association's most valuable player, with 412 runs and 23 wickets. There were also strong showings in those PCA rankings from English all-rounders Samit Patel of Nottinghamshire, Tom Smith of Lancashire and Kent's Darren Stevens. Northamptonshire's long-locked, headbanded Jack Brooks proved an economical seamer, at 6.25 an over.

There were 11 centuries in total, including Adams's 100 not out against Glamorgan (the first in county Twenty20 without a six) and a remarkable 101 not out for Surrey's 19-year-old Jason Roy against Kent at Beckenham. But, curiously, only six resulted in victory for the centurion's team. And there was a tie when Herschelle Gibbs made his hundred against Northamptonshire. It was no ordinary tie, though. Northamptonshire required 13 to win from the last ball against Yorkshire. Nicky Boje was facing, Rich Pyrah bowling medium-pace. He delivered a high full toss, called a no-ball (worth two runs), which Boje hit for six. Not a free hit, but still another delivery, which Boje smashed for four.

The best of the centuries was probably Scott Styris's unbeaten 106 from only 50 balls for Essex against Surrey at Chelmsford. Chasing 188 to win under lights, they had made just 65 for two at the halfway stage. And when Ravi Bopara fell, they needed another 113 from 8.5 overs. But Styris launched a violent assault until 22 were required from the last over, bowled by Symonds. Remarkably, five balls sufficed.

Of the top 50 aggregate run-makers, only Pollard and Durham's New Zealander Ross Taylor possessed higher strike-rates than Test wicketkeeper Matt Prior (169.08). Omitted not only from England's one-day side, but also from England Lions, Prior returned to Sussex, asked to open and vowed to expand his range of shots. "Stand there and react," his temporary team-mate, the Kiwi Brendon McCullum, told him. And Prior did, finding the leg-side boundary with a regularity that belied all previous perceptions of him as a purely off-side player.

There was also invention. Essex's James Foster often stood beside or just outside off stump, and then, at the last second, leapt across his stumps to smear the ball away on the leg side. The emergence of the slower-ball bouncer led to some novel fields, often with all four mandatory infielders being placed on the off side and four boundary riders stationed to leg. Off-spinners frequently bowled the first over. Glamorgan's canny veteran, Robert Croft, was by far the best – only he and Sussex's Yardy, of regular bowlers, had an economy-rate below six. Kent even played a "home" game at The Oval, attracting a crowd of 7,620 against Essex.

There were linguistic innovations too. The ECB sold Welsh-language television rights to S4C, who covered five of Glamorgan's home games with relatively decent viewing figures. The presence of the broadcasters allowed line decisions to be adjudicated by a third umpire, whose verdict appeared on the big screen in Welsh. This led to confusion. For Gloucestershire's Chris Taylor, utter bemusement gave way to relief when the penny finally dropped. "Heb Fod Mas" meant not out; others were not so lucky when "Mas" (out) appeared on the screen.

Mostly, though, players were just down and out after 16 matches.

Prize money

£200,000 (+£120,000 from 2009 Twenty20 Cup) for winners: HAMPSHIRE.

£84,000 (+£34,000) for runners-up: SOMERSET.

£27,000 (–£13,000) for losing semi-finalists: ESSEX, NOTTINGHAMSHIRE.

£5,000 (no change) for losing quarter-finalists: LANCASHIRE, NORTHAMPTONSHIRE, SUSSEX, WARWICKSHIRE.

Match-award winners received £2,000 (+£500) in the final, £1,000 (+£500) in the semi-finals, £500 (+£250) in the quarter-finals and £250 (+£50) in group games.

Until 2009, awards were also made on the basis of performances throughout the group stages. No such awards were made in 2010.

FINAL DIVISION TABLES

North Division	Played	Won	Lost	Tied	No result	Points	NRR
WARWICKSHIRE	16	11	4	0	1	23	0.40
NOTTINGHAMSHIRE	16	10	4	2	0	22	0.64
LANCASHIRE	16	9	6	0	1	19	0.47
NORTHAMPTONSHIRE	16	7	6	3	0	17	−0.16
Derbyshire.	16	6	8	0	2	14	−0.15
Yorkshire	16	6	9	1	0	13	−0.12
Leicestershire	16	6	9	0	1	13	−0.23
Durham	16	4	8	0	4	12	−0.29
Worcestershire	16	5	10	0	1	11	−0.65

South Division	Played	Won	Lost	Tied	No result	Points	NRR
SOMERSET	16	11	5	0	0	22	0.41
ESSEX	16	10	6	0	0	20	0.39
SUSSEX	16	9	7	0	0	18	0.60
HAMPSHIRE	16	8	8	0	0	16	0.38
Surrey	16	8	8	0	0	16	0.18
Middlesex	16	8	8	0	0	16	0.01
Kent	16	7	9	0	0	14	−0.16
Glamorgan	16	6	10	0	0	12	−0.97
Gloucestershire	16	5	11	0	0	10	−0.94

Where two or more counties finished with an equal number of points, the positions were decided by (a) most points in head-to-head matches (b) net run-rate (runs scored per over minus runs conceded per over) (c) most wickets taken per balls bowled in matches achieving a result.

FRIENDS PROVIDENT T20 AVERAGES, 2010

BATTING (250 runs, average 31.00)

		M	I	NO	R	HS	100s	50s	Avge	SR	4	6
1	R. N. ten Doeschate (*Essex*) . .	6	6	1	296	102	1	1	59.20	177.24	21	19
2	D. J. Hussey (*Notts*).	17	17	5	524	81*	0	3	43.66	142.00	34	19
3	A. J. Hall (*Northants*)	17	16	10	252	40*	0	0	42.00	111.50	21	3
4	A. McGrath (*Yorks*).	12	10	4	251	73*	0	1	41.83	110.57	18	5
5	D. I. Stevens (*Kent*).	14	13	4	369	52*	0	2	41.00	149.39	32	14
6	N. D. McKenzie (*Hants*).	17	17	6	440	73	0	5	40.00	123.94	48	5
7	L. R. P. L. Taylor (*Durham*) . .	11	9	1	315	80*	0	2	39.37	173.07	24	23
8	†J. H. K. Adams (*Hants*)	19	19	2	668	101*	2	2	39.29	132.27	78	17
9	†J. E. C. Franklin (*Glos*)	15	15	3	470	90	0	2	39.16	130.19	40	15
10	†A. N. Cook (*Essex*)	11	11	1	388	73	0	3	38.80	132.42	40	7
11	W. J. Durston (*Derbys*)	16	15	3	445	111	1	2	37.08	129.36	42	13
12	J. W. A. Taylor (*Leics*)	14	14	3	407	62*	0	4	37.00	136.12	30	13
13	H. H. Gibbs (*Yorks*).	15	15	3	443	101*	1	2	36.91	148.16	43	16
14	M. R. Ramprakash (*Surrey*) . .	11	11	2	331	63*	0	3	36.77	116.54	35	7
15	†T. C. Smith (*Lancs*).	17	17	2	543	92*	0	3	36.20	119.60	53	10
16	†S. M. Ervine (*Hants*)	19	19	6	470	74*	0	3	36.15	146.41	49	12
17	S. B. Styris (*Essex*)	15	13	2	392	106*	1	1	35.63	161.98	23	24
18	†M. J. Cosgrove (*Glam*)	16	16	0	562	89	0	4	35.12	132.23	65	14
19	O. A. Shah (*Middx*)	16	15	3	421	80	0	3	35.08	110.20	35	13
20	M. J. Prior (*Sussex*)	14	14	1	443	117	1	2	34.07	169.08	53	14
21	†J. A. Morkel (*Durham*)	15	11	3	272	48	0	0	34.00	128.90	20	9
22	R. S. Bopara (*Essex*)	16	16	2	473	105*	1	2	33.78	128.88	46	16
23	†D. J. Malan (*Middx*)	16	16	5	364	86	0	1	33.09	130.00	25	15

		M	I	NO	R	HS	100s	50s	Avge	SR	4	6
24	†P. A. Jaques (*Worcs*)	14	13	3	330	78*	0	2	33.00	131.47	39	5
25	J. C. Hildreth (*Somerset*)	19	19	5	459	77*	0	2	32.78	110.60	49	3
26	D. L. Maddy (*Warwicks*)	17	17	3	456	88	0	1	32.57	132.55	46	18
27	K. A. Pollard (*Somerset*)	17	16	5	354	89*	0	2	32.18	175.24	19	29
28	{J. L. Denly (*Kent*)	12	12	0	382	65	0	1	31.83	115.75	49	3
	{†A. W. Gale (*Yorks*)	14	14	2	382	65*	0	4	31.83	128.61	43	9
30	†M. E. Trescothick (*Somerset*)	19	19	1	572	83	0	6	31.77	157.14	72	22

BOWLING (16 wickets)

		Style	O	M	R	W	BB	4W/i	Avge	SR	ER
1	A. C. Thomas (*Somerset*)	RFM	72.5	3	460	33	3-11	0	13.93	13.24	6.31
2	D. R. Briggs (*Hants*)	SLA	67	0	445	31	3-5	0	14.35	12.96	6.64
3	K. A. Pollard (*Somerset*)	RM	58.2	0	438	29	4-15	1	15.10	12.06	7.50
4	R. D. B. Croft (*Glam*)	OB	57.5	0	343	22	3-19	0	15.59	15.77	5.93
5	W. P. U. J. C. Vaas (*Northants*)	LFM	57.3	1	364	23	3-16	0	15.82	15.00	6.33
6	S. D. Parry (*Lancs*)	SLA	60	0	427	26	4-28	1	16.42	13.84	7.11
7	A. U. Rashid (*Yorks*)	LBG	61	0	428	26	4-20	1	16.46	14.07	7.01
8	K. H. D. Barker (*Warwicks*)	LFM	48.3	0	350	21	4-19	1	16.66	13.85	7.21
9	Danish Kaneria (*Essex*)	LBG	42.3	1	291	17	3-32	0	17.11	15.00	6.84
10	C. T. Tremlett (*Surrey*)	RFM	60	1	411	24	3-17	0	17.12	15.00	6.85
11	T. M. J. Smith (*Middx*)	SLA	39.5	0	311	18	5-24	1	17.27	13.27	7.80
12	D. J. Pattinson (*Notts*)	RFM	50	1	353	20	4-19	1	17.65	15.00	7.06
13	S. I. Mahmood (*Lancs*)	RFM	53	0	430	23	4-21	1	18.69	13.82	8.11
14	J. D. Shantry (*Worcs*)	LM	49	1	345	18	3-23	0	19.16	16.33	7.04
15	R. M. Pyrah (*Yorks*)	RM	58	0	408	21	3-12	0	19.42	16.57	7.03
16	S. J. Cook (*Kent*)	RFM	57	1	413	21	3-13	0	19.66	16.28	7.24
17	Imran Tahir (*Warwicks*)	LBG	61	1	401	20	3-14	0	20.05	18.30	6.57
18	S. R. Patel (*Notts*)	SLA	58	0	377	17	3-26	0	22.17	20.47	6.50
19	H. M. C. M. Bandara (*Kent*)	LBG	48	0	384	17	3-14	0	22.58	16.94	8.00
20	T. D. Groenewald (*Derbys*)	RFM	50.2	1	375	16	3-18	0	23.43	18.87	7.45
21	N. M. Carter (*Warwicks*)	LFM	60	0	383	16	3-28	0	23.93	22.50	6.38
22	S. M. Ervine (*Hants*)	RFM	44	1	386	16	4-12	1	24.12	16.50	8.77
23	B. J. Phillips (*Somerset*)	RFM	60	1	466	19	3-33	0	24.52	18.94	7.76
24	T. J. Murtagh (*Middx*)	RFM	48.2	2	393	16	3-24	0	24.56	18.12	8.13
25	R. S. Bopara (*Essex*)	RM	54	0	397	16	3-13	0	24.81	20.25	7.35
26	M. J. Hoggard (*Leics*)	RFM	54.5	0	465	18	3-19	0	25.83	18.27	8.48
27	P. T. Collins (*Middx*)	LFM	54	0	422	16	3-27	0	26.37	20.25	7.81
28	A. J. Hall (*Northants*)	RFM	48.5	0	423	16	2-8	0	26.43	18.31	8.66
29	D. P. Nannes (*Notts*)	LF	58.5	0	466	17	2-20	0	27.41	20.76	7.92
30	C. P. Wood (*Hants*)	LFM	65.1	1	551	20	3-27	0	27.55	19.55	8.45
31	C. J. C. Wright (*Essex*)	RFM	66	0	609	21	4-25	1	29.00	18.85	9.22

LEADING WICKETKEEPERS

Dismissals	M		Dismissals	M	
15 (13 ct, 2 st)	11	J. C. Buttler (*Somerset*)	13 (9 ct, 4 st)	11	T. R. Ambrose (*Warwicks*)
15 (14 ct, 1 st)	15	S. M. Davies (*Surrey*)	13 (9 ct, 4 st)	11	N. J. O'Brien (*Northants*)
14 (11 ct, 3 st)	15	P. Mustard (*Durham*)	13 (7 ct, 6 st)	15	P. A. Nixon (*Leics*)
14 (8 ct, 6 st)	16	M. A. Wallace (*Glam*)	13 (4 ct, 9 st)	18	J. S. Foster (*Essex*)

Note: J. C. Buttler played another eight matches as an outfielder and took six more catches.

LEADING FIELDERS

Ct	M			Ct	M	
13	17	S. J. Croft (*Lancs*)		11	17	A. G. Botha (*Warwicks*)
12	14	J. du Toit (*Leics*)		10	14	J. M. Vince (*Hants*)
11	15	G. M. Smith (*Derbys*)				

Note: Nine outfielders held nine catches: A. J. Blake (*Kent*), G. R. Breese (*Durham*), R. Clarke (*Warwicks*), D. J. Hussey (*Notts*), S. I. Mahmood (*Lancs*), S. C. Moore (*Lancs*), T. C. Smith (*Lancs*), S. J. Walters (*Surrey*), G. G. White (*Notts*).

NORTH DIVISION

DERBYSHIRE

At Derby, June 9 (floodlit). **Warwickshire won by three wickets. Derbyshire 120-4** (20 overs) (G. M. Smith 38, R. J. Peterson 35*); ‡**Warwickshire 123-7** (19.2 overs) (I. R. Bell 66). *MoM*: I. R. Bell. *Attendance*: 1,079. *On a torpid pitch, Ian Bell's quality set him apart. As Derbyshire trudged to 120-4, Chris Woakes allowed only a single from his last two overs to produce Warwickshire's thriftiest four-over return of 1-9. In reply, they were 25-3 in the sixth over, but Bell's 66 from 56 balls tipped the balance.*

At Derby, June 13. **No result. Derbyshire 172-3** (19 overs) (L. E. Bosman 57, W. J. Durston 71*) v ‡**Durham**. *Attendance*: 1,085. *Derbyshire's new opening pair, Loots Bosman and Wes Durston, followed their 79 in Nottingham two days before with a stand of 90 from 55 balls. Derbyshire were four runs short of their highest Twenty20 total at Derby when rain arrived.*

At Derby, June 17 (floodlit). **Nottinghamshire won by six wickets. ‡Derbyshire 152-7** (20 overs) (G. T. Park 66); **Nottinghamshire 153-4** (18 overs) (M. J. Wood 51*, D. J. Hussey 65; C. K. Langeveldt 3-36). *MoM*: D. J. Hussey. *Attendance*: 2,575. *Captain David Hussey made light work of chasing victory with 65 from 34 balls as he and the sturdy Matthew Wood added 95 at ten an over for the third wicket. Derbyshire had earlier stuttered to 2-3 from the first eight balls before Garry Park's admirable 66 secured a respectable score.*

At Derby, June 21 (floodlit). **Derbyshire won by six wickets. Worcestershire 127-7** (20 overs) (M. M. Ali 67); ‡**Derbyshire 128-4** (19.2 overs) (L. E. Bosman 34, G. T. Park 41*). *MoM*: M. M. Ali. *Attendance*: 1,224. *Moeen Ali's one-man show could not prevent the fifth of six consecutive Worcestershire defeats. Having hit 67 while his team-mates managed 55 between them, he made Derbyshire work hard with 2-14 in four overs of tidy off-spin. But a sensible fourth-wicket stand of 64 in ten overs between Park and Robin Peterson saw Derbyshire through.*

At Chesterfield, July 2. **Leicestershire won by 16 runs. ‡Leicestershire 212-5** (20 overs) (B. J. Hodge 39, W. I. Jefferson 83); **Derbyshire 196-8** (20 overs) (J. L. Sadler 39, P. S. Jones 40; M. J. Hoggard 3-38). *MoM*: W. I. Jefferson. *Attendance*: 1,359. *Colossal blows from the towering Will Jefferson brought 83 off 33 balls, eight of them smashed for six, and left no margin for error in the chase, even on such a fast-scoring ground. Derbyshire sprinted to 56-0, but four wickets crashed in 11 balls, three to Matthew Hoggard, and the task proved too stiff.*

At Chesterfield, July 4. **Derbyshire won by five wickets. ‡Lancashire 132-7** (20 overs) (G. D. Cross 65*; T. D. Groenewald 3-18); **Derbyshire 135-5** (18.1 overs) (G. T. Park 50). *MoM*: T. D. Groenewald. *Attendance*: 2,357. *Lancashire were in tatters at 22-5 after Tim Groenewald grabbed wickets in each of his first three overs. Gareth Cross gave them something to bowl at with an unbeaten 65, his highest score in any cricket for almost three years, but 50 from Park left Derbyshire comfortable winners.*

At Derby, July 16 (floodlit). **Northamptonshire won by 43 runs. Northamptonshire 159-4** (20 overs) (D. J. Sales 39, E. Chigumbura 35*); ‡**Derbyshire 116** (18.5 overs) (E. Chigumbura 4-14). *MoM*: E. Chigumbura. *Attendance*: 1,944. *Given the opportunity to book their place in the quarter-finals for the first time since 2005, Derbyshire failed dismally to rise to the occasion and were left to hope for favours from others. Elton Chigumbura, the Zimbabwe captain, shot out four men in 15 balls as they plummeted from 50-2 to 76-8 in a crucial win for Northamptonshire.*

At Derby, July 18. **Yorkshire won by six wickets. ‡Derbyshire 137-7** (20 overs) (W. J. Durston 39, R. J. Peterson 32*); **Yorkshire 138-4** (19.2 overs) (A. W. Gale 55, G. S. Ballance 48*). *MoM*: A. W.

Gale. *Attendance: 2,436. Derbyshire could not claim the win they needed, so results elsewhere became academic. The game's one significant stand, 85 for the third wicket between Andrew Gale and Gary Ballance, proved ample for Yorkshire.*

Derbyshire away matches

June 2: beat Leicestershire by 11 runs.
June 3: beat Yorkshire by 65 runs.
June 11: lost to Nottinghamshire by five wickets.
June 20: beat Northamptonshire by nine runs.

June 25: lost to Warwickshire by six wickets.
June 27: lost to Worcestershire by eight wickets.
July 11: beat Lancashire by seven runs.
July 14: no result v Durham.

DURHAM

At Chester-le-Street, June 4. **Lancashire won by 23 runs. ‡Lancashire 179-4** (20 overs) (T. C. Smith 44, S. C. Moore 83*); **Durham 156-8** (20 overs) (P. Mustard 47; S. J. Croft 3-18). *MoM:* S. C. Moore. *Attendance:* 8,768. County debuts: L. R. P. L. Taylor (Durham); S. M. Katich (Lancashire). *In front of Riverside's record crowd for a county match, the new name of Emirates Durham International Cricket Ground was unveiled. But there was no change in Durham's traditional struggles against Twenty20 spin. At 77-2 and needing 103 more from 58 balls, there was hope, but Lancashire had played a third spinner in Steven Croft, and his three wickets proved decisive. Stephen Moore's unbeaten 83 earlier came off 52 balls, in a match that featured 14 bowlers.*

At Chester-le-Street, June 6. **Durham v ‡Worcestershire. Abandoned.**

At Chester-le-Street, June 14. **Durham won by 71 runs. ‡Durham 225-2** (20 overs) (P. Mustard 65, I. D. Blackwell 37, L. R. P. L. Taylor 80*, D. M. Benkenstein 35*); **Leicestershire 154** (17.2 overs) (J. du Toit 39, J. W. A. Taylor 38; P. D. Collingwood 4-13). *MoM:* L. R. P. L. Taylor. *Attendance:* 2,397. *For the second time in four days, Durham bettered their highest-ever total, and Ross Taylor's unbeaten 80 from 33 balls with nine sixes became their highest individual score. His stand of 117* in 45 balls with Dale Benkenstein was also a new county best, 81 of them plundered from the final four overs. Desperately hitting out in reply, Leicestershire lost four of their last five wickets in 13 balls from Paul Collingwood, playing only his sixth Twenty20 match for Durham.*

At Chester-le-Street, June 18. **Durham won by six wickets. ‡Yorkshire 131-8** (20 overs) (A. McGrath 34*); **Durham 132-4** (15.1 overs) (L. R. P. L. Taylor 49, D. M. Benkenstein 57*). *MoM:* D. M. Benkenstein. *Attendance:* 3,017. *Yorkshire reached 54-1 after six overs, but the next five produced only 13 runs. Tino Best reduced Durham to 1-2 before Taylor and Benkenstein put on 101 in 11 overs, Benkenstein hitting four sixes in a competition-best 57*.*

At Chester-le-Street, June 20. **Nottinghamshire won by 11 runs. ‡Nottinghamshire 186-4** (20 overs) (A. D. Brown 73*, S. R. Patel 51); **Durham 175-5** (20 overs) (L. R. P. L. Taylor 33, D. M. Benkenstein 40). *MoM:* A. D. Brown. *Attendance:* 5,722. *A controversial boundary catch proved decisive. Durham needed 53 off five overs with six wickets standing when Benkenstein pulled to deep square leg. Alex Hales took the catch but staggered over the rope, throwing the ball skywards as he did so. He recovered to complete the catch, but, with no TV cameras, there was no evidence that the catch was clean. The umpires were unable to give Benkenstein out, but he walked across to speak to Hales, who told him he was certain the catch was legitimate. Benkenstein departed for 40 and later said: "I just feel that's the way the game should be played." Nottinghamshire belted 125 from their last ten overs, with Ali Brown going from 14 to 73* and Samit Patel making 51 in a stand of 112.*

At Chester-le-Street, July 2. **Warwickshire won by five wickets. Durham 117-8** (20 overs) (J. A. Morkel 48, G. R. Breese 30*; Imran Tahir 3-19); **‡Warwickshire 120-5** (18 overs) (J. O. Troughton 34). *MoM:* Imran Tahir. *Attendance:* 3,089. *Imran Tahir's hat-trick in his first over (the 12th) reduced Durham to 51-7. He bowled Gordon Muchall with a googly, Will Smith drove to mid-on and left-hander Ben Harmison edged another googly to slip. Despite run-outs from consecutive balls at the reply's same stage, Warwickshire revived from 69-4.*

At Chester-le-Street, July 14. **No result. Durham 110-2** (13 overs) (P. Mustard 70*) v **‡Derbyshire.** *Attendance:* 2,440. *Phil Mustard's unbeaten 70 off 39 balls was his highest in Twenty20 cricket, but torrential rain after 48 minutes effectively ended Durham's slim hopes of a quarter-final place.*

At Chester-le-Street, July 18. **Northamptonshire won by seven wickets. ‡Durham 130-5** (20 overs) (M. D. Stoneman 36, J. A. Morkel 35*); **Northamptonshire 133-3** (17.5 overs) (R. A. White 63,

A. G. Wakely 35). *MoM:* R. A. White. *Attendance:* 3,143. *Northamptonshire needed a win to be sure of the group's last qualifying spot, while Durham played for pride only. They managed one six in an uninspired 130-5, and Rob White's 63 calmly took Northamptonshire through.*

Durham away matches

June 10: lost to Yorkshire by nine wickets.	June 25: lost to Nottinghamshire by four wickets.
June 11: beat Warwickshire by 15 runs.	June 26: lost to Northamptonshire by 30 runs.
June 13: no result v Derbyshire.	July 9: beat Worcestershire by three runs.
June 22: lost to Lancashire by 50 runs.	July 16: abandoned v Leicestershire.

LANCASHIRE

At Manchester, June 9. **Lancashire won by 69 runs.** ‡**Lancashire 157-5** (20 overs) (T. C. Smith 67; W. P. U. J. C. Vaas 3-32); **Northamptonshire 88** (17.5 overs) (S. C. Kerrigan 3-17). *MoM:* S. C. Kerrigan. *Attendance:* 2,164. *County club:* L. Vincent (Northamptonshire). *Northamptonshire suffered a spectacular collapse, plummeting from 42-1 to 57-7 in 27 balls. As so often at Old Trafford, spin did the damage: Lancashire's three seamers bowled just six overs between them. Simon Kerrigan returned 3-17 in his second Twenty20 match, backed by fellow young left-armer Steven Parry and Steven Croft, who had converted from medium-pace to off-spin. Earlier, Tom Smith's 67 was a Twenty20 best.*

At Manchester, June 11. **Leicestershire won by 14 runs.** ‡**Leicestershire 141-6** (20 overs) (J. G. E. Benning 45, J. du Toit 31; S. D. Parry 3-26); **Lancashire 127-9** (20 overs) (T. C. Smith 48, S. M. Katich 30; M. J. Hoggard 3-19). *MoM:* B. J. Hodge. *Attendance:* 3,112. *Lancashire were hoist with their own petard as batsmen capitulated to spin on another slow pitch. Claude Henderson and Brad Hodge shared 4-35 from eight overs after Lancashire, chasing 142, had reached 63-1 in the tenth.*

At Manchester, June 20. **Lancashire won by five wickets.** ‡**Warwickshire 126-6** (20 overs) (J. O. Troughton 42*); **Lancashire 127-5** (19.5 overs) (T. C. Smith 51; Imran Tahir 3-18). *MoM:* T. C. Smith. *Attendance:* 4,814. *Gareth Cross seized a dramatic win by striking Keith Barker for six off the penultimate ball. Tom Smith passed 40 for the fifth time in six completed games, but Imran Tahir, with 3-18, slowed the reply. When Smith fell, Lancashire needed 12 from seven balls. Cross hit the first for four but did not face again until two balls remained, while only a wide and a single accrued. Cue Cross to clear the ropes.*

At Manchester, June 22. **Lancashire won by 50 runs.** ‡**Lancashire 187-8** (20 overs) (S. J. Croft 68, S. M. Katich 36, N. L. McCullum 32*; S. J. Harmison 5-41); **Durham 137** (18.4 overs) (L. E. Plunkett 31; S. D. Parry 4-28). *MoM:* S. D. Parry. *Attendance:* 2,915. *Steve Harmison became the first bowler in 2010 to claim five wickets or more in a domestic Twenty20 innings. However, it was the most expensive such feat by seven runs, and couldn't stop Croft making 68. Oddly, two further instances followed, both against Kent, in the next two days. But it was Parry's maiden four-for that proved more telling as Durham staggered to 137 all out.*

At Manchester, July 5. **Lancashire won by 46 runs. Lancashire 170-5** (20 overs) (T. C. Smith 92*, M. J. Chilton 34); ‡**Worcestershire 124** (18.4 overs) (S. T. Jayasuriya 54; G. Chapple 3-36, T. C. Smith 3-12, S. D. Parry 3-19). *MoM:* T. C. Smith. *Attendance:* 2,722. *Tom Smith lost two partners for ducks before he faced a ball, but he batted throughout the innings for a career-best 92*. Worcestershire, on 73-1, needed 98 more at 8.5 an over, but Parry removed Sanath Jayasuriya for 54, and the last eight clattered in 29 balls. Uniquely in 2010, three bowlers claimed three wickets in the same innings, Glen Chapple for the first time.*

At Manchester, July 9. **Lancashire won by five wickets.** ‡**Yorkshire 162-8** (20 overs) (A. Lyth 56, H. H. Gibbs 51; S. I. Mahmood 3-30, S. D. Parry 3-17); **Lancashire 163-5** (19 overs) (S. C. Moore 59, S. J. Croft 36, P. J. Horton 37*; R. M. Pyrah 3-33). *MoM:* S. D. Parry. *Attendance:* 11,898. *A Friday evening sell-out created a buzz lacking from other home games, but Yorkshire squandered Herschelle Gibbs's inspired start when they mustered only 43 from their last seven overs. Parry pegged them back from 119-2 before Stephen Moore raced off in the reply. Lancashire retained control, completing their highest successful run-chase at Old Trafford.*

At Manchester, July 11. **Derbyshire won by seven runs.** ‡**Derbyshire 163-6** (20 overs) (W. J. Durston 39); **Lancashire 156-6** (20 overs) (T. C. Smith 38, S. J. Croft 38; T. D. Groenewald 3-32). *MoM:* T. D. Groenewald. *Attendance:* 3,916. *Tim Groenewald snatched three key Lancashire wickets* *for the second time in a week to secure Derbyshire's first win at Old Trafford in all formats for seven years. Lancashire were 93-1, needing 71 from 56 balls, when Smith was run out. With 13 wanted, Charl Langeveldt produced a masterful last over, taking a wicket and conceding five singles.*

At Manchester, July 14. **Lancashire won by nine wickets** (D/L method). ‡**Nottinghamshire 138-7** (20 overs) (A. D. Hales 83); **Lancashire 83-1** (8.2 overs) (S. C. Moore 51*). MoM: S. C. Moore. *Attendance:* 2,601. *Lancashire joined Nottinghamshire in the quarter-finals after a game that would undoubtedly have been abandoned without Old Trafford's expensive new drains. In a bizarre innings, Alex Hales hit 83 as his colleagues mustered 44 between them, facing four spinners and just six overs of seam. After rain, Moore made short work of the adjusted target of 81 in ten overs.*

Lancashire away matches

June 4: beat Durham by 23 runs.
June 13: no result v Warwickshire.
June 15: lost to Nottinghamshire by 26 runs.
June 17: lost to Yorkshire by 17 runs.

June 25: beat Leicestershire by six wickets.
July 4: lost to Derbyshire by five wickets.
July 15: lost to Northamptonshire by 11 runs.
July 18: beat Worcestershire by seven runs.

LEICESTERSHIRE

At Leicester, June 2. **Derbyshire won by 11 runs. Derbyshire 165-5** (20 overs) (L. E. Bosman 39, G. M. Smith 30); ‡**Leicestershire 154-8** (20 overs) (A. B. McDonald 67; P. S. Jones 3-20). MoM: A. B. McDonald. *Attendance:* 3,030. *County debut:* L. E. Bosman. *Steffan Jones took a Twenty20-best 3-20 as Derbyshire capably defended a total of 165-5. Australian all-rounder Andrew McDonald kept Leicestershire in the hunt with 67 from 50 balls, but they could not sustain the momentum in the closing overs.*

At Leicester, June 18. **Northamptonshire won by ten runs.** Reduced to 18 overs a side. ‡**Northamptonshire 166-4** (18 overs) (W. P. U. J. C. Vaas 50, N. Boje 54*); **Leicestershire 156-6** (18 overs) (W. I. Jefferson 53, J. W. A. Taylor 38). MoM: W. P. U. J. C. Vaas. *Attendance:* 1,477. *County debut:* E. Chigumbura (Northamptonshire). *South Africans Nicky Boje and Andrew Hall, county captains past and present, smashed 51 from the final three overs for Northamptonshire in an onslaught that proved decisive. Chaminda Vaas, one of eight bowlers used, added 2-24 to his earlier 50 as they just defended their total. Niall O'Brien, the Northamptonshire wicketkeeper, had been playing for Ireland against Australia in Dublin the previous day, and reported back to his county later than agreed. He did not bat in Northamptonshire's innings. The club suspended him for their next two matches, and stripped him of the vice-captaincy.*

At Leicester, June 20. **Yorkshire won by nine wickets.** ‡**Leicestershire 148-8** (20 overs) (B. J. Hodge 43, J. W. A. Taylor 60); **Yorkshire 150-1** (17.1 overs) (A. W. Gale 65*, J. A. Rudolph 53). MoM: A. W. Gale. *Attendance:* 3,618. *A stand of 103 in 68 balls between openers Andrew Gale and Jacques Rudolph confirmed that Leicestershire's total was well below par. James Taylor made a maiden Twenty20 fifty, but Yorkshire breezed to victory.*

At Leicester, June 25. **Lancashire won by six wickets.** ‡**Leicestershire 176-6** (20 overs) (J. du Toit 69, J. W. A. Taylor 61; S. I. Mahmood 3-46); **Lancashire 180-4** (19.3 overs) (T. C. Smith 32, S. J. Croft 42, P. J. Horton 30*, S. M. Katich 41*). MoM: T. C. Smith. *Attendance:* 2,466. *Jacques du Toit made 69 and Taylor 61 from only 37 balls to raise Leicestershire hopes, but Brad Hodge's off-spin conceded 15 runs in the first over of the reply. His fellow-Australian, Simon Katich, hit a blistering, 41* from 19 balls as Lancashire sped home.*

At Leicester, July 4. **Nottinghamshire won by seven wickets.** ‡**Leicestershire 182-3** (20 overs) (B. J. Hodge 103, J. W. A. Taylor 56*); **Nottinghamshire 185-3** (18.3 overs) (A. D. Brown 55, M. J. Wood 61). MoM: B. J. Hodge. *Attendance:* 2,795. *County debut:* S. L. Elstone (Nottinghamshire). *Hodge became the third Leicestershire batsman to hit a Twenty20 century but, in a campaign in which they never won at home, to no avail. Quiet at first, he hit his second fifty from 15 balls and shared a 121-run, third-wicket stand with Taylor, whose fifty was his fourth in six innings. It mattered not. Ali Brown and Matthew Wood savaged poor bowling to race to fifties of their own, scoring at nearly 11 an over in a 74-run stand for the second wicket.*

At Leicester, July 7. **Worcestershire won by three wickets. Leicestershire 142-8** (20 overs) (M. M. Ali 3-19); ‡**Worcestershire 146-7** (19 overs) (P. A. Jaques 32; B. J. Hodge 3-26). MoM: M. M. Ali. *Attendance:* 1,768. *Leicestershire were in sight of ending their miserable home run when*

Worcestershire were reduced to 112-7, chasing 143. But Gareth Andrew wielded the long-handled Mongoose bat to devastating effect, and his 27* from 11 balls brought another defeat.

At Leicester, July 16. **Leicestershire v Durham. Abandoned.**

At Leicester, July 18. **Warwickshire won by eight runs. Warwickshire 137-7** (20 overs) (D. L. Maddy 41*); **‡Leicestershire 129-6** (20 overs). *MoM:* C. R. Woakes. *Attendance:* 2,109. *Leicestershire failed to break their home duck at the last attempt, though the task had seemed moderate. Darren Maddy contrived 41 from 29 balls, but his old county floundered. Chris Woakes claimed 2-16 with the new ball, and acceleration never came.*

Leicestershire away matches

June 8: beat Northamptonshire by 12 runs.
June 11: beat Lancashire by 14 runs.
June 14: lost to Durham by 71 runs.
June 23: beat Warwickshire by 32 runs.

June 27: beat Yorkshire by six runs.
July 2: beat Derbyshire by 16 runs.
July 11: lost to Worcestershire by six wickets.
July 15: beat Nottinghamshire by 23 runs (D/L).

NORTHAMPTONSHIRE

At Northampton, June 8 (floodlit). **Leicestershire won by 12 runs.** Reduced to 18 overs a side. **‡Leicestershire 149-8** (18 overs) (A. B. McDonald 49, C. W. Henderson 32); **Northamptonshire 137-9** (18 overs) (M. B. Loye 39; M. N. Malik 4-25). *MoM:* C. W. Henderson. *Attendance:* 2,074. *Nadeem Malik grabbed four wickets in seven balls as Northamptonshire, needing 44, crashed from 106-3 to 120-7. By 128-9, they had lost five men in 12 balls. Malik's 4-25 was not his Twenty20 best, but it contrasted decisively with the 19 runs off Lee Daggett in Leicestershire's final over.*

At Northampton, June 11 (floodlit). **Northamptonshire won by 21 runs. ‡Northamptonshire 143-8** (20 overs) (W. P. U. J. C. Vaas 54, N. J. O'Brien 31); **Worcestershire 122-8** (20 overs). *MoM:* W. P. U. J. C. Vaas. *Attendance:* 2,547. *After three defeats, Northamptonshire's first win owed most to Chaminda Vaas, an inspired choice as new opener. Dropped twice, he belted a maiden Twenty20 fifty from 39 balls on a sterile pitch, adding 71 in nine overs with Niall O'Brien for the second wicket. With James Middlebrook taking 2-12, Vaas bowled only three overs, claiming 2-13 as Worcestershire failed to cope.*

At Northampton, June 20. **Derbyshire won by nine runs. ‡Derbyshire 109-9** (20 overs) (N. Boje 3-20); **Northamptonshire 100-8** (20 overs) (A. G. Wakely 37; G. T. Park 3-11). *MoM:* G. T. Park. *Attendance:* 2,567. *In a freakish game, Garry Park dismissed Alex Wakely, David Willey and David Murphy in five balls to set up a remarkable win. Northamptonshire needed 26 from 19 balls at 84-4 when Wakely fell for 37. He was the sole batsman, of 21 who tried, to venture past 28 on another resentful pitch. With him departed home hopes.*

At Northampton, June 26. **Northamptonshire won by 30 runs. ‡Northamptonshire 164-5** (20 overs) (W. P. U. J. C. Vaas 73, N. J. O'Brien 37); **Durham 134** (18.2 overs) (W. P. U. J. C. Vaas 3-23). *MoM:* W. P. U. J. C. Vaas. *Attendance:* 2,362. *The irrepressible Vaas shone again, establishing another career-best (73) and sharing a stand of 91 with O'Brien after David Sales had gone to the opening ball. He then claimed 3-23 as no Durham batsman reached 25. At 89-4, they needed nearly ten an over, but Sales ran out Dale Benkenstein to end a threatening 37-run stand with Albie Morkel, whom Vaas removed two overs later.*

At Northampton, July 2 (floodlit). **Tied. ‡Yorkshire 180-3** (20 overs) (H. H. Gibbs 101*, J. M. Bairstow 32*); **Northamptonshire 180-5** (20 overs) (D. J. Sales 49, W. P. U. J. C. Vaas 53). *MoM:* H. H. Gibbs. *Attendance:* 3,179. *A stunning maiden Twenty20 century from Herschelle Gibbs was matched by an extraordinary finish that belonged to a ripping yarn. With 13 needed off the last ball, Rich Pyrah conceded two extras for a no-ball which Nicky Boje gleefully swatted for six. He then hit the extra delivery to the midwicket boundary and the match was tied. There were three ties in 2010: mercurial Northamptonshire were party to all. But they should probably have won this game. At 161-3, they needed 20 from 11 balls, only for Anthony McGrath to strike twice in the 19th over, and just five came from the six balls before the climax. For Gibbs, defeat would have been an injustice: his 101* from 53 balls was simply magnificent and, with Jonny Bairstow, he added 73 from Yorkshire's final five overs.*

At Northampton, July 9 (floodlit). **Warwickshire won by six wickets. ‡Northamptonshire 146-8** (20 overs) (S. D. Peters 39, A. G. Wakely 41; C. R. Woakes 3-21); **Warwickshire 147-4** (18.1

overs) (D. L. Maddy 30, K. H. D. Barker 46, T. R. Ambrose 30*; E. Chigumbura 3-19). *MoM:* K. H. D. Barker. *Attendance: 3,749. Although Elton Chigumbura claimed three wickets in four balls, including Keith Barker's for 46 off 28 balls, Warwickshire, at 93-4, needed only 54 more at less than a run a ball, and calmly completed victory.*

At Northampton, July 11. **Tied. ‡Nottinghamshire 144-7** (20 overs) (S. R. Patel 40, D. J. Hussey 41; D. J. Willey 3-33); **Northamptonshire 144-8** (20 overs) (W. P. U. J. C. Vaas 47). *MoM:* W. P. U. J. C. Vaas. *Attendance: 2,101. The second tie in 20 days between these teams came amid controversy. One of Northamptonshire's speciality collapses, this one from 107-3, culminated in three run-outs when eight runs were needed from the final five balls. The first saw Andrew Hall dismissed after appearing to be impeded by the bowler, Dirk Nannes. "They stuck to their guns that they wanted the run-out and there wasn't much we could do about it," Hall said. Jack Brooks hit the last ball for two to level the scores.*

At Northampton, July 15 (floodlit). **Northamptonshire won by 11 runs. Northamptonshire 170-4** (20 overs) (R. A. White 80); **‡Lancashire 159-6** (20 overs) (G. D. Cross 41*). *MoM:* R. A. White. *Attendance: 3,345. Rob White's 80 set up the win that boosted home hopes of qualification. Lancashire slipped to 109-6, Wakely holding a breathtaking one-handed catch at long-on, and, although Gareth Cross and Sajid Mahmood did their best to belt 62 from the last 22 balls, they managed only 50.*

Northamptonshire away matches

June 3: lost to Warwickshire by eight wickets.
June 9: lost to Lancashire by 69 runs.
June 13: beat Yorkshire by 14 runs (D/L).
June 18: beat Leicestershire by ten runs.

June 22: tied with Nottinghamshire.
June 25: lost to Worcestershire by nine wickets.
July 16: beat Derbyshire by 43 runs.
July 18: beat Durham by seven wickets.

NOTTINGHAMSHIRE

At Nottingham, June 11. **Nottinghamshire won by five wickets. ‡Derbyshire 192-6** (20 overs) (L. E. Bosman 39, W. J. Durston 111); **Nottinghamshire 193-5** (17 overs) (A. D. Hales 69, A. D. Brown 32, S. R. Patel 62*; G. M. Smith 3-34). *MoM:* W. J. Durston. *Attendance: 6,434. Alex Hales's fifty, from 16 balls, was then the second-fastest in English Twenty20 cricket, and a bravura follow-up from Samit Patel eclipsed a brilliant hundred from Wes Durston as almost 400 runs were scored in the match. Durston's seven sixes included a reverse-sweep off Patel, and his century came in 51 balls. This looked pedestrian as Hales began the reply, and Patel kept up the charge, romping home with three overs to spare.*

At Nottingham, June 13. **Nottinghamshire won by six wickets. ‡Worcestershire 150-7** (20 overs) (M. M. Ali 67, D. K. H. Mitchell 34*); **Nottinghamshire 155-4** (16.1 overs) (S. R. Patel 63, D. J. Hussey 34*). *MoM:* S. R. Patel. *Attendance: 6,160. Stuart Broad (on his Nottinghamshire 20-over debut), Dirk Nannes and Ryan Sidebottom conceded only nine boundaries in their 12 allotted overs as Worcestershire's batsmen were blitzed by pace. Patel maintained his good form with another fifty, and David Hussey finished the match with a straight six.*

At Nottingham, June 15. **Nottinghamshire won by 26 runs. Nottinghamshire 157-7** (20 overs) (A. D. Hales 35, D. J. Hussey 44; S. I. Mahmood 4-21); **‡Lancashire 131** (18.5 overs) (T. C. Smith 43; S. R. Patel 3-26). *MoM:* S. R. Patel. *Attendance: 5,674. Sajid Mahmood, cleverly varying his pace for a Twenty20-best, restricted Nottinghamshire to 157-7, but they showed they could defend as well as chase. Patel took three wickets in five balls to halt Lancashire's good start, and the hostility of Broad and Darren Pattinson did the rest.*

At Nottingham, June 22. **Tied. ‡Northamptonshire 121-7** (20 overs) (A. G. Wakely 43, A. J. Hall 40*; D. J. Pattinson 4-19); **Nottinghamshire 121** (20 overs) (M. J. Wood 41, S. J. Mullaney 53; W. P. U. J. C. Vaas 3-16). *MoM:* D. J. Pattinson. *Attendance: 5,546. With scores level, Nottinghamshire's last two batsmen were both run out as Andrew Hall produced yorkers for the final two balls to secure a remarkable tie. Chaminda Vaas, moving to a Twenty20 career-best, took three wickets in his first two overs in a slump to 23-4. But Steven Mullaney, eighth out, ensured that five were needed from as many balls when Hall undid him. Hall then allowed a boundary, but nothing more. Earlier, Pattinson's maiden Twenty20 four-for held Northamptonshire to an apparently inadequate score.*

At Nottingham, June 25. **Nottinghamshire won by four wickets. Durham 155-9** (20 overs) (P. Mustard 35); ‡**Nottinghamshire 159-6** (19.3 overs) (M. J. Wood 36, D. J. Hussey 47*). *MoM*: D. J. Hussey. *Attendance*: 7,244. *Cool finishing from David Hussey and Graeme White decided the game. Patel had conceded just 15 from his four overs in Durham's 155-9, but Nottinghamshire declined to 96-6, needing 56 from the last five overs, 36 from three. White launched Liam Plunkett for a straight six as the 18th over cost 16, and Hussey hit Steve Harmison for another six, leading the way home.*

At Nottingham, June 27. **Nottinghamshire won by 32 runs.** ‡**Nottinghamshire 149-6** (20 overs) (S. R. Patel 38, D. J. Hussey 56; N. M. Carter 3-28); **Warwickshire 117** (19.5 overs) (G. G. White 3-22). *MoM*: S. R. Patel. *Attendance*: 5,632. *Patel and Hussey cannily steered Nottinghamshire to a par total on a grudging pitch in use for a third time. Warwickshire showed no such wit and were all out for 117.*

At Nottingham, July 15. **Leicestershire won by 23 runs** (D/L method). **Leicestershire 145-5** (20 overs) (W. I. Jefferson 33, A. B. McDonald 58*); ‡**Nottinghamshire 107-9** (16.4 overs) (A. B. McDonald 5-13). *MoM*: A. B. McDonald. *Attendance*: 5,936. *Nottinghamshire's unbeaten run at home was ended by a thoroughbred solo effort from Andrew McDonald, who top-scored on a slow pitch with a well-judged 58*, before exploiting conditions on his way to a maiden five-wicket haul. Nottinghamshire were 64-3 in the ninth over before McDonald's medium-pace instigated a collapse. Rain, which had already revised their target to 141 from 19 overs, returned to end the game.*

At Nottingham, July 17. **Nottinghamshire won by seven wickets.** ‡**Yorkshire 112-7** (20 overs) (L. J. Hodgson 39*); **Nottinghamshire 116-3** (15.4 overs) (S. R. Patel 40, D. J. Hussey 37*). *MoM*: S. R. Patel. *Attendance*: 7,012. *Out of the running for the quarter-finals, Yorkshire fielded a youthful side that failed to adapt to a pitch being used for a third time in ten days. Only Lee Hodgson's tenacity on his Twenty20 debut averted their lowest-ever total, but defeat was never in doubt.*

Nottinghamshire away matches

June 10: beat Worcestershire by six wickets.
June 16: lost to Warwickshire by five wickets.
June 17: beat Derbyshire by six wickets.
June 20: beat Durham by 11 runs.
June 24: lost to Yorkshire by seven wickets.
July 4: beat Leicestershire by seven wickets.
July 11: tied with Northamptonshire.
July 14: lost to Lancashire by nine wickets (D/L).

WARWICKSHIRE

At Birmingham, June 3. **Warwickshire won by eight wickets.** ‡**Northamptonshire 147-5** (20 overs) (M. B. Loye 54; Imran Tahir 3-14); **Warwickshire 151-2** (14.1 overs) (D. L. Maddy 88, J. O. Troughton 41*). *MoM*: D. L. Maddy. *Attendance*: 3,716. *Darren Maddy and Mal Loye, veterans who between them played just one Twenty20 game in 2009 because of injury, dominated proceedings. It was Maddy who prevailed. In his first game in the competition since the 2008 quarter-final, he cracked 80 of his 88 runs in boundaries to hasten a walkover and leave Loye upstaged, despite a ninth Twenty20 fifty.*

At Birmingham, June 11. **Durham won by 15 runs. Durham 215-6** (20 overs) (I. D. Blackwell 79, L. R. P. L. Taylor 64); ‡**Warwickshire 200-7** (20 overs) (I. R. Bell 85, J. O. Troughton 33; S. J. Harmison 4-30). *MoM*: I. D. Blackwell. *Attendance*: 2,718. *Warwickshire were beset by Ross Taylor and Ian Blackwell, who pummelled 113 in 58 balls as Durham charged past 200 for the first time. Until bettered by Taylor three days later, Blackwell's 79 was their individual best. Now, though, Taylor clobbered 64, including 26 in five balls from Imran Tahir. Ian Bell's revenge was 85 from 47 balls, taking the reply to 166-2 until he fell to Steve Harmison, whose late four-wicket burst cut Warwickshire short.*

At Birmingham, June 13. **No result. Warwickshire 196-9** (20 overs) (I. J. L. Trott 42, N. M. Carter 39, J. O. Troughton 66; N. L. McCullum 3-31); ‡**Lancashire 3-0** (1 over). *Attendance*: 4,420. *County debut: N. L. McCullum. The pitch used against Durham was still full of runs, but Neil Carter's early aggression and Jim Troughton's 66, a Twenty20 best, were annulled by rain.*

At Birmingham, June 16. **Warwickshire won by five wickets.** ‡**Nottinghamshire 176-6** (20 overs) (D. J. Hussey 81*); **Warwickshire 178-5** (18.5 overs) (I. J. L. Trott 46, N. M. Carter 35, R. Clarke 34*). *MoM*: D. J. Hussey. *Attendance*: 3,680. *Nottinghamshire suffered their first defeat in the competition, a ragged display in the field hinting at fatigue caused by five matches in seven days. David Hussey's 81* from 42 balls, his English Twenty20 best, revived them from 40-4. But*

Warwickshire paced their reply after a rampaging start from Carter and Jonathan Trott, who put on 74 from 40 balls.

At Birmingham, June 23. **Leicestershire won by 32 runs.** ‡Leicestershire 172-6 (20 overs) (B. J. Hodge 54, J. du Toit 40, W. I. Jefferson 50; K. H. D. Barker 3-29); **Warwickshire 140** (16.5 overs) (C. W. Henderson 3-33). *MoM:* M. A. G. Boyce. *Attendance:* 4,015. Matt Boyce's remarkable contribution as twelfth man, running out Carter, Troughton and Tim Ambrose, secured him the match award. Boyce was pressed into service after Will Jefferson, who made 50 from 31 balls, jabbed a ball on to his ankle. Brad Hodge offered a less painful 54.

At Birmingham, June 25. **Warwickshire won by six wickets.** Derbyshire 148-7 (20 overs) (G. M. Smith 30, J. L. Sadler 38*); ‡**Warwickshire 152-4** (20 overs) (I. J. L. Trott 44, J. O. Troughton 58). *MoM:* J. O. Troughton. *Attendance:* 2,789. Warwickshire managed an unlikely last-gasp victory despite requiring eight off two balls. Charl Langeveldt bowled five wides from what should have been the penultimate ball and Maddy then scrambled two to level the scores before straight-driving the last for four. Trott, cautiously, and Troughton, more fluently, had earlier guided the chase.

At Birmingham, July 14. **Warwickshire won by 14 runs.** Warwickshire 145-8 (20 overs) (R. Clarke 39; D. J. Wainwright 3-32, S. A. Patterson 3-25); ‡Yorkshire 131 (19.5 overs) (A. Lyth 31; K. H. D. Barker 4-19). *MoM:* K. H. D. Barker. *Attendance:* 3,888. With 15 needed from four balls, Keith Barker curtailed debate with a hat-trick. Both sides struggled on a worn pitch: Warwickshire were 93-7 in the 16th over; Yorkshire 99-7 at the same stage. But Rikki Clarke and Chris Woakes – who faced 12 balls, hit two for six and reached 27* – oversaw 52 more for Warwickshire from 25 balls, while Yorkshire managed only 32 before their peremptory end.

At Birmingham, July 16. **Warwickshire won by nine runs.** Reduced to 15 overs a side. Warwickshire 112-4 (15 overs) (I. J. L. Trott 53*); ‡Worcestershire 103-7 (15 overs) (A. N. Kervezee 35). *MoM:* S. A. Piolet. *Attendance:* 5,970. Trott, the one opening batsman in the match to survive his first ball, helped Warwickshire secure a home quarter-final with a polished 53*. Barker followed his hat-trick two days earlier with an immediate success to make it four in four, but Worcestershire reached 72-3. Needing 41 from 33 balls, they lost three men in successive overs, two to Steffan Piolet, and quietly petered out.

Warwickshire away matches

June 9: beat Derbyshire by three wickets.
June 18: beat Worcestershire by nine wickets.
June 20: lost to Lancashire by five wickets.
June 27: lost to Nottinghamshire by 32 runs.

July 2: beat Durham by five wickets.
July 4: beat Yorkshire by 34 runs.
July 9: beat Northamptonshire by six wickets.
July 18: beat Leicestershire by eight runs.

WORCESTERSHIRE

At Worcester, June 4. **Worcestershire won by 21 runs.** ‡Worcestershire 208-7 (20 overs) (V. S. Solanki 30, P. A. Jaques 30, S. P. D. Smith 34, J. G. Cameron 51*; A. U. Rashid 3-32); **Yorkshire 187-7** (20 overs) (A. McGrath 39, A. U. Rashid 34). *MoM:* J. G. Cameron. *Attendance:* 3,691. *County debut:* S. P. D. Smith. The tone was set when off-spinner Azeem Rafiq went for 18 in the first over. James Cameron, a Zimbabwean left-hander on Twenty20 debut, made an unbeaten 51 as Worcestershire topped 200. In his first appearance in England, two days after his 21st birthday, the Australian Steve Smith hit 34 and added two wickets as Yorkshire failed to spark.

At Worcester, June 10. **Nottinghamshire won by six wickets.** Worcestershire 113-9 (20 overs) (S. J. Mullaney 3-12); ‡**Nottinghamshire 114-4** (14 overs) (A. D. Hales 66*). *MoM:* A. D. Hales and S. J. Mullaney. *Attendance:* 1,888. *County debut:* D. P. Nannes (Nottinghamshire). Only Gareth Andrew's three sixes off Paul Franks in their last over carried Worcestershire past 100 after Steven Mullaney's tight seam claimed 3-12. Alex Hales, opening, raced to 66 off 49 balls to seize victory in appalling light with six overs to spare.

At Worcester, June 18. **Warwickshire won by nine wickets.** ‡Worcestershire 118-9 (20 overs) (J. K. Manuel 31); **Warwickshire 121-1** (16.2 overs) (I. J. L. Trott 72*, D. L. Maddy 44*). *MoM:* I. J. L. Trott. *Attendance:* 2,866. *County debut:* S. T. Jayasuriya (Worcestershire). A second-wicket stand of exactly 100* in 14 overs from Jonathan Trott and Darren Maddy waltzed Warwickshire home at their leisure. Worcestershire's one consolation, in another crushing loss, was that teenager Jack Manuel, the England Under-19 left-hander, top-scored with 31.

At Worcester, June 25. **Worcestershire won by nine wickets. ‡Northamptonshire 140-5** (20 overs) (N. J. O'Brien 34, A. G. Wakely 31, E. Chigumbura 39*; M. M. Ali 3-25); **Worcestershire 142-1** (14.2 overs) (P. A. Jaques 47*, S. T. Jayasuriya 87). *MoM:* S. T. Jayasuriya. *Attendance:* 2,437. *Worcestershire ended a run of six successive Twenty20 defeats as Sanath Jayasuriya, just five days short of his 41st birthday, hit 87 off 45 balls with five sixes. Jayasuriya's opening stand of 138 with Phil Jaques came at 9.74 per over. In contrast, Northamptonshire were stunted from the outset as Jack Shantry conceded only six in his three-over new-ball spell.*

At Worcester, June 27. **Worcestershire won by eight wickets. Derbyshire 147-7** (20 overs) (W. J. Durston 77; J. D. Shantry 3-23, J. G. Cameron 3-22); **‡Worcestershire 148-2** (15.1 overs) (P. A. Jaques 70*, M. M. Ali 45). *MoM:* P. A. Jaques. *Attendance:* 1,162. *Jaques saw Worcestershire comfortably home with 70* from 42 balls, but England's World Cup clash with Germany kept attendance down. Shantry impressed those who were there, taking three wickets in four balls and ensuring that Wes Durston's 77 supplied more than half Derbyshire's total.*

At Worcester, July 9. **Durham won by three runs. Durham 144-6** (20 overs) (M. D. Stoneman 46, B. A. Stokes 44); **‡Worcestershire 141-8** (20 overs) (S. T. Jayasuriya 45; G. R. Breese 3-14). *MoM:* G. R. Breese. *Attendance:* 2,442. *A blazing opening stand of 51, in which Jaques made seven, apparently put Worcestershire on course. But four men went in 29 balls, three to Gareth Breese including Jayasuriya, who passed 2,000 Twenty20 runs in his 45. Ultimately, 11 were needed from four balls but two wickets fell in immediate succession. Mark Stoneman, on Twenty20 debut, earlier top-scored with 46.*

At Worcester, July 11. **Worcestershire won by six wickets. Leicestershire 171-4** (20 overs) (B. J. Hodge 70, P. A. Nixon 44*); **‡Worcestershire 172-4** (19 overs) (P. A. Jaques 78*, V. S. Solanki 51). *MoM:* P. A. Jaques. *Attendance:* 1,535. *Brad Hodge reached 3,000 Twenty20 runs, but was upstaged by fellow-Australian Phil Jaques. Paul Nixon's unbeaten 44 from 16 balls took Leicestershire to 171-4 after Hodge was run out for 70. Jaques, however, perfectly weighted his reply, batting through for 78 and adding 94 for the third-wicket in 11 overs with Solanki before ending the game with a six.*

At Worcester, July 18. **Lancashire won by seven runs. Lancashire 198-6** (20 overs) (T. C. Smith 40, S. J. Croft 88); **‡Worcestershire 191-7** (20 overs) (M. M. Ali 72, D. K. H. Mitchell 39). *MoM:* S. J. Croft. *Attendance:* 2,238. *Lancashire had secured a quarter-final, but Worcestershire, with more defeats in the eight seasons of Twenty20 than any other county except Glamorgan, maintained standards to finish last. After Steven Croft's career-best 88 for the visitors, Worcestershire needed 17 from 11 balls with six wickets intact. But Moeen Ali's 72 from 39 balls, another Twenty20-best, was wasted when Sajid Mahmood struck twice in the 19th over.*

Worcestershire away matches

June 6: abandoned v Durham.
June 11: lost to Northamptonshire by 21 runs.
June 13: lost to Nottinghamshire by six wickets.
June 21: lost to Derbyshire by six wickets.

June 22: lost to Yorkshire by 104 runs.
July 5: lost to Lancashire by 46 runs.
July 7: beat Leicestershire by three wickets.
July 16: lost to Warwickshire by nine runs.

YORKSHIRE

At Leeds, June 3. **Derbyshire won by 65 runs. Derbyshire 222-5** (20 overs) (L. E. Bosman 94, C. F. Hughes 65, J. L. Sadler 31*; C. J. McKay 4-33); **‡Yorkshire 157** (17.5 overs) (J. A. Rudolph 34, H. H. Gibbs 36; G. M. Smith 3-19). *MoM:* L. E. Bosman. *Attendance:* 4,921. *County debuts:* H. H. Gibbs, C. J. McKay. *Loots Bosman's township side in Kimberley is named "Yorkshire" after David Bairstow's days there as coach. He showed little deference to the late keeper's old county, however, thrashing 94 from 50 balls. Bosman added 141 for the second wicket with Chesney Hughes, who eventually fell for 65 to Clint McKay during what would have been a hat-trick had not a wide interrupted the three wickets. But the total was already beyond Yorkshire's originals.*

At Leeds, June 10. **Yorkshire won by nine wickets. Durham 156-7** (20 overs) (L. R. P. L. Taylor 31, B. A. Stokes 32, J. A. Morkel 33; A. U. Rashid 3-23); **‡Yorkshire 160-1** (16 overs) (A. W. Gale 60*, H. H. Gibbs 76*). *MoM:* H. H. Gibbs. *Attendance:* 2,934. *Yorkshire tore home in one withering hour of batting after an all-wicket county-record stand of 137*. Andrew Gale and Herschelle Gibbs made light work of a seemingly difficult task on a seaming pitch, Gibbs taking command with 76* from 39 balls. And Gale was no shrinking violet, either.*

At Leeds, June 13. **Northamptonshire won by 14 runs** (D/L method). ‡**Northamptonshire 151-7** (20 overs) (L. Vincent 38, A. J. Hall 31*; A. U. Rashid 3-23); **Yorkshire 51-4** (7.5 overs) (J. A. Brooks 3-24). MoM: J. A. Brooks. Attendance: 3,726. *Adil Rashid's third consecutive three-for was squandered when Yorkshire lost batsmen in a vain attempt to achieve par before rain. Jack Brooks's three scalps were his first in Twenty20 cricket.*

At Leeds, June 17. **Yorkshire won by 17 runs.** ‡**Yorkshire 155-6** (20 overs) (A. W. Gale 34, A. McGrath 73*); **Lancashire 138** (19.1 overs) (P. J. Horton 30; S. A. Patterson 4-30). MoM: A. McGrath. Attendance: 9,259. *Yorkshire were cheered by Anthony McGrath's career-best 73* and by a late burst from Steven Patterson that sealed a hard-fought win. But others opened the door. Lancashire were 46-1 from six overs when Gibbs ran out Paul Horton, the first of five to fall for 52 as the reply was stifled by spin. With 34 needed from 17 balls, Patterson then struck three times in the 18th over, seizing a maiden four-for.*

At Leeds, June 22. **Yorkshire won by 104 runs.** ‡**Yorkshire 213-7** (20 overs) (A. Lyth 59, H. H. Gibbs 40, J. M. Bairstow 49*); **Worcestershire 109** (16.5 overs) (D. K. H. Mitchell 34; R. M. Pyrah 3-12, Azeem Rafiq 3-23). MoM: A. Lyth. Attendance: 2,745. *Having made five ducks in his previous eight Twenty20 innings, Adam Lyth returned for the injured Jacques Rudolph and promptly lashed the then joint third-fastest fifty (18 balls) in competition history, his first 48 coming in boundaries (nine fours and two sixes). Rich Pyrah and Azeem Rafiq each took three wickets, and Yorkshire completed their biggest win by runs in Twenty20 cricket.*

At Leeds, June 24. **Yorkshire won by seven wickets.** ‡**Nottinghamshire 158-7** (20 overs) (A. D. Hales 62, S. R. Patel 41); **Yorkshire 162-3** (18.2 overs) (A. Lyth 43, A. McGrath 38*, G. L. Brophy 31*). MoM: A. McGrath. Attendance: 3,438. *Once Alex Hales and Samit Patel were parted after a 70-run third-wicket stand, Yorkshire applied the brakes with the ball before cantering to a third straight win.*

At Leeds, June 27. **Leicestershire won by six runs.** ‡**Leicestershire 175-4** (20 overs) (J. G. E. Benning 41, J. W. A. Taylor 62*; A. U. Rashid 4-20); **Yorkshire 169-8** (20 overs) (A. W. Gale 52, J. M. Bairstow 40; N. L. Buck 3-20). MoM: J. W. A. Taylor. Attendance: 3,312. *Seeking a six to tie the match off the final ball, Pyrah was caught on the boundary off Matthew Hoggard, a former mentor. James Taylor's startling 62* from 28 balls dealt largely in sixes and singles after Rashid, with career-best figures, had claimed all four Leicestershire wickets. This proved less telling than the new-ball burst of 19-year-old Nathan Buck. Inflicting damage that neither Gale nor Jonny Bairstow could fully repair, he dismissed three men in ten balls.*

At Leeds, July 4. **Warwickshire won by 34 runs.** ‡**Warwickshire 155-8** (20 overs) (D. L. Maddy 33, K. H. D. Barker 35; R. M. Pyrah 3-22); **Yorkshire 121-9** (20 overs) (A. Lyth 34; A. G. Botha 3-16). MoM: A. G. Botha. Attendance: 4,704. *Yorkshire "celebrated" using the £21m new Carnegie pavilion for the first time by staging a match which had no redeeming features and will quickly be forgotten.*

Yorkshire away matches

June 4: lost to Worcestershire by 21 runs.
June 18: lost to Durham by six wickets.
June 20: beat Leicestershire by nine wickets.
July 2: tied with Northamptonshire.

July 9: lost to Lancashire by five wickets.
July 14: lost to Warwickshire by 14 runs.
July 17: lost to Nottinghamshire by seven wickets.
July 18: beat Derbyshire by six wickets.

SOUTH DIVISION

ESSEX

At Chelmsford, June 2 (floodlit). **Kent won by six wickets. Essex 167-9** (20 overs) (R. N. ten Doeschate 98); ‡**Kent 170-4** (18.4 overs) (G. O. Jones 54, D. I. Stevens 49*). MoM: R. N. ten Doeschate. Attendance: 4,993. *County debut: H. M. C. M. Bandara (Kent). Despite Ryan ten Doeschate's 98 from 47 balls, it was Darren Stevens who grasped victory. Opening the bowling, he claimed both Essex openers by the end of his first over before ten Doeschate led the revival. Stevens, though, was not to be denied: his 49* took Kent across the line with eight balls to spare.*

At Chelmsford, June 11 (floodlit). **Glamorgan won by seven wickets.** ‡**Essex 191-6** (20 overs) (R. N. ten Doeschate 37, J. S. Foster 54*; R. D. B. Croft 3-22); **Glamorgan 192-3** (17.4 overs)

(M. J. Cosgrove 89, T. L. Maynard 66*). *MoM:* M. J. Cosgrove. *Attendance:* 4,927. *Glamorgan, hitting 73% of their runs off the bat in boundaries, made nonsense of a challenging target, winning with 14 balls left after Mark Cosgrove and Tom Maynard added 97 in 50 balls for the third wicket. Mark Pettini, who fell to the game's first ball, later stood down from Twenty20 cricket, passing the captaincy to James Foster, the wicketkeeper.*

At Chelmsford, June 25 (floodlit). **Essex won by six wickets.** Surrey 187-6 (20 overs) (S. M. Davies 89, M. R. Ramprakash 35; Danish Kaneria 3-32); ‡**Essex 188-4** (19.5 overs) (S. B. Styris 106*, T. J. Phillips 30). *MoM:* S. B. Styris. *Attendance:* 6,060. *An amazing assault by Scott Styris stole the match for Essex after Steve Davies's career-best 89 had apparently made Surrey safe. Needing 65 from four overs, Styris surged into overdrive and began the final over, from Andrew Symonds, requiring 22 more. He hit a maiden Twenty20 century from 49 balls, struck an eighth six off the next, and Essex triumphed with a ball to spare.*

At Chelmsford, June 29 (floodlit). **Sussex won by 17 runs.** ‡Sussex 174-5 (20 overs) (M. J. Prior 50); **Essex 157-9** (20 overs) (M. L. Pettini 59, J. C. Mickleburgh 32). *MoM:* M. J. Prior. *Attendance:* 4,280. *A top-of-the-table clash hung in the balance until a spectacular Essex decline. At 90-0, they needed 85 from 56 balls, but Mark Pettini fell for 59, prompting a crash to 139-9. Earlier, Matt Prior's 50 from 28 balls gave Sussex a racing start.*

At Chelmsford, July 4. **Essex won by three wickets.** ‡Hampshire 161-6 (20 overs) (J. H. K. Adams 32, N. Pothas 59); **Essex 163-7** (19.5 overs) (G. W. Flower 54). *MoM:* G. W. Flower. *Attendance:* 3,955. *Playing three spinners, Essex held Hampshire to 90-5 by the 14th over, but Nic Pothas's 59 carried them to 161-6. Grant Flower, with 54, had victory in sight, but was the first of four to fall in a 16-ball slump to 154-7. With eight needed from five balls, however, Jaik Mickleburgh took Essex home.*

At Chelmsford, July 11. **Somerset won by six wickets.** ‡Essex 173-6 (20 overs) (R. S. Bopara 105*); **Somerset 177-4** (19.1 overs) (M. E. Trescothick 78, J. C. Hildreth 43). *MoM:* M. E. Trescothick. *Attendance:* 3,708. *Ravi Bopara became the third Essex player to bat through all 20 overs of a Twenty20 innings, saving special punishment for Kieron Pollard. But his maiden Twenty20 hundred was not enough. Marcus Trescothick passed 75 for the third successive innings as Somerset won with ease.*

At Chelmsford, July 15 (floodlit). **Essex won by seven wickets.** Gloucestershire 162-5 (20 overs) (A. P. R. Gidman 30, C. D. J. Dent 31); ‡**Essex 167-3** (18.4 overs) (A. N. Cook 73, R. S. Bopara 59). *MoM:* A. N. Cook. *Attendance:* 3,967. *A first-wicket stand of 119 in 14 overs made the target a formality for Essex. Alastair Cook reached 73 from 53 balls after Bopara went for 59.*

At Chelmsford, July 18. **Middlesex won by 11 runs.** Middlesex 173-7 (20 overs) (D. A. Warner 37, G. K. Berg 41, B. J. M. Scott 43*); ‡**Essex 162-6** (20 overs) (S. B. Styris 42, J. S. Foster 35*). *MoM:* G. K. Berg. *Attendance:* 4,531. *County debut:* A. Carter (Essex). *Five successive boundaries by David Warner off Maurice Chambers sparked a frank exchange of views before umpire Martin Bodenham, a former football referee, and Essex captain James Foster stepped between them. Gareth Berg and Ben Scott added 63 in 43 balls for the fifth wicket to swell a target Essex never neared, though Styris and Foster, aiming for 70 off five overs, managed 58.*

Essex away matches

June 10: beat Surrey by nine runs.	June 23: beat Gloucestershire by 66 runs.
June 13: lost to Middlesex by five runs.	June 27: beat Hampshire by nine wickets.
June 16: beat Somerset by ten runs.	July 9: beat Kent by four wickets.
June 19: beat Glamorgan by nine wickets.	July 16: beat Sussex by five wickets.

GLAMORGAN

At Cardiff, June 4 (floodlit). **Glamorgan won by six wickets.** ‡Gloucestershire 148-6 (20 overs) (J. E. C. Franklin 42; J. Allenby 3-23); **Glamorgan 151-4** (19.1 overs) (J. Allenby 54, G. P. Rees 32*). *MoM:* J. Allenby. *Attendance:* 7,242. *County debut:* S. W. Tait (Glamorgan). *A record crowd saw Jim Allenby produce a match-winning performance with three wickets and 54 runs as Glamorgan made controlled progress to their target. Shaun Tait, the Australia fast bowler, conceded only 19 runs on his debut but Ian Butler, the New Zealander signed as Gloucestershire's specialist, fell for a duck and went for 47 in the reply.*

At Cardiff, June 8 (floodlit). **Glamorgan won by seven wickets.** ‡Hampshire 114-9 (20 overs) (M. A. Carberry 34); Glamorgan 115-3 (19.2 overs) (J. Allenby 52*). *MoM*: J. Allenby. *Attendance*: 2,838. *County debut*: D. T. Christian (Hampshire). *Glamorgan's decision to open the bowling with two off-spinners on a used pitch was vindicated as Hampshire failed to recover from a poor start. Tait, though wicketless, blunted their progress and bowled one ball at 92mph. In the chase, Allenby earned a second match award in five nights for his 52*.*

At Cardiff, June 13. **Sussex won by three wickets.** ‡Glamorgan 143-6 (20 overs) (T. L. Maynard 35, G. P. Rees 35); Sussex 144-7 (18.5 overs) (L. J. Wright 39). *MoM*: L. J. Wright. *Attendance*: 3,666. *Reigning champions Sussex completed their fifth win of the season and a record-equalling 13th consecutive victory in domestic Twenty20 cricket. Pursuing 144, they faltered at 46-4 in the eighth over, but Luke Wright hit 39 from 21 balls with three sixes, and Chris Nash took over when Wright fell at 99-5.*

At Cardiff, June 19 (floodlit). **Essex won by nine wickets.** ‡Glamorgan 94-9 (20 overs) (R. S. Bopara 3-13); Essex 95-1 (13.1 overs) (R. S. Bopara 42, A. N. Cook 42*). *MoM*: R. S. Bopara. *Attendance*: 4,710. *Essex strolled home with almost seven overs in hand as Glamorgan lost a third successive game – after winning their first three. They crashed from 47-0 to 65-8 in 43 bemused balls, before passing the lowest total in the competition of 67, made by Sussex in 2004. Danish Kaneria produced the most economical figures (4–1–11–2) of any bowler against Glamorgan, and Ravi Bopara took 3-13. He then dominated an opening stand of 73 which settled the issue.*

At Cardiff, June 26. **Glamorgan won by seven wickets.** ‡Middlesex 166-2 (20 overs) (S. A. Newman 48, N. J. Dexter 40*, D. J. Malan 40*); Glamorgan 167-3 (18.5 overs) (M. J. Cosgrove 33, J. Allenby 45, T. L. Maynard 63*). *MoM*: T. L. Maynard. *Attendance*: 4,012. *Both Neil Dexter, who became Middlesex's third captain of the tournament, and Dawid Malan made exactly the same score, 40* from 26 balls, but Tom Maynard's 63* from 38 was more explosive still, and Glamorgan ended a run of four defeats. Maynard came in after an opening stand of 56 in 35 balls and added 54 with Allenby.*

At Cardiff, July 9 (floodlit). **Glamorgan won by ten runs.** Glamorgan 164-8 (20 overs) (M. J. Cosgrove 76, J. Allenby 34, J. W. M. Dalrymple 33); ‡Surrey 154-8 (20 overs) (S. J. Walters 53*; J. W. M. Dalrymple 3-25). *MoM*: M. J. Cosgrove. *Attendance*: 4,514. *Mark Cosgrove went on to 76 after an opening stand of 75 in 52 balls that underlay a challenging total. Glamorgan's spinners, led by Robert Croft, who took a wicket with the first legitimate ball, never allowed Surrey to take control, and Stewart Walters's maiden Twenty20 fifty was in vain.*

At Cardiff, July 14 (floodlit). **Somerset won by seven wickets** (D/L method). ‡Glamorgan 116-7 (20 overs) (T. L. Maynard 39; M. L. Turner 3-25); Somerset 92-3 (11.5 overs) (M. E. Trescothick 54*). *MoM*: M. E. Trescothick. *Attendance*: 2,349. *Marcus Trescothick, striking Tait for 14 in his first over, charged to his fourth successive fifty and passed 1,500 Twenty20 runs. A shower interrupted Somerset's reply in the ninth over; on the resumption, they needed another 44 from 50 balls with eight men standing.*

At Cardiff, July 16. **Kent won by 14 runs** (D/L method). Kent 158-9 (20 overs) (J. L. Denly 30); ‡Glamorgan 95-3 (14.4 overs) (M. J. Cosgrove 54). *MoM*: M. J. Cosgrove. *Attendance*: 2,310. *Although Croft took a wicket in the first over of the innings for the sixth time in 16 games, Kent's total always looked competitive. Glamorgan were left short of the D/L par score of 109 when rain ended play after Cosgrove's 54 had taken him to 562 Twenty20 runs for the summer. Neither side progressed to the quarter-finals.*

Glamorgan away matches

June 11: beat Essex by seven wickets.
June 15: lost to Middlesex by 84 runs.
June 23: lost to Sussex by 53 runs.
June 28: lost to Somerset by six wickets.

July 1: lost to Hampshire by 54 runs.
July 2: lost to Gloucestershire by eight wickets.
July 4: beat Surrey by five wickets.
July 11: lost to Kent by six wickets.

GLOUCESTERSHIRE

At Gloucester, June 11. **Sussex won by seven wickets.** Gloucestershire 166-8 (20 overs) (C. G. Taylor 35); ‡Sussex 168-3 (15.5 overs) (M. J. Prior 90*). *MoM*: M. J. Prior. *Attendance*: 2,657. *Matt Prior, opening, led Sussex to a fourth successive win with a commanding 90* off 49 balls as*

Gloucestershire were overhauled with ease. Their 166-8 was never going to be enough once Prior, smarting at being left out of England's one-day squad, raced from the blocks.

At Gloucester, June 13. **Kent won by 36 runs.** Kent 217 (19.5 overs) (J. L. Denly 48, R. W. T. Key 44, A. J. Blake 33); ‡**Gloucestershire 181** (19.5 overs) (W. T. S. Porterfield 43, C. G. Taylor 67; M. T. Coles 3-48, S. J. Cook 3-22). *MoM:* S. J. Cook. *Attendance:* 2,550. *Short outground boundaries delighted Rob Key and Joe Denly, who put on 87 from 50 balls to set up Kent's formidable total. Gloucestershire, in contrast, slid to 94-6, and Chris Taylor's 67 off 36 balls was in vain.*

At Bristol, June 19. **Hampshire won by seven wickets.** ‡**Gloucestershire 68** (17.5 overs) (S. M. Ervine 4-12); **Hampshire 69-3** (7.3 overs). *MoM:* S. M. Ervine. *Attendance:* 1,998. *Paltry Championship scores had been the norm in Bristol, and nothing changed for Twenty20: Gloucestershire were shot out for 68. The No. 11 arrived to squeeze a final single that prevented their equalling the worst total in county Twenty20. As Sean Ervine took 4-12, Alex Gidman regretted his decision to bat: "I'm just lost for words and a bit confused," he offered later.*

At Bristol, June 23. **Essex won by 66 runs.** ‡**Essex 184-4** (20 overs) (A. N. Cook 38, M. J. Walker 66, S. B. Styris 41); **Gloucestershire 118** (17.3 overs) (C. D. J. Dent 31, C. G. Taylor 32). *MoM:* M. J. Walker. *Attendance:* 1,665. *Essex found no problem defending an aggressive 184-4 after the home bowlers had struggled for accuracy. Matthew Walker made a Twenty20-best 66, sharing 82 for the third wicket in 44 balls with Scott Styris, who bounded to 41. Gloucestershire then failed to reach the 19th over for the second time in five days.*

At Bristol, June 27. **Gloucestershire won by four runs.** Gloucestershire 153-6 (20 overs) (H. J. H. Marshall 52*, A. P. R. Gidman 42); ‡**Middlesex 149-7** (20 overs) (D. J. Malan 44). *MoM:* H. J. H. Marshall. *Attendance:* 1,106. *The occasional leg-spin of Aaron Redmond, their latest New Zealand recruit, aided Richard Dawson as Gloucestershire turned to spin for their first home win. The pair took 3-46 combined, stalling Middlesex's advance. With 12 needed, Dawid Malan fell for 44 to the first ball of the last over, and they finished just short. Hamish Marshall had earlier added 94 for the fourth wicket in 64 balls with Gidman, the core of a winning score.*

At Bristol, July 2. **Gloucestershire won by eight wickets.** ‡**Glamorgan 153-7** (20 overs) (M. A. Wallace 34, T. L. Maynard 36, J. W. M. Dalrymple 38; S. P. Kirby 3-17); **Gloucestershire 154-2** (15.3 overs) (A. J. Redmond 33, W. T. S. Porterfield 65). *MoM:* W. T. S. Porterfield. *Attendance:* 2,398. *Will Porterfield dominated an alliance of Ulster and Otago that effectively won the game by the reply's eighth over. Captaining the side, he belted 65 from 27 balls in a 94-run stand, fellow-opener Redmond going on to 33. Steve Kirby's Twenty20-best of 3-17 had earlier limited Glamorgan to 153-7.*

At Bristol, July 16. **Somerset won by six wickets.** Gloucestershire 152-9 (20 overs) (A. P. R. Gidman 31, H. J. H. Marshall 45, C. D. J. Dent 30; K. A. Pollard 3-36); ‡**Somerset 156-4** (16.5 overs) (P. D. Trego 46, Z. de Bruyn 37, K. A. Pollard 30*). *MoM:* P. D. Trego. *Attendance:* 5,769. *Peter Trego followed figures of 2-29 by hitting 44 in fours or sixes out of 46 from 17 balls. Although Somerset were 67-3 when he fell, they glided past Gloucestershire and into the quarter-finals, to be hailed by Gidman, the opposing skipper, as "world-class at Twenty20".*

At Bristol, July 18. **Surrey won by six wickets.** Gloucestershire 147-9 (20 overs) (W. T. S. Porterfield 37, J. E. C. Franklin 33; C. T. Tremlett 3-18); ‡**Surrey 150-4** (11.5 overs) (R. J. Hamilton-Brown 48, S. M. Davies 73). *MoM:* S. M. Davies. *Attendance:* 1,728. *Demoralised Gloucestershire finished bottom of the group after their 11th defeat. Steve Davies reached 50 in 19 balls on his way to 73, sharing an opening stand of 112 that sealed the match for Surrey. Chris Tremlett had earlier taken two wickets in his first 13 balls, but Gloucestershire reached 89-2, only to plummet to 115-7.*

Gloucestershire away matches

June 4: lost to Glamorgan by six wickets.
June 8: beat Surrey by ten wickets.
June 16: beat Sussex by eight runs.
June 18: lost to Somerset by six wickets.

June 25: lost to Hampshire by 28 runs.
July 4: lost to Kent by 12 runs.
July 11: beat Middlesex by six wickets.
July 15: lost to Essex by seven wickets.

HAMPSHIRE

At Southampton, June 3 (floodlit). **Hampshire won by five wickets.** ‡**Kent 114-9** (20 overs) (D. I. Stevens 36); **Hampshire 117-5** (19.4 overs) (S. M. Ervine 31). *MoM:* C. P. Wood. *Attendance:* 4,288. *County debut: Abdul Razzaq (Hampshire). Only Darren Stevens scored more than 15 as Kent blamed heavy traffic on the way to the Rose Bowl for lethargic batting. Chris Wood, a 19-year-old left-arm seamer from Basingstoke, took two wickets on his competition debut and also ran out Stevens. Hampshire won with two balls to spare, though the result was never at issue.*

At Southampton, June 11 (floodlit). **Somerset won by seven wickets.** **Somerset 104-7** (20 overs) (Z. de Bruyn 32*); ‡**Hampshire 97** (19.2 overs) (J. H. K. Adams 61; K. A. Pollard 3-15). *MoM:* A. C. Thomas. *Attendance:* 3,733. *Hampshire were docked two points from the 2011 competition for a pitch of "excessive unevenness". Chasing 105 and needing 12 off four overs, they lost their last six wickets for four runs and showed significant unevenness of their own: Jimmy Adams made 61, but nobody else passed eight. Alfonso Thomas had figures of 4–2–5–2.*

At Southampton, June 13. **Hampshire won by ten runs.** ‡**Hampshire 201-2** (20 overs) (J. H. K. Adams 101*, S. M. Ervine 54*); **Surrey 191-9** (20 overs) (M. R. Ramprakash 61; C. P. Wood 3-30). *MoM:* J. H. K. Adams. *Attendance:* 4,230. *Kevin Pietersen, temporarily released by the ECB, made his first Hampshire appearance for two years – and later announced he was leaving. He hit 15 from ten balls, but was overshadowed by Adams, who reached his first Twenty20 century from 64 balls, sharing in a stand of 144 in 12 overs with Sean Ervine.*

At Southampton, June 25 (floodlit). **Hampshire won by 28 runs.** ‡**Hampshire 205-5** (20 overs) (J. M. Vince 77, N. D. McKenzie 55); **Gloucestershire 177** (19.5 overs) (J. E. C. Franklin 46, C. D. J. Dent 63; C. P. Wood 3-27, D. R. Briggs 3-31). *MoM:* J. M. Vince. *Attendance:* 4,398. *County debut: A. J. Redmond (Gloucestershire). James Vince, playing in only his third Twenty20 match, dominated proceedings with 77 from 46 balls. He added 110 for the third wicket with Neil McKenzie. James Franklin and Chris Dent led a bold Gloucestershire riposte, but the last six wickets fell for 13.*

At Southampton, June 27. **Essex won by nine wickets.** ‡**Hampshire 159-8** (20 overs) (J. H. K. Adams 31, S. M. Ervine 74*); **Essex 164-1** (18 overs) (R. S. Bopara 94*, M. J. Walker 33*). *MoM:* R. S. Bopara. *Attendance:* 2,494. *Ravi Bopara's 94* off 65 balls, his Twenty20 best, helped Essex to a walkover. He upstaged Ervine's unsupported hand of 74* earlier, putting on 71 for the first wicket with Alastair Cook and an unbroken 93 with Matt Walker, before finishing the match with a six.*

At Southampton, July 1 (floodlit). **Hampshire won by 54 runs.** ‡**Hampshire 199-5** (20 overs) (J. H. K. Adams 100*, J. M. Vince 39; H. T. Waters 3-30); **Glamorgan 145-9** (20 overs) (M. J. Cosgrove 33, M. A. Wallace 42*; D. R. Briggs 3-27). *MoM:* J. H. K. Adams. *Attendance:* 3,953. *Adams became only the second batsman to score two Twenty20 centuries in the same domestic season, following Cameron White of Somerset in 2006. He reached three figures in the last over, from 61 balls. Mark Cosgrove soon hit three sixes in reply, but was the first to go in a collapse from 44-1 to 116-9.*

At Southampton, July 16 (floodlit). **Middlesex won by eight wickets.** ‡**Hampshire 99** (17.5 overs) (M. A. Carberry 34; T. M. J. Smith 3-26); **Middlesex 100-2** (14.2 overs) (D. A. Warner 43). *MoM:* T. M. J. Smith. *Attendance:* 5,300. *Tom Smith, the left-arm spinner, took three wickets, held a catch and ran out Dominic Cork as Hampshire lost their last nine batsmen for 56. David Warner and Neil Dexter made light of a meagre target with an opening stand of 57.*

At Southampton, July 18. **Hampshire won by 45 runs.** **Hampshire 195-5** (20 overs) (J. H. K. Adams 30, N. D. McKenzie 67*, M. A. Carberry 36; S. M. Ervine 32); ‡**Sussex 150** (19 overs) (C. D. Nash 32). *MoM:* N. D. McKenzie. *Attendance:* 5,211. *Hampshire pipped Middlesex and Surrey for a place in the quarter-finals on superior net run-rate. McKenzie's unbeaten fifty was supported by three late sixes from Ervine, who hammered 32 from 12 balls. Never in it, Sussex subsided to their fourth successive defeat, their sixth in seven.*

Hampshire away matches

June 8: lost to Glamorgan by seven wickets.
June 18: lost to Sussex by nine wickets.
June 19: beat Gloucestershire by seven wickets.
June 22: lost to Surrey by 11 runs.

July 2: beat Kent by 45 runs.
July 4: lost to Essex by three wickets.
July 9: lost to Somerset by six wickets.
July 10: beat Middlesex by six wickets.

KENT

At Tunbridge Wells, June 9. **Sussex won by four wickets. Kent 163-5** (20 overs) (G. O. Jones 32, D. I. Stevens 52*); ‡**Sussex 166-6** (19.4 overs) (M. J. Prior 47, M. H. Yardy 36*). *MoM:* D. I. Stevens. *Attendance:* 4,533. *County debut:* B. B. McCullum (Sussex). *In a tense finish at a packed outground, Mike Yardy pulled a slow bouncer from Azhar Mahmood to the boundary and Sussex won with two balls to spare. After playing out a maiden in a sedate start, Kent relied on Darren Stevens's 52* from 30 balls. But Matt Prior's dash and Yardy's nous took Sussex to a third straight win.*

At Canterbury, June 11. **Middlesex won by six wickets. Kent 183-6** (20 overs) (J. L. Denly 44, M. van Jaarsveld 50, D. I. Stevens 34, G. O. Jones 39; P. T. Collins 3-38); ‡**Middlesex 185-4** (19 overs) (A. C. Gilchrist 106, N. J. Dexter 45). *MoM:* A. C. Gilchrist. *Attendance:* 2,126. *County debut:* D. A. Warner (Middlesex). *Adam Gilchrist, named as emergency skipper following Shaun Udal's mid-afternoon abdication, responded with a 47-ball century that saw Middlesex home with an over in hand, and which was the eventual winner of the Walter Lawrence award for the season's fastest hundred. Though Kent set an asking rate of 9.2 per over, Gilchrist's 68-minute display, with ten fours and seven sixes, denied all hope.*

At Beckenham, June 20. **Somerset won by 84 runs. Somerset 189-4** (20 overs) (J. C. Hildreth 77*, J. C. Buttler 48*); ‡**Kent 105** (18.3 overs) (A. C. Thomas 3-15, K. A. Pollard 4-15). *MoM:* J. C. Hildreth. *Attendance:* 2,967. *A fifth-wicket stand of 80* from 37 balls between James Hildreth, with a competition-best 77*, and 19-year-old wicketkeeper Jos Buttler (48* off 22 balls) set a target beyond a feeble Kent. Kieron Pollard, Somerset's Trinidadian import, claimed a maiden Twenty20 four-for.*

At Beckenham, June 23. **Surrey won by 38 runs. ‡Surrey 201-4** (20 overs) (S. M. Davies 42, J. J. Roy 101*, A. Symonds 31); **Kent 163-8** (20 overs) (M. van Jaarsveld 82, Azhar Mahmood 34; A. Symonds 5-18). *MoM:* J. J. Roy. *Attendance:* 1,764. *Jason Roy, a 19-year-old without first-class experience playing only his third Twenty20 game, became the first Surrey batsman to score a Twenty20 hundred. Durban-born but educated at Whitgift School, he hit 101* from 57 balls and added 63 from 27 with Andrew Symonds. Symonds went on to a career-best 5-18 as Kent capitulated despite Martin van Jaarsveld's 82, another Twenty20 best.*

At Canterbury, July 2. **Hampshire won by 45 runs. ‡Hampshire 139** (19.5 overs) (S. M. Ervine 44; H. M. C. M. Bandara 3-14, M. van Jaarsveld 3-25); **Kent 94** (16.3 overs) (S. P. Jones 3-20, D. R. Briggs 3-5). *MoM:* S. P. Jones. *Attendance:* 1,982. *Remarkable figures from slow left-armer Danny Briggs helped rout Kent for 94, their last eight wickets managing 40. His 4-0-5-3, welcome enough in any cricket, exploited a bone-dry pitch and upstaged the 6-39 that Malinga Bandara and van Jaarsveld, with leg-spin and off-spin, shared as Hampshire made 139. "I didn't bowl one bad ball," said Briggs, a 19-year-old from the Isle of Wight.*

At Canterbury, July 4. **Kent won by 12 runs. ‡Kent 165-9** (20 overs) (J. L. Denly 44, M. van Jaarsveld 59; D. A. Payne 3-25); **Gloucestershire 153** (19.2 overs) (J. E. C. Franklin 40; H. M. C. M. Bandara 3-27). *MoM:* M. van Jaarsveld. *Attendance:* 2,072. *Despite David Payne's competition-best 3-25, Kent built a winning total around van Jaarsveld's 27-ball fifty. At 82-2, Gloucestershire needed 84 from 63 balls, but lost five wickets in five overs for 28 runs, three of them to Bandara.*

At The Oval, July 9. **Essex won by four wickets. ‡Kent 171-6** (20 overs) (J. L. Denly 35, D. I. Stevens 50*); **Essex 174-6** (19.4 overs) (A. N. Cook 51, M. L. Pettini 51). *MoM:* A. N. Cook. *Attendance:* 6,482. *Kent risked members' ire by hiring The Oval for a "home" fixture, but attracted their best crowd of the campaign. The faithful still had little to cheer. Restricted to 73-4 from 12 overs, Kent relied on Darren Stevens for a final 171-6, his 50* coming from 26 balls. But Alastair Cook and Mark Pettini both made 51 from 36 balls, as Essex saw Kent from the premises.*

At Canterbury July 11. **Kent won by six wickets. ‡Glamorgan 126-6** (20 overs) (M. J. Cosgrove 36, J. W. M. Dalrymple 33*; H. M. C. M. Bandara 3-15); **Kent 130-4** (19.1 overs) (J. L. Denly 36, Azhar Mahmood 30*; R. D. B. Croft 3-19). *MoM:* Azhar Mahmood. *Attendance:* 1,666. *Hopes of a fourth successive finals day had all but gone by the time Kent wrapped up only their second home win. Bandara's leg-breaks just outperformed Robert Croft's off-spin, but the Sri Lankan was better supported in holding Glamorgan to 126-6. Kent barely broke sweat overhauling it.*

Kent away matches

June 2: beat Essex by six wickets.
June 3: lost to Hampshire by five wickets.
June 13: beat Gloucestershire by 36 runs.
June 18: lost to Surrey by 15 runs (D/L).

June 24: lost to Middlesex by 13 runs.
June 27: beat Sussex by 27 runs.
July 16: beat Glamorgan by 14 runs (D/L).
July 18: beat Somerset by 59 runs.

MIDDLESEX

At Lord's, June 3 (floodlit). **Sussex won by 28 runs.** ‡Sussex 146-6 (20 overs) (D. R. Smith 49, M. H. Yardy 37*; P. T. Collins 3-27); **Middlesex 118-6** (20 overs). *MoM:* M. H. Yardy. *Attendance:* 16,576. *County debuts:* A. C. Gilchrist, P. R. Stirling (Middlesex). *They flocked to Lord's for Middlesex's first match, no doubt encouraged by perfect weather and by Adam Gilchrist's debut for the county. Unfortunately, Gilchrist lasted only three balls and scored just two. A Sussex total of 146 seemed below par but, stifled by Mike Yardy's 2-14, the Middlesex reply never got going.*

At Lord's, June 9 (floodlit). **Somerset won by five wickets.** ‡**Middlesex 155-6** (20 overs) (E. J. G. Morgan 48*; K. A. Pollard 3-26); **Somerset 158-5** (17.5 overs) (K. A. Pollard 89*). *MoM:* K. A. Pollard. *Attendance:* 10,132. *County debut:* K. A. Pollard. *After further chagrin for Gilchrist, with a seven-ball duck, it was Kieron Pollard who supplied the ferocious hitting in Somerset's reply. Igniting the innings from 31-4, he found 70 in fours and sixes alone as 89* from 45 balls sped them home. One of his hits off Shaun Udal came within seven or eight feet of clearing the Pavilion. Earlier, only Eoin Morgan managed any fluency, with 48* from 30 balls.*

At Lord's, June 13. **Middlesex won by five runs. Middlesex 200-6** (20 overs) (N. J. Dexter 43, O. A. Shah 35); ‡**Essex 195-8** (20 overs) (M. J. Walker 30, R. N. ten Doeschate 102; P. T. Collins 3-28). *MoM:* R. N. ten Doeschate. *Attendance:* 11,271. *Ryan ten Doeschate improved on his 98, made 11 days before, with a maiden Twenty20 century, from 52 balls, but once again it failed to win the match for Essex. They fell just short of the 23 they needed from eight balls when he departed. In a triumph of the collective over the spectacular, Middlesex mustered five scores between 21 and 43.*

At Richmond, June 15. **Middlesex won by 84 runs. Middlesex 213-4** (20 overs) (A. C. Gilchrist 51, O. A. Shah 30, E. J. G. Morgan 79*); ‡**Glamorgan 129** (17 overs) (J. Allenby 30; T. M. J. Smith 4-23, S. D. Udal 3-24). *MoM:* E. J. G. Morgan. *Attendance:* 2,511. *Gilchrist's original contract was to play only in Middlesex's five matches at Lord's, but, having played for Richmond as a 17-year-old, he asked to appear. He delighted a capacity crowd with a 29-ball fifty, followed by a catch and two stumpings. Morgan outpaced him in his 79*, and Glamorgan tried eight bowlers. None had the success of spinners Udal and Tom Smith, who shared seven wickets.*

At Lord's, June 17 (floodlit). **Surrey won by nine wickets.** ‡**Middlesex 128-9** (20 overs) (O. A. Shah 44*; G. J. Batty 4-23); **Surrey 130-1** (17 overs) (R. J. Hamilton-Brown 73*, M. R. Ramprakash 36*). *MoM:* G. J. Batty. *Attendance:* 16,317. *Rory Hamilton-Brown's 73* from 49 balls walked Surrey home with just one man lost. Earlier, Gareth Batty gained his maiden Twenty20 four-for, and only Owais Shah scored more than 15.*

At Lord's, June 24 (floodlit). **Middlesex won by 13 runs.** ‡**Middlesex 154-6** (20 overs) (D. J. Malan 41); **Kent 141-7** (20 overs) (R. W. T. Key 42; T. M. J. Smith 5-24). *MoM:* T. M. J. Smith. *Attendance:* 14,082. *County debut:* S. A. Shaw (Kent). *The unsung 22-year-old Tom Smith stopped Kent in their tracks. They were 54-0 after 40 balls when Smith, a left-arm spinner at his third county, broke through and seized five wickets in a slump to 113-6, two stumped by Gilchrist. It was his first five-for in all cricket.*

At Uxbridge, July 10. **Hampshire won by six wickets.** ‡**Middlesex 164-7** (20 overs) (O. A. Shah 80); **Hampshire 165-4** (18.3 overs) (J. H. K. Adams 64, M. A. Carberry 41). *MoM:* O. A. Shah. *Attendance:* 2,642. *Middlesex completed their home programme with a weekend at Uxbridge, and the first of the two matches did not augur well. Only Shah, with a Twenty20-best 80 from 52 balls, made any impression with the bat. Jimmy Adams and Michael Carberry put on 89 in nine overs for the first wicket, and Hampshire eased to their target.*

At Uxbridge, July 11. **Gloucestershire won by six wickets.** ‡**Middlesex 185-8** (20 overs) (D. J. Malan 86, N. J. Dexter 38; S. P. Kirby 3-29); **Gloucestershire 188-4** (19.2 overs) (W. T. S. Porterfield 64, J. E. C. Franklin 51*). *MoM:* W. T. S. Porterfield. *Attendance:* 1,633. *This was almost a rerun of the day before. Now, though, it was Dawid Malan who made Middlesex's runs, with six* *sixes in his 44-ball 86. Once again the visitors enjoyed a rampant opening stand – 78 from six overs – and the rest was relatively easy.*

Middlesex away matches

June 11: beat Kent by six wickets.
June 26: lost to Glamorgan by seven wickets.
June 27: lost to Gloucestershire by four runs.
July 2: beat Sussex by five wickets.

July 4: lost to Somerset by 79 runs.
July 8: beat Surrey by seven wickets.
July 16: beat Hampshire by eight wickets.
July 18: beat Essex by 11 runs.

SOMERSET

At Taunton, June 12. **Surrey won by 21 runs.** Surrey 160-7 (20 overs) (M. R. Ramprakash 59, Younis Khan 59; A. C. Thomas 3-27); ‡Somerset 139-8 (20 overs) (J. C. Hildreth 54*, K. A. Pollard 42). *MoM:* M. R. Ramprakash. *Attendance:* 5,930. *Somerset handed out hard hats to spectators to promote their explosive batting line-up, but only Kieron Pollard came off as, needing 44 from 23 balls, they slumped from 117-3 to 139-8. Mark Ramprakash and Younis Khan earlier rescued the visitors from 47-4 with a stand of 84 in 49 balls, despite Ramprakash suffering a painful blow to the foot.*

At Taunton, June 16. **Essex won by ten runs.** ‡Essex 177-7 (20 overs) (M. J. Walker 35, R. N. ten Doeschate 48*; A. C. Thomas 3-24); Somerset 167-9 (20 overs) (M. E. Trescothick 40, N. R. D. Compton 71). *MoM:* N. R. D. Compton. *Attendance:* 5,510. *Ryan ten Doeschate was averaging almost 74 in five Twenty20 innings when he tore a calf muscle attempting a quick single. The injury took the gloss off an unlikely Essex win after Somerset collapsed spectacularly again. At 145-2, they needed 33 from 29 balls but lost seven wickets for 21, David Masters and Chris Wright bowling intelligently at the death.*

At Taunton, June 18. **Somerset won by six wickets.** ‡Gloucestershire 199-8 (20 overs) (H. J. H. Marshall 45, S. D. Snell 50; B. J. Phillips 3-33, A. C. Thomas 3-41); Somerset 200-4 (18.5 overs) (Z. de Bruyn 95*, K. A. Pollard 54). *MoM:* Z. de Bruyn. *Attendance:* 4,920. *Zander de Bruyn shed his image as an accumulator in a 46-ball, 106-run stand with Pollard. Both cracked five sixes, setting up victory from 56-3. Steve Snell's 25-ball 50 helped Gloucestershire to a challenging total, but their bowling lacked discipline, Vikram Banerjee sending down five wides in conceding 54 runs.*

At Taunton, June 25. **Somerset won by seven wickets.** Sussex 159 (19 overs) (M. J. Prior 36, C. D. Nash 44; A. C. Thomas 3-29, K. A. Pollard 3-16); ‡Somerset 161-3 (18.4 overs) (M. E. Trescothick 50, P. D. Trego 41, J. C. Hildreth 37*, Z. de Bruyn 30*). *MoM:* Z. de Bruyn. *Attendance:* 6,196. *Matt Prior hit two sixes and two fours in the opening over of the game, from Mark Turner. But from 57-1 in 4.1 overs, Sussex lost five wickets for ten runs. A total of 159 was soon made inadequate by Marcus Trescothick's first fifty of the campaign.*

At Taunton, June 28. **Somerset won by six wickets.** ‡Glamorgan 138 (19.5 overs) (M. J. Cosgrove 75; A. C. Thomas 3-11, M. Kartik 3-18); Somerset 139-4 (18.4 overs) (N. R. D. Compton 40, J. C. Hildreth 45). *MoM:* A. C. Thomas. *Attendance:* 5,265. *Mark Cosgrove played a lone hand in the Glamorgan innings and came within four balls of batting the entire 20 overs. Nobody else reached 15 as the wily South African, Alfonso Thomas, took three wickets for the sixth consecutive game. Pollard's 19 comprised three sixes and a single, quelling any fears of a collapse.*

At Taunton, July 4. **Somerset won by 79 runs.** Somerset 204-5 (20 overs) (M. E. Trescothick 83, J. C. Hildreth 48); ‡Middlesex 125 (17.4 overs) (J. G. Thompson 32; M. Kartik 3-37). *MoM:* M. E. Trescothick. *Attendance:* 6,471. *County debut:* J. G. Thompson. *Left-arm spinner Murali Kartik shone against his old Middlesex team-mates after conceding 24 runs from his first eight balls. He claimed three successive wickets to start a terminal decline from 73-1. Trescothick's 83, earlier, came off 38 balls, fast even by Twenty20 norms: all but 15 arrived in sixes and fours.*

At Taunton, July 9. **Somerset won by six wickets.** ‡Hampshire 216-5 (20 overs) (N. D. McKenzie 73, S. M. Ervine 53); Somerset 220-4 (18 overs) (M. E. Trescothick 78, P. D. Trego 72*). *MoM:* M. E. Trescothick. *Attendance:* 7,479. *Having warmed up in the previous match, Trescothick now hit the fastest fifty in all domestic Twenty20 cricket. It took 13 balls, five of which went for six, and another for four in a chilling 17-minute onslaught. Peter Trego's promotion to open the batting saw the pair put together a century stand in 6.3 overs as Somerset breezed past a target of 217.*

Abdul Razzaq suffered most: in county Twenty20, only two bowlers have conceded more than his 64 runs. The total of 436 was the second-highest in county Twenty20.

At Taunton, July 18. **Kent won by 59 runs.** ‡**Kent 141** (19.5 overs) (J. L. Denly 65, D. I. Stevens 39; A. C. Thomas 3-21); **Somerset 82** (16.5 overs) (S. J. Cook 3-13, J. C. Tredwell 3-13). *MoM:* D. I. Stevens. *Attendance:* 7,511. *Already assured a home quarter-final, Somerset were shot out for their lowest Twenty20 score, chasing a modest target. Alfonso Thomas took his wicket tally to 31, enhancing his position as the competition's top bowler, but couldn't prevent Joe Denly and Darren Stevens making the only significant scores.*

Somerset away matches

June 1: lost to Sussex by 52 runs.
June 9: beat Middlesex by five wickets.
June 11: beat Hampshire by seven runs.
June 20: beat Kent by 84 runs.

July 2: lost to Surrey by 39 runs.
July 11: beat Essex by six wickets.
July 14: beat Glamorgan by seven wickets.
July 16: beat Gloucestershire by six wickets.

SURREY

At The Oval, June 8. **Gloucestershire won by ten wickets.** Surrey 97 (18.1 overs) (R. J. Hamilton-Brown 41; I. G. Butler 3-8); ‡**Gloucestershire 98-0** (9.5 overs) (W. T. S. Porterfield 47*, J. E. C. Franklin 41*). *MoM:* I. G. Butler. *Attendance:* 4,429. *County debut:* A. Symonds (Surrey). *Surrey were booed off after total capitulation. They lost their first five wickets for 17 runs in 34 balls, Ian Butler making the most of seaming conditions. Despite Rory Hamilton-Brown's counter-blast, they managed only 97, three run-outs adding to the debacle. Will Porterfield and James Franklin flogged a dispirited attack to take victory in 38 minutes.*

At The Oval, June 10 (floodlit). **Essex won by nine runs.** Essex 121-8 (20 overs); ‡**Surrey 112-7** (20 overs) (R. S. Bopara 3-13). *MoM:* R. S. Bopara. *Attendance:* 12,410. *County debut:* S. B. Styris (Essex). *A modest target was beyond Surrey, who lost all momentum on a dead pitch after Ravi Bopara claimed Andrew Symonds and Younis Khan in successive balls of the eighth over. At 50-4, Usman Afzaal arrived to muster 12 from 26 balls.*

At The Oval, June 18. **Surrey won by 15 runs** (D/L method). **Surrey 150-7** (20 overs) (S. J. Walters 42, A. Symonds 62; D. I. Stevens 3-17); ‡**Kent 81-5** (12.5 overs) (D. I. Stevens 33*). *MoM:* A. Symonds. *Attendance:* 6,274. *Surrey launched a violent assault from Symonds, who reached fifty in 24 balls and crunched seven sixes, the biggest into the second floor of the pavilion. From 35-4 in the eighth over, Symonds found an ally in Stewart Walters, adding 95 from 64 balls. Only Darren Stevens threatened in reply, and Kent were well behind par when rain arrived.*

At The Oval, June 20. **Sussex won by 39 runs.** Sussex 158-7 (20 overs) (B. B. McCullum 34, C. D. Nash 32*); ‡**Surrey 119** (19.5 overs) (S. M. Davies 35; C. B. Keegan 3-11). *MoM:* W. A. T. Beer. *Attendance:* 7,256. *Of two leg-spinners, Will Beer proved the key when he cut down Symonds and Steve Davies in five balls after Surrey had reached 64-2. The target was never again in sight. Chris Schofield's leg-breaks had earlier undone Brendon McCullum and Dwayne Smith in their muscular pomp, but Sussex rallied from 99-4 to a defensible score.*

At The Oval, June 22. **Surrey won by 11 runs.** ‡**Surrey 200-8** (20 overs) (S. M. Davies 60, A. Symonds 63; S. M. Ervine 3-28); **Hampshire 189-6** (20 overs) (J. H. K. Adams 46, J. M. Vince 43, N. D. McKenzie 52*). *MoM:* S. M. Davies. *Attendance:* 6,741. *County debut:* S. P. Jones (Hampshire). *Simon Jones took the field for the first time since August 2008, but may have rued the decision. He went for 25 in his first over, ending with figures of 4–0–53–1. Fifties came in 18 balls for Davies and 27 for Symonds as Surrey reached 200. At 117-3 from 12 overs, Hampshire were on course, but Neil McKenzie's 52* from 28 balls lacked late support.*

At The Oval, July 2 (floodlit). **Surrey won by 39 runs.** ‡**Surrey 171-6** (20 overs) (M. R. Ramprakash 34, J. J. Roy 74); **Somerset 132-9** (20 overs) (C. T. Tremlett 3-17). *MoM:* J. J. Roy. *Attendance:* 8,787. *For the second time in three games, Jason Roy proved irrepressible. The teenager followed his hundred against Kent at Beckenham with 74 from 50 balls. Somerset's goose was all but cooked by the reply's fourth over, Chris Tremlett finding high pace and Matthew Spriegel striking twice in three balls in a crash to 18-4.*

At The Oval, July 4. **Glamorgan won by five wickets.** ‡Surrey 168-4 (20 overs) (M. R. Ramprakash 63*, S. J. Walters 31*); **Glamorgan 172-5** (19.3 overs) (T. L. Maynard 78*). *MoM:* T. L. Maynard. *Attendance:* 5,758. *Glamorgan slumped to 46-3 and, at 78-4, still needed ten an over. But Tom Maynard surged home with 78* off 43 balls. Surrey went the other way. Putting on 68 for the first wicket in 34 balls, they might have managed more than 168-4. Mark Ramprakash batted through the innings for 63*.*

At The Oval, July 8 (floodlit). **Middlesex won by seven wickets.** ‡Surrey 120-8 (20 overs) (G. C. Wilson 36*; T. M. J. Smith 3-16); **Middlesex 121-3** (18 overs) (N. J. Dexter 62*, O. A. Shah 32). *MoM:* N. J. Dexter. *Attendance:* 15,668. *A polished 62* from Neil Dexter took Middlesex to easy victory. Two of Surrey's top three had earlier run themselves out, and Tom Smith, the left-arm spinner, did for the imports, Symonds and Younis Khan, in four balls as they sank to 62-6.*

Surrey away matches

June 12: beat Somerset by 21 runs.
June 13: lost to Hampshire by ten runs.
June 17: beat Middlesex by nine wickets.
June 23: beat Kent by 38 runs.

June 25: lost to Essex by six wickets.
July 9: lost to Glamorgan by five wickets.
July 11: beat Sussex by eight wickets.
July 18: beat Gloucestershire by six wickets.

SUSSEX

At Hove, June 1 (floodlit). **Sussex won by 52 runs. Sussex 155-7** (20 overs) (M. W. Goodwin 30, L. J. Wright 39); ‡**Somerset 103** (17.1 overs) (C. Kieswetter 47; R. J. Kirtley 3-3). *MoM:* L. J. Wright. *Attendance:* 6,264. *There were echoes of the 2009 final as Somerset folded, losing six wickets for 13 in five overs to record what was then their lowest Twenty20 total. Sussex had also collapsed after openers Luke Wright and Murray Goodwin put on 58, Wright snapping a bat with one drive that still found the boundary. But, in damp conditions, Sussex had enough to defend.*

At Hove, June 16 (floodlit). **Gloucestershire won by eight runs. Gloucestershire 178-4** (20 overs) (J. E. C. Franklin 90, H. J. H. Marshall 37); ‡**Sussex 170-9** (20 overs) (B. B. McCullum 46, M. W. Goodwin 31, J. S. Gatting 30*; A. J. Ireland 3-35). *MoM:* J. E. C. Franklin. *Attendance:* 4,452. *Despite the tight result, Sussex never really threatened to beat the record of 13 straight wins set by Surrey in 2004 and which Sussex had equalled at Cardiff. Defeat was likely after James Franklin's clean hitting brought a Twenty20 career-best. Brendon McCullum made a bid to outshine his fellow Kiwi, until he fell in the reply's tenth over at 83-2, but Gloucestershire fielded ferociously and conceded no extras until the last over.*

At Hove, June 18. **Sussex won by nine wickets.** ‡Hampshire 132-8 (20 overs) (J. H. K. Adams 31, N. D. McKenzie 40, N. Pothas 32); **Sussex 136-1** (11.4 overs) (B. B. McCullum 59*, M. W. Goodwin 76*). *MoM:* M. W. Goodwin. *Attendance:* 3,815. *England's World Cup football match in Cape Town badly affected the gate, although stayaways wouldn't have missed much as Sussex won seven minutes after kick-off. Hampshire never recovered from an early collapse, and their inexperienced attack was laid waste by Goodwin and McCullum with 135 in 65 balls, an all-wicket Sussex record.*

At Hove, June 23 (floodlit). **Sussex won by 53 runs. Sussex 239-5** (20 overs) (M. J. Prior 117, C. D. Nash 60*); ‡Glamorgan 186-5 (20 overs) (M. J. Cosgrove 43, J. W. M. Dalrymple 46*). *MoM:* M. J. Prior. *Attendance:* 3,581. *Glamorgan captain Jamie Dalrymple's belief that Sussex would struggle without Mike Yardy and Luke Wright was made to look foolish, particularly by Matt Prior, whose maiden Twenty20 century, from 48 balls, eventually included 90 in fours and sixes. Chris Nash's 21-ball fifty swelled the total to 239, the third-highest in the competition's history, and Glamorgan never came close. On a chastening night for bowlers, James Harris's figures equalled the then fourth-worst in county Twenty20 games (4–0–61–0).*

At Hove, June 27. **Kent won by 27 runs.** ‡Kent 194-1 (20 overs) (J. L. Denly 38, R. W. T. Key 98*, M. van Jaarsveld 53*); **Sussex 167-9** (20 overs) (M. J. Prior 44; M. T. Coles 3-30). *MoM:* R. W. T. Key. *Attendance:* 4,954. *Sussex felt Rob Key, not Joe Denly, should have been run out when both openers were stranded at the same end; Key made the most of his reprieve with 98 off 55 balls, a Twenty20-best. Sloppy fielding cost Sussex at least 20 runs and, once Prior had gone, Kent were in command, their 20-year-old seamer Matt Coles prospering at the end.*

At Hove, July 2 (floodlit). **Middlesex won by five wickets.** ‡Sussex 140-9 (20 overs) (O. P. Rayner 41*; T. J. Murtagh 3-24, T. Henderson 3-25); **Middlesex 143-5** (19.2 overs) (S. A. Newman 30, O. A. Shah 34). *MoM:* T. J. Murtagh. *Attendance: 5,212. After Tim Murtagh's three-wicket burst in the third over, Sussex slumped to 76-8 before Ollie Rayner oversaw an improbable 64 from the last six overs. Middlesex found their chase tough on a dry pitch and, at 96-4, needed 45 from 28 balls, but Chad Keegan conceded 16 in the penultimate over against his old county.*

At Arundel, July 11. **Surrey won by eight wickets.** ‡Sussex 121-8 (20 overs); **Surrey 122-2** (18.2 overs) (R. J. Hamilton-Brown 87*). *MoM:* R. J. Hamilton-Brown. *Attendance: 7,000. Rory Hamilton-Brown, badly dropped on four, made his former team-mates suffer as he hit a Twenty20-best off 66 balls; results elsewhere guaranteed Sussex a quarter-final berth. The start was delayed 20 minutes to accommodate a packed crowd, but most were heading home well before the end. Sussex lost a wicket in each of the game's first four overs and never really made a match of it.*

At Hove, July 16 (floodlit). **Essex won by five wickets.** ‡Sussex 185-4 (20 overs) (M. W. Goodwin 55, M. H. Yardy 76*); **Essex 188-5** (19.2 overs) (R. S. Bopara 39, A. N. Cook 63, S. B. Styris 52*; W. A. T. Beer 3-19). *MoM:* S. B. Styris. *Attendance: 6,778. Crowd trouble at the end forced police to put several youths on the train back to Essex, but couldn't sour a wonderful game. Mike Yardy's career-best set a stiff target which Sussex seemed likely to defend with Will Beer, one of eight bowlers, claimed three scalps with his leg-breaks. But, needing 27 from 12 balls, Essex roared home in eight as Scott Styris finished with four sixes in 52*.*

Sussex away matches

June 3: beat Middlesex by 28 runs.
June 9: beat Kent by four wickets.
June 11: beat Gloucestershire by seven wickets.
June 13: beat Glamorgan by three wickets.

June 20: beat Surrey by 39 runs.
June 25: lost to Somerset by seven wickets.
June 29: beat Essex by 17 runs.
July 18: lost to Hampshire by 45 runs.

QUARTER-FINALS

At Birmingham, July 26. **Hampshire won by five wickets.** Warwickshire 153-5 (20 overs) (D. L. Maddy 44, T. R. Ambrose 31*; D. R. Briggs 3-29); ‡Hampshire 154-5 (19.5 overs) (Abdul Razzaq 33, J. M. Vince 66*). *MoM:* J. M. Vince. *Attendance: 4,053. Hampshire fielded three 19-year-olds and another who had just turned 20. Slow left-armer Danny Briggs stifled Warwickshire to carry his season's tally to 27 wickets, the most by a spinner, and fellow-teenager James Vince hit an unbeaten 66 to win with a ball to spare. For Hampshire, finals day had at last arrived; for Warwickshire, a sixth quarter-final in seven seasons had yet again been wasted.*

At Nottingham, July 26 (floodlit). **Nottinghamshire won by 13 runs.** Nottinghamshire 141-9 (20 overs) (A. D. Brown 31, M. J. Wood 36; Yasir Arafat 4-34); ‡Sussex 128-7 (20 overs) (D. J. Pattinson 3-17). *MoM:* S. J. Mullaney. *Attendance: 8,558. Nottinghamshire's irresistible form at home continued as they defended a below-par total. Tight bowling from Samit Patel and Steven Mullaney pushed the champions behind the asking-rate and, at 106-4, they needed 36 from 21 balls. Andrew Hodd, Murray Goodwin and Yasir Arafat then fell for three runs in eight balls, the last two to Darren Pattinson, and Sussex's reign ended.*

At Taunton, July 27. **Somerset won by seven wickets.** ‡Northamptonshire 112-6 (20 overs) (S. D. Peters 40*); **Somerset 115-3** (17 overs) (C. Kieswetter 33, P. D. Trego 30). *MoM:* M. Kartik and A. V. Suppiah. *Attendance: 7,165. The run-out of Chaminda Vaas without facing a ball in the opening over set the tone for a poor Northamptonshire display. Left-arm spinners Murali Kartik and Arul Suppiah extracted turn from an unusually responsive Taunton one-day pitch, with 2-29 in their combined eight overs. Chasing 113, Somerset were never tested.*

At Chelmsford, July 27 (floodlit). **Essex won by eight wickets.** Lancashire 183-6 (20 overs) (T. C. Smith 35, P. J. Horton 44, S. I. Mahmood 34; C. J. C. Wright 4-25); ‡Essex 184-2 (19.1 overs) (M. L. Pettini 81, M. J. Walker 74*). *MoM:* M. L. Pettini and M. J. Walker. *Attendance: 5,571. An Essex-record second-wicket stand of 147 in 92 balls between Mark Pettini and Matt Walker overcame a challenging target. Requiring 75 from the last six overs, and 20 from the final two after the pair were parted, they inflicted Lancashire's third successive Twenty20 quarter-final defeat. Stephen Moore, earlier out first ball, suffered a shoulder injury in the field that ended his season. The match ended at 11.16 p.m.*

SEMI-FINAL

HAMPSHIRE v ESSEX

At Southampton, August 14 (floodlit). Hampshire won by six wickets. Toss: Hampshire. County debut: D. J. Bravo.

At 79 without loss in the ninth over, and Cook's confidence starting to return after recent England failures, Essex were eyeing a score of 200 on a true pitch. But Cook, scoring almost exclusively on the leg side, flicked an indifferent ball from Christian to short fine leg where Briggs, one of three Hampshire teenagers, held the catch. And it was Briggs's left-arm spin, modelled on Daniel Vettori's, that wrested the game from Essex. He used a bold variety of flight and pace to remove the dangerous Bopara, the threatening (if rusty) ten Doeschate and the well-set Pettini in the space of nine balls. When a long-range direct hit from the 20-year-old Wood did for Bravo – controversially signed up purely for finals day at a reported cost of £10,000 – Essex were in danger of squandering a perfect start, before Walker and Foster briefly regrouped. The Hampshire reply followed a similar path: they coasted to 67 for none in the ninth over before a second mid-innings totter. With four overs left, Essex's disciplined bowling – especially Bopara's nagging medium-pace – had lifted the asking-rate above ten. But the course then changed: Ervine smashed Bravo for a four and a six to settle nerves and, with McKenzie keeping a cool head while Carberry's fleetness of foot turned ones into twos, Hampshire sped into the final as the heavens opened.

Man of the Match: D. R. Briggs.

Attendance (for all three matches on finals day): 22,353.

Essex

		B	4	6
M. L. Pettini *b 11*	55	43	7	0
A. N. Cook *c 1 b 7*	38	22	3	2
R. S. Bopara *c 10 b 11*	2	5	0	0
R. N. ten Doeschate *c 3 b 11*	1	4	0	0
D. J. Bravo *run out*	5	8	0	0
M. J. Walker *c 7 b 9*	18	21	1	0
*†J. S. Foster *c 8 b 7*	15	11	3	0
G. W. Flower *not out*	8	6	0	0
D. D. Masters *not out*	0	0	0	0
B 1, l-b 2, w 11	14			

6 overs: 48-0   (20 overs) 156-7

1/79 2/84 3/97 4/106 5/111 6/135 7/154

Danish Kaneria and C. J. C. Wright did not bat.

Cork 4–0–22–0; Wood 4–0–40–1; Abdul Razzaq 4–0–23–0; Christian 4–0–39–2; Briggs 4–0–29–3.

Hampshire

		B	4	6
J. H. K. Adams *c 1 b 3*	34	32	2	1
Abdul Razzaq *c 3 b 11*	44	31	6	1
J. M. Vince *st 7 b 11*	15	15	1	0
S. M. Ervine *b 5*	21	14	1	1
N. D. McKenzie *not out*	19	15	2	0
M. A. Carberry *not out*	17	9	2	0
B 2, l-b 1, w 4	7			

6 overs: 45-0   (19.2 overs) 157-4

1/67 2/99 3/101 4/127

D. T. Christian, *D. G. Cork, C. P. Wood, †A. M. Bates and D. R. Briggs did not bat.

Masters 4–0–21–0; Bravo 4–0–46–1; Wood 3.2–0–30–1; Danish Kaneria 4–0–30–1; Bopara 4–0–27–1.

Umpires: R. J. Bailey and N. A. Mallender.   Third umpire: R. K. Illingworth.

NOTTINGHAMSHIRE v SOMERSET

At Southampton, August 14 (floodlit). Somerset won by three runs (D/L method). Toss: Nottinghamshire.

Most neutrals had hoped this would be the final. Certainly, a clash between West Country strokemakers and East Midlands strike bowlers had everything except the weather, which barged in like some gate-crashing drunk at a garden party. Chasing a revised target of 152 from 16 overs, Nottinghamshire were just ahead at the start of the 13th: they needed another 41 runs from four overs and, with rain falling, were one in front on Duckworth/Lewis. Patel then walloped Trego for what

Caught in time: Kieron Pollard's boundary catch swings the second semi-final Somerset's way.

seemed a certain six. But Pollard steamed round from long-on, leapt impossibly high, held a breath-taking overhead catch and, somehow, kept his balance as he landed millimetres inside the boundary. Come the end of the over, the rain had become stair rods, the game was abandoned – and Somerset were in the final. The old saw that "catches win matches" had never been truer: without Pollard's leap Nottinghamshire would have had six more runs, and edged home by three. Earlier, Trescothick enthralled the crowd with a transcendent innings: his placement was sublime, his power awesome. His eventual departure – beaten in the air by Swann – brought a wobble, but, in 19-year-old Buttler, Somerset had the man for the moment. Mixing strokes with slogs, he smashed Broad for 4, 6, 4 in the 18th over and Sidebottom for 15 in the last. A shower nibbled four overs from Nottinghamshire's reply, which then began at a lick before two wickets for Thomas in the fifth over seemed to confirm Somerset's superiority. But, as the skies grew black, Patel and Hussey rebuilt. A fraction more timing – and elevation – from Patel, and the match would have been Nottinghamshire's.

Man of the Match: J. C. Buttler.

Somerset

		B	4	6
*M. E. Trescothick st 6 b 1	60	28	9	2
†C. Kieswetter c 2 b 9	14	18	0	1
P. D. Trego b 4	2	5	0	0
J. C. Hildreth c and b 1	19	19	0	0
Z. de Bruyn run out	4	9	0	0
K. A. Pollard not out	23	18	2	0
J. C. Buttler not out	55	23	6	2
L-b 3, w 2	5			

6 overs: 54-1   (20 overs) 182-5

1/50 2/56 3/90 4/101 5/107

A. V. Suppiah, B. J. Phillips, A. C. Thomas and M. Kartik did not bat.

Sidebottom 4–0–45–0; Nannes 3–0–30–0; Broad 4–0–44–1; Patel 4–0–20–1; Swann 4–0–24–2; Mullaney 1–0–16–0.

Nottinghamshire

		B	4	6
G. P. Swann c 5 b 6	11	9	0	1
A. D. Brown c 6 b 10	19	12	2	0
A. D. Hales b 10	11	8	2	0
S. R. Patel c 6 b 3	39	26	3	3
*D. J. Hussey not out	27	21	2	0
†C. M. W. Read not out	3	3	0	0
L-b 3, w 2, n-b 2	7			

5 overs: 48-3   (13 overs) 117-4

1/33 2/45 3/47 4/111

M. J. Wood, S. J. Mullaney, S. C. J. Broad, R. J. Sidebottom and D. P. Nannes did not bat.

Thomas 3–0–23–2; Phillips 2–0–21–0; Pollard 2–0–19–1; Kartik 3–0–28–0; Suppiah 1–0–9–0; Trego 2–0–14–1.

Umpires: R. K. Illingworth and N. J. Llong.   Third umpire: N. A. Mallender.

FINAL

HAMPSHIRE v SOMERSET

At Southampton, August 14 (floodlit). Hampshire won by virtue of losing fewer wickets. Toss: Somerset.

This astonishing match was the consummate riposte to those who claim the shortest form of the game is too fleeting to allow fortunes to ebb and flow. Twenty20 cricket, they argue, is wholly predictable. At around 11 p.m., as fireworks lit up the night sky to mark the end of an utterly compelling day's entertainment, there should also have been the sight of late-night snacking as critics ate their words.

In essence, the final was a tale of two last overs. And the true value of the first, bowled by the wily Cork, was not clear until the end of the second, which, for sheer drama, defied belief. Hampshire, it seemed, had done the heavy lifting, and reached the home stretch needing just 11 runs from 12 balls. But McKenzie, coolness personified in compiling his fifty, top-edged a short ball from Phillips, and Carberry nervily followed three deliveries later. With the ever-threatening Thomas bowled out and Pollard in hospital, Trescothick gives the last over to de Bruyn, unused during the semi-final...

Hampshire are 166 for five, and eight runs will do it – seven if they don't lose two wickets (the first tie-breaker is fewer wickets lost, the second the six-over score, and Hampshire's is better). Christian, newly arrived at the crease, swings at the first delivery, but connects with thin air. The batsmen scramble a bye to give the strike to Ervine, who misses the second, shifting the advantage Somerset's way. Hampshire need seven to be sure, four balls left. Ervine top-edges another short delivery, and the ball arcs over Kieswetter for a fluky two. Five needed from three. Yet another short ball produces another swish and miss, but Kieswetter is standing back – and with his throw failing to hit the stumps the pair pinch a frantic bye. Four from two (though three should probably be enough for Hampshire); Christian on strike.

As the Rose Bowl crackles with tension, Trescothick slows things down by asking to replace the ball – an intriguing request since this one, changed just four overs ago, has been kind to Somerset. But a sopping outfield turns it into a bar of soap, and a dry replacement is easier to grip. The delay

Heading for trouble? Dan Christian survives Zander de Bruyn's lbw shout, but flirts with disaster as he leaves his crease.

cranks up the pressure on Christian. Yet he middles the inevitable short ball and tears off. They make two. One from the last ball will tie the scores and win it for Hampshire.

But Christian has not simply pulled the ball; he has pulled a hamstring and needs a runner. And it's not just the batsman in trouble: there are no markings on any adjacent pitch. At 10.45, Nigel Gray, the groundsman, rushes out, paint pot in hand. Gray's housekeeping completed, Kieswetter stands up to the stumps for the final ball and, eventually, the match can reach a conclusion. One hell of a conclusion. A run, and Hampshire can celebrate; a wicket, and Somerset's triumph.

De Bruyn raps Christian on the pad, there's a huge appeal, and the batsmen – all three of them – run. The ball is heading for somewhere near the edge of leg stump; it is a decent shout, but it does not sway umpire Rob Bailey. Even the hobbling Christian, in the melee forgetting he has a runner, reaches the non-striker's end, sparking an invasion by the delirious Hampshire team. And then they stop.

In the umpteenth example of cricket's magnificent ability to unearth the unexpected, the game is not over. Law 29.2 (e) states that "When a batsman with a runner is striker, his ground is always that at the wicketkeeper's end." The umpires know this, though crucially the players do not. Christian's progress down the pitch keeps the game in play, even when he reaches the non-striker's end – and Somerset have an age in which to break the stumps he has unwisely abandoned. When the umpires see this is not about to happen, the game is at last over, and Hampshire can resume their victory invasion.

Eons before – or so it seemed – Trescothick chose to bat, knowing a damp and dewy outfield would make bowling awkward later on. He looked in ominous touch until, for once, his timing failed him, and he miscued to midwicket when trying to hit over the top. Kieswetter took up where his captain left off, Kieswetter worked on scratchy beginnings to become increasingly polished and, at 97 for one in the 12th over, Somerset were buoyant. But a one-handed boundary catch by Ervine dismissed Trego, and Buttler, promoted after earlier outshining Pollard, could not conjure a reprise.

Pollard, not to be outshone twice, had hit 19 from five balls when Cork began the last over with Somerset 170 for four and targeting 190. Six waspish balls later, Somerset had added just three – from a dropped chance – and lost two wickets. Full-length deliveries accounted for both wickets, either side of a surprise bouncer which shot between Pollard's visor and grille, gashing him above the eye and ending his involvement in the game. That over handed the initiative to Hampshire, who built on it through an explosive opening stand. That in turn allowed the older heads of McKenzie and Ervine to ease back slightly as the target approached.

Then the fall of wickets brought the rise of self-doubt, and the delicious, enthralling climax. And the bottom line was that a young and unfancied Hampshire side – without the experienced quartet of Pietersen (omitted after revealing his intention to leave the county), Mascarenhas, Lumb and Pothas (all injured) – were the first to win the Twenty20 on home soil.

Man of the Match: N. D. McKenzie.

Somerset

		B	4	6
*M. E. Trescothick c 7 b 2	19	8	0	2
C. Kieswetter c 6 b 7	71	59	6	2
P. D. Trego c 5 b 11	33	24	3	1
J. C. Hildreth c 7 b 2	12	14	0	0
J. C. Buttler c 3 b 8	5	7	0	0
K. A. Pollard retired hurt	22	7	1	2
Z. de Bruyn not out	0	0	0	0
A. V. Suppiah c 10 b 8	0	1	0	0
B. J. Phillips not out	0	1	0	0
L-b 1, w 8, n-b 2	11			

6 overs: 47-1   (20 overs)   173-6

1/41 2/97 3/145 4/149 5/173 6/173

A. C. Thomas and M. Kartik did not bat.

Pollard retired hurt at 173-5.

Cork 4–0–24–2; Wood 4–0–51–0; Abdul Razzaq 4–0–37–2; Christian 4–0–30–1; Briggs 4–0–30–1.

Hampshire

		B	4	6
J. H. K. Adams b 8	34	24	3	1
Abdul Razzaq c 2 b 3	33	19	6	1
J. M. Vince run out	0	1	0	0
N. D. McKenzie c 1 b 9	52	39	3	1
S. M. Ervine not out	44	31	7	0
M. A. Carberry c 2 b 9	0	2	0	0
D. T. Christian not out	3	4	0	0
B 2, l-b 4, w 1	7			

6 overs: 62-1   (20 overs)   173-5

1/60 2/62 3/84 4/163 5/164

*D. G. Cork, C. P. Wood, †A. M. Bates and D. R. Briggs did not bat.

Thomas 4–0–23–0; Phillips 4–0–44–2; de Bruyn 3–0–29–0; Trego 4–0–38–1; Kartik 4–0–27–0; Suppiah 1–0–6–1.

Umpires: R. J. Bailey and R. K. Illingworth.   Third umpire: N. J. Llong.

CLYDESDALE BANK 40, 2010

Review by Paul Edwards

To judge by its scheduling and the number of games required for its completion, the new Clydesdale Bank 40 might have been designed with the objective of failing to capture the public's imagination. As it turned out, the tournament reached a memorable climax courtesy of Ian Bell's wonderful century in a gripping final; yet the fact that it happened at a less than half-full Lord's epitomised a competition in which the players did their best only after the planners had done their worst. And a 40-over event did little to prepare English cricketers for the World Cup in 2011. It wasn't just the length of the innings: there were few matches under lights, for good or ill; no ball change after 34 overs, a key phase of 50-over cricket; and shorter powerplays (eight overs then two lots of four, rather than ten overs then two lots of five).

The protracted group stage made the least sense. The Netherlands were added to the sides who competed in the 2009 Friends Provident Trophy, until Ireland threw a spanner in the works by declining the ECB's invitation to participate – effectively their first year away from county cricket since 1979. Ireland's absence forced the cobbling together of the Unicorns (an unpaid squad of club players without first-class contracts) to bring the numbers up to

Night star: Ian Bell shone brightest in Lord's first floodlit final.

21 teams, divided into three groups of seven with each playing the others home and away. Only the three group winners and the second-placed side with the most points qualified for the semis. Thus, 126 games were played to reduce 21 teams to four.

By early August, two or three counties dominated each septet, leaving more than half the teams with the task of fulfilling fixtures in the knowledge that they had little or no chance of progressing in the competition. Some played consistently good cricket and yet failed to make the last four. Gloucestershire, for whom James Franklin scored 511 runs, won nine of their 12 games in Group B, yet gained nothing but professional pride for their pains. A condensed group stage and the addition of quarter-finals would have removed some of these problems. Such a scheme is planned – but not until 2012.

Graham Morris

Maintaining the paying public's interest was not easy. The group games were played in two tranches, mainly to ensure that the lucrative Friends Provident T20 took pride of place in June and July. But in order to give the county treasurers' over-fattened cash cow the sweetest pasture, as many as six CB40 matches per county were squeezed between April 25 and May 31, a period already crammed full of Championship matches. Understandably, coaches sometimes opted to prioritise four-day cricket and rest older players, particularly the bowlers, whom they wanted to keep match-fit throughout the season. It was something of a bleak portent that when the CB40 was officially launched at Whitgift School, Lancashire rested their captain Glen Chapple. He featured in only three matches, and by late July Lancashire were using the competition to blood promising youngsters. They were not alone. "The schedule was lined up to make Twenty20 the jewel in the crown in the middle of the season," said their coach Peter Moores. "The Championship got stuck either side, and the CB40 got stuck with it. We had so much cricket in those first six weeks, and certain players couldn't play in all the matches. It made sense to prioritise."

Attendances were variable. Sussex's six home group games, of which two were played prior to the Twenty20, attracted an aggregate of just 14,827 spectators. Admittedly rain prevented any play in their match against Glamorgan – one of only seven games not to reach a positive outcome in a benign summer – but the gate for their match against Surrey at Hove (3,836) was boosted by the appearance of Kevin Pietersen, who made a century in the only tie of the competition. As might have been expected, crowds were often good at Taunton, where a limited-overs match usually brings the Somerset fans down James Street in strong numbers; however, the semi-final against Essex was not a sell-out. Healthy attendances were reported from outgrounds at Scarborough, Colwyn Bay and Guildford, and it was a delight to see county cricket played again at Exmouth, Bournemouth and Leek. Perhaps supporters were tempted to club grounds by the knowledge that they would not resemble building sites, a fate which befell a number of Test match venues in 2010. The sound of willow on leather may be cricket's hoariest cliché, but it still knocks spots off the clang of mallet on transom.

While many games in the CB40's first season would be quickly forgotten, at least four players had cause to remember the competition with fondness. Somerset's Alfonso Thomas proved he remained one of the most intelligent seamers in the country by taking 27 wickets, although this was unlikely to have been much consolation as he sat in the Lord's dressing-room on September 18 reflecting on the savage triple disappointment his team had suffered in 2010. His team-mate Jos Buttler, who turned 20 in September, had the highest strike-rate and hit the most sixes, besides keeping wicket or fielding outstandingly.

Jacques Rudolph marked his last season with Yorkshire by passing 50 nine times in 13 innings and converting four of those scores into centuries. If the South African's 861 runs at 95.66 earned him the unofficial accolade of CB40 cricketer of the year, the most heart-warming tale belonged to 29-year-old Wes Durston. Released by Somerset at the end of 2009, he made the most of his

Unicorns – unsigned, unpaid, undaunted

JOSH KNAPPETT

Having finished with Worcestershire in 2009 at the age of 24, I still believed I had a huge amount to offer as a wicketkeeper-batsman who worked hard without bundles of style or pizzazz. Then I heard rumours of an amateur team playing in the CB40 with the big boys, and got an invite to the first Unicorns trial at Edgbaston. After fortnightly training sessions under Phil Oliver, while I worked full-time for a sales company in London, I managed to get my name and number on the back of a shirt. A start.

Game 1: v Surrey at The Oval. The Unicorns – mainly guys from Minor Counties and ex-pros trying to get back in – had no fear and were eager to show their capabilities after being dismissed as "cannon fodder". Rained off – gutted! Game 2: Hove v Sussex. Lost, but competed. Ultimately their experience with bat and ball at the end of both innings was the biggest difference. My sense of belonging at this level began when I caught Matt Prior from a delivery bowled by Tom Mees – a skyer which would have comfortably won the hang-time competition on TV's "Cricket AM"!

Bournemouth for a home game v Glamorgan. Without an established fan-base, creating a MCG Boxing Day buzz was going to be difficult. However, a few hundred to a thousand usually turned up. I went in at No. 3, never having batted there before, but soon revelled in the chance to build an innings – luxury! Keith Parsons, our experienced ex-Somerset captain, hit 89, and 231 was enough. Cosgrove, 64 off 40 balls, all but took the game from us, but a leg-side wide from Zimbabwean born medium-pacer Glenn Querl was enough to give me a stumping. To the critics' surprise, our first victory over the big guns.

Then back to Sussex, and the highest run-chase in 40-over cricket – by the Unicorns! Sussex made 325 on a good wicket at a sunny Arundel. Welcome Wes Durston: 117 off 68 balls, while I made 90 off 84 at the other end: together we added 165 in 18 overs. Parsons got the 'Corns home with six wickets and three balls to spare. Against a county of Sussex's calibre, and five international bowlers to boot. Not bad for amateurs! (Except Durston signed for Derbyshire and did not play for us again.)

Victory number three – against Worcestershire, my ex-employers, at Kidderminster, my old club side – couldn't have been sweeter. Mike O'Shea crashed 90 from 64 balls. In the return at New Road I walked in to small applause. A hundred balls later I dragged on a slower-ball bouncer from close friend Gareth Andrew. Nine short! Still, getting clapped from crease to changing-room at my former home was a career highlight.

The season finished at Colwyn Bay with a home game against Lancashire. Kyle Hogg hit 13 from the last over to snatch victory from the grasps of the unsigned – and unpaid. We didn't even get a win bonus. But I finished with 364 runs – *and a share in a world record*.

opportunity to put himself in the shop window by clubbing 117 from 68 balls in the Unicorns' six-wicket defeat of Sussex at Arundel. It earned Durston a Twenty20 deal with Derbyshire, and he was later awarded a full contract until the end of the 2012 season – by when the CB40 may have evolved into a format befitting one of English cricket's leading competitions.

FINAL GROUP TABLES

Group A

	Played	Won	Lost	Tied	No result	Points	NRR
SOMERSET	12	10	2	0	0	20	1.49
Sussex	12	7	3	1	1	16	0.90
Surrey	12	6	4	1	1	14	0.00
Lancashire	12	6	6	0	0	12	−0.31
Worcestershire	12	4	8	0	0	8	−0.19
Unicorns	12	3	7	0	2	8	−0.47
Glamorgan	12	2	8	0	2	5†	−1.58

Group B

	Played	Won	Lost	Tied	No result	Points	NRR
YORKSHIRE	12	10	2	0	0	20	0.38
ESSEX	12	9	2	0	1	19	0.31
Gloucestershire	12	9	3	0	0	18	0.65
Derbyshire	12	4	8	0	0	8	−0.03
Northamptonshire	12	4	8	0	0	8	−0.03
Middlesex	12	3	7	0	2	8	−0.44
Netherlands	12	1	10	0	1	3	−0.99

Group C

	Played	Won	Lost	Tied	No result	Points	NRR
WARWICKSHIRE	12	9	3	0	0	18	0.31
Kent	12	7	3	0	2	16	0.77
Nottinghamshire	12	7	4	0	1	15	0.34
Hampshire	12	6	6	0	0	12	0.00
Durham	12	5	6	0	1	11	0.26
Leicestershire	12	4	8	0	0	8	−0.22
Scotland	12	2	10	0	0	4	−1.22

† *Glamorgan's total includes a one-point penalty for preparing a sub-standard pitch during the 2009 Friends Provident Trophy.*

Where two or more counties finished with an equal number of points, the positions were decided by (a) most wins (b) most points in head-to-head matches (c) net run-rate (runs scored per over minus runs conceded per over) (d) most wickets taken per balls bowled in matches achieving a result.

Prize money

£150,000 (no change from 2009 Friends Provident Trophy) for winners: WARWICKSHIRE.
£75,000 (−£25,000) for runners-up: SOMERSET.
£25,000 (no change) for losing semi-finalists: ESSEX, YORKSHIRE.
In 2010, there was no financial reward for winning individual matches.

CLYDESDALE BANK 40 AVERAGES, 2010

BATTING (300 runs at 45.00)

	M	I	NO	R	HS	100s	50s	Avge	SR	4	6
1 †J. A. Rudolph (*Yorks*)	13	13	4	861	124*	4	5	95.66	91.79	82	4
2 R. S. Bopara (*Essex*)	6	6	2	308	88*	0	2	77.00	95.35	33	7
3 I. J. L. Trott (*Warwicks*)	8	8	2	460	103	1	4	76.66	83.18	50	0
4 †J. E. C. Franklin (*Glos*)	12	12	5	511	133*	2	2	73.00	91.74	30	10
5 J. C. Hildreth (*Somerset*)	14	14	5	627	100*	1	5	69.66	110.19	58	7

		M	I	NO	R	HS	100s	50s	Avge	SR	4	6
6	G. W. Flower (*Essex*)	12	11	3	527	116	2	2	65.87	95.64	42	2
7	I. R. Bell (*Warwicks*)	9	9	0	554	107	1	6	61.55	106.53	52	10
8	†S. M. Davies (*Surrey*)	9	9	1	485	101	1	4	60.62	128.98	59	11
9	S. C. Moore (*Lancs*)	7	7	1	335	118	2	1	55.83	107.71	46	5
10	M. van Jaarsveld (*Kent*)	11	11	4	388	104*	1	4	55.42	101.04	36	5
11	J. C. Buttler (*Somerset*).	14	13	5	440	90*	0	4	55.00	153.84	40	19
12	S. J. Croft (*Lancs*).	12	11	3	425	93*	0	4	53.12	96.81	37	10
13	A. McGrath (*Yorks*)	12	11	3	414	77*	0	4	51.75	89.41	35	4
14	M. P. O'Shea (*Unicorns*) . . .	8	7	0	355	90	0	3	50.71	93.17	29	10
15	W. L. Madsen (*Derbys*)	10	10	2	404	71*	0	4	50.50	95.28	22	7
16	†M. J. Cosgrove (*Glam*)	10	8	0	397	88	0	5	49.62	120.30	50	8
17	†J. H. K. Adams (*Hants*).	11	11	1	496	131	1	4	49.60	95.56	40	11
18	K. A. Parsons (*Unicorns*) . . .	11	10	2	388	89	0	3	48.50	87.98	28	6
19	J. L. Denly (*Kent*)	11	11	1	467	102*	1	2	46.70	79.42	48	5
20	S. R. Patel (*Notts*)	12	11	1	467	108*	1	3	46.70	95.50	47	9
21	M. R. Ramprakash (*Surrey*) . .	9	9	2	326	85*	0	2	46.57	99.08	23	5
22	J. W. A. Taylor (*Leics*)	12	12	3	407	103*	1	3	45.22	89.64	27	6

† *Left-handed batsman.*

BOWLING (12 wickets at 25.00)

		Style	O	M	R	W	BB	4W/i	Ave	SR	ER
1	M. T. Coles (*Kent*)	RFM	25	2	150	14	4-47	1	10.71	10.28	6.00
2	H. M. C. M. Bandara (*Kent*) .	LBG	33	1	143	13	5-35	0	11.00	15.23	4.33
3	D. A. Payne (*Glos*)	LFM	36.5	3	179	16	7-29	1	11.18	13.81	4.85
4	C. Rushworth (*Durham*) . . .	RFM	52	7	226	15	3-6	0	15.06	20.80	4.34
5	A. C. Thomas (*Somerset*). . .	RFM	81.1	2	430	27	4-34	2	15.92	18.03	5.29
6	M. Kartik (*Somerset*)	SLA	69.3	1	321	20	4-30	1	16.05	20.85	4.61
7	W. B. Rankin (*Warwicks*) . .	RFM	41.4	0	244	15	4-34	1	16.26	16.66	5.85
8	L. M. Daggett (*Northants*) . .	RFM	71	7	330	20	4-17	1	16.50	21.30	4.64
9	C. W. Henderson (*Leics*) . . .	SLA	42	2	219	12	4-25	1	18.25	21.00	5.21
10	P. T. Collins (*Middx*)	LFM	45.4	1	244	13	4-25	1	18.76	21.07	5.34
11	Z. de Bruyn (*Somerset*)	RM	47.2	0	291	15	3-27	0	19.40	18.93	6.14
12	Imran Tahir (*Warwicks*)	LBG	81	1	431	22	5-41	1	19.59	22.09	5.32
13	R. J. Kirtley (*Sussex*)	RFM	72.4	2	476	24	4-30	3	19.83	18.16	6.55
14	C. P. Wood (*Hants*)	RFM	71.1	4	368	18	4-33	1	20.44	23.72	5.17
15	S. J. Mullaney (*Notts*)	RM	53	1	280	13	3-24	0	21.53	24.46	5.28
16	J. Lewis (*Glos*)	RFM	67	4	350	16	3-3	0	21.87	25.12	5.22
17	S. A. Patterson (*Yorks*).	RFM	92	4	470	21	6-32	0	22.38	26.28	5.10
18	S. P. Kirby (*Glos*)	RFM	73	5	400	17	3-41	0	23.52	25.76	5.47
19	R. M. Pyrah (*Yorks*)	RM	81	1	484	20	4-24	2	24.20	24.30	5.97
20	B. J. Phillips (*Somerset*). . . .	RFM	83.5	4	466	19	4-31	1	24.52	26.47	5.55
21	W. T. Owen (*Glam*)	RFM	49	1	320	13	5-49	0	24.61	22.61	6.53

GROUP A

GLAMORGAN

At Cardiff, April 25. **Somerset won by 38 runs** (D/L method). ‡**Somerset 224-5** (39 overs) (N. R. D. Compton 73, J. C. Hildreth 68*; D. S. Harrison 3-54); **Glamorgan 186** (37.1 overs) (M. J. Cosgrove 31, T. L. Maynard 48; B. J. Phillips 3-26, A. C. Thomas 3-27). *County debut:* D. O. Brown (Glamorgan). *An aggressive innings by Nick Compton, who scored a one-day hundred for Middlesex on this ground the previous year, rescued Somerset in a match reduced to 39 overs a side. Once Tom Maynard was sixth out with the score at 132, Glamorgan were never likely to succeed.*

At Cardiff, May 9. **Glamorgan won by five wickets.** Worcestershire 256-6 (40 overs) (V. S. Solanki 55, P. A. Jaques 110, D. K. H. Mitchell 33*); ‡Glamorgan 259-5 (38.3 overs) (M. J. Cosgrove 86, J. Allenby 30, G. P. Rees 51*, D. O. Brown 31*; J. G. Cameron 4-44). *The match was decided when Gareth Rees and David Brown milked 52 runs from Glamorgan's batting powerplay,* *left-hander Rees repeatedly reverse-sweeping the seamers to the vacant third-man boundary. Phil Jaques followed a pair in the Championship against Leicestershire with a century, succumbing to the final ball of Worcestershire's innings.*

At Cardiff, May 21 (day/night). **Surrey won by two wickets. ‡Glamorgan 223-8** (40 overs) (M. J. Cosgrove 61, T. L. Maynard 64); **Surrey 227-8** (38.4 overs) (M. R. Ramprakash 40, C. P. Schofield 64*). *Glamorgan were compromised when Mark Cosgrove and Jim Allenby needlessly sacrificed their wickets after a rousing opening stand of 88. With Surrey 126-6 in the 26th over, Glamorgan appeared in control, but Chris Schofield and Gareth Batty added 53 to set up Surrey's third win of the competition.*

At Swansea, July 25. **Glamorgan won by three wickets. ‡Sussex 203-7** (40 overs) (C. D. Nash 85, M. W. Goodwin 45; W. T. Owen 3-35, D. A. Cosker 4-33); **Glamorgan 205-7** (39.2 overs) (J. Allenby 61, M. A. Wallace 32, B. J. Wright 34). *Glamorgan did well to chase 204 on a tricky pitch in the absence of Cosgrove, who dislocated a finger in the field. Sussex had been well placed at 165-3, but stuttered against Dean Cosker. Allenby ensured a brisk response, and a partnership of 60 between Mark Wallace and Ben Wright settled the issue. Several members of a South Wales Premier League club, Ynysygerwn, were banned from attending home games for abusive chanting; Glamorgan also prevented two of their contracted players from appearing for the club in future.*

At Colwyn Bay, August 8. **Lancashire won by eight wickets. Glamorgan 211-9** (40 overs) (B. J. Wright 79, M. A. Wallace 38, R. D. B. Croft 53*; T. C. Smith 3-49); **‡Lancashire 213-2** (37.2 overs) (T. C. Smith 61, K. R. Brown 32, S. J. Croft 93*). *Steven Croft eased Lancashire to a consolation win. From 29-5, Wright had led a superb Glamorgan recovery with his highest one-day score. An elderly couple from Stockport, Carole and Mike Russell, were refused entry to the ground when a steward, searching their bags, confiscated two small metal spoons. "Our friend gave us some strawberries and cream and two spoons to eat them with," said Mrs Russell. "The spoons didn't belong to us, so I couldn't risk leaving them, and we decided not to go in." The steward cited ECB rules; Glamorgan issued an apology four days after the match.*

At Cardiff, August 20 (day/night). **Glamorgan v ‡Unicorns. Abandoned.**

Glamorgan away matches

May 2: lost to Lancashire by seven wickets.
May 16: lost to Unicorns by 58 runs.
August 4: lost to Surrey by 39 runs (D/L).

August 22: lost to Worcestershire by 178 runs.
August 25: no result v Sussex.
September 4: lost to Somerset by 249 runs.

LANCASHIRE

At Manchester, May 2. **Lancashire won by seven wickets. ‡Glamorgan 271-4** (40 overs) (J. Allenby 40, M. J. Cosgrove 50, J. W. M. Dalrymple 31, T. L. Maynard 103*); **Lancashire 275-3** (37.2 overs) (T. C. Smith 33, A. G. Prince 102*, S. J. Croft 84*). *A Lancashire victory looked a pipe dream until Steven Croft joined Ashwell Prince for a stand of 186*, foiling Glamorgan in fading light. Prince's 102* was just his second one-day hundred, three months after he scored his first. Tom Maynard went one run better in just 68 deliveries.*

At Manchester, May 3. **Somerset won by 42 runs. Somerset 235** (39.2 overs) (A. V. Suppiah 80, P. D. Trego 38; D. B. L. Powell 4-49); **‡Lancashire 193** (37.5 overs) (P. J. Horton 59, S. C. Moore 51; B. J. Phillips 3-28, A. C. Thomas 4-34). *Alfonso Thomas and Ben Phillips swarmed all over Lancashire, whose last six wickets tumbled for 20 runs in 22 balls: aside from the run-out of Stephen Parry, all fell to the experienced and resourceful pairing. Somerset's own batting inadequacies were shielded by Arul Suppiah's career-best score and by a 31-ball cameo from Peter Trego.*

At Manchester, May 23. **Surrey won by eight wickets. ‡Lancashire 165** (39.3 overs) (M. J. Chilton 68, L. D. Sutton 47; A. Nel 3-29, J. W. Dernbach 3-29); **Surrey 166-2** (23.5 overs) (R. J. Hamilton-Brown 65, S. M. Davies 82*). *On a fast, bouncy pitch, Lancashire utterly failed to cope with Andre Nel, Chris Tremlett and Jade Dernbach, lurching to 39-5 and losing their last five wickets for just 18. Between those positions came a doughty stand of 108 between Mark Chilton and Luke Sutton, but even their graft could not test Surrey, whose openers dashed to 113 in reply.*

At Manchester, July 24. **Lancashire won by nine wickets. ‡Unicorns 143** (39.5 overs); **Lancashire 144-1** (26.4 overs) (K. R. Brown 65*, S. J. Croft 39*). *Unicorns debuts: C. Brown, N. C. Saker,*

E. G. C. Young. *Lancashire made five changes to the team that had lost to Surrey two months earlier, signalling their intention to use the rest of the CB40 to blood younger players. Left-arm spinner Stephen Parry produced another eye-catching spell, and Karl Brown's 65* off 80 balls was a career-high.*

At Manchester, August 3 (day/night). **Sussex won by four wickets.** ‡**Lancashire 244-7** (40 overs) (T. C. Smith 34, P. J. Horton 69, K. W. Hogg 36*; R. J. Kirtley 3-35); **Sussex 248-6** (39.2 overs) (E. C. Joyce 46, J. S. Gatting 71, M. H. Yardy 46*, A. J. Hodd 30). *Joe Gatting freed his arms, and Michael Yardy oversaw a well-timed chase under floodlights, in a match that effectively marked the end of Daren Powell's Lancashire career. In addition to leaking runs – including ten to Chris Nash off his first two balls – he attracted derision from the crowd for a couple of shocking and costly errors in the field.*

At Liverpool, September 4. **Lancashire won by four wickets.** ‡**Worcestershire 258-6** (40 overs) (A. N. Kervezee 111, D. K. H. Mitchell 40; G. Keedy 4-41); **Lancashire 260-6** (39.1 overs) (K. R. Brown 41, S. J. Croft 60, L. A. Procter 64*, J. Clark 32). *County debut:* J. Clark. *Old Trafford was hosting the rock group Muse for the evening, so Lancashire made a rare one-day trip to Aigburth. It encouraged a healthy crowd and an exciting finish in which Luke Procter steered a youthful team to victory. Alexei Kervezee's hundred was his first in one-day cricket for Worcestershire.*

Lancashire away matches

April 25: lost to Surrey by two wickets (D/L).
May 9: lost to Sussex by 39 runs.
May 16: beat Worcestershire by nine wickets.

August 8: beat Glamorgan by eight wickets.
August 16: lost to Somerset by 115 runs.
August 30: beat Unicorns by two wickets.

SOMERSET

At Taunton, May 9. **Somerset won by seven wickets.** ‡**Unicorns 233-8** (40 overs) (J. G. Thompson 36, M. P. O'Shea 61, W. J. Durston 31, K. A. Parsons 53; D. G. Wright 3-43, B. J. Phillips 3-40); **Somerset 234-3** (36.5 overs) (A. V. Suppiah 36, Z. de Bruyn 106*, J. C. Hildreth 84*). *Unicorns debut:* C. T. Peploe. *Keith Parsons and Wes Durston prospered on their return to Taunton, but the Unicorns could not seriously inconvenience their old county. From 9-2, Somerset were spared any embarrassment by Zander de Bruyn's polished century and a savage 54-ball blitz from James Hildreth.*

At Taunton, May 15. **Somerset won by four wickets.** ‡**Sussex 291-8** (40 overs) (M. J. Prior 64, M. A. Thornely 67, M. W. Goodwin 64; D. G. Wright 3-66, A. C. Thomas 3-40); ‡**Somerset 295-6** (38.3 overs) (M. E. Trescothick 61, Z. de Bruyn 33, J. C. Hildreth 100*, J. C. Buttler 69). *Almost 600 runs were plundered by the two pre-competition favourites as Somerset celebrated the opening of the newly developed Colin Atkinson Pavilion. They reached their target remarkably comfortably due to Hildreth and Jos Buttler's exhilarating fifth-wicket stand of 158, Hildreth waltzing to a 66-ball century.*

At Bath, May 23. **Somerset won by 71 runs. Somerset 235-9** (40 overs) (C. Kieswetter 52, Z. de Bruyn 55, B. J. Phillips 51*); ‡**Worcestershire 164** (32.4 overs) (M. L. Turner 4-36). *After 15 years of trying, Ben Phillips scored a maiden one-day fifty, boosting Somerset's modest score as spectators basked in the Recreation Ground sunshine. Mark Turner's opening ball to Vikram Solanki at the start of Worcestershire's pursuit was a brute, gloved to gully, and he marked his first appearance of the season with four wickets.*

At Taunton, August 16 (day/night). **Somerset won by 115 runs.** ‡**Somerset 245-4** (40 overs) (N. R. D. Compton 59, J. C. Hildreth 72*, J. C. Buttler 64*); **Lancashire 130** (29.4 overs) (M. Kartik 4-30). *County debut:* G. S. Montgomery (Lancashire). *Lancashire offered feeble resistance on a turning pitch perfectly suited to Murali Kartik, who ran through the middle order. Hildreth and Buttler again combined to devastating effect in the last ten overs of Somerset's innings.*

At Taunton, August 29. **Somerset won by 64 runs** (D/L method). **Somerset 290-6** (36 overs) (C. Kieswetter 79, Z. de Bruyn 54, J. C. Hildreth 38, J. C. Buttler 87); ‡**Surrey 227** (31.4 overs) (S. J. Walters 45, M. R. Ramprakash 73, M. N. W. Spriegel 48*, J. W. Dernbach 31). *A rejuvenated Craig Kieswetter was eclipsed by Buttler, whose 46-ball 87 confirmed him as one of the country's brightest prospects. Mark Ramprakash, Stewart Walters and Matthew Spriegel offered brief hope for Surrey, but their last six wickets fell for 61 runs.*

SOMERSET v GLAMORGAN

At Taunton, September 4. Somerset won by 249 runs. Toss: Somerset.

Jos Buttler came within two blows of overtaking Graham Rose's world record for the fastest List A century, but on 90 not out from 33 balls – Rose had taken 36, also for Somerset – Buttler lost the strike. However, Glamorgan's David Harrison (8–0–100–0) did reach the swiftest hundred in English domestic one-day cricket; only Bardo Fransman, who conceded 103 for South Western Districts against Northerns at Oudtshoorn in 2009-10, has a worse eight-over return. Peter Trego almost doubled his previous best in crashing Somerset to their highest 40-over total. Phillips then ran through the Glamorgan top order to complete the annihilation – the biggest margin of victory in a 40-over game – and secure a home semi-final.

Somerset

*M. E. Trescothick c Rees b Owen	22		†J. C. Buttler not out	90	
P. D. Trego c Wright b Owen	147		L-b 5, w 5, n-b 2	12	
N. R. D. Compton c Wallace b Owen	6				
Z. de Bruyn c Maynard b Cosker	33		1/48 (1) 2/62 (3)	(4 wkts, 40 overs)	368
J. C. Hildreth not out	58		3/123 (4) 4/251 (2)		

A. V. Suppiah, B. J. Phillips, A. C. Thomas, M. Kartik and M. L. Turner did not bat.

Harrison 8–0–100–0; Jones 8–0–74–0; Owen 8–0–69–3; Allenby 5–0–43–0; Cosker 8–0–30–1; Bragg 1–0–15–0; Maynard 2–0–32–0.

Glamorgan

G. P. Rees b Thomas	0		A. J. Jones c Trego b de Bruyn	5	
J. Allenby c Hildreth b Phillips	11		D. S. Harrison st Buttler b Kartik	12	
W. D. Bragg c Trego b Phillips	16		D. A. Cosker not out	1	
D. O. Brown c Suppiah b Phillips	1		B 1, l-b 4, w 1, n-b 6	12	
T. L. Maynard c Trescothick b Phillips	18				
B. J. Wright b de Bruyn	36		1/0 (1) 2/14 (2) 3/28 (4)	(23.3 overs)	119
*†M. A. Wallace b Kartik	2		4/41 (3) 5/53 (5) 6/59 (7)		
W. T. Owen c Hildreth b Kartik	5		7/71 (8) 8/95 (9) 9/117 (6) 10/119 (10)		

Thomas 3–0–9–1; Phillips 6–0–31–4; Turner 5–0–17–0; Kartik 5.3–0–23–3; de Bruyn 4–0–34–2.

Umpires: N. G. C. Cowley and S. J. O'Shaughnessy.

Somerset away matches

April 25: beat Glamorgan by 38 runs (D/L).
May 3: beat Lancashire by 42 runs.
July 25: beat Surrey by 94 runs.

August 8: beat Unicorns by three wickets.
August 22: lost to Sussex by 17 runs (D/L)
August 30: lost to Worcestershire by 49 runs.

SURREY

At Whitgift School, Croydon, April 25. **Surrey won by two wickets** (D/L method). **Lancashire 290-6** (40 overs) (S. C. Moore 118, A. G. Prince 48, S. J. Croft 44, M. J. Chilton 32); ‡**Surrey 285-8** (38.5 overs) (R. J. Hamilton-Brown 92, S. M. Davies 50, U. Afzaal 43). County debut: D. B. L. Powell (Lancashire). *The match chosen to launch the new competition produced a grandstand finish, with Iftikhar Anjum edging Sajid Mahmood's penultimate ball to the boundary as Surrey overhauled a revised target of 283 from 39 overs. Stephen Moore made the most of Whitgift's short boundaries with 14 fours and three sixes in 96 balls, but Lancashire's total was exposed when Rory Hamilton-Brown raced Surrey to 169 from their first 20 overs. Andre Nel's latest outburst at officialdom, storming off after being run out late in the innings, earned him a two-match ban from the ECB.*

At The Oval, May 2. **Surrey v Unicorns. Abandoned.** *Persistent rain overnight and through the morning delayed the first appearance of the Unicorns. Two ex-county bowlers, David Burton and Carl Greenidge, had withdrawn from their squad prior to the match in protest at not being paid.*

At The Oval, July 25. **Somerset won by 94 runs.** ‡**Somerset 303-5** (40 overs) (M. E. Trescothick 69, Z. de Bruyn 89, J. C. Hildreth 68); **Surrey 209** (35.1 overs) (M. R. Ramprakash 42, M. N. W. Spriegel 53, C. T. Tremlett 31; M. Kartik 3-40). *Both teams started unbeaten, but Somerset floored Surrey in style on a perfect surface. Marcus Trescothick set the tone with seven fours in eight balls; Zander de Bruyn and James Hildreth forged on with a fourth-wicket stand worth 145 as Surrey's bowlers were flogged. Their response hit trouble immediately and was all but over at 148-7.*

At The Oval, August 4 (day/night). **Surrey won by 39 runs** (D/L method). Reduced to 38 overs a side. **Surrey 386-3** (38 overs) (R. J. Hamilton-Brown 115, S. M. Davies 88, M. R. Ramprakash 85*, M. N. W. Spriegel 56*); ‡**Glamorgan 187-5** (20 overs) (M. J. Cosgrove 88, J. W. M. Dalrymple 54*; G. J. Batty 3-44). *County debut: S. P. Cheetham (Surrey). Driven on with zeal by their young captain Hamilton-Brown, who faced just 69 balls, Surrey went 11 runs beyond the world record 40-over total they set at Scarborough in 1994 under Alec Stewart. And they did so in only 38 overs against a poor Glamorgan attack – matched by shoddy outfielding and catching – who must have regretted Jamie Dalrymple's decision to bowl in such easy batting conditions. A storm reduced Glamorgan's task to a still-formidable 227 in 20 overs; Mark Cosgrove, in a fifth consecutive half-century, slammed 88 before holing out, attempting his fourth six, from his 55th ball.*

At Guildford, August 8. **Sussex won by six wickets.** ‡**Surrey 252** (39.5 overs) (R. J. Hamilton-Brown 31, S. J. Walters 88, M. R. Ramprakash 33, M. N. W. Spriegel 30; R. J. Kirtley 4-60, C. J. Liddle 4-49); **Sussex 256-4** (38.2 overs) (E. C. Joyce 37, C. D. Nash 62, M. H. Yardy 66*, A. J. Hodd 46*). *Michael Yardy's limited-overs expertise assured victory in front of a packed Guildford Festival crowd. The asking-rate rose to nine an over with five remaining, but Yardy and Andrew Hodd had delayed the batting powerplay, and they cannily utilised the short boundaries.*

At The Oval, September 1 (day/night). **Worcestershire won by 90 runs.** ‡**Worcestershire 376-6** (40 overs) (M. M. Ali 41, V. S. Solanki 129, G. M. Andrew 104, D. K. H. Mitchell 35*; J. W. Dernbach 3-64); **Surrey 286** (36.4 overs) (R. J. Hamilton-Brown 80, K. P. Pietersen 38, C. P. Schofield 37, C. T. Tremlett 38; S. H. Choudhry 4-54). *County debut: K. P. Pietersen. Having broken their own 40-over world record, Surrey almost lost it within a month. No bowler escaped punishment as Vikram Solanki, who needed 89 balls for his 129, was outpaced by Gareth Andrew, who faced 60; his hundred was a first in professional cricket – for him and for the heavy-bottomed Mongoose MMi3 bat he wielded throughout. Kevin Pietersen made his Surrey debut after the ECB hastily arranged a loan deal: his solitary over cost 17, and he watched from 22 yards as Hamilton-Brown thrashed seven boundaries. Both fell to left-arm spinner Shaaiq Choudhry as an unlikely chase subsided – and with it Surrey's hopes of qualification.*

Surrey away matches

May 3: beat Worcestershire by 30 runs (D/L).
May 21: beat Glamorgan by two wickets.
May 23: beat Lancashire by eight wickets.

August 22: beat Unicorns by 66 runs.
August 29: lost to Somerset by 64 runs (D/L).
September 4: tied with Sussex.

SUSSEX

At Hove, May 3. **Sussex won by 44 runs. Sussex 255-8** (40 overs) (C. D. Nash 81, M. W. Goodwin 56); ‡**Unicorns 211** (38.2 overs) (C. P. Murtagh 31, J. G. Thompson 43, M. P. O'Shea 44, W. J. Durston 51; R. J. Kirtley 4-35). *Unicorns debuts: J. S. Ahmed, W. J. Durston, N. D. Hancock, J. P. T. Knappett, T. Mees, J. S. Miles, C. P. Murtagh, M. P. O'Shea, K. A. Parsons, R. G. Querl, J. G. Thompson. The Unicorns were well placed in their first fixture to survive the weather until their last six wickets fell in 14 balls, all to James Kirtley and Naved-ul-Hasan. For Sussex, only Chris Nash and Murray Goodwin, who passed 10,000 List A runs, had the measure of a two-paced pitch.*

At Hove, May 9. **Sussex won by 39 runs.** ‡**Sussex 245-7** (40 overs) (M. J. Prior 36, A. J. Hodd 91, R. S. C. Martin-Jenkins 32); **Lancashire 206** (37.5 overs) (P. J. Horton 30, S. J. Croft 32, L. D. Sutton 31*; Naved-ul-Hasan 3-37). *Andrew Hodd's one-day featured five successive boundaries off Glen Chapple and lasted just 65 balls; he established a strong score on a used surface later exploited with relish by Ollie Rayner and Monty Panesar.*

At Hove, July 19 (day/night). **Sussex won by 159 runs.** ‡**Sussex 313-6** (40 overs) (E. C. Joyce 117, L. J. Wright 95; J. D. Shantry 3-54); **Worcestershire 154** (33 overs) (S. H. Choudhry 39; R. J. Kirtley 3-33). *In his last game before retiring Robin Martin-Jenkins helped Sussex to a convincing* *win. The crowd gave him a standing ovation before and after a cameo 18* from 13 balls, and willed him to finish off Worcestershire in his second spell. Though a wicket proved elusive, he was serenaded with "He's old, he's posh, he's got loads of dosh… RMJ." A sublime hundred from Ed Joyce and Luke Wright's adroit use of the batting powerplay – during which he hit six fours and a six – left Worcestershire too much to do.*

At Horsham, August 22. **Sussex won by 17 runs** (D/L method). Reduced to 20 overs a side. **Somerset 216-7** (20 overs) (M. E. Trescothick 67, C. Kieswetter 45, P. D. Trego 50; L. J. Wright 3-41); ‡**Sussex 177-4** (15 overs) (E. C. Joyce 35, M. H. Yardy 66*). *After a three-hour delay, a patient audience witnessed 40 fours and 18 sixes in 35 overs – and Somerset's first defeat. The consensus was that conditions were the worst either team had experienced, so Michael Yardy's shot selection was especially good. He added a match-winning 91 in 43 balls with Joe Gatting before heavy rain and bad light – car headlights pierced the gloom – brought an early end.*

At Hove, August 25 (day/night). **Sussex v Glamorgan. Abandoned.**

At Hove, September 4. **Tied.** ‡**Surrey 240** (38.3 overs) (J. J. Roy 60, K. P. Pietersen 116; R. J. Kirtley 3-61); **Sussex 240-8** (40 overs) (C. D. Nash 53, M. W. Goodwin 81, O. P. Rayner 35*; J. W. Dernbach 3-44). *County debut: Z. S. Ansari (Surrey). Kevin Pietersen looked the part as he scored his first hundred in any format for 18 months and his first in domestic one-day cricket for seven years. His six sixes included two back to back off Kirtley, who eventually yorked him to enjoy a suitable finale to his county career. Sussex took 14 from the final over to square the game, Rayner hitting Tim Linley's last ball for four. Pietersen's presence drew an attendance of 3,836, Sussex's highest of the competition.*

Sussex away matches

April 25: beat Worcestershire by five wickets.
May 15: lost to Somerset by four wickets.
May 23: lost to Unicorns by six wickets.

July 25: lost to Glamorgan by three wickets.
August 3: beat Lancashire by four wickets.
August 8: beat Surrey by six wickets.

UNICORNS

At Bournemouth, May 16. **Unicorns won by 58 runs. Unicorns 231-8** (40 overs) (J. G. Thompson 36, J. P. T. Knappett 65, K. A. Parsons 89; W. T. Owen 5-49); ‡**Glamorgan 173** (35 overs) (M. J. Cosgrove 64). *Unicorns debuts: Arfan Akram, S. M. Park. Glamorgan's dreadful batting made them the Unicorns' first scalp. Mark Cosgrove was the only county batsman to seem unflustered and, after he was third out for a dashing 64 at 79 in the 13th over, they subsided limply.*

At Arundel, May 23. **Unicorns won by six wickets.** ‡**Sussex 325-4** (40 overs) (E. C. Joyce 45, C. D. Nash 53, L. J. Wright 38, M. W. Goodwin 92*, M. H. Yardy 36, J. S. Gatting 55*); **Unicorns 327-4** (39.3 overs) (J. G. Thompson 39, J. P. T. Knappett 90, W. J. Durston 117, K. A. Parsons 41*). *Sussex were on the receiving end of a scintillating maiden hundred by Wes Durston, the sort of career-reviving innings for which the Unicorns might have been conceived. Their pursuit on a benign pitch and an "outfield like glass" – according to captain Keith Parsons – was the highest score batting second in 40-over cricket. It was quite a comedown for Michael Yardy and Luke Wright after England's World Twenty20 celebrations in Barbados. Immediately after the game, Derbyshire called Durston to offer him a contract for the Friends Provident T20.*

At Kidderminster, July 25. **Unicorns won by three wickets. Worcestershire 277-7** (40 overs) (Shakib Al Hasan 72, D. K. H. Mitchell 70, J. G. Cameron 58; J. S. Miles 3-49); ‡**Unicorns 280-7** (39.4 overs) (J. G. Thompson 54, M. P. O'Shea 90, K. A. Parsons 47). *Worcestershire lost their seventh match out of seven, this time inside their own borders. Initially undone by Jonathan Miles, once of Kidderminster Victoria CC, Worcestershire needed a 113-run revival between Shakib Al Hasan and Daryl Mitchell. Their efforts proved insufficient as the Unicorns built strong partnerships around Mike O'Shea.*

At Exmouth, August 8. **Somerset won by three wickets. Unicorns 166-9** (40 overs) (M. P. O'Shea 40; Z. de Bruyn 3-27); ‡**Somerset 169-7** (36.2 overs) (C. Kieswetter 30, N. R. D. Compton 64; R. G. Querl 4-41). *Unicorns debut: T. G. Sharp. Somerset continued unbeaten. Marcus Trescothick unleashed his bowlers with success, and Craig Kieswetter and Nick Compton shared a leisurely 67 to ensure a middle-order wobble was irrelevant.*

At Wormsley, August 22. **Surrey won by 66 runs.** ‡**Surrey 273-4** (40 overs) (R. J. Hamilton-Brown 52, S. M. Davies 101, S. J. Walters 78*); **Unicorns 207-8** (40 overs) (M. P. O'Shea 65, N. C. Saker 40*; S. P. Cheetham 4-32). *Unicorns debut: Atiq-ur-Rehman. Nine days before his recall to the England one-day squad, Steve Davies struck his fifth century in the format to keep alive Surrey's hopes of a semi-final.*

At Colwyn Bay, August 30. **Lancashire won by two wickets.** Unicorns 253-7 (40 overs) (J. P. T. Knappett 64, K. A. Parsons 84*; Extras 30; L. A. Procter 3-29); ‡**Lancashire 254-8** (40 overs) (K. R. Brown 64, P. J. Horton 63, S. J. Croft 51, K. W. Hogg 35*; N. D. Hancock 5-64). *With Lancashire cruising towards their target at 115-0, the Unicorns turned to Neil Hancock, a left-arm spinner born in Casino, New South Wales, as a last throw of the dice. He produced a career-best 5-64 as the county slipped to 207-6, before Kyle Hogg finally provided some gumption. Hogg hit 12 of the 13 runs required from Jonathan Miles's final over of the match, including a straight six, to deny the Unicorns a fourth win.*

Unicorns away matches

May 2: no result v Surrey.
May 3: lost to Sussex by 44 runs.
May 9: lost to Somerset by seven wickets.

July 24: lost to Lancashire by nine wickets.
August 20: no result v Glamorgan.
August 29: lost to Worcestershire by five wickets.

WORCESTERSHIRE

At Worcester, April 25. **Sussex won by five wickets.** Worcestershire 144-9 (40 overs) (M. M. Ali 38; R. J. Kirtley 4-30); ‡**Sussex 145-5** (23.1 overs) (C. D. Nash 33, M. J. Prior 37, R. S. C. Martin-Jenkins 35*; C. D. Whelan 3-34). *Sussex began by winning at the scene of their 2009 Pro40 triumph. Worcestershire went into decline after replays suggested an erroneous lbw decision against Phil Jaques, the first of three wickets in one James Kirtley over. Sussex were in some trouble at 91-5, but Robin Martin-Jenkins and Andrew Hodd's stand of 54* prevented further alarm.*

At Worcester, May 3. **Surrey won by 30 runs** (D/L method). **Worcestershire 235-7** (40 overs) (P. A. Jaques 78, A. N. Kervezee 39, D. K. H. Mitchell 35, J. G. Cameron 48*; Iftikhar Anjum 3-39); ‡**Surrey 191-3** (31 overs) (S. M. Davies 81, U. Afzaal 51*; M. N. W. Spiegel 31*). *Steve Davies returned to New Road to warm applause; not so another former Worcestershire player, Gareth Batty, who was loudly jeered when he came on to bowl. Davies survived a chance on 12 to plunder 81 from 55 balls, leaving Surrey well ahead when rain set in.*

At Worcester, May 16. **Lancashire won by nine wickets.** ‡**Worcestershire 208-8** (40 overs) (V. S. Solanki 45, M. M. Ali 31, J. G. Cameron 41; S. I. Mahmood 4-40); **Lancashire 211-1** (34.3 overs) (P. J. Horton 78*, S. C. Moore 105*). *The dominant figure in Worcestershire's thumping defeat was Stephen Moore, a third big name to have left over the winter. His partnership of 191* with Paul Horton was Lancashire's highest in the tournament.*

At Worcester, August 22. **Worcestershire won by 178 runs.** ‡**Worcestershire 296-5** (40 overs) (M. M. Ali 121, V. S. Solanki 51, A. N. Kervezee 37, G. M. Andrew 66*); **Glamorgan 118** (26.1 overs) (M. S. Mason 3-38, Shakib Al Hasan 4-32). *Matt Mason ripped out three wickets in an unchanged eight-over spell, confirming Worcestershire's first win at their eighth attempt. An initially out-of-sorts Moeen Ali needed 22 balls to find the boundary; but he raced from 50 to three figures in 19 deliveries – and would have scored even quicker had the match been played six weeks later. Twice he was denied a maximum when the long-on fielder Tom Maynard backed beyond the ropes, caught and threw the ball back into the field of play while airborne. Quick-witted and legal Maynard's actions may have been, but they were outlawed under changes made to Law 19 that came into effect on October 1 (see page 1224).*

At Worcester, August 29. **Worcestershire won by five wickets.** Reduced to 37 overs a side. **Unicorns 181-9** (37 overs) (J. P. T. Knappett 91; J. D. Shantry 3-33, G. M. Andrew 4-30); ‡**Worcestershire 184-5** (35 overs) (M. M. Ali 40, V. S. Solanki 39). *Worcestershire exacted revenge for defeat in the "away" fixture at Kidderminster with a stronger bowling display. They overcame an impressive 91 from their former wicketkeeper Josh Knappett, who in three seasons on their books never played a one-day match for them.*

At Worcester, August 30. **Worcestershire won by 49 runs.** ‡**Worcestershire 255-9** (40 overs) (M. M. Ali 50, Shakib Al Hasan 91; A. C. Thomas 4-49); **Somerset 206-9** (40 overs) (C. Kieswetter

107, P. D. Trego 35; J. D. Shantry 3-45). *Craig Kieswetter's only hundred of the season was his first since a one-day international in Chittagong in March. One of his Bangladeshi opponents that day, Shakib Al Hasan, was Worcestershire's star performer, though he injured his hip in the course of his aggressive 69-ball innings and was unable to bowl. His absence barely mattered as Alan Richardson and Jack Shantry reduced Somerset to 41-5, and it was asking too much of Kieswetter to salvage victory from such depths.*

Worcestershire away matches

May 9: lost to Glamorgan by five wickets.
May 23: lost to Somerset by 71 runs.
July 19: lost to Sussex by 159 runs.

July 25: lost to Unicorns by three wickets.
September 1: beat Surrey by 90 runs.
September 4: lost to Lancashire by four wickets.

GROUP B

DERBYSHIRE

At Leek, May 3. **Essex won by five wickets** (D/L method). **Derbyshire 299-7** (40 overs) (C. J. L. Rogers 41, C. F. Hughes 55, W. L. Madsen 66, G. T. Park 43; G. R. Napier 3-54); ‡**Essex 248-5** (27.2 overs) (R. N. ten Doeschate 109*, J. C. Mickleburgh 34, J. S. Foster 31*). *County debut:* C. S. Martin (Essex). *Derbyshire marked their return to the Staffordshire moorlands after 18 years with their highest total in 40-over cricket, but lost a contest transformed by Ryan ten Doeschate. Rain between innings adjusted Essex's target to 247 in 30 overs; they were soon 27-3, but ten Doeschate unleashed five fours and eight sixes – one hitting the roof of an occupied portaloo – to reach his hundred in 59 balls.*

At Derby, May 30. **Netherlands won by seven wickets. Derbyshire 206** (40 overs) (C. J. L. Rogers 73; P. M. Seelaar 3-39); ‡**Netherlands 209-3** (39.2 overs) (M. G. Dighton 110*, B. Zuiderent 42*). *County debut:* W. J. Durston (Derbyshire). *Australian Michael Dighton's inability to contribute a major innings in half a season with Derbyshire in 2007 cost him an extended stay, but he returned to score a match-winning hundred for the Netherlands.*

At Derby, July 20 (day/night). **Gloucestershire won by one run** (D/L method). ‡**Derbyshire 225-8** (40 overs) (C. J. L. Rogers 40, W. J. Durston 34, W. L. Madsen 65; A. J. Ireland 3-46); **Gloucestershire 125-5** (28.3 overs) (W. T. S. Porterfield 38, A. P. R. Gidman 45). *Chris Taylor's clip for two to midwicket was the decisive last word in an unsatisfactory finale. In constant but not worsening drizzle, Gloucestershire needed 23 from 15 balls, but the umpires led the teams off after Taylor's shot, leaving them just ahead of the Duckworth/Lewis par score.*

At Chesterfield, August 8. **Yorkshire won by eight runs. Yorkshire 276-6** (40 overs) (J. A. Rudolph 105, A. Lyth 91, A. McGrath 31*; G. G. Wagg 3-56); ‡**Derbyshire 268-8** (40 overs) (C. F. Hughes 54, W. L. Madsen 65, G. T. Park 30). *County debut:* S. J. Adshead (Derbyshire). *Jacques Rudolph survived an early chance to complete another century; days later it was announced he would captain the Titans upon his return to South Africa. Thanks largely to his second-wicket partnership of 144 with Adam Lyth, Yorkshire's formidable total at the fast-scoring Queen's Park proved beyond Derbyshire.*

At Derby, August 24 (day/night). **Derbyshire won by 81 runs** (D/L method). **Derbyshire 192-7** (38 overs) (W. L. Madsen 71*; P. T. Collins 3-42); ‡**Middlesex 110** (27.3 overs) (N. J. Dexter 30; G. G. Wagg 3-22, M. H. A. Footitt 3-20). *Neil Dexter's decision to bowl on a damp wicket looked a good one when Derbyshire slipped to 49-4 in the 14th over, but Wayne Madsen anchored the recovery. Rain made the game a 38-over affair, with Middlesex's target revised down a smidgin to 192, but they fell well short against penetrative seam bowling from Graham Wagg and Mark Footitt.*

At Derby, August 30. **Northamptonshire won by five wickets.** ‡**Derbyshire 171** (39.3 overs) (C. F. Hughes 55, D. J. Redfern 37; L. M. Daggett 3-38, A. J. Hall 3-32, J. D. Middlebrook 3-34); **Northamptonshire 172-5** (37 overs) (S. D. Peters 53*, J. D. Middlebrook 57*). *A tight, low-scoring encounter was tipped in Northamptonshire's favour by James Middlebrook. His disciplined off-spin removed three of the Derbyshire top five, and the first one-day half-century of his career, in an unbroken sixth-wicket stand of 96 with Stephen Peters, clinched the win.*

Derbyshire away matches

April 25: lost to Gloucestershire by 51 runs.
May 7: beat Northamptonshire by five wickets.
May 9: lost to Yorkshire by 100 runs.

July 30: beat Netherlands by seven wickets.
August 22: beat Essex by 85 runs.
September 4: lost to Middlesex by seven wickets.

ESSEX

At Chelmsford, April 25. **Yorkshire won by ten wickets. Essex 232-9** (40 overs) (M. L. Pettini 51, G. W. Flower 113*; T. L. Best 4-46); ‡**Yorkshire 233-0** (35.5 overs) (A. W. Gale 125*, J. A. Rudolph 101*). *County debut: T. L. Best. Yorkshire opened their campaign with a withering victory. Essex underachieved on a true strip, but could barely have foreseen Andrew Gale and Jacques Rudolph sauntering to centuries in a partnership just nine short of the Yorkshire all-wicket record. Tino Best cleaned up Alastair Cook with his sixth ball in county cricket.*

At Chelmsford, May 9. **Essex won by 42 runs. Essex 267** (40 overs) (A. N. Cook 37, G. W. Flower 116, R. N. ten Doeschate 84; D. A. Payne 7-29); ‡**Gloucestershire 225** (37.3 overs) (W. T. S. Porterfield 65, H. J. H. Marshall 39, S. D. Snell 57; T. J. Phillips 4-37). *With his second century of the tournament, Grant Flower established a winning platform in a stand of 166 with Ryan ten Doeschate; together they broke Essex's fourth-wicket record. But the headlines were stolen by David Payne, a 19-year-old left-arm pace bowler from Poole playing his first Gloucestershire match of the season. He took five wickets in six balls, including four in four in the final over of the innings. Adding to the mayhem, Chris Martin signed off his overseas duties by being run out off the last delivery. Not even Mike Procter claimed seven in a one-day match for Gloucestershire, but their batsmen could not rouse themselves to comparable heights.*

FOUR WICKETS IN FOUR BALLS IN LIST A MATCHES

A. Ward	Derbyshire v Sussex at Derby....................................	1970
S. M. Pollock	Warwickshire v Leicestershire at Birmingham...................	1996
V. C. Drakes	Nottinghamshire v Warwickshire at Nottingham.................	1999
S. L. Malinga	Sri Lanka v South Africa at Providence, Guyana................	2006-07
D. A. Payne	**Gloucestershire v Essex at Chelmsford**.......................	**2010**

At Southend, August 8. **Essex won by five wickets.** ‡**Northamptonshire 215-6** (40 overs) (M. B. Loye 55, D. J. Sales 36, S. D. Peters 46); **Essex 216-5** (38.3 overs) (R. S. Bopara 42, M. J. Walker 39, A. J. Wheater 55*, M. A. Comber 52*). *County debut: C. A. L. Davis (Northamptonshire). Essex were wobbling at 100-5 until Adam Wheater and Michael Comber, both aged 20, took command with an unbroken stand in 16.3 overs. Christian Davis, at 17 years 301 days, became the youngest player to represent Northamptonshire since David Sales in 1994.*

At Colchester, August 22. **Derbyshire won by 85 runs. Derbyshire 253-5** (40 overs) (C. F. Hughes 45, G. M. Smith 46, W. J. Durston 72*, W. L. Madsen 35, G. G. Wagg 36*); ‡**Essex 168** (32.3 overs) (G. W. Flower 53, M. J. Walker 32; J. Needham 3-36, R. J. Peterson 3-38). *Derbyshire claimed a surprise win over Essex, who were still smarting from Championship defeat by Somerset here two days earlier. They allowed Wes Durston and Graham Wagg to plunder 50 from the final three overs, and later lost their last seven wickets for 30, collapsing to spinners Jake Needham and Robin Peterson.*

At Chelmsford, August 29. **Essex won by eight wickets** (D/L method). ‡**Netherlands 51-3** (16 overs) (D. D. Masters 3-11); **Essex 77-2** (8 overs) (M. L. Pettini 31, R. S. Bopara 43*). *David Masters's frugal seven-over spell and the intervention of rain disrupted the Dutch innings. Essex achieved a laughably simple target – 74 from 16 overs – in half their allocation. Ravi Bopara bludgeoned 28 from off-spinner Mohammad Kashif's only over to conclude the match.*

At Chelmsford, September 2 (day/night). **Essex won by seven wickets.** ‡**Middlesex 189-7** (40 overs) (D. J. Malan 38, N. J. Dexter 48*); **Essex 193-3** (33.3 overs) (R. S. Bopara 68, G. W. Flower 81*). *Although five of the Middlesex top six reached 20, none could force the pace. They were to rue a dropped catch by Tom Scollay off Steven Finn when Bopara had just 14. Capitalising on his good fortune, he joined Flower in a defining stand of 114 for the third wicket.*

Essex away matches

May 2: no result v Middlesex.
May 3: beat Derbyshire by five wickets.
May 21: beat Netherlands by one run.

July 25: beat Northamptonshire by nine wickets.
August 23: beat Gloucestershire by six wickets.
September 4: beat Yorkshire by seven wickets.

GLOUCESTERSHIRE

At Bristol, April 25. **Gloucestershire won by 51 runs. Gloucestershire 230-5** (40 overs) (J. E. C. Franklin 133*, A. P. R. Gidman 35, C. G. Taylor 32); ‡**Derbyshire 179** (35.3 overs) (C. J. L. Rogers 37, J. L. Sadler 41; S. P. Kirby 3-44). *Opening for Gloucestershire in one-day cricket for the first time, James Franklin responded with the best score of his career, thrashing 13 boundaries in 121 balls. Derbyshire never recovered from losing four of their middle order for 26 runs, two to Chris Taylor's unassuming off-spin.*

At Bristol, May 23. **Gloucestershire won by seven runs.** ‡**Gloucestershire 192-9** (40 overs) (A. P. R. Gidman 61, S. D. Snell 41; A. J. Hall 4-39); **Northamptonshire 185-7** (40 overs) (D. J. Sales 59*, A. J. Hall 37; J. Lewis 3-45). *Northamptonshire needed 14 from two overs to win, but Anthony Ireland and Jon Lewis varied their pace cannily to keep David Sales off strike. Gloucestershire had earlier been baled out by Alex Gidman, ninth out for a patient 61 from 86 balls.*

At Cheltenham, July 29. **Gloucestershire won by 65 runs. Gloucestershire 294-6** (40 overs) (A. P. R. Gidman 64, J. E. C. Franklin 42, H. J. H. Marshall 42, C. G. Taylor 83*); ‡**Yorkshire 229** (35.3 overs) (A. Lyth 84, T. T. Bresnan 58; S. P. Kirby 3-41, R. K. J. Dawson 3-41). *Escaping from a seam-dominated Bristol, Gidman and Taylor gorged themselves as Yorkshire's unbeaten record went up in smoke. A century partnership between Adam Lyth and Tim Bresnan kept Yorkshire interested until Steve Kirby dismissed both in successive overs.*

At Cheltenham, August 8. **Gloucestershire won by three wickets.** ‡**Middlesex 299-8** (40 overs) (J. A. Simpson 82, O. A. Shah 111, G. K. Berg 43, S. D. Udal 33*); **Gloucestershire 302-7** (39.5 overs) (H. J. H. Marshall 44, C. G. Taylor 85, S. D. Snell 95; T. J. Murtagh 3-76). *County debut: E. G. C. Young (Gloucestershire). Lewis smashed 20 from Tim Murtagh's last over to complete a remarkable turnaround. Labouring at 100-4 in the 18th over, Gloucestershire were resuscitated by Taylor and Steve Snell, who rattled 158 from the ensuing 19. They perished within three balls, Snell five shy of a maiden hundred. Middlesex had appeared to be cruising while Owais Shah compiled his 13th one-day century.*

At Bristol, August 23 (day/night). **Essex won by six wickets. Gloucestershire 184-8** (40 overs) (J. E. C. Franklin 70*, S. D. Snell 32; C. J. C. Wright 3-43); ‡**Essex 188-4** (39 overs) (M. L. Pettini 37, R. S. Bopara 45, G. W. Flower 45, M. J. Walker 32). *In an uninspiring but decisive contest, Essex overtook their nearest challengers to the best runners-up spot. Gloucestershire owed much to Franklin, the only batsman to adapt properly to a pedestrian wicket. Though Ravi Bopara was aggrieved at being given out caught behind off David Payne, he tellingly enjoyed significantly greater support.*

At Bristol, August 30. **Gloucestershire won by nine wickets.** ‡**Netherlands 191** (39.5 overs) (M. G. Dighton 51, W. Barresi 39; D. A. Payne 3-33); **Gloucestershire 192-1** (36.3 overs) (A. P. R. Gidman 104*, J. E. C. Franklin 77*). *William Porterfield was out to the first ball of the reply, caught trying to run Berend Westdijk down to third man. It was Gloucestershire's only hindrance as they swept to a five-day double over the bottom side. Gidman reached his only century of the season from 112 balls.*

Gloucestershire away matches

May 9: lost to Essex by 42 runs.
May 14: beat Middlesex by 77 runs.
July 20: beat Derbyshire by one run (D/L).

August 11: lost to Yorkshire by 23 runs.
August 26: beat Netherlands by 54 runs.
September 4: beat Northamptonshire by 82 runs.

MIDDLESEX

At Lord's, May 2. **Middlesex v Essex. Abandoned.**

At Lord's, May 14 (day/night). **Gloucestershire won by 77 runs. ‡Gloucestershire 246-9** (40 overs) (J. N. Batty 54, H. J. H. Marshall 85; P. T. Collins 3-46); **Middlesex 169** (31.3 overs) (O. A. Shah 32, D. J. Malan 42; A. J. Ireland 3-36). *Only two Gloucestershire batsmen passed 21, Jon Batty scoring the first of his two fifties in a wretched first year with his new county. Their score was nevertheless comfortably beyond Middlesex's capabilities.*

At Lord's, May 16. **No result. ‡Middlesex 185-4** (32.3 overs) (O. A. Shah 74*, G. K. Berg 53) v **Netherlands.** *Heavy rain thwarted Middlesex, for whom Owais Shah had engineered a strong position.*

At Lord's, July 25. **Yorkshire won by eight wickets. ‡Middlesex 183-9** (40 overs) (G. K. Berg 40, T. E. Scollay 32; A. Shahzad 4-34); **Yorkshire 184-2** (37 overs) (A. W. Gale 39, J. A. Rudolph 86*, A. Lyth 34). *A crowd of 3,300 came to see Yorkshire's first appearance at Lord's since July 1998, but Middlesex brought little to the occasion. Only Gareth Berg held firm against the England pair, Tim Bresnan and Ajmal Shahzad, and Middlesex's bowling was scarcely better, with 14 wides helping Jacques Rudolph to the winning post.*

At Lord's, August 5 (day/night). **Northamptonshire won by 49 runs. Northamptonshire 264-5** (40 overs) (M. B. Loye 66, R. I. Newton 41, D. J. Sales 84, S. D. Peters 40); **‡Middlesex 215** (39.5 overs) (J. A. Simpson 48; J. D. Middlebrook 3-41). *The experiment of promoting wicketkeeper John Simpson to open was the only decision to work for Middlesex, whose semi-final hopes burned out under the floodlights. Mal Loye hauled four sixes over square leg in customary fashion, despite clearly being hindered by a back problem, and David Sales administered further blows.*

At Lord's, September 4. **Middlesex won by seven wickets.** Derbyshire 195-9 (40 overs) (C. F. Hughes 64, W. L. Madsen 39, G. G. Wagg 48*; T. M. J. Smith 3-26); **‡Middlesex 196-3** (38.1 overs) (S. A. Newman 90, O. A. Shah 58*). *With qualification out of the question, Middlesex discovered form at last. Tom Smith held the success of Chesney Hughes's partners, before the vastly more experienced Shah guided Middlesex to victory with his 45th one-day half-century, to go with 12 hundreds, in his 224th and final one-day innings for the county.*

Middlesex away matches

April 25: beat Northamptonshire by seven wickets.
May 23: beat Netherlands by 46 runs.
August 8: lost to Gloucestershire by three wickets.

August 22: lost to Yorkshire by five runs.
August 24: lost to Derbyshire by 81 runs (D/L).
September 2: lost to Essex by seven wickets.

NETHERLANDS

At Amstelveen, May 21. **Essex won by one run. Essex 218-8** (40 overs) (J. C. Mickleburgh 46, M. J. Walker 71; P. M. Seelaar 3-31); **‡Netherlands 217-6** (40 overs) (E. S. Szwarczynski 75, B. Zuiderent 56). *County cricket made its return to continental Europe, but Chris Wright ensured there was no accompanying fairytale. The Netherlands needed six from the final over; Wright limited them to four, with Mudassar Bukhari run out off the final ball. Their downfall was triggered by national team-mate Ryan ten Doeschate, who ran out Eric Szwarczynski to end a stand of 103 with Bas Zuiderent, who was lbw to Graham Napier's next ball.*

At Amstelveen, May 23. **Middlesex won by 46 runs. ‡Middlesex 241-5** (40 overs) (N. J. Dexter 40, S. A. Newman 122); **Netherlands 195** (36.4 overs) (M. G. Dighton 85, T. L. W. Cooper 30; P. T. Collins 4-25, T. J. Murtagh 3-39). *Scott Newman was the dominant figure in a humdrum Middlesex win, taking the lead in a 112-run opening stand with Neil Dexter.*

At Schiedam, July 30. **Derbyshire won by seven wickets. Netherlands 181-9** (40 overs) (B. Zuiderent 31, Mudassar Bukhari 69*; M. H. A. Footitt 3-27, P. S. Jones 3-27); **‡Derbyshire 182-3** (37 overs) (C. J. L. Rogers 56, C. F. Hughes 72). *Derbyshire, the only team to lose to the Netherlands in the competition, became the first county to play on grass at the Excelsior 20 club. Mudassar Bukhari's display of fierce hitting kindled Dutch hopes, swiftly extinguished by Derbyshire's 111-run opening stand.*

At Schiedam, August 1. **Yorkshire won by five wickets. Netherlands 154-9** (40 overs) (R. M. Pyrah 4-24); ‡**Yorkshire 158-5** (36 overs) (A. W. Gale 32, J. M. Bairstow 46*). *Jonny Bairstow appeared to be playing in a different match from everybody else. On a slow pitch, Steven Patterson completed a spell of 8–2–9–0, though from 64-6, the Netherlands squeezed out another 90. Peter Borren (8–3–18–2), proved almost as adept at containing Yorkshire, at least until Bairstow arrived to hit 46* from 48 balls and provide some relief from the torpor.*

At Hazelaarweg, Rotterdam, August 22. **Northamptonshire won by 32 runs** (D/L method). **Northamptonshire 150-5** (27 overs) (A. G. Wakely 35); ‡**Netherlands 106-9** (22 overs) (B. Zuideret 35). *This match was fun only for Duckworth/Lewis aficionados. In an innings split into three parts and ultimately shorn by 13 overs, Northamptonshire reached 150-5. After several interruptions the Netherlands discovered that a further 70 would be required from six overs, which proved far too demanding.*

At Hazelaarweg, Rotterdam, August 26. **Gloucestershire won by 54 runs.** Reduced to 10 overs a side. **Gloucestershire 122-3** (10 overs) (W. T. S. Porterfield 46, J. E. C. Franklin 45*); ‡**Netherlands 68-6** (10 overs) (J. Lewis 3-3). *That any play was possible was a compliment to the groundstaff at VOC Rotterdam. Starting just before six o'clock, William Porterfield and James Franklin launched a ferocious onslaught, and Jon Lewis, on his 35th birthday, instantly killed the chase with three wickets in two overs.*

Netherlands away matches

May 15: lost to Yorkshire by four wickets.
May 16: no result v Middlesex.
May 30: beat Derbyshire by seven wickets.

May 31: lost to Northamptonshire by 119 runs.
August 29: lost to Essex by eight wickets (D/L).
August 30: lost to Gloucestershire by nine wickets.

NORTHAMPTONSHIRE

At Northampton, April 25. **Middlesex won by seven wickets.** ‡**Northamptonshire 146** (35.4 overs) (D. J. Sales 56; I. E. O'Brien 4-41); **Middlesex 148-3** (32.3 overs) (D. J. Malan 31*, G. K. Berg 43*). *County debuts:* J. D. Middlebrook (Northamptonshire); J. H. Davey, T. S. Roland-Jones, T. M. J. Smith (Middlesex). *Beaten by Northamptonshire in an extraordinary Championship finish the previous day, Middlesex gained instant revenge through Iain O'Brien's destructive spell. Only David Sales, playing his first one-day innings since September 2008, offered serious resistance. The result was confirmed by an 85-run stand between Dawid Malan and Gareth Berg, both former Northamptonshire Premier League players.*

At Northampton, May 7 (day/night). **Derbyshire won by five wickets.** ‡**Northamptonshire 230-6** (40 overs) (N. J. O'Brien 52, M. B. Loye 35, N. Boje 36; T. Lungley 3-41); **Derbyshire 234-5** (38.4 overs) (C. J. L. Rogers 47, C. F. Hughes 41, R. J. Peterson 51, W. L. Madsen 37, G. M. Smith 30; L. M. Daggett 3-48). *The first match under Wantage Road's newly installed floodlights failed to produce a celebratory result for Northamptonshire. It later emerged that three of the six 48-metre high pylons had been put in the wrong position. Niall O'Brien, returning from the World Twenty20, was prised out after seven boundaries, and Derbyshire's top five all contributed to a skilful chase.*

At Northampton, May 31. **Northamptonshire won by 119 runs.** ‡**Northamptonshire 238-7** (40 overs) (D. J. Sales 62, N. Boje 38, R. A. White 51, D. Murphy 31*; M. B. S. Jonkman 3-34); **Netherlands 119** (30.2 overs) (B. Zuideret 32; L. M. Daggett 4-17, N. Boje 3-10). *Fresh from defeating Derbyshire, Netherlands anticipated another memorable day when Mark Jonkman removed Mal Loye and Vishal Tripathi with the new ball. Their hopes soon nosedived during Sales and Nicky Boje's 99-run stand, and were snuffed out by Lee Daggett.*

At Northampton, July 25. **Essex won by nine wickets.** ‡**Northamptonshire 198-9** (40 overs) (R. I. Newton 66); **Essex 199-1** (33.2 overs) (M. L. Pettini 58, R. S. Bopara 88*, G. W. Flower 35*). *Left out of England's squad for the First Test against Pakistan in the morning, Ravi Bopara took out his frustration on Northamptonshire's bowlers with 88* from 89 balls. Northamptonshire wasted the healthy position established by opener Rob Newton, who top-scored with a maiden one-day fifty.*

At Northampton, August 31 (day/night). **Yorkshire won by four wickets.** ‡**Northamptonshire 204-8** (40 overs) (R. I. Newton 35, R. A. White 61; T. T. Bresnan 3-40); **Yorkshire 207-6** (38.3 overs) (J. A. Rudolph 54, A. McGrath 70; J. A. Brooks 3-41). *County debut:* R. I. Keogh (Northamptonshire). *Yorkshire's nervy win confirmed their semi-final place, but a defeated side* *featuring five players aged 21 or under had reason to be proud. One of them, Newton, prospered early on, although it took 61 from 68 balls by the 30-year-old Rob White to set Yorkshire a competitive target. After Jacques Rudolph's demise ended a 90-run partnership, Anthony McGrath calmly steered them home.*

At Northampton, September 4. **Gloucestershire won by 82 runs.** ‡**Gloucestershire 268-4** (40 overs) (J. E. C. Franklin 108*, C. G. Taylor 105); **Northamptonshire 186-9** (40 overs) (M. B. Loye 43, S. D. Peters 56; D. A. Payne 4-34). *Once James Franklin and Chris Taylor were in, Gloucestershire looked nothing other than certainties to win handsomely, yet they were denied a last-four spot by Essex's victory at Headingley. Remarkably, Taylor's hundred was his first in one-day cricket in 152 attempts; Franklin had scored 300 runs in four CB40 innings without being dismissed.*

Northampronshire away matches

May 2: lost to Yorkshire by 35 runs (D/L).
May 23: lost to Gloucestershire by seven runs.
August 5: beat Middlesex by 49 runs.

August 8: lost to Essex by five wickets.
August 22: beat Netherlands by 32 runs (D/L).
August 30: beat Derbyshire by five wickets.

YORKSHIRE

At Scarborough, May 2. **Yorkshire won by 35 runs** (D/L method). **Yorkshire 240-3** (30 overs) (A. W. Gale 35, J. A. Rudolph 83, A. McGrath 77*); ‡**Northamptonshire 118** (15.2 overs) (R. A. White 69; R. M. Pyrah 3-18). *Resuming after an innings-long stand of 233 at Chelmsford, Andrew Gale and Jacques Rudolph added another 61 before Gale fell to David Lucas. Anthony McGrath was even more fluent, hitting seven fours and two sixes. Conditions were very bleak by the time Northamptonshire came to bat, and only Rob White offered any hope in a forlorn chase of 154 in 16 overs.*

At Leeds, May 9. **Yorkshire won by 100 runs.** ‡**Yorkshire 241-4** (40 overs) (A. Lyth 38, A. McGrath 40, G. L. Brophy 93*); **Derbyshire 141** (31.5 overs) (C. J. L. Rogers 37, G. T. Park 31, J. L. Sadler 37; S. A. Patterson 6-32). *Yorkshire were already well on course for a third consecutive victory when Steve Patterson returned with an 11-ball burst of 5-5, securing him Yorkshire's eighth-best figures in one-day cricket. Gerard Brophy also contributed a career-high score.*

At Leeds, May 15. **Yorkshire won by four wickets. Netherlands 200-8** (40 overs) (M. G. Dighton 62, Mudassar Bukhari 49*; T. L. Best 3-43, S. A. Patterson 3-34); ‡**Yorkshire 204-6** (39.3 overs) (A. W. Gale 38, J. A. Rudolph 83*). *Returning to English domestic cricket after four seasons away, the Netherlands pushed the group leaders right to the last. Rudolph hit the winning boundary with three balls remaining, a patient 100-ball innings continuing a phenomenal run.*

At Leeds, August 11 (day/night). **Yorkshire won by 23 runs.** ‡**Yorkshire 247-5** (40 overs) (A.W. Gale 61, A. McGrath 76, G. L. Brophy 33); **Gloucestershire 224** (38.4 overs) (A. P. R. Gidman 48, W. T. S. Porterfield 53, H. J. H. Marshall 53; R. M. Pyrah 4-43). *Yorkshire avenged their defeat at Cheltenham to establish a four-point lead in the group. Former Yorkshire players Richard Dawson and Steve Kirby had a hand in all home wickets to fall, but a return of 4-43 and two run-outs for Rich Pyrah stymied Gloucestershire after a spirited start.*

At Scarborough, August 22. **Yorkshire won by five runs.** ‡**Yorkshire 250-6** (40 overs) (A. W. Gale 36, J. A. Rudolph 124*, A. McGrath 68; T. J. Murtagh 3-35, T. S. Roland-Jones 3-55); **Middlesex 245-8** (40 overs) (S. A. Newman 77, N. J. Dexter 56*; A. U. Rashid 3-28). *A game dominated by Yorkshire was almost pulled out of the fire by Neil Dexter, who required six from the final ball to tie. McGrath kept him to a single, after a ninth-wicket stand with Toby Roland-Jones had realised 50* in six overs. Rudolph scored his third hundred of the competition.*

At Leeds, September 4. **Essex won by seven wickets. Yorkshire 209-8** (40 overs) (J. A. Rudolph 59, G. L. Brophy 52, J. M. Bairstow 30; D. D. Masters 4-41); ‡**Essex 211-3** (36.3 overs) (M. L. Pettini 82, A. N. Cook 101*). *Alastair Cook's unbeaten century, after an opening alliance of 161 with Mark Pettini, ensured Essex simple passage into semi-finals for which Yorkshire had already qualified. In moving to 755 runs in 12 innings, Rudolph overtook by two Yorkshire's previous highest aggregate in a single one-day tournament, set by Darren Lehmann in the 2001 Norwich Union League.*

Yorkshire away matches

April 25: beat Essex by ten wickets.
July 25: beat Middlesex by eight wickets.
July 29: lost to Gloucestershire by 65 runs.

August 1: beat Netherlands by five wickets.
August 8: beat Derbyshire by eight runs.
August 31: beat Northamptonshire by four wickets.

GROUP C

DURHAM

At Chester-le-Street, April 25. **Durham won by 149 runs. Durham 264-6** (40 overs) (P. Mustard 74, B. W. Harmison 52, B. A. Stokes 34); ‡**Hampshire 115** (23 overs) (W. R. S. Gidman 4-36). *Durham's score looked little better than par, but the Hampshire reply was pitiful against a heavily depleted attack. Most of Will Gidman's four wickets resulted from rash strokes.*

At Chester-le-Street, May 23. **Leicestershire won by seven wickets.** ‡**Durham 189-9** (40 overs) (B. W. Harmison 48, G. J. Muchall 43, G. R. Breese 42; S. J. Cliff 3-27); **Leicestershire 190-3** (26 overs) (A. B. McDonald 46, J. du Toit 64, P. A. Nixon 33*). *Durham, with Phil Mustard now installed as captain, struggled against the miserly Matthew Hoggard and Sam Cliff, spluttering to 68-4 after 20 overs. By comparison, Leicestershire flew out of the blocks, bringing up 71 by the eighth over, with Jacques du Toit needing just 25 balls to reach 50.*

At Chester-le-Street, July 25. **Nottinghamshire won by five wickets. Durham 181-8** (40 overs) (G. J. Muchall 77); ‡**Nottinghamshire 182-5** (35.5 overs) (A. D. Hales 96*, S. R. Patel 46). *The match slipped from Durham's grasp when Alex Hales, on two, was dropped by second slip Gareth Breese off Chris Rushworth. Hales and Samit Patel added 86 runs in 13 overs, meaning only 25 were needed in ten when Patel was stumped. Mitch Claydon prolonged matters by taking two wickets, but Hales remained steadfast on 96* from 113 balls.*

At Chester-le-Street, August 22. **Durham won by five wickets. Warwickshire 243-8** (40 overs) (V. Chopra 70, N. M. Carter 35, J. O. Troughton 48*; M. E. Claydon 3-51); ‡**Durham 244-5** (38.2 overs) (P. Mustard 90, B. W. Harmison 35, G. J. Muchall 49*). *Mustard emerged from a lean run with 90 off 72 balls, while Gordon Muchall proved the perfect finisher. Varun Chopra and Darren Maddy progressed too slowly in the middle overs for Warwickshire, who, aside from Neil Carter and Chris Woakes, bowled poorly.*

At Chester-le-Street, August 29. **Durham won by 63 runs** (D/L method). **Durham 157** (35 overs) (K. J. Coetzer 35, G. R. Breese 34; M. A. Parker 3-27); ‡**Scotland 94** (29.3 overs) (C. Rushworth 3-6, I. D. Blackwell 3-22). *Durham were in trouble when Matthew Parker, who had played for their Second Eleven, moved the ball away from the left-handers to claim the first three wickets. They could rest easy when Scotland collapsed more alarmingly to 44-6. In a good game for wicket-keepers, Douglas Lockhart claimed the first five Durham wickets, while Mustard completed three stumpings off Ian Blackwell.*

At Chester-le-Street, September 4. **Kent won by 31 runs.** ‡**Kent 144** (39.1 overs) (J. L. Denly 71; C. Rushworth 3-26, N. Killeen 3-24); **Durham 113** (33.3 overs) (B. W. Harmison 34; J. C. Tredwell 4-20). *County debuts: A. J. Ball, P. B. Muchall (Kent). With nothing at stake Durham brought back Neil Killeen and announced he would retire after the match, ending a 15-year career; Kent handed a debut to triallist Paul Muchall, who had spent three years in Durham's Academy. Joe Denly's 71 showed batting was not as difficult as his colleagues made it look, and somehow 144 proved sufficient. When Gordon Muchall sliced a drive at his brother's otherwise expensive medium-pace, it sparked Durham's collapse from 54-2.*

Durham away matches

May 2: no result v Kent.
May 3: beat Leicestershire by 21 runs (D/L).
May 9: lost to Warwickshire by seven wickets.

July 31: beat Scotland by 47 runs (D/L).
August 8: lost to Hampshire by six wickets.
August 30: lost to Nottinghamshire by three runs.

HAMPSHIRE

At Southampton, May 2. **Nottinghamshire won by 35 runs.** Reduced to 24 overs a side. **Nottinghamshire 180-7** (24 overs) (H. M. Amla 33, A. D. Hales 41, C. M. W. Read 30; D. G. Cork 3-30); ‡**Hampshire 145-7** (24 overs) (N. D. McKenzie 32, L. A. Dawson 47*; S. J. Mullaney 3-24). *County debut:* H. M. R. K. B. Herath (Hampshire). *Steven Mullaney's burst of 3–0–5–3 in only his second appearance for Nottinghamshire proved pivotal in a rain-ruined encounter. Three wickets in ten balls for Dominic Cork kept Hampshire interested, but there was no way back after they slipped to 63-5.*

At Southampton, May 14 (day/night). **Warwickshire won by seven wickets.** ‡**Hampshire 211-8** (40 overs) (J. M. Vince 30, S. M. Ervine 35, N. D. McKenzie 62*, L. A. Dawson 30); **Warwickshire 212-3** (35.4 overs) (I. J. L. Trott 96*, I. R. Bell 71). *Neil McKenzie held Warwickshire at bay in a battling effort, though Jonathan Trott and Ian Bell made light of their target in a second-wicket stand of 155. Trott batted through the innings to finish four adrift of a second successive century.*

At Southampton, May 30. **Hampshire won by 31 runs.** ‡**Hampshire 237-9** (40 overs) (J. H. K. Adams 57, S. M. Ervine 43, N. D. McKenzie 41, N. Pothas 34; G. Goudie 3-54, R. D. Berrington 4-47); **Scotland 206** (39.4 overs) (R. O. Hussain 42, G. J. Bailey 90; J. A. Tomlinson 3-33, C. P. Wood 3-32). *Omer Hussain and George Bailey put on 118 for the second wicket to encourage Scotland's hopes, dampened later when four wickets tumbled for ten runs. Hampshire were 6-2 before Jimmy Adams and Sean Ervine started their recovery with a tenth-wicket stand of 84.*

At Southampton, August 8. **Hampshire won by six wickets.** ‡**Durham 205-8** (40 overs) (M. J. Di Venuto 37, B. W. Harmison 30, D. M. Benkenstein 33, B. A. Stokes 31*); **Hampshire 207-4** (34.5 overs) (M. J. Lumb 75, J. H. K. Adams 86; D. M. Benkenstein 3-27). *Hampshire's victory was a formality once Michael Lumb and Adams shared 150 for the first wicket.*

At Southampton, August 17 (day/night). **Hampshire won by two wickets** (D/L method). ‡**Leicestershire 176-8** (35 overs) (J. du Toit 45, M. A. G. Boyce 37, T. J. New 30; C. P. Wood 3-39); **Hampshire 177-8** (32.5 overs) (N. D. McKenzie 51*, L. A. Dawson 30; M. N. Malik 4-40). *County debut:* B. A. C. Howell (Hampshire). *Three days on from their Friends Provident T20 finals day nail-biter on this ground, McKenzie scrambled Hampshire home in another tight, rain-affected scrap to prolong hopes of a second trophy. He built vital stands with Michael Carberry and Liam Dawson, staving off Nadeem Malik to claim victory with 13 balls left.*

At Southampton, August 29. **Kent won by 20 runs.** ‡**Kent 241-5** (40 overs) (M. van Jaarsveld 104*, G. O. Jones 40); **Hampshire 221** (38.5 overs) (J. H. K. Adams 74, P. J. Hughes 32, M. A. Carberry 57; M. T. Coles 4-45, H. M. C. M. Bandara 3-25). *County debut:* P. J. Hughes. *Matt Coles took four wickets in nine balls during the 34th and 36th overs, boosting Kent's qualification hopes at the expense of Hampshire, who had been sailing at 85-0. Kent's score was built around Martin van Jaarsveld's century, completed in the last over of the innings.*

Hampshire away matches

April 25: lost to Durham by 149 runs.
May 16: lost to Nottinghamshire by 12 runs.
May 22: beat Warwickshire by 130 runs.

July 25: beat Kent by two wickets.
August 21: beat Scotland by eight wickets.
September 4: lost to Leicestershire by 14 runs.

KENT

At Canterbury, April 25. **Warwickshire won by six wickets.** Kent 246-6 (40 overs) (J. L. Denly 80, M. van Jaarsveld 58, D. I. Stevens 55); ‡**Warwickshire 247-4** (37.5 overs) (I. J. L. Trott 54, I. R. Bell 88, J. O. Troughton 56*). *Warwickshire began their campaign in imposing style. Missing James Tredwell and Amjad Khan, Kent lacked sufficient firepower or control to defend even a strong total, and Ian Bell reserved much of his punishment for Dewald Nel, who leaked 70 in 7.5 overs on a miserable home debut.*

At Canterbury, May 2. **Kent v Durham. Abandoned.**

At Canterbury, May 31. **Kent won by 58 runs.** Kent 249-7 (40 overs) (A. J. Blake 81*, Azhar Mahmood 44); ‡**Scotland 191-7** (40 overs) (G. J. Bailey 70, N. F. I. McCallum 45; A. Khan 3-32). *Wearing their retro powder-blue and burgundy kit for the first time since 1993, Kent completed the* *double over Scotland inside ten days. Alex Blake's 81 from 56 balls roused Kent from a lacklustre opening and contributed to a sixth-wicket stand of 102 with Azhar Mahmood that left Scotland too many to chase.*

At Canterbury, July 25. **Hampshire won by two runs. Hampshire 238-7** (40 overs) (M. J. Lumb 50, J. M. Vince 49, N. D. McKenzie 40, M. A. Carberry 46; J. C. Tredwell 3-40, M. T. Coles 3-59); ‡**Kent 236-4** (40 overs) (J. L. Denly 102*, M. van Jaarsveld 73; D. G. Cork 3-56). *Hampshire went against the wishes of the England management in declining to play Kevin Pietersen, so it was perhaps just as well that Dominic Cork held his nerve in a last-ball finish. Joe Denly and Martin van Jaarsveld's second-wicket stand of 136 had distilled Kent's task to 13 from Cork's final over. Denly chipped a single from the first ball to reach 100 in 107 balls – his only competitive century of the season – before Azhar clubbed a boundary, a two and a single. Denly dug out Cork's sublime yorker and was unable to reach the ropes from his sixth delivery.*

At Canterbury, August 8. **Kent won by eight wickets.** ‡**Leicestershire 148** (30.1 overs) (J. G. E. Benning 37; H. M. C. M. Bandara 5-35, M. van Jaarsveld 3-23); **Kent 150-2** (26.1 overs) (J. L. Denly 39, M. van Jaarsveld 56*). *Having flown to 41-0 in four overs, Leicestershire were bamboozled by Bandara in his only five-wicket return of the summer, two to sharp stumpings by Geraint Jones, who then helped van Jaarsveld rush Kent to their quickest win of the year.*

At Canterbury, August 22. **Kent won by 42 runs.** Reduced to 16 overs a side. **Kent 135-3** (16 overs) (D. I. Stevens 49*); ‡**Nottinghamshire 93-9** (16 overs) (M. T. Coles 3-7). *A three-and-a-half-hour rain delay forced a shortened match which Nottinghamshire barely contested. Kent sprinted along at more than eight an over, Darren Stevens leading the spree with three sixes. Though Alex Hales, who hit 21, did his best, Matt Coles took three wickets in the penultimate over.*

Kent away matches

May 8: no result v Nottinghamshire.
May 16: lost to Warwickshire by six wickets.
May 22: beat Scotland by nine wickets.

August 29: beat Hampshire by 20 runs.
August 30: beat Leicestershire by six wickets.
September 4: beat Durham by 31 runs.

LEICESTERSHIRE

At Leicester, April 25. **Leicestershire won by 47 runs. Leicestershire 282-6** (40 overs) (W. I. Jefferson 55, J. du Toit 141, P. A. Nixon 37); ‡**Nottinghamshire 235** (37 overs) (A. D. Hales 46, H. M. Amla 53, S. R. Patel 59, S. J. Mullaney 41; W. A. White 6-29). *County debuts: S. J. Mullaney, G. G. White (Nottinghamshire). Jacques du Toit, a British-qualified South African unaffected by the Kolpak exodus, struck his second one-day century for Leicestershire, batting through until eight balls from the end. Nottinghamshire's challenge reached 96-0, but was checked by Matthew Hoggard and halted by the unlikely figure of Wayne White, who claimed a career-best 6-29 with his medium-pace.*

At Leicester, May 3. **Durham won by 21 runs** (D/L method). Reduced to 37 overs a side. ‡**Durham 156-4** (26 overs) (I. D. Blackwell 35, B. W. Harmison 45; W. R. Smith 50*); **Leicestershire 154-8** (26 overs) (W. I. Jefferson 45, W. A. White 36; C. Rushworth 3-29). *Durham won comfortably, even though errors in calculating the Duckworth/Lewis target gave Leicestershire too generous a target. After rain limited Durham's innings to 26 overs, Leicestershire were set 176, also from 26 overs, when it should have been 181. The mistake was the match manager's: he used the previous year's D/L tables rather than new software – distributed before the season – which took into account quicker scoring-rates. He also neglected to consult the scorers. Durham's video analyst noticed the discrepancy, but not before the players had taken the field for the second innings, so the umpires were obliged to inform captain Will Smith that the incorrect figure would have to stand. In the event, Leicestershire never looked like threatening it and folded miserably. Smith could look back on his 33-ball 50, his only competitive half-century of a torrid summer, as the telling contribution.*

At Leicester, May 16. **Scotland won by four wickets. ‡Leicestershire 217-7** (40 overs) (J. du Toit 55, J. W. A. Taylor 51, P. A. Nixon 34; G. Goudie 3-45); **Scotland 218-6** (39.4 overs) (G. J. Bailey 54, R. D. Berrington 51). *Scotland debut: N. J. W. Laidlaw. Scotland thoroughly deserved to win their first match of the tournament. George Bailey and Richie Berrington kept them ahead of the game, and the deciding blows came from Neil McCallum, whose 27* from 19 balls included a towering six off Hoggard.*

At Leicester, July 25. **Warwickshire won by 25 runs. Warwickshire 272-8** (40 overs) (N. M. Carter 101, I. J. Westwood 47, A. G. Botha 42; J. W. A. Taylor 4-61); ‡**Leicestershire 247-6** (40 overs) (J. G. E. Benning 46, J. W. A. Taylor 103*, M. A. G. Boyce 33). *James Taylor took four wickets with his seldom-seen leg-spin, but the runs he conceded in his six overs helped Neil Carter thrash Warwickshire to a position they never relinquished. Taylor's calmer century, brought up with his 95th and last ball, prevented a cakewalk.*

At Leicester, August 30. **Kent won by six wickets. Leicestershire 182** (38.1 overs) (M. A. G. Boyce 41, T. J. New 47*; M. T. Coles 3-27); ‡**Kent 185-4** (33.2 overs) (J. L. Denly 40, R. W. T. Key 45, D. I. Stevens 42*, A. J. Blake 41*). *Kent were barely stretched, though wins for Warwickshire and Nottinghamshire on the same day ended their semi-final hopes. Leicestershire's score was confirmed as inadequate when Rob Key and Joe Denly shared 86 for Kent's first wicket. Though 14 wickets went down in the match, not a single catch was taken.*

At Leicester, September 4. **Leicestershire won by 14 runs.** ‡**Leicestershire 241-3** (40 overs) (J. G. E. Benning 62, J. du Toit 84, J. W. A. Taylor 34, J. J. Cobb 43*); **Hampshire 227-9** (40 overs) (J. M. Vince 62, S. M. Ervine 35, N. D. McKenzie 46, M. A. Carberry 36; H. F. Gurney 5-24). *Harry Gurney's devastating late spell closed out Leicestershire's first home win in the CB40 since the opening day. The match was deliciously poised with Hampshire 202-4 at the start of the 36th over, but Gurney claimed four wickets for three in nine balls to end with the finest figures of his one-day career.*

Leicestershire away matches

May 2: lost to Warwickshire by 41 runs (D/L).   August 17: lost to Hampshire by two wickets (D/L).
May 23: beat Durham by seven wickets.   August 22: lost to Scotland by 12 runs (D/L).
August 8: lost to Kent by eight wickets.   August 29: beat Nottinghamshire by four runs.

NOTTINGHAMSHIRE

At Nottingham, May 8. **No result.** Reduced to 10 overs a side. **Kent 78-2** (6.1 overs) (R. W. T. Key 44) v ‡**Nottinghamshire.** *The rain would not permit even a short thrash to be completed. Rob Key and Joe Denly blasted 73 before falling to Steven Mullaney.*

At Nottingham, May 16. **Nottinghamshire won by 12 runs.** ‡**Nottinghamshire 265-8** (40 overs) (A. D. Hales 46, S. R. Patel 108*, A. D. Brown 43; S. M. Ervine 3-43); **Hampshire 253-7** (40 overs) (S. M. Ervine 96, M. A. Carberry 35, N. Pothas 40). *Samit Patel's perfectly judged century left Hampshire still searching for their first win in any competition, nine matches into the season. Patel, hitting the spinners inside-out over cover with aplomb, also claimed the crucial wicket of Sean Ervine, holing out at long-on as the run-rate climbed.*

At Nottingham, August 8. **Nottinghamshire won by 75 runs.** ‡**Nottinghamshire 260-5** (40 overs) (S. R. Patel 48, D. J. Hussey 80, C. M. W. Read 69*); **Scotland 185** (38.4 overs) (M. M. Iqbal 31, D. R. Lockhart 37; P. J. Franks 3-22). *Nottinghamshire's victory turned out to be comfortable, which seemed unlikely when they lost their top three in the first 11 overs. Patel steadied the ship with David Hussey, who then combined with Chris Read to blaze 115 from the last ten overs. The chase was never on for Scotland, who lost their first four wickets in the space of five overs.*

At Nottingham, August 12 (day/night). **Nottinghamshire won by seven wickets.** Reduced to 16 overs a side. **Warwickshire 81-6** (16 overs); ‡**Nottinghamshire 82-3** (8 overs) (D. J. Hussey 34*). *The meeting of the group's top two proved a thorough mismatch. Ryan Sidebottom conceded only 12 from his four overs, and none of Warwickshire's batsmen could break free. They were made to look slightly silly by Patel and Hussey, who smashed 34* off 12 balls to finish the game in half their allocation.*

At Nottingham, August 29. **Leicestershire won by four runs. Leicestershire 219-7** (40 overs) (J. W. A. Taylor 58, M. A. G. Boyce 60, T. J. New 33*; J. T. Ball 3-32); ‡**Nottinghamshire 215-9** (40 overs) (A. C. Voges 71*, C. M. W. Read 32; M. J. Hoggard 3-43). *Leicestershire's youngsters combined to harm their neighbours' semi-final hopes. Jake Ball, Nottinghamshire's 19-year-old seamer, bowled with accuracy and lift before Matt Boyce and James Taylor put on 114 together. Familiar failings at the top of the Nottinghamshire order left Adam Voges with just too much to do.*

At Nottingham, August 30. **Nottinghamshire won by three runs.** ‡Nottinghamshire 257-7 (40 overs) (A. Patel 38, S. R. Patel 75, S. L. Elstone 30, C. M. W. Read 66*); **Durham 254-8** (40 overs) (B. W. Harmison 46, G. J. Muchall 47, B. A. Stokes 39, I. D. Blackwell 30; R. J. Sidebottom 3-45, D. J. Pattinson 3-70). *Narrow victory over a youthful Durham side secured Nottinghamshire the chance of a shoot-out for top spot with Warwickshire. Two amateurish mix-ups led to run-outs in the first three overs, but Patel and Read repaired the damage. Durham misjudged their run-chase: they needed 16 from four balls, and not even Scott Borthwick's four and a hooked six by Chris Rushworth could manage that.*

Nottinghamshire away matches

April 25: lost to Leicestershire by 47 runs.
May 2: beat Hampshire by 35 runs.
May 23: beat Scotland by 43 runs.

July 25: beat Durham by five wickets.
August 22: lost to Kent by 42 runs.
September 4: lost to Warwickshire by seven wickets.

SCOTLAND

At Edinburgh, May 22. **Kent won by nine wickets.** ‡Scotland 180-6 (40 overs) (R. D. Berrington 68, N. F. I. McCallum 41; S. J. Cook 3-39); **Kent 183-1** (30.2 overs) (J. L. Denly 38, R. W. T. Key 67*, M. van Jaarsveld 72*). *Scotland were on a high after their opening victory at Grace Road, but Kent easily avenged their defeat here in 2009.*

At Edinburgh, May 23. **Nottinghamshire won by 43 runs.** ‡Nottinghamshire 256-6 (40 overs) (A. D. Hales 69, M. J. Wood 60, S. R. Patel 61; G. Goudie 3-56); **Scotland 213** (35.3 overs) (G. M. Hamilton 42, R. R. Watson 48, R. D. Berrington 54; G. G. White 5-35). *Scotland debut: F. R. J. Coleman. Nottinghamshire's total ultimately proved too daunting, even after Gavin Hamilton and Ryan Watson put on a rapid 83 for Scotland's first wicket and Richie Berrington hit his third half-century. In a career-best performance, left-arm spinner Graeme White sent back Scotland's top five, three of them to return catches.*

At Glasgow, July 31. **Durham won by 47 runs** (D/L method). Durham 189-7 (30 overs) (M. J. Di Venuto 63, B. A. Stokes 39, D. M. Benkenstein 34; G. Goudie 4-51); ‡Scotland 145-9 (30 overs) (G. M. Hamilton 64; I. D. Blackwell 3-35). *Scotland's move along the M8 to Clydesdale's Titwood ground ushered in their worst weekend of the season. Despite Hamilton grinding out a half-century against the second of his old counties, the Scots could not sufficiently repair their collapse against the new ball.*

At Glasgow, August 1. **Warwickshire won by seven wickets.** ‡Scotland 95 (29.4 overs) (C. R. Woakes 3-16); **Warwickshire 97-3** (21 overs) (D. L. Maddy 43*). *Warwickshire marched on, while Scotland plumbed their nadir by slumping to 95 all out. They looked in little trouble reaching 29-0 before a three-wicket burst by Chris Woakes opened the floodgates.*

At Aberdeen, August 21. **Hampshire won by eight wickets.** ‡Scotland 164 (39.2 overs) (G. J. Bailey 43; C. P. Wood 4-33); **Hampshire 165-2** (31.2 overs) (J. H. K. Adams 74*, S. M. Ervine 63). *Mannofield Park hosted a county for the first time in 25 years. Hampshire may wish to return rather sooner. Much of the damage was caused by Chris Wood, who curtailed the dangerous George Bailey. Jimmy Adams and Sean Ervine put on 121 for the second wicket; it was Adams's third century stand of the competition.*

At Aberdeen, August 22. **Scotland won by 12 runs** (D/L method). ‡Scotland 166-9 (40 overs) (R. D. Berrington 46; C. W. Henderson 4-25); **Leicestershire 101-7** (21 overs) (J. G. E. Benning 42). *Hamilton's swansong proved a happy one as Scotland beat Leicestershire for the second time, with a little assistance from Duckworth/Lewis. Hamilton's final contribution before retiring was 23 from 44 balls. When rain produced a target of 114 in 21 overs, Leicestershire choked against keen fielding and spin bowling. All was not right in their camp: the following day it emerged that players and staff had written to the board requesting the removal of the club chairman, Neil Davidson, alleging he had interfered in selection.*

Scotland away matches

May 16: beat Leicestershire by four wickets.
May 30: lost to Hampshire by 31 runs.
May 31: lost to Kent by 58 runs.

August 8: lost to Nottinghamshire by 75 runs.
August 29: lost to Durham by 63 runs (D/L).
August 30: lost to Warwickshire by four wickets.

WARWICKSHIRE

At Birmingham, May 2. **Warwickshire won by 41 runs** (D/L method). **Warwickshire 321-7** (40 overs) (I. J. L. Trott 33, N. M. Carter 68, I. R. Bell 72, T. R. Ambrose 31*, C. R. Woakes 49*); ‡**Leicestershire 235-7** (34.1 overs) (J. W. A. Taylor 92*, P. A. Nixon 40; Imran Tahir 3-47). *Warwickshire's total surpassed their previous 40-over best, set at Colchester in 1982, and was topped and tailed by breathless innings from Neil Carter and Chris Woakes, who needed just 16 balls to bludgeon 49*, with four fours and four sixes. James Taylor replied in more cultured fashion, but was denied the chance of a century when the umpires led the players off in murky conditions.*

At Birmingham, May 9. **Warwickshire won by seven wickets.** ‡**Durham 200-9** (40 overs) (P. Mustard 61; D. L. Maddy 3-25); **Warwickshire 201-3** (35 overs) (I. J. L. Trott 103, J. O. Troughton 66*). *Jonathan Trott punished Durham with a clinical hundred, his first since the 2009 Ashes Test at The Oval. Steve Harmison was returning from a back problem, but with seven bowlers absent, Durham lacked the nous to contain Trott and Jim Troughton, who added 117 for the third wicket.*

At Birmingham, May 16. **Warwickshire won by six wickets.** Kent 192-9 (40 overs) (R. W. T. Key 87, R. S. Ferley 52; W. B. Rankin 4-34); ‡**Warwickshire 194-4** (35.1 overs) (I. R. Bell 55, D. L. Maddy 43*). *Ian Bell's composed half-century guided Warwickshire to another comfortable win. Boyd Rankin took three wickets in five balls to leave Kent 57-5; they partially recovered through an eighth-wicket stand of 87 between Rob Key and Rob Ferley, whose maiden fifty in senior cricket arrived in his 24th and final one-day innings for Kent; he was released in July.*

At Birmingham, May 22. **Hampshire won by 130 runs.** ‡**Hampshire 341-6** (40 overs) (J. H. K. Adams 131, M. A. Carberry 103, S. M. Ervine 48); **Warwickshire 211** (31.3 overs) (I. J. L. Trott 60, I. R. Bell 41; C. P. Wood 3-56, S. M. Ervine 4-39). *Centuries by Michael Carberry and Jimmy Adams, his first in limited-overs matches, ended Warwickshire's run of 16 games without defeat in 40-over cricket. They had never conceded a higher total. Warwickshire's innings was enlivened when water sprayed from one of Edgbaston's underground water sprinklers. Head groundsman Steve Rouse was the culprit: he had switched it on in a mischievous attempt to douse umpire George Sharp, a former opponent in his playing days. "I thought George was looking a bit hot and bothered and needed cooling down," Rouse explained. "But with a left-hand/right-hand combination at the crease it was difficult to get the timing right and he wasn't at square leg when the sprinkler came on."*

At Birmingham, August 30. **Warwickshire won by four wickets.** Scotland 267-4 (40 overs) (G. J. Bailey 123*, R. D. Berrington 82; K. H. D. Barker 4-33); ‡**Warwickshire 268-6** (37 overs) (N. M. Carter 81, K. H. D. Barker 40, D. L. Maddy 74, R. Clarke 49*; R. T. Lyons 3-39). *Prospects of an upset looked good when George Bailey and Richie Berrington plundered 198 in 24 overs, Scotland's highest partnership against a first-class county. Bailey, the Tasmania and Australia A captain, needed just 90 deliveries to score 123*. But Carter came out swinging, and Maddy and Rikki Clarke made good on his aggression with a sixth-wicket stand of 111.*

At Birmingham, September 4. **Warwickshire won by seven wickets.** ‡**Nottinghamshire 192** (38.4 overs) (A. D. Hales 34, A. C. Voges 54, C. M. W. Read 35; Imran Tahir 4-27); **Warwickshire 194-3** (36.5 overs) (I. J. L. Trott 84*, N. M. Carter 32, I. R. Bell 50). *Warwickshire prevailed in a winner-takes-all clash, although Nottinghamshire made their priorities obvious by resting several players before the Championship match with Yorkshire. They were unpicked by Imran Tahir, whose victims included Voges and Read following the innings' only meaningful stand. Bell, captaining Warwickshire for the first time, marked his comeback after eight weeks out with a broken foot to score a fluent 50, a hint of greater achievements to come.*

Warwickshire away matches

April 25: beat Kent by six wickets.
May 14: beat Hampshire by seven wickets.
July 25: beat Leicestershire by 25 runs.

August 1: beat Scotland by seven wickets.
August 12: lost to Nottinghamshire by seven wickets.
August 22: lost to Durham by five wickets.

SEMI-FINALS

SOMERSET v ESSEX

At Taunton, September 11. Somerset won by 95 runs. Toss: Somerset.

Marcus Trescothick, whose off-side driving and two pull-driven sixes brought him 79 from 62 balls, never let Essex into the game. Neither their bowling nor their fielding could restrain Trescothick or his successors: Buttler hit 36 from 18 balls and Suppiah (playing because de Bruyn was busy in the Twenty20 Champions League in South Africa) 42 from 20. It was Grant Flower's last game for Essex after six seasons; aged 39 he was their best fielder. When Essex chased, he was eventually given run out after prolonged analysis of television replays. Tempers frayed when Phillips, in his follow-through, accidentally got in the way of ten Doeschate; and later when Buttler pulled off a second brilliant run-out from the deep to dismiss Palladino. When Palladino made an indecent gesture, Kieswetter gave him a verbal send-off, for which they were both penalised. But the occasion, watched by a less than capacity crowd, was subdued overall.

Man of the Match: M. E. Trescothick.

Somerset

*M. E. Trescothick b Wright	79	B. J. Phillips not out	8
†C. Kieswetter c Flower b Palladino	8		
P. D. Trego c and b Danish Kaneria	33	W 3, n-b 2	5
N. R. D. Compton c Pettini b Masters	55		
J. C. Hildreth c Palladino b Danish Kaneria	46	1/32 (2) 2/113 (3) (6 wkts, 40 overs) 312
J. C. Buttler lbw b ten Doeschate	36	3/141 (1) 4/217 (5)
A. V. Suppiah not out	42	5/247 (4) 6/269 (6)

A. C. Thomas, M. Kartik and M. L. Turner did not bat.

Masters 8–0–58–1; Palladino 6–0–56–1; Wright 7–0–43–1; ten Doeschate 6–0–66–1; Danish Kaneria 8–0–41–2; Flower 5–0–48–0.

Essex

M. L. Pettini c Turner b Thomas	0	A. P. Palladino run out	2
A. N. Cook c Trescothick b Phillips	10	C. J. C. Wright c Phillips b Turner	0
R. N. ten Doeschate run out	22	Danish Kaneria not out	1
G. W. Flower run out	39	L-b 4, w 2, n-b 2	8
M. J. Walker c Thomas b Kartik	39		
*†J. S. Foster c Buttler b Thomas	58	1/0 (1) 2/33 (2) 3/33 (3) (29.3 overs) 217
A. J. Wheater lbw b Kartik	36	4/88 (4) 5/139 (5) 6/208 (6)
D. D. Masters b Trego	2	7/213 (7) 8/216 (9) 9/216 (10) 10/217 (8)

Thomas 6–0–47–2; Phillips 6–0–48–1; Turner 3–0–18–1; Kartik 8–1–40–2; Trego 4.3–0–35–1; Suppiah 2–0–25–0.

Umpires: N. G. B. Cook and P. Willey. Third umpire: M. A. Gough.

Scarborough fairest: Jacques Rudolph hits his fourth hundred of the tournament, but cannot prevent Yorkshire losing to Warwickshire.

Christopher Lee, Getty Images

YORKSHIRE v WARWICKSHIRE

At Scarborough, September 11. Warwickshire won by four wickets (D/L method). Toss: Warwickshire.

Jacques Rudolph, the star performer throughout the competition, became the first Yorkshire player to score four one-day centuries in a season. His 861 runs would have given him an average above 100 had he not been run out off the final ball. Despite Rudolph's brilliance and the frenetic support he received from Brophy and Bairstow, Warwickshire's team effort told in the end. They curbed Yorkshire's quick start by bowling 13 consecutive boundary-less overs, and their top four all contributed significantly in pursuit of a slightly revised target; Chopra benefited from a stinging drop at short extra cover by Gale, and Bell survived a sharp return drive to McGrath. It was a late blast from Maddy, with successive sixes off Patterson and two fours in the penultimate over, from McGrath, which hauled Warwickshire over the line with seven balls remaining. The outcome was a matter of regret to most in the 5,100 crowd at North Marine Road, hosting its first knockout semi-final since 1969. Headingley was staging a one-day international the next day, and, since the television cameras were there rather than at Scarborough, there was no match award.

Yorkshire

*A. W. Gale c Clarke b Barker	....	30
J. A. Rudolph run out	....	106
A. Lyth c Maddy b Botha	....	10
A. McGrath c Johnson b Imran Tahir	.....	9
†G. L. Brophy c Troughton b Barker	......	64
J. M. Bairstow not out	....	26
B 4, l-b 3, w 3, n-b 2	....	12

1/73 (1) 2/91 (3)   (5 wkts, 37 overs) 257
3/114 (4) 4/213 (5)
5/257 (2)

A. U. Rashid, R. M. Pyrah, A. Shahzad, B. W. Sanderson and S. A. Patterson did not bat.

Carter 8–1–58–0; Woakes 6–0–52–0; Barker 7–0–53–2; Botha 8–0–40–1; Imran Tahir 6–1–38–1; Maddy 2–0–9–0.

Warwickshire

V. Chopra c McGrath b Patterson	76	A. G. Botha not out		1
N. M. Carter lbw b Sanderson	40			
K. H. D. Barker c Brophy b Pyrah	34	L-b 2, w 2		4
*I. R. Bell c Bairstow b Rashid	57			
J. O. Troughton c Rudolph b Rashid	2	1/65 (2) 2/117 (3)	(6 wkts, 35.5 overs)	260
D. L. Maddy not out	34	3/203 (4) 4/206 (5)		
R. Clarke b Patterson	12	5/216 (1) 6/250 (7)		

C. R. Woakes, †R. M. Johnson and Imran Tahir did not bat.

Shahzad 8–0–59–0; Patterson 7–0–63–2; Sanderson 2–0–20–1; Rashid 8–0–43–2; Pyrah 5–0–34–1; McGrath 5.5–0–39–0.

Umpires: R. J. Bailey and R. T. Robinson.

FINAL

SOMERSET v WARWICKSHIRE

James Coyne

At Lord's, September 18 (day/night). Warwickshire won by three wickets. Toss: Warwickshire.

A final marred by muddled thinking was settled by comfortably the clearest mind at Lord's. Ian Bell's virtually flawless hundred as captain, which single-handedly steered Warwickshire from 20 for two to within one run of victory, was another hurdle triumphantly cleared by a batsman transformed over the previous 12 months. "In one-day cricket, I probably haven't played better," Bell reflected. Few quibbled, certainly not the England selectors, who immediately recalled him for the final throes of the ill-tempered series against Pakistan. The enhanced model had become mature and ruthless. With 22 needed from three overs, Trescothick returned in desperation to Turner, indisputably the weak link in Somerset's attack; his short and wide bowling proved cannon fodder for a man merrily ripping up an outdated caricature. Bell repeatedly backed away to leg, swung, and put faith in his strengthened upper body, racing from 85 to 107 in six balls, each boundary accompanied by a clenched fist.

This diminished fixture suffered again at the hands of those charged with promoting it. Scheduling the event only a week after the two finalists had been confirmed made it a hard enough sell when sandwiched between two London one-day internationals, at the tail-end of a saturated calendar. A start time of three o'clock ensured MCC their first floodlit final, yet betrayed staggering disregard for the watching public, many of whom wisely packed extra layers for warmth. Hoteliers in London were also rubbing their hands – with glee: Woakes hit the winning run at 8.40, ten minutes after the last train for Taunton had pulled out of Paddington station. Although the ECB had belatedly woken up to a mess of their own creation and subsidised 14 coachloads of Somerset supporters at £5 a head, most voted with their feet and stayed away. *Wisden* has never recorded a lower attendance in the 48-year history of a Lord's final.

Put in by Bell on a bouncy, newly prepared pitch, Somerset's menacing top three miscued short balls, but consolation came via Compton and the industrious Hildreth, keen to scamper in adding 95 for the fourth wicket. Compton went one step too far when a doomed single to the alert Trott at point sold his partner's wicket; though at 176 for four with the batting powerplay still in their pocket for the remaining nine overs, this team would usually sprint out of sight. Not here. Tahir, making his swansong appearance for his 17th first-class side, switched to the Pavilion End and took five for nine in 14 balls – a devastating and ultimately decisive sequence. Suddenly Bell's determination to keep his trump card away from the nuisance of evening dew looked very shrewd. A fatigued Somerset had to defend a mere 199 – uncharted territory for them in the competition, and doubly tough with emotions still raw from seeing the Championship lost just 48 hours earlier. To their credit, Thomas and Phillips circled the wagons for a last hurrah, and when Trott was third out, nibbling behind, Somerset appeared in danger of winning a trophy. Bell abruptly dashed such heady ambitions.

Man of the Match: I. R. Bell.   *Attendance:* 13,952.

Warwickshire's No. 1: Imran Tahir gains the desired verdict from umpire Richard Kettleborough, and Jos Buttler becomes the first of Tahir's five wickets.

Somerset

*M. E. Trescothick c Woakes b Barker	21	A. C. Thomas not out	6
†C. Kieswetter c Barker b Carter	37	M. Kartik st Johnson b Imran Tahir	3
P. D. Trego c Clarke b Barker	11	M. L. Turner c Clarke b Carter	8
N. R. D. Compton lbw b Imran Tahir	60	W 5, n-b 2	7
J. C. Hildreth run out	44		
J. C. Buttler lbw b Imran Tahir	0	1/41 (1) 2/62 (3) 3/81 (2)　(39 overs) 199
A. V. Suppiah b Imran Tahir	1	4/176 (5) 5/176 (6) 6/178 (7)
B. J. Phillips c Bell b Imran Tahir	1	7/179 (4) 8/180 (8) 9/187 (10) 10/199 (11)

Carter 6–0–40–2; Woakes 8–1–31–0; Barker 7–0–33–2; Botha 8–0–39–0; Imran Tahir 8–0–41–5; Maddy 2–0–15–0.

Warwickshire

I. J. L. Trott c Kieswetter b Phillips	17	A. G. Botha not out	4
N. M. Carter c Trego b Phillips	5	C. R. Woakes not out	1
K. H. D. Barker c Turner b Thomas	3	B 1, l-b 2, n-b 2	5
*I. R. Bell c Buttler b Thomas	107		
J. O. Troughton c Kieswetter b Thomas	30	1/12 (2) 2/20 (3)　(7 wkts, 39 overs) 200
D. L. Maddy c Kartik b Turner	9	3/39 (1) 4/118 (5)
R. Clarke c Hildreth b Trego	19	5/135 (6) 6/164 (7) 7/199 (4)

†R. M. Johnson and Imran Tahir did not bat.

Thomas 8–1–33–3; Phillips 8–0–24–2; Turner 7–0–71–1; Kartik 8–0–27–0; Trego 7–0–36–1; Suppiah 1–0–6–0.

Umpires: P. J. Hartley and R. A. Kettleborough.　Third umpire: R. T. Robinson.

THE UNIVERSITIES, 2010

RALPH DELLOR AND STEPHEN LAMB

CAMBRIDGE MCCU v SURREY

At Cambridge, April 3–5. Drawn. Toss: Cambridge MCCU. First-class debuts: C. E. H. Hopkins, C. M. Park. County debut: S. M. Davies.

Cambridge restricted Surrey to 183 for five after putting them in, but then Davies and Gareth Batty – both recruits from Worcestershire – shared a stand of 155 to dampen the students' optimism. Davies made 122 at a run a ball, with 16 fours; his century, completed on the second morning, was the earliest in any English summer. (April 3 was also the earliest start date for the first-class season, discounting MCC v Durham in Abu Dhabi, which began five days before and included two hundreds.) Peter Turnbull, a tall medium-pacer from Pontypridd took a maiden five-for. Nine batsmen from Cambridge MCC University – the team suffixes had been changed from "UCCE" to reflect MCC's sponsorship of university cricket – reached double figures in the first innings, but only Adam Wheater, the Essex reserve wicketkeeper, made a half-century. Brown and Harinath extended Surrey's lead before a declaration set Cambridge an unlikely 244 in just over a session.

Close of play: First day, Surrey 326-5 (Davies 94, Batty 59); Second day, Cambridge MCCU 212-8 (Lotay 24, Turnbull 1).

Surrey

A. Harinath c Gray b Turnbull	3	– (2) not out	50
M. J. Brown lbw b Turnbull	17	– (1) c Gray b Turnbull	47
M. N. W. Spriegel lbw b Turnbull	35		
U. Afzaal b Woolley	66		
*R. J. Hamilton-Brown c Lotay b Hopkins	36		
†S. M. Davies not out	122		
G. J. Batty lbw b Turnbull	67		
S. C. Meaker lbw b Woolley	18		
T. M. Jewell not out	4		
B 1, l-b 4, n-b 12	17	L-b 6, n-b 2	8

1/15 (1) 2/28 (2) (7 wkts dec, 83 overs) 385   1/105 (1) (1 wkt dec, 27.2 overs) 105
3/124 (3) 4/162 (4)
5/183 (5) 6/338 (7) 7/378 (8)

T. E. Linley and J. W. Dernbach did not bat.

Woolley 20-1-110-1; Turnbull 27-9-92-5; Hopkins 14-3-66-1; Park 6-0-36-0; Brown 12-0-45-0; Lotay 4-0-31-0. *Second Innings*—Woolley 7-0-26-0; Turnbull 13.2-2-40-1; Hopkins 7-0-33-0.

Cambridge MCCU

A. S. Ansari lbw b Dernbach	20	– not out	26
A. J. P. Joslin lbw b Linley	1	– c Davies b Dernbach	11
S. K. Gray b Linley	22	– not out	19
†A. J. Wheater c Batty b Dernbach	52		
*N. T. Lee b Dernbach	7		
F. A. Brown lbw b Jewell	30		
J. D. S. Lotay not out	34		
R. J. J. Woolley lbw b Meaker	17		
C. M. Park lbw b Hamilton-Brown	13		
P. T. Turnbull lbw b Dernbach	12		
C. E. H. Hopkins b Batty	14		
B 3, l-b 11, w 5, n-b 6	25	L-b 1, w 1	2

1/10 (2) 2/47 (3) 3/49 (1) 4/63 (5) (91.2 overs) 247   1/23 (2) (1 wkt, 19 overs) 58
5/135 (6) 6/152 (4) 7/185 (8)
8/209 (9) 9/228 (10) 10/247 (11)

Dernbach 21–6–42–4; Linley 23–9–41–2; Meaker 18–3–58–1; Jewell 10–2–31–1; Batty 14.2–3–44–1; Hamilton-Brown 5–0–17–1. *Second Innings—*Dernbach 5–3–4–1; Meaker 4–1–29–0; Batty 4–1–14–0; Linley 5–3–5–0; Afzaal 1–0–5–0.

Umpires: P. K. Baldwin and D. J. Millns.

At Derby, April 3–5. DERBYSHIRE v LOUGHBOROUGH MCCU. Abandoned.

DURHAM MCCU v LANCASHIRE

At Durham, April 3–5. Abandoned.
   Persistent bad weather meant the match was called off on April 1.

At Chelmsford, April 3–5. LEEDS/BRADFORD MCCU drew with ESSEX.

At Bristol, April 3–5. CARDIFF MCCU drew with GLOUCESTERSHIRE.

OXFORD MCCU v NORTHAMPTONSHIRE

At Oxford, April 3–5. Drawn. Toss: Oxford MCCU. First-class debuts: S. S. Agarwal, D. O. Conway, B. R. W. Stebbings; T. Brett, V. Tripathi.
   Rain permitted only 81 overs over the first two days, sentencing the match to a draw, although one notable aspect was Northamptonshire's reversal of the counties' usual inclination to treat these fixtures as batting practice. In their only lengthy warm-up match ahead of their opening Championship game, they spent the majority of the time in the field. After Vishal Tripathi made a half-century on debut, Eddie Abel and Ed Young – the brother of the 2007 and 2008 Oxford captain Peter – hit maiden fifties for the students, who went into the lead by 76. Jasper Davies, a 17-year-old from Rushden Town CC, was allowed to keep wicket for Northamptonshire on the final day after an injury to Paul Harrison.
   Close of play: First day, Northamptonshire 72-3 (Loye 8, White 2); Second day, Oxford MCCU 34-1 (Abel 11, Sharma 1).

Northamptonshire

S. D. Peters c Young b Sharma	24	V. Tripathi not out	55
†P. W. Harrison c Martin b Conway	11	B 7, l-b 2, w 2, n-b 10	21
M. B. Loye not out	42		
A. G. Wakely lbw b Milligan	13	1/26 (2) 2/45 (1) (4 wkts dec, 65 overs)	168
*R. A. White c Watson b Conway	2	3/68 (4) 4/81 (5)	

D. J. Willey, D. S. Lucas, J. A. Brooks, L. M. Daggett and T. Brett did not bat.

Conway 21–8–36–2; Milligan 15.2–4–49–1; Bradshaw 9–2–17–0; Sharma 9–3–14–1; Agarwal 7–1–29–0; Young 1–1–0–0; Watson 3–0–14–0.

Oxford MCCU

E. Abel c Wakely b Brooks	60	S. S. Agarwal not out	1
*J. Martin c White b Brooks	22	B 11, l-b 4, w 1	16
R. Sharma lbw b Brooks	1		
D. P. Bradshaw b Lucas	34	1/29 (2) 2/35 (3) (5 wkts dec, 94 overs)	244
E. G. C. Young b Willey	79	3/123 (4) 4/125 (1)	
†R. G. Coughtrie not out	31	5/241 (5)	

M. J. C. Watson, M. J. Milligan, D. O. Conway and B. R. W. Stebbings did not bat.

Daggett 18–1–49–0; Lucas 18–5–45–1; Brooks 22–7–33–3; Brett 17–6–38–0; Willey 15–5–47–1; Tripathi 4–0–17–0.

Umpires: M. J. D. Bodenham and S. J. Malone.

DURHAM MCCU v NOTTINGHAMSHIRE

At Durham, April 10–12. Drawn. Toss: Nottinghamshire. First-class debuts: L. A. Blackaby, L. E. Durandt, D. C. A. Newton, L. A. Patel, C. G. W. Roper. County debuts: H. M. Amla, N. J. Edwards.

Nottinghamshire, fielding a strong team that included their new overseas signing Hashim Amla, gave an inexperienced Durham side a torrid first day in the field, running up 505 in 108 overs, led by centuries from Shafayat and Wagh, who put on 200. The students responded in kind, if more sedately, batting throughout the next day; Greg Smith, who had played ten Championship matches for Leicestershire, reached a maiden first-class hundred, hitting 13 fours and four sixes. He was captaining Durham in place of Tom Westley, playing for Essex at Chelmsford. Nottinghamshire came close to an entire reversal of their batting order in the second innings; Franks began his successful experiment as an opening batsman and scored 114 in 97 balls, including 19 fours, as they took their lead back to 505 before a token declaration.

Close of play: First day, Nottinghamshire 505-5 (Brown 37, Read 16); Second day, Durham MCCU 272-9 (Gale 22, Glover 0).

Nottinghamshire

N. J. Edwards c Morgan b Glover	23	– st Morgan b Gale	43
B. M. Shafayat c Roper b Gale	159		
M. A. Wagh c Durandt b Waters	100		
H. M. Amla lbw b Glover	86		
S. R. Patel b Gale	72	– c Gale b Waters	37
A. D. Brown not out	37	– (8) not out	21
*†C. M. W. Read not out	16	– (4) c Glover b Gale	13
P. J. Franks (did not bat)		– (2) b Harper	114
L. J. Fletcher (did not bat)		– (3) c Waters b Roper	15
D. J. Pattinson (did not bat)		– (6) lbw b Harper	8
R. J. Sidebottom (did not bat)		– (7) not out	22
B 5, l-b 3, w 2, n-b 2	12	B 1, l-b 9, w 6, n-b 2	18

1/40 (1) 2/240 (3)   (5 wkts dec, 108 overs) 505   1/102 (1)   (6 wkts dec, 50 overs) 291
3/317 (2) 4/451 (5)   2/145 (3) 3/170 (4)
5/453 (4)   4/216 (2) 5/226 (6) 6/242 (5)

Glover 19–5–82–2; Roper 19–0–114–0; Harper 25–0–117–0; Gale 31–1–126–2; Waters 13–3–47–1; Blackaby 1–0–11–0. *Second Innings*—Glover 10–1–33–0; Harper 12–0–89–2; Roper 13–2–74–1; Gale 12–0–67–2; Waters 3–0–18–1.

Durham MCCU

S. R. Waters c Edwards b Fletcher	18	– c Shafayat b Franks	4
L. E. Durandt c Edwards b Sidebottom	14	– not out	20
*G. P. Smith c Read b Sidebottom	114	– not out	29
D. C. A. Newton lbw b Sidebottom	0		
L. A. Blackaby c Shafayat b Pattinson	38		
L. A. Patel c Shafayat b Patel	26		
†C. F. D. Morgan lbw b Fletcher	16		
G. M. Harper lbw b Pattinson	3		
D. J. Gale c Brown b Patel	37		
C. G. W. Roper lbw b Fletcher	0		
J. C. Glover not out	4		
L-b 12, w 1, n-b 8	21		

1/34 (1) 2/52 (2) 3/56 (4)   (103 overs) 291   1/8 (1)   (1 wkt, 16 overs) 53
4/138 (5) 5/223 (6) 6/238 (8) 7/241 (8)
8/266 (7) 9/272 (10) 10/291 (9)

Sidebottom 18–4–48–3; Pattinson 16–5–52–2; Fletcher 20–8–39–3; Patel 29–8–77–2; Franks 18–3–59–0; Brown 2–0–4–0. *Second Innings*—Franks 6–1–24–1; Fletcher 5–1–16–0; Patel 5–1–13–0.

Umpires: M. A. Gough and N. A. Mallender.

At Canterbury, April 10–12. LOUGHBOROUGH MCCU drew with KENT.

At Taunton Vale, April 10–12. CARDIFF MCCU lost to SOMERSET by 385 runs.

OXFORD MCCU v HAMPSHIRE

At Oxford, April 15–17. Drawn. Toss: Hampshire. First-class debuts: A. M. Bates, C. P. Wood.

Oxford tried eight bowlers, but could not prevent Hampshire – for whom the Test batsmen Carberry and McKenzie put on 221 in 53 overs – gambolling beyond 400 on the first day. A dogged 265-minute innings from captain Jak Martin, who shared a similarly adhesive stand of 124 with Duncan Bradshaw, kept Hampshire at arm's length until 19-year-old left-arm seamer Chris Wood broke the students' resistance by taking five wickets on first-class debut. A declaration midway through the final day set Oxford 339 and a county victory looked likely at 85 for six, 11 overs after tea, before Sam Agarwal dug in for 80 minutes, in concert with David Smith for the last half-hour.

Close of play: First day, Oxford MCCU 11-1 (Martin 3, Watson 1); Second day, Hampshire 28-1 (Dawson 17, Ervine 6).

Hampshire

M. A. Carberry c Smith b Bradshaw	164	
L. A. Dawson c Coughtrie b Conway	32	– (1) c Coughtrie b Bradshaw 86
N. D. McKenzie not out	141	
C. C. Benham c Coughtrie b Bradshaw	5	– (2) c Young b Bradshaw 5
J. M. Vince not out	46	– (4) not out 50
*S. M. Ervine (did not bat)		– (3) c Agarwal b Conway 32
†A. M. Bates (did not bat)		– (5) not out 0
L-b 6, n-b 10	16	B 3 3

1/72 (2) 2/293 (1)   (3 wkts dec, 92.3 overs) 404   1/13 (2)   (3 wkts dec, 47.5 overs) 176
3/303 (4)   2/62 (3) 3/168 (1)

H. Riazuddin, C. P. Wood, D. J. Balcombe and D. R. Briggs did not bat.

Conway 22–3–92–1; Milligan 17–2–84–0; Sharma 12–3–48–0; Agarwal 14–1–53–0; Young 11–1–52–0; Bradshaw 13–2–45–2; Watson 3–0–19–0; Smith 0.3–0–5–0. *Second Innings—* Milligan 10–4–26–0; Conway 11–2–41–1; Bradshaw 10–1–41–2; Agarwal 4–0–21–0; Sharma 8.5–0–22–0; Young 4–0–22–0.

Oxford MCCU

B. R. W. Stebbings c Bates b Wood	7	
*J. Martin c Dawson b Briggs	81	– c Benham b Ervine 10
M. J. C. Watson c Bates b Balcombe	4	– (7) b Wood 0
R. Sharma lbw b Balcombe	0	– (3) c Bates b Balcombe 21
D. P. Bradshaw c Bates b Riazuddin	63	– (4) c Bates b Riazuddin 19
E. G. C. Young c Benham b Wood	60	– (5) b Briggs 28
†R. G. Coughtrie b Wood	3	– (1) lbw b Wood 0
S. S. Agarwal lbw b Wood	0	– (6) not out 16
D. T. Smith c Benham b Ervine	4	– (8) not out 12
M. J. Milligan b Wood	3	
D. O. Conway not out	0	
L-b 8, w 1, n-b 8	17	B 1, l-b 2, n-b 2 5

1/7 (1) 2/30 (3) 3/34 (4) 4/158 (5)   (93.1 overs) 242   1/0 (1) 2/31 (3)   (6 wkts, 39 overs) 111
5/179 (2) 6/200 (7) 7/200 (8)   3/45 (4) 4/53 (4)
8/230 (9) 9/241 (10) 10/242 (6)   5/84 (5) 6/85 (7)

Balcombe 23–9–54–2; Wood 20.1–7–54–5; Briggs 12–3–20–1; Riazuddin 11–4–29–1; Ervine 10–2–26–1; Dawson 12–2–42–0; Carberry 4–2–9–0; Vince 1–1–0–0. *Second Innings*—Wood 10–1–30–2; Balcombe 9–1–37–1; Ervine 7–1–24–1; Riazuddin 2–2–0–1; Briggs 7–3–12–1; Dawson 3–2–4–0; Carberry 1–0–1–0.

Umpires: N. L. Bainton and V. A. Holder.

At Kidderminster, April 15–17. LEEDS/BRADFORD MCCU lost to WORCESTERSHIRE by 250 runs.

CAMBRIDGE MCCU v LEICESTERSHIRE

At Cambridge, April 21–23. Drawn. Toss: Leicestershire. First-class debuts: B. J. Ackland, R. L. Hesketh.

Another impressive new-ball spell from Turnbull allowed Cambridge to claim Leicestershire's first three wickets for 47. But the students were frustrated by a partnership of 132 between Taylor and du Toit, who struck a career-best 154. Adam Wheater and Rob Woolley – who faced 62 balls and hit ten fours – both made 55, but the rest of Cambridge's batting underachieved as they trailed by 212. That was increased to a distant 497, Jefferson scoring 101 in his 151-run opening stand with Naik before retiring. The students lost only one wicket in the 45 overs possible and held on comfortably. Ben Ackland, born in Nuneaton but an Ireland Under-19 batsman, took three hours over his maiden fifty.

Close of play: First day, Leicestershire 411-7 (Naik 48, Malik 35); Second day, Leicestershire 151-0 (Jefferson 101, Naik 45).

Leicestershire

*W. I. Jefferson c Wheater b Turnbull	23	– retired hurt	101
M. A. G. Boyce b Turnbull	11		
J. J. Cobb lbw b Turnbull	1	– not out	55
J. W. A. Taylor lbw b Hopkins	56		
J. du Toit lbw b Brown	154	– (4) lbw b Brown	0
†T. J. New lbw b Woolley	12	– (5) not out	44
W. A. White c Hesketh b Brown	48		
J. K. H. Naik not out	48	– (2) c Park b Brown	72
M. N. Malik not out	35		
B 4, l-b 3, w 1, n-b 15	23	B 2, l-b 3, w 2, n-b 6	13

1/24 (2) 2/28 (3) (7 wkts dec, 98 overs) 411   1/205 (2) (2 wkts dec, 62 overs) 285
3/47 (1) 4/179 (4) 5/212 (6) 6/317 (7) 7/318 (5)   2/205 (4)

S. J. Cliff and H. F. Gurney did not bat.

In the second innings Jefferson retired hurt at 151.

Woolley 23–3–83–1; Turnbull 24–4–97–3; Hopkins 21–3–97–1; Park 9–0–53–0; Ansari 2–1–4–0; Brown 19–0–70–2. *Second Innings*—Turnbull 15–3–35–0; Woolley 12–0–61–0; Hopkins 8–2–48–0; Park 10–0–37–0; Brown 14–0–79–2; Hesketh 2–0–17–0; Ackland 1–0–3–0.

Cambridge MCCU

†A. J. Wheater c White b Gurney	55	– c sub (A. C. F. Wyatt) b Gurney	19
B. J. Ackland c Naik b Cliff	0	– not out	51
S. K. Gray c du Toit b Malik	8	– not out	35
*N. T. Lee c Cobb b Naik	39		
F. A. Brown c New b White	0		
C. M. Park c New b Naik	6		
R. L. Hesketh c New b White	1		
R. J. J. Woolley not out	55		
P. T. Turnbull c New b Naik	0		
A. S. Ansari b Naik	4		
C. E. H. Hopkins c du Toit b Malik	8		
B 7, l-b 4, w 8, n-b 4	23	B 5, l-b 4, n-b 2	11

1/4 (2) 2/31 (3) 3/82 (1) 4/92 (5) (61.2 overs) 199   1/33 (1) (1 wkt, 45 overs) 116
5/128 (4) 6/129 (7) 7/135 (6)
8/135 (9) 9/178 (10) 10/199 (11)

Malik 16.2–3–50–2; Cliff 12–4–29–1; Gurney 12–5–32–1; White 10–0–53–2; Naik 11–4–24–4. *Second Innings*—Malik 10–1–28–0; Cliff 9–2–25–0; Gurney 8–2–24–1; White 8–2–14–0; Naik 8–4–9–0; Cobb 2–1–7–0.

Umpires: M. A. Gough and G. D. Lloyd.

DURHAM MCCU v DURHAM

At Durham, May 5–7. Drawn. Toss: Durham. First-class debut: M. J. Richardson.

Stoneman's century – his first since September 2007 – prevented potential embarrassment for the County Champions at the hands of the local student side, enjoying their finest season for several years. Westley returned to lead Durham MCCU, and took four wickets with his off-spin, as did slow left-armer Dan Gale. Seren Waters, who had played one-day internationals for Kenya, and Luc Durandt began the reply with assurance. But rain washed out the second day, and vandals then ripped the covers during the night, ending any chance of play on the last.

Close of play: First day, Durham MCCU 46-0 (Waters 25, Durandt 19); Second day, No play.

Durham

M. D. Stoneman b Westley	118	M. Davies c Atkinson b Gale	0
K. J. Coetzer lbw b Roper	22	S. J. Harmison c Waters b Gale	7
*W. R. Smith c Morgan b Gale	57	L. Evans not out	4
G. J. Muchall c Morgan b Westley	12	B 1, l-b 6, w 8, n-b 6	21
B. W. Harmison lbw b Gale	21		
G. R. Breese c Morgan b Westley	14	1/42 (2) 2/169 (3) (93.3 overs) 324
S. G. Borthwick c Harper b Westley	46	3/227 (1) 4/228 (4) 5/248 (6) 6/284 (5)
†M. J. Richardson run out	2	7/291 (8) 8/298 (9) 9/314 (10) 10/324 (7)

Glover 16–2–65–0; Roper 10–1–61–1; Harper 12–1–42–0; Gale 35–7–94–4; Westley 20.3–5–55–4.

Durham MCCU

S. R. Waters not out	25
L. E. Durandt not out	19
N-b 2	2
(no wkt, 16 overs)	46

*T. Westley, G. P. Smith, L. A. Blackaby, †J. J. Atkinson, C. F. D. Morgan, G. M. Harper, D. J. Gale, C. G. W. Roper and J. C. Glover did not bat.

S. J. Harmison 5–1–18–0; Davies 3–2–9–0; Evans 2–0–11–0; Breese 3–1–5–0; Borthwick 3–1–3–0.

Umpires: N. G. B. Cook and G. D. Lloyd.

At Cardiff, May 5–7. CARDIFF MCCU lost to GLAMORGAN by 215 runs.

At Weetwood, Leeds, May 10–12 (not first-class). **Drawn.** ‡Leeds/Bradford MCCU **108** (S. A. Piolet 3-28) **and 250-5 dec** (B. T. Slater 100*, D. A. Clarke 34, J. A. Hawley 48; K. H. D. Barker 3-21); **Warwickshire 180** (V. Chopra 40, D. L. Maddy 37, A. G. Botha 40, R. M. Johnson 31; A. C. Williamson 3-21) **and 111-6** (V. Chopra 33, A. G. Botha 63*; A. C. Williamson 6-59). *Left-hander Ben Slater batted over five and a half hours for his century. Warwickshire were set 179 to win in the final session, but Darren Maddy and James Ord were both out for ducks as slow left-armer Craig Williamson (who, like Slater, had played for Derbyshire Second Eleven) took all six wickets to fall.*

At Leeds, May 10–12. LOUGHBOROUGH MCCU drew with YORKSHIRE.

CAMBRIDGE MCCU v SUSSEX

At Cambridge, May 12–14. Sussex won by 84 runs. Toss: Cambridge MCCU. First-class debuts: P. H. Hughes, M. H. Taylor; M. S. Chadwick, L. J. Hatchett, M. W. Machan.

Rob Woolley's medium-pace caused Sussex early alarms, reducing them to 24 for three, though an unbeaten century from Joyce underpinned a strong revival. Nash's declaration paid immediate dividends, as Cambridge lost five quick wickets before Craig Park (brother of Derbyshire all-rounder Garry) organised a recovery. Sussex built hastily on their lead of 96, with wicketkeeper Ben Brown reaching his maiden first-class hundred shortly before a second declaration set Cambridge 350 to win in more than a day. They lost Akbar Ansari second ball, but resisted stoutly until after tea, despite Rayner bowling skilfully to add to his pair of half-centuries. Nick Lee survived for 108 balls before becoming Joe Gatting's maiden victim in senior cricket.

Close of play: First day, Cambridge MCCU 84-5 (Park 18, Ashok 15); Second day, Cambridge MCCU 25-1 (Hughes 7, Ackland 15).

Sussex

†B. C. Brown c Park b Woolley	1	– (2) not out	110
*C. D. Nash lbw b Woolley	4	– (1) c Ashok b Turnbull	18
E. C. Joyce not out	135	– b Woolley	13
J. S. Gatting b Woolley	0	– c Ashok b Lotay	31
M. W. Machan c Ackland b Park	6	– c Gray b Park	5
O. P. Rayner b Lotay	54	– not out	67
R. G. Aga not out	66		
B 2, l-b 3, n-b 6	11	B 4, l-b 2, w 1, n-b 2	9

1/1 (1) 2/24 (2) 3/24 (4) (5 wkts dec, 67 overs) 277
4/43 (5) 5/133 (6)

1/19 (1) (4 wkts dec, 61 overs) 253
2/42 (3) 3/105 (4) 4/112 (5)

W. A. T. Beer, J. E. Anyon, M. S. Chadwick and L. J. Hatchett did not bat.

Turnbull 14–3–33–0; Woolley 15–3–73–3; Park 11–1–34–1; Taylor 6–1–39–0; Lotay 18–1–72–1; Ashok 2–0–15–0; Ansari 1–0–6–0. *Second Innings*—Woolley 12–1–41–1; Turnbull 15–1–69–1; Park 13–2–59–1; Lotay 15–2–43–1; Taylor 6–0–35–0.

Cambridge MCCU

A. S. Ansari c Brown b Aga	13	– lbw b Anyon	0
P. H. Hughes lbw b Aga	5	– c and b Rayner	32
B. J. Ackland b Anyon	5	– c Gatting b Rayner	37
†S. K. Gray c Joyce b Hatchett	20	– c Aga b Rayner	27
*N. T. Lee lbw b Chadwick	2	– c Nash b Gatting	63
C. M. Park c Brown b Beer	72	– b Rayner	0
A. Ashok c Brown b Hatchett	24	– c Joyce b Nash	23
R. J. J. Woolley lbw b Rayner	18	– (9) b Hatchett	27
P. T. Turnbull lbw b Beer	0	– (10) c Nash b Hatchett	13
J. D. S. Lotay st Brown b Rayner	4	– (8) lbw b Anyon	5
M. H. Taylor not out	4	– not out	16
B 8, l-b 4, n-b 2	14	B 7, l-b 14, w 1	22

1/20 (2) 2/21 (1) 3/32 (3) 4/51 (4) (57.5 overs) 181
5/51 (5) 6/123 (7) 7/173 (8)
8/173 (6) 9/173 (9) 10/181 (10)

1/0 (1) 2/65 (2) (97.2 overs) 265
3/92 (3) 4/119 (4)
5/119 (6) 6/191 (5) 7/197 (7)
8/206 (8) 9/248 (9) 10/265 (10)

Anyon 15–2–40–1; Aga 13–4–29–2; Hatchett 10–3–28–2; Chadwick 9–1–41–1; Rayner 5.5–1–16–2; Beer 5–0–15–2. *Second Innings*—Anyon 20–10–31–2; Aga 14–5–32–0; Chadwick 10–1–33–0; Rayner 24–5–62–4; Beer 13–4–35–0; Gatting 5–2–19–1; Nash 7–2–11–1; Hatchett 4.2–1–21–2.

Umpires: S. J. Malone and J. F. Steele.

OXFORD MCCU v MIDDLESEX

At Oxford, May 25–27. Middlesex won by 101 runs. Toss: Middlesex. First-class debuts: M. R. Barnard, A. F. Jeavons, S. J. V. Watkins; J. H. Davey, T. R. G. Hampton, R. H. Patel, S. W. Poynter, T. S. Roland-Jones, A. M. Rossington, K. S. Toor.

With their first-team squad gearing up for the Friends Provident T20 by playing Berkshire, Middlesex fielded seven debutants, which made for an evenly matched encounter. Two of those with first-class experience prospered with the bat: Robson made an accomplished 204, with 27 fours, putting on 192 with Aberdeen-born newcomer Josh Davey, then 175 with Dan Housego, who called a halt when he reached his maiden century. Aaron Jeavons led a competent Oxford reply before they declared 122 behind. With the notable exception of Davey, Middlesex found it hard going against Dan Pascoe's left-arm spin, though their lead of 308 with two sessions remaining was more than sufficient. Jak Martin composed a spirited 65, but the students never threatened an upset.

Close of play: First day, Oxford MCCU 36-0 (Stebbings 25, Jeavons 11); Second day, Middlesex 70-2 (Davey 40, Toor 15).

Middlesex

J. H. Davey run out	72	– c Martin b Pascoe	54
S. D. Robson c Milligan b Conway	204	– (6) c and b Pascoe	18
*D. M. Housego not out	102	– (5) c and b Pascoe	6
A. B. London not out	7	– (2) b Sharma	10
A. M. Rossington (did not bat)		– (3) c Coughtrie b Conway	1
K. S. Toor (did not bat)		– (4) b Pascoe	15
†S. W. Poynter (did not bat)		– c Jeavons b Barnard	42
T. S. Roland-Jones (did not bat)		– c Milligan b Pascoe	15
D. Evans (did not bat)		– c and b Pascoe	0
R. H. Patel (did not bat)		– not out	19
T. R. G. Hampton (did not bat)		– not out	1
B 9, l-b 3, n-b 2	14	L-b 1, n-b 4	5

1/192 (1) 2/367 (2)   (2 wkts dec, 96.1 overs) 399

1/20 (2)   (9 wkts dec, 65 overs) 186
2/31 (3) 3/70 (4)
4/78 (5) 5/106 (6) 6/109 (1)
7/139 (8) 8/141 (9) 9/184 (7)

Conway 13–1–56–1; Barnard 14.1–3–50–0; Sharma 13–1–47–0; Milligan 10–0–46–0; Pascoe 21–3–74–0; Watson 11–0–50–0; Watkins 14–1–64–0. *Second Innings*—Barnard 8–4–14–1; Sharma 9–2–25–1; Conway 9–3–24–1; Pascoe 22–4–68–6; Watson 14–2–45–0; Watkins 3–0–9–0.

Oxford MCCU

B. R. W. Stebbings lbw b Evans	25	– b Roland-Jones	12
A. F. Jeavons c Poynter b Patel	62	– c Poynter b Hampton	4
R. Sharma c Rossington b Patel	44	– c Poynter b Davey	36
*J. Martin run out	17	– c Roland-Jones b Patel	65
†R. G. Coughtrie c Robson b London	43	– (6) b Patel	7
M. J. C. Watson c Robson b Patel	0	– (7) b Toor	22
D. C. Pascoe not out	31	– (8) not out	33
S. J. V. Watkins not out	46	– (5) b Davey	8
M. J. Milligan (did not bat)		– run out	4
D. O. Conway (did not bat)		– c Davey b Roland-Jones	6
M. R. Barnard (did not bat)		– lbw b Evans	0
B 1, l-b 5, w 1, n-b 2	9	B 2, l-b 6, n-b 2	10

1/36 (1) 2/124 (3)   (6 wkts dec, 88 overs) 277

1/15 (1) 2/17 (2)   (64.5 overs) 207
3/140 (4) 4/156 (4)
5/156 (6) 6/224 (5)
3/96 4/104 (5)
5/125 (6) 6/147 (3) 7/172 (7)
8/184 (9) 9/198 (10) 10/207 (11)

Evans 13–3–59–1; Roland-Jones 14–3–46–0; Hampton 7–1–27–0; Davey 5–0–24–0; Patel 25–7–52–3; Toor 16–2–48–0; London 8–3–15–1. *Second Innings*—Evans 7.5–2–14–1; Roland-Jones 10–4–11–2; Hampton 7–2–15–1; Patel 22–1–82–2; Toor 9–0–36–1; Davey 9–0–41–2.

Umpires: V. A. Holder and J. S. Wilson.

THE UNIVERSITY MATCHES, 2010

At Oxford, June 4 (not first-class). **Oxford University won by 53 runs. ‡Oxford University 178-2** (20 overs) (D. A. King 41, S. S. Agarwal 88, R. Sharma 33*); **Cambridge University 125** (18.4 overs) (F. A. Brown 38; D. C. Pascoe 3-7). *Sam Agarwal hit 88 in 58 balls for Oxford, who recorded their first victory in the Twenty20 Varsity Match: Cambridge won the first, in 2008, while the second was a no result.*

At Lord's, July 4 (not first-class). **Cambridge University won by five wickets. Oxford University 270-9** (50 overs) (A. S. Sharma 51, N. A. Meadows 67, D. C. Pascoe 42); **‡Cambridge University 271-5** (47.5 overs) (A. Ashok 34, A. S. Ansari 54, M. C. Rosenberg 61, F. A. Brown 37*). *A fourth-wicket stand of 99 in 15 overs between Akbar Ansari and the Johannesburg-born former Leicestershire batsman Marc Rosenberg set up Cambridge's victory, although both were out in quick succession. Frankie Brown and Gus Kennedy (29*) then added 64* in less than seven overs. Oxford had been 142-5 before the Australian pair of Nick Meadows (who went to 50 in 41 balls) and Dan Pascoe delivered a strong target through a 112-run partnership. Cambridge reduced Oxford's lead to 9–7 in the one-day Varsity series.*

OXFORD UNIVERSITY v CAMBRIDGE UNIVERSITY

At Oxford, July 6–9. Oxford University won by an innings and 28 runs. Toss: Oxford University. First-class debuts: J. A. Lodwick, N. A. Meadows, A. J. D. Scott, A. S. Sharma; D. M. Goodwin, J. M. Greenwood, A. D. J. Kennedy.

The Varsity Match was a delight for statisticians, and a nightmare for Light Blue supporters. Raj Sharma won the toss on what looked to be a batsman's paradise – and it was, as Dan King and Sam Agarwal demonstrated by sprinting to 259 in just 56 overs, eclipsing Oxford's record opening stand against Cambridge, the 243 between Kingsmill Key and William Rashleigh at Lord's in 1886. When the persistent Irish leg-spinner Michael Taylor finally broke through, King and Avinash Sharma – one of seven players making their first-class debut in the match – piled on a further 149 before King fell in the evening, after hitting 25 fours. Oxford declared before lunch on the second day in an impregnable position. Dan Pascoe, a postgraduate criminology student from Canberra, took his five wickets in a ten-over spell, while his spin partner, the Hong Kong-born Alex Scott, picked up four with his leg-breaks. Cambridge followed on 368 in arrears despite Phil Hughes's resolute 74, and although Hughes again stood defiant, putting on 168 with Anand Ashok, Oxford's spinners had the last word. Scott took four more wickets, while Sam Agarwal claimed five with his off-breaks as Oxford won on the final afternoon.

Close of play: First day, Oxford University 475-2 (A. S. Sharma 124, Kruger 28); Second day, Cambridge University 191-4 (Owen 24, Kennedy 9); Third day, Cambridge University 227-2 (Hughes 83, Hesketh 8).

Oxford University

†D. A. King c Kennedy b Taylor	189	N. A. Meadows c Greenwood b Taylor	38
S. S. Agarwal lbw b Taylor	117	B 14, l-b 2, w 5, n-b 2, p 5	28
A. S. Sharma not out	185		
N. Kruger c Timms b Taylor	48	1/259 (2) (5 wkts dec, 129.5 overs)	611
*R. Sharma c Kennedy b Goodwin	6	2/408 (1) 3/522 (4) 4/539 (5) 5/611 (6)	

D. C. Pascoe, T. E. Bryan, J. A. Lodwick, A. J. D. Scott and L. A. Dingle did not bat.

Goodwin 35–6–142–1; Greenwood 19–1–97–0; Hopkins 11–1–61–0; Ashok 11–2–52–0; Timms 11–0–51–0; Taylor 38.5–3–161–4; Ansari 3–0–22–0; Hesketh 1–0–4–0.

Cambridge University

R. T. Timms lbw b Scott	36	– c King b Agarwal	30
P. H. Hughes c Kruger b Scott	74	– lbw b Scott	87
A. Ashok c Meadows b Scott	17	– c A. S. Sharma b Pascoe	93
R. L. Hesketh lbw b Dingle	17	– c Meadows b Scott	20
F. G. Owen lbw b Pascoe	24	– c King b Scott	9
†A. D. J. Kennedy c Meadows b Pascoe	14	– not out	48
D. M. Goodwin b Pascoe	8	– (8) c A. S. Sharma b Agarwal	18
M. H. Taylor lbw b Pascoe	10	– (9) c R. Sharma b Agarwal	12
C. E. H. Hopkins c Lodwick b Pascoe	5	– (10) lbw b Agarwal	7
J. M. Greenwood not out	23	– (11) c Meadows b Agarwal	1
*A. S. Ansari c Kruger b Scott	1	– (7) c Bryan b Scott	2
W 2, n-b 12	14	L-b 11, n-b 2	13

1/110 (1) 2/128 (3) 3/143 (2)   (103.5 overs) 243
4/169 (4) 5/191 (5) 6/199 (7)
7/206 (6) 8/214 (9) 9/224 (8) 10/243 (11)

1/45 (1) 2/213 (3)   (121.1 overs) 340
3/235 (2) 4/252 (4)
5/261 (5) 6/269 (7) 7/304 (8)
8/324 (9) 9/338 (10) 10/340 (11)

Dingle 13–3–36–1; R. Sharma 13–5–25–0; Agarwal 28–9–68–0; Lodwick 5–1–24–0; Pascoe 30–18–38–5; Scott 14.5–2–52–4. *Second Innings*—Dingle 6–0–37–0; R. Sharma 3–0–7–0; Agarwal 27.1–7–78–5; Lodwick 13–3–36–0; Pascoe 34–12–65–1; Scott 33–6–95–4; Bryan 5–1–11–0.

Umpires: M. R. Benson and S. J. O'Shaughnessy.

This was the 165th University Match, a first-class fixture dating back to 1827. Cambridge have won 57 and Oxford 54, with 54 drawn. It was played at Lord's until 2000.

MCC UNIVERSITIES CHAMPIONSHIP, 2010

	Played	Won	Lost	1st-inns wins	1st-inns losses	Drawn/ no result	Bonus points	Points
Durham	5	0	0	4	0	1	39	83*
Loughborough	5	0	0	3	2	0	26	53.5*
Leeds/Bradford	5	0	0	2	3	0	34	53.5*
Oxford	5	0	0	1	1	3	27	52
Cardiff	5	0	0	1	3	1	32	47
Cambridge	5	0	0	1	3	1	32	47

* *Durham were deducted 1pt for a slow-over-rate; Loughborough were deducted 2.5pts and Leeds/Bradford 0.5pts.*

Outright win = 17pts; 1st-innings win in a drawn match = 10pts; no result on 1st innings = 5pts; abandoned = 5pts. Bonus points were available for batting and bowling.

WINNERS

2001	Loughborough	2005	Loughborough	2009	Leeds/Bradford
2002	Loughborough	2006	Oxford	2010	Durham
2003	Loughborough	2007	Cardiff/Glamorgan		
2004	Oxford	2008	Loughborough		

MCC UNIVERSITIES CHALLENGE FINAL

At Lord's, June 25 (not first-class). **Durham won by 159 runs.** ‡Durham **328-6** (50 overs) (S. R. Waters 111, G. P. Smith 97, Extras 44; P .R. Groves 3-60); **Loughborough 169** (36.5 overs) (P. R. Groves 50; D. J. Gale 5-22, G. M. Harper 3-48). *Durham, who had topped the two-day MCCU table, added an emphatic victory in the one-day challenge final after Seren Waters and Greg Smith put on 193 for the second wicket. Loughborough slipped to 101-9 before No. 11 Peter Groves spanked five sixes and four fours in a 31-ball half-century.*

MCC IN 2010

STEPHEN FAY

Lord's in 2010 was a sombre place, even though it staged three Tests for the first time since 1912. In the quiet of the Pavilion, MCC's management and committee members started to feel anxious about the future, with only one Test to come in 2012.

The closest Lord's came to capacity last summer was England's one-day international against Australia (27,425). Gate receipts from Tests against Bangladesh and Pakistan were almost £3m lower than two Tests in 2009, yet the ECB insisted on a bigger share of the gate. Having substantially outbid Cardiff for a West Indies Test in 2012, MCC were informed that the game would go to Wales to encourage geographical spread. The bidding process has been a commercial success, but no one at the ECB seemed to question whether higher ticket prices might be strangling the golden goose. In February 2011, a group from the Test match grounds, led by MCC chief executive Keith Bradshaw, succeeded in renegotiating the bidding system from the old "blind" auction to packages of set fees from 2013.

Bad news did not kill off enterprise. Under their "Spirit of Cricket" banner, MCC sponsored the entertaining short series between Australia and Pakistan, which produced the extra Test for MCC members. MCC broke even on the Test, but the spot-fixing scandal means a prompt return by Pakistan to Lord's will not be encouraged. In December, MCC's World Cricket Committee offered their own suggestions to combat such vices: amending the Laws to forbid corruption; the legalising of betting markets in India; and most controversially, the use of lie-detector tests, even though evidence obtained from a polygraph is considered inadmissible in most courts of law.

Since MCC share profits with Middlesex from Twenty20 county matches at Lord's, they agreed to help with the cost of hiring Adam Gilchrist, but revenue from five games in 2010 was less than from three in 2009. Moreover, the drama of the domestic one-day final at Lord's was deflated by inept scheduling. MCC's game against the Champion County returns to Abu Dhabi in 2011, where the pink balls will bear a white seam, after some players experienced trouble seeing the green stitching last year.

Preparatory work on the ambitious "Vision for Lord's" development scheme was slowed by the state of the economy. Initially, the idea was to pay for the first stage by selling MCC's share of the land bordering Wellington Road for residential development. But as half this profit would go to Rifkind Levy, who outbid MCC for the land a decade ago, the club is contemplating a more modest, self-financing strategy to increase ground capacity by 3,000. Whatever the outcome, MCC had decided to play a long game.

It is easy to forget that MCC are a cricket club, but they arranged 446 out-matches in 2010, winning 180 and losing 140; 84 were drawn, four tied and 38 abandoned or cancelled. Women's teams scheduled 28 matches, winning 19, losing and drawing three apiece, with three abandoned or cancelled.

From Riverside to desert: the English season starts with Durham's game against MCC at Abu Dhabi.

MCC v DURHAM

DEREK PRINGLE

At Abu Dhabi, March 29–April 1. Durham won by 311 runs. Toss: Durham. First-class debut: B. A. Stokes.

By holding their match against the Champion County under floodlights in Abu Dhabi using a pink cricket ball, MCC shifted three pillars of the first-class game at a stroke. This was only the fifth time a pink ball had been used in first-class cricket (after four matches in the West Indies earlier in the year). It was a cerise Kookaburra, with green stitching, rather than a Dukes of an altogether lighter pink. MCC had borne the cost of development by scientists at Imperial College London of a ball that could be seen clearly by players and spectators (on TV and at the match) for at least 80 overs, and specifically under floodlights. Given the alarming decline in Test crowds in most countries, MCC were keen to see if the trend could be arrested by playing part of the match at night. Their close ties with the Abu Dhabi Cricket Club, owners of the impressive Sheikh Zayed Stadium, provided the perfect laboratory. But if they were hoping for feedback from the public, they were disappointed: no one was there bar a gaggle of about 60 Durham supporters, the parents of a few players and a handful of officials from various cricketing bodies.

The match itself did little to promote this type of pink ball. The first one was used for 90.3 overs, by which point much of the dye had worn off, and the second-division players representing MCC did not put up enough of a fight in their two innings to test subsequent balls rigorously. As in standard one-day "white ball" cricket, the twilight period compromised its visibility. Di Venuto, maker of the season's first hundred, reported problems with seeing the ball's green stitching through the air. "No disrespect to the spinners here, but against the top international spinners, who can turn the ball both ways, if you can't pick up the seam that is going to be pretty hard work," he said. The ICC, based in neighbouring Dubai, sent general manager Dave Richardson, and he too struck a cautious note. "MCC have been great in initiating trials around the world, but before we look at these projects we need to establish, from a scientific point of view, what makes sense," Richardson said. "The [pink] balls that have been developed so far are still a long way off being able to last 80 overs. They just get too dirty. The beauty of the red ball is that it keeps its colour even when it's old."

Durham's victory, in little over three days, suggested a third successive Championship title might be theirs providing the fast bowlers stayed fit. In stifling heat, Di Venuto monopolised the strike, racing to 131 out of 181 before charging Middlebrook in search of a 22nd boundary. Ben Stokes had come and gone for a spunky fifty on debut by the time Coetzer missed a straight one, ending his career-best four-session marathon. MCC were dismal in response: Steve Harmison's fiery opening spell had them six for three and, 297 behind on first innings, they would have been made to follow on had this been a Championship match. Scott Borthwick took the opportunity to experiment with his googlies, claiming eight of MCC's last 14 wickets.

Close of play: First day, Durham 329-3 (Coetzer 123, Blackwell 13); Second day, Durham 7-2 (Smith 4, Blackwell 3); Third day, MCC 156-7 (Murtagh 27, Lewis 32).

Durham

M. J. Di Venuto st Foster b Middlebrook	 131				
K. J. Coetzer lbw b Malan	... 172	– (7) not out	... 52
*W. R. Smith c Newman b Middlebrook	... 13	– (1) b Lewis	... 11
D. M. Benkenstein b Cosker	... 41	– (3) lbw b Kirby	... 0
I. D. Blackwell c Sales b Kirby	... 13	– (4) c Malan b Cosker	... 26
B. A. Stokes c Newman b Middlebrook	... 51	– lbw b Gidman	... 7
†P. Mustard not out	... 23	– (5) c Taylor b Middlebrook	... 50
S. G. Borthwick c Sales b Malan	... 0	– (2) c Foster b Kirby	... 0
C. D. Thorp c and b Malan	... 0	– (8) not out	... 79
M. E. Claydon c Gidman b Malan	... 0		
B 4, l-b 9, n-b 2	... 15	L-b 3	... 3

1/181 (1) 2/203 (3)	(9 wkts dec, 138 overs)	459
3/295 (4) 4/330 (5) 5/411 (6)		
6/457 (2) 7/457 (8) 8/459 (9) 9/459 (10)		

1/0 (2)	(6 wkts dec, 58 overs)	228
2/0 (3) 3/33 (1)		
4/43 (4) 5/74 (6) 6/103 (5)		

S. J. Harmison did not bat.

Lewis 12–3–34–0; Murtagh 19–2–91–0; Kirby 20–7–48–1; Middlebrook 35–4–118–3; Gidman 11–3–36–0; Cosker 29–6–77–1; Malan 6–1–20–4; Taylor 6–0–22–0. *Second Innings*—Murtagh 8–1–28–0; Kirby 6–2–10–2; Lewis 4–0–19–1; Cosker 9–2–19–1; Gidman 4–1–18–1; Middlebrook 8–2–22–1; Malan 12–0–68–0; Taylor 7–0–41–0.

MCC

S. A. Newman lbw b Thorp	... 0	– b Harmison	... 5
D. J. Malan c Borthwick b Thorp	... 41	– c sub (M. D. Stoneman) b Blackwell	... 13
D. J. Sales lbw b Harmison	... 4	– lbw b Blackwell	... 3
J. W. A. Taylor c Mustard b Harmison	... 0	– c Coetzer b Borthwick	... 39
*A. P. R. Gidman c Mustard b Stokes	... 29	– b Blackwell	... 17
†J. S. Foster c and b Thorp	... 26	– lbw b Borthwick	... 6
J. D. Middlebrook not out	... 11	– c Smith b Borthwick	... 9
T. J. Murtagh c Benkenstein b Borthwick	... 21	– not out	... 55
J. Lewis c Di Venuto b Borthwick	... 0	– c Mustard b Blackwell	... 32
D. A. Cosker b Borthwick	... 1	– lbw b Harmison	... 14
S. P. Kirby b Borthwick	... 13	– lbw b Borthwick	... 16
B 4, l-b 8, n-b 4	... 16	B 3, n-b 2	... 5

1/1 (1) 2/6 (3) 3/6 (4) 4/41 (5)	(45.5 overs)	162
5/102 (6) 6/103 (2) 7/132 (8)		
8/132 (9) 9/142 (10) 10/162 (11)		

1/7 (1) 2/16 (3) 3/21 (2)	(59 overs)	214
4/45 (5) 5/74 (6) 6/90 (7)		
7/97 (4) 8/156 (9) 9/179 (10) 10/214 (11)		

Harmison 9–2–37–2; Thorp 10–7–25–3; Claydon 10–3–31–0; Stokes 4–0–14–1; Blackwell 8–2–16–0; Borthwick 4.5–0–27–4. *Second Innings*—Claydon 6–1–22–0; Harmison 11–2–39–2; Blackwell 25–8–70–4; Stokes 5–1–23–0; Borthwick 12–1–57–4.

Umpires: B. Dudleston and R. T. Robinson.

THE MINOR COUNTIES, 2010

PHILIP AUGUST

In autumn 2009, the ECB asked the Minor Counties Cricket Association to organise and fund a team from recreational cricket to fill out their new domestic 40-over competition in 2010. MCCA viewed the Clydesdale Bank 40 – as it became known – as an excellent opportunity for Minor County cricketers and others to pit their wits against first-class opposition. They accepted the invitation, and the Unicorns were born (see page 656).

The former Warwickshire batsman Phil Oliver was appointed coach, and an exhaustive selection process began to draw a squad of players from Minor Counties, ECB Premier Leagues, MCC Young Cricketers and the Universities. Keith Parsons, the ex-Somerset batsman now playing for Cornwall, was appointed captain; apart from him, not a single Unicorn received a fee to play. Former first-class players working in the media predicted a litany of uncompetitive games, but only at Old Trafford in late July were they truly outclassed, and by successfully pursuing 326 to beat Sussex at Arundel, they pulled off the highest run-chase in 40-over cricket.

Though they comfortably lost both the Championship and Trophy finals, Lincolnshire were the Minor County of 2010. They were an abrasive side, applying pressure in the field to batsmen and umpires alike. In Brett Houston, they possessed the leading wicket-taker with 36; from an awkward bustling left-arm style, he went at just 2.42 runs an over from 258.4 overs. Dorset won the Championship after a ten-year gap, while Shropshire's victory in the Knockout Trophy final at Riverside ended a 37-year wait since their only other silverware, the 1973 Championship.

The age profile of all teams continues to fall. Minor County cricket has become a young man's game, in spite of the widely held view that it is a resting place for the old. Most counties produce cricketers for their neighbouring first-class academies, and are always anxious to select them in three-day cricket, though all too often young players are required for 50-over friendlies or age-group cricket for their academy. Surely they would be better served developing their games in a competitive and adult environment.

Minor County cricket provided not only Wes Durston, via Wiltshire, with a path back to the first-class game, but also Tony Palladino, who took 19 wickets in three outings for Suffolk before his recall by Essex. Steve Adshead, released by Gloucestershire in 2009, hit more than 500 runs for Herefordshire, and was playing for Derbyshire by the end of the season.

Dorset headed into the final round of Western Division matches eight points behind Berkshire, but ten wickets for captain Tom Hicks at Bournemouth defeated Wales early on the third day. Dorset's imminent success forced **Berkshire** to declare in their game at Truro, since bonus points alone would not be enough to keep them top. They set **Cornwall** 263 in a day, but lost by three wickets following a fine unbeaten 111 by Tom Sharp. Berkshire badly missed slow left-armer Chris Peploe, who won the Frank Edwards award for his 16 wickets at 11.25, from just two matches, against Herefordshire and Shropshire.

He pipped another left-arm spinner, Dorset's 19-year-old Jack Leach, who, also in two games, took 20 at 11.30, including 13 for 148 on debut against Herefordshire.

Wales, who always field a very young side, went winless throughout the season, as did **Wiltshire**, but **Herefordshire**, after four seasons with the wooden spoon, won twice and finished seventh. **Shropshire's** youthful team came eighth, despite Ed Foster and Chris Murtagh scoring more than 500 runs each, and Andy Gray taking 28 wickets and scoring 318. **Cheshire**, losing finalists in 2009, were twice bowled out cheaply by Dorset in a key game at Bournemouth.

Matthew Thompson, at 18 years and 206 days, became the youngest **Devon** batsman to score a century – 122 against Herefordshire – while Lloyd Sabin became the youngest **Oxfordshire** debutant, at 16 years and 26 days, against Wales at Pontarddulais.

Before the final round began, any of the top four could have won the Eastern Division, though Suffolk held a slender five-point advantage. The contenders were all playing each other, adding further spice. **Lincolnshire** won a vital toss against Bedfordshire at Grantham, bowled them out in damp conditions, with Brett Houston taking eight for 49 in 32.1 overs, and won the match comfortably. That result put Cumberland out of the title race but, in a rain-affected encounter at Sedbergh, they still set **Suffolk** a chase of 383. Suffolk's game attempt ended 49 runs short with one wicket left, and Lincolnshire won the group by nine points.

Cumberland enjoyed a much-improved season under Gary Pratt (once of Durham, and Ricky Ponting run-out fame), who led the way with 542 runs. They suffered considerable bad luck: aside from failing to take Suffolk's last wicket, they drew against Norfolk with the scores level when No. 8 Graham Dawson was run out attempting the vital run, and suffered the only washout of the competition.

Bedfordshire captain Ollie Clayson received the Wilfred Rhodes Trophy for the best batting average, 77.66. Along the way, his half-century inspired his side to chase down 402 and beat **Staffordshire** by two wickets at Luton. In Bedfordshire's next game, against Northumberland, Clayson smashed 147 not out to overhaul a target of 381, also by two wickets. The match was caught up in the police hunt for Raoul Moat, who, after an earlier fatal shooting, injured PC David Rathband at a roundabout in East Denton, a short distance from Benwell Hill CC, on Sunday July 4. Players and officials trying to reach the ground for the first day's play were held up by blockades, police stopped by to use the toilets, and helicopters hovered overhead.

Neither Hertfordshire nor **Buckinghamshire**, the 2009 champions, won a game, though **Hertfordshire**, led by Andy Lewis's 168, fell 19 runs short in a brave chase of 436 at Bedford School. **Cambridgeshire**, whose batting collapsed alarmingly at Bury St Edmunds and Jesmond, won fewer bonus points than anyone and languished in mid-table. **Northumberland** were hamstrung by four draws, but their crushing innings victory over Cambridgeshire did feature the season's only double-hundred, from Gary Scott. No side scored more than **Norfolk's** seven centuries – by Trevor Ward, James Spelman and Sam Arthurton – but they could not summon the same bowling strength, and also drew four.

MINOR COUNTIES CHAMPIONSHIP, 2010

Eastern Division	P	W	L	D	A	Bonus points Batting	Bowling	Total points
Lincolnshire	6	4	1	1	0	15	24	107
Suffolk	6	3	0	3	0	14	24	98
Cumberland	6	2	0	3*	1	13	18	87
Bedfordshire	6	3	2	1	0	13	21	86
Northumberland	6	1	1	4	0	19	24	75
Cambridgeshire	6	2	2	1	1	8	20	72
Norfolk	6	1	1	4	0	16	22	70
Staffordshire	6	1	4	1	0	15	21	56
Buckinghamshire	6	0	2	4	0	15	20	51
Hertfordshire	6	0	4	2	0	13	22	43

Western Division

	P	W	L	D	A	Bonus points Batting	Bonus points Bowling	Total points
Dorset	6	3	0	3	0	17	24	101
Berkshire	6	3	2	1	0	20	22	94
Oxfordshire	6	3	1	2	0	11	24	91
Cheshire	6	3	2	1	0	18	19	89
Cornwall	6	2	0	4	0	12	23	83
Devon	6	2	2	2	0	18	24	80§
Herefordshire	6	2	3	1	0	15	21	72
Shropshire	6	1	3	2	0	13	23	60
Wales	6	0	3	3	0	10	20	40§
Wiltshire	6	0	3	3	0	10	20	40§

Final: Dorset beat Lincolnshire by 135 runs.

Win = 16pts; draw = 4pts; abandoned = 6pts.

* *Cumberland received 8pts batting second against Norfolk in a drawn match with scores level.*
§ *Two points deducted for a slow over-rate.*

LEADING AVERAGES, 2010

BATTING (350 runs in 5 completed innings, average 45.00)

	M	I	NO	R	HS	100s	Avge
O. J. Clayson (*Bedfordshire*)	6	11	2	699	156*	3	77.66
T. G. Sharp (*Cornwall*)	6	8	2	417	114	2	69.50
J. M. Spelman (*Norfolk*)	6	11	1	668	158	3	66.80
D. R. J. Cranfield-Thompson (*Bucks*)	6	9	3	392	100*	1	65.33
T. R. Ward (*Norfolk*)	6	11	1	636	127	4	63.60
J. R. Levitt (*Wiltshire*)	4	8	0	491	112	2	61.37
G. J. Pratt (*Cumberland*)	5	9	0	542	169	2	60.22
R. I. Kaufman (*Oxfordshire*)	5	9	0	535	144	1	59.44
C. P. Murtagh (*Shropshire*)	6	12	3	524	126*	2	58.22
G. M. Scott (*Northumberland*)	6	10	0	579	203	2	57.90
E. J. Foster (*Shropshire*)	5	10	1	519	120	1	57.66
C. W. Boroughs (*Herefordshire*)	6	11	2	509	140*	2	56.55
B. H. D. Mordt (*Berkshire*)	6	10	2	440	106*	1	55.00
J. J. McLean (*Berkshire*)	6	11	1	546	182	2	54.60
J. J. Bess (*Devon*)	6	11	3	426	88*	0	53.25
L. F. Dixon (*Cheshire*)	6	9	0	439	169	1	48.77
Ikramullah (*Cumberland*)	5	9	1	382	107*	1	47.75
B. L. Spendlove (*Cheshire*)	6	11	2	427	136	1	47.44
M. J. Symington (*Northumberland*)	6	10	0	471	122	1	47.10
P. G. Cook (*Lincolnshire*)	7	11	0	513	127	2	46.63
D. F. Lye (*Devon*)	6	10	0	463	165	1	46.30
S. J. Adshead (*Herefordshire*)	6	12	1	507	110	1	46.09

BOWLING (15 wickets at 25.00)

	O	M	R	W	BB	5W/i	Avge
C. T. Peploe (*Berkshire*)	78.5	28	180	16	6-53	2	11.25
M. J. Leach (*Dorset*)	102.3	37	226	20	7-70	3	11.30
L. C. Ryan (*Oxfordshire*)	162.4	43	470	29	6-46	3	16.20
A. L. Osmond (*Lincolnshire*)	160.3	36	460	28	4-39	0	16.42
M. A. Sharp (*Cumberland*)	101	38	281	17	6-78	1	16.52
A. P. Palladino (*Suffolk*)	111	23	321	19	6-69	2	16.89
T. S. Anning (*Devon*)	119.2	36	339	20	5-28	1	16.95
B. W. Houston (*Lincolnshire*)	258.4	79	627	36	8-49	2	17.41
T. C. Hicks (*Dorset*)	184.4	54	474	27	7-54	1	17.55
D. J. Rutherford (*Northumberland*)	145.2	42	311	17	5-42	2	18.29

	O	M	R	W	BB	5W/i	Avge
C. T. Griffiths (*Herefordshire*)	156.4	39	432	23	6-77	2	18.78
M. J. Metcalfe (*Dorset*)	157.2	44	434	22	7-53	1	19.72
T. G. Sharp (*Cornwall*)	101	36	482	23	5-71	1	20.95
A. J. Jones (*Wales*)	117.1	19	409	19	6-55	1	21.52
I. E. Bishop (*Devon*)	197.5	52	555	25	7-74	2	22.20
D. T. Rowe (*Oxfordshire*)	115	27	423	19	6-33	1	22.26
M. J. Symington (*Northumberland*)	249.1	62	740	33	6-61	2	22.42
J. M. Fawcett (*Cheshire*)	135.5	39	364	16	4-35	0	22.75
C. Brown (*Norfolk*)	196.5	46	610	26	4-38	0	23.46
G. R. Willott (*Staffordshire*)	160	37	497	21	6-79	2	23.66
S. F. Stanway (*Buckinghamshire*)	198.1	37	613	25	4-58	0	24.52
C. Bradley (*Devon*)	138.3	35	369	15	6-34	1	24.60
C. R. Griggs (*Bedfordshire*).	163.5	39	568	23	4-54	0	24.69

CHAMPIONSHIP FINAL

At Dean Park, Bournemouth, September 5–8. **Dorset won by 135 runs.** ‡Dorset 245 (80.3 overs) (C. G. W. Morgan 49, G. R. Treagus 80*; A. R. K. Onyon 4-96, B. W. Houston 5-52) **and 262** (94.5 overs) (N. G. Park 33, M. J. Metcalfe 36, E. G. Denham 71, Extras 36), **Lincolnshire 254** (85.3 overs) (V. Atri 118; M. T. C. Waller 4-96) **and 118** (47.2 overs) (L. R. Andrews 35; M. J. Leach 6-21). *Man of the Match:* V. Atri. *Dorset made full use of home advantage by playing two front-line spinners, Jack Leach and Max Waller, both on Somerset's books. The pair took 11 wickets between them, and Leach demolished Lincolnshire in 17.2 overs of slow left-arm on the last day. Dorset were ensured a substantial first innings by No. 4 Glyn Treagus, who stayed unbeaten from 174 balls, but they slipped from 134-2 to 245 against tight bowling from Brett Houston. Vikram Atri played some superb wristy drives on a difficult pitch and, when he was ninth out, a last-wicket stand of 39 helped Lincolnshire scrape a small lead. At the fall of Dorset's seventh wicket they were ahead by just 150, but Matt Metcalfe (forced off the field through a back injury on the first day) and Ed Denham rattled off 82 in 23 overs, leaving Lincolnshire needing to repeat their first-innings score to win, which proved far beyond them.*

RECENT MINOR COUNTIES CHAMPIONS

1985	Cheshire	1995	Devon	2003	Lincolnshire
1986	Cumberland	1996	Devon	2004	{ Bedfordshire
1987	Buckinghamshire	1997	Devon		{ Devon
1988	Cheshire	1998	Staffordshire	2005	{ Cheshire
1989	Oxfordshire	1999	Cumberland		{ Suffolk
1990	Hertfordshire	2000	Dorset	2006	Devon
1991	Staffordshire	2001	{ Cheshire	2007	Cheshire
1992	Staffordshire		{ Lincolnshire	2008	Berkshire
1993	Staffordshire	2002	{ Herefordshire	2009	Buckinghamshire
1994	Devon		{ Norfolk	2010	Dorset

A full list of previous Champions can be found on pages 915–16 of Wisden 2008.

MCCA KNOCKOUT TROPHY FINAL

At Chester-le-Street, August 11. **Shropshire won by seven wickets.** ‡Lincolnshire 249-6 (50 overs) (M. C. Dobson 33, M. P. Dowman 35, P. G. Cook 50, L. R. Andrews 52*, O. E. Burford 30*); **Shropshire 251-3** (44.5 overs) (E. J. Foster 95*, J. D. Whitney 30, J. Leach 67*, Extras 31). *Man of the Match:* E. J. Foster. *Shropshire sent down 16 wides; the usually reliable Lincolnshire attack surpassed them with 24. Lincolnshire never fully recovered from a pedestrian start, even if their unbroken seventh-wicket pair took 77 from the last ten overs. Ed Foster carried his bat while anchoring Shropshire's reply, and put on a decisive 139* with Joseph Leach to secure their county's first MCCA Trophy.*

A full list of previous winners can be found on page 905 of Wisden 2010.

SECOND ELEVEN CHAMPIONSHIP, 2010

Michael Vockins

Second Eleven cricket in 2010 was, again, a mixture of tradition and innovation. Surrey beat Warwickshire by 70 runs in the four-day final, played at Wormsley in early September, to win the Championship. Surrey owed much to a century in each innings from opening batsman Stewart Walters.

The Championship comprised all 18 counties, MCC Young Cricketers and an MCC Universities XI: 20 teams competing in two groups of ten. First-class County Championship playing conditions applied, apart from an increased daily quota of overs (partially compensating for three days' play rather than four). Warwickshire convincingly won the North Division with six wins, Darren Maddy scoring 252 in one of them. Surrey's five – together with a handsome 35 batting points – eased them ahead of Somerset in the South.

In the 50-over Second Eleven Trophy, Essex beat Lancashire by 14 runs to win the final at Chelmsford, having seen off Nottinghamshire and Middlesex respectively in the semi-finals. Mervyn Westfield, the fast bowler under suspicion for spot-fixing in a Pro40 game in 2009, bowled Essex to the title, a month after he had been released from his professional contract.

The major talking point was the introduction of a Knockout Competition of split innings, in which each team's allocation of 40 overs was divided into two phases of 20 – with a pink ball. The idea was not revolutionary: split innings had been proposed before as a way to prevent one-day matches drifting to predictable conclusions. In 2009, the ICC discussed trialling the format at domestic level, and won Sachin Tendulkar's support. "Today, we can tell the result of close to 75% of matches after the toss. We know how conditions will affect the two teams," he said. "(Split innings) are not too dependent on the toss. If it's a day/night match, then both teams will have to bat under lights."

The format generated considerable interest and, sometimes, exciting cricket. However, by season's end the overall reaction was mixed. The extra tactical demands were embraced by some, while others felt that domination of the first half often led to a tedious second. When a side batting first lost early wickets and began to rebuild, their momentum was broken when they reached the 20-over cut-off, so the argument ran. If a team batted well in its first 20, then the second 20 had little relevance.

Sophisticated arrangements for the revision of overs (in the event of weather interruptions) were not seriously tested as the competition was played mostly in good weather. Overall, it was a worthy experiment which, for the moment, will not be continued as the ECB waits on Cricket Australia, and the outcome of their own split-innings venture in the 45-over Ryobi Cup.

The merits of the pink ball were largely confirmed, especially the Kookaburra, which displayed the best characteristics of the white ball. It will be used in Second Eleven Trophy games in 2011, when the season will more closely mirror the first-class game, with the Championship, a Trophy competition of 40 overs, and a midsummer Twenty20 tournament.

SECOND ELEVEN CHAMPIONSHIP, 2010

North Division

	P	W	L	D	Bonus points Bat	Bonus points Bowl	Pen	Total points
Warwickshire (10)	9	6	2	1	23	35	0	157
Durham (4)	9	4	1	4	29	34	0	139
Lancashire (1)	9	5	3	1	25	28	0	136
Leicestershire (8)	9	4	1	4	28	31	0	135
MCC Young Cricketers (7)	9	3	4	2	22	24	0	100
Worcestershire (5)	9	2	3	4	23	28	0	95
Nottinghamshire (3)	9	2	4	3	23	28	0	92
Derbyshire (6)	9	2	5	2	13	35	0	86
Yorkshire (2)	9	2	4	3	18	27	0	86
Glamorgan (9)	9	1	4	4	21	30	0	79

South Division

	P	W	L	D	Bonus points Bat	Bonus points Bowl	Pen	Total points
Surrey (1)	9	5	1	3	35	28	0	152
Somerset (7)	9	5	3	1	25	35	0	143
Gloucestershire (6)	9	4	2	3	26	31	0	130
Sussex (4)	9	4	3	2	24	33	-0.5	126.5
Northamptonshire (9)	9	3	4	2	20	33	0	107
Middlesex (3)	9	2	3	4	32	31	0	107
MCC Universities (10)	9	2	1	6	24	24	0	98
Essex (8)	9	2	2	5	27	26	-3	97
Hampshire (2)	9	1	5	3	19	27	0	71
Kent (5)	9	0	4	5	24	29	0	68

2009 positions are shown in brackets.

Win = 16pts; draw = 3pts.

Essex and Sussex were deducted points for a slow over-rate.

LEADING AVERAGES, 2010

BATTING (400 runs in 6 completed innings, average 45.00)

	M	I	NO	R	HS	100	Avge
M. J. Richardson (*Durham*)	9	13	5	562	159*	2	70.25
K. Turner (*Durham*)	8	14	3	740	137*	3	67.27
M. A. Thornely (*Sussex*)	5	10	1	574	124*	2	63.77
R. J. Burns (*MCCU, Hampshire, Surrey*)	8	11	1	635	166	3	63.50
L. J. Evans (*Surrey, Warwickshire*)	9	15	2	808	186	4	62.15
J. K. Maunders (*Essex*)	5	7	0	423	195	1	60.42
W. M. Goodwin (*Lancashire*)	6	9	2	421	133	2	60.14
T. E. Scollay (*Middlesex*)	7	8	0	478	179	1	59.75
R. I. Newton (*Northamptonshire*)	7	10	1	535	134	2	59.44
N. D. Pinner (*Worcestershire*)	9	17	1	922	164	3	57.62
W. D. Bragg (*Glamorgan*)	6	11	0	630	127	2	57.27
B. A. Godleman (*Essex*)	5	9	1	443	137	2	55.37
A. Harinath (*Surrey*)	5	8	0	428	166	3	53.50
D. P. Bradshaw (*MCCU*)	7	12	3	480	103	1	53.33
J. E. Root (*Yorkshire*)	6	11	1	514	169	2	51.40
S. D. Robson (*Middlesex*)	6	10	2	409	146	1	51.12
J. J. Roy (*Surrey*)	7	12	0	583	180	2	48.58
J. I. Pope (*Leicestershire*)	9	13	1	576	126	2	48.00
R. J. H. Lett (*Somerset*)	7	14	1	608	159	2	46.76
B. C. Brown (*Sussex*)	7	12	0	556	117	2	46.33

BOWLING (20 wickets, average 30.00)

	O	M	R	W	BB	5W/i	Avge
L. M. Daggett (*Northamptonshire*)	101.2	24	287	23	7-29	1	12.47
S. G. Borthwick (*Durham*).	110.5	22	328	21	4-38	0	15.61
C. P. Ashling (*Glamorgan*)	118.3	21	348	22	7-51	1	15.81
W. A. T. Beer (*Sussex*).	97.1	20	319	20	7-48	2	15.95
D. A. Burton (*Surrey, Northamptonshire*) . .	121.3	53	556	32	6-52	3	17.37
S. A. Piolet (*Warwickshire*)	232.5	48	751	43	7-75	4	17.46
S. D. Parry (*Lancashire*).	199.4	30	609	33	6-94	1	18.45
H. F. Gurney (*Leicestershire*).	143.5	37	398	20	3-18	0	19.90
G. S. Randhawa (*Yorkshire*).	231.2	51	645	32	6-98	1	20.15
A. J. Dibble (*Somerset*)	134.2	30	412	20	8-21	1	20.60
J. E. Anyon (*Sussex*).	118.0	17	424	20	5-20	2	21.20
T. W. Allin (*Warwickshire*)	154.5	33	538	24	6-53	1	22.41
R. H. Patel (*Middlesex*)	168.5	25	617	27	6-110	3	22.85
A. S. Welsh (*MCCU*)	147.2	37	507	22	4-73	0	23.04
G. G. White (*Nottinghamshire*)	230.2	59	610	26	6-36	2	23.46
S. P. Cheetham (*Lancashire*)	136.3	25	507	21	5-62	1	24.14
M. T. C. Waller (*Somerset*)	222.0	44	626	25	5-51	1	25.04
G. S. Montgomery (*Lancashire*)	189.4	38	616	22	4-43	0	28.00
C. J. Russell (*Worcestershire*)	208.4	34	732	25	5-56	1	29.28

CHAMPIONSHIP FINAL

At Wormsley, September 7–10. **Surrey won by 70 runs.** ‡**Surrey 369** (110.5 overs) (S. J. Walters 103, Z. S. Ansari 78, Extras 62; A. S. Miller 4-62) **and 263** (81.2 overs) (S. J. Walters 116; P. M. Best 4-93); **Warwickshire 360** (120.3 overs) (J. E. Ord 76, K. H. D. Barker 90, C. S. MacLeod 59; T. E. Linley 6-62) **and 202** (40.2 overs) (J. E. Ord 79).

SECOND ELEVEN TROPHY, 2010

Final

At Chelmsford, September 13. **Essex won by 14 runs.** ‡**Essex 271-9** (50 overs) (B. A. Godleman 43, T. Westley 39, T. J. Phillips 56*, A. S. T. West 36, Extras 36; S. P. Cheetham 3-43, S. D. Parry 3-37); **Lancashire 257** (49.4 overs) (W. M. Goodwin 82, A. P. Agathagelou 53; M. S. Westfield 4-48).

SECOND ELEVEN KNOCKOUT COMPETITION, 2010

Final

At Horsham, June 21. **Sussex won by 137 runs. Sussex 307-7** (40 overs; 141-2 after 20 overs) (M. A. Thornely 102, E. C. Joyce 53, B. C. Brown 93); ‡**Derbyshire 170** (30.2 overs; 111-4 after 20 overs) (W. L. Madsen 97; M. S. Panesar 4-45).

LEAGUE CRICKET, 2010

Geoffrey Dean

It was gratifying that the title of the oldest league in the world, the **Birmingham & District League**, should be clinched on the final day of the season by a superb performance from an English leg-spinner. In a winner-takes-all encounter between Shrewsbury and Kidderminster Victoria, Elliot Green returned the second-best figures by a bowler in the league in 2010, nine for 77, to secure Shrewsbury's first championship. Set 197 to win, home side Kidderminster were bowled out for 159. Green finished with 46 victims, only three behind the league's leading wicket-taker, Barnt Green captain and former England one-day all-rounder Dougie Brown, who also managed 404 runs. Shrewsbury captain Ed Foster was the highest run-scorer in the league with 788.

There was another dramatic last-day finish further up the M6 in the **Cheshire County League**, where Nantwich also won their first title, narrowly pipping Hyde, who had started the final round of matches with a two-point lead. The weather was not kind to them, however, for while Nantwich were charging to 265 for seven from 51 overs to give themselves time to bowl Oxton out, Hyde were frustrated by rain against Bramhall. After the visitors had struggled to 190 for seven from 52 overs, Hyde were left with only 14 overs to get the runs. They finished on 141 for four at 7.50 p.m. The news was conveyed to the jubilant Nantwich team, for whom the New Zealand Test batsman Lou Vincent broke the league record with 1,207 runs in the season. Vincent struck six hundreds, the last being 173, the highest score of the day, against Oxton; he capped an outstanding all-round effort that day by claiming four for 34. Hyde, unbeaten since May 8, had to be content with second place.

York captain Marcus Wood lifted the **Yorkshire Premier League** trophy for the fourth successive season. "We've a good set of young lads who've done very well at key times," he said. "Whenever we've needed to win games, somebody's played a vital part and won it for us. It's been a good team effort with some outstanding individuals." Duncan Snell and Simon Mason both passed 1,000 runs, while slow left-armer Daniel Woods finished with 87 wickets in all competitions, well supported by fellow-spinner Tom Pringle.

Lullington Park became the eighth different club to win the **Derbyshire Premier League** in 11 seasons, while Bourne clinched the **Lincolnshire League** title on the penultimate weekend, thanks to a match-winning nine for 37 from Mark Dixon, as Hartsholme were shot out for 62. Both Preston Nomads in **Sussex** and Sidmouth in **Devon** made it a hat-trick of championships, but St Just's remarkable run of six successive **Cornwall Premier League** titles finally came to an end when Paul beat them by four wickets to become champions for the first time. Ealing were **Middlesex Premier League** champions for a sixth consecutive year.

As Premier League cricket enters its 13th year, the premier family, which has numbered 25 since 2003, has long been comfortable with its size. The only

A declaration of intent

GEOFFREY DEAN

The Surrey Championship, traditionally one of the strongest leagues in the country, is showing signs that it could again nurture the sort of talent that underpinned Surrey's trio of County Championships between 1999 and 2002. Those sides contained a bevy of homegrown players such as Stewart, Thorpe, Butcher, Brown and Ward, as well as the Bicknell and Hollioake brothers. Today's class are not yet as well-known, but Jason Roy and Tom Lancefield are two highly promising products of a league prospering under its new format. Roy conjured the innings of the season when he hammered a 35-ball century for champions Reigate Priory in their win at Wimbledon.

For the first nine years of Premier League cricket, the Surrey Championship played only declaration matches, 120 overs in length with the side batting first unable to go beyond 66 overs. In 2008, however, the Southern Premier League's format was adopted, with 50-over contests occupying the first and last months of the season and declaration cricket sandwiched in between over the longer summer days. The theory was that young players would develop limited-overs skills, and sides needing victories in the final run-in would not be frustrated by draws. Chris Murtagh, the Reigate Priory captain, believed the change had been welcomed by players throughout the league. The start times for some 50-over matches were shifted in 2010 from 11.30 a.m. to 12.30 p.m., so that those games ending soon after 5 p.m. stretched until 6 p.m. or later to ensure club bar takings were not affected.

While certain other leagues have found that too many declaration matches end in draws, those in the Surrey Championship were notable for the high percentage of results. In 2010, no side drew more than two of their nine declaration games, with Reigate, Wimbledon and Banstead winning six. Three sides won two and lost four. Murtagh felt the unusually high number of positive finishes was due not so much to result pitches as to the points system; a win brought 13 points and a losing draw (worked out on run-rate) just one. With a winning draw worth only four points, captains were prepared to risk losing in order to win, declaring earlier.

Andy Packham, the president of the Surrey Championship executive committee, said he could not remember seeing a poor pitch all season. Murtagh, a batsman, felt there was variance in quality of surfaces. "Some clubs have good wickets, some don't," he said. "The fact that lots of bowlers averaged under 20 this year and not many batsmen over 40 suggests the quality of pitches is not quite as good as we'd like. But 50-over games remove the incentive for a club to produce a result pitch." Alex Richards of Reigate still managed to average 88.80, winning four matches single-handedly, in Murtagh's view. Graham Grace's 848 runs helped Wimbledon climb from bottom of the table in early June to top by mid-July following six successive declaration-match victories. Reigate, however, won six of their last seven to clinch their fourth title in six years.

modification in 2010 was a new **SWALEC Premier League**, an amalgamation of the old South Wales Cricket League and those from Glamorgan and Monmouthshire. Seven counties – Durham, Hampshire, Lancashire, Northamptonshire, Nottinghamshire, Sussex and Yorkshire – now have academy or board teams competing in a local Premier League. "Counties are now fully aware of the benefits of premier leagues," said Paul Bedford, the ECB's head of non-first-class operations. "Those that do not are recognising that academy and Second Eleven players need to play a leading role at individual clubs." In short, Premier League cricket continues to serve the county game well.

Chris Aspin writes: There were two outstanding feats by amateur bowlers in the Lancashire Leagues. Jonathan Fielding took 113 wickets at 10.32 to steer Ramsbottom to their first Lancashire League championship since 1992; and in the Central Lancashire League, Oldham's Mel Whittle bowled 553 overs of swing and seam – 100 more than anyone else – to take exactly 100 wickets at 18.72. He was 63 years old, and playing his 49th and final season. As well as bowling virtually unchanged, Whittle found time to be club chairman and groundsman. On his final day, needing five wickets for his 100, he was working on the square at 7 a.m., though because of poor weather he wasn't expecting any cricket against Middleton. Then the umpires agreed to a 37-over game, and he walked out to a guard of honour. He took the crucial fifth wicket – his 11th five-for of the season – with two overs remaining. When asked why he hadn't pressed on for a 50th season, Whittle, a landscape gardener, replied: "The standard's slipped too far."

With world-class professionals rarely available or affordable these days, amateurs contributed significantly in both competitions. In the **Lancashire League**, Ramsbottom won 23 of their 26 matches, the most ever, and Fielding was the first amateur to take 100 wickets since Tommy Lowe in 1939. Steve Dearden claimed 75 for runners-up Haslingden, the club's best haul since 1908, and his 609 runs made him the top all-rounder. The leading run-maker was 19-year-old Ammer Mirza, who scored 930 runs for Church, including three centuries, just ahead of Todmorden's South African pro David Wiese, whose 924 included 140 against Nelson followed up by eight for 56. Haslingden amassed 340 for seven against Accrington, then dismissed them for 48 to win by a record 292 runs.

Fluctuating fortunes and mounting drama marked Ramsbottom's Worsley Cup semi-final against Burnley. Ramsbottom were eight for four (all caught behind by Chris Burton) when Fielding joined South African Faf du Plessis in a stand of 191. Du Plessis, the former Lancashire all-rounder, reached 111 before he was caught and bowled by Titans team-mate Farhaan Behardien. Ramsbottom finished on 249 for nine and, when Burnley slid to 148 for eight, the outcome seemed certain. But Behardien added 93 for the ninth wicket with Graham Lalor, who contributed five. It was growing dark as Behardien battered his way to 175; then du Plessis had his revenge when he caught and bowled him. Burnley needed nine off nine balls and managed six. Ramsbottom were clear favourites to win the final but lost after Colne, next to bottom in the league, bowled them out for 113.

During Rawtenstall's home game against Enfield, a ball hit out of the ground struck a car; the driver got out, picked it up and drove off with it. The replacement came to an unusual end, too, when another six landed in a tree, and the ball could not be dislodged.

Norden won the **Central Lancashire League**, with their professional Michael Price contributing 1,662 runs and 72 wickets. Runners-up Milnrow lifted the Lees Wood Cup. Their pro, Kuldeep Diwan, took 100 wickets at 11.66, while team-mates Maxwell Power, Paul Winrow and Alex Schofield passed 1,000 runs. Clinton Perren headed the professional averages with 1,813 at 86.33 for Littleborough. Crompton failed to reach 100 in nine matches, while their friendly bowling allowed four opponents to reach 300: Luke Procter, Royton's pro, hammered 198 not out against them, and Middleton's stand-in pro Michael Smith an unbeaten 193.

ECB PREMIER LEAGUE TABLES, 2010

Birmingham & District Premier Cricket League

	P	W	L	Pts
Shrewsbury	22	12	4	310
Knowle & Dorridge	22	10	2	295
Kidderminster Victoria	22	10	5	288
Barnt Green	22	6	7	249
Wellington	22	6	7	227
Himley	22	3	8	224
Wolverhampton	22	5	7	220
Smethwick	22	5	5	219
Moseley	22	6	7	218
Walsall	22	5	9	215
Kenilworth Wardens	22	6	6	214
Walmley	22	4	11	177

Cornwall Premier League

	P	W	L	Pts
Paul	18	13	3	285
St Just	18	9	5	252
Truro	18	9	6	241
Callington	18	8	6	238
St Austell	18	8	5	237
Grampound Road	18	9	5	236
Werrington	18	8	5	225
Falmouth	18	8	8	206
Newquay	18	3	13	128
Penzance	18	0	17	78

Cheshire County Cricket League

	P	W	L	Pts
Nantwich	22	12	6	382
Hyde	22	11	2	367
Neston	22	10	7	360
Alderley Edge	22	10	3	352
Oulton Park	22	10	7	351
Oxton	22	10	9	336
Chester Boughton Hall	22	7	9	311
Urmston	22	6	10	297
Toft	22	5	9	287
Didsbury	22	8	8	286
Bowdon	22	5	9	281
Bramhall	22	2	17	167

Derbyshire Premier League

	P	W	L	Pts
Lullington Park	22	13	4	413
Ockbrook & Borrowash	22	13	2	397
Sandiacre Town	22	11	5	383
Chesterfield	22	8	7	323
Spondon	22	4	7	289
Alvaston & Boulton	22	7	9	285
Quarndon	22	5	6	282
Ilkeston Rutland	22	6	8	244
Dunstall	22	6	7	242
Alfreton	22	5	7	236
Matlock	22	5	7	231
Elvaston	22	0	14	131

Devon Cricket League

	P	W	L	Pts
Sidmouth	**18**	**14**	**1**	**311**
North Devon	18	10	2	285
Plymouth	18	5	4	225
Bovey Tracey	18	6	6	213
Bradninch	18	7	8	213
Budleigh Salterton	18	6	6	198
Paignton	18	5	7	183
Plympton	18	3	7	177
Exeter	18	3	9	156
Braunton	18	3	12	137

East Anglian Premier Cricket League

	P	W	L	Pts
Cambridge Granta	**22**	**11**	**2**	**398**
Saffron Walden	22	11	1	390
Swardeston	22	9	4	365
Vauxhall Mallards	22	6	3	310
Horsford	22	7	5	304
Great Witchingham	22	7	6	296
Burwell	22	7	9	293
Bury St Edmunds	22	7*	8	292
Clacton-on-Sea	22	4	6	232
Norwich	22	2	10	220
Halstead	22	2*	10	176
Fakenham	22	1	10	175

* Plus one tie.

Essex Premier League

	P	W	L	Pts
Brentwood	**18**	**13**	**3**	**302**
Wanstead	18	10	3	265
Chelmsford	18	10	5	244
Loughton	18	7	7	224
Hainault & Clayhall	18	6	6	207
Colchester & East Essex	18	6	6	207
Woodford Wells	18	6	7	203
Ilford	18	5	8	182
Upminster	18	4	9	169
Gidea Park & Romford	18	0	13	93

Home Counties Premier Cricket League

	P	W	L	Pts
Henley	**18**	**8**	**2**	**297**
Welwyn Garden City	18	8	4	281
Oxford	18	7	4	266
Tring Park	18	7	5	262
Banbury	18	7	6	241
High Wycombe	18	5	6	239
Radlett	18	5	6	219
Harpenden	18	4	7	194
Potters Bar	18	4	8	194
Aston Rowant	18	3	10	179

Kent Cricket League

	P	W	L	Pts
Bromley	**18**	**10**	**3**	**242**
Hartley	18	9	3	238
St Lawrence & Highland Court	18	9	5	210
The Mote	18	8	5	202
Bexley	18	7	7	197
Bickley Park	18	7	5	189
Sevenoaks Vine	18	6	9	175
Tunbridge Wells	18	5	10	161
Lordswood	18	5	6	145
Gore Court	18	0	13	84

Leicestershire County Cricket League

	P	W	L	Pts
Market Harborough	**22**	**10**	**1**	**359**
Loughborough Town	22	11	4	350
Barrow Town	22	8	5	342
Kibworth	22	9	4	327
Syston Town	22	10	9	307
Kegworth Town	22	7	7	292
Stoughton & Thurnby	22	6	8	283
Sileby Town	22	8	9	282
Leicester Ivanhoe	22	5	8	260
Lutterworth	22	4	6	254
Ashby Hastings	22	3	14	187
Narborough & Littlethorpe	22	2	12	181

Lincolnshire Cricket Board Premier League

	P	W	L	Pts	Avge
Bourne	**18**	**12**	**5**	**273**	**15.16**
Sleaford	17	11	5	244	14.35
Lindum	18	9*	7	236	13.11
Bracebridge Heath	16	9	7	205	12.81
Skegness	19	12	7	230	12.10
Nettleham	17	7	6	205	12.05
Market Deeping	17	8	6	200	11.76
Grimsby Town	19	3*	8	204	10.73
Louth	17	5†	7	166	9.76
Boston	17	6	10	165	9.70
Woodhall Spa	18	5	10	164	9.11
Hartsholme	17	2	11	134	7.88

* Plus one tie. † Plus two ties.

Liverpool & District Cricket Competition

	P	W	L	Pts
Lytham	**22**	**14**	**4**	**369**
Ormskirk	22	13	5	350
New Brighton	22	11	4	324
Highfield	22	11	8	313
Colwyn Bay	22	10	7	283
Bootle	22	9	6	281
Hightown	22	8	9	257
Newton-le-Willows	22	7	12	241
Northern	22	6	7	235
Northop Hall	22	7	11	232
Wallasey	22	3	12	172
Prestatyn	22	2	16	119

Middlesex County Cricket League

	P	W	L	Pts
Ealing	**18**	**11**	**3**	**120**
Teddington	18	10	4	107
Eastcote	18	7	3	93
Brondesbury	18	7	4	83
Hampstead	18	7	8	73
Finchley	18	6	8	67
Stanmore	18	5	7	62
Twickenham	18	5	7	59
Shepherds Bush	18	4	8	49
Acton	18	2	12	27

Northamptonshire Cricket League

	P	W	L	Pts
Finedon Dolben	**22**	**16**	**3**	**471**
Peterborough Town	22	15	2	471
Northampton Saints	22	11	3	415
Old Northamptonians	22	10	3	370
Rushton	22	7	8	292
Wollaston	22	5	7	261
Stony Stratford	22	6	8	255
Rushden Town	22	6	10	233
Northants Cricket Academy	22	5	6	233
Brixworth	22	5	10	229
Burton Latimer	22	3	14	197
Wellingborough Town	22	1	16	138

North East Premier Cricket League

	P	W	L	Pts
Chester-le-Street	**22**	**14**	**1**	**474**
South Northumberland	22	14	3	465
Benwell Hill	22	8	3	355
Durham Cricket Academy	22	8	6	328
Blaydon	22	7	6	320
Newcastle	22	6	9	268
Stockton	22	5	7	244
Gateshead Fell	22	6	8	244
Sunderland	22	5	9	230
Hetton Lyons	22	4	11	246
South Shields	22	5	12	195
Tynemouth	22	3	10	182

*Northern Cricket League

	P	W	L	Pts
Leyland	**25**	**17**	**2**	**265**
Barrow	25	16	4	256
St Annes	25	15	4	236
Darwen	25	10	7	209
Blackpool	25	11	6	199
Morecambe	25	10	9	182
Lancaster	25	8	6	180
Netherfield	25	8	8	164
Lancashire Cricket Board	13	3	7	152†
Fleetwood	25	4	12	143
Kendal	25	3	11	138
Carnforth	25	4	15	126
Preston	25	4	10	124
Chorley	25	3	15	103

* ECB-approved but not a Premier League.
† Lancashire Cricket Board played only 13 games; their final position was obtained by multiplying their 79 points by 25 and divided by 13.

North Staffs & South Cheshire League

	P	W	L	Pts
Little Stoke	**22**	**13**	**3**	**361**
Audley	22	10	9	308
Stone	22	9	9	296
Burslem	22	10	9	293
Longton	22	9	7	290
Knypersley	22	9	10	285
Porthill Park	22	8	9	277
Wood Lane	22	7	9	254
Barlaston	22	9	10	251
Hem Heath	22	6	8	251
Elworth	22	6	8	248
Moddershall	22	5	10	199

North Wales Premier League

	P	W	L	Pts
Llandudno	**22**	**19**	**1**	**512**
Bangor	22	11	6	353
Pontblyddyn	22	10*	6	329
Connah's Quay	22	10*	6	327
Mold	22	10	10	308
Menai Bridge	22	8	9	298
St Asaph	22	11	10	294
Brymbo	22	8	9	273
Mochdre	22	4	10	256
Hawarden Park	22	4	12	249
Llanrwst	22	5	13	217
Chirk	22	4	12	206

* Plus one tie.

Nottinghamshire Cricket Board Premier League

	P	W	L	Pts
Clifton Village	22	12	3	347
West Indian Cavaliers	22	12	3	312
Cuckney.	22	8	5	304
Papplewick & Linby	22	8	5	287
Kimberley Institute	22	7	6	266
Caythorpe	22	6	6	259
Notts Cricket Board.	22	5	6	243
Mansfield Hosiery Mills . .	22	8	7	234
Welbeck Colliery	22	6	9	222
Wollaton	22	6	9	201
Radcliffe-on-Trent	22	3	11	168
Attenborough.	22	1	12	133

Southern Premier Cricket League

	P	W	L	Pts	Avge
Bournemouth	15	10	3	267	17.80
South Wiltshire	15	7	4	214	14.26
Hampshire Academy	17	10	3	237	13.94
St Cross Symondians	15	6	7	182	12.13
Alton	15	6	7	178	11.86
Totton & Eling	16	7	6	184	11.50
Bashley	15	6*	5	168	11.20
Havant	15	4*	5	155	10.33
Lymington	16	3	11	140	8.75
Ventnor	15	2	10	100	6.66

* Plus one tie.

Surrey Championship

	P	W	L	Pts
Reigate Priory	18	12	3	144
Wimbledon	18	10	6	121
Sunbury	18	9	6	108
Banstead	18	9	5	97
Ashtead	18	7	8	87
Weybridge	18	6	7	80
Guildford	18	6	7	73
Sutton	18	5	11	64
Cobham Avorians	18	5	10	58
Malden Wanderers	18	4	10	45

Sussex Cricket League

	P	W	L	Pts
Preston Nomads	19	13	2	441
Horsham	19	11	3	412
Brighton & Hove	19	8	5	357
Sussex Cricket Board	10	4	4	357†
Chichester Prior Park	19	7	4	313
East Grinstead	19	7	5	299
Hastings & St Leonard's				
Priory	19	5	8	291
Three Bridges	19	5	10	284
Eastbourne	19	5	8	265
Cuckfield	19	4	11	261
Bexhill	19	2	11	219

† Sussex Cricket Board played only ten games; their actual points total was multiplied by 1.9.

SWALEC Premier Cricket League

	P	W	L	Pts	Avge
Sully Centurions . .	16	10	0	303	18.93
Pontarddulais	14	6	5	197	14.07
Newport	16	6	5	224	14.00
Port Talbot	15	6	4	202	13.46
Cardiff	16	4	5	205	12.81
Ynysygerwn	16	5	5	204	12.75
Ammanford	15	6	6	189	12.60
Swansea	15	4	8	159	10.60
St Fagans	16	4*	8	169	10.56
Usk	15	3*	8	136	9.06

* Plus one tie.

West of England Premier League

	P	W	L	Pts
Bath	18	9	0	450
Bridgwater	18	8	3	379
Taunton St Andrews	18	8	4	370
Frocester	18	6	3	347
Corsham	18	6	5	308
Taunton Deane	18	6	7	272
Weston-super-Mare	18	4	7	258
Bristol	18	5	8	246
Taunton	18	1	7	180
Glastonbury	18	1	10	132

Yorkshire ECB County Premier League

	P	W	L	Pts
York	26	17	0	181
Barnsley	26	14	1	153
Yorkshire Academy	26	14	5	136
Scarborough	26	11	5	123
Rotherham Town	26	11	9	115
Castleford	26	10	4	114
Harrogate	26	10	11	92
Doncaster Town	26	8	8	82
Cleethorpes	26	4	10	74
Sheffield Collegiate	26	5	10	74
Driffield Town	26	7	11	73
Appleby Frodingham	26	5	12	64
Hull & YPI	26	4	17	39
Sheffield United	26	4	17	36

The following leagues do not have ECB Premier League status:

LANCASHIRE LEAGUES

Lancashire League

	P	W	L	Pts
Ramsbottom............	26	23	3	264
Haslingden.............	26	20	5	237
East Lancs............	26	17	8	211
Todmorden	26	17	8	209
Church................	26	16	9	185
Nelson................	26	14	10	180
Rawtenstall	26	13*	12	180
Burnley	26	12	13	161
Lowerhouse............	26	10	15	151
Accrington.............	26	9	17	130
Enfield................	26	8*	16	110†
Rishton	26	6	20	98
Colne	26	5	20	80
Bacup.................	26	5	19	68

* Includes tie.　† 12pts deducted for "contractual irregularity".

Central Lancashire League

	P	W	L	Pts
Norden	30	25	4	125
Milnrow...............	30	23	6	112
Rochdale	30	21	7	106
Heywood	30	19	8	104
Clifton	30	18	9	95
Littleborough...........	30	17	9	95
Werneth...............	30	14	13	82
Monton & Weaste.......	30	13	14	74
Middleton	30	11	16	68
Unsworth.............	30	11	15	62
Radcliffe	30	10	19	57
Walsden..............	30	9	19	52
Ashton	30	9	19	51
Oldham	30	10	18	45†
Royton...............	30	6	22	39
Crompton.............	30	5	23	29

† 15pts deducted for fielding ineligible player.

OTHER LEAGUE WINNERS, 2010

Airedale & Wharfedale	Burley
Bolton Association	Little Hulton
Bolton League	Farnworth
Bradford	Pudsey Congs
Cambridgeshire	Camden
Central Yorkshire	Wrenthorpe
Durham County	Kimblesworth
Durham Senior	Boldon
Hertfordshire	Totteridge Millhillians
Huddersfield	Honley
Lancashire County	Denton West
Merseyside	Huyton
Norfolk Alliance	Downham Town
North Essex	Mistley
N. Lancs & Cumbria	Furness
Northumberland & Tyneside Senior	Swalwell
N. Yorks & S. Durham	Middlesbrough
Pembrokeshire	Cresselly
Quaid-e-Azam	Keighley RZM
Ribblesdale	Clitheroe
Saddleworth	Bamford Fieldhouse
Shropshire	Madeley
South Wales Association	Mumbles
South Yorkshire	Whitley Hall
Two Counties	Sudbury
Warwickshire	Handsworth
West Wales	Aberystwyth
Worcestershire	Barnards Green
York Senior	Dunnington

CLUB CHAMPIONSHIP AND COCKSPUR CUP, 2010

PAUL EDWARDS

After a couple of seasons characterised by flux and uncertainty (see *Wisden 2010*, page 919), English club cricketers now have two well-established national trophies for which they can compete.

The ECB National Club Championship celebrated its 42nd year in 2010 with a clutch of high-quality matches leading to the final at Derby, while the considerably younger Cockspur Cup offered players the chance to display their burgeoning 20-over expertise. Both competitions were well supported and, in the early part of the season at least, blessed by good weather. "I'd like to think they're twin peaks," said Paul Bedford, the ECB's head of non-first-class operations.

The team of the year were South Northumberland, also known as "South North Bulls". Five days after winning the national knockout, they narrowly failed to add the Cockspur to their already heaving trophy cabinet when they lost to Swardeston, from Norfolk, in a memorable final at the Rose Bowl.

Yet South North's achievement in reaching the last stage of two national competitions, while still fulfilling their league commitments, bears witness that the area is one of the strongholds of recreational cricket. In 2010, the club ran a total of 17 teams for its members, around 400 of whom were juniors. Success on the scale their club enjoyed in 2010 is built on sheer hard work and long-term investment.

Swardeston, of the East Anglian Premier League, needed a wonderful innings by 20-year-old Peter Lambert to carry off the trophy. Having helped his team defeat Wimbledon in the first semi-final with 33 from 27 balls, Lambert hit five sixes in his 72 not out in the final. His strokes lost little in comparison to Eoin Morgan's century in the one-day international on the same ground 24 hours earlier. Lambert's innings set a target too stiff for the early-morning favourites, and the competitive English season ended with Swardeston's claret-and-blue-clad players cavorting under the Hampshire floodlights in uninhibited delight, an image symbolising the rapid changes taking place in the club game.

In future years, the ECB are keen to welcome clubs whose busy schedules have previously deterred them from entering the Cockspur, or worse, withdrawing from the competition in the later stages.

"There's more work to do to accommodate leagues who have full Sunday programmes," said Bedford. "I don't want teams dropping out, and if that means we have single matches on a Friday night instead of regional finals days, that's fine by us."

If Lord's is again unavailable to host the 2011 national knockout final, the ECB aim to find a venue like Derby, ready and willing to stage the event; and, depending upon TV commitments, the hope is that Cockspur finals day will be hosted by a Test match ground. For elite club cricketers, the rewards for excellence are sweet indeed.

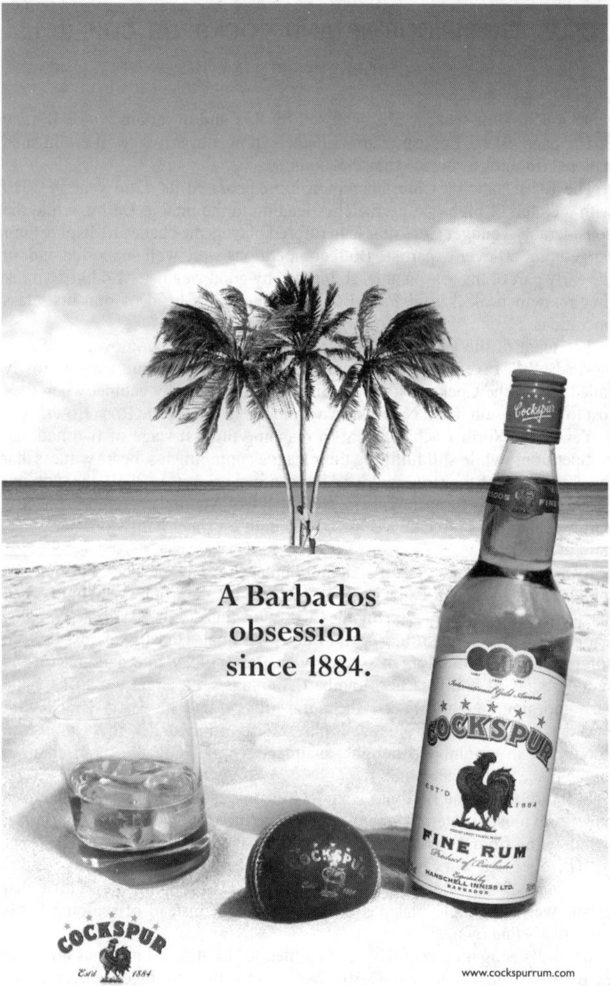
A Barbados
obsession
since 1884.
COCKSPUR
FINE RUM
COCKSPUR
Est'd 1884
FINE RUM
www.cockspurrum.com
DRINKAWARE.CO.UK

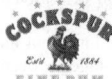

ECB NATIONAL CLUB CHAMPIONSHIP FINAL

EALING v SOUTH NORTHUMBERLAND

At Derby, September 18. South Northumberland won by five runs (D/L method) Toss: Ealing.

South Northumberland won the title for the second time in five years, and did so in circumstances which may trouble Ealing's cricketers for a long time. Needing exactly four an over to beat their powerful opponents from the North-East, Ealing had recovered from 33 for four to 113 for five when drizzle forced the players off the field. With captain David Holt and Chris Wakefield batting well, Ealing, whose line-up contained eight former colts, had a fair chance of scoring the 67 runs they needed in the remaining 13.5 overs. Crucially, though, they were a trifle behind on Duckworth/Lewis. The rain toyed with the players, easing for a few moments, only to mock their optimism by returning in greater force. Ealing's misfortune did not sour South Northumberland's victory, nor did it take the gloss off a fine individual display from Steve Humble. The 33-year-old all-rounder, also Man of the Match in the 2006 final, made 40 off 39 balls to ensure a defendable total; he then accounted for Simon Hawk and Mylo Wilkin as the seamers made inroads on a wicket offering help.

Man of the Match: S. Humble.

South Northumberland

A. T. Heather c Hawk b Tahir Afridi	0	L. J. Crozier lbw b Patel			0
S. Jobson c M. Wilkin b Tahir Afridi	1	J. R. Wightman b Patel			0
C. J. Hewison b Parry	33	R. M. Brook not out			0
†A. D. Cragg c Holt b Hawk	41	B 1, l-b 2, w 20, n-b 3			26
*J. A. Graham c Fallis b Parry	11				
J. N. Miller c Jones b Peploe	16	1/0 (1) 2/18 (2) 3/89 (4) (35.1 overs)			179
C. J. Hooker c Hawk b Patel	11	;4/95 (3) 5/120 (5) 6/131 (6)			
S. Humble b Hawk	40	;7/164 (7) 8/171 (9) 9/179 (10) 10/179 (8)			

Tahir Afridi 6–0–40–2; O. Wilkin 4–0–32–0; Hawk 8.1–1–34–2; Parry 6–0–22–2; Peploe 5–0–27–1; Patel 6–1–21–3.

Ealing

S. L. J. M. Hawk c Cragg b Humble	0	C. Wakefield not out			23
P. D. J. Fallis b Wightman	6				
†M. Wilkin lbw b Humble	20	B 1, l-b 5, w 15, n-b 2			23
*D. R. Holt not out	32				
C. T. Peploe lbw b Wightman	0	1/0 (1) 2/26 (3) (5 wkts, 31.1 overs)			113
H. Jones c Brook b Hooker	9	;3/33 (4) 4/33 (5) 5/68 (6)			

S. Patel, L. J. Parry, O. Wilkin and Tahir Afridi did not bat.

Humble 7–1–29–2; Wightman 6–0–24–2; Crozier 9–0–23–0; Hooker 5–1–15–1; Brook 4.1–0–16–0.

Umpires: A. Davies and G. W. W. Wood. Referee: G. Hornbuckle.

A full list of winners from the start of the competition in 1969 appears in Wisden 2005, *page 941.*

COCKSPUR CUP FINALS DAY

Semi-finals

At Southampton, September 23. **Swardeston won by nine runs.** ‡**Swardeston 103-9** (20 overs) (P. A. Lambert 33); **Wimbledon 94-9** (20 overs).

At Southampton, September 23. **South Northumberland won by 20 runs.** ‡**South Northumberland 107-8** (20 overs); **Bootle 87-6** (20 overs).

Final

At Southampton, September 23 (floodlit). **Swardeston won by 11 runs.** ‡**Swardeston 129-8** (20 overs) (P. A. Lambert 72*; S. Humble 3-12); **South Northumberland 118-6** (20 overs) (J. A. Graham 34).

NPOWER VILLAGE CUP, 2010

Benj Moorehead

It all ended at Lord's with the dancing, jumping figure of a bald 55-year-old farmer from Sessay, the North Yorkshire parish whose cricketers won the Village Cup at the 39th attempt.

John Flintoff has played in every year bar one since the competition began in 1972. As a 21-year-old he was injured for the 1976 Lord's final, when Sessay were beaten by Cornish club Troon. Eight years later Sessay narrowly lost in the semi-finals: "the most disappointing day of my life". Thereafter Flintoff had to settle for the village green. Then in June he was summoned from the second team to the Cup eleven because of an injury, and wouldn't let go of his place. Lord's was his. And he was in the middle to help knock off the last 18 runs, filling with ecstasy the emptiness of 34 years of disappointment.

What a contrast the finalists were. Sessay, their Lord's first-timers beaming in blazers; Shipton-under-Wychwood, the Oxfordshire club of whom seven had played a Lord's final at least once and were hoping to join Troon and St Fagans as triple winners. Hunger trumped experience on this occasion.

Sessay's triumph was in no small part due to Matthew Till, a stocky opening bat in a sunhat who crouches low in his stance and dangles his bat like a red rag to bowlers. Then he bullies. Till hit a club-record 201 off 108 balls (22 fours, 11 sixes) against Barton in the early rounds. Shipton were driven on by the runs of Andy Hemming, 719 in all, including a double-hundred.

The final was a balm to Lord's, exactly two weeks on from the no-ball accusations which had sullied the Pakistan Test. In the evening sunshine idle spectators ambled in front of the Pavilion, from where outgoing MCC president John Barclay announced: "This is the real thing!" It felt like release.

From Kintore, in Aberdeenshire, to Constantine, 25 miles east of Land's End, 273 teams were stripped down through 32 regional groups and five national rounds. Other stories flickered without bubbling to the surface quite like Flintoff's. Fifteen-year-old Curtly Slatter, christened so because of his father's admiration for West Indian fast bowlers, scored two hundreds in two days for the Oxfordshire club Great & Little Tew, including one in the Cup against Kingston Bagpuize.

Troon, whose tin-miners won the inaugural Village Cup but who haven't reached the final since 1983, woke from their slumber, but lost to Shipton in the quarter-finals. They had only returned to the competition after relegation from the Cornish Premier League had made them eligible under Village Cup rules. Promotion back to their top tier means Troon cannot enter in 2011. Ahsad Sayed – or "Waqar" as he is known at Fillongley, the semi-finalists from Warwickshire – scored 239 runs and took 21 wickets.

The Cup turns 40 in 2012, and sponsorship remains precarious. You need only glimpse the pavilion walls around the country, on which hang photographs toasting a famous year in this competition, or at the triumph of John Flintoff, to see the colour it brings to village cricket, and how it would be missed.

FINAL

SESSAY v SHIPTON-UNDER-WYCHWOOD

At Lord's, September 12. Sessay won by seven wickets. Toss: Sessay.

This was a batsman's final. Both teams reached 200 with wickets in hand, but the difference lay in their approach. True to their Lord's know-how, Shipton-under-Wychwood settled for a score not much beyond 200 in the knowledge that no one had overhauled more than 221 in a Village Cup final – only for Sessay to respond with a refreshing freedom that took no regard of such things. As the day began, Sessay's disciplined new-ball bowlers, Richard Till and Stuart Peirse, forced the Shipton openers to show caution over adventure. Only when the pace came off the ball did Andy Hemming score freely; he was deftly caught down the leg side by wicketkeeper Nick Harrison, and it took a berserker's innings – 38 off 13 balls with five sixes – from weighty left-hander Jason Hunt to guide Shipton to what, history said, would be enough. But Sessay were uncowed: Mark Wilkie and Matthew Till put on 127 for the first wicket, Till's run-a-ball fifty including 11 fours. All his shots went along the ground – and he played all the shots. By the 21st over Shipton were using their seventh bowler, and their field-settings were changing shape like helpless military formations. First Wilkie, fluent yet patient, and then Nick Thorne nursed Sessay to within reach of their target, setting up the moment of fulfilment for the folk hero, John Flintoff.

Man of the Match: M. Wilkie.

Shipton-under-Wychwood

A. P. Hemming c Harrison b R. C. Till	59	T. F. King not out	1
C. A. Brain b Langstaff	33	B 4, l-b 7, w 13, n-b 1	25
S. A. Bates not out	46		
T. J. Senior c Harrison b Peirse	18	1/88 (2) 2/126 (1) (5 wkts, 40 overs) 227
J. M. Hunt st Harrison b Wilkie	38	3/151 (4) 4/200 (5)
*P. Hemming b Peirse	7	5/224 (6)

C. J. Lambert, C. P. Panter, S. Miller and †P. N. Jennings did not bat.

Peirse 9–1–39–2; R. J. Till 9–1–48–1; Langstaff 9–0–45–1; Wilkie 8–0–37–1; M. C. Till 5–0–47–0.

Sessay

M. Wilkie c Brain b P. Hemming	78
M. C. Till c Senior b P. Hemming	56
N. J. Thorne st Jennings b Hunt	42
†N. J. Harrison not out	22
J. B. Flintoff not out	13
L-b 5, w 10, n-b 2	17

1/127 (2) 2/159 (1)   (3 wkts, 37.1 overs) 228
3/210 (3)

J. K. Spencer, C. J. Till, R. J. Till, S. M. Peirse, J. P. Watson and *S. J. Langstaff did not bat.

Panter 8.1–2–35–0; Lambert 2–0–21–0; Brain 2–0–20–0; Miller 9–1–51–0; Hunt 5–0–32–1; P. Hemming 9–0–51–2; King 2–0–13–0.

Umpires: K. A. Little and L. R. Strout.

RECENT WINNERS

2001	Ynystawe (Glamorgan)	2006	Houghton Main (Yorkshire)
2002	Shipton-under-Wychwood (Oxfordshire)	2007	Woodhouse Grange (Yorkshire)
2003	Shipton-under-Wychwood (Oxfordshire)	2008	Valley End (Surrey)
2004	Sully Centurions (Glamorgan)	2009	Glynde & Beddingham (Sussex)
2005	Sheriff Hutton Bridge (Yorkshire)	2010	Sessay (Yorkshire)

A full list of winners from the start of the competition in 1972 appears in Wisden 2005, *page 944.*

DISABILITY CRICKET

Spreading the word – and field

PAUL EDWARDS

In June 2010, the ICC held their first game-development conference call devoted entirely to disability cricket. In some quarters the event might prompt cynical comments about the activities of bureaucrats, but for disabled cricketers around the world it could prove to have far-reaching benefits. ICC officials discussed all aspects of the disabled game, and focused particularly on the need for closer cooperation between governing bodies and disability cricket groups in member countries. The result of these consultations should be that blind or deaf cricketers, and those coping with learning or physical disabilities, begin to feel they are an integral part of the game in their respective countries, with access to more resources and playing more matches at a higher standard.

For Ian Martin, the ECB's national disability cricket manager, June's meeting was a personal triumph – although he would be the last person to view it in those terms. The ECB continues to lead the way in encouraging disabled players to feel part of the wider cricket family, and Martin has been charged with updating other Full Members of the ICC on the global picture of disability cricket. This work was recognised in October, when the ECB was shortlisted in the Sports Award and Martin for Person of the Year in the Royal Association for Disability and Rehabilitation awards.

Administrative activity and acclaim has had its effect on the field. More disabled cricket is being played throughout the UK, and in September the ECB asked the development staff of each county board to provide evidence of how they were promoting the role of disabled people in cricket.

At a national level, 2010 was a mixed year. The third Deaf World Cup had to be cancelled, for the second year in a row, because host country New Zealand were not satisfied that an appropriate level of sponsorship had been achieved. In spite of two double-hundreds by Nathan Foy, England Blind suffered a 3–0 whitewash to Pakistan in April's one-day series in Sharjah, and also lost the Twenty20 match. Foy made another century in the home one-day series against India, but could not prevent another 3–0 defeat (with one washout). Nevertheless, Foy, the 2009 Disabled Cricketer of the Year, is now only ten shy of the 3,000-run landmark in international matches and he remains a credit to the sport. Chris Edwards, from the Wirral, won the 2010 Disabled Cricketer of the Year prize, for his performances in last year's Learning Disability Tri-Nations.

The ECB hopes that June's appointment of four head coaches to work with each of the disability squads (Physical Disability, Learning Disability, Blind, Deaf) will raise levels of performance, as England seek to keep pace with the ever-improving teams turned out by other nations.

ENGLAND UNDER-19 v SRI LANKA UNDER-19

PATRICK KIDD

Under-19 Tests (2): England 1, Sri Lanka 1
Under-19 one-day internationals (5): England 2, Sri Lanka 2
Under-19 Twenty20 internationals (2): England 1, Sri Lanka 1

It seemed that 2010 was the year of the twit, as an increasing number of sportsmen took advantage of the endless possibilities to embarrass themselves in 140 characters or fewer on the social networking website Twitter. Kevin Pietersen, who posted a foul-mouthed rant after being dropped from England's one-day side, was the most notable senior player to be reminded of his responsibilities. But the comments left by Azeem Rafiq, after he was dropped as captain of England Under-19, may have the most damaging consequences.

An ECB disciplinary committee ordered Rafiq, the Yorkshire all-rounder, to be suspended from all cricket for a month and to pay £500 costs after ruling that he had breached the code of conduct with his ill-judged and abusive comments about John Abrahams, the England Under-19 manager. Abrahams had decided to leave Rafiq out of the Second Test against Sri Lanka Under-19, despite his making 82 in the opening match at Northampton, for unspecified "inappropriate conduct" that is believed to have involved breaking a curfew.

Rafiq's response was to write "What a fucking farsee" on Twitter – one assumes he meant "farce" – followed by some crass invective aimed at Abrahams and the ECB. He renewed his attack on Abrahams the following day. Although Rafiq took the comments down once he realised anyone could read them, they had already been "retweeted" by others and brought to the attention of his employers. Yorkshire did not select Rafiq for their first team – and barely for their second – during the rest of the season.

Abrahams rose above the abuse and said he thought "the summer went really well" on the pitch. He could be encouraged by the character England showed in coming from behind to share all three series. "The ECB decided that Under-19 players who were getting regular first-team cricket would be better served by staying with their counties," said Abrahams. "This deprived the team of seven possible first-choice players, but those selected did a really good job. It was very satisfying." Paul Best, the Warwickshire slow left-armer, replaced Rafiq as captain and proved a shrewd and mature leader.

As Abrahams is keen to point out, the Under-19 set-up has become very successful at developing senior international players. Of the 34 who left to tour Australia in the winter with either England or the Performance Programme, 24 had played for the Under-19s. It makes the announcement that there will be no Under-19 Tests for England in summer 2011 all the more disappointing and perplexing. South Africa will come for a three-week tour that features seven one-day internationals as preparation for the 2012 Under-19 World Cup.

Lewis Gregory, the Somerset all-rounder, led a 17-man squad to Sri Lanka at the start of 2011 for two Tests and five one-day internationals. They were accompanied by Tim Boon, who left his position at Leicestershire to become the fourth England Under-19 coach in just over a year (and took the title of England Development Programme head coach). Adrian Birrell, the former Ireland coach, worked with the Under-19s in the summer series, and will continue with the Under-17s. Abrahams pledged that any county coach who wanted to further develop his skills would be welcome as an assistant with future England Under-19 squads.

SRI LANKA UNDER-19 TOURING PARTY

*K. P. C. M. Peiris, M. L. R. Buddika, V. S. de Mel, M. A. P. Fernando, M. D. Gunathilleke, W. M. C. Jayampathi, P. L. M. Jayarathne, D. H. Jayasinghe, K. P. N. M. Karunanayake, A. K. K. Y. Lanka, K. A. S. N. Rajaguru, D. D. M. Rajakaruna, P. B. B. Rajapaksa, R. L. B. Rambukwella, K. D. K. Vithanage. *Manager:* C. T. M. Devaraj. *Coach:* M. N. Nawaz.

At Loughborough, July 18–19. **Drawn. ‡ECB Elite Player Development XI 162** (45.2 overs) and **249-7 dec** (61.2 overs) (A. W. R. Barrow 80, Z. S. Ansari 57, A. M. Rossington 51); **Sri Lanka Under-19 237-6 dec** (60 overs) (M. L. R. Buddika 61) and **169-7** (33 overs) (P. B. B. Rajapaksa 50). *The ECB XI (effectively England Under-18s) named 12 players and Sri Lanka 15; in each case, 11 could bat and 11 field. The home side fought back from a poor first innings and denied Sri Lanka the last six runs needed to win their tour opener. Somerset's Alex Barrow and Zafar Ansari of Surrey proved their first major obstacle with 117 for the second wicket, and three strikes in the last three overs of the match conclusively slowed Sri Lanka's pursuit of 175.*

ENGLAND v SRI LANKA

First Under-19 Test

At Northampton, July 21–24. Sri Lanka Under-19 won by 199 runs. Toss: England Under-19.

Sri Lanka twice ran through England's lower order to seize the initiative in the series. When England were 112 for five in the ninth over after tea on the last day, chasing a nominal 369, they hoped to escape with a draw. But the dismissal of Azeem Rafiq – in what proved his final innings at Under-19 level – sparked England's gradual disintegration. Jack Manuel, the last recognised batsman, was eighth out, caught and bowled by Charith Jayampathi, and Sri Lanka completed victory with half an hour to spare. With no Sri Lankan passing 52 in the first innings, it appeared 287 would be a little skimpy. England were just eight behind when Ateeq Javid and Rafiq (who raced to 50 in 62 balls) took their record sixth-wicket stand to 156, but seamers Sanitha de Mel and Chathura Peiris swept up the last five wickets for seven runs. Spearheaded by Bhanuka Rajapaksa, Sri Lanka built an unassailable lead. Peiris advanced from 13 to 66 on the final morning, and declared four overs before lunch, when Denuwan Rajakaruna was out for 45. De Mel dealt immediate blows to England's top order, and emerged with six for 97 from the match.

Close of play: First day, England Under-19 14-0 (Root 1, Bell-Drummond 7); Second day, England Under-19 255-5 (Javid 79, Azeem Rafiq 73); Third day, Sri Lanka Under-19 269-6 (Rajakaruna 13, Peiris 13).

Sri Lanka Under-19

A. K. K. Y. Lanka c Javid b Sheikh	0	– c Javid b Sheikh	4
R. L. B. Rambukwella c Manuel b Dunn	34	– b Dunn	31
P. B. B. Rajapaksa c and b Gregory	45	– c Wells b Azeem Rafiq	97
M. L. R. Buddika c Sheikh b Gregory	11	– c Rouse b Sheikh	27
K. D. K. Vithanage c Rouse b Azeem Rafiq	52	– c Manuel b Ball	48
K. P. N. M. Karunanayake c Gregory b Dunn	6	– c Rouse b Ball	22
†D. D. M. Rajakaruna c Root b Wells	44	– c Manuel b Root	45
*K. P. C. M. Peiris not out	46	– b Root	66
W. M. C. Jayampathi b Gregory	20	– lbw b Root	6
K. A. S. N. Rajaguru b Dunn	4	– not out	2
V. S. de Mel b Dunn	0		
B 9, l-b 3, w 1, n-b 12	25	B 8, l-b 8, w 2, n-b 1	19

1/0 (1) 2/74 (2) 3/92 (4) 4/101 (3) (84.4 overs) 287
5/154 (6) 6/174 (5) 7/241 (7)
8/280 (9) 9/285 (10) 10/287 (11)

1/9 (1) (9 wkts dec, 107.2 overs) 367
2/83 (2) 3/147 (4)
4/193 (3) 5/233 (5) 6/250 (6)
7/352 (8) 8/360 (9) 9/367 (7)

Sheikh 9–0–48–1; Dunn 15.4–5–50–4; Ball 10–1–51–0; Gregory 17–6–39–3; Azeem Rafiq 23–8–68–1; Wells 10–3–19–1. *Second Innings*—Sheikh 11–2–44–2; Dunn 18–3–67–1; Gregory 19–3–65–0; Root 6.2–0–20–3; Ball 16–2–41–2; Azeem Rafiq 34–7–103–1; Wells 3–0–11–0.

England Under-19

J. E. Root c Lanka b Jayampathi	40	– c Rajakaruna b de Mel	31
D. J. Bell-Drummond c Rambukwella b Jayampathi	32	– c Rajapaksa b de Mel	1
L. Gregory lbw b Peiris	13	– c Vithanage b de Mel	5
L. W. P. Wells c Rajapaksa b Jayampathi	0	– c de Mel b Rajaguru	26
A. Javid c Peiris b de Mel	90	– lbw b Rajaguru	2
J. K. Manuel c Rajakaruna b Peiris	0	– c and b Jayampathi	39
*Azeem Rafiq b de Mel	82	– c Vithanage b de Mel	16
†A. P. Rouse lbw b Peiris	1	– b Peiris	5
J. T. Ball c Rajakaruna b Peiris	4	– b Jayampathi	12
A. Sheikh c Rajakaruna b Peiris	0	– c Karunanayake b Rajaguru	12
M. P. Dunn not out	0	– not out	0
B 7, l-b 8, w 7, n-b 7	24	B 5, l-b 9, w 5, n-b 1	20

1/77 (2) 2/78 (1) 3/78 (4) (82.1 overs) 286
4/123 (3) 5/123 (6) 6/279 (7)
7/282 (8) 8/286 (9) 9/286 (10) 10/286 (5)

1/2 (2) 2/10 (3) (62.1 overs) 169
3/65 (4) 4/71 (5)
5/75 (1) 6/112 (7) 7/125 (8)
8/149 (6) 9/161 (9) 10/169 (10)

Jayampathi 23–3–94–3; de Mel 14.1–6–48–2; Peiris 18–4–44–5; Rajapaksa 6–0–25–0; Rajaguru 14–0–44–0; Rambukwella 7–0–21–0. *Second Innings*—Peiris 16–5–36–1; de Mel 20–7–49–4; Rajaguru 16.1–2–51–3; Jayampathi 8–4–16–2; Buddika 2–1–3–0.

Umpires: N. A. Mallender and R. T. Robinson.

ENGLAND v SRI LANKA

Second Under-19 Test

At Scarborough, July 27–30. England Under-19 won by six wickets. Toss: Sri Lanka Under-19.

England recovered superbly to square the series in the final match, as they would in the Twenty20 and one-day international series that followed. They were indebted to a marvellous fourth-wicket stand of 174 in 61 overs between Warwickshire's Ateeq Javid, and Daniel Bell-Drummond, of Kent; their task was made a smidgin easier when the umpires awarded England five penalty runs at lunch on the last day because of suspicious markings on the ball. Sri Lanka, though dismayed and protesting their innocence, did not emulate Pakistan at The Oval in 2006 by refusing to play on. They were, however, affected mentally, to judge from their body language. When Javid was out to his 198th ball, England required only 22 to win in 46 minutes, and Jack Manuel decided to finish the match in a hurry. He swept his first ball for six and struck two more fours, denying Bell-Drummond, the youngest member of the squad at 16, a possible and well-deserved hundred. Paul Best, in his first and last Test as captain, removed five of Sri Lanka's top six on the opening day, and then made 37 in two and a half hours as England eked out a slight lead. Three wickets in 15 balls for Jacob Ball rocked Sri Lanka's second innings. The last six batsmen assembled 203 between them, but England gave away just a single extra, and were up to the task in the chase.

Close of play: First day, Sri Lanka Under-19 298-8 (Jayampathi 12, Rajaguru 22); Second day, England Under-19 223-6 (Best 27, A. J. Ball 1); Third day, Sri Lanka Under-19 171-7 (Fernando 44, Jayampathi 17).

Sri Lanka Under-19

K. P. N. M. Karunanayake lbw b Best	90	– lbw b J. T. Ball	5
R. L. B. Rambukwella c Gregory b J. T. Ball	10	– (4) lbw b J. T. Ball	1
P. B. B. Rajapaksa lbw b Best	47	– c Gregory b Payne	0
M. L. R. Buddika lbw b Best	4	– (2) c A. J. Ball b J. T. Ball	14
K. D. K. Vithanage c Rouse b Best	6	– b Best	53
†D. D. M. Rajakaruna c and b Best	35	– c Root b Best	16
M. A. P. Fernando b Payne	39	– lbw b J. T. Ball	49
*K. P. C. M. Peiris b Root	22	– c Rouse b Best	20
W. M. C. Jayampathi c Wells b J. T. Ball	31	– c Rouse b J. T. Ball	25
K. A. S. N. Rajaguru b Payne	22	– not out	11
V. S. de Mel not out	0	– c Rouse b Gregory	29
B 4, l-b 6, w 1	11	L-b 1	1

1/29 (2) 2/124 (3) 3/134 (4)   (98.3 overs) 317   1/10 (1) 2/19 (2)   (65 overs) 224
4/154 (5) 5/178 (1) 6/207 (6)   3/20 (4) 4/20 (3) 5/67 (6)
7/244 (8) 8/269 (7) 9/317 (9) 10/317 (10)   6/108 (5) 7/148 (8) 8/183 (7)
9/184 (9) 10/224 (11)

J. T. Ball 21–4–61–2; Payne 24.3–3–108–2; A. J. Ball 12–2–33–0; Gregory 10–3–24–0; Best 22–5–53–5; Root 4–0–12–1; Wells 5–1–16–0. *Second Innings*—J. T. Ball 16–5–64–5; Payne 18–1–59–1; A. J. Ball 2–0–14–0; Gregory 7–0–28–1; Best 18–4–53–3; Root 4–2–5–0.

England Under-19

J. E. Root lbw b Jayampathi	24	– c Rajakaruna b Peiris	0
D. J. Bell-Drummond lbw b Peiris	5	– not out	88
L. Gregory c Rajapaksa b Peiris	0	– c Rajapaksa b de Mel	5
L. W. P. Wells b Buddika	54	– c Rajakaruna b Peiris	4
A. Javid b Peiris	33	– lbw b Buddika	89
J. K. Manuel c Rambukwella b Peiris	57	– not out	18
*P. M. Best c Rajaguru b Peiris	37		
A. J. Ball lbw b Peiris	18		
†A. P. Rouse b Rajaguru	17		
D. A. Payne c Rajapaksa b de Mel	18		
J. T. Ball not out	26		
B 3, l-b 13, w 6, n-b 10	32	B 4, l-b 1, w 6, n-b 1, p 5	17

1/17 (2) 2/17 (3) 3/46 (1)   (107.3 overs) 321   1/5 (1)   (4 wkts, 71.3 overs) 221
4/124 (5) 5/161 (4) 6/214 (6)   2/16 (3) 3/25 (4)
7/251 (8) 8/261 (7) 9/283 (9) 10/321 (10)   4/199 (5)

Peiris 28–5–79–6; de Mel 25.3–6–70–1; Jayampathi 18–4–58–1; Rajaguru 17–1–65–1; Buddika 13–5–26–1; Fernando 6–3–7–0. *Second Innings*—Peiris 14–3–49–2; de Mel 10–0–40–1; Jayampathi 4–0–18–0; Rajaguru 25–2–55–0; Rajapaksa 13–4–23–0; Buddika 5.3–0–26–1.

Umpires: M. R. Benson and P. Willey.

At Chester-le-Street, August 2 (floodlit). **First Twenty20 international. Sri Lanka Under-19 won by nine wickets.** ‡**England Under-19 107** (18.3 overs) (K. P. C. M. Peiris 3-20); **Sri Lanka Under-19 109-1** (13.4 overs) (P. B. B. Rajapaksa 54*, R. L. B. Rambukwella 36). *Bhanuka Rajapaksa bowled a tidy spell of medium-pace (4–0–19–2), and then bludgeoned three fours and five sixes in 29 balls. His opening partnership of 75 in 7.4 overs with Ramith Rambukwella confirmed a thrashing.*

At Chester-le-Street, August 3 (floodlit). **Second Twenty20 international. England Under-19 won by 46 runs. England Under-19 164-4** (20 overs) (J. K. Manuel 31, J. E. Root 59*, L. Gregory 55); ‡**Sri Lanka Under-19 118** (18 overs) (K. D. K. Vithanage 48, M. D. Gunathilleke 31; J. E. Root 3-17, J. A. Thorpe 3-21). *Jack Manuel needed only 18 balls to reach 31, and Joe Root and Luke Gregory forged on in a second-wicket partnership of 103. Root set an England Under-19 record in Twenty20 internationals by scoring a half-century and taking three wickets, although this was only their sixth match in the format.*

At Sleaford, August 5. **Sri Lanka Under-19 won by 60 runs. Sri Lanka Under-19 186** (42.4 overs) (A. K. K. Y. Lanka 33, D. D. M. Rajakuruna 33, M. A. P. Fernando 30*); ‡**England Under-17 126** (35.2 overs) (S. J. Thakor 59, V. S. de Mel 4-11). *England Under-17 named 12 players and Sri Lanka 15; in each case, 11 could bat and 11 field. Shiv Thakor, who was run out, was the only player on either side to make a fifty. Sanitha de Mel's wickets came in six overs at the start of the innings. Thakor prevented de Mel from taking a hat-trick.*

At Cambridge, August 7. **First one-day international. England Under-19 won by three wickets. Sri Lanka Under-19 207-7** (50 overs) (M. D. Gunathilleke 83*); ‡**England Under-19 208-7** (49.2 overs) (J. E. Root 48, A. W. R. Barrow 50, L. W. P. Wells 39*). *England reduced Sri Lanka to 90-6 and 116-7, but then Dhanushka Gunathilleke shared 91 with de Mel (29*). Alex Barrow and Luke Wells came together with England 135-4, and together knocked off 55 of the 73 needed. Barrow hit only two boundaries in his 96-ball innings.*

At Arundel, August 9. **Second one-day international. Sri Lanka Under-19 won by five wickets.** ‡**England Under-19 175** (49.4 overs) (L. Gregory 87; V. S. de Mel 3-23, K. A. S. N. Rajaguru 3-33); **Sri Lanka Under-19 176-5** (34.3 overs) (P. B. B. Rajapaksa 46, K. D. K. Vithanage 51*). *No. 3 Luke Gregory was last out, with no other England batsman making more than Wells's 20. Sri Lanka were 125-5 but Kithuruwan Vithanage and Akshu Fernando (29*) saw them home.*

At Arundel, August 10. **Third one-day international. No result.** Reduced to 31 overs a side. **Sri Lanka Under-19 58-1** (11.4 overs) v ‡**England Under-19.** *A second shower caused play to be abandoned, after Rumesh Buddika (29*) and Rajapaksa (24*) had taken their stand to 50*.*

At Canterbury, August 12. **Fourth one-day international. Sri Lanka Under-19 won by 11 runs.** ‡**Sri Lanka Under-19 221** (49.1 overs) (R. L. B. Rambukwella 68, K. D. K. Vithanage 45; D. A. Payne 3-46); **England Under-19 210** (49 overs) (L. W. P. Wells 47; P. L. M. Jayarathne 3-43). *For the third time on this tour, Sri Lanka opened a one-match lead with one to play. They were set up brilliantly by Rambukwella and Vithanage, who added 94 for the third wicket in 22 overs. Manuel and Root set off at six an over, but only Wells could press on beyond Root's 26.*

At Canterbury, August 13. **Fifth one-day international. England Under-19 won by 51 runs.** ‡**England Under-19 184** (48.2 overs) (J. K. Manuel 69; P. L. M. Jayarathne 3-22); **Sri Lanka Under-19 125** (34.1 overs) (M. P. Dunn 3-15, D. A. Payne 4-40). *Matt Dunn and David Payne reduced Sri Lanka to 43-5 before rain. Although both were recorded by the broadcasters as breaking 90mph, the best ball of the day was a slow yorker from Payne which bowled opener Buddika. There was an interesting ethical discussion about the behaviour of Best, the England captain, as rain started to fall in the 20th over. With the covers being readied and England well ahead on Duckworth/ Lewis, Best appeared to deliberately drop a catch off Denuwan Rajakaruna, so ensuring the completion of the 20 overs necessary for a result. However, after a 94-minute stoppage, play resumed, and Sri Lanka were set a revised target of 177 from 41 overs. They blazed another 82 in 14 before being bowled out at 6.54 p.m. England celebrated levelling the series, but the post-tour report by Sri Lanka's team manager Muttaiah Devaraj, leaked to a Sri Lankan newspaper, appeared to explain the tourists' pell-mell batting – and cast doubt on the real value of England's achievement. Having been assured by his board that the return flight with Oman Air would wait at Heathrow for up to two hours, Devaraj learned during the match that it would leave on schedule, at 10.35 p.m. Faced with a rush-hour coach journey on the M25, Devaraj said he asked his batsmen to hit out or get out. Despite it being Friday 13th, they made the flight.*

YOUTH CRICKET, 2010

Patrick Kidd

The route into the England dressing-room tends to involve a meeting with the former manager of the Bee Gees. In the early 1980s, David English, who was awarded a CBE in the Queen's Birthday Honours in 2010 for services to cricket and charity, wrote a book called *The Bunbury Tails* about rabbits playing cricket against the cats from Whisker Town, whose manager was Chairman Miaow. From this came the idea for forming a charity team of celebrities from showbusiness, the Bunburys, and a spin-off festival for under-15s.

The Bunbury Festival celebrates its 25th anniversary in 2011 and English, who has raised £14m for charity through the Bunburys, will again be there to deliver a pep talk to the stars of tomorrow. James Anderson presented the caps at the 24th festival, in Chester, in which more than 50 boys played for four regions in a round-robin tournament.

"The award [the CBE] makes me feel immensely proud," said English. "So does the fact that 13 of England's current Ashes squad played in the Bunbury Festival as 15-year-olds." Some 60 Bunbury boys have gone on to play Test cricket for England, the most recent of them Steve Finn, who played at the festival in 2004. "It's where the boys cut their teeth and first play at a higher level."

The identification of talented young players who can be fast-tracked into the national side now begins at under-13 level with an emerging player programme that the ECB has initiated for all first-class and Minor Counties. From this, regional squads are formed for the Bunbury Festival and then the best players enter the England age-group programme, a four-year scheme culminating in the under-19s.

Surrey, for all their lack of senior success, appear to be developing a golden generation. Their under-15s won the national title, having won at under-14 and under-13 level in previous years. Four of the team (captain Richard O'Grady, David Buck, Jack Winslade and Charlie O'Brien) had played in all three years. With no national under-16 competition, many of them will step up a level and try to win the Under-17 County Cup in 2011.

Chance to Shine, the charity which aims to revive cricket in state schools, reached a major landmark in its fifth year. Rachel Sanders, aged 11, from St Thomas Primary School in Exeter, became the one millionth child to participate in a Chance to Shine session, which operated last year in 3,700 state primary and secondary schools.

England Under-17 won a triangular tournament with the Ireland and Scotland Development XIs at Loughborough in August. Adam Rossington scored 122 as England chased 288 in 45 overs to win their first match against Scotland, while the second was ended by rain. Sam Wood, who scored 102 not out, shared an unbeaten fourth-wicket stand of 169 with Graham Clark to beat Ireland, but England lost the second meeting by three wickets. The Under-17s will be coached throughout the winter by the ECB, and were due to attend a training camp in Port Elizabeth in February half-term.

A 15-man England Under-18 squad toured India early in 2010, where they were coached in Bangalore by Michael Vaughan. Their summer highlight was two 50-over victories against county second elevens. Jack Taylor, who made his Gloucestershire debut in August, took four for 46 and Daniel Bell-Drummond, of Kent, made 88 as they beat Nottinghamshire by seven wickets. Kent's Adam Ball, and Lewis Gregory, of Somerset, then shared an eighth-wicket stand of 132 in a one-wicket win over Derbyshire.

Winners of age-group competitions: Boys – Under-17 County Championship Middlesex. **Under-17 County Cup** Kent. **Under-15 County Cup** Surrey. **Under-14 County Cup** Yorkshire. **Under-15 ECB National Club Championship** Wanstead. **Under-13 Club Competition** Newport. **ASDA Kwik Cricket** Bispham Drive Junior School, Nottinghamshire. **Bunbury Festival** London & East. **Girls – Under-13, 15 and 17** all won by Kent. **Lady Taverners Under-15 Outdoor** Wirksworth CC. **Under-15 Indoor** Ilkley Grammar School. **Under-13 Outdoor** Burton Latimer CC. **Under-13 Indoor** Colston's School. **ASDA Girls** Oakley C of E Junior School, Hampshire.

SCHOOLS CRICKET, 2010

REVIEW BY DOUGLAS HENDERSON

The most striking development of the 2010 summer was the introduction of the National Schools Twenty20 tournament. Most participating schools came from the private sector. However, several state schools joined in, and some, such as The Judd, performed with distinction. There had been a similar competition, promoted by Rumsey Travel, involving some 60 schools, but this was the first year of a truly national tournament contested by the great majority of establishments appearing in these pages. For assorted reasons, the first year included only English sides. The winners were Millfield, who defeated Bedford in the final. The other semi-finalists on a glorious June day at Lord's were Abingdon and Shrewsbury.

Another welcome feature of the summer was the continuation of 2009's good weather, with many schools reporting a season that included not a single complete washout. What chance a third in succession?

Limited-overs games tend to dominate the fixture list, but the format did produce at least one astonishing match. Solihull, batting first on their home ground, rattled up 408 for five in 50 overs against Nottingham High School; Chris Williamson led the assault with 263, having never scored a century before. He was eventually run out after hitting 12 sixes and 29 fours. Nottingham were unfazed by the scale of the task and, with one over and one wicket left, needed 12 to win. But from the third ball of the final over the last man was stumped, eight short of the target. The aggregate of 809 runs is believed to be a record for a limited-overs schools match.

Nottingham were also involved in a remarkable match in that endangered species, the two-day declaration game. They called a halt at a comparatively modest 333 for seven against Wellingborough, who then closed their reply at 484 for five, from just 69 overs; Jack Johnson agonisingly fell on 199. The game petered out into a slightly dull draw, but it was clearly a considerable batting display.

Two batsmen to have had an inkling of how Johnson must have felt were Hugo Darby of Bradfield and Radley's Wilf Marriott. Darby was undefeated on 99 with one run required, but the match ended when the Free Foresters bowler delivered a wide; Marriott suffered the ignominy of being run out just one from a century.

Sedbergh benefited from having a magnificent pair of slow bowlers. Left-arm spinner Tim Raglan claimed 48 wickets, while off-spinner Charlie Thwaytes took 46. They were the top two wicket-takers in the 2010 season. Sedbergh played 20 matches, and of 200 possible wickets, their attack claimed 195. Oundle also possessed a talented slow left-armer: Jack Oughtred grabbed 40 wickets in the season, including all ten for 48 against The Perse. The following week he hit a century against Eton. Others to take 40 wickets or more were Arthur Jones of Malvern, Alex Colville of St George's Weybridge, Jake Lintott from Queen's Taunton and Radley's Andrew Tinsley.

Will Vanderspar of Eton, the fourth *Young Wisden* Cricketer of the Year. Previous winners were Jonny Bairstow, James Taylor and Jos Buttler.

Alexander Russell of Adams Grammar School finished with a remarkable average: despite bowling only 22 overs in a short season of just eight games, he took 11 wickets at 7.27. Others to average below ten were Tim Raglan, Lewis Catlow of Ipswich, Joseph Schindler of Cranbrook, Arnold's Tom Hessey, Harry Rouse of Kingswood, Merchiston Castle's Rakeeb Patel, Ben Ladd-Gibbon from Clayesmore and Fred van den Bergh of Whitgift.

Will Vanderspar, captaining Eton in his fifth year in the team, was the leading run-scorer with 1,286. He ended an illustrious school career with 4,268 runs. Oakham's Tom Fell, still only in his GCSE year, was close behind with 1,242. Zafar Ansari, from Hampton, scored 1,111 and averaged 101; he hit 179 against Eton. In all, six batsmen passed 1,000 runs for the season. Rory Osmond, Oundle's captain, totalled 3,135 runs in four years.

King's Taunton continued their strong showing: Alex Barrow, the 2010 captain, averaged 160.60; his opening partner, Craig Meschede, was not too far behind with 105. Another outstanding player was Freddie Coleman of Strathallan, with an average of 139.20. Two other notable performers, if with slightly quirky figures, were Ashville's James Kempley, whose average reached 186 after being dismissed just twice in 12 innings, and Craig Atherton of Adams Grammar, who hit 156 runs in two innings. Since he was unbeaten on 114 in one, he averaged 156.

Double-hundreds are more common than they used to be, and one reason – not as improbable as it might seem – is the rise of limited-overs cricket. In the traditional format of declaration matches, where draws remain a possibility, the team batting first gain little by running up a total so daunting that the opposition shut up shop. But in limited-overs games runs are the only currency, and it's not possible to have too many. Meschede twice reached 200 for King's

Taunton; Vanderspar of Eton, Shiv Thakor and Henry Hughes, both of Uppingham, and Chris Williamson of Solihull all did so once.

Dulwich were the outstanding school: in a very strong circuit they won 19 of their 21 games. (They also shone at the Sir Garfield Sobers tournament in Barbados where they reached the final.) Denstone, Trent, King's Taunton, Abingdon, Sedbergh and Bromsgrove all prevailed in at least 80% of their matches. Denstone remained unbeaten; King's Taunton, Winchester, Hymers, Felsted, The Perse and Adams Grammar lost only once.

For his magnificent contribution to his side's batting, the winner of the *Young Wisden* Schools Cricketer of the Year is Will Vanderspar. There were many strong candidates, with Zafar Ansari, Alex Barrow and Craig Meschede all making cogent cases; but Vanderspar, who plays on perhaps the toughest schools circuit of them all, was the leading run-scorer in the land. He scored his runs with the freedom of batsmen in the Golden Age, advancing down the pitch to drive the new ball and disrupting the bowler like a MacLaren, although he was a Harrovian, or Lionel Palairet. When he stepped up a grade, if only a small one, his strokeplay against Cambridge University was superlative. He can bowl too, at lively pace, but has been hampered by injury. Attached to Middlesex, he might not pursue a career in the game like the other Wisden Schools Cricketers of the Year, but Vanderspar in terms of skill and achievement to date is a worthy successor.

Two years ago, the Schools Cricket Committee of the HMC (the body representing most leading independent schools in the UK) circulated a paper which, they requested, should be handed to umpires. This asked the officials to enforce Law 42 – and specifically the section stating that captains have a responsibility to ensure the game is played not only within the Laws, but in accordance with the Spirit of Cricket. This appears to have had an effect in concentrating the minds of young players, with several schools suggesting on-field behaviour has improved. The ECB is determined to press players at the highest level to show a good example to the young. Without that example, the old saw "It's not cricket" will lose all resonance.

Douglas Henderson is the current editor of Schools Cricket Online (www. schoolscricketonline.co.uk).

Full coverage of the 2010 Eton v Harrow match can be found on the wisden website (wisden.com/almanacklinks).

Schools who wish to be considered for inclusion in *Wisden* should email the deputy editor: hugh.chevallier@wisden.com. State schools and girls' schools are especially welcome.

Note: The following tables cover only those schools listed in the Schools A–Z section.

LEADING BATSMEN IN SCHOOLS CRICKET – 500 runs at 65.00

	I	NO	Runs	HS	100s	Avge
A. W. R. Barrow (*King's College, Taunton*)	11	6	803	168*	4	160.60
F. R. J. Coleman (*Strathallan School*)	8	3	696	140*	4	139.20
C. A. J. Meschede (*King's College, Taunton*)	11	2	946	216*	3	105.11
Z. S. Ansari (*Hampton School*)	14	3	1,111	179	7	101.00
S. B. Ward (*Ipswich School*)	14	5	890	171*	3	98.88

	I	*NO*	*Runs*	*HS*	*100s*	*Avge*
W. T. Root (*Worksop College*)	14	5	868	151	4	96.44
M. K. Phillips (*Ratcliffe College*)	11	3	724	160*	4	90.50
B . P. Wilson (*Barnard Castle School*)	9	3	537	151*	3	89.50
M. L. Swift (*Wrekin College*)	13	5	703	112*	1	87.87
J. M. Kettleborough (*Bedford School*)	17	4	1,085	145	6	83.46
C. J. Beech (*Denstone College*)	14	4	831	158*	3	83.10
A. T. Alleyne (*Dulwich College*)	18	7	909	153*	4	82.63
M. J. Winter (*Cheadle Hulme School*)	15	3	976	136*	3	81.33
G. J. Brothwood (*Cheltenham College*)	12	3	730	142*	2	81.11
S. J. Thakor (*Uppingham School*)	14	3	889	219*	3	80.81
A. J. Robertson (*Gordonstoun School*)	11	3	644	136*	3	80.50
W. G. R. Vanderspar (*Eton College*)	20	4	1,286	204*	6	80.37
R. J. McClellan (*RGS, Guildford*)	14	5	685	106*	1	76.11
S. A. Moss (*Wells Cathedral School*)	14	5	675	133*	2	75.00
O. J. D. Swann (*Trent College*)	9	1	591	139	3	73.87
S. Mount (*King Edward's School, Bath*)	13	4	663	148*	4	73.66
S. F. G. Bullen (*Filton College*)	8	1	509	143	2	72.71
C. H. Portz (*Winchester College*)	18	4	999	108	4	71.35
U. A. Qureshi (*Marlborough College*)	13	3	713	112	3	71.30
G. R. Thurstance (*Bedford Modern School*)	16	4	849	133*	3	70.75
N. A. T. Watkins (*Abingdon School*)	13	3	705	136*	2	70.50
T. J. Ravenscroft (*Elizabeth College, Guernsey*)	13	3	697	129	2	69.70
J. B. Lintott (*Queen's College, Taunton*)	16	1	1,045	136	2	69.66
T. C. Fell (*Oakham School*)	22	4	1,242	181*	4	69.00
C. L. Lawlor (*Monmouth School*)	15	0	1,034	137	4	68.93
B. A. Letts (*Haberdashers' Aske's*)	15	5	687	143	2	68.70
N. G. R. Cooper (*RGS, Guildford*)	16	6	685	155*	1	68.50
W. M. Langmead (*Cranleigh School*)	18	4	947	138*	2	67.64
D. J. Bell-Drummond (*Millfield School*)	17	2	982	136*	4	65.46
L. D. McManus (*Claysmore School*)	13	4	588	117*	1	65.33

MOST WICKETS IN SCHOOLS CRICKET – 25 wickets at 16.00

	O	*M*	*R*	*W*	*BB*	*Avge*
L. J. Catlow (*Ipswich School*)	141.2	14	228	27	7-55	8.44
T. D. Raglan (*Sedbergh School*)	145.1	31	461	48	4-16	9.60
F. O. E. van den Bergh (*Whitgift School*)	102.2	23	311	32	5-6	9.71
T. Moore (*Brentwood School*)	108	22	334	31	6-16	10.77
Z. S. Ansari (*Hampton School*)	132.3	25	337	31	6-33	10.87
A. D. W. Tinsley (*Radley College*)	135.4	16	436	40	7-29	10.90
T. Q. McGeer (*Oratory School*)	116	14	340	30	6-27	11.33
R. G. Craze (*Kimbolton School*)	96	12	365	32	4-27	11.40
N. A. T. Watkins (*Abingdon School*)	115	17	355	31	5-35	11.45
C. W. Thwaytes (*Sedbergh School*)	143.2	19	532	46	5-12	11.56
A. Tillcock (*Trent College*)	102	8	390	32	4-24	12.18
S. E. J. Thornton (*Oratory School*)	142	19	404	32	5-17	12.62
B. W. Kemp (*St Edmund's School, Canterbury*)	99.5	8	383	30	4-12	12.76
M. Paynter (*Monkton Combe School*)	142	24	473	37	5-23	12.78
J. B. Lintott (*Queen's College, Taunton*)	144	16	513	40	6-72	12.82
J. Wainman (*Leeds Grammar School*)	124	21	419	32	6-28	13.09
A. Shinwari (*Whitgift School*)	105	19	370	28	6-33	13.21
B. Chohan (*Hampton School*)	120.1	20	414	31	5-19	13.35
B. D. H. Stevens (*Winchester College*)	174.5	40	508	38	4-21	13.36
D. T. Brown (*Manchester Grammar School*)	130	27	410	30	4-21	13.66
P. A. Baker (*Merchiston Castle School*)	117	15	397	29	4-14	13.68
T. M. Bird (*King's School, Worcester*)	140	29	465	33	3-10	14.09
T. P. A. Davies (*Monkton Combe School*)	161	22	527	37	7-43	14.24
A. J. Marjoribanks (*Felsted School*)	125.3	20	388	27	4-6	14.37
J. W. Howe (*St John's School, Leatherhead*)	135	9	479	33	4-29	14.51
A. K. Colville (*St George's College, Weybridge*)	159.4	18	597	41	5-40	14.56

	O	M	R	W	BB	Avge
A. M. Dobb (*Worksop College*)	128	12	453	31	5-39	14.61
C. C. Farrant (*Sevenoaks School*)	116	16	461	31	7-20	14.87
T. M. Nugent (*Oratory School*)	126	12	376	25	5-34	15.04
M. P. Dawe (*RGS, Guildford*)	126.1	9	558	37	4-25	15.08
M. E. Hobden (*Eastbourne College*)	139	31	481	31	6-30	15.51
M. J. Dawes (*City of London Freemen's School*)	135.4	26	405	26	6-33	15.57

OUTSTANDING SEASONS – minimum 10 matches

	P	W	L	T	D	A	%W
Dulwich College	21	19	1	0	1	0	90.48
Denstone College	14	12	0	1	1	0	85.71
King's College, Taunton	14	12	1	0	1	0	85.71
Trent College	14	12	2	0	0	0	85.71
Abingdon School	16	13	3	0	0	1	81.25
Sedbergh School	20	16	3	0	1	0	80.00
Bromsgrove School	15	12	3	0	0	1	80.00
Winchester College	18	14	1	0	3	2	77.78
Hampton School	18	14	2	0	2	0	77.78
Bancroft's School	18	14	3	0	1	0	77.78
Cranbrook School	17	13	3	0	1	0	76.47
Westminster School	17	13	3	0	1	0	76.47
Royal Grammar School, Worcester	20	15	3	0	2	0	75.00
Radley College	16	12	3	0	1	0	75.00
Repton School	16	12	3	0	1	0	75.00
Filton College	12	9	3	0	1	0	75.00

SCHOOLS A–Z

In the results line, A = abandoned without a ball bowled. An asterisk next to a name indicates captain. Schools provide their own report and averages. The qualification for the averages is 150 runs or ten wickets.

Abingdon School
P16 W13 L3 A1

Masters i/c C. R. Burnand/D. C. Shirazi   **Coach** D. C. Shirazi

Abingdon had an excellent season, winning 81% of their games and reaching the National Twenty20 semi-finals at Lord's. Nathaniel Watkins and Joshua Smith were the mainstays of the batting while Sasha Barras and Joshua Bull had fine first seasons with the ball.

Batting N. A. T. Watkins* 705 at 70.50; J. W. G. Smith 583 at 64.77; J. H. Edwards 266 at 44.33; H. R. Grant 388 at 43.11; W. G. Sensecall 217 at 31.00; J. W. Channon 191 at 23.87.

Bowling N. A. T. Watkins 31 at 11.45; J. W. G. Smith 14 at 16.71; A. D. P. Barras 22 at 20.13; J. C. E. Bull 17 at 21.64.

Adams Grammar School
P8 W6 L1 D1 A1

Master i/c S. D. Blount

Adams GS had a gratifying season, beating Ellesmere, Wymondham College, Solihull and St Joseph's College. The only defeat came against a strong Shrewsbury.

Batting C. Atherton* 156 at 156.00.

Bowling A. Russell 11 at 7.27.

Aldenham School
P13 W3 L10

Master i/c M. I. Yeabsley   **Coach** D. J. Goodchild

The side won just three games against other schools. Rishi Batra was the pick of the bowlers, while Matthew Lench was the leading batsman. An annual John Dewes Invitational XI was established in which both John Emburey and Paul Weekes played.

Batting G. M. Stear 197 at 39.40; H. J. Ripper 239 at 26.55; B. I. Boothby 208 at 23.11; M. O. Lench 252 at 21.00; W. E. C. Collier 203 at 20.30.

Bowling R. Batra 18 at 20.16; S. Shah* 10 at 21.00; T. R. Bayley 10 at 30.00.

Alleyn's School
P14 W8 L3 T1 D2

Master i/c R. N. Ody   **Coach** P. E. Edwards

An enjoyable and successful season resulted in eight wins from 14 games. The team were well led by Matthew Syrett who had a fine season with the bat, passing 50 on eight occasions.

Batting M. A. S. Syrett* 600 at 46.15; J. W. Mayes 266 at 20.46; A. M. A. Senn 273 at 18.20.

Bowling I. R. S. Taylor 18 at 13.27; A. M. A. Senn 20 at 14.05; M. A. S. Syrett 16 at 16.06; D. L. Petrides 10 at 19.10; R. J. Balfour 15 at 20.00; J. E. Miller 12 at 21.41; D. L. Forde 10 at 21.90.

Ampleforth College
P17 W5 L6 D6

Master i/c G. D. Thurman

A very young side played some terrific cricket and, under the careful captaincy of Will Prest, will have learned a huge amount for future seasons.

Batting C. J. Ramsay 281 at 40.14; W. D. Prest* 507 at 33.80; F. Black 377 at 25.13; H. Barnard 289 at 24.08; E. J. Robinson 319 at 21.26; J. E. Ainscough 167 at 12.84.

Bowling J. S. Prest 22 at 18.22; J. E. Ainscough 23 at 25.82; C. J. Ramsay 15 at 26.53; C. R. Hawkesworth 14 at 32.35; N. J. Macauley 13 at 40.23.

Ardingly College
P14 W10 L3 D1

Masters i/c R. A. King/N. J. Tester   **Coach** C. E. Waller

Following an enjoyable and successful tour to Cape Town, the College had a most pleasing season, winning more than 70% of their matches. The opening bowling attack of Joshua Higgins and Abidine Sakande was outstanding.

Batting J. S. Howard 376 at 34.18; H. O. Sims 328 at 29.81; J. D. Higgins 374 at 28.76; T. G. Howard 223 at 27.87; H. I. Clark 314 at 24.15; H. W. Tye 233 at 19.41; A. M. H. Pollard 163 at 18.11.

Bowling A. Sakande 15 at 15.60; J. D. Higgins 23 at 18.26; J. D. H. Hong* 12 at 23.66.

Arnold School
P6 W4 L2

Master i/c M. L. Evans   **Coach** A. J. McKeown

The team had a wonderful run during May, losing only to MCC and enjoying wins over Rossall, Kirkham GS, KEQMS Lytham and Birkenhead. Team captain Nathan Bolus led superbly, with Ben Perkins and all-rounder Tom Hessey in particularly good form.

Batting T. J. Hessey 241 at 48.20.

Bowling T. J. Hessey 12 at 9.00; B. H. Perkins 10 at 16.60.

Ashville College
P15 W10 L4 T1

Master i/c J. R. Goldthorp

Ashville had their best season for many years, with a winning streak of ten games following a tie. They played some excellent cricket and came out on top in several tight finishes. Ned Hammond led by example, scoring the only century, and encouraged the newcomers in the team to play a full part.

Batting J. O. Kempley 372 at 186.00; N. P. Hammond* 663 at 60.27; M. R. J. Johnson 385 at 35.00; J. M. W. Hare 415 at 31.92; O. P. Mitchell 187 at 15.58.

Bowling N. P. Hammond 24 at 16.16; J. M. W. Hare 21 at 19.57; M. R. J. Johnson 19 at 20.36; W. E. Hammond 20 at 21.15; R. M. B. Simms 11 at 26.45.

Bancroft's School
P18 W14 L3 D1

Master i/c J. K. Lever

Gareth James's outstanding all-round contribution sustained a successful season, with only one defeat by another school. He was well supported by the batting of Nigel Jacob and captain Rishabh Shah, and the bowling of Neville Jacob and Rahul Patel.

Batting R. A. Shah* 578 at 64.22; G. O. James 590 at 59.00; N. Jacob 683 at 52.53; N. P. Jacob 344 at 24.57.

Bowling R. S. Patel 23 at 13.43; M. J. Tann 20 at 14.95; G. O. James 22 at 19.50; N. Jacob 10 at 21.20; N. P. Jacob 23 at 23.26; L. Sathananthan 11 at 28.90.

Barnard Castle School
P10 W1 L7 D2

Master i/c B. C. Usher   **Coach** J. W. Lister

A very young and inexperienced side relied heavily on runs from John Huck and Ben Wilson. Kit Wilson, in Year 9, showed some promise with the ball, but in general control in the field was a real problem.

Batting B. P. Wilson* 537 at 89.50; J. R. Huck 365 at 73.00; B. P. Upton 191 at 31.83.
Bowling K. S. Wilson 11 at 26.36; B. P. Upton 12 at 26.50; B. P. Wilson 11 at 26.72.

Bedford Modern School   P16 W8 L2 D6
Master i/c N. J. Chinneck
Bedford Modern had a profitable season that included the notable scalps of Haileybury, Stowe and Haberdashers' Aske's. George Thurstance, the captain, was outstanding and played for Bedfordshire and Northamptonshire seconds.
Batting G. R. Thurstance* 849 at 70.75; B. Naik 377 at 31.41; C. D. Wood 271 at 30.11; J. Nicklin 316 at 28.72; R. A. Cunningham 323 at 26.91; H. P. Thurstance 284 at 25.81.
Bowling A. J. Walker 34 at 19.85; M. P. Kraus 15 at 23.46; G. R. Thurstance 22 at 24.95; F. R. Wilson 14 at 29.85; N. J. O'Quinn 13 at 35.69.

Bedford School   P17 W10 L5 D2 A1
Master i/c P. Sherwin   **Coach** D. W. Randall
The highlight of the season was the National Twenty20 final at Lord's. James Kettleborough captained well and batted with class as the side experienced tense victories against Oakham and Haileybury, but suffered last-over defeats by The Perse, Tonbridge and Harrow.
Batting J. M. Kettleborough* 1,085 at 83.46; C. A. L. Davis 560 at 62.22; R. J. T. Wharton 503 at 45.72; S. Kumar 523 at 37.35; J. H. T. McDuell 260 at 23.63; C. G. Smart 173 at 19.22.
Bowling V. V. S. Sohal 15 at 20.60; H. C. Banks 13 at 20.76; M. W. Edmunds 19 at 21.57; C. A. L. Davis 17 at 25.41.

Beechen Cliff School   P9 W4 L4 D1
Master i/c E. J. Wilmot   **Coach** M. J. Thorburn
Some excellent performances were capped by a rare victory against MCC that included an impressive 106 not out from Tom Weaver. Mixed form in the Peak Sports League was less encouraging.
Batting T. Weaver 204 at 68.00; O. Canning 263 at 43.83; C. E. Mackenzie 249 at 35.57.
Bowling J. Self 13 at 18.76; J. Price 10 at 20.50.

Belfast Royal Academy   P11 W4 L7
Masters i/c M. C. W. Harte/J. McCombe   **Coach** M. R. Shields
This was a slightly disappointing season, perhaps reflective of the side's youthful composition. Notable achievements include opening batsman Jordan McClurkin's 103 not out against Regent House and Matthew Palmer's fourth season in the first team, his second as captain.
Batting J. R. J. McClurkin 251 at 27.88; D. M. McFadden 200 at 25.00.
Bowling R. J. R. Martin 16 at 11.37; A. T. A. Montgomery 15 at 14.53; M. J. Palmer 12 at 18.16.

Birkenhead School   P15 W9 L6 A1
Master i/c P. N. Lindberg   **Coach** G. J. Rickman
James Hassall guided an inexperienced side to a greatly improved season after 2009's disappointing results. He also led the batting by scoring over 500 runs and was ably supported by wicketkeeper William Lamb and talented Under-16 all-rounders Ashley Davis and Oliver Hearn.
Batting A. Hind 190 at 63.33; J. Hassall* 539 at 38.50; W. Lamb 463 at 35.61; T. Bills 191 at 31.83; A. Davis 258 at 28.66; O. Hearn 300 at 23.07; J. Hillyer 182 at 20.22.
Bowling P. Benc 10 at 14.80; A. Davis 15 at 17.00; N. Hearn 10 at 24.00; O. Hearn 13 at 29.30.

Bishop's Stortford College   P8 W1 L6 D1
Master i/c M. Drury   **Coach** J. Kirton
A very young side worked hard through a difficult season, and the experience gained will serve them well in the coming years. With junior sides winning regularly, the future looks promising.
Batting A. Palmer 242 at 34.57; F. Hiard* 153 at 21.85.
Bowling S. Sterenborg 11 at 20.09; A. Mozumdar 10 at 26.10.

Bloxham School   P13 W5 L5 D3 A2
Master i/c R. W. F. Hastings   **Coach** A. D. Jones
Good performances against some strong opposition resulted in a decent term's cricket. Sam Ryan scored runs and captained effectively, helped by telling contributions from Scott de Weymarn and Thomas Gurney.
Batting S. E. Ryan* 506 at 46.00; S. A. de Weymarn 297 at 33.00.
Bowling B. Williams 22 at 14.09; T. Stephenson 21 at 14.33.

Blundell's School
P17 W10 L7

Master i/c R. J. Turner   **Coach** C. L. L. Gabbitass

Mixed form and fortunes characterised the season, although more games were won than lost. Performances during successful festivals at Malvern and Marlborough bode well for future years.

Batting C. R. Grainger 421 at 28.06; T. A. H. Lett 251 at 27.88; N. R. Menheneott 301 at 27.36; H. J. D. McDowell* 265 at 24.09; B. G. Goss 231 at 23.10; Z. G. Bess 277 at 21.30; J. A. Rossiter 187 at 20.77.

Bowling N. R. Menheneott 17 at 22.76; J. Lilly D'Cruz 13 at 24.69; M. J. Goss 10 at 24.80; H. N. Folland 12 at 25.16; M. G. Hague 11 at 28.63; T. E. Cole 10 at 29.20.

Bradfield College
P19 W6 L13

Master i/c M. S. Hill   **Coach** J. R. Wood

After an encouraging start, a young side learned quite how merciless 50-over cricket can be. Jonathan Gaffney's eight for 54 and Paul Woodford's 147 not out were highlights, and both will be expected to contribute heavily in 2011.

Batting H. R. Darby 424 at 32.61; C. N. Gaur 391 at 30.07; L. D. Glover 255 at 28.33; R. F. Higgins 382 at 27.28; P. A. Woodford 414 at 23.00; R. Wijeratne 263 at 21.91; P. E. Williams 244 at 20.33; J. J. Gaffney 182 at 14.00.

Bowling J. J. Gaffney 31 at 17.96; G. E. Graham* 23 at 26.73; T. J. Allen 17 at 28.70; G. C. Smith 11 at 32.00; M. F. E. Glenn 10 at 36.10.

Bradford Grammar School
P17 W9 L5 D3

Master i/c A. G. Smith   **Coach** S. A. Kellett

The team enjoyed a rewarding year. The success was very much a team effort, though the remarkably reliable batting of Arkam Asif was vital. Also in fine form was opening bowler Ravi Prasad in his debut season.

Batting M. A. Asif 626 at 48.15; A. E. Browne 407 at 33.91; N. Devesher 158 at 26.33; S. Rashid 363 at 25.92; J. C. R. Wadkin 185 at 23.12; S. J. G. Connor 216 at 21.60; G. F. M. O'Hara 176 at 14.66.

Bowling G. F. M. O'Hara 10 at 14.80; S. Rashid 22 at 16.63; R. A. Prasad 26 at 17.26; W. P. F. Vickers 16 at 27.06; M. A. Asif 13 at 30.15; R. R. Misra 13 at 34.23.

Brentwood School
P16 W8 L7 D1 A3

Master i/c B. R. Hardie

An inexperienced team matured as the season unfolded. The captain Tom Moore bowled quickly and demonstrated good control for his 30 wickets. The best of eight victories was a thrilling run-chase against MCC.

Batting G. W. C. Balmford 548 at 49.81; J. Mowll 193 at 48.25; J. S. Welham 182 at 45.50; R. Hassan 368 at 33.45; C. J. Sutherland 464 at 33.14; K. S. Velani 212 at 19.27; E. J. Hardy 164 at 14.90.

Bowling T. Moore 31 at 10.77; T. Patterson 16 at 22.43; K. S. Velani 10 at 24.50; R. Hassan 16 at 27.68; H. J. D. Levy 16 at 30.75.

Brighton College
P14 W6 L5 T1 D2

Master i/c Miss A. L. Walker   **Coach** N. J. Buoy

Skipper Adam Davies guided a very young side with skill – and also averaged over 50 with the bat. Wins over Gordonstoun and a strong MCC team, together with a tied match against Eastbourne, were the highlights.

Batting A. R. Davies* 652 at 50.15; A. W. C. Chapman 514 at 36.71; J. N. Thornley 255 at 23.18; H. Richards 177 at 13.61; E. Kalidasan 159 at 11.35.

Bowling C. R. Davies 32 at 16.40; Y. Bahemou 19 at 17.42; J. N. Thornley 17 at 22.70; E. Kalidasan 14 at 32.57.

Bristol Grammar School
P17 W6 L11

Master i/c R. S. Jones   **Coach** K. R. Blackburn

Andraes Moeller provided the high point of the season with a scintillating 188 against Taunton. Solid batting contributions from the captain Charlie Killick, and the consistent Sam Brewer and Will Godfrey, were the key to most of the side's success.

Batting S. A. Brewer 552 at 36.80; A. Moeller 540 at 36.00; C. R. Killick* 473 at 31.53; W. F. Godfrey 276 at 21.23; L. C. Luscombe 170 at 15.45.

Andraes Moeller, from Bristol Grammar, after scoring 188 against Taunton.

Bowling T. I. Barrington 16 at 24.81; J. H. Fairs 16 at 26.93; C. R. Killick 12 at 34.33; G. F. J. Bacon 11 at 36.09; S. A. Brewer 10 at 47.40; L. C. Luscombe 11 at 48.36.

Bromsgrove School
P15 W12 L3 A1

Master i/c D. J. Fallows
A series of excellent results were topped by fantastic wins against MCC and a strong Worcester Gents side, but there were also three disappointing defeats. Ben Cox closed his school account in good form, and leaves after signing a contract with Worcestershire.
Batting J. P. Webb* 566 at 47.16; O. B. Cox 311 at 44.42; M. Wyres 336 at 37.33; B. Huxley 165 at 33.00; J. Dudley 204 at 20.40; A. J. G. Clegg 203 at 20.30; J. R. Evans 231 at 19.25; N. Chana 243 at 18.69; M. M. Nawaz 175 at 13.46.
Bowling J. P. Webb 24 at 15.58; J. Dudley 23 at 15.78; M. J. Cox 17 at 16.94; M. M. Nawaz 26 at 17.34; N. Chana 12 at 18.33; M. Wyres 14 at 24.35.

Bryanston School
P16 W8 L5 D3 A1

Master i/c B. J. Lawes
Coach P. J. Norton
Joe Weld was the outstanding player with 600 runs at an average over 42. He was shadowed by skipper Oliver d'Erlanger-Bertrand, who hit 140 not out and took 23 wickets. Mitch Wilson, on Gloucestershire's books, bowled with real pace to gain 21 wickets, and added zest to the attack.
Batting J. J. R. Weld 601 at 42.92; H. P. Turpie 268 at 29.77; O. A. d'Erlanger-Bertrand* 430 at 28.66; S. G. Fry 413 at 27.53; H. H. Mayhew 189 at 21.00; M. J. Wilson 228 at 16.28.
Bowling M. J. Wilson 21 at 15.52; O. A. d'Erlanger-Bertrand 23 at 18.21; G. E. Dickson 18 at 22.11; J. J. R. Weld 12 at 29.16; C. J. Dickson 11 at 31.81; S. G. Fry 10 at 47.10.

Canford School
P12 W4 L8

Master i/c B. C. Edgell
Coach M. Griggs
It was a slightly disappointing season for Canford, with only four victories. However, the team were ably led by Tom Darby, who gathered 328 runs and claimed 14 wickets. The outstanding individual performance came from Harry Anstee, who scored 102 against Sherborne.

Batting T. W. E. Darby* 328 at 46.85; B. C. W. Upton 312 at 39.00; H. Anstee 225 at 37.50;
R. Triniman 202 at 22.44; W. J. Connor 214 at 19.45.
Bowling T. W. E. Darby 14 at 16.64; R. A. G. Graham 20 at 23.05; M. S. M. W. Senior 17 at 23.11.

Charterhouse
P15 W4 L10 D1

Master i/c M. P. Bicknell

Runs were hard to come by in an unrewarding season. Only centuries from Charlie Evans in the first
match and Shevantha de Soysa in the last lifted the gloom. The highlight was the consistently fine
left-arm spin of Andrew Corridan.
Batting T. M. Gallyer 394 at 26.26; C. Evans 389 at 25.93; S. T. de Soysa 276 at 25.09; J. E. Ryder-
Smith 228 at 19.00; A. W. Rozier-Pamplin 279 at 18.60; C. E. R. Kimmins 204 at 17.00; J. P.
Hornby* 236 at 15.73.
Bowling T. M. Gallyer 21 at 24.23; E. M. Birkett 10 at 25.70; A. G. Corridan 24 at 29.66; J. E.
Ryder-Smith 13 at 35.92; J. C. Gonszor 12 at 36.83; C. E. R. Kimmins 10 at 38.60.

Cheadle Hulme School
P17 W8 L8 D1

Master i/c J. C. Winter

Skipper Matthew Marfani and Matthew Winter, at the top of the order, both scored prodigiously to
create a sound platform that was not always exploited. However, three Under-15s, Harry Whitaker,
Drew Carswell and Andrew Jackson, bowled with real promise in a young side that achieved as
many wins as losses.
Batting M. J. Winter 976 at 81.33; M. A. Marfani* 890 at 55.62; A. Agarwal 305 at 33.88; A. J.
Jackson 207 at 23.00; H. J. B. Taylor 312 at 20.80.
Bowling H. J. Whitaker 13 at 14.69; D. Carswell 17 at 20.94; M. J. Winter 15 at 25.06; B. A. J.
Lambert 13 at 32.23; A. Agarwal 11 at 32.90; A. J. Jackson 11 at 35.90.

Cheltenham College
P18 W13 L2 D3

Master i/c M. W. Stovold   **Coach** M. P. Briers

An outstanding season concluded with a win-rate of 72%. The side were admirably led by James
Croft, with Guy Mitchell (four centuries) and Guy Brothwood (two) scoring the bulk of the runs.
Tom Ward headed the bowling, with Ben Ringrose the most promising young player.
Batting G. J. Brothwood 730 at 81.11; G. J. Mitchell 749 at 57.61; J. W. Croft* 523 at 40.23;
G. D. L. Sandbach 428 at 32.92; A. M. Mason 318 at 31.80; B. J. Ringrose 212 at 30.28; A. T. A.
Ross 170 at 28.33.
Bowling T. W. Ward 24 at 17.25; J. H. Law 21 at 21.09; B. J. Ringrose 20 at 21.25; B. W. Hayward
14 at 23.21; A. M. Mason 20 at 25.00; G. J. Brothwood 16 at 27.12.

Chigwell School
P14 W6 L7 D1

Master i/c F. A. Griffith

The bowlers stole the honours with some excellent individual performances. Thomas Gibbs took six
for 20 against Colchester RGS; Christopher Stephens was the leading wicket-taker; and Asim
Shamsudin bowled economically. Christopher Briggs carried the batting, averaging over 60.
Seventeen-year-old Beth MacGregor was selected for the England Women's Twenty20 team in Sri
Lanka.
Batting C. D. A. Briggs 498 at 62.25; E. MacGregor 157 at 31.40; N. W. Brown 291 at 26.45; N. D.
Morse 167 at 15.18.
Bowling A. Shamsudin 10 at 16.40; C. N. Stephens 19 at 16.52; A. Chopra 10 at 25.20; T. J. Gibbs
15 at 26.93.

Chislehurst & Sidcup Grammar School
P6 W2 L4 A3

Master i/c R. Wallbridge   **Coach** I. B. Willmott

Term started with a good win against Borden that saw the captain, Mathew Kilbey, score his maiden
school century. Hopes were high but, despite admirable spirit, further successes were hard to find.
Batting M. Kilbey* 291 at 72.75.
Bowling No one took ten wickets. The leading bowler was C. A. Nash, who took nine at 18.44.

Cheadle Hulme's Matthew Winter (*left*) and Matthew Marfani put on 248 for the first wicket against Birkenhead; they shared five other century opening stands.

Christ College, Brecon
P9 L7 T1 D1 A1

Master i/c C. J. Webber   **Coach** P. Brett

This was a disappointing summer as far as results were concerned, though a young squad, all returning next year, will have gained useful experience.

Batting R. S. Lovering 288 at 41.14; T. W. Burton* 249 at 35.57.

Bowling No one took ten wickets. The leading bowler was S. D. Abbott, who took eight at 28.50.

Christ's College, Finchley
P12 W3 L8 D1 A1

Master i/c S. S. Goldsmith

A positive approach was never going to be enough for a young side, relying heavily on four senior players, to negotiate a tough fixture list successfully. Visitors from abroad were Afrikaanse High School from Pretoria and the Delhi Blues, for whom former Indian Test player Sanjeev Sharma took four wickets. Among the more bizarre statistics of the season was winning every single toss and using seven different wicketkeepers.

Batting B. A. Pujara 386 at 35.09; D. V. Jaichand* 266 at 26.60; R. V. Thakkar 161 at 14.63.

Bowling F. Azam 12 at 14.50; R. V. Thakkar 11 at 23.54; B. A. Pujara 11 at 26.54.

Christ's Hospital
P16 W9 L5 D2

Master i/c H. P. Holdsworth   **Coach** T. E. Jesty

This was a season of good, positive cricket. There were excellent centuries for 14-year-old Luke Hansford against Reigate GS, and Stuart Whittingham against St Peter's, York. Very well led by Alex Marsh and his vice-captain Alex Satterfield, the side played particularly well after exams, with seamers Sebastian Streeting and Max Haywood excelling. Four consecutive matches went to the last over.

Batting S. G. Whittingham 471 at 47.10; C. P. Williams 468 at 46.80; A. D. Satterfield 530 at 33.12; L. W. Hansford 402 at 26.80; A. P. Marsh* 338 at 24.14; C. B. J. Kowszun 158 at 17.55.

Bowling M. F. Haywood 27 at 19.96; S. A. A. Streeting 28 at 20.32; S. G. Whittingham 15 at 20.60; A. D. Satterfield 15 at 24.86; A. P. Marsh 12 at 25.33.

City of London Freemen's School
P22 W10 L11 D1 A1

Master i/c J. G. Moore   **Coach** N. M. Stewart

A shortage of senior batsmen made competitive totals elusive. Pleasing wins, however, came against Tiffin, Caterham and King's Bruton. Fred Davies led the way with the bat, while a balanced spin attack, coupled with accurate seam bowling from Michael Dawes, held opposition batsmen in check.

Batting F. H. Davies 600 at 30.00; J. J. Lewis-Oliver 306 at 25.50; J. D. E. Hutter 426 at 23.66; M. E. Dawes 229 at 14.31; G. Seymour 202 at 13.46; W. J. D. Culhane* 154 at 11.84; E. Walton 188 at 11.05.

Bowling J. J. Lewis-Oliver 21 at 12.33; M. J. Dawes 26 at 15.57; M. E. Dawes 21 at 16.28; W. J. D. Culhane 37 at 17.70; F. H. Davies 15 at 23.73; R. O'Brien 14 at 25.85.

Clayesmore School   P14 W7 L5 D2
Master i/c D. I. Rimmer   **Coach** P. M. Warren
Lewis McManus was the team's pivotal player, batting and keeping wicket with efficiency and flair. Early runs from the brothers Chris and Rob Morey, McManus and Toby Sutton were rarely followed up, making matches closer than necessary.
Batting L. D. McManus 588 at 65.33; C. J. Morey 231 at 57.75; B. I. Ladd-Gibbon 227 at 37.83; R. D. Morey 344 at 34.40; W. F. Morgan 183 at 22.87; T. J. Sutton 202 at 22.44.
Bowling B. I. Ladd-Gibbon 19 at 9.57; W. F. Morgan 16 at 22.56; H. J. Beardsley 17 at 23.17; G. J. Slinger 12 at 23.50; J. W. Green 12 at 29.16.

Clifton College   P14 W7 L7
Master i/c J. C. Bobby   **Coach** P. W. Romaines
After a very successful pre-season tour to Barbados, much was expected of the 2010 squad. In the end, a season that promised much never quite delivered. Highlights were wins over MCC, Monmouth, Sherborne and Bromsgrove – and reaching the West Final of the National Twenty20.
Batting C. A. M. Walker* 609 at 50.75; F. R. H. John 477 at 39.75; J. E. V. Barnes 335 at 30.45; M. W. Cornish 251 at 27.88; G. R. M. Kinsey 201 at 22.33; B. M. Figueiredo 172 at 21.50; L. E. V. Durrans 218 at 19.81.
Bowling G. A. Harris 12 at 29.33; C. A. M. Walker 20 at 29.70; R. E. Miller 16 at 30.56; L. R. Watson 10 at 36.50; M. W. Cornish 12 at 37.91; W. J. M. Barrett 11 at 40.54.

Colfe's School   P20 W9 L10 D1 A1
Master i/c G. S. Clinton
Performances from an extremely inexperienced side were, as expected, somewhat uneven. Future results should improve as some talented boys mature.
Batting F. Frazer 337 at 33.70; J. Potter* 418 at 32.15; D. Patel 161 at 23.00; E. A. Thompson 208 at 16.00; M. J. Selvey-Clinton 211 at 15.07; M. Stiddard 155 at 12.91; J. Carmichael 178 at 11.07.
Bowling A. Patel 12 at 15.16; M. Stiddard 14 at 15.28; J. Powerie 11 at 19.63; H. Furze 10 at 19.70; S. Roffo 13 at 24.15.

Colston's School   P13 W4 L9
Master i/c T. A. H. Williams   **Coach** D. V. Lawrence
A total of four victories from 13 fixtures was rather disappointing, even for a youthful and inexperienced side. But this squad has potential, and Colston's cricket should be exciting in 2011.
Batting M. N. Thatcher 469 at 36.07; O. D. King-Sorrell 372 at 28.61.
Bowling M. Evans 12 at 11.33; S. Cockram 11 at 23.00; O. D. King-Sorrell 10 at 28.30.

Cranbrook School   P17 W13 L3 D1 A2
Master i/c A. J. Presnell   **Coach** R. Leslie
Cranbrook relished their best season for decades with a record number of wins. Tom Seagrim was the stand-out individual in a good all-round team. Stuart Underwood and Bertie Berger guided a very young side including opening bowler Finn Hulbert, a Year 9.
Batting T. A. Seagrim 761 at 54.35; T. W. Carr 184 at 26.28; S. Underwood* 183 at 20.33; T. Berger 166 at 18.44; N. A. Manser 218 at 18.16; E. Berger 212 at 17.66.
Bowling J. Schindler 19 at 8.57; E. Berger 22 at 13.72; F. A. Hulbert 21 at 15.57.

Cranleigh School   P17 W8 L7 D2
Master i/c J. S. Ross   **Coach** S. D. Welch
In a season that improved after a difficult start, highlights were victories over Charterhouse and MCC. William Langmead excelled: his aggregate of 947 runs was a school record.
Batting W. M. Langmead 947 at 67.64; D. Allan* 599 at 46.07; J. A. L. Scriven 528 at 44.00; O. J. Davies 529 at 35.26; M. Burgess 300 at 30.00; J. C. Austin 353 at 23.53; O. J. Cross 205 at 20.50.
Bowling J. F. Cordy-Redden 24 at 21.66; J. G. Richards 27 at 22.59; O. J. Cross 15 at 25.20; J. A. L. Scriven 13 at 27.61; O. J. Davies 12 at 34.83.

Culford School
P9 W5 L3 D1 A1

Master i/c A. H. Marsh

Culford's relatively inexperienced side enjoyed a fine season. Having struggled through the early fixtures, the younger players began to find their feet – and finished the term with three straight wins.
Batting B. Shepperson 305 at 43.57; F. Preston 199 at 28.42.
Bowling B. Shepperson 24 at 12.25; J. Shepherd 12 at 15.91.

Dame Allan's School
P12 W7 L5

Master i/c J. A. Benn   **Coach** W. P. Hudson

An excellent first half of the season resulted in only one defeat, but after exams the availability of several key players was patchy. Alex Gray and Assad Mohammed excelled with the bat, and Ben Smith had a solid all-round season.
Batting A. Mohammed 244 at 34.85; A. Gray 332 at 30.18; B. Smith 173 at 21.62.
Bowling A. Mohammed 12 at 14.75; D. Hill 10 at 17.30; B. Smith 15 at 18.86; J. D. Richardson* 11 at 23.00.

Dauntsey's School
P16 W9 L7

Master i/c A. J. Palmer   **Coach** S. Cloete

There was no shortage of runs on dry wickets, with 15-year-old Jack Mynott outstanding. Although opening bowlers James Duckworth and Dave Probert had good strike-rates, the change bowling lacked control. A refurbished and extended pavilion, plus the laying of a fourth square, enhanced the facilities.
Batting J. M. A. Mynott 726 at 51.85; J. M. Tomlinson 351 at 43.87; E. J. Duckworth 219 at 36.50; N. H. T. Hargreaves 470 at 36.15; K. Patrick 319 at 31.90; A. H. R. Harvey 211 at 26.37; A. M. P. Jones 267 at 24.27; D. W. T. Thomas 242 at 18.61; B. D. Rostand 232 at 17.84.
Bowling D. J. Probert 23 at 14.43; J. R. Duckworth* 30 at 16.36; A. H. R. Harvey 11 at 42.45.

Dean Close School
P16 W6 L9 D1

Master i/c B. P. Price   **Coach** R. J. Cunliffe

The 2010 season was memorable for the hard work and commitment shown by the team. They bounced back from a disappointing start, and enjoyed a superb cricket week in which they won four matches, including a wonderful victory over MCC.
Batting L. R. Brignull* 656 at 50.46; A. T. Parker 257 at 25.70; T. E. Warren 340 at 24.28; S. P. Slabbert 337 at 24.07; R. J. McInnes-Gibbons 172 at 19.11; J. W. Ford 172 at 14.33.
Bowling T. E. Warren 16 at 21.00; R. J. McInnes-Gibbons 13 at 22.69; S. P. Slabbert 16 at 23.37; J. J. Drewett 10 at 27.80.

Denstone College
P14 W12 T1 D1

Master i/c Miss J. R. Morris

Under captain Chris Beech, who contributed three centuries, Denstone remained unbeaten throughout a memorable season. Aneesh Kapil enjoyed his role as strike bowler, while spinners Jack Warren and Greg Chance stifled opponents' batting.
Batting C. J. Beech* 831 at 83.10; R. J. Morgan 308 at 38.50; A. Kapil 278 at 30.88; T. K. J. Bamford 352 at 29.33; J. G. M. Bamford 244 at 24.40; J. J. Moran 186 at 18.60.
Bowling A. Kapil 21 at 10.95; G. T. Chance 14 at 14.78; J. S. Warren 15 at 23.80; D. D. Burnett 10 at 26.80.

Dr Challoner's Grammar School
P11 W7 L3 D1

Master i/c D. J. Colquhoun

The team had a splendid summer, with captain Jack Shiel leading the way with the bat; Sam Westaway also contributed well as a classy wicketkeeper and opening batsman. Jack Rogers headed the bowling and improved dramatically during the campaign.
Batting J. J. Shiel* 436 at 54.50; S. A. Westaway 213 at 35.50; M. J. Rance 229 at 32.71; A. D. Morgan 186 at 31.00; S. J. Bracey 151 at 25.16; G. J. Emery 181 at 22.62.
Bowling J. S. Rogers 17 at 12.05; I. S. Khan 17 at 18.64; R. G. Knudsen 10 at 20.80.

Dollar Academy
P12 W6 L5 D1

Master i/c J. G. A. Frost

A reasonably successful season contained notable wins against Glenalmond and Fettes College. Jamie McCann took 20 wickets, and Scotland Under-17 representatives Peter Ross and all-rounder Scott Weir performed with great credit.

Batting P. A. Ross* 472 at 78.66; C. J. W. Smith 248 at 35.42; S. D. Weir 264 at 29.33.
Bowling J. R. McCann 20 at 12.20; S. R. Bell 13 at 12.30; S. D. Weir 14 at 19.57.

Dover College
P13 W5 L5 T2 D1 A1
Master i/c G. R. Hill
Convincing and pleasing batting – there were three centuries and 15 fifty partnerships – backed by solid bowling resulted in an entertaining and enjoyable term. The side showed excellent spirit and, with eight returning for 2011, that should continue.
Batting J. Harrison-Dring 441 at 63.00; M. G. Jay* 557 at 50.63; T. L. P. Waya 213 at 21.30.
Bowling J. Deverson 16 at 10.00; J. G. R. Woods 24 at 15.50; M. G. Jay 19 at 19.21; J. P. Whybrow 11 at 21.00; C. S. E. Engelbretson 13 at 21.23.

Downside School
P13 W5 L7 T1
Master i/c D. A. Grass   Coach P. Lawrence
High points of an encouraging campaign were the tied game with Milton Abbey and a hugely enjoyable festival at Malvern. Luke Hickey's accomplished century was the outstanding individual performance.
Batting W. D. J. Mostyn 244 at 27.11; L. B. Hickey* 249 at 24.90; H. C. D. Waddington 199 at 22.11; H. E. P. Jennings 152 at 19.00.
Bowling T. B. Doe 15 at 10.06; F. A. M. Mercer 17 at 17.82; H. C. D. Waddington 16 at 22.50; A. T. Gilbert 16 at 25.93.

Duke of York's Royal Military School
P13 W5 L6 T2
Master i/c S. Salisbury   Coach M. J. Dobson
With several younger players coming to prominence, a strong and stable side should develop over the next three years. Michael Thompson and Jack Adkins both have the capability to transform matches.
Batting M. P. Thompson* 499 at 45.36; H. S. C. Catmur 286 at 40.85; C. Gauchan 207 at 17.25; W. J. Calter 151 at 15.10.
Bowling J. M. Boxall 19 at 23.42; J. I. B. Adkins 15 at 29.53; M. P. Thompson 13 at 33.92.

Dulwich College
P21 W19 L1 D1
Master i/c D. J. Cooper   Coach C. W. J. Athey
On the most difficult of circuits the team won every schools game, drew with MCC and lost narrowly in a pre-season match to the OA Cricketer Cup XI; a truly incredible season. Will MacVicar broke the batting record held since 1929, and Anthony Alleyne, with another two years left in the side, was a very impressive all-rounder. The College reached the final of the Sir Garfield Sobers festival in Barbados, only the third UK school to do so in 24 years.
Batting A. T. Alleyne 909 at 82.63; W. A. MacVicar* 1,045 at 55.00; T. J. Deasy 857 at 45.10; J. F. Kelleher 339 at 42.37; A. J. Corbin 664 at 36.88; S. A. R. Northcote-Green 277 at 30.77.
Bowling A. T. Alleyne 27 at 18.40; H. E. F. Cullum 34 at 18.41; P. Patel 27 at 18.51; W. A. MacVicar 34 at 19.85; H. G. S. Munton 28 at 21.92.

Durham School
P16 W8 L7 D1 A1
Master i/c M. B. Fishwick
A squad ably captained by James Ritzema improved steadily as the term progressed, with youngsters showing sound promise for 2011. Highlights were the successful run-chases against Barnard Castle (264 from 39 overs), RGS Newcastle (168 from 32) and Durham County Under-17s (229 from 39).
Batting J. R. Ritzema* 618 at 41.20; L. Hall 428 at 28.53; D. G. Jaques 283 at 25.72; R. B. Burdon 228 at 25.33; A. Arif 215 at 21.50; G. F. C. Robinson 256 at 18.28; S. J. Hardy 176 at 17.60.
Bowling J. J. Gaff 21 at 16.52; B. P. Simpson 17 at 20.76; R. B. Burdon 11 at 22.18; L. Hall 17 at 29.35.

Eastbourne College
P14 W6 L4 T1 D3
Master i/c M. J. Banes   Coach M. M. Patel
Peter Wooldridge led well as a Year 12 boy, and Matt Hobden was impressive with the new ball, taking three five-wicket hauls in the last five games, including six against a strong MCC team. Seven of the regular side return for 2011.
Batting H. J. H. Finzel 473 at 43.00; P. J. Wooldridge* 536 at 38.28; S. C. Garratt 434 at 33.38; T. W. M. Caffyn 277 at 30.77; G. A. Hopkins 179 at 25.57; O. P. Smith 235 at 23.50.

Bowling M. E. Hobden 31 at 15.51; B. N. Saunders 17 at 19.82; F. H. Voorspuy 15 at 20.93; P. J. Wooldridge 18 at 22.00; S. C. Garratt 22 at 31.22.

The Edinburgh Academy
P15 W6 L9

Master i/c M. J. D. Allingham

The highlight of a mixed season was battling through to the Lothian Schools Cup final and chasing 235 to beat Loretto.

Batting A. R. M. Muir 374 at 34.00; N. C. G. Hunt 357 at 29.75; J. D. Munro* 165 at 15.00.

Bowling J. G. Connor 15 at 12.60; A. S. F. Rive 19 at 16.78; J. D. Munro 20 at 17.50; R. J. S. Cumming 16 at 18.87; N. C. G. Hunt 11 at 29.18.

Elizabeth College, Guernsey
P12 W7 L5 A1

Master i/c M. E. Kinder

The season ended on a high, with six consecutive victories, including success against Victoria College, Jersey and Worth School, in a two-day game. Tim Ravenscroft, the captain, scored two centuries in three days to end his career with 1,887 runs and a highest score of 152 not out.

Batting T. J. Ravenscroft* 697 at 69.70; N. R. Waldron 191 at 31.83; J. J. Kirk 359 at 29.91; W. G. Thompson 324 at 27.00; H. G. Player 178 at 17.80; A. D. Hindle 150 at 15.00.

Bowling J. N. L. Wilkes-Green 12 at 15.66; T. M. Kirk 18 at 19.88; T. J. Still 11 at 25.63; T. J. Ravenscroft 11 at 34.00.

Ellesmere College
P11 W6 L3 D2 A2

Master i/c P. J. Hayes   **Coach** R. Jones

Jordan Evans scored an important century in the victory over Rydal Penrhos, while Raunak Jain, James Williams and Ben Spaven all provided significant runs. The highlight of the season was the defeat of Hurstpierpoint in which 15-year-old Dewi Jones removed three of their top four batsmen in just 11 deliveries.

Batting R. Jain 318 at 53.00; J. Williams 283 at 40.42; J. W. Evans* 354 at 39.33; B. Spaven 163 at 32.60.

Bowling R. Jain 13 at 14.00; D. P. Jones 11 at 16.18; R. L. Hayes 11 at 16.72; J. W. Evans 11 at 24.90.

Eltham College
P17 W7 L6 T1 D3 A1

Master i/c E. T. Thorogood   **Coach** D. DeBeer/R. W. Hills

Eltham were slightly disappointed with their season: although winning more games than they lost, they had hoped for better. Top run-scorer Chris Harden returns as skipper for 2011, along with seven team-mates.

Batting C. M. Harden 545 at 41.92; D. R. Giles 514 at 32.12; C. S. Speller 391 at 26.06; R. L. M. Fleming 287 at 22.07; J. R. Robertson 216 at 21.60.

Bowling F. J. M. Simpson 15 at 13.60; E. M. Forshaw 20 at 16.70; S. T. Hardy 10 at 18.50; D. R. Giles 18 at 23.05; J. R. Robertson 16 at 24.93.

Emanuel School
P12 W7 L5

Master i/c P. A. King   **Coach** M. L. Roberts

After a highly successful training camp at La Manga, the side enjoyed another winning season, securing victories over many local rivals. Skipper Sam Hawley led by example, finishing with good bowling and batting averages. Cricket at Emanuel continues to grow.

Batting S. M. Hawley* 252 at 42.00; J. W. Lampier 339 at 33.90; S. Mufid 234 at 33.42.

Bowling S. Mufid 17 at 12.05; V. N. Patel 16 at 15.31; H. Thaker 16 at 17.50; S. M. Hawley 16 at 18.43; P. E. Lufkin 12 at 24.75.

Enfield Grammar School
P15 W5 L5 D5

Master i/c M. S. Alder

Captained by Matthew Shore, who developed a fine team spirit, a youthful side grew in confidence and recorded excellent results, including an end-of-season draw against MCC. The majority of the side return, so hopes are high.

Batting M. Barrell 277 at 27.70; H. F. Allen 154 at 25.66; A. R. Blaby 268 at 24.36; J. M. Naughton 230 at 20.90; R. B. Quinlan 189 at 17.18; M. W. T. Shore* 152 at 15.20.

Bowling G. T. Bridges 14 at 16.78; M. W. T. Shore 13 at 22.07; M. T. Barrell 11 at 25.27; J. C. Smith 11 at 30.36.

Epsom College
P10 W2 L4 D4

Master i/c M. D. Hobbs   **Coach** N. R. Taylor

A season of rebuilding saw the side contain only two Year 13s and five Year 11s. Josh Allen, who hit a splendid 85 not out against the Old Boys, was the leading run-scorer, while Tom Williams and Nikhil Waugh, the captain, spearheaded the bowling. There were good wins against MCC and Lord Wandsworth College.

Batting M. Van Wyk 181 at 45.25; J. E. J. Allen 225 at 28.12; R. G. Malcolm 193 at 27.57.

Bowling No one took ten wickets. The leading bowler was N. Waugh*, who took nine at 24.77.

Eton College
P20 W8 L9 D3

Master i/c R. R. Montgomerie   **Coach** J. M. Rice

Eton's season finished with a win in the Silk Trophy when teamwork finally shone through, but too often the opposition found batting comfortable on excellent pitches. Will Vanderspar broke his own school batting record, scoring 1,286 runs, and taking his aggregate to 4,268 runs.

Batting W. G. R. Vanderspar* 1,286 at 80.37; A. S. Sangha 593 at 42.35; T. W. Shaw 500 at 41.66; E. D. Oram 352 at 25.14; E. W. C. Gross 378 at 23.62; J. J. Ballantine Dykes 236 at 19.66; H. L. Hayes 262 at 15.41.

Bowling J. Warburton 23 at 22.82; H. L. Hayes 13 at 29.46; G. V. C. Tidbury 20 at 35.00; A. S. Sangha 16 at 38.31.

Felsted School
P18 W10 L1 D7

Master i/c C. S. Knightley   **Coach** J. E. R. Gallian

The captain Alex Marjoribanks and Stephen Drain proved a successful new-ball pairing, but it was the youthful Jake Foley who finished as top wicket-taker. Youngsters Joshua Wells and Joshua Hunter-Jordan formed a successful partnership at the top of the order, but overall the campaign was a team effort, with competition for places tough.

Batting J. Wells 685 at 45.66; J. Hunter-Jordan 602 at 40.13; L. Paternott 507 at 39.00; O. Ekers 389 at 38.90; A. H. J. Ross 305 at 25.41; A. J. Marjoribanks* 162 at 14.72.

Bowling A. J. Marjoribanks 27 at 14.37; C. H. George 21 at 15.76; L. Paternott 18 at 15.88; J. Foley 30 at 17.63; S. Drain 22 at 18.72.

Fettes College
P14 W7 L7

Master i/c C. S. Thomson   **Coach** A. B. Russell

After a promising start – five wins in six games – a mid-term stutter undermined batsmen's confidence, and doubts set in. However, Henry Edwards was the exception, maintaining good form.

Batting H. R. Edwards 435 at 48.33; J. A. Collister 252 at 22.90; S. Wickramasuriya 202 at 18.36; W. D. R. Philip* 197 at 17.90.

Bowling W. A. Edwards 17 at 12.70; W. D. R. Philip 16 at 15.93; S. Wickramasuriya 20 at 17.85; C. N. Giffin 14 at 20.57.

Filton College
P12 W9 L2 D1

Master i/c T. H. C. Hancock

Filton enjoyed a successful campaign, losing only two matches all season. The batting was particularly solid, with Steve Bullen and Matthew Kinchin scoring five hundreds between them. Matt Carpenter, a hostile opening bowler, was the pick of the attack.

Batting M. J. Kinchin 474 at 79.00; S. F. G. Bullen 509 at 72.71; A. D. Taylor 153 at 51.00; S. Mustafa 259 at 43.16; P. J. Robbins 226 at 28.25; R. J. Thorpe 182 at 26.00.

Bowling C. L. C. Blakemore 10 at 22.00; M. E. Carpenter 11 at 22.18; A. Khan 12 at 22.75.

Forest School
P18 W10 L5 D3 A1

Master i/c S. J. Foulds   **Coach** S. Turner

With batting underpinned by the consistency of Jonathan Das and with variety in the bowling, a relatively young side had a fine season. Stuart Turner retired after 24 distinguished seasons at the helm of Forest cricket.

Batting J. J. Das 656 at 50.46; C. C. S. Wong 343 at 26.38; J. Akbar 177 at 22.12; T. A. Perkins 236 at 21.45; J. D. Lloyd 331 at 20.68; W. Smith 308 at 20.53; N. A. Knight 296 at 18.50; C. J. Campbell* 210 at 17.50.

Bowling T. Qazi 24 at 12.33; J. Akbar 24 at 16.37; G. N. Summers 25 at 16.72; C. C. S. Wong 28 at 18.28.

Framlingham College
P12 W4 L8

Master i/c P. W. Jarvis

Robbie Bridgstock was the leading light, with sound averages in both disciplines. There was top-notch support from Lee Buckingham and Tom Claydon, but inexperience was a heavy burden.
Batting R. Bridgstock 504 at 50.40; K. N. Williman 221 at 27.62; T. W. Claydon 301 at 25.08; C. A. J. Garrard* 257 at 21.41; C. T. O. Precious 171 at 17.10.
Bowling R. Bridgstock 12 at 17.83; L. M. Buckingham 13 at 28.92; T. W. Claydon 11 at 35.00.

George Watson's College
P12 W6 L6 A1

Master i/c I. Geddes
Coach M. J. Leonard

Talent was not enough to overcome inconsistent performances and fluctuating availability. Bowling, led by Fraser Sands, was the stronger suit, and youngster Chris Cash continues to thrive.
Batting A. D. Chalmers* 284 at 35.50; S. R. H. Mullins 318 at 35.33; Z. M. Yusaf 314 at 34.88.
Bowling C. A. Cash 23 at 10.21; A. D. Chalmers 13 at 15.69; S. R. H. Mullins 17 at 15.70; F. J. Sands 18 at 17.33.

The Glasgow Academy
P10 W4 L5 D1

Master i/c S. G. Weston
Coach V. Hariharan

A youthful side grew in confidence as the season progressed and certainly saved the best for last: an exciting eight-run win over Stewart's Melville in a low-scoring game.
Batting A. L. Lloyd 336 at 37.33; L. H. Hill 231 at 33.00.
Bowling A. M. W. Johnson 17 at 10.64; H. M. Chaudhry 13 at 13.76; L. H. Hill 11 at 18.18.

The High School of Glasgow
P12 W6 L6

Master i/c D. N. Barrett
Coaches N. R. Clarke/K. J. A. Robertson

Another very encouraging season saw every scheduled game played. Wins came against all the other Glasgow independent schools, as well as Stewart's Melville and Strathallan. The captain Phil Revie scored the first century in five seasons.
Batting P. D. J. Bell 158 at 39.50; C. J. McNaught 276 at 27.60; A. R. I. Umeed 188 at 26.85; P. K. Revie* 167 at 18.55; C. L. McInteer 156 at 15.60.
Bowling C. J. McNaught 11 at 15.72; M. R. Ralston 15 at 18.86; C. L. McInteer 16 at 20.43; A. R. I. Umeed 10 at 22.40.

Glenalmond College
P9 W2 L7 A1

Master i/c M. J. Davies

Despite a brief resurgence in mid-season, this was a disappointing campaign, where a lack of consistent runs placed a potentially penetrative bowling attack under pressure. A good nucleus remains for 2011.
Batting G. B. F. Russell 174 at 19.33; T. S. J. Robertson 160 at 17.77.
Bowling T. S. J. Robertson 14 at 18.00; B. P. D. King 10 at 19.30.

Gordonstoun School
P13 W7 L4 T1 D1 A5

Master i/c C. J. Barton
Coach R. Denyer

The season was badly hit by cold, damp weather in May, causing the cancellation of several games. However, some positive cricket was played, with Nathan Roberts, who later played for Sussex seconds, leading the attack; Jonathan Robertson scored three excellent centuries on the North Lawn.
Batting A. J. Robertson 644 at 80.50; N. J. Roberts 485 at 60.62; J. T. Marnie* 492 at 44.72; R. Amin 349 at 38.77; F. Amin 156 at 22.28.
Bowling J. R. Barton 15 at 17.00; N. J. Roberts 18 at 17.50; F. Amin 13 at 25.69.

Gresham's School
P15 W3 L9 D3

Master i/c P. J. Watson
Coach S. Noster

Results picked up as the season progressed, and hopes are high for 2011; most of the squad return. Sam Ward, the captain, and Frankie Sutton held the batting together, each scoring 104 against The Leys.
Batting S. G. Ward* 429 at 30.64; F. C. Sutton 419 at 29.92; B. Stromberg 204 at 17.00; H. G. Blackiston 191 at 11.92.
Bowling K. Pereira 19 at 17.26; B. Stromberg 22 at 22.72; H. J. M. P. Knapp 10 at 24.10; W. F. Templeman 11 at 40.45.

Beth MacGregor played for Chigwell firsts and later represented England Women in a Twenty20 series against Sri Lanka. Hampton's skipper, Zafar Ansari, hit 1,111 runs and took 31 wickets with his left-arm spin.

Haberdashers' Aske's Boys' School
P18 W10 L5 D3 A6

Master i/c S. D. Charlwood   **Coaches** D. H. Kerry/D. I. Yeabsley

After an indifferent start and the cancellation of several games due to exams, the season ended on a high, with victory against previously unbeaten Bancroft's. This was followed by a triumphant tour to Devon, where all four games were won, and middle-order batsman Basil Letts discovered the form of his life. Doug Yeabsley completed 45 years' service at the school.

Batting B. A. Letts 687 at 68.70; K. A. Patel 663 at 39.00; J. P. Miller 337 at 37.44; T. W. Edrich* 454 at 30.26; T. K. Malde 261 at 23.72; N. N. Selvakumar 271 at 20.84.

Bowling S. Patel 22 at 15.18; K. Setia 10 at 20.20; S. A. Schusman 24 at 24.00; B. Z. Cherkas 19 at 29.73; T. W. Edrich 16 at 34.37.

Haileybury
P13 W6 L6 D1 A1

Master i/c M. J. Cawdron   **Coach** G. P. Howarth

Huge progress was made by a young and inexperienced side as the season unwound. Sam Boothby was the leading light among the bowlers, and a strong batting line-up, with three centurions, returns next summer.

Batting C. E. Stewart 389 at 55.57; H. A. P. Hughes D'Aeth 507 at 39.00; T. H. Billings 369 at 26.35; R. W. J. Dawes* 253 at 25.30; J. W. Satt 270 at 20.76.

Bowling S. J. Boothby 24 at 18.00; J. Alibhai 19 at 22.63; O. Stirling 10 at 34.50; R. W. J. Dawes 14 at 38.42.

Hampton School
P18 W14 L2 D2

Master i/c D. E. Peel   **Coach** A. M. Banerjee

Arguably Hampton's strongest-ever side had an outstanding season, with a 180-run victory over Eton the highlight. Skipper Zafar Ansari scored over 1,100 runs, including seven centuries, and took 31 wickets. Vice-captain Bilal Chohan also claimed 31 wickets.

Batting Z. S. Ansari* 1,111 at 101.00; B. Chohan 432 at 86.40; T. D. Walker 467 at 51.88; N. T. Prowse 379 at 34.45; M. R. Main 208 at 29.71; M. W. G. Nichols 203 at 25.37; C. Madoc-Jones 371 at 24.73.

Bowling Z. S. Ansari 31 at 10.87; M. W. G. Nichols 14 at 13.14; C. M. Bryant 21 at 13.19; B. Chohan 31 at 13.35; A. L. Pindar 11 at 25.72.

Harrow School

P17 W10 L5 D2 A1

Master i/c S. J. Halliday   **Coach** S. A. Jones

Youth was no bar to the team enjoying a successful season. Yunus Sert, Robbie White and Mikey Cousens held the batting together, while Douglas Pratt was the key bowler. The fine win over Eton at Lord's was the highlight.

Batting Y. M. Sert 668 at 55.66; M. E. Cousens 565 at 47.08; R. G. White 535 at 41.15; C. J. Baird 392 at 23.05; H. C. J. Cousens 186 at 20.66; N. M. T. Castleman 279 at 18.60; T. W. Pearson-Jones* 206 at 17.16; G. M. O. Bunting 152 at 16.88.

Bowling T. W. Pearson-Jones 15 at 13.66; D. T. P. Pratt 32 at 18.31; Y. M. Sert 20 at 22.75; G. M. O. Bunting 21 at 26.04; T. M. N. Faber 13 at 43.84.

The Harvey Grammar School

P14 W8 L6 A2

Master i/c N. Bristow   **Coach** P. M. Castle

The team relished a rewarding season, but faltered when leading batsman Jamie Keeler suffered a serious back injury. The high point was a seven-wicket win over the XL Club, when the school chased 207.

Batting J. A. Keeler 215 at 71.66; T. D. Payne* 267 at 53.40; J. M. Hemphrey 395 at 35.90; B. A. Tosland 219 at 24.33; A. Bill 163 at 13.58.

Bowling J. M. Hemphrey 22 at 13.72; A. Bill 13 at 23.00; J. Sheppard 10 at 24.90.

Highgate School

P14 W6 L8

Master i/c A. G. Tapp   **Coach** S. Patel

Highgate could not quite make it three wins in a row in the Middlesex Under-19 Cup. But they did contest the semi-finals, and had an enjoyable end-of-season tour to Guernsey. Captain Ali Buchanan ended his career having played almost 70 games for the first team.

Batting A. J. Buchanan* 288 at 22.15; A. P. Thomas 197 at 19.70; P. Dave 169 at 18.77; C. T. S. Yorke-Starkey 156 at 17.33; N. E. Friend 162 at 16.20.

Bowling N. E. Friend 24 at 17.33; C. T. S. Yorke-Starkey 11 at 18.18; L. E. B. Masefield 14 at 21.21; R. A. Blackshaw 15 at 24.93; H. T. R. Lambert 10 at 34.40.

Hurstpierpoint College

P19 W7 L12

Master i/c G. J. Haines   **Coach** N. J. K. Creed

A superb start to the season included important wins in the local Twenty20 competition. Unfortunately, exams led to a fluctuation in availability, and the side struggled to perform after June.

Batting J. R. C. Barclay 680 at 35.78; J. Parsons* 516 at 27.15; G. N. Wisdom 300 at 23.07; T. H. Moses 157 at 22.42; O. J. Meredith 157 at 22.42; B. J. Gayler 249 at 20.75; R. J. Noble 161 at 14.63.

Bowling J. Newland 20 at 18.55; T. H. Moses 14 at 19.00; J. R. C. Barclay 18 at 23.61; J. Parsons 24 at 25.16; T. H. Blake 11 at 34.63.

Hymers College

P11 W4 L1 T1 D5

Master i/c G. Tipping

Hymers's season was laced with excitement as game after game produced a tight finish. In none of the victories were more than two wickets standing at the end. Captain Daniel Leather orchestrated a great season.

Batting M. Yousuff 256 at 32.00; G. W. Lound 174 at 21.75; S. C. A. Hammersley 215 at 21.50.

Bowling M. Yousuff 12 at 14.08; N. J. Leather 10 at 15.90; M. P. Fitzpatrick 10 at 20.80; J. M. Brocklebank 14 at 22.42; D. W. E. Leather* 10 at 23.80.

Ipswich School

P16 W8 L4

Master i/c A. K. Golding   **Coach** R. E. East

The batting was dominated by Sasha Ward (three hundreds) and Ashwin Raj (two). Tom Sinclair batted productively, while left-arm spinner Lewis Catlow led the bowling. Seven of the team will reappear in 2011, and there are many promising players in the wings.

Batting S. B. Ward 890 at 98.88; A. Raj* 717 at 55.15; F. C. R. Ward 155 at 38.75; T. Sinclair 390 at 32.50; H. W. M. Gravell 327 at 27.25.

Bowling L. J. Catlow 27 at 8.44; A. Bhatt 13 at 15.84; R. G. Sexton 16 at 25.06; K. Patel 11 at 36.36.

John Lyon School
P18 W10 L7 T1

Master i/c I. R. Parker   **Coach** C. T. Peploe

There were notable wins over Harrow A and Merchant Taylors' Northwood, but overall results were mixed. The team was captained by wicketkeeper Debashis Biswas. Alex Fraser, son of Angus, made his debut.

Batting M. D. T. Hoy 428 at 32.92; A. C. Sloan 200 at 25.00; F. G. Grist 318 at 24.46; A. K. Patel 262 at 20.15; O. J. B. Marsh 237 at 18.23.

Bowling B. M. Makwana 17 at 18.76; O. J. B. Marsh 19 at 20.89; A. C. M. Fraser 10 at 23.90; A. C. Sloan 19 at 24.94; A. K. Patel 13 at 28.92.

The Judd School
P12 W8 L2 D2 A1

Master i/c D. W. Joseph

Showing adaptability and a positive approach, the side prospered both in the National Twenty20, where they reached the regional final, and in the longer forms of the game. Special praise should go to openers Tom and Chris Williams, who both averaged over 40.

Batting T. D. Williams 442 at 44.20; C. M. Williams 342 at 42.75; G. I. G. Willis 187 at 37.40; W. Bryce-Borthwick 237 at 33.85; H. J. Blamey* 170 at 28.33; M. R. Thompson 174 at 19.33.

Bowling C. M. Williams 15 at 12.40; M. R. Thompson 16 at 13.56; M. W. T. Barnes 11 at 14.27; R. J. Pulsford 14 at 14.57; G. I. G. Willis 10 at 14.90; W. E. Needham 12 at 16.91.

Kimbolton School
P14 W8 L4 D2 A2

Master i/c T. Webley   **Coach** P. S. Coverdale

A fine season, with wins against Eton seconds, Wisbech and Ratcliffe. Guven Kooner scored 737 runs, including a majestic century against Carey GS from Melbourne. Leg-spinner Robert Craze was in superb form, grabbing 32 wickets at under 12.

Batting G. M. Kooner 737 at 56.69; G. F. Richards* 467 at 46.70; R. G. Craze 441 at 40.09; R. J. Lowin 398 at 33.16; T. A. Hilliard 383 at 31.91; D. A. Wright 280 at 21.53.

Bowling R. G. Craze 32 at 11.40; R. J. Lowin 16 at 15.62; J. D. Kenmir 14 at 18.57; H. J. Winterton 10 at 21.00; C. D. Macgregor 10 at 29.50.

King Edward VI School, Southampton
P10 W7 L3

Master i/c M. G. M. Mixer   **Coach** C. R. Surry

An experienced team – losing nine players for 2011 – flourished. Results might have been even better if the bowlers had recaptured the form of last season. A new era will require younger players to take more responsibility.

Batting A. M. Wilkinson 278 at 39.71; C. P. R. Ratcliffe 187 at 37.40; J. E. Cook 296 at 37.00; S. J. McCormick-Cox 232 at 33.14; T. M. McCormick-Cox* 294 at 32.66.

Bowling R. S. N. Warrick 12 at 15.41.

King Edward VII & Queen Mary's School Lytham
P13 L10 D3

Master i/c J. A. Liggett   **Coach** A. Uz Zaman

A youthful side worked very hard without tangible reward, but showed flashes of improvement throughout. Highlights were Matthew Cartmell's six for 72 against King's Macclesfield and a staunch effort from Peter Mackay, who opened the batting against Abingdon, and fell to the final ball of the 50th over for 104.

Batting M. P. Cartmell 230 at 25.55; B. P. Saunders 161 at 20.12; A. J. Yates 238 at 19.83; M. P. Sworder 235 at 19.58; P. D. Mackay 205 at 17.08; A. McWilliam-Grey 151 at 16.77; K. S. O'Hanlon* 176 at 14.66.

Bowling K. S. O'Hanlon 10 at 23.50; M. P. Cartmell 13 at 25.84; A. J. Yates 13 at 36.76; J. Brown 11 at 41.18.

King Edward's School, Bath
P16 W10 L5 D1

Master i/c P. J. McComish   **Coach** M. R. Howarth

First-rate performances at the start and finish of the campaign were marred only during the exam period. Sam Mount struck four centuries and averaged over 70, Will Collier scored consistently and bowled with pace, and all-rounder Olly Metcalfe hit a debut hundred.

Batting S. Mount 663 at 73.66; J. W. Collier* 562 at 43.23; O. Metcalfe 391 at 32.58; W. Wales 182 at 15.16.

Bowling J. Weare 13 at 14.00; S. Mount 18 at 19.00; R. Morgan 10 at 19.30; J. W. Collier 15 at 24.06; O. Metcalfe 11 at 25.63.

Craig Meschede, from King's Taunton, en route to a double-hundred against Monmouth.

King Edward's School, Birmingham
P20 W6 L13 D1

Master i/c L. M. Roll   **Coach** D. Collins

The season got off to a poor start and, although some decent performances followed, the team failed to realise their full potential. However, many boys gained experience of senior cricket and should prosper in the future.

Batting J. P. P. Cornick 537 at 35.80; N. C. Roberts 384 at 27.42; H. K. Ismail* 421 at 26.31; A. P. Sonsale 235 at 26.11; T. P. Lilburn 221 at 22.10; R. Maini 306 at 21.85.

Bowling S. J. B. Hobbs 22 at 17.81; J. E. Khanna 25 at 18.76; W. M. H. Chesner 12 at 19.33; R. J. Wigley 16 at 21.93; H. K. Ismail 15 at 34.53.

King Henry VIII School
P18 W7 L7 D4 A2

Master i/c A. M. Parker

Promise began to translate into results as a talented side turned around a shaky start to the summer. The captain Darun Kaliray was well supported by two excellent young all-rounders, Steven Abbey and Amar Kalsi.

Batting S. D. Abbey 418 at 32.15; S. R. Lucas 323 at 23.07; A. S. Kalsi 245 at 20.41; R. H. Arnold 157 at 19.62; G. W. Sunter 250 at 19.23; D. A. S. Kaliray* 282 at 18.80.

Bowling S. D. Abbey 18 at 17.05; K. K. Sharma 15 at 19.60; A. S. Kalsi 18 at 22.55; K. S. Punian 14 at 30.00.

King's College, Taunton
P14 W12 L1 D1

Master i/c P. D. Lewis   **Coach** D. Breakwell

This was another hugely successful season: King's won the West of England Schools league; there were two double-hundreds from Craig Meschede; and a triple-century partnership was scored against Monmouth. All this and just one fixture lost all summer!

Batting A. W. R. Barrow 803 at 160.60; C. A. J. Meschede 946 at 105.11; A. K. M. Brown 379 at 54.14; T. Barrett 159 at 53.00; M. Lenygon 358 at 44.75.

Bowling C. A. J. Meschede 21 at 13.47; A. W. R. Barrow 16 at 17.87; T. Barrett 19 at 25.26; N. A. Smith 16 at 26.00.

King's College School, Wimbledon
P18 W7 L11 A1

Master i/c T. P. Howland   Coach G. P. Butcher

With the senior boys missing due to exams, the first half of term was difficult. At full strength, however, this was a good side. Alex Hunt, batting at No. 7, scored an outstanding 115 not out while chasing down 320 against Lord Wandsworth College; it included a last-wicket stand of 60 at eight an over.

Batting A. P. Hunt 317 at 35.22; A. R. Hawkins-Hooker 392 at 30.15; J. R. T. Churchman 151 at 21.57; E. C. Goldsmith* 210 at 21.00; T. C. Rawlinson 312 at 20.80.

Bowling T. C. Rawlinson 18 at 23.38; S. J. Holland 14 at 24.50; A. P. Hunt 14 at 24.92; M. A. Sheikh 12 at 26.66.

The King's School, Canterbury
P14 W6 L3 T1 D4

Master i/c R. A. L. Singfield   Coach M. A. Ealham

Batting was the school's strength: five players scored over 250 runs. Wicketkeeper Charles MacLeod captained the side intelligently and led by example, thrice claiming five victims in a match.

Batting J. W. Hearn 273 at 45.50; J. S. Masters 343 at 42.87; C. A. R. MacLeod* 352 at 35.20; O. E. Robinson 265 at 29.44; N. P. Hands 226 at 22.60; M. N. Healy 258 at 21.50; T. J. Dixey 188 at 20.88.

Bowling L. M. Anglin 19 at 23.15; T. J. Dixey 15 at 25.20; S. R. Attwood 10 at 28.90.

The King's School, Chester
P19 W11 L7 D1 A1

Masters i/c S. Neal and T. R. Hughes   Coach N. R. Walker

In a season largely undisturbed by the weather, the side usually prospered when at full strength. Three batsmen made hundreds: Arthur Thomas hit 154 not out and Oliver Thompson an unbeaten 153. Thompson, the leading wicket-taker, will captain a largely unchanged squad in 2011.

Batting A. W. Leech* 408 at 51.00; O. E. J. Thompson 746 at 46.62; A. A. Thomas 372 at 41.33; G. M. Coppack 484 at 32.26; J. S. Benson 348 at 31.63; M. J. Torr 352 at 29.33; H. F. J. Peel 206 at 25.75.

Bowling J. S. Benson 11 at 17.00; J. L. A. F. Oldman 13 at 21.07; R. C. Benson 20 at 21.85; H. F. J. Peel 12 at 24.33; O. E. J. Thompson 21 at 25.61; L. G. Robinson 12 at 30.00.

The King's School, Ely
P15 W2 L12 D1

Master i/c K. G. Shaw

King's played positive cricket without getting the results they deserved. The highlight was undoubtedly young Chris Aniskowicz's blistering batting: he scored 129 in 42 balls against Kimbolton and averaged over 40 for the season.

Batting C. H. J. Aniskowicz 395 at 43.88; J. J. E. Sivier 296 at 19.73; T. C. G. Sweeney 179 at 16.27; S. A. Montague-Fuller* 209 at 14.92; D. J. Wallis 188 at 13.42.

Bowling S. A. Montague-Fuller 14 at 31.28; T. C. G. Sweeney 14 at 34.85.

The King's School in Macclesfield
P19 W12 L6 D1 A1

Master i/c S. Moores   Coach A. Kennedy

Runs were gratifyingly spread about with 11 batsmen scoring fifties, though only Tim Saxon made a hundred. Jonathan Marsden, who skippers again in 2011, had an excellent summer with 35 wickets and 271 runs.

Batting B. J. Marsden 574 at 47.83; A. J. Hodgson 606 at 40.40; T. S. Foreman 459 at 32.78; A. T. Thomson 376 at 31.33; J. T. A. Knowles 208 at 29.71; L. Kennedy 165 at 27.50; J. Marsden* 271 at 27.10; M. P. Jones 185 at 26.42; T. J. Saxon 256 at 21.33; J. O. Stanley 189 at 21.00; G. T. W. Drury 193 at 19.30.

Bowling J. Marsden 35 at 17.00; T. J. Saxon 28 at 21.35; J. Stubbs 18 at 27.38; A. J. Hodgson 16 at 29.18; T. S. Foreman 18 at 35.16.

King's School, Rochester
P12 W6 L6

Master i/c W. E. Smith   Coach C. H. Page

Following an uncertain start, the side eventually made sound progress. Harri Ashdown led well in his fifth season in the senior team. Dominic Saunders and Arthur McCormick scored heavily, while Alistair Saunders spearheaded the bowling.

Batting D. A. Saunders 483 at 53.66; A. E. McCormick 445 at 40.45; H. F. J. Ashdown* 278 at 27.80; A. Poddar 172 at 24.57; F. Forward 228 at 22.80; G. W. Rumbelow 151 at 18.87.

Bowling A. C. Saunders 22 at 18.90; D. A. W. Saunders 17 at 20.64; G. W. Rumbelow 17 at 25.11.

The King's School, Tynemouth
P11 W3 L5 D3 A1

Masters i/c W. Ryan/P. J. Nicholson   **Coach** R. M. Fearon

In an unexceptional side, several younger players caught the eye: seam-bowling all-rounder Sami Chaudhary blasted his runs from the lower order and took important wickets with the new ball, while Ben Richardson, showing belated form, made two hundreds in his last three innings.

Batting M. S. U. Chaudhary 264 at 66.00; B. J. Richardson 379 at 42.11; R. D. Sidney-Wilmot 369 at 41.00; S. J. Robson* 158 at 19.75.

Bowling M. S. U. Chaudhary 18 at 15.33; M. Fearon 15 at 16.26; S. J. Robson 10 at 31.20.

King's School, Worcester
P20 W7 L13

Master i/c D. P. Iddon   **Coach** A. A. D. Gillgrass

Despite some heavy defeats, a young side began to play well towards the end of the season. The captain Tom Bird did his best, contributing 492 runs and 33 wickets, and Sam Harris scored productively at times. Twelve-year-old Josh Tongue did not look out of his depth.

Batting S. Harris 781 at 41.10; T. P. Mills 558 at 32.82; T. M. Bird* 492 at 30.75; J. Doorbar 300 at 25.00; H. H. Patel 248 at 16.53; H. W. Iddon 160 at 13.33.

Bowling T. M. Bird 33 at 14.09; T. J. Wilde 24 at 24.41; H. W. Iddon 16 at 38.12; D. J. Lewis 11 at 45.90.

Kingston Grammar School
P15 W5 L8 D2 A1

Master i/c J. E. K. Schofield

The season offered so much during the first half, with excellent performances against Tiffin, MCC and Reed's. But the half-term break came at the wrong time, and momentum was lost. However, there is some real talent, and the future should be bright.

Batting G. Morris 334 at 27.83; T. R. A. Huxford 186 at 20.66; A. M. Harper 197 at 19.70; A. H. Jenkins 210 at 19.09; G. N. Sams 197 at 17.90; J. H. G. Baverstock 185 at 16.81; T. J. Beaumont* 218 at 15.57; O. M. Clements 168 at 12.92.

Bowling T. R. A. Huxford 21 at 15.14; J. E. Tetlow 16 at 23.43; G. Morris 13 at 24.15.

Kingswood School, Bath
P11 W6 L4 T1

Master i/c J. O. Brown

Kingswood's form improved as the summer progressed, with captain Euan Gordon leading the side with flair. The Rouse brothers, Harry (16) and Tim (14), were key players with both bat and ball. The highlight was the win over MCC, thanks to a brilliant 137 from Nick Prettejohn.

Batting N. G. Prettejohn 333 at 47.57; H. P. Rouse 339 at 33.90; T. D. Rouse 199 at 28.42; E. Gordon* 337 at 28.08; S. J. Morris 150 at 18.75.

Bowling H. P. Rouse 16 at 9.00; T. H. Simpson 12 at 15.91; W. A. Mackenzie 15 at 18.73; T. D. Rouse 13 at 26.30.

Kirkham Grammar School
P12 W6 L5 D1

Master i/c M. A.Whalley   **Coach** N. S. Passenger

A young Kirkham side, led by Kieran Marmion, had an excellent season. Marmion scored 553 runs, took 21 wickets and thoughtfully guided the team to more victories than defeats. Nine of the squad return for 2011.

Batting K. D. Marmion* 533 at 41.00; B. M. Jones 222 at 22.20; A. Galley 305 at 20.33.

Bowling A. Galley 13 at 14.00; F. Burnie 14 at 15.07; K. D. Marmion 21 at 16.95; D. L. Egelstaff 17 at 20.23; M. Mollinga 10 at 20.90.

Lancaster Royal Grammar School
P14 W6 L2 D6 A3

Master i/c I. W. Ledward   **Coach** I. D. Whitehouse

The reward for tackling a more challenging fixture list was the advancement of many younger players, who should be a force to be reckoned with in 2011. Mark Walling guided the side superbly and scored over 880 runs, with sterling support from Charlie Rossiter, who had a superb RGS Festival. Pace bowler Dan Whitehouse led the attack while 15-year-old off-spinner Tom Whitehouse also enjoyed success.

Batting M. A. Walling* 821 at 45.61; A. R. Metcalfe 164 at 41.00; C. E. Rossiter 570 at 33.52; M. J. Mollinga 312 at 31.20; J. A. Ralston 342 at 24.42; S. Moorby 349 at 23.26; J. A. Brown 172 at 19.11; T. Deakin 282 at 16.58.

Bowling A. R. Metcalfe 10 at 17.90; M. J. Mollinga 18 at 20.55; M. J. Sharp 15 at 21.13; A. Stevens 10 at 21.40; D. W. Whitehouse 31 at 21.93; J. Brown 12 at 26.75; T. D. Whitehouse 20 at 28.15.

Lancing College
P18 W6 L10 T1 D1

Master i/c C. P. E. Crowe
Coach C. M. Mole

A mixed season of results was punctuated by excellent individual and team performances. George Welsby was the pick of the bowlers and was ably supported by Jack Bradshaw. Jamie Betts made his maiden senior century, firing 139 not out against Portsmouth GS.

Batting J. E. R. Betts 358 at 32.54; M. G. Mills 193 at 27.57; G. R. T. Holman* 217 at 19.72; J. A. Cobbold 255 at 19.61; H. A. L. Loughton 177 at 17.70.

Bowling O. H. Rogers 11 at 15.90; G. Welsby 25 at 17.52; J. D. H. Bradshaw 12 at 24.91.

Latymer Upper School
P11 W1 L9 D1

Master i/c G. E. Cooper
Coaches T. Biddle/B. Taylor

The team, somewhat hamstrung by the loss of key players from 2009, battled well without much reward. Highlights included beating Mill Hill, and seeing Marcus Burling and Robbie Burnett score maiden hundreds.

Batting R. D. Burnett 162 at 54.00; E. L. McKenzie 194 at 21.55; M. G. Burling 226 at 20.54; M. D. Brewer 202 at 18.36; S. D. Conacher* 182 at 16.54.

Bowling No one took ten wickets. The leading bowler was A. T. M. Jones, who took nine at 27.55.

The Grammar School at Leeds
P14 W6 L6 D2

Master i/c S. H. Dunn

Following a very successful Easter tour to Sri Lanka, a youthful squad performed with great confidence and enthusiasm. James Wainman was the pick with bat and ball throughout the season.

Batting C. Rice 184 at 61.33; L. Johnson 377 at 47.12; J. C. Wainman 405 at 36.81; F. M. S. Kamstra 289 at 28.90.

Bowling J. C. Wainman 32 at 13.09; W. Sweeting 13 at 17.53.

Leicester Grammar School
P8 W1 L7 A1

Master i/c L. Potter

Injury and irregular availability had a real influence on performance. Robert Berkeley showed character, opening the batting and keeping wicket with great success.

Batting A. M. McGuinn 156 at 22.28; R. Berkeley 171 at 21.37; R. J. Clarke* 153 at 19.12.

Bowling No one took ten wickets. The leading bowler was R. J. Clarke, who took eight at 29.75.

The Leys School
P13 W7 L2 D4 A1

Master i/c B. A. Barton
Coach J. D. R. Benson

An enthusiastic approach gained positive results. James Lee led the attack well, though the key was outstanding fielding. Against St Paul's, the season culminated in a record 210-run partnership between James Latham and Andrew Laws; both scored centuries.

Batting J. M. Latham 543 at 45.25; P. D. Miller 338 at 37.55; A. J. Gale 391 at 35.54; A. Laws* 269 at 29.88.

Bowling J. A. Lee 21 at 15.90; W. E. McGahey 11 at 18.09; A. Laws 10 at 31.20; A. J. Gale 11 at 34.27.

Lord Wandsworth College
P15 W5 L10

Master i/c A. Williams
Coach C. C. Hicks

A frustrating season seemed full of missed opportunities, with the side contriving to lose games they should really have won. Andrew House's total of 750 runs was a striking achievement.

Batting A. J. House 750 at 62.50; R. A. Heywood 340 at 42.50; G. H. Breddy 343 at 34.30; C. S. Arundel 286 at 19.06.

Bowling T. J. B. Salmon 24 at 21.25; C. S. Arundel 24 at 23.75; J. A. Dow 19 at 25.05; J. W. Hopkin 15 at 32.66.

Loughborough Grammar School
P13 W7 L6

Master i/c H. T. Tunnicliffe
Coach M. I. Gidley

The side was smartly led by Jack Williamson, who averaged over 60. Highlights included wins against MCC and Old Loughburians, but there were inconsistent days – and results were mixed.

Batting J. A. Williamson* 492 at 61.50; J. W. Purvis 453 at 45.30; S. A. Patel 532 at 40.92; J. D. Orchiston 391 at 39.10; K. K. Ross 307 at 34.11; A. J. Morris 202 at 25.25.

Bowling D. Bathia 13 at 21.69; R. C. Purohit 21 at 23.04; J. A. Williamson 11 at 27.27; S. A. Patel 15 at 33.40; A. J. Morris 11 at 37.18.

Magdalen College School
P16 W3 L10 D3 A1

Master i/c R. G. Gilbert

A superb win against Rugby showed much promise, but finishing off opponents was always a problem. Encouraging form from Jai-Hin Patel, whose wicketkeeping and batting shone through, masked disappointing returns from other talented players.

Batting J-H. Patel 425 at 32.69; I. A. Khan 239 at 29.87; H. Anderson-Elliott 229 at 28.62; T. Hogan 394 at 28.14; G. Rendall 307 at 23.61; E. A. Shaw 256 at 19.69; C. Beeson 156 at 13.00.

Bowling C. Morton 17 at 24.11; J. Brodley 15 at 35.20; I. A. Khan 15 at 35.66; S. Robins 13 at 41.76.

Malvern College
P24 W11 L7 T1 D5

Master i/c T. P. Newman   **Coaches** T. W. Roberts/M. A. Hardinges

Winning 11 games was a superb achievement for a youthful team. Odge Davey was magnificent with three centuries in his 872 runs, and 15-year-old Tom Kohler-Cadmore batted fluently in scoring 680. The bowling was dominated by spin: Arthur Jones with 44 wickets was the pick.

Batting O. J. Davey 872 at 45.89; T. Kohler-Cadmore 680 at 34.00; S. P. Harwood 384 at 29.53; H. T. B. Sinclair* 283 at 28.30; C. W. F. Lacey 448 at 22.40; C. S. Harwood 198 at 16.50; B. D. M. Bartlett 158 at 10.53.

Bowling T. Kohler-Cadmore 23 at 13.95; A. G. T. Jones 44 at 16.93; S. P. Harwood 21 at 22.14; W. S. Wright 29 at 24.82; W. Meredith 25 at 26.60; C. S. Harwood 21 at 31.38.

The Manchester Grammar School
P19 W14 L3 D2

Master i/c D. Moss

Following a pre-season tour to the West Indies, MGS had an excellent season guided by Daniel Brown, who scored over 900 runs and took 30 wickets. Alex Platts was another key all-rounder, and the batting was strong down the order.

Batting D. T. Brown* 905 at 64.64; A. T. Platts 608 at 40.53; S. Qasim 466 at 35.84; M. R. Tully 337 at 33.70; E. C. Bullock 423 at 28.20; A. A. Sheikh 185 at 26.42; J. E. Lowe 217 at 24.11.

Bowling A. T. Platts 13 at 11.15; D. T. Brown 30 at 13.66; A. J. Dagnall 15 at 14.26; A. T. Read 21 at 19.09; J. J. Brierley 31 at 19.61; M. R. Tully 17 at 26.23; C. D. Wyche 18 at 26.61.

Marlborough College
P13 W7 L4 D2

Master i/c N. E. Briers   **Coach** R. M. Ratcliffe

There were impressive wins against Wellington, Sherborne, Bradfield, St Edward's, Haileybury, MCC and Wiltshire Under-17s. The two-day Colours Match against Rugby was drawn. Uzi Qureshi, the captain, represented Gloucestershire seconds.

Batting U. A. Qureshi* 713 at 71.30; S. T. Swift 204 at 40.80; O. R. D. Logan 289 at 28.90; W. D. N. von Behr 316 at 26.33; A. L. D. Kidwell 289 at 24.08.

Bowling M. I. Sangster 26 at 18.30; J. D. Bunting 12 at 20.41; W. D. N. von Behr 15 at 26.80; A. L. M. Cary 19 at 30.36.

Merchant Taylors' School, Crosby
P19 W13 L4 D2

Master i/c Rev. D. Smith   **Coach** S. P. Sutcliffe

Merchant Taylors' had a splendid time, winning a record 13 matches. Lawrence Armstrong, who scored prolifically and bowled very effectively, was a very able skipper. James Morrissey also made a fine all-round contribution, as did Stephen Lucas. MCC were beaten for the first time in many years.

Batting L. T. E. Armstrong* 757 at 54.07; S. Lucas 543 at 36.20; J. J. Morrissey 540 at 33.75; R. E. Metcalf 179 at 29.83; A. P. D. Rigby 206 at 25.75; B. J. Wilson 235 at 21.36; M. Thompson 198 at 18.00.

Bowling A. P. D. Rigby 11 at 17.18; S. Lucas 21 at 23.09; L. T. E. Armstrong 20 at 24.50; J. J. Morrissey 20 at 24.70; J. G. Bell 12 at 31.91.

Merchant Taylors' School, Northwood
P13 W4 L4 D5

Master i/c A. J. Booth   **Coach** H. C. Latchman

With youngsters unable to compensate for underperforming senior players, the season was rather disappointing. Jonathan Phillips scored 126 to help beat MCC, and Will Magie had an excellent time with the bat. Ashil Shah looks a real prospect.

Batting W. M. Magie 374 at 53.42; J. T. Phillips 284 at 31.55; O. Wilkin* 188 at 26.85; R. M. Patel 187 at 23.37; I. K. Shah 246 at 22.36.

Bowling O. Wilkin 12 at 13.83; M. J. Grant 14 at 19.42; J. T. Phillips 10 at 20.30; R. D. Marsh 14 at 23.57; I. K. Shah 11 at 24.36.

Merchiston Castle School
P17 W12 L4 D1

Master i/c C. W. Swan   **Coach** S. C. Gilmour

In 13 matches against other schools, Merchiston prevailed in ten. Kyle Smith scored 638 runs and was one of four to score centuries. In June, Ollie Hairs opened Scotland's innings against India A.

Batting D. D. Duff 468 at 46.80; K. M. Smith* 638 at 39.87; P. A. Baker 580 at 38.66; D. J. Voas 513 at 32.06; P. J. S. Legget 307 at 21.92.

Bowling R. Patel 17 at 9.47; P. A. Baker 29 at 13.68; P. J. S. Legget 22 at 17.27; A. Maxwell 13 at 24.84; K. M. Smith 19 at 25.94.

Mill Hill School
P11 W2 L7 D2 A2

Master i/c I. J. F. Hutchinson   **Coach** N. R. Hodgson

The season was a little frustrating, with the hugely talented Adam Rossington unavailable for several fixtures. The captain, Rohun Davda, and senior player Miftah Ibrahim rose to the challenge, with Nikhil Lalwani the pick of the promising group of emerging youngsters.

Batting A. M. Rossington 341 at 85.25; M. Ibrahim 257 at 28.55.

Bowling R. Davda 14 at 13.92; N. Lalwani 13 at 18.00.

Millfield School
P19 W10 L7 D2 A1

Master i/c R. M. Ellison   **Coaches** M. R. Davis/R. L. Cook

A young team had a successful season against strong opposition. Highlights included Daniel Bell-Drummond's consistent batting – he was later signed by Kent – and retaining the National Schools Twenty20 title at Lord's.

Batting D. J. Bell-Drummond 982 at 65.46; J. Pinn 391 at 43.44; H. M. Thomas* 336 at 37.33; F. J. L. Gabbitass 196 at 21.77; W. H. Jenkins 266 at 20.46; D. E. Smith 156 at 19.50; H. R. C. Ellison 157 at 15.70; T. P. Wheater 203 at 15.61; S. R. O'Neill 198 at 15.23.

Bowling D. M. Hancock 29 at 17.37; T. P. Wheater 17 at 17.47; F. J. L. Gabbitass 18 at 20.77; D. J. Bell-Drummond 16 at 24.43; S. R. O'Neill 18 at 24.72; J. Pinn 10 at 29.70.

Monkton Combe School
P18 W10 L5 D3

Master i/c P. R. Wickens   **Coaches** P. Burke/M. B. Abington

A record ten wins and victory in the Bath Schools League were largely due to Ed Vickers, Mike Salmon and Toby Davies each scoring over 500 runs. Davies also took 37 wickets, as did pace bowler Matt Paynter.

Batting E. Vickers 504 at 42.00; T. P. A. Davies* 539 at 38.50; M. Salmon 512 at 34.13; J. Arney 281 at 31.22; B. Halle 176 at 29.33; B. Stupples 210 at 21.00.

Bowling M. Paynter 37 at 12.78; T. P. A. Davies 37 at 14.24; J. Adams 19 at 20.42; O. Millard 12 at 35.00.

Monmouth School
P16 W10 L5 D1 A1

Master i/c A. J. Jones   **Coach** G. I. Burgess

Chris Lawlor became the first batsman in the school's history to score 1,000 runs in a season. Andrew Leering won the Rob Hastings-Trew match award versus the OMs. Term ended with victory in the Castle Festival.

Batting C. L. Lawlor 1,034 at 68.93; M. J. Lovett 424 at 47.11; J. P. Grey 459 at 32.78; M. C. Backhouse 222 at 31.71; A. Leering 260 at 26.00; M. J. L. Scarr* 400 at 25.00.

Bowling A. Leering 26 at 16.88; M. J. L. Scarr 31 at 17.09; M. J. Lovett 20 at 18.65; A. Thomas 10 at 27.70; J. M. O. Scarr 11 at 30.81.

Newcastle-under-Lyme School
P13 W1 L10 D2

Master i/c G. M. Breen

Newcastle-under-Lyme had no one capable of building an innings, and so lost a record number of matches. It was ironic that against MCC, Benjamin Crome and George Mellor broke the school ninth-wicket record, with a stand of 67.

Batting T. W. Fuller 200 at 20.00; M. A. Spooner 187 at 15.58.

Bowling P. Nalwaya* 18 at 22.27; J. P. Wright 13 at 30.84.

Oakham's Tom Fell smashed the school batting record with 1,242 runs. Slow left-armer Jack Oughtred, from Oundle, bewildered The Perse batsmen to take ten for 48.

Nottingham High School
P17 W5 L10 D2
Master i/c S. A. J. Boswell   **Coach** I. Rose

The inability to take wickets at crucial times led to a difficult season. Several batsmen scored freely, with Sam Storey, skipper in 2011, ahead of the rest. Richard Brierley bowled an incredible spell of leg-spin against Bedford Modern, returning a season's-best seven for 26, and finished the top wicket-taker.

Batting J. S. Taylor 598 at 46.00; P. Sidhu 498 at 41.50; S. E. Storey 705 at 41.47; S. J. Johnson 607 at 40.46; J. S. Godrich 330 at 25.38; F. Sail 218 at 24.22.

Bowling R. W. Brierley 24 at 19.45; S. E. Storey 15 at 23.73; S. J. Johnson 14 at 24.14; C. F. C. Lea 12 at 29.16; A. D. Tosar 14 at 36.14; L. G. Robinson 12 at 42.75.

Oakham School
P23 W12 L9 D2 A1
Master i/c F. C. Hayes   **Coach** P. A. J. DeFreitas

The previous season's youth policy seemed to have borne fruit, though the batting still needs to develop consistency and the bowling incision if this young side are to prosper fully. Tom Fell, in his GCSE year, far exceeded the school record by scoring 1,242 runs at 69.00; he hit another 135 runs in Twenty20 matches.

Batting T. C. Fell 1,242 at 69.00; C. A. French 223 at 31.85; A. T. A. Martin 505 at 29.70; W. H. R. Edwards 437 at 21.85; L. M. D. Spears 296 at 21.14; J. C. Keywood 256 at 19.69; J. A. D. McCormack 153 at 19.12; B. D. Jacob-Farnsworth 205 at 17.08; H. G. Foster 165 at 13.75.

Bowling A. T. A. Martin 26 at 21.69; G. Maybury 24 at 24.54; J. H. A. Spence* 14 at 27.78; H. G. Foster 19 at 28.47; C. M. Billows 18 at 34.50; J. C. Keywood 15 at 35.06; C. A. French 10 at 36.80; B. D. Jacob-Farnsworth 11 at 44.27.

The Oratory School
P21 W13 L5 T3
Master i/c S. C. B. Tomlinson

With most players in their final year, the side produced excellent, good-spirited cricket, recording some deserved victories along the way. There were notable individual performances from wicketkeeper Tom Huysinga and Trevor McGeer, an all-rounder.

Batting T. Q. McGeer 465 at 35.76; T. J. Huysinga* 408 at 34.00; C. Whittaker 360 at 30.00; S. E. J. Thornton 355 at 31.84; M. P. G. Evans 226 at 25.11; J-C. Arnold 221 at 24.55.

Bowling T. Q. McGeer 30 at 11.33; S. E. J. Thornton 32 at 12.62; T. M. Nugent 25 at 15.04; C. Whittaker 14 at 15.42; C. De Verteuil 18 at 19.88.

Oundle School
P22 W10 L8 D4

Master i/c J. R. Wake   **Coach** van der Merwe Genis

Rory Osmond, the captain, scored 920 at 57.50 and ended his four-year career with 3,135 runs. Slow left-arm spinner Jack Oughtred achieved the rare feat of taking all ten wickets against The Perse (22–6–48–10). He and off-spinner Harry Ramsden claimed the all-round honours. Highlights of a curate's-egg season were wins against Shrewsbury, Radley, Uppingham and South Africa's Hilton College.

Batting R. T. Osmond* 920 at 57.50; J. Oughtred 524 at 34.93; H. D. Ramsden 466 at 27.41; T. M. A. Bishop 492 at 27.33; J. G. T. Johansen 407 at 27.13; G. H. Hodgkinson 273 at 19.50.

Bowling J. Oughtred 40 at 17.17; H. D. Ramsden 33 at 24.63; J. G. T. Johansen 12 at 26.66; W. P. Street 24 at 27.50; S. T. Olver 11 at 28.90; H. J. Spencer 12 at 30.33.

Pangbourne College
P14 W6 L6 D2

Master i/c C. G. Sutton   **Coach** J. J. C. Lewis

This was an encouraging season for Pangbourne that lacked only consistency. The team started very well, and could rely on runs from Phil Walden, Rupert Lewis and Scott Addyman. Guy Ashby was the stand-out bowler with his left-arm swing, and the future looks secure in the hands of youngsters such as off-spinner Louis Bearn.

Batting T. J. Lightfoot 197 at 39.40; S. T. Addyman 308 at 34.22; P. T. Walden* 390 at 32.50; R. A. A. Lewis 300 at 30.00; B. H. Tooze 177 at 22.12; G. W. M. Ashby 223 at 17.15; C. G. Bonwell 150 at 13.63.

Bowling G. W. M. Ashby 19 at 18.00; R. A. A. Lewis 14 at 20.78; M. P. H. Riley 12 at 24.16.

The Perse School
P9 W5 L1 D3 A1

Master i/c D. G. Roots   **Coach** D. C. Collard

The Perse had a productive summer, losing only one match out of nine played. Ben Creese was outstanding as captain and with bat and ball. He received telling support from Peter Richer, Alex Swan and wicketkeeper Micky Franklin. A last-ball victory over Bedford was the highlight.

Batting B. T. Creese* 410 at 51.25; P. G. Richer 301 at 37.62; G. C. Skinner 155 at 31.00.

Bowling B. T. Creese 20 at 16.60; A. E. Swan 16 at 22.25; P. G. Richer 19 at 23.57.

Plymouth College
P12 W8 L4 A1

Master i/c S. J. Vorster   **Coach** J. R. Mears

The season, dominated by Plymouth batsmen, resulted in consistently big scores. Unfortunately, the bowlers often lacked the firepower to trouble opponents, though dynamic fielding and catching helped offset this.

Batting G. Stephenson 229 at 45.80; A. J. Hill 268 at 38.28; J. R. E. Luffman* 366 at 36.60; H. J. Bennett 297 at 29.70; C. C. P. Cload 150 at 15.00.

Bowling H. J. Bennett 15 at 17.86; O. Mulberry 15 at 26.13.

Pocklington School
P15 W3 L9 D3 A2

Master i/c D. Byas

A season of mixed fortunes: the local derbies against Hymers and St Peter's were very closely fought. Chris Suddaby captained the team adeptly, hitting most runs and claiming most wickets; he received sterling support from Roger Moorhouse, James Flint and Peter Massie.

Batting C. Suddaby 491 at 37.76; R. Moorhouse 282 at 23.50; J. Flint 245 at 22.27; I. Green 234 at 18.00; W. Axup 158 at 11.28.

Bowling P. Massie 16 at 18.31; C. Suddaby 22 at 22.00; L. Smith 13 at 22.84.

Portsmouth Grammar School
P20 W14 L6 A2

Master i/c S. J. Curwood   **Coach** R. J. Maru

Three boys scored more than 450 runs and carried the side to success. Jacob George struck two centuries. The bowlers, headed by Robert Gibson, worked extremely well as a unit, with six taking 15 wickets or more.

Batting J. George 681 at 48.64; T. P. Finneran 196 at 39.20; R. A. M. Gibson 454 at 34.92; C. J. Stone 497 at 33.13; J. Collings-Wells 248 at 22.54; M. D. Walker 294 at 21.00; T. J. Seebold 234 at 18.00; C. G. O. Prentice* 163 at 14.81.

Bowling C. J. Stone 18 at 15.55; J. G. M. Scott 16 at 21.12; R. D. Tusler 17 at 23.64; R. A. M. Gibson 20 at 25.90; C. G. O. Prentice 18 at 27.38; C. W. Harding 15 at 35.80.

Prior Park College

P13 W8 L4 D1

Master i/c S. J. Capon   **Coach** M. D. Browning

The most successful summer in many years saw Seth Tapsfield and Edward Robinson leading the averages again, but fine team performances throughout were the key. Edward Singleton excelled as captain.

Batting B. S. Tapsfield 525 at 40.38; E. J. M. Singleton* 403 at 31.00; E. J. M. Borton 242 at 20.16; A. J. Barnes 182 at 16.54; E. Robinson 162 at 16.20.

Bowling E. Robinson 24 at 10.70; P. G. S. Borton 16 at 17.87; E. J. M. Borton 14 at 19.07; B. S. Tapsfield 10 at 25.50.

Queen Elizabeth Grammar School, Wakefield

P15 W6 L8 D1

Master i/c I. A. Wolfenden

The senior side had variable fortunes in an often challenging – but ultimately profitable – season, culminating with a summer festival and tour to St Lucia.

Batting J. Sleightholme* 631 at 57.36; S. Douglas 269 at 33.62; D. Hoyle 188 at 26.85; F. Fox 152 at 21.71; N. Busby 212 at 17.66; R. Knowles 159 at 12.23.

Bowling J. Sleightholme 10 at 30.20; S. Douglas 11 at 33.18; R. Knowles 13 at 36.38.

Queen Elizabeth's Hospital

P12 W4 L8 A1

Master i/c P. E. Joslin   **Coach** D. C. Forder

Teejay Coles guided the side well through an enjoyable season for all. Mike Willmott was again top wicket-taker and run-scorer.

Batting M. T. Willmott 377 at 34.27; E. M. Piercy 156 at 31.20; J. W. Barnsley 234 at 23.40; T. Coles* 172 at 21.50.

Bowling T. P. Ware 13 at 12.00; E. M. Piercy 10 at 16.80; M. T. Willmott 17 at 18.70.

Queen's College, Taunton

P17 W9 L6 T1 D1 A1

Master i/c A. S. Free   **Coach** D. R. Bates

Jake Lintott became only the second player to hit 1,000 runs in a season at the school. Other highlights were his hat-trick in a one-wicket defeat by MCC, and Will Steward's fine 118 at Taunton. George Musgrave contributed strongly with bat and ball.

Batting J. B. Lintott* 1,045 at 69.66; W. E. Steward 627 at 39.18; G. H. Musgrave 511 at 34.06; J. S. Kohler 355 at 27.30; M. J. Steward 179 at 12.78.

Bowling J. B. Lintott 40 at 12.82; O. M. L. Webb 18 at 19.50; M. J. Steward 15 at 33.73; G. W. A. Pike 15 at 35.06; G. H. Musgrave 15 at 37.20.

Radley College

P16 W12 L3 D1

Master i/c J. R. W. Beasley   **Coach** A. R. Wagner

This side, led with steel-eyed determination and tactical maturity by Hector Freyne, relished many resounding victories. Excellent in the field, the squad had a powerful team spirit, and displayed real depth in batting and bowling.

Batting N. R. T. Gubbins 582 at 44.76; H. A. Freyne* 437 at 43.70; O. J. Thornton 229 at 38.16; A. G. Hearne 491 at 35.07; W. W. J. Marriott 397 at 28.35; N. G. M. Ramsay 155 at 22.14; S. P. J. Aldridge 215 at 19.54; J. M. Wynne-Griffith 242 at 18.61.

Bowling A. D. W. Tinsley 40 at 10.90; A. Wallis 24 at 17.70; A. A. K. Low 16 at 20.31; W. W. J. Marriott 16 at 24.68; N. G. M. Ramsay 14 at 29.92.

Ratcliffe College

P12 W5 L5 D2 A2

Master i/c R. M. Hughes   **Coach** E. O. Woodcock

In a somewhat inconsistent season for Ratcliffe, the batting relied heavily on Michael Phillips, whose 724 runs included four sparkling hundreds. Tom Smith, having led the batting in 2009, now dominated the bowling, taking 20 wickets with his fast-medium seamers.

Batting M. K. Phillips 724 at 90.50; T. R. Smith 217 at 24.11; H. F. G. Spillane* 221 at 22.10.

Bowling T. R. Smith 20 at 16.60.

Reed's School

P19 W5 L8 D6 A1

Master i/c M. R. Dunn   **Coach** K. T. Medlycott

Although smartly captained by Toby Tarrant, who with Simon Sweeney formed a formidable opening attack, the team should have completed more victories. But promise was shown by a young batting line-up featuring Rory Woolston and Alex Redmayne.

Batting K. Kapoor 538 at 38.42; R. J. Woolston 520 at 37.14; A. J. S. Redmayne 629 at 37.00; M. A. Macpherson 258 at 32.25; H. Breimyr 178 at 25.42; S. A. C. Sweeney 454 at 25.22; J. A. Malthouse 180 at 22.50; R. G. Davis 302 at 20.13; L. R. Simon 179 at 17.90.
Bowling K. Kapoor 17 at 23.11; S. A. C. Sweeney 24 at 23.58; T. C. Tarrant* 35 at 24.02; R. J. Woolston 18 at 37.94.

Reigate Grammar School
P14 W6 L8 A1
Master i/c E. M. Wesson   **Coach** J. E. Benjamin
It was pleasing to finish a campaign, which fluctuated between mediocrity and exciting achievement, so strongly. A fine Twenty20 record of six wins from seven starts showed that the shorter game suited many of the players. Will Irving completed four years in the team – and was an astute captain.
Batting W. G. O. Irving* 423 at 35.25; W. C. F. Fry 454 at 34.92; C. M. Steedman 403 at 31.00; H. P. Elsey 183 at 16.63.
Bowling B. J. Baker 16 at 18.25; W. G. O. Irving 21 at 20.52; N. J. Gunning 14 at 26.85.

Repton School
P16 W12 L3 D1
Master i/c I. M. Pollock   **Coaches**: H. B. Dytham/J. A. Afford
Much of this season's triumph was down to two spinners, Matt Sanderson and Tom Cosford, and the top four batsmen. Varied bowling options and competence down the order often proved crucial.
Batting S. R. Graham 547 at 54.70; T. P. Cosford 555 at 46.25; E. Ikin 549 at 45.75; C. G. Murrall* 433 at 30.92; M. J. S. Jacques 337 at 28.08; M. W. Sanderson 214 at 21.40.
Bowling M. W. Sanderson 25 at 17.20; A. Ahmed 16 at 17.31; T. P. Cosford 23 at 19.95; H. Eldred 12 at 20.66; E. Ikin 16 at 30.18.

Rossall School
P18 W9 L8 T1
Master i/c T. L. N. Root
A very successful pre-season tour to St Kitts helped to mould the side into a competitive and committed unit. All-rounders Toby Lester and Luke Williams, both Lancashire youth players, showed blossoming skills. Nine of the squad return in 2011.
Batting L. C. W. Williams 446 at 31.85; P. Rimmer 190 at 31.66; C. J. Metcalfe* 383 at 23.93; J. R. Wilson 268 at 22.33; C. T. Hough 210 at 19.09; H. Southern 186 at 15.50; T. J. Lester 216 at 14.40.
Bowling S. Bhuyan 10 at 11.70; L. C. W. Williams 21 at 12.95; C. J. Metcalfe 17 at 15.52; C. P. Andrews 18 at 16.55; T. J. Lester 25 at 18.44; J. R. Wilson 14 at 22.21.

The Royal Grammar School, Guildford
P16 W11 L4 D1 A1
Master i/c S. B. R. Shore   **Coach** M. A. Lynch
A determined flourish at the end of term, with nine wins from the last ten games, saw Guildford declared joint winners of the RGS Festival. Performances included 401 for five in 50 overs, an opening partnership of 243, an unbeaten 155 for captain Nick Cooper, and Morgan Dawe taking an impressive 37 wickets.
Batting R. J. McClellan 685 at 76.11; N. G. R. Cooper* 685 at 68.50; A. N. Goodchild 227 at 37.83; A. D. Z. Brown 528 at 37.71; T. J. Barnardo 437 at 31.21; C. F. Warren 171 at 19.00.
Bowling M. P. Dawe 37 at 15.08; G. J. P. Neal-Smith 10 at 16.80; A. D. Z. Brown 17 at 20.70; C. F. Warren 15 at 22.46; C. H. Hunt 11 at 28.81; R. J. McClellan 13 at 33.69.

The Royal Grammar School, Worcester
P20 W15 L3 D2
Master i/c M. D. Wilkinson   **Coach** P. J. Newport
Tom Williams captained a good all-round side very perceptively. A highly successful season included a huge win over King's, and culminated in sharing the honours at the RGS Festival at Colchester. With only four leaving, there is much promise for the future.
Batting T. J. P. Williams* 543 at 45.25; O. J. Steele 333 at 41.62; D. A. Hagger 663 at 39.00; A. Pollock 528 at 37.71; A. S. N. Curtis 641 at 33.73; Z. W. Turley 421 at 32.38; E. J. Pollock 445 at 31.78.
Bowling A. A. Dilley 15 at 17.00; A. Pollock 37 at 17.16; P. E. O'Driscoll 23 at 20.60; W. G. French 13 at 21.76; E. J. Pollock 19 at 25.26; A. S. N. Curtis 19 at 29.21.

Royal Hospital School
P14 W9 L4 D1
Master i/c T. D. Topley   **Coach** D. W. Hawkley
A run of seven wins was the high point for a competitive side. Reece Topley took all-round duties in his stride with able support from Ben Allday and Ben Rutledge. The youthful bowlers offer RHS appreciable hope for the years to come.

Batting R. J. W. Topley 385 at 32.08; B. N. Allday 261 at 26.10; B. W. G. Rutledge 314 at 24.15; F. Seccombe* 233 at 21.18.
Bowling R. J. W. Topley 21 at 14.47; C. Stuart 14 at 16.71; G. Paton 17 at 18.64.

Rugby School   P24 W11 L7 D6
Master i/c M. J. Semmence   **Coach** G. B. Brent
Following a successful tour of India, the team had a fine season that included wins against MCC, Warwick, Uppingham, Stowe and Malvern. Joe Moxham made 756 runs, including four hundreds, while fifth-former Jake Kings combined 711 runs with 39 wickets for his off-spin.
Batting J. B. Kings 711 at 39.50; J. L. Moxham 756 at 37.80; G. R. Mackenzie 594 at 29.70; T. H. Clarke 471 at 29.43; G. E. O. Terry 242 at 24.20; K. T. Cutter 304 at 21.71; D. A. Mackenzie 161 at 20.12; T. P. McKibbin 369 at 19.42.
Bowling T. H. Clarke 26 at 18.92; G. R. Mackenzie 32 at 19.31; J. B. Kings 39 at 20.74; J. M. Barker 20 at 23.40; R. H. Inamdar 18 at 24.38; K. T. Cutter 12 at 25.50; G. E. O. Terry 11 at 25.63; D. A. Mackenzie 12 at 41.08.

Rydal Penrhos   P9 W2 L7
Master i/c M. T. Leach
Despite some poor results overall, improved team and individual performances towards the end of term were pleasing. With only one player leaving, hopes are brighter for 2011.
Batting M. J. D. Kitchen* 213 at 26.62; D. Parry 193 at 24.12.
Bowling No one took ten wickets. The leading bowler was B. Walsh, who took eight at 34.50.

Ryde School with Upper Chine   P13 W9 L4
Master i/c C. Sutton
This was another excellent season for Ryde. A total of nine victories, as well as winning the Milton Abbey Twenty20 competition, suggests there is much more to come from this squad. Once again, the captain Toby Jackson and Cameron Mitchell had superb seasons.
Batting C. G. Grant 222 at 44.40; T. A. Jackson* 567 at 43.61; C. J. Mitchell 394 at 39.40; J. S. Cutting 276 at 25.09.
Bowling T. A. Groves 14 at 20.64; C. J. Mitchell 17 at 22.00; B. A. McEwen 10 at 26.00; J. C. Leggett 10 at 30.40; T. A. Jackson 10 at 33.90.

St Albans School   P14 W4 L9 D1
Master i/c C. C. Hudson   **Coach** M. C. Ilott
Victories were thin on the ground, but there was real encouragement in the performance of George Scott, who, aged 14 years and three months, became the school's youngest centurion: he needed just 52 balls to reach three figures against Enfield GS.
Batting H. J. J. Stairmand 420 at 38.18; J. E. Scott 444 at 37.00; A. Rajah 336 at 30.54; B. J. Hudson* 347 at 28.91; K. Hassani 301 at 27.36; G. Scott 256 at 23.27.
Bowling T. W. Kight 21 at 23.33; A. S. Kulkarni 14 at 25.21.

St Edmund's School, Canterbury   P16 W10 L5 D1 A1
Master i/c A. R. Jones   **Coach** H. L. Alleyne
With several new faces demonstrating real potential, the term could be viewed with pleasure. At times, though, a lack of composure proved costly, resulting in some disappointing defeats, especially in the County Cup final. The squad retains its depth and balance for 2011.
Batting R. J. Stone 606 at 40.40; M. Anglin 327 at 36.33; B. J. Pape* 541 at 36.06; H. J. Callaway 317 at 28.81; B. W. Kemp 180 at 20.00.
Bowling B. W. Kemp 30 at 12.76; B. J. Pape 24 at 15.12; A. J. Higson 15 at 20.06; R. T. Penn 17 at 21.82; R. J. Stone 13 at 25.00.

St Edward's School, Oxford   P23 W8 L8 D7
Master i/c M. A. Stephenson   **Coaches** R. W. J. Howitt/C. J. L. Sandbach
Alex Smith guided his side shrewdly and scored three superb centuries. Jasper Joyce was an immaculate wicketkeeper, while Jamie Fraser led the bowling attack skilfully. The emergence of some exciting prospects bodes well.
Batting A. D. Smith* 901 at 42.90; H. A. Coles 488 at 27.11; B. A. Taylor 266 at 22.16; G. E. J. Chaffer 243 at 18.71; J. L. Joyce 350 at 17.50; F. Beg 210 at 17.50; F. J. Kerr-Dineen 176 at 11.73; O. P. Smith 158 at 11.28.

Bowling R. J. Wise 24 at 17.87; A. S. Hargreaves 20 at 20.80; M. A. Hammond 19 at 30.15; J. R. Fraser 16 at 31.75; R. S. Shipperley 13 at 49.92.

St George's College, Weybridge
P19 W9 L7 D3
Master i/c M. T. Harrison   **Coach** J. R. P. Heath

Will Grant, with over 700 runs, and Alex Colville, by taking 41 wickets, rewrote two College records that had survived for more than 20 years. They, and Nick Kent, will form the backbone of the 2011 side. Five leave after contributing 245 appearances between them: an exodus of great experience.
Batting W. R. Grant 728 at 45.50; T. P. Cross 543 at 36.20; J. D. McKinlay 508 at 26.73; A. M. Stanley 341 at 21.31; B. O. Rooney 264 at 20.30; S. M. Cox* 223 at 17.15.
Bowling A. K. Colville 41 at 14.56; N. O. Kent 32 at 16.78; B. G. C. Scott 28 at 18.00; A. M. Stanley 16 at 21.31; R. G. F. Snowball 15 at 23.20.

St John's School, Leatherhead
P15 W11 L4 A1
Master i/c G. I. Macmillan   **Coach** I. Trott

An exceptionally young team, well led by Benjamin Frost, recorded 11 good wins. The strength of the side lay in the bowling. Six boys, including the stand-out player Adam Dyson, return for a further two seasons.
Batting A. Dyson 178 at 35.60; B. Frost* 488 at 34.85; J. Prichard 421 at 32.38; S. Roberts 269 at 26.90; W. Lander 191 at 23.87; R. Heald 232 at 23.20; J. W. Howe 274 at 22.83; S. Kiff 195 at 21.66.
Bowling A. Dyson 21 at 13.28; J. W. Howe 33 at 14.51; W. Lander 21 at 16.52; S. Kiff 12 at 16.75; J. Lander 11 at 18.00; O. Glanville 22 at 23.90.

St Lawrence College
P8 W1 L7
Master i/c T. Moulton   **Coach** S. M. Simmons

Robert Newbery was a consistent run-scorer, but generally the batsmen struggled to support good work from the bowlers, leading to a disappointing season. Patrick Collins gave a cutting edge with the new ball.
Batting R. W. Newbery 229 at 38.16; R. A. Jones 152 at 19.00.
Bowling W. P. C. Collins 12 at 15.75; D. C. Whittle* 11 at 19.45; R. W. Newbery 12 at 19.75.

St Paul's School
P17 W12 L2 D3 A1
Master i/c M. G. Howat   **Coach** A. G. J. Fraser

St Paul's had one of their finest campaigns in many years. More games were won than in any season since the early 1950s. The team came second in the 50/40 League. Alastair Edmonds was an excellent captain and consistent opening batsman.
Batting S. J. Cato 473 at 52.55; N. R. Edmonds 205 at 51.25; A. S. Edmonds* 638 at 45.57; T. R. R. Schneider 410 at 31.53; H. W. Browne 210 at 30.00; F. J. G. Light 338 at 24.14.
Bowling S. J. Cato 17 at 17.76; C. M. Berkett 27 at 20.14; J. H. Walker 10 at 22.20; R. D. Majithia 11 at 28.63.

St Peter's School, York
P18 W9 L3 D6
Master i/c D. Kirby

A record of nine wins was a very good effort from the St Peter's squad. The core of the team was the three all-rounders: Will Peet, Joe Halstead and skipper Harry Booth. Oliver Burdass was an effective opening batsman.
Batting H. T. R. Booth* 734 at 43.17; J. J. D. Robinson 254 at 42.33; J. J. Halstead 593 at 37.06; O. C. Burdass 558 at 32.82; S. P. Ash 307 at 25.58; W. T. Peet 272 at 24.72; W. G. Stephen 284 at 20.28; H. D. Lynde 223 at 15.92.
Bowling W. T. Peet 35 at 18.60; H. T. R. Booth* 33 at 21.18; J. J. Halstead 22 at 21.18; C. J. Brown 11 at 39.09.

Sedbergh School
P20 W16 L3 D1
Master i/c C. P. Mahon   **Coach** C. G. Siller

An inexperienced side exceeded expectations and established a school record of 16 victories. The main strengths lay in a well-balanced attack that took 195 of the 200 wickets available from 20 games. Spinners Tim Raglan and Charlie Thwaytes were outstanding throughout, taking 94 wickets between them.

Sedbergh's spinners were the two most successful bowlers in the country. Charlie Thwaytes (*left*) took 46 wickets, and Tim Raglan claimed 48.

Batting D. W. Bell* 917 at 61.13; W. Chapples 743 at 57.15; J. J. McCluskie 355 at 39.44; S. M. Dutton 450 at 32.14; T. A. Benn 278 at 23.16.
Bowling T. D. Raglan 48 at 9.60; C. W. Thwaytes 46 at 11.56; H. M. R. Peterson 22 at 15.18; W. Chapples 21 at 17.90; B. N. Davis 18 at 18.83; J. J. McCluskie 16 at 20.18.

Sevenoaks School
P19 W9 L8 D2
Master i/c C. J. Tavaré   **Coach** P. J. Hulston
Wins against Haileybury (Ben Richardson 102 not out), Hurstpierpoint (Charlie Farrant seven for 20), and Judd (Tom Nickols 98 not out), were an indication of how well the team could play in an up-and-down summer. Dom Makepeace topped the batting averages and kept wicket admirably.
Batting D. W. Makepeace 347 at 31.54; B. A. Richardson* 362 at 30.16; T. R. Nickols 358 at 27.53; J. P. Hulston 256 at 23.27; C. C. Farrant 344 at 22.93; M. C. Thorpe 337 at 22.46.
Bowling C. C. Farrant 31 at 14.87; C. B. Carter-Leno 18 at 17.83; B. A. Richardson* 15 at 23.93; E. T. Woodhouse-Darry 14 at 24.28; W. P. Gill 12 at 31.75; J. P. Hulston 10 at 34.90.

Sherborne School
P16 W10 L5 D1 A1
Master i/c R. W. Hill   **Coach** A. Willows
In an excellent all-round season, Theo Cooke was the foremost performer with the bat and, as captain, he set high standards in all departments. Spinners Ferg Taylor and Theo Grainzevelles took 56 wickets between them. Charlie Carline made 15 catches and five stumpings.
Batting T. S. C. Cooke* 631 at 45.07; C. E. H. Carline 223 at 27.87; C. J. Peatfield 260 at 26.00; C. A. L. Leach 307 at 25.58; H. J. Wildsmith 238 at 21.63; F. E. Taylor 258 at 21.50; W. A. A. Selfe 210 at 21.00; T. Grainzevelles 314 at 20.93.
Bowling F. E. Taylor 29 at 17.31; H. E. Fielder 11 at 17.90; T. Grainzevelles 27 at 19.18; W. A. A. Selfe 12 at 33.91.

Shiplake College

P15 W10 L3 D2

Master i/c A. D. Dix   **Coach** S. Cane-Hardy

Once the experienced quartet of captain Oliver Gould, Ross Ritchie, James Black and James Luscombe came to the fore, the season turned out well. The team were superbly led, and contained some talented Year 11 players such as wicketkeeper Ben Francis (15 stumpings and nine catches).

Batting R. M. Ritchie 220 at 44.00; J. R. Black 291 at 41.57; T. J. P. Luscombe 262 at 37.42; O. W. Gould* 281 at 28.10; B. Francis 324 at 27.00; J. A. Wood 312 at 26.00; M. Thomas 204 at 17.00; H. Laflin 150 at 12.50.

Bowling R. M. Ritchie 20 at 17.20; O. W. Gould 18 at 19.05; H. Grummitt 14 at 20.42; J. R. Black 13 at 24.30; I. A. S. Brown 11 at 24.36.

Shrewsbury School

P20 W14 L5 D1

Master i/c A. S. Barnard   **Coach** A. P. Pridgeon

Heavy scoring throughout the term from skipper Alex Blofield, David Lloyd, Ben Price and Ben Williams gave the team a solid platform for many victories. Losing a second successive National Twenty20 semi-final to Millfield and a final-day defeat by Eton in the Silk Trophy were relative low points in a season of sustained high quality.

Batting D. L. Lloyd 696 at 63.27; B. L. C. Price 736 at 46.00; B. Williams 487 at 37.46; A. D. Blofield 590 at 36.87; S. J. Barnard 321 at 35.66; J. G. Hudson Williams 334 at 33.40; M. J. Cull 398 at 30.61; S. G. Leach 578 at 28.90.

Bowling S. J. Barnard 15 at 20.40; J. G. Hudson Williams 19 at 20.68; H. G. Lewis 24 at 21.41; D. L. Lloyd 18 at 23.44; J. N. Aston 20 at 24.70; A. D. Blofield 27 at 27.11.

Silcoates School

P17 W3 L13 D1

Master i/c G. M. Roberts   **Coach** E. R. Hudson

This was essentially a pleasing season for a hard-working and enthusiastic group of young cricketers who deserved better results. The highlight was the two-wicket victory against King's Tynemouth, when Silcoates knocked off 283 with four balls to spare.

Batting J. S. Langrick* 360 at 25.71; M. T. Butel 263 at 17.53; W. Fraine 165 at 16.50.

Bowling J. S. Langrick 16 at 14.75; T. G. Godlington 11 at 17.54.

Simon Langton Grammar School

P10 W4 L4 D2 A1

Master i/c R. H. Green

After a pre-season tour to St Lucia, the prospects for the summer looked encouraging. But four excellent wins – bolstered by two centuries from John Ewart, plus some good fielding and bowling – were countered by four inexplicable batting collapses that led to defeat.

Batting J. P. R. Ewart 294 at 49.00.

Bowling J. M. C. Pearson* 12 at 11.41; R. T. Smith 11 at 14.36; W. D. Lock 11 at 25.09.

Solihull School

P21 W10 L8 D3 A2

Master i/c D. L. Hemp

Given the scant experience of the squad, the season turned out well. There were some memorable performances, especially Chris Williamson's 263 against Nottingham HS. Dominic Harding played consistently well, striking four centuries.

Batting D. G. Harding 997 at 58.64; C. Williamson* 823 at 39.19; J. Carey 261 at 26.10; J. Lucas 308 at 23.69; M. J. Bacon 355 at 20.88; J. J. Coleman 416 at 20.80; D. Brotherhood 205 at 17.08.

Bowling D. Brotherhood 14 at 21.71; J. Carey 12 at 28.50; M. Sinha 25 at 30.44; C. Williamson 22 at 39.90; C. Wood 10 at 40.60; J. J. Coleman 16 at 51.75.

Stamford School

P17 W7 L9 D1 A2

Master i/c D. G. Colley   **Coach** E. J. Wilson

This was a nearly season: the number of defeats did not truly reflect the ability of a developing team. A fine hundred by Louis Grimoldby, and a splendid undefeated 123 from captain Tom Williams in the victory over MCC, were highlights.

Batting G. Hook 340 at 85.00; T. N. Williams* 551 at 45.91; L. Grimoldby 384 at 42.66; B. J. P. Mhlanga 349 at 31.72; J. R. Bolus 284 at 31.55; T. P. Anders 237 at 19.75; J. Williams 183 at 18.30.

Bowling H. Charlton 12 at 18.66; J. C. Oakley 18 at 23.94; A. Emerson 10 at 33.00; J. Williams 13 at 34.84; P. J. Wilson 11 at 36.00.

Stewart's Melville College, Edinburgh

P16 W8 L6 D2 A1

Master i/c A. Ranson

The season contained plenty of ups and a few downs. Thomas Beattie, Mohammed Ahmed, and 13-year-old Michael Miller all enjoyed a profitable summer.
Batting T. J. Beattie 367 at 24.46; I. Mackie 219 at 21.90; M. Miller 185 at 16.81; M. Ahmed 235 at 16.78; A. T. Dry 181 at 16.45; M. G. Bunker 159 at 13.25.
Bowling M. Miller 19 at 11.36; M. Ahmed 20 at 12.95; S. C. Doherty 11 at 19.00; B. C. J. Doherty 15 at 20.13; A. J. Warnock 11 at 24.09; A. T. Dry 13 at 25.61.

Stockport Grammar School

P8 W3 L5

Master i/c R. Young   **Coach** D. J. Makinson

After a tough start, this young side made excellent progress, resulting in one of the more successful campaigns of recent years. The batsmen dominated, with opener Robert Griffiths leading the way. Key bowler Stephen Dickie had a superb debut season.
Batting R. Griffiths 242 at 34.57; D. J. Wright 178 at 25.42; D. I. Isherwood 175 at 25.00; T. Isherwood* 154 at 19.25.
Bowling S. P. A. Dickie 12 at 16.58.

Stowe School

P23 W11 L7 T1 D4 A1

Master i/c J. A. Knott   **Coach** C. J. Townsend

Jon Gurney's side enjoyed an excellent season, beating Oundle, Radley and Oakham, and winning their own Twenty20 festival. Ali Birkby had a superb summer, compiling 1,000 runs and adding 25 wickets, too. Fifteen-year-old Ben Duckett gathered over 850 runs and made 30 dismissals.
Batting A. F. B. Birkby 1,013 at 59.58; B. M. Duckett 852 at 47.33; J. A. Olley 392 at 24.50; J. J. C. MacDonald 325 at 20.31; J. K. W. Sainsbury-Bow 166 at 18.44; B. Curley 156 at 17.33; B. T. Sutton 237 at 13.16.
Bowling J. A. Olley 13 at 18.61; J. K. W. Sainsbury-Bow 33 at 19.75; W. J. B. Berner 23 at 23.00; H. R. C. Rudd 10 at 23.80; A. F. B. Birkby 28 at 24.28; J. H. Gurney* 26 at 26.34; B. T. Paine 12 at 31.58.

Strathallan School

P14 W7 L6 D1

Master i/c R. H. Fitzsimmons

An odd season, notable for Freddie Coleman's record four centuries, the debut of 14-year-old leg-spinner Grant Doig and, at one stage, three sets of brothers in the side. Keith Wigley also scored a century against the XL Club, while older brother Paul, and Declan Norrie, each grabbed 24 wickets.
Batting F. R. J. Coleman* 696 at 139.20; D. J. Hoogerbrugge 259 at 37.00; N. A. G. Farrar 239 at 34.14; K. G. J. Wigley 225 at 20.45; C. D. R. Donald 208 at 18.90.
Bowling F. R. J. Coleman 10 at 17.20; P. G. E. Wigley 24 at 17.87; D. J. Norrie 24 at 20.29; K. G. J. Wigley 11 at 22.72; N. A. G. Farrar 12 at 23.41; G. R. T. Doig 12 at 28.75.

Sutton Valence School

P17 W11 L5 D1

Master i/c W. D. Buck   **Coach** V. J. Wells

Tyler Griffin, Ali Neale and Chris Vernon all played for the Kent Academy and for Kent Premier League clubs. Raw pace from Robbie Palmer and intelligent bowling from Miles Henslow stood out in a young attack.
Batting A. D. G. Neale 565 at 40.35; C. R. G. Vernon 685 at 40.29; T. J. Griffin* 606 at 37.87; B. J. Woodmansee 333 at 33.30; H. C. S. Galpin 297 at 24.75.
Bowling T. J. Griffin 24 at 15.54; M. T. Henslow 21 at 16.52; R. M. Palmer 17 at 18.58; M. N. Murray 10 at 20.30; A. D. G. Neale 23 at 24.21; H. C. S. Galpin 10 at 26.30.

Taunton School

P16 W8 L7 D1

Master i/c S. T. Hogg   **Coach** H. K. C. Todd

Led by quick-bowling, hard-hitting all-rounder William Gater, Taunton enjoyed several fine victories. Thomas Abell has now scored over 1,500 runs before entering the sixth form. The bowling and fielding were less consistent than in recent years, allowing opponents to score more freely.
Batting T. B. Abell 735 at 61.25; J. J. Debenham 434 at 39.45; G. A. Cook 237 at 29.62; W. H. Gater* 293 at 26.63; H. G. Popplewell 290 at 22.30; R. P. Glover 196 at 19.60.
Bowling R. P. Glover 18 at 18.16; H. G. Popplewell 24 at 18.54; W. H. Gater 19 at 21.73; J. J. Debenham 12 at 39.33.

Tiffin School
P22 W7 L13 D2

Master i/c M. J. Williams

A season of rebuilding meant Tiffin endured a difficult start, although results picked up, with six wins from the last nine games. With no single batsman dominating, runs were generally hard to find; there is a healthy clutch of bowlers for 2011.

Batting K. S. Toor 390 at 26.00; K. A. Gor 266 at 20.46; G. M. Liyanage 285 at 16.76; B. A. Khan* 274 at 16.11; N. Thevarajan 185 at 13.21; M. M. Khan 222 at 11.68.

Bowling S. S. Sandher 14 at 15.28; C. F. Belcher 23 at 18.47; G. M. Liyanage 30 at 21.93; P. K. Patel 25 at 25.84.

Tonbridge School
P16 W10 L4 D2

Master i/c A. R. Whittall   **Coaches** J. P. Arscott/I. Baldock

Tonbridge retained the Cowdrey Cup to crown a fine year. Victories in school fixtures came against Charterhouse, Eton, Harrow, Wellington, Radley, Eastbourne, Bedford, Cranleigh, and St Peter's Adelaide. Once again, the leading run-scorer was Tom Elliott with 832 runs. He also captained the side with great awareness. Fabian Cowdrey scored 632 runs and was the leading wicket-taker.

Batting T. C. Elliott* 832 at 59.42; F. K. Cowdrey 632 at 48.61; C. J. A. Paget 393 at 35.72; J. J. Payne 416 at 34.66; T. P. W. Harvey 308 at 25.66; C. F. Munton 294 at 22.61.

Bowling F. K. Cowdrey 30 at 17.76; J. L. Cowdrey 13 at 21.07; T. M. S. Jenner 15 at 23.86; T. F. J. Coldman 26 at 24.61; T. P. W. Harvey 12 at 33.58.

Trent College
P14 W12 L2

Master i/c O. J. Clayson   **Coach** D. Hartley

This was a truly fantastic season in all forms of the game. Trent reached the quarter-final of the National Twenty20 and lost only two longer matches. Oli Swann, Nick Halley and Adam Tillcock contributed many outstanding performances.

Batting O. J. D. Swann* 591 at 73.87; A. Tillcock 399 at 39.90; T. J. Young 371 at 30.91.

Bowling A. Tillcock 32 at 12.18; N. Halley 20 at 18.80.

Truro School
P11 W3 L5 D3

Master i/c A. D. Lawrence

Batting C. Purchase 244 at 61.00; M. Manuell* 200 at 28.57.

Bowling T. Child 13 at 15.92.

University College School
P15 W5 L9 D1

Master i/c S. M. Bloomfield   **Coach** W. G. Jones

Victories over St Edmund's, Aldenham, St Benedict's, Forest and KEQMS Lytham were the bright spots of a largely frustrating term. A varied and useful bowling attack often had to defend small targets: the batsmen lacking patience and determination.

Batting J. Pilgrim 301 at 27.36; T. B. Bradshaw 268 at 24.36; E. J. Lowe* 251 at 22.81; G. S. Bennetts 226 at 22.60; B. N. Brodie 172 at 14.33.

Bowling C. C. Diebitsch 12 at 19.33; E. J. Lowe* 18 at 25.16; G. S. Bennetts 14 at 26.57; O. G. Chapman 18 at 30.16; K. Y. Patel 10 at 34.30.

Uppingham School
P16 W7 L5 T2 D2 A2

Master i/c C. P. Simmons   **Coach** T. R. Ward

A hugely eventful season included a tour to the UAE, two tied matches (MCC and Yarra GS) and two pupils scoring double-centuries. Henry Hughes broke the school batting record with 229 against Shrewsbury, while Shiv Thakor continues to thrive.

Batting S. J. Thakor 889 at 80.81; H. C. D. Hughes 892 at 59.46; B. G. D. Stewart 267 at 24.27; S. J. Foster* 213 at 23.66; T. C. Moxon 229 at 19.08.

Bowling P. E. D. Morrissey 29 at 22.58; S. J. Thakor 25 at 24.60; G. T. G. Weller 17 at 28.94.

Victoria College, Jersey
P16 W7 L8 D1

Master i/c M. D. Smith   **Coach** C. E. Minty

Victoria made history in 2010 by entering the Jersey Premier League for the first time, as well as playing their more traditional fixtures. The batting highlight was an excellent 125 by Aidan McGuire, who will be captain in 2011. Steven Blackburn took 22 wickets despite missing the first six weeks of the season with injury. The College won four out of five fixtures on their annual tour to England.

Batting A. M. McGuire 538 at 44.83; L. E. W. Gallichan 250 at 35.71; D. L. McAviney 480 at 34.28; T. N. de la Haye* 346 at 26.61; C. J. Bodenstein 336 at 22.40; W. T. Falle 205 at 20.50; A. X. Noel 153 at 19.12; C. F. Bisson 250 at 17.85.
Bowling S. T. Blackburn 22 at 19.54; A. X. Noel 17 at 24.35; C. J. Bodenstein 16 at 26.87; C. P. F. Bisson 14 at 27.35; L. E. W. Gallichan 12 at 31.50.

Warwick School
P16 W9 L7

Master i/c G. A. Tedstone — **Coach** S. R. G. Francis
The results were a vast improvement on last year's. Expectations were for batting weakness, yet Jonathan Byrd, George Tedstone and Thomas Williams all scored over 400 runs, while Peter Walters continued to bowl with an economy-rate of less than 3.50.
Batting G. Tedstone 431 at 35.91; T. A. Williams 458 at 32.71; J. R. Byrd 401 at 26.73; B. J. Howard 297 at 21.21; S. J. Hooper 199 at 19.90; T. O. J. Edwards* 168 at 18.66; T. J. M. Glanfield 162 at 16.20.
Bowling S. Lyall 20 at 16.70; J. R. Byrd 19 at 19.68; T. O. J. Edwards 15 at 20.53; P. J. Walters 18 at 21.94; J. M. Atkins 13 at 26.07; O. J. Lunel 15 at 30.00.

Wellingborough School
P13 W5 L5 D3 A1

Master i/c G. E. Houghton — **Coach** N. K. Knight
A season of mixed fortunes saw the second half of term bring considerably more success than the first. Fifteen-year-old Charlie Macdonell scored his maiden senior century, while Jack Johnson fell one short of a double-hundred in the last game of the summer.
Batting J. W. Johnson 376 at 94.00; P. Patel* 616 at 56.00; W. Kiddle 220 at 27.50; C. M. Macdonell 314 at 26.16; J. C. T. Collins 325 at 25.00.
Bowling P. Patel 22 at 20.81; J. C. T. Collins 15 at 30.53; W. C. Knibbs 12 at 33.66.

Wellington College
P22 W9 L11 D2

Master i/c G. D. Franklin — **Coach** M. T. Boobbyer
Wins over Sedbergh, Cranleigh and Charterhouse were highlights of a fair season. Tom Wood led with intelligence, and was stoutly supported by Max Tulley and by promising all-rounder Will Leith. James Brooks shone behind the stumps and, with Angus Boobbyer, scored invaluable runs.
Batting M. W. A. Tulley 442 at 34.00; J. P. P. Brooks 564 at 33.17; A. T. Boobbyer 583 at 29.15; J. B. Rendell 359 at 25.64; W. R. G. Leith 523 at 24.90; C. J. Nurse 370 at 21.76; W. O. E. Barker 298 at 18.62; T. J. Wood* 312 at 17.33.
Bowling W. T. G. Membrey 16 at 20.25; M. W. A. Tulley 19 at 23.31; W. R. G. Leith 33 at 25.12; C. D. James 15 at 30.80; T. J. Wood* 19 at 31.15; W. E. Miller 11 at 34.09; W. O. E. Barker 11 at 40.18.

Wellington School
P7 W4 L3 A1

Master i/c M. H. Richards
The school ended the term on a high note, achieving two wins in their last three fixtures. Lack of composure at crucial moments denied them more victories, but the team played a positive brand of cricket, particularly after the exam period. With all but two players leaving, rebuilding is a priority.
Batting C. F. Davies 263 at 43.83; J. E. Brown 295 at 42.14; L. R. Corbin-O'Grady 154 at 19.25; M. C. M. Capaldi* 151 at 18.87.
Bowling J. E. Brown 10 at 15.80; J. C. Carson 10 at 17.80; M. C. M. Capaldi 10 at 22.10.

Wells Cathedral School
P14 W9 L4 T1

Master i/c R. J. Newman — **Coach** C. R. Keast
Success in 2010 was achieved through the individual performances of all-rounder Simon Moss, the outstanding leadership of captain Harry Keevil, and a strong team ethic.
Batting S. A. Moss 675 at 75.00; D. G. Nancekievill 476 at 43.27; D. C. Gray 304 at 25.33; R. W. Shelton 158 at 15.80; H. G. Keevil* 157 at 14.27; N. C. Jarman 151 at 12.58.
Bowling C. C. Martin 16 at 14.12; J. H. Killen 14 at 16.00; H. G. Keevil 26 at 17.69; S. A. Moss 21 at 20.57; G. E. Killen 17 at 24.52.

West Buckland School
P15 W10 L2 D2 A1

Master i/c D. R. Ford — **Coach** M. T. Brimson
Under the shrewd stewardship of Will Popplewell, another excellent season was dominated by the batting of Tom Mitcham and the Overton twins, Craig and Jamie. The squad was balanced by a varied bowling attack, including the improving off-spin of Harry Booker.

Batting C. Overton 464 at 58.00; J. Overton 347 at 49.57; T. M. Mitcham 482 at 48.20; H. Briggs 237 at 33.85; H. Booker 258 at 28.66.

Bowling J. Overton 14 at 15.92; H. Booker 18 at 17.72; G. D. H. Long-Howell 12 at 19.66; J. Popplewell 15 at 21.86.

Westminster School
P17 W13 L3 D1

Master i/c J. D. Kershen   Coach P. N. Weekes

A second consecutive record-breaking year brought more wins than for any previous Westminster team. Highlights were the Barbados tour, the victory – and Ollie Wood's century – against MCC, and Leo Nelson-Jones's seven for two against John Lyon. Captain Keval Patel was outstanding, and was ably assisted by fellow all-rounder Alex Stewart and by Tom Fitzsimons with the ball.

Batting K. A. Patel* 491 at 40.91; A. D. Stewart 201 at 40.20; O. W. G. Wood 550 at 36.66; F. F. B. Spoliar 376 at 26.85; J. P. Burdell 245 at 20.41; H. G. McNeill Adams 190 at 17.27.

Bowling L. R. Nelson-Jones 20 at 11.75; K. A. Patel 30 at 17.03; T. R. Fitzsimons 26 at 18.19; O. W. Jones 14 at 20.14; A. D. Stewart 10 at 31.40.

Whitgift School
P15 W10 L3 D2

Master i/c D. M. Ward   Coach N. M. Kendrick

Ten victories made the season a resounding success. Bowling was the strength of the side, with opponents shot out for under 100 on five occasions. Thirty-two wickets from Fred van den Bergh and 28 from Aman Shinwari demonstrated the firepower that few sides could contain.

Batting M. J. Laidman 300 at 50.00; J. G. Ledger 206 at 41.20; G. Heyns 206 at 41.20; G. Gandy 436 at 39.63; T. C. J. Woodrow 236 at 26.22; H. Ledger 163 at 23.28.

Bowling F. O. E. van den Bergh 32 at 9.71; A. Shinwari 28 at 13.21; G. Heyns 10 at 20.40.

Winchester College
P18 W14 L1 D3 A2

Master i/c G. J. Watson   Coaches B. L. Reed/P. N. Gover

Winchester's highlights included successive wins against Harrow and a seven-wicket defeat of Eton. Led convincingly by Ben Stevens and Christian Portz, the key to success was the ability of the whole squad to contribute when required.

Batting C. H. Portz 999 at 71.35; O. C. H. Mills 686 at 52.76; B. D. H. Stevens* 532 at 31.29; B. A. Brown 309 at 28.09; J. A. R. Parker 183 at 26.14; J. J. B. Gidley 228 at 17.53; C. T. Bowden 154 at 17.11.

Bowling C. J. K. Evans-Gordon 12 at 12.00; B. D. H. Stevens 38 at 13.36; J. T. E. Essex 19 at 19.21; B. A. Brown 19 at 20.10; O. C. H. Mills 11 at 23.81; E. R. Bath 15 at 28.93.

Wolverhampton Grammar School
P13 W7 L5 D1 A1

Master i/c T. King   Coach N. H. Crust

The team can look back on a largely successful season in which they endeavoured to play positively and enjoy their cricket. This mindset was thanks to the excellent leadership of Chris Bate. Michael Jones takes over next year, having offered plenty with both bat and ball.

Batting J. S. Nurpuri 150 at 37.50; N. K. Bandurak 163 at 32.60; M. I. Jones 346 at 31.45; O. P. Wagstaff 338 at 30.72; D. J. Powner 233 at 29.12; W. F. Nield 231 at 25.66; C. L. Bate* 179 at 16.27.

Bowling M. I. Jones 19 at 21.94; B. C. Willis 11 at 36.45.

Woodbridge School
P11 W4 L6 D1 A1

Master i/c D. A. Brous

The term saw many extraordinary performances, both collective and individual, not least Joseph Youngs's 108 versus MCC. The batsmen generally prospered, while the bowlers continued to deliver good line and length. The squad maintained an exemplary positive attitude on and off the field.

Batting W. J. Hawkins 249 at 35.57; J. J. Youngs 337 at 33.70; J. A. Rowett 276 at 27.60; T. J. B. Dobree 188 at 17.09.

Bowling H. C. Apperley* 11 at 33.81; J. J. Youngs 11 at 35.45.

Woodhouse Grove School
P15 W9 L4 D2

Master i/c R. I. Frost   Coach A. Sidebottom

Woodhouse Grove relished a successful pre-season tour to Antigua and St Lucia, where they won five out of six matches. Alex Hewitt, Oliver Hardaker and Lahiru Dissanayaka were selected for Yorkshire Schools Under-19s, and Ryan Sharrocks for the North of England Under-15 team. Hardaker's total of 690 runs was the second-highest in the school's history.

Batting O. J. Hardaker 690 at 57.50; C. T. Fairbank 653 at 54.41; A. G. S. Hewitt* 451 at 41.00; T. J. Cummins 322 at 29.27; L. C. Dissanayaka 382 at 25.46.
Bowling G. P. Marsden 12 at 15.75; A. G. S. Hewitt 25 at 17.08; L. C. Dissanayaka 15 at 18.73; M. J. Worrall 11 at 25.45; A. T. Fox 15 at 25.46; J. A. Hartley 16 at 25.50; R. C. Sharrocks 15 at 30.73.

Worksop College
P17 W10 L3 D4

Master i/c I. C. Parkin **Coach** A. Kettleborough

A committed approach saw the team reach the last eight of the National Twenty20 competition. Will Root dominated the batting in all competitions and represented Yorkshire seconds. Adam Dobb captained with tremendous flair and also led Nottinghamshire Under-17s to the national two-day final. Brett Hutton played second-team cricket for Nottinghamshire.
Batting W. T. Root 868 at 96.44; B. A. Hutton 491 at 44.63; K. J. H. Spence 170 at 42.50; J. B. Smith 172 at 34.40; A. M. Dobb* 469 at 33.50; J. A. Schofield 223 at 27.87; C. J. Smith 290 at 22.30.
Bowling A. M. Dobb 31 at 14.61; J. B. Smith 15 at 14.80; B. A. Hutton 17 at 21.00; C. J. Smith 13 at 24.46.

Worth School
P13 W4 L8 D1

Master i/c R. Chaudhuri

The summer began promisingly, but after half-term the side lost momentum. Greg Russell, Theo Rivers, Joe Rivers and Mathew Donegan performed well.
Batting G. A. Russell 346 at 34.60; M. J. P. Donegan* 261 at 20.07; T. L. Rivers 245 at 18.84.
Bowling T. L. Rivers 14 at 25.57.

Wrekin College
P14 W7 L3 D4 A2

Master i/c M. de Weymarn **Coach** N. P. Benwell

Considering the squad's lack of experience, results were far better than expected. All but the skipper were from the lower years, including two Year 9s. Wicketkeeper-captain Matthew Swift got the very best from his squad – which included four leg-spinners – and improved his own batting as well.
Batting M. L. Swift* 703 at 87.87; T. A. J. Saunders 543 at 45.25; J. Shaw 334 at 30.36; O. W. Holt 218 at 27.25; H. de Abreu 153 at 21.85; R. A. C. Blackie 243 at 18.69.
Bowling H. de Abreu 20 at 11.45; S. J. Evans 12 at 12.83; O. W. Holt 10 at 17.10; J. Shaw 16 at 21.00; T. M. Grainger 14 at 24.36; H. R. C. Dawson 16 at 28.81.

Wycliffe College
P17 W2 L12 D3 A1

Master i/c M. J. Kimber

The commitment and contributions from skipper Ed Price were the high points in an otherwise disappointing term. Poor shot selection from the batsmen – and the bowlers' inability to maintain control – did not help. However, a limited squad proved themselves committed to the cause.
Batting E. C. H. Price* 376 at 26.85; C. L. Williams-Camp 262 at 15.41; G. Mason 177 at 14.75; W. J. L. Hewer 203 at 13.53.
Bowling E. C. H. Price 22 at 20.00; N. W. Morris 18 at 29.44; R. W. J. Woodmason 18 at 29.50; M. Freeman-Inglis 15 at 30.80; C. L. Williams-Camp 11 at 34.00.

YOUNG WISDEN SCHOOLS CRICKETER OF THE YEAR

2008	Jonathan Bairstow	St Peters School, York/Yorkshire
2009	James Taylor	Shrewsbury School/Leicestershire
2010	Jos Buttler	Kings College, Taunton/Somerset
2011	**Will Vandarspar**	**Eton College/Middlesex**

WOMEN'S CRICKET, 2010

Sarah Potter

ENGLAND v NEW ZEALAND, 2010

One-day internationals (5): England 3, New Zealand 2
Twenty20 internationals (3): England 1, New Zealand 2

Barely six months on from England's year of world domination, their most successful captain of all time, Charlotte Edwards, was fielding questions about "reality checks" and "a crisis of confidence". The damage had been done in the Caribbean, first with unexpected series defeats by West Indies in November, then at the World Twenty20 tournament in May, where holders England exited at the group stage. In short, they needed a win ahead of winter tours of Sri Lanka and Australia, and Edwards urged her players to step up and move forward. The visit of New Zealand (again defeated finalists in the World Twenty20) would show if England's graph had indeed peaked.

Three Twenty20 internationals preceded men's matches in the Friends Provident Trophy, and were televised live by Sky Sports. New Zealand appeared a tad jet-lagged in Chelmsford's sunshine as Lydia Greenway, who had helped lift England to 150 for five, claimed four catches and engineered a run-out. But the tourists came from behind to win the series after two tight victories in successive days. The big-hitting Suzie Bates, a 22-year-old from Otago who played basketball in the 2008 Olympics, was the destroyer-in-chief at Southampton, despite a career-best 73 from Sarah Taylor, while at Hove, Nicola Browne injected New Zealand's innings with the boost it needed, then claimed a wicket and three catches.

Both sides warmed up for their 50-over series by thrashing Ireland in Leicestershire. Moving on to Taunton, New Zealand rattled up 231, but Edwards responded with 70 and Katherine Brunt (recently named England's Woman Cricketer of the Year) was at her fiery best, taking three wickets and hitting the winning runs. Two days later, Bates's all-round excellence pulled New Zealand level again – three late-order wickets followed by an unbeaten 75.

Jenny Gunn's career-best five for 31 swung the third game England's way at Derby. New Zealand captain Aimee Watkins rescued her side from 108 for six, but big partnerships from openers Sarah Taylor and Heather Knight and then Gunn and Greenway saw England home under the lights. Mean and miserly bowling gave England a comprehensive victory – and an unassailable 3–1 series lead – at Barnsley, staging its first international. Brunt, on her home ground, led the dismantling of the tourists' suddenly fragile batting; the two Taylors, Sarah and Claire, ensured victory with 23 balls to spare.

There were women aplenty in the Lord's Pavilion at the final game, many wearing splashes of pink, and a "Strawberry Tea" stand as England and MCC supported Breast Cancer Care. The star of the day was New Zealand's Erin Bermingham, who captured a career-best four for 35, before a century stand between Amy Satterthwaite and Sara McGlashan secured a consolation win. Though disappointed with this finale, England's head coach Mark Lane professed himself happy with the bigger picture, describing the one-day series victory against a strong New Zealand side as "close, hard-fought, well-planned and well-deserved".

Greenway was named Player of the Series for her 150 runs at 75 in four matches, and moved up six places to eighth in the ICC's batting rankings; Claire Taylor remained third, just ahead of Sarah Taylor and Edwards. Brunt moved up to second in the bowling and was shortlisted for the ICC Women's Cricketer of the Year award, won by Shelley Nitschke of Australia in October.

Nicky Shaw announced her retirement after the Twenty20 series, aged 28. Her seam bowling had claimed 76 wickets in all formats in 11 years playing for England, but she will be remembered best for replacing Gunn minutes before the World Cup final at North Sydney in March 2009, and downing New Zealand with four for 34.

NEW ZEALAND TOURING PARTY

*A. L. Watkins, S. W. Bates, E. M. Bermingham, K. E. Broadmore, N. J. Browne, S. F. M. Devine, N. C. Dodd, L. R. Doolan, M. F. Fahey, S. J. McGlashan, E. C. Perry, R. H. Priest, S. E. A. Ruck, A. E. Satterthwaite. *Coach:* G. R. Stead.

ENGLAND v NEW ZEALAND

At Chelmsford, June 29. **First Twenty20 international: England won by 37 runs.** ‡**England 150-5** (20 overs) (C. M. Edwards 46, S. C. Taylor 34); **New Zealand 113** (18.5 overs) (D. N. Wyatt 3-12). *Player of the Match:* L. S. Greenway. *Lydia Greenway followed a 17-ball 23* with four catches in the field, a record in women's Twenty20 internationals, and a run-out; New Zealand collapsed from 100-4.*

At Southampton, July 1. **Second Twenty20 international: New Zealand won by four runs.** ‡**New Zealand 147-8** (20 overs) (S. W. Bates 68, S. J. McGlashan 47; D. Hazell 3-19); **England 143-8** (20 overs) (S. J. Taylor 73; S. E. A. Ruck 3-15). *Player of the Match:* S. W. Bates. *Suzie Bates, who hit eight fours and two sixes in a career-best 68 from 55 balls, set up a series-levelling victory by adding 105 with Sara McGlashan (47 in 33 balls).*

At Hove, July 2. **Third Twenty20 international: New Zealand won by nine runs.** ‡**New Zealand 124-8** (20 overs) (D. Hazell 3-16); **England 115-8** (20 overs) (S. F. M. Devine 3-26, L. R. Doolan 3-26). *Player of the Match:* N. J. Browne. *Player of the Series:* S. W. Bates. *Nicola Browne scored 22 in 14 balls then had a hand in dismissing four of England's top five – one bowled, three caught – to ensure that New Zealand won the series 2–1.*

At Taunton, July 10. **First one-day international: England won by one wicket.** ‡**New Zealand 231-8** (50 overs) (M. F. Fahey 61, A. E. Satterthwaite 38, S. F. M. Devine 50; K. H. Brunt 3-31); **England 234-9** (49.3 overs) (H. C. Knight 32, C. M. Edwards 70, J. L. Gunn 31, L. A. Marsh 31; N. J. Browne 3-31, L. R. Doolan 3-41). *Player of the Match:* K. H. Brunt. *Katherine Brunt started the match by trapping opener Natalie Dodd in her second over, and finished it by hitting the winning runs with one wicket and three balls to spare.*

At Taunton, July 12. **Second one-day international: New Zealand won by four wickets.** ‡**England 208-9** (50 overs) (S. C. Taylor 66, L. S. Greenway 40; S. W. Bates 3-27); **New Zealand 211-6** (47.5 overs) (S. W. Bates 75*; L. A. Marsh 3-34). *One-day international debut:* E. M. Bermingham. *Player of the Match:* S. W. Bates. *Suzie Bates took three wickets with her medium-pace and then saw her side home, hitting seven fours in her 75*.*

At Derby, July 15 (day/night). **Third one-day international: England won by six wickets.** New Zealand 220-9 (50 overs) (L. R. Doolan 34, A. L. Watkins 68; J. L. Gunn 5-31); ‡**England 223-4** (48.4 overs) (S. J. Taylor 64, H. C. Knight 42, L. S. Greenway 45*, J. L. Gunn 37*). *Player of the*

Match: J. L. Gunn. *Jenny Gunn took five wickets in an international for the first time before Aimee Watkins hit a 65-ball 68. Sarah Taylor and Heather Knight opened with 108; Lydia Greenway and Gunn completed victory by adding 83.*

At Barnsley, July 17. **Fourth one-day international: England won by nine wickets.** ‡New Zealand **136-9** (50 overs) (A. L. Watkins 42; K. H. Brunt 3-31); **England 139-1** (46.1 overs) (S. J. Taylor 49*, S. C. Taylor 51*). *Player of the Match:* S. J. Taylor. *England secured the series after Katherine Brunt claimed three wickets on her home ground; Sarah and Claire Taylor shared an unbeaten stand of 98.*

At Lord's, July 20. **Fifth one-day international: New Zealand won by six wickets.** ‡England **176-9** (50 overs) (H. C. Knight 34, L. S. Greenway 65; E. M. Bermingham 4-35); **New Zealand 178-4** (46.4 overs) (A. E. Satterthwaite 59, S. J. McGlashan 65*). *Player of the Match:* E. M. Bermingham. *Player of the Series:* L. S. Greenway. *New Zealand pulled the one-day series back to 3–2. Erin Bermingham's career-best 4-35 trumped Lydia Greenway's highest one-day international score; Amy Satterthwaite and Sara McGlashan added 109 for the fourth wicket.*

IRELAND v NEW ZEALAND

At Kibworth, July 4. **One-day international: New Zealand won by 159 runs. New Zealand 296-8** (50 overs) (L. R. Doolan 33, M. F. Fahey 59, E. C. Perry 70, R. H. Priest 36*; C. J. Metcalfe 3-54); ‡**Ireland 137** (44.4 overs) (J. A. Whelan 36; L. R. Doolan 3-7). *One-day international debuts:* L. Delany, K. J. Garth, M. V. Waldron (Ireland); E. C. Perry (New Zealand). *Liz Perry scored 70 in 69 balls on her one-day debut; later, off-spinner Lucy Doolan had figures of 5–2–7–3.*

ENGLAND v IRELAND

At Kibworth, July 7. **One-day international: England won by 147 runs.** ‡**England 274-7** (50 overs) (C. M. Edwards 72, L. A. Marsh 67); **Ireland 127** (49.2 overs) (L. Delany 43). *One-day international debut:* L. N. McCarthy (Ireland). *Laura Marsh scored a maiden international fifty, adding 54 with Charlotte Edwards and 60 with Danielle Hazell.*

Other tour games

At Kibworth, July 5. **MCC won by two wickets. Ireland 270-7** (50 overs) (C. M. A. Shillington 88, I. M. H. C. Joyce 50, K. J. Garth 34*, Extras 40; A. J. Macleod 3-51); ‡**MCC 271-8** (48.4 overs) (A. J. Macleod 45, A. Potgieter 108, Extras 51; I. M. H. C. Joyce 3-64).

At Kibworth, July 7. **New Zealanders won by six wickets. England Academy 190** (49.5 overs) (C. M. G. Atkins 63, F. C. Wilson 30, S. E. Rowe 38; A. E. Satterthwaite 4-43); ‡**New Zealanders 193-4** (35.3 overs) (M. F. Fahey 53, S. W. Bates 59).

ENGLISH WOMEN'S CRICKET, 2010

The County Championship ended in the last-gasp, winner-takes-all drama now routinely supplied by Kent and Sussex, who have monopolised the title since 2003. Defending champions Kent had a six-point advantage entering the final match, at Horsham. But ruthless bowling, spearheaded by Izi Noakes, whose four victims included England captain Charlotte Edwards, meant Sussex needed only 133. Caroline Atkins completed a fine all-round performance with 57 not out, and Sussex clinched the title by cantering to a six-wicket victory with nearly 12 overs to spare.

Middlesex pipped Essex by one point to win the second division; in the third, Wales achieved their second successive promotion. Netherlands took the fourth division, their points adjusted to reflect the fact that they (and Ireland in the fifth division) played opponents only once, whereas all other teams played home and away. Kent swept the board in the age-group finals: their Under-13s beat Lancashire, the Under-15s Hampshire and, sweetest of all, the Under-17s showed no frailties against a strong Sussex.

The Women's Twenty20 Cup, truncated by bad weather in 2009, reached a proper conclusion with a finals day in Bishop's Stortford. Lissie MacLeod, a 16-year-old selected for the England Women's Academy, showed her maturity in a well-paced 61 which set up Berkshire's victory over Yorkshire.

Northern Division winners Ransome & Marles lost their second successive Premier League final against the Southern champions, in this case Reading. On a green pitch at Bishop's Stortford, they managed 85; even so, England's Katherine Brunt claimed five for nine – exactly matching Reading's 15-year-old Linsey Smith – and threatened to snatch the game away, until England batsman Claire Taylor grittily saw her side home.

Once again there was no senior Super Fours, but the Rubies won the junior tournament. Twickenham, defeated finalists in 2009's inaugural Women's Cricket Southern League Super Eight Twenty20, beat Hursley Park this time.

LV= COUNTY CHAMPIONSHIP, 2010

50-over league

Division One

	Played	Won	Lost	No result	Bonus Points Batting	Bonus Points Bowling	Points	Avge Pts
Sussex	10	8	2	0	21	39	140	14.00
Kent.	10	7	3	0	29	33	132	13.20
Berkshire	10	6	4	0	22	27	109	10.90
Yorkshire.	10	5	5	0	24	29	103	10.30
Nottinghamshire . . .	10	2	8	0	17	25	62	6.20
Somerset	10	2	8	0	20	20	60	6.00

Division Two

	Played	Won	Lost	No result	Bonus Points Batting	Bonus Points Bowling	Points	Avge Pts
Middlesex	10	8	2	0	29	35	144	14.40
Essex	10	8	2	0	29	34	143	14.30
Warwickshire	10	6	4	0	23	33	116	11.60
Surrey	10	5	4	1	18	28	96	10.66
Cheshire	10	2	7	1	18	26	64	7.11
Worcestershire	10	0	10	0	8	27	35	3.50

Division Three

	Played	Won	Lost	No result	Bonus Points Batting	Bonus Points Bowling	Points	Avge Pts
Wales.	10	8	2	0	21	32	133	13.30
Staffordshire	10	6	3	1	23	35	118	13.11
Lancashire	10	6	3	1	18	35	113	12.55
Devon	10	7	3	0	23	32	125	12.50
Scotland.	10	2	8	0	11	23	54	5.40
Hampshire.	10	0	10	0	16	22	38	3.80

Division Four

	Played	Won	Lost	No result	Bonus Points Batting	Bowling	Points	Avge Pts
Netherlands	5	4	1	0	14	19	73	14.60
Derbyshire	9	6	3	0	21	33	114	12.66
Northamptonshire . .	9	5	4	0	17	30	97	10.77
Hertfordshire	9	4	3	2	13	22	75	10.71
Durham	9	4	4	1	16	23	79	9.87
Cornwall	9	0	8	1	7	13	20	2.50

Win = 10pts. Up to four batting and four bonus points are available to each team in each match. Final points are divided by the number of matches played (excluding no results) to calculate the average number of points.

Division Five

East: Cambridgeshire and Huntingdonshire avge pts 16.60, Norfolk 10.80, Oxfordshire 7.83, Suffolk 5.00.
North: Leicestershire and Rutland avge pts 15.71, Ireland 14.75, Cumbria 8.71, Shropshire 8.57, Northumberland 3.28.
South and West: Gloucestershire avge pts 14.50, Wiltshire 12.83, Dorset 10.33, Buckinghamshire 1.66.

ECB TWENTY20 CUP, 2010

Semi-finals

At Bishop's Stortford, September 18. **Berkshire won by 29 runs. Berkshire 135-4** (20 overs) (S. C. Taylor 65*); ‡**Kent 106** (19.1 overs) (J. Turner 3-12).

At Bishop's Stortford, September 18. **Yorkshire won by ten wickets. Sussex 78-5** (20 overs) (A. L. Walker 36); ‡**Yorkshire 81-0** (15.3 overs) (K. H. Brunt 45*).

Third-place play-off

At Bishop's Stortford, September 18. **Sussex won by four wickets.** ‡**Kent 90** (17.5 overs) (J. O. Elphick 4-13); **Sussex 93-6** (19 overs).

Final

At Bishop's Stortford, September 18. **Berkshire won by 46 runs.** ‡**Berkshire 173-7** (20 overs) (H. C. Knight 30, A. J. Macleod 61, S. C. Taylor 33; H. Buck 3-38); **Yorkshire 127-5** (20 overs) (K. H. Brunt 32, D. Hazell 45*). *Berkshire's 16-year-old Lissie MacLeod hit 61 in 46 balls; even the England pair Katherine Brunt and Danielle Hazell could not guide Yorkshire to a target of 174.*

ECB PREMIER LEAGUE FINAL, 2010

At Bishop's Stortford, September 4. **Reading won by three wickets. Ransome & Marles 85** (31.4 overs) (D. V. Gardner 3-42, L. C. N. Smith 5-9); ‡**Reading 86-7** (39.2 overs) (K. H. Brunt 5-9). *Fifteen-year-old left-arm seamer Linsey Smith and Katherine Brunt both took 5-9, but Smith ended up on top as Claire Taylor (17* in 68 balls) steered Reading home with more than ten overs to spare.*

CRICKET IN IRELAND, 2010

Another Stirling performance

IAN CALLENDER

Ireland extended their sequence of winning at least one trophy every year since 2005, but they will look back on 2010 as one of missed opportunities. Success in Division One of the World Cricket League confirmed their status as the top Associate, and victory in the last match of their series in Harare in September kept Ireland above Zimbabwe in the world one-day rankings. The battle for tenth place could become increasingly important in the next few years if the ICC insist on inviting only ten teams to the 2015 World Cup.

Encouragingly, Ireland reserved their best performances for one-day internationals. Of 17 matches they won 11, including a victory over Bangladesh, while they lost to Australia by only 39 runs and to Zimbabwe by two wickets and three wickets. All three defeats could be put in the near-miss category, as could the abandoned game against England in the World Twenty20.

Fourth place in the Intercontinental Cup was disappointing, but two rain-ruined games proved vital, and Ireland's hold on the trophy they had won three times running was fatally loosened when they lost to Afghanistan in Sri Lanka. That game in Dambulla, the start of a record 44 during 2010, was Ireland's first since the retirement of long-serving off-spinner Kyle McCallan. They were also without injured bowlers Boyd Rankin and Regan West, yet it was a batting collapse which led to defeat. Only 20 wickets had fallen on the first three days for 921 runs, but Ireland lost ten in two sessions. Afghanistan won with 15 balls to spare to complete Ireland's first Intercontinental Cup defeat since August 2004, the last time McCallan did not play.

Ireland moved on to Colombo to play a quadrangular 20-over tournament with Canada, Afghanistan and Sri Lanka A before the World Twenty20 qualifiers in the UAE. Ireland's only victory in Sri Lanka came against Afghanistan, who then dominated the qualifying tournament. Ireland, though, did win four games to confirm their place in the Caribbean.

In the West Indies, the scene of Ireland's amazing World Cup run in 2007, the batting proved to be a problem. They were shot out for 68 in their first match by the hosts, though there were positives in the bowling and fielding – 17-year-old slow left-armer George Dockrell took three for 16 – and these were maintained four days later when England were restricted to 120 for eight. Eoin Morgan, in his first match against his former team-mates, top-scored with 45. Ireland scented an upset which would have eliminated the eventual champions, but rain had the last laugh.

The first home match of the year was against Australia at Clontarf, in glorious weather and in front of a capacity 4,500 crowd. It was the perfect setting for the mother of all upsets… and it might have been. After Australia were restricted to 231 for nine, William Porterfield and Paul Stirling had 80 on the board in 11 overs. But three wickets fell in as many overs, and from 137 for three – and less than 100 needed – six more wickets clattered for 19.

West Indies A easily won their two games in Belfast. With Porterfield playing for Gloucestershire and Trent Johnston injured, Kevin O'Brien emulated his father Brendan and older brother Niall by captaining Ireland. Rory McCann, a wicketkeeper from Instonians, and Albert van der Merwe, a South African-born off-spinner from The Hills club in Dublin, made debuts.

The next stop was the Netherlands for the World Cricket League and, despite the absence of their four county players and the injured Andre Botha, Ireland won all six games with something to spare. Andrew Balbirnie, an all-rounder from Pembroke and Ireland's captain at the Under-19 World Cup in January, made his full debut against Scotland, and kept his place for the final, in which Kevin O'Brien won the match award for his unbeaten 98.

Boosted by the return of Porterfield, Rankin, Niall O'Brien and Gary Wilson, it was a confident Irish side which took on Bangladesh in two one-day internationals in Belfast in July. The first game was Ireland's 750th all told, and their 50th official ODI; they reached their target of 235 with plenty to spare to complete their first win over a Test-playing nation since 2007. Porterfield became the first to score eight centuries in all matches for Ireland, but Bangladesh, helped by Porterfield's decision to bat on an overcast morning, fought back to square the series.

The season was completed by the three remaining Intercontinental Cup matches, and seven accompanying one-day internationals. Allan Eaglestone, the 30-year-old Pembroke opening bowler, made his debut against the Netherlands in Dublin, taking four wickets in the second innings as Ireland won before lunch on the third day: they also won the one-day series 2–0.

Paul Stirling played the innings of the year, against Canada in Toronto. He was on course to become only the second man, after Sachin Tendulkar, to hit an ODI double-century, but fell for 177, easily the highest by a non-Test player. The previous day Ireland had lost to a fellow Associate for the first time in 17 games, when Canada won a rain-reduced match by six wickets. Also in Toronto, McCann held nine catches, an Ireland record, as they beat Canada in the Intercontinental Cup.

Slim hopes of a fourth successive appearance in the Intercontinental final vanished in Harare, where Ireland conceded their highest total: the Zimbabwe XI made 590, though Ireland easily batted out for the draw. In the three-match one-day series that followed, however, poor batting led to a 2–1 defeat.

Dockrell finished his first season with 49 wickets, behind Kevin O'Brien's 50 and Johnston's record 58 as Ireland ended the year with 21 wins, 20 defeats, two draws and the no-result against England. Stirling scored 1,189 runs in the year, comfortably an Irish record; Andrew White made 1,003. White, Porterfield and the O'Brien brothers all passed 3,000 career runs for Ireland, while Johnston became the sixth bowler to take 200 wickets.

Merrion won their first Irish Cup, beating Railway Union, the Leinster Senior Cup winners, in the final. In the NCU, North Down won the league and cup double for the fifth time in ten years, while Strabane won the North West League title and lost in the cup final to Brigade, from Londonderry.

Winners of Irish Leagues and Cups
Bob Kerr Irish Senior Cup Merrion. **Leinster League** North County. **Leinster Cup** Railway Union. **Munster League** Cork County. **Munster Cup** Cork County. **Northern Union League** North Down. **Northern Union Cup** North Down. **North West League** Strabane. **North West Cup** Brigade.

ONE-DAY INTERNATIONALS IN IRELAND IN 2010

Ireland v Australia

At Dublin, June 17, 2010. **Australia won by 39 runs.** ‡**Australia 231-9** (50 overs) (T. D. Paine 81, R. T. Ponting 33, C. L. White 42; K. J. O'Brien 3-43); **Ireland 192** (42 overs) (W. T. S. Porterfield 39, P. R. Stirling 36, A. R. Cusack 30, J. F. Mooney 38; J. R. Hopes 5-14). MoM: J. R. Hopes. *Australia's batsmen struggled to get the ball away on a slow pitch, and a shock looked on the cards when William Porterfield launched Ireland's chase with three fours in the first over, from Ryan Harris. Porterfield and his fellow-opener Paul Stirling added 80 in the first 11 overs, but then Harris and Hauritz applied the brakes, before James Hopes prevented the possibility of an upset, taking five wickets in nine economical overs. The only previous time these sides had met in a one-day international was in the 2007 World Cup, when Australia won by nine wickets.*

Ireland v Bangladesh

At Belfast, July 15, 2010. **First one-day international: Ireland won by seven wickets. Bangladesh 234-9** (50 overs) (Junaid Siddique 100, Shakib Al Hasan 50; W. B. Rankin 3-43); ‡**Ireland 235-3** (45 overs) (W. T. S. Porterfield 108, P. R. Stirling 52, A. R. Cusack 45*). MoM: W. T. S. Porterfield. *Five days after beating England, Bangladesh slipped to embarrassing defeat. Junaid Siddique struck his maiden one-day international hundred – he hit nine fours from 123 balls – but had little support other than from Shakib Al Hasan, who helped add 107 for the fourth wicket. But Ireland, contesting their 50th official one-day international (excluding four abandonments), were never in trouble: William Porterfield glided to his fifth one-day hundred – his first against a Test-playing country – adding 118 for the first wicket with Paul Stirling and 90 for the second with Alex Cusack.*

At Belfast, July 16, 2010. **Second one-day international: Bangladesh won by six wickets** (D/L method). ‡**Ireland 189-9** (46 overs) (G. C. Wilson 60; Shafiul Islam 4-59); **Bangladesh 191-4** (37.4 overs) (Tamim Iqbal 74, Jahurul Islam 34, Shakib Al Hasan 33*). MoM: Shafiul Islam. *Rain before the start reduced this to a 49-over match, then another shower after just seven balls lopped a further three overs off each side's quota. Bangladesh squared the series with a comfortable victory, overhauling their target – which remained 190 from 46 overs – with 50 balls to spare. Ireland lost both openers with 13 on the board, and only a resolute innings from Gary Wilson, who hit six fours from 64 balls, took them close to 200. It never looked enough once Tamim Iqbal got going.*

Ireland v Netherlands

At Dublin, August 16, 2010. **First one-day international: Ireland won by 70 runs. Ireland 275-6** (50 overs) (G. C. Wilson 113, P. R. Stirling 40, A. R. Cusack 45); ‡**Netherlands 205** (45.1 overs) (T. L. W. Cooper 68, P. M. Seelaar 34*; K. J. O'Brien 3-18, A. R. White 4-44). *One-day international debut: T. J. Heggelman (Netherlands). Gary Wilson, opening in the absence of William Porterfield on county duty, hit his maiden one-day international century, with ten fours from 147 balls. He put on 82 with Paul Stirling and then 118 for the second wicket with Alex Cusack, as Ireland built a total that proved well beyond the Netherlands, despite another fine innings from Tom Cooper.*

At Dublin, August 18, 2010. **Second one-day international: Ireland won by nine wickets.** ‡**Netherlands 125** (47.2 overs) (P. M. Seelaar 34); **Ireland 129-1** (20.3 overs) (G. C. Wilson 48*, P. R. Stirling 62). *Ireland wrapped up the short series 2–0 with almost 30 overs to spare. Paul Stirling kick-started the chase with 62 from 36 balls, including six fours and five sixes, four of them in off-spinner Adeel Raja's only over, which cost 26 (666116).*

For Ireland's matches in the Intercontinental Cup in 2010, see page 1165.

CRICKET IN SCOTLAND, 2010

From Hamilton to Berrington

WILLIAM DICK

Scotland took some encouraging steps towards restoring their position as one of the leading ICC Associates during 2010, during which the national side reached two major finals. The Scots had fallen in the rankings after failing to reach the final stages of either the World Twenty20 in 2010 or the World Cup in 2011, but a new-look side showed improvement overall during the year.

It started with an impressive performance at the World Cricket League in July. Led by new captain Gordon Drummond after Gavin Hamilton stood down, the Scots defeated the Netherlands (the hosts), Canada, Afghanistan and Kenya to gain a place in the final. There, though, they were unable to take advantage of a position of strength against old foes Ireland.

It was not only in the one-day format that improvement was evident: Drummond's side ended the year with Scotland's first appearance in the Intercontinental Cup final since they won it in 2004. The showdown with Afghanistan was only secured when Zimbabwe forfeited the points from the decisive qualifying match (the Scots refused to travel to Harare on government advice, and Zimbabwe declined a neutral venue, as originally mooted).

Earlier in the competition the Scots had beaten Canada, Kenya and the Netherlands, and enjoyed the best of a draw against the holders Ireland, so they were entitled to feel they had made the Dubai final on merit. Once again, though, the last hurdle proved insurmountable: Scotland failed to cash in on a first-innings lead, instead collapsing to 82 all out in their second innings. It was the worst possible time to record their lowest-ever Intercontinental Cup total, and Afghanistan lost just three wickets in knocking off 124 for victory.

Scotland's most impressive performance of the year came in the first of two limited-overs encounters with the touring India A team at Titwood in Glasgow at the end of June. Fears beforehand that these might be mismatches appeared justified when Scotland collapsed to 64 for seven in response to India A's 276 for nine – but what followed represented one of the most remarkable run-chases in the history of Scottish cricket. An eighth-wicket stand of 174 between Richie Berrington and Moneeb Iqbal served first to restore pride and then to allow dreams of an unthinkable victory. Berrington departed for 106 – his maiden international century – with Scotland 40 short and facing probable, if glorious, failure. But Iqbal continued to 67, his finest innings for Scotland, while last man Gordon Goudie, who had earlier claimed four wickets, bludgeoned an unbeaten 26 to seal a thrilling one-wicket victory with three balls to spare. India A restored order with a 152-run victory in the second game, led by a century from their captain Cheteshwar Pujara.

Hamilton relinquished the captaincy after Scotland's one-day international against England in June, and announced his retirement from all international cricket towards the end of the season. The tributes were appropriately warm for a great servant of the Scottish game, who will always be remembered for his fine efforts at the 1999 World Cup. Hamilton, who turned 36 in September, played 38 official one-day internationals for Scotland – and one Test for England, in South Africa in 1999-2000, during a county career which included stints with Yorkshire and Durham. He was originally an all-rounder, but although his nippy medium-pacers eventually seized up he remained a dependable batsman who scored two centuries in one-day internationals as an opener and two more in first-class cricket. Hamilton gave Scottish fans many happy memories, so it seemed fitting that his team-mates gave him a winning send-off by beating Leicestershire in the Clydesdale Bank 40 competition.

That victory at Aberdeen completed a double over Leicestershire, but they were the only wins in the CB40, although another highlight came in the final match of the season at Edgbaston: Berrington and the Australian George Bailey produced a fourth-wicket stand of 198 before Warwickshire – the eventual champions – chased down 267. Berrington, who was awarded a full-time Cricket Scotland contract following Dewald Nel's departure to Kent, achieved the distinction of scoring three consecutive half-centuries against county opposition, and could be the next Scot to head south of the border.

There was further encouragement at youth level, where Scotland's Under-19 and U-15 sides won European titles.

Domestically, Grange from Edinburgh won their seventh SNCL title – the last in the old format, after a vote for reorganisation meant that a Premiership and Championship, each of 16 teams, will replace the old structure of three divisions of ten teams. Uddingston claimed their second Scottish Cup, while Carlton were convincing winners of the Murgitroyd Twenty20 Cup.

Winners of Scottish Leagues and Cups
Premier Division Grange. **First Division** Arbroath. **Second Division** Dumfries. **Scottish Cup** Uddingston. **Murgitroyd Twenty20 Cup** Carlton. **Regional Tri-Series40** Caledonian Highlanders. **Regional Tri-Series Big Bash** Caledonian Highlanders.

ONE-DAY INTERNATIONALS IN SCOTLAND IN 2010

SCOTLAND v ENGLAND

Scyld Berry

At Edinburgh, June 19, 2010. England won by seven wickets. Toss: Scotland.
 This game served to warm England up for their one-day internationals against Australia – and to illustrate the gap in standard between Scotland and Ireland, who had been able to stretch England in more than one format. The only home batsman to attack England's steady bowling on a true batting pitch was Kyle Coetzer, who plays occasionally for Durham. After being very close to leg-before to his first ball, from Anderson, Coetzer hit as many fours – eight – as all his team-mates put together. Strauss and Kieswetter began with 121 from 15 overs as Kieswetter "went on" and passed 50, which he was not to do against Australia. The only home bowler to stem the flow was the off-spinner Majid Haq, the sole representative from Scotland's large – and largely untapped – Asian community. There was no match award.

Scotland

*G. M. Hamilton st Kieswetter b Swann....	48	G. D. Drummond not out	8
R. R. Watson c Swann b Anderson	0	R. T. Lyons b Shahzad	1
K. J. Coetzer c and b Yardy............	51		
J. H. Davey lbw b Yardy..............	4	B 1, l-b 6, w 8	15
R. D. Berrington c Broad b Yardy........	3		
N. F. I. McCallum c Swann b Collingwood	22	1/1 (2) 2/87 (3) 3/101 (4) (49.5 overs)	211
†D. R. Lockhart b Shahzad	46	4/108 (5) 5/121 (1) 6/148 (6)	
M. A. Parker lbw b Swann	2	7/157 (8) 8/199 (9) 9/209 (7)	
R. M. Haq b Anderson.	11	10/211 (11) 10 overs: 42-1	

Anderson 9–0–43–2; Shahzad 9.5–2–31–2; Broad 8–0–49–0; Yardy 10–0–41–3; Swann 10–0–29–2; Collingwood 3–0–11–1.

England

*A. J. Strauss c McCallum b Haq	61
†C. Kieswetter c Coetzer b Lyons.........	69
K. P. Pietersen c Watson b Haq..........	17
P. D. Collingwood not out..............	38
E. J. G. Morgan not out...............	24
B 2, l-b 1, w 1	4

1/121 (1) 2/147 (2)   (3 wkts, 33.4 overs) 213
3/151 (3)   10 overs: 75-0

L. J. Wright, M. H. Yardy, G. P. Swann, S. C. J. Broad, A. Shahzad and J. M. Anderson did not bat.

Drummond 5–0–26–0; Parker 3–0–26–0; Coetzer 2–0–23–0; Davey 2–0–25–0; Lyons 10–0–64–1; Haq 10–0–35–2; Berrington 1.4–0–11–0.

Umpires: Aleem Dar and I. N. Ramage.   Referee: J. Srinath.

Scotland v Bangladesh

At Glasgow, July 19, 2010. **Scotland v Bangladesh. Abandoned.** *Heavy rain prevented any play at Titwood.*

Bangladesh v Netherlands

At Glasgow, July 20, 2010. **Netherlands won by six wickets.** Reduced to 30 overs a side. **Bangladesh 199-7** (30 overs) (Imrul Kayes 52, Junaid Siddique 31, Jahurul Islam 41; P. W. Borren 3-30); ‡**Netherlands 200-4** (28.5 overs) (E. S. Szwarczynski 67, B. Zuiderent 35*, W. Barresi 64*). *Bangladesh suffered another embarrassing defeat, in a rain-affected match. Although Tamim Iqbal left early on, they reached 132-2 in the 18th over, and should have made more than 199. Eric Szwarczynski clattered seven fours and three sixes in his 54-ball innings, and although he departed at the end of the 15th over, making it 104-4, the fifth-wicket pair saw the Dutch home. Both faced 43 balls, but whereas Bas Zuiderent did not manage a four (he did hit one six) Wesley Barresi reached the ropes 11 times, including the winning boundary off Shafiul Islam.*

Scotland v Afghanistan

At Ayr, August 16, 2010. **First one-day international: Afghanistan won by nine wickets.** ‡**Scotland 224-9** (50 overs) (D. F. Watts 55, G. M. Hamilton 31, G. D. Drummond 35*; Shapoor Zadran 3-69); **Afghanistan 225-1** (31 overs) (Karim Sadiq 114*, Mohammad Shahzad 100*). *After losing Noor Ali to the eighth ball of their reply, Afghanistan steamrollered to victory through a second-wicket partnership of 218* between Karim Sadiq, who made his first one-day international hundred, and Mohammad Shahzad, whose third century included 15 fours and came from just 72 balls. Earlier, Scotland slipped to 24-3, and needed a last-wicket stand of 44* between Gordon Drummond and Dewald Nel (11*) to make it past 200.*

At Ayr, August 17, 2010. **Second one-day international: Scotland won by six wickets.**
‡**Afghanistan 120** (40.2 overs) (Samiullah Shenwari 46; J. H. Davey 5-9); **Scotland 121-4** (33.5
overs) (D. F. Watts 55*, R. D. Berrington 33). *One-day international debuts:* R. Flannigan (Scotland);
Noor-ul-Haq (Afghanistan). *Gavin Hamilton, who had stepped down as captain earlier in the year,
announced his retirement from international cricket after this match: he scored 1,231 runs in 38
one-day internationals for Scotland – and also played a Test for England in 1999-2000. He went out
with a win, as Scotland squared the short series. Afghanistan's batting, so impressive in the first
match, imploded this time after Karim Sadiq fell to the first ball of the match, from new skipper
Gordon Drummond; they were 49-6 after 15 overs before a partial recovery. Josh Davey, a 20-year-
old Middlesex batsman bowling medium-pace, recorded Scotland's best figures in one-day
internationals (previously John Blain's 5-22 against the Netherlands in 2008). Although Hamilton
soon departed for two, his opening partner Fraser Watts played the anchor role as the Scots wrapped
up victory with 97 balls to spare.*

For Scotland's matches in the Intercontinental Cup in 2010, see page 1165.

CRICKET IN THE NETHERLANDS, 2010

The flying-in Dutchmen

DAVID HARDY

A year is a long time in cricket. In 2009 the Dutch were celebrating their historic Twenty20 victory over England at Lord's: 12 months later several of that team had faded from view. The captain Jeroen Smits, Darron Reekers and Edgar Schiferli all retired from international cricket. Ryan ten Doeschate and Alexei Kervezee played very little in 2010, mainly due to county commitments. Daan van Bunge decided, for the second time, to give more priority to things other than cricket. Tom de Grooth and left-arm spinner Pieter Seelaar lost form, while Dirk Nannes went off to play for Australia. Of the eleven Lord's heroes, only two – all-rounder Peter Borren, who took over the captaincy from Smits, and batsman Bas Zuiderent – maintained reasonable form and consistency in 2010.

And therein lies a big clue to the performances of the Dutch national team in 2010. There were a record 34 matches in the year, of which only nine were won – three Twenty20s, two in the World Cricket League, three other 50-over games and one in the English CB40 competition – against 24 lost (including the other 11 CB40 games and all four four-day Intercontinental Cup matches) and one abandoned.

Central contracts were awarded for the first time, but only three were full-time – to Borren, de Grooth and Eric Szwarczynski – and 12 part-time. The commitment required of the players, the majority thus part-time, was huge, once all the travelling, training and preparation were added to the 46 match-days. It remains a virtual impossibility for part-time professionals to perform consistently at the highest level if they have to juggle national-team commitments with work, study or a private life.

Another problem was that ten Doeschate and Kervezee played only 21 out of a possible 68 matches between them. Ten Doeschate was still named as the ICC's Associate Player of the Year: in his only four-day match, against Kenya, he achieved a double-century and five wickets in an innings for the second time in his first-class career (he also did it against Canada, again in the Intercontinental Cup, in 2006-07), mirroring the achievements of, among others, Sir Garfield Sobers and W. G. Grace.

In a year of underachievement for the national team, the biggest disappointment was not qualifying for the World Twenty20 in the Caribbean. A surprise defeat by hosts United Arab Emirates in the group stage was crucial, as this result was carried into the Super Fours, where heavy defeat by Ireland ended Dutch hopes, even though they beat Afghanistan, the other qualifiers.

The first division of the World Cricket League (50-over matches for the top six Associate nations) was held in the Netherlands for the first time, but home advantage counted for little: fourth place was a disappointment.

Fast bowler Mark Jonkman, 24, was the leading wicket-taker in the WCL, but during the tournament his bowling action was reported by the umpires. In August he was sent to Western Australia for scientific tests: every delivery exceeded the ICC tolerance threshold of 15 degrees of elbow-flexion, and Jonkman was suspended from international cricket pending remedial work. His identical twin, Maurits, took his place in the Dutch team. The two are extremely difficult to tell apart: in the CB40 programme the same photograph was used by mistake for both players, but no one noticed.

After retiring from playing, Jeroen Smits took up a new job as High Performance Adviser, one of his tasks being to search for high-quality cricketers with Dutch qualifications. In 2010 he unearthed three: Tom Cooper (from Australia), Derek de Boorder (New Zealand) and Brad Kruger (South Africa). The most successful was Cooper, from South Australia, who was the leading run-scorer in the WCL with 408. A few eyebrows were raised in traditional Dutch cricket circles about this policy of recruiting players from afar, which inevitably led to a diminishing number of local born-and-raised players in the national team.

Tasmania's Michael Dighton, the player-coach at VOC Rotterdam, was the one permitted overseas player in the squad for the CB40: it was the first time since 2005 that the Netherlands had taken part in the English county season. After an excellent start – two of the first three matches, against Yorkshire and Essex, were narrowly lost in the last over, and Derbyshire were beaten in the fifth match, when Dighton exacted revenge on his former employers with a match-winning 110 not out – the campaign fell away badly, the last seven matches all being lost.

All was not doom and gloom, however, as Bangladesh were surprisingly beaten in a one-off one-day international in Glasgow in July. Crucially, this was the one match of the year that counted towards the official one-day world rankings, in which the Netherlands now stood 12th.

Of similar concern to the question of imports is the dearth of young players coming through the junior ranks. Two 18-year-olds did distinguish themselves for VRA Amstelveen: Emile van den Berg played decisive match-winning innings in both the 50-over play-off and Twenty20 finals, while Vinoo Tewarie confirmed his outstanding talent in that same 50-over final, taking three for 19 in ten overs of leg-spin. But the performances of the national age-group teams were uninspiring. It is some years since a Dutch youth team got the better of Ireland at any level, and recently Scotland have often won too – but in 2010 the Under-15s lost to Denmark, and even to Guernsey, in the European Championship (in which the Netherlands just managed to avoid the wooden spoon on home soil), while the Under-19s lost to Jersey. The youth programme is in need of a major overhaul, with more intensive training and coaching of paramount importance. Dutch cricket's new chief executive Richard Cox has identified this as one of his major tasks.

Among other priorities identified by Cox early in 2010, soon after his appointment, were central contracts, finding new sponsors and more grass squares. He achieved considerable success on all three counts. Contracts were indeed signed; a number of small-scale sponsors were found for both the men's and women's national teams (but, crucially, no large sponsor for Dutch cricket as a whole); and two new grass squares came into use, at VCC Voorburg and Excelsior 20 in Schiedam, bringing the nationwide total to seven (at six clubs). It came as no surprise that the new pitches were either slow or irregular in bounce, but there are now more grass squares in the Netherlands than ever before, which should encourage more clubs to follow suit.

In the premier league, reduced from ten teams to eight and renamed the *Topklasse*, Excelsior 20 and VRA Amstelveen, who had won eight championships apiece over the last 20 seasons, fought out the play-off final for the second successive year: this time VRA emerged victorious. They also won the Twenty20 Cup to complete the double, as Excelsior had done in 2009. Excelsior had finished as league leaders, and boasted the leading run-scorer (their Australian professional Ed Cowan, with 762 at 63.50) and the leading wicket-taker (Usman Malik, for the second season running, with 37 at 12.89 this time).

The Dutch Women's team, which has an extremely narrow base of only 11 teams to pick from, continued to do well, gaining promotion once again in the ECB County Championship, from the fourth division to the third. They also beat Scotland in the European Championship, thus ensuring a place in the World Cup Qualifier in Bangladesh in 2011, and also defeated a strong ECB Development XI at the same tournament. Unfortunately, later in the year in South Africa they lost all their matches when they came up against some of the world's best teams, but a world ranking of tenth at the end of 2010 – still higher than the men! – is something of which to be proud.

ONE-DAY INTERNATIONALS IN THE NETHERLANDS IN 2010

Netherlands v Scotland

At Rotterdam, June 15, 2010. **Netherlands won by six wickets.** ‡Scotland 235-6 (50 overs) (G. I. Maiden 31, R. D. Berrington 84, D. R. Lockhart 31*); **Netherlands 236-4** (49.3 overs) (A. N. Kervezee 32, T. L. W. Cooper 80*, R. N. ten Doeschate 90). *MoM:* T. L. W. Cooper. *One-day international debuts:* T. L. W. Cooper (Netherlands); J. H. Davey, G. I. Maiden, P. L. Mommsen, M. A. Parker (Scotland). *Tom Cooper, an aggressive right-hander from South Australia, made a fine start to his international career, putting on 158 with Ryan ten Doeschate and anchoring his adopted country to a last-over victory.*

ICC WORLD CRICKET LEAGUE DIVISION ONE

1. Ireland 2. Scotland 3. Afghanistan

Ireland confirmed their standing as the leading Associate side in one-day internationals, maintaining a 100% record in Division One of the ICC's World Cricket League. The matches were crammed into a ten-day period in July, and the occasionally fickle Dutch weather relented enough to allow all the games to be completed.

The tournament's batting star was Tom Cooper, an Australian who qualifies for a Dutch passport through his mother. He made the only century, and finished with 408 runs from his six matches, over 100 more than the next man, Canada's Ashish Bagai (284). Ireland's bowling depth was exemplified by two of their bowlers – Alex Cusack and 17-year-old George Dockrell – being among the four who took ten wickets. The others were two of the fastest bowlers on display, Hamid Hassan of Afghanistan and the Dutchman Mark Jonkman, whose bowling action was reported during the tournament.

Ireland won despite some leading players – including captain William Porterfield and wicketkeeper Niall O'Brien – being absent on county duty. The Netherlands found it more difficult to do without their star all-rounder Ryan ten Doeschate, who was injured.

FINAL TABLE

	Played	Won	Lost	Points	Net run-rate
Ireland	5	5	0	10	0.91
Scotland	5	4	1	8	0.17
Afghanistan	5	3	2	6	–0.10
Netherlands	5	2	3	4	0.31
Canada	5	1	4	2	–0.44
Kenya	5	0	5	0	–0.91

At Voorburg, July 1, 2010. **Afghanistan won by six wickets.** ‡Canada 257-7 (50 overs) (H. Patel 43, A. Bagai 82, A. S. Hansra 30*, U. Bhatti 32, Extras 34; Samiullah Shenwari 3-43); **Afghanistan 258-4** (48.4 overs) (Noor Ali Zadran 50, Mohammad Shahzad 57, Nawroz Mangal 70*). *MoM:* Nawroz Mangal. *One-day international debut: A. S. Hansra. Afghanistan's captain Nawroz Mangal hit 70* from 58 balls to take his side home.*

At Rotterdam, July 1, 2010. **Ireland won by seven wickets.** Kenya 163 (45.3 overs) (A. A. Obanda 40, C. O. Obuya 30); ‡Ireland 164-3 (39.5 overs) (P. R. Stirling 87, A. R. Cusack 59*). *MoM:* A. R. Cusack. *One-day international debuts: J. D. Hall, N. G. Jones, R. D. McCann (Ireland); J. O. Ngoche, F. N. Otieno (Kenya). Off-spinner James Ngoche joined his brothers Shem Ngoche, Nehemiah Odhiambo and Lameck Onyango as an international (only Odhiambo was also playing here). Ireland eased to a comfortable victory thanks to a second-wicket stand of 127 in 28 overs between Paul Stirling and Alex Cusack, who had earlier taken 2-29 as Kenya were restricted to a modest total.*

At Amstelveen, July 1, 2010. **Scotland won by one wicket.** ‡Netherlands 234-6 (50 overs) (T. L. W. Cooper 87, W. Barresi 35, B. Zuiderent 55*); **Scotland 235-9** (49.5 overs) (R. D. Berrington 37, M. M. Iqbal 63, G. D. Drummond 33*; Mudassar Bukhari 3-31). *MoM:* T. L. W. Cooper. *One-day international debuts: W. Barresi (Netherlands); O. J. Hairs (Scotland). Tom Cooper followed 80* in his first one-day international the previous month with 87 from 130 balls this time, but it was not quite enough: Scotland's last pair squeaked them home. They had needed ten off ten balls, and reduced that to three off two when Gordon Drummond was dropped close in by Tom de Grooth: the batsmen took a single. The last scheduled delivery, from Mark Jonkman, was called wide, which levelled the scores – but Drummond and Ross Lyons, thinking it was the final ball, had already reeled off for a bye. The ball was rolled back to Jonkman, who missed the stumps with his lunge, and Scotland had won.*

At Rotterdam, July 3–4, 2010. **Ireland won by 39 runs.** ‡Ireland 237-9 (50 overs) (K. J. O'Brien 44, A. D. Poynter 78, A. R. White 31, D. T. Johnston 42*; Hamid Hassan 3-44); **Afghanistan 198** (47.1 overs) (Shabir Noori 38; A. R. Cusack 5-20). *Player of the Match: A. D. Poynter. Rain set in after the Ireland innings, and Afghanistan batted on the reserve day.*

At Amstelveen, July 3, 2010. **Scotland won by 69 runs** (D/L method). ‡Scotland 236-4 (50 overs) (G. I. Maiden 30, R. D. Berrington 67, N. F. I. McCallum 89*); **Canada 126-9** (26 overs) (H. Patel 37; G. Goudie 3-18). *MoM:* N. F. I. McCallum. *Two rain interruptions during Canada's innings meant their target was revised to 196 in 26 overs, but they never got close.*

At Voorburg, July 3, 2010. **Netherlands won by 117 runs.** Netherlands 229 (49.2 overs) (A. N. Kervezee 92, T. L. W. Cooper 67; J. K. Kamande 4-36); ‡Kenya 112 (30 overs). *MoM:* A. N. Kervezee. *Alexei Kervezee hit 11 fours and a six from 89 balls, and put on 123 for the second wicket with Tom Cooper, who made his third half-century in his first three one-day internationals, an unprecedented feat. Kenya collapsed from 80-3 to 112 all out.*

At Amstelveen, July 5, 2010. **Afghanistan won by one wicket.** ‡Kenya 233-7 (50 overs) (M. A. Ouma 40, C. O. Obuya 60, R. R. Patel 34, T. M. Odoyo 52*; N. N. Odhiambo 3-53). **Afghanistan 234-9** (50 overs) (Samiullah Shenwari 82, Mohammad Nabi 47; N. N. Odhiambo 3-53). *MoM:* M. A. Ouma. *Kenya finally showed some batting form, with Thomas Odoyo's 52* coming from just 33* *balls. Led by Samiullah Shenwari, who hit nine fours from 118 balls, Afghanistan closed in on victory – but, with the scores level and two balls remaining, Hamid Hassan skied a catch off Jimmy Kamande. The batsmen had crossed, so No. 11 Shapoor Zadran didn't have to face the vital last ball: instead Khaliq Dad (18*) swept the winning run.*

At Voorburg, July 5, 2010. **Ireland won by five wickets. Scotland 117** (47.2 overs) (N. F. I. McCallum 49); **‡Ireland 120-5** (34.2 overs) (P. R. Stirling 37, K. J. O'Brien 41*). MoM: K. J. O'Brien. *One-day international debut: A. Balbirnie (Ireland). Scotland were 40-5 in the 20th over, and limped along at less than 2.5 per over. Ireland also stumbled at the start, losing the debutant Andrew Balbirnie and Alex Cusack to successive balls from Matthew Parker to be 12-2, but Kevin O'Brien stopped the rot, passing 1,000 runs in one-day internationals during his 84-ball innings.*

At Rotterdam, July 5, 2010. **Netherlands won by seven wickets. ‡Canada 168** (49.1 overs) (G. E. F. Barnett 34, A. Bagai 71; M. B. S. Jonkman 3-39, B. P. Kruger 3-21); **Netherlands 169-3** (42.4 overs) (E. S. Szwarczynski 84*, T. L. W. Cooper 39, B. Zuiderent 35*). MoM: E. S. Szwarczynski. *One-day international debut: B. P. Kruger (Netherlands). Eric Szwarczynski batted for 121 balls and his highest score in one-day internationals to anchor his side past winless Canada's modest total. He put on 91 with Tom Cooper, who finally failed to reach 50, in his fourth match.*

At Amstelveen, July 7, 2010. **Ireland won by five wickets. ‡Canada 154-9** (50 overs) (N. R. Kumar 38); **Ireland 155-5** (39.1 overs) (P. R. Stirling 35, K. J. O'Brien 43*, J. F. Mooney 44*). MoM: K. J. O'Brien. *Unbeaten Ireland were in some trouble at 92-5 in the 24th over, but a stand of 63* between Kevin O'Brien and John Mooney took them to another victory.*

At Rotterdam, July 7, 2010. **Scotland won by six runs. ‡Scotland 172-8** (50 overs) (D. F. Watts 50, M. M. Iqbal 36; T. M. Odoyo 3-43, J. O. Ngoche 3-18); **Kenya 166** (48.4 overs) (A. A. Obanda 39, J. K. Kamande 34; M. A. Parker 4-33). MoM: M. A. Parker. *One-day international debut: D. S. Wesonga (Kenya). Kenya's bowling was opened by Thomas Odoyo and his nephew Nelson Odhiambo, and later the slow-bowling Ngoche brothers – Shem (left-arm) and James (off-breaks) – delivered their 20 overs for just 51 runs. Kenya looked set fair at 94-4, but lost five for 21 before a determined last-wicket stand of 51 in nine overs between Nelson Odhiambo (29) and James Ngoche (21*) left them just short. Fraser Watts's 92-ball 50 was the only half-century of the game.*

At Voorburg, July 7, 2010. **Afghanistan won by six wickets. Netherlands 202-8** (50 overs) (T. L. W. Cooper 101; Khaliq Dad 3-30); **‡Afghanistan 203-4** (42.3 overs) (Mohammad Shahzad 55, Nawroz Mangal 67*). MoM: T. L. W. Cooper. *Tom Cooper continued the phenomenal start to his international career, completing his first century and taking the aggregate from his first five one-day matches to 374, well clear of the previous record of 328 by England's Allan Lamb in 1982. But again he had little support, and Afghanistan eased to victory after a wobble left them 110-4. The bowling action of the Netherlands' fast bowler Mark Jonkman was reported to the ICC after the match: he was allowed to continue playing in this tournament, but following tests later in the year he was suspended from international cricket.*

At Rotterdam, July 9, 2010. **Scotland won by two wickets. ‡Afghanistan 141** (47.1 overs) (Mohammad Shahzad 34, Nawroz Mangal 38*; R. T. Lyons 3-21); **Scotland 142-8** (43.5 overs) (D. F. Watts 46). MoM: D. F. Watts. *One-day international debut: Javed Ahmadi (Afghanistan). Scotland ensured that they, rather than Afghanistan, would reach the final – although they ultimately made heavy weather of what seemed a simple task after reaching 134-5, chasing 142. Three wickets for five runs set Scottish nerves jangling, but Moneeb Iqbal and Gordon Goudie stood firm. Earlier Afghanistan had also failed to push on after reaching 98-4 in 32 overs.*

At Schiedam, July 9, 2010. **Canada won by six wickets. Kenya 153** (45.2 overs) (M. A. Ouma 38; H. S. Baidwan 3-24); **‡Canada 154-4** (35.5 overs) (A. Bagai 61*). MoM: H. S. Baidwan. *Neither side had won any of their four previous games, but it was Kenya whose misery continued with a fifth defeat: they seemed to be in with a shout after reducing Canada to 71-4, but Ashish Bagai and Zubin Surkari (23*) took their side over the finish line with 85 balls to spare.*

At Amstelveen, July 9, 2010. **Ireland won by 39 runs. ‡Ireland 177** (48.2 overs) (P. R. Stirling 33, J. F. Mooney 54; M. B. S. Jonkman 3-28, B. P. Loots 3-16); **Netherlands 138** (38.5 overs) (P. W. Borren 47; G. H. Dockrell 4-35, P. R. Stirling 4-11). MoM: P. R. Stirling. *One-day international debuts: B. P. Loots; A. van der Merwe (Ireland). Ireland completed a 100% qualifying record despite dipping to 57-5 in the 22nd over. Earlier, the Dutch debutant medium-pacer Bernard Loots had dismissed James Hall with his second ball in international cricket, and Kevin O'Brien with his third. But the dependable John Mooney again lifted Ireland to a respectable total.*

Final

At Amstelveen, July 10, 2010. **Ireland won by six wickets. Scotland 232** (48.5 overs) (D. F. Watts 98, P. L. Mommsen 80, G. D. Drummond 30); ‡**Ireland 233-4** (44.5 overs) (P. R. Stirling 32, K. J. O'Brien 98*, A. R. White 79). *MoM:* K. J. O'Brien. *Scotland seemed to be in control while Fraser Watts and Preston Mommsen were going well in an opening partnership of 141, but after Mommsen fell in the 31st over six more wickets went down in the next ten: from 169-7 Scotland regrouped thanks to captain Gordon Drummond, but their eventual total was slightly disappointing. It looked better when Ireland lurched from 37-0 to 51-3, but a stand of 160 between Kevin O'Brien and Andrew White, who hit 11 fours, settled the destination of the trophy.*

Third-place Play-off

At Rotterdam, July 10, 2010. **Afghanistan won by five wickets. ‡Netherlands 218-5** (50 overs) (T. L. W. Cooper 96, W. Barresi 51*); **Afghanistan 219-5** (46 overs) (Mohammad Shahzad 82, Asghar Stanikzai 64). *MoM:* T. L. W. Cooper. *It was a familiar story for the hosts: Tom Cooper batted well, falling just short of his second century of the tournament, but they lost again – Afghanistan rarely looked troubled despite the early loss of both openers, and completed victory with four overs to spare. Cooper was named Player of the Tournament after scoring 408 runs at an average of 68.00.*

Fifth-place Play-off

At Schiedam, July 10, 2010. **Canada won by three wickets. Kenya 190** (50 overs) (C. O. Obuya 34, T. M. Odoyo 39, D. S. Wesonga 33; Rizwan Cheema 3-39); ‡**Canada 194-7** (49.2 overs) (A. Bagai 39, Z. E. Surkari 49). *MoM:* Z. E. Surkari. *Canada won the wooden-spoon match by overhauling Kenya's modest total in the last over. Canada had looked in some trouble at 81-5 after 27 overs, but Ashish Bagai and Zubin Surkari steadied the ship with a stand of 85 in 18 overs.*

For the Netherlands' matches in the Intercontinental Cup in 2010, see page 1165.

PART FIVE

Overseas Cricket

WORLD CRICKET IN 2010

Decline and fall

SIMON WILDE

The story of the year was one of failure rather than success. It had been obvious for some time that Australia were no longer the lean, mean fighting machine they had once been, but they had remained a highly competitive side. Indeed, in the first few months of 2010 little happened to suggest this was not still the case. Until their World Twenty20 final defeat by England in Barbados on May 16, Australia's results bore the hallmark of a team every bit as mighty as their predecessors: of 30 games in all formats, they had won 26 and lost two.

This only made the collapse, when it came, all the more striking. They won only six more matches all year, at one point were beaten in seven straight games (a sequence equalling the worst in their history), and by the end of the Sydney Test in the first week of 2011 had lost six Tests out of eight, an indignity they had not endured for a quarter of a century. If their 2–0 defeat in India was no great surprise, the humiliating manner in which they lost the Ashes series to England at home certainly was. Only once before – when Australia trounced South Africa in 1935-36 – had any home side suffered three innings defeats in the same series.

Ricky Ponting, the captain in Tests and one-day internationals, and Michael Clarke, who led the Twenty20 side, scored just two centuries between them after mid-February; and in Tests throughout the year the team lost their wickets more cheaply than everyone bar West Indies, Bangladesh and Pakistan. But if the batting creaked, the wheels all but came off the bowling attack, which by Sydney had conceded totals of 490, 517 for one, 620 for five, 513 and 644 in the space of six Tests. By ordering an inquiry into what had gone wrong, Cricket Australia entered post-Ashes territory previously reserved for the Poms.

With Australia sliding into mid-table anonymity, a three-way argument appeared to be developing between India, South Africa and England as to who might replace them as the world's best all-round team. India and England did not meet in any format, but South Africa played out some close-fought contests with both. Having started the year by drawing a Test series with England that began in December 2009, South Africa went on to draw 1–1 with India away and at home, letting leads slip on both occasions. The Test series in South Africa – where India finally came away with a share of the spoils after being beaten on all four previous visits – produced cricket of epic quality as Sachin Tendulkar and Dale Steyn, the leading batsman and fast bowler of the year, traded blows. The one-day series were also enthralling viewing, with India twice winning by one run – at Jaipur and, in January 2011, at Johannesburg.

The open nature of this three-way battle promised to create some welcome interest in Test cricket, with England hosting India in 2011 and South Africa in 2012, and the ICC having confirmed plans to stage an inaugural world Test

Heavyweight clash... As 2010 turns to 2011, India and South Africa struggle for Test supremacy; Sachin Tendulkar leads the fight for India.

championship in 2013, in which the top four teams in the rankings would take part (a one-day league spread over four years was also announced).

Outside icon events such as the Ashes, Test attendances remained a concern. India's victory at Durban during a holiday period was watched by fewer than 36,000, and when England entertained Bangladesh in Manchester and Pakistan in Birmingham neither gate reached 30,000, low figures for England. The English season had typically attracted at least 550,000 for seven Tests, but in 2010 the aggregate figure slumped to 450,000 for eight, including two "neutral" matches between Pakistan and Australia. The economic recession may have been one factor, England's decision also to stage five one-day internationals against Australia another (these drew a combined gate of 100,000).

Taking all formats together, England were arguably the team of the year. They won the World Twenty20 to lift their first global limited-overs tournament, pulled off a spectacular Test series win in Australia, and created a world record by winning 11 successive events (including a one-off international against Scotland). This run ended when Australia held them 1–1 in a two-match Twenty20 series early in 2011, although not before England had set another record by winning their eighth straight Twenty20 international.

England enjoyed easier pickings than most – 24 of their 42 matches were against Bangladesh and a dysfunctional Pakistan team – but the way they crushed Australia suggested a team operating on a rarefied level. Their bowlers claimed 250 Test wickets – only India with 214 also topped 200 – and they were the only team to achieve a collective bowling average of under 30. Graeme Swann was the world's leading Test wicket-taker with 64, while James Anderson came in third on 57, only three behind Steyn. Swann's success was unusual, as the overall average for spinners was 40.56, the highest for ten years.

England's batsmen also discovered a taste for big scores, individually topping 150 seven times, more than any other side, while as a team they achieved in the space of 16 Tests – from their final match of 2009 to their first of 2011 – their third-highest total in South Africa, their second-biggest in Asia and their highest in Australia.

MOST SUCCESSIVE SERIES WINS IN ALL FORMATS

11	**England (4 Test series, 5 ODI series, 2 Twenty20 series)**	**2010–2011**
10	South Africa (5 Test series, 5 ODI series)	2000–2001
10	Australia (5 Test series, 5 ODI series)	2002–2003
9	West Indies (4 Test series, 5 ODI series)	1983–1985
9	Pakistan (3 Test series, 6 ODI series)	2001–2002
9	Australia (2 Test series, 5 ODI series, 2 Twenty20)	2009–2010
8	England (all Tests)	1884–1890

South Africa were also a hard team to beat. Probably they should have converted some of their four drawn Test series into wins. The difficulty was that although they possessed the best new-ball pair – Steyn and Morne Morkel, who took 109 Test wickets between them – they lacked a match-winning spinner and struggled to finish off opponents. Their first-choice option Paul Harris took just 23 wickets in ten Tests at an average of 50.65 and a strike-rate of 120.3, but there were hopes that the problem might ease once Lahore-born Imran Tahir completed his qualification for 2011.

South Africa's batting was formidable. Jacques Kallis, Hashim Amla and A. B. de Villiers all averaged over 75 in Tests, and de Villiers set a national record with 278 not out against Pakistan in Abu Dhabi, which staged a Test for the first time. Amla was the only batsman worldwide to score 1,000 runs in both Tests and one-day internationals, and his ten centuries in the calendar year had been bettered only twice – by Tendulkar with 12 in 1998 and Ponting with 11 in 2003. South Africa were the only team to average more than six runs per over in one-day internationals (6.01, with India next on 5.50), in part because they made good use of the powerplays.

India, their enthusiasm for Test cricket fired by their status as the No. 1 ranked side, had one of their best years in the five-day game, winning three series, drawing three and losing none. As India possessed the most influential voice in the corridors of power, with Sharad Pawar the ICC president, it was heartening to see them add two Tests to a tour by Australia originally scheduled only to include one-day internationals. India won both matches, despite Australia scoring 428 and 478 in the two first innings.

If India want to remain competitive, they might need to encourage the production of more result pitches on their own grounds. Between 2006 and 2010, no country witnessed more draws than India, while of regular venues only Pakistan also saw wickets cost more than 40 apiece. In all Tests for 2010, runs per wicket topped 34 for only the third time, after 1989 and 2009.

As India played 12 of their 14 Tests on generally docile subcontinental surfaces, their batsmen made hay, never more so than during a tedious encounter with Sri Lanka in Colombo, where the respective first innings were not completed until the fifth morning. Tendulkar and Virender Sehwag both topped 1,400 Test runs for the year: Tendulkar's haul of 1,562 was the best by any Indian, and he also became the first man ever to score a double-century in a one-day international, with 200 not out against South Africa at Gwalior in February. Given the testing conditions for bowling in which he operated, among the finest performances of the year was Zaheer Khan's 47 Test wickets at 21.97 apiece. India's next-best bowler, Harbhajan Singh, picked up his 43 wickets at 40.69 each.

THE HIGHEST-SCORING TEST GROUNDS, 2006–2010

	Tests	Results	% Results	Runs	Wickets	Average
Lahore	4	1	25.00	3,984	78	**51.08**
Ahmedabad	3	1	33.33	3,730	79	**47.22**
Colombo (SSC)	8	4	50.00	9,719	213	**45.63**
Bangalore	3	1	33.33	4,207	96	**43.82**
Bridgetown	3	2	66.66	3,708	85	**43.62**
Adelaide	5	3	60.00	6,315	147	**42.96**

Minimum: three matches. The lowest runs-per-wicket average for a ground staging three or more Tests in this period was 23.23, in three matches (all with positive results) at Kingston.

Research: Andrew Samson

With the calendar having to accommodate the World Twenty20 as well as the IPL (during the 45 days of which only four Tests and five one-day internationals were staged elsewhere), the 50-over international took something of a back seat in 2010. India still played more of them than any other team, but only once since 1995 had they played fewer than the 27 they did now.

Unlike England and South Africa, India remained firmly opposed to the Decision Review System, which had been introduced on an optional basis in November 2009. It was used in the Ashes for the first time, and generally worked well. It caused the occasional dispute – Ponting was fined 40% of his match fee in Melbourne for arguing with Aleem Dar about how it had been used after an Australian appeal against Kevin Pietersen – but it usually helped take the heat out of player–umpire relations. The ICC announced that the DRS would be used at the 2011 World Cup, but India remained adamant that they would not use it in any bilateral Test series.

Sri Lanka, who beat India six times in ten one-day internationals, were a match for most sides, but they faced a challenge to remain competitive without Muttiah Muralitharan, their greatest match-winner. Murali made one of the most dramatic of all departures from the Test arena when he announced that the first match of the series against India at Galle would be his last, then took the eight wickets he needed to become the first man to reach 800 Test scalps, completing his side's victory with the vital wicket. He said he would continue to play one-dayers until the 2011 World Cup, and signed off from Australia – a destination that had brought him little joy over the years – by helping his team beat their hosts in one Twenty20 and two 50-over games. In an extraordinary match at Melbourne, Sri Lanka won after sliding to 107 for eight, chasing 240. Angelo Mathews and Lasith Malinga added 132 for the ninth wicket, a record in all one-day internationals, before Murali joyfully struck the winning boundary.

USING THE POWERPLAYS

Scoring in the optional batting powerplay during one-day internationals in 2010:

	Overs	Runs	Wickets	Average	Runs/over
India	92	751	23	32.65	**8.16**
Australia	91.3	744	25	29.76	**8.13**
New Zealand	72.1	580	22	26.36	**8.03**
South Africa	72.5	579	18	32.16	**7.94**
West Indies	43.5	336	11	30.54	**7.66**
Pakistan	77.1	581	43	13.51	**7.52**
England	49.1	370	23	16.08	**7.52**
Sri Lanka	76.3	567	26	21.80	**7.41**
Bangladesh	73.1	527	36	14.63	**7.20**
Zimbabwe	59	409	25	16.36	**6.93**

Note: Includes all completed 50-overs internationals between Full Members of the ICC in 2010.

Research: Andrew Samson

Sri Lanka lost their hold on third place in the Test rankings after failing to beat West Indies in a rain-ravaged series scheduled outside their normal season, in November and December. In more favourable conditions Sri Lanka would surely have prevailed, as West Indies had not won a match of any description outside the Caribbean since June 2009, and their bowling attack was suffering its worst year in more than half a century, taking their wickets at more than 45 each. That said, Chris Gayle did make 333, the highest score by any visiting batsman in Sri Lanka, in the First Test.

Even by their own turbulent standards, Pakistan had a chaotic and unhappy year. After losing every international match on tour in Australia, several players were blacklisted. Then, unable to stage matches at home because of the security crisis within Pakistan, they were indebted to the generosity and co-operation of other national boards who agreed to them playing elsewhere. They held a "home" series against Australia in England (two Tests, two Twenty20s) and another against South Africa in Abu Dhabi and Dubai (two Tests, five one-day internationals, two Twenty20s).

This was not, therefore, a good time for a corruption scandal to break, as it did during the Lord's Test against England, with allegations of spot-fixing. With Pakistan officials seemingly in denial over the seriousness of the situation facing their country's cricket, relations with the ECB and ICC neared breaking point.

Despite moving on to a fourth Test captain for the year in Misbah-ul-Haq, even without their three suspended players Pakistan managed to hold South Africa to two Test draws in the Middle East, where a close-run one-day series went down to the final match before South Africa prevailed 3–2. Despite this, Pakistan were beaten 31 times in all, making this the worst year in their history not only in terms of scandal but also statistics. The only thing they won – apart from shaming headlines – was a Twenty20 series against Australia in England.

New Zealand's misdemeanours were confined to the field, but they also had a shockingly bad time. They beat Bangladesh at home, but that was their last joy until the final week of the year when they saw off Pakistan in a Twenty20 series. Traditionally a capable one-day team, New Zealand won just six matches out of 21, the nadir coming late on when they were trounced 4–0 in Bangladesh and 5–0 in India, leaving their captain Daniel Vettori's argument that 50-overs series were tediously long looking like sour grapes rather than constructive criticism.

TWENTY20: THE WINNING FACTORS

In the 46 Twenty20 internationals played during 2010:

		%
The team bowling most dot balls won	34	73.91
The team taking most wickets won	32	69.56
The team scoring more runs in the first six overs won	32	69.56
The team hitting most fours won	30	65.21
The team hitting most sixes won	27	58.69
The team taking most wickets in the first six overs won	23	50.00
The team scoring most singles won	13	28.26

Note: Includes all completed 20-overs internationals between Full Members of the ICC in 2010 (excluding ties).

Research: Andrew Samson

Bangladesh's clean sweep over New Zealand was an eye-catching feather in their cap, and suggested they might be capable of more giant-killing on home soil at the World Cup. This was only their second series win against major opposition, following their victory over a weakened West Indies side in 2009, and they pulled off another coup by beating England for the first time in any international match, in a 50-over game at Bristol in July.

Zimbabwe's situation continued to improve, with more players returning to the fold and good coaches being attracted to key positions. The team played 13 one-day internationals against major opposition, as opposed to three in 2009, and by beating India twice and Sri Lanka once reached the final of a triangular one-day tournament involving two front-line sides for the first time since the NatWest Series final at Lord's in 2000.

TEST MATCHES IN 2010

	Tests	Won	Lost	Drawn	% won	% lost	% drawn
England	14	9	3	2	**64.28**	21.42	14.28
India	14	8	3	3	**57.14**	21.42	21.42
Australia	12	6	5	1	**50.00**	41.66	8.33
South Africa	11	5	2	4	**45.45**	18.18	36.36
Pakistan	10	2	6	2	**20.00**	60.00	20.00
Sri Lanka	6	1	1	4	**16.66**	16.66	66.66
New Zealand	6	1	3	2	**16.66**	50.00	33.33
West Indies	6	0	2	4	**0.00**	33.33	66.66
Bangladesh	7	0	7	0	**0.00**	100.00	0.00
Totals	43	32	32	11	**74.41**	74.41	25.58

Zimbabwe did not play any Test matches in 2010.

ONE-DAY INTERNATIONALS IN 2010

	ODIs	Won	Lost	NR	% won	% lost
South Africa	16	12	4	0	**75.00**	25.00
Sri Lanka	22	15	6	1	**71.42**	28.57
England	17	12	5	0	**70.58**	29.41
Australia	25	16	8	1	**66.66**	33.33
Ireland	17	11	6	0	**64.70**	35.29
India	27	17	10	0	**62.96**	37.03
Afghanistan	13	7	6	0	**53.84**	46.15
Scotland	10	5	5	0	**50.00**	50.00
Netherlands	12	5	7	0	**41.66**	58.33
West Indies	17	6	10	1	**37.50**	62.50
Canada	11	4	7	0	**36.36**	63.63
Zimbabwe	20	7	13	0	**35.00**	65.00
Bangladesh	27	9	18	0	**33.33**	66.66
New Zealand	21	6	14	1	**30.00**	70.00
Pakistan	18	5	13	0	**27.77**	72.22
Kenya	11	3	8	0	**27.27**	72.72
Totals	142	140	140	2		

For one-day internationals, the % won and lost excludes no-results.

RELIANCE MOBILE ICC TEST CHAMPIONSHIP

(As at January 19, 2011)

		Matches	Points	Rating
1	India	42	5,357	128
2	South Africa	36	4,228	117
3	England	45	5,165	115
4	Sri Lanka	27	2,951	109
5	Australia	43	4,583	107
6	Pakistan	29	2,615	90
7	West Indies	25	2,128	85
8	New Zealand	32	2,482	78
9	Bangladesh	19	131	7

RELIANCE MOBILE ICC ONE-DAY CHAMPIONSHIP

(As at December 31, 2010)

		Matches	Points	Rating
1	Australia	36	4,595	128
2	India	39	4,713	121
3	Sri Lanka	33	3,892	118
4	South Africa	25	2,873	115
5	England	28	3,147	112
6	Pakistan	27	2,704	100
7	New Zealand	29	2,651	91
8	West Indies	18	1,207	67
9	Bangladesh	32	2,121	66
10	Ireland	11	425	39
11	Zimbabwe	34	1,272	37
12	Netherlands	6	103	17
13	Kenya	8	1	0

RELIANCE MOBILE ICC RANKINGS

Introduced in 1987, the Rankings have been backed by various sponsors, but were taken over by the International Cricket Council in January 2005. They rank cricketers on a scale up to 1,000 on their performances in Tests. The rankings take into account playing conditions, the quality of the opposition and the result of the matches. In August 1998, a similar set of rankings for one-day internationals was added.

The leading ten batsmen and bowlers in the Test Rankings on January 19, 2011, were:

Rank	Batsmen	Points	Rank	Bowlers	Points
1	{ S. R. Tendulkar (*India*)	883	1	D. W. Steyn (*South Africa*)	899
	{ J. H. Kallis (*South Africa*)	883	2	G. P. Swann (*England*)	793
3	K. C. Sangakkara (*Sri Lanka*)	882	3	J. M. Anderson (*England*)	776
4	I. J. L. Trott (*England*)	826	4	M. Morkel (*South Africa*)	751
5	A. N. Cook (*England*)	803	5	Zaheer Khan (*India*)	748
6	V. Sehwag (*India*)	790	6	M. G. Johnson (*Australia*)	727
7	D. P. M. D. Jayawardene (*Sri Lanka*)	781	7	Mohammad Asif (*Pakistan*)	723
8	S. Chanderpaul (*West Indies*)	779	8	Harbhajan Singh (*India*)	672
9	V. V. S. Laxman (*India*)	774	9	Shakib Al Hasan (*Bangladesh*)	648
10	T. T. Samaraweera (*Sri Lanka*)	763	10	Mohammad Aamer (*Pakistan*)	632

The leading ten batsmen and bowlers in the One-Day International Rankings on Dec 31, 2010 were:

Rank	Batsmen	Points	Rank	Bowlers	Points
1	H. M. Amla (*South Africa*)	854	1	D. L. Vettori (*New Zealand*)	728
2	A. B. de Villiers (*South Africa*)	809	2	Abdur Razzak (*Bangladesh*)	675
3	M. E. K. Hussey (*Australia*)	796	3	{ R. W. Price (*Zimbabwe*)	669
4	M. S. Dhoni (*India*)	767		{ G. P. Swann (*England*)	669
5	V. Kohli (*India*)	751	5	Shakib Al Hasan (*Bangladesh*)	668
6	C. H. Gayle (*West Indies*)	738	6	S. C. J. Broad (*England*)	662
7	T. M. Dilshan (*Sri Lanka*)	731	7	K. M. D. N. Kulasekara (*Sri Lanka*)	651
8	S. Chanderpaul (*West Indies*)	710	8	D. E. Bollinger (*Australia*)	645
9	J. H. Kallis (*South Africa*)	708	9	J. M. Anderson (*England*)	635
10	G. Gambhir (*India*)	706	10	P. Kumar (*India*)	618

In October 2008, the ICC launched a set of rankings for women cricketers, based on one-day international performances because of the paucity of women's Test cricket. The ICC said it hoped to raise the profile of the women's game by identifying where the leading players stood, and to add further competition and context to their achievements.

The leading ten batsmen and bowlers in the Women's One-Day International Rankings on December 31, 2010, were:

Rank	Batsmen	Points	Rank	Bowlers	Points
1	M. Raj (*India*)	823	1	J. Goswami (*India*)	777
2	S. Nitschke (*Australia*)	689	2	S. Nitschke (*Australia*)	747
3	S. C. Taylor (*England*)	680	3	K. H. Brunt (*England*)	724
4	S. R. Taylor (*West Indies*)	655	4	L. C. Sthalekar (*Australia*)	714
5	S. J. Taylor (*England*)	605	5	R. Dhar (*India*)	698
6	C-Z. Brits (*South Africa*)	572	6	L. A. Marsh (*England*)	679
7	A. J. Blackwell (*Australia*)	569	7	H. L. Colvin (*England*)	638
8	L. C. Sthalekar (*Australia*)	567	8	N. J. Browne (*New Zealand*)	623
9	C. M. Edwards (*England*)	552	9	E. A. Perry (*Australia*)	598
10	L. S. Greenway (*England*)	530	10	J. L. Gunn (*England*)	582

INTERNATIONAL AVERAGES

TEST AVERAGES IN CALENDAR YEAR 2010

BATTING (300 runs, average 30.00)

	T	I	NO	R	HS	100s	Avge	SR	Ct/St
T. T. Samaraweera (SL)	6	8	4	457	137*	1	114.25	51.58	1
†K. C. Sangakkara (SL)	6	9	2	695	219	3	99.28	61.07	6
J. H. Kallis (SA)	11	19	4	1,198	201*	6	79.86	54.01	16
S. R. Tendulkar (I)	14	23	3	1,562	214	7	78.10	55.90	2
H. M. Amla (SA)	11	19	3	1,249	253*	5	78.06	53.05	12
A. B. de Villiers (SA)	11	18	5	996	278*	3	76.61	58.45	17
B. B. McCullum (NZ).........	6	12	2	758	225	3	75.80	62.43	11/1
V. V. S. Laxman (I)	11	18	4	939	143*	2	67.07	51.82	9
I. J. L. Trott (E).............	14	24	4	1,325	226	4	66.25	49.44	7
I. R. Bell (E)	10	14	2	786	138	2	65.50	52.26	6
V. Sehwag (I)	14	25	2	1,422	173	5	61.82	90.80	10
†Tamim Iqbal (B)	7	14	0	837	151	3	59.78	80.71	3
†A. N. Cook (E)	14	24	2	1,287	235*	6	58.50	54.76	10
†C. H. Gayle (WI)............	6	9	0	525	333	1	58.33	70.09	3
†S. Chanderpaul (WI)	6	9	2	394	166	1	56.28	38.10	2
†N. T. Paranavitana (SL)	6	10	2	433	111	2	54.12	43.91	3
†G. C. Smith (SA)............	11	18	0	971	183	4	53.94	57.42	11
†M. E. K. Hussey (A).........	12	22	3	967	195	1	50.89	50.73	14
D. P. M. D. Jayawardene (SL) ...	6	8	0	407	174	1	50.87	52.65	13
M. J. Guptill (NZ)...........	5	10	1	452	189	1	50.22	46.45	3
†S. M. Katich (A).............	9	18	1	796	106	2	46.82	47.12	3
R. Dravid (I)	12	20	2	771	191	3	42.83	44.56	12
S. R. Watson (A).............	11	22	1	897	126	1	42.71	50.30	12
Mahmudullah (B)............	7	14	1	545	115	1	41.92	61.79	3
M. S. Dhoni (I)	13	19	1	749	132*	1	41.61	55.48	41/7
K. P. Pietersen (E)	14	22	2	831	227	1	41.55	62.20	11
M. J. Prior (E)..............	14	20	4	640	102*	1	40.00	61.47	54/2
L. R. P. L. Taylor (NZ).......	6	11	0	433	138	1	39.36	71.45	7
B. J. Haddin (A)	8	14	2	465	136	1	38.75	61.02	28/1
†B. P. Nash (WI).............	6	8	0	302	114	1	37.75	53.73	2
Azhar Ali (P)...............	8	16	2	528	92*	0	37.71	38.70	3
R. T. Ponting (A)	12	23	1	813	209	1	36.95	56.93	16
M. J. Clarke (A)	12	21	0	771	168	2	36.71	53.47	15
Mushfiqur Rahim (B)	7	14	1	461	101	1	35.46	45.41	11/5
M. V. Boucher (SA)	10	12	1	389	95	0	35.36	54.71	34
A. N. Petersen (SA)	8	15	0	529	100	1	35.26	53.54	5
†Junaid Siddique (B)	6	12	0	416	106	1	34.66	40.46	5
†A. J. Strauss (E)	12	20	1	657	110	1	34.57	52.06	17
M. Vijay (I)................	7	11	0	376	139	1	34.18	46.82	4
†Salman Butt (P)..............	8	16	0	543	102	1	33.93	51.22	0
†S. K. Raina (I)..............	8	12	1	373	120	1	33.90	57.20	9
†Shakib Al Hasan (B).........	7	14	0	464	100	1	33.14	59.03	0
†G. Gambhir (I)	10	18	2	524	116	1	32.75	59.74	5
†A. G. Prince (SA)	11	15	4	350	78*	0	31.81	37.15	9
†T. G. McIntosh (NZ).........	6	12	0	374	102	1	31.16	38.87	3

BOWLING (10 wickets, average 55.00)

	Style	O	M	R	W	BB	5W/i	Avge	SR
C. T. Tremlett (E)...........	RF	75.5	15	247	13	5-87	1	19.00	35.00
D. W. Steyn (SA)	RF	390.1	80	1,285	60	7-51	4	21.41	39.01
Zaheer Khan (I).............	LFM	311.5	62	1,033	47	7-87	2	21.97	39.80
Mohammad Aamer (P).......	LFM	251.5	54	737	33	6-84	2	22.33	45.78

	Style	O	M	R	W	BB	5W/i	Avge	SR
J. M. Anderson (E)	RFM	463	120	1,309	57	6-17	3	22.96	48.73
M. Morkel (SA)	RF	387.1	100	1,179	49	5-20	3	24.06	47.40
R. J. Harris (A)	RF	154.1	32	488	20	6-47	1	24.40	46.25
G. P. Swann (E)	OB	576	121	1,662	64	6-65	6	25.96	54.00
S. T. Finn (E)	RFM	304.4	64	1,207	46	6-125	3	26.23	39.73
K. A. J. Roach (WI)	RF	134	24	431	16	5-100	1	26.93	50.25
S. R. Watson (A).	RFM	162.5	32	514	19	6-33	2	27.05	51.42
D. E. Bollinger (A)	LFM	237.5	46	815	30	5-28	1	27.16	47.56
S. L. Malinga (SL)	RF	72	6	273	10	5-50	1	27.30	43.20
Mohammad Asif (P).........	RFM	303.1	68	903	33	6-41	2	27.36	55.12
T. T. Bresnan (E)	RFM	168	54	470	17	4-50	0	27.64	59.29
P. M. Siddle (A)	RFM	177.3	43	526	19	6-54	2	27.68	56.05
J. Botha (SA)	OB	132	27	395	13	4-56	0	30.38	60.92
S. J. Benn (WI).............	SLA	197.4	36	526	16	6-81	2	32.87	74.12
M. G. Johnson (A)	LF	381	68	1,367	40	6-38	3	34.17	57.15
Saeed Ajmal (P)............	OB	187.1	27	550	15	5-82	1	36.66	74.86
I. Sharma (I)	RFM	323.4	56	1,240	33	4-43	0	37.57	58.84
S. C. J. Broad (E)	RFM	332.4	79	980	26	4-38	0	37.69	76.76
B. A. W. Mendis (SL).......	OB/LBG	213.3	29	650	17	6-169	1	38.23	75.35
D. L. Vettori (NZ).	SLA	360.3	68	999	26	5-135	1	38.42	83.19
T. G. Southee (NZ).	RFM	154	28	545	14	4-61	0	38.92	66.00
Shakib Al Hasan (B)........	SLA	348.4	62	1,053	27	5-62	2	39.00	77.48
S. Randiv (SL)	OB	175.3	28	567	14	5-82	1	40.50	75.21
Harbhajan Singh (I)	OB	612	103	1,750	43	5-59	1	40.69	85.39
N. M. Hauritz (A)	OB	261.4	54	909	22	5-53	1	41.31	71.36
B. W. Hilfenhaus (A)	RFM	262.5	61	745	18	4-57	0	41.38	87.61
A. Mishra (I)...............	LBG	212	29	633	15	4-92	0	42.20	84.80
P. P. Ojha (I)	SLA	504.4	103	1,439	33	4-107	0	43.60	91.75
Umar Gul (P)	RFM	269	38	921	21	4-61	0	43.85	76.85
J. H. Kallis (SA)	RFM	199.1	45	574	12	2-36	0	47.83	99.58
S. Sreesanth (I)	RFM	198.2	22	772	16	3-45	0	48.25	74.37
Danish Kaneria (P)..........	LBG	196.4	18	791	16	5-151	1	49.43	73.75
P. L. Harris (SA).	SLA	461.3	113	1,165	23	3-76	0	50.65	120.39
Shahadat Hossain (B)	RFM	165	16	676	13	5-71	2	52.00	76.15
C. S. Martin (NZ)	RFM	207	33	731	14	5-63	1	52.21	88.71

MOST DISMISSALS BY A WICKETKEEPER

Dis		T		Dis		T	
56	(54 ct, 2 st)	14	M. J. Prior (E)	27	(27 ct)	6	Kamran Akmal (P)
48	(41 ct, 7 st)	13	M. S. Dhoni (I)	17	(16 ct, 1 st)	4	T. D. Paine (A)
34	(34 ct)	10	M. V. Boucher (SA)	16	(11 ct, 5 st)	7	Mushfiqur Rahim (B)
29	(28 ct, 1 st)	8	B. J. Haddin (A)				

MOST CATCHES IN THE FIELD

Ct	T		Ct	T	
22	12	P. D. Collingwood (E)	16	11	J. H. Kallis (SA)
17	12	A. J. Strauss (E)	16	12	R. T. Ponting (A)
17	14	G. P. Swann (E)	15	12	M. J. Clarke (A)
16†	10	A. B. de Villiers (SA)	14	12	M. E. K. Hussey (A)

† *De Villiers also made one catch in one match as wicketkeeper.*

ONE-DAY INTERNATIONAL AVERAGES IN CALENDAR YEAR 2010

BATTING (500 runs, average 30.00)

	M	I	NO	R	HS	100s	50s	Avge	SR	4	6
A. B. de Villiers (SA)	16	16	4	964	114*	5	4	80.33	102.11	67	19
H. M. Amla (SA)	15	15	1	1,058	129	5	4	75.57	104.23	106	6
T. L. W. Cooper (NL)	10	10	1	589	101	1	5	65.44	71.30	55	1
A. Bagai (Can)	11	11	2	539	91*	0	6	59.88	71.29	49	1
J. H. Kallis (SA)	12	12	2	593	104*	1	6	59.30	89.30	36	7
†A. J. Strauss (E)	14	14	0	806	154	2	6	57.57	95.95	89	12
†G. Gambhir (I)	14	14	2	670	138*	2	3	55.83	93.96	79	1
M. J. Clarke (A)	19	19	5	777	111*	1	5	55.50	79.36	45	4
†E. J. G. Morgan (E)	17	17	4	691	110*	3	2	53.15	93.88	62	9
T. M. Dilshan (SL)	20	20	2	921	110	3	4	51.16	98.92	124	7
†K. C. Sangakkara (SL)	17	17	2	726	74	0	7	48.40	84.41	81	1
V. Kohli (I)	25	24	3	995	118	3	7	47.38	85.11	90	4
Mohammad Shahzad (Afg)	12	12	1	517	118	2	3	47.00	93.32	61	6
M. S. Dhoni (I)	18	17	4	600	101*	1	3	46.15	78.94	52	9
†M. E. K. Hussey (A)	24	23	5	825	79	0	6	45.83	91.56	54	6
P. R. Stirling (Ire)	17	17	0	771	177	1	5	45.35	90.59	87	17
C. L. White (A)	25	23	4	848	105	1	6	44.63	84.46	60	20
D. P. M. D. Jayawardene (SL)	15	15	3	509	108	1	4	42.41	79.90	51	2
B. R. M. Taylor (Z)	20	20	2	723	145*	2	3	40.16	79.27	63	5
†S. K. Raina (I)	24	21	5	631	106	1	3	39.43	97.22	58	10
R. G. Sharma (I)	15	14	1	504	114	2	1	38.76	86.00	34	7
L. R. P. L. Taylor (NZ)	20	19	1	676	95	0	7	37.55	81.05	48	20
†W. U. Tharanga (SL)	22	22	3	707	118*	1	5	37.21	73.79	85	3
S. R. Watson (A)	21	21	0	771	69	0	7	36.71	88.41	87	14
R. T. Ponting (A)	22	22	1	771	106	1	6	36.71	82.63	73	9
T. Taibu (Z)	18	18	2	574	78	0	5	35.87	68.41	31	3
P. D. Collingwood (E)	16	16	2	500	95	0	4	35.71	70.52	26	8
†Junaid Siddique (B)	17	17	1	568	100	1	4	35.50	75.43	49	4
†Tamim Iqbal (B)	23	23	0	776	125	1	5	33.73	96.15	90	17
Shahid Afridi (P)	18	18	0	601	124	2	0	33.38	144.12	54	27
†Shakib Al Hasan (B)	27	27	3	787	106	1	5	32.79	80.14	70	2
†Imrul Kayes (B)	27	27	0	867	101	1	6	32.11	67.15	88	7
Mahmudullah (B)	24	22	6	507	64*	0	2	31.68	69.26	38	3

BOWLING (15 wickets, average 30.00)

	Style	O	M	R	W	BB	4W/i	Avge	SR	ER
R. J. Harris (A)	RF	130.5	13	607	40	5-19	3	15.17	19.62	4.63
G. P. Swann (E)	OB	123	1	523	28	4-37	2	18.67	26.35	4.25
N. L. T. C. Perera (SL)	RFM	80.4	5	416	22	5-28	2	18.90	22.00	5.15
C. J. McKay (A)	RFM	110	11	529	27	5-33	2	19.59	24.44	4.80
H. S. Baidwan (Can)	RM	74	8	317	16	3-24	0	19.81	27.75	4.28
Hamid Hassan (Afg)	RFM	78.2	7	320	16	4-26	1	20.00	29.37	4.08
S. L. Malinga (SL)	RF	87	2	369	18	5-34	1	20.50	29.00	4.24
K. J. O'Brien (Ire)	RM	126.4	11	542	25	3-18	0	21.68	30.40	4.27
D. T. Johnston (Ire)	RM	123.5	15	436	20	2-18	0	21.80	37.15	3.52
D. J. Bravo (WI)	RFM	71.2	3	339	15	4-21	1	22.60	28.53	4.75
M. Morkel (SA)	RF	84.1	4	434	19	4-21	2	22.84	26.57	5.15
M. B. S. Jonkman (NL)	RFM	74.4	8	367	16	3-24	0	22.93	28.00	4.91
S. R. Watson (A)	RFM	102.2	4	512	22	4-36	1	23.27	27.90	5.00
D. E. Bollinger (A)	LFM	150	16	655	28	4-28	1	23.39	32.14	4.36
Samiullah Shenwari (Afg)	LBG	121.3	7	488	20	4-31	1	24.40	36.45	4.01
S. C. J. Broad (E)	RFM	143	6	746	30	4-44	3	24.86	28.60	5.21

	Style	O	M	R	W	BB	4W/i	Avge	SR	ER
L. L. Tsotsobe (SA)	LFM	91.4	7	427	17	4-27	1	25.11	32.35	4.65
N. N. Odhiambo (Ken)	RM	78.4	7	382	15	3-16	0	25.46	31.46	4.85
D. L. Vettori (NZ)	SLA	140	3	539	21	3-32	0	25.66	40.00	3.85
Shakib Al Hasan (B.)	SLA	249	8	1,196	46	4-33	3	26.00	32.47	4.80
K. D. Mills (NZ)	RFM	93.4	7	505	19	4-41	1	26.57	29.57	5.39
G. H. Dockrell (Ire.)	SLA	128.5	10	532	20	4-35	1	26.60	38.65	4.12
A. J. McKay (NZ)	LFM	98.3	5	512	19	4-62	1	26.94	31.10	5.19
K. A. Pollard (WI)	RM	96.4	4	497	18	3-27	0	27.61	32.22	5.14
M. G. Johnson (A)	LF	103.3	5	512	18	4-51	1	28.44	34.50	4.94
D. J. G. Sammy (WI)	RM	100	8	427	15	4-26	1	28.46	40.00	4.27
P. Kumar (I)	RFM	111	14	553	19	3-34	0	29.10	35.05	4.98
Umar Gul (P)	RFM	70.1	2	439	15	6-42	2	29.26	28.06	6.25

MOST DISMISSALS BY A WICKETKEEPER

Dis		M		Dis		M	
35	(33 ct, 2 st)	16	B. J. Haddin (A)	21	(8 ct, 13 st)	18	T. Taibu (Z)
31	(27 ct, 4 st)	17	K. C. Sangakkara (SL)	18	(18 ct)	14	D. Ramdin (WI)
30†	(19 ct, 11 st)	24	Mushfiqur Rahim (B)	16†	(16 ct)	9	B. B. McCullum (NZ)
23	(19 ct, 4 st)	18	M. S. Dhoni (I)	16†	(13 ct, 3 st)	11	Mohammad Shahzad (Afg)
22†	(21 ct, 1 st)	13	A. B. de Villiers (SA)	15	(12 ct, 3 st)	10	A. F. Buurman (NL)

† *Mushfiqur Rahim also played one match when not keeping wicket but held no catches; de Villiers also made one catch in three matches, McCullum three in six, and Mohammad Shahzad one in one when not keeping wicket.*

MOST CATCHES IN THE FIELD

Ct	M		Ct	M	
16	20	L. R. P. L. Taylor (NZ)	11	24	M. E. K. Hussey (A)
12	27	Shakib Al Hasan (B)	11	25	C. L. White (A)
11	14	A. J. Strauss (E)	10	14	D. J. G. Sammy (WI)
11	17	A. R. White (Ire)	10	17	P. R. Stirling (Ire)
11	22	R. T. Ponting (A)			

TWENTY20 INTERNATIONAL AVERAGES IN CALENDAR YEAR 2010

BATTING (150 runs, average 20.00)

	M	I	NO	R	HS	100s	50s	Avge	SR	4	6
S. O. Tikolo (Ken)	4	4	3	152	56*	0	2	152.00	142.05	20	3
K. P. Pietersen (E)	8	8	3	353	73*	0	3	70.60	134.22	31	10
†M. E. K. Hussey (A)	9	8	4	231	60*	0	1	57.75	169.85	21	9
†S. K. Raina (I)	7	7	1	319	101	1	2	53.16	151.18	31	11
†E. J. G. Morgan (E)	11	11	5	315	67*	0	2	52.50	132.91	32	8
†J-P. Duminy (SA)	11	10	4	276	96*	0	1	46.00	130.80	21	12
D. P. M. D. Jayawardene (SL)	9	9	1	343	100	1	2	42.87	156.62	36	12
B. B. McCullum (NZ)	10	10	3	287	116*	1	1	41.00	141.37	33	11
C. J. Chibhabha (Z)	4	4	0	158	59	0	2	39.50	131.66	18	5
†Salman Butt (P)	8	8	1	267	73	0	2	38.14	125.94	33	4
J. H. Kallis (SA)	6	6	0	224	73	0	2	37.33	116.66	7	11
C. L. White (A)	15	14	5	306	85*	0	2	34.00	141.01	18	19
Umar Akmal (P)	18	17	2	441	64	0	3	29.40	123.18	28	17
D. J. Hussey (A)	15	14	2	350	59	0	2	29.16	125.89	23	13
Kamran Akmal (P)	11	11	0	317	73	0	3	28.81	132.08	34	10
†G. C. Smith (SA)	11	11	0	316	58	0	1	28.72	125.39	38	7
Noor Ali Zadran (Afg)	7	7	0	199	50	0	1	28.42	91.70	15	1
C. Kieswetter (E)	9	9	0	244	63	0	1	27.11	117.87	23	12

	M	I	NO	R	HS	100s	50s	Avge	SR	4	6
†K. C. Sangakkara (SL)	9	9	1	205	68	0	1	25.62	101.99	16	6
†D. A. Warner (A)	15	15	0	373	72	0	2	24.86	156.72	36	22
S. R. Watson (A)	13	13	0	293	81	0	3	24.41	152.60	20	19
A. B. de Villiers (SA)	9	9	1	194	53	0	1	24.25	111.49	5	9
M. J. Clarke (A)	15	13	0	272	67	0	1	22.66	103.81	20	4
S. B. Styris (NZ)	9	8	0	178	45	0	0	22.25	129.92	16	7
M. J. Guptill (NZ)	11	10	1	200	54	0	1	22.22	111.11	18	8
Mohammad Shahzad (Afg)	8	8	1	154	65*	0	1	22.00	102.66	11	2
H. Masakadza (Z)	7	7	0	153	72	0	1	21.85	93.29	13	3
†W. T. S. Porterfield (Ire)	8	8	1	152	46	0	0	21.71	122.58	22	2
T. M. Dilshan (SL)	9	9	2	151	41	0	0	21.57	94.37	19	1
L. R. P. L. Taylor (NZ)	13	11	2	191	44	0	0	21.22	106.70	9	8
†C. H. Gayle (WI)	8	8	0	163	98	0	1	20.37	134.71	13	10
B. J. Haddin (A)	13	12	1	224	47	0	0	20.36	119.78	20	7

BOWLING (10 wickets)

	Style	O	M	R	W	BB	4W/i	Avge	SR	ER
S. B. Styris (NZ)	RM	17	0	80	10	3-5	0	8.00	10.20	4.70
A. C. Botha (Ire)	RM	24	0	142	13	3-14	0	10.92	11.07	5.91
G. H. Dockrell (Ire)	SLA	24.3	0	132	12	4-20	1	11.00	12.25	5.38
C. K. Langeveldt (SA)	RFM	19	0	135	12	4-19	1	11.25	9.50	7.10
G. P. Swann (E)	OB	37	1	217	19	3-14	0	11.42	11.68	5.86
Hamid Hassan (Afg)	RFM	29.1	0	170	14	3-21	0	12.14	12.50	5.82
D. J. G. Sammy (WI)	RM	27.3	0	175	14	5-26	1	12.50	11.78	6.36
D. T. Johnston (Ire)	RM	32	2	178	13	4-22	1	13.69	14.76	5.56
Mohammad Aamer (P)	LFM	31	1	206	14	3-23	0	14.71	13.28	6.64
S. W. Tait (A)	RF	51.4	2	324	22	3-13	0	14.72	14.09	6.27
D. P. Nannes (A)	LF	53	2	403	27	4-18	1	14.92	11.77	7.60
M. Morkel (SA)	RF	29	2	183	12	4-20	1	15.25	14.50	6.31
J. Botha (SA)	OB	32	0	200	13	3-22	0	15.38	14.76	6.25
A. Nehra (I)	LFM	20	0	156	10	3-19	0	15.60	12.00	7.80
N. L. McCullum (NZ)	OB	43	0	267	17	4-16	1	15.70	15.17	6.20
S. C. J. Broad (E)	RFM	36.5	0	237	13	2-18	0	18.23	17.00	6.43
Mohammad Nabi (Afg)	OB	28	1	208	11	3-23	0	18.90	15.27	7.42
Saeed Ajmal (P)	OB	61.1	0	419	22	4-26	1	19.04	16.68	6.85
M. G. Johnson (A)	LF	46.2	1	310	16	3-15	0	19.37	17.37	6.69
R. J. Sidebottom (E)	LFM	32.3	2	235	12	3-23	0	19.58	16.25	7.23
S. L. Malinga (SL)	RF	31.2	0	228	11	3-12	0	20.72	17.09	7.27
S. P. D. Smith (A)	LBG	42.3	1	333	16	3-20	0	20.81	15.93	7.83
Shoaib Akhtar (P)	RF	30	3	249	11	3-38	0	22.63	16.36	8.30
T. G. Southee (NZ)	RFM	31	1	259	11	5-18	1	23.54	16.90	8.35
Shahid Afridi (P)	LBG	58.5	0	398	16	4-14	1	24.87	22.06	6.76

MOST DISMISSALS BY A WICKETKEEPER

Dis		M			Dis		M	
15	(5 ct, 10 st)	11	Kamran Akmal (P)		10	(9 ct, 1 st)	6	D. Ramdin (WI)
12	(8 ct, 4 st)	13	B. J. Haddin (A)		8	(3 ct, 5 st)	8	N. J. O'Brien (Ire)

MOST CATCHES IN THE FIELD

Ct	M			Ct	M	
12	14	S. P. D. Smith (A)		9	13	N. L. McCullum (NZ)
12	15	D. A. Warner (A)		8	9	M. E. K. Hussey (A)
10	15	D. J. Hussey (A)		8	11	G. C. Smith (SA)
10	15	Umar Akmal (P)				

† *Umar Akmal also made three catches and one stumping in three matches when keeping wicket.*

INDEX OF TEST MATCHES

Five earlier 2009-10 Test series – India v Sri Lanka, New Zealand v Pakistan, Australia v West Indies, South Africa v England, and Australia v Pakistan – appeared in *Wisden 2010*.

ENGLAND v PAKISTAN, 2010

INDIA v AUSTRALIA, 2010-11

INDIA v NEW ZEALAND, 2010-11

PAKISTAN v SOUTH AFRICA, 2010-11

SRI LANKA v WEST INDIES, 2010-11

AUSTRALIA v ENGLAND, 2010-11

SOUTH AFRICA v INDIA, 2010-11

ICC WORLD TWENTY20, 2010

Tony Cozier

1. England   2. Australia   3= Pakistan and Sri Lanka

To Paul Collingwood it was "a massive achievement, right up there with last year's Ashes win". To Haroon Lorgat it was "a truly memorable event which showcased the unique culture and passion for cricket in the Caribbean".

Their euphoria following the third ICC World Twenty20 tournament was fully understandable, if generated from different perspectives. Collingwood, England's short-term, short-game captain, had just led his team to their first global trophy after 35 years of failure and frustration in nine World Cups, six editions of the Champions Trophy and two World Twenty20 tournaments.

Lorgat, the ICC's chief executive, was speaking with as much relief as elation; the event did realise one of its aims, to atone for the universally reviled 2007 World Cup, the first major ICC event staged in the region, which smothered "the unique culture and passion for cricket in the Caribbean" with its security-obsessed organisation.

England's triumph, the culmination of a campaign virtually flawless after the qualifying stage, was all the sweeter as the opponents they thoroughly outplayed in the final were their oldest rivals, Australia, who were denied the only global title still eluding them. For England, it was compensation for the 6–1 thrashing in the one-day series that had followed their recapture of Ashes the previous summer. It was appropriate that it should be at Bridgetown's Kensington Oval, long since the favoured overseas venue for England's supporters, who transformed the stands into a Caribbean Wembley with a sea of St George flags. When Collingwood, whose unassuming leadership was one of the influential factors in the success, clubbed the winning run, the delight of his team-mates who dashed on to embrace him was unconfined.

As the trophy was lifted and the champagne sprayed on the victors, somewhere in the hospitality boxes ICC and West Indies Cricket Board officials were also popping corks in celebration. Julian Hunte, the WICB president, declared that his people had "every reason to be proud... for pulling it off in such spectacular fashion".

It was in striking contrast to the shambles of the last World Cup, when the rain-reduced final on the same ground ended in disarray and darkness, and the predecessors of Lorgat and Hunte – Malcolm Speed and Ken Gordon – were roundly booed by spectators angered by the overbearing regulations that undermined the eagerly awaited event.

An intense promotional campaign, under the slogan "Bring It", clearly achieved its purpose. Spectators heeded the call – even when made by a reserved Welshman, ICC president David Morgan – to "bring your musical instruments, your songs and cheers, your flags, banners and colourful costumes". Nor, with prices slashed by more than half, did they have to fork out an average month's wage for tickets, as they did three years before.

A palpable hit: Caribbean crowds returned to cricket after the disastrous 2007 World Cup.

The Caribbean touch was most distinctive as steel bands melodiously rendered the national anthems of the teams before each match; not everyone appreciated the incessant beating of drums and blowing of horns and conch shells that followed. "It's not a fête in there, it's madness," wrote B. C. Pires in *The Nation* of Barbados after one match at Kensington Oval. "I've been in quieter sheeting-iron factories. You leave cricket feeling you've been beaten inside and out." At the Beausejour Stadium in St Lucia, reporters in the open-air press box had to seek the hush of the toilet for mobile-phone contact with their offices.

Such a cacophony did not explain the empty seats at many matches. Lorgat claimed that the ICC "recognised the need to involve all the local people", but this was hardly possible when the first of the two daily matches usually started at 9.30 a.m. Only three of the 27 games in the men's competition were played in the evening under lights (available at each venue), which would have been ideal for a few hours of all-action Twenty20 after work or school.

The reason for the early starts was to accommodate prime-time viewing in the major television markets of India and the UK. Given the vast sums paid by Sony for the rights, it brooked no argument, but it did limit local involvement. For all that, the general assessment coincided with that of Lorgat and Hunte.

Indisputably the two best teams arrived at the final. If there were none of the upsets that enliven any major sporting event, the presence of Afghanistan among the game's elite for the first time was a fairytale in itself. The canny left-arm spin of the youngest participant, 17-year-old Irishman George Dockrell, also caught the imagination – and the interest of Somerset; his combined returns against West Indies and England were 8–0–35–3. The two Associate qualifiers, Afghanistan and Ireland, departed in the first round as expected, along with Bangladesh and Zimbabwe. Of the eight Full Members that survived, England at last proved to be the best.

There were no new trick shots, such as Tillekeratne Dilshan's daring over-the-shoulder "starfish" in England a year earlier; instead, Sri Lanka's Mahela Jayawardene and India's Suresh Raina proved that conventional strokeplay can be just as effective. Both made stylish hundreds in the opening round, the first in the tournament since Chris Gayle's 117 for West Indies against South Africa at the start of the inaugural event in 2007-08.

The three grounds presented contrasting conditions testing everyone's adaptability. The National Stadium at Providence was similar to the old Bourda with its slow turn and low bounce, but Guyana's notorious equatorial weather caused the contentious use of the Duckworth/Lewis method in three of its six first-round matches, with another washed out before achieving a result. Not a ball was lost at Beausejour, where bowlers gained little from the bland pitches, or at Kensington Oval, where bouncer-shy batsmen (notably India's) were exposed on true, lively surfaces.

England mastered all conditions, even though their one defeat was at Providence and they qualified for the Super Eights without actually winning – they tied on one point with Ireland but had a better run-rate. It was a misleading preface to their subsequent unbeaten advance to the title.

Collingwood rightly complained about the calculations of Duckworth/Lewis in their opening defeat. England had amassed 191 for five from their 20 overs, but West Indies easily achieved a reduced target of 60 from six. England believed a similarly unfair formula had led to their elimination from the 2009 tournament when they lost to West Indies at The Oval, and Collingwood was fed up with it: "95% of the time when you get 191 on the board you are going to win the game," he fumed. "Unfortunately Duckworth/Lewis seems to have other ideas and brings the equation completely the other way." Frank Duckworth, the retired mathematical scientist who devised the system with statistician Tony Lewis, immediately responded with a strong defence. It was true that West Indies had eased their own path by scoring 30 without loss from the 14 balls possible before the rain-break.

The following day, Ireland restricted England to 120 for eight (their only lower score in Twenty20 internationals was 111 against South Africa at Trent Bridge in 2009), but were denied the chance of an upset when rain arrived in the fourth over of their reply. As they had been routed for 68 by West Indies in their previous match, Ireland might have found even such a modest target out of reach, but they made their exit wondering.

There were no problems for England, from Duckworth/Lewis or from anyone else, once they moved on to Barbados and St Lucia. They were not pressed by Pakistan, South Africa and New Zealand in the Super Eights, and completed seven-wicket victories in the semi-final (against Sri Lanka) and the final with overs to spare. Such dominance was matched by no side in either 2007-08 or 2009.

England's success was based primarily on constant selection. Their team changed only once, to allow Kevin Pietersen's return to London to be with his wife for the birth of their first child. It meant a settled order, batting and bowling. England were not once bowled out, and only twice did they call on more than five bowlers, and then only for a solitary over (Luke Wright's

Final flourish: man of the tournament Kevin Pietersen takes the aerial route; Brad Haddin follows the trajectory.

brought the wicket of the dangerous Cameron White in the final). Their self-confidence rose conspicuously with every match.

Coach Andy Flower's batting tactics involved an initial blitz aimed at maximising runs from the six opening powerplay overs, and bowling that had the right balance. The batting belligerence was entrusted to a completely new opening combination – left-hander Michael Lumb (son of the more staid Yorkshire batsman Richard) and wicketkeeper Craig Kieswetter – with Pietersen the enforcer at No. 3. Bothered by injury and lack of form for more than a year, Pietersen was back to his best and ended up as Man of the Tournament. The combined aggregate of these three – 607 runs in seven matches – was compiled off 467 balls and included 21 sixes and 62 fours. When they did not deliver and the innings wobbled at 66 for four against New Zealand (the match Pietersen missed), Eoin Morgan and Wright put things right with a partnership of 52; earlier, it was the same pair's 95 from 9.2 overs that had propelled the total to 191 against West Indies.

Lumb, Kieswetter and Pietersen were born, raised and learned their cricket in South Africa, and Morgan in Ireland, prompting former England captain Mike Atherton, who is now chief cricket writer at *The Times*, to echo the widely held view that "Collingwood's team would not have gone down in English folklore... People do not generally regard this England team as an 'English' team." Others noted that, until Pietersen was second out in the match against South Africa, the only men on the field not born in South Africa were the umpires, Aleem Dar of Pakistan and the London-born Steve Davis of Australia. It was a puzzling point; England's teams have long included players who were born, and developed their early cricket, in other lands.

The bowling was entrusted to the seam and swing of Stuart Broad, Tim Bresnan and Ryan Sidebottom, and the contrasting spin of the crafty Graeme Swann and the flat, left-arm darts of Michael Yardy, all indubitably English. A "slow bouncer" was one of the pace bowlers' collective innovations. The bowlers were supported by outstanding catching and ground fielding and never conceded more than New Zealand's 149 for six against England.

Australia played under a new captain, following Ricky Ponting's decision to forgo the Twenty20 game; it was clear that Michael Clarke was still feeling his way. His own returns were so meagre (92 runs off 114 balls) that he acknowledged afterwards he was "not up to scratch". Yet despite having to claw themselves out of more than one hole, his team entered the final with the only 100% record, as they had done in their last two World Cup campaigns.

Even in the absence of Brett Lee, a late withdrawal with an arm injury, their attack was heavily based on pace – Shaun Tait and left-armers Mitchell Johnson and Dirk Nannes (the Dutchman of the 2009 tournament, now playing for his native country, and the leading wicket-taker with 14). What spin there was came mainly from Steven Smith, a blond 20-year-old from Sydney whose curling leg-breaks inevitably, but unfairly, invoked comparisons with another more illustrious blond tweaker from Down Under. Smith is no Shane Warne and his batting is likely to be his stronger suit, but he still bagged 11 wickets; only Nannes had more. Australia bowled out the opposition in their first five matches, before failing to do so in the semi and final.

Unusually, Australia's top-order batting was wobbly. But time and again Mike Hussey restored the situation, after which the fast men usually did their thing. Hussey was there with Smith to pull them round from 65 for six to 141 for seven against Bangladesh and, with White, to turn 67 for five into 168 without another wicket lost against Sri Lanka. But no innings in the tournament came close to matching his intervention in the semi-final against the dangerous Pakistanis. The contest looked as good as over, with Australia 158 for seven, needing 34 off the last two overs to overhaul Pakistan's imposing 191 for six. That was reduced to 18 off the last over; after a single by Johnson, Hussey finished it with a ball to spare, clouting off-spinner Saeed Ajmal for 6646. Apart from two leg-byes and Johnson's run, Hussey made 36 of the 39 scored off those 11 deliveries, his 60 requiring just 24 balls.

Australia again found themselves in a corner in the final at eight for three and 45 for four. Another Hussey, this time David, pushed it up to 147, first with White and then with older brother Mike, but that was never enough to prevent England claiming the trophy. It was left to the Australian women to restore national pride later in the evening.

Like Australia, **Pakistan** – the 2007-08 finalists and 2009 champions – were under a new captain. Shahid Afridi was an unlikely choice emerging from the internal upheavals in the wake of their dismal tour of Australia (when he was banned for biting the ball) and they remained as erratic as ever. Their fielding was at times extraordinarily bad – Ajmal dropped three catches within the first five overs against England – but, after early losses to Australia, England and New Zealand (by one run off the last ball), they somehow scraped into the semi by beating South Africa and, but for Hussey's hurricane, would have reached their third straight final.

Pakistan missed the experience, if not the influence, of their debarred former captains Younis Khan and Mohammad Yousuf, and the cutting edge of Umar Gul, the injured yorker specialist who was one of the principal reasons for their 2009 triumph. Their runs came from the top, from left-handed opener Salman Butt and the Akmal brothers, their wickets mainly from spin. Before his pasting from Hussey, Ajmal was among the tournament's most economical bowlers; his 11 wickets were the joint second-most. Afridi's all-round form, so decisive in England a year earlier, dipped significantly – 91 runs, four wickets – and he ran himself out first ball against England.

Three days before Hussey stole a place in the final from Pakistan, and at the same Beausejour Stadium, similar last-over drama sent **Sri Lanka** through to the last four and India on their way home to the usual recriminations. With three needed off the final ball of the match, Chamara Kapugedera hoisted Ashish Nehra into the stand at point, which was to secure their date with England.

Promoted to the unaccustomed position of opener (the result of a successful experiment in the IPL), Jayawardene was the tournament's highest run-scorer with 302, but his form dipped sharply after he hit 81, 100 and 98 not out in Sri Lanka's first three matches. Dilshan, the Man of the Tournament in 2009, managed only 71 in six matches this time, while Muttiah Muralitharan struggled with a groin injury that eventually ended his involvement. Sri Lanka thus had to depend too heavily on too few players, mainly the impressive young all-rounder Angelo Mathews, and in the semi-final they were no match for a rampant England.

TEAM PERFORMANCES

Performances for teams that qualified for the second group stage. Figures include matches in the preliminary group stage.

	For				Against			
	Runs	Wickets	Avge	Runs/ over	Runs	Wickets	Avge	Runs/ over
England.......	1,063	37	28.72	8.06	774	40	19.35	7.14
Australia	1,137	44	25.84	8.36	937	59	15.88	7.28
Pakistan.......	947	42	22.54	7.89	960	42	22.85	8.04
Sri Lanka......	885	37	23.91	7.60	769	30	25.63	7.62
New Zealand...	614	29	21.17	6.97	674	34	19.82	7.14
South Africa ...	747	33	22.63	7.54	739	36	20.52	7.69
West Indies	610	35	17.42	7.19	718	31	23.16	7.72
India	755	32	23.59	8.16	807	29	27.82	8.07

Muralitharan aimed to continue until the 2011 World Cup, hosted in part by Sri Lanka, but his long-time team-mate Sanath Jayasuriya's prospects were less certain. Age – he turned 41 in June – and the distraction of a new political career seemed to take their toll. His six innings brought him just 15 runs, and in one game he came in down at No. 8.

India and **South Africa**, in the top three of both Test and one-day rankings, began among the most fancied contenders; they finished among the also-rans. Mahendra Singh Dhoni blamed his team's losses in all three Super Eight matches, after winning both first-round games (an exact repeat of their 2009 showing), on the excessive travelling and the mandatory parties in the IPL, which ended less than a week before their Caribbean campaign. India didn't even bother to have a warm-up game. South Africa's all-rounder Albie Morkel cited history as the reason for another of their failures. "One got the impression that everyone felt the pressure as we had not won a major tournament in 12 years," he said (their only global trophy was the inaugural Champions Trophy, then called the Wills International Cup, in 1998-99).

There were more basic reasons for India's demise than IPL excesses. According to the Indian media, coach Gary Kirsten complained that, at 42, he was fitter than some of the players; certainly there seemed to be a lot more of Yuvraj Singh (who made only 74 runs in five innings) than during his devastating performance in India's inaugural triumph in 2007-08. Kirsten's mood could not have improved after a widely reported altercation in a St Lucia restaurant between some of his charges and irate Indian fans following the loss to Sri Lanka; the Indian board issued show-cause notices to several players, demanding that they explain themselves.

Kirsten would probably have handled short-pitched fast bowling a bit better, too. As in 2009, India's best player of pace, Virender Sehwag, was missing through a shoulder injury; those expected to fill the breach were

Sir Viv volunteered his services

once more undermined by pace and bounce, losing to Australia and West Indies in two matches at Bridgetown. Sunil Gavaskar recommended special sessions to deal with the problem; Sir Viv Richards volunteered his services as consultant.

India had been more comfortable in St Lucia, where their first-round victory over South Africa, based on Raina's 101, strengthened their status as one of the favourites. But their critical weakness was exposed in those games in Bridgetown. There, too, the South Africans were further deflated, losing heavily to England. The last time the two teams met in Barbados, in the 2007 World Cup, England had been jeered by their thousands of travelling supporters after a humbling defeat with more than 30 overs to spare; now they revelled in the reversal. South Africa's subsequent loss to Pakistan was not surprising.

Usually credible contenders, **New Zealand** didn't get enough from their main men this time. No one managed 100 runs in their five matches, no one more than seven wickets. Since they were laden with as many as seven IPL players, there might have been something in Dhoni's theory after all. New Zealand did scrape to the two closest victories, by two wickets with one ball remaining against Sri Lanka, and by one run off the last ball against Pakistan – but Super Eight losses to South Africa and England knocked them out.

West Indies were simply not good enough, prompting Gayle to issue yet another apology to the long-suffering local public for the failure to improve on a similarly inadequate performance in the World Cup on home soil three years earlier. But realistically only cock-eyed optimists expected much more from them. West Indies entered the tournament after losing both Twenty20 matches and all four completed 50-over internationals in Australia in February, followed by another Twenty20 loss and an unconvincing one-day series win at home to Zimbabwe. They conceded two of the five highest totals (England's 191 and Sri Lanka's 195), were aided by Duckworth/Lewis in beating England, and had only one individual innings over 30, Gayle's 98 off 66 balls against India. However, they were quick to use Kensington Oval to their advantage in the same game.

Disappointment at the hosts' capitulation to Australia before a packed Beausejour Stadium in their last match was compounded by the first-ball dismissal of St Lucia's sole representative, Darren Sammy, who had shone with a fine all-round performance in the opening match against Ireland.

Bangladesh could not survive a tough first-round group, losing to Pakistan and Australia, whose early exit in 2009 meant they were unseeded. **Zimbabwe** had three former captains – Heath Streak, David Houghton and Alistair Campbell – back in management roles following their return from self-imposed exile, and victories over Australia and Pakistan in warm-up matches seemed to indicate the value of the preceding limited-overs series against West Indies in the Caribbean. But their collapse to 84 all out against New Zealand was more the cause of their immediate elimination than the Duckworth/Lewis method that ultimately determined the outcome of both their matches.

Ireland failed to repeat their shocks in making it through to the Super Eight rounds in the 2007 World Cup and the 2009 World Twenty20. Their hopes unravelled in their first match when they were skittled for 68, the tournament's lowest total. That they had earlier contained West Indies to 138 for nine – and England to 120 for eight four days later – was little consolation.

It was **Afghanistan**'s inaugural appearance on the world stage. Their enthusiasm and potential were as obvious as their inexperience and their need for more exposure against stronger teams in a variety of conditions. They were rattled by South Africa's bounce at Bridgetown but, as they moved from 32 for eight to 80 all out, Mirwais Ashraf struck one of the longest sixes of the tournament, off Albie Morkel, on to the roof of the Sobers Pavilion. Fast bowler Hamid Hassan's full-length accuracy made him the meanest of all the bowlers on view, his four wickets from seven overs taken at an average of 7.25 and an economy-rate of 4.14.

At the end – after only 17 days, against the seven protracted weeks of the 2007 World Cup – the BBC cricket correspondent Jonathan Agnew's view was that the event "brought a smile back to West Indies cricket". While the ICC and the WICB congratulated themselves on getting it right this time, there were no happy West Indian faces to be found following another let-down by their men's team, a failure accentuated by the advance of their fast-improving women in reaching their semi-final.

The smiles were, at last, all English.

ICC WORLD TWENTY20 STATISTICS

Leading run-scorers

	M	I	NO	R	HS	50s	Avge	SR	4	6
D. P. M. D. Jayawardene (SL).......	6	6	1	302	100	2	60.40	159.78	29	11
K. P. Pietersen (E)................	6	6	2	248	73*	2	62.00	137.77	24	7
†Salman Butt (P).................	6	6	1	223	73	2	44.60	131.17	26	4
C. Kieswetter (E).................	7	7	0	222	63	1	31.71	116.84	20	11
†S. K. Raina (I)...................	5	5	0	219	101	1	43.80	146.00	22	8
†M. E. K. Hussey (A)...............	7	6	4	188	60*	1	94.00	175.70	14	9
†E. J. G. Morgan (E)...............	7	7	2	183	55	1	36.60	128.87	16	5
C. L. White (A)...................	7	7	3	180	85*	1	45.00	146.34	10	12
Kamran Akmal (P).................	6	6	0	180	73	2	30.00	120.80	19	6
D. J. Hussey (A).................	7	7	1	179	59	2	29.83	130.65	8	10
J. H. Kallis (SA).................	5	5	0	171	73	1	34.20	116.32	6	8
S. R. Watson (A).................	7	7	0	163	81	2	23.28	146.84	10	11
Umar Akmal (P).................	6	5	1	155	56*	2	38.75	143.51	6	10
A. B. de Villiers (SA).............	5	5	1	153	53	1	38.25	122.40	4	8
†D. A. Warner (A).................	7	7	0	150	72	1	21.42	148.51	13	10

Best strike-rates – most runs scored per 100 balls

	SR	Runs		SR	Runs
M. E. K. Hussey (A)........	175.70	188	D. A. Warner (A)	148.51	150
J. A. Morkel (SA)........	160.78	82	S. R. Watson (A)	146.84	163
D. P. M. D. Jayawardene (SL) .	159.78	302	C. L. White (A)............	146.34	180
C. H. Gayle (WI)	157.14	132	S. K. Raina (I).............	146.00	219
R. G. Sharma (I)..........	155.55	84	Umar Akmal (P)............	143.51	155
M. S. Dhoni (I)..........	149.12	85	M. J. Lumb (E).............	141.23	137

Minimum 75 runs.

Leading wicket-takers

	Style	O	M	R	W	BB	4W/i	Avge	SR	ER
D. P. Nannes (A)...........	LF	26	1	183	14	4-18	1	13.07	11.14	7.03
C. K. Langeveldt (SA)	RFM	16	0	104	11	4-19	1	9.45	8.72	6.50
S. P. D. Smith (A)..........	LBG	23	1	163	11	3-20	0	14.81	12.54	7.08
Saeed Ajmal (P)	OB	22.2	0	169	11	4-26	1	15.36	12.18	7.56
G. P. Swann (E)	OB	22	0	144	10	3-24	0	14.40	13.20	6.54
M. G. Johnson (A)	LF	22.2	0	145	10	3-15	0	14.50	13.40	6.49
A. Nehra (I)................	LFM	20	0	156	10	3-19	0	15.60	12.00	7.80
R. J. Sidebottom (E)..........	LFM	21.3	0	160	10	3-23	0	16.00	12.90	7.44
S. W. Tait (A)..............	RF	23.4	2	131	9	3-20	0	14.55	15.77	5.53
M. Morkel (SA).............	RF	15	0	119	8	4-20	1	14.87	11.25	7.93
S. C. J. Broad (E)	RFM	20.5	0	140	8	2-21	0	17.50	15.62	6.72
Mohammad Aamer (P)........	LFM	23	1	152	8	3-23	0	19.00	17.25	6.60

Most economical bowlers – runs per over

	ER	Overs		ER	Overs
N. O. Miller (WI)	5.25	12	J. H. Kallis (SA)	6.40	15
D. J. G. Sammy (WI)	5.26	13.4	K. A. J. Roach (WI)	6.41	12
S. W. Tait (A).............	5.53	23.4	M. G. Johnson (A)	6.49	22.2
D. L. Vettori (NZ)...........	5.68	19.1	C. K. Langeveldt (SA)	6.50	16
Harbhajan Singh (I)..........	6.15	20	S. J. Benn (WI)	6.50	12

Minimum 10 overs.

Leading wicketkeepers

	Dis	M		Dis	M
Kamran Akmal (P)	9 (3 ct, 6 st)	6	B. J. Haddin (A)	5 (3 ct, 2 st)	5
M. S. Dhoni (I)	7 (6 ct, 1 st)	5	C. Kieswetter (E)	5 (4 ct, 1 st)	7
M. V. Boucher (SA)	5 (all ct)	3	D. Ramdin (WI)	5 (all ct)	7

Leading fielders – most catches

	Ct	M
M. E. K. Hussey (A)	8	7
D. A. Warner (A)	8	7
Umar Akmal (P)	7	6

NATIONAL SQUADS

* Captain. ‡ Did not play in ICC World Twenty20.

Afghanistan **Nawroz Mangal, Asghar Stanikzai, Dawlat Ahmadzai, Hamid Hassan, Karim Sadiq, Mirwais Ashraf, Mohammad Nabi, Mohammad Shahzad, ‡Nasratullah, Noor Ali, Raees Ahmadzai, Samiullah Shenwari, ‡Shabir Noori, ‡Shafiqullah, Shapoor Zadran. *Coach:* Kabir Khan.

Australia **M. J. Clarke, ‡D. T. Christian, B. J. Haddin, R. J. Harris, ‡N. M. Hauritz, D. J. Hussey, M. E. K. Hussey, M. G. Johnson, D. P. Nannes, ‡T. D. Paine, S. P. D. Smith, S. W. Tait, D. A. Warner, S. R. Watson, C. L. White. *Coach:* T. J. Nielsen.
  B. Lee was originally selected, but injured his arm and was replaced by Harris.

Bangladesh **Shakib Al Hasan, Abdur Razzak, Aftab Ahmed, Imrul Kayes, Jahurul Islam, Mahmudullah, Mashrafe bin Mortaza, Mohammad Ashraful, Mushfiqur Rahim, Naeem Islam, ‡Rubel Hossain, Shafiul Islam, Suhrawadi Shuvo, ‡Syed Rasel, Tamim Iqbal. *Coach:* J. D. Siddons.

England **P. D. Collingwood, ‡J. M. Anderson, R. S. Bopara, T. T. Bresnan, S. C. J. Broad, C. Kieswetter, M. J. Lumb, E. J. G. Morgan, K. P. Pietersen, ‡A. Shahzad, R. J. Sidebottom, G. P. Swann, ‡J. C. Tredwell, L. J. Wright, M. H. Yardy. *Coach:* A. Flower.

India **M. S. Dhoni, P. P. Chawla, G. Gambhir, Harbhajan Singh, R. A. Jadeja, K. D. Karthik, P. Kumar, A. Nehra, Y. K. Pathan, S. K. Raina, R. G. Sharma, M. Vijay, R. Vinay Kumar, Yuvraj Singh, Zaheer Khan. *Coach:* G. Kirsten.
  V. Sehwag was originally selected, but withdrew with a shoulder injury and was replaced by Vijay. Kumar injured his side after two matches and was replaced by ‡U. T. Yadav.

Ireland **W. T. S. Porterfield, A. C. Botha, ‡P. Connell, A. R. Cusack, G. H. Dockrell, D. T. Johnston, ‡N. G. Jones, ‡G. E. Kidd, J. F. Mooney, K. J. O'Brien, N. J. O'Brien, W. B. Rankin, P. R. Stirling, ‡A. R. White, G. C. Wilson. *Coach:* P. V. Simmons.

New Zealand **D. L. Vettori, S. E. Bond, I. G. Butler, M. J. Guptill, G. J. Hopkins, B. B. McCullum, N. L. McCullum, K. D. Mills, ‡R. J. Nicol, J. D. P. Oram, A. J. Redmond, J. D. Ryder, T. G. Southee, S. B. Styris, L. R. P. L. Taylor. *Coach:* M. J. Greatbatch.

Pakistan **Shahid Afridi, Abdul Razzaq, Abdur Rehman, Fawad Alam, ‡Hammad Azam, Kamran Akmal, Khalid Latif, Misbah-ul-Haq, Mohammad Aamer, Mohammad Asif, Mohammad Hafeez, Mohammad Sami, Saeed Ajmal, Salman Butt, Umar Akmal. *Coach:* Waqar Younis.
  Umar Gul and Yasir Arafat were originally selected, but injured their shoulder and calf respectively during the pre-tournament training camp in Lahore, and were replaced by Abdur Rehman and Mohammad Sami.

South Africa **G. C. Smith, L. E. Bosman, J. Botha, M. V. Boucher, A. B. de Villiers, J-P. Duminy, H. H. Gibbs, J. H. Kallis, R. K. Kleinveldt, C. K. Langeveldt, J. A. Morkel, M. Morkel, D. W. Steyn, ‡J. Theron, R. E. van der Merwe. *Coach:* C. J. P. G. van Zyl.

Sri Lanka **K. C. Sangakkara, L. D. Chandimal, T. M. Dilshan, C. U. Jayasinghe, S. T. Jayasuriya, D. P. M. D. Jayawardene, C. K. Kapugedera, K. M. D. N. Kulasekara, S. L. Malinga, A. D. Mathews, B. A. W. Mendis, M. Muralitharan, N. L. T. C. Perera, S. Randiv, U. W. M. B. C. A. Welagedara. *Coach:* T. H. Bayliss.
  Muralitharan suffered a groin injury during the tournament and was replaced by M. T. T. Mirando.

West Indies *C. H. Gayle, S. J. Benn, D. J. Bravo, S. Chanderpaul, N. Deonarine, A. D. S. Fletcher, W. W. Hinds, N. O. Miller, K. A. Pollard, D. Ramdin, R. Rampaul, K. A. J. Roach, D. J. G. Sammy, R. R. Sarwan, J. E. Taylor. *Coach:* O. D. Gibson.

Zimbabwe *P. Utseya, A. M. Blignaut, ‡C. J. Chibhabha, E. Chigumbura, C. K. Coventry, A. G. Cremer, C. R. Ervine, G. A. Lamb, T. Maruma, H. Masakadza, C. B. Mpofu, R. W. Price, ‡V. Sibanda, T. Taibu, B. R. M. Taylor. *Coach:* A. R. Butcher.

Match reports by Julian Guyer

GROUP A

BANGLADESH v PAKISTAN

At Gros Islet, St Lucia, May 1, 2010. Pakistan won by 21 runs. Toss: Pakistan. Twenty20 international debuts: Imrul Kayes, Suhrawadi Shuvo; Mohammad Sami.

Pakistan, shorn of several star players for disciplinary reasons after their wretched tour of Australia, and having just lost a warm-up match to Zimbabwe, nonetheless began the defence of their title in sound fashion. Victory was built around an opening stand of 142 in 16 overs between Kamran Akmal and Salman Butt. Both made 73, although surprisingly it was the more orthodox Butt who scored the quicker. It was then the third-highest partnership in all Twenty20 internationals, and just three shy of the tournament record, by West Indies openers Chris Gayle and Devon Smith against South Africa in 2007-08. A third-wicket stand of 91 between Mohammad Ashraful, less reckless than usual, and Shakib Al Hasan kept Bangladesh in the game, before the recalled Mohammad Sami, making his Twenty20 debut nine years after his first Test, took two wickets in an over to settle any lingering doubts.

Man of the Match: Salman Butt.

Pakistan		B	4	6
†Kamran Akmal *c 11 b 4*	73	55	8	1
Salman Butt *b 10*	73	46	8	2
*Shahid Afridi *c 5 b 4*	9	9	0	0
Abdul Razzaq *not out*	6	5	0	0
Misbah-ul-Haq *not out*	8	5	0	0
L-b 2, w 1	3			
6 overs: 47-0 (20 overs)	172-3			

1/142 2/156 3/158

Mohammad Hafeez, Umar Akmal, Fawad Alam, Mohammad Aamer, Mohammad Sami and Saeed Ajmal did not bat.

Mashrafe bin Mortaza 4–0–39–0; Abdur Razzak 4–0–41–0; Shafiul Islam 4–0–25–1; Naeem Islam 2–0–18–0; Shakib Al Hasan 4–0–27–2; Suhrawadi Shuvo 1–0–12–0; Mohammad Ashraful 1–0–8–0.

Bangladesh		B	4	6
Tamim Iqbal *c and b 6*	19	18	3	0
Imrul Kayes *c 5 b 9*	0	2	0	0
Mohammad Ashraful *c 1 b 9*	65	49	4	3
*Shakib Al Hasan *c 7 b 10*	47	31	3	2
Mahmudullah *c 9 b 10*	0	3	0	0
Naeem Islam *not out*	10	9	1	0
†Mushfiqur Rahim *c 11 b 10*	4	3	0	0
Mashrafe bin Mortaza *st 1 b 11*	1	3	0	0
Suhrawadi Shuvo *not out*	1	3	0	0
W 3, n-b 1	4			
6 overs: 36-2 (20 overs)	151-7			

1/1 2/31 3/122 4/123 5/140 6/145 7/150

Shafiul Islam and Abdur Razzak did not bat.

Mohammad Aamer 4–0–16–2; Mohammad Sami 4–0–29–3; Mohammad Hafeez 3–0–28–1; Abdul Razzaq 2–0–23–0; Saeed Ajmal 3–0–18–1; Shahid Afridi 4–0–37–0.

Umpires: E. A. R. de Silva and R. J. Tucker.   Third umpire: S. K. Tarapore.

AUSTRALIA v PAKISTAN

At Gros Islet, St Lucia, May 2, 2010. Australia won by 34 runs. Toss: Australia.

Australia made clear their determination to secure the one trophy that had so far eluded them with a thoroughly professional entrance into the tournament, whereas Pakistan produced a shoddy fielding display. Watson, on 11, was dropped one-handed by Misbah-ul-Haq off a chip to midwicket; he went on to make 81 before falling lbw to Saeed Ajmal. Watson and David Hussey, badly dropped by Salman Butt at long-off on 18, took Australia to a total that looked more than enough, even when Mohammad Aamer, bowling with admirable accuracy, finished the innings with a five-wicket maiden: Haddin was caught at short third man, Johnson yorked, Hussey run out attempting a bye to the keeper, as was Smith next ball; Tait missed the fifth and was bowled off his pads by the last. Kamran Akmal was out to the first legitimate ball of the reply, and Pakistan declined to their 11th successive defeat by Australia in all forms of international cricket.

Man of the Match: S. R. Watson.

Australia

		B	4	6
D. A. Warner *c 4 b 10*........	26	18	4	1
S. R. Watson *lbw b 11*	81	49	7	4
*M. J. Clarke *b 3*.............	2	3	0	0
D. J. Hussey *c 8 b 11*	53	29	2	5
M. E. K. Hussey *run out*.......	17	8	1	1
C. L. White *c 8 b 11*	9	7	0	0
†B. J. Haddin *c 10 b 9*.........	1	2	0	0
M. G. Johnson *b 9*............	0	1	0	0
S. P. D. Smith *run out*........	0	1	0	0
D. P. Nannes *not out*..........	0	1	0	0
S. W. Tait *b 9*	0	2	0	0
W 1, n-b 1..............	2			

6 overs: 55-1   (20 overs)   191

1/51 2/64 3/162 4/164 5/181 6/191 7/191 8/191 9/191

Mohammad Aamer 4–1–23–3; Mohammad Hafeez 4–0–47–1; Mohammad Sami 4–0–54–1; Shahid Afridi 4–0–33–0; Saeed Ajmal 4–0–34–3.

Pakistan

		B	4	6
†Kamran Akmal *c 9 b 10*	0	1	0	0
Salman Butt *c 4 b 11*..........	15	10	3	0
Mohammad Hafeez *c 5 b 8*.....	12	14	3	0
Umar Akmal *c 5 b 9*..........	18	14	0	1
Misbah-ul-Haq *c 3 b 10*	41	31	1	2
*Shahid Afridi *b 11*...........	33	24	3	1
Abdul Razzaq *c 1 b 10*........	1	2	0	0
Fawad Alam *c 3 b 8*	16	11	1	1
Mohammad Aamer *c 9 b 4*.....	2	3	0	0
Mohammad Sami *not out*	5	5	0	0
Saeed Ajmal *b 11*	4	6	0	0
L-b 1, w 8, n-b 1............	10			

6 overs: 49-3   (20 overs)   157

1/1 2/28 3/34 4/70 5/117 6/120 7/132 8/146 9/151

Nannes 4–0–41–3; Tait 4–0–20–3; Johnson 4–0–21–2; Watson 3–0–24–0; D. J. Hussey 2–0–12–1; Clarke 1–0–14–0; Smith 2–0–24–1.

Umpires: E. A. R. de Silva and S. K. Tarapore.   Third umpire: M. Erasmus.

AUSTRALIA v BANGLADESH

At Bridgetown, Barbados, May 5, 2010. Australia won by 27 runs. Toss: Australia. Twenty20 international debut: Jahurul Islam.

Australia collapsed to 65 for six inside 13 overs, on a pitch of far greater bounce and pace than the one in St Lucia. But, not for the first time, Mike Hussey revived them with a well-constructed 47. He found a useful ally in Steven Smith, who showed judgment beyond his 20 years, in a stand of 74 that proved the decisive partnership of the match. Any lingering thoughts that Bangladesh might cause an upset ended as they failed to cope with the pace of Tait and Nannes, collapsing to 15 for four in the fourth over. Nannes went on to four for 18, Australia's best figures in Twenty20 internationals.

Man of the Match: M. E. K. Hussey.

Australia

		B	4	6
D. A. Warner *c 3 b 4*	16	11	2	1
S. R. Watson *c 3 b 10*	4	7	0	0
*M. J. Clarke *c 8 b 2*	16	21	0	1
†B. J. Haddin *c 9 b 11*	6	9	0	0
D. J. Hussey *c 6 b 10*	9	13	0	0
C. L. White *b 4*	8	11	0	0
M. E. K. Hussey *not out*	47	29	4	1
S. P. D. Smith *run out*	27	18	1	2
R. J. Harris *not out*	2	1	0	0
B 1, l-b 1, w 4	6			

6 overs: 35-2   (20 overs) 141-7

1/16 2/21 3/37 4/52 5/57 6/65 7/139

S. W. Tait and D. P. Nannes did not bat.

Mashrafe bin Mortaza 4–0–28–2; Shafiul Islam 4–0–34–0; Shakib Al Hasan 4–0–24–2; Abdur Razzak 4–0–29–1; Mohammad Ashraful 4–0–24–1.

Bangladesh

		B	4	6
Imrul Kayes *c 5 b 10*	0	6	0	0
Mohammad Ashraful *c 10 b 11*	0	3	0	0
Aftab Ahmed *c 1 b 11*	1	3	0	0
*Shakib Al Hasan *c 7 b 8*	28	28	0	1
Mahmudullah *c 7 b 11*	2	3	0	0
†Mushfiqur Rahim *c 7 b 5*	24	25	2	1
Naeem Islam *c 8 b 5*	7	6	0	1
Jahurul Islam *c 3 b 11*	18	12	1	1
Shafiul Islam *b 8*	16	13	1	1
Mashrafe bin Mortaza *b 9*	6	5	1	0
Abdur Razzak *not out*	3	8	0	0
L-b 4, w 5	9			

6 overs: 27-4   (18.4 overs) 114

1/4 2/4 3/13 4/15 5/63 6/70 7/81 8/100 9/106

Tait 4–2–15–1; Nannes 4–0–18–4; Clarke 1–0–12–0; Harris 3.4–0–28–1; Smith 4–0–29–2; D. J. Hussey 2–0–8–2.

Umpires: Aleem Dar and B. R. Doctrove.   Third umpire: R. E. Koertzen.
Group referee: R. S. Madugalle.

GROUP B

NEW ZEALAND v SRI LANKA

At Providence, Guyana, April 30, 2010. New Zealand won by two wickets. Toss: Sri Lanka. Twenty20 international debuts: L. D. Chandimal, U. W. M. B. C. A. Welagedara.

A masterclass in timing on the slowest of pitches by Jayawardene – he scored from 42 of the 51 deliveries he faced – was surpassed by New Zealand's collective determination. Only Ryder adjusted remotely as well as Jayawardene, until his side were carried home by a couple of sixes from Oram (off Mendis as he bowled too quickly), Vettori's calmness, and the toughness of Nathan McCullum: after 20 were needed off the last two overs and ten from the last, he powered the penultimate ball, from Malinga, over long-off for six. McCullum also took the new ball and a wicket with his off-spin, and added three catches in the deep, while his more-heralded brother, Brendon, made a duck.

Man of the Match: N. L. McCullum.

Sri Lanka

		B	4	6
D. P. M. D. Jayawardene *c 9 b 10*	81	51	8	2
T. M. Dilshan *b 7*	3	19	0	0
*†K. C. Sangakkara *b 5*	4	11	0	0
L. D. Chandimal *c 4 b 9*	29	23	1	1
C. K. Kapugedera *c 9 b 11*	11	10	0	1
A. D. Mathews *c 9 b 11*	3	6	0	0
S. T. Jayasuriya *not out*	0	0	0	0
L-b 3, w 1	4			

6 overs: 36-1   (20 overs) 135-6

1/35 2/44 3/103 4/124 5/135 6/135

S. L. Malinga, M. Muralitharan, B. A. W. Mendis and U. W. M. B. C. A. Welagedara did not bat.

New Zealand

		B	4	6
B. B. McCullum *c 8 b 6*	0	4	0	0
J. D. Ryder *b 9*	42	27	3	2
M. J. Guptill *b 7*	19	24	1	1
L. R. P. L. Taylor *c 6 b 9*	9	15	0	0
S. B. Styris *b 10*	17	21	1	0
*D. L. Vettori *run out*	17	15	1	0
J. D. P. Oram *b 11*	15	6	0	2
†G. J. Hopkins *run out*	1	1	0	0
N. L. McCullum *not out*	16	6	1	1
T. G. Southee *not out*	0	0	0	0
B 2, w 1	3			

6 overs: 40-1   (19.5 overs) 139-8

1/0 2/62 3/66 4/86 5/96 6/116 7/117 8/133

S. E. Bond did not bat.

N. L. McCullum 3–0–17–1; Bond 4–0–35–2; Southee 4–0–21–1; Oram 3–0–23–1; Vettori 4–0–23–0; Styris 2–0–13–1.

Mathews 2–1–7–1; Welagedara 2–0–21–1; Mendis 4–0–34–1; Malinga 3.5–0–33–0; Muralitharan 4–0–25–2; Jayasuriya 4–0–17–1.

Umpires: S. J. Davis and R. E. Koertzen.   Third umpire: B. R. Doctrove.

SRI LANKA v ZIMBABWE

At Providence, Guyana, May 3, 2010. Sri Lanka won by 14 runs (D/L method). Toss: Sri Lanka. Twenty20 international debuts: N. L. T. C. Perera, S. Randiv; C. K. Coventry, C. R. Ervine.

While the supposed power-hitters struggled, Jayawardene played more classically, starting in the first over when he stroked Mpofu back over his head for an elegant straight six. He reached the fourth century in Twenty20 internationals – the second in two days – from 63 deliveries before holing out to his 64th. Zimbabwe, who had recorded impressive wins over Australia and Pakistan in their warm-ups, stuck to their task gamely in the field, but a lengthy shower after just one over of their reply left them with a target of 104 from 11 overs. Their batsmen did not manage a single boundary in the play possible before rain set in again, ending the match just after the five-over cut-off for a result and ensuring Sri Lanka's victory. Had Taibu been given out lbw from the fifth ball of the fifth over – he was almost run out too by the bowler, Randiv – there might not have been time for a new batsman to come in and the points would have been shared.

Man of the Match: D. P. M. D. Jayawardene.

Sri Lanka

		B	4	6
D. P. M. D. Jayawardene *c 8 b 10*	100	64	10	4
T. M. Dilshan *c 11 b 5*	2	4	0	0
N. L. T. C. Perera *c 5 b 7*	23	19	1	2
*†K. C. Sangakkara *c 10 b 8*	3	7	0	0
L. D. Chandimal *c 11 b 9*	9	8	0	1
A. D. Mathews *c 4 b 7*	4	6	0	0
C. K. Kapugedera *c 1 b 10*	13	6	0	2
S. T. Jayasuriya *not out*	3	3	0	0
S. L. Malinga *not out*	2	3	0	0
L-b 5, w 9	14			

6 overs: 59-1   (20 overs) 173-7

1/24 2/80 3/96 4/113 5/138 6/166 7/166

S. Randiv and B. A. W. Mendis did not bat.

Mpofu 3–0–27–0; Price 4–0–31–2; Chigumbura 2–0–21–1; Lamb 4–0–34–2; Utseya 4–0–32–1; Cremer 3–0–23–1.

Zimbabwe

		B	4	6
H. Masakadza *run out*	4	6	0	0
†T. Taibu *not out*	12	13	0	0
B. R. M. Taylor *not out*	11	11	0	0
W 2	2			

3 overs: 15-1   (5 overs)   29-1

1/10

C. R. Ervine, E. Chigumbura, C. K. Coventry, G. A. Lamb, A. G. Cremer, *P. Utseya, R. W. Price and C. B. Mpofu did not bat.

Mendis 2–0–9–0; Malinga 1–0–6–0; Jayasuriya 1–0–8–0; Randiv 1–0–6–0.

Umpires: B. R. Doctrove and I. J. Gould.   Third umpire: S. J. Davis.

NEW ZEALAND v ZIMBABWE

At Providence, Guyana, May 4, 2010. New Zealand won by seven runs (D/L method). Toss: New Zealand. Twenty20 international debut: A. M. Blignaut.

On a desperately slow pitch offering turn for those prepared to flight the ball, Zimbabwe were bundled out of the game, and the tournament. After they breezed to 58 for one in the seventh over, Masakadza's departure sparked a collapse of five wickets for five runs; Nathan McCullum's off-spin claimed three victims in the ninth over. There was no recovery: Styris's stifling medium-pace prompted further panic, and he too filched three in an over. Ryder fell slogging, but Brendon McCullum, who became the first to score 1,000 runs in Twenty20 internationals, ensured Kiwi noses were ahead of Duckworth/Lewis when the rain arrived.

Man of the Match: N. L. McCullum.

Zimbabwe

		B	4	6
†T. Taibu *c 7 b 10*	21	14	3	0
H. Masakadza *run out*	20	20	2	0
A. M. Blignaut *b 6*	8	8	1	0
E. Chigumbura *c 3 b 9*	3	4	0	0
C. R. Ervine *st 8 b 9*	1	5	0	0
C. K. Coventry *c and b 9*	0	2	0	0
G. A. Lamb *not out*	14	21	0	0
T. Maruma *c 3 b 5*	4	11	0	0
A. G. Cremer *b 5*	0	1	0	0
*P. Utseya *lbw b 5*	0	1	0	0
R. W. Price *b 6*	2	4	0	0
B 1, l-b 1, w 9	11			

6 overs: 54-1   (15.1 overs)   **84**

1/36 2/58 3/60 4/62 5/62 6/63 7/73 8/74 9/74

N. L. McCullum 4–0–16–3; Bond 3–0–20–0; Southee 2–0–18–1; Oram 1–0–13–0; Vettori 3.1–0–10–2; Styris 2–0–5–3.

New Zealand

		B	4	6
B. B. McCullum *not out*	22	26	2	0
J. D. Ryder *c 1 b 10*	2	11	0	0
M. J. Guptill *not out*	6	12	0	0
W 6	6			

6 overs: 26-1   (8.1 overs)   **36-1**

1/7

L. R. P. L. Taylor, S. B. Styris, *D. L. Vettori, J. D. P. Oram, †G. J. Hopkins, N. L. McCullum, T. G. Southee and S. E. Bond did not bat.

Utseya 4–1–21–1; Price 4–0–14–0; Lamb 0.1–0–1–0.

Umpires: Asad Rauf and S. J. Davis.   Third umpire: I. J. Gould.   Group referee: A. G. Hurst.

GROUP C

AFGHANISTAN v INDIA

At Gros Islet, St Lucia, May 1, 2010. India won by seven wickets. Toss: India. Twenty20 international debut: M. Vijay.

When Afghanistan collapsed to 29 for three inside six overs, it seemed the romance of their journey to the Caribbean – exemplified by the way in practice they had applauded the local steel band for playing the Afghan national anthem – was about to be outweighed by criticism of the ICC for giving them a chance to compete among cricket's elite. In that context, opener Noor Ali's 50 was, in its way, the most important innings of the tournament, as it helped vindicate Afghanistan's inclusion. Driving through the off side in the style of many a subcontinental master, he was well supported in a fourth-wicket stand of 68 by Asghar Stanikzai, who smote three sixes. Theirs, though, were the only double-figure scores of an innings which did at least last the full 20 overs. In what was to be a theme of the tournament, Nehra demonstrated the value of left-arm pace bowling with three cheap wickets. After the early loss of Gambhir, India reached their modest target with more than five overs to spare.

Man of the Match: A. Nehra.

Afghanistan

		B	4	6
Noor Ali c 5 b 11	50	48	4	0
Karim Sadiq c 5 b 11	0	4	0	0
†Mohammad Shahzad c 5 b 11...	6	5	1	0
*Nawroz Mangal c 1 b 7.......	5	11	1	0
Asghar Stanikzai c 10 b 9	30	33	0	3
Mohammad Nabi c 5 b 9	0	3	0	0
Raees Ahmadzai not out	5	5	0	0
Samiullah Shenwari run out	7	6	1	0
Hamid Hassan c 11 b 10.......	6	5	1	0
Shapoor Zadran not out	0	0	0	0
L-b 3, w 3	6			

6 overs: 29-3   (20 overs)   115-8

1/6 2/22 3/29 4/97 5/97 6/97 7/107 8/114

Dawlat Ahmadzai did not bat.

Kumar 3–0–14–2; Nehra 4–0–19–3; Zaheer Khan 3–0–24–1; Jadeja 4–1–15–1; Yuvraj Singh 1–0–4–0; Harbhajan Singh 4–0–24–0; Pathan 1–0–12–0.

India

		B	4	6
G. Gambhir c 6 b 11	4	6	0	0
M. Vijay c 10 b 9	48	46	2	3
S. K. Raina lbw b 8	18	13	1	1
Yuvraj Singh not out	23	22	0	1
*†M. S. Dhoni not out	15	6	0	2
L-b 1, w 3, n-b 4	8			

6 overs: 47-2   (14.5 overs)   116-3

1/19 2/46 3/101

Y. K. Pathan, R. A. Jadeja, Harbhajan Singh, P. Kumar, Zaheer Khan and A. Nehra did not bat.

Dawlat Ahmadzai 2–0–21–1; Shapoor Zadran 2–0–6–0; Mohammad Nabi 3–0–33–0; Samiullah Shenwari 2–0–11–1; Karim Sadiq 2–0–22–0; Hamid Hassan 3–0–8–1; Nawroz Mangal 0.5–0–14–0.

Umpires: Aleem Dar and M. Erasmus.   Third umpire: S. J. A. Taufel.

INDIA v SOUTH AFRICA

At Gros Islet, St Lucia, May 2, 2010. India won by 14 runs. Toss: South Africa. Twenty20 international debut: P. P. Chawla.

Suresh Raina became only the third player to make a Twenty20 international hundred as India made light of Graeme Smith's mischievous suggestion they might struggle to play two matches in as many days. Yet South Africa's captain might still have been smiling at the end had not Raina been reprieved on five when he was caught at mid-off from what turned out to be a no-ball from Morne Morkel. It was the definitive expensive error: Raina hurtled to his century in only 59 balls, with five sixes and nine fours. The 18th over, from pace bowler Kleinveldt, cost 25 as Raina followed three successive fours – over long-on, through extra cover and straight down the ground – by hoisting the final ball for six over long-off. He started the 20th over with 95 and off strike but, facing the third ball, completed his hundred and inflicted more misery on the brothers Morkel by striking a delivery from Albie that pitched on middle and off for six over midwicket – though he was caught on the boundary next ball. In comparison, South Africa started irrationally slowly, not reaching 50 until the ninth over. Kallis and Smith's second-wicket stand of 97 looked ponderous, and their side were never truly in the hunt.

Man of the Match: S. K. Raina.

India

		B	4	6
K. D. Karthik *c 3 b 1*	16	17	2	0
M. Vijay *c 6 b 9*	0	1	0	0
S. K. Raina *c 4 b 5*	101	60	9	5
Yuvraj Singh *c 3 b 9*	37	30	3	2
Y. K. Pathan *c 8 b 10*	11	7	0	1
*†M. S. Dhoni *not out*	16	6	1	1
Harbhajan Singh *not out*	0	0	0	0
W 4, n-b 1	5			

6 overs: 36-2   (20 overs) 186-5

1/4 2/32 3/120 4/163 5/178

R. A. Jadeja, P. P. Chawla, P. Kumar and A. Nehra did not bat.

Kleinveldt 4–0–48–2; Steyn 4–0–24–1; M. Morkel 4–0–32–0; J. A. Morkel 3–0–39–1; Kallis 4–0–30–1; van der Merwe 1–0–13–0.

South Africa

		B	4	6
J. H. Kallis *c 8 b 9*	73	54	3	3
L. E. Bosman *c 9 b 5*	8	14	0	0
*G. C. Smith *run out*	36	28	1	2
A. B. de Villiers *c 9 b 11*	31	15	1	3
J. A. Morkel *c 7 b 5*	12	7	0	1
†M. V. Boucher *not out*	4	2	0	0
J-P. Duminy *not out*	4	1	1	0
B 1, l-b 2, n-b 1	4			

6 overs: 32-1   (20 overs) 172-5

1/21 2/118 3/128 4/152 5/167

R. E. van der Merwe, R. K. Kleinveldt, D. W. Steyn and M. Morkel did not bat.

Harbhajan Singh 4–0–33–0; Kumar 1–0–3–0; Nehra 4–0–27–1; Pathan 4–0–42–2; Chawla 3–0–27–1; Jadeja 4–0–37–0.

Umpires: Aleem Dar and S. J. A. Taufel.   Third umpire: R. J. Tucker.

AFGHANISTAN v SOUTH AFRICA

At Bridgetown, Barbados, May 5, 2010 (day/night). South Africa won by 59 runs. Toss: Afghanistan.

Afghanistan bowled splendidly but their batsmen – understandably given that they had been playing the likes of Jersey only a year or two earlier – were overwhelmed by South Africa's short-pitched bowling, especially from the giant Morne Morkel. For Afghanistan Hamid Hassan, red headband and all, looked every inch the image of a fast bowler, and his mood may not have been improved by being the sixth bowler tried. He responded with three wickets, having Kallis caught behind, Boucher plumb lbw and Duminy well caught in the covers by captain Nawroz Mangal. But it was not long before Hamid was out in the middle again, as Afghanistan slumped to 32 for eight in the eighth over. A record-breaking rout, if not a comprehensive defeat, was then averted: Hamid lofted Albie Morkel's first ball over long-off for six in an innings suffused with spirited defiance.

Man of the Match: M. Morkel.

South Africa

		B	4	6
*G. C. Smith *c 4 b 7*	27	14	4	1
L. E. Bosman *run out*	0	1	0	0
J. H. Kallis *c 3 b 10*	34	33	0	2
A. B. de Villiers *st 3 b 4*	17	21	1	1
J-P. Duminy *c 4 b 10*	25	21	0	2
†M. V. Boucher *lbw b 10*	4	6	0	0
J. A. Morkel *c 4 b 11*	23	17	2	1
R. E. van der Merwe *not out*	2	6	0	0
D. W. Steyn *not out*	1	1	0	0
L-b 4, w 2	6			

6 overs: 49-2   (20 overs) 139-7

1/13 2/45 3/77 4/84 5/90 6/133 7/137

M. Morkel and C. K. Langeveldt did not bat.

Afghanistan

		B	4	6
Noor Ali *c 6 b 9*	0	3	0	0
Karim Sadiq *c 4 b 10*	2	8	0	0
†Mohammad Shahzad *c 6 b 9*	2	6	0	0
*Nawroz Mangal *c 3 b 10*	1	4	0	0
Asghar Stanikzai *c 9 b 11*	3	6	0	0
Raees Ahmadzai *c 6 b 10*	4	2	1	0
Mohammad Nabi *c 5 b 10*	0	5	0	0
Samiullah Shenwari *run out*	11	12	0	1
Mirwais Ashraf *b 11*	23	25	1	2
Hamid Hassan *c 3 b 11*	22	21	1	2
Shapoor Zadran *not out*	1	6	0	0
L-b 1, w 8, n-b 2	11			

6 overs: 23-6   (16 overs) 80

1/1 2/5 3/7 4/8 5/12 6/14 7/25 8/32 9/65

Shapoor Zadran 3–0–29–1; Mirwais Ashraf 2–0–18–0; Mohammad Nabi 4–0–33–1; Samiullah Shenwari 4–0–14–0; Nawroz Mangal 3–0–20–1; Hamid Hassan 4–0–21–3.

Steyn 3–0–6–2; Langeveldt 4–0–12–3; M. Morkel 3–0–20–4; van der Merwe 4–0–21–0; J. A. Morkel 2–0–20–0.

Umpires: I. J. Gould and S. J. A. Taufel.   Third umpire: B. R. Doctrove.
Group referee: R. S. Madugalle.

Emmanuel Durand, AFP/Getty Images

The one that didn't get away: Afghanistan's Hamid Hassan has Mark Boucher lbw.

GROUP D

WEST INDIES v IRELAND

At Providence, Guyana, April 30, 2010 (day/night). West Indies won by 70 runs. Toss: West Indies.

An impassioned all-round performance from Darren Sammy saved the hosts from embarrassment. West Indies had taken several wrong options against the precocious left-arm spin of 17-year-old George Dockrell, trying to hit him straight on the very slow pitch and not sweeping him. But Sammy counter-attacked from 93 for six by going after Ireland's opening bowlers, the only two who put much pace on the ball. He followed up with three wickets and four catches: the first was an inspiring one – very low and fast to his right – when Bravo (captaining in place of Gayle, who had a buttock strain) posted a second slip for the second ball of Ireland's innings after Porterfield had edged the first through there for four. The Irish batsmen found the pace of Roach and Rampaul too much under lights, and Sammy mopped up.

Man of the Match: D. J. G. Sammy.

West Indies

		B	4	6
A. D. S. Fletcher *c 6 b 11*	19	22	1	0
S. Chanderpaul *c 5 b 10*	14	12	2	0
*D. J. Bravo *c and b 4*	18	10	0	2
R. R. Sarwan *c 5 b 11*	24	26	1	0
N. Deonarine *c 3 b 11*	10	16	0	0
†D. Ramdin *c 3 b 10*	1	2	0	0
D. J. G. Sammy *c 1 b 9*	30	17	2	2
K. A. Pollard *c and b 9*	8	6	1	0
N. O. Miller *not out*	2	2	0	0
R. Rampaul *c 9 b 4*	8	8	0	0
L-b 2, w 1, n-b 1	4			

6 overs: 43-2   (20 overs)   138-9

1/19 2/43 3/77 4/77 5/83 6/93 7/125 8/127 9/138

K. A. J. Roach did not bat.

Rankin 4–0–35–2; Johnston 4–0–36–0; K. J. O'Brien 1–0–8–0; Cusack 3–0–19–2; Stirling 2–0–15–0; Dockrell 4–0–16–3; Botha 2–0–7–2.

Ireland

		B	4	6
*W. T. S. Porterfield *c 7 b 11*	4	2	1	0
P. R. Stirling *c 7 b 10*	0	4	0	0
†N. J. O'Brien *c 6 b 10*	6	5	1	0
A. R. Cusack *c 7 b 10*	2	4	0	0
G. C. Wilson *c 7 b 3*	17	34	0	0
K. J. O'Brien *c 1 b 7*	9	16	1	0
D. T. Johnston *b 3*	5	10	0	0
J. F. Mooney *lbw b 9*	1	3	0	0
A. C. Botha *not out*	4	11	0	0
W. B. Rankin *c 6 b 7*	1	5	0	0
G. H. Dockrell *c 6 b 7*	0	6	0	0
L-b 8, w 11	19			

6 overs: 31-4   (16.4 overs)   68

1/4 2/7 3/11 4/16 5/39 6/55 7/56 8/61 9/64

Roach 4–0–12–1; Rampaul 3–0–17–3; Bravo 2–0–5–2; Miller 4–0–18–1; Sammy 3.4–0–8–3.

Umpires: Asad Rauf and B. F. Bowden.   Third umpire: A. L. Hill.

WEST INDIES v ENGLAND

At Providence, Guyana, May 3, 2010. West Indies won by eight wickets (D/L method). Toss: West Indies. Twenty20 international debuts: C. Kieswetter, M. J. Lumb.

For the second time in less than a year England seemed to get the rough end of the Duckworth/Lewis calculations and lost to West Indies in the World Twenty20. Their consolation was that, unlike at The Oval the previous June, this defeat did not eliminate them. England's new-look side had run up an impressive 191 for five on the sluggish Providence pitch, with Lumb and Kieswetter starting brightly before Morgan and Wright swung to good effect at the end. Morgan picked Bravo up into the wind, high over the longer square-leg boundary, for one of 11 sixes in the innings to go with just ten fours. England looked to be in charge… but the rain that had truncated Sri Lanka v Zimbabwe earlier in the day returned. West Indies had sprinted to 30 without loss from 2.2 overs before the heavens opened, and there was just time afterwards for six overs: the target was reduced to 60, or a further 30 from 22 balls. Although Pollard fell to his first delivery, stumped off a wide, Fletcher's four as Broad strayed down leg in the final over all but settled it.

Man of the Match: D. J. G. Sammy.

England

		B	4	6
M. J. Lumb *b 1*	28	18	4	0
†C. Kieswetter *lbw b 9*	26	14	1	3
K. P. Pietersen *c 5 b 8*	24	20	1	1
*P. D. Collingwood *b 8*	6	8	0	0
E. J. G. Morgan *c 3 b 7*	55	35	3	3
L. J. Wright *not out*	45	27	1	4
T. T. Bresnan *not out*	0	0	0	0
B 1, l-b 1, w 3, n-b 2	7			

6 overs: 60-1   (20 overs)   191-5

1/36 2/66 3/81 4/88 5/183

M. H. Yardy, G. P. Swann, S. C. J. Broad and R. J. Sidebottom did not bat.

West Indies

		B	4	6
*C. H. Gayle *c 8 b 9*	25	12	2	2
S. Chanderpaul *not out*	15	13	0	1
K. A. Pollard *st 2 b 9*	0	0	0	0
†A. D. S. Fletcher *not out*	12	10	1	0
W 8	8			

2.2 overs: 30-0   (5.5 overs)   60-2

1/41 2/42

R. R. Sarwan, N. Deonarine, D. J. Bravo, D. J. G. Sammy, N. O. Miller, S. J. Benn and R. Rampaul did not bat.

Benn 3–0–23–0; Rampaul 3–0–52–0; Gayle 1–0–11–1; Miller 4–0–29–1; Sammy 4–0–22–2; Bravo 4–0–36–1; Pollard 1–0–16–0. | Sidebottom 1–0–15–0; Swann 2–0–24–2; Bresnan 1–0–7–0; Yardy 1–0–6–0; Broad 0.5–0–8–0.

Umpires: A. L. Hill and R. E. Koertzen.   Third umpire: B. F. Bowden.

ENGLAND v IRELAND

At Providence, Guyana, May 4, 2010. No result. Toss: Ireland.

Rain, which Collingwood had blamed for England's defeat the day before, now gave them safe passage into the Super Eights, without a win: they tied on one point with Ireland but had a better run-rate. After some lion-hearted bowling and fielding, the men in green would have fancied a tilt at 121, though on this most grudging of pitches their brittle batting might not have held firm. There was irony in that the one England batsman to come to terms with the conditions was born and raised in Dublin: when these teams met on the same ground in the 2007 World Cup, Eoin Morgan was playing for Ireland. Now he tempered his improvisation with caution, treating his fellow-Dubliner Dockrell with deserved respect and slowly steering his adopted side back from the abyss at 49 for four. Johnston, more than twice Dockrell's age at 36 and even cannier, conceded only 14 from his four overs and ran out Yardy with a direct hit from wide mid-on. Ireland's reply, interrupted after eight balls, began quietly but, just after the resumption, Lumb pulled off a miraculous run-and-dive catch at deep square to dismiss Stirling. The bellicose Niall O'Brien counter-attacked with successive fours, but the Guyanese rain would have none of it.

England

	B	4	6
M. J. Lumb c 10 b 6	14	11	3	0
†C. Kieswetter run out	13	17	0	0
K. P. Pietersen c 8 b 6	9	18	0	0
*P. D. Collingwood c 9 b 7	0	3	0	0
E. J. G. Morgan c 5 b 9	45	37	5	0
L. J. Wright c 1 b 10	20	24	0	1
T. T. Bresnan c 8 b 10	5	6	1	0
G. P. Swann not out	7	5	0	0
M. H. Yardy run out	0	0	0	0
S. C. J. Broad not out	0	0	0	0
L-b 4, w 2, n-b 1	7			

6 overs: 32-3   (20 overs) 120-8

1/24 2/32 3/32 4/49 5/90 6/109 7/115 8/118

R. J. Sidebottom did not bat.

Rankin 4–0–25–2; Johnston 4–0–14–1; K. J. O'Brien 3–0–22–2; Dockrell 4–0–19–0; Botha 4–0–29–1; Cusack 1–0–7–0.

Ireland

	B	4	6
*W. T. S. Porterfield not out	4	10	0	0
P. R. Stirling c 1 b 11	0	6	0	0
†N. J. O'Brien not out.	9	5	2	0
W 1	1			

1/4   (3.3 overs)   14-1

A. R. Cusack, G. C. Wilson, K. J. O'Brien, D. T. Johnston, J. F. Mooney, A. C. Botha, W. B. Rankin and G. H. Dockrell did not bat.

Bresnan 2–0–5–0; Sidebottom 1.3–0–9–1.

Umpires: B. F. Bowden and A. L. Hill.   Third umpire: Asad Rauf.   Group referee: A. G. Hurst.

FINAL GROUP TABLES

Group A	Played	Won	Lost	No result	Points	Net run-rate
AUSTRALIA	2	2	0	0	4	1.52
PAKISTAN.................	2	1	1	0	2	–0.32
Bangladesh	2	0	2	0	0	–1.20

Group B	Played	Won	Lost	No result	Points	Net run-rate
NEW ZEALAND	2	2	0	0	4	0.42
SRI LANKA	2	1	1	0	2	0.35
Zimbabwe	2	0	2	0	0	−1.59

Group C	Played	Won	Lost	No result	Points	Net run-rate
INDIA	2	2	0	0	4	1.49
SOUTH AFRICA	2	1	1	0	2	1.12
Afghanistan..................	2	0	2	0	0	−2.44

Group D	Played	Won	Lost	No result	Points	Net run-rate
WEST INDIES	2	2	0	0	4	2.78
ENGLAND	2	0	1	1	1	−0.45
Ireland	2	0	1	1	1	−3.50

GROUP E

ENGLAND v PAKISTAN

At Bridgetown, Barbados, May 6, 2010. England won by six wickets. Toss: England.

Pietersen's well-paced 73 not out saw England to their opening win of the tournament with three balls to spare. Pakistan once again handicapped themselves with a wretched fielding display that saw five catches dropped, three of them by Saeed Ajmal in the first five overs. His worst error was his first when, fielding at mid-on, he dropped Kieswetter before he had scored; after catching the ball, he apparently lost control trying to throw it up in celebration. But Ajmal's mixture of off-breaks and doosras did trouble England, and he was given the responsibility – rare for a spinner – of the final over. Pietersen, reprieved on 34 when a drive off Ajmal was tipped over the boundary for six by Fawad Alam at long-off, completed his fifty with a straight six off Shahid Afridi. Earlier, Broad and Yardy both bowled efficiently. Pakistan's day was summed up by Afridi's first-ball run-out attempting a non-existent single to Wright in the covers; his partner, Umar Akmal, did not even try to run.

Man of the Match: K. P. Pietersen.

Pakistan

		B	4	6
†Kamran Akmal *c 2 b 10*	15	18	2	1
Salman Butt *c 4 b 9*..........	34	26	3	1
Mohammad Hafeez *c 10 b 8*....	18	14	2	0
Umar Akmal *c 3 b 11*	30	25	2	1
*Shahid Afridi *run out*	0	1	0	0
Misbah-ul-Haq *b 8*	13	14	0	1
Abdul Razzaq *c 7 b 11*	10	9	0	1
Fawad Alam *c 2 b 10*	1	3	0	0
Mohammad Aamer *c 8 b 7*	3	7	0	0
Saeed Ajmal *not out*	13	5	1	1
Mohammad Asif *not out*.......	0	0	0	0
B 1, w 7, n-b 2	10			

6 overs: 44-1   (20 overs) 147-9

1/31 2/71 3/77 4/77 5/102 6/118 7/120 8/132 9/132

Sidebottom 3–0–28–2; Bresnan 4–0–36–1; Broad 4–0–25–2; Yardy 4–0–19–2; Swann 4–0–28–1; Collingwood 1–0–10–0.

England

		B	4	6
M. J. Lumb *st 1 b 10*..........	25	13	3	1
†C. Kieswetter *c 4 b 7*........	25	27	3	1
K. P. Pietersen *not out*	73	52	8	2
*P. D. Collingwood *c 4 b 5*......	16	15	1	0
E. J. G. Morgan *b 10*..........	5	7	1	0
L. J. Wright *not out*...........	1	3	0	0
L-b 3, w 3	6			

6 overs: 45-1   (19.3 overs) 151-4

1/44 2/65 3/125 4/140

T. T. Bresnan, M. H. Yardy, G. P. Swann, S. C. J. Broad and R. J. Sidebottom did not bat.

Abdul Razzaq 3–0–22–1; Mohammad Asif 4–0–43–0; Mohammad Aamer 4–0–25–0; Saeed Ajmal 3.3–0–18–2; Mohammad Hafeez 1–0–12–0; Shahid Afridi 4–0–28–1.

Umpires: B. F. Bowden and R. E. Koertzen.   Third umpire: S. J. A. Taufel.   Referee: A. G. Hurst.

Sky Sports

Sky Sports

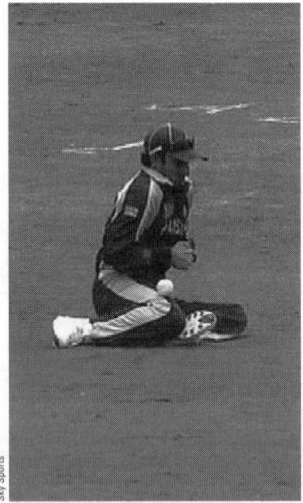

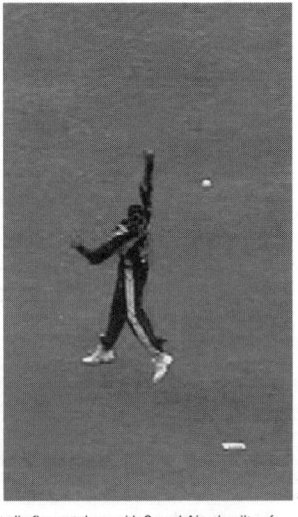

Losing their grip... Defending champions Pakistan let slip five catches, with Saeed Ajmal guilty of three drops: he reprieved Craig Kieswetter twice (*above*), on nought and two, and Michael Lumb (*below*) on 23.

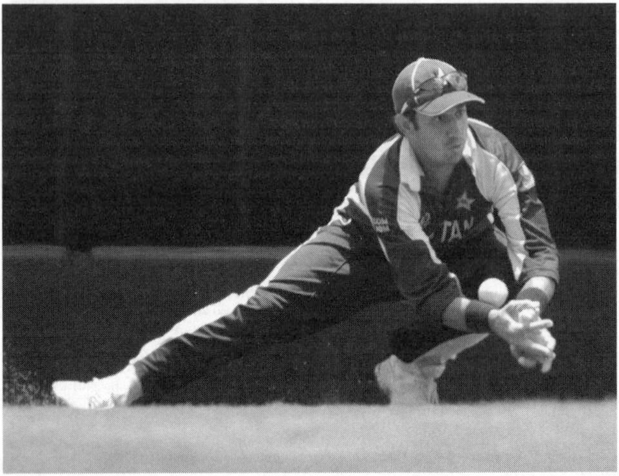

Philip Brown

NEW ZEALAND v SOUTH AFRICA

At Bridgetown, Barbados, May 6, 2010. South Africa won by 13 runs. Toss: South Africa.

Albie Morkel's rapid 40 off 18 balls helped give South Africa enough runs to play with: he proved equally adept at depositing left-arm spinner Vettori over long-off for six or striking paceman Southee for three sixes in an over. But while the sight of a hard-hitting South African was no surprise, the return of off-spinner Botha, who took two top-order wickets, suggested they were slowly weaning themselves off pace alone. However, it needed a fine catch by the diving Gibbs to get rid of the danger man Brendon McCullum in New Zealand's first over. With 27 needed off six balls, Albie Morkel came on for his only over and was promptly flicked for four by Vettori – but Morkel kept his head and the target became an impossible 22 off three balls. Nathan McCullum's six over deep cover arrived too late.

Man of the Match: J. A. Morkel.

South Africa		*B*	*4*	*6*
J. H. Kallis *c 11 b 7*	31	26	1	2
*G. C. Smith *c 3 b 11*	14	12	2	0
H. H. Gibbs *c 1 b 8*	30	24	1	2
A. B. de Villiers *not out*	47	39	1	2
J. A. Morkel *run out*	40	18	0	5
†M. V. Boucher *not out*	0	1	0	0
B 6, w 2	8			

6 overs: 48-1   (20 overs)   170-4

1/40 2/55 3/97 4/169

J-P. Duminy, J. Botha, D. W. Steyn, M. Morkel and C. K. Langeveldt did not bat.

N. L. McCullum 4–0–35–1; Bond 4–0–33–0; Southee 3–0–39–1; Oram 3–0–22–1; Vettori 4–0–21–0; Styris 2–0–14–0.

New Zealand		*B*	*4*	*6*
B. B. McCullum *c 3 b 11*	6	5	1	0
J. D. Ryder *c 4 b 8*	33	28	2	2
M. J. Guptill *c 5 b 8*	18	19	3	0
L. R. P. L. Taylor *c 3 b 10*	19	16	1	1
S. B. Styris *c 3 b 11*	13	12	2	0
†G. J. Hopkins *c 9 b 10*	18	13	0	2
J. D. P. Oram *lbw b 9*	0	2	0	0
N. L. McCullum *not out*	26	17	3	1
*D. L. Vettori *not out*	10	10	1	0
L-b 7, w 5, n-b 2	14			

6 overs: 39-1   (20 overs)   157-7

1/7 2/51 3/67 4/87 5/109 6/110 7/123

S. E. Bond and T. G. Southee did not bat.

Langeveldt 4–0–39–2; Steyn 4–0–25–1; M. Morkel 4–0–27–2; Kallis 4–0–23–0; Botha 3–0–23–2; J. A. Morkel 1–0–13–0.

Umpires: Aleem Dar and S. J. Davis.   Third umpire: B. R. Doctrove.   Referee: A. G. Hurst.

NEW ZEALAND v PAKISTAN

At Bridgetown, Barbados, May 8, 2010. New Zealand won by one run. Toss: Pakistan.

One of the tournament's few close matches left Pakistan on the brink of elimination, the only team in the group without a point. Both sides found unlikely heroes: left-armer Abdur Rehman, in his first international match for two and a half years, was one of several spinners who bowled splendidly as New Zealand were restricted to 133. Later, when Shahid Afridi fell to the recalled seamer Butler in a middle-order collapse, Pakistan were 58 for five: but some typically aggressive hitting from Abdul Razzaq, allied to sensible strokeplay from Salman Butt – transformed from bit-part player to top-order mainstay – swung the game back their way. Then Nathan McCullum persuaded Razzaq to hole out to deep midwicket and, come the final over, the target was 11. Butt swung and missed at Butler's first and third balls, but collected boundaries off the second and fourth: a neat summation of how the game's balance of power had shifted throughout. Pakistan needed two from the last delivery, with Rehman on strike. He swung at a leg-side delivery from Butler and made good contact… but the ball flew straight to Guptill at deep square.

Man of the Match: I. G. Butler.

New Zealand

		B	4	6
B. B. McCullum *c 11 b 8*	33	29	5	0
J. D. Ryder *c 8 b 11*	7	8	1	0
M. J. Guptill *c 4 b 8*	2	10	0	0
L. R. P. L. Taylor *c 1 b 11*	3	7	0	0
*D. L. Vettori *run out*	38	34	1	2
S. B. Styris *b 6*	21	17	1	1
†G. J. Hopkins *c 8 b 6*	2	7	0	0
N. L. McCullum *not out*	12	9	0	1
I. G. Butler *not out*	0	0	0	0
L-b 2, w 12, n-b 1	15			

6 overs: 41-1   (20 overs) 133-7

1/34 2/41 3/55 4/58 5/98 6/104 7/127

K. D. Mills and S. E. Bond did not bat.

Mohammad Aamer 3–0–20–0; Mohammad Sami 3–0–25–2; Abdur Rehman 3–0–19–2; Mohammad Hafeez 3–0–11–0; Shahid Afridi 4–0–29–2; Saeed Ajmal 4–0–27–0.

Pakistan

		B	4	6
†Kamran Akmal *b 10*	5	8	0	0
Salman Butt *not out*	67	54	8	1
Mohammad Hafeez *c 7 b 11*....	8	4	2	0
Umar Akmal *c 7 b 10*	0	1	0	0
Misbah-ul-Haq *lbw b 9*	3	13	0	0
*Shahid Afridi *c 8 b 9*	11	9	1	0
Abdul Razzaq *c 4 b 8*	29	29	1	3
Abdur Rehman *c 3 b 9*	2	3	0	0
B 1, l-b 1, w 4, n-b 1	7			

6 overs: 35-3   (20 overs) 132-7

1/15 2/24 3/25 4/42 5/58 6/111 7/132

Mohammad Aamer, Saeed Ajmal and Mohammad Sami did not bat.

Bond 4–0–28–1; Mills 4–0–33–2; Butler 4–1–19–3; Vettori 4–0–31–0; N. L. McCullum 4–0–19–1.

Umpires: B. R. Doctrove and I. J. Gould.   Third umpire: R. E. Koertzen.
Referee: R. S. Madugalle.

ENGLAND v SOUTH AFRICA

At Bridgetown, Barbados, May 8, 2010. England won by 39 runs. Toss: England.

Kieswetter and Pietersen, both of whom might have been playing for South Africa, took the game away from their former countrymen with a stand of 94 in a match where, with Lumb acting as England's other opener, the only man on the field at the start who was born in England was Australian umpire Steve Davis. Steyn, arguably the world's leading quick bowler, was treated with disdain in four overs that went for an extraordinary 50 runs. Pietersen struck him for a huge six over long-on, just after casually advancing down the pitch to drive him for four. Kieswetter had had a lucky escape on seven, when he edged one straight to third man, only for the mortified Morne Morkel to discover that he had overstepped the crease and struck with a no-ball, just as he had during Suresh Raina's century for India a week earlier. South Africa's reply was suffocated by spin as Swann and the unheralded Yardy shared five wickets. Yardy even outdid Swann by taking a wicket first ball (Swann had to wait until his fourth) thanks to a glorious leap by Sidebottom at short fine leg which sent back Gibbs. Sidebottom ended the match with an over to spare. Another win, another award for Pietersen – but England's talisman was now heading home for the birth of his first child.

Man of the Match: K. P. Pietersen.

England

	B	4	6
M. J. Lumb *lbw b 8*	3	4	0	0
†C. Kieswetter *c 9 b 6*	41	42	3	2
K. P. Pietersen *c 1 b 8*	53	33	8	1
*P. D. Collingwood *c 7 b 10*	14	9	0	2
E. J. G. Morgan *c 4 b 11*	21	14	3	0
L. J. Wright *b 11*	0	2	0	0
T. T. Bresnan *b 10*	13	13	1	0
M. H. Yardy *not out*	8	5	1	0
G. P. Swann *not out*	1	1	0	0
L-b 3, w 7, n-b 4	14			

6 overs: 65-1   (20 overs)   168-7

1/4 2/98 3/113 4/124 5/137 6/148 7/162

S. C. J. Broad and R. J. Sidebottom did not bat.

Botha 4–0–15–2; Steyn 4–0–50–0; M. Morkel 4–0–40–2; Langeveldt 4–0–34–2; Kallis 3–0–15–0; Duminy 1–0–11–1.

South Africa

	B	4	6
*G. C. Smith *c 1 b 9*	19	24	2	0
J. H. Kallis *c 3 b 10*	11	13	0	1
H. H. Gibbs *c 11 b 8*	8	8	1	0
A. B. de Villiers *c 4 b 9*	5	9	0	0
J. A. Morkel *b 8*	0	2	0	0
J-P. Duminy *c 8 b 11*	39	25	2	2
†M. V. Boucher *c 5 b 9*	9	11	0	0
J. Botha *c and b 11*	12	12	0	1
D. W. Steyn *c 5 b 10*	5	6	0	0
M. Morkel *b 11*	1	2	0	0
C. K. Langeveldt *not out*	2	3	0	0
B 2, l-b 9, w 6, n-b 1	18			

6 overs: 34-1   (19 overs)   129

1/19 2/34 3/44 4/46 5/53 6/90 7/111 8/125 9/126

Sidebottom 4–0–23–3; Bresnan 3–0–14–0; Broad 4–0–26–2; Yardy 4–0–31–2; Swann 4–0–24–3.

Umpires: Aleem Dar and S. J. Davis.   Third umpire: S. J. A. Taufel.   Referee: A. G. Hurst.

PAKISTAN v SOUTH AFRICA

At Gros Islet, St Lucia, May 10, 2010. Pakistan won by 11 runs. Toss: Pakistan.

Pakistan somehow found a way to win and stay alive in the tournament, having been 18 for three; South Africa departed, having snatched defeat from the jaws of victory as they succumbed to spin. If there was something stereotypical about both sides' play, it still made for an absorbing match. The Akmal brothers stopped the rot with a stand of 51 in six overs; van der Merwe bore the brunt as both Kamran and Umar slog-swept him for a couple of sixes. Umar was finally caught on the long-on boundary off the admirable Langeveldt, attempting his fifth six, after adding 61 in six overs with Shahid Afridi who contributed a brisk 30. Abdur Rehman enticed Smith to hole out to mid-on, but Pakistan, defending 148, had precious few runs to play with. De Villiers looked as if he might get his side home before an audacious scoop off Saeed Ajmal was skied to the wicketkeeper. South Africa needed a not-impossible 17 off the last over, but three singles followed before Botha was stumped – Ajmal's fourth wicket.

Man of the Match: Umar Akmal.

Pakistan

	B	4	6
†Kamran Akmal *c 1 b 9*	37	33	3	2
Salman Butt *c 2 b 10*	2	4	0	0
Khalid Latif *c 10 b 3*	7	9	1	0
Mohammad Hafeez *lbw b 11*	1	5	0	0
Umar Akmal *c 1 b 11*	51	33	2	4
*Shahid Afridi *b 11*	30	18	4	1
Abdul Razzaq *not out*	11	10	0	0
Misbah-ul-Haq *c 4 b 11*	3	7	0	0
Abdur Rehman *not out*	2	1	0	0
L-b 1, w 3	4			

6 overs: 19-3   (20 overs)   148-7

1/6 2/14 3/18 4/69 5/130 6/132 7/143

Mohammad Aamer and Saeed Ajmal did not bat.

South Africa

	B	4	6
H. H. Gibbs *c 8 b 7*	3	9	0	0
*G. C. Smith *c 6 b 9*	13	13	1	0
J. H. Kallis *c 8 b 11*	22	21	2	0
A. B. de Villiers *c 1 b 11*	53	41	1	2
J-P. Duminy *c 3 b 9*	3	5	0	0
†M. V. Boucher *lbw b 11*	12	14	1	0
J. A. Morkel *not out*	7	7	0	0
J. Botha *st 1 b 11*	19	8	4	0
R. E. van der Merwe *not out*	2	2	0	0
L-b 1, w 2	3			

6 overs: 32-2   (20 overs)   137-7

1/12 2/23 3/56 4/68 5/101 6/113 7/135

D. W. Steyn and C. K. Langeveldt did not bat.

Morkel 4–0–28–0; Steyn 4–0–26–1; Langeveldt 4–0–19–4; Kallis 4–0–28–1; Botha 2–0–13–0; van der Merwe 2–0–33–1.

Abdul Razzaq 3–0–16–1; Mohammad Aamer 4–0–33–0; Abdur Rehman 4–0–35–2; Mohammad Hafeez 1–0–5–0; Shahid Afridi 4–0–21–0; Saeed Ajmal 4–0–26–4.

Umpires: B. R. Doctrove and I. J. Gould.   Third umpire: B. F. Bowden.   Referee: A. G. Hurst.

ENGLAND v NEW ZEALAND

At Gros Islet, St Lucia, May 10, 2010. England won by three wickets. Toss: New Zealand.

England, already through to the semi-finals, enjoyed the satisfaction of winning a game that was closer than it ought to have been, and doing so without the absent Pietersen, in London for the birth of his son Dylan. As a consequence England knocked New Zealand out and ensured that Pakistan, on net run-rate, joined them in qualifying for the last four. The bowlers again did well, restricting New Zealand to 149; Brendon McCullum once more failed to make a big score after getting in. But Lumb missed a sweep at Vettori and was lbw, then Collingwood was deceived by Styris's slower ball, and England were 66 for four. Morgan, whose 40 included an extraordinary one-handed six off Styris over wide long-on, kept New Zealand at bay, but he could not finish the job: that was left to Bresnan, who had earlier been the most economical of England's bowlers and now ended the match with five balls to spare by pulling Mills for four.

Man of the Match: T. T. Bresnan.

New Zealand		B	4	6
B. B. McCullum *c 2 b 9*	33	32	4	0
J. D. Ryder *b 7*	9	11	2	0
A. J. Redmond *c 10 b 9*	16	15	0	1
L. R. P. L. Taylor *c 7 b 11* ...	44	33	0	2
S. B. Styris *c 6 b 10*	31	19	3	1
†G. J. Hopkins *b 10*	1	2	0	0
N. L. McCullum *not out*	3	5	0	0
*D. L. Vettori *not out*	4	4	0	0
L-b 5, w 2, n-b 1	8			
6 overs: 39-1 (20 overs)	149-6			

1/30 2/59 3/65 4/127 5/133 6/141

I. G. Butler, K. D. Mills and S. E. Bond did not bat.

Bresnan 4–0–20–1; Sidebottom 4–0–35–1; Broad 4–0–33–2; Swann 4–0–31–2; Yardy 4–0–25–0.

England		B	4	6
†C. Kieswetter *c 7 b 10*........	15	12	1	1
M. J. Lumb *lbw b 8*..........	32	21	4	1
R. S. Bopara *c 4 b 5*	9	10	1	0
*P. D. Collingwood *c 1 b 5*.....	3	6	0	0
E. J. G. Morgan *c 8 b 11*.......	40	34	4	1
L. J. Wright *c 10 b 11*........	24	17	3	0
T. T. Bresnan *not out*	23	11	3	0
M. H. Yardy *c 9 b 7*	0	2	0	0
G. P. Swann *not out*	1	2	0	0
L-b 5, w 1	6			
6 overs: 57-1 (19.1 overs)	153-7			

1/24 2/60 3/60 4/66 5/118 6/142 7/146

S. C. J. Broad and R. J. Sidebottom did not bat.

N. L. McCullum 4–0–37–1; Bond 4–0–29–2; Mills 3.1–0–32–1; Vettori 4–0–24–1; Styris 3–0–16–2; Butler 1–0–10–0.

Umpires: S. J. Davis and S. J. A. Taufel.   Third umpire: Aleem Dar.   Referee: R. S. Madugalle.

GROUP F

AUSTRALIA v INDIA

At Bridgetown, Barbados, May 7, 2010. Australia won by 49 runs. Toss: India.

Australia reinforced the widespread belief that India were vulnerable against fast bowling on a pitch with some bounce; their opening bowlers shared six wickets in an innings where only Sharma passed 13. India's fate was all but sealed when Nannes beat both Vijay and Gambhir for pace in his second over, then Raina top-edged Tait almost vertically – Clarke and Warner collided as they ran in to take the catch, but Clarke held on. Warner had earlier given Australia a strong start with a commanding 72, and they ought to have made 200. Both Warner and Watson, who put on 104 in 11 overs, struck the

MOST SIXES IN A TWENTY20 INTERNATIONAL INNINGS

17	South Africa	v England at Centurion	2009-10
16	**Australia**	**v India at Bridgetown**	**2010**
14	Australia	v England at Sydney	2006-07
14	**Australia**	**v Pakistan at Gros Islet, St Lucia**	**2010**
13	India	v New Zealand at Christchurch	2008-09

slow left-armer Jadeja for three successive sixes, the luckless bowler conceding six in a row split between two overs. Watson's three leg-side blows came from the last three balls of the fourth over, then Warner followed suit when Jadeja returned for the tenth.

Man of the Match: D. A. Warner.

Australia

	B	4	6
S. R. Watson *b 7* 54	32	1	6
D. A. Warner *c 6 b 5* 72	42	2	7
D. J. Hussey *c 1 b 11* 35	22	3	2
†B. J. Haddin *st 6 b 5* 8	7	0	1
C. L. White *not out* 5	6	0	0
M. E. K. Hussey *b 11* 8	10	0	0
S. P. D. Smith *not out* 1	1	0	0
W 1 1			

6 overs: 53-0   (20 overs)   184-5

1/104 2/142 3/166 4/172 5/183

*M. J. Clarke, M. G. Johnson, S. W. Tait and
D. P. Nannes did not bat.

Harbhajan Singh 4–1–15–0; Nehra 4–0–31–2;
Jadeja 2–0–38–0; Zaheer Khan 4–0–45–0;
Pathan 4–0–35–1; Yuvraj Singh 2–0–20–2.

India

	B	4	6
M. Vijay *c 5 b 11* 2	7	0	0
G. Gambhir *c 6 b 11* 9	10	2	0
S. K. Raina *c 8 b 10* 5	5	1	0
R. G. Sharma *not out* 79	46	4	6
Yuvraj Singh *b 11* 1	2	0	0
*†M. S. Dhoni *c 3 b 7* 2	8	0	0
Y. K. Pathan *c 2 b 9* 1	5	0	0
R. A. Jadeja *run out* 4	5	0	0
Harbhajan Singh *c 3 b 1* 13	11	1	1
Zaheer Khan *c 8 b 10* 9	6	0	1
A. Nehra *b 10* 0	1	0	0
L-b 1, w 9 10			

6 overs: 24-4   (17.4 overs)   135

1/10 2/12 3/17 4/23 5/37 6/42 7/50 8/97 9/133

Nannes 4–0–25–3; Tait 3.4–0–21–3; Watson
3–0–31–1; Johnson 3–0–23–1; Smith
4–0–34–1.

Umpires: B. F. Bowden and B. R. Doctrove. Third umpire: I. J. Gould.
Referee: R. S. Madugalle.

WEST INDIES v SRI LANKA

At Bridgetown, Barbados, May 7, 2010. Sri Lanka won by 57 runs. Toss: Sri Lanka.

That artistry could have a place in Twenty20 batsmanship was demonstrated by another sublime innings from Jayawardene, who unselfishly passed up the chance to become the first man to score two hundreds at this level. Concerns that he needed more support were dealt with by Sangakkara, who made 68. They put on 166, the second-highest partnership in all Twenty20 internationals, just behind the 170 of Graeme Smith and Loots Bosman opening for South Africa against England in November 2009. Sangakkara was dropped before scoring by Gayle, who appeared to see the slip chance all the way, and again on 27. Jayawardene was missed twice, on 65 and 66, off Benn; first Fletcher missed a stumping, and then, in an incident that might have embarrassed a school side, when the ball was skied behind, he exchanged blank looks with Hinds at short third man as the chance fell safe. Fletcher had been keeping wicket after Denesh Ramdin was dropped to fit in another batsman; Ramdin was recalled for the last two games. Under scoreboard pressure, West Indies lost key batsmen Chanderpaul and Gayle in the space of three balls, and it was all they could do to bat out their 20 overs.

Man of the Match: D. P. M. D. Jayawardene.

Sri Lanka

		B	4	6
D. P. M. D. Jayawardene *not out*	98	56	9	4
S. T. Jayasuriya *c 9 b 11*	6	10	1	0
*†K. C. Sangakkara *c 6 b 4*	68	49	5	3
C. K. Kapugedera *b 11*	6	4	1	0
T. M. Dilshan *not out*	4	1	1	0
B 1, l-b 1, w 11	13			

6 overs: 47-1   (20 overs) 195-3

1/7 2/173 3/191

A. D. Mathews, N. L. T. C. Perera,
M. Muralitharan, S. L. Malinga, B. A. W.
Mendis and K. M. D. N. Kulasekara did not bat.

Roach 4–0–27–2; Taylor 3–0–28–0; Bravo
3–0–36–1; Benn 4–0–41–0; Sammy
2–0–23–0; Pollard 4–0–38–0.

West Indies

		B	4	6
*C. H. Gayle *c 6 b 11*	5	4	1	0
S. Chanderpaul *c 4 b 6*	11	9	1	1
R. R. Sarwan *c and b 10*	28	33	2	0
D. J. Bravo *c 6 b 9*	23	23	3	0
†A. D. S. Fletcher *b 9*	16	18	2	0
K. A. Pollard *c 4 b 10*	9	10	1	0
D. J. G. Sammy *lbw b 9*	2	3	0	0
W. W. Hinds *lbw b 10*	5	7	1	0
J. E. Taylor *not out*	16	9	2	0
S. J. Benn *not out*	6	4	1	0
L-b 7, w 10	17			

6 overs: 41-2   (20 overs) 138-8

1/22 2/23 3/76 4/82 5/99 6/110 7/116 8/122

K. A. J. Roach did not bat.

Kulasekara 4–0–27–1; Mathews 2–0–13–1;
Mendis 4–0–24–3; Perera 2–0–13–0;
Muralitharan 4–0–26–0; Malinga 4–0–28–3.

Umpires: R. E. Koertzen and S. J. A. Taufel.   Third umpire: Aleem Dar.   Referee: A. G. Hurst.

WEST INDIES v INDIA

At Bridgetown, Barbados, May 9, 2010. West Indies won by 14 runs. Toss: India.

Gayle's leg-side hitting propelled his side to a total which proved beyond India; again, their batsmen struggled against the short stuff, of which there was a lot. Gayle was narrowly run out in the final over, when his bat bounced off the ground as he slid back for his 99th run to keep the strike, but he had done enough. Two of his seven sixes ended up on stand roofs, though he was dropped on 46 when Dhoni and Pathan collided under a skyer near square leg. India were not helped when umpire Bowden gave Sharma out caught – by the recalled Ramdin – off what the batsman claimed was his forearm (he was later fined for protesting too much). But only Raina and Dhoni made much headway against the bouncing ball, and a home victory was sealed at the start of the 19th over when Bravo lasered a throw from long-on to run Dhoni out.

Man of the Match: C. H. Gayle.

West Indies

		B	4	6
*C. H. Gayle *run out*	98	66	5	7
S. Chanderpaul *c 6 b 10*	23	29	2	0
D. J. G. Sammy *c 1 b 9*	19	10	2	1
K. A. Pollard *c 7 b 11*	17	11	0	2
D. J. Bravo *c 4 b 10*	1	2	0	0
R. R. Sarwan *c 4 b 10*	0	1	0	0
W. W. Hinds *not out*	0	0	0	0
†D. Ramdin *not out*	4	2	1	0
L-b 4, w 2, n-b 1	7			

6 overs: 31-0   (20 overs) 169-6

1/80 2/119 3/160 4/163 5/164 6/165

J. E. Taylor, S. J. Benn and K. A. J. Roach did
not bat.

India

		B	4	6
M. Vijay *c 4 b 3*	7	14	0	0
G. Gambhir *c 8 b 11*	15	14	3	0
S. K. Raina *c 3 b 1*	32	25	4	1
R. G. Sharma *c 8 b 4*	5	8	1	0
Yuvraj Singh *c 2 b 10*	12	14	1	0
*†M. S. Dhoni *run out*	29	18	2	2
Y. K. Pathan *c 7 b 9*	17	10	0	2
Harbhajan Singh *c 5 b 11*	14	10	1	1
R. A. Jadeja *not out*	5	6	0	0
A. Nehra *c 10 b 5*	0	2	0	0
Zaheer Khan *not out*	0	1	0	0
L-b 2, w 15, n-b 2	19			

6 overs: 33-2   (20 overs) 155-9

1/12 2/27 3/38 4/80 5/81 6/114 7/139 8/150
9/152

Harbhajan Singh 4–0–16–0; Zaheer Khan 4–0–36–1; Nehra 4–0–35–3; Pathan 4–0–28–0; Raina 2–0–23–0; Jadeja 2–0–27–1.

Sammy 3–0–16–1; Taylor 4–0–24–1; Roach 4–0–38–2; Bravo 4–0–28–1; Pollard 2–0–23–1; Gayle 2–0–22–1; Benn 1–0–2–1.

Umpires: B. F. Bowden and S. J. A. Taufel.   Third umpire: S. J. Davis.   Referee: J. J. Crowe.

AUSTRALIA v SRI LANKA

At Bridgetown, Barbados, May 9, 2010. Australia won by 81 runs. Toss: Australia.

Australia lost four wickets before the end of the fifth over, and another in the 11th during an impressive spell by the off-spinner Suraj Randiv, who was playing instead of the injured Muttiah Muralitharan. But White and Mike Hussey piled on 101, a sixth-wicket record in Twenty20 internationals, in the last nine overs to ensure a decent total. White collected successive sixes off Welagedara, before the pair plundered 31 – 29 of them to Hussey – off Malinga's final two overs. Sri Lanka also lost quick wickets, but there was no comeback for them against some rapid bowling from Nannes and Tait, while Johnson, no slouch himself, took two important wickets in his first over. Steven Smith's leg-spin then slowed down the later order, and Sri Lanka never looked like getting close.

Man of the Match: C. L. White.

Australia		B	4	6
S. R. Watson *b* 5	1	4	0	0
D. A. Warner *c 1 b* 8	9	12	1	0
†B. J. Haddin *c 2 b* 5	15	10	3	0
*M. J. Clarke *b* 8	14	20	0	0
D. J. Hussey *st 3 b* 8	0	1	0	0
C. L. White *not out*	85	49	6	6
M. E. K. Hussey *not out*	39	26	4	1
L-b 2, w 1, n-b 2	5			
6 overs: 33-4 (20 overs)	168-5			

1/2 2/20 3/30 4/30 5/67

S. P. D. Smith, M. G. Johnson, S. W. Tait and D. P. Nannes did not bat.

Mathews 4–0–24–2; Welagedara 4–0–40–0; Randiv 4–0–20–3; Malinga 4–0–40–0; Mendis 4–0–42–0.

Sri Lanka		B	4	6
D. P. M. D. Jayawardene *c 8 b 11*	9	6	0	1
S. T. Jayasuriya *lbw b 11*	5	14	0	0
*†K. C. Sangakkara *c 3 b 10*	2	3	0	0
T. M. Dilshan *c 6 b 9*	20	12	2	1
A. D. Mathews *c 7 b 9*	8	4	2	0
L. D. Chandimal *st 3 b 8*	19	24	1	0
C. K. Kapugedera *b 8*	12	15	1	0
S. Randiv *run out*	2	2	0	0
S. L. Malinga *c 8 b 4*	1	8	0	0
B. A. W. Mendis *b 9*	1	7	0	0
U. W. M. B. C. A. Welagedara *not out*	2	3	0	0
L-b 2, w 4	6			
6 overs: 45-3 (16.2 overs)	87			

1/16 2/18 3/26 4/48 5/49 6/73 7/83 8/83 9/84

Nannes 3–0–19–2; Tait 2–0–10–1; Watson 3–0–27–0; Johnson 3.2–0–15–3; Smith 4–1–12–2; Clarke 1–0–2–1.

Umpires: I. J. Gould and R. E. Koertzen.   Third umpire: B. R. Doctrove.   Referee: J. J. Crowe.

INDIA v SRI LANKA

At Gros Islet, St Lucia, May 11, 2010. Sri Lanka won by five wickets. Toss: India. Twenty20 international debut: R. Vinay Kumar.

Sri Lanka knocked India out before the end of the match, and then ensured they stayed in the hunt themselves by winning off the very last ball. India had been well placed for a big score – 90 for one at halfway – but Sri Lanka's bowlers, with Malinga to the fore, restricted them to 73 runs from the second ten overs. After making 163, India had to restrict their opponents to less than 144 to progress on net run-rate. A rare failure for Jayawardene followed by Jayasuriya's duck left Sri Lanka in dire straits at six for two, but Sangakkara and Mathews led the recovery with 46 apiece. When Kapugedera struck a full toss from the debutant medium-pacer Vinay Kumar for six off the penultimate ball of the 19th over, India (who lost all three of their Super Eight matches) were out. Kapugedera repeated the dose next ball, leaving 13 to win off the last over. Mathews smashed Nehra's first ball for six, but he was run out off the fifth by Nehra's direct hit. That left Kapugedera needing three off the last ball: he carved Nehra for six over cover, sparking debate about the damage the IPL was doing to the Indian national side.

Man of the Match: A. D. Mathews.

India

		B	4	6
K. D. Karthik *c and b 10*	13	12	2	0
G. Gambhir *c 4 b 10*	41	32	3	0
S. K. Raina *c 1 b 1*	63	47	7	1
*†M. S. Dhoni *not out*	23	19	0	1
Yuvraj Singh *c 1 b 11*	1	2	0	0
Y. K. Pathan *c 6 b 7*	13	9	2	0
B 1, l-b 1, w 6, n-b 1	9			

6 overs: 52-1   (20 overs)   163-5

1/30 2/96 3/144 4/147 5/163

R. G. Sharma, Harbhajan Singh, P. P. Chawla, R. Vinay Kumar and A. Nehra did not bat.

Mathews 3–0–29–0; Perera 3–0–15–1; Mirando 4–0–41–2; Malinga 4–0–25–2; Randiv 3–0–25–0; Dilshan 2–0–14–0; Jayasuriya 1–0–12–0.

Sri Lanka

		B	4	6
D. P. M. D. Jayawardene *c 6 b 11*	4	3	1	0
S. T. Jayasuriya *c 1 b 10*	0	5	0	0
T. M. Dilshan *c 5 b 6*	33	26	5	0
*†K. C. Sangakkara *b 10*	46	33	2	3
A. D. Mathews *run out*	46	37	3	2
C. K. Kapugedera *not out*	37	16	2	3
N. L. T. C. Perera *not out*	0	0	0	0
L-b 1	1			

6 overs: 41-2   (20 overs)   167-5

1/4 2/6 3/49 4/105 5/161

C. U. Jayasinghe, S. Randiv, S. L. Malinga and M. T. T. Mirando did not bat.

Nehra 4–0–44–1; Vinay Kumar 4–0–30–2; Harbhajan Singh 4–0–35–0; Pathan 3–0–23–1; Chawla 4–0–28–0; Yuvraj Singh 1–0–6–0.

Umpires: Aleem Dar and S. J. Davis.   Third umpire: I. J. Gould.   Referee: A. G. Hurst.

WEST INDIES v AUSTRALIA

At Gros Islet, St Lucia, May 11, 2010 (day/night). Australia won by six wickets. Toss: West Indies.

West Indies departed their own stage in feeble fashion as Australia eased into the semi-finals with their fifth straight win of the tournament, incidentally ensuring Sri Lanka's progress. Bowled out for 105, the hosts – and their supporters – lost heart after Gayle, who got off the mark with a first-ball boundary after a wide, was bowled by the second legal delivery from the in-form Nannes. Bravo, run out backing up, was blameless in his exit, but several others, operating on a policy of hit out or get out, never gave themselves a chance, and leg-spinner Smith helped himself to three cheap wickets. That Australia took nearly 17 overs to reach their target somehow made the agony worse. West Indies' performance was summed up when Gayle ended the game by bowling a bouncer that went for five wides.

Man of the Match: S. P. D. Smith.

West Indies

		B	4	6
*C. H. Gayle b 11		4	2	1	0
S. Chanderpaul c 5 b 9		24	18	4	0
R. R. Sarwan c 1 b 5		26	31	2	0
D. J. Bravo run out		6	9	0	0
N. Deonarine c 7 b 8		0	2	0	0
†D. Ramdin b 2		1	2	0	0
K. A. Pollard st 4 b 8		13	14	1	1
D. J. G. Sammy c and b 8		0	1	0	0
J. E. Taylor c 9 b 5		3	7	0	0
N. O. Miller not out		10	13	0	0
S. J. Benn b 2		9	16	0	1
L-b 4, w 4, n-b 1		9			

6 overs: 40-2   (19 overs) 105

1/5 2/39 3/52 4/56 5/60 6/77 7/77 8/82 9/85

Nannes 3–0–19–1; Tait 3–0–12–0; Watson 2–0–13–1; Johnson 4–0–22–2; Smith 4–0–20–3; Clarke 2–0–12–0; D. J. Hussey 1–0–3–2.

Australia

		B	4	6
D. A. Warner c 1 b 9		25	12	4	1
S. R. Watson b 11		5	7	0	0
*M. J. Clarke run out		16	24	0	0
†B. J. Haddin c 8 b 1		42	46	5	0
D. J. Hussey not out		10	9	1	0
C. L. White not out		0	0	0	0
W 11		11			

6 overs: 37-2   (16.2 overs) 109-4

1/31 2/31 3/78 4/104

M. E. K. Hussey, S. P. D. Smith, M. G. Johnson, S. W. Tait and D. P. Nannes did not bat.

Taylor 4–0–47–1; Benn 4–1–12–1; Miller 4–0–16–0; Bravo 1–0–11–0; Deonarine 2–0–15–0; Sammy 1–0–3–0; Gayle 0.2–0–5–1.

Umpires: B. F. Bowden and R. E. Koertzen.   Third umpire: S. J. Davis.   Referee: R. S. Madugalle.

FINAL SUPER EIGHT TABLES

Group E

	Played	Won	Lost	No result	Points	Net run-rate
ENGLAND	3	3	0	0	6	0.96
PAKISTAN	3	1	2	0	2	0.04
New Zealand	3	1	2	0	2	–0.37
South Africa	3	1	2	0	2	–0.61

Group F

	Played	Won	Lost	No result	Points	Net run-rate
AUSTRALIA	3	3	0	0	6	2.73
SRI LANKA	3	2	1	0	4	–0.33
West Indies	3	1	2	0	2	–1.28
India	3	0	3	0	0	–1.11

SEMI-FINALS

ENGLAND v SRI LANKA

At Gros Islet, St Lucia, May 13, 2010. England won by seven wickets. Toss: Sri Lanka.

Conventional wisdom had it that Sri Lanka, the losing finalists from 2009, would give England a stern test. But from the moment Sidebottom's impressively accurate first ball had Jayasuriya caught at second slip by Collingwood, England were in complete and – almost shockingly – total command. There was no looser either from Broad, whose first ball bounced from the flat pitch and had Jayawardene caught behind, shortly after he scored his 300th run of the tournament. When Swann had Sangakkara caught by Pietersen, running to long-off, Sri Lanka were 47 for four in the ninth over. The slow bouncers of Sidebottom and Broad puzzled their batsmen, and England encountered precious little resistance until the 18th over: Bresnan bowled three wides and Mathews kept chipping twos to leg, where England's fielders in front of square were on the boundary. After Kieswetter and Lumb knocked up 68 in eight overs, new father Pietersen celebrated his return to the squad in style, ending the match with a six and a four off Malinga, and four overs to spare. But victory, which carried England into their first final in a global tournament since the Champions Trophy of 2004, belonged to the bowlers.

Man of the Match: S. C. J. Broad.

Sri Lanka

		B	4	6
D. P. M. D. Jayawardene *c 1 b 10*	10	9	1	0
S. T. Jayasuriya *c 4 b 11*	1	4	0	0
T. M. Dilshan *c 6 b 7*	9	8	2	0
*†K. C. Sangakkara *c 3 b 9*	16	19	2	0
A. D. Mathews *run out*	58	45	3	1
C. K. Kapugedera *c 7 b 10*	16	27	2	0
N. L. T. C. Perera *not out*	7	8	0	0
C. U. Jayasinghe *not out*	2	1	0	0
L-b 1, w 7, n-b 1	9			

6 overs: 38-3   (20 overs)   **128-6**

1/7 2/20 3/26 4/47 5/93 6/126

S. Randiv, S. L. Malinga and B. A. W. Mendis
did not bat.

Bresnan 4–0–41–1; Sidebottom 4–0–24–1;
Broad 4–0–21–2; Swann 4–0–20–1; Yardy
4–0–21–0.

England

		B	4	6
†C. Kieswetter *b 10*	39	29	5	2
M. J. Lumb *b 7*	33	26	4	1
K. P. Pietersen *not out*	42	26	3	2
*P. D. Collingwood *c 4 b 7*	10	13	0	0
E. J. G. Morgan *not out*	2	2	0	0
L-b 4, w 2	6			

6 overs: 47-0   (16 overs)   **132-3**

1/68 2/80 3/113

L. J. Wright, T. T. Bresnan, M. H. Yardy, G. P.
Swann, S. C. J. Broad and R. J. Sidebottom did
not bat.

Dilshan 1–0–5–0; Mendis 4–0–19–0; Randiv
3–0–27–0; Mathews 1–0–10–0; Malinga
4–0–33–1; Jayasuriya 1–0–15–0; Perera
2–0–19–2.

Umpires: Aleem Dar and S. J. A. Taufel.   Third umpire: S. J. Davis.   Referee: A. G. Hurst.

AUSTRALIA v PAKISTAN

At Gros Islet, St Lucia, May 14, 2010. Australia won by three wickets. Toss: Australia.

Pakistan played some superb cricket, yet still suffered their 12th consecutive defeat by
Australia in all formats. It was Mike Hussey, in the best Australian tradition of refusing to
give up, who turned the contest on its head with a stunning unbeaten 60. When he came to
the crease in the 13th over, after his brother David's dismissal, his side were 105 for five,
chasing 192. But in the space of 24 balls, off which he hit six sixes and three fours, Hussey
lifted them to victory after White had steadied the innings with a well-made 43. With three
overs left Australia needed 48, but 14 came from Saeed Ajmal's over and 16 from
Mohammad Aamer's, leaving 18 to get. Shahid Afridi entrusted the final over to Ajmal,
as he had done for most of the tournament. Johnson took a single off the first ball, then

In full flow: Mike Hussey slams another six as Australia somehow overcome Pakistan in the semi-
finals.

Philip Brown

Hussey took over as Ajmal fired the ball in from over and round the wicket. Hussey pulled him for six, struck him over long-on for six more, brought the scores level with a four past point, then thumped another six for good measure, sealing victory with a ball to spare. Hussey did actually play himself in and, until the very end, his shot-making was essentially orthodox. Earlier, the Akmal brothers made fifties as Australia's previously dominating quick bowlers were put in their place, and even Pakistan's fielding was vastly improved. No wonder coach Waqar Younis said afterwards: "All you can do is just smile about it."

Man of the Match: M. E. K. Hussey.

Pakistan

		B	*4*	*6*
†Kamran Akmal *c 1 b 9*	50	34	6	2
Salman Butt *c 1 b 8*	32	30	4	0
Umar Akmal *not out*	56	35	2	4
*Shahid Afridi *c 3 b 5*	8	9	0	0
Khalid Latif *c 1 b 11*	13	6	1	1
Abdul Razzaq *run out*	12	7	0	1
Misbah-ul-Haq *run out*	0	0	0	0
B 10, l-b 1, w 9	20			

6 overs: 40-0   (20 overs) 191-6

1/82 2/89 3/114 4/145 5/189 6/191

Mohammad Hafeez, Saeed Ajmal, Abdur Rehman and Mohammad Aamer did not bat.

Nannes 4–1–32–1; Tait 4–0–25–0; Johnson 4–0–37–1; Watson 2–0–26–0; Smith 2–0–23–1; D. J. Hussey 3–0–24–1; Clarke 1–0–13–0.

Australia

		B	*4*	*6*
D. A. Warner *c 3 b 11*	0	2	0	0
S. R. Watson *c 10 b 11*	16	9	2	1
†B. J. Haddin *st 1 b 10*	25	20	2	1
*M. J. Clarke *st 1 b 4*	17	19	2	0
D. J. Hussey *c and b 10*	13	9	0	1
C. L. White *c 8 b 11*	43	31	0	5
M. E. K. Hussey *not out*	60	24	3	6
S. P. D. Smith *st 1 b 9*	5	4	1	0
M. G. Johnson *not out*	5	3	1	0
L-b 7, w 5, n-b 1	13			

6 overs: 53-2   (19.5 overs) 197-7

1/1 2/26 3/58 4/62 5/105 6/139 7/144

S. W. Tait and D. P. Nannes did not bat.

Mohammad Aamer 4–0–35–3; Abdul Razzaq 2–0–22–0; Abdur Rehman 4–0–33–2; Saeed Ajmal 3.5–0–46–1; Shahid Afridi 4–0–34–1; Mohammad Hafeez 2–0–20–0.

Umpires: B. R. Doctrove and I. J. Gould.   Third umpire: B. F. Bowden.   Referee: R. S. Madugalle.

FINAL

AUSTRALIA v ENGLAND

At Bridgetown, Barbados, May 16, 2010. England won by seven wickets. Toss: England.

England ended their 35-year wait for a global trophy in such commanding style that their supporters were entitled to ask "What took you so long?" Here they seized control right from the start and never relented. Their new-ball bowlers kept Australia down to 24 for three in the powerplay – easily their lowest of the tournament – and made judicious use of the quicker and slower bouncer. Then Swann, using the prevailing breeze, bowled a brilliant four-over spell which cost just 17 and ensured a chaseable target which England knocked off with panache.

Collingwood chose to bowl first, and had to wait only three balls for a wicket. Kieswetter had been caught off a no-ball and dropped several times in the tournament, and saw his good fortune continue with the gloves after Sidebottom lured Watson into playing outside off stump: Kieswetter failed to hold the fast-travelling nick, but the ball fell perfectly to Swann at first slip. Clarke was unable to gain momentum – his 27, his highest of the tournament, took as many balls – and he called Warner for a homicidal single: the vast improvement in England's fielding under Richard Halsall's coaching was embodied in Lumb's direct hit from cover to dismiss Warner. Haddin was given out caught down the leg side off Sidebottom and, although it was a dubious decision, Haddin did himself no favours with visible dissent (he was later fined). After 13 balls, Australia were eight for three. David Hussey and White mauled Yardy, taking 21 off his third over but Wright dismissed White in his only over of the tournament, allowing Collingwood to bask in an inspired bowling change.

The early loss of Lumb twanged English nerves, but Kieswetter and Pietersen put on 111, one short of England's all-wicket Twenty20 record. After some playing and missing at short balls, not even a problem with the sightscreen behind Nannes, which halted play, could disturb Kieswetter. The ball before the hold-up he flicked for four, and he cover-drove the next for four more. His fifty completed, there were shades of Ricky Ponting in the 2003 World Cup final in the way he struck a one-handed six over square leg off Nannes. Pietersen, meanwhile, was imperious, driving Tait over long-off for six.

Eventually both went departed in quick succession, but that paved the way for Collingwood to collect the winning runs off Watson, who was battered so much in his three overs that he might have been an English pie-chucker. Thousands of surprised and delighted England fans acclaimed Collingwood as he became their first male captain to raise a world cup, at the 18th attempt.

Man of the Match: C. Kieswetter. *Man of the Tournament:* K. P. Pietersen.

Australia

		B	4	6
S. R. Watson *c 9 b 11*	2	3	0	0
D. A. Warner *run out*	2	4	0	0
*M. J. Clarke *c 4 b 9*	27	27	2	0
†B. J. Haddin *c 2 b 11*	1	2	0	0
D. J. Hussey *run out*	59	54	2	2
C. L. White *c 10 b 6*	30	19	4	1
M. E. K. Hussey *not out*	17	10	2	0
S. P. D. Smith *not out*	1	2	0	0
B 1, l-b 2, w 4, n-b 1	8			

6 overs: 24-3   (20 overs)   147-6

1/2 2/7 3/8 4/45 5/95 6/142

M. G. Johnson, S. W. Tait and D. P. Nannes did not bat.

Sidebottom 4–0–26–2; Bresnan 4–0–35–0; Broad 4–0–27–0; Swann 4–0–17–1; Yardy 3–0–34–0; Wright 1–0–5–1.

England

		B	4	6
M. J. Lumb *c 5 b 10*	2	4	0	0
†C. Kieswetter *b 9*	63	49	7	2
K. P. Pietersen *c 2 b 8*	47	31	4	1
*P. D. Collingwood *not out*	12	5	1	1
E. J. G. Morgan *not out*	15	13	0	1
L-b 1, w 8	9			

6 overs: 41-1   (17 overs)   148-3

1/7 2/118 3/121

L. J. Wright, T. T. Bresnan, M. H. Yardy, G. P. Swann, S. C. J. Broad and R. J. Sidebottom did not bat.

Nannes 4–0–29–0; Tait 3–0–28–1; Johnson 4–0–27–1; Smith 3–0–21–1; Watson 3–0–42–0.

Umpires: Aleem Dar and B. R. Doctrove. Third umpire: B. F. Bowden. Referee: R. S. Madugalle.

ICC WORLD TWENTY20 WINNERS

2007-08	India
2009	Pakistan
2010	England

ICC WOMEN'S WORLD TWENTY20, 2010

1. Australia   2. New Zealand   3= India and West Indies

When the pundits predicted that England would win the World Twenty20 in May 2010, it was the women they had in mind. The previous year, Charlotte Edwards's team had secured the World Cup, the World Twenty20 and the Ashes in the space of five months. Despite some setbacks in the West Indies in November, on a tour intended to accustom the players to local conditions, they returned to the Caribbean as favourites – only to go out at the first stage, while England's men won an unexpected triumph.

The women's reverses could hardly have been closer. In their opening game, **England** tied with Australia after 20 overs, and in the eliminator; the game was awarded to Australia because they hit its only six. Next, England lost to West Indies by just two runs, and that ended the defence of their title. Their batsmen finally found form to crush South Africa in a dead match. "We've played some brilliant cricket over the last two years," said head coach Mark Lane, "but we've come across a bit of a stumbling block in the West Indies. The standard of women's cricket has really kicked on over the last 12 months."

With England out, an Australasian final looked likely. Australia and New Zealand reached Barbados unbeaten – indeed, New Zealand had won nine successive Twenty20s, starting with five against Australia away and at home. After losing two finals to England in 2009, **New Zealand** fancied their chances here, but a low-scoring game featuring only four boundaries apiece left them bridesmaids again. Still, their seamer Nicola Browne was Player of the Tournament, and Sara McGlashan the leading scorer with 147.

Avenging the honour of their men

It was **Australia** who lifted the trophy, avenging the honour of their men (who lost to England earlier in the day) and securing their first global title for five years by defending a seemingly inadequate 106. Ellyse Perry's pace claimed a wicket in each of her first three overs, and in her fourth, the last of the innings, she prevented Sophie Devine from scoring the boundary that might have won the game – or forced an eliminator over, as against England.

India remained one of the leading women's sides, thanks to the runs of Mithali Raj and the off-spin of Diana David, which saw them into the last four in St Lucia (as in 2009, the women's semis and final were played on the same days and grounds as the men's). The surprise success was **West Indies**, who had clearly benefited more than England from their series in November. Deandra Dottin gave them a stunning start against South Africa, reaching the first century in women's Twenty20 internationals in just 38 balls – though in their next three games she managed only one run. Their victory over England earned them a semi-final, where they came up short against New Zealand. But the remaining teams – **South Africa**, **Sri Lanka** and **Pakistan** – had yet to kick on from 2009.

Group A

At Basseterre, St Kitts, May 5, 2010. **West Indies won by 17 runs. West Indies 175-5** (20 overs) (D. J. S. Dottin 112*); ‡**South Africa 158-4** (20 overs) (S. A. Fritz 58, C-Z. Brits 43). *Twenty20 international debut: C. L. Tryon (South Africa). Player of the Match: D. J. S. Dottin. Coming in at 52-4 – after 16-year-old Chloe Tryon took a wicket with her first ball in international cricket – 18-year-old Deandra Dottin became the first woman to score a century in Twenty20 internationals. She did so in 38 balls, beating the men's record of 50 balls; her second fifty took just 13, and in all she faced 45, hitting seven fours and nine sixes, and added 118, a fifth-wicket record at this level, with Shanel Daley (ten).*

At Basseterre, May 5, 2010. **Tied. Australia won by virtue of hitting more sixes.** ‡**England 104** (17.3 overs) (S. J. Taylor 46; L. C. Sthalekar 3-29); **Australia 104** (19.4 overs). *Player of the Match: L. C. Sthalekar. Only Sarah Taylor made any headway in England's innings, while Claire Taylor, the Player of the Tournament in 2009, was run out without facing a ball. But Australia crumbled in turn to 63-7 until the tail forced a tie. The teams could not be separated on the eliminator over – both scored 6-2 – but Australia were declared winners because they had hit one six (by Jess Cameron) and England none (though England had 11 fours to Australia's eight).*

At Basseterre, May 7, 2010. **Australia won by 24 runs. Australia 155** (19.3 overs) (S. Nitschke 44, L. J. Poulton 39; S. Ismail 3-30, S. Loubser 3-22); ‡**South Africa 131-7** (20 overs) (M. du Preez 53*). *Player of the Match: S. Nitschke. Left-handed opener Shelley Nitschke hit 44 in 32 balls, with seven fours, to lead Australia to 101-2 in the 12th over before she became one of three victims for Sunette Loubser's off-spin, and her team faltered. But Nitschke returned as a slow left-armer to take two top-order wickets, and Mignon du Preez's 53 in 46 balls could not give South Africa sufficient momentum.*

At Basseterre, May 7, 2010. **West Indies won by two runs. West Indies 122-8** (20 overs) (J. B. Nero 32; L. A. Marsh 3-17); ‡**England 120-9** (20 overs) (S. J. Taylor 33, C. M. Edwards 31). *Player of the Match: A. Mohammed. Hosts West Indies secured their place in the semi-finals and knocked out reigning champions England in another nail-biting finish. Chasing 123, openers Sarah Taylor and Charlotte Edwards were well on course with 65 in nine overs. But off-spinner Anisa Mohammed removed them with successive deliveries; Dottin (who had followed her century against South Africa with a first-ball duck) also struck with successive balls in the next over, and England were suddenly 66-4. Lydia Greenway fought back with an unbeaten run-a-ball 26, but a stumping and a run-out in the final over ended England's hopes.*

At Basseterre, May 9, 2010. **England won by 56 runs.** ‡**England 141-6** (20 overs) (L. A. Marsh 33, L. S. Greenway 34*); **South Africa 85** (17 overs) (N. J. Shaw 3-17, D. N. Wyatt 4-11). *Player of the Match: D. N. Wyatt. Too late, England rediscovered their form and completed one of the biggest wins of the tournament. Greenway steered them to a defensible 141, before Nicki Shaw's medium-pace and Danielle Wyatt's off-spin wrecked South Africa's reply. Wyatt achieved the tournament's best return – 4-11 – in her only match. It was South Africa's 12th consecutive Twenty20 defeat.*

At Basseterre, May 9, 2010. **Australia won by nine runs. Australia 133-7** (20 overs) (S. F. Daley 3-31, A. Mohammed 3-17); ‡**West Indies 124-7** (20 overs) (S. R. Taylor 58*). *Player of the Match: S. R. Taylor. Like their men's team, Australia finished the group stage with a 100% record, thanks to a solid all-round performance. For West Indies, Daley and Mohammed picked up three wickets apiece and Stafanie Taylor batted through the innings for 58 in 54 balls, though Dottin suffered another first-ball duck.*

Group B

At Basseterre, St Kitts, May 6, 2010. **Sri Lanka won by one run.** ‡**Sri Lanka 108** (19.3 overs); **Pakistan 107** (20 overs) (Bismah Maroof 42). *Twenty20 international debut: Nida Dar (Pakistan). Player of the Match: Bismah Maroof. Debutant Nida Dar's two wickets triggered Sri Lanka's collapse from 66-1, but Pakistan's reply slumped to 65-6. Only Bismah Maroof stood firm, until she became one of five run-outs in the innings; the last one, off the final ball, gave Sri Lanka the narrowest possible victory. Pakistan off-spinner Javeria Khan was reported by the umpires for a suspect action, and in July the ICC suspended her from bowling in international cricket.*

At Basseterre, May 6, 2010. **New Zealand won by ten runs.** ‡**New Zealand 139-8** (20 overs) (S. W. Bates 32; D. P. David 4-27); **India 129-8** (20 overs) (M. Raj 44). *Player of the Match: S. W. Bates.*

New Zealand owed much to Rachel Priest, who scored 20 in 12 balls after coming in at an uncertain 96-6. India struggled to 56-4 before Mithali Raj, with 44 in 36 balls, and Amita Sharma, with 28* in 16, hit out to reduce the margin of defeat.

At Basseterre, May 8, 2010. **India won by nine wickets.** ‡**Pakistan 104-6** (20 overs) (Sana Mir 35; P. Roy 3-19); **India 106-1** (16.4 overs) (P. G. Raut 54*, M. Raj 33*). *Twenty20 international debut:* Sania Khan (Pakistan). *Player of the Match:* P. G. Raut. *India coasted to victory, reducing Pakistan to 29-4 in the seventh over and losing only one wicket – to a run-out – as they knocked off the runs with 20 balls to spare, led by Punam Raut's run-a-ball fifty.*

At Basseterre, May 8, 2010. **New Zealand won by 47 runs.** ‡**New Zealand 154-7** (20 overs) (S. W. Bates 50, S. J. McGlashan 31; C. R. Seneviratne 4-21); **Sri Lanka 107-8** (20 overs). *Twenty20 international debut:* E. C. Perry (New Zealand). *Player of the Match:* S. W. Bates. *New Zealand secured their place in the semi-finals. Suzie Bates was their top scorer again, hitting six fours in her 43-ball 50, and most of her team-mates contributed until seamer Chamani Seneviratne claimed three wickets in the final over. Sri Lanka never looked like achieving a target of 155.*

At Basseterre, May 10, 2010. **New Zealand won by six wickets.** ‡**Pakistan 65-9** (20 overs) (N. J. Browne 4-15); **New Zealand 71-4** (8.2 overs). *Twenty20 international debuts:* Rabia Shah, Sadia Yousuf (Pakistan). *Player of the Match:* N. J. Browne. *New Zealand swept home with 11.4 overs to spare after restricting Pakistan to a mere 3.25 runs an over. Nicola Browne's four wickets left them on 30-5, which became 30-7 in the next over, though they just lasted out their full 20.*

At Basseterre, May 10, 2010. **India won by 71 runs.** ‡**India 144-3** (20 overs) (S. Naik 59, M. Raj 52*); **Sri Lanka 73-9** (20 overs) (H. M. D. Rasangika 31*; D. P. David 4-12). *Player of the Match:* S. Naik. *India joined New Zealand in the last four after another huge win. Sulakshana Naik and Mithali Raj set up their total by adding 86 in 10.3 overs for the second wicket, before off-spinner Diana David reduced Sri Lanka to 19-6 in the seventh over; Deepika Rasangika batted out time.*

GROUP TABLES

Group A	Played	Won	Lost	Points	Net run-rate
AUSTRALIA	3	3	0	6	0.55
WEST INDIES	3	2	1	4	0.16
England.	3	1	2	2	0.90
South Africa	3	0	3	0	−1.61

Group B	Played	Won	Lost	Points	Net run-rate
NEW ZEALAND . . .	3	3	0	6	2.51
INDIA.	3	2	1	4	1.42
Sri Lanka.	3	1	2	2	−1.95
Pakistan.	3	0	3	0	−1.73

Semi-finals

At Gros Islet, St Lucia, May 13, 2010 (floodlit). **Australia won by seven wickets.** ‡**India 119-5** (20 overs) (P. G. Raut 44); **Australia 123-3** (18.5 overs) (A. J. Blackwell 61, L. J. Poulton 30*). *Player of the Match:* A. J. Blackwell. *Australia made sure of the final after keeping up the pressure on India, who lost three wickets in the 17th over, two of them to run-outs. Captain Alex Blackwell took Australia most of the way to victory, with eight fours in her 49-ball 61; Leah Poulton hit the winning runs with seven balls to spare.*

At Gros Islet, St Lucia, May 14, 2010 (floodlit). **New Zealand won by 56 runs. New Zealand 180-5** (20 overs) (S. J. McGlashan 84); ‡**West Indies 124-8** (20 overs) (S. R. Taylor 40; A. L. Watkins 3-26). *Player of the Match:* S. J. McGlashan. *New Zealand completed a record ninth consecutive win in women's Twenty20 internationals after piling up the biggest total of the tournament. Sara McGlashan hit six fours and two sixes in 55 balls, and added 93 in just 8.3 overs with Sophie Devine. Taylor tried to respond in kind, with three fours and two sixes in 33 balls, but West Indies stumbled to 76-4 and they could not keep up with the rate.*

FINAL

AUSTRALIA v NEW ZEALAND

At Bridgetown, Barbados, May 16, 2010 (day/night). Australia won by three runs. Toss: Australia.

Australia's women restored national pride, with several of the men, who had earlier lost to England, cheering them on from the stands – though a disappointing batting effort suggested a double defeat until Ellyse Perry proved too quick for the New Zealanders. Alex Blackwell chose to bat, but Australia were 20 for three when she was caught at gully, after facing seven dot balls from Nicola Browne, who bowled straight through for 4–1–11–2. At 72 for six, New Zealand seemed to be completely on top. A late fightback from Sarah Elliott and Lisa Sthalekar helped Australia past 100; it hardly seemed enough. New Zealand, however, struggled even more. A terrible mix-up led to Sara McGlashan's run-out; then Perry had Suzie Bates caught at mid-off in her first over, and bowled Amy Satterthwaite in her second. The chase looked hopeless at 36 for five, but Sophie Devine and Browne added 41, the game's biggest stand. After Perry returned and removed Browne, New Zealand needed 29 from two overs. Hitting four and six off Rene Farrell, Devine made that 14 from six balls. But she could not get the boundary she needed off Perry. A four from the last ball would have tied the scores and triggered an eliminator over; though Devine drove it hard and straight, Perry – a football international – deflected it to the mid-on fielder with her boot, and New Zealand managed only a single.

Player of the Match: E. A. Perry.   *Player of the Series:* N. J. Browne.

Australia		B	4	6
E. J. Villani *c 3 b 7*	6	10	1	0
S. Nitschke *lbw b 11*	3	5	0	0
L. J. Poulton *c 2 b 4*	20	28	1	0
*A. J. Blackwell *c 4 b 7*	0	7	0	0
J. E. Cameron *b 10*	14	24	0	0
S. J. Elliott *not out*	19	20	0	0
†A. J. Healy *run out*	10	10	0	0
L. C. Sthalekar *b 4*	18	13	2	0
R. M. Farrell *c 2 b 9*	3	4	0	0
L-b 1, w 11, n-b 1	13			

6 overs: 24-3   (20 overs) 106-8

1/10 2/14 3/20 4/50 5/51 6/72 7/99 8/106

E. A. Perry and C. R. Smith did not bat.

Ruck 3–0–18–1; Browne 4–1–11–2; Watkins 4–0–17–0; Devine 3–0–21–2; Broadmore 2–0–15–1; Doolan 4–0–23–1.

New Zealand		B	4	6
S. W. Bates *c 6 b 10*	18	23	0	1
*A. L. Watkins *c 4 b 11*	2	5	0	0
S. J. McGlashan *run out*	1	4	0	0
S. F. M. Devine *not out*	38	35	1	1
A. E. Satterthwaite *b 10*	4	8	0	0
†R. H. Priest *c 4 b 2*	5	16	0	0
N. J. Browne *c 7 b 10*	20	25	1	0
E. C. Perry *not out*	4	4	0	0
L-b 3, w 8	11			

6 overs: 24-3   (20 overs) 103-6

1/16 2/19 3/24 4/29 5/36 6/77

L. R. Doolan, K. E. Broadmore and S. E. A. Ruck did not bat.

Farrell 4–0–31–0; Smith 4–0–22–1; Nitschke 4–0–10–1; Perry 4–0–18–3; Sthalekar 4–0–19–0.

Umpires: E. A. R. de Silva and M. Erasmus. Third umpire: Asad Rauf. Referee: A. J. Pycroft.

ICC WOMEN'S WORLD TWENTY20 WINNERS

2009	England	2010	Australia

THE ICC UNDER-19 WORLD CUP, 2009-10

Charles Randall

1. Australia   2. Pakistan   3. West Indies   4. Sri Lanka

High summer in New Zealand produced one of the coldest January months on record in South Island, and blighted much of the Under-19 World Cup based at Christchurch, a stand-in venue after Kenya's preparations fell behind schedule. The last ten days coincided with the annual World Buskers Festival for circus acts in the city. Night-time rain and a cruel Antarctic south wind made conditions unpleasant for players, umpires, coaches and clowns alike. The sunniest day was reserved for the final, when Australia joined India and Pakistan as two-time champions by winning the seventh ICC-organised tournament since 1998. (The only previous comparable age-group tournament took place in 1987-88, when Australia won the restricted World Youth Cup in Adelaide during the Australian Bicentenary celebrations.)

The four first-class grounds in the Christchurch area – at Lincoln University, Hagley Oval, The Village Green, and the satellite town of Rangiora – all offered seaming pitches for the knockout stages. So many a Plan A must have been scrapped as all-out assaults on the new ball were shown to work less well than orthodox build-ups. Seam bowlers, especially tall men such as Josh Hazlewood, of Australia, and Jason Holder, the 6ft 7in Barbadian, naturally fared very well, and left-armers such as David Payne of England, Chathura Peiris, the Sri Lanka captain, and India's Saurav Netravalkar proved hard to get away. Generally, top-order batting tended to go missing when it mattered. Those who made runs under pressure stood out: the Australia captain Mitchell Marsh, son of former Test player Geoff; Babar Azam, 15, a heavy scorer for Pakistan; and the calm West Indies opener Kraigg Brathwaite. The most prolific was Dominic Hendricks, an aggressive left-handed opener from Johannesburg. He was named Man of the Tournament.

Afghanistan arrived weakened by the disappearance of five players and their coach at the qualifying tournament in Toronto the previous September. The New Zealand immigration authorities took special precautions. All countries had to surrender their passports, and a close eye was kept on the Afghans. The players were given minders during leisure hours in the final week, and their last match in Napier, against the USA, was switched from Nelson Park to McLean Park for no obvious reason apart from McLean's status as an enclosed venue. Though Noor-ul-Haq and Hashmatullah Shaidi, a gifted 15-year-old left-hander, did well with the bat, Afghanistan finished last in the play-offs in their debut World Cup.

The Sussex professional cricket manager, Mark Robinson, was given responsibility for England on his first representative assignment, with county colleague Carl Hopkinson as assistant. His charges, captained by Yorkshire all-rounder Azeem Rafiq, won their group after becoming the first England side to beat India in an Under-19 World Cup, with a well-deserved 31-run victory. Four previous teams had failed since 1998, and four years ago, in Colombo, India had beaten a team captained by Moeen Ali by a humiliating 234 runs, so the televised victory at Lincoln University reclaimed some pride. A powerful century from Durham left-hander Ben Stokes repaired early damage caused by Netravalkar.

Sadly for England, the India match proved to be their high point of the tournament. In the quarter-finals, West Indies inflicted an 18-run upset at Rangiora, in a match reduced to 36 overs by a soggy outfield. England gifted a succession of early wickets and had no answer to Holder, who finished with five for 19. The England players sat stunned in the tent after the game, and tears were shed. The ICC had held a briefing session for the players in the Crowne Plaza Hotel before their first game, covering corruption and a zero tolerance on drugs. The ICC chief executive Haroon Lorgat described it as a "finishing school" for future internationals, but nothing could prepare England for their sudden, sickening exit. Aside from hard, focused training and advice, there was little Robinson could do with a fragile top order who rarely did themselves justice. Robinson believed that, compared to "physically stronger" players from rugby-playing nations in the southern hemisphere, England were at a natural disadvantage. A tooth abcess limited the influence of Jos Buttler, the first-choice wicketkeeper-batsman, and openers Joe Root and Chris Dent seldom fired. James Vince, the pivotal batsman highly rated at Hampshire, started with 76 not out against Hong Kong but faded, with each subsequent innings lower than the previous. He still led the English batting with 192 runs in his six innings, including play-off matches, well behind the leaders, headed by Hendricks with 391 and Brathwaite with 335.

Much was expected of New Zealand. They boasted an accomplished first-class batsman in Corey Anderson and two members of the Bracewell dynasty – Doug and Michael were nephews of former Test off-spinner and national coach John Bracewell. Their quest for a second final was ended by old rivals Australia, in front of a crowd of more than 1,500 at Rangiora.

Two off-spinners, Rushan Jaleel of Sri Lanka, and Riyazkhan Pathan of Canada, were reported for suspect bowling actions during the tournament.

Group A

At Lincoln (Bert Sutcliffe Oval), January 15, 2010. **India won by eight wickets. Afghanistan 118** (49.2 overs) (Noor-ul-Haq 61); ‡**India 122-2** (25.2 overs) (Mandeep Singh 51*). *A captain's innings from Noor-ul-Haq marked Afghanistan's debut at this level.*

At Lincoln (Bert Sutcliffe Oval), January 16, 2010. **England won by nine wickets. Hong Kong 185** (48.5 overs) (Nizakat Khan 65); ‡**England 186-1** (30.1 overs) (J. E. Root 70*, J. M. Vince 76*). *Nizakat Khan scored 65 in 69 balls.*

At Christchurch (Hagley Oval), January 17, 2010. **India won by nine wickets.** Reduced to 34 overs a side. **Hong Kong 143** (33.5 overs); ‡**India 147-1** (24 overs) (K. L. Rahul 62*, M. A. Agarwal 63). *Hong Kong opener Alex Smith was run out without facing.*

At Christchurch (Village Green), January 18, 2010. **England won by nine wickets. Afghanistan 126** (47.2 overs); ‡**England 127-1** (25.5 overs) (C. D. J. Dent 53*). *Hashmatullah Shaidi, at 15 the youngest player in the tournament, top-scored for Afghanistan with 41.*

At Christchurch (Hagley Oval), January 19, 2010. **Afghanistan won by eight wickets. Hong Kong 137** (35.1 overs) (Zakiullah 5-34); ‡**Afghanistan 141-2** (31 overs) (Javed Ahmadi 90*). *Afghanistan cruised to victory in the meeting of two debutant countries. Javed Ahmadi, a refugee-camp player in Pakistan, hit nine fours and three sixes in 98 balls.*

At Lincoln (Bert Sutcliffe Oval), January 21, 2010. **England won by 31 runs. England 246-8** (50 overs) (B. A. Stokes 100); ‡**India 215** (46.4 overs). *England won the group, with Ben Stokes (born in Christchurch) reaching his century in 87 balls, with four fours and six sixes.*

England 6pts, India 4pts, Afghanistan 2pts, Hong Kong 0pts.

Group B

At Queenstown, January 15, 2010. **South Africa won by five wickets. Ireland 216-6** (50 overs) (B. J. Ackland 66, L. T. Nelson 55); ‡**South Africa 220-5** (43.4 overs) (S. Smith 67*). *Ireland recovered from 36-4 through a fifth-wicket stand of 117 between Ben Ackland and Lee Nelson.*

At Queenstown, January 16, 2010. **Australia won by 108 runs. ‡Australia 262** (49.3 overs) (T. M. Beaton 73); **USA 154** (41.2 overs) (A. Mohammed 70; A. C. McDermott 4-29). *Alister McDermott, son of former Australia fast bowler Craig, helped beat off spirited opposition.*

At Queenstown, January 17, 2010. **Australia won by 209 runs. Australia 274-5** (50 overs) (T. M. Beaton 53, A. R. Keath 88, T. J. Armstrong 73*); ‡**Ireland 65** (24.2 overs) (N. D. Buchanan 4-16). *Ireland slid to a humiliating defeat, the heaviest by runs in the tournament.*

At Queenstown, January 18, 2010. **South Africa won by eight wickets. USA 163** (49.5 overs); ‡**South Africa 166-2** (35.1 overs) (D. A. Hendricks 75*, C. N. Ackermann 64*). *Dominic Hendricks and Colin Ackermann shared 130* for the third wicket.*

At Queenstown, January 19, 2010. **Ireland won by five wickets. ‡USA 217** (48.1 overs) (S. R. Taylor 57, Saqib Saleem 62); **Ireland 218-5** (43.5 overs) (P. R. Stirling 114). *Paul Stirling restored some Irish pride with 114 off 102 balls.*

At Queenstown, January 20, 2010. **South Africa won by two wickets. ‡Australia 276-7** (50 overs) (A. R. Keath 64, J. S. Floros 96); **South Africa 278-8** (49.4 overs) (D. A. Hendricks 94). *South Africa sneaked home in one of the competition's best contests. Jason Floros's 96 took just 97 balls; Hendricks responded with 94 from 99.*

South Africa 6pts, Australia 4pts, Ireland 2pts, USA 0pts.

Group C

At Christchurch (Village Green), January 15, 2010. **Canada won by ten runs. ‡Canada 201-7** (50 overs) (Usman Limbada 90); **Zimbabwe 191** (49.4 overs) (D. Mazhawidza 75). *Canada's first victory in any Under-19 World Cup began a disappointing tournament for Zimbabwe.*

At Lincoln (No. 3), January 16, 2010. **New Zealand won by nine wickets. Canada 128** (29.3 overs); ‡**New Zealand 130-1** (19.1 overs). *Doug Bracewell, son of former New Zealand seamer Brendon, won the match award for his 3-31, and Jimmy Neesham hit 47* in 20 deliveries to hasten victory.*

At Lincoln (Bert Sutcliffe Oval), January 17, 2010. **Sri Lanka won by eight wickets.** Reduced to 34 overs a side. **Zimbabwe 121** (33.3 overs) (W. M. C. Jayampathi 4-26); ‡**Sri Lanka 122-2** (24.2 overs). *Tinotenda Mutombodzi (42*) restored Zimbabwe from 20-6.*

At Lincoln (No. 3), January 18, 2010. **Sri Lanka won by 134 runs. Sri Lanka 276-6** (50 overs) (P. B. B. Rajapaksa 68); ‡**Canada 142** (39.3 overs) (H. Patel 69; K. P. C. M. Peiris 5-25). *Hiral Patel took 3-45 and top-scored for Canada, who were wrecked by left-arm seamer Chathura Peiris.*

At Lincoln (Bert Sutcliffe Oval), January 19, 2010. **New Zealand won by seven wickets. Zimbabwe 135** (42.2 overs); ‡**New Zealand 140-3** (25.3 overs) (H. K. P. Boam 58, T. W. M. Latham 57*). *New Zealand's openers settled the match with 116 in 20 overs.*

At Christchurch (Village Green), January 20, 2010. **New Zealand won by seven wickets. Sri Lanka 195** (49.1 overs) (M. D. Gunathilleke 69); ‡**New Zealand 196-3** (43.2 overs) (H. K. P. Boam 85*). *Kasun Madushanka accounted for just five of his last-wicket stand of 59 with Dhanushka Gunathilleke, who finished on 69 from 71 balls. Harry Boam finished with 172 runs in the group stage.*

New Zealand 6pts, Sri Lanka 4pts, Canada 2pts, Zimbabwe 0pts.

Group D

At Palmerston North, January 15, 2010. **Pakistan won by 40 runs. Pakistan 297-7** (50 overs) (Babar Azam 129); ‡**West Indies 257** (46.5 overs) (K. C. Brathwaite 92*, T. Griffith 84). *Babar Azam hit the competition's highest score, but was briefly upstaged by Guyanese left-hander Trevon Griffith, who bludgeoned 84 (with 11 fours and three sixes) out of a 120-run opening stand with Kraigg Brathwaite. West Indies collapsed against spin.*

At Palmerston North, January 16, 2010. **Bangladesh won by five wickets** (D/L method). ‡**Papua New Guinea 191-9** (46 overs) (T. P. Ura 70; Abul Hasan 4-22); **Bangladesh 190-5** (27.2 overs) (Sabbir Rahman 51*). *Bangladesh were 77-4, chasing a revised target of 189 in 46 overs, when Sabbir Rahman arrived.*

At Palmerston North, January 17, 2010. **West Indies won by one run.** ‡**West Indies 249-8** (50 overs) (A. S. Creary 55); **Bangladesh 248** (49.4 overs) (Sabbir Rahman 53, Tasamul Haque 54). *Griffith was run out by partner Brathwaite off the first ball of the match without facing. With Bangladesh needing two to win from four deliveries, with two wickets in hand, Tasamul Haque was bowled for 54, and last man Shaker Ahmed was run out next ball attempting a bye to wicketkeeper Shane Dowrich.*

At Palmerston North, January 18, 2010. **Pakistan won by six wickets.** ‡**Papua New Guinea 99** (37.3 overs) (Usman Qadir 4-35); **Pakistan 100-4** (18.1 overs).

At Palmerston North, January 19, 2010. **West Indies won by five wickets. Papua New Guinea 187** (50 overs) (S. Bau 50; Y. Cariah 4-37); ‡**West Indies 188-5** (35.4 overs) (K. C. Brathwaite 82, S. O. Dowrich 84*). *Brathwaite and Shane Dowrich put on 118 for the fifth wicket.*

At Palmerston North, January 20, 2010. **Pakistan won by four wickets.** ‡**Bangladesh 250-5** (50 overs) (Anamul Haque 55, Mahmudul Hasan 63); **Pakistan 251-6** (49.5 overs) (Ahmed Shehzad 52, Babar Azam 91). *Pakistan needed 39 to win off two overs, and Mohammad Waqas cruelly eliminated Bangladesh on his debut with 34* off 14 balls.*

Pakistan 6pts, West Indies 4pts, Bangladesh 2pts, Papua New Guinea 0pts.

Quarter-Finals

At Rangiora, January 23, 2010. **West Indies won by 18 runs.** Reduced to 36 overs a side. **West Indies 166** (34.4 overs) (K. C. Brathwaite 69, A. S. Creary 52; D. A. Payne 4-19); ‡**England 148** (33.1 overs) (J. O. Holder 5-19). *West Indies lost their last eight wickets for 31 runs. England's final three succumbed in seven balls, all to the giant Jason Holder.*

At Lincoln (Bert Sutcliffe Oval), January 23, 2010. **Pakistan won by two wickets.** Reduced to 23 overs a side. **India 114-9** (23 overs) (Fayyaz Butt 4-27); ‡**Pakistan 117-8** (22.3 overs). *Hammad Azam's 21 over the last six overs squeezed Pakistan through from a rain-ruined match.*

At Rangiora, January 24, 2010. **Australia won by 62 runs.** ‡**Australia 232-8** (50 overs) (M. R. Marsh 53); **New Zealand 170** (43.2 overs). *Brilliant New Zealand fielding, including direct-hit run-outs by Boam and Michael Bracewell, was a feature, but Australia's bowlers were ruthlessly efficient.*

At Lincoln (Bert Sutcliffe Oval), January 24, 2010. **Sri Lanka won by 146 runs** (D/L method). **Sri Lanka 293-8** (50 overs) (P. B. B. Rajapaksa 79); ‡**South Africa 145** (36.4 overs) (W. M. C. Jayampathi 4-31). *Chasing 292 in 49 overs, South Africa flopped spectacularly to left-arm quick Charith Jayampathi. They never recovered from Sri Lanka's batting onslaught, with Bhanuka Rajapaksa hitting 79 off 78 balls.*

Semi-Finals

At Lincoln (Bert Sutcliffe Oval), January 25, 2010. **Pakistan won by four wickets. West Indies 212-8** (50 overs) (K. C. Brathwaite 85, S. O. Dowrich 55); ‡**Pakistan 213-6** (48.3 overs) (Hammad Azam 92*). *Azam's 92 in 93 balls from No. 6 rescued Pakistan superbly from 49-4 in the 20th over.*

At Lincoln (Bert Sutcliffe Oval), January 27, 2010. **Australia won by two wickets.** ‡**Sri Lanka 205** (48.2 overs) (M. A. P. Fernando 52; J. R. Hazlewood 4-26); **Australia 206-8** (48.3 overs) (M. R. Marsh 97, T. I. F. Triffitt 50). *Australia edged another thriller. Sri Lanka's last five wickets added 173, and Australia were 93-5 before Mitchell Marsh and wicketkeeper Tom Triffitt put on 78.*

FINAL

AUSTRALIA v PAKISTAN

At Lincoln (Bert Sutcliffe Oval), January 30, 2010. Australia won by 25 runs. Toss: Pakistan.

Australia chiselled out an excellent victory in a tense affair, televised live by ESPN Star Sports for a huge worldwide audience. The highest individual score was only 44, a run-a-ball bash by Kane Richardson at No. 8 for Australia. Raza Hasan, a left-arm spinner, was the pick of the Pakistan attack, though he took only one wicket, his fizzing delivery having Alex Keath caught at slip. In reply, Luke Doran, another left-armer, removed three top-order batsmen with variations of flight and spin. If the game hinged on one incident, it was the dismissal of Hammad Azam for a duck. This resourceful all-rounder had been a proven match-winner, and Josh Hazlewood, Australia's best bowler, was summoned as soon as Azam reached the crease at 110 for four; the result was an impatient slash and a fatal nick. After that there was no way back for Pakistan, and Hazlewood returned to mop up the innings. This was the second time the Lincoln University ground had hosted this ICC event, and, as in 2001-02, Australia took the title.

Man of the Match: J. R. Hazlewood.   *Man of the Series:* D. A. Hendricks (South Africa).

Australia

N. J. Maddinson lbw b Fayyaz Butt		0
T. M. Beaton c Babar Azam b Sarmad Bhatti		5
*M. R. Marsh c Mohammad Waqas		
b Fayyaz Butt .		7
A. R. Keath c Rameez Aziz b Raza Hasan .		25
J. S. Floros run out		35
T. J. Armstrong b Sarmad Bhatti		37
†T. I. F. Triffitt c Mohammad Waqas		
b Babar Azam .		21
K. W. Richardson c Ahmed Shehzad		
b Sarmad Bhatti .		44

J. R. Hazlewood run out		5
L. A. Doran not out		9
A. C. McDermott not out.		3
L-b 2, w 14		16
1/2 (1) 2/10 (2)	(9 wkts, 50 overs)	207
3/23 (3) 4/80 (5)		
5/82 (4) 6/127 (7) 7/189 (8)		
8/189 (6) 9/199 (9)	10 overs: 48-3	

Fayyaz Butt 7–0–37–2; Sarmad Bhatti 8–0–33–3; Raza Hasan 10–3–21–1; Hammad Azam 2–0–23–0; Usman Qadir 10–0–35–0; Ahmed Shehzad 7–0–22–0; Babar Azam 6–0–34–1.

Pakistan

Babar Azam c Triffitt b Doran		28
Ahsan Ali c Beaton b Hazlewood		2
Ahmed Shehzad lbw b Doran		36
*Azeem Ghumman b Floros		41
Rameez Aziz b Doran		23
Hameed Azam c Triffitt b Hazlewood		0
†Mohammad Waqas c Hazlewood b Keath		21
Sarmad Bhatti b Hazlewood		10
Usman Qadir c Triffitt b McDermott		9

Raza Hasan c Triffitt b Hazlewood		10
Fayyaz Butt not out		4
W 3, n-b 3		6
1/15 (2) 2/69 (3) 3/74 (1)	(46.4 overs)	182
4/110 (5) 5/111 (6) 6/130 (7)		
7/156 (4) 8/166 (8) 9/168 (9)		
10/182 (10)	10 overs: 42-1	

Hazlewood 8.4–1–30–4; McDermott 8–0–50–1; Richardson 7–1–20–0; Armstrong 2–0–13–0; Doran 10–1–32–3; Floros 8–1–19–1; Keath 3–0–18–1.

Umpires: H. D. P. K. Dharmasena and R. A. Kettleborough.   Third umpire: B. G. Jerling.
Referee: J. J. Crowe.

UNDER-19 WORLD CUP WINNERS

1987-88	AUSTRALIA beat Pakistan by five wickets at Adelaide.
1997-98	ENGLAND beat New Zealand by seven wickets at Johannesburg.
1999-2000	INDIA beat Sri Lanka by six wickets at Colombo (SSC).
2001-02	AUSTRALIA beat South Africa by seven wickets at Lincoln (Bert Sutcliffe Oval).
2003-04	PAKISTAN beat West Indies by 25 runs at Dhaka.
2005-06	PAKISTAN beat India by 38 runs at Colombo (RPS).
2007-08	INDIA beat South Africa by 12 runs (D/L method) at Kuala Lumpur.
2009-10	AUSTRALIA beat Pakistan by 25 runs at Lincoln (Bert Sutcliffe Oval).

Third-place Play-off

At Christchurch (Village Green), January 29, 2010. **West Indies won by four wickets. Sri Lanka 291-6** (50 overs) (D. D. M. Rajakaruna 94, M. D. U. S. Jayasundera 77); ‡**West Indies 294-6** (48.3 overs) (J. R. C. Campbell 77, Y. Cariah 110*). *Denuwan Rajakaruna and Udara Jayasundera opened with 174, comfortably the highest partnership of the tournament.*

Fifth-place Play-offs

Semi-finals: At Christchurch (Hagley Oval), January 25, 2010. **India won by seven wickets.** ‡**England 176** (49.2 overs) (J. C. Buttler 78; A. L. Menaria 4-35); **India 179-3** (36.4 overs) (P. Akshath Reddy 94). *England's fifth defeat by India in six Under-19 World Cup meetings.*

At Lincoln (No. 3), January 25, 2010. **South Africa won by nine wickets. New Zealand 250** (49.4 overs) (J. D. S. Neesham 64, C. J. Anderson 64); ‡**South Africa 252-1** (48.1 overs) (J. R. Richards 67, D. A. Hendricks 107*, D. J. White 72*).

Final: At Lincoln (No. 3), January 27, 2010. **South Africa won by six wickets.** ‡**India 235-9** (50 overs) (H. S. Bhatia 56, Zahid Ali 98); **South Africa 237-4** (48.5 overs) (D. A. Hendricks 63, D. J. White 77, C. N. Ackermann 52*). *Graham Hume's 3-31 gave the South African seamer 13 wickets for the tournament.*

Seventh-place Play-off

At Christchurch (Village Green), January 26, 2010. **New Zealand won by two wickets. England 228-9** (50 overs); ‡**New Zealand 232-8** (49.4 overs) (C. Cachopa 64, C. J. Anderson 50, L. V. van Beek 51*). *Six England batsmen passed 20, but none went further than Jack Manuel's 43.*

Ninth-place Play-offs

Quarter-finals: At Napier (McLean Park), January 23, 2010. **No result.** Reduced to 23 overs a side. ‡**USA 13-0** (3 overs) **v Canada.** *Canada qualified for the ninth-place play-off semi-final on account of their better record in the group stage.*

At Napier (Nelson Park), January 23, 2010. **Ireland won by seven wickets** (D/L method). Reduced to 32 overs a side. **Zimbabwe 102** (26.2 overs) (C. A. Young 4-14); ‡**Ireland 110-3** (20.2 overs) (P. R. Stirling 65). *Ireland chased a revised 110 in 27 overs.*

At Napier (Nelson Park), January 24, 2010. **Papua New Guinea won by 30 runs. Papua New Guinea 173-9** (50 overs) (S. Eno 55*; Aftab Alam 6-33); ‡**Afghanistan 143** (37.3 overs) (R. C. Haoda 5-34). *Aftab Alam was the only bowler in the event to take a six-for.*

At Napier (McLean Park), January 24, 2010. **Bangladesh won by four wickets.** ‡**Hong Kong 156** (49 overs) (Nizakat Khan 56*; Shaker Ahmed 4-26); **Bangladesh 157-6** (40.4 overs).

Semi-finals: At Palmerston North, January 25, 2010. **Canada v Ireland. Abandoned.** *Ireland qualified for the ninth-place play-off final on account of their better record in the group stage.*

At Palmerston North, January 26, 2010. **Bangladesh won by 168 runs. ‡Bangladesh 253** (49.4 overs) (Saikat Ali 61, Noor Hossain 66); **Papua New Guinea 85** (32.5 overs) (Noor Hossain 4-11).

Final: At Napier (McLean Park), January 28, 2010. **Bangladesh won by 195 runs. Bangladesh 307-8** (50 overs) (Mominul Haque 81, Mahmudul Hasan 52; A. Balbirnie 4-59); **‡Ireland 112** (38.5 overs). *Bangladesh were the only side to breach 300, and Kamrul Islam wrapped up the match with a hat-trick.*

Eleventh-place Play-off

At Napier (Nelson Park), January 28, 2010. **Canada won by two wickets. ‡Papua New Guinea 145** (47.1 overs) (H. Siaka 50); **Canada 146-8** (49.1 overs). *Papua New Guinea's Raymond Haoda finished with 15 wickets, more than anyone else.*

Thirteenth-place Play-offs

Semi-finals: At Napier (McLean Park), January 25, 2010. **Hong Kong won by four wickets.** Reduced to 32 overs a side. **‡Afghanistan 151-5** (32 overs) (Noor-ul-Haq 61); **Hong Kong 153-6** (30.1 overs) (Irfan Ahmed 68, Waqas Barkat 57*; Aftab Alam 4-31).

At Napier (Nelson Park), January 25, 2010. **Zimbabwe won by five wickets.** Reduced to 41 overs a side. **USA 115** (33.1 overs); **‡Zimbabwe 119-5** (29 overs) (Saqib Saleem 4-38).

Final: At Napier (McLean Park), January 27, 2010. **Zimbabwe won by 137 runs. Zimbabwe 235-8** (50 overs); **‡Hong Kong 98** (36.4 overs) (N. Mushangwe 4-18). *Natsai Mushangwe won his second consecutive match award.*

Fifteenth-place Play-off

At Napier (McLean Park), January 27, 2010. **USA won by nine wickets. ‡Afghanistan 86** (32.2 overs); **USA 87-1** (14.2 overs).

AUSTRALIAN CRICKET, 2010

A year of losses

Peter English

Australia ended their worst period since the mid-1980s without the Ashes, Ricky Ponting or any of the revered Test eminence earned over the previous 15 years. Michael Clarke, the stand-in captain for the first match of 2011, denied the game in the country was in crisis, but there was no other way to describe it. For the first time since Mike Gatting's men visited in 1986-87, Australia were beaten at home in an Ashes series. But they weren't just beaten. The 3–1 loss included a trio of innings defeats, at Adelaide, Melbourne and Sydney, the most Australia had ever suffered in the same series. On the morning that England sealed the victory at the SCG, the *Sydney Morning Herald* labelled the current side "The Worst XI". Actually the country has had worse teams, but none has ever been swept aside so brutally.

In the immediate aftermath of the Ashes, Cricket Australia's senior figures seemed determined not to accept blame for a summer destined for trouble from the moment the selectors, impersonating their England counterparts of the

AUSTRALIA IN 2010

	Played	Won	Lost	Drawn/No result
Tests	12	6	5	1
One-day internationals	25	16	8	1
Twenty20 internationals	15	10	5	–

DECEMBER		
JANUARY	3 Tests, 5 ODIs and 1 T20I (h) v Pakistan	(see *Wisden 2010*, page 1055)
FEBRUARY	5 ODIs and 2 T20Is (h) v West Indies	(page 846)
MARCH	2 Tests, 5 ODIs and 2 T20Is (a) v New Zealand	(page 983)
APRIL		
MAY	World Twenty20 (in West Indies)	(page 797)
JUNE	1 ODI (a) v Ireland	(page 770)
JULY	5 ODIs (a) v England	(page 303)
	2 Tests and 2 T20Is (a) (in England) v Pakistan	(page 310)
AUGUST		
SEPTEMBER		
OCTOBER	2 Tests and 3 ODIs (a) v India	(page 926)
NOVEMBER	3 ODIs and 1 T20I (h) v Sri Lanka	(page 853)
DECEMBER		
JANUARY	5 Tests, 7 ODIs and 2 T20Is (h) v England	(page 210)
FEBRUARY		

For a review of Australian domestic cricket from the 2009-10 season, see page 870.

1990s, chose a 17-man squad for the First Test. As it happened, 17 players were used by Australia, but not the ones originally picked, as the previously conservative decision-makers suddenly panicked. A couple of hours after Andrew Strauss lifted the urn, Australia's selection chairman Andrew Hilditch said his panel had done "a very good job", although he could not actually give any examples of the successes. The greatest waste occurred with the overlooking of the off-spinner Nathan Hauritz who, despite being the most potent of the 11 slow bowlers called on since Shane Warne retired in 2007, was not used at all in the Ashes series. Instead, two fringe slow left-armers – Xavier Doherty and Michael Beer – and the leg-spinning all-rounder Steve Smith were employed, and managed four wickets between them. The lack of options became so bad that after the Second Test there was a concerted public campaign – it was always going to fail – to bring back the 41-year-old Warne.

Clarke was so impressed by England's performances that he called for Australia to copy the model during the rebuilding phase, but the board's leaders showed a greater tendency to contract the diseases of the Old Enemy's previous regimes, such as inquiries and stopgap measures. James Sutherland, Cricket Australia's chief executive, attempted to outline what a review of the Ashes loss would entail, but was hamstrung because any review had to be approved by the board, which itself was under review. It was clear that change was required from the boardroom to club level, which was suffering from an exodus of senior players, causing the weakening of its traditionally uncompromising standards.

Like Hilditch, Sutherland did not take any responsibility for the side's inability to regain the urn, preferring to pay tribute to England's exceptional displays. Sutherland also praised the coach, Tim Nielsen, whose support staff were thoroughly out-thought by Andy Flower's shrewd back-room. "He's doing a great job with the development of players," said Sutherland of Nielsen, whose contract had been extended to 2013 before the series started. Yet Nielsen, who has been in charge since 2007, could name only three players – Michael Hussey, Shane Watson and Peter Siddle – who had improved over the previous six months while the side suffered a series of record-breaking defeats. "If we sit back and look at the series results it would be easy to say none of us have [improved]," Nielsen conceded. Despite the magnitude of the loss and the serious flaws in performance, there were no off-field sackings, and nobody walked away. Only the players, it seemed, had let the country down.

Ponting, whose position came under increasing scrutiny as he struggled with the bat – he made only 113 runs in four Ashes matches – broke his finger at the end of the Third Test at Perth. It was the venue for Australia's only victory, which came via a wind blowing perfectly for Mitchell Johnson's devastating swing. Johnson surged to nine wickets in the match, but had it not been for the Barmy Army targeting him repeatedly, he would have been anonymous for the remainder of the series. Clarke, like his skipper, struggled for runs. At the SCG he became Australia's 43rd Test captain, but a long-term reign was not assured. Only Hussey, who held the team together for the first three matches and finished with 570 runs in the series, Watson and Brad Haddin deserved to be satisfied with their performances.

Australia's year started with a seemingly miraculous victory over Pakistan at Sydney, where Hussey's unbeaten 134 helped turn a first-innings deficit of 206 into a 36-run win. That result, and the entire tour, soon became tainted by suggestions of match-fixing. Australia's players and officials maintained they won the game fair and square, and the ACSU did not find anything untoward. After a 2–0 triumph over New Zealand, most notable for Clarke's tunnel vision in making a century after a very public break-up with his fiancée, Australia went to the World Twenty20 and were beaten in the final by a younger, more energetic and committed England.

Ponting, who had given up the 20-over game, was back in charge for the Test series against Pakistan in England in July. The series, played in seaming and swinging conditions, ended in a 1–1 draw. Australia were in control until dismissed for 88 in their first innings in the Second Test at Leeds, another example of the batting frailties. Defeats in both Tests in India followed, including a painful one-wicket miss which showed their growing inability to finish opponents off. Despite repeated claims that all was healthy, Australia lost seven successive matches in all forms of the game between July and October, an international sequence not known since the 1880s.

The home one-day series against Sri Lanka – four limited-overs games squeezed in before the Ashes – was contested in almost empty stadiums amid

Graham Morris

Where do we go from here? Ricky Ponting at Adelaide.

heavy criticism over the meaninglessness of it all. Australia lost the first three of those too (a Twenty20 and two 50-over games), but when they won the dead rubber at Brisbane, dismissing Sri Lanka for 115, the players wrongly insisted they were back. The Test victory at Perth was Australia's only other win until the end of the Ashes series, and briefly delayed an understanding of the full scale of the country's woes.

In reality, it was a year of losses on and off the field. Cricket Australia's administrators suffered a major embarrassment when they were forced to withdraw the nomination of John Howard, the former prime minister, as the ICC's president-elect. The joint choice of Cricket Australia and New Zealand Cricket, he was expected to become president in 2012. Like most long-standing political leaders, Howard had been a divisive figure during 11 years in charge of his country, but the two boards did not expect the rejection of their candidate. The matter did not even get to a vote in June after representatives from six countries signed a letter requesting another candidate. "Even in private discussions they are very reluctant to give a reason," said a disappointed Howard. His staunch opposition to the regime of Robert Mugabe and his 2004 comment that Muttiah

Muralitharan was a "chucker" were key reasons (although Zimbabwe were not one of the signatories to the letter). A lack of experience in cricket administration was also cited, although that has rarely been a prerequisite for ICC office. The Australia and New Zealand boards were furious that they had been outmanoeuvred, and refused to remove Howard's nomination until it became clear there was no alternative. Alan Isaac, New Zealand Cricket's chairman, was installed and approved without incident in August.

Cricket Australia decided in August to revisit the split-innings one-day format in the hope it would be embraced internationally in time for the 2015 World Cup. Worried by declining crowds for one-day internationals, the board passed the changes for a domestic trial in 2010-11 despite it being hugely unpopular with the players, 78% of whom were against the concept before it started. The ICC were not interested in the 45-over, four-innings format, a version of which was first trialled in Australia in 1994-95. A similar experiment was ditched after a season in England's Second Eleven competition in 2009. There were some early close encounters, but before Christmas the Australian Cricketers' Association was already starting to lobby to have it replaced.

The domestic Twenty20 tournament provided an 80% increase in crowds, to an average of 18,000 per fixture in 2009-10, and the success led to plans for an expanded eight-team league for 2011-12. The new competition will involve regional sides instead of the traditional state-based teams which have been part of the Australian game ever since it became established in the late 19th century.

Cricket Australia were slow to embrace Twenty20 when it began in England in 2003, but after realising its popularity they have been desperate to be involved. The board are a major shareholder in the Champions League Twenty20, and they put that competition above the Test side when they made Hussey and Doug Bollinger stay on with their Chennai Super Kings franchise until the final in South Africa in September, giving them only two days' preparation for the Test series against top-ranked India. "It is a fact of life that scheduling of elite cricket will create tough decisions from time to time," said Sutherland. Hussey complained about the decision and subsequently remained out of form until the Ashes, while Bollinger strained a stomach muscle with Australia desperately close to victory at Mohali. Australia lost that Test and the series, and Bollinger's fitness remained an issue for the rest of the summer.

The appointment of Greg Chappell as Cricket Australia's first full-time selector came in August, as he reprised the role he first accepted in the country's last playing crisis in the mid-1980s. His elevation resulted in Merv Hughes being replaced after five years of mixing his judgments with the hosting of overseas tour groups. Officially, the 62-year-old Chappell was the national talent manager. But as the public face of the regularly scorned four-man panel, he quickly began looking more decisive than Hilditch, the chairman since 2006 and whose contract was due to expire at the end of the World Cup. He was keen to continue in his part-time role, even though he had presided over the Test team's slide from first to fifth. Despite his insistence that the selectors had done a "very good job", Hilditch and his panel were major players in Australia's dramatic and ugly fall.

AUSTRALIA v WEST INDIES, 2009-10

Daniel Brettig

One-day internationals (5): Australia 4, West Indies 0
Twenty20 internationals (2): Australia 2, West Indies 0

Anyone who saw Pakistan's 2009-10 tour disintegrate had to hope West Indies would produce something more edifying when they returned to Australia for seven limited-overs matches to round off the summer. The West Indians had already done well, to a degree, in the pre-Christmas Tests, when their captain Chris Gayle conjured up centuries at Adelaide and Perth as contrasting as they were arresting (details in *Wisden 2010*). Meanwhile Kemar Roach's bowling, all speed and flash, had unsettled the Australian captain, Ricky Ponting.

Expectations rose after a startling display against the Prime Minister's XI. The West Indians hammered 399 for five in 45 overs – Gayle 146 from 89 balls. But he confessed he was not, actually, in great shape: "I'm struggling, to be honest… It might be a surprising thing to say, but I know myself and I know when I'm at my best… I really need to hit a few more balls."

Though Gayle soon reverted to a showman's bravado, predicting his side would win the one-day series 4–1, his earlier comments turned out to be gloomily prescient. He passed 14 only once more on the tour, and was dismissed four times by a surging Doug Bollinger. The team, lacking Shivnarine Chanderpaul, Dwayne Bravo, Ramnaresh Sarwan and Jerome Taylor through various injuries, repeatedly folded, as Australia summarily brushed them aside. Only Kieron Pollard, acclimatised by a successful stint for South Australia in the domestic Twenty20, consistently held his own.

It said much for the home attack's dominance that no West Indian specialist batsman averaged 25 in the 50-over games, leaving all-rounders Pollard (42.50) and Dwayne Smith (43.33) to fight some impossible rearguards. The bowlers were a little more respectable, but all conceded more than five an over.

By contrast, the Australians had nary a weak link. Bollinger's triumphs over Gayle epitomised his rise from the fringes to lead the attack. Ryan Harris's international breakthrough – which had started with a bang when he claimed 13 wickets in three games against Pakistan in January – slowed only slightly. The batting was led by Ponting, hungry for runs after a lean summer. Of the others, James Hopes made a vain bid for a Twenty20 recall, achieving a strike-rate of 159, while Michael Clarke, despite plenty of starts, appeared to be decelerating – a trend which was to cost his team in the World Twenty20 final. But he did lead them to two emphatic T20 victories here.

Australia completed the home season unbeaten, but those watching were not entirely enthused. Overkill seemed the only explanation for sparse crowds as the international summer ran deep into February. The MCG recorded its lowest attendance for an Australia–West Indies one-day international in the second game there; on the same day, almost twice as many people went to the nearby Docklands stadium for a pre-season Australian Rules football match.

WEST INDIAN TOURING PARTY

*C. H. Gayle, N. Deonarine, T. M. Dowlin, W. W. Hinds, N. O. Miller, R. S. Morton, B. P. Nash, K. A. Pollard, R. Ramdin, R. Rampaul, K. A. J. Roach, D. J. G. Sammy, L. M. P. Simmons, D. R. Smith, G. C. Tonge. *Coach:* D. Williams.

D. J. Bravo was originally selected, but broke his thumb while playing for Victoria in the Australian domestic Twenty20 competition, and was replaced by Hinds.

Note: The Tests and other matches from West Indies' tour of Australia in November–December 2009 were reported in *Wisden 2010*, pages 1044–54.

At Canberra, February 4, 2010 (not first-class). **West Indians won by 90 runs** (D/L method). **West Indians 399-5** (45 overs) (C. H. Gayle 146, T. M. Dowlin 72, L. M. P. Simmons 70*, K. A. Pollard 36, Extras 31; A. R. Keath 4-71); ‡**Prime Minister's XI 312-7** (45 overs) (T. D. Paine 36, T. L. W. Cooper 160*; N. O. Miller 3-51). *Chris Gayle blasted 14 fours (three off the first three balls of the match from James Pattinson, whose nine overs cost 91) and eight sixes in 89 balls; he put on 234 for the first wicket with Travis Dowlin before being first out in the 29th over. Showers delayed the start, and later interrupted the West Indian innings, limiting it to 45 overs; the PM's XI target was eventually revised to a dizzying 403. Tom Cooper, of South Australia (and, not long afterwards, the Netherlands), struck 14 fours and six sixes from 120 balls, but the home team – captained by Matthew Hayden, who made 13 at No. 6 – fell well short.*

AUSTRALIA v WEST INDIES

First One-Day International

At Melbourne, February 7, 2010 (day/night). Australia won by 113 runs. Toss: West Indies.

Australia immediately dampened prospects of a competitive series by trouncing the visitors without slipping out of first gear. That the home batsmen could lose their way in the middle overs yet still produce a total the West Indians were incapable of approaching made for a dreary spectacle, watched by one of the MCG's smallest crowds (25,463) for a limited-overs match involving Australia. Watson and Ponting played crisply in a second-wicket stand of 85, before their dismissals in quick succession briefly raised hopes of a manageable chase. Pollard's three wickets arrived through some crafty medium-pace variations on a pitch that slowed up. Replying in the twilight, Gayle managed one boundary before miscuing a pull at the pacy Bollinger to be well caught by Johnson running back from mid-off. With Harris maintaining his prolific wicket-taking from the preceding one-day series with Pakistan, the innings soon unravelled. Simmons scratched around for more than an hour and a half, and Pollard again looked a cricketer of substance, but it was a dreadful start to the series.

Man of the Match: S. R. Watson.

Australia

S. R. Watson c Morton b Gayle	59	N. M. Hauritz not out		6
S. E. Marsh c Ramdin b Smith	20	R. J. Harris not out		2
*R. T. Ponting b Pollard	49	B 4, l-b 9, w 10		23
M. J. Clarke c Ramdin b Pollard	18			
C. L. White c Ramdin b Roach	22	1/50 (2) 2/135 (1)	(8 wkts, 50 overs)	256
M. E. K. Hussey c Ramdin b Rampaul	28	3/144 (3) 4/179 (4)		
†B. J. Haddin c and b Pollard	8	5/189 (5) 6/210 (7)		
M. G. Johnson b Rampaul	21	7/241 (6) 8/254 (8)	10 overs: 50-0	

D. E. Bollinger did not bat.

Roach 10–1–41–1; Rampaul 8–0–43–2; Smith 8–0–42–1; Miller 8–0–40–0; Gayle 6–0–32–1; Pollard 10–0–45–3.

West Indies

*C. H. Gayle c Johnson b Bollinger	7	R. Rampaul c Marsh b Hauritz	3
R. S. Morton c Haddin b Harris	3	K. A. J. Roach not out	0
T. M. Dowlin c White b Bollinger	1		
L. M. P. Simmons c Haddin b Watson	29	B 4, l-b 7, w 11	22
N. Deonarine c Ponting b Johnson	19		
K. A. Pollard c Johnson b Hauritz	31	1/11 (1) 2/12 (2) 3/12 (3) (34.2 overs)	143
†D. Ramdin b Harris	17	4/44 (5) 5/108 (6) 6/111 (4)	
D. R. Smith c Watson b Hauritz	7	7/135 (8) 8/136 (7) 9/143 (9)	
N. O. Miller c Haddin b Harris	4	10/143 (10) 10 overs: 34-3	

Bollinger 6–3–18–2; Harris 9–1–24–3; Johnson 7–0–31–1; Watson 6–0–31–1; Hauritz 6.2–0–28–3.

Umpires: B. F. Bowden and B. N. J. Oxenford. Third umpire: P. R. Reiffel.

AUSTRALIA v WEST INDIES

Second One-Day International

At Adelaide, February 9, 2010 (day/night). Australia won by eight wickets. Toss: West Indies.

This match essentially ended after its first ball, with which Bollinger pinned Gayle in front. West Indies' dire start in the previous match was outdone – 16 for four this time, against 12 for three – in front of a crowd of 8,378, the smallest ever to watch Australia in a limited-overs match at the Adelaide Oval. The next four all passed 20, but it was not enough to prolong the innings beyond the 40th over, on a pitch of no particular venom. After Watson scored yet another half-century in his summer of plenty, it was left to Ponting to complete Australia's tenth successive one-day victory over West Indies (dating back to November 2006), with nearly half the overs remaining.

Man of the Match: D. E. Bollinger.

West Indies

*C. H. Gayle lbw b Bollinger	0	R. Rampaul run out	18
R. S. Morton lbw b Bollinger	4	K. A. J. Roach not out	0
T. M. Dowlin c Haddin b McKay	2		
L. M. P. Simmons c Haddin b Bollinger	1	L-b 4, w 4, n-b 3	11
N. Deonarine lbw b Johnson	23		
†D. Ramdin c Haddin b Watson	30	1/0 (1) 2/11 (3) 3/11 (2) (39.4 overs)	170
K. A. Pollard c Johnson b Bollinger	32	4/16 (4) 5/62 (5) 6/77 (6)	
D. R. Smith c Hussey b McKay	43	7/114 (7) 8/125 (9) 9/170 (10)	
N. O. Miller c Marsh b Hauritz	6	10/170 (8) 10 overs: 24-4	

Bollinger 8–2–28–4; Johnson 8–0–36–1; McKay 7.4–1–33–2; Watson 6–1–24–1; Hauritz 10–0–45–1.

Australia

S. R. Watson c Ramdin b Roach	53	
S. E. Marsh b Smith	27	
*R. T. Ponting not out	57	
M. J. Clarke not out	27	
W 6, n-b 1	7	
1/51 (2) (2 wkts, 26.3 overs)	171	
2/99 (1) 10 overs: 57-1		

C. L. White, M. E. K. Hussey, †B. J. Haddin, M. G. Johnson, N. M. Hauritz, C. J. McKay and D. E. Bollinger did not bat.

Roach 6–0–44–1; Rampaul 6–0–36–0; Smith 4–0–28–1; Miller 5–0–24–0; Pollard 4–0–28–0; Deonarine 1.3–0–11–0.

Umpires: B. F. Bowden and B. N. J. Oxenford. Third umpire: P. R. Reiffel.

AUSTRALIA v WEST INDIES

Third One-Day International

At Sydney, February 12, 2010 (day/night). No result. Toss: West Indies.

West Indies' best performance of the series was unluckily cut short by the sort of showers common in Sydney in mid-February. Australia, who had rested Watson, also lost Marsh to back trouble, leaving the opening duties in the unfamiliar hands of Paine and Voges. Both fell to deliveries that shaped into them, and what followed was a muddled innings in the face of some decent bowling. Rampaul was incisive if expensive, while Pollard was the most disciplined and impressive. Clarke's 46 occupied 74 balls, and included only one four and 34 singles. Whether West Indies' batsmen would have been capable of chasing the modest target they had been set is a matter for conjecture. Rain interrupted after five balls of their reply; after a two-hour delay the sides emerged again, the target reduced to 151 off 24 overs – but the resumption lasted only one ball before the rain returned.

Australia

†T. D. Paine b Rampaul	16		R. J. Harris c Pollard b Rampaul	21
A. C. Voges lbw b Smith	8		D. E. Bollinger not out	0
*R. T. Ponting b Sammy	22			
M. J. Clarke c Ramdin b Sammy	46		L-b 5, w 12	17
C. L. White c Ramdin b Pollard	17			
M. E. K. Hussey b Smith	44		1/28 (1) 2/30 (2) 3/78 (3) (49.5 overs)	225
J. R. Hopes c Deonarine b Rampaul	30		4/107 (5) 5/144 (4) 6/194 (6)	
M. G. Johnson c Pollard b Smith	2		7/198 (7) 8/202 (9) 9/206 (8)	
N. M. Hauritz b Rampaul	2		10/225 (10)	10 overs: 39-2

Rampaul 9.5–0–61–4; Smith 10–0–45–3; Sammy 10–0–46–2; Pollard 9–2–26–1; Miller 10–0–35–0; Gayle 1–0–7–0.

West Indies

*C. H. Gayle not out	0
T. M. Dowlin not out	0
B 4, w 2	6
(no wkt, 1 over)	6

L. M. P. Simmons, N. Deonarine, W. W. Hinds, †D. Ramdin, K. A. Pollard, D. R. Smith, D. J. G. Sammy, N. O. Miller and R. Rampaul did not bat.

Bollinger 1–0–2–0.

Umpires: B. F. Bowden and B. N. J. Oxenford. Third umpire: P. R. Reiffel.

AUSTRALIA v WEST INDIES

Fourth One-Day International

At Brisbane, February 14, 2010 (day/night). Australia won by 50 runs. Toss: West Indies.

A series Australia had never looked in danger of losing was secured when Ponting delivered a consummate century – his 29th in one-day internationals but first in 17 games at Brisbane – to an appreciative crowd of 20,088. West Indies showed a willingness to dive around in the field, removing Watson and Paine with superb catches. White added 131 with his captain in an expertly measured partnership, shrugging off a blow to the jaw from Pollard on 35. Later Voges, Hussey and especially Hopes (42 off 21 balls) sent the fielders scurrying to all parts with some intelligent shots. Ponting's century maintained his most productive touch of the summer, and helped to build the highest one-day international total at the Gabba (previously India's 303 for four in 2003-04). Gayle hinted at a decent chase, hurrying to 34 from 21 balls, but when he touched a good one from his nemesis Bollinger the innings subsided again. No other home bowler particularly distinguished himself, allowing Pollard and Dwayne Smith to add 102 and a sheen of respectability.

Man of the Match: R. T. Ponting.

Australia

S. R. Watson c Hinds b Smith	26
†T. D. Paine c Pollard b Sammy	24
*R. T. Ponting c Rampaul b Smith	106
C. L. White c Sammy b Miller	63
A. C. Voges c Miller b Rampaul	16
M. E. K. Hussey b Pollard	23
J. R. Hopes c Smith b Sammy	42

M. G. Johnson not out 7
R. J. Harris not out. 0
L-b 11, w 6 17

1/43 (1) 2/95 (2)   (7 wkts, 50 overs) 324
3/226 (4) 4/252 (5)
5/252 (3) 6/304 (6) 7/318 (7)   10 overs: 65-1

N. M. Hauritz and D. E. Bollinger did not bat.

Smith 8–0–59–2; Rampaul 10–0–68–1; Sammy 8–0–44–2; Pollard 7–0–45–1; Miller 10–0–55–1; Gayle 1–0–9–0; Deonarine 6–0–33–0.

West Indies

*C. H. Gayle c Paine b Bollinger	34
T. M. Dowlin c Paine b Harris	8
L. M. P. Simmons c Hauritz b Hopes	1
N. Deonarine c Harris b Hauritz	53
W. W. Hinds run out	20
†D. Ramdin b Bollinger	15
K. A. Pollard c Hussey b Johnson	62
D. R. Smith not out	59

D. J. G. Sammy b Harris 0
N. O. Miller not out. 5

B 2, l-b 6, w 9 17

1/44 (2) 2/44 (1)   (8 wkts, 50 overs) 274
3/55 (3) 4/100 (5) 5/127 (4)
6/146 (6) 7/248 (7) 8/265 (9)   10 overs: 55-2

R. Rampaul did not bat.

Bollinger 10–1–44–2; Harris 10–0–64–2; Hopes 6–1–39–1; Johnson 10–0–55–1; Hauritz 10–1–47–1; Voges 4–0–17–0.

Umpires: B. F. Bowden and P. R. Reiffel.   Third umpire: B. N. J. Oxenford.

AUSTRALIA v WEST INDIES

Fifth One-Day International

At Melbourne, February 19, 2010 (day/night). Australia won by 125 runs. Toss: Australia. One-day international debut: S. P. D. Smith.

Australia stuck to the script, again overwhelming West Indies with bat and ball. They matched their Brisbane total exactly, with Hopes reprising his Gabba assault on an attack that watched aghast as their fielders turfed five catches. Bollinger dismissed Gayle for the fourth time in four completed matches, miscuing to cover immediately after top-edging a pair of sixes. As usual, the major middle-order resistance was offered by Pollard; as usual, the rest melted away without much of a quarrel, though Sammy hit the debutant Steve Smith's leg-spin for three sixes. Amid continued debate about whether this unrewarding series had done the game any good, Ponting pointed with pride at the summer's limited-overs ledger that read played ten, won nine, lost none. "One-day cricket tends to bring a lot of teams closer together, and we haven't allowed that to happen," he said. But the crowd of 15,538 was even lower than for the previous Melbourne encounter.

Man of the Match: J. R. Hopes.   Man of the Series: R. T. Ponting.

Australia

S. R. Watson c Smith b Sammy	51
†B. J. Haddin b Pollard	32
*R. T. Ponting c Ramdin b Pollard	61
M. J. Clarke c Deonarine b Rampaul	47
C. L. White c Ramdin b Rampaul	22
A. C. Voges not out	45

J. R. Hopes not out 57
L-b 4, w 4, n-b 1 9

1/81 (1) 2/88 (2)   (5 wkts, 50 overs) 324
3/192 (3) 4/206 (4)
5/242 (5)   10 overs: 60-0

S. P. D. Smith, R. J. Harris, C. J. McKay and D. E. Bollinger did not bat.

Rampaul 10–0–68–2; Smith 8–0–55–0; Miller 8–0–60–0; Sammy 10–0–51–2; Pollard 9–0–59–2; Gayle 3–0–17–0; Deonarine 2–0–10–0.

West Indies

*C. H. Gayle c Clarke b Bollinger	14	N. O. Miller c Clarke b McKay	22
T. M. Dowlin lbw b Bollinger	0	R. Rampaul st Haddin b Smith	4
N. Deonarine b Harris	4		
K. A. Pollard c Smith b Hopes	45	W 5	5
W. W. Hinds c Smith b Harris	5		
L. M. P. Simmons c Clarke b Bollinger	29	1/1 (2) 2/17 (1) 3/19 (3) (36.5 overs)	199
D. R. Smith run out	21	4/39 (5) 5/80 (4) 6/118 (7)	
†D. Ramdin lbw b Smith	3	7/124 (6) 8/135 (8) 9/190 (10)	
D. J. G. Sammy not out	47	10/199 (11)	10 overs: 45-4

Bollinger 7–1–33–3; Harris 7–2–26–2; McKay 7–1–35–1; Hopes 6–0–27–1; Smith 9.5–0–78–2.

Umpires: B. F. Bowden and B. N. J. Oxenford. Third umpire: P. R. Reiffel.
Series referee: J. Srinath.

AUSTRALIA v WEST INDIES

First Twenty20 International

At Hobart, February 21, 2010 (floodlit). Australia won by 38 runs. Toss: Australia. Twenty20 international debut: N. Deonarine.

Hobart's first floodlit international attracted a capacity crowd of 15,575, who saw the home batsmen score briskly in fits and starts before their pacemen blew the West Indians out of Bellerive with a trio of fiery spells. Australia showed off their game plan for the World Twenty20 in the Caribbean: Watson and Warner swung lustily in the first six powerplay overs, eventually cracking half a dozen sixes between them, and after a mid-innings stumble Haddin strong-armed 37 from only 16 balls to take the total comfortably beyond mediocrity. What followed was as lop-sided as most of the 50-over series, but the unbridled speed of Nannes, Tait and Johnson made it a far more thrilling spectacle. Tait beat Gayle for pace, then found spiteful bounce to account for Deonarine and his own South Australian team-mate Pollard. The sixth wicket fell in the tenth over, and the subsequent recovery by Morton and Ramdin served only to narrow the margin of defeat.

Man of the Match: S. W. Tait.

Australia		B	4	6
S. R. Watson c 8 b 1	37	19	1	4
D. A. Warner c and b 7	49	32	6	2
*M. J. Clarke c 10 b 4	12	9	1	0
D. J. Hussey c 11 b 1	1	3	0	0
C. L. White c 4 b 10	15	20	0	0
T. R. Birt st 8 b 10	13	10	2	0
†B. J. Haddin not out	37	16	2	2
M. G. Johnson c and b 9	4	7	0	0
S. P. D. Smith c 8 b 7	8	5	1	0
W 2, n-b 1	3			

6 overs: 58-0   (20 overs) 179-8

1/83 2/86 3/95 4/106 5/128 6/129 7/151 8/179

S. W. Tait and D. P. Nannes did not bat.

Deonarine 2–0–17–0; Miller 4–0–20–2; Sammy 3–0–36–1; Roach 2–0–30–0; Smith 3–0–38–2; Gayle 2–0–15–2; Pollard 4–0–23–1.

West Indies		B	4	6
*C. H. Gayle b 10	5	5	1	0
L. M. P. Simmons c 10 b 11	5	6	1	0
N. Deonarine c 1 b 10	0	1	0	0
K. A. Pollard c 7 b 10	12	9	2	0
W. W. Hinds c 1 b 8	11	14	1	0
R. S. Morton c 9 b 11	40	41	3	0
D. R. Smith c 9 b 8	4	6	0	0
†D. Ramdin c 4 b 11	44	26	7	0
D. J. G. Sammy not out	3	4	0	0
N. O. Miller not out	11	8	1	0
L-b 2, w 4	6			

6 overs: 40-4   (20 overs) 141-8

1/12 2/12 3/14 4/26 5/46 6/53 7/126 8/126

K. A. J. Roach did not bat.

Nannes 4–0–21–3; Tait 4–0–30–3; Johnson 4–0–28–2; Hussey 1–0–4–0; Smith 3–0–23–0; Clarke 2–0–19–0; Watson 2–0–14–0.

Umpires: B. N. J. Oxenford and P. R. Reiffel. Third umpire: R. J. Tucker.

AUSTRALIA v WEST INDIES

Second Twenty20 International

At Sydney, February 23, 2010 (floodlit). Australia won by eight wickets. Toss: West Indies. Twenty20 international debuts: D. T. Christian, R. J. Harris.

West Indies were handed the best of the conditions for this final match, but cobbled together only 138. The Australians broadened their talent base by including the prolific limited-overs wicket-taker Ryan Harris and the 26-year-old Daniel Christian, a potentially explosive all-rounder of indigenous heritage. He enjoyed a useful cameo, claiming two inexpensive wickets (the first courtesy of Steve Smith's stunning catch, diving at deep square to account for Dowlin) then striking the winning four. Centre-stage, though, was held by Warner and Watson, who obliterated the bowling so thoroughly that the century was raised inside eight overs; 24 runs, including three sixes, came from the first of the innings, bowled by Roach. Warner's seven sixes helped him to the second-fastest half-century in Twenty20 internationals – 18 balls – and ensured an early finish, though the summer had already dragged on far too deeply into February. The only other time Australia had gone unbeaten through a home summer, since the introduction of regular one-day internationals in the late 1970s, was in 2000-01, when West Indies lost all five Tests before sharing ten one-day defeats with Zimbabwe.

Man of the Match: D. A. Warner.

West Indies

		B	4	6
*C. H. Gayle c 8 b 11	12	14	1	1
T. M. Dowlin c 8 b 4	31	32	3	0
R. S. Morton c 7 b 11	0	1	0	0
K. A. Pollard b 1	5	9	0	0
W. W. Hinds run out	0	2	0	0
D. R. Smith c 2 b 4	8	10	0	0
N. Deonarine not out	36	29	4	0
†D. Ramdin c 2 b 10	9	12	0	0
D. J. G. Sammy not out	26	11	1	2
L-b 5, w 6	11			

6 overs: 35-2   (20 overs) 138-7

1/26 2/27 3/50 4/51 5/63 6/77 7/98

N. O. Miller and K. A. J. Roach did not bat.

Tait 4–0–27–1; Harris 4–0–27–2; Johnson 4–0–22–0; Watson 3–0–15–1; Christian 4–0–29–2; Smith 1–0–13–0.

Australia

		B	4	6
S. R. Watson not out	62	33	4	4
D. A. Warner c 4 b 10	67	29	5	7
†B. J. Haddin c 3 b 10	6	6	1	0
D. T. Christian not out	4	2	1	0
W 3	3			

6 overs: 83-0   (11.4 overs) 142-2

1/99 2/138

*M. J. Clarke, D. J. Hussey, C. L. White, S. P. D. Smith, M. G. Johnson, S. W. Tait and R. J. Harris did not bat.

Roach 2–0–33–0; Sammy 1–0–14–0; Smith 1–0–9–0; Deonarine 2–0–18–0; Miller 3.4–0–56–2; Pollard 2–0–12–0.

Umpires: B. N. J. Oxenford and R. J. Tucker.   Third umpire: P. R. Reiffel.
Series referee: J. Srinath.

AUSTRALIA v SRI LANKA, 2010-11

Daniel Brettig

One-day internationals (3): Australia 1, Sri Lanka 2
Twenty20 international (1): Australia 0, Sri Lanka 1

Australia's limited-overs cricketers had nary a moment to catch breath or reset body-clock upon their return from India. Within a matter of days they were reassembling to face Sri Lanka in a home series squeezed in ahead of the Ashes because the World Cup early in 2011 left no room for it after facing England.

This seemed as much of a shock to the Australian public as it did to the players: the crowds – with the exception of a decent turnout for the Twenty20 match at Perth – were among the sparsest ever seen in Melbourne, Sydney and Brisbane. Admitting to the "disappointing" attendances, Cricket Australia's marketeers spun the line that internationals so early in the season had the effect of placing cricket on the national agenda. This was true, but not for the reasons they intended.

The Sri Lankan tourists proved themselves comfortably the more settled, not to mention accomplished, of the two sides, and won the first three internationals in some style to leave Ricky Ponting and his vice-captain Michael Clarke lost for words. They had good reason to be speechless after the Melbourne match, which was surrendered from a position of such strength that it was possible to wonder whether the Australians had completely lost their once-clinical ability to close out a contest.

There was plenty to admire about Sri Lanka's personnel and approach, which brought them their first series win in Australia, and put them second in the ICC rankings behind their hosts. It also gave Muttiah Muralitharan the joy and closure of success on his final playing visit to these shores, the first in 1995-96 having been the source of so much pain and anger after he was no-balled for throwing. No one was required to play more than one significant innings with the bat, but the contributions of Angelo Mathews at Melbourne and Upul Tharanga at Sydney were defining. Thisara Perera was the most prominent bowler, his intelligent swing and seam mirrored with less individual lustre by team-mates.

For the Australians only two batsmen scored half-centuries and only one bowler managed five wickets – slim returns that betrayed a lack of focus and cohesion. Ponting had always been scheduled to skip the third match of the one-day series to get some rest, but he also missed the first because of a family bereavement. Though some ground was regained in the last match, where the left-arm fast bowling of 20-year-old Mitchell Starc caught the eye, it was scant consolation for what had gone before. It all meant that Australia's players entered the Ashes needing to convince the public of their ability, rather than being roared on from the start with the haughty enthusiasm of old. It was quite a change.

SRI LANKAN TOURING PARTY

*K. C. Sangakkara, L. D. Chandimal, T. M. Dilshan, C. R. D. Fernando, D. P. M. D. Jayawardene, C. K. Kapugedera, K. M. D. N. Kulasekara, S. L. Malinga, A. D. Mathews, B. M. A. J. Mendis, M. Muralitharan, N. L. T. C. Perera, K. T. G. D. Prasad, S. Randiv, L. P. C. Silva, W. U. Tharanga. *Coach:* T. H. Bayliss.

At Brisbane, October 22, 2010 (day/night). **Sri Lankans won by 112 runs.** ‡**Sri Lankans 301-7** (50 overs) (C. K. Kapugedera 35, K. C. Sangakkara 110, L. P. C. Silva 75; B. Laughlin 3-54); **Queensland 189** (36.1 overs) (C. P. Simpson 31, C. A. Lynn 31, C. A. Philipson 69; K. T. G. D. Prasad 3-43, C. R. D. Fernando 4-41). *Both sides chose from 12 players, of whom 11 could bat and 11 field. The Sri Lankans, after a slow start (30-2), relied on Sangakkara, who hit ten fours and five sixes – one of which brought up his hundred. Queensland were never in the hunt after slipping from 45-0 to 51-4, with Dammika Prasad taking three of the wickets.*

At Sydney, October 24, 2010 (day/night). **New South Wales v Sri Lankans. Abandoned.** *Rain prevented any play, and the match was called off at 5.19 p.m.*

At Sydney (Blacktown Olympic Park Oval), October 27, 2010 (floodlit). **Sri Lankans won by 22 runs** (D/L method). ‡**Sri Lankans 167-4** (20 overs) (D. P. M. D. Jayawardene 59); **New South Wales 100-2** (14 overs) (P. J. Hughes 30, U. T. Khawaja 32*). *Both sides chose from 12 players, of whom 11 could bat and 11 field. The start of this Twenty20 match at a new ground to the west of Sydney was delayed by 15 minutes after the Sri Lankan team bus was held up in traffic. A rain delay early in NSW's innings revised their target to 123 in 14 overs.*

AUSTRALIA v SRI LANKA

Twenty20 International

At Perth, October 31, 2010 (floodlit). Sri Lanka won by seven wickets. Toss: Australia. Twenty20 international debuts: J. W. Hastings, C. J. McKay.

A well-prepared Sri Lankan side dealt a hiding to an Australian team still acclimatising six days after returning from India. It was Australia's first home Twenty20 international defeat, after ten victories. Clarke chose to bat, but found his side in major trouble against an accurate and varied attack. Warner was unable to make a firm connection with any of his agricultural swings and skied a catch, while Clarke pulled convulsively and was miraculously caught one-handed by Fernando, who had seemingly misjudged the flight. Demoted to No. 3, Watson fell as Warner had, then Hussey and White were defeated by sharper bounce than they expected. From 43 for five the rest of the innings was a salvage operation; just as they looked set for 150, Smith and Haddin were undone within three balls by Randiv's cagey off-breaks, and 133 was an unsatisfactory total. Jayawardene and Dilshan made a punchy start to the chase, then Sangakkara played with his customary authority to oversee the conclusion. Perera finished the match by smashing Smith over long-on for six, four and six.

Man of the Match: S. Randiv.

Australia

		B	4	6
D. A. Warner *c 5 b 11*	2	8	0	0
*M. J. Clarke *c 11 b 5*	16	19	1	1
S. R. Watson *c 10 b 5*	4	7	0	0
D. J. Hussey *c 4 b 8*	7	10	0	0
C. L. White *c 4 b 9*	8	10	0	0
†B. J. Haddin *c 6 b 8*	35	30	3	1
S. P. D. Smith *st 4 b 8*	34	23	3	1
J. W. Hastings *run out*	15	8	2	0
C. J. McKay *not out*	6	6	1	0
W 5, n-b 1	6			

6 overs: 27-2   (20 overs)   133-8

1/12 2/22 3/30 4/31 5/43 6/109 7/110 8/133

P. M. Siddle and D. P. Nannes did not bat.

Sri Lanka

		B	4	6
D. P. M. D. Jayawardene *c 6 b 10*	24	16	5	0
T. M. Dilshan *st 6 b 7*	41	34	6	0
L. D. Chandimal *lbw b 11*	2	3	0	0
*†K. C. Sangakkara *not out*	44	43	6	0
N. L. T. C. Perera *not out*	17	4	1	2
L-b 3, w 3, n-b 1	7			

6 overs: 57-2   (16.3 overs)   135-3

1/35 2/42 3/113

A. D. Mathews, C. K. Kapugedera, S. Randiv, S. L. Malinga, M. Muralitharan and C. R. D. Fernando did not bat.

Fernando 4–0–29–1; Malinga 4–0–26–1; Muralitharan 4–0–31–0; Perera 4–0–22–2; Randiv 4–0–25–3.

McKay 4–1–19–0; Nannes 3–0–28–1; Siddle 4–0–34–1; Hastings 3–0–18–0; Smith 2.3–0–33–1.

Umpires: B. N. J. Oxenford and P. R. Reiffel.   Third umpire: S. D. Fry.   Referee: B. C. Broad.

AUSTRALIA v SRI LANKA

First One-Day International

At Melbourne, November 3, 2010 (day/night). Sri Lanka won by one wicket. Toss: Australia. One-day international debut: X. J. Doherty.

Sri Lanka conjured victory from a position so dire that to say Australia had the match all but won would be to understate their position. The visitors needed another 133 when their eighth wicket went down in the 26th over, but a fearless stand between Mathews and his unlikely ally Malinga accounted for all but the last run, which came when a jubilant Muralitharan glanced Watson to the fine-leg fence. It was a ninth-wicket record in one-day internationals, beating the 126 by Kapil Dev and Syed Kirmani in a similar turnaround in India's World Cup match against Zimbabwe at Tunbridge Wells in 1983. Mathews made a vibrant 77, while Malinga – who had scored his maiden Test fifty only four months previously – now added his first one-day half-century and finished with 56 from 48 balls. Australia's total was mediocre on a fair pitch, particularly after reaching a promising 85 for one. But they lost three wickets for as many runs to Perera's clever fast-medium, and Hussey sweated 91 balls for only one boundary to set a modest target. That soon appeared gargantuan when debutant slow left-armer Xavier Doherty turned a trickle of Sri Lankan wickets into a torrent: he slid his second ball unerringly into the front pad of Jayawardene before bowling Sangakkara behind his legs with one that turned expansively. Mathews and Malinga took advantage of opponents who relaxed too soon: Johnson and Siddle were particularly culpable.

Man of the Match: A. D. Mathews.

Australia

S. R. Watson c Silva b Malinga	10	J. W. Hastings b Perera	16
†B. J. Haddin c Dilshan b Perera	49	X. J. Doherty not out	3
*M. J. Clarke c Sangakkara b Perera	27	B 1, l-b 5, w 4	10
M. E. K. Hussey not out	71		
C. L. White b Perera	0	1/30 (1) 2/85 (3) (8 wkts, 50 overs) 239
S. E. Marsh c Sangakkara b Randiv	31	3/88 (2) 4/88 (5)
S. P. D. Smith c Sangakkara b Perera	12	5/155 (6) 6/178 (7)
M. G. Johnson b Kulasekara	10	7/204 (8) 8/235 (9) 10 overs: 48-1

P. M. Siddle did not bat.

Malinga 10–0–39–1; Kulasekara 10–0–60–1; Perera 8–0–46–5; Muralitharan 9–0–36–0; Randiv 9–0–35–1; Dilshan 4–0–17–0.

Sri Lanka

W. U. Tharanga run out	3	S. L. Malinga run out	56
T. M. Dilshan c Hussey b Siddle	7	M. Muralitharan not out	4
*K. C. Sangakkara b Doherty	49		
D. P. M. D. Jayawardene lbw b Doherty	19	B 2, w 12	14
L. P. C. Silva c Watson b Doherty	4		
A. D. Mathews not out	77	1/10 (2) 2/19 (1) (9 wkts, 44.2 overs) 243
N. L. T. C. Perera b Johnson	0	3/73 (4) 4/84 (5)
S. Randiv run out	10	5/84 (3) 6/86 (7) 7/107 (8)
K. M. D. N. Kulasekara lbw b Doherty	0	8/107 (9) 9/239 (10) 10 overs: 57-2

Johnson 10–1–68–1; Siddle 8–0–51–1; Watson 6.2–0–39–0; Hastings 6–0–27–0; Doherty 10–1–46–4; Smith 3–0–8–0; Clarke 1–0–2–0.

Umpires: M. Erasmus and P. R. Reiffel.   Third umpire: B. N. J. Oxenford.

Robert Cianflone, Getty Images

Never say die: Angelo Mathews lofts a six in his triumphant innings at Melbourne.

AUSTRALIA v SRI LANKA

Second One-Day International

At Sydney, November 5, 2010 (day/night). Sri Lanka won by 29 runs (D/L method). Toss: Sri Lanka.

Disturbed more by rain than their opponents, Sri Lanka won their first series victory of any kind in Australia on a night of misery for the home side, whose defeat was their seventh in succession in all formats, in front of a crowd of only 11,495. After winning a useful toss, the Sri Lankans constructed the foundations of a strong total against an attack that was diligent but far from spiky.

Tharanga played with good sense and the occasional flashing stroke and deserved a century, only to be denied his chance by two rain delays that reduced and then closed the innings. Australia's revised target of 244 in 39 overs – later reduced to 240 in 38 by another brief shower – looked distant from the moment Haddin, leaving a yawning gap between bat and pad, was bowled by Kulasekara. The chase was a series of starts, the rate climbing all the time, and Sri Lanka's beguiling variety of pace and spin kept the batsmen off balance on a greasy surface. The last real hope was extinguished when, in one over from Randiv, Johnson was run out and Smith neatly stumped. McKay was bowled by Malinga to give every Sri Lankan bowler a wicket: a neat encapsulation of how victory had gone to the better balanced team.

Man of the Match: W. U. Tharanga.

Sri Lanka

W. U. Tharanga not out................	86
T. M. Dilshan lbw b Hauritz	47
D. P. M. D. Jayawardene lbw b Watson	5
*†K. C. Sangakkara c McKay b Watson	45
A. D. Mathews not out	17
B 2, l-b 3, w 8	13

1/98 (2) 2/116 (3)   (3 wkts, 41.1 overs) 213
3/186 (4)   10 overs: 49-0

L. P. C. Silva, N. L. T. C. Perera, S. Randiv, K. M. D. N. Kulasekara, M. Muralitharan and S. L. Malinga did not bat.

Siddle 7.1–1–31–0; McKay 8–1–42–0; Johnson 7–0–43–0; Hauritz 9–0–48–1; Smith 2–0–10–0; Watson 8–0–34–2.

Australia

S. R. Watson lbw b Muralitharan	40	C. J. McKay b Malinga	6
†B. J. Haddin b Kulasekara..............	1	P. M. Siddle not out..................	9
*R. T. Ponting c Silva b Perera	10		
M. J. Clarke c Muralitharan b Perera.....	25		
C. L. White b Kulasekara	35	B 1, l-b 5, w 3	9
M. E. K. Hussey c Mathews b Muralitharan	15	1/3 (2) 2/32 (3) 3/78 (1) (37.4 overs) 210
S. P. D. Smith st Sangakkara b Randiv	33	4/80 (4) 5/112 (6) 6/155 (5)
M. G. Johnson run out.................	23	7/189 (8) 8/189 (7) 9/199 (9)
N. M. Hauritz c Perera b Randiv	4	10/210 (10) 8 overs: 32-2

Malinga 7.4–0–34–1; Kulasekara 8–1–48–2; Perera 8–0–39–2; Muralitharan 7–0–30–2; Randiv 7–0–53–2.

Umpires: M. Erasmus and B. N. J. Oxenford.   Third umpire: P. R. Reiffel.

AUSTRALIA v SRI LANKA

Third One-Day International

At Brisbane, November 7, 2010 (day/night). Australia won by eight wickets. Toss: Sri Lanka.

Australia fired out Sri Lanka in 32 overs on a lively pitch to claim a comfortable victory and some solace from the series, in front of a crowd of only 9,037 – the lowest for a one-day international involving Australia at the Gabba. McKay accounted for most of the top order, gaining plenty of bounce and just enough seam to defeat batsmen who may have felt their job completed when the series was clinched at Sydney. Much of the later damage was done by 20-year-old Mitchell Starc, who bowled with slippery pace and a higher and more reliable action than the senior left-armer Johnson. Australia's chase was swift and efficient; Clarke gained some touch before the first Ashes Test on this ground later in the month with a series of crisp boundaries. Despite Australia's margin of victory here, the sight of Sri Lanka hoisting the trophy gave them a sobering reminder of the shortcomings uncovered over the previous three matches.

Man of the Match: C. J. McKay.   *Man of the Series:* S. L. Malinga.

Sri Lanka

W. U. Tharanga lbw b Watson	28	S. L. Malinga c Ferguson b Starc 2
T. M. Dilshan c Hussey b McKay	1	C. R. D. Fernando not out 2
*†K. C. Sangakkara c Haddin b McKay	0	
D. P. M. D. Jayawardene c White b McKay	0	L-b 10, w 14, n-b 1 25
L. P. C. Silva b Starc	33	
A. D. Mathews b Starc	9	1/8 (2) 2/8 (3) 3/14 (4) (32 overs) 115
B. M. A. J. Mendis c Haddin b Starc	5	4/50 (1) 5/81 (6) 6/92 (7)
S. Randiv b McKay	7	7/95 (5) 8/103 (9) 9/112 (8)
N. L. T. C. Perera c Smith b McKay	3	10/115 (10) 10 overs: 39-3

McKay 9–1–33–5; Johnson 5–0–17–0; Watson 5–0–11–1; Starc 9–0–27–4; Doherty 4–0–17–0.

Australia

S. R. Watson c Mathews b Fernando	15
†B. J. Haddin c and b Fernando	31
*M. J. Clarke not out	50
M. E. K. Hussey not out	6
L-b 1, w 10, n-b 6	17

1/35 (1)   (2 wkts, 21.4 overs) 119
2/84 (2)   10 overs: 63-1

C. L. White, C. J. Ferguson, S. P. D. Smith, M. G. Johnson, C. J. McKay, X. J. Doherty and M. A. Starc did not bat.

Malinga 6–0–31–0; Fernando 8–0–47–2; Perera 4.4–1–19–0; Mendis 1–0–10–0; Randiv 2–0–11–0.

Umpires: M. Erasmus and P. R. Reiffel.   Third umpire: B. N. J. Oxenford.
Series referee: B. C. Broad.

THE COMMONWEALTH BANK SERIES, 2010-11

SIMON BRIGGS

One-day internationals (7): Australia 6, England 1
Twenty20 internationals (2): Australia 1, England 1

Cricket Australia based their marketing campaign for the Commonwealth Bank Series around the 40th anniversary of the first official one-day international, which was staged after a rain-ruined Test on January 5, 1971. In honour of that impromptu game of 40 eight-ball overs – an innovation that *Wisden* declined to report in full – the stadium DJs played '70s rock music while Channel 9's presenters pulled on flares and mullet wigs.

Unfortunately, these seven – seven! – 50-over games never fully lived up to their billing as a celebration of the art form. Modern batsmen may be able to clear the boundary with greater ease and consistency than John Edrich and Ian Chappell, the top scorers in that inaugural match. But they have also learned to tick over through the middle overs, a period that often left the crowd more interested in the beach balls being batted around the stands than what was happening in the middle.

Then there was England's failure to translate their focus and form from the Ashes to the thrashes. Despite the 6–1 scoreline against them – one which replicated the result of the one-day series that followed the home Ashes victory in 2009 – they were actually only a couple of dropped catches and silly run-outs away from giving Australia a closer run. But it was the error count that killed them. To take one example, Jonathan Trott's failure to catch Shane Watson in the first 50-over match at Melbourne allowed him to push on to an unbeaten 161, and reverse the momentum of the whole summer. England made their three highest totals against Australia in Australia – but only one of them proved enough.

Given their unfortunate position, sandwiched between the Ashes and the World Cup, these limited-overs games were always going to feel like an afterthought – a money-spinning addendum tacked on to what had already been a lucrative Ashes tour. This impression was redoubled by Australia's dominance, which was interrupted by just one lonely England victory at the Adelaide Oval (a happy hunting ground for Andrew Strauss's men on this trip, with wins at Test, Twenty20 and 50-over level).

But then, the scoreline in this series was always going to be of limited significance, coming as it did after one of the great Test series of the modern era. Even as the results stacked up against him, Strauss felt able to sit in the sun at the WACA, as England prepared for the final match, and say "Regardless of what happens tomorrow, it is going to be an enjoyable plane journey home."

There were plenty of subplots bubbling under the surface. The most significant related to the injury epidemic that took out half a dozen players on

---

For coverage of the Ashes Test series, see page 210.

each side at some stage or other. The rate of attrition was so high that, as the players jockeyed for a starting berth at the World Cup, even the team physios must have reckoned they had a shot.

Mike Hussey's torn hamstring, Eoin Morgan's broken finger and Tim Bresnan's calf strain were probably the most alarming setbacks. But Graeme Swann, Paul Collingwood, Ajmal Shahzad and Chris Tremlett also pulled up for England, while Australia lost Nathan Hauritz, Xavier Doherty, Steve Smith and Shaun Marsh.

With both sets of selectors forced into "experiment" mode, no one pressed his case better than Trott. A couple of mistakes in the field couldn't take the gloss off his series return of 375 runs at 62.50, which included two centuries, one of them 137. His prolific showing was all the more timely because he was not thought to be in England's eleven at the start of the series; only Paul Collingwood's dramatic loss of form allowed him a chance. Although Trott is not a natural boundary-hitter – and came out of the series still without a single six from any of his 183 one-day internationals – he made a virtue of the most basic skill in batting: staying in.

If Trott nailed down the No. 3 position, England's opening partnership was a problem area, averaging just under 27 in the series. On January 19, the decision day for the World Cup squads, they opted for a surprise change in the wicketkeeper-opener position. Steve Davies, the man who had worn England's non-stick gloves since September, was unceremoniously dumped to allow Matt Prior to resume his former spot. This was England's tenth change of tack behind the stumps since the previous World Cup, but the shift was not conspicuously successful. Prior contributed 99 runs in five knocks at No. 2 before Morgan's finger injury required Davies to return for the final match at Perth. He made an inglorious duck, and it was Kevin Pietersen who became Strauss's opening partner in the World Cup.

Before the 50-over series, Davies had also played in the two Twenty20 internationals, both of which went down to the last ball. At Adelaide, England were indebted to the debutant Chris Woakes for sealing their eighth consecutive 20-over victory – a record for the format. Afterwards, captain Collingwood opined that "I can't see too many teams coming close to that in the future." Then, at Melbourne, some feckless batting handed Cameron White his first victory as Australia's new Twenty20 captain (Michael Clarke had resigned from the post at the end of the Sydney Test), and gave a hint of the disappointments to come over the next three weeks.

The beginning of the 50-over series brought a new storyline into play: Clarke's struggle to persuade the public that he was a worthy Australian leader. The origins of the popular animus against Clarke are hard to discern, except that his image as a wide boy contrasts with the grittiness of his predecessors. But he also came into the pyjama leg of the tour in appalling form. He eked out a painful 36 from 57 balls in the first match, while Watson was going ballistic at the other end, and earned a few heckles from the MCG crowd. These grew into jeers and even boos as Clarke scratched around in the next three matches: an "un-Australian" response from the spectators, in the words of former fast-bowling firebrand Rodney Hogg.

The low point came in Hobart, when a cheeky teenager gatecrashed the pre-match press conference and gave Clarke some unsolicited career advice, telling him to "play [the ball] in front of your nose and under your eyes". But the runs finally began to flow in the fifth and sixth matches, as a relieved Clarke top-scored both times to set up two more Australian victories. Having rediscovered his touch, he sat out the final game at the WACA, along with his best batsman and bowler (Watson and the revitalised Brett Lee). This brought more chuntering from Perth's cricket lovers, who complained that they were being short-changed, even though Australia's back-ups were still good enough to wallop England by 57 runs. It's not easy being Australia's captain in times of turmoil, even when you're handing the Poms a bashing.

ENGLAND TOURING PARTY

*A. J. Strauss (Middlesex), J. M. Anderson (Lancashire), I. R. Bell (Warwickshire), T. T. Bresnan (Yorkshire), P. D. Collingwood (Durham), S. M. Davies (Surrey), S. T. Finn (Middlesex), E. J. G. Morgan (Middlesex), K. P. Pietersen (Surrey), M. J. Prior (Sussex), A. Shahzad (Yorkshire), G. P. Swann (Nottinghamshire), J. C. Tredwell (Kent), C. T. Tremlett (Surrey), I. J. L. Trott (Warwickshire), C. R. Woakes (Warwickshire), L. J. Wright (Sussex), M. H. Yardy (Sussex).

For the two Twenty20 internationals which started this leg of the tour, Collingwood captained in place of Strauss. C. Kieswetter (Somerset) was originally selected, but developed an abscess and was replaced by M. J. Lumb (Hampshire). Finn, who was not originally selected for the limited-overs matches, stayed with the team as cover for Anderson, who returned home briefly and missed the Twenty20s and the first three one-day internationals. Bresnan (calf), Collingwood (back), Morgan (fractured finger), Shahzad (hamstring), Swann (back) and Tremlett (side) all suffered injuries during the one-day series and returned home early. L. E. Plunkett (Durham) joined the team from the England Lions' tour of West Indies in time to play in the last match.

Coach: A. Flower. *Assistant coach:* R. G. Halsall. *Bowling coach:* D. J. Saker. *Additional coach:* Mushtaq Ahmed. *Team operations manager:* P. A. Neale. *Team analyst:* G. J. Broad. *Physiotherapist:* B. Langley. *Strength and conditioning:* H. R. Bevan. *Team doctor:* Dr M. J. Stone. *Massage therapist:* M. E. S. Saxby. *Security manager:* R. C. Dickason. *Security assistant:* S. Dickason. *Media relations manager:* R. C. Evans.

At Canberra, January 10, 2011 (day/night). **England won by seven wickets** (D/L method). ‡**Prime Minister's XI 254-9** (43 overs) (T. D. Paine 50, C. J. Ferguson 39, D. T. Christian 53; A. Shahzad 3-61, M. H. Yardy 3-33); **England XI 225-3** (33.3 overs) (I. R. Bell 124*, I. J. L. Trott 48). *Two interruptions for rain reduced England's target to 223 from 35 overs, and a fine century from Bell – who hit 13 fours and a six from 102 balls in all – sent them into the internationals in an optimistic frame of mind. Bell put on 82 for the first wicket in 11.3 overs with Davies (24), then 98 in 16 overs with Trott. The PM's XI had been hamstrung by Yardy, who had 2-10 after five overs.*

AUSTRALIA v ENGLAND

First Twenty20 International

At Adelaide, January 12, 2011 (floodlit). England won by one wicket. Toss: Australia. Twenty20 international debuts: A. J. Finch; C. R. Woakes.

England's panic-stricken run-chase was rescued by Chris Woakes, a 21-year-old debutant who maintained a cooler head than any of his team-mates. Woakes had actually been picked for his bowling, but arrived at 130 for seven, with Watson on a hat-trick, and 28 still needed from 27 balls. He put down an early marker, pulling his fourth ball – from the super-speedy Tait – for a spectacular six. Then, as his colleagues continued to combust spontaneously at the other end, he flicked the final ball over midwicket for the single that sealed England's narrow win. The result was hard on Watson, who struck Swann's first three deliveries for sixes on his way to 59, then took four for 15 in his four overs.

Man of the Match: S. R. Watson. *Attendance:* 32,205.

Australia

		B	4	6
D. A. Warner c 11 b 8	30	28	5	0
S. R. Watson b 8	59	31	6	3
D. J. Hussey b 7	28	27	1	1
*C. L. White c 3 b 9	6	9	0	0
A. J. Finch not out	15	14	1	0
S. P. D. Smith not out	15	11	1	0
B 1, l-b 1, w 2	4			

6 overs: 41-0   (20 overs)   157-4

1/83 2/92 3/115 4/133

†T. D. Paine, S. N. J. O'Keefe, M. G. Johnson, B. Lee and S. W. Tait did not bat.

Woakes 4–0–34–1; Shahzad 4–0–25–0; Bresnan 4–0–28–1; Yardy 4–0–28–2; Swann 4–0–40–0.

England

		B	4	6
I. R. Bell c 6 b 9	27	17	4	1
†S. M. Davies c 4 b 10	4	2	1	0
K. P. Pietersen c 3 b 8	25	11	3	1
*P. D. Collingwood c 7 b 3	16	20	2	0
E. J. G. Morgan c 3 b 2	43	33	5	1
L. J. Wright lbw b 11	0	2	0	0
T. T. Bresnan c 10 b 2	11	11	1	0
M. H. Yardy c 7 b 2	0	1	0	0
C. R. Woakes not out	19	15	1	1
G. P. Swann b 2	6	5	0	0
A. Shahzad not out	0	3	0	0
L-b 5, w 2	7			

6 overs: 64-3   (20 overs)   158-9

1/16 2/49 3/63 4/99 5/104 6/130 7/130 8/141 9/154

Tait 4–0–40–1; Lee 4–0–41–1; Johnson 4–0–27–1; O'Keefe 2–0–16–1; Watson 4–0–15–4; Hussey 2–0–14–1.

Umpires: S. D. Fry and B. N. J. Oxenford.   Third umpire: P. R. Reiffel.

AUSTRALIA v ENGLAND

Second Twenty20 International

At Melbourne, January 14, 2011 (floodlit). Australia won by four runs. Toss: Australia.

Another newcomer made the difference – this time a human wardrobe named Finch. Playing only his second international, the hulking Aaron Finch – from Colac in up-country Victoria – heaved a slew of boundaries in his 53 from 33 balls, which revived a faltering Australian innings. England's winning streak then petered out, owing to an erratic batting display from their top six. A target of 148 should have been within their compass after Bell and Davies had shared a rollicking opening stand of 60 in 7.2 overs. But Bell missed a wild heave at Johnson, and even Woakes – with another composed late hand – could not quite bale out a leaky middle order this time.

Man of the Match: A. J. Finch.   *Attendance:* 58,837.

Australia

		B	4	6
D. A. Warner c 3 b 9	30	26	3	0
S. R. Watson c 5 b 8	17	10	0	2
†T. D. Paine c 4 b 10	21	12	2	1
D. J. Hussey c 8 b 9	8	16	0	0
*C. L. White lbw b 10	0	2	0	0
A. J. Finch not out	53	33	4	2
S. P. D. Smith c 4 b 11	13	18	0	0
S. N. J. O'Keefe b 7	1	2	0	0
M. G. Johnson not out	1	1	0	0
L-b 2, w 1	3			

6 overs: 57-1   (20 overs)   147-7

1/37 2/63 3/72 4/74 5/80 6/131 7/138

B. Lee and S. W. Tait did not bat.

Woakes 3–0–29–1; Shahzad 3–0–34–1; Bresnan 4–0–27–1; Swann 4–0–19–2; Yardy 4–0–19–2; Pietersen 2–0–17–0.

England

		B	4	6
I. R. Bell b 9	39	30	3	0
†S. M. Davies c 1 b 2	29	26	2	0
K. P. Pietersen c 5 b 9	1	2	0	0
*P. D. Collingwood c 1 b 2	6	10	0	0
E. J. G. Morgan c 6 b 9	14	21	1	0
L. J. Wright c 7 b 11	18	15	1	0
T. T. Bresnan not out	15	12	0	0
C. R. Woakes not out	11	6	0	1
L-b 2, w 6, n-b 2	10			

6 overs: 50-0   (20 overs)   143-6

1/60 2/62 3/74 4/88 5/111 6/113

M. H. Yardy, G. P. Swann and A. Shahzad did not bat.

Tait 4–0–39–1; Lee 4–0–29–0; Watson 4–0–17–2; Johnson 4–0–29–3; Hussey 4–0–18–0; O'Keefe 1–0–9–0.

Umpires: B. N. J. Oxenford and P. R. Reiffel.   Third umpire: S. D. Fry.
Series referee: R. S. Madugalle.

Shifting the momentum of the summer: Shane Watson drives Australia to victory in the opening one-day international.

AUSTRALIA v ENGLAND

First One-Day International

At Melbourne, January 16, 2011 (day/night). Australia won by six wickets. Toss: England.

A cathartic innings from Watson released the frustration of his nearly-man Test series, during which he had passed 50 four times without once reaching three figures. This time he just kept going and going until he had an unbeaten 161, the fifth-highest one-day international score by an Australian. Watson's broad-chested drives were the highlight of one of the most dominant knocks England had ever encountered. Dropped off a difficult chance by Trott at mid-on when 44, he bludgeoned 12 fours and four sixes and, though he peppered the arc between long-on and midwicket, he also had the touch to score heavily behind the wicket. With little support, Watson contributed well over half his side's runs as they successfully chased 294 – the highest England had made against Australia on their own territory. The English innings had been helped along by a rash of fielding errors: Haddin missed three stumpings, while Davies used up four lives before finally falling for an unconvincing 42. Their top-scorer was Pietersen, returning to the one-day side after being dropped for the home series against Pakistan and replacing the out-of-form Collingwood. But after clubbing three sixes off the spinners, Pietersen ran himself out for 78, just when an individual hundred – and a team score of at least 320 – had looked within his grasp. After the match, Watson admitted that his mind had been distracted from cricket in the lead-up to the game, because of the floodwaters inundating his native Queensland town of Ipswich.

Man of the Match: S. R. Watson.   *Attendance:* 34,854.

England

*A. J. Strauss c Clarke b Lee	63	A. Shahzad not out 8
†S. M. Davies b D. J. Hussey	42	C. T. Tremlett c Haddin b Johnson 7
I. J. L. Trott c Haddin b D. J. Hussey	6	
K. P. Pietersen run out	78	B 2, l-b 1, w 14, n-b 1 18
I. R. Bell c Clarke b Smith	23	
E. J. G. Morgan c White b Smith	8	1/90 (2) 2/100 (3) (49.4 overs) 294
M. H. Yardy c M. E. K. Hussey b Bollinger	9	3/131 (1) 4/174 (5) 5/186 (6)
T. T. Bresnan c Doherty b Lee	28	6/236 (7) 7/257 (4) 8/271 (8)
G. P. Swann c Doherty b Johnson	4	9/278 (9) 10/294 (11) 10 overs: 70-0

Lee 9–0–43–2; Bollinger 9–0–57–1; D. J. Hussey 6–0–42–2; Johnson 7.4–0–53–2; Watson 8–0–44–0; Doherty 7–0–40–0; Smith 3–0–12–2.

Australia

S. R. Watson not out	161	C. L. White not out	25
†B. J. Haddin c Shahzad b Swann	39	L-b 6, w 3, n-b 1	10
*M. J. Clarke c Shahzad b Bresnan	36		
S. P. D. Smith c Yardy b Shahzad	5	1/110 (2) 2/213 (3) (4 wkts, 49.1 overs) 297	
M. E. K. Hussey c Tremlett b Bresnan	21	3/220 (4) 4/244 (5) 10 overs: 62-0	

D. J. Hussey, M. G. Johnson, B. Lee, X. J. Doherty and D. E. Bollinger did not bat.

Bresnan 10–0–71–2; Tremlett 10–0–67–0; Shahzad 9.1–0–51–1; Yardy 9–0–53–0; Swann 10–0–42–1; Trott 1–0–7–0.

Umpires: B. F. Bowden and B. N. J. Oxenford.   Third umpire: A. L. Hill.
Referee: R. S. Madugalle.

AUSTRALIA v ENGLAND

Second One-Day International

At Hobart, January 21, 2011 (day/night). Australia won by 46 runs. Toss: England.

Having been under lock and key at 33 for four, and later 142 for eight, Australia slipped past England's jailers thanks to a late stand of 88, their highest for the ninth wicket in one-day internationals. Aggravating for the tourists, one of the partners was Bollinger, whose best score in any 50-over match, international or otherwise, had previously been seven. This time, Bollinger rode his luck to belt 30 from as many balls, while Marsh – only called up as cover for Mike Hussey, who had ripped his hamstring in the previous match – made a magnificent 110 from No. 6. England's seamers, particularly Tremlett, had been impeccable with the new ball, but spinner Yardy went the distance as Marsh unfurled some ferocious slog-sweeps in his second one-day international hundred. The fired-up Bollinger then claimed four for 28 – including Pietersen for a golden duck – as England's top order were blown away. The match was notable for a further series of injuries, as Hauritz dislocated his shoulder, Bresnan tore a calf muscle, and Tait limped off with a thigh problem.

Man of the Match: S. E. Marsh.   *Attendance:* 15,125.

Australia

S. R. Watson b Shahzad	5	D. E. Bollinger c Shahzad b Tremlett	30
†B. J. Haddin b Shahzad	5	S. W. Tait not out	0
*M. J. Clarke c Bell b Bresnan	10		
C. L. White c and b Yardy	45	L-b 7, w 8	15
D. J. Hussey c Strauss b Tremlett	8		
S. E. Marsh c Bell b Tremlett	110	1/6 (1) 2/15 (2) 3/21 (3) (48.2 overs) 230	
S. P. D. Smith b Shahzad	0	4/33 (5) 5/133 (4) 6/136 (7)	
N. M. Hauritz c Trott b Bresnan	2	7/140 (8) 8/142 (9) 9/230 (10)	
B. Lee b Yardy	0	10/230 (6) 10 overs: 21-3	

Shahzad 10–1–43–3; Tremlett 9.2–0–22–3; Bresnan 9–1–37–2; Trott 3–0–16–0; Tredwell 8–0–44–0; Yardy 9–1–61–2.

England

*A. J. Strauss lbw b Bollinger	19	A. Shahzad run out	2
†M. J. Prior c Watson b Lee	0	C. T. Tremlett not out	1
I. J. L. Trott c Hussey b Smith	32		
K. P. Pietersen b Bollinger	0	L-b 6, w 13, n-b 1	20
I. R. Bell c Smith b Lee	32		
E. J. G. Morgan c Tait b Watson	21	1/12 (2) 2/36 (1) 3/36 (4) (45 overs) 184	
M. H. Yardy run out	22	4/83 (3) 5/96 (5) 6/140 (6)	
T. T. Bresnan c Watson b Bollinger	19	7/147 (7) 8/178 (8) 9/180 (9)	
J. C. Tredwell lbw b Bollinger	16	10/184 (10) 10 overs: 41-3	

Lee 9–0–39–2; Tait 5.5–0–30–0; Bollinger 9–0–28–4; Watson 9–0–32–1; Hauritz 8–0–36–0; Smith 2–0–5–1; Clarke 0.1–0–0–0; Hussey 2–0–8–0.

Umpires: A. L. Hill and P. R. Reiffel.   Third umpire: B. F. Bowden.
Referee: J. Srinath.

AUSTRALIA v ENGLAND

Third One-Day International

At Sydney, January 23, 2011 (day/night). Australia won by four wickets. Toss: England. One-day international debut: C. R. Woakes.

The strain of a long tour was evident in a poor match that featured cheap dismissals on both sides. Batting first, England should have made better use of an advantageous toss, but only Trott established himself, and even he was content to bunt singles for most of his innings, apparently waiting for someone to crash a few boundaries at the other end. Nobody did, and when Tremlett was dozily run out in the 48th over, failing to ground his bat, England were all out for 214 with Trott still there on 84. Australia maintained the tension as four of their top five failed to reach double figures, but Haddin's bumptious 54 and David Hussey's more sure-footed 68 not out took them home. The standard of batting was so bad that, for once, the match award went to a bowler: Lee, for his three for 27.

Man of the Match: B. Lee.   Attendance: 36,072.

England

*A. J. Strauss run out	23	A. Shahzad c White b Lee		4
†M. J. Prior lbw b Lee	0	C. T. Tremlett run out		1
I. J. L. Trott not out	84			
I. R. Bell c and b Watson	10	L-b 3, w 6, n-b 1		10
E. J. G. Morgan c Clarke b Hussey	30			
P. D. Collingwood b Doherty	1	1/1 (2) 2/38 (1) 3/61 (4)	(48 overs)	214
M. H. Yardy c and b Doherty	7	4/118 (5) 5/119 (6) 6/130 (7)		
L. J. Wright c Haddin b Hastings	32	7/179 (8) 8/199 (9) 9/208 (10)		
C. R. Woakes c Haddin b Lee	12	10/214 (11)	10 overs: 47-2	

Lee 8–0–27–3; Bollinger 8–0–36–0; Hastings 10–0–51–1; Watson 6–0–17–1; Smith 3–0–19–0; Doherty 10–0–37–2; Hussey 3–0–24–1.

Australia

S. R. Watson b Tremlett	9	J. W. Hastings not out		18
†B. J. Haddin c Woakes b Collingwood	54			
S. E. Marsh lbw b Shahzad	6	L-b 7, w 11		18
*M. J. Clarke c Yardy b Woakes	9			
C. L. White lbw b Collingwood	7	1/10 (1) 2/27 (3)	(6 wkts, 46 overs)	215
D. J. Hussey not out	68	3/59 (4) 4/92 (5)		
S. P. D. Smith c Yardy b Tremlett	26	5/100 (2) 6/163 (7)	10 overs: 53-2	

B. Lee, X. J. Doherty and D. E. Bollinger did not bat.

Shahzad 10–0–45–1; Tremlett 9–0–50–2; Woakes 7–0–31–1; Wright 2–0–12–0; Yardy 10–0–45–0; Collingwood 8–0–25–2.

Umpires: G. A. V. Baxter and P. R. Reiffel.   Third umpire: A. L. Hill.
Referee: J. Srinath.

AUSTRALIA v ENGLAND

Fourth One-Day International

At Adelaide, January 26, 2011 (day/night). England won by 21 runs. Toss: England.

Lifting themselves briefly out of their end-of-tour malaise, England did at least stave off the embarrassment of losing the series in the shortest possible time by winning on Australia Day. The catalyst was a bold 67 from opener Prior, who had failed to score in the previous two matches. He struck the ball with panache in a stand of 113 with Trott, who reprised his anchorman role from the previous game, and went on to register his second one-day international hundred. When strong finishing from Yardy and Collingwood carried England to 299, they had broken their record against Australia in Australia for the second time in the series. This time, it was enough. Watson threatened again, with a classy 64, but acceleration proved tricky in the middle overs when England turned to their dibbly-dobbly medium-pacers. Trott, who had never taken a wicket in 14 previous one-day internationals, completed a strong all-round performance with figures of two for 31.

Man of the Match: I. J. L. Trott.   *Attendance:* 34,393.

England

*A. J. Strauss c Haddin b Lee	8	A. Shahzad c Watson b Hussey		4
†M. J. Prior c Doherty b Smith	67	C. T. Tremlett not out		0
I. J. L. Trott b Hussey	102	L-b 4, w 12		16
K. P. Pietersen c Marsh b Smith	12			
I. R. Bell c Haddin b Smith	0	1/23 (1) 2/136 (2)	(8 wkts, 50 overs)	299
E. J. G. Morgan c Lee b Hussey	24	3/158 (4) 4/158 (5)		
P. D. Collingwood c White b Hussey	27	5/224 (3) 6/227 (6)		
M. H. Yardy not out	39	7/283 (7) 8/294 (9)	10 overs: 65-1	

J. M. Anderson did not bat.

Lee 8–0–68–1; Bollinger 9–0–55–0; Watson 5–0–29–0; Hastings 7–0–45–0; Doherty 10–0–44–0; Smith 7–0–33–3; Hussey 4–0–21–4.

Australia

S. R. Watson c Prior b Shahzad	64	J. W. Hastings c Strauss b Anderson		1
†B. J. Haddin c Strauss b Tremlett	20	B. Lee not out		39
S. E. Marsh c and b Anderson	1	B 4, l-b 8, w 7, n-b 1		20
*M. J. Clarke b Collingwood	15			
C. L. White c Yardy b Trott	44	1/32 (2) 2/33 (3)	(7 wkts, 50 overs)	278
D. J. Hussey c Bell b Trott	28	3/87 (4) 4/116 (1)		
S. P. D. Smith not out	46	5/176 (6) 6/199 (5) 7/201 (8)	10 overs: 45-2	

X. J. Doherty and D. E. Bollinger did not bat.

Anderson 10–1–57–2; Shahzad 10–0–58–1; Tremlett 10–0–62–1; Collingwood 7–0–22–1; Yardy 6–0–36–0; Trott 7–0–31–2.

Umpires: M. Erasmus and S. D. Fry.   Third umpire: G. A. V. Baxter.
Referee: J. Srinath.

AUSTRALIA v ENGLAND

Fifth One-Day International

At Brisbane, January 30, 2011 (day/night). Australia won by 51 runs. Toss: Australia. One-day international debut: S. T. Finn.

Woakes caught the eye again by claiming six for 45 – the second-best bowling figures by an Englishman, and the best overseas. But his was a lone hand as England surrendered the series with their feeblest all-round performance of the entire tour. Australia's innings was scratchy, punctuated as it was by batsmen clipping the accurate Woakes straight to fielders. But Clarke's first half-century since the Adelaide Test helped them towards 249 – about par on a bouncy Gabba pitch. England's reply was soon in tatters. They lost their top three in the space of eight balls, including linchpin Trott for a first-ball duck as he flicked the pacy Lee to short fine leg. Pietersen's 40 – which ended when he was duped by a slow bouncer from Hastings and pulled to mid-on – was the top score as England subsided to 128 for eight, although a few lusty blows from Finn (whose 35 on debut was the highest innings by an England No. 11 in one-day internationals) helped add some respectability to the scorecard.

Man of the Match: C. R. Woakes.   *Attendance:* 30,651.

Australia

S. R. Watson c Collingwood b Woakes	16	B. Lee c sub (L. J. Wright) b Woakes	0	
†B. J. Haddin b Finn	37	D. E. Bollinger run out	6	
S. E. Marsh c Strauss b Collingwood	16			
*M. J. Clarke c Strauss b Woakes	54	B 2, l-b 3, w 11, n-b 1	17	
C. L. White c Prior b Woakes	16			
D. J. Hussey b Woakes	34	1/48 (1) 2/72 (2) 3/96 (3)	(49.3 overs) 249	
S. P. D. Smith not out	24	4/113 (5) 5/178 (6) 6/190 (4)		
M. G. Johnson b Anderson	16	7/212 (8) 8/128 (9) 9/234 (10)		
J. W. Hastings c Collingwood b Woakes	13	10/249 (11)	10 overs: 50-1	

Anderson 10–1–42–1; Shahzad 8–1–46–0; Finn 10–0–61–1; Woakes 10–0–45–6; Collingwood 10–1–36–1; Trott 1.3–0–14–0.

England

*A. J. Strauss c Smith b Bollinger	3	J. M. Anderson not out	20	
†M. J. Prior b Lee	14	S. T. Finn b Watson	35	
I. J. L. Trott c Bollinger b Lee	0			
K. P. Pietersen c Lee b Hastings	40	L-b 2, w 4, n-b 7	13	
I. R. Bell b Hastings	36			
E. J. G. Morgan c Johnson b Smith	2	1/20 (2) 2/20 (1) 3/22 (3)	(45.3 overs) 198	
P. D. Collingwood c Hastings b Watson	18	4/95 (4) 5/98 (6) 6/103 (5)		
C. R. Woakes c Haddin b Watson	8	7/128 (7) 8/128 (8) 9/145 (9)		
A. Shahzad c Haddin b Bollinger	9	10/198 (11)	10 overs: 45-3	

Lee 7–0–21–2; Bollinger 9–1–57–2; Johnson 8–1–29–0; Hastings 9–0–35–2; Smith 8–0–29–1; Watson 4.3–1–25–3.

Umpires: Asad Rauf and R. J. Tucker.   Third umpire: M. Erasmus.
Referee: J. Srinath.

AUSTRALIA v ENGLAND

Sixth One-Day International

At Sydney, February 2, 2011 (day/night). Australia won by two wickets. Toss: England.

Another record for England, whose 333 for six was their best on Australian soil, although it was surpassed by the fourth-highest successful run-chase in one-day internationals; and more runs for Trott, who continued his prolific tour with 137. Only Robin Smith had played a bigger individual innings for England against Australia, 167 not out at Edgbaston in 1993: England lost that one too. Trott arrived in the eighth over and ticked along almost imperceptibly at first. He faced 126 balls in all, working 64 for singles, and allowing only 37 to pass without scoring. But on a swelteringly hot and humid evening, all this legwork left him with severe cramp, which forced him to use a runner once he had reached his hundred. When England bowled, Woakes opened with a wide half-volley which Watson drove for four, and then fired five wides down the leg side, so that Australia had nine runs after one legitimate ball. From that moment, the chase was always on, as every man in the top seven – including the promoted Johnson – reached 20. Clarke confirmed his return to form with a commanding 82 from 70 balls, although his run-out in the 48th over left Hastings to scramble Australia over the line with an inside-edge past the stumps for four. It was the highest total England had made to lose a match – and the highest in any one-day international not to contain a six – while it was Australia's best when batting second. Anderson's figures of 10–0–91–1, meanwhile, were the second-most expensive by an England bowler.

Man of the Match: I. J. L. Trott. *Attendance:* 19,479.

England

*A. J. Strauss c Hussey b Smith	63	C. R. Woakes not out	0
†M. J. Prior b Johnson	18		
I. J. L. Trott c and b Tait	137	B 1, l-b 4, w 6, n-b 2	13
K. P. Pietersen c Smith b Lee	29		
I. R. Bell c Clarke b Tait	45	1/41 (2) 2/121 (1) (6 wkts, 50 overs)	333
E. J. G. Morgan c Tait b Watson	21	3/189 (4) 4/293 (5)	
P. D. Collingwood not out	7	5/319 (6) 6/330 (3) 10 overs: 46-1	

M. H. Yardy, J. M. Anderson and S. T. Finn did not bat.

Lee 9–1–66–1; Tait 10–0–59–2; Johnson 6–0–43–1; Hastings 7–0–48–0; Hussey 4–0–25–0; Smith 7–0–40–1; Clarke 1–0–7–0; Watson 6–0–40–1.

Australia

S. R. Watson c Strauss b Yardy	51	J. W. Hastings not out	7
†B. J. Haddin c Trott b Anderson	20	B. Lee not out	2
C. J. Ferguson run out	46	W 11	11
M. G. Johnson st Prior b Pietersen	57		
*M. J. Clarke run out	82	1/71 (2) 2/87 (1) (8 wkts, 49.2 overs)	334
C. L. White c Morgan b Finn	20	3/166 (3) 4/194 (4)	
D. J. Hussey c Prior b Finn	38	5/224 (6) 6/314 (7)	
S. P. D. Smith run out	0	7/317 (8) 8/327 (5) 10 overs: 78-1	

S. W. Tait did not bat.

Woakes 9.2–0–73–0; Anderson 10–0–91–1; Finn 10–0–51–2; Yardy 10–0–47–1; Pietersen 6–0–43–1; Trott 4–0–29–0.

Umpires: M. Erasmus and D. J. Harper. Third umpire: Asad Rauf.
Referee: J. Srinath.

AUSTRALIA v ENGLAND

Seventh One-Day International

At Perth, February 6, 2011. Australia won by 57 runs. Toss: Australia. One-day international debut: J. J. Krejza.

Australia rested three of their highest-profile players – Clarke, Watson and Lee. When combined with the ever-extending injury list, this left them with a virtual shadow squad. Still, Australia's second-string side was easily good enough to wallop an increasingly dispirited England. For the tourists, Liam Plunkett came in after a 40-hour journey from St Kitts, but Morgan was missing after X-rays revealed the broken finger on his left hand which would keep him out of the World Cup. England bowled satisfactorily, no more, on a classic WACA trampoline. They reduced Australia to 103 for four, but – as at Hobart – could not find the critical wicket that would have opened up the tail, as they lacked an attacking spinner. Voges, a Perth boy who knew the local conditions intimately, played some crunching cuts in his unbeaten 80 from 72 balls, and his stand of 95 with David Hussey left England chasing 280. They lost both openers for ducks, and their entire top five by the 15th over. Despite a defiant 60 not out from the hardy Yardy, it was never going to be a happy ending for Strauss's men.

Man of the Match: A. C. Voges. *Attendance:* 18,736.
Man of the Series: S. R. Watson.

Australia

T. D. Paine lbw b Plunkett	5	J. W. Hastings c Wright b Anderson	6
†B. J. Haddin c Finn b Yardy	27	J. J. Krejza not out	6
C. J. Ferguson c Strauss b Anderson	15	L-b 11, w 19	30
*C. L. White c and b Yardy	24		
D. J. Hussey c Bell b Plunkett	60	1/16 (1) 2/35 (3) (7 wkts, 50 overs)	279
A. C. Voges not out	80	3/72 (2) 4/103 (4)	
M. G. Johnson c Prior b Anderson	26	5/198 (5) 6/243 (7) 7/263 (8) 10 overs: 36-2	

S. W. Tait and D. E. Bollinger did not bat.

Anderson 10–1–48–3; Plunkett 10–0–49–2; Finn 10–1–57–0; Wright 9–0–47–0; Yardy 10–0–59–2; Trott 1–0–8–0.

England

*A. J. Strauss b Tait	0	S. T. Finn b Tait	0
†S. M. Davies c Haddin b Bollinger	0	J. M. Anderson c Haddin b Hastings	4
I. J. L. Trott c Hussey b Johnson	14		
K. P. Pietersen c Krejza b Johnson	26	L-b 3, w 19, n-b 5	27
I. R. Bell c Tait b Johnson	8		
M. J. Prior c Hussey b Krejza	39	1/0 (1) 2/5 (2) 3/48 (3) (44 overs)	222
M. H. Yardy not out	60	4/56 (4) 5/64 (5) 6/119 (6)	
L. J. Wright c Bollinger b Krejza	24	7/152 (8) 8/200 (9) 9/200 (10)	
L. E. Plunkett c Haddin b Tait	20	10/222 (11) 10 overs: 55-3	

Tait 8–1–48–3; Bollinger 7–0–45–1; Johnson 7–0–18–3; Hastings 9–0–39–1; Krejza 9–0–53–2; Hussey 4–0–16–0.

Umpires: Asad Rauf and P. R. Reiffel.   Third umpire: M. Erasmus.
Referee: J. Srinath.

DOMESTIC CRICKET IN AUSTRALIA, 2009-10

PETER ENGLISH

Victoria remained Australia's most accomplished domestic outfit, lifting the Sheffield Shield and Twenty20 trophies. With a line-up of seasoned talent who had limited appeal to the national selectors, their only blemish was losing the 50-over final to Tasmania.

David Hussey, the Shield's leading run-scorer with 970 at 57, produced a superb 168 in the five-day final at the MCG, where Cameron White let his men bat on to 591 in the second innings before setting Queensland an impossible 640; Victoria dismissed them for 182 to claim back-to-back first-class trophies for the first time in 30 years. Their 28th title came despite the decision of Brad Hodge and Dirk Nannes to retire from first-class cricket, to prevent domestic clashes with the IPL. Hodge exited in December, with 10,474 Shield runs in 140 matches, and Nannes even earlier.

Both continued in the shorter formats and helped Victoria win the Twenty20 final against South Australia, the early pace-setters: Aiden Blizzard led the batting with 42 from 19 balls, and the hosts were overpowered after captain Graham Manou was dismissed by Nannes off the first ball of their reply. Victoria, who have won four of the five Big Bash tournaments, earned a second shot at the lucrative Champions League, after going out in the semi-finals in October 2009. South Australia qualified alongside them for the next tournament, in South Africa.

The inaugural Champions League in India was won by **New South Wales**. But back in Australia their results were inconsistent, despite an enviable list of talented young players. The Blues unearthed an exciting core of fast bowlers in Josh Hazlewood, Trent Copeland and Mitchell Starc, while leg-spinning all-rounder Steve Smith combined 772 Shield runs with 21 wickets and gained national recognition. Phillip Hughes returned from his Ashes disappointment with 953 runs, winning a couple more Test caps; Usman Khawaja, another fine prospect, scored three first-class hundreds. But the bright flashes could not push New South Wales above third in any competition.

Queensland exceeded expectations in a season of rebuilding. They relied heavily on wicketkeeper Chris Hartley, the Shield Player of the Year for his 827 runs and 44 dismissals, and Ben Cutting, a tall right-arm fast bowler, who topped the wicket-takers' list with 46. Another promising arrival was Cameron Boyce, a 20-year-old leg-spinner, who collected seven wickets in the Shield final. But the Gabba is rarely a kind environment for emerging slow bowlers.

Tom Moody's third fruitless campaign as coach of **Western Australia** ended his tenure; Mickey Arthur, who had resigned as South Africa's coach, succeeded him. Arthur faced a difficult job lifting a squad that has struggled for unity and runs, although Luke Ronchi, the aggressive wicketkeeper-batsman, re-emerged from the struggles that followed his brief spell in Australia's limited-overs sides.

Tasmania lost the stalwart Dan Marsh, son of Rod, to retirement. He had scored 7,449 first-class runs in 14 seasons with the state, led them to their first Shield win in 2006-07, and was part of three domestic 50-over triumphs, including their victory in February. George Bailey performed solidly, with 692 runs in his first year as captain, but Ed Cowan, recruited from New South Wales, was the batting leader with 957. Tasmania also picked up former one-day international Mark Cosgrove in the off-season.

Cosgrove had been cut by a suddenly ruthless **South Australia**, despite scoring 511 in eight Shield matches. Tired of perennial underachievement, the Redbacks also changed captains after finishing last in the Shield and one-day tournaments, and chose Michael Klinger to replace Manou.

Cricket Australia trialled pink balls in a handful of Second Eleven fixtures, without the success needed to expand the experiment. They were hoping for better results when they tried out split-innings matches in the 2010-11 one-day competition.

FIRST-CLASS AVERAGES, 2009-10

BATTING (500 runs, average 35.00)

	M	I	NO	R	HS	100s	Avge	Ct/St
S. P. D. Smith (*New South Wales*)	8	13	3	772	177	4	77.20	17
†U. T. Khawaja (*New South Wales*)	7	12	1	698	132*	3	63.45	5
M. Klinger (*South Australia*)	10	19	5	886	207*	2	63.28	7
S. R. Watson (*Australia*)	6	11	1	609	120*	1	60.90	11
M. J. Clarke (*New South Wales & Australia*)	7	12	2	588	166	2	58.80	9
D. J. Hussey (*Victoria*)	10	17	0	970	174	3	57.05	14
†M. E. K. Hussey (*Australia*)	6	11	2	502	134*	1	55.77	8
†P. J. Hughes (*New South Wales & Australia*)	11	19	0	990	192	3	52.10	8
R. T. Ponting (*Australia*)	6	11	1	514	209	1	51.40	5
†E. J. M. Cowan (*Tasmania*)	11	20	1	963	225	3	50.68	7
†C. J. L. Rogers (*Victoria*)	9	15	2	641	149	2	49.30	4
†S. M. Katich (*New South Wales & Australia*)	11	18	1	829	108	2	48.76	10
†M. S. Wade (*Victoria*)	11	17	3	677	96	0	48.35	32/1
L. Ronchi (*Western Australia*)	10	17	2	716	148	3	47.73	42/2
†C. D. Hartley (*Queensland*)	12	20	2	839	125	2	46.61	49/1
G. J. Bailey (*Tasmania*)	10	18	1	742	115	2	43.64	10
†M. J. Cosgrove (*South Australia*)	8	14	2	511	105	2	42.58	6
C. J. Borgas (*South Australia*)	8	14	2	504	164*	1	42.00	1
†P. A. Jaques (*New South Wales*)	10	17	1	636	131	1	39.75	3
N. Jewell (*Victoria*)	11	19	0	682	96	0	35.89	6
A. J. Doolan (*Tasmania*)	10	18	0	642	135	2	35.66	7
J. D. Smith (*South Australia*)	10	19	1	641	116	1	35.61	4

BOWLING (20 wickets)

	Style	O	M	R	W	BB	5W/i	Avge
D. G. Wright (*Victoria*)	RFM	218.3	79	502	35	5-37	2	14.34
T. A. Copeland (*New South Wales*)	RFM	234.1	76	615	35	8-92	3	17.57
D. E. Bollinger (*New South Wales & Australia*)	LFM	235.1	51	695	34	5-68	2	20.44
B. C. J. Cutting (*Queensland*)	RFM	335.3	76	1,100	46	6-37	3	23.91
L. W. Feldman (*Queensland*)	RFM	249.2	61	791	33	5-32	1	23.96
B. A. Knowles (*Western Australia*)	RFM	214.1	39	750	30	4-32	0	25.00
C. R. Swan (*Queensland*)	RFM	276.1	75	793	31	5-26	1	25.58
J. W. Hastings (*Victoria*)	RFM	337.2	88	941	36	4-30	0	26.13
N. M. Hauritz (*Australia*)	OB	245.4	47	778	29	5-53	2	26.82

	Style	O	M	R	W	BB	5W/i	Avge
M. G. Johnson (*Australia*)	LF	221.2	43	785	29	5-103	1	27.06
B. Geeves (*Tasmania*)	RFM	203	53	571	21	5-106	1	27.19
S. J. Magoffin (*Western Australia*)	RFM	348	112	853	31	6-44	2	27.51
A. B. McDonald (*Victoria*)	RM	329.1	90	839	29	4-37	0	28.93
P. R. George (*South Australia*)	RFM	364.5	101	1,096	36	8-84	1	30.44
M. G. Hogan (*Western Australia*)	RFM	247.4	64	711	23	5-83	1	30.91
S. H. Walter (*Queensland*)	LFM	174.2	35	641	20	6-121	1	32.05
B. E. McGain (*Victoria*)	LBG	266	48	845	26	4-41	0	32.50
D. T. Christian (*South Australia*)	RFM	261.4	62	818	25	5-24	1	32.72
D. J. Pattinson (*Victoria*)	RFM	228.2	47	736	22	3-15	0	33.45
M. A. Starc (*New South Wales*)	LFM	199	39	718	21	5-74	1	34.19
T. P. Macdonald (*Tasmania*)	RFM	299.2	73	863	20	3-65	0	43.15
S. P. D. Smith (*New South Wales*)	LBG	219.1	29	932	21	7-64	1	44.38

SHEFFIELD SHIELD, 2009-10

	Played	Won	Lost	Drawn	1st-inns points	Points	Quotient
Victoria	10	6	1	3	6	41*	1.185
Queensland	10	5	2	3	2	32	1.001
New South Wales	10	4	3	3	2	26	1.392
Western Australia	10	2	6	2	8	20	0.984
Tasmania	10	2	4	4	6	17*	0.737
South Australia	10	2	5	3	4	16	0.840

Final: Victoria beat Queensland by 457 runs.

* 1pt deducted for slow over-rate.

Outright win = 6pts; lead on first-innings in a drawn or lost game = 2pts.

Quotient = runs per wicket scored divided by runs per wicket conceded.

At Adelaide, October 13–16, 2009. **South Australia won by nine wickets.** ‡Tasmania 236 and 184; South Australia 345 (J. D. Smith 116) and 76-1. *South Australia 6pts.*

At Perth, October 13–16, 2009. **Drawn. Western Australia 406-9 dec** (M. J. North 107; S. H. Walter 6-121) **and 132-1;** ‡Queensland 458 (R. A. Broad 103). *Queensland 2pts. Ryan Broad scored his third century in successive Shield matches.*

At Adelaide, October 30–November 2, 2009. **Drawn.** ‡South Australia 292 and 340-3 (D. J. Harris 166*); **Victoria 643-9 dec** (C. J. L. Rogers 149, B. J. Hodge 195, A. B. McDonald 114). *Victoria 2pts. A week after returning from the Champions League in India, Victoria's batsmen readjusted to the longer game, their first four wickets putting on 102, 181, 85 and 137 – a total of 505 in 108.5 overs, including 450 on the second day. But Daniel Harris, who batted for eight hours ten minutes, and Cullen Bailey (91) added 200 for South Australia's third wicket to help save the match.*

At Brisbane, November 1–4, 2009. **Queensland won by an innings and seven runs.** ‡Tasmania 156 and 219 (B. C. J. Cutting 6-37); **Queensland 382** (G. C. Batticciotto 101; B. Geeves 5-106). *Queensland 6pts, Tasmania –1pt. Tasmania were 27-5 on the first morning after choosing to bat, and later lost their last six second-innings wickets for 30 to suffer an innings defeat.*

At Sydney, November 3–6, 2009. **Drawn.** ‡Western Australia 499-8 dec (W. M. Robinson 141, L. Ronchi 148) **and 24-2; New South Wales 402** (S. M. Katich 108). *Western Australia 2pts.*

At Adelaide, November 8–11, 2009. **Drawn.** ‡South Australia 477-5 dec (C. J. Borgas 164*) **and 159-2 dec;** Queensland 308 and 228-5. *South Australia 2pts. Cameron Borgas, playing only because of Mark Cosgrove's hamstring injury, hit 17 fours and five sixes in a career-best 164*.*

At Sydney, November 17–20, 2009. **Drawn.** ‡New South Wales 420-8 dec (M. J. Clarke 106) **and 208-5;** Tasmania 482 (G. J. Bailey 112, D. J. Marsh 134). *Tasmania 2pts.*

At Melbourne, November 17–20, 2009. **Victoria won by seven wickets.** Western Australia 277 (A. C. Voges 114*) **and 227;** ‡Victoria 246 and 259-3 (C. J. L. Rogers 110). *Victoria 6pts, Western*

Australia 2pts. Chris Rogers scored his fifth century in consecutive first-class matches, for Derbyshire and Victoria.

At Hobart, November 24–27, 2009. **Drawn. Tasmania 389** (E. J. M. Cowan 225; P. R. George 8-84) **and 129-4; ‡South Australia 363.** *Tasmania 2pts. Ed Cowan hit 33 fours and a six in his maiden double-hundred and added 240 for the fourth wicket with Dan Marsh (90). Peter George took 11-131 in the match; his 8-84 was a ground record.*

At Melbourne, November 27–29, 2009. **Victoria won by an innings and 50 runs. Victoria 378** (D. J. Hussey 174); **‡Queensland 195 and 133.** *Victoria 6pts.*

At Perth, November 27–29, 2009. **New South Wales won by eight wickets. Western Australia 131 and 245** (D. E. Bollinger 5-68); **‡New South Wales 274 and 106-2.** *New South Wales 6pts. In Western Australia's first innings, the only score over 22 was 59* from debutant Mitchell Marsh, son of Test player Geoff, playing alongside his brother, one-day international player Shaun. New South Wales collected their first points of the season under first-time captain Stuart Clark.*

At Hobart, December 8–11, 2009. **Tasmania won by one wicket. Western Australia 442-8 dec** (L. J. C. Towers 124, L. Ronchi 122) **and 201-4 dec; ‡Tasmania 296-5 dec** (A. J. Doolan 135) **and 351-9** (E. J. M. Cowan 152). *Tasmania 6pts, Western Australia 2pts. Tasmania inflicted Western Australia's third consecutive defeat off the last ball of this match. Their ninth wicket fell at the start of the final over, with six required; No. 10 Brady Jones hit fours off the last two deliveries.*

At Melbourne, December 10–13, 2009. **Victoria won by six wickets. South Australia 517-6 dec** (M. Klinger 207*, M. J. Cosgrove 103) **and 109-2 dec; ‡Victoria 246-6 dec and 384-4.** *Victoria 6pts, South Australia 2pts. Brad Hodge ended his first-class career by scoring 61 in the run-chase that sealed Victoria's third consecutive win. He retired as the state's leading run-scorer with 11,350. Earlier, brothers James and Darren Pattinson (the one-off England player) shared the new ball for Victoria for the first time, while their former batsman Michael Klinger scored his second double-century and Mark Cosgrove passed 5,000 first-class runs as he scored 103 out of a third-wicket stand of 152 with him.*

At Brisbane, December 11–14, 2009. **Queensland won by nine wickets. ‡New South Wales 451-5 dec** (U. T. Khawaja 132*, S. P. D. Smith 102*) **and 184; Queensland 468** (C. D. Hartley 125; M. A. Starc 5-74) **and 168-1.** *Queensland 6pts. Steve Smith scored a run-a-ball maiden hundred, but Queensland completed a comfortable win despite slumping to 84-5 in their first innings in reply to 451 before Chris Hartley led the recovery.*

At Newcastle, December 18–21, 2009. **Drawn. ‡New South Wales 390-8 dec** (P. J. Hughes 122) **and 306-3 dec** (P. A. Jaques 131, U. T. Khawaja 107); **Victoria 311 and 144-5.** *New South Wales 2pts. Tailenders Steve O'Keefe and Mitchell Starc added 124* for the ninth wicket in New South Wales's first innings; in their second, Phil Jaques, who passed 12,000 first-class runs, and Usman Khawaja added 213 for the second wicket.*

At Adelaide, December 18–21, 2009. **Western Australia won by 104 runs. ‡Western Australia 401 and 198-2 dec** (S. E. Marsh 108*); **South Australia 249-6 dec** (M. Klinger 109*) **and 246.** *Western Australia 6pts.*

At Sydney, January 29–February 1, 2010. **Queensland won by 168 runs. Queensland 335** (L. A. Carseldine 109; T. A. Copeland 8-92) **and 252** (R. A. Broad 129); **‡New South Wales 243** (B. C. J. Cutting 5-82) **and 176** (L. W. Feldman 5-32). *Queensland 6pts. First-class debutant Trent Copeland, a 23-year-old seamer, took 8-92 (10-149 in the match), the second-best analysis on Sheffield Shield debut after 8-12 by Clarrie Grimmett for Victoria against South Australia in 1923-24, and the best in the first innings. But Luke Feldman, in his third first-class game, took 9-81 in the match to win it for Queensland.*

At Hobart, January 29–February 1, 2010. **Drawn. Victoria 297 and 340** (R. J. Quiney 153); **‡Tasmania 262 and 207-5** (E. J. M. Cowan 108*). *Victoria 2pts.*

At Hobart, February 8–11, 2010. **Drawn. ‡Queensland 326** (W. J. Townsend 121; A. R. Griffith 5-85) **and 338** (C. D. Hartley 112); **Tasmania 427** (G. J. Bailey 115; B. C. J. Cutting 6-90) **and 121-5.** *Tasmania 2pts.*

At Perth, February 8–11, 2010. **South Australia won by two wickets. Western Australia 284 and 189** (D. T. Christian 5-24); **‡South Australia 380-9 dec** (M. G. Hogan 5-83) **and 94-8.** *South*

Australia 6pts. Daniel Christian set up South Australia's victory with a first-innings 71 and nine wickets in the match, but their pursuit of 94 to win was almost derailed by Brad Knowles's 7–2–32–4.

At Melbourne, February 12–15, 2010. **Victoria won by six wickets. New South Wales 225** (D. G. Wright 5-37) **and 387** (P. J. Hughes 149, S. P. D. Smith 124); ‡**Victoria 418** (A. B. McDonald 120) **and 200-4.** *Victoria 6pts.*

At Adelaide, February 19–22, 2010. **New South Wales won by an innings and 174 runs.** ‡**New South Wales 565-6 dec** (P. J. Hughes 192, P. J. Forrest 141, B. J. Rohrer 115*); **South Australia 288 and 103** (T. A. Copeland 5-31). *New South Wales 6pts. In South Australia's second innings, Josh Hazlewood had figures of 11–7–10–2.*

At Perth, February 19–22, 2010. **Tasmania won by 70 runs. Tasmania 261** (S. J. Magoffin 6-44) **and 246;** ‡**Western Australia 233 and 204.** *Tasmania 6pts. Western Australian wicketkeeper Luke Ronchi held nine catches in the match.*

At Brisbane, February 22–25, 2010. **Queensland won by one wicket. Victoria 316** (J. R. Hopes 5-66) **and 104;** ‡**Queensland 170 and 252-9.** *Queensland 6pts, Victoria 1pt. Chasing 251, Queensland were 174-8 at the end of the third day, when 17 wickets fell; Chris Swan and Luke Feldman saw them home with a last-wicket stand of 58, inflicting Victoria's only defeat of the season.*

At Brisbane, March 3–6, 2010. **Queensland won by 94 runs. Queensland 160 and 237-6 dec** (W. J. Townsend 114*); ‡**South Australia 72** (C. R. Swan 5-26) **and 231.** *Queensland 6pts. Rain permitted only 8.1 overs on the first day, then 20 wickets fell on the second afternoon. Wade Townsend scored the third century of his debut season, while Chris Swan and Luke Feldman took eight wickets apiece.*

At Hobart, March 3–6, 2010. **New South Wales won by 216 runs.** ‡**New South Wales 468-6 dec** (S. P. D. Smith 177) **and 246; Tasmania 303** (A. J. Doolan 100; T. A. Copeland 5-56) **and 214.** *New South Wales 6pts. Trent Copeland took five or more in an innings for the third time in his first four first-class matches.*

At Perth, March 3–6, 2010. **Victoria won by 54 runs. Victoria 199 and 378;** ‡**Western Australia 274 and 249** (L. Ronchi 115). *Victoria 6pts, Western Australia 2pts.*

At Sydney, March 10–12, 2010. **New South Wales won by an innings and 39 runs.** ‡**New South Wales 550-9 dec** (U. T. Khawaja 102, S. P. D. Smith 100, P. M. Nevill 105); **South Australia 267 and 244** (M. J. Cosgrove 105; S. P. D. Smith 7-64). *New South Wales 6pts. Steve Smith scored his fourth century of the season, and followed up with a career-best 16–4–64–7, while Trent Copeland ended his debut season with 35 wickets from five matches. New South Wales's third consecutive win was South Australia's third consecutive defeat.*

At Brisbane, March 10–12, 2010. **Western Australia won by three wickets. Western Australia 286 and 109-7;** ‡**Queensland 106 and 285** (C. A. Lynn 139; S. J. Magoffin 5-27). *Western Australia 6pts. Chris Lynn, a 19-year-old in his second first-class game, reached his maiden century with a six.*

At Melbourne, March 10–12, 2010. **Victoria won by an innings and 46 runs.** ‡**Tasmania 222** (D. G. Wright 5-49) **and 114; Victoria 382** (A. J. Finch 102, D. J. Hussey 140). *Victoria 6pts. Aaron Finch and David Hussey added 212 for the third wicket – Victoria's biggest stand of the season.*

FINAL

VICTORIA v QUEENSLAND

At Melbourne, March 17–21, 2010. Victoria won by 457 runs. Toss: Victoria.

Amid rumours that the Sheffield Shield final could be abolished to make room for more Twenty20 cricket, Victoria completed one of the most decisive victories in the 28 finals to date, and retained the trophy. A year earlier, a draw against second-placed Queensland had been enough to win the title; this time, against the same opponents, they recorded their third-biggest winning margin by runs, and their best since 1926-27. That seemed unlikely just after lunch on the opening day. Already unsettled by the absence of opener Chris Rogers, who had a broken hand, Victoria collapsed to 75 for six on a pitch offering early help. They were rescued by the tail, led by wicketkeeper Matthew Wade; the last four wickets added 230, with Wade narrowly missing his century. Only Ryan Broad offered prolonged resistance for Queensland on the second day, maintaining his focus despite playing and missing. But Victoria pulled well ahead when they batted again, the top order compensating for their earlier failures. All the first five reached 60, but the standout innings was David Hussey's, a five-hour 168 in 198 balls, with 18 fours and four sixes. The visitors' most encouraging performance came from 20-year-old leg-spinner Cameron Boyce, who claimed six for 181 in his second first-class match. Cameron White finally declared on the fourth evening, setting Queensland a notional 640; another leg-spinner, Bryce McGain, bowled them out on the fifth afternoon.

Man of the Match: M. S. Wade.   *Attendance:* 7,798.

Close of play: First day, Victoria 286-9 (Pattinson 14, McGain 0); Second day, Queensland 199-6 (Simpson 15, Cutting 1); Third day, Victoria 273-2 (Finch 54, Hussey 63); Fourth day, Queensland 29-0 (Broad 9, Townsend 16).

Victoria

R. J. Quiney c Hartley b Swan	15	– (2) b Boyce	73
N. Jewell b Swan	7	– (1) c Simpson b Boyce	70
A. J. Finch c Lynn b Feldman	26	– run out	63
D. J. Hussey c Simpson b Hopes	8	– c Carseldine b Cutting	168
*C. L. White b Cutting	10	– b Boyce	89
A. B. McDonald c Simpson b Feldman	0	– not out	41
†M. S. Wade c Cutting b Hopes	96	– c Feldman b Boyce	20
J. W. Hastings c Hopes b Boyce	47	– st Hartley b Boyce	26
D. G. Wright b Swan	42	– c Hartley b Boyce	13
D. J. Pattinson c Townsend b Cutting	25	– not out	6
B. E. McGain not out	7		
L-b 8, w 2, n-b 12	22	B 5, l-b 11, w 3, n-b 3	22

1/24 (1) 2/33 (2) 3/46 (4) 4/60 (3)   (98.5 overs) 305
5/60 (6) 6/75 (5) 7/161 (8)
8/245 (9) 9/285 (10) 10/305 (10)

1/154 (2)   (8 wkts dec, 146 overs) 591
2/155 (1) 3/311 (3) 4/481 (4) 5/481 (5)
6/524 (7) 7/561 (8) 8/581 (9)

Swan 24–6–65–3; Cutting 21.5–4–59–2; Hopes 22–8–43–2; Feldman 15–3–46–2; Simpson 5–2–25–0; Boyce 11–1–59–1. *Second Innings*—Swan 32–4–113–0; Cutting 23–6–87–1; Feldman 26–4–108–0; Simpson 17–4–58–0; Boyce 44–6–181–6; Lynn 4–0–28–0.

Queensland

W. J. Townsend b Pattinson	1	– (2) b McGain	19
R. A. Broad b McGain	82	– (1) c Wade b Pattinson	14
L. A. Carseldine c McDonald b Wright	7	– lbw b Hastings	75
C. A. Lynn lbw b McDonald	40	– b McGain	21
J. R. Hopes c Hussey b McDonald	17	– absent hurt	
†C. D. Hartley lbw b McGain	24	– not out	29
*C. P. Simpson lbw b Wright	16	– (5) c Wade b Pattinson	0
B. C. J. Cutting not out	35	– (7) c Hastings b McGain	6
C. R. Swan b Hastings	10	– (8) c Wade b Hastings	4
L. W. Feldman c Quiney b Hastings	4	– (9) lbw b Hastings	0
C. J. Boyce b McDonald	4	– (10) lbw b McGain	0
B 4, l-b 8, n-b 5	17	B 10, l-b 3, w 1	14

1/3 (1) 2/14 (2) 3/73 (4) 4/93 (5)   (97.4 overs) 257
5/158 (6) 6/195 (2) 7/220 (7)
8/243 (9) 9/249 (10) 10/257 (11)

1/37 (2) 2/45 (1)   (58.4 overs) 182
3/107 (4) 4/108 (5)
5/155 (3) 6/162 (7)
7/179 (8) 8/179 (9) 9/182 (10)

Wright 21.4–10–48–2; Pattinson 17–3–53–1; McDonald 26.4–9–64–3; Hastings 18.2–2–51–2; McGain 14.5–5–29–2. *Second Innings*—Pattinson 11–0–47–2; McDonald 8–3–23–0; McGain 25.4–4–70–4; Hastings 10–3–25–3; White 3–2–3–0; Hussey 1–0–1–0.

Umpires: S. D. Fry and B. N. J. Oxenford.   Third umpire: I. H. Lock.
Referee: R. J. Evans.

CHAMPIONS

Sheffield Shield		
1892-93	Victoria	
1893-94	South Australia	
1894-95	Victoria	
1895-96	New South Wales	
1896-97	New South Wales	
1897-98	Victoria	
1898-99	Victoria	
1899-1900	New South Wales	
1900-01	Victoria	
1901-02	New South Wales	
1902-03	New South Wales	
1903-04	New South Wales	
1904-05	New South Wales	
1905-06	New South Wales	
1906-07	New South Wales	
1907-08	Victoria	
1908-09	New South Wales	
1909-10	South Australia	
1910-11	New South Wales	
1911-12	New South Wales	
1912-13	South Australia	
1913-14	New South Wales	
1914-15	Victoria	
1915-19	No competition	
1919-20	New South Wales	
1920-21	New South Wales	
1921-22	Victoria	
1922-23	New South Wales	
1923-24	Victoria	
1924-25	Victoria	
1925-26	New South Wales	
1926-27	South Australia	
1927-28	Victoria	
1928-29	New South Wales	
1929-30	Victoria	
1930-31	Victoria	
1931-32	New South Wales	
1932-33	New South Wales	
1933-34	Victoria	
1934-35	Victoria	
1935-36	South Australia	
1936-37	Victoria	
1937-38	New South Wales	
1938-39	South Australia	
1939-40	New South Wales	
1940-46	No competition	
1946-47	Victoria	
1947-48	Western Australia	
1948-49	New South Wales	
1949-50	New South Wales	
1950-51	Victoria	
1951-52	New South Wales	
1952-53	South Australia	
1953-54	New South Wales	
1954-55	New South Wales	
1955-56	New South Wales	
1956-57	New South Wales	
1957-58	New South Wales	
1958-59	New South Wales	
1959-60	New South Wales	
1960-61	New South Wales	
1961-62	New South Wales	
1962-63	Victoria	
1963-64	South Australia	
1964-65	New South Wales	
1965-66	New South Wales	
1966-67	Victoria	
1967-68	Western Australia	
1968-69	South Australia	
1969-70	Victoria	
1970-71	South Australia	
1971-72	Western Australia	
1972-73	Western Australia	
1973-74	Victoria	
1974-75	Western Australia	
1975-76	South Australia	
1976-77	Western Australia	
1977-78	Western Australia	
1978-79	Victoria	
1979-80	Victoria	
1980-81	Western Australia	
1981-82	South Australia	
1982-83	New South Wales*	
1983-84	Western Australia	
1984-85	New South Wales	
1985-86	New South Wales	
1986-87	Western Australia	
1987-88	Western Australia	
1988-89	Western Australia	
1989-90	New South Wales	
1990-91	Victoria	
1991-92	Western Australia	
1992-93	New South Wales	
1993-94	New South Wales	
1994-95	Queensland	
1995-96	South Australia	
1996-97	Queensland*	
1997-98	Western Australia	
1998-99	Western Australia*	
Pura Milk Cup		
1999-2000	Queensland	
Pura Cup		
2000-01	Queensland	
2001-02	Queensland	
2002-03	New South Wales*	
2003-04	Victoria	
2004-05	New South Wales*	
2005-06	Queensland	
2006-07	Tasmania	
2007-08	New South Wales	
Sheffield Shield		
2008-09	Victoria	
2009-10	Victoria	

New South Wales have won the title 45 times, Victoria 28, Western Australia 15, South Australia 13, Queensland 6, Tasmania 1.

* Second in table but won final. Finals were introduced in 1982-83.

FORD RANGER CUP, 2009-10

50-over league plus final

	Played	Won	Lost	Bonus points	Points	Net run-rate
Victoria	10	6	4	1	25	0.18
Tasmania	10	6	4	0	24	0.13
New South Wales	10	5	5	1	21	−0.10
Queensland	10	5	5	1	21	0.17
Western Australia	10	4	6	2	18	−0.07
South Australia	10	4	6	1	17	−0.35

Final

At Melbourne, February 28, 2010 (day/night). **Tasmania won by 110 runs.** ‡Tasmania **304-6** (50 overs) (T. D. Paine 100); **Victoria 194** (42.1 overs) (G. J. Denton 5-45). *Tim Paine, who faced 118 balls and batted into the 47th over, put on 132 for Tasmania's first wicket with Michael Dighton and 111 for the third with Ed Cowan. Gerard Denton reduced Victoria to 35-3 by the tenth over. Though captain Andrew McDonald and wicketkeeper Matthew Wade put on 82 for the fifth wicket, Tasmania grabbed the last six for 22 runs in 5.2 overs. It was the fourth time running that Victoria had been losing finalists in this competition.*

KFC TWENTY20 BIG BASH, 2009-10

20-over league plus final

	Played	Won	Lost	Points	Net run-rate
South Australia	5	4	1	8	0.74
Queensland	5	3	2	6	1.00
Victoria	5	3	2	6	−0.86
Western Australia	5	2	3	4	0.68
New South Wales	5	2	3	4	−0.76
Tasmania	5	1	4	2	−0.72

Teams tied on points were separated on net run-rate.

Play-off

At Brisbane, January 19, 2010 (floodlit). **Victoria won by six wickets.** ‡Queensland **149-5** (20 overs); **Victoria 150-4** (18.5 overs). *Attendance: 11,806. Queensland wicketkeeper Ben Dunk hit 70* in 40 balls with six fours and two sixes, but David Hussey steered Victoria into the final with 60* in 39 balls.*

Final

At Adelaide, January 23, 2010 (floodlit). **Victoria won by 48 runs.** ‡Victoria **166-7** (20 overs); **South Australia 118-9** (20 overs). *Attendance: 17,722. Victoria's Aiden Blizzard won the match award for his 42* off 19 balls, with three fours and three sixes. Dirk Nannes began South Australia's innings by dismissing captain Graham Manou first ball, and his figures of 4–1–8–1 were the most economical in the tournament's history. Victoria won the Twenty20 title for the fourth time in its five seasons.*

BANGLADESH CRICKET, 2010

Something to write home about

UTPAL SHUVRO

Although Bangladesh lost all of their seven Test matches, they had one of their better years in 2010. To understand this paradox, one has to remember Bangladesh's Test history and look beyond the win–lose equation. For a team that had only three wins in their first ten years in Test cricket – and those against seriously understrength opposition – it is obvious that they would look for some positives, even in defeat. And there were plenty of positives in 2010, particularly in the batting.

For the first time, Bangladesh passed 400 twice in a year. The first one (408) was in New Zealand, where the batsmen had struggled on two previous tours. Bangladesh also recorded their highest innings in England – 382 at Lord's, two months after making 419 against them at Mirpur. The batting improvement was also reflected in the number of centuries scored: in 61 Tests prior to 2010 there were only 15 centuries, but in 2010 there were seven in seven matches.

BANGLADESH IN 2010

	Played	Won	Lost	Drawn/No result
Tests	7	–	7	–
One-day internationals	27	9	18	–
Twenty20 internationals	3	–	3	–

JANUARY	Triangular ODI tournament (h) v India and Sri Lanka	(page 881)
	2 Tests (h) v India	(page 884)
FEBRUARY	1 Test, 3 ODIs and 1 T20I (a) v New Zealand	(page 976)
MARCH }	2 Tests and 3 ODIs (h) v England	(page 890)
APRIL		
MAY	World Twenty20 (in West Indies)	(page 797)
JUNE }	2 Tests (a) v England	(page 283)
	Asia Cup (in Sri Lanka)	(page 1076)
	3 ODIs (a) v England	(page 283)
JULY	2 ODIs (a) v Ireland	(page 770)
	1 ODI (a) v Scotland: 1 ODI (a) (in Scotland) v Netherlands	(page 777)
AUGUST		
SEPTEMBER		
OCTOBER	5 ODIs (h) v New Zealand	(page 903)
NOVEMBER		
DECEMBER	5 ODIs (h) v Zimbabwe	(page 906)

For a review of Bangladesh domestic cricket from the 2009-10 season, see page 907.

Underdogs bite back: Shakib Al Hasan holds the trophy after a 4–0 whitewash against New Zealand in October 2010.

Four partnership records were broken, the highlight being the first double-century stand in Bangladesh's Test history, by Tamim Iqbal and Junaid Siddique against India at Mirpur in January. In 14 innings, they were bundled out for less than 200 only once (by England at Old Trafford). It might not seem much to write home about, but for Bangladesh these were obvious signs of improvement.

Considering the gradual upturn, it was a pity that Bangladesh's Test year was over by early June. Tamim must have been the most disappointed. The dashing opener was in terrific form: he scored three hundreds and six half-centuries – passing 50 in five consecutive innings – in his 14 attempts. Exactly a third of Bangladesh's 27 scores of 50 or more came from Tamim's flashing blade.

More important than the runs he made, though, was the way he scored them. In his three Test centuries – 151 against India at Mirpur, then 103 and 108 against England – he reached his hundred in 101, 94 and 100 balls respectively, and were the fastest three scored by a Bangladeshi batsman. He often reminded spectators of Virender Sehwag with his audacious strokeplay at the top of the innings. Interestingly, among batsmen who scored more than 300 Test runs in 2010, only Sehwag had a better strike-rate than Tamim.

Recognition also came. Tamim became the first Bangladeshi to be selected as one of *Wisden's* Cricketers of the Year: those blazing back-to-back centuries at Lord's and Old Trafford were hard to ignore. He was also named as *The Wisden Cricketer* magazine's Test cricketer of the year.

In the one-day arena, Bangladesh reserved their best till last. After a slow start – defeat in the first 14 games – they won seven of the last eight matches they played in 2010. As the World Cup loomed in their own backyard, it was a real confidence-booster – nothing more so than the whitewash they inflicted on New Zealand. Bangladesh had never won even two consecutive matches against fully fledged opposition before, so winning four out of four against New Zealand came as a pleasant surprise to a legion of cricket fans, who rejoiced in this unexpected glory.

Bangladesh enjoyed another significant moment in their one-day history when they beat England for the first time, at Bristol in July. England were the last Test team to fall to Bangladesh, and the cycle was completed. But the glory of this win was tarnished almost immediately, with defeats by Ireland and the Netherlands.

If Tamim was the best performer in Test cricket, Shakib Al Hasan was the shining star in one-day internationals. For the second year running, he was the top-ranked all-rounder in the ICC one-day rankings. He played like No. 1 too. Shakib was the highest wicket-taker in one-day internationals in 2010 with 46 (Ryan Harris of Australia was next with 40), and also scored nearly 800 runs.

Bangladesh lost all three of their Twenty20 internationals, with defeats by Pakistan and Australia sending them out of the World Twenty20 in the West Indies at the first group stage.

The captaincy remained a hot topic throughout the year. Shakib, the stopgap choice, wanted the job long-term, while the board seemed to be waiting for Mashrafe bin Mortaza to regain fitness. Mortaza was out for more than eight months after injuring his knee in the Caribbean in 2009. Shakib captained the side in his absence with some success, but had to give way when Mortaza came back. Then, after Mortaza again injured his ankle against New Zealand in October, Shakib took over once more. Finally, the board had to give Shakib what he wanted, and named him as captain for 2011, with Tamim as his deputy. Shakib and Tamim are the best of friends, and have now been entrusted with the job of taking Bangladesh to the next level.

IDEA CUP, 2009-10

Utpal Shuvro

1. Sri Lanka   2. India   3. Bangladesh

There was an air of predictability about this hastily arranged tournament; with hosts Bangladesh failing to upset any apple-carts, it quickly became obvious that India and Sri Lanka would indeed contest the final. It was the latest instalment of a seemingly never-ending saga: the 22nd one-day international between the two teams in 19 months. India might have had the better record, winning 13 of those matches, but their fallibility in finals cropped up again, and Kumar Sangakkara lifted the Idea Cup.

The toss was such an important factor that the captains might have thought about practising it; since it was midwinter in Dhaka, dew, rather than skill with bat or ball, proved decisive. The tournament consisted entirely of day/night games, and in the evening life became very difficult for the bowling side, especially the spinners, as they struggled to grip the ball. All the matches were won by the team batting second. After the first three, the start was brought forward by half an hour, but it made little difference.

The final was relatively free of dew, although it might have had an indirect influence: the Indians played some indiscreet shots, thinking that they needed a big total in case their bowlers struggled again.

Still, Sri Lanka were worthy champions. They came with a relatively inexperienced team, lacking Sanath Jayasuriya (omitted) and Muttiah Muralitharan (injured). Lasith Malinga and Ajantha Mendis were dropped after modest performances on the preceding tour of India, while Mahela Jayawardene, originally rested, was called up mid-tournament after further injuries. But the newcomers saw all this as an opportunity. With Sangakkara leading from the front – he scored half-centuries in four of Sri Lanka's five matches – his side turned the tables on the favourites, themselves without Sachin Tendulkar, who gave the trip a miss.

NATIONAL SQUADS

Bangladesh *Shakib Al Hasan, Abdur Razzak, Aftab Ahmed, Imrul Kayes, Mahmudullah, Mohammad Ashraful, Mushfiqur Rahim, Naeem Islam, Raqibul Hasan, Rubel Hossain, Shafiul Islam, Shahadat Hossain, Shahriar Nafees, Syed Rasel, Tamim Iqbal. *Coach:* J. D. Siddons.
Mashrafe bin Mortaza, originally named as captain, was omitted on fitness grounds. Nazmul Hossain was selected but injured a thigh muscle and was replaced by Shahadat Hossain.

India *M. S. Dhoni, A. B. Dinda, G. Gambhir, Harbhajan Singh, R. A. Jadeja, K. D. Karthik, V. Kohli, A. Mishra, A. Nehra, S. K. Raina, V. Sehwag, R. G. Sharma, S. Sreesanth, S. Tyagi, Yuvraj Singh, Zaheer Khan. *Coach:* G. Kirsten.

Sri Lanka *K. C. Sangakkara, H. M. C. M. Bandara, T. M. Dilshan, S. H. T. Kandamby, K. M. D. N. Kulasekara, R. A. S. Lakmal, M. T. T. Mirando, N. L. T. C. Perera, M. Pushpakumara, S. Randiv, T. T. Samaraweera, L. P. C. Silva, W. U. Tharanga, H. D. R. L. Thirimanne, U. W. M. B. C. A. Welagedara. *Coach:* T. H. Bayliss.
L. D. Chandimal, D. P. M. D. Jayawardene and M. L. Udawatte joined the squad after injuries to Dilshan (groin), Pushpakumara (shoulder) and Silva (fractured thumb).

At Mirpur, January 4, 2010 (day/night). **Sri Lanka won by seven wickets. Bangladesh 260-7** (50 overs) (Tamim Iqbal 40, Mohammad Ashraful 75, Mushfiqur Rahim 35, Mahmudullah 45); ‡**Sri Lanka 261-3** (44.5 overs) (T. M. Dilshan 104, K. C. Sangakkara 74, T. T. Samaraweera 41*). *Sri Lanka 4pts. One-day international debut: Shafiul Islam (Bangladesh). MoM: T. M. Dilshan. Shakib Al Hasan complained that excessive dew made conditions "unplayable and unfit to play"; Bangladesh's four spinners found it almost impossible to grip the ball after Sangakkara condemned them to bowl second. Dilshan, who hit ten international centuries in 2009, started 2010 with another, including 12 fours, though a tweaked groin muscle meant he needed a runner late on, and he missed the next two matches. Mohammad Ashraful played responsibly for 94 deliveries, and Bangladesh's batting powerplay brought them 43 runs before Naeem Islam smashed 20 off the final over, from Suranga Lakmal.*

At Mirpur, January 5, 2010 (day/night). **Sri Lanka won by five wickets. India 279-9** (50 overs) (V. Sehwag 47, Yuvraj Singh 74, M. S. Dhoni 37, S. K. Raina 35, R. A. Jadeja 39; U. W. M. B. C. A. Welagedara 5-66); ‡**Sri Lanka 283-5** (48 overs) (W. U. Tharanga 30, K. C. Sangakkara 60, T. T. Samaraweera 105*, N. L. T. C. Perera 36*). *Sri Lanka 4pts. One-day international debut: H. D. R. L. Thirimanne (Sri Lanka). MoM: T. T. Samaraweera. Left-armer Chanaka Welagedara derailed India's batting with a maiden international five-for, and Thilan Samaraweera scored a controlled unbeaten century. But Sri Lanka still needed 54 from 39 balls when 20-year-old left-hander Thissara Perera came to the crease, for only his second international innings, and hammered 36 from 15 balls, with six fours and a six, to clinch victory with two overs to spare. He had earlier removed the dangerous pair of Dhoni and Yuvraj Singh after they had added 99. India's last five overs saw only 20 runs and four wickets.*

At Mirpur, January 7, 2010 (day/night). **India won by six wickets. ‡Bangladesh 296-6** (50 overs) (Tamim Iqbal 60, Imrul Kayes 70, Raqibul Hasan 40*, Mahmudullah 60*); **India 297-4** (47.3 overs) (V. Kohli 91, M. S. Dhoni 101*, S. K. Raina 51*). *India 4pts. MoM: M. S. Dhoni. Despite the persistent problems with dew, Shakib Al Hasan batted, fearing India might score 350 in perfect batting conditions. Bangladesh made their highest total against a major Test side, with Tamim Iqbal scorching to 60 in 42 balls with ten fours and a six. India slipped to 51-3 before Dhoni and Kohli's watchful stand of 152 in 26 overs. Kohli, using a runner because of cramp, just missed a century; Dhoni, dropped by Shakib off his own bowling on 61, reached his seventh one-day hundred two balls before Raina hit the winning runs.*

At Mirpur, January 8, 2010 (day/night). **Sri Lanka won by nine wickets. Bangladesh 249-9** (50 overs) (Imrul Kayes 42, Raqibul Hasan 43, Shakib Al Hasan 47, Mushfiqur Rahim 32); ‡**Sri Lanka 252-1** (42.5 overs) (W. U. Tharanga 118*, D. P. M. D. Jayawardene 108). *Sri Lanka 4pts. MoM: W. U. Tharanga. Sri Lanka reached the final with their third victory, making light of a target of 250 as both openers scored centuries and shared a stand of 215. Tharanga hit 18 fours and Mahela Jayawardene (recently arrived as a reinforcement) 13. Bangladesh's batting powerplay saw them lose a wicket in each of the five overs (43rd–47th) while adding 32. This match, and all later ones, started half an hour early in an attempt to counteract the evening dew. But Shakib still tried seven bowlers by the 14th over as they struggled to grip the ball.*

At Mirpur, January 10, 2010 (day/night). **India won by eight wickets. ‡Sri Lanka 213** (46.1 overs) (T. M. Dilshan 33, K. C. Sangakkara 68, S. Randiv 56; Zaheer Khan 3-38, A. Mishra 3-40); **India 214-2** (32.4 overs) (K. D. Karthik 48, G. Gambhir 71, V. Kohli 71*). *India 5pts. MoM: Zaheer Khan. Already in the final, Sri Lanka decided to give their bowlers experience of the dewy conditions by batting first – but faltered after an audacious 17-ball 33 by Dilshan, returning from injury. At 66-5 in the 14th over – when Zaheer Khan had 5–2–9–2 – it seemed the match might end before any dew fell. Sangakkara and Randiv rallied with resilient fifties, but 213 looked inadequate. Karthik thumped 48 from 40 balls, then Gambhir (dropped in successive overs from Thushara Mirando) and Kohli helped India romp home and gain a bonus point.*

At Mirpur, January 11, 2010 (day/night). **India won by six wickets. Bangladesh 247-6** (50 overs) (Shakib Al Hasan 85, Mahmudullah 64*); ‡**India 249-4** (43 overs) (K. D. Karthik 34, G. Gambhir 41, V. Kohli 102*, M. S. Dhoni 32). *India 4pts. MoM: V. Kohli. Bangladesh made a poor start and, although Shakib added 106 with Mahmudullah, an upset never looked likely. Kohli continued his recent run of form with the fifth score above 50 in his last six innings. Reprieved when Mohammad Ashraful dropped him off Syed Rasel on 83, and again when Mushfiqur Rahim missed a stumping off Shakib, he reached his second one-day international hundred shortly before the end.*

India 13pts, Sri Lanka 12pts, Bangladesh 0pts. India and Sri Lanka qualified for the final.

FINAL

INDIA v SRI LANKA

At Mirpur, January 13, 2010 (day/night). Sri Lanka won by four wickets. Toss: Sri Lanka.

The match almost went the distance, but in fact India all but blew their chances inside the first 11 overs. Kulasekara and Welagedara, gaining some extra bounce, had already taken two wickets apiece before Sehwag ended a 27-ball onslaught by feathering an intended upper-cut to the keeper. That left his side in tatters at 60 for five. Raina repaired the damage with a fighting century – his third in one-day internationals, though his first since the previous two came in the space of four days against Hong Kong and Bangladesh in June 2008. But Sri Lanka were always favourites to overhaul a total of 245, even after Tharanga departed third ball for his second consecutive duck. Dilshan and Sangakkara put on 93, then Jayawardene anchored the victory push. Going into the 49th over, bowled by Sreesanth, he had hit only two fours from 78 balls; but a miscued pull, a better-timed one and a sumptuous cover-drive meant Jayawardene ended the match with three successive boundaries. Although the expected dew did not materialise and the spinners kept the brakes on, India still had problems in the bowling department, as Nehra limped off with a groin injury in his second over. The result continued their poor form in multi-team competitions: of 19 tournaments in which they had reached the finals since 2000, they had won only three.

Man of the Match: K. M. D. N. Kulasekara.   *Man of the Series:* K. C. Sangakkara.

India

V. Sehwag c Sangakkara b Kulasekara	42	A. Nehra not out	2
G. Gambhir b Kulasekara	0	S. Sreesanth b Perera	4
V. Kohli c Sangakkara b Welagedara	2		
Yuvraj Singh c Samaraweera b Welagedara	0	L-b 4, w 6	10
*†M. S. Dhoni c Sangakkara b Kulasekara	14		
S. K. Raina b Welagedara	106	1/1 (2) 2/4 (3) 3/16 (4) (48.2 overs)	245
R. A. Jadeja lbw b Dilshan	38	4/47 (5) 5/60 (1) 6/166 (7)	
Harbhajan Singh lbw b Randiv	11	7/213 (8) 8/233 (9) 9/237 (6)	
Zaheer Khan c Samaraweera b Kulasekara	16	10/245 (11)	10 overs: 58-4

Kulasekara 10–0–48–4; Welagedara 10–1–53–3; Mirando 6–1–26–0; Randiv 9–0–47–1; Perera 8.2–0–49–1; Dilshan 5–0–18–1.

Sri Lanka

W. U. Tharanga c Kohli b Nehra	0	S. Randiv run out	17
T. M. Dilshan c Dhoni b Yuvraj Singh	49	N. L. T. C. Perera not out	6
*†K. C. Sangakkara c Sehwag		L-b 1, w 4, n-b 1	6
b Harbhajan Singh	55		
D. P. M. D. Jayawardene not out	71	1/0 (1) 2/93 (2) (6 wkts, 48.3 overs)	249
T. T. Samaraweera b Jadeja	27	3/109 (3) 4/157 (5)	
S. H. T. Kandamby lbw b Harbhajan Singh	18	5/189 (6) 6/228 (7)	10 overs: 64-1

K. M. D. N. Kulasekara, M. T. T. Mirando and U. W. M. B. C. A. Welagedara did not bat.

Nehra 1.2–0–2–1; Sreesanth 9.3–0–72–0; Kohli 1.4–0–12–0; Zaheer Khan 10–0–51–0; Harbhajan Singh 10–0–41–2; Yuvraj Singh 9–0–41–1; Jadeja 7–0–29–1.

Umpires: Enamul Haque and I. J. Gould.   Third umpire: Sharfuddoula.
Series referee: A. J. Pycroft.

BANGLADESH v INDIA, 2009-10

UTPAL SHUVRO

Test matches (2): Bangladesh 0, India 2

When the top team in the ICC Test rankings meet the bottom team in a two-match series, what happens? A 2–0 clean sweep would be the obvious answer, and that was exactly what India achieved on their fourth Test tour of Bangladesh.

India had dethroned South Africa from the top of the table by beating Sri Lanka in December 2009. They had already led the one-day rankings, in September, but it was the first time they had been recognised as the No. 1 Test team, and Mahendra Singh Dhoni's men were determined to celebrate in style.

Dhoni missed the First Test at Chittagong after injuring his back during practice, and the dashing opener Virender Sehwag took over as captain. He was responsible for adding some spice to a low-key series when he declared Bangladesh "ordinary" and predicted a cakewalk for his team. His bluntness came without provocation in the pre-Test press conference, when a journalist asked a routine question about whether Bangladesh had the ability to surprise India. With the same nonchalance he shows in despatching balls to the boundary, Sehwag replied, "No. They can surprise you in one-dayers, but not in Tests. They can't take 20 wickets. They are an ordinary side."

Not surprisingly, his comment caused a stir among his opponents. Home captain Shakib Al Hasan refused to be drawn into the battle of words, but later admitted he had used it to motivate his team. When India found themselves 213 for eight at the end of the first day of the series, it seemed Sehwag might have done the young Bangladeshis a good turn.

India would have been embarrassed if Sachin Tendulkar had not come to the rescue, for the umpteenth time, with yet another unbeaten hundred. The Little Master duly completed another century in the Second Test; he headed the run-scoring list as well as the series averages with 264 at 132. Tendulkar made only 18 in the first Test between these countries – Bangladesh's inaugural match in November 2000. But he has more than made up for that with five centuries in the next six Tests. Every time he has reached 50, he has gone on to a century. Zaheer Khan, though, was named Man of the Series for his 15 wickets.

Even if there was the ignominy of another whitewash, there were some encouraging signs for Bangladesh, with left-handed opener Tamim Iqbal at the forefront. His cavalier approach to batting prompted his coach, Jamie Siddons, to label him "Bangladesh's Sehwag", and his strokeful 151 in the Second Test was the innings of the series.

Mushfiqur Rahim and Mahmudullah also shone with the bat, but they were Nos 7 and 8 in the batting line-up. Bangladesh desperately needed someone in the top order to complement Tamim if they were to present a sustained challenge to the established Test teams.

INDIAN TOURING PARTY

*M. S. Dhoni, R. Dravid, G. Gambhir, Harbhajan Singh, K. D. Karthik, V. V. S. Laxman, A. Mishra, P. P. Ojha, V. Sehwag, I. Sharma, S. Sreesanth, S. R. Tendulkar, S. Tyagi, M. Vijay, Yuvraj Singh, Zaheer Khan. *Coach:* G. Kirsten.

Details of India's matches in the Idea Cup with Bangladesh and Sri Lanka can be found in that section (page 881).

BANGLADESH v INDIA

First Test Match

At Chittagong, January 17–21, 2010. India won by 113 runs. Toss: Bangladesh. Test debut: Shafiul Islam.

Spurred on by the comment of India's acting-captain Sehwag that they were an "ordinary" side, not capable of taking 20 wickets, Bangladesh hit back by putting India in and shooting them out for 243. Given Bangladesh's previous record, one might say Sehwag was not unjustifiably rude, but naturally it was not taken well by his hosts, and he may have felt bewildered by their response. In five previous Tests between the sides, India's lowest all-out total was 429, better than Bangladesh's highest, 400. Over the course of the match, the loudest cheers from the home players and the crowd were unsurprisingly reserved for Sehwag's dismissals. He scored 52 and 45 – not bad, but it seemed a failure because he had set himself such lofty standards.

HUNDREDS IN MOST CONSECUTIVE TEST MATCHES

6 in 6	D. G. Bradman (Australia) . . . . . . 3 v England 1936-37	3 in England 1938
6 in 5*	Mohammad Yousuf (Pakistan) . . . 2 in England 2006	4 v West Indies 2006-07
5 in 5	J. H. Kallis (South Africa) . . . . . . 4 v West Indies 2003-04	1 in New Zealand 2003-04
5 in 5	**G. Gambhir (India)**. . . . . **2 in New Zealand 2008-09**	**2 v Sri Lanka 2009-10**
	1 in Bangladesh 2009-10	

* Mohammad Yousuf scored six hundreds in five Tests (with two in the Third Test v West Indies).

In fact, Bangladesh were on the verge of taking 20 wickets when Sehwag (captaining India for the third time in a Test, after Mahendra Singh Dhoni was ruled out by a back strain) declared with eight down, maybe to avoid the embarrassment of eating his words. By then, however, India's victory was all but assured, as they had set a target of 415.

The first three days were a seesaw battle: only one run separated the sides on first innings. But that was where Bangladesh lost the plot, by not taking advantage of India's stumble to build a significant lead. It was highly improbable that the tourists' mighty batting would fail twice running. Nor did it. Gambhir led the way with his fifth hundred in consecutive Tests, matching Jacques Kallis and Mohammad Yousuf; only Don Bradman has achieved centuries in six successive Tests.

Gambhir's performance was not without blemish. He was dropped on 55, by Imrul Kayes at short leg off Shakib Al Hasan. Bangladesh's catching was horrible throughout the match. Kayes also dropped Tendulkar, at first slip this time, off Shafiul Islam on the first day, when he was on 16. Had that been taken, India would have been 111 for five. Tendulkar made full use of his escape to reach his 44th Test hundred on the second morning; he had already become the first batsman to score 13,000 Test runs, on the opening day, when he had notched another record just by stepping on to the field for his 266th Test innings (beating Allan Border's 265). He scored an unbeaten 105 out of 164 added after his arrival in the 16th over. India had lost both openers, including Sehwag, in the space of three balls, and worse was to come as pacer Shahadat Hossain and left-arm spinner Shakib reduced them to 150 for six; when they wound India up next morning, it was the 52nd time a pair of bowlers had claimed five wickets apiece in the same Test innings.

Though India's bowling was more of a combined effort, there was an uncanny similarity between the two teams' first innings. Bangladesh's collapse, like India's, started in the 15th over. India lost three wickets for six runs on the first afternoon; Bangladesh lost three for five on the second. Both days were hampered by fog and bad light, which caused play to begin an hour and a half late; on the second, only 24.5 overs were possible.

Bangladesh's challenge was collapsing at 98 for six on the third day, when Mushfiqur Rahim and Mahmudullah came to the rescue with a stand of 108. In the second innings, Mushfiqur came to the fore again with some dashing strokeplay. He was only 62 when the ninth wicket fell, but scored 39 from his next 28 balls to complete a maiden Test century in 112 balls with his 17th four (there was also one six), just before he was last out on the final afternoon. It was the fastest hundred by a Bangladeshi batsman, until the next match.

Debutant fast bowler Shafiul had not done much with the ball, but achieved a remarkable batting feat. Though he scored only 14 runs in two innings, he got off the mark with a six off leg-spinner Mishra both times, and was believed to be the first player whose first two scoring shots in Test cricket went for six.

Man of the Match: S. R. Tendulkar.

Close of play: First day, India 213-8 (Tendulkar 76, Sharma 1); Second day, Bangladesh 59-3 (Mohammad Ashraful 0, Raqibul Hasan 1); Third day, India 122-1 (Gambhir 47, Mishra 24); Fourth day, Bangladesh 67-2 (Tamim Iqbal 23, Mohammad Ashraful 16).

India

G. Gambhir c Mushfiqur Rahim b Shahadat Hossain	23	– c Shahriar Nafees b Shafiul Islam	116
*V. Sehwag c Tamim Iqbal b Shakib Al Hasan	52	– c Raqibul Hasan b Shakib Al Hasan	45
R. Dravid b Shahadat Hossain	4	– (4) run out	24
S. R. Tendulkar not out	105	– (5) lbw b Rubel Hossain	16
V. V. S. Laxman st Mushfiqur Rahim b Shakib Al Hasan	7	– (6) not out	69
Yuvraj Singh c Rubel Hossain b Shakib Al Hasan	12	– (7) c Mohammad Ashraful b Shahadat Hossain	25
†K. D. Karthik c Raqibul Hasan b Shahadat Hossain	0	– (8) c Rubel Hossain b Mahmudullah	27
A. Mishra lbw b Shahadat Hossain	14	– (3) c Tamim Iqbal b Mahmudullah	50
Zaheer Khan c Raqibul Hasan b Shakib Al Hasan	11	– b Shakib Al Hasan	20
I. Sharma c Mushfiqur Rahim b Shahadat Hossain	1	– not out	7
S. Sreesanth c Imrul Kayes b Shakib Al Hasan	1		
B 1, l-b 6, w 1, n-b 5	13	B 1, l-b 5, w 3, n-b 2	14

1/79 (2) 2/79 (1) 3/85 (3)   (70.5 overs) 243   1/90 (2)   (8 wkts dec, 87 overs) 413
4/107 (5) 5/149 (6) 6/150 (7)   2/188 (3) 3/233 (1)
7/182 (8) 8/209 (9) 9/230 (10) 10/243 (11)   4/245 (4) 5/272 (5) 6/313 (7)
                                    7/362 (8) 8/394 (9)

Shafiul Islam 9–1–41–0; Shahadat Hossain 18–2–71–5; Rubel Hossain 10–0–40–0; Shakib Al Hasan 29.5–0–62–5; Mahmudullah 3–0–17–0. *Second Innings*—Shafiul Islam 15–0–87–1; Shahadat Hossain 16–1–53–1; Rubel Hossain 15–0–94–1; Shakib Al Hasan 27–2–112–2; Mahmudullah 13–0–52–2; Mohammad Ashraful 1–0–9–0.

Bangladesh

Tamim Iqbal b Zaheer Khan	31	– c Dravid b Sehwag	52
Imrul Kayes lbw b Zaheer Khan	23	– c Karthik b Zaheer Khan	1
Shahriar Nafees c Laxman b Sharma	4	– c Sehwag b Sharma	21
Mohammad Ashraful c Dravid b Sharma	2	– c Dravid b Sharma	27
Raqibul Hasan c Karthik b Sreesanth	17	– lbw b Sharma	13
*Shakib Al Hasan c Sehwag b Zaheer Khan	17	– c Sehwag b Mishra	17
†Mushfiqur Rahim c Sehwag b Mishra	44	– c sub (P. P. Ojha) b Mishra	101
Mahmudullah c Karthik b Sreesanth	69	– c Karthik b Zaheer Khan	20
Shahadat Hossain c Yuvraj Singh b Mishra	11	– b Mishra	24
Shafiul Islam c Yuvraj Singh b Mishra	6	– c and b Mishra	8
Rubel Hossain not out	0	– not out	4
B 4, l-b 1, w 1, n-b 12	18	B 4, l-b 3, n-b 6	13
	242		**301**

1/53 (2) 2/58 (3) 3/58 (1) 4/68 (4)   (65.2 overs) 242
5/89 (6) 6/98 (5) 7/206 (7) 8/228 (9)
9/235 (8) 10/242 (10)

1/8 (2) 2/47 (3)   (75.2 overs) 301
3/79 (4) 4/97 (5)
5/135 (1) 6/145 (6) 7/170 (8)
8/230 (9) 9/258 (10) 10/301 (7)

Zaheer Khan 20–4–54–3; Sreesanth 11–1–55–2; Sharma 13–3–47–2; Mishra 16.2–2–66–3; Yuvraj Singh 5–1–15–0. *Second Innings*—Zaheer Khan 20–5–90–2; Sreesanth 12.2–0–53–0; Sharma 15–4–48–3; Mishra 22.2–3–92–4; Sehwag 4–1–7–1; Yuvraj Singh 1.4–1–4–0.

Umpires: B. F. Bowden and M. Erasmus.   Third umpire: Enamul Haque, sen.

BANGLADESH v INDIA

Second Test Match

At Mirpur, January 24–27, 2010. India won by ten wickets. Toss: Bangladesh.

This match saw some dramatic turns. Tendulkar and Dravid shared their fourth double-century stand in Test cricket, while Bangladesh – between collapses – registered their first, thanks to Tamim Iqbal's brilliant counter-attacking 151. Mahmudullah was unlucky to miss a maiden Test hundred, while Tendulkar scored his 45th. But in the end the memory that lingered was of left-armer Zaheer Khan's destructive spell of reverse swing on the fourth day, which put Bangladesh in total disarray from a relatively promising position.

At 290 for three, only 21 behind, they fancied giving India something to chase. Then spinners Harbhajan Singh and Ojha broke through, and Zaheer, who had spent most of the morning in a back-brace and bowled only two short spells, returned just before lunch to take three wickets in four balls. Raqibul Hasan shouldered arms to one that came in and shattered the stumps; Mahmudullah was done by late movement, with second slip Vijay diving to his left for a superb catch; and Shafiul Islam was bowled. Suddenly Bangladesh had lost six for 14 and were eyeing an innings defeat.

MOST CENTURY STANDS BY A PAIR OF TEST BATSMEN

100 stands	Inns		
19	129	**R. Dravid/S. R. Tendulkar (India)**	**1996–2010-11**
16	148	C. G. Greenidge/D. L. Haynes (West Indies)	1977-78–1990-91
16	76	M. L. Hayden/R. T. Ponting (Australia)	2000-01–2008-09
15	39	J. B. Hobbs/H. Sutcliffe (England)	1924–1930
14	122	M. L. Hayden/J. L. Langer (Australia)	1996-97–2006-07
14	48	J. L. Langer/R. T. Ponting (Australia)	1998-99–2006-07
12	71	S. C. Ganguly/S. R. Tendulkar (India)	1996–2008-09
12	81	D. P. M. D. Jayawardene/K. C. Sangakkara (Sri Lanka)	2000-01–2010-11
12	58	B. C. Lara/R. R. Sarwan (West Indies)	2000–2006-07
12	101	A. J. Strauss/A. N. Cook (England)	2006–2010-11

That was avoided, but only just. Mushfiqur Rahim struck a couple of fours before Zaheer bowled Rubel Hossain with his third ball after lunch. The lead was a single run, and India came out needing two to win. They didn't have to play a shot. Shakib Al Hasan's second ball went for two byes to give India their fifth successive series win, a national record.

Zaheer had already taken all the three wickets that fell the previous afternoon; his final spell of four for nought in eight deliveries gave him a Test-best seven for 87, his first ten-wicket haul, and the match and series awards. Mahendra Singh Dhoni confessed he had been contemplating taking the second new ball when Zaheer started his magic with the old one.

Bangladesh had been on the back foot from the beginning, losing five wickets on the opening morning after electing to bat. Though Imrul Kayes, who fell to the game's seventh delivery, was lost to umpire Bowden's misjudgment – a crooked finger declared him caught behind when the ball brushed his thigh pad – most perished through lacking the discipline required to grind it out. Mohammad Ashraful was the prime example, storming to 39 from 30 balls before making a headless-chicken charge at Ojha's left-arm spin and being stumped.

Mahmudullah was the exception. He came in at 106 for six, which was soon 127 for seven, but added a further 106 with the three pace bowlers, of which his own contribution was 84. He was stranded four short of a deserved century.

Bangladesh's fielding woes continued, and again Tendulkar was the main beneficiary – dropped on 27 and 53 by Raqibul, first at gully off Rubel and then at point off Shahadat Hossain. The second chance came just after Dravid and Tendulkar had completed their 17th century stand in Test cricket, from 117 partnerships in all. It was a record by a single pair, putting them ahead of West Indies' Greenidge and Haynes, and Australia's Hayden and Ponting. Both went on to hundreds, and they took their stand to 222 before Shahadat's bouncer broke it, and Dravid's jaw. The ball didn't lift as he expected, and crashed into his face; he was taken to hospital, where he stayed overnight as a precaution.

Gambhir's pursuit of Bradman's record of centuries in six successive Tests had also been cut short by a bouncer, when Shafiul's snorter put him in a tangle and he was caught behind for 68. He had the consolation of emulating West Indian great Viv Richards by scoring fifties in 11 consecutive Tests.

With Yuvraj Singh nursing a wrist injury, Dhoni declared once he was out at lunch on the third day, 311 ahead. But Bangladesh fought back through an onslaught from Tamim, who raced to 50 from 49 balls and his hundred from 101 – beating Mushfiqur's the previous week as Bangladesh's fastest in Tests. He advanced to a career-best 151 from 183, with 18 fours and three sixes. Tamim found an ally in Junaid Siddique; they added 200, an all-wicket national record. But both departed just before stumps on the third evening, caught behind in consecutive overs from Zaheer – who was to finish the job the following day.

Man of the Match: Zaheer Khan.   *Man of the Series:* Zaheer Khan.
Close of play: First day, India 69-0 (Gambhir 26, Sehwag 41); Second day, India 459-5 (Dhoni 22); Third day, Bangladesh 228-3 (Shahadat Hossain 2, Mohammad Ashraful 2).

Bangladesh

Tamim Iqbal b Zaheer Khan	0	– c Dhoni b Zaheer Khan	151
Imrul Kayes c Dhoni b Sharma	0	– c sub (K. D. Karthik) b Zaheer Khan	5
Junaid Siddique c Dhoni b Zaheer Khan	7	– c Dhoni b Zaheer Khan	55
Mohammad Ashraful st Dhoni b Ojha	39	– (5) c Dhoni b Ojha	25
Raqibul Hasan c Dravid b Sharma	4	– (6) b Zaheer Khan	5
*Shakib Al Hasan c Dhoni b Zaheer Khan	34	– (7) c Gambhir b Ojha	7
†Mushfiqur Rahim lbw b Sharma	30	– (8) not out	10
Mahmudullah not out	96	– (9) c Vijay b Zaheer Khan	0
Shahadat Hossain st Dhoni b Ojha	8	– (4) c sub (A. Mishra)	
		b Harbhajan Singh	40
Shafiul Islam c Dravid b Sharma	9	– b Zaheer Khan	0
Rubel Hossain b Harbhajan Singh	4	– b Zaheer Khan	0
L-b 2	2	B 7, l-b 5, w 2	14

1/0 (2) 2/4 (1) 3/13 (3) 4/44 (5)   (73.5 overs) 233   1/19 (2) 2/219 (3)   (90.3 overs) 312
5/51 (4) 6/106 (7) 7/127 (6)   3/222 (1) 4/290 (4)
8/155 (9) 9/213 (10) 10/233 (11)   5/291 (5) 6/301 (7) 7/304 (6) 8/304 (9)
                                                                 9/304 (10) 10/312 (11)

Zaheer Khan 19–3–62–3; Sharma 18–3–66–4; Ojha 16–1–49–2; Harbhajan Singh 18.5–3–48–1; Yuvraj Singh 2–0–6–0. *Second Innings*—Zaheer Khan 20.3–2–87–7; Sharma 15–2–50–0; Harbhajan Singh 26–7–75–1; Ojha 22–4–77–2; Sehwag 7–2–11–0.

India

G. Gambhir c Mushfiqur Rahim b Shafiul Islam	68	– (2) not out	0
V. Sehwag c Mushfiqur Rahim b Shahadat Hossain	56	– (1) not out	0
R. Dravid retired hurt	111		
S. R. Tendulkar c Imrul Kayes b Shakib Al Hasan	143		
M. Vijay c Mahmudullah b Shakib Al Hasan	30		
*†M. S. Dhoni st Mushfiqur Rahim b Raqibul Hasan	89		
Harbhajan Singh c Mushfiqur Rahim b Shafiul Islam	13		
Zaheer Khan c Shahadat Hossain b Shafiul Islam	0		
I. Sharma c Mushfiqur Rahim			
b Mohammad Ashraful	13		
P. P. Ojha not out	1		
B 3, l-b 6, w 1, n-b 10	20	B 2	2

1/103 (2) 2/146 (1)   (8 wkts dec, 133 overs) 544   (no wkt, 0.2 overs) 2
3/421 (4) 4/436 (5)
5/459 (7) 6/467 (8) 7/518 (9) 8/544 (6)

Yuvraj Singh did not bat.

In the first innings Dravid retired hurt at 368.

Shafiul Islam 23–1–86–3; Shahadat Hossain 22–2–91–1; Rubel Hossain 28–1–115–0; Shakib Al Hasan 34–3–118–2; Mohammad Ashraful 9–0–38–1; Mahmudullah 15–0–78–0; Junaid Siddique 1–0–9–0; Raqibul Hasan 1–1–0–1. *Second Innings*—Shakib Al Hasan 0.2–0–0–0.

Umpires: B. F. Bowden and M. Erasmus.   Third umpire: Sharfuddoula.
Series referee: A. J. Pycroft.

BANGLADESH v ENGLAND, 2009-10

David Hopps

Test matches (2): Bangladesh 0, England 2
One-day internationals (3): Bangladesh 0, England 3

Andrew Strauss's decision to miss England's tour of the Middle East and Bangladesh and opt instead for rest and recuperation ahead of a year of non-stop cricket attracted predictable criticism. A former England captain or two were among those expressing misgivings that Strauss should play so fast and loose with the job. There was even talk of the supposed disrespect to Bangladesh – some of it from people who had been routinely disrespecting Bangladeshi cricket for years. Others, however, were more sympathetic. It seemed sensible that, if the proliferation of international cricket made occasional rest for top players inevitable, then the England captain, with the most demanding job of all, should not be excluded. For Strauss to rest ahead of an English summer, an Ashes winter, and the World Cup on the subcontinent had a persuasive logic about it.

If it was contestable whether England would feel the benefit of Strauss's sabbatical – short-term disruption for medium-term gain was how he argued it – there was no doubt that Alastair Cook, his replacement as captain, was well served. Cook began the tour with a reputation as a future England captain that had been bestowed upon him too easily for comfort: he had no experience of the role at Essex and had never built a reputation as a deep thinker in the dressing-room. There were times, notably the first morning of the Second Test, as Tamim Iqbal was running amok, when Cook's inexperience was apparent. But he was a popular and even-handed skipper of a squad that he led with great equanimity. His batting, in all forms of the game, grew in authority with the responsibility thrust upon him. Cook could be proud of his achievements and the manner in which he conducted himself. His coach, Andy Flower, asserted immediately after the tour: "I think he has done brilliantly."

After sharing two Twenty20 matches against Pakistan in Dubai, England had a clean sweep in Bangladesh, winning all three one-day internationals and both Tests. They protected, for the moment, the last remaining 100% win record against Bangladesh. They could have done no more, yet the praise was muted, because of Bangladesh's cricketing reputation. England's visit felt part international tour, part cricket aid. They had never been as vociferous as Australia in questioning Bangladesh's right to Test status, but they had not toured there for seven years, an absence which had been silently dismissive.

In England's absence, Bangladeshi cricket had slowly begun to mature. They took both Tests, in Chittagong and Mirpur, a suburb of Dhaka, deep into the final day. At the new national stadium in Mirpur, they were about ten overs away from saving the match, and arguably deserved to do so. England overcame them gradually, after many sessions of attritional cricket. Bangladesh's batting, aided by docile home surfaces, had become more resilient;

Stu Forster, Getty Images

Part international tour, part cricket aid: boys prepare to man the scoreboard during England's visit.

under the influence of a dedicated and talented captain, Shakib Al Hasan, and Australian coach Jamie Siddons, they scrapped for all they were worth. But when the series was over, they had only two more defeats to show for their efforts, their record standing at 57 losses and three victories (one against Zimbabwe, two against a second-string West Indies) in 66 Tests.

England were supported by a large backroom staff offering coaching advice, fitness plans, fielding routines, psychological guidance, massages, computer analysis, rehydration techniques, pills and potions, but still had to work hard to conquer a Bangladesh side who had to make do with only three bowling machines in the entire country. Siddons had also had to struggle with the fallout from the rebel Indian Cricket League. Bangladesh cricket's relative poverty had made them easy prey for the ICL's promise of rich pickings, but India, aggressively protecting the official IPL, ensured that Bangladesh's 14 ICL players were heavily punished, with a ten-year ban. It was revoked months before England's arrival after the ICL withered away.

But Bangladesh's story is also one of individual achievement in the face of hardship. Shakib had become the third-ranked all-rounder in Test cricket, and the first in one-day internationals. He had first held a proper cricket ball when he was nearly 15, after playing tape-ball cricket on waste ground in his home town of Magura. Eight years on, as the Second Test reached its final stages, Shakib seemed to be resisting England almost single-handedly. When he was last out for 96, stumped off James Tredwell's off-spin as he sought a lofted straight hit, few would have wished upon him such ill luck.

The tour had the usual successes and disappointments. Of the five fast bowlers originally chosen for Bangladesh, only Stuart Broad played in the Tests. Ryan Sidebottom and Graham Onions succumbed to injury. Steve Finn and Tim Bresnan, both late additions, were favoured for the Tests rather than two original picks: Ajmal Shahzad, who had his moments in one-day cricket, and Liam Plunkett, who finished gym-toned, but achieved little else in an inactive and dispiriting winter. Finn – variously stated to be 6ft 8in or 6ft 7in – struggled to maintain his menace in discouraging conditions, but still showed enough to invite speculation as to whether he could play a central role on quicker and bouncier pitches in Australia the following winter. Bresnan, built like a rugby centre, had never looked fitter, and was named as the best seamer on tour by Flower, who liked his grounded and disciplined approach. He survived the heat of the subcontinent surprisingly well. "I don't sweat much," he explained. "When I was a kid my mum used to keep the central heating up."

Broad was afflicted by back trouble, enough for one tabloid to conduct a survey of Chittagong mattresses; his batting had deteriorated, with talk of him becoming a Test No. 7 temporarily forgotten; and he looked in need of a break. With England still searching for a bowling coach to replace Ottis Gibson, who had taken charge of West Indies, the fast-bowling group had to revert to self-tuition as they tried to master the skills of reverse swing. (Shortly after the tour, David Saker was appointed as Gibson's replacement.)

Cook had most reason for satisfaction among the batsmen, with a century in each Test. Michael Carberry's Test debut in Chittagong was solid enough, although Jonathan Trott replaced him as opener in Mirpur when England abandoned their policy of six specialist batsmen. Kevin Pietersen became entangled in technical uncertainty against left-arm spinners, but after phone calls to former England coach Duncan Fletcher, among others, he responded with dedicated net practice, better balance, a determination to play them more through the off side, and a recovery of form. Paul Collingwood and Ian Bell, in the Tests, and Eoin Morgan and Craig Kieswetter, in the one-day internationals, all made hundreds.

Long before the end of the tour, it felt right that England were in Bangladesh. It felt right not just because the matches – clean sweep or not – were competitive, but because their presence brought so much pleasure. In such insensitive, financially driven times, that was something to cherish.

ENGLAND TOURING PARTY

*A. N. Cook (Essex), I. R. Bell (Warwickshire), T. T. Bresnan (Yorkshire), S. C. J. Broad (Nottinghamshire), M. A. Carberry (Hampshire), P. D. Collingwood (Durham), S. M. Davies (Surrey), S. T. Finn (Middlesex), K. P. Pietersen (Hampshire), L. E. Plunkett (Durham), M. J. Prior (Sussex), A. Shahzad (Yorkshire), G. P. Swann (Nottinghamshire), J. C. Tredwell (Kent), I. J. L. Trott (Warwickshire), L. J. Wright (Sussex).

G. Onions (Durham) and R. J. Sidebottom (Nottinghamshire) were originally selected, but Sidebottom pulled out with an injury after the first one-day international, and Onions went home before the Test series. For the one-day internationals preceding the Tests, J. E. Denly (Kent), C. Kieswetter (Somerset) and E. J. G. Morgan (Middlesex) replaced Bell, Carberry, Davies and Finn.

Coach: A. Flower. *Assistant coaches:* R. G. Halsall; *(one-day leg only)* B. N. French and G. A. Gooch. *Team operations manager:* P. A. Neale. *Team analyst:* N. A. Leamon. *Physiotherapist:* K. A. Russell. *Physiologist:* H. R. Bevan. *Team doctor:* Dr M. Stone. *Team psychologist:* Dr M. Bawden. *Massage therapist:* M. E. S. Saxby. *Security officers:* R. C. Dickason and S. Dickason. *Media relations manager:* M. Ward.

Details of England's matches against England Lions and Pakistan in the UAE can be found on page 1004.

At Fatullah, February 23, 2010. **England XI won by 112 runs. England XI 370-7** (50 overs) (A. N. Cook 56, C. Kieswetter 143, P. D. Collingwood 109; Tapash Baisya 3-72); ‡**Bangladesh Cricket Board XI 258-9** (50 overs) (Nasiruddin Faruque 37, Raqibul Hasan 41, Naeem Islam 40, Sharifullah 47; G. P. Swann 4-44). *A week after qualifying for England by residence, Craig Kieswetter hit 143 from 123 balls, with 13 fours and six sixes, though he was dropped four times. He put on 127 in 21 overs with Alastair Cook; then, after seamer Alauddin Babu trapped Cook and Kevin Pietersen lbw with successive deliveries on his senior debut, another 125 in 16 overs with Paul Collingwood, who hit 109 from 74 balls, with six fours and six sixes.*

At Fatullah, February 25, 2010. **England XI won by seven wickets.** Reduced to 37 overs a side. ‡**Bangladesh Cricket Board XI 151-8** (37 overs) (Tanveer Haider 35, Alauddin Babu 43*); **England XI 155-3** (25.2 overs) (A. N. Cook 52, M. J. Prior 64*). *The Board XI collapsed to 80-7 in the 22nd over after overnight rain delayed the start by two hours. Cook retired out for a run-a-ball fifty; later, the umpire reprieved Matt Prior (playing as a batsman while Kieswetter kept wicket) when he holed out on 51, ruling that he had been distracted by loud music from the stands. Prior remained to steer the England XI home with nearly 12 overs to spare.*

BANGLADESH v ENGLAND

First One-Day International

At Mirpur, February 28, 2010 (day/night). England won by six wickets. Toss: England. One-day international debut: C. Kieswetter.

England gave Cook a winning start in his first one-day international in charge as they defeated Bangladesh with four overs to spare. Cook was ambitious to prove that he had a future in the one-day side, and batted confidently, making 64 from 68 balls before he was ruled lbw by umpire Nadir Shah to an off-spinner from Naeem Islam that seemed to be slipping down the leg side. His vice-captain, Collingwood, rounded things off with an untroubled 75 not out. An England victory in their first one-day international in Bangladesh for seven years had looked far from assured during a typically unrestrained assault by the pinch-hitting prankster, Tamim Iqbal, who was dropped at cover by Morgan off Sidebottom on ten and went on to thrash 125 from 120 balls. He fell in the final powerplay, walking extravagantly across his stumps to be bowled behind his legs by Broad. Why the IPL franchises ignored him was a mystery. Craig Kieswetter, on his one-day debut for England, might have gone for nought when he edged Shakib Al Hasan's left-arm spin through the legs of wicketkeeper Mushfiqur Rahim.

Man of the Match: Tamim Iqbal.

Bangladesh

Tamim Iqbal b Broad	125		Abdur Razzak c Cook b Sidebottom	2
Imrul Kayes c Wright b Bresnan	15		Shafiul Islam not out	11
Junaid Siddique c Kieswetter b Broad	0			
Aftab Ahmed run out	2		L-b 4, w 5, n-b 1	10
*Shakib Al Hasan c Prior b Swann	12			
†Mushfiqur Rahim run out	22		1/63 (2) 2/71 (3) 3/82 (4) (45.4 overs)	228
Mahmudullah c Collingwood b Swann	0		4/112 (5) 5/146 (6) 6/146 (7)	
Naeem Islam c Morgan b Wright	25		7/209 (8) 8/214 (9) 9/214 (1)	
Mashrafe bin Mortaza lbw b Swann	4		10/228 (10) 10 overs: 68-1	

Sidebottom 7.4–0–46–1; Bresnan 9–0–48–1; Broad 9–2–46–2; Swann 10–0–32–3; Collingwood 7–1–39–0; Pietersen 2–0–9–0; Wright 1–0–4–1.

England

*A. N. Cook lbw b Naeem Islam	64	†M. J. Prior not out	30
C. Kieswetter st Mushfiqur Rahim			
b Naeem Islam	19		
K. P. Pietersen c Junaid Siddique		B 4, l-b 1, w 2	7
b Shakib Al Hasan	1		
P. D. Collingwood not out	75	1/73 (2) 2/74 (3) (4 wkts, 46 overs)	229
E. J. G. Morgan c Aftab Ahmed		3/96 (1)	
b Naeem Islam	33	4/184 (5) 10 overs: 63-0	

L. J. Wright, T. T. Bresnan, S. C. J. Broad, G. P. Swann and R. J. Sidebottom did not bat.

Mashrafe bin Mortaza 6–0–37–0; Shafiul Islam 2–0–11–0; Shakib Al Hasan 10–1–42–1; Abdur Razzak 10–1–41–0; Naeem Islam 10–0–49–3; Mahmudullah 8–0–44–0.

Umpires: Nadir Shah and R. J. Tucker.   Third umpire: Sharfuddoula.

BANGLADESH v ENGLAND

Second One-Day International

At Mirpur, March 2, 2010 (day/night). England won by two wickets. Toss: England. One-day international debuts: Suhrawadi Shuvo; J. C. Tredwell.

A nerveless hundred by Eoin Morgan brought England victory with seven balls to spare, and with it the series. Bangladesh made orderly progress to 260 for six, their highest total against England in ten one-day internationals. Armed with five spinners, they defended it with spirit, only for Morgan to score 110 from 104 balls – his first century for England, following one for Ireland three years earlier. He survived a good lbw appeal from Mahmudullah on five, but thereafter reverse-swept with elan. The return of Shafiul Islam's pace gave him final impetus: he won the match with a slog-sweep for six. Broad, who had back trouble, was poised to bat with a runner at No. 11. Cook had put Bangladesh in; the last 16 one-day internationals here had been won by the side batting second, the last 11 under lights, when the surface was sharpened by evening dew. The only member of England's one-day squad excluded from a provisional 30 for the World Twenty20, Cook retorted with his first six in one-day internationals, a slog-sweep against Mahmudullah. Slow left-armer Abdur Razzak passed Mashrafe bin Mortaza – who pulled out of the series after being omitted from this game – as Bangladesh's leading one-day wicket-taker when he dismissed Collingwood.

Man of the Match: E. J. G. Morgan.

Bangladesh

Tamim Iqbal c Cook b Broad	30	Suhrawadi Shuvo not out	14
Imrul Kayes c Collingwood b Swann	63		
Aftab Ahmed b Bresnan	4	B 5, l-b 2, w 7	14
†Mushfiqur Rahim c Wright b Bresnan	76		
*Shakib Al Hasan c and b Swann	14	1/46 (1) 2/56 (3) (6 wkts, 50 overs)	260
Mahmudullah b Bresnan	27	3/146 (2) 4/166 (5)	
Naeem Islam not out	18	5/211 (4) 6/235 (6) 10 overs: 52-1	

Abdur Razzak, Shafiul Islam and Rubel Hossain did not bat.

Bresnan 10–0–51–3; Broad 6–0–34–1; Swann 10–0–52–2; Wright 9–0–38–0; Tredwell 10–0–52–0; Collingwood 5–0–26–0.

England

*A. N. Cook c Mushfiqur Rahim		T. T. Bresnan lbw b Mahmudullah	0
b Shakib Al Hasan .	60	G. P. Swann b Shakib Al Hasan	2
C. Kieswetter c Imrul Kayes b Shafiul Islam	4	J. C. Tredwell not out	2
K. P. Pietersen lbw b Abdur Razzak	18	B 4, l-b 3, w 2	9
P. D. Collingwood lbw b Abdur Razzak ...	7		
E. J. G. Morgan not out...............	110	1/5 (2) 2/52 (3) (8 wkts, 48.5 overs)	261
†M. J. Prior lbw b Abdur Razzak	42	3/68 (4) 4/108 (1) 5/198 (6)	
L. J. Wright b Shakib Al Hasan..........	7	6/223 (7) 7/224 (8) 8/229 (9) 10 overs: 52-2	

S. C. J. Broad did not bat.

Shafiul Islam 6.5–0–55–1; Rubel Hossain 6–0–30–0; Abdur Razzak 10–0–52–3; Naeem Islam 6–0–41–0; Shakib Al Hasan 10–2–32–3; Mahmudullah 7–0–30–1; Suhrawadi Shuvo 3–0–14–0.

Umpires: Nadir Shah and R. J. Tucker.   Third umpire: Sharfuddoula.

BANGLADESH v ENGLAND

Third One-Day International

At Chittagong, March 5, 2010. England won by 45 runs. Toss: Bangladesh. One-day international debut: A. Shahzad.

Craig Kieswetter's maiden international hundred gave England ample statistical proof that they should take him to the imminent World Twenty20 in the Caribbean. It was an innings that spoke of adaptability as he adjusted his explosive, pinch-hitting style to combat a quintet of Bangladesh spinners, with slow bowlers in tandem on a slow surface by the ninth over. A convincing total of 284 for five and a comfortable win gave England the series 3–0, but Bangladesh had proved spirited and worthy one-day hosts. Meanwhile, Pietersen had cause for introspection: this was his tenth one-day international innings without a fifty, a fallibility against left-arm spinners increasingly vexing him. Bangladesh's reply began badly when Ajmal Shahzad, on his one-day England debut, dismissed Tamim Iqbal third ball – a first-over feat Shahzad had also achieved on his Twenty20 debut against Pakistan in Dubai. When Shakib Al Hasan suffered an unfortunate lbw decision against Pietersen, defeat looked inevitable. In the absence of the injured Broad and Sidebottom, Bresnan bowled with Yorkshire gumption in the powerplays for his best international figures to date.

Man of the Match: C. Kieswetter.   *Man of the Series:* E. J. G. Morgan.

England

*A. N. Cook c Mushfiqur Rahim		L. J. Wright not out	32
b Shakib Al Hasan .	32	T. T. Bresnan not out.................	6
C. Kieswetter b Abdur Razzak	107		
K. P. Pietersen lbw b Abdur Razzak	22	L-b 3, w 10	13
P. D. Collingwood c Abdur Razzak			
b Suhrawadi Shuvo .	36	1/59 (1) 2/96 (3) (5 wkts, 50 overs)	284
E. J. G. Morgan c Tamim Iqbal		3/170 (4) 4/237 (2)	
b Shafiul Islam .	36	5/257 (5) 10 overs: 50-0	

†M. J. Prior, A. Shahzad, G. P. Swann and L. E. Plunkett did not bat.

Shafiul Islam 5–0–35–1; Rubel Hossain 6–0–62–0; Abdur Razzak 10–0–40–2; Shakib Al Hasan 10–0–45–1; Naeem Islam 7–0–36–0; Suhrawadi Shuvo 10–1–45–1; Mahmudullah 2–0–18–0.

Bangladesh

Tamim Iqbal c Bresnan b Shahzad	0	Shafiul Islam c Prior b Bresnan	0
Imrul Kayes c Prior b Bresnan	17	Rubel Hossain not out	2
Aftab Ahmed run out	46		
†Mushfiqur Rahim c Bresnan b Swann	40	L-b 3, w 14	17
*Shakib Al Hasan lbw b Pietersen	38		
Mahmudullah c Cook b Bresnan	33	1/0 (1) 2/40 (2) (9 wkts, 50 overs) 239
Naeem Islam c Wright b Swann	18	3/96 (3) 4/125 (4) 5/162 (5)
Suhrawadi Shuvo c Shahzad b Bresnan	11	6/204 (7) 7/211 (6) 8/228 (8)
Abdur Razzak not out	17	9/228 (10) 10 overs: 40-2

Shahzad 9–0–55–1; Bresnan 9–1–28–4; Wright 2–0–16–0; Plunkett 2–0–12–0; Collingwood 10–0–51–0; Swann 10–0–38–2; Pietersen 8–0–36–1.

Umpires: Enamul Haque and R. J. Tucker.   Third umpire: Sharfuddoula.
Series referee: J. J. Crowe.

At Chittagong, March 7–9, 2010 (not first-class). **Drawn. ‡Bangladesh A 202** (Raqibul Hasan 107*; J. C. Tredwell 6-95) **and 362-6 dec** (Junaid Siddique 37, Raqibul Hasan 51, Mohammad Ashraful 30, Saghir Hossain 51, Shuvagoto Hom 91*, Dolar Mahmud 66*); **England XI 281-7 dec** (I. J. L. Trott 101, I. R. Bell 48, M. J. Prior 73*) **and 185-5** (A. N. Cook 42, M. A. Carberry 35, T. T. Bresnan 36; Mohammad Ashraful 3-76). *This match lost its first-class status on the second day when England allowed Bangladesh A to replace injured medium-pacer Syed Rasel with Mahbubul Alam; the tourists later introduced Steve Davies to keep wicket in the second innings. Jonathan Trott arrested a modest run with a fluent hundred, batting with unwavering concentration until he retired out. That could not be said for Kevin Pietersen, who fell cheaply – for two runs – to left-arm spin for the fourth time in eight days. Raqibul Hasan seemed to have played himself back into Bangladesh's Test side, only to make a rash and emotional decision to retire at the age of 22, apparently upset by his omission from the limited-overs squad. He quickly changed his mind, but was given a three-month suspension. England's declaration bowling on the final day conceded 189 in nine overs to stage-manage more batting practice. James Tredwell's off-spin claimed eight wickets but he was still omitted for the First Test at the same ground. Steve Finn and Tim Bresnan pushed ahead of fellow-seamers Ajmal Shahzad and Liam Plunkett.*

BANGLADESH v ENGLAND

First Test Match

At Chittagong, March 12–16, 2010. England won by 181 runs. Toss: Bangladesh. Test debuts: M. A. Carberry, S. T. Finn.

Graeme Swann became the first specialist England off-spinner to take ten wickets in a Test since Jim Laker as Bangladesh were finally dispensed with by 181 runs, but it was midway through the fifth afternoon before England could celebrate the fruits of their labours. Comprehensively outplayed on the opening two days, Bangladesh resisted gamely, assisted by a soporific pitch and England's reliance upon only four main bowlers, which convinced Cook not to enforce the follow-on despite a lead of 303. "To my mind, the follow-on is overrated," he said. Considering the side's balance, stultifying heat and an unresponsive pitch which failed to deteriorate, he had a point.

Swann, England's sole spinner, bowled with enormous heart and finished with match figures of ten for 217, continuing an extraordinary entry into Test cricket. Fifty-four years had passed since Laker famously routed Australia at Old Trafford, although all-rounder Tony Greig was bowling off-spin when he took 13 wickets against West Indies at Port-of-Spain in 1973-74. Swann's efforts were tarnished by a verbal last-day send-off to Junaid Siddique, whose stubborn forward-defensive had become etched on the mind during a 385-minute innings of 106. But Swann had bowled with great skill, he had the grace to offer an immediate apology, and his frustration usefully illustrated the fact that by then England were too exhausted to win in style. Junaid could take pride in that.

Flawed diamond: Mushfiqur Rahim rues the attempted six that brought his downfall.

There is something about Asia's cricketing outposts that brings peace to Cook. Four years earlier he had made a hundred on Test debut in Nagpur, and here, in the unprepossessing surroundings of the Zohur Ahmed Chowdhury Stadium, he added another hundred in his first Test as captain. Despite fielding four spinners, Bangladesh had put England in, hoping in vain for early moisture; Cook was 158 not out when the first day ended, his placid and meticulous approach attuned to a languorous day during which freight trains rumbled past so slowly that, if they were bearing newspapers from Dhaka, they were probably carrying headlines about Bangladesh's elevation to Test status ten years earlier. Cook reached his hundred with only his fourth Test six, though his second of this innings, a thumping slog-sweep off Mahmudullah.

Michael Carberry, skittish on debut, was lbw sweeping; Trott was given caught off his helmet, hooking; Pietersen's reassessment of his technique against left-arm spin paid dividends as he played handsomely through the off side before, on 99, the old vulnerability inconveniently returned and Abdur Razzak bowled him. England, 374 for three at the close, added another 225 at 4.6 an over as they rushed to a declaration 40 minutes before tea on the second day. Cook hit what was then a career-best 173 before he mis-pulled Mahmudullah's turning long-hop, after nearly seven hours at the crease. Collingwood made a four-hour 145, his tenth (and, as it turned out, his last) Test hundred.

Bangladesh were soon in trouble. Tamim Iqbal, a batsman seemingly oblivious to Test cricket's restrictive traditions, breezed past 1,000 runs in his 29th innings, but five colleagues had gone by the close, and there was to be no repeat of Tamim's ebullient strokeplay next morning; Bresnan bowled him when he had added only five to his overnight 81. Mushfiqur Rahim, forever spritely, and Naeem Islam then summoned a record Bangladesh eighth-wicket stand of 113. Carberry's brilliant chase and return ran out Naeem, and Swann cleaned up the tail in the next three balls – one of them a blinding one-handed catch at midwicket by Tredwell, who was on the field for that one delivery after Cook went off. But by then Cook's interest in a follow-on had drained away. Of England's three pace bowlers, Broad had been prone to back trouble, Steve Finn was on debut and Bresnan's Test pedigree was unproven; Cook could at least give them a rest.

England played positively in search of a second declaration. The loss of three wickets as the third day approached its end was negligent, but they rattled off another 78 at almost a run a ball on the fourth morning, Bell advancing his freakish Test average against Bangladesh to 350. Swann then took over proceedings: Tamim was bowled with a perfect off-spinner and, when Shakib Al Hasan swept at a ball too full for the shot and was adjudged lbw, Bangladesh were five down for 110. With tea still 20 minutes away, England sensed a quick kill.

MOST WICKETS IN A TEST BY AN ENGLAND OFF-SPINNER

19-90 (9-37, 10-53)	J. C. Laker	v Australia at Manchester	1956
14-102 (7-28, 7-74)	W. Bates	v Australia at Melbourne	1882-83
13-156 (8-86, 5-70)	A. W. Greig	v West Indies at Port-of-Spain	1973-74
12-101 (7-52, 5-49)	R. Tattersall	v South Africa at Lord's	1951
11-113 (5-58, 6-55)	J. C. Laker	v Australia at Leeds	1956
10-119 (4-64, 6-55)	J. C. Laker	v South Africa at The Oval	1951
10-217 (5-90, 5-127)	**G. P. Swann**	**v Bangladesh at Chittagong**	**2009-10**

By lunch on the following day, however, they had made no further progress. Junaid, 22 in years and Test average, and Mushfiqur ground out 167 in 70 overs. In the England dressing-room, video statisticians produced comforting figures suggesting that the sixth-wicket pair had played false shots at more than 10% of deliveries, but that did not capture their determination. Though Junaid's technique was not easy on the eye, his battling qualities were evident as he accumulated a maiden Test hundred. Swann finally forced him to edge a comfortable catch to first slip just after lunch. Mushfiqur's wicketkeeping had been lacking, but as a keeper-batsman he was a diamond; he was searching for a straight six to bring up his own hundred when Swann deceived him in the flight, tempting him down the pitch for virtually the first time. Fittingly, Swann took the final wicket, too, his tenth, Carberry taking a slick catch at midwicket to dismiss Naeem.

Man of the Match: G. P. Swann.

Close of play: First day, England 374-3 (Cook 158, Collingwood 32); Second day, Bangladesh 154-5 (Tamim Iqbal 81, Shahadat Hossain 0); Third day, England 131-5 (Bell 0, Prior 0); Fourth day, Bangladesh 191-5 (Junaid Siddique 68, Mushfiqur Rahim 47).

England

*A. N. Cook c and b Mahmudullah	173	– c Aftab Ahmed b Mahmudullah	39
M. A. Carberry lbw b Mahmudullah	30	– lbw b Abdur Razzak	34
I. J. L. Trott c Mushfiqur Rahim b Rubel Hossain	39	– c Junaid Siddique b Shakib Al Hasan	14
K. P. Pietersen b Abdur Razzak	99	– lbw b Shakib Al Hasan	32
P. D. Collingwood c Tamim Iqbal b Abdur Razzak	145	– c Mahmudullah b Abdur Razzak	3
I. R. Bell c Rubel Hossain b Shakib Al Hasan	84	– not out	39
†M. J. Prior not out	0	– c Shahadat Hossain b Shakib Al Hasan	7
G. P. Swann (did not bat)		– c Junaid Siddique b Shakib Al Hasan	32
B 6, l-b 9, w 3, n-b 11	29	B 5, l-b 2, n-b 2	9

1/72 (2) 2/149 (3)	(6 wkts dec, 138.3 overs) 599	1/65 (1) (7 wkts dec, 49.3 overs) 209
3/319 (4) 4/412 (1)		2/87 (3) 3/126 (4)
5/596 (5) 6/599 (6)		4/130 (2) 5/131 (5) 6/144 (7) 7/209 (8)

S. C. J. Broad, T. T. Bresnan and S. T. Finn did not bat.

Shahadat Hossain 17–2–73–0; Rubel Hossain 19–0–97–1; Shakib Al Hasan 34.3–4–133–1; Naeem Islam 12–1–42–0; Mahmudullah 23–1–78–2; Abdur Razzak 31–1–157–2; Aftab Ahmed 1–0–2–0; Tamim Iqbal 1–0–2–0. *Second Innings*—Shahadat Hossain 6–0–19–0; Rubel Hossain 6–1–28–0; Mahmudullah 8–0–26–1; Naeem Islam 3–0–14–0; Shakib Al Hasan 16.3–1–62–4; Abdur Razzak 10–2–53–2.

Bangladesh

Tamim Iqbal b Bresnan	86	– b Swann	14
Imrul Kayes c Prior b Broad	4	– c Prior b Finn	23
Junaid Siddique c and b Broad	7	– c Collingwood b Swann	106
Aftab Ahmed c Bell b Swann	1	– c Prior b Bresnan	26
Mahmudullah c Collingwood b Swann	51	– b Bresnan	5
*Shakib Al Hasan b Swann	4	– lbw b Swann	4
Shahadat Hossain c Collingwood b Finn	14	– (10) c Prior b Bresnan	12
†Mushfiqur Rahim c sub (J. C. Tredwell) b Swann	79	– (7) b Swann	95
Naeem Islam run out	38	– (8) c Carberry b Swann	36
Abdur Razzak not out	0	– (9) lbw b Broad	1
Rubel Hossain b Swann	0	– not out	0
B 1, l-b 12, w 1, n-b 1	15	B 2, l-b 7	9

1/13 (2) 2/27 (3) 3/51 (4)	(90.3 overs) 296	1/33 (1) 2/45 (2) (124 overs) 331
4/145 (5) 5/149 (6) 6/159 (1)		3/99 (4) 4/105 (5)
7/183 (7) 8/296 (9) 9/296 (8) 10/296 (11)		5/110 (6) 6/277 (3) 7/294 (7)
		8/301 (9) 9/327 (10) 10/331 (8)

Broad 21–4–70–2; Bresnan 25–10–72–1; Swann 29.3–8–90–5; Finn 14.5–5–48–1; Pietersen 1–0–3–0. *Second Innings*—Broad 24–7–65–1; Bresnan 24–7–63–3; Finn 18–7–47–1; Swann 49–11–127–5; Pietersen 7–1–15–0; Trott 2–0–5–0.

Umpires: A. L. Hill and R. J. Tucker. Third umpire: Enamul Haque.

BANGLADESH v ENGLAND

Second Test Match

At Mirpur, March 20–24, 2010. England won by nine wickets. Toss: Bangladesh. Test debuts: Jahurul Islam; J. C. Tredwell.

Alastair Cook could contentedly claim that he had got the job done. England needed another fifth-day finish, but won an attritional Test by a comfortable margin. Still only 25, Cook rounded things off with his 12th Test hundred, a measured and increasingly relaxed affair. A long winter ended with him wreathed in smiles, but England's pleasure had been hard-earned.

The Test started on Tamim Iqbal's 21st birthday, and he treated its opening moments licentiously, taking something normally sedate and slightly forbidding, and making it wild and intoxicating. He was dropped by Cook, leaping at mid-on, in the ninth over, and then ran riot: England had five boundary fielders by the end of the first hour. No Test batsman, not even Virender Sehwag, matches him for sheer effrontery. No batsman had struck a century before lunch on the first day of a Test since Majid Khan against New Zealand at Karachi in 1976-77; Tamim came close. He had 85 from 71 balls and lunch was still half an hour away when he swept at James Tredwell and the ball ran down the leg side off top edge and forearm for Prior to hold the catch. Kent off-spinner Tredwell, who had bowled his first ball in Test cricket at 114 for one in the 17th over, had his first Test wicket in a manner he had not imagined. "He has no fear," he said of Tamim.

If Cook is one day hailed as an authoritative England captain, he will surely look back at the start of the second day and wince. As Bangladesh chanced their arm, extending their overnight 330 for eight by another 89 runs, his fields defied logic. Dispensing with a third man followed a well-beaten path, but there had rarely been a more extreme example, as Naeem Islam and Shafiul Islam happily carved in that direction. It felt like England's lowest point of a long winter. Bangladesh's 419 was their third-highest Test score.

Tredwell had predicted (inaccurately, it turned out) that the pitch's cracks could turn into "platelets" as the match wore on. With only five specialist batsmen, England were suddenly under pressure. Trott's grim but invaluable resistance turned an embarrassing morning into a day of unremitting tedium. In India, the third year of the IPL had begun, to

Carefree, careworn: Alastair Cook experiences the ups and downs of the game.

its usual hype; in England the ECB were predicting the financial collapse of the game if the Ashes returned, as proposed, to free-to-air TV. But, however worthy, nobody would have paid 100 taka – or £1 – to show the highlights of this. Trott fulfilled an unfamiliar opener's role after England omitted Carberry in favour of a second spinner. He took 33 balls to get off the mark – one fewer than Tamim needed to reach 50 – and had laboured for 64 overs to be 64 by the close. A small crowd examined sunburn or inner selves. Trott concluded the day, appropriately, by ducking a bouncer. He was out early next morning in equally passive fashion, bowled by Shakib Al Hasan off front pad and elbow.

His resistance had an aim: an England first-innings lead. They eventually led by 77 runs, guided there by Bell, whose tenth Test hundred – 138 in a shade under seven hours, marked by lissom footwork against the spinners – finally removed a statistic repeatedly aired to devalue his career. This was the first time he made a Test century without another batsman paving the way by reaching one before him, the implication being that he never did it when conditions were at their toughest. "I've put a few things to bed," he said. "I can't say it's an unfair stat; it's a stat." On this occasion, it was Bell who paved the way for Bresnan almost to reach a maiden Test hundred, on his promotion to No. 7. He batted for over five hours, not blocking and bashing, but patiently working the spinners around like a proper batsman.

Bangladesh's captain, Shakib, again carried the fight, 66 overs of slow left-arm bringing four for 124, all his victims from the top six. Trott found him particularly difficult to score against, managing only ten runs from six scoring shots in the 81 balls Shakib bowled him.

England faced another hard slog as they slowly dismantled Bangladesh's second innings. Tredwell's presence alongside Swann proved essential: they bowled 64 of the 102 overs, and each finished with six wickets in the match. Tamim was less impressive second time around, dropped three times in making 52. Trott's inexplicable miss at backward point – off Tredwell, when Tamim was 47 – was surely one of the great England missed catches of all time. Jahurul Islam, who had made a duck in his first innings, emulated team-mate Shafiul Islam against India in January when his first two scoring shots in Test cricket were sixes. But it was Shakib, again, who did Bangladesh cricket proud. He was last out for 96, drawn down the pitch by Tredwell as he sought a lofted six to bring what would have been his second Test hundred.

HIGHEST TEST TOTALS BY BANGLADESH

488	v Zimbabwe at Chittagong (won by 226 runs)	2004-05
427	v Australia at Fatullah (lost by three wickets)	2005-06
419	**v England at Mirpur (lost by nine wickets)**	**2009-10**
416	v West Indies at Gros Islet, St Lucia (drawn)	2003-04
413	v Sri Lanka at Mirpur (lost by 107 runs)	2008-09
408	**v New Zealand at Hamilton (lost by 121 runs)**	**2009-10**
400	v India at Dhaka (lost by nine wickets)	2000-01

Media attention turned on Broad, who had worked hard on the technique of reverse swing and now claimed the benefit. He first produced a big inswinger against Mushfiqur Rahim and slumped, hands on knees, when umpire Tony Hill refused his appeal. Another inswinger bowled Mushfiqur next ball and, arguably out of nothing more sinister than elation and momentary confusion, he swung round to appeal. Some interpreted that as petulance, but Broad suffered no punishment from the referee.

The run-chase – 209 in 54 overs – was straightforward, as Tredwell's prediction of a last-day minefield never materialised. Cook's second hundred of the series came confidently, and Pietersen, bound for Royal Challengers Bangalore in the IPL, even practised a few switch-hits in his unbeaten 74 from 79 balls. England's supremacy had rarely looked so marked.

Man of the Match: Shakib Al Hasan.   *Man of the Series:* G. P. Swann.

Close of play: First day, Bangladesh 330-8 (Naeem Islam 33, Shafiul Islam 8); Second day, England 171-3 (Trott 64, Bell 25); Third day, England 440-8 (Bresnan 74, Tredwell 0); Fourth day, Bangladesh 172-6 (Shakib Al Hasan 25, Shafiul Islam 0).

Bangladesh

Tamim Iqbal c Prior b Tredwell	85	– c Broad b Swann	52
Imrul Kayes c Finn b Broad	12	– b Broad	4
Junaid Siddique lbw b Swann	39	– c and b Tredwell	34
Jahurul Islam lbw b Swann	0	– b Swann	43
Mahmudullah c Collingwood b Finn	59	– c Prior b Bresnan	6
*Shakib Al Hasan lbw b Tredwell	49	– st Prior b Tredwell	96
†Mushfiqur Rahim c Prior b Bresnan	30	– b Broad	3
Naeem Islam not out	59	– (9) c Pietersen b Tredwell	3
Abdur Razzak lbw b Swann	3	– (10) lbw b Finn	8
Shafiul Islam c Prior b Bresnan	53	– (8) c Trott b Tredwell	28
Rubel Hossain c Prior b Swann	17	– not out	0
B 1, l-b 10, n-b 2	13	L-b 3, w 5	8

1/53 (2) 2/119 (1) 3/122 (4)   (117.1 overs) 419
4/167 (3) 5/226 (5) 6/254 (6)
7/301 (7) 8/314 (9) 9/388 (10) 10/419 (11)

1/23 (2) 2/86 (1)   (102 overs) 285
3/110 (3) 4/130 (5)
5/156 (4) 6/169 (7) 7/232 (8)
8/258 (9) 9/275 (10) 10/285 (6)

Broad 18–5–69–1; Bresnan 21–7–57–2; Swann 36.1–5–114–4; Finn 10–2–61–1; Tredwell 31–5–99–2; Collingwood 1–0–8–0. *Second Innings*—Broad 16–2–72–2; Bresnan 13–2–34–1; Tredwell 34–8–82–4; Finn 9–3–21–1; Swann 30–7–73–2.

England

*A. N. Cook c Imrul Kayes b Abdur Razzak	21	– not out	109
I. J. L. Trott b Shakib Al Hasan	64	– run out	19
K. P. Pietersen c Imrul Kayes b Shakib Al Hasan	45	– not out	74
P. D. Collingwood lbw b Rubel Hossain	0		
I. R. Bell c Jahurul Islam b Shakib Al Hasan	138		
†M. J. Prior b Shakib Al Hasan	62		
T. T. Bresnan st Mushfiqur Rahim b Abdur Razzak	91		
G. P. Swann run out	6		
S. C. J. Broad lbw b Mahmudullah	3		
J. C. Tredwell st Mushfiqur Rahim b Abdur Razzak	37		
S. T. Finn not out	0		
B 9, l-b 12, w 1, n-b 7	29	B 2, l-b 4, n-b 1	7

1/29 (1) 2/105 (3) 3/107 (4) (173.3 overs) 496 1/42 (2) (1 wkt, 44 overs) 209
4/174 (2) 5/272 (6) 6/415 (5)
7/426 (8) 8/434 (9) 9/481 (7) 10/496 (10)

Shafiul Islam 14–3–45–0; Abdur Razzak 39.3–8–132–3; Shakib Al Hasan 66–27–124–4; Mahmudullah 20–4–53–1; Rubel Hossain 26–4–88–1; Naeem Islam 7–0–29–0; Tamim Iqbal 1–0–4–0. *Second Innings*—Shafiul Islam 6–0–22–0; Abdur Razzak 15–0–67–0; Shakib Al Hasan 8–0–31–0; Mahmudullah 7–1–38–0; Rubel Hossain 4–0–26–0; Naeem Islam 4–0–19–0.

Umpires: A. L. Hill and R. J. Tucker. Third umpire: Nadir Shah. Series referee: J. J. Crowe.

BANGLADESH v NEW ZEALAND, 2010-11

Utpal Shuvro

One-day internationals (5): Bangladesh 4, New Zealand 0

Bangladesh's team and supporters had become wearily accustomed to the term "whitewash" over the often painful years since they were elevated to Test status. In this series, though, the other side was on the receiving end for a change: Bangladesh won all four completed matches, to send New Zealand home to an embarrassing inquest before their impending tour of India.

It was a result few had predicted, and the whole country rejoiced. Bangladesh's leading daily newspaper headlined it "Banglawash". The players were hailed as national heroes, and the prime minister feted them with cash prizes, housing plots and cars.

Bangladesh's previous-best series result was winning 3–0 in the Caribbean in 2009, but West Indies were much depleted by a player revolt. There were similarities between the two series, though: as in the Caribbean the regular captain Mashrafe bin Mortaza was injured right at the start, and Shakib Al Hasan stepped in to lead his side to a historic success.

And how he led! Shakib, with his brilliance with the bat and ball, was the difference between the two sides. The series was hyped as a duel between him and the visiting captain Daniel Vettori, but Shakib won the contest hands down, scoring more runs (213 at 71) and taking more wickets (11 at 15.90) than anyone on either side. Vettori had nothing but praise for his opposite number: "He has done a fantastic job, and he has captained the side as well. Bangladesh definitely has one of the best players in the world in Shakib."

But Vettori was clearly devastated by the result. "It's incredibly disappointing, as we came here with high hopes of preparing for the World Cup and to win games," he said. "To be staring down the barrel of a 4–0 scoreline is really disappointing." Mark Greatbatch, New Zealand's coach, was rather less diplomatic, observing afterwards that his team had "played like dicks". Once the team returned from India, Greatbatch was moved sideways, and John Wright took over as coach.

Vettori's shock was understandable. Before this series Bangladesh had managed to beat New Zealand only once in 17 meetings: this thrashing was not only beyond Vettori's imagination, but beyond that of the most patriotic Bangladeshi supporter too. Shakib, though, had been courageous enough to predict it after his side took an unbeatable lead in the third match (the second was rained off). "Now 4–0 is very much possible," he declared – and he walked the talk.

The series win brought Bangladesh within a whisker of West Indies in the ICC one-day rankings. Both had 67 points, though Bangladesh remained fractionally behind in ninth when the decimal points were taken into account.

NEW ZEALAND TOURING PARTY

*D. L. Vettori, H. K. Bennett, G. D. Elliott, B. B. McCullum, N. L. McCullum, A. J. McKay, K. D. Mills, A. J. Redmond, J. D. Ryder, T. G. Southee, S. L. Stewart, L. R. P. L. Taylor, D. R. Tuffey, B-J. Watling, K. S. Williamson. Coach: M. J. Greatbatch.

At Savar (BKSP), October 1, 2010. **Bangladesh Cricket Board XI v New Zealanders. Abandoned.** *No play was possible after a fortnight of heavy rain.*

At Savar (BKSP), October 3, 2010. **Bangladesh Cricket Board XI v New Zealanders. Abandoned.** *More rain meant the second warm-up match was called off a day in advance.*

At Mirpur, October 5, 2010. **First one-day international: Bangladesh won by nine runs** (D/L method). ‡**Bangladesh 228** (49.3 overs) (Shahriar Nafees 35, Junaid Siddique 30, Shakib Al Hasan 58; K. D. Mills 3-44); **New Zealand 200-8** (37 overs) (B. B. McCullum 61, L. R. P. L. Taylor 42; Shakib Al Hasan 4-41). *MoM:* Shakib Al Hasan. *Shakib's all-round brilliance was instrumental in only Bangladesh's second win over New Zealand in 18 one-day internationals. He spanked 58 from 51 balls to lift his side to a competitive total, then took four wickets, including a crucial double strike in the 15th over to remove Brendon McCullum, who had clattered 61 from 45 balls, and Elliott. Rain stopped play for 45 minutes immediately after that: New Zealand's target was revised to 210 from 37 overs. It boiled down to 21 off the last two, whereupon Shakib bowled an outstanding over, giving away just three runs and dismissing Nathan McCullum. Shakib had taken over captaincy duties after Mashrafe bin Mortaza – on his 27th birthday – sprained his ankle when he slipped at the start of his second over and limped out of the series.*

At Mirpur, October 8, 2010. **Second one-day international: abandoned.** *Persistent rain in the two days prior to the match left the outfield soaked, and play was abandoned soon after 11 a.m.*

At Mirpur, October 11, 2010. **Third one-day international: Bangladesh won by seven wickets. New Zealand 173** (42.5 overs) (J. D. Ryder 33, L. R. P. L. Taylor 62*; Suhrawadi Shuvo 3-14); ‡**Bangladesh 177-3** (40 overs) (Imrul Kayes 50, Shahriar Nafees 73). *MoM:* Suhrawadi Shuvo. *Bangladesh completed back-to-back wins over major, full-strength opposition for the first time, mainly thanks to their three left-arm spinners, who took 6-106 between them in 29 overs. The best was the least known: Suhrawadi Shuvo, 21, in only his fifth one-day international, mesmerised the batsmen for outstanding figures of 10–2–14–3. After the nippy Shafiul Islam had removed Brendon McCullum in the first over, only Taylor put up much resistance. He added 72 for the eighth wicket with Kyle Mills (26), but was then left stranded when the last three wickets fell without addition in the space of six balls. The result was never in doubt after Imrul Kayes and Shahriar Nafees opened with a stand of 127, Bangladesh's best for any wicket against New Zealand.*

At Mirpur, October 14, 2010. **Fourth one-day international: Bangladesh won by nine runs. Bangladesh 241** (48.1 overs) (Imrul Kayes 37, Shakib Al Hasan 106, Mahmudullah 37; H. K. Bennett 3-44); ‡**New Zealand 232** (49.3 overs) (K. S. Williamson 108, N. L. McCullum 33; Shakib Al Hasan 3-54). *MoM:* Shakib Al Hasan. *One-day international debut:* H. K. Bennett. *Bangladesh sealed a historic series win, with Shakib again at the forefront. His fifth century, the most by a Bangladeshi in one-day internationals, was a rescue act after they slipped to 44-3 in the eighth over. New Zealand were also in trouble at 80-5, but Williamson's first hundred in one-day internationals took the match down to the wire. Williamson, who had scored only 13 runs in four previous innings, batted with a runner after suffering from cramp on the way to becoming New Zealand's youngest one-day century-maker, at 20. He kept hopes alive till the final over: with 16 needed, he took six from Shafiul Islam's first two balls, but then holed out at deep midwicket. The stadium erupted with joy, and Shakib described the win as the sweetest of his career.*

BANGLADESH v NEW ZEALAND

Fifth One-Day International

At Mirpur, October 17, 2010. Bangladesh won by three runs. Toss: Bangladesh.

Bangladesh completed their whitewash by winning a pulsating match which reminded everyone that one-day games don't necessarily have to be high-scoring to be a great spectacle. It was a thriller of the highest order, in which the pendulum kept swinging till the last. New Zealand eventually needed eight from the final over, with their last pair at the wicket. Mills dispatched Rubel Hossain's first ball – a full toss on the pads – to the fine-leg boundary, but Rubel, who had earlier taken New Zealand's first three wickets, bounced back with two terrific yorkers, the second sending Mills's leg stump flying. Bangladesh had earlier been bundled out for 174, losing their last six wickets for 44 against some rejuvenated bowling. But good work by New Zealand's bowlers was undone by the catastrophic collapse of their top order: by the seventh over they were reeling at 20 for five. Elliott and Vettori, dropped at slip early on, regrouped in a stand of 86, but after Vettori fell to an outstanding running catch by Shafiul Islam at deep midwicket Bangladesh pressed on, and just managed to complete their historic clean sweep.

Man of the Match: Rubel Hossain. *Man of the Series:* Shakib Al Hasan.

Bangladesh

Imrul Kayes lbw b Vettori	34	Shafiul Islam not out		5
Shahriar Nafees lbw b McKay	11	Rubel Hossain c Watling b Mills		2
Junaid Siddique c Vettori b Mills	10			
Raqibul Hasan b Vettori	6	B 1, l-b 7, w 9		17
*Shakib Al Hasan c Williamson b Elliott	36			—
†Mushfiqur Rahim b Elliott	29	1/15 (2) 2/32 (3) 3/69 (4) (44.2 overs)		174
Mahmudullah lbw b Vettori	19	4/77 (1) 5/132 (5) 6/144 (6)		
Suhrawadi Shuvo c B. B. McCullum b Mills	3	7/161 (8) 8/163 (7) 9/168 (9)		
Abdur Razzak c B. B. McCullum b McKay	2	10/174 (11)	10 overs: 53-2	

Mills 8.2–0–36–3; McKay 9–0–34–2; Bennett 8–1–29–0; Vettori 10–0–32–3; N. L. McCullum 5–0–27–0; Elliott 4–2–8–2.

New Zealand

†B. B. McCullum c Shakib Al Hasan		N. L. McCullum b Shakib Al Hasan		4
b Rubel Hossain	4	K. D. Mills b Rubel Hossain		33
J. D. Ryder lbw b Rubel Hossain	4	A. J. McKay lbw b Abdur Razzak		0
B-J. Watling run out	1	H. K. Bennett not out		0
L. R. P. L. Taylor b Abdur Razzak	3			
K. S. Williamson c Raqibul Hasan		B 6, l-b 1, w 13		20
b Rubel Hossain	0			
*D. L. Vettori c Shafiul Islam		1/8 (1) 2/10 (2) 3/14 (3) (49.3 overs)		171
b Shakib Al Hasan	43	4/16 (5) 5/20 (4) 6/106 (6)		
G. D. Elliott c Rubel Hossain		7/119 (8) 8/145 (7) 9/145 (10)		
b Suhrawadi Shuvo	59	10/171 (9)	10 overs: 34-5	

Shafiul Islam 5–0–23–0; Rubel Hossain 9.3–1–25–4; Abdur Razzak 10–2–34–2; Mahmudullah 7–0–18–0; Shakib Al Hasan 10–1–35–2; Suhrawadi Shuvo 8–0–29–1.

Umpires: Aleem Dar and Nadir Shah. Third umpire: Sharfuddoula.
Series referee: J. Srinath.

BANGLADESH v ZIMBABWE, 2010-11

One-day internationals (5): Bangladesh 3, Zimbabwe 1

These two teams rounded off their World Cup preparations with a one-day series in which slow, spin-friendly pitches kept the runs down – in the four matches possible Zimbabwe managed four totals between 181 and 209. They did win the first game, helped by four run-outs, but Bangladesh then came from behind to take the series with three relatively straightforward victories.

Slow left-armer Abdur Razzak took 13 wickets, including a hat-trick, to continue his fine record against Zimbabwe at home; after this series, he had taken 41 wickets in 15 one-day internationals at 12.14.

ZIMBABWE TOURING PARTY

*E. Chigumbura, R. E. Butterworth, R. W. Chakabva, C. J. Chibhabha, A. G. Cremer, K. M. Dabengwa, C. R. Ervine, H. Masakadza, S. W. Masakadza, K. O. Meth, C. B. Mpofu, R. W. Price, T. Taibu, B. R. M. Taylor, P. Utseya. *Coach:* A. R. Butcher.

At Savar (BKSP No. 2 Ground), November 29, 2010. **Bangladesh Cricket Board XI won by 29 runs.** ‡Bangladesh Cricket Board XI 223-9 (50 overs) (Fazle Mahmud 30, Asif Ahmed 46, Saghir Hossain 49; C. B. Mpofu 3-37, K. O. Meth 4-46); **Zimbabweans 194** (46.1 overs) (T. Taibu 32; Noor Hossain 3-40). *Each team nominated 13 players, 11 batting, 11 fielding.*

At Mirpur, December 1, 2010. **First one-day international: Zimbabwe won by nine runs. Zimbabwe 209** (49 overs) (R. W. Chakabva 45, C. R. Ervine 41; Abdur Razzak 4-41); ‡**Bangladesh 200** (49 overs) (Imrul Kayes 41, Shakib Al Hasan 63; C. B. Mpofu 3-25). *MoM:* C. B. Mpofu. *Zimbabwe's total did not look big enough to trouble a Bangladesh side fresh from whitewashing New Zealand, but four run-outs derailed their progress, and although Shakib Al Hasan glued the innings together his departure in the 48th over proved fatal.*

At Mirpur, December 3, 2010. **Second one-day international: Bangladesh won by six wickets. Zimbabwe 191** (46.2 overs) (K. M. Dabengwa 30, C. R. Ervine 42*, P. Utseya 32; Abdur Razzak 5-30, Shakib Al Hasan 4-39); ‡**Bangladesh 194-4** (39.4 overs) (Tamim Iqbal 44, Junaid Siddique 53, Raqibul Hasan 65). *MoM:* Abdur Razzak. *Bangladesh squared the series, this time having little difficulty overhauling another modest target. Abdur Razzak ended Zimbabwe's innings with a hat-trick – Bangladesh's second in one-day internationals, after Shahadat Hossain, also against Zimbabwe, in 2006 – to dismiss Utseya, Price and Mpofu.*

At Mirpur, December 6, 2010. **Third one-day international: Bangladesh won by 65 runs. Bangladesh 246-7** (50 overs) (Imrul Kayes 33, Shakib Al Hasan 73, Mushfiqur Rahim 63; P. Utseya 4-38); ‡**Zimbabwe 181** (48.1 overs) (P. Utseya 67; Shafiul Islam 4-43, Abdur Razzak 4-14). *MoM:* Abdur Razzak. *Bangladesh shrugged off the first-over loss of Tamim Iqbal for a duck to reach the highest total of the series, mainly thanks to a fifth-wicket stand of 116 between Shakib and Mushfiqur Rahim. Zimbabwe plummeted to 47-6, and only a defiant 101-ball rearguard from Utseya – captain again in the absence of Chigumbura with a groin strain – held Bangladesh up for long.*

At Chittagong, December 10, 2010. **Fourth one-day international: abandoned.** *Heavy overnight rain prevented any play.*

At Chittagong, December 12, 2010. **Fifth one-day international: Bangladesh won by six wickets.** ‡**Zimbabwe 188-6** (50 overs) (C. R. Ervine 46, T. Taibu 64; Shakib Al Hasan 3-58); **Bangladesh 189-4** (43 overs) (Tamim Iqbal 95, Junaid Siddique 56*). *MoM:* Tamim Iqbal. Man of the Series: Abdur Razzak. *Ervine and Taibu, who put on 95, rescued Zimbabwe from 21-3 in the 11th over, but the eventual total was insufficient to trouble Bangladesh, who completed a 3–1 series win. Tamim thrashed seven sixes and five fours from 96 balls – the rest of the batsmen in the match managed only ten boundaries between them – and put on 136 with Junaid Siddique. Razzak finished with 13 wickets in the series at 8.92, to follow 15 at 11.46 in a similar home series against Zimbabwe the previous year.*

DOMESTIC CRICKET IN BANGLADESH, 2009-10

UTPAL SHUVRO

The real drama of the domestic season took place before a ball was bowled, when Bangladesh's leading players threatened to strike over changes in the format of the National Cricket League, the country's only first-class tournament.

Although most experts felt Bangladesh cricketers needed more exposure to the longer game, to improve on their abysmal Test record, the Bangladesh Cricket Board made the bizarre decision to reduce the number of four-day matches. Instead of the six divisional teams (picked by the national selectors) playing each other home and away, they played each other once in a preliminary phase, before the top four met again in a Super Four, leading to a final. The previous format guaranteed each team ten games; now, the maximum was nine, for the finalists, and the two teams failing to reach the Super Four had just five. The BCB argued that the home-and-away format produced too many meaningless matches, and that the new plan would increase competitiveness. All matches were staged on neutral grounds to avoid home advantage – and spectator involvement.

The final resolved a personal battle

It did not go down well with the players. Under the banner of the Cricketers' Welfare Association of Bangladesh, leading players threatened to boycott the league unless the board restored the old format and increased match fees. These had risen from 10,000 taka (£93) to 12,000 (£111) for four-day games, but the CWAB wanted 35,000 taka (£325).

The BCB took a firm stand against the threat, and declared that the tournament would go on with those players willing to continue. After several days at loggerheads, the cricketers succumbed to the pressure, but the start of the National Cricket League was delayed for two weeks.

Though the format changed, the winners did not: **Rajshahi** retained their crown by thwarting the challenge of **Chittagong**, who were fourth in the first phase but won all three Super Four games to reach the final. **Sylhet**, though boasting quite a few national players, yet again fared miserably; for the third successive season, they failed to win a match, and this time they lost all five.

The first first-class final for seven years, and the first five-day match in Bangladeshi domestic cricket – intended to prepare players for Tests – promised excitement but was disappointing, with only two and a half innings completed in the five days; the teams scored 1,086 runs between them at just 2.5 an over. Rajshahi gained the crucial first-innings lead and, knowing that was enough to clinch the championship, kept on batting on the docile surface.

The final also resolved a personal battle between Faisal Hossain of Chittagong, who started it as the league's leading scorer, with 852 to the 789 of his nearest rival, Rajshahi's Jahurul Islam. Faisal was still ahead after the first innings, but Jahurul overtook him in a second-innings century, his fourth of the season. He was rewarded with a Test debut against England ten days later. Faisal got some solace when he was named the player of the tournament; as well as his 880 runs, he took 16 wickets with his left-arm spin. In addition to the leading scorer Rajshahi had the leading wicket-taker, slow left-armer Saqlain Sajib, who claimed 54. Habibul Bashar, Bangladesh's former captain and highest Test run-scorer, announced his retirement from all cricket in March. He had finished with a century in his last match.

In April, Rajshahi added the inaugural Twenty20 trophy to their first-class title, defeating Khulna in the final. The one-day National League was not held, due to time constraints. The most popular one-day competition, the Dhaka Premier League, was a cracker, with the title decided by the last ball of the last match: Mohammedan won after eight years' drought, defeating arch-rivals Abahani, who won the Premier Twenty20.

FIRST-CLASS AVERAGES, 2009-10

BATTING (350 runs, average 30.00)

	M	I	NO	R	HS	100s	Avge	Ct/St
Jahurul Islam (*Rajshahi & Bangladesh*).	10	17	1	1,008	139	4	63.00	12
Shuvagoto Hom (*Dhaka*)	7	12	2	601	166*	1	60.10	5
†Tamim Iqbal (*Bangladesh*)	4	8	0	471	151	1	58.87	3
†Faisal Hossain (*Chittagong*)	9	16	1	880	154	2	58.66	12
Farhad Hossain (*Rajshahi*)	9	15	1	797	159	3	56.92	12
Habibul Bashar (*Khulna*)	4	7	0	396	103	1	56.57	1
Mushfiqur Rahim (*Bangladesh*)	4	8	1	392	101	1	56.00	7/4
†Taposh Ghosh (*Khulna*)	6	11	3	381	150*	1	47.62	2
Nazimuddin (*Chittagong*)	8	15	2	613	205	2	47.15	3
Anisur Rahman (*Rajshahi*)	8	11	1	441	151*	1	44.10	4
Tushar Imran (*Khulna*)	6	11	1	380	109	1	38.00	3
Gazi Salahuddin (*Chittagong*)	9	16	1	565	88	0	37.66	10
Saghir Hossain (*Khulna*)	8	14	1	428	79	0	32.92	27/1
Shamsur Rahman (*Dhaka*)	7	13	1	372	134	1	31.00	5
Marshall Ayub (*Dhaka*)	8	15	1	427	72	0	30.50	3

BOWLING (20 wickets)

	Style	O	M	R	W	BB	5W/i	Avge
Syed Rasel (*Khulna*)	LM	147	36	455	25	5-60	1	18.20
Mohammad Shahzada (*Rajshahi*)	RFM	114.3	20	365	20	6-62	1	18.25
Saqlain Sajib (*Rajshahi*)	SLA	353.2	69	1,059	54	7-29	5	19.61
Dolar Mahmud (*Khulna*)	RFM	155.3	30	495	25	5-57	1	19.80
Mohammad Sharif (*Dhaka*)	RFM	235	55	813	41	5-34	3	19.82
Talha Jubair (*Dhaka*)	RM	163.2	27	600	30	7-59	1	20.00
Arafat Salahuddin (*Barisal*)	RFM	145.1	39	438	21	6-68	1	20.85
Elias Sunny (*Chittagong*)	SLA	360.4	81	938	42	6-47	2	22.33
Suhrawadi Shuvo (*Rajshahi*)	SLA	167.1	28	538	24	6-93	3	22.41
Robiul Islam (*Khulna*)	RFM	147	27	571	23	5-30	2	24.82
Kamrul Islam (*Chittagong*)	LFM	274	62	887	30	4-31	0	29.56

NATIONAL CRICKET LEAGUE FIRST PHASE, 2009-10

					1st-inns	Bonus points			Net
	Played	Won	Lost	Drawn	points	Batting	Bowling	Points	run-rate
Rajshahi	5	3	1	1	2	19	20	67	0.14
Dhaka	5	3	0	2	2	6	20	56	−0.29
Khulna	5	3	2	0	0	8	18	50	0.10
Chittagong	5	2	2	1	0	5	19	42	0.09
Barisal	5	2	3	0	0	4	20	40	0.11
Sylhet	5	0	5	0	0	3	17	20	−0.26

In the first phase, each of the six teams played each other once. In the second phase, the top four teams played each other again, and their results and points from the first phase were carried through to the final table.

NATIONAL CRICKET LEAGUE SECOND PHASE, 2009-10

					1st-inns	Bonus points			Net
	Played	Won	Lost	Drawn	points	Batting	Bowling	Points	run-rate
Rajshahi	8	3	2	3	4	24	31	89	−0.00
Chittagong	8	5	2	1	0	11	31	84	0.25
Dhaka	8	3	2	3	4	11	32	77	−0.16
Khulna	8	4	3	1	0	11	29	74	−0.02

Final: Rajshahi drew with Chittagong but claimed the title by virtue of their first-innings lead.

Win = 8pts; draw = 2pts; first-innings lead in a drawn match = 2pts. First-innings bonus points were awarded as follows: one point for the first 200 runs and then for 251, 301 and 351; one point for the fifth wicket taken and then for the sixth, eighth and tenth.

First phase

At Khulna, January 14–17, 2010. **Chittagong won by 122 runs. Chittagong 200 and 269** (Sohag Gazi 5-63); ‡**Barisal 239** (Asif Ahmed 108) **and 108.** *Chittagong 13pts, Barisal 5pts.*

At Rajshahi, January 14–16, 2010. **Dhaka won by eight wickets. Khulna 132 and 220** (Talha Jubair 7-59); ‡**Dhaka 120 and 236-2.** *Dhaka 12pts, Khulna 4pts. Dhaka won despite being 57-8 on the first day; Mohammad Sharif, who had retired hurt, returned to add 52 with Mosharraf Hossain.*

At Fatullah, January 14–16, 2010. **Rajshahi won by an innings and 139 runs. Rajshahi 529-7 dec** (Jahurul Islam 139, Naeem Islam 123*); ‡**Sylhet 144** (Saqlain Sajib 7-29) **and 246** (Rajin Saleh 112; Saqlain Sajib 6-84). *Rajshahi 16pts, Sylhet 2pts. Rajshahi's total was the highest of the tournament, and slow left-armer Saqlain Sajib's 13-113 the best match return.*

At Khulna, January 20–22, 2010. **Dhaka won by ten wickets. Barisal 89** (Mohammad Sharif 5-34) **and 250** (Asif Ahmed 121); ‡**Dhaka 295 and 48-0.** *Dhaka 14pts, Barisal 4pts.*

At Savar, January 20–22, 2010. **Rajshahi won by an innings and 131 runs. Chittagong 184** (Saqlain Sajib 5-33) **and 109** (Suhrawadi Shuvo 5-36); ‡**Rajshahi 424** (Farhad Hossain 159). *Rajshahi 16pts, Chittagong 4pts.*

At Bogra, January 20–23, 2010. **Khulna won by 49 runs. Khulna 242 and 226;** ‡**Sylhet 272 and 147.** *Khulna 13pts, Sylhet 6pts.*

At Fatullah, January 26–29, 2010. **Khulna won by 179 runs.** ‡**Khulna 332** (Arafat Salahuddin 6-68) **and 232-8 dec; Barisal 202 and 183** (Murad Khan 6-64). *Khulna 15pts, Barisal 5pts.*

At Rajshahi, January 26–28, 2010. **Chittagong won by eight wickets. Sylhet 207 and 141;** ‡**Rajshahi 227 and 123-2.** *Chittagong 13pts, Sylhet 6pts.*

At Chittagong, January 26–29, 2010. **Drawn.** ‡**Dhaka 195** (Saqlain Sajib 7-85) **and 440-9 dec** (Shamsur Rahman 134); **Rajshahi 375** (Jahurul Islam 115, Farhad Hossain 157; Mohammad Sharif 5-100) **and 105-3.** *Dhaka 6pts, Rajshahi 2pts. Saqlain Sajib took seven in an innings for the second time in three games. Jahurul Islam and Farhad Hossain added 217 for Rajshahi's third wicket as Dhaka tried ten bowlers, including the keeper.*

At Khulna, February 2–3, 2010. **Barisal won by eight wickets. Sylhet 65** (Shafaq Al Zabir 5-30) **and 193;** ‡**Barisal 230 and 31-2.** *Barisal 13pts, Sylhet 4pts. Sylhet's 65, the lowest total of the season, stretched across 40 overs.*

At Bogra, February 2–5, 2010. **Drawn. Chittagong 350** (Faisal Hossain 154; Mohammad Sharif 5-102) **and 442-9 dec** (Nazimuddin 205; Arafat Sunny 5-87); ‡**Dhaka 351** (Shuvagoto Hom 166*) **and 93-3.** *Chittagong 9pts, Dhaka 12pts. Nazimuddin scored the only double-hundred of this tournament, and added 258 for Chittagong's sixth wicket with Arman Hossain (97).*

At Chittagong, February 2–5, 2010. **Rajshahi won by an innings and 28 runs.** ‡**Khulna 184** (Saqlain Sajib 6-53) **and 295** (Taposh Ghosh 150*; Suhrawadi Shuvo 6-93); **Rajshahi 507-6 dec** (Farhad Hossain 135, Anisur Rahman 151*). *Rajshahi 16pts, Khulna 2pts. Farhad Hossain scored his third century in successive matches. Taposh Ghosh carried his bat in Khulna's second innings.*

At Khulna, February 8–11, 2010. **Barisal won by five wickets. Rajshahi 336** (Suhrawadi Shuvo 151) **and 183** (Jahurul Islam 113); ‡**Barisal 244 and 278-5.** *Barisal 13pts, Rajshahi 7pts.*

At Rajshahi, February 8–11, 2010. **Khulna won by 446-9 dec. Khulna 184** (Tushar Imran 109, Habibul Bashar 103; Elias Sunny 5-86) **and 95-2;** ‡**Chittagong 199 and 340.** *Khulna 16pts, Chittagong 3pts. Former Test captain Habibul Bashar hit a century in what he later declared was his last first-class match; he added 186 for the fourth wicket with Tushar Imran.*

At Bogra, February 8–10, 2010. **Dhaka won by three wickets. Sylhet 172 and 98;** ‡**Dhaka 91** (Nasir Hossain 5-28, Maisuqur Rahman 5-19) **and 181-7.** *Dhaka 12pts, Sylhet 4pts. Nineteen wickets fell on the first day and 16 on the second.*

Second phase

At Bogra, February 15–17, 2010. **Chittagong won by 25 runs. ‡Chittagong 198** (Suhrawadi Shuvo 5-36) **and 250** (Faisal Hossain 100); **Rajshahi 258 and 165** (Elias Sunny 6-47). *Chittagong 12pts, Rajshahi 6pts. Chasing 191, Rajshahi collapsed from 128-2; slow left-armer Elias Sunny took the last six wickets, including a hat-trick to complete victory.*

At Chittagong, February 15–18, 2010. **Khulna won by 229 runs. Khulna 244 and 325; ‡Dhaka 111** (Robiul Islam 5-30) **and 229** (Robiul Islam 5-62). *Khulna 13pts, Dhaka 4pts.*

At Khulna, February 22–25, 2010. **Chittagong won by 218 runs. Chittagong 312 and 330-9 dec** (Nazimuddin 136); **‡Dhaka 239** (Mehrab Hossain 101) **and 185.** *Chittagong 15pts, Dhaka 5pts.*

At Savar, February 22–25, 2010. **Drawn. Rajshahi 269-9 dec** (Nasir Hossain 122) **and 221-6;** **‡Khulna 243** (Mohammad Shahzada 6-62). *Khulna 6pts, Rajshahi 10pts.*

At Bogra, February 28–March 3, 2010. **Chittagong won by three wickets. Khulna 241 and 268;** **‡Chittagong 308** (Syed Rasel 5-60) **and 204-7** (Dolar Mahmud 5-57). *Chittagong 15pts, Khulna 5pts. Chittagong won all three of their second-phase matches to join Rajshahi in the final.*

At Khulna, February 28–March 3, 2010. **Drawn. Dhaka 400-8 dec** (Nadimuddin 147) **and 151-8;** **‡Rajshahi 241 and 404-7 dec** (Sabbir Rahman 100*). *Dhaka 12pts, Rajshahi 6pts. Rajshahi's Saqlain Sajib took his 50th wicket of the season. His team-mate Nasir Hossain was called up to Bangladesh's one-day squad against England during the game, and Mohammad Shahzada replaced him as a full substitute.*

Final

At Mirpur, March 6–10, 2010. **Drawn. Rajshahi won the title by virtue of their first-innings lead. Rajshahi 372 and 413-5 dec** (Jahurul Islam 117); **‡Chittagong 301.** *Rajshahi batted for most of the first two days (169 overs) at 2.2 an over, and Chittagong were almost as bad at 2.4. Having gained first-innings lead, Rajshahi batted out time, stepping up to a dizzy three an over; Jahurul Islam scored his fourth century of the season to finish the tournament with 965 runs and earn a Test call.*

NATIONAL CRICKET LEAGUE WINNERS

†1999-2000	Chittagong	2002-03	Khulna	2006-07	Dhaka
2000-01	Biman Bangladesh Airlines	2003-04	Dhaka	2007-08	Khulna
2001-02	Dhaka	2004-05	Dhaka	2008-09	Rajshahi
		2005-06	Rajshahi	2009-10	Rajshahi

†The National Cricket League was not first-class in 1999-2000.
Dhaka have won the title four times, Rajshahi three times, Khulna twice, Biman Bangladesh Airlines and Chittagong once each. In 1999-2000, the competition was not first class.

DESTINY GROUP NATIONAL CRICKET LEAGUE T20, 2009-10

	Played	Won	Lost	Points	Net run-rate
Dhaka..............	5	5	0	10	1.11
Sylhet..............	5	4	1	8	0.39
Rajshahi............	5	2	3	4	−0.37
Khulna..............	5	2	3	4	0.39
Chittagong..........	5	1	4	2	−0.83
Barisal..............	5	1	4	2	−0.77

Semi-finals: Khulna beat Sylhet by six wickets; Rajshahi beat Dhaka by 12 runs.

Final

At Mirpur, April 21, 2010. **Rajshahi won by six wickets. ‡Khulna 161-6** (20 overs); **Rajshahi 163-4** (19.2 overs). *Rajshahi collected their second title of the season after Shuvagoto Hom and Qaiser Abbas added 109 in 14 overs for their fourth wicket.*

INDIAN CRICKET, 2010

Expert series-levellers

ANAND VASU

By the Chinese Zodiac, 2010 was the Year of the Tiger. Courage, power, passion, loyalty… these are the traditional values of the tiger. The Chinese are yet to make a serious foray into cricket, but for the Indian game, though, 2010 was characterised by something much more mundane, yet equally valuable: recovery.

On and off the field, it was a year in which Indian cricket scrambled to undo what was done unto it. There were serious challenges but, mercifully, nothing that could not be rectified with swift intervention. On the field, the results were only a whisker short of spectacular. In 2010 India played 14 Tests, winning eight and losing only three, none of which cost them a series. India last lost a Test series in August 2008, and none since Mahendra Singh Dhoni took over soon after that.

However, they don't start well. In 2010 alone, India lost the first Test of a series on three occasions – to South Africa at Nagpur in February, Sri Lanka

INDIA IN 2010

	Played	Won	Lost	Drawn/No result
Tests	14	8	3	3
One-day internationals	27	17	10	–
Twenty20 internationals	7	4	3	–

JANUARY	Triangular ODI tournament (a) in Bangladesh	(page 881)
	2 Tests (a) v Bangladesh	(page 884)
FEBRUARY	2 Tests and 3 ODIs (h) v South Africa	(page 915)
MARCH		
APRIL		
MAY	World Twenty20 (in West Indies)	(page 797)
JUNE }	Triangular ODI tournament (a) in Zimbabwe	(page 1146)
	2 T20Is (a) v Zimbabwe	(page 1149)
	Asia Cup (in Sri Lanka)	(page 1076)
JULY	3 Tests (a) v Sri Lanka	(page 1080)
AUGUST	Triangular ODI tournament (a) in Sri Lanka	(page 1090)
SEPTEMBER		
OCTOBER	2 Tests and 3 ODIs (h) v Australia	(page 926)
NOVEMBER		
DECEMBER }	3 Tests and 5 ODIs (h) v New Zealand	(page 936)
JANUARY	3 Tests, 5 ODIs and 1 T20I (a) v South Africa	(page 1040)

For a review of Indian domestic cricket from the 2009-10 season, see page 961.

at Galle in July, and to South Africa again at Centurion in December. Each time, they bounced back to force a win and square the series 1–1.

It doesn't take a forensic analyst to pick out the common thread in these performances. In the innings win over South Africa at Kolkata, V. V. S. Laxman made an unbeaten 143. At the Saravanamuttu Oval in Colombo, when India got home by five wickets after chasing 257 on a wearing fifth-day pitch, Laxman had 103 not out. And at Durban, where the seamer-friendly conditions had traditionally defeated India's brightest batting stars, it was Laxman's 96 – in a game where the next-best score on either side was 39 – that allowed India to seal an 87-run win.

For too long Laxman, who will turn 37 in November, was denied the respect he deserved. Compliments on his elegant, exotic style of play, pleasing to the eye at a time when the focus seems to be on hitting the ball out of the ground, miss the point. Laxman's value to India is not confined merely to the genteel way in which he bats. The steel he takes to the crease when he walks out to bat, the calming influence he has on those not as abundantly gifted, and the knack he has for building partnerships with tailend batsmen of non-existent skill have been integral to India's fortunes.

Statistically, Laxman has never been able to match the feats of some of his run-hungry team-mates. In 2010, though, he had 939 runs from 11 Tests at an average of 67, a return most batsmen would be mighty pleased with. What did rankle, though, even for someone who bats at No. 6 and with the tail a lot, was his conversion rate: only two hundreds to go with seven half-centuries, two of which were more than 90. "I would have had more satisfaction if I had had more hundreds. I am quite happy with my average – batting at No. 5 or 6 for a long time, averaging almost 48 is quite good," explained Laxman. "But I have 48 fifties and only 16 hundreds, so the conversion rate has not been good, for various reasons. I always feel the conversion rate should have been two-thirds."

Laxman says this not because he is worried about how his numbers will stack up by the time he retires, but because it represents, in some ways, promise unfulfilled. In many ways, this has been the story of Indian cricket until recently. The team would win the odd Test away from home, but never consistently enough to stave off series defeat. In the last three years this has changed, and a lot of it, both at individual and team level, has to do with security and stability. "When I look back, there were a lot of times when I was unnecessarily put in a position where I had to take the pressure of retaining my place in the squad," says Laxman. "Obviously, once you have that in mind, the way you play changes. Since Anil Kumble took over in 2007, I've been more relaxed and the insecurity is not there. Starting with Anil, and followed by M. S. Dhoni taking over as captain, and then Gary Kirsten as coach, that insecurity is not there and we can concentrate totally on the job in hand."

In 2010, limited-overs cricket took a back seat for once. While this is surprising, given that the year preceded the staging of the World Cup in the subcontinent, it is easily explained. The Indian board, keen to give the team every opportunity to retain its No. 1 ranking in the ICC's Test table, rescheduled at least two series, against Australia and South Africa at home, cutting one-day

Plenty to smile about: V. V. S. Laxman and Sachin Tendulkar enjoyed 2010.

internationals and fitting in extra Test matches. The Australian Tests were both nail-biters, but India prevailed, thanks in no small part to another Laxman epic at Mohali, where he held the chase together with the tail in breathtaking fashion.

The limited-overs results were a mixed bag, with India winning 17 of their 27 matches, but the bare statistics say little about how the team did. With a constant need to balance the workload of key players, India often rested senior ones, and even sent something approaching an A team, led by Suresh Raina, to Zimbabwe. The chief beneficiary of this rotation policy was Sachin Tendulkar, who played just two one-day internationals, both against South Africa, but made them count. At Gwalior in February, India chose to bat first, and Tendulkar made 200 not out, becoming the first man to reach the mark in a one-day international. In the middle of having his best year in 22 seasons of Test cricket (1,562 runs at an average of 78), Tendulkar managed to make a mark in one-dayers as well.

Off the field, the year was marked by more recoveries. The BCCI, under severe fire for the way Lalit Modi had handled the Indian Premier League, fought to restore some sense of stability. Various governmental agencies probed the IPL, a chain of events set off when bidding was opened for two new teams, and resulted in the resignation of a cabinet minister. Multiple investigations were opened against Modi, who was subsequently stripped of all posts in the IPL and the BCCI.

As part of its clean-up, the board summarily expelled the Rajasthan Royals and the Kings XI Punjab from the IPL, a move that was successfully challenged in the courts. However, the two teams had to provide some weighty financial guarantees, which they did in the nick of time to be part of the 2011 IPL player auction.

The one situation in which the board did not have its way was the extension of the contract of Gary Kirsten, the national coach, who decided he would step down after the 2011 World Cup. Kirsten said he wanted to return home to Cape Town to spend more time with his young sons, and turned down the offer of an extension. Kirsten, along with Paddy Upton (the physiotherapist, who also spends a lot of time on the mental side of the game), had worked with the Indian team for three years, during their most successful sustained run in Tests. The board did not immediately name a successor, saying that the process would be started after the World Cup.

The staging of the World Cup provided its own set of challenges, key among those being the readiness of grounds to host the matches. Delhi's Ferozeshah Kotla had been up against it ever since a one-dayer against Sri Lanka late in 2009 was called off soon after the start because of a pitch that was rated "dangerous" and "unfit" by the referee, Chris Broad. A 12-month suspension of international status followed, and the ICC's pitches expert Andy Atkinson oversaw the ground's rehabilitation. Elsewhere, construction deadlines were missed at Eden Gardens in Kolkata and Mumbai's Wankhede Stadium. Eventually, the ICC took the prestigious India–England game away from Kolkata and moved it to Bangalore instead.

In many ways, 2010 marked the return of Indian cricket to more restrained ways, with talk focusing on the performances of the Test team rather than multimillion-dollar IPL deals.

INDIA v SOUTH AFRICA, 2009-10

KEN BORLAND

Test matches (2): India 1, South Africa 1
One-day internationals (3): India 2, South Africa 1

The top two teams in the ICC Test rankings met in a brief Test series hastily tacked on to what had been planned as a limited-overs tour. South Africa had originally been due to play seven, then five, one-day internationals. But, after India reached No. 1 in the Test rankings late in 2009 and it became apparent that they did not have enough Tests scheduled for 2010 to keep their crown, two were included at the expense of a couple of one-day games.

The tourists arrived in India without their coach, Mickey Arthur, who had resigned four days before their departure when he and the South African board disagreed on the way forward. Despite having to adjust to the temporary management team of former international fast bowler Corrie van Zyl and ex-captain Kepler Wessels – both known for advocating a disciplined but aggressive approach – the South Africans were quickly into their stride.

India went into the First Test at Nagpur with a depleted side after several batsmen suffered injuries, and Dale Steyn took full advantage, slicing through the inexperienced middle order with a devastating spell of reverse-swing bowling rated among the best ever seen in India. Hashim Amla – in sublime form throughout the tour – and Jacques Kallis had already set up an imposing total, and South Africa ended up winning by an innings.

However, even more heroics from Amla, dismissed only once in more than 23 hours of batting over two Tests, could not save his side in the Second Test at Kolkata. South Africa suffered a spectacular collapse of their own on the first evening, and India rammed home the advantage with centuries from Virender Sehwag, Sachin Tendulkar, the returning V. V. S. Laxman and the captain Mahendra Singh Dhoni. It was only the fourth time a team had lost a Test by an innings and then won the next match of the series by an innings.

With the No. 1 Test ranking safely in their pockets, India's focus turned to the one-day games, in which South Africa were led by Kallis after Graeme Smith returned home to rest a broken little finger. India kept their nerve to win the first match by one run, despite the South African tail mounting a fierce comeback; Tendulkar took centre-stage in the second with an inspired double-century, which not only established a new benchmark in one-day internationals but also ensured the series win.

TURNING THE TABLES

Innings victories for opposing sides in consecutive Tests of the same series (* = home team):
India* (inns and 70 runs at Delhi) v Pakistan (inns and 43 runs at Lucknow). 1952-53
England (inns and 93 runs at Sydney) v Australia* (inns and nine runs at Adelaide). 1965-66
West Indies (inns and 55 runs at Leeds) v England* (inns and 34 runs at The Oval) 1966
South Africa (inns and six runs at Nagpur) v India* (inns and 57 runs at Kolkata) . . . **2009-10**

SOUTH AFRICAN TOURING PARTY

*G. C. Smith, H. M. Amla, J. Botha, M. V. Boucher, A. B. de Villiers. J-P. Duminy, P. L. Harris, J. H. Kallis, R. McLaren, M. Morkel, W. D. Parnell, A. N. Petersen, A. G. Prince, D. W. Steyn, L. L. Tsotsobe. *Coach:* C. J. P. G. van Zyl.

After the Tests, Smith went home to an injured finger; for the one-day series that followed, Kallis took over as captain. Harris, McLaren and Prince also returned home and were replaced by L. L. Bosman, H. H. Gibbs, C. K. Langeveldt, J. A. Morkel and R. E. van der Merwe.

At Nagpur, February 2–3, 2010 (not first-class). **Drawn. ‡Indian Board President's XI 318** (M. K. Pandey 43, A. M. Nayar 100, S. Dhawan 70; M. Morkel 3-24, W. D. Parnell 3-66); **South Africans 354** (A. G. Prince 42, G. C. Smith 45, H. M. Amla 72, J. H. Kallis 63, J-P. Duminy 39; R. Ashwin 3-96, P. P. Chawla 4-88). *The President's XI named 14 players and the South Africans their entire squad of 15, though only 11 could bat and 11 field. Abhishek Nayar, who hit 16 fours, added 181 with Shikhar Dhawan after the home side had been 114-6. Both Kallis (who hit 50 in boundaries) and Amla retired out. This match was played at the old VCA Ground, used for internationals up to 2007-08, rather than the VCA Stadium inaugurated in 2008-09 which hosted the Test that followed.*

INDIA v SOUTH AFRICA

First Test Match

At Jamtha, Nagpur, February 6–9, 2010. South Africa won by an innings and six runs. Toss: South Africa. Test debuts: S. Badrinath, W. P. Saha.

Skill applied with patience often pays off in India, and South Africa showed these qualities in abundance in a memorable match for Amla and Steyn. Amla batted over 11 hours to compile the highest score for South Africa against India, beating de Villiers's 217 not out at Ahmedabad on the previous tour in April 2008. Steyn then ripped the heart out of India's batting in an astonishing spell on the way to career-best figures and South Africa's first ten-wicket haul in the subcontinent outside Bangladesh.

The match played out in front of disappointing crowds – Nagpur's new stadium is impressive, but unpopular with the locals as it is some way out of town. India were without Rahul Dravid (broken cheekbone), V. V. S. Laxman (finger) and Yuvraj Singh (wrist); when Rohit Sharma missed his Test debut after twisting an ankle in the warm-ups, reserve wicketkeeper Wriddhiman Saha had to play as a batsman alongside fellow new cap Subramanian Badrinath and the inexperienced Murali Vijay. India still made a useful start. Zaheer Khan took advantage of cool, cloudy conditions to remove Prince and Smith in successive overs during an opening spell of 6–4–2–2. The struggling Prince suffered a tough call, being caught off his arm-guard. With the umpire decision review system not being used for this series (the Indian board and the broadcasters were unable to reach agreement about the cost), there was no reprieve.

But if India thought they had their challengers on the run, Kallis quickly put them right as he breezed to a no-nonsense half-century, while Amla was solid. Kallis did not allow Harbhajan Singh to settle, hammering him for six and four with slog-sweeps from successive balls, and minutes later unveiled a sublime cover-drive for four. With Amla using his marvellous wrists to manipulate the ball all around the ground, Harbhajan failed to bowl a maiden on the first day. Leg-spinner Mishra had a nasty habit of bowling long-hops, Ishant Sharma failed to threaten, and India relied almost entirely on Zaheer.

Kallis soon completed a masterful hundred – out of South Africa's 149 for two. His 34th Test century put him joint third on the all-time list with Sunil Gavaskar and Brian Lara, behind only Ricky Ponting (39) and Tendulkar (then 45). Amla also reached three figures – his eighth hundred in Tests – ten overs before stumps, when South Africa were a commanding 291 for two.

Arko Datta, Reuters

Unquenchable: Hashim Amla's thirst for runs was the defining feature of South Africa's tour.

They resumed cautiously, with the prospect of Kallis's first Test double-hundred dominating talk. But he remained comfortably the most prolific Test batsman without one when Harbhajan obtained extra bounce and turn, and a bat-pad catch looped to short leg. The catcher, Vijay, had failed to hold a similar chance six overs earlier when Amla, on 149, had come down the pitch to Harbhajan. Kallis may have missed his elusive milestone, but the innings was memorable: he came in at six for two against the world's top-ranked side and added 340 with Amla, South Africa's best stand for any wicket against India, and the fifth-highest in any Test in India. Later on, Amla also showed more flair, regularly coming down the pitch to the spinners and even reverse-sweeping.

De Villiers was similarly daring and reached 53 before Sehwag beat him in the air. Harbhajan claimed a second wicket when he trapped Duminy leg-before on the sweep, but Amla was remorseless, showing tremendous shot selection and powers of concentration. He extended his maiden Test double-century to 253 not out – stretched over 675 minutes, the second-longest innings for South Africa after the current Indian coach Gary Kirsten's 878-minute marathon against England at Durban in 1999-2000 – before Smith's declaration gave his bowlers four overs before stumps and two bites of the new ball.

India began briskly, but lost Gambhir to the seventh ball of the third day and Vijay three overs later. Vijay was undone by superb bowling by Steyn, who followed up several away-swingers with an in-ducker; the batsman shouldered arms and was bowled. Sehwag had played in typically carefree style, but the cheap loss of Tendulkar, to a killer away-swinger from Steyn, caused him to rein himself in, and he reached lunch with 63. Sehwag lifted the pace again in the afternoon, however, receiving valuable support from the debutant Badrinath, and achieved a rousing century from 134 balls – only to depart two overs later, managing to pick out deep cover during an erratic over from Parnell.

Badrinath completed a gritty fifty before tea, by which time India were 221 for four, but he and Dhoni fell in the first seven balls of the final session, opening the way for Steyn's sensational burst. Harris spun a delivery out of the leg-side rough to Dhoni, who padded up, and the ball bounced up off his body, on to the gloves and then off the bat to slip.

The ball had been changed shortly before tea, and Steyn found the replacement to his liking, reverse-swinging it back into the batsmen at venomous speed. India's first innings was wrapped up in just 7.4 overs after the interval, Steyn taking five for three in 22 deliveries to finish with seven for 51.

Smith consulted with his bowlers before enforcing the follow-on, but the decision was soon proved correct. Morkel, who had dismissed Gambhir in the first innings from around the wicket with a ball that nipped away, this time bowled him in the second over with one that jagged back in. A flurry of four fours from Sehwag was ended by a slip catch off Steyn, and India were still 259 behind going into the fourth day.

It took a top-class century from Tendulkar, his 46th in Tests, for thoughts of a fifth day even to be contemplated. It was the 100th time in his lengthy Test career that he had reached 50, and he was imperious square of the wicket on both sides. Neither Vijay nor Badrinath lasted long on the fourth morning, during which Harris frustrated the batsmen by bowling over the wicket and some distance outside leg stump. This line also accounted for Tendulkar, the over after he had achieved his hundred; he missed a sweep and the ball hit him on the pad, ran up his leg and was then dragged back on to the stumps by his arms. Harris had the good grace to call the dismissal "unplanned".

Harris did deserve credit, though, for Dhoni's wicket, caught bat-pad, and he should have had Saha before that, when a rebound off his bat to silly point went undetected. Busy innings from Harbhajan and Zaheer complemented Saha's defiance – he batted for two and a half hours to make up for a first-innings duck – and took India past 300, but the final say went once again to Steyn, whose rapid inswingers quickly accounted for Saha and Mishra when he returned to the attack late in the day.

Man of the Match: H. M. Amla.

Close of play: First day, South Africa 291-2 (Amla 115, Kallis 159); Second day, India 25-0 (Gambhir 12, Sehwag 9); Third day, India 66-2 (Vijay 27, Tendulkar 15).

South Africa

*G. C. Smith b Zaheer Khan	6	D. W. Steyn not out		0
A. G. Prince c Dhoni b Zaheer Khan	0			
H. M. Amla not out	253	B 8, l-b 6, n-b 9		25
J. H. Kallis c Vijay b Harbhajan Singh	173			
A. B. de Villiers c Badrinath b Sehwag	53	1/5 (2) 2/6 (1)	(6 wkts dec, 176 overs)	558
J-P. Duminy lbw b Harbhajan Singh	9	3/346 (4) 4/454 (5)		
†M. V. Boucher c Mishra b Zaheer Khan	39	5/476 (6) 6/554 (7)		

W. D. Parnell, P. L. Harris and M. Morkel did not bat.

Zaheer Khan 31–7–96–3; Sharma 28–4–85–0; Harbhajan Singh 46–1–166–2; Mishra 53–5–140–0; Sehwag 18–1–55–1.

India

G. Gambhir c Boucher b Morkel	12	– b Morkel	1
V. Sehwag c Duminy b Parnell	109	– c Smith b Steyn	16
M. Vijay b Steyn	4	– c Morkel b Harris	32
S. R. Tendulkar c Boucher b Steyn	7	– b Harris	100
S. Badrinath c Prince b Steyn	56	– c Boucher b Parnell	6
*†M. S. Dhoni c Kallis b Harris	6	– c de Villiers b Harris	25
W. P. Saha b Steyn	0	– lbw b Harris	36
Harbhajan Singh lbw b Steyn	8	– lbw b Parnell	39
Zaheer Khan b Steyn	2	– c Harris b Kallis	33
A. Mishra b Steyn	0	– b Steyn	0
I. Sharma not out	0	– not out	0
B 14, l-b 6, w 5, n-b 4	29	B 15, l-b 8, w 6, n-b 2	31

1/31 (1) 2/40 (3) 3/56 (4)   (64.4 overs) 233
4/192 (2) 5/221 (6) 6/221 (5) 7/222 (7)
8/226 (9) 9/228 (10) 10/233 (8)

1/1 (1) 2/24 (2)   (107.1 overs) 319
3/96 (3) 4/122 (5)
5/192 (4) 6/209 (6) 7/259 (8)
8/318 (9) 9/318 (7) 10/319 (10)

Steyn 16.4–6–51–7; Morkel 15–4–58–1; Harris 17–2–39–1; Parnell 7–1–31–1; Kallis 6–0–14–0; Duminy 3–0–20–0. *Second Innings*—Steyn 18.1–1–57–3; Morkel 21–6–65–1; Parnell 13–2–58–2; Harris 38–17–76–3; Kallis 12–3–19–1; Duminy 5–0–21–0.

Umpires: S. J. Davis and I. J. Gould.   Third umpire: A. M. Saheba.

INDIA v SOUTH AFRICA

Second Test Match

At Kolkata, February 14–18, 2010. India won by an innings and 57 runs. Toss: South Africa. Test debut: A. N. Petersen.

Revenge was swift for India after their Nagpur mauling, but South Africa made it easier with an astonishing collapse on the first evening. They had raced to 200 for one in the 45th over, with Amla and Alviro Petersen in firm control – Amla piling on the misery for India as he raced to a sublime century off just 124 balls, while Petersen proved his credentials with a quality hundred on debut. Then a fiery second spell from Sharma changed the mood before Zaheer Khan and Harbhajan Singh turned the innings on its head.

Petersen came into the side when back trouble ended Mark Boucher's run of 54 successive Tests (de Villiers took the gloves). He was unfazed by the early loss of his opening partner Smith, who played despite the broken little finger which kept him out of the subsequent one-day series but knew little about a superb ball from Zaheer that came back a considerable distance. Petersen fought his way to only the third century on debut for South Africa after those by Andrew Hudson (1991-92) and Jacques Rudolph (2002-03). Crucially, he fell in the next over as he chased a delivery that Zaheer angled across him. Even more importantly, given his record-breaking form, Amla fell four balls after tea, edging a misguided pull at a Zaheer bouncer that was outside off stump and going further away. Amla was rather fortunate to have reached three figures: he was badly dropped by Laxman at slip when 60, and on 76 sliced Harbhajan just out of reach of the diminutive Mishra at mid-off.

Once Zaheer had removed Petersen and Amla, Harbhajan put India on top with a superb spell, while an inspired Sharma kept the pressure on from the other end. Harbhajan bowled a better line than at Nagpur, and the middle order crumbled in the Eden Gardens cauldron. Kallis reverted to the default sweep, and Laxman claimed a rousing catch running back from slip towards fine leg. Prince and Duminy, both out of form, fell to successive balls in Harbhajan's next over, getting their pads in the way of the variation that goes straight on.

From 218 for one South Africa had crashed alarmingly, not helped by the run-out of de Villiers, whose over-exuberance caused Steyn to panic; Zaheer claimed a thrilling direct hit to make it 254 for seven. Harris and Steyn fell cheaply before bad light brought India's fightback to a temporary halt. As the match had been in South Africa's control, with a rare series win in India beckoning, it seemed legitimate to ask whether they had suffered another of their infamous "chokes".

Parnell and Morkel added 30 next morning before Zaheer claimed his fourth wicket. There was still over an hour to go to lunch, and South Africa had high hopes of early

The leveller: Harbhajan Singh removes Morne Morkel to square the two-Test series at one-all.

breakthroughs on a firm pitch with swing possible in the murky atmosphere – but Sehwag had other ideas. He blasted 39, with seven fours and a six, from his first 20 balls, and was 52 by the interval.

By then, however, Sehwag had lost two partners – the first without warning, when he sent Gambhir back too late to beat some excellent fielding from Petersen. An intense spell from Morkel accounted for Vijay and also saw Sehwag dropped by Duminy at first slip. But after lunch Sehwag and Tendulkar cruised along at five an over thanks to fluent, attacking strokeplay. If Sehwag was the brutal axeman, crashing anything remotely wide through the off side and hitting powerfully off his pads, Tendulkar was the precise surgeon, showing clinical timing and placement, and incredible touch, in his 47th Test hundred.

Sehwag made the most of his earlier let-off – and a missed stumping by de Villiers off Harris at 129 – as he plundered 165 from just 174 balls with 23 fours and two sixes. In the end, though, he fell lamely, driving a well-flighted delivery from part-time off-spinner Duminy straight to extra cover.

Harris had Tendulkar caught at slip in the next over and, when Steyn returned to bowl Badrinath, South Africa had grabbed three wickets for five runs at the end of the day. With the second new ball due after four overs next morning, they needed more of the same to fight their way back into contention – but instead fluffed three half-chances before lunch, while nightwatchman Mishra proved an irritation. Laxman (back after missing the previous Test with a finger injury) and Dhoni then kicked on remorselessly, reaching centuries as they steered India to their highest total against South Africa during an unbeaten seventh-wicket stand of 259, an Indian record, beating 235 by Ravi Shastri and Syed Kirmani against England at Bombay in 1984-85. Harris was prevented from bowling the over-the-wicket line outside leg stump he had used at Nagpur as umpire Ian Gould called wides.

Dhoni ended the numbed visitors' suffering in the field with 11 scheduled overs left in the day, but bad light meant just five balls were possible. The weather helped South Africa

MOST RUNS IN A TWO-TEST SERIES

Runs	Average			
571	190.33	S. T. Jayasuriya	Sri Lanka v India	1997-98
563	563.00	W. R. Hammond	England v New Zealand	1932-33
540	270.00	A. Flower.	Zimbabwe v India.	2000-01
510	170.00	D. P. M. D. Jayawardene	Sri Lanka v South Africa	2006
501	250.50	M. L. Hayden.	Australia v Zimbabwe	2003-04
490	**490.00**	**H. M. Amla**.	**South Africa v India**.	**2009-10**
469	234.50	T. T. Samaraweera.	Sri Lanka v Pakistan.	2008-09

further overnight, a wet outfield preventing play for an hour and a half on the fourth morning. Bad light and rain cost another 95 minutes before tea, and only one over was possible in the final session. But Mishra finally made his mark, claiming the big wickets of Smith, with his first delivery, and Kallis, who edged a gem of a leg-break. On the final morning Mishra also removed de Villiers, who failed to read the googly, while Harbhajan was starting to make his presence felt at the other end.

South Africa slumped to 180 for seven, still 167 behind. But magnificent was the only word for Amla, who tried gamely to save the Test with the aid of the tail. Parnell batted for 101 minutes before Sharma was recalled and had him caught at mid-on, followed by Harris in the slips. Last man Morkel miraculously survived over an hour, and the Eden Gardens crowd grew desperate as the close loomed. Sehwag kicked the ball over the boundary in an attempt to deny Amla – who had strolled a single – the strike at the end of an over, but the umpires correctly awarded five penalty runs for unfair fielding.

Just nine mandatory balls remained (although there were still 16 minutes of play left) when Harbhajan answered the crowd's prayers, turning a delivery past Morkel's inside edge to render Amla's heroics redundant. He had completed his second century of the match, the tenth of his Test career, and his eventual series average of 490 had been bettered only by Wally Hammond, who made 563 runs for once out, also in two Tests, for England in New Zealand in 1932-33.

Man of the Match: H. M. Amla.   *Man of the Series:* H. M. Amla.

Close of play: First day, South Africa 266-9 (Parnell 2, Morkel 3); Second day, India 342-5 (Laxman 9, Mishra 1); Third day, South Africa 6-0 (Smith 5, Petersen 1); Fourth day, South Africa 115-3 (Amla 49, Prince 0).

South Africa

*G. C. Smith b Zaheer Khan	4	– lbw b Mishra	20
A. N. Petersen c Dhoni b Zaheer Khan	100	– c Badrinath b Harbhajan Singh . . .	21
H. M. Amla c Dhoni b Zaheer Khan	114	– not out	123
J. H. Kallis c Laxman b Harbhajan Singh	10	– c Dhoni b Mishra	20
†A. B. de Villiers run out.	12	– (6) lbw b Mishra	3
A. G. Prince lbw b Harbhajan Singh	1	– (5) c Sharma b Harbhajan Singh	23
J-P. Duminy lbw b Harbhajan Singh	1	– lbw b Harbhajan Singh.	6
D. W. Steyn lbw b Mishra	5	– lbw b Harbhajan Singh.	1
P. L. Harris c Dhoni b Sharma.	1	– (10) c sub (K. D. Karthik) b Sharma .	4
W. D. Parnell lbw b Zaheer Khan	12	– (9) c Harbhajan Singh b Sharma	22
M. Morkel not out	11	– lbw b Harbhajan Singh.	12
B 1, l-b 4, w 10, n-b 11	26	B 6, l-b 5, w 1, n-b 8, p 5 . . .	35

1/9 (1) 2/218 (2) 3/229 (3) 4/251 (4) (85 overs) 296
5/253 (6) 6/253 (7) 7/254 (5) 8/255 (9)
9/261 (8) 10/296 (10)

1/36 (1) 2/54 (2) (131.3 overs) 290
3/111 (4) 4/158 (5)
5/164 (6) 6/172 (7) 7/180 (8)
8/250 (9) 9/264 (10) 10/290 (11)

Zaheer Khan 22–5–90–4; Sharma 18–3–67–1; Mishra 21–3–70–1; Harbhajan Singh 24–2–64–3. *Second Innings*—Zaheer Khan 6–0–32–0; Harbhajan Singh 48.3–23–59–5; Sharma 25–5–84–2; Mishra 40–12–78–3; Sehwag 10–2–20–0; Tendulkar 2–1–1–0.

India

G. Gambhir run out	25	*†M. S. Dhoni not out	132
V. Sehwag c Prince b Duminy	165		
M. Vijay c de Villiers b Morkel	7	B 6, l-b 9, w 13, n-b 8	36
S. R. Tendulkar c Kallis b Harris	106		
V. V. S. Laxman not out	143	1/73 (1) 2/82 (3) (6 wkts dec, 153 overs)	643
S. Badrinath b Steyn	1	3/331 (2) 4/335 (4)	
A. Mishra c Kallis b Morkel	28	5/336 (6) 6/384 (7)	

Harbhajan Singh, Zaheer Khan and I. Sharma did not bat.

Steyn 30–5–115–1; Morkel 26–3–115–2; Parnell 20–1–103–0; Kallis 12–1–40–0; Harris 50–5–182–1; Duminy 15–0–73–1.

Umpires: S. J. Davis and I. J. Gould.   Third umpire: S. K. Tarapore.

Series referee: A. J. Pycroft.

INDIA v SOUTH AFRICA

First One-Day International

At Jaipur, February 21, 2010 (day/night). India won by one run. Toss: South Africa.

Unlikely batting heroes Parnell and Steyn almost saved their top order's blushes with a ninth-wicket stand of 65 in 38 balls. Steyn lashed two sixes in one Raina over, and both men cleared the boundary in the penultimate over, from Nehra, to leave South Africa needing ten from the last to snatch victory. Praveen Kumar hit Steyn's leg stump with the second ball, several replays finally proved Tendulkar had saved a four near the long-leg rope off the fifth, and the sixth was a wide. So it boiled down to three needed from one ball, but Parnell could only slice it to third man for a single. Kallis, the stand-in captain, was the one recognised batsman who married composure to strokeplay, batting into the 43rd over in a 97-ball innings. Gibbs and Bosman made a rapid start but got themselves out when well set; so did de Villiers, as Jadeja bowled his slow left-armers superbly on a beige pitch to restrict the middle order. India's innings had turned sour after bowler Langeveldt's deflection at the non-striker's end ran out Sehwag. Raina stopped the rot and, with the tail's help, pushed India to safety. Nehra had two lucky moments: he should have been given run out before scoring, but a subdued appeal was not referred to the TV umpire; and, in the final over, Langeveldt sent a yorker crashing into his off stump, but the bails did not fall and the ball ricocheted to the boundary for four.

Man of the Match: R. A. Jadeja.

India

V. Sehwag run out	46	A. Nehra not out	16
S. R. Tendulkar run out	4	S. Sreesanth not out	0
K. D. Karthik c Petersen b Langeveldt	44		
*†M. S. Dhoni c Morkel b Kallis	26	L-b 7, w 13	20
V. Kohli c Gibbs b Morkel	31		
S. K. Raina c Boucher b Kallis	58	1/10 (2) 2/89 (1) (9 wkts, 50 overs)	298
Y. K. Pathan c Kallis b Parnell	18	3/116 (3) 4/138 (4)	
R. A. Jadeja c Boucher b Kallis	22	5/204 (5) 6/231 (7) 7/260 (6)	
P. Kumar run out	13	8/274 (8) 9/292 (9)	
		10 overs: 58-1	

Steyn 10–1–46–0; Parnell 9–0–69–1; Langeveldt 10–0–48–1; Morkel 8–0–59–1; Botha 6–0–40–0; Kallis 7–0–29–3.

South Africa

L. E. Bosman b Kumar	29		D. W. Steyn b Kumar	35
H. H. Gibbs c Kohli b Jadeja	27		C. K. Langeveldt not out	4
*J. H. Kallis b Sreesanth	89			
A. B. de Villiers b Jadeja	25		B 1, l-b 4, w 8	13
A. N. Petersen run out	9			
J. A. Morkel lbw b Nehra	2		1/58 (1) 2/64 (2) 3/109 (4) (50 overs)	297
†M. V. Boucher c Dhoni b Sreesanth	5		4/134 (5) 5/142 (6) 6/161 (7)	
J. Botha lbw b Pathan	10		7/180 (8) 8/225 (3) 9/290 (10)	
W. D. Parnell run out	49		10/297 (9) 10 overs: 60-1	

Kumar 8–0–46–2; Nehra 10–0–67–1; Sreesanth 9–1–74–2; Jadeja 10–2–29–2; Pathan 10–0–51–1; Raina 3–0–25–0.

Umpires: A. M. Saheba and S. K. Tarapore. Third umpire: S. S. Hazare.

INDIA v SOUTH AFRICA

Second One-Day International

At Gwalior, February 24, 2010 (day/night). India won by 153 runs. Toss: India.

Sachin Tendulkar produced a dazzling display of top-class strokeplay to become the first man to score a double-century in a one-day international, and sealed India's series victory. He needed just 147 balls, having reached his 46th one-day hundred (to go with 47 in Tests) in 90, and he collected 25 fours and three sixes. From the outset, Tendulkar looked on course for something special. After the early loss of Sehwag, he raced to his fifty in 37 balls, driving superbly square of the wicket; with Karthik ensuring his senior partner had plenty of strike, India breezed to 219 for two in the 34th over. Tendulkar had 124 at that stage, and he forged on remorselessly, his placement so perfect, his timing so precise that South Africa were simply blown away. Dhoni's pyrotechnics – seven fours and four

TENDULKAR'S 200, BALL BY BALL

```
0000    4402    14    01    004020    04001    2421    1    4104    1    0004[†]1    0020    11
2040    410    1    211    011    014    111    00410    0100    1200    11    00101    11
0111[‡]    40410    1    001    614    11    040041    1140    404    4[§]1    401    021    116
146    124    1    211    221    101    01    1[¶]
```

50 dot balls, 56 singles, 13 twos, 25 fours, 3 sixes. There were three overs in which Tendulkar did not face a ball.

† 51 from 37 balls; ‡ 100 from 90 balls; § 151 from 118 balls; ¶ 200 from 147 balls.

sixes off 35 balls – ensured the innings ended in a blur, even though cramp meant Tendulkar was running out of puff towards the end. He passed the previous one-day international record of 194 (shared by Saeed Anwar of Pakistan and Zimbabwe's Charles Coventry) in the 46th over, before being briefly becalmed as Dhoni flailed away. But a single steered behind point off the third ball of the final over brought up the historic 200, amid a tremendous hullabaloo from the capacity crowd. South Africa's batsmen had little stomach for the daunting chase, focusing too much on the overall target rather than building partnerships, although de Villiers made an excellent century, full of elegant drives.

Man of the Match: S. R. Tendulkar.

All hail the Little Master: Sachin Tendulkar leaves the field after becoming the first man to hit a double-hundred in one-day internationals.

India

V. Sehwag c Steyn b Parnell	9
S. R. Tendulkar not out	200
K. D. Karthik c Gibbs b Parnell	79
Y. K. Pathan c de Villiers b van der Merwe	36
*†M. S. Dhoni not out	68
L-b 3, w 5, n-b 1	9

1/25 (1) 2/219 (3) (3 wkts, 50 overs) 401
3/300 (4) 10 overs: 74-1

V. Kohli, S. K. Raina, R. A. Jadeja, P. Kumar, A. Nehra and S. Sreesanth did not bat.

Steyn 10–0–89–0; Parnell 10–0–95–2; van der Merwe 10–0–62–1; Langeveldt 10–0–70–0; Duminy 5–0–38–0; Kallis 5–0–44–0.

South Africa

H. M. Amla c Nehra b Sreesanth	34	D. W. Steyn b Sreesanth	0
H. H. Gibbs b Kumar	7	C. K. Langeveldt c Nehra b Jadeja	12
R. E. van der Merwe c Raina b Sreesanth	12		
*J. H. Kallis b Nehra	11	L-b 5, w 8, n-b 4	17
A. B. de Villiers not out	114		
A. N. Petersen b Jadeja	9	1/17 (2) 2/47 (3) 3/61 (1) (42.5 overs)	248
J-P. Duminy lbw b Pathan	0	4/83 (4) 5/102 (6) 6/103 (7)	
†M. V. Boucher lbw b Pathan	14	7/134 (8) 8/211 (9) 9/216 (10)	
W. D. Parnell b Nehra	18	10/248 (11)	10 overs: 81-3

Kumar 5–0–31–1; Nehra 8–0–60–2; Sreesanth 7–0–49–3; Jadeja 8.5–0–41–2; Pathan 9–1–37–2; Sehwag 5–0–25–0.

Umpires: I. J. Gould and S. K. Tarapore. Third umpire: S. S. Hazare.

INDIA v SOUTH AFRICA

Third One-Day International

At Ahmedabad, February 27, 2010 (day/night). South Africa won by 90 runs. Toss: South Africa. One-day international debuts: A. Mithun, M. Vijay.

De Villiers's furious 58-ball century, the seventh-fastest in one-day internationals – only Boucher, in 44 balls against Zimbabwe in 2006-07, had made a quicker one for South Africa – led to a flurry of runs in the closing overs of the innings. With Kallis improvising elegantly in the later stages of his own century (his last 74 came from 48 balls) the final five overs produced 78 runs as India's inexperienced attack struggled. The visitors had rectified their error in the first one-dayer, and opened with Amla, whose inspired form continued; he and the dazzling Bosman, who hit four sixes, piled on 113 in 15.4 overs. Facing such a huge target, India's batsmen plodded along. Raina's clean hitting in the batting powerplay was the only real threat to the South Africans, who were hungry for victory after their pride had been grievously wounded at Gwalior.

Man of the Match: A. B. de Villiers.   *Man of the Series:* S. R. Tendulkar.

South Africa

L. E. Bosman c Jadeja b Pathan	....	68
H. M. Amla c Vijay b Jadeja	....	87
*J. H. Kallis not out	....	104
A. B. de Villiers not out	....	102
L-b 2, n-b 2	....	4

1/113 (1)   (2 wkts, 50 overs) 365
2/192 (2)   10 overs: 70-0

H. H. Gibbs, †M. V. Boucher, J. Botha, R. E. van der Merwe, D. W. Steyn, M. Morkel and L. L. Tsotsobe did not bat.

Sreesanth 9–0–83–0; Tyagi 8–0–59–0; Mithun 8–0–63–0; Jadeja 10–0–53–1; Pathan 10–0–66–1; Kohli 2–0–11–0; Sharma 3–0–28–0.

India

K. D. Karthik c Amla b Steyn	....	11
M. Vijay c Boucher b Tsotsobe	....	25
V. Kohli c Boucher b Steyn	....	57
R. G. Sharma c Tsotsobe b Botha	......	48
*†M. S. Dhoni c Boucher b Steyn	....	9
S. K. Raina c sub (W. D. Parnell) b Botha	.	49
Y. K. Pathan c Steyn b Tsotsobe	......	5
R. A. Jadeja c Boucher b Tsotsobe	....	36
S. Sreesanth lbw b van der Merwe	....	1
A. Mithun st Boucher b van der Merwe	...	24
S. Tyagi not out	....	1
L-b 5, w 4	....	9

1/22 (1) 2/40 (2) 3/135 (4)   (44.3 overs) 275
4/156 (5) 5/157 (3) 6/179 (7)
7/233 (6) 8/237 (9) 9/273 (10)
10/275 (8)   10 overs: 60-2

Steyn 8–1–37–3; Tsotsobe 9.3–0–58–3; Morkel 7–0–48–0; van der Merwe 10–0–47–2; Botha 10–0–80–2.

Umpires: I. J. Gould and S. S. Hazare.   Third umpire: S. K. Tarapore.
Series referee: A. J. Pycroft.

INDIA v AUSTRALIA, 2010-11

Daniel Brettig

Test matches (2): India 2, Australia 0
One-day internationals (3): India 1, Australia 0

There were many reasons why India's two-Test series against Australia should have been unexceptional. The matches were themselves afterthoughts, thrown into the schedule in place of four of the seven limited-overs matches which the Indian board had originally planned.

Neither team assembled with great preparation behind them. Two players from each side – Mahendra Singh Dhoni and Suresh Raina for India, Mike Hussey and Doug Bollinger for Australia – had only the most rudimentary familiarisation after being kept in South Africa until four days before the First Test by the financial imperatives of Twenty20. And the Australians were not considered capable of great things, being inexperienced and having their eyes on the home Ashes summer that followed. Even their captain Ricky Ponting departed for India saying he was not expecting miracles.

Yet there was one reason to look forward to the series in spite of it all. No one over the past decade has done Test cricket better than these two sides, whether in moments of high drama or intense discord. And so it was to prove again, as India retained the Border–Gavaskar Trophy.

As in 2000-01, the matches were played against a backdrop of questions about cricket's integrity, following an August as gloomy for cricket as 1914's had been for Europe. At the same time Twenty20 hung threateningly over the series, in the form of the Champions League in South Africa, a tournament which caused considerable rancour among the Australians. Hussey and Bollinger were contracted to Chennai Super Kings, but could have been withdrawn from the later stages at Cricket Australia's behest. As part-owners of the event, however, Australian administrators decided to rate their financial investment above the preparations of their Test team, and so the players were compelled to stay on, alongside Dhoni and Raina, in what proved to be the winning team. This would have ramifications in particular for Bollinger, who arrived in India short of adequate preparation for long spells, and suffered an abdominal strain which removed him from the attack for most of the vital final day of the Mohali Test, and kept him on the sidelines for Bangalore. Hussey's handicaps were more technical than physical, resulting in four innings symptomatic of a batsman struggling to locate the correct gears for Test cricket.

For all that, the epic First Test played out as though both sides were well prepared and quite evenly matched. Australia's batsmen were led boldly by Shane Watson, while Ponting provided welcome evidence that the fire to resume the batting mastery of his prime years was undimmed. Things were less certain lower down, as Michael Clarke demonstrated by scavenging a paltry 35 runs in four innings, and at No. 6 Marcus North maintained his maddening tendency for feast or famine with scores of 0, 10, 128 and 3. The

Off and running: Sachin Tendulkar near the start of his Bangalore double-hundred.

future was given a considerably brighter tone by the young wicketkeeper Tim Paine, again deputising while Brad Haddin recovered from a stubborn elbow complaint. Paine was solid, less flashy than Haddin, and his two first innings of 92 and 59 showed the sort of grit needed by his team at times of uncertainty. Each time he was aided by a more free-scoring partner at the other end, and Paine should be a man to build the middle order around in years to come.

The runs Australia could score counted for little if their bowlers were unable to find a way through the best batting line-up in contemporary Test cricket, and it was here that India would ultimately overwhelm the visitors. Sachin Tendulkar's bat appeared to widen the closer he inched towards his 40th year, and here it proved virtually impassable. The Australians escaped relatively lightly at Mohali by dismissing him for 98 and 38, but in Bangalore, Tendulkar would respond by delivering the series to his homeland by compiling 214 and an unbeaten 53 to collect the winning runs. He gave scarcely a chance in either innings. By contrast to the ever-present Tendulkar, V. V. S. Laxman was restricted by back problems to one telling contribution. But it arrived when most desperately needed, and maintained the near-mystical power he holds over the Australians.

Virender Sehwag's unproductive series – 113 runs in his four innings – was a victory for Australia's planners, who had reasoned that a short-pitched attack would keep the combustible opener as quiet as was possible. Mitchell Johnson and Ben Hilfenhaus played the role of spoiler well, although Johnson could not always land the ball where he wanted. Less successful were the plans devised by and for the slow bowler Nathan Hauritz, who found himself helpless at times against the home batsmen. In consultation with Ponting, Hauritz had attempted to change his angle to the crease and shape on the ball to be more closely in line with the Indian off-spinner Harbhajan Singh, but as a result found himself neither as accurate nor as penetrating as he had been at times in Australia the previous summer. He spent the series tinkering with his action and approach while trying to do his best in Test matches – a place no bowler would wish to be.

While the Australians did their best to cope with conditions they did not enjoy, the Indian attack revelled in local knowledge. Zaheer Khan swung the new ball a little and the old ball a lot, and his work in tandem with Sreesanth on the fourth and fifth days at Bangalore set up victory, with vicious movement in both directions. Between times Harbhajan and Pragyan Ojha did their best to keep things quiet, building pressure and occasionally claiming wickets with sharp turn.

Australia's defeat at Bangalore meant a 0–2 scoreline, a drop to fifth in the world rankings, and a sequence of consecutive Test defeats (three, including the one by Pakistan at Headingley in July) not seen from them since 1988-89. They also lost the only one-day game spared by the rain. Ponting, though, returned home in a mood of optimism: his players had, after all, just taken part in an exceptional series. "It's just what the international game needed, to see cricket played like this," he said after India's breathless one-wicket victory at Mohali. "All the people who have watched this game around the world will be thinking some good things about the game of cricket now."

AUSTRALIAN TOURING PARTY

*R. T. Ponting, D. E. Bollinger, M. J. Clarke, P. R. George, N. M. Hauritz, B. W. Hilfenhaus, P. J. Hughes, M. E. K. Hussey, M. G. Johnson, S. M. Katich, M. J. North, T. D. Paine, J. L. Pattinson, S. P. D. Smith, M. A. Starc, S. R. Watson. *Coach:* T. J. Nielsen.

J. R. Hazlewood was originally selected, but withdrew with a back injury and was replaced by Pattinson and Starc. Pattinson himself injured his back in practice, and was replaced by J. W. Hastings, who stayed on for the remainder of the tour. For the limited-overs internationals which followed the Tests, C. J. Ferguson, J. R. Hopes, C. J. McKay, S. E. Marsh, D. A. Warner and C. L. White replaced George, Hilfenhaus, Hughes, Johnson, Katich, North, Ponting and Watson. Clarke took over as captain.

At Chandigarh (Sector 16 Stadium), September 25–27, 2010. **Drawn. ‡Australians 505** (S. R. Watson 115, S. M. Katich 104 ret hurt, R. T. Ponting 42, M. J. Clarke 44, M. J. North 124 ret hurt, T. D. Paine 45; P. P. Ojha 3-67) **and 187-6 dec.** (S. R. Watson 104*; P. P. Chawla 3-64); **Indian Board President's XI 177** (P. P. Chawla 82; B. W. Hilfenhaus 5-47) **and 174-0** (A. M. Rahane 113*, C. A. Pujara 52*). *Although Australia's front-line batsmen all made runs, there were signs that they would not be entirely at home against India. Watson contributed two of the tourists' four centuries: the others came from Katich, who eventually retired with what he thought was a bruised thumb (only when he returned home was a fracture diagnosed), and North, who also retired, pleading a back strain after an enterprising innings. The Board President's XI sank to 90-6 before Piyush Chawla at No. 7 played a resolute innings. Ponting preferred batting practice to the follow-on, but only Watson took advantage: he hit 34 fours across his two innings. The eventual declaration left a nominal target of 516: Ajinkya Rahane led the reply with a hundred of his own, putting on 165* with Cheteshwar Pujara once Shikhar Dhawan retired hurt after being hit near the ear by a Hilfenhaus bouncer.*

INDIA v AUSTRALIA

First Test Match

At Mohali, October 1–5, 2010. India won by one wicket. Toss: Australia.

India scrambled to the narrowest of their 106 Test victories despite requiring 92 runs at the time the eighth wicket went down. That they did so was thanks to yet another miraculous performance by V. V. S. Laxman, a man who produces the impossible on a regular basis against Australia. This time he managed it with the impediment of back spasms so serious that he had been unable to bat until No. 10 in the first innings.

VERY VERY SPECIAL AGAINST AUSTRALIA

V. V. S. Laxman's Test record:

	T	I	NO	Runs	HS	100s	50s	Avge
v Australia	25	46	5	2,279	281	6	11	55.58
(in India)	**14**	**25**	**4**	**1,198**	**281**	**2**	**8**	**57.04**
(in Australia)	11	21	1	1,081	178	4	3	54.05
v other countries	95	152	26	5,624	154*	10	38	44.63
v all countries	120	198	31	7,903	281	16	49	47.32

Of Laxman's 25 Tests against Australia, India have won nine and lost ten. Figures correct to March 31, 2011.

Laxman would still have fallen short without an ally, and he found a perfect foil on the final day in Ishant Sharma, who took on the air of no less a tail-end tormentor than Test double-centurion Jason Gillespie. Ponting was unable to call on his most incisive bowler, Bollinger, after the most poorly timed of muscle strains, and fell into the trap of not trying to dismiss Laxman while pressing too hard against his junior partner, thus allowing Sharma to collect his share of runs while soaking up plenty of the strike.

Johnson did shake Sharma up with short balls, but only 11 runs were needed when Hilfenhaus finally dismissed him, lbw to an off-cutter that would have missed leg stump (once again, the Decision Review System was not in use as the ICC and the Indian board bickered over who should pay for it).

Ojha has few pretensions as a batsman and even fewer as a sprinter, and Laxman lost his characteristic cool, wildly urging his partner to run harder, even threatening to use his bat as punishment. These comedic gesticulations did little to ease the tension, and what turned out to be the final over of the match began with six required and last man Ojha on strike. Johnson whirred one at middle stump, Ojha was struck on the pad and the Australians went up as one. Their shock at umpire Bowden's refusal – he was to argue forcefully for an inside edge – quickly turned to grief when the substitute Steve Smith at point threw for the run-out and screamed in exasperation when no one on the leg side was around to back up. The resultant four overthrows left only two runs to win, and two leg-yes a couple of balls later did the trick.

The game – only the 12th Test to end in victory by a single wicket – was rightly celebrated as one of the greatest of the modern era, at a time when it was most needed. Australia's despair at the finish could be alleviated somewhat by the fact they had performed far better than anyone had a right to expect against the world's best team on their home turf.

Back on the first morning Ponting had won what was thought to be a critical toss, but Australia's ability to capitalise on it would have been severely compromised had Sehwag at gully clung on to a high chance from Watson's loose drive off the second ball of the match. But he dropped it, and Watson went on to a century that was arresting for its early outburst of shots then admirable for its later control. Katich – who went into the match

Cutting it fine: Pragyan Ojha, V. V. S. Laxman and Suresh Raina after India's one-wicket victory.

with exactly the same number of runs (3,981) from the same number of Tests (52) as Hussey – was hampered by the thumb he injured in the warm-up game, but Ponting fired off a handsome array of strokes, including the pull shot that had often been his downfall in recent times, to help take his team to 154 for one. With Sharma off the field owing to a jarred knee, Australia might have been expected to take advantage, but they were instead forced to graft and fight for the rest of the day against Ojha and Harbhajan Singh, and a spell of typically venomous reverse swing from Zaheer Khan.

An overnight score of 224 for five required significant addition, and the young wicketkeeper Paine made sure those runs were found. Struggling to score early on, he was helped greatly by the breezy hitting of Johnson, and looked deserving of a maiden Test century before he edged Zaheer low to second slip, where Laxman appeared to aggravate his back in taking the catch. Sehwag's response to a total of some heft was to blaze, and he thrilled a small crowd by galloping to 59 in 54 balls as Australia's fielders experienced the mixture of a spectator's joy and an opponent's bewilderment. Though Sehwag would exit before stumps, attempting to work a short one from Johnson to leg, his efforts lent India's innings a momentum they would retain for most of the third day.

Dravid had shown fine touch himself on the second evening and, having narrowly survived a searching morning spell by Hilfenhaus, would go on to support Tendulkar, before Raina added to Australian frustrations with an innings of good shots and better fortune. Meanwhile Tendulkar pushed inexorably towards a century, and by the time he reached 98 there seemed no other possibility. But then a strange thing happened: Tendulkar played across an off-break from North and was lbw, prompting an outpouring of relief from the tourists that quickly turned to whoops of delight as the last five wickets went down for 23. Johnson, fast and straight, did most of the damage, while Hauritz was rewarded for a difficult day with two late wickets, including a very lame-looking Laxman.

This unthreatening image stuck with the Australians, and it was possible that some of them expected ten Indians rather than 11 as they went about setting a target. Watson was once more in the ascendant against the new ball, but the return of Sharma and an apparent quickening of the pitch – it had started slow, due to heavy rains during its preparation, before beginning to harden – brought about another dramatic change of fortune. Trying to pull when he might have cut, Watson dragged on, then Ponting miscued to a short backward square leg placed adroitly by Dhoni. And though Clarke enjoyed a theatrical reprieve first ball when he flicked to short midwicket but was called back as umpire Bowden checked on a possible no-ball from Sharma, he did not make the most of it, flinching at a short ball and lobbing a gentle catch to Dhoni.

These wickets allowed Harbhajan and Ojha to weave a web around the rest of the batting and, it must be said, the umpires. From 87 without loss the Australians lost all ten wickets for 105.

With only 216 needed for victory, the 17 overs remaining on the fourth day presented India with the chance either to get closer or get out, and four batsmen got out. Hilfenhaus claimed three of them, including Gambhir unluckily given lbw to a delivery that would have been missing off stump had the batsman not diverted its path via the inside edge, while Sehwag glided a riser to gully. Bollinger had been the best Australian bowler when wickets were proving difficult to come by in the first innings, and he again defeated Dravid by angling the ball across.

The final day dawned with India needing 161 runs and Australia six wickets. It was five when Hauritz had the nightwatchman Zaheer pouched at slip, but the requirement was soon being drastically reduced by Tendulkar and Laxman, who was now appearing much supple. He was nonetheless fortunate that Ponting had not persisted with a second slip when an edge off Bollinger flashed through at catchable height. Using all the placement, power and wristy artistry he is known for, Laxman was energised by the occasion, and a delectable back-foot cover-drive took the requirement beneath 100. Tendulkar was cramped and caught from the bowling of Bollinger, however, and after Dhoni was run out in a muddle with Laxman's runner (Raina), Harbhajan fended lamely to slip and the Australians mistakenly felt that the day was theirs.

Laxman was the man of the hour – but not, strangely, the Man of the Match, which went to Zaheer for his eight wickets. Ponting spoke gracefully in defeat, and ruefully of his side's growing propensity for near misses: "That's really the only thing I've been thinking about since walking off the ground – South Africa in Australia last time, First Test in Cardiff in the last Ashes series," he said. "It's disappointing that we haven't been able to nail some of those really crucial moments that define champion teams." Champion teams – and champion players. Laxman is certainly one of those.

Man of the Match: Zaheer Khan.

Close of play: First day, Australia 224-5 (Watson 101, Paine 1); Second day, India 110-2 (Dravid 21, Sharma 0); Third day, India 405; Fourth day, India 55-4 (Tendulkar 10, Zaheer Khan 5).

Australia

S. R. Watson c Gambhir b Harbhajan Singh	126	– b Sharma	56
S. M. Katich lbw b Zaheer Khan	6	– c Dhoni b Ojha	37
*R. T. Ponting run out	71	– c Raina b Sharma	4
M. J. Clarke c Dravid b Harbhajan Singh	14	– c Dhoni b Sharma	4
M. E. K. Hussey lbw b Zaheer Khan	17	– lbw b Harbhajan Singh	28
M. J. North b Zaheer Khan	0	– c sub (C. A. Pujara) b Harbhajan Singh	10
†T. D. Paine c Laxman b Zaheer Khan	92	– c sub (C. A. Pujara) b Ojha	9
M. G. Johnson c Dhoni b Zaheer Khan	47	– c Dhoni b Zaheer Khan	3
N. M. Hauritz c Gambhir b Harbhajan Singh	9	– b Zaheer Khan	9
B. W. Hilfenhaus not out	20	– b Zaheer Khan	6
D. E. Bollinger c Sharma b Ojha	0	– not out	5
B 4, l-b 9, n-b 13	26	B 12, l-b 4, n-b 5	21

1/13 (2) 2/154 (3) 3/172 (4) (151.4 overs) 428
4/218 (5) 5/222 (6) 6/275 (1)
7/357 (8) 8/373 (9) 9/427 (7) 10/428 (11)

1/87 (1) 2/91 (3) (60.5 overs) 192
3/96 (4) 4/138 (2)
5/154 (5) 6/165 (6) 7/165 (7)
8/170 (8) 9/183 (9) 10/192 (10)

Zaheer Khan 30–7–94–5; Sharma 11.4–1–71–0; Ojha 51.4–16–113–1; Harbhajan Singh 49–12–114–3; Sehwag 9.2–1–23–0. *Second Innings*—Zaheer Khan 11.5–1–43–3; Sharma 9–2–34–3; Harbhajan Singh 23–7–40–2; Ojha 17–1–59–2.

India

G. Gambhir lbw b Johnson	25	–	lbw b Hilfenhaus	0
V. Sehwag c Clarke b Johnson	59	–	c Hussey b Hilfenhaus	17
R. Dravid c Paine b Bollinger	77	–	c Paine b Bollinger	13
I. Sharma b Bollinger	18	–	(10) lbw b Hilfenhaus	31
S. R. Tendulkar lbw b North	98	–	c Hussey b Bollinger	38
S. K. Raina lbw b Johnson	86	–	(5) c North b Hilfenhaus	0
*†M. S. Dhoni c Watson b Johnson	14	–	(8) run out	2
Harbhajan Singh c Paine b Johnson	0	–	(9) c Ponting b Bollinger	2
Zaheer Khan b Hauritz	6	–	(6) c Clarke b Hauritz	10
V. V. S. Laxman c Clarke b Hauritz	2	–	(7) not out	73
P. P. Ojha not out	0	–	not out	5
B 5, l-b 13, w 1, n-b 1	20		B 10, l-b 8, w 6, n-b 1	25

1/81 (1) 2/106 (2) 3/151 (4)   (108.1 overs) 405   1/0 (1)   (9 wkts, 58.4 overs) 216
4/230 (3) 5/354 (5) 6/382 (7)   2/31 (3) 3/48 (2)
7/382 (8) 8/399 (9) 9/401 (6) 10/405 (10)   4/48 (5) 5/76 (6) 6/119 (4)
                                                               7/122 (8) 8/124 (9) 9/205 (10)

Hilfenhaus 25–2–100–0; Bollinger 16–2–49–2; Johnson 20–5–64–5; Hauritz 29.1–4–116–2; Watson 6–0–19–0; North 12–3–39–1. *Second Innings*—Hilfenhaus 19–3–57–4; Bollinger 8–0–32–3; Johnson 16.4–2–50–0; Hauritz 9–1–45–1; North 4–0–8–0; Watson 2–0–6–0.

Umpires: B. F. Bowden and I. J. Gould. Third umpire: S. S. Hazare.

INDIA v AUSTRALIA

Second Test Match

At Bangalore, October 9–13, 2010. India won by seven wickets. Toss: Australia. Test debuts: C. A. Pujara; P. R. George.

Until an hour before lunch on the final day, the Second Test matched the First for quality and fluctuations. It did not quite carry through to the same kind of desperate conclusion, because India were finally able to shake a tenacious Australia. The debutant Cheteshwar Pujara, in concert with fellow batting aspirant Murali Vijay, effectively won the game for India with a partnership of 72 that was brief but ferocious, resulting in a 2–0 series scoreline for the triumphant hosts. If this was harsh on Australia, who fought so well throughout, it was not unwarranted. India's experienced players were more consistent across the two matches, and on the final day the young batsmen imposed themselves in a way their touring contemporaries could only wish to emulate. Pujara, a 22-year-old right-hander from Saurashtra, had finally been included in India's squad after a mountain of domestic runs: he averaged 60 before this match and had a first-class triple-century to his name, and now he replaced the injured Laxman.

For the second time in the series Australia had the advantage of batting first, and for the second time they went close to surrendering it with some inattentive batting. Watson and Katich were untroubled despite noticeable new-ball swing under overcast skies, and put on 99 before Katich cut at Harbhajan Singh and was taken at slip. Ponting was again in decent touch, reaching the outskirts of a century only to squander it by missing a straight ball from the part-time spin of Raina and gifting him a distinguished first Test wicket. North needed a score to make his place safe for the Ashes series, and responded with a fluent contribution in a city he had visited on pre-season tours with Western Australia.

Taking a confident stride forward and timing the ball sweetly down the ground, North showed the array of his talents with help from the doughty Paine, and their concentration took Australia towards 478. As with Clarke at Mohali, Paine was reprieved by a check for a no-ball after he edged Sreesanth behind.

Early incisions were made by the Australian attack when India batted. Sehwag swatted to deep square and Dravid again edged a ball slanted towards the cordon, but they were to prove the last wickets for more than six hours. Tendulkar, who passed 14,000 Test runs with a four off Hauritz through the covers, found a sprightly ally in Vijay, and together they made the touring attack look very pedestrian. In the case of Hauritz the batsmen's contempt was plain, and Tendulkar swung him for six on 93 and 99 with all the assurance of a man who knew precisely what his quarry was doing, or not doing, with the SG ball. Vijay had a more torrid time against Australia's debutant, the gangling seamer Peter George from Adelaide, but held firm for a maiden Test hundred as he and Tendulkar added 308. Johnson broke the stand by coaxing an edge from Vijay, and in the same over conjured a shooter from nowhere to defeat the unfortunate Pujara, who had sat padded up awaiting his chance through 90.3 overs, the longest wait for any Test debutant.

Tendulkar went on and on, converting his 49th Test hundred into his sixth double on the fourth morning, and taking India seemingly beyond the point of danger, before he was out to George, who found some old-ball swing to get an inside edge on to the stumps. George admitted to some shock at the identity of his first wicket, but it was the 19th time Tendulkar had been dismissed by a debutant. The unexpected success brought another twist, as five wickets went down for nine runs in eight overs. Watson and George delivered the only significant spells of reverse swing by Australian bowlers in the series, and Hauritz salvaged something from his earlier torment by collecting Dhoni and last man Sreesanth. For all Tendulkar's dominance, India led by only 17.

Australia's effort to set a target was to mirror Mohali, a firm start giving way to quick wickets. Clarke completed a miserable series when he stretched forward to Ojha, was beaten by the turn and misjudged the position of his back foot, holding his forward stroke as Dhoni removed the bails. For a time it appeared Ponting would deliver his team the lead they required, playing with more authority than he had usually managed in India. However Zaheer Khan and Sreesanth (replacing the injured Ishant Sharma) summoned treacherous amounts of reverse on the fourth evening, and Ponting was lbw to limit his contribution to that of a masterpiece in miniature. The tail offered only nuisance value, and a target of 207 required plenty of early wickets to become defendable.

The Australians had one when Paine moved sharply to his right to claim an edge from Sehwag, and were surprised when Pujara was promoted ahead of Dravid at No. 3. Wrongly sensing an easy wicket, they bowled like gamblers rather than misers, allowing Pujara and Vijay to capitalise nervelessly. Hauritz entered the attack and was taken for 22 runs in two overs before lunch, while back in Australia Shane Warne wondered loudly at the wisdom of his field settings. Pujara, too, would express his lack of regard for the tactics employed – "They didn't know what they were trying to do," he said later – but in truth the weary Australians were never given a chance by the sheer quality of the batting that confronted them. Vijay played inside Watson to be lbw, and Pujara did the same to be bowled by Hauritz, but the remaining runs were gleaned, fittingly, by Tendulkar.

All this was watched and cheered across five days at the Chinnaswamy Stadium by one of the largest and most buoyant Test crowds witnessed in India this century, a pointed lesson about the importance of wise venue choices for the continued health of Test cricket. India's captain, Dhoni, is no great traditionalist, but he had it right here. "Maybe some of these centres where people come up to see Test matches can be given preference over some other centres where people don't come in large numbers," he said. "After all, if taken in the right sense, we are the performers in the circus, but you need the circus to be full."

Man of the Match: S. R. Tendulkar.   *Man of the Series:* S. R. Tendulkar.

Close of play: First day, Australia 285-5 (North 43, Paine 8); Second day, India 128-2 (Vijay 42, Tendulkar 44); Third day, India 435-5 (Tendulkar 191, Dhoni 11); Fourth day, Australia 202-7 (Johnson 7, Hauritz 8).

Australia

S. R. Watson c Dhoni b Ojha	57	– lbw b Ojha	32
S. M. Katich c Dravid b Harbhajan Singh	43	– c Dhoni b Harbhajan Singh	24
*R. T. Ponting lbw b Raina	77	– lbw b Zaheer Khan	72
M. J. Clarke c Raina b Harbhajan Singh	14	– st Dhoni b Ojha	3
M. E. K. Hussey c Sehwag b Zaheer Khan	34	– lbw b Ojha	20
M. J. North c Sreesanth b Harbhajan Singh	128	– b Harbhajan Singh	3
†T. D. Paine st Dhoni b Ojha	59	– c Dhoni b Sreesanth	23
M. G. Johnson lbw b Ojha	0	– b Zaheer Khan	11
N. M. Hauritz run out	17	– not out	21
B. W. Hilfenhaus not out	16	– b Sreesanth	0
P. R. George st Dhoni b Harbhajan Singh	2	– c Dhoni b Zaheer Khan	0
B 9, l-b 12, w 1, n-b 9	31	B 1, l-b 5, w 3, n-b 5	14

1/99 (2) 2/113 (1) 3/132 (4)   (141 overs) 478   1/58 (1)   (75.2 overs) 223
4/198 (5) 5/256 (3) 6/405 (7)   2/58 (2) 3/65 (4)
7/415 (8) 8/458 (6) 9/459 (9) 10/478 (11)   4/126 (5) 5/131 (6) 6/181 (3) 7/185 (7)
                                      8/217 (9) 9/218 (10) 10/223 (11)

Zaheer Khan 23–5–84–1; Sreesanth 21–1–79–0; Ojha 42–7–120–3; Harbhajan Singh 43–3–148–4; Sehwag 4–1–7–0; Raina 8–1–19–1. *Second Innings*—Zaheer Khan 11.2–1–41–3; Sreesanth 14–2–48–2; Ojha 25–5–57–3; Harbhajan Singh 21–2–63–2; Sehwag 4–0–8–0.

India

M. Vijay c Paine b Johnson	139	– lbw b Watson	37
V. Sehwag c Johnson b Hilfenhaus	30	– c Paine b Hilfenhaus	7
R. Dravid c North b Johnson	1	– (5) not out	21
S. R. Tendulkar b George	214	– not out	53
C. A. Pujara lbw b Johnson	4	– (3) b Hauritz	72
S. K. Raina c Hilfenhaus b Clarke	32		
*†M. S. Dhoni c Clarke b Hauritz	30		
Harbhajan Singh c Ponting b Watson	4		
Zaheer Khan c Clarke b George	1		
P. P. Ojha not out	0		
S. Sreesanth lbw b Hauritz	0		
B 6, l-b 26, w 8	40	B 8, l-b 5, w 4	17

1/37 (2) 2/38 (3) 3/346 (1)   (144.5 overs) 495   1/17 (2)   (3 wkts, 45 overs) 207
4/350 (5) 5/411 (6) 6/486 (4)   2/89 (1) 3/146 (3)
7/491 (8) 8/494 (9) 9/495 (7) 10/495 (11)

Hilfenhaus 31–6–77–1; Johnson 28–2–105–3; George 21–3–48–2; Hauritz 39.5–4–153–2; Clarke 8–0–27–1; Watson 12–2–35–1; Katich 5–0–18–0. *Second Innings*—Hilfenhaus 7–0–27–1; Johnson 14–4–42–0; Hauritz 12–0–76–1; George 7–0–29–0; Watson 5–0–20–1.

Umpires: B. F. Bowden and I. J. Gould. Third umpire: A. M. Saheba.
Series referee: B. C. Broad.

INDIA v AUSTRALIA

First One-Day International

At Kochi, October 17, 2010. Abandoned.
Torrential rains in the lead-up did for this match at a ground built for football. They would also ruin the third match of the series in Goa at a venue of similarly inadequate drainage. Both sides took the opportunity to rest key players: Ponting, Watson and Johnson had flown home to Australia, while Tendulkar, Harbhajan Singh and Zaheer Khan were among India's absentees. The Australian squad bore a particularly experimental look because of the selectors' desire to test new options ahead of the 2011 World Cup on the subcontinent, but the weather thwarted most of their good intentions.

INDIA v AUSTRALIA

Second One-Day International

At Visakhapatnam, October 20, 2010 (day/night). India won by five wickets. Toss: India. One-day international debuts: S. Dhawan; S. S. Tiwary; J. W. Hastings, M. A. Starc.

A century from Kohli and a savage 71 from 47 balls by Raina allowed India to roll up a seemingly strong Australian total with seven balls to spare. Dhoni had chosen to field, rightly reckoning that a slightly tacky pitch would improve with age. Australia's batsmen struggled against the new ball: only 51 runs came from the first 15 overs. Things picked up from there, as Hussey showed growing fluency to encourage the reinvigoration of acting-captain Clarke after a horrid Test series. Hussey's departure to a tired stroke cleared the stage for White, who swung lustily to clear the fence six times in his 49-ball onslaught. Clarke also struck a rare six in his fifth one-day hundred, and against some mediocre bowling they collared 84 runs from the final five overs. India lost early wickets to McKay, who with 12 previous one-day caps was the nominal leader of an exceptionally inexperienced Australian pace attack: his second ball accounted for the debutant Shikhar Dhawan, a left-hander from Delhi. But Kohli pushed the Indians home, helped first by Yuvraj Singh then by Raina, who did with fours what White had earlier done with sixes. John Hastings, a burly seamer and a Victoria team-mate of White and McKay, showed decent control to collect two wickets on debut: Mitchell Starc, a left-arm fast bowler from New South Wales, was rather more expensive.

Man of the Match: V. Kohli.

Australia

S. E. Marsh b Nehra	. . . .	0
†T. D. Paine c Vinay Kumar b Nehra	. . . . . .	9
*M. J. Clarke not out	. . . .	111
M. E. K. Hussey lbw b Ashwin	. . . .	69
C. L. White not out	. . . .	89
L-b 10, w 1	. . . .	11

1/11 (1) 2/16 (2)   (3 wkts, 50 overs) 289
3/160 (4)   10 overs: 30-2

S. P. D. Smith, J. R. Hopes, N. M. Hauritz, J. W. Hastings, M. A. Starc and C. J. McKay did not bat.

P. Kumar 9–1–51–0; Nehra 10–1–57–2; Vinay Kumar 9–1–71–0; Ashwin 9–0–34–1; Yuvraj Singh 10–0–48–0; Raina 3–0–18–0.

India

S. Dhawan b McKay	. . . .	0
M. Vijay c Paine b McKay	. . . .	15
V. Kohli c Hopes b Hastings	. . . .	118
Yuvraj Singh b McKay	. . . .	58
S. K. Raina not out	. . . .	71
*†M. S. Dhoni b Hastings	. . . .	0

S. S. Tiwary not out. 12
B 8, l-b 1, w 9 18

1/0 (1) 2/35 (2)   (5 wkts, 48.5 overs) 292
3/172 (4) 4/256 (3)
5/257 (6)   10 overs: 40-2

R. Ashwin, P. Kumar, A. Nehra and R. Vinay Kumar did not bat.

McKay 10–0–55–3; Starc 8.5–0–51–0; Hastings 10–1–44–2; Hopes 7–0–56–0; Hauritz 10–0–54–0; Smith 3–0–23–0.

Umpires: B. F. Bowden and S. K. Tarapore. Third umpire: S. Asnani. Series referee: B. C. Broad.

INDIA v AUSTRALIA

Third One-Day International

At Margao, October 24, 2010. Abandoned.

A sodden outfield forced another abandonment in Goa, giving India the series 1–0. About the only brief source of excitement for a disappointed crowd came when one of the stadium's wheeled sightscreens slipped on the wet ground and fell forward, narrowly missing two of the groundstaff.

Man of the Series: V. Kohli.

INDIA v NEW ZEALAND, 2010-11

SRIRAM VEERA

Test matches (3): India 1, New Zealand 0
One-day internationals (5): India 5, New Zealand 0

There was an unpromising preamble to the Test series. New Zealand arrived in India still licking their wounds from an embarrassing one-day whitewash by Bangladesh. Their coach Mark Greatbatch had flogged them publicly, saying that they had "played like dicks" there. India, meanwhile, were ranked No. 1 in the Test table and were expected to roll over their eighth-ranked opponents. If the Kiwis couldn't handle Bangladesh's spinners, how were they supposed to cope with Harbhajan Singh? The rest of the pre-Test talk revolved around the supposed certainty of Sachin Tendulkar's 50th hundred – he went into the series with 49 – and few gave New Zealand any chance. Even Greatbatch said beforehand that two draws would be a good result. And he got them, as his side competed superbly in the first two Tests before – perhaps subconsciously feeling they had achieved their coach's aim – capitulating in the Third.

New Zealand nearly stunned India in the First Test, and comfortably drew the Second. Three factors turned their batting fortunes around: Brendon McCullum settled very quickly as a specialist opener after renouncing the wicketkeeping gloves, Jesse Ryder shone on his comeback from injury, and 20-year-old Kane Williamson, who marked his Test debut at Ahmedabad with a fine century, added stability to the middle order. Chris Martin bowled the spell of his life on a docile track in the First Test, and suddenly it was India on the back foot.

However, New Zealand ruined all their good efforts in the final Test. Their captain Daniel Vettori had said his side would be judged on how they fared in it – but they froze. The second-innings collapse on a turning track was understandable, but the first-day debacle, against an Indian attack lacking the injured Zaheer Khan, was surprising. It is tempting to suggest that New Zealand do well as underdogs but, the moment they are on an even keel with their opponents, they freeze. Favourites in Bangladesh, they were crushed. Expected to go down tamely to India, they reached Nagpur with their reputations enhanced, only to surrender meekly.

The one-day series, by contrast, followed the expected pattern: India won all five games, despite resting several senior players ahead of their South African tour and the World Cup, including the captain Mahendra Singh Dhoni. Gautam Gambhir stood in, and began his captaincy career with five wins out of five – and two centuries. It meant that New Zealand had lost their last 11 completed one-day internationals, including the whitewash in Bangladesh.

On the debit side, Ross Taylor failed to convert his starts, Vettori's bowling was steady but his batting was inconsistent, while the left-arm seamer Andy McKay was impressive but played only in the Third Test.

A couple of positives emerged for India. Gambhir, who had scored only 65 runs in his previous four Tests, hit his first half-century for ten months in the Second Test; Rahul Dravid, who had averaged a modest 34.60 in 2010 before this, hit two centuries, as did Harbhajan Singh, the first No. 8 to score back-to-back hundreds, his first in Tests. The biggest disappointment was Suresh Raina. Everyone expected him to beef up his statistics against New Zealand, and that his real battle would be on the South African tour; but he slipped up, too often caught hanging too far back in the crease against the seamers in anticipation of the short ball, and getting into trouble against fuller deliveries. And Tendulkar's 50th century? That had to wait, after his four innings in the Tests brought him 126 runs, with a highest of 61.

NEW ZEALAND TOURING TEAM

*D. L. Vettori, B. J. Arnel, H. K. Bennett, M. J. Guptill, G. J. Hopkins, B. B. McCullum, T. G. McIntosh, A. J. McKay, C. S. Martin, J. S. Patel, J. D. Ryder, T. G. Southee, L. R. P. L. Taylor, B-J. Watling, K. S. Williamson. *Coach:* M. J. Greatbatch.

Bennett injured his groin during the First Test, and was replaced by J. E. C. Franklin. For the one-day internationals which followed the Tests, G. D. Elliott, J. M. How, N. L. McCullum, K. D. Mills, S. B. Styris and D. R. Tuffey replaced Arnel, Guptill, McIntosh, McKay, Martin, Patel and Watling. Ryder was originally selected for the one-day series, but injured his calf during the Tests and was replaced by Franklin. Tuffey strained a bicep muscle during the first one-day international and returned home, but was not replaced.

TEST MATCH AVERAGES

INDIA – BATTING AND FIELDING

	T	I	NO	R	HS	100s	50s	Avge	Ct/St
Harbhajan Singh	3	4	1	315	115	2	1	105.00	0
V. Sehwag	3	5	1	398	173	1	3	99.50	3
R. Dravid	3	4	0	341	191	2	0	85.25	1
V. V. S. Laxman	3	4	0	217	91	0	2	54.25	3
†G. Gambhir	3	5	1	167	78	0	2	41.75	1
M. S. Dhoni	3	4	0	144	98	0	1	36.00	8/2
S. R. Tendulkar	3	4	0	126	61	0	1	31.50	0
S. Sreesanth	3	4	2	30	24	0	0	15.00	0
†S. K. Raina	3	4	0	26	20	0	0	6.50	3
Zaheer Khan	2	3	0	8	7	0	0	2.66	0

Played in three Tests: †P. P. Ojha 11, 9*, 0. Played in one Test: I. Sharma 7* (1 ct).

BOWLING

	Style	O	M	R	W	BB	5W/i	Avge
I. Sharma	RFM	24.2	6	58	7	4-43	0	8.28
S. K. Raina	OB	35	6	97	5	2-1	0	19.40
Zaheer Khan	LFM	67.1	17	167	7	4-69	0	23.85
P. P. Ojha	SLA	167	38	449	12	4-107	0	37.41
Harbhajan Singh	OB	152.3	26	420	10	4-76	0	42.00
S. Sreesanth	RFM	94	15	354	8	3-121	0	44.25

Also bowled: M. S. Dhoni (RM) 1–0–5–0; V. Sehwag (OB) 1–0–7–0; S. R. Tendulkar (RM/OB/LB) 4–0–23–0.

NEW ZEALAND – BATTING AND FIELDING

	T	I	NO	R	HS	100s	50s	Avge	Ct
B. B. McCullum	3	6	1	370	225	1	1	74.00	3
†J. D. Ryder	3	5	0	274	103	1	2	54.80	0
K. S. Williamson	3	5	0	212	131	1	1	42.40	0
M. J. Guptill	2	4	0	109	85	0	1	27.25	2
L. R. P. L. Taylor	3	5	0	136	56	0	1	27.20	3
†T. G. McIntosh	3	6	0	163	102	1	0	27.16	0
T. G. Southee	2	4	0	90	38	0	0	22.50	0
†D. L. Vettori	3	5	0	91	41	0	0	18.20	2
G. J. Hopkins	3	5	1	44	14	0	0	11.00	6
C. S. Martin	3	4	2	8	3*	0	0	4.00	0

Played in one Test: B. J. Arnel 6*, 1* (1 ct); †H. K. Bennett 4; A. J. McKay 5, 20*; J. S. Patel 14 (1 ct); B-J. Watling 6, 2* (2 ct).

BOWLING

	Style	O	M	R	W	BB	5W/i	Avge
C. S. Martin	RFM	108	23	307	9	5-63	1	34.11
D. L. Vettori	SLA	200.3	34	512	14	5-135	1	36.57
T. G. Southee	RFM	66	11	224	4	3-119	0	56.00
J. S. Patel	OB	52	7	207	3	3-135	0	69.00

Also bowled: B. J. Arnel (RFM) 29–6–90–0; H. K. Bennett (RF) 15–2–47–0; M. J. Guptill (OB) 12–0–60–0; B. B. McCullum (RM) 6–1–18–0; A. J. McKay (LFM) 31–5–120–1; J. D. Ryder (RM) 17–4–56–1; L. R. P. L. Taylor (OB) 9. 4–2–29–2; K. S. Williamson (OB) 34–0–143–2.

INDIA v NEW ZEALAND

First Test Match

At Ahmedabad, November 4–8, 2010. Drawn. Toss: India. Test debuts: H. K. Bennett, K. S. Williamson.

Chris Martin breathed some life into a comatose Test with an intoxicating spell of inswing bowling. India were tottering at 15 for five on the fourth evening, but their crisis man, Laxman, added 163 with Harbhajan Singh, who hit his maiden hundred, to force a draw.

It was an unbelievable turnaround after bat had dominated ball for almost four days. India racked up 487 then New Zealand replied with 459, and the game looked dead and buried before Martin stirred himself into producing perhaps the most inspired spell of his career. He knocked out Gambhir, Dravid, Tendulkar and Raina in a magical first spell of 9–6–15–4, and returned later to dismiss Dhoni, which left India tottering at 65 for six and facing a night of discontent.

However, they got out of jail on the final day through two contrasting innings. Harbhajan counter-punched his way out of trouble, the spirit of his knock captured in two moments: there was a gap of about seven feet between short cover and short extra, and he smacked a length delivery from Martin right between them. Ballsy or foolhardy? Secondly, when India were 135 for six, and still at least an hour's batting short of safety, Harbhajan twice walked down the pitch and tried to swipe Martin to the on side. Both times Laxman had a chat with him. The second delivery after that was short and outside off, and Harbhajan upper-cut it to the boundary. He became only the second No. 8 to score a half-century and a hundred in the same Test, after Eric Dalton of South Africa at The Oval in 1935. If Harbhajan batted with a dash of insouciance, Laxman flowed like a gentle river, and India eventually escaped.

The drama on the fourth evening and the final day was in contrast to the first few days. On the first day, Sehwag collected 173 from 199 balls, and Dravid slowly dragged himself back into form with a sedate 104, his 30th Test century, as India reached 329 for three. The first night was spent wondering whether Tendulkar would make his 50th Test hundred, but neither he nor Laxman converted his start, and India meandered to a large total.

The third day featured New Zealand's batsmen healing themselves after a nightmarish Bangladesh tour, where they were whitewashed 4–0 in the one-day series. McCullum, who had decided to stop keeping wicket in Tests and played as an opener, made 65, but it was Ryder and the 20-year-old debutant Kane Williamson who really sparkled. Ryder, making his comeback after an elbow injury and yet another indiscretion off the field, hit a serene 103. His foot movement was minimal but precise, the backlift was short, and he showed good solidity in defence and conviction in attack. Williamson, who batted for six and a half hours, became the eighth and youngest New Zealander to make a century in his first Test. New Zealand's other debutant, fast bowler Hamish Bennett, was not so lucky: he suffered a groin strain on the first day and went home.

The match appeared to be heading towards a tame draw before Martin kicked it alive in dramatic fashion although, in the end, the lifeless surface won the day. Harbhajan was given the match award, but admitted that the real hero was Martin, who bowled his heart out on a flat wicket.

Man of the Match: Harbhajan Singh.

Close of play: First day, India 329-3 (Tendulkar 13, Laxman 7); Second day, New Zealand 69-2 (McCullum 38, Taylor 18); Third day, New Zealand 331-5 (Williamson 87); Fourth day, India 82-6 (Laxman 34, Harbhajan Singh 12).

India

G. Gambhir b Ryder	21	– c Hopkins b Martin	0
V. Sehwag b Vettori	173	– run out	1
R. Dravid b Martin	104	– c Hopkins b Martin	1
S. R. Tendulkar c and b Patel	40	– b Martin	12
V. V. S. Laxman lbw b Patel	40	– lbw b Vettori	91
S. K. Raina c McCullum b Williamson	3	– c Taylor b Martin	0
*†M. S. Dhoni c Watling b Vettori	10	– b Martin	22
Harbhajan Singh c Hopkins b Vettori	69	– c Watling b Taylor	115
Zaheer Khan b Vettori	1	– lbw b Vettori	0
P. P. Ojha lbw b Patel	11	– not out	9
S. Sreesanth not out	2	– c Hopkins b Taylor	4
B 5, l-b 2, w 1, n-b 5	13	B 10, n-b 1	11

1/60 (1) 2/297 (3) 3/317 (3) (151.5 overs) 487
4/383 (4) 5/392 (6) 6/392 (5)
7/410 (7) 8/412 (9) 9/478 (10) 10/487 (8)

1/0 (1) 2/1 (2) (102.4 overs) 266
3/2 (3) 4/15 (4) 5/15 (6)
6/65 (7) 7/228 (5) 8/228 (9)
9/260 (8) 10/266 (11)

Martin 24–5–75–1; Bennett 15–2–47–0; Vettori 54.5–12–118–4; Ryder 17–4–56–1; Patel 29–6–135–3; Williamson 12–0–49–1. *Second Innings*—Martin 27–8–63–5; Vettori 38–8–81–2; Patel 23–1–72–0; Williamson 4–0–18–0; Taylor 4.4–2–4–2; McCullum 6–1–18–0.

New Zealand

T. G. McIntosh c Dhoni b Zaheer Khan	0	– lbw b Zaheer Khan	0
B. B. McCullum st Dhoni b Ojha	65	– not out	11
B-J. Watling b Ojha	6	– not out	2
L. R. P. L. Taylor c Laxman b Harbhajan Singh	56		
J. D. Ryder lbw b Sreesanth	103		
K. S. Williamson c Laxman b Ojha	131		
*D. L. Vettori c Dhoni b Raina	41		
†G. J. Hopkins lbw b Ojha	14		
J. S. Patel b Sreesanth	14		
H. K. Bennett b Zaheer Khan	4		
C. S. Martin not out	3		
B 5, l-b 12, n-b 5	22	B 4, w 5	9

1/8 (1) 2/27 (3) 3/131 (4) (165.4 overs) 459   1/4 (1)   (1 wkt, 10 overs) 22
4/137 (2) 5/331 (5) 6/417 (6)
7/417 (7) 8/445 (8) 9/445 (9) 10/459 (10)

Zaheer Khan 28.4–6–70–2; Sreesanth 26–2–88–2; Ojha 53–14–107–4; Harbhajan Singh 43–7–112–1; Sehwag 1–0–7–0; Raina 12–1–42–1; Tendulkar 2–0–16–0. *Second Innings*—Zaheer Khan 4–2–7–1; Sreesanth 1–0–4–0; Ojha 3–2–1–0; Raina 1–0–1–0; Dhoni 1–0–5–0.

Umpires: S. J. Davis and H. D. P. K. Dharmasena.   Third umpire: S. K. Tarapore.

INDIA v NEW ZEALAND

Second Test Match

Nagraj Gollapudi

At Uppal, Hyderabad, November 12–16, 2010. Drawn. Toss: New Zealand.

Like the previous Test, this one came alive on the fourth day. New Zealand started it needing to wipe out India's lead of 122, which they did without breaking sweat as McCullum and McIntosh dominated the bowling, and cleared the deficit in 35 overs. This was the first time New Zealand's openers had shared a century partnership since 2004, and both men were in dominant mood.

Shortly before tea, an umpiring blunder denied McIntosh a fifty to go with his first-innings century, as he was adjudged caught off bat and pad when replays showed no contact with the bat. India bounced back with three further wickets, but McCullum, whose splendid strokeplay had lit up the day, battled hard for his third century in five Tests in 2010, remaining unbeaten and calming the visitors' nerves.

If India held hopes of victory next morning, McCullum dashed them with gusto, beginning in circumspect fashion before charging the bowlers with contempt, using his trademark "McScoop" shot to good effect as he raced to his maiden double-century. Dhoni packed the leg-side field, so McCullum unleashed a reverse scoop to beat the trap. India paid dearly for dropping him on 148 – the lead was 185 at the time – when the substitute Cheteshwar Pujara failed to latch on to a chance at short leg off Harbhajan Singh. Otherwise McCullum was in complete command, batting for 543 minutes in all, and hitting 22 fours and four sixes from 308 balls. He found an able lieutenant in Williamson, who started the final morning with three fours in four balls. Unfortunately he also fell to an erroneous decision, declared lbw to Harbhajan when the ball was clearly missing leg stump: he had looked set to become only the seventh batsman to make centuries in his first two Tests.

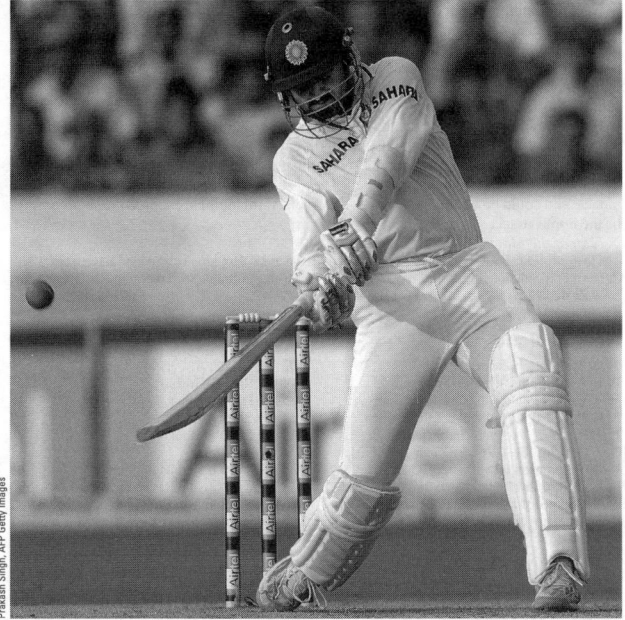

Giving it some air: Harbhajan Singh powers towards his second successive hundred.

It mattered little, as McCullum had ensured the only result possible was a draw. Indeed, the draw became a stronger possibility with every passing day at the Rajiv Gandhi International Stadium at Uppal, the 101st ground to stage Test cricket – the 21st in India and the second in Hyderabad, after the Lal Bahadur Shastri Stadium, which last hosted a Test in December 1988. A scathing appraisal came from the disappointed Harbhajan: "It would need ten days to get a result on such pitches."

On the first morning Vettori made some correct calls: deciding to bat; retaining McIntosh, who had bagged a pair in Ahmedabad; and replacing Watling with Guptill. McIntosh countered the cunning Zaheer Khan patiently before cashing in on the blandness of the rest of the attack to become only the 17th batsman to log a century in the Test after a pair. At the other end Guptill edged a lovely outswinger from Sreesanth to the keeper when he had only five, but was reprieved when umpire Dharmasena checked whether it had been a no-ball. Guptill recovered well and was unlucky to fall close to the end of the second session, as he neared a deserved century built on exquisite drives.

India bounced back next morning as Zaheer and Harbhajan combined well, and the last seven wickets went down for 97. Sehwag started the reply in Dravidesque mode – he scored just two runs off his first 23 balls – before switching to his usual style. Along with Gambhir, who hit a scratchy fifty, Sehwag pulled India back – but four short of his century he tried to slog-sweep Vettori and was bowled. Gambhir left in the next over, and New Zealand were in control again.

Next day India were in danger of losing the plot at 336 for seven – still 14 adrift – with all their specialist batsmen out. But Harbhajan showed his growing pedigree as a batsman: initially he shielded Sreesanth from the strike, then opened his shoulders to smack a power-filled century, hitting seven sixes in all. He stitched together a hundred partnership with Sreesanth, only India's third for the last wicket, and also became the first No. 8 to score back-to-back centuries in Tests.

But if Harbhajan's batting stats were superb, his bowling ones were atrocious for him: by the end of the match he had taken just six wickets in the series at a cost of 305 runs. The Indian bowlers in general did not seem to have any alternative plans to dislodge New Zealand's batsmen once they had settled. The absence of Zaheer, who pulled an abdominal muscle and could bowl only 7.3 overs in the crucial third innings, exposed the shortcomings of the home attack.

Man of the Match: B. B. McCullum.

Close of play: First day, New Zealand 258-4 (Ryder 22, Hopkins 0); Second day, India 178-2 (Dravid 7, Tendulkar 11); Third day, India 436-9 (Harbhajan Singh 85, Sreesanth 14); Fourth day, New Zealand 237-4 (McCullum 124, Williamson 12).

New Zealand

T. G. McIntosh b Zaheer Khan	102	– c sub (C. A. Pujara) b Ojha	49
B. B. McCullum c Dhoni b Sreesanth	4	– c Raina b Sreesanth	225
M. J. Guptill lbw b Ojha	85	– b Ojha	18
L. R. P. L. Taylor c Dhoni b Zaheer Khan	24	– b Sreesanth	7
J. D. Ryder c Laxman b Harbhajan Singh	70	– c Dhoni b Raina	20
†G. J. Hopkins lbw b Zaheer Khan	4	– (8) not out	11
K. S. Williamson lbw b Zaheer Khan	4	– (6) lbw b Harbhajan Singh	69
*D. L. Vettori lbw b Harbhajan Singh	11	– (7) c Dravid b Raina	23
T. G. Southee st Dhoni b Harbhajan Singh	10	– b Sreesanth	11
B. J. Arnel not out	6	– not out	1
C. S. Martin c Sehwag b Harbhajan Singh	3		
B 2, l-b 20, w 1, n-b 4	27	B 4, l-b 3, w 2, n-b 5	14

1/4 (2) 2/151 (3) 3/206 (4)   (117.3 overs) 350   1/125 (1)   (8 wkts dec, 135 overs) 448
4/253 (1) 5/269 (6) 6/287 (7)   2/174 (3) 3/187 (4)
7/312 (8) 8/331 (5) 9/338 (9) 10/350 (11)   4/221 (5) 5/345 (6) 6/396 (7)
                                                             7/431 (2) 8/447 (9)

Zaheer Khan 27–8–69–4; Sreesanth 21–1–88–1; Harbhajan Singh 35.3–10–76–4; Ojha 27–4–80–1; Raina 7–2–15–0. *Second Innings*—Zaheer Khan 7.3–1–21–0; Sreesanth 27–5–121–3; Ojha 47.3–14–137–2; Harbhajan Singh 38–3–117–1; Tendulkar 2–0–7–0; Raina 13–2–38–2.

India

G. Gambhir c Hopkins b Southee	54	– not out	14
V. Sehwag b Vettori	96	– not out	54
R. Dravid lbw b Southee	45		
S. R. Tendulkar c Taylor b Vettori	13		
V. V. S. Laxman lbw b Martin	74		
S. K. Raina c Guptill b Vettori	20		
*†M. S. Dhoni c McCullum b Vettori	14		
Harbhajan Singh not out	111		
Zaheer Khan c Arnel b Southee	7		
P. P. Ojha run out	0		
S. Sreesanth lbw b Vettori	24		
B 4, l-b 8, w 1, n-b 1	14		

1/160 (2) 2/160 (1) 3/184 (4)   (143.4 overs) 472   (no wkt, 17 overs) 68
4/259 (3) 5/311 (6) 6/326 (5)
7/336 (7) 8/355 (9) 9/367 (10)
10/472 (11)

Martin 29–6–87–1; Southee 33–6–119–3; Arnel 24–5–79–0; Vettori 49.4–7–135–5; Williamson 7–0–31–0; Taylor 1–0–9–0. *Second Innings—*Southee 4–0–11–0; Arnel 5–1–11–0; Guptill 5–0–33–0; Taylor 3–0–13–0.

　　Umpires: H. D. P. K. Dharmasena and S. J. A. Taufel.　　Third umpire: A. M. Saheba.

INDIA v NEW ZEALAND

Third Test Match

At Jamtha, Nagpur, November 20–23, 2010. India won by an innings and 198 runs. Toss: New Zealand. Test debut: A. J. McKay.

　　India went into the final match with the series all square, and their reputation as the top-ranked Test team at stake. New Zealand were upbeat after refreshing performances in the first two Tests, and the final one looked like being a well-fought encounter. But that proved a mirage, as New Zealand collapsed in their first innings for 193, a position from which they couldn't recover. India seized a 373-run lead, and went on to clinch a simple win.

　　New Zealand's problems started even before the first ball: McCullum tweaked his back during catching practice just before the toss, and couldn't open the innings. Then the team that had batted so well in the previous two Tests went down as if they had been shot. Sreesanth started the slide, producing a cracking leg-cutter to remove Guptill, then bursting one through the gap between McIntosh's bat and pad. Ishant Sharma – replacing the injured Zaheer Khan – extracted some extra bounce and occasional movement, and the middle order surrendered.

　　Fears that the visitors would self-destruct completely were allayed by the under-the-weather pair of Ryder (who had injured his calf in the First Test) and McCullum. Ryder made 59 before he edged a flighted Harbhajan delivery to slip, where Raina snapped up a smart catch to leave New Zealand 124 for seven. Southee helped save his side's blushes with a breezy 38, but 193 was never going to be enough.

　　The pitch was flat, the bowling insipid, and Dravid piled on the agony by making 191 in nine and a half hours after the openers had provided a fiery start. Even the usually dependable Vettori had a disappointing day as the Indians indulged themselves. There was no respite on the third day, either: Dravid never quite reached the fluency of which he is capable, but remained patient enough to keep working the angles, while Dhoni took the attack by the scruff of the neck and hit a rapid 98. His contest with Vettori was the highlight of the day. Dhoni ruled out the lbws by rarely getting his front pad across: he moved back and forward according to the length, and looked to be in complete control until cramp forced him to bat with a runner (Raina). Sensing an opportunity, Vettori persuaded the lunging Dhoni to scoop a return catch, but by then he had propelled India towards a big lead.

　　New Zealand didn't put up much of a fight in the second innings either, and slid to defeat with a day to spare. The ball turned and bounced on the fourth day, and with two umpiring decisions – Guptill and Taylor were the unlucky victims – going against them, they had little chance to save the game. On a pitch that helped the spinners, India were all over New Zealand like a rash. The ball kicked and spat, and the visitors didn't have the technique to cope. Only Southee, who biffed three more sixes, passed 30 as the spinners shared seven wickets to lead India to a series win.

　　Man of the Match: R. Dravid.　　*Man of the Series:* Harbhajan Singh.
　　Close of play: First day, New Zealand 148-7 (McCullum 34, Southee 7); Second day, India 292-2 (Dravid 69, Tendulkar 57); Third day, New Zealand 24-1 (McCullum 15, Hopkins 1).

New Zealand

T. G. McIntosh b Sreesanth	4	– lbw b Harbhajan Singh	8
M. J. Guptill c Dhoni b Sreesanth	6	– (4) lbw b Ojha	0
L. R. P. L. Taylor lbw b Sharma	20	– (5) c sub (C. A. Pujara) b Harbhajan Singh	29
J. D. Ryder c Raina b Harbhajan Singh	59	– (6) c Sharma b Raina	22
K. S. Williamson c Sehwag b Ojha	0	– (7) b Sharma	8
*D. L. Vettori b Sharma	3	– (8) lbw b Raina	13
†G. J. Hopkins c Raina b Ojha	7	– (3) c Gambhir b Harbhajan Singh	8
B. B. McCullum c Dhoni b Sharma	40	– (2) lbw b Ojha	25
T. G. Southee c Sehwag b Ojha	38	– b Sharma	31
A. J. McKay b Sharma	5	– not out	20
C. S. Martin not out	2	– b Sharma	0
B 1, l-b 5, n-b 3	9	B 10, l-b 1	11

1/11 (2) 2/16 (1) 3/42 (3) 4/43 (5) (66.3 overs) 193
5/51 (6) 6/82 (7) 7/124 (4) 8/159 (8)
9/165 (10) 10/193 (9)

1/18 (1) 2/38 (2) (51.2 overs) 175
3/38 (4) 4/62 (3)
5/93 (5) 6/110 (7) 7/123 (6)
8/124 (8) 9/175 (9) 10/175 (11)

Sreesanth 12–4–28–2; Sharma 18–4–43–4; Ojha 19.3–2–57–3; Harbhajan Singh 17–2–59–1. *Second Innings*—Sreesanth 7–3–25–0; Sharma 6.2–2–15–3; Ojha 17–2–67–2; Harbhajan Singh 19–4–56–3; Raina 2–1–1–2.

India

G. Gambhir c Taylor b Southee	78	I. Sharma not out	7
V. Sehwag c and b Vettori	74	S. Sreesanth not out	0
R. Dravid c Guptill b Williamson	191	B 12, l-b 5, w 4, n-b 1	22
S. R. Tendulkar c Hopkins b McKay	61		
V. V. S. Laxman b Martin	12	1/113 (2) (8 wkts dec, 165 overs) 566	
S. K. Raina c sub (B.-J. Watling) b Vettori	3	2/192 (1) 3/296 (4)	
*†M. S. Dhoni c and b Vettori	98	4/309 (5) 5/328 (6) 6/521 (7)	
Harbhajan Singh c McCullum b Martin	20	7/549 (3) 8/562 (8)	

P. P. Ojha did not bat.

Martin 28–4–82–2; Southee 29–5–94–1; McKay 31–5–120–1; Vettori 58–7–178–3; Williamson 11–0–45–1; Guptill 7–0–27–0; Taylor 1–0–3–0.

Umpires: N. J. Llong and S. J. A. Taufel. Third umpire: S. S. Hazare.
Series referee: R. S. Madugalle.

ONE-DAY INTERNATIONAL MATCH REPORTS BY
NAGRAJ GOLLAPUDI

INDIA v NEW ZEALAND

First One-Day International

At Guwahati, November 28, 2010. India won by 40 runs. Toss: New Zealand. One-day international debut: W. P. Saha.

Gambhir made a victorious debut as captain after Kohli's century – his second in successive international innings, following 118 against Australia at Visakhapatnam the previous month – helped India to a challenging target. It might have been even higher, but they struggled badly at the end, losing their last six wickets for 26 in 5.1 overs. Ashwin's smart off-spin during the powerplays, which brought him the big wickets of Guptill and Taylor, seemed to seal New Zealand's fate, but Mills and Nathan McCullum created some anxious moments for India with a gritty stand of 67 for the ninth wicket. Sreesanth returned to claim both with successive deliveries, to secure a comfortable victory just before darkness set in. Vettori, who had bowled more than 200 overs in the Tests, missed this match to rest a back niggle.

Man of the Match: V. Kohli.

India

M. Vijay c Hopkins b Tuffey	29	S. Sreesanth c How b Mills	4
*G. Gambhir c How b McKay	38	M. M. Patel not out	1
V. Kohli c How b McKay	105		
Yuvraj Singh c Hopkins b Tuffey	42	B 1, l-b 1, w 8, n-b 1	11
S. K. Raina c How b Mills	13		
Y. K. Pathan c Taylor b Mills	29	1/44 (1) 2/92 (2) 3/180 (4) (49 overs) 276		
†W. P. Saha c Hopkins b McKay	4	4/220 (5) 5/250 (3) 6/256 (7)		
R. Ashwin c and b McKay	0	7/256 (8) 8/257 (9) 9/275 (6)		
A. Nehra run out	0	10/276 (10) 10 overs: 58-1		

Mills 10–0–42–3; Tuffey 8–0–56–2; McKay 10–1–62–4; Elliott 5–0–24–0; McCullum 9–0–53–0; Styris 6–0–26–0; Williamson 1–0–11–0.

New Zealand

M. J. Guptill c Patel b Ashwin	30	K. D. Mills c Saha b Sreesanth	32
J. M. How c Vijay b Nehra	9	A. J. McKay not out	0
K. S. Williamson c Saha b Yuvraj Singh	25		
*L. R. P. L. Taylor c Patel b Ashwin	66	L-b 1, w 3	4
S. B. Styris c Pathan b Yuvraj Singh	10		
G. D. Elliott c Pathan b Sreesanth	5	1/32 (2) 2/46 (1) 3/113 (3) (45.2 overs) 236		
D. R. Tuffey c Raina b Yuvraj Singh	4	4/131 (5) 5/136 (6) 6/144 (7)		
†G. J. Hopkins c Pathan b Ashwin	16	7/157 (4) 8/169 (8) 9/236 (9)		
N. L. McCullum c Gambhir b Sreesanth	35	10/236 (10) 10 overs: 46-2		

Nehra 9–0–44–1; Sreesanth 5.2–0–30–3; Ashwin 10–1–50–3; Patel 8–0–39–0; Yuvraj Singh 10–0–43–3; Pathan 2–0–24–0; Raina 1–0–5–0.

Umpires: N. J. Llong and S. K. Tarapore.   Third umpire: S. S. Hazare.

INDIA v NEW ZEALAND

Second One-Day International

At Jaipur, December 1, 2010 (day/night). India won by eight wickets. Toss: India.

Gambhir made the right call, putting New Zealand in on a slow pitch with low bounce. His attack then bowled the right lengths to push back the diffident batsmen. Guptill hung around for 102 deliveries and, although Styris later made his 59 at better than a run a ball New Zealand's total looked too small. It soon looked even smaller as Gambhir bounced back to form, shifting gears effortlessly in the company of the versatile Kohli, who seemed set for a third successive century before he mistimed a pull. He wouldn't have been too bothered, as his captain hurried India over the finish line with his eighth century in one-day internationals: Gambhir hit 18 fours in all, three of them off successive balls from McKay.

Man of the Match: G. Gambhir.

New Zealand

M. J. Guptill c Saha b Ashwin	70	K. D. Mills b Sreesanth	13
J. M. How c Saha b Sreesanth	5	T. G. Southee not out	2
K. S. Williamson b Patel	29	L-b 5, w 6	11
L. R. P. L. Taylor c Kohli b Pathan	15		
S. B. Styris c Saha b Sreesanth	59	1/14 (2) 2/64 (3) (8 wkts, 50 overs) 258		
*D. L. Vettori b Sreesanth	31	3/96 (4) 4/161 (1)		
†G. J. Hopkins not out	11	5/219 (5) 6/219 (6)		
N. L. McCullum run out	12	7/243 (8) 8/256 (9) 10 overs: 40-1		

A. J. McKay did not bat.

Nehra 9–1–45–0; Sreesanth 9–1–47–4; Patel 8–0–34–1; Ashwin 10–0–52–1; Yuvraj Singh 9–1–48–0; Pathan 4–0–23–1; Raina 1–0–4–0.

India

M. Vijay b Vettori	33
*G. Gambhir not out	138
V. Kohli c Taylor b McKay	64
Yuvraj Singh not out	16
W 8	8

1/87 (1)   (2 wkts, 43 overs) 259
2/203 (3)   10 overs: 52-0

S. K. Raina, Y. K. Pathan, †W. P. Saha, R. Ashwin, A. Nehra, S. Sreesanth and M. M. Patel did not bat.

McCullum 9–0–37–0; Mills 7–0–49–0; McKay 7–0–59–1; Styris 3–0–20–0; Vettori 8–0–32–1; Southee 5–0–33–0; Williamson 4–0–29–0.

Umpires: S. S. Hazare and N. J. Llong.   Third umpire: S. Asnani.

INDIA v NEW ZEALAND

Third One-Day International

At Vadodara, December 4, 2010. India won by nine wickets. Toss: India.

India won with consummate ease, and clinched the series at the earliest opportunity. Their task was helped by New Zealand's batsmen retreating into their shells. Put in again by Gambhir, they admittedly had to counter early-morning moisture, which offered good seam movement to Zaheer Khan and Patel, but no one seized control as the score declined to 106 for seven. An even heavier defeat was avoided by an intelligent stand of 94 between Franklin and Nathan McCullum, but the target was nowhere near big enough to worry the in-form pair of Gambhir and Kohli, who battered the bowling again, maintaining India's unbeaten home season. Gambhir strode to his second successive century, hitting 16 fours this time, the pick a classical on-drive off Mills early on.

Man of the Match: G. Gambhir.

New Zealand

M. J. Guptill run out	12	N. L. McCullum c Gambhir b Ashwin	43
B. B. McCullum c Vijay b Zaheer Khan	0	K. D. Mills run out	15
K. S. Williamson lbw b Patel	21	B 1, l-b 10, w 15	26
L. R. P. L. Taylor c Saha b Zaheer Khan	4		
S. B. Styris c Yuvraj Singh b Ashwin	22	1/2 (2) 2/19 (1) (9 wkts, 50 overs) 224
J. E. C. Franklin not out	72	3/34 (4) 4/49 (3)	
*D. L. Vettori c Yuvraj Singh b Pathan	3	5/77 (5) 6/96 (7) 7/106 (8)	
†G. J. Hopkins c Yuvraj Singh b Pathan	6	8/200 (9) 9/224 (10)	10 overs: 32-2

A. J. McKay did not bat.

Zaheer Khan 8–2–31–2; Nehra 8–1–38–0; Patel 10–0–28–1; Ashwin 9–1–49–2; Pathan 8–0–27–2; Jadeja 7–0–40–0.

India

M. Vijay run out		30
*G. Gambhir not out		126
V. Kohli not out		63
L-b 5, w 5		10

1/115 (1)   (1 wkt, 39.3 overs) 229
                        10 overs: 73-0

Yuvraj Singh, R. A. Jadeja, Y. K. Pathan, †W. P. Saha, R. Ashwin, A. Nehra, Zaheer Khan and M. M. Patel did not bat.

Mills 6–0–39–0; McKay 6.3–0–42–0; Franklin 4–0–34–0; Vettori 9–0–41–0; N. L. McCullum 8–0–36–0; Styris 6–0–32–0.

Umpires: R. A. Kettleborough and S. K. Tarapore.   Third umpire: S. S. Hazare.

INDIA v NEW ZEALAND

Fourth One-Day International

At Bangalore, December 7, 2010 (day/night). India won by five wickets. Toss: India.

On a wet and chilly evening Yusuf Pathan decided to correct the impression that he was just a 20-over Goliath. It came at an important time, too, as India were in deep trouble chasing a lofty 316. It seemed that New Zealand were finally on the verge of their first victory since August, after Franklin's superb unbeaten 98, which included three sixes and a dozen fours. Pathan entered at 108 for four, and started the repair job with Rohit Sharma. They put on 80, but when rain stopped play for an hour India – behind on Duckworth/Lewis at the time – still needed 113 from 14 overs. Pathan had 48 from 49 balls at the break, and reached his half-century by swatting the first ball after the resumption, from Vettori, for six. He did not just indulge in power hitting; in an over that cost 21, he also flicked Mills to fine leg for consecutive fours, having spotted that the fielder was squarer than usual. A massive pulled six – his sixth of seven – off McKay brought up his maiden one-day international century, from just 79 balls. Not long afterwards he secured India's victory with seven deliveries to spare.

Man of the Match: Y. K. Pathan.

New Zealand

M. J. Guptill c Yuvraj Singh b Nehra	30	K. D. Mills b Pathan		1
†B. B. McCullum c Sharma b Ashwin	42	N. L. McCullum not out		13
J. M. How c Pathan b Nehra	4	L-b 8, w 12		20
L. R. P. L. Taylor lbw b Ashwin	44			
S. B. Styris c Tiwary b Pathan	46	1/62 (1) 2/70 (3) (7 wkts, 50 overs)		315
J. E. C. Franklin not out	98	3/91 (2) 4/170 (5)		
*D. L. Vettori b Pathan	17	5/210 (4) 6/249 (7) 7/251 (8) 10 overs: 70-1		

T. G. Southee and A. J. McKay did not bat.

Zaheer Khan 8–0–40–0; Kumar 7–0–42–0; Ashwin 10–0–66–2; Nehra 9–1–70–2; Yuvraj Singh 3–0–21–0; Pathan 9–0–49–3; Sharma 4–0–19–0.

India

*G. Gambhir c Guptill b McKay	27	S. S. Tiwary not out		37
†P. A. Patel c sub (K. S. Williamson)		B 4, l-b 3, w 8, n-b 2		17
b N. L. McCullum	53			
V. Kohli c Mills b McKay	0	1/67 (1) 2/68 (3) (5 wkts, 48.5 overs)		321
Yuvraj Singh c How b N. L. McCullum	20	3/103 (4) 4/108 (2)		
R. G. Sharma c Vettori b Southee	44	5/188 (5)		10 overs: 68-2
Y. K. Pathan not out	123			

R. Ashwin, A. Nehra, Zaheer Khan and P. Kumar did not bat.

Mills 10–1–65–0; Southee 10–0–64–1; McKay 7–0–63–2; N. L. McCullum 7.5–0–38–2; Styris 4–1–27–0; Vettori 10–0–57–0.

Umpires: R. A. Kettleborough and A. M. Saheba.   Third umpire: S. Asnani.

INDIA v NEW ZEALAND

Fifth One-Day International

At Chennai, December 10, 2010 (day/night). India won by eight wickets. Toss: New Zealand.

India finished only their second 5–0 series whitewash – they also did it to England in 2008-09, in a series originally scheduled for seven matches – as the hapless tourists crumbled without any fight. Guptill departed in the first over, and it was all downhill from then on. New Zealand's 103 from only 27 overs was their lowest one-day total against India, who took just 76 minutes to finish the drubbing. The reply started badly, with the in-form pair of Gambhir and Kohli departing quickly, but Parthiv Patel and Yuvraj Singh did the needful in an unbroken stand of 97. For India, playing a virtual second-string side (several senior players were resting for the South African tour which followed), this was a huge shot in the arm with the World Cup round the corner. But New Zealand – who had now lost their last 11 completed one-day internationals, including four to Bangladesh – were in disarray. Vettori admitted: "India scored over us because they struck a balance in every department, in the Tests as well as the one-day series."

Man of the Match: Yuvraj Singh.   *Man of the Series:* G. Gambhir.

New Zealand

M. J. Guptill c P. A. Patel b Kumar	0	K. D. Mills c Tiwary b Ashwin	4	
†B. B. McCullum lbw b Nehra	14	T. G. Southee c Sharma b Ashwin	0	
J. M. How b Yuvraj Singh	23			
L. R. P. L. Taylor c P. A. Patel b Nehra	9	W 2	2	
S. B. Styris lbw b Ashwin	24			
J. E. C. Franklin not out	17	1/0 (1) 2/14 (2) 3/28 (4) (27 overs) 103		
G. D. Elliott lbw b Yuvraj Singh	0	4/71 (3) 5/73 (5) 6/74 (7)		
*D. L. Vettori c Yuvraj Singh b Pathan	9	7/90 (8) 8/98 (9) 9/103 (10)		
N. L. McCullum c Yuvraj Singh b Pathan	1	10/103 (11) 10 overs: 47-3		

Kumar 6–1–20–1; Nehra 5–0–34–2; M. M. Patel 3–0–9–0; Ashwin 8–1–24–3; Yuvraj Singh 2–0–5–2; Pathan 3–0–11–2.

India

*G. Gambhir c B. B. McCullum		
b N. L. McCullum	0	
†P. A. Patel not out	56	
V. Kohli c Taylor b Vettori	2	
Yuvraj Singh not out	42	
L-b 2, w 5	7	

1/0 (1)   (2 wkts, 21.1 overs) 107
2/10 (3)   10 overs: 47-2

R. G. Sharma, Y. K. Pathan, S. S. Tiwary, R. Ashwin, A. Nehra, P. Kumar and M. M. Patel did not bat.

N. L. McCullum 6–1–26–1; Vettori 6–0–30–1; Styris 4–0–7–0; Mills 1–0–15–0; Elliott 4.1–0–27–0.

Umpires: R. A. Kettleborough and A. M. Saheba.   Third umpire: S. Asnani.
Series referee: R. S. Mahanama.

THE INDIAN PREMIER LEAGUE, 2009-10

Nagraj Gollapudi

"I've played this game for 20-odd years. I've seen Sachin Tendulkar smash bowlers all around the park plenty of times, and I've seen some wonderful players, but this is probably the best innings I've ever seen." So said Shane Warne, the Rajasthan Royals captain, about Yusuf Pathan's 37-ball century against Mumbai Indians on the second day of the third IPL. He couldn't stop gushing, even though his side had lost by four runs.

It was a ridiculous statement; even Warne, the agent provocateur nonpareil, should have known he was not giving a pep talk in the dugout but making a declaration to the world. But hyperbole was one of the strongest bricks that the IPL's architect, Lalit Modi, used while constructing the league. Since day one, the likes of Warne have been strengthening that foundation.

Modi made it clear nothing would stop him turning the IPL into the first global Asian sporting brand. In the weeks before the third tournament, he stressed that his only goal was "reach, reach, reach". So he signed a one-year deal with ITV, which itself was returning to high-profile cricket broadcasting in the UK after a generation. Even considering the matches were shown on ITV4, a free-to-air channel, the broadcasts proved a raging success – a daily average of 400,000 viewers was ten times the figure achieved by Setanta, the pay-TV network which had bagged the original rights in 2008 but collapsed in 2009, leaving the IPL without a UK broadcaster for its second season.

Modi could only smile back at the enraged cricket purists in England. No matter what the die-hard fanatics thought about the quality, the numbers revealed that a lot more people were interested in watching the bling of the IPL compared to the staid cricket being played by England in Bangladesh (their tour overlapped with the first part of IPL3).

There was a further boost when Modi signed a two-year deal to stream the matches 15 minutes after they finished. They were screened on the Google-owned YouTube in all countries bar the United States. According to the *New York Times*, "about 50 million viewers tuned in to YouTube's IPL channel, 25% more than Google executives said they expected when they signed the deal in January. Approximately 40% of those viewers were outside India."

Several new sponsors were added, including one for the controversial after-hours party: here players would mingle with a select group of fans, who had to buy the invitations at premium prices – but Modi knew the idol-worshipping Indian fan would stop at nothing. More money was brought to the table when Modi found another 150 seconds of commercial space by throwing ads between deliveries mid-over. For the purist this was the final slap; already the screen space was partially obscured by vertical ads that cut the size of the live picture.

Still, nothing could deter the crowds thronging to the 12 venues. It was clear that Indian fans had dearly missed the IPL the previous year when it was displaced to South Africa. Now the show was back in town, they were willing to brave the heat, the moths, and even – in Bangalore towards the end of the tournament – a bomb scare. Two of what the police called "low-intensity" devices exploded around the Chinnaswamy Stadium – one at an entrance and another a few hundreds yards away – and the match between Royal Challengers Bangalore and Mumbai Indians was delayed. But the teams remained mostly unaffected, as their bosses personally assured the players, especially the overseas contingent, that it was safe to stay and play.

On the field, Sachin Tendulkar was the star. He had opted out of India's national 20-over side three years previously, saying Twenty20 was a format more appropriate for youngsters, but now he added another chapter to his ever-evolving career by playing some traditional cricket with a calm pulse to set up most of **Mumbai Indians'** 11 victories. Tendulkar finished as the tournament's highest run-getter with 618 at 48, including five half-centuries, and four match awards, not to forget the Man of the Series gong. His success and tactical nous drove his Mumbai team-mate Harbhajan Singh to suggest that his captain should reconsider his decision not to play Twenty20 for his country.

Tendulkar was touched by Harbhajan's sentiment, but remained happy to allow Mahendra Singh Dhoni to safeguard India's fortunes. Dhoni, captaining **Chennai Super Kings**, again proved a smart strategist, fielding three spinners in the crucial semi-final, and before that throwing the new ball to off-spinner Ravichandran Ashwin, whose alliance with the left-arm pace of Doug Bollinger put Chennai back on the tracks after a terrible start. Before Bollinger arrived in India to make his IPL debut, Chennai had lost five of their first eight matches, but once he was paired up with Ashwin – the most economical regular bowler in the tournament – they choked the flow of runs in the crucial powerplay overs, shifting the momentum towards Chennai, who finished with six wins in their final eight games.

He screamed in ecstasy and punched at his jaw

But Chennai's, and the IPL's, most stunning picture materialised in Dharmasala, where Dhoni cracked a swashbuckling half-century, including 30 off the final two overs, to help his side become the only team to make the semi-finals in each of the IPL's three seasons. It was a must-win game, so, after Dhoni hit the winning back-to-back sixes off Irfan Pathan, he screamed in ecstasy to release all his pent-up energy while he punched manically at his jaw. A week later he brought his slow bowlers on early again to stifle Mumbai's batsmen in the final, helping Chennai lift the IPL crown for the first time.

Although the standard of the fielding – and perhaps overall – was lower than in the first two IPLs, there were more hold-your-breath moments for the photo album. Justin Kemp's backward-running, twisting, one-handed clincher on the ropes to dismiss Virender Sehwag in Chennai's match against Delhi Daredevils was one of the best catches; in the same game Matthew Hayden walked out with the long-handled, short-bodied Mongoose bat and thrashed Delhi into submission, thereby giving the bat-maker priceless exposure. For Bangalore, Robin Uthappa's muscularity oozed through powerful hits over the shortened boundaries, but it was his switch-hits that lingered more in the memory, because of their effortlessness. Competing with Kemp for best catch of the tournament was David Hussey of Kolkata; it also came against Delhi. Paul

Collingwood hit a flat-batted stroke which seemed to be sailing over long-on; Hussey took a couple of steps backwards, jumped up, was on the other side of the rope as he parried the ball back while still airborne, then sprang back on to the field to complete a stupendous effort.

Of the other teams, the most disappointing were **Delhi Daredevils**, who on paper boasted one of the most fearsome batting line-ups. They started well, but subsequently looked out of sorts, and fragmented. **Royal Challengers Bangalore**, runners-up in IPL2, stayed in contention till the semis but, once Jacques Kallis grew tired after a long summer and failed to provide an opening burst, their middle order struggled.

The **Deccan Chargers** captain Adam Gilchrist fell away with the bat. After making 149 runs in his first four innings, his remaining 12 knocks produced only 140, with seven single-figure scores. The defending champions did still reach the last four – they had to win their last five league games to do it – with much credit going to Andrew Symonds and Rohit Sharma for their sensible batting. **Rajasthan Royals**, who lost match-winners such as Graeme Smith and Dimitri Mascarenhas to injury early on, again relied heavily on Warne, but at 40 even he couldn't overcome the inaugural champions' misfortunes on his own. He finished with 11 wickets at 27, and an economy-rate of 7.62. The New Zealand fast bowler Shane Bond was bagged by **Kolkata Knight Riders** for the princely sum of $750,000, but didn't do much (nine wickets in eight games) for the IPL's most popular team, owned by Bollywood heart-throb Shah Rukh Khan and led by Bengal's favourite son, Sourav Ganguly.

But it was **Kings XI Punjab**, one of the more successful teams of the league's first two seasons, who plummeted to the bottom, mainly because of the failure of Yuvraj Singh (255 runs in 14 games with a highest score of 43), while Kumar Sangakkara, who replaced him as captain, had a subdued time too. Tom Moody, one of the best coaches around, said Yuvraj's slump was down to a wrist injury, but he knew his star player was below par in fitness, batting, fielding and even attitude. Yuvraj maintained a relaxed attitude off the pitch as well: at a meeting with the Dalai Lama in Dharmasala he asked him what his favourite sport was (table tennis).

Among those seeking the meaning of life beyond cricket in the Tibetan head monk's summer palace was Modi himself. The couple of hundred fans who lined the steep and narrow path leading to it instantly recognised Modi, on the verge of a descent into turbulent times. India's tax authorities had found irregularities in the ownership structure of the Kochi franchise (one of two new entrants for IPL4, the second being a Pune side fronted by the Sahara Group, India's team sponsors) after Modi himself, in a reckless moment that ultimately proved his downfall, had posted the individual stakes of Kochi's various owners on Twitter. That exposed the involvement of Shashi Tharoor, a minister in India's federal government, who had to resign within days.

Modi himself soon hit rock bottom as the government revealed that "all aspects of the IPL" were under investigation. None of the BCCI's functionaries attended the final, not even the secretary, N. Srinivasan, owner of the victorious Chennai team. After the presentations Modi was handed a letter of suspension from the board, and an inquiry began into the many allegations.

IPL STATISTICS

Leading run-scorers

	M	I	NO	Runs	HS	50s	Avge	SR	4s	6s
S. R. Tendulkar (*Mumbai Indians*)	15	15	2	618	89*	5	47.53	132.61	86	3
J. H. Kallis (*Royal Challengers Bangalore*).	16	16	4	572	89*	6	47.66	115.78	67	9
†S. K. Raina (*Chennai Super Kings*)	16	16	5	520	83*	4	47.27	142.85	45	22
†S. C. Ganguly (*Kolkata Knight Riders*)	14	14	1	493	88	4	37.92	117.66	58	15
M. Vijay (*Chennai Super Kings*)	15	15	2	458	127	3	35.23	156.84	36	26
D. P. M. D. Jayawardene (*Kings XI Punjab*) . . .	13	13	3	439	110*	2	43.90	147.31	55	11
A. Symonds (*Deccan Chargers*)	16	16	2	429	54	4	30.64	125.80	35	18
†S. S. Tiwary (*Mumbai Indians*)	16	15	1	419	61	3	29.92	135.59	29	18
R. G. Sharma (*Deccan Chargers*)	16	12	2	404	73	3	28.85	133.77	36	14
N. V. Ojha (*Rajasthan Royals*)	14	14	2	377	94*	2	31.41	132.28	42	15
R. V. Uthappa (*Royal Challengers B'lore*)	16	14	2	374	68*	1	31.16	171.55	21	27
†K. C. Sangakkara (*Kings XI Punjab*)	13	12	0	357	56	2	29.75	138.91	47	5
V. Sehwag (*Delhi Daredevils*)	14	14	0	356	75	3	25.42	163.30	47	14
A. T. Rayudu (*Mumbai Indians*)	14	14	1	356	55*	2	27.38	144.71	34	13
S. Badrinath (*Chennai Super Kings*)	16	15	4	356	55*	2	32.36	117.49	41	5

There were four centuries: 127 by M. Vijay (Chennai v Rajasthan), 110 by D. P. M. D. Jayawardene
(Punjab v Kolkata), 107* by D. A. Warner (Delhi v Kolkata) and 100 by Y. K. Pathan (Rajasthan v
Mumbai). The highest strike-rate for anyone scoring more than 100 runs was 185.71 by K. A. Pollard
(273 runs for Mumbai Indians).*

Leading wicket-takers

	Style	O	M	R	W	BB	4W/i	Avge	SR	ER
P. P. Ojha (*Deccan Chargers*)	SLA	58.5	0	429	21	3-26	0	20.42	16.80	7.29
A. Mishra (*Delhi Daredevils*).	LBG	53	0	363	17	3-25	0	21.35	18.70	6.84
Harbhajan Singh (*Mumbai Indians*)	OB	53.3	1	377	17	3-31	0	22.17	18.88	7.04
A. Kumble (*Royal Challengers Bangalore*) . . .	LBG	63.2	0	407	17	4-16	1	23.94	22.35	6.42
R. Vinay Kumar (*Royal Chall'rs B'lore*) . . .	RM	46.1	0	396	16	4-40	1	24.75	17.31	8.57
K. A. Pollard (*Mumbai Indians*)	RM	37	0	274	15	3-17	0	18.26	14.80	7.40
M. Muralitharan (*Chennai Super Kings*) . . .	OB	48	0	329	15	3-16	0	21.93	19.20	6.85
S. L. Malinga (*Mumbai Indians*)	RF	49	0	344	15	4-22	1	22.93	19.60	7.02
Zaheer Khan (*Mumbai Indians*)	LFM	48.2	1	376	15	3-21	0	25.06	19.33	7.77
D. W. Steyn (*Royal Challengers B'lore*) . . .	RF	59	1	406	15	3-18	0	27.06	23.60	6.88
I. K. Pathan (*Kings XI Punjab*)	LFM	46.2	0	426	15	3-24	0	28.40	18.53	9.19
R. J. Harris (*Deccan Chargers*)	RF	30.4	0	233	14	3-18	0	16.64	13.14	7.59
S. B. Jakati (*Chennai Super Kings*)	SLA	38	1	291	13	2-17	0	22.38	17.53	7.65
R. Ashwin (*Chennai Super Kings*)	OB	48	0	293	13	3-16	0	22.53	22.15	6.10
R. P. Singh (*Deccan Chargers*)	LFM	42	0	370	13	3-17	0	28.46	19.38	8.80
J. H. Kallis (*Royal Challengers B'lore*)	RFM	57	1	476	13	2-3	0	36.61	26.30	8.35

*There were three other bowlers who took four wickets in an innings: D. E. Bollinger (4-13, Chennai
v Deccan), A. D. Mathews (4-19, Kolkata v Bangalore) and S. K. Warne (4-21, Rajasthan v Deccan).
The best economy-rate by a bowler bowling at least ten overs was Ashwin's 6.10; the best not listed
above was 6.31 by W. P. U. J. C. Vaas (9 wickets in 22 overs for Deccan Chargers).*

Leading wicketkeepers

Dis	M	Dis	M
13 (9 ct, 4 st)	16 A. C. Gilchrist (*Deccan*)	11 (5 ct, 6 st)	13 M. S. Dhoni (*Chennai*)
12 (6 ct, 6 st)	14 K. D. Karthik (*Delhi*)	11 (6 ct, 5 st)	13 K. C. Sangakkara (*Punjab*)

Leading fielders – most catches

Ct	M		Ct	M	
12	16	A. Symonds (*Deccan*)	10	16	S. K. Raina (*Chennai*)
11	15	M. Vijay (*Chennai*)			

INDIAN PREMIER LEAGUE, 2009-10

20-over league plus knockout

	Played	Won	Lost	Points	Net run-rate
MUMBAI INDIANS...................	14	10	4	20	1.08
DECCAN CHARGERS................	14	8	6	16	−0.29
CHENNAI SUPER KINGS.............	14	7	7	14	0.27
ROYAL CHALLENGERS BANGALORE ...	14	7	7	14	0.21
Delhi Daredevils....................	14	7	7	14	0.02
Kolkata Knight Riders................	14	7	7	14	−0.34
Rajasthan Royals....................	14	6	8	12	−0.51
Kings XI Punjab	14	4	10	8	−0.47

Chennai Super Kings and Royal Challengers Bangalore qualified for the semi-finals ahead of Delhi Daredevils and Kolkata Knight Riders, who were level on points, by virtue of their net run-rate.

All games were played partially or entirely under floodlights.

At Dr D. Y. Patil Sports Academy, Mumbai, March 12, 2010. **Kolkata Knight Riders won by 11 runs. Kolkata Knight Riders 161-4** (20 overs) (O. A. Shah 58*, A. D. Mathews 65*); ‡**Deccan Chargers 150-7** (20 overs) (A. C. Gilchrist 54). MoM: A. D. Mathews. *Angelo Mathews and Owais Shah resurrected Kolkata's hopes, putting on 130 after Chaminda Vaas started the third IPL tournament with two wickets in the first four balls. Despite the customary breezy start from Adam Gilchrist (54 from 35 balls), the defending champions were beaten in an otherwise drab match.*

At Brabourne Stadium, Mumbai, March 13, 2010. **Mumbai Indians won by four runs.** ‡**Mumbai Indians 212-6** (20 overs) (S. S. Tiwary 53, A. T. Rayudu 55); **Rajasthan Royals 208-7** (20 overs) (Y. K. Pathan 100, P. Dogra 41). MoM: Y. K. Pathan. *Yusuf Pathan smashed the second-fastest century in Twenty20 cricket – after Andrew Symonds's in 34 balls for Kent in 2004 – from just 37 balls, with eight sixes and nine fours. But even he couldn't lift the 2008 champions past Mumbai's highest IPL total to date, which owed much to an enterprising fourth-wicket stand of 110 in 10.3 overs between Ambati Rayudu and Saurabh Tiwary, who paced their innings superbly – something Rajasthan's batsmen, Pathan apart, failed to do.*

At Mohali, March 13, 2010. **Delhi Daredevils won by five wickets. Kings XI Punjab 142-9** (20 overs) (R. S. Bopara 56); ‡**Delhi Daredevils 146-5** (19.5 overs) (G. Gambhir 72, M. Manhas 31*). MoM: G. Gambhir. *After Dirk Nannes and Farveez Maharoof suffocated Punjab's batsmen, Delhi captain Gautam Gambhir saved his side's blushes with a hard-working half-century, enough to secure victory with a ball to spare despite three early wickets.*

At Kolkata, March 14, 2010. **Kolkata Knight Riders won by seven wickets. Royal Challengers Bangalore 135-7** (20 overs) (J. H. Kallis 65*, A. D. Mathews 4-19); ‡**Kolkata Knight Riders 136-3** (19.2 overs) (B. J. Hodge 50, M. K. Tiwary 50). MoM: M. K. Tiwary. *Kolkata continued the upbeat start to their campaign: after overcoming the defending champions in their first match, they now recorded a resounding victory over the previous season's runners-up.*

At Chennai, March 14, 2010. **Deccan Chargers won by 31 runs.** ‡**Deccan Chargers 190-4** (20 overs) (A. C. Gilchrist 38, H. H. Gibbs 45, A. Symonds 50); **Chennai Super Kings 159-9** (20 overs) (M. S. Dhoni 42, J. A. Morkel 42*; W. P. U. J. C. Vaas 3-21). MoM: W. P. U. J. C. Vaas. *The old hands carved out an easy win: Adam Gilchrist batted like a speeding bullet (38 from 17 balls), Herschelle Gibbs and Andrew Symonds strengthened the foundation, then Chaminda Vaas's gentle swing accounted for Chennai's top order.*

At Ahmedabad, March 15, 2010. **Delhi Daredevils won by six wickets. Rajasthan Royals 141-6** (20 overs) (A. A. Jhunjhunwala 53*); ‡**Delhi Daredevils 142-4** (17.1 overs) (V. Sehwag 75). MoM: V. Sehwag. *Ahmedabad became Rajasthan's second home-base after Jaipur, but the hosts had a* *forgettable start on the moth-filled Motera ground as Virender Sehwag thrashed a blistering 34-ball 75 – eight fours, five sixes – to ease Delhi to their second successive win. Shane Warne was left pondering not only a second defeat but also the loss of two important lieutenants – Graeme Smith and Dimitri Mascarenhas, forced out of the tournament with injuries.*

At Bangalore, March 16, 2010. **Royal Challengers Bangalore won by eight wickets. ‡Kings XI Punjab 203-3** (20 overs) (R. S. Bopara 77, M. S. Bisla 75); **Royal Challengers Bangalore 204-2** (18.5 overs) (M. K. Pandey 38, J. H. Kallis 89*, R. V. Uthappa 51). *MoM:* J. H. Kallis. *A formidable total, set up by a stroke-filled opening stand of 129 in 14 overs between Ravi Bopara and Manvinder Bisla, was not enough for Punjab; they were left dazed by Jacques Kallis, who paced the chase cleverly, and some imperious batting from Robin Uthappa, who turned the tide by taking 25 off a Sreesanth over.*

At Kolkata, March 16, 2010. **Chennai Super Kings won by 55 runs. ‡Chennai Super Kings 164-3** (20 overs) (M. Vijay 33, S. Badrinath 43*, M. S. Dhoni 66*); **Kolkata Knight Riders 109** (19.2 overs) (J. M. Kemp 3-12). *MoM:* M. S. Dhoni. *Kolkata's victory run was broken as none of their batsmen showed the patience, the nerve, the ability to stitch a partnership... all characteristics of Dhoni's cleverly crafted 33-ball innings, which had lifted Chennai from a desperate 59-3 at halfway.*

At Delhi, March 17, 2010. **Mumbai Indians won by 98 runs. Mumbai Indians 218-7** (20 overs) (S. R. Tendulkar 63, S. S. Tiwary 61, A. T. Rayudu 34); **‡Delhi Daredevils 120** (16.3 overs). *MoM:* S. R. Tendulkar. *Mumbai raised their highest total again and registered the season's biggest victory in terms of runs, after Tendulkar (who hit 11 fours from 32 balls) and Saurabh Tiwary caned the bowling. Delhi's star-studded batting failed to respond in kind.*

At Bangalore, March 18, 2010. **Royal Challengers Bangalore won by ten wickets. Rajasthan Royals 92** (19.5 overs) (P. Kumar 3-18, A. Kumble 3-9); **‡Royal Challengers Bangalore 93-0** (10.4 overs) (M. K. Pandey 42*, J. H. Kallis 44*). *MoM:* J. H. Kallis. *Praveen Kumar grabbed the only hat-trick of the tournament during his spell of 4–0–18–3, but that was the one good memory for Rajasthan, who slumped to their third successive loss, with 56 balls to spare. This was the only ten-wicket victory in IPL3.*

At Delhi, March 19, 2010. **Chennai Super Kings won by five wickets. ‡Delhi Daredevils 185-6** (20 overs) (V. Sehwag 74, M. Manhas 32*); **Chennai Super Kings 190-5** (19.1 overs) (M. L. Hayden 93, S. K. Raina 49*). *MoM:* M. L. Hayden. *Virender Sehwag bolted out of the blocks with 74 from 38 balls – ten fours and three sixes – only to be stopped by a spectacular one-handed overhead catch by Justin Kemp at long-off. Then Matthew Hayden fashioned an equally belligerent response, utilising the much-hyped Mongoose bat's supposed extra power as he zipped to 93 from just 43 deliveries, with nine fours and seven sixes.*

At Cuttack, March 19, 2010. **Deccan Chargers won by six runs. Deccan Chargers 170-7** (20 overs) (A. C. Gilchrist 33, A. Symonds 53); **‡Kings XI Punjab 164-8** (20 overs) (R. S. Bopara 38, I. K. Pathan 60). *MoM:* A. Symonds. *Punjab's slide continued, their top order flopping once again as the Chargers recorded their first IPL victory over the Kings XI. It was set up by some manic hitting from Gilchrist in the first three overs (33 from 12 balls), before a more measured half-century from Symonds. That proved too much: the target swelled to 67 from 24 balls, and although some pyrotechnics from Irfan Pathan reduced that to 19 from the final over, he was out to its first ball.*

At Ahmedabad, March 20, 2010. **Rajasthan Royals won by 34 runs. ‡Rajasthan Royals 168-7** (20 overs) (F. Y. Fazal 31, A. A. Jhunjhunwala 45, A. C. Voges 37*); **Kolkata Knight Riders 134-5** (20 overs) (B. J. Hodge 36, S. C. Ganguly 33). *MoM:* A. A. Jhunjhunwala. *In their attempt to preserve wickets Kolkata choked fatally: they ignored the mounting run-rate, and Shane Warne's side took advantage to seal their first win of the season.*

At Brabourne Stadium, Mumbai, March 20, 2010. **Royal Challengers Bangalore won by seven wickets. ‡Mumbai Indians 151-9** (20 overs) (D. W. Steyn 3-26, R. Vinay Kumar 3-25); **Royal Challengers Bangalore 155-3** (19.1 overs) (M. K. Pandey 40, J. H. Kallis 66*). *MoM:* J. H. Kallis. *Vinay Kumar, the highest first-class wicket-taker of the Indian domestic season with 53, removed Ambati Rayudu, Sachin Tendulkar and Dwayne Bravo in the 11th over: it was enough to ensure Mumbai's first defeat of the tournament.*

At Cuttack, March 21, 2010. **Deccan Chargers won by ten runs. ‡Deccan Chargers 171-6** (20 overs) (H. H. Gibbs 31, A. Symonds 35, R. G. Sharma 45); **Delhi Daredevils 161-9** (20 overs) (D. A. Warner 52, K. D. Karthik 46; A. Symonds 3-21). *MoM:* A. Symonds. *Once David Warner was run out after a solid half-century, Delhi's batting misfired against some tight bowling from*

Symonds. He had stood strong earlier after Gilchrist went for 24, and later passed the baton to Rohit Sharma. It was Deccan's third successive victory, and Delhi's third straight defeat, all coming while their captain Gautam Gambhir was out with a groin injury.

At Chennai, March 21, 2010. **Kings XI Punjab won after eliminator over following a tie. Kings XI Punjab 136-8** (20 overs) (I. K. Pathan 39, Yuvraj Singh 43; M. Muralitharan 3-16); ‡**Chennai Super Kings 136-7** (20 overs) (P. A. Patel 57, M. L. Hayden 33). *MoM:* J. Theron. *Punjab snatched a lucky win in the "super over" decider, but in reality this match was a lame affair, both teams' middle orders being woeful. Chennai needed only 16 off the final 17 balls, and then ten off the last over – but Albie Morkel and Ravichandran Ashwin struggled against Irfan Pathan, even though he seemed to be inviting the drive. Rusty Theron delivered an excellent super over – Chennai had managed only nine runs in five balls, when they lost their second wicket – before Yuvraj Singh hit the winning runs off Muttiah Muralitharan.*

At Brabourne Stadium, Mumbai, March 22, 2010. **Mumbai Indians won by seven wickets. ‡Kolkata Knight Riders 155-3** (20 overs) (C. H. Gayle 75, S. C. Ganguly 31, O. A. Shah 31); **Mumbai Indians 156-3** (18.3 overs) (S. R. Tendulkar 71*, S. S. Tiwary 30). *MoM:* S. R. Tendulkar. *Kolkata scored 62 off their last six overs, but even Chris Gayle, who faced 60 balls, had failed to press the accelerator significantly before that, and they were at least 20 runs below par, which allowed Mumbai to complete a relaxed victory; they logged 50 in just 4.2 overs.*

At Bangalore, March 23, 2010. **Royal Challengers Bangalore won by 36 runs. Royal Challengers Bangalore 171-5** (20 overs) (R. V. Uthappa 68*; M. Muralitharan 3-25); ‡**Chennai Super Kings 135-7** (20 overs) (M. L. Hayden 32, S. Badrinath 31; R. Vinay Kumar 4-40). *MoM:* R. V. Uthappa. *For Bangalore, Kallis was finally dismissed after scoring 283 runs in five innings, but Uthappa ransacked 23 off five balls in the penultimate over from Lakshmipathy Balaji, and in all collected 39 off his last ten balls as Bangalore galloped from 119 after 17 overs to 171. Chennai, already without the injured Dhoni, suffered a mortal blow when Hayden was run out by a brilliant underarm throw from Rahul Dravid.*

At Mohali, March 24, 2010. **Rajasthan Royals won by 31 runs. Rajasthan Royals 183-5** (20 overs) (M. J. Lumb 41, F. Y. Fazal 45, A. C. Voges 45*); ‡**Kings XI Punjab 152** (19.1 overs) (M. S. Bisla 35; S. W. Tait 3-22). *MoM:* A. C. Voges. *Punjab's chase got off to a blistering start, blasting 76 runs in the powerplay – the highest in the tournament in the first six overs – but once the top order departed Rajasthan took control.*

At Bangalore, March 25, 2010. **Delhi Daredevils won by 17 runs. Delhi Daredevils 183-4** (20 overs) (D. A. Warner 33, A. B. de Villiers 45, K. M. Jadhav 50*); ‡**Royal Challengers Bangalore 166-9** (20 overs) (M. K. Pandey 39, V. Kohli 38*). *MoM:* K. M. Jadhav. *David Warner's assault – he outpaced Virender Sehwag with 33 out of 44 in the first 3.2 overs – gave Delhi early impetus, which the debutant Kedar Jadhav further strengthened. Bangalore were never in the hunt, and slipped to their first home defeat as Delhi ended their three-match losing streak.*

At Brabourne Stadium, Mumbai, March 25, 2010. **Mumbai Indians won by five wickets. Chennai Super Kings 180-2** (20 overs) (S. K. Raina 83*, S. Badrinath 55*); ‡**Mumbai Indians 181-5** (19 overs) (S. Dhawan 56, S. R. Tendulkar 72). *MoM:* S. R. Tendulkar. *For the first time since the first match Mumbai's bowling misfired, allowing Suresh Raina and Subramaniam Badrinath to repair the early loss of the openers and stitch together an unbeaten 142-run stand to set a formidable target. But Tendulkar and Shikhar Dhawan got Mumbai halfway home inside nine overs, virtually ensuring victory.*

At Ahmedabad, March 26, 2010. **Rajasthan Royals won by eight wickets. ‡Deccan Chargers 148-9** (20 overs) (R. G. Sharma 49; S. W. Tait 3-22); **Rajasthan Royals 151-2** (15.4 overs) (M. J. Lumb 45, Y. K. Pathan 73*). *MoM:* Y. K. Pathan. *Warne cleverly worked his bowlers around to restrict the Chargers to a below-par total, which Rajasthan knocked off easily thanks to a sound start from Michael Lumb and a blitz by Yusuf Pathan, who smashed eight sixes (and two fours) in his 34-ball stay for an eye-popping strike-rate of 214.70.*

At Mohali, March 27, 2010. **Kolkata Knight Riders won by 39 runs. ‡Kolkata Knight Riders 183-5** (20 overs) (S. C. Ganguly 50, M. K. Tiwary 75*); **Kings XI Punjab 144-6** (20 overs) (K. C. Sangakkara 30). *MoM:* M. K. Tiwary. *Sourav Ganguly played the anchor with a composed half-century, before Manoj Tiwary took up the cudgels: he hit 21 from the final over. Punjab's aimless batting was exposed once again, and the experiment of opening with Yuvraj Singh did not pay off as he was out for 24.*

At Ahmedabad, March 28, 2010. **Rajasthan Royals won by 17 runs. ‡Rajasthan Royals 177-8** (20 overs) (M. J. Lumb 30, N. V. Ojha 80); **Chennai Super Kings 160-6** (20 overs) (M. Vijay 42). *MoM:* N. V. Ojha. *Rajasthan shocked the pre-tournament favourites to record their fourth successive win after three defeats: the hero this time was Naman Ojha. His highest IPL score so far (49 balls, six fours, five sixes) set a challenging target for Chennai, who failed to escape from the maze that Warne built.*

At Dr D. Y. Patil Sports Academy, Mumbai, March 28, 2010. **Mumbai Indians won by 41 runs. Mumbai Indians 172-7** (20 overs) (S. R. Tendulkar 55, Harbhajan Singh 49*; R. P. Singh 3-31); **‡Deccan Chargers 131** (17.4 overs) (R. G. Sharma 45; Harbhajan Singh 3-34, Zaheer Khan 3-21, S. L. Malinga 3-12). *MoM:* Harbhajan Singh. *Harbhajan stunned the Chargers with a flamboyant 18-ball effort – including eight fours and two sixes – at the end of the innings to help Mumbai from a perilous 119-7. After Gilchrist fell second ball, Deccan were never in touch.*

At Delhi, March 29, 2010. **Delhi Daredevils won by 40 runs. ‡Delhi Daredevils 177-4** (20 overs) (D. A. Warner 107*, P. D. Collingwood 53); **Kolkata Knight Riders 137-9** (20 overs) (C. H. Gayle 30). *MoM:* D. A. Warner. *Warner lived up to his billing as the pocket rocket with a thunderous century (69 balls in all, with nine fours and five sixes), his first in the IPL and the second of this tournament. Warner was unfazed by wickets falling in each of the first three overs, or by a dangerously slow turner at the Feroz Shah Kotla: his stand of 128 with the equally resolute Paul Collingwood proved vital.*

At Brabourne Stadium, Mumbai, March 30, 2010. **Mumbai Indians won by four wickets. Kings XI Punjab 163** (20 overs) (S. E. Marsh 57; Zaheer Khan 3-34, S. L. Malinga 4-22); **‡Mumbai Indians 164-6** (19.3 overs) (S. Dhawan 50, S. S. Tiwary 31; R. S. Bopara 3-31). *MoM:* S. L. Malinga. *The final over began with six needed; with three balls remaining, Brett Lee's wide went racing to the boundary to seal Mumbai's win, and Punjab's sixth defeat in seven. Lasith Malinga had earlier bowled ferociously to restrict Punjab to a par score despite a half-century from Shaun Marsh, in his first match of the tournament, and 21 extras, the most in the season.*

At Chennai, March 31, 2010. **Chennai Super Kings won by five wickets. ‡Royal Challengers Bangalore 161-4** (20 overs) (J. H. Kallis 52, V. Kohli 34); **Chennai Super Kings 162-5** (18.5 overs) (M. Vijay 78, S. K. Raina 40*). *MoM:* M. Vijay. *Kevin Pietersen, in his first game of the tournament, contributed a handy 23* at the end of Bangalore's innings, but it was not enough. Murali Vijay gave himself a birthday present a day early with a robust performance that included six sixes as Chennai halted their slide.*

At Delhi, March 31, 2010. **Delhi Daredevils won by 67 runs. ‡Delhi Daredevils 188-6** (20 overs) (G. Gambhir 43, K. D. Karthik 69; S. Narwal 3-36); **Rajasthan Royals 121** (17.4 overs) (A. Mishra 3-25). *MoM:* K. D. Karthik. *Rajasthan were in the reckoning when Delhi were 67-4 in the ninth over, but Dinesh Karthik rescued them, initially in concert with his fit-again captain Gambhir. Karthik clobbered six fours and four sixes from only 38 balls to push his side up to second.*

At Kolkata, April 1, 2010. **Kolkata Knight Riders won by 24 runs. ‡Kolkata Knight Riders 181-6** (20 overs) (S. C. Ganguly 88, D. J. Hussey 31); **Deccan Chargers 157-5** (20 overs) (H. H. Gibbs 50, A. Symonds 45). *MoM:* S. C. Ganguly. *In front of an adoring full house at Eden Gardens, Sourav Ganguly turned the clock back to his glory years, with 88 from 54 balls (nine fours, five sixes) to put Kolkata in command. His opposing captain Gilchrist was less lucky: he missed a couple of easy stumpings, then failed to reach double figures for the third match running.*

At Mohali, April 2, 2010. **Royal Challengers Bangalore won by six wickets. ‡Kings XI Punjab 181-5** (20 overs) (K. C. Sangakkara 45, R. S. Bopara 42*, Yuvraj Singh 36); **Royal Challengers Bangalore 184-4** (19.1 overs) (K. P. Pietersen 66*, V. Kohli 42). *MoM:* K. P. Pietersen. *A combination of mature batting, woeful fielding (several easy catches went down) and some terrible bowling at the death helped Bangalore to an easy win. Pietersen reined himself in, but his stand of 76 with Virat Kohli kept his side in the hunt; then, with 48 needed from the final four overs, Uthappa flayed the out-of-sorts Brett Lee for 19 in an over costing 25.*

At Chennai, April 3, 2010. **Chennai Super Kings won by 23 runs. ‡Chennai Super Kings 246-5** (20 overs) (M. Vijay 127, M. L. Hayden 34, J. A. Morkel 62); **Rajasthan Royals 223-5** (20 overs) (M. J. Lumb 37, N. V. Ojha 94*, S. R. Watson 60). *MoM:* M. Vijay. *This was a day for records: Chennai's 246 was the highest total in IPL history, after they pillaged 155 off the final ten overs. Murali Vijay zipped to 127, the highest score of this tournament, facing only 56 balls and hitting 11 sixes and eight fours; his stand of 152 with Albie Morkel was three short of the all-wicket IPL record. Rajasthan held their nerve, with Naman Ojha sprinting to one of the most inspired innings of the* *tournament. He and Shane Watson threatened a miracle – but Doug Bollinger, making his IPL debut, doused the challenge by bowling straight, finishing with 2-15 from his four overs.*

At Brabourne Stadium, Mumbai, April 3, 2010. **Mumbai Indians won by 63 runs. ‡Mumbai Indians 178-5** (20 overs) (S. R. Tendulkar 35, S. S. Tiwary 44, A. T. Rayudu 55*; P. P. Ojha 3-26); **Deccan Chargers 115** (18.2 overs). MoM: A. T. Rayudu. *Ambati Rayudu and Saurabh Tiwary's fourth-wicket stand of 65, after the spinners Pragyan Ojha and Rahul Sharma had picked up three quick wickets following the powerplay, ensured a total too tall for the Chargers.*

At Kolkata, April 4, 2010. **Kings XI Punjab won by eight wickets. ‡Kolkata Knight Riders 200-3** (20 overs) (S. C. Ganguly 36, C. H. Gayle 88, M. K. Tiwary 35); **Kings XI Punjab 204-2** (18.2 overs) (D. P. M. D. Jayawardene 110*, K. C. Sangakkara 38, Yuvraj Singh 33*). MoM: D. P. M. D. Jayawardene. *Chris Gayle had made only 24 from as many balls by halfway, but woke up to shake and stir Punjab, smiting four successive sixes off a Ravi Bopara over that ended up costing 33. He finished with eight sixes in his 88 from 42 balls. Kolkata reached 200, but Mahela Jayawardene, opening in the place of the injured Shaun Marsh, captivated Eden Gardens with some sumptuous strokeplay in his maiden Twenty20 century.*

At Delhi, April 4, 2010. **Delhi Daredevils won by 37 runs. ‡Delhi Daredevils 184-5** (20 overs) (D. A. Warner 33, V. Sehwag 35, P. D. Collingwood 75*); **Royal Challengers Bangalore 147-9** (20 overs) (J. H. Kallis 54; A. Mishra 3-32, P. Sangwan 3-22). MoM: P. D. Collingwood. *Collingwood consolidated the early momentum of openers Sehwag and Warner, stealing the limelight with a wonderfully paced innings, which included seven sixes. Delhi's total proved enough on a placid pitch which favoured the slow bowlers: leg-spinner Amit Mishra became the holder of the purple cap for most wickets (he had 14; the leading run-scorer gets an orange one) as Bangalore slipped behind the required rate.*

At Nagpur, April 5, 2010. **Rajasthan Royals won by two runs. ‡Rajasthan Royals 159** (19.5 overs) (F. Y. Fazal 36, S. R. Watson 58; R. P. Singh 3-17); **Deccan Chargers 157** (19.5 overs) (A. C. Gilchrist 34, R. G. Sharma 73; S. K. Trivedi 3-16, S. K. Warne 4-21). MoM: S. K. Warne. *Despite Warne's best Twenty20 bowling figures, the Chargers still stood on the brink of victory, needing only six from the final six balls to pass a modest target… but Siddharth Trivedi, fired up by the screaming Warne at mid-off, delivered a near-flawless over in which three wickets fell, concluding with the dangerous Rohit Sharma.*

At Chennai, April 6, 2010. **Chennai Super Kings won by 24 runs. ‡Chennai Super Kings 165-4** (20 overs) (M. L. Hayden 35, M. S. Dhoni 31, S. Badrinath 30*); **Mumbai Indians 141-9** (20 overs) (S. R. Tendulkar 45, Harbhajan Singh 33). MoM: S. K. Raina. *Chennai stuttered to a decent total, but Mumbai struggled once Tendulkar was forced to retire after the ninth over by severe cramps and dehydration on a humid evening. He returned later, but the task was beyond even him as the table-toppers tasted defeat.*

At Jaipur, April 7, 2010. **Rajasthan Royals won by nine wickets. ‡Kings XI Punjab 153-6** (20 overs) (D. P. M. D. Jayawardene 44); **Rajasthan Royals 157-1** (15 overs) (M. J. Lumb 83, N. V. Ojha 44*). MoM: M. J. Lumb. *Back in Jaipur for the first time in nearly two years, Rajasthan maintained their 100% record there, with Michael Lumb (83 from 43 balls) despatching quick and slow bowlers alike and raising their 50 in 3.5 overs with his eighth four (of 16, two sixes). He was ably supported by Naman Ojha, and victory came with five overs remaining.*

At Kolkata, April 7, 2010. **Kolkata Knight Riders won by 14 runs. ‡Kolkata Knight Riders 181-3** (20 overs) (S. C. Ganguly 56, C. H. Gayle 40, A. D. Mathews 46*); **Delhi Daredevils 167-8** (20 overs) (V. Sehwag 64, G. Gambhir 47). MoM: S. C. Ganguly. *Ganguly played the winning hand here: first with a calm half-century that was a perfect foil to the aggression of Gayle, then in the field where, showing uncharacteristic agility at mid-off, he smartly picked up a firm stroke and ran out Gambhir to break a stand of 99 with Sehwag and stymie the fightback.*

At Bangalore, April 8, 2010. **Deccan Chargers won by seven wickets. Royal Challengers Bangalore 184-6** (20 overs) (J. H. Kallis 68, V. Kohli 58); **‡Deccan Chargers 186-3** (19.2 overs) (A. C. Gilchrist 32, T. L. Suman 78*, A. Symonds 53*). MoM: T. L. Suman. *The Chargers' death bowling was exposed once again as Bangalore fought back from 68-4 after 10.1 overs and stole 92 off the final 36 balls. But Tirumalasetti Suman chose the occasion to display his pedigree, steadily opening up before Andrew Symonds led the final push. Deccan picked up the first of the five successive wins they now needed to make the semis.*

At Mohali, April 9, 2010. **Kings XI Punjab won by six wickets.** ‡**Mumbai Indians 154-9** (20 overs) (A. T. Rayudu 33, J-P. Duminy 35; I. K. Pathan 3-29, P. P. Chawla 3-24); **Kings XI Punjab 158-4** (19.2 overs) (A. B. Barath 33, D. P. M. D. Jayawardene 31, K. C. Sangakkara 56). *MoM:* K. C. Sangakkara. *Eyes had rolled in India when Piyush Chawla was picked as their second spinner for the World Twenty20, but he answered his critics, triggering the Mumbai upper-order collapse with three wickets in successive overs from his leg-breaks.*

At Nagpur, April 10, 2010. **Deccan Chargers won by six wickets.** ‡**Chennai Super Kings 138-8** (20 overs) (S. K. Raina 52; R. J. Harris 3-18); **Deccan Chargers 139-4** (19.1 overs) (T. L. Suman 55). *MoM:* R. J. Harris. *Suman starred for the second match running with another half-century, this time a more composed one, to overhaul a small target on a hot afternoon on another slow pitch.*

At Bangalore, April 10, 2010. **Royal Challengers Bangalore won by seven wickets.** Kolkata Knight Riders **160-9** (20 overs) (S. C. Ganguly 33, C. H. Gayle 34, B. B. McCullum 45; R. Vinay Kumar 3-23); ‡**Royal Challengers Bangalore 162-3** (17.1 overs) (R. Dravid 52, R. V. Uthappa 50*). *MoM:* R. Vinay Kumar. *Kolkata got off to a blazing start, but Vinay Kumar played a vital hand in restricting the total, which was overhauled without much bother by the controlled aggression of Dravid, with his first fifty of the season, and another example of the brutal force of Uthappa, whose 50* came from 22 balls.*

At Delhi, April 11, 2010. **Kings XI Punjab won by seven wickets.** ‡**Delhi Daredevils 111** (19.4 overs) (I. K. Pathan 3-24); **Kings XI Punjab 112-3** (18.4 overs) (D. P. M. D. Jayawardene 38, K. C. Sangakkara 33). *MoM:* P. P. Chawla. *Delhi's top order faltered, the middle crumbled, and Punjab chased down a small target without much fuss.*

At Jaipur, April 11, 2010. **Mumbai Indians won by 37 runs. Mumbai Indians 174-5** (20 overs) (S. R. Tendulkar 89*, J-P. Duminy 31; S. R. Watson 3-37); ‡**Rajasthan Royals 137-8** (20 overs) (A. P. Dole 30). *MoM:* S. R. Tendulkar. *The previous time Mumbai had played in Jaipur, in 2008, they lost the match and the opportunity to make the semis – but Tendulkar made sure there would be no repeat, batting through for his fifth half-century, to offset the early inroads made by Watson, who snatched three wickets in his first two overs. Rajasthan slipped to their first defeat at this ground in their ninth game.*

At Nagpur, April 12, 2010. **Deccan Chargers won by 13 runs. Deccan Chargers 151-6** (20 overs) (R. G. Sharma 51, M. D. Mishra 41; D. W. Steyn 3-18); ‡**Royal Challengers Bangalore 138** (19.4 overs) (R. Dravid 49, R. V. Uthappa 34). *MoM:* H. S. Bansal. *This was a low-scoring thriller: Dale Steyn returned to the ground where he took 10-108 in a Test in February and began a top-order collapse with three wickets in his first two overs, but his side stuttered through the chase. They reached the last two overs needing 18 with four wickets left. Although Uthappa was still there, Harmeet Singh Bansal bowled him with a clever slower delivery, and all four wickets went for four runs to keep the Chargers' semi-final hopes alive.*

At Brabourne Stadium, Mumbai, April 13, 2010. **Mumbai Indians won by 39 runs.** ‡**Mumbai Indians 183-4** (20 overs) (S. R. Tendulkar 30, S. S. Tiwary 38, K. A. Pollard 45*); **Delhi Daredevils 144-7** (20 overs) (D. A. Warner 31, A. B. McDonald 33*). *MoM:* K. A. Pollard. *Kieron Pollard unleashed his ferocious power with three sixes in a 25-run final over from Andrew McDonald, to offset a sedate start: 75 came in the final five overs. Delhi started brightly, but the later batsmen failed to keep up the momentum. Mumbai were the first team to reach the semi-finals, which they had never managed previously in the IPL.*

At Chennai, April 13, 2010. **Chennai Super Kings won by nine wickets.** ‡**Kolkata Knight Riders 139-8** (20 overs) (A. D. Mathews 48; R. Ashwin 3-16); **Chennai Super Kings 143-1** (13.3 overs) (M. Vijay 50*, S. K. Raina 78*). *MoM:* R. Ashwin. *For the second match running, off-spinner Ravichandran Ashwin took the new ball and grabbed two wickets in an over. Kolkata never really recovered from 22-4 after six overs (the lowest powerplay score of the season). In reply, Murali Vijay and Suresh Raina shared a rapid unbroken partnership of 137 in 13 overs.*

At Jaipur, April 14, 2010. **Royal Challengers Bangalore won by five wickets.** ‡**Rajasthan Royals 130-6** (20 overs) (A. S. Raut 32*); **Royal Challengers Bangalore 132-5** (15.4 overs) (K. P. Pietersen 62). *MoM:* K. P. Pietersen. *Pietersen's 24-ball fifty was the solitary highlight of an otherwise forgettable encounter, in which Rajasthan never had any control, their batsmen like rabbits in the headlights against some disciplined bowling.*

At Chennai, April 15, 2010. **Delhi Daredevils won by six wickets.** ‡**Chennai Super Kings 112-9** (20 overs) (S. Badrinath 30; A. Nehra 3-26); **Delhi Daredevils 113-4** (18.4 overs) (G. Gambhir 57*).

MoM: G. Gambhir. *At 38-4, chasing a modest target on a humid day, Delhi seemed to have imploded – but Gambhir and Mithun Manhas fought dehydration and Dhoni's clever field-placing to chalk up a hard-fought victory which had seemed a formality after Chennai equalled their lowest IPL score.*

At Dharmasala, April 16, 2010. **Deccan Chargers won by five wickets. Kings XI Punjab 174-3** (20 overs) (D. P. M. D. Jayawardene 93*, K. C. Sangakkara 52); ‡**Deccan Chargers 178-5** (19.1 overs) (T. L. Suman 43, R. G. Sharma 68*). *MoM:* R. G. Sharma. *On one of the most beautiful cricket grounds in the world, Rohit Sharma kept calm to carve a spectacular half-century. Jayawardene had earlier stroked 93* from 62 balls as an opener.*

At Bangalore, April 17, 2010. **Mumbai Indians won by 57 runs. Mumbai Indians 191-4** (20 overs) (R. McLaren 40, A. T. Rayudu 46, J-P. Duminy 42*); ‡**Royal Challengers Bangalore 134-9** (20 overs) (V. Kohli 37; K. A. Pollard 3-28). *MoM:* R. McLaren. *Two explosions around the Chinnaswamy Stadium reportedly injured eight people. After an hour-long delay Bangalore conceded a big total, then never looked like overhauling it.*

At Kolkata, April 17, 2010. **Kolkata Knight Riders won by eight wickets. ‡Rajasthan Royals 132-9** (20 overs) (S. R. Watson 44; J. D. Unadkat 3-26); **Kolkata Knight Riders 133-2** (16.1 overs) (S. C. Ganguly 75*, C. A. Pujara 45*). *MoM:* J. D. Unadkat. *Left-armer Jaidev Unadkat from Saurashtra, only 18 and rated by Wasim Akram as an emerging talent even though he had not played a first-class match, showed impressive pace and control to put Rajasthan on the back foot: they never made it on to the front.*

At Dharmasala, April 18, 2010. **Chennai Super Kings won by six wickets. Kings XI Punjab 192-3** (20 overs) (S. E. Marsh 88*, K. C. Sangakkara 33, I. K. Pathan 44*); ‡**Chennai Super Kings 195-4** (19.4 overs) (S. K. Raina 46, S. Badrinath 53, M. S. Dhoni 54*). *MoM:* M. S. Dhoni. *Chennai needed to win to qualify for the semis for the third straight season, and their captain Dhoni rose to the occasion with a pumped-up half-century, remembered for his emotional celebration (an upper-cut to the jaw) after he blasted 30 runs off the final two overs to overhaul a steep target, which owed much to Shaun Marsh's calculated assault (88 from 57 balls). But the afternoon, which started with the players being blessed by the Dalai Lama, belonged to Dhoni.*

At Delhi, April 18, 2010. **Deccan Chargers won by 11 runs. ‡Deccan Chargers 145-7** (20 overs) (A. Symonds 54); **Delhi Daredevils 134-7** (20 overs) (P. D. Collingwood 51*). *MoM:* A. Symonds. *Gilchrist's men achieved the fifth successive victory they needed for an unlikely semi-final berth. Symonds resurrected the Chargers' innings, then Chaminda Vaas used his vast experience, smartly changing the pace. Two of Rohit Sharma's three catches were blinders, and Delhi failed to recover.*

At Kolkata, April 19, 2010. **Kolkata Knight Riders won by nine wickets. ‡Mumbai Indians 133-8** (20 overs) (S. S. Tiwary 46); **Kolkata Knight Riders 135-1** (17.3 overs) (S. C. Ganguly 42, B. B. McCullum 57*). *MoM:* M. Kartik. *Kolkata secured an easy victory in the only dead rubber of the third IPL season, against an understrength Mumbai team lacking Tendulkar and four other regulars ahead of the semi-final.*

Semi-finals

At Dr D. Y. Patil Sports Academy, Mumbai, April 21, 2010. **Mumbai Indians won by 35 runs. ‡Mumbai Indians 184-5** (20 overs) (A. T. Rayudu 40, S. S. Tiwary 52*, K. A. Pollard 33*); **Royal Challengers Bangalore 149-9** (20 overs) (L. R. P. L. Taylor 31*; K. A. Pollard 3-17). *MoM:* K. A. Pollard. *Two big fellas – Saurabh Tiwary and Kieron Pollard – played the axemen to slay the Bangalore bowlers with a mixture of brute force and clever placement, plundering 77 in the final five overs after only 26 had come in the previous five. Bangalore lost their big hitters Pietersen and Uthappa by halfway, and Ross Taylor couldn't rescue them on his own as Mumbai reached the final for the first time.*

At Dr D. Y. Patil Sports Academy, Mumbai, April 22, 2010. **Chennai Super Kings won by 38 runs. ‡Chennai Super Kings 142-7** (20 overs) (S. Badrinath 37, M. S. Dhoni 30; R. J. Harris 3-29); **Deccan Chargers 104** (19.2 overs) (D. E. Bollinger 4-13). *MoM:* D. E. Bollinger. *This was a lame affair, and the Chargers could blame only themselves for a hopeless response to a modest Chennai total. Gilchrist continued his horrible batting form – only 45 runs in his last six innings – and the menacing Bollinger ended the champions' hopes of retaining their title.*

Third-place play-off

At Dr D. Y. Patil Sports Academy, Mumbai, April 24, 2010. **Royal Challengers Bangalore won by nine wickets. ‡Deccan Chargers 82** (18.3 overs) (Anirudh Singh 40; A. Kumble 4-16); **Royal Challengers Bangalore 86-1** (13.5 overs) (R. Dravid 35*). *MoM:* A. Kumble. *In probably the most one-sided match of the tournament, the Chargers embarrassed themselves by logging the lowest total of the season, with nine single-digit scores.*

FINAL

MUMBAI INDIANS v CHENNAI SUPER KINGS

At Dr D. Y. Patil Sports Academy, Mumbai, April 25, 2010 (floodlit). Chennai Super Kings won by 22 runs. Toss: Chennai Super Kings.

After a scratchy start, Raina settled down to cobble together a match-turning fourth-wicket stand of 72 with Dhoni, his captain. Finally Raina hit the accelerator to help Chennai reach 168, the highest total in the three IPL finals so far. It soon became a mountain for Mumbai, as they committed a tactical faux pas by batting Nayar, Harbhajan Singh and Duminy ahead of the dangerous Pollard – who underlined the blunder when he did come in, with 55 needed from the final 18 deliveries, and blasted 22 in the next over from Bollinger. Pollard threatened to make the evening his own, but fell to a smart piece of thinking by Dhoni, who put Hayden almost in line with the bowler's arm at straight mid-off; Pollard obligingly popped the ball straight to him.

Man of the Match: S. K. Raina. *Man of the Series:* S. R. Tendulkar.

Chennai Super Kings		*B*	*4*	*6*
M. Vijay *c 6 b 11*	26	19	1	2
M. L. Hayden *c 5 b 8*	17	31	1	1
S. K. Raina *not out*	57	35	3	3
S. Badrinath *c 10 b 11*	14	11	2	0
*†M. S. Dhoni *c 11 b 9*	22	15	2	1
J. A. Morkel *run out*	15	6	1	1
A. Srikkanth *not out*	6	3	1	0
L-b 3, w 8	11			

6 overs: 40-0   (20 overs)   168-5

1/44 2/47 3/67 4/139 5/157

R. Ashwin, S. B. Jakati, D. E. Bollinger and M. Muralitharan did not bat.

Harbhajan Singh 4–0–30–0; Malinga 4–0–33–0; Zaheer Khan 4–0–34–1; Fernando 4–0–23–2; Pollard 4–0–45–1.

Mumbai Indians		*B*	*4*	*6*
S. Dhawan *c 5 b 10*	0	8	0	0
*S. R. Tendulkar *c 1 b 9*	48	45	7	0
A. M. Nayar *run out*	27	26	1	2
Harbhajan Singh *lbw b 3*	1	2	0	0
†A. T. Rayudu *run out*	21	14	1	1
S. S. Tiwary *c 3 b 9*	0	2	0	0
J-P. Duminy *c 9 b 11*	6	7	0	0
K. A. Pollard *c 2 b 6*	27	10	3	2
Zaheer Khan *run out*	1	3	0	0
S. L. Malinga *not out*	1	1	0	0
C. R. D. Fernando *not out*	2	2	0	0
B 1, l-b 6, w 5	12			

6 overs: 33-1   (20 overs)   146-9

1/1 2/67 3/73 4/99 5/100 6/114 7/142 8/142 9/143

Ashwin 4–1–24–0; Bollinger 4–0–31–1; Morkel 3–0–20–1; Muralitharan 4–0–17–1; Jakati 3–0–26–2; Raina 2–0–21–1.

Umpires: R. E. Koertzen and S. J. A. Taufel.   Third umpire: S. Ravi.
Referee: S. Venkataraghavan.

IPL FINALS

2007-08	RAJASTHAN ROYALS beat Chennai Super Kings by three wickets in Mumbai.
2008-09	DECCAN CHARGERS beat Royal Challengers Bangalore by six runs at Johannesburg.
2009-10	CHENNAI SUPER KINGS beat Mumbai Indians by 22 runs in Mumbai.

DOMESTIC CRICKET IN INDIA, 2009-10

R. Mohan

Indian cricket did not summer well in 2010. The Indian Premier League's image took a hit, through the alleged machinations of its commissioner, Lalit Modi, while Team India made an early exit from the World Twenty20 in the Caribbean. The Twenty20 format remained the most popular in India, but its administration and practitioners were no longer in such favour. Though the third IPL season was a financial hit, its playing standards were questioned after the top Indian stars flopped in the ICC's global event.

Meanwhile, in the traditional Ranji and Duleep domestic finals, two remarkably close contests made many fans proud. For the second year running, Wasim Jaffer led both Mumbai and West Zone to victory, but the Ranji final had its second-closest finish, when Mumbai retained their title by a mere six runs on the fourth afternoon against Karnataka.

In the Duleep final, **West Zone** achieved the biggest successful fourth-innings run-chase in first-class history, passing a target of 536 with three wickets to spare. Though Yusuf Pathan rode his luck scoring 210 not out, following a first-innings 108, he evoked the striking prowess and destructive capabilities of modern batsmen bred on 20-over cricket's compulsory aggression. Typecast as a Twenty20 specialist, Pathan demonstrated how quickly such players could gather runs in the longer format. **South Zone** were left ruing their abysmal catching, however; he was dropped at least five times. When he feared running out of partners, Pathan struck successive sixes to reach his double-century, and finished the job himself.

Security concerns in Hyderabad, in the wake of agitation for a separate state, saw the Duleep final begin behind closed doors before the police agreed to allow spectators in. The need for watchfulness has become part of the Indian environment; bomb blasts around the Bangalore stadium during the IPL highlighted the kind of lives now lived in Asia.

The Ranji final had been a more joyous affair, played in the ancient royal city of Mysore in front of capacity crowds, who urged home team **Karnataka** to stop **Mumbai** winning their

> Blame it on
> modern cricket
> and television

39th title. In keeping with the lively thinking characteristic of cricket in Karnataka, a greentop led to some exciting first-innings action favouring the fast bowlers. As the pitch settled, so did the batsmen's nerves, but in the end the home side's failure to keep their cool against the second new ball cost them the game. Chasing 338 after conceding a lead of 103, Karnataka had rallied round a century from Manish Pandey; they were in sight of victory, needing 42 with four wickets in hand. But the Mumbai quicks' aggressive body language and sledging seemed to put them off, as nervous batsmen kept swiping across the line at the new ball. Ill feeling between the teams spilled over when Mumbai's celebrating players gestured at the crowd. Blame it on modern cricket and the poor example set by international teams on television.

Karnataka's Test star Rahul Dravid, who was touring Bangladesh during the Ranji final, called for more space between first-class matches – it was often only three days – so that bowlers were not run into the ground looking for outright results on slow pitches in a hot country. He also questioned the amount of cricket, at all levels. The crowding of the domestic calendar was illustrated by the fact that there were six different competitions in three different formats over just five months. Respected as a voice of reason, Dravid signed off by reiterating the need for true sporting pitches, which might prevent the dip in performance when Indians play international cricket on bouncy surfaces – a weakness once again exposed in the Caribbean. More than one IPL coach blamed low domestic standards for their own team's poor showing.

FIRST-CLASS AVERAGES, 2009-10

BATTING (600 runs)

	M	I	NO	R	HS	100s	Avge	Ct/St
R. Dravid (*Karnataka & India*)	7	11	3	909	209*	3	113.62	12
V. Sehwag (*Rest & India*)	6	8	0	791	293	4	98.87	1
†S. S. Tiwary (*Jharkhand & East Zone*)	6	9	2	615	136	3	87.85	5
C. A. Pujara (*Saurashtra & West Zone*)	6	10	1	741	204*	2	82.33	1
R. G. Sharma (*Mumbai & West Zone*)	8	10	1	718	309*	3	79.77	2
†D. S. Jadhav (*Assam & East Zone*)	8	10	2	631	165*	3	78.87	4
K. D. Karthik (*Tamil Nadu & South Zone*)	7	10	0	776	183	4	77.60	15/2
Sunny Singh (*Haryana*)	6	9	1	617	312	3	77.12	4
M. Vijay (*Tamil Nadu, Rest & India*)	9	12	0	770	154	2	64.16	7
G. Satish (*Karnataka & South Zone*)	8	13	2	698	141	2	63.45	5
A. M. Rahane (*Mumbai & West Zone*)	11	17	3	887	265*	3	63.35	1
†P. A. Patel (*Gujarat & West Zone*)	8	13	0	813	166	3	62.53	24/1
†C. R. Pathak (*Saurashtra & West Zone*)	7	12	0	735	138	3	61.25	9
†A. M. Nayar (*Mumbai & West Zone*)	8	11	1	610	259	2	61.00	3
M. K. Pandey (*Karnataka & South Zone*)	10	16	0	956	194	4	59.75	14
S. Badrinath (*Tamil Nadu, S. Zone, Rest & India*)	10	14	0	800	250	3	57.14	7
†A. Mukund (*Tamil Nadu & South Zone*)	9	14	0	689	257	2	49.21	6
†U. Kaul (*Punjab & North Zone*)	9	15	2	625	123	1	48.07	24
Wasim Jaffer (*Mumbai & West Zone*)	13	19	2	801	165*	3	47.11	17
M. Kaif (*Uttar Pradesh & Central Zone*)	10	17	2	684	202*	2	45.60	10
Parvinder Singh (*Uttar Pradesh & Central Zone*)	10	16	0	682	122	4	42.62	2
K. B. Arun Karthik (*Tamil Nadu & South Zone*)	10	15	0	637	118	1	42.46	11
K. B. Pawan (*Karnataka & South Zone*)	10	17	1	651	152	2	40.68	7
S. O. Kukreja (*Mumbai*)	11	17	1	617	122	1	38.56	4

BOWLING (25 wickets)

	Style	O	M	R	W	BB	5W/i	Avge
A. Konwar (*Assam*)	OB	251.3	51	542	31	6-72	2	17.48
S. V. Bahutule (*Assam*)	LBG	239.2	58	536	28	6-61	2	19.14
Pankaj Singh (*Rajasthan & Central Zone*)	RM	223.4	47	638	32	7-56	2	19.93
R. Vinay Kumar (*Karnataka & South Zone*)	RM	340.4	75	1,058	53	8-32	3	19.96
I. K. Pathan (*Baroda & West Zone*)	LFM	170	21	647	31	5-100	1	20.87
M. S. Gony (*Punjab & North Zone*)	RM	229	47	702	33	5-21	2	21.27
A. N. Ahmed (*Assam & East Zone*)	RFM	244.4	79	615	28	5-40	3	21.96
V. Malik (*Himachal Pradesh & North Zone*)	RM	275.2	81	726	33	6-33	2	22.00
A. Mithun (*Karnataka & South Zone*)	RFM	336.1	56	1,210	52	6-71	3	23.26
L. Ablash (*Punjab*)	RM	259.5	47	860	36	6-79	3	23.88
R. R. Bose (*Bengal & East Zone*)	RFM	233.5	50	748	30	5-18	2	24.93
C. Ganapathy (*Tamil Nadu & South Zone*)	RM	253	69	682	25	5-61	2	27.28
Iqbal Abdulla (*Mumbai*)	SLA	359.1	89	978	35	4-48	0	27.94
P. P. Chawla (*Uttar Pradesh & Central Zone*)	LBG	321.2	55	1,059	36	5-73	1	29.41
D. S. Kulkarni (*Mumbai & West Zone*)	RFM	367	96	983	33	5-58	1	29.78
A. Absolem (*Hyderabad & South Zone*)	RM	278.5	52	865	29	5-89	2	29.82
Dhiraj Kumar (*Orissa*)	SLA	216.3	31	751	25	4-29	0	30.04
Zaheer Khan (*Mumbai & India*)	LFM	229.2	44	835	27	5-72	1	30.92
S. M. Fallah (*Maharashtra*)	LM	226.3	34	807	26	8-98	2	31.03
R. P. Singh (*Uttar Pradesh & Central Zone*)	LFM	367.5	85	1,113	35	4-47	0	31.80
S. Aravind (*Karnataka & South Zone*)	LM	300.5	67	973	30	5-49	1	32.43
P. Awana (*Delhi & North Zone*)	RM	264.1	43	950	29	5-40	1	32.75
R. Aushik Srinivas (*Tamil Nadu & South Zone*)	SLA	289.1	78	839	25	7-107	1	33.56

IRANI CUP, 2009-10

Ranji Trophy Champions (Mumbai) v Rest of India

At Nagpur, October 1–5, 2009. **Drawn.** Rest of India won by virtue of their first-innings lead. ‡**Rest of India 260 and 352-4** (A. Mukund 126); **Mumbai 230** (M. M. Patel 5-70). *Rest of India claimed the Irani Cup for the fourth year running after the fifth day was abandoned because of a waterlogged outfield. Abhinav Mukund and Murali Vijay (91) opened their second innings with 227 as the Rest batted on to avoid any risk of a run-chase. Test bowler Sreesanth was fined 60% of his match fee after a row with Mumbai's Dhawal Kulkarni.*

RANJI TROPHY, 2009-10

Elite Group A	P	W	L	D	Pts		Elite Group B	P	W	L	D	Pts
Tamil Nadu	7	2	0	5	26		Karnataka	6	4	0	2	28
Punjab	7	2	1	4	19		Uttar Pradesh	6	2	1	3	18
Mumbai	7	1	0	6	19		Delhi	6	2	1	3	16
Railways	7	1	0	6	14		Baroda	6	2	1	3	15
Orissa	7	0	1	6	12		Bengal	6	1	1	4	11
Himachal Pradesh	7	1	3	3	10		Saurashtra	6	0	3	3	7
Gujarat	7	1	3	3	10		Maharashtra	6	0	4	2	4
Hyderabad	7	0	0	7	7							

The top three from each Group were joined in the quarter-finals by the Plate semi-final winners.

Quarter-finals: Assam drew with Uttar Pradesh; Delhi drew with Tamil Nadu; Haryana drew with Mumbai; Karnataka drew with Punjab. Uttar Pradesh, Delhi, Mumbai and Karnataka reached the semi-finals by virtue of their first-innings leads.

Semi-finals: Karnataka drew with Uttar Pradesh; Mumbai drew with Delhi. Karnataka and Mumbai reached the final by virtue of their first-innings leads.

Final: Mumbai beat Karnataka by six runs.

Plate Group A	P	W	L	D	Pts		Plate Group B	P	W	L	D	Pts
Assam	5	1	1	3	13		Haryana	4	2	0	2	17
Tripura	5	1	1	3	12		Andhra	4	1	1	2	10
Vidarbha	5	1	0	4	11		Madhya Pradesh	4	1	0	3	9
Goa	5	0	0	5	11		Jammu and Kashmir	4	1	2	1	6
Jharkhand	5	0	0	5	9		Kerala	4	0	2	2	2
Rajasthan	5	1	2	2	7							

Services were expelled from Plate Group B after refusing to travel to Kashmir.

Semi-finals: Assam beat Andhra by five wickets; Haryana drew with Tripura but advanced by virtue of their first-innings lead.

No final was held, as Assam and Haryana advanced to the Elite League quarter-finals; they were also promoted to the Elite League in 2010-11 (replacing Hyderabad and Maharashtra).

Outright win = 5pts; lead on first innings in a drawn match = 3pts; deficit on first innings in a drawn match = 1pt; abandoned or very little play = 1pt each; win by an innings or ten wickets = 1 bonus pt. Teams tied on points were ranked on most wins, and then on quotient (runs scored per wicket divided by runs conceded per wicket).

Elite League Group A

At Ahmedabad (Sardar Vallabhbhai Patel), November 3–6, 2009. **Gujarat won by 159 runs.** ‡**Gujarat 270 and 301-6 dec** (N. K. Patel 107); **Orissa 192 and 220.** *Gujarat 5pts.*

At Secunderabad, November 3–6, 2009. **Drawn.** ‡**Hyderabad 328 and 189** (A. K. Thakur 5-22); **Himachal Pradesh 350** (P. Dogra 123) **and 136-8** (P. P. Ojha 5-52). *Hyderabad 1pt, Himachal Pradesh 3pts.*

At Chandigarh, November 3–6, 2009. **Drawn. ‡Punjab 259** (R. Inder Singh 104) **and 311-7; Mumbai 471-9 dec** (R. R. Powar 125*). *Punjab 1pt, Mumbai 3pts. No. 9 Ramesh Powar added 163 for Mumbai's eighth wicket with Onkar Khanwilkar (87).*

At Delhi (Karnail Singh), November 3–6, 2009. **Drawn. ‡Railways 327** (S. B. Bangar 163*) **and 178-2; Tamil Nadu 337** (S. Badrinath 111). *Railways 1pt, Tamil Nadu 3pts. Tamil Nadu's Abhinav Mukund, who had previously bowled a single first-class over in his career, took 3-5 in 2.4 overs in Railways' first innings.*

At Ahmedabad (Sardar Vallabhbhai Patel), November 10–13, 2009. **Drawn. ‡Gujarat 343** (P. A. Patel 166) **and 165-4** (J. D. Desai 108); *Tamil Nadu 419-8 dec. Gujarat 1pt, Tamil Nadu 3pts.*

At Mumbai (Brabourne), November 10–13, 2009. **Drawn. Mumbai 307-4 dec** (Wasim Jaffer 165*); **‡Orissa 243-8.** *Mumbai 1pt, Orissa 1pt.*

At Mohali, November 10–13, 2009. **Drawn. Punjab 221** (M. P. Arjun 6-47) **and 307-9 dec** (V. Bhalla 116*; Abdul Khader 5-101); **‡Hyderabad 193 and 254-7.** *Punjab 3pts, Hyderabad 1pt. Pankaj Dharmani (Punjab) became the seventh man to pass 7,000 Ranji runs. Vishwas Bhalla scored 116* on first-class debut, after coming in at 92-5.*

At Delhi (Karnail Singh), November 10–13, 2009. **Drawn. ‡Railways 419** (T. P. Singh 102; Sarandeep Singh 7-120); **Himachal Pradesh 145-4.** *Railways 1pt, Himachal Pradesh 1pt.*

At Hyderabad, November 17–20, 2009. **Drawn. ‡Hyderabad 236** (S. K. Trivedi 5-39) **and 2-0; Gujarat 536** (P. A. Patel 105, R. H. Bhatt 186). *Hyderabad 1pt, Gujarat 3pts.*

At Mumbai (Bandra Kurla), November 17–20, 2009. **Mumbai won by 85 runs. Mumbai 162** (V. Malik 6-33) **and 335-7 dec** (A. B. Agarkar 102*); **‡Himachal Pradesh 246 and 166.** *Mumbai 5pts.*

At Bhubaneswar, November 17–20, 2009. **Drawn. Railways 307-8 dec; ‡Orissa 132-4.** *Orissa 1pt, Railways 1pt.*

At Amritsar, November 17–20, 2009. **Tamil Nadu won by an innings and 45 runs. ‡Punjab 228 and 248** (R. Ashwin 5-116); **Tamil Nadu 521-9 dec** (M. Vijay 148, K. D. Karthik 117). *Tamil Nadu 6pts.*

At Dharmasala, November 24–27, 2009. **Tamil Nadu won by 91 runs. ‡Tamil Nadu 293-8 dec** (R. Ashwin 107*) **and 319; Himachal Pradesh 366 and 155** (C. Ganapathy 5-61). *Tamil Nadu 5pts.*

At Hyderabad, November 24–27, 2009. **Drawn. Orissa 276 and 243-5 dec; ‡Hyderabad 199 and 205-9.** *Hyderabad 1pt, Orissa 3pts.*

At Mohali, November 24–27, 2009. **Punjab won by an innings and 32 runs. Gujarat 160** (L. Ablash 6-79) **and 252; ‡Punjab 444** (T. Kohli 118; S. G. Yadav 6-123). *Punjab 6pts.*

At Delhi (Karnail Singh), November 24–27, 2009. **Drawn. ‡Railways 187 and 309; Mumbai 284** (R. G. Sharma 101; M. Kartik 5-81) **and 69-0.** *Railways 1pt, Mumbai 3pts.*

At Valsad, December 1–4, 2009. **Railways won by an innings and five runs. Gujarat 91 and 295** (N. K. Patel 102); **‡Railways 391** (S. B. Bangar 109). *Railways 6pts.*

At Hyderabad, December 1–4, 2009. **Drawn. ‡Hyderabad 266 and 276-6; Mumbai 521-2 dec** (S. O. Kukreja 122, A. M. Rahane 265*, Wasim Jaffer 107*). *Hyderabad 1pt, Mumbai 3pts. Ajinkya Rahane, who scored his second double-century, added 258 for Mumbai's second wicket with Sahil Kukreja, and 236* in 42 overs for the third with Wasim Jaffer.*

At Sambalpur, December 1–4, 2009. **Drawn. ‡Tamil Nadu 361** (K. B. Arun Karthik 118) **and 375-8** (K. D. Karthik 152); **Orissa 327** (S. S. Das 119). *Orissa 1pt, Tamil Nadu 3pts.*

At Mohali, December 1–3, 2009. **Punjab won by eight wickets. Himachal Pradesh 197** (M. S. Gony 5-47) **and 82** (M. S. Gony 5-21); **‡Punjab 186** (V. Malik 5-68) **and 97-2.** *Punjab 5pts.*

At Surat, December 8–10, 2009. **Himachal Pradesh won by six wickets. Gujarat 234 and 87** (M. Sharma 5-31); **‡Himachal Pradesh 182** (S. K. Trivedi 6-32) **and 141-4.** *Himachal Pradesh 5pts.*

At Hyderabad, December 8–11, 2009. **Drawn. Railways 305** (A. Absolem 5-89) **and 363-5** (T. P. Singh 100*); **‡Hyderabad 303.** *Hyderabad 1pt, Railways 3pts.*

At Mumbai (Bandra Kurla), December 8–11, 2009. **Drawn. ‡Tamil Nadu 501** (S. Badrinath 250, C. Ganapathy 126) **and 255-3** (M. Vijay 154); **Mumbai 366** (Wasim Jaffer 141; R. Aushik Srinivas

7-107). *Mumbai 1pt, Tamil Nadu 3pts. Subramaniam Badrinath batted 11 hours 11 minutes for his fourth and highest double-hundred. He and Chandrasekharan Ganapathy came together at 50-5 and added 329 for Tamil Nadu's sixth wicket. Later, 16-year-old slow left-armer Aushik Srinivas bowled a spell of 8.1–4–11–6 as Mumbai collapsed from 336-4 to 366 all out.*

At Chandigarh, December 8–11, 2009. **Drawn. Orissa 283** (L. Ablash 6-110) **and 247-8 dec** (L. Ablash 5-73); ‡**Punjab 177** (B. C. Mohanty 6-65) **and 192-4.** *Punjab 1pt, Orissa 3pts.*

At Dharmasala, December 15–18, 2009. **Drawn. Himachal Pradesh 125 and 486** (V. A. Indulkar 165); ‡**Orissa 316** (H. M. Das 144; M. Sharma 5-102) **and 183-8** (A. K. Thakur 6-38). *Himachal Pradesh 1pt, Orissa 3pts.*

At Hyderabad, December 15–18, 2009. **Drawn. Hyderabad 347** (A. T. Rayudu 106) **and 148-2** (Abhinav Kumar 103*); ‡**Tamil Nadu 785** (A. Mukund 257, S. Badrinath 122, C. Ganapathy 126; A. Absolem 5-114). *Hyderabad 1pt, Tamil Nadu 3pts. Shashank Nag was dismissed by the first ball of the match. Abhinav Mukund batted for nine hours 27 minutes for his second double-hundred and added 259 for the third wicket with Badrinath. There were six individual fifties in the innings, which at 785 was the eighth-highest in Ranji history; off-spinner Vishal Sharma had figures of 54–7–215–0. Hyderabad were relegated to the Plate League for the first time while Tamil Nadu topped their group.*

At Mumbai (Brabourne), December 15–18, 2009. **Drawn. Mumbai 648-6 dec** (S. H. Marathe 144, R. G. Sharma 309*) **and 180-2**; ‡**Gujarat 502** (P. A. Patel 149, B. D. Thaker 122). *Mumbai 3pts, Gujarat 1pt. Rohit Sharma converted his second double-century into a maiden triple, hitting 38 fours and four sixes. He added 342 for Mumbai's fourth wicket with Sushant Marathe. Leg-spinner Salil Yadav conceded 201 in 50 overs. In reply, Parthiv Patel and Bhavik Thaker put on 266 for Gujarat's fourth wicket.*

At Delhi (Karnail Singh), December 15–18, 2009. **Drawn. ‡Railways 276** (R. Sharma 6-92) **and 230-4** (S. B. Bangar 115*); **Punjab 401** (U. Kaul 123). *Railways 1pt, Punjab 3pts.*

Elite League Group B

At Vadodara (Moti Bagh), November 3–6, 2009. **Drawn. ‡Delhi 591** (S. Dhawan 224); **Baroda 326** (S. Narwal 5-71) **and 233-4.** *Baroda 1pt, Delhi 3pts. Shikhar Dhawan's maiden double-century lasted ten hours 38 minutes. Delhi wicketkeeper Punit Bisht took seven catches in Baroda's first innings (equalling the record for catches by an Indian keeper), and two more when they followed on.*

At Pune, November 3–6, 2009. **Bengal won by seven wickets. ‡Maharashtra 179** (R. R. Bose 5-67) **and 319** (H. H. Khadiwale 114; R. R. Bose 5-57); **Bengal 325 and 175-3.** *Bengal 5pts.*

At Meerut (Bhamashah), November 3–6, 2009. **Karnataka won by 185 runs. Karnataka 405** (M. K. Pandey 194) **and 311-5 dec; ‡Uttar Pradesh 279** (A. Mithun 6-86) **and 252** (A. Mithun 5-95). *Karnataka 5pts. Rahul Dravid (97) and Manish Pandey joined forces at 27-3 and added 273 for Karnataka's fourth wicket. Abhimanyu Mithun, a 20-year-old seamer, took 11-181 on first-class debut, including a second-innings hat-trick.*

At Kolkata (Eden Gardens), November 10–13, 2009. **Drawn. Baroda 307 and 458-8** (S. S. Parab 154); ‡**Bengal 293.** *Bengal 1pt, Baroda 3pts. Sourav Ganguly passed 15,000 first-class runs during his 76 for Bengal.*

At Delhi (Roshanara), November 10–13, 2009. **Drawn. Delhi 154** (R. Vinay Kumar 8-32) **and 277** (S. Dhawan 100; S. Aravind 5-71); ‡**Karnataka 260 and 149-6.** *Delhi 1pt, Karnataka 3pts. Vinay Kumar took 11-102 in the match, including 8-32, the best innings return of the season.*

At Rajkot (Madhavrao Scindia), November 10–13, 2009. **Drawn. ‡Uttar Pradesh 395** (S. S. Shukla 119, Parvinder Singh 122; R. V. Dhruve 5-107) **and 148-9 dec;** **Saurashtra 267 and 155-5.** *Saurashtra 1pt, Uttar Pradesh 3pts.*

At Mysore, November 17–20, 2009. **Drawn. Bengal 324** (R. B. Banerjee 107) **and 213-6;** ‡**Karnataka 523-9 dec** (K. B. Pawan 134, A. A. Verma 157, C. M. Gautam 108*; S. S. Lahiri 5-157). *Karnataka 3pts, Bengal 1pt. Kolar Pawan and Amit Verma added 249 for Karnataka's third wicket.*

At Rajkot (Madhavrao Scindia), November 17–20, 2009. **Drawn. ‡Saurashtra 544-3 dec** (S. H. Kotak 103, C. A. Pujara 204*, R. A. Jadeja 122*); **Maharashtra 289 and 162-5** (K. M. Jadhav

111*). *Saurashtra 3pts, Maharashtra 1pt. Cheteshwar Pujara scored his second double-hundred and added 272* for the fourth wicket with Ravi Jadeja, exactly doubling Saurashtra's total.*

At Mohan Nagar, November 17–20, 2009. **Drawn. ‡Baroda 234 and 331; Uttar Pradesh 240 and 8-1.** *Uttar Pradesh 3pts, Baroda 1pt.*

At Kolkata (Eden Gardens), November 24–27, 2009. **Drawn. Saurashtra 650-9 dec** (C. R. Pathak 118, S. D. Jogiyani 103); **‡Bengal 456** (A. S. Das 144, M. K. Tiwary 107) **and 135-1.** *Bengal 1pt, Saurashtra 3pts. Chirag Pathak and Sagar Jogiyani opened with 206 for Saurashtra's first wicket. In reply, Arindam Das and Manoj Tiwary put on 201 for Bengal's third.*

At Pune, November 24–27, 2009. **Karnataka won by an innings and 128 runs. Maharashtra 105** (R. Vinay Kumar 5-40) **and 320** (A. R. Bawne 136); **‡Karnataka 553-4 dec** (K. B. Pawan 152, G. Satish 141, A. A. Verma 150*). *Karnataka 6pts. Kolar Pawan and Ganesh Satish added 284 for Karnataka's second wicket.*

At Lucknow, November 24–27, 2009. **Uttar Pradesh won by an innings and 22 runs. ‡Uttar Pradesh 536-7 dec** (T. M. Srivastava 109, Parvinder Singh 108); **Delhi 202 and 312** (V. Kohli 145). *Uttar Pradesh 6pts. Punit Bisht (79) and Virat Kohli added 207 for Delhi's third wicket to delay defeat.*

At Vadodara (Moti Bagh), December 1–3, 2009. **Karnataka won by an innings and 102 runs. Karnataka 488** (M. K. Pandey 110); **‡Baroda 153 and 233.** *Karnataka 6pts. Karnataka's third win made them the first team to reach the quarter-finals.*

At Delhi (Roshanara), December 1–4, 2009. **Delhi won by eight wickets. Saurashtra 328** (C. R. Pathak 138) **and 214; ‡Delhi 383** (P. Bisht 120; J. A. Odedra 6-92) **and 161-2.** *Delhi 5pts.*

At Pune, December 1–4, 2009. **Drawn. Maharashtra 292** (P. Kumar 6-68) **and 338-9 dec** (P. P. Chawla 5-73); **‡Uttar Pradesh 208** (K. R. Adhav 5-24) **and 391-7** (Parvinder Singh 100). *Maharashtra 3pts, Uttar Pradesh 1pt.*

At Vadodara (Moti Bagh), December 8–9, 2009. **Baroda won by seven wickets. Saurashtra 127** (M. M. Patel 5-48) **and 137; ‡Baroda 124** (J. A. Odedra 5-28) **and 145-3.** *Baroda 5pts. Baroda captain Irfan Pathan led them to a two-day win, taking seven wickets in the match, and then scoring 65* in 45 balls in the final innings.*

At Delhi (Roshanara), December 8–11, 2009. **Delhi won by ten wickets. Delhi 419** (M. Manhas 170; S. M. Fallah 5-121) **and 112-0; ‡Maharashtra 163** (P. Awana 5-40) **and 364** (A. R. Bawne 118; P. Sangwan 5-107). *Delhi 6pts. Mithun Manhas and Rajat Bhatia (99) added 256 for Delhi's fourth wicket.*

At Kanpur (Modi), December 8–10, 2009. **Uttar Pradesh won by three wickets. Bengal 193 and 104** (Bhuvneshwar Singh 5-27); **‡Uttar Pradesh 62** (R. R. Bose 5-18) **and 236-7.** *Uttar Pradesh 5pts. Uttar Pradesh won to reach the quarter-finals, despite being bowled out for 62 on the second day, when 22 wickets fell.*

At Kolkata (Jadavpur), December 15–18, 2009. **Drawn. ‡Bengal 522** (S. C. Ganguly 152, W. P. Saha 120, L. R. Shukla 132) **and 223-3** (A. S. Das 102*); **Delhi 378** (P. Bisht 128*; I. Saxena 5-72). *Bengal 3pts, Delhi 1pt. Sourav Ganguly and Wriddhiman Saha joined forces at 43-4 on the first morning to add 249 for Bengal's fifth wicket. Ganguly later announced that he was retiring from first-class cricket, with 15,243 runs at 44.18 in 246 matches.*

At Pune, December 15–18, 2009. **Baroda won by seven wickets. Maharashtra 288** (H. H. Khadiwale 111) **and 207; ‡Baroda 395** (C. C. Williams 129, S. A. Gaekwad 118; S. M. Fallah 8-98) **and 101-3.** *Baroda 5pts. Connor Williams and Shatrunjay Gaekwad added 214 for Baroda's third wicket. Samad Fallah took a hat-trick split over two innings, but defeat relegated his team to the Plate League. Baroda would have reached the quarter-finals, ahead of Delhi, had they secured the bonus point for winning without losing a second-innings wicket.*

At Rajkot (Khandheri), December 15–18, 2009. **Karnataka won by six wickets. ‡Saurashtra 216 and 407; Karnataka 384** (G. Satish 120) **and 241-4.** *Karnataka 5pts.*

Quarter-finals

At Guwahati (NE Frontier Railway), December 24–27, 2009. **Drawn.** Uttar Pradesh qualified for the semi-finals by virtue of their first-innings lead. ‡**Uttar Pradesh 213** (A. Konwar 5-79) **and 272** (D. S. Goswami 5-57); **Assam 149 and 259-8** (A. A. Muzumdar 119*).

At Delhi (Palam), December 24–27, 2009. **Drawn.** Delhi qualified for the semi-finals by virtue of their first-innings lead. **Tamil Nadu 463** (A. Srikkanth 113; V. Mishra 5-112) **and 27-0;** ‡**Delhi 490-8 dec** (G. Chhabra 100).

At Rohtak, December 24–27, 2009. **Drawn.** Mumbai qualified for the semi-finals by virtue of their first-innings lead. ‡**Mumbai 400** (A. M. Rahane 143) **and 334-7** (A. M. Rahane 101*); **Haryana 164.** *Ajinkya Rahane scored a century in each innings.*

At Mysore, December 24–27, 2009. **Drawn.** Karnataka qualified for the semi-finals by virtue of their first-innings lead. **Punjab 300 and 367-6 dec;** ‡**Karnataka 378** (M. K. Pandey 115) **and 42-1.**

Semi-finals

At Bangalore (Chinnaswamy), January 3–6, 2010. **Drawn.** Karnataka qualified for the final by virtue of their first-innings lead. ‡**Karnataka 575-7 dec** (R. Dravid 209*) **and 247-8 dec** (C. M. Gautam 100*); **Uttar Pradesh 208 and 22-1.** *Rahul Dravid scored his tenth double-hundred and shared century stands for the fourth, sixth, seventh and eighth wickets to set up a decisive first-innings lead of 367.*

At Mumbai (Brabourne), January 3–6, 2010. **Drawn.** Mumbai qualified for the final by virtue of their first-innings lead. ‡**Mumbai 500** (A. M. Nayar 156) **and 187** (V. Mishra 6-49); **Delhi 211** (R. R. Powar 5-47) **and 160-4.** *Off-spinner Ramesh Powar wound up Delhi's first innings with a spell of 5.3–3–9–5, Mumbai's first five-wicket return of the season. Though 17-year-old slow left-armer Vikas Mishra responded with a career-best 6-49, a first-innings lead of 289 was enough to ensure Mumbai's passage to the final.*

Final

At Mysore, January 11–14, 2010. **Mumbai won by six runs.** ‡**Mumbai 233 and 234** (A. Mithun 6-71); **Karnataka 130** (A. M. Salvi 5-31) **and 331** (M. K. Pandey 144; A. B. Agarkar 5-81). *Karnataka's batting let them down at the last as they were bowled out for 130 in their first innings, exactly half their previous lowest all-out total of the season. With Mumbai's top order also underperforming, Karnataka eventually needed 338 in the fourth innings to win. Despite being 46-3, they were back on track while Ganesh Satish (75) and Manish Pandey (whose century helped him overtake Mumbai's Ajinkya Rahane as the leading Ranji scorer, in his second season) added 209 for the fourth wicket. Then the remaining seven wickets fell for 76, with a day to spare; the last pair needed 16, but managed just nine. Wasim Jaffer maintained his record of never losing a Ranji match as Mumbai captain (he had won nine and drawn 11 of his 20 in charge), while Karnataka had still never beaten Mumbai in a first-class game. Two Mumbai players were fined 50% of their match fees – Ajit Agarkar for dissent when given run out while practising a shot, and Dhawan Kulkarni for shaking his fist in the opposing batsmen's faces.*

RANJI TROPHY WINNERS

1934-35	Bombay	1944-45	Bombay	1954-55	Madras
1935-36	Bombay	1945-46	Holkar	1955-56	Bombay
1936-37	Nawanagar	1946-47	Baroda	1956-57	Bombay
1937-38	Hyderabad	1947-48	Holkar	1957-58	Baroda
1938-39	Bengal	1948-49	Bombay	1958-59	Bombay
1939-40	Maharashtra	1949-50	Baroda	1959-60	Bombay
1940-41	Maharashtra	1950-51	Holkar	1960-61	Bombay
1941-42	Bombay	1951-52	Bombay	1961-62	Bombay
1942-43	Baroda	1952-53	Holkar	1962-63	Bombay
1943-44	Western India	1953-54	Bombay	1963-64	Bombay

1964-65	Bombay	1980-81	Bombay	1996-97	Mumbai
1965-66	Bombay	1981-82	Delhi	1997-98	Karnataka
1966-67	Bombay	1982-83	Karnataka	1998-99	Karnataka
1967-68	Bombay	1983-84	Bombay	1999-2000	Mumbai
1968-69	Bombay	1984-85	Bombay	2000-01	Baroda
1969-70	Bombay	1985-86	Delhi	2001-02	Railways
1970-71	Bombay	1986-87	Delhi	2002-03	Mumbai
1971-72	Bombay	1987-88	Hyderabad	2003-04	Mumbai
1972-73	Bombay	1988-89	Tamil Nadu	2004-05	Railways
1973-74	Karnataka	1989-90	Delhi	2005-06	Uttar Pradesh
1974-75	Bombay	1990-91	Bengal	2006-07	Mumbai
1975-76	Bombay	1991-92	Haryana	2007-08	Delhi
1976-77	Bombay	1992-93	Delhi	2008-09	Mumbai
1977-78	Karnataka	1993-94	Punjab	2009-10	Mumbai
1978-79	Delhi	1994-95	Bombay		
1979-80	Delhi	1995-96	Bombay		
			Karnataka		

Bombay/Mumbai have won the Ranji Trophy 39 times, Delhi 7, Karnataka 6, Baroda 5, Holkar 4, Bengal, Hyderabad, Madras/Tamil Nadu, Maharashtra and Railways 2, Haryana, Nawanagar, Punjab, Uttar Pradesh and Western India 1.

Plate League Group A

At Guwahati (NE Frontier Railway), November 3–6, 2009. **Rajasthan won by 95 runs.** ‡Rajasthan **228** (G. K. Khoda 106) **and 256** (V. A. Saxena 103*; A. N. Ahmed 5-57); Assam 189 and 200 (Pankaj Singh 7-64). *Rajasthan 5pts. Amol Muzumdar, who had recently left Mumbai for Assam, passed Amarjit Kaypee's record of 7,623 as the leading Ranji run-scorer.*

At Ranchi, November 3–6, 2009. **Drawn.** Jharkhand 431 (S. S. Tiwary 136) **and 167-3;** ‡Tripura **438** (N. S. Shetty 104). *Jharkhand 1pt, Tripura 3pts.*

At Nagpur, November 3–6, 2009. **Drawn.** ‡Goa **474** (A. Ratra 121, S. S. Bandekar 100) **and 203-8 dec** (A. A. Wakhare 5-65); Vidarbha 338 and 83-1. *Vidarbha 1pt, Goa 3pts.*

At Margao, November 10–13, 2009. **Drawn.** Assam 177-5 v ‡Goa. *Goa 1pt, Assam 1pt.*

At Ranchi, November 10–13, 2009. **Drawn.** Jharkhand 292 and 155-9 (U. T. Yadav 6-40); ‡Vidarbha 248. *Jharkhand 3pts, Vidarbha 1pt.*

At Agartala, November 10–13, 2009. **Tripura won by one wicket.** Rajasthan 102 (W. A. Mota 6-26) **and 206** (S. D. Chowdhury 5-35); ‡Tripura **179** (M. S. Khatri 6-49) **and 130-9.** *Tripura 5pts.*

At Guwahati (Nehru), November 17–20, 2009. **Drawn.** ‡Jharkhand 261 (S. V. Bahutule 5-53) **and 247** (S. S. Tiwary 121); Assam 298 and 99-9. *Assam 3pts, Jharkhand 1pt. Chasing 211, Assam lost their ninth wicket to the last ball of the match.*

At Margao, November 17–20, 2009. **Drawn.** Goa 338 (S. A. Asnodkar 136) **and 212-9;** ‡Rajasthan 225. *Goa 3pts, Rajasthan 1pt.*

At Nagpur, November 17–20, 2009. **Drawn.** Vidarbha 222 and 217-6 dec; ‡Tripura 151 and 73-4. *Vidarbha 3pts, Tripura 1pt.*

At Guwahati (Nehru), December 1–3, 2009. **Assam won by an innings and 55 runs.** ‡Assam 331 (D. S. Jadhav 114; T. K. Chanda 5-65); Tripura 104 (A. N. Ahmed 5-40) **and 172** (A. N. Ahmed 5-43). *Assam 6pts. Abu Nechim Ahmed took 10-83 in the match to secure an innings win that lifted Assam from the bottom to the top of their group.*

At Dhanbad, December 1–4, 2009. **Drawn.** ‡Goa 561-8 dec (A. Ratra 170*); Jharkhand 303 (S. Prasad 106) **and 205-3.** *Jharkhand 1pt, Goa 3pts. Goa's 561-8 was their highest first-class total. In reply, Sachin Prasad scored 106 on first-class debut.*

At Jaipur (K. L. Saini), December 1–4, 2009. **Vidarbha won by 129 runs.** ‡Vidarbha 238 and 271-9 dec; Rajasthan 244 (A. A. Wakhare 6-56) **and 136** (A. A. Wakhare 5-45). *Vidarbha 5pts.*

At Guwahati (Nehru), December 8–11, 2009. **Drawn.** Assam 392-8 dec (D. S. Jadhav 111, Tarjinder Singh 117); ‡Vidarbha 240 (A. Konwar 6-72) **and 99-7.** *Assam 3pts, Vidarbha 1pt.*

At Dhanbad, December 8–11, 2009. **Drawn.** ‡Rajasthan 246 (S. Nadeem 6-74) **and** 375 (V. A. Saxena 115, N. S. Doru 104; R. Shukla 5-90); **Jharkhand 368-9 dec** (M. S. Vardhan 108, S. S. Tiwary 103; Pankaj Singh 7-56) **and 41-0.** *Jharkhand 3pts, Rajasthan 1pt. Vineet Saxena and Nikhil Doru added 229 for the third wicket in Rajasthan's second innings.*

At Agartala, December 8–11, 2009. **Drawn. Goa 201;** ‡**Tripura 280-7.** *Tripura 3pts, Goa 1pt.*

Plate League Group B

At Srinagar, November 3–6, 2009. **Jammu and Kashmir v Services. Cancelled.** *Services refused to travel to Kashmir for security reasons, and were suspended from the tournament, with their remaining four scheduled fixtures also cancelled.*

At Thalassery, November 3–6, 2009. **Drawn.** ‡Andhra 442 (B. A. Sumanth 117, K. S. Sahabuddin 120) **and 46-0; Kerala 336** (G. V. S. Prasad 5-100). *Kerala 1pt, Andhra 3pts.*

At Indore (Emerald HS), November 3–6, 2009. **Drawn. Haryana 546** (Sunny Singh 312) **and 244-0** (R. Dewan 133*, A. Rawat 100*); ‡**Madhya Pradesh 434** (J. S. Saxena 142). *Madhya Pradesh 1pt, Haryana 3pts. Sunny Singh, whose previous best score was 137, batted for seven minutes short of eight hours, hitting 44 fours and seven sixes, in Haryana's first-ever triple-hundred; only one of his team-mates reached 50 in the first innings, though he added 143 for the ninth wicket with Sanjay Badhwar (22). In their second innings, openers Rahul Dewan and Ankit Rawat put on 244* in 54.2 overs.*

At Srinagar, November 10–13, 2009. **Drawn. Haryana 225** (Sunny Singh 105) **and 57-3;** ‡**Jammu and Kashmir 179.** *Jammu and Kashmir 1pt, Haryana 3pts. This was the first first-class game played in Srinagar for five years, but cricket's comeback was badly affected by rain, with only eight overs possible on the first two days.*

At Indore (Maharani Usharaje), November 10–13, 2009. **Drawn. Madhya Pradesh 172-1 v** ‡**Kerala.** *Madhya Pradesh 1pt, Kerala 1pt.*

At Vijayawada, November 17–20, 2009. **Drawn.** ‡**Madhya Pradesh 308-5 dec; Andhra 145-6.** *Andhra 1pt, Madhya Pradesh 1pt.*

At Jammu, November 17–19, 2009. **Jammu and Kashmir won by 194 runs. Jammu and Kashmir 164** (S. K. Cheruvathur 6-31) **and 244;** ‡**Kerala 133 and 81** (Abid Nabi 5-27). *Jammu and Kashmir 5pts.*

At Anantapur, December 1–4, 2009. **Haryana won by 123 runs.** ‡**Haryana 170** (T. Atchuti Rao 5-43) **and 298** (J. Sharma 110); **Andhra 138 and 207.** *Haryana 5pts. A low-scoring match was effectively settled by a last-wicket stand of 114 between No. 9 Joginder Sharma and Sanjay Badhwar (who contributed 17) in Haryana's second innings.*

At Indore (Maharani Usharaje), December 1–4, 2009. **Madhya Pradesh won by an innings and 48 runs. Jammu and Kashmir 171** (T. P. Sudhindra 5-39) **and 300;** ‡**Madhya Pradesh 519** (D. Bundela 153, M. D. Mishra 131; Abid Nabi 5-148). *Madhya Pradesh 6pts. Devendra Bundela and Mohnish Mishra added 226 for Madhya Pradesh's sixth wicket.*

At Anantapur, December 8–10, 2009. **Andhra won by ten wickets. Andhra 318 and 22-0;** ‡**Jammu and Kashmir 147 and 192.** *Andhra 6pts.*

At Rohtak, December 8–10, 2009. **Haryana won by an innings and 85 runs.** ‡**Kerala 93 and 205** (S. Badhwar 5-69); **Haryana 383** (Sunny Singh 140). *Haryana 6pts.*

Plate League Semi-finals

At Guwahati (Nehru), December 15–18, 2009. **Assam won by five wickets.** ‡**Andhra 214 and 241** (S. V. Bahutule 6-61); **Assam 327** (D. S. Jadhav 165*) **and 132-5.** *Dheeraj Jadhav carried his bat through Assam's first innings for his third century in successive innings. Team-mate Sairaj Bahutule took his 600th first-class wicket.*

At Rohtak, December 15–18, 2009. **Drawn.** *Haryana qualified for the Elite quarter-finals by virtue of their first-innings lead.* **Haryana 265** (T. K. Chanda 5-56) **and 478-6** (A. Rawat 114*, S. Rana 163*); ‡**Tripura 193** (A. Mishra 5-41).

Assam and Haryana advanced to the quarter-finals of the Ranji Elite League.

DULEEP TROPHY, 2009-10

Four-day knockout for five zonal teams

Quarter-final

At Amritsar, January 19–22, 2010. **Drawn.** Central Zone qualified for the semi-finals by virtue of their first-innings lead. **Central Zone 480-8 dec** (M. Kaif 202*, Parvinder Singh 113); ‡**East Zone 290** (M. K. Tiwary 102*). *Fog and bad light affected all four days, but Central Zone had time to bowl out East Zone to secure first-innings lead. Their captain, Mohammad Kaif, led them from 9-3 to 480 with a maiden double-hundred, adding 164 for the fourth wicket with Suresh Raina (98) and 184 for the fifth with Parvinder Singh.*

Semi-finals

At Rajkot (Madhavrao Scindia), January 26–29, 2010. **Drawn.** West Zone qualified for the semi-finals by virtue of their first-innings lead. ‡**West Zone 769** (A. M. Nayar 259, R. R. Powar 109) **and 345-7** (C. A. Pujara 110, R. G. Sharma 116); **North Zone 294.** *Abhishek Nayar hit 38 fours and five sixes in his maiden double-hundred; there were six more individual fifties in West Zone's first innings. North Zone were 7-3 by the fifth over of their reply, and conceded a lead of 475, but West chose to sit on their advantage rather than enforcing the follow-on.*

At Indore (Maharani Usharaje), January 26–29, 2010. **South Zone won by five wickets. Central Zone 333** (M. Kaif 112; R. Vinay Kumar 5-102) **and 252** (R. Ashwin 6-67); ‡**South Zone 295** (P. Kumar 5-82) **and 293-5.** *South Zone fought back to reach the final after conceding first-innings lead and being 72-3 chasing 291, thanks to fifties from captain Subramaniam Badrinath, Manish Pandey and Ravichandran Ashwin, who hit 59* in 44 balls to complete victory.*

Final

At Hyderabad, February 2–6, 2010. **West Zone won by three wickets.** ‡**South Zone 400** (K. D. Karthik 183; I. K. Pathan 5-100) **and 386-9 dec** (K. D. Karthik 150; D. S. Kulkarni 5-58); **West Zone 251** (Y. K. Pathan 108; C. Ganapathy 5-75) **and 541-7** (C. R. Pathak 130, Y. K. Pathan 210*). *West Zone pulled off the highest successful run-chase in first-class history, beating Central Province's 513-9 against Southern Province in Sri Lanka in 2003-04. Yusuf Pathan led the pursuit of 536 with a maiden double-century, including 19 fours and ten sixes in 190 balls, though he was dropped five times and needed his brother to run for him from 144 onwards. Both he and South Zone's Dinesh Karthik scored twin centuries. Karthik scored 150-plus in each innings, and added 247 with Muralidharan Gautam (88) for the fifth wicket in South Zone's second innings; Pathan reached his first-innings century in 71 balls and the second one in 84. No spectators were admitted on the first two days, apparently for fear that political tensions in Andhra Pradesh would lead to crowd trouble, but the authorities relented for the last three days, claiming that the problem had been civil works on the ground.*

DEODHAR TROPHY, 2009-10

50-over knockout

Quarter-final

At Vadodara (Moti Bagh), March 6, 2010. **Central Zone won by seven wickets. South Zone 222** (47.4 overs); ‡**Central Zone 225-3** (39.1 overs).

Semi-finals

At Vadodara (Moti Bagh), March 7, 2010. **North Zone won by eight wickets. East Zone 210** (48.2 overs) (B. Sharma 5-36); ‡**North Zone 211-2** (37.5 overs).

At Vadodara (Moti Bagh), March 8, 2010. **West Zone won by 216 runs. West Zone 335-8** (50 overs); ‡**Central Zone 119** (29.4 overs). *Ajinkya Rahane and Cheteshwar Pujara added 154 in 32 overs for West Zone's second wicket before Yusuf Pathan smashed 59 in 24 balls, with six sixes and* *four fours, and Ravi Jadeja 42 from 18 balls. Jadeja went on to wrap up Central Zone's innings with more than 20 overs to spare, with figures of 4.4–0–8–4.*

Final

At Vadodara (Moti Bagh), March 9, 2010. **North Zone won by 49 runs. North Zone 267-9** (50 overs); ‡**West Zone 218** (38 overs) (M. Sharma 5-59). *West Zone's Yusuf Pathan played another whirlwind innings, with nine sixes and three fours in his 80 from 39 balls, but could not swing the game as North Zone claimed the title with 12 overs to spare.*

N. K. P. SALVE CHALLENGER TROPHY, 2009-10

50-over mini-league plus final

Final

At Nagpur, October 11, 2009 (day/night). **India Red won by seven wickets. India Blue 84** (27.1 overs); ‡**India Red 85-3** (20.3 overs). *The entire match lasted only 47.4 overs, less than half its allocated span, after India Blue's collapse.*

VIJAY HAZARE TROPHY, 2009-10

50-over league plus knockout

Semi-finals

At Vadodara (Moti Bagh), February 27, 2010. **Bengal won by four wickets. Karnataka 230-9** (50 overs); ‡**Bengal 231-6** (49 overs). *Karnataka sank to 130-8 before a 93-run stand between Muralidharan Gautam and Sreesanth Aravind, but Manoj Tiwary steered Bengal to their third successive final.*

At Rajkot (Madhavrao Scindia), February 27, 2010. **Tamil Nadu won by 134 runs. ‡Tamil Nadu 348-5** (50 overs) (A. Mukund 130); **Madhya Pradesh 214** (43.1 overs). *Abhinav Mukund, who hit 12 fours and a six in 137 balls, put on 177 for Tamil Nadu's first wicket with Anirudh Srikkanth and 99 for the second with Subramaniam Badrinath.*

Final

At Ahmedabad (Sardar Patel), March 2, 2010. **Tamil Nadu won by 29 runs. ‡Tamil Nadu 379-6** (50 overs) (M. Vijay 103); **Bengal 350-8** (50 overs). *Tamil Nadu retained the title after their top order piled up another huge total; the final surge came from captain Dinesh Karthik's 47-ball 88, with 11 fours and three sixes. They scored 68 from the five-over batting powerplay, whereas Bengal managed only 38, and suffered their third successive defeat in the Vijay Hazare final.*

SYED MUSHTAQ ALI TROPHY, 2009-10

20-over league plus knockout

Semi-finals

At Indore (Maharani Usharaje), March 15, 2010. **Maharashtra won by three wickets. Tamil Nadu 153-5** (20 overs); ‡**Maharashtra 154-7** (19.4 overs).

At Indore (Maharani Usharaje), March 15, 2010. **Hyderabad won by five wickets. ‡Delhi 157-8** (20 overs); **Hyderabad 158-5** (19 overs).

Final

At Indore (Maharani Usharaje), March 16, 2010 (floodlit). **Maharashtra won by 19 runs. Maharashtra 119** (18.4 overs); ‡**Hyderabad 100** (20 overs).

NEW ZEALAND CRICKET, 2010

Twelve wasted months

LYNN MCCONNELL

Twelve wasted months: that has to be the verdict on one of the most lamentable periods of New Zealand's inconsistent cricket history. After the sacking of coach Andy Moles in November 2009, the nation's cricket was placed under the control of captain Daniel Vettori. Admirable as Vettori's acceptance of this responsibility may have been – and he did win the first Test of his regime, against Pakistan at Dunedin – the problem he faced was apparent as early as the Second Test, which resulted in a heavy loss. New Zealand's age-old inability to string two good performances together exposed the obvious shortcomings of asking the side's best player to take control of preparation,

NEW ZEALAND IN 2010

	Played	Won	Lost	Drawn/No result
Tests	6	1	3	2
One-day internationals	21	6	14	1
Twenty20 internationals	13	8	5	–

selection and leadership. It may have been the norm in days gone by, but in the modern world it was never going to last.

The former Test batsman Mark Greatbatch, now an experienced coach, joined the side – ostensibly as a batting coach who would be a mentor for Vettori, but the lines of responsibility became blurred. After a year of predictable confusion, successive one-day whitewashes by Bangladesh (4–0; one game was rained off) and India (5–0) precipitated an internal review by New Zealand Cricket. Ex-captain Martin Crowe and recently retired fast bowler Shane Bond joined a high-powered independent committee chaired by the former Test slow left-armer Stephen Boock, now NZC's deputy chairman.

One of the committee's first tasks was to conduct a post-tour review after the visit to India. Greatbatch was relegated to batting coach at the NZC High Performance Centre, Vettori was removed from the selection panel, and John Wright stepped into the head coach role, looking to perform for his own country in the way that he succeeded with India at the turn of the century, and during his own distinguished playing career. Wright, like Vettori, would not be a part of the selection panel, which was entrusted to Greatbatch, Glenn Turner and Lance Cairns. Thus ended one of the more contentious aspects of the team administration over the previous 12 months.

At the same time it was announced that the support structure surrounding the team would also be significantly reduced, as Wright looked to put his own people in place. Many were left wondering why such a review could not have been held 12 months earlier, when Moles departed, to ensure that Wright's skills were brought to bear much sooner. But it was clear Wright had some concerns with the structure surrounding the side and was not prepared for anything other than the final say.

There was more administrative ineptitude when New Zealand were party to the controversial decision to nominate former Australian Prime Minister John Howard as the region's candidate for the ICC vice-presidency, supposedly for his diplomatic qualities. New Zealand had initially wanted past NZC chairman Sir John Anderson, who enjoyed respect at ICC level. A special committee, weighted in Australia's favour, eventually broke the deadlock between the two countries, but Howard was rejected by ICC members. New Zealand went back to Anderson, who declined the role, and it fell to Alan Isaac, almost by default. He was replaced as NZC chairman by Chris Moller, previously chief executive of the New Zealand Rugby Union.

It was hoped that the turmoil did not further distract players – especially senior figures – who should have been focused on raising standards on the pitch. A key performer was Brendon McCullum, particularly in Tests, of which there were just six in 2010. He scored 758 runs at 75.80 with three centuries, including his first double, in the Second Test in India. But playing more than 50 Tests, most as wicketkeeper, had taken its toll of his back, and he decided during 2010 that he would play as a specialist batsman (though he continued to keep in limited-overs matches). McCullum's innovation in the shorter forms saw him hit an audacious century, New Zealand's first in Twenty20 internationals, from just 50 balls against Australia at Christchurch in February, a match New Zealand won in the "super over".

Daniel in the lion's den: Vettori and Mark Greatbatch (*left*) plot strategy on their tour of India.

Martin Guptill continued to show top-order promise: his 189 against Bangladesh at Hamilton was a notable maiden Test century but, like Ross Taylor, he needs to achieve more big scores. Taylor struggled in India, appearing to be the player most affected by the changing tempos of the various formats. Tim McIntosh's advance as an opener continued, with a second Test century, but he still lacked a permanent partner. Great hope centred on Kane Williamson, a 20-year-old from Northern Districts who started with a fine 131 on debut to help save the First Test against India at Ahmedabad. His all-round qualities suggest a long career if he is allowed to flourish in a consistent batting line-up. Jesse Ryder was confined by various aches and strains to only three Tests and three 50-over games, but that was still sufficient to demonstrate his importance.

Vettori decided to give up the captaincy in all formats after the World Cup. As a bowler, he dominated the returns in both Tests and one-dayers, and his economy-rate was unyielding in the shorter form. But he needs greater support at Test level, where a lack of penetration has been a permanent defect post-Bond, who retired in May, a month before his 35th birthday. Chris Martin has been valiant, but Tim Southee had an up-and-down year. The signs are not especially bright that relief will quickly be forthcoming.

The year started comfortably enough. New Zealand hosted Bangladesh, and it was soon clear that in spite of their shortcomings the home team would be untroubled. New Zealand were in a spot of bother at 19 for two in the first one-day international, but recovered to reach 336, and went on to win the series 3–0. Bangladesh did highlight the inadequacies of the bowling attack when scoring 408 in reply to New Zealand's 553 for seven in the solitary Test. New Zealand's innings featured a stand of 336 between Guptill and McCullum, the third-highest for the sixth wicket in all Tests. Bangladesh were left 404 for victory but were dismissed for 282: it was the first time New Zealand had ever won a Test after declaring twice.

Australia's visit was always going to be a more significant trial. After the Twenty20 games were shared 1–1 – thanks largely to McCullum's brilliant 56-ball 116 not out – Australia were pushed to a 3–2 win in the one-dayers. Hopes were high for a tight tussle in the Tests, but they proved misplaced. New Zealand were decisively outplayed, losing the First Test after following on. They did gain a narrow lead in the Second Test, but Simon Katich's century turned the tide and another heavy defeat followed.

New Zealand then failed to reach the semi-finals of the World Twenty20, after being beaten by England in the deciding qualifying game. The top-order batting did not fire, while Gareth Hopkins's role as a specialist wicketkeeper was a throwback to more leisurely times.

A trip to Zimbabwe, scheduled for June, was called off, with NZC blaming "the collapse of Zimbabwe's health system and the unstable environment". Having said that, New Zealand's A team toured there in October.

After the trauma of the one-day losses in Bangladesh, there were fears of how New Zealand would cope against the powerful Indian Test side. However, determination prevailed on slow pitches and the tourists drew the first two Tests with some honour, only to succumb to an innings defeat in the last.

The year finished with another visit by Pakistan, which started with three Twenty20 matches just after Christmas. New Zealand won those 2–1 but, once the New Year began, Pakistan shaded the Test and one-day series.

NEW ZEALAND v BANGLADESH, 2009-10

Don Cameron

Test match (1): New Zealand 1, Bangladesh 0
One-day internationals (3): New Zealand 3, Bangladesh 0
Twenty20 international (1): New Zealand 1, Bangladesh 0

When the Bangladeshis opened their short tour by scratching together only 78 runs in a Twenty20 international at Hamilton, many New Zealanders graciously hoped they would improve. Just as many morbidly worried that this was only the first humiliation, and they had a point. Bangladesh lost the three one-day games that followed, and finished where they started, losing a one-off Test at Hamilton.

Yet Shakib Al Hasan, only 22 but a mature all-rounder and captain, was entitled to leave the Test field with pride. Several of his men had cast away the nervous nightmare of that Twenty20 match to play bravely on the same ground two weeks later. Shakib's own batting shone like a beacon in the Test. In the first innings Bangladesh were on the edge of disaster, six down and 357 behind, when he was joined by Mahmudullah, a strapping 24-year-old, who finally left in a trail of glory at 402 for nine, with 115 from 177 balls. Shakib fell 13 short of a maiden hundred then, but raced to the landmark on the final day.

Tamim Iqbal – an 18-year-old dasher when he toured New Zealand two years earlier – still started the innings like a cavalry charge. Imrul Kayes picked up a one-day hundred, and the lively keeper, Mushfiqur Rahim, scored 86 in a one-man attempt to win at Dunedin. Rubel Hossain, aged 20, had a five-wicket bag in the Test; something of a spendthrift, he also conceded 166 from 29 overs, but could become decidedly quick. It was unlucky that the senior seamer, Mashrafe bin Mortaza, who had hoped to prove his fitness after knee surgery, pulled out with a fever. At 26, he was the second-oldest man picked, but would have led the attack with grit and speed.

The Bangladeshis were already stronger than on their previous tour; they competed in the one-day internationals and came out of the Test with honour. But they needed to play more five-day Tests, or four-day tour matches. Their talent has been reared on one-day cricket in its varied versions – none designed for building long innings. A more wide-awake team would have bowled first in the Twenty20 game: they were barely off the plane, and should have made their first uncertain steps on the outfield, not at the crease. Perhaps misled by misty rain and low clouds, they did bowl first in the Test at Hamilton, where the pitch contains little mischief these days. Though New Zealand were three down at lunch, the tourists must have envied the way Martin Guptill and Brendon McCullum worked their way clear with a stand of 339. Still, Bangladesh fought nobly for their first-innings 408, the kind of high-water mark they must aim for.

New Zealand had reshaped their management team just before the tour: Mark Greatbatch was appointed coach, three months after the senior players had forced out Andy Moles. Since then, captain Daniel Vettori had effectively been coach and chief selector, and he retained his influence. But Guptill credited Greatbatch with advancing his career. Aucklanders were understandably proud of Guptill, a tall, hard-working youngster who had become the first New Zealander to score a century on one-day debut (against West Indies, a year earlier), despite losing three toes in an accident involving a forklift truck when 13 years old. But his form had been inconsistent for a man of his skill, spirit and athleticism, and he tended to be regarded as an opening batsman, though his early history had him at No. 3 or 4.

The promising debut of breezy young opener B-J. Watling (who had left his native South Africa aged ten) against Pakistan in December, and the domestic runs piled up by yeoman Peter Ingram – whatever the flaws in his footwork, or absence of it – offered the chance for a reshuffle. Ingram opened with McCullum in the one-dayers, and came in at first drop in the Test. With Ross Taylor the boss-figure at No. 4, Guptill was moved down to No. 5, away from the new ball. His maiden Test hundred, followed by an unbeaten fifty, rewarded the change of policy.

BANGLADESHI TOURING PARTY

*Shakib Al Hasan, Abdur Razzak, Aftab Ahmed, Imrul Kayes, Junaid Siddique, Mahmudullah, Mohammad Ashraful, Mushfiqur Rahim, Naeem Islam, Nazmul Hossain, Raqibul Hasan, Rubel Hossain, Shafiul Islam, Shahadat Hossain, Tamim Iqbal. *Coach:* J. D. Siddons.
Mashrafe bin Mortaza was originally selected, but a fever prevented him from joining the tour.

NEW ZEALAND v BANGLADESH

Twenty20 International

At Hamilton, February 3, 2010 (floodlit). New Zealand won by ten wickets. Toss: Bangladesh. Twenty20 international debuts: P. J. Ingram; Shafiul Islam.

Hamilton did its best to turn on a tropical night, with sunshine giving way to steamy evening humidity, and Bangladesh risked batting first. It was a disaster: they collapsed for their lowest Twenty20 score. Tamim Iqbal looked lively, but fell quickly; after a brief rally by Aftab Ahmed and Mohammad Ashraful, the tourists lost their next four wickets in just ten balls. The spin of Vettori and Nathan McCullum, plus the accuracy of the burly Tuffey, kept them tumbling. It would have been even worse without Raqibul Hasan, last out for 18. New Zealand openers Brendon McCullum and 31-year-old debutant Peter Ingram rubbed acid in the wounds, blithely reaching the target in the ninth over, though both were dropped.

Man of the Match: D. L. Vettori.

Bangladesh

	B	4	6
Tamim Iqbal c 1 b 11	14	9	3	0
Mohammad Ashraful c 7 b 8	11	14	1	0
Aftab Ahmed b 9	12	14	1	1
*Shakib Al Hasan b 6	3	5	0	0
†Mushfiqur Rahim lbw b 8	0	1	0	0
Mahmudullah c 9 b 6	11	23	1	0
Naeem Islam b 5	5	11	0	0
Raqibul Hasan c 7 b 5	18	13	2	1
Shahadat Hossain st 1 b 8	1	3	0	0
Shafiul Islam c 4 b 11	1	9	0	0
Nazmul Hossain not out	0	3	0	0
L-b 2	2			

6 overs: 39-2   (17.3 overs)   78

1/18 2/37 3/41 4/42 5/42 6/57 7/59 8/64 9/72

Tuffey 4–0–16–2; Southee 2–0–15–0; Franklin 1–0–8–1; Vettori 4–1–6–3; N. L. McCullum 4–0–15–2; Oram 2.3–0–16–2.

New Zealand

	B	4	6
†B. B. McCullum not out	56	27	7	2
P. J. Ingram not out	20	23	3	0
L-b 2, w 1	3			

6 overs: 49-0   (8.2 overs)   79-0

M. J. Guptill, L. R. P. L. Taylor, J. D. P. Oram, N. L. McCullum, G. J. Hopkins, *D. L. Vettori, J. E. C. Franklin, T. G. Southee and D. R. Tuffey did not bat.

Shahadat Hossain 3–0–28–0; Nazmul Hossain 2–0–18–0; Shafiul Islam 1–0–7–0; Shakib Al Hasan 2–0–16–0; Aftab Ahmed 0.2–0–8–0.

Umpires: G. A. V. Baxter and C. B. Gaffaney.
Third umpire: E. A. Watkin.   Referee: A. G. Hurst.

NEW ZEALAND v BANGLADESH

First One-Day International

At Napier, February 5, 2010 (day/night). New Zealand won by 146 runs. Toss: New Zealand. One-day international debuts: P. J. Ingram, A. J. McKay.

The McLean Park pitch is the hardest in the land, and New Zealand's favourite, so there was no nonsense about inserting Bangladesh after their drubbing two nights before. McCullum and Guptill went by the seventh over, but the stocky opener Ingram was on his home ground and made the most of it. He and Taylor weighed in with fifties, and Oram at last rediscovered his old verve, smashing eight fours and five sixes; he hit 83 from 40 balls as the batting powerplay brought 82 runs. Shafiul Islam deserved praise for extracting four wickets from the carnage. The tourists sprinted away at seven an over, with Tamim Iqbal striking ten fours, but once the opening stand was broken only Mahmudullah's run-a-ball flurry held up New Zealand; Bangladesh's innings went quietly to its end with six overs to spare.

Man of the Match: J. D. P. Oram.

New Zealand

†B. B. McCullum run out	0
P. J. Ingram c Mohammad Ashraful b Shafiul Islam	69
M. J. Guptill c Raqibul Hasan b Shahadat Hossain	2
L. R. P. L. Taylor c Mahmudullah b Naeem Islam	51
J. E. C. Franklin c Mushfiqur Rahim b Shafiul Islam	2
N. T. Broom run out	71
*D. L. Vettori st Mushfiqur Rahim b Shakib Al Hasan	32

J. D. P. Oram b Shafiul Islam	83
T. G. Southee b Shafiul Islam	0
D. R. Tuffey not out	10
A. J. McKay not out	3
B 1, l-b 2, w 10	13

1/1 (1) 2/19 (3)   (9 wkts, 50 overs) 336
3/117 (2) 4/120 (5)
5/135 (4) 6/187 (7) 7/310 (6)
8/310 (9) 9/328 (8)   10 overs: 37-2

Shahadat Hossain 9–2–56–1; Nazmul Hossain 9–1–78–0; Shafiul Islam 10–0–68–4; Shakib Al Hasan 9–0–62–1; Naeem Islam 10–0–51–1; Mahmudullah 3–0–18–0.

Bangladesh

Tamim Iqbal c McCullum b Vettori	62	Shafiul Islam c Taylor b Guptill		11
Imrul Kayes c McCullum b McKay	33	Nazmul Hossain not out		0
Mohammad Ashraful c McCullum b McKay	5			
Raqibul Hasan lbw b Vettori	9	B 2, l-b 2, w 9, n-b 2		15
*Shakib Al Hasan c Southee b Vettori	8			
†Mushfiqur Rahim c McCullum b Tuffey	8	1/71 (2) 2/84 (3) 3/118 (4) (43.5 overs)		190
Mahmudullah c McKay b Oram	23	4/119 (1) 5/133 (5) 6/144 (6)		
Naeem Islam c McCullum b Guptill	15	7/167 (7) 8/173 (9) 9/190 (8)		
Shahadat Hossain c Franklin b Oram	1	10/190 (10)	10 overs: 68-0	

Tuffey 7–1–39–1; Southee 7–0–34–0; McKay 8–0–40–2; Oram 9–0–33–2; Vettori 10–0–33–3; Guptill 2.5–0–7–2.

Umpires: R. A. Kettleborough and E. A. Watkin. Third umpire: G. A. V. Baxter.

NEW ZEALAND v BANGLADESH

Second One-Day International

At University Oval, Dunedin, February 8, 2010. New Zealand won by five wickets. Toss: New Zealand.

Bangladesh seemed to be heading for another thrashing when New Zealand's new-ball bowlers were given first use of a helpful pitch and cross-field breeze; after 23 overs of the first one-day international at the University Oval, Bangladesh were tottering at 46 for six. Suddenly the bonny little wicketkeeper Mushfiqur Rahim revealed an astonishing range of boundary strokes. They brought him eight fours and three sixes as he raced to 86 from 107 balls, sharing a century stand with Naeem Islam and giving Bangladesh's total modest respectability. In New Zealand's reply, Shafiul Islam bowled McCullum on nine, but Ingram and Guptill steadied the ship before Taylor sailed it home with a merry 78 from 52 balls, including six fours and five sixes.

Man of the Match: L. R. P. L. Taylor.
Close of play:.

Bangladesh

Tamim Iqbal c McCullum b McKay	1	Shahadat Hossain not out		16
Imrul Kayes run out	9	Shafiul Islam not out		1
Mohammad Ashraful c and b Tuffey	1	B 2, l-b 1, w 5		8
Aftab Ahmed c McCullum b Butler	10			
*Shakib Al Hasan b McKay	0	1/5 (1) 2/11 (2) (8 wkts, 50 overs)		183
†Mushfiqur Rahim lbw b Butler	86	3/14 (3) 4/23 (5)		
Mahmudullah run out	8	5/25 (4) 6/46 (7)		
Naeem Islam b Butler	43	7/147 (8) 8/166 (6)	10 overs: 15-3	

Rubel Hossain did not bat.

Tuffey 9–1–55–1; McKay 10–3–17–2; Butler 10–2–43–3; Oram 7–1–24–0; Vettori 10–0–25–0; Franklin 4–0–16–0.

New Zealand

†B. B. McCullum b Shafiul Islam	9	N. T. Broom lbw b Shafiul Islam		0
P. J. Ingram c Mushfiqur Rahim		*D. L. Vettori not out		4
b Rubel Hossain	28	L-b 3, w 9, n-b 2		14
M. J. Guptill b Rubel Hossain	32			
L. R. P. L. Taylor c Mahmudullah		1/9 (1) 2/52 (3) (5 wkts, 27.3 overs)		185
b Shafiul Islam	78	3/100 (2) 4/179 (4)		
J. E. C. Franklin not out	20	5/180 (6)	10 overs: 54-2	

J. D. P. Oram, I. G. Butler, D. R. Tuffey and A. J. McKay did not bat.

Shahadat Hossain 7–0–38–0; Shafiul Islam 7–0–49–3; Rubel Hossain 9.3–0–68–2; Shakib Al Hasan 3–0–13–0; Naeem Islam 1–0–14–0.

Umpires: A. L. Hill and R. A. Kettleborough.   Third umpire: C. B. Gaffaney.

NEW ZEALAND v BANGLADESH

Third One-Day International

At Christchurch, February 11, 2010 (day/night). New Zealand won by three wickets. Toss: New Zealand.

The reshaping of Lancaster Park for the 2011 Rugby World Cup had left some of the midwicket boundaries insanely short, but ideal for one-day batsmen. At last, Bangladesh started to look like a serviceable team. Though Tamim Iqbal was bowled in the first over (after hitting two fours), his partner Imrul Kayes settled down as the very solid foundation for the rest of the innings. He batted into the 48th over, completing a maiden international century with 11 fours, though he had little useful support after Shakib Al Hasan was fourth out at 183 with 12 overs left, and 241 for nine was hardly a dominating total. For once Taylor did not flourish, but Guptill led the way, scoring at a run a ball with nine fours and three sixes, until he became one of Shakib's career-best four victims. The hefty New Zealand tail reached victory with five overs to spare.

Man of the Match: M. J. Guptill.

Bangladesh

Tamim Iqbal b Southee	8	
Imrul Kayes b Vettori	101	
Aftab Ahmed c Southee b McKay	18	
Mohammad Ashraful c McCullum b Oram	31	
*Shakib Al Hasan c Taylor b Southee	36	
†Mushfiqur Rahim lbw b Vettori	4	
Mahmudullah b Vettori	6	
Naeem Islam c Ingram b Southee	10	
Shahadat Hossain run out	4	
Shafiul Islam not out	2	
B 4, l-b 3, w 12, n-b 2	21	

1/8 (1) 2/41 (3)   (9 wkts, 50 overs) 241
3/99 (4) 4/183 (5)
5/205 (6) 6/221 (7)
7/234 (2) 8/234 (8) 9/241 (9)   10 overs: 49-2

Rubel Hossain did not bat.

Southee 10–2–37–3; McKay 8–0–48–1; Butler 8–0–58–0; Oram 6–1–23–1; Vettori 10–0–42–3; Franklin 5–0–18–0; Guptill 3–0–8–0.

New Zealand

†B. B. McCullum b Rubel Hossain	19	
P. J. Ingram b Shakib Al Hasan	25	
M. J. Guptill c Tamim Iqbal b Shakib Al Hasan	91	
L. R. P. L. Taylor st Mushfiqur Rahim b Shakib Al Hasan	3	
*D. L. Vettori c Aftab Ahmed b Mahmudullah	34	
N. T. Broom b Shakib Al Hasan	18	
J. D. P. Oram c Shakib Al Hasan b Naeem Islam	12	
J. E. C. Franklin not out	19	
I. G. Butler not out	13	
L-b 6, w 2, n-b 2	10	

1/37 (1) 2/75 (2)   (7 wkts, 44.5 overs) 244
3/89 (4) 4/160 (5)
5/195 (3) 6/204 (6) 7/210 (7)   10 overs: 73-1

T. G. Southee and A. J. McKay did not bat.

Shahadat Hossain 5.5–0–39–0; Shafiul Islam 8–1–46–0; Rubel Hossain 10–0–55–1; Shakib Al Hasan 10–0–33–4; Naeem Islam 8–0–32–1; Mahmudullah 3–0–33–1.

Umpires: G. A. V. Baxter and R. A. Kettleborough.   Third umpire: E. A. Watkin.
Series referee: A. G. Hurst.

NEW ZEALAND v BANGLADESH

Test Match

At Hamilton, February 15–19. New Zealand won by 121 runs. Toss: Bangladesh. Test debut: P. J. Ingram.

This Test, tucked away on a comfy little field in a pleasantly large country town, may not have shaken the cricket world, but for at least two players, Martin Guptill and visiting captain Shakib Al Hasan, it may have been a stepping stone to a higher level.

Rain delayed the start by an hour, and Shakib put New Zealand in. They declined to 158 for five on the first afternoon, with three men caught off the lively Rubel Hossain. Then Guptill was joined by McCullum in what became a match-winning partnership of 339 – a New Zealand record for the sixth wicket (beating 246 by Jeff Crowe and Richard Hadlee in Colombo in 1986-87), their third-best stand for any wicket, and only 12 runs short of the sixth-wicket record in all Tests. McCullum, further from the dizzy delights of the top five, showed a tenacity and willpower not always apparent, and reached the highest innings by a New Zealand wicketkeeper. But though McCullum scored more quickly, Guptill was the dominant man, with a steady hand on the tiller; sound defence melded smoothly with classical front-foot driving as he reached his maiden Test hundred, batting nearly seven and a half hours before he gave Rubel a first five-wicket Test haul.

HIGHEST TEST PARTNERSHIPS FOR NEW ZEALAND

467 for 3rd	A. H. Jones and M. D. Crowe v Sri Lanka at Wellington.	1990-91
387 for 1st	G. M. Turner and T. W. Jarvis at Georgetown.	1971-72
339 for 6th	**M. J. Guptill and B. B. McCullum v Bangladesh at Hamilton**	**2009-10**
276 for 1st	C. S. Dempster and J. E. Mills v England at Wellington	1929-30
271 for 4th	L. R. P. L. Taylor and J. D. Ryder v India at Napier	2008-09
256 for 8th	S. P. Fleming and J. E. C. Franklin v South Africa at Cape Town	2005-06
253 for 8th	N. J. Astle and A. C. Parore v Australia at Perth	2001-02
246* for 6th	J. J. Crowe and R. J. Hadlee v Sri Lanka at Colombo (CCC).	1986-87

New Zealand declared at tea on 553, and must have expected to make Bangladesh follow on. But Tamim Iqbal charged to 50 in 39 balls that evening and, though five wickets fell before lunch on the third day, with Bangladesh still 357 behind, the pitch became more and more amiable, while the bowlers looked as though they expected, rather than demanded, wickets. The runs flowed steadily, especially against the spinners, as Shakib and Mahmudullah counter-attacked, batting throughout the second session and adding 145, a record for Bangladesh's seventh wicket. Just after tea, Shakib was given out, caught behind. Although the catch was not referred, replays suggested it had not carried. Mahmudullah remained, to avert the follow-on, complete a maiden Test century and take Bangladesh past 400. He batted more than three hours, and hit 17 fours and two sixes in all.

Shakib ran out Watling with a direct hit before the close, the first of three run-outs involving McIntosh, who was the top scorer in New Zealand's second innings. Guptill followed his century with 56 not out, and Vettori's second declaration left Bangladesh nearly four sessions to score 404.

They had the time, but not the firepower. Vettori brought himself on in the sixth over, and his fourth ball removed Tamim; Bangladesh were already five down by the close. Shakib fought back valiantly, but without real hope, sharing significant partnerships with Mushfiqur Rahim and, again, Mahmudullah. At one point, Shakib hit four fours and two sixes in nine deliveries from Vettori, then lifted a third six off Patel. He reached the third maiden century in this Test immediately after lunch; at 127 balls, it was the fastest of the game's four hundreds. Shakib seemed to wobble at the knees with excitement, and Southee bowled him two balls later. New Zealand completed victory soon afterwards. But both teams had cause for satisfaction, with Shakib and Guptill maybe a little closer to the threshold of fulfilment.

Man of the Match: M. J. Guptill.

Close of play: First day, New Zealand 258-5 (Guptill 80, McCullum 58); Second day, Bangladesh 87-1 (Tamim Iqbal 56, Junaid Siddique 3); Third day, New Zealand 9-1 (McIntosh 5, Ingram 2); Fourth day, Bangladesh 88-5 (Shakib Al Hasan 0, Mushfiqur Rahim 10).

New Zealand

T. G. McIntosh c Imrul Kayes b Shafiul Islam	7	– (2) run out	89
B-J. Watling c Junaid Siddique b Rubel Hossain	13	– (1) run out	1
P. J. Ingram c Shahadat Hossain b Rubel Hossain	42	– run out	13
L. R. P. L. Taylor c Mushfiqur Rahim b Rubel Hossain	40	– c Imrul Kayes b Mahmudullah	51
M. J. Guptill c Mushfiqur Rahim b Rubel Hossain	189	– not out	56
*D. L. Vettori b Shakib Al Hasan	10	– c Mohammad Ashraful b Mahmudullah	13
†B. B. McCullum b Rubel Hossain	185	– not out	19
D. R. Tuffey not out	31		
J. S. Patel not out	12		
B 1, l-b 10, w 5, n-b 8	24	B 5, l-b 2, w 6, n-b 3	16

1/17 (1) 2/57 (2)   (7 wkts dec, 135 overs) 553   1/2 (1)   (5 wkts dec, 71 overs) 258
3/66 (3) 4/126 (4) 5/158 (6)   2/52 (3) 3/124 (4)
6/497 (7) 7/525 (5)   4/196 (2) 5/227 (6)

T. G. Southee and C. S. Martin did not bat.

Shahadat Hossain 24–1–136–0; Shafiul Islam 31–2–111–1; Rubel Hossain 29–1–166–5; Shakib Al Hasan 37–6–89–1; Aftab Ahmed 4–0–10–0; Mahmudullah 7–0–21–0; Mohammad Ashraful 3–0–9–0. *Second Innings*—Shahadat Hossain 11–2–32–0; Shafiul Islam 14–3–47–0; Shakib Al Hasan 15–1–44–0; Rubel Hossain 12–0–44–0; Mahmudullah 19–1–84–2.

Bangladesh

Tamim Iqbal c McCullum b Southee	68	– c Tuffey b Vettori	30
Imrul Kayes c Taylor b Vettori	28	– b Patel	29
Junaid Siddique c Taylor b Martin	21	– b Martin	8
Aftab Ahmed c Taylor b Tuffey	33	– run out	8
Mohammad Ashraful c Watling b Tuffey	12	– lbw b Vettori	2
*Shakib Al Hasan c McCullum b Martin	87	– b Southee	100
†Mushfiqur Rahim c Guptill b Vettori	7	– c McIntosh b Tuffey	22
Mahmudullah lbw b Vettori	115	– c Tuffey b Patel	42
Shahadat Hossain c McCullum b Martin	13	– not out	17
Shafiul Islam not out	12	– c McCullum b Southee	13
Rubel Hossain run out	0	– c McIntosh b Southee	0
B 4, l-b 1, w 7	12	B 4, l-b 1, w 6	11

1/79 (2) 2/118 (1) 3/132 (3)   (97.3 overs) 408   1/35 (1) 2/51 (3)   (76 overs) 282
4/162 (5) 5/179 (4) 6/196 (7)   3/72 (4) 4/78 (5) 5/78 (2)
7/341 (6) 8/362 (9) 9/402 (8) 10/408 (11)   6/157 (7) 7/225 (8) 8/252 (6)
                                           9/282 (10) 10/282 (11)

Martin 25–2–116–3; Southee 16–2–62–1; Patel 10–3–53–0; Tuffey 18–2–84–2; Vettori 28.3–7–88–3. *Second Innings*—Martin 12–1–48–1; Southee 11–4–41–3; Vettori 24–6–80–2; Tuffey 12–5–33–1; Patel 17–2–75–2.

Umpires: R. E. Koertzen and R. J. Tucker.   Third umpire: S. J. A. Taufel.   Referee: A. G. Hurst.

NEW ZEALAND v AUSTRALIA, 2009-10

REVIEW BY DON CAMERON

Test matches (2): Australia 2, New Zealand 0
One-day internationals (5): Australia 3, New Zealand 2
Twenty20 internationals (2): New Zealand 1, Australia 1

Although Australia had yet to regain the power and panache of the Warne, McGrath and Gilchrist era, Ricky Ponting was drilling his troops into battle order for the Ashes during the southern summer. After unbeaten home series against West Indies and Pakistan, they arrived in New Zealand, where they encountered a little more resistance in the limited-overs series, but easily won both Tests – pushing New Zealand's last Test win against them, in 1992-93, ever further into the background. Nevertheless, it was Ponting's team-building that was the tour's strong point.

After winning the first Twenty20 match, Australia were apparently slaughtered in the second when opener Brendon McCullum scored 116 from 56 balls, hitting eight sixes around the small Christchurch ground – and risking his own facial demolition by flicking good-length balls, even yorkers, over his left shoulder to the boundary behind the keeper where long-stops once lurked. But the tourists fought back for a tie, resolved in New Zealand's favour by an eliminator over.

If this defeat, and another in the first one-day international thanks to a brave fightback by New Zealand No. 7 Scott Styris, baffled the Australians, they gave no sign that their armour had been dented. Ponting realised the pitches were true, but slower than at home. They marched steadily to victory in the next three matches to take the series – and, in the peculiar Australian custom, forgot to win the "dead" last one-dayer.

By now the Australians were familiar with the various strengths of the more dangerous New Zealand players (realistically only McCullum and Ross Taylor as batsmen and Daniel Vettori among the bowlers), while Ponting had at least seven batsmen in form and a potent trio of fast bowlers – Mitchell Johnson, Doug Bollinger and Ryan Harris – all bowling at 140kph-plus (over 87mph). He also had the gods on his side, winning the toss in all five one-day internationals and both Tests.

He must have known that, on the good-natured pitches New Zealand seemed determined to provide, his fast bowlers would dominate, whereas the home side's honest medium-fast men presented no danger, and Vettori would be a threat only in the unlikely event of the wicket deteriorating.

The First Test on a placid Basin Reserve pitch followed the script: Australia batted first, and Michael Clarke and Marcus North shared a 253-run stand while a ferocious Wellington gale further embarrassed the New Zealand bowlers. Facing the hurdle of Australia's first-innings 459, New Zealand declined steadily, but managed to prolong the agony until lunch on the fifth day. By contrast, in the Second Test at Hamilton, Australia's batting lacked concentration on the first day – all out for 231 – but they rallied, controlled the flow for the next three days and again won by lunch on the fifth.

Ponting left New Zealand knowing he had an established Test team with strong reserves in every department except spin. Simon Katich, Clarke and North were the most successful batsmen of the series, with Phil Hughes and all-rounder Shane Watson on the fringe; Brad Haddin was a fine wicketkeeper with a healthy taste for runs. The fast bowling squad offered three different styles – Ryan Harris the orthodox right-armer, Doug Bollinger the left-armer with a splendidly high action, and Mitchell Johnson the left-armer who might not always keep his arm high, but seemed most likely to get the right-hander's outside edge. This trio took 33 of Australia's 40 Test victims, on pitches that were not especially fast nor giving any extraordinary lift or sideways movement. In the Twenty20 games, they had the added pace of Shaun Tait and Dirk Nannes, who had both abandoned first-class cricket.

Nathan Hauritz took four Test wickets at 65 each, and reinforcing the spin attack was obviously a work in progress. Steve Smith, a jaunty youngster, played Twenty20 cricket on tour and at home during the summer and appeared a promising leg-spinner; Ponting retained him in the Test squad for experience rather than giving him a rushed entrée to the top level.

Sadly, New Zealand's Test performances were relentlessly exposed by the Australians. The absence of Shane Bond, who left for the IPL after the one-day series, and Iain O'Brien, who had moved to England, took the shine from the bowling; Jesse Ryder missed almost the whole season through injury, and the main run-gatherers were Taylor, Vettori and McCullum. Tim Southee, regarded as a promising new-ball prospect, showed international class only when he knocked the middle out of Australia's first innings at Hamilton – perhaps helped by a replacement ball that was required in mid-innings.

Before he left, Ponting tried to offer New Zealand some solace. He had, he said, learned his cricket in Tasmania, which was always the poor relation compared with the giants on the mainland. "So I know how you New Zealanders feel, when things go wrong for you." Was that a tear in the eye of the hard-bitten little scrapper? Not likely.

AUSTRALIAN TOURING PARTY

*R. T. Ponting, D. E. Bollinger, M. J. Clarke, B. J. Haddin, R. J. Harris, N. M. Hauritz, P. J. Hughes, M. E. K. Hussey, M. G. Johnson, S. M. Katich, C. J. McKay, M. J. North, S. P. D. Smith, S. R. Watson. *Coach:* T. J. Nielsen.

P. R. George was called into the Test squad as cover for Harris, while Hughes, Katich and North did not arrive until the Test series. Clarke was captain during the Twenty20 games, with Ponting taking over once he arrived for the one-day internationals along with Bollinger and McKay. C. L. White took part in the Twenty20 and one-day series but not the Tests; T. R. Birt, D. T. Christian, D. J. Hussey, D. P. Nannes, S. W. Tait and D. A. Warner were in the Twenty20 squad only, and G. J. Bailey, J. R. Hopes and A. C. Voges only in the one-day squad. Smith was in the Twenty20 and Test parties but not the one-day squad. S. E. Marsh was selected for both limited-overs squads, but withdrew unfit.

LIMITED-OVERS INTERNATIONAL REPORTS BY WILL SWANTON

NEW ZEALAND v AUSTRALIA

First Twenty20 International

At Wellington (Westpac Stadium), February 26, 2010 (floodlit). Australia won by six wickets. Toss: New Zealand.

The fastest pace trio in world cricket – Tait, Nannes and Johnson – all sent the radar gun past 150kph, and bullets through New Zealand's batsmen. The Australians had just ended their home summer undefeated, and this trip did nothing to halt their momentum. They won with six wickets to spare and barely a hair out of place after New Zealand were skittled for 118. Watson's confident body language when bowling earned the ire of local supporters, who directed a stream of less than complimentary chanting at him, but he and the dynamic Warner silenced them by clubbing 28 runs off the first two overs of their reply. Putting in the big-hitting Johnson, coming off his three for 19, at No. 4 was a failure – Australia slipped to 39 for three – but the target was so small that they settled into a patient chase and reached it with four overs, an eternity in Twenty20, to spare.

Man of the Match: M. G. Johnson.

New Zealand		B	4	6
B. B. McCullum *c 7 b 10*	2	4	0	0
P. J. Ingram *b 4*	2	10	0	0
M. J. Guptill *c 2 b 4*	30	29	4	0
L. R. P. L. Taylor *lbw b 4*	9	9	1	0
J. E. C. Franklin *c 9 b 10*	43	42	2	2
†G. J. Hopkins *c 7 b 2*	21	13	2	1
J. D. P. Oram *c 2 b 11*	1	2	0	0
N. L. McCullum *c 5 b 11*	1	2	0	0
*D. L. Vettori *run out*	3	5	0	0
D. R. Tuffey *c 7 b 2*	0	3	0	0
S. E. Bond *not out*	1	1	0	0
B 3, l-b 1, w 1	5			

6 overs: 29-2   (20 overs) 118

1/2 2/13 3/33 4/54 5/104 6/109 7/111 8/113 9/117

Tait 4–0–21–2; Nannes 4–0–22–2; Johnson 4–0–19–3; Smith 2–0–9–0; Hussey 1–0–6–0; Watson 4–0–23–2; Christian 1–0–14–0.

Australia		B	4	6
D. A. Warner *b 11*	19	10	2	1
S. R. Watson *lbw b 9*	19	12	4	0
*M. J. Clarke *not out*	18	26	1	0
M. G. Johnson *b 11*	1	3	0	0
D. J. Hussey *c 3 b 8*	46	36	5	0
C. L. White *not out*	11	9	1	1
W 5	5			

6 overs: 47-3   (16 overs) 119-4

1/38 2/38 3/39 4/106

†B. J. Haddin, D. T. Christian, S. P. D. Smith, S. W. Tait and D. P. Nannes did not bat.

Bond 4–0–32–2; Tuffey 2–0–27–0; Vettori 4–0–13–1; Oram 2–0–15–0; N. L. McCullum 3–0–21–1; Guptill 1–0–11–0.

Umpires: G. A. V. Baxter and B. F. Bowden.   Third umpire: E. A. Watkin.

NEW ZEALAND v AUSTRALIA

Second Twenty20 International

At Christchurch, February 28, 2010 (floodlit). New Zealand won after an eliminator over, following a tie. Toss: New Zealand.

A nerve-jangling, spine-tingling, jaw-dropping thriller was highlighted by a rollicking century from New Zealand's Brendon McCullum and decided by a "super over" after the scores were tied. McCullum's unbeaten 116, off 56 balls, was only the second century in a Twenty20 international, and one run short of Chris Gayle's record. It was a daring exhibition, brave and inventive, with ramp shots off the express Tait flying for boundaries over wicketkeeper Haddin's head – one, off a 155kph missile, almost defied belief. New Zealand's total of 214 was a tall order, but Clarke and White nearly stretched the reply far enough, with Clarke run out trying for a winning third run off the final ball. Southee bowled a tight eliminator over, conceding only six runs; Tait was profligate, coughing up two wides before Guptill ended proceedings by striking the third legitimate delivery for four.

Man of the Match: B. B. McCullum.

New Zealand

		B	4	6
B. B. McCullum *not out*	116	56	12	8
P. J. Ingram *b 10*	0	2	0	0
M. J. Guptill *c 7 b 9*	17	17	3	0
L. R. P. L. Taylor *run out*	6	9	1	0
J. E. C. Franklin *c 3 b 7*	7	8	1	0
†G. J. Hopkins *hit wkt b 11*	36	17	3	2
J. D. P. Oram *b 10*	0	3	0	0
N. L. McCullum *not out*	14	9	1	1
L-b 12, w 5, n-b 1	18			

6 overs: 62-1   (20 overs)   214-6

1/10 2/62 3/69 4/77 5/145 6/164

*D. L. Vettori, S. E. Bond and T. G. Southee did not bat.

Tait 4–0–40–2; Nannes 4–0–51–1; Harris 4–1–40–1; Hussey 3–0–21–1; Smith 3–0–24–1; Christian 2–0–26–0.

Australia

		B	4	6
D. A. Warner *c 11 b 10*	20	10	3	1
†B. J. Haddin *c 2 b 5*	47	36	4	2
*M. J. Clarke *run out*	67	45	5	2
D. J. Hussey *b 5*	10	6	2	0
C. L. White *not out*	64	26	5	5
L-b 1, w 2, n-b 3	6			

6 overs: 53-1   (20 overs)   214-4

1/27 2/100 3/132 4/214

T. R. Birt, S. P. D. Smith, D. T. Christian, R. J. Harris, S. W. Tait and D. P. Nannes did not bat.

Bond 4–0–27–1; Southee 4–0–44–0; Oram 4–0–52–0; Vettori 4–0–41–0; Franklin 3–0–32–2; N. L. McCullum 1–0–17–0.

Eliminator over: **Australia 6-1** (1 over) (White 4*, Warner 0, Haddin 2*; Southee 1–0–6–1); **New Zealand 9-0** (0.3 overs) (B. B. McCullum 1*, Guptill 5*, Extras 3; Tait 0.3–0–9–0).

Umpires: C. B. Gaffaney and A. L. Hill.   Third umpire: G. A. V. Baxter.
Series referee: R. S. Madugalle.

NEW ZEALAND v AUSTRALIA

First One-Day International

At Napier, March 3, 2010 (day/night). New Zealand won by two wickets. Toss: Australia.

Johnson and Styris were fined after a heated mid-pitch exchange during New Zealand's run-chase. Johnson was accused of head-butting – though head-tapping would be more accurate, as he lightly made contact with the peak of Styris's helmet. There was nothing gentle about their war of words, however, or the competitive feeling between the teams. Styris, who had been pegged for twelfth-man duties, became the local hero when Vettori pulled out with a neck injury. The ever-reliable Hussey had made a polished run-a-ball 59 as Australia reached a highly respectable 275 for eight. Then Styris came out swinging: he hammered 49 from 34 balls and sealed the win with a six over long-off from Bollinger. He raised his arms, roared – and shook hands with Johnson. It was a dream night for first-time captain Taylor, thrown into the job by Vettori's last-minute withdrawal. His 70 from 71 balls helped to mould the result, which ended Australia's run of 13 one-day games without defeat.

Man of the Match: L. R. P. L. Taylor.

Australia

S. R. Watson *c Ingram b Oram*	45
†B. J. Haddin *b Bond*	12
*R. T. Ponting *c Guptill b Franklin*	44
M. J. Clarke *c B. B. McCullum b Tuffey*	22
C. L. White *b Tuffey*	33
M. E. K. Hussey *b Bond*	59
J. R. Hopes *b Southee*	33
M. G. Johnson *not out*	21
N. M. Hauritz *c sub (N. L. McCullum)* b Tuffey	4
R. J. Harris *not out*	0
B 1, w 1	2

1/50 (2) 2/58 (1)   (8 wkts, 50 overs) 275
3/100 (4) 4/148 (3)
5/172 (5) 6/244 (7)
7/252 (6) 8/268 (9)   10 overs: 62-2

D. E. Bollinger did not bat.

Southee 8–0–66–1; Bond 10–1–50–2; Oram 7–0–29–1; Tuffey 10–0–58–3; Franklin 9–0–44–1; Styris 6–0–27–0.

New Zealand

†B. B. McCullum b Bollinger	45	T. G. Southee run out	2
P. J. Ingram c Hussey b Johnson	40	S. E. Bond not out	11
M. J. Guptill c Watson b Hopes	9	L-b 10, w 2	12
*L. R. P. L. Taylor c Hussey b Watson	70		
J. E. C. Franklin c Haddin b Hauritz	12	1/75 (2) 2/90 (1)	(8 wkts, 49.2 overs) 281
N. T. Broom b Bollinger	19	3/106 (3) 4/175 (5)	
S. B. Styris not out	49	5/204 (4) 6/207 (6)	
D. R. Tuffey b Harris	12	7/234 (8) 8/246 (9)	10 overs: 64-0

J. D. P. Oram did not bat.

Harris 10–1–57–1; Bollinger 9.2–0–58–2; Johnson 10–1–46–1; Hopes 6–0–40–1; Watson 9–0–47–1; Clarke 2–0–8–0; Hauritz 3–0–15–1.

Umpires: A. L. Hill and R. E. Koertzen.   Third umpire: C. B. Gaffaney.

NEW ZEALAND v AUSTRALIA

Second One-Day International

At Auckland, March 6, 2010. Australia won by 12 runs (D/L method). Toss: Australia.

Now public enemy No. 1 after his altercation with Styris, Johnson was booed when he came to the crease, and escorted by two security men at the end of Australia's innings; later, his every touch of the ball, every bowling spell, triggered obscene chants. But he thrived, claiming four for 51 as Australia levelled the series. He appeared to enjoy the banter, no doubt aware that any combativeness with spectators would make things worse, but began his spell by kissing his Australian badge and celebrated his wickets with passion. Fifties from Haddin, White and Hussey forged Australia's 273 for seven. Johnson nipped the threat of danger man McCullum in the bud, caught behind by Haddin for 24, and a rain-break revised New Zealand's target to 266 in 45 overs. An inventive, unorthodox but wonderfully entertaining 49-ball 70 from Vettori (playing only because his deputy, Taylor, had a bad leg) was good viewing without threatening to turn the game – even if he did grab the match award for the losing dressing-room.

Man of the Match: D. L. Vettori.

Australia

S. R. Watson c Guptill b Tuffey	47	J. R. Hopes run out	29
†B. J. Haddin c and b Vettori	53	M. G. Johnson not out	16
*R. T. Ponting c B. B. McCullum b Vettori	1	W 6	6
M. J. Clarke c Guptill b Bond	11		
C. L. White c B. B. McCullum b Franklin	54	1/73 (1) 2/79 (3)	(7 wkts, 50 overs) 273
M. E. K. Hussey c sub (N. L. McCullum)		3/114 (2) 4/116 (4)	
b Bond	56	5/217 (5) 6/238 (6) 7/273 (7)	10 overs: 43-0

N. M. Hauritz, R. J. Harris and D. E. Bollinger did not bat.

Bond 10–1–42–2; Southee 10–0–57–0; Franklin 4.3–0–35–1; Tuffey 9–1–64–1; Vettori 10–0–43–2; Styris 6.3–0–32–0.

New Zealand

B. B. McCullum c Haddin b Johnson	24	S. E. Bond b Johnson	6
P. J. Ingram lbw b Harris	14	T. G. Southee not out	4
M. J. Guptill c Haddin b Watson	18		
N. T. Broom lbw b Harris	0	L-b 2, w 11, n-b 1	14
J. E. C. Franklin c Haddin b Johnson	2		
S. B. Styris c Ponting b Hauritz	46	1/27 (1) 2/43 (2) 3/43 (4)	(43.2 overs) 253
†G. J. Hopics c Bollinger b Watson	35	4/46 (5) 5/89 (3) 6/131 (6)	
*D. L. Vettori b Harris	70	7/176 (7) 8/213 (9)	
D. R. Tuffey c White b Johnson	20	9/239 (10) 10/253 (8)	10 overs: 46-3

Bollinger 8–0–63–0; Harris 8.2–0–34–3; Johnson 9–1–51–4; Watson 5–0–33–2; Hopes 6–0–29–0; Hauritz 7–0–41–1.

Umpires: B. F. Bowden and R. E. Koertzen.   Third umpire: G. A. V. Baxter.

NEW ZEALAND v AUSTRALIA

Third One-Day International

At Hamilton, March 9, 2010 (day/night). Australia won by six wickets. Toss: Australia.

Australian wicketkeeper Haddin was having a golden run with the gloves: his recent appearances were dotted with diving, full-stretch, one-handed catches off his side's speedsters. But this time he shone with the blade, compiling his second one-day international century to put Australia ahead in emphatic style. Ponting raised eyebrows by electing to bowl but, by the end of the night, he had won 20 victories from the 24 one-day internationals where he had opted to field (compared with 63 from the 87 one-day games where he chose to bat), and his firm preference in Tests for batting first. He had been goading his top-order batsmen into converting good starts and fifties into big scores and centuries; Haddin followed orders, with flowing strokeplay and perfect timing, for five sixes and seven fours from 121 balls. Ponting got to watch it from the other end, contributing 69 to their imposing 151-run stand.

Man of the Match: B. J. Haddin.

New Zealand

B. B. McCullum b Bollinger	23	T. G. Southee b Harris		1
P. J. Ingram c Haddin b Harris	5	M. J. Mason not out		2
M. J. Guptill c White b Johnson	21			
L. R. P. L. Taylor c Hussey b Watson	62	B 1, l-b 1, w 6, n-b 2		10
N. T. Broom c Watson b Johnson	24			
S. B. Styris c Harris b Watson	41	1/7 (2) 2/45 (1) 3/55 (3)	(46.2 overs)	245
†G. J. Hopkins c Watson b Harris	45	4/126 (5) 5/146 (4) 6/213 (6)		
*D. L. Vettori run out	0	7/213 (8) 8/240 (7) 9/243 (10)		
S. E. Bond c Haddin b Johnson	11	10/245 (9)	10 overs: 55-2	

Harris 7–0–48–3; Bollinger 8–1–39–1; Johnson 9.2–1–41–3; Hauritz 8–0–40–0; Hopes 8–0–49–0; Watson 6–0–26–2.

Australia

S. R. Watson run out	15	A. C. Voges not out		13
†B. J. Haddin st Hopkins b Vettori	110	L-b 2, w 4, n-b 1		7
*R. T. Ponting c Taylor b Mason	69			
M. E. K. Hussey c Ingram b Southee	9	1/25 (1) 2/176 (3)	(4 wkts, 47.2 overs)	248
C. L. White not out	25	3/190 (4) 4/230 (2)	10 overs: 39-1	

J. R. Hopes, M. G. Johnson, N. M. Hauritz, R. J. Harris and D. E. Bollinger did not bat.

Bond 8–1–43–0; Southee 10–0–43–1; Mason 10–0–68–1; Vettori 10–0–36–1; Styris 7.2–0–43–0; Guptill 2–0–13–0.

Umpires: Asad Rauf and B. F. Bowden.   Third umpire: E. A. Watkin.

NEW ZEALAND v AUSTRALIA

Fourth One-Day International

At Auckland, March 11, 2010 (day/night). Australia won by six wickets (D/L method). Toss: Australia. One-day international debut: S. L. Stewart.

Australia ignored the rain and complexities of the Duckworth/Lewis method to retain the Chappell–Hadlee Trophy in convincing fashion. In a match New Zealand needed to dominate to keep the series alive, they came up with almost nothing, and the series was over as a contest. Asked to bat first again, they lasted barely 44 overs in making a paltry 238. The big wet reduced Australia's chase to 200 from 34 overs and, despite a couple of wickets from Vettori, White made an unbeaten 50 to guide them home and earn the match award. Earlier, off-spinner Hauritz grabbed three for 46 as New Zealand's batting crumbled. They had started their innings powerfully, flying to 63 without loss in the eighth over, and finished it just as well, with Tuffey smacking 34 off 17 balls with four sixes, three of them in a row off Hauritz – which proves how weak the middle was.

Man of the Match: C. L. White.

New Zealand

B. B. McCullum c White b Hauritz	61	S. E. Bond c Hauritz b Johnson	19
M. J. Guptill c Ponting b Watson	30	T. G. Southee not out	1
L. R. P. L. Taylor c Hussey b Hopes	15		
S. L. Stewart c Watson b Hauritz	4	L-b 9, w 13, n-b 2	24
S. B. Styris c and b Hopes	8		
*D. L. Vettori lbw b Johnson	12	1/63 (2) 2/120 (3) (44.1 overs)	238
†G. J. Hopkins c Haddin b Watson	20	3/128 (4) 4/130 (1) 5/152 (5)	
J. E. C. Franklin b Hauritz	10	6/154 (6) 7/177 (8) 8/213 (7)	
D. R. Tuffey c and b Harris	34	9/236 (9) 10/238 (10) 10 overs: 65-1	

Harris 7–1–37–1; Bollinger 5–0–34–0; Johnson 8.1–0–40–2; Watson 6–1–34–2; Hopes 10–0–38–2; Hauritz 8–0–46–3.

Australia

S. R. Watson lbw b Vettori	32	M. E. K. Hussey not out	28
†B. J. Haddin c Styris b Bond	0	L-b 6, w 2	8
*R. T. Ponting lbw b Vettori	50		
C. L. White not out	50	1/2 (2) 2/84 (1) (4 wkts, 31.1 overs)	202
A. C. Voges c Vettori b Franklin	34	3/85 (3) 4/150 (5) 7 overs: 37-1	

J. R. Hopes, M. G. Johnson, N. M. Hauritz, R. J. Harris and D. E. Bollinger did not bat.

Bond 6–0–28–1; Southee 5.1–0–55–0; Tuffey 5–0–38–0; Vettori 7–1–29–2; Styris 5–0–20–0; Franklin 3–0–26–1.

Umpires: Asad Rauf and G. A. V. Baxter.   Third umpire: C. B. Gaffaney.

NEW ZEALAND v AUSTRALIA

Fifth One-Day International

At Wellington (Westpac Stadium), March 13, 2010 (day/night). New Zealand won by 51 runs. Toss: Australia.

In a dead rubber, Australia managed a lifeless pursuit of victory; it was third time unlucky for Ponting as he decided to chase again. New Zealand's 241 was a moderate total but the tourists capitulated to a staggering degree, seven single-figure scores leading to a 51-run defeat. The Kiwis were heading for a pride-saving triumph as soon as Bond, the chief destroyer with four for 26, sent Haddin and Ponting on their way with successive balls in the seventh over. Ponting was stunned to be given caught behind off a searing first-up bouncer; replays suggested the ball had gone closer to the scalp Bond was after than bat or glove, making clear contact with his helmet and nothing else. Southee provided great support for Bond, with four middle-order victims including Hussey, who had done his best to get Australia out of their pickle. In this new age, rather than taking his sizzling form into the upcoming Tests, Bond boarded a flight for India to take up his IPL contract.

Man of the Match: T. G. Southee.

New Zealand

B. B. McCullum c Ponting b McKay	1
M. J. Guptill run out	7
L. R. P. L. Taylor c Bollinger b Watson ...	30
S. L. Stewart c Haddin b Johnson	6
S. B. Styris b Hopes.	55
*D. L. Vettori b Bollinger	28
†G. J. Hopkins c Haddin b Hauritz	26
N. L. McCullum c and b Johnson	17

D. R. Tuffey c Ponting b McKay 36
S. E. Bond not out 6
L-b 3, w 19, n-b 7 29

1/21 (1) 2/25 (2)   (9 wkts, 50 overs) 241
3/32 (4) 4/85 (3)
5/153 (5) 6/155 (6) 7/186 (7)
8/214 (8) 9/241 (9)   10 overs: 43-3

T. G. Southee did not bat.

McKay 10–1–57–2; Bollinger 9–2–37–1; Johnson 10–0–42–2; Watson 8–1–31–1; Hauritz 7–0–43–1; Hopes 6–0–28–1.

Australia

S. R. Watson c Taylor b N. L. McCullum..	53
†B. J. Haddin c Southee b Bond	17
*R. T. Ponting c Hopkins b Bond	0
C. L. White c Vettori b Southee	6
A. C. Voges c Hopkins b Southee	5
M. E. K. Hussey b Southee	46
J. R. Hopes c Guptill b Vettori	40
M. G. Johnson c sub (J. E. C. Franklin) b Southee .	6

N. M. Hauritz c Styris b Bond........... 9
C. J. McKay c Southee b Bond 2
D. E. Bollinger not out 1
L-b 1, w 4 5

1/27 (2) 2/27 (3) 3/46 (4)   (46.1 overs) 190
4/72 (5) 5/96 (1) 6/146 (6)
7/157 (8) 8/186 (9)
9/186 (7) 10/190 (10)   10 overs: 37-2

Bond 9.1–1–26–4; Tuffey 8–0–41–0; Vettori 10–1–39–1; Southee 9–0–36–4; N. L. McCullum 8–0–31–1; Styris 2–0–16–0.

Umpires: Asad Rauf and G. A. V. Baxter.   Third umpire: E. A. Watkin.
Series referee: R. S. Madugalle.

NEW ZEALAND v AUSTRALIA

First Test Match

Will Swanton

At Wellington (Basin Reserve), March 19–23, 2010. Australia won by ten wickets. Toss: Australia. Test debuts: B. J. Arnel; R. J. Harris.

Much ado about plenty. Young daredevil Phillip Hughes received an unexpected opportunity when Shane Watson, recent winner of the Allan Border Medal for Australia's player of the year, was ruled out on the first morning by a hip strain. Hughes went on to seal Australia's emphatic win with a slightly crazed 86 on the final day. His madcap knock was a fitting conclusion to a Test where players cast aside personal dramas, form slumps, the breakdown of video technology and freakish weather.

North entered the match on Test cricket's version of death row, after struggling for most of the Australian summer. He came out and hit the most flawless of centuries, a five-hour gem, as though he didn't even know the vultures had been circling. His captain deserved, and received, enormous credit. Ponting had encouraged North throughout the lead-up, working side by side with him in the nets on his technique and his confidence. North's first net session had been a shocker, but the change in his fortunes after Ponting's overtime was marked.

Vice-captain Clarke was suffering problems of another kind; he had flown back to Australia halfway through the one-day series, on a trip which ended with the announcement that his high-profile engagement to a Sydney model was over. When he rejoined the tour – criticism from past players for having left it ringing in his ears – he looked like a shell

Escape from death row: Marcus North guides the ball past B-J. Watling en route to a crucial hundred, 12 innings on from his last.

of his former self. But the first person to greet him in the foyer of the team hotel was Ponting. They shook hands, hugged, laughed and disappeared to Ponting's room for a pep talk. Clarke emerged a reinvigorated soul, reached a hundred on the first day, and went on to his highest Test score while adding 253 for the fifth wicket with North.

Australia declared at 459 for five, and New Zealand were skittled for 157 with Bollinger, a true and endearing character, bouncing back from an ordinary one-day series with five for 28. Celebrating his fifth wicket, he meant to kiss the Australian crest on his shirt but kissed the wrong side – planting his lips on the logo for Victoria Bitter beer. Ponting enforced the follow-on and the Kiwis made a better fist of it, especially on the fourth day, when windy Wellington became so windy it was a minor miracle the entire city wasn't blown out to sea.

Gusts of up to 150kph were recorded during New Zealand's second innings, and for a while video replay equipment was unavailable. When McCullum was 52, the Australians tried to refer an lbw appeal to the Decision Review System, but the tracking cameras were shaking too much to project the path of the ball reliably so he continued to get the benefit of the doubt. The HotSpot cameras had to be taken down altogether, a light roller started moving on its own, and a groundsman, clinging to the covers for dear life, was nearly thrown into the sightscreen as the weather turned feral.

Hauritz bowled 49 overs of off-spin into the wind for three wickets, and debutant paceman Ryan Harris also toiled manfully, claiming three of his four victims pushing into the gale. Dynamo McCullum's century took the hosts to the respectability of 407, but their first innings had been such a disaster that it was too little much too late.

Hughes and Katich hustled out and reached 106 without loss, the youngster throwing himself out of his shoes with every attacking shot. His unbeaten 86 came from just 75 balls. Katich, with 18 from 65, played second fiddle to perfection – a job requiring just as much skill as first fiddle. The Australians took a commanding lead in the two-Test series.

Clarke won the match award, but Ponting deserved one for his input behind the scenes. Not only had his coaching rescued North's career; he had given Clarke, whose head was spinning after his personal dramas dominated front and back pages, support and mateship. Australia had Clarke to thank for their dominance. And Clarke was indebted to his captain.

Man of the Match: M. J. Clarke.

Close of play: First day, Australia 316-4 (Clarke 100, North 52); Second day, New Zealand 108-4 (Guptill 19, Vettori 42); Third day, New Zealand 187-5 (Vettori 18, McCullum 4); Fourth day, New Zealand 369-6 (McCullum 94, Tuffey 23).

Australia

P. J. Hughes c Taylor b Arnel	20	– not out	86
S. M. Katich lbw b Arnel	79	– not out	18
*R. T. Ponting run out	41		
M. E. K. Hussey c Watling b Martin	4		
M. J. Clarke st McCullum b Vettori	168		
M. J. North not out	112		
†B. J. Haddin not out	11		
B 2, l-b 15, w 2, n-b 5	24	N-b 2	2

1/25 (1) 2/104 (3)   (5 wkts dec, 131 overs) 459   (no wkt, 23 overs) 106
3/115 (4) 4/176 (2)
5/429 (5)

M. G. Johnson, N. M. Hauritz, R. J. Harris and D. E. Bollinger did not bat.

Martin 30–3–115–1; Southee 19–4–68–0; Arnel 26–4–89–2; Tuffey 22–7–49–0; Vettori 33–5–111–1; Guptill 1–0–10–0. *Second Innings*—Martin 6–0–43–0; Arnel 10–2–31–0; Vettori 7–1–32–0.

New Zealand

T. G. McIntosh c Hussey b Harris	9	– (2) c Katich b Hauritz	83
B-J. Watling lbw b Bollinger	0	– (1) lbw b Bollinger	33
P. J. Ingram run out	5	– c Haddin b Bollinger	1
L. R. P. L. Taylor c North b Bollinger	21	– lbw b Hauritz	25
M. J. Guptill c Haddin b Bollinger	30	– c North b Harris	6
*D. L. Vettori c Ponting b Harris	46	– b Hauritz	77
†B. B. McCullum c Harris b Bollinger	24	– c Clarke b Harris	104
D. R. Tuffey run out	0	– not out	47
T. G. Southee c Haddin b Johnson	5	– c Clarke b Harris	0
B. J. Arnel c Ponting b Bollinger	0	– lbw b Harris	3
C. S. Martin not out	0	– b Johnson	1
L-b 4, w 2, n-b 11	17	B 1, l-b 14, w 1, n-b 11	27

1/3 (2) 2/14 (3) 3/31 (1) 4/43 (4)   (59.1 overs) 157   1/70 (1) 2/78 (3)   (134.5 overs) 407
5/112 (6) 6/148 (7) 7/148 (5)   3/115 (4) 4/136 (5)
8/154 (8) 9/156 (10) 10/157 (9)   5/183 (2) 6/309 (6) 7/388 (7)
                                                           8/392 (9) 9/396 (10) 10/407 (11)

Bollinger 13–4–28–5; Harris 17–4–42–2; Johnson 11.1–5–38–1; Hauritz 14–4–39–0; North 4–1–6–0. *Second Innings*—Bollinger 27–3–80–2; Harris 24–3–77–4; Johnson 29.5–7–107–1; Hauritz 49–16–119–3; North 5–2–9–0.

Umpires: Asad Rauf and I. J. Gould.   Third umpire: Aleem Dar.

NEW ZEALAND v AUSTRALIA

Second Test Match

DON CAMERON

At Hamilton, March 27–31. Australia won by 176 runs. Toss: Australia.

Vettori made an excellent start to his 100th Test, on his home ground, when he took four wickets and ran out Ponting on the opening day, and a whirlwind hundred from Taylor gave New Zealand first-innings lead on the second. But the game slipped away as the Australian batsmen, led by Katich, regained control and Johnson found a final burst of pace. The ultimate outcome mimicked Wellington: a crushing home defeat before lunch on the last day.

New Zealand recalled Sinclair yet again to replace the out-of-form Ingram, and off-spinner Patel for Tuffey, nursing a broken hand, while Watson, recovered from his hip injury, returned to open for Australia in place of Hughes. Otherwise it seemed little had changed. Ponting won his seventh consecutive toss on this tour and claimed first use of a firm, batsman-friendly pitch; Martin, supposedly New Zealand's spearhead, was no sharper than at Wellington. But the first change in the script came after half an hour, when Watson played an ugly heave at a harmless ball from Southee and the tall Arnel pulled down the catch at deepish mid-on.

An hour later Ponting, who had been settling in, off-drove Patel in his first over; Vettori picked up at mid-off, and his brilliant throw hit the stumps. It was Ponting's 13th run-out in Tests; he headed the list one ahead of Allan Border, Matthew Hayden and Rahul Dravid. The painstaking left-handers, Katich and Hussey, took Australia to 129 for two before Southee had Hussey caught behind. Not normally a bowler who snarls at the batsman's throat or threatens the outside edge, Southee suddenly found his outswinger, apparently aided by a replacement ball. He swung back to hold a return catch from Haddin and trapped North lbw. Vettori had Katich crisply caught at short leg, for the only half-century, and then swooped through the tail: the last seven fell for 59. The formidable Australians were all out for 231 and, though Bollinger bowled McIntosh in New Zealand's first over, home hearts were happy at stumps.

The madness was maintained on the second sunny day, but this time both teams had their share of the spectacular. Bollinger, Harris and Johnson were fast and adroit enough to extract some magic from the amiable pitch and, had the catching been half as good, Australia's fightback would have been even more effective. But the day belonged to the effervescent Taylor, assisted by the fielders' failure to gather the flying snicks skidding from his top edge towards third man; he was dropped three times. Taylor drove with equal profit, and his favourite swipe to midwicket brought a steady flow of boundaries. While wickets tumbled at the other end, he bolted to 50 in 34 balls and cantered on to New Zealand's fastest Test century, from 81 balls, beating Vettori's 82 at Harare in 2005-06. Next, he lifted Hauritz for three successive sixes in an over costing 25. By the time the explosions ceased, he had hit four sixes and 19 fours – exactly 100 in boundaries – from 104 balls. On 138, umpire Asad Rauf initially gave him not out caught behind, but the decision was overturned on review. Apart from Taylor, Watling managed a solid 46 and Southee had a 15-ball slog, but no one else passed 15; Sinclair made a predictably small score against superior bowling odds.

Still, New Zealand were 33 runs to the good. Australia regained the lead just before bad light stopped play, but took their time to recover command. Vettori made a furious lbw appeal for the second ball of the third day; Rauf gave Watson out, but he was reprieved on referral. Watson and Katich began to right the slightly battered Australian craft, and they were 85 without hurt – Katich prim, Watson restraining his usual boldness – when Southee had Watson caught, top-edging to Watling at deep midwicket. Alarm bells must have rung when the same pair removed Ponting, whose only scoring shot went for six. Australia were 91 for two, only 58 in profit; another wicket could have spelled disaster.

But the Katich–Hussey recovery slowly restored what should have been the status quo – home bowlers struggling on the too-friendly pitch, Australia building an impregnable wall of runs. Katich did not even hit a four for 137 balls; his fifty, needing 177, was more than five times slower than Taylor's. He reached his hundred just before tea, though he and Hussey were both out just after, having added 155. Clarke and North took over in a partnership worth 142, and the tempo speeded up on the fourth morning before Ponting halted the slaughter at 511 for eight.

New Zealand had five sessions to pursue an unlikely 479, and worked hard that afternoon, but had lost half their side by the close. Johnson took the first three, including the prize wicket of Taylor, and next day claimed the last three in successive overs to finish with ten in the match. Guptill had survived nearly three and a half hours, and Southee struck out again for 45 off 25 balls. But by lunch the Australians' early vulnerability was forgotten as they cruised home with 176 runs to spare.

Man of the Match: M. G. Johnson.

Close of play: First day, New Zealand 19-1 (Watling 6, Sinclair 8); Second day, Australia 35-0 (Watson 28, Katich 6); Third day, Australia 333-4 (Clarke 42, North 42); Fourth day, New Zealand 185-5 (Guptill 29, McCullum 19).

Australia

S. R. Watson c Arnel b Southee..............	12 –	c Watling b Southee.............. 65
S. M. Katich c Watling b Vettori............	88 –	c McCullum b Arnel 106
*R. T. Ponting run out	22 –	c Watling b Southee.............. 6
M. E. K. Hussey c McCullum b Southee........	22 –	c McCullum b Arnel 67
M. J. Clarke c Southee b Patel............	28 –	lbw b Arnel 63
M. J. North lbw b Southee	9 –	c McCullum b Vettori 90
†B. J. Haddin c and b Southee.............	12 –	b Patel........................ 48
M. G. Johnson c McIntosh b Vettori	0 –	c Patel b Vettori 0
N. M. Hauritz not out	12 –	not out 41
R. J. Harris lbw b Vettori	10 –	not out 18
D. E. Bollinger b Vettori	4	
B 4, l-b 6, n-b 2	12	B 2, l-b 1, n-b 4 7

1/25 (1) 2/63 (3) 3/129 (4)　　　(74.3 overs) 231   1/85 (1)　(8 wkts dec, 153 overs) 511
4/172 (5) 5/180 (2) 6/199 (7)　　　　　　　　　　　2/91 (3) 3/246 (4)
7/200 (8) 8/200 (6) 9/217 (10) 10/231 (11)　　　4/247 (2) 5/389 (5) 6/443 (6)
　　　　　　　　　　　　　　　　　　　　　　　　　　7/443 (8) 8/453 (7)

Martin 12–3–42–0; Southee 19–3–61–4; Arnel 12–2–53–0; Vettori 19.3–5–36–4; Patel 12–2–29–1. *Second Innings*—Martin 14–1–60–0; Southee 23–4–89–2; Arnel 26–6–77–3; Vettori 48–10–140–2; Patel 39–8–141–1; Sinclair 3–2–1–0.

New Zealand

T. G. McIntosh b Bollinger	4 –	(2) b Johnson 19
B-J. Watling b Bollinger	46 –	(1) c Haddin b Johnson 24
M. S. Sinclair b Johnson	11 –	lbw b Clarke 29
L. R. P. L. Taylor c Haddin b Bollinger.........	138 –	c Haddin b Johnson 22
M. J. Guptill c Ponting b Harris	4 –	c Ponting b Johnson 58
*D. L. Vettori c Haddin b Harris	15 –	lbw b Hauritz 22
†B. B. McCullum c Ponting b Johnson	5 –	c Hussey b Bollinger 51
J. S. Patel c Ponting b Johnson..............	7 –	c North b Bollinger 3
T. G. Southee not out	22 –	c Clarke b Johnson 45
B. J. Arnel c Haddin b Johnson	7 –	c Haddin b Johnson 0
C. S. Martin b Harris	0 –	not out 5
W 1, n-b 4	5	B 12, l-b 10, n-b 2 24

1/4 (1) 2/30 (3) 3/114 (2)　　　(63.3 overs) 264   1/40 (2) 2/53 (1)　(91.1 overs) 302
4/143 (5) 5/167 (6) 6/193 (7) 7/234 (8)　　　　　3/107 (4) 4/119 (3)
8/236 (4) 9/263 (10) 10/264 (11)　　　　　　　　5/152 (6) 6/239 (7) 7/249 (8)
　　　　　　　　　　　　　　　　　　　　　　　　　　8/273 (5) 9/295 (10) 10/302 (9)

Bollinger 14–3–57–3; Harris 15.3–3–50–3; Johnson 16–2–59–4; Hauritz 13–1–68–0; Watson 5–1–30–0. *Second Innings*—Bollinger 16–2–87–2; Harris 14–3–38–0; Watson 6–2–18–0; Johnson 20.1–6–73–6; Clarke 16–4–27–1; Hauritz 17.5–5–37–1; North 2–2–0–0.

Umpires: Aleem Dar and Asad Rauf.　Third umpire: I. J. Gould.
Series referee: J. Srinath.

DOMESTIC CRICKET IN NEW ZEALAND, 2009-10

Don Cameron

The 2009-10 season saw the return of the Plunket Shield, after 34 seasons in which New Zealand's first-class tournament bore the names of sponsors. Though the change came when the last sponsor pulled out, NZC chief executive Justin Vaughan declared that the naming rights for the four-day competition would no longer be for sale, and the old shield was brought out of a museum in Wellington to be presented to the latest champions, **Northern Districts**.

At the same time, the first-class format was revised; after six seasons in which teams played eight league matches (one full round before the top three played the bottom three a second time) followed by a final, it reverted to a home-and-away round-robin league, with each side playing ten matches. There was no final.

Northern headed the table from start to finish, winning six games and losing only two, under the leadership of Jamie Marshall. They also retained the 50-over title, beating table-leaders Auckland in the final. Seamer Graeme Aldridge was the season's leading first-class wicket-taker, while wicketkeeper Peter McGlashan claimed a world record when he took 12 catches in one game.

Nominally, Northern Districts can call on the services of the country's captain and finest player, Daniel Vettori, but he represented them only in the Twenty20 competition. Vettori hogged the national cricket awards, presented in September 2010, winning Player of the Year for the fourth time in six, plus the trophies for the "most meritorious" first-class bowler and one-day international bowler (he was also nominated as a batsman and an all-rounder). But his only first-class cricket came in six home Tests. He has been playing at the top level since he was 18, and turned 32 in January 2011; shoulder injuries are a worry, and he rested during a triangular one-day series with Sri Lanka and India in August 2010.

> Vettori hogged the national cricket awards

That series marked the international debut of another Northern Districts player, Kane Williamson, just two days after his 20th birthday. Over the previous two home summers he had been the outstanding teenage batsman, and he was twice named his team's player of the year.

Williamson was the leading scorer in the 2009-10 domestic one-day competition, with two unbeaten centuries among his 621 runs; he also passed 600, with another two hundreds, in the Plunket Shield. The New Zealand cricketing public waited anxiously to see whether he could make the step up, after starting his international career with a couple of ducks.

A revamped Twenty20 tournament, now called the HRV Cup, was expanded from eight rounds to ten; with New Zealand's international players available throughout, plus overseas signings, it attracted 4,000 to 5,000 to late-afternoon games, often at suburban grounds. The final, between **Central Districts** and **Auckland** at the picturesque if modestly sized Pukekura Park, witnessed some thrilling batting. Put in, Central were given a quick start by the rugged Peter Ingram before Ross Taylor – New Zealand's best batsman of the season – and Kieran Noema-Barnett stole the show. They put on 133 in only 53 balls: Taylor smashed eight sixes and five fours to finish with 80 from 30 balls. Central scored 206, a shell-shocked Auckland only 128.

Central Districts put on another remarkable batting performance when they were set 443 to win in the final innings of a Plunket Shield game at Wellington: their opening pair responded with 428, and Ingram scored an unbeaten 245 which helped him earn an international debut in February. Earlier in the same game, Wellington's Luke Woodcock reached 220 not out as he put on 225 for the ninth wicket with Ili Tugaga; he was to finish as the season's leading first-class scorer, only 12 short of his thousand.

FIRST-CLASS AVERAGES, 2009-10

BATTING (600 runs)

	M	I	NO	R	HS	100s	Avge	Ct/St
S. L. Stewart (*Canterbury*)	8	14	3	812	227*	3	73.81	2
N. T. Broom (*Otago*)	7	10	1	608	196	3	67.55	11
†L. J. Woodcock (*Wellington*)	10	20	5	988	220*	1	65.86	4
C. D. Cumming (*Otago*)	9	16	1	924	160	4	61.60	10
P. J. Ingram (*C. Districts & New Zealand*)	9	17	2	916	245*	3	61.06	5
R. A. Jones (*Auckland*)	10	17	1	953	170*	4	59.56	7
M. S. Sinclair (*C. Districts & New Zealand*) ..	10	17	2	818	165	3	54.53	8
L. R. P. L. Taylor (*C. Districts & N. Zealand*) .	7	13	0	693	138	1	53.30	13
B. B. McCullum (*Otago & New Zealand*) ..	7	13	1	607	185	2	50.58	23/2
J. G. Myburgh (*Canterbury*)	9	15	0	758	120	2	50.53	6
†T. G. McIntosh (*Auckland & New Zealand*) ...	10	20	2	889	171	1	49.38	11
M. H. W. Papps (*Canterbury*)	10	20	1	927	180	4	48.78	14
K. S. Williamson (*Northern Districts*)........	10	15	2	614	192	2	47.23	12
J. M. How (*Central Districts*)	9	17	1	695	176	1	43.43	12
†C. J. Merchant (*Wellington*)	10	20	1	764	108	2	40.21	6
N. R. Parlane (*Wellington*)...............	10	20	1	763	193	2	40.15	11
P. G. Fulton (*Canterbury & New Zealand*)	10	19	1	691	172	1	38.38	9

BOWLING (20 wickets)

	Style	O	M	R	W	BB	5W/i	Avge
G. W. Aldridge (*Northern Districts*)........	RFM	291.3	68	968	42	6-49	3	23.04
B. J. Arnel (*N. Districts & New Zealand*) ..	RFM	309.1	95	818	34	6-18	2	24.05
E. P. Thompson (*Central Districts*)	LFM	278.1	62	819	34	5-64	3	24.08
S. R. Wells (*Otago*).....................	RM	148.3	28	513	21	5-26	2	24.42
M. J. Mason (*Central Districts*)	RFM	264.1	67	758	30	5-42	2	25.26
T. G. Southee (*N. Districts & N. Zealand*) ..	RFM	200	49	594	23	8-27	1	25.82
I. E. O'Brien (*Wellington & New Zealand*) ..	RFM	188.3	35	560	21	5-75	1	26.66
M. D. Bates (*Auckland*)	LM	356.5	92	1,016	37	6-55	3	27.45
W. C. McSkimming (*Otago*)	RM	207.5	51	653	23	5-17	1	28.39
B. C. Hiini (*Canterbury*)	RFM	231.3	59	674	22	4-34	0	30.63
N. Wagner (*Otago*)	LFM	301.4	46	1,047	28	4-62	0	37.39
N. B. Beard (*Otago*)	SLA	364.3	72	1,033	27	6-107	1	38.25
M. J. Tugaga (*Wellington*)	RFM	209.1	33	887	23	5-77	1	38.56
D. L. Vettori (*New Zealand*).............	SLA	312	84	851	22	4-36	0	38.68
J. S. Patel (*Wellington & New Zealand*)	OB	396.3	113	1,078	26	4-48	0	41.46
C. S. Martin (*Canterbury & New Zealand*)	RFM	392	68	1,355	32	4-35	0	42.34

PLUNKET SHIELD, 2009-10

	Played	Won	Lost	Drawn	1st-inns points	Points	Net avge runs per wkt
Northern Districts	10	6	2	2	16	52	7.86
Canterbury	10	4	3	3	12	36	7.12
Central Districts	10	4	3	3	8	32	−5.23
Otago	10	3	3	4	10	28	−3.00
Auckland.................	10	3	5	2	6	24	1.26
Wellington	10	2	6	2	8	20	−6.97

Outright win = 6pts; lead on first innings = 2pts. Net average runs per wicket is calculated by subtracting average runs conceded per wicket from average runs scored per wicket.

At Napier (Nelson Park), November 10–13, 2009. **Drawn. ‡Auckland 403** (A. P. de Boorder 125*) **and 232-3; Central Districts 418-9 dec** (M. S. Sinclair 165). *Central Districts 2pts. England batsman Ravi Bopara played Auckland's first five Plunket Shield games.*

At Dunedin (University Oval), November 10–12, 2009. **Northern Districts won by ten wickets. Otago 88** (B. J. Arnel 6-18) **and 334** (C. D. Cumming 126); ‡**Northern Districts 410** (J. A. F. Yovich 128*) **and 13-0.** *Northern Districts 8pts. Northern Districts began their campaign by winning with a day to spare, after bowling Otago out for what would remain the season's lowest total; Brent Arnel had career-best figures of 10–3–18–6.*

At Wellington, November 10–13, 2009. **Drawn.** ‡**Wellington 214 and 262** (L. M. Burtt 5-57); **Canterbury 222** (I. E. O'Brien 5-75) **and 191-6.** *Canterbury 2pts. Canterbury slumped to 91-6 on the final day but held on for the draw.*

At Rangiora, November 17–20, 2009. **Canterbury won by 115 runs. Canterbury 440** (P. G. Fulton 172; S. R. Wells 5-75) **and 265-5 dec;** ‡**Otago 235 and 355.** *Canterbury 8pts.*

At Whangarei, November 17–19, 2009. **Northern Districts won by nine wickets. Central Districts 94** (G. W. Aldridge 6-49) **and 310** (G. W. Aldridge 5-96); ‡**Northern Districts 279** (M. J. Mason 5-94) **and 129-1.** *Northern Districts 8pts. For the second match running, Northern Districts won in three days after dismissing their opponents in double figures on the first day. Graeme Aldridge claimed a career-best 11-145, and wicketkeeper Peter McGlashan made 12 catches (six in each innings), a world record; only Wayne James, with 11 catches and two stumpings for Matabeleland v Mashonaland Country Districts in 1995-96, had made more dismissals in a match.*

At Wellington, November 17–20, 2009. **Wellington won by 99 runs. Wellington 356** (J. M. Brodie 103) **and 280-5 dec** (C. J. Merchant 108); ‡**Auckland 274-9 dec** (R. A. Jones 101) **and 263.** *Wellington 8pts.*

At Christchurch (Village Green), November 24–27, 2009. **Drawn.** ‡**Canterbury 540** (M. H. W. Papps 107, J. G. Myburgh 120, C. Z. Harris 105) **and 133-1 dec;** Auckland **392-7 dec** (S. B. Styris 112) **and 160-4.** *Canterbury 2pts.*

At Napier (Nelson Park), November 24–27, 2009. **Drawn. Otago 534-8 dec** (S. B. Haig 153, N. T. Broom 196; E. P. Thompson 5-122) **and 133-8;** ‡**Central Districts 190** (S. R. Wells 5-26) **and 517** (P. J. Ingram 135). *Otago 2pts. Shaun Haig and Neil Broom scored career-bests as they added 306 for the third wicket, enabling Otago to enforce the follow-on, though they then stumbled to 133-8 chasing 174.*

At Hamilton, November 24–27, 2009. **Wellington won by 38 runs. Wellington 263** (T. G. Southee 8-27) **and 304** (B. J. Arnel 5-47); ‡**Northern Districts 281 and 248.** *Wellington 6pts, Northern Districts 2pts. Despite Tim Southee's 25–12–27–8, the best return of the season, and a second-innings collapse to 33-5, Wellington halted Northern Districts' bid for a third straight win.*

At Auckland (Colin Maiden Park), December 3–6, 2009. **Northern Districts won by 55 runs. Northern Districts 290-3 dec** (B-J. Watling 136) **and forfeited second innings;** ‡**Auckland forfeited first innings and 235.** *Northern Districts 8pts. Other teams alleged collusion between the captains to contrive a result – illegal in this tournament – when they both forfeited an innings. Only 40 overs were bowled on the first three days, in which Northern Districts scored 82-0. The captains said they had acted independently, with Gareth Hopkins pointing out that he was desperate for a win: Auckland remained pointless after four matches.*

At Rangiora, December 3–5, 2009. **Central Districts won by ten wickets. Central Districts 325** (L. M. Burtt 5-108) **and 28-0;** ‡**Canterbury 171 and 180** (M. J. Mason 5-42). *Central Districts 8pts.*

At Queenstown, December 3–6, 2009. **Otago won by nine wickets.** ‡**Wellington 391-6 dec** (S. J. Rhodes 142*) **and 203; Otago 471-9 dec** (N. T. Broom 136, S. R. Wells 115*) **and 124-1.** *Otago 8pts. Stewart Rhodes scored 142* on first-class debut.*

At Auckland (Colin Maiden Park), December 12–15, 2009. **Otago won by five wickets. Auckland 229** (W. C. McSkimming 5-17) **and 354** (J. A. Raval 134); ‡**Otago 270** (M. D. Bates 5-83) **and 316-5** (N. T. Broom 152*). *Otago 8pts. Auckland had no points at the halfway mark of this tournament, and were 16 behind fifth place.*

At Hamilton, December 12–14, 2009. **Canterbury won by ten wickets. Northern Districts 205 and 111** (C. J. Anderson 5-22); ‡**Canterbury 289** (J. G. Myburgh 107) **and 31-0.** *Canterbury 8pts.*

At Wellington, December 12–15, 2009. **Central Districts won by nine wickets. Wellington 440-9 dec** (L. J. Woodcock 220*, M. J. Tugaga 103) **and 207-4 dec;** ‡**Central Districts 205 and 445-1** (P. J. Ingram 245*, J. M. How 176). *Central Districts 6pts, Wellington 2pts. Luke Woodcock more* *than doubled his previous best during a 225-run ninth-wicket stand with Ili Tugaga. Central Districts were set a target of 443 in 113 overs; Peter Ingram, whose 245* was the highest score of the season, and Jamie How responded with an opening stand of 428, a New Zealand first-wicket record, and they won with more than an hour to spare.*

At Auckland (Colin Maiden Park), February 25–28, 2010. **Auckland won by ten wickets. Wellington 477** (S. J. Rhodes 124; G. S. Shaw 5-101) **and 122; ‡Auckland 480-3 dec** (T. G. McIntosh 171, R. A. Jones 107) **and 121-0.** *Auckland 8pts. After the New Year break Auckland claimed their first points of the season, bowling out Wellington cheaply after the first two innings totalled 957-13; Tim McIntosh and Richard Jones added 212 for Auckland's second wicket.*

At Rangiora, February 25–28, 2010. **Drawn. ‡Canterbury 558-4 dec** (R. J. Nicol 134, S. L. Stewart 161*, D. G. Brownlie 112*) **and 85-1; Northern Districts 726** (H. J. H. Marshall 170, J. A. H. Marshall 178*). *Northern Districts 2pts. Northern Districts scored only the third total of 700-plus in New Zealand first-class cricket, with both Marshall twins reaching 170 and all 11 batsmen in double figures. Earlier, Dean Brownlie scored 112* on first-class debut while adding 236* for Canterbury's fifth wicket with Shanan Stewart.*

At Invercargill, February 25–28, 2010. **Drawn. Central Districts 355** (M. S. Sinclair 122) **and 95-5; ‡Otago 330** (A. J. Redmond 136; E. P. Thompson 5-64). *Central Districts 2pts.*

At New Plymouth, March 4–7, 2010. **Central Districts won by one wicket. ‡Central Districts 414 and 361-9; Canterbury 223** (E. P. Thompson 5-68) **and 551-5 dec** (S. L. Stewart 227*, C. F. K. van Wyk 178*). *Central Districts 8pts. Canterbury were 94-4 following on – still 97 behind – before Shanan Stewart and Kruger van Wyk added 379*. The declaration set Central Districts a target of 361 in 74 overs; last man 17-year-old Adam Milne, making his first-class debut as a full substitute for Michael Mason (like Stewart called up by New Zealand during the game), hit the winning runs with two balls to spare.*

At Dunedin (University Oval), March 4–7, 2010. **Otago won by 24 runs. Otago 387** (C. D. Cumming 102) **and 208-3 dec; ‡Auckland 238-7 dec and 333** (N. B. Beard 6-107). *Otago 8pts. Auckland lost their last six for 39 chasing 358.*

At Wellington, March 4–6, 2010. **Northern Districts won by nine wickets. Wellington 193** (G. W. Aldridge 6-57) **and 248; ‡Northern Districts 400** (K. S. Williamson 170) **and 44-1.** *Northern Districts 8pts.*

At Napier (McLean Park), March 12–15, 2010. **Central Districts won by seven wickets. Wellington 250** (D. A. J. Bracewell 5-47) **and 207; ‡Central Districts 232** (M. J. Tugaga 5-77) **and 228-3.** *Central Districts 6pts, Wellington 2pts.*

At Whangarei, March 12–14, 2010. **Northern Districts won by ten wickets. ‡Auckland 227 and 188; Northern Districts 410** (K. S. Williamson 192) **and 9-0.** *Northern Districts 8pts. Kane Williamson batted throughout the second day's 98 overs, and raised his career-best score for the second week running.*

At Queenstown, March 12–15, 2010. **Canterbury won by 158 runs. Canterbury 315 and 340-5 dec** (M. H. W. Papps 122); **‡Otago 221 and 276** (T. D. Astle 5-55). *Canterbury 8pts. Todd Astle bowled Canterbury to victory after coming in as a full substitute for Chris Martin, called up by New Zealand.*

At Auckland (Colin Maiden Park), March 20–23, 2010. **Auckland won by an innings and 93 runs. ‡Central Districts 269 and 273** (M. S. Sinclair 129; M. D. Bates 5-71); **Auckland 635-6 dec** (R. A. Jones 123, G. J. Hopkins 201, A. K. Kitchen 116, C. de Grandhomme 106*). *Auckland 8pts. Auckland celebrated their second win of the season in style after four of their batsmen reached centuries; captain Gareth Hopkins completed a maiden double, and added 206 for the fifth wicket with Anaru Kitchen.*

At Rangiora, March 20–23, 2010. **Canterbury won by five wickets. Wellington 176 and 447** (N. R. Parlane 137, J. E. C. Franklin 162; T. D. Astle 5-118); **‡Canterbury 318** (S. L. Stewart 101) **and 306-5.** *Canterbury 8pts.*

At Whangarei, March 20–23, 2010. **Drawn. Northern Districts 465-9 dec** (B. S. Wilson 107) **and 212-7; ‡Otago 576-8 dec** (C. D. Cumming 160, D. J. Broom 119). *Otago 2pts. Darren Broom scored 119 on first-class debut, and added 247 for Otago's second wicket with Craig Cumming.*

At Auckland (Colin Maiden Park), March 29–April 1, 2010. **Auckland won by seven wickets. Canterbury 203** (M. H. W. Papps 104; M. D. Bates 6-55) **and 485** (M. H. W. Papps 180; R. R. Sherlock 7-133); ‡**Auckland 352** (T. D. Astle 6-103) **and 337-3** (R. A. Jones 170*, R. A. Young 126*). *Auckland 8pts. Auckland claimed a third win after Richard Jones and Reece Young shared an unbroken 241-run partnership for their fourth wicket.*

At Napier (McLean Park), March 29–April 1, 2010. **Northern Districts won by six wickets. Central Districts 217 and 531-7 dec** (P. J. Ingram 178); ‡**Northern Districts 342** (P. D. McGlashan 115) **and 411-4** (H. J. H. Marshall 108, B. S. Wilson 101*). *Northern Districts 8pts. Northern Districts made sure of the Plunket Shield when they took first-innings points, but rounded off their season by scoring 411 in the fourth innings to complete their sixth win.*

At Wellington, March 29–April 1, 2010. **Drawn. Wellington 389** (J. D. Ryder 103) **and 402-3 dec** (N. R. Parlane 193, C. J. Merchant 101*); ‡**Otago 192** (S. R. Wells 102*) **and 344-7** (C. D. Cumming 103). *Wellington 2pts. Otago wicketkeeper Derek de Boorder made eight catches in Wellington's first innings, a national record and one short of the world record. Jesse Ryder scored 103 in his only appearance of the season. Neal Parlane narrowly missed a maiden double-century, adding 251 with Cameron Merchant for Wellington's third wicket.*

CHAMPIONS

Plunket Shield				
1921-22	Auckland	1955-56	Canterbury	1984-85	Wellington
1922-23	Canterbury	1956-57	Wellington	1985-86	Otago
1923-24	Wellington	1957-58	Otago	1986-87	Central Districts
1924-25	Otago	1958-59	Auckland	1987-88	Otago
1925-26	Wellington	1959-60	Canterbury	1988-89	Auckland
1926-27	Auckland	1960-61	Wellington	1989-90	Wellington
1927-28	Wellington	1961-62	Wellington	1990-91	Auckland
1928-29	Auckland	1962-63	Northern Districts	1991-92	Central Districts / Northern Districts
1929-30	Wellington	1963-64	Auckland	1992-93	Northern Districts
1930-31	Canterbury	1964-65	Canterbury	1993-94	Canterbury
1931-32	Wellington	1965-66	Wellington	1994-95	Auckland
1932-33	Otago	1966-67	Central Districts	1995-96	Auckland
1933-34	Auckland	1967-68	Central Districts	1996-97	Canterbury
1934-35	Canterbury	1968-69	Auckland	1997-98	Canterbury
1935-36	Wellington	1969-70	Otago	1998-99	Central Districts
1936-37	Auckland	1970-71	Central Districts	1999-2000	Northern Districts
1937-38	Auckland	1971-72	Otago	2000-01	Wellington
1938-39	Auckland	1972-73	Wellington		
1939-40	Auckland	1973-74	Wellington	*State Championship*	
1940–45	No competition	1974-75	Otago	2001-02	Auckland
1945-46	Canterbury			2002-03	Auckland
1946-47	Auckland	*Shell Trophy*		2003-04	Wellington
1947-48	Otago	1975-76	Canterbury	2004-05	Auckland
1948-49	Canterbury	1976-77	Otago	2005-06	Central Districts
1949-50	Wellington	1977-78	Auckland	2006-07	Northern Districts
1950-51	Otago	1978-79	Otago	2007-08	Canterbury
1951-52	Canterbury	1979-80	Northern Districts	2008-09	Auckland
1952-53	Otago	1980-81	Auckland		
1953-54	Central Districts	1981-82	Wellington	*Plunket Shield*	
1954-55	Wellington	1982-83	Wellington	2009-10	Northern Districts
		1983-84	Canterbury		

Auckland have won the title outright 22 times, Wellington 20, Canterbury 15, Otago 13, Central Districts 7, Northern Districts 6. Central Districts and Northern Districts also shared the title once.

NZC ONE-DAY COMPETITION, 2009-10

50-over league plus knockout

	Played	Won	Lost	Tied	Bonus points	Points	Net run-rate
Auckland	8	5	2	1	2	24	0.59
Northern Districts	8	5	3	0	1	21	0.13
Canterbury	8	4	3	1	1	19	−0.04
Central Districts	8	4	4	0	1	17	0.56
Otago	8	3	5	0	1	13	−0.41
Wellington	8	2	6	0	0	8	−0.9c

Preliminary finals

1st v 2nd: Auckland beat Northern Districts by eight wickets to qualify for final. **3rd v 4th:** Central Districts beat Canterbury by six wickets. **Final play-off:** Northern Districts beat Central Districts by 83 runs to qualify for final.

Final

At Auckland (Colin Maiden Park), February 21, 2010. **Northern Districts won by 21 runs. Northern Districts 304-3** (50 overs) (B-J. Watling 145*); ‡**Auckland 283-9** (50 overs) (K. S. Williamson 5-51).

B-J. Watling batted throughout Northern Districts' 50 overs, for his highest one-day score, hitting 16 fours and two sixes in 158 balls. He added 163 for the second wicket with Kane Williamson, who later returned career-best figures with his off-spin.

HRV CUP, 2009-10

20-over league plus final

	Played	Won	Lost	No result	Points	Net run-rate
Central Districts	10	7	3	0	28	0.30
Auckland	10	6	4	0	24	0.49
Otago	10	5	3	2	24	0.27
Northern Districts	10	5	5	0	20	0.53
Wellington	10	3	5	2	16	−0.87
Canterbury	10	2	8	0	8	−0.85

Auckland qualified for the final ahead of Otago because they won six victories to Otago's five.

Final

At New Plymouth, January 31, 2010. **Central Districts won by 78 runs. Central Districts 206-6** (20 overs); ‡**Auckland 128** (16.1 overs).

Ross Taylor hit 80 in 30 balls, with five fours and eight sixes, and added 133 in nine overs for Central's fourth wicket with Kieran Noema-Barnett (49 in 28 balls).

PAKISTAN CRICKET, 2010

A triumph for the paranoid

OSMAN SAMIUDDIN

Perhaps Pakistan cricket should begin to organise itself along the lines of the Chinese calendar. If 2006 was the Year of Hair, 2007 the Year of Woolmer, 2008 the Year of No Test, and 2009 the Year of Lahore, then 2010 can only be known as the Year of the Spot-Fix.

Ultimately this year was a dirty triumph for the paranoid. All the creeping growth of rumour and speculation and confusion over the last decade was first fuelled by the board's inquiry into the disastrous tour of Australia which began the year. The committee's meetings, recorded on camera, were leaked – and it wasn't pretty. Coaches Intikhab Alam and Aqib Javed suspected their own

PAKISTAN IN 2010

	Played	Won	Lost	Drawn/No result
Tests	10	2	6	2
One-day internationals	18	5	13	–
Twenty20 internationals	18	6	12	–

DECEMBER / JANUARY	3 Tests, 5 ODIs and 1 T20I (a) v Australia	(see *Wisden 2010*, page 1055)
FEBRUARY	2 T20Is (h) (in UAE) v England	(page 1004)
MARCH		
APRIL		
MAY	World Twenty20 (in West Indies)	(page 797)
JUNE	Asia Cup (in Sri Lanka)	(page 1076)
JULY	2 Tests and 2 T20Is (h) (in England) v Australia	(page 310)
AUGUST / SEPTEMBER	4 Tests, 5 ODIs and 2 T20Is (a) v England	(page 322)
OCTOBER / NOVEMBER	2 Tests, 5 ODIs and 2 T20Is (h) (in UAE) v South Africa	(page 1007)
DECEMBER / JANUARY / FEBRUARY	2 Tests, 6 ODIs and 3 T20Is (a) v New Zealand	(see *Wisden 2012*)

For a review of Pakistan domestic cricket from the 2009-10 season, see page 1021.

players of deliberate underperformance. Seven were punished, and four banned, though these punishments were rescinded a few months later.

But it all found release in those three no-balls at the Lord's Test in August. Now every slog, wide, no-ball, dropped catch, run-out, loss, win, any and every thing will for ever fall under a scanner of revitalised paranoia.

That was the bad news. But the spot-fixing scandal didn't just deprive Pakistan of three vital players in Salman Butt, Mohammad Aamer and Mohammad Asif – although the loss of a potential long-term captain and arguably the world's best new-ball pair cannot be oversold. The really bad news was that the fallout also pushed Pakistan cricket to the very precipice of existence.

The PCB's initial reaction to the *News of the World* sting operation was typical of this administration, but probably wouldn't have been out of place from any of the last few administrations: a bumbling, incoherent denial. Noises were made about conspiracies before outrageously incendiary accusations were hurled at England. The ECB was, at that point, a lone ally in world cricket. It left Pakistan friendless and homeless, and at one stage – make no mistake – suspension of their membership of the ICC, or at least that of their chairman, was a very real possibility.

After those critical ICC meetings in October, however, the PCB – with much steering from the ICC's reconstituted task force, headed by

Plenty to think about: Ijaz Butt in October 2010, after apologising to the ECB.

Giles Clarke – pulled itself back a little. Ijaz Butt stopped talking so publicly, and a raft of anti-corruption and disciplinary measures were implemented.

Subhan Ahmed has also been promoted to the position of chief executive officer, to take the limelight, pressure and burden off Ijaz, who was increasingly becoming a one-man board. Subhan is an indigenous PCB product, and that is a *good* thing. If there is a job in the board he hasn't done since the mid 1990s, it must be because it doesn't exist, and this is a gradual, deserved progression. That he is immensely respected, trusted and liked by the ICC, a man they can and do work with, is doubly important.

Under his direction, some dynamism emerged. The Quaid-e-Azam Trophy, Pakistan's premier first-class tournament, has always lacked shape and identity, but Subhan pushed through a first-ever day/night final, with an orange ball. It was a left-field, decidedly modern piece of administration, and the ICC, keen to trial floodlit first-class games to pave the way for day/night Tests eventually, were suitably impressed. Soon, as the year turned, the board were also to hold the first meeting of the general body in nearly a decade, a key requirement of the constitution.

But, as the strange flight of Zulqarnain Haider from Dubai to London showed, calamity is never far away. Haider zipped off on the morning of a deciding one-day international against South Africa, claiming he had been first approached and then threatened by a bookie during the series. The seriousness of his claims receded as questions over his motives increased but, in the light of the Lord's Test, it was still a disaster.

Other equally grave problems remained. After the summer's shenanigans, England cannot, for now, be considered as a home venue. The UAE remains geographically feasible, but poses logistical and financial problems. Sri Lanka and England are scheduled to play full series against Pakistan soon, and it is likely that the UAE again will be "home". This administration – led by Subhan – is at least more realistic about when any international cricket will return to Pakistan, acceptance being the first step to rehabilitation.

That there was at least enough on the field to distract occasionally from all the troubles was some consolation. If there still wasn't a Test or one-day international series win in 2010 – Pakistan hadn't won a Test series since November 2006 or a one-day series since November 2008 – there were plenty of moments to reaffirm that cricket without Pakistan would be a less colourful arena. And finally, early in 2011, they won a series of each kind in New Zealand.

Test wins over Australia – the first in 15 years – and England in England, a drawn series with South Africa, and a semi-final run in the World Twenty20 would be a fair collection in any year. In one which began with that dysfunctional whitewash, where four top players were briefly banned, and concluded with the aftermath of the England tour, in which three more were lost, it is actually remarkable.

Indeed, it is frightening to think what might have been achieved had Pakistan managed to synchronise their bowling riches from the English summer with the batting growth seen later in the year in the UAE. Or if they had had one Test captain rather than four. Or one coach. Or one chief selector. It has ever been thus. Most importantly, that strange, uncontrollable collective spirit was still present, evidenced in outstanding one-day comebacks against England and South Africa. And with the emergence of players such as Azhar Ali, and the reintroduction of Wahab Riaz, that strange, uncontrollable method of bringing out talent was also working.

After four of the worst years any side could have, there is deep comfort in that knowledge.

PAKISTAN v ENGLAND IN THE UAE, 2009-10

David Hopps

Twenty20 internationals (2): Pakistan 1, England 1

The seeds of England's World Twenty20 triumph in the Caribbean in May 2010 were sown in Abu Dhabi in February. They played two 20-over internationals there against the reigning champions, Pakistan, before travelling on for their tour of Bangladesh. And one of the key incidents took place in a warm-up game against their own second team, England Lions, who won off the last ball of the match. The Lions' victory identified their South African-born opening batsmen, Craig Kieswetter and Michael Lumb, as claimants for promotion; their case grew stronger as the senior side's openers, Jonathan Trott and particularly Joe Denly, failed to click. Events in the West Indies might have turned out differently if Stuart Broad had not badly missed Kieswetter off Ryan Sidebottom when he was four; Broad failed to lay a hand on the ball at mid-off, and Kieswetter, who had qualified as a full England player only the day before, went on to 81, and was soon added to the one-day squad in Bangladesh.

Pakistan, falling back on the United Arab Emirates as a refuge after being shorn of cricket in their own country because of terrorism, had just lost all nine international matches on their tour of Australia, and they made it ten in a row in the first game with England, when the batting of Eoin Morgan and Kevin Pietersen offered another pointer to future success in the Caribbean. But the short series was squared when Abdul Razzaq steered Pakistan to their first win since the Wellington Test in early December.

Shoaib Malik was captain for both Twenty20 games even though Shahid Afridi returned for the second, following his two-match ban for biting the ball (see *Wisden 2010*, page 1071). Mohammad Asif was unable to play because he had been banned from the UAE.

NATIONAL SQUADS

Pakistan *Shoaib Malik, Abdul Razzaq, Fawad Alam, Imran Farhat, Imran Nazir, Khalid Latif, Mohammad Talha, Saeed Ajmal, Sarfraz Ahmed, Shahid Afridi, Umar Akmal, Umar Gul, Wahab Riaz, Yasir Arafat. *Coach:* Ijaz Ahmed.

England *P. D. Collingwood, T. T. Bresnan, S. C. J. Broad, A. N. Cook, J. L. Denly, E. J. G. Morgan, K. P. Pietersen, L. E. Plunkett, M. J. Prior, A. Shahzad, R. J. Sidebottom, G. P. Swann, J. C. Tredwell, I. J. L. Trott, L. J. Wright. *Coach:* A. Flower.

At Abu Dhabi, February 17, 2010 (floodlit). **England Lions won by five wickets. ‡England XI 157-6** (20 overs) (L. J. Wright 42*, M. J. Prior 33; A. U. Rashid 3-22); **England Lions 158-5** (20 overs) (M. J. Lumb 58*, C. Kieswetter 81). *In front of empty terraces at the Sheikh Zayed Stadium, England Lions completed a last-ball victory in this warm-up match. Craig Kieswetter struck 81 from 66 balls, the day after officially qualifying for England, and put on 86 for the first wicket in 11 overs with Michael Lumb, another Johannesburg-born player. When Lumb retired hurt, after being hit on the head by a Broad bouncer, the Lions stuttered, but he returned, face bloodied, to add another 20 with Kieswetter and finally won the game with fours off the last two balls. On the same day, Pakistan lost to Pakistan A by seven wickets in a 20-over 13-a-side match.*

PAKISTAN v ENGLAND

First Twenty20 International

At Dubai, February 19, 2010 (floodlit). England won by seven wickets. Toss: Pakistan. Twenty20 international debut: Sarfraz Ahmed.

England's Twenty20 captain, Paul Collingwood, had been emphatic that Craig Kieswetter and Michael Lumb would get no immediate promotion after starring in the England Lions' defeat of the senior side in Abu Dhabi. But that policy immediately looked unconvincing as the incumbents, Denly and Trott, made five runs between them in this game. Pakistan's 129 for eight was a modest total even allowing for a bouncy, two-paced pitch. All the same, England's seven-wicket win with nine balls to spare was edgier than it sounds. They were 18 for three in the fifth over before Pietersen, showing a glimpse of improved form after a disappointing South African tour, and Morgan, who hit 67 in 51 balls, shared a stand of 112, an England all-wicket record in this format. World Twenty20 champions Pakistan still seemed bedevilled by in-fighting after their disastrous tour of Australia, and also lacked the dangerous Shahid Afridi, who was serving the last match of a ban for a ball-biting episode in Perth.

Man of the Match: E. J. G. Morgan.

Pakistan

		B	4	6
Imran Nazir c 2 b 8	2	15	0	0
Imran Farhat run out	14	13	3	0
Khalid Latif c 6 b 7	4	6	0	0
Umar Akmal c 8 b 10	13	12	1	0
*Shoaib Malik c 4 b 10	33	26	3	0
Fawad Alam c 6 b 8	23	23	0	1
Abdul Razzaq c 8 b 9	22	15	1	1
†Sarfraz Ahmed c 8 b 9	5	5	1	0
Yasir Arafat not out	9	4	2	0
Umar Gul not out	1	2	0	0
L-b 1, w 1, n-b 1	3			

6 overs: 25-2   (20 overs) 129-8

1/9 2/20 3/26 4/39 5/86 6/106 7/115 8/119

Saeed Ajmal did not bat.

Sidebottom 4–0–21–0; Bresnan 4–0–30–2; Broad 4–0–23–2; Wright 4–0–27–1; Swann 3–0–18–2; Collingwood 1–0–9–0.

England

		B	4	6
I. J. L. Trott b 7	4	10	0	0
J. L. Denly c 2 b 9	1	3	0	0
K. P. Pietersen not out	43	43	3	0
*P. D. Collingwood run out	0	4	0	0
E. J. G. Morgan not out	67	51	7	2
B 1, l-b 5, w 9	15			

6 overs: 25-3   (18.3 overs) 130-3

1/7 2/10 3/18

†M. J. Prior, L. J. Wright, S. C. J. Broad, T. T. Bresnan, G. P. Swann and R. J. Sidebottom did not bat.

Abdul Razzaq 4–0–24–1; Yasir Arafat 4–0–18–1; Shoaib Malik 3–0–28–0; Saeed Ajmal 4–0–18–0; Umar Gul 3.3–0–36–0.

Umpires: E. A. R. de Silva and H. D. P. K. Dharmasena.   Third umpire: Enamul Haque.

PAKISTAN v ENGLAND

Second Twenty20 International

At Dubai, February 20, 2010 (floodlit). Pakistan won by four wickets. Toss: Pakistan. Twenty20 international debut: A. Shahzad.

Pakistan finally found solace after a run of ten defeats in all formats, beating England with an over to spare to tie the series. Abdul Razzaq struck an unbeaten 46 from 18 balls, with five sixes, including two straight hits off Ajmal Shahzad in the final over. Shahzad, who had become the first Yorkshireman of Asian background to represent his county in 2004, had earlier taken two wickets with his first five balls in international cricket; he and Swann, with three for 14 in his four overs, reduced Pakistan to 78 for five before Razzaq arrived. The addition of Kieswetter to England's one-day party in Bangladesh (prematurely leaked by the Bangladesh Cricket Board) focused further attention on their current failing opening combination. Denly, bowled through the gate by Yasir Arafat, had now totalled 20 runs in five Twenty20 attempts, while Trott's 39 from 51 balls lacked sufficient impetus; he was run out when Pietersen, who scored an impressive 62 in 40 balls, was trying to force the pace.

Man of the Match: Abdul Razzaq. *Man of the Series:* G. P. Swann.

England

		B	4	6
I. J. L. Trott *run out*	39	51	3	0
J. L. Denly *b 8*	5	10	0	0
K. P. Pietersen *lbw b 11*	62	40	4	3
E. J. G. Morgan *c 4 b 10*	9	6	0	1
L. J. Wright *c 5 b 8*	13	8	0	1
*P. D. Collingwood *not out*	11	4	0	1
T. T. Bresnan *c 1 b 8*	0	1	0	0
†M. J. Prior *not out*	1	1	0	0
W 7, n-b 1	8			

6 overs: 39-1   (20 overs) 148-6

1/12 2/110 3/120 4/125 5/144 6/144

S. C. J. Broad, G. P. Swann and A. Shahzad did not bat.

Abdul Razzaq 4–0–17–0; Yasir Arafat 4–0–32–3; Shahid Afridi 4–0–27–0; Saeed Ajmal 4–0–29–1; Umar Gul 4–0–43–1.

Pakistan

		B	4	6
Imran Nazir *c 7 b 11*	4	3	1	0
Imran Farhat *c 9 b 11*	0	2	0	0
Umar Akmal *c 4 b 10*	36	41	3	0
*Shoaib Malik *st 8 b 10*	13	16	2	0
Shahid Afridi *c 4 b 10*	8	9	1	0
Fawad Alam *c 4 b 8*	28	20	2	0
Abdul Razzaq *not out*	46	18	0	5
Yasir Arafat *not out*	5	5	0	0
B 4, l-b 3, w 2	9			

6 overs: 39-2   (19 overs) 149-6

1/4 2/4 3/40 4/64 5/78 6/126

†Sarfraz Ahmed, Umar Gul and Saeed Ajmal did not bat.

Shahzad 4–0–38–2; Bresnan 3–0–25–0; Broad 4–0–24–1; Swann 4–1–14–3; Wright 2–0–21–0; Collingwood 2–0–20–0.

Umpires: E. A. R. de Silva and Enamul Haque.   Third umpire: H. D. P. K. Dharmasena.
Series referee: R. S. Madugalle.

England Lions won a three-match Twenty20 series with Pakistan A in Sharjah and Abu Dhabi 2–1, before Pakistan A won a three-match 50-over series in Dubai 2–1. See page 1019.

PAKISTAN v SOUTH AFRICA IN THE UAE, 2010-11

NEIL MANTHORP

Test matches (2): Pakistan 0, South Africa 0
One-day internationals (5): Pakistan 2, South Africa 3
Twenty20 internationals (2): Pakistan 0, South Africa 2

Zulqarnain Haider's dramatic abandonment of this tour 48 hours after the fourth one-day international dominated the news headlines of a series which had done much to generate interest. Sadly, a lot of it was less than positive.

Some of South Africa's senior players had indicated their reluctance to play against "tainted" opposition in unfamiliar climes following Pakistan's controversial tour of England, but threats of a revolt were quashed by Cricket South Africa, who indicated that the Future Tours Programme would not be compromised except at the ICC's instigation.

Haider played a small but crucial role in Pakistan's series-levelling victory in the fourth one-day game in Dubai, and attracted some attention by the vigour of his fist-pumping celebration afterwards. Pakistan had looked like squandering a last-minute chance of victory, but Haider kept a cool head and won the game. Two days later he requested his passport from the team management on the pretext of needing it to buy a SIM-card for his mobile phone, but instead he purchased an airline ticket and boarded a plane for London, where he informally sought asylum.

The ICC offered "support" for Haider, whose initial accounts of the threats made against him were vague. Some said this was understandable; others suggested he had a tendency to be drawn towards the media spotlight. His team-mates, oddly, said nothing at all. Pakistan's sports minister, though, pronounced him a coward.

Haider's first statement was to a Pakistani TV station – a sign, according to sceptics, that he was an attention-seeker. He said he could not trust the ICC's Anti-Corruption and Security Unit, which drew an understandably defensive response from the game's global administrators.

Further details gradually emerged during Haider's subsequent time in England. He claimed he had been told to "lose the game" and that there had been "threats". Ten days later his family, in Lahore, said he had received death threats. Haider's initial assertion that he was concerned about his family's safety drew more flak from doubters who questioned his decision to flee to London rather than Pakistan. If he was a genuine whistle-blower, they said, then he would have been more specific with his allegations, as Rashid Latif had been in the 1990s when naming his own captain, Salim Malik, among others, as being involved in match-fixing. Yet Haider's concerns all along, he claimed, were for his own safety rather than about the actions of his team-mates. He said he did not tell them because he wanted to protect them. Once again, doubters suggested that his public actions did little to protect anyone.

Whatever emerges in the future, it must be considered against the background of Haider's career. While some sniffed at his credentials, he had been identified five years previously as a potential international, and had been waiting for his chance at the top level. No 24-year-old would wantonly abandon an international career so eagerly and patiently awaited.

After an engaging one-day series, the Haider imbroglio continued to bubble, interest in it being maintained when the two Tests which followed provided the entertainment value of sleeping tablets. The groundstaff and administrators at the new Test grounds in Dubai and Abu Dhabi were understandably keen to prolong the contests and prove that reasonable conditions could be produced in the Gulf, but the pitches might as well have been made of concrete; the players endured conditions virtually unchanged from first to fifth day.

Pakistan, the "home" nation, gained most from the series – as it should be. Seamer Tanvir Ahmed claimed six wickets on debut in the Second Test, just weeks away from his 32nd birthday, while several others would have regarded their careers advanced despite the modest overall results – notably Misbah-ul-Haq, Pakistan's latest Test captain, who was recalled to the side at 36: his undefeated 76 ensured that the First Test was drawn, and he made two more half-centuries in the Second.

South Africa were set back as far as the Test rankings were concerned – and understandably frustrated – but were grateful for the workout ahead of the so-called Test championship decider between themselves and top-ranked India less than a month later.

The logistical exercise of splitting a full tour between Dubai and Abu Dhabi was a great success. Not only were the teams and management happy with their travel and security arrangements, but the sight of almost 20,000 packing the Dubai stadium for the fourth one-dayer was ample proof that the game need not be played in a vacuum in the region. The Tests were, it's true, played in front of just a couple of hundred people – but, with winter temperatures pushing into the high thirties and the shortage of entertainment on offer, that showed discerning good sense from the local Pakistani community rather than lack of interest.

Inevitably, though, the tour will be remembered for the flight of Zulqarnain Haider. Self-sacrificing hero and martyr in the fight against corruption? Over-sensitive, confused and indulgent? Frightened into a panic? It may be years before the full story emerges.

NATIONAL SQUADS

Pakistan *Misbah-ul-Haq, Abdur Rehman, Asad Shafiq, Azhar Ali, Imran Farhat, Mohammad Hafeez, Mohammad Sami, Mohammad Yousuf, Saeed Ajmal, Tanvir Ahmed, Taufeeq Umar, Umar Akmal, Umar Gul, Younis Khan, Zulqarnain Haider. *Coach:* Waqar Younis.

Danish Kaneria was originally selected, but was refused clearance to play by the Pakistan board; Mohammad Hafeez, originally selected only for the limited-overs matches, replaced him for the Tests which followed. Sohail Tanvir was also originally chosen for the Tests, but did not travel due to a knee injury. For the limited-overs matches which preceded the Tests, Abdul Razzaq, Fawad Alam, Shahid Afridi, Shahzaib Hasan, Shoaib Akhtar and Wahab Riaz replaced Azhar Ali, Mohammad Sami, Sohail Tanvir and Taufeeq Umar; Afridi was as captain. Younis Khan joined the squad after the Twenty20 internationals, while Mohammad Yousuf, originally selected for the whole tour, missed the Twenty20 internationals with a groin strain, played in the last one-day international, then aggravated the injury and returned home before the Tests. Zulqarnain Haider left the tour after the fourth one-day international, and was replaced by Adnan Akmal for the Tests. Wahab Riaz injured his side during the First Test and returned home.

South Africa *G. C. Smith, H. M. Amla, J. Botha, M. V. Boucher, A. B. de Villiers, J-P. Duminy, P. L. Harris, J. H. Kallis, M. Morkel, W. D. Parnell, A. N. Petersen, A. G. Prince, D. W. Steyn, L. L. Tsotsobe. *Coach:* C. J. P. G. van Zyl.

For the limited-overs matches which preceded the Tests, L. E. Bosman (Twenty20 matches only), C. A. Ingram, C. K. Langeveldt (50-overs matches only), D. A. Miller, J. A. Morkel, R. J. Peterson and J. Theron replaced Boucher, Harris, Petersen and Prince. Botha captained in the Twenty20 internationals.

PAKISTAN v SOUTH AFRICA

First Twenty20 International

At Abu Dhabi, October 26, 2010 (floodlit). South Africa won by six wickets. Toss: Pakistan.

Shahid Afridi belted 25 from his first six balls, then gave his wicket away, and with it went Pakistan's chances of posting a competitive total. Afridi smashed Botha over long-on for three sixes, but perished attempting a fourth. Misbah-ul-Haq tried to anchor the innings, but the eventual target was modest. South Africa themselves wobbled at 26 for three in the sixth over – Shoaib Akhtar took two wickets in four balls – but the mini-crisis was maturely handled by Duminy and the impressive Ingram, who put on 66 in ten overs to put their side back on course. However, the impression lingered that it was a contest shorn of drama by Afridi's tendency to abuse rather than use his talent. This match was a late addition to the original itinerary, to raise money for the victims of the Pakistan flood disaster.

Man of the Match: J-P. Duminy.

Pakistan		B	4	6
Shahzaib Hasan *c 4 b 11*	9	14	0	0
Imran Farhat *c 1 b 11*	10	8	2	0
Mohammad Hafeez *c 5 b 8*	13	17	2	0
Umar Akmal *c 8 b 7*	14	21	1	0
*Shahid Afridi *c 2 b 8*	25	7	1	3
Misbah-ul-Haq *not out*	27	32	2	1
Abdul Razzaq *b 8*	4	5	0	0
†Zulqarnain Haider *c 4 b 9*	1	4	0	0
Umar Gul *c 1 b 11*	0	5	0	0
Saeed Ajmal *run out*	4	7	0	0
Shoaib Akhtar *run out*	3	2	0	0
L-b 1, w 5, n-b 3	9			

6 overs: 43-2   (19.5 overs) 119

1/16 2/38 3/46 4/75 5/84 6/90 7/91 8/92 9/99

J. A. Morkel 4–0–28–1; Tsotsobe 4–0–16–3; M. Morkel 4–1–18–1; Theron 3.5–0–25–0; Botha 4–0–31–3.

South Africa		B	4	6
G. C. Smith *b 3*	13	12	3	0
L. E. Bosman *c 2 b 11*	2	4	0	0
†A. B. de Villiers *b 11*	0	3	0	0
J-P. Duminy *c 4 b 10*	41	46	5	0
C. A. Ingram *not out*	46	38	4	2
D. A. Miller *not out*	13	7	3	0
L-b 3, w 2	5			

6 overs: 29-3   (18.2 overs) 120-4

1/16 2/16 3/26 4/92

J. A. Morkel, *J. Botha, M. Morkel, J. Theron and L. L. Tsotsobe did not bat.

Shoaib Akhtar 4–1–29–2; Abdul Razzaq 2–0–20–0; Mohammad Hafeez 3–0–10–1; Umar Gul 3.2–0–17–0; Saeed Ajmal 4–0–18–1; Shahid Afridi 2–0–23–0.

Umpires: Ahsan Raza and Asad Rauf.   Third umpire: Nadeem Ghauri.

PAKISTAN v SOUTH AFRICA

Second Twenty20 International

At Abu Dhabi, October 27, 2010 (floodlit). South Africa won by six wickets. Toss: Pakistan.

Early wickets forced Pakistan to consolidate – they were 29 for three in the sixth over – but they were never able to accelerate in the face of some smart seam bowling from Theron, who took three wickets in the last over, and Tsotsobe. Disaster was avoided by Misbah-ul-Haq and Abdul Razzaq, but for the second match running the eventual total was at least 30 short of par. Smith grafted to 38 before he was stumped: at that point 57 were still needed from 40 balls, and Ingram again showed his big-hitting potential to lift his side towards what eventually became a comfortable victory.

Man of the Match: J. Theron. *Man of the Series:* J. Botha.

Pakistan

		B	4	6
Shahzaib Hasan *c 8 b 11*	6	6	1	0
Imran Farhat *b 11*	9	12	1	0
Mohammad Hafeez *b 9*	14	9	2	0
Misbah-ul-Haq *c 7 b 10*	33	38	2	1
Umar Akmal *run out*	5	4	1	0
*Shahid Afridi *c 1 b 10*	3	3	0	0
Abdul Razzaq *c 10 b 7*	25	29	0	2
†Zulqarnain Haider *b 10*	17	17	1	0
Umar Gul *b 10*	0	1	0	0
Saeed Ajmal *not out*	1	1	0	0
L-b 3, w 4	7			

6 overs: 35-3   (20 overs) 120-9

1/9 2/29 3/29 4/36 5/39 6/84 7/119 8/119 9/120

Shoaib Akhtar did not bat.

J. A. Morkel 4–0–31–1; Tsotsobe 4–0–20–2; M. Morkel 4–1–22–1; Botha 4–0–17–0; Theron 4–0–27–4.

South Africa

		B	4	6
G. C. Smith *st 8 b 10*	38	42	4	0
L. E. Bosman *lbw b 6*	11	16	2	0
†A. B. de Villiers *c 2 b 3*	11	15	0	0
J-P. Duminy *not out*	20	16	0	2
C. A. Ingram *c 5 b 11*	31	17	4	1
D. A. Miller *not out*	6	6	0	0
L-b 2, w 6	8			

6 overs: 38-0   (18.4 overs) 125-4

1/38 2/63 3/68 4/109

J. A. Morkel, *J. Botha, M. Morkel, J. Theron and L. L. Tsotsobe did not bat.

Shoaib Akhtar 4–0–36–1; Umar Gul 3.4–0–32–0; Mohammad Hafeez 4–0–19–1; Shahid Afridi 4–0–13–1; Saeed Ajmal 3–0–23–1.

Umpires: Asad Rauf and Nadeem Ghauri.   Third umpire: Ahsan Raza.
Series referee: A. J. Pycroft.

PAKISTAN v SOUTH AFRICA

First One-Day International

At Abu Dhabi, October 29, 2010 (day/night). South Africa won by eight wickets. Toss: Pakistan. One-day international debut: Zulqarnain Haider.

Pakistan's top order were somnambulant on a perfect batting surface, crawling to 140 for one after 30 overs. Mohammad Hafeez nibbled his way to 68 from 84 balls, and Younis Khan was no more urgent during his 54 from 75. That might still have presaged a score of 270–300, but a collapse set in against bowling which was good but not outstanding; Tsotsobe took three quick wickets to finish with splendid figures, and Pakistan limped to 203. Smith retired hurt in the sixth over, as a precaution after being rapped on the hand by a Shoaib Akhtar bouncer, but subsequently South Africa had more trouble with the conditions than the Pakistan bowling: Kallis ended up on a drip after cramping up with dehydration and a stomach ailment shortly before victory was secured with more than ten overs to spare.

Man of the Match: L. L. Tsotsobe.

Pakistan

Asad Shafiq *c Amla b Tsotsobe*	19
Mohammad Hafeez *c Langeveldt b Botha*	68
Younis Khan *lbw b Botha*	54
Misbah-ul-Haq *c Ingram b Tsotsobe*	14
Fawad Alam *b Langeveldt*	9
*Shahid Afridi *c Smith b Tsotsobe*	1
Abdul Razzaq *c de Villiers b Tsotsobe*	2
†Zulqarnain Haider *not out*	12
Umar Gul *c de Villiers b Morkel*	3

Saeed Ajmal *run out*	3
Shoaib Akhtar *c Miller b Langeveldt*	6
L-b 4, w 8	12

1/26 (1) 2/140 (2) 3/157 (3)   (49 overs) 203
4/165 (4) 5/167 (6) 6/173 (7)
7/177 (5) 8/183 (9) 9/196 (10)
10/203 (11)   10 overs: 32-1

Langeveldt 10–1–47–2; Tsotsobe 10–3–27–4; Morkel 8–0–32–1; Kallis 6–0–22–0; Botha 10–0–40–2; Duminy 5–0–31–0.

South Africa

*G. C. Smith retired hurt	18		C. A. Ingram not out	12
H. M. Amla lbw b Saeed Ajmal	35		L-b 7, w 6, n-b 2	15
J. H. Kallis retired hurt	66			
†A. B. de Villiers c and b Saeed Ajmal	51		1/70 (2)	(2 wkts, 39.3 overs) 207
J-P. Duminy not out	10		2/147 (4)	10 overs: 55-0

Smith retired hurt at 29 and Kallis at 188.

D. A. Miller, J. Botha, M. Morkel, C. K. Langeveldt and L. L. Tsotsobe did not bat.

Shoaib Akhtar 8–0–46–0; Umar Gul 6.3–0–34–0; Mohammad Hafeez 1–0–14–0; Shahid Afridi 10–0–36–0; Saeed Ajmal 10–1–42–2; Abdul Razzaq 4–0–28–0.

Umpires: Asad Rauf and R. J. Tucker.   Third umpire: Zameer Haider.

PAKISTAN v SOUTH AFRICA

Second One-Day International

At Abu Dhabi, October 31, 2010 (day/night). Pakistan won by one wicket. Toss: South Africa.

Abdul Razzaq single-handedly manufactured one of the most unlikely international victories with an unbeaten 109 from 72 balls, which featured no fewer than ten sixes to go with seven fours. Chasing 287, Pakistan seemingly had no chance at 228 for seven with only 5.5 overs remaining… yet Razzaq dominated the closing stages to such an extent that the last three batsmen between them contributed only one run to an amazing victory: Shoaib Akhtar faced a solitary delivery during the tenth-wicket stand of 32 from 14 balls. Razzaq even turned down half a dozen runs in the final couple of overs, so intent was he on hitting boundaries and keeping the strike. Pakistan had once again been wayward in the field, allowing Ingram to reach his second century in just his fourth one-day international innings after Amla had given South Africa a flying start with 65 from 62 balls. The final total, though, was disappointing after reaching 232 for four with 7.1 overs to go. Still, all seemed well for South Africa until Razzaq terrified their experienced seamers into delivering a stream of full tosses and hittable length balls. Three sixes in the 47th over, from Langeveldt, made the impossible possible, then Razzaq heaved Albie Morkel for two more sixes over midwicket in the final over before carving the winning four through the covers with one ball to spare.

Man of the Match: Abdul Razzaq.

South Africa

H. M. Amla lbw b Shahid Afridi	65		M. Morkel not out	1
R. J. Peterson b Abdul Razzaq	6		C. K. Langeveldt not out	4
C. A. Ingram lbw b Wahab Riaz	100		B 1, l-b 5, w 5	11
†A. B. de Villiers b Shahid Afridi	29			
J-P. Duminy c Fawad Alam b Shoaib Akhtar	54		1/24 (2) 2/108 (1)	(8 wkts, 50 overs) 286
D. A. Miller c and b Wahab Riaz	6		3/194 (4) 4/216 (3)	
J. A. Morkel b Mohammad Hafeez	1		5/232 (6) 6/236 (7)	
*J. Botha run out	9		7/263 (8) 8/281 (5)	10 overs: 62-1

L. L. Tsotsobe did not bat.

Shoaib Akhtar 10–1–57–1; Abdul Razzaq 5–1–37–1; Mohammad Hafeez 10–0–49–1; Wahab Riaz 10–0–43–2; Shahid Afridi 10–0–59–2; Saeed Ajmal 5–0–35–0.

Pakistan

Asad Shafiq c M. Morkel b Langeveldt....	1	Saeed Ajmal run out	1
Mohammad Hafeez c de Villiers b Botha..	30	Shoaib Akhtar not out	0
Younis Khan lbw b Langeveldt..........	18		
Misbah-ul-Haq lbw b Peterson	17	L-b 3, w 5, n-b 2	10
Fawad Alam c J. A. Morkel b Langeveldt .	48		
*Shahid Afridi c Ingram b Tsotsobe	49	1/8 (1) 2/31 (3) (9 wkts, 49.5 overs) 289	
Abdul Razzaq not out	109	3/58 (4) 4/70 (2)	
†Zulqarnain Haider run out	6	5/136 (6) 6/217 (5) 7/228 (8)	
Wahab Riaz run out...................	0	8/254 (9) 9/257 (10) 10 overs: 36-2	

Langeveldt 10–0–75–3; Tsotsobe 10–1–39–1; M. Morkel 10–0–39–0; J. A. Morkel 4.5–0–52–0; Peterson 7–0–40–1; Botha 8–0–41–1.

Umpires: Aleem Dar and R. J. Tucker.   Third umpire: Nadeem Ghauri.

PAKISTAN v SOUTH AFRICA

Third One-Day International

At Dubai, November 2, 2010 (day/night). South Africa won by two runs. Toss: Pakistan.

Despite an error-strewn finish – two dropped catches, two sets of overthrows and a no-ball in the last couple of overs – South Africa overall made marginally fewer mistakes than their opponents, and just held on to regain the series lead. Any one of those blunders could, and probably should, have cost South Africa the game, which would have been very hard on Amla, who produced a masterclass in adapting to the conditions (the Dubai pitch was underprepared to preserve it for three games in a week, and was consequently slow and awkward): his unbeaten 119 from 126 balls, with nine fours, was quite brilliant. It was his sixth century in one-day internationals, but his fifth of 2010. For Pakistan, Imran Farhat's 47 from 86 deliveries was too slow – he managed just one boundary – and Fawad Alam's unbeaten 59 from 67 balls wasn't quite enough. Their running between wickets was also wretched, and the shot selection left much to be desired too. Theron and Morne Morkel somehow found enough good deliveries in the final two overs, but South Africa's mistakes should have been more costly.

Man of the Match: H. M. Amla.

South Africa

H. M. Amla not out	119	*J. Botha b Shoaib Akhtar..............	15
J. H. Kallis b Shoaib Akhtar	0	M. Morkel c Fawad Alam b Wahab Riaz ..	2
C. A. Ingram c and b Shoaib Akhtar	4	J. Theron run out	5
†A. B. de Villiers st Zulqarnain Haider			
b Shahid Afridi.	19	L-b 1, w 11, n-b 1	13
J-P. Duminy c Zulqarnain Haider			
b Mohammad Hafeez.	26	1/9 (2) 2/15 (3) (9 wkts, 50 overs) 228	
D. A. Miller b Mohammad Hafeez	6	3/57 (4) 4/116 (5)	
J. A. Morkel c Mohammad Hafeez		5/126 (6) 6/163 (7) 7/201 (8)	
b Shahid Afridi.	19	8/211 (9) 9/228 (10) 10 overs: 37-2	

L. L. Tsotsobe did not bat.

Shoaib Akhtar 10–1–39–3; Abdul Razzaq 5–1–19–0; Wahab Riaz 10–1–46–1; Saeed Ajmal 6–0–36–0; Shahid Afridi 10–0–53–2; Mohammad Hafeez 9–0–34–2.

Pakistan

Imran Farhat run out	47	Saeed Ajmal b Theron	2
Mohammad Hafeez c Botha b Tsotsobe	4	Shoaib Akhtar not out	1
Younis Khan c Botha b M. Morkel	0		
Asad Shafiq run out	43	L-b 13, w 5, n-b 1	19
*Shahid Afridi c de Villiers b M. Morkel	7		
Fawad Alam not out	59	1/12 (2) 2/13 (3) (9 wkts, 50 overs) 226	
Abdul Razzaq c de Villiers b Kallis	12	3/98 (1) 4/108 (5)	
†Zulqarnain Haider c Amla b M. Morkel	11	5/121 (4) 6/148 (7) 7/176 (8)	
Wahab Riaz c de Villiers b M. Morkel	21	8/209 (9) 9/225 (10) 10 overs: 23-2	

M. Morkel 10–1–47–4; Tsotsobe 10–1–28–1; Kallis 7–0–30–1; Theron 8–0–49–1; Botha 10–0–42–0; Duminy 5–0–17–0.

Umpires: Aleem Dar and R. J. Tucker.   Third umpire: Zameer Haider.

PAKISTAN v SOUTH AFRICA

Fourth One-Day International

At Dubai, November 5, 2010 (day/night). Pakistan won by one wicket. Toss: South Africa.

A well-paced 92 by the fit-again Smith laid the foundation for what should have been a much larger total, but his troops, particularly de Villiers, were over-cautious and failed to recognise how much the conditions had improved from the previous match. If Botha had not played the reverse sweep to good effect in an entertaining 28 from 15 balls at the end, the total would have been even more modest after Abdur Rehman's canny left-arm spin applied a strong handbrake. Chasing 275, Pakistan looked buried at 220 for seven with just 7.3 overs left, despite Younis Khan's mature, wristy 73 from 115 balls, which contained a solitary boundary. The late revival was sparked by an unlikely late alliance between Wahab Riaz, who smashed 18 from ten balls, and Zulqarnain Haider, who made 19 from 22, including the winning single as the penultimate delivery was squeezed behind square. Haider's fist-pumping celebration at clinching an unlikely victory to square the series assumed greater significance when, a few days later, he left the tour secretly amid claims of match-fixing and death threats.

Man of the Match: Younis Khan.

South Africa

*G. C. Smith lbw b Mohammad Hafeez	92	D. A. Miller b Wahab Riaz	0
H. M. Amla c Imran Farhat b Shoaib Akhtar	10	J. Botha not out	28
J. H. Kallis c Asad Shafiq b Mohammad Hafeez	15	B 1, l-b 4, w 11, n-b 1	17
†A. B. de Villiers c Mohammad Hafeez b Shoaib Akhtar	49	1/35 (2) 2/62 (3) (6 wkts, 50 overs) 274	
J-P. Duminy b Wahab Riaz	36	3/156 (1) 4/191 (4)	
C. A. Ingram not out	27	5/226 (5) 6/226 (7) 10 overs: 50-1	

W. D. Parnell, D. W. Steyn and M. Morkel did not bat.

Shoaib Akhtar 9–0–51–2; Abdul Razzaq 5–0–30–0; Wahab Riaz 9–0–61–2; Mohammad Hafeez 7–0–37–2; Shahid Afridi 10–0–51–0; Abdur Rehman 10–0–39–0.

Pakistan

Imran Farhat lbw b Morkel	2	Wahab Riaz run out	18
Mohammad Hafeez lbw b Steyn	42	Shoaib Akhtar not out	0
Younis Khan b Morkel	73		
Asad Shafiq run out	36	L-b 4, w 12, n-b 1	17
Fawad Alam c Miller b Kallis	6		
*Shahid Afridi c Parnell b Botha	29	1/6 (1) 2/64 (2) (9 wkts, 49.5 overs) 275	
Abdul Razzaq c de Villiers b Morkel	33	3/120 (4) 4/131 (5)	
Abdur Rehman run out	0	5/171 (6) 6/220 (3) 7/220 (8)	
†Zulqarnain Haider not out	19	8/244 (7) 9/272 (10) 10 overs: 64-2	

Morkel 10–0–48–3; Parnell 8.5–0–53–0; Steyn 10–0–79–1; Botha 10–0–42–1; Kallis 9–0–40–1; Duminy 2–0–9–0.

Umpires: D. J. Harper and Zameer Haider. Third umpire: Ahsan Raza.

PAKISTAN v SOUTH AFRICA

Fifth One-Day International

At Dubai, November 8, 2010 (day/night). South Africa won by 57 runs. Toss: South Africa.

A solid effort from the South African batsmen, who finally accepted that the pitch was, in fact, very good, saw them push well past 300, although Kallis and de Villiers were able to score their runs at a comfortable pace – they put on 121 in 23 overs – only because Amla had slashed and flicked his 62 from 47 balls in dazzling style before departing at the end of the 15th over. Duminy applied the garnish with 59 from just 41 balls; the old showman Shoaib Akhtar, who had shone fitfully in all four previous matches, suffered considerably this time, conceding 77 from just seven overs. Pakistan started brightly, the openers putting on 82 in 12.2 overs, but the game again seemed well and truly over when they then dipped to 119 for five – Kallis followed his fine innings with three wickets in 13 balls – before another late rally, this time led by Umar Akmal (showing few ill-effects from having to keep wicket after Zulqarnain Haider's hasty departure), briefly raised hopes of another late turnaround. But in reality the target was far too distant, and after Akmal fell in the 41st over South Africa eventually claimed the series 3–2 with something to spare. It was the fifth one-day series between these two countries, and South Africa had won all five.

Man of the Match: J. H. Kallis. Man of the Series: H. M. Amla.

South Africa

H. M. Amla c Shoaib Akhtar b Shahid Afridi	62		J. Botha not out	28
*G. C. Smith c Shahid Afridi b Shoaib Akhtar	14			
J. H. Kallis c Wahab Riaz b Shahid Afridi	83		B 1, l-b 3, w 5	9
†A. B. de Villiers c Younis Khan b Mohammad Hafeez	61		1/37 (2) 2/98 (1)	(5 wkts, 50 overs) 317
J-P. Duminy not out	59		3/219 (4) 4/227 (3)	
C. A. Ingram run out	1		5/228 (6)	10 overs: 73-1

R. J. Peterson, D. W. Steyn, M. Morkel and L. L. Tsotsobe did not bat.

Shoaib Akhtar 7–0–77–1; Abdul Razzaq 3–0–18–0; Abdur Rehman 10–0–33–0; Shahid Afridi 10–0–59–2; Mohammad Hafeez 10–0–47–1; Wahab Riaz 8–0–64–0; Younis Khan 2–0–15–0.

Pakistan

Shahzaib Hasan c Morkel b Kallis	39		Abdur Rehman not out	9
Mohammad Hafeez c Kallis b Botha	59		Shoaib Akhtar b Peterson	1
Younis Khan c de Villiers b Kallis	3			
Mohammad Yousuf c de Villiers b Kallis	3		W 13	13
Fawad Alam c de Villiers b Steyn	1			
†Umar Akmal c Smith b Steyn	60		1/82 (1) 2/90 (3) 3/96 (4)	(44.5 overs) 260
*Shahid Afridi st de Villiers b Peterson	24		4/101 (5) 5/119 (2) 6/166 (7)	
Abdul Razzaq c Botha b Tsotsobe	39		7/226 (6) 8/245 (9) 9/252 (8)	
Wahab Riaz c Morkel b Peterson	9		10/260 (11)	10 overs: 66-0

Steyn 8–0–47–2; Tsotsobe 9–0–47–1; Morkel 7–0–45–0; Kallis 5–0–30–3; Botha 7–0–49–1; Peterson 8.5–0–42–3.

Umpires: D. J. Harper and Nadeem Ghauri. Third umpire: Zameer Haider.
Series referee: A. J. Pycroft.

TEST MATCH REPORTS BY PATRICK COMPTON

PAKISTAN v SOUTH AFRICA

First Test Match

At Dubai, November 12–16, 2010. Drawn. Toss: South Africa. Test debut: Adnan Akmal.

On the third afternoon, after quickly finishing off Pakistan's first innings and claiming a 132-run lead, South Africa had high hopes of winning the first-ever Test at Dubai. The match had moved along briskly in its first half, with both teams making good starts before suffering near-identical collapses: South Africa lost their last seven wickets for 73, Pakistan theirs for 72.

This was puzzling, because the pitch played well throughout at the Dubai International Cricket Stadium – which became the 102nd Test ground just a few hours after Uppal in Hyderabad became the 101st, the first time two Test grounds had been christened on the same day. Indeed before the match, the Australian groundsman Tony Hemming predicted that, while he couldn't be sure exactly what would happen, the wicket would certainly go the distance. How right he was.

Smith and Petersen survived some difficult moments in an otherwise productive opening session, with Umar Gul and Wahab Riaz getting some seam and swing movement from the new ball in the humidity. As the conditions eased after lunch, so the batsmen took complete charge. After featuring in an opening partnership of 153, Smith completed his 22nd Test century – a world-record 20th as captain – while Kallis and Amla made impressive half-centuries as South Africa reached 311 for three by the close. Amla eventually provided a notable first Test catch to 25-year-old Adnan Akmal, who had been summoned from Lahore to become the third Akmal brother to keep wicket for Pakistan during 2010, following Kamran (who was overlooked for this tour) and Umar, who stood in for the preceding one-day international after Zulqarnain Haider's moonlight flit.

Hemming had predicted that early humidity would encourage lively first sessions throughout the game, and sure enough South Africa were all out for 380 shortly after lunch on the second day, a respectable total but considerably fewer than they would have expected given their fine start. Pakistan, whose side showed seven changes from their previous Test (against England at Lord's in August), then started well themselves, reaching a promising 144 for two by the close, with Mohammad Hafeez in particularly belligerent form as he and Taufeeq Umar – in his first Test for more than four years – profited from some loose bowling to collect 60 from the first nine overs. But next morning Pakistan replicated South Africa's collapse, to be bowled out for 248, the lanky Morkel collecting his third Test five-for after Botha's off-spin had claimed three early wickets.

With Riaz off the field suffering from a side strain, South Africa built effortlessly on their lead. Batting can seldom have looked easier in a Test as Amla and Kallis took their stand to an unbroken 242, a record for South Africa's third wicket against Pakistan. In successive overs Amla reached his 11th Test century, and Kallis his 36th. (They clearly enjoy batting together: it was their eighth hundred partnership in Tests, including two of more than 300.) Smith declared on the fourth afternoon once the lead reached 450. By the close, Steyn and Botha had disposed of Pakistan's openers, but Amla warned that his side still "faced a long, hard day at the office", and he was proved right.

As it turned out, they managed only one wicket – that of Azhar Ali – on the final day. Younis Khan and Pakistan's new captain Misbah-ul-Haq, who delightedly declared the draw a "gift for the nation", batted their side to safety.

If Pakistan's ambitions never went beyond earning a draw, the disappointed South Africans could point to two fielding lapses on the fifth morning that destroyed whatever hope they might have had of winning. In the fourth over, Younis drove loosely at Steyn and edged towards first slip. Boucher, sensing the ball might land in front of the fielder, dived to his right, but spilled a chance he would normally have taken comfortably. Then, shortly before lunch, Misbah pushed forward to Harris and offered Amla at forward short leg an easier opportunity than the one he had taken off the same batsman in the same position in the first innings – but this one went down.

Younis, in his first Test for more than 15 months, offered another chance shortly after lunch, a difficult one to Kallis at slip, but otherwise he batted serenely through the rest of the day, combining watchful defence with bursts of aggression in his 17th Test century – his third against South Africa, all in successive matches – as Pakistan reached their highest fourth-innings total in any Test. It was, nevertheless, a sterile end to a match that had promised much: only three wickets fell on the last two days.

Man of the Match: Younis Khan.

Close of play: First day, South Africa 311-3 (Kallis 53, Harris 0); Second day, Pakistan 144-2 (Azhar Ali 12, Younis Khan 21); Third day, South Africa 139-2 (Amla 44, Kallis 32); Fourth day, Pakistan 109-2 (Azhar Ali 37, Younis Khan 11).

South Africa

*G. C. Smith c Taufeeq Umar b Wahab Riaz	100	– (2) lbw b Saeed Ajmal 34
A. N. Petersen c Younis Khan b Abdur Rehman	67	– (1) lbw b Abdur Rehman 26
H. M. Amla c Adnan Akmal b Wahab Riaz	80	– not out 118
J. H. Kallis c Adnan Akmal b Saeed Ajmal	73	– not out 135
P. L. Harris c Younis Khan b Umar Gul	0	
A. B. de Villiers b Umar Gul	5	
A. G. Prince lbw b Umar Gul	1	
†M. V. Boucher lbw b Abdur Rehman	9	
J. Botha b Abdur Rehman	10	
D. W. Steyn not out	10	
M. Morkel lbw b Saeed Ajmal	10	
B 9, l-b 2, w 1, n-b 3	15	B 1, l-b 2, w 1, n-b 1 5

1/153 (2) 2/190 (1) 3/307 (3)   (123 overs) 380   1/47 (1)   (2 wkts dec, 95 overs) 318
4/318 (5) 5/327 (6) 6/329 (7)   2/76 (2)
7/345 (8) 8/347 (4) 9/363 (9) 10/380 (11)

Umar Gul 30–4–100–3; Wahab Riaz 18–3–61–2; Abdur Rehman 32–2–101–3; Saeed Ajmal 35–6–95–2; Mohammad Hafeez 1–0–1–0; Younis Khan 7–2–11–0. *Second Innings*—Umar Gul 18–0–73–0; Younis Khan 3–0–15–0; Abdur Rehman 36–5–105–1; Mohammad Hafeez 11–3–20–0; Saeed Ajmal 27–2–102–1.

Pakistan

Mohammad Hafeez c Smith b Harris	60	– c Botha b Steyn 34
Taufeeq Umar lbw b Morkel	42	– c Kallis b Botha 22
Azhar Ali c Amla b Morkel	56	– b Harris 63
Younis Khan c de Villiers b Botha	35	– not out 131
*Misbah-ul-Haq c Amla b Botha	9	– not out 76
Umar Akmal c Steyn b Botha	4	
†Adnan Akmal c Boucher b Steyn	10	
Abdur Rehman c de Villiers b Morkel	1	
Umar Gul not out	12	
Wahab Riaz c Boucher b Morkel	5	
Saeed Ajmal c Boucher b Morkel	2	
L-b 12	12	B 6, l-b 4, w 5, n-b 2 17

1/105 (1) 2/111 (2) 3/176 (4)   (95 overs) 248   1/41 (1)   (3 wkts, 117 overs) 343
4/196 (5) 5/202 (6) 6/220 (7) 7/225 (8)   2/75 (2) 3/157 (3)
8/228 (3) 9/246 (10) 10/248 (11)

Steyn 18–3–58–1; Morkel 21–7–54–5; Harris 25–7–47–1; Kallis 8–3–16–0; Botha 23–6–61–3. *Second Innings*—Steyn 22–6–82–1; Morkel 22–4–46–0; Harris 31–10–57–1; Botha 38–7–138–1; Kallis 4–2–10–0.

Umpires: E. A. R. de Silva and D. J. Harper. Third umpire: Ahsan Raza.

PAKISTAN v SOUTH AFRICA

Second Test Match

At Abu Dhabi, November 20–24, 2010. Drawn. Toss: Pakistan. Test debuts: Asad Shafiq, Tanvir Ahmed.

Pakistan made a serious assault on South Africa's top order after they put them in on a green-tinged pitch at the Sheikh Zayed Stadium, which became Test cricket's 103rd ground. Their chief weapon was almost a local: Tanvir Ahmed, the 31-year-old Karachi seamer making his Test debut after an injury to Wahab Riaz, was born in Kuwait.

Test cricket must have seemed simple to Tanvir after he claimed wickets in his first two overs (Petersen with his third ball and Amla with his eighth), followed by Smith, South Africa's captain, with the first ball of his sixth over.

With the moist pitch having encouraged seam and swing for the first hour, Pakistan were sitting pretty. But from 33 for three, Kallis and de Villiers counter-attacked and, by the end of a rollicking first session – by some distance the most entertaining of the series – the batsmen had cracked 17 fours and two sixes, and the score had shot to 114 from just 25 overs.

It was the normally cautious Kallis who led the charge. His 37th century was at the time his fastest in Tests, and it came from just 135 balls as his team shrugged off that faltering start. He and de Villiers shared a stand of 179, their tenth century partnership in Tests. Once Kallis went, though, it was the AB show. In conditions that had eased after that atypical first hour, de Villiers showed a mature relish for building the big innings. Well supported by the lower order, he batted for a minute over ten hours for 278 not out, the highest Test innings for South Africa. Some criticised Smith for denying him a possible triple-century, but not de Villiers himself: "I want to dedicate that innings to Graeme. I thought he should have declared even earlier than he did, but he insisted that he wouldn't until I'd had the chance to break his record [of 277]. That's a measure of him as a man and a captain."

Pakistan's encouraging start seemed a long time ago, though they must have gained comfort from Tanvir's performance: after his early success he persevered to finish with six for 120, figures bettered on debut for Pakistan only by Mohammad Zahid (seven for 66 against New Zealand in 1996-97), Mohammad Nazir (seven for 99, also against New Zealand, in 1969-70) and Arif Butt (six for 89 against Australia in 1964-65). But all the Pakistan attack came unstuck against the last pair, whose unbeaten stand of 107 passed by four South Africa's only previous hundred partnership, by Tuppy Owen-Smith and Sandy Bell at Headingley in 1929.

Pakistan faced a grim battle to secure a draw, but with the pitch continuing to stroke the batsmen's egos and stoke their averages, they avoided the follow-on with some ease. Azhar Ali, with his third consecutive fifty, was particularly impressive; Asad Shafiq, a 24-year-old from Karachi, made an assured 61 on debut; and Misbah-ul-Haq, following his key partnership with Younis Khan on the final day of the First Test, was rock-solid again.

South Africa, for whom Smith did not bat after injuring his thumb in the field, built on their lead of 150. Amla, opening in his place, struck a scintillating 62 in 64 balls, but the South Africans, after dominating this Test and the series, were not going to risk letting Pakistan in by the back door. In the end, the declaration set them a distant 354 from 82 overs. They suffered a hiccough shortly after lunch when Harris and Botha picked up three wickets in eight balls as the batsmen played for non-existent turn and fell leg-before, but the South Africans never looked likely to take all ten.

After the match, Kallis claimed that pitches such as those in Dubai and Abu Dhabi represented a danger to the health of Test cricket, which relied on a balance of power between bat and ball. Pakistan, though, had fewer complaints after emerging with a hard-earned draw.

Man of the Match: A. B. de Villiers.   *Man of the Series:* J. H. Kallis.

Close of play: First day, South Africa 311-5 (de Villiers 120, Boucher 26); Second day, Pakistan 59-1 (Taufeeq Umar 16, Azhar Ali 34); Third day, Pakistan 317-6 (Misbah-ul-Haq 77, Abdur Rehman 0); Fourth day, South Africa 173-4 (Prince 27, Boucher 13).

South Africa

*G. C. Smith c Adnan Akmal b Tanvir Ahmed	10	
A. N. Petersen c Misbah-ul-Haq b Tanvir Ahmed..	2	– (1) c Younis Khan b Abdur Rehman . 35
H. M. Amla c Adnan Akmal b Tanvir Ahmed.....	4	– (2) b Abdur Rehman 62
J. H. Kallis b Tanvir Ahmed	105	– c Taufeeq Umar b Mohammad Hafeez 10
A. B. de Villiers not out...................	278	– (3) lbw b Abdur Rehman 25
A. G. Prince c Asad Shafiq b Mohammad Hafeez..	32	– (5) not out.................... 47
†M. V. Boucher b Tanvir Ahmed	45	– (6) b Umar Gul................ 15
J. Botha b Abdur Rehman	12	– (7) not out................... 7
D. W. Steyn c Mohammad Hafeez b Abdur Rehman	27	
P. L. Harris c Adnan Akmal b Tanvir Ahmed.....	19	
M. Morkel not out	35	
B 6, l-b 1, w 2, n-b 6	15	L-b 1, n-b 1 2

1/2 (2) 2/6 (3) 3/33 (1) (9 wkts dec, 153 overs) 584
4/212 (4) 5/268 (6) 6/341 (7)
7/383 (8) 8/442 (9) 9/477 (10)

1/81 (1) (5 wkts dec, 55 overs) 203
2/113 (2) 3/130 (3)
4/148 (4) 5/182 (6)

Umar Gul 36–6–137–0; Tanvir Ahmed 28–6–120–6; Mohammad Sami 24–1–101–0; Younis Khan 3–1–11–0; Abdur Rehman 50–9–150–2; Mohammad Hafeez 12–0–58–1. *Second Innings*—Umar Gul 7–0–32–1; Tanvir Ahmed 5–1–29–0; Abdur Rehman 22–1–81–3; Mohammad Sami 5–0–28–0; Mohammad Hafeez 16–4–32–1.

Pakistan

Mohammad Hafeez lbw b Steyn	2	– lbw b Harris 34
Taufeeq Umar c Amla b Kallis	43	– lbw b Botha 30
Azhar Ali c Smith b Steyn.................	90	– not out 28
Younis Khan c Amla b Steyn...............	14	– lbw b Harris 0
*Misbah-ul-Haq lbw b Steyn...............	77	– not out 58
Asad Shafiq c Kallis b Harris..............	61	
†Adnan Akmal c Amla b Harris.............	17	
Abdur Rehman lbw b Botha	60	
Umar Gul lbw b Harris..................	21	
Tanvir Ahmed c Prince b Morkel............	30	
Mohammad Sami not out.................	2	
B 5, l-b 8, w 2, n-b 2	17	L-b 2, w 1.............. 3

1/2 (1) 2/119 (2) 3/153 (4) (144.1 overs) 434
4/156 (3) 5/263 (6) 6/309 (7)
7/317 (5) 8/353 (9) 9/412 (10) 10/434 (8)

1/66 (2) (3 wkts, 67 overs) 153
2/66 (1) 3/66 (3)

Steyn 30–8–98–4; Morkel 33–13–94–1; Kallis 21–6–77–1; Botha 14.1–3–54–1; Harris 46–17–98–3. *Second Innings*—Steyn 13–2–40–0; Morkel 11–3–29–0; Harris 23–14–28–2; Kallis 2–0–13–0; Botha 17–4–40–1; Petersen 1–0–1–0.

Umpires: E. A. R. de Silva and D. J. Harper.   Third umpire: Nadeem Ghauri.
Series referee: A. J. Pycroft.

PAKISTAN A v ENGLAND LIONS IN THE UAE, 2009-10

One-day matches (3): Pakistan A 2, England Lions 1
Twenty20 matches (3): Pakistan A 1, England Lions 2

For England's aspirant one-day players, a fortnight of cricket in the Gulf made eminent good sense. The heat and slow-turning dustbowls provided several Lions players with a logical lead-in to England's tour of Bangladesh, which began later in February. And with the senior England and Pakistan teams stopping off in Dubai for two Twenty20 internationals, Andy Flower could cast his eye over the highest concentration of English-qualified talent conceivable.

The World Twenty20 was the most pressing priority, but the 2011 World Cup, a seven-week behemoth on the subcontinent, was also lumbering into view, 12 months away. "International cricket is very intense now – you can't guess whether a player is good enough from domestic cricket," reasoned Geoff Miller, the national selector. "There has to be a step between."

Craig Kieswetter encountered little trouble bridging the gap, even if, for the opening three games, he was still not eligible to play for the full England team. The day after he qualified through residency, Kieswetter smashed 81 – to beat England, no less. South African in birth and approach, he believed his powerful straight-hitting was influenced by a childhood grounding in field hockey. "I am not a slogger. But usually I just swing from the hip as hard as I can," he said, only half-joking. By weight of runs – 279 in five innings – and the fearless manner in which he made them, Kieswetter won his battle against Steven Davies (the pair alternated wicketkeeping duties in the Twenty20 matches). Flower had seen little of Kieswetter before, and his glovework was clearly a work in progress, but he was shoehorned into the England one-day squad which flew on to Dhaka.

Kieswetter and James Tredwell left before the Lions' 50-over series, which exposed traditional frailties. The batsmen coped well in the opening powerplays, even against Pakistan A's accomplished left-arm quick, Wahab Riaz. But Ian Bell aside, they had insufficient method to combat three spinners in the middle overs. Graham Thorpe, the new Lions batting coach, and one of England's finest players of spin in recent memory, had plenty of work on his hands.

ENGLAND LIONS TOURING PARTY

*A. W. Gale (Yorkshire), I. R. Bell (Warwickshire), M. A. Carberry (Hampshire), S. M. Davies (Surrey), S. T. Finn (Middlesex), C. Kieswetter (Somerset), S. P. Kirby (Gloucestershire), M. J. Lumb (Hampshire), S. I. Mahmood (Lancashire), A. U. Rashid (Yorkshire), J. W. A. Taylor (Leicestershire), J. C. Tredwell (Kent), P. D. Trego (Somerset), D. J. Wainwright (Yorkshire), C. R. Woakes (Warwickshire).

C. Kieswetter and J. C. Tredwell transferred to the senior England one-day squad for the tour of Bangladesh after the England v England Lions match on February 17.

Coach: D. Parsons. *Manager:* G. A. M. Jackson. *Batting coach:* G. P. Thorpe. *Fast bowling coach:* K. J. Shine. *Media relations manager:* R. C. Evans. *Physiotherapist:* M. Young. *Physiologist:* M. Spivey. *Analyst:* M. Bourne.

At Sharjah, February 10, 2010. **England Lions won by 52 runs. ‡England Lions 184-5** (20 overs) (C. Kieswetter 31, M. J. Lumb 42, I. R. Bell 37*); **United Arab Emirates A 132-7** (20 overs) (I. Sampath 33; J. C. Tredwell 3-22). *UAE A were 51-0 in the sixth over before James Tredwell removed Indika Sampath with his second ball, and swiftly killed the chase.*

At Sharjah, February 12, 2010. **England Lions won by seven wickets. Pakistan A 156-7** (20 overs) (Shahzaib Hasan 57); **‡England Lions 159-3** (17.4 overs) (C. Kieswetter 77*, I. R. Bell 48; Wahab Riaz 3-34). *Craig Kieswetter, playing as a specialist batsman with Steven Davies keeping wicket, ran out Shahzaib Hasan from mid-off, and then thumped eight fours and four sixes in a 52-ball assault. His third-wicket stand with the daintier Ian Bell – who denied Wahab Riaz a hat-trick – came to 115.*

At Sharjah, February 14, 2010. **England Lions won by eight wickets. Pakistan A 106** (19.5 overs) (A. U. Rashid 3-13); **‡England Lions 107-2** (16.1 overs) (C. Kieswetter 40*, I. R. Bell 32*). *The Lions claimed their first series victory since March 2007, in Bangladesh. On a used, sticky pitch, Kieswetter proved he could adapt his game, hitting only four boundaries. He also made two stumpings off Adil Rashid. Together with Tredwell (who opened the bowling), Rashid suffocated Pakistan A by conceding just 25 runs from their eight overs combined.*

At Abu Dhabi, February 16, 2010. **Pakistan A won by four wickets. England Lions 146-4** (20 overs) (C. Kieswetter 50, A. W. Gale 36*); **‡Pakistan A 149-6** (19.5 overs) (Asad Shafiq 31, Umair Khan 49; S. P. Kirby 3-33). *Kieswetter marked the day of his qualification for England with 50 from 32 balls, taking his tally to 198 runs in four innings on tour. Others struggled against fine death bowling. Third-wicket pair Asad Shafiq and Umair Khan added 61 for Pakistan A, and Tanvir Ahmed swiped the penultimate ball, a wide full toss from Sajid Mahmood, for the winning runs.*

At Abu Dhabi, February 17, 2010. ENGLAND LIONS beat ENGLAND by five wickets (see Pakistan v England in the UAE, page 1004).

At Dubai, February 22, 2010 (day/night). **Pakistan A won by 83 runs. Pakistan A 179** (47.5 overs) (Mohammad Hafeez 51, Aamer Sajjad 39; D. J. Wainwright 3-26); **‡England Lions 96** (34.3 overs) (I. R. Bell 46*; Raza Hasan 3-16, Abdur Rehman 4-25). *With Tredwell now in Bangladesh, David Wainwright came in and produced a career-best performance. Pakistan A's own left-arm spinners, Raza Hasan and Abdur Rehman, proved even more destructive on a two-paced pitch under lights, sweeping up the last nine wickets for 56 runs in 22 overs, with the help of off-spinner Mohammad Hafeez (4–0–8–2). Only No. 3 Bell resisted with any success.*

At Dubai, February 24, 2010 (day/night). **England Lions won by three wickets. Pakistan A 231** (50 overs) (Umair Khan 61, Aamer Sajjad 32, Navid Yasin 32); **‡England Lions 232-7** (49 overs) (M. J. Lumb 110, J. W. A. Taylor 61; Wahab Riaz 3-52, Raza Hasan 3-45). *Lumb demonstrated superb concentration amid bouts of cramp, batting from the first to the 49th over for his third and highest one-day hundred. He eventually became the first of two wickets in consecutive Riaz deliveries. Chris Woakes was run out off the fifth ball of the same over, before Wainwright scrambled a leg-bye to level the series.*

At Dubai, February 26, 2010 (day/night). **Pakistan A won by 70 runs. ‡Pakistan A 213-9** (50 overs) (Asad Shafiq 52, Naved Yasin 46, Yasir Shah 51; C. R. Woakes 4-38); **England Lions 143** (40.1 overs) (M. J. Lumb 30, I. R. Bell 30; Raza Hasan 3-13, Abdur Rehman 3-24). *A sandstorm disrupted training the previous day, but did not delay play in the series decider. Hafeez broke the established pattern at the toss by choosing to bat. Woakes tore in and reduced Pakistan A to 33-4 on his way to career-best figures, but Shafiq organised a fine recovery, and the tidy Yorkshire pair of Rashid and Wainwright were limited to one wicket apiece. Faced with 34 overs of spin, the Lions floundered. Raza's habit of whistling to himself in the outfield amused the watching English players, but there were few smiles when the 17-year-old, with just two first-class matches to his name, removed Andrew Gale for the third successive occasion, setting in motion the Lions' collapse from 43-1 to 143 all out.*

DOMESTIC CRICKET IN PAKISTAN, 2009-10

Abid Ali Kazi

With the national team forced to play all their matches abroad for security reasons, there was no international cricket in Pakistan for the first time since 1992-93, and the domestic tournaments were the only cricket on offer at home.

The 2009-10 season produced a world record when Rafatullah Mohmand, who scored an unbeaten triple-hundred, and Aamer Sajjad added 580 runs for WAPDA's second wicket against Sui Southern Gas in the Quaid-e-Azam Trophy. They beat the second-wicket record of 576 set by Sanath Jayasuriya and Roshan Mahanama for Sri Lanka against India in Colombo in 1997-98; the only higher stand for any wicket in first-class cricket also came in a Colombo Test, when Kumar Sangakkara and Mahela Jayawardene added 624 for Sri Lanka's third wicket against South Africa in 2006. The PCB rewarded both Rafatullah and Sajjad with cash prizes and medals. There had been another huge partnership only weeks earlier, when Misbah-ul-Haq and Usman Arshad put on 479 for Sui Northern Gas against Lahore Shalimar, the second-highest fifth-wicket stand in all first-class cricket.

Sajjad was the leading run-scorer of the season, with 1,435 at 68, but in 2009-10 he was one of seven batsmen who passed 1,000, compared with a single one in 2008-09, though the number of domestic first-class matches was exactly the same. But bowlers also raised their performance, with Tanvir Ahmed taking 97 wickets for Quaid-e-Azam champions Karachi Blues, and slow left-armer Zulfiqar Babar just behind on 96, including all ten in an innings for Multan against Islamabad.

The Quaid-e-Azam Trophy was contested in the same format by the same 22 teams as in 2008-09, with none promoted or relegated. As before, the departmental teams were restricted to Group A, ensuring that a regional team would reach the final via Group B. **Karachi Blues** duly headed their group and won a low-scoring final when Mohammad Sami and Tanvir Ahmed, bowling unchanged, shot out **Habib Bank** for 66 on the third day of the five scheduled. In a reversion to form, the PCB planned a shake-up of the competition in 2010-11, reintroducing two divisions with promotion and relegation.

Defending Quaid-e-Azam champions **Sialkot** missed out after finishing second to Karachi Blues in their group, and reached the final of the one-day RBS Cup only to fold against **Sui Northern Gas**. But Sialkot Stallions won the Twenty20 title for the fifth time in a row, comfortably defeating **Faisalabad Wolves**.

Sui Northern Gas also won the first-class Pentangular Cup, which retained its format but was contested by different teams. For the past two seasons, this had been a competition for four provincial sides (Sind, Punjab, Baluchistan and NWFP) and a Federal Areas team; in 2009-10, the top two teams from each Quaid-e-Azam Trophy group were joined by a fifth side called The Rest. Habib Bank reached their second first-class final of the season but succumbed

The domestic struggle

Qamar Ahmed

The success of any team at international level depends a lot on how professionally the domestic game is run, and how well it is looked after by those in charge. From the 1960s Pakistan's cricket has enjoyed spells of efficient administration. Now, though, the war against the Taliban in Afghanistan, and resultant insurgencies within Pakistan, mean that uncertainty reigns in every part of society – including sport. The attack on the Sri Lankan team bus in Lahore in March 2009, which has been blamed on the so-called "Punjabi Taliban", was a severe blow. No international teams have toured since, and World Cup matches scheduled for Pakistan in early 2011 were moved.

Domestic cricket has suffered badly. With Pakistan forced to play all their games abroad, most of the national players are away so often that they hardly appear at domestic level, and the decline in standards is obvious. Karachi – whose sides have won 19 national titles under various names over the years – is the biggest loser. Actually, the regional teams have been up against it since the early 1960s, when commercial organisations joined the big competitions with their own sides: players were lured away by the promise of employment and a career. There have also been allegations of players bribing their way into teams, or even threatening local officials with guns.

The recent troubles have only made this situation worse. "It is difficult to field a balanced side these days," admits Mohammad Sami, the Test bowler who led Karachi Blues to the Quaid-e-Azam Trophy in 2009-10 and now captains Karachi Whites. "We keep on losing players to teams run by banks and airlines who not only provide employment but also better facilities for practice and travel. Whereas those teams travel by air to domestic tournaments, we are given train expenses only – it's not ideal, or a safe mode of travelling, because of the security fears that always lurk round the corner. We have to put in money from our own pockets to pay the difference to travel by air."

The financial rewards are slim for those not employed by banks or airlines. Players in Division One matches are paid Rs 10,000 (£75) per match besides their daily allowance – "a pittance" according to Sami. Division Two players get only half that fee. The umpires receive Rs 2,500 a day (£18) from the PCB, and the referees Rs 3,000 (£22).

The Blues' and the Whites' first-round matches in 2010-11 had to be postponed after a series of targeted killings in Karachi. Crowds are virtually non-existent. I watched two later first-class games in the city; no more than 20 people were in sight, and a couple of those were uniformed security men.

There is one faint glimmer of light, though: for most of the matches in the domestic Twenty20 competition, played in Lahore in October 2010, the Gaddafi Stadium was packed to near-capacity, and the final, between Karachi Dolphins and Lahore Lions, had a full house.

to Sui Northern – who had pressed them hard in the first half of the Quaid-e-Azam tournament, winning their first six games, before slipping back when they could not conjure a win from the last four.

Oddly, the provincial sides now abandoned for the first-class version continued to compete for the Pentangular One-Day Cup, in which **Sind Dolphins** won all their league games and the final against **Baluchistan Bears**.

FIRST-CLASS AVERAGES, 2009-10

BATTING (700 runs, average 37.00)

	M	I	NO	R	HS	100s	Avge	Ct
Aamer Sajjad (*WAPDA & The Rest*)	14	25	4	1,435	289	5	68.33	10
†Naved Yasin (*Multan & The Rest*)	12	20	1	1,230	154	6	64.73	10
Mohammad Ayub (*Sialkot*)	14	23	3	1,193	179*	4	59.65	6
Khalid Latif (*Karachi Blues*)	10	17	2	878	254*	3	58.53	2
Afsar Nawaz (*Karachi Whites*)	10	17	2	826	121*	1	55.06	8
Zeeshan Butt (*Faisalabad*)	10	17	1	866	221	3	54.12	11
Naved Ashraf (*Rawalpindi*)	9	15	1	714	230*	1	51.00	2
Asad Shafiq (*Karachi Blues*)	15	28	3	1,244	147*	4	49.76	13
Faisal Khan (*Sialkot*)	9	16	1	713	202*	1	47.53	12
†Umair Khan (*Islamabad & The Rest*)	14	26	1	1,175	194	3	47.00	8
†Kashif Siddiq (*Lahore Ravi & The Rest*)	12	22	2	925	178	3	46.25	11
Usman Arshad (*Sui Northern Gas*)	14	22	3	857	183	2	45.10	19
†Adnan Raees (*Abbottabad*)	9	17	1	704	200*	3	44.00	9
†Saeed Anwar (*KRL & The Rest*)	13	24	3	919	126	2	43.76	8
Hasan Raza (*Habib Bank*)	16	26	1	1,087	124	2	43.48	22
Abid Ali (*Lahore Shalimar & The Rest*)	11	21	1	853	91	0	42.65	13
†Naeemuddin (*Sui Northern Gas*)	12	22	3	809	139	1	42.57	5
†Taufeeq Umar (*Habib Bank*)	11	20	2	756	154*	3	42.00	7
Saeed Bin Nasir (*Sui Southern Gas & The Rest*)	14	24	0	986	129	3	41.08	14
Mohammad Hafeez (*Sui Northern Gas*)	15	27	0	1,043	110	1	38.62	17
Majid Jahangir (*Sialkot*)	14	25	2	859	124	2	37.34	18
Kamran Younis (*Sialkot*)	12	21	1	741	182	2	37.05	12
Naved Khan (*Karachi Whites & The Rest*) . .	11	20	1	703	120	2	37.00	10

BOWLING (40 wickets, average 27.00)

	Style	O	M	R	W	BB	5W/i	Avge
Samiullah Khan (*Sui Northern Gas*)	LFM	249	49	715	45	7-55	5	15.88
Zulfiqar Babar (*Multan & The Rest*)	SLA	626.1	144	1,613	96	10-143	9	16.80
Abdur Rehman (*Habib Bank*)	SLA	571.5	148	1,493	88	6-52	5	16.96
Rashid Latif (*Rawalpindi*)	RFM	325.4	86	940	53	9-42	4	17.73
Tanvir Ahmed (*Karachi Blues*)	RFM	509.1	58	1,962	97	8-53	8	20.22
Mohammad Rameez (*R'pindi & The Rest*)	RFM	507	124	1,602	79	8-27	9	20.27
Mohammad Sami (*Karachi Blues*)	RFM	286.4	45	855	41	6-38	2	20.85
Aizaz Cheema (*PIA*)	RFM	284.5	68	845	40	6-75	2	21.12
Imran Ali (*Sui Northern Gas*)	RFM	301.5	72	865	40	6-87	2	21.62
Nasrullah Khan (*Islamabad*)	LFM	287.1	49	1,022	47	5-54	2	21.74
Tabish Khan (*Karachi Whites & The Rest*)	RFM	515	99	1,819	77	7-72	7	23.62
Shehzad Azam (*Islamabad*)	RFM	283.2	31	1,170	49	7-36	3	23.87
Junaid Khan (*Abbottabad & The Rest*) . . .	LFM	562.1	96	1,795	75	7-94	7	23.93
Naved Arif (*Sialkot*)	LFM	314.4	57	993	41	5-42	2	24.21
Tariq Haroon (*Karachi Blues*)	RM	334.5	70	1,122	46	6-127	2	24.39
Sarmad Anwar (*Habib Bank*)	RFM	296.5	42	990	40	7-33	2	24.75
Arun Lal (*Quetta & The Rest*)	RFM	342.4	65	1,145	46	7-87	3	24.89
Asad Ali (*Sui Northern Gas*)	RFM	450.2	108	1,386	54	7-98	4	25.66
Mohammad Talha (*National Bank & Rest*)	RFM	303.2	33	1,175	45	5-37	2	26.11
Yasir Shah (*Sui Northern Gas*)	LB	370.1	75	1,081	41	6-40	1	26.36
Mohammad Irshad (*Lahore Ravi*)	RFM	316.3	61	1,134	43	6-42	3	26.37
Bilawal Bhatti (*Sialkot*)	RFM	380.1	75	1,326	50	6-94	3	26.52
Mohammad Naved (*Lahore Shalimar & Rest*)	RFM	350	67	1,118	42	6-114	3	26.61

QUAID-E-AZAM TROPHY, 2009-10

Group A	P	W	L	D	Pts
Habib Bank.........	10	8	1	1	66
Sui Northern Gas	10	6	2	2	48
National Bank	10	5	3	2	48
PIA	10	4	2	4	45
WAPDA	10	4	1	5	42
ZTBL	10	4	2	4	42
Karachi Whites	10	4	5	1	36
KRL	10	2	3	5	21
Sui Southern Gas	10	1	4	5	12
Pakistan Customs	10	1	9	0	9
Lahore Shalimar	10	0	7	3	0

Group B	P	W	L	D	Pts
Karachi Blues	10	6	1	3	60
Sialkot.............	10	5	1	4	51
Rawalpindi	10	5	2	3	48
Islamabad	10	4	3	3	39
Multan.............	10	4	3	3	36
Lahore Ravi	10	3	3	4	30
Faisalabad	10	2	2	6	30
Peshawar...........	10	2	5	3	18
Hyderabad..........	10	1	5	4	18
Quetta	10	2	5	3	15
Abbottabad	10	1	5	4	15

PIA = Pakistan International Airlines; WAPDA = Water and Power Development Authority; ZTBL = Zarai Taraqiati Bank Limited (formerly ADBP); KRL = Khan Research Laboratories.

Final: Karachi Blues beat Habib Bank by 141 runs.

Outright win = 6pts; lead on first innings in a won or drawn game = 3pts. Teams tied on points are ranked on most wins, then fewest losses, and then on net run-rate (runs conceded per over from runs scored per over).

Group A

At Karachi (National Bank), October 10–12, 2009. **Habib Bank won by seven wickets. Karachi Whites 190** (Danish Kaneria 5-72) **and 172** (Danish Kaneria 6-59); ‡**Habib Bank 306** (Imran Farhat 141; Tabish Khan 7-72) **and 57-3.** *Habib Bank 9pts.*

At Karachi (National Stadium), October 10–13, 2009. **Drawn. KRL 468** (Azhar Ali 108, Mohammad Wasim 105; Tahir Khan 5-150) **and 34-1;** ‡**PIA 517-6 dec** (Khurram Manzoor 241). *PIA 3pts. Khurram Manzoor batted 11 hours 52 minutes for his third and highest double-hundred.*

At Lahore (Gaddafi Stadium), October 10–13, 2009. **National Bank won by an innings and 46 runs. Lahore Shalimar 239 and 250;** ‡**National Bank 535-6 dec** (Salman Butt 177, Fawad Alam 126). *National Bank 9pts.*

At Karachi (UBL), October 10–13, 2009. **Sui Southern Gas won by eight wickets.** ‡**Pakistan Customs 85** (Sohail Khan 6-34) **and 340; Sui Southern Gas 187 and 239-2** (Asif Zakir 122*). *Sui Southern Gas 9pts.*

At Faisalabad (Iqbal Stadium), October 10–13, 2009. **Sui Northern Gas won by six wickets. WAPDA 215 and 258** (Asad Ali 6-38); ‡**Sui Northern Gas 147 and 329-4.** *Sui Northern Gas 6pts.*

At Karachi (National Stadium), October 16–19, 2009. **Habib Bank won by 235 runs. Habib Bank 222 and 384-9 dec** (Taufeeq Umar 154*; Mohammad Irfan 7-113); ‡**KRL 130 and 241** (Saeed Anwar 122*). *Habib Bank 9pts. Saeed Anwar carried his bat through KRL's second innings.*

At Karachi (Southend CC), October 16–18, 2009. **Karachi Whites won by 253 runs. Karachi Whites 234 and 213;** ‡**Pakistan Customs 106** (Tabish Khan 5-51) **and 88** (Ali Mudassar 6-61). *Karachi Whites 9pts.*

At Lahore (LCCA), October 16–19, 2009. **ZTBL won by 97 runs. ZTBL 264 and 308-7 dec** (Sohail Tanvir 116); ‡**Lahore Shalimar 165 and 310.** *ZTBL 9pts.*

At Lahore (Gaddafi Stadium), October 16–19, 2009. **Drawn. WAPDA 133** (Mohammad Asif 5-35) **and 413** (Aamer Sajjad 139, Bilal Khilji 161); ‡**National Bank 321** (Fawad Alam 154*) **and 156-7.** *National Bank 3pts. Naved-ul-Hasan, playing for WAPDA, took his 500th first-class wicket. Aamer Sajjad and Bilal Khilji, joining forces at 69-4, added 208 for WAPDA's fifth wicket.*

At Karachi (UBL), October 16–19, 2009. **Drawn. PIA 320** (Sohail Khan 5-102) **and 277-5 dec** (Khurram Manzoor 117); ‡**Sui Southern Gas 153** (Najaf Shah 6-39) **and 296-4** (Saeed Bin Nasir 126, Rizwan Ahmed 117*). *PIA 3pts.*

At Lahore (Gaddafi Stadium), October 22–25, 2009. **Drawn. WAPDA 411** (Ahmed Said 101) **and 316-6; ‡Habib Bank 354** (Saleem Elahi 178*). *WAPDA 3pts.*

At Karachi (National Stadium), October 22–24, 2009. **KRL won by an innings and 107 runs. Karachi Whites 87** (Mohammad Irfan 5-27) **and 314** (Mohammad Irfan 6-96); **‡KRL 508-8 dec** (Ali Khan 117*). *KRL 9pts.*

At Lahore (LCCA), October 22–25, 2009. **Sui Northern Gas won by an innings and 53 runs. Sui Northern Gas 609-6 dec** (Misbah-ul-Haq 284, Usman Arshad 183); **‡Lahore Shalimar 296 and 260** (Asad Ali 5-64). *Sui Northern Gas 9pts. Misbah-ul-Haq and Usman Arshad added 479, the second-highest fifth-wicket stand in first-class history. Misbah scored his sixth and highest double-century from 327 balls, with four sixes and 39 fours.*

At Faisalabad (Iqbal Stadium), October 22–23, 2009. **National Bank won by nine wickets. ZTBL 115** (Mohammad Asif 5-35) **and 201** (Mohammad Talha 5-37); **‡National Bank 292** (Kamran Akmal 109) **and 28-1.** *National Bank 9pts.*

At Karachi (National Bank), October 22–25, 2009. **PIA won by ten wickets. Pakistan Customs 227 and 142** (Aizaz Cheema 5-26); **‡PIA 323 and 47-0.** *PIA 9pts.*

At Lahore (Gaddafi Stadium), October 28–31, 2009. **Habib Bank won by four wickets. National Bank 412** (Qaiser Abbas 124*) **and 139; ‡Habib Bank 353** (Taufeeq Umar 114) **and 199-6.** *Habib Bank 6pts.*

At Karachi (National Stadium), October 28–31, 2009. **PIA won by ten wickets. Karachi Whites 192 and 276; ‡PIA 432-5 dec** (Khurram Manzoor 133) **and 40-0.** *PIA 9pts.*

At Rawalpindi (KRL), October 28–31, 2009. **ZTBL won by two wickets. KRL 259** (Zahoor Elahi 105; Junaid Nadir 6-60) **and 215; ‡ZTBL 243 and 235-8** (Yasir Arafat 6-67). *ZTBL 6pts.*

At Lahore (LCCA), October 28–30, 2009. **WAPDA won by six wickets. Lahore Shalimar 173 and 210; ‡WAPDA 227** (Mohammad Saeed 6-82) **and 157-4.** *WAPDA 9pts. WAPDA wicketkeeper Ahmed Said made ten catches in the match.*

At Sheikhupura, October 28–30, 2009. **Sui Northern Gas won by an innings and 115 runs. Sui Southern Gas 160** (Samiullah Khan 5-41) **and 182** (Mohammad Hafeez 5-63); **‡Sui Northern Gas 457** (Ali Waqas 147; Shakeel-ur-Rehman 5-105). *Sui Northern Gas 9pts.*

At Islamabad (Marghzar), November 3–6, 2009. **Habib Bank won by 83 runs. Habib Bank 257** (Kashif Daud 6-94) **and 149** (Kashif Daud 6-52); **‡ZTBL 167 and 156** (Sarmad Anwar 6-70). *Habib Bank 9pts.*

At Rawalpindi (KRL), November 3–6, 2009. **Sui Northern Gas won by six wickets. KRL 198** (Asad Ali 5-32) **and 180; ‡Sui Northern Gas 293** (Jaffar Nazir 5-45) **and 87-4.** *Sui Northern Gas 9pts.*

At Muridke, November 3–5, 2009. **Pakistan Customs won by eight wickets. Lahore Shalimar 114** (Mohammad Hussain 5-7) **and 244** (Sohail Idrees 104*; Mohammad Iftikhar 5-68); **‡Pakistan Customs 296** (Mohammad Naved 5-87) **and 63-2.** *Pakistan Customs 9pts. Slow left-arm Mohammad Hussain's first-innings figures were 6.3–1–7–5.*

At Faisalabad (Iqbal Stadium), November 3–6, 2009. **National Bank won by an innings and 68 runs. Sui Southern Gas 182** (Uzair-ul-Haq 5-40) **and 191** (Uzair-ul-Haq 6-65); **‡National Bank 441-5 dec** (Nasir Jamshed 108, Umar Amin 147). *National Bank 9pts. Nasir Jamshed and Umar Amin opened with 236 for National Bank's first wicket.*

At Lahore (Gaddafi Stadium), November 3–6, 2009. **WAPDA won by 141 runs. WAPDA 138 and 333-9 dec; ‡PIA 193** (Sarfraz Ahmed 5-40, Azharullah 5-68) **and 137.** *WAPDA 6pts. There were two Sarfraz Ahmeds in this match; the PIA captain and wicketkeeper made ten catches over WAPDA's two innings, but they did not include his namesake, who dismissed him twice.*

At Rawalpindi (KRL), November 9–12, 2009. **Habib Bank won by an innings and 14 runs. Sui Southern Gas 141 and 144; ‡Habib Bank 299-8 dec.** *Habib Bank 9pts.*

At Lahore (Gaddafi Stadium), November 9–12, 2009. **Drawn. Lahore Shalimar 257 and 364-9 dec** (Tabish Khan 6-110); **‡Karachi Whites 520-8 dec** (Naved Khan 120). *Karachi Whites 3pts. Lahore Shalimar were 182-7 in their second innings, still 81 short of averting an innings defeat which would* *have been their sixth consecutive loss, before tailenders Saad Nasim (86) and Mohammad Saeed (96) added 181 to save the game.*

At Faisalabad (Iqbal Stadium), November 9–12, 2009. **PIA won by 25 runs. PIA 179 and 256** (Wasim Khan 5-71); ‡**National Bank 170 and 240** (Anwar Ali 6-113). *PIA 9pts. Anwar Ali took a hat-trick in National Bank's second innings.*

At Islamabad (Marghzar), November 9–12, 2009. **Sui Northern Gas won by ten wickets. Pakistan Customs 169 and 160** (Samiullah Khan 7-55); ‡**Sui Northern Gas 307-8 dec** (Usman Salahuddin 116, Adnan Akmal 120; Tahir Mughal 5-101) **and 23-0.** *Sui Northern Gas 9pts. Coming together at 82-5, Usman Salahuddin and Adnan Akmal added 219 for Sui Northern's sixth wicket.*

At Gujranwala (Jinnah Stadium), November 9–12, 2009. **Drawn. WAPDA 446-8 dec** (Adil Nisar 104); ‡**ZTBL 248-6.**

At Islamabad (Diamond), November 15–18, 2009. **Sui Northern Gas won by 73 runs. Sui Northern Gas 245 and 256** (Abdur Rehman 5-72); ‡**Habib Bank 249** (Asad Ali 7-98) **and 179** (Samiullah Khan 6-32). *Sui Northern Gas 6pts. Sui Northern Gas pulled ahead of Habib Bank at the top of the group table with their sixth win in six games, but it was to be their last in this tournament.*

At Karachi (National Bank), November 15–18, 2009. **WAPDA won by one wicket. Karachi Whites 170 and 310;** ‡**WAPDA 222** (Tabish Khan 6-90) **and 260-9.** *WAPDA 9pts.*

At Rawalpindi (KRL), November 15–18, 2009. **Drawn. KRL 353** (Mohammad Talha 5-72) **and 272-5** (Mohammad Wasim 100*); ‡**National Bank 398** (Imran Javed 167, Naumanullah 110; Nauman Ali 5-51). *National Bank 3pts. Imran Javed and Naumanullah added 263 for National Bank's fourth wicket.*

At Lahore (Gaddafi Stadium), November 15–18, 2009. **Drawn. Sui Southern Gas 422-6 dec** (Azeem Ghumman 183, Saeed Bin Nasir 101) **and 183-5 dec;** ‡**Lahore Shalimar 307 and 217-6.** *Sui Southern Gas 3pts.*

At Islamabad (Marghzar), November 15–18, 2009. **ZTBL won by 26 runs. ZTBL 358** (Zulqarnain Haider 161) **and 183-8 dec;** ‡**Pakistan Customs 212** (Kashif Daud 6-67) **and 303.** *ZTBL 9pts. Zulqarnain Haider, scoring a career-best 161 from No. 7, and Rehan Riaz (26) added 158 for ZTBL's ninth wicket.*

At Islamabad (Marghzar), November 21–23, 2009. **Habib Bank won by ten wickets. PIA 224** (Abdur Rehman 6-52) **and 123;** ‡**Habib Bank 347** (Hasan Raza 124) **and 4-0.** *Habib Bank 9pts.*

At Karachi (National Stadium), November 21–23, 2009. **Karachi Whites won by nine wickets. Karachi Whites 404** (Adnan Rasool 5-93) **and 160-1** (Naved Khan 103*); ‡**Sui Northern Gas 199** (Tabish Khan 6-112) **and 364** (Misbah Khan 5-101). *Karachi Whites 9pts. Karachi Whites made Sui Northern Gas follow on and ended their winning run.*

At Islamabad (National Ground), November 21–23, 2009. **National Bank won by an innings and 23 runs. Pakistan Customs 157 and 196** (Uzair-ul-Haq 6-67); ‡**National Bank 376-7 dec** (Rashid Riaz 101, Qaiser Abbas 136*). *National Bank 9pts.*

At Lahore (Gaddafi Stadium), November 21–24, 2009. **Drawn. Sui Southern Gas 264 and 302-9** (Wajid Ali 143); ‡**ZTBL 345.** *ZTBL 3pts.*

At Rawalpindi (KRL), November 22–25, 2009. **Drawn. WAPDA 462** (Rafatullah Mohmand 148; Mohammad Irfan 5-188) **and 195-4 dec** (Asif Hussain 100*); ‡**KRL 304 and 39-2.** *WAPDA 3pts.*

At Islamabad (Diamond), December 3–6, 2009. **Habib Bank won by five wickets. Pakistan Customs 238 and 234** (Sarmad Anwar 7-33); ‡**Habib Bank 320** (Humayun Farhat 156) **and 153-5.** *Habib Bank 9pts.*

At Karachi (UBL), December 3–6, 2009. **ZTBL won by six wickets. Karachi Whites 232** (Iftikhar Anjum 5-44) **and 338** (Zohaib Khan 5-57); ‡**ZTBL 397** (Zohaib Khan 143, Shahid Yousuf 104; Tabish Khan 7-121) **and 174-4.** *ZTBL 9pts. Zohaib Khan and Shahid Yousuf added 202 for ZTBL's third wicket. Tabish Khan took four wickets in four balls, split between two overs at the end of ZTBL's first innings.*

At Lahore (Gaddafi Stadium), December 3–6, 2009. **Drawn. KRL 502-7 dec** (Saeed Anwar 126, Mohammad Wasim 123); ‡**Lahore Shalimar 316** (Jaffar Nazir 5-95) **and 257-8** (Nauman Ali 5-26). *KRL 3pts.*

At Gujranwala (Jinnah Stadium), December 3–6, 2009. **Drawn. Sui Northern Gas 265 and 272** (Aizaz Cheema 6-75); ‡**PIA 328** (Yasir Hameed 180; Imran Ali 6-87) **and 119-2.** *PIA 3pts.*

At Sheikhupura, December 3–6, 2009. **Drawn. Sui Southern Gas 466** (Saeed Bin Nasir 129); ‡**WAPDA 671-2** (Rafatullah Mohmand 302*, Aamer Sajjad 289). *WAPDA 3pts. Rafatullah Mohmand and Aamer Sajjad added 580, a second-wicket world record and the second-highest for any first-class wicket, in a stand lasting eight hours 43 minutes. Rafatullah, who batted ten hours 47 minutes in all, scored his first triple-hundred (and second double). Sajjad a maiden double-century.*

At Karachi (National Bank), December 9–12, 2009. **Karachi Whites won by an innings and 87 runs. National Bank 198 and 201;** ‡**Karachi Whites 486** (Fazal Subhan 107, Afsar Nawaz 121*). *Karachi Whites 9pts. Karachi's left-arm seamer, Zohaib Shera, claimed a hat-trick on first-class debut to reduce National Bank's second innings to 9-4.*

At Rawalpindi (KRL), December 9–12, 2009. **Drawn. Sui Southern Gas 137** (Yasir Ali 5-43) **and 315** (Asif Zakir 109); ‡**KRL 352-5 dec** (Azhar Ali 153*) **and 32-2.** *KRL 3pts.*

At Lahore (Gaddafi Stadium), December 9–12, 2009. **PIA won by nine wickets. Lahore Shalimar 177** (Anwar Ali 6-62) **and 225** (Nauman Alavi 5-42); ‡**PIA 303** (Mohammad Naved 5-84) **and 100-1.** *PIA 9pts.*

At Islamabad (Diamond), December 9–12, 2009. **WAPDA won by four wickets. Pakistan Customs 120** (Azharullah 5-51) **and 398;** ‡**WAPDA 391-6 dec** (Bilal Khilji 150, Ali Azmat 128*; Zeeshan Nadir 5-101) **and 128-6** (Zeeshan Nadir 6-63). *WAPDA 9pts. Bilal Khilji and Ali Azmat added 253 for WAPDA's sixth wicket.*

At Gujranwala (Jinnah Stadium), December 9–12, 2009. **Drawn.** ‡**Sui Northern Gas 233 and 283-6** (Saleem Mughal 102*); **ZTBL 270** (Zohaib Khan 114*). *ZTBL 3pts. Zohaib Khan carried his bat through ZTBL's innings, batting throughout the third day.*

At Karachi (Southend CC), December 15–18, 2009. **Karachi Whites won by seven wickets. Sui Southern Gas 293** (Rizwan Ahmed 113) **and 182;** ‡**Karachi Whites 253 and 223-3.** *Karachi Whites 6pts.*

At Rawalpindi (KRL), December 15–17, 2009. **KRL won by nine wickets. Pakistan Customs 197 and 137;** ‡**KRL 176** (Zeeshan Nadir 5-58) **and 160-1.** *KRL 6pts.*

At Lahore (Gaddafi Stadium), December 15–17, 2009. **Habib Bank won by 117 runs.** ‡**Habib Bank 141** (Hasan Dar 7-53) **and 263** (Mohammad Naved 6-114); **Lahore Shalimar 149** (Kamran Hussain 7-25) **and 138** (Abdur Rehman 5-36). *Habib Bank 6pts. Habib Bank won despite being reduced to 30-7 on the first day. Left-arm seamer Kamran Hussain took four wickets with consecutive balls in Lahore Shalimar's first innings, all with the score on 111.*

At Faisalabad (Iqbal Stadium), December 15–18, 2009. **National Bank won by nine wickets. Sui Northern Gas 259** (Usman Arshad 105) **and 150** (Qaiser Abbas 5-20); ‡**National Bank 202** (Yasir Shah 6-40) **and 208-1.** *National Bank 6pts.*

At Islamabad (Diamond), December 15–18, 2009. **Drawn. PIA 273 and 379-5 dec** (Kamran Sajid 133); ‡**ZTBL 373 and 76-1.** *ZTBL 3pts.*

Group B

At Abbottabad, October 10–13, 2009. **Drawn. Abbottabad 251 and 247;** ‡**Quetta 243 and 183-7** (Adnan Raees 5-20). *Abbottabad 3pts. Arun Lal took a hat-trick in Abbottabad's first innings, and Riaz Kail was out obstructing the field in their second.*

At Islamabad (Diamond), October 10–13, 2009. **Drawn. Islamabad 438 and 382-8 dec** (Umair Khan 143); ‡**Hyderabad 466** (Shahid Qambrani 150*; Shehzad Azam 5-142) **and 304-7** (Sharjeel Khan 135). *Hyderabad 3pts. Twenty-year-old left-hander Sharjeel Khan scored a century on first-class debut in a match which saw 1,590 runs scored for 35 wickets.*

At Lahore (LCCA), October 10–12, 2009. **Multan won by an innings and 31 runs. Lahore Ravi 206** (Zulfiqar Babar 5-84) **and 149** (Zulfiqar Babar 6-46); ‡**Multan 386** (Naved Yasin 103*; Junaid Zia 5-90). *Multan 9pts.*

At Sialkot (Jinnah Stadium), October 10–12, 2009. **Sialkot won by an innings and four runs.** ‡**Faisalabad 136** (Bilawal Bhatti 5-48) **and 220; Sialkot 360** (Majid Jahangir 124, Mohammad Ayub 129). *Sialkot 9pts.*

At Rawalpindi (KRL), October 11–13, 2009. **Karachi Blues won by an innings and 251 runs. Karachi Blues 458** (Khalid Latif 254*); ‡**Peshawar 141** (Atif Maqbool 5-33) **and 66** (Tanvir Ahmed 6-29). *Karachi Blues 9pts. Khalid Latif carried his bat for 254, his maiden double-century, through Karachi Blues' innings, and easily outscored both Peshawar totals added together.*

At Abbottabad, October 16–19, 2009. **Karachi Blues won by 200 runs. Karachi Blues 335** (Khalid Latif 103, Ali Asad 113; Junaid Khan 7-94) **and 262-4 dec** (Asad Shafiq 103*); ‡**Abbottabad 238** (Tanvir Ahmed 5-86) **and 159** (Tanvir Ahmed 8-53). *Karachi Blues 9pts. Tanvir Ahmed took 13-139 in the match.*

At Faisalabad (Iqbal Stadium), October 16–19, 2009. **Drawn. Multan 237 and 287;** ‡**Faisalabad 188** (Abdur Rauf 5-76) **and 235-6.** *Multan 3pts. Imran Ali carried his bat for 90* through Faisalabad's first innings.*

At Islamabad (Diamond), October 16–18, 2009. **Rawalpindi won by an innings and 190 runs.** ‡**Rawalpindi 531** (Naved Ashraf 230*); ‡**Hyderabad 96** (Mohammad Rameez 5-42) **and 245.** *Rawalpindi 9pts. Naved Ashraf scored 230*, his maiden double-century, in 219 balls, with six sixes and 25 fours.*

At Muridke, October 16–19, 2009. **Drawn. Lahore Ravi 328** (Kashif Siddiq 178) **and 134-5;** ‡**Sialkot 271.** *Lahore Ravi 3pts.*

At Islamabad (National Ground), October 16–18, 2009. **Peshawar won by ten wickets. Quetta 207 and 62** (Imran Khan 6-29); ‡**Peshawar 213 and 59-0.** *Peshawar 9pts.*

At Abbottabad, October 22–25, 2009. **Abbottabad won by 217 runs. Abbottabad 420** (Adnan Raees 159) **and 295** (Lal Kumar 7-100); ‡**Hyderabad 283** (Khalid Usman 5-51) **and 215** (Junaid Khan 6-89). *Abbottabad 9pts.*

At Sargodha, October 22–25, 2009. **Drawn. Peshawar 232** (Ahmed Hayat 5-47) **and 459-6** (Fawad Ali 110, Sajjad Ahmed 117*, Azam Jan 110); ‡**Faisalabad 316.** *Faisalabad 3pts. Sajjad Ahmed and Azam Jan added 201 for Peshawar's sixth wicket.*

At Islamabad (Diamond), October 22–25, 2009. **Karachi Blues won by two wickets. Karachi Blues 396** (Sheharyar Ghani 159) **and 197-8;** ‡**Islamabad 236 and 356** (Tanvir Ahmed 6-104). *Karachi Blues 9pts. Asad Shafiq (89) and Sheharyar Ghani added 226 for Karachi Blues' third wicket.*

At Islamabad (National Ground), October 22–24, 2009. **Rawalpindi won by an innings and 192 runs. Rawalpindi 529** (Babar Naeem 117, Fawad Hussain 150); ‡**Quetta 148** (Mohammad Rameez 5-83, Rashid Latif 5-29) **and 189** (Rashid Latif 6-50). *Rawalpindi 9pts.*

At Sialkot (Jinnah Stadium), October 22–25, 2009. **Drawn.** ‡**Multan 278 and 331** (Naved Yasin 122); **Sialkot 279** (Zulfiqar Babar 7-97) **and 146-5.** *Sialkot 3pts.*

At Abbottabad, October 28–30, 2009. **Sialkot won by 136 runs. Sialkot 237** (Majid Jahangir 116; Junaid Khan 5-70) **and 184** (Armaghan Elahi 5-64); ‡**Abbottabad 178** (Naved Arif 7-66) **and 107** (Faisal Rasheed 5-58). *Sialkot 9pts.*

At Faisalabad (Iqbal Stadium), October 28–31, 2009. **Drawn.** ‡**Faisalabad 321 and 254-3 dec** (Zeeshan Butt 145*); **Lahore Ravi 269** (Zulqarnain 5-91) **and 166-8.** *Faisalabad 3pts.*

At Muridke, October 28–31, 2009. **Hyderabad won by 62 runs.** ‡**Hyderabad 284** (Mohammad Awais 113; Imran Khan 6-85) **and 281** (Mohammad Fayyaz 6-54); **Peshawar 197** (Mir Ali 5-80) **and 306** (Mohammad Fayyaz 100; Hanif-ur-Rehman 6-65). *Hyderabad 9pts.*

At Islamabad (Diamond), October 28–31, 2009. **Quetta won by 20 runs. Quetta 163 and 303;** ‡**Islamabad 215 and 231** (Arun Lal 5-62). *Quetta 6pts.*

At Islamabad (Diamond), October 28–30, 2009. **Rawalpindi won by 77 runs. Rawalpindi 271 and 161** (Tanvir Ahmed 7-70); ‡**Karachi Blues 152** (Mohammad Rameez 6-50) **and 203** (Rashid Latif 7-69). *Rawalpindi 9pts. Tanvir Ahmed finished on the losing side despite taking 10-170 in the match and hitting 50 in 27 balls from No. 9 as Karachi Blues went down on the third day.*

At Islamabad (Diamond), November 3–6, 2009. **Islamabad won by an innings and 70 runs. Islamabad 485** (Ashar Zaidi 129); ‡**Faisalabad 309 and 106** (Shehzad Azam 7-36). *Islamabad 9pts.*

At Karachi (National Stadium), November 3–6, 2009. **Karachi Blues won by 25 runs. Karachi Blues 377 and 167** (Rizwan Haider 5-74); ‡**Multan 229** (Naved Yasin 113) **and 290** (Mohammad Sami 5-48). *Karachi Blues 9pts.*

At Lahore (LCCA), November 3–6, 2009. **Drawn. Hyderabad 379 and 346-9;** ‡**Lahore Ravi 348** (Kashif Siddiq 121). *Hyderabad 3pts.*

At Islamabad (National Ground), November 3–5, 2009. **Rawalpindi won by 75 runs. Peshawar 263** (Mohammad Rameez 5-89) **and 77** (Mohammad Rameez 8-27); ‡**Rawalpindi 81** (Riaz Afridi 6-31) **and 334.** *Rawalpindi 6pts. Rawalpindi won their fourth successive victory, despite scoring 81 in their first innings and following on, thanks to 19-year-old pace bowler Mohammad Rameez, who took 13-116 and bowled out Peshawar for 77 on the third day.*

At Sialkot (Jinnah Stadium), November 3–5, 2009. **Sialkot won by nine wickets.** ‡**Quetta 213 and 156; Sialkot 354** (Kamran Younis 182; Arun Lal 7-87) **and 16-1.** *Sialkot 9pts. Kamran Younis and Ahmed Butt (94) added 222 for Sialkot's sixth wicket.*

At Abbottabad, November 9–12, 2009. **Drawn. Abbottabad 111** (Nauman Habib 5-40, Riaz Afridi 5-70) **and 364-6 dec** (Adnan Raees 200*); ‡**Peshawar 81** (Junaid Khan 6-43) **and 217-4.** *Abbottabad 3pts. Peshawar were dismissed in double figures for the third time in a month. Adnan Raees scored his second double-hundred.*

At Sargodha, November 9–12, 2009. **Faisalabad won by eight wickets. Faisalabad 350 and 82-2;** ‡**Quetta 167** (Zahoor Khan 5-55) **and 264** (Shoaib Khan 102; Ijaz Ahmed 5-59). *Faisalabad 9pts.*

At Hyderabad (Niaz Stadium), November 9–11, 2009. **Multan won by an innings and five runs. Hyderabad 194** (Rizwan Haider 5-60) **and 254;** ‡**Multan 453** (Naved Yasin 111). *Multan 9pts.*

At Islamabad (Diamond), November 9–12, 2009. **Drawn. Rawalpindi 237 and 252-5 dec;** ‡**Islamabad 151** (Rashid Latif 9-42) **and 176-3.** *Rawalpindi 3pts. Rashid Latif (not the former Test keeper) took the last nine wickets of Islamabad's first innings plus the first two of their second.*

At Karachi (National Stadium), November 9–12, 2009. **Karachi Blues won by 312 runs. Karachi Blues 297** (Shahzaib Hasan 127; Mohammad Irshad 5-59) **and 311** (Asad Shafiq 147*); ‡**Lahore Ravi 190** (Tanvir Ahmed 5-65) **and 106** (Mohammad Sami 5-40). *Karachi Blues 9pts.*

At Islamabad (National Ground), November 15–18, 2009. **Islamabad won by 37 runs. Islamabad 256** (Riaz Afridi 5-104) **and 292** (Azam Khan 5-45); ‡**Peshawar 156** (Nasrullah Khan 5-54) **and 355** (Azam Jan 115). *Islamabad 9pts.*

At Lahore (LCCA), November 15–17, 2009. **Lahore Ravi won by ten wickets.** Quetta 220 and 108; ‡**Lahore Ravi 268** (Arshad Khan 5-85) **and 63-0.** *Lahore Ravi 9pts.*

At Okara, November 15–18, 2009. **Multan won by seven wickets. Abbottabad 300** (Adnan Raees 110) **and 204** (Zulfiqar Babar 5-58); ‡**Multan 275** (Mohammad Hafeez 105) **and 233-3** (Gulraiz Sadaf 118*). *Multan 6pts.*

At Sialkot (Jinnah Stadium), November 15–18, 2009. **Sialkot won by 158 runs. Sialkot 107** (Mohammad Rameez 6-43) **and 493-9 dec** (Mohammad Ayub 179*); ‡**Rawalpindi 215 and 227** (Nayyer Abbas 5-37). *Sialkot 6pts. Sialkot won despite sinking to 53-9 on the first day, when 16 wickets fell; No. 10 Naved Arif rescued their first innings with 49.*

At Karachi (National Stadium), November 16–19, 2009. **Drawn.** ‡**Karachi Blues 401** (Ahmed Hayat 5-87) **and 307-5 dec** (Asad Shafiq 108*, Wajihuddin 100*); **Faisalabad 360** (Tariq Haroon 6-127) **and 59-3.** *Karachi Blues 3pts.*

At Hyderabad (Niaz Stadium), November 21–24, 2009. **Drawn. Hyderabad 301 and 462-5** (Sharjeel Khan 120, Nasrullah Memon 144); ‡**Faisalabad 465** (Zeeshan Butt 161, Naved Latif 105; Sajjad Ali 6-104). *Faisalabad 3pts.*

At Islamabad (Diamond), November 21–23, 2009. **Islamabad won by 420 runs.** ‡**Islamabad 182 and 419** (Umair Khan 194; Junaid Khan 7-175); **Abbottabad 100** (Shehzad Azam 5-65) **and 81** (Rauf Akbar 5-32). *Islamabad 9pts. Umair Khan's career-best 194 outscored both Abbottabad* *innings put together, enabling Islamabad to complete a massive win despite stumbling to 35-5 on the first day.*

At Lahore (LCCA), November 21–24, 2009. **Drawn. Rawalpindi 271** (Aamer Hayat 6-29) **and 165-8; ‡Lahore Ravi 378-9 dec** (Sohail Ahmed 111). *Lahore Ravi 3pts.*

At Okara, November 21–23, 2009. **Quetta won by 114 runs. Quetta 305** (Zulfiqar Babar 5-76) **and 106** (Ansar Javed 6-34); **‡Multan 178** (Jalat Khan 6-35) **and 119.** *Quetta 9pts. Bismillah Khan, promoted from No. 9, carried his bat for 63* through Quetta's second innings.*

At Sialkot (Jinnah Stadium), November 21–24, 2009. **Drawn. ‡Peshawar 295** (Mohammad Idrees 102; Bilawal Bhatti 6-94) **and 383-3** (Israrullah 136); **Sialkot 522-2 dec** (Faisal Khan 202*, Mohammad Ayub 166*). *Sialkot 3pts. Faisal Khan, who scored a maiden double-century, and Mohammad Ayub added 284* for Sialkot's third wicket.*

At Faisalabad (Iqbal Stadium), December 3–6, 2009. **Faisalabad won by 181 runs. Faisalabad 333 and 202; ‡Rawalpindi 191 and 163.** *Faisalabad 9pts.*

At Mirpur Khas, December 3–5, 2009. **Karachi Blues won by an innings and 259 runs. Karachi Blues 552-7 dec** (Asad Shafiq 145, Wajihuddin 142); **‡Hyderabad 123** (Mohammad Sami 5-56, Tanvir Ahmed 5-60) **and 170.** *Karachi Blues 9pts. Asad Shafiq and Wajihuddin added 252 for Karachi Blues' third wicket.*

At Muridke, December 3–6, 2009. **Lahore Ravi won by five wickets. Abbottabad 283** (Aamer Hayat 6-77) **and 161** (Aamer Hayat 5-59); **‡Lahore Ravi 259 and 186-5.** *Lahore Ravi 6pts.*

At Multan (Cricket Stadium), December 3–6, 2009. **Multan won by an innings and 124 runs. ‡Peshawar 217** (Tahir Maqsood 5-76) **and 197** (Zulfiqar Babar 6-37); **Multan 538-6 dec** (Rameez Alam 222*, Naved Yasin 154). *Multan 9pts. Rameez Alam, with a maiden double-century, and Naved Yasin added 280 for Multan's fourth wicket.*

At Sialkot (Jinnah Stadium), December 3–6, 2009. **Islamabad won by 37 runs. Islamabad 401** (Ashar Zaidi 202; Naved Arif 5-109) **and 155** (Faisal Rasheed 5-45); **‡Sialkot 302 and 217** (Nasrullah Khan 5-70). *Islamabad 9pts. Ashar Zaidi scored a maiden double-hundred and added 241 for the sixth wicket with Naeed Anjum (77).*

At Islamabad (National Ground), December 9–12, 2009. **Drawn. Rawalpindi 201** (Junaid Khan 5-98) **and 238-7 dec** (Naved Malik 116*; Junaid Khan 5-100); **‡Abbottabad 190** (Sadaf Hussain 5-51) **and 52-4.** *Rawalpindi 3pts.*

At Hyderabad (Niaz Stadium), December 9–12, 2009. **Sialkot won by nine wickets. Sialkot 461** (Mohammad Ayub 142) **and 27-1; ‡Hyderabad 178** (Bilawal Bhatti 5-63) **and 309** (Faisal Rasheed 5-66). *Sialkot 9pts.*

At Karachi (National Stadium), December 9–12, 2009. **Drawn. ‡Karachi Blues 309** (Shahzaib Hasan 119; Nazar Hussain 5-93) **and 324-3 dec** (Ali Asad 100*, Khalid Latif 158); **Quetta 139 and 407-6** (Shoaib Khan 111*). *Karachi Blues 3pts. Ali Asad and Khalid Latif added 225 for Karachi Blues' third wicket, to set up a target of 495; Quetta were 183-5 but Arun Lal (98) and Shoaib Khan saved the game by adding 224 to carry them past 400.*

At Lahore (LCCA), December 9–12, 2009. **Peshawar won by 51 runs. Peshawar 236** (Sajjad Ahmed 104*; Mohammad Irshad 5-50) **and 199** (Mohammad Irshad 6-42); **‡Lahore Ravi 207 and 177** (Imran Khan 5-39). *Peshawar 9pts.*

At Multan (Cricket Stadium), December 9–12, 2009. **Drawn. Multan 352** (Naved Yasin 131) **and 332-5 dec** (Rameez Alam 119*); **‡Islamabad 418** (Ashar Zaidi 130*; Zulfiqar Babar 10-143) **and 58-3.** *Islamabad 3pts. Slow left-armer Zulfiqar Babar became the fourth Pakistani to take all ten wickets (nine caught and one bowled) in a first-class innings, the day after his 31st birthday.*

At Sargodha, December 15–18, 2009. **Drawn. Abbottabad 339** (Zahoor Khan 5-83) **and 236-4; ‡Faisalabad 510** (Zeeshan Butt 221, Ijaz Ahmed 149). *Faisalabad 3pts. Zeeshan Butt, with a maiden double-century, and Ijaz Ahmed added 302 for Faisalabad's fifth wicket.*

At Mirpur Khas, December 15–18, 2009. **Drawn. ‡Quetta 280 and 283** (Naeem-ur-Rehman 5-56); **Hyderabad 296** (Hanif-ur-Rehman 123; Arun Lal 6-81) **and 213-8.** *Hyderabad 3pts.*

At Karachi (National Stadium), December 15–18, 2009. **Drawn. Sialkot 316** (Kamran Younis 107) **and 445; ‡Karachi Blues 216 and 378-4.** *Sialkot 3pts.*

At Lahore (LCCA), December 15–18, 2009. **Lahore Ravi won by ten wickets. Lahore Ravi 448** (Kashif Siddiq 112, Sohail Ahmed 103; Kamran Hussain 5-101) **and 24-0;** ‡Islamabad 145 (Junaid Zia 6-48) **and 326.** *Lahore Ravi 9pts.*

At Multan (Cricket Stadium), December 15–17, 2009. **Rawalpindi won by an innings and 25 runs.** Multan 108 (Mohammad Rameez 8-46) **and 208** (Mohammad Rameez 5-86); ‡**Rawalpindi 341** (Babar Naeem 101). *Rawalpindi 9pts. Mohammad Rameez took eight wickets in an innings and 13 in the match for the second time in the season.*

Final

At Karachi (National Stadium), December 21–23, 2009. **Karachi Blues won by 141 runs.** ‡**Karachi Blues 215 and 187;** Habib Bank 195 (Taufeeq Umar 100*; Tanvir Ahmed 5-85) **and 66** (Mohammad Sami 6-38). *Seventeen wickets fell on the opening day. Taufeeq Umar carried his bat through Habib Bank's first innings, but could do nothing to save them in their second. Needing 208 to win, they folded inside 21 overs as Mohammad Sami (just called up for Pakistan's tour of Australia, after two years out of favour for joining the unofficial Indian Cricket League) and Tanvir Ahmed (the tournament's leading wicket-taker) bowled unchanged. Younis Khan, playing for Habib Bank after resigning the Pakistan captaincy, scored 11 runs in the match. Karachi Blues claimed the title with two days to spare.*

QUAID-E-AZAM TROPHY WINNERS

1953-54	Bahawalpur	1976-77	United Bank	1994-95	Karachi Blues
1954-55	Karachi	1977-78	Habib Bank	1995-96	Karachi Blues
1956-57	Punjab	1978-79	National Bank	1996-97	Lahore City
1957-58	Bahawalpur	1979-80	PIA	1997-98	Karachi Blues
1958-59	Karachi	1980-81	United Bank	1998-99	Peshawar
1959-60	Karachi	1981-82	National Bank	1999-2000	PIA
1961-62	Karachi Blues	1982-83	United Bank	2000-01	Lahore City Blues
1962-63	Karachi A	1983-84	National Bank	2001-02	Karachi Whites
1963-64	Karachi Blues	1984-85	United Bank	2002-03	PIA
1964-65	Karachi Blues	1985-86	Karachi	2003-04	Faisalabad
1966-67	Karachi Blues	1986-87	National Bank	2004-05	Peshawar
1968-69	Lahore	1987-88	PIA	2005-06	Sialkot
1969-70	PIA	1988-89	ADBP	2006-07	Karachi Urban
1970-71	Karachi Blues	1989-90	PIA	2007-08	Sui Northern Gas
1972-73	Railways	1990-91	Karachi Whites	2008-09	Sialkot
1973-74	Railways	1991-92	Karachi Whites	2009-10	Karachi Blues
1974-75	Punjab A	1992-93	Karachi Whites		
1975-76	National Bank	1993-94	Lahore City		

The competition has been contested sometimes by regional teams, sometimes by departments, and sometimes by a mixture of the two. Karachi teams have won the Quaid-e-Azam Trophy 19 times, PIA 6, National Bank 5, Lahore teams and United Bank 4, Bahawalpur, Peshawar, Punjab, Railways and Sialkot 2, ADBP, Faisalabad, Habib Bank and Sui Northern Gas 1.

RBS PENTANGULAR CUP, 2009-10

	Played	Won	Lost	Drawn	1st-inns points	Points	Net run-rate
Sui Northern Gas	4	3	0	1	9	27	0.22
Habib Bank	4	2	0	2	12	24	0.08
The Rest.	4	2	1	1	6	18	0.63
Karachi Blues.	4	1	3	0	0	6	−0.74
Sialkot	4	0	4	0	0	0	−0.38

Final: Sui Northern Gas beat Habib Bank by seven wickets.

Outright win = 6pts; lead on first innings in a won or drawn game = 3pts. Net run-rate is calculated by subtracting runs conceded per over from runs scored per over.

At Karachi (National Bank), January 2–5, 2010. **Drawn. Habib Bank 250** (Hasan Raza 102) **and 260; ‡Sui Northern Gas 245** (Irfan Fazil 5-56) **and 186-4.** *Habib Bank 3pts. Shan Masood carried his bat for a career-best 98* through Habib Bank's second innings.*

At Karachi (National Stadium), January 2–5, 2010. **Karachi Blues won by 60 runs. ‡Karachi Blues 188 and 304; Sialkot 210** (Tariq Haroon 5-66) **and 222.** *Karachi Blues 6pts.*

At Karachi (National Bank), January 7–10, 2010. **Sui Northern Gas won by nine wickets. ‡Karachi Blues 272 and 197** (Imran Ali 5-34); **Sui Northern Gas 400** (Mohammad Hafeez 110) **and 70-1.** *Sui Northern Gas 9pts.*

At Karachi (National Stadium), January 7–10, 2010. **The Rest won by 207 runs. The Rest 412** (Aamer Sajjad 119) **and 304-9 dec; ‡Sialkot 345** (Tabish Khan 5-96) **and 164.** *The Rest 9pts.*

At Karachi (National Bank), January 13–16, 2010. **Drawn. The Rest 142 and 428** (Aamer Sajjad 134*; Abdur Rehman 5-113); **‡Habib Bank 238** (Mohammad Rameez 5-86) **and 299-7.** *Habib Bank 3pts.*

At Hyderabad (Niaz Stadium), January 13–15, 2010. **Sui Northern Gas won by seven wickets. Sialkot 78** (Samiullah Khan 5-25) **and 268; ‡Sui Northern Gas 269 and 79-3.** *Sui Northern Gas 9pts. Sialkot were 20-6, and then 40-9, before No. 10 Bilawal Bhatti reduced the scale of their humiliation by hitting 33.*

At Karachi (National Stadium), January 19–22, 2010. **Habib Bank won by 120 runs. Habib Bank 421 and 239; ‡Sialkot 243** (Abdur Rehman 5-86) **and 297.** *Habib Bank 9pts.*

At Hyderabad (Niaz Stadium), January 19–21, 2010. **The Rest won by an innings and 167 runs. Karachi Blues 198 and 210** (Zulfiqar Babar 7-56); **‡The Rest 575-5 dec** (Umair Khan 115, Aamer Sajjad 200*). *The Rest 9pts. Aamer Sajjad scored his third century in successive matches, and his second double, in 263 balls, seven weeks after the first.*

At Karachi (National Stadium), January 25–27, 2010. **Habib Bank won by nine wickets. Karachi Blues 187** (Mohammad Aslam 7-37) **and 214; ‡Habib Bank 337 and 66-1.** *Habib Bank 9pts.*

At Karachi (National Bank), January 25–28, 2010. **Sui Northern Gas won by 43 runs. Sui Northern Gas 321** (Naeemuddin 139) **and 198** (Zulfiqar Babar 7-55); **‡The Rest 286 and 190.** *Sui Northern Gas 9pts. Slow left-armer Zulfiqar Babar took seven in an innings for the second match running, and the fourth time in this season. But The Rest lost their last five wickets for 14 runs as they chased 234, and Sui Northern Gas's third successive win put them in the final with Habib Bank.*

Final

At Karachi (National Stadium), January 31–February 4, 2010. **Sui Northern Gas won by seven wickets. Habib Bank 484 and 105** (Samiullah Khan 5-16); **‡Sui Northern Gas 368 and 223-3.** *Habib Bank took a 116-run lead, thanks to their lower order, who added 239 for the last four wickets; Humayun Farhat hit 80 in 63 balls, with seven sixes and four fours. But Samiullah Khan ran through their second innings, enabling Sui Northern to come from behind; captain Misbah-ul-Haq steered them home with 12 fours and four sixes in his 89*.*

PENTANGULAR CUP WINNERS

1973-74	PIA	1982-83	Habib Bank	1995-96	United Bank
1974-75	National Bank	1984-85	United Bank	2005-06	National Bank
1975-76	PIA	1985-86	PACO	2006-07	Habib Bank
1976-77	PIA	1986-87	PIA	2007-08	Sind
1980-81	PIA	1990-91	United Bank	2008-09	North West FP
1981-82	Habib Bank	1994-95	National Bank	2009-10	Sui Northern Gas

RBS CUP, 2009-10

Four 50-over leagues plus knockout

Semi-finals

At Lahore (Gaddafi Stadium), February 21, 2010. **Sialkot Stallions won by six wickets. Multan Tigers 282-9** (50 overs); ‡**Sialkot Stallions 283-4** (45.3 overs) (Kamran Younis 127). *Kamran Younis steered Sialkot towards the final with 127 in 123 balls, including 15 fours and two sixes.*

At Faisalabad (Iqbal Stadium), February 21, 2010. **Sui Northern Gas won by 181 runs.** ‡**Sui Northern Gas 297-6** (50 overs); **National Bank 116** (29.2 overs).

Final

At Lahore (Gaddafi Stadium), February 23, 2010. **Sui Northern Gas won by 132 runs.** ‡**Sui Northern Gas 284-7** (50 overs) (Misbah-ul-Haq 119*); **Sialkot Stallions 152** (39.5 overs). *Sui Northern captain Misbah-ul-Haq hit 119* in 109 balls with nine fours and a six, and added 111 for the third wicket with Naeemuddin (84), to secure Sui Northern Gas's second trophy of the season.*

RBS PENTANGULAR CUP, 2009-10

50-over league plus final

Final

At Karachi (National Stadium), April 29, 2010. **Sind Dolphins won by 78 runs.** ‡**Sind Dolphins 270-6** (50 overs); **Baluchistan Bears 192** (43.5 overs). *Baluchistan slid to 73-8 in the 20th over before Abid Ali (63) and Abdur Rauf (55) added 110 for their ninth wicket, but they could only reduce the margin of Sind's victory.*

RBS TWENTY20 CUP, 2009-10

Four 20-over leagues plus knockout

Semi-finals

At Karachi (National Stadium), March 6, 2010 (floodlit). **Faisalabad Wolves won by 45 runs. Faisalabad Wolves 211-5** (20 overs) (Mohammad Hafeez 100); ‡**Lahore Lions 166-9** (20 overs). *Mohammad Hafeez hit the only century of the tournament in 53 balls with 16 fours and two sixes, and put on 117 in 11.4 overs with Asif Hussain (54) for the first wicket. Faisalabad's total was the only one to reach 200 in this competition.*

At Karachi (National Stadium), March 6, 2010 (floodlit). **Sialkot Stallions won by seven runs.** ‡**Sialkot Stallions 149-7** (20 overs); **Karachi Dolphins 142** (18.3 overs). *Karachi's run-chase had a curious start when they reached 81-6 in 12 overs, having scored 49 of those runs in the first, fourth and fifth overs, and only 32 in the other nine.*

Final

At Karachi (National Stadium), March 7, 2010 (floodlit). **Sialkot Stallions won by five wickets.** ‡**Faisalabad Wolves 109-9** (20 overs); **Sialkot Stallions 110-5** (16.3 overs). *Sialkot secured their fifth successive Twenty20 title with 21 balls to spare.*

SOUTH AFRICAN CRICKET, 2010

Close to the summit ...

COLIN BRYDEN

Several high-scoring batsmen and two outstanding fast bowlers took South Africa close to the summit of Test cricket during 2010. At crucial moments, however, an alarming fragility was revealed. The chance of a rare series win in India was squandered, Pakistan could not be put away during a series on neutral ground in the United Arab Emirates, while an innings win in the First Test at home to India was followed by a costly batting collapse in the Second. A team once proud of its indomitability at home had to be satisfied with a share of the honours against India – the third successive time South Africa had failed to win a home series, following a loss to Australia in 2008-09 and a draw against England the following season.

SOUTH AFRICA IN 2010

	Played	Won	Lost	Drawn/No result
Tests	11	5	2	4
One-day internationals	16	12	4	–
Twenty20 internationals	11	8	3	–

NOVEMBER		
DECEMBER	4 Tests, 5 ODIs and 2 T20Is (h) v England	(see *Wisden 2010*, page 1269)
JANUARY		
FEBRUARY	2 Tests and 3 ODIs (a) v India	(page 915)
MARCH		
APRIL		
MAY	World Twenty20 (in West Indies)	(page 797)
JUNE	3 Tests, 5 ODIs and 2 T20Is (a) v West Indies	(page 1122)
JULY		
AUGUST		
SEPTEMBER		
OCTOBER	3 ODIs and 2 T20Is (h) v Zimbabwe	(page 1038)
NOVEMBER	2 Tests, 5 ODIs and 2 T20Is (a) (in UAE) v Pakistan	(page 1007)
DECEMBER		
JANUARY	3 Tests, 5 ODIs and 1 T20I (h) v India	(page 1040)

For a review of South African domestic cricket from the 2009-10 season, see page 1060.

South Africa performed solidly in one-day internationals, with some new young talent emerging, and were strong in Twenty20 internationals too, except when it really mattered – during the World Twenty20 in the West Indies.

Mickey Arthur and Mike Procter lost their jobs as coach and convenor of selectors after the drawn home Test series against England at the beginning of the year, while Graeme Smith loosened his grip on the captaincy by handing over to Johan Botha for Twenty20 internationals and announcing he would step aside as one-day captain after the World Cup.

In a book published later in the year, Arthur alleged that both past president Norman Arendse and current president Dr Mtutuzeli Nyoka had interfered with team selection. Arthur suggested that Nyoka's complaint that there was no black African in the team for the final Test against England had led to him losing his job.

Corrie van Zyl, the former South African fast bowler who had recently been appointed head of CSA's high performance programme, was made interim coach through to the end of the 2011 World Cup. CSA's chief executive Gerald Majola headed an interim selection committee, which included ex-captain Kepler Wessels, until the former Test opener Andrew Hudson was appointed convenor in May.

Arthur resigned on January 26, less than a week before South Africa started their tour of India. Despite the upheavals, they won the First Test at Nagpur by an innings on the back of 253 not out by Hashim Amla and ten wickets from Dale Steyn. After a good start in the Second Test at Kolkata, and despite two more centuries by Amla, South Africa achieved the unwanted distinction of becoming only the fourth team to win and lose consecutive Test matches by an innings.

In the return series in December, South Africa crushed India by an innings at Centurion. This may have led to a degree of arrogance in the players, who were not convinced that India deserved to be ranked No. 1 in Test cricket, as they had risen to the top without playing any major series outside Asia. Needing to win all three Tests to take over the top ranking, South Africa crashed back to earth in the Second Test at Durban, collapsing to 131 all out in the first innings on the way to an 87-run defeat.

Three of South Africa's batsmen averaged over 76 in Test cricket during the year, led by Jacques Kallis (79.86) and Amla, who both scored more than 1,000 runs, while AB de Villiers fell just four short. All three made double-centuries, with de Villiers setting a new national record when he made 278 not out against Pakistan in Abu Dhabi. In his next match de Villiers reached a century against India at Centurion in 75 balls, 20 faster than the previous-quickest hundred by a South African. In the same match, Kallis turned his 38th hundred into a long-awaited first double-century, and he added two more hundreds in the drawn final Test.

Steyn had another outstanding year, taking 60 wickets at 21.41, with seven for 51 (ten for 108 in the match) against India at Nagpur. The tall Morne Morkel, established as Steyn's new-ball partner, took 49 wickets at 24.06, and by the end of the year they were first and third in the ICC's Test bowling rankings.

Before the fall: Dr Mtutuzeli Nyoka (*left*) and Gerald Majola (*right*) with Makhaya Ntini at the announcement of his retirement from international cricket.

Beyond the new-ball pair, however, the bowling resources were thin: slow left-armer Paul Harris was the next-highest wicket-taker with 23, but they cost him more than 50 apiece. If Steyn or Morkel did not break through, South Africa struggled to bowl teams out. Imran Tahir, the much-travelled Pakistan-born leg-spinner and a prolific wicket-taker, acquired South African citizenship at the end of the year, and was immediately selected for the World Cup.

Amla and de Villiers carried their Test form into one-day internationals, scoring 1,058 runs (average 75.57) and 964 (80.33) respectively, both hitting five centuries and scoring at better than a run a ball over the course of the year. Amla, once regarded as a Test specialist, was a revelation as a one-day opener, able to set up big totals with classical strokeplay.

Two young left-handers, Colin Ingram and David Miller, made promising international starts: Ingram hit two centuries in his first four one-day innings, and Miller proved to be a hard-hitting "finisher" in the mould of a Lance Klusener.

By year's end, however, there was no certainty about South Africa's best one-day bowling combination, and there remained an alarming tendency to leak large numbers of runs in the powerplay overs late in an innings.

In South Africa, the issue of race is seldom far from the surface, and the loss of form and subsequent retirement of Makhaya Ntini left a gap in the team for a credible black African player to satisfy the politicians. The player chosen was Lonwabo Tsotsobe, a left-arm pace bowler. He topped the bowling averages in a one-day series against Pakistan, but his lack of genuine speed was a concern: he took only three wickets at 84.66 in his first three Tests. Tsotsobe was, however, one of the few South Africans to shine in the defeat by India at Durban, his five wickets representing a distinguished line-up – Tendulkar, Dravid, Sehwag, Dhoni and Pujara.

South Africa again staged a big international tournament, the Champions League Twenty20, but it was followed by controversy over bonuses paid to key staff, notably chief executive Majola (1.7m Rand, or around £143,000) and chief operating officer Don McIntosh (R1.4m), for their efforts in making a success of the Indian Premier League and the Champions Trophy, which were both staged in South Africa in 2009.

It transpired that the bonuses had not been authorised by CSA's remuneration committee. A statement issued nine days before the AGM in August announced that an independent review committee would look into the matter. In the end, though, Majola was cleared by an internal review which found he had been guilty of no more than "an error of judgment" in not making full disclosure of the bonus payments. He was cleared of all charges of financial impropriety, but was told to repay R28,000 of CSA funds that had been spent on travel for his children. This led to criticism by three former directors, all of whom lost their places at the AGM, that the decision "appears to be at odds with the facts and information available to us". It also led to Nyoka falling out with Majola, claiming his chief executive had lied to him. The CSA board sided with Majola, and a special meeting in February 2011 passed a vote of no confidence in Nyoka, who was deposed as president.

One of the departing directors, treasurer Hentie van Wyk, reported before the voting that CSA made a healthy profit of R138.8m for the 2009-10 financial year. But there was a setback for CSA when Standard Bank announced it would not renew their 13-year sponsorship of South African cricket, worth about R100m a year, when the current contract expired in May 2011. The bank's decision was announced on the same day that CSA released the result of its inquiry into Majola's conduct, but this may have been coincidence because Standard Bank, which had earlier announced they intended to cut staff because of the financial downturn, also withdrew from two major football sponsorships.

Although SABC, the national broadcaster, continued to screen home international matches, the host-broadcaster role switched to the pay channel SuperSport. A significant change was that CSA sold only the rights to SuperSport while retaining ownership of the production.

SOUTH AFRICA v ZIMBABWE, 2010-11

One-day internationals (3): South Africa 3, Zimbabwe 0
Twenty20 internationals (2): South Africa 2, Zimbabwe 0

After installing a new-look administration featuring several former players, and gaining some encouraging results, Zimbabwe embarked on their tour of South Africa in October with a new optimism – and an old face in Grant Flower, who made a brief international return after more than six years. He had recently agreed to become Zimbabwe's batting coach, but his form in limited-overs cricket for Essex in 2010 persuaded the selectors to ask him to play as well, only for him to retire in January 2011, aged 40.

However, the on-field improvement did not extend to beating South Africa, something Zimbabwe have managed only twice in 34 one-day internationals, and not since they won at Flower's adopted home of Chelmsford in the 1999 World Cup and again at Durban the following winter. South Africa swept all five international matches on this short tour, despite resting several senior players and trying a new Twenty20 captain, Johan Botha.

Flower's comeback was low-key. After a short delay in Zimbabwe with visa problems he sat out the Twenty20s, then made 35 runs in the first two one-day internationals before being left out of the third as the step back up from county cricket proved a big one. He was overshadowed by Brendan Taylor, who hit 182 runs, including a valiant 145 not out in the first 50-over match.

South Africa's batting was predictably too strong for the tourists' limited attack, and they had two century-makers in each of the one-day internationals, including debutant Colin Ingram in the first. Ingram, a left-hander from Warriors, was one of two newcomers to catch the eye: fast-medium bowler Juan "Rusty" Theron took three wickets in his first one-day international and five in the second, in front of his home-town crowd at Potchefstroom.

ZIMBABWEAN TOURING PARTY

*E. Chigumbura, C. J. Chibhabha, C. K. Coventry, A. G. Cremer, K. M. Dabengwa, C. R. Ervine, G. W. Flower, H. Masakadza, S. W. Masakadza, C. B. Mpofu, I. A. Nicolson, E. C. Rainsford, T. Taibu, B. R. M. Taylor, P. Utseya, S. C. Williams. *Coach:* A. R. Butcher.

Coventry returned home after the Twenty20 internationals, while Ervine and Williams joined the team for the one-day internationals that followed.

At Bloemfontein, October 8, 2010 (floodlit). **First Twenty20 international: South Africa won by seven wickets.** ‡Zimbabwe 168-4 (20 overs) (H. Masakadza 72, C. J. Chibhabha 52); **South Africa 169-3** (15.5 overs) (G. C. Smith 58, L. E. Bosman 33, J-P. Duminy 35*, D. A. Miller 36*). MoM: G. C. Smith. *Twenty20 international debuts:* C. A. Ingram, J. Theron (South Africa). *South Africa won the first Twenty20 international between these sides with some ease, even though Zimbabwe made a useful total, based on a stand of 76 between Masakadza and Chibhabha, whose 29-ball fifty was his country's fastest in this format. Smith (relieved of the captaincy) and Bosman replied with 90 in seven overs, and although three wickets fell in the nineties – including Smith's for 58 from just 29 balls – the left-handers Duminy and David Miller had few alarms.*

At Kimberley, October 10, 2010. **Second Twenty20 international: South Africa won by eight runs.** ‡South Africa 194-6 (20 overs) (G. C. Smith 46, J-P. Duminy 96*); Zimbabwe 186-7 (20 overs) (B. R. M. Taylor 59, C. J. Chibhabha 59). MoM: J-P. Duminy. *Led by sparkling innings from*

Taylor and Chibhabha, Zimbabwe almost overcame South Africa's imposing total. With eight balls and five wickets remaining, they needed 16, but the dangerous Chigumbura was run out; Rusty Theron removed Shingirai Masakadza two balls later, and only six runs came from the final over. Earlier, Duminy had thrashed South Africa's highest individual score in a Twenty20 international, 21 runs coming in the last over, from the listless Mpofu, whose four overs cost 59 in all.

At Bloemfontein, October 15, 2010 (day/night). **First one-day international: South Africa won by 64 runs.** ‡**South Africa 351-6** (50 overs) (H. M. Amla 110, C. A. Ingram 124, D. A. Miller 51; S. W. Masakadza 4-86); **Zimbabwe 287-6** (50 overs) (H. Masakadza 30, B. R. M. Taylor 145*; J. Theron 3-62). *MoM:* C. A. Ingram. *One-day international debuts:* C. A. Ingram, J. Theron (South Africa). *A defiant innings from Taylor, who faced 136 balls and hit 12 fours, lifted Zimbabwe to a big total – but they were never really on terms with the asking-rate after South Africa had passed 350. Their innings featured centuries from Amla – his fourth in one-day internationals – and one for Colin Ingram, a 25-year-old left-hander from the Warriors franchise, who became only the sixth batsman to score a hundred in his first one-day international: his 124 – from 126 balls with eight fours and two sixes – had been bettered on debut only by Desmond Haynes for West Indies in 1977-78. Miller, another young left-hander, rounded off the innings with 51 from 31 balls. The 39-year-old Grant Flower, already the holder of the Zimbabwean record for most one-day international caps (219 before this), made his first appearance since March 2004. Like all the other Zimbabweans who batted, Flower made it into double figures (he scored 13), but no one could stay with Taylor long enough. Only three higher individual scores had been made in unsuccessful run-chases, the highest Sachin Tendulkar's 175 against Australia at Hyderabad in November 2009.*

CENTURY ON ONE-DAY INTERNATIONAL DEBUT

D. L. Amiss	103	England v Australia at Manchester.	1972
D. L. Haynes	148	West Indies v Australia at St John's.	1977-78
A. Flower	115*	Zimbabwe v Sri Lanka at New Plymouth	1991-92
Saleem Elahi	102*	Pakistan v Sri Lanka at Gujranwala	1995-96
M. J. Guptill	122*	New Zealand v West Indies at Auckland	2008-09
C. A. Ingram	**124***	**South Africa v Zimbabwe at Bloemfontein**	**2010-11**

Amiss also scored a century in his last one-day international.

At Potchefstroom, October 17, 2010. **Second one-day international: South Africa won by eight wickets.** ‡**Zimbabwe 268** (48.2 overs) (B. R. M. Taylor 32, T. Taibu 78; J. Theron 5-44); **South Africa 273-2** (39 overs) (H. M. Amla 110, G. C. Smith 40, A. B. de Villiers 101*). *MoM:* J. Theron. *Once again Zimbabwe batted consistently throughout and made a reasonable score – and again it wasn't enough, as South Africa cantered past their target with 11 overs to spare. Amla reprised his 110 of two days previously, the main help this time coming in a stand of 139 with de Villiers, who, seemingly unaffected by having to keep wicket as well, hurtled to his own hundred from just 72 balls, with five sixes and five fours. Earlier, Rusty Theron, the 25-year-old Warriors seamer, took three late wickets to finish with five, in only his second one-day international. Coming in off a short run, and often going wide on the crease, Theron generally angled the ball in, and collected three wickets through catches to the keeper, while Chigumbura played on and Cremer missed a slower delivery.*

At Benoni, October 22, 2010 (day/night). **Third one-day international: South Africa won by 272 runs.** ‡**South Africa 399-6** (50 overs) (J-P. Duminy 129, A. B. de Villiers 109, J. A. Morkel 37, D. A. Miller 33*); **Zimbabwe 127** (29 overs) (J. Theron 3-18). *MoM:* J-P. Duminy. *Man of the Series:* A. B. de Villiers. *South Africa completed their clean sweep in thumping style, falling just short of 400, with two players scoring centuries for the third match running. This time it was Duminy, whose clean striking brought him four straight sixes, and de Villiers, whose second successive hundred took only 91 balls. They put on 219, a South African third-wicket record, in 32 overs, and caned all the bowlers – particularly the inexperienced new-ball pair of Shingirai Masakadza (10-0-95-2) and Ian Nicolson (7-0-74-1), while one of leg-spinner Cremer's overs cost 18. Zimbabwe were never likely to threaten such a target, but on a good pitch they should have lasted longer than 29 overs; the only resistance came from Taibu and Ervine, in a stand of 47, but Botha gated both in his first over. The only bigger defeat by runs in one-day internationals was when Ireland lost to New Zealand by 290 at Aberdeen in July 2008. Zimbabwe's previous-biggest thrashing – 212 runs – came courtesy of South Africa, at Centurion 11 months before.*

SOUTH AFRICA v INDIA, 2010-11

NEIL MANTHORP

Test matches (3): South Africa 1, India 1
One-day internationals (5): South Africa 3, India 2
Twenty20 international (1): South Africa 0, India 1

A hard-fought, often intense and frequently enthralling series, both in the Tests and one-dayers, left a mutual sense of satisfaction. Supporters and neutral observers were allowed to say so in public, although pride precluded the players on either side from admitting as much.

The Test series was shared; India won what amounted to an exhibition Twenty20 game; and South Africa shaded the 50-over series. But, shamelessly to use the greatest cliché, the game itself was the biggest winner.

The popularity of the Ashes gives Englishmen and Australians a distorted view of the health of Test cricket. The reality for the rest of the world is that it is clinging to life by the slenderest of threads, and that thread could well snap should India fall down the rankings and become mediocre again. The plutocrats at the Indian board would quickly divert their allegiance and return to the monotonous stream of more lucrative limited-overs games that India used to play; Test cricket would, once again, be relegated to the status of "unavoidable chore".

Gary Kirsten's success as India's head coach could be measured in many ways, but the most important, for the rest of the world, was to change the way the Indian players approached the concept of "team" – and to guide them from a Test ranking of fourth when he was appointed to No. 1.

Nonetheless, belief in India's durability – not to mention the long-term health of Test cricket – would have suffered a crushing blow if the tourists had been hammered in South Africa, as they had been on previous tours. Even though they had competed strongly in England and Australia, sceptics believed that South Africa, with its bouncy tracks and bouncer-happy fast bowlers, would be unconquerable for India. It was their final frontier.

Kirsten's ability to communicate with his bosses in their unique diplo-speak resulted in his arriving in Cape Town eight days before the First Test with most of the squad, while a virtual shadow team finished a one-day series against New Zealand back home. There were no warm-up fixtures scheduled, but Kirsten's plan was for each of the specialist batsmen to hit "somewhere between two and three thousand balls each on South African soil before the First Test".

It was all so well planned. How could anything possibly go wrong? Kirsten even threw in a bit of extra incentive in the form of a declaration that the team could justifiably call itself "one of India's greatest" if they won.

But they were hammered in the First Test at Centurion, even though Sachin Tendulkar made his 50th Test century. Afterwards, Kirsten's long-time friend and assistant, Paddy Upton, spoke of his theory that the Indian collective psyche precluded its sports teams from producing their best performances unless they were in retaliation. Like the nation's army, Upton concluded, India's sportsmen were generally very laid-back until provoked. But the backlash could be fierce. It sounded desperately optimistic, given the nature of the defeat as much as the size of it, but it was remarkably prophetic, as India bounced back to square the series at Durban, despite an unpromising start.

The first four days of the decider at Cape Town, where Tendulkar produced century No. 51, were rip-snortingly good. Both sides looked like winning at various stages, before they sagged back into their corners on the fifth day and settled for the draw.

There was much talk afterwards about the need for longer series between the two countries, and Cricket South Africa duly announced that future series would consist of at least four Tests. They did not, however, add the rider "... provided India agree to it when the time comes". After all, CSA stated before the series that they would be making use of the Decision Review System, only to back down, tails embarrassingly curled between legs, when the Indian board objected. Sachin Tendulkar knows he prospers more than most from umpiring decisions made in the world of human error rather than technology.

INDIAN TOURING TEAM

*M. S. Dhoni, R. Dravid, G. Gambhir, Harbhajan Singh, V. V. S. Laxman, P. P. Ojha, C. A. Pujara, S. K. Raina, W. P. Saha, V. Sehwag, I. Sharma, S. Sreesanth, S. R. Tendulkar, J. D. Unadkat, M. Vijay, U. T. Yadav, Zaheer Khan. *Coach:* G. Kirsten.

For the limited-overs matches that followed the Tests, R. Ashwin, P. P. Chawla, V. Kohli, P. Kumar, A. Nehra, M. M. Patel, Y. K. Pathan, R. G. Sharma and Yuvraj Singh replaced Dravid, Gambhir, Laxman, Ojha, Pujara, Saha, Sehwag, Unadkat, Yadav and Zaheer. Gambhir and Sehwag were originally selected for the one-day squad, but suffered shoulder and arm injuries during the Tests and were replaced by R. G. Sharma and Vijay. Kumar aggravated an elbow injury during the Twenty20 international and returned home, to be replaced by I. Sharma. Tendulkar tweaked a hamstring in the second one-day international and left the tour, and was replaced by P. A. Patel.

TEST MATCH AVERAGES

SOUTH AFRICA – BATTING AND FIELDING

	T	I	NO	R	HS	100s	50s	Avge	Ct
J. H. Kallis	3	5	2	498	201*	3	0	166.00	5
H. M. Amla	3	5	0	250	140	1	1	50.00	4
†A. G. Prince	3	4	1	121	47	0	0	40.33	5
A. B. de Villiers	3	5	0	201	129	1	0	40.20	5
A. N. Petersen	3	5	0	170	77	0	1	34.00	1
†G. C. Smith	3	5	0	143	62	0	1	28.60	3
M. V. Boucher	3	4	1	72	55	0	1	24.00	14
†M. Morkel	3	4	0	66	28	0	0	16.50	0
D. W. Steyn	3	4	0	43	32	0	0	10.75	1
L. L. Tsotsobe	3	4	1	16	8*	0	0	5.33	1
P. L. Harris	3	4	0	14	7	0	0	3.50	2

BOWLING

	Style	O	M	R	W	BB	5W/i	Avge
D. W. Steyn............	RF	124	31	367	21	6-50	2	17.47
M. Morkel.............	RF	122	28	361	15	5-20	1	24.06
J. H. Kallis.............	RFM	40	8	124	3	1-20	0	41.33
L. L. Tsotsobe...........	LFM	96	20	342	7	3-43	0	48.85
P. L. Harris	SLA	112	35	257	4	2-88	0	64.25

Also bowled: A. N. Petersen (RM) 4–0–14–0; G. C. Smith (OB) 4–0–27–0.

INDIA – BATTING AND FIELDING

	T	I	NO	R	HS	100s	50s	Avge	Ct
S. R. Tendulkar.........	3	6	2	326	146	2	0	81.50	0
†G. Gambhir............	2	4	0	242	93	0	3	60.50	1
V. V. S. Laxman........	3	6	1	196	96	0	1	39.20	0
M. S. Dhoni	3	5	0	179	90	0	1	35.80	13
V. Sehwag	3	6	0	144	63	0	1	24.00	2
R. Dravid	3	6	0	120	43	0	0	20.00	1
Harbhajan Singh........	3	5	0	93	40	0	0	18.60	0
Zaheer Khan	2	3	0	50	27	0	0	16.66	0
C. A. Pujara	2	3	0	31	19	0	0	10.33	6
I. Sharma	3	5	1	25	23	0	0	6.25	0
S. Sreesanth	3	5	2	7	4*	0	0	2.33	2

Played in one Test: †S. K. Raina 1, 5; J. D. Unadkat 1*, 1; M. Vijay 19, 9 (1 ct).

BOWLING

	Style	O	M	R	W	BB	5W/i	Avge
Zaheer Khan	LFM	79.5	13	246	10	3-36	0	24.60
Harbhajan Singh........	OB	137.2	13	444	15	7-120	1	29.60
S. Sreesanth	RFM	99	6	376	9	5-114	1	41.77
I. Sharma	RFM	92.4	11	337	7	2-77	0	48.14

Also bowled: S. K. Raina (OB) 7–0–77–0; S. R. Tendulkar (RM/OB/LB) 13–1–66–1; J. D. Unadkat (LFM) 26–4–101–0.

SOUTH AFRICA v INDIA

First Test Match

At Centurion, December 16–20, 2010. South Africa won by an innings and 25 runs. Toss: South Africa. Test debut: J. D. Unadkat.

India enjoyed the considerable consolation of Sachin Tendulkar's 50th Test century, but were otherwise wretched and were duly thrashed. Every team has bad days, of course – or even four consecutive ones, as was the case in this match – but what made the defeat so hard to bear was its nature. Meek and submissive, just as had been the case with previous Indian teams in South Africa, and just as they had sworn would not be the case this time.

Torrential rain produced flash floods in town, but the match was still able to start only four hours late under grey, overcast skies and on a pitch offering decent but not lavish assistance to the seamers. The tourists were flung instantly on to the back foot – literally and metaphorically – by a single shot of the utmost stupidity, played by Sehwag before he had scored. He disregarded that most unusual of field placements, third man, and slashed wildly at a full, wide delivery from Steyn which flew perfectly into the hands of Amla, who was clearly not stationed there to save runs.

Tendulkar briefly but beautifully counter-attacked until a Steyn delivery swung too fast and too late for him, but it was Steyn's new-ball partner, Morkel, who enjoyed the greater success, with a career-best five for 20 which flattered him not a bit. Making full use of his height and bowling regularly in excess of 150kph (93mph), he hit the seam constantly and enthralled his home crowd with three spells of previously unattained control and pressure in which he looked able, even likely, to take a wicket with every delivery.

Exactly as forecast, the second day dawned hot and sunny. India really did have the worst of conditions with bat and ball, but it still wasn't enough to excuse their ineptitude in either discipline. Smith and Petersen were measured and assured during their century opening partnership – but also untested; neither was required to work hard or look for runs, because there was a steady supply on offer. But their scoring-rate of four an over was made to look pedestrian by the carnage which followed.

Amla initially set the tone during a third-wicket stand of 230 with Kallis, but soon found that his more illustrious partner was not only keeping up but outscoring him. Amla was at his quintessential best, buffering bursts of scoring with reflective periods, almost as though he was wary of being greedy.

Kallis, meanwhile, was on a mission. His 130-ball century was the fastest of the 38 in his Test career, and he maintained almost the same pace in slaying the albatross around his neck, the much talked-about lack of a double-century. It finally arrived with a glance to the fine-leg boundary off Jayder Unadkat – his 15th four, to go with five sixes – from 267 balls, in a shade under six and a half hours.

The dressing-room balcony was a picture of riotous celebration, characterised by a Smith grin which was too big for his face, while on the field Kallis managed to maintain a degree of decorum… just. After looking heavenwards and dedicating the elusive double to his late father, Henry, he acknowledged his team-mates' delight by playing a golf shot with his bat. It later transpired that the reclusive South African billionaire Johann Rupert had offered him honorary life membership at his exclusive luxury resort of Leopard Creek on the border of the Kruger National Park. Effectively it meant free golf for Kallis (and all his mates) at one of the continent's finest resort courses.

Where's the albatross? Jacques Kallis practises his golf swing after hitting his maiden Test double-hundred.

The irony of the innings itself, however, was that it was completely over-shadowed as a spectacle – by Kallis's own admission – by what was happening at the other end, where de Villiers was shattering the record for the fastest Test century by a South African. He was helped by an exhausted and dispirited mainstream attack, and the introduction of Raina, whose off-breaks would have looked out of their depth in the Indian Under-15 team. Or the Uttar Pradesh Under-15s, for that matter. De Villiers – who had made South Africa's highest individual score in the previous Test, against Pakistan – was playing virtual trick shots in between spanking terrible deliveries over the fence. It may have been one-sided, but there could be no arguing with the precision and viciousness with which de Villiers handled the bowlers in reaching 100 from just 75 deliveries, fully 20 quicker than South Africa's previous-fastest (where balls faced are known), by Denis Lindsay, Shaun Pollock and Jonty Rhodes. Unadkat, a 19-year-old left-arm medium-pacer from Saurashtra, had taken 13 wickets on his first-class debut earlier in 2010, but found Test cricket somewhat harder.

India's second innings was much better than their first. It couldn't have been worse. Gambhir fought hard and Sehwag belatedly showed that he was capable of tempering his aggression, making 63. Dravid was typically stoic, then Dhoni added 172 with the imperious Tendulkar, whose milestone 50th Test century received the attention and adulation it deserved despite all the other records which had preceded it in this match. Necessity determined what it was: an innings full of skill and discipline rarely seen before against Steyn and Morkel. Such was the effect of his technique that Steyn admitted that he had "given up trying to get him out once he'd reached about 40. I was just attacking the other guy."

South Africa were cock-a-hoop at the scale of their victory, and speculation was sky-high about the possibility of completing a 3–0 clean sweep and usurping India at the top of the Test rankings. Nobody foresaw what was to happen just six days later.

Man of the Match: J. H. Kallis.

Close of play: First day, India 136-9 (Dhoni 33, Unadkat 1); Second day, South Africa 366-2 (Amla 116, Kallis 102); Third day, India 190-2 (Dravid 28, Sharma 7); Fourth day, India 454-8 (Tendulkar 107, Sreesanth 3).

India

G. Gambhir c Harris b Morkel	5 – lbw b Steyn	80
V. Sehwag c Amla b Steyn	0 – c Smith b Harris	63
R. Dravid lbw b Morkel	14 – c Boucher b Morkel	43
S. R. Tendulkar lbw b Steyn	36 – (5) not out	111
V. V. S. Laxman b Steyn	7 – (6) c de Villiers b Tsotsobe	8
S. K. Raina c Prince b Kallis	1 – (7) c Harris b Kallis	5
*†M. S. Dhoni lbw b Morkel	33 – (8) c Boucher b Steyn	90
Harbhajan Singh run out	27 – (9) c Kallis b Harris	1
I. Sharma c Kallis b Morkel	0 – (4) c Amla b Steyn	23
S. Sreesanth c Steyn b Morkel	0 – c de Villiers b Morkel	3
J. D. Unadkat not out	1 – c Prince b Steyn	1
L-b 6, w 3, n-b 3	12	B 13, l-b 5, w 8, n-b 5	31

1/1 (2) 2/24 (1) 3/27 (3) 4/66 (5) (38.4 overs) 136
5/67 (6) 6/71 (4) 7/110 (8) 8/110 (9)
9/116 (10) 10/136 (7)

1/137 (2) 2/170 (1) (128.1 overs) 459
3/214 (4) 4/242 (3)
5/256 (6) 6/277 (7) 7/449 (8)
8/450 (9) 9/456 (10) 10/459 (11)

Steyn 10·1–1–34–3; Morkel 12.4–5–20–5; Tsotsobe 9–2–50–0; Kallis 6–1–20–1; Harris 1–0–6–0. *Second Innings*—Steyn 30.1–6–105–4; Morkel 31–6–94–2; Tsotsobe 24–3–98–1; Harris 30–5–88–2; Kallis 13–3–56–1.

South Africa

*G. C. Smith c Dhoni b Harbhajan Singh	62
A. N. Petersen c Gambhir b Harbhajan Singh	77
H. M. Amla c Dhoni b Sharma	140
J. H. Kallis not out	201
A. B. de Villiers c Dhoni b Sharma	129
B 2, l-b 3, w 2, n-b 4	11

1/111 (1) (4 wkts dec, 130.1 overs) 620
2/166 (2) 3/396 (3)
4/620 (5)

A. G. Prince, †M. V. Boucher, D. W. Steyn, P. L. Harris, M. Morkel and L. L. Tsotsobe did not bat.

Sreesanth 24–1–97–0; Sharma 27.1–2–120–2; Unadkat 26–4–101–0; Harbhajan Singh 36–2–169–2; Raina 7–0–77–0; Tendulkar 10–1–51–0.

Umpires: S. J. Davis and I. J. Gould.   Third umpire: S. George.

SOUTH AFRICA v INDIA

Second Test Match

Anand Vasu

At Durban, December 26–29, 2010. India won by 87 runs. Toss: South Africa.

After their implosion at Centurion, India threatened to live up to their reputation as poor travellers, especially in South Africa, when they arrived in Durban. Greeted by the greenest Kingsmead pitch in recent memory, and weakened by an injury to Gautam Gambhir (struck on the left hand in the nets the day before the match, aggravating an injury picked up in Centurion), the Indian team were in a familiar position of weakness. What happened next stunned the sceptics, and left even the optimists confused.

When Dhoni lost the toss – for the 12th time in 13 Tests in 2010 – South Africa had their tails up and a lively pitch to exploit. Overnight and morning rains juiced up the pitch just a touch, but when Vijay, Gambhir's replacement, and Virender Sehwag put together a streaky stand of 43, home hopes slipped a little.

Then Steyn, swinging the ball at great pace, only occasionally banging it into the hard surface for variation, got rid of both openers, and an early pattern emerged: India's batsmen would all get starts, but none could push on past the thirties. Dravid poked outside off, Tendulkar played a loose shot, and Laxman, who had resisted hard for 38, watched in horror as a powerful pull off Steyn was somehow plucked out of the air one-handed by Tsotsobe at midwicket. India ended the day at 183 for six, seemingly well on track to emulate their predecessors in South Africa, who frequently followed up a first-game rout with a poor series.

The sun shone in patches on the second day and the pitch appeared to ease, giving little sign of the carnage that would follow. A combination of opportunistic bowling and poor batting resulted in a dramatic day on which 18 wickets fell, and every player from both sides came to the batting crease at one time or another.

India's first innings did not extend long into the second day: 205 looked well short of par, with Steyn picking up his 15th five-for in only 45 Tests. What followed was a passage of play that few could have foreseen. Zaheer Khan roughed up Smith, then got lucky against Petersen, the ball trickling on to the stumps from the outside of the left pad. Kallis, backing up too far, was beaten by a straight drive from Amla that brushed the bowler Ishant Sharma's hand and hit the stumps at the non-striker's end. At 67 for three, South Africa were vulnerable, if hardly in trouble. But de Villiers received a peach from Sreesanth, then Harbhajan Singh got in on the act, trapping Amla in front essaying a half-hearted sweep.

From then on, the South Africans weren't quite sure whether to attack or defend, and Harbhajan made full use of the extra bounce on offer, polishing off the tail to end with four for ten from 7.2 overs. With an entirely unexpected lead of 74, the Indian batsmen rejoined battle. Once again, though, while the conviction was evident and the intent positive, the juice in the pitch ensured that run-scoring was never a formality. While batsmen got starts and occasionally played fluently, danger was never far away. At 56 for four, India were close to handing back whatever advantage they had, with only the redoubtable Laxman showing any signs of ease at the crease.

Wickets fell at regular intervals, but Laxman would not relent. Coming down hard on anything short, he attacked where his team-mates had been tentative. Laxman was reunited with Zaheer at 148 for seven – the exact score at which they came together at Johannesburg in 2006, when India won their first Test on South African soil. In an exact repeat, the pair again added 70, Laxman advancing stealthily towards his first hundred in South Africa. But it was not to be: at 96, just after trying (and failing) to hit Harris for six, Laxman wafted at Steyn to be the last man out.

South Africa, faced with a target of 303, were relying heavily on Amla and Kallis – and Sreesanth took care of both. Amla, cutting at a wide delivery that bounced a touch, provided a low catch to Dhoni, while Kallis was unlucky to receive the ball of the series. Climbing from a good length and jagging back into the right-hander, a Sreesanth special crashed into glove even as Kallis leapt into the air in a forlorn attempt to get out of the way. Sehwag gleefully accepted the catch at gully, and then and there the game was sealed.

Man of the Match: V. V. S. Laxman.

Close of play: First day, India 183-6 (Dhoni 20, Harbhajan Singh 15); Second day, India 92-4 (Laxman 23, Pujara 10); Third day, South Africa 111-3 (Kallis 12, de Villiers 17).

India

V. Sehwag c Kallis b Steyn	25	– c Boucher b Tsotsobe	32
M. Vijay c Boucher b Steyn	19	– c Amla b Morkel	9
R. Dravid c Boucher b Steyn	25	– c Boucher b Tsotsobe	2
S. R. Tendulkar c Kallis b Tsotsobe	13	– c de Villiers b Steyn	6
V. V. S. Laxman c Tsotsobe b Steyn	38	– c Boucher b Steyn	96
C. A. Pujara c Boucher b Tsotsobe	19	– b Morkel	10
*†M. S. Dhoni c Petersen b Steyn	35	– c Boucher b Tsotsobe	21
Harbhajan Singh c de Villiers b Steyn	21	– c Kallis b Morkel	4
Zaheer Khan c Boucher b Morkel	0	– c de Villiers b Harris	27
I. Sharma not out	1	– c Amla b Kallis	0
S. Sreesanth c Boucher b Morkel	0	– not out	0
B 1, l-b 2, w 4, n-b 2	9	B 8, l-b 4, w 9	21

1/43 (1) 2/48 (2) 3/79 (4)   (65.1 overs) 205   1/42 (1) 2/44 (2)   (70.5 overs) 228
4/117 (3) 5/130 (5) 6/156 (6)   3/48 (3) 4/56 (4)
7/190 (8) 8/193 (9) 9/205 (10) 10/205 (11)   5/93 (6) 6/141 (7)
                                          7/148 (8) 8/218 (9)
                                          9/223 (10) 10/228 (5)

Steyn 19–6–50–6; Morkel 19.1–3–68–2; Tsotsobe 11–3–40–2; Kallis 8–2–18–0; Harris 8–1–26–0. *Second Innings*—Steyn 15.5–1–60–2; Morkel 15–1–47–3; Tsotsobe 13–3–43–3; Kallis 13–2–30–1; Harris 14–2–36–1.

South Africa

A. N. Petersen b Zaheer Khan	24	– (2) c Pujara b Harbhajan Singh	26
*G. C. Smith c Dhoni b Zaheer Khan	9	– (1) c Dhoni b Sreesanth	37
H. M. Amla lbw b Harbhajan Singh	33	– c Dhoni b Sreesanth	16
J. H. Kallis run out	10	– c Sehwag b Sreesanth	17
A. B. de Villiers c Dhoni b Sreesanth	0	– lbw b Harbhajan Singh	33
A. G. Prince b Zaheer Khan	13	– not out	39
†M. V. Boucher not out	16	– lbw b Zaheer Khan	1
D. W. Steyn c Dravid b Harbhajan Singh	1	– c Pujara b Zaheer Khan	10
P. L. Harris c Pujara b Harbhajan Singh	0	– b Zaheer Khan	7
M. Morkel c Harbhajan Singh b Sharma	10	– c Dhoni b Sharma	20
L. L. Tsotsobe c Vijay b Harbhajan Singh	0	– run out	0
L-b 2, w 1, n-b 12	15	L-b 1, n-b 8	9

1/23 (2) 2/46 (1) 3/67 (4) 4/74 (5)   (37.2 overs) 131   1/63 (1) 2/82 (2)   (72.3 overs) 215
5/96 (3) 6/100 (6) 7/103 (8)   3/82 (3) 4/123 (4)
8/103 (9) 9/127 (10) 10/131 (11)   5/136 (5) 6/143 (7)
                                          7/155 (8) 8/182 (9)
                                          9/215 (10) 10/215 (11)

Zaheer Khan 13–2–36–3; Sreesanth 8–0–41–1; Sharma 9–2–42–1; Harbhajan Singh 7.2–2–10–4. *Second Innings*—Zaheer Khan 17–3–57–3; Sharma 11.3–0–36–1; Sreesanth 14–2–45–3; Harbhajan Singh 29–5–70–2; Tendulkar 1–0–6–0.

Umpires: Asad Rauf and S. J. Davis.   Third umpire: J. D. Cloete.

SOUTH AFRICA v INDIA

Third Test Match

ANAND VASU

At Cape Town, January 2–6, 2011. Drawn. Toss: India.

When the First Test ended, South Africa were speaking enthusiastically about winning the series 3–0. After the stunning reversal at Durban, India piped up, renewing hopes of breaking their jinx by winning their first Test series in South Africa. At picturesque Newlands, neither team could force the issue in the end, leaving the series tied at 1–1.

For India, the result was acceptable on one level, as it was the first time they had come to South Africa and not lost. But Dhoni conceded that it was also a golden opportunity missed, as the core members of this team – Tendulkar, Dravid, Laxman and Zaheer Khan – were unlikely to be around for the next such tour.

When the game began, with Dhoni winning the toss for a change and deciding to bowl, India were presented with their first challenge. In overcast conditions, and with grey clouds hanging around for most of the first day, their fast bowlers needed to lift themselves and pile the pressure on, but they were found wanting. Zaheer, Sharma and Sreesanth all threatened occasionally, but never consistently, and once again it was Kallis who emphasised his immense value with an innings of astute judgment and eyeball-grabbing technical poise.

After the opening batsmen were dealt with fairly swiftly, Amla came at the Indians, attacking with fluency. He and Kallis added 72 for the third wicket, before an ambitious pull resulted in Amla's downfall. While Dhoni's bowl-first approach was fully justified, conditions were not nearly as helpful as they had been at Centurion or Durban, and when South Africa ended the first day with 232 for four they had done more than enough to negate the disadvantage of losing the toss.

> The contest was a match-up between Tendulkar and Steyn

The second day dawned bright and sunny, and the pitch temporarily quickened, benefiting from the baking effect of a hot summer's day. Sreesanth, marshalling his talent productively, asked many questions, but none was difficult enough to trip Kallis up. He overcame the opposition and the pitch to collect his 39th Test hundred, one he would later rate as among his best efforts technically. Kallis reaffirmed his position in the sport's pantheon, and soaked up the admiration of an adoring home crowd. But, more importantly, his 161 – in 459 minutes, from 291 balls with 19 fours – bound the innings together, pushing the total to a healthy 362.

India needed to show similar resolution to stay in touch, but what followed was the now-familiar top-order wobble, with Sehwag falling to yet another poor stroke and Dravid running himself out to make it 28 for two. Gambhir and Tendulkar were asked to repair the damage, and it was only a generous slice of luck and some dogged determination that helped them move towards safety, ending the day with 142 for two. Gambhir was dropped twice, and Tendulkar was put down at second slip by de Villiers: each time the unfortunate bowler was Tsotsobe.

The third-day contest was reduced largely to the match-up between Tendulkar and Steyn, whose sustained, high-quality swing bowling at great pace was a feature of the series. Getting the ball to move from lines that did not allow the batsmen the luxury of shouldering arms, Steyn induced so much playing and missing that he was very unlucky not to end with more wickets in the series than he did (21). But Tendulkar, taking a leaf out of Kallis's book, refused to be perturbed by several close shaves, and negotiated each ball on merit. His 51st century lifted the total towards 364, aided by a stand of 176 with Gambhir and a late flourish from Harbhajan Singh. India led by two, and the match was reduced to a second-innings shoot-out.

Harbhajan set to work on a surface that was starting to show signs of wear and tear, and exploited the occasionally variable bounce that the rough afforded, pegging South Africa back to 64 for four to raise hopes of an unlikely Indian win.

But, once again, Kallis towered above all around him, neither yielding nor taking a backward step, and forced India to work exceptionally hard to earn each wicket. At 130 for six, when Boucher joined Kallis, India were within one wicket of the clear favourites. But the quick bowlers, especially Sharma, bowled into Boucher's pads, and he raced to a half-century, adding 103 with Kallis, whose 109 – characterised by his decisive reverse-sweeping against Harbhajan – made him the first South African to score two centuries in a Test twice. It was his 40th Test hundred, putting him ahead of Ricky Ponting and behind only Tendulkar.

India were left with 90 overs to survive for the draw, as they were never likely to score quickly enough to reach their target of 340. Harbhajan had been India's workhorse, sending down 38 overs for seven for 120, figures which only he himself had bettered for India against South Africa.

On the final day, Sehwag – restricted by a shoulder injury which saw him miss the ensuing one-day matches – completed a disappointing series (only 144 runs from six innings) when he outside-edged to first slip, whereupon India slammed down the shutters. Gambhir survived for more than four and a half hours for 64, while Tendulkar was uncharacteristically restrained in making 14 from 91 balls. When the captains shook hands little more than an hour into the final session, India had reached 166 for three at a shade above two an over.

Man of the Match: J. H. Kallis. *Man of the Series:* J. H. Kallis.

Close of play: First day, South Africa 232-4 (Kallis 81, Prince 28); Second day, India 142-2 (Gambhir 65, Tendulkar 49); Third day, South Africa 52-2 (Petersen 22, Amla 0); Fourth day, South Africa 341.

South Africa

A. N. Petersen c Dhoni b Sharma	21	– (2) lbw b Harbhajan Singh	22
*G. C. Smith lbw b Zaheer Khan	6	– (1) lbw b Harbhajan Singh	29
H. M. Amla c Pujara b Sreesanth	59	– (4) b Harbhajan Singh	2
J. H. Kallis c Dhoni b Zaheer Khan	161	– (5) not out	109
A. B. de Villiers c Dhoni b Sreesanth	26	– (6) b Zaheer Khan	13
A. G. Prince b Sreesanth	47	– (7) c Sreesanth b Sharma	22
†M. V. Boucher c Dhoni b Sreesanth	0	– (8) lbw b Tendulkar	55
D. W. Steyn c Pujara b Zaheer Khan	0	– (9) c sub (M. Vijay) b Harbhajan Singh	32
M. Morkel c Dhoni b Sreesanth	8	– (10) c Sreesanth b Harbhajan Singh	28
P. L. Harris c Pujara b Sharma	7	– (3) lbw b Harbhajan Singh	0
L. L. Tsotsobe not out	8	– c Sehwag b Harbhajan Singh	8
B 1, l-b 6, w 1, n-b 11	19	L-b 7, w 2, n-b 12	21

1/17 (2) 2/34 (1) 3/106 (3)   (112.5 overs) 362   1/50 (1) 2/52 (3)   (102 overs) 341
4/164 (5) 5/262 (6) 6/262 (7)   3/53 (2) 4/64 (4)
7/272 (8) 8/283 (9) 9/310 (10) 10/362 (4)   5/98 (6) 6/130 (7)
7/233 (8) 8/287 (9)
9/333 (10) 10/341 (11)

Zaheer Khan 29.5–6–89–3; Sreesanth 29–0–114–5; Sharma 27–6–77–2; Harbhajan Singh 27–3–75–0. *Second Innings*—Zaheer Khan 20–2–64–1; Sreesanth 24–3–79–0; Sharma 18–1–62–1; Harbhajan Singh 38–1–120–7; Tendulkar 2–0–9–1.

India

G. Gambhir c Boucher b Harris	93	– c Boucher b Steyn	64
V. Sehwag c Smith b Steyn	13	– c Smith b Morkel	11
R. Dravid run out	5	– c Prince b Tsotsobe	31
S. R. Tendulkar b Morkel	146	– not out	14
V. V. S. Laxman run out	15	– not out	32
C. A. Pujara lbw b Steyn	2		
*†M. S. Dhoni c Prince b Steyn	0		
Harbhajan Singh c sub (J-P. Duminy) b Steyn	40		
Zaheer Khan c Prince b Morkel	23		
I. Sharma c Boucher b Steyn	1		
S. Sreesanth not out	4		
L-b 20, w 1, n-b 1	22	B 7, w 5, n-b 2	14

1/19 (2) 2/28 (3) 3/204 (1) (117.1 overs) 364 1/27 (2) (3 wkts, 82 overs) 166
4/235 (5) 5/237 (6) 6/247 (7) 2/106 (3) 3/120 (1)
7/323 (8) 8/341 (4) 9/350 (10) 10/364 (9)

Steyn 31–11–75–5; Morkel 29.1–7–106–2; Tsotsobe 26–5–82–0; Harris 29–8–72–1; Petersen 2–0–9–0. *Second Innings*—Steyn 18–6–43–1; Morkel 15–6–26–1; Tsotsobe 13–4–29–1; Harris 30–19–29–0; Smith 4–0–27–0; Petersen 2–0–5–0.

Umpires: I. J. Gould and S. J. A. Taufel.   Third umpire: B. G. Jerling.
Series referee: A. J. Pycroft.

SOUTH AFRICA v INDIA

Twenty20 International

At Moses Mabhida Stadium, Durban, January 9, 2011. India won by 21 runs. Toss: India. Twenty20 international debut: M. M. Patel.

The organisers certainly didn't lack ambition: they successfully aimed to assemble the largest crowd ever to watch a cricket match on the African continent. They had three pegs on which to hang their ambitions: a celebration of the arrival of the first indentured-labourer Indians in the country 150 years earlier, the final appearance of the officially retired Makhaya Ntini in a South African shirt… and the really big one, which put most of the 50,000 bums on seats – a post-match concert by Bollywood superstar (and Kolkata Knight Riders owner) Shah Rukh Khan.

Just visiting the architecturally magnificent stadium, built for the 2010 football World Cup and named after a prominent former politician, was an event in itself. The square boundaries were shorter than ICC regulations dictate and the one-off pitch played like the strip of bare rolled mud that it was, but it hardly mattered.

Sportainment, South African style: the Moses Mabhida Stadium hosts its first international match.

The extravaganza was a tremendous success. Even the match itself, fourth on the priority list, wasn't too bad. Ntini, unfortunately, showed why he had retired, but it simply didn't matter. He was cheered all afternoon, if not quite as much as Shah Rukh was later in the evening. South Africa never really threatened India's total, despite a whirlwind innings from opener Morne van Wyk on the day he had been ignored in the IPL auction. Afterwards, South Africa's politicians and administrators liked to believe they had proved it was not just India which did "sportainment", and there was talk about making it an annual event.

Man of the Match: R. G. Sharma.

India

		B	4	6
V. Kohli *b 7*	28	19	5	0
M. Vijay *c 1 b 9*	14	12	3	0
R. G. Sharma *c 11 b 5*	53	34	5	2
Yuvraj Singh *run out*	12	13	1	0
Y. K. Pathan *b 10*	6	8	0	0
S. K. Raina *c 6 b 10*	41	23	2	3
*†M. S. Dhoni *not out*	10	11	0	0
L-b 1, w 3	4			

6 overs: 57-1   (20 overs)   168-6

1/18 2/67 3/109 4/110 5/136 6/168

R. Ashwin, P. Kumar, A. Nehra and M. M. Patel did not bat.

Parnell 4–0–25–1; Ntini 4–0–46–0; Theron 4–0–39–2; Peterson 3–0–20–0; Botha 3–0–25–1; Duminy 2–0–12–1.

South Africa

		B	4	6
M. N. van Wyk *c 10 b 9*	67	39	5	5
H. M. Amla *b 10*	1	3	0	0
C. A. Ingram *c 9 b 11*	2	8	0	0
†A. B. de Villiers *run out*	14	10	2	0
J-P. Duminy *lbw b 4*	0	2	0	0
D. A. Miller *lbw b 5*	10	8	0	1
*J. Botha *c 3 b 10*	25	22	1	1
R. J. Peterson *c 1 b 5*	2	6	0	0
W. D. Parnell *c 5 b 8*	14	16	1	0
J. Theron *not out*	1	4	0	0
M. Ntini *not out*	1	2	0	0
B 4, l-b 3, w 3	10			

6 overs: 59-2   (20 overs)   147-9

1/6 2/31 3/88 4/89 5/93 6/108 7/120 8/141 9/144

Kumar 3–0–17–1; Nehra 4–0–22–2; Patel 2–0–26–1; Ashwin 4–0–33–1; Yuvraj Singh 4–0–20–1; Pathan 3–0–22–2.

Umpires: M. Erasmus and B. G. Jerling.   Third umpire: J. D. Cloete.   Referee: B. C. Broad.

SOUTH AFRICA v INDIA

First One-Day International

At Kingsmead, Durban, January 12, 2011 (day/night). South Africa won by 135 runs. Toss: South Africa.

One-sided one-dayers can be very boring, and this was no exception. Amla spanked 50 from 36 balls to ignite the South African innings, and a fourth-wicket stand of 131 in 22 overs between de Villiers and Duminy – including 45 in the five-over batting powerplay, called early – gave it stability. But wickets kept tumbling, and what should have been a total well in excess of 300 eventually fell 11 short. Oddly, India's front-line bowlers were initially very expensive, and it was the part-timers, expected to be a liability, who put the brakes on. Kohli showed touches of class during his 54, but Tsotsobe quickly had Tendulkar caught at third man with a clever bouncer, and added the last three to finish with four for 31. Steyn made the first breakthrough then, in the 30th over, ended India's hopes by dismissing Kohli. Morkel, meanwhile, proved almost unplayable and finished with two for 12 from his five overs.

Man of the Match: L. L. Tsotsobe.

South Africa

*G. C. Smith c Sharma b Nehra	11	D. W. Steyn c Yuvraj Singh b Zaheer Khan	7	
H. M. Amla c Harbhajan Singh b Patel	50	M. Morkel b Zaheer Khan	0	
C. A. Ingram c Nehra b Patel	5	L. L. Tsotsobe not out	1	
†A. B. de Villiers c Harbhajan Singh		B 1, l-b 8, w 4	13	
b Sharma.	76			
J-P. Duminy lbw b Sharma	73	1/21 (1) 2/72 (3) (9 wkts, 50 overs)	289	
D. A. Miller b Raina	9	3/82 (2) 4/213 (4)		
J. Botha b Harbhajan Singh	23	5/226 (6) 6/244 (5) 7/266 (7)		
W. D. Parnell not out	21	8/285 (9) 9/286 (10) 10 overs: 63-1		

Zaheer Khan 10–0–44–2; Nehra 6–0–61–1; Patel 7–1–36–2; Harbhajan Singh 10–0–56–1; Yuvraj Singh 6–0–32–0; Sharma 7–0–30–2; Raina 4–0–21–1.

India

M. Vijay lbw b Steyn	1	A. Nehra b Tsotsobe	1	
S. R. Tendulkar c Steyn b Tsotsobe	7	M. M. Patel not out	1	
V. Kohli c Smith b Steyn	54			
R. G. Sharma c de Villiers b Morkel	11	B 4, w 10	14	
Yuvraj Singh b Smith b Morkel	2			
*†M. S. Dhoni run out	25	1/3 (1) 2/13 (2) 3/41 (4) (35.4 overs)	154	
S. K. Raina c Ingram b Tsotsobe	32	4/43 (5) 5/95 (6) 6/128 (3)		
Harbhajan Singh b Parnell	0	7/129 (8) 8/148 (7)		
Zaheer Khan c Duminy b Tsotsobe	6	9/153 (10) 10/154 (9) 10 overs: 41-2		

Steyn 6–0–29–2; Tsotsobe 8.4–0–31–4; Morkel 5–0–12–2; Parnell 7–0–25–1; Botha 7–0–46–0; Duminy 2–0–7–0.

Umpires: M. Erasmus and S. J. A. Taufel.   Third umpire: B. G. Jerling.

SOUTH AFRICA v INDIA

Second One-Day International

At Johannesburg, January 15, 2011 (day/night). India won by one run. Toss: India.

Low-scoring matches are often the most exciting, and this was an edge-of-your-seat thriller. It didn't look that way when South Africa were 119 for three after 24 overs, seemingly cruising to their target of 191. It took a couple of dreadful shots to start the rot, and once the innings had become infected, it was incurable. Duminy slogged the part-time off-spinner Rohit Sharma to long-on, and Smith had his off stump knocked back eight overs later for what had been a stabilising 77, during which he passed 6,000 runs in one-day internationals. Nonetheless, South Africa were still favourites with 39 required, five wickets in hand and far more overs than were necessary. Even after Zaheer Khan removed Miller and Botha in the space of five balls, only 14 runs were eventually needed to win with three wickets left. But Steyn ran himself out, and Morkel and Parnell were both caught at point cutting Munaf Patel, who was mobbed by his team-mates and picked up the match award. His final two wicket-taking deliveries were both nervous military-medium long-hops: such is the margin between success and failure. Tendulkar tweaked a hamstring during his innings, and returned home as a precautionary measure ahead of the World Cup.

Man of the Match: M. M. Patel.

India

M. Vijay c Morkel b Tsotsobe.	16	A. Nehra c Botha b Steyn	1
S. R. Tendulkar b Botha	24	M. M. Patel not out	6
V. Kohli run out	22		
Yuvraj Singh c Steyn b Tsotsobe	53	L-b 4, w 3	7
*†M. S. Dhoni b Tsotsobe	38		
S. K. Raina lbw b Tsotsobe.	11	1/21 (1) 2/63 (3) 3/67 (2) (47.2 overs) 190
R. G. Sharma lbw b Morkel.	9	4/150 (4) 5/169 (6) 6/172 (5)
Harbhajan Singh c Miller b Morkel.	3	7/177 (8) 8/179 (9) 9/184 (7)
Zaheer Khan c Tsotsobe b Steyn.	0	10/190 (10) 10 overs: 28-1

Steyn 9.2–1–35–2; Tsotsobe 10–2–22–4; Parnell 7–0–43–0; Morkel 8–0–32–2; Botha 10–0–35–1; Duminy 3–0–19–0.

South Africa

H. M. Amla c Dhoni b Patel	4	D. W. Steyn run out.	6
*G. C. Smith b Patel	77	M. Morkel c sub (Y. K. Pathan) b Patel . . .	6
C. A. Ingram lbw b Harbhajan Singh	25	L. L. Tsotsobe not out	1
†A. B. de Villiers c Dhoni b Nehra	8	L-b 5, w 1	6
J-P. Duminy c Vijay b Sharma	13		
D. A. Miller c sub (P. P. Chawla)		1/7 (1) 2/66 (3) 3/77 (4) (43 overs) 189
b Zaheer Khan.	27	4/120 (5) 5/152 (2) 6/160 (6)
J. Botha lbw b Zaheer Khan	4	7/163 (7) 8/177 (9) 9/188 (10)
W. D. Parnell c Yuvraj Singh b Patel	12	10/189 (8) 10 overs: 55-1

Zaheer Khan 9–0–37–2; Patel 8–0–29–4; Nehra 7–1–44–1; Harbhajan Singh 10–0–32–1; Raina 6–0–27–0; Sharma 2–0–12–1; Yuvraj Singh 1–0–3–0.

Umpires: B. G. Jerling and S. J. A. Taufel.   Third umpire: J. D. Cloete.

SOUTH AFRICA v INDIA

Third One-Day International

At Cape Town, January 18, 2011 (day/night). India won by two wickets. Toss: South Africa. One-day international debut: F. du Plessis.

India crashed to 93 for five in response to a modest total of 220, and looked out of the contest. They were dragged back into it by Raina and Yusuf Pathan, who added 75 for the sixth wicket, and even moved from underdogs to favourites when Pathan launched Botha for three straight sixes in four balls in the 30th over. But Morkel and Steyn claimed two quick wickets, including Pathan slicing to third man, and it was left to the tail to find another 39 runs. They did not inspire confidence against a fired-up pace attack on an uneven and two-paced surface, but Harbhajan Singh and Zaheer Khan played and missed to great effect against the good balls; Zaheer made enough contact to collect two fours, while Harbhajan smashed two timely off-side sixes, off Parnell and Morkel. It was just enough to squeak the visitors home. Earlier, South Africa had suffered their own early wobble to 90 for four before a cool, highly impressive 60 from the debutant Faf du Plessis restored order during a partnership of 110 with Duminy.

Man of the Match: Y. K. Pathan.

South Africa

*G. C. Smith c Kohli b Harbhajan Singh . . .	43	M. Morkel not out	0
H. M. Amla b Zaheer Khan	16	L. L. Tsotsobe run out	0
C. A. Ingram c Kohli b Harbhajan Singh . .	10		
†A. B. de Villiers c Zaheer Khan b Pathan . .	16	W 4	4
J-P. Duminy b Zaheer Khan	52		
F. du Plessis c Kohli b Patel	60	1/31 (2) 2/49 (3) 3/83 (4) (49.2 overs) 220
J. Botha b Zaheer Khan	9	4/90 (1) 5/200 (6) 6/202 (5)		
W. D. Parnell run out	5	7/207 (8) 8/216 (9) 9/219 (7)		
D. W. Steyn c Raina b Patel	5	10/220 (11)	10 overs: 39-1

Zaheer Khan 9.2–2–43–3; Patel 10–1–42–2; Nehra 7–0–42–0; Harbhajan Singh 9–1–23–2; Pathan 6–0–27–1; Yuvraj Singh 6–0–30–0; Sharma 1–0–5–0; Raina 1–0–8–0.

India

R. G. Sharma b Morkel	23	Zaheer Khan c Smith b Tsotsobe	14
M. Vijay c and b Steyn	1	A. Nehra not out	6
V. Kohli c de Villiers b Morkel	28	L-b 5, w 6	11
Yuvraj Singh lbw b Duminy	16		
*†M. S. Dhoni c de Villiers b Botha	5	1/4 (2) 2/56 (3) (8 wkts, 48.2 overs) 223
S. K. Raina c de Villiers b Morkel	37	3/61 (1) 4/69 (5)		
Y. K. Pathan c Morkel b Steyn	59	5/93 (4) 6/168 (6)		
Harbhajan Singh not out	23	7/182 (7) 8/208 (9)	10 overs: 36-1

M. M. Patel did not bat.

Steyn 10–1–31–2; Tsotsobe 10–0–41–1; Parnell 8–0–53–0; Morkel 10–0–28–3; Botha 7.2–1–48–1; Duminy 2–0–9–1; du Plessis 1–0–8–0.

Umpires: J. D. Cloete and S. J. A. Taufel.   Third umpire: S. George.

SOUTH AFRICA v INDIA

Fourth One-Day International

At Port Elizabeth, January 21, 2011 (day/night). South Africa won by 48 runs (D/L method). Toss: South Africa.

South Africa's batsmen judged the pitch better than the curator, who swore it would be "worth at least 300". As it transpired it was particularly awkward for batting, and hard work was the order of the day – unless you were Amla, whose wristy strength and ability to play the ball impossibly late enabled him to conjure attacking strokes. From 106 for one South Africa dipped alarmingly to 118 for five, but Amla's flying start gave Duminy and Botha the time to rebuild sensibly, leading to a very competitive total. Amla passed 2,000 one-day international runs in only his 40th innings, breaking the previous record of 45 by Zaheer Abbas and Kevin Pietersen. Kohli was outstanding in reply, hitting seven fours and two sixes from 92 balls, but nobody else looked comfortable, and when rain ended proceedings the target was simply out of sight, allowing South Africa to level the series.

Man of the Match: J-P. Duminy.

South Africa

H. M. Amla run out	64	R. J. Peterson run out	31
*G. C. Smith c Harbhajan Singh b Nehra . . .	18	D. W. Steyn not out	4
M. N. van Wyk c Kohli b Yuvraj Singh . . .	15	B 1, l-b 1, w 10, n-b 2	14
†A. B. de Villiers c Dhoni b Yuvraj Singh . .	3		
J-P. Duminy not out	71	1/57 (2) 2/106 (3) (7 wkts, 50 overs) 265
F. du Plessis run out	1	3/111 (1) 4/115 (4)		
J. Botha st Dhoni b Yuvraj Singh	44	5/118 (6) 6/188 (7) 7/242 (8)	10 overs: 54-0

M. Morkel and L. L. Tsotsobe did not bat.

Zaheer Khan 9–1–55–0; M. M. Patel 8–1–49–0; Nehra 6–0–27–1; Harbhajan Singh 10–0–61–0; Yuvraj Singh 8–0–34–3; Sharma 2–0–6–0; Raina 3–0–13–0; Pathan 4–0–18–0.

India

R. G. Sharma c Duminy b Tsotsobe	1	Harbhajan Singh not out	3
P. A. Patel lbw b Tsotsobe	11		
V. Kohli not out	87	L-b 2, w 2	4
Yuvraj Singh c Smith b Botha	12		
S. K. Raina st de Villiers b Peterson	20	1/1 (1) 2/32 (2)	(6 wkts, 32.5 overs) 142
*†M. S. Dhoni c du Plessis b Peterson	2	3/49 (4) 4/112 (5)	
Y. K. Pathan c de Villiers b Morkel	2	5/123 (6) 6/128 (7)	10 overs: 32-2

Zaheer Khan, A. Nehra and M. M. Patel did not bat.

Steyn 4–0–15–0; Tsotsobe 6–1–25–2; Morkel 6–1–13–1; Botha 6.5–0–27–1; Peterson 8–0–46–2; du Plessis 1–0–5–0; Duminy 1–0–9–0.

Umpires: J. D. Cloete and S. J. A. Taufel.   Third umpire: B. G. Jerling.

SOUTH AFRICA v INDIA

Fifth One-Day International

At Centurion, January 23, 2011. South Africa won by 33 runs (D/L method). Toss: India.

Yusuf Pathan turned what had looked to be a lost cause into a thriller with a breathtaking century, which resurrected India from a hopeless position. They were 119 for eight, in pursuit of a revised target of 268 in 46 overs, but Pathan's eight fours and eight sixes, from just 70 balls, left South Africa's attack gasping for breath. Zaheer Khan once again found a way to survive, and the ninth-wicket pair added 100 in less than 13 overs. When Pathan finally lost his head and slogged Morkel almost vertically, India still needed 49. Pathan's animated self-beration showed what all the players felt: "He threw the game away at the end," said Smith. Earlier, Amla had again defied a pitch which confused almost everyone else. He moved from 20 to 53 entirely in singles, and his unbeaten 116 was completed in the face of an embarrassing slide in which five wickets tumbled for eight runs in ten balls, after a rain-break sliced four overs off the innings. It was enough – just – to give South Africa the series 3–2, despite Pathan's heroic counter-blast.

Man of the Match: H. M. Amla.   *Man of the Series:* M. Morkel.

South Africa

*G. C. Smith c Pathan b Zaheer Khan	7	M. Morkel run out	0
H. M. Amla not out	116	L. L. Tsotsobe not out	0
M. N. van Wyk c and b Yuvraj Singh	56		
†A. B. de Villiers st Dhoni b Yuvraj Singh	11	L-b 6, w 5	11
J-P. Duminy c and b M. M. Patel	35		
F. du Plessis b M. M. Patel	8	1/16 (1) 2/113 (3)	(9 wkts, 46 overs) 250
J. Botha c Dhoni b M. M. Patel	2	3/129 (4) 4/231 (5)	
R. J. Peterson b Zaheer Khan	4	5/242 (6) 6/244 (7) 7/250 (8)	
D. W. Steyn run out	0	8/250 (9) 9/250 (10)	10 overs: 53-1

Zaheer Khan 9–1–47–2; M. M. Patel 8–0–50–3; Chawla 7–0–32–0; Harbhajan Singh 8–0–33–0; Pathan 2–0–10–0; Yuvraj Singh 8–0–45–2; Sharma 2–0–14–0; Raina 2–0–13–0.

India

P. A. Patel c du Plessis b Morkel	38	Zaheer Khan c Morkel b Tsotsobe	24
R. G. Sharma b Tsotsobe	5	M. M. Patel not out	4
V. Kohli c de Villiers b Morkel	2		
*†M. S. Dhoni b Smith b Morkel	5	L-b 2, w 7, n-b 2	11
Yuvraj Singh c Duminy b Steyn	8		
S. K. Raina c Morkel b Steyn	11	1/21 (2) 2/31 (3) 3/45 (4)	(40.2 overs) 234
Y. K. Pathan c du Plessis b Morkel	105	4/60 (1) 5/60 (5) 6/74 (6)	
Harbhajan Singh c Duminy b Botha	13	7/98 (8) 8/119 (9) 9/219 (7)	
P. P. Chawla b Peterson	8	10/234 (10)	9 overs: 49-3

Steyn 9–1–32–2; Tsotsobe 7.2–0–57–2; Morkel 8–0–52–4; Botha 8–0–33–1; Peterson 7–0–45–1; du Plessis 1–0–13–0.

Umpires: B. G. Jerling and S. J. A. Taufel.   Third umpire: S. George.   Series referee: B. C. Broad.

AIRTEL CHAMPIONS LEAGUE TWENTY20, 2010-11

Ken Borland

The Chennai Super Kings' telling combination of international stars and some of India's finest talent carried them to the second Champions League title, giving the IPL winners good reason to proclaim themselves the kings of Twenty20 at domestic level.

The second staging of the richest tournament in cricket – Chennai earned themselves $US2.5m for their triumph – was held in South Africa, the hosts for the inaugural World Twenty20 and the second IPL. Local fans were able to enjoy a thrilling run by the Eastern Cape Warriors, who made it all the way to the final before coming undone against the Chennai spin duo of Muttiah Muralitharan and Ravichandran Ashwin.

Chennai's opener Murali Vijay was the leading run-scorer in the tournament with 294. Suresh Raina, with 203, and Mike Hussey supported him in a powerful top three, and Mahendra Singh Dhoni provided his usual inspiration with the bat and as captain. Off-spinners Muralitharan and Ashwin were the only bowlers to take more than ten wickets in the tournament and were well backed by Chennai's faster men Albie Morkel, Doug Bollinger and Lakshmipathy Balaji.

The Warriors, who ceded the services of Jacques Kallis to the Bangalore Royal Challengers, finished second to Chennai in the closely contested Group A, and were inspired by their captain, Davy Jacobs, who powered his way to 286 runs in six innings. Johan Botha and Nicky Boje – international spinners present and past – operated extremely well in tandem for the Warriors, but the team's lack of quality in depth showed in the final.

The event was enthusiastically received by South Africans, especially younger fans, and had the best possible start when the Highveld Lions, the weaker of the two home teams, upset the star-studded Mumbai Indians in the opening game after Sachin Tendulkar's brilliance seemed to have made sure of victory.

Mumbai's array of big names – Tendulkar, Dwayne Bravo, J-P. Duminy, Harbhajan Singh, Lasith Malinga and Zaheer Khan – failed to fire consistently, although Bravo's fellow-Trinidadian Kieron Pollard proved himself the most lethal batsman in this format, ending the competition with 127 runs at a strike-rate of 201.58.

Mumbai could beat only Guyana (who lost all their matches) and Bangalore, by two runs in a wonderful contest that ebbed and flowed in Durban, as Mumbai's involvement in the tournament ended before the semi-final stage.

Victoria – semi-finalists in the first incarnation of this tournament in India (last year's champions, New South Wales, did not qualify) – were unfortunate: they matched Chennai and the Warriors by winning three of their four Group A matches, but were eliminated because of their inferior run-rate.

Raina came to the fore with his blazing 94 not out from just 48 balls as Chennai beat Bangalore in a rain-reduced match in the first semi-final, while

Jacobs and Colin Ingram seized early control for the Warriors in the other semi against previously undefeated South Australia. Left-arm seamer Lonwabo Tsotsobe then struck twice in his second over, allowing Boje and Botha to strangle the rest of the batting.

In the final, though, the roles were reversed, as the Warriors struggled against spin, leading to a mediocre match in which the outcome was seldom in doubt.

There were no English teams this time, as the event clashed with the end of the county season.

CHAMPIONS LEAGUE TWENTY20, 2010-11

Group A	Played	Won	Lost	Points	Net run-rate
CHENNAI SUPER KINGS	4	3	1	6	2.05
WARRIORS	4	3	1	6	0.58
Victoria	4	3	1	6	0.36
Wayamba	4	1	3	2	−1.12
Central Districts	4	0	4	0	−1.84

Group B	Played	Won	Lost	Points	Net run-rate
SOUTH AUSTRALIA	4	4	0	8	0.58
ROYAL CHALLENGERS BANGALORE	4	2	2	4	0.75
Lions	4	2	2	4	0.40
Mumbai Indians	4	2	2	4	0.22
Guyana	4	0	4	0	−2.08

Group A

At Port Elizabeth, September 11, 2010. **Warriors won by seven wickets.** ‡Wayamba 153-9 (20 overs) (H. G. J. M. Kulatunga 59, M. D. K. J. Perera 39; J. Theron 3-23); **Warriors 156-3** (18.2 overs) (C. A. Ingram 34, J. P. Kreusch 37*, M. V. Boucher 40*). *MoM:* J. Theron. *Rusty Theron removed Mahela Jayawardene second ball and Mahela Udawatte with the last ball of the first over.*

At Durban, September 11, 2010 (floodlit). **Chennai Super Kings won by 57 runs.** ‡Chennai Super Kings 151-4 (20 overs) (S. Badrinath 52*, A. Srikkanth 42); **Central Districts 94** (18.1 overs) (D. A. J. Bracewell 30; L. Balaji 3-20). *MoM:* S. Badrinath. *Central Districts were 44-6 in the 11th over; Muttiah Muralitharan took 2-15 in his four overs, and Doug Bollinger 2-10 from 3.1.*

At Port Elizabeth, September 13, 2010 (floodlit). **Warriors won by 28 runs.** ‡Warriors 158-6 (20 overs) (D. J. Jacobs 59, M. V. Boucher 31); **Victoria 130-9** (20 overs) (J. Theron 3-22). *MoM:* D. J. Jacobs. *Davy Jacobs hit 59 from 39 balls, with nine fours and a six.*

At Centurion, September 15, 2010. **Victoria won by seven wickets.** ‡Central Districts 165-5 (20 overs) (J. M. How 77*); **Victoria 166-3** (19.4 overs) (A. J. Finch 93*). *MoM:* A. J. Finch. *Peter Ingram was out to the first ball of the match. Aaron Finch faced 60 balls and hit 11 fours and three sixes, one of which (off Doug Bracewell) ended the match.*

At Centurion, September 15, 2010 (floodlit). **Chennai Super Kings won by 97 runs.** Chennai Super Kings 200-3 (20 overs) (M. Vijay 68, S. K. Raina 87); **Wayamba 103** (17.1 overs) (J. A. Morkel 3-22, R. Ashwin 4-18). *MoM:* S. K. Raina. *Murali Vijay and Suresh Raina (who hit six fours and six sixes from 44 balls) put on 137 for the second wicket in 12 overs.*

At Port Elizabeth, September 18, 2010. **Warriors won by six wickets.** ‡Central Districts 175-3 (20 overs) (J. M. How 88*, K. Noema-Barnett 53*); **Warriors 181-4** (19.1 overs) (D. J. Jacobs 74, A. G. Prince 64). *MoM:* D. J. Jacobs. *After Jamie How and Kieran Noema-Barnett put on 100* in 10.1 overs, Davy Jacobs (who hit six sixes and five fours) and Ashwell Prince countered with an opening stand of 147 in 15.4.*

At Port Elizabeth, September 18, 2010 (floodlit). **Victoria won one-over eliminator after tied match.** ‡Chennai Super Kings 162-6 (20 overs) (M. Vijay 73); **Victoria 162** (20 overs) (A. J. Finch

41, M. S. Wade 31, D. J. Hussey 51; S. K. Raina 4-26). *MoM: A. J. Finch. After Bryce McGain was run out from the final ball of the match proper to force a tie, Victoria scored 23 runs – 22 by David Hussey, who swiped the last two balls for six – from Ravichandran Ashwin's "super over". Chennai could manage only 13 off Clint McKay.*

At Centurion, September 20, 2010 (floodlit). **Victoria won by eight wickets.** ‡**Wayamba 106** (16.3 overs) (D. P. M. D. Jayawardene 51, J. Mubarak 51; P. M. Siddle 4-29); **Victoria 108-2** (13.2 overs) (A. J. Finch 38*, D. J. Hussey 47*). *MoM: P. M. Siddle. Wayamba were 81-2 at halfway, but lost their last eight wickets for 25 in 39 balls, Peter Siddle taking 4-7 in his last two overs.*

At Port Elizabeth, September 22, 2010. **Wayamba won by 74 runs.** ‡**Wayamba 144-6** (20 overs) (J. Mubarak 30); **Central Districts 70** (15.3 overs) (I. Udana 3-22, B. A. W. Mendis 3-14). *MoM: I. Udana. With consecutive deliveries left-arm medium-pacer Isuru Udana had Brad Patton caught behind, Mathew Sinclair stumped off a wide, and bowled George Worker to complete a hat-trick from two legal balls (believed to be unique in senior cricket). Then slow left-armer Rangana Herath returned the most economical figures of the tournament (4–0–7–2).*

At Port Elizabeth, September 22, 2010 (floodlit). **Chennai Super Kings won by ten runs.** ‡**Chennai Super Kings 136-6** (20 overs) (M. E. K. Hussey 50, M. Vijay 35, M. S. Dhoni 31*; J. P. Kreusch 3-19); **Warriors 126-8** (20 overs) (D. J. Jacobs 32; R. Ashwin 3-24). *MoM: M. E. K. Hussey. Chennai made sure of qualifying by ending Warriors' unbeaten record, their spinners taking seven of the eight wickets (the other was a run-out) as they defended a modest total. Despite defeat, Warriors also qualified for the semi-finals.*

Group B

At Johannesburg, September 10, 2010 (floodlit). **Lions won by nine runs. Lions 186-5** (20 overs) (J. D. Vandiar 71, N. D. McKenzie 56*; S. L. Malinga 3-33); ‡**Mumbai Indians 177-6** (20 overs) (S. Dhawan 32, S. R. Tendulkar 69, J-P. Duminy 30). *MoM: J. D. Vandiar. Mumbai seemed to be in control as Shikhar Dhawan and Sachin Tendulkar (42 balls, nine fours) put on 83 for the first wicket in 9.5 overs, but the later batsmen could not maintain the required rate.*

At Centurion, September 12, 2010. **South Australia won by 11 runs. South Australia 178-6** (20 overs) (M. Klinger 78, C. J. Ferguson 47); ‡**Lions 167-8** (20 overs) (A. N. Petersen 56; S. W. Tait 3-36). *MoM: M. Klinger. Michael Klinger's 78 from 48 balls with six fours and five sixes – and his third-wicket stand of 97 with Callum Ferguson, whose 47 came from 27 balls – underpinned the Redbacks' total.*

At Centurion, September 12, 2010 (floodlit). **Royal Challengers Bangalore won by nine wickets. Guyana 103** (20 overs) (C. D. Barnwell 30; J. H. Kallis 3-16); ‡**Royal Challengers Bangalore 106-1** (12.2 overs) (J. H. Kallis 43*, R. Dravid 33). *MoM: J. H. Kallis. Bangalore knocked off their modest target with 7.4 overs to spare.*

At Durban, September 14, 2010 (floodlit). **South Australia won by five wickets.** ‡**Mumbai Indians 180-7** (20 overs) (A. T. Rayudu 38, S. S. Tiwary 44, K. A. Pollard 36); **South Australia 182-5** (19.3 overs) (M. Klinger 50, D. J. Harris 56). *MoM: D. J. Harris. Openers Michael Klinger and Daniel Harris put on 112 in 13.3 overs as the Redbacks paced their substantial chase to perfection; Tom Cooper (19* from five balls) supplied the finishing touches with a six and a four in the last over, from Harbhajan Singh.*

At Durban, September 16, 2010 (floodlit). **Mumbai Indians won by 31 runs.** ‡**Mumbai Indians 184-4** (20 overs) (S. Dhawan 39, S. R. Tendulkar 48, K. A. Pollard 72*; D. Bishoo 3-34); **Guyana 153-6** (20 overs) (R. R. Sarwan 46). *MoM: K. A. Pollard. Guyana's gentle attack restricted Mumbai to 99-3 after 15 overs, before Pollard's 72* from just 30 balls, with nine sixes (including three in one Esuan Crandon over), killed off Guyana's hopes.*

At Durban, September 17, 2010 (floodlit). **South Australia won by eight wickets.** ‡**Royal Challengers Bangalore 154** (19.5 overs) (L. R. P. L. Taylor 46, D. du Preez 46; D. T. Christian 4-23); **South Australia 155-2** (18.3 overs) (D. J. Harris 57, M. Klinger 69*). *MoM: M. Klinger. Bangalore were 7-2 after eight balls, before Ross Taylor and Dillon du Preez organised a revival – but South Australia's openers continued their good form, this time putting on 124 in 14.2 overs.*

At Johannesburg, September 19, 2010. **Lions won by nine wickets. Guyana 148-9** (20 overs) (S. A. Jacobs 34; E. O'Reilly 4-27); ‡**Lions 149-1** (15.1 overs) (A. N. Petersen 57*, R. Cameron 78*). *MoM: E. O'Reilly. After Ethan O'Reilly slowed Guyana down, Alviro Petersen and Richard*

Cameron (who hit six sixes and five fours from 42 balls) took their side home with a stand of 133* in 12.3 overs.

At Durban, September 19, 2010 (floodlit). **Mumbai Indians won by two runs. ‡Mumbai Indians 165-7** (20 overs) (S. Dhawan 41, S. S. Tiwary 38*; D. W. Steyn 3-26); **Royal Challengers Bangalore 163-5** (20 overs) (R. Dravid 71*, V. Kohli 47). MoM: D. J. Bravo. *Rahul Dravid (58 balls, eight fours) anchored Bangalore's innings, and Virat Kohli (47 from 24 balls) provided the late fireworks – but, with three needed from the final delivery, Kohli was caught behind off Zaheer Khan. For Mumbai, Dwayne Bravo hit 29 from 17 balls and had figures of 4–0–23–2.*

At Johannesburg, September 21, 2010. **South Australia won by 15 runs. South Australia 191-6** (20 overs) (C. J. Ferguson 55, C. J. Borgas 48); **‡Guyana 176-7** (20 overs) (R. N. Ramdeen 35, R. R. Sarwan 70, S. A. Jacobs 32; D. J. Harris 3-33). MoM: C. J. Ferguson. *South Australia maintained their 100% record with a comfortable victory over winless Guyana.*

At Johannesburg, September 21, 2010 (floodlit). **Royal Challengers Bangalore won by six wickets. ‡Lions 159-6** (20 overs) (A. N. Petersen 45, N. D. McKenzie 39); **Royal Challengers Bangalore 160-4** (19 overs) (M. K. Pandey 44, R. Dravid 33, V. Kohli 49*). MoM: V. Kohli. *With Anil Kumble whipping through his four overs for only 13 runs, Bangalore kept the Warriors to a modest total, and pipped them (and Mumbai) to a semi-final place on run-rate.*

Semi-finals

At Durban, September 24, 2010 (floodlit). **Chennai Super Kings won by 52 runs** (D/L method). **‡Chennai Super Kings 174-4** (17 overs) (M. Vijay 41, S. K. Raina 94*); **Royal Challengers Bangalore 123** (16.2 overs) (M. K. Pandey 52; D. E. Bollinger 3-27). MoM: S. K. Raina. *Suresh Raina smashed 94* from 48 balls, with six sixes and five fours. Rain early in the match meant Bangalore's target was increased to 176 from 17 overs, and they were never in contention once Doug Bollinger and Albie Morkel (3–0–13–1) reduced them to 12-3.*

At Centurion, September 25, 2010 (floodlit). **Warriors won by 30 runs. ‡Warriors 175-6** (20 overs) (D. J. Jacobs 61, C. A. Ingram 46; D. J. Harris 3-18); **South Australia 145-7** (20 overs) (C. J. Ferguson 71). MoM: D. J. Jacobs. *Davy Jacobs hit ten fours and a six from 41 balls to propel his side to a total which the previously unbeaten Redbacks never approached, despite Callum Ferguson's 49-ball 71.*

FINAL

CHENNAI SUPER KINGS v WARRIORS

At Johannesburg, September 26, 2010 (floodlit). Chennai Super Kings won by eight wickets. Toss: Warriors.

The Warriors, from South Africa's Eastern Cape, had reached the final through a combination of teamwork and inspiring contributions from their captain Davy Jacobs – but this proved insufficient against the international pedigree of the Chennai Super Kings, who added the Champions League title to the IPL crown they had collected earlier in the year. Chennai's bowlers, all internationals, made regular inroads once Jacobs missed a reverse sweep and departed for a forthright 34, then Hussey and Vijay all but ensured victory with an opening stand of 103 in 14.5 overs. Fittingly, it was left to Chennai's captain, Dhoni, to round things off in style, hitting Theron for four to win the match with six balls to spare, after clouting him straight for six and four earlier in the same over.

Man of the Match: M. Vijay.   *Man of the Series:* R. Ashwin.

Warriors

		B	4	6
*D. J. Jacobs *lbw b 8*..........	34	21	8	0
A. G. Prince *b 10*	6	9	0	0
C. A. Ingram *c 3 b 5*	16	23	1	0
J. P. Kreusch *c 3 b 11*	17	17	1	0
†M. V. Boucher *b 11*	5	11	0	0
J. Botha *c 6 b 8*	7	10	0	0
C. A. Thyssen *c 6 b 11*	25	18	3	1
N. Boje *not out*	8	10	0	0
J. Theron *not out*	2	1	0	0
L-b 4, w 4	8			

6 overs: 47-2   (20 overs) 128-7

1/39 2/45 3/73 4/81 6/111 7/125

M. Ntini and L. L. Tsotsobe did not bat.

Bollinger 4–0–33–1; Morkel 4–0–31–1; Ashwin 4–0–16–2; Balaji 4–0–28–0; Muralitharan 4–0–16–3.

Chennai Super Kings

		B	4	6
M. E. K. Hussey *not out*	51	46	3	0
M. Vijay *c 4 b 8*	58	53	6	2
S. K. Raina *c 6 b 10*	2	3	0	0
*†M. S. Dhoni *not out*..........	17	12	2	1
L-b 1, w 3	4			

6 overs: 39-0   (19 overs) 132-2

1/103 2/107

J. A. Morkel, A. Srikkanth, S. Badrinath, R. Ashwin, L. Balaji, D. E. Bollinger and M. Muralitharan did not bat.

Ntini 4–0–30–1; Tsotsobe 3–0–14–0; Theron 4–0–40–0; Botha 4–0–18–0; Boje 4–0–29–1.

Umpires: Aleem Dar and R. E. Koertzen.   Third umpire: M. Erasmus.   Referee: R. S. Madugalle.

WINNERS

2009-10 New South Wales Blues	2010-11 Chennai Super Kings

DOMESTIC CRICKET IN SOUTH AFRICA, 2009-10

COLIN BRYDEN

It was perhaps a sign of the times that the Cape Cobras won the South African domestic first-class competition for the first time – and promptly fired their coach.

Barely six months earlier, Shukri Conrad had been hailed for guiding them to the semi-finals of the inaugural Champions League Twenty20 competition, netting $US500,000 in prize money. Yet in April, Western Cape Cricket announced that Conrad would not be offered a new contract and "a fresh face was needed to take the Cobras to the next level"; the much-travelled Richard Pybus was appointed in July.

The Cobras had won three titles during Conrad's five seasons, including the 45-over competition in 2006-07 and the lucrative Twenty20 crown in 2008-09. If nothing else, his sacking was a clear indication that the prestige of first-class success no longer outranked the financial rewards flowing from the limited-overs game, particularly Twenty20. This was underlined when Warriors coach Russell Domingo was named Coach of the Year at the annual Cricket South Africa awards; while the Cobras had satisfied the purists, the Warriors from the Eastern Cape had scooped the money, lifting the MTN40 and Standard Bank Pro20 titles.

The MTN shrank from 45 to 40 overs a side. Teams were allowed 12 players and two five-over batting powerplays were introduced, on top of ten overs for the bowling team. With half the overs now powerplays, totals actually rose, despite the sorter innings – the average runs per over increased by almost one to 6.15 – and crowds grew by 10%, but it was hard to see the changes helping national selectors find the right players for 50-over internationals. For 2010-11, there was a single five-over batting powerplay but, surprisingly, teams expanded to 13 a side, further reducing the need for balance.

In the four-day SuperSport Series, the **Cape Cobras** lost one and drew three of their opening four matches before pulling away to win the remaining six. A key factor was the fast-medium bowling of all-rounder Vernon Philander, the tournament's leading wicket-taker with 45 at 14. It was a remarkable turnaround. Discarded by the national selectors in 2008, he was briefly relegated to the amateur Western Province team in October. The Cobras' attack had strength in depth, with pace bowlers Rory Kleinveldt, Francois Plaatjies and Charl Langeveldt backing up Philander; left-arm spinner Robin Peterson proved a good acquisition from the Warriors, while the leg-spin of Alistair Gray was a useful bonus. Gray and Andrew Puttick were reliable openers, and the left-handed Stiaan van Zyl was one of the country's more promising young batsmen.

Van Zyl's 696 runs at 58 proved insignificant, however, against the feats of three more young men, Rilee Rossouw, Dean Elgar and Stephen Cook, who all scored over 1,000 runs, though their teams, the **Eagles** and the **Lions**, had little success. Left-handers Rossouw and Elgar scored four and five centuries respectively for the Eagles. The 20-year-old Rossouw hit an astonishing 319 off 291 balls on the opening day of his last match, against the Titans, and shared a South African all-wicket record of 480 with Elgar. Cook, son of former Test player Jimmy, had set a national first-class record in October, when he made 390 for the Lions against the Warriors in 838 minutes, the fourth-longest innings in cricket history.

Defending champions the **Titans** finished runners-up after two remarkable comeback wins, beating the Lions after conceding 562 and trailing by 194 on first innings, then defeating the Eagles, who had made 570 for nine including Rossouw's 319; by following up with 64 in the second innings, Rossouw achieved the dubious distinction of scoring the most runs for a beaten side anywhere in the world. The **Dolphins** finished bottom of the SuperSport and Pro20 tables but reached the MTN final.

The **Warriors** were aided by their international stars in the closing stages of both limited-overs competitions, but performed consistently to get into contention without them. Colin Ingram, another young talent, was the leading run-scorer in both tournaments; the Warriors also had the best-balanced attack, with left-armers Lonwabo Tsotsobe and Wayne Parnell plus right-armers Makhaya Ntini and Rusty Theron providing pace, and Johan Botha and Nicky Boje quality slow bowling.

Eastern Province won the first-class amateur competition, now played in a single 14-team league, and **Northerns** the one-day title.

FIRST-CLASS AVERAGES, 2009-10

BATTING (700 runs, average 40.00)

	M	I	NO	R	HS	100s	Avge	Ct/St
B. J. Pelser (*North West*)	11	20	10	1,003	163*	4	100.30	8
S. C. Cook (*Lions & Gauteng*)	18	30	4	1,642	390	5	63.15	22
†D. Elgar (*Eagles & Free State*)	12	22	3	1,193	189*	5	62.78	8
†J. A. Beukes (*Free State*)	12	20	8	700	120*	1	58.33	14
D. J. van Wyk (*Eagles & Free State*)	13	23	3	1,159	153	4	57.95	15
†R. R. Rossouw (*Eagles & Free State*)	13	22	0	1,261	319	4	57.31	15
W. Bossenger (*Griqualand West*)	13	20	5	844	168	3	56.26	36/1
†S. van Zyl (*Cape Cobras & Boland*)	12	19	3	872	167*	3	54.50	7
†J. J. Pienaar (*Titans & Easterns*)	12	19	2	907	154	3	53.35	2
N. D. McKenzie (*Lions*)	10	16	1	798	140	3	53.20	9
U-K. J. Birkenstock (*Boland*)	9	17	2	774	112	2	51.60	3
J. T. Smuts (*Warriors & Eastern Province*) . . .	14	26	4	1,134	150*	4	51.54	3
M. Y. Vallie (*Western Province*)	12	21	3	865	119	3	48.05	4
M. L. Price (*Eastern Province*)	12	21	1	953	179	2	47.65	12
H. E. van der Dussen (*Northerns*)	13	22	3	904	124	3	47.57	10
R. R. Hendricks (*Eagles & Griqualand West*) .	14	24	3	974	133	3	46.38	13
A. P. Agathagelou (*North West*)	13	26	1	1,076	158	4	43.04	27
†K. R. Smuts (*Eastern Province*)	13	21	2	816	102	2	42.94	7
A. J. A. Gray (*Cape Cobras & W. Province*) . .	19	32	2	1,281	127	3	42.70	28
J. Booysen (*Easterns*)	12	19	1	764	145	2	42.44	12
J. F. Mostert (*North West*)	11	22	3	806	163*	2	42.42	1
†C. Pietersen (*Eagles & Griqualand West*)	16	23	2	886	140	1	42.19	8
J. C. Kent (*Dolphins & KwaZulu-Natal*)	13	23	6	715	158*	2	42.05	8
†J. G. Strydom (*South Western Districts*)	13	26	1	1,032	134	2	41.28	11

BOWLING (30 wickets, average 35.00)

	Style	O	M	R	W	BB	5W/i	Avge
V. D. Philander (*Cape Cobras & W. Province*)	RFM	324.1	89	765	59	5-16	3	12.96
Q. Friend (*Dolphins & KwaZulu-Natal*)	RFM	297.5	67	847	50	6-45	3	16.94
L. M. G. Masekela (*Titans & Northerns*)	RFM	263	72	810	41	5-69	1	19.75
J. Louw (*Dolphins & Cape Cobras*)	RFM	318	96	758	38	6-50	1	19.94
M. Morkel (*Titans & South Africa*)	RF	277.2	56	796	38	5-75	1	20.94
M. A. Mashimbyi (*Titans & Northerns*)	RFM	308.5	90	876	41	6-31	2	21.36
T. Shamsi (*Lions & Gauteng*)	SLC	316	52	1,082	50	6-89	2	21.64
D. D. G. Baartman (*South Western Districts*) . .	RFM	279.4	74	859	39	4-39	0	22.02
Imran Tahir (*Titans & Easterns*)	LBG	436.4	74	1,498	67	7-82	8	22.35
R. C. Williams (*Eastern Province*)	RFM	316.1	59	1,125	50	7-60	3	22.50
L. Klazinga (*Namibia*)	RFM	332	47	1,108	48	6-70	3	23.08
S. de Kock (*Border*)	SLA	313.2	53	1,049	45	8-64	3	23.31
S. von Berg (*Titans & Northerns*)	LBG	323.2	57	1,144	49	6-34	4	23.34
R. J. Peterson (*Cape Cobras*)	SLA	234.4	55	709	30	5-45	3	23.63
W. A. Deacon (*Lions & North West*)	LFM	380.2	87	1,263	52	6-75	2	24.28
A. C. R. Birch (*Warriors & Eastern Province*) .	RFM	299.2	58	952	38	5-42	1	25.05
S. A. Nowak (*Northerns*)	RFM	262	62	863	33	5-32	1	26.15
K. A. Maharaj (*Dolphins & KwaZulu-Natal*) . .	SLA	274.4	42	941	34	5-30	1	27.67
G. C. Viljoen (*Titans & Easterns*)	RFM	343	45	1,279	46	6-55	3	27.80
A. J. A. Gray (*Cape Cobras & W. Province*) . .	LBG	245.4	38	905	30	4-27	0	30.16

	Style	O	M	R	W	BB	5W/i	Avge
K. Nipper (*KwaZulu-Natal Inland*)	SLA	264.1	39	1,027	34	5-143	1	30.20
A. A. Temoor (*Western Province*)	LBG	285.4	49	965	31	5-31	1	31.12
C. J. D. de Villiers (*Eagles & Free State*)	RFM	304.1	51	1,059	33	4-36	0	32.09
P. L. Harris (*Titans & South Africa*)	SLA	390.5	85	1,102	34	6-54	3	32.41

Averages include CSA Provincial Three-Day Challenge matches played in Namibia.

SUPERSPORT SERIES, 2009-10

	Played	Won	Lost	Drawn	Bonus points Batting	Bowling	Points
Cape Cobras	10	6	1	3	37.72	33	130.72
Titans	10	5	2	3	36.28	26	112.28
Lions	10	2	4	4	45.44	35	100.44
Eagles	10	2	4	4	47.44	25	86.44*
Warriors	10	3	5	2	28.12	25	83.12
Dolphins	10	2	4	4	26.18	29	75.18

* 6pts deducted for slow over-rate.

Outright win = 10pts. Bonus points awarded for the first 100 overs of each team's first innings. One batting point was awarded for the first 150 runs and 0.02 of a point for every subsequent run. One bowling point was awarded for the third wicket taken and for every subsequent two.

At Bloemfontein, September 17–20, 2009. **Drawn. ‡Cape Cobras 573-8 dec** (A. G. Puttick 118, R. E. Levi 137) **and 60-0; Eagles 527** (D. Elgar 112, R. R. Rossouw 115). *Eagles 6.26pts, Cape Cobras 5.54pts.*

At Kimberley, September 24–27, 2009. **Eagles won by eight wickets. ‡Lions 485-8 dec** (A. N. Petersen 128, N. D. McKenzie 109) **and 165-9 dec; Eagles 312** (W. A. Deacon 6-75) **and 339-2** (D. Elgar 189*, H. H. Dippenaar 101*). *Eagles 16.22pts, Lions 9.4pts. Alviro Petersen scored his third century in successive innings spanning two seasons. On the final day, Dean Elgar and Boeta Dippenaar added a match-winning 264* for Eagles' third wicket.*

At Benoni, September 24–27, 2009. **Titans won by 179 runs. ‡Titans 222 and 285; Cape Cobras 180** (N. E. Mbhalati 5-56) **and 148** (P. L. Harris 6-54). *Titans 16.44pts, Cape Cobras 5.6pts.*

At Durban, October 1–4, 2009. **Drawn. Dolphins 233 and 128-3; ‡Titans 164** (Y. A. Abdulla 5-62). *Dolphins 6.66pts, Titans 5.28pts.*

At Randjesfontein, October 1–4, 2009. **Drawn. ‡Warriors 474** (A. Jacobs 119, J. P. Kreusch 130) **and 102-2; Lions 395-7 dec** (J. D. Vandiar 128*). *Lions 6.7pts, Warriors 7.5pts.*

At Benoni, October 8, 2009. **Drawn. ‡Warriors 17-1 v Titans.** *The match was called off after seven overs because of an unfit pitch, which was too soft in the landing area for bowlers running in from the southern end. It was replayed at Port Elizabeth in November.*

At Port Elizabeth, October 15–18, 2009. **Warriors won by 43 runs. ‡Warriors 174** (Q. Friend 5-28) **and 254** (J. Botha 109); **Dolphins 147** (J. Theron 5-27) **and 238.** *Warriors 15.48pts, Dolphins 4pts.*

At Centurion, October 22–25, 2009. **Drawn. ‡Titans 315** (J. A. Morkel 102; J. Louw 6-50) **and 263-8 dec; Dolphins 288 and 209-4.** *Titans 8.26pts, Dolphins 6.76pts. Johann Louw took 10-99 in the match.*

At East London, October 22–25, 2009. **Drawn. Warriors 532** (A. G. Prince 154); **‡Lions 690-9** (S. C. Cook 390, T. L. Tsolekile 141). *Warriors 6.58pts, Lions 5.1pts. Stephen Cook's 390 was the highest individual score in South African cricket, beating 337* by Daryll Cullinan for Transvaal v Northern Transvaal in 1993-94, and the 12th-highest in all first-class cricket. It was his 14th century, but only the second double. He and his father Jimmy (313* for Somerset v Glamorgan in 1990) became the first father and son to score triple-hundreds. Cook batted for two minutes short of 14 hours – the fourth-longest innings in first-class history – and hit 54 fours and a single six from 648 balls. He added 365, a national sixth-wicket record, with Thami Tsolekile, whose 141 was his first century for five years, to help Lions reach 690, the third-highest total in South African cricket (all three have come in the 21st century). England spinner Monty Panesar played for Lions in this and their next five games.*

At Cape Town, November 12–15, 2009. **Drawn. ‡Lions 416** (V. B. van Jaarsveld 123) **and 194-2 dec** (A. N. Petersen 122*); **Cape Cobras 332** (A. Nel 5-64) **and 135-7.** *Cape Cobras 5.86pts, Lions 8.28pts. Vaughn van Jaarsveld reached 100 in 81 balls; in all, he hit 13 fours and six sixes in 90 balls.*

At Pietermaritzburg, November 12–15, 2009. **Drawn. ‡Eagles 178 and 203-3** (D. Elgar 110*); **Dolphins 375** (A. M. Amla 134). *Dolphins 8.2pts, Eagles 4.56pts.*

At Port Elizabeth, November 12–14, 2009. **Titans won by ten wickets. ‡Titans 403** (P. J. Malan 115) **and 41-0; Warriors 214** (P. L. Harris 5-49) **and 227.** *Titans 18.92pts, Warriors 4.28pts. This was the replay of the abandoned game of October 8; it was transferred to Warriors' home ground, but the original hosts, Titans, completed a crushing win.*

At Durban, November 19–22, 2009. **Drawn. Dolphins 237; ‡Cape Cobras 329-2** (A. G. Puttick 169*). *Dolphins 2.74pts, Cape Cobras 8.58pts.*

At East London, November 19–22, 2009. **Warriors won by six wickets. Eagles 391-4 dec** (H. H. Dippenaar 112*) **and 273-6 dec** (R. R. Hendricks 109); **‡Warriors 315-3 dec** (J. T. Smuts 150*) **and 353-4** (A. G. Prince 136). *Warriors 15.3pts, Eagles 6.82pts.*

At Paarl, November 26–28, 2009. **Cape Cobras won by nine wickets. ‡Warriors 143 and 143; Cape Cobras 240 and 47-1.** *Cape Cobras 16.8pts, Warriors 4pts.*

At Bloemfontein, November 26–29, 2009. **Drawn. ‡Eagles 404** (D. Elgar 110; P. Joubert 6-89) **and 345** (R. R. Rossouw 139); **Titans 468** (J. A. Rudolph 192, F. Behardien 106; G. A. Vries 6-92) **and 79-1.** *Eagles 6.36pts, Titans 7.52pts.*

At Johannesburg, November 26–29, 2009. **Dolphins won by five wickets. ‡Lions 359** (N. D. McKenzie 140) **and 226; Dolphins 353 and 235-5** (L. E. Bosman 100*). *Dolphins 18.06pts, Lions 8.12pts.*

At Cape Town, December 3–5, 2009. **Cape Cobras won by 106 runs. Cape Cobras 231 and 226** (A. J. A. Gray 113); **‡Eagles 220** (V. D. Philander 5-58) **and 131** (R. J. Peterson 5-60). *Cape Cobras 16.62pts, Eagles 6.4pts. Cape Cobras captain Justin Kemp took seven catches in the field.*

At Potchefstroom, December 3–6, 2009. **Lions won by an innings and 216 runs. ‡Lions 550-7 dec** (V. B. van Jaarsveld 135, Z. de Bruyn 144); **Titans 134 and 200.** *Lions 19.54pts, Titans 1pt.*

At Paarl, December 10–12, 2009. **Cape Cobras won by an innings and 72 runs. Titans 240 and 108; ‡Cape Cobras 420** (R. J. Peterson 100). *Cape Cobras 17.52pts, Titans 4.8pts.*

At Durban, December 10–13, 2009. **Warriors won by 88 runs. Warriors 248** (Q. Friend 5-59) **and 96-6 dec; ‡Dolphins 70-0 dec and 186** (G. J-P. Kruger 5-71). *Warriors 12.96pts, Dolphins 4pts.*

At Johannesburg, December 10–13, 2009. **Drawn. ‡Lions 368 and 301-6 dec; Eagles 337 and 114-3.** *Lions 8.52pts, Eagles 7.46pts.*

At Kimberley, December 16–19, 2009. **Dolphins won by six runs. Dolphins 236 and 258** (D. A. Miller 108*); **‡Eagles 327 and 161** (Q. Friend 6-45). *Dolphins 15.72pts, Eagles 8.3pts. Quinton Friend became the second Dolphins seamer in the 2009-10 season (after Johann Louw in October) to take 10-99 in a SuperSport match; on the final day, he took five wickets in three overs as Eagles collapsed from 143-3 chasing 168.*

At Johannesburg, December 16–19, 2009. **Cape Cobras won by four wickets. ‡Lions 202 and 308** (R. J. Peterson 5-70); **Cape Cobras 296** (R. Frylinck 5-78) **and 215-6.** *Cape Cobras 17.92pts, Lions 6.04pts.*

At Port Elizabeth, December 16–19, 2009. **Titans won by 229 runs. ‡Titans 343** (H. G. Kuhn 160*) **and 401-7 dec** (B. D. Snijman 128); **Warriors 370 and 145.** *Titans 16.86pts, Warriors 7.82pts.*

At Cape Town, March 18–21, 2010. **Cape Cobras won by ten wickets. Cape Cobras 477-8 dec** (A. G. Puttick 180, S. van Zyl 157) **and 29-0; ‡Dolphins 276 and 225.** *Cape Cobras 17.34pts, Dolphins 4.34pts. Andrew Puttick and Stiaan van Zyl added 271 for Cape Cobras' second wicket.*

At Bloemfontein, March 18–21, 2010. **Eagles won by an innings and 15 runs. ‡Eagles 609-9 dec** (R. R. Hendricks 133, R. R. Rossouw 123); **Warriors 260** (J. J. van der Wath 5-54) **and 334** (J. T. Smuts 100; P. V. Mpitsang 5-50). *Eagles 20.68pts, Warriors 5.2pts. Reeza Hendricks and Rilee*

Rossouw added 246 for Eagles' second wicket as Warriors conceded 600-plus for the second time in the season.

At Benoni, March 18–21, 2010. **Titans won by two wickets. ‡Lions 562-8 dec** (N. D. McKenzie 103) **and 114** (G. C. Viljoen 5-57); **Titans 368 and 311-8.** *Titans 16.4pts, Lions 10.14pts. In Lions' first innings, Andre Nel hit 50* in 27 balls, with five sixes and two fours.*

At Durban, March 25–27, 2010. **Lions won by ten wickets. ‡Dolphins 185 and 234; Lions 415** (S. C. Cook 119; M. Shezi 7-45) **and 7-0.** *Lions 18.6pts, Dolphins 4.7pts. Twenty-year-old left-arm wrist-spinner Tabraiz Shamsi (Gauteng and Lions) took five wickets to become only the second South African to take 50 wickets in his maiden first-class season (after Pienaar Anker of Boland in 1981-82).*

At Centurion, March 25–28, 2010. **Titans won by two wickets. ‡Eagles 570-9 dec** (D. Elgar 161, R. R. Rossouw 319) **and 164; Titans 546-9 dec** (G. H. Bodi 159) **and 190-8.** *Titans 16.8pts, Eagles 9.38pts. On the first day Rilee Rossouw became the youngest South African to reach a triple-hundred, at 20 years 196 days, and the fastest, in 276 balls – less than half the 569 taken by Stephen Cook earlier in the season. He finished with the third-highest score in South African cricket, and in all hit 47 fours and eight sixes in 291 balls and 345 minutes; his previous best was just 139. It gave him a record 1,125 runs in the SuperSport season. Rossouw added 480 for Eagles' second wicket with fellow left-hander Dean Elgar (who batted nearly an hour longer for barely half the runs), an all-wicket South African record. But when Titans completed an unexpected win Rossouw ended the game as first-class cricket's highest individual scorer over two innings in a losing cause, with 383 runs in all; the 480-run stand was also a record for a losing team. Titans wicketkeeper Mangaliso Moselhe made five catches in each innings, including Rossouw twice.*

At Port Elizabeth, March 25–27, 2010. **Cape Cobras won by an innings and 117 runs. ‡Warriors 110** (V. D. Philander 5-40) **and 142** (R. J. Peterson 5-45); **Cape Cobras 369** (S. van Zyl 167*). *Cape Cobras 18.94pts, Warriors 4pts. Cape Cobras' sixth successive victory secured their first SuperSport title.*

CHAMPIONS

Currie Cup			
1889-90	Transvaal	1947-48	Natal
1890-91	Kimberley	1950-51	Transvaal
1892-93	Western Province	1951-52	Natal
1893-94	Western Province	1952-53	Western Province
1894-95	Transvaal	1954-55	Natal
1896-97	Western Province	1955-56	Western Province
1897-98	Western Province	1958-59	Transvaal
1902-03	Transvaal	1959-60	Natal
1903-04	Transvaal	1960-61	Natal
1904-05	Transvaal	1962-63	Natal
1906-07	Transvaal	1963-64	Natal
1908-09	Western Province	1965-66	{ Natal
1910-11	Natal		{ Transvaal
1912-13	Natal	1966-67	Natal
1920-21	Western Province	1967-68	Natal
	{ Transvaal	1968-69	Transvaal
1921-22	{ Natal	1969-70	{ Transvaal
	{ Western Province		{ Western Province
1923-24	Transvaal	1970-71	Transvaal
1925-26	Transvaal	1971-72	Transvaal
1926-27	Transvaal	1972-73	Transvaal
1929-30	Transvaal	1973-74	Natal
1931-32	Western Province	1974-75	Western Province
1933-34	Natal	1975-76	Natal
1934-35	Transvaal	1976-77	Natal
1936-37	Natal	1977-78	Western Province
1937-38	{ Natal	1978-79	Transvaal
	{ Transvaal	1979-80	Transvaal
1946-47	Natal	1980-81	Natal
		1981-82	Western Province

1982-83	Transvaal	*SuperSport Series*	
1983-84	Transvaal	1996-97	Natal
1984-85	Transvaal	1997-98	Free State
1985-86	Western Province	1998-99	Western Province
1986-87	Transvaal	1999-2000	Gauteng
1987-88	Transvaal	2000-01	Western Province
1988-89	Eastern Province	2001-02	KwaZulu-Natal
1989-90	{ Eastern Province	2002-03	Easterns
	{ Western Province	2003-04	Western Province
		2004-05	{ Dolphins
Castle Cup			{ Eagles
1990-91	Western Province	2005-06	{ Dolphins
1991-92	Eastern Province		{ Titans
1992-93	Orange Free State	2006-07	Titans
1993-94	Orange Free State	2007-08	Eagles
1994-95	Natal	2008-09	Titans
1995-96	Western Province	2009-10	Cape Cobras

Transvaal/Gauteng have won the title outright 25 times, Natal/KwaZulu-Natal 21, Western Province 18, Orange Free State/Free State 3, Eastern Province and Titans 2, Cape Cobras, Eagles, Easterns and Kimberley 1. The title has been shared seven times as follows: Transvaal 4, Natal and Western Province 3, Dolphins 2, Eagles, Eastern Province and Titans 1.

From 1971-72 to 1990-91, the non-white South African Cricket Board of Control (later the South African Cricket Board) organised its own three-day tournaments. These are now recognised as first-class (see *Wisden 2006*, pages 79–80). A list of winners appears in *Wisden 2007*, page 1346.

CSA PROVINCIAL THREE-DAY CHALLENGE, 2009-10

					Bonus points		
	Played	Won	Lost	Drawn	Batting	Bowling	Points
Eastern Province	13	8	1	4	61.76	49	190.76
Gauteng	13	6	1	5†	61.88	46	167.88
Northerns	13	5	2	6	60.96	50	160.96
Easterns	13	5	2	6	58.16	42	150.16
Western Province	13	5	5	3	46.30	50	146.30
South Western Districts	13	4	5	4	44.82	47	131.82
Griqualand West	13	3	2	8	55.02	44	129.02
North West	13	2	1	10	60.80	43	122.80*
Free State	13	2	3	7†	54.64	42	115.64*
KwaZulu-Natal	13	3	3	7	39.88	44	113.88
Boland	13	2	5	5†	41.80	42	103.80
Namibia	13	1	6	6	41.92	45	96.92
Border	13	1	7	4†	40.34	43	93.34
KwaZulu-Natal Inland	13	0	4	7‡	39.26	36	75.26

† *Plus one match abandoned.* ‡ *Plus two matches abandoned.* * *1pt deducted for slow over-rate.*

Outright win = 10pts.

Bonus points awarded for the first 85 overs of each team's first innings. One bonus batting point was awarded for the first 100 runs and 0.02 of a point for every subsequent run. One bonus bowling point was awarded for the second wicket taken and for every subsequent two up to eight.
Each team's first innings was restricted to 85 overs, except that, if the first team was bowled out inside 85 overs, their unused overs were added to the second team's allocation.

At Bloemfontein, October 1–3, 2009. **Drawn.** ‡**North West 345-5** (A. P. Agathagelou 118, M. Akoojee 142) **and 179** (A. J. Pienaar 5-27); **Free State 258-9 and 62-1.** *Free State 6.16pts, North West 9.9pts. Andrea Agathagelou and Muhammad Akoojee added 220 for North West's second wicket on the opening day.*

At Pietermaritzburg, October 1–3, 2009. **Drawn. KwaZulu-Natal Inland 250-6** (G. N. Addicott 104) **and 124-3;** ‡**Western Province 266.** *KwaZulu-Natal Inland 8pts, Western Province 7.32pts.*

At Paarl, October 8–10, 2009. **Drawn. Boland 192** (F. S. Holtzhausen 6-29) **and 331-2 dec** (E. C. Kriek 149, U-K. J. Birkenstock 101*); **‡Griqualand West 219** (G. L. Cloete 103) **and 110-3.** *Boland 6.84pts, Griqualand West 7.38pts. Gihan Cloete was the third-youngest South African to score a first-class century, at 17 years five days (after Daryll Cullinan and Graeme Pollock, who both did so while 16). There were more maiden centuries in Boland's second innings, for Emile Kriek and debutant Uwe-Karl Birkenstock.*

At East London, October 8–10, 2009. **Drawn. ‡Northerns 333-9** (P. J. Malan 168) **and 87-1; Border 219** (L. M. G. Masekela 5-69). *Border 7.38pts, Northerns 9.66pts.*

At Bloemfontein, October 8–10, 2009. **Drawn. ‡Namibia 311-6** (C. G. Williams 122) **and 289-7 dec** (S. F. Burger 123*); **Free State 312** (L. Klazinga 5-67) **and 83-1.** *Free State 8.24pts, Namibia 9.22pts.*

At Johannesburg (ABSA Oval), October 8–10, 2009. **Drawn. ‡Gauteng 438-6** (S. C. Cook 116, D. J. Vilas 135*) **and 278-2 dec** (J. Symes 147*); **Eastern Province 338-6** (M. B. A. Smith 108) **and 122-1.** *Gauteng 10.76pts, Eastern Province 8.76pts.*

At Pietermaritzburg, October 8–10, 2009. **Drawn. KwaZulu-Natal Inland 171 and 184; ‡KwaZulu-Natal 309 and 17-0.** *KwaZulu-Natal Inland 5.42pts, KwaZulu-Natal 8.6pts.*

At Kimberley, October 15–17, 2009. **Drawn. Griqualand West 165** (R. N. Manyande 5-29) **and 288-5 dec; ‡Namibia 168** (C. Pietersen 5-34) **and 245-8.** *Griqualand West 6.3pts, Namibia 6.36pts.*

At Cape Town (Northerns-Goodwood Oval), October 15–17, 2009. **Western Province won by five wickets. South Western Districts 280-8** (S. E. Avontuur 123) **and 228** (A. A. Temoor 5-31); **‡Western Province 236-9** (N. G. Brouwers 5-83) **and 274-5** (A. J. A. Gray 123). *Western Province 17.72pts, South Western Districts 8.6pts.*

At Port Elizabeth (ABSA Oval), October 22–24, 2009. **Drawn. ‡Eastern Province 244** (W. L. Coetsee 5-84) **and 217; North West 220-6 and 108-4.** *Eastern Province 6.88pts, North West 7.24pts.*

At Bloemfontein, October 22–24, 2009. **Drawn. ‡Free State 244 and 271-6 dec; Boland 226 and 177-2.** *Free State 7.88pts, Boland 7.52pts.*

At Johannesburg (Old Edwardians A Ground), October 22–24, 2009. **Gauteng won by an innings and 18 runs. Gauteng 352-7** (S. Burger 101*); **‡Border 124** (S. Burger 5-13) **and 210.** *Gauteng 20.04pts, Border 4.48pts.*

At Durban, October 22–24, 2009. **Northerns won by an innings and 54 runs. ‡KwaZulu-Natal 144 and 73; Northerns 271.** *Northerns 18.42pts, KwaZulu-Natal 5.88pts.*

At Pietermaritzburg, October 22–24, 2009. **Drawn. KwaZulu-Natal Inland 300-4** (C. A. H. Barron 109, D. J. Watson 103*) **and 212-2** (M. Olivier 101*); **‡Griqualand West 223-7 dec** (R. R. Hendricks 112*). *KwaZulu-Natal Inland 8pts, Griqualand West 5.46pts. Chad Barron scored 109 on first-class debut.*

At Windhoek, October 22–24, 2009. **Drawn. Namibia 219** (G. C. Viljoen 5-54) **and 418-5** (R. van Schoor 141); **‡Easterns 430-8** (J. J. Pienaar 154; L. P. van der Westhuizen 5-90). *Namibia 6.38pts, Easterns 10.42pts.*

At East London (Buffalo Flats), October 29–31, 2009. **Western Province won by four wickets. Border 258 and 279** (K. D. Bennett 112*); **‡Western Province 359-9** (S. de Kock 5-87) **and 179-6.** *Western Province 18.68pts, Border 7.16pts.*

At Port Elizabeth, October 29–31, 2009. **Eastern Province won by 188 runs. Eastern Province 345-2** (J. T. Smuts 134) **and 223-5 dec** (M. B. A. Smith 100); **‡Free State 206 and 174** (L. Meyer 5-33). *Eastern Province 19.9pts, Free State 4.12pts. Athenkosi Dyili of Eastern Province became only the 12th wicketkeeper and the first South African to make eight dismissals in a first-class innings. He took eight catches as Free State were bowled out on the final day, and ten in the match.*

At Windhoek, October 29–30, 2009. **Boland won by ten wickets. ‡Namibia 215** (C. H. Raubenheimer 6-65) **and 134; Boland 324 and 26-0.** *Boland 18.98pts, Namibia 6.3pts.*

At Potchefstroom (Witrand Cricket Field), October 29–31, 2009. **Drawn. North West 375-6** (J. F. Mostert 161*) **and 297-7 dec** (B. J. Pelser 109*); **‡KwaZulu-Natal Inland 337-5** (M. Olivier 133) **and 129-7.** *North West 8.5pts, KwaZulu-Natal Inland 8.74pts.*

At Oudtshoorn, October 29–31, 2009. **Easterns won by 216 runs. Easterns 321-7** (J. J. Pienaar 112) **and 293-4 dec** (J. J. Pienaar 135, J. Booysen 103); ‡**South Western Districts 172 and 226** (Imran Tahir 5-79). *Easterns 19.42pts, South Western Districts 5.44pts. Cobus Pienaar scored 112 in 115 balls in Easterns' first innings, and 135 in 145 in the second, to make it three centuries in successive innings; in between, he took 4-25 in South Western Districts' first innings.*

At Port Elizabeth (ABSA Oval), November 5–7, 2009. **Eastern Province won by eight wickets.** ‡**Griqualand West 334** (W. Bossenger 129; S. R. Harmer 5-111) **and 327-7 dec** (A. P. McLaren 125*); **Eastern Province 345-7** (K. R. Smuts 102) **and 318-2** (M. L. Price 138*). *Eastern Province 19.66pts, Griqualand West 7.68pts. Off-spinner Simon Harmer took 5-111 on first-class debut.*

At Chatsworth, November 5–7, 2009. **Drawn. ‡KwaZulu-Natal 278-4 dec** (B. G. Barnes 100) **and 224-5** (J. C. Kent 100*); **Boland 211 and 195-8.** *KwaZulu-Natal 8.56pts, Boland 5.22pts.*

At Potchefstroom, November 5–7, 2009. **Drawn. North West 273** (V. D. Philander 5-16) **and 291-8** (J. F. Mostert 163*); ‡**Western Province 287-9** (M. Y. Vallie 107, V. D. Philander 102). *North West 6.46pts, Western Province 8.52pts. Vernon Philander's first-innings figures were 18–9–16–5; later, he and Yaseen Vallie added 208 for Western Province's sixth wicket.*

At Pretoria, November 5–7, 2009. **Northerns won by nine wickets. Free State 212 and 260;** ‡**Northerns 336 and 140-1.** *Northerns 19.48pts, Free State 7.24pts.*

At Oudtshoorn, November 5–6, 2009. **Gauteng won by seven runs. ‡Gauteng 206 and 92** (W. C. Hantam 5-53); **South Western Districts 189** (U. Govender 5-30) **and 102.** *Gauteng 17.12pts, South Western Districts 6.78pts.*

At Paarl, November 12–14, 2009. **Boland v KwaZulu-Natal Inland. Abandoned!**

At East London (Buffalo Flats), November 12–14, 2009. **Griqualand West won by nine wickets.** ‡**Griqualand West 407** (W. Bossenger 168) **and 48-1; Border 182** (G. R. de Wee 5-15) **and 270** (C. Pietersen 5-51). *Griqualand West 21.14pts, Border 6.64pts. Wendell Bossenger and Charl Pietersen (91) added 234 for Griquas' sixth wicket.*

At Port Elizabeth (ABSA Oval), November 12–14, 2009. **Drawn. South Western Districts 324-7** (J. G. Strydom 134, W. C. Hantam 102) **and 447-9** (R. E. Hillermann 140*; C. R. Dolley 5-151); ‡**Eastern Province 325-7** (W. E. Bell 100*). *Eastern Province 8.5pts, South Western Districts 8.48pts.*

At Benoni, November 12–13, 2009. **Easterns won by an innings and 96 runs. ‡North West 177** (Imran Tahir 5-53) **and 100** (Imran Tahir 5-34); **Easterns 373** (V. C. M. Mazibuko 6-108). *Easterns 19.54pts, North West 5.54pts. Leg-spinner Imran Tahir's ten wickets took him to 400 in his first-class career.*

At Windhoek, November 12–14, 2009. **Drawn. ‡Namibia 252 and 397-7** (G. J. Rudolph 118); **Gauteng 332-9 dec** (L. Klazinga 6-70). *Namibia 6.04pts, Gauteng 9.06pts.*

At Benoni, November 19–21, 2009. **Drawn. ‡KwaZulu-Natal 73-2 v Easterns.** *Easterns 1pt.*

At Alberton, November 19–21, 2009. **Gauteng v Free State. Abandoned.**

At Kimberley, November 19–21, 2009. **Griqualand West won by 107 runs. ‡Griqualand West 210 and 307** (C. Pietersen 140; M. W. Olivier 6-97); **Western Province 270 and 140** (R. Pietersen 7-41). *Griqualand West 16.2pts, Western Province 8.28pts. In Griquas' second innings, Charl Pietersen and Adrian McLaren (76) added 213 for the sixth wicket.*

At Pietermaritzburg, November 19–21, 2009. **KwaZulu-Natal Inland v Border. Abandoned.**

At Oudtshoorn, November 19–21, 2009. **South Western Districts won by eight wickets. ‡Northerns 174 and 278; South Western Districts 328-9** (P. A. Stuurman 108) **and 128-2.** *South Western Districts 17.7pts, Northerns 5.48pts.*

At Potchefstroom, December 17–19, 2009. **Drawn. North West 341-9** (B. J. Pelser 163*) **and 265;** ‡**South Western Districts 425-7 and 121-8.** *North West 8.82pts, South Western Districts 11.5pts. Sammy-Joe Avontuur (90) and Neil Bredenkamp (91) opened South Western Districts' first innings with a stand of 201.*

At Benoni, December 20–22, 2009. **Easterns won by three wickets. ‡Boland 327-9** (U-K. J. Birkenstock 112; Imran Tahir 5-114) **and 255** (Imran Tahir 7-82); **Easterns 315 and 268-7.** *Easterns 19.3pts, Boland 9.54pts. Leg-spinner Imran Tahir took 12-196 in the match.*

At Johannesburg (Old Edwardians A Ground), December 20–22, 2009. **KwaZulu-Natal won by one wicket. ‡Gauteng 188 and 128** (S. Mlongo 5-35); **KwaZulu-Natal 189 and 130-9.** *KwaZulu-Natal 16.78pts, Gauteng 6.76pts.*

At Paarl, January 7–9, 2010. **Eastern Province won by 182 runs. ‡Eastern Province 248 and 200-9 dec; Boland 116 and 150** (A. C. R. Birch 5-42). *Eastern Province 17.96pts, Boland 5.32pts. Andrew Birch ended the match with a hat-trick.*

At Pietermaritzburg, January 7–9, 2010. **Drawn. KwaZulu-Natal Inland 259** (Imran Tahir 5-105) **and 352-5 dec** (B. Moses 119); **‡Easterns 317 and 91-4.** *KwaZulu-Natal Inland 8.18pts, Easterns 9.34pts.*

At Windhoek, January 7–9, 2010. **Drawn. ‡Border 275-7 and 213-7 dec; Namibia 193 and 216-9.** *Namibia 5.86pts, Border 8.5pts.*

At Potchefstroom, January 7–9, 2010. **Drawn. ‡North West 308** (R. Pietersen 6-65) **and 329-8 dec** (B. J. Pelser 117*); **Griqualand West 339-7** (W. Bossenger 133*) **and 73-1.** *North West 8.16pts, Griqualand West 9.4pts. In North West's second innings, Brett Pelser and Jimmy Kgamadi (98) added 204 for the sixth wicket.*

At Oudtshoorn, January 7–9, 2010. **Drawn. ‡KwaZulu-Natal 177 and 301** (R. E. Hillermann 5-55); **South Western Districts 288** (J. G. Strydom 102) **and 147-7.** *South Western Districts 8.66pts, KwaZulu-Natal 6.54pts.*

At Stellenbosch, January 14–16, 2010. **Northerns won by 326 runs. Northerns 360-5** (H. E. van der Dussen 124, P. J. Malan 109) **and 219-4 dec** (J. F. le Clus 103); **‡Boland 122** (M. A. Mashimbyi 6-31) **and 131.** *Northerns 20.2pts, Boland 3.44pts.*

At East London, January 14–16, 2010. **Eastern Province won by five wickets. Border 290-9 and 187** (R. C. Williams 6-52); **‡Eastern Province 298-9 and 180-5.** *Eastern Province 18.96pts, Border 8.8pts.*

At Benoni, January 14–16, 2010. **Drawn. ‡Easterns 361-6** (J. Booysen 145) **and 52-2; Gauteng 351-4** (T. Bavuma 152*, S. Burger 138*). *Easterns 8.22pts, Gauteng 9.02pts. Temba Bavuma and Shane Burger added 270* for Gauteng's fifth wicket, halted only by the 85-over limit on first innings.*

At Chatsworth, January 14–16, 2010. **Western Province won by an innings and 95 runs. ‡KwaZulu-Natal 131** (G. R. Rabie 5-29) **and 180; Western Province 406-7** (M. Y. Vallie 113). *Western Province 17.82pts, KwaZulu-Natal 3.62pts.*

At Bloemfontein, January 21–23, 2010. **Drawn. ‡Free State 374-7** (D. J. van Wyk 153) **and 26-0; KwaZulu-Natal Inland 288-9** (G. N. Addicott 104). *Free State 10.48pts, KwaZulu-Natal Inland 7.76pts.*

At Kimberley, January 21–23, 2010. **Griqualand West won by seven wickets. South Western Districts 187 and 195** (J. Coetzee 5-64); **‡Griqualand West 262 and 121-3.** *Griqualand West 18.24pts, South Western Districts 6.74pts.*

At Durban, January 21–23, 2010. **KwaZulu-Natal won by 155 runs. KwaZulu-Natal 267-9** (J. C. Kent 158*) **and 206-3 dec** (K. Zondo 100*); **‡Namibia 151** (K. A. Maharaj 5-30) **and 167.** *KwaZulu-Natal 18.34pts, Namibia 6.02pts.*

At Pretoria, January 21–23, 2010. **Drawn. Northerns 352-9** (R. Bhayat 6-110); **‡North West 147** (S. von Berg 5-43) **and 389-3** (A. P. Agathagelou 136*, M. Akoojee 123, C. Jonker 100*). *Northerns 10.04pts, North West 5.94pts.*

At Cape Town (Northerns-Goodwood Oval), January 21–23, 2010. **Gauteng won by 146 runs. Gauteng 324-7 and 216-3 dec** (J. Symes 110); **‡Western Province 114 and 280** (T. Shamsi 6-89). *Gauteng 19.48pts, Western Province 4.28pts.*

At Paarl, January 28–30, 2010. **Drawn. ‡Boland 309-9** (S. van Zyl 161; N. Bredenkamp 5-41) **and 237-4 dec** (O. A. Ramela 104); **South Western Districts 170 and 302-6** (N. Bredenkamp 116). *Boland 9.18pts, South Western Districts 6.4pts.*

At East London (Buffalo Flats), January 28–30, 2010. **Free State won by an innings and one run. Border 205** (D. du Preez 5-19) **and 100** (D. du Preez 6-31); **‡Free State 306-8** (D. J. van Wyk 119). *Free State 18.34pts, Border 5.1pts.*

At Port Elizabeth, January 28–30, 2010. **Eastern Province won by 221 runs. Eastern Province 264 and 239-4 dec** (K. R. Smuts 101*); ‡**Namibia 209-8 and 73** (R. C. Williams 6-24). *Eastern Province 18.28pts, Namibia 7.18pts.*

At Pretoria, January 28–30, 2010. **Easterns won by six wickets. Northerns 225** (J. J. Pienaar 5-40) **and 248** (Imran Tahir 5-105); ‡**Easterns 239** (S. von Berg 5-105) **and 240-4** (T. M. Bodibe 100*). *Easterns 17.78pts, Northerns 7.5pts.*

At Port Elizabeth, February 4–5, 2010. **Eastern Province won by an innings and 96 runs. Easterns 145** (R. C. Williams 7-60) **and 168;** ‡**Eastern Province 409** (M. L. Price 179; Imran Tahir 5-117). *Eastern Province 19.42pts, Easterns 2.9pts. Michael Price and Kelly Smuts (95) added 226 for Eastern Province's fourth wicket, more than Easterns managed in either innings.*

At Johannesburg, February 4–6, 2010. **Drawn.** ‡**North West 260 and 136-5; Gauteng 391-4 dec** (S. C. Cook 168*). *Gauteng 10.78pts, North West 6.2pts.*

At Kimberley, February 4–6, 2010. **Drawn. Griqualand West 343-8 and 252-8 dec;** ‡**Free State 262-9 and 169-4.** *Griqualand West 9.86pts, Free State 8.24pts.*

At Pretoria, February 4–6, 2010. **Northerns won by an innings and 75 runs.** ‡**Namibia 155** (S. von Berg 6-34) **and 88** (S. von Berg 5-30); **Northerns 318.** *Northerns 19.16pts, Namibia 6.1pts.*

At Benoni, February 11–13, 2010. **Border won by two wickets. Easterns 286-8** (J. C. Fourie 113*) **and 137** (S. de Kock 5-27); ‡**Border 187** (G. C. Viljoen 6-55) **and 237-8.** *Border 16.74pts, Easterns 8.72pts.*

At Potchefstroom, February 11–13, 2010. **Drawn.** ‡**North West 411-5** (A. P. Agathagelou 158) **and 192-8 dec; KwaZulu-Natal 214 and 297-4.** *North West 11.22pts, KwaZulu-Natal 5.28pts.*

At Oudtshoorn, February 11–12, 2010. **South Western Districts won by five wickets.** ‡**KwaZulu-Natal Inland 136** (S. F. Grobler 5-38) **and 112** (R. Botha 6-26); **South Western Districts 153 and 96-5.** *South Western Districts 16.06pts, KwaZulu-Natal Inland 5.72pts. Eighteen-year-old seamer Rian Botha took 6-26 on first-class debut.*

At Cape Town (Durbanville), February 11–13, 2010. **Drawn. Northerns 316-9** (C. F. Schoeman 100) **and 190;** ‡**Western Province 272-8** (R. C. C. Canning 116; M. A. Mashimbyi 5-81) **and 131-5.** *Western Province 8.44pts, Northerns 9.32pts.*

At Kimberley, February 18–19, 2010. **Gauteng won by an innings and 22 runs.** ‡**Griqualand West 161** (J. T. Mafa 6-44) **and 122; Gauteng 305.** *Gauteng 18.6pts, Griqualand West 6.22pts.*

At Oudtshoorn, February 18–20, 2010. **South Western Districts won by 134 runs. South Western Districts 220** (S. F. Grobler 106) **and 247** (B. C. de Wett 108; S. de Kock 8-64); ‡**Border 200 and 133.** *South Western Districts 17.4pts, Border 7pts. Slow left-armer Shaun de Kock took 12-93 in the match.*

At Cape Town, February 18–20, 2010. **Western Province won by eight wickets.** ‡**Free State 356-8 and 164** (A. Mgijima 5-24); **Western Province 394-8** (M. Y. Vallie 119) **and 129-2.** *Western Province 20.88pts, Free State 10.12pts.*

At East London, February 25–27, 2010. **Drawn.** ‡**Boland 260 and 43-0; Border 422-5 dec** (S. de Kock 100*). *Border 11.28pts, Boland 6.2pts.*

At Bloemfontein, February 25–27, 2010. **Free State won by eight wickets. Free State 364-5** (D. J. van Wyk 134, J. A. Beukes 120*) **and 78-2;** ‡**South Western Districts 143 and 295.** *Free State 20.28pts, South Western Districts 3.86pts.*

At Durban, February 25–27, 2010. **Drawn. Griqualand West 154** (K. J. Abbott 6-42) **and 121-1;** ‡**KwaZulu-Natal 314-8 dec** (B. G. Barnes 157). *KwaZulu-Natal 8.36pts, Griqualand West 4.08pts.*

At Pietermaritzburg, February 25–27, 2010. **Gauteng won by ten wickets.** ‡**KwaZulu-Natal Inland 186** (J. Symes 6-61) **and 177** (T. Shamsi 5-72); **Gauteng 349-6** (D. Conway 123*) **and 15-0.** *Gauteng 17.68pts, KwaZulu-Natal Inland 5.72pts.*

At Pretoria, February 25–27, 2010. **Drawn. Northerns 268** (H. E. van der Dussen 114; S. R. Harmer 5-68) **and 92-5;** ‡**Eastern Province 185.** *Northerns 8.36pts, Eastern Province 6.7pts.*

At Cape Town (Durbanville), February 25–27, 2010. **Namibia won by eight wickets. Western Province 70 and 286** (M. D. Walters 110; L. Klazinga 5-50); ‡**Namibia 327** (B. E. Hendricks 5-52) **and 32-2.** *Namibia 19.02pts, Western Province 4pts.*

At Paarl, March 4–6, 2010. **North West won by 242 runs.** ‡**North West 307-8** (C. Jonker 100) **and 238-5 dec** (A. P. Agathagelou 105); **Boland 202** (C. H. Morris 5-44) **and 101.** *North West 19.14pts, Boland 7.04pts.*

At Benoni, March 4–6, 2010. **Drawn. Easterns 300-9;** ‡**Free State 148-5.** *Easterns 7pts, Free State 5.96pts.*

At Kimberley, March 4–6, 2010. **Drawn. Griqualand West 332-8;** ‡**Northerns 209.** *Griqualand West 9.64pts, Northerns 7.18pts.*

At Windhoek, March 4–6, 2010. **Drawn. Namibia 112 and 290;** ‡**KwaZulu-Natal Inland 275 and 102-8** (C. G. Williams 5-41). *Namibia 3.24pts, KwaZulu-Natal Inland 6.54pts.*

At Cape Town, March 4–6, 2010. **Western Province won by one wicket. Eastern Province 305 and 241-7 dec;** ‡**Western Province 166** (L. Meyer 5-38) **and 384-9** (A. J. A. Gray 127). *Western Province 16.32pts, Eastern Province 9.1pts.*

At Benoni, March 11–12, 2010. ‡**Western Province won by seven wickets.** ‡**Western Province 197 and 102; Easterns 235 and 66-3.** *Easterns 17.7pts, Western Province 6.94pts.*

At Johannesburg, March 11–13, 2010. **Gauteng won by seven wickets.** ‡**Boland 194** (G. I. Hume 5-44) **and 88; Gauteng 208** (S. C. Cook 117*; J. L. Ontong 5-62) **and 77-3.** *Gauteng 17.16pts, Boland 6.88pts.*

At Durban, March 11–13, 2010. **Eastern Province won by four wickets. KwaZulu-Natal 244-9 and 251;** ‡**Eastern Province 220 and 278-6** (J. T. Smuts 130*; C. A. Flowers 5-92). *Eastern Province 17.4pts, KwaZulu-Natal 7.88pts.*

At Windhoek, March 11–13, 2010. **South Western Districts won by 33 runs. South Western Districts 110 and 339;** ‡**Namibia 267-8 dec and 149.** *South Western Districts 14.2pts, Namibia 7.94pts.*

At Potchefstroom, March 11–13, 2010. **Drawn. North West 340-7 and 209-5 dec;** ‡**Border 139** (W. A. Deacon 5-27) **and 224-6.** *North West 9.8pts, Border 4.78pts.*

At East London (Buffalo Flats), March 18–19, 2010. **KwaZulu-Natal won by 69 runs. KwaZulu-Natal 217 and 149;** ‡**Border 124 and 173.** *KwaZulu-Natal 17.34pts, Border 5.48pts.*

At Port Elizabeth, March 18–20, 2010. **Eastern Province won by 150 runs. Eastern Province 312-5** (R. R. Jeggels 104*) **and 270-6 dec;** ‡**KwaZulu-Natal Inland 255-8 and 177.** *Eastern Province 19.24pts, KwaZulu-Natal Inland 6.1pts.*

At Pretoria, March 18–20, 2010. **Drawn.** ‡**Northerns 217 and 365** (H. E. van der Dussen 101, D. Hewitt 103); **Gauteng 421-6 dec** (D. Conway 128, S. Burger 112*) **and 112-8.** *Northerns 6.34pts, Gauteng 11.42pts. In Gauteng's first innings, Devon Conway and Shane Burger added 227 for the fifth wicket; in Northerns' second, Douglas Hewitt scored 103 on first-class debut, during a second-wicket stand of 189 with Rassie van der Dussen.*

At Bloemfontein, March 25–27, 2010. **Drawn.** ‡**Free State 329-9 and 220-6 dec** (D. J. van Wyk 114); **KwaZulu-Natal 185 and 142-8.** *Free State 9.58pts, KwaZulu-Natal 6.7pts.*

At Kimberley, March 25–27, 2010. **Drawn. Griqualand West 271 and 128-5 dec;** ‡**Easterns 306-8** (R. A. du Plessis 112) **and 8-0.** *Griqualand West 7.42pts, Easterns 8.82pts.*

At Pietermaritzburg, March 25–27, 2010. **Northerns won by ten wickets.** ‡**KwaZulu-Natal Inland 154** (S. A. Nowak 5-32) **and 274** (G. N. Addicott 106); **Northerns 360-7 dec** (K. Nipper 5-143) **and 69-0.** *Northerns 19.82pts, KwaZulu-Natal Inland 5.08pts.*

At Potchefstroom, March 25–27, 2010. **North West won by 76 runs. North West 194 and 350-7 dec** (B. J. Pelser 110*, C. H. Morris 145); ‡**Namibia 213** (K. M. Vardhan 5-25) **and 255** (W. L. Coetsee 5-78). *North West 16.88pts, Namibia 7.26pts. North West were 96-6 in their second innings, only 77 ahead, before Brett Pelser and Chris Morris added 249 for their seventh wicket.*

At Cape Town, March 25–26, 2010. **Boland won by six wickets. Western Province 205 and 119** (C. J. August 9-37); ‡**Boland 232 and 93-4.** *Boland 17.64pts, Western Province 7.1pts.*

Twenty-year-old Yaseen Vallie of Western Province scored 92 and eight to finish with 865 first-class runs, a South African record for a debut season. In the second innings, he was one of nine victims for left-arm seamer Clayton August, who took 13-106 in the match.*

MTN DOMESTIC CHAMPIONSHIP, 2009-10

40-over league plus knockout

	Played	Won	Lost	No result	Bonus points	Points	Net run-rate
Titans	10	7	1	2	2	34	0.59
Cape Cobras	10	7	2	1	3	33	0.58
Warriors	10	5	5	0	1	20*	0.00
Dolphins	10	3	6	1	0	14	−0.27
Eagles	10	3	7	0	1	13	−0.01
Lions........................	10	3	7	0	0	12	−0.80

* 1pt deducted for slow over-rate.

Semi-finals

At Paarl, January 22, 2010 (day/night). **Warriors won by nine runs. ‡Warriors 274-4** (40 overs); **Cape Cobras 265-8** (40 overs).

At Centurion, January 24, 2010. **Dolphins won by 15 runs. Dolphins 251-6** (40 overs); **‡Titans 236-9** (40 overs).

Final

At East London, January 29, 2010 (day/night). **Warriors won by 71 runs. ‡Warriors 299-4** (40 overs) (A. G. Prince 128); **Dolphins 228** (36.4 overs).

STANDARD BANK PRO20 SERIES, 2009-10

	Played	Won	Lost	No result	Bonus points	Points	Net run-rate
Warriors	5	4	1	0	0	16	−0.07
Titans	5	3	1	1	1	15	1.11
Lions........................	5	3	2	0	0	11*	−0.17
Cape Cobras	5	2	3	0	1	9	0.15
Eagles	5	2	3	0	0	8	−0.05
Dolphins	5	0	4	1	0	1*	−0.74

* 1pt deducted for slow over-rate.

Semi-finals

Lions won their best-of-three semi-finals against Titans 2–0; Warriors beat Cape Cobras 2–0.

Final

At Port Elizabeth, March 12, 2010 (day/night). **Warriors won by 82 runs. ‡Warriors 186-2** (20 overs); **Lions 104** (17.5 overs).

CSA PROVINCIAL ONE-DAY CHALLENGE, 2009-10

40-over league

	Played	Won	Lost	Tied	No result	Bonus points	Points	Net run-rate
Northerns	13	9	2	0	2	5	45	0.80
Gauteng	13	8	5	0	0	6	38	0.78
Eastern Province	13	7	5	1	0	3	34	0.58
Griqualand West	13	7	4	0	2	2	34	0.15
Border	13	7	4	1	1	0	33	−0.58
Free State	13	7	5	0	1	3	32*	0.27
North West...............	13	7	6	0	0	4	30†	−0.66
Boland	13	6	5	0	2	2	30	0.22
KwaZulu-Natal............	13	6	6	0	1	3	29	0.23
Western Province..........	13	5	7	0	1	2	24	0.51
South Western Districts	13	5	7	1	0	0	23	−0.51
KwaZulu-Natal Inland	13	4	8	0	1	2	20	−0.03
Easterns	13	4	9	0	0	0	16	−0.59
Namibia	13	1	10	1	1	1	10	−1.14

* 1pt deducted for slow over-rate.   † 2pts deducted for slow over-rate.

SRI LANKAN CRICKET, 2010

Board games

Sa'adi Thawfeeq

The retirement of Muttiah Muralitharan, after becoming the first bowler to take 800 Test wickets, and the shock sacking of assistant coach Chandika Hathurusinghe, who was being groomed to take over as head coach of the national team, were the features of an otherwise quiet year for Sri Lanka.

Muralitharan closed a glorious chapter when he finally quit Test cricket with a record haul of wickets. Being the fighter he is, Muralitharan set himself to get the last eight he needed for 800 in the First Test against India at Galle in July: he not only achieved what he wanted but also bowled his country to victory, as he had done umpteen times before during his illustrious career. Galle gave him a 21-gun salute, which is normally reserved for visiting heads of state.

SRI LANKA IN 2010

	Played	Won	Lost	Drawn/ No result
Tests	6	1	1	4
One-day internationals	22	15	6	1
Twenty20 internationals	9	5	4	–

JANUARY	Triangular ODI tournament (a) in Bangladesh	(page 881)
FEBRUARY		
MARCH		
APRIL		
MAY	World Twenty20 (in West Indies)	(page 797)
	2 T20Is v New Zealand (in USA)	(page 1157)
JUNE	Triangular ODI tournament (a) in Zimbabwe	(page 1146)
	Asia Cup (in Sri Lanka)	(page 1076)
JULY	3 Tests (h) v India	(page 1080)
AUGUST	Triangular ODI tournament (h) v India and New Zealand	(page 1090)
SEPTEMBER		
OCTOBER		
NOVEMBER	3 ODIs and 1 T20I (a) v Australia	(page 853)
DECEMBER	3 Tests (h) v West Indies	(page 1093)

Reports from Sri Lanka's home ODI series against West Indies in January 2011 will appear in *Wisden 2012*.

For a review of Sri Lankan domestic cricket from the 2009-10 season, see page 1102.

Muralitharan's Test retirement, following that of Chaminda Vaas, left Sri Lanka in a new era with plenty of promising bowlers, both pace and spin, but no experienced spearhead. The fact that during 2010 Lasith Malinga became only the third Sri Lankan to reach 100 Test wickets – in almost 30 years of Test status – underlined the country's reliance on Murali and Vaas, who took more than 2,000 wickets between them in all international cricket. The batting, however, was formidably strong in all formats, as Kumar Sangakkara and Mahela Jayawardene were supported by some very promising talent, most notably Angelo Mathews.

Hathurusinghe, the former Test batsman and A-team coach, was only 18 months into his job when he was given the boot because he disobeyed Somachandra de Silva, the former Test leg-spinner who is now the chairman of the Sri Lankan board. Hathurusinghe had been given permission by both manager Anura Tennekoon and head coach Trevor Bayliss to leave ahead of the one-day tri-series final in Zimbabwe in June, to take a coaching course in Australia financed by Sri Lanka Cricket. But SLC dismissed him, saying he had disobeyed de Silva's order not to leave Zimbabwe until the final was over. Even a letter of support from Sangakkara, pointing out Hathurusinghe's immense value to the side ahead of the World Cup, fell on deaf ears. During his short time with the national team Hathurusinghe helped several players improve their individual skills and outlook. He sought greener pastures, and took his family to Australia to start afresh.

Cricket in Sri Lanka continued to be run by a government-appointed interim committee for the 11th consecutive year, with no signs of an election. This frustrated some of the member clubs. One, the United Southern Sports Club, went to the extent of filing a fundamental-rights petition against the board, calling for elections. They claimed that the Minister of Sport had misused his powers by continuing to have an interim committee run the board's affairs. The case has been put off twice.

These allegations came after the new sports minister, Chandrasiri Bandara Ratnayake, first accused Sri Lanka Cricket of being the third-most corrupt institution in the country after Education and Police, and then, two days later, reappointed the same interim committee, with only a few minor changes. The only good thing the minister did during his brief six-month tenure before being replaced was to appoint the former World Cup hero Aravinda de Silva to head the national selection committee.

De Silva accepted the position on condition that there would no political interference with selection. His World Cup-winning team-mate Sanath Jayasuriya, who had been hoping to make one final appearance in a World Cup at 41, was elected a Member of Parliament. Jayasuriya polled 74,352 votes to win his seat in his home town of Matara, in the Southern Province – but he failed to hold on to his place in the national one-day team.

Board chairman Somachandra de Silva continued to attract much criticism from the media about his close connections with Sri Lanka's president. De Silva also invited a lot more criticism when he appointed two of his nephews to the World Cup Secretariat. This committee had the big responsibility of completing Sri Lanka's three Cup venues, the total cost amounting to more

Eranga Jayawardena, AP/PA

And then there was one: with Trevor Bayliss (*left*) and Muttiah Muralitharan (*right*) due to quit after the 2011 World Cup, much responsibility will fall on Kumar Sangakkara.

than three billion rupees. The construction was constantly behind schedule, but the board convinced the public that World Cup matches could be staged at the venues by playing two of the three West Indies Tests in them at the end of the year, even though building work was still taking place at the Premadasa Stadium in Colombo and the new Pallakele ground near Kandy. However, attempts to host two one-day internationals against West Indies at the third World Cup venue, the new ground in Hambantota, failed when bad weather forced the postponement of the one-day series to late January 2011.

Meanwhile, Sri Lanka Cricket expanded the number of contracted players, from 24 to 74 in 2009, then to 100 a year later. This was done with the intention of ensuring that the contracted players were committed full-time professionals. The contracts were in two categories: National (30 players) and Provincial (70). The contracts ranged between US$120,000 to US$400 per annum per player, and cost Sri Lanka Cricket $2.5m annually.

The board has effectively contracted out its provincial tournaments to a Singapore-based entertainment company called Somerset Ventures. The plan is to revamp the domestic Interprovincial Twenty20 tournament on the same lines as the IPL, by allowing foreign players to participate, and attempting to attract overseas sponsorship, to reach a much wider audience.

Sri Lanka Cricket was also left with the task of head-hunting for a new coach – in the absence of Hathurusinghe – when the Australian Trevor Bayliss, who took over in 2007, decided to step down after the World Cup. Under Bayliss, Sri Lanka won their maiden one-day series in Australia late in 2010, the main feature being a stunning record ninth-wicket stand of 132 between Mathews and Malinga to turn the first game at Melbourne on its head.

ASIA CUP, 2010

SA'ADI THAWFEEQ

1. India   2. Sri Lanka   3. Pakistan   4. Bangladesh

India won the Asia Cup for the first time since April 1995, after having one of those days in the final where everything went right. Sri Lanka had just beaten them in the last qualifying match, but when it counted India held all the aces.

All the matches were played at the Rangiri Dambulla Stadium. Ever since it was built in 2001, there had been criticism of the low output of the floodlights and the strong crosswinds that are quite common in this part of central Sri Lanka. These factors meant that toss-winning captains had usually batted first, to avoid having to chase under lights with the ball darting around. Mahendra Singh Dhoni was no exception in the final here, and his side ran up the impressive total of 268. When Sri Lanka's first five wickets tumbled for 51 the contest was effectively over: India ended Sri Lanka's recent domination of the Asia Cup, which they had won on the previous two occasions, in 2004 and 2008.

India's victory against a full-strength home team was even more creditable as they were lacking Sachin Tendulkar (who was rested), Yuvraj Singh (omitted) and Virender Sehwag, who pulled his hamstring in the second match and missed the rest of the tournament. Sehwag's replacement, Dinesh Karthik, played a crucial innings in the final and collected the match award.

The previous two Asia Cup tournaments had included Hong Kong and the United Arab Emirates, but the crowded schedule meant this time there was no room for the minnows, and the whole thing was crammed into a nine-day window. Even that was only possible because Pakistan and Bangladesh made late changes to the itineraries of their tours of England, a fact acknowledged by Ashraful Huq, the chief executive of the Asian Cricket Council.

It didn't do those two sides much good: Pakistan lost their first two matches before handing Bangladesh a third successive drubbing in the final qualifying game. Pakistan, under their new captain Shahid Afridi, did play some excellent cricket – Afridi himself hammered two typically aggressive centuries, and was named player of the tournament – but they inexplicably lost the initiative at crucial stages of their matches against Sri Lanka and India. Chasing a modest 243 in the first match, against Sri Lanka, Pakistan lost their first four wickets for 32, and their last four for 21. Against India they were 196 for four in the 38th over but 267 all out – and Pakistan still had a chance until Harbhajan Singh pulled a short ball from Mohammad Aamer for six in the final over.

Controversy had erupted during Pakistan's first match, when Aamer was seemingly caught on camera using a mobile phone in the dressing-room area, in contravention of ICC regulations, as he waited to bat, with his helmet on. Team manager Yawar Saeed launched an investigation, which concluded that the pictures were misleading and that Aamer was not using a mobile outside his helmet.

NATIONAL SQUADS

Sri Lanka *K. C. Sangakkara, T. M. Dilshan, H. M. R. K. B. Herath, D. P. M. D. Jayawardene, S. H. T. Kandamby, C. K. Kapugedera, K. M. D. N. Kulasekara, M. F. Maharoof, S. L. Malinga, A. D. Mathews, M. Muralitharan, S. Randiv, T. T. Samaraweera, W. U. Tharanga, U. W. M. B. C. A. Welagedara. *Coach:* T. H. Bayliss.

Bangladesh *Shakib Al Hasan, Abdur Razzak, Imrul Kayes, Jahurul Islam, Junaid Siddique, Mahmudullah, Mashrafe bin Mortaza, Mohammad Ashraful, Mushfiqur Rahim, Naeem Islam, Rubel Hossain, Shafiul Islam, Suhrawadi Shuvo, Syed Rasel, Tamim Iqbal. *Coach:* J. D. Siddons.

India *M. S. Dhoni, R. Ashwin, A. B. Dinda, G. Gambhir, Harbhajan Singh, R. A. Jadeja, V. Kohli, P. Kumar, A. Nehra, P. P. Ojha, S. K. Raina, V. Sehwag, R. G. Sharma, S. S. Tiwary, Zaheer Khan. *Coach:* G. Kirsten.

Sehwag injured his hamstring during the match against Pakistan, and was replaced by K. D. Karthik.

Pakistan *Shahid Afridi, Abdul Razzaq, Abdur Rehman, Asad Shafiq, Imran Farhat, Kamran Akmal, Mohammad Aamer, Mohammad Asif, Saeed Ajmal, Salman Butt, Shahzaib Hasan, Shoaib Akhtar, Shoaib Malik, Umar Akmal, Umar Amin. *Coach:* Waqar Younis.

At Dambulla, June 15, 2010 (day/night). **Sri Lanka won by 16 runs.** ‡**Sri Lanka 242-9** (50 overs) (K. C. Sangakkara 42, D. P. M. D. Jayawardene 54, A. D. Mathews 55; Shoaib Akhtar 3-41); **Pakistan 226** (47 overs) (Umar Akmal 30, Shahid Afridi 109; S. L. Malinga 5-34). *Sri Lanka 4pts. MoM:* Shahid Afridi. *One-day international debuts:* Shahzaib Hasan, Umar Amin (Pakistan). *Pakistan did not chase down an unexceptional target, in spite of a brilliant century from their captain. After Salman Butt was bowled in Pakistan's second over, their batting was in the hands of two debutants, who put their team behind the clock: Shahzaib Hasan made 11 off 33 balls and Umar Amin seven from 26. From 32-4, Shahid Afridi lifted his side close to victory, hammering 109 from 76 balls, with eight fours and seven sixes, five of them off Muralitharan, whose ten overs cost 71. Afridi put on 73 with Umar Akmal, but no one else could stay for long, and when he finally fell – he was struggling with cramp and was well caught behind by Sangakkara off Murali to make it 205-7 – 38 were needed from 9.1 overs, a task that proved beyond the tail with Malinga bowling fast and straight. Earlier, Shoaib Akhtar, in his first international match for 13 months, had taken three wickets to restrict Sri Lanka.*

At Dambulla, June 16, 2010 (day/night). **India won by six wickets.** ‡**Bangladesh 167** (34.5 overs) (Imrul Kayes 37, Mushfiqur Rahim 30; V. Sehwag 4-6); **India 168-4** (30.4 overs) (G. Gambhir 82, M. S. Dhoni 38*). *India 5pts. MoM:* G. Gambhir. *Bangladesh hurtled out of the blocks, with Tamim Iqbal falling for 22 to make it 35-1 after 17 balls, then Imrul Kayes and Mohammad Ashraful (20) took the score to 81 in the 14th over. But Bangladesh lost their sixth wicket at 160 and their last four all at 167, with Sehwag's flighted off-breaks bringing him the remarkable figures of 2.5–0–6–4. With Gambhir anchoring the chase, India shrugged off the loss of Virat Kohli and Rohit Sharma to successive balls in the 15th over to claim a bonus point.*

At Dambulla, June 18, 2010 (day/night). **Sri Lanka won by 126 runs.** ‡**Sri Lanka 312-4** (50 overs) (W. U. Tharanga 54, T. M. Dilshan 71, K. C. Sangakkara 52, D. P. M. D. Jayawardene 43, A. D. Mathews 42*, C. K. Kapugedera 37*); **Bangladesh 186** (40.2 overs) (Tamim Iqbal 51, Junaid Siddique 38; T. M. Dilshan 3-37). *Sri Lanka 5pts. MoM:* T. M. Dilshan. *Every Sri Lankan who batted made more than 36 to set up the first total of more than 300 in one-day internationals on this ground, then Bangladesh again imploded after a decent start (77-1 in the 14th over). Sri Lanka claimed the bonus point, and confirmed their place in the final, with something to spare. Dilshan followed 71 from 51 balls – which included 11 fours and a six which won him a $1,500 prize for hitting a particular advertising hoarding – with three wickets with his off-breaks.*

At Dambulla, June 19, 2010 (day/night). **India won by three wickets.** ‡**Pakistan 267** (49.3 overs) (Salman Butt 74, Shoaib Malik 39, Shahid Afridi 32, Kamran Akmal 51; P. Kumar 3-53); **India 271-7** (49.5 overs) (G. Gambhir 83, M. S. Dhoni 56, S. K. Raina 34; Saeed Ajmal 3-56). *India 4pts. MoM:* G. Gambhir. *India won a seesaw battle with a ball to spare to clinch their place in the final, and render the two remaining group games meaningless. India looked sure to win while Gambhir and Dhoni were putting on 98, but they slipped from 180-2 to 219-6. They eventually needed 16 from the last two overs with four wickets standing: Suresh Raina eased the pressure by smashing Shoaib Akhtar for six, then was run out in the final over with six still needed – but Harbhajan Singh hoisted* *the fifth ball of Mohammad Aamer's last over into the crowd at midwicket. Virender Sehwag injured his hamstring during his innings of ten and missed the rest of the tournament.*

At Dambulla, June 21, 2010 (day/night). **Pakistan won by 139 runs.** ‡**Pakistan 385-7** (50 overs) (Imran Farhat 66, Shahzaib Hasan 50, Umar Akmal 50, Shahid Afridi 124; Shafiul Islam 3-95); **Bangladesh 246-5** (50 overs) (Tamim Iqbal 34, Imrul Kayes 66, Junaid Siddique 97). *Pakistan 5pts.* MoM: Shahid Afridi. *One-day international debuts: Jahurul Islam (Bangladesh), Asad Shafiq (Pakistan). Shahid Afridi's second violent century of the tournament – this one came off only 53 balls, and he hit 17 fours and four sixes in all – set up Pakistan's highest total in one-day internationals, beating 371-4 against Sri Lanka in Nairobi in October 1996, in the match in which Afridi blasted the fastest one-day international hundred of all (37 balls) in his maiden innings. Afridi passed Sanath Jayasuriya (270) as the leading one-day six-hitter during his onslaught. It was predictably far too much for Bangladesh, who slipped to their third heavy defeat of the tournament despite a stand of 160 between Imrul Kayes and Junaid Siddique, who just missed his first one-day hundred. This was Pakistan's eighth one-day international in 2010, but their first victory.*

At Dambulla, June 22, 2010 (day/night). **Sri Lanka won by seven wickets. India 209** (42.3 overs) (K. D. Karthik 40, R. G. Sharma 69, M. S. Dhoni 41; M. F. Maharoof 5-42); ‡**Sri Lanka 211-3** (37.3 overs) (W. U. Tharanga 38, K. C. Sangakkara 73, D. P. M. D. Jayawardene 53*). *Sri Lanka 5pts. MoM: M. F. Maharoof. Both sides rested some players ahead of the final two days later: one of Sri Lanka's replacements, Maharoof (who had missed the previous match), complicated matters for his selectors by taking five wickets – including a hat-trick to send back Ravindra Jadeja, Praveen Kumar and Zaheer Khan, all for ducks – as India nosedived from 189-4 to 189-8, and then 209 all out.*

Sri Lanka 14pts, India 9pts, Pakistan 5pts, Bangladesh 0pts.

FINAL

SRI LANKA v INDIA

At Dambulla, June 24, 2010 (day/night). India won by 81 runs. Toss: India.

Sri Lanka may have topped the qualifying table, but India came up with an excellent all-round performance in the final to win the Asia Cup for the first time since 1994-95. They controlled the match from the start, reaching an impressive total of 268 after winning the toss. The top-scorer was Karthik, who had joined the team in mid-tournament after Virender Sehwag tweaked a hamstring. His nine fours included four in six balls – three of them sweetly timed off-side drives – from Maharoof, India's destroyer in the last group game but ineffective this time. Sri Lanka's batting, so consistent in the earlier matches, was then swept aside by India's seamers, who used the blustery conditions well to reduce them to 51 for five. Kumar started the slide in the first over, persuading Dilshan to mis-pull his second ball tamely to mid-on. Kandamby and Kapugedera repaired some of the damage in a stand of 53, but when Kandamby was stranded after trying a non-existent run to Kohli in the covers there was little to come. Left-armer Nehra was the pick of the bowlers, picking up three early wickets in the space of eight balls. "It was a good toss to win – conditions were ideal for batting," admitted Dhoni. "It got a bit slower as the game progressed and started doing a bit under the lights, and the fast bowlers made the most of it."

Man of the Match: K. D. Karthik. *Man of the Series:* Shahid Afridi.

India

G. Gambhir run out	15	Harbhajan Singh not out	7
K. D. Karthik c Jayawardene b Kandamby	66		
V. Kohli c Sangakkara b Malinga	28	B 2, l-b 7, w 9, n-b 1	19
*†M. S. Dhoni c Kulasekara b Kandamby	38		
R. G. Sharma c Maharoof b Kulasekara	41	1/38 (1) 2/100 (3) (6 wkts, 50 overs)	268
S. K. Raina lbw b Malinga	29	3/146 (2) 4/167 (4)	
R. A. Jadeja not out	25	5/217 (6) 6/249 (5)	10 overs: 53-1

P. Kumar, Zaheer Khan and A. Nehra did not bat.

Kulasekara 9–0–44–1; Malinga 10–0–57–2; Maharoof 6–0–41–0; Mathews 3–1–16–0; Muralitharan 10–0–34–0; Kandamby 7–0–37–2; Dilshan 5–0–30–0.

Sri Lanka

W. U. Tharanga b Zaheer Khan	16	S. L. Malinga c Jadeja b Nehra	7
T. M. Dilshan c Harbhajan Singh b Kumar	0	M. Muralitharan c Dhoni b Jadeja	2
*†K. C. Sangakkara c Zaheer Khan b Nehra	17		
D. P. M. D. Jayawardene c Dhoni b Nehra	11	B 4, l-b 3, w 9, n-b 2	18
A. D. Mathews c Dhoni b Nehra	0		
S. H. T. Kandamby run out	31	1/5 (2) 2/31 (1) 3/50 (4) (44.4 overs)	187
C. K. Kapugedera not out	55	4/50 (5) 5/51 (3) 6/104 (6)	
M. F. Maharoof c Dhoni b Zaheer Khan	10	7/132 (8) 8/168 (9) 9/177 (10)	
K. M. D. N. Kulasekara st Dhoni b Jadeja	20	10/187 (11)	10 overs: 42-2

Kumar 9–1–29–1; Zaheer Khan 8–2–36–2; Nehra 9–0–40–4; Harbhajan Singh 9–0–30–0; Kohli 3–0–16–0; Jadeja 6.4–0–29–2.

Umpires: B. F. Bowden and B. R. Doctrove.   Third umpire: Ahsan Raza.
Series referee: A. J. Pycroft.

SRI LANKA v INDIA, 2010

Sa'adi Thawfeeq

Test matches (3): Sri Lanka 1, India 1

Muttiah Muralitharan had previously intimated that he would bow out from Test cricket at the end of 2010, after a home series against West Indies. But after the Sri Lankan board addressed a shortage of Test cricket by arranging another series against India in the middle of the year, he decided that the First Test at Galle would be his last, although he would be available for one-day cricket until the 2011 World Cup.

This set up an intriguing scenario, as he went into the match with 792 Test wickets, and the whole of Sri Lanka praying that he would claim the eight scalps he needed for 800. It was a close-run thing, but in the end Muralitharan's Test career had the fairytale ending the nation craved: the landmark wicket ended India's resistance and set up a ten-wicket victory.

Following that heady triumph, Sri Lanka were expected to clinch the series at the Sinhalese Sports Club in Colombo, but the pitch was a shirtfront which produced a stack of runs and a high-scoring draw. The benign track helped India's batsmen back into form: they ran up a total of 707, then kicked on to win the final Test and square the series. Left-hander Suresh Raina, who had played 98 one-day internationals for India without winning a Test cap, finally got into the side, and started with a forthright 120 in the Second Test and 62 in the Third.

Sri Lanka, who had relied on Muralitharan's vicious spin for most of their victories over the previous 18 years, soon realised that in future success would not come as consistently. Like Australia when Glenn McGrath and Shane Warne both quit the scene, Sri Lanka had lost their most potent bowling weapons – Murali and Chaminda Vaas – in 12 months. Between them they accounted for 1,155 Test wickets.

The second part of this series was therefore the start of a new era for Sri Lankan cricket. Muralitharan's exit meant that both sides were short on bowling quality: India were without Sreesanth and Zaheer Khan, both injured, and Harbhajan Singh was not fully fit after being laid low by viral flu at the start of the tour, while Ishant Sharma appeared to have mislaid the nip that had seamed back in to Ricky Ponting. It was left to India's back-up spinners, Pragyan Ojha and Amit Mishra – and the off-breaks of Virender Sehwag – to shape their victory in the final Test. Sehwag topped India's averages with seven wickets at 27, to emphasise their bowling problems.

Sri Lanka passed 500 in the first two Tests, and their only batting failure came in the second innings of the Third, when they were bundled out for 267. That left India 257 to win, a tricky target which V. V. S. Laxman made look relatively simple.

As India had lost their previous two Test series in Sri Lanka, this drawn rubber was almost a triumph for them.

Eranga Jayawardena, AP/PA Photos

One man, who fought for 800: Muttiah Muralitharan has Pragyan Ojha caught by regular accomplice Mahela Jayawardene with his last delivery in Test cricket.

INDIAN TOURING PARTY

*M. S. Dhoni, R. Dravid, G. Gambhir, Harbhajan Singh, V. V. S. Laxman, A. Mishra, A. Mithun, P. P. Ojha, M. M. Patel, S. K. Raina, W. P. Saha, V. Sehwag, I. Sharma, S. R. Tendulkar, M. Vijay, Yuvraj Singh. *Coach:* G. Kirsten.

S. Sreesanth and Zaheer Khan were originally selected, but suffered knee and shoulder injuries respectively and were replaced by Patel and Mithun.

TEST MATCH AVERAGES

SRI LANKA – BATTING AND FIELDING

	T	I	NO	R	HS	100s	50s	Avge	Ct/St
T. T. Samaraweera	3	5	3	306	137*	1	2	153.00	0
†K. C. Sangakkara	3	5	1	467	219	2	1	116.75	6
†N. T. Paranavitana	3	6	1	292	111	2	0	58.40	2
D. P. M. D. Jayawardene	3	5	0	288	174	1	1	57.60	9
T. M. Dilshan	3	6	1	215	68*	0	2	43.00	3
A. D. Mathews	3	3	0	91	45	0	0	30.33	0
S. L. Malinga	2	3	0	83	64	0	1	27.66	0
H. A. P. W. Jayawardene	3	3	0	36	27	0	0	12.00	5/2

Played in two Tests: B. A. W. Mendis 3, 78 (1 ct); S. Randiv 8, 6; U. W. M. B. C. A. Welagedara 4, 4* (1 ct). Played in one Test: †H. M. R. K. B. Herath 80*; M. Muralitharan 5*; C. R. D. Fernando and K. T. G. D. Prasad did not bat.

BOWLING

	Style	O	M	R	W	BB	5W/i	Avge
M. Muralitharan	OB	61.4	8	191	8	5-63	1	23.87
S. L. Malinga	RF	72	6	273	10	5-50	1	27.30
S. Randiv	OB	127.1	25	384	11	5-82	1	34.90
T. M. Dilshan	OB	43	7	119	3	3-56	0	39.66
B. A. W. Mendis.	OB/LBG	107	14	346	6	4-172	0	57.66

Also bowled: C. R. D. Fernando (RFM) 31.2–1–116–1; H. M. R. K. B. Herath (SLA) 45–4–122–1; A. D. Mathews (RFM) 27–4–74–1; K. T. G. D. Prasad (RFM) 22–2–101–0; U. W. M. B. C. A. Welagedara (LFM) 44.3–5–234–2.

INDIA – BATTING AND FIELDING

	T	I	NO	R	HS	100s	50s	Avge	Ct
†S. K. Raina	2	3	1	223	120	1	1	111.50	4
S. R. Tendulkar	3	5	0	390	203	1	2	78.00	2
V. V. S. Laxman	3	5	1	279	103*	1	2	69.75	3
V. Sehwag.	3	5	0	348	109	2	1	69.60	1
M. Vijay	2	3	0	99	58	0	1	33.00	1
M. S. Dhoni.	3	4	0	128	76	0	1	32.00	6
A. Mithun	3	4	0	120	46	0	0	30.00	1
I. Sharma.	3	5	1	75	31*	0	0	25.00	1
R. Dravid.	3	5	0	95	44	0	0	19.00	3
†P. P. Ojha.	3	4	2	35	18*	0	0	17.50	0
Harbhajan Singh	2	3	0	10	8	0	0	3.33	1

Played in one Test: †G. Gambhir 2, 0; A. Mishra 40 (1 ct); †Yuvraj Singh 52, 5.

BOWLING

	Style	O	M	R	W	BB	5W/i	Avge
V. Sehwag	OB	59	1	193	7	3-51	0	27.57
A. Mishra.	LBG	59.2	4	187	4	3-47	0	46.75
I. Sharma	RFM	99	19	432	7	3-72	0	61.71
A. Mithun	RFM	92	12	372	6	4-105	0	62.00
P. P. Ojha.	SLA	164	31	515	8	4-115	0	64.37

Also bowled: Harbhajan Singh (OB) 87.5–8–304–2; S. K. Raina (OB) 5–0–21–0.

Details of India's matches against Sri Lanka, Bangladesh and Pakistan in the one-day Asia Cup in June may be found in that section (page 1076).

At Colombo (Colts), July 13–15, 2010. **Drawn. ‡Sri Lanka Board President's XI 514-9 dec** (W. U. Tharanga 110, H. D. R. L. Thirimanne 66, S. H. T. Kandamby 101, T. T. Samaraweera 102, L. D. Chandimal 47*, Extras 35; P. P. Ojha 5-153) **and 260-6** (H. D. R. L. Thirimanne 102, L. D. Chandimal 69; P. P. Ojha 3-85); **Indians 291** (G. Gambhir 89, Yuvraj Singh 118; B. A. W. Mendis 6-67). *Upul Tharanga, who hit 20 fours and two sixes, dominated an opening stand of 188 with Lahiru Thirimanne, then Thilina Kandamby and Thilan Samaraweera put on 180 for the third wicket; at the end of a boiling hot first day the President's XI had 432-5. The Indians had familiar problems against Ajantha Mendis (omitted from the First Test squad), although Yuvraj Singh hit six sixes and 11 fours in a counter-attacking innings from No. 6. Samaraweera chose not to enforce the follow-on, and his side batted through the third day, with Thirimanne collecting the hundred he missed in the first innings.*

SRI LANKA v INDIA

First Test Match

At Galle, July 18–22, 2010. Sri Lanka won by ten wickets. Toss: Sri Lanka. Test debut: A. Mithun.

Galle was all agog for Muttiah Muralitharan's farewell Test appearance, with the entire stadium and its neighbourhood decorated with cut-outs depicting him and banners reflecting his performances. Muralitharan came to his final Test requiring eight wickets to become the first to take 800 – he said beforehand that he had given himself one match to make it a challenge. At the start, everything went according to plan: Sangakkara won the toss, chose to bat on a bone-dry pitch and, despite the loss of the second day to rain, Sri Lanka ran up a strong total, leaving India under pressure to bat out the final two days.

The time lost to the weather meant that for Sri Lanka to win – and probably for Muralitharan to make it to 800 – they had to bowl India out twice. They looked on course to do that when the tourists made only 276 in their first innings, with Murali stretching his record number of Test five-fors to 67. India followed on, and the man of the moment made it to 799 by dismissing Yuvraj Singh and Harbhajan Singh as the score lurched to 197 for seven. But India were not going to serve up No. 800 on a platter: Muralitharan had to toil through 23.4 further overs – during which he twice narrowly failed to run out one of the last pair – before Ojha edged him low to slip, where Mahela Jayawardene dived to his left for the catch. It was his 77th catch off Muralitharan's bowling, a Test record for a bowler and non-wicketkeeper, 22 ahead of Anil Kumble and Rahul Dravid.

MOST FIVE-FORS AND TEN-FORS IN TEST CRICKET

5W/i	T		10W/m	T	
67	133	M. Muralitharan (SL/World)	22	133	M. Muralitharan (SL/World)
37	145	S. K. Warne (Australia)	10	145	S. K. Warne (Australia)
36	86	R. J. Hadlee (New Zealand)	9	86	R. J. Hadlee (New Zealand)
35	132	A. Kumble (India)	8	132	A. Kumble (India)
29	124	G. D. McGrath (Australia)	7	27	S. F. Barnes (England)
27	102	I. T. Botham (England)	7	37	C. V. Grimmett (Australia)
25	104	Wasim Akram (Pakistan)	7	70	D. K. Lillee (Australia)
24	27	S. F. Barnes (England)	6	86	D. L. Underwood (England)
24	87	Harbhajan Singh (India)	6	88	Imran Khan (Pakistan)

The entire stadium erupted. Muralitharan was given a 21-gun salute, an honour normally reserved for visiting heads of state. He was carried around the field by his team-mates to the cheers of spectators. It was a momentous occasion for Murali and his family, who were present to witness this unique piece of cricket history.

Earlier, the first day had ended prematurely because of rain, with Sri Lanka already sitting pretty thanks to a maiden Test century from opener Tharanga Paranavitana, and another from Sangakkara. Showers had been forecast throughout the match, and a massive downpour the following morning prevented any play. By the time the game restarted on the third day there were serious doubts over whether sufficient time remained for Sri Lanka to make enough runs and take 20 Indian wickets – or, more importantly for most locals, about whether Muralitharan would have time to claim his eight.

India made early inroads when play did resume. Paranavitana was caught behind in the second over, and three more wickets went down before lunch, but an eighth-wicket partnership of 115 between Herath and Malinga, playing his first Test for 31 months after a knee injury had sapped his stamina, stopped the rot. Both made their highest first-class scores as they frustrated the Indian bowlers on a placid pitch. Malinga hit nine fours and two sixes before top-edging a pull to fine leg, while Herath, batting with great assurance, struck ten fours and a six in his unbeaten 80. Muralitharan was greeted by fireworks, and an Indian guard of honour, when he came out for a brief knock, before Sangakkara declared at tea. Karnataka's 20-year-old pace bowler, Abhimanyu Mithun, making his debut, ended with four of the eight wickets to fall.

India started badly, losing Gambhir second ball, and even a brilliant century from Sehwag, his 20th in Tests, failed to avert the follow-on. He hit 19 fours and a six before chasing a wide one from Welagedara and edging to first slip for 109 in 118 balls. India fought back in the second innings, principally during a third-wicket stand of 119 between Dravid and Tendulkar, but a fiery spell from Malinga accounted for both in successive overs as Sri Lanka – and Muralitharan – edged closer to victory and glory. In the end Sri Lanka needed 95 to win, and they reached their target shortly after tea on the final day.

Man of the Match: S. L. Malinga.

Close of play: First day, Sri Lanka 256-2 (Paranavitana 110, D. P. M. D. Jayawardene 8); Second day, No play; Third day, India 140-3 (Sehwag 85, Laxman 18); Fourth day, India 181-5 (Laxman 9).

Sri Lanka

N. T. Paranavitana c Dhoni b Sharma	111	– not out	23
T. M. Dilshan c Dhoni b Mithun	25	– not out	68
*K. C. Sangakkara c Tendulkar b Sehwag	103		
D. P. M. D. Jayawardene lbw b Sharma	48		
T. T. Samaraweera lbw b Mithun	0		
A. D. Mathews c Laxman b Sharma	41		
†H. A. P. W. Jayawardene lbw b Mithun	27		
H. M. R. K. B. Herath not out	80		
S. L. Malinga c Harbhajan Singh b Mithun	64		
M. Muralitharan not out	5		
B 2, l-b 9, n-b 5	16	W 1, n-b 4	5
1/55 (2) 2/236 (3) (8 wkts dec, 124 overs)	520	(no wkt, 14.1 overs)	96
3/259 (1) 4/260 (5)			
5/322 (4) 6/344 (6) 7/393 (7) 8/508 (9)			

U. W. M. B. C. A. Welagedara did not bat.

Sharma 28–5–145–3; Mithun 28–3–105–4; Harbhajan Singh 30–4–98–0; Ojha 28–1–115–0; Sehwag 10–0–46–1. *Second Innings*—Mithun 5–0–33–0; Sharma 4–0–28–0; Ojha 3–0–11–0; Harbhajan Singh 2.1–0–24–0.

India

G. Gambhir lbw b Malinga	2	– c H. A. P. W. Jayawardene b Malinga	0
V. Sehwag c Paranavitana b Welagedara	109	– c D. P. M. D. Jayawardene	
		b Welagedara	31
R. Dravid run out	18	– c Sangakkara b Malinga	44
S. R. Tendulkar lbw b Muralitharan	8	– lbw b Malinga	84
V. V. S. Laxman c Dilshan b Muralitharan	22	– run out	69
Yuvraj Singh c D. P. M. D. Jayawardene		– c D. P. M. D. Jayawardene	
b Muralitharan	52	b Muralitharan	5
*†M. S. Dhoni b Muralitharan	33	– b Malinga	4
Harbhajan Singh st H. A. P. W. Jayawardene			
b Herath	2	– lbw b Muralitharan	8
I. Sharma not out	5	– (10) not out	31
P. P. Ojha c D. P. M. D. Jayawardene		– (11) c D. P. M. D. Jayawardene	
b Muralitharan	3	b Muralitharan	13
A. Mithun b Muralitharan	8	– (9) lbw b Malinga	25
B 1, l-b 1, w 2, n-b 10	14	B 5, l-b 9, w 2, n-b 8	24
1/2 (1) 2/68 (3) 3/101 (4) 4/169 (2) (65 overs)	276	1/0 (1) 2/42 (2) (115.4 overs)	338
5/178 (5) 6/252 (7) 7/259 (6) 8/259 (8)		3/161 (3) 4/172 (4)	
9/266 (10) 10/276 (11)		5/181 (6) 6/186 (7) 7/197 (8)	
		8/246 (9) 9/314 (5) 10/338 (11)	

Malinga 13–0–55–2; Welagedara 11–1–69–1; Herath 18–1–62–1; Mathews 5–0–19–0; Muralitharan 17–1–63–5; Dilshan 1–0–6–0. *Second Innings*—Malinga 17–2–50–5; Welagedara 10–2–43–1; Herath 27–3–60–0; Mathews 7–3–13–0; Muralitharan 44.4–7–128–3; Dilshan 10–1–30–0.

Umpires: D. J. Harper and R. J. Tucker.   Third umpire: T. H. Wijewardene.

SRI LANKA v INDIA

Second Test Match

At Colombo (SSC), July 26–30, 2010. Drawn. Toss: Sri Lanka. Test debuts: S. Randiv; S. K. Raina.

After the Lord Mayor's Show of the First Test, the Second was a bore-draw. A pitch with less life than a dodo provided little interest, with batsmen piling up massive scores against hapless bowlers. The match may have produced two double-centuries, another three hundreds and a 99, but overall it was a poor advertisement for Test cricket. Anurudda Polonowita, Sri Lanka's national groundsman, countered criticism by arguing that both sides were weak in bowling but brilliant in batting.

MOST ONE-DAY INTERNATIONALS BEFORE TEST DEBUT

ODIs pre-debut		Test debut		ODI debut
98	**S. K. Raina (India)**	**v Sri Lanka at Colombo (SSC)** .	**2010**	**2005**
94	A. Symonds (Australia)	v Sri Lanka at Galle	2003-04	1998-99
76	A. C. Gilchrist (Australia)	v Pakistan at Brisbane	1999-2000	1996-97
73	Yuvraj Singh (India)	v New Zealand at Mohali	2003-04	2000-01
66	Shahid Afridi (Pakistan)	v Australia at Karachi	1998-99	1996-97
60	R. R. Singh (India)	v Zimbabwe at Harare	1998-99	1988-89
55	G. R. Larsen (New Zealand)	v England at Nottingham	1994	1989-90

J. R. Hopes (Australia) has played 84 one-day internationals from 2004-05 to 2010 without making a Test appearance, the current record for a player from a Test country.

Research by: Nirav Malavi

Unusually for a winning team, Sri Lanka changed all four specialist bowlers. Muttiah Muralitharan must have been delighted he had retired before encountering this pitch; Malinga, who had helped him bowl Sri Lanka to victory at Galle, was forced out when his knee flared up; and the selectors omitted Herath and Welagedara. The man given the thankless task of replacing Muralitharan was Suraj Randiv, formerly known as Mohamed Suraj, a 25-year-old off-spinner from Matara. India also had two enforced changes: Gambhir (knee injury) and Yuvraj Singh (fever) gave way to Vijay and Suresh Raina, who finally made his Test debut after 98 one-day internationals.

Batsmen soon took the upper hand. Sri Lanka again piled up runs, eventually calling a halt at 642 for four: everyone who came to the crease passed 50 and, had openers Paranavitana and Dilshan – who hit Sharma for four successive fours in the fourth over – added one more run, all four partnerships would have been worth 100 or more. Paranavitana, whose first ten Tests had not produced a century, now made his second in two matches, putting on 174 with Sangakkara, who added 193 more with Mahela Jayawardene. Sangakkara purred on to his third century in consecutive Test innings, and his seventh double-century in Tests, equalling Wally Hammond: only Don Bradman (12) and Brian Lara (nine) lay ahead. In all, he batted for 399 minutes, and hit 29 fours from 335 balls. Jayawardene completed his tenth Test hundred at the SSC to surpass Bradman's record of nine at a single ground (Melbourne).

India's openers provided an ideal platform of 165 in 36 overs. Sehwag missed his second century in successive matches by a whisker, going for an adventurous drive on 99 and presenting Randiv with a distinguished first Test victim. He was only the third man to be stumped for 99 in a Test, following Maqsood Ahmed (Pakistan v India at Lahore, 1954-55) and John Wright (New Zealand v England at Christchurch, 1991-92). Vijay fell to Mendis's googly in the next over, and shortly afterwards Randiv trapped Dravid lbw. Sri Lanka had taken three for eight, but that was their high point: the next five sessions were dominated by the visiting batsmen. Wicketkeeper Prasanna Jayawardene missed a straightforward chance above his head, off Fernando, when Tendulkar had 29, and it proved an expensive miss, with Tendulkar advancing to his 48th Test hundred and the fifth double of his illustrious career.

The debutant left-hander Raina benefited from batting with the master, helping him add 256, an Indian fifth-wicket record against Sri Lanka. Raina, previously seen as a one-day specialist, knuckled down for nearly five hours, hitting 12 fours plus a six. He was the 12th Indian to score a century on Test debut, but the first since Sehwag in November 2001. Dilshan enlivened dull proceedings on the fourth evening, grabbing three wickets with his part-time off-spin. He finally ended Tendulkar's eight-and-a-half hour marathon at 203, from 347 balls with a six and 23 fours, when the keeper did hold another chance; he added Harbhajan Singh for a duck in the same over; and then took a brilliant return catch to dismiss Dhoni.

India's last-wicket pair proved just how docile the pitch was, batting without discomfort to add 38 in 27 overs on the final morning before Fernando finally had Sharma caught at gully, shortly before lunch. A total of 707 was the highest by a visiting team in a Test in Sri Lanka, and it was only the fourth time in Tests that both sides reached 600 in their first innings – all, except the Manchester Ashes Test of 1964, within 18 months. Randiv conceded 222, a record for a bowler on Test debut; only fellow off-spinners Jason Krejza of Australia (against India in 2008-09) and Omari Banks of West Indies (against Australia in 2002-03) had previously gone for more than 200, and only England's Tom Cartwright (77 against Australia in 1964) had bowled more overs in an innings in his first Test than Randiv's 73.

Sri Lanka batted out time to preserve their 1–0 series lead.

Man of the Match: K. C. Sangakkara.

Close of play: First day, Sri Lanka 312-2 (Sangakkara 130, D. P. M. D. Jayawardene 13); Second day, India 95-0 (Vijay 22, Sehwag 64); Third day, India 382-4 (Tendulkar 108, Raina 66); Fourth day, India 669-9 (Sharma 10, Ojha 0).

Sri Lanka

N. T. Paranavitana b Sharma	100	– c Laxman b Harbhajan Singh	34
T. M. Dilshan c Laxman b Ojha	54	– c Sharma b Mithun	14
*K. C. Sangakkara c Dravid b Sehwag	219	– not out	42
D. P. M. D. Jayawardene c Raina b Harbhajan Singh	174	– lbw b Sehwag	5
T. T. Samaraweera not out	76	– not out	10
B 4, l-b 8, w 2, n-b 5	19	B 8, l-b 8, n-b 8	24

1/99 (2) 2/273 (1)   (4 wkts dec, 159.4 overs) 642   1/50 (2)   (3 wkts dec, 45 overs) 129
3/466 (3) 4/642 (4)   2/73 (1) 3/97 (4)

A. D. Mathews, †H. A. P. W. Jayawardene, K. T. G. D. Prasad, S. Randiv, B. A. W. Mendis and C. R. D. Fernando did not bat.

Mithun 23–5–117–0; Sharma 23–5–102–1; Ojha 46–9–172–1; Harbhajan Singh 42.4–4–147–1; Sehwag 20–0–71–1; Raina 5–0–21–0. _Second Innings_—Mithun 6–1–17–1; Sharma 4–0–31–0; Sehwag 9–1–17–1; Harbhajan Singh 13–0–35–1; Ojha 13–6–13–0.

India

M. Vijay lbw b Mendis	58		A. Mithun b Mendis	41
V. Sehwag st H. A. P. W. Jayawardene			I. Sharma c Sangakkara b Fernando	27
b Randiv	99		P. P. Ojha not out	18
R. Dravid lbw b Randiv	3			
S. R. Tendulkar c H. A. P. W. Jayawardene			B 9, l-b 7, w 4, n-b 13	33
b Dilshan	203			
V. V. S. Laxman lbw b Mendis	29		1/165 (2) 2/169 (1)	(225.2 overs) 707
S. K. Raina c Sangakkara b Mendis	120		3/173 (3) 4/241 (5)	
*†M. S. Dhoni c and b Dilshan	76		5/497 (6) 6/592 (4) 7/592 (8)	
Harbhajan Singh c Sangakkara b Dilshan	0		8/643 (7) 9/668 (9) 10/707 (10)	

Prasad 22–2–101–0; Fernando 31.2–1–116–1; Mathews 9–1–24–0; Randiv 73–16–222–2; Mendis 63–10–172–4; Dilshan 27–6–56–3.

Umpires: D. J. Harper and R. J. Tucker.   Third umpire: R. Martinesz.

SRI LANKA v INDIA

Third Test Match

At Colombo (PSS), August 3–7, 2010. India won by five wickets. Toss: Sri Lanka.

If the previous match was a downright bore, this one had all the ingredients that make Test cricket the ultimate test of character. India emerged victorious to square the series as Laxman guided them to what had looked a tricky target, assisted by Tendulkar, whose 169th appearance lifted him past Australia's Steve Waugh as the world's most capped Test player.

Malinga and Welagedara returned to bolster Sri Lanka's bowling, while India replaced Harbhajan Singh, who had been struggling against indifferent form and a side strain, with the leg-spinner Amit Mishra. Sangakkara won his third straight toss, and again decided to bat. But the pitch had a lot more for bowlers than the SSC's featherbed. It helped the seamers early on, and allowed some spin later in the day. Sharma seamed and swung the ball, and removed Paranavitana in the fourth over. Dilshan was unluckily run out thanks to a sharp piece of fielding: thinking of a single, he stepped out of his crease after playing a no-ball from Ojha, and Vijay at silly point flicked the ball back to Dhoni, who broke the stumps with Dilshan's bat still in the air. Sri Lanka fought back to end the day at 293 for four. Samaraweera, 65 overnight, went on to an unbeaten six-hour 137 but, after Mathews helped him add 89 for the fifth wicket (the highest partnership of the innings), Sri Lanka lost their last six for 95, with Sharma and slow left-armer Ojha claiming seven wickets between them.

India started well, and ended the second day at 180 for two with Sehwag poised for his 21st Test hundred, which he duly reached next morning off just 90 balls when he pulled Randiv for his 18th four. Soon afterwards, he played a loose shot against the same bowler and gave a simple catch to mid-off. Sehwag passed 7,000 runs during his 79th Test: only Wally Hammond got there in fewer innings (131 to Sehwag's 134; Don Bradman was famously stranded four short of 7,000 after 80 innings). Tendulkar had gone earlier, when he edged behind in the day's first over, making Malinga only the third Sri Lankan bowler to reach a century of Test wickets, after Muralitharan's 800 and Chaminda Vaas's 355.

Sri Lanka reduced India to 350 for seven, but were again thwarted by the tail: the last three wickets added 86 valuable runs to manufacture a slender first-innings lead of 11. Then Sri Lanka were pushed on to the back foot by Sehwag's seemingly innocuous off-breaks, losing both openers cheaply by the close. The fourth morning was all drama, as India came roaring back. Sri Lanka's strong batting line-up buckled for the first time in the series, losing six for 62 in a dramatic session, with the spinners in charge. It was no fault of the pitch but poor batting that caused the batsmen's downfall.

At 125 for eight, an overall lead of only 114, Sri Lanka looked down and out. Then Samaraweera found an unlikely ally in Mendis; they staged a superb rearguard action, batting throughout the afternoon session to frustrate the Indian bowling and putting on 118, a ninth-wicket Test record for Sri Lanka. The stand was finally broken by the second new ball: Samaraweera attempted to pull Mithun, but gloved a catch to Dhoni for a defiant 83. Mendis had just completed his maiden first-class fifty: in all he batted nearly three hours and hit a six and ten fours – most of them accompanied by an engaging smile – before he finally mistimed a drive off Mishra to short extra cover.

By the end of the day the match was nicely poised. India needed 257 to square the series, but Randiv, who opened the bowling, had snapped up three wickets to leave them struggling at 53 for three. In his first over Sehwag edged to slip before scoring; Dravid did not last long before playing on; and Vijay was caught by Mahela Jayawardene at backward short leg. He stood his ground, challenging the validity of the catch, but had to leave after the decision was upheld by the TV umpire.

Sri Lanka dropped Tendulkar again – and this time it probably cost them the Test. He had made 18 when he was put down by Dilshan, at forward short leg off Randiv, in the eighth over of the final day. That would have been 67 for five. Instead, Tendulkar went on to a valuable 54, taking his partnership with Laxman to 109 as India pushed towards victory. The stand was finally broken after Laxman, who had been batting beautifully, suffered back spasms: he did not retire, but play halted while he received treatment before resuming with a runner. Three balls later, Tendulkar gloved a sweep off Randiv to the wicketkeeper. At this point, with half the side out (all to Randiv), India still needed 86 – but Raina joined Laxman and put the Indian dressing-room at ease.

The pair slowly but surely reached the target, with Laxman completing a courageous century – his 16th in Tests – despite batting in a lot of discomfort in the second half of his innings, which lasted 149 balls in all. Raina finished the match by smashing Welagedara over long-on for six. It was Sri Lanka's first defeat at this venue in eight Tests since Pakistan won in August 1994.

Man of the Match: V. V. S. Laxman.   *Man of the Series:* V. Sehwag.

Close of play: First day, Sri Lanka 293-4 (Samaraweera 65, Mathews 26); Second day, India 180-2 (Sehwag 97, Tendulkar 40); Third day, Sri Lanka 45-2 (Sangakkara 12, Randiv 0); Fourth day, India 53-3 (Tendulkar 11, Sharma 2).

Sri Lanka

N. T. Paranavitana c Dhoni b Sharma	8	– c Dhoni b Sehwag	16
T. M. Dilshan run out	41	– c Vijay b Sehwag	13
*K. C. Sangakkara c Sehwag b Ojha	75	– c Raina b Ojha	28
D. P. M. D. Jayawardene lbw b Ojha	56	– (5) c Dravid b Ojha	5
T. T. Samaraweera not out	137	– (6) c Dhoni b Mithun	83
A. D. Mathews lbw b Ojha	45	– (7) c Tendulkar b Mishra	5
†H. A. P. W. Jayawardene lbw b Ojha	9	– (8) lbw b Mishra	0
S. Randiv c Dravid b Sehwag	8	– (4) lbw b Ojha	6
S. L. Malinga c and b Mishra	4	– lbw b Mishra	15
B. A. W. Mendis c Raina b Sharma	3	– c Raina b Mishra	78
U. W. M. B. C. A. Welagedara c Dhoni b Sharma	4	– not out	4
B 8, l-b 4, w 7, n-b 16	35	L-b 4, w 4, n-b 6	14

1/15 (1) 2/102 (2) 3/157 (3)   (138 overs) 425   1/32 (1) 2/39 (2)   (85.2 overs) 267
4/241 (4) 5/330 (6) 6/359 (7)   3/63 (4) 4/77 (5)
7/381 (8) 8/386 (9) 9/421 (10) 10/425 (11)   5/78 (3) 6/87 (7) 7/87 (8)
                                                        8/125 (9) 9/243 (6) 10/267 (10)

Mithun 22–2–78–0; Sharma 23–6–72–3; Mishra 42–3–140–1; Ojha 46–10–115–4; Sehwag 5–0–8–1. *Second Innings*—Mithun 8–1–22–1; Sharma 17–3–54–0; Ojha 28–5–89–3; Sehwag 15–0–51–3; Mishra 17.2–1–47–3.

India

M. Vijay c Mendis b Malinga	14	– c D. P. M. D. Jayawardene b Randiv . 27
V. Sehwag c Welagedara b Randiv	109	– c D. P. M. D. Jayawardene b Randiv . 0
R. Dravid lbw b Mathews	23	– b Randiv . 7
S. R. Tendulkar c H. A. P. W. Jayawardene b Malinga	41	– c H. A. P. W. Jayawardene b Randiv . 54
V. V. S. Laxman c D. P. M. D. Jayawardene b Mendis	56	– (6) not out . 103
S. K. Raina c Sangakkara b Mendis	62	– (7) not out . 41
*†M. S. Dhoni c H. A. P. W. Jayawardene b Malinga	15	
A. Mithun c D. P. M. D. Jayawardene b Randiv	46	
A. Mishra c Dilshan b Randiv	40	
I. Sharma c Paranavitana b Randiv	8	– (5) c Sangakkara b Randiv . 4
P. P. Ojha not out	1	
B 6, l-b 6, w 1, n-b 8	21	B 5, l-b 6, w 2, n-b 9 . 22

1/49 (1) 2/92 (3) 3/183 (4) (106.1 overs) 436 1/10 (2) (5 wkts, 68.3 overs) 258
4/199 (2) 5/304 (5) 6/321 (6) 2/27 (3) 3/49 (1)
7/350 (7) 8/414 (8) 9/433 (9) 10/436 (10) 4/62 (5) 5/171 (4)

Malinga 30–3–119–3; Welagedara 15–0–88–0; Mendis 30–4–109–2; Mathews 4–0–13–1; Randiv 25.1–6–80–4; Dilshan 2–0–15–0. *Second Innings*—Malinga 12–1–49–0; Randiv 29–3–82–5; Mathews 2–0–5–0; Welagedara 8.3–2–34–0; Mendis 14–0–65–0; Dilshan 3–0–12–0.

Umpires: S. J. A. Taufel and R. J. Tucker. Third umpire: H. D. P. K. Dharmasena.
Series referee: A. J. Pycroft.

Details of India's matches against Sri Lanka and New Zealand in the triangular one-day international series in August may be found in that section (page 1090).

MICROMAX CUP IN SRI LANKA, 2010

SA'ADI THAWFEEQ

1. Sri Lanka   2. India   3. New Zealand

Sri Lanka ended India's recent superiority in one-day internationals at home with a comprehensive win in the final of the tri-nation Micromax Cup in Dambulla in August.

The floodlights, which had caused some concern during the Asia Cup on the same ground two months previously, were improved to some extent: the wattage on the eight towers was increased from 1,000–1,100 to 1,300–1,400. Even so, some of the players complained it was still too dark.

The Sri Lankans antagonised the Indians in one of the qualifying matches, when Suraj Randiv – on the urging of his team-mate Tillekeratne Dilshan – bowled a deliberate no-ball to deprive Virender Sehwag of a century when India needed just one to win. Sehwag hit it for six, but the no-ball ended the match, so the runs off the bat did not count and he was stranded on 99. The Sri Lankan board ordered an immediate inquiry into this unsporting act: Randiv was banned for one match, and both he and Dilshan lost their match fees.

The incident dented the camaraderie that had previously existed between the two teams – who by the end of this tournament had had 43 international matches of all types against each other since July 2008 – and one Indian player voiced the feelings of his team when he stated before the final that they were determined to beat the daylights out of the hosts for what they had done to Sehwag. However, come the final it was Kumar Sangakkara and his team who had the last laugh: Dilshan carved out a match-winning hundred to end India's run of four consecutive one-day series victories in Sri Lanka.

It would have been doubly embarrassing for Sri Lanka if they had lost, as they were the only full-strength team on view. India, with half an eye on the World Cup early in 2011, began a policy of rotating their key players, several of whom were rested for this tournament, while New Zealand were also understrength: Daniel Vettori was given a rest (Ross Taylor captained instead) while Brendon McCullum also had a break after playing 208 successive international matches in all formats since September 2004.

NATIONAL SQUADS

Sri Lanka *K. C. Sangakkara, T. M. Dilshan, C. R. D. Fernando, H. M. R. K. B. Herath, D. P. M. D. Jayawardene, C. K. Kapugedera, K. M. D. N. Kulasekara, S. L. Malinga, A. D. Mathews, B. A. W. Mendis, N. L. T. C. Perera, S. Randiv, T. T. Samaraweera, L. P. C. Silva, W. U. Tharanga. *Coach:* T. H. Bayliss.

India *M. S. Dhoni, R. Ashwin, R. A. Jadeja, K. D. Karthik, V. Kohli, P. Kumar, A. Mithun, A. Nehra, P. P. Ojha, M. M. Patel, S. K. Raina, V. Sehwag, I. Sharma, R. G. Sharma, S. S. Tiwary, Yuvraj Singh. *Coach:* G. Kirsten.
  Patel was not part of the original squad but was added after injuries to other bowlers.

New Zealand *L. R. P. L. Taylor, G. D. Elliott, M. J. Guptill, G. J. Hopkins, P. J. Ingram, N. L. McCullum, A. J. McKay, K. D. Mills, J. D. P. Oram, J. S. Patel, T. G. Southee, S. B. Styris, D. R. Tuffey, B-J. Watling, K. S. Williamson. *Coach:* M. J. Greatbatch.

J. D. Ryder was originally selected, but injured his elbow and was replaced by Ingram.

At Dambulla, August 10, 2010 (day/night). **New Zealand won by 200 runs.** ‡New Zealand 288 (48.5 overs) (L. R. P. L. Taylor 95, S. B. Styris 89; P. Kumar 3-43, A. Nehra 4-47); India 88 (29.3 overs) (D. R. Tuffey 3-34). *New Zealand 5pts. MoM:* L. R. P. L. Taylor. *One-day international debut:* K. S. Williamson (New Zealand). *India slumped to their fifth-lowest all-out total in one-day internationals, and their fourth-heaviest defeat by runs. Apart from the openers, and Ravindra Jadeja who made 20 in an hour at No. 7, no one reached double figures as they failed to handle the bounce under the lights. Earlier, New Zealand's highly rated 20-year-old batsman Kane Williamson had started his international career with a duck, to make it 28-3 as the ball swung, but Taylor and Styris added 190, a New Zealand one-day international record for the fourth wicket.*

At Dambulla, August 13, 2010 (day/night). **Sri Lanka won by three wickets.** ‡New Zealand 192 (48.1 overs) (B-J. Watling 55, N. L. McCullum 36; S. L. Malinga 3-35, A. D. Mathews 3-36); Sri Lanka 195-7 (40.5 overs) (W. U. Tharanga 70, K. C. Sangakkara 48, T. T. Samaraweera 36*; K. D. Mills 4-41). *Sri Lanka 4pts. MoM:* W. U. Tharanga. *One-day international debut:* B-J. Watling. *Malinga, who had taken his 100th Test wicket (Sachin Tendulkar) the previous week, now made it 100 in one-day internationals as well when he dismissed Guptill with the third delivery of the day. Kane Williamson collected his second successive duck – echoing the poor start his hero, Tendulkar, made in one-day internationals – and B-J. Watling's debut half-century was not enough to ensure a competitive total. Tharanga anchored the chase with a well-paced 70 off 109 balls, and nine fours. At 162-3 Sri Lanka looked set for a wider margin of victory, but they lost four wickets for 18 in 15 balls in an unsuccessful attempt to win before the end of the 40th over and collect the bonus point.*

At Dambulla, August 16, 2010 (day/night). **India won by six wickets.** ‡Sri Lanka 170 (46.1 overs) (T. M. Dilshan 45, S. Randiv 43; P. P. Ojha 3-36); India 171-4 (34.3 overs) (V. Sehwag 99*). *India 5pts. MoM:* V. Sehwag. *Sehwag smashed 99* off 100 balls as India roared back with a convincing win. He cracked 11 fours and two sixes as India won quickly enough to earn a valuable bonus point, although they were an unconvincing 91-4 before Dhoni joined Sehwag in a partnership of 80* in 79 balls. The match ended in controversy: with the scores level Sehwag was denied a century when Randiv, egged on by Dilshan, bowled a deliberate no-ball which gave India victory – Sehwag smashed it for six, but the runs off the bat did not count. Randiv was suspended for one match, and both he and Dilshan were fined their match fees by the Sri Lankan board. Earlier, Tharanga had fallen to the first ball of the match, and Sri Lanka never really recovered after slipping to 44-4.*

At Dambulla, August 19–20, 2010 (day/night). **No result.** Sri Lanka 203-3 (43.4 overs) (T. M. Dilshan 44, K. C. Sangakkara 40, D. P. M. D. Jayawardene 59*, L. P. C. Silva 41*) v ‡New Zealand. *Sri Lanka 2pts, New Zealand 2pts. Rain ruled out any play on the scheduled day – a toss, which New Zealand won (they would have batted), was the only action all afternoon – and when the teams reconvened next day only 43.4 overs were possible before the heavens opened again. Another toss was held, and Taylor won it again – this time deciding to bowl. Sri Lanka's otherwise unremarkable innings was enlivened in the 27th over by an angry exchange when Sangakkara bumped into bowler Nathan McCullum while trying to ground his bat: referee Alan Hurst later cleared Sangakkara of any offence. Then Kyle Mills was prevented from bowling the 39th over after he bowled a practice delivery in contravention of Law 17.1: the umpires banned him from bowling for half an hour (in the event the match ended before that) and the over was delivered by Oram.*

At Dambulla, August 22, 2010 (day/night). **Sri Lanka won by eight wickets.** ‡India 103 (33.4 overs) (Yuvraj Singh 38; N. L. T. C. Perera 5-28); Sri Lanka 104-2 (15.1 overs) (D. P. M. D. Jayawardene 33, T. M. Dilshan 35). *Sri Lanka 5pts. MoM:* N. L. T. C. Perera. *The tall (6ft 1in) all-rounder Thisara Perera bowled Sri Lanka into the final with his first five-for in international cricket. Making full use of his height, he seamed and swung the ball around on a two-paced pitch as India crumbled for 103. Yuvraj Singh top-scored, once belting Perera for six over long-off, but he finally fell to a debatable lbw decision. Randiv returned after his one-match ban – and wasn't needed to bowl. Sri Lanka made short work of the target: Jayawardene, promoted to open, and Dilshan raced to 79 off 56 balls before both fell to successive balls from Ishant Sharma. Sri Lanka wasted no time by calling for the batting powerplay early on, and easily earned the bonus point which guaranteed they headed the table. They won with 34.5 overs to spare: India had never been so soundly beaten by that measure in a one-day international before.*

At Dambulla, August 25, 2010 (day/night). **India won by 105 runs.** ‡**India 223** (46.3 overs) (V. Sehwag 110, M. S. Dhoni 38; T. G. Southee 4-49, N. L. McCullum 3-35); **New Zealand 118** (30.1 overs) (K. D. Mills 52; P. Kumar 3-34, M. M. Patel 3-21). *India 5pts. MoM:* V. Sehwag. *Sehwag smashed 110 off 93 balls to propel India into the final. He stood tall as wickets tumbled, crashing 16 fours (three in succession off Mills, including his 1,000th in one-day internationals) and a six. After 13 overs, India were 66-4 – the four batsmen out made 15 between them – before Dhoni helped Sehwag add 107, but then another four fell for eight in 26 balls. New Zealand began their chase disastrously, losing Guptill in the third over, and although Kane Williamson (13) finally got off the mark in international cricket they were floundering at 53-8, before some lusty hits from Mills – who reached 50 from 32 balls, with three sixes and seven fours – dragged them to three figures.*

Sri Lanka 11pts, India 10pts, New Zealand 7pts.

FINAL

SRI LANKA v INDIA

At Dambulla, August 28, 2010 (day/night). Sri Lanka won by 74 runs. Toss: Sri Lanka.

A brilliant century from Dilshan – his eighth in one-day internationals, but his first in 62 matches at home – helped his side to a crushing victory that ended India's run of one-day success in Sri Lanka: they had won their last four tournaments here, including the four-nation Asia Cup two months before. Dilshan hit 12 fours and a six off 115 balls as Sri Lanka reached an imposing 299. He shared a run-a-ball opening stand of 121 with Jayawardene, who became the third Sri Lankan, after Aravinda de Silva and Sanath Jayasuriya, to make 9,000 runs in one-day internationals. Sangakkara hit a classy 71 from 62 balls before falling just after the final over of the powerplay. Then, under lights, India lost the key wicket of Sehwag in the sixth over: run out by a direct hit from Kapugedera at backward point while attempting a leg-bye after a confident lbw appeal by Kulasekara. Although Dhoni fought hard, facing 100 balls for his 67, his side were never on terms after that.

Man of the Match: T. M. Dilshan. *Man of the Series:* V. Sehwag.

Sri Lanka

D. P. M. D. Jayawardene c Karthik b I. Sharma .	39	N. L. T. C. Perera c Dhoni b Patel.	6
T. M. Dilshan c I. Sharma b Kumar	110	S. Randiv run out.	4
W. U. Tharanga c Dhoni b Yuvraj Singh . .	6	K. M. D. N. Kulasekara not out.	0
*†K. C. Sangakkara c R. G. Sharma b Patel .	71	L-b 12, w 12	24
C. K. Kapugedera c Karthik b Nehra	12		
A. D. Mathews c R. G. Sharma b I. Sharma	1	1/121 (1) 2/132 (3) (8 wkts, 50 overs) 299	
L. P. C. Silva not out	26	3/217 (2) 4/242 (5) 5/258 (6)	
		6/261 (4) 7/294 (8) 8/298 (9) 10 overs: 52-0	

S. L. Malinga did not bat.

Kumar 10–0–72–1; Patel 9–1–43–2; Nehra 10–0–60–1; I. Sharma 8–0–54–2; Yuvraj Singh 8–0–37–1; Sehwag 5–0–21–0.

India

V. Sehwag run out.	28	A. Nehra c Perera b Mathews	2
K. D. Karthik c Sangakkara b Malinga	0	M. M. Patel not out	0
V. Kohli c Mathews b Perera	37		
Yuvraj Singh c Sangakkara b Perera	26	B 4, l-b 1, w 8, n-b 4	17
*†M. S. Dhoni b Randiv.	67		
S. K. Raina c Dilshan b Randiv.	29	1/9 (2) 2/38 (1) 3/88 (4) (46.5 overs) 225	
R. G. Sharma st Sangakkara b Randiv	5	4/109 (3) 5/158 (6) 6/177 (7)	
P. Kumar b Malinga	14	7/201 (8) 8/210 (9) 9/224 (10)	
I. Sharma b Perera	0	10/225 (5) 10 overs: 55-2	

Malinga 9–0–49–2; Kulasekara 9–0–47–0; Mathews 10–0–48–1; Perera 9–2–36–3; Randiv 9.5–1–40–3.

Umpires: Asad Rauf and E. A. R. de Silva.   Third umpire: T. H. Wijewardene.
Series referee: A. G. Hurst.

SRI LANKA v WEST INDIES, 2010-11

TONY COZIER

Test matches (3): Sri Lanka 0, West Indies 0

Through November and into December 2010, Sri Lanka's heaviest and most widespread rainfall in 18 years caused flash floods and landslides that displaced an estimated 300,000 people. It so ruined West Indies' tour that fewer than half the allocated overs (656.2 of 1,350) could be bowled in the three Tests, none of which came close to a positive result. But for covers that protected the entire outfield at the three venues, and more than 150 diligent groundstaff, there would have been even less play.

Finally, after considerable vacillation and at considerable financial loss, Sri Lanka Cricket, with the agreement of the West Indies Cricket Board, decided to end the tour before the scheduled five one-day internationals (and one Twenty20 game). It was a relief to all concerned; the utter unreadiness of the three venues being prepared for the approaching World Cup exacerbated the situation. The Premadasa Stadium in Colombo, the Pallekele Stadium outside Kandy and the new Mahinda Rajapakse Stadium (named in honour of Sri Lanka's president) in the southern town of Hambantota, where the first two abandoned one-day internationals were supposed to have been played, were little more than building sites. During the Second and Third Tests, a smattering of spectators – never many more than a thousand – were restricted to the few areas not under construction or repair. West Indies' coach Ottis Gibson derided the facilities as "obviously not up to staging international cricket".

West Indies were only a day into their opening warm-up match when 490mm (19.3 inches) of rain inundated Colombo in the space of 15 hours. Sri Lanka's captain Kumar Sangakkara was one of the many caught up; he and his wife, Yehali, watched their abandoned vehicle swept away as they waded waist-high to safety.

Sangakkara's later concern was "the frustration of sitting in the dressing-room and watching the rain". It was frustrating for both teams. Sri Lanka were keen to assess their bowling in the first series since the Test retirement of Muttiah Muralitharan, and in the absence of their fiery round-arm slinger, Lasith Malinga, who was being kept in cotton wool for the World Cup. West Indies were under a new captain, having replaced Chris Gayle with Darren Sammy, and without their long-serving No. 3, Ramnaresh Sarwan, contentiously omitted on grounds of attitude and fitness.

Gayle and Sangakkara provided the two major individual performances. Gayle's second Test triple-century, his 333 at Galle, was an immediate and unmistakable statement that, whatever his status following his rejection of a retainer contract and dismissal as captain, he remained crucial to West Indies' strength; Sangakkara's 150 in Colombo, fashioned from a shaky 34 for three on a tricky first-day pitch, confirmed his quality and elevated him, if briefly, to the top of the ICC's rankings for Test batsmen.

It never rains but it pours: groundstaff were kept busy throughout the series.

Such performances from two well-established batsmen revealed nothing especially new; others were more instructive. Sammy endured an unsettling introduction to what has become one of the most insecure posts in the game: he was out first ball on debut as captain, made two and eight in his next two innings, and had only two wickets to show from 59 overs. Along with the team management, he had to deal with the personal trauma of the Dominican off-spinner Shane Shillingford, whose suspect action was reported by the umpires after the First Test. Subsequent tests confirmed the worst: his average elbow-flexion was 17 degrees, two above the ICC's legal limit, leading to a suspension from bowling until it was corrected.

More positive for West Indies was the advance of two of their young brigade. Fast bowler Kemar Roach, 22, with only seven Tests behind him before the tour, was a worthy Man of the Series. He carried the attack virtually on his own, taking ten wickets, seven from the top six in the order. Darren Bravo, 21, the half-brother of Dwayne, marked his first appearances in Test cricket with three classy half-centuries from the demanding No. 3 position. He is a cousin of Brian Lara, a relationship uncannily reflected in his mannerisms and, more importantly, his left-handed strokeplay. He will find it impossible to dismiss the comparison; on the early evidence, he was unlikely to be spoiled by it.

With doubts over the longevity of Malinga, Farveez Maharoof and Dilhara Fernando, Sri Lanka continued their search for fast bowlers. All but five of the 29 West Indian wickets that fell in the series went to the varied spin of Ajantha Mendis, Rangana Herath, Suraj Randiv and Tillekeratne Dilshan, but Suranga Lakmal, 23, slim and of lively pace, made a favourable impression when he was brought in after a lacklustre showing by Dammika Prasad and Thilan Thushara Mirando in the First Test.

For both teams, the one-day internationals were supposed to be the last before the World Cup. For that main reason, West Indies returned to Sri Lanka in late January 2011 and lost a one-day series reduced to three matches 2–0.

WEST INDIAN TOURING PARTY

*D. J. G. Sammy, A. B. Barath, C. S. Baugh, S. J. Benn, D. J. Bravo, D. M. Bravo, S. Chanderpaul, C. H. Gayle, B. P. Nash, N. T. Pascal, K. A. J. Roach, A. D. Russell, S. Shillingford, D. S. Smith, D. C. Thomas. *Coach:* O. D. Gibson.

For the five one-day internationals and one Twenty20 international that were aborted after the Tests, K. A. Edwards, N. O. Miller, K. A. Pollard and R. Rampaul arrived in Sri Lanka to replace Nash, Pascal and Shillingford.

TEST MATCH AVERAGES

SRI LANKA – BATTING AND FIELDING

	T	I	NO	R	HS	100s	50s	Avge	Ct
†K. C. Sangakkara	3	4	1	228	150	1	1	76.00	0
T. T. Samaraweera	3	3	1	151	80	0	2	75.50	1
†N. T. Paranavitana	3	4	1	141	95	0	1	47.00	1
D. P. M. D. Jayawardene	3	3	0	119	59	0	2	39.66	4
A. D. Mathews	3	3	1	57	27	0	0	28.50	2
T. M. Dilshan	3	4	0	84	54	0	1	21.00	0

Played in three Tests: H. A. P. W. Jayawardene 58, 34 (1 ct, 3 st); B. A. W. Mendis 4, 2. Played in two Tests: †H. M. R. K. B. Herath 24* (1 ct); R. A. S. Lakmal did not bat. Played in one Test: K. M. D. N. Kulasekera 17; †M. T. T. Mirando 4*; K. T. G. D. Prasad 47; S. Randiv 12; C. R. D. Fernando did not bat.

BOWLING

	Style	O	M	R	W	BB	5W/i	Avge
T. M. Dilshan	OB	20	3	43	3	2-4	0	14.33
H. M. R. K. B. Herath	SLA	47	9	130	7	4-54	0	18.57
B. A. W. Mendis	OB/LBG	106.3	15	304	11	6-169	1	27.63
R. A. S. Lakmal	RFM	35.3	6	132	3	2-84	0	44.00
S. Randiv	OB	48.2	3	183	3	3-183	0	61.00

Also bowled: C. R. D. Fernando (RFM) 15-2-72-1; K. M. D. N. Kulasekera (RFM) 11-5-17-1; A. D. Mathews (RFM) 15-6-45-0; M. T. T. Mirando (LFM) 21-4-79-0; K. T. G. D. Prasad (RFM) 30-3-116-0.

WEST INDIES – BATTING AND FIELDING

	T	I	NO	R	HS	100s	50s	Avge	Ct
†C. H. Gayle	3	4	0	366	333	1	0	91.50	1
†D. M. Bravo	3	4	1	206	80	0	3	68.66	1
†B. P. Nash	3	3	0	160	67	0	2	53.33	1
†S. Chanderpaul	3	4	1	94	54	0	1	31.33	0
C. S. Baugh	3	3	1	60	50	0	1	30.00	3
A. B. Barath	2	3	0	61	50	0	1	20.33	0
D. J. Bravo	3	3	0	25	20	0	0	8.33	2
D. J. G. Sammy	3	3	0	10	8	0	0	3.33	3

Played in three Tests: K. A. J. Roach 3, 12* (1 ct). Played in two Tests: †S. J. Benn 0, 29*; S. Shillingford 1, 5* (2 ct). Played in one Test: A. D. Russell 3; †D. S. Smith 55; N. T. Pascal did not bat.

BOWLING

	Style	O	M	R	W	BB	5W/i	Avge
K. A. J. Roach	RF	69.2	10	245	10	5-100	1	24.50
D. J. Bravo	RFM	50.2	11	156	3	1-8	0	52.00
S. Shillingford	OB	78.2	7	275	5	4-123	0	55.00

Also bowled: S. J. Benn (SLA) 21–4–66–1; C. H. Gayle (OB) 1–0–3–0; B. P. Nash (LM) 5–0–21–1; A. D. Russell (RF) 23–2–104–1; D. J. G. Sammy (RM) 59–13–151–2.

At Colombo (SSC), November 10–12, 2010 (not first-class). **Drawn.** ‡**West Indians 176** (S. Chanderpaul 33, B. P. Nash 62); U. W. M. B. C. A. Welagedara 3-37, H. M. C. M. Bandara 3-39); **Sri Lanka Cricket President's XI 59-3** (H. D. R. L. Thirimanne 30). *There was no play on the last two days (rain and a flooded outfield). Each team nominated 12 players, 11 batting, 11 fielding.*

SRI LANKA v WEST INDIES

First Test Match

At Galle, November 15–19, 2010. Drawn. Toss: West Indies. Test debuts: D. M. Bravo, A. D. Russell.

In his first Test since being replaced as captain, Gayle joined the elite company of Don Bradman, Brian Lara and Virender Sehwag in scoring two triple-centuries in Tests, his 333 adding to 317 against South Africa in Antigua in 2005. The extravagant celebrations that marked the self-styled Mr Cool's arrival at his 13th Test century, midway through the opening day, revealed its personal significance; after raising his bat he dropped to his knees, then lay flat on his back for so long it appeared he might have injured himself. On his feet again, he moved past another hundred and then another on his way to the highest score by a West Indian in a Test outside the Caribbean.

It was clearly a calculated response to those who had interpreted his rejection of the board's retainer contract a few weeks earlier as further evidence of his previously stated preference for the more lucrative shorter formats, and to others who might have doubted his pledge to fully support his successor, Darren Sammy.

Gayle's marathon of seven minutes short of 11 hours secured a position from which West Indies, even with their inexperienced bowling, could dominate. He put on 110 with Barath, 196 with the younger Bravo, Darren, who made a polished 58 on debut, and 167 with Nash, the new vice-captain. Then Roach's full-length pace and Shillingford's varied off-spin, from an action later reported by the umpires as suspect, chipped away at the Sri Lankan batting. Sammy eventually had the satisfaction of enforcing the follow-on in his first Test at the helm, when Prasanna Jayawardene swept Shillingford to deep square with Sri Lanka just three runs away from safety.

By then, time was running short following the loss of the last 67 overs of the third day to the weather. The limitations of West Indies' bowling – and more uncooperative weather – allowed Sri Lanka comfortably to bat their way to safety before drizzle and darkness ended the stalemate at the final tea interval.

Already without the recently retired Muralitharan, Sri Lanka rested the fragile Malinga ahead of the approaching World Cup, which further weakened their attack. Sangakkara was pointedly critical of his bowlers' lack of discipline on the first day when, after spending 19 balls over his first run, Gayle plundered 26 fours and eight sixes (erasing the

Making hay while the sun shines: Chris Gayle hits out during his Galle triple-hundred.

previous West Indian record of seven in an innings he jointly held with Viv Richards, Gordon Greenidge and Lara). He was less commanding when he resumed next morning with 219. There was a narrow escape thanks to the DRS after an lbw appeal to the first ball of the day, by Mendis. Gayle was even luckier at 287; surprised by Prasad's bouncer, he prodded a catch to extra-cover only for umpire Richard Kettleborough, who had an excellent first Test, to check with his colleague monitoring the TV replay in case he had missed a front-foot no-ball. Asad Rauf confirmed that he had, and Gayle carried on.

With Gayle and Nash entrenched at 559 for three, there was nothing to suggest that West Indies would not amass 700 if they chose. But suddenly, after his first 54 overs had yielded a solitary wicket, Mendis's magic returned with mesmerising effect. As six wickets tumbled for 21, he snared five for 12 in 23 balls. Among them were Gayle, defeated by his 437th delivery, which spun between bat and pad into off stump, and Sammy, clueless about a googly to his first ball as captain. Gayle had added just eight fours and a six to his first-day tally. His first hundred, completed with a four and two sixes in the same Randiv over, needed 116 balls and his second 105; he spent 172 overs his third.

As they set out on their first goal to prevent the follow-on, Sri Lanka immediately lost Dilshan to the Jamaican fast bowler Andre Russell's second ball in Test cricket. West Indies strengthened their grip when Roach despatched Paranavitana in the second over of the third day. In spite of the inexperience of their main bowlers, some assured batting by the lower order and Prasad's breezy run-a-ball 47 near the end, West Indies made the opposition follow on in a Test for the first time since 2005. Paranavitana and Dilshan dispelled any Sri Lankan doubts with an opening partnership of 102 second time round that carried into the final morning. Dilshan and Sangakkara fell in successive overs to Roach within 25 minutes of the resumption, but after that West Indies could remove only Paranavitana, taken at slip five short of his hundred, before the deficit was erased. Mahela Jayawardene tapped a return catch just before the weather closed in for the last time.

Man of the Match: C. H. Gayle.

Close of play: First day, West Indies 362-2 (Gayle 219, Chanderpaul 20); Second day, Sri Lanka 54-1 (Paranavitana 10, Sangakkara 33); Third day, Sri Lanka 165-3 (D. P. M. D. Jayawardene 51, Samaraweera 11); Fourth day, Sri Lanka 89-0 (Paranavitana 44, Dilshan 44).

West Indies

C. H. Gayle b Mendis	333	
A. B. Barath c D. P. M. D. Jayawardene		
b Randiv	50	
D. M. Bravo c Samaraweera b Mendis	58	
S. Chanderpaul c D. P. M. D. Jayawardene		
b Randiv	32	
B. P. Nash lbw b Mendis	64	
D. J. Bravo lbw b Mendis	5	
†C. S. Baugh not out	8	
*D. J. G. Sammy b Mendis	0	

A. D. Russell b Mendis 2
S. Shillingford st H. A. P. W. Jayawardene
b Randiv . 1

B 2, l-b 6, w 7, n-b 12 27

1/110 (2)   (9 wkts dec, 163.2 overs) 580
2/306 (3) 3/392 (4)
4/559 (5) 5/565 (6) 6/566 (1)
7/566 (8) 8/579 (9) 9/580 (10)

K. A. J. Roach did not bat.

Mirando 21–4–79–0; Prasad 30–3–116–0; Mendis 59–6–169–6; Randiv 48.2–3–183–3; Dilshan 3–0–15–0; Mathews 2–0–10–0.

Sri Lanka

N. T. Paranavitana b Roach	10	– c Sammy b Shillingford	95	
T. M. Dilshan c Shillingford b Russell	0	– b Roach	54	
*K. C. Sangakkara b D. J. Bravo	73	– c Sammy b Roach	4	
D. P. M. D. Jayawardene c Baugh b Roach	59	– c and b Nash	58	
T. T. Samaraweera run out	52	– not out	19	
A. D. Mathews c Sammy b Shillingford	27	– not out	5	
†H. A. P. W. Jayawardene c Roach b Shillingford	58			
S. Randiv b Shillingford	12			
K. T. G. D. Prasad c Russell b Shillingford	47			
B. A. W. Mendis c D. M. Bravo b Roach	4			
M. T. T. Mirando not out	4			
B 8, l-b 8, w 3, n-b 13	32	L-b 1, w 4, n-b 1	6	

1/6 (2) 2/61 (1) 3/132 (3)   (95.2 overs) 378
4/193 (4) 5/227 (5) 6/264 (6)
7/295 (8) 8/367 (9) 9/374 (10) 10/378 (7)

1/102 (2)   (4 wkts, 81.2 overs) 241
2/110 (3) 3/197 (1)
4/233 (4)

Roach 19–2–75–3; Russell 15–1–73–1; Shillingford 33.2–3–123–4; Sammy 11–2–41–0; D. J. Bravo 16–4–47–1; Gayle 1–0–3–0. *Second Innings*—Roach 17–3–55–2; Russell 8–1–31–0; D. J. Bravo 12.2–1–40–0; Shillingford 30–4–79–1; Sammy 9–2–14–0; Nash 5–0–21–1.

Umpires: S. J. Davis and R. A. Kettleborough.   Third umpire: Asad Rauf.

SRI LANKA v WEST INDIES

Second Test Match

At Colombo (RPS), November 23–27, 2010. Drawn. Toss: Sri Lanka. Test debut: R. A. S. Lakmal.

On winning the toss, Sangakkara pondered his options like a schoolboy faced with a tricky exam question. His uncertainty was prompted by a newly laid pitch and weeks of rain; he eventually chose to bat, a misjudgment that was evident as Sri Lanka stumbled to 34 for three after 14 overs on a surface more Chester-le-Street than Colombo.

Missed from a tough slip catch by Sammy off Roach when two, Sangakkara spent six and three-quarter hours putting matters right. He offered a difficult leg-side chance to wicketkeeper Baugh off Dwayne Bravo at 118, before he was finally taken by Gayle, diving at first slip, off Sammy. A six and 18 fours were the main scoring shots in an assured innings. His partnership of 170 with Samaraweera and contributions down the order shifted the pressure on to West Indies, who were hindered by the choice of left-arm spinner Benn over Russell. It meant Sammy took the new ball for the first time in Tests, extending himself to 17 consecutive overs of tame medium-pace on the reduced opening day. Without incisive support, Roach deserved even better than his five for 100.

Darren Bravo's exquisite strokeplay, strikingly similar to his cousin Brian Lara's, yielded four sixes and five fours and made light of West Indies' precarious position at 77 for three before Sangakkara remembered Dilshan's partnership-breaking reputation. He dismissed Nash, after a stand of 83, with his tenth ball and Bravo with his 12th, to Herath's leaping catch at cover from an unbecoming slog. At 165 for five, two testing days lay ahead for West Indies. The weather eased their worries; the fourth was completely lost, and no play was possible until after lunch on the fifth. Once Baugh took them past the follow-on requirement, they were safe.

Man of the Match: K. C. Sangakkara.

Close of play: First day, Sri Lanka 84-3 (Sangakkara 25, Samaraweera 26); Second day, Sri Lanka 294-5 (Sangakkara 135, H. A. P. W. Jayawardene 12); Third day, West Indies 165-5 (D. J. Bravo 1, Baugh 4); Fourth day, No play.

Sri Lanka

N. T. Paranavitana c D. J. Bravo b Roach	16	– not out	20
T. M. Dilshan b Roach	4	– c Baugh b D. J. Bravo	26
*K. C. Sangakkara c Gayle b Sammy	150	– not out	1
D. P. M. D. Jayawardene b Sammy	2		
T. T. Samaraweera c Shillingford b D. J. Bravo	80		
A. D. Mathews c Baugh b Roach	25		
†H. A. P. W. Jayawardene b Benn	34		
K. M. D. N. Kulasekara c D. J. Bravo b Roach	17		
H. M. R. K. B. Herath not out	24		
B. A. W. Mendis b Roach	2		
B 4, l-b 12, w 14, n-b 3	33	B 5, l-b 4, w 1	10

1/10 (2) 2/31 (1)   (9 wkts dec, 115.2 overs) 387   1/55 (2)   (1 wkt dec, 15 overs) 57
3/34 (4) 4/204 (5) 5/273 (6)
6/325 (3) 7/349 (7) 8/383 (8) 9/387 (10)

R. A. S. Lakmal did not bat.

Roach 28.2–5–100–5; Sammy 35–8–80–2; D. J. Bravo 18–5–61–1; Benn 19–4–57–1; Shillingford 15–0–73–0. *Second Innings*—Roach 5–0–15–0; Sammy 4–1–16–0; D. J. Bravo 4–1–8–1; Benn 2–0–9–0.

West Indies

C. H. Gayle c Mathews b Lakmal	30	– c D. P. M. D. Jayawardene b Dilshan	3
A. B. Barath lbw b Kulasekara	3	– lbw b Mendis	8
D. M. Bravo c Herath b Dilshan	80	– not out	0
S. Chanderpaul lbw b Mendis	8	– not out	0
B. P. Nash lbw b Dilshan	29		
D. J. Bravo st H. A. P. W. Jayawardene b Herath	20		
†C. S. Baugh b Herath	50		
*D. J. G. Sammy c Mathews b Lakmal	2		
S. J. Benn c Paranavitana b Herath	0		
S. Shillingford not out	5		
K. A. J. Roach b Mendis	3		
L-b 5, n-b 8	13	N-b 1	1

1/7 (2) 2/51 (1) 3/77 (4) 4/160 (5)   (71.3 overs) 243   1/9 (2) 2/11 (1)   (2 wkts, 11 overs) 12
5/161 (3) 6/205 (6) 7/208 (8)
8/209 (9) 9/240 (7) 10/243 (11)

Mendis 16.3–1–56–2; Lakmal 16–1–84–2; Kulasekara 11–5–17–1; Herath 23–3–76–3; Mathews 3–2–1–0; Dilshan 2–0–4–2. *Second Innings*—Lakmal 2–0–7–0; Dilshan 5–2–4–1; Mendis 3–2–1–1; Herath 1–1–0–0.

Umpires: Asad Rauf and R. A. Kettleborough.   Third umpire: S. J. Davis.

SRI LANKA v WEST INDIES

Third Test Match

At Pallekele, December 1–5, 2010. Drawn. Toss: Sri Lanka.

The Muttiah Muralitharan Stadium, Test cricket's 104th venue, a half-hour drive from Kandy's city centre, had a sensational initiation as Gayle, just two matches after his Galle triple-century, was dismissed by the first ball, lbw to Lakmal. It was only the third ground – the first outside India – to witness a wicket to its first ball in a Test, following Jullundur (Mohsin Khan dismissed by Kapil Dev in 1983-84) and Jaipur (Sunil Gavaskar by Imran Khan in 1986-87). The start was delayed by an hour and ten minutes, and the rains that had flooded much of the country and disrupted the tour from the start were never far away. There was no play on the third and fifth days, and each of the others was appreciably shortened, allowing only 103.3 overs all told.

Another sparkling innings by Darren Bravo and Herath's probing left-arm spin were the highlights of what play there was. On Gayle's swift dismissal, the younger Bravo filled the breach with such composure that he might have been playing a Saturday afternoon game for his Queen's Park club in Port-of-Spain. As he stroked his way to the third half-century of his debut series, his confidence helped settle Devon Smith, drafted in for his first Test for 18 months after the late withdrawal of Barath with flu. They added 115, and Chanderpaul and Nash 99, but none of the four left-handers carried on past the sixties.

Before the rain intervened again, Chanderpaul's dismissal set off a familiar clatter of wickets. Five fell for 33, four in succession to Herath, before Benn and Roach held firm as the series splashed to its inevitable soggy end at ten to one on the fourth afternoon.

Man of the Series: K. A. J. Roach.

Close of play: First day, West Indies 134-2 (D. M. Bravo 63, Chanderpaul 11); Second day, West Indies 244-5 (Nash 62, Baugh 0); Third day, No play; Fourth day, West Indies 303-8 (Benn 29, Roach 12).

West Indies

C. H. Gayle lbw b Lakmal	0	†C. S. Baugh lbw b Herath		2
D. S. Smith lbw b Mendis	55	*D. J. G. Sammy lbw b Herath		8
D. M. Bravo lbw b Fernando	68	S. J. Benn not out		29
S. Chanderpaul c D. P. M. D. Jayawardene		K. A. J. Roach not out		12
b Mendis.	54	L-b 4, w 1, n-b 3		8
B. P. Nash c H. A. P. W. Jayawardene				
b Herath.	67	1/0 (1) 2/115 (2) (8 wkts, 103.3 overs)		303
D. J. Bravo st H. A. P. W. Jayawardene		3/142 (3) 4/241 (4)		
b Herath.	0	5/242 (6) 6/252 (5) 7/253 (7) 8/274 (8)		

N. T. Pascal did not bat.

Lakmal 17.3–5–41–1; Mathews 10–4–34–0; Dilshan 10–1–20–0; Fernando 15–2–72–1; Mendis 28–6–78–2; Herath 23–5–54–4.

Sri Lanka

N. T. Paranavitana, T. M. Dilshan, *K. C. Sangakkara, D. P. M. D. Jayawardene, T. T. Samaraweera, A. D. Mathews, †H. A. P. W. Jayawardene, H. M. R. K. B. Herath, B. A. W. Mendis, C. R. D. Fernando and R. A. S. Lakmal.

Umpires: Asad Rauf and B. N. J. Oxenford. Third umpire: R. J. Tucker.
Series referee: A. G. Hurst.

Reports of the rearranged one-day series will appear in Wisden 2012.

ASSOCIATES T20 SERIES

As part of their preparation for the World Twenty20 Qualifier, Afghanistan, Canada and Ireland took part in a quadrangular 20-over tournament in Sri Lanka in February 2010. The fourth team was Sri Lanka A, who included several players with Test or other international experience: they won all three of their matches.

Only the games played by Afghanistan, Canada and Ireland against each other were official Twenty20 internationals.

At Colombo (PSS), February 1, 2010. **Sri Lanka A won by nine wickets. Canada 93-6** (20 overs) (S. Prasanna 3-13); **‡Sri Lanka A 94-1** (13 overs) (T. A. M. Siriwardana 54*, J. K. Silva 35*). *After making three stumpings in Canada's innings, the Sri Lanka A captain Kaushal Silva shared a stand of 80* with Milinda Siriwardana which brought victory with seven overs unused.*

At Colombo (PSS), February 1, 2010. **Ireland won by five wickets. ‡Afghanistan 121-9** (20 overs) (Raees Ahmadzai 33*; D. T. Johnston 4-22, A. C. Botha 3-14); **Ireland 124-5** (18.1 overs) (W. T. S. Porterfield 46). *Twenty20 international debuts:* Asghar Stanikzai, Dawlat Ahmadzai, Hamid Hassan, Karim Sadiq, Mohammad Nabi, Mohammad Shahzad, Nawroz Mangal, Raees Ahmadzai, Samiullah Shenwari, Shafiqullah, Shapoor Zadran (Afghanistan); G. H. Dockrell (Ireland). *Afghanistan's first Twenty20 international ended in defeat, after they were restricted to a total which Ireland had few problems in surpassing. George Dockrell, a 17-year-old slow left-armer from the Leinster club in Dublin, started his international career with figures of 4–0–11–2.*

At Colombo (SSC), February 3, 2010. **Canada won by four runs. Canada 176-3** (20 overs) (H. Patel 88*, Rizwan Cheema 34, A. Bagai 42; A. C. Botha 3-35); **‡Ireland 172-8** (20 overs) (N. J. O'Brien 50, U. Bhatti 3-26). *Twenty20 international debuts:* T. C. Bastiampillai, S. Keshvani, Khurram Chauhan, H. Patel, Usman Limbada (Canada); P. S. Eaglestone, G. E. Kidd (Ireland). *Ireland's tag as the leading Associate nation at the short-form game took a jolt when Canada ran up a big total, led by the 18-year-old debutant Hiral Patel's 88* from 61 balls: he matched Rizwan Cheema shot for shot in an opening stand of 68, then put on 101 in ten overs with Ashish Bagai. Only the Australians Ricky Ponting (98*) and David Warner (89) had made higher scores on Twenty20 international debut. Despite a 34-ball half-century from Niall O'Brien, Ireland fell just short when the task of making 12 from the final over proved beyond them.*

At Colombo (SSC), February 3, 2010. **Sri Lanka A won by 69 runs. ‡Sri Lanka A 175-5** (20 overs) (M. L. Udawatte 103*, J. K. Silva 31; Hamid Hassan 3-26); **Afghanistan 106-8** (20 overs) (Mohammad Shahzad 56). *Mahela Udawatte faced 67 balls, and hit eight fours and three sixes: he put on 82 in eight overs with Kaushal Silva. Afghanistan were 67-7 before Mohammad Shahzad (who was out to the last ball of the match) and Mirwais Ashraf (25*) put on 39.*

At Colombo (SSC), February 4, 2010. **Afghanistan won by five wickets. ‡Canada 140-6** (20 overs) (A. Bagai 53); **Afghanistan 143-5** (19.5 overs) (Karim Sadiq 42, Noor Ali Zadran 31; H. S. Baidwan 3-23). *Twenty20 international debuts:* Mirwais Ashraf, Noor Ali Zadran (Afghanistan). *An opening stand of 66 in 9.3 overs between Karim Sadiq and Noor Ali set up Afghanistan's eventual narrow victory.*

At Colombo (SSC), February 4, 2010. **Sri Lanka A won by five wickets. ‡Ireland 174-6** (20 overs) (P. R. Stirling 43, N. J. O'Brien 59); **Sri Lanka A 178-5** (18.2 overs) (H. C. U. Jayasinghe 41*). *Sri Lanka A made it three wins out of three, although Ireland ran them close: the A team were 110-5 in the tenth over, but Chinthaka Jayasinghe and Jeevan Mendis (29*) took them home.*

Sri Lanka A 6pts, Afghanistan 2pts, Canada 2pts, Ireland 2pts.

DOMESTIC CRICKET IN SRI LANKA, 2009-10

Sa'adi Thawfeeq

Chilaw Marians defied the odds to emerge as Premier League champions in 2009-10, overcoming the handicap of not having a ground or a clubhouse of their own to outshine more famous and influential clubs. It was their maiden first-class title, though they were runners-up in 2005-06; in 2004-05 they were Twenty20 champions and shared the limited-overs title with Tamil Union.

It was not until the final day of their final league game, against Moors, that Chilaw Marians were crowned champions. Interruptions by rain threatened to prevent them gaining enough points to displace Nondescripts from the top of Tier A. All they required was first-innings lead but, after Moors had managed a respectable 260 on a rain-restricted first day, Marians slumped to 157 for five on the second, and were 238 for seven on the last. But their eighth-wicket pair, wicketkeeper Suresh Niroshan and left-arm spinner Dinuka Hettiarachchi, dragged them into the lead amid wild cheers from their supporters.

"The game of cricket needs luck, and it certainly was with us in our final match, and throughout the season," said their coach Mahesh Weerasinghe. The captain, Mahela Udawatte – one of six Marian batsmen to pass 400 runs – argued that the club had made the most of their individual talent, a blend of experience and youth (they had won four Under-23 championships in the 2000s). Hettiarachchi, who had played a single Test in 2000-01, was the competition's leading wicket-taker with 66 at just under 19 apiece; 36 of them came in a run of three successive wins.

Chilaw Marians finished just over four points ahead of **Nondescripts**, who won five matches to their four and had a stranglehold on the table for much of the season; Nondescripts were convincing winners of the Under-23 tournament. Back in the first-class Premier League, the Tier B champions were **Lankan**, another club facing similar disadvantages to those of Chilaw Marians, who finished less than half a point above **Seeduwa Raddoluwa**; only Lankan were promoted as **Army** and **Moors** came down, with Tier A reverting to 11 teams. **Tamil Union** won the Premier limited-overs tournament.

Rain prevented a ball from being bowled on any of the four days of the final of the Interprovincial Tournament, which had seen two totals of 700-plus in the qualifying games. **Basnahira North** and **Basnahira South** were proclaimed joint champions. **Kandurata**, led by national captain Kumar Sangakkara, won the Interprovincial limited-overs championship, while **Wayamba** claimed the Twenty20 title for the third time running and qualified for the Champions League again.

Bloomfield off-spinner Suraj Mohamed followed T. M. Dilshan's path by changing his name, to Suraj Randiv, in 2009; like Dilshan, the change seemed to bring him luck. Randiv's 67 first-class wickets helped him break into the national team as the legendary Muttiah Muralitharan fought for fitness approaching the end of a glorious career. Another promising off-spinner, Sachithra Senanayake of Sinhalese, was unlucky not to win similar recognition after being a reliable wicket-taker for the past three domestic seasons. His reward for 72 scalps was a tour of Australia with Sri Lanka A; he claimed a career-best eight for 70 against Australia A at Brisbane.

Two former Sri Lanka Under-19 cricketers, Lahiru Thirimanne, who scored 1,020 first-class runs at 51 for Ragama and Basnahira South, and wicketkeeper-batsman Dinesh Chandimal, with 895 runs and 37 dismissals for Nondescripts and Ruhuna, also made the senior national team. Saracens opener Geeth Alwis recorded the season's highest individual score when he compiled 219 against Colombo.

Sajith Fernando, a reputable all-rounder first with Colts and latterly with Tamil Union, announced his retirement from first-class cricket. He had scored over 10,000 runs in a 16-year career, the only modern Sri Lankan to do so without winning a national cap.

FIRST-CLASS AVERAGES, 2009-10

BATTING (600 runs, average 40.00)

	M	I	NO	R	HS	100s	Avge	Ct/St
J. K. Silva (*Sinhalese & Basnahira North*)..........	10	15	4	745	158	2	67.72	23/4
N. A. N. N. Perera (*Burgher*).....................	8	15	1	818	211	3	58.42	9
†F. D. M. Karunaratne (*Sinhalese & Bas North*)......	13	22	1	1,186	185	2	56.47	12
S. I. de Saram (*Ragama & Ruhuna*)..................	9	16	3	691	119*	2	53.15	14
‡B. M. A. J. Mendis (*Tamil Union & Kandurata*)......	15	22	6	846	153*	2	52.87	17
L. D. Chandimal (*Nondescripts & Ruhuna*)...........	13	18	1	895	164	3	52.64	31/6
†H. D. R. L. Thirimanne (*Ragama & Bas Sth*)........	12	22	2	1,020	148	3	51.00	8
L. J. P. Gunaratne (*Chilaw Marians & Bas Sth*)......	15	20	2	911	130	1	50.61	14
A. R. S. Silva (*Colts & Basnahira North*)...........	11	15	2	654	155	1	50.30	13
K. H. R. K. Fernando (*Moors & Basnahira Sth*)......	9	14	1	645	115	1	49.61	5
S. C. Serasinghe (*Tamil Union & Basnahira Nth*).....	14	22	5	837	126	2	49.23	5
H. G. J. M. Kulatunga (*Colts & Wayamba*)..........	12	16	1	725	158	3	48.33	6
†J. R. G. Namal (*Burgher*)........................	9	15	2	628	154	2	48.30	8
†W. G. R. K. Alwis (*Saracens & Ruhuna*)............	15	23	1	1,016	219	3	46.18	4
A. K. Perera (*Nondescripts & Basnahira North*)......	12	15	1	626	178	1	44.71	9
S. Leelaratne (*Navy*).............................	9	17	2	667	84*	0	44.46	13
†T. A. M. Siriwardene (*Chilaw M & Bas Sth*)........	12	19	3	703	151*	1	43.93	11
L. P. C. Silva (*Bloomfield & Basnahira South*)......	15	25	1	1,035	145	3	43.12	19
N. M. N. P. Nawela (*Moors & Kandurata*)..........	15	24	1	985	115	2	42.82	5
H. A. P. W. Jayawardene (*Bloomfield & Bas Sth*).....	10	16	1	619	155	2	41.26	20/4

BOWLING (30 wickets, average 25.00)

	Style	O	M	R	W	BB	5W/i	Avge
N. C. K. Liyanage (*Singha*).....................	LFM	185.5	36	583	39	6-29	4	14.94
R. M. G. K. Sirisoma (*Lankan*).................	SLA	315.4	75	790	52	7-53	5	15.19
K. S. N. Karunadasa (*Navy*)...................	OB	203.2	31	686	44	7-111	4	15.59
T. M. U. S. Karunaratne (*Seeduwa Raddoluwa*)....	OB	248.5	37	845	50	7-146	5	16.90
G. A. S. Perera (*Panadura*)....................	SLA	241.1	60	530	30	6-29	3	17.66
A. A. C. E. Athukorala (*Burgher*)...............	RFM	169.1	27	584	33	7-78	2	17.69
S. C. D. Boralessa (*Colombo & Bas North*).......	SLA	391	59	1,326	72	9-47	3	18.41
D. G. R. Dhammika (*Seeduwa Raddoluwa*).......	SLA	211.3	53	631	34	6-41	1	18.55
C. A. M. Madusanka (*Burgher*).................	SLA	215.1	29	783	42	5-39	4	18.64
H. M. C. M. Bandara (*Ragama & Bas South*)......	LBG	313.2	49	1,029	55	7-74	3	18.70
S. Madanayake (*Sebastianites*)..................	SLA	269.5	53	722	37	5-32	1	19.51
W. T. Abeyratne (*Lankan*).....................	OB	230.4	40	715	35	5-47	2	20.42
S. Randiv (*Bloomfield & Kandurata*).............	OB	380.5	57	1,384	67	9-109	7	20.65
H. M. R. K. B. Herath (*Moors & Wayamba*)......	SLA	205.4	26	666	31	5-68	3	21.48
D. Hettiarachchi (*Chilaw Marians & Bas Sth*).....	SLA	434.4	52	1,498	69	8-66	6	21.71
T. D. D. Darshanapriya (*Ragama & Bas Nth*)....	RFM	196.4	24	699	32	6-71	2	21.84
C. K. B. Kulasekara (*Nondescripts & Ruhuna*).....	RFM	249.2	30	950	43	5-50	1	22.09
N. C. Komasaru (*Nondescripts & Ruhuna*)........	SLA	386	66	1,166	50	5-52	3	23.32
S. M. S. M. Senanayake (*Sinhalese & Ruhuna*)....	OB	530.1	74	1,690	72	8-117	7	23.47

PREMIER LEAGUE, 2009-10

Tier A	P	W	L	D	Pts	Tier B	P	W	L	D	Pts
Chilaw Marians CC	11	4	0	7	107.675	Lankan CC	9	4	0	5	102.175
Nondescripts CC......	11	5	0	6	103.460	Seeduwa Raddoluwa SC.	9	4	0	5	101.695
Colts CC	11	4	1	6	82.315	Navy SC	9	2	2	5	78.510
Sinhalese SC.........	11	1	0	10	79.900	Panadura SC	9	2	1	6	72.015
Badureliya SC........	11	2	3	6	79.540	Burgher RC..........	9	1	2	6	66.620
Tamil Union C & AC ...	11	1	2	8	76.315	Singha SC	9	3	3	3	64.430
Bloomfield C & AC	11	2	2	7	73.800	Police SC...........	9	1	1	7	62.360
Ragama CC..........	11	0	3	8	72.590	Air Force SC	9	1	3	5	47.555
Saracens SC	11	2	3	6	63.915	Moratuwa SC	9	0	1	8	39.740
Colombo CC	11	2	2	7	62.640	Sebastianites C & AC...	9	0	5	4	33.735
Army SC	11	1	5	5	41.435						
Moors SC	11	0	3	8	39.695						

Lankan were promoted to Tier A, replacing Army and Moors. Antonians replaced Moratuwa and Sebastianites in Tier B.

Outright win = 12pts; lead on first innings in a drawn game = 8pts. Bonus points were awarded as follows: 0.1pt for each wicket taken and 0.005pt for each run scored, up to 400 runs per innings.

Tier A

At Panagoda (Army), October 2–4, 2009. **Drawn.** ‡Chilaw Marians 173-5 dec; **Army 73-7.** *Army 0.865pts, Chilaw Marians 1.565pts.*

At Colombo (Bloomfield), October 2–4, 2009. **Drawn. Saracens 194** (S. Randiv 5-65); ‡**Bloomfield 186-8.** *Bloomfield 1.93pts, Saracens 1.77pts.*

At Colombo (CCC), October 2–4, 2009. **Drawn. Sinhalese 138-4 v** ‡**Colombo.** *Colombo 0.4pts, Sinhalese 0.69pts.*

At Colombo (Colts), October 2–4, 2009. **Colts won by eight wickets. Ragama 117 and 232** (M. D. K. Perera 6-78); ‡**Colts 277-6 dec and 74-2.** *Colts 15.755pts, Ragama 2.545pts. Harvir Baidwan, a 22-year-old Indian-born Canadian international, helped to set up Colts' victory with figures of 11.5–5–16–4 on first-class debut.*

At Colombo (Moors), October 2–4, 2009. **Drawn. Moors 244-6 v** ‡**Tamil Union.** *Moors 1.22pts, Tamil Union 0.6pts.*

At Colombo (NCC), October 2–4, 2009. **Nondescripts won by an innings and 13 runs. Nondescripts 251;** ‡**Badureliya 131 and 107.** *Nondescripts 15.255pts, Badureliya 2.19pts.*

At Katunayake, October 9–11, 2009. **Drawn.** ‡Chilaw Marians 236 (W. G. H. N. Premaratne 5-58) **and 304-4 dec; Ragama 297 and 127-5.** *Chilaw Marians 4.2pts, Ragama 11.52pts. Ragama's Indika de Saram, a former international batsman, passed 10,000 first-class runs.*

At Colombo (CCC), October 9–11, 2009. **Drawn.** ‡**Saracens 445** (W. G. R. K. Alwis 219) **and 83-4; Colombo 404** (W. M. M. W. E. V. Gangoda 5-81). *Colombo 3.4pts, Saracens 11.415pts. Left-handed opener Geeth Alwis scored a maiden double-hundred on the first day, hitting 27 fours in 259 balls, and added 175 for Saracens' seventh wicket with Dasun Randika (69).*

At Colombo (Colts), October 9–11, 2009. **Drawn. Sinhalese 372** (F. D. M. Karunaratne 147; P. D. R. L. Perera 5-102) **and 241-6** (K. T. G. D. Prasad 103*); ‡**Colts 370** (M. R. D. G. Mapa Bandara 104*). *Colts 3.45pts, Sinhalese 12.065pts. Dammika Prasad hit 103* in 81 balls, with ten fours and six sixes, on the final day.*

At Colombo (Moors), October 9–11, 2009. **Drawn.** ‡**Bloomfield 318 and 189; Moors 215 and 248-6.** *Moors 4.315pts, Bloomfield 12.135pts.*

At Colombo (NCC), October 9–11, 2009. **Nondescripts won by an innings and 168 runs.** ‡**Nondescripts 458-8 dec** (A. K. Perera 178); **Army 116** (W. G. R. L. Wijenayake 5-37) **and 174** (W. G. R. L. Wijenayake 5-66). *Nondescripts 16pts, Army 2.25pts. Angelo Perera, a 19-year-old who scored a maiden hundred in his second first-class game, and Akalanka Ganegama (93) added 193 for Nondescripts' seventh wicket and 144 for the eighth with Tharaka Kottehewa.*

At Colombo (PSS), October 9–11, 2009. **Badureliya won by 19 runs. Badureliya 238 and 217; ‡Tamil Union 251 and 185.** *Badureliya 16.275pts, Tamil Union 4.18pts.*

At Colombo (Bloomfield), October 16–18, 2009. **Bloomfield won by an innings and 90 runs. ‡Badureliya 183** (D. M. G. S. Dissanayake 5-29) **and 218** (S. Randiv 5-109); **Bloomfield 491-7 dec** (D. M. G. S. Dissanayake 205). *Bloomfield 16pts, Badureliya 2.705pts. Shanuka Dissanayake converted only the third century of his 14-year career into a maiden double.*

At Colombo (CCC), October 16–18, 2009. **Drawn. Moors 332** (D. N. Hunukumbura 116, K. H. R. K. Fernando 115) **and 134** (S. C. D. Boralessa 9-47); **Colombo 275** (H. M. R. K. B. Herath 5-86) **and 150-8.** *Colombo 4.125pts, Moors 12.13pts. Slow left-armer Sohan Boralessa's 9-47 was the best return of the season; he took 13-122 in the match.*

At Colombo (Colts), October 16–18, 2009. **Drawn. ‡Chilaw Marians 442** (D. N. A. Athulathmudali 153) **and 197-5** (M. M. D. N. R. G. Perera 102*); **Colts 346** (A. R. S. Silva 155). *Colts 3.23pts, Chilaw Marians 11.985pts. Amal Athulathmudali hit 153, his maiden century, in 127 balls, with eight fours and nine sixes, and put on 201 for Chilaw Marians' first wicket with Mahela Udawatte.*

At Colombo (NCC), October 16–18, 2009. **Drawn. ‡Ragama 347 and 330-5** (S. I. de Saram 100*); **Nondescripts 297** (L. D. Chandimal 138; S. A. D. U. Indrasiri 5-103). *Nondescripts 2.985pts, Ragama 12.385pts. Ten Nondescripts players, including wicketkeeper Dinesh Chandimal, bowled in Ragama's second innings.*

At Colombo (SSC), October 16–18, 2009. **Drawn. ‡Sinhalese 367** (W. M. M. W. E. V. Gangoda 5-65) **and 342-8** (T. T. Samaraweera 131); **Saracens 281** (K. T. G. D. Prasad 5-45). *Sinhalese 12.545pts, Saracens 3.205pts.*

At Colombo (PSS), October 16–18, 2009. **Tamil Union won by seven wickets. ‡Army 245 and 266; Tamil Union 417-7 dec** (B. M. A. J. Mendis 153*) **and 97-3.** *Tamil Union 16.485pts, Army 3.555pts. Sachithra Serasinghe (84) and Jeewan Mendis added 221 for Tamil Union's fifth wicket.*

At Panadura, October 23–25, 2009. **Badureliya won by ten wickets. ‡Saracens 200 and 187** (A. A. S. Silva 7-73); **Badureliya 366** (K. R. N. U. Perera 123*; W. M. M. W. E. V. Gangoda 5-126) **and 24-0.** *Badureliya 15.95pts, Saracens 2.935pts. Badureliya were 244-9 before last pair Ranesh Perera, with a maiden hundred, and Himesh Silva (48) added 122 for the tenth wicket.*

At Colombo (Bloomfield), October 23–25, 2009. **Bloomfield won by five wickets. Army 251 and 231** (S. Randiv 9-109); **‡Bloomfield 216** (S. Randiv 112) **and 267-5** (L. P. C. Silva 112*). *Bloomfield 16.415pts, Army 3.91pts. Suraj Randiv took 13-187 and scored a maiden century. The only wicket he did not claim in the first innings was a run-out.*

At Colombo (CCC), October 23–25, 2009. **Chilaw Marians won by ten wickets. ‡Colombo 167 and 245; Chilaw Marians 403-7 dec** (T. A. M. Siriwardene 151*) **and 10-0.** *Chilaw Marians 16.05pts, Colombo 2.76pts.*

At Colombo (Colts), October 23–25, 2009. **Nondescripts won by six wickets. Colts 170 and 224** (N. C. Komasaru 5-52); **‡Nondescripts 200 and 199-4** (M. F. Maharoof 115*). *Nondescripts 15.995pts, Colts 3.37pts.*

At Colombo (NCC), October 23–25, 2009. **Drawn. Ragama 361** (H. D. R. L. Thirimanne 107; M. Pushpakumara 5-79) **and 268-8** (S. C. Liyanagunawardene 5-89); **‡Tamil Union 318** (T. D. D. Darshanpriya 6-71). *Ragama 12.145pts, Tamil Union 3.39pts.*

At Colombo (SSC), October 23–25, 2009. **Sinhalese won by an innings and 83 runs. Sinhalese 466-7 dec** (S. H. Fernando 103, S. H. T. Kandamby 102); **‡Moors 135 and 248** (S. M. S. M. Senanayake 5-76). *Sinhalese 16pts, Moors 2.615pts.*

At Panagoda (Army), October 30–November 1, 2009. **Saracens won by 43 runs. ‡Saracens 172 and 185** (B. A. W. Mendis 6-64); **Army 161** (W. R. D. Wimaladarma 8-68) **and 153** (W. G. R. K. Alwis 6-36). *Saracens 15.785pts, Army 3.57pts.*

At Colombo (Thurstan), October 30–November 1, 2009. **Drawn. ‡Bloomfield 336** (H. A. P. W. Jayawardene 115); **Ragama 62-0.** *Bloomfield 1.68pts, Ragama 1.31pts.*

At Colombo (Moors), October 30–November 1, 2009. **Drawn. ‡Moors 178 and 204-5 dec; Badureliya 202** (H. M. R. K. B. Herath 5-68) **and 61-6.** *Moors 3.51pts, Badureliya 10.815pts.*

At Colombo (NCC), October 30–November 1, 2009. **Drawn. Nondescripts 551-9 dec** (W. U. Tharanga 155, L. D. Chandimal 164) **and 100-0;** ‡**Colombo 398** (W. M. B. Perera 123; N. C. Komasaru 5-90). *Nondescripts 11.5pts, Colombo 2.89pts. Upul Tharanga and Yohan de Silva (80) set Nondescripts on their way to their highest total with an opening stand of 207. Nineteen-year-old Dinesh Chandimal scored his third century, 164 in 168 balls with 17 fours and five sixes, in his seventh first-class match.*

At Colombo (SSC), October 30–November 1, 2009. **Drawn. Sinhalese 171** (N. T. Paranavitana 103) **and 283-7 dec;** ‡**Chilaw Marians 210** (S. M. S. M. Senanayake 5-71) **and 122-4.** *Sinhalese 3.67pts, Chilaw Marians 11.36pts.*

At Colombo (PSS), October 30–November 1, 2009. **Drawn.** ‡**Tamil Union 320 and 116-3; Colts 283.** *Tamil Union 11.18pts, Colts 2.715pts.*

At Colombo (PSS), November 6–8, 2009. **Drawn.** ‡**Ragama 136-4 v Badureliya.** *Badureliya 0.4pts, Ragama 0.68pts.*

At Colombo (Bloomfield), November 6–8, 2009. **Drawn. Bloomfield 191-4 v** ‡**Colts.** *Bloomfield 0.955pts, Colts 0.4pts.*

At Colombo (Colts), November 6–8, 2009. **Drawn. Chilaw Marians 305** (W. R. D. Wimaladarma 5-106); ‡**Saracens 146-5.** *Chilaw Marians 2.025pts, Saracens 1.73pts.*

At Colombo (CCC), November 6–8, 2009. **Drawn.** ‡**Tamil Union 193; Colombo 111-4.** *Colombo 1.555pts, Tamil Union 1.365pts.*

At Colombo (Moors), November 6–8, 2009. **Drawn. Moors 257-5 v** ‡**Army.** *Moors 1.285pts, Army 0.5pts.*

At Colombo (NCC), November 6–8, 2009. **Drawn.** ‡**Nondescripts 312** (S. M. S. M. Senanayake 8-117); **Sinhalese 102-6.** *Nondescripts 2.16pts, Sinhalese 1.51pts. With six Sinhalese players touring India with the national team, coach Avishka Gunawardene came out of retirement to play his first match in 21 months, and scored 20* in 24 balls before rain ended the match.*

At Panagoda (Army), November 13–15, 2009. **Drawn.** ‡**Colts 144-6 v Army.** *Army 0.6pts, Colts 0.72pts.*

At Colombo (CCC), November 13–15, 2009. **Drawn. Bloomfield 246** (L. P. C. Silva 130); ‡**Colombo 5-1.** *Colombo 1.025pts, Bloomfield 1.33pts.*

At Colombo (Moors), November 13–15, 2009. **Drawn. Moors 91** (H. G. D. Nayanakantha 5-37); ‡**Ragama 64-5.** *Moors 0.955pts, Ragama 1.32pts. Indika de Saram held five catches in the field in Moors' first innings.*

At Colombo (NCC), November 13–15, 2009. **Drawn. Nondescripts 265;** ‡**Chilaw Marians 48-3.** *Nondescripts 1.625pts, Chilaw Marians 1.24pts.*

At Colombo (PSS), November 13–15, 2009. **Drawn. Tamil Union 94-4 v** ‡**Sinhalese.** *Tamil Union 0.47pts, Sinhalese 0.4pts.*

At Panagoda (Army), November 27–29, 2009. **Army won by six wickets.** ‡**Ragama 229** (W. R. Palleguruge 5-44) **and 83** (S. Prasanna 5-26); **Army 152** (T. D. D. Darshanpriya 5-41) **and 161-4.** *Army 15.565pts, Ragama 2.96pts.*

At Colombo (CCC), November 27–29, 2009. **Drawn. Badureliya 242** (S. C. D. Boralessa 8-111); ‡**Colombo 380** (K. R. N. U. Perera 5-103). *Colombo 10.9pts, Badureliya 2.21pts.*

At Colombo (Colts), November 27–29, 2009. **Colts won by an innings and nine runs. Saracens 166 and 231** (W. G. R. K. Alwis 115; S. Weerakoon 5-84); ‡**Colts 406-5 dec** (H. G. J. M. Kulatunga 158). *Colts 16pts, Saracens 2.485pts.*

At Colombo (Moors), November 27–29, 2009. **Drawn.** ‡**Moors 396-8 dec; Nondescripts 356-7** (K. Y. de Silva 164, D. H. S. Pradeep 104). *Moors 2.68pts, Nondescripts 2.58pts. Yohan de Silva and Susantha Pradeep added 245 for Nondescripts' second wicket.*

At Colombo (SSC), November 27–29, 2009. **Drawn.** ‡**Sinhalese 264 and 280** (S. Randiv 5-99); **Bloomfield 376** (L. P. C. Silva 145; S. M. S. M. Senanayake 7-157) **and 133-4.** *Sinhalese 4.12pts, Bloomfield 12.545pts.*

At Colombo (PSS), November 27–29, 2009. **Chilaw Marians won by seven wickets. Chilaw Marians 299 and 104-3; ‡Tamil Union 124** (D. Hettiarachchi 6-40) **and 275.** *Chilaw Marians 16.015pts, Tamil Union 3.295pts. Dinuka Hettiarachchi took a hat-trick in Tamil Union's second innings to finish with 10-123 in the match.*

At Panagoda (Army), December 4–6, 2009. **Drawn. ‡Army 178** (M. R. C. N. Bandaratilleke 6-65) **and 200-8; Badureliya 244.** *Army 2.89pts, Badureliya 11.02pts.*

At Katunayake, December 4–6, 2009. **Chilaw Marians won by 16 runs. ‡Chilaw Marians 124** (S. Randiv 8-50) **and 188** (S. Randiv 5-69); **Bloomfield 149** (D. Hettiarachchi 5-72) **and 147** (D. Hettiarachchi 8-66). *Chilaw Marians 15.56pts, Bloomfield 3.48pts. Suraj Randiv and Dinuka Hettiarachchi each took 13 wickets in the match, Randiv for the second time in the season, as Chilaw Marians displaced Nondescripts at the top of the table for the first time.*

At Colombo (Colts), December 4–6, 2009. **Colts won by 235 runs. ‡Colts 182 and 363** (T. M. I. Mutaliph 125, H. G. J. M. Kulatunga 101; S. C. D. Boralessa 5-147); **Colombo 141** (S. Weerakoon 5-54) **and 169** (S. Weerakoon 5-62). *Colts 16.725pts, Colombo 3.55pts.*

At Colombo (Moors), December 4–6, 2009. **Saracens won by six wickets. Moors 108** (W. R. D. Wimaladarma 5-27) **and 284-9 dec** (S. Kalavitigoda 124; W. R. D. Wimaladarma 5-127); **‡Saracens 231** (J. U. Chaturanga 5-45) **and 163-4.** *Saracens 15.87pts, Moors 3.36pts.*

At Colombo (NCC), December 4–6, 2009. **Drawn. ‡Nondescripts 143 and 219** (S. C. Liyanagunawardene 5-63); **Tamil Union 167 and 170-4.** *Nondescripts 3.21pts, Tamil Union 11.685pts.*

At Colombo (SSC), December 4–6, 2009. **Drawn. ‡Sinhalese 283 and 237; Ragama 352** (M. N. Mazahir 104) **and 40-1.** *Sinhalese 3.7pts, Ragama 11.96pts.*

At Katunayake, December 11–13, 2009. **Chilaw Marians won by nine wickets. ‡Badureliya 69** (D. Hettiarachchi 6-25) **and 416** (T. P. Attanayake 113; D. Hettiarachchi 7-201); **Chilaw Marians 359 and 131-1.** *Chilaw Marians 16.45pts, Badureliya 3.445pts. Dinuka Hettiarachchi wound up Badureliya in 25 overs on the first morning, and finished with 13 wickets for the second time in successive matches and 36 wickets in his last three games – all of which Chilaw Marians won.*

At Colombo (Bloomfield), December 11–13, 2009. **Nondescripts won by seven wickets. ‡Bloomfield 219** (N. C. Komasaru 5-82) **and 127** (C. K. B. Kulasekara 5-50); **Nondescripts 236 and 115-3.** *Nondescripts 15.755pts, Bloomfield 3.03pts.*

At Colombo (NCC), December 11–13, 2009. **Colombo won by 31 runs. Colombo 178 and 201** (J. Mubarak 110); **‡Ragama 190 and 158** (S. S. Pathirana 5-57). *Colombo 15.895pts, Ragama 3.74pts.*

At Colombo (Colts), December 11–13, 2009. **Colts won by five wickets. Colts 411** (N. L. T. C. Perera 113*) **and 196-5; ‡Moors 168** (N. L. T. C. Perera 5-69) **and 436** (S. Weerakoon 5-158). *Colts 16.98pts, Moors 4.34pts.*

At Colombo (SSC), December 11–13, 2009. **Drawn. ‡Sinhalese 216 and 308** (S. Prasanna 8-123); **Army 209** (S. M. S. M. Senanayake 6-79) **and 245-8.** *Sinhalese 12.42pts, Army 4.27pts.*

At Colombo (PSS), December 11–13, 2009. **Drawn. Tamil Union 319** (S. C. Serasinghe 126; W. R. D. Wimaladarma 8-107) **and 349-6** (A. D. Gunawardene 130; W. R. D. Wimaladarma 5-152); **‡Saracens 256.** *Tamil Union 12.34pts, Saracens 2.88pts. Rakitha Wimaladarma took ten or more wickets for the third time in five matches.*

At Panagoda (Army), December 18–20, 2009. **Colombo won by 136 runs. ‡Colombo 164** (S. Prasanna 5-55) **and 264; Army 147 and 145.** *Colombo 16.14pts, Army 3.46pts.*

At Colombo (Bloomfield), December 18–20, 2009. **Drawn. Bloomfield 195 and 305-3 dec** (M. T. Gunaratne 126); **‡Tamil Union 227 and 178-8.** *Bloomfield 4.3pts, Tamil Union 11.325pts.*

At Colombo (NCC), December 18–20, 2009. **Nondescripts won by six wickets. ‡Saracens 247 and 230; Nondescripts 270 and 209-4.** *Nondescripts 16.395pts, Saracens 3.785pts. Nondescripts finished their programme seven points ahead of Chilaw Marians – who had a game in hand.*

At Colombo (SSC), December 18–20, 2009. **Drawn. Sinhalese 506** (W. L. P. Fernando 102, K. P. S. P. Karunanayake 172) **and 356-1** (L. A. H. N. Perera 153*, S. H. Fernando 100*); **‡Badureliya 314** (S. M. S. M. Senanayake 6-110). *Sinhalese 12.78pts, Badureliya 2.67pts. No. 7*

Shalika Karunanayake hit a career-best 172 in 164 balls, with 15 fours and nine sixes; Badureliya wicketkeeper Dilshan Vitharana did not concede a single bye in Sinhalese's total of 506.

At Colombo (Colts), December 26–28, 2009. **Drawn.** ‡**Badureliya 372-9 dec** (T. M. N. Sampath 158) **and 200-6; Colts 294** (D. F. Arnolda 5-64). *Colts 2.97pts, Badureliya 11.86pts.*

At Colombo (Moors), December 26–28, 2009. **Drawn. Moors 260 and 257-9** (D. Hettiarachchi 5-106); ‡**Chilaw Marians 265-7 dec.** *Moors 3.285pts, Chilaw Marians 11.225pts. Despite interruptions from the rain, Chilaw Marians achieved first-innings lead on the final day, which gave them enough points for their maiden first-class title.*

At Colombo (NCC), December 26–28, 2009. **Drawn. Ragama 375-7 dec** (H. D. R. L. Thirimanne 144) **and 230-2** (S. I. de Saram 119*); ‡**Saracens 231** (H. M. C. M. Bandara 7-74). *Ragama 12.025pts, Saracens 2.055pts. Indika de Saram hit 119* in 94 balls, with nine fours and eight sixes, on the final day.*

CHAMPIONS

Lakspray Trophy		1994-95	Bloomfield C & AC	2001-02	Colts CC
1988-89	Nondescripts CC		Sinhalese SC	2002-03	Moors SC
	Sinhalese SC	1995-96	Colombo SC	2003-04	Bloomfield C & AC
1989-90	Sinhalese SC	1996-97	Bloomfield C & AC	2004-05	Colts CC
		1997-98	Sinhalese SC	2005-06	Sinhalese SC
P. Saravanamuttu Trophy				2006-07	Colombo CC
1990-91	Sinhalese SC	*Premier League*		2007-08	Sinhalese SC
1991-92	Colts CC	1998-99	Bloomfield C & AC	2008-09	Colts CC
1992-93	Sinhalese SC	1999-2000	Colts CC	2009-10	Chilaw Marians
1993-94	Nondescripts CC	2000-01	Nondescripts CC		

Sinhalese have won the title outright 6 times, Colts 5, Bloomfield 3, Colombo and Nondescripts 2, Chilaw Marians and Moors 1. Sinhalese have also shared the title twice, and Bloomfield and Nondescripts once each.

Tier B

At Colombo (Air Force), October 2–4, 2009. **Drawn.** ‡**Air Force 152; Panadura 220-7.** *Air Force 1.46pts, Panadura 10.1pts.*

At Colombo (Burgher), October 2–4, 2009. **Drawn. Burgher 168 and 92-0;** ‡**Sebastianites 247** (W. M. P. N. Wanasinghe 108). *Burgher 2.3pts, Sebastianites 10.235pts.*

At Katunayake, October 2–4, 2009. **Lankan won by four wickets. Singha 233** (W. T. Abeyratne 5-61) **and 101;** ‡**Lankan 179 and 159-6.** *Lankan 15.69pts, Singha 3.27pts.*

At Moratuwa, October 2–4, 2009. **Drawn. Police 311-7 dec** (P. H. K. S. Nirmala 104*); ‡**Moratuwa 52-0.** *Moratuwa 0.96pts, Police 1.555pts.*

At Welisara, October 2–4, 2009. **Drawn. Seeduwa Raddoluwa 322;** ‡**Navy 172 and 184-4.** *Navy 2.78pts, Seeduwa Raddoluwa 11.01pts.*

At Colombo (Air Force), October 9–11, 2009. **Lankan won by 166 runs.** ‡**Lankan 415-8 dec** (B. A. R. S. Priyadarshana 123) **and 224-8 dec** (D. H. A. Isanka 6-51); **Air Force 266 and 207.** *Lankan 17.12pts, Air Force 3.965pts.*

At Panadura, October 9–11, 2009. **Drawn. Moratuwa 306 and 273-4** (R. S. R. de Zoysa 111*); ‡**Panadura 223** (H. G. P. Ranaweera 5-61). *Panadura 2.515pts, Moratuwa 11.895pts.*

At Colombo (Thurstan), October 9–11, 2009. **Drawn.** ‡**Seeduwa Raddoluwa 320** (C. A. M. Madusanka 5-74) **and 109-7; Burgher 411-8 dec** (N. A. N. N. Perera 211; T. M. U. S. Karunaratne 5-99). *Seeduwa Raddoluwa 2.945pts, Burgher 11.7pts. Opener Nimesh Perera converted only the second century of his eight-year career into a maiden double.*

At Colombo (Air Force), October 16–18, 2009. **Drawn.** ‡**Navy 255 and 299; Air Force 204 and 236-6.** *Air Force 4.2pts, Navy 12.37pts.*

At Moratuwa, October 16–18, 2009. **Drawn.** ‡**Moratuwa 264** (R. M. G. K. Sirisoma 7-53) **and 251-6; Lankan 431** (P. B. Ediriweera 125). *Moratuwa 3.575pts, Lankan 11.6pts.*

At Panadura, October 16–18, 2009. **Panadura won by five wickets.** ‡**Panadura 282 and 123-5; Sebastianites 125** (G. A. S. Perera 6-29) **and 279** (H. D. N. de Silva 7-33). *Panadura 16.025pts, Sebastianites 3.52pts. Leg-spinner Nilantha Cooray had figures of 5.2–3–2–4 as he made Sebastianites follow on.*

At Colombo (Police), October 16–18, 2009. **Burgher won by 104 runs. Burgher 297** (N. A. N. N. Perera 113) **and 190** (R. G. D. Sanjeewa 6-36); ‡**Police 254 and 129.** *Burgher 16.435pts, Police 3.915pts.*

At Colombo (Air Force), October 23–25, 2009. **Singha won by 222 runs.** ‡**Singha 241** (D. H. A. Isanka 5-77) **and 260-8 dec; Air Force 133 and 146** (S. K. C. Randunu 6-60). *Singha 16.505pts, Air Force 3.195pts.*

At Colombo (Burgher), October 23–25, 2009. **Drawn.** ‡**Burgher 263** (J. R. G. Namal 142*; G. A. S. Perera 5-71) **and 255-6** (I. C. D. Perera 113*); **Panadura 266.** *Burgher 3.59pts, Panadura 10.93pts.*

At Welisara, October 23–25, 2009. **Navy won by an innings and 75 runs.** ‡**Navy 390; Moratuwa 179 and 136** (B. M. D. K. Mendis 5-42). *Navy 15.95pts, Moratuwa 2.575pts.*

At Colombo (Police), October 23–25, 2009. **Drawn. Seeduwa Raddoluwa 391 and 130-1;** ‡**Police 328.** *Police 2.74pts, Seeduwa Raddoluwa 11.605pts.*

At Moratuwa, October 23–25, 2009. **Lankan won by 101 runs.** ‡**Lankan 268 and 226** (M. T. P. Fernando 5-70); **Sebastianites 256** (R. M. G. K. Sirisoma 7-91) **and 137** (W. T. Abeyratne 5-47). *Lankan 16.47pts, Sebastianites 3.965pts.*

At Colombo (Air Force), October 30–November 1, 2009. **Seeduwa Raddoluwa won by nine wickets. Air Force 221** (T. M. U. S. Karunaratne 6-52) **and 179;** ‡**Seeduwa Raddoluwa 267 and 134-1.** *Seeduwa Raddoluwa 16.005pts, Air Force 3.1pts. Air Force wicketkeeper Marlon Fernando made five catches and two stumpings in the first innings.*

At Katunayake, October 30–November 1, 2009. **Drawn.** ‡**Burgher 216** (W. J. S. D. Perera 5-35) **and 123-6; Lankan 366.** *Burgher 2.695pts, Lankan 11.43pts.*

At Panadura, October 30–November 1, 2009. **Drawn.** ‡**Police 210** (G. A. S. Perera 5-28) **and 201-7; Panadura 313.** *Panadura 11.265pts, Police 3.055pts.*

At Moratuwa, October 30–November 1, 2009. **Drawn.** ‡**Navy 219 and 273** (M. D. U. S. Jayasundera 102); **Sebastianites 190** (B. M. D. K. Mendis 5-55) **and 145-8.** *Sebastianites 3.675pts, Navy 12.26pts. Eighteen-year-old left-hander Udara Jayasundera scored 102 on first-class debut.*

At Colombo (Burgher), November 6–8, 2009. **Drawn. Singha 176 and 42-0;** ‡**Burgher 203** (G. R. Perera 101). *Burgher 10.015pts, Singha 2.09pts.*

At Welisara, November 6–8, 2009. **Drawn.** ‡**Navy 151 and 157-5; Police 177** (K. S. N. Karunadasa 6-60). *Navy 2.54pts, Police 10.385pts.*

At Panadura, November 6–8, 2009. **Drawn.** ‡**Panadura 187-4 v Lankan.** *Panadura 0.935pts, Lankan 0.4pts.*

At Moratuwa, November 6–8, 2009. **Drawn. Sebastianites 69** (D. M. A. D. Karunaratne 6-33) **and 31-1;** ‡**Air Force 94** (W. M. P. N. Wanasinghe 5-42, S. Madanayake 5-32). *Sebastianites 1.5pts, Air Force 9.57pts. A rain-shortened first day saw 18 wickets fall for 161 runs in 61.3 overs, with only two men reaching 20; further rain prevented a result.*

At Colombo (Thurstan), November 6–8, 2009. **Drawn.** ‡**Moratuwa 144; Seeduwa Raddoluwa 139-7.** *Seeduwa Raddoluwa 1.695pts, Moratuwa 1.42pts.*

At Moratuwa, November 13–15, 2009. **Drawn. Moratuwa 262-9 v** ‡**Sebastianites.** *Moratuwa 1.31pts, Sebastianites 0.9pts.*

At Welisara, November 13–15, 2009. **Drawn.** ‡**Navy 139 and 61-2; Panadura 114** (S. Chamika 5-58). *Navy 10pts, Panadura 1.77pts.*

At Colombo (Police), November 13–15, 2009. **Drawn. Singha 172** (W. C. K. Ramanayake 5-53); ‡**Police 212-5.** *Police 10.06pts, Singha 1.36pts.*

At Colombo (Thurstan), November 13–15, 2009. **Drawn. ‡Lankan 129 and 39-0; Seeduwa Raddoluwa 266.** *Seeduwa Raddoluwa 10.33pts, Lankan 1.84pts.*

At Moratuwa, November 20–22, 2009. **Drawn. ‡Moratuwa 200-8 dec; Singha 123-7.** *Moratuwa 1.7pts, Singha 1.415pts.*

At Colombo (Burgher), November 27–29, 2009. **Drawn. Moratuwa 335** (L. T. A. de Silva 127; A. A. C. E. Athukorala 7-78) **and 246** (C. A. M. Madusanka 5-72); **‡Burgher 405** (J. R. G. Namal 154) **and 115-9** (H. G. P. Ranaweera 6-52). *Burgher 12.575pts, Moratuwa 4.805pts. Raju Namal hit a run-a-ball 154 with 14 fours and seven sixes.*

At Welisara, November 27–29, 2009. **Lankan won by seven wickets. ‡Navy 147** (R. M. G. K. Sirisoma 5-38) **and 241** (R. M. G. K. Sirisoma 7-74); **Lankan 320 and 70-3.** *Lankan 15.95pts, Navy 3.24pts.*

At Panadura, November 27–29, 2009. **Panadura won by 54 runs. ‡Panadura 172** (H. W. M. Kumara 5-34) **and 219** (N. C. K. Liyanage 5-68); **Singha 167 and 170** (M. N. R. Cooray 5-65). *Panadura 15.955pts, Singha 3.685pts.*

At Colombo (Police), November 27–29, 2009. **Drawn. Air Force 348** (R. G. D. Sanjeewa 5-55) **and 53-1; ‡Police 394.** *Police 11.07pts, Air Force 3.005pts.*

At Moratuwa, November 27–29, 2009. **Seeduwa Raddoluwa won by 46 runs. ‡Seeduwa Raddoluwa 136 and 242-7 dec; Sebastianites 137** (T. M. U. S. Karunaratne 5-58) **and 195** (D. G. R. Dhammika 6-41). *Seeduwa Raddoluwa 15.89pts, Sebastianites 3.36pts.*

At Colombo (Burgher), December 4–6, 2009. **Navy won by six wickets. Burgher 235** (S. Chamika 5-88, K. S. N. Karunadasa 5-67) **and 143** (K. S. N. Karunadasa 5-48); **‡Navy 226** (A. A. C. E. Athukorala 5-52) **and 153-4.** *Navy 15.895pts, Burgher 3.29pts.*

At Colombo (Police), December 4–6, 2009. **Drawn. Police 201** (S. H. S. M. K. Silva 7-52) **and 190** (R. M. G. K. Sirisoma 6-58); **‡Lankan 213 and 122-4.** *Police 3.355pts, Lankan 11.675pts. Lankan finished their nine matches 17 points ahead of nearest rivals Seeduwa Raddoluwa, who had a game in hand.*

At Colombo (Bloomfield), December 4–6, 2009. **Singha won by 168 runs. ‡Singha 115** (W. G. C. D. Ranaweera 5-37) **and 247** (H. B. D. Fernando 5-60); **Sebastianites 115 and 79** (N. C. K. Liyanage 6-29). *Singha 15.81pts, Sebastianites 2.97pts. Sebastianites were bowled out for under 80 for the second time in a month, with left-arm seamer Nevil Liyanage completing a hat-trick.*

At Colombo (Thurstan), December 4–6, 2009. **Seeduwa Raddoluwa won by ten wickets. Panadura 141** (W. K. G. Dilruk 5-34) **and 163; ‡Seeduwa Raddoluwa 291 and 14-0.** *Seeduwa Raddoluwa 15.525pts, Panadura 2.52pts.*

At Moratuwa, December 6–8, 2009. **Drawn. ‡Air Force 237 and 164; Moratuwa 300.** *Moratuwa 11.5pts, Air Force 3.005pts.*

At Colombo (Air Force), December 11–13, 2009. **Air Force won by seven runs. Air Force 141** (C. A. M. Madusanka 5-39) **and 270** (C. A. M. Madusanka 5-89); **‡Burgher 168 and 236.** *Air Force 16.055pts, Burgher 4.02pts.*

At Welisara, December 14–16, 2009. **Singha won by 137 runs. Singha 188 and 244** (H. H. R. Kavinga 129; K. S. N. Karunadasa 7-111); **‡Navy 148** (N. C. K. Liyanage 6-36) **and 147** (N. A. C. T. Perera 5-51). *Singha 16.16pts, Navy 3.475pts. Singha opener Rishan Kavinga hit 129 in 112 balls, with 18 fours and two sixes.*

At Colombo (Police), December 11–13, 2009. **Police won by six wickets. Sebastianites 183 and 259** (Y. A. N. Mendis 5-106); **‡Police 314** (R. G. D. Sanjeewa 124) **and 131-4.** *Police 16.225pts, Sebastianites 3.61pts.*

At Colombo (Ananda), December 18–20, 2009. **Seeduwa Raddoluwa won by 111 runs. ‡Seeduwa Raddoluwa 238 and 300** (K. M. Fernando 121; N. C. K. Liyanage 5-82); **Singha 164** (T. M. U. S. Karunaratne 6-79) **and 263** (T. M. U. S. Karunaratne 7-146). *Seeduwa Raddoluwa 16.69pts, Singha 4.135pts. Seeduwa Raddoluwa's victory, set up by off-spinner Umesh Karunaratne who took 13-225, almost closed the 17-point gap on tier leaders Lankan; had they scored 97 more runs, they and not Lankan would have won promotion.*

INTERPROVINCIAL TOURNAMENT, 2009-10

	Played	Won	Lost	Drawn	1st-inns points	Batting	Bowling	Points
Basnahira North	4	2	0	2	8	9.830	6.0	47.830
Basnahira South	4	2	2	0	0	10.025	6.5	40.525
Ruhuna	4	1	2	1	8	8.345	5.7	34.045
Kandurata	4	0	1	3	16	7.590	4.5	28.090
Wayamba	4	1	1	2	0	7.105	4.6	23.705

Final: Basnahira North drew with Basnahira South and shared the title.

Outright win = 12pts; lead on first innings in a drawn game = 8pts. Bonus points were awarded as follows: 0.1pt for each wicket taken and 0.005pt for each run scored, up to 400 runs per innings

At Colombo (Moors), March 18–21, 2010. **Drawn. ‡Basnahira North 530 and 209-4; Kandurata 727** (N. M. N. P. Nawela 113, T. T. Samaraweera 214, B. M. A. J. Mendis 150). *Basnahira North 4.045pts, Kandurata 11.4pts. Replying to Basnahira North's 530, Kandurata's 727 was the third-highest first-class total on Sri Lankan soil, and the highest in domestic cricket. Captain Thilan Samaraweera, who scored his fourth double-hundred, and Jeewan Mendis added 274 for their fifth wicket.*

At Pallekele, March 18–20, 2010. **Wayamba won by seven wickets. ‡Basnahira South 120 and 352** (H. M. R. K. B. Herath 5-129); **Wayamba 249 and 226-3** (H. G. J. M. Kulatunga 100*). *Wayamba 16.375pts, Basnahira South 3.66pts. Jeevantha Kulatunga steered Wayamba to a three-day win with 100* in 101 balls.*

At Colombo (Bloomfield), March 25–28, 2010. **Basnahira South won by five wickets. Kandurata 179** (H. M. C. M. Bandara 5-40) **and 302; ‡Basnahira South 300 and 182-5** (S. Randiv 5-87). *Basnahira South 16.41pts, Kandurata 3.905pts.*

At Galle, March 25–28, 2010. **Basnahira North won by an innings and 108 runs. ‡Basnahira North 538-9 dec** (E. M. G. D. Y. Munaweera 153, S. C. Serasinghe 117, J. K. Silva 108). *Ruhuna 301* (L. D. Chandimal 109) **and 129.** *Basnahira North 16pts, Ruhuna 3.05pts. Dilshan Munaweera, who hit eight sixes and 12 fours in his maiden hundred, and Sachithra Serasinge added 210 for Basnahira North's second wicket.*

At Moratuwa, April 3–6, 2010. **Basnahira North won by eight wickets. Basnahira South 224 and 259** (K. T. G. D. Prasad 6-74); **‡Basnahira North 321** (E. M. G. D. Y. Munaweera 136) **and 165-2.** *Basnahira North 16.43pts, Basnahira South 3.615pts. Dilshan Munaweera hit 136 in 109 balls, with 21 fours and a six; none of his team-mates reached 30 in that innings.*

At Colombo (Colts), April 3–6, 2010. **Ruhuna won by an innings and 63 runs. Wayamba 161 and 235; ‡Ruhuna 459** (W. G. R. K. Alwis 123). *Ruhuna 16pts, Wayamba 2.98pts. Off-spinner Sachithra Senanayake set up Ruhuna's innings win with a career-best 89 in 108 balls plus four wickets in each innings.*

At Moratuwa, April 22–25, 2010. **Drawn. Basnahira North 598** (F. D. M. Karunaratne 185, J. K. Silva 158) **and 71-3; ‡Wayamba 292** (M. G. Vandort 100). *Basnahira North 11.355pts, Wayamba 2.76pts. Basnahira North passed 500 for the third time in four matches to end the qualifying rounds on top of the table; Dimuth Karunaratne and Kaushal Silva added 306 for their third wicket.*

At Colombo (PSS), April 22–25, 2010. **Drawn. Kandurata 271** (N. M. N. P. Nawela 115) **and 44-0; ‡Ruhuna 402-6 dec** (T. M. N. Sampath 154). *Kandurata 2.175pts, Ruhuna 11pts.*

At Colombo (Colts), May 6–9, 2010. **Basnahira South won by 449 runs. Basnahira South 720** (H. D. R. L. Thirimanne 148, L. J. P. Gunaratne 130, H. A. P. W. Jayawardene 155, H. M. C. M. Bandara 108) **and 168-8 dec** (S. M. S. M. Senanayake 5-47); **‡Ruhuna 180 and 259** (H. M. C. M. Bandara 5-96). *Basnahira South 16.84pts, Ruhuna 3.995pts. Basnahira South almost matched Kandurata's record domestic total of 727 scored in March, after scoring 440-6 in 90 overs on the opening day. Lahiru Thirimanne and Janaka Gunaratne (who hit 130 in 131 balls) added 208 for their third wicket; Malinga Bandara scored a maiden century – 108 in 94 balls, with five fours and seven sixes – from No. 9 and, had Charith Jayampathi made four more runs, there would have been five hundreds in the innings. Despite a first-innings lead of 540, Basnahira South waived the follow-on and set a target of 709; unlike Kandurata they converted their superiority into victory, which put them in the final.*

At Kandy, May 6–9, 2010. **Drawn.** ‡**Wayamba 258; Kandurata 322-3** (B. M. A. J. Mendis 134*, G. A. S. K. Gangodawila 103*). *Kandurata 10.61pts, Wayamba 1.59pts. Jeewan Mendis and Sanjaya Gangodawila added 202* for Kandurata's fourth wicket but were unable to continue when the last day was washed out.*

Final

At Colombo (SSC), May 13–16, 2010. **Basnahira North v Basnahira South. Abandoned.** Basnahira North and Basnahira South shared the title.

INTERPROVINCIAL CHAMPIONS

1989-90	Western Province	2003-04	Central Province
1990-91	Western Province City	2004-05	North Central Province
1991-92	Western Province North	2008-09	Basnahira North
1993-94	Western Province City	2009-10 {	Basnahira North
1994-95	Western Province City		Basnahira South

PREMIER LIMITED-OVERS TOURNAMENT, 2009-10

50-over league plus knockout

The Tier A semi-finals (Chilaw Marians v Colts and Sinhalese v Tamil Union) and Tier B semi-finals (Lankan v Panadura and Sebastianites v Seeduwa Raddoluwa) were all abandoned. Chilaw Marians and Tamil Union reached the Tier A final and Panadura and Seeduwa Raddoluwa the Tier B final by virtue of their better positions in the qualifying table.

Tier A Final

At Colombo (SSC), December 1, 2009. **Tamil Union won by 63 runs** (D/L method). ‡**Tamil Union 234** (49.2 overs); **Chilaw Marians 143-8** (36 overs). *When play ended, Chilaw Marians needed to have scored 207 to win.*

Tier B Final

At Colombo (SSC), November 25, 2009. **Seeduwa Raddoluwa won by seven runs** (D/L method). Reduced to 40 overs a side. ‡**Panadura 175** (38.5 overs); **Seeduwa Raddoluwa 92-2** (23.2 overs). *The match, already shortened, was halted when Seeduwa Raddoluwa needed to have scored 86 to win.*

INTERPROVINCIAL LIMITED-OVER TOURNAMENT, 2009-10

50-over league plus knockout

	Played	Won	Lost	No result	Bonus points	Points	Net run-rate
Ruhuna	5	3	1	1	2	16	1.27
Kandurata	5	3	2	0	3	15	1.03
Wayamba	5	3	2	0	2	14	0.54
Basnahira South	5	2	2	1	0	10	–1.03
Basnahira North	5	2	3	0	2	10	0.04
Sri Lanka Cricket Combined XI	5	1	4	0	1	5	–1.53

Semi-finals

At Moratuwa, February 19, 2010. **Ruhuna won by 39 runs.** ‡**Ruhuna 228** (48.3 overs); **Basnahira South 189** (47 overs).

At Colombo (NCC), February 19, 2010. **Kandurata won by nine wickets. Wayamba 123** (23.4 overs) (M. T. T. Mirando 5-39); ‡**Kandurata 124-1** (20.1 overs).

Final

At Moratuwa, February 21, 2010. **Kandurata won by three wickets.** ‡**Ruhuna 263-7** (50 overs); **Kandurata 264-7** (49.1 overs). *Kandurata captain Kumar Sangakkara helped to secure the title with 76 in 79 balls, including six fours and two sixes.*

INTERPROVINCIAL TWENTY20 TOURNAMENT, 2009-10

	Played	Won	Lost	No result	Bonus points	Points	Net run-rate
Wayamba	5	5	0	0	1	21	1.05
Ruhuna	5	3	2	0	0	12	0.39
Kandurata	5	2	2	1*	1	11	0.20
Basnahira South	5	2	2	1*	1	11	−0.42
Basnahira North	5	2	3	0	1	9	0.37
Sri Lanka Cricket Combined XI	5	0	5	0	0	0	−1.72

* *The match between Basnahira South and Kandurata was originally listed as a win for Basnahira South; after a dispute over the scores which suggested Kandurata might have won, the tournament committee ruled that it should be recorded as a no result, with two points each.*

Semi-finals

At Moratuwa, March 6, 2010. **Wayamba won by nine wickets. Basnahira South 117** (18.4 overs); ‡**Wayamba 122-1** (13.3 overs).

At Moratuwa, March 6, 2010. **Ruhuna won by seven wickets. Kandurata 102** (18.3 overs); ‡**Ruhuna 106-3** (9.4 overs).

Final

At Moratuwa, March 7, 2010. **Wayamba won by 95 runs. Wayamba 208-8** (20 overs); ‡**Ruhuna 113** (13.2 overs). *Wayamba won the Twenty20 title for the third time running after Mahela Jayawardene hit 91 in 49 balls, with ten fours and six sixes, and Ajantha Mendis claimed 4-9 in 3.2 overs.*

WEST INDIAN CRICKET, 2010

New initiatives, old story

TONY COZIER

Confronted once again by a familiar string of depressing results, the West Indies Cricket Board introduced new initiatives and promised more to follow in a glossy magazine-style document called "Transforming West Indies Cricket".

"West Indies cricket is emerging from a challenging period which included issues with the 2007 ICC World Cup, the demise of the Stanford investment in the game, an underperforming men's team, commercial disputes and even player strikes," it pronounced. "The West Indies Cricket Board is undertaking a complete strategic, operational and staffing review covering all areas of activity and seeking to re-establish West Indies cricket as a dominant force in the world game."

Such sentiments came against the background of losses in all 14 one-day and Twenty20 internationals, away and at home, against Australia in February

WEST INDIES IN 2010

	Played	Won	Lost	Drawn/No result
Tests	6	–	2	4
One-day internationals	17	6	10	1
Twenty20 internationals	10	3	7	–

JANUARY		
FEBRUARY	5 ODIs and 2 T20Is (a) v Australia	(page 846)
MARCH	5 ODIs and 1 T20I (h) v Zimbabwe	(page 1117)
APRIL	1 ODI (h) v Canada; 1 ODI (h) v Ireland	(page 1121)
MAY	World Twenty20 (in West Indies)	(page 797)
JUNE	3 Tests, 5 ODIs and 2 T20Is (h) v South Africa	(page 1122)
JULY		
AUGUST		
SEPTEMBER		
OCTOBER		
NOVEMBER	3 Tests (a) v Sri Lanka	(page 1093)
DECEMBER		

Reports from West Indies' ODI series in Sri Lanka in January 2011 will appear in *Wisden 2012*.
For a review of West Indian domestic cricket from the 2009-10 season, see page 1137.

and South Africa in May and June, and two defeats and a high-scoring draw in the Tests against the Proteas. Such disappointments were not tempered by beating Zimbabwe 4–1 in a one-day series at home in May, and three inconclusive rain-ruined Tests in Sri Lanka at the end of the year.

Even the satisfaction of a successful hosting of the ICC's third World Twenty20 championship in May – the plaudits were in marked contrast to the criticism that followed the World Cup three years earlier – was offset by the team's failure, as in that World Cup, to advance past the Super Eight stage. "Those who don't think we have to change are just fooling themselves," said the board's chief executive, Ernest Hilaire. It seemed a self-evident truth, but he would have known not to expect everything to go smoothly.

The two most contentious issues involved four of the most high-profile players. There was an inevitable furore after Ramnaresh Sarwan, a former captain and a proven batsman in 83 Tests over the previous ten years, was excluded from both the list of those given retainer contracts in November and the tour of Sri Lanka a few weeks later. The board's forthright explanation charged Sarwan with an "extremely indifferent attitude and sporadic approach towards fitness". One Guyana Cricket Board official called the decision "a national disgrace". Satisfied that Sarwan had acted on the message and was again ready, the selectors brought him back for the 2011 World Cup.

Denesh Ramdin, almost ever-present as wicketkeeper since 2005, was another to lose his contract. His form, both behind and in front of the stumps, had been patchy but, in the tradition of West Indian insularity, Trinidad and Tobago Cricket Board president Azim Bassarath and T&T's Minister of Sport Anil Roberts demanded reasons; the board considered none necessary.

Chris Gayle, the captain since 2007, and Dwayne Bravo, the vice-captain, were offered contracts, at the highest level, worth US$120,000. But, seduced by the rapidly expanding number of lucrative domestic Twenty20 tournaments around the world, they chose not to sign, becoming free agents instead (or so they thought: the board reminded them that they had to obtain No Objection Certificates to play elsewhere). It effectively eliminated them from their leadership positions and pitchforked St Lucia's Darren Sammy, a borderline all-rounder with only eight Tests since his debut in 2007, into the captaincy. Gayle's response was to amass 333 in his next Test, in Sri Lanka. But he was strangely left on the shelf in the subsequent IPL auction, and his immediate future appeared to lie exclusively with West Indies, contract or no contract.

The regional first-class tournament reverted to one round after one season of a home-and-away format. It was a reduction that especially displeased the West Indies Players Association (WIPA), but the schedule for 2011 was extended, with the inclusion of the England Lions as one of the eight teams and by adding semi-finals and a final after the qualifying games. The board chose to invest more heavily in the A team, with a tour (the first in four years) to Bangladesh, Ireland and England in the summer and a home series against Pakistan in November. It made it plain that such concentration would continue, providing emerging players with early exposure to international cricket.

The board's decision to spend $3m of its 2010-11 budget of $41m on the second, still unsponsored, Caribbean T20 Championship in January, a sum

Worrying outlook: new captain Darren Sammy follows old captain Chris Gayle from the field, Galle, November 2010.

bumped up by the inclusion of Canada and, for the first time, English counties Hampshire and Somerset, was also criticised by WIPA, whose director Michael Hall described it as "a spending spree". Board president Julian Hunte accepted that the tournament would initially operate at a loss; he saw its formative stages as "purely as an investment in a platform for our players to showcase their wares" to the international television viewership, guaranteed through a three-year deal with ESPN. One of those who showcased his wares most strongly in the 2011 event was Marlon Samuels: six months after completing his two-year ICC suspension for involvement with an Indian bookmaker, the graceful Jamaican made an early case for reinstatement to the West Indies team, finishing as the leading scorer.

After years of procrastination, the WICB's High Performance Center was opened at the University of the West Indies campus in June. Headed by Toby Radford, the former Middlesex coach, it had an initial intake of 15 players between the ages of 18 and 22. Early returns on a brief visit to Toronto in the summer and in the regional 50-overs tournament in October were encouraging.

Recognising the belated growth, and strength, of women's cricket, evident in West Indies' semi-final place in the World Twenty20, the WICB placed six female players under contract for the first time. Among them were opener Stafanie Taylor, who rose to second in the ICC's batting ratings, and Deandra Dottin, who smashed a century – the first in women's Twenty20 internationals – during the World Twenty20, a few weeks before her 19th birthday. Performances in a six-nation ICC tournament in South Africa and in limited-overs matches on a later brief tour of India confirmed the improvement. Such progress by their male counterparts was long overdue.

WEST INDIES v ZIMBABWE, 2009-10

TONY COZIER

One-day internationals (5): West Indies 4, Zimbabwe 1
Twenty20 international (1): West Indies 0, Zimbabwe 1

Two teams glued to the lower rungs of the ICC one-day ratings simply marked time on Zimbabwe's brief tour of West Indies, their first outside Africa and the Indian subcontinent since the 2007 World Cup in the Caribbean.

Neither side learned much about themselves in the six limited-overs matches. The sequence was similar to their previous encounter, in Zimbabwe two years earlier, when Zimbabwe won the first match only to lose the next three. This time, just three days after their players returned from crushing defeat in their one-day series in Australia, West Indies were beaten in the first two matches before finding their land legs to take the next four.

Apart from their overwhelming victory by 141 runs in the second 50-over game, West Indies' performances were unconvincing. Patience and batting technique – in the absence of the injured Ramnaresh Sarwan – were tested to the limit by Zimbabwe's many spinners on turning pitches. Ottis Gibson's first venture since his appointment as West Indian head coach, following the abortive stints of the Australians Bennett King and John Dyson, would have alerted him to the daunting task ahead.

Once Chris Gayle returned after taking a break from the Twenty20 international, he found himself burdened with the responsibility of providing early momentum to innings that often subsided after his dismissal. More significant than his three half-centuries were his heated comments after the loss in the first one-day international: "When you do crap, it's definitely crap and there is no excuse," the usually super-cool captain fumed. "Guys have to take responsibility out there in the middle. It is just sad and disappointing."

He identified three of the "guys" at fault as Dwayne Smith, who was promptly discarded for the series, Denesh Ramdin, who was dropped for the next match, and Kieron Pollard, who did nothing to indicate he was worth the US$790,000 IPL contract he had signed a month earlier.

Amid the struggles of others, the Guyana left-hander Narsingh Deonarine dealt competently with the varied Zimbabwean spin through quick feet and a level head. Twice his presence was vital as West Indies made mountains out of molehill targets.

Against batting even shakier than his own team's, and in spite of slow pitches, Kemar Roach confirmed the value of genuine pace in any form of the game. His colleagues were capable enough, but only once were they able to convert Zimbabwe's top-order meltdowns into complete routs.

Zimbabwe were also under new guidance. After ending their protracted self-imposed exiles over differences with the board, three former captains were back in management positions: Alistair Campbell was chief selector, Heath Streak bowling coach and Dave Houghton batting consultant. During the tour,

Alan Butcher, the one-Test England batsman, was appointed head coach. Their stated aim was to regain, within 18 months, the Test status their board voluntarily forsook in 2006; this trip was seen as the first step.

Given the conditions they encountered, they understandably opted to stack their hand with their strongest suit, spin. The seasoned left-armer Ray Price bowled as economically as usual, while Graeme Cremer looked a very competent leg-spinner. As a consequence, the quick bowlers had little chance to prove their worth, confined to 30 overs between them in the five one-day internationals.

The bespectacled opener Vusi Sibanda made 95 as Zimbabwe won the first one-dayer, in Providence; there were other half-centuries from Tatenda Taibu, Elton Chigumbura (whose all-round talent earned him a contract with Northamptonshire midway through the tour) and, in surprisingly his only match, Charles Coventry. But repeatedly Zimbabwe had to recover from early disasters.

It would have been more useful for them to have encountered true, hard pitches as a test of their all-round strength. The problem is that such conditions are presently rare anywhere in the Caribbean, a worry for West Indies as much as anyone else.

ZIMBABWEAN TOURING PARTY

*P. Utseya, E. Chigumbura, C. K. Coventry, A. G. Cremer, K. M. Jarvis, G. A. Lamb, T. Maruma, H. Masakadza, S. W. Masakadza, S. Matsikenyeri, C. B. Mpofu, R. W. Price, V. Sibanda, T. Taibu, B. R. M. Taylor. *Interim coach:* W. R. Chawaguta.

At St Augustine, Trinidad, February 26, 2010. **Zimbabweans won by five runs. ‡Zimbabweans 281** (49.2 overs) (H. Masakadza 38, T. Taibu 107); **University of West Indies Vice-Chancellor's XI 276-8** (50 overs) (K. C. Brathwaite 80, N. Parris 73).

The Vice-Chancellor's XI looked set for victory after the Barbadians Kraigg Brathwaite and Nekoli Parris put on 136 for the third wicket, but in the end they fell just short. Earlier Tatenda Taibu faced 92 balls and hit 11 fours and a six in his 107.

WEST INDIES v ZIMBABWE

Twenty20 International

At Port-of-Spain, Trinidad, February 28, 2010. Zimbabwe won by 26 runs. Toss: Zimbabwe. Twenty20 international debuts: A. B. Barath, D. M. Bravo; G. A. Lamb, S. W. Masakadza.

Given the new ball, the beanpole left-arm spinner Benn bowled Sibanda with the first delivery of the match and removed Taibu, Matsikenyeri and Taylor in his first three overs, all four without scoring (there were eight ducks in all in the match, a Twenty20 international record). At 11 for four halfway through the fifth over, Zimbabwe's swift demise seemed certain. However, on an unsatisfactory pitch, offering encouraging turn to the spinners (of which West Indies had only Benn), Hamilton Masakadza and Chigumbura led a partial revival with contrasting innings. Masakadza's 44 occupied 57 balls, Chigumbura's 34 only 19; in total, 29 runs came from the last two overs, even though three of Sammy's five wickets came in the last. Without Gayle (who asked for the match off) and Dwayne Bravo (fractured thumb), West Indies laboured against Zimbabwe's spin – only two overs, late on, were delivered by medium-pacers. In an extraordinarily inept batting display they managed only one six and two fours between them on the way to West Indies' lowest total in a Twenty20 international; leg-spinner Cremer collected the match award for his three wickets, which included Pollard and Darren Bravo with successive balls.

Man of the Match: A. G. Cremer.

Zimbabwe

		B	4	6
V. Sibanda b 10	0	1	0	0
H. Masakadza c 6 b 8	44	57	3	1
†T. Taibu lbw b 10	0	7	0	0
S. Matsikenyeri c 6 b 10.....	0	2	0	0
B. R. M. Taylor b 10..........	0	3	0	0
G. A. Lamb b 8	11	28	0	0
E. Chigumbura c 1 b 8	34	19	2	2
A. G. Cremer b 9.............	2	3	0	0
S. W. Masakadza c 4 b 8......	0	2	0	0
*P. Utseya b 8	0	1	0	0
R. W. Price not out	0	0	0	0
L-b 6, w 4, n-b 4	14			

6 overs: 13-4   (19.5 overs)   105

1/0 2/0 3/0 4/11 5/51 6/74 7/98 8/104 9/104

Benn 4-2-6-4; Roach 4-1-15-0; Rampaul 4-0-28-1; Pollard 4-0-24-0; Sammy 3.5-0-26-5.

West Indies

		B	4	6
A. B. Barath b 11	8	19	1	0
S. Chanderpaul lbw b 6	20	30	1	0
A. D. S. Fletcher c 9 b 10	0	2	0	0
K. A. Pollard b 8............	1	4	0	0
D. M. Bravo lbw b 8	0	1	0	0
*†D. Ramdin not out	23	36	1	0
D. R. Smith c 10 b 6	12	15	0	1
D. J. G. Sammy b 8...........	2	4	0	0
R. Rampaul not out	3	9	0	0
W 10.....................	10			

6 overs: 21-1   (20 overs)   79-7

1/21 2/24 3/32 4/32 5/39 6/57 7/65

S. J. Benn and K. A. J. Roach did not bat.

Utseya 4-0-12-1; Price 4-1-18-1; Cremer 4-0-11-3; Lamb 4-0-14-2; Matsikenyeri 1-0-10-0; Taylor 1-0-1-0; Chigumbura 1-0-7-0; S. W. Masakadza 1-0-6-0.

Umpires: C. R. Duncan and N. A. Malcolm.   Third umpire: G. E. Greaves.
Referee: R. S. Mahanama.

At Providence, Guyana, March 4, 2010. **First one-day international: Zimbabwe won by two runs.** ‡**Zimbabwe 254-5** (50 overs) (H. Masakadza 41, V. Sibanda 95, T. Taibu 56); **West Indies 252-9** (50 overs) (C. H. Gayle 57, A. B. Barath 50, S. Chanderpaul 70; S. W. Masakadza 3-36). *MoM:* V. Sibanda. *One-day international debuts:* A. B. Barath (West Indies); G. A. Lamb, S. W. Masakadza (Zimbabwe). *West Indies needed 15 off the final over, which was boldly given to the debutant Shingirai Masakadza (Hamilton's brother), whose previous two overs had cost 24; when Nikita Miller hit the first three balls for six, four and one, the rest seemed straightforward. But Masakadza kept his head, while Dwayne Smith and Benn didn't, falling to the fourth and fifth balls, then Roach could only scramble a single off the last. Sibanda's 95 from 162 deliveries – and his partnerships of 67 with Hamilton Masakadza and 100 with the sprightly Taibu – was the foundation of Zimbabwe's challenging total; he finally fell to a rapid Roach yorker which broke his bat on the way through to the stumps. Chigumbura's 27 off 22 balls saw to it that the last five overs, including the batting powerplay, yielded 52. Gayle and Barath set West Indies on course with an opening stand of 99, but once they were dismissed only Chanderpaul's run-a-ball 70 escaped Gayle's post-match wrath.*

At Providence, Guyana, March 6, 2010. **Second one-day international: West Indies won by four wickets.** ‡**Zimbabwe 206** (49.5 overs) (B. R. M. Taylor 47, T. Taibu 31, E. Chigumbura 50; K. A. J. Roach 3-37, N. O. Miller 4-43); **West Indies 208-6** (47.5 overs) (C. H. Gayle 88, N. Deonarine 65*). *MoM:* N. Deonarine. *Batsmen toiled again on a slow, turning pitch; West Indies needed Deonarine's unruffled 65* from 85 balls to square the series after Gayle fell for 88 to Cremer's googly in the 42nd over. Slow left-armer Nikita Miller returned his best figures for West Indies, but the brakes were applied more by the off-spin of Gayle (10–0–25–1). Taylor and Taibu spent 14.1 overs adding 59 before Chigumbura's typically aggressive 50 and his partnership of 73 with Greg Lamb (23) helped inch Zimbabwe past 200.*

At Arnos Vale, St Vincent, March 10, 2010. **Third one-day international: West Indies won by 141 runs. West Indies 245-9** (50 overs) (C. H. Gayle 33, A. B. Barath 35, S. Chanderpaul 58); ‡**Zimbabwe 104** (31.5 overs) (H. Masakadza 35; K. A. J. Roach 3-28, D. J. G. Sammy 4-26). *MoM:* D. J. G. Sammy. *Zimbabwe's last nine wickets tumbled for 53 in 22 overs, and only the final pair took them into three figures. West Indies' innings was built around Chanderpaul's diligent 58 off 76 balls but, on another sluggish pitch, impatient batsmen kept offering their wickets to Zimbabwe's spin-based attack. While Masakadza and Taylor were scoring at five an over – they put on 51 for the second wicket – a close match seemed in prospect, but Sammy removed them both, then he and the other pacemen scythed through some limp batting.*

At Arnos Vale, St Vincent, March 12, 2010. **Fourth one-day international: West Indies won by four wickets. Zimbabwe 141** (48.2 overs) (E. Chigumbura 42; D. J. Bravo 4-21); ‡**West Indies 142-6** (34.3 overs) (C. H. Gayle 32, N. Deonarine 32*; A. G. Cremer 3-34). *MoM:* D. J. Bravo. *Sent in on a pitch that encouraged the home bowlers with its bounce and movement, Zimbabwe were 62-6 after 19 overs, and in severe danger of another heavy defeat as Rampaul and Bravo made inroads. But Chigumbura responded in typically forthright fashion, hitting three sixes and two fours in his 42; he dominated a partnership of 41 with Cremer, whose impressive leg-spin then made West Indies fight hard to reach their modest target. Barath and Gayle put on 46 in just 6.1 overs for the first wicket but, as in the second match, it required Deonarine's composure to carry West Indies to the victory that clinched the series.*

At Arnos Vale, St Vincent, March 14, 2010. **Fifth one-day international: West Indies won by four wickets. Zimbabwe 161** (50 overs) (C. K. Coventry 56; D. J. G. Sammy 3-33); ‡**West Indies 165-6** (27.4 overs) (C. H. Gayle 63, K. A. Pollard 36). *MoM:* C. H. Gayle. *Man of the Series:* C. H. Gayle. *Zimbabwe had to overcome another appalling start – they were 25-5 after 15.4 overs and 63-6 after 25.1 – to stay in contention. In his only match of the series, Coventry batted enterprisingly for 56 off 88 balls, while Lamb and Cremer made useful contributions to ensure that all 50 overs were used up. As Gayle lashed two sixes and eight fours in 63 off 41 balls, West Indies' victory seemed a formality, but after he hoisted a catch to long-off the batting again faltered against spin, until Pollard's strong-arm methods – 36 off 20 balls, with three sixes and three fours – settled the issue.*

OTHER INTERNATIONAL CRICKET IN THE WEST INDIES

West Indies v Canada

At Kingston, April 13, 2010. **One-day international: West Indies won by 208 runs.** ‡**West Indies 316-4** (50 overs) (A. D. S. Fletcher 48, S. Chanderpaul 101, D. M. Bravo 74, R. R. Sarwan 47*, N. Deonarine 31); **Canada 108** (39.2 overs) (U. Bhatti 32*; N. O. Miller 3-15). *MoM:* S. Chanderpaul. *One-day international debut:* P. A. Desai (Canada). *West Indies continued their preparations for the World Twenty20 with a crushing victory, led by Chanderpaul's 11th one-day international century: he and Darren Bravo added 143 for the second wicket in 23 overs. Canada dipped to 61-7 after 17 overs, and only a determined 78-ball innings from No. 8 Umar Bhatti inched them into three figures. Canada also played three other matches on their short tour, losing a 50-over game to Jamaica and Twenty20 matches to Jamaica and a strong West Indies XI, led by Darren Sammy.*

Jamaica v Ireland

At Spanish Town, Jamaica, April 3–5, 2010. **Drawn.** ‡**Jamaica 339** (D. P. Hyatt 55, T. L. Lambert 68, D. E. Bernard 102; P. Connell 4-77) **and 314-7 dec** (D. P. Hyatt 53, B. A. Parchment 83, A. D. Russell 108*); **Ireland 275** (P. R. Stirling 65, N. J. O'Brien 62, A. R. Cusack 53; A. D. Russell 4-41, A. M. A. Dewar 4-81). *Andre Russell followed up his best bowling in first-class cricket with a maiden century – from 62 balls, with nine sixes and seven fours – as all 11 Ireland players bowled as the match drifted towards a draw on the final day. Ireland's short tour also included 20- and 50-over matches against Jamaica, an official one-day international (see below), and three Twenty20 games against a West Indies XI, who won all three matches.*

West Indies v Ireland

At Kingston, April 15, 2010. **One-day international: West Indies won by six wickets** (D/L method). ‡**Ireland 219** (50 overs) (P. R. Stirling 51, N. J. O'Brien 49, K. J. O'Brien 54; D. E. Bernard 3-32); **West Indies 213-4** (44 overs) (R. R. Sarwan 100*, N. Deonarine 57). *MoM:* R. R. Sarwan. *One-day international debut:* G. H. Dockrell (Ireland). *Rain early in West Indies' reply – by which time they were teetering at 9-2 after 5.2 overs – meant their target was revised to 213 from 45 overs. Sarwan calmly ensured victory with an over to spare, hitting 11 fours in his fourth one-day international century and putting on 111 in 17 overs with Deonarine for the fourth wicket.*

WEST INDIES v SOUTH AFRICA, 2010

CRAIG COZIER

Test matches (3): West Indies 0, South Africa 2
One-day internationals (5): West Indies 0, South Africa 5
Twenty20 internationals (2): West Indies 0, South Africa 2

A series that started only a few days after the highly successful World Twenty20 carnival in the Caribbean was always likely to be an anticlimax, and so it proved – at least for the home side. South Africa swiftly put yet another world tournament let-down behind them, producing the kind of consistently clinical cricket that had led to their flirting with the No. 1 ranking in all forms of the game over the previous two years.

West Indies, who like South Africa failed to qualify for the knockout stage of the World Twenty20 (despite home advantage, just as in the 2007 World Cup), caved in at key moments and failed to win a match of any duration. They came closest in the shorter formats, throwing away favourable positions in the second Twenty20 game and the final one-day international, which meant they lost all seven limited-overs matches. They avoided the whitewash in the Tests mainly through a featherbed of a pitch at St Kitts that consigned the second match to a run-soaked draw almost from the first delivery.

Low attendances, except for the two one-day internationals in Dominica, reflected a surfeit of cricket, public disenchantment with their team's continuing struggles, and a clash with the football World Cup, not necessarily in that order.

Crucial injuries handicapped West Indies, who lacked the reserve strength of the South Africans. Fidel Edwards (back) and Adrian Barath (leg) missed all the matches with long-term ailments, while Ramnaresh Sarwan ruptured a hamstring and Jerome Taylor damaged his hip early on.

The gulf in quality between the sides was more obvious in the Tests. Dale Steyn and Morne Morkel, polar opposites in stature and style, made for an uncomfortable new-ball proposition, and exposed some technically ill-equipped batsmen. Steyn, lean and always mean, earned the series award for his 15 wickets, which came via a combination of controlled aggression and each-way reverse swing. Morkel, 6ft 6in tall, obtained steepling bounce, even on uncooperative pitches, which brought him most of his 14 wickets.

Of the visiting batsmen, Graeme Smith, Jacques Kallis and A. B. de Villiers prospered against the inexperienced home attack. De Villiers was prolific throughout, even when burdened with the added responsibility of keeping wicket in the limited-overs games, as South Africa prepared for life after Mark Boucher. Still only 33, Boucher accepted the tactical demotion through gritted teeth, and at Warner Park had the satisfaction of claiming an unprecedented 500th Test victim.

Smith and Kallis enhanced already glowing reputations, while in the first and last Tests Ashwell Prince's solidity helped restore faltering innings. Such

Arms and the man: Mark Boucher became the first wicketkeeper to make 500 Test dismissals.

successes were counterbalanced by the regression of Alviro Petersen and J-P. Duminy, whose faltering form cost him his Test place.

Left-arm spinner Paul Harris sent down 46 more overs than any of his team-mates in the Tests, although his was a holding role rather than an attacking one. Off-spinner Johan Botha, picked at Bridgetown for his third Test after more than two years out, made an immediate impact with his remedied action; he seemed unlikely to wait as long again for his next opportunity.

West Indies' lone star was, almost inevitably, Shivnarine Chanderpaul, who continued to compile impressive numbers in his 36th year. His 22nd Test century, occupying six hours in Warner Park's generous environment, was as predictable as those of Smith, Kallis and de Villiers preceding it.

Kemar Roach led the attack gamely, but was hindered by back-up – Ravi Rampaul and the debutants Nelon Pascal and Brandon Bess – which was woefully short of experience and class. What quality there was came from Sulieman Benn's left-arm spin, but his performance was once again tarnished by poor behaviour – he received his second ICC Code of Conduct suspension in a few months, and was also sent off the field by Chris Gayle in the fourth one-day international after refusing an instruction to bowl over the wicket.

A previously uneventful series came to a bitter end over the last two days. Steyn was fined his full match fee by Jeff Crowe for spitting in Benn's direction after his dismissal, prompting Benn's angry incursion into the South African dressing-room which led to his ban. And the final images were of a mid-pitch flare-up between Roach and Kallis, which cost Roach half his match fee.

It was an explosive and unseemly end – if not an entirely surprising one – to a long season for both teams.

SOUTH AFRICAN TOURING PARTY

*G. C. Smith, H. M. Amla, J. Botha, M. V. Boucher, A. B. de Villiers, J-P. Duminy, P. L. Harris, J. H. Kallis, R. McLaren, M. Morkel, A. N. Petersen, A. G. Prince, D. W. Steyn, L. L. Tsotsobe. *Coach:* C. J. P. G. van Zyl.

For the Twenty20 and one-day internationals which started the tour, L. E. Bosman, C. K. Langeveldt, D. A. Miller and R. E. van der Merwe replaced Harris and Prince. W. D. Parnell was originally selected for the whole tour, but failed to recover from a groin injury; he was replaced by Miller for the limited-overs matches.

TEST MATCH AVERAGES

WEST INDIES – BATTING AND FIELDING

	T	I	NO	R	HS	100s	50s	Avge	Ct/St
†S. Chanderpaul	3	5	1	300	166	1	1	75.00	2
D. J. Bravo	3	5	0	166	61	0	2	33.20	4
†N. Deonarine	3	5	0	163	65	0	1	32.60	1
†C. H. Gayle	3	5	0	159	73	0	2	31.80	2
†B. P. Nash	3	5	0	142	114	1	0	28.40	1
†R. Rampaul	2	3	1	49	31	0	0	24.50	4
†S. J. Benn	3	5	0	101	42	0	0	20.20	1
D. Ramdin	3	5	1	63	27	0	0	15.75	3/1
S. Shillingford	3	5	0	59	27	0	0	11.80	5
K. A. J. Roach	2	3	1	11	8	0	0	5.50	1
T. M. Dowlin	2	3	0	15	10	0	0	5.00	1

Played in one Test: B. J. Bess 11*, 0; N. T. Pascal 2, 10 (1 ct); D. M. Richards 0, 17 (1 ct).

BOWLING

	Style	O	M	R	W	BB	5W/i	Avge
S. J. Benn	SLA	176.4	32	460	15	6-81	2	30.66
K. A. J. Roach	RF	64.4	14	186	6	3-22	0	31.00
S. Shillingford	OB	163	16	521	9	3-96	0	57.88

Also bowled: B. J. Bess (RFM) 13–0–92–1; D. J. Bravo (RFM) 76.4–25–180–2; N. Deonarine (OB) 3–0–20–0; T. M. Dowlin (OB) 1–0–3–0; C. H. Gayle (OB) 3–1–4–1; B. P. Nash (LM) 13–4–18–0; N. T. Pascal (RF) 17–2–59–0; R. Rampaul (RFM) 45–9–149–0.

SOUTH AFRICA – BATTING AND FIELDING

	T	I	NO	R	HS	100s	50s	Avge	Ct
A. B. de Villiers	3	6	4	331	135*	1	2	165.50	4
†A. G. Prince	3	4	2	160	78*	0	2	80.00	2
J. H. Kallis	3	6	2	283	110	1	1	70.75	4
†G. C. Smith	3	6	0	371	132	1	2	61.83	2
M. V. Boucher	3	3	0	103	69	0	1	34.33	10
D. W. Steyn	3	3	0	63	39	0	0	31.50	1
A. N. Petersen	3	6	0	151	52	0	1	25.16	4
H. M. Amla	3	6	0	122	44	0	0	20.33	1

Played in three Tests: P. L. Harris 10, 11 (1 ct); †M. Morkel 2, 9. Played in two Tests: L. L. Tsotsobe 3*. Played in one Test: J. Botha 9 (1 ct).

BOWLING

	Style	O	M	R	W	BB	5W/i	Avge
J. Botha	OB	39.5	7	102	7	4-56	0	14.57
D. W. Steyn	RF	82.3	17	272	15	5-29	1	18.13
M. Morkel	RF	83.2	26	265	14	4-19	0	18.92
J. H. Kallis	RFM	56.1	13	166	5	2-36	0	33.20
P. L. Harris	SLA	129.3	19	358	5	2-91	0	71.60

Also bowled: A. N. Petersen (RM) 7–1–21–1; G. C. Smith (OB) 0.3–0–4–0; L. L. Tsotsobe (LFM) 49–15–106–2.

WEST INDIES v SOUTH AFRICA

First Twenty20 International

At North Sound, Antigua, May 19, 2010. South Africa won by 13 runs. Toss: West Indies. Twenty20 international debut: A. N. Petersen.

The Sir Vivian Richards Stadium returned to the international roster rather sooner than expected, when the West Indian board decided to move the first four tour matches from Port-of-Spain after a general election was called in Trinidad for May 24. An ICC inspection team rubber-stamped the decision, ending the ban imposed after the sandy debacle of England's abandoned ten-ball Test in February 2009. There were no issues with the outfield this time, but an unpredictable pitch contributed to a low-scoring contest. Both teams were eager to erase their disappointments in the World Twenty20, which had ended only three days earlier, but the thousand or so spectators witnessed a bizarre start as Bosman walked for a leg-side catch behind even as umpire Duncan signalled wide. Kallis's experience shone through as he guided his side to a competitive total. West Indies' pursuit never took off once McLaren removed both openers, although Pollard threatened briefly before a yorker ensured the chase petered out. McLaren's five for 19, including an underarm stumping by the experimental wicketkeeper de Villiers standing back, was the second-best return in this format.

Man of the Match: R. McLaren.

South Africa

		B	4	6
*G. C. Smith *st 2 b 8*	37	31	3	1
L. E. Bosman *c 2 b 9*	7	12	0	0
J. H. Kallis *c 4 b 6*	53	45	1	3
†A. B. de Villiers *c 9 b 6*	11	14	0	0
J-P. Duminy *b 11*	0	1	0	0
J. Botha *c 2 b 11*	0	2	0	0
A. N. Petersen *run out*	6	7	1	0
R. McLaren *not out*	6	6	0	0
R. E. van der Merwe *not out*	4	3	0	0
L-b 3, w 4, n-b 5	12			

6 overs: 33-1   (20 overs)   136-7

1/15 2/88 3/111 4/115 5/115 6/122 7/127

D. W. Steyn and C. K. Langeveldt did not bat.

12th man: H. M. Amla.

Roach 4–0–25–2; Taylor 3–0–16–1; Benn 3–0–20–0; Sammy 2–0–11–0; Bravo 1–0–14–0; Gayle 1–0–12–0; Miller 2–0–13–1; Pollard 4–0–22–2.

West Indies

		B	4	6
*C. H. Gayle *c 1 b 8*	14	16	2	0
†A. D. S. Fletcher *c 4 b 8*	0	3	0	0
D. J. Bravo *c 12 b 6*	20	22	2	0
R. R. Sarwan *c 7 b 9*	13	20	1	0
N. Deonarine *st 4 b 6*	0	0	0	0
K. A. Pollard *b 8*	27	17	2	1
D. J. G. Sammy *st 4 b 8*	17	28	1	0
N. O. Miller *c 4 b 11*	5	6	0	0
J. E. Taylor *run out*	7	2	0	1
S. J. Benn *c 12 b 8*	4	4	1	0
K. A. J. Roach *not out*	3	2	0	0
L-b 1, w 11, n-b 1	13			

6 overs: 31-2   (19.5 overs)   123

1/14 2/28 3/48 4/50 5/52 6/88 7/99 8/111 9/120

Van der Merwe 3–0–17–1; Steyn 4–0–23–0; McLaren 3.5–0–19–5; Langeveldt 3–0–31–1; Kallis 2–0–13–0; Botha 4–0–19–2.

Umpires: C. R. Duncan and N. A. Malcolm.   Third umpire: C. E. Mack.

WEST INDIES v SOUTH AFRICA

Second Twenty20 International

At North Sound, Antigua, May 20, 2010. South Africa won by one run. Toss: West Indies. Twenty20 international debut: D. A. Miller.

On another challenging pitch, South Africa slipped to 59 for five in the 13th over before the 20-year-old left-hander David Miller, not long off the plane after a successful tour of Bangladesh with the A-team, smacked his sixth ball for six, and quickly added another. Botha was more measured during their stand of 57 from 42 balls, which set up a decent target. Gayle fell in Steyn's first over and Fletcher soon followed, but Bravo and Chanderpaul added 68 in 12 overs: when Chanderpaul gloved a reverse sweep off Botha, West Indies needed 44 from 32 deliveries. Botha then held a spiralling catch off Bravo, and eventually 15 were wanted from McLaren's final over. Sammy managed two fours (one all-run), but West Indies couldn't hold their nerve to seal the deal. Deonarine was run out seeking a second off the penultimate ball, and Taylor could only squeeze a single off the last when three were needed.

Man of the Match: J. Botha.

South Africa		*B*	*4*	*6*
*G. C. Smith *b 9*		15	18	2 0
L. E. Bosman *c 2 b 9*		0	3	0 0
†A. B. de Villiers *c 3 b 7*		19	17	1 1
J-P. Duminy *c 2 b 7*		13	20	1 0
A. N. Petersen *lbw b 10*		8	12	0 0
D. A. Miller *run out*		33	26	0 2
J. Botha *c 6 b 9*		23	22	0 2
R. McLaren *not out*		1	2	0 0
B 1, l-b 5, w 2		8		

6 overs: 32-2   (20 overs)   120-7

1/6 2/27 3/42 4/57 5/59 6/116 7/120

D. W. Steyn, M. Morkel and L. L. Tsotsobe did not bat.

Roach 4–0–24–0; Taylor 4–1–14–3; Benn 3–0–26–1; Bravo 4–0–20–0; Sammy 4–0–16–2; Pollard 1–0–14–0.

West Indies		*B*	*4*	*6*
*C. H. Gayle *lbw b 9*		0	2	0 0
†A. D. S. Fletcher *c 3 b 10*		4	11	0 0
D. J. Bravo *c 7 b 10*		40	42	1 2
S. Chanderpaul *c 3 b 7*		29	37	2 1
K. A. Pollard *c 9 b 7*		12	13	1 0
R. R. Sarwan *c 8 b 7*		6	6	1 0
D. J. G. Sammy *not out*		12	6	1 0
N. Deonarine *run out*		3	2	0 0
J. E. Taylor *not out*		1	1	0 0
B 5, l-b 2, w 5		12		

6 overs: 17-2   (20 overs)   119-7

1/4 2/9 3/77 4/87 5/97 6/99 7/118

S. J. Benn and K. A. J. Roach did not bat.

Steyn 4–0–18–1; Tsotsobe 4–0–28–0; Morkel 4–0–15–2; Botha 4–0–22–3; McLaren 4–0–29–0.

Umpires: C. R. Duncan and N. A. Malcolm.   Third umpire: G. E. Greaves.
Series referee: R. S. Mahanama.

WEST INDIES v SOUTH AFRICA

First One-Day International

At North Sound, Antigua, May 22, 2010. South Africa won by 66 runs (D/L method). Toss: West Indies. One-day international debut: D. A. Miller.

South Africa's formidable total was built around an unfussed second one-day international hundred from Amla, while de Villiers strode to his third in successive innings – the fourth batsman to do this after Zaheer Abbas, Saeed Anwar and Herschelle Gibbs. The tourists had looked shaky at 57 for two after Bravo's double strike removed Smith and Kallis, but Amla – who passed 1,000 runs in one-dayers in 24 innings, a record for a South African – quickly regained the initiative in a partnership of 129 in 25 overs with the equally fluent de Villiers. West Indies' target was raised slightly to 282, as rain shortly after the start had reduced this to a 48-over match, but it made no difference: though six of the top seven reached double figures, Gayle's 45 was the highest in a morale-sapping defeat. Morkel removed the three leading scorers.

Man of the Match: H. M. Amla.

South Africa

H. M. Amla b Rampaul	102	R. McLaren c Gayle b Taylor	1
*G. C. Smith b Ramdin c Bravo	18	D. W. Steyn not out	2
J. H. Kallis c Rampaul b Bravo	1	L-b 2, w 10, n-b 1	13
†A. B. de Villiers c Sarwan b Taylor	102		
J-P. Duminy b Rampaul	15	1/53 (2) 2/57 (3) (7 wkts, 48 overs) 280	
D. A. Miller not out	23	3/186 (1) 4/240 (5)	
J. Botha b Bravo	3	5/259 (4) 6/265 (7) 7/268 (8) 10 overs: 62-2	

M. Morkel and L. L. Tsotsobe did not bat.

Taylor 10–0–62–2; Rampaul 10–1–46–2; Sammy 2–0–25–0; Bravo 10–0–40–3; Miller 7–0–46–0; Gayle 5–0–27–0; Pollard 3–0–19–0; Deonarine 1–0–13–0.

West Indies

A. D. S. Fletcher c Kallis b Steyn	3	J. E. Taylor lbw b Botha	0
*C. H. Gayle c Botha b Morkel	45	R. Rampaul c Smith b Tsotsobe	3
D. J. Bravo c de Villiers b McLaren	15		
R. R. Sarwan b Morkel	38	L-b 2, w 6, n-b 1	9
N. Deonarine c Kallis b Botha	26		
†D. Ramdin b Steyn	17	1/4 (1) 2/44 (3) 3/69 (2) (44.1 overs) 215	
K. A. Pollard c McLaren b Morkel	44	4/130 (5) 5/140 (4) 6/192 (6)	
D. J. G. Sammy c Kallis b McLaren	2	7/197 (8) 8/203 (8)	
N. O. Miller not out	13	9/205 (10) 10/215 (11) 10 overs: 49-2	

Steyn 8–0–37–2; Tsotsobe 6.1–0–34–1; McLaren 9–1–37–2; Morkel 8–1–40–3; Botha 10–0–47–2; Kallis 3–0–18–0.

Umpires: D. J. Harper and N. A. Malcolm.   Third umpire: C. R. Duncan.

WEST INDIES v SOUTH AFRICA

Second One-Day International

At North Sound, Antigua, May 24, 2010. South Africa won by 17 runs. Toss: South Africa.

With the outcome seemingly already settled, Sammy blasted six sixes and two fours in an unbeaten 58 from 24 balls – but South Africa held off the late surge to secure victory. Their lofty total was built on successive partnerships of 89, 79 and 71: Amla followed his century two days earlier with some more classic strokeplay for 92 off 95 balls, while Kallis, in his 300th one-day international, contributed 85 off 89. West Indies' chase was suffocated by the early loss of Gayle, to Morkel, and Sarwan, to a pulled hamstring; he resumed later but was out first ball, and missed the rest of South Africa's tour. Dale Richards stroked 51 in his first international for eight months, but the required rate soared. Bravo made a defiant 74, but when he and the limping Sarwan departed to successive balls it looked all over at 236 for eight. However, Sammy – dropped off Morkel when two – kept his team in the hunt. His fifty arrived off 20 balls, West Indies' fastest (beating Brian Lara's 23 balls against Canada in the 2003 World Cup), but his efforts fell short as his last two partners were run out in the frenetic final stages.

Man of the Match: H. M. Amla.

South Africa

*G. C. Smith b Miller	37	R. McLaren not out	8
H. M. Amla c Richards b Taylor	92	B 1, l-b 4, w 5	10
J. H. Kallis c Richards b Pollard	85		
†A. B. de Villiers c Taylor b Pollard	41	1/89 (1) 2/168 (2) (5 wkts, 50 overs) 300	
D. A. Miller not out	26	3/239 (4) 4/276 (3)	
A. N. Petersen lbw b Taylor	1	5/278 (6) 10 overs: 54-0	

J. Botha, D. W. Steyn, M. Morkel and L. L. Tsotsobe did not bat.

Taylor 9–0–50–2; Rampaul 8–0–58–0; Bravo 10–0–63–0; Miller 2.5–0–19–1; Gayle 7.1–0–41–0; Sammy 5–0–25–0; Pollard 8–0–39–2.

West Indies

*C. H. Gayle c McLaren b Morkel	26	R. Rampaul run out	5
D. M. Richards b Kallis	51	N. O. Miller run out	0
R. R. Sarwan c de Villiers b Botha	6		
N. Deonarine c Miller b Tsotsobe	7	B 1, l-b 6, w 12	19
D. J. Bravo c Kallis b Steyn	74		
K. A. Pollard c Botha b Morkel	29	1/40 (1) 2/77 (4) 3/119 (2) (48.1 overs)	283
J. E. Taylor b Morkel	6	4/182 (6) 5/189 (7) 6/200 (8)	
†D. Ramdin run out	2	7/236 (5) 8/236 (3) 9/283 (10)	
D. J. G. Sammy not out	58	10/283 (11) 10 overs: 40-0	

Sarwan, when 6, retired hurt at 50 and resumed at 236-7.

Steyn 10–0–59–1; Tsotsobe 9–1–53–1; Morkel 9.1–2–58–3; McLaren 7–1–41–0; Botha 10–0–58–1; Kallis 3–0–7–1.

Umpires: C. R. Duncan and D. J. Harper.   Third umpire: C. E. Mack.

WEST INDIES v SOUTH AFRICA

Third One-Day International

At Roseau, Dominica, May 28, 2010. South Africa won by 67 runs. Toss: South Africa.

Morkel's career-best figures made up for his side's disappointing batting, and ensured a crushing victory, with 12 overs to spare, to seal the series. West Indies' pursuit of a modest 225 was in high gear at 59 for one in the 12th over before Morkel changed the course of the match, removing Richards and Darren Bravo in the space of four deliveries: after four overs he had two for five. Once Chanderpaul was out, the rest of the batting surrendered meekly. Taylor typified West Indian fatalism when he casually trotted through for a single only to be run out by Steyn's direct hit from mid-on. Only Dwayne Bravo was blameless, undone by a vicious Steyn bouncer that he fended to the wicketkeeper. South Africa's innings had promised much more after a third successive half-century opening from Amla and Smith, but Pollard's three wickets and Benn's direct hit to run out de Villiers from long-off after a fine 70 sparked a collapse, the last five wickets tumbling for 18 runs.

Man of the Match: A. B. de Villiers.

South Africa

H. M. Amla b Benn	34	M. Morkel c D. M. Bravo b Pollard	14
*G. C. Smith lbw b D. J. Bravo	29	C. K. Langeveldt not out	0
J. H. Kallis c Sammy b Benn	31		
†A. B. de Villiers run out	70	L-b 2	2
A. N. Petersen b Pollard	16		
D. A. Miller c Ramdin b Taylor	5	1/53 (1) 2/91 (2) 3/113 (3) (47.2 overs)	224
J. Botha c and b D. J. Bravo	18	4/153 (5) 5/162 (6) 6/206 (8)	
R. McLaren c Richards b Pollard	5	7/207 (4) 8/207 (9) 9/223 (10)	
D. W. Steyn b Rampaul	0	10/224 (7) 10 overs: 53-1	

Botha, when 15, retired hurt at 197 and resumed at 207-8.

Taylor 8–0–39–1; Rampaul 10–0–45–1; Benn 10–0–43–2; D. J. Bravo 8.2–0–40–2; Sammy 5–0–28–0; Pollard 6–1–27–3.

West Indies

*C. H. Gayle c Kallis b Langeveldt	16	S. J. Benn c McLaren b Morkel	17
D. M. Richards c Kallis b Morkel	28	R. Rampaul c Botha b Morkel	7
S. Chanderpaul c de Villiers b Kallis	24		
D. M. Bravo lbw b Morkel	1	B 4, l-b 3, w 5	12
D. J. Bravo c de Villiers b Steyn	13		
K. A. Pollard c Petersen b Langeveldt	10	1/29 (1) 2/59 (2) 3/63 (4) (38 overs)	157
D. J. G. Sammy c de Villiers b Langeveldt	14	4/87 (3) 5/93 (5) 6/116 (6)	
†D. Ramdin not out	15	7/118 (7) 8/118 (9) 9/147 (10)	
J. E. Taylor run out	0	10/157 (11) 10 overs: 48-1	

Steyn 7–1–19–1; Langeveldt 7–0–30–3; McLaren 5–0–34–0; Morkel 7–0–21–4; Botha 6–0–29–0; Kallis 6–0–17–1.

Umpires: B. R. Doctrove and D. J. Harper. Third umpire: C. R. Duncan.

WEST INDIES v SOUTH AFRICA

Fourth One-Day International

At Roseau, Dominica, May 30, 2010. South Africa won by seven wickets. Toss: West Indies.

Amla's magnificent 129 off 115 balls, his second century of the series, guided South Africa to a victory that always seemed likely, although it required a scampered single off the final ball. Amla paced the pursuit of a demanding 304 beautifully, hitting two sixes and nine mainly off-side fours. When, visibly drained by the stifling heat and humidity, he departed in the 38th over, de Villiers and Duminy maintained the momentum; a routine win seemed assured with seven required from the last two overs and seven wickets standing. But to the backdrop of deafening anticipation from a packed Windsor Park crowd, Rampaul yielded only four off the penultimate over, and Dwayne Bravo followed with a miserly final six balls. With one needed from the last delivery, West Indies could have salvaged a tie, but Sammy at short midwicket fumbled when a clean pick-up might have run de Villiers out. Home chances were diminished as Benn was limited to four overs. Only at the post-match presentation was the reason revealed: Gayle said he had sent his left-arm spinner off the field when he refused to bowl over the wicket, defiance that cost him his match fee. West Indies' best batting of the series was led by Chanderpaul and Richards, with late acceleration from the Bravo brothers. It should have been enough.

Man of the Match: H. M. Amla.

West Indies

D. M. Richards c Smith b Tsotsobe	59	D. E. Bernard not out		13
*C. H. Gayle c Duminy b Morkel	29			
S. Chanderpaul c Tsotsobe b McLaren	66	B 1, l-b 8, w 10		19
D. J. Bravo b Tsotsobe	46			
D. M. Bravo not out	45	1/64 (2) 2/115 (1)	(6 wkts, 50 overs)	303
K. A. Pollard b Langeveldt	26	3/191 (4) 4/223 (3)		
D. J. G. Sammy b Langeveldt	0	5/282 (6) 6/282 (7)	10 overs: 60-0	

†D. Ramdin, S. J. Benn and R. Rampaul did not bat.

Langeveldt 8–0–59–2; Tsotsobe 8–0–48–2; Morkel 8–0–56–1; McLaren 10–1–45–1; Kallis 5–1–27–0; Botha 10–0–50–0; Duminy 1–0–9–0.

South Africa

*G. C. Smith b D. J. Bravo	23
H. M. Amla c Bernard b Pollard	129
J. H. Kallis c sub (T. M. Dowlin) b Gayle	51
†A. B. de Villiers not out	57
J-P. Duminy not out	32
L-b 6, w 6	12

1/59 (1) 2/178 (3)	(3 wkts, 50 overs)	304
3/224 (2)	10 overs: 64-1	

D. A. Miller, J. Botha, R. McLaren, M. Morkel, C. K. Langeveldt and L. L. Tsotsobe did not bat.

Bernard 4–0–25–0; Rampaul 9–0–58–0; D. J. Bravo 7–0–41–1; Sammy 7–0–34–0; Benn 4–0–22–0; Gayle 10–0–60–1; Pollard 9–0–58–1.

Umpires: B. R. Doctrove and D. J. Harper. Third umpire: N. A. Malcolm.

WEST INDIES v SOUTH AFRICA

Fifth One-Day International

At Port-of-Spain, Trinidad, June 3, 2010. South Africa won by one wicket. Toss: West Indies.

South Africa completed their third successive 5–0 series sweep against West Indies, and their 11th straight one-day international victory over them. But they needed last man Tsotsobe's winning boundary in the final over to do it, after almost fluffing their lines. Pursuing 253, they seemed to be coasting at 163 for three in the 31st over: Amla had pushed his aggregate for the series to 402, while Kallis and Duminy compiled comfortable fifties. Then wickets started falling and, although Dwayne Bravo's death bowling was wayward, the departures of Botha and McLaren left South Africa eight down, needing 17 off the final two overs. A hip injury to Taylor kept Bravo in the hot seat; he conceded ten from his first five balls, but grabbed the ninth wicket with his last. In the pulsating final over, van der Merwe swatted Pollard's first ball for four before Tsotsobe, in his first one-day international innings, carved the winning runs through the covers. Earlier, West Indies were indebted to contrasting half-centuries by Chanderpaul (67 off 104 balls) and Deonarine (a run-a-ball 53). Darren Bravo was supposedly caught in the covers by the flying Boucher, whose 292nd one-day international was the first in which he did not keep wicket. Muscular hitting by Pollard and Sammy helped raise 90 from the last ten overs, but the total always looked a little below par.

Man of the Match: J. H. Kallis. *Man of the Series:* H. M. Amla.

West Indies

D. M. Richards c Kallis b Tsotsobe	19	D. J. G. Sammy not out	19
*C. H. Gayle c Smith b McLaren	12		
S. Chanderpaul lbw b Botha	67	L-b 4, w 8, n-b 2	14
D. M. Bravo c Boucher b van der Merwe	17		
D. J. Bravo b Tsotsobe	26	1/22 (1) 2/45 (2) (6 wkts, 50 overs) 252	
N. Deonarine not out	53	3/96 (4) 4/137 (5)	
K. A. Pollard c Smith b Kallis	25	5/161 (3) 6/219 (7) 10 overs: 44-1	

D. E. Bernard, †D. Ramdin and J. E. Taylor did not bat.

Langeveldt 8–0–48–0; Tsotsobe 7–1–31–2; McLaren 7–0–46–1; Kallis 6–0–38–1; Botha 10–0–48–1; van der Merwe 10–1–27–1; Duminy 2–0–10–0.

South Africa

H. M. Amla run out	45	C. K. Langeveldt c Ramdin b D. J. Bravo	6
*G. C. Smith c Ramdin b D. J. Bravo	12	L. L. Tsotsobe not out	4
J. H. Kallis c Ramdin b Gayle	57		
†A. B. de Villiers c Chanderpaul b Gayle	13	L-b 1, w 14	15
J-P. Duminy b Taylor	51		
M. V. Boucher c Chanderpaul b Pollard	6	1/40 (2) 2/76 (1) (9 wkts, 49.4 overs) 255	
J. Botha c Bernard b Pollard	24	3/105 (4) 4/163 (3)	
R. McLaren run out	12	5/175 (6) 6/211 (5) 7/234 (7)	
R. E. van der Merwe not out	10	8/235 (8) 9/246 (10) 10 overs: 53-1	

Taylor 8–0–36–1; Bernard 5–0–30–0; D. J. Bravo 10–0–73–2; Sammy 4–0–24–0; Gayle 10–1–38–2; Deonarine 3–0–11–0; Pollard 9.4–0–42–2.

Umpires: D. J. Harper and N. A. Malcolm. Third umpire: G. E. Greaves.
Series referee: R. S. Mahanama.

At Sir Frank Worrell Ground, St Augustine, Trinidad, June 6–7, 2010 (not first-class). **Drawn.**
‡**South Africans 347-7 dec** (G. C. Smith 41, A. N. Petersen 65, H. M. Amla 44, A. B. de Villiers 53, J-P. Duminy 51, M. V. Boucher 51*); **Trinidad & Tobago 18-1.**

Both sides chose from 14 players, of whom 11 could bat and 11 field. The South Africans batted throughout the first day: only three wickets fell to bowlers, as Amla, de Villiers and Duminy all retired out while Smith, the first to go, was run out. Rain allowed T&T only 4.4 overs on the second day.

WEST INDIES v SOUTH AFRICA

First Test Match

At Port-of-Spain, Trinidad, June 10–13, 2010. South Africa won by 163 runs. Toss: South Africa. Test debuts: N. T. Pascal, S. Shillingford; L. L. Tsotsobe.

The pace and hostility of Steyn and Morkel, even on a benign pitch, were too much for a fragile West Indian team which had just been beaten in all seven limited-overs matches. Despite persistent rain wiping out all but 34 overs of the first day, South Africa surged to victory with a day to spare.

West Indies went in with a depleted line-up as their injury list lengthened. The first-choice fast bowlers Fidel Edwards (in long-term recovery after an operation on a slipped disc), Jerome Taylor (persistent hip pain) and Kemar Roach (ruled out the day before the match with a sore ankle) were all missing, leaving the attack in the hands of Benn (12 Tests), Ravi Rampaul (three) and two debutants, fast bowler Nelon Pascal from Grenada and Dominican off-spinner Shane Shillingford. The batting was also weakened through the absence of Ramnaresh Sarwan, who had a strained hamstring, and opener Adrian Barath, with a damaged calf. South Africa resisted the temptation to include off-spinner Johan Botha, and gave left-arm seamer Lonwabo Tsotsobe his first Test cap instead.

Their height may have evoked memories of a bygone era of giant fast bowlers, but ironically six-footers Benn and Shillingford represented the rarity of two front-line spinners in a West Indies Test team. They used the early turn to good effect, sharing the wickets as South Africa slipped to 107 for five on the second morning, before the middle order repaired the damage to set up a respectable total. When de Villiers and Prince, taken at leg slip in Gayle's solitary over, were out in quick succession after a restorative stand of 122, Boucher and the markedly improved Steyn put on 86. Benn claimed his second Test five-for, while Shillingford, whose opportunities had previously been restricted by doubts over his delivery, made a strong impression.

However, West Indies' competitiveness evaporated on the third morning with a spectacular batting collapse. Morkel used his height to good advantage to prise out the top three with short deliveries within the first hour. Dowlin deflected to first slip; Nash, up at No. 3 in Sarwan's absence, tried to pull away but gloved to the keeper (a dismissal confirmed through the Decision Review System, which continued to create more doubts than certainties); while Gayle under-edged a pull into his stumps to round off a spell of three for none in eight balls.

Chanderpaul and Deonarine, left-handers from Guyana both, arrested the early slide, but Steyn revved up after lunch to destroy the innings: the last seven wickets tumbled for 31 once Chanderpaul gloved a nasty lifter which ballooned to Boucher. Steyn bowled Benn to claim his 200th wicket in his 39th Test; only Clarrie Grimmett (36), Dennis Lillee and Waqar Younis (both 38) had got there in fewer matches. Steyn took five wickets for two runs in 16 balls and, although the last pair inched West Indies into three figures, it was still their lowest total in 23 Tests against South Africa.

Smith waived the follow-on, despite a lead of 250, and proceeded to consolidate his team's position against a lethargic attack; he himself fell ten short of a cheap century, bowled by Benn behind his legs. During much of his 173-minute innings, the few dozen spectators in the Trini Posse Stand had their backs to the game, choosing to watch England's football World Cup struggle against the United States on television in the bar instead.

The declaration arrived an hour into the fourth day, the target an improbable 457 in five and a half sessions. Gayle's 73 led a steelier West Indian display, but Morkel and Steyn were again superb. A late flourish from the tail threatened to take play into the final day but, after Smith claimed the extra half-hour, Steyn fittingly ended the contest with his eighth wicket of the match, when Pascal under-edged an attempted pull into his stumps.

Man of the Match: D. W. Steyn.

Close of play: First day, South Africa 70-3 (Kallis 6, Harris 0); Second day, South Africa 352; Third day, South Africa 155-2 (Smith 79, Kallis 40).

South Africa

*G. C. Smith c Bravo b Shillingford	23	– b Benn	90
A. N. Petersen lbw b Shillingford	31	– lbw b Benn	22
H. M. Amla lbw b Benn	2	– c Deonarine b Shillingford	5
J. H. Kallis lbw b Shillingford	28	– lbw b Benn	40
P. L. Harris c Shillingford b Benn	10		
A. B. de Villiers c Ramdin b Benn	68	– (5) not out	19
A. G. Prince c Dowlin b Gayle	57	– (6) not out	16
†M. V. Boucher c Pascal b Bravo	69		
D. W. Steyn st Ramdin b Benn	39		
M. Morkel b Benn	2		
L. L. Tsotsobe not out	3		
B 9, l-b 4, w 1, n-b 6	20	B 6, l-b 3, n-b 5	14

1/55 (1) 2/60 (3) 3/68 (2) (129.4 overs) 352
4/91 (5) 5/107 (4) 6/229 (7) 7/238 (6)
8/324 (9) 9/330 (10) 10/352 (8)

1/56 (2) (4 wkts dec, 62 overs) 206
2/79 (3) 3/157 (4)
4/178 (1)

Rampaul 19–3–56–0; Pascal 11–1–32–0; Bravo 16.4–6–33–1; Benn 47–9–120–5; Shillingford 35–4–96–3; Gayle 1–0–2–1. *Second Innings*—Rampaul 6–2–21–0; Pascal 6–1–27–0; Benn 25–3–74–3; Shillingford 21–2–66–1; Bravo 4–1–9–0.

West Indies

*C. H. Gayle b Morkel	6	– lbw b Morkel	73
T. M. Dowlin c Smith b Morkel	4	– lbw b Morkel	1
B. P. Nash c Boucher b Morkel	1	– c Boucher b Steyn	13
S. Chanderpaul c Boucher b Steyn	26	– c de Villiers b Kallis	15
N. Deonarine b Steyn	29	– lbw b Steyn	23
D. J. Bravo c Boucher b Morkel	1	– c Prince b Harris	49
†D. Ramdin not out	25	– c de Villiers b Tsotsobe	9
S. Shillingford lbw b Steyn	0	– c Petersen b Harris	27
S. J. Benn b Steyn	0	– lbw b Petersen	42
R. Rampaul b Steyn	0	– not out	18
N. T. Pascal c Petersen b Kallis	2	– b Steyn	10
B 2, l-b 3, w 2, n-b 1	8	B 11, l-b 2	13

1/7 (2) 2/9 (3) 3/12 (1) 4/71 (4) (47.1 overs) 102
5/72 (6) 6/72 (5) 7/72 (8) 8/75 (9)
9/75 (10) 10/102 (11)

1/2 (2) 2/39 (3) (80.3 overs) 293
3/94 (4) 4/114 (1)
5/152 (5) 6/192 (6) 7/194 (7)
8/260 (9) 9/264 (8) 10/293 (11)

Steyn 14–5–29–5; Morkel 13–7–19–4; Tsotsobe 8–0–18–0; Harris 6–1–25–0; Kallis 6.1–2–6–1. *Second Innings*—Steyn 15.3–1–65–3; Morkel 12–3–49–2; Tsotsobe 13–5–20–1; Harris 26.3–3–91–2; Kallis 11–3–49–1; Smith 0.3–0–4–0; Petersen 2–1–2–1.

Umpires: Asad Rauf and S. J. Davis. Third umpire: S. J. A. Taufel.
Referee: R. S. Mahanama.

WEST INDIES v SOUTH AFRICA

Second Test Match

At Basseterre, St Kitts, June 18–22, 2010. Drawn. Toss: South Africa.

At the toss for only the second Test played at Warner Park, Gayle called the grassless, straw-coloured pitch "a road". And after five days of dour batsman-dominated cricket that drew just a few hundred spectators and did Test cricket no favours, no one could argue.

Smith's 132 was the first of five centuries in the match, setting up the platform for a formidable total. Kallis and de Villiers duly followed the captain's lead to three figures; Chanderpaul, inevitably, and Nash responded for West Indies, but there was no point to the contest from as early as midway through the third day.

Dropped at 79 and 112, Smith became the third South African to reach 7,000 Test runs, with successive sixes off Deonarine's part-time off-spin, before a sweep off the same bowler carried him to his 21st Test century. Amla, who survived an edge to Gayle off Roach when 14, helped grind down the West Indians in a second-wicket stand of 112. He fell when well set, snapped up at slip off Shillingford, while Smith, dragging on a pull at Roach, just failed to last the day.

Kallis and de Villiers were in no mood to ignore such favourable conditions. Each passed his hundred on the second day, notching further personal landmarks along the way. Kallis leapfrogged Steve Waugh (10,927) on the Test run-scorers' list on the first day, and later joined Tendulkar, Lara, Ponting, Dravid and Border in passing 11,000. Yet again he could not convert a century (this was his 35th in Tests) into that elusive double, top-edging a sweep at Shillingford. De Villiers, enjoying the freedom lent by the scoreboard, produced the most enterprising batting; his 135 required 168 balls and included six of the 15 sixes in the innings on what it claimed to be Test cricket's smallest outfield. One of them, off Benn, took him to three figures.

The death knell of the contest

Shillingford, the unlucky bowler when Chanderpaul at square leg and wicketkeeper Ramdin let Smith off, was again accurate and probing; his 52 overs were significantly more than he had ever bowled in an innings, a load that took its toll in the Third Test a few days later. Roach, back from injury, worked up threatening pace (he occasionally unsettled Kallis, once hitting him on the helmet), but was plagued by no-balls, delivering a dozen in all.

When West Indies batted, Morkel continued his habit of striking with the new ball as Dowlin sparred to third slip. Gayle and Deonarine consolidated with a stand of 93, but the innings was at the crossroads at 151 for three just after lunch on the third day before Chanderpaul and Nash, left-handers of similar stature and method, stifled any anxiety with a counter-attacking stand of 220 in 200 minutes. Chanderpaul rose after he was felled by Steyn's bouncer when five to register his 15th Test century at home (against seven away). Nash, watched by his parents, wife and infant son, over from their home in Australia, arrived at his second, off 129 balls, a couple of overs later. He fell after tea to de Villiers's direct hit from short third man.

West Indies, four down and trailing by only 119, had the momentum entering the fourth day, yet retreated into an ultra-cautious approach, aided and abetted by South Africa's own negative tactics. Already shunned by an uninterested public, such cricket sounded the death knell for the contest and further undermined the status of the five-day game.

Chanderpaul used up another 93 balls compiling 15 more runs, and the normally ebullient Bravo spent much of his 215-ball innings kicking away Harris's left-arm over-the-wicket deliveries, which were pitched well outside leg stump. The pair occupied 26 overs adding 39 in the morning session. Suddenly, the tempo perked up; four wickets fell for 15, among them Chanderpaul and Bravo to Harris, before Benn and Rampaul slashed and swatted to good effect against the third new ball. West Indies had the trifling satisfaction of a three-run lead; more significant was Boucher becoming the first man to make 500 dismissals in Tests, with a catch off Morkel to dismiss Rampaul.

South Africa's batsmen enjoyed a glorified net session over the last day, to ensure their retention of the Sir Vivian Richards Trophy.

Man of the Match: S. Chanderpaul.

Close of play: First day, South Africa 296-3 (Kallis 45, de Villiers 7); Second day, West Indies 86-1 (Gayle 42, Deonarine 33); Third day, West Indies 424-4 (Chanderpaul 151, Bravo 21); Fourth day, South Africa 23-0 (Smith 13, Petersen 8).

South Africa

*G. C. Smith b Roach	132	– c Ramdin b Shillingford	46
A. N. Petersen c Roach b Shillingford	52	– b Bravo	39
H. M. Amla c Bravo b Shillingford	44	– c sub (D. J. G. Sammy) b Shillingford	41
J. H. Kallis c Rampaul b Shillingford	110	– not out	62
A. B. de Villiers not out	135	– not out	31
A. G. Prince c Gayle b Benn	9		
†M. V. Boucher run out	17		
D. W. Steyn not out	20		
L-b 5, w 2, n-b 17	24	B 1, l-b 1, w 13, n-b 1	16

1/99 (2) 2/211 (3)   (6 wkts dec, 147 overs) 543   1/74 (1)   (3 wkts dec, 94 overs) 235
3/283 (1) 4/421 (4)   2/131 (3) 3/131 (2)
5/442 (6) 6/490 (7)

P. L. Harris, M. Morkel and L. L. Tsotsobe did not bat.

Roach 22–4–72–1; Rampaul 18–4–65–0; Benn 30–3–124–1; Bravo 18–2–58–0; Shillingford 52–4–193–3; Deonarine 3–0–20–0; Nash 4–0–6–0. *Second Innings*—Roach 13–3–33–0; Rampaul 2–0–7–0; Benn 28–4–61–0; Shillingford 30–5–80–2; Bravo 11–4–37–1; Nash 9–4–12–0; Dowlin 1–0–3–0.

West Indies

*C. H. Gayle b Morkel	50	R. Rampaul c Boucher b Morkel	31
T. M. Dowlin c de Villiers b Morkel	10	K. A. J. Roach not out	1
N. Deonarine b Steyn	65		
S. Chanderpaul c and b Harris	166	B 1, l-b 7, w 7, n-b 7	22
B. P. Nash run out	114		
D. J. Bravo c Boucher b Harris	53	1/13 (2) 2/106 (1) (181.1 overs) 546
†D. Ramdin c Petersen b Tsotsobe	1	3/151 (3) 4/371 (5)
S. Shillingford c de Villiers b Kallis	7	5/471 (4) 6/476 (7) 7/486 (6)
S. J. Benn c Kallis b Morkel	26	8/486 (8) 9/545 (10) 10/546 (9)

Steyn 29–4–105–1; Morkel 34.1–9–116–4; Tsotsobe 28–10–68–1; Harris 62–9–165–2; Kallis 23–7–65–1; Petersen 5–0–19–0.

Umpires: Asad Rauf and S. J. A. Taufel.   Third umpire: S. J. Davis.
Referee: J. J. Crowe.

WEST INDIES v SOUTH AFRICA

Third Test Match

At Bridgetown, Barbados, June 26–29, 2010. South Africa won by seven wickets. Toss: West Indies. Test debut: B. J. Bess.

Once again, brittle West Indian batting contributed to another hefty defeat against clinical opponents, this one being completed half an hour before lunch on the fourth day. South Africa thus took the series 2–0, and made the overall score 9–0 in ten international matches on their tour. But the outcome was sullied by incidents on the last two days, on and off the field, which resulted in heavy fines for Steyn and Roach, and Benn's second suspension in six months under the ICC's Code of Conduct.

As Steyn walked away after he was bowled by Roach in the first innings, he spat in the direction of the taunting Benn, who had laughed derisively as he passed. Steyn's coarse response drew a fine of his complete match fee from Jeff Crowe. But Benn hadn't let the matter rest, entering the South Africans' dressing-room during lunch to accost players and management. His punishment, following a complaint from the South Africans, was a suspension of one Test (or two limited-overs games, whichever came next). Not long before, Benn had been banned for two one-day internationals for his part in an on-field altercation with Mitchell Johnson and Brad Haddin during the Perth Test in December

Flashpoint: umpire Simon Taufel speaks to Chris Gayle after Sulieman Benn (*left*) clashed with Dale Steyn.

2009. Here, on the fourth morning, as South Africa coasted to their tiny target, there was an animated exchange between Roach and Kallis. Crowe blamed Roach for "an unpleasant altercation" in which he had to be pulled away by one of his fellow players, and fined him half his match fee.

South Africa had balanced their attack by replacing fast bowler Tsotsobe with the off-spinner Botha, who was making his first Test appearance since 2008: it was the first time South Africa had gone into a Test with two specialist spinners since October 2003 in Pakistan. Botha's clever variations turned out to be as effective as the pace of Steyn, Morkel and Kallis, and his seven wickets earned him the match award.

The usual calm of the toss was interrupted by a flurry of activity as West Indies learned that a late neck injury had eliminated Pascal from the chosen team. Short of experienced replacements, they hurriedly summoned the beanpole Brandon Bess, the 22-year-old Guyana paceman, for his debut: he was at the recently opened High Performance Centre just down the Spring Garden Highway at the University of the West Indies Cave Hill campus, and arrived shortly after the start.

Gayle's decision to bat came unstuck from as early as the fourth over when Richards, in his first Test of the series, fell to Morkel without scoring; next over Gayle himself played on for the third time in three matches. Chanderpaul and Deonarine promised a recovery with 55 for the third wicket, before Kallis's brilliant left-handed slip catch off Chanderpaul got Botha into his groove to lead to a middle-order meltdown.

Bravo and Ramdin fought back, adding 76, but a lively spell from Kallis prevented a full recovery. Two down at the close, South Africa were stuttering next day against Benn, at 145 for five, in spite of Smith's dominant 70; de Villiers rode some early fortune after Gayle chose not to use the TV review to challenge legitimate claims for his dismissal at eight (a thin edge off Roach) and 42 (lbw to Bess), and gradually took control in a partnership of 134 with Prince. De Villiers fell just before the close, but Prince stretched the lead to 115 with some dour resistance on the third morning before running out of partners.

After his altercation with Benn, a fired-up Steyn quickly scotched any notions of a West Indian fightback with a three-wicket burst that accounted for Richards and Deonarine with successive deliveries and Gayle four overs later. Chanderpaul, in his accustomed role on a sinking ship, supplied an unbeaten four-hour 71, but Botha again ripped through the middle, and only Chanderpaul's seventh-wicket partnership of 53 with Shillingford carried the contest into the fourth day. Roach's hostility, which brought him three wickets, enlivened South Africa's short victory chase – but it also boiled over in his ugly mid-pitch confrontation with Kallis.

Man of the Match: J. Botha.   *Man of the Series:* D. W. Steyn.

Close of play: First day, South Africa 46-2 (Smith 35, Harris 2); Second day, South Africa 285-6 (Prince 55, Boucher 4); Third day, West Indies 134-7 (Chanderpaul 57, Benn 4).

West Indies

*C. H. Gayle b Steyn	20	– c Boucher b Steyn	10
D. M. Richards lbw b Morkel	0	– c Petersen b Steyn	17
N. Deonarine b Botha	46	– c Prince b Steyn	0
S. Chanderpaul c Kallis b Botha	22	– not out	71
B. P. Nash lbw b Botha	2	– c Kallis b Botha	12
D. J. Bravo c Smith b Steyn	61	– b Harris	2
†D. Ramdin c Steyn b Kallis	27	– c Prince b Botha	1
S. Shillingford c Botha b Kallis	0	– lbw b Botha	25
S. J. Benn c Amla b Botha	24	– b Morkel	9
K. A. J. Roach c Boucher b Steyn	2	– c Boucher b Morkel	8
B. J. Bess not out	11	– c Kallis b Morkel	0
B 4, l-b 7, w 5	16	B 1, l-b 1, w 1, n-b 3	6

1/12 (2) 2/21 (1) 3/76 (4) 4/90 (5)   (73.5 overs) 231   1/27 (2) 2/27 (3)   (65.1 overs) 161
5/105 (3) 6/181 (7) 7/187 (8)   3/36 (1) 4/70 (5) 5/74 (6)
8/204 (6) 9/207 (10) 10/231 (9)   6/75 (7) 7/128 (8) 8/151 (9)
                                                   9/161 (10) 10/161 (11)

Steyn 13–3–37–3; Morkel 10–2–48–1; Kallis 12–1–36–2; Botha 19.5–2–56–4; Harris 19–3–43–0. *Second Innings*—Steyn 11–4–36–3; Morkel 14.1–5–33–3; Harris 16–3–34–1; Botha 20–5–46–3; Kallis 4–0–10–0.

South Africa

*G. C. Smith c Richards b Benn	70	– c Chanderpaul b Roach	10
A. N. Petersen c Chanderpaul b Roach	1	– b Roach	6
H. M. Amla c Nash b Benn	5	– c Benn b Roach	25
P. L. Harris c Gayle b Bess	11		
J. H. Kallis b Benn	43	– (4) not out	0
A. B. de Villiers c Ramdin b Benn	73	– (5) not out	4
A. G. Prince not out	78		
†M. V. Boucher run out	17		
J. Botha lbw b Benn	9		
D. W. Steyn b Roach	4		
M. Morkel c Bravo b Benn	9		
B 5, l-b 6, w 7, n-b 8	26	W 2, n-b 2	4

1/17 (2) 2/41 (3) 3/60 (4)   (134.4 overs) 346   1/14 (1)   (3 wkts, 8.4 overs) 49
4/122 (1) 5/145 (5) 6/279 (6)   2/29 (2) 3/45 (3)
7/312 (8) 8/326 (9) 9/333 (10) 10/346 (11)

Roach 25–6–59–2; Bess 9–0–65–1; Shillingford 25–2–85–0; Benn 46.4–13–81–6; Bravo 27–12–43–0; Gayle 2–1–2–0. *Second Innings*—Roach 4.4–1–22–3; Bess 4–0–27–0.

Umpires: S. J. Davis and S. J. A. Taufel.   Third umpire: Asad Rauf.
Referee: J. J. Crowe.

DOMESTIC CRICKET IN THE WEST INDIES, 2009-10

HAYDN GILL

Jamaica completed a rare hat-trick of first-class titles in 2009-10, the first by a West Indian regional side for 30 years. It was a deserved success, achieved on the back of another solid team effort, though it emphasised a sad lack of competitiveness among most of their rivals.

While Jamaica had breezed their way to the title in 2008-09, their triumph was far tougher this time; they had to wait until the last match of the short first-class season, despite winning five of their six games. The previous year's expanded structure, which had featured home and away rounds for the first time in four years, once more made way for a familiar shortened and largely inadequate schedule, in which the seven teams played each other only once. There was an innovation whereby in each round the three fixtures were played in the same territory. Four matches were staged partly under floodlights and with a pink ball: the first time this combination had been used in a first-class match anywhere in the world, although both white and orange balls had been tried before.

Jamaica galloped to victories in their first four games, but were stopped in their tracks by a surprise defeat against Barbados, the only other team still in contention. That put Barbados nine points clear at the top, with their full quota of matches complete; Jamaica needed nothing less than a win from their game in hand. They duly sealed their hat-trick of titles with an innings victory over Trinidad & Tobago.

Under the astute captaincy of Tamar Lambert, they owed their championship largely to a varied bowling attack that never conceded 300. Tall leg-spinner Odean Brown claimed a career-best eight-wicket haul among his 30 scalps – the second-most in the tournament. In tandem with slow left-armer Nikita Miller, he was a constant threat. The continued vulnerability of regional batsmen to the slower stuff was highlighted by the fact that spinners provided nine of the top ten wicket-takers, headed by Trinidadian leg-spinner Imran Khan, with 41. If Jamaica's batting was not overwhelmingly dominant, they had useful contributions from most players at some stage. The batsman who stood out, however, was 33-year-old Wavell Hinds, whose 330 runs in three matches, at an average of 110, earned him an international recall after more than three years.

> Guyana were in the cellar with Windwards

Barbados rebounded from a disappointing 2008-09 to finish second. They won four matches and boasted four batsmen – Dale Richards, Ryan Hinds, Jason Haynes and Kirk Edwards – among the tournament's six leading run-scorers, plus the top fast bowler, Pedro Collins. **Leeward Islands** retained third place, but a measure of inconsistency was reflected by two wins and three defeats.

Trinidad & Tobago, the dominant team in the shorter forms of the game in recent seasons, again failed to live up to expectations in the longer form and came fourth; disappointingly their young rising talents, Adrian Barath and Darren Bravo, were limited to one match each because of injuries. A couple of centuries from Denesh Ramdin put him on top of the averages, with 340 at 113, before he left for Australia with West Indies. **Combined Campuses & Colleges**, playing their third season in the regional first-class competition, were again up and down and lost four matches. **Windward Islands** dropped from second to finish joint bottom, but had the only batsman to top 500 runs in Devon Smith. Off-spinner Shane Shillingford landed 28 wickets and an eventual Test call-up.

Guyana were in the cellar with Windwards, but had the satisfaction of winning the inaugural non-Stanford Caribbean Twenty20 tournament, in July 2010, with a remarkable one-wicket victory over Barbados in the final; Jonathan Foo saw them home with a ball to spare. Guyana had also been finalists in the 50-over competition back in November, but Trinidad & Tobago retained their title.

FIRST-CLASS AVERAGES, 2009-10

BATTING (250 runs, average 25.00)

	M	I	NO	R	HS	100s	Avge	Ct/St
D. Ramdin (*Trinidad & Tobago*)	3	6	3	340	166*	2	113.33	6/1
†W. W. Hinds (*Jamaica*)	3	4	1	330	151	1	110.00	2
R. S. Morton (*Leeward Islands*)	2	4	0	287	108	1	71.75	1
†D. S. Smith (*Windward Islands*)	6	11	0	546	193	2	49.63	13
A. D. S. Fletcher (*Windward Islands*)	5	10	1	431	80	0	47.88	3
D. M. Richards (*Barbados*)	6	12	2	457	67	0	45.70	14
†R. O. Hinds (*Barbados*)	6	11	1	446	139	1	44.60	5
D. P. Hyatt (*Jamaica*)	5	8	0	321	104	1	40.12	4
†J. A. M. Haynes (*Barbados*)	6	11	0	432	83	0	39.27	3
K. A. Edwards (*Barbados*)	6	11	0	425	90	0	38.63	5
R. N. Lewis (*Windward Islands*)	6	10	2	308	82*	0	38.50	3
C. S. Baugh (*Jamaica*)	7	10	1	315	124	1	35.00	11/1
†J. C. Guillen (*Trinidad & Tobago*)	6	12	0	419	134	1	34.91	10
†A. B. Fudadin (*Guyana*)	5	9	0	301	78	0	33.44	6
D. E. Bernard (*Jamaica*)	6	8	0	260	102	1	32.50	6
B. A. Parchment (*Jamaica*)	6	10	0	323	109	1	32.30	7
D. J. Pagon (*Jamaica*)	7	12	1	346	80	0	31.45	3
O. A. C. Banks (*Leeward Islands*)	6	11	0	319	60	0	29.00	3
M. V. Hodge (*Leeward Islands*)	6	12	2	288	61	0	28.80	9
†O. J. Phillips (*Campuses & Colleges*)	6	12	1	309	88	0	28.09	8
K. A. Stoute (*Barbados*)	6	10	0	264	74	0	26.40	2
R. Chandrika (*Guyana*)	6	12	1	280	65	0	25.45	2
†S. Ganga (*Trinidad & Tobago*)	6	12	1	275	99	0	25.00	9

BOWLING (15 wickets)

	Style	O	M	R	W	BB	5W/i	Avge
T. L. Lambert (*Jamaica*)	OB	86.4	23	176	16	8-42	1	11.00
N. O. Miller (*Jamaica*)	SLA	161.5	63	283	22	7-28	2	12.86
L. S. Baker (*Leeward Islands*)	RFM	123.2	25	347	23	8-31	2	15.08
I. Khan (*Trinidad & Tobago*)	LBG	222.4	36	672	41	7-71	3	16.39
P. T. Collins (*Barbados*)	LFM	175	50	456	26	5-32	2	17.53
K. Kantasingh (*Campuses & Colleges*)	SLA	207.4	61	525	29	6-29	3	18.10
O. A. C. Banks (*Leeward Islands*)	OB	154.2	33	467	24	7-41	2	19.45
R. A. Austin (*Campuses & Colleges*)	OB	212.1	53	529	27	7-42	2	19.59
R. N. Lewis (*Windward Islands*)	LBG	197.2	37	567	27	5-81	1	21.00
O. V. Brown (*Jamaica*)	LBG	248.4	64	668	30	8-54	3	22.26
D. E. Bernard (*Jamaica*)	RFM	122.4	28	341	15	6-40	1	22.73
A. Martin (*Leeward Islands*)	LBG	233.1	85	488	21	4-55	0	23.23
A. S. Jaggernauth (*Trinidad & Tobago*)	OB	250.1	51	668	27	5-47	1	24.74
R. O. Hinds (*Barbados*)	SLA	191	48	409	16	5-59	1	25.56
E. A. Crandon (*Guyana*)	RFM	134.3	28	393	15	5-39	1	26.20
S. Shillingford (*Windward Islands*)	OB	286.5	56	740	28	6-98	1	26.42
D. Bishoo (*Guyana*)	LBG	215.1	34	656	24	5-45	2	27.33
T. L. Best (*Barbados*)	RF	112	11	477	17	6-65	2	28.05
V. Permaul (*Guyana*)	OB	182.1	36	533	17	5-91	1	31.35

WICB PRESIDENT'S TROPHY

	Played	Won	Lost	Drawn	1st-inns points	Points
Jamaica	6	5	1	0	0	60
Barbados	6	4	0	2	3	57
Leeward Islands.	6	2	3	1	7	34
Trinidad & Tobago	6	2	2	2	3	33
Combined Campuses & Colleges	6	2	4	0	0	24
Windward Islands	6	1	4	1	7	22
Guyana	6	1	3	2	4	22

Win = 12pts; draw = 3pts; first-innings lead in a drawn match = 3pts; first-innings lead in a lost match = 4pts; no first-innings lead in a drawn match = 1pt each.

At Kingston (Kensington Park), Jamaica, January 8–11, 2010. **Drawn. ‡Leeward Islands 236 and 216** (P. T. Collins 5-36, R. O. Hinds 5-59); **Barbados 229 and 158-7.** *Barbados 3pts, Leeward Islands 6pts.*

At Montego Bay, Jamaica, January 8–11, 2010. **Combined Campuses & Colleges won by 151 runs. Combined Campuses & Colleges 234 and 148-5 dec; ‡Trinidad & Tobago 107** (K. Kantasingh 6-29) **and 124** (K. Kantasingh 6-55). *Combined Campuses & Colleges 12pts. Slow left-arm Kavesh Kantasingh took six wickets in each innings, the first a career-best.*

At Spanish Town, Jamaica, January 8–11, 2010. **Jamaica won by six wickets. Windward Islands 181** (N. O. Miller 7-28) **and 251; ‡Jamaica 335 and 98-4.** *Jamaica 12pts. Slow left-arm Nikita Miller's first-innings figures were 26.1–14–28–7.*

At Charlestown, Nevis, January 15–18, 2010. **Barbados won by eight wickets. ‡Combined Campuses & Colleges 213 and 187** (K. A. J. Roach 7-23); **Barbados 301 and 100-2.** *Barbados 12pts.*

At North Sound, Antigua, January 15–18, 2010 (day/night). **Drawn. ‡Trinidad & Tobago 416** (L. M. P. Simmons 107, D. Ramdin 109*) **and 199-8 dec; Guyana 273** (I. Khan 5-96) **and 265-5** (N. Deonarine 104*). *Guyana 3pts, Trinidad & Tobago 6pts. This was the first first-class day/night match in the Caribbean.*

At Basseterre, St Kitts, January 15–18, 2010. **Jamaica won by seven wickets. ‡Leeward Islands 188 and 216** (R. S. Morton 108; O. V. Brown 6-88); **Jamaica 379-8 dec and 27-3.** *Jamaica 12pts.*

At Bridgetown (Kensington Oval), Barbados, January 22–25, 2010. **Drawn. Trinidad & Tobago 271 and 412** (J. C. Guillen 134, D. Ramdin 166*); **‡Barbados 386** (R. O. Hinds 139; I. Khan 7-71) **and 193-8.** *Barbados 6pts, Trinidad & Tobago 3pts. Sherwin Ganga was run out one short of a maiden hundred in Trinidad & Tobago's first innings, but Justin Guillen achieved one in their second.*

At Bridgetown (Three Ws Oval), Barbados, January 22–24, 2010. **Windward Islands won by nine wickets. ‡Combined Campuses & Colleges 158 and 198; Windward Islands 286** (D. S. Smith 122; J. P. Bennett 5-86) **and 71-1.** *Windward Islands 12pts.*

At St Philip, Barbados, January 22–25, 2010. **Jamaica won by an innings and 27 runs. Jamaica 429** (W. W. Hinds 151, C. S. Baugh 124; V. Permaul 5-91); **‡Guyana 166** (N. O. Miller 6-42) **and 236** (D. E. Bernard 6-40). *Jamaica 12pts. This was the first first-class match played at Foursquare Park at St Philip in Barbados. Wavell Hinds (13 fours and six sixes in 317 balls) and Carlton Baugh (13 fours and three sixes in 133 balls) added 232 in 198 minutes for the seventh wicket.*

At Bridgetown (Kensington Oval), Barbados, January 29–February 1, 2010 (day/night). **Barbados won by 98 runs. ‡Barbados 287** (S. Shillingford 6-98) **and 292-7 dec; Windward Islands 307** (L. A. S. Sebastien 143) **and 174** (T. L. Best 5-41). *Barbados 12pts, Windward Islands 4pts. All three matches in this round were won by the team who trailed on first innings.*

At Bridgetown (Three Ws Oval), Barbados, January 29–31, 2010. **Combined Campuses & Colleges won by five wickets. Guyana 271 and 162** (R. A. Austin 7-42); **‡Combined Campuses & Colleges 239 and 195-5.** *Combined Campuses & Colleges 12pts, Guyana 4pts.*

At St Philip, Barbados, January 29–February 1, 2010. **Trinidad & Tobago won by 45 runs. Trinidad & Tobago 176** (W. W. Cornwall 5-27) **and 226; ‡Leeward Islands 201 and 156.** *Leeward Islands 4pts, Trinidad & Tobago 12pts. Mali Richards, who had previously played first-class cricket for Oxford and MCC, made his debut for Leewards, his father Viv's old team. His opening partner, Montcin Hodge, carried his bat for 54 in Leewards' first innings.*

At Providence, Guyana, February 12–15, 2010 (day/night). **Jamaica won by 29 runs. ‡Jamaica 202** (R. A. Austin 5-59) **and 164; Combined Campuses & Colleges 161** (O. V. Brown 8-54) **and 176** (T. L. Lambert 8-42). *Jamaica 12pts. Leg-spinner Odean Brown and off-spinner Tamar Lambert each took a career-best eight in an innings and ten in the match to complete Jamaica's fourth straight win. Of the 40 wickets, 36 fell to spin, three to fast bowler Kevin McClean and one to a run-out.*

At Albion, Guyana, February 12–15, 2010. **Barbados won by 58 runs. ‡Barbados 403** (D. Bishoo 5-75) **and 154-9 dec** (D. Bishoo 5-45); **Guyana 229** (T. L. Best 6-65) **and 270.** *Barbados 12pts.*

At Georgetown (Bourda), Guyana, February 12–15, 2010. **Leeward Islands won by 53 runs. ‡Leeward Islands 325 and 198; Windward Islands 204** (O. A. C. Banks 7-41) **and 266** (O. A. C. Banks 6-113). *Leeward Islands 12pts. Off-spinner Omari Banks claimed a career-best 7-41, and 13-154 in all, which took him past 200 first-class wickets. Nelon Pascal finally scored his first runs of the season in Windwards' second innings, after four ducks and two unbeaten noughts.*

At St Augustine, Trinidad, February 19–21, 2010. **Barbados won by ten wickets. ‡Jamaica 226** (C. R. Edwards 6-41) **and 120** (P. T. Collins 5-32); **Barbados 293 and 54-0.** *Barbados 12pts. Barbados inflicted Jamaica's only defeat of the tournament with a day to spare to leapfrog to the top of the table.*

At Couva, Trinidad, February 19–22, 2010. **Guyana won by five wickets. ‡Leeward Islands 192** (E. A. Crandon 5-39) **and 192; Guyana 287** (S. Chanderpaul 105*) **and 99-5.** *Guyana 12pts. Shivnarine Chanderpaul's 52nd hundred helped Guyana to complete their first win in this tournament for nearly two years.*

At Port-of-Spain, Trinidad, February 19–22, 2010. **Trinidad & Tobago won by 155 runs. ‡Trinidad & Tobago 263** (R. N. Lewis 5-81) **and 297-6 dec; Windward Islands 188 and 217** (A. S. Jaggernauth 5-47). *Trinidad & Tobago 12pts.*

At Gros Islet, St Lucia, February 19–22, 2010. **Leeward Islands won by ten wickets. Leeward Islands 227** (K. Kantasingh 5-69) **and 40-0; ‡Combined Campuses & Colleges 65** (L. S. Baker 8-31) **and 200** (L. S. Baker 5-52). *Leeward Islands 12pts. Lionel Baker became the third bowler in three weeks to take eight in an innings against Campuses & Colleges. His career-best 8-31 skittled them inside 26 overs; he finished with 13-83 as Leewards won on the third morning. For Campuses & Colleges, Kavesh Kantasingh recorded his fourth and fifth ducks of the season; his ten first-class innings also included one 0*.*

At St Andrew's, Grenada, February 26–28, 2010. **Jamaica won by an innings and 72 runs. Jamaica 379** (B. A. Parchment 109, D. P. Hyatt 104; I. Khan 7-124); **‡Trinidad & Tobago 144** (O. V. Brown 5-46) **and 163.** *Jamaica 12pts. Jamaican openers Brenton Parchment and Danza Hyatt – who hit ten fours and five sixes in a maiden century – put on 200, more than Trinidad & Tobago managed in either innings, paving the way for a decisive win which secured their third successive first-class title with a day to spare.*

At St George's (Queen's Park New), Grenada, February 26–March 1, 2010. **Drawn. Guyana 452** (R. R. Sarwan 116) **and 83-1; ‡Windward Islands 462** (D. S. Smith 193). *Guyana 6pts, Windward Islands 3pts. Devon Smith's 193 was the highest score of the season, occupying almost eight hours; he hit 25 fours. Team-mate Devendra Bishoo emulated Kantasingh with his sixth score of nought in the season, five of them ducks.*

REGIONAL CHAMPIONS

Shell Shield					
1965-66	Barbados	1969-70	Trinidad	1974-75	Guyana
1966-67	Barbados	1970-71	Trinidad	1975-76 {	Trinidad
1967-68	No competition	1971-72	Barbados		Barbados
1968-69	Jamaica	1972-73	Guyana	1976-77	Barbados
		1973-74	Barbados	1977-78	Barbados

1978-79	Barbados	1990-91	Barbados	2000-01	Barbados
1979-80	Barbados	1991-92	Jamaica	2001-02	Jamaica
1980-81	Combined Islands	1992-93	Guyana		
1981-82	Barbados	1993-94	Leeward Islands	*Carib Beer Cup*	
1982-83	Guyana	1994-95	Barbados	2002-03	Barbados
1983-84	Barbados	1995-96	Leeward Islands	2003-04	Barbados
1984-85	Trinidad & Tobago	1996-97	Barbados	2004-05	Jamaica
1985-86	Barbados			2005-06	Trinidad & Tobago
1986-87	Guyana	*President's Cup*		2006-07	Barbados
		1997-98 {	Leeward Islands	2007-08	Jamaica
Red Stripe Cup			Guyana		
1987-88	Jamaica	*Busta Cup*		*President's Trophy*	
1988-89	Jamaica	1998-99	Barbados	2008-09	Jamaica
1989-90	Leeward Islands	1999-2000	Jamaica	2009-10	Jamaica

Barbados have won the title outright 19 times, Jamaica 10, Guyana 5, Trinidad/Trinidad & Tobago 4, Leeward Islands 3, Combined Islands 1. Barbados, Guyana, Leeward Islands and Trinidad have also shared the title.

WEST INDIES CRICKET BOARD CUP, 2009-10

50-over league plus knockout

Zone A	P	W	L	NR	Pts	**Zone B**	P	W	L	NR	Pts
Trinidad & Tobago	3	1	0	2	7	Guyana	3	2	0	1	9
Campuses & Colleges	3	1	0	2	6	Barbados	3	1	1	1	5
Windward Islands	3	0	1	2	2	West Indies Under-19	3	0	1	2	2
Jamaica	3	0	1	2	2	Leeward Islands	3	0	1	2	2

Semi-finals

At Providence, Guyana, November 2, 2009 (day/night). **Trinidad & Tobago won by two wickets.** ‡**Barbados 229** (49.5 overs) (D. J. Bravo 6-46); **Trinidad & Tobago 230-8** (49.2 overs). *The Barbados openers put on 85 before Dwayne Bravo parted them in the 21st over and went on to take six wickets, his best one-day figures. Captain Daren Ganga completed victory with 79*, though he hit only three fours in 105 balls.*

At Providence, Guyana, November 3, 2009 (day/night). **Guyana won by six wickets.** ‡**Combined Campuses & Colleges 151** (48.3 overs); **Guyana 152-4** (40.3 overs). *Off-spinner Royston Crandon (4-25) bowled Campuses & Colleges out cheaply, and Shivnarine Chanderpaul steered them home with four fours and a six in his unbeaten 50.*

Final

At Providence, Guyana, November 5, 2009 (day/night). **Trinidad & Tobago won by 81 runs.** ‡**Trinidad & Tobago 286-6** (50 overs); **Guyana 205** (45.3 overs). *Darren Bravo and Daren Ganga put on 92 in 17 overs for Trinidad & Tobago's third wicket before Kieron Pollard hit 57 in 50 balls, with four fours and three sixes. Pollard went on to take three wickets and a catch as Trinidad & Tobago retained the 50-over title.*

CARIBBEAN T20, 2010

Zone A	P	W	L	NR	Pts	NRR	**Zone B**	P	W	L	NR	Pts	NRR
Trinidad & Tobago	3	3	0	0	12	1.86	Barbados	3	2	0	1	9	0.97
Jamaica	3	2	1	0	8	0.31	Guyana	3	2	0	1	9	0.36
Leeward Islands	3	0	2	1	1	–0.73	Campuses & Colleges	3	0	2	1	1	–0.16
Canada	3	0	2	1	1	–2.56	Windward Islands	3	0	2	1	1	–1.18

Semi-finals

At Port-of-Spain, Trinidad, July 30, 2010 (floodlit). **Guyana won by four runs.** Reduced to 19 overs a side. **Guyana 175-7** (19 overs); ‡**Trinidad & Tobago 171** (18.5 overs). *Dwayne Bravo hit 55 in 20 balls, including six sixes, for Trinidad, but could not secure a home win.*

At Port-of-Spain, Trinidad, July 30, 2010 (floodlit). **Barbados won by six wickets.** ‡**Jamaica 153-9** (20 overs); **Barbados 154-4** (18.5 overs). *Danza Hyatt hit a Twenty20-best 89 in 50 balls for Jamaica, with eight sixes and four fours – but to no avail.*

Third-place play-off

At Port-of-Spain, Trinidad, July 31, 2010 (floodlit). **Trinidad & Tobago won by ten wickets** (D/L method). Reduced to 14 overs a side. ‡**Jamaica 94-7** (14 overs); **Trinidad & Tobago 89-0** (10.1 overs). *Trinidad & Tobago's target was revised to 89 in 13 overs.*

Final

At Port-of-Spain, Trinidad, July 31, 2010 (floodlit). **Guyana won by one wicket.** ‡**Barbados 134-5** (20 overs); **Guyana 135-9** (19.5 overs). *Guyana were reeling at 85-8, 50 runs short with 21 balls remaining, before 19-year-old Jonathan Foo masterminded the recovery. He hit 42* off 17 balls, and last man Devendra Bishoo scored two runs off the penultimate ball to complete victory.*

ZIMBABWEAN CRICKET, 2010

Looking to Test themselves

MEHLULI SIBANDA

The Zimbabwean board announced during 2010 that they aimed to return to Test cricket in 2011, after voluntarily pulling out of the longer version of the game in 2006. The move was prompted by a strong domestic first-class set-up, in which a number of foreign stars signed up to play for the five franchises set up in 2009. Another reason was the good performance by the Zimbabwe XI side in the ICC Intercontinental Cup, in which they ended up undefeated, and might have gone through to the final had Zimbabwe Cricket not forfeited the last match when Scotland asked for it to be played at a neutral venue.

In the year building up to the World Cup, Zimbabwe played 20 one-day and seven Twenty20 internationals. They won seven of the 50-over games, but only one of the Twenty20s. However, unlike in recent years when the victories tended to come against the likes of Bangladesh and Kenya, this time Zimbabwe beat India, Sri Lanka and West Indies.

The year started with Zimbabwe looking for a new coach to replace the inexperienced local man Walter Chawaguta. A number of names were thrown

ZIMBABWE IN 2010

	Played	Won	Lost	Drawn/No result
One-day internationals	20	7	13	–
Twenty20 internationals	7	1	6	–

JANUARY		
FEBRUARY ⎫	5 ODIs and 1 T20I (a) v West Indies	(page 1117)
MARCH ⎭		
APRIL		
MAY	World Twenty20 (in West Indies)	(page 797)
JUNE ⎱	Triangular ODI tournament (h) v India and Sri Lanka	(page 1146)
	2 T20Is (h) v India	(page 1149)
JULY		
AUGUST		
SEPTEMBER	3 ODIs (h) v Ireland	(page 1150)
OCTOBER	3 ODIs and 2 T20Is (a) v South Africa	(page 1038)
NOVEMBER		
DECEMBER	5 ODIs (a) v Bangladesh	(page 906)

For a review of Zimbabwean domestic cricket from the 2009-10 season, see page 1151.

Planning the return journey: Alan Butcher and Elton Chigumbura hope Zimbabwe are playing Tests before the end of 2011.

Pavel Rahman, AP/PA

around, and on the eve of the team's tour of West Indies the once-capped England batsman Alan Butcher was unveiled. Chawaguta was still in charge for the West Indian tour, where Zimbabwe won the only Twenty20 game and also lifted the first one-day international before losing their way and eventually going down 4–1. Butcher took over for the World Twenty20 in the Caribbean, where Zimbabwe lost their group matches to Sri Lanka and New Zealand after shock wins over Australia and Pakistan in the warm-ups.

Off-spinner Prosper Utseya, who had captained since 2006, stepped down after the World Twenty20. All-rounder Elton Chigumbura took over. His first assignment was the home tri-series against India and Sri Lanka, who both sent weakened teams, which allowed Zimbabwe to record some morale-boosting victories and book a place in the final, where they lost to Sri Lanka.

Zimbabwe then hosted Ireland, scraping a 2–1 win after three close games. Soon after that there was a far tougher challenge: a tour to South Africa. Zimbabwe showed some fight, despite losing both Twenty20 matches, and kept things tight in the first two 50-over games before collapsing in the third to lose by 272 runs, the second-biggest defeat by runs in one-day internationals.

Grant Flower came home to take up a position as Zimbabwe's batting coach, and was also rather surprisingly persuaded to make an international return at 39. He did play in two of the one-dayers in South Africa, but met with little success and retired from all cricket not long afterwards.

The final engagement of 2010 – and the last before the World Cup – was a trip to Bangladesh, where a one-day series was lost 3–1.

Brendan Taylor was the star performer for Zimbabwe with the bat during the year, racking up 723 runs in 20 innings, including a fine rearguard 145 not out against South Africa at Bloemfontein in October. Former skipper Tatenda Taibu scored 574 runs at 35.

Chigumbura clearly did not enjoy the cares of captaincy. In his early days he was always liable to chip in with crucial runs in the middle order, in addition to being a reliable fast-medium bowler. But now he lost it as a bowler, picking up just eight wickets in 2010, at an average above 50. He felt the pressure as early as his first day as captain, leaking 36 runs in just two overs against India at Bulawayo. Chigumbura did make 368 runs, to finish 2010 as the third-highest run-scorer – but he never reached 50 after taking over the captaincy.

Left-hander Craig Ervine made a promising start to his international career, his unbeaten 67 on debut securing victory against India, and he ended the year with 324 runs. It briefly looked as if Ervine's older brother, Sean, would be returning to Zimbabwe colours, but after being named in the World Cup squad he pulled out, preferring to stay with Hampshire.

Hamilton Masakadza, who had been Zimbabwe's leading scorer in 2009 with over 1,000 one-day runs, had a disappointing year, managing only 323 at 19, and he was ultimately omitted from the World Cup.

Utseya, who played in all Zimbabwe's 20 one-day internationals, emerged as the leading bowler with 18 wickets. He also rediscovered his batting touch, ending up with 276 runs at a fine average of 30. Leg-spinner Graeme Cremer took 15 wickets, the lanky fast bowler Christopher Mpofu 14, and newcomer Shingirai Masakadza – Hamilton's brother – took 11, as did the long-serving left-arm spinner Ray Price.

The talented but controversial batsman Mark Vermeulen was not selected for Zimbabwe at all during 2010, and it appears that his international career might really be over this time. After a number of disciplinary issues, including several open clashes with former national coach Robin Brown, the Bulawayo-based Matabeleland Tuskers decided not to renew Vermeulen's contract for 2010-11. He fell out with Brown to such an extent that he was relegated to the Tuskers B team. Vermeulen moved to Mutare, and the Mountaineers, where he settled down and performed well with the bat.

Overall, Zimbabwe were inconsistent, as shown by the defeat by Ireland and the failure to win the series against Bangladesh after having beaten West Indies, India and Sri Lanka earlier in the year. Most of the players are still struggling to stamp their authority on the game, even though several of them have been around for five years or more and played around 100 one-day internationals.

MICROMAX CUP IN ZIMBABWE, 2010

Mehluli Sibanda

1. Sri Lanka   2. Zimbabwe   3. India

Although Sri Lanka won the tournament in the end, with a clinical performance in the final, Zimbabwe had much to cheer after beating India twice and Sri Lanka once to finish top of the qualifying table. Their only defeat before the final came in a rain-reduced game. It was a fine start for Zimbabwe's new coach, the former Surrey and England batsman Alan Butcher, and their new captain, Elton Chigumbura, who had taken over just before the tournament when Prosper Utseya stood down.

Admittedly India and Sri Lanka did choose to rest several leading players. Both were also under new leadership, in their cases temporary: Tillekeratne Dilshan captained Sri Lanka, while Suresh Raina led India's one-day side before he had even played in a Test.

Zimbabwe started by defeating India and, after a sobering defeat by Sri Lanka, conquered India again, the first time they had ever beaten them in successive one-day internationals. Sri Lanka then beat India, to ensure they would play Zimbabwe in the final. The last round-robin game was a dress rehearsal for that, and Brendan Taylor ensured Zimbabwe went in with the psychological edge by scoring a century: he was later named Man of the Series after scoring 295 runs at 73.75. But he could not maintain his form in the final, which Sri Lanka won with something to spare. Dilshan, who made a sparkling hundred in the decider, ended up as the tournament's leading run-scorer with 328 at 109.33: the leading bowler was another Sri Lankan, Suraj Randiv, with six wickets.

If Dilshan made sure the cup was safely in Sri Lankan hands when he left Zimbabwe, rather less care was taken as the team arrived home. When the official welcoming party was delayed, the players made their own way from Katunayake airport, but left the crystal trophy behind them. It was later returned to Sri Lanka Cricket.

NATIONAL SQUADS

Zimbabwe *E. Chigumbura, A. M. Blignaut, C. J. Chibhabha, C. K. Coventry, A. G. Cremer, C. R. Ervine, G. A. Lamb, H. Masakadza, C. B. Mpofu, R. W. Price, E. C. Rainsford, V. Sibanda, T. Taibu, B. R. M. Taylor, P. Utseya. *Coach:* A. R. Butcher.

India *S. K. Raina, R. Ashwin, A. B. Dinda, R. A. Jadeja, K. D. Karthik, V. Kohli, A. Mishra, N. V. Ojha, P. P. Ojha, Pankaj Singh, Y. K. Pathan, R. G. Sharma, M. Vijay, R. Vinay Kumar, U. Yadav. *Coach:* G. Kirsten.

Vinay Kumar injured his knee in practice before India's second match, and was replaced by A. Mithun.

Sri Lanka *T. M. Dilshan, L. D. Chandimal, C. R. D. Fernando, C. K. Kapugedera, K. M. D. N. Kulasekara, A. D. Mathews, B. A. W. Mendis, B. M. A. J. Mendis, M. T. T. Mirando, N. L. T. C. Perera, S. Randiv, T. T. Samaraweera, L. P. C. Silva, W. U. Tharanga, H. D. R. L. Thirimanne. *Coach:* T. H. Bayliss.

At Bulawayo, May 28, 2010. **Zimbabwe won by six wickets.** ‡India 285-5 (50 overs) (R. G. Sharma 114, S. K. Raina 37, R. A. Jadeja 61*); **Zimbabwe 289-4** (48.2 overs) (H. Masakadza 46, B. R. M. Taylor 81, C. R. Ervine 67*, C. K. Coventry 32). *Zimbabwe 4pts. MoM:* B. R. M. Taylor. *One-day international debuts:* C. R. Ervine (Zimbabwe); A. B. Dinda, R. Vinay Kumar, U. Yadav (India). *Rohit Sharma's first century in one-day internationals, and his fifth-wicket stand of 132 with Jadeja, lifted India to a total they thought would be enough. But in the face of some solid batting, it wasn't. Masakadza and Taylor piled on 88 in the first 13 overs; later, after Taylor's 103-ball vigil finally ended, the debutant Craig Ervine anchored the chase. It was left to Chigumbura, in his first match as Zimbabwe's captain, to top-edge the winning boundary over the wicketkeeper with ten balls to spare. They had only once chased a higher score to win (290-4 against West Indies at Chester-le-Street in 2000). It was Zimbabwe's first victory over India in a one-day international since March 2002: India had won all ten matches in the interim.*

At Bulawayo, May 30, 2010. **India won by seven wickets.** Sri Lanka 242 (49.5 overs) (T. M. Dilshan 61, A. D. Mathews 75, N. L. T. C. Perera 32); **‡India 243-3** (43.3 overs) (V. Kohli 82, R. G. Sharma 101*). *India 4pts. MoM:* R. G. Sharma. *Rohit Sharma hit his second century in three days, and this time it did bring his side victory. He put on 154 for the third wicket with Kohli as India made light of a modest target.*

At Bulawayo, June 1, 2010. **Sri Lanka won by nine wickets.** Zimbabwe 118 (24.5 overs) (H. Masakadza 62; S. Randiv 3-23); **‡Sri Lanka 119-1** (15.2 overs) (W. U. Tharanga 40, T. M. Dilshan 60*). *Sri Lanka 5pts. MoM:* S. Randiv. *One-day international debuts:* L. D. Chandimal, B. M. A. J. Mendis (Sri Lanka). *Zimbabwe's delight at beating India in their first match seemed a distant memory after they were thrashed by Sri Lanka in a match reduced to 26 overs a side by rain. "Frankly, today we were rubbish," said their new coach Alan Butcher. Only Masakadza, who faced 69 balls, scored more than 11 in Zimbabwe's disappointing total, then Sri Lanka's openers Tharanga and Dilshan sprinted to 86 in 10.5 overs.*

At Harare, June 3, 2010. **Zimbabwe won by seven wickets.** India 194-9 (50 overs) (K. D. Karthik 33, R. A. Jadeja 51; G. A. Lamb 3-45); **‡Zimbabwe 197-3** (38.2 overs) (H. Masakadza 66, B. R. M. Taylor 74). *Zimbabwe 5pts. MoM:* B. R. M. Taylor. *Zimbabwe completed the double over India with a superb all-round performance. India started solidly, openers Karthik and Murali Vijay (21 in 56 balls) putting on 58 in 16 overs, but wickets fell regularly once they were separated. Led by an opening stand of 128 between Masakadza and Taylor, Zimbabwe skipped home quickly enough to earn a bonus point. They had never before beaten India in successive one-day internationals.*

At Harare, June 5, 2010. **Sri Lanka won by six wickets.** India 268-9 (50 overs) (V. Kohli 68, Y. K. Pathan 44, R. G. Sharma 32, R. Ashwin 38; M. T. T. Mirando 3-57); **‡Sri Lanka 270-4** (48.2 overs) (L. D. Chandimal 111, C. K. Kapugedera 42, B. M. A. J. Mendis 35*). *Sri Lanka 4pts. MoM:* L. D. Chandimal. *One-day international debuts:* R. Ashwin, N. V. Ojha, Pankaj Singh (India). *A century from Dinesh Chandimal, in only his second one-day international, ensured Sri Lanka would be in the final while India would not. Chandimal, 20, usurped his team-mate Upul Tharanga as Sri Lanka's youngest one-day international centurion: he hit six fours and five sixes from 118 balls, and put on 114 for the third wicket with Kapugedera. When they were out, Jeevan Mendis (also playing his second match) and Thilan Samaraweera (28*) added 55* in 7.2 overs.*

At Harare, June 7, 2010. **Zimbabwe won by eight wickets.** Sri Lanka 236 (47.5 overs) (W. U. Tharanga 69, T. M. Dilshan 78); **‡Zimbabwe 240-2** (47.5 overs) (B. R. M. Taylor 119*, C. J Chibhabha 58, T. Taibu 42*). *Zimbabwe 4pts. MoM:* B. R. M. Taylor. *Zimbabwe put in another impressive all-round performance, which ensured they topped the qualifying table. Their successful chase was founded on a second-wicket stand of 134 between Taylor, who went on to his second one-day international hundred, and Chibhabha. Earlier, Zimbabwe's spinners applied the brakes after Tharanga and Dilshan's opening stand reached 122 in the 21st over.*

Zimbabwe 13pts, Sri Lanka 9pts, India 4pts.

FINAL

ZIMBABWE v SRI LANKA

At Harare, June 9, 2010. Sri Lanka won by nine wickets. Toss: Sri Lanka.

Local hopes were high after Zimbabwe had topped the qualifying table, but dipped when Dilshan won the toss and decided to bowl first: all seven matches in this tournament were won by the side batting second. Masakadza and Taylor, who had been very consistent in the previous games, fell cheaply this time as Kulasekara and Fernando kept it tight with the new ball. Taibu dug in for 71 from 93 balls, but his only significant help came from Greg Lamb in a stand of 90. Zimbabwe needed to make early inroads if Sri Lanka were to struggle chasing only four an over, but instead Tharanga and Dilshan flew out of the blocks, bringing up their century partnership in 16.2 overs. By the time they were separated, in the 26th over, the match was all but decided. Fittingly it was Dilshan, Sri Lanka's stand-in captain, who hit the winning boundary, shortly after completing his seventh one-day international hundred. This was Rudi Koertzen's 209th and last one-day international as an umpire.

Man of the Match: T. M. Dilshan. *Man of the Series:* B. R. M. Taylor.

Zimbabwe

H. Masakadza c Chandimal b Kulasekara. .	4	P. Utseya not out	10
B. R. M. Taylor c Samaraweera b Fernando	19	R. W. Price c Dilshan b B. A. W. Mendis. .	0
†T. Taibu c Kapugedera b Fernando	71	C. B. Mpofu run out	6
C. R. Ervine run out	9	L-b 2, w 8	10
G. A. Lamb b B. M. A. J. Mendis	37		
*E. Chigumbura c Dilshan b B. A. W. Mendis	10	1/11 (1) 2/29 (2) 3/49 (4) (49 overs) 199	
C. K. Coventry c Tharanga		4/139 (3) 5/155 (6) 6/163 (5)	
b B. M. A. J. Mendis .	18	7/178 (7) 8/189 (8) 9/190 (10)	
A. G. Cremer b Fernando	5	10/199 (11) 10 overs: 30-2	

Kulasekara 7–2–17–1; Fernando 9–0–36–3; B. A. W. Mendis 10–1–44–2; Mathews 4–0–14–0; Randiv 8–0–36–0; B. M. A. J. Mendis 9–0–36–2; Dilshan 2–0–14–0.

Sri Lanka

W. U. Tharanga run out	72
*T. M. Dilshan not out	108
†L. D. Chandimal not out	16
L-b 2, w 5	7
1/160 (1) (1 wkt, 34.4 overs) 203	
10 overs: 63-0	

A. D. Mathews, C. K. Kapugedera, T. T. Samaraweera, B. M. A. J. Mendis, K. M. D. N. Kulasekara, S. Randiv, C. R. D. Fernando and B. A. W. Mendis did not bat.

Mpofu 5–0–36–0; Chigumbura 5–0–28–0; Price 7–0–34–0; Lamb 6–0–24–0; Cremer 4.4–0–27–0; Utseya 6–0–44–0; Masakadza 1–0–8–0.

Umpires: R. E. Koertzen and R. B. Tiffin. Third umpire: O. Chirombe.
Series referee: J. J. Crowe.

ZIMBABWE v INDIA, 2010

Twenty20 internationals (2): Zimbabwe 0, India 2

After losing to Sri Lanka in the final of the preceding triangular series, India remained in Harare for a week to play two Twenty20 internationals, the first on Zimbabwean soil. Despite missing several senior players India won both matches reasonably comfortably, with their stand-in captain Suresh Raina making 100 runs for once out.

INDIAN TOURING PARTY

*S. K. Raina, R. Ashwin, P. P. Chawla, A. B. Dinda, R. A. Jadeja, K. D. Karthik, V. Kohli, A. Mishra, N. V. Ojha, P. P. Ojha, Pankaj Singh, Y. K. Pathan, R. G. Sharma, M. Vijay, R. Vinay Kumar, U. Yadav. *Coach:* G. Kirsten.

From the team which had contested the preceding tri-series, Chawla replaced A. Mithun, while Vinay Kumar returned after missing the tri-series (for which he was originally selected) with a knee injury.

At Harare, June 12, 2010. **First Twenty20 international: India won by six wickets. Zimbabwe 111-9** (20 overs) (C. J. Chibhabha 40, C. R. Ervine 30; R. Vinay Kumar 3-24); ‡**India 112-4** (15 overs) (Y. K. Pathan 37*). *MoM:* Y. K. Pathan. *Twenty20 international debuts:* E. C. Rainsford (Zimbabwe); R. Ashwin, V. Kohli, N. V. Ojha (India). *India won the first Twenty20 international ever played in Zimbabwe. The home side collapsed after reaching a promising 73-3 at halfway: the last seven wickets crashed for 38 as India's spinners took control, and Pragyan Ojha finished with 4–0–11–2. India lost both openers cheaply, Chris Mpofu dismissing Murali Vijay for five and Naman Ojha for two, but Yusuf Pathan finished the game off with five overs to spare, hitting three sixes and two fours from 24 balls.*

At Harare, June 13, 2010. **Second Twenty20 international: India won by seven wickets. Zimbabwe 140-5** (20 overs) (T. Taibu 45*); ‡**India 144-3** (18 overs) (M. Vijay 46, S. K. Raina 72*). *MoM:* S. K. Raina. *Man of the Series:* S. K. Raina. *Twenty20 international debuts:* T. L. Chatara (Zimbabwe); A. Mishra (India). *Zimbabwe struggled to get going, and had made only 74-3 after 15 overs before some improvisation from Taibu helped almost to double the score. But India wrapped up the short series with something to spare, Raina anchoring the chase with 72* from 44 balls.*

ZIMBABWE v IRELAND, 2010-11

One-day internationals (3): Zimbabwe 2, Ireland 1

Ireland stayed on in Harare after their Intercontinental Cup match against a Zimbabwe XI (see page 1167) to contest three one-day internationals against the full Zimbabwe side. They were all close-run affairs: the first went to the last ball, the home side clinched the series with a three-wicket win in the second, before Ireland completed a consolation victory in the last.

There was a successful return to Zimbabwe colours after more than a year for the fast bowler Ed Rainsford. He won the first match with a last-ball six, and also took ten wickets overall, including five in the third game. Ireland's leading bowler was the 18-year-old slow left-armer George Dockrell, who claimed seven wickets and maintained a miserly economy-rate of 3.83 runs per over.

IRELAND TOURING PARTY

*W. T. S. Porterfield, A. C. Botha, G. H. Dockrell, A. Eastwood, D. T. Johnston, N. G. Jones, J. F. Mooney, K. J. O'Brien, N. J. O'Brien, A. D. Poynter, P. R. Stirling, A. van der Merwe, A. R. White, G. C. Wilson. *Coach:* P. V. Simmons.

At Harare, September 26, 2010. **Zimbabwe won by two wickets. Ireland 200** (47.3 overs) (A. R. White 47, G. C. Wilson 69; E. C. Rainsford 4-23); **‡Zimbabwe 206-8** (50 overs) (T. Taibu 62, E. Chigumbura 41; G. H. Dockrell 3-27). *MoM:* E. C. Rainsford. *Zimbabwe started the final over needing six to win, and scored five off the first five balls from Kevin O'Brien before Ed Rainsford (who had survived a confident run-out appeal from the previous delivery) settled the match by pulling a six off the last ball, a full toss. Ireland earlier recovered from 22-4 thanks to a stand of 115 between Andrew White and Gary Wilson. Hamilton Masakadza fell to the first ball of the reply, but Zimbabwe were held together by Taibu, who hit just three fours from 106 balls.*

At Harare, September 28, 2010. **Zimbabwe won by three wickets. Ireland 238-9** (50 overs) (P. R. Stirling 52, K. J. O'Brien 73*, D. T. Johnston 30); **‡Zimbabwe 239-7** (48.5 overs) (B. R. M. Taylor 71, T. Taibu 41, E. Chigumbura 32*). *MoM:* B. R. M. Taylor. *When Zimbabwe dipped to 192-7 in the 43rd over chasing 239, Ireland looked set to level the series – but Elton Chigumbura and Graeme Cremer batted sensibly, taking their side home with an unbroken stand of 47 in 39 balls.*

At Harare, September 30, 2010. **Ireland won by 20 runs. Ireland 244** (49.4 overs) (W. T. S. Porterfield 46, K. J. O'Brien 34, A. R. White 41, J. F. Mooney 55; E. C. Rainsford 5-36); **‡Zimbabwe 224** (47.4 overs) (S. C. Williams 74, S. W. Masakadza 45*; K. J. O'Brien 3-27, G. H. Dockrell 3-41). *MoM:* J. F. Mooney. *One-day international debut: I. A. Nicolson (Zimbabwe). Ireland dipped to 128-6 before Andrew White and John Mooney started a recovery with a stand of 66. Zimbabwe lost Hamilton Masakadza in the first over and Brendan Taylor in the third to be 3-2, and although Sean Williams batted calmly, collecting nine fours from 86 balls, he received little support. Zimbabwe were 164-9 before a last-wicket stand of 60 between Shingirai Masakadza and the debutant fast bowler Ian Nicolson (whose contribution was 14) worried the Irish a little – but they eventually completed a satisfying consolation victory.*

DOMESTIC CRICKET IN ZIMBABWE, 2009-10

JOHN WARD

Zimbabwean cricket is on its way back. In a highly successful eight-month season, the country's top players had more domestic cricket than ever before, and the standard was a vast improvement on recent years.

The revival began with the decision of Zimbabwe Cricket's managing director, Ozias Bvute – blamed, along with board president Peter Chingoka, for a series of disasters – to invite back experienced people to rebuild the game. Most responded readily. The key figure was former national captain Alistair Campbell, appointed chairman of selectors and of the cricket committee. Campbell urged others to join him, including another ex-captain, Heath Streak, to coach. Cynics described all this as window-dressing, and said these whites had no power, but it was manifestly untrue: Campbell testified that he had been given a free hand in selection, with no pressure of any sort, and that all his committee's recommendations were accepted.

Players returning included Andy Blignaut, Terry Duffin, Dion Ebrahim, Gavin Ewing, Douglas Hondo, Greg Lamb, Mluleki Nkala, Raymond Price and Brendan Taylor. The most spectacular reappearance was Sean Ervine's, with 208 and 160 in his first match. Besides Streak, Andy Waller and Grant Flower returned as coaches. One former England player, Alan Butcher, was appointed national team coach; another, Chris Silverwood, came as player-coach to Mashonaland Eagles.

Domestic cricket was restructured, with franchises, based on the South African system, replacing provinces. The Logan Cup reverted to five teams (Southerns had been dropped in 2008-09), based in the five main cricketing centres. On the face of it little changed apart from the names, but they represented new identities: each franchise was responsible for nurturing cricket in a neighbouring, largely rural province. An ambitious programme was drawn up, with each franchise playing the others three times, a minimum of 12 first-class matches (there was also a final). The aim was to prepare players thoroughly in the longer game and to expedite a return to Test cricket.

In recent years there had been serious problems with interprovincial facilities, but most were resolved. The grounds were in good condition, although the two Test centres in Harare and Bulawayo were inevitably best. The standard of scoring greatly improved, but there were still concerns about the inexperience of some umpires; Matabeleland Tuskers complained that Taylor had refused to walk for a blatant catch, the umpires declined to give him out, and he went on to a century.

Recognising a serious imbalance caused by most top players living in Harare, the provincial chairmen negotiated a deal assigning many of them (subject to their agreement) to the smaller provinces. Franchises were also encouraged to engage foreign professionals, to raise the tournament's standards. Kenyans Steve Tikolo and Thomas Odoyo signed for Southern Rocks, and former Northamptonshire wicketkeeper Riki Wessels for Mid West Rhinos.

Mashonaland Eagles still proved the strongest team. Led by all-rounder Elton Chigumbura (appointed national captain in May 2010) they lost only one first-class match, when they rested players after reaching the final. Their bowling had real depth; their batting was less stable, despite Lamb and Forster Mutizwa being among five who scored 1,000 runs, a new landmark in Zimbabwean cricket.

Mid West Rhinos showed their keen fighting spirit when they had Mashonaland in serious trouble at 36 for five on the last afternoon of the final, though they could not force the victory they needed to take the title. Captain Vusi Sibanda scored a remarkable nine centuries in ten first-class matches – a record for any batsman in a non-English season – and finished with 1,612 runs at 73, while Taylor also passed 1,000. Leg-spinner Graeme Cremer was the Logan Cup's leading wicket-taker with 59. **Mountaineers** were kept out of the final after a surprise home defeat by Mid West. They had a strong core in the Churchill School quartet of Hamilton Masakadza (who averaged 74), Tatenda Taibu, Stuart Matsikenyeri and Prosper Utseya, backed up by the promising Shingi Masakadza and leg-spinning all-rounder Timycen Maruma – whose 64 first-class wickets set another seasonal record.

Despite a strong team on paper, including many former "rebels", **Matabeleland Tuskers** were plagued by injuries, loss of form, inconsistent selection and, it was rumoured, dissension in the ranks. The future of batsman Mark Vermeulen, whose psychological problems had seemed to be behind him, became uncertain again: he was twice suspended for serious misbehaviour. **Southern Rocks**, based in Masvingo, the youngest of Zimbabwe's main cricket centres, failed to win a first-class match, even when Ervine made his spectacular return.

A 50-over tournament – the Faithwear Metbank Cup – ran concurrently with the Logan Cup, although each franchise played the others twice instead of three times. Mountaineers headed the table and won a thrilling, low-scoring final in Mutare, with Mid West the losers again.

As far as public support was concerned, the highlight of the season was the Stanbic Bank Twenty20. Played over nine days, morning and afternoon, at Harare Sports Club, with Namibia's Desert Vipers as a sixth team, it was superbly marketed: the final day was watched by almost 10,000 spectators, more than at most internationals and certainly a domestic record. In the end the critical experience of Hamilton Masakadza and Taibu in playing before large crowds saw Mountaineers home in their first limited-overs final of the season, after Mashonaland crumbled under the pressure.

Unfortunately the success of the domestic season was not yet mirrored by the national side, which will be necessary to maintain the surge of interest. But it was a huge step in the right direction. A season earlier, it appeared there was no light at the end of the tunnel; afterwards, that light seemed only a few steps away.

Note: Mashonaland Eagles correspond to the previous season's Northerns, Matabeleland Tuskers to Westerns, Mid West Rhinos to Centrals (previously Midlands), Mountaineers to Easterns (previously Manicaland) and Southern Rocks to Southerns (previously Masvingo).

FIRST-CLASS AVERAGES, 2009-10

BATTING (600 runs, average 30.00)

	M	I	NO	R	HS	100s	Avge	Ct/St
H. Masakadza (*Mountaineers*)	11	18	3	1,111	188	4	74.06	6
V. Sibanda (*Mid West Rhinos & Zim. XI*)	14	26	4	1,612	215	9	73.27	15
B. R. M. Taylor (*Mid West Rhinos*)	10	18	2	1,058	217	5	66.12	13
G. A. Lamb (*Mashonaland Eagles*)	12	19	2	1,050	171	3	61.76	8
F. Mutizwa (*Mashonaland Eagles & Zim. XI*)	14	25	5	1,149	190	3	57.45	18/2
T. Taibu (*Mountaineers & Zim. XI*)	10	17	0	899	172	2	52.88	30/2
A. G. Cremer (*Mid West Rhinos*)	11	18	4	738	94	0	52.71	10
E. Chigumbura (*Mashonaland Eagles*)	10	16	1	756	105	1	50.40	8
D. D. Ebrahim (*Matabeleland Tuskers*)	10	16	0	746	114	1	46.62	7
†K. M. Dabengwa (*Matabeleland Tuskers*)	9	14	0	646	158	2	46.14	3
S. Matsikenyeri (*Mountaineers*)	11	17	1	710	110	1	44.37	4
G. M. Strydom (*Mata'land Tuskers & Zim. XI*)	12	18	0	651	89	0	36.16	6
R. W. Chakabva (*Mash'land Eagles & Zim. XI*)	14	22	0	739	111	1	33.59	36/4
R. E. Butterworth (*Mashonaland Eagles*)	12	21	1	608	109	2	30.40	6

BOWLING (20 wickets, average 30.00)

	Style	O	M	R	W	BB	5W/i	Avge
K. O. Meth (*Matabeleland Tuskers*)	RM	223.3	70	561	29	5-26	1	19.34
T. Maruma (*Mountaineers & Zim. XI*).....	LBG	362.4	54	1,260	64	6-40	7	19.68
E. C. Rainsford (*Mid West Rhinos & Zim. XI*)	RFM	319.2	62	871	40	6-66	3	21.77
E. Chigumbura (*Mashonaland Eagles*)	RFM	313.4	71	949	41	4-49	0	23.14
R. W. Price (*Mashonaland Eagles*)	SLA	437	152	838	35	5-57	1	23.94
T. N. Garwe (*Mash'land Eagles & Zim. XI*)	RFM	267.5	62	848	33	5-43	1	25.69
P. Utseya (*Mountaineers*)...............	OB	368.5	94	801	30	5-28	1	26.70
S. W. Masakadza (*Mountaineers & Zim. XI*)	RM	365.2	69	1,225	45	6-54	1	27.22
C. B. Mpofu (*Mata'land Tuskers & Zim. XI*)	RFM	362.4	75	1,156	41	5-52	2	28.19
A. G. Cremer (*Mid West Rhinos*)	LBG	547.4	115	1,668	59	8-92	5	28.27

LOGAN CUP, 2009-10

	Played	Won	Lost	Drawn	Bonus points Batting	Bowling	Points	Net run-rate
Mashonaland Eagles	12	6	1	5	38	40	168	0.39
Mid West Rhinos	12	4	1	7	28	35	145	0.09
Mountaineers	12	3	3	6	31	46	143	0.13
Matabeleland Tuskers ..	12	3	5	4	34	39	127	0.22
Southern Rocks	12	0	6	6	19	35	90	−0.91

Final: Mashonaland Eagles drew with Mid West Rhinos but won the Logan Cup by virtue of heading the table.

Win = 10pts; draw = 6pts. Bonus points awarded for the first 100 overs of each team's first innings. One bonus batting point was awarded for the first 175 runs and another point for each further 50. One bonus bowling point was awarded for the third wicket taken and every subsequent two.

At Harare, September 14–17, 2009. **Drawn. Mashonaland Eagles 317 and 271;** ‡**Mountaineers 493-7 dec** (H. Masakadza 188) **and 45-7.** *Mashonaland Eagles 10pts, Mountaineers 13pts. Hamilton Masakadza's career-best 188 helped Mountaineers to a 176-run lead – but, needing 96 to win in 12 overs, they slumped to 45-7.*

At Kwekwe, September 14–17, 2009. **Mid West Rhinos won by 135 runs. Mid West Rhinos 319** (V. Sibanda 130) **and 286-5 dec** (F. Kasteni 101*); ‡**Matabeleland Tuskers 234** (A. G. Cremer 5-74) **and 236.** *Mid West Rhinos 17pts, Matabeleland Tuskers 5pts. Vusi Sibanda's record run began with only the second century of his career, and his first on Zimbabwean soil (he scored 122 at Chittagong in 2004-05).*

At Kwekwe, September 22–25, 2009. **Drawn.** ‡**Mid West Rhinos 344** (F. Kasteni 100, B. R. M. Taylor 79; C. T. Mutombodzi 7-84) **and 370-9; Mashonaland Eagles 380** (F. Mutizwa 156*; A. G. Cremer 5-160). *Mid West Rhinos 12pts, Mashonaland Eagles 12pts. Friday Kasteni and Brendan Taylor added 204 for the third wicket.*

At Mutare, September 22–25, 2009. **Mountaineers won by eight wickets. Southern Rocks 250** (T. Maruma 5-37) **and 211** (T. Maruma 5-61); ‡**Mountaineers 287 and 180-2.** *Mountaineers 16pts, Southern Rocks 6pts. Southern Rocks were 43-7 in their second innings, then 101-9, before Alester Maregwede and Hilary Matanga added 110 for the last wicket.*

At Country Club, Harare, September 30–October 3, 2009. **Mashonaland Eagles won by 234 runs. Mashonaland Eagles 357 and 260-9 dec;** ‡**Southern Rocks 159 and 224** (R. W. Price 5-57). *Mashonaland Eagles 17pts, Southern Rocks 4pts.*

At Queens, Bulawayo, September 30–October 3, 2009. **Mountaineers won by 204 runs. Mountaineers 203 and 393-6 dec** (H. Masakadza 172*); ‡**Matabeleland Tuskers 191 and 201** (T. Maruma 5-67). *Mountaineers 15pts, Matabeleland Tuskers 5pts.*

At Queens, Bulawayo, October 14–17, 2009. **Mashonaland Eagles won by six wickets.** ‡**Matabeleland Tuskers 237** (A. M. Manyumwa 5-41) **and 227; Mashonaland Eagles 419** (R. E.

Butterworth 109, R. W. Chakabva 111) **and 46-4.** *Mashonaland Eagles 17pts, Matabeleland Tuskers 4pts. Former England bowler Chris Silverwood, now Mashonaland coach, played in this and their next match; he took 3-47 in the first innings.*

At Masvingo, October 14–17, 2009. **Drawn. ‡Southern Rocks 299** (E. C. Rainsford 5-60) **and 385-6 dec** (E. Chauluka 113*); **Mid West Rhinos 290** (V. Sibanda 107) **and 189-4** (V. Sibanda 101*). *Southern Rocks 13pts, Mid West Rhinos 13pts. Vusi Sibanda scored twin centuries for the second time in successive matches (following his 209 and 116* v Kenya – see Wisden 2010 p 1456).*

At Mutare, October 22–25, 2009. **Mid West Rhinos won by 19 runs. Mid West Rhinos 136** (T. Maruma 6-40) **and 416** (V. Sibanda 215); **‡Mountaineers 303** (J. Mawudzi 105; D. R. Higgins 6-93) **and 230** (D. R. Higgins 5-58). *Mid West Rhinos 13pts, Mountaineers 7pts. Jethro Mawudzi scored 105 on first-class debut. Sibanda's career-best 215 was his second double-hundred in three weeks. Leg-spinners Timycen Maruma and Dylon Higgins took 21 wickets between them.*

At Masvingo, October 22–25, 2009. **Matabeleland Tuskers won by an innings and 214 runs. ‡Matabeleland Tuskers 554-9 dec** (T. Duffin 144); **Southern Rocks 141 and 199.** *Matabeleland Tuskers 18pts, Southern Rocks 1pt. This was the first first-class win for a Matabeleland side since April 2007, when they won under the name Westerns.*

At Queens, Bulawayo, November 16–19, 2009. **Drawn. ‡Matabeleland Tuskers 418** (C. K. Coventry 100; A. G. Cremer 7-124); **Mid West Rhinos 207** (V. Sibanda 111; C. B. Mpofu 5-52) **and 419-7** (M. H. Wessels 114, B. R. M. Taylor 168). *Matabeleland Tuskers 14pts, Mid West Rhinos 10pts. Sibanda's seventh hundred in six first-class matches (11 innings) made him the first batsman to score 1,000 in a Zimbabwean season, beating Grant Flower's 983 in 12 games in 1994-95, but failed to avert the follow-on.*

At Mutare, November 16–19, 2009. **Mashonaland Eagles won by six wickets. Mountaineers 291** (S. Matsikenyeri 110) **and 249** (K. M. Jarvis 6-60); **‡Mashonaland Eagles 315 and 227-4.** *Mashonaland Eagles 17pts, Mountaineers 7pts.*

At Harare, November 24–27, 2009. **Mashonaland Eagles won by six wickets. Mid West Rhinos 312** (V. Sibanda 153) **and 269;** **‡Mashonaland Eagles 406** (F. Mutizwa 190) **and 176-4.** *Mashonaland Eagles 18pts, Mid West Rhinos 5pts.*

At Masvingo, November 24–27, 2009. **Drawn. Mountaineers 350** (H. Matanga 5-98) **and 145-4 dec; ‡Southern Rocks 237** (T. Maruma 6-100). *Southern Rocks 10pts, Mountaineers 12pts.*

At Mutare, December 2–5, 2009. **Drawn. Matabeleland Tuskers 195; ‡Mountaineers 348-6.** *Mountaineers 14pts, Matabeleland Tuskers 9pts.*

At Masvingo, December 2–5, 2009. **Drawn. Southern Rocks 321 and 104-8; ‡Mashonaland Eagles 512-8 dec** (F. Mutizwa 113, G. A. Lamb 106; N. B. Mahwire 5-92). *Southern Rocks 9pts, Mashonaland Eagles 13pts.*

At Harare, December 10–13, 2009. **Mashonaland Eagles won by nine wickets. ‡Matabeleland Tuskers 217 and 153** (T. N. Garwe 5-43); **Mashonaland Eagles 307 and 66-1.** *Mashonaland Eagles 17pts, Matabeleland Tuskers 5pts.*

At Kwekwe, December 10–13, 2009. **Drawn. ‡Mid West Rhinos 185; Southern Rocks 0-0.** *Mid West Rhinos 7pts, Southern Rocks 10pts.*

At Queens, Bulawayo, January 4–6, 2010. **Matabeleland Tuskers won by an innings and 87 runs. Southern Rocks 149 and 220; ‡Matabeleland Tuskers 456-5 dec** (C. K. Coventry 100*). *Matabeleland Tuskers 20pts, Southern Rocks 2pts.*

At Kwekwe, January 4–7, 2010. **Drawn. Mid West Rhinos 202** (S. W. Masakadza 6-54) **and 94-1; ‡Mountaineers 362-9 dec** (H. Masakadza 155; E. C. Rainsford 5-83). *Mid West Rhinos 8pts, Mountaineers 13pts. Hamilton Masakadza and Tatenda Taibu (95) added 235 for Mountaineers' third wicket.*

At Harare, January 13–16, 2010. **Drawn. Mashonaland Eagles 266 and 264** (P. Masvaure 101); **‡Mountaineers 241 and 190-4.** *Mashonaland Eagles 12pts, Mountaineers 12pts.*

At Kwekwe, January 13–16, 2010. **Mid West Rhinos won by eight wickets. ‡Matabeleland Tuskers 337-8 dec** (K. M. Dabengwa 158) **and 240; Mid West Rhinos 408** (V. Sibanda 131, B. R. M. Taylor 104; K. O. Meth 5-26) **and 172-2.** *Mid West Rhinos 17pts, Matabeleland Tuskers*

5pts. Sibanda's 131 was his ninth century of the season, in ten first-class matches and 17 innings. No other batsman had scored more than eight in a non-English season.

At Kwekwe, January 20–23, 2010. **Drawn. Mashonaland Eagles 376** (G. A. Lamb 171) **and 204** (A. G. Cremer 8-92); ‡**Mid West Rhinos 286-9 dec** and **168-5.** *Mid West Rhinos 13pts, Mashonaland Eagles 14pts. Leg-spinner Graeme Cremer claimed a career-best 12-203 in the match.*

At Mutare, January 20–23, 2010. **Mountaineers won by an innings and 114 runs. Southern Rocks 263** (T. Maruma 5-107) **and 185** (P. Utseya 5-28); ‡**Mountaineers 562-9 dec** (H. Masakadza 183, S. W. Masakadza 100*). *Mountaineers 18pts, Southern Rocks 3pts. Southern Rocks conceded 500-plus for the third time in the season. For Mountaineers, Hamilton Masakadza scored his fourth century of the tournament, all of them over 150, while his brother Shingi reached a maiden hundred from 79 balls with seven fours and three sixes, adding 141* with Prosper Utseya for the ninth wicket.*

At Harare, January 27–30, 2010. **Mashonaland Eagles won by an innings and 19 runs. Southern Rocks 188 and 68;** ‡**Mashonaland Eagles 275-9 dec.** *Mashonaland Eagles 17pts, Southern Rocks 5pts. Southern Rocks suffered their third successive innings defeat after being bowled out for 68, the season's lowest total; slow left-armer Ray Price returned figures of 20–10–21–4.*

At Queens, Bulawayo, January 27–30, 2010. **Drawn. Matabeleland Tuskers 236 and 303-8 dec** (D. D. Ebrahim 114); ‡**Mountaineers 265** (T. Mupariwa 6-52) **and 104-4.** *Matabeleland Tuskers 12pts, Mountaineers 12pts.*

At Queens, Bulawayo, February 3–6, 2010. **Matabeleland Tuskers won by seven wickets. Matabeleland Tuskers 425-8 dec** (K. M. Dabengwa 136) **and 142-3;** ‡**Mashonaland Eagles 264 and 300** (R. E. Butterworth 102; C. B. Mpofu 5-75). *Matabeleland Tuskers 19pts, Mashonaland Eagles 4pts. Already through to the final, Mashonaland rested four top players and suffered their only first-class defeat of the season.*

At Masvingo, February 3–6, 2010. **Drawn.** ‡**Mid West Rhinos 267** (M. N. Waller 124) **and 443-5 dec** (B. R. M. Taylor 217); **Southern Rocks 374** (S. M. Ervine 208; A. G. Cremer 5-125) **and 278-8** (S. M. Ervine 160). *Southern Rocks 14pts, Mid West Rhinos 12pts. Sean Ervine returned to Zimbabwean cricket with two huge centuries, including a maiden double. Coming in at 13-4 in the first innings, he put on 178 with his brother Craig; on the final day, he scored another 160 to end Southern Rocks' losing run. In between, Brendan Taylor scored his own maiden double-hundred, and added 235 for Mid West's second wicket with Innocent Chikunya.*

At Mutare, March 23–25, 2010. **Mid West Rhinos won by eight wickets. Mountaineers 212 and 230;** ‡**Mid West Rhinos 338** (M. N. Waller 117; T. L. Chatara 5-42) **and 106-2.** *Mid West Rhinos 18pts, Mountaineers 4pts. Victory lifted Mid West Rhinos ahead of Mountaineers to join Mashonaland in the final.*

At Masvingo, March 23–26, 2010. **Drawn. Matabeleland Tuskers 260 and 397;** ‡**Southern Rocks 431** (C. R. Ervine 108, R. Mutumbami 100) **and 136-8.** *Southern Rocks 13pts, Matabeleland Tuskers 11pts.*

Final

At Harare, March 30–April 3, 2010. **Drawn. Mashonaland Eagles won the Logan Cup by virtue of heading the qualifying table. Mid West Rhinos 364** (B. R. M. Taylor 131) **and 335-6 dec** (M. H. Wessels 108*); ‡**Mashonaland Eagles 451** (G. A. Lamb 159, E. Chigumbura 105; E. C. Rainsford 6-66) **and 67-5.** *Mid West captain Vusi Sibanda took his record season's aggregate to 1,612 runs at 73.27, but was overshadowed by four centuries, including team-mate Brendan Taylor's fifth of the season. In reply, Greg Lamb and Elton Chigumbura added 211 for Mashonaland's fifth wicket, helping to build a lead which seemed enough to ensure them the Logan Cup – until the final afternoon, when they were set 249 and slid to 36-5 against Taurai Muzarabani and Graeme Cremer. The Eagles hung on for 27 overs to secure the draw and the title.*

LOGAN CUP WINNERS

1993-94	Mashonaland U-24	1999-2000	Mashonaland	2005-06	No competition
1994-95	Mashonaland	2000-01	Mashonaland	2006-07	Easterns
1995-96	Matabeleland	2001-02	Mashonaland	2007-08	Northerns
1996-97	Mashonaland	2002-03	Mashonaland	2008-09	Easterns
1997-98	Mashonaland	2003-04	Mashonaland	2009-10	Mashonaland Eagles
1998-99	Matabeleland	2004-05	Mashonaland		

Mashonaland/Mashonaland Eagles have won the title ten times, Matabeleland and Easterns twice, Mashonaland U-24 and Northerns once each.

FAITHWEAR METBANK ONE-DAY COMPETITION, 2009-10

50-over league plus knockout

	Played	Won	Lost	No result	Bonus points	Points	Net run-rate
Mountaineers	8	6	1	1	2	28	0.78
Mid West Rhinos	8	5	3	0	0	20	0.07
Mashonaland Eagles.	8	3	3	2	0	16	−0.02
Southern Rocks	8	3	4	1	0	14	−0.29
Matabeleland Tuskers	8	1	7	0	0	4	−0.48

Semi-finals

At Kwekwe, April 7, 2010. **Mid West Rhinos won by two wickets. Mashonaland Eagles 221-9** (50 overs); ‡**Mid West Rhinos 222-8** (46.3 overs).

At Mutare, April 7, 2010. **Mountaineers won by seven wickets. Southern Rocks 131** (39.5 overs); ‡**Mountaineers 134-3** (19.5 overs).

Final

At Mutare, April 10, 2010. **Mountaineers won by three wickets. Mid West Rhinos 144** (35.5 overs); ‡**Mountaineers 149-7** (37.5 overs). *An ice-cool 83-run partnership between Prosper Utseya and Shingi Masakadza took the Mountaineers from 66-7 to their target.*

STANBIC BANK TWENTY20, 2009-10

	Played	Won	Lost	No result	Points	Net run-rate
Mashonaland Eagles.	5	4	1	0	8	1.06
Mountaineers	5	3	2	0	6	−0.40
Desert Vipers (Namibia)	5	2	2	1	5	0.32
Matabeleland Tuskers	5	2	2	1	5	−0.61
Mid West Rhinos	5	2	3	0	4	−0.22
Southern Rocks	5	1	4	0	2	−0.24

Third-place play-off

At Harare, February 20, 2010. **Desert Vipers won by 35 runs. ‡Desert Vipers 126-7** (20 overs); **Matabeleland Tuskers 91** (18.3 overs).

Final

At Harare, February 20, 2010. **Mountaineers won by nine wickets. Mashonaland Eagles 105** (18.4 overs); ‡**Mountaineers 106-1** (17.3 overs).
 Mountaineers captain Hamilton Masakadza saw his team to the title with 64* from 55 balls.

NEW ZEALAND v SRI LANKA IN THE USA, 2010

Twenty20 internationals (2): New Zealand 1, Sri Lanka 1

An ambitious initiative by the USA Cricket Association led to New Zealand and Sri Lanka travelling to Florida shortly after the World Twenty20 in the West Indies for a short series of Twenty20 internationals in May. It was the first time two Test-playing countries had contested official international matches in the United States: more may follow as a result of a three-year agreement between the American and New Zealand boards. The US national team and Jamaica also played matches there at the same time.

The crowds were small, limited mainly to Sri Lankan expatriates, and excitement in the matches themselves was kept to a minimum by a slow, spongy turf pitch at the Central Broward Regional Park Stadium in Lauderhill (which is inland of Fort Lauderdale and just north of Miami). The losing side in both matches was bowled out for less than 100, and the highest individual score of the weekend was 36 not out.

This was originally planned to be a three-match series starting on a Thursday night, but problems with the floodlights and ticket sales reduced it to a weekend double-header. "The original match was scheduled under lights," said Don Lockerbie, the US board's chief executive at the time. "We wanted to move it to the afternoon, but that's tough to pull off in an American working week." Kumar Sangakkara, Sri Lanka's captain, admitted that the pitches could have been better, but remained upbeat about the experiment: "The ground facilities are pretty good, there's great seating, and the atmosphere is brilliant to play cricket in."

NATIONAL SQUADS

New Zealand *D. L. Vettori, I. G. Butler, M. J. Guptill, G. J. Hopkins, B. B. McCullum, N. L. McCullum, A. J. McKay, K. D. Mills, R. J. Nicol, J. D. P. Oram, A. J. Redmond, T. G. Southee, S. B. Styris, L. R. P. L. Taylor. *Coach:* M. J. Greatbatch.

S. E. Bond was originally selected, but announced his retirement and was replaced by McKay. J. D. Ryder was also originally chosen, but withdrew with an elbow injury and was not replaced.

Sri Lanka *K. C. Sangakkara, L. D. Chandimal, T. M. Dilshan, H. C. U. Jayasinghe, S. T. Jayasuriya, D. P. M. D. Jayawardene, C. K. Kapugedera, K. M. D. N. Kulasekara, S. L. Malinga, A. D. Mathews, B. A. W. Mendis, M. T. T. Mirando, N. L. T. C. Perera, S. Randiv, U. W. M. B. C. A. Welagedara. *Coach:* T. H. Bayliss.

NEW ZEALAND v SRI LANKA

First Twenty20 International

At Lauderhill, May 22, 2010. New Zealand won by 28 runs. Toss: New Zealand. Twenty20 international debuts: A. J. McKay, R. J. Nicol.

All New Zealand's batsmen found scoring difficult on a spongy pitch, but the Sri Lankans had even more trouble: after Mahela Jayawardene fell to the second ball of the reply, only Sangakkara and Mathews (who took 16 from the ninth over, bowled by Nathan McCullum) reached double figures, and it was left to the last-wicket pair to inch them past their previous-lowest Twenty20 international total of 87. Styris collected the match award after taking two wickets in his second over and another in his third, and then flew to Fiji for his wedding.

Man of the Match: S. B. Styris.

New Zealand		B	4	6
†B. B. McCullum *c 4 b 8*	18	13	2	1
A. J. Redmond *c 10 b 4*	8	10	1	0
R. J. Nicol *b 9*	10	15	1	0
L. R. P. L. Taylor *run out*	27	30	3	0
S. B. Styris *b 11*	10	12	0	0
*D. L. Vettori *not out*	21	16	1	0
M. J. Guptill *b 11*	10	10	0	0
N. L. McCullum *c 1 b 10*	9	12	0	0
K. D. Mills *not out*	2	2	0	0
L-b 1, w 4	5			

6 overs: 33-2   (20 overs) 120-7

1/25 2/27 3/51 4/71 5/77 6/94 7/113

T. G. Southee and A. J. McKay did not bat.

Mathews 3–0–17–1; Kulasekara 3–0–22–1; Malinga 4–0–25–1; Randiv 2–0–12–1; Perera 4–0–25–0; Mendis 4–0–18–2.

12th man J. D. P. Oram.

Sri Lanka		B	4	6
D. P. M. D. Jayawardene *c 1 b 9*	0	2	0	0
T. M. Dilshan *b 9*	6	7	1	0
*†K. C. Sangakkara *c 5 b 6*	17	25	1	0
A. D. Mathews *c 12 b 5*	27	31	1	1
C. K. Kapugedera *c 2 b 5*	7	11	0	0
C. U. Jayasinghe *not out*	9	20	0	0
N. L. T. C. Perera *c 8 b 5*	3	5	0	0
K. M. D. N. Kulasekara *run out*	6	7	1	0
S. Randiv *c 1 b 11*	6	4	1	0
S. L. Malinga *run out*	0	2	0	0
B. A. W. Mendis *b 11*	2	5	0	0
B 1, l-b 4, w 3, n-b 1	9			

6 overs: 25-2   (19.4 overs) 92

1/0 2/20 3/48 4/62 5/62 6/69 7/78 8/85 9/85

Mills 4–0–17–2; McKay 3.4–0–20–2; Southee 3–0–10–0; N. L. McCullum 2–0–19–0; Vettori 4–0–11–1; Styris 3–0–10–3.

Umpires: M. Erasmus and I. J. Gould.   Third umpire: R. J. Tucker.

NEW ZEALAND v SRI LANKA

Second Twenty20 International

At Lauderhill, May 23, 2010. Sri Lanka won by seven wickets. Toss: New Zealand.

Another treacly track posed problems for the batsmen, and this time it was the New Zealanders who struggled more. They slumped to 13 for five in the fifth over – Kulasekara, mostly bowling off-cutters, took three wickets in his first over and followed that with a maiden to Hopkins – before Vettori and Nathan McCullum shared a stand of 45, which ended when Vettori was given out caught behind, although he suggested his bat had hit the pitch rather than the ball as he tried to sweep Mendis. Malinga polished off the innings with three wickets in four balls; the last two, from consecutive deliveries, both sent the off stump flying. New Zealand's total was their lowest in Twenty20 internationals (previously 99 against Pakistan at The Oval in 2009). Sri Lanka made sure they did not lose early wickets, and had all but ensured victory by the ten-over stage at 58 for one. Perera then fell to a stunning leaping catch by Rob Nicol on the long-on boundary, but Dilshan anchored his team to victory. A squared series was unsatisfactory for at least one American cricket fan, Sham Samaroo, who hijacked the PA system and announced there would be a "super-over" decider. Vettori waved his hands in refusal.

Man of the Match: K. M. D. N. Kulasekara.   Man of the Series: D. L. Vettori.

New Zealand

		B	4	6
B. B. McCullum *b 9*	1	7	0	0
A. J. Redmond *lbw b 9*	1	2	0	0
L. R. P. L. Taylor *lbw b 5*	5	5	0	0
R. J. Nicol *lbw b 9*	0	1	0	0
*D. L. Vettori *c 4 b 11*	27	24	2	0
†G. J. Hopkins *run out*	1	8	0	0
N. L. McCullum *not out*	36	39	2	0
J. D. P. Oram *c 6 b 10*	3	7	0	0
K. D. Mills *lbw b 11*	0	2	0	0
T. G. Southee *b 10*	4	9	0	0
A. J. McKay *b 10*	0	1	0	0
W 3	3			

6 overs: 17-5   (17.3 overs)   81

1/3 2/4 3/4 4/8 5/13 6/58 7/67 8/68 9/81

Mathews 4–0–22–1; Kulasekara 3–1–4–3; Malinga 2.3–0–12–3; Mendis 4–0–19–2; Jayasuriya 1–0–12–0; Perera 2–0–8–0; Dilshan 1–0–4–0.

Sri Lanka

		B	4	6
D. P. M. D. Jayawardene *c 1 b 8*	17	12	2	1
T. M. Dilshan *not out*	33	49	2	0
N. L. T. C. Perera *c 4 b 7*	24	17	2	1
*†K. C. Sangakkara *st 6 b 7*	5	11	0	0
A. D. Mathews *not out*	0	4	0	0
B 1, w 2	3			

6 overs: 29-1   (15.3 overs)   82-3

1/19 2/63 3/80

C. K. Kapugedera, S. T. Jayasuriya, L. D. Chandimal, K. M. D. N. Kulasekara, S. L. Malinga and B. A. W. Mendis did not bat.

Mills 3–0–18–0; McKay 2–0–11–0; Oram 2–0–3–1; N. L. McCullum 4–0–15–2; Vettori 2–0–10–0; Southee 1–0–15–0; Nicol 1.3–0–9–0.

Umpires: M. Erasmus and R. J. Tucker.   Third umpire: I. J. Gould.
Series referee: A. J. Pycroft.

ICC WORLD TWENTY20 QUALIFIER

1. Afghanistan 2. Ireland 3. UAE 4. Netherlands

The eight leading Associate teams assembled in the UAE in February 2010 to fight it out for the two places available at the top table – the imminent World Twenty20 in the West Indies. Afghanistan completed their improbable rise by winning the tournament to qualify for their first senior global event, while Ireland confirmed their high standing by taking the other place with some ease. Ireland's two defeats came against Afghanistan, in the qualifying stage and in the final. Only those matches involving the six nations with full one-day international status were considered official, meaning that the games played by the UAE and the USA (a controversial addition to the tournament anyway, for marketing reasons: their overall ranking did not merit their inclusion) do not count in the records for Twenty20 internationals.

Group A

At Abu Dhabi, February 9, 2010. **USA won by six wickets.** ‡Scotland 120-7 (20 overs) (G. M. Hamilton 41); **USA** 121-4 (19.1 overs) (C. D. Wright 62, L. J. Cush 41). *MoM:* C. D. Wright.

At Dubai, February 9, 2010. **Afghanistan won by 13 runs. Afghanistan** 139-8 (20 overs) (Noor Ali Zadran 42, Mohammad Nabi 43*); ‡**Ireland** 126 (19.2 overs) (W. T. S. Porterfield 35; Karim Sadiq 3-15). *MoM:* Mohammad Nabi.

At Abu Dhabi, February 10, 2010. **Afghanistan won by 14 runs. Afghanistan** 131-7 (20 overs) (Noor Ali Zadran 42, Mohammad Shahzad 30; K. J. Coetzer 3-25); ‡Scotland 117-9 (20 overs) (G. M. Hamilton 32, N. F. I. McCallum 38; Hamid Hassan 3-32). *MoM:* Noor Ali Zadran.

At Abu Dhabi, February 10, 2010. **Ireland won by 78 runs.** ‡Ireland 202-4 (20 overs) (W. T. S. Porterfield 45, N. J. O'Brien 84, A. R. Cusack 46); **USA** 124-6 (20 overs) (A. Thyagarajan 72*; P. Connell 4-14). *MoM:* N. J. O'Brien. *Niall O'Brien hit ten fours and two sixes from 50 balls, and put on 83 with William Porterfield and 89 with Alex Cusack. Paul Connell and Trent Johnston (2-17) reduced the USA to 25-6 (they were 8-4 in the third over) before a stand of 99* between Aditya Thyagarajan, who hit 11 fours, and Orlando Baker (28*).*

At Dubai, February 11, 2010. **Afghanistan won by 29 runs.** ‡Afghanistan 135-4 (20 overs) (Nawroz Mangal 30); **USA** 106-7 (20 overs) (Hamid Hassan 3-14). *MoM:* Hamid Hassan.

At Dubai, February 11, 2010 (floodlit). **Ireland won by 37 runs.** ‡Ireland 136-7 (20 overs); **Scotland** 99 (18.3 overs) (K. J. Coetzer 43, G. D. Drummond 35; D. T. Johnston 3-20). *MoM:* D. T. Johnston. *In a low-scoring match eight Irishmen reached ten, but no one passed 20 (Gary Wilson and Andrew White both made 19). Then Scotland were 12-5 before Kyle Coetzer and Gordon Drummond put on 62 – but they were the only batsmen to make double figures.*

Afghanistan 6pts, Ireland 4pts, USA 2pts, Scotland 0pts.

Group B

At Abu Dhabi, February 9, 2010. **UAE won by 15 runs.** ‡UAE 165-5 (20 overs) (Arfan Haider 59, Saqib Ali 31); **Kenya** 150-5 (20 overs) (M. A. Ouma 39, C. O. Obuya 42*). *MoM:* Arfan Haider.

At Dubai, February 9, 2010 (floodlit). **Netherlands won by six wickets.** ‡Canada 142-7 (20 overs) (G. E. F. Barnett 36, I. S. Billcliff 37); **Netherlands** 146-4 (19.1 overs) (A. N. Kervezee 39, B. Zuiderent 43*). *MoM:* B. Zuiderent. *Twenty20 international debuts:* I. S. Billcliff (Canada); A. F. Buurman (Netherlands). *Canada's captain and opener Rizwan Cheema retired hurt after being hit in the face by the third ball he received.*

At Dubai, February 10, 2010. **Kenya won by nine wickets. Canada** 138-9 (20 overs) (Rizwan Cheema 32, G. E. F. Barnett 30, A. Bagai 36; N. N. Odhiambo 3-16); ‡Kenya 141-1 (14.5 overs) (A. A. Obanda 79, S. O. Tikolo 50*). *MoM:* A. A. Obanda. *Twenty20 international debut:* Arsalan Qadir (Canada). *Canada's former captain John Davison fell first ball for his second duck of the* *tournament. Alex Obanda, who hit 11 fours and a six, and Steve Tikolo all but ensured victory with 126 in 12.4 overs for Kenya's first wicket.*

At Dubai, February 10, 2010 (floodlit). **UAE won by six wickets. Netherlands 164-8** (20 overs) (D. L. S. van Bunge 76, P. W. Borren 32*; Qasim Zubair 5-24); ‡**UAE 168-4** (18.5 overs) (Naeemuddin Islam 60*, Khurram Khan 52*). *MoM:* Naeemuddin Islam. *The UAE's reply was tottering at 67-4 before Naeemuddin Islam and captain Khurram Khan put on 101* in 11.2 overs.*

At Abu Dhabi, February 11, 2010. **UAE won by 42 runs. UAE 142-7** (20 overs) (Arfan Haider 46, Saqib Ali 43; Khurram Chauhan 3-20); ‡**Canada 100** (15.5 overs). *MoM:* Saqib Ali. *John Davison finally survived the first over, only to be out for eight in the second.*

At Abu Dhabi, February 11, 2010. **Netherlands won by seven wickets. Kenya 130** (19.4 overs) (C. O. Obuya 33, J. K. Kamande 42; Mudassar Bukhari 4-33, P. M. Seelaar 4-19); ‡**Netherlands 133-3** (19.1 overs) (A. N. Kervezee 33, E. S. Szwarczynski 45). *MoM:* P. M. Seelaar. *Twenty20 international debuts:* M. B. S. Jonkman, Mohammad Kashif (Netherlands).

UAE 6pts, Netherlands 4pts, Kenya 2pts, Canada 0pts.

Super Fours

At Dubai, February 12, 2010. **Netherlands won by four wickets. Afghanistan 128-9** (20 overs); ‡**Netherlands 132-6** (18.5 overs) (A. N. Kervezee 39; Mohammad Nabi 3-23). *MoM:* R. N. ten Doeschate. *After pulling him 1-15 from two overs and pulling off one of four run-outs in the Afghan innings, Ryan ten Doeschate took his team home with 24* from 20 balls.*

At Dubai, February 12, 2010. **Ireland won by 22 runs.** ‡**Ireland 152-7** (20 overs) (N. J. O'Brien 46; Qadar Nawaz 3-23); **UAE 130** (19.1 overs) (Saqib Ali 63; A. R. Cusack 3-19). *MoM:* A. R. Cusack. *Despite Saqib Ali's 63 from 49 balls, the UAE never recovered from 17-3 after 13 balls of their reply.*

At Dubai, February 13, 2010. **Afghanistan won by four wickets.** ‡**UAE 100-9** (20 overs) (Mohammad Nabi 3-17); **Afghanistan 101-6** (19.3 overs) (Noor Ali Zadran 38*). *MoM:* Noor Ali Zadran. *UAE made another poor start in what became a low-scoring game, slumping to 11-3 before Saqib Ali (24) top-scored again. Afghanistan looked set for a straightforward victory at 88-3 in the 18th over, but lost three wickets for 12 before Noor Ali inched them over the line and into the World Twenty20 in the West Indies.*

At Dubai, February 13, 2010. **Ireland won by 65 runs.** ‡**Ireland 151-6** (20 overs) (A. R. Cusack 65); **Netherlands 86** (15.3 overs) (R. N. ten Doeschate 32; G. H. Dockrell 4-20). *MoM:* A. R. Cusack. *Ireland made sure of a place in the World Twenty20 proper with a comfortable victory. The Netherlands lost two wickets in the first over of their chase, and subsided to 86 all out, with George Dockrell taking four late wickets.*

Super Fours table

	Played	Won	Lost	Points	Net Run-Rate
IRELAND	3	2	1	4	1.17
AFGHANISTAN	3	2	1	4	0.10
UAE	3	1	2	2	−0.24
Netherlands	3	1	2	2	−1.10

The top two teams in each group progressed to the Super Fours, where they played the qualifiers from the other group. The result from the match against the other qualifier from the original group was carried forward to the Super Fours table.

Final

At Dubai, February 13, 2010 (floodlit). **Afghanistan won by eight wickets.** ‡**Ireland 142-8** (20 overs) (Nawroz Mangal 3-23); **Afghanistan 147-2** (17.3 overs) (Karim Sadiq 34, Mohammad Shahzad 65*). *MoM:* Mohammad Shahzad. *Man of the Series:* A. R. Cusack. *Twenty20 international debut:* N. G. Jones (Ireland). *Ireland lost wickets too regularly to reach a commanding total, and Afghanistan overhauled their target with some ease, Mohammad Shahzad completing victory with a six off Paul Connell to go with six fours from 46 balls.*

OTHER A-TEAM TOURS

BANGLADESH A v SOUTH AFRICA A, 2010

South Africa A, captained by Thami Tsolekile, toured Bangladesh in April–May 2010. They won a two-match first-class series against Bangladesh A 2–0, and beat West Indies A in the final of the Tri-Nation one-day series.

At Mirpur, April 23–26, 2010. **South Africa A won by an innings and four runs.** ‡**Bangladesh A** 346 (Shahriar Nafees 45, Shamsur Rahman 84, Nazimuddin 48, Farhad Hossain 38, Noor Hossain 49; S. van Zyl 4-37) **and 326** (Shahriar Nafees 51, Shamsur Rahman 38, Nazimuddin 82, Faisal Hossain 51, Saghir Hossain 44; D. Elgar 3-68); **South Africa A 676-9 dec** (D. Elgar 48, A. N. Petersen 116, J. D. Vandiar 51, H. G. Kuhn 191, T. L. Tsolekile 140, J. J. van der Wath 30, Extras 36; Faisal Hossain 5-183). *Johan van der Wath made his first South African representative appearance since the lifting of his ICL-related ban. One of his three victims, captain Junaid Siddique, injured his hand at slip, ending his involvement in the series. South Africa A plundered their highest total abroad, with Heino Kuhn and Tsolekile adding 283 for the sixth wicket.*

At Savar (BKSP No. 2 Ground), April 29–May 2, 2010. **South Africa A won by 185 runs.** ‡**South Africa A 482** (A. N. Petersen 92, R. R. Rossouw 81, H. G. Kuhn 48, T. L. Tsolekile 111, V. D. Philander 39*, P. L. Harris 39; Faisal Hossain 3-111, Noor Hossain 4-146) **and 143-3 dec** (A. N. Petersen 40, R. R. Rossouw 68); **Bangladesh A 275** (Shamsur Rahman 89, Nazimuddin 53, Faisal Hossain 37; P. L. Harris 6-90) **and 225** (Mehrab Hossain 41, Shamsur Rahman 57, Faisal Hossain 43; P. L. Harris 3-85). *Paul Harris, flown in ahead of this match, chipped away for his ninth first-class six-for. Shamsur Rahman, captaining Bangladesh A, batted for a total of six hours 24 minutes, but received significant support only from his second-wicket partners: Nazimuddin helped add 106 in the first innings, and Mehrab Hossain 87 in the second.*

BANGLADESH A v WEST INDIES A, 2010

West Indies A, captained by Travis Dowlin, toured Bangladesh in May 2010. They lost to South Africa A in the final of the Tri-Nation one-day series, and won a two-match first-class series against Bangladesh A 1–0.

At Mirpur, May 17–20, 2010. **West Indies A won by 114 runs.** ‡**West Indies A 285** (D. S. Smith 30, T. M. Dowlin 75, D. M. Bravo 102, B. P. Nash 44; Suhrawadi Shuvo 6-124) **and 269-6 dec** (D. S. Smith 62, T. M. Dowlin 32, K. A. Edwards 72, D. M. Bravo 37; Suhrawadi Shuvo 3-104); **Bangladesh A 125** (Nazimuddin 33; S. Shillingford 4-30) **and 315** (Shahriar Nafees 133, Saghir Hossain 47, Suhrawadi Shuvo 64*; L. S. Baker 3-70, O. V. Brown 3-60). *Darren Bravo (who made a century and three fifties in the tri-series) sauntered to 102 in 137 balls, before becoming the first of seven wickets for 45 runs. Suhrawadi Shuvo took three in five balls of the 69th over. Bangladesh A then surrendered nine for 68. In a doomed pursuit of 430, Shahriar Nafees scored his first century since November 2007, 90 of his 133 coming in boundaries.*

At Savar (BKSP No. 2 Ground), May 23–26, 2010. **Drawn.** ‡**West Indies A 268** (B. P. Nash 99*, C. A. K. Walton 70; Syed Rasel 5-59, Suhrawadi Shuvo 5-85) **and 109-3** (O. J. Phillips 47*, B. P. Nash 32*); **Bangladesh A 272** (Nazimuddin 72, Faisal Hossain 100, Saghir Hossain 35; S. Shillingford 3-82, O. V. Brown 3-79). *West Indies A led by 105 with seven wickets in hand, but the last day was washed out. In the first innings, Brendan Nash struck only eight boundaries and was stranded unbeaten on 99 when No. 11 Nelon Pascal completed Syed Rasel's five-for. Shuvo removed four of Nash's middle-order colleagues. Bangladesh A owed their slender lead to Nazimuddin, fifth out at 130, and Faisal Hossain, who struck four fours and five sixes in 199 balls.*

AUSTRALIA A v SRI LANKA A, 2010

Sri Lanka A toured Australia in June–July 2010. Captained by Thilina Kandamby, they lost two first-class matches against Australia A, and lost a three-day warm-up (non-first-class) against the Australian Cricket Academy by one wicket. Captained by Chamara Kapugedera, they beat Australia A 2–1 in a four-match one-day series at Townsville.

At Brisbane (Allan Border Field), June 18–21, 2010. **Australia A won by 107 runs. ‡Australia A 208** (S. N. J. O'Keefe 61, B. W. Hilfenhaus 42; S. M. S. M. Senanayake 8-70) **and 318** (M. Klinger 32, U. T. Khawaja 30, G. J. Bailey 87, S. N. J. O'Keefe 47, B. W. Hilfenhaus 50; S. M. S. M. Senanayake 3-110, K. T. G. D. Prasad 3-59); **Sri Lanka A 103** (S. N. J. O'Keefe 7-35) **and 316** (N. T. Paranavitana 47, L. D. Chandimal 54, J. K. Silva 47, L. P. C. Silva 58, C. K. B. Kulasekara 33; B. W. Hilfenhaus 5-63, P. R. George 5-84). *Ben Hilfenhaus scored a maiden fifty and took the last five wickets on his comeback from seven months out with tendonitis of the knee; his success won him a Test recall for Australia's series against Pakistan in England. But on a sticky winter wicket, his thunder was stolen by two spinners. Sachithra Senanayake single-handedly had Australia A 92-6, and went on to take career-best innings and match figures (11-180). Steve O'Keefe's seven wickets salvaged an ultimately decisive first-innings lead of 105.*

At Townsville, June 25–27, 2010. **Australia A won by an innings and 17 runs. ‡Sri Lanka A 78** (P. R. George 4-13, A. B. McDonald 3-17) **and 307** (H. D. R. L. Thirimanne 47, L. P. C. Silva 92, C. K. B. Kulasekara 56; B. W. Hilfenhaus 3-60, J. L. Pattinson 3-59); **Australia A 402-4 dec** (E. J. M. Cowan 126, U. T. Khawaja 69, G. J. Bailey 154*, P. J. Forrest 31). *Only Dinesh Chandimal (12) and Nadeera Nawela (27) reached double figures in Sri Lanka A's first innings. Ed Cowan and Usman Khawaja ground out 141, before George Bailey freed his arms to hit 14 fours and six sixes in 138 balls before calling off the slaughter. Chamara Silva's 92 took 100 balls.*

SRI LANKA A v SOUTH AFRICA A, 2010

South Africa A, captained by Thami Tsolekile, toured Sri Lanka in August–September 2010. They drew two first-class matches against Sri Lanka A, and beat them in the final of the one-day tri-series (which also involved Pakistan A). They also drew a two-day warm-up against a Sri Lanka Board XI, and won a one-day warm-up against a Sri Lanka Development XI.

At Pallekele, August 10–13, 2010. **Drawn. South Africa A 419** (D. Elgar 74, R. R. Rossouw 131, J. D. Vandiar 68, H. G. Kuhn 87; S. M. S. M. Senanayake 3-90, S. Prasanna 3-74) **and 280-5 dec** (D. Elgar 105, S. van Zyl 81, H. G. Kuhn 51*); **‡Sri Lanka A 326** (J. K. Silva 84, S. H. T. Kandamby 34, L. J. P. Gunaratne 122; Q. Friend 4-68) **and 175-2** (F. D. M. Karunaratne 52, H. D. R. L. Thirimanne 67, L. D. Chandimal 39*). *Three hundreds and eight fifties were scored in the second first-class game staged at Pallekele. The stands were still being constructed ahead of its inaugural Test against West Indies in December and World Cup matches in 2011.*

At Colombo (SSC), August 16–19, 2010. **Drawn. ‡South Africa A 345** (D. Elgar 174, V. D. Philander 34; L. J. P. Gunaratne 3-60) **and 220-6** (S. C. Cook 52, D. Elgar 78, H. G. Kuhn 33*; B. M. A. J. Mendis 5-74); **Sri Lanka A 543-4 dec** (F. D. M. Karunaratne 184, L. D. Chandimal 244, J. K. Silva 70*). *This was the Sinhalese Sports Club's first first-class match since Sri Lanka and India made 1,349 first-innings runs combined in their July Test. Dean Elgar entrenched himself for 11 hours 45 minutes in all, moving to 431 runs in the series. Dinesh Chandimal, aged 20, scored a maiden double-hundred, sharing 369 in 108 overs with Dinuth Karunaratne.*

SRI LANKA A v PAKISTAN A, 2010

Pakistan A, captained by Azeem Ghumman, toured Sri Lanka in August–September 2010. They failed to reach the final of the one-day tri-series (won by South Africa A), and lost a two-match first-class series against Sri Lanka A 1–0. They also won a one-day warm-up against the Sri Lanka Academy.

At Galle, September 9–12, 2010. **Drawn. Sri Lanka A 308-3 dec** (F. D. M. Karunaratne 51, J. K. Silva 124*, S. H. T. Kandamby 100*); **‡Pakistan A 222-5** (Khurram Manzoor 45, Azeem Ghumman 42, Aamer Sajjad 51*, Naeem Anjum 53*; S. M. S. M. Senanayake 5-40). *Kaushal Silva and Thilina Kandamby's stand of 209* straddled all four days (rain permitted just 87 overs on the first three). When Pakistan A did bat, off-spinner Sachithra Senanayake reduced them to 124-5.*

At Hambantota, September 15–17, 2010. **Sri Lanka A won by 39 runs. Sri Lanka A 97** (B. M. A. J. Mendis 40; Junaid Khan 4-33, Hammad Azam 4-19) **and 175** (L. D. Chandimal 46, S. H. T. Kandamby 32; Junaid Khan 5-50, Zulfiqar Babar 4-38); **‡Pakistan A 94** (R. A. S. Lakmal 4-33, S. M. S. M. Senanayake 5-35) **and 139** (Hammad Azam 40; B. M. A. J. Mendis 5-32). *Twenty-two wickets tumbled on the opening day, no batsman scored a fifty, and the game was over in seven sessions; Hambantota certainly offered a break from the Sri Lankan norm on its first-class debut.*

Officials rushed to absolve the surface of blame, less than three months before it was due to host its first full international. "Not a single ball misbehaved, nor was any unplayable," said Ranjit Fernando, a national selector. "Both teams have been playing on very placid pitches in Colombo, and when the ball did a little bit they were found wanting." All out in 32 overs, Sri Lanka A somehow scrambled a three-run lead, Senanayake delivering his latest lethal spell of off-spin (in six A "Tests" in 2010, he took 33 wickets). Pakistan A needed 179 to win, but dipped terminally from 115-5, when Jeewan Mendis had Hammad Azam lbw for 40 from 81 balls, the longest stay of the match.

ZIMBABWE A v NEW ZEALAND A, 2010-11

New Zealand A, captained by James Franklin, toured Zimbabwe in October 2010, the first New Zealand side to visit since their board suspended bilateral relations in 2005. They won a three-match first-class series against Zimbabwe A 2–0, and drew a two-day warm-up against Mountaineers.

At Harare (Sports Club), October 7–10, 2010. **Drawn. New Zealand A 426** (J. M. How 92, D. R. Flynn 162, G. J. Hopkins 50*; N. Ncube 3-47, M. N. Waller 3-57) **and 280-5 dec** (T. G. McIntosh 31, J. E. C. Franklin 107*, G. J. Hopkins 73); ‡**Zimbabwe A 365-7 dec** (S. J. Marillier 46, V. Sibanda 38, C. R. Ervine 55, M. N. Waller 35, R. W. Chakabva 103*, T. Maruma 59; J. E. C. Franklin 3-36, N. B. Beard 4-87) **and 243-5** (T. M. K. Mawoyo 125*, V. Sibanda 42). *Two adventurous declarations could not defeat a grudging pitch. Daniel Flynn attacked for an 83-ball hundred and pressed on to his career-best score, featuring five sixes. Vusi Sibanda declared 61 behind on the third afternoon, upon Regis Chakabva reaching his century. From 65-4, Franklin and Gareth Hopkins averted danger in a stand of 132. Tino Mawoyo carried his bat to surpass his career-best first-class score by one, a week after making 208* for Mountaineers in the two-day warm-up on this ground.*

At Harare (Country Club), October 14–17, 2010. **New Zealand A won by ten wickets. ‡New Zealand A 526-8 dec** (T. G. McIntosh 58, J. M. How 115, M. J. Guptill 46, J. E. C. Franklin 47, R. A. Young 76, G. J. Hopkins 100*, Extras 30; N. Ncube 3-87) **and 18-0; Zimbabwe A 256** (M. N. Waller 53, F. Mutizwa 47, T. Maruma 62*; C. S. Martin 4-46, J. E. C. Franklin 5-22) **and 287** (T. M. K. Mawoyo 31, S. J. Marillier 50, F. Mutizwa 35, R. W. Chakabva 46, T. Maruma 37; B. J. Arnel 8-81). *New Zealand A's top seven clicked, and Chris Martin's opening spell claimed Stephan Marillier and Sibanda for ducks in successive balls. Franklin then swung through a resistant tail to enforce the follow-on. Brent Arnel (wicketless in the first innings) had the ball moving off the straight in his maiden eight-for.*

At Harare (Country Club), October 21–23, 2010. **New Zealand A won by nine wickets. Zimbabwe A 186** (C. S. Martin 4-41, G. W. Aldridge 3-42) **and 189** (T. M. K. Mawoyo 62, T. Maruma 43*; B. J. Arnel 3-47); ‡**New Zealand A 208** (G. J. Hopkins 69; T. Panyangara 3-52, M. T. Chinouya 3-44, T. N. Garwe 3-45) **and 168-1** (T. G. McIntosh 76*, P. J. Ingram 63). *Zimbabwe A, blown away in 55 overs, were delirious when they had New Zealand A 93-6, but would be frustrated by Hopkins, who eked 103 out of the next three wickets; he later completed a fine stumping of Chakabva. The fall of Mawoyo, who grew increasingly careless, sparked the hosts' slide from 116-4.*

WEST INDIES A v PAKISTAN A, 2010-11

Pakistan A, captained by Faisal Iqbal, toured the West Indies in November 2010. They won a five-match one-day series against West Indies A 2–1 (with two matches tied), and drew two first-class matches.

At Kingstown, St Vincent, November 18–21, 2010. **Drawn. West Indies A 305-3 dec** (K. O. A. Powell 50, K. C. Brathwaite 130, K. A. Edwards 94; Zulfiqar Babar 3-122); ‡**Pakistan A 156-1** (Khurram Manzoor 100*). *In the 104.3 overs possible on the first two days, 17-year-old Kraigg Brathwaite ground out a maiden hundred. He returned after a third-day washout to press on to 130 from 414 balls. Khurram Manzoor required just 153 to reach his century.*

At Kingstown, St Vincent, November 24–27, 2010. **Drawn. ‡Pakistan A 261** (Khurram Manzoor 104, Umair Khan 41, Shan Masood 44; V. Permaul 3-68) **and 261-7** (Khurram Manzoor 85, Faisal Iqbal 48, Yasir Arafat 35*, Yasir Shah 30*; O. V. Brown 4-100); **West Indies A 357** (K. O. A. Powell 98, A. B. Fudadin 37, J. L. Carter 48, O. V. Brown 66; Zulfiqar Babar 3-111, Yasir Shah 5-143). *Pakistan A were twice propped up by Manzoor: his hundred steered them to 203-4 (a position they squandered), and 85 from 295 balls cleared a deficit of 96 and the path to safety. The two Pakistani spinners accounted for 85 of 120 overs, taking eight wickets.*

ICC INTERCONTINENTAL CUP, 2009–10

The fifth edition of the ICC's ambitious first-class tournament for the leading non-Test nations climaxed in Dubai, where Afghanistan's rise continued with a three-day victory over Scotland in a low-scoring game. Things had looked promising for the Scots – winners of the inaugural competition in 2004 – when they took a narrow lead on first innings, but then they were bowled out for just 82, leaving Afghanistan a simple target.

Scotland had reached the final after being awarded full points from their last qualifying match, against the Zimbabwe XI. Scotland originally agreed to travel to Harare, but withdrew on advice from the British government: the Zimbabweans might have claimed the points and reached the final, but agreed to forfeit the match. Zimbabwe Cricket's managing director Ozias Bvute explained: "We feel the Intercontinental Cup is a significant competition in Scotland's development and therefore important that it gets the full benefits associated with playing in it." On the face of it this was a magnanimous gesture, although some suspected that the Zimbabweans wanted to avoid the possibility of an embarrassing defeat – either at the hands of the Scots or in the final – which might have harmed their prospects of a return to Test cricket. The ICC, which had suggested a neutral venue (as for all Afghanistan's "home" games), reluctantly accepted the Zimbabwean decision, but warned against a repeat.

Afghanistan had a less troubled route to the final, winning all four of their matches in 2010 to qualify with some ease. Their victories included scoring 494 to beat Canada in Sharjah – rather bad luck on the Canadians (who finished without a win) after they had run up 566 in their first innings. Afghanistan's amazing chase included an undefeated 214 from Mohammad Shahzad. This was one of three double-centuries in the 2009–10 tournament, the others coming from Ryan ten Doeschate, in the only match he managed for the Netherlands, and Zimbabwe's Vusi Sibanda (see page 1456 of *Wisden 2010*).

Ireland, winners of the three previous tournaments, were handicapped this time by the weather and the patchy availability of senior players, several of whom had county contracts. Regular captain William Porterfield managed only three matches and wicketkeeper Niall O'Brien two; fast bowler Boyd Rankin played none, through a mixture of county commitments and injuries.

For 2011–12, the Intercontinental Cup reverts to an eight-team competition (without Zimbabwe, but with two additional teams); the Shield is abolished.

FINAL TABLE

	Played	Won	Lost	Drawn	1st-inns Lead	Points
AFGHANISTAN	6	5	0	1	4	97
SCOTLAND	6	4	1	1	5	89
Zimbabwe XI	6	3	1	2	4	72
Ireland	6	2	1	3	3	55
Kenya	6	2	3	1	3	43
Netherlands	6	0	5	1	2	15
Canada	6	0	5	1	1	9

Win = 14pts. Tie = 7pts. Draw with more than ten hours lost to weather = 7pts. Draw with less than ten hours lost to the weather = 3pts. First-innings lead = 6pts. Tie on first innings = 3pts. Abandoned = 10pts. Teams finishing level on points separated by (a) most outright wins (b) most first-innings leads and (c) the higher net runs-per-wicket ratio.

Note: For matches played in this tournament during 2009 see *Wisden 2010* page 1455.

At Dambulla, January 21–24, 2010. **Afghanistan won by seven wickets.** ‡Ireland 405 (W. T. S. Porterfield 78, G. C. Wilson 53, A. R. Cusack 39, N. J. O'Brien 58, J. F. Mooney 58*; Hamid Hassan 3-91, Samiullah Shenwari 4-75) **and** 202 (D. T. Johnston 63*; Dawlat Ahmadzai 5-52, Mohammad Nabi 4-33); **Afghanistan 474** (Noor Ali Zadran 53, Shabir Noori 85, Nawroz Mangal 84, Mohammad Shahzad 88, Asghar Stanikzai 39, Mohammad Nabi 64; A. R. White 4-99, A. C. Botha 3-44) **and 137-3** (Noor Ali Zadran 57, Mohammad Shahzad 42*). *Afghanistan 20pts. Trent Johnston biffed 63* from No. 9 after Ireland were 101-7 in their second innings and only 32 ahead, but could not prevent a defeat which harmed Ireland's chances of defending their title (they had drawn both their matches in this tournament during 2009).*

At Nairobi (Gymkhana), January 25–28, 2010. **Scotland won by eight wickets.** Kenya 91 (C. O. Obuya 40; G. D. Drummond 3-18, R. D. Berrington 3-13) **and 323** (H. A. Varaiya 44, C. O. Obuya 38, S. O. Tikolo 34, M. A. Ouma 130; J. D. Nel 5-107, R. M. Haq 3-46); ‡**Scotland 306** (M. Q. Sheikh 108, R. D. Berrington 80; N. N. Odhiambo 3-60) **and 110-2** (K. J. Coetzer 34, D. R. Lockhart 51*). *Scotland 20pts. Scotland took charge on the opening day, shooting Kenya out in 49.1 overs – only opener Maurice Ouma (22) and Collins Obuya made double figures – then moving in to the lead before the end of the day. A patient stand of 102 in 39 overs between Qasim Sheikh, who hit 19 fours, and Richie Berrington stretched the advantage, and only a battling century from skipper Ouma (down the order at No. 6, he hit 21 fours and a six from 209 balls) prevented an innings defeat.*

At Sharjah, February 20–23, 2010. **Afghanistan won by six wickets.** ‡Canada 566 (S. Jyoti 32, T. C. Bastiampillai 55, N. R. Kumar 74, A. Bagai 93, S. Dhaniram 130, Umar Bhatti 31, H. Patel 36, Extras 34; Mirwais Ashraf 3-103, Samiullah Shenwari 4-118) **and 191-4 dec** (T. C. Bastiampillai 73, S. Jyoti 35*); **Afghanistan 264** (Shabir Noori 60, Karim Sadiq 32, Mohammad Nabi 48*; N. R. Kumar 3-58) **and 494-4** (Karim Sadiq 42, Noor Ali Zadran 52, Mohammad Shahzad 214*, Nawroz Mangal 70, Mohammad Nabi 80). *Afghanistan 14pts, Canada 6pts. Afghanistan pulled off a remarkable victory after trailing by 302 on first innings and being set 494 to win: with 18-year-old Mohammad Shahzad scoring a memorable double-century – he hit 16 fours from 258 balls, in 328 minutes – they sailed home with 14 balls to spare. It was the ninth-biggest successful run-chase in first-class history: the largest – West Zone's 541-7 to beat South Zone in India's Duleep Trophy final – had happened less then three weeks previously. Earlier, 41-year-old Sunil Dhaniram's third first-class century was the major contribution to Canada's big score – only 11 higher first-innings totals have resulted in defeat.*

At Nairobi (Gymkhana), February 20–23, 2010. **Kenya won by five wickets.** ‡Netherlands 385 (A. N. Kervezee 42, R. N. ten Doeschate 212*, P. W. Borren 44, Extras 31; N. N. Odhiambo 3-101, E. Otieno 4-57) **and 367-6 dec** (A. N. Kervezee 89, E. S. Szwarczynski 93, N. A. Statham 62*; E. Otieno 3-59); **Kenya 433** (D. O. Obuya 115, C. O. Obuya 89, M. A. Ouma 52, J. K. Kamande 75, N. N. Odhiambo 50*; M. B. S. Jonkman 3-54, R. N. ten Doeschate 5-104) **and 320-5** (D. O. Obuya 58, R. R. Patel 87, C. O. Obuya 79, A. A. Obanda 40). *Kenya 20pts. Ryan ten Doeschate made the most of what turned out to be his only appearance in this competition in 2010, clattering seven sixes and 22 fours in an unbeaten 212. But he had little support, and a second-wicket stand of 203 from the Obuya brothers helped Kenya take a narrow lead. After the Dutch openers Alexei Kervezee and Eric Szwarczynski put on 187, Peter Borren's declaration left the home side needing 320 in 64 overs: they got home with 12 balls to spare. After this match ten Doeschate had scored 1,285 runs in eight Intercontinental Cup games, at an average of 142.77, with seven centuries.*

At Deventer, June 10–13, 2010. **Scotland won by four wickets.** Netherlands 210 (S. T. de Bruin 32, W. P. Diepeveen 72*; M. A. Parker 4-63, R. M. Haq 3-45) **and 257** (E. S. Szwarczynski 62, P. W. Borren 109, P. M. Seelaar 30*; M. A. Parker 3-56, R. D. Berrington 3-48); ‡**Scotland 391** (R. D. Berrington 82, N. F. I. McCallum 51, G. I. Maiden 40, M. A. Parker 65, R. M. Haq 30, G. Goudie 44*, Extras 30; P. M. Seelaar 3-54) **and 77-6** (N. F. I. McCallum 34*, R. M. Haq 34*; M. B. S. Jonkman 5-21). *Scotland 20pts. An aggressive century by the home captain Peter Borren – he hammered five sixes to go with 11 fours in his 109 – avoided an innings defeat and set Scotland a modest target of 77... which looked mountainous when they lurched to 18-6, with fast bowler Mark Jonkman taking 5-10 in 45 balls. But Neil McCallum and Majid Haq took the Scots home without further alarms.*

At Amstelveen, July 25–28, 2010. **Zimbabwe XI won by 137 runs.** ‡**Zimbabwe XI 298** (S. Matsikenyeri 44, C. R. Ervine 145, R. W. Chakabva 34*; B. A. Westdijk 4-46, P. W. Borren 3-61) **and 305-5 dec** (S. Matsikenyeri 68, V. Sibanda 88, C. R. Ervine 59*, R. W. Chakabva 54*); **Netherlands 186** (W. Barresi 81, P. M. Seelaar 40*; N. Mushangwe 3-47) **and 280** (E. S. Szwarczynski 72, W. Barresi 33, P. M. Seelaar 81*, P. W. Borren 38; T. Maruma 3-44). *Zimbabwe XI 20pts. A Zimbabwean side containing five seasoned internationals proved too strong for the home side, Craig Ervine following his third first-class hundred with an undefeated half-century. Captain Vusi Sibanda hit a cultured 88 in the second innings after a golden duck in the first.*

At King City, August 2–4, 2010. **Zimbabwe XI won by an innings and 73 runs. Canada 129** (H. Patel 32, Rizwan Cheema 46*; E. C. Rainsford 3-45, T. L. Chatara 3-21) **and 149** (Hamza Tariq 39; S. W. Masakadza 5-58, T. L. Chatara 3-18); ‡**Zimbabwe XI 351** (C. R. Ervine 177, S. W. Masakadza 35, Extras 30; Umar Bhatti 6-98). *Zimbabwe XI 20pts. Craig Ervine carried on his fine form of the previous week in Holland, hitting 16 fours and three sixes in his career-best score. Canada, missing some regular players, struggled with the bat.*

At Dublin (Rathmines), August 11–13, 2010. **Ireland won by an innings and 84 runs.** ‡**Netherlands 188** (W. P. Diepeveen 41, P. W. Borren 39, T. J. Heggelman 30; G. H. Dockrell 4-36, A. van der Merwe 3-25) **and 136** (P. W. Borren 37; A. W. Eastwood 4-62, D. T. Johnston 3-41, A. van der Merwe 3-15); **Ireland 408** (A. R. Cusack 43, K. J. O'Brien 41, A. R. White 144, J. F. Mooney 107; Mohammad Kashif 5-53). *Ireland 20pts. A sixth-wicket partnership of 221 between Andrew White and John Mooney, who completed his maiden first-class hundred, lifted Ireland to a total that proved too much for the Dutch, who slipped to their fifth successive defeat in the competition.*

At Ayr, August 11–14, 2010. **Afghanistan won by 229 runs. Afghanistan 435** (Noor Ali Zadran 36, Karim Sadiq 67, Mohammad Shahzad 54, Asghar Stanikzai 93, Samiullah Shenwari 102) **and 249-5 dec** (Karim Sadiq 40, Mohammad Shahzad 105*, Asghar Stanikzai 36); ‡**Scotland 139** (J. D. Nel 36; Hamid Hassan 6-40) **and 316** (R. Flannigan 32, E. F. Chalmers 67, M. M. Iqbal 42, M. A. Parker 42, Extras 43; Hamid Hassan 5-114). *Afghanistan 20pts. In what turned out to be a dress rehearsal for the final, Scotland were comprehensively outplayed, and never seriously threatened a lofty target of 546. In the first innings their middle order was destroyed by fast bowler Hamid Hassan, whose figures included a spell of three wickets in five balls. He finished the match with 11 wickets, despite an ankle injury: "The doctor told me not to bowl, but I wanted to, so he bandaged my ankle up to my knee."*

At Toronto, August 31–September 3, 2010. **Ireland won by six wickets.** ‡**Canada 120** (A. W. Eastwood 3-30, D. T. Johnston 5-23) **and 316** (R. Gunasekera 47, Z. E. Surkari 72, A. Bagai 90, Khurram Chauhan 59; A. C. Botha 3-25, K. J. O'Brien 5-39); **Ireland 261** (P. R. Stirling 45, A. C. Botha 39, K. J. O'Brien 57, A. R. White 84; H. Osinde 5-68) **and 176-4** (A. C. Botha 61, A. R. White 59*). *Ireland 20pts. Ireland kept their hopes of retaining the trophy alive with a comfortable victory: they took charge in the third over of the match, when Allan Eastwood dismissed both Canadian openers, then Trent Johnston took three wickets in four balls as the score dipped from 58-2 to 60-6. A ninth-wicket stand of 121 between Ashish Bagai and Khurram Chauhan extended Ireland's eventual target to 176, but they eased home inside an hour on the fourth morning.*

At Harare, September 20–23, 2010. **Drawn.** ‡**Ireland 465** (W. T. S. Porterfield 51, K. J. O'Brien 71, A. R. White 102, G. C. Wilson 47, J. F. Mooney 87, G. H. Dockrell 30*; S. W. Masakadza 5-107, N. Mushangwe 3-106) **and 151-4** (W. T. S. Porterfield 66, N. J. O'Brien 41, G. C. Wilson 35*); **Zimbabwe XI 590** (S. J. Marillier 47, S. C. Williams 178, K. M. Dabengwa 140, R. W. Chakabva 54, F. Mutizwa 47*, Extras 42; D. T. Johnston 4-118, K. J. O'Brien 4-104). *Zimbabwe XI 9pts, Ireland 3pts. Ireland's chances of retaining their crown finally disappeared when they failed to win. Both sides' batting proved strong: Ireland recovered from 172-5 to make 465, then a stand of 237 between Sean Williams, who hit 24 fours, and Keith Dabengwa underpinned the strong Zimbabwean response.*

At Nairobi (Gymkhana), October 2–5, 2010. **Afghanistan won by 167 runs.** ‡**Afghanistan 464** (Karim Sadiq 55, Mohammad Shahzad 72, Nawroz Mangal 168, Samiullah Shenwari 45, Mirwais Ashraf 80*; N. N. Odhiambo 3-80, E. Otieno 4-99) **and 207** (Javed Ahmadi 55, Nawroz Mangal 33; E. Otieno 4-44, J. O. Ngoche 5-39); **Kenya 160** (S. R. Waters 73, R. G. Aga 36; Hamid Hassan 5-70, Samiullah Shenwari 3-9) **and 344** (D. O. Obuya 79, C. O. Obuya 52, S. O. Tikolo 55, M. A. Ouma 68, T. M. Odoyo 37*; Hamid Hassan 6-87). *Afghanistan 20pts. Afghanistan confirmed their place in the final with a clinical victory over Kenya. They scored 440-6 on the opening day – Nawroz Mangal, who hit 23 fours and a six in all, reached his maiden first-class hundred – then shot Kenya out for 160, with only opener Seren Waters holding them up for long. With plenty of time remaining,*

Mangal waived the follow-on: Kenya's eventual target was a distant 512 and, despite some consistent middle-order contributions, they never got close. Their captain, Maurice Ouma, resigned after the match.

At Harare, October 13–16, 2010. **Zimbabwe XI v Scotland. Scotland won by forfeiture.** *Scotland 20pts. The Zimbabwean board agreed to forfeit the match after the Scotland team was advised not to travel to Harare by the British government. The points ensured that Scotland qualified for the final ahead of the Zimbabwe XI.*

Final

At Dubai (International Stadium), December 2–4, 2010. **Afghanistan won by seven wickets.** ‡**Scotland 212** (N. F. I. McCallum 104*, S. J. S. Smith 36; Hamid Hassan 5-45, Mirwais Ashraf 3-53) **and 82** (Hamid Hassan 3-39, Samiullah Shenwari 3-15, Mirwais Ashraf 3-8); **Afghanistan 171** (Karim Sadiq 34, Nawroz Mangal 56; M. A. Parker 3-56, R. M. Haq 3-49) **and 124-3** (Shabir Noori 35, Mohammad Shahzad 56*). *MoM:* Hamid Hassan. *Afghanistan won the Intercontinental Cup for the first time, most of the credit going to their attack: fast bowler Hamid Hassan delivered an unbroken spell of 22 overs on the first day despite a leg injury; he ended the drawn-out tournament with 43 wickets at an average of 19.18. In their first innings Scotland were reduced to 97-8 before Neil McCallum, who hit 17 fours, and wicketkeeper Simon Smith put on 107 for the ninth wicket, lifting the Scots to a total which proved enough for a slender first-innings lead. But there was no such revival in their second innings, in which only opener Fraser Watts (28) scored more than 11: Afghanistan were left with a modest target, which they reached before tea on the third day of the scheduled five.*

ICC INTERCONTINENTAL CUP FINALS

2004	SCOTLAND beat Canada by an innings and 84 runs at Sharjah.
2005	IRELAND beat Kenya by six wickets at Windhoek.
2006–07	IRELAND beat Canada by an innings and 115 runs at Leicester.
2007–08	IRELAND beat Namibia by nine wickets at Port Elizabeth.
2009–10	AFGHANISTAN beat Scotland by seven wickets at Dubai.

ICC INTERCONTINENTAL SHIELD, 2009–10

Namibia became the first winners of the ICC's second-tier competition for the non-Test-playing nations – and maybe the only winners as the ICC later decided to shelve it. Namibia had lost to the United Arab Emirates in their first match in the tournament (see *Wisden 2010*), but won their three remaining matches, including the final against the UAE in Dubai.

There were some encouraging performances from Uganda, but Bermuda's fall from the heady heights of World Cup qualification in 2007 continued apace: they lost all their matches by wide margins and failed to earn a single point, the nadir coming when they were bowled out for 56 at home in Hamilton by the UAE.

FINAL TABLE

					1st-inns	
	Played	Won	Lost	Drawn	Lead	Points
NAMIBIA	3	2	1	0	3	46
UNITED ARAB EMIRATES	3	2	0	1	1	37
Uganda	3	1	1	1	2	29
Bermuda	3	0	3	0	0	0

Win = 14pts. Tie = 7pts. Draw with more than ten hours lost to weather = 7pts. Draw with less than ten hours lost to the weather = 3pts. First-innings lead = 6pts. Tie on first innings = 3pts. Abandoned = 10pts. Teams finishing level on points separated by (a) most outright wins (b) most first-innings leads and (c) the higher net runs-per-wicket ratio.

Note: For matches played in this tournament during 2009 see *Wisden 2010* page 1457.

At Abu Dhabi, January 20–23, 2010. **Drawn. United Arab Emirates 361** (Arshad Ali 33, Khurram Khan 87, Naeemuddin Aslam 152; F. Nsubuga 3-76) **and 282-9 dec** (Arshad Ali 130, Saqib Ali 77; F. Nsubuga 3-100); ‡**Uganda 373** (R. G. Mukasa 46, A. S. Kyobe 49, A. M. Baig 51, L. Sematimba 89, R. Ssemanda 41, B. Musoke 40, F. Nsubuga 37; Amjad Javed 4-48, Fayyaz Ahmed 3-74) **and 79-6** (Qasim Zubair 3-16). *UAE 3pts, Uganda 9pts. Set 271 in 43 overs, Uganda hung on despite crashing to 36-5.*

At Windhoek (Wanderers), April 3–5, 2010. **Namibia won by an innings and 185 runs.** ‡**Bermuda 214** (C. R. Foggo 34, D. L. Hemp 52, S. D. Outerbridge 46, I. H. Romaine 34; T. Verwey 5-46) **and 184** (D. L. Hemp 65; L. Klazinga 5-45); **Namibia 583-8 dec** (R. van Schoor 157, E. Steenkamp 206, C. Williams 110*, T. Verwey 35, Extras 36; M. O. Jones 3-141). *Namibia 20pts. Bermuda, for whom Malachi Jones bagged a pair, were overwhelmed by an opening stand of 374 between 19-year-old Raymond van Schoor and Ewald Steenkamp, 20. David Hemp, the former Glamorgan captain, led from the front with two half-centuries, but Bermuda still lost by an innings.*

At National Stadium, Hamilton, July 5–7, 2010. **United Arab Emirates won by nine wickets.** ‡**Bermuda 56** (E. H. S. N. Silva 3-4) **and 332** (C. R. Foggo 60, S. D. Outerbridge 62, D. L. Hemp 84, I. H. Romaine 48; Ahmed Raza 4-55); **United Arab Emirates 356-6 dec** (Abdul Rehman 65, Arshad Ali 126, Saqib Ali 34, S. P. Patil 37, Amjad Ali 36*; R. J. Trott 3-96, J. Gilbert 3-85) **and 35-1.** *UAE 20pts. Bermuda finished a disastrous campaign pointless after a third heavy defeat. This time they were shot out in 31.3 overs on the first day: opener Chris Foggo made 29, more than half their eventual total, but no one else hit more than six. The UAE led by 136 by the end of the first day, retained the initiative and, despite a vastly improved batting display by Bermuda in their second innings, claimed a place in the final.*

At Windhoek (United), September 18–21, 2010. **Namibia won by ten wickets. Uganda 329** (A. M. Baig 40, B. Musoke 59, L. Sematimba 106; C. Williams 5-90) **and 295** (R. G. Mukasa 121, L. Sematimba 54; L. Klazinga 3-42); ‡**Namibia 609** (R. van Schoor 31, E. Steenkamp 87, S. F. Burger 68, C. Williams 82, L. J. Burger 30, G. Snyman 86, L. P. van der Westhuizen 50, T. Verwey 73, L. Klazinga 48*; C. Waiswa 3-123) **and 16-0.** *Namibia 20pts. Namibia confirmed their place in the final after a consistent batting display in which everyone reached double figures but no one passed 100: their 609 was the highest first-class total not to include an individual century, beating Madhya Pradesh's 605 against Haryana at Rajnandgaon in the 1998-99 Ranji Trophy. The Ugandans batted reasonably well themselves, both Lawrence Sematimba and Roger Mukasa recording their maiden first-class hundreds.*

Final

At Dubai (ICC Global Academy), December 2–5, 2010. **Namibia won by six wickets. United Arab Emirates 79** (Naeemuddin Aslam 38; K. B. Burger 7-38) **and 427** (Naeemuddin Aslam 48, Arshad Ali 50, Saqib Ali 160*, S. P. Patil 94; L. Klazinga 3-98, S. F. Burger 5-80); ‡**Namibia 320** (E. Steenkamp 66, S. F. Burger 73, C. G. Williams 116, L. P. van der Westhuizen 34; Arshad Ali 3-46) **and 187-4** (E. Steenkamp 35, C. G. Williams 113*; Amjad Javed 3-54). *MoM:* C. G. Williams. *Namibia won the Intercontinental Shield, although they had to work harder than they might have expected after bowling the UAE out in 25.3 overs on the first day and then running up a lead of 241. Saqib Ali, who batted for 581 minutes and hit 19 fours, led the UAE's second-innings resistance, and his sixth-wicket stand of 172 with Swapnil Patil at least ensured that Namibia would have a target to chase. They eventually needed 187 and, although they lost two quick wickets, a second attacking century of the match from their captain, Craig Williams, took Namibia home.*

INDIA WOMEN v ENGLAND WOMEN, 2009-10

One-day internationals (5): India 3, England 2
Twenty20 internationals (3): India 1, England 2

England's women arrived in India looking for their first one-day series win there; in three previous bilateral tours, they had lost 12 one-day internationals and won only three, and had finished on top only in a Test series in 1995-96. As the Women's World Cup and Twenty20 champions, they were hopeful of turning that record round, but they could not quite manage it, though the 3–2 margin was closer than on their two last visits, and they did win the Twenty20 series which followed. All four of their international victories came in the final over.

England's most recent tour had been to the Caribbean, where, in the absence of two of their leading batsmen, Claire Taylor and Sarah Taylor, they had suffered unexpected series defeats by West Indies. Sarah did return for this trip, but was forced home by injury after the first international. Though captain Charlotte Edwards and opener Ebony-Jewel Rainford-Brent passed 100 runs in the one-day series, the batting sometimes looked fragile without the Taylors, and England lacked a top-class spinner with Holly Colvin also unavailable.

The 50-over series was dominated by the batting of Mithali Raj, who scored a half-century in every innings (she did not bat in the third game) to finish with 287 at 143.50, consolidating her position at the top of the ICC batting rankings. By the end of the series India's captain, Jhulan Goswami, had risen to first place in the bowling list, thanks to her 11 wickets; slow left-armer Gouher Sultana claimed 12.

England's spirits were lifted by their victory in the 20-over series, their last competitive cricket before they attempted to defend their World Twenty20 title in the West Indies in May. But overall India had fared slightly better throughout the tour, which was to prove a pointer to events in the Caribbean.

ENGLAND TOURING PARTY

*C. M Edwards (Kent), C. M. G. Atkins (Sussex), T. T. Beaumont (Kent), K. H. Brunt (Yorkshire), L. S. Greenway (Kent), I. T. Guha (Berkshire), J. L. Gunn (Nottinghamshire), D. Hazell (Yorkshire), L. A. Marsh (Sussex), B. L. Morgan (Middlesex), E-J. C-L. R. C. Rainford-Brent (Surrey), N. J. Shaw (Surrey), A. Shrubsole (Somerset), S. J. Taylor (Sussex), D. N. Wyatt (Staffordshire). *Coach:* M. G. Lane.

H. C. Knight (Berkshire) was called up when Taylor went home injured.

At Bangalore, February 17, 2010. **England XI won by 141 runs.** ‡England XI 273-9 (50 overs) (S. J. Taylor 52, L. S. Greenway 81, J. L. Gunn 32); **BCCI President's XI 132** (41.2 overs) (B. Mandlik 33; C. M. Edwards 3-14).

At Bangalore, February 19, 2010. **First one-day international: India won by 35 runs.** ‡India 199-5 (50 overs) (M. Raj 62, P. Roy 69*); **England 164** (45 overs) (E-J. C-L. R. C. Rainford-Brent 64, L. S. Greenway 35; J. Goswami 3-16, G. Sultana 3-26). *The teams observed a minute's silence in memory of former England player Audrey Collins, who had died aged 94. England needed 55 from the last 11 overs, with six wickets in hand, but lost all six for 19.*

At Bangalore, February 21, 2010. **Second one-day international: England won by three runs.** ‡England 183-8 (50 overs) (J. L. Gunn 64; G. Sultana 4-30); **India 180** (49.3 overs) (M. Raj 91*,

A. Sharma 40; K. H. Brunt 5-22). *Katherine Brunt's career-best 5-22 reduced India to 16-4, effectively 22-5 when Thirush Kamini retired hurt. But Mithali Raj and Amita Sharma swung the game round as they added 106 – only for India's last four wickets to fall for seven runs.*

At Visakhapatnam, February 24, 2010. **Third one-day international: India won by seven wickets. England 130** (49.2 overs) (R. Dhar 4-19); ‡**India 133-3** (40.5 overs) (P. G. Raut 44, A. Chopra 61*). *One-day international debut: S. Dabir (India). England made a poor start and were 54-4 after 24 overs, with Rumeli Dhar on her way to career-best figures, whereas Punam Raut and Anjum Chopra opened with 97 in 32 overs. India won with nine overs to spare; for once, Mithali Raj was not needed.*

At Visakhapatnam, February 26, 2010. **Fourth one-day international: India won by five wickets. England 152-9** (50 overs) (C. M. Edwards 57*; J. Goswami 3-34, P. Dimri 3-18); ‡**India 156-5** (44.4 overs) (M. Raj 84*). *India made sure of the series with a match to go when Mithali Raj steered them to another comfortable victory, striking 13 fours in her 123-ball 84, after disciplined bowling had restricted England's scoring again.*

At Mumbai (Bandra Kurla), March 1, 2010. **Fifth one-day international: England won by two wickets. India 206-9** (50 overs) (M. Raj 50, H. Kaur 84, S. Dabir 31*; N. J. Shaw 3-34); ‡**England 210-8** (49.5 overs) (H. C. Knight 49). *One-day international debuts: H. C. Knight, D. N. Wyatt (England). Player of the Series: M. Raj. Katherine Brunt and Nicky Shaw reduced India to 26-4 in the 14th over. Though Mithali Raj, with her fourth successive half-century, and Harmanpreet Kaur, with a maiden fifty, rallied them, England secured a consolation win with a ball to spare. Their chase was led by Heather Knight, who scored 49 on her international debut, and completed by Danielle Wyatt's 28* in 26 balls.*

At Mumbai (Bandra Kurla), March 4, 2010. **First Twenty20 international: England won by two wickets. India 125-5** (20 overs) (M. Raj 30); ‡**England 126-8** (20 overs) (J. L. Gunn 34; S. Dabir 3-23). *Twenty20 international debuts: S. Dabir, B. Mandlik (India); D. N. Wyatt (England). England entered the last over needing six runs, with four wickets in hand, but lost two wickets in the first three balls before Nicky Shaw scrambled the winning runs off the final delivery, thanks to an overthrow. The match's 13 wickets included five run-outs and three stumpings.*

At Mumbai (Bandra Kurla), March 6, 2010. **Second Twenty20 international: India won by 30 runs.** ‡**India 126-7** (20 overs) (S. Naik 36, H. Kaur 33; D. Hazell 3-20, L. A. Marsh 3-29); **England 96** (19.2 overs) (P. G. Raut 3-12). *Twenty20 international debut: D. P. David (India). England lost their last seven wickets for 18 runs in the final five overs. Punam Raut's off-spin earned three wickets, but she was later reported for a suspect action.*

At Mumbai (Bandra Kurla), March 8, 2010. **Third Twenty20 international: England won by five wickets. India 125-4** (20 overs) (H. Kaur 30*); ‡**England 126-5** (19.2 overs) (L. A. Marsh 46*; G. Sultana 3-26). *England won the series 2–1, despite losing their top three batsmen for 23 by the fourth over; Laura Marsh saw them home with 46* in 53 balls.*

SRI LANKA WOMEN v ENGLAND WOMEN, 2010-11

One-day internationals (2): Sri Lanka 0, England 1
Twenty20 internationals (3): Sri Lanka 0, England 3

England faced more obstruction from the weather than from their opponents on a short visit to Sri Lanka in November 2010. Severe flooding in Colombo caused a couple of changes of date and venue – in the end, all the matches except one were staged at the Nondescripts ground – while rain ended the second one-day international and washed out the second Twenty20 game (replayed the following morning). But England won all the matches they did play, and faced serious resistance only in the first one-day international, when Sri Lanka recovered from a mid-innings collapse and needed six to win from the last two balls, and made none.

With wicketkeeper-batsman Sarah Taylor and bowlers Katherine Brunt and Holly Colvin unavailable, England took the opportunity to blood some of their Academy players ahead of their tour of Australia in January. The tour was also intended to prepare the squad for the next World Twenty20, to be held in Sri Lanka in 2012.

Captain Charlotte Edwards set a women's record when she appeared in her 142nd one-day international since her debut in 1997 – she played her first Test the previous year, aged 16 – passing Karen Rolton's 141 matches for Australia. Though she had only one significant innings, she claimed ten cheap wickets in her four matches. Off-spinner Danielle Hazell collected 11 wickets, and vice-captain Jenny Gunn was the leading batsman, with 121 runs at 40 over the course of the tour. "I really wish we were going to Australia tomorrow," said Gunn.

ENGLAND TOURING PARTY

*C. M Edwards (Kent), L. S. Greenway (Kent), L. P. Griffiths (Cheshire), I. T. Guha (Berkshire), J. L. Gunn (Nottinghamshire), D. Hazell (Yorkshire), H. C. Knight (Berkshire), E. MacGregor (Essex), L. A. Marsh (Sussex), B. L. Morgan (Middlesex), S. E. Rowe (Kent), A. Shrubsole (Somerset), S. C. Taylor (Berkshire), F. C. Wilson (Somerset), D. N. Wyatt (Staffordshire). *Coach:* M. G. Lane.

At Colombo (NCC), November 15, 2010. **First one-day international: England won by five runs. England 192** (49.4 overs) (S. C. Taylor 73, J. L. Gunn 39; H. M. D. Rasangika 4-38); ‡**Sri Lanka 187-9** (50 overs) (P. R. C. S. Kumarihami 32, A. C. Jayangani 30, L. E. Kaushalya 32; D. Hazell 3-22). *One-day international debuts: D. G. D. R. Dharmasiri (Sri Lanka); L. P. Griffiths, F. C. Wilson (England). Player of the Match:* S. C. Taylor. *Seven of England's batsmen fell in single figures, but Claire Taylor's 73 in 93 balls – her 30th half-century in one-day internationals – helped them reach 192, and Sri Lanka stumbled to 86-5 after an opening stand of 64. Eshani Kaushalya led a recovery and they needed six runs from the last two balls of the game: Jenny Gunn dismissed Deepika Rasangika and finished with a dot ball.*

At Colombo (PSS), November 17, 2010. **Second one-day international: No result.** Reduced to 38 overs a side. **Sri Lanka 173-8** (38 overs) (A. C. Jayangani 37; C. M. Edwards 4-30); ‡**England 30-1** (9.1 overs). *One-day international debut: S. Ravikumar. Charlotte Edwards became the most capped player in women's one-day international cricket, in her 142nd game, and celebrated with her best figures for England in any format, but rain, which had already shortened the match, returned to end it, giving England a 1–0 victory in the short series.*

At Colombo (NCC), November 19, 2010. **First Twenty20 international: England won by eight wickets.** ‡**Sri Lanka 95-8** (20 overs) (C. M. Edwards 3-21); **England 99-2** (15.4 overs) (C. M. Edwards 48*). *Twenty20 international debuts:* E. MacGregor, S. E. Rowe, F. C. Wilson (England). *Player of the Match:* C. M. Edwards. *Charlotte Edwards followed her best bowling in this format by guiding England to victory with more than four overs in hand.*

At Colombo (NCC), November 21, 2010. **Second Twenty20 international: Sri Lanka v England. Abandoned.**

At Colombo (NCC), November 22, 2010. **Second Twenty20 international (replay): England won by 17 runs. England 114** (19.5 overs) (L. A. Marsh 30); ‡**Sri Lanka 97** (20 overs). *Twenty20 international debuts:* K. R. S. Fernando, S. Ravikumar (Sri Lanka); H. C. Knight (England). *Player of the Match:* L. A. Marsh. *This match was a replay of the previous day's abandoned game; Jenny Gunn led England to a series-clinching victory as Charlotte Edwards rested. Again Sri Lanka failed to reach three figures in their 20 overs.*

At Colombo (NCC), November 22, 2010. **Third Twenty20 international: England won by 89 runs.** ‡**England 160-5** (20 overs) (J. L. Gunn 69); **Sri Lanka 71** (18.3 overs) (D. Hazell 3-14). *Player of the Match:* J. L. Gunn. *In their second game of the day, England completed a 3–0 series whitewash. Sri Lanka struggled again as only Dilani Manodara (25*) and Extras (11) managed double figures. Jenny Gunn hit 69 in 46 balls, with four fours and three sixes; she also took a wicket and three catches.*

CRICKET IN AFGHANISTAN, 2010

Climbing beyond base camp

SHAHID HASHMI

Afghanistan's rise in the cricket world continued apace during 2010: a silver medal in the Asian Games in China and winning the ICC Intercontinental Cup capped another stunning year.

Even the American Secretary of State Hillary Clinton hailed the growth of cricket in Afghanistan: "I might suggest that if we are searching for a model of how to meet tough international challenges with skill, dedication and teamwork, we need only look to the Afghan national cricket team," she said in May 2010. "Afghanistan did not even have a cricket team a decade ago. And last month, the team made it to the World Twenty20 championships featuring the best teams in the world, and that's incredible progress."

Those seeds of progress were sown in 2009, when Afghanistan narrowly failed to qualify for the 2011 World Cup, after surprising everyone by winning the fifth, fourth and third divisions of the World Cricket League in quick succession – triumphs which prompted President Hamid Karzai to support and fund the Afghanistan Cricket Board. Early in 2010 Afghanistan put missing out on the 50-over World Cup behind them by winning the World Twenty20 qualifying competition, earning a place in the third edition of the 20-over global championship. And although they did not trouble the bigger nations in the Caribbean, it was still an important outing which gave the side their first taste of top-level cricket.

For fast-improving paceman Hamid Hassan, 23, the rise has been stupendous. "Getting the chance to play India and South Africa at the World Twenty20 in the Caribbean was amazing," he said, "and beating Pakistan at the Asian Games and securing a silver medal was one of the greatest moments of my career." Pakistan fielded a largely youthful team.

Still, the post-World Twenty20 period wasn't as smooth as expected. Inspiring coach Kabir Khan, a former Pakistan fast bowler, fell out with the board about payments and quit. But Afghanistan found another able coach in Rashid Latif – the former Pakistan wicketkeeper and captain. He did make some changes: "I introduced training camps in Afghanistan, which were not happening in the past, when the camps were held in Pakistan, India, Sri Lanka and Dubai. My point was that to motivate the youngsters and produce new players we needed to play more in Afghanistan. I saw that the youth was very keen and enthusiastic – even more than in India and Pakistan. However, with fewer playing fields in the country, they were found playing on the streets."

One thing that does hamper Afghanistan's progress is the lack of facilities at home, especially grounds. All-rounder Mohammad Nabi, who took over from Nawroz Mangal as captain late in the year, admitted after the Asian Games final defeat by Bangladesh: "With a successful year behind us now, it should be enough inspiration to our administrators to start building playing facilities so that more and more young players can be attracted toward this game."

This is being addressed: while the national team was busy at the Asian Games, the administration was busy laying the foundation stone of the Kabul National Cricket Stadium. The ground, to be built with funds from the United States Agency for International Development, is expected to be completed by July 2011, with space for 6,000 spectators. "It's a historic occasion," said Karl Eikenberry, the US ambassador to Afghanistan. "This project will provide a safe venue to Afghan youth and the national team to play for years to come."

Mohammad Omer Zakhiwal, the Afghanistan board's chief executive, enthused: "Because of the national team's exceptional success, cricket in Afghanistan is gaining popularity. The growing number of players includes not only men, but women as well. More than 100 young women are currently playing cricket in Kabul, and the board is about to create a national women's cricket team for the Asian Elite Cup Tournament in February 2011."

Zakhiwal, the country's finance minister, added: "Cricket in Afghanistan is more than a game. It is a means for bringing Afghan youth from different backgrounds together. It has become a source of pride for ordinary Afghans, and an example of their resolve and determination. It is a game that can contribute positively to peace and stability in our country."

AFGHANISTAN'S "HOME" ONE-DAY INTERNATIONALS IN 2010

Afghanistan v Canada in Sharjah

At Sharjah, February 16, 2010 (day/night). **First one-day international: Afghanistan won by one run. Afghanistan 289-6** (50 overs) (Noor Ali Zadran 114, Mohammad Shahzad 118, Nawroz Mangal 32; Khurram Chauhan 4-39); ‡**Canada 288-8** (50 overs) (T. C. Bastiampillai 33, Rizwan Cheema 61, A. Bagai 91*, S. Dhaniram 56; Samiullah Shenwari 4-31). *MoM:* Mohammad Shahzad. *One-day international debuts:* Aftab Alam (Afghanistan); Usman Limbada (Canada). *Noor Ali and Mohammad Shahzad piled on 205 for the second wicket to set up an imposing total, but Canada made a noble effort, led from the front by Rizwan Cheema, who blasted 61 from 35 balls, with 11 fours and two sixes. Ashish Bagai carried on the fight, and it all boiled down to the last ball, from Mohammad Nabi: with four needed, Khurram Chauhan hit it away for two but was run out attempting the third run which would have tied the match.*

At Sharjah, February 18, 2010 (day/night). **Second one-day international: Canada won by four wickets. Afghanistan 177** (43.1 overs) (Mohammad Nabi 62; Khurram Chauhan 4-43); ‡**Canada 178-6** (39.2 overs) (A. Bagai 52). *MoM:* Khurram Chauhan. *One-day international debuts:* Shabir Noori (Afghanistan); N. R. Kumar (Canada). *Canada squared the short series with a comfortable victory, set up by the opening burst from Pakistan-born medium-pacer Khurram Chauhan: he dismissed Shafiqullah and Mohammad Shahzad for ducks in his first over as the Afghans slumped to 4-3, and later 38-5.*

For Afghanistan's matches in the Intercontinental Cup in 2010, see page 1165.

CRICKET IN CANADA, 2010

Putting a brave face on it

Faraz Sarwat

The year started on an optimistic note, with news that the big-hitting Canadian opener Rizwan Cheema was to be included in the IPL player auction. Sadly, although Cheema made the shortlist, which meant that at least one franchise had shown an interest, in the end he was left on the shelf. And Canadian cricket stayed there for much of the year, despite their new motto "The Dream Is Alive", which had been added to the national board's logo.

In January Canada set off for the Under-19 World Cup in New Zealand with a team that contained several players who had already represented the senior team or were on the verge of national selection. After they beat Zimbabwe, the president of Cricket Canada, Ranjit Saini, sent out a rambling email describing the win as "the single biggest honour that our volunteer coaches and staffs may achieve". But Canada went on to lose all but one of their remaining games, beating only Papua New Guinea. Before upsetting Zimbabwe, they had already lost to Hong Kong.

By March, Saini was embroiled in allegations of misappropriation of funds from his time as the head of the Maple Leaf Cricket Club near Toronto, which hosted Pakistan, Sri Lanka and Zimbabwe for a Twenty20 tournament in 2008. Saini denied any wrongdoing; a police investigation was ongoing.

Shortly after this, Canada formally declined to host the 2012 edition of the Under-19 World Cup, which the ICC had awarded them in 2007. Many had wondered about Canada's suitability and readiness for such a prestigious tournament, but throwing in the towel two years early was still seen as a sign of incompetence by some. The most extreme reaction came from Pandit Maharaj, the president of Maple Leaf CC, which would have hosted most of the matches: he went on hunger strike to pressure the ICC to give the tournament back to Canada. He toughed it out for a week before better sense prevailed.

Ontario remains the heartland of the game in Canada, with more than 80% of the games played in the country said to take place there. The local governing body, headed by Saini's rival Mike Kendall, remained openly critical of what it saw as Cricket Canada's mismanagement. In 2010, the Ontario Cricket Association invited Rod Marsh and Mudassar Nazar from the ICC Global Academy to hold a four-day training camp in Toronto. Tellingly, Scotiabank – which had pulled its sponsorship of Cricket Canada in November 2009 – chose to support the camp. But Cricket Canada all but boycotted the visit, which meant no national players took part, and Marsh and Mudassar had to make do with an enthusiastic group of youngsters.

For the first time since 2005, a 50-overs championship was staged in 2010. Maddeningly, though, it was held the week the national team was in the West

Indies, getting mauled in the Caribbean's domestic Twenty20 tournament. Without Canada's best players, the national championship proved another missed opportunity for genuine context when evaluating the national player pool. The bad blood between the two led to Cricket Canada rejecting the OCA's team and selecting its own Ontario side – which still proved good enough to win. In response the OCA threatened legal action, which never materialised. But a few weeks later, after much constitutional wrangling over jurisdiction, Cricket Canada expelled the OCA and recognised another body as the representative of Ontario cricket. This time the OCA did serve legal papers: that affair rumbled on too.

Teams from Bermuda and the West Indies High Performance Center arrived in Toronto in mid-September to play in something ill-advisedly called "The Summer Cricket Festival". Hurricane Igor soon sent Bermuda packing, and the tournament fizzled out, though not before the board deemed it a success.

And finally, to round off an indifferent year, the Canadian team was sent to India in November to play against club sides to get a taste of conditions ahead of the World Cup. Virtually every game was lost, but the tour was still hailed as a success – and great preparation for the Cup – even though core players such as Rizwan Cheema, John Davison, Geoff Barnett, Khurram Chauhan and Umar Bhatti were not there. It remains unclear whether Cricket Canada's pronouncements are an effort to put a brave face on what continues to be shambolic governance, or whether they believe their own spin. The dream may be alive, but the time to wake up has long since passed.

ONE-DAY INTERNATIONALS IN CANADA IN 2010

Canada v Ireland

At Toronto, September 6, 2010. **First one-day international: Canada won by four runs** (D/L method). ‡**Ireland 175-9** (35 overs) (P. R. Stirling 35, J. F. Mooney 47; Khurram Chauhan 3-25); **Canada 163-4** (33 overs) (R. Gunasekera 71, A. Bagai 64). *MoM:* R. Gunasekera. *Ireland's weakened side, lacking any county players, slipped to defeat in a rain-affected match. The start was delayed for three and a half hours, turning it into a 35-over match, and bad light ended the game two overs early. By then Canada were just ahead on Duckworth/Lewis calculations, thanks to a third-wicket stand of 140 in 29 overs between Ruvindu Gunasekera, in only his second one-day international, and Ashish Bagai.*

At Toronto, September 7, 2010. **Second one-day international: Ireland won by 92 runs. Ireland 325-8** (50 overs) (P. R. Stirling 177, A. D. Poynter 30; H. S. Baidwan 3-60, A. S. Hansra 3-27); ‡**Canada 233** (46.3 overs) (R. Gunasekera 59, A. Bagai 44, Z. E. Surkari 32; A. van der Merwe 5-49). *MoM:* P. R. Stirling. *Ireland squared the series in style, their chunky 20-year-old opener Paul Stirling sprinting to the highest score in a one-day international by a player from a non-Test country (previously Kennedy Otieno's 144 for Kenya v Bangladesh in Nairobi in 1997-98). Stirling faced 134 balls and hit 21 fours and five sixes, three of them straight back over the head of slow left-armer Parth Desai, who took 1-77 in ten overs. Canada never threatened the required rate: Cape Town-born off-spinner Albert van der Merwe took five wickets in his fifth match for Ireland.*

For Canada's matches in the Intercontinental Cup in 2010, see page 1165.

CRICKET IN KENYA, 2010

New broom in Nairobi

MARTIN WILLIAMSON

Kenya's cricket continued its gradual decline in 2010, with poor performances on the field and lingering unrest off it, although the appointment of Tom Sears as its new chief executive in June at least put in place someone with the drive to turn things round – if he can overcome the prevailing culture of self-interest.

The blame for the ongoing malaise has to be shared around. The legacy of the time when the Kenyan Cricket Association squandered money and momentum are at the heart of the problem, but in the five years since Cricket Kenya assumed control it has been slow to rebuild grass-roots cricket. The players often seem too willing to expect the rewards of professionalism without the work that comes with it.

Outside the World Cricket League in the Netherlands in July, Kenya played only five one-day internationals, all in Nairobi, plus a smattering of Twenty20 games, and had to make do with matches against Indian state teams and regional neighbours. Maintaining a fully professional side was increasingly hard to justify, especially when the biggest fight many players showed came in June, when they went on strike for more money, egged on by former players, including the disgraced former captain Maurice Odumbe.

The matter was swiftly and firmly resolved, but not in time to salvage a short tour of England which had been arranged by well-wishers there. It cost Cricket Kenya $50,000 and no end of lost goodwill, and fuelled the constant sniping of the mischief-making local media.

A ludicrous attempt by the women's team to push for more money on the eve of a tournament in Nairobi a few months later highlighted the depth of the problem facing the board. Just like the men, the ladies performed abjectly.

For the men the nadir came, perhaps unsurprisingly, just after their strike, when they finished bottom of the World Cricket League Division One, the premier competition for Associates which they had won three years previously. Kenya lost all six matches, often by humiliating margins, finally ending any pretence that they were one of the leading non-Test nations. Shortly after that two youthful Indian state sides, Gujarat and Baroda, visited Nairobi and underlined how far Kenya had sunk during a series of one-sided games.

There were glimmers of hope, as several young players began to make their mark in a side overshadowed for far too long by the old guard. The selectors took a pragmatic decision to stick with a mixture of old and new for the World Cup, but after that changes will surely come.

The appointment of Sears might be a watershed. As someone with plenty of experience of handling struggling organisations, gained from his time with Derbyshire and Worcestershire, he is not one to resist a challenge. His first job was to resolve the strike: rarely has a honeymoon been so brief.

High on his agenda was the reality that Kenya, like all Associates, will be increasingly marginalised in the coming years as a result of ICC's decision effectively to exclude them from the World Cup by limiting future competitions to ten teams. The hectic international schedule will also mean that matches against Test-playing countries may become a thing of the past. "We all know what it is about," Sears said. "It's about power, it is about money and it is about votes – and it is a disgrace. The ICC don't seem to have the teeth or will to confront the parties that don't want the Associates to compete on not even an even footing, but on any footing. What's the point of putting funding into Kenya or Ireland if we don't know what we are striving to achieve?"

On the home front he quickly identified reforms. Plans are underway for a structure which will identify and encourage the best young players through schools cricket. Sears also recognised the inadequacies of the local leagues and the often poor standard of cricket, and the planned launch of elite limited-overs and Twenty20 competitions can only help bridge the chasm between the domestic and international games. It will not be easy, given the rampant self-interest of clubs and some administrators, but it is vital.

Kanbis, whose six-year stranglehold over the NPCA League was ended in 2009, regained their title. Tellingly, the club provided almost no players to the national squad. If Sears and Cricket Kenya have their way, it could be the last time that this is seen as the country's premier competition.

ONE-DAY INTERNATIONALS IN KENYA IN 2010

Kenya v Netherlands

At Nairobi (Gymkhana), February 16, 2010. **First one-day international: Kenya won by six wickets. Netherlands 219-9** (50 overs) (R. N. ten Doeschate 109*; E. Otieno 3-39); ‡**Kenya 221-4** (34.5 overs) (D. O. Obuya 32, R. R. Patel 92, A. A. Obanda 61). *One-day international debuts:* S. O. Ngoche, N. M. Odhiambo (Kenya); T. J. G. Gruijters (Netherlands). *The Kenyan debutant Shem Ngoche is the brother of Nehemiah (N. N.) Odhiambo, who also played in this match, and the former Kenyan fast bowler Lameck Onyango; two sisters have played for the national women's team too. Kenya's other debutant here, Nelson Mandela Odhiambo, is not related, though he is the nephew of long-serving all-rounder Thomas Odoyo. Ryan ten Doeschate clouted four sixes and ten fours in his third one-day international century, but had little support – none of the last seven in the order made double figures. Kenya eased to their target with 91 balls to spare, thanks largely to a second-wicket stand of 126 between Rakep Patel, with his highest one-day score, and Alex Obanda.*

At Nairobi (Gymkhana), February 18, 2010. **Second one-day international: Netherlands won by 80 runs. Netherlands 200** (48.4 overs) (B. Zuiderent 56, A. F. Buurman 30*; N. N. Odhiambo 3-35, H. A. Varaiya 4-33); ‡**Kenya 120** (32 overs) (J. K. Kamande 42; Mudassar Bukhari 3-17, M. B. S. Jonkman 3-24). *The Netherlands convincingly squared the series, thanks in part to their opening bowlers: Mudassar Bukhari had David Obuya caught behind from the third ball of the innings, and Kenya were 22-3 when the pacy Mark Jonkman bowled Alex Obanda. Jimmy Kamande organised something of a recovery, but the last five wickets fell for 15. Earlier Ryan ten Doeschate was out for nine, after making 216 runs since his previous dismissal in one-day internationals.*

Kenya v Afghanistan

At Nairobi (Gymkhana), October 7, 2010. **First one-day international: Kenya won by 92 runs.** ‡**Kenya 180** (46.2 overs) (S. O. Tikolo 57, J. K. Kamande 31; Mirwais Ashraf 4-35, Hamid Hassan 4-26); **Afghanistan 88** (27.5 overs) (Noor Ali Zadran 41; N. N. Odhiambo 3-16). *Steve Tikolo, in his first one-day international for almost a year, added solidity to the Kenyan batting. Still, their total looked flimsy – until Afghanistan collapsed. Only Karim Sadiq (19) and Noor Ali, who put on*

32 for the first wicket, made double figures as all ten wickets subsided for 56 inside 20 overs. Kenya's new captain was Jimmy Kamande, after Maurice Ouma resigned following heavy defeat to Afghanistan in the Intercontinental Cup matches that preceded this series.

At Nairobi (Gymkhana), October 9, 2010. **Second one-day international: Afghanistan won by six wickets.** ‡Kenya **139** (41 overs) (T. Mishra 32, M. A. Ouma 31*; Samiullah Shenwari 3-29); **Afghanistan 143-4** (27 overs) (Mohammad Shahzad 37, Asghar Stanikzai 55*). *One-day international debuts: Abdulla, Izatullah Dawlatzai (Afghanistan). Afghanistan levelled the series with an emphatic victory after Kenya's batting failed again, despite the reassuring presence of another returnee, 23-year-old Tanmay Mishra, playing his first match since the 2007 World Cup after a spell at university in India. Afghanistan's reply began badly – they were 19-2 with Noor Ali also retired hurt – but Mohammad Shahzad and Asghar Stanikzai made sure of victory.*

At Nairobi (Gymkhana), October 11, 2010. **Third one-day international: Kenya won by eight wickets.** ‡Afghanistan **188** (43 overs) (Javed Ahmadi 35, Mohammad Nabi 60); Kenya **189-2** (41.3 overs) (A. A. Obanda 77, C. O. Obuya 86*). *Kenya took the series 2–1 with their best batting display for some time: Alex Obanda and Collins Obuya took them to the brink of victory with a second-wicket stand of 143. Earlier, Afghanistan's batsmen had struggled again: they were 118-7, but Mohammad Nabi top-scored with 60 from No. 7.*

KENYA T20 TRI-SERIES

As part of their preparation for the World Twenty20 Qualifier, Scotland took part in a triangular 20-over tournament in Kenya early in 2010. The third team was Uganda, whose matches did not count as official Twenty20 internationals.

At Nairobi (Gymkhana), January 30, 2010. **Kenya won by eight wickets. Uganda 123-9** (20 overs); ‡Kenya **127-2** (17.2 overs) (S. O. Tikolo 63, A. A. Obanda 31*).

At Nairobi (Gymkhana), January 31, 2010. **Scotland won after an eliminator over, following a tie.** ‡Scotland **109-8** (20 overs) (H. Senyondo 3-20); Uganda **109** (20 overs) (A. S. Kyobe 51*; R. T. Lyons 3-28). *Uganda scored 6-1 in their "super over", bowled by Majid Haq, then Scotland collected ten runs from the first four deliveries by Joseph Nsubuga.*

At Nairobi (Gymkhana), February 1, 2010. **Kenya won by ten wickets. Scotland 109-9** (20 overs) (J. K. Kamande 3-28); ‡Kenya **110-0** (12.3 overs) (D. O. Obuya 60*, S. O. Tikolo 46*). *Twenty20 international debuts: S. O. Ngoche (Kenya); G. Goudie, R. T. Lyons, S. J. S. Smith (Scotland). Scotland struggled into three figures – Majid Haq top-scored with 21* from No. 9 – then Kenya's openers knocked off the runs with 45 balls to spare.*

At Nairobi (Gymkhana), February 2, 2010. **Kenya won by 14 runs. Kenya 186-3** (20 overs) (A. A. Obanda 43, C. O. Obuya 79*, M. A. Ouma 39); ‡Uganda **172-9** (20 overs) (R. G. Mukasa 66; N. M. Odhiambo 4-25). *Collins Obuya faced 45 balls, hitting three fours and seven of Kenya's 14 sixes.*

At Nairobi (Gymkhana), February 3, 2010. **Scotland won by 56 runs. Scotland 163-4** (20 overs) (K. J. Coetzer 64, D. F. Watts 73); ‡Uganda **107-9** (20 overs) (A. M. Baig 38). *Kyle Coetzer and Fraser Watts, who both hit three sixes, put on 130 for the second wicket in 14 overs.*

At Nairobi (Gymkhana), Nairobi, February 4, 2010. **Kenya won by ten wickets. Scotland 123** (19.2 overs) (J. H. Stander 45; N. N. Odhiambo 5-20); ‡Kenya **126-0** (14.3 overs) (D. O. Obuya 65*, S. O. Tikolo 56*). *Twenty20 international debut: N. M. Odhiambo (Kenya). For the second time in four days Kenya thrashed Scotland without losing a wicket. This time the Scots were 38-5 before Jan Stander oversaw a minor recovery, but David Obuya and Steve Tikolo had few problems during another century partnership. Kenya finished the tournament with a 100% record and eight points, to Scotland's four; Uganda finished pointless, despite some encouraging performances.*

For Kenya's matches in the Intercontinental Cup in 2010, see page 1165.

CRICKET ROUND THE WORLD

COMPILED BY TONY MUNRO

There was inevitable criticism of the ICC following their decision, in October 2010, to limit the 2015 World Cup to ten teams, four fewer than contested the 2011 tournament. When it was also announced the World Twenty20 would be increased to 16 teams from 2012, critics argued this was insufficient compensation for the loss of a clear path to full membership of the ICC and, with it, the possibility of Test status for the game's 95 Associate and Affiliate Members. And while the method of choosing the ten participants for 2015 remained unclear, there was also doubt over the future of the popular World Cricket League, the structure through which the World Cup's non-Test-playing nations are currently chosen.

WORLD CRICKET LEAGUE

Ireland confirmed their status as the best side below Test level when they remained unbeaten to win the six-team Division One tournament in Amsterdam in July. Robbed of the services of their county professionals, plus the injured Andre Botha, Ireland's coach – the former West Indies batsman Phil Simmons – had prepared for disappointment by predicting victory for Afghanistan. But the Afghans fielded poorly when the sides met, allowing Ireland – boosted by 78 from Andrew Poynter – to reach 237 for nine from their 50 overs before Alex Cusack's haul of five for 20 restricted Afghanistan to 198 in reply. Ireland went on to beat Scotland in the final by six wickets thanks to an undefeated 98 from Kevin O'Brien. Elsewhere, Kenya's participation came under threat when their players went on strike ahead of the tournament following a contractual dispute, a move that led to the cancellation of a brief tour to England. Their eventual participation was a predictable let-down: they lost every game.

The United States began 2010 in Division Five, enjoyed successive promotions, then dropped back to Division Four following defeats at the Division Three tournament in Hong Kong in January 2011 to Denmark, a Papua New Guinea side coached by former Australia seamer Andy Bichel, and Italy. The Americans' only defeat in Division Five had come at the hands of Singapore, who were later denied promotion in controversial circumstances when the game at Kirtipur between the hosts, Nepal, and the USA was disrupted by the home crowd with the Americans homing in on victory. With all three sides heading for equal points and a net run-rate calculation to determine which two would gain promotion, the crowd held up play for 45 minutes after Nepalese off-spinner Sanjay Regmi had been hit for three sixes in an over. That left the USA, needing 163 in 37.4 overs to knock Nepal out, on 150 for five after 32. But the hold-up, which involved spectators damaging a wall in search of material to hurl on to the outfield, prompted a recalculation. Set a revised target of 157 from 46 overs, the USA completed victory nine balls after the resumption, leaving Nepal – third on net run-rate before the interruption – now ahead of Singapore by 0.0035 of a run. The ICC launched an investigation, but found no justification for Singapore's complaint. "The decision has really put our cricket back a few years," said the Singapore captain, Munish Arora. While Jersey and Fiji were demoted to Division Six, USA and Nepal moved up a tier, with the Americans then gaining instant qualification to Division Three after losing only one game out of five, against Italy, who were also promoted. The Nepalese finished third following a careless loss to the youthful Tanzanians. The Division Three tournament in Hong Kong then brought promotion for the hosts and Papua New Guinea, while USA and Denmark were relegated. The first staging of Division Eight brought victory for the hosts, Kuwait, while Germany and Vanuatu retained their newly won WCL status. TONY MUNRO

BELGIUM

When Jack Richards, the Ashes-winning former England wicketkeeper who now lives in Antwerp, was appointed director of excellence by the Belgian Cricket Federation, his brightest prospect looked to be Rob Sehmi, who learned his cricket in Belgium but played for Kent Under-14s in 2010. Rob also represented the Under-17 national side, although the team finished a disappointing sixth at the European Championships on the Isle of Man. Back home, amid growing interest from Flemish schools, ES Mol won the schools trophy, while the university at Leuven launched a club of its own; two other new clubs – Kempen Tigers and Meise – are entering the leagues. Women's cricket is developing too, and Francesca Moore beat off junior rivals from both genders to be named most promising player for 2010. Meanwhile, the ladies of Royal Brussels CC reformed under Lucy Hess to provide excellent cricket against sides from Paris, and took part in a sun-drenched Ladies' Day involving eight teams and 12 nationalities in mid-July. In a sometimes disorganised men's game, more Twenty20 will be played in 2011, while at national level Belgium were set to host the European Twenty20 Division Two competition. Cricket here retains a multinational feel, despite the growing Flemish interest. The Pakistani community staged a well-supported sixes competition in aid of flood victims back home, and mobilised everyone from Commonwealth embassy staff and local hockey players to their compatriot night-shop assistants. Belgium was also the first stop-off point for charity cyclist Oli Broom (www.cyclingtotheashes.com) en route from London to Brisbane for the first Ashes Test. Like the many teams who visit Belgium each year, Oli enjoyed the fantastic beer; we strive – not always successfully – to provide equally memorable cricket. COLIN WOLFE

CHINA

Historic though it may yet come to be seen, the first international cricket match in this country – between the women of China and Malaysia – was an underwhelming affair. Five hundred school and college students were bussed in to watch the sport make its Asian Games debut, but that wasn't enough to remove the cavernous feel of the brand-new 6,000-seat Guanggong Stadium in Guangzhou. The PA system did its best, barking out cues for cheers and applause at the relevant moments; and the spectators dutifully obliged – until about the tenth over, when the cheers tapered off in a collective bout of apparent confusion. The Chinese cricketers, though, were marginally less clueless, compiling a 55-run win – including a composed 47 from the vice-captain, Sun Huan, an ex-footballer – on their way to the semi-finals. But the men's team, despite the presence as adviser of the former Pakistan captain Javed Miandad, easily lost both their games, to Malaysia and Pakistan. The batting was feeble: only teenager Li Jian, who hit three fours while making 14, looked even remotely confident as the home side collapsed to 55 for nine in their 20 overs. Even so, the presence of the sport in the Games could turn out to be a watershed for Chinese cricket. Helped by a mid-tournament lecture about the difference between a "run" and a "point" from the secretary of the Chinese Cricket Association, Liu Rongyao, local journalists brought cricket to a wider audience than ever before, and there were subtle hints of promise from the players themselves: some crafty leg-spin here, a spot of elegant strokeplay there, and better than expected pace bowling. Requests from both Miandad – who was among those advocating the senior Pakistan national side use China as their home away from home – and the CCA for more time seemed justified: over half the team in the game against Pakistan were under 22. Reassuringly, there was none of the laughter that had greeted the men's performances at an Asian Cricket Council event in 2009. RANAJIT DAM

DENMARK

In September 2010, Danish cricket lost Peter S. Hargreaves, one of its unstinting supporters and for many years *Wisden's* Denmark correspondent (see Obituaries, p 189). The fortunes of Hargreaves's adopted nation showed little sign of improvement. At the European Championships in July, Denmark suffered defeats to hosts Jersey and A teams from Ireland, Scotland and the Netherlands, and they then finished bottom of the World Cricket League Division Three in Hong Kong in January 2011, despite victory over the USA. In between, the Club Cricket Conference, coached by former Kent spinner Min Patel, visited Copenhagen, and won the single Twenty20 match. But a young Denmark XI took the one-day series 2–1. On the domestic front, national captain Michael Pedersen inspired Herning to a second successive Danish Championship title. He scored 47 and took five for 17 to help beat Svanholm by 77 runs in a low-scoring play-off shortened by rain. In straitened times, an overhauled Danish Cricket Federation pledged to keep a lid on spending, but coaches pressed ahead with the Integration Project, taking cricket into schools and youth clubs in an attempt to address Denmark's enduring problem of persuading different ethnic groups to play together.

FALKLAND ISLANDS

The Falklands' participation in their first ICC international series, the three-team American Division Four tournament in Mexico in June, also produced a maiden international win, by 39 runs over Costa Rica. A collapse to 31 all out against the hosts was less auspicious, but a degree of dishevelment was forgivable: most of the team's equipment had been accidentally offloaded in Punta Arenas, in southern Chile, and only caught up with the players on the day of departure from Mexico. Both opposition teams generously lent us their kit, and captain Elliott Taylforth was sufficiently inspired to take four wickets in five balls against Costa Rica. Meanwhile, Kevin Clapp's five-wicket haul against Mexico earned him a free night out in Mexico City at the expense of his team-mates. The season had started poorly when the Commander British Forces XI beat HE The Governor's XI 3–0 to retain the South Atlantic Ashes. There was, though, a silver lining: three successive triumphs meant the CBF XI gained permanent ownership of the odd-looking trophy – purportedly depicting the hatching of a phoenix egg – and the commissioning of a new piece of silverware. In July, the team travelled to Scotland to take part in the Festival of the Three Falklands at the beautiful Scroggie Park along with Falkland CC (Fife), who were celebrating their 150th anniversary, and Falkland CC (Berkshire). Fife's hospitality was outstanding, the ceilidh memorable and, although the Islands lost comfortably to the side from Berkshire, they beat the locals in a rain-affected ten-over slog to claim the Drysdale Cup, kindly donated by Karen Drysdale, grand-daughter of a former Fife captain. ROGER DIGGLE

GIBRALTAR

The Gibraltar Cricket Association marked its 50th anniversary with the production of a special 96-page brochure and the visit of an MCC side in November, although bad weather marred the trip's highlight – a rare day/night game, which finished as a Duckworth/Lewis win for MCC. Fortunes were little better in the international arena: the national side lost all their matches in Guernsey in July, and in November were relegated from the World Cricket League Division Eight in Kuwait. The Under-17s, meanwhile, managed only one victory in the Isle of Man. But more and more youngsters are coming into the game, and 99% of Gibraltarian players are now indigenous. Barbarians, a new club, lifted all three major domestic trophies, while touring sides from the UK continued to visit the Rock. In March, local cricketer and now Gibraltar's cricket development officer, Mark Bacarese, won the Sky Sports coaching award, and the GCA is now in the process of becoming a board. The Association's chairman, Tom Finlayson, announced his retirement after 30 years' service. T. J. FINLAYSON

HONG KONG

The 2010 Hong Kong Sixes tournament reached a remarkable climax when Australian pair David Warner and Ryan Carters belted 48 off the last over of the final to defeat Pakistan by two wickets. Australia had needed 46 off Imran Nazir's final eight-ball over, but – with the help of numerous extras – achieved the feat with a ball to spare amid scenes of near-delirium. It was the second successive nailbiter at the Kowloon Cricket Club following South Africa's last-ball win over surprise finalists Hong Kong in 2009. The hosts had beaten New Zealand, Australia, Sri Lanka, England and South Africa themselves (twice) en route to the final, only for the South Africans to gain revenge with a last-ball six. Perhaps the highlight for Hong Kong sides in 2010 was the presence of the Under-19s at the World Cup in New Zealand, where they finished 14th of 16. But that achievement was surpassed in early 2011 when the men's team qualified for World Cricket League Division Two. The Division Three tournament, hosted in Hong Kong, began badly for the hosts with defeats by the USA and Oman, but three straight wins – against Denmark, Italy and Papua New Guinea – earned Hong Kong a place in the final, where they beat the Papuans. We also bade farewell to Terry Smith, our long-standing president, who decided it was time to step down, and welcomed his successor, Captain Shahzada Saleem Ahmed, while rebranding ourselves as Hong Kong Cricket. JOHN CRIBBIN

ISRAEL

The year began splendidly when Israel received the ICC's coveted Spirit of Cricket award in honour of its project involving children from the Bedouin towns of Beersheba, the so-called "Capital of the Negev" (the desert in the south of the country), and Hura. The project is the product of tireless work by George Sheader, the youth development officer in the south, and involves using cricket to bring together people from different backgrounds. The senior side performed reasonably well in the European Division Two competition in Guernsey, but not even excellent wins over Gibraltar and Germany could make up for the careless three-run defeat in the first game against Norway after Israel needed 14 with five wickets in hand. Despite that, Eshkol Solomon compiled the competition's highest score, 120 against Gibraltar, and Josh Evans, a promising 17-year-old, took nine wickets in 42 overs of tidy leg-spin. Raanana – boasting six players under 21 – won their first national league title in 20 years under the leadership of former national captain Steven Shein, while the T20 cup was won by Sri Lanka Jerusalem, who, along with Sri Lanka Tel Aviv, were promoted to the A Division. Improvements were made to the fields in Eilat, Dimona and Beersheba, and a modern lecture room with sophisticated camera equipment was installed in the Beersheba clubhouse with the help of the European Cricket Council. Youth cricket is flourishing under the direction of Herschel Gutman, with numbers trebling and women's cricket taking off. Action cricket, played indoors on basketball courts with games lasting 90 minutes, has been introduced on Thursday and Saturday nights: 13 teams take part and the competition has been hailed in the local press. On December 12, a group of 35 Palestinian scholars, aged between eight and 12, from the West Bank villages of Samoa and Yaata travelled to Beersheba to meet fellow students from Yerucham and Dimona. For four hours, the boys and girls – who had never met before – played cricket together, and will continue to meet once a month in a project put together by the Israel Cricket Association, Al Quds and the Peres Centre for Peace. The project is being financed by an anonymous donor from England. STANLEY PERLMAN

LUXEMBOURG

Cricket has made substantial progress here since Luxembourg last featured in these pages seven years ago. The Luxembourg Cricket Federation league now includes seven teams, the latest addition being Arcelor Mittal CC, while the country's original club, Optimists CC, continues to perform steadily in the Belgian League; Star CC were the 2010 national champions. The LCF winter indoor league is now over ten years old and attracts players of all ages and abilities on Sunday afternoons. Luxembourg's national team performed well at the most recent European Division Four tournament, in Cyprus in 2009, achieving wins over Slovenia and Finland, but losing by one wicket to Austria, the winning run scrambled as a catch was being dropped. In June 2010, Luxembourg had its first taste of international T20 cricket in a tournament organised by the Dutch board. Games against France, Belgium and Netherlands A ended in honourable defeat, though Luxembourg were the only team to bowl out France, the eventual winners. Lower down the ladder, the Optimists Under-15 team were crowned unbeaten champions in their first season in the Belgian League, and junior teams went on successful tours to Denmark, Switzerland and France. The one-week junior training academy in July has become an established event and in 2010 was attended by 40 boys and girls of all ages, who were able to take advantage of a Level 3 coach from the UK and excellent facilities at the Pierre Werner ground just outside Luxembourg City. BRYAN ROUSE

MALI

Asked whether I really do play cricket in Mali, I can confidently reply: "Yes!" Pushed on what the cricket is actually like, I may resort to: "Ah, well…" Mali became an ICC Affiliate member in 2005, but the participation of our men's and Under-17 teams in the sub-regional championships in Gambia in 2007 and Nigeria in 2008 failed to produce a single win; frustratingly, the tournament has not taken place since. Nevertheless, Mali did win its first regional ICC trophy in 2010 – for professionalism and efficiency as Best New Administration. It's just a shame the facilities lag behind. We are still playing on sand and rock, basketball courts and football pitches, still using locally made equipment, and still sponsorless. And, with little cricket broadcast on accessible media, it remains difficult for Malians to pick up the game. There are, though, glimmers of hope. After three annual National Cricket Championships involving teams from Bamako – the current champions – Segou and Sikasso, the sport has reached seven of the eight Malian regions, including the city of Tombouctou, the French rendition of Timbuktu. There are also a small number of Malians working as full- and part-time cricket administrators or coaches. But the urgent need is to build simple, accessible, cricket grounds, initially in Bamako. And, yes, I have coached cricket in Timbuktu! PHIL WATSON

NAMIBIA

The highlight of the year was Namibia's victory in the final of the Intercontinental Shield over UAE in Dubai in December 2010. Kola Burger set Namibia up with figures of seven for 38 as the hosts were skittled for 79, before a pair of hundreds from Craig Williams sealed a comprehensive six-wicket win – itself justification in part for the awarding of eight professional contracts. There was success, too, for the Under-19s, who qualified for their 2012 World Cup without losing a match; Gerhard Lotter and Wian Van Vuuren both graduated to the senior side. Cricket Namibia was the global winner of the ICC's Best Development Programme in recognition of a partnership with UNICEF that uses cricket to draw attention to the plight of vulnerable and abused women and children. More than 1,000 boys and girls receive coaching, as well as life-skills advice, every week. Elsewhere, four new turf outfields and practice wickets have been constructed, with Sparta Cricket Club, an attractive ground in the middle of the desert, likely to be favoured by touring teams. LAURIE PIETERS

NORWAY

Norwegian cricket was honoured when the former England off-spinner John Emburey agreed to coach the Under-19 side on its first tour, to Scotland. Emburey proved inspirational to a team captained by Waqas Ahmed, son of Munawar, who had led the senior side in their maiden international match, in Austria in 2000. And although none of the three matches against the Scottish Academy sides was won, rain robbed the Norwegians of near-certain victory in the first game. Back home, 37 senior clubs competed in four divisions and there were also Under-19 and Under-17 leagues. Nord CC won the Elite Division while the overall Norwegian Master Champions were Nation CC. Friends CC earned promotion from Division One, as well as winning the Twenty20 tournament and finishing runners-up to Nation in the Masters Cup. The earliest cricket of the year was the first indoor six-a-side tournament in Bergen on the south-west coast of Norway, where a field of 24 teams delayed the finish until 1.50 a.m., with Bergen crowned champions. At the European Championships Division Two, Norway won two and lost three, with every game bar the 109-run defeat to Guernsey closely contested. BOB GIBB

PANAMA

The Panamanian season reached a nerve-jangling climax at the Clayton Sports City venue, only a stone's throw from the Miraflores Locks on the Panama Canal. Watched by a 9,000-strong crowd made up of the country's Indian community, Dadabhai CC reached the last ball of their championship final against Ahir CC needing six to win with one wicket left. Incredibly, rookie Asif Dassu made light of the tension to hit what was widely regarded as one of the biggest blows ever struck in Panamanian cricket to seal victory for his side. But the sport here still suffers from a lack of proper venues, a problem that prompted the Panamian Cricket Association to meet with Pandeportes, the national sport institute, who agreed to provide help in setting up two state-of-the-art cricket facilities in the nation's capital, Panama City. The recent establishment of a domestic second division tournament,

comprising six teams (and possibly nine from 2011) has boosted the game's standing.
SALEH BHANA

PERU

As the world's second-largest desert city behind Cairo, Lima was proud to maintain its sequence of never having lost a moment's play to rain since cricket began here in 1859. Among other developments, this meteorological certainty allowed the sport to be reintroduced to four schools in the Peruvian capital, and the first Lima Interschools Trophy – involving students of both genders – took place in November. Peru also hosted the inaugural South America Under-13 Championships, in April, when Chile beat Argentina in the final. Lima's four club teams – Kiteflyers, Eidgenossen, Chak De ("Let's go" in Punjabi) and the Lima Cricket and Football Club – contested various Twenty20, six- and eight-a-side tournaments through the year, while the annual Easter tournament was run on national lines: the Lima Llamas (comprising mainly British and Australian players) versus Chak De (Lima-based south Asians) versus Tacna Tigers (south Asian miners based in the country's south). Tacna also stay active with regular games against Iquique, a city across the border in Chile. MILES BUESST

SOLOMON ISLANDS

The revival of cricket in the Solomon Islands – where it had thrived during British colonial rule and beyond independence in 1978 – was not exactly top of the agenda when the Regional Assistance Mission to Solomon Islands (RAMSI) was invited here to restore law and order following the ethnic conflicts of 1998–2003. But the appointment as Prime Minister in January 2009 of Dr Derek Sikua, an avid sports fan, changed all that. Following his impassioned plea to the Special Coordinator of the RAMSI, cricket was reborn with a game in mid-2009 between the PM's XI and the Special Coordinator's XI, with Dr Sikua sending down the first ball. A four-team competition was organised, with Twenty20 widely agreed to be the way forward in the consistently hot conditions. Two of the teams are made up of RAMSI police, military and civilian personnel while the other two, the Barbarians and the Wanderers, draw on a range of local and imported talent. The inaugural competition in 2009 was won by the RAMSI military outfit but, in an upset, the civilian team, the RAMSI Crocs, claimed the title in 2010. Games are played every Sunday on a concrete-based wicket covered by a grass-coloured mat at King George VI Secondary School in Honiara. The grass grows quickly in the tropical rain, and mowing is an irregular phenomenon: many a glorious drive has ended up trickling into the covers for a single. As a result, the aerial route is popular, especially among the Solomon Islanders, most of whom believe a straight bat is an unhappy bat. Lost balls are an occupational hazard. GRAEME WILSON

SUDAN

As cricket's remote outposts go, Sudan is among the remotest. Although the country has several of the pre-requisites for a thriving cricket culture – year-round sunshine and historical ties with Britain – the sport has never really caught on with the locals, leaving it largely in the hands of the expats. Friendlies are played between the British Embassy, students at the Khartoum International Community School and their parents, and the DAL Group, a local conglomerate, allowing a variety of Anglo-Saxons, Australasians, Canadians and others to play for the 20 or so overs that seem sensible in the unforgiving heat. Several groups from the subcontinent also play improvised matches on the uneven ground of outer Omdurman, while the presence of Indian, Pakistani and Bangladeshi battalions in the United Nations Mission here has taken social matches to such unlikely places as Juba and Kadugli. But the result of the referendum in January 2011, when the overwhelming majority of Southern Sudan voted for independence, could yet prove significant. If the newly independent south follows in the footsteps of Rwanda by applying for membership of the Commonwealth and the East African Community, what better way to show its bona fides than by establishing the roots of a cricketing culture? Since the region's most famous sportsman, basketball player Luol Deng, typifies the height and build of his people, it is tempting to conclude that any fast-bowling attack could prove quite a lively proposition. TONY BRENNAN

TURKEY

When Syed Mahmud, an economics professor at Bilkent University, decided he was going to try to promote cricket in Turkey, it felt like nothing short of heretical in a country that worships football. But with Mahmud's hard work, the support of his university and of the many expats living here, a dream has become a reality. Now the chief executive of Turkey's cricket board, Mahmud oversees a structure comprising eight senior teams, divided into two leagues, and five junior sides, who mainly play Kwik cricket but also take part in a couple of hard-ball tournaments. A lack of manpower has been a problem, but there are now 13 ACO Level 1 umpires and ten ECB Level 1 coaches in Turkey, six of them native Turks. The sport here is mainly played in Ankara – at Bilkent University itself – and Istanbul. Cricket may be dominated by south Asian expats, but an increasing number of indigenous Turks are now showing an interest too. SOHAIB TARIQ MIAN

UKRAINE

Cricket is putting down roots in Europe's largest country thanks to the efforts of Pakistani-born businessman Mohammad Zahoor. The enigmatic Mr Zahoor's calm smile and few words belie a business acumen that helped him survive Ukraine's cut-throat 1990s to rank in 2010 as one of the country's richest men, emerging from the steel industry with an estimated fortune of $1bn. Now he is dedicating himself to a number of pet projects, including the *Kyiv Post* newspaper, the career of his wife, Ukrainian pop diva Kamaliya... and cricket. Zahoor wants Ukraine to send a cricket team to the 2020 Olympics, but has no illusions about the size of the task: current estimates suggest there are no more than 800 players in this country of 42 million. And the village-green tournaments Zahoor has hosted in Kyiv reveal that almost all of them hail from the subcontinent, with less than a handful of Ukrainian-born players. But the Asian presence could serve as a bridgehead for the game; and the lack of a summer sport in eastern Europe during the football off-season could help cricket spread. Zahoor, a British citizen, has found support from unlikely quarters. The British ambassador, Leigh Turner, says the introduction of cricket could help nurture a culture of fair play and serve as an antidote to Ukraine's endemic corruption. John Illingworth, meanwhile, nephew of former England captain Ray, has settled here and captains Kyiv Cricket Club. Another colourful local fan is Sean Carr – son-in-law of former prime minister Yulia Tymoshenko, Ukraine's famous blonde-and-braided Iron Lady. Carr, a tattooed and leathered English biker – when he is not racing his Harley-Davidson across Ukraine's wide steppes – often attends Zahoor's events. GRAHAM STACK

UNITED STATES

While America's cricketers turned in some memorable performances on the field, there was no shortage of drama off it. The follies continued with rifts in the board, the resignation of First Vice-President Nabeel Ahmed, and the sacking of chief executive Don Lockerbie. In other words, business as usual at the USA Cricket Association. After a disappointing performance at the World Twenty20 Qualifiers in the UAE in February, the men's team travelled straight to Nepal for Division Five of the World Cricket League. In a must-win round-robin match, USA overcame the distraction of a crowd riot to defeat the hosts and clinch promotion. Captain Steve Massiah finished as the tournament's leading scorer with 289 runs and four fifties in six matches, while pace bowler Kevin Darlington led the wicket-takers with 14. In August, the men returned to action in Italy for Division Four. Sushil Nadkarni was named player of the tournament as USA defeated the hosts in the final, so it was disappointing when they were immediately relegated in Hong Kong in January 2011. In between, the team went to Bermuda for the ICC Americas Division One tournament in May. And while they relinquished their hold on the 50-over title to Canada, USA exacted revenge on their northern neighbours to win the event's inaugural Twenty20 championship. During the tour, Aditya Thyagarajan hit USA's highest score of the year, 159 from only 119 balls against Argentina, while Nadkarni produced their quickest hundred on record, finishing 101 not out in a 54-ball demolition of the Cayman Islands. In July, the women's team travelled to Toronto for a three-match 50-over series, and pulled off a clean sweep over Canada to secure a spot in the 2013 Women's World Cup Qualifier, due to be held in Bangladesh in November 2011. However, these were all foreign successes. The biggest event to take place on US soil was the arrival of New Zealand and Sri Lanka in Florida in May for a pair of Twenty20 matches. Unfortunately, poor pitches and an even poorer turnout was not the advertisement Lockerbie had in mind when he threw the doors open for business with his "Destination USA" project. After failing to secure a major sponsorship deal by November's National Championships, Lockerbie was out of a job. PETER DELLA PENNA

VIETNAM

First played in Vietnam in the mid-20th century, cricket was formalised with the establishment of the Hanoi Cricket Club only in 1993. It is largely played by English and Australian expats as the country has no officially recognised organisation for cricket, and in 2006 the Saigon Cricket Association (SCA) was formed, with six teams, divided mainly along national lines, contesting a 25-over Sunday tournament running from October to May. The SCA was renamed the Vietnam Cricket Association in 2009 in an attempt to ease our passage into the Asian Cricket Council. But it has proved difficult to cultivate local cricketing talent. Most Vietnamese, encouraged not to get a sun tan as it may lower their social standing, try to avoid direct sunlight during the middle hours of the day – a cultural phenomenon reflected by the amount of whitening agents in cosmetics, sunscreens and moisturisers. But one of the best-known expats to have played in the tournament is Peter Brown, grandson of Bill, who toured England in 1948 with Don Bradman's Invincibles. Over 60 years after his grandfather was infamously "Mankaded" in the Sydney Test, Peter suffered the same fate playing for the Saigon Australian club against the Indian Sports club of Saigon.   The VCA organises an international sixes tournament in February and March each year, attracting teams from around south-east Asia, including Thailand, Malaysia, Singapore, Hong Kong and the Philippines. It is also open to local teams from other cities where the game is not established. TERRY GORDON

TOURNAMENTS CONTESTED BY NON-TEST NATIONS, 2009-10 TO JAN 2011

Competition	Winner	Runner-up	Others
World T20 Qualifier	Afghanistan	Ireland	UAE, Netherlands, USA, Kenya, Scotland, Canada
WCL Division One	Ireland	Scotland	Afghanistan, Netherlands, Canada, Kenya
WCL Division Three....	PNG	Hong Kong	Oman, Italy, USA, Denmark
WCL Division Four	USA	Italy	Nepal, Tanzania, Cayman Islands, Argentina
WCL Division Five.....	Nepal	USA	Bahrain, Singapore, Jersey, Fiji

Competition	Winner	Runner-up	Others
WCL Division Eight	Kuwait	Germany	Vanuatu, Zambia, Suriname, Gibraltar, Bahamas
Africa Division Two	Swaziland	Zambia	Ghana, Mozambique, Sierra Leone, Malawi
Africa Division Three . . .	Malawi	Sierra Leone	Rwanda, Gambia, Lesotho
Americas Division One . .	Canada	USA	Bermuda, Argentina, Cayman Islands, Bahamas
Americas Division One (T20)	USA	Canada	Cayman Islands, Bermuda, Bahamas, Argentina
Americas Division Two .	Bahamas	Suriname	Panama, Turks & Caicos Islands, Brazil
Americas Division Three	Brazil	Belize	Chile, Peru
Americas Division Four .	Mexico	Falkland Islands	Costa Rica
Americas Division Four (T20)	Mexico	Costa Rica	Falkland Islands
Asian CC Elite Trophy . .	Afghanistan	Nepal	Hong Kong, Malaysia, Oman, UAE, Kuwait, Bhutan, Singapore
Asian CC T20	Afghanistan	UAE	Oman, Kuwait, Nepal, Singapore, Malaysia, Saudi Arabia, Qatar, Hong Kong, Bahrain, China
European CC Division One	Jersey	Ireland A	Scotland A, Netherlands A, Denmark, Italy
European CC Division Two	Guernsey	Germany	France, Norway, Israel, Gibraltar

All tournaments scheduled as 50-over competitions unless indicated as T20 games.

PART SIX

Law and Administration

OFFICIAL BODIES

INTERNATIONAL CRICKET COUNCIL

The ICC are world cricket's governing body. They are responsible for managing the playing conditions and Code of Conduct for international fixtures, expanding the game and organising the major international tournaments, including the World Cup and World Twenty20. Their mission statement says the ICC "will lead by promoting and protecting the game, and its unique spirit" and "optimising their commercial rights and properties for the benefit of their members".

Ten national governing bodies are currently Full Members of the ICC; full membership qualifies a nation (or geographic area) to play official Test matches. A candidate for full membership must meet a number of playing and administrative criteria, after which elevation is decided by a vote among existing Full Members. There are also currently 35 Associate Members (non-Test-playing nations or geographic areas where cricket is firmly established and organised) and 60 Affiliate Members (other countries or geographic areas where the ICC recognise that cricket is played in accordance with the Laws).

The ICC were founded in 1909 as the Imperial Cricket Conference by three Foundation Members: England, Australia and South Africa. Other countries (or geographic areas) became Full Members and thus acquired Test status as follows: India, New Zealand and West Indies in 1926, Pakistan in 1952, Sri Lanka in 1981, Zimbabwe in 1992 and Bangladesh in 2000. South Africa ceased to be a member on leaving the Commonwealth in 1961, but were re-elected as a Full Member in 1991.

In 1965, the Conference were renamed the International Cricket Conference and new rules permitted the election of countries from outside the Commonwealth for the first time. The first Associate Members (Fiji and USA), who had diluted voting rights, were admitted. However, Foundation Members retained a veto over all resolutions. In 1989, the Conference were again renamed without changing their initials. The new International Cricket Council adopted revised rules, aimed at producing an organisation which could make a larger number of binding decisions, rather than simply make recommendations to national governing bodies. In 1993, the Council, which had previously been administered by MCC, gained their own secretariat and chief executive, though their headquarters remained at Lord's. The category of Foundation Member was abolished.

In 1997, the Council became an incorporated body, with an executive board, and a president instead of a chairman. The ICC remained at Lord's, with a commercial base in Monaco, until August 2005, when after 96 years they moved to Dubai in the United Arab Emirates, which offered organisational and tax advantages.

Officers

President: S. G. R. Pawar. *Vice-President:* A. R. Isaac. *Chief Executive:* H. Lorgat.

Chairs of Committees – Chief Executives' Committee: H. Lorgat. *Cricket:* C. H. Lloyd. *Audit:* A. H. M. Mustafa Kamal. *Governance Review:* J. R. Hunte. *Development:* H. Lorgat. *Code of Conduct Commission:* M. J. Beloff, QC. *Women's Committee:* B. Timmer. *Finance and Commercial Affairs:* A. R. Isaac. *Medical Committee:* Dr P. R. Harcourt. *Anti-Corruption and Security Unit:* Sir Ronnie Flanagan.

Executive Board: The president, president-elect and chief executive sit on the board *ex officio*. They are joined by P. F. Chingoka (Zimbabwe), C. G. Clarke (England), J. J. Clarke (Australia), D. S. de Silva (Sri Lanka), J. R. Hunte (West Indies), Ijaz Butt (Pakistan), A. K. Khan (South Africa), I. Khwaja (Singapore), S. V. Manohar (India), C. J. D. Moller (New Zealand), A. H. M. Mustafa Kamal (Bangladesh), C. K. Oliver (Scotland), N. Speight (Bermuda). I. S. Bindra (ICC Principal Advisor) also attends board meetings.

Chief Executives' Committee: The chairman, president and cricket committee chairman sit on the Chief Executives' Committee *ex officio*. They are joined by the chief executives of the ten Full

Member boards and three Associate Member boards: D. G. Collier (England), J. A. Cribbin (Hong Kong), W. Deutrom (Ireland), F. Erasmus (Namibia), E. Hilaire (West Indies), M. G. Majola (South Africa), Manzoor Ahmed (Bangladesh), W. Mukondiwa (Zimbabwe), N. Ranatunga (Sri Lanka), N. Srinivasan (India), J. A. Sutherland (Australia), J. T. C. Vaughan (New Zealand), Zakir Khan (Pakistan).

General Manager – Cricket: D. J. Richardson. *General Manager – Commercial:* D. C. Jamieson. *Anti-Corruption and Security Unit General Manager:* R. Sawani. *Acting Global Development Manager:* T. L. Anderson. *Chief Financial Officer:* Faisal Hasnain. *Head of Legal and Company Secretary:* D. Becker. *Member Services Manager:* J. Long. *Human Resources and Administration Manager:* S. K. Banerjee. *Head of Media and Communications Manager:* C. R. Gibson.

Constitution

President: S. G. R. Pawar of India became president in June 2010, and A. R. Isaac of New Zealand is due to succeed him in 2012.

Chief Executive: Appointed by the Council. In 2008, H. Lorgat succeeded M. W. Speed, who had served for seven years.

Membership

Full Members: Australia, Bangladesh, England, India, New Zealand, Pakistan, South Africa, Sri Lanka, West Indies and Zimbabwe.

Associate Members*: Argentina (1974), Belgium (2005), Bermuda (1966), Botswana (2005), Canada (1968), Cayman Islands (2002), Denmark (1966), Fiji (1965), France (1998), Germany (1999), Gibraltar (1969), Guernsey (2005), Hong Kong (1969), Ireland (1993), Israel (1974), Italy (1995), Japan (2005), Jersey (2007), Kenya (1981), Kuwait (2005), Malaysia (1967), Namibia (1992), Nepal (1996), Netherlands (1966), Nigeria (2002), Papua New Guinea (1973), Scotland (1994), Singapore (1974), Tanzania (2001), Thailand (2005), Uganda (1998), United Arab Emirates (1990), USA (1965), Vanuatu (1995), Zambia (2003).

Affiliate Members*: Afghanistan (2001), Austria (1992), Bahamas (1987), Bahrain (2001), Belize (1997), Bhutan (2001), Brazil (2002), Brunei (1992), Bulgaria (2008), Cameroon (2007), Chile (2002), China (2004), Cook Islands (2000), Costa Rica (2002), Croatia (2001), Cuba (2002), Cyprus (1999), Czech Republic (2000), Estonia (2008), Falkland Islands (2007), Finland (2000), Gambia (2002), Ghana (2002), Greece (1995), Indonesia (2001), Iran (2003), Isle of Man (2004), Lesotho (2001), Luxembourg (1998), Malawi (2003), Maldives (2001), Mali (2005), Malta (1998), Mexico (2004), Morocco (1999), Mozambique (2003), Myanmar (2006), Norway (2000), Oman (2000), Panama (2002), Peru (2007), Philippines (2000), Portugal (1996), Qatar (1999), Rwanda (2003), St Helena (2001), Samoa (2000), Saudi Arabia (2003), Seychelles (2010), Sierra Leone (2002), Slovenia (2005), South Korea (2001), Spain (1992), Suriname (2002), Swaziland (2007), Sweden (1997), Switzerland (1985), Tonga (2000), Turkey (2008), Turks & Caicos Islands (2002).

* Year of election shown in parentheses.

Full Members: The governing body for cricket (recognised by the ICC) of a country, or countries associated for cricket purposes, or a geographical area, from which representative teams are qualified to play official Test matches.

Associate Members: The governing body for cricket (recognised by the ICC) of a country, or countries associated for cricket purposes, or a geographical area, which does not qualify as a Full Member but where cricket is firmly established and organised.

Affiliate Members: The governing body for cricket (recognised by the ICC) of a country, or countries associated for cricket purposes, or a geographical area (which is not part of one of those already constituted as a Full or Associate Member) where the ICC recognise that cricket is played in accordance with the Laws of Cricket. Five Affiliate Member representatives have the right to attend or vote at the ICC annual conference.

Addresses

ICC: Street 69, Dubai Sports City, Emirates Road, PO Box 500 070, Dubai, United Arab Emirates (+971 4382 8800; fax +971 4382 8600; website www.icc-cricket.yahoo.net; email enquiry@icc-cricket.com).

Australia: Cricket Australia, 60 Jolimont Street, Jolimont, Victoria 3002 (+61 3 9653 9999; fax +61 3 9653 9922; website www.cricket.com.au; email penquiries@cricket. com.au).

Bangladesh: Bangladesh Cricket Board, Sher-e-Bangla National Cricket Stadium, Mirpur, Dhaka 1216 (+880 2 803 1101; fax +880 2 803 1199; website www. tigercricket.com; email info@bcb-cricket.com).

England: England and Wales Cricket Board (see below).

India: Board of Control for Cricket in India, Cricket Centre, 2nd Floor, Wankhede Stadium, D Road, Churchgate, Mumbai 400 020 (+91 22 2289 8800; fax +91 22 2289 8801; website www.bcci.tv; email bcci@vsnl.com and cricketboard@gmail.com).

New Zealand: New Zealand Cricket, PO Box 958, Level 6, 164 Hereford Street, Christchurch (+64 3 366 2964; fax +64 3 365 7491; website www.blackcaps.co.nz; email info@nzcricket.org.nz).

Pakistan: Pakistan Cricket Board, Gaddafi Stadium, Ferozpur Road, Lahore 54600 (+92 42 571 7231; fax +92 42 571 1860; website www.pcb.com.pk; email mail@pcb.com.pk).

South Africa: Cricket South Africa, Wanderers Club, PO Box 55009, 21 North Street, Illovo, Northlands 2116 (+27 11 880 2810; fax +27 11 880 6578; website www.cricket.co.za; email info@cricket.co.za).

Sri Lanka: Sri Lanka Cricket, 35 Maitland Place, Colombo 07000 (+94 112 681 601; fax +94 114 722 236; website www.srilankacricket.lk; email info@srilankacricket.lk).

West Indies: West Indies Cricket Board, PO Box 616 W, Factory Road, St John's, Antigua (+1 268 481 2450; fax +1 268 481 2498; website www.windiescricket.com; email wicb@windiescricket.com).

Zimbabwe: Zimbabwe Cricket, PO Box 2739, 28 Maiden Drive, Highlands, Harare (+263 4 788 090; fax +263 4 788 094; website www.zimcricket.org; email info@zimcricket.org).

Note: Full contact details for all Associate and Affiliate Members may be found at the ICC website www.icc-cricket.yahoo.net/the-icc/icc_members/overview.php.

ENGLAND AND WALES CRICKET BOARD

The England and Wales Cricket Board (ECB) became responsible for the administration of all cricket – professional and recreational – in England and Wales on January 1, 1997. They took over the functions of the Cricket Council, the Test and County Cricket Board and the National Cricket Association which had run the game in England and Wales since 1968. In 2005, a new constitution was approved which streamlined and modernised the governance of English cricket. The Management Board of 18 directors was replaced by a Board of Directors numbering 12, with three appointed by the first-class counties and two by the county boards. In 2010, this expanded to 14, with the appointment of the ECB's first two women directors.

Officers

Chairman: C. G. Clarke. *Deputy Chairman:* D. L. Amiss. *Chief Executive:* D. G. Collier.

Board of Directors: C. G. Clarke (*chairman*), D. L. Amiss, D. G. Collier, M. V. Fleming, C. Graves, B. W. Havill, Lady Heyhoe-Flint, N. R. A. Hilliard, R. Jackson, I. N. Lovett, Lord Morris of Handsworth, J. B. Pickup, J. Stichbury, P. G. Wright.

Chairmen of Committees – Cricket: P. G. Wright. *Commercial:* C. G. Clarke. *Recreational Assembly:* J. B. Pickup. *Audit:* I. N. Lovett. *Remuneration:* N. R. A. Hilliard. *Discipline:* G. Elias, QC.

Managing Director, England Cricket: H. Morris. *Managing Director, Cricket Partnerships:* M. W. Gatting. *Managing Director, Events and County Business:* G. Hollins. *Finance Director:* B. W. Havill. *Director of Marketing and Communications:* S. Elworthy. *Director of Public Policy and International Relations:* P. French. *Director of England Cricket:* J. D. Carr. *Commercial Director:* J. Perera. *Head of Information Technology:* C. Hoad. *General Manager of Communications,*

Publications and New Media: A. J. Walpole. *England Teams Media Manager:* J. D. Avery. *Head of Women's Cricket:* C. J. Connor. *Head of Operations (First-class cricket):* A. Fordham. *Cricket Operations Manager (Non-first-class cricket):* P. Bedford. *National Selector:* G. Miller.

ECB: D. G. Collier, Lord's Ground, London NW8 8QZ (020 7432 1200; fax 020 7286 5583; website www.ecb.co.uk).

THE MARYLEBONE CRICKET CLUB

The Marylebone Cricket Club evolved out of the White Conduit Club in 1787, when Thomas Lord laid out his first ground in Dorset Square. Their members revised the Laws in 1788 and gradually took responsibility for cricket throughout the world. However, they relinquished control of the game in the UK in 1968 and the International Cricket Council finally established their own secretariat in 1993. MCC still own Lord's and remain the guardian of the Laws. They call themselves "a private club with a public function" and aim to support cricket everywhere, especially at grassroots level and in countries where the game is least developed.

Patron: HER MAJESTY THE QUEEN

Officers

President: 2010-11 – C. D. A. Martin-Jenkins. *Club Chairman:* O. H. J. Stocken. *Treasurer:* L. J. Dowley. *Trustees:* J. M. Brearley, Sir Timothy Rice, A. W. Wreford. *Hon. Life Vice-Presidents:* Lord Bramall, D. G. Clark, E. R. Dexter, G. H. G. Doggart, T. W. Graveney, Lord Griffiths, D. J. Insole, M. E. L. Melluish, Sir Oliver Popplewell, D. R. W. Silk, J. J. Warr, J. C. Woodcock.

Secretary and Chief Executive: K. Bradshaw. *Deputy Secretary:* C. Maynard. *Assistant Secretaries – Cricket and Estates:* J. P. Stephenson. *Legal:* H. A-M. Roper-Curzon. *Finance:* S. J. M. Gibb. *Marketing and Catering:* J. D. Robinson. *Vision for Lord's Project Director:* D. N. Batts.

MCC Committee: J. R. T. Barclay, P. R. Carroll, S. Dyson, D. J. C. Faber, M. V. Fleming, C. A. Fry, M. W. Gatting, Lady Heyhoe-Flint, G. W. Jones, P. L. O. Leaver, Sir John Major, T. J. G. O'Gorman. The president, club chairman, treasurer and committee chairmen are on the committee *ex officio*.

Chairmen of Committees – Arts and Library: A. I. Lack. *Cricket:* M. G. Griffith. *Estates:* B. N. Gorst. *Finance:* L. J. Dowley. *Membership and General Purposes:* N. M. Peters. *World Cricket:* A. R. Lewis.

MCC: The Secretary and Chief Executive, Lord's Ground, London NW8 8QN (020 7616 8500; email reception@mcc.org.uk; website www.lords.org/mcc. Tickets 020 7432 1000; fax 020 7616 8700; email ticketing@mcc.org.uk).

PROFESSIONAL CRICKETERS' ASSOCIATION

The Professional Cricketers' Association were formed in 1967 (as the Cricketers' Association) to be the collective voice of first-class professional players and enhance and protect their interests. During the 1970s, they succeeded in establishing pension schemes and a minimum wage. In the last decade their strong commercial operations and greater funding from the ECB have increased their services to current and past players, including education, legal, financial and benevolent help.

President: Sir Ian Botham. *Chairman:* V. S. Solanki. *Vice-President – Benevolent Trust:* D. A. Graveney. *Non-Executive Group Chairman:* A. W. Wreford. *Non-Executive Director:* M. Wheeler. *Chief Executive:* A. J. Porter. *Assistant Chief Executive:* J. D. Ratcliffe. *Legal Director:* I. T. Smith. *Commercial Director:* J. M. Grave. *Commercial Manager:* P. J. Prichard. *Commercial Assistant:* A. R. Phipps. *Events and Fundraising Manager:* L. A. Michael. *Team England Account Manager:* E. M. Barnes. *Team England Assistant:* E. T. Cadwell. *Player Services Executive:* A. Prosser.

PCA: Unit 3, Utopia Village, 7 Chalcot Road, London NW1 8LH (020 7449 4221; fax 020 7586 8520; email events@thepca.co.uk; website www.thepca.co.uk).

THE LAWS IN 2010

FRASER STEWART

In May 2010, MCC members gave approval to certain Law changes that are now incorporated into the fourth edition of the 2000 Code of Laws, which came into effect on October 1, 2010.

Changes to Laws 3.8 and 3.9 mean that the umpires will no longer "offer the light" to the batting side. MCC felt the decision to stay on or come off the field was often made on tactical grounds based on what best suited the batting side, rather than for safety or visibility. In poor light (and the same is to apply in poor conditions of ground or weather), the umpires will suspend play only when they consider it to be unreasonable or dangerous.

After witnessing seemingly ever-increasing athleticism from fielders on the boundary, MCC also felt a change to Law 19 would be sensible. It was thought to be wrong to allow a fielder, seeing a ball flying over his head, to retreat beyond the boundary and then to jump up and parry the ball back towards the field of play. The change to Law 19.4(i) requires that the fielder who first makes contact with the ball must do so when some part of his person is grounded within the boundary or, if he is airborne, that his final contact with the ground before touching the ball was within the boundary.

The issue of whether or not cramp should be considered an injury or illness was mentioned last year. The ICC's medical committee have since decreed that cramp should be so considered. So a batsman suffering from cramp may now, if he wishes, request a runner or retire hurt. MCC will not add anything so specific to the Laws, but are content for this interpretation to be adopted at lower levels of the game.

As usual, the professional game produced a number of talking points in relation to the Laws. One such was Jonathan Trott's routine before facing each ball, which has led to complaints from some opponents about his not being ready. Law 42.10 requires that "in normal circumstances, the striker should always be ready to take strike when the bowler is ready to start his run-up". Umpires must take all circumstances into account before deciding whether the batsman is wasting time by taking longer than is reasonable. Repeatedly marking a guard or having an extravagant pre-facing routine must not delay the bowler. If the umpires feel that the Law has been breached, a first and final warning is given to the batting side. This warning applies to the entire team, not just to the batsman who caused the offence. For each further incident of time-wasting by the batting side, five penalty runs are awarded to the fielding side. MCC are unaware of any official warnings being issued to Trott.

The final ball of the Friends Provident T20 final at the Rose Bowl in 2010 produced an excellent example of how a sound knowledge of the Laws is essential. Hampshire needed two runs to win, although one would have been enough as they had lost fewer wickets. The striker, Dan Christian, had a runner. The ball hit him on the pads, and all three Hampshire players set off for a run, including the injured Christian, who later claimed that he simply acted out of habit. The ball evaded the Somerset in-fielders, and all three Hampshire players (injured striker, non-striker and runner) ended up at the opposite end from where they had started.

There followed a few confusing seconds in which none of the players seemed to know who had won. Law 29.2(e) clarifies that the injured striker's ground always remains at the wicketkeeper's end. Law 2.8(c) shows he can be run out at that end, no matter where the other two are. It makes no difference whether he is an inch or 22 yards out of his ground. A Somerset fielder simply needed to put the wicket down at the wicketkeeper's end: had that happened, Christian would have been given run out on appeal and no run would have been scored. But no such attempt was made, and eventually the umpires called "Time", with Hampshire being credited with the vital run. After the match, the legitimacy of the run was questioned by some. But both the runner and the non-striker had completed a single. Any run they complete will count unless there is a subsequent run-out of the injured striker at the wicketkeeper's end. As no such run-out was attempted, even after a deliberate pause by the umpires before calling "Time", the run did count.

Another interesting incident occurred during the Trent Bridge Test of 2010. Kevin Pietersen backed away, claiming to be distracted, just as Mohammad Asif was entering his delivery stride. Asif delivered the ball normally and Pietersen, from about two feet outside leg stump, took a half-hearted swing at the ball, not in self-defence. The ball was caught at mid-off and there was an appeal. There are two relevant Laws that come into play here, 23.4(b)(v) and (vi). In the first of these, if the striker is not ready to receive the ball, the umpire is to call "Dead ball" – but only if there is no attempt to play the ball. Subsection (vi) requires the umpire to call dead ball if the striker is distracted while he is preparing to receive or receiving a delivery. Then the striker is protected even if he does play the ball. Pietersen was distracted, rather than not ready, and so the fact that he played at the ball was not relevant.

Virender Sehwag of India was denied a century in controversial circumstances during a one-day international in Sri Lanka in August. He was on 99 with the scores level. The bowler delivered a no-ball (deliberately), which Sehwag hit for six. However, the umpire correctly ruled that the six did not count, as the run from the no-ball completed the match. Law 21.6 states: "As soon as a result is reached... the match is at an end. Nothing that happens thereafter, except as in Law 42.17(b) (penalty runs), shall be regarded as part of it." Furthermore, Law 24.12 states: "A penalty of one run shall be awarded instantly on the call of no-ball." Consequently, the match was already at an end before Sehwag was able to hit the ball. It was unfortunate for Sehwag, but the Laws are clear. The same principle applies if the striker is stumped off a wide when the scores are level. Although not called until later, the ball is a wide from the instant of delivery, and the run for it counts from that point. Hence the result is reached before the stumping can take place.

Always keen to protect and promote the Spirit of Cricket, MCC were heartened by a directive from the ECB, applicable in county cricket but which should also affect lower levels of the game, which reminded players that a throw by the bowler towards a striker who has not left his ground is an unfair act. The ECB described such pieces of fielding as "unwarranted aggressive behaviour which carries with it the very real prospect of injury to the batsman", and continued: "Where there is no genuine run-out attempt, such behaviour is totally unacceptable." Umpires at all levels can report players under Laws 42.2 and 42.18 – there is no punishment that can be handed out during the game, but the appropriate governing body can deal with the report as it sees fit.

In addition to these high-profile incidents, MCC received many requests for interpretations of bizarre incidents, including one where a boundary was prevented when the ball hit a water bottle that had been left on the outfield by a fielder. This scenario counts as illegal fielding, under Law 41.2, as the bottle had been placed there wilfully by a fielder. Five penalty runs are awarded, plus any runs for a no-ball or a wide, together with any runs completed by the batsmen and, if they have crossed, the run in progress when the incident occurred. If, however, the bottle had been thrown on to the field by a spectator, the ball hitting it would simply be treated as an accident and the ball would remain in play.

Full details of the changes to the Laws, including a video, are available on MCC's website (www.lords.org).

Fraser Stewart is laws manager at MCC.

PREFACE TO THE LAWS

The game of cricket has been governed by a series of Codes of Law for over 250 years. These Codes have been subject to additions and alterations recommended by the governing authorities of the time. Since its formation in 1787, the Marylebone Cricket Club has been recognised as the sole authority for drawing up the Code and for all subsequent amendments. The club also holds the world copyright.

The basic Laws of Cricket have stood remarkably well the test of over 250 years of playing the game. It is thought the real reason for this is that cricketers have traditionally been prepared to play in the spirit of the game as well as in accordance with the Laws.

In 2000, MCC revised and rewrote the Laws for the new millennium. In this Code, the major innovation was the introduction of the Spirit of Cricket as a Preamble to the Laws. Whereas in the past it was assumed that the implicit spirit of the game was understood and accepted by all those involved, MCC felt it right to put into words some clear guidelines, which help to maintain the unique character and enjoyment of the game. The other aims were to dispense with the Notes, to incorporate all the points into the Laws and to remove, where possible, any ambiguities, so that captains, players and umpires could continue to enjoy the game at whatever level they might be playing. MCC consulted widely with all the Full Member countries of the International Cricket Council, the governing body of the game. There was close consultation with the Association of Cricket Umpires and Scorers. The club also brought in umpires and players from all round the world.

This latest version, The Laws of Cricket (2000 Code 4th Edition – 2010) includes several necessary amendments arising from experience and practical application of the Code around the world since October 2000.

Significant dates in the history of the Laws are as follows:

1700	Cricket was recognised as early as this date.
1744	The earliest known Code was drawn up by certain "Noblemen and Gentlemen" who used the Artillery Ground in London.
1755	The Laws were revised by "Several Cricket Clubs, particularly the Star and Garter in Pall Mall".
1774	A further revision was produced by "a Committee of Noblemen and Gentlemen of Kent, Hampshire, Surrey, Sussex, Middlesex and London at the Star and Garter".
1786	A further revision was undertaken by a similar body of Noblemen and Gentlemen of Kent, Hampshire, Surrey, Sussex, Middlesex and London.
1788	The first MCC Code of Laws was adopted on May 30.
1835	A new Code of Laws was approved by the MCC committee on May 19.
1884	After consultation with cricket clubs worldwide, important alterations were incorporated in a new version approved at an MCC special general meeting on April 21.
1947	A new Code of Laws was approved at an MCC SGM on May 7. The main changes were aimed at achieving clarification and better arrangement of the Laws and their interpretations. This did not, however, exclude certain definite alterations which were designed to provide greater latitude in the conduct of the game as required by the widely differing conditions in which cricket was played.
1979	After five editions of the 1947 Code, a further revision was begun in 1974 with the aim being to remove certain anomalies, consolidate various Amendments and Notes, and to achieve greater clarity and simplicity. The new Code of Laws was approved at an MCC SGM on November 21.
1992	A second edition of the 1980 Code was produced, incorporating all the amendments which were approved during the intervening 12 years.
2000	A new Code of Laws, including a Preamble defining the Spirit of Cricket, was approved on May 3, 2000.

Many queries on the Laws, which apply equally to women's cricket as to men's, are sent to MCC for decision every year. MCC, as the accepted guardian of the Laws, have always been prepared to answer the queries and to give interpretations on certain conditions, which will be readily understood.

(a) In the case of league or competition cricket, the enquiry must come from the committee responsible for organising the league or competition. In other cases, enquiries should be initiated by a representative officer of a club, or of an umpires' association on behalf of his or her committee, or by a master or mistress in charge of school cricket.

(b) MCC reserve the right not to answer queries which they consider to be frivolous.

(c) The enquiry must not be connected in any way with a bet or wager.

Lord's Cricket Ground   K. Bradshaw
London NW8 8QN   Secretary & Chief Executive MCC
May 5, 2010

CONTENTS

Appendices A–D can be found at www.lords.org/laws-and-spirit/laws-of-cricket/laws

THE LAWS OF CRICKET

THE PREAMBLE – The Spirit of Cricket

Cricket is a game that owes much of its unique appeal to the fact that it should be played not only within its Laws but also within the Spirit of the Game. Any action which is seen to abuse this spirit causes injury to the game itself. The major responsibility for ensuring the spirit of fair play rests with the captains.

1. There are two Laws which place the responsibility for the team's conduct firmly on the captain.

Responsibility of captains

The captains are responsible at all times for ensuring that play is conducted within the Spirit of the Game as well as within the Laws.

Player's conduct

In the event of a player failing to comply with instructions by an umpire, or criticising by word or action the decisions of an umpire, or showing dissent, or generally behaving in a manner which might bring the game into disrepute, the umpire concerned shall in the first place report the matter to the other umpire and to the player's captain, and instruct the latter to take action.

2. Fair and unfair play

According to the Laws the umpires are the sole judges of fair and unfair play.
The umpires may intervene at any time and it is the responsibility of the captain to take action where required.

3. The umpires are authorised to intervene in cases of

- Time wasting
- Damaging the pitch
- Dangerous or unfair bowling
- Tampering with the ball
- Any other action that they consider to be unfair

4. The Spirit of the Game involves respect for

- Your opponents
- Your own captain and team
- The role of the umpires
- The game and its traditional values

5. It is against the Spirit of the Game

- To dispute an umpire's decision by word, action or gesture
- To direct abusive language towards an opponent or umpire
- To indulge in cheating or any sharp practice, for instance:

    (a) to appeal knowing that the batsman is not out

    (b) to advance towards an umpire in an aggressive manner when appealing

    (c) to seek to distract an opponent either verbally or by harassment with persistent clapping or unnecessary noise under the guise of enthusiasm and motivation of one's own side

6. Violence

There is no place for any act of violence on the field of play.

7. Players

Captains and umpires together set the tone for the conduct of a cricket match. Every player is expected to make an important contribution to this.

The players, umpires and scorers in a game of cricket may be of either gender and the Laws apply equally to both. The use, throughout the text, of pronouns indicating the male gender is purely for brevity. Except where specifically stated otherwise, every provision of the Laws is to be read as applying to women and girls equally as to men and boys.

LAW 1 THE PLAYERS

1. Number of players

A match is played between two sides, each of eleven players, one of whom shall be captain. By agreement a match may be played between sides of fewer than, or more than, eleven players, but not more than eleven players may field at any time.

2. Nomination of players

Each captain shall nominate his players in writing to one of the umpires before the toss. No player may be changed after the nomination without the consent of the opposing captain.

3. Captain

If at any time the captain is not available, a deputy shall act for him.

    (a) If a captain is not available during the period in which the toss is to take place, then the deputy must be responsible for the nomination of the players, if this has not already been done, and for the toss. See 2 above and Law 12.4 (The toss).

    (b) At any time after the nomination of the players, only a nominated player can act as deputy in discharging the duties and responsibilities of the captain as stated in these Laws.

4. Responsibility of captains

The captains are responsible at all times for ensuring that play is conducted within the spirit and traditions of the game as well as within the Laws. See The Preamble – The Spirit of Cricket and Law 42.1 (Fair and unfair play – responsibility of captains).

LAW 2 SUBSTITUTES AND RUNNERS; BATSMAN OR FIELDER LEAVING THE FIELD; BATSMAN RETIRING; BATSMAN COMMENCING INNINGS

1. Substitutes and runners

    (a) If the umpires are satisfied that a nominated player has been injured or become ill since the nomination of the players, they shall allow that player to have

        (i) a substitute acting for him in the field.

        (ii) a runner when batting.

Any injury or illness that occurs at any time after the nomination of the players until the conclusion of the match shall be allowable, irrespective of whether play is in progress or not.

    (b) The umpires shall have discretion to allow, for other wholly acceptable reasons, a substitute fielder or a runner to act for a nominated player, at the start of the match, or at any subsequent time.

    (c) A player wishing to change his shirt, boots, etc. shall leave the field to do so. No substitute shall be allowed for him.

2. Objection to substitutes

The opposing captain shall have no right of objection to any player acting as a substitute on the field, nor as to where the substitute shall field. However, no substitute shall act as wicket-keeper. See 3 below.

3. Restrictions on role of substitutes

A substitute shall not be allowed to bat, bowl or act as wicket-keeper. Note also Law 1.3(b) (Captain).

4. A player for whom a substitute has acted

A nominated player is allowed to bat, bowl or field even though a substitute has previously acted for him.

5. Fielder absent or leaving the field

If a fielder fails to take the field with his side at the start of the match or at any later time, or leaves the field during a session of play,

(a) the umpire shall be informed of the reason for his absence.

(b) he shall not thereafter come on to the field of play during a session of play without the consent of the umpire. See 6 below. The umpire shall give such consent as soon as is practicable.

(c) if he is absent for 15 minutes of playing time or longer, he shall not be permitted to bowl thereafter, subject to (i), (ii) or (iii) below, until he has been on the field for at least the length of playing time for which he was absent.

    (i) Absence or penalty for time absent shall not be carried over into a new day's play.

    (ii) If, in the case of a follow-on or forfeiture, a side fields for two consecutive innings, this restriction shall, subject to (i) above, continue as necessary into the second innings, but shall not otherwise be carried over into a new innings.

    (iii) The time lost for an unscheduled break in play shall be counted as time on the field of play for any fielder who comes on to the field at the resumption of play after the break. See Law 15.1 (An interval).

6. Player returning without permission

If a player comes on to the field of play in contravention of 5(b) above and comes into contact with the ball while it is in play,

(a) the ball shall immediately become dead and the umpire shall award 5 penalty runs to the batting side. Additionally, runs completed by the batsmen shall be scored together with the run in progress if they had already crossed at the instant of the offence. The ball shall not count as one of the over.

(b) the umpire shall inform the other umpire, the captain of the fielding side, the batsmen and, as soon as practicable, the captain of the batting side of the reason for this action.

(c) the umpires together shall report the occurrence as soon as possible after the match to the Executive of the fielding side and to any Governing Body responsible for the match, who shall take such action as is considered appropriate against the captain and the player concerned.

7. Runner

The player acting as a runner for a batsman shall be a member of the batting side and shall, if possible, have already batted in that innings. The runner shall wear external protective equipment equivalent to that worn by the batsman for whom he runs and shall carry a bat.

8. Transgression of the Laws by a batsman who has a runner

(a) A batsman's runner is subject to the Laws. He will be regarded as a batsman except where there are specific provisions for his role as a runner. See 7 above and Law 29.2 (Which is a batsman's ground).

(b) A batsman who has a runner will suffer the penalty for any infringement of the Laws by his runner as if he had been himself responsible for the infringement. In particular he will be out if his runner is out under any of Laws 33 (Handled the ball), 37 (Obstructing the field) or 38 (Run out).

(c) When a batsman who has a runner is striker he remains himself subject to the Laws and will be liable to the penalties that any infringement of them demands.

Additionally, if he is out of his ground when the wicket at the wicket-keeper's end is fairly put down by the action of a fielder then, notwithstanding (b) above and irrespective of the position of the non-striker and the runner,

  (i) notwithstanding the provisions of Law 38.2(e), he is out Run out except as in (ii) below. Sections (a), (b), (c) and (d) of Law 38.2 (Batsman not Run out) shall apply.

  (ii) he is out Stumped if the delivery is not a No ball and the wicket is fairly put down by the wicket-keeper without the intervention of another fielder. However, Law 39.3 (Not out Stumped) shall apply.

If he is thus dismissed, runs completed by the runner and the other batsman before the wicket is put down shall be disallowed. However, any runs for penalties awarded to either side shall stand. See Law 18.6 (Runs awarded for penalties). The non-striker shall return to his original end.

(d) When a batsman who has a runner is not the striker

  (i) he remains subject to Laws 33 (Handled the ball) and 37 (Obstructing the field) but is otherwise out of the game.

  (ii) he shall stand where directed by the striker's end umpire so as not to interfere with play.

  (iii) he will be liable, notwithstanding (i) above, to the penalty demanded by the Laws should he commit any act of unfair play.

9. Batsman retiring

A batsman may retire at any time during his innings when the ball is dead. The umpires, before allowing play to proceed shall be informed of the reason for a batsman retiring.

(a) If a batsman retires because of illness, injury or any other unavoidable cause, he is entitled to resume his innings subject to (c) below. If for any reason he does not do so, his innings is to be recorded as "Retired – not out".

(b) If a batsman retires for any reason other than as in (a) above, he may resume his innings only with the consent of the opposing captain. If for any reason he does not resume his innings it is to be recorded as "Retired – out".

(c) If after retiring a batsman resumes his innings, it shall be only at the fall of a wicket or the retirement of another batsman.

10. Commencement of a batsman's innings

Except at the start of a side's innings, a batsman shall be considered to have commenced his innings when he first steps on to the field of play, provided "Time" has not been called. The innings of the opening batsmen, and that of any new batsman on the resumption of play after a call of "Time", shall commence at the call of "Play".

LAW 3 THE UMPIRES

1. Appointment and attendance

Before the match, two umpires shall be appointed, one for each end, to control the game as required by the Laws, with absolute impartiality. The umpires shall be present on the ground and report to the Executive of the ground at least 45 minutes before the scheduled start of each day's play.

2. Change of umpire

An umpire shall not be changed during the match, other than in exceptional circumstances, unless he is injured or ill. If there has to be a change of umpire, the replacement shall act only as striker's end umpire unless the captains agree that he should take full responsibility as an umpire.

3. Agreement with captains

Before the toss the umpires shall

(a) ascertain the hours of play and agree with the captains

(i) the balls to be used during the match. See Law 5 (The ball).

(ii) times and durations of intervals for meals and times for drinks intervals. See Law 15 (Intervals).

(iii) the boundary of the field of play and allowances for boundaries. See Law 19 (Boundaries).

(iv) any special conditions of play affecting the conduct of the match.

(b) inform the scorers of agreements in (ii), (iii) and (iv) above.

4. To inform captains and scorers

Before the toss the umpires shall agree between themselves and inform both captains and both scorers

(i) which clock or watch and back-up time piece is to be used during the match.

(ii) whether or not any obstacle within the field of play is to be regarded as a boundary. See Law 19 (Boundaries).

5. The wickets, creases and boundaries

Before the toss and during the match, the umpires shall satisfy themselves that

(a) the wickets are properly pitched. See Law 8 (The wickets).

(b) the creases are correctly marked. See Law 9 (The bowling, popping and return creases).

(c) the boundary of the field of play complies with the requirements of Laws 19.1 (The boundary of the field of play) and 19.2 (Defining the boundary – boundary marking).

6. Conduct of the game, implements and equipment

Before the toss and during the match, the umpires shall satisfy themselves that

(a) the conduct of the game is strictly in accordance with the Laws.

(b) the implements of the game conform to the following

(i) Law 5 (The ball).

(ii) externally visible requirements of Law 6 (The bat) and Appendix E.

(iii) either Laws 8.2 (Size of stumps) and 8.3 (The bails) or, if appropriate, Law 8.4 (Junior cricket).

(c) (i) no player uses equipment other than that permitted. See Appendix D. Note particularly therein the interpretation of "protective helmet".

(ii) the wicket-keeper's gloves comply with the requirements of Law 40.2 (Gloves).

7. Fair and unfair play

The umpires shall be the sole judges of fair and unfair play.

8. Fitness for play

(a) It is solely for the umpires together to decide whether

    either   conditions of ground, weather or light

    or   exceptional circumstances

mean that it would be dangerous or unreasonable for play to take place.
Conditions shall not be regarded as either dangerous or unreasonable merely because they are not ideal.

(b) Conditions shall be regarded as dangerous if there is actual and foreseeable risk to the safety of any player or umpire.

(c) Conditions shall be regarded as unreasonable if, although posing no risk to safety, it would not be sensible for play to proceed.

9. Suspension of play in dangerous or unreasonable conditions

(a) All references to ground include the pitch. See Law 7.1 (Area of pitch).

(b) If at any time the umpires together agree that the conditions of ground, weather or light, or any other circumstances are dangerous or unreasonable, they shall immediately suspend play, or not allow play to start or to recommence.

(c) When there is a suspension of play it is the responsibility of the umpires to monitor conditions. They shall make inspections as often as appropriate, unaccompanied by any players or officials. Immediately the umpires together agree that the conditions are no longer dangerous or unreasonable they shall call upon the players to resume play.

10. Position of umpires

Each umpire shall stand where he can best see any act upon which his decision may be required. Subject to this over-riding consideration, the bowler's end umpire shall stand where he does not interfere with either the bowler's run up or the striker's view.

The striker's end umpire may elect to stand on the off side instead of the on side of the pitch, provided he informs the captain of the fielding side, the striker and the other umpire of his intention to do so.

11. Umpires changing ends

The umpires shall change ends after each side has had one completed innings. See Law 12.3 (Completed innings).

12. Consultation between umpires

All disputes shall be determined by the umpires. The umpires shall consult with each other whenever necessary. See also Law 27.6 (Consultation by umpires).

13. Informing the umpires

Throughout the Laws, wherever the umpires are to receive information from captains or other players, it will be sufficient for one umpire to be so informed and for him to inform the other umpire.

14. Signals

(a) The following code of signals shall be used by umpires.

  (i) Signals made while the ball is in play

Dead ball	– by crossing and re-crossing the wrists below the waist.
No ball	– by extending one arm horizontally.
Out	– by raising an index finger above the head. (If not out, the umpire shall call "Not out".)
Wide	– by extending both arms horizontally.

  (ii) When the ball is dead, the bowler's end umpire shall repeat the signals above, with the exception of the signal for "Out", to the scorers.

(iii) The signals listed below shall be made to the scorers only when the ball is dead.

Boundary 4	– by waving an arm from side to side finishing with the arm across the chest.
Boundary 6	– by raising both arms above the head.
Bye	– by raising an open hand above the head.
Commencement of last hour	– by pointing to a raised wrist with the other hand.
Five penalty runs awarded to the batting side	– by repeated tapping of one shoulder with the opposite hand.
Five penalty runs awarded to the fielding side	– by placing one hand on the opposite shoulder.
Leg bye	– by touching a raised knee with the hand.
New ball	– by holding the ball above the head.
Revoke last signal	– by touching both shoulders, each with the opposite hand.
Short run	– by bending one arm upwards and touching the nearer shoulder with the tips of the fingers.

All these signals are to be made by the bowler's end umpire except that for Short run, which is to be signalled by the umpire at the end where short running occurs. However, the bowler's end umpire shall be responsible both for the final signal of Short run to the scorers and for informing them as to the number of runs to be recorded.

(b) The umpire shall wait until each signal to the scorers has been separately acknowledged by a scorer before allowing play to proceed.

15. Correctness of scores

Consultation between umpires and scorers on doubtful points is essential. The umpires shall, throughout the match, satisfy themselves as to the correctness of the number of runs scored, the wickets that have fallen and, where appropriate, the number of overs bowled. They shall agree these with the scorers at least at every interval, other than a drinks interval, and at the conclusion of the match. See Laws 4.2 (Correctness of scores), 21.8 (Correctness of result) and 21.10 (Result not to be changed).

LAW 4   THE SCORERS

1. Appointment of scorers

Two scorers shall be appointed to record all runs scored, all wickets taken and, where appropriate, number of overs bowled.

2. Correctness of scores

The scorers shall frequently check to ensure that their records agree. They shall agree with the umpires, at least at every interval, other than drinks intervals, and at the conclusion of the match, the runs scored, the wickets that have fallen and, where appropriate, the number of overs bowled. See Law 3.15 (Correctness of scores).

3. Acknowledging signals

The scorers shall accept all instructions and signals given to them by umpires. They shall immediately acknowledge each separate signal.

LAW 5   THE BALL

1. Weight and size

The ball, when new, shall weigh not less than $5^1/_2$oz/155.9g, nor more than $5^3/_4$oz/163g, and shall measure not less than $8^{13}/_{16}$in/22.4cm, nor more than 9in/22.9cm in circumference.

2. Approval and control of balls

(a) All balls to be used in the match, having been approved by the umpires and captains, shall be in the possession of the umpires before the toss and shall remain under their control throughout the match.

(b) The umpire shall take possession of the ball in use at the fall of each wicket, at the start of any interval and at any interruption of play.

3. New ball

Unless an agreement to the contrary has been made before the match, either captain may demand a new ball at the start of each innings.

4. New ball in match of more than one day's duration

In a match of more than one day's duration, the captain of the fielding side may demand a new ball after the prescribed number of overs has been bowled with the old one. The Governing Body for cricket in the country concerned shall decide the number of overs applicable in that country, which shall not be less than 75 overs.

The umpire shall inform the other umpire and indicate to the batsmen and the scorers whenever a new ball is taken into play.

5. Ball lost or becoming unfit for play

If, during play, the ball cannot be found or recovered or the umpires agree that it has become unfit for play through normal use, the umpires shall replace it with a ball which has had wear comparable with that which the previous ball had received before the need for its replacement. When the ball is replaced the umpire shall inform the batsmen and the fielding captain.

6. Specifications

The specifications as described in 1 above shall apply to men's cricket only. The following specifications will apply to

    (i) *Women's cricket*
        Weight: – from $4^{15}/_{16}$oz/140g to $5^5/_{16}$oz/151g
        Circumference: – from $8^1/_4$in/21.0cm to $8^7/_8$in/22.5cm

    (ii) *Junior cricket*   – Under 13
        Weight: – from $4^{11}/_{16}$oz/133g to $5^1/_{16}$oz/144g
        Circumference: – from $8^1/_{16}$in/20.5cm to $8^{11}/_{16}$in/22.0cm

LAW 6   THE BAT

1. The bat

The bat consists of two parts, a handle and a blade.

2. Measurements

All provisions in sections 3 to 6 below are subject to the measurements and restrictions stated in Appendix E.

3. The handle

(a) One end of the handle is inserted into a recess in the blade as a means of joining the handle and the blade. The part of the handle that is then wholly outside the blade is defined to be the upper portion of the handle. It is a straight shaft for holding the bat. The remainder of the handle is its lower portion used purely for joining the blade and the handle together. It is not part of the blade but, solely in interpreting 5 and 6 below, references to the blade shall be considered to extend also to the lower portion of the handle where relevant.

(b) The handle is to be made principally of cane and/or wood, glued where necessary and bound with twine along the upper portion.

(c) Providing 7 below is not contravened, the upper portion may be covered with materials solely to provide a surface suitable for gripping. Such covering is an addition and is not part of the bat. Note, however, 8 below.

(d) Notwithstanding 4(c) and 5 below, both the twine binding and the covering grip may extend beyond the junction of the upper and lower portions, to cover part of the shoulders as defined in Appendix E.

4. The blade

(a) The blade comprises the whole of the bat apart from the handle as defined above. The blade has a face, a back, a toe, sides and shoulders. See Appendix E.

(b) The blade shall consist solely of wood.

(c) No material may be placed on or inserted into either the blade or the lower portion of the handle other than as permitted in 3(d) above and 5 and 6 below, together with the minimal adhesives or adhesive tape used solely for fixing these items, or for fixing the handle to the blade.

5. Covering the blade

All bats may have commercial identifications on the blade. Type A and Type B bats may have no other covering on the blade except as permitted in 6 below. Type C bats may have a cloth covering on the blade. This may be treated as specified in 6 below.

Such covering is additional to the blade and is not part of the bat. Note, however, 8 below.

6. Protection and repair

Providing neither 4 above nor 7 below is contravened,

(a) solely for the purposes of

    either (i) protection from surface damage to the face, sides and shoulders of the blade

    or   (ii) repair to the blade after damage

material that is not rigid, either at the time of its application to the blade or subsequently, may be placed on these surfaces. Any such material shall not extend over any part of the back of the blade except in the case of (ii) above and then only when it is applied as a continuous wrapping covering the damaged area.

(b) solid material may be inserted into the blade for repair after damage other than surface damage. Additionally, for protection from damage, for Types B and C, material may be inserted at the toe and/or along the sides, parallel to the face of the blade.

    The only material permitted for any insertion is wood with minimal essential adhesives.

(c) to prevent damage to the toe, material may be placed on that part of the blade but shall not extend over any part of the face, back or sides of the blade.

(d) the surface of the blade may be treated with non-solid materials to improve resistance to moisture penetration and/or mask natural blemishes in the appearance of the wood. Save for the purpose of giving a homogeneous appearance by masking natural blemishes, such treatment must not materially alter the colour of the blade.

Any materials referred to in (a), (b), (c) or (d) above are additional to the blade and not part of the bat. Note, however, 8 below.

7. Damage to the ball

(a) For any part of the bat, covered or uncovered, the hardness of the constituent materials and the surface texture thereof shall not be such that either or both could cause unacceptable damage to the ball.

(b) Any material placed on any part of the bat, for whatever purpose, shall similarly not be such that it could cause unacceptable damage to the ball.

(c) For the purposes of this Law, unacceptable damage is deterioration greater than normal wear and tear caused by the ball striking the uncovered wooden surface of the blade.

8. Contact with the ball

In these Laws,

(a) reference to the bat shall imply that the bat is held in the batsman's hand or a glove worn on his hand, unless stated otherwise.

(b) contact between the ball and

    either   (i) the bat itself

    or   (ii) the batsman's hand holding the bat

    or   (iii) any part of a glove worn on the batsman's hand holding the bat

    or   (iv) any additional materials permitted under 3, 5 or 6 above

shall be regarded as the ball striking or touching the bat or being struck by the bat.

LAW 7   THE PITCH

1. Area of pitch

The pitch is a rectangular area of the ground 22 yds/20.12m in length and 10ft/3.05m in width. It is bounded at either end by the bowling creases and on either side by imaginary lines, one each side of the imaginary line joining the centres of the two middle stumps, each parallel to it and 5ft/1.52m from it. See Laws 8.1 (Width and pitching) and 9.2 (The bowling crease).

2. Fitness of pitch for play

The umpires shall be the sole judges of the fitness of the pitch for play. See Laws 3.8 (Fitness for play) and 3.9 (Suspension of play in dangerous or unreasonable conditions)

3. Selection and preparation

Before the match, the Ground Authority shall be responsible for the selection and preparation of the pitch. During the match, the umpires shall control its use and maintenance.

4. Changing the pitch

The pitch shall not be changed during the match unless the umpires decide that it is dangerous or unreasonable for play to continue on it and then only with the consent of both captains.

5. Non-turf pitches

In the event of a non-turf pitch being used, the artificial surface shall conform to the following measurements.

    Length   a minimum of 58ft/17.68m

    Width   a minimum of 6ft/1.83m

See Law 10.8 (Non-turf pitches).

LAW 8   THE WICKETS

1. Width and pitching

Two sets of wickets shall be pitched opposite and parallel to each other at a distance of 22yds/ 20.12m between the centres of the two middle stumps. Each set shall be 9in/22.86cm wide and shall consist of three wooden stumps with two wooden bails on top. See Appendix A.

2. Size of stumps

The tops of the stumps shall be 28in/71.1cm above the playing surface and shall be dome shaped except for the bail grooves. The portion of a stump above the playing surface shall be cylindrical apart from the domed top, with circular section of diameter not less than 1³/₈in/3.49cm nor more than 1¹/₂in/3.81cm.

3. The bails

(a) The bails, when in position on top of the stumps,

    (i) shall not project more than $^1/_2$in/1.27cm above them.

    (ii) shall fit between the stumps without forcing them out of the vertical.

(b) Each bail shall conform to the following specifications. See Appendix A.

Overall length	$4^5/_{16}$in/10.95cm
Length of barrel	$2^1/_8$in /5.40cm
Longer spigot	$1^3/_8$in/3.49cm
Shorter spigot	$^{13}/_{16}$in/2.06cm

4. Junior cricket

In junior cricket, the same definitions of the wickets shall apply subject to the following measurements being used.

Width	8in/20.32cm
Pitched for under 13	21yds/19.20m
Pitched for under 11	20yds/18.29m
Pitched for under 9	18yds/16.46m
Height above playing surface	27in/68.58cm

Each stump

Diameter	not less than $1^1/_4$in/3.18cm nor more than $1^3/_8$in/3.49cm

Each bail

Overall	$3^{13}/_{16}$in/9.68cm
Barrel	$1^{13}/_{16}$in/4.60cm
Longer spigot	$1^1/_4$in/3.18 cm
Shorter spigot	$^3/_4$in/1.91cm

5. Dispensing with bails

The umpires may agree to dispense with the use of bails, if necessary. If they so agree then no bails shall be used at either end. The use of bails shall be resumed as soon as conditions permit. See Law 28.4 (Dispensing with bails).

LAW 9   THE BOWLING, POPPING AND RETURN CREASES

1. The creases

A bowling crease, a popping crease and two return creases shall be marked in white, as set out in 2, 3 and 4 below, at each end of the pitch. See Appendix B.

2. The bowling crease

The bowling crease, which is the back edge of the crease marking, shall be the line through the centres of the three stumps at that end. It shall be 8 ft 8 in/2.64 m in length, with the stumps in the centre.

3. The popping crease

The popping crease, which is the back edge of the crease marking, shall be in front of and parallel to the bowling crease and shall be 4ft/1.22m from it. The popping crease shall be marked to a minimum of 6ft/1.83m on either side of the imaginary line joining the centres of the two middle stumps and shall be considered to be unlimited in length.

4. The return creases

The return creases, which are the inside edges of the crease markings, shall be at right angles to the popping crease at a distance of 4ft 4in/1.32m either side of the imaginary line joining the centres of the two middle stumps. Each return crease shall be marked from the popping crease to a minimum of 8ft/2.44m behind it and shall be considered to be unlimited in length.

LAW 10   PREPARATION AND MAINTENANCE OF THE PLAYING AREA

1. Rolling

The pitch shall not be rolled during the match except as permitted in (a) and (b) below.

(a) Frequency and duration of rolling
During the match the pitch may be rolled at the request of the captain of the batting side, for a period of not more than seven minutes, before the start of each innings, other than the first innings of the match, and before the start of each subsequent day's play. See (d) below.

(b) Rolling after a delayed start
In addition to the rolling permitted above, if, after the toss and before the first innings of the match, the start is delayed, the captain of the batting side may request that the pitch be rolled for not more than seven minutes. However, if the umpires together agree that the delay has had no significant effect on the state of the pitch, they shall refuse such request for rolling of the pitch.

(c) Choice of rollers
If there is more than one roller available the captain of the batting side shall choose which one is to be used.

(d) Timing of permitted rolling
The rolling permitted (maximum seven minutes) before play begins on any day shall be started not more than 30 minutes before the time scheduled or rescheduled for play to begin. The captain of the batting side may, however, delay the start of such rolling until not less than 10 minutes before the time scheduled or rescheduled for play to begin, should he so wish.

(e) Insufficient time to complete rolling
If, when a captain declares an innings closed, or forfeits an innings, or enforces the follow-on, there is insufficient time for the pitch to be rolled for seven minutes, or if there is insufficient time for any other reason, the batting captain shall nevertheless be permitted to exercise his option to have such rolling. The time by which the start of the innings is delayed on that account shall be taken out of normal playing time.

2. Clearing debris from the pitch

(a) The pitch shall be cleared of any debris

   (i) before the start of each day's play. This shall be after the completion of mowing and before any rolling, not earlier than 30 minutes nor later than ten minutes before the time or any rescheduled time for start of play.

   (ii) between innings. This shall precede rolling if any is to take place.

   (iii) at all intervals for meals.

(b) The clearance of debris in (a) above shall be done by sweeping, except where the umpires consider that this may be detrimental to the surface of the pitch. In this case the debris must be cleared from that area by hand, without sweeping.

(c) In addition to (a) above, debris may be cleared from the pitch by hand, without sweeping, before mowing and whenever either umpire considers it necessary.

3. Mowing

(a) Responsibility for mowing
All mowings which are carried out before the match shall be the sole responsibility of the Ground Authority.

All subsequent mowings shall be carried out under the supervision of the umpires.

(b) The pitch and outfield

In order that throughout the match the ground conditions should be as nearly the same for both sides as possible,

    (i) the pitch

    (ii) the outfield

shall be mown on each day of the match on which play is expected to take place, if ground and weather conditions permit.

If, for reasons other than conditions of ground or weather, complete mowing of the outfield is not possible, the Ground Authority shall notify the captains and umpires of the procedure to be adopted for such mowing during the match.

(c) Timing of mowing

    (i) Mowing of the pitch on any day shall be completed not later than 30 minutes before the time scheduled or rescheduled for play to begin on that day, before any sweeping prior to rolling. If necessary, debris may be removed from the pitch before mowing, by hand, without sweeping. See 2(c) above.

    (ii) Mowing of the outfield on any day shall be completed not later than 15 minutes before the time scheduled or rescheduled for play to begin on that day.

4. Watering the pitch

The pitch shall not be watered during the match.

5. Re-marking creases

Creases shall be re-marked whenever either umpire considers it necessary.

6. Maintenance of footholes

The umpires shall ensure that the holes made by the bowler and batsmen are cleaned out and dried whenever necessary to facilitate play. In matches of more than one day's duration, the umpires shall allow, if necessary, the re-turfing of footholes made by the bowler in his delivery stride, or the use of quick-setting fillings for the same purpose.

7. Securing of footholds and maintenance of pitch

During play, umpires shall allow the players to secure their footholds by the use of sawdust provided that no damage to the pitch is caused and that Law 42 (Fair and unfair play) is not contravened.

8. Non-turf pitches

Wherever appropriate, the provisions set out in 1 to 7 above shall apply.

LAW 11   COVERING THE PITCH

1. Before the match

The use of covers before the match is the responsibility of the Ground Authority and may include full covering if required. However, the Ground Authority shall grant suitable facility to the captains to inspect the pitch before the nomination of their players and to the umpires to discharge their duties as laid down in Laws 3 (The umpires), 7 (The pitch), 8 (The wickets), 9 (The bowling, popping and return creases) and 10 (Preparation and maintenance of the playing area).

2. During the match

The pitch shall not be completely covered during the match unless provided otherwise by regulations or by agreement before the toss.

3. Covering the bowlers' run ups

Whenever possible, the bowlers' run ups shall be covered in inclement weather, in order to keep them dry. Unless there is agreement for full covering under 2 above the covers so used shall not extend further than 5ft/1.52m in front of each popping crease.

4. Removal of covers

(a) If after the toss the pitch is covered overnight, the covers shall be removed in the morning at the earliest possible moment on each day that play is expected to take place.

(b) If covers are used during the day as protection from inclement weather, or if inclement weather delays the removal of overnight covers, they shall be removed promptly as soon as conditions allow.

LAW 12   INNINGS

1. Number of innings

(a) A match shall be one or two innings for each side according to agreement reached before the match.

(b) It may be agreed to limit any innings to a number of overs or to a period of time. If such an agreement is made then

  (i) in a one innings match a similar agreement shall apply to both innings.

  (ii) in a two innings match similar agreements shall apply to

    either the first innings of each side

    or   the second innings of each side

    or   both innings of each side.

For both one innings and two innings matches, the agreement must also include criteria for determining the result when neither of Laws 21.1 (A Win – two innings match) or 21.2 (A Win – one innings match) applies.

2. Alternate innings

In a two innings match each side shall take their innings alternately except in the cases provided for in Law 13 (The follow-on) or in Law 14.2 (Forfeiture of an innings).

3. Completed innings

A side's innings is to be considered as completed if

        (a) the side is all out

  or (b) at the fall of a wicket or the retirement of a batsman, further balls remain to be bowled but no further batsman is available to come in

  or (c) the captain declares the innings closed

  or (d) the captain forfeits the innings

  or (e) in the case of an agreement under 1(b) above,

        either (i) the prescribed number of overs has been bowled

        or   (ii) the prescribed time has expired

  as appropriate.

4. The toss

The captains shall toss for the choice of innings, on the field of play and in the presence of one or both of the umpires, not earlier than 30 minutes, nor later than 15 minutes before the scheduled or any rescheduled time for the match to start. Note, however, the provisions of Law 1.3 (Captain).

5. Decision to be notified

As soon as the toss is completed, the captain of the side winning the toss shall notify the opposing captain and the umpires of his decision to bat or to field. Once notified, the decision cannot be changed.

LAW 13   THE FOLLOW-ON

1. Lead on first innings

(a) In a two innings match of five days or more, the side which bats first and leads by at least 200 runs shall have the option of requiring the other side to follow their innings.

(b) The same option shall be available in two innings matches of shorter duration with the minimum leads as follows.

   (i) 150 runs in a match of three or four days;

   (ii) 100 runs in a two-day match;

   (iii) 75 runs in a one-day match.

2. Notification

A captain shall notify the opposing captain and the umpires of his intention to take up this option. Law 10.1(e) (Insufficient time to complete rolling) shall apply.

3. First day's play lost

If no play takes place on the first day of a match of more than one day's duration, 1 above shall apply in accordance with the number of days remaining from the actual start of the match. The day on which play first commences shall count as a whole day for this purpose, irrespective of the time at which play starts.

Play will have taken place as soon as, after the call of "Play", the first over has started. See Law 22.2 (Start of an over).

LAW 14   DECLARATION AND FORFEITURE

1. Time of declaration

The captain of the side batting may declare an innings closed, when the ball is dead, at any time during the innings.

2. Forfeiture of an innings

A captain may forfeit either of his side's innings at any time before the commencement of that innings. A forfeited innings shall be considered to be a completed innings.

3. Notification

A captain shall notify the opposing captain and the umpires of his decision to declare or to forfeit an innings. Law 10.1(e) (Insufficient time to complete rolling) shall apply.

LAW 15   INTERVALS

1. An interval

The following shall be classed as intervals.

   (i) The period between close of play on one day and the start of the next day's play.

   (ii) Intervals between innings.

   (iii) Intervals for meals.

   (iv) Intervals for drinks.

   (v) Any other agreed interval.

All these intervals shall be considered as scheduled breaks for the purposes of Law 2.5 (Fielder absent or leaving the field).

2. Agreement of intervals

(a) Before the toss

(i) the hours of play shall be established.

(ii) except as in (b) below, the timing and duration of intervals for meals shall be agreed.

(iii) the timing and duration of any other interval under 1(v) above shall be agreed.

(b) In a one-day match no specific time need be agreed for the tea interval. It may be agreed instead to take this interval between innings.

(c) Intervals for drinks may not be taken during the last hour of the match, as defined in Law 16.6 (Last hour of match – number of overs). Subject to this limitation, the captains and umpires shall agree the times for such intervals, if any, before the toss and on each subsequent day not later than ten minutes before play is scheduled to start.

See also Law 3.3 (Agreement with captains).

3. Duration of intervals

(a) An interval for lunch or tea shall be of the duration agreed under 2(a) above, taken from the call of "Time" before the interval until the call of "Play" on resumption after the interval.

(b) An interval between innings shall be ten minutes from the close of an innings until the call of "Play" for the start of the next innings, except as in 4, 6 and 7 below.

4. No allowance for interval between innings

In addition to the provisions of 6 and 7 below,

(a) if an innings ends when ten minutes or less remains before the time agreed for close of play on any day, there shall be no further play on that day. No change shall be made to the time for the start of play on the following day on account of the ten minute interval between innings.

(b) if a captain declares an innings closed during an interruption in play of more than ten minutes duration, no adjustment shall be made to the time for resumption of play on account of the ten minute interval between innings, which shall be considered as included in the interruption. Law 10.1(e) (Insufficient time to complete rolling) shall apply.

(c) if a captain declares an innings closed during any interval other than an interval for drinks, the interval shall be of the agreed duration and shall be considered to include the ten minute interval between innings. Law 10.1(e) (Insufficient time to complete rolling) shall apply.

5. Changing agreed times of intervals

If, at any time during the match,

either playing time is lost through adverse conditions of ground, weather or light or in exceptional circumstances.

or the players have occasion to leave the field other than at a scheduled interval,

the time of the lunch interval or of the tea interval may be changed if the two umpires and both captains so agree, providing the requirements of 3 above and 6, 7, 8 and 9(c) below are not contravened.

6. Changing agreed time for lunch interval

(a) If an innings ends when ten minutes or less remains before the agreed time for lunch, the interval shall be taken immediately. It shall be of the agreed length and shall be considered to include the ten minute interval between innings.

(b) If because of adverse conditions of ground, weather or light, or in exceptional circumstances, a stoppage occurs when ten minutes or less remains before the agreed time for lunch, then, notwithstanding 5 above, the interval shall be taken immediately. It shall be of the agreed length. Play shall resume at the end of this interval or as soon after as conditions permit.

(c) If the players have occasion to leave the field for any reason when more than ten minutes remains before the agreed time for lunch then, unless the umpires and captains together agree to alter it, lunch will be taken at the agreed time.

7. Changing agreed time for tea interval

(a) (i) If an innings ends when 30 minutes or less remains before the agreed time for tea, the interval shall be taken immediately. It shall be of the agreed length and shall be considered to include the ten minute interval between innings.

(ii) If, when 30 minutes remains before the agreed time for tea, an interval between innings is already in progress, play will resume at the end of the ten minute interval, if conditions permit.

(b) (i) If, because of adverse conditions of ground, weather or light, or in exceptional circumstances, a stoppage occurs when 30 minutes or less remains before the agreed time for tea, then unless

either there is an agreement to change the time for tea, as permitted in 5 above

or the captains agree to forgo the tea interval, as permitted in 10 below

the interval shall be taken immediately. The interval shall be of the agreed length. Play shall resume at the end of the interval or as soon after as conditions permit.

(ii) If a stoppage is already in progress when 30 minutes remains before the agreed time for tea, 5 above will apply.

8. Tea interval – nine wickets down

If either nine wickets are already down when two minutes remains to the agreed time for tea, or the ninth wicket falls within this two minutes, or at any time up to and including the final ball of the over in progress at the agreed time for tea, then, notwithstanding the provisions of Law 16.5(b) (Completion of an over), tea will not be taken until the end of the over that is in progress 30 minutes after the originally agreed time for tea, unless the players have cause to leave the field of play or the innings is completed earlier.

For the purposes of this section of Law, the retirement of a batsman is not to be considered equivalent to the fall of a wicket.

9. Intervals for drinks

(a) If on any day the captains agree that there shall be intervals for drinks, the option to take such drinks shall be available to either side. Each interval shall be kept as short as possible and in any case shall not exceed five minutes.

(b) Unless, as permitted in 10 below, the captains agree to forgo it, a drinks interval shall be taken at the end of the over in progress when the agreed time is reached. If, however, a wicket falls or a batsman retires within five minutes of the agreed time then drinks shall be taken immediately. No other variation in the timing of drinks intervals shall be permitted except as provided for in (c) below.

(c) If an innings ends or the players have to leave the field of play for any other reason within 30 minutes of the agreed time for a drinks interval, the umpires and captains together may rearrange the timing of drinks intervals in that session.

10. Agreement to forgo intervals

At any time during the match, the captains may agree to forgo the tea interval or any of the drinks intervals. The umpires shall be informed of the decision.

When play is in progress, the batsmen at the wicket may deputise for their captain in making an agreement to forgo a drinks interval in that session.

11. Scorers to be informed

The umpires shall ensure that the scorers are informed of all agreements about hours of play and intervals and of any changes made thereto as permitted under this Law.

LAW 16   START OF PLAY; CESSATION OF PLAY

1. Call of "Play"

The bowler's end umpire shall call "Play" at the start of the match and on the resumption of play after any interval or interruption.

2. Call of "Time"

The bowler's end umpire shall call "Time" when the ball is dead on the cessation of play before any interval or interruption and at the conclusion of the match. See Laws 23.3 (Call of "Over" or "Time") and 27 (Appeals).

3. Removal of bails

After the call of "Time", the bails shall be removed from both wickets.

4. Starting a new over

Another over shall always be started at any time during the match, unless an interval is to be taken in the circumstances set out in 5 below, if, walking at his normal pace, the umpire has arrived at his position behind the stumps at the bowler's end before the time agreed for the next interval, or for the close of play, has been reached.

5. Completion of an over

Other than at the end of the match,

(a) if the agreed time for an interval is reached during an over, the over shall be completed before the interval is taken, except as provided for in (b) below.

(b) when less than two minutes remains before the time agreed for the next interval, the interval will be taken immediately if

either (i) a batsman is dismissed or retires

or (ii) the players have occasion to leave the field

whether this occurs during an over or at the end of an over. Except at the end of an innings, if an over is thus interrupted it shall be completed on the resumption of play.

6. Last hour of match – number of overs

When one hour of playing time of the match remains, according to the agreed hours of play, the over in progress shall be completed. The next over shall be the first of a minimum of 20 overs which must be bowled, provided that a result is not reached earlier and provided that there is no interval or interruption in play.

The bowler's end umpire shall indicate the commencement of this 20 overs to the players and to the scorers. The period of play thereafter shall be referred to as the last hour, whatever its actual duration.

7. Last hour of match – interruptions of play

If there is an interruption in play during the last hour of the match, the minimum number of overs to be bowled shall be reduced from 20 as follows.

(a) The time lost for an interruption is counted from the call of "Time" until the time for resumption as decided by the umpires.

(b) One over shall be deducted for every complete three minutes of time lost.

(c) In the case of more than one such interruption, the minutes lost shall not be aggregated; the calculation shall be made for each interruption separately.

(d) If, when one hour of playing time remains, an interruption is already in progress

(i) only the time lost after this moment shall be counted in the calculation

(ii) the over in progress at the start of the interruption shall be completed on resumption and shall not count as one of the minimum number of overs to be bowled.

(e) If, after the start of the last hour, an interruption occurs during an over, the over shall be completed on resumption of play. The two part-overs shall between them count as one over of the minimum number to be bowled.

8. Last hour of match – intervals between innings

If an innings ends so that a new innings is to be started during the last hour of the match, the interval starts with the end of the innings and is to end ten minutes later.

(a) If this interval is already in progress at the start of the last hour then, to determine the number of overs to be bowled in the new innings, calculations are to be made as set out in 7 above.

(b) If the innings ends after the last hour has started, two calculations are to be made, as set out in (c) and (d) below. The greater of the numbers yielded by these two calculations is to be the minimum number of overs to be bowled in the new innings.

(c) Calculation based on overs remaining.

　(i) At the conclusion of the innings, the number of overs that remain to be bowled, of the minimum in the last hour, to be noted.

　(ii) If this is not a whole number it is to be rounded up to the next whole number.

　(iii) Three overs, for the interval, to be deducted from the resulting number to determine the number of overs still to be bowled.

(d) Calculation based on time remaining.

　(i) At the conclusion of the innings, the time remaining until the agreed time for close of play to be noted.

　(ii) Ten minutes, for the interval, to be deducted from this time to determine the playing time remaining.

　(iii) A calculation to be made of one over for every complete three minutes of the playing time remaining, plus one more over if a further part of three minutes remains.

9. Conclusion of match

The match is concluded

(a) as soon as a result as defined in sections 1, 2, 3, 4 or 5(a) of Law 21 (The result) is reached.

(b) as soon as both

　　(i) the minimum number of overs for the last hour are completed

　and (ii) the agreed time for close of play is reached

unless a result is reached earlier.

(c) in the case of an agreement under Law 12.1(b) (Number of innings), as soon as the final innings is completed as defined in Law 12.3(e) (Completed innings).

(d) if, without the match being concluded, either as in (a) or in (b) or in (c) above, the players leave the field for adverse conditions of ground, weather or light, or in exceptional circumstances, and no further play is possible.

10. Completion of last over of match

The over in progress at the close of play on the final day shall be completed unless

either　(i) a result has been reached

or　　(ii) the players have occasion to leave the field. In this case there shall be no resumption of play except in the circumstances of Law 21.9 (Mistakes in scoring) and the match shall be at an end.

11. Bowler unable to complete an over during last hour of match

If, for any reason, a bowler is unable to complete an over during the last hour, Law 22.8 (Bowler incapacitated or suspended during an over) shall apply. The separate parts of such an over shall count as one over of the minimum to be bowled.

LAW 17   PRACTICE ON THE FIELD

1. Practice on the pitch

There shall be no practice of any kind, at any time on any day of the match, on the pitch or on either of the two strips parallel and immediately adjacent to the pitch, one on either side of it, each of the same dimensions as the pitch.

2. Practice on the rest of the square

There shall be no practice of any kind on any other part of the square on any day of the match, except before the start of play or after the close of play on that day. Practice before the start of play

(a) must not continue later than 30 minutes before the scheduled time or any rescheduled time for play to start on that day.

(b) shall not be allowed if the umpires consider that it will significantly impair the surface of the square.

3. Practice on the outfield

(a) All forms of practice are permitted on the outfield before the start of play or after the close of play on any day

or during the lunch and tea intervals

or between innings

providing the umpires are satisfied that such practice will not cause significant deterioration in the condition of the outfield.

Such practice must not continue later than five minutes before the time for play to commence or to resume.

(b) Between the call of Play and the call of "Time"

(i) no one may participate in practice of any kind on the field of play, even from outside the boundary, except the fielders as defined in Appendix D and the batsmen at the wicket. Any player involved in practice contravening this Law shall be considered to have himself contravened the Law and will be subject to the penalty in 4 below.

(ii) there shall be no bowling or batting practice on the outfield. Bowling a ball, using arm action only, to a player in the outfield is not to be regarded as bowling practice but shall be subject to (b)(iii) and (c) below. However, a bowler deliberately bowling a ball thus on to the ground will contravene Law 42.3 (The match ball – changing its condition).

(iii) other practice shall be permitted, subject to the restriction in (i) and (ii) above,

either at the fall of a wicket.

or during other gaps in play for legitimate activities, such as adjustment of the sight-screen.

(c) (i) Practice at the fall of a wicket must cease as soon as the incoming batsman steps on to the square.

(ii) Practice during other legitimate gaps in play must not continue beyond the minimum time required for the activity causing the gap in play.

If these time restrictions are not observed, umpires shall apply the procedures of Law 42.9 (Time wasting by the fielding side).

4. Penalty for contravention

If a player contravenes 1, 2, 3(b)(i) or 3(b)(ii) above, he shall not be allowed to bowl until

either at least one hour has elapsed

or there has been at least 30 minutes of playing time

since the contravention, whichever is sooner.

If the contravention is by the bowler during an over, he shall not be allowed to complete that over. It shall be completed by another bowler, who shall neither have bowled any part of the previous over nor be allowed to bowl any part of the next over.

5. Trial run up

A bowler is permitted to have a trial run up subject to the provisions of 3 and 4 above.

LAW 18   SCORING RUNS

1. A run

The score shall be reckoned by runs. A run is scored

(a) so often as the batsmen, at any time while the ball is in play, have crossed and made good their ground from end to end.

(b) when a boundary is scored. See Law 19 (Boundaries).

(c) when penalty runs are awarded. See 6 below.

(d) when Lost ball is called. See Law 20 (Lost ball).

2. Runs disallowed

Notwithstanding 1 above, or any other provisions elsewhere in these Laws, the scoring of runs or awarding of penalties will be subject to any provisions that may be applicable, for the disallowance of runs or for the non-award of penalties.

3. Short runs

(a) A run is short if a batsman fails to make good his ground in turning for a further run.

(b) Although a short run shortens the succeeding one, the latter if completed shall not be regarded as short. A striker setting off for his first run from in front of his popping crease may do so also without penalty.

4. Unintentional short runs

Except in the circumstances of 5 below,

(a) if either batsman runs a short run, the umpire concerned shall, unless a boundary is scored, call and signal "Short run" as soon as the ball becomes dead and that run shall not be scored.

(b) if, after either or both batsmen run short, a boundary is scored the umpire concerned shall disregard the short running and shall not call or signal "Short run".

(c) if both batsmen run short in one and the same run, this shall be regarded as only one short run.

(d) if more than one run is short then, subject to (b) and (c) above, all runs so called shall not be scored.

If there has been more than one short run, the umpire shall inform the scorers as to the number of runs to be recorded.

5. Deliberate short runs

(a) Notwithstanding 4 above, if either umpire considers that either or both batsmen deliberately run short at his end, the umpire concerned shall, when the ball is dead, inform the other umpire of what has occurred. The bowler's end umpire shall then

(i) warn both batsmen that the practice is unfair and indicate that this is a first and final warning. This warning shall apply throughout the innings. The umpire shall so inform each incoming batsman.

(ii) whether a batsman is dismissed or not, disallow all runs to the batting side from that delivery other than any runs awarded for penalties.

(iii) return the batsmen to their original ends.

(iv) inform the captain of the fielding side and, as soon as practicable, the captain of the batting side of the reason for this action.

(v) inform the scorers as to the number of runs to be recorded.

(b) If there is any further instance of deliberate short running by any batsman in that innings, the umpire concerned shall, when the ball is dead, inform the other umpire of what has occurred and the procedure set out in (a) (ii), (iii) and (iv) above shall be repeated. Additionally the bowler's end umpire shall

(i) award five penalty runs to the fielding side

(ii) inform the scorers as to the number of runs to be recorded

(iii) together with the other umpire report the occurrence as soon as possible after the match to the Executive of the batting side and to any Governing Body responsible for the match, who shall take such action as is considered appropriate against the captain and the player or players concerned.

6. Runs awarded for penalties

Runs shall be awarded for penalties under 5 above and Laws 2.6 (Player returning without permission), 24 (No ball), 25 (Wide ball), 41.2 (Fielding the ball), 41.3 (Protective helmets belonging to the fielding side), and 42 (Fair and unfair play).

7. Runs scored for boundaries

Runs shall be scored for boundary allowances under Law 19 (Boundaries).

8. Runs scored for Lost ball

Runs shall be scored when Lost ball is called under Law 20 (Lost ball).

9. Runs scored when a batsman is dismissed

When a batsman is dismissed, any runs for penalties awarded to either side shall stand. No other runs shall be credited to the batting side, except as follows. If a batsman is

(a) dismissed Handled the ball, the batting side shall also score the runs completed before the offence.

(b) dismissed Obstructing the field, the batting side shall also score the runs completed before the offence.

If, however, the obstruction prevented a catch from being made, no runs other than penalties shall be scored.

(c) dismissed Run out, the batting side shall also score the runs completed before the wicket was put down.

If, however, a striker who has a runner is himself dismissed Run out, no runs other than penalties shall be scored. See Law 2.8 (Transgression of the Laws by a batsman who has a runner).

10. Runs scored when the ball becomes dead other than at the fall of a wicket

When the ball becomes dead for any reason other than the fall of a wicket, or is called dead by an umpire, unless there is specific provision otherwise in the Laws,

(a) any runs for penalties awarded to either side shall be scored. Note, however, the provisions of Laws 26.3 (Leg byes not to be awarded) and 41.4 (Penalty runs not to be awarded).

(b) additionally the batting side shall be credited with

(i) all runs completed by the batsmen before the incident or call

and (ii) the run in progress if the batsmen had already crossed at the instant of the incident or call. Note specifically, however, the provisions of Laws 34.4(c) (Runs scored from ball lawfully struck more than once) and 42.5(f) (Deliberate distraction or obstruction of batsman).

11. Batsman returning to original end

(a) When a batsman is dismissed, the not out batsman shall return to his original end

    (i) if the striker is himself Run out in the circumstances of Law 2.8(c) (Transgression of the Laws by a batsman who has a runner).

    (ii) for all other methods of dismissal other than those in 12(a) below.

(b) Other than at the fall of a wicket, the batsmen shall return to their original ends in the cases of, and only in the cases of,

    (i) a boundary.

    (ii) disallowance of runs for any reason.

    (iii) a decision by the batsmen at the wicket to do so under Law 42.5(g) (Deliberate distraction or obstruction of batsman).

12. Batsman returning to wicket he has left

(a) When a batsman is dismissed

    (i) Caught, Handled the ball or Obstructing the field,

    (ii) Run out other than as in 11(a) above,

the not out batsman shall return to the wicket he has left, but only if the batsmen had not already crossed at the instant of the incident causing the dismissal.

(b) Except in the cases of 11(b) above, if while a run is in progress the ball becomes dead for any reason other than the dismissal of a batsman, or is called dead by an umpire, the batsmen shall return to the wickets they had left, but only if they had not already crossed in running when the ball became dead.

LAW 19 BOUNDARIES

1. The boundary of the field of play

(a) Before the toss the umpires shall agree the boundary of the field of play with both captains. The boundary shall if possible be marked along its whole length.

(b) The boundary shall be agreed so that no part of any sight-screen is within the field of play.

(c) An obstacle or person within the field of play shall not be regarded as a boundary unless so decided by the umpires before the toss. See Law 3.4 (To inform captains and scorers).

2. Defining the boundary – boundary marking

(a) Wherever practicable the boundary shall be marked by means of a white line or a rope along the ground.

(b) If the boundary is marked by means of a white line,

    (i) the inside edge of the line shall be the boundary edge.

    (ii) a flag, post or board used merely to highlight the position of a line marked on the ground must be placed outside the boundary edge and is not itself to be regarded as defining or marking the boundary. Note, however, the provisions of (c) below.

(c) If a solid object is used to mark the boundary, it must have an edge or a line to constitute the boundary edge.

    (i) For a rope, which includes any similar object of curved cross section, lying on the ground, the boundary edge will be the line formed by the innermost points of the rope along its length.

    (ii) For a fence, which includes any similar object in contact with the ground but with a flat surface projecting above the ground, the boundary edge will be the base line of the fence.

(d) If the boundary edge is not defined as in (b) or (c) above, the umpires and captains must agree before the toss what line will be the boundary edge. Where there is no physical marker for a section of boundary, the boundary edge shall be the imaginary straight line on the ground joining the two nearest marked points of the boundary edge.

(e) If a solid object used to mark the boundary is disturbed for any reason during play then, if possible, it shall be restored to its original position as soon as the ball is dead. If it is not possible then,

(i) if some part of the fence or other marker has come within the field of play, that part shall be removed from the field of play as soon as the ball becomes dead.

(ii) the line where the base of the fence or marker originally stood shall define the boundary edge.

3. Scoring a boundary

(a) A boundary shall be scored and signalled by the bowler's end umpire whenever, while the ball is in play, in his opinion,

(i) the ball touches the boundary, or is grounded beyond the boundary.

(ii) a fielder with some part of his person in contact with the ball, touches the boundary or has some part of his person grounded beyond the boundary.

(b) The phrases "touches the boundary" and "touching the boundary" shall mean contact with

either (i) the boundary edge as defined in 2 above

or (ii) any person or obstacle within the field of play which has been designated a boundary by the umpires before the toss.

(c) The phrase "grounded beyond the boundary" shall mean contact with

either (i) any part of a line or solid object marking the boundary except its boundary edge

or (ii) the ground beyond the boundary edge

or (iii) any object in contact with the ground beyond the boundary edge.

4. Ball beyond the boundary

A ball may be caught, subject to the provisions of Law 32, or fielded after it has crossed the boundary, provided that

(i) the first contact with the ball is by a fielder either with some part of his person grounded within the boundary, or whose final contact with the ground before touching the ball was within the boundary.

(ii) neither the ball, nor any fielder in contact with the ball, touches or is grounded beyond, the boundary at any time during the act of making the catch or of fielding the ball.

The act of making the catch, or of fielding the ball, shall start from the time when the ball first comes into contact with some part of a fielder's person and shall end when a fielder obtains complete control both over the ball and over his own movement and has no part of his person touching or grounded beyond the boundary.

5. Runs allowed for boundaries

(a) Before the toss, the umpires shall agree with both captains the runs to be allowed for boundaries. In deciding the allowances, the umpires and captains shall be guided by the prevailing custom of the ground.

(b) Unless agreed differently under (a) above, the allowances for boundaries shall be six runs if the ball having been struck by the bat pitches beyond the boundary, but otherwise four runs. These allowances shall still apply even though the ball has previously touched a fielder. See also (c) below.

(c) The ball shall be regarded as pitching beyond the boundary and six runs shall be scored if a fielder

(i) has any part of his person touching the boundary or grounded beyond the boundary when he catches the ball.

(ii) catches the ball and subsequently touches the boundary or grounds some part of his person beyond the boundary while carrying the ball but before completing the catch. See Law 32 (Caught).

6. Runs scored

When a boundary is scored,

    (a) any runs for penalties awarded to either side shall be scored.

    (b) the batting side, except in the circumstances of 7 below, shall additionally be awarded whichever is the greater of

        (i) the allowance for the boundary

        (ii) the runs completed by the batsmen together with the run in progress if they had already crossed at the instant the boundary is scored.

    (c) When the runs in (ii) above exceed the boundary allowance they shall replace the boundary for the purposes of Law 18.12 (Batsman returning to wicket he has left).

7. Overthrow or wilful act of fielder

If the boundary results from an overthrow or from the wilful act of a fielder the runs scored shall be

        (i) any runs for penalties awarded to either side

and   (ii) the allowance for the boundary

and (iii) the runs completed by the batsmen, together with the run in progress if they had already crossed at the instant of the throw or act.

Law 18.12(b) (Batsman returning to wicket he has left) shall apply as from the instant of the throw or act.

LAW 20   LOST BALL

1. Fielder to call "Lost ball"

If a ball in play cannot be found or recovered, any fielder may call "Lost ball". The ball shall then become dead. See Law 23.1 (Ball is dead). Law 18.12(b) (Batsman returning to wicket he has left) shall apply as from the instant of the call.

2. Ball to be replaced

The umpires shall replace the ball with one which has had wear comparable with that which the previous ball had received before it was lost or became irrecoverable. See Law 5.5 (Ball lost or becoming unfit for play).

3. Runs scored

    (a) Any runs for penalties awarded to either side shall be scored.

    (b) The batting side shall additionally be awarded

      either (i) the runs completed by the batsmen, together with the run in progress if they had already crossed at the instant of the call,

      or   (ii) six runs,

    whichever is the greater.

These shall be credited to the striker if the ball has been struck by the bat, but otherwise to the total of Byes, Leg-byes, No-balls or Wides as the case may be.

LAW 21   THE RESULT

1. A win – two innings match

The side which has scored a total of runs in excess of that scored in the two completed innings of the opposing side shall win the match. See Law 12.3 (Completed innings). Note also 6 below.

2. A win – one innings match

The side which has scored in its one innings a total of runs in excess of that scored by the opposing side in its one completed innings shall win the match. See Law12.3 (Completed innings). Note also 6 below.

3. Umpires awarding a match

Notwithstanding any agreement under Law 12.1(b) (Number of innings),

    (a) a match shall be lost by a side which

        either (i) concedes defeat

        or   (ii) in the opinion of the umpires refuses to play

    and the umpires shall award the match to the other side.

    (b) if an umpire considers that an action by any player or players might constitute a refusal by either side to play then the umpires together shall ascertain the cause of the action. If they then decide together that this action does constitute a refusal to play by one side, they shall so inform the captain of that side. If the captain persists in the action the umpires shall award the match in accordance with (a) above.

    (c) if action as in (b) above takes place after play has started and does not constitute a refusal to play,

        (i) playing time lost shall be counted from the start of the action until play recommences, subject to Law 15.5 (Changing agreed times for intervals).

        (ii) the time for close of play on that day shall be extended by this length of time, subject to Law 3.9 (Suspension of play in dangerous or unreasonable conditions).

        (iii) if applicable, no overs shall be deducted during the last hour of the match solely on account of this time.

4. Matches in which there is an agreement under Law 12.1(b)

For any match in which there is an agreement under Law 12.1(b) (Number of innings), if the result is not determined in any of the ways stated in 1, 2 or 3 above, then the result shall be as laid down in that agreement.

5. All other matches – A tie or draw

    (a) **A tie**

        The result of a match shall be a tie when the scores are equal at the conclusion of play, but only if the side batting last has completed its innings.

    (b) **A draw**

        A match which is concluded as defined Law 16.9 (Conclusion of match), without being determined in any of the ways stated in (a) above or in 1, 2, or 3, above, shall count as a draw.

6. Winning hit or extras

    (a) As soon as a result is reached as defined in 1, 2, 3, 4 or 5(a) above, the match is at an end. Nothing that happens thereafter, except as in Law 42.17(b) (Penalty runs), shall be regarded as part of it. Note also 9 below.

    (b) The side batting last will have scored enough runs to win only if its total of runs is sufficient without including any runs completed by the batsmen before the completion of a catch, or the obstruction of a catch, from which the striker can be dismissed.

    (c) If a boundary is scored before the batsmen have completed sufficient runs to win the match, the whole of the boundary allowance shall be credited to the side's total and, in the case of a hit by the bat, to the striker's score.

7. Statement of result

If the side batting last wins the match without losing all its wickets, the result shall be stated as a win by the number of wickets still then to fall.

If, without having scored a total of runs in excess of the total scored by the opposing side, the side batting last has lost all its wickets, but as the result of an award of five penalty runs its total of runs is then sufficient to win, the result shall be stated as a win to that side by Penalty runs.

If the side fielding last wins the match, the result shall be stated as a win by runs.

If the match is decided by one side conceding defeat or refusing to play, the result shall be stated as Match Conceded or Match Awarded, as the case may be.

8. Correctness of result

Any decision as to the correctness of the scores shall be the responsibility of the umpires. See Law 3.15 (Correctness of scores).

9. Mistakes in scoring

If, after the players and umpires have left the field in the belief that the match has been concluded, the umpires discover that a mistake in scoring has occurred which affects the result then, subject to 10 below, they shall adopt the following procedure.

(a) If, when the players leave the field, the side batting last has not completed its innings and

either (i) the number of overs to be bowled in the last hour, or in that innings, has not been completed

or   (ii) the agreed time for close of play, or for the end of the innings, has not been reached

then, unless one side concedes defeat, the umpires shall order play to resume.

Unless a result is reached sooner, play will then continue, if conditions permit, until the prescribed number of overs has been completed and either time for close of play has been reached or the allotted time for the innings has expired, as appropriate. The number of overs and time remaining shall be taken as they were at the call of "Time" for the supposed conclusion of the match. No account shall be taken of the time between that moment and the resumption of play.

(b) If, at this call of "Time", the overs have been completed and no playing time remains, or if the side batting last has completed its innings, the umpires shall immediately inform both captains of the necessary corrections to the scores and to the result.

10. Result not to be changed

Once the umpires have agreed with the scorers the correctness of the scores at the conclusion of the match – see Laws 3.15 (Correctness of scores) and 4.2 (Correctness of scores) – the result cannot thereafter be changed.

LAW 22   THE OVER

1. Number of balls

The ball shall be bowled from each end alternately in overs of six balls.

2. Start of an over

An over has started when the bowler starts his run up or, if he has no run up, his action for the first delivery of that over.

3. Validity of balls

(a) A ball shall not count as one of the six balls of the over unless it is delivered, even though, as in Law 42.15 (Bowler attempting to run out non-striker before delivery) a batsman may be dismissed or some other incident occurs without the ball having been delivered.

(b) A ball delivered by the bowler shall not count as one of the six balls of the over

    (i) if it is called dead, or is to be considered dead, before the striker has had an opportunity to play it. See Law 23.6 (Dead Ball; ball counting as one of over).

    (ii) if it is called dead in the circumstances of Law 23.4(b)(vi) (Umpire calling and signalling Dead ball). Note also the special provisions of Law 23.4(b)(v).

    (iii) if it is a No ball. See Law 24 (No ball).

    (iv) if it is a Wide. See Law 25 (Wide ball).

    (v) when 5 penalty runs are awarded to the batting side under any of Laws 2.6 (Player returning without permission), 41.2 (Fielding the ball), 42.4 (Deliberate attempt to distract striker), or 42.5 (Deliberate distraction or obstruction of batsman).

(c) Any deliveries other than those listed in (a) and (b) above shall be known as valid balls. Only valid balls shall count towards the 6 balls of the over.

4. Call of "Over"

When six valid balls have been bowled and when the ball becomes dead, the umpire shall call "Over" before leaving the wicket. See also Law 23.3 (Call of "Over" or "Time").

5. Umpire miscounting

(a) If the umpire miscounts the number of valid balls, the over as counted by the umpire shall stand.

(b) If, having miscounted, the umpire allows an over to continue after six valid balls have been bowled, he may subsequently call "Over" as the ball becomes dead after any delivery, even if that delivery is not a valid ball.

6. Bowler changing ends

A bowler shall be allowed to change ends as often as desired, provided he does not bowl two overs consecutively, nor bowl parts of each of two consecutive overs, in the same innings.

7. Finishing an over

(a) Other than at the end of an innings, a bowler shall finish an over in progress unless he is incapacitated or is suspended under any of the Laws.

(b) If for any reason, other than the end of an innings, an over is left uncompleted at the start of an interval or interruption, it shall be completed on resumption of play.

8. Bowler incapacitated or suspended during an over

If for any reason a bowler is incapacitated while running up to deliver the first ball of an over, or is incapacitated or suspended during an over, the umpire shall call and signal "Dead ball". Another bowler shall complete the over from the same end, provided that he does not bowl two overs consecutively, nor bowl parts of each of two consecutive overs, in that innings.

LAW 23   DEAD BALL

1. Ball is dead

(a) The ball becomes dead when

    (i) it is finally settled in the hands of the wicket-keeper or of the bowler.

    (ii) a boundary is scored. See Law 19.3 (Scoring a boundary).

    (iii) a batsman is dismissed. The ball will be deemed to be dead from the instant of the incident causing the dismissal.

    (iv) whether played or not it becomes trapped between the bat and person of a batsman or between items of his clothing or equipment.

    (v) whether played or not it lodges in the clothing or equipment of a batsman or the clothing of an umpire.

    (vi) it lodges in a protective helmet worn by a fielder.

(vii) there is an award of penalty runs under either of Laws 2.6 (Player returning without permission) or 41.2 (Fielding the ball). The ball shall not count as one of the over.

(viii) there is contravention of Law 41.3 (Protective helmets belonging to the fielding side).

(ix) Lost ball is called. See Law 20 (Lost ball).

(b) The ball shall be considered to be dead when it is clear to the bowler's end umpire that the fielding side and both batsmen at the wicket have ceased to regard it as in play.

2. Ball finally settled

Whether the ball is finally settled or not is a matter for the umpire alone to decide.

3. Call of Over or Time

Neither the call of Over (see Law 22.4), nor the call of Time (see Law 16.2) is to be made until the ball is dead, either under 1 above or under 4 below.

4. Umpire calling and signalling "Dead ball"

(a) When the ball has become dead under 1 above, the bowler's end umpire may call and signal "Dead ball" if it is necessary to inform the players.

(b) Either umpire shall call and signal "Dead ball" when

(i) he intervenes in a case of unfair play.

(ii) a serious injury to a player or umpire occurs.

(iii) he leaves his normal position for consultation.

(iv) one or both bails fall from the striker's wicket before the striker has had the opportunity of playing the ball.

(v) the striker is not ready for the delivery of the ball and, if the ball is delivered, makes no attempt to play it. Provided the umpire is satisfied that the striker had adequate reason for not being ready, the ball shall not count as one of the over.

(vi) the striker is distracted by any noise or movement or in any other way while he is preparing to receive, or receiving a delivery. This shall apply whether the source of the distraction is within the game or outside it. Note also (vii) below. The ball shall not count as one of the over.

(vii) there is an instance of a deliberate attempt to distract under either of Laws 42.4 (Deliberate attempt to distract striker) or 42.5 (Deliberate distraction or obstruction of batsman). The ball shall not count as one of the over.

(viii) the bowler drops the ball accidentally before delivery.

(ix) the ball does not leave the bowler's hand for any reason other than an attempt to run out the non-striker before entering his delivery stride. See Law 42.15 (Bowler attempting to run out non-striker before delivery).

(x) he is required to do so under any of the Laws not included above.

5. Ball ceases to be dead

The ball ceases to be dead – that is, it comes into play – when the bowler starts his run up or, if he has no run up, his bowling action.

6. Dead ball; ball counting as one of over

(a) When a ball which has been delivered is called dead or is to be considered dead then, other than as in (b) below,

(i) it will not count in the over if the striker has not had an opportunity to play it.

(ii) it will be a valid ball if the striker has had an opportunity to play it, unless No ball or Wide has been called, except in the circumstances of 4(b)(vi) above and Laws 2.6 (Fielder returning without permission), 41.2 (Fielding the ball), 42.4 (Deliberate attempt to distract striker) and 42.5 (Deliberate distraction or obstruction of batsman).

(b) In 4(b)(v) above, the ball will not count in the over only if both conditions of not attempting to play the ball and having an adequate reason for not being ready are met. Otherwise the delivery will be a valid ball.

LAW 24 NO-BALL

1. Mode of delivery

(a) The umpire shall ascertain whether the bowler intends to bowl right handed or left handed, over or round the wicket, and shall so inform the striker.

It is unfair if the bowler fails to notify the umpire of a change in his mode of delivery. In this case the umpire shall call and signal "No-ball".

(b) Underarm bowling shall not be permitted except by special agreement before the match.

2. Fair delivery – the arm

For a delivery to be fair in respect of the arm the ball must not be thrown. See 3 below.

Although it is the primary responsibility of the striker's end umpire to assess the fairness of a delivery in this respect, there is nothing in this Law to debar the bowler's end umpire from calling and signalling "No-ball" if he considers that the ball has been thrown.

(a) If, in the opinion of either umpire, the ball has been thrown, he shall call and signal "No-ball" and, when the ball is dead, inform the other umpire of the reason for the call.

The bowler's end umpire shall then

(i) caution the bowler. This caution shall apply throughout the innings.

(ii) inform the captain of the fielding side of the reason for this action.

(iii) inform the batsmen at the wicket of what has occurred.

(b) If, after such caution, either umpire considers that, in that innings, a further delivery by the same bowler is thrown, the procedure set out in (a) above shall be repeated, indicating to the bowler that this is a final warning. This warning shall also apply throughout the innings.

(c) If either umpire considers that, in that innings, a further delivery by the same bowler is thrown, he shall call and signal "No-ball" and when the ball is dead inform the other umpire of the reason for the call. The bowler's end umpire shall then

(i) direct the captain of the fielding side to suspend the bowler forthwith. The over shall, if applicable, be completed by another bowler, who shall neither have bowled the previous over or part thereof nor be allowed to bowl any part of the next over.

The bowler thus suspended shall not bowl again in that innings.

(ii) inform the batsmen at the wicket and, as soon as practicable, the captain of the batting side of the occurrence.

(d) The umpires together shall report the occurrence as soon as possible after the match to the Executive of the fielding side and to any governing body responsible for the match, who shall take such action as is considered appropriate against the captain and the bowler concerned.

3. Definition of fair delivery – the arm

A ball is fairly delivered in respect of the arm if, once the bowler's arm has reached the level of the shoulder in the delivery swing, the elbow joint is not straightened partially or completely from that point until the ball has left the hand. This definition shall not debar a bowler from flexing or rotating the wrist in the delivery swing.

4. Bowler throwing towards striker's end before delivery

If the bowler throws the ball towards the striker's end before entering his delivery stride, either umpire shall call and signal "No-ball". See Law 42.16 (Batsmen stealing a run). However, the procedure stated in 2 above of caution, informing, final warning, action against the bowler and reporting shall not apply.

5. Fair delivery – the feet

For a delivery to be fair in respect of the feet, in the delivery stride

(a) the bowler's back foot must land within and not touching the return crease appertaining to his stated mode of delivery.

(b) the bowler's front foot must land with some part of the foot, whether grounded or raised

(i) on the same side of the imaginary line joining the two middle stumps as the return crease described in (a) above

and (ii) behind the popping crease.

If the bowler's end umpire is not satisfied that all of these three conditions have been met, he shall call and signal "No-ball".

6. Ball bouncing more than twice or rolling along the ground

The umpire shall call and signal "No-ball" if a ball which he considers to have been delivered, without having previously touched bat or person of the striker,

either (i) bounces more than twice

or (ii) rolls along the ground

before it reaches the popping crease.

7. Ball coming to rest in front of striker's wicket

If a ball delivered by the bowler comes to rest in front of the line of the striker's wicket, without having previously touched the bat or person of the striker, the umpire shall call and signal "No-ball" and immediately call and signal "Dead ball".

8. Call of "No-ball" for infringement of other Laws

In addition to the instances above, "No-ball" is to be called and signalled as required by the following

Law 40.3	– Position of wicket-keeper.
Law 41.5	– Limitation of on side fielders.
Law 41.6	– Fielders not to encroach on pitch.
Law 42.6	– Dangerous and unfair bowling.
Law 42.7	– Dangerous and unfair bowling – action by the umpire.
Law 42.8	– Deliberate bowling of high full pitched balls.

9. Revoking a call of "No-ball"

An umpire shall revoke his call of "No-ball" if the ball does not leave the bowler's hand for any reason.

10. No-ball to over-ride Wide

A call of "No-ball" shall override the call of "Wide ball" at any time. See Laws 25.1 (Judging a Wide) and 25.3 (Call and signal of Wide ball).

11. Ball not dead

The ball does not become dead on the call of "No-ball".

12. Penalty for a No-ball

A penalty of one run shall be awarded instantly on the call of "No-ball". Unless the call is revoked, the penalty shall stand even if a batsman is dismissed. It shall be in addition to any other runs scored, any boundary allowance and any other runs awarded for penalties.

13. Runs resulting from a No-ball – how scored

The one run penalty shall be scored as a No-ball extra. If other penalty runs have been awarded to either side these shall be scored as stated in Law 42.17 (Penalty runs). Any runs completed by the batsmen or any boundary allowance shall be credited to the striker if the ball has been struck with the bat; otherwise they shall also be scored as No-ball extras.

Apart from any award of 5 penalty runs, all runs resulting from a No-ball, whether as No-ball extras or credited to the striker, shall be debited against the bowler.

14. No-ball not to count

A No-ball shall not count as one of the over. See Law 22.3 (Validity of balls).

15. Out from a No-ball

When "No-ball" has been called, neither batsman shall be out under any of the Laws except 33 (Handled the ball), 34 (Hit the ball twice), 37 (Obstructing the field) or 38 (Run out).

LAW 25   WIDE BALL

1. Judging a Wide

(a) If the bowler bowls a ball, not being a No ball, the umpire shall adjudge it a Wide if, according to the definition in (b) below, in his opinion the ball passes wide of the striker where he is and which also would have passed wide of him standing in a normal guard position.

(b) The ball will be considered as passing wide of the striker unless it is sufficiently within his reach for him to be able to hit it with his bat by means of a normal cricket stroke.

2. Delivery not a Wide

The umpire shall not adjudge a delivery as being a Wide

(a) if the striker, by moving,

either   (i) causes the ball to pass wide of him, as defined in 1(b) above

or   (ii) brings the ball sufficiently within his reach to be able to hit it by means of a normal cricket stroke.

(b) if the ball touches the striker's bat or person.

3. Call and signal of "Wide ball"

(a) If the umpire adjudges a delivery to be a Wide he shall call and signal "Wide ball" as soon as the ball passes the striker's wicket. It shall, however, be considered to have been a Wide from the instant of delivery, even though it cannot be called Wide until it passes the striker's wicket.

(b) The umpire shall revoke the call of "Wide ball" if there is then any contact between the ball and the striker's bat or person.

(c) The umpire shall revoke the call of "Wide ball" if a delivery is called a No ball. See Law 24.10 (No ball to over-ride Wide).

4. Ball not dead

The ball does not become dead on the call of "Wide ball".

5. Penalty for a Wide

A penalty of one run shall be awarded instantly on the call of "Wide ball". Unless the call is revoked (see 3(b) and (c) above), this penalty shall stand even if a batsman is dismissed, and shall be in addition to any other runs scored, any boundary allowance and any other runs awarded for penalties.

6. Runs resulting from a Wide – how scored

All runs completed by the batsmen or a boundary allowance, together with the penalty for the Wide, shall be scored as Wide balls. Apart from any award of five penalty runs, all runs resulting from a Wide shall be debited against the bowler.

7. Wide not to count

A Wide shall not count as one of the over. See Law 22.3 (Validity of balls).

8. Out from a Wide

When Wide ball has been called, neither batsman shall be out under any of the Laws except 33 (Handled the ball), 35 (Hit wicket), 37 (Obstructing the field), 38 (Run out) or 39 (Stumped).

LAW 26 BYE AND LEG BYE

1. Byes

If the ball, delivered by the bowler, not being a No-ball or a Wide, passes the striker without touching his bat or person, any runs completed by the batsmen from that delivery, or a boundary allowance, shall be credited as Byes to the batting side.

2. Leg byes

(a) If a ball delivered by the bowler first strikes the person of the striker, runs shall be scored only if the umpire is satisfied that the striker has

either   (i)   attempted to play the ball with his bat

or   (ii) tried to avoid being hit by the ball.

(b) If the umpire is satisfied that either of these conditions has been met runs shall be scored as follows.

(i) If there is

either   no subsequent contact with the striker's bat or person,

or   only inadvertent contact with the striker's bat or person,

runs completed by the batsmen or a boundary allowance shall be credited to the striker in the case of subsequent contact with his bat but otherwise to the batting side as in (c) below.

(ii) If the striker wilfully makes a lawful second strike, Laws 34.3 (Ball lawfully struck more than once) and 34.4 (Runs scored from ball lawfully struck more than once) shall apply.

(c) The runs in (b)(i) above, unless credited to the striker, shall,

(i) if the delivery is not a No-ball, be scored as Leg byes.

(ii) if No-ball has been called, be scored together with the penalty for the No-ball, as No-ball extras.

3. Leg byes not to be awarded

If in the circumstance of 2(a) above the umpire considers that neither of the conditions (i) and (ii) therein has been met, then Leg byes shall not be awarded. The batting side shall not be credited with any runs from that delivery apart from the one run penalty for a No-ball if applicable. Moreover, no other penalties arising from that delivery shall be awarded to the batting side. The following procedure shall be adopted.

(a) If no run is attempted but the ball reaches the boundary, the umpire shall call and signal "Dead ball", and disallow the boundary.

(b) If runs are attempted and if

(i) neither batsman is dismissed and the ball does not become dead for any other reason, the umpire shall call and signal "Dead ball" as soon as one run is completed or the ball reaches the boundary. The run or boundary shall be disallowed. The batsmen shall return to their original ends.

(ii) before one run is completed or the ball reaches the boundary, a batsman is dismissed, or the ball becomes dead for any other reason, all the provisions of the Laws will apply, except that no runs and no penalties shall be credited to the batting side, other than the penalty for a No ball if applicable.

LAW 27   APPEALS

1. Umpire not to give batsman out without an appeal

Neither umpire shall give a batsman out, even though he may be out under the Laws, unless appealed to by a fielder. This shall not debar a batsman who is out under any of the Laws from leaving his wicket without an appeal having been made. Note, however, the provisions of 7 below.

2. Batsman dismissed

A batsman is dismissed if

either (a) he is given out by an umpire, on appeal

or   (b) he is out under any of the Laws and leaves his wicket as in 1 above.

3. Timing of appeals

For an appeal to be valid, it must be made before the bowler begins his run up or, if he has no run up, his bowling action to deliver the next ball, and before "Time" has been called.

The call of "Over" does not invalidate an appeal made prior to the start of the following over, provided Time has not been called. See Laws 16.2 (Call of "Time") and 22.2 (Start of an over).

4. Appeal "How's That?"

An appeal "How's That?" covers all ways of being out.

5. Answering appeals

The striker's end umpire shall answer all appeals arising out of any of Laws 35 (Hit wicket), 39 (Stumped) or 38 (Run out) when this occurs at the wicket-keeper's end. The bowler's end umpire shall answer all other appeals.

When an appeal is made, each umpire shall answer on any matter that falls within his jurisdiction.

When a batsman has been given "Not out", either umpire may answer an appeal, made in accordance with 3 above, if it is on a further matter and is within his jurisdiction.

6. Consultation by umpires

Each umpire shall answer appeals on matters within his own jurisdiction. If an umpire is doubtful about any point that the other umpire may have been in a better position to see, he shall consult the latter on this point of fact and shall then give the decision. If, after consultation, there is still doubt remaining, the decision shall be "Not out".

7. Batsman leaving his wicket under a misapprehension

An umpire shall intervene if satisfied that a batsman, not having been given out, has left his wicket under a misapprehension that he is out. The umpire intervening shall call and signal Dead ball to prevent any further action by the fielding side and shall recall the batsman.

8. Withdrawal of an appeal

The captain of the fielding side may withdraw an appeal only if he obtains the consent of the umpire within whose jurisdiction the appeal falls. He must do so before the outgoing batsman has left the field of play. If such consent is given, the umpire concerned shall, if applicable, revoke his decision and recall the batsman.

9. Umpire's decision

An umpire may alter his decision provided that such alteration is made promptly. This apart, an umpire's decision, once made, is final.

LAW 28   THE WICKET IS DOWN

1. Wicket put down

(a) The wicket is put down if a bail is completely removed from the top of the stumps, or a stump is struck out of the ground,

> (i) by the ball,

> or (ii) by the striker's bat if he is holding it or by any part of his bat that he is holding,

> or (iii) notwithstanding the provisions of Law 6.8(a), by the striker's bat in falling if he has let go of it, or by any part of his bat becoming detached,

> or (iv) by the striker's person or by any part of his clothing or equipment becoming detached from his person,

> or (v) by a fielder with his hand or arm, providing that the ball is held in the hand or hands so used, or in the hand of the arm so used.

> The wicket is also put down if a fielder strikes or pulls a stump out of the ground in the same manner.

(b) The disturbance of a bail, whether temporary or not, shall not constitute its complete removal from the top of the stumps, but if a bail in falling lodges between two of the stumps this shall be regarded as complete removal.

2. One bail off

If one bail is off, it shall be sufficient for the purpose of putting the wicket down to remove the remaining bail or to strike or pull any of the three stumps out of the ground, in any of the ways stated in 1 above.

3. Remaking wicket

If a wicket is broken or put down while the ball is in play, it shall not be remade by an umpire until the ball is dead. See Law 23 (Dead ball). Any fielder may, however, while the ball is in play,

> (i) replace a bail or bails on top of the stumps.

> (ii) put back one or more stumps into the ground where the wicket originally stood.

4. Dispensing with bails

If the umpires have agreed to dispense with bails in accordance with Law 8.5 (Dispensing with bails), it is for the umpire concerned to decide whether or not the wicket has been put down.

(a) After a decision to play without bails, the wicket has been put down if the umpire concerned is satisfied that the wicket has been struck by the ball, by the striker's bat, person or items of his clothing or equipment as described in 1(a) (ii), (iii) or (iv) above, or by a fielder in the manner described in 1(a)(v) above.

(b) If the wicket has already been broken or put down, (a) above shall apply to any stump or stumps still in the ground. Any fielder may replace a stump or stumps, in accordance with 3 above, in order to have an opportunity of putting the wicket down.

LAW 29   BATSMAN OUT OF HIS GROUND

1. When out of his ground

(a) A batsman shall be considered to be out of his ground unless his bat or some part of his person is grounded behind the popping crease at that end.

(b) Notwithstanding (a) above, if a running batsman, having grounded some part of his foot behind the popping crease, continues running further towards the wicket at that end and beyond, then any subsequent total loss of contact with the ground of both his person and his bat during his continuing forward momentum shall not be interpreted as being out of his ground.

2. Which is a batsman's ground?

(a) If only one batsman is within a ground

(i) it is his ground

(ii) it remains his ground even if he is later joined there by the other batsman.

(b) If both batsmen are in the same ground and one of them subsequently leaves it, (a)(i) above applies.

(c) If there is no batsman in either ground, then each ground belongs to whichever batsman is nearer to it, or, if the batsmen are level, to whichever batsman was nearer to it immediately prior to their drawing level.

(d) If a ground belongs to one batsman then, unless there is a striker who has a runner, the other ground belongs to the other batsman, irrespective of his position.

(e) When a batsman who has a runner is striker, his ground is always at the wicket-keeper's end. However, (a), (b), (c) and (d) above will still apply, but only to the runner and the non-striker, so that that ground will also belong to either the non-striker or the runner, as the case may be.

3. Position of non-striker

The non-striker, when standing at the bowler's end, should be positioned on the opposite side of the wicket to that from which the ball is being delivered, unless a request to do otherwise is granted by the umpire.

LAW 30   BOWLED

1. Out Bowled

(a) The striker is out *Bowled* if his wicket is put down by a ball delivered by the bowler, not being a No ball, even if it first touches his bat or person.

(b) Notwithstanding (a) above he shall not be out Bowled if before striking the wicket the ball has been in contact with any other player or an umpire. He will, however, be subject to Laws 33 (Handled the ball), 37 (Obstructing the field), 38 (Run out) and 39 (Stumped).

2. Bowled to take precedence

The striker is out Bowled if his wicket is put down as in 1 above, even though a decision against him for any other method of dismissal would be justified.

LAW 31   TIMED OUT

1. Out Timed out

(a) After the fall of a wicket or the retirement of a batsman, the incoming batsman must, unless Time has been called, be in position to take guard or for his partner to be ready to receive the next ball within 3 minutes of the dismissal or retirement. If this requirement is not met, the incoming batsman will be out, *Timed out*.

(b) In the event of protracted delay in which no batsman comes to the wicket, the umpires shall adopt the procedure of Law 21.3 (Umpires awarding a match). For the purposes of that Law the start of the action shall be taken as the expiry of the 3 minutes referred to above.

2. Bowler does not get credit

The bowler does not get credit for the wicket.

LAW 32   CAUGHT

1. Out Caught

The striker is out *Caught* if a ball delivered by the bowler, not being a No-ball, touches his bat without having previously been in contact with any fielder, and is subsequently held by a fielder as a fair catch before it touches the ground.

2. Caught to take precedence

If the criteria of 1 above are met and the striker is not out Bowled, then he is out Caught, even though a decision against either batsman for another method of dismissal would be justified.

3. A fair catch

A catch shall be considered to have been fairly made if

    (a) throughout the act of making the catch

        (i) any fielder in contact with the ball is within the field of play. See 4 below.

        (ii) the ball is at no time in contact with any object grounded beyond the boundary.

    The act of making the catch shall start from the time when the ball in flight comes into contact with some part of a fielder's person other than a protective helmet, and shall end when a fielder obtains complete control both over the ball and over his own movement.

    (b) the ball is hugged to the body of the catcher or accidentally lodges in his clothing or, in the case of the wicket-keeper only, in his pads. However, it is not a fair catch if the ball lodges in a protective helmet worn by a fielder. See Law 23 (Dead ball).

    (c) the ball does not touch the ground even though the hand holding it does so in effecting the catch.

    (d) a fielder catches the ball after it has been lawfully struck more than once by the striker, but only if it has not been grounded since first being struck.

    (e) a fielder catches the ball after it has touched an umpire, another fielder or the other batsman. However, it is not a fair catch if the ball has previously touched a protective helmet worn by a fielder. The ball will then remain in play.

    (f) a fielder catches the ball in the air after it has crossed the boundary provided that

        (i) he has no part of his person touching or grounded beyond the boundary at any time while he is contact with the ball.

        (ii) the ball has not been grounded beyond the boundary. See Law 19.3 (Scoring a boundary).

Note also Law 19.4 (Ball beyond the boundary)

    (g) the ball is caught off an obstruction within the boundary provided the obstruction had not been designated a boundary by the umpires before the toss.

4. Fielder within the field of play

    (a) A fielder is not within the field of play if he has any part of his person touching, or grounded beyond, the boundary. See Law 19.3 (Scoring a boundary).

    (b) Six runs shall be scored if a fielder

        (i) has any part of his person touching, or grounded beyond, the boundary when he catches the ball.

        (ii) catches the ball and subsequently touches the boundary or grounds some part of his person beyond the boundary while carrying the ball but before completing the catch.

See Laws 19.3 (Scoring a boundary) and 19.5 (Runs allowed for boundaries).

5. No runs to be scored

If the striker is dismissed Caught, runs from that delivery completed by the batsmen before the completion of the catch shall not be scored but any runs for penalties awarded to either side shall stand. Law 18.12 (Batsman returning to wicket he has left) shall apply from the instant of the completion of the catch.

LAW 33   HANDLED THE BALL

1. Out Handled the ball

(a) Either batsman is out *Handled the ball* if he wilfully touches the ball while in play with a hand or hands not holding the bat unless he does so with the consent of a fielder.

(b) Either batsman is out under this Law if, while the ball is in play, and without the consent of a fielder, he uses his hand or hands not holding the bat to return the ball to any fielder.

2. Not out Handled the ball

Notwithstanding 1(a) above, a batsman will not be out under this Law if he handles the ball to avoid injury.

3. Runs scored

If either batsman is dismissed Handled the ball, runs completed by the batsmen before the offence shall be scored, together with any runs for penalties awarded to either side. See Laws 18.6 (Runs awarded for penalties) and 18.9 (Runs scored when a batsman is dismissed).

4. Bowler does not get credit

The bowler does not get credit for the wicket.

LAW 34   HIT THE BALL TWICE

1. Out Hit the ball twice

(a) The striker is out *Hit the ball twice* if, while the ball is in play, it strikes any part of his person or is struck by his bat and, before the ball has been touched by a fielder, he wilfully strikes it again with his bat or person, other than a hand not holding the bat, except for the sole purpose of guarding his wicket. See 3 below and Laws 33 (Handled the ball) and 37 (Obstructing the field).

(b) For the purpose of this Law "struck" or "strike" shall include contact with the person of the striker.

2. Not out Hit the ball twice

Notwithstanding 1(a) above, the striker will not be out under this Law if

      (i) he strikes the ball a second or subsequent time in order to return the ball to any fielder. Note, however, the provisions of Law 37.4 (Returning the ball to a fielder).

      (ii) he wilfully strikes the ball after it has touched a fielder. Note, however the provisions of Law 37.1 (Out Obstructing the field).

3. Ball lawfully struck more than once

Solely in order to guard his wicket and before the ball has been touched by a fielder, the striker may lawfully strike the ball a second or subsequent time with his bat, or with any part of his person other than a hand not holding the bat.

Notwithstanding this provision, he may not prevent the ball from being caught by striking the ball more than once in defence of his wicket. See Law 37.3 (Obstructing a ball from being caught).

4. Runs scored from ball lawfully struck more than once

When the ball is lawfully struck more than once, as permitted in 3 above, only the first strike is to be considered in determining whether runs are to be permitted and if so how they are to be recorded.

(a) If on the first strike, the umpire is satisfied that

either   (i)   the ball first struck the bat

or   (ii)   the striker attempted to play the ball with his bat

or   (iii)   the striker attempted to avoid being hit by the ball,

then the batting side shall be credited with any runs for penalties that may be applicable.

(b) Additionally, if the conditions in (a) above are met then, if they result from overthrows and only if they result from overthrows, runs completed by the batsmen or a boundary will be scored. They shall be credited to the striker if the first strike was with the bat. If the first strike was on the person of the striker they shall be recorded as Leg byes or No ball extras as appropriate. See Law 26.2 (Leg byes).

(c) If the conditions in (a) above are met and there is no overthrow until after the batsmen have started to run but before one run is completed,

(i)   only subsequent completed runs or a boundary shall be scored. For the purposes of this clause and (iii) below, the first run shall count as a completed run if and only if the batsmen had not already crossed at the instant of the throw.

(ii)   if in these circumstances the ball goes to the boundary from the throw then, notwithstanding the provisions of Law 19.7 (Overthrow or wilful act of fielder), only the boundary allowance shall be scored.

(iii)   if the ball goes to the boundary as the result of a further overthrow, then runs completed by the batsman after the first throw but before this final throw shall be added to the boundary allowance. The run in progress at the first throw will count as a completed run only if the batsmen had not already crossed at that instant. The run in progress at the final throw shall count as a completed run only if the batsmen had already crossed at that instant. Law 18.12 (Batsman returning to wicket he has left) shall apply as from the instant of the final throw.

(d) If, in the opinion of the umpire, none of the conditions in (a) above are met then, whether there is an overthrow or not, the batting side shall not be credited with any runs from that delivery apart from the penalty for a No ball if applicable. Moreover, no other runs for penalties shall be awarded to the batting side.

5. Ball lawfully struck more than once – action by the umpire

If no runs are to be permitted, either in the circumstances of 4(d) above, or because there has been no overthrow, and

(a) if no run is attempted but the ball reaches the boundary, the umpire shall call and signal "Dead ball" and disallow the boundary.

(b) if the batsmen run and

(i)   neither batsman is dismissed and the ball does not become dead for any other reason, the umpire shall call and signal "Dead ball" as soon as one run is completed or the ball reaches the boundary. The run or boundary shall be disallowed. The batsmen shall return to their original ends.

or (ii)   a batsman is dismissed, or if for any other reason the ball becomes dead before one run is completed or the ball reaches the boundary, all the provisions of the Laws will apply except that the award of penalties to the batting side shall be as laid down in 4(a) or 4(d) above, as appropriate.

6. Bowler does not get credit

The bowler does not get credit for the wicket.

LAW 35   HIT WICKET

1. Out Hit wicket

(a) The striker is out *Hit wicket* if, after the bowler has entered his delivery stride and while the ball is in play, his wicket is put down either by the striker's bat or by his person as described in Law 28

    either   (i)   in the course of any action taken by him in preparing to receive or in receiving a delivery,

    or   (ii)   in setting off for his first run immediately after playing or playing at the ball,

    or   (iii)   if he makes no attempt to play the ball, in setting off for his first run, providing that in the opinion of the umpire this is immediately after he has had the opportunity of playing the ball,

    or   (iv)   in lawfully making a second or further stroke for the purpose of guarding his wicket within the provisions of Law 34.3 (Ball lawfully struck more than once).

(b) If the striker puts his wicket down in any of the ways described in Law 28.1(a)(ii) and (iii) (Wicket put down) before the bowler has entered his delivery stride, either umpire shall call and signal "Dead ball".

2. Not out Hit wicket

Notwithstanding 1 above, the striker is not out under this Law should his wicket be put down in any of the ways referred to in 1 above if

(a) it occurs after he has completed any action in receiving the delivery, other than in 1(a)(ii), (iii) and (iv) above.

(b) it occurs when he is in the act of running, other than setting off immediately for his first run.

(c) it occurs when he is trying to avoid being run out or stumped.

(d) it occurs when he is trying to avoid a throw in at any time.

(e) the bowler after entering his delivery stride does not deliver the ball. In this case either umpire shall immediately call and signal "Dead ball". See Law 23.3 (Umpire calling and signalling "Dead ball").

(f) the delivery is a No-ball.

LAW 36   LEG BEFORE WICKET

1. Out LBW

The striker is out *LBW* in the circumstances set out below.

       (a) The bowler delivers a ball, not being a No ball

and (b) the ball, if it is not intercepted full pitch, pitches in line between wicket and wicket or on the off side of the striker's wicket

and (c) the ball not having previously touched his bat, the striker intercepts the ball, either full pitch or after pitching, with any part of his person

and (d) the point of impact, even if above the level of the bails,

       either   (i)   is between wicket and wicket

       or   (ii)   if the striker has made no genuine attempt to play the ball with his bat, is either between wicket and wicket or outside the line of the off stump.

and (e) but for the interception, the ball would have hit the wicket.

2. Interception of the ball

(a) In assessing points (c), (d) and (e) in 1 above, only the first interception is to be considered.

(b) In assessing point (e) in 1 above, it is to be assumed that the path of the ball before interception would have continued after interception, irrespective of whether the ball might have pitched subsequently or not.

3. Off side of wicket

The off side of the striker's wicket shall be determined by the striker's stance at the moment the ball comes into play for that delivery. See Appendix D.

LAW 37   OBSTRUCTING THE FIELD

1. Out Obstructing the field

Either batsman is out *Obstructing the field* if he wilfully obstructs or distracts the fielding side by word or action.

Furthermore, it shall be regarded as obstruction if while the ball is in play either batsman wilfully, and without the consent of a fielder, strikes the ball with his bat or person, other than a hand not holding the bat, after the ball has been touched by a fielder. This shall apply whether or not there is any disadvantage to the fielding side. See 4 below.

2. Accidental obstruction

It is for either umpire to decide whether any obstruction or distraction is wilful or not. He shall consult the other umpire if he has any doubt.

3. Obstructing a ball from being caught

The striker is out should wilful obstruction or distraction by either batsman prevent a catch being made.

This shall apply even though the striker causes the obstruction in lawfully guarding his wicket under the provisions of Law 34.3 (Ball lawfully struck more than once).

4. Returning the ball to a fielder

Either batsman is out Obstructing the field if, without the consent of a fielder and while the ball is in play, he uses his bat or person, other than a hand not holding the bat, to return the ball to any fielder.

5. Runs scored

If either batsman is dismissed Obstructing the field, runs completed by the batsmen before the offence shall be scored, together with any runs for penalties awarded to either side. See Laws 18.6 (Runs awarded for penalties) and 18.9 (Runs scored when a batsman is dismissed).

If, however the obstruction prevents a catch from being made, runs completed by the batsmen before the offence shall not be scored, but any runs for penalties awarded to either side shall stand.

6. Bowler does not get credit

The bowler does not get credit for the wicket.

LAW 38   RUN OUT

1. Out Run out

(a) Either batsman is out *Run out*, except as in 2 below, if, at any time while the ball is in play,

    (i) he is out of his ground

and (ii) his wicket is fairly put down by the action of a fielder.

(b) (a) above shall apply even though No ball has been called and whether or not a run is being attempted, except in the circumstances of 2(e) below.

2. Batsman not Run out

Notwithstanding 1 above, a batman is not out Run out if

(a) he has been within his ground and has subsequently left it to avoid injury, when the wicket is put down.
Note also the provisions of Law 29.1(b) (When out of his ground)

(b) the ball has not subsequently been touched by a fielder, after the bowler has entered his delivery stride, before the wicket is put down.

(c) the ball, having been played by the striker, or having come off his person, directly strikes a protective helmet worn by a fielder and without further contact with him or any other fielder rebounds directly on to the wicket. However, the ball remains in play and either batsman may be Run out in the circumstances of 1 above if a wicket is subsequently put down.

(d) he is out Stumped. See Law 39.1(b) (Out Stumped).

(e) No ball has been called

    and (i) he is out of his ground not attempting a run

    and (ii) the wicket is fairly put down by the wicket-keeper without the intervention of another fielder.

3. Which batsman is out

The batsman out in the circumstances of 1 above is the one whose ground is at the end where the wicket is put down. See Laws 2.8 (Transgression of the Laws by a batsman who has a runner) and 29.2 (Which is a batsman's ground).

4. Runs scored

If either batsman is dismissed Run out, the run in progress when the wicket is put down shall not be scored, but runs completed by the batsmen shall stand, together with any runs for penalties awarded to either side. See Laws 18.6 (Runs awarded for penalties) and 18.9 (Runs scored when a batsman is dismissed).

If, however, a striker who has a runner is himself dismissed Run out, runs completed by the runner and the other batsman before the wicket is put down shall not be scored, but any runs for penalties awarded to either side shall stand. See Law 2.8 (Transgression of the Laws by a batsman who has a runner).

5. Bowler does not get credit

The bowler does not get credit for the wicket.

LAW 39   STUMPED

1. Out Stumped

(a) The striker is out *Stumped*, except as in 3 below, if

    (i) a ball which is not a No ball is delivered

    and (ii) he is out of his ground, other than as in 3(a) below

    and (iii) he has not attempted a run

    when (iv) his wicket is fairly put down by the wicketkeeper without the intervention of another fielder. Note, however Laws 2.8(c) (Transgression of the Laws by a batsman who has a runner) and 40.3 (Position of wicketkeeper).

(b) The striker is out Stumped if all the conditions of (a) above are satisfied, even though a decision of Run out would be justified.

2. Ball rebounding from wicketkeeper's person

(a) If the wicket is put down by the ball, it shall be regarded as having been put down by the wicketkeeper if the ball

   (i) rebounds on to the stumps from any part of the wicketkeeper's person or equipment other than a protective helmet

   or (ii) has been kicked or thrown on to the stumps by the wicketkeeper.

(b) If the ball touches a protective helmet worn by the wicketkeeper, the ball is still in play but the striker shall not be out Stumped. He will, however, be liable to be Run out in these circumstances if there is subsequent contact between the ball and any fielder. Note, however, 3 below.

3. Not out Stumped

(a) Notwithstanding 1 above, the striker will not be out Stumped if he has left his ground to avoid injury, when his wicket is put down.

(b) If the striker is not out Stumped he may, except in the circumstances of Law 38.2(e), be out Run out if the conditions of Law 38 (Run out) apply.

LAW 40   THE WICKETKEEPER

1. Protective equipment

The wicketkeeper is the only fielder permitted to wear gloves and external leg guards. If he does so these are to be regarded as part of his person for the purposes of Law 41.2 (Fielding the ball). If by his actions and positioning it is apparent to the umpires that he will not be able to discharge his duties as a wicketkeeper, he shall forfeit this right and also the right to be recognised as a wicketkeeper for the purposes of Laws 32.3 (A fair catch), 39 (Stumped), 41.1 (Protective equipment), 41.5 (Limitation of on-side fielders) and 41.6 (Fielders not to encroach on pitch).

2. Gloves

If, as permitted under 1 above, the wicketkeeper wears gloves, they shall have no webbing between the fingers except joining index finger and thumb, where webbing may be inserted as a means of support. If used, the webbing shall be

(a) a single piece of non-stretch material which, although it may have facing material attached, shall have no reinforcements or tucks.

(b) such that the top edge of the webbing

   (i) does not protrude beyond the straight line joining the top of the index finger to the top of the thumb.

   (ii) is taut when a hand wearing the glove has the thumb fully extended.

See Appendix C.

3. Position of wicketkeeper

The wicketkeeper shall remain wholly behind the wicket at the striker's end from the moment the ball comes into play until

(a) a ball delivered by the bowler

   either (i) touches the bat or person of the striker

   or   (ii) passes the wicket at the striker's end

or (b) the striker attempts a run.

In the event of the wicketkeeper contravening this Law, the striker's end umpire shall call and signal No ball as soon as possible after the delivery of the ball.

4. Movement by wicketkeeper

It is unfair if the wicketkeeper standing back makes a significant movement towards the wicket after the ball comes into play and before it reaches the striker. In the event of such unfair movement by the wicketkeeper, either umpire shall call and signal "Dead ball".

It will not be considered a significant movement if the wicketkeeper moves a few paces forward for a slower delivery.

5. Restriction on actions of wicketkeeper

If, in the opinion of either umpire, the wicketkeeper interferes with the striker's right to play the ball and to guard his wicket, Law 23.4(b)(vi) (Umpire calling and signalling "Dead ball") shall apply.

If, however, either umpire considers that the interference by the wicketkeeper was wilful, then Law 42.4 (Deliberate attempt to distract striker) shall also apply.

6. Interference with wicketkeeper by striker

If, in playing at the ball or in the legitimate defence of his wicket, the striker interferes with the wicketkeeper, he shall not be out except as provided for in Law 37.3 (Obstructing a ball from being caught).

LAW 41   THE FIELDER

1. Protective equipment

No fielder other than the wicketkeeper shall be permitted to wear gloves or external leg guards. In addition, protection for the hand or fingers may be worn only with the consent of the umpires.

2. Fielding the ball

A fielder may field the ball with any part of his person, but if, while the ball is in play, he wilfully fields it otherwise,

    (a)   the ball shall immediately become dead.

  and (b) the umpire shall

      (i) award five penalty runs to the batting side.

      (ii) The penalty for a No-ball or a Wide shall stand. Additionally, runs completed by the batsmen shall be credited to the batting side, together with the run in progress if the batsmen had already crossed at the instant of the offence.

      (iii) inform the other umpire and the captain of the fielding side of the reason for this action.

      (iv) inform the batsmen and, as soon as practicable, the captain of the batting side of what has occurred.

    (c) The ball shall not count as one of the over.

    (d) The umpires together shall report the occurrence as soon as possible after the match to the Executive of the fielding side and to any Governing Body responsible for the match, who shall take such action as is considered appropriate against the captain and the player or players concerned.

3. Protective helmets belonging to the fielding side

Protective helmets, when not in use by fielders, should, if above the surface, be placed only on the ground behind the wicket-keeper and in line with both sets of stumps. If a protective helmet belonging to the fielding side is on the ground within the field of play, and the ball while in play strikes it, the ball shall become dead, and 5 penalty runs shall then be awarded to the batting side, in addition to the penalty for a No-ball or a Wide, if applicable.

Additionally runs completed by the batsmen before the ball strikes the protective helmet shall be scored, together with the run in progress if the batsmen had already crossed at the instant of the ball striking the protective helmet. See Law 18.10 (Runs scored when the ball becomes dead other than at the fall of a wicket).

4. Penalty runs not to be awarded

Notwithstanding 2 and 3 above, if from the delivery by the bowler, the ball first struck the person of the striker and, if in the opinion of the umpire, the striker

    Neither   (i) attempted to play the ball with his bat

    Nor   (ii) tried to avoid being hit by the ball,

then no award of five penalty runs shall be made and no other runs or penalties shall be credited to the batting side except the penalty for a No-ball, if applicable.

If runs are attempted, the umpire should follow the procedure laid down in Law 26.3 (Leg byes not to be awarded).

5. Limitation of on side fielders

At the instant of the bowler's delivery there shall not be more than two fielders, other than the wicket-keeper, behind the popping crease on the on side. A fielder will be considered to be behind the popping crease unless the whole of his person whether grounded or in the air is in front of this line.

In the event of infringement of this Law by any fielder, the striker's end umpire shall call and signal "No-ball".

6. Fielders not to encroach on pitch

While the ball is in play and until the ball has made contact with the striker's bat or person, or has passed the striker's bat, no fielder, other than the bowler, may have any part of his person grounded on or extended over the pitch.

In the event of infringement of this Law by any fielder other than the wicketkeeper, the bowler's end umpire shall call and signal "No-ball" as soon as possible after delivery of the ball. Note, however, Law 40.3 (Position of wicketkeeper).

7. Movement by fielders

Any significant movement by any fielder after the ball comes into play, and before the ball reaches the striker, is unfair. In the event of such unfair movement, either umpire shall call and signal "Dead ball". Note also the provisions of Law 42.4 (Deliberate attempt to distract striker).

8. Definition of significant movement

    (a) For close fielders anything other than minor adjustments to stance or position in relation to the striker is significant.

    (b) In the outfield, fielders are permitted to move towards the striker or the striker's wicket, provided that 5 above is not contravened. Anything other than slight movement off line or away from the striker is to be considered significant.

    (c) For restrictions on movement by the wicketkeeper see Law 40.4 (Movement by wicket-keeper).

LAW 42   FAIR AND UNFAIR PLAY

1. Fair and unfair play – responsibility of captains

The responsibility lies with the captains for ensuring that play is conducted within the spirit and traditions of the game, as described in The Preamble – The Spirit of Cricket, as well as within the Laws.

2. Fair and unfair play – responsibility of umpires

The umpires shall be the sole judges of fair and unfair play. If either umpire considers an action, not covered by the Laws, to be unfair he shall intervene without appeal and, if the ball is in play, call and signal "Dead ball" and implement the procedure as set out in 18 below. Otherwise umpires shall not interfere with the progress of play without appeal except as required to do so by the Laws.

3. The match ball – changing its condition

(a) Any fielder may

   (i) polish the ball provided that no artificial substance is used and that such polishing wastes no time.

   (ii) remove mud from the ball under the supervision of the umpire.

   (iii) dry a wet ball on a piece of cloth.

(b) It is unfair for anyone to rub the ball on the ground for any reason, to interfere with any of the seams or the surface of the ball, to use any implement, or to take any other action whatsoever which is likely to alter the condition of the ball, except as permitted in (a) above.

(c) The umpires shall make frequent and irregular inspections of the ball.

(d) If the umpires together agree that the deterioration in the condition of the ball is greater than is consistent with the use it has received, they shall consider that there has been a contravention of this Law. They shall

   (i) change the ball forthwith. It shall be for the umpires to decide on the replacement ball. It shall, in their opinion, have had wear comparable to that which the previous ball had received immediately prior to the contravention.

Additionally the bowler's end umpire shall

   (ii) award 5 penalty runs to the batting side.

   (iii) inform the batsmen that the ball has been changed.

   (iv) inform the captain of the fielding side that the reason for the action was the unfair interference with the ball.

   (v) inform the captain of the batting side as soon as practicable of what has occurred.

   (vi) together with the other umpire report the occurrence as soon as possible after the match to the executive of the fielding side and to any governing body responsible for the match, who shall take such action as is considered appropriate against the captain and team concerned.

(e) If the umpires together agree that there has been any further instance in that innings of greater deterioration in the condition of the ball than is consistent with the use it has received, they shall

   (i) repeat the procedure in (d)(i), (ii) and (iii) above

Additionally the bowler's end umpire shall

   (ii) inform the captain of the fielding side of the reason for the action taken and direct him to suspend the bowler forthwith who delivered the immediately preceding ball. The bowler thus suspended shall not be allowed to bowl again in that innings.

   If applicable, the over shall be completed by another bowler, who shall neither have bowled any part of the previous over, nor be allowed to bowl any part of the next over.

   (iii) inform the captain of the batting side as soon as practicable of what has occurred.

   (iv) together with the other umpire report the further occurrence as soon as possible after the match to the executive of the fielding side and to any governing body responsible for the match, who shall take such action as is considered appropriate against the captain and team concerned.

4. Deliberate attempt to distract striker

It is unfair for any fielder deliberately to attempt to distract the striker while he is preparing to receive or receiving a delivery.

(a) If either umpire considers that any action by a fielder is such an attempt, at the first instance he shall immediately call and signal "Dead ball" and inform the other umpire of the reason for the call. The bowler's end umpire shall

   (i) warn the captain of the fielding side that the action is unfair and indicate that this is a first and final warning.

   (ii) inform the batsmen of what has occurred.

Neither batsman shall be dismissed from that delivery. The ball shall not count as one of the over.

(b) If there is any further such deliberate attempt by any fielder in that innings, the procedures, other than warning, as set out in (a) above shall apply. Additionally, the bowler's end umpire shall

    (i) award five penalty runs to the batting side.

    (ii) inform the captain of the fielding side and, as soon as practicable, the captain of the batting side of the reason for the action.

    (iii) together with the other umpire report the occurrence as soon as possible after the match to the Executive of the fielding side and to any Governing Body responsible for the match, who shall take such action as is considered appropriate against the captain and the player or players concerned.

5. Deliberate distraction or obstruction of batsman

In addition to 4 above, it is unfair for any fielder wilfully to attempt, by word or action, to distract or obstruct either batsman after the striker has received the ball.

(a) It is for either one of the umpires to decide whether any distraction or obstruction is wilful or not.

(b) If either umpire considers that a fielder has caused or attempted to cause such a distraction or obstruction, he shall immediately call and signal "Dead ball" and inform the other umpire of the reason for the call.

(c) Neither batsman shall be dismissed from that delivery.

Additionally

(d) The bowler's end umpire shall

    (i) award five penalty runs to the batting side.

    (ii) inform the captain of the fielding side of the reason for this action and as soon as practicable inform the captain of the batting side.

(e) The ball shall not count as one of the over.

(f) Runs completed by the batsmen before the offence shall be scored, together with any runs for penalties awarded to either side. Additionally, the run in progress shall be scored whether or not the batsmen had already crossed at the instant of the offence.

(g) The batsmen at the wicket shall decide which of them is to face the next delivery.

(h) The umpires together shall report the occurrence as soon as possible after the match to the executive of the fielding side and to any governing body responsible for the match, who shall take such action as is considered appropriate against the captain and player or players concerned.

6. Dangerous and unfair bowling

(a) Bowling of fast short pitched balls

    (i) The bowling of fast short pitched balls is dangerous and unfair if the bowler's end umpire considers that by their repetition and taking into account their length, height and direction they are likely to inflict physical injury on the striker irrespective of the protective equipment he may be wearing. The relative skill of the striker shall be taken into consideration.

    (ii) Any delivery which, after pitching, passes or would have passed over head height of the striker standing upright at the popping crease, although not threatening physical injury, shall be included with bowling under (i) above, both when the umpire is considering whether the bowling of fast short pitched balls has become dangerous and unfair and after he has so decided. The umpire shall call and signal "No-ball" for each such delivery.

(b) Bowling of high full pitched balls

    (i) Any delivery, other than a slow paced one, which passes or would have passed on the full above waist height of the striker standing upright at the popping crease is to be deemed dangerous and unfair, whether or not it is likely to inflict physical injury on the striker.

(ii) A slow delivery which passes or would have passed on the full above shoulder height of the striker standing upright at the popping crease is to be deemed dangerous and unfair, whether or not it is likely to inflict physical injury on the striker.

7. Dangerous and unfair bowling – action by the umpire

(a) As soon as the bowler's end umpire decides under 6(a) above that the bowling of fast short pitched balls has become dangerous and unfair, or, except as in 8 below, there is an instance of dangerous and unfair bowling as defined in 6(b) above, he shall call and signal "No-ball". When the ball is dead, he shall caution the bowler, inform the other umpire, the captain of the fielding side and the batsmen of what has occurred. This caution shall apply throughout the innings.

(b) If there is any further instance of dangerous and unfair bowling by the same bowler in that innings, the umpire shall repeat the above procedure and indicate to the bowler that this is a final warning. This warning shall also apply throughout the innings.

(c) Should there be any further repetition by the same bowler in that innings, the umpire shall call and signal "No-ball" and

(i) when the ball is dead direct the captain to suspend the bowler forthwith and inform the other umpire of the reason for this action. The bowler thus suspended shall not be allowed to bowl again in that innings.

If applicable, the over shall be completed by another bowler, who shall neither have bowled any part of the previous over, nor be allowed to bowl any part of the next over.

Additionally he shall

(ii) report the occurrence to the batsmen and, as soon as practicable, to the captain of the batting side.

(iii) together with the other umpire report the occurrence as soon as possible after the match to the executive of the fielding side and to any governing body responsible for the match, who shall take such action as is considered appropriate against the captain and bowler concerned.

8. Deliberate bowling of high full-pitched balls

If the umpire considers that a bowler deliberately bowled a high full-pitched ball, deemed to be dangerous and unfair as defined in 6(b) above, then the caution and warning prescribed in 7 above shall be dispensed with. The umpire shall

(a) (i) call and signal "No-ball".

(ii) when the ball is dead direct the captain of the fielding side to suspend the bowler forthwith. The bowler thus suspended shall not be allowed to bowl again in that innings.

If applicable, the over shall be completed by another bowler, who shall neither have bowled any part of the previous over, nor be allowed to bowl any part of the next over.

(iii) inform the other umpire of the reason for this action.

(b) report the occurrence to the batsmen and, as soon as practicable, to the captain of the batting side.

(c) together with the other umpire report the occurrence as soon as possible after the match to the executive of the fielding side and to any governing body responsible for the match, who shall take such action as is considered appropriate against the captain and bowler concerned.

9. Time-wasting by the fielding side

It is unfair for any fielder to waste time.

(a) If either umpire considers that the progress of an over is unnecessarily slow, or time is being wasted in any other way, by the captain of the fielding side or by any other fielder, at the first instance the umpire concerned shall

(i) if the ball is in play, call and signal "Dead-ball".

(ii) inform the other umpire of what has occurred.

(b) The bowler's end umpire shall then

    (i) warn the captain of the fielding side, indicating that this is a first and final warning.

    (ii) inform the batsmen of what has occurred.

(c) If either umpire considers that there is any further waste of time in that innings by any fielder, he shall

    (i) if the ball is in play, call and signal "Dead ball".

    (ii) inform the other umpire of what has occurred.

The bowler's end umpire shall

    (iii) either, if the waste of time is not during an over, award five penalty runs to the batting side and inform the captain of the fielding side of the reason for this action

    or,   if the waste of time is during the course of an over, direct the captain of the fielding side to suspend the bowler forthwith. The bowler thus suspended shall not be allowed to bowl again in that innings.

If applicable, the over shall be completed by another bowler, who shall neither have bowled any part of the previous over, nor be allowed to bowl any part of the next over.

    (iv) inform the batsmen and, as soon as is practicable, the captain of the batting side of what has occurred.

    (v) together with the other umpire report the occurrence as soon as possible after the match to the executive of the fielding side and to any governing body responsible for the match, who shall take such action as is considered appropriate against the captain and team concerned.

10. Batsman wasting time

It is unfair for a batsman to waste time. In normal circumstances, the striker should always be ready to take strike when the bowler is ready to start his run up.

(a) Should either batsman waste time by failing to meet this requirement, or in any other way, the following procedure shall be adopted. At the first instance, either before the bowler starts his run up or when the ball becomes dead, as appropriate, the umpire shall

    (i) warn both batsmen and indicate that this is a first and final warning. This warning shall apply throughout the innings. The umpire shall so inform each incoming batsman.

    (ii) inform the other umpire of what has occurred.

    (iii) inform the captain of the fielding side and, as soon as practicable, the captain of the batting side of what has occurred.

(b) If there is any further time wasting by any batsman in that innings, the umpire shall, at the appropriate time while the ball is dead

    (i) award five penalty runs to the fielding side.

    (ii) inform the other umpire of the reason for this action.

    (iii) inform the other batsman, the captain of the fielding side and, as soon as practicable, the captain of the batting side of what has occurred.

    (iv) together with the other umpire report the occurrence as soon as possible after the match to the executive of the batting side and to any governing body responsible for the match, who shall take such action as is considered appropriate against the captain and player or players and, if appropriate, team concerned.

11. Damaging the pitch – area to be protected

(a) It is incumbent on all players to avoid unnecessary damage to the pitch. A player will be deemed to be causing avoidable damage if either umpire considers that his presence on the pitch is without reasonable cause.

It is unfair to cause deliberate damage to the pitch.

(b) An area of the pitch, to be referred to as "the protected area", is defined as that area contained within a rectangle bounded at each end by imaginary lines parallel to the popping creases and 5ft/1.52m front of each, and on the sides by imaginary lines, one each side of the imaginary line joining the centres of the two middle stumps, each parallel to it and 1ft/30.48cm from it.

12. Bowler running on protected area after delivering the ball

(a) A bowler will contravene this Law if he runs on to the protected area, either after delivering the ball or, if he fails to release the ball, after the completion of his delivery swing and delivery stride. See 11 above, Law 23.4(viii) (Umpire calling and signalling "Dead ball") and Appendix D.

(b) If, as defined in (a) above, the bowler contravenes this Law, at the first instance and when the ball is dead, the umpire shall

(i) caution the bowler and inform the other umpire of what has occurred.

This caution shall apply throughout the innings.

(ii) inform the captain of the fielding side and the batsmen of what has occurred.

(c) If, in that innings, the same bowler again contravenes this Law, the umpire shall repeat the above procedure indicating that this is a final warning. This warning shall also apply throughout the innings.

(d) If in that innings the same bowler contravenes this Law a third time, the umpire shall,

(i) when the ball is dead, direct the captain of the fielding side to suspend the bowler forthwith.

The bowler thus suspended shall not be allowed to bowl again in that innings.
If applicable, the over shall be completed by another bowler, who shall neither have bowled any part of the previous over, nor be allowed to bowl any part of the next over.

(ii) inform the other umpire of the reason for this action.

(iii) inform the batsmen and, as soon as practicable, the captain of the batting side of what has occurred.

(iv) together with the other umpire report the occurrence as soon as possible after the match to the executive of the fielding side and to any governing body responsible for the match, who shall take such action as is considered appropriate against the captain and bowler concerned.

13. Fielder damaging the pitch

(a) If any fielder causes avoidable damage to the pitch, other than as in 12(a) above, at the first instance the umpire seeing the contravention shall, when the ball is dead, inform the other umpire. The bowler's end umpire shall then

(i) caution the captain of the fielding side and indicate that this is a first and final warning. This warning shall apply throughout the innings.

(ii) inform the batsmen of what has occurred.

(b) If, in that innings, there is any further instance of avoidable damage to the pitch, by any fielder, the umpire seeing the contravention shall, when the ball is dead, inform the other umpire. The bowler's end umpire shall then

(i) award five penalty runs to the batting side.

Additionally he shall

(ii) inform the fielding captain of the reason for this action.

(iii) inform the batsmen and, as soon as practicable, the captain of the batting side of what has occurred.

(iv) together with the other umpire report the occurrence as soon as possible after the match to the executive of the fielding side and to any governing body responsible for the match, who shall take such action as is considered appropriate against the captain and player or players concerned.

14. Batsman damaging the pitch

(a) If either batsman causes avoidable damage to the pitch, at the first instance the umpire seeing the contravention shall, when the ball is dead, inform the other umpire of the occurrence. The bowler's end umpire shall then

(i) warn both batsmen that the practice is unfair and indicate that this is a first and final warning. This warning shall apply throughout the innings. The umpire shall so inform each incoming batsman.

(ii) inform the captain of the fielding side and, as soon as practicable, the captain of the batting side of what has occurred.

(b) If there is any further instance of avoidable damage to the pitch by any batsman in that innings, the umpire seeing the contravention shall, when the ball is dead, inform the other umpire of the occurrence. The bowler's end umpire shall then

(i) disallow all runs to the batting side from that delivery other than the penalty for a No-ball or a Wide, if applicable.

(ii) additionally, award five penalty runs to the fielding side.

(iii) return the batsmen to their original ends.

(iv) inform the captain of the fielding side and, as soon as practicable, the captain of the batting side of what has occurred.

(c) The umpires together shall report the occurrence as soon as possible after the match to the executive of the batting side and to any governing body for the match who shall take such action as is considered appropriate against the captain and player or players concerned.

15. Bowler attempting to run out non-striker before delivery

The bowler is permitted, before entering his delivery stride, to attempt to run out the non-striker. Whether the attempt is successful or not, the ball shall not count as one of the over.

If the bowler fails in an attempt to run out the non-striker, the umpire shall call and signal "Dead ball" as soon possible.

16. Batsman stealing a run

It is unfair for the batsmen to attempt to steal a run during the bowler's run up. Unless the bowler attempts to run out either batsman – see 15 above and Law 24.4 (Bowler throwing towards striker's end before delivery) – the umpire shall

(i) call and signal "Dead ball" as soon as the batsmen cross in such an attempt.

(ii) inform the other umpire of the reason for this action.

(iii) return the batsmen to their original ends.

(iv) award five penalty runs to the fielding side.

(v) inform the batsmen, the captain of the fielding side and, as soon as practicable, the captain of the batting side, of the reason for this action.

(vi) together with the other umpire report the occurrence as soon as possible after the match to the executive of the batting side and to any governing body responsible for the match, who shall take such action as is considered appropriate against the captain and players concerned.

17. Penalty runs

(a) When penalty runs are awarded to either side, when the ball is dead the umpire shall signal the penalty runs to the scorers. See Law 3.14 (Signals).

(b) Notwithstanding the provisions, of Law 21.6 (Winning hit or extras), penalty runs shall be awarded in each case where the Laws require the award.

Note, however, that the restrictions on awarding penalty runs, in Laws 26.3 (Leg byes not to be awarded), 34.4 (Runs scored from ball lawfully struck more than once) and Law 41.6 (Penalty runs not to be awarded), will apply.

(c) When five penalty runs are awarded to the batting side under any of Laws 2.6 (Player returning without permission), 41.2 (Fielding the ball), or 41.3 (Protective helmets belonging to the fielding side) or under 3, 4, 5, 9 or 13 above, then

    (i) they shall be scored as penalty extras and shall be in addition to any other penalties.

    (ii) they are awarded when the ball is dead and shall not be regarded as runs scored from either the immediately preceding delivery or the immediately following delivery, and shall be in addition to any runs from those deliveries.

    (iii) the batsmen shall not change ends solely by reason of the five run penalty.

(d) When five penalty runs are awarded to the fielding side, under Law 18.5(b) (Deliberate short runs), or under 10, 14 or 16 above, they shall be added as penalty extras to that side's total of runs in its most recently completed innings. If the fielding side has not completed an innings, the five penalty runs shall be added to the score in its next innings.

18. Players' conduct

If there is any breach of the Spirit of the Game

    either in the case of an unfair action not covered by the Laws, under 2 above,

    or   by a player

        either failing to comply with the instructions of an umpire

        or   criticising an umpire's decisions by word or action

        or   showing dissent

        or   generally behaving in a manner which might bring the game into disrepute,

the umpire concerned shall immediately report the matter to the other umpire.
The umpires together shall

    (i) inform the player's captain of the occurrence, instructing the latter to take action.

    (ii) warn him of the gravity of the offence, and tell him it will be reported to higher authority.

    (iii) report the occurrence as soon as possible after the match to the Executive of the player's team and to any Governing Body responsible for the match, who shall take such action as is considered appropriate against the captain and player or players and, if appropriate, team concerned.

Appendices A–D can be found at www.lords.org/laws-and-spirit/laws-of-cricket/laws

APPENDIX E – THE BAT: LAW 6

All Law references are to sections of Law 6

Categories of bat – Types A, B and C are bats conforming to Law 6, sections 1 to 8 inclusive. Bats which do not qualify for any of the three categories are not recognised in the Laws. Type A bats may be used at any level. Bats of Type B or Type C and any other bats may be used only at or below levels determined by the Governing Body for cricket in the country concerned.

The blade – The face of the blade is its main striking surface. The back is the opposite surface.

The shoulders, sides and toe are the remaining surfaces, separating the face and the back. The shoulders, one on each side of the handle, are along that portion of the blade between the first entry point of the handle and the point at which the blade first reaches its full width.

The toe is the surface opposite to the shoulders taken as a pair.

The sides, one each side of the blade, are along the rest of the blade, between the toe and the shoulders.

Adhesives – Throughout, adhesives are permitted only where essential and only in minimal quantity.

Materials in handle – As a proportion of the total volume of the handle, materials other than cane, wood or twine are restricted to one-tenth for Types A and B and one-fifth for Type C. Such materials must not project more than 3.25in/8.26cm into the lower portion of the handle.

Binding and covering of handle – The permitted continuation beyond the junction of the upper and lower portions of the handle is restricted to a maximum, measured along the length of the handle, of

2.5in/6.35cm for the twine binding
2.75in/6.99cm for the covering grip.

Length and width

(a) The overall length of the bat, when the lower portion of the handle is inserted, shall not be more than 38in/96.5cm.

(b) The width of the bat shall not exceed 4.25in/10.8cm at its widest part.

(c) Permitted coverings, repair material and toe guards, not exceeding their specified thicknesses, may be additional to the dimensions above.

Length of handle – Except for bats of size 6 and less, the handle shall not exceed 52% of the overall length of the bat.

Covering of blade – The cloth covering permitted for Type C bats shall be of thickness not exceeding 0.012in/0.3mm before treatment as in 6.6(d).

Protection and repair of blade – The material permitted in 6.6(a) shall not exceed 0.04in/1mm in thickness. In 6.6(a)(ii), the repair material shall not extend along the length of the blade more than 0.79in/2cm in each direction beyond the limits of the damaged area. Where used as a continuous binding, any overlapping shall not breach the maximum of 0.04in/1mm in total thickness.

In 6.6(d), the use of non-solid material which when dry forms a hard layer more than 0.004in/0.1mm in thickness is not permitted.

Toe and side inserts – The wood used must not be more than 0.3in/0.89cm in thickness.
The toe insert shall not extend from the toe more than 2.5in/6.35cm up the blade at any point.
Neither side insert may extend from the edge more than 1in/2.54cm across the blade at any point.

Toe protection – The maximum permitted thickness of protective material placed on the toe of the blade is 0.12in/3mm.

Commercial identifications – These identifications may not exceed 0.008in/0.2mm in thickness. On the back of the blade they must occupy no more than 50% of the surface. On the face of the blade, they must be confined within the top 9in/22.86cm, measured from the bottom of the grip.

REGULATIONS OF THE INTERNATIONAL CRICKET COUNCIL

Extracts

1. Classification of Official Cricket

A. Test matches

Test matches are those which:

    (a) are played in accordance with the ICC standard Test match playing conditions and other ICC regulations pertaining to Test matches; and

    (b) are between

        (i) teams selected by Full Members of the ICC as representative of the member countries (Full Member teams).

        (ii) a Full Member team and a composite team selected by the ICC as representative of the best players from the rest of the world.

B. One-day internationals

One-day international matches are those which:

    (a) are played in accordance with the ICC standard one-day international playing conditions and other ICC regulations pertaining to one-day internationals; and

    (b) are between

        (i) any teams participating in and as part of the World Cup or Champions Trophy.

        (ii) Full Member teams.

        (iii) a Full Member team and any of the top six Associate/Affiliates.

        (iv) any of the top six Associate/Affiliates.

        (v) a Full Member team (or top six Associate/Affiliate) and a composite team selected by the ICC as representative of the best players from the rest of the world.

Note: The identity of the top six Associate/Affiliate teams will be determined through the World Cup Qualifier tournament. The ICC will determine the precise point during the tournament at which the new top six shall take effect.

C. Twenty20 international matches

Twenty20 international matches are those which:

    (a) are played in accordance with the ICC standard Twenty20 international playing conditions and other ICC regulations pertaining to Twenty20 matches; and

    (b) are between

        (i) any teams participating in and as part of the World Twenty20 Championship.

        (ii) Full Member teams.

        (iii) a Full Member team and any of the Associate/Affiliate Member teams whose matches have been granted one-day international status (i.e. the top six Associates/ Affiliates).

        (iv) any of the top six Associates/Affiliates.

D. Other Official Internationals

Any limited-overs match between Associate/Affiliate international teams other than those already classified as one-day/Twenty20 internationals, if played as part of a global or regional ICC event or competition, or agreed with and under the auspices of the ICC Development Programme/High Performance Programme.

E. First-class matches

First-class matches are those matches of three or more days' duration between two sides of 11 players played on natural turf pitches and substantially conforming to ICC standard playing conditions.

Full Members may, if they wish, introduce playing regulations allowing the 11 playing members of a side to be changed after the start of a match without the match forgoing its first-class status, provided any such changes relate solely to a player's call-up to or release from international duty. No playing members of a side in a first-class match may be replaced for reasons of tactics or injury.

Rules

(a) The status of all matches in an official ICC competition shall be decided by the ICC. For matches outside official ICC competitions (b) and (c) shall apply.

(b) Full Members of the ICC shall decide the status of matches of three or more days' duration played in their countries.

(c) in matches of three or more days' duration played in countries which are not Full Members of the ICC

(i) if only one team comes from a Full Member country or both teams come from the same Full Member country then that country shall decide the status; otherwise

(ii) if both teams come from different Full Member countries then the status shall be decided by agreement between those countries if possible; otherwise

(iii) the ICC shall decide.

Notes: Governing bodies agree that the interest of first-class cricket will be served by ensuring that first-class status is not accorded to any match in which one or other of the teams taking part cannot on a strict interpretation of the definitions be adjudged first-class.

Decisions regarding awarding a match first-class status should whenever possible be taken prior to its commencement, failing which as soon as possible thereafter. Where a decision regarding first-class status has already been made, including in respect of all matches played prior to these classifications taking effect, any subsequent reversal of a decision (i.e. to upgrade a match to first-class status or downgrade it from first-class status) shall be permitted only in exceptional circumstances, and then only with the approval of the ICC.

First-Class Status

The following matches of three or more days' duration shall be regarded as first-class, subject to the provisions of the first-class match definition being complied with. The list below is not exhaustive and is merely indicative of the matches which would fall into the first-class definition.

(a) Test matches.

(b) ICC Intercontinental Cup matches.

(c) Matches played by A-teams of Full Member countries against teams and judged first-class (including other A-teams).

(d) **In all Full Member Countries:** Matches against teams adjudged first-class played by official touring teams.

(e) **In England and Wales:** (i) County Championship matches between counties; (ii) MCC v any first-class county; (iii) Oxford University v Cambridge University; (iv) Cambridge, Durham, Loughborough and Oxford MCCUs v any first-class county.

(f) **In Australia:** Sheffield Shield matches between states.

(g) **In South Africa:** (i) SuperSport Series matches between franchises; (ii) Provincial three-day competition matches between provinces.

(h) **In West Indies:** Regional four-day competition matches between countries and Combined Campuses & Colleges.

(i) **In New Zealand:** Plunket Shield matches between provinces.

(j) **In India:** (i) Ranji Trophy matches between states; (ii) Duleep Trophy matches between zones; (iii) Irani Trophy match (winner of previous Ranji Trophy against Rest of India).

(k) **In Pakistan:** (i) Quaid-e-Azam Trophy (Grade I) matches between regions and departments; (ii) Pentangular Cup matches between leading teams from the other first-class tournaments.

(l) **In Sri Lanka:** (i) Premier League Division I matches between clubs; (ii) Interprovincial Tournament matches between provinces.

(m) **In Zimbabwe:** Logan Cup matches between areas.

(n) **In Bangladesh:** National Cricket League matches between divisions.

F. List A limited-overs matches

Any one-day international or limited-overs match scheduled for one day's duration and of one innings of a minimum 40 overs per side, played at least at state, county or provincial level in a Full Member country or as an official match of a touring Test team against at least state, county or provincial level teams and accorded List A limited-overs status by the relevant governing bodies. A match will still be regarded as List A limited-overs even if reduced by bad weather or for other reasons to fewer than 40 overs per side.

G. List A Twenty20 matches

Any Twenty20 international or limited-overs match scheduled for one day's duration and of one innings with a limit of 20 overs per side played at least at state, county or provincial level in a Full Member country or as an official match of a touring Test team against at least state, county or provincial level teams and accorded List A Twenty20 status by the relevant governing bodies.

Rules: The rules on who should decide the status of matches of one day's duration are the same as those for first-class matches (above).

Note: List A matches should be those one-day matches played at the highest domestic level. Matches that are primarily arranged as festival, friendly or practice matches and outside of any competitive structure should not qualify as List A matches.

H. Other matches

Other cricket played under the auspices of a Member country may be classified by such Member country as Official Cricket, including but not limited to:

(a) matches between the A-teams, National Academy or age-group teams of member countries.

(b) all other matches played as part of a competition or tournament held under the auspices of a member including club cricket, schools, age groups and university cricket.

(c) Matches between Members not covered in the above regulations on Tests, one-day/Twenty20/other official internationals (these matches are not subject to ICC officials' arrangements, qualification rules and/or the ICC Code of Conduct and playing conditions).

(d) Any senior or junior national teams playing in matches as prescribed in (c) above shall be known as, and affixed with, an "XI", "A-team", "Representative Side" or similar title.

Notes: Matches involving an A-team or age-group team shall not be classified as Tests, one-day internationals or Twenty20 internationals. Matches involving age-group teams up to and including Under-19 shall not be classified as first-class cricket.

In case of any disputes arising from these Rules, failing unanimous agreement being reached between the disputing parties, the chief executive of the ICC shall refer the matter to the ICC disputes resolution committee for its final and binding determination.

2. Player eligibility qualification criteria

A. Core qualification criteria

A player shall be qualified to play for a country where he satisfies at least one of the following:

(a) Born in the country.

(b) A national of the country (demonstrated by possession of a valid passport).

(c) Resident in the country for at least 183 days in each of the preceding seven years

(d) Resident in the country for at least 183 days in each of the preceding four years (some restrictions for Associates and Affiliates detailed below).

B. Additional development criteria for Associate/Affiliate Members

Where a player is seeking to qualify for an Associate or Affiliate Member, he must also satisfy at least one of the following criteria:

(a) He has played a minimum of 50% of of the domestic league matches his club team were scheduled to play in any three of the five preceding years.

(b) He has spent a cumulative total of at least 100 days doing cricket work in the country in the immediately preceding five years.

(c) He has previously represented that country at Under-19 level or above after satisfying ICC development criteria or similar requirements under previous eligibility regulations.

C. Representing more than one country

Nothing shall prohibit a player from representing more than one country during his career. However

(a) Where a player is seeking to qualify for a Full Member of the ICC, he must not have played an international match for any other Full Member during the immediately preceding four years.

(b) Where a player is seeking to qualify for an Associate or Affiliate Member, he must not have played an international match for any other country (irrespective of its membership status) during the immediately preceding four years.

(c) No player shall be entitled to seek to qualify for a different country more than once, unless the second qualification is for the same country for which he originally played.

Note: No restrictions shall apply to any player seeking to qualify to play for a Full Member where he has previously played an international match for an Associate or Affiliate Member.

D. Selection restrictions for Affiliate/Associate Members

(a) Except as described in (b) below,

    (i) Associate and Affiliate Members may not select more than two players in any team who qualify under A(d).

    (ii) Associates and Affiliates may not select more than two players in any team who have formerly represented a Full Member at Under-19 level or above.

(b) For Associate and Affiliate members, when playing a Full Member or in a tournament involving Full Member(s), or when playing any one-day international, or when playing in the World Cup Qualifier, the selection restrictions in (a) above and the additional development criteria in Section B do not apply.

E. Further note

The ICC's Exceptional Circumstances Committee may recommend that an exemption be granted (by the ICC's cricket committee chairman) from full compliance with any of the core qualification criteria and/or additional development criteria upon consideration of an application that exceptional circumstances exist to justify such exemption.

ICC CODES OF CONDUCT

The ICC Code of Conduct, first introduced in 1991, was divided into three Codes in 2009. These are the Code of Conduct, the Anti-Corruption Code, and the Anti-Racism Code. There is also an Anti-Doping Code. Full details of their scope and application, offences under the Codes, disciplinary procedures, sanctions and appeals may be found on the ICC website at http://icc-cricket.yahoo.net/rules_and_regulations.php.

CRIME AND PUNISHMENT

ICC Code of Conduct – Breaches and Penalties in 2009-10 to 2010-11

Harbhajan Singh   India v Bangladesh, Second Test at Mirpur.
Kicked advertising board after misfield. Reprimanded by A. J. Pycroft.

M. G. Johnson   Australia v New Zealand, First One-Day International at Napier.
Deliberate and inappropriate physical contact with opponent. Fined 60% of match fee by R. S. Madugalle.

S. B. Styris   New Zealand v Australia, First One-Day International at Napier.
Verbal exchange with opponent. Fined 15% of match fee by R. S. Madugalle.

J. D. Siddons (coach)   Bangladesh v England, Second Test at Mirpur.
Dissent when umpires turned down Bangladesh appeals. Fined 10% of match fee by J. J. Crowe.

R. G. Sharma   India v West Indies, World Twenty20 international at Bridgetown.
Dissent at umpire's decision when given out. Fined 15% of match fee by J. J. Crowe.

B. J. Haddin   Australia v England, World Twenty20 final at Bridgetown.
Dissent at umpire's decision when given out. Fined 10% of match fee by R. S. Madugalle.

K. A. Pollard   West Indies v South Africa, Second One-Day International at North Sound.
Impeded the bowler as he ran towards non-striker's end. Fined 25% of match fee by R. S. Mahanama.

D. W. Steyn   South Africa v West Indies, Third Test at Bridgetown.
Spat at opponent after being dismissed. Fined 100% of match fee by J. J. Crowe.

K. A. J. Roach   West Indies v South Africa, Third Test at Bridgetown.
Altercation with batsman after hitting him on helmet with bouncer. Fined 50% of match fee by J. J. Crowe.

S. J. Benn   West Indies v South Africa, Third Test at Bridgetown.
Entered South African dressing-room to argue with opponents. Banned for one Test by J. J. Crowe.

S. C. J. Broad   England v Pakistan, Second Test at Birmingham.
Threw ball at batsman. Fined 50% of match fee by R. S. Madugalle.

V. Kohli   India v New Zealand, Tri-Series one-day international at Dambulla.
Dissent at umpire's decision when given out. Fined 15% of match fee by A. G. Hurst.

M. Vijay   India v Australia, Second Test at Bangalore.
Displayed too many logos on his batting pads. Officially reprimanded by B. C. Broad.

R. T. Ponting   Australia v England, Fourth Test at Melbourne.
Argued with umpires when batsman given not out. Fined 40% of match fee by R. S. Madugalle.

S. Sreesanth   India v South Africa, Third Test at Cape Town.
Kicked the boundary rope after two lbw appeals turned down. Fined 10% of match fee by A. J. Pycroft.

M. S. Dhoni   India v South Africa, Third Test at Cape Town.
Failed to ensure team met minimum over-rate. Fined 60% of match fee by A. J. Pycroft.

Note: Details of these and seven further breaches which took place in Associate Member matches may be found on the ICC website (www.icc-cricket.com).

INTERNATIONAL UMPIRES' PANELS

In 1993, the International Cricket Council formed an international umpires' panel, containing at least two officials from each Full Member. A third-country umpire from this panel stood with a "home" umpire, not necessarily from the panel, in every Test from February 1994 onwards. In March 2002, an elite panel of umpires was appointed; two elite umpires were to stand in all Tests from April 2002, and at least one in every one-day international. A supporting panel of international umpires was created to provide cover at peak times in the Test schedule, and to provide a second umpire in one-day internationals. The ICC also appointed specialist third umpires to give rulings from TV replays. The panels are sponsored by Emirates Airlines.

At the end of 2010, the following umpires were on the elite panel: Aleem Dar (Pakistan), Asad Rauf (Pakistan), B. F. Bowden (New Zealand), S. J. Davis (Australia), E. A. R. de Silva (Sri Lanka), B. R. Doctrove (West Indies), M. Erasmus (South Africa), I. J. Gould (England), D. J. Harper (Australia), A. L. Hill (New Zealand), S. J. A. Taufel (Australia) and R. J. Tucker (Australia).

The international panel consisted of G. A. V. Baxter (New Zealand), O. Chirombe (Zimbabwe), J. D. Cloete (South Africa), H. D. P. K. Dharmasena (Sri Lanka), C. R. Duncan (West Indies), Enamul Haque (Bangladesh), C. B. Gaffaney (New Zealand), B. G. Jerling (South Africa), R. A. Kettleborough (England), N. J. Llong (England), N. A. Malcolm (West Indies), R. Martinesz (Sri Lanka), Nadeem Ghauri (Pakistan), Nadir Shah (Bangladesh), B. N. J. Oxenford (Australia), P. R. Reiffel (Australia), A. M. Saheba (India), S. K. Tarapore (India), R. B. Tiffin (Zimbabwe) and Zamir Haider (Pakistan).

The specialist third umpires were Ahsan Raza (Pakistan), S. Asnani (India), B. G. Frost (New Zealand), S. D. Fry (Australia), S. George (South Africa), G. E. Greaves (West Indies), S. S. Hazare (India), R. K. Illingworth (England), C. E. Mack (West Indies), Sharfuddoula (Bangladesh) and T. H. Wijewardene (Sri Lanka).

There is also an Associate and Affiliate international panel, consisting of N. G. Bagh (Denmark), R. Dill (Bermuda), M. Hawthorne (Ireland), J. J. Luck (Namibia), B. B. Pradhan (Nepal), S. S. Prasad (Singapore), I. N. Ramage (Scotland), Shahul Hameed (Indonesia), R. P. Smith (Cyprus), T. G. van Schalkwyk (Namibia) and C. Young (Cayman Islands).

ICC REFEREES' PANEL

In 1991, the International Cricket Council formed a panel of referees to enforce their Code of Conduct for Tests and one-day internationals, to impose penalties for slow over-rates, breaches of the Code and other ICC regulations, and to support the umpires in upholding the conduct of the game. In March 2002, the ICC launched an elite panel of referees, on full-time contracts, to act as their independent representatives in all international cricket.

At the end of 2010, the panel consisted of B. C. Broad (England), J. J. Crowe (New Zealand), A. G. Hurst (Australia), R. S. Madugalle (Sri Lanka), R. S. Mahanama (Sri Lanka), A. J. Pycroft (Zimbabwe) and J. Srinath (India). The panel is sponsored by Emirates Airlines.

ENGLISH UMPIRES FOR 2011

First-Class: R. J. Bailey, N. L. Bainton, M. R. Benson, M. J. D. Bodenham, N. G. B. Cook, N. G. Cowley, J. H. Evans, S. C. Gale, S. A. Garratt, M. A. Gough, I. J. Gould, P. J. Hartley, R. K. Illingworth, T. E. Jesty, R. A. Kettleborough, N. J. Llong, J. W. Lloyds, N. A. Mallender, D. J. Millns, S. J. O'Shaughnessy, R. T. Robinson, G. Sharp, J. F. Steele, P. Willey. *Reserves:* P. K. Baldwin, I. Dawood, M. A. Eggleston, R. Evans, A. Hicks, G. D. Lloyd, S. J. Malone, M. J. Saggers, B. V. Taylor, A. G. Wharf .

Minor Counties: J. Attridge, P. K. Baldwin, S. F. Bishopp, M. L. Brown, A. Bullock, G. I. Callaway, A. Clark, K. T. Coburn, T. Cox, A. Davies, B. J. Debenham, M. Dixon, A. D'Leny, M. Dobbs, R. G. Eagleton, M. A. Eggleston, H. Evans, R. Evans, P. Gardner, D. J. Gower, M. D. Gumbley, A. Hicks, M. J. Izzard, J. H. James, R. N. Johnson, C. D. Jones, P. W. Joy, D. M. Koch, S. J. Malone, P. W. Matten, S. Nelson, R. J. Newham, G. Parker, C. T. Puckett, D. Pyke, J. G. Reed, B. W. Reidy, I. Royle, P. A. Sadler, M. I. Southerton, R. M. Sutton, R. W. Tolchard, B. S. Toombs, T. J. Urben, S. Waterhouse, C. Watts, M. C. White, J. Wilkinson.

THE DUCKWORTH/LEWIS METHOD

In 1997, the ECB's one-day competitions adopted a new method to revise targets in interrupted games, devised by Frank Duckworth of the Royal Statistical Society and Tony Lewis of the University of the West of England. The method was gradually taken up by other countries and, in 1999, the ICC decided to incorporate it into the standard playing conditions for one-day internationals.

The system aims to preserve any advantage that one team has established before the interruption. It uses the idea that teams have two resources from which they make runs – an allocated number of overs, and ten wickets. It also takes into account when the interruption occurs, because of the different scoring-rates typical of different stages of an innings. Traditional run-rate calculations relied only on the overs available, and ignored wickets lost.

After modifications, the system now uses one table with 50 rows, covering matches of any length up to 50 overs, and ten columns, from nought to nine wickets down. Each figure in the table gives the percentage of the total runs in an innings that would, on average, be scored with a certain number of overs left and wickets lost. If a match is shortened before it begins, for instance to 33 overs a side, the figure for 33 overs and ten wickets remaining would be the starting point. The same table is used for Twenty20 cricket, starting with the row for 20 overs remaining.

If overs are lost, the table is used to calculate the percentage of runs the team would be expected to score in those missing overs. This is obtained by reading off the figure for the number of overs left and wickets down when play stops and subtracting from it the corresponding figure for the number of overs remaining when it resumes. If the suspension of play occurs between innings, and the second team's allocation of overs is reduced, then their target is obtained by calculating the appropriate percentage for the reduced number of overs with all ten wickets standing. For instance, if the second team's innings halves from 50 overs to 25, the table shows that they still have 66.5% of their resources left, so have to beat two-thirds of the first team's total, rather than half.

If the first innings is complete and the second innings is interrupted or prematurely terminated, the score to be beaten is reduced by the percentage of the innings lost. In the World Cup match between South Africa and Sri Lanka at Durban on March 3, 2003, South Africa's run-chase was ended by rain after 45 overs, when they were 229 for six. The Duckworth/Lewis tables showed that, with five overs left and four wickets standing, South Africa had used 85.7% of their run-scoring resources, and 14.3% remained unused. Multiplying Sri Lanka's 50-over total, 268, by 85.7% produced a figure of 229.67. This was rounded down to 229 to give the par score (the runs needed to tie), and the target to win became par plus one – 230 in 45 overs. Under old-fashioned average run-rate per over, the target would have been 242; South Africa benefited because they had preserved wickets into the final stages. (If they had lost one more wicket, par would have been 233; two fewer, 226.)

The system also covers interruptions to the first innings, multiple interruptions and innings terminated by rain. The tables were revised slightly in 2002, taking account of rising scoring-rates; the average 50-over total in a one-day international is now taken to be 235, rather than 225.

The version known as the "Professional Edition" was introduced into one-day internationals from October 1, 2003, and subsequently into several national one-day competitions. Based on a more advanced mathematical formula (it is entirely computerised), in effect it adjusts the tables to make allowance for the different scoring-rates that emerge in matches with above-average first-innings scores. The former version, now known as "Standard Edition", has been retained for use where computers are not available and at lower levels of the game.

POWERPLAYS

In the first ten "powerplay" overs of an uninterrupted one-day international innings (first six overs in a Twenty20 international), only two fieldsmen may be positioned outside the area marked by two semi-circles of 30-yard (27.43 metres) radius behind each set of stumps, joined by straight lines parallel to the pitch. In one-day internationals, there must also be two "close" (and stationary) fielders in this initial period.

After the first mandatory ten-over powerplay in an uninterrupted one-day international, two further blocks of five overs each must be claimed by the respective captains (or the batsmen at the crease in the case of the batting side). During these overs, a maximum of three players may be stationed outside the 30-yard area. If either team chooses not to take the powerplay available to them, the umpires will enforce it at the latest available point in the innings (so, in an uninterrupted innings, an unclaimed powerplay would begin at the start of the 46th over).

At all other times no more than five fieldsmen are permitted outside the 30-yard area. In matches affected by the weather, the number of overs in each powerplay is reduced in proportion to the overall reduction of overs.

MEETINGS AND DECISIONS, 2010

ICC EXECUTIVE BOARD

The ICC Executive Board met in Dubai on February 10–11. They agreed to conduct research into other sports and entertainment, and in particular to investigate floodlit Test cricket, to help a working party provide greater context to Tests, one-day and Twenty20 internationals outside the major ICC events.

A review of categories of ICC membership was approved in advance of Cricket Ireland's planned application for Full Membership.

David Richardson, the ICC general manager for cricket, reported that in 13 recent Tests which used the Decision Review System the number of correct decisions had increased from 91.3% to 97.44%. Further technological improvements were to be discussed with broadcasters.

The board unanimously accepted the recommendations of a security task force set up after the Lahore attack in March 2009; every Full Member was to appoint a full-time security manager, and introduce minimum standards and best-practice guidelines for safety and security.

There were progress reports from the World Twenty20 tournament, to be held in the West Indies in May, and the World Cup, in the subcontinent in early 2011. Offers to host the 2013 Champions Trophy were invited. The ANZ Stadium in Sydney was approved as an international venue. The board considered relocating from Dubai to Lord's, but were not ready to make a decision.

The board congratulated those involved in the ICC Centenary celebrations and praised the legacy projects, particularly the Cricket Hall of Fame, and the Think Wise initiative raising awareness of AIDS.

ECB SPONSORSHIP DEAL

The ECB announced on February 15 that Clydesdale Bank had signed a three-year deal to sponsor the new domestic 40-over competition for the 18 first-class counties, Scotland, the Netherlands and an ECB Recreational XI, later renamed the Unicorns. The tournament would be known as the Clydesdale Bank 40, and most matches would take place on Sunday afternoons.

ICC CHIEF EXECUTIVES' COMMITTEE

The ICC Chief Executives' Committee met in Dubai on March 9–10 and were updated on developing a context for international cricket and the commercial impact of the proposed Future Tours Programme 2012–2020, and on the implementation of the Decision Review System in 14 Tests over the past four months. Afterwards, members of the committee, key broadcasters, leading technology suppliers, umpire representatives and staff held a two-day DRS workshop, covering protocols for broadcasters and umpires, playing conditions, the preferred technology, the cost of providing equipment at all Tests, and whether it should be used in the 2011 World Cup.

ICC EXECUTIVE BOARD

At an ICC Executive Board meeting in Dubai on April 19–20, Lord Condon, chairman of the Anti-Corruption and Security Unit, reported that all recommendations on safety and security made after the Lahore attack in 2009 had been accepted; all Full Members had appointed security directors and the ICC had appointed a full-time security manager, Sean

Carroll from Australia. The only recommendation still to be implemented was a series of mandatory security standards for international cricket, to be presented to the board in June.

The board endorsed contingency plans to ensure that all players, officials and television crews could reach the Caribbean for the World Twenty20 by the end of April, despite disruption to air travel in Europe caused by a volcanic eruption in Iceland (which forced ECB representatives David Morgan and Giles Clarke to take part in this meeting by teleconference).

It was agreed that prize money for the World Cup in 2011 should be set at a record \$US10m to reflect the importance of the ICC's flagship competition.

Following Cricket Canada's decision to withdraw as hosts of the Under-19 World Cup in 2012, the ICC invited proposals from other members.

ICC president David Morgan said he and chief executive Haroon Lorgat would visit Zimbabwe in June to investigate the implementation of the Zimbabwe Task Team's 35 recommendations, and to discuss progress in reconstructing domestic cricket and prospects for Zimbabwe's return to Test cricket within the next two years. The board reiterated their desire for Pakistan to continue playing, albeit at away or neutral venues because of security concerns, and noted the importance of resuming fixtures between Pakistan and India as soon as possible.

ENGLAND PERFORMANCE SQUAD

On April 20, the ECB announced a 27-man England Performance Squad for the summer. The England coach would have the right to withdraw any of these players from domestic cricket. The squad consisted of 11 players already on 12-month ECB contracts running from October 2009: England captain Andrew Strauss, James Anderson, Ian Bell, Stuart Broad, Paul Collingwood, Alastair Cook, Graham Onions, Kevin Pietersen, Matt Prior, Ryan Sidebottom and Graeme Swann; seven on increment contracts: Ravi Bopara, Tim Bresnan, Eoin Morgan, Adil Rashid, Owais Shah, Jonathan Trott and Luke Wright; and nine others: Michael Carberry, Joe Denly, Steven Finn, Craig Kieswetter, Michael Lumb, Liam Plunkett, Ajmal Shahzad, James Tredwell and Michael Yardy. All except Lumb had already appeared for England.

ECB BOARD AGM

On April 22, the ECB's AGM decided that the ECB Board would expand from 12 members to 14, with the addition of a representative of women's cricket and an extra independent representative.

The AGM acknowledged the issue facing the nine "Category A" grounds – The Oval, Edgbaston, Headingley, Lord's, Old Trafford, Riverside, The Rose Bowl, the Swalec Stadium and Trent Bridge – who were concerned about the long-term viability of the current Test venues. The grounds had invested substantial capital in developing their stadiums, and suffered financial pressure through the current bidding process for major matches; they were anxious for an acceptable return on their investment. A working party drawn from chief executives of Category A counties had been set up as part of a strategic review into the changing cricket landscape, and would deliver recommendations to the ECB. Chairman Giles Clarke said the ECB would support these venues in ensuring long-term financial viability.

ICC ANTI-CORRUPTION AND SECURITY UNIT CHAIRMAN

On May 4, the ICC announced that Sir Ronnie Flanagan, the former Home Office Chief Inspector of Constabulary who was previously chief constable of the Northern Ireland police, would become chairman of the ICC Anti-Corruption and Security Unit in June, when Lord Condon retired after ten years in the role.

MCC ANNUAL GENERAL MEETING

The 223rd AGM of the Marylebone Cricket Club was held at Lord's on May 5, with the president, John Barclay, in the chair. He announced that his successor, from October, would be Christopher Martin-Jenkins, the writer and broadcaster. Resolutions were passed increasing members' entrance fees and annual subscriptions and amending various rules of the club. Membership of the club on December 31, 2009, totalled 22,465, made up of 17,926 full members, 3,998 associate members, 315 honorary members, 151 senior members and 75 out-match members. There were 9,898 candidates awaiting election to Full membership; in 2009, 467 vacancies arose.

The meeting also approved several changes to the Laws of Cricket, including umpires no longer "offering the light" to batsmen; at least one umpire being present at the toss; a limit on bowlers practising deliveries on the field to warm up; the boundary catch ruling; the bowler's front-foot ruling; and penalties for batsmen damaging the pitch. MCC members agreed to cede authority on passing new Laws to the MCC Laws subcommittee and the main committee.

ICC DEVELOPMENT COMMITTEE

The ICC Development Committee met in Jakarta on June 10 and decided to expand the tournament for Associate and Affiliate Members seeking to qualify for the 2012 World Twenty20 in Sri Lanka to include 16 teams – the six currently enjoying one-day/Twenty20 international status plus ten qualifiers from regional Twenty20 events. The committee also pledged $US2m towards major cricket facilities developments in the six top-ranked Associates/Affiliates, China, the USA and a member nominated by each of the Africa, East Asia-Pacific and Europe regions, plus any Associate or Affiliate scheduled to host certain ICC events.

ICC ANNUAL MEETINGS

The ICC annual conference took place in Singapore on June 27–July 1.

Sharad Pawar succeeded David Morgan as ICC president on the final day. But the Executive Board decided there was insufficient support for the nomination of former Australian prime minister John Howard as vice-president, made by Cricket Australia and New Zealand Cricket under the regional rotation process. The two countries were asked to nominate a new candidate by August 31.

The board approved 13 recommendations on the use of the Decision Review System in Tests and the World Cup. It was agreed that the host country would determine whether to use the DRS in home Test series (after consulting the visiting country). It would be used in the 2011 World Cup if agreement could be reached with broadcaster ESPN Star Sports and the host countries (Bangladesh, India and Sri Lanka), and if there was sufficient technology available to operate it in a global event. Preliminary findings of an investigation into DRS problems in the Johannesburg Test between South Africa and England in January 2010 cleared third umpire Daryl Harper on the grounds that a technical failure had adversely affected the information he received while making his decision.

The Chief Executives' Committee and Governance Review Committee considered the playing structure for international cricket and its implications for ICC membership. This included a discussion on the events programme post-2015; the frequency and format of global events, and qualification for those events; and the introduction of Test and one-day international leagues.

The Champions Trophy 2013 was awarded to the England and Wales Cricket Board. The Seychelles Cricket Association became the 105th member of the ICC, as an Affiliate.

On July 16, in a follow-up to the annual meeting, the ICC agreed a set of "whereabouts" rules to support out-of-competition drug testing under their Anti-Doping Code, to come into effect on August 1. Earlier there had been concerns that the need to file information on their whereabouts might infringe players' privacy. The rules established an international registered testing pool of players who would be required to submit information on their whereabouts, as well as a national player pool, for whom other "cricket whereabouts" information would be provided.

MCC WORLD CRICKET COMMITTEE

The MCC World Cricket Committee met at Lord's on July 1–2. After a presentation from former Zimbabwean captain Andy Flower, the committee recommended a fact-finding mission to Zimbabwe to gauge its suitability as a touring venue in 2011.

They expressed their belief that it was time to play day/night Test cricket, with a pink ball, in countries where Test attendances had dropped markedly. This followed the successful trial of pink balls at the MCC v Champion County match in Abu Dhabi in March. They argued that Test cricketers should still wear white clothing, to maintain the game's traditions and to keep it distinct from limited-overs formats. The committee also called for the introduction of a World Test Championship, to provide a wider context for each Test series; Test pitches offering a fair balance between bat and ball; financial rewards to ensure Test cricket was an attractive proposition for players; and investment in marketing Test cricket to improve crowd and television audiences. Research into televised cricket viewing patterns in India indicated that only 11% of all cricket watched in India was Test cricket, down from 33% in 2004.

After work with scientists and manufacturers to develop durable coloured cricket balls, the committee concluded that these balls were ready for use in domestic and international cricket. They said a pink ball could remove the need for a mandatory ball-change after 34 overs of a 50-over match, thus bringing back the skill of reverse swing bowling at the end of an innings.

After three years of the IPL, Rahul Dravid described how the IPL franchises had learned to maximise their brand and reach new markets. He was concerned, however, that parents of talented children were asking coaches to teach them Twenty20 skills only, in the hope of securing an IPL contract; he felt that the best IPL cricketers were those with the skills to play all forms of the game. The committee believed the IPL had been a great success in capturing the public imagination, but were concerned about the proliferation of fixtures in the IPL and other Twenty20 tournaments at the expense of longer forms.

ICC VICE-PRESIDENT

On August 9, the ICC endorsed the nomination of Alan Isaac to serve as ICC vice-president until 2012, when he would succeed Sharad Pawar as president. Isaac was put forward by Cricket Australia and New Zealand Cricket after their earlier nomination of John Howard did not receive support. A businessman and corporate governance practitioner, Isaac stepped down as New Zealand Cricket's chairman after two years in the post.

ICC CHIEF EXECUTIVES' COMMITTEE

The Chief Executives' Committee met in Cape Town on September 13–14 and endorsed a series of recommendations on the context for international cricket within the Future Tours Programme after 2012. They proposed that the programme should consist of a Test league, in which the top four teams would qualify for a play-off every four years from 2013, and a one-day international league, independent of the World Cup, initially running from April 2011 until April 2014, when the one-day champions would be crowned. They also recommended that the ICC Board should consider a ten-team format for the World Cup, from 2015, and a 16-team format for the World Twenty20, from 2012, with the women's event continuing to run alongside the men's. A Twenty20 international rankings table should be introduced as soon as justifiable.

After recent discussions at the elite umpires and referees seminar, it was clarified that players should be allowed to leave the field due to bad light only when conditions were considered dangerous or unreasonable; they should not go off when ground floodlights deemed adequate before the series were switched on.

The committee also discussed the need to ensure that Test pitches provided a fair balance between bat and ball, and approved a revised guideline to the ICC pitch and outfield monitoring process.

There was a detailed progress report on preparations for the 2011 World Cup and an update on progress in developing the ICC strategic plan for 2011 to 2015.

The committee recommended a wide-ranging and, if necessary, independent review of current ICC anti-corruption measures, and supported the ICC's action after recent spot-fixing allegations at the Lord's Test between England and Pakistan.

ENGLAND CENTRAL CONTRACTS

On September 23, at the same time as the announcement of the Ashes party, the ECB awarded 11 England central contracts running for 12 months from October 1, 2010, to James Anderson, Ian Bell, Stuart Broad, Paul Collingwood, Alastair Cook, Steve Finn, Kevin Pietersen, Matt Prior, Andrew Strauss, Graeme Swann and Jonathan Trott. Compared with September 2010, Finn and Trott had replaced Graham Onions and Ryan Sidebottom. Incremental contracts were awarded again to Ravi Bopara, Tim Bresnan, Eoin Morgan, Luke Wright and Mike Yardy. Adil Rashid and Owais Shah were dropped from the list. Players on incremental contracts receive a one-off ECB payment on top of their county salary, whereas centrally contracted players are paid by the ECB rather than their county. Incremental contracts can be earned by amassing 20 appearance points between October and September (five points for a Test, two for a Twenty20 or one-day international); Finn and Yardy had been awarded incremental contracts on this basis in June 2010.

ECB/PCA CONTRACTS DEAL

On October 11, the ECB and the Professional Cricketers' Association announced agreement on arrangements for England contracts until September 2013 (a period including two Ashes series and the World Cup). While individual central contracts would continue to be offered for 12-month periods, a framework was settled covering remuneration and a comprehensive set of agreements on playing and management matters. The ECB said it would continue to offer additional rewards to players for successful team performances.

ICC EXECUTIVE BOARD

The ICC Executive Board met in Dubai on October 12–13, and received an update on spot-fixing allegations against three Pakistan players during a recent tour of England. The board promised to work with the Pakistan Cricket Board to protect the integrity of the game and restore confidence, and committed to an independent review of the ICC's anti-corruption measures. Members agreed to undertake independent inquiries into any substantive allegations of corruption within their domestic game, unless there were already credible disciplinary processes within their constitutions. The chairman of the Anti-Corruption Security Unit, Sir Ronnie Flanagan, and its general manager, Ravi Sawani, updated the board on the unit's competency-based education process; a request that the ICC anti-corruption code be mirrored by all members; the investigation of a player accreditation scheme; the employment of regular team managers; establishing an ethic of accountability within teams; increased interaction with betting companies; and sports integrity units.

The board issued advice on players' individual and collective obligations to uphold the game's integrity. The PCB were required to conduct a thorough review of player integrity issues across all authorised cricket in Pakistan and report back to the ICC's Pakistan Task Team within 30 days, and to encourage players to provide any relevant information to the ACSU in confidence, with co-operation a mitigating factor in the consideration of appropriate sanctions. The PCB were told to desist from any actions which might put them in a conflict of interest over allegations that were the subject of disciplinary proceedings, and from making public comments and disclosing confidential information undermining the integrity, reputation and image of the game and/or ongoing disciplinary or criminal investigation/proceedings.

After investigating allegations about the one-day international between England and Pakistan at The Oval on September 17, the ACSU concluded there was currently no compelling evidence against individual players or support staff.

The board approved the Chief Executives' Committee recommendations of September 13–14 on the Future Tours Programme after 2012, including the Test and one-day leagues, the formats for the World Cup and World Twenty20, and Twenty20 international rankings. Discussion of performance-related ranking and qualification for ICC global events should be considered by the ICC Governance Committee.

The board heard reports from Asian Cricket Council chief executive Ashraful Huq on cricket development in China, and from New Zealand chief executive Justin Vaughan on progress in the USA.

The host countries for the 2011 World Cup confirmed that the Decision Review System should be used, subject to the reliability of ball-tracking technology. The board agreed that Hot Spot technology would be used in the semi-finals and final. The possibility of sponsorship for the DRS would be explored.

It was decided that the ICC headquarters should remain in Dubai, and the matter of relocation to London was closed.

ECB BOARD MEETING AND DOMESTIC SCHEDULE

On November 17 the ECB Board supported the initial recommendations of the schedule working party, chaired by chief executive David Collier and including representatives of the Professional Cricketers' Association as well the counties, which had been reviewing the domestic programme for 2012 onwards. The working party said the volume of domestic cricket should be reduced by eight to 12 days to enable a coherent and balanced domestic schedule; the Clydesdale Bank 40 competition should be played in four pools of five leading to quarter-finals, and the match format should mirror that of one-day international cricket, which was to be reviewed by the ICC after the 2011 World Cup. The board agreed to conduct detailed research with cricket supporters and partners to provide objective analysis for the recommendations, to be considered at the next board meeting in February.

ICC EXECUTIVE BOARD

On November 21 the ICC Executive Board met via teleconference for an update on the Pakistan Cricket Board's progress in conjunction with the ICC's Pakistan Task Team in implementing the steps required by the ICC Board to preserve the integrity of cricket. The PCB had begun to carry out requirements including establishing an integrity committee and appointing an integrity officer. The board agreed that all members should introduce anti-corruption codes for their domestic cricket, mirroring the ICC code, by April 2011. They noted the Task Team's work to support the PCB in carrying out reforms to restore confidence in the game's administration in Pakistan, while reiterating that team selection was solely the responsibility of the PCB, which should ensure that their selection policies were appropriate.

ICC CHIEF EXECUTIVES' COMMITTEE

The ICC Chief Executives' Committee met in Dubai on November 30–December 1 and asked the working group on establishing Test and one-day international leagues to begin drawing up rules, regulations and points systems. It was intended that the one-day league should commence straight after the 2011 World Cup.

With the Decision Review System approved for use in the World Cup, the committee agreed that members could use the DRS in bilateral one-day internationals before the tournament, providing further exposure to the system for players, officials and technology suppliers. Its long-term use in one-day internationals would be decided after the World Cup.

The committee received an update on the Anti-Corruption and Security Unit review and were reminded of the need to implement domestic anti-corruption codes by April 2011.

PART SEVEN

Records and Registers

FEATURES OF 2010

In the past, *Wisden* has run separate lists of the statistical features of the English and overseas seasons (e.g. 2007 and 2006-07). These have now been combined in a single list of statistical features of the calendar year. Because the section now covers the calendar year, some of the features listed occurred in matches reported in *Wisden 2010* and some will be reported in *Wisden 2012*; these items are indicated by [w10] or [w12].

Double-Hundreds (63)

	Mins	Balls	4s	6s		
333	665	437	34	9	C. H. Gayle	West Indies v Sri Lanka (First Test) at Galle.
319	345	291	47	8	R. R. Rossouw	Eagles v Titans at Centurion.
301*	812	582	36	3	A. Chopra	Rajasthan v Maharashtra at Nasik. [w12]
278*	601	418	23	6	A. B. de Villiers	S Africa v Pakistan (Second Test) at Abu Dhabi. [w12]
268	423	351	33	6	Kamran Akmal	National Bank v Faisalabad at Sargodha. [w12]
261	369	270	38	3	R. W. T. Key	Kent v Durham at Canterbury.
259	474	389	38	5	A. M. Nayar	West Zone v North Zone at Rajkot.
254	445	360	31	5	Ahmed Shehzad	Habib Bank v Faisalabad at Faisalabad. [w12]
253*	675	473	22	0	H. M. Amla	South Africa v India at Nagpur.
251*	343	250	29	3	D. J. Hussey	Nottinghamshire v Yorkshire at Leeds.
250	481	371	35	3	L. R. Shukla	Bengal v Assam at Kolkata. [w12]
248	495	350	35	1	†M. R. Ramprakash	Surrey v Northamptonshire at The Oval.
244	528	401	20	4	L. D. Chandimal	Sri Lanka A v South Africa A at Colombo.
237*	382	333	29	5	†S. M. Ervine	Hampshire v Somerset at Southampton.
235*	630	428	26	0	A. N. Cook	England v Australia (First Test) at Brisbane.
233*	596	405	20	2	M. K. Tiwary	Bengal v Saurashtra at Rajkot. [w12]
232	579	409	27	1	A. Mukund	Tamil Nadu v Saurashtra at Rajkot. [w12]
232	356	244	25	4	Awais Zia	Pakistan TV v State Bank of Pakistan at Islamabad. [w12]
228*	459	389	35	0	J. A. Rudolph	Yorkshire v Durham at Leeds.
228*	300	230	23	7	M. E. Trescothick	Somerset v Essex at Colchester.
227*	454	346	26	4	S. L. Stewart	Canterbury v Central Districts at New Plymouth.
227	428	308	33	1	K. P. Pietersen	England v Australia (Second Test) at Adelaide.
226	490	349	20	0	I. J. L. Trott	England v Bangladesh (First Test) at Lord's.
225	543	308	22	4	B. B. McCullum	New Zealand v India (Second Test) at Hyderabad.
223	564	395	26	1	†M. R. Ramprakash	Surrey v Middlesex at The Oval.
219*	540	397	28	1	Asif Zakir	Karachi Whites v Abbottabad at Abbottabad. [w12]
219	399	335	29	0	K. C. Sangakkara	Sri Lanka v India (Second Test) at Colombo.
217	276	207	24	8	B. R. M. Taylor	Mid West Rhinos v Southern Rocks at Masvingo.
217	321	220	29	3	G. C. Smith	Cape Cobras v Lions at Randjesfontein. [w12]
214*	328	258	16	0	Mohammad Shahzad	Afghanistan v Canada at Sharjah.
214		355	21	0	T. T. Samaraweera	Kandurata v Basnahira North at Colombo.
214	547	363	22	2	†S. R. Tendulkar	India v Australia (Second Test) at Bangalore.
214	461	294	32	0	U. T. Khawaja	New South Wales v South Australia at Adelaide. [w12]
214	411	279	26	4	M. D. Mishra	Madhya Pradesh v Hyderabad at Secunderabad. [w12]
212*		282	22	7	R. N. ten Doeschate	Netherlands v Kenya at Nairobi.
211*	534	417	19	0	Haris Sohail	ZTBL v National Bank at Sialkot. [w12]
210*	331	190	19	10	Y. K. Pathan	West Zone v South Zone at Hyderabad.
209*	500	340	26	1	R. Dravid	Karnataka v Uttar Pradesh at Bangalore.
209	528	354	25	0	R. T. Ponting	Australia v Pakistan (Third Test) at Hobart. [w10]
208*	513	355	34	1	C. A. Pujara	India A v West Indies A at Croydon.
208*	505	371	24	3	H. Masakadza	Mountaineers v Mid West Rhinos at Kwekwe. [w12]
208	383	274	22	3	†S. M. Ervine	Southern Rocks v Mid West Rhinos at Masvingo.
206*	343	271	28	0	J. W. A. Taylor	Leicestershire v Middlesex at Leicester.
206		282	18	1	E. Steenkamp	Namibia v Bermuda at Windhoek.
205	308	289	30	1	Nazimuddin	Chittagong v Dhaka at Bogra.

Mins	Balls	4s	6s		
204*	302	194	28	5	Yuvraj Singh . . . . . . Rest of India v Mumbai at Jaipur. [w12]
204*	348	248	30	1	A. Ratra . . . . Goa v Rajasthan at Jaipur. [w12]
204	324	253	27	0	S. D. Robson . . . . . Middlesex v Oxford UCCE at Oxford.
203*	436	326	22	1	N. T. Broom . . . . Otago v Northern Districts at Queenstown. [w12]
203*	450	313	26	0	Yashpal Singh . . . . . Services v Maharashtra at Delhi. [w12]
203	516	347	23	1	†S. R. Tendulkar . . . India v Sri Lanka (Second Test) at Colombo.
202*	551	366	23	1	M. Kaif . . . . Central Zone v East Zone at Amritsar.
201*	324	223	20	4	Wajid Ali . . . . Abbottabad v Quetta at Abbottabad. [w12]
201*	389	270	15	5	J. H. Kallis . . . . South Africa v India (First Test) at Centurion.
201	455	334	23	0	G. J. Hopkins . . . . . Auckland v Central Districts at Auckland.
200*	354	263	28	0	Aamer Sajjad . . . . . The Rest v Karachi Blues at Hyderabad. [w12]
200*	291	255	27	3	A. T. Rayudu . . . . . Baroda v Orissa at Cuttack. [w12]
200*	383	257	23	3	R. G. Sharma . . . . . Mumbai v Bengal at Kolkata. [w12]
200*	486	333	30	0	I. R. Jaggi . . . . Jharkhand v Hyderabad at Ranchi. [w12]
200*	273	201	13	9	J-P. Duminy . . . . . . Cape Cobras v Dolphins at Paarl. [w12]
200*	235	150	26	4	Khalid Latif . . . . . . Karachi Whites v Abbottabad at Abbottabad. [w12]
200	442	322	27	0	C. J. L. Rogers . . . . Derbyshire v Surrey at The Oval.
200	384	313	21	1	Shoaib Malik . . . . . PIA v Faisalabad at Faisalabad. [w12]

† *Ervine, Ramprakash and Tendulkar each scored two double-hundreds.*

Hundred on First-Class Debut

114	Abdul Jabbar	Karachi Whites v Hyderabad at Karachi. [w12]
108	Asif Ahmed	Barisal v Chittagong at Khulna.
	He also scored 121 in his second match, Barisal v Dhaka at Khulna.	
119	D. J. Broom	Otago v Northern Districts at Whangarei.
112*	D. G. Brownlie	Canterbury v Northern Districts at Rangiora.
103	D. Hewitt	Northerns v Gauteng at Pretoria.
113	N. J. Maddinson	New South Wales v South Australia at Adelaide. [w12]
106	G. B. Podder	Orissa v Baroda at Cuttack. [w12]
144	B. P. Sandeep	Hyderabad v Jharkhand at Ranchi. [w12]
185*	A. S. Sharma	Oxford University v Cambridge University at Oxford.
130	S. M. Swain	Services v Kerala at Delhi. [w12]

Three Hundreds in Successive Innings

H. M. Amla (South Africa)	253*	v India (First Test) at Nagpur.
	114 and 123*	v India (Second Test) at Kolkata.
D. Bundela (Madhya Pradesh)	106*	v Rajasthan at Jaipur. [w12]
	145	v Jharkhand at Indore. [w12]
	121	v Hyderabad at Secunderabad. [w12]
H. H. Kanitkar (Rajasthan)	100*	v Maharashtra at Nasik. [w12]
Kanitkar's third hundred was	113	v Mumbai at Jaipur. [w12]
scored in January 2011.	100*	v Tamil Nadu at Jaipur. [w12]
D. K. H. Mitchell (Worcestershire)	104 and 134*	v Gloucestershire at Cheltenham.
	165*	v Glamorgan at Colwyn Bay.
K. C. Sangakkara (Sri Lanka)	137	v India (Third Test) at Mumbai.
	103	v India (First Test) at Galle.
	219	v India (Second Test) at Colombo.
S. R. Watson (Australians)	115 and 104*	v Indian Board President's XI at Chandigarh.
	126	v India (First Test) at Mohali.
C. G. Williams (Namibia)	144	v Boland at Paarl. [w12]
	116 and 113*	v United Arab Emirates at Dubai. [w12]

Hundred in Each Innings of a Match

Ahmed Shehzad	123 109*	Habib Bank v Sialkot at Sialkot. [w12]
H. M. Amla	114 123*	South Africa v India (Second Test) at Kolkata.
R. S. Bopara	142 102	Essex v Yorkshire at Chelmsford.
M. A. Carberry	162 107	Hampshire v Durham at Basingstoke.
S. M. Ervine	208 160	Southern Rocks v Mid West Rhinos at Masvingo.
K. D. Karthik	183 150	South Zone v West Zone at Hyderabad.
A. B. McDonald	100 107*	Victoria v New South Wales at Sydney. [w12]
W. L. Madsen	109 105	Derbyshire v Surrey at Chesterfield.
D. K. H. Mitchell	104 134*	Worcestershire v Gloucestershire at Cheltenham.
M. H. W. Papps	104 180	Canterbury v Auckland at Auckland.
Y. K. Pathan	108 210*	West Zone v South Zone at Hyderabad.
M. R. Ramprakash	223 103*	Surrey v Middlesex at The Oval.
C. J. L. Rogers	200 140*	Derbyshire v Surrey at The Oval.
Shoaib Malik	102 156	PIA v Sialkot at Sialkot. [w12]
D. J. van Wyk	111 178	KwaZulu-Natal v Border at Durban. [w12]
Wasim Jaffer	138 103*	Mumbai v Saurashtra at Mumbai. [w12]
S. R. Watson	115 104*	Australians v Indian Board President's XI at Chandigarh.
M. H. Wessels	105 101*	Mid West Rhinos v Matabeleland Tuskers at Bulawayo. [w12]
C. G. Williams	116 113*	Namibia v United Arab Emirates at Dubai. [w12]

Carrying Bat through Completed Innings

S. C. Cook	117*	Gauteng (208) v Boland at Johannesburg.
M. J. Di Venuto	117*	Durham (213) v Yorkshire at Chester-le-Street.
M. V. Hodge	54*	Leeward Islands (201) v Trinidad & Tobago at St Philip.
Shan Masood	98*	Habib Bank (260) v Sui Northern Gas at Karachi.
Taposh Ghosh	150*	Khulna (295) v Rajshahi at Chittagong.
I. J. Westwood	82*	Warwickshire (197) v Lancashire at Manchester.
Yasir Hameed	171*	ZTBL (361) v Habib Bank at Rawalpindi. [w12]

Hundred before Lunch

A. B. de Villiers	119*	South Africa v India (First Test) at Centurion (3rd day).
M. H. W. Papps	104*	Canterbury v Auckland at Auckland (1st day).
S. P. D. Smith	71* to 177	New South Wales v Tasmania at Hobart (2nd day).

300 Runs in a Day

R. R. Rossouw	319	Eagles v Titans at Centurion.

Most Sixes in an Innings

10	Y. K. Pathan (210*)	West Zone v South Zone at Hyderabad.
10	Y. K. Pathan (195)	Baroda v Haryana at Rohtak. [w12]
10	A. D. Russell (108*)	Jamaica v Ireland at Spanish Town.
9	J-P. Duminy (200*)	Cape Cobras v Dolphins at Paarl. [w12]
9	C. H. Gayle (333)	West Indies v Sri Lanka (First Test) at Galle.
9	A. P. McLaren (146)	Griqualand West v Western Province at Cape Town. [w12]

Most Runs in Boundaries

	4s	*6s*		
236	47	8	R. R. Rossouw (319)	Eagles v Titans at Centurion.

Longest Innings

Mins

812	A. Chopra (301*)	Rajasthan v Maharashtra at Nasik. [W12]
675	H. M. Amla (253*)	South Africa v India (First Test) at Nagpur.
665	C. H. Gayle (333)	West Indies v Sri Lanka (First Test) at Galle.
635	J. H. K. Adams (194)	Hampshire v Lancashire at Liverpool.
630	A. N. Cook (235*)	England v Australia (First Test) at Brisbane.
601	A. B. de Villiers (278*).	South Africa v Pakistan (Second Test) at Abu Dhabi.

Unusual Dismissals

Stumped by a Substitute

T. E. Linley (16) st S. D. Snell. . . . . Surrey v Gloucestershire at Bristol.

First-Wicket Partnership of 100 in Each Innings

169	121*	J. A. Raval/T. G. McIntosh, Auckland v Wellington at Auckland.
163	103	A. J. Strauss/S. A. Newman, Middlesex v Surrey at The Oval.
125	131	S. J. Marillier/C. J. Chibhabha (1st inns)/T. Chitongo (2nd inns), Southern Rocks v Mashonaland Eagles at Masvingo. [W12]
107	136	Farrukh Shehzad/Asif Hussain, Faisalabad v ZTBL at Sargodha. [W12]

Highest Wicket Partnerships

First Wicket

374	R. van Schoor/E. Steenkamp, Namibia v Bermuda at Windhoek.
337	Saeed Anwar/Ali Naqvi, KRL v Karachi Whites at Karachi. [W12]
333	G. C. Smith/A. G. Puttick, Cape Cobras v Lions at Randjesfontein. [W12]
294	E. C. Joyce/C. D. Nash, Sussex v Derbyshire at Horsham.
283	A. G. Puttick/J. A. Gray, Cape Cobras v Warriors at East London. [W12]
273	C. J. L. Rogers/W. L. Madsen, Derbyshire v Northamptonshire at Northampton.
259	D. A. King/S. S. Agarwal, Oxford University v Cambridge University at Oxford.

Second Wicket

480†	D. Elgar/R. R. Rossouw, Eagles v Titans at Centurion.
371	Ahmed Shehzad/Salim Elahi, Habib Bank v Faisalabad at Faisalabad. [W12]
333	F. D. M. Karunaratne/L. D. Chandimal, Sri Lanka A v South Africa A at Colombo.
329*	A. N. Cook/I. J. L. Trott, England v Australia (First Test) at Brisbane.
314	M. A. Carberry/M. J. Lumb, Hampshire v Durham at Basingstoke.
272	R. W. T. Key/G. O. Jones, Kent v Loughborough UCCE at Canterbury.
271	A. G. Puttick/S. van Zyl, Cape Cobras v Dolphins at Cape Town.
251	N. R. Parlane/C. J. Merchant, Wellington v Otago at Wellington.

Third Wicket

340	H. M. Amla/J. H. Kallis, South Africa v India (First Test) at Nagpur.
318	A. Mukund/S. Badrinath, Tamil Nadu v Saurashtra at Rajkot. [W12]
308	M. Vijay/S. R. Tendulkar, India v Australia (Second Test) at Bangalore.
306	F. D. M. Karunaratne/J. K. Silva, Basnahira North v Wayamba at Moratuwa.
279	C. C. Williams/Y. K. Pathan, Baroda v Haryana at Rohtak. [W12]
265	P. J. Hughes/P. J. Forrest, New South Wales v South Australia at Adelaide.
265	A. Chopra/R. D. Bist, Rajasthan v Maharashtra at Nasik. [W12]
255	A. Mukund/S. Badrinath, Tamil Nadu v Railways at Chennai. [W12]

275 runs were put on by R. Dravid, S. R. Tendulkar and M. Vijay for India's third wicket v Bangladesh at Mirpur; Dravid retired hurt after 222 runs had been added.

Fourth Wicket

360* J. W. A. Taylor/A. B. McDonald, Leicestershire v Middlesex at Leicester.
352 R. T. Ponting/M. J. Clarke, Australia v Pakistan (Third Test) at Hobart. [W10]
332* Asif Zakir/Khalid Latif, Karachi Whites v Abbottabad at Abbottabad. [W12]
310* A. Ratra/R. V. Keni, Goa v Rajasthan at Jaipur. [W12]
278 J. H. K. Adams/J. M. Vince, Hampshire v Yorkshire at Scarborough.
266 O. A. Shah/N. J. Dexter, Middlesex v Leicestershire at Leicester.
260 B. A. Sumanth/A. G. Pradeep, Andhra v Services at Anantapur. [W12]
254 M. A. Carberry/N. D. McKenzie, Hampshire v Kent at Southampton.
253 A. V. Suppiah/J. C. Hildreth, Somerset v Kent at Canterbury.

Fifth Wicket

339 J. C. Mickleburgh/J. S. Foster, Essex v Durham at Chester-le-Street.
289 Mohammad Ayub/Mansoor Amjad, Sialkot v Karachi Blues at Karachi. [W12]
274 T. T. Samaraweera/B. M. A. J. Mendis, Kandurata v Basnahira North at Colombo.
270* T. Bavuma/S. Burger, Gauteng v Easterns at Benoni.
256 S. R. Tendulkar/S. K. Raina, India v Sri Lanka (Second Test) at Colombo.
253* I. R. Jaggi/S. P. Gautam, Jharkhand v Hyderabad at Ranchi. [W12]
253 M. J. Clarke/M. J. North, Australia v New Zealand (First Test) at Wellington.
252 N. T. Broom/D. J. Broom, Otago v Northern Districts at Queenstown. [W12]

Sixth Wicket

417† W. P. Saha/L. R. Shukla, Bengal v Assam at Kolkata. [W12]
379*† S. L. Stewart/C. F. K. van Wyk, Canterbury v Central Districts at New Plymouth.
339 M. J. Guptill/B. B. McCullum, New Zealand v Bangladesh (Only Test) at Hamilton.
328 M. K. Pandey/C. M. Gautam, Karnataka v Orissa at Bangalore. [W12]
307 M. E. K. Hussey/B. J. Haddin, Australia v England (First Test) at Brisbane.
283 H. G. Kuhn/T. L. Tsolekile, South Africa A v Bangladesh A at Mirpur.
270 D. I. Stevens/J. C. Tredwell, Kent v Nottinghamshire at Tunbridge Wells.
258 Nazimuddin/Arman Hossain, Chittagong v Dhaka at Bogra.

Seventh Wicket

259* V. V. S. Laxman/M. S. Dhoni, India v South Africa (Second Test) at Kolkata.
249 B. J. Pelser/C. H. Morris, North West v Namibia at Potchefstroom.
237 A. D. Brown/C. M. W. Read, Nottinghamshire v Durham at Nottingham.
232 W. W. Hinds/C. S. Baugh, Jamaica v Guyana at St Philip.
225 M. W. Goodwin/R. S. C. Martin-Jenkins, Sussex v Derbyshire at Derby.
218 A. G. Pradeep/D. Sivakumar, Andhra v Kerala at Anantapur. [W12]
209 M. K. Tiwary/S. S. Lahiri, Bengal v Saurashtra at Rajkot. [W12]
193* Usman Salahuddin/Saad Nasim, Lahore Shalimar v Peshawar at Mardan. [W12]
188 N. R. D. Compton/T. N. Garwe, Mashonaland Eagles v Southern Rocks at Harare. [W12]
187 C. F. K. van Wyk/D. A. J. Bracewell, Central Districts v Wellington at Napier. [W12]
183 M. N. W. Spriegel/S. C. Meaker, Surrey v Bangladeshis at The Oval.
183 Sajjad Ahmed/Riaz Afridi, Peshawar v Pakistan Television at Peshawar. [W12]

Eighth Wicket

332† I. J. L. Trott/S. C. J. Broad, England v Pakistan (Fourth Test) at Lord's.
197 A. M. Nayar/R. R. Powar, West Zone v North Zone at Rajkot.
165 A. B. Agarkar/Iqbal Abdulla, Mumbai v Saurashtra at Mumbai. [W12]
164 M. W. Goodwin/Naved-ul-Hasan, Sussex v Leicestershire at Hove.
161 Lal Kumar/Kashif Bhatti, Hyderabad v Quetta at Hyderabad. [W12]

Ninth Wicket

141 S. W. Masakadza/P. Utseya, Mountaineers v Southern Rocks at Mutare.

Tenth Wicket

123 T. D. Groenewald/P. S. Jones, Derbyshire v Worcestershire at Worcester.
118 A. Nel/J. W. Dernbach, Surrey v Northamptonshire at Northampton.
118 A. G. Botha/Imran Tahir, Warwickshire v Kent at Birmingham.
107* A. B. de Villiers/M. Morkel, South Africa v Pakistan (Second Test) at Abu Dhabi.
105 Harbhajan Singh/S. Sreesanth, India v New Zealand (Second Test) at Hyderabad.
103 C. R. Woakes/Imran Tahir, Warwickshire v Hampshire at Birmingham.

† *National record.*

Most Wickets in an Innings

9-37	C. J. August	Boland v Western Province at Cape Town.
9-37	S. T. Finn	Middlesex v Worcestershire at Worcester.
9-68	B. L. Barends	KwaZulu-Natal Inland v Northerns at Pietermaritzburg. [W12]
9-108	Yasir Arafat	KRL v State Bank of Pakistan at Rawalpindi. [W12]
8-10	D. L. Chahar	Rajasthan v Hyderabad at Jaipur (*on first-class debut*). [W12]
8-25	A. Gqamane	Border v Griqualand West at East London. [W12]
8-31	L. S. Baker	Leeward Islands v Combined Campuses & Colleges at Gros Islet.
8-32	Pankaj Singh	Rajasthan v Tripura at Kota. [W12]
8-35	D. J. Pattinson	Victoria v Western Australia at Perth. [W12]
8-40	Jaffar Nazir	KRL v Peshawar at Mardan. [W12]
8-42	T. L. Lambert	Jamaica v Combined Campuses & Colleges at Providence.
8-52	S. C. J. Broad	Nottinghamshire v Warwickshire at Birmingham.
8-54	O. V. Brown	Jamaica v Combined Campuses & Colleges at Providence.
8-64	S. de Kock	Border v South Western Districts at Oudtshoorn.
8-70	S. M. S. M. Senanayake	Sri Lanka A v Australia A at Brisbane.
8-81	B. J. Arnel	New Zealand A v Zimbabwe A at Harare. [W12]
8-82	Ahmed Jamal	Abbottabad v State Bank of Pakistan at Abbottabad. [W12]
8-83	Riaz Afridi	Peshawar v Abbottabad at Swabi. [W12]
8-85	Abdur Rauf	Multan v Faisalabad at Bahawalpur. [W12]
8-92	A. G. Cremer	Mid West Rhinos v Mashonaland Eagles at Kwekwe.
8-92	T. A. Copeland	New South Wales v Queensland at Sydney.
8-99	Danish Kaneria	Habib Bank v ZTBL at Rawalpindi. [W12]
8-105	G. C. Viljoen	Easterns v Northerns at Benoni. [W12]
8-114	Imran Tahir	Warwickshire v Durham at Birmingham.

Most Wickets in a Match

14-52	Pankaj Singh	Rajasthan v Tripura at Kota. [W12]
14-106	S. T. Finn	Middlesex v Worcestershire at Worcester.
13-83	L. S. Baker	Leeward Islands v Combined Campuses & Colleges at Gros Islet.
13-94	W. L. Coetsee	North West v Easterns at Potchefstroom.
13-103	J. D. Unadkat	India A v West Indies A at Leicester (*on first-class debut*).
13-106	C. J. August	Boland v Western Province at Cape Town.
13-113	Saqlain Sajib	Rajshahi v Sylhet at Fatullah.
13-144	C. R. Swan	Queensland v South Australia at Brisbane. [W12]
13-154	O. A. C. Banks	Leeward Islands v Windward Islands at Georgetown.
13-176	Ahmed Raza	Multan v Sui Northern Gas at Multan. [W12]
12-32	A. Gqamane	Border v Griqualand West at East London. [W12]
12-64	D. L. Chahar	Rajasthan v Hyderabad at Jaipur (*on first-class debut*). [W12]
12-84	K. Kantasingh	Combined Campuses & Colls v Trinidad & Tobago at Montego Bay.
12-85	Waqas Ahmed	Sialkot v Multan at Okara. [W12]
12-89	Aizaz Cheema	PIA v Habib Bank at Faisalabad. [W12]
12-93	S. de Kock	Border v South Western Districts at Oudtshoorn.
12-103	W. C. Hantam	South Western Districts v Namibia at Oudtshoorn. [W12]
12-107	B. L. Barends	KwaZulu-Natal Inland v Northerns at Pietermaritzburg. [W12]
12-107	Jaffar Nazir	KRL v Peshawar at Mardan. [W12]
12-115	Aamer Hayat	Lahore Shalimar v Lahore Ravi at Lahore. [W12]
12-151	Riaz Afridi	Peshawar v Abbottabad at Swabi. [W12]
12-155	Saad Altaf	Pakistan Television v Hyderabad at Hyderabad. [W12]
12-159	Imran Tahir	Dolphins v Titans at Durban. [W12]
12-176	Atif Maqbool	Karachi Whites v Quetta at Karachi. [W12]
12-203	A. G. Cremer	Mid West Rhinos v Mashonaland Eagles at Kwekwe.

Outstanding Innings Analyses

7.3–2–10–8	D. L. Chahar	Rajasthan v Hyderabad at Jaipur (*on first-class debut*). [W12]
6–3–14–7	J. E. C. Franklin	Gloucestershire v Derbyshire at Bristol.
7–4–5–5	J. P. Faulkner	Tasmania v South Australia at Hobart. [W12]

Hat-Tricks (9)

A. C. R. Birch . . . . Eastern Province v Boland at Paarl.
S. J. Coyte . . . . New South Wales v Queensland at Brisbane. [W12]
R. D. B. Croft. . . . . Glamorgan v Gloucestershire at Cheltenham.
Elias Sunny . . . . Chittagong v Rajshahi at Bogra.
A. Gqamane . . . . Border v Griqualand West at East London. [W12]
A. J. Hall . . . . Northamptonshire v Glamorgan at Northampton.
Prince Abbas . . . . Sialkot v Multan at Okara. [W12]
P. M. Siddle . . . . Australia v England (First Test) at Brisbane.
J. C. Tredwell. . . . . Kent v Yorkshire at Leeds.

Most Wicketkeeping Dismissals in an Innings

8 (8ct). . . . . . . D. C. de Boorder   Otago v Wellington at Wellington.
7 (7ct). . . . . . . Kamran Akmal   National Bank v WAPDA at Sialkot. [W12]
7 (7ct). . . . . . . Kashif Mahmood   Lahore Shalimar v Abbottabad at Abbottabad. [W12]
6 (6ct). . . . . . . S. R. Adair   Eastern Province v Western Province at Cape Town.
6 (6ct). . . . . . . Ali Hasnain   Multan v Sui Northern Gas at Multan. [W12]
6 (5ct, 1st) . . . Anop Santosh   PIA v Islamabad at Islamabad. [W12]
6 (6ct). . . . . . . J. Austin-Smellie   Wellington v Central Districts at Napier. [W12]
6 (6ct). . . . . . . S. M. Davies   England Lions v Bangladeshis at Derby.
6 (5ct, 1st) . . . A. Z. M. Dyili   Eastern Province v KwaZulu-Natal Inland at Port Elizabeth.
6 (6ct). . . . . . . Gauhar Ali   Peshawar v Quetta at Peshawar. [W12]
6 (6ct). . . . . . . C. D. Hartley   Queensland v Tasmania at Hobart.
6 (6ct). . . . . . . C. D. Hartley   Queensland v Western Australia at Brisbane.
6 (6ct). . . . . . . Kamran Akmal   National Bank v Sui Northern Gas at Faisalabad. [W12]
6 (6ct). . . . . . . Kashif Mahmood   Lahore Shalimar v Lahore Ravi at Lahore. [W12]
6 (5ct, 1st) . . . U. Kaul   Punjab v Uttar Pradesh at Meerut. [W12]
6 (6ct). . . . . . . T. P. Ludeman   South Australia v New South Wales at Sydney.
6 (6ct). . . . . . . Mohammad Kashif   Islamabad v National Bank at Islamabad. [W12]
6 (6ct). . . . . . . M. Mosehle   Easterns v Border at Benoni.
6 (6ct). . . . . . . P. M. Nevill   New South Wales v Tasmania at Hobart.
6 (6ct). . . . . . . M. J. Prior   England v Australia (Fourth Test) at Melbourne.
6 (6ct). . . . . . . C. M. W. Read   Nottinghamshire v Essex at Chelmsford.
6 (5ct, 1st) . . . T. L. Tsolekile   Lions v Dolphins at Johannesburg (1st inns). [W12]
6 (6ct). . . . . . . T. L. Tsolekile   Lions v Dolphins at Johannesburg (2nd inns). [W12]
6 (6ct). . . . . . . R. van Schoor   Namibia v Eastern Province at Port Elizabeth.

Most Wicketkeeping Dismissals in a Match

12 (12ct). . . . . Kashif Mahmood   Lahore Shalimar v Abbottabad at Abbottabad. [W12]
12 (11ct, 1st) . T. L. Tsolekile   Lions v Dolphins at Johannesburg. [W12]
10 (9ct, 1st) . . D. C. de Boorder   Otago v Wellington at Wellington.
10 (10ct). . . . . Gauhar Ali   Peshawar v Quetta at Peshawar. [W12]
10 (10ct). . . . . Hanif Malik   Sui Northern Gas v Islamabad at Islamabad. [W12]
10 (10ct). . . . . M. Mosehle   Titans v Eagles at Centurion.
9 (9ct). . . . . . Ali Hasnain   Multan v Sui Northern Gas at Multan. [W12]
9 (9ct). . . . . . M. V. Boucher   South Africa v India (Second Test) at Durban.
9 (9ct). . . . . . Fawad Khan   Abbottabad v Peshawar at Swabi. [W12]
9 (9ct). . . . . . B. J. Haddin   Australia v Pakistan (Second Test) at Sydney. [W10]
9 (9ct). . . . . . R. D. McCann   Ireland v Canada at Toronto.
9 (9ct). . . . . . D. Murphy   Northamptonshire v Glamorgan at Northampton.
9 (9ct). . . . . . Naeem Anjum   Pakistan Television v State Bank of Pakistan at Islamabad. [W12]
9 (9ct). . . . . . L. Ronchi   Western Australia v Tasmania at Perth.

Five Catches in an Innings in the Field

N. J. Edwards . . . . Nottinghamshire v Kent at Nottingham.
C. D. Hartley . . . . Queensland v Western Australia at Brisbane. [w12]

Six Catches in a Match in the Field

C. de Grandhomme . . . . . Auckland v Canterbury at Christchurch. [w12]
C. J. L. Rogers . . . . Derbyshire v Surrey at Chesterfield.
E. Steenkamp . . . . Namibia v Easterns at Windhoek. [w12]

No Byes Conceded in Total of 500 or More

S. H. Marathe . . . . Mumbai v Rest of India (668) at Jaipur. [w12]
P. Mustard . . . . Durham v Yorkshire (610-6 dec) at Leeds.
S. D. Jogiyani . . . . Saurashtra v Bengal (569-7) at Rajkot. [w12]
T. P. Ludeman . . . . South Australia v New South Wales (565-6 dec) at Adelaide.
T. P. Ludeman . . . . South Australia v New South Wales (550-9 dec) at Sydney.
D. Ramdin . . . . West Indies v South Africa (543-6 dec) (Second Test) at Basseterre.
T. D. Paine . . . . Australia A v England XI (523) at Hobart. [w12]
D. Smit . . . . Dolphins v Cape Cobras (515-5 dec) at Paarl. [w12]
M. S. Dhoni . . . . Indians v Sri Lanka Board President's XI (514-9 dec) at Colombo.
T. L. Tsolekile . . . . Lions v Titans (513) at Potchefstroom. [w12]
Mushfiqur Rahim . . . . Bangladesh v England (505) (First Test) at Lord's.
W. P. Saha . . . . Indian Board President's XI v Australians (505) at Chandigarh. [w12]

Highest Innings Totals

769 . . . . West Zone v North Zone at Rajkot.
727 . . . . Kandurata v Basnahira North at Colombo.
726 . . . . Northern Districts v Canterbury at Rangiora.
720 . . . . Basnahira South v Ruhuna at Colombo.
707 . . . . India v Sri Lanka (Second Test) at Colombo.
676-9 dec . . . South Africa A v Bangladesh A at Mirpur.
668 . . . . Rest of India v Mumbai at Jaipur. [w12]
643-6 dec . . . India v South Africa (Second Test) at Kolkata.
642-4 dec . . . Sri Lanka v India (Second Test) at Colombo.
641-7 dec . . . Rajasthan v Maharashtra at Nasik. [w12]
635-6 dec . . . Auckland v Central Districts at Auckland.
621-8 dec . . . Mumbai v Bengal at Kolkata. [w12]
620-4 dec . . . South Africa v India (First Test) at Centurion.
620-5 dec . . . England v Australia (Second Test) at Adelaide.
620-7 dec . . . Surrey v Northamptonshire at The Oval.
611-5 dec . . . Oxford University v Cambridge University at Oxford.
610-6 dec . . . Yorkshire v Durham at Leeds.
609-7 dec . . . Mid West Rhinos v Southern Rocks at Masvingo. [w12]
609-9 dec . . . Eagles v Warriors at Bloemfontein.
609 . . . . Namibia v Uganda at Windhoek. [w12]
604 . . . . Maharashtra v Jammu and Kashmir at Jammu. [w12]

Lowest Innings Totals

21	Hyderabad v Rajasthan at Jaipur. [W12]
44	Derbyshire v Gloucestershire at Bristol.
45	Quetta v KRL at Rawalpindi. [W12]
55	South Australia v Tasmania at Hobart. [W12]
55	Tripura v Rajasthan at Kota. [W12]
56	Bermuda v United Arab Emirates at Hamilton.
57	Sui Northern Gas v Islamabad at Islamabad. [W12]
59	Nottinghamshire v Yorkshire at Nottingham.
61	Vidarbha v Maharashtra at Nasik. [W12]
63†	Multan v Sialkot at Okara. [W12]
64	Karachi Blues v ZTBL at Karachi. [W12]
65	Sylhet v Barisal at Khulna.
65	Combined Campuses & Colleges v Leeward Islands at Gros Islet.
65	KwaZulu-Natal Inland v Namibia at Windhoek. [W12]
65	Hyderabad v Karachi Whites at Karachi. [W12]
65	Multan v Karachi Blues at Karachi. [W12]
66	Middlesex v Worcestershire at Lord's.
68†	Southern Rocks v Mashonaland Eagles at Harare.
70	Western Province v Namibia at Cape Town.
70	Gloucestershire v Derbyshire at Bristol.
71	Leicestershire v Glamorgan at Leicester.
71	Gujarat v Delhi at Delhi. [W12]
72	South Australia v Queensland at Brisbane.
72	Pakistan v England (Second Test) at Birmingham.
72	Multan v PIA at Okara. [W12]
73	Namibia v Eastern Province at Port Elizabeth.
73	Tripura v Jharkhand at Agartala. [W12]
74	Pakistan v England (Fourth Test) at Lord's.
75	Queensland v New South Wales at Brisbane. [W12]
75	Lahore Ravi v KRL at Lahore. [W12]

† *One batsman absent hurt.*

Highest Fourth-Innings Totals

541-7	West Zone v South Zone at Hyderabad (set 536) *(world record to win)*.
494-4	Afghanistan v Canada at Sharjah (set 494).
420	Mumbai v Rest of India at Jaipur (set 782). [W12]
411-4	Northern Districts v Central Districts at Napier (set 407).

Match Aggregate of 1,500 Runs

1,749 for 33	Rest of India (668 and 387-3 dec) v Mumbai (274 and 420) at Jaipur. [W12]
1,578 for 36	South Zone (400 and 386-9 dec) v West Zone (251 and 541-7) at Hyderabad.
1,549 for 34	Central Districts (414 and 361-9) v Canterbury (223 and 551-5 dec) at New Plymouth.
1,515 for 28	Canada (566 and 191-4 dec) v Afghanistan (264 and 494-4) at Sharjah.
1,505 for 31	Netherlands (385 and 367-6 dec) v Kenya (433 and 320-5) at Nairobi.
1,501 for 32	New Zealand (553-7 dec and 258-5 dec) v Bangladesh (408 and 282) (Only Test) at Hamilton.
1,501 for 31	Central Districts (217 and 531-7 dec) v Northern Districts (342 and 411-4) at Napier.

Matches Dominated by Batting (1,200 runs at 80 runs per wicket)

1,369 for 15 (91.26) Canterbury (558-4 dec and 85-1) v Northern Districts (726) at Rangiora.
1,478 for 17 (86.94) Sri Lanka (642-4 dec and 129-3 dec) v India (707) (Second Test) at Colombo.

Four Individual Hundreds in an Innings

India (643-6 dec) v South Africa (Second Test) at Kolkata.
Auckland (635-6 dec) v Central Districts at Auckland.
Basnahira South (720) v Ruhuna at Colombo.
Sussex (576-3 dec) v Derbyshire at Horsham.

Seven Individual Hundreds in a Match

India v South Africa (Second Test) at Kolkata.

Most Individual Fifties in an Innings

7 West Zone (769) v North Zone at Rajkot.
6 Eagles (609-9 dec) v Warriors at Bloemfontein.
6 Lions (562-8 dec) v Titans at Benoni.
6 Namibia (609) v Uganda at Windhoek. [W12]
6 Rest of India (668) v Mumbai at Jaipur. [W12]
6 Goa (583) v Jharkhand at Porvorim. [W12]
6 Karnataka (537-4) v Uttar Pradesh at Kanpur. [W12]

Large Margin of Victory

Victoria (305 and 591-8 dec) v Queensland (257 and 182) at Melbourne by 457 runs.
Basnahira South (720 and 168-8 dec) v Ruhuna (180 and 259) at Colombo by 449 runs.

Win after Following On

Tasmania (251 and 177) lost to South Australia (55 and 416) at Hobart by 43 runs. [W12]

Eleven Bowlers in an Innings

Ireland v Jamaica (314-7 dec) at Spanish Town.

Most Extras in an Innings

b	l-b	w	n-b	
83	41	11	6	25	Rajasthan (641-7 dec) v Maharashtra at Nasik. [w12]
76	6	19	13	38	Gloucestershire (242) v Derbyshire at Derby.
69	20	26	15	8	Middlesex (442-8 dec) v Northamptonshire at Northampton.
61	13	10	13	25	State Bank of Pakistan (553-9 dec) v Lahore Shalimar at Lahore. [w12]
61	13	18	1	29	PIA (401-9 dec) v Sui Northern Gas at Islamabad. [w12]
59	17	0	7	35	Hampshire (553-7 dec) v Kent at Southampton.
58	26	11	1	20	West Indies A (563) v India A at Croydon.
58	8	10	1	39	PIA (352) v Habib Bank at Faisalabad. [w12]
55	27	11	1	16	Sussex (429) v Derbyshire at Derby.
55	20	15	3	17	Rawalpindi (430) v ZTBL at Rawalpindi. [w12]
54	8	13	1	32	Lancashire (398) v Hampshire at Liverpool.
54	21	18	6	9	Karnataka (537-4) v Uttar Pradesh at Kanpur. [w12]
52	21	20	7	4	Rajasthan (589) v Mumbai at Jaipur. [w12]

Career Aggregate Milestones

20,000 runs.	M. W. Goodwin, M. E. K. Hussey.
15,000 runs.	D. P. M. D. Jayawardene, R. W. T. Key, V. S. Solanki.
10,000 runs.	H. M. Amla, A. N. Cook, Z. de Bruyn, G. Gambhir, E. C. Joyce, Mohammad Yousuf, A. A. Muzumdar, S. D. Peters, C. M. W. Read, G. C. Smith, I. J. L. Trott.
500 wickets	Abdur Rauf, Imran Tahir, Jaffar Nazir, M. Kartik, D. L. Vettori.
500 dismissals	J. S. Foster, H. A. P. W. Jayawardene.

RECORDS

COMPILED BY PHILIP BAILEY

This section covers
- first-class records to December 31, 2010 (page 1287).
- List A one-day records to December 31, 2010 (page 1326).
- List A Twenty20 records to December 31, 2010 (page 1329).
- Test records to January 19, 2011, the end of the New Zealand v Pakistan series (page 1331).
- Test records series by series (page 1373).
- one-day international records to December 31, 2010 (page 1459).
- Twenty20 international records to December 31, 2010 (page 1470).
- miscellaneous other records to December 31, 2010 (page 1473).
- women's Test and one-day international records to December 31, 2010 (page 1477).

The sequence
- Test series records begin with those involving England, arranged in the order their opponents entered Test cricket (Australia, South Africa, West Indies, New Zealand, India, Pakistan, Sri Lanka, Zimbabwe, Bangladesh). Next come all remaining series involving Australia, then South Africa – and so on until Zimbabwe v Bangladesh records appear on pages 000–000.

Notes
- Unless otherwise stated, all records apply only to first-class cricket. This is considered to have started in 1815, after the Napoleonic War.
- mid-year seasons taking place outside England are given simply as 2002, 2003, etc.
- (E), (A), (SA), (WI), (NZ), (I), (P), (SL), (Z) or (B) indicates the nationality of a player or the country in which a record was made.
- in career records, dates in italic indicate seasons embracing two different years (i.e. non-English seasons). In these cases, only the first year is given, e.g. *2008* for 2008-09.

See also
- up-to-date Test records on www.cricinfo.com and at www.cricketarchive.co.uk/Archive/Records/Tests/index.html.
- Features of 2010 (page 1270).

CONTENTS

FIRST-CLASS RECORDS

BATTING RECORDS

BOWLING RECORDS

ALL-ROUND RECORDS

WICKETKEEPING RECORDS

FIELDING RECORDS

TEAM RECORDS

LIST A ONE-DAY RECORDS

LIST A TWENTY20 RECORDS

TEST RECORDS

BATTING RECORDS

BOWLING RECORDS

ALL-ROUND RECORDS

WICKETKEEPING RECORDS

FIELDING RECORDS

TEAM RECORDS

PLAYERS

UMPIRES

TEST SERIES

ONE-DAY INTERNATIONAL RECORDS

TWENTY20 INTERNATIONAL RECORDS

MISCELLANEOUS RECORDS

WOMEN'S TEST AND OTHER INTERNATIONAL RECORDS

FIRST-CLASS RECORDS

Note: Throughout this section, bold type denotes performances in the calendar year 2010 or, in career figures, players who appeared in first-class cricket in that year.

BATTING RECORDS

HIGHEST INDIVIDUAL INNINGS

In the history of first-class cricket, there have been **179** individual scores of 300 or more:

501*	B. C. Lara	Warwickshire v Durham at Birmingham	1994
499	Hanif Mohammad	Karachi v Bahawalpur at Karachi	1958-59
452*	D. G. Bradman	NSW v Queensland at Sydney	1929-30
443*	B. B. Nimbalkar	Maharashtra v Kathiawar at Poona	1948-49
437	W. H. Ponsford	Victoria v Queensland at Melbourne	1927-28
429	W. H. Ponsford	Victoria v Tasmania at Melbourne	1922-23
428	Aftab Baloch	Sind v Baluchistan at Karachi	1973-74
424	A. C. MacLaren	Lancashire v Somerset at Taunton	1895
405*	G. A. Hick	Worcestershire v Somerset at Taunton	1988
400*	B. C. Lara	West Indies v England at St John's	2003-04
394	Naved Latif	Sargodha v Gujranwala at Gujranwala	2000-01
390	S. C. Cook	Lions v Warriors at East London	2009-10
385	B. Sutcliffe	Otago v Canterbury at Christchurch	1952-53
383	C. W. Gregory	NSW v Queensland at Brisbane	1906-07
380	M. L. Hayden	Australia v Zimbabwe at Perth	2003-04
377	S. V. Manjrekar	Bombay v Hyderabad at Bombay	1990-91
375	B. C. Lara	West Indies v England at St John's	1993-94
374	D. P. M. D. Jayawardene	Sri Lanka v South Africa at Colombo	2006
369	D. G. Bradman	South Australia v Tasmania at Adelaide	1935-36
366	N. H. Fairbrother	Lancashire v Surrey at The Oval	1990
366	M. V. Sridhar	Hyderabad v Andhra at Secunderabad	1993-94
365*	C. Hill	South Australia v NSW at Adelaide	1900-01
365*	G. S. Sobers	West Indies v Pakistan at Kingston	1957-58
364	L. Hutton	England v Australia at The Oval	1938
359*	V. M. Merchant	Bombay v Maharashtra at Bombay	1943-44
359	R. B. Simpson	NSW v Queensland at Brisbane	1963-64
357	R. Abel	Surrey v Somerset at The Oval	1899
357	D. G. Bradman	South Australia v Victoria at Melbourne	1935-36
356	B. A. Richards	South Australia v Western Australia at Perth	1970-71
355*	G. R. Marsh	Western Australia v South Australia at Perth	1989-90
355	B. Sutcliffe	Otago v Auckland at Dunedin	1949-50
353	V. V. S. Laxman	Hyderabad v Karnataka at Bangalore	1999-2000
352	W. H. Ponsford	Victoria v NSW at Melbourne	1926-27
350	Rashid Israr	Habib Bank v National Bank at Lahore	1976-77
345	C. G. Macartney	Australians v Nottinghamshire at Nottingham	1921
344*	G. A. Headley	Jamaica v Lord Tennyson's XI at Kingston	1931-32
344*	M. W. Goodwin	Sussex v Somerset at Taunton	2009
344	W. G. Grace	MCC v Kent at Canterbury	1876
343*	P. A. Perrin	Essex v Derbyshire at Chesterfield	1904
342	J. L. Langer	Somerset v Surrey at Guildford	2006
341	G. H. Hirst	Yorkshire v Leicestershire at Leicester	1905
341	C. M. Spearman	Gloucestershire v Middlesex at Gloucester	2004
340*	D. G. Bradman	NSW v Victoria at Sydney	1928-29
340	S. M. Gavaskar	Bombay v Bengal at Bombay	1981-82
340	S. T. Jayasuriya	Sri Lanka v India at Colombo	1997-98
339	D. S. Lehmann	Yorkshire v Durham at Leeds	2006
338*	R. C. Blunt	Otago v Canterbury at Christchurch	1931-32
338	W. W. Read	Surrey v Oxford University at The Oval	1888

337*	Pervez Akhtar	Railways v Dera Ismail Khan at Lahore.............	1964-65
337*	D. J. Cullinan	Transvaal v Northern Transvaal at Johannesburg	1993-94
337	Hanif Mohammad	Pakistan v West Indies at Bridgetown.............	1957-58
336*	W. R. Hammond	England v New Zealand at Auckland.............	1932-33
336	W. H. Ponsford	Victoria v South Australia at Melbourne...........	1927-28
335*	M. W. Goodwin	Sussex v Leicestershire at Hove...................	2003
334*	M. A. Taylor	Australia v Pakistan at Peshawar................	1998-99
334	D. G. Bradman	Australia v England at Leeds....................	1930
333	K. S. Duleepsinhji	Sussex v Northamptonshire at Hove...............	1930
333	G. A. Gooch	England v India at Lord's......................	1990
333	**C. H. Gayle**	**West Indies v Sri Lanka at Galle**..............	**2010-11**
332	W. H. Ashdown	Kent v Essex at Brentwood.....................	1934
331*	J. D. Robertson	Middlesex v Worcestershire at Worcester..........	1949
331*	M. E. K. Hussey	Northamptonshire v Somerset at Taunton..........	2003
329*	M. E. K. Hussey	Northamptonshire v Essex at Northampton.........	2001
329	Inzamam-ul-Haq	Pakistan v New Zealand at Lahore................	2002
325*	H. L. Hendry	Victoria v New Zealanders at Melbourne...........	1925-26
325	A. Sandham	England v West Indies at Kingston................	1929-30
325	C. L. Badcock	South Australia v Victoria at Adelaide.............	1935-36
324*	D. M. Jones	Victoria v South Australia at Melbourne...........	1994-95
324	J. B. Stollmeyer	Trinidad v British Guiana at Port-of-Spain.........	1946-47
324	Waheed Mirza	Karachi Whites v Quetta at Karachi...............	1976-77
323	A. L. Wadekar	Bombay v Mysore at Bombay....................	1966-67
323	D. Gandhi	Bengal v Assam at Gauhati.....................	1998-99
322*	M. B. Loye	Northamptonshire v Glamorgan at Northampton......	1998
322	E. Paynter	Lancashire v Sussex at Hove....................	1937
322	I. V. A. Richards	Somerset v Warwickshire at Taunton..............	1985
321	W. L. Murdoch	NSW v Victoria at Sydney......................	1881-82
320	R. Lamba	North Zone v West Zone at Bhilai................	1987-88
319	Gul Mahomed	Baroda v Holkar at Baroda.....................	1946-47
319	C. J. L. Rogers	Northamptonshire v Gloucestershire at Northampton ..	2006
319	V. Sehwag	India v South Africa at Chennai..................	2007-08
319	**R. R. Rossouw**	**Eagles v Titans at Centurion**....................	**2009-10**
318*	W. G. Grace	Gloucestershire v Yorkshire at Cheltenham..........	1876
317	W. R. Hammond	Gloucestershire v Nottinghamshire at Gloucester	1936
317	K. R. Rutherford	New Zealanders v D. B. Close's XI at Scarborough ...	1986
317	C. H. Gayle	West Indies v South Africa at St John's............	2004-05
316*	J. B. Hobbs	Surrey v Middlesex at Lord's....................	1926
316*	V. S. Hazare	Maharashtra v Baroda at Poona.................	1939-40
316	R. H. Moore	Hampshire v Warwickshire at Bournemouth.........	1937
315*	T. W. Hayward	Surrey v Lancashire at The Oval.................	1898
315*	P. Holmes	Yorkshire v Middlesex at Lord's..................	1925
315*	A. F. Kippax	NSW v Queensland at Sydney...................	1927-28
315*	G. A. Hick	Worcestershire v Durham at Worcester.............	2002
315	M. A. Wagh	Warwickshire v Middlesex at Lord's...............	2001
315	J. L. Langer	Somerset v Middlesex at Taunton................	2007
314*	C. L. Walcott	Barbados v Trinidad at Port-of-Spain.............	1945-46
314*	Wasim Jaffer	Mumbai v Saurashtra at Rajkot..................	1996-97
313*	S. J. Cook	Somerset v Glamorgan at Cardiff.................	1990
313*	Raqibul Hasan	Barisal v Sylhet at Fatullah	2006-07
313	H. Sutcliffe	Yorkshire v Essex at Leyton....................	1932
313	W. V. Raman‡	Tamil Nadu v Goa at Panjim....................	1988-89
313	Younis Khan	Pakistan v Sri Lanka at Karachi.................	2008-09
312*	W. W. Keeton	Nottinghamshire v Middlesex at The Oval†.........	1939
312*	J. M. Brearley	MCC Under-25 v North Zone at Peshawar.........	1966-67
312	R. Lamba	Delhi v Himachal Pradesh at Delhi...............	1994-95
312	J. E. R. Gallian	Lancashire v Derbyshire at Manchester............	1996
312	Sunny Singh	Haryana v Madhya Pradesh at Indore	2009-10
311*	G. M. Turner	Worcestershire v Warwickshire at Worcester	1982
311*	J. P. Crawley	Hampshire v Nottinghamshire at Southampton	2005
311	J. T. Brown	Yorkshire v Sussex at Sheffield	1897

311	R. B. Simpson	Australia v England at Manchester	1964
311	Javed Miandad	Karachi Whites v National Bank at Karachi	1974-75
311	G. C. Smith	Somerset v Leicestershire at Taunton	2005
310*	J. H. Edrich	England v New Zealand at Leeds	1965
310*	M. E. K. Hussey	Northamptonshire v Gloucestershire at Bristol	2002
310	H. Gimblett	Somerset v Sussex at Eastbourne	1948
309*	S. P. James	Glamorgan v Sussex at Colwyn Bay	2000
309*	H. D. Ackerman	Leicestershire v Glamorgan at Cardiff	2006
309*	R. G. Sharma	Mumbai v Gujarat at Mumbai	2009-10
309	V. S. Hazare	The Rest v Hindus at Bombay	1943-44
309	V. Sehwag	India v Pakistan at Multan	2003-04
308*	F. M. M. Worrell	Barbados v Trinidad at Bridgetown	1943-44
308	D. Mongia	Punjab v Jammu and Kashmir at Jullundur	2000-01
307*	T. N. Lazard	Boland v W. Province at Worcester, Cape Province	1993-94
307	M. C. Cowdrey	MCC v South Australia at Adelaide	1962-63
307	R. M. Cowper	Australia v England at Melbourne	1965-66
306*	A. Ducat	Surrey v Oxford University at The Oval	1919
306*	E. A. B. Rowan	Transvaal v Natal at Johannesburg	1939-40
306*	D. W. Hookes	South Australia v Tasmania at Adelaide	1986-87
306*	S. R. Nair	Kerala v Services at Palakkad	2007-08
306	M. H. Richardson	New Zealanders v Zimbabwe A at Kwekwe	2000-01
306	S. M. Katich	New South Wales v Queensland at Sydney	2007-08
305*	F. E. Woolley	MCC v Tasmania at Hobart	1911-12
305*	F. R. Foster	Warwickshire v Worcestershire at Dudley	1914
305*	W. H. Ashdown	Kent v Derbyshire at Dover	1935
305*	P. Dharmani	Punjab v Jammu and Kashmir at Ludhiana	1999-2000
304*	A. W. Nourse	Natal v Transvaal at Johannesburg	1919-20
304*	P. H. Tarilton	Barbados v Trinidad at Bridgetown	1919-20
304*	E. D. Weekes	West Indians v Cambridge University at Cambridge	1950
304	R. M. Poore	Hampshire v Somerset at Taunton	1899
304	D. G. Bradman	Australia v England at Leeds	1934
303*	W. W. Armstrong	Australians v Somerset at Bath	1905
303*	Mushtaq Mohammad	Karachi Blues v Karachi University at Karachi	1967-68
303*	Abdul Azeem	Hyderabad v Tamil Nadu at Hyderabad	1986-87
303*	S. Chanderpaul	Guyana v Jamaica at Kingston	1995-96
303*	G. A. Hick	Worcestershire v Hampshire at Southampton	1997
303*	D. J. Sales	Northamptonshire v Essex at Northampton	1999
303*	N. V. Knight	Warwickshire v Middlesex at Lord's	2004
303*	J. C. Hildreth	Somerset v Warwickshire at Taunton	2009
302*	P. Holmes	Yorkshire v Hampshire at Portsmouth	1920
302*	W. R. Hammond	Gloucestershire v Glamorgan at Bristol	1934
302*	Arjan Kripal Singh‡	Tamil Nadu v Goa at Panjim	1988-89
302*	B. J. Hodge	Leicestershire v Nottinghamshire at Nottingham	2003
302*	C. A. Pujara	Saurashtra v Orissa at Rajkot	2008-09
302*	Rafatullah Mohmand	WAPDA v Sui Southern Gas at Sheikhupura	2009-10
302	W. R. Hammond	Gloucestershire v Glamorgan at Newport	1939
302	L. G. Rowe	West Indies v England at Bridgetown	1973-74
301*	E. H. Hendren	Middlesex v Worcestershire at Dudley	1933
301*	V. V. S. Laxman	Hyderabad v Bihar at Jamshedpur	1997-98
301*	P. G. Fulton	Canterbury v Auckland at Christchurch	2002-03
301*	J. P. Crawley	Hampshire v Nottinghamshire at Nottingham	2004
301*	D. S. Lehmann	South Australia v Western Australia at Adelaide	2005-06
301*	M. R. Ramprakash	Surrey v Northamptonshire at The Oval	2006
301*	**A. Chopra**	**Rajasthan v Maharashtra at Nasik**	**2010-11**
301	W. G. Grace	Gloucestershire v Sussex at Bristol	1896
301	Wasim Jaffer	Mumbai v Saurashtra at Chennai	2008-09
300*	V. T. Trumper	Australians v Sussex at Hove	1899
300*	F. B. Watson	Lancashire v Surrey at Manchester	1928
300*	Imtiaz Ahmed	PM's XI v Commonwealth XI at Bombay	1950-51
300*	G. K. Khoda	Central Zone v South Zone at Panaji	2000-01
300*	M. L. Love	Queensland v Victoria at Melbourne (Junction Oval)	2003-04

300*	Shoaib Khan	Peshawar v Quetta at Peshawar	2003-04
300*	Bazid Khan	Rawalpindi v Hyderabad at Hyderabad	2004-05
300*	S. S. Das	Orissa v Jammu and Kashmir at Cuttack	2006-07
300*	A. Mukund	Tamil Nadu v Maharashtra at Nasik.	2008-09
300	J. T. Brown	Yorkshire v Derbyshire at Chesterfield	1898
300	D. C. S. Compton	MCC v N. E. Transvaal at Benoni	1948-49
300	R. Subba Row	Northamptonshire v Surrey at The Oval	1958
300	Ramiz Raja	Allied Bank v Habib Bank at Lahore.	1994-95
300	Yasir Hameed	NWFP v Baluchistan at Peshawar	2007-08

† *Played at The Oval because Lord's was required for Eton v Harrow.*
‡ *W. V. Raman and Arjan Kripal Singh scored triple-hundreds in the same innings, a unique occurrence.*

DOUBLE-HUNDRED ON DEBUT

227	T. Marsden	Sheffield & Leicester v Nottingham at Sheffield.	1826
207	N. F. Callaway†	New South Wales v Queensland at Sydney	1914-15
240	W. F. E. Marx	Transvaal v Griqualand West at Johannesburg	1920-21
200*	A. Maynard	Trinidad v MCC at Port-of-Spain	1934-35
232*	S. J. E. Loxton	Victoria v Queensland at Melbourne.	1946-47
215*	G. H. G. Doggart	Cambridge University v Lancashire at Cambridge . . .	1948
202	J. Hallebone	Victoria v Tasmania at Melbourne	1951-52
230	G. R. Viswanath	Mysore v Andhra at Vijayawada.	1967-68
260	A. A. Muzumdar	Bombay v Haryana at Faridabad	1993-94
209*	A. Pandey	Madhya Pradesh v Uttar Pradesh at Bhilai	1995-96
210*	D. J. Sales	Northants v Worcestershire at Kidderminster	1996
200*	M. J. Powell	Glamorgan v Oxford University at Oxford	1997

† *In his only first-class innings. He was killed in action in France in 1917.*

TWO SEPARATE HUNDREDS ON DEBUT

148	and 111	A. R. Morris	New South Wales v Queensland at Sydney	1940-41
152	and 102*	N. J. Contractor	Gujarat v Baroda at Baroda	1952-53
132*	and 110	Aamer Malik	Lahore A v Railways at Lahore	1979-80
130	and 100*	Noor Ali	Afghanistan v Zimbabwe XI at Mutare	2009

TWO DOUBLE-HUNDREDS IN A MATCH

| A. E. Fagg . . . . | 244 | 202* | Kent v Essex at Colchester. . . . . | 1938 |

TRIPLE-HUNDRED AND HUNDRED IN A MATCH

| G. A. Gooch. . . . . | 333 | 123 | England v India at Lord's. . . . . | 1990 |

DOUBLE-HUNDRED AND HUNDRED IN A MATCH

In addition to Fagg and Gooch, there have been **57** further instances of a batsman scoring a double-hundred and a hundred in the same first-class match. The most recent are:

B. C. Lara	221	130	West Indies v Sri Lanka at Colombo		2001-02
Minhazul Abedin	210	110	Chittagong v Dhaka at Mymensingh		2001-02
A. T. Rayudu	210	159*	Hyderabad v Andhra at Secunderabad		2002-03
H. H. Kanitkar	112	207*	Maharashtra v Services at Aurangabad		2003-04
M. J. Horne	118	209*	Auckland v Northern Districts at Auckland		2003-04
S. A. Newman	117	219	Surrey v Glamorgan at The Oval		2005
P. A. Jaques	240	117	Australia A v India A at Cairns		2006
C. J. L. Rogers	128	222*	Northamptonshire v Somerset at Taunton		2006
M. W. Goodwin	119	205*	Sussex v Surrey at Hove		2007
Younis Khan	106	202*	Yorkshire v Hampshire at Southampton		2007
V. Sibanda	209	116*	Zimbabwe XI v Kenya at Kwekwe		2009-10
S. M. Ervine	**208**	**160**	**Southern Rocks v MW Rhinos at Masvingo**		**2009-10**
C. J. L. Rogers	**200**	**140***	**Derbyshire v Surrey at The Oval**		**2010**
M. R. Ramprakash	**223**	**103***	**Surrey v Middlesex at The Oval**		**2010**

Notes: Zaheer Abbas achieved the feat four times, for Gloucestershire between 1976 and 1981, and was not out in all eight innings. M. R. Hallam did it twice for Leicestershire, in 1959 and 1961; N. R. Taylor twice for Kent, in 1990 and 1991; G. A. Gooch for England in 1990 (see above) and Essex in 1994; M. W. Goodwin twice for Sussex, in 2001 and 2007; and C. J. L. Rogers for Northamptonshire in 2006 and for Derbyshire in 2010.

TWO SEPARATE HUNDREDS IN A MATCH MOST TIMES

R. T. Ponting	8	J. B. Hobbs	6	M. L. Hayden	5
Zaheer Abbas	8	G. M. Turner	6	G. A. Hick	5
W. R. Hammond	7	C. B. Fry	5		
M. R. Ramprakash	7	G. A. Gooch	5		

Current players only:

S. G. Law	4	J. P. Crawley	3	M. van Jaarsveld	3
C. J. L. Rogers	4	A. N. Petersen	3		

Notes: W. Lambert scored 107 and 157 for Sussex v Epsom at Lord's in 1817, and it was not until W. G. Grace made 130 and 102* for South of the Thames v North of the Thames at Canterbury in 1868 that the feat was repeated.

FIVE HUNDREDS OR MORE IN SUCCESSION

D. G. Bradman (1938-39)	6	B. C. Lara (1993-94/1994)	5
C. B. Fry (1901)	6	P. A. Patel (2007/2007-08)	5
M. J. Procter (1970-71)	6	E. D. Weekes (1955-56)	5
M. E. K. Hussey (2003)	5		

Notes: Bradman also scored four hundreds in succession twice, in 1931-32 and 1948/1948-49; W. R. Hammond did it in 1936-37 and 1945/1946, and H. Sutcliffe in 1931 and 1939.

Current players only:

S. Badrinath (2007/2007-08)	4	S. R. Tendulkar (1994-95)	4
Ijaz Ahmed, jun. (1994-95)	4	Yasir Hameed (2002-03/2003)	4
V. Sibanda (2009-10)	4	Younis Khan (1999-2000)	4

Notes: T. W. Hayward (Surrey v Nottinghamshire and Leicestershire), D. W. Hookes (South Australia v Queensland and New South Wales) and V. Sibanda (Zimbabwe XI v Kenya and Mid West v Southern Rocks) are the only players to score two hundreds in each of two successive matches. Hayward scored his in six days, June 4-9, 1906.

The most fifties in consecutive innings is ten — by E. Tyldesley in 1926, by D. G. Bradman in the 1947-48 and 1948 seasons and by R. S. Kaluwitharana in 1994-95.

MOST HUNDREDS IN A SEASON

D. C. S. Compton (1947)	18	W. R. Hammond (1937)	13
J. B. Hobbs (1925)	16	T. W. Hayward (1906)	13
W. R. Hammond (1938)	15	E. H. Hendren (1923)	13
H. Sutcliffe (1932)	14	E. H. Hendren (1927)	13
G. Boycott (1971)	13	E. H. Hendren (1928)	13
D. G. Bradman (1938)	13	C. P. Mead (1928)	13
C. B. Fry (1901)	13	H. Sutcliffe (1928)	13
W. R. Hammond (1933)	13	H. Sutcliffe (1931)	13

Since 1969 (excluding G. Boycott – above)

G. A. Gooch (1990)	12	M. R. Ramprakash (1995)	10
S. J. Cook (1991)	11	M. R. Ramprakash (2007)	10
Zaheer Abbas (1976)	11	G. M. Turner (1970)	10
G. A. Hick (1988)	10	Zaheer Abbas (1981)	10
H. Morris (1990)	10		

Note: The most achieved outside England is **nine by V. Sibanda in Zimbabwe (2009-10)**, followed by eight by D. G. Bradman in Australia (1947-48), D. C. S. Compton (1948-49), R. N. Harvey and A. R. Morris (both 1949-50) all three in South Africa, M. D. Crowe in New Zealand (1986-87), Asif Mujtaba in Pakistan (1995-96), V. V. S. Laxman in India (1999-2000) and M. G. Bevan in Australia (2004-05).

MOST DOUBLE-HUNDREDS IN A SEASON

D. G. Bradman (1930)	6	W. R. Hammond (1933)	4
K. S. Ranjitsinhji (1900)	5	W. R. Hammond (1934)	4
E. D. Weekes (1950)	5	E. H. Hendren (1929-30)	4
Arun Lal (1986-87)	4	V. M. Merchant (1944-45)	4
C. B. Fry (1901)	4	G. M. Turner (1971-72)	4

Current players only:

A. Chopra (2007-08)	3	D. S. Jadhav (2003-04)	3
R. Dravid (2003-04)	3	P. A. Jaques (2006)	3
B. J. Hodge (2004)	3	M. R. Ramprakash (1995)	3
M. E. K. Hussey (2001)	3		

Note: R. Dravid scored his three double-hundreds in three different countries; P. A. Jaques scored his in two.

MOST DOUBLE-HUNDREDS IN A CAREER

D. G. Bradman	37	C. P. Mead	13	**R. Dravid**	**10**
W. R. Hammond	36	W. H. Ponsford	13	M. W. Gatting	10
E. H. Hendren	22	J. T. Tyldesley	13	S. M. Gavaskar	10
M. R. Ramprakash	**17**	P. Holmes	12	J. Hardstaff, jun	10
H. Sutcliffe	17	Javed Miandad	12	V. S. Hazare	10
C. B. Fry	16	J. L. Langer	12	B. J. Hodge	10
G. A. Hick	16	R. B. Simpson	12	I. V. A. Richards	10
J. B. Hobbs	16	J. W. Hearne	11	A. Shrewsbury	10
C. G. Greenidge	14	L. Hutton	11	R. T. Simpson	10
K. S. Ranjitsinhji	14	D. S. Lehmann	11	G. M. Turner	10
G. A. Gooch	13	V. M. Merchant	11	Zaheer Abbas	10
W. G. Grace	13	A. Sandham	11		
B. C. Lara	13	G. Boycott	10		

MOST HUNDREDS IN A CAREER

(50 or more)

		Total	Total Inns	100th 100 Season	Inns	400+	300+	200+
1	J. B. Hobbs..........	197	1,315	1923	821	0	1	16
2	E. H. Hendren	170	1,300	1928-29	740	0	1	22
3	W. R. Hammond	167	1,005	1935	680	0	4	36
4	C. P. Mead	153	1,340	1927	892	0	0	13
5	G. Boycott	151	1,014	1977	645	0	0	10
6	H. Sutcliffe.........	149	1,088	1932	700	0	1	17
7	F. E. Woolley.......	145	1,532	1929	1,031	0	1	9
8	G. A. Hick	136	871	1998	574	1	3	16
9	L. Hutton	129	814	1951	619	0	1	11
10	G. A. Gooch........	128	990	1992-93	820	0	1	13
11	W. G. Grace........	126	1,493	1895	1,113	0	3	13
12	D. C. S. Compton...	123	839	1952	552	0	1	9
13	T. W. Graveney	122	1,223	1964	940	0	0	7
14	D. G. Bradman	117	338	1947-48	295	1	6	37
15	I. V. A. Richards	114	796	1988-89	658	0	1	10
16	**M. R. Ramprakash...**	**113**	**729**	**2008**	**676**	**0**	**1**	**17**
17	Zaheer Abbas	108	768	1982-83	658	0	0	10
18	{ A. Sandham	107	1,000	1935	871	0	1	11
	{ M. C. Cowdrey.....	107	1,130	1973	1,035	0	1	3
20	T. W. Hayward......	104	1,138	1913	1,076	0	1	8
21	{ G. M. Turner	103	792	1982	779	0	1	10
	{ J. H. Edrich........	103	979	1977	945	0	1	4
23	{ L. E. G. Ames	102	951	1950	916	0	0	9
	{ E. Tyldesley........	102	961	1934	919	0	0	7
	{ D. L. Amiss	102	1,139	1986	1,081	0	0	3

Notes: In the above table, 200+, 300+ and 400+ include all scores above those figures.

E. H. Hendren, D. G. Bradman and I. V. A. Richards scored their 100th hundreds in Australia; G. A. Gooch scored his in India. His record includes his century in South Africa in 1981-82, which is no longer accepted by the ICC. Zaheer Abbas scored his 100th in Pakistan. Zaheer Abbas and G. Boycott did so in Test matches.

J. W. Hearne	96	S. R. Waugh	79	M. G. Bevan	68
C. B. Fry	94	**S. R. Tendulkar**	**77**	D. C. Boon	68
M. W. Gatting	94	K. F. Barrington	76	R. E. Marshall	68
C. G. Greenidge......	92	J. G. Langridge	76	R. N. Harvey	67
A. J. Lamb	89	C. Washbrook	76	P. Holmes	67
A. I. Kallicharran ...	87	H. T. W. Hardinge ...	75	J. D. Robertson	67
W. J. Edrich........	86	R. Abel	74	P. A. Perrin	66
R. B. Kanhai	86	G. S. Chappell	74	K. C. Wessels	66
J. L. Langer	86	D. Kenyon	74	B. C. Lara	65
G. S. Sobers........	86	K. S. McEwan	74	S. J. Cook	64
J. T. Tyldesley......	86	Majid Khan.........	73	T. M. Moody	64
P. B. H. May	85	**R. T. Ponting**	**73**	R. G. Pollock	64
R. E. S. Wyatt	85	Mushtaq Mohammad...	72	R. T. Simpson	64
J. Hardstaff, jun	83	J. O'Connor	72	K. W. R. Fletcher ...	63
D. S. Lehmann......	82	W. G. Quaife	72	**M. W. Goodwin**....	**63**
S. M. Gavaskar	81	K. S. Ranjitsinhji.....	72	R. T. Robinson	63
M. E. Waugh........	81	D. Brookes..........	71	**R. Dravid**	**62**
Javed Miandad......	80	M. D. Crowe	71	G. Gunn............	62
M. Leyland	80	A. C. Russell	71	S. J. Barnett	61
B. A. Richards......	80	A. R. Border	70	D. L. Haynes	61
M. L. Hayden	79	D. Denton	69	R. A. Smith	61
S. G. Law...........	79	C. L. Hooper	69	V. S. Hazare	60
C. H. Lloyd	79	M. J. K. Smith	69	G. H. Hirst.........	60

R. B. Simpson	60	D. M. Jones	55	N. Hussain	52
P. F. Warner	60	**J. H. Kallis**	**55**	J. E. Morris	52
I. M. Chappell	59	D. B. Vengsarkar	55	D. W. Randall	52
A. L. Hassett	59	W. Watson	55	J. Cox	51
W. Larkins	59	M. A. Atherton	54	E. R. Dexter	51
M. P. Maynard	59	M. Azharuddin	54	B. J. Hodge	51
A. Shrewsbury	59	J. P. Crawley	54	**S. M. Katich**	**51**
J. G. Wright	58	D. J. Insole	54	J. M. Parks	51
A. E. Fagg	58	W. W. Keeton	54	**M. van Jaarsveld**	**51**
P. H. Parfitt	58	W. Bardsley	53	W. W. Whysall	51
W. Rhodes	58	B. F. Davison	53	B. C. Broad	50
M. J. Di Venuto	**57**	A. E. Dipper	53	G. Cox, jun	50
P. N. Kirsten	57	D. I. Gower	53	H. E. Dollery	50
L. B. Fishlock	56	G. L. Jessop	53	K. S. Duleepsinhji	50
A. Jones	56	**V. V. S. Laxman**	**53**	M. T. G. Elliott	50
C. A. Milton	56	H. Morris	53	H. Gimblett	50
C. W. J. Athey	55	James Seymour	53	W. M. Lawry	50
S. Chanderpaul	**55**	Shafiq Ahmad	53	Sadiq Mohammad	50
C. Hallows	55	E. H. Bowley	52	F. B. Watson	50
Hanif Mohammad	55	D. B. Close	52		
M. E. K. Hussey	**55**	A. Ducat	52		

Other Current Players

In addition to the above, the following who played in 2010 have scored 30 or more hundreds.

A. D. Brown	46	P. A. Jaques	36	K. C. Sangakkara	32
D. P. M. D. Jayawardene	45	V. Sehwag	36	S. Sriram	32
C. J. L. Rogers	45	Younis Khan	35	H. M. Amla	31
R. W. T. Key	43	D. M. Benkenstein	34	M. J. North	31
M. E. Trescothick	43	Hasan Raza	34	A. G. Prince	31
Wasim Jaffer	43	H. H. Dippenaar	33	R. R. Sarwan	31
M. B. Loye	42	Ijaz Ahmed	33	G. C. Smith	31
D. J. Hussey	40	T. T. Samaraweera	33	M. A. Wagh	31
B. F. Smith	40	U. Afzaal	32	Zahoor Elahi	31
K. P. Pietersen	39	I. R. Bell	32	A. N. Cook	30
J. A. Rudolph	39	G. Gambhir	32	T. M. Dilshan	30
O. A. Shah	39	S. C. Ganguly	32	D. L. Hemp	30
A. J. Strauss	38	A. McGrath	32	M. S. Sinclair	30
N. D. McKenzie	37	Misbah-ul-Haq	32		

MOST RUNS IN A SEASON

	Season	I	NO	R	HS	100s	Avge
D. C. S. Compton	1947	50	8	3,816	246	18	90.85
W. J. Edrich	1947	52	8	3,539	267*	12	80.43
T. W. Hayward	1906	61	8	3,518	219	13	66.37
L. Hutton	1949	56	6	3,429	269*	12	68.58
F. E. Woolley	1928	59	4	3,352	198	12	60.94
H. Sutcliffe	1932	52	7	3,336	313	14	74.13
W. R. Hammond	1933	54	5	3,323	264	13	67.81
E. H. Hendren	1928	54	7	3,311	209*	13	70.44
R. Abel	1901	68	8	3,309	247	7	55.15

Notes: 3,000 in a season has been surpassed on 19 other occasions (a full list can be found in *Wisden* 1999 and earlier editions). W. R. Hammond, E. H. Hendren and H. Sutcliffe are the only players to achieve the feat three times. K. S. Ranjitsinhji was the first batsman to reach 3,000 in a season, with 3,159 in 1899. M. J. K. Smith (3,245 in 1959) and W. E. Alley (3,019 in 1961) are the only players except those listed above to have reached 3,000 since World War II.

W. G. Grace scored 2,739 runs in 1871 – the first batsman to reach 2,000 runs in a season. He made ten hundreds including two double-hundreds, with an average of 78.25 in all first-class matches.

The highest aggregate in a season since the reduction of County Championship matches in 1969 is 2,755 by S. J. Cook (42 innings) in 1991, and the last batsman to achieve 2,000 was M. R. Ramprakash (2,026 in 2007).

2,000 RUNS IN A SEASON MOST TIMES

J. B. Hobbs	17	F. E. Woolley	13	C. P. Mead	11
E. H. Hendren	15	W. R. Hammond	12	T. W. Hayward	10
H. Sutcliffe	15	J. G. Langridge	11		

Note: Since the reduction of County Championship matches in 1969, G. A. Gooch is the only batsman to have reached 2,000 runs in a season five times.

1,000 RUNS IN A SEASON MOST TIMES

Includes overseas tours and seasons

W. G. Grace	28	A. Jones	23	G. Gunn	20
F. E. Woolley	28	T. W. Graveney	22	T. W. Hayward	20
M. C. Cowdrey	27	W. R. Hammond	22	G. A. Hick	20
C. P. Mead	27	D. Denton	21	James Langridge	20
G. Boycott	26	J. H. Edrich	21	**M. R. Ramprakash**	**20**
J. B. Hobbs	26	G. A. Gooch	21	A. Sandham	20
E. H. Hendren	25	W. Rhodes	21	M. J. K. Smith	20
D. L. Amiss	24	D. B. Close	20	C. Washbrook	20
W. G. Quaife	24	K. W. R. Fletcher	20		
H. Sutcliffe	24	M. W. Gatting	20		

Notes: F. E. Woolley reached 1,000 runs in 28 consecutive seasons (1907–1938), C. P. Mead in 27 (1906–1936).

Outside England, 1,000 runs in a season has been reached most times by D. G. Bradman (in 12 seasons in Australia).

Three batsmen have scored 1,000 runs in a season in each of four different countries: G. S. Sobers in West Indies, England, India and Australia; M. C. Cowdrey and G. Boycott in England, South Africa, West Indies and Australia.

HIGHEST AGGREGATES OUTSIDE ENGLAND

	Season	I	NO	R	HS	100s	Avge
In Australia D. G. Bradman	1928-29	24	6	1,690	340*	7	93.88
In South Africa J. R. Reid	1961-62	30	2	1,915	203	7	68.39
In West Indies E. H. Hendren	1929-30	18	5	1,765	254*	6	135.76
In New Zealand M. D. Crowe	1986-87	21	3	1,676	175*	8	93.11
In India C. G. Borde	1964-65	28	3	1,604	168	6	64.16
In Pakistan Saadat Ali	1983-84	27	1	1,649	208	4	63.42
In Sri Lanka R. P. Arnold	1995-96	24	3	1,475	217*	5	70.23
In Zimbabwe **V. Sibanda**	**2009-10**	**26**	**4**	**1,612**	**215**	**9**	**73.27**
In Bangladesh Minhazul Abedin	2001-02	15	1	1,012	210	3	72.28

Note: In more than one country, the following aggregates of over 2,000 runs have been recorded:

M. Amarnath (P/I/WI)	1982-83	34	6	2,234	207	9	79.78
J. R. Reid (SA/A/NZ)	1961-62	40	2	2,188	203	7	57.57
S. M. Gavaskar (I/P)	1978-79	30	6	2,121	205	10	88.37
R. B. Simpson (I/P/A/WI)	1964-65	34	4	2,063	201	8	68.76
M. H. Richardson (Z/SA/NZ)	2000-01	34	3	2,030	306	4	65.48

LEADING BATSMEN IN AN ENGLISH SEASON

(Qualification: 8 completed innings)

Season	Leading scorer	Runs	Avge	Top of averages	Runs	Avge
1946	D. C. S. Compton	2,403	61.61	W. R. Hammond	1,783	84.90
1947	D. C. S. Compton	3,816	90.85	D. C. S. Compton	3,816	90.85
1948	L. Hutton	2,654	64.73	D. G. Bradman	2,428	89.92
1949	L. Hutton	3,429	68.58	J. Hardstaff	2,251	72.61
1950	R. T. Simpson	2,576	62.82	E. D. Weekes	2,310	79.65
1951	J. D. Robertson	2,917	56.09	P. B. H. May	2,339	68.79
1952	L. Hutton	2,567	61.11	D. S. Sheppard	2,262	64.62
1953	W. J. Edrich	2,557	47.35	R. N. Harvey	2,040	65.80
1954	D. Kenyon	2,636	51.68	D. C. S. Compton	1,524	58.61
1955	D. J. Insole	2,427	42.57	D. J. McGlew	1,871	58.46
1956	T. W. Graveney	2,397	49.93	K. Mackay	1,103	52.52
1957	T. W. Graveney	2,361	49.18	P. B. H. May	2,347	61.76
1958	P. B. H. May	2,231	63.74	P. B. H. May	2,231	63.74
1959	M. J. K. Smith	3,245	57.94	V. L. Manjrekar	755	68.63
1960	M. J. K. Smith	2,551	45.55	R. Subba Row	1,503	55.66
1961	W. E. Alley	3,019	56.96	W. M. Lawry	2,019	61.18
1962	J. H. Edrich	2,482	51.70	R. T. Simpson	867	54.18
1963	J. B. Bolus	2,190	41.32	G. S. Sobers	1,333	47.60
1964	T. W. Graveney	2,385	54.20	K. F. Barrington	1,872	62.40
1965	J. H. Edrich	2,319	62.67	M. C. Cowdrey	2,093	63.42
1966	A. R. Lewis	2,198	41.47	G. S. Sobers	1,349	61.31
1967	C. A. Milton	2,089	46.42	K. F. Barrington	2,059	68.63
1968	B. A. Richards	2,395	47.90	G. Boycott	1,487	64.65
1969	J. H. Edrich	2,238	69.93	J. H. Edrich	2,238	69.93
1970	G. M. Turner	2,379	61.00	G. S. Sobers	1,742	75.73
1971	G. Boycott	2,503	100.12	G. Boycott	2,503	100.12
1972	Majid Khan	2,074	61.00	G. Boycott	1,230	72.35
1973	G. M. Turner	2,416	67.11	G. M. Turner	2,416	67.11
1974	R. T. Virgin	1,936	56.94	C. H. Lloyd	1,458	63.39
1975	G. Boycott	1,915	73.65	R. B. Kanhai	1,073	82.53
1976	Zaheer Abbas	2,554	75.11	Zaheer Abbas	2,554	75.11
1977	I. V. A. Richards	2,161	65.48	G. Boycott	1,701	68.04
1978	D. L. Amiss	2,030	53.42	C. E. B. Rice	1,871	66.82
1979	K. C. Wessels	1,800	52.94	G. Boycott	1,538	102.53
1980	P. N. Kirsten	1,895	63.16	A. J. Lamb	1,797	66.55
1981	Zaheer Abbas	2,306	88.69	Zaheer Abbas	2,306	88.69
1982	A. I. Kallicharran	2,120	66.25	G. M. Turner	1,171	90.07
1983	K. S. McEwan	2,176	64.00	I. V. A. Richards	1,204	75.25
1984	G. A. Gooch	2,559	67.34	C. G. Greenidge	1,069	82.23
1985	G. A. Gooch	2,208	71.22	I. V. A. Richards	1,836	76.50
1986	C. G. Greenidge	2,035	67.83	C. G. Greenidge	2,035	67.83
1987	G. A. Hick	1,879	52.19	M. D. Crowe	1,627	67.79
1988	G. A. Hick	2,713	77.51	R. A. Harper	622	77.75
1989	S. J. Cook	2,241	60.56	D. M. Jones	1,510	88.82
1990	G. A. Gooch	2,746	101.70	G. A. Gooch	2,746	101.70
1991	S. J. Cook	2,755	81.02	C. L. Hooper	1,501	93.81
1992	{ P. D. Bowler	2,044	65.93	Salim Malik	1,184	78.93
	{ M. A. Roseberry	2,044	56.77			

Season	Leading scorer	Runs	Avge	Top of averages	Runs	Avge
1993	G. A. Gooch	2,023	63.21	D. C. Boon	1,437	75.63
1994	B. C. Lara	2,066	89.82	J. D. Carr	1,543	90.76
1995	M. R. Ramprakash ..	2,258	77.86	M. R. Ramprakash	2,258	77.86
1996	G. A. Gooch	1,944	67.03	S. C. Ganguly	762	95.25
1997	S. P. James	1,775	68.26	G. A. Hick	1,524	69.27
1998	J. P. Crawley	1,851	74.04	J. P. Crawley	1,851	74.04
1999	S. G. Law	1,833	73.32	S. G. Law	1,833	73.32
2000	D. S. Lehmann	1,477	67.13	M. G. Bevan	1,124	74.93
2001	M. E. K. Hussey	2,055	79.03	D. R. Martyn	942	104.66
2002	I. J. Ward	1,759	62.82	R. Dravid	773	96.62
2003	S. G. Law	1,820	91.00	S. G. Law	1,820	91.00
2004	R. W. T. Key	1,896	79.00	R. W. T. Key	1,896	79.00
2005	O. A. Shah	1,728	66.46	M. E. K. Hussey	1,074	76.71
2006	M. R. Ramprakash ...	2,278	103.54	M. R. Ramprakash	2,278	103.54
2007	M. R. Ramprakash ...	2,026	101.30	M. R. Ramprakash	2,026	101.30
2008	S. C. Moore	1,451	55.80	T. Frost	1,003	83.58
2009	M. E. Trescothick	1,817	75.70	M. R. Ramprakash	1,350	90.00
2010	**M. R. Ramprakash ..**	**1,595**	**61.34**	**J. C. Hildreth ....**	**1,440**	**65.45**

Notes: The highest average recorded in an English season was 115.66 (2,429 runs, 26 innings) by D. G. Bradman in 1938.

In 1953, W. A. Johnston averaged 102.00 from 17 innings, 16 not out.

MOST RUNS

Dates in italics denote the first half of an overseas season; i.e. *1945* denotes the 1945-46 season.

		Career	R	I	NO	HS	100s	Avge
1	J. B. Hobbs.........	1905–1934	61,237	1,315	106	316*	197	50.65
2	F. E. Woolley	1906–1938	58,969	1,532	85	305*	145	40.75
3	E. H. Hendren.......	1907–1938	57,611	1,300	166	301*	170	50.80
4	C. P. Mead	1905–1936	55,061	1,340	185	280*	153	47.67
5	W. G. Grace	1865–1908	54,896	1,493	105	344	126	39.55
6	W. R. Hammond	1920–1951	50,551	1,005	104	336*	167	56.10
7	H. Sutcliffe	1919–1945	50,138	1,088	123	313	149	51.95
8	G. Boycott	1962–1986	48,426	1,014	162	261*	151	56.83
9	T. W. Graveney	1948–*1971*	47,793	1,223	159	258	122	44.91
10	G. A. Gooch	1973–2000	44,846	990	75	333	128	49.01
11	T. W. Hayward	1893–1914	43,551	1,138	96	315*	104	41.79
12	D. L. Amiss	1960–1987	43,423	1,139	126	262*	102	42.86
13	M. C. Cowdrey......	1950–1976	42,719	1,130	134	307	107	42.89
14	A. Sandham	1911–*1937*	41,284	1,000	79	325	107	44.82
15	G. A. Hick	*1983*–2008	41,112	871	84	405*	136	52.23
16	L. Hutton	1934–1960	40,140	814	91	364	129	55.51
17	M. J. K. Smith	1951–1975	39,832	1,091	139	204	69	41.84
18	W. Rhodes	1898–1930	39,802	1,528	237	267*	58	30.83
19	J. H. Edrich........	1956–1978	39,790	979	104	310*	103	45.47
20	R. E. S. Wyatt	1923–1957	39,405	1,141	157	232	85	40.04
21	D. C. S. Compton....	1936–1964	38,942	839	88	300	123	51.85
22	E. Tyldesley........	1909–1936	38,874	961	106	256*	102	45.46
23	J. T. Tyldesley	1895–1923	37,897	994	62	295*	86	40.66
24	K. W. R. Fletcher....	1962–1988	37,665	1,167	170	228*	63	37.77
25	C. G. Greenidge	1970–1992	37,354	889	75	273*	92	45.88
26	J. W. Hearne.......	1909–1936	37,252	1,025	116	285*	96	40.98
27	L. E. G. Ames......	1926–1951	37,248	951	95	295	102	43.51
28	D. Kenyon	1946–1967	37,002	1,159	59	259	74	33.63
29	W. J. Edrich	1934–1958	36,965	964	92	267*	86	42.39
30	J. M. Parks	1949–1976	36,673	1,227	172	205*	51	34.76
31	M. W. Gatting	1975–1998	36,549	861	123	258	94	49.52
32	D. Denton..........	1894–1920	36,479	1,163	70	221	69	33.37

		Career	R	I	NO	HS	100s	Avge
33	G. H. Hirst	1891–1929	36,323	1,215	151	341	60	34.13
34	I. V. A. Richards	1971–1993	36,212	796	63	322	114	49.40
35	A. Jones	1957–1983	36,049	1,168	72	204*	56	32.89
36	W. G. Quaife	1894–1928	36,012	1,203	185	255*	72	35.37
37	R. E. Marshall	1945–1972	35,725	1,053	59	228*	68	35.94
38	G. Gunn	1902–1932	35,208	1,061	82	220	62	35.96
39	D. B. Close	1949–1986	34,994	1,225	173	198	52	33.26
40	Zaheer Abbas	1965–1986	34,843	768	92	274	108	51.54
41	**M. R. Ramprakash** .	**1987–2010**	**34,839**	**729**	**91**	**301***	**113**	**54.60**
42	J. G. Langridge.	1928–1955	34,380	984	66	250*	76	37.45
43	G. M. Turner	1964–1982	34,346	792	101	311*	103	49.70
44	C. Washbrook.	1933–1964	34,101	906	107	251*	76	42.67
45	M. Leyland	1920–1948	33,660	932	101	263	80	40.50
46	H. T. W. Hardinge . . .	1902–1933	33,519	1,021	103	263*	75	36.51
47	R. Abel	1881–1904	33,124	1,007	73	357*	74	35.46
48	A. I. Kallicharran	1966–1990	32,650	834	86	243*	87	43.64
49	A. J. Lamb	1972–1995	32,502	772	108	294	89	48.94
50	C. A. Milton	1948–1974	32,150	1,078	125	170	56	33.73
51	J. D. Robertson.	1937–1959	31,914	897	46	331*	67	37.50
52	J. Hardstaff, jun	1930–1955	31,847	812	94	266	83	44.35
53	James Langridge.	1924–1953	31,716	1,058	157	167	42	35.20
54	K. F. Barrington	1953–1968	31,714	831	136	256	76	45.63
55	C. H. Lloyd	1963–1986	31,232	730	96	242*	79	49.26
56	Mushtaq Mohammad .	1956–1985	31,091	843	104	303*	72	42.07
57	C. B. Fry	1892–1921	30,886	658	43	258*	94	50.22
58	D. Brookes	1934–1959	30,874	925	70	257	71	36.10
59	P. Holmes	1913–1935	30,573	810	84	315*	67	42.11
60	R. T. Simpson.	1944–1963	30,546	852	55	259	64	38.32
61	L. G. Berry	1924–1951	30,225	1,056	57	232	45	30.25
61	K. G. Suttle.	1949–1971	30,225	1,064	92	204*	49	31.09
63	P. A. Perrin	1896–1928	29,709	918	91	343*	66	35.92
64	R. B. Kanhai	1954–1981	29,250	675	83	256	86	49.40
65	P. F. Warner	1894–1929	29,028	875	75	244	60	36.28
66	J. O'Connor	1921–1939	28,764	903	79	248	72	34.90
67	Javed Miandad	1973–1993	28,647	631	96	311	80	53.44
68	T. E. Bailey	1945–1967	28,641	1,072	215	205	28	33.42
69	K. J. Barnett	1979–2002	28,593	784	76	239*	61	40.38
70	D. W. Randall.	1972–1993	28,456	827	81	237	52	38.14
71	J. L. Langer	1991–2009	28,382	622	57	342	86	50.23
72	E. H. Bowley	1912–1934	28,378	859	47	283	52	34.94
73	B. A. Richards	1964–1982	28,358	576	58	356	80	54.74
74	G. S. Sobers	1952–1974	28,315	609	93	365*	86	54.87
75	A. E. Dipper	1908–1932	28,075	865	69	252*	53	35.27
76	D. G. Bradman	1927–1948	28,067	338	43	452*	117	95.14
77	J. H. Hampshire	1961–1984	28,059	924	112	183*	43	34.55
78	P. B. H. May.	1948–1963	27,592	618	77	285*	85	51.00
79	R. T. Robinson	1978–1999	27,571	739	85	220*	63	42.15
80	B. F. Davison	1967–1987	27,453	766	79	189	53	39.96
81	Majid Khan.	1961–1984	27,444	700	62	241	73	43.01
82	A. C. Russell	1908–1930	27,358	717	59	273	71	41.57
83	E. G. Hayes	1896–1926	27,318	896	48	276	48	32.21
84	A. E. Fagg	1932–1957	27,291	803	46	269*	58	36.05
85	James Seymour.	1900–1926	27,237	911	62	218*	53	32.08
86	W. Larkins	1972–1995	27,142	842	54	252	59	34.44
87	A. R. Border.	1976–1995	27,131	625	97	205	70	51.38
88	S. G. Law	1988–2009	27,080	601	65	263	79	50.52
89	P. H. Parfitt.	1956–1973	26,924	845	104	200*	58	36.33
90	M. E. Waugh	1985–2003	26,855	591	75	229*	81	52.04
91	G. L. Jessop	1894–1914	26,698	855	37	286	53	32.63
92	K. S. McEwan	1972–1991	26,628	705	67	218	74	41.73

		Career	R	I	NO	HS	100s	Avge
93	D. E. Davies	1924–1954	26,564	1,032	80	287*	32	27.90
94	A. Shrewsbury	1875–1902	26,505	813	90	267	59	36.65
95	M. J. Stewart	1954–1972	26,492	898	93	227*	49	32.90
96	C. T. Radley	1964–1987	26,441	880	134	200	46	35.44
97	D. I. Gower	1975–1993	26,339	727	70	228	53	40.08
98	C. E. B. Rice	1969–1993	26,331	766	123	246	48	40.95
99	A. J. Stewart	1981–2003	26,165	734	81	271*	48	40.06
100	R. A. Smith	1980–2003	26,155	717	87	209*	61	41.51

Note: Some works of reference provide career figures which differ from those in this list, owing to the exclusion or inclusion of matches recognised or not recognised as first-class by *Wisden*.

Other Current Players with 20,000 Runs

	Career	R	I	NO	HS	100s	Avge
M. J. Di Venuto	1991–2010	23,974	556	41	254*	57	46.55
S. R. Tendulkar	1988–2010	23,425	440	47	248*	77	59.60
R. Dravid	1990–2010	22,410	465	64	270	62	55.88
R. T. Ponting	1992–2010	21,332	436	55	257	73	55.98
M. E. K. Hussey	1994–2010	20,651	434	43	331*	55	52.81
M. W. Goodwin	1994–2010	20,381	461	38	344*	63	48.18

HIGHEST CAREER AVERAGE

(Qualification: 10,000 runs)

Avge		Career	I	NO	R	HS	100s
95.14	D. G. Bradman	1927–1948	338	43	28,067	452*	117
71.22	V. M. Merchant	1929–1951	229	43	13,248	359*	44
67.46	Ajay Sharma	1984–2000	166	16	10,120	259*	38
65.18	W. H. Ponsford	1920–1934	235	23	13,819	437	47
64.99	W. M. Woodfull	1921–1934	245	39	13,388	284	49
59.60	**S. R. Tendulkar**	**1988–2010**	**440**	**47**	**23,425**	**248***	**77**
58.24	A. L. Hassett	1932–1953	322	32	16,890	232	59
58.19	V. S. Hazare	1934–1966	365	45	18,621	316*	60
57.83	D. S. Lehmann	1987–2007	479	33	25,795	339	82
57.32	M. G. Bevan	1989–2006	400	66	19,147	216	68
57.22	A. F. Kippax	1918–1935	256	33	12,762	315*	43
56.83	G. Boycott	1962–1986	1,014	162	48,426	261*	151
56.55	C. L. Walcott	1941–1963	238	29	11,820	314*	40
56.37	K. S. Ranjitsinhji	1893–1920	500	62	24,692	285*	72
56.22	R. B. Simpson	1952–1977	436	62	21,029	359	60
56.10	W. R. Hammond	1920–1951	1,005	104	50,551	336*	167
56.02	M. D. Crowe	1979–1995	412	62	19,608	299	71
55.98	**R. T. Ponting**	**1992–2010**	**436**	**55**	**21,332**	**257**	**73**
55.88	**R. Dravid**	**1990–2010**	**465**	**64**	**22,410**	**270**	**62**
55.51	L. Hutton	1934–1960	814	91	40,140	364	129
55.34	E. D. Weekes	1944–1964	241	24	12,010	304*	36
55.27	**D. J. Hussey**	**2002–2010**	**240**	**25**	**11,885**	**275**	**40**
55.11	S. V. Manjrekar	1984–1997	217	31	10,252	377	31
54.87	G. S. Sobers	1952–1974	609	93	28,315	365*	86
54.74	B. A. Richards	1964–1982	576	58	28,358	356	80
54.67	R. G. Pollock	1960–1986	437	54	20,940	274	64
54.63	**J. H. Kallis**	**1993–2010**	**384**	**54**	**18,029**	**201***	**55**
54.60	**M. R. Ramprakash**	**1987–2010**	**729**	**91**	**34,839**	**301***	**113**
54.49	**G. Gambhir**	**1999–2010**	**205**	**20**	**10,082**	**233***	**32**
54.26	**S. Chanderpaul**	**1991–2010**	**428**	**76**	**19,101**	**303***	**55**
54.24	F. M. M. Worrell	1941–1964	326	49	15,025	308*	39
54.05	A. Flower	1986–2006	372	69	16,379	271*	49

Note: G. A. Headley (*1927–1954*) scored 9,921 runs, average 69.86.

FASTEST FIFTIES

Minutes

11	C. I. J. Smith (66)	Middlesex v Gloucestershire at Bristol	1938
13	Khalid Mahmood (56)	Gujranwala v Sargodha at Gujranwala............	2000-01
14	S. J. Pegler (50)	South Africans v Tasmania at Launceston........	1910-11
14	F. T. Mann (53)	Middlesex v Nottinghamshire at Lord's........	1921
14	H. B. Cameron (56)	Transvaal v Orange Free State at Johannesburg.....	1934-35
14	C. I. J. Smith (52)	Middlesex v Kent at Maidstone	1935

Note: The number of balls taken to achieve fifties was rarely recorded until recently. C. I. J. Smith's two fifties (above) may have taken only 12 balls each. Khalid Mahmood reached his fifty in 15 balls.

Fifties scored in contrived circumstances and with the bowlers' compliance are excluded from the above list, including the fastest of them all, in 8 minutes (13 balls) by C. C. Inman, Leicestershire v Nottinghamshire at Nottingham, 1965, and 10 minutes by G. Chapple, Lancashire v Glamorgan at Manchester, 1993.

FASTEST HUNDREDS

Minutes

35	P. G. H. Fender (113*)	Surrey v Northamptonshire at Northampton	1920
40	G. L. Jessop (101)	Gloucestershire v Yorkshire at Harrogate	1897
40	Ahsan-ul-Haq (100*)	Muslims v Sikhs at Lahore.....................	1923-24
42	G. L. Jessop (191)	Gentlemen of South v Players of South at Hastings .	1907
43	A. H. Hornby (106)	Lancashire v Somerset at Manchester	1905
43	D. W. Hookes (107)	South Australia v Victoria at Adelaide	1982-83
44	R. N. S. Hobbs (100)	Essex v Australians at Chelmsford.............	1975

Notes: The fastest recorded authentic hundred in terms of balls received was scored off 34 balls by D. W. Hookes (above). Research of the scorebook has shown that P. G. H. Fender scored his hundred from between 40 and 46 balls. He contributed 113 to an unfinished sixth-wicket partnership of 171 in 42 minutes with H. A. Peach.

E. B. Alletson (Nottinghamshire) scored 189 out of 227 runs in 90 minutes against Sussex at Hove in 1911. It has been estimated that his last 139 runs took 37 minutes.

Hundreds scored in contrived circumstances and with the bowlers' compliance are excluded, including the fastest of them all, in 21 minutes (27 balls) by G. Chapple, Lancashire v Glamorgan at Manchester, 1993, 24 minutes (27 balls) by M. L. Pettini, Essex v Leicestershire at Leicester, 2006, and 26 minutes (36 balls) by T. M. Moody, Warwickshire v Glamorgan at Swansea, 1990.

FASTEST DOUBLE-HUNDREDS

Minutes

113	R. J. Shastri (200*)	Bombay v Baroda at Bombay	1984-85
120	G. L. Jessop (286)	Gloucestershire v Sussex at Hove	1903
120	C. H. Lloyd (201*)	West Indians v Glamorgan at Swansea	1976
130	G. L. Jessop (234)	Gloucestershire v Somerset at Bristol	1905
131	V. T. Trumper (293)	Australians v Canterbury at Christchurch	1913-14

FASTEST TRIPLE-HUNDREDS

Minutes

181	D. C. S. Compton (300)	MCC v North Eastern Transvaal at Benoni	1948-49
205	F. E. Woolley (305*)	MCC v Tasmania at Hobart	1911-12
205	C. G. Macartney (345)	Australians v Nottinghamshire at Nottingham......	1921
213	D. G. Bradman (369)	South Australia v Tasmania at Adelaide	1935-36

MOST RUNS IN A DAY BY ONE BATSMAN

390*	B. C. Lara	Warwickshire v Durham at Birmingham	1994
345	C. G. Macartney	Australians v Nottinghamshire at Nottingham	1921
334	W. H. Ponsford	Victoria v New South Wales at Melbourne	1926-27
333	K. S. Duleepsinhji	Sussex v Northamptonshire at Hove	1930
331*	J. D. Robertson	Middlesex v Worcestershire at Worcester	1949
325*	B. A. Richards	South Australia v Western Australia at Perth	1970-71

Note: These scores do not necessarily represent the complete innings. See page 1287.

There have been another **14** instances of a batsman scoring 300 runs in a day, most recently **319 by R. R. Rossouw, Eagles v Titans at Centurion in 2009-10** (see *Wisden 2003*, pages 278–279, for full list).

LONGEST INNINGS

Hrs	Mins			
16	55	R. Nayyar (271)	Himachal Pradesh v Jammu and Kashmir at Chamba	1999-2000
16	10	Hanif Mohammad (337)	Pakistan v West Indies at Bridgetown	1957-58
		Hanif believes he batted 16 hours 39 minutes.		
14	38	G. Kirsten (275)	South Africa v England at Durban	1999-2000
13	58	S. C. Cook (390)	Lions v Warriors at East London	2009-10
13	41	S. S. Shukla (178*)	Uttar Pradesh v Tamil Nadu at Nagpur.	2008-09
13	**32**	**A. Chopra (301*)**	**Rajasthan v Maharashtra at Nasik**	**2010-11**
13	19	S. T. Jayasuriya (340)	Sri Lanka v India at Colombo.	1997-98
13	17	L. Hutton (364)	England v Australia at The Oval.	1938

1,000 RUNS IN MAY

	Runs	Avge
W. G. Grace, May 9 to May 30, 1895 (22 days)	1,016	112.88
Grace was 46 years old.		
W. R. Hammond, May 7 to May 31, 1927 (25 days)	1,042	74.42
Hammond scored his 1,000th run on May 28, thus equalling Grace's record of 22 days.		
C. Hallows, May 5 to May 31, 1928 (27 days)	1,000	125.00

1,000 RUNS IN APRIL AND MAY

	Runs	Avge
T. W. Hayward, April 16 to May 31, 1900	1,074	97.63
D. G. Bradman, April 30 to May 31, 1930	1,001	143.00
On April 30 Bradman was 75 not out.		
D. G. Bradman, April 30 to May 31, 1938	1,056	150.85
Bradman scored 258 on April 30, and his 1,000th run on May 27.		
W. J. Edrich, April 30 to May 31, 1938	1,010	84.16
Edrich was 21 not out on April 30. All his runs were scored at Lord's.		
G. M. Turner, April 24 to May 31, 1973	1,018	78.30
G. A. Hick, April 17 to May 29, 1988	1,019	101.90
Hick scored a record 410 runs in April, and his 1,000th run on May 28.		

MOST RUNS SCORED OFF AN OVER

(All instances refer to six-ball overs)

36	G. S. Sobers	off M. A. Nash, Nottinghamshire v Glamorgan at Swansea (six sixes)...	1968
36	R. J. Shastri	off Tilak Raj, Bombay v Baroda at Bombay (six sixes)......	1984-85
34	E. B. Alletson	off E. H. Killick, Nottinghamshire v Sussex at Hove (46604446; including two no-balls)................................	1911
34	F. C. Hayes	off M. A. Nash, Lancashire v Glamorgan at Swansea (646666)	1977
34†	A. Flintoff	off A. J. Tudor, Lancashire v Surrey at Manchester (64444660; including two no-balls)................................	1998
34	C. M. Spearman	off S. J. P. Moreton, Gloucestershire v Oxford UCCE at Oxford (666646).. *This was Moreton's first over in first-class cricket.*	2005
32	I. T. Botham	off I. R. Snook, England XI v Central Districts at Palmerston North (466466)..	1983-84
32	P. W. G. Parker	off A. I. Kallicharran, Sussex v Warwickshire at Birmingham (466664)..	1982
32	I. R. Redpath	off N. Rosendorff, Australians v Orange Free State at Bloemfontein (666644)................................	1969-70
32	C. C. Smart	off G. Hill, Glamorgan v Hampshire at Cardiff (664664)...	1935
32	Khalid Mahmood	off Naved Latif, Gujranwala v Sargodha at Gujranwala (666662)..	2000-01

† Altogether 38 runs were scored off this over, the two no-balls counting for two extra runs each under ECB regulations.

Notes: The following instances have been excluded because of the bowlers' compliance: 34 – M. P. Maynard off S. A. Marsh, Glamorgan v Kent at Swansea, 1992; 34 – G. Chapple off P. A. Cottey, Lancashire v Glamorgan at Manchester, 1993; 34 – F. B. Touzel off F. J. J. Viljoen, Western Province B v Griqualand West at Kimberley, 1993-94. Chapple scored a further 32 off Cottey's next over.

There were 35 runs off an over received by A. T. Reinholds off H. T. Davis, Auckland v Wellington at Auckland 1995-96, but this included 16 extras and only 19 off the bat.

In a match against KwaZulu-Natal at Stellenbosch in 2006-07, W. E. September (Boland) conceded 34 in an over: 27 to M. Bekker, six to K. Smit, plus one no-ball.

In a match against Canterbury at Christchurch in 1989-90, R. H. Vance (Wellington) deliberately conceded 77 runs in an over of full tosses which contained 17 no-balls and, owing to the umpire's understandable miscalculation, only five legitimate deliveries.

The greatest number of runs scored off an eight-ball over is 34 (40446664) by R. M. Edwards off M. C. Carew, Governor-General's XI v West Indians at Auckland, 1968-69.

MOST SIXES IN AN INNINGS

16	A. Symonds (254*)	Gloucestershire v Glamorgan at Abergavenny.......	1995
15	J. R. Reid (296)	Wellington v Northern Districts at Wellington.......	1962-63
14	Shakti Singh (128)	Himachal Pradesh v Haryana at Dharmsala.........	1990-91
14	D. J. Hussey (275)	Nottinghamshire v Essex at Nottingham.............	2007
13	Majid Khan (147*)	Pakistanis v Glamorgan at Swansea...............	1967
13	C. G. Greenidge (273*)	D. H. Robins' XI v Pakistanis at Eastbourne........	1974
13	C. G. Greenidge (259)	Hampshire v Sussex at Southampton..............	1975
13	G. W. Humpage (254)	Warwickshire v Lancashire at Southport...........	1982
13	R. J. Shastri (200*)	Bombay v Baroda at Bombay....................	1984-85
12	Gulfraz Khan (207)	Railways v Universities at Lahore................	1976-77
12	I. T. Botham (138*)	Somerset v Warwickshire at Birmingham..........	1985
12	R. A. Harper (234)	Northamptonshire v Gloucestershire at Northampton .	1986
12	D. M. Jones (248)	Australians v Warwickshire at Birmingham.........	1989
12	U. N. K. Fernando (160)	Sinhalese SC v Sebastianites C and AC at Colombo ..	1990-91
12	D. N. Patel (204)	Auckland v Northern Districts at Auckland.........	1991-92
12	W. V. Raman (206)	Tamil Nadu v Kerala at Madras..................	1991-92
12	G. D. Lloyd (241)	Lancashire v Essex at Chelmsford................	1996

12	Wasim Akram (257*)	Pakistan v Zimbabwe at Sheikhupura	1996-97
12	S. I. de Saram (188)	Ragama v Badureliya at Colombo	2007-08
12	K. J. O'Brien (171*)	Ireland v Kenya at Nairobi	2008
12	H. G. J. M. Kulatunga (234)	Colts v Ragama at Colombo	2008-09

Note: F. B. Touzel (128*) hit 13 sixes for Western Province B v Griqualand West in contrived circumstances at Kimberley in 1993-94.

MOST SIXES IN A MATCH

| 20 | A. Symonds (254*, 76) | Gloucestershire v Glamorgan at Abergavenny | 1995 |
| 17 | W. J. Stewart (155, 125) | Warwickshire v Lancashire at Blackpool | 1959 |

MOST SIXES IN A SEASON

80	I. T. Botham	1985		49	I. V. A. Richards	1985
66	A. W. Wellard	1935		48	A. W. Carr	1925
57	A. W. Wellard	1936		48	J. H. Edrich	1965
57	A. W. Wellard	1938		48	A. Symonds	1995
51	A. W. Wellard	1933				

MOST BOUNDARIES IN AN INNINGS

	4s/6s			
72	62/10	B. C. Lara (501*)	Warwickshire v Durham at Birmingham	1994
68	68/–	P. A. Perrin (343*)	Essex v Derbyshire at Chesterfield	1904
65	64/1	A. C. MacLaren (424)	Lancashire v Somerset at Taunton	1895
64	64/–	Hanif Mohammad (499)	Karachi v Bahawalpur at Karachi	1958-59
57	52/5	J. H. Edrich (310*)	England v New Zealand at Leeds	1965
57	52/5	Naved Latif (394)	Sargodha v Gujranwala at Gujranwala	2000-01
55	55/–	C. W. Gregory (383)	NSW v Queensland at Brisbane	1906-07
55	53/2	G. R. Marsh (355*)	W. Australia v S. Australia at Perth	1989-90
55	51/3†	S. V. Manjrekar (377)	Bombay v Hyderabad at Bombay	1990-91
55	52/3	D. S. Lehmann (339)	Yorkshire v Durham at Leeds	2006
55	54/1	D. K. H. Mitchell (298)	Worcestershire v Somerset at Taunton	2009
55	54/1	S. C. Cook (390)	Lions v Warriors at East London	2009-10
55	**47/8**	**R. R. Rossouw (319)**	**Eagles v Titans at Centurion**	**2009-10**
54	53/1	G. H. Hirst (341)	Yorkshire v Leicestershire at Leicester	1905
53	53/–	A. W. Nourse (304*)	Natal v Transvaal at Johannesburg	1919-20
53	45/8	K. R. Rutherford (317)	New Zealanders v D. B. Close's XI at Scarborough	1986
53	51/2	V. V. S. Laxman (353)	Hyderabad v Karnataka at Bangalore	1999-2000
53	52/1	M. W. Goodwin (335*)	Sussex v Leicestershire at Hove	2003
52	47/5	N. H. Fairbrother (366)	Lancashire v Surrey at The Oval	1990
52	50/2	C. J. L. Rogers (319)	Northamptonshire v Gloucestershire at Northampton	2006
51	51/–	W. G. Grace (344)	MCC v Kent at Canterbury	1876
51	44/7‡	C. G. Macartney (345)	Australians v Notts at Nottingham	1921
51	50/1	B. B. Nimbalkar (443*)	Maharashtra v Kathiawar at Poona	1948-49
51	49/2	G. A. Hick (315*)	Worcestershire v Durham at Worcester	2002
51	50/1	Salman Butt (290)	Punjab v Federal Areas at Lahore	2007-08
51	44/7	Sunny Singh (312)	Haryana v Madhya Pradesh at Indore	2009-10
50	47/–‡	A. Ducat (306*)	Surrey v Oxford U. at The Oval	1919
50	46/4	D. G. Bradman (369)	S. Australia v Tasmania at Adelaide	1935-36
50	35/15	J. R. Reid (296)	Wellington v N. Districts at Wellington	1962-63
50	42/8	I. V. A. Richards (322)	Somerset v Warwickshire at Taunton	1985
50	50/–	Shoaib Khan (300*)	Peshawar v Quetta at Peshawar	2003-04

† *Plus one five.*
‡ *Plus three fives.*

PARTNERSHIPS OVER 500

624	for 3rd	K. C. Sangakkara (287) and D. P. M. D. Jayawardene (374), Sri Lanka v South Africa at Colombo	2006
580	for 2nd	Rafatullah Mohmand (302*) and Aamer Sajjad (289), WAPDA v Sui Southern Gas at Sheikhupura	2009-10
577	for 4th	V. S. Hazare (288) and Gul Mahomed (319), Baroda v Holkar at Baroda	1946-47
576	for 2nd	S. T. Jayasuriya (340) and R. S. Mahanama (225), Sri Lanka v India at Colombo	1997-98
574*	for 4th	F. M. M. Worrell (255*) and C. L. Walcott (314*), Barbados v Trinidad at Port-of-Spain	1945-46
561	for 1st	Waheed Mirza (324) and Mansoor Akhtar (224*), Karachi Whites v Quetta at Karachi	1976-77
555	for 1st	P. Holmes (224*) and H. Sutcliffe (313), Yorkshire v Essex at Leyton	1932
554	for 1st	J. T. Brown (300) and J. Tunnicliffe (243), Yorkshire v Derbyshire at Chesterfield	1898
520*	for 5th	C. A. Pujara (302*) and R. A. Jadeja (232*), Saurashtra v Orissa at Rajkot	2008-09
502*	for 4th	F. M. M. Worrell (308*) and J. D. C. Goddard (218*), Barbados v Trinidad at Bridgetown	1943-44

HIGHEST PARTNERSHIPS FOR EACH WICKET

The following lists include all stands above 400; otherwise the top ten for each wicket.

First Wicket

561	Waheed Mirza and Mansoor Akhtar, Karachi Whites v Quetta at Karachi	1976-77
555	P. Holmes and H. Sutcliffe, Yorkshire v Essex at Leyton	1932
554	J. T. Brown and J. Tunnicliffe, Yorkshire v Derbyshire at Chesterfield	1898
490	E. H. Bowley and J. G. Langridge, Sussex v Middlesex at Hove	1933
464	R. Sehgal and R. Lamba, Delhi v Himachal Pradesh at Delhi	1994-95
462	M. Vijay and A. Mukund, Tamil Nadu v Maharashtra at Nasik	2008-09
459	Wasim Jaffer and S. K. Kulkarni, Mumbai v Saurashtra at Rajkot	1996-97
456	E. R. Mayne and W. H. Ponsford, Victoria v Queensland at Melbourne	1923-24
451*	S. Desai and R. M. H. Binny, Karnataka v Kerala at Chikmagalur	1977-78
431	M. R. J. Veletta and G. R. Marsh, Western Australia v South Australia at Perth	1989-90
428	J. B. Hobbs and A. Sandham, Surrey v Oxford University at The Oval	1926
428	P. J. Ingram and J. M. How, Central Districts v Wellington at Wellington	2009-10
425*	L. V. Garrick and C. H. Gayle, Jamaica v West Indies B at Montego Bay	2000-01
424	I. J. Siedle and J. F. W. Nicolson, Natal v Orange Free State at Bloemfontein	1926-27
421	S. M. Gavaskar and G. A. Parkar, Bombay v Bengal at Bombay	1981-82
418	Kamal Najamuddin and Khalid Alvi, Karachi v Railways at Karachi	1980-81
415	N. D. McKenzie and G. C. Smith, South Africa v Bangladesh at Chittagong	2007-08
413	V. Mankad and Pankaj Roy, India v New Zealand at Madras	1955-56
410	V. Sehwag and R. Dravid, India v Pakistan at Lahore	2005-06
406*	D. J. Bicknell and G. E. Welton, Notts v Warwickshire at Birmingham	2000
405	C. P. S. Chauhan and M. S. Gupte, Maharashtra v Vidarbha at Poona	1972-73
403	Rizwan-uz-Zaman and Shoaib Mohammad, PIA v Hyderabad at Hyderabad	1999-2000

Second Wicket

580	Rafatullah Mohmand and Aamer Sajjad, WAPDA v Sui Southern Gas at Sheikhupura	2009-10
576	S. T. Jayasuriya and R. S. Mahanama, Sri Lanka v India at Colombo	1997-98
480	**D. Elgar and R. R. Rossouw, Eagles v Titans at Centurion**	**2009-10**
475	Zahir Alam and L. S. Rajput, Assam v Tripura at Gauhati	1991-92
465*	J. A. Jameson and R. B. Kanhai, Warwicks v Gloucestershire at Birmingham	1974

455	K. V. Bhandarkar and B. B. Nimbalkar, Maharashtra v Kathiawar at Poona....	1948-49
451	W. H. Ponsford and D. G. Bradman, Australia v England at The Oval	1934
446	C. C. Hunte and G. S. Sobers, West Indies v Pakistan at Kingston	1957-58
448	C. C. Bradfield and J. D. C. Bryant, E. Province v North West at Potchefstroom	2002-03
438	M. S. Atapattu and K. C. Sangakkara, Sri Lanka v Zimbabwe at Bulawayo	2003-04
431	Yasir Hameed and Asad Shafiq, NWFP v Baluchistan at Peshawar.	2007-08
429*	J. G. Dewes and G. H. G. Doggart, Cambridge U. v Essex at Cambridge	1949
426	Arshad Pervez and Mohsin Khan, Habib Bank v Income Tax at Lahore	1977-78
417	K. J. Barnett and T. A. Tweats, Derbyshire v Yorkshire at Derby	1997
415	A. Jadeja and S. V. Manjrekar, Indians v Bowl XI at Springs	1992-93
403	G. A. Gooch and P. J. Prichard, Essex v Leicestershire at Chelmsford	1990

Third Wicket

624	K. C. Sangakkara and D. P. M. D. Jayawardene, Sri Lanka v South Africa at Colombo	2006
467	A. H. Jones and M. D. Crowe, New Zealand v Sri Lanka at Wellington	1990-91
459	C. J. L. Rogers and M. J. North, Western Australia v Victoria at Perth	2006-07
456	Khalid Irtiza and Aslam Ali, United Bank v Multan at Karachi	1975-76
451	Mudassar Nazar and Javed Miandad, Pakistan v India at Hyderabad.	1982-83
445	P. E. Whitelaw and W. N. Carson, Auckland v Otago at Dunedin.	1936-37
438*	G. A. Hick and T. M. Moody, Worcestershire v Hampshire at Southampton ...	1997
436*	D. L. Maddy and B. J. Hodge, Leics v Loughborough UCCE at Leicester	2003
436	S. S. Das and S. S. Raul, Orissa v Bengal at Baripada.	2001-02
436	J. B. Stollmeyer and G. E. Gomez, Trinidad v British Guiana at Port-of-Spain .	1946-47
429*	J. A. Rudolph and H. H. Dippenaar, South Africa v Bangladesh at Chittagong .	2003
424*	W. J. Edrich and D. C. S. Compton, Middlesex v Somerset at Lord's.	1948
417	G. A. Hick and B. F. Smith, Worcestershire v Gloucestershire at Worcester....	2004
413	D. J. Bicknell and D. M. Ward, Surrey v Kent at Canterbury	1990
410*	R. S. Modi and L. Amarnath, India in England v The Rest at Calcutta	1946-47
409	V. V. S. Laxman and R. Dravid, South Zone v West Zone at Surat	2000-01
408	S. Oberoi and D. R. Fox, Oxford U. v Cambridge U. at Cambridge	2005
406*	R. S. Gavaskar and S. J. Kalyani, Bengal v Tripura at Agartala.	1999-2000
405	A. Jadeja and A. S. Kaypee, Haryana v Services at Faridabad.	1991-92
404	M. R. Ramprakash and S. J. Walters, Surrey v Leicestershire at The Oval	2009
403	M. R. Ramprakash and M. A. Butcher, Surrey v Sussex at Hove	2007

Fourth Wicket

577	V. S. Hazare and Gul Mahomed, Baroda v Holkar at Baroda	1946-47
574*	C. L. Walcott and F. M. M. Worrell, Barbados v Trinidad at Port-of-Spain	1945-46
502*	F. M. M. Worrell and J. D. C. Goddard, Barbados v Trinidad at Bridgetown ...	1943-44
470	A. I. Kallicharran and G. W. Humpage, Warwicks v Lancs at Southport	1982
462*	D. W. Hookes and W. B. Phillips, South Australia v Tasmania at Adelaide	1986-87
448	R. Abel and T. W. Hayward, Surrey v Yorkshire at The Oval	1899
437	D. P. M. D. Jayawardene and T. T. Samaraweera, Sri Lanka v Pakistan at Karachi	2008-09
436	S. Abbas Ali and P. K. Dwevedi, Madhya Pradesh v Railways at Indore	1997-98
425*	A. Dale and I. V. A. Richards, Glamorgan v Middlesex at Cardiff	1993
424	I. S. Lee and S. O. Quin, Victoria v Tasmania at Melbourne	1933-34
411	P. B. H. May and M. C. Cowdrey, England v West Indies at Birmingham	1957
410	G. Abraham and P. Balan Pandit, Kerala v Andhra at Palghat	1959-60
402	W. Watson and T. W. Graveney, MCC v British Guiana at Georgetown	1953-54
402	R. B. Kanhai and K. Ibadulla, Warwicks v Notts at Nottingham	1968

Fifth Wicket

520*	C. A. Pujara and R. A. Jadeja, Saurashtra v Orissa at Rajkot	2008-09
479	Misbah-ul-Haq and Usman Arshad, Sui Northern Gas v Lahore Shalimar at Lahore	2009-10
464*	M. E. Waugh and S. R. Waugh, New South Wales v Western Australia at Perth	1990-91

420	Mohammad Ashraful and Marshall Ayub, Dhaka v Chittagong at Chittagong ..	2006-07
410*	A. Chopra and S. Badrinath, India A v South Africa A at Delhi	2007-08
405	S. G. Barnes and D. G. Bradman, Australia v England at Sydney	1946-47
401	M. B. Loye and D. Ripley, Northamptonshire v Glamorgan at Northampton .	1998
397	W. Bardsley and C. Kelleway, New South Wales v South Australia at Sydney...	1920-21
393	E. G. Arnold and W. B. Burns, Worcestershire v Warwickshire at Birmingham.	1909
391	A. Malhotra and S. Dogra, Delhi v Services at Delhi......................	1995-96

Sixth Wicket

487*	G. A. Headley and C. C. Passailaigue, Jamaica v Lord Tennyson's XI at Kingston..	1931-32
428	W. W. Armstrong and M. A. Noble, Australians v Sussex at Hove	1902
417	**W. P. Saha and L. R. Shukla, Bengal v Assam at Kolkata**	**2010-11**
411	R. M. Poore and E. G. Wynyard, Hampshire v Somerset at Taunton..........	1899
379	**S. L. Stewart and C. F. K. van Wyk, Canterbury v C. Dists at New Plymouth**	**2010-11**
376	R. Subba Row and A. Lightfoot, Northamptonshire v Surrey at The Oval	1958
372*	K. P. Pietersen and J. E. Morris, Nottinghamshire v Derbyshire at Derby	2001
371	V. M. Merchant and R. S. Modi, Bombay v Maharashtra at Bombay	1943-44
365	B. C. Lara and R. D. Jacobs, West Indians v Australia A at Hobart...........	2000-01
365	S. C. Cook and T. L. Tsolekile, Lions v Warriors at East London	2009-10

Seventh Wicket

460	Bhupinder Singh, jun. and P. Dharmani, Punjab v Delhi at Delhi	1994-95
347	D. St E. Atkinson and C. C. Depeiza, West Indies v Australia at Bridgetown...	1954-55
344	K. S. Ranjitsinhji and W. Newham, Sussex v Essex at Leyton	1902
340	K. J. Key and H. Philipson, Oxford University v Middlesex at Chiswick Park ..	1887
336	F. C. W. Newman and C. R. N. Maxwell, Sir Julien Cahn's XI v Leicestershire at Nottingham...	1935
335	C. W. Andrews and E. C. Bensted, Queensland v New South Wales at Sydney .	1934-35
325	G. Brown and C. H. Abercrombie, Hampshire v Essex at Leyton	1913
323	E. H. Hendren and L. F. Townsend, MCC v Barbados at Bridgetown.........	1929-30
315	D. M. Benkenstein and O. D. Gibson, Durham v Yorkshire at Leeds	2006
308	Waqar Hassan and Imtiaz Ahmed, Pakistan v New Zealand at Lahore	1955-56

Eighth Wicket

433	A. Sims and V. T. Trumper, A. Sims' Aust. XI v Canterbury at Christchurch...	1913-14
332	**I. J. L. Trott and S. C. J. Broad, England v Pakistan at Lord's** ...	**2010**
313	Wasim Akram and Saqlain Mushtaq, Pakistan v Zimbabwe at Sheikhupura....	1996-97
292	R. Peel and Lord Hawke, Yorkshire v Warwickshire at Birmingham	1896
291	R. S. C. Martin-Jenkins and M. J. G. Davis, Sussex v Somerset at Taunton	2002
270	V. T. Trumper and E. P. Barbour, New South Wales v Victoria at Sydney	1912-13
268	S. Sriram and M. R. Srinivas, Tamil Nadu v Punjab at Mohali	2002-03
263	D. R. Wilcox and R. M. Taylor, Essex v Warwickshire at Southend..........	1946
257	N. Pothas and A. J. Bichel, Hampshire v Gloucestershire at Cheltenham	2005
256	S. P. Fleming and J. E. C. Franklin, New Zealand v S. Africa at Cape Town ...	2005-06

Ninth Wicket

283	A. Warren and J. Chapman, Derbyshire v Warwickshire at Blackwell	1910
268	J. B. Commins and N. Boje, South Africa A v Mashonaland at Harare........	1994-95
251	J. W. H. T. Douglas and S. N. Hare, Essex v Derbyshire at Leyton	1921
249*†	A. S. Srivastava and K. Seth, Madhya Pradesh v Vidarbha at Indore	2000-01
246	T. T. Bresnan and J. N. Gillespie, Yorkshire v Surrey at The Oval	2007
245	V. S. Hazare and N. D. Nagarwalla, Maharashtra v Baroda at Poona	1939-40
244*	Arshad Ayub and M. V. Ramanamurthy, Hyderabad v Bihar at Hyderabad	1986-87
239	H. B. Cave and I. B. Leggat, Central Districts v Otago at Dunedin	1952-53

233	I. J. L. Trott and J. S. Patel, Warwickshire v Yorkshire at Birmingham.........	2009
232	C. Hill and E. Walkley, South Australia v New South Wales at Adelaide......	1900-01

† *276 unbeaten runs were scored for this wicket in two separate partnerships; after Srivastava retired hurt, Seth and N. D. Hirwani added 27.*

Tenth Wicket

307	A. F. Kippax and J. E. H. Hooker, New South Wales v Victoria at Melbourne..	1928-29
249	C. T. Sarwate and S. N. Banerjee, Indians v Surrey at The Oval.............	1946
239	Aqeel Arshad and Ali Raza, Lahore Whites v Hyderabad at Lahore.........	2004-05
235	F. E. Woolley and A. Fielder, Kent v Worcestershire at Stourbridge........	1909
233	Ajay Sharma and Maninder Singh, Delhi v Bombay at Bombay.............	1991-92
230	R. W. Nicholls and W. Roche, Middlesex v Kent at Lord's................	1899
228	R. Illingworth and K. Higgs, Leicestershire v Northamptonshire at Leicester...	1977
219	D. J. Thorneley and S. C. G. MacGill, NSW v Western Australia at Sydney	2004-05
218	F. H. Vigar and T. P. B. Smith, Essex v Derbyshire at Chesterfield........	1947
214	N. V. Knight and A. Richardson, Warwickshire v Hampshire at Birmingham ..	2002

Note: There have been only 11 last-wicket stands of 200 or more, the 11th being 211 by M. Ellis and T. J. Hastings for Victoria v South Australia at Melbourne in 1902-03.

UNUSUAL DISMISSALS

Handled the Ball

There have been **56** instances in first-class cricket. The most recent are:

G. A. Gooch	England v Australia at Manchester.................	1993
A. C. Waller	Mashonaland CD v Mashonaland Under-24 at Harare..........	1994-95
K. M. Krikken	Derbyshire v Indians at Derby.............................	1996
A. Badenhorst	Eastern Province B v North West at Fochville................	1998-99
S. R. Waugh	Australia v India at Chennai..............................	2000-01
M. P. Vaughan	England v India at Bangalore..............................	2001-02
Tushar Imran	Bangladesh A v Jamaica at Spanish Town....................	2001-02
Al Sahariar	Dhaka v Chittagong at Dhaka.............................	2003-04
Junaid Zia	Rawalpindi v Lahore at Lahore............................	2003-04
D. J. Watson	Dolphins v Eagles at Bloemfontein........................	2004-05
M. Zondeki	Cape Cobras v Eagles at Bloemfontein.....................	2006-07
L. N. Mosena	Free State v Limpopo at Bloemfontein.....................	2006-07

Obstructing the Field

There have been **21** instances in first-class cricket. T. Straw of Worcestershire was given out for obstruction v Warwickshire in both 1899 and 1901. The last occurrence in England involved L. Hutton of England v South Africa at The Oval in 1951. The most recent are:

Arshad Ali	Sukkur v Quetta at Quetta..............................	1983-84
H. R. Wasu	Vidarbha v Rajasthan at Akola...........................	1984-85
Khalid Javed	Railways v Lahore at Lahore.............................	1985-86
C. Binduhewa	Singha SC v Sinhalese SC at Colombo.....................	1990-91
S. J. Kalyani	Bengal v Orissa at Calcutta..............................	1994-95
R. C. Rupasinghe	Rio v Kurunegala Youth at Colombo.......................	2001-02
K. N. S. Fernando	Lankan v Army at Welisara...............................	2006-07
H. R. Jadhav	Baroda v Uttar Pradesh at Baroda........................	2006-07
Riaz Kail	Abbottabad v Quetta at Abbottabad........................	2009-10

Hit the Ball Twice

There have been **21** instances in first-class cricket. The last occurrence in England involved J. H. King of Leicestershire v Surrey at The Oval in 1906. The most recent are:

Aziz Malik	Lahore Division v Faisalabad at Sialkot......................	1984-85
Javed Mohammad	Multan v Karachi Whites at Sahiwal	1986-87
Shahid Pervez	Jammu and Kashmir v Punjab at Srinagar	1986-87
Ali Naqvi	PNSC v National Bank at Faisalabad.......................	1998-99
A. George	Tamil Nadu v Maharashtra at Pune	1998-99
Maqsood Raza	Lahore Division v PNSC at Sheikhupura....................	1999-2000
D. Mahajan	Jammu and Kashmir v Bihar at Jammu	2005-06

Timed Out

There have been **four** instances in first-class cricket:

A. Jordaan	Eastern Province v Transvaal at Port Elizabeth (SACB match)....	1987-88
H. Yadav	Tripura v Orissa at Cuttack.................................	1997-98
V. C. Drakes	Border v Free State at East London	2002-03
A. J. Harris	Nottinghamshire v Durham UCCE at Nottingham.............	2003

BOWLING RECORDS

TEN WICKETS IN AN INNINGS

In the history of first-class cricket, there have been **80** instances of a bowler taking all ten wickets in an innings:

	O	M	R		
E. Hinkly (Kent)				v England at Lord's.............	1848
*J. Wisden (North)				v South at Lord's...............	1850
V. E. Walker (England)	43	17	74	v Surrey at The Oval	1859
V. E. Walker (Middlesex).......	44.2	5	104	v Lancashire at Manchester ...	1865
G. Wootton (All England)	31.3	9	54	v Yorkshire at Sheffield	1865
W. Hickton (Lancashire)........	36.2	19	46	v Hampshire at Manchester	1870
S. E. Butler (Oxford)..........	24.1	11	38	v Cambridge at Lord's	1871
James Lillywhite (South)	60.2	22	129	v North at Canterbury	1872
A. Shaw (MCC)	36.2	8	73	v North at Lord's.............	1874
E. Barratt (Players)	29	11	43	v Australians at The Oval	1878
G. Giffen (Australian XI)	26	10	66	v The Rest at Sydney	1883-84
W. G. Grace (MCC)	36.2	17	49	v Oxford University at Oxford ...	1886
G. Burton (Middlesex)	52.3	25	59	v Surrey at The Oval...........	1888
†A. E. Moss (Canterbury).	21.3	10	28	v Wellington at Christchurch ...	1889-90
S. M. J. Woods (Cambridge U.) ..	31	6	69	v Thornton's XI at Cambridge ...	1890
T. Richardson (Surrey)	15.3	3	45	v Essex at The Oval	1894
H. Pickett (Essex)	27	11	32	v Leicestershire at Leyton	1895
E. J. Tyler (Somerset)	34.3	15	49	v Surrey at Taunton...........	1895
W. P. Howell (Australians)	23.2	14	28	v Surrey at The Oval...........	1899
C. H. G. Bland (Sussex)	25.2	10	48	v Kent at Tonbridge	1899
J. Briggs (Lancashire)..........	28.5	7	55	v Worcestershire at Manchester ..	1900
A. E. Trott (Middlesex)	14.2	5	42	v Somerset at Taunton	1900
A. Fielder (Players)	24.5	1	90	v Gentlemen at Lord's	1906
E. G. Dennett (Gloucestershire) .	19.4	7	40	v Essex at Bristol	1906
A. E. E. Vogler (E. Province)	12	2	26	v Griqualand W. at Johannesburg.	1906-07
C. Blythe (Kent)	16	7	30	v Northants at Northampton	1907
J. B. King (Philadelphia)........	18.1	7	53	v Ireland at Haverford‡........	1909
A. Drake (Yorkshire)	8.5	0	35	v Somerset at Weston-s-Mare....	1914
W. Bestwick (Derbyshire)	19	2	40	v Glamorgan at Cardiff.........	1921

	O	M	R		
A. A. Mailey (Australians)	28.4	5	66	v Gloucestershire at Cheltenham. . .	1921
C. W. L. Parker (Glos.)	40.3	13	79	v Somerset at Bristol.	1921
T. Rushby (Surrey)	17.5	4	43	v Somerset at Taunton	1921
J. C. White (Somerset)	42.2	11	76	v Worcestershire at Worcester	1921
G. C. Collins (Kent)	19.3	4	65	v Nottinghamshire at Dover	1922
H. Howell (Warwickshire)	25.1	5	51	v Yorkshire at Birmingham	1923
A. S. Kennedy (Players)	22.4	10	37	v Gentlemen at The Oval	1927
G. O. B. Allen (Middlesex)	25.3	10	40	v Lancashire at Lord's	1929
A. P. Freeman (Kent)	42	9	131	v Lancashire at Maidstone	1929
G. Geary (Leicestershire)	16.2	8	18	v Glamorgan at Pontypridd.	1929
C. V. Grimmett (Australians)	22.3	8	37	v Yorkshire at Sheffield	1930
A. P. Freeman (Kent)	30.4	8	53	v Essex at Southend	1930
H. Verity (Yorkshire)	18.4	6	36	v Warwickshire at Leeds	1931
A. P. Freeman (Kent)	36.1	9	79	v Lancashire at Manchester	1931
V. W. C. Jupp (Northants)	39	6	127	v Kent at Tunbridge Wells	1932
H. Verity (Yorkshire)	19.4	16	10	v Nottinghamshire at Leeds	1932
T. W. Wall (South Australia)	12.4	2	36	v New South Wales at Sydney . . .	1932-33
T. B. Mitchell (Derbyshire)	19.1	4	64	v Leicestershire at Leicester	1935
J. Mercer (Glamorgan)	26	10	51	v Worcestershire at Worcester	1936
T. W. J. Goddard (Glos.)	28.4	4	113	v Worcestershire at Cheltenham . . .	1937
T. F. Smailes (Yorkshire)	17.1	5	47	v Derbyshire at Sheffield.	1939
E. A. Watts (Surrey)	24.1	8	67	v Warwickshire at Birmingham . . .	1939
*W. E. Hollies (Warwickshire)	20.4	4	49	v Notts at Birmingham	1946
J. M. Sims (East)	18.4	2	90	v West at Kingston	1948
T. E. Bailey (Essex)	39.4	9	90	v Lancashire at Clacton.	1949
J. K. Graveney (Glos.)	18.4	2	66	v Derbyshire at Chesterfield	1949
R. Berry (Lancashire)	36.2	9	102	v Worcestershire at Blackpool	1953
S. P. Gupte (President's XI)	24.2	7	78	v Combined XI at Bombay	1954-55
J. C. Laker (Surrey)	46	18	88	v Australians at The Oval	1956
J. C. Laker (England)	51.2	23	53	v Australia at Manchester	1956
G. A. R. Lock (Surrey)	29.1	18	54	v Kent at Blackheath.	1956
K. Smales (Nottinghamshire)	41.3	20	66	v Gloucestershire at Stroud.	1956
P. M. Chatterjee (Bengal)	19	11	20	v Assam at Jorhat	1956-57
J. D. Bannister (Warwickshire)	23.3	11	41	v Comb. Services at Birmingham§ .	1959
A. J. G. Pearson (Cambridge U.)	30.3	8	78	v Leics at Loughborough	1961
N. I. Thomson (Sussex)	34.2	19	49	v Warwickshire at Worthing	1964
P. J. Allan (Queensland)	15.6	3	61	v Victoria at Melbourne	1965-66
I. J. Brayshaw (W. Australia)	17.6	4	44	v Victoria at Perth	1967-68
Shahid Mahmood (Karachi Whites)	25	5	58	v Khairpur at Karachi	1969-70
E. E. Hemmings (International XI)	49.3	14	175	v West Indies XI at Kingston	1982-83
P. Sunderam (Rajasthan)	22	5	78	v Vidarbha at Jodhpur.	1985-86
S. T. Jefferies (W. Province)	22.5	7	59	v Orange Free State at Cape Town . .	1987-88
Imran Adil (Bahawalpur)	22.5	3	92	v Faisalabad at Faisalabad	1989-90
G. P. Wickremasinghe (Sinhalese)	19.2	5	41	v Kalutara at Colombo	1991-92
R. L. Johnson (Middlesex)	18.5	6	45	v Derbyshire at Derby	1994
Naeem Akhtar (Rawalpindi B)	21.3	10	28	v Peshawar at Peshawar	1995-96
A. Kumble (India)	26.3	9	74	v Pakistan at Delhi	1998-99
D. S. Mohanty (East Zone)	19	5	46	v South Zone at Agartala	2000-01
O. D. Gibson (Durham)	17.3	1	47	v Hampshire at Chester-le-Street . .	2007
M. W. Olivier (Warriors)	26.3	4	65	v Eagles at Bloemfontein	2007-08
Zulfiqar Babar (Multan)	39.4	3	143	v Islamabad at Multan.	2009-10

Note: In addition, the following instances were achieved in 12-a-side matches:

E. M. Grace (MCC)	32.2	7	69	v Gents of Kent at Canterbury . . .	1862
W. G. Grace (MCC)	46.1	15	92	v Kent at Canterbury.	1873
†D. C. S. Hinds (A. B. St Hill's XII)	19.1	6	36	v Trinidad at Port-of-Spain	1900-01

* J. Wisden and W. E. Hollies achieved the feat without the direct assistance of a fielder. Wisden's ten were all bowled; Hollies bowled seven and had three lbw.

† On debut in first-class cricket. ‡ Pennsylvania. § Mitchells & Butlers Ground.

OUTSTANDING BOWLING ANALYSES

	O	M	R	W		
H. Verity (Yorkshire)	19.4	16	10	10	v Nottinghamshire at Leeds	1932
G. Elliott (Victoria)	19	17	2	9	v Tasmania at Launceston	1857-58
Ahad Khan (Railways)	6.3	4	7	9	v Dera Ismail Khan at Lahore	1964-65
J. C. Laker (England)	14	12	2	8	v The Rest at Bradford	1950
D. Shackleton (Hampshire)	11.1	7	4	8	v Somerset at Weston-s-Mare	1955
E. Peate (Yorkshire)	16	11	5	8	v Surrey at Holbeck	1883
K. M. Dabengwa (Westerns)	4.4	3	1	7	v Northerns at Harare	2006-07
F. R. Spofforth (Australians)	8.3	6	3	7	v England XI at Birmingham	1884
W. A. Henderson (NE Transvaal)	9.3	7	4	7	v OFS at Bloemfontein	1937-38
Rajinder Goel (Haryana)	7	4	4	7	v Jammu and Kashmir at Chandigarh	1977-78
N. W. Bracken (NSW)	7	5	4	7	v South Australia at Sydney	2004-05
V. I. Smith (South Africans)	4.5	3	1	6	v Derbyshire at Derby	1947
S. Cosstick (Victoria)	21.1	20	1	6	v Tasmania at Melbourne	1868-69
Israr Ali (Bahawalpur)	11	10	1	6	v Dacca U. at Bahawalpur	1957-58
A. D. Pougher (MCC)	3	3	0	5	v Australians at Lord's	1896
G. R. Cox (Sussex)	6	6	0	5	v Somerset at Weston-s-Mare	1921
R. K. Tyldesley (Lancashire)	5	5	0	5	v Leicestershire at Manchester	1924
P. T. Mills (Gloucestershire)	6.4	6	0	5	v Somerset at Bristol	1928

MOST WICKETS IN A MATCH

19-90	J. C. Laker	England v Australia at Manchester	1956
17-48†	C. Blythe	Kent v Northamptonshire at Northampton	1907
17-50	C. T. B. Turner	Australians v England XI at Hastings	1888
17-54	W. P. Howell	Australians v Western Province at Cape Town	1902-03
17-56	C. W. L. Parker	Gloucestershire v Essex at Gloucester	1925
17-67	A. P. Freeman	Kent v Sussex at Hove	1922
17-89	W. G. Grace	Gloucestershire v Nottinghamshire at Cheltenham	1877
17-89	F. C. L. Matthews	Nottinghamshire v Northants at Nottingham	1923
17-91	H. Dean	Lancashire v Yorkshire at Liverpool	1913
17-91†	H. Verity	Yorkshire v Essex at Leyton	1933
17-92	A. P. Freeman	Kent v Warwickshire at Folkestone	1932
17-103	W. Mycroft	Derbyshire v Hampshire at Southampton	1876
17-106	G. R. Cox	Sussex v Warwickshire at Horsham	1926
17-106†	T. W. J. Goddard	Gloucestershire v Kent at Bristol	1939
17-119	W. Mead	Essex v Hampshire at Southampton	1895
17-137	W. Brearley	Lancashire v Somerset at Manchester	1905
17-137	J. M. Davison	Canada v USA at Fort Lauderdale	2004
17-159	S. F. Barnes	England v South Africa at Johannesburg	1913-14
17-201	G. Giffen	South Australia v Victoria at Adelaide	1885-86
17-212	J. C. Clay	Glamorgan v Worcestershire at Swansea	1937

† *Achieved in a single day.*

Note: H. Arkwright took 18-96 for MCC v Gentlemen of Kent in a 12-a-side match at Canterbury in 1861.

There have been 57 instances of a bowler taking 16 wickets in an 11-a-side match, the most recent being 16-189 by Sohail Khan for Sui Southern Gas v WAPDA at Karachi, 2007-08.

FOUR WICKETS WITH CONSECUTIVE BALLS

There have been **37** instances in first-class cricket. R. J. Crisp achieved the feat twice, for Western Province in 1931-32 and 1933-34. A. E. Trott took four in four balls and another hat-trick in the same innings for Middlesex v Somerset in 1907, his benefit match. Occurrences since the Second World War:

F. Ridgway	Kent v Derbyshire at Folkestone	1951
A. K. Walker‡	Nottinghamshire v Leicestershire at Leicester	1956
D. Robins†	South Australia v New South Wales at Adelaide	1965-66
S. N. Mohol	President's XI v Combined XI at Poona	1965-66
P. I. Pocock	Surrey v Sussex at Eastbourne	1972
S. S. Saini†	Delhi v Himachal Pradesh at Delhi	1988-89
D. Dias	W. Province (Suburbs) v Central Province at Colombo	1990-91
Ali Gauhar	Karachi Blues v United Bank at Peshawar	1994-95
K. D. James§	Hampshire v Indians at Southampton	1996
G. P. Butcher	Surrey v Derbyshire at The Oval	2000
Fazl-e-Akbar	PIA v Habib Bank at Lahore	2001-02
C. M. Willoughby	Cape Cobras v Dolphins at Durban	2005-06
Tabish Khan	Karachi Whites v ZTBL at Karachi	2009-10
Kamran Hussain	Habib Bank v Lahore Shalimar at Lahore	2009-10

† *Not all in the same innings.*

‡ *Having bowled Firth with the last ball of the first innings, Walker achieved a unique feat by dismissing Lester, Tompkin and Smithson with the first three balls of the second.*

§ *James also scored a century, a unique double.*

Notes: In their match with England at The Oval in 1863, Surrey lost four wickets in the course of a four-ball over from G. Bennett.

Sussex lost five wickets in the course of the final (six-ball) over of their match with Surrey at Eastbourne in 1972. P. I. Pocock, who had taken three wickets in his previous over, captured four more, taking in all seven wickets with 11 balls, a feat unique in first-class matches. (The eighth wicket fell to a run-out.)

HAT-TRICKS

Double Hat-Trick

Besides Trott's performance, which is mentioned in the preceding section, the following instances are recorded of players having performed the hat-trick twice in the same match, Rao doing so in the same innings.

A. Shaw	Nottinghamshire v Gloucestershire at Nottingham	1884
T. J. Matthews	Australia v South Africa at Manchester	1912
C. W. L. Parker	Gloucestershire v Middlesex at Bristol	1924
R. O. Jenkins	Worcestershire v Surrey at Worcester	1949
J. S. Rao	Services v Northern Punjab at Amritsar	1963-64
Amin Lakhani	Combined XI v Indians at Multan	1978-79

Five Wickets in Six Balls

W. H. Copson	Derbyshire v Warwickshire at Derby	1937
W. A. Henderson	N.E. Transvaal v Orange Free State at Bloemfontein	1937-38
P. I. Pocock	Surrey v Sussex at Eastbourne	1972
Yasir Arafat	Rawalpindi v Faisalabad at Rawalpindi	2004-05

Yasir Arafat's five wickets were spread across two innings and interrupted only by a no-ball.

Most Hat-Tricks

D. V. P. Wright	7	R. G. Barlow	4	T. G. Matthews	4
T. W. J. Goddard	6	Fazl-e-Akbar	4	M. J. Procter	4
C. W. L. Parker	6	A. P. Freeman	4	T. Richardson	4
S. Haigh	5	J. T. Hearne	4	F. R. Spofforth	4
V. W. C. Jupp	5	J. C. Laker	4	F. S. Trueman	4
A. E. G. Rhodes	5	G. A. R. Lock	4		
F. A. Tarrant	5	G. G. Macaulay	4		

Current players only:

Asad Ali	2	S. J. Harmison	2	P. D. R. L. Perera	2
D. G. Cork	2	M. J. Hoggard	2	C. M. Willoughby	2
Elias Sunny	2	G. J-P. Kruger	2		
J. E. C. Franklin	2	M. Ntini	2		

Hat-Trick on Debut

There have been **18** instances in first-class cricket. Occurrences since the Second World War:

J. C. Treanor	New South Wales v Queensland at Brisbane	1954-55
V. B. Ranjane	Maharashtra v Saurashtra at Poona	1956-57
Arshad Khan	Dacca University v East Pakistan B at Dacca	1957-58
N. Fredrick	Ceylon v Madras at Colombo	1963-64
J. S. Rao	Services v Jammu and Kashmir at Delhi	1963-64
Mehboodullah	Uttar Pradesh v Madhya Pradesh at Lucknow	1971-72
R. O. Estwick	Barbados v Guyana at Bridgetown	1982-83
S. A. Ankola	Maharashtra v Gujarat at Poona	1988-89
J. Srinath	Karnataka v Hyderabad at Secunderabad	1989-90
S. P. Mukherjee	Bengal v Hyderabad at Secunderabad	1989-90
S. M. Harwood	Victoria v Tasmania at Melbourne	2002-03
P. Connell	Ireland v Netherlands at Rotterdam	2008
A. Mithun	Karnataka v Uttar Pradesh at Meerut	2009-10
Zohaib Shera	Karachi Whites v National Bank at Karachi	2009-10

Notes: R. R. Phillips (Border) took a hat-trick in his first over in first-class cricket (v Eastern Province at Port Elizabeth, 1939-40) having previously played in four matches without bowling.

    J. S. Rao took two more hat-tricks in his next match.

250 WICKETS IN A SEASON

	Season	O	M	R	W	Avge
A. P. Freeman	1928	1,976.1	423	5,489	304	18.05
A. P. Freeman	1933	2,039	651	4,549	298	15.26
T. Richardson	1895‡	1,690.1	463	4,170	290	14.37
C. T. B. Turner	1888†	2,427.2	1,127	3,307	283	11.68
A. P. Freeman	1931	1,618	360	4,307	276	15.60
A. P. Freeman	1930	1,914.3	472	4,632	275	16.84
T. Richardson	1897‡	1,603.4	495	3,945	273	14.45
A. P. Freeman	1929	1,670.5	381	4,879	267	18.27
W. Rhodes	1900	1,553	455	3,606	261	13.81
J. T. Hearne	1896‡	2,003.1	818	3,670	257	14.28
A. P. Freeman	1932	1,565.5	404	4,149	253	16.39
W. Rhodes	1901	1,565	505	3,797	251	15.12

† *Indicates 4-ball overs.*   ‡ *5-ball overs.*

Notes: In four consecutive seasons (1928-31), A. P. Freeman took 1,122 wickets, and in eight consecutive seasons (1928-35), 2,090 wickets. In each of these eight seasons he took over 200 wickets.

    T. Richardson took 1,005 wickets in four consecutive seasons (1894-97).

    The earliest date by which any bowler has taken 100 wickets in an English season is June 12, achieved by J. T. Hearne in 1896 and C. W. L. Parker in 1931, when A. P. Freeman did it on June 13.

200 WICKETS IN A SEASON MOST TIMES

A. P. Freeman	8	J. T. Hearne	3	T. Richardson	3
C. W. L. Parker	5	G. A. Lohmann	3	M. W. Tate	3
T. W. J. Goddard	4	W. Rhodes	3	H. Verity	3

Notes: A. P. Freeman reached 200 wickets in eight successive seasons – 1928 to 1935 – including 304 in 1928.

The last bowler to reach 200 wickets in a season was G. A. R. Lock (212 in 1957).

100 WICKETS IN A SEASON MOST TIMES

(Includes overseas tours and seasons)

W. Rhodes	23	C. W. L. Parker	16	G. H. Hirst	15
D. Shackleton	20	R. T. D. Perks	16	A. S. Kennedy	15
A. P. Freeman	17	F. J. Titmus	16		
T. W. J. Goddard	16	J. T. Hearne	15		

Notes: D. Shackleton reached 100 wickets in 20 successive seasons – 1949 to 1968.

Since the reduction of County Championship matches in 1969, D. L. Underwood (five times) and J. K. Lever (four times) are the only bowlers to have reached 100 wickets in a season more than twice. The highest aggregate in a season since 1969 is 134 by M. D. Marshall in 1982.

100 WICKETS IN A SEASON OUTSIDE ENGLAND

W		Season	Country	R	Avge
116	M. W. Tate	1926-27	India/Ceylon	1,599	13.78
113	Kabir Khan	1998-99	Pakistan	1,706	15.09
107	Ijaz Faqih	1985-86	Pakistan	1,719	16.06
106	C. T. B. Turner	1887-88	Australia	1,441	13.59
106	R. Benaud	1957-58	South Africa	2,056	19.39
105	Murtaza Hussain	1995-96	Pakistan	1,882	17.92
104	S. F. Barnes	1913-14	South Africa	1,117	10.74
104	Sajjad Akbar	1989-90	Pakistan	2,328	22.38
103	Abdul Qadir	1982-83	Pakistan	2,367	22.98

LEADING BOWLERS IN AN ENGLISH SEASON

(Qualification: 10 wickets in 10 innings)

Season	Leading wicket-taker	Wkts	Avge	Top of averages	Wkts	Avge
1946	W. E. Hollies	184	15.60	A. Booth	111	11.61
1947	T. W. J. Goddard	238	17.30	J. C. Clay	65	16.44
1948	J. E. Walsh	174	19.56	J. C. Clay	41	14.17
1949	R. O. Jenkins	183	21.19	T. W. J. Goddard	160	19.18
1950	R. Tattersall	193	13.59	R. Tattersall	193	13.59
1951	R. Appleyard	200	14.14	R. Appleyard	200	14.14
1952	J. H. Wardle	177	19.54	F. S. Trueman	61	13.78
1953	B. Dooland	172	16.58	C. J. Knott	38	13.71
1954	B. Dooland	196	15.48	J. B. Statham	92	14.13
1955	G. A. R. Lock	216	14.49	R. Appleyard	85	13.01
1956	D. J. Shepherd	177	15.36	G. A. R. Lock	155	12.46
1957	G. A. R. Lock	212	12.02	G. A. R. Lock	212	12.02
1958	G. A. R. Lock	170	12.08	H. L. Jackson	143	10.99
1959	D. Shackleton	148	21.55	J. B. Statham	139	15.01
1960	F. S. Trueman	175	13.98	J. B. Statham	135	12.31
1961	J. A. Flavell	171	17.79	J. A. Flavell	171	17.79
1962	D. Shackleton	172	20.15	C. Cook	58	17.13
1963	D. Shackleton	146	16.75	C. C. Griffith	119	12.83
1964	D. Shackleton	142	20.40	J. A. Standen	64	13.00

Season	Leading wicket-taker	Wkts	Avge	Top of averages	Wkts	Avge
1965	D. Shackleton	144	16.08	H. J. Rhodes	119	11.04
1966	D. L. Underwood	157	13.80	D. L. Underwood	157	13.80
1967	T. W. Cartwright	147	15.52	D. L. Underwood	136	12.39
1968	R. Illingworth	131	14.36	O. S. Wheatley	82	12.95
1969	R. M. H. Cottam	109	21.04	A. Ward	69	14.82
1970	D. J. Shepherd	106	19.16	Majid Khan	11	18.81
1971	L. R. Gibbs	131	18.89	G. G. Arnold	83	17.12
1972	{ T. W. Cartwright	98	18.64	I. M. Chappell	10	10.60
	{ B. Stead	98	20.38			
1973	B. S. Bedi	105	17.94	T. W. Cartwright	89	15.84
1974	A. M. E. Roberts	119	13.62	A. M. E. Roberts	119	13.62
1975	P. G. Lee	112	18.45	A. M. E. Roberts	57	15.80
1976	G. A. Cope	93	24.13	M. A. Holding	55	14.38
1977	M. J. Procter	109	18.04	R. A. Woolmer	19	15.21
1978	D. L. Underwood	110	14.49	D. L. Underwood	110	14.49
1979	{ D. L. Underwood	106	14.85	J. Garner	55	13.83
	{ J. K. Lever	106	17.30			
1980	R. D. Jackman	121	15.40	J. Garner	49	13.93
1981	R. J. Hadlee	105	14.89	R. J. Hadlee	105	14.89
1982	M. D. Marshall	134	15.73	R. J. Hadlee	61	14.57
1983	{ J. K. Lever	106	16.28	Imran Khan	12	7.16
	{ D. L. Underwood	106	19.28			
1984	R. J. Hadlee	117	14.05	R. J. Hadlee	117	14.05
1985	N. V. Radford	101	24.68	R. M. Ellison	65	17.20
1986	C. A. Walsh	118	18.17	M. D. Marshall	100	15.08
1987	N. V. Radford	109	20.81	R. J. Hadlee	97	12.64
1988	F. D. Stephenson	125	18.31	M. D. Marshall	42	13.16
1989	{ D. R. Pringle	94	18.64	T. M. Alderman	70	15.64
	{ S. L. Watkin	94	25.09			
1990	N. A. Foster	94	26.61	I. R. Bishop	59	19.05
1991	Waqar Younis	113	14.65	Waqar Younis	113	14.65
1992	C. A. Walsh	92	15.96	C. A. Walsh	92	15.96
1993	S. L. Watkin	92	22.80	Wasim Akram	59	19.27
1994	M. M. Patel	90	22.86	C. E. L. Ambrose	77	14.45
1995	A. Kumble	105	20.40	A. A. Donald	89	16.07
1996	C. A. Walsh	85	16.84	C. E. L. Ambrose	43	16.67
1997	A. M. Smith	83	17.63	A. A. Donald	60	15.63
1998	C. A. Walsh	106	17.31	V. J. Wells	36	14.27
1999	A. Sheriyar	92	24.70	Saqlain Mushtaq	58	11.37
2000	G. D. McGrath	80	13.21	C. A. Walsh	40	11.42
2001	R. J. Kirtley	75	23.32	G. D. McGrath	40	15.60
2002	{ M. J. Saggers	83	21.51	C. P. Schofield	18	18.38
	{ K. J. Dean	83	23.50			
2003	Mushtaq Ahmed	103	24.65	Shoaib Akhtar	34	17.05
2004	Mushtaq Ahmed	84	27.59	D. S. Lehmann	15	17.40
2005	S. K. Warne	87	22.50	M. Muralitharan	36	15.00
2006	Mushtaq Ahmed	102	19.91	Naved-ul-Hasan	35	16.71
2007	Mushtaq Ahmed	90	25.66	Harbhajan Singh	37	18.54
2008	J. A. Tomlinson	67	24.76	M. Davies	41	14.63
2009	Danish Kaneria	75	23.69	G. Onions	69	19.95
2010	**A. R. Adams**	**68**	**22.17**	**J. K. H. Naik**	**35**	**17.68**

1,500 WICKETS

Dates in italics denote the first half of an overseas season; i.e. *1970* denotes the 1970-71 season.

		Career	W	R	Avge
1	W. Rhodes	1898–1930	4,187	69,993	16.71
2	A. P. Freeman	1914–1936	3,776	69,577	18.42
3	C. W. L. Parker	1903–1935	3,278	63,817	19.46
4	J. T. Hearne	1888–1923	3,061	54,352	17.75

		Career	W	R	Avge
5	T. W. J. Goddard	1922–1952	2,979	59,116	19.84
6	W. G. Grace	1865–1908	2,876	51,545	17.92
7	A. S. Kennedy	1907–1936	2,874	61,034	21.23
8	D. Shackleton...............	1948–1969	2,857	53,303	18.65
9	G. A. R. Lock..............	1946–*1970*	2,844	54,709	19.23
10	F. J. Titmus...............	1949–1982	2,830	63,313	22.37
11	M. W. Tate................	1912–1937	2,784	50,571	18.16
12	G. H. Hirst	1891–1929	2,739	51,282	18.72
13	C. Blythe	1899–1914	2,506	42,136	16.81
14	D. L. Underwood...........	1963–1987	2,465	49,993	20.28
15	W. E. Astill	1906–1939	2,431	57,783	23.76
16	J. C. White................	1909–1937	2,356	43,759	18.57
17	W. E. Hollies	1932–1957	2,323	48,656	20.94
18	F. S. Trueman..............	1949–1969	2,304	42,154	18.29
19	J. B. Statham	1950–1968	2,260	36,999	16.37
20	R. T. D. Perks.............	1930–1955	2,233	53,770	24.07
21	J. Briggs.................	1879–1900	2,221	35,431	15.95
22	D. J. Shepherd	1950–1972	2,218	47,302	21.32
23	E. G. Dennett	1903–1926	2,147	42,571	19.82
24	T. Richardson..............	1892–1905	2,104	38,794	18.43
25	T. E. Bailey	1945–1967	2,082	48,170	23.13
26	R. Illingworth..............	1951–1983	2,072	42,023	20.28
27 {	N. Gifford.................	1960–1988	2,068	48,731	23.56
	F. E. Woolley.............	1906–1938	2,068	41,066	19.85
29	G. Geary..................	1912–1938	2,063	41,339	20.03
30	D. V. P. Wright............	1932–1957	2,056	49,307	23.98
31	J. A. Newman..............	1906–1930	2,032	51,111	25.15
32	†A. Shaw	1864–1897	2,027	24,580	12.12
33	S. Haigh	1895–1913	2,012	32,091	15.94
34	H. Verity	1930–1939	1,956	29,146	14.90
35	W. Attewell	1881–1900	1,951	29,896	15.32
36	J. C. Laker	1946–*1964*	1,944	35,791	18.41
37	A. V. Bedser...............	1939–1960	1,924	39,279	20.41
38	W. Mead..................	1892–1913	1,916	36,388	18.99
39	A. E. Relf.................	1900–1921	1,897	39,724	20.94
40	P. G. H. Fender	1910–1936	1,894	47,458	25.05
41	J. W. H. T. Douglas	1901–1930	1,893	44,159	23.32
42	J. H. Wardle	1946–*1967*	1,846	35,027	18.97
43	G. R. Cox.................	1895–1928	1,843	42,136	22.86
44	G. A. Lohmann	1884–*1897*	1,841	25,295	13.73
45	J. W. Hearne..............	1909–1936	1,839	44,926	24.42
46	G. G. Macaulay	1920–1935	1,837	32,440	17.65
47	M. S. Nichols..............	1924–1939	1,833	39,666	21.63
48 {	J. B. Mortimore	1950–1975	1,807	41,904	23.18
	C. A. Walsh	*1981–2000*	1,807	39,233	21.71
50	C. Cook	1946–1964	1,782	36,578	20.52
51	R. Peel	1882–1899	1,752	28,442	16.23
52	H. L. Jackson	1947–1963	1,733	30,101	17.36
53	J. K. Lever	1967–1989	1,722	41,772	24.25
54	T. P. B. Smith.............	1929–1952	1,697	45,059	26.55
55	J. Southerton	1854–1879	1,681	24,290	14.44
56	A. E. Trott	*1892*–1911	1,674	35,317	21.09
57	A. W. Mold	1889–1901	1,673	26,010	15.54
58	T. G. Wass	1896–1920	1,666	34,092	20.46
59	V. W. C. Jupp..............	1909–1938	1,658	38,166	23.01
60	C. Gladwin................	1939–1958	1,653	30,265	18.30
61	M. D. Marshall.............	*1977–1995*	1,651	31,548	19.10
62	W. E. Bowes	1928–1947	1,639	27,470	16.76
63	A. W. Wellard	1927–1950	1,614	39,302	24.35
64	J. E. Emburey..............	1973–1997	1,608	41,958	26.09

		Career	W	R	Avge
65	P. I. Pocock	1964–1986	1,607	42,648	26.53
66	N. I. Thomson	1952–1972	1,597	32,867	20.58
67 {	J. Mercer	1919–1947	1,591	37,210	23.38
	G. J. Thompson	1897–1922	1,591	30,058	18.89
69	J. M. Sims	1929–1953	1,581	39,401	24.92
70 {	T. Emmett	1866–1888	1,571	21,314	13.56
	Intikhab Alam	1957–1982	1,571	43,474	27.67
72	B. S. Bedi	1961–1981	1,560	33,843	21.69
73	W. Voce	1927–1952	1,558	35,961	23.08
74	A. R. Gover	1928–1948	1,555	36,753	23.63
75 {	T. W. Cartwright	1952–1977	1,536	29,357	19.11
	K. Higgs	1958–1986	1,536	36,267	23.61
77	James Langridge	1924–1953	1,530	34,524	22.56
78	J. A. Flavell	1949–1967	1,529	32,847	21.48
79	E. E. Hemmings	1966–1995	1,515	44,403	29.30
80 {	C. F. Root	1910–1933	1,512	31,933	21.11
	F. A. Tarrant	1898–1936	1,512	26,450	17.49
82	R. K. Tyldesley	1919–1935	1,509	25,980	17.21

† *The figures for A. Shaw exclude one wicket for which no analysis is available.*

Note: Some works of reference provide career figures which differ from those in this list, owing to the exclusion or inclusion of matches recognised or not recognised as first-class by *Wisden*.

Current Players with 1,000 Wickets

	Career	W	R	Avge
M. Muralitharan	1989–2010	1,374	26,997	19.64
R. D. B. Croft	1989–2010	1,133	39,995	35.30

ALL-ROUND RECORDS

REMARKABLE ALL-ROUND MATCHES

V. E. Walker	20*	108	10-74	4-17	England v Surrey at The Oval	1859
W. G. Grace	104		2-60	10-49	MCC v Oxford University at Oxford .	1886
G. Giffen	271		9-96	7-70	South Australia v Victoria at Adelaide	1891-92
B. J. T. Bosanquet	103	100*	3-75	8-53	Middlesex v Sussex at Lord's	1905
G. H. Hirst	111	117*	6-70	5-45	Yorkshire v Somerset at Bath	1906
F. D. Stephenson	111	117	4-105	7-117	Notts v Yorkshire at Nottingham	1988

Note: E. M. Grace, for MCC v Gentlemen of Kent in a 12-a-side match at Canterbury in 1862, scored 192* and took 5-77 and 10-69.

HUNDRED AND HAT-TRICK

G. Giffen, Australians v Lancashire at Manchester	1884
W. E. Roller, Surrey v Sussex at The Oval. *Unique instance of 200 and hat-trick.*	1885
W. B. Burns, Worcestershire v Gloucestershire at Worcester	1913
V. W. C. Jupp, Sussex v Essex at Colchester	1921
R. E. S. Wyatt, MCC v Ceylonese at Colombo	1926-27
L. N. Constantine, West Indians v Northamptonshire at Northampton	1928
D. E. Davies, Glamorgan v Leicestershire at Leicester	1937
V. M. Merchant, Dr C. R. Pereira's XI v Sir Homi Mehta's XI at Bombay	1946-47
M. J. Procter, Gloucestershire v Essex at Westcliff-on-Sea	1972
M. J. Procter, Gloucestershire v Leicestershire at Bristol	1979
K. D. James, Hampshire v Indians at Southampton. *Unique instance of 100 and four wickets in four balls*	1996
J. E. C. Franklin, Gloucestershire v Derbyshire at Cheltenham	2009

THE DOUBLE

The double was traditionally regarded as 1,000 runs and 100 wickets in an English season. The feat became exceptionally rare after the reduction of County Championship matches in 1969.

Remarkable Seasons

	Season	R	W		Season	R	W
G. H. Hirst	1906	2,385	208	J. H. Parks	1937	3,003	101

1,000 Runs and 100 Wickets

W. Rhodes	16	W. G. Grace	8	F. J. Titmus	8
G. H. Hirst	14	M. S. Nichols	8	F. E. Woolley	7
V. W. C. Jupp	10	A. E. Relf	8	G. E. Tribe	7
W. E. Astill	9	F. A. Tarrant	8		
T. E. Bailey	8	M. W. Tate	8†		

† *M. W. Tate also scored 1,193 runs and took 116 wickets on the 1926-27 MCC tour of India and Ceylon.*

Note: R. J. Hadlee (1984) and F. D. Stephenson (1988) are the only players to perform the feat since the reduction of County Championship matches in 1969. A complete list of those performing the feat before then may be found on page 202 of the 1982 *Wisden*. T. E. Bailey (1959) was the last player to achieve 2,000 runs and 100 wickets in a season; M. W. Tate (1925) the last to reach 1,000 runs and 200 wickets. Full lists may be found in *Wisdens* up to 2003.

Wicketkeeper's Double

The only wicketkeepers to achieve 1,000 runs and 100 dismissals in a season were L. E. G. Ames (1928, 1929 and 1932, when he scored 2,482 runs) and J. T. Murray (1957).

WICKETKEEPING RECORDS

MOST DISMISSALS IN AN INNINGS

9 (8ct, 1st)	Tahir Rashid	Habib Bank v PACO at Gujranwala	1992-93
9 (7ct, 2st)	W. R. James*	Matabeleland v Mashonaland CD at Bulawayo	1995-96
8 (all ct)	A. T. W. Grout	Queensland v Western Australia at Brisbane	1959-60
8 (all ct)†	D. E. East	Essex v Somerset at Taunton	1985
8 (all ct)	S. A. Marsh‡	Kent v Middlesex at Lord's	1991
8 (6ct, 2st)	T. J. Zoehrer	Australians v Surrey at The Oval	1993
8 (7ct, 1st)	D. S. Berry	Victoria v South Australia at Melbourne	1996-97
8 (7ct, 1st)	Y. S. S. Mendis	Bloomfield v Kurunegala Youth at Colombo	2000-01
8 (7ct, 1st)	S. Nath§	Assam v Tripura at Guwahati	2001-02
8 (all ct)	J. N. Batty¶	Surrey v Kent at The Oval	2004
8 (all ct)	Golam Mabud	Sylhet v Dhaka at Dhaka	2005-06
8 (all ct)	A. Z. M. Dyili	Eastern Province v Free State at Port Elizabeth	2009-10
8 (all ct)	**D. C. de Boorder**	**Otago v Wellington at Wellington**	**2009-10**

There have been **84** further instances of seven dismissals in an innings. R. W. Taylor achieved the feat three times, and G. J. Hopkins, Kamran Akmal, S. A. Marsh, K. J. Piper, Shahin Hossain and Wasim Bari twice. One of Marsh's two instances was of eight dismissals – see above. A fuller list can be found in *Wisdens* before 2004. The most recent occurrences are:

7 (all ct)	W. A. Seccombe	Queensland v New South Wales at Brisbane	2001-02
7 (all ct)	M. G. Croy	Otago v Auckland at Auckland	2001-02
7 (all ct)	Wasim Ahmed	Dadu v PWD at Karachi	2002-03
7 (all ct)	S. G. Clingeleffer	Tasmania v Western Australia at Perth	2003-04
7 (6ct, 1st)	C. O. Browne	Barbados v Jamaica at Kingston	2003-04
7 (all ct)	Adnan Akmal	Lahore Blues v Karachi Blues at Karachi	2004-05
7 (all ct)	G. J. Hopkins	New Zealand A v South Africa A at Centurion	2004-05

7 (all ct)	Mohammad Kashif	Rawalpindi v Multan at Multan	2004-05
7 (all ct)	T. L. Tsolekile	Western Province Boland v Dolphins at Durban ..	2004-05
7 (all ct)	M. S. Dhoni	East Zone v Central Zone at Gwalior	2004-05
7 (all ct)	Shahin Hossain	Barisal v Rajshahi at Rajshahi.	2004-05
7 (all ct)	G. J. Hopkins	New Zealand A v Sri Lanka A at Kandy	2005-06
7 (all ct)	D. H. Yagnik	Rajasthan v Saurashtra at Rajkot.	2005-06
7 (all ct)	N. Pothas	Hampshire v Lancashire at Manchester	2006
7 (6ct, 1st)	Shahin Hossain	Barisal v Dhaka at Dhaka	2006-07
7 (all ct)	B. B. J. Griggs	Central Districts v Northern Districts at Hamilton	2007-08
7 (all ct)	C. D. Hartley	Queensland v New South Wales at Brisbane	2007-08
7 (all ct)	L. D. Sutton	Lancashire v Yorkshire at Leeds.	2008
7 (all ct)	Jamal Anwar	Federal Areas v Punjab at Islamabad	2008-09
7 (all ct)	Kamran Akmal	National Bank v Habib Bank at Karachi.	2008-09
7 (all ct)	Sarfraz Ahmed	PIA v Habib Bank at Karachi	2008-09
7 (all ct)	P. A. Browne	Barbados v Windward Islands at Bridgetown.	2008-09
7 (all ct)	P. Bisht	Delhi v Baroda at Vadodara	2009-10
7 (5ct, 2st)	S. M. Fernando	Air Force v Seeduwa Raddoluwa at Colombo	2009-10
7 (all ct)	**Kashif Mahmood**	**Lahore Shalimar v Abbottabad at Abbottabad.**	**2010-11**
7 (all ct)	**Kamran Akmal**	**National Bank v WAPDA at Sialkot**	**2010-11**

* W. R. James also scored 99 and 99 not out.   *† The first eight wickets to fall.*
‡ S. A. Marsh also scored 108 not out.   *§ On his only first-class appearance.*
¶ J. N. Batty also scored 129.

WICKETKEEPERS' HAT-TRICKS

W. H. Brain, Gloucestershire v Somerset at Cheltenham, 1893 – three stumpings off successive balls from C. L. Townsend.

G. O. Dawkes, Derbyshire v Worcestershire at Kidderminster, 1958 – three catches off successive balls from H. L. Jackson.

R. C. Russell, Gloucestershire v Surrey at The Oval, 1986 – three catches off successive balls from C. A. Walsh and D. V. Lawrence (2).

MOST DISMISSALS IN A MATCH

13 (11ct, 2st)	W. R. James*	Matabeleland v Mashonaland CD at Bulawayo....	1995-96
12 (8ct, 4st)	E. Pooley	Surrey v Sussex at The Oval	1868
12 (9ct, 3st)	D. Tallon	Queensland v New South Wales at Sydney	1938-39
12 (9ct, 3st)	H. B. Taber	New South Wales v South Australia at Adelaide. . .	1968-69
12 (all ct)	P. D. McGlashan	Northern Districts v Central Districts at Whangarei	2009-10
12 (11ct, 1st)	**T. L. Tsolekile**	**Lions v Dolphins at Johannesburg**	**2010-11**
12 (all ct)	**Kashif Mahmood**	**Lahore Shalimar v Abbottabad at Abbottabad.**	**2010-11**
11 (all ct)	A. Long	Surrey v Sussex at Hove	1964
11 (all ct)	R. W. Marsh	Western Australia v Victoria at Perth	1975-76
11 (all ct)	D. L. Bairstow	Yorkshire v Derbyshire at Scarborough.	1982
11 (all ct)	W. K. Hegg	Lancashire v Derbyshire at Chesterfield	1989
11 (all ct)	A. J. Stewart	Surrey v Leicestershire at Leicester	1989
11 (all ct)	T. J. Nielsen	South Australia v Western Australia at Perth.	1990-91
11 (10ct, 1st)	I. A. Healy	Australians v N. Transvaal at Verwoerdburg.	1993-94
11 (all ct)	K. J. Piper	Warwickshire v Derbyshire at Chesterfield	1994
11 (all ct)	D. S. Berry	Victoria v Pakistanis at Melbourne	1995-96
11 (10ct, 1st)	W. A. Seccombe	Queensland v Western Australia at Brisbane.	1995-96
11 (all ct)	R. C. Russell	England v South Africa (2nd Test) at Johannesburg	1995-96
11 (10ct, 1st)	D. S. Berry	Victoria v South Australia at Melbourne	1996-97

11 (all ct)	Wasim Yousufi	Peshawar v Bahawalpur at Peshawar............	1997-98
11 (all ct)	Aamer Iqbal	Pakistan Customs v Karachi Whites at Karachi....	1999-2000
11 (10ct, 1st)	S. Nath†	Assam v Tripura at Guwahati	2001-02
11 (all ct)	Wasim Ahmed	Dadu v PWD at Karachi	2002-03
11 (7ct, 4st)	J. N. Batty	Surrey v Lancashire at Manchester	2004
11 (7ct, 4st)	M. S. Dhoni	India A v Zimbabwe Select XI at Harare........	2004
11 (all ct)	Adnan Akmal	Lahore Blues v Karachi Blues at Karachi	2004-05
11 (9ct, 2st)	M. S. Bisla	Himachal Pradesh v Saurashtra at Dharmasala	2004-05

* W. R. James also scored 99 and 99 not out.   † On his only first-class appearance.

100 DISMISSALS IN A SEASON

128 (79ct, 49st)	L. E. G. Ames 1929	104 (82ct, 22st)	J. T. Murray...... 1957
122 (70ct, 52st)	L. E. G. Ames 1928	102 (69ct, 33st)	F. H. Huish 1913
110 (63ct, 47st)	H. Yarnold....... 1949	102 (95ct, 7st)	J. T. Murray...... 1960
107 (77ct, 30st)	G. Duckworth 1928	101 (62ct, 39st)	F. H. Huish 1911
107 (96ct, 11st)	J. G. Binks 1960	101 (85ct, 16st)	R. Booth 1960
104 (40ct, 64st)	L. E. G. Ames 1932	100 (91ct, 9st)	R. Booth 1964

Note: L. E. G. Ames achieved the two highest stumping totals in a season: 64 in 1932, and 52 in 1928.

1,000 DISMISSALS

Dates in italics denote the first half of an overseas season; i.e. *1914* denotes the 1914-15 season.

			Career	*M*	*Ct*	*St*
1	R. W. Taylor	1,649	1960–1988	639	1,473	176
2	J. T. Murray	1,527	1952–1975	635	1,270	257
3	H. Strudwick	1,497	1902–1927	675	1,242	255
4	A. P. E. Knott..............	1,344	1964–1985	511	1,211	133
5	R. C. Russell	1,320	1981–2004	465	1,192	128
6	F. H. Huish	1,310	1895–1914	497	933	377
7	B. Taylor.................	1,294	1949–1973	572	1,083	211
8	S. J. Rhodes	1,263	1981–2004	440	1,139	124
9	D. Hunter	1,253	1889–1909	548	906	347
10	H. R. Butt................	1,228	1890–1912	550	953	275
11	J. H. Board	1,207	1891–*1914*	525	852	355
12	H. Elliott.................	1,206	1920–1947	532	904	302
13	J. M. Parks	1,181	1949–1976	739	1,088	93
14	R. Booth.................	1,126	1951–1970	468	948	178
15	L. E. G. Ames	1,121	1926–1951	593	703	418†
16	D. L. Bairstow.............	1,099	1970–1990	459	961	138
17	G. Duckworth..............	1,096	1923–1947	504	753	343
18	H. W. Stephenson	1,082	1948–1964	462	748	334
19	J. G. Binks	1,071	1955–1975	502	895	176
20	T. G. Evans	1,066	1939–1969	465	816	250
21	A. Long	1,046	1960–1980	452	922	124
22	G. O. Dawkes.............	1,043	1937–1961	482	895	148
23	R. W. Tolchard.............	1,037	1965–1983	483	912	125
24	W. L. Cornford.............	1,017	1921–1947	496	675	342

† Record.

Current Players with 500 Dismissals

		Career	M	Ct	St
956	P. A. Nixon	1989–2010	351	889	67
747	C. M. W. Read	1997–2010	239	707	40
710	M. V. Boucher..................	1995–2010	200	674	36
637	N. Pothas	1993–2010	210	592	45
620	J. N. Batty	1994–2010	206	553	67
596	Kamran Akmal	1997–2010	161	550	46
528	J. S. Foster	2000–2010	174	484	44
503	H. A. P. W. Jayawardene............	1997–2010	183	418	85

Note: Some of these figures include catches taken in the field.

FIELDING RECORDS

excluding wicketkeepers

MOST CATCHES IN AN INNINGS

7	M. J. Stewart	Surrey v Northamptonshire at Northampton	1957
7	A. S. Brown	Gloucestershire v Nottinghamshire at Nottingham	1966

MOST CATCHES IN A MATCH

10	W. R. Hammond†	Gloucestershire v Surrey at Cheltenham	1928
8	W. B. Burns	Worcestershire v Yorkshire at Bradford	1907
8	F. G. Travers	Europeans v Parsees at Bombay	1923-24
8	A. H. Bakewell	Northamptonshire v Essex at Leyton.	1928
8	W. R. Hammond	Gloucestershire v Worcestershire at Cheltenham	1932
8	K. J. Grieves	Lancashire v Sussex at Manchester.....................	1951
8	C. A. Milton	Gloucestershire v Sussex at Hove	1952
8	G. A. R. Lock	Surrey v Warwickshire at The Oval	1957
8	J. M. Prodger	Kent v Gloucestershire at Cheltenham	1961
8	P. M. Walker	Glamorgan v Derbyshire at Swansea	1970
8	Masood Anwar	Rawalpindi v Lahore Division at Rawalpindi	1983-84
8	M. C. J. Ball	Gloucestershire v Yorkshire at Cheltenham	1994
8	J. D. Carr	Middlesex v Warwickshire at Birmingham................	1995
8	G. A. Hick	Worcestershire v Essex at Chelmsford	2005
8	A. P. McLaren	Eagles v Lions at Johannesburg.......................	2007-08

† *Hammond also scored a hundred in each innings.*

MOST CATCHES IN A SEASON

78	W. R. Hammond..........	1928	69	P. M. Walker.............	1960
77	M. J. Stewart.............	1957	66	J. Tunnicliffe.............	1895
73	P. M. Walker.............	1961	65	W. R. Hammond..........	1925
71	P. J. Sharpe	1962	65	P. M. Walker.............	1959
70	J. Tunnicliffe.............	1901	65	D. W. Richardson	1961
69	J. G. Langridge	1955			

Note: The most catches by a fielder since the reduction of County Championship matches in 1969 is 49 by C. J. Tavaré in 1978.

750 CATCHES

Dates in italics denote the first half of an overseas season; i.e. *1970* denotes the 1970-71 season.

		Career	M			Career	M
1,018	F. E. Woolley....	1906–1938	979	784	J. G. Langridge...	1928–1955	574
887	W. G. Grace.....	1865–1908	879	764	W. Rhodes......	1898–1930	1,107
830	G. A. R. Lock....	1946–*1970*	654	758	C. A. Milton.....	1948–1974	620
819	W. R. Hammond .	1920–1951	634	754	E. H. Hendren....	1907–1938	833
813	D. B. Close......	1949–1986	786				

Note: The most catches by a current player is 379 by M. J. Di Venuto (*1991*–2010).

TEAM RECORDS

HIGHEST INNINGS TOTALS

1,107	Victoria v New South Wales at Melbourne	1926-27
1,059	Victoria v Tasmania at Melbourne...........................	1922-23
952-6 dec	Sri Lanka v India at Colombo.............................	1997-98
951-7 dec	Sind v Baluchistan at Karachi.............................	1973-74
944-6 dec	Hyderabad v Andhra at Secunderabad.......................	1993-94
918	New South Wales v South Australia at Sydney	1900-01
912-8 dec	Holkar v Mysore at Indore...............................	1945-46
912-6 dec†	Tamil Nadu v Goa at Panjim..............................	1988-89
910-6 dec	Railways v Dera Ismail Khan at Lahore......................	1964-65
903-7 dec	England v Australia at The Oval...........................	1938
900-6 dec	Queensland v Victoria at Brisbane..........................	2005-06
887	Yorkshire v Warwickshire at Birmingham....................	1896
868†	North Zone v West Zone at Bhilai..........................	1987-88
863	Lancashire v Surrey at The Oval	1990
855-6 dec†	Bombay v Hyderabad at Bombay...........................	1990-91
850-7 dec	Somerset v Middlesex at Taunton	2007
849	England v West Indies at Kingston..........................	1929-30
843	Australians v Oxford & Cambridge U P & P at Portsmouth	1893
839	New South Wales v Tasmania at Sydney	1898-99
826-4	Maharashtra v Kathiawar at Poona..........................	1948-49
824	Lahore Greens v Bahawalpur at Lahore......................	1965-66
821-7 dec	South Australia v Queensland at Adelaide....................	1939-40
815	New South Wales v Victoria at Sydney	1908-09
811	Surrey v Somerset at The Oval	1899
810-4 dec	Warwickshire v Durham at Birmingham	1994
807	New South Wales v South Australia at Adelaide	1899-1900
806-8 dec	Victoria v Queensland at Melbourne	2008-09
805	New South Wales v Victoria at Melbourne	1905-06
803-4 dec	Kent v Essex at Brentwood.	1934
803	Non-Smokers v Smokers at East Melbourne	1886-87
802-8 dec	Karachi Blues v Lahore City at Peshawar	1994-95
802	New South Wales v South Australia at Sydney	1920-21
801-8 dec	Derbyshire v Somerset at Taunton	2007
801	Lancashire v Somerset at Taunton	1895
798	Maharashtra v Northern India at Poona	1940-41
793	Victoria v Queensland at Melbourne	1927-28
791-6 dec	Karnataka v Bengal at Calcutta............................	1990-91
791	Nottinghamshire v Essex at Chelmsford.	2007
790-3 dec	West Indies v Pakistan at Kingston.........................	1957-58
786	New South Wales v South Australia at Adelaide	1922-23
785	Tamil Nadu v Hyderabad at Hyderabad	2009-10
784	Baroda v Holkar at Baroda	1946-47
783-8 dec	Hyderabad v Bihar at Secunderabad.	1986-87
781-7 dec	Northamptonshire v Nottinghamshire at Northampton	1995

781	Lancashire v Warwickshire at Birmingham	2003
780-8	Punjab v Delhi at Delhi	1994-95
777	Canterbury v Otago at Christchurch	1996-97
775	New South Wales v Victoria at Sydney	1881-82

† *Tamil Nadu's total of 912-6 dec included 52 penalty runs from their opponents' failure to meet the required bowling rate. North Zone's total of 868 included 68, and Bombay's total of 855-6 dec included 48.*

Note: The highest total in a team's second innings is 770 by New South Wales v South Australia at Adelaide in 1920-21.

HIGHEST FOURTH-INNINGS TOTALS

654-5	England v South Africa at Durban	1938-39
	After being set 696 to win. The match was left drawn on the tenth day.	
604	Maharashtra (*set 959 to win*) v Bombay at Poona.	1948-49
576-8	Trinidad (*set 672 to win*) v Barbados at Port-of-Spain	1945-46
572	New South Wales (*set 593 to win*) v South Australia at Sydney.	1907-08
541-7	**West Zone (*won*) v South Zone at Hyderabad**	**2009-10**
529-9	Combined XI (*set 579 to win*) v South Africans at Perth	1963-64
518	Victoria (*set 753 to win*) v Queensland at Brisbane	1926-27
513-9	Central Province (*won*) v Southern Province at Kandy.	2003-04
507-7	Cambridge University (*won*) v MCC and Ground at Lord's.	1896
506-6	South Australia (*won*) v Queensland at Adelaide	1991-92
503-4	South Zone (*won*) v England A at Gurgaon	2003-04
502-6	Middlesex (*won*) v Nottinghamshire at Nottingham.	1925
502-8	Players (*won*) v Gentlemen at Lord's	1900
500-7	South African Universities (*won*) v Western Province at Stellenbosch	1978-79

MOST RUNS IN A DAY (ONE SIDE)

721	Australians (721) v Essex at Southend (1st day).	1948
651	West Indians (651-2) v Leicestershire at Leicester (1st day)	1950
649	New South Wales (649-7) v Otago at Dunedin (2nd day)	1923-24
645	Surrey (645-4) v Hampshire at The Oval (1st day).	1909
644	Oxford U. (644-8) v H. D. G. Leveson Gower's XI at Eastbourne (1st day) . . .	1921
640	Lancashire (640-8) v Sussex at Hove (1st day).	1937
636	Free Foresters (636-7) v Cambridge U. at Cambridge (1st day).	1938
625	Gloucestershire (625-6) v Worcestershire at Dudley (2nd day)	1934

MOST RUNS IN A DAY (BOTH SIDES)

(excluding the above)

685	North (169-8 and 255-7), South (261-8 dec) at Blackpool (2nd day).	1961
666	Surrey (607-4), Northamptonshire (59-2) at Northampton (2nd day).	1920
665	Rest of South Africa (339), Transvaal (326) at Johannesburg (1st day).	1911-12
663	Middlesex (503-4), Leicestershire (160-2) at Leicester (2nd day)	1947
661	Border (201), Griqualand West (460) at Kimberley (1st day).	1920-21
649	Hampshire (570-8), Somerset (79-3) at Taunton (2nd day)	1901

HIGHEST AGGREGATES IN A MATCH

Runs	Wkts		
2,376	37	Maharashtra v Bombay at Poona	1948-49
2,078	40	Bombay v Holkar at Bombay	1944-45
1,981	35	South Africa v England at Durban	1938-39
1,945	18	Canterbury v Wellington at Christchurch	1994-95
1,929	39	New South Wales v South Australia at Sydney	1925-26
1,911	34	New South Wales v Victoria at Sydney	1908-09
1,905	40	Otago v Wellington at Dunedin	1923-24

In Britain

Runs	Wkts		
1,815	28	Somerset v Surrey at Taunton	2002
1,808	20	Sussex v Essex at Hove	1993
1,795	34	Somerset v Northamptonshire at Taunton	2001
1,723	31	England v Australia at Leeds	1948
1,706	23	Hampshire v Warwickshire at Southampton	1997
1,683	14	Middlesex v Glamorgan at Southgate	2005
1,665	33	Warwickshire v Yorkshire at Birmingham	2002
1,659	13	Somerset v Middlesex at Taunton	2007
1,655	25	Derbyshire v Nottinghamshire at Derby	2001
1,650	19	Surrey v Lancashire at The Oval	1990

LOWEST INNINGS TOTALS

12†	Oxford University v MCC and Ground at Oxford	1877
12	Northamptonshire v Gloucestershire at Gloucester	1907
13	Auckland v Canterbury at Auckland	1877-78
13	Nottinghamshire v Yorkshire at Nottingham	1901
14	Surrey v Essex at Chelmsford	1983
15	MCC v Surrey at Lord's	1839
15†	Victoria v MCC at Melbourne	1903-04
15†	Northamptonshire v Yorkshire at Northampton	1908
15	Hampshire v Warwickshire at Birmingham	1922
	Following on, Hampshire scored 521 and won by 155 runs.	
16	MCC and Ground v Surrey at Lord's	1872
16	Derbyshire v Nottinghamshire at Nottingham	1879
16	Surrey v Nottinghamshire at The Oval	1880
16	Warwickshire v Kent at Tonbridge	1913
16	Trinidad v Barbados at Bridgetown	1942-43
16	Border v Natal at East London (first innings)	1959-60
17	Gentlemen of Kent v Gentlemen of England at Lord's	1850
17	Gloucestershire v Australians at Cheltenham	1896
18	The Bs v England at Lord's	1831
18†	Kent v Sussex at Gravesend	1867
18	Tasmania v Victoria at Melbourne	1868-69
18†	Australians v MCC and Ground at Lord's	1896
18	Border v Natal at East London (second innings)	1959-60
19	Sussex v Surrey at Godalming	1830
19†	Sussex v Nottinghamshire at Hove	1873
19	MCC and Ground v Australians at Lord's	1878
19	Wellington v Nelson at Nelson	1885-86
19	Matabeleland v Mashonaland at Harare	2000-01

† *One man absent.*

Note: At Lord's in 1810, The Bs, with one man absent, were dismissed by England for 6.

LOWEST TOTALS IN A MATCH

| 34 | (16 and 18) Border v Natal at East London. | 1959-60 |
| 42 | (27 and 15) Northamptonshire v Yorkshire at Northampton. | 1908 |

Note: Northamptonshire batted one man short in each innings.

LOWEST AGGREGATE IN A COMPLETED MATCH

Runs	Wkts		
85	11†	Quetta v Rawalpindi at Islamabad.	2008-09
105	31	MCC v Australians at Lord's.	1878

† *Both teams forfeited their first innings.*

Note: The lowest aggregate in a match in which the losing team was bowled out twice since 1900 is 157 for 22 wickets, Surrey v Worcestershire at The Oval, 1954.

LARGEST VICTORIES

Largest Innings Victories

Inns and 851 runs	Railways (910-6 dec) v Dera Ismail Khan at Lahore	1964-65
Inns and 666 runs	Victoria (1,059) v Tasmania at Melbourne	1922-23
Inns and 656 runs	Victoria (1,107) v New South Wales at Melbourne	1926-27
Inns and 605 runs	New South Wales (918) v South Australia at Sydney	1900-01
Inns and 579 runs	England (903-7 dec) v Australia at The Oval	1938
Inns and 575 runs	Sind (951-7 dec) v Baluchistan at Karachi	1973-74
Inns and 527 runs	New South Wales (713) v South Australia at Adelaide	1908-09
Inns and 517 runs	Australians (675) v Nottinghamshire at Nottingham	1921

Largest Victories by Runs Margin

685 runs	New South Wales (235 and 761-8 dec) v Queensland at Sydney	1929-30
675 runs	England (521 and 342-8 dec) v Australia at Brisbane	1928-29
638 runs	New South Wales (304 and 770) v South Australia at Adelaide	1920-21
609 runs	Muslim Commercial Bank (575 and 282-0 dec) v WAPDA at Lahore.	1977-78
585 runs	Sargodha (336 and 416) v Lahore Municipal Corporation at Faisalabad.	1978-79
573 runs	Sinhalese (395-7 dec and 350-2 dec) v Sebastianites at Colombo	1990-91
571 runs	Victoria (304 and 649) v South Australia at Adelaide	1926-27
562 runs	Australia (701 and 327) v England at The Oval	1934
556 runs	Nondescripts (397-8 dec and 313-6 dec) v Matara at Colombo	1998-99

Victory Without Losing a Wicket

Lancashire (166-0 dec and 66-0) beat Leicestershire by ten wickets at Manchester	1956
Karachi A (277-0 dec) beat Sind A by an innings and 77 runs at Karachi	1957-58
Railways (236-0 dec and 16-0) beat Jammu and Kashmir by ten wickets at Srinagar	1960-61
Karnataka (451-0 dec) beat Kerala by an innings and 186 runs at Chikmagalur	1977-78

Notes: There have been **29** wins by an innings and 400 runs or more, the most recent being an innings and 415 runs by Islamabad v Quetta at Islamabad in 2008-09.

There have been **18** wins by 500 runs or more, the most recent being 533 runs by Chilaw Marians v Rio at Colombo in 2001-02.

There have been **32** wins by a team losing only one wicket, the most recent being by Rawalpindi v Quetta at Islamabad in 2008-09.

TIED MATCHES

Since 1948, a tie has been recognised only when the scores are level with all the wickets down in the fourth innings. There have been **32** instances since then, including two Tests (see Test record section); Sussex have featured in five of those, Essex and Kent in four each.

The most recent instances are:

Bahawalpur v Peshawar at Bahawalpur...	1988-89
Wellington v Canterbury at Wellington..	1988-89
Sussex v Kent at Hove...	1991
Nottinghamshire v Worcestershire at Nottingham............................	1993
Somerset v West Indies A at Taunton...	†2002
Warwickshire v Essex at Birmingham..	2003
Worcestershire v Zimbabweans at Worcester................................	2003

† *Somerset (453) made the highest total to tie a first-class match.*

MATCHES COMPLETED ON FIRST DAY

(Since 1946)

Derbyshire v Somerset at Chesterfield, June 11................................	1947
Lancashire v Sussex at Manchester, July 12....................................	1950
Surrey v Warwickshire at The Oval, May 16	1953
Somerset v Lancashire at Bath, June 6 (H. F. T. Buse's benefit).............	1953
Kent v Worcestershire at Tunbridge Wells, June 15	1960

SHORTEST COMPLETED MATCHES

Balls

121	Quetta (forfeit and 41) v Rawalpindi (forfeit and 44-1) at Islamabad	2008-09
350	Somerset (35 and 44) v Middlesex (86) at Lord's	1899
352	Victoria (82 and 57) v Tasmania (104 and 37-7) at Launceston	1850-51
372	Victoria (80 and 50) v Tasmania (97 and 35-2) at Launceston	1853-54
419*	England XI (82 and 26) v Australians (76 and 33-6) at Aston.................	1884
425	Derbyshire (180-0 dec and forfeit) v Northamptonshire (forfeit and 181-2) at Northampton	1992
432	Victoria (78 and 67) v Tasmania (51 and 25) at Hobart	1857-58
435	Northamptonshire (4-0 dec and 86) v Yorkshire (4-0 dec and 88-5) at Bradford ..	1931
442*	Wellington (31 and 48) v Nelson (73 and 7-1) at Nelson	1887-88
445	Glamorgan (272-1 dec and forfeit) v Lancashire (forfeit and 51) at Liverpool	1997
450	Bengal Governor's XI (33 and 59) v Maharaja of Cooch-Behar's XI (138) at Calcutta	1917-18

* *Match completed on first day.*

LIST A ONE-DAY RECORDS

List A is a concept intended to provide an approximate equivalent in one-day cricket of first-class status. It was introduced by the Association of Cricket Statisticians and Historians and is now recognised by the ICC, with a separate category for Twenty20 cricket. Further details are available at stats.acscricket.com/ListA/Description.html. List A games comprise:

(a) One-day internationals.
(b) Other international matches (e.g. A-team internationals).
(c) Premier domestic one-day tournaments in Test-playing countries.
(d) Official tourist matches against the main first-class teams (e.g. counties, states, provinces and national Board XIs).

The following matches are excluded:

(a) Matches originally scheduled as less than 40 overs per side (e.g. Twenty20 games).
(b) World Cup warm-up games.
(c) Tourist matches against teams outside the major domestic competitions (e.g. universities).
(d) Festival games and pre-season friendlies.

Notes: This section covers one-day cricket to December 31, 2010. Bold type denotes performances in the calendar year 2010 or, in career figures, players who appeared in List A cricket in that year.

BATTING RECORDS

HIGHEST INDIVIDUAL INNINGS

268	A. D. Brown	Surrey v Glamorgan at The Oval	2002
222*	R. G. Pollock	Eastern Province v Border at East London	1974-75
207	Mohammad Ali	Pakistan Customs v DHA at Sialkot	2004-05
206	A. I. Kallicharran	Warwickshire v Oxfordshire at Birmingham	1984
204*	Khalid Latif	Karachi Dolphins v Quetta Bears at Karachi	2008-09
203	A. D. Brown	Surrey v Hampshire at Guildford	1997
202*	A. Barrow	Natal v SA African XI at Durban	1975-76
201*	R. S. Bopara	Essex v Leicestershire at Leicester	2008
201	V. J. Wells	Leicestershire v Berkshire at Leicester	1996
200*	**S. R. Tendulkar**	**India v South Africa at Gwalior**	**2009-10**

MOST RUNS

	Career	M	I	NO	R	HS	100s	Avge
G. A. Gooch	1973–1997	614	601	48	22,211	198*	44	40.16
G. A. Hick	*1983–2008*	651	630	96	22,059	172*	40	41.30
S. R. Tendulkar	*1989–2009*	529	516	55	21,150	**200***	57	45.87
I. V. A. Richards	1973–1993	500	466	61	16,995	189*	26	41.96
C. G. Greenidge	1970–1992	440	436	33	16,349	186*	33	40.56
S. T. Jayasuriya	*1989–2010*	548	533	25	15,806	189	31	31.11
A. J. Lamb	1972–1995	484	463	63	15,658	132*	19	39.14
D. L. Haynes	1976–1996	419	416	44	15,651	152*	28	42.07
K. J. Barnett	1979–2005	527	500	54	15,564	136	17	34.89
S. C. Ganguly	*1989–2009*	431	415	43	15,531	183	31	41.75
R. T. Ponting	*1992–2010*	424	415	50	15,438	164	33	42.29
R. Dravid	*1992–2009*	444	411	55	15,147	153	21	42.54
M. G. Bevan	1989–2006	427	385	124	15,103	157*	13	57.86

HIGHEST PARTNERSHIP FOR EACH WICKET

326*	for 1st	Ghulam Ali and Sohail Jaffer, PIA v ADBP at Sialkot	2000-01
331	for 2nd	S. R. Tendulkar and R. Dravid, India v New Zealand at Hyderabad . . .	1999-2000
309*	for 3rd	T. S. Curtis and T. M. Moody, Worcestershire v Surrey at The Oval . .	1994
275*	for 4th	M. Azharuddin and A. Jadeja, India v Zimbabwe at Cuttack	1997-98
267*	for 5th	Minhazul Abedin and Khaled Mahmud, Bangladeshis v Bahawalpur at Karachi.	1997-98
226	for 6th	N. J. Llong and M. V. Fleming, Kent v Cheshire at Bowdon	1999
203*	for 7th	S. H. T. Kandamby and H. M. R. K. B. Herath, Sri Lanka A v South Africa A at Benoni	2008-09
203	for 8th	Shahid Iqbal and Haaris Ayaz, Karachi Whites v Hyderabad at Karachi	1998-99
155	for 9th	C. M. W. Read and A. J. Harris, Notts v Durham at Nottingham	2006
106*	for 10th	I. V. A. Richards and M. A. Holding, West Indies v England at Manchester.	1984

BOWLING RECORDS

BEST BOWLING ANALYSES

8-15	R. L. Sanghvi	Delhi v Himachal Pradesh at Una	1997-98
8-19	W. P. U. J. C. Vaas	Sri Lanka v Zimbabwe at Colombo	2001-02
8-20*	D. T. Kottehewa	Nondescripts v Ragama at Colombo	2007-08
8-21	M. A. Holding	Derbyshire v Sussex at Hove	1988
8-26	K. D. Boyce	Essex v Lancashire at Manchester.	1971
8-30	G. D. R. Eranga	Burgher v Army at Colombo	2007-08
8-31	D. L. Underwood	Kent v Scotland at Edinburgh	1987
8-43	S. W. Tait	South Australia v Tasmania at Adelaide	2003-04
8-52	**K. A. Stoute**	**West Indies A v Lancashire at Manchester**	**2010**
8-66	S. R. G. Francis	Somerset v Derbyshire at Derby	2004

* *Including two hat-tricks.*

MOST WICKETS

	Career	M	B	R	W	BB	4W/i	Avge
Wasim Akram.	1984–2003	594	29,719	19,303	881	5-10	46	21.91
A. A. Donald.	1985–2003	458	22,856	14,942	684	6-15	38	21.84
Waqar Younis.	1988–2003	412	19,841	15,098	675	7-36	44	22.36
J. K. Lever	1968–1990	481	23,208	13,278	674	5-8	34	19.70
M. Muralitharan. . . .	**1991–2010**	**436**	**22,898**	**14,703**	**656**	**7-30**	**28**	**22.41**
J. E. Emburey.	1975–2000	536	26,399	16,811	647	5-23	26	25.98
I. T. Botham	1973–1993	470	22,899	15,264	612	5-27	18	24.94

WICKETKEEPING AND FIELDING RECORDS

MOST DISMISSALS IN AN INNINGS

8	(all ct)	D. J. S. Taylor	Somerset v Combined Universities at Taunton . . .	1982
8	(5ct, 3st)	S. J. Palframan	Boland v Easterns at Paarl	1997-98
8	(all ct)	D. J. Pipe	Worcestershire v Hertfordshire at Hertford	2001
7	(6ct, 1st)	R. W. Taylor	Derbyshire v Lancashire at Manchester	1975
7	(4ct, 3st)	Rizwan Umar	Sargodha v Bahawalpur at Sargodha	1991-92
7	(all ct)	A. J. Stewart	Surrey v Glamorgan at Swansea.	1994
7	(all ct)	I. Mitchell	Border v Western Province at East London	1998-99
7	(6ct, 1st)	M. K. P. B. Kularatne	Galle v Colts at Colombo	2001-02
7	(5ct, 2st)	T. R. Ambrose	Warwickshire v Middlesex at Birmingham	2009
7	(3ct, 4st)	W. A. S. Niroshan	Chilaw Marians v Saracens at Katunayake.	2009-10

MOST CATCHES IN AN INNINGS IN THE FIELD

5	V. J. Marks	Combined Universities v Kent at Oxford...............	1976
5	J. M. Rice	Hampshire v Warwickshire at Southampton..............	1978
5	A. J. Kourie	Transvaal v Western Province at Johannesburg...........	1979-80
5	J. N. Rhodes	South Africa v West Indies at Bombay.................	1993-94
5	J. W. Wilson	Otago v Auckland at Dunedin	1993-94
5	K. C. Jackson	Boland v Natal at Durban..........................	1995-96
5	Mohammad Ramzan	PNSC v PIA at Karachi	1998-99
5	Amit Sharma	Punjab v Jammu and Kashmir at Ludhiana	1999-2000
5	B. E. Young	South Australia v Tasmania at Launceston.............	2001-02
5	Hasnain Raza	Bahawalpur v Pakistan Customs at Karachi.............	2002-03
5	D. J. Sales	Northamptonshire v Essex at Northampton..............	2007
5	L. N. Mosena	Free State v North West at Bloemfontein..............	2007-08

TEAM RECORDS

HIGHEST INNINGS TOTALS

496-4	(50 overs)	Surrey v Gloucestershire at The Oval.....................	2007
443-9	(50 overs)	Sri Lanka v Netherlands at Amstelveen	2006
438-5	(50 overs)	Surrey v Glamorgan at The Oval	2002
438-9	(49.5 overs)	South Africa v Australia at Johannesburg.................	2005-06
434-4	(50 overs)	Australia v South Africa at Johannesburg.................	2005-06
429	(49.5 overs)	Glamorgan v Surrey at The Oval	2002
424-5	(50 overs)	Buckinghamshire v Suffolk at Dinton....................	2002
418-5	(50 overs)	South Africa v Zimbabwe at Potchefstroom................	2006-07
414-7	(50 overs)	India v Sri Lanka at Rajkot	2009-10
413-4	(60 overs)	Somerset v Devon at Torquay.........................	1990
413-5	(50 overs)	India v Bermuda at Port-of-Spain	2006-07
412-4	(50 overs)	United Arab Emirates v Argentina at Windhoek	2007-08
412-6	**(50 overs)**	**Madhya Pradesh v Railways at Indore**..................	**2009-10**
411-6	(50 overs)	Yorkshire v Devon at Exmouth........................	2004
411-8	(50 overs)	Sri Lanka v India at Rajkot	2009-10
410-5	(50 overs)	Canterbury v Otago at Timaru	2009-10
409-6	(50 overs)	Trinidad & Tobago v North Windward Islands at Kingston....	2001-02
408-4	(50 overs)	KRL v Sialkot at Sialkot	2002-03
406-5	(60 overs)	Leicestershire v Berkshire at Leicester	1996
405-4	(50 overs)	Queensland v Western Australia at Brisbane	2003-04
404-3	(60 overs)	Worcestershire v Devon at Worcester....................	1987
403-3	(50 overs)	Somerset v Scotland at Taunton	2009
402-2	(50 overs)	New Zealand v Ireland at Aberdeen	2008
401-3	**(50 overs)**	**India v South Africa at Gwalior**......................	**2009-10**
401-7	(50 overs)	Gloucestershire v Buckinghamshire at Wing	2003

LOWEST INNINGS TOTALS

18	(14.3 overs)	West Indies Under-19 v Barbados at Blairmont	2007-08
23	(19.4 overs)	Middlesex v Yorkshire at Leeds	1974
30	(20.4 overs)	Chittagong v Sylhet at Dhaka	2002-03
31	(13.5 overs)	Border v South Western Districts at East London...........	2007-08
34	(21.1 overs)	Saurashtra v Mumbai at Mumbai	1999-2000
35	(18 overs)	Zimbabwe v Sri Lanka at Harare	2003-04
36	(25.4 overs)	Leicestershire v Sussex at Leicester	1973
36	(18.4 overs)	Canada v Sri Lanka at Paarl	2002-03
38	(15.4 overs)	Zimbabwe v Sri Lanka at Colombo	2001-02
39	(26.4 overs)	Ireland v Sussex at Hove............................	1985
39	(15.2 overs)	Cape Cobras v Eagles at Paarl *(one man absent)*	2008-09

LIST A TWENTY20 RECORDS

Notes: This section covers Twenty20 cricket to December 31, 2010. Bold type denotes performances in the calendar year 2010 or, in career figures, players who appeared in Twenty20 cricket in that year.

BATTING RECORDS

HIGHEST INDIVIDUAL INNINGS

158*	B. B. McCullum	Kolkata Knight Riders v Bangalore Royal Challengers at Bangalore............................	2007-08
152*	G. R. Napier	Essex v Sussex at Chelmsford........................	2008
141*	C. L. White	Somerset v Worcestershire at Worcester................	2006
127	**M. Vijay**	**Chennai Super Kings v Rajasthan Royals at Chennai......**	**2009-10**
124*	M. J. Lumb	Hampshire v Essex at Southampton....................	2009
117*	A. Symonds	Deccan Chargers v Rajasthan Royals at Hyderabad.......	2007-08
117	C. H. Gayle	West Indies v South Africa at Johannesburg.............	2007-08
117	**M. J. Prior**	**Sussex v Glamorgan at Hove.......................**	**2010**
116*	G. A. Hick	Worcestershire v Northamptonshire at Luton............	2004
116*	I. J. Thomas	Glamorgan v Somerset at Taunton....................	2004
116*	C. L. White	Somerset v Gloucestershire at Taunton.................	2006
116*	M. E. K. Hussey	Chennai Superstars v Kings XI Punjab at Mohali..........	2007-08
116*	**B. B. McCullum**	**New Zealand v Australia at Christchurch..............**	**2009-10**
115	Imran Farhat	Lahore Eagles v Multan Tigers at Karachi...............	2005-06
115	S. E. Marsh	Kings XI Punjab v Rajasthan Royals at Mohali...........	2007-08

MOST RUNS

	Career	M	I	NO	R	HS	100s	Avge
D. J. Hussey.............	2004–*2010*	133	128	25	3,388	100*	1	32.89
B. J. Hodge..............	2003–*2010*	107	104	13	3,303	106	2	36.29
B. B. McCullum..........	2004–*2010*	99	98	13	2,716	158*	3	31.95
L. R. P. L. Taylor........	2005–*2010*	101	95	17	2,563	111*	1	32.85
H. H. Gibbs..............	2003–*2010*	105	103	9	2,476	101*	1	26.34
S. B. Styris..............	2004–*2010*	109	103	10	2,256	106*	1	24.25
G. C. Smith..............	2003–*2010*	75	75	6	2,216	105	1	32.11
J-P. Duminy.............	2003–*2010*	89	85	22	2,210	99*	0	35.07
K. C. Sangakkara.........	2004–*2010*	80	76	6	2,182	94	0	31.17
O. A. Shah...............	2003–*2010*	89	85	17	2,160	80	0	31.76
D. P. M. D. Jayawardene...	2004–*2010*	89	86	16	2,154	110*	2	30.77
D. A. Warner.............	2006–*2010*	82	82	3	2,154	107*	1	27.26
I. J. L. Trott.............	2003–*2010*	76	71	16	2,081	86*	0	37.83
S. T. Jayasuriya..........	2004–*2010*	92	91	6	2,052	114*	1	24.14
S. K. Raina..............	2006–*2010*	70	67	12	2,046	101	1	37.20

HIGHEST PARTNERSHIP FOR EACH WICKET

175	for 1st	V. S. Solanki and G. A. Hick, Worcs v Northants at Kidderminster......	2007
186	for 2nd	J. L. Langern and C. L. White, Somerset v Gloucestershire at Taunton....	2006
162	for 3rd	Abdul Razzaq and Nasir Jamshed, Lahore Lions v Quetta Bears at Lahore....	2009
140*	for 4th {	N. L. McCullum and A. D. Mascarenhas, Otago v Canterbury at Dunedin.	2008-09
		E. Chigumbura and C. Zhuwao, Northerns v Centrals at Bulawayo.....	2009
149	for 5th	Y. V. Takawale and S. V. Bahutule, Maharashtra v Gujarat at Mumbai...	2006-07
104	for 6th	D. J. Hussey and W. P. Saha, Kolkata Knight Riders v Kings XI Punjab at Mohali..	2007-08
99*	**for 7th**	**A. Thyagarajan and O. M. Baker, USA v Ireland at Abu Dhabi......**	**2009-10**
78	for 8th	R. S. A. Palliyaguruge and J. G. N. Priyantha, Saracens v Chilaw Marians at Colombo..	2006-07
59*	for 9th	G. Chapple and P. J. Martin, Lancashire v Leicestershire at Leicester.....	2003
59	for 10th	H. H. Streak and J. E. Anyon, Warwickshire v Worcs at Birmingham....	2005

BOWLING RECORDS

BEST BOWLING ANALYSES

6-14	Sohail Tanvir	Rajasthan Royals v Chennai Superstars at Jaipur.........	2007-08
6-15	S. R. Abeywardene	Panadura v Air Force at Colombo	2005-06
6-21	A. J. Hall	Northamptonshire v Worcestershire at Northampton.......	2008
6-24	T. J. Murtagh	Surrey v Middlesex at Lord's	2005
6-25	Irfanuddin	Karachi Dolphins v Sialkot Stallions at Karachi	2005-06
6-25	M. G. Dighton	Tasmania v Queensland at Toowoomba..................	2006-07
6-28	**I. G. Butler**	**Otago v Auckland at Dunedin**	**2009-10**

MOST WICKETS

	Career	M	B	R	W	BB	4W/i	Avge
D. P. Nannes	*2007–2010*	94	2,100	2,464	125	4-11	5	19.71
J. A. Morkel	*2003–2010*	133	2,263	3,033	108	4-30	2	28.08
Yasir Arafat	*2005–2010*	86	1,777	2,298	106	4-17	5	21.67
A. J. Hall	*2003–2010*	79	1,573	1,995	101	6-21	3	19.75
A. C. Thomas	*2003–2010*	82	1,578	1,892	99	4-27	1	19.11
Shahid Afridi	*2004–2010*	81	1,760	1,865	98	4-11	4	19.03
M. Muralitharan .	*2005–2010*	73	1,686	1,732	95	4-16	3	18.23
T. Henderson	*2003–2010*	84	1,824	2,195	93	4-29	1	23.60
Umar Gul	*2004–2010*	62	1,322	1,521	92	5-6	7	16.53
Azhar Mahmood .	*2003–2010*	81	1,658	2,004	91	4-20	2	22.02
G. R. Napier	*2003–2010*	67	1,419	1,720	90	4-10	1	19.11

WICKETKEEPING AND FIELDING RECORDS

MOST DISMISSALS IN AN INNINGS

7 (all ct)   E. F. M. U. Fernando Lankan v Moors at Colombo 2005-06

MOST CATCHES IN AN INNINGS IN THE FIELD

5   Manzoor Ilahi   Jammu and Kashmir v Delhi at Delhi............... **2010-11**

Twenty-one further fielders have made four catches in an innings in the field.

TEAM RECORDS

HIGHEST INNINGS TOTALS

260-6	(20 overs)	Sri Lanka v Kenya at Johannesburg......................	2007-08
250-3	(20 overs)	Somerset v Gloucestershire at Taunton	2006
246-5	**(20 overs)**	**Chennai Super Kings v Rajasthan Royals at Chennai** ...	**2009-10**
245-4	(20 overs)	Nondescripts v Air Force at Colombo	2005-06
243-2	**(20 overs)**	**Karachi Dolphins v Lahore Eagles at Lahore**.............	**2010-11**
242-3	(20 overs)	Essex v Sussex at Chelmsford	2008
241-6	(20 overs)	South Africa v England at Centurion.....................	2009-10
240-5	(20 overs)	Chennai Superstars v Kings XI Punjab at Mohali	2007-08

LOWEST INNINGS TOTALS

30	(11.1 overs)	Tripura v Jharkhand at Dhanbad..........................	2009-10
47	(14.3 overs)	Titans v Eagles at Centurion............................	2003-04
58	(15.1 overs)	Rajasthan Royals v Royal Challengers Bangalore at Cape Town ...	2008-09
58	**(12.5 overs)**	**Andhra v Hyderabad at Secunderabad**	**2010-11**
59	(12.1 overs)	Army v Sinhalese at Colombo	2006-07
59	**(11.5 overs)**	**Mountaineers v Mashonaland Eagles at Harare**............	**2009-10**

TEST RECORDS

Notes: This section covers all Tests up to January 19, 2011.
Throughout this section, bold type denotes performances since January 1, 2010, or, in career figures,
players who have appeared in Test cricket since that date.

BATTING RECORDS

HIGHEST INDIVIDUAL INNINGS

400*	B. C. Lara	West Indies v England at St John's	2003-04
380	M. L. Hayden	Australia v Zimbabwe at Perth	2003-04
375	B. C. Lara	West Indies v England at St John's	1993-94
374	D. P. M. D. Jayawardene	Sri Lanka v South Africa at Colombo (SSC)	2006
365*	G. S. Sobers	West Indies v Pakistan at Kingston	1957-58
364	L. Hutton	England v Australia at The Oval	1938
340	S. T. Jayasuriya	Sri Lanka v India at Colombo (RPS)	1997-98
337	Hanif Mohammad	Pakistan v West Indies at Bridgetown	1957-58
336*	W. R. Hammond	England v New Zealand at Auckland	1932-33
334*	M. A. Taylor	Australia v Pakistan at Peshawar	1998-99
334	D. G. Bradman	Australia v England at Leeds	1930
333	G. A. Gooch	England v India at Lord's	1990
333	**C. H. Gayle**	**West Indies v Sri Lanka at Galle**	**2010-11**
329	Inzamam-ul-Haq	Pakistan v New Zealand at Lahore	2002
325	A. Sandham	England v West Indies at Kingston	1929-30
319	V. Sehwag	India v South Africa at Chennai	2007-08
317	C. H. Gayle	West Indies v South Africa at St John's	2004-05
313	Younis Khan	Pakistan v Sri Lanka at Karachi	2008-09
311	R. B. Simpson	Australia v England at Manchester	1964
310*	J. H. Edrich	England v New Zealand at Leeds	1965
309	V. Sehwag	India v Pakistan at Multan	2003-04
307	R. M. Cowper	Australia v England at Melbourne	1965-66
304	D. G. Bradman	Australia v England at Leeds	1934
302	L. G. Rowe	West Indies v England at Bridgetown	1973-74
299*	D. G. Bradman	Australia v South Africa at Adelaide	1931-32
299	M. D. Crowe	New Zealand v Sri Lanka at Wellington	1990-91
293	V. Sehwag	India v Sri Lanka at Mumbai (BS)	2009-10
291	I. V. A. Richards	West Indies v England at The Oval	1976
291	R. R. Sarwan	West Indies v England at Bridgetown	2008-09
287	R. E. Foster	England v Australia at Sydney	1903-04
287	K. C. Sangakkara	Sri Lanka v South Africa at Colombo (SSC)	2006
285*	P. B. H. May	England v West Indies at Birmingham	1957
281	V. V. S. Laxman	India v Australia at Kolkata	2000-01
280*	Javed Miandad	Pakistan v India at Hyderabad	1982-83
278*	**A. B. de Villiers**	**South Africa v Pakistan at Abu Dhabi**	**2010-11**
278	D. C. S. Compton	England v Pakistan at Nottingham	1954
277	B. C. Lara	West Indies v Australia at Sydney	1992-93
277	G. C. Smith	South Africa v England at Birmingham	2003
275*	D. J. Cullinan	South Africa v New Zealand at Auckland	1998-99
275	G. Kirsten	South Africa v England at Durban	1999-2000
275	D. P. M. D. Jayawardene	Sri Lanka v India at Ahmedabad	2009-10
274*	S. P. Fleming	New Zealand v Sri Lanka at Colombo (PSS)	2003
274	R. G. Pollock	South Africa v Australia at Durban	1969-70
274	Zaheer Abbas	Pakistan v England at Birmingham	1971
271	Javed Miandad	Pakistan v New Zealand at Auckland	1988-89
270*	G. A. Headley	West Indies v England at Kingston	1934-35
270	D. G. Bradman	Australia v England at Melbourne	1936-37
270	R. Dravid	India v Pakistan at Rawalpindi	2003-04
270	K. C. Sangakkara	Sri Lanka v Zimbabwe at Bulawayo	2003-04

268	G. N. Yallop	Australia v Pakistan at Melbourne	1983-84
267*	B. A. Young	New Zealand v Sri Lanka at Dunedin	1996-97
267	P. A. de Silva	Sri Lanka v New Zealand at Wellington	1990-91
267	Younis Khan	Pakistan v India at Bangalore	2004-05
266	W. H. Ponsford	Australia v England at The Oval	1934
266	D. L. Houghton	Zimbabwe v Sri Lanka at Bulawayo	1994-95
262*	D. L. Amiss	England v West Indies at Kingston	1973-74
262	S. P. Fleming	New Zealand v South Africa at Cape Town	2005-06
261*	R. R. Sarwan	West Indies v Bangladesh at Kingston	2003-04
261	F. M. M. Worrell	West Indies v England at Nottingham	1950
260	C. C. Hunte	West Indies v Pakistan at Kingston	1957-58
260	Javed Miandad	Pakistan v England at The Oval	1987
259	G. M. Turner	New Zealand v West Indies at Georgetown	1971-72
259	G. C. Smith	South Africa v England at Lord's	2003
258	T. W. Graveney	England v West Indies at Nottingham	1957
258	S. M. Nurse	West Indies v New Zealand at Christchurch	1968-69
257*	Wasim Akram	Pakistan v Zimbabwe at Sheikhupura	1996-97
257	R. T. Ponting	Australia v India at Melbourne	2003-04
256	R. B. Kanhai	West Indies v India at Calcutta	1958-59
256	K. F. Barrington	England v Australia at Manchester	1964
255*	D. J. McGlew	South Africa v New Zealand at Wellington	1952-53
254	D. G. Bradman	Australia v England at Lord's	1930
254	V. Sehwag	India v Pakistan at Lahore	2005-06
253*	**H. M. Amla**	**South Africa v India at Nagpur**	**2009-10**
253	S. T. Jayasuriya	Sri Lanka v Pakistan at Faisalabad	2004-05
251	W. R. Hammond	England v Australia at Sydney	1928-29
250	K. D. Walters	Australia v New Zealand at Christchurch	1976-77
250	S. F. A. F. Bacchus	West Indies v India at Kanpur	1978-79
250	J. L. Langer	Australia v England at Melbourne	2002-03

Note: The highest individual innings for Bangladesh is 158* by Mohammad Ashraful against India at Chittagong in 2004-05.

HUNDRED ON TEST DEBUT

C. Bannerman (165*)	Australia v England at Melbourne	1876-77
W. G. Grace (152)	England v Australia at The Oval	1880
H. Graham (107)	Australia v England at Lord's	1893
†K. S. Ranjitsinhji (154*)	England v Australia at Manchester	1896
†P. F. Warner (132*)	England v South Africa at Johannesburg	1898-99
†R. A. Duff (104)	Australia v England at Melbourne	1901-02
§R. E. Foster (287)	England v Australia at Sydney	1903-04
G. Gunn (119)	England v Australia at Sydney	1907-08
†R. J. Hartigan (116)	Australia v England at Adelaide	1907-08
†H. L. Collins (104)	Australia v England at Sydney	1920-21
W. H. Ponsford (110)	Australia v England at Sydney	1924-25
A. A. Jackson (164)	Australia v England at Adelaide	1928-29
†G. A. Headley (176)	West Indies v England at Bridgetown	1929-30
J. E. Mills (117)	New Zealand v England at Wellington	1929-30
Nawab of Pataudi sen. (102)	England v Australia at Sydney	1932-33
B. H. Valentine (136)	England v India at Bombay	1933-34
†L. Amarnath (118)	India v England at Bombay	1933-34
†P. A. Gibb (106)	England v South Africa at Johannesburg	1938-39
S. C. Griffith (140)	England v West Indies at Port-of-Spain	1947-48
A. G. Ganteaume (112)	West Indies v England at Port-of-Spain	1947-48
†J. W. Burke (101*)	Australia v England at Adelaide	1950-51
P. B. H. May (138)	England v South Africa at Leeds	1951
R. H. Shodhan (110)	India v Pakistan at Calcutta	1952-53
B. H. Pairaudeau (115)	West Indies v India at Port-of-Spain	1952-53

†O. G. Smith (104)	West Indies v Australia at Kingston	1954-55
A. G. Kripal Singh (100*)	India v New Zealand at Hyderabad	1955-56
C. C. Hunte (142)	West Indies v Pakistan at Bridgetown	1957-58
C. A. Milton (104*)	England v New Zealand at Leeds	1958
†A. A. Baig (112)	India v England at Manchester	1959
Hanumant Singh (105)	India v England at Delhi	1963-64
Khalid Ibadulla (166)	Pakistan v Australia at Karachi	1964-65
B. R. Taylor (105)	New Zealand v India at Calcutta	1964-65
K. D. Walters (155)	Australia v England at Brisbane	1965-66
J. H. Hampshire (107)	England v West Indies at Lord's	1969
†G. R. Viswanath (137)	India v Australia at Kanpur	1969-70
G. S. Chappell (108)	Australia v England at Perth	1970-71
‡L. G. Rowe (214, 100*)	West Indies v New Zealand at Kingston	1971-72
A. I. Kallicharran (100*)	West Indies v New Zealand at Georgetown	1971-72
R. E. Redmond (107)	New Zealand v Pakistan at Auckland	1972-73
†F. C. Hayes (106*)	England v West Indies at The Oval	1973
†C. G. Greenidge (107)	West Indies v India at Bangalore	1974-75
†L. Baichan (105*)	West Indies v Pakistan at Lahore	1974-75
G. J. Cosier (109)	Australia v West Indies at Melbourne	1975-76
S. Amarnath (124)	India v New Zealand at Auckland	1975-76
Javed Miandad (163)	Pakistan v New Zealand at Lahore	1976-77
†A. B. Williams (100)	West Indies v Australia at Georgetown	1977-78
†D. M. Wellham (103)	Australia v England at The Oval	1981
†Salim Malik (100*)	Pakistan v Sri Lanka at Karachi	1981-82
K. C. Wessels (162)	Australia v England at Brisbane	1982-83
W. B. Phillips (159)	Australia v West Indies at Perth	1983-84
¶M. Azharuddin (110)	India v England at Calcutta	1984-85
D. S. B. P. Kuruppu (201*)	Sri Lanka v New Zealand at Colombo (CCC)	1986-87
†M. J. Greatbatch (107*)	New Zealand v England at Auckland	1987-88
M. E. Waugh (138)	Australia v England at Adelaide	1990-91
A. C. Hudson (163)	South Africa v West Indies at Bridgetown	1991-92
R. S. Kaluwitharana (132*)	Sri Lanka v Australia at Colombo (SSC)	1992-93
D. L. Houghton (121)	Zimbabwe v India at Harare	1992-93
P. K. Amre (103)	India v South Africa at Durban	1992-93
†G. P. Thorpe (114*)	England v Australia at Nottingham	1993
G. S. Blewett (102*)	Australia v England at Adelaide	1994-95
S. C. Ganguly (131)	India v England at Lord's	1996
†Mohammad Wasim (109*)	Pakistan v New Zealand at Lahore	1996-97
Ali Naqvi (115)	Pakistan v South Africa at Rawalpindi	1997-98
Azhar Mahmood (128*)	Pakistan v South Africa at Rawalpindi	1997-98
M. S. Sinclair (214)	New Zealand v West Indies at Wellington	1999-2000
†Younis Khan (107)	Pakistan v Sri Lanka at Rawalpindi	1999-2000
Aminul Islam (145)	Bangladesh v India at Dhaka	2000-01
†H. Masakadza (119)	Zimbabwe v West Indies at Harare	2001
T. T. Samaraweera (103*)	Sri Lanka v India at Colombo (SSC)	2001
Taufeeq Umar (104)	Pakistan v Bangladesh at Multan	2001-02
†Mohammad Ashraful (114) . . .	Bangladesh v Sri Lanka at Colombo (SSC)	2001-02
V. Sehwag (105)	India v South Africa at Bloemfontein	2001-02
L. Vincent (104)	New Zealand v Australia at Perth	2001-02
S. B. Styris (107)	New Zealand v West Indies at St George's	2002
J. A. Rudolph (222*)	South Africa v Bangladesh at Chittagong	2003
‡Yasir Hameed (170, 105)	Pakistan v Bangladesh at Karachi	2003
†D. R. Smith (105*)	West Indies v South Africa at Cape Town	2003-04
A. J. Strauss (112)	England v New Zealand at Lord's	2004
M. J. Clarke (151)	Australia v India at Bangalore	2004-05
†A. N. Cook (104*)	England v India at Nagpur	2005-06
M. J. Prior (126*)	England v West Indies at Lord's	2007
M. J. North (117)	Australia v South Africa at Johannesburg	2008-09
†Fawad Alam (168)	Pakistan v Sri Lanka at Colombo (PSS)	2009
†I. J. L. Trott (119)	England v Australia at The Oval	2009
Umar Akmal (129)	Pakistan v New Zealand at Dunedin	2009-10

†A. B. Barath (104)	West Indies v Australia at Brisbane	2009-10
A. N. Petersen (100)	**South Africa v India at Kolkata**	**2009-10**
S. K. Raina (120)	India v Sri Lanka at Colombo (SSC)	2010
K. S. Williamson (131)	New Zealand v India at Ahmedabad	2010-11

† *In his second innings of the match.*

‡ *L. G. Rowe and Yasir Hameed are the only batsmen to score a hundred in each innings on debut.*

§ *R. E. Foster (287, 19) and L. G. Rowe (214, 100*) are the only batsmen to score 300 runs in their debut Tests.*

¶ *M. Azharuddin is the only batsman to score hundreds in each of his first three Tests.*

Notes: L. Amarnath and S. Amarnath were father and son.

Ali Naqvi and Azhar Mahmood achieved the feat in the same innings.

Only Bannerman, Houghton and Aminul Islam scored hundreds in their country's first Test.

TRIPLE-HUNDRED AND HUNDRED IN A TEST

G. A. Gooch (England) . . . .   333 and 123 v India at Lord's 1990

The only instance in first-class cricket. M. A. Taylor (Australia) scored 334* and 92 v Pakistan at Peshawar in 1998-99.

DOUBLE-HUNDRED AND HUNDRED IN A TEST

K. D. Walters (Australia)	242 and 103 v West Indies at Sydney	1968-69
S. M. Gavaskar (India)	124 and 220 v West Indies at Port-of-Spain	1970-71
†L. G. Rowe (West Indies)	214 and 100* v New Zealand at Kingston	1971-72
G. S. Chappell (Australia)	247* and 133 v New Zealand at Wellington	1973-74
B. C. Lara (West Indies)	221 and 130 v Sri Lanka at Colombo (SSC)	2001-02

† *On Test debut.*

TWO SEPARATE HUNDREDS IN A TEST

S. M. Gavaskar (I)	3	G. A. Gooch (E)	1	J. Moroney (A)	1
R. T. Ponting (A)	**3**	C. G. Greenidge (WI) . .	1	A. R. Morris (A)	1
A. R. Border (A)	2†	A. P. Gurusinha (SL) . .	1	E. Paynter (E)	1
G. S. Chappell (A)	2	W. R. Hammond (E) . . .	1	L. G. Rowe (WI)	1¶
P. A. de Silva (SL)	2‡	Hanif Mohammad (P) . .	1	A. C. Russell (E)	1
R. Dravid (I)	**2**	V. S. Hazare (I)	1	R. B. Simpson (A)	1
M. L. Hayden (A)	2	G. P. Howarth (NZ) . . .	1	G. S. Sobers (WI)	1
G. A. Headley (WI)	2	**P. J. Hughes (A)**	**1**	A. J. Stewart (E)	1
H. Sutcliffe (E)	2	Inzamam-ul-Haq (P) . . .	1	**A. J. Strauss (E)**	**1**
C. L. Walcott (WI)	2§	Javed Miandad (P)	1	M. E. Trescothick (E) . .	1
H. M. Amla (SA)	**1**	A. H. Jones (NZ)	1	G. M. Turner (NZ)	1
W. Bardsley (A)	1	D. M. Jones (A)	1	M. P. Vaughan (E)	1
D. G. Bradman (A)	1	R. B. Kanhai (WI)	1	Wajahatullah Wasti (P) .	1
I. M. Chappell (A)	1	G. Kirsten (SA)	1	K. D. Walters (A)	1
D. C. S. Compton (E) . .	1	B. C. Lara (WI)	1	S. R. Waugh (A)	1
T. M. Dilshan (SL)	**1**	A. Melville (SA)	1	E. D. Weekes (WI)	1
A. Flower (Z)	1	L. R. D. Mendis (SL) . . .	1	**Yasir Hameed (P)**	**1¶**
G. W. Flower (Z)	1	B. Mitchell (SA)	1		
		Mohammad Yousuf (P)	**1**		

† *A. R. Border scored 150* and 153 against Pakistan in 1979-80 to become the first to score 150 in each innings of a Test match.*

‡ *P. A. de Silva scored 138* and 103* against Pakistan in 1996-97 to become the first to score two not-out hundreds in a Test match.*

§ *C. L. Walcott scored twin hundreds twice in one series, against Australia in 1954-55.*

¶ *L. G. Rowe's and Yasir Hameed's two hundreds were on Test debut.*

MOST DOUBLE-HUNDREDS

D. G. Bradman (A)	12	**D. P. M. D. Jayawardene (SL)**	**6**	S. M. Gavaskar (I)	4
B. C. Lara (WI)	9	**V. Sehwag (I)**	**6**	C. G. Greenidge (WI)	4
W. R. Hammond (E)	7	**S. R. Tendulkar (I)**	**6**	L. Hutton (E)	4
K. C. Sangakkara (SL)	**7**	**R. Dravid (I)**	**5**	**Mohammad Yousuf (P)**	**4**
M. S. Atapattu (SL)	6	**R. T. Ponting (A)**	**5**	**G. C. Smith (SA)**	**4**
Javed Miandad (P)	6	G. S. Chappell (A)	4	Zaheer Abbas (P)	4

MOST HUNDREDS

S. R. Tendulkar (I)	**51**	S. Chanderpaul (WI)	22	M. D. Crowe (NZ)	17
J. H. Kallis (SA)	**40**	M. C. Cowdrey (E)	22	A. C. Gilchrist (A)	17
R. T. Ponting (A)	**39**	W. R. Hammond (E)	22	**K. P. Pietersen (E)**	**17**
S. M. Gavaskar (I)	34	**V. Sehwag (I)**	**22**	D. B. Vengsarkar (I)	17
B. C. Lara (WI)	34	**G. C. Smith (SA)**	**22**	**Younis Khan (P)**	**17**
S. R. Waugh (A)	32	D. C. Boon (A)	21	M. S. Atapattu (SL)	16
R. Dravid (I)	**31**	R. N. Harvey (A)	21	M. A. Atherton (E)	16
M. L. Hayden (A)	30	G. Kirsten (SA)	21	**A. N. Cook (E)**	**16**
D. G. Bradman (A)	29	K. F. Barrington (E)	20	S. C. Ganguly (I)	16
D. P. M. D. Jayawardene (SL)	**28**	P. A. de Silva (SL)	20	**V. V. S. Laxman (I)**	**16**
A. R. Border (A)	27	G. A. Gooch (E)	20	R. B. Richardson (WI)	16
G. S. Sobers (WI)	26	M. E. Waugh (A)	20	H. Sutcliffe (E)	16
Inzamam-ul-Haq (P)	25	C. G. Greenidge (WI)	19	G. P. Thorpe (E)	16
G. S. Chappell (A)	24	L. Hutton (E)	19	J. B. Hobbs (E)	15
Mohammad Yousuf (P)	**24**	C. H. Lloyd (WI)	19	R. B. Kanhai (WI)	15
K. C. Sangakkara (SL)	**24**	**A. J. Strauss (E)**	**19**	Salim Malik (P)	15
Javed Miandad (P)	23	M. A. Taylor (A)	19	R. R. Sarwan (WI)	15
J. L. Langer (A)	23	D. I. Gower (E)	18	A. J. Stewart (E)	15
M. Azharuddin (I)	22	D. L. Haynes (WI)	18	C. L. Walcott (WI)	15
G. Boycott (E)	22	M. P. Vaughan (E)	18	K. D. Walters (A)	15
		D. C. S. Compton (E)	17	E. D. Weekes (WI)	15

Note: The most hundreds for Zimbabwe is 12 by A. Flower, and the most for Bangladesh is **5** by **Mohammad Ashraful**.

MOST HUNDREDS AGAINST ONE TEAM

D. G. Bradman	19	Australia v England	**S. R. Tendulkar**	**11**	**India v Australia**
S. M. Gavaskar	13	India v West Indies	G. S. Sobers	10	West Indies v England
J. B. Hobbs	12	England v Australia	S. R. Waugh	10	Australia v England

MOST DUCKS

C. A. Walsh (WI)	43	M. Dillon (WI)	26	S. J. Harmison (E)	21
G. D. McGrath (A)	35	**Danish Kaneria (P)**	**25**	M. Ntini (SA)	21
S. K. Warne (A)	34	D. K. Morrison (NZ)	24	Waqar Younis (P)	21
M. Muralitharan (SL)	**33**	B. S. Chandrasekhar (I)	23	**Zaheer Khan (I)**	**21**
C. S. Martin (NZ)	**29**	M. S. Atapattu (SL)	22	M. A. Atherton (E)	20
C. E. L. Ambrose (WI)	26	S. R. Waugh (A)	22	B. S. Bedi (I)	20

CARRYING BAT THROUGH TEST INNINGS

(Figures in brackets show team's total)

A. B. Tancred	26*	(47)	South Africa v England at Cape Town	1888-89
J. E. Barrett	67*	(176)†	Australia v England at Lord's	1890
R. Abel	132*	(307)	England v Australia at Sydney	1891-92
P. F. Warner	132*	(237)†	England v South Africa at Johannesburg	1898-99

W. W. Armstrong	159*	(309)	Australia v South Africa at Johannesburg	1902-03
J. W. Zulch	43*	(103)	South Africa v England at Cape Town	1909-10
W. Bardsley	193*	(383)	Australia v England at Lord's	1926
W. M. Woodfull	30*	(66)§	Australia v England at Brisbane	1928-29
W. M. Woodfull	73*	(193)‡	Australia v England at Adelaide	1932-33
W. A. Brown	206*	(422)	Australia v England at Lord's	1938
L. Hutton	202*	(344)	England v West Indies at The Oval	1950
L. Hutton	156*	(272)	England v Australia at Adelaide	1950-51
Nazar Mohammad¶	124*	(331)	Pakistan v India at Lucknow	1952-53
F. M. M. Worrell	191*	(372)	West Indies v England at Nottingham	1957
T. L. Goddard	56*	(99)	South Africa v Australia at Cape Town	1957-58
D. J. McGlew	127*	(292)	South Africa v New Zealand at Durban	1961-62
C. C. Hunte	60*	(131)	West Indies v Australia at Port-of-Spain	1964-65
G. M. Turner	43*	(131)	New Zealand v England at Lord's	1969
W. M. Lawry	49*	(107)	Australia v India at Delhi	1969-70
W. M. Lawry	60*	(116)‡	Australia v England at Sydney	1970-71
G. M. Turner	223*	(386)	New Zealand v West Indies at Kingston	1971-72
I. R. Redpath	159*	(346)	Australia v New Zealand at Auckland	1973-74
G. Boycott	99*	(215)	England v Australia at Perth	1979-80
S. M. Gavaskar	127*	(286)	India v Pakistan at Faisalabad	1982-83
Mudassar Nazar¶	152*	(323)	Pakistan v India at Lahore	1982-83
S. Wettimuny	63*	(144)	Sri Lanka v New Zealand at Christchurch	1982-83
D. C. Boon	58*	(103)	Australia v New Zealand at Auckland	1985-86
D. L. Haynes	88*	(211)	West Indies v Pakistan at Karachi	1986-87
G. A. Gooch	154*	(252)	England v West Indies at Leeds	1991
D. L. Haynes	75*	(176)	West Indies v England at The Oval	1991
A. J. Stewart	69*	(175)	England v Pakistan at Lord's	1992
D. L. Haynes	143*	(382)	West Indies v Pakistan at Port-of-Spain	1992-93
M. H. Dekker	68*	(187)	Zimbabwe v Pakistan at Rawalpindi	1993-94
M. A. Atherton	94*	(228)	England v New Zealand at Christchurch	1996-97
G. Kirsten	100*	(239)	South Africa v Pakistan at Faisalabad	1997-98
M. A. Taylor	169*	(350)	Australia v South Africa at Adelaide	1997-98
G. W. Flower	156*	(321)	Zimbabwe v Pakistan at Bulawayo	1997-98
Saeed Anwar	188*	(316)	Pakistan v India at Calcutta	1998-99
M. S. Atapattu	216*	(428)	Sri Lanka v Zimbabwe at Bulawayo	1999-2000
R. P. Arnold	104*	(231)	Sri Lanka v Zimbabwe at Harare	1999-2000
Javed Omar	85*	(168)†‡	Bangladesh v Zimbabwe at Bulawayo	2000-01
V. Sehwag	201*	(329)	India v Sri Lanka at Galle	2008
S. M. Katich	131*	(268)	Australia v New Zealand at Brisbane	2008-09
C. H. Gayle	165*	(317)	West Indies v Australia at Adelaide	2009-10
Imran Farhat	117*	(223)	Pakistan v New Zealand at Napier	2009-10

† *On debut*   ‡ *One man absent.*   § *Two men absent.*   ¶ *Father and son.*

Notes: G. M. Turner (223*) holds the record for the highest score by a player carrying his bat through a Test innings. He is also the youngest player to do so, being 22 years 63 days old when he first achieved the feat (1969).

D. L. Haynes, who is alone in achieving this feat on three occasions, also opened the batting and was last man out in each innings for West Indies v New Zealand at Dunedin, 1979-80.

750 RUNS IN A SERIES

	T	I	NO	R	HS	100s	Avge		
D. G. Bradman	5	7	0	974	334	4	139.14	A v E	1930
W. R. Hammond	5	9	1	905	251	4	113.12	E v A	1928-29
M. A. Taylor	6	11	1	839	219	2	83.90	A v E	1989
R. N. Harvey	5	9	0	834	205	4	92.66	A v SA	1952-53
I. V. A. Richards	4	7	0	829	291	3	118.42	WI v E	1976
C. L. Walcott	5	10	0	827	155	5	82.70	WI v A	1954-55
G. S. Sobers	5	8	2	824	365*	3	137.33	WI v P	1957-58

	T	I	NO	R	HS	100s	Avge		
D. G. Bradman	5	9	0	810	270	3	90.00	A v E	1936-37
D. G. Bradman	5	5	1	806	299*	4	201.50	A v SA	1931-32
B. C. Lara	5	8	0	798	375	2	99.75	WI v E	1993-94
E. D. Weekes	5	7	0	779	194	4	111.28	WI v I	1948-49
†S. M. Gavaskar ...	4	8	3	774	220	4	154.80	I v WI	1970-71
A. N. Cook.......	**5**	**7**	**1**	**766**	**235***	**3**	**127.66**	**E v A**	**2010-11**
B. C. Lara	6	10	1	765	179	3	85.00	I v I	1995
Mudassar Nazar ...	6	8	2	761	231	4	126.83	P v I	1982-83
D. G. Bradman	5	8	0	758	304	2	94.75	A v E	1934
D. C. S. Compton .	5	8	0	753	208	4	94.12	E v SA	1947
‡G. A. Gooch	3	6	0	752	333	3	125.33	E v I	1990

† *Gavaskar's aggregate was achieved in his first Test series.*

‡ *G. A. Gooch is alone in scoring 1,000 runs in Test cricket during an English season with 1,058 runs in 11 innings against New Zealand and India in 1990.*

MOST RUNS IN A CALENDAR YEAR

	T	I	NO	R	HS	100s	Avge	Year
Mohammad Yousuf (P)......	11	19	1	1,788	202	9	99.33	2006
I. V. A. Richards (WI)......	11	19	0	1,710	291	7	90.00	1976
G. C. Smith (SA).........	15	25	2	1,656	232	6	72.00	2008
S. R. Tendulkar (I)........	**14**	**23**	**3**	**1,562**	**214**	**7**	**78.10**	**2010**
S. M. Gavaskar (I)	18	27	1	1,555	221	5	59.80	1979
R. T. Ponting (A).........	15	28	5	1,544	207	6	67.13	2005
R. T. Ponting (A).........	11	18	3	1,503	257	6	100.20	2003
J. L. Langer (A)..........	14	27	0	1,481	215	5	54.85	2004
M. P. Vaughan (E)........	14	26	2	1,481	197	6	61.70	2002
V. Sehwag (I)............	14	27	1	1,462	319	3	56.23	2008

Notes: M. Amarnath reached 1,000 runs in 1983 on May 3.

The only batsman to score 1,000 runs in a year before World War II was C. Hill of Australia: 1,061 in 1902.

M. L. Hayden (Australia) scored 1,000 runs in each year from 2001 to 2005.

MOST RUNS

1 **S. R. Tendulkar**	**14,692**		21 M. E. Waugh (Australia)........	8,029
2 **R. T. Ponting (Australia)**	**12,363**		22 **V. V. S. Laxman (India)**.....	**7,903**
3 **R. Dravid (India/World)**......	**12,063**		23 M. A. Atherton (England)......	7,728
4 B. C. Lara (West Indies/World) ..	11,953		24 J. L. Langer (Australia)	7,696
5 **J. H. Kallis (South Africa/World)**	**11,947**		25 **V. Sehwag (India/World)**.....	**7,694**
6 A. R. Border (Australia)	11,174		26 M. C. Cowdrey (England)......	7,624
7 S. R. Waugh (Australia)	10,927		27 C. G. Greenidge (West Indies) ..	7,558
8 S. M. Gavaskar (India)	10,122		28 **Mohammad Yousuf (Pakistan)** .	**7,530**
9 **D. P. M. D. Jayawardene (SL)**..	**9,527**		29 M. A. Taylor (Australia).......	7,525
10 **S. Chanderpaul (West Indies)** ..	**9,063**		30 C. H. Lloyd (West Indies)	7,515
11 G. A. Gooch (England).........	8,900		31 D. L. Haynes (West Indies)	7,487
12 Javed Miandad (Pakistan).......	8,832		32 **G. C. Smith (South Africa/World)** .	**7,457**
13 Inzamam-ul-Haq (Pakistan/World) .	8,830		33 D. C. Boon (Australia)	7,422
14 M. L. Hayden (Australia)	8,625		34 G. Kirsten (South Africa)	7,289
15 I. V. A. Richards (West Indies)....	8,540		35 W. R. Hammond (England)	7,249
16 A. J. Stewart (England).........	8,463		36 S. C. Ganguly (India)	7,212
17 **K. C. Sangakkara (Sri Lanka)** ..	**8,244**		37 S. P. Fleming (New Zealand) ...	7,172
18 D. I. Gower (England)	8,231		38 G. S. Chappell (Australia)......	7,110
19 G. Boycott (England)	8,114		39 D. G. Bradman (Australia)	6,996
20 G. S. Sobers (West Indies)	8,032		40 S. T. Jayasuriya (Sri Lanka)	6,973

MOST RUNS FOR EACH COUNTRY

ENGLAND

		T	I	NO	R	HS	100s	Avge
1	G. A. Gooch	118	215	6	8,900	333	20	42.58
2	A. J. Stewart	133	235	21	8,463	190	15	39.54
3	D. I. Gower	117	204	18	8,231	215	18	44.25
4	G. Boycott	108	193	23	8,114	246*	22	47.72
5	M. A. Atherton	115	212	7	7,728	185*	16	37.69
6	M. C. Cowdrey	114	188	15	7,624	182	22	44.06
7	W. R. Hammond	85	140	16	7,249	336*	22	58.45
8	L. Hutton	79	138	15	6,971	364	19	56.67
9	K. F. Barrington	82	131	15	6,806	256	20	58.67
10	G. P. Thorpe	100	179	28	6,744	200*	16	44.66
11	**A. J. Strauss**	**82**	**147**	**6**	**6,084**	**177**	**19**	**43.14**
12	M. E. Trescothick	76	143	10	5,825	219	14	43.79
13	D. C. S. Compton	78	131	15	5,807	278	17	50.06
14	N. Hussain	96	171	16	5,764	207	14	37.18
15	M. P. Vaughan	82	147	9	5,719	197	18	41.44
16	**K. P. Pietersen**	**71**	**123**	**6**	**5,666**	**227**	**17**	**48.42**
17	J. B. Hobbs	61	102	7	5,410	211	15	56.94
18	I. T. Botham	102	161	6	5,200	208	14	33.54
19	J. H. Edrich	77	127	9	5,138	310*	12	43.54
20	**A. N. Cook**	**65**	**115**	**7**	**5,130**	**235***	**16**	**47.50**
21	T. W. Graveney	79	123	13	4,882	258	11	44.38
22	A. J. Lamb	79	139	10	4,656	142	14	36.09
23	H. Sutcliffe	54	84	9	4,555	194	16	60.73
24	P. B. H. May	66	106	9	4,537	285*	13	46.77
25	E. R. Dexter	62	102	8	4,502	205	9	47.89
26	M. W. Gatting	79	138	14	4,409	207	10	35.55
27	A. P. E. Knott	95	149	15	4,389	135	5	32.75
28	M. A. Butcher	71	131	7	4,288	173*	8	34.58
29	**P. D. Collingwood**	**68**	**115**	**10**	**4,259**	**206**	**10**	**40.56**
30	R. A. Smith	62	112	15	4,236	175	9	43.67
31	**I. R. Bell**	**62**	**106**	**11**	**4,192**	**199**	**12**	**44.12**

AUSTRALIA

		T	I	NO	R	HS	100s	Avge
1	**R. T. Ponting**	**152**	**259**	**28**	**12,363**	**257**	**39**	**53.51**
2	A. R. Border	156	265	44	11,174	205	27	50.56
3	S. R. Waugh	168	260	46	10,927	200	32	51.06
4	M. L. Hayden	103	184	14	8,625	380	30	50.73
5	M. E. Waugh	128	209	17	8,029	153*	20	41.81
6	J. L. Langer	105	182	12	7,696	250	23	45.27
7	M. A. Taylor	104	186	13	7,525	334*	19	43.49
8	D. C. Boon	107	190	20	7,422	200	21	43.65
9	G. S. Chappell	87	151	19	7,110	247*	24	53.86
10	D. G. Bradman	52	80	10	6,996	334	29	99.94
11	R. N. Harvey	79	137	10	6,149	205	21	48.41
12	A. C. Gilchrist	96	137	20	5,570	204*	17	47.60
13	K. D. Walters	74	125	14	5,357	250	15	48.26
14	I. M. Chappell	75	136	10	5,345	196	14	42.42
15	M. J. Slater	74	131	7	5,312	219	14	42.83
16	W. M. Lawry	67	123	12	5,234	210	13	47.15
17	R. B. Simpson	62	111	7	4,869	311	10	46.81
18	**M. J. Clarke**	**69**	**114**	**12**	**4,742**	**168**	**14**	**46.49**
19	I. R. Redpath	66	120	11	4,737	171	8	43.45
20	**M. E. K. Hussey**	**59**	**103**	**12**	**4,650**	**195**	**13**	**51.09**

		T	I	NO	R	HS	100s	Avge
21	K. J. Hughes	70	124	6	4,415	213	9	37.41
22	D. R. Martyn	67	109	14	4,406	165	13	46.37
23	I. A. Healy.	119	182	23	4,356	161*	4	27.39
24	**S. M. Katich**	**56**	**99**	**6**	**4,188**	**157**	**10**	**45.03**

SOUTH AFRICA

		T	I	NO	R	HS	100s	Avge
1	**J. H. Kallis**	**144†**	**244**	**37**	**11,864**	**201***	**40**	**57.31**
2	**G. C. Smith**	**90†**	**157**	**9**	**7,445**	**277**	**22**	**50.30**
3	G. Kirsten	101	176	15	7,289	275	21	45.27
4	H. H. Gibbs	90	154	7	6,167	228	14	41.95
5	**M. V. Boucher**	**138†**	**194**	**23**	**5,295**	**125**	**5**	**30.96**
6	**A. B. de Villiers**	**66**	**113**	**13**	**4,741**	**278***	**12**	**47.41**
7	D. J. Cullinan	70	115	12	4,554	275*	14	44.21

† J. H. Kallis also scored 44 and 39*, G. C. Smith 12 and 0, and M. V. Boucher 0 and 17 for the ICC World XI v Australia in the Super Series Test of 2005-06.

WEST INDIES

		T	I	NO	R	HS	100s	Avge
1	B. C. Lara	130†	230	6	11,912	400*	34	53.17
2	**S. Chanderpaul**	**129**	**219**	**34**	**9,063**	**203***	**22**	**48.98**
3	I. V. A. Richards	121	182	12	8,540	291	24	50.23
4	G. S. Sobers	93	160	21	8,032	365*	26	57.78
5	C. G. Greenidge	108	185	16	7,558	226	19	44.72
6	C. H. Lloyd	110	175	14	7,515	242*	19	46.67
7	D. L. Haynes	116	202	25	7,487	184	18	42.29
8	**C. H. Gayle**	**91**	**159**	**6**	**6,373**	**333**	**13**	**41.65**
9	R. B. Kanhai	79	137	6	6,227	256	15	47.53
10	R. B. Richardson	86	146	12	5,949	194	16	44.39
11	C. L. Hooper	102	173	15	5,762	233	13	36.46
12	R. R. Sarwan	83	146	8	5,759	291	15	41.73
13	E. D. Weekes	48	81	5	4,455	207	15	58.61
14	A. I. Kallicharran	66	109	10	4,399	187	12	44.43
15	R. C. Fredericks	59	109	7	4,334	169	8	42.49

† B. C. Lara also scored 5 and 36 for the ICC World XI v Australia in the Super Series Test of 2005-06.

NEW ZEALAND

		T	I	NO	R	HS	100s	Avge
1	S. P. Fleming.	111	189	10	7,172	274*	9	40.06
2	M. D. Crowe.	77	131	11	5,444	299	17	45.36
3	J. G. Wright	82	148	7	5,334	185	12	37.82
4	N. J. Astle	81	137	10	4,702	222	11	37.02
5	**D. L. Vettori**	**104†**	**159**	**22**	**4,159**	**140**	**6**	**30.35**

† D. L. Vettori also scored 8* and 0 for the ICC World XI v Australia in the Super Series Test of 2005-06.

INDIA

		T	I	NO	R	HS	100s	Avge
1	**S. R. Tendulkar**	**177**	**290**	**32**	**14,692**	**248***	**51**	**56.94**
2	**R. Dravid**	**149†**	**257**	**29**	**12,040**	**270**	**31**	**52.80**
3	S. M. Gavaskar	125	214	16	10,122	236*	34	51.12
4	**V. V. S. Laxman**	**120**	**198**	**31**	**7,903**	**281**	**16**	**47.32**
5	**V. Sehwag**	**86†**	**148**	**6**	**7,611**	**319**	**22**	**53.59**
6	S. C. Ganguly	113	188	17	7,212	239	16	42.17
7	D. B. Vengsarkar	116	185	22	6,868	166	17	42.13
8	M. Azharuddin	99	147	9	6,215	199	22	45.03
9	G. R. Viswanath	91	155	10	6,080	222	14	41.93
10	Kapil Dev	131	184	15	5,248	163	8	31.05
11	M. Amarnath	69	113	10	4,378	138	11	42.50

† *R. Dravid also scored 0 and 23, and V. Sehwag also scored 76 and 7, for the ICC World XI v Australia in the Super Series Test of 2005-06.*

PAKISTAN

		T	I	NO	R	HS	100s	Avge
1	Javed Miandad	124	189	21	8,832	280*	23	52.57
2	Inzamam-ul-Haq	119†	198	22	8,829	329	25	50.16
3	**Mohammad Yousuf**	**90**	**156**	**12**	**7,530**	**223**	**24**	**52.29**
4	Salim Malik	103	154	22	5,768	237	15	43.69
5	**Younis Khan**	**67**	**119**	**8**	**5,617**	**313**	**17**	**50.60**
6	Zaheer Abbas	78	124	11	5,062	274	12	44.79
7	Mudassar Nazar	76	116	8	4,114	231	10	38.09
8	Saeed Anwar	55	91	2	4,052	188*	11	45.52

† *Inzamam-ul-Haq also scored 1 and 0 for the ICC World XI v Australia in the Super Series Test of 2005-06.*

SRI LANKA

		T	I	NO	R	HS	100s	Avge
1	**D. P. M. D. Jayawardene**	**116**	**190**	**13**	**9,527**	**374**	**28**	**53.82**
2	**K. C. Sangakkara**	**94**	**156**	**12**	**8,244**	**287**	**24**	**57.25**
3	S. T. Jayasuriya	110	188	14	6,973	340	14	40.07
4	P. A. de Silva	93	159	11	6,361	267	20	42.97
5	M. S. Atapattu	90	156	15	5,502	249	16	39.02
6	A. Ranatunga	93	155	12	5,105	135*	4	35.69
7	H. P. Tillekeratne	83	131	25	4,545	204*	11	42.87
8	**T. T. Samaraweera**	**63**	**98**	**17**	**4,395**	**231**	**12**	**54.25**

ZIMBABWE

		T	I	NO	R	HS	100s	Avge
1	A. Flower	63	112	19	4,794	232*	12	51.54

BANGLADESH

No player has scored 4,000 Test runs for Bangladesh. The highest total is:

	T	I	NO	R	HS	100s	Avge
Habibul Bashar	50	99	1	3,026	113	3	30.87

CAREER AVERAGE OVER 50

(Qualification: 20 innings)

Avge		T	I	NO	R	HS	100s
99.94	D. G. Bradman (A).	52	80	10	6,996	334	29
61.53	**I. J. L. Trott (E)**	**18**	**30**	**4**	**1,600**	**226**	**5**
60.97	R. G. Pollock (SA)	23	41	4	2,256	274	7
60.83	G. A. Headley (WI)	22	40	4	2,190	270*	10
60.73	H. Sutcliffe (E)	54	84	9	4,555	194	16
59.23	E. Paynter (E)	20	31	5	1,540	243	4
58.67	K. F. Barrington (E)	82	131	15	6,806	256	20
58.61	E. D. Weekes (WI)	48	81	5	4,455	207	15
58.45	W. R. Hammond (E)	85	140	16	7,249	336*	22
57.78	G. S. Sobers (WI)	93	160	21	8,032	365*	26
57.43	**J. H. Kallis (SA/World)**	**145**	**246**	**38**	**11,947**	**201***	**40**
57.25	**K. C. Sangakkara (SL)**	**94**	**156**	**12**	**8,244**	**287**	**24**
56.94	J. B. Hobbs (E)	61	102	7	5,410	211	15
56.94	**S. R. Tendulkar (I)**	**177**	**290**	**32**	**14,692**	**248***	**51**
56.68	C. L. Walcott (WI)	44	74	7	3,798	220	15
56.67	L. Hutton (E)	79	138	15	6,971	364	19
55.00	E. Tyldesley (E)	14	20	2	990	122	3
54.25	**T. T. Samaraweera (SL)**	**63**	**98**	**17**	**4,395**	**231**	**12**
54.20	C. A. Davis (WI)	15	29	5	1,301	183	4
54.20	V. G. Kambli (I)	17	21	1	1,084	227	4
53.86	G. S. Chappell (A)	87	151	19	7,110	247*	24
53.82	**D. P. M. D. Jayawardene (SL)** . .	**116**	**190**	**13**	**9,527**	**374**	**28**
53.81	A. D. Nourse (SA)	34	62	7	2,960	231	9
53.51	**R. T. Ponting (A)**	**152**	**259**	**28**	**12,363**	**257**	**39**
53.43	**V. Sehwag (I/World)**	**87**	**150**	**6**	**7,694**	**319**	**22**
52.88	B. C. Lara (WI/World)	131	232	6	11,953	400*	34
52.57	Javed Miandad (P)	124	189	21	8,832	280*	23
52.44	**R. Dravid (I/World)**	**150**	**259**	**29**	**12,063**	**270**	**31**
52.29	Mohammad Yousuf (P)	90	156	12	7,530	223	24
51.62	J. Ryder (A)	20	32	5	1,394	201*	3
51.54	A. Flower (Z)	63	112	19	4,794	232*	12
51.33	**G. Gambhir (I)**	**38**	**68**	**5**	**3,234**	**206**	**9**
51.12	S. M. Gavaskar (I)	125	214	16	10,122	236*	34
51.09	**M. E. K. Hussey (A)**	**59**	**103**	**12**	**4,650**	**195**	**13**
51.06	S. R. Waugh (A)	168	260	46	10,927	200	32
50.73	M. L. Hayden (A)	103	184	14	8,625	380	30
50.60	**Younis Khan (P)**	**67**	**119**	**8**	**5,617**	**313**	**17**
50.56	A. R. Border (A)	156	265	44	11,174	205	27
50.23	I. V. A. Richards (WI)	121	182	12	8,540	291	24
50.06	D. C. S. Compton (E)	78	131	15	5,807	278	17

HIGHEST PERCENTAGE OF TEAM'S RUNS OVER TEST CAREER

(Qualification: 20 Tests)

	Tests	Runs	Team Runs	% of Team Runs
D. G. Bradman (Australia)	52	6,996	28,810	24.28
G. A. Headley (West Indies)	22	2,190	10,239	21.38
B. C. Lara (West Indies)	131	11,953	63,328	18.87
L. Hutton (England)	79	6,971	38,440	18.13
J. B. Hobbs (England)	61	5,410	30,211	17.90
A. D. Nourse (South Africa)	34	2,960	16,659	17.76

	Tests	Runs	Team Runs	% of Team Runs
E. D. Weekes (West Indies)	48	4,455	25,667	17.35
B. Mitchell (South Africa)	42	3,471	20,175	17.20
H. Sutcliffe (England)	54	4,555	26,604	17.12
B. Sutcliffe (New Zealand)	42	2,727	16,158	16.87

The percentage shows the proportion of a team's runs scored by that player in all Tests in which he played, including team runs in innings in which he did not bat.

FASTEST FIFTIES

Minutes

27	Mohammad Ashraful	Bangladesh v India at Mirpur	2007
28	J. T. Brown	England v Australia at Melbourne	1894-95
29	S. A. Durani	India v England at Kanpur	1963-64
30	E. A. V. Williams	West Indies v England at Bridgetown	1947-48
30	B. R. Taylor	New Zealand v West Indies at Auckland	1968-69
31	W. J. O'Reilly	Australia v South Africa at Johannesburg	1935-36
32	R. Benaud	Australia v West Indies at Kingston	1954-55
32	W. J. Cronje	South Africa v Sri Lanka at Centurion	1997-98

The fastest fifties in terms of balls received (where recorded) are:

Balls

24	J. H. Kallis	South Africa v Zimbabwe at Cape Town	2004-05
26	Shahid Afridi	Pakistan v India at Bangalore	2004-05
26	Mohammad Ashraful	Bangladesh v India at Mirpur	2007
27	Yousuf Youhana	Pakistan v South Africa at Cape Town	2002-03
28	E. A. V. Williams	West Indies v England at Bridgetown	1947-48
28	I. T. Botham	England v India at Delhi	1981-82
29	B. Yardley	Australia v West Indies at Bridgetown	1977-78
29	T. G. Southee	New Zealand v England at Napier	2007-08
30	Kapil Dev	India v Pakistan at Karachi	1982-83
30	T. M. Dilshan	Sri Lanka v New Zealand at Galle	2009
31	A. Ranatunga	Sri Lanka v India at Kanpur	1986-87
31	W. J. Cronje	South Africa v Sri Lanka at Centurion	1997-98
32	I. V. A. Richards	West Indies v India at Kingston	1982-83
32	I. T. Botham	England v New Zealand at The Oval	1986
32	V. Sehwag	India v England at Chennai	2008-09
32	Umar Akmal	Pakistan v New Zealand at Wellington	2009-10

FASTEST HUNDREDS

Minutes

70	J. M. Gregory	Australia v South Africa at Johannesburg	1921-22
75	G. L. Jessop	England v Australia at The Oval	1902
78	R. Benaud	Australia v West Indies at Kingston	1954-55
80	J. H. Sinclair	South Africa v Australia at Cape Town	1902-03
81	I. V. A. Richards	West Indies v England at St John's	1985-86
86	B. R. Taylor	New Zealand v West Indies at Auckland	1968-69

The fastest hundreds in terms of balls received (where recorded) are:

Balls

56	I. V. A. Richards	West Indies v England at St John's	1985-86
57	A. C. Gilchrist	Australia v England at Perth	2006-07
67	J. M. Gregory	Australia v South Africa at Johannesburg	1921-22
69	S. Chanderpaul	West Indies v Australia at Georgetown	2002-03
70	C. H. Gayle	West Indies v Australia at Perth	2009-10
71	R. C. Fredericks	West Indies v Australia at Perth	1975-76
74	Majid Khan	Pakistan v New Zealand at Karachi	1976-77

74	Kapil Dev	India v Sri Lanka at Kanpur	1986-87
74	M. Azharuddin	India v South Africa at Calcutta	1996-97
75	**A. B. de Villiers**	**South Africa v India at Centurion**	**2010-11**
76	G. L. Jessop.	England v Australia at The Oval.	1902

FASTEST DOUBLE-HUNDREDS

Minutes

214	D. G. Bradman	Australia v England at Leeds	1930
217	N. J. Astle	New Zealand v England at Christchurch.	2001-02
223	S. J. McCabe.	Australia v England at Nottingham	1938
226	V. T. Trumper.	Australia v South Africa at Adelaide	1910-11
234	D. G. Bradman	Australia v England at Lord's	1930
240	W. R. Hammond.	England v New Zealand at Auckland	1932-33
241	S. E. Gregory	Australia v England at Sydney	1894-95
245	D. C. S. Compton	England v Pakistan at Nottingham	1954

The fastest double-hundreds in terms of balls received (where recorded) are:

Balls

153	N. J. Astle	New Zealand v England at Christchurch.	2001-02
168	V. Sehwag.	India v Sri Lanka at Mumbai (BS)	2009-10
182	V. Sehwag.	India v Pakistan at Lahore.	2005-06
194	V. Sehwag.	India v South Africa at Chennai	2007-08
211	H. H. Gibbs.	South Africa v Pakistan at Cape Town	2002-03
212	A. C. Gilchrist.	Australia v South Africa at Johannesburg. . . .	2001-02
220	I. T. Botham	England v India at The Oval	1982
221	**C. H. Gayle**	**West Indies v Sri Lanka at Galle**	**2010-11**
222	V. Sehwag.	India v Pakistan at Multan.	2003-04
227	V. Sehwag.	India v Sri Lanka at Galle	2008
229	P. A. de Silva	Sri Lanka v Bangladesh at Colombo (PSS). . .	2002

FASTEST TRIPLE-HUNDREDS

Minutes

| 288 | W. R. Hammond. . . . . | England v New Zealand at Auckland . . . . . . | 1932-33 |
| 336 | D. G. Bradman . . . . | Australia v England at Leeds . . . . | 1930 |

The fastest triple-hundred in terms of balls received (where recorded) is:

Balls

| 278 | V. Sehwag. . . . . | India v South Africa at Chennai . . . . | 2007-08 |

MOST RUNS SCORED OFF AN OVER

28	B. C. Lara (466444)	off R. J. Peterson	WI v SA at Johannesburg . .	2003-04
27	Shahid Afridi (666621)	off Harbhajan Singh	P v I at Lahore	2005-06
26	C. D. McMillan (444464)	off Younis Khan	NZ v P at Hamilton	2000-01
26	B. C. Lara (406664)	off Danish Kaneria	WI v P at Multan	2006-07
26	M. G. Johnson (446066)	off P. L. Harris	A v SA at Johannesburg . . .	2009-10

MOST RUNS IN A DAY

309	D. G. Bradman.	Australia v England at Leeds	1930
295	W. R. Hammond	England v New Zealand at Auckland	1932-33
273	D. C. S. Compton	England v Pakistan at Nottingham	1954
271	D. G. Bradman.	Australia v England at Leeds	1934

MOST SIXES IN A CAREER

A. C. Gilchrist (A)	100	**C. H. Gayle (WI)**	**75**
B. C. Lara (WI)	88	**R. T. Ponting (A)**	**72**
C. L. Cairns (NZ)	87	C. H. Lloyd (WI)	70
J. H. Kallis (SA/World)	**86**	I. T. Botham (E)	67
V. Sehwag (I/World)	**85**	C. G. Greenidge (WI)	67
I. V. A. Richards (WI)	84	**S. R. Tendulkar (I)**	**64**
A. Flintoff (E/World)	82	C. L. Hooper (WI)	63
M. L. Hayden (A)	82	Kapil Dev (I)	61

SLOWEST INDIVIDUAL BATTING

0	in 101 minutes	G. I. Allott, New Zealand v South Africa at Auckland	1998-99
4*	in 110 minutes	Abdul Razzaq, Pakistan v Australia at Melbourne	2004-05
7	in 123 minutes	G. Miller, England v Australia at Melbourne	1978-79
9	in 132 minutes	R. K. Chauhan, India v Sri Lanka at Ahmedabad	1993-94
10*	in 133 minutes	T. G. Evans, England v Australia at Adelaide	1946-47
12	in 140 minutes	R. Dravid, India v England at The Oval	2007
14*	in 165 minutes	D. K. Morrison, New Zealand v England at Auckland	1996-97
18	in 194 minutes	W. R. Playle, New Zealand v England at Leeds	1958
19*	in 217 minutes	M. D. Crowe, New Zealand v Sri Lanka at Colombo (SSC)	1983-84
25	in 242 minutes	D. K. Morrison, New Zealand v Pakistan at Faisalabad	1990-91
29*	in 277 minutes	R. C. Russell, England v South Africa at Johannesburg	1995-96
35	in 332 minutes	C. J. Tavaré, England v India at Madras	1981-82
60	in 390 minutes	D. N. Sardesai, India v West Indies at Bridgetown	1961-62
62	in 408 minutes	Ramiz Raja, Pakistan v West Indies at Karachi	1986-87
68	in 458 minutes	T. E. Bailey, England v Australia at Brisbane	1958-59
99	in 505 minutes	M. L. Jaisimha, India v Pakistan at Kanpur	1960-61
105	in 575 minutes	D. J. McGlew, South Africa v Australia at Durban	1957-58
114	in 591 minutes	Mudassar Nazar, Pakistan v England at Lahore	1977-78
146*	in 655 minutes	M. J. Greatbatch, New Zealand v Australia at Perth	1989-90
163	in 720 minutes	Shoaib Mohammad, Pakistan v New Zealand at Wellington	1988-89
201*	in 777 minutes	D. S. B. P. Kuruppu, Sri Lanka v New Zealand at Colombo (CCC)	1986-87
275	in 878 minutes	G. Kirsten, South Africa v England at Durban	1999-2000
337	in 970 minutes	Hanif Mohammad, Pakistan v West Indies at Bridgetown	1957-58

SLOWEST HUNDREDS

557 minutes	Mudassar Nazar, Pakistan v England at Lahore	1977-78
545 minutes	D. J. McGlew, South Africa v Australia at Durban	1957-58
535 minutes	A. P. Gurusinha, Sri Lanka v Zimbabwe at Harare	1994-95
516 minutes	J. J. Crowe, New Zealand v Sri Lanka at Colombo (CCC)	1986-87
500 minutes	S. V. Manjrekar, India v Zimbabwe at Harare	1992-93
488 minutes	P. E. Richardson, England v South Africa at Johannesburg	1956-57

Notes: The slowest hundred for any Test in England is 458 minutes (329 balls) by K. W. R. Fletcher, England v Pakistan, The Oval, 1974.

The slowest double-hundred in a Test was scored in 777 minutes (548 balls) by D. S. B. P. Kuruppu for Sri Lanka v New Zealand at Colombo (CCC), 1986-87, on his debut.

PARTNERSHIPS OVER 400

624	for 3rd	K. C. Sangakkara (287)/D. P. M. D. Jayawardene (374)..................	SL v SA	Colombo (SSC)	2006
576	for 2nd	S. T. Jayasuriya (340)/R. S. Mahanama (225)	SL v I	Colombo (RPS)	1997-98
467	for 2nd	A. H. Jones (186)/M. D. Crowe (299)	NZ v SL	Wellington	1990-91
451	for 2nd	W. H. Ponsford (266)/D. G. Bradman (244) .	A v E	The Oval	1934
451	for 3rd	Mudassar Nazar (231)/Javed Miandad (280*)	P v I	Hyderabad	1982-83
446	for 2nd	C. C. Hunte (260)/G. S. Sobers (365*)	WI v P	Kingston	1957-58
438	for 2nd	M. S. Atapattu (249)/K. C. Sangakkara (270)	SL v Z	Bulawayo	2003-04
437	for 4th	D. P. M. D. Jayawardene (240)/T. T. Samaraweera (231)	SL v P	Karachi	2008-09
429*	for 3rd	J. A. Rudolph (222*)/H. H. Dippenaar (177*)	SA v B	Chittagong	2003
415	for 1st	N. D. McKenzie (226)/G. C. Smith (232) ...	SA v B	Chittagong	2007-08
413	for 1st	V. Mankad (231)/Pankaj Roy (173)........	I v NZ	Madras	1955-56
411	for 4th	P. B. H. May (285*)/M. C. Cowdrey (154)..	E v WI	Birmingham	1957
410	for 1st	V. Sehwag (254)/R. Dravid (128*)	I v P	Lahore	2005-06
405	for 5th	S. G. Barnes (234)/D. G. Bradman (234)....	A v E	Sydney	1946-47

Notes: 415 runs were added for the third wicket for India v England at Madras in 1981-82 by D. B. Vengsarkar (retired hurt), G. R. Viswanath and Yashpal Sharma. 408 runs were added for the first wicket for India v Bangladesh at Mirpur in 2007 by K. D. Karthik (retired hurt), Wasim Jaffer (retired hurt), R. Dravid and S. R. Tendulkar.

HIGHEST PARTNERSHIPS FOR EACH WICKET

The following lists include all stands above 300; otherwise the top ten for each wicket.

First Wicket

415	N. D. McKenzie (226)/G. C. Smith (232)	SA v B	Chittagong	2007-08
413	V. Mankad (231)/Pankaj Roy (173)	I v NZ	Madras	1955-56
410	V. Sehwag (254)/R. Dravid (128*)	I v P	Lahore	2005-06
387	G. M. Turner (259)/T. W. Jarvis (182)	NZ v WI	Georgetown	1971-72
382	W. M. Lawry (210)/R. B. Simpson (201)	A v WI	Bridgetown	1964-65
368	G. C. Smith (151)/H. H. Gibbs (228)	SA v P	Cape Town	2002-03
359	L. Hutton (158)/C. Washbrook (195)	E v SA	Johannesburg	1948-49
338	G. C. Smith (277*)/H. H. Gibbs (179)	SA v E	Birmingham	2003
335	M. S. Atapattu (207*)/S. T. Jayasuriya (188)	SL v P	Kandy	2000
329	G. R. Marsh (138)/M. A. Taylor (219)	A v E	Nottingham	1989
323	J. B. Hobbs (178)/W. Rhodes (179)	E v A	Melbourne	1911-12
301	G. C. Smith (139)/H. H. Gibbs (192)	SA v WI	Centurion	2003-04

Second Wicket

576	S. T. Jayasuriya (340)/R. S. Mahanama (225)	SL v I	Colombo (RPS)	1997-98
451	W. H. Ponsford (266)/D. G. Bradman (244).......	A v E	The Oval	1934
446	C. C. Hunte (260)/G. S. Sobers (365*)...........	WI v P	Kingston	1957-58
438	M. S. Atapattu (249)/K. C. Sangakkara (270)......	SL v Z	Bulawayo	2003-04
382	L. Hutton (364)/M. Leyland (187)	E v A	The Oval	1938
369	J. H. Edrich (310*)/K. F. Barrington (163)........	E v NZ	Leeds	1965
351	G. A. Gooch (196)/D. I. Gower (157)............	E v A	The Oval	1985
344*	S. M. Gavaskar (182*)/D. B. Vengsarkar (157*) ...	I v WI	Calcutta	1978-79
331	R. T. Robinson (148)/D. I. Gower (215)..........	E v A	Birmingham	1985
331	C. H. Gayle (317)/R. R. Sarwan (127)	WI v SA	St John's	2004-05

329*	A. N. Cook (235*)/I. J. L. Trott (135*)	E v A	**Brisbane**	**2010-11**
315*	H. H. Gibbs (211*)/J. H. Kallis (148*).	SA v NZ	Christchurch	1998-99
314	G. Gambhir (179)/R. Dravid (136).	I v E	Mohali	2008-09
301	A. R. Morris (182)/D. G. Bradman (173*)	A v E	Leeds	1948

Third Wicket

624	K. C. Sangakkara (287)/			
	D. P. M. D. Jayawardene (374).	SL v SA	Colombo (SSC)	2006
467	A. H. Jones (186)/M. D. Crowe (299).	NZ v SL	Wellington	1990-91
451	Mudassar Nazar (231)/Javed Miandad (280*)	P v I	Hyderabad	1982-83
429*	J. A. Rudolph (222*)/H. H. Dippenaar (177*)	SA v B	Chittagong	2003
397	Qasim Omar (206)/Javed Miandad (203*)	P v SL	Faisalabad	1985-86
370	W. J. Edrich (189)/D. C. S. Compton (208)	E v SA	Lord's	1947
363	Younis Khan (163)/Mohammad Yousuf (192)	P v E	Leeds	2006
352*‡	Ijaz Ahmed, sen. (211)/Inzamam-ul-Haq (200*)	P v SL	Dhaka	1998-99
341	E. J. Barlow (201)/R. G. Pollock (175).	SA v A	Adelaide	1963-64
340	**H. M. Amla (253*)/J. H. Kallis (173).**	**SA v I**	**Nagpur**	**2009-10**
338	E. D. Weekes (206)/F. M. M. Worrell (167).	WI v E	Port-of-Spain	1953-54
336	V. Sehwag (309)/S. R. Tendulkar (194*)	I v P	Multan	2003-04
330	H. M. Amla (176*)/J. H. Kallis (186).	SA v NZ	Johannesburg	2007-08
324	Younis Khan (267)/Inzamam-ul-Haq (184)	P v I	Bangalore	2004-05
323	Aamir Sohail (160)/Inzamam-ul-Haq (177)	P v WI	Rawalpindi	1997-98
319	A. Melville (189)/A. D. Nourse (149).	SA v E	Nottingham	1947
319	Younis Khan (199)/Mohammad Yousuf (173).	P v I	Lahore	2005-06
316†	G. R. Viswanath (222)/Yashpal Sharma (140)	I v E	Madras	1981-82
315	R. T. Ponting (206)/D. S. Lehmann (160).	A v WI	Port-of-Spain	2002-03
311	K. C. Sangakkara (222*)/D. P. M. D. Jayawardene (165)	SL v B	Kandy	2007
308	R. B. Richardson (154)/I. V. A. Richards (178)	WI v A	St John's	1983-84
308	G. A. Gooch (333)/A. J. Lamb (139)	E v I	Lord's	1990
308	**M. Vijay (139)/S. R. Tendulkar (214)**	**I v A**	**Bangalore**	**2010-11**
303	I. V. A. Richards (232)/A. I. Kallicharran (97).	WI v E	Nottingham	1976
303	M. A. Atherton (135)/R. A. Smith (175).	E v WI	St John's	1993-94

† *415 runs were scored for this wicket in two separate partnerships; D. B. Vengsarkar retired hurt when he and Viswanath had added 99 runs.*

‡ *366 runs were scored for this wicket in two separate partnerships; Inzamam retired ill when he and Ijaz had added 352 runs.*

Fourth Wicket

437	D. P. M. D. Jayawardene (240)/			
	T. T. Samaraweera (231)	SL v P	Karachi	2008-09
411	P. B. H. May (285*)/M. C. Cowdrey (154)	E v WI	Birmingham	1957
399	G. S. Sobers (226)/F. M. M. Worrell (197*).	WI v E	Bridgetown	1959-60
388	W. H. Ponsford (181)/D. G. Bradman (304).	A v E	Leeds	1934
353	S. R. Tendulkar (241*)/V. V. S. Laxman (178)	I v A	Sydney	2003-04
352	**R. T. Ponting (209)/M. J. Clarke (166)**	**A v P**	**Hobart**	**2009-10**
350	Mushtaq Mohammad (201)/Asif Iqbal (175)	P v NZ	Dunedin	1972-73
336	W. M. Lawry (151)/K. D. Walters (242)	A v WI	Sydney	1968-69
322	Javed Miandad (153*)/Salim Malik (165)	P v E	Birmingham	1992
320	J. N. Gillespie (201*)/M. E. K. Hussey (182).	A v B	Chittagong	2005-06
310	P. D. Collingwood (206)/K. P. Pietersen (158).	E v A	Adelaide	2006-07

Fifth Wicket

405	S. G. Barnes (234)/D. G. Bradman (234).	A v E	Sydney	1946-47
385	S. R. Waugh (160)/G. S. Blewett (214)	A v SA	Johannesburg	1996-97
376	V. V. S. Laxman (281)/R. Dravid (180).	I v A	Kolkata	2000-01

332*	A. R. Border (200*)/S. R. Waugh (157*)	A v E	Leeds	1993
327	J. L. Langer (144)/R. T. Ponting (197)	A v P	Perth	1999-2000
322†	B. C. Lara (213)/J. C. Adams (94)	WI v A	Kingston	1998-99
303	R. Dravid (233)/V. V. S. Laxman (148)	I v A	Adelaide	2003-04
300	S. C. Ganguly (239)/Yuvraj Singh (169)	I v P	Bangalore	2007-08
293	C. L. Hooper (233)/S. Chanderpaul (140)	WI v I	Georgetown	2001-02
281	Javed Miandad (163)/Asif Iqbal (166)	P v NZ	Lahore	1976-77
281	S. R. Waugh (199)/R. T. Ponting (104)	A v WI	Bridgetown	1998-99

† *344 runs were scored for this wicket in two separate partnerships; P. T. Collins retired hurt when he and Lara had added 22 runs.*

Sixth Wicket

351	D. P. M. D. Jayawardene (275)/ H. A. P. W. Jayawardene (154*)	SL v I	Ahmedabad	2009-10
346	J. H. Fingleton (136)/D. G. Bradman (270)	A v E	Melbourne	1936-37
339	**M. J. Guptill (189)/B. B. McCullum (185)**	**NZ v B**	**Hamilton**	**2009-10**
317	D. R. Martyn (133)/A. C. Gilchrist (204*)	A v SA	Johannesburg	2001-02
307	**M. E. K. Hussey (195)/B. J. Haddin (136)**	**A v E**	**Brisbane**	**2010-11**
298*	D. B. Vengsarkar (164*)/R. J. Shastri (121*)	I v A	Bombay	1986-87
282*	B. C. Lara (400*)/R. D. Jacobs (107*)	WI v E	St John's	2003-04
281	G. P. Thorpe (200*)/A. Flintoff (137)	E v NZ	Christchurch	2001-02
279	M. L. Hayden (153)/A. Symonds (156)	A v E	Melbourne	2006-07
274*	G. S. Sobers (163*)/D. A. J. Holford (105*)	WI v E	Lord's	1966

Seventh Wicket

347	D. St E. Atkinson (219)/C. C. Depeiza (122)	WI v A	Bridgetown	1954-55
308	Waqar Hassan (189)/Imtiaz Ahmed (209)	P v NZ	Lahore	1955-56
259*	**V. V. S. Laxman (143*)/M. S. Dhoni (132*)**	**I v SA**	**Kolkata**	**2009-10**
248	Yousuf Youhana (203)/Saqlain Mushtaq (101*)	P v NZ	Christchurch	2000-01
246	D. J. McGlew (255*)/A. R. A. Murray (109)	SA v NZ	Wellington	1952-53
235	R. J. Shastri (142)/S. M. H. Kirmani (102)	I v E	Bombay	1984-85
225	C. L. Cairns (158)/J. D. P. Oram (90)	NZ v SA	Auckland	2003-04
223*	H. A. P. W. Jayawardene (120*)/ W. P. U. J. C. Vaas (100*)	SL v B	Colombo (SSC)	2007
221	D. T. Lindsay (182)/P. L. van der Merwe (76)	SA v A	Johannesburg	1966-67
217	K. D. Walters (250)/G. J. Gilmour (101)	A v NZ	Christchurch	1976-77
217	V. V. S. Laxman (130)/A. Ratra (115*)	I v WI	St John's	2001-02

Eighth Wicket

332	**I. J. L. Trott (184)/S. C. J. Broad (169)**	**E v P**	**Lord's**	**2010**
313	Wasim Akram (257*)/Saqlain Mushtaq (79)	P v Z	Sheikhupura	1996-97
256	S. P. Fleming (262)/J. E. C. Franklin (122*)	NZ v SA	Cape Town	2005-06
253	N. J. Astle (156*)/A. C. Parore (110)	NZ v A	Perth	2001-02
246	L. E. G. Ames (137)/G. O. B. Allen (122)	E v NZ	Lord's	1931
243	R. J. Hartigan (116)/C. Hill (160)	A v E	Adelaide	1907-08
217	T. W. Graveney (165)/J. T. Murray (112)	E v WI	The Oval	1966
173	C. E. Pellew (116)/J. M. Gregory (100)	A v E	Melbourne	1920-21
170	D. P. M. D. Jayawardene (237)/ W. P. U. J. C. Vaas (69)	SL v SA	Galle	2004
168	R. Illingworth (107)/P. Lever (88*)	E v I	Manchester	1971
168	H. H. Streak (127*)/A. M. Blignaut (91)	Z v WI	Harare	2003-04

Ninth Wicket

195	M. V. Boucher (78)/P. L. Symcox (108).	SA v P	Johannesburg	1997-98
190	Asif Iqbal (146)/Intikhab Alam (51).	P v E	The Oval	1967
180	J-P. Duminy (166)/D. W. Steyn (76)	SA v A	Melbourne	2008-09
163*	M. C. Cowdrey (128*)/A. C. Smith (69*)	E v NZ	Wellington	1962-63
161	C. H. Lloyd (161*)/A. M. E. Roberts (68)	WI v I	Calcutta	1983-84
161	Zaheer Abbas (82*)/Sarfraz Nawaz (90).	P v E	Lahore	1983-84
154	S. E. Gregory (201)/J. McC. Blackham (74).	A v E	Sydney	1894-95
151	W. H. Scotton (90)/W. W. Read (117)	E v A	The Oval	1884
150	E. A. E. Baptiste (87*)/M. A. Holding (69)	WI v E	Birmingham	1984
149	P. G. Joshi (52*)/R. B. Desai (85).	I v P	Bombay	1960-61

Tenth Wicket

151	B. F. Hastings (110)/R. O. Collinge (68*)	NZ v P	Auckland	1972-73
151	Azhar Mahmood (128*)/Mushtaq Ahmed (59)	P v SA	Rawalpindi	1997-98
133	Wasim Raja (71)/Wasim Bari (60*)	P v WI	Bridgetown	1976-77
133	S. R. Tendulkar (248*)/Zaheer Khan (75)	I v B	Dhaka	2004-05
130	R. E. Foster (287)/W. Rhodes (40*)	E v A	Sydney	1903-04
128	K. Higgs (63)/J. A. Snow (59*)	E v WI	The Oval	1966
127	J. M. Taylor (108)/A. A. Mailey (46*)	A v E	Sydney	1924-25
124	J. G. Bracewell (83*)/S. L. Boock (37).	NZ v A	Sydney	1985-86
120	R. A. Duff (104)/W. W. Armstrong (45*).	A v E	Melbourne	1901-02
118	N. J. Astle (222)/C. L. Cairns (23*)	NZ v E	Christchurch	2001-02

HIGHEST PARTNERSHIPS FOR EACH COUNTRY

ENGLAND

359	for 1st	L. Hutton (158)/C. Washbrook (195)	v SA	Johannesburg	1948-49
382	for 2nd	L. Hutton (364)/M. Leyland (187)	v A	The Oval	1938
370	for 3rd	W. J. Edrich (189)/D. C. S. Compton (208) . . .	v SA	Lord's	1947
411	for 4th	P. B. H. May (285*)/M. C. Cowdrey (154) . . .	v WI	Birmingham	1957
254	for 5th	K. W. R. Fletcher (113)/A. W. Greig (148) . . .	v I	Bombay	1972-73
281	for 6th	G. P. Thorpe (200*)/A. Flintoff (137)	v NZ	Christchurch	2001-02
197	for 7th	M. J. K. Smith (96)/J. M. Parks (101*).	v WI	Port-of-Spain	1959-60
332	**for 8th**	**I. J. L. Trott (184)/S. C. J. Broad (169).** . . .	**v P**	**Lord's**	**2010**
163*	for 9th	M. C. Cowdrey (128*)/A. C. Smith (69*)	v NZ	Wellington	1962-63
130	for 10th	R. E. Foster (287)/W. Rhodes (40*)	v A	Sydney	1903-04

AUSTRALIA

382	for 1st	W. M. Lawry (210)/R. B. Simpson (201)	v WI	Bridgetown	1964-65
451	for 2nd	W. H. Ponsford (266)/D. G. Bradman (244). . .	v E	The Oval	1934
315	for 3rd	R. T. Ponting (206)/D. S. Lehmann (160)	v WI	Port-of-Spain	2002-03
388	for 4th	W. H. Ponsford (181)/D. G. Bradman (304). . .	v E	Leeds	1934
405	for 5th	S. G. Barnes (234)/D. G. Bradman (234)	v E	Sydney	1946-47
346	for 6th	J. H. Fingleton (136)/D. G. Bradman (270) . . .	v E	Melbourne	1936-37
217	for 7th	K. D. Walters (250)/G. J. Gilmour (101)	v NZ	Christchurch	1976-77
243	for 8th	R. J. Hartigan (116)/C. Hill (160).	v E	Adelaide	1907-08
154	for 9th	S. E. Gregory (201)/J. McC. Blackham (74) . .	v E	Sydney	1894-95
127	for 10th	J. M. Taylor (108)/A. A. Mailey (46*)	v E	Sydney	1924-25

SOUTH AFRICA

415	for 1st	N. D. McKenzie (226)/G. C. Smith (232).....	v B	Chittagong	2007-08
315*	for 2nd	H. H. Gibbs (211*)/J. H. Kallis (148*).....	v NZ	Christchurch	1998-99
429*	for 3rd	J. A. Rudolph (222*)/H. H. Dippenaar (177*) .	v B	Chittagong	2003
249	for 4th	J. H. Kallis (177)/G. Kirsten (137)..........	v WI	Durban	2003-04
267	for 5th	J. H. Kallis (147)/A. G. Prince (131)	v WI	St John's	2004-05
271	for 6th	A. G. Prince (162*)/M. V. Boucher (117)	v B	Centurion	2008-09
246	for 7th	D. J. McGlew (255*)/A. R. A. Murray (109) ..	v NZ	Wellington	1952-53
150	for 8th {	N. D. McKenzie (103)/S. M. Pollock (111) ...	v SL	Centurion	2000-01
		G. Kirsten (130)/M. Zondeki (59)............	v E	Leeds	2003
195	for 9th	M. V. Boucher (78)/P. L. Symcox (108)	v P	Johannesburg	1997-98
107*	**for 10th**	**A. B. de Villiers (278*)/M. Morkel (35*)... **	**v P**	**Abu Dhabi**	**2010-11**

WEST INDIES

298	for 1st	C. G. Greenidge (149)/D. L. Haynes (167)....	v E	St John's	1989-90
446	for 2nd	C. C. Hunte (260)/G. S. Sobers (365*).......	v P	Kingston	1957-58
338	for 3rd	E. D. Weekes (206)/F. M. M. Worrell (167)..	v E	Port-of-Spain	1953-54
399	for 4th	G. S. Sobers (226)/F. M. M. Worrell (197*)..	v E	Bridgetown	1959-60
322	for 5th†	B. C. Lara (213)/J. C. Adams (94)	v A	Kingston	1998-99
282*	for 6th	B. C. Lara (400*)/R. D. Jacobs (107*).......	v E	St John's	2003-04
347	for 7th	D. St E. Atkinson (219)/C. C. Depeiza (122) .	v A	Bridgetown	1954-55
148	for 8th	J. C. Adams (101*)/F. A. Rose (69)	v Z	Kingston	1999-2000
161	for 9th	C. H. Lloyd (161*)/A. M. E. Roberts (68) ...	v I	Calcutta	1983-84
106	for 10th	C. L. Hooper (178*)/C. A. Walsh (30).......	v P	St John's	1992-93

† 344 runs were added between the fall of the 4th and 5th wickets: P. T. Collins retired hurt when he and Lara had added 22 runs.

NEW ZEALAND

387	for 1st	G. M. Turner (259)/T. W. Jarvis (182)	v WI	Georgetown	1971-72
241	for 2nd	J. G. Wright (116)/A. H. Jones (143)	v E	Wellington	1991-92
467	for 3rd	A. H. Jones (186)/M. D. Crowe (299)	v SL	Wellington	1990-91
271	for 4th	L. R. P. L. Taylor (151)/J. D. Ryder (201) ...	v I	Napier	2008-09
222	for 5th	N. J. Astle (141)/C. D. McMillan (142)	v Z	Wellington	2000-01
339	**for 6th**	**M. J. Guptill (189)/B. B. McCullum (185). ..**	**v B**	**Hamilton**	**2009-10**
225	for 7th	C. L. Cairns (158)/J. D. P. Oram (90).......	v SA	Auckland	2003-04
256	for 8th	S. P. Fleming (262)/J. E. C. Franklin (122*) ..	v SA	Cape Town	2005-06
136	for 9th	I. D. S. Smith (173)/M. C. Snedden (22)	v I	Auckland	1989-90
151	for 10th	B. F. Hastings (110)/R. O. Collinge (68*)	v P	Auckland	1972-73

INDIA

413	for 1st	V. Mankad (231)/Pankaj Roy (173)	v NZ	Madras	1955-56
344*	for 2nd	S. M. Gavaskar (182*)/D. B. Vengsarkar (157*) .	v WI	Calcutta	1978-79
336	for 3rd†	V. Sehwag (309)/S. R. Tendulkar (194*).....	v P	Multan	2003-04
353	for 4th	S. R. Tendulkar (241*)/V. V. S. Laxman (178) ..	v A	Sydney	2003-04
376	for 5th	V. V. S. Laxman (281)/R. Dravid (180)	v A	Kolkata	2000-01
298*	for 6th	D. B. Vengsarkar (164*)/R. J. Shastri (121*)..	v A	Bombay	1986-87
259	**for 7th**	**V. V. S. Laxman (143*)/M. S. Dhoni (132*) .**	**v SA**	**Kolkata**	**2009-10**
161	for 8th	A. Kumble (88)/M. Azharuddin (109)	v SA	Calcutta	1996-97
149	for 9th	P. G. Joshi (52*)/R. B. Desai (85)	v P	Bombay	1960-61
133	for 10th	S. R. Tendulkar (248*)/Zaheer Khan (75)	v B	Dhaka	2004-05

†415 runs were scored for India's 3rd wicket v England at Madras in 1981-82, in two partnerships: D. B. Vengsarkar and G. R. Viswanath put on 99 before Vengsarkar retired hurt, then Viswanath and Yashpal Sharma added a further 316.

PAKISTAN

298	for 1st	Aamir Sohail (160)/Ijaz Ahmed, sen. (151) . . .	v WI	Karachi	1997-98
291	for 2nd	Zaheer Abbas (274)/Mushtaq Mohammad (100)	v E	Birmingham	1971
451	for 3rd	Mudassar Nazar (231)/Javed Miandad (280*) .	v I	Hyderabad	1982-83
350	for 4th	Mushtaq Mohammad (201)/Asif Iqbal (175) . .	v NZ	Dunedin	1972-73
281	for 5th	Javed Miandad (163)/Asif Iqbal (166)	v NZ	Lahore	1976-77
269	for 6th	Mohammad Yousuf (223)/Kamran Akmal (154)	v E	Lahore	2005-06
308	for 7th	Waqar Hassan (189)/Imtiaz Ahmed (209)	v NZ	Lahore	1955-56
313	for 8th	Wasim Akram (257*)/Saqlain Mushtaq (79) . .	v Z	Sheikhupura	1996-97
190	for 9th	Asif Iqbal (146)/Intikhab Alam (51).	v E	The Oval	1967
151	for 10th	Azhar Mahmood (128*)/Mushtaq Ahmed (59)	v SA	Rawalpindi	1997-98

SRI LANKA

335	for 1st	M. S. Atapattu (207*)/S. T. Jayasuriya (188). .	v P	Kandy	2000
576	for 2nd	S. T. Jayasuriya (340)/R. S. Mahanama (225) .	v I	Colombo (RPS)	1997-98
624	for 3rd	K. C. Sangakkara (287)/			
		D. P. M. D. Jayawardene (374).	v SA	Colombo (SSC)	2006
437	for 4th	D. P. M. D. Jayawardene (240)/			
		T. T. Samaraweera (231)	v P	Karachi	2008-09
280	for 5th	T. T. Samaraweera (138)/T. M. Dilshan (168) .	v B	Colombo (PSS)	2005-06
351	for 6th	D. P. M. D. Jayawardene (275)/			
		H. A. P. W. Jayawardene (154*)	v I	Ahmedabad	2009-10
223*	for 7th	H. A. P. W. Jayawardene (120*)/			
		W. P. U. J. C. Vaas (100*)	v B	Colombo (SSC)	2007
170	for 8th	D. P. M. D. Jayawardene (237)/			
		W. P. U. J. C. Vaas (69)	v SA	Galle	2004
118	**for 9th**	**T. T. Samaraweera (83)/B. A. W. Mendis (78)**	**v I**	**Colombo (PSS)**	**2010**
79	for 10th	W. P. U. J. C. Vaas (68*)/M. Muralitharan (43)	v A	Kandy	2003-04

ZIMBABWE

164	for 1st	D. D. Ebrahim (71)/A. D. R. Campbell (103) .	v WI	Bulawayo	2001
135	for 2nd	M. H. Dekker (68*)/A. D. R. Campbell (75) . .	v P	Rawalpindi	1993-94
194	for 3rd	A. D. R. Campbell (99)/D. L. Houghton (142).	v SL	Harare	1994-95
269	for 4th	G. W. Flower (201*)/A. Flower (156)	v P	Harare	1994-95
277*	for 5th	M. W. Goodwin (166*)/A. Flower (100*)	v P	Bulawayo	1997-98
165	for 6th	D. L. Houghton (121)/A. Flower (59).	v I	Harare	1992-93
154	for 7th	H. H. Streak (83*)/A. M. Blignaut (92)	v WI	Harare	2001
168	for 8th	H. H. Streak (127*)/A. M. Blignaut (91)	v WI	Harare	2003-04
87	for 9th	P. A. Strang (106*)/B. C. Strang (42).	v P	Sheikhupura	1996-97
97*	for 10th	A. Flower (183*)/H. K. Olonga (11)	v I	Delhi	2000-01

BANGLADESH

185	**for 1st**	**Tamim Iqbal (103)/Imrul Kayes (75)**	**v E**	**Lord's**	**2010**
200	**for 2nd**	**Tamim Iqbal (151)/Junaid Siddique (55)** . . .	**v I**	**Mirpur**	**2009-10**
130	for 3rd	Javed Omar (119)/Mohammad Ashraful (77) .	v P	Peshawar	2003
120	for 4th	Habibul Bashar (77)/Manjural Islam Rana (35)	v WI	Kingston	2003-04
144	for 5th	Mehrab Hossain (83)/Mushfiqur Rahim (79) . .	v NZ	Chittagong	2008-09
191	for 6th	Mohammad Ashraful (129*)/			
		Mushfiqur Rahim (80).	v SL	Colombo (PSS)	2007
145	**for 7th**	**Shakib Al Hasan (87)/Mahmudullah (115)** . .	**v NZ**	**Hamilton**	**2009-10**
113	**for 8th**	**Mushfiqur Rahim (79)/Naeem Islam (38)** . . .	**v E**	**Chittagong**	**2009-10**
77	for 9th	Mashrafe bin Mortaza (79)/			
		Shahadat Hossain (31)	v I	Chittagong	2007
69	for 10th	Mohammad Rafique (65)/			
		Shahadat Hossain (3*)	v A	Chittagong	2005-06

UNUSUAL DISMISSALS

Handled the Ball

W. R. Endean	South Africa v England at Cape Town	1956-57
A. M. J. Hilditch	Australia v Pakistan at Perth	1978-79
Mohsin Khan	Pakistan v Australia at Karachi	1982-83
D. L. Haynes	West Indies v India at Bombay	1983-84
G. A. Gooch	England v Australia at Manchester	1993
S. R. Waugh	Australia v India at Chennai	2000-01
M. P. Vaughan	England v India at Bangalore	2001-02

Obstructing the Field

L. Hutton	England v South Africa at The Oval	1951

Note: There have been no cases of Hit the Ball Twice or Timed Out in Test cricket.

BOWLING RECORDS

MOST WICKETS IN AN INNINGS

10-53	J. C. Laker	England v Australia at Manchester	1956
10-74	A. Kumble	India v Pakistan at Delhi	1998-99
9-28	G. A. Lohmann	England v South Africa at Johannesburg	1895-96
9-37	J. C. Laker	England v Australia at Manchester	1956
9-51	M. Muralitharan	Sri Lanka v Zimbabwe at Kandy	2001-02
9-52	R. J. Hadlee	New Zealand v Australia at Brisbane	1985-86
9-56	Abdul Qadir	Pakistan v England at Lahore	1987-88
9-57	D. E. Malcolm	England v South Africa at The Oval	1994
9-65	M. Muralitharan	Sri Lanka v England at The Oval	1998
9-69	J. M. Patel	India v Australia at Kanpur	1959-60
9-83	Kapil Dev	India v West Indies at Ahmedabad	1983-84
9-86	Sarfraz Nawaz	Pakistan v Australia at Melbourne	1978-79
9-95	J. M. Noreiga	West Indies v India at Port-of-Spain	1970-71
9-102	S. P. Gupte	India v West Indies at Kanpur	1958-59
9-103	S. F. Barnes	England v South Africa at Johannesburg	1913-14
9-113	H. J. Tayfield	South Africa v England at Johannesburg	1956-57
9-121	A. A. Mailey	Australia v England at Melbourne	1920-21
8-7	G. A. Lohmann	England v South Africa at Port Elizabeth	1895-96
8-11	J. Briggs	England v South Africa at Cape Town	1888-89
8-24	G. D. McGrath	Australia v Pakistan at Perth	2004-05
8-29	S. F. Barnes	England v South Africa at The Oval	1912
8-29	C. E. H. Croft	West Indies v Pakistan at Port-of-Spain	1976-77
8-31	F. Laver	Australia v England at Manchester	1909
8-31	F. S. Trueman	England v India at Manchester	1952
8-34	I. T. Botham	England v Pakistan at Lord's	1978
8-35	G. A. Lohmann	England v Australia at Sydney	1886-87
8-38	L. R. Gibbs	West Indies v India at Bridgetown	1961-62
8-38	G. D. McGrath	Australia v England at Lord's	1997
8-43†	A. E. Trott	Australia v England at Adelaide	1894-95
8-43	H. Verity	England v Australia at Lord's	1934
8-43	R. G. D. Willis	England v Australia at Leeds	1981
8-45	C. E. L. Ambrose	West Indies v England at Bridgetown	1989-90
8-46	M. Muralitharan	Sri Lanka v West Indies at Kandy	2005
8-51	D. L. Underwood	England v Pakistan at Lord's	1974
8-52	V. Mankad	India v Pakistan at Delhi	1952-53
8-53	G. B. Lawrence	South Africa v New Zealand at Johannesburg	1961-62
8-53†	R. A. L. Massie	Australia v England at Lord's	1972
8-53	A. R. C. Fraser	England v West Indies at Port-of-Spain	1997-98

8-55	V. Mankad	India v England at Madras	1951-52
8-56	S. F. Barnes	England v South Africa at Johannesburg	1913-14
8-58	G. A. Lohmann	England v Australia at Sydney	1891-92
8-58	Imran Khan	Pakistan v Sri Lanka at Lahore	1981-82
8-59	C. Blythe	England v South Africa at Leeds	1907
8-59	A. A. Mallett	Australia v Pakistan at Adelaide	1972-73
8-60	Imran Khan	Pakistan v India at Karachi	1982-83
8-61†	N. D. Hirwani	India v West Indies at Madras	1987-88
8-61	M. G. Johnson	Australia v South Africa at Perth	2008-09
8-64†	L. Klusener	South Africa v India at Calcutta	1996-97
8-65	H. Trumble	Australia v England at The Oval	1902
8-68	W. Rhodes	England v Australia at Melbourne	1903-04
8-69	H. J. Tayfield	South Africa v England at Durban	1956-57
8-69	Sikander Bakht	Pakistan v India at Delhi	1979-80
8-70	S. J. Snooke	South Africa v England at Johannesburg	1905-06
8-70	M. Muralitharan	Sri Lanka v England at Nottingham	2006
8-71	G. D. McKenzie	Australia v West Indies at Melbourne	1968-69
8-71	S. K. Warne	Australia v England at Brisbane	1994-95
8-71	A. A. Donald	South Africa v Zimbabwe at Harare	1995-96
8-72	S. Venkataraghavan	India v New Zealand at Delhi	1964-65
8-75†	N. D. Hirwani	India v West Indies at Madras	1987-88
8-75	A. R. C. Fraser	England v West Indies at Bridgetown	1993-94
8-76	E. A. S. Prasanna	India v New Zealand at Auckland	1975-76
8-79	B. S. Chandrasekhar	India v England at Delhi	1972-73
8-81	L. C. Braund	England v Australia at Melbourne	1903-04
8-83	J. R. Ratnayeke	Sri Lanka v Pakistan at Sialkot	1985-86
8-84†	R. A. L. Massie	Australia v England at Lord's	1972
8-84	Harbhajan Singh	India v Australia at Chennai	2000-01
8-85	Kapil Dev	India v Pakistan at Lahore	1982-83
8-86	A. W. Greig	England v West Indies at Port-of-Spain	1973-74
8-86	J. Srinath	India v Pakistan at Calcutta	1998-99
8-87	M. G. Hughes	Australia v West Indies at Perth	1988-89
8-87	M. Muralitharan	Sri Lanka v India at Colombo (SSC)	2001
8-92	M. A. Holding	West Indies v England at The Oval	1976
8-94	T. Richardson	England v Australia at Sydney	1897-98
8-97	C. J. McDermott	Australia v England at Perth	1990-91
8-103	I. T. Botham	England v West Indies at Lord's	1984
8-104†	A. L. Valentine	West Indies v England at Manchester	1950
8-106	Kapil Dev	India v Australia at Adelaide	1985-86
8-107	B. J. T. Bosanquet	England v Australia at Nottingham	1905
8-107	N. A. Foster	England v Pakistan at Leeds	1987
8-108	S. C. G. MacGill	Australia v Bangladesh at Fatullah	2005-06
8-109	P. A. Strang	Zimbabwe v New Zealand at Bulawayo	2000-01
8-112	G. F. Lawson	Australia v West Indies at Adelaide	1984-85
8-126	J. C. White	England v Australia at Adelaide	1928-29
8-141	C. J. McDermott	Australia v England at Manchester	1985
8-141	A. Kumble	India v Australia at Sydney	2003-04
8-143	M. H. N. Walker	Australia v England at Melbourne	1974-75
8-164	Saqlain Mushtaq	Pakistan v England at Lahore	2000-01
8-215†	J. J. Krejza	Australia v India at Nagpur	2008-09

† *On Test debut.*

Note: The best for Bangladesh is 7-36 by Shakib Al Hasan against New Zealand at Chittagong in 2008-09.

OUTSTANDING BOWLING ANALYSES

	O	M	R	W		
J. C. Laker (E)	51.2	23	53	10	v Australia at Manchester	1956
A. Kumble (I)	26.3	9	74	10	v Pakistan at Delhi	1998-99
G. A. Lohmann (E)	14.2	6	28	9	v South Africa at Johannesburg	1895-96
J. C. Laker (E)	16.4	4	37	9	v Australia at Manchester	1956

	O	M	R	W		
G. A. Lohmann (E)	9.4	5	7	8	v South Africa at Port Elizabeth	1895-96
J. Briggs (E)	14.2	5	11	8	v South Africa at Cape Town	1888-89
S. J. Harmison (E)	12.3	8	12	7	v West Indies at Kingston	2003-04
J. Briggs (E)	19.1	11	17	7	v South Africa at Cape Town	1888-89
M. A. Noble (A)	7.4	2	17	7	v England at Melbourne	1901-02
W. Rhodes (E)	11	3	17	7	v Australia at Birmingham	1902
J. J. C. Lawson (WI)	6.5	4	3	6	v Bangladesh at Dhaka	2002-03
A. E. R. Gilligan (E)	6.3	4	7	6	v South Africa at Birmingham	1924
M. J. Clarke (A)	6.2	0	9	6	v India at Mumbai.............	2004-05
S. Haigh (E)	11.4	6	11	6	v South Africa at Cape Town	1898-99
Shoaib Akhtar (P)	8.2	4	11	6	v New Zealand at Lahore	2002
D. L. Underwood (E)	11.6	7	12	6	v New Zealand at Christchurch. ...	1970-71
S. L. V. Raju (I)	17.5	13	12	6	v Sri Lanka at Chandigarh	1990-91
H. J. Tayfield (SA)	14	7	13	6	v New Zealand at Johannesburg ...	1953-54
C. T. B. Turner (A)	18	11	15	6	v England at Sydney...........	1886-87
M. H. N. Walker (A)	16	8	15	6	v Pakistan at Sydney	1972-73
E. R. H. Toshack (A)	2.3	1	2	5	v India at Brisbane	1947-48
H. Ironmonger (A)	7.2	5	6	5	v South Africa at Melbourne......	1931-32
T. B. A. May (A)	6.5	3	9	5	v West Indies at Adelaide	1992-93
Pervez Sajjad (P)	12	8	5	4	v New Zealand at Rawalpindi	1964-65
K. Higgs (E)	9	7	5	4	v New Zealand at Christchurch.....	1965-66
P. H. Edmonds (E)	8	6	6	4	v Pakistan at Lord's	1978
J. C. White (E)	6.3	2	7	4	v Australia at Brisbane	1928-29
J. H. Wardle (E)	5	2	7	4	v Australia at Manchester	1953
R. Appleyard (E)	6	3	7	4	v New Zealand at Auckland	1954-55
R. Benaud (A)	3.4	3	0	3	v India at Delhi..............	1959-60

WICKET WITH FIRST BALL IN TEST CRICKET

Batsman dismissed

A. Coningham	A. C. MacLaren	A v E	Melbourne	1894-95
W. M. Bradley	F. Laver	E v A	Manchester	1899
E. G. Arnold	V. T. Trumper	E v A	Sydney	1903-04
G. G. Macaulay	G. A. L. Hearne	E v SA	Cape Town	1922-23
M. W. Tate	M. J. Susskind	E v SA	Birmingham	1924
M. Henderson	E. W. Dawson	NZ v E	Christchurch	1929-30
H. D. Smith	E. Paynter	NZ v E	Christchurch	1932-33
T. F. Johnson	W. W. Keeton	WI v E	The Oval	1939
R. Howorth	D. V. Dyer	E v SA	The Oval	1947
Intikhab Alam	C. C. McDonald	P v A	Karachi	1959-60
R. K. Illingworth	P. V. Simmons	E v WI	Nottingham	1991
N. M. Kulkarni	M. S. Atapattu	I v SL	Colombo (RPS) ...	1997-98
M. K. G. C. P. Lakshitha	Mohammad Ashraful	SL v B	Colombo (SSC)	2002

HAT-TRICKS

F. R. Spofforth	Australia v England at Melbourne	1878-79
W. Bates	England v Australia at Melbourne	1882-83
J. Briggs	England v Australia at Sydney	1891-92
G. A. Lohmann	England v South Africa at Port Elizabeth ...	1895-96
J. T. Hearne	England v Australia at Leeds	1899
H. Trumble	Australia v England at Melbourne	1901-02
H. Trumble	Australia v England at Melbourne	1903-04
T. J. Matthews† .... } Australia v South Africa at Manchester		1912
T. J. Matthews .... }		
M. J. C. Allom‡.......	England v New Zealand at Christchurch	1929-30
T. W. J. Goddard	England v South Africa at Johannesburg	1938-39
P. J. Loader..........	England v West Indies at Leeds	1957
L. F. Kline...........	Australia v South Africa at Cape Town	1957-58

W. W. Hall	West Indies v Pakistan at Lahore	1958-59
G. M. Griffin	South Africa v England at Lord's	1960
L. R. Gibbs	West Indies v Australia at Adelaide	1960-61
P. J. Petherick‡	New Zealand v Pakistan at Lahore	1976-77
C. A. Walsh§	West Indies v Australia at Brisbane	1988-89
M. G. Hughes§	Australia v West Indies at Perth	1988-89
D. W. Fleming‡	Australia v Pakistan at Rawalpindi	1994-95
S. K. Warne	Australia v England at Melbourne	1994-95
D. G. Cork	England v West Indies at Manchester	1995
D. Gough	England v Australia at Sydney	1998-99
Wasim Akram¶	Pakistan v Sri Lanka at Lahore	1998-99
Wasim Akram¶	Pakistan v Sri Lanka at Dhaka	1998-99
D. N. T. Zoysa‖	Sri Lanka v Zimbabwe at Harare	1999-2000
Abdul Razzaq	Pakistan v Sri Lanka at Galle	2000
G. D. McGrath	Australia v West Indies at Perth	2000-01
Harbhajan Singh	India v Australia at Kolkata	2000-01
Mohammad Sami	Pakistan v Sri Lanka at Lahore	2001-02
J. J. C. Lawson§	West Indies v Australia at Bridgetown	2002-03
Alok Kapali	Bangladesh v Pakistan at Peshawar	2003
A. M. Blignaut	Zimbabwe v Bangladesh at Harare	2003-04
M. J. Hoggard	England v West Indies at Bridgetown	2003-04
J. E. C. Franklin	New Zealand v Bangladesh at Dhaka	2004-05
I. K. Pathan‖	India v Pakistan at Karachi	2005-06
R. J. Sidebottom	England v New Zealand at Hamilton	2007-08
P. M. Siddle	**Australia v England at Brisbane**	**2010-11**

† *T. J. Matthews did the hat-trick in each innings of the same match.*
‡ *On Test debut.*
§ *Not all in the same innings.*
¶ *Wasim Akram did the hat-trick in successive matches.*
‖ *D. N. T. Zoysa did the hat-trick in the match's second over; I. K. Pathan in the match's first over.*

FOUR WICKETS IN FIVE BALLS

M. J. C. Allom	England v New Zealand at Christchurch	1929-30
	On debut, in his eighth over: W-WWW	
C. M. Old	England v Pakistan at Birmingham	1978
	Sequence interrupted by a no-ball: WW-WW	
Wasim Akram	Pakistan v West Indies at Lahore (*WW-WW*)	1990-91

MOST WICKETS IN A TEST

19-90	J. C. Laker	England v Australia at Manchester	1956
17-159	S. F. Barnes	England v South Africa at Johannesburg	1913-14
16-136†	N. D. Hirwani	India v West Indies at Madras	1987-88
16-137†	R. A. L. Massie	Australia v England at Lord's	1972
16-220	M. Muralitharan	Sri Lanka v England at The Oval	1998
15-28	J. Briggs	England v South Africa at Cape Town	1888-89
15-45	G. A. Lohmann	England v South Africa at Port Elizabeth	1895-96
15-99	C. Blythe	England v South Africa at Leeds	1907
15-104	H. Verity	England v Australia at Lord's	1934
15-123	R. J. Hadlee	New Zealand v Australia at Brisbane	1985-86
15-124	W. Rhodes	England v Australia at Melbourne	1903-04
15-217	Harbhajan Singh	India v Australia at Chennai	2000-01
14-90	F. R. Spofforth	Australia v England at The Oval	1882
14-99	A. V. Bedser	England v Australia at Nottingham	1953
14-102	W. Bates	England v Australia at Melbourne	1882-83

14-116	Imran Khan	Pakistan v Sri Lanka at Lahore	1981-82
14-124	J. M. Patel	India v Australia at Kanpur	1959-60
14-144	S. F. Barnes	England v South Africa at Durban	1913-14
14-149	M. A. Holding	West Indies v England at The Oval	1976
14-149	A. Kumble	India v Pakistan at Delhi	1998-99
14-191	W. P. U. J. C. Vaas	Sri Lanka v West Indies at Colombo (SSC)	2001-02
14-199	C. V. Grimmett	Australia v South Africa at Adelaide	1931-32

† *On Test debut.*

Note: The best for South Africa is 13-132 by M. Ntini against West Indies at Port-of-Spain, 2004-05, for Zimbabwe 11-255 by A. G. Huckle against New Zealand at Bulawayo, 1997-98, and for Bangladesh 12-200 by Enamul Haque, jun. against Zimbabwe at Dhaka, 2004-05.

MOST BALLS BOWLED IN A TEST

S. Ramadhin (West Indies) sent down 774 balls in 129 overs against England at Birmingham, 1957. It was the most delivered by any bowler in a Test, beating H. Verity's 766 for England against South Africa at Durban, 1938-39. In this match Ramadhin also bowled the most balls (588) in a Test or first-class innings, since equalled by Arshad Ayub, Hyderabad v Madhya Pradesh at Secunderabad, 1991-92.

MOST WICKETS IN A SERIES

	T	R	W	Avge		
S. F. Barnes	4	536	49	10.93	England v South Africa	1913-14
J. C. Laker	5	442	46	9.60	Australia v England	1956
C. V. Grimmett	5	642	44	14.59	Australia v South Africa	1935-36
T. M. Alderman	6	893	42	21.26	Australia v England	1981
R. M. Hogg	6	527	41	12.85	Australia v England	1978-79
T. M. Alderman	6	712	41	17.36	Australia v England	1989
Imran Khan	6	558	40	13.95	Pakistan v India	1982-83
S. K. Warne	5	797	40	19.92	Australia v England	2005
A. V. Bedser	5	682	39	17.48	England v Australia	1953
D. K. Lillee	6	870	39	22.30	Australia v England	1981
M. W. Tate	5	881	38	23.18	England v Australia	1924-25
W. J. Whitty	5	632	37	17.08	Australia v South Africa	1910-11
H. J. Tayfield	5	636	37	17.18	South Africa v England	1956-57
A. E. E. Vogler	5	783	36	21.75	South Africa v England	1909-10
A. A. Mailey	5	946	36	26.27	Australia v England	1920-21
G. D. McGrath	6	701	36	19.47	Australia v England	1997
G. A. Lohmann	3	203	35	5.80	England v South Africa	1895-96
B. S. Chandrasekhar	5	662	35	18.91	India v England	1972-73
M. D. Marshall	5	443	35	12.65	West Indies v England	1988

Notes: The most for New Zealand is 33 by R. J. Hadlee against Australia in 1985-86, for Sri Lanka 30 by M. Muralitharan against Zimbabwe in 2001-02, for Zimbabwe 22 by H. H. Streak against Pakistan in 1994-95 (all in three Tests), and for Bangladesh 18 by Enamul Haque, jun. against Zimbabwe in 2004-05 (two Tests).

75 WICKETS IN A CALENDAR YEAR

	T	R	W	Avge	5W/i	10W/m	Year
S. K. Warne (A)	15	2,114	96	22.02	6	2	2005
M. Muralitharan (SL)	11	1,521	90	16.89	9	5	2006
D. K. Lillee (A)	13	1,781	85	20.95	5	2	1981
A. A. Donald (SA)	14	1,571	80	19.63	7	–	1998
M. Muralitharan (SL)	12	1,699	80	21.23	7	4	2001
J. Garner (WI)	15	1,604	77	20.83	4	–	1984
Kapil Dev (I)	18	1,739	75	23.18	5	1	1983
M. Muralitharan (SL)	10	1,463	75	19.50	7	3	2000

MOST WICKETS

1	**M. Muralitharan (SL/World)**	.... **800**
2	S. K. Warne (Australia)	 708
3	A. Kumble (India)	 619
4	G. D. McGrath (Australia)	 563
5	C. A. Walsh (West Indies)	 519
6	Kapil Dev (India)	 434
7	R. J. Hadlee (New Zealand)	 431
8	S. M. Pollock (South Africa)	 421
9	Wasim Akram (Pakistan)	 414
10	C. E. L. Ambrose (West Indies)	 405
11	**Harbhajan Singh (India)**	.... **393**
12	M. Ntini (South Africa)	 390
13	I. T. Botham (England)	 383
14	M. D. Marshall (West Indies)	 376
15	Waqar Younis (Pakistan)	 373

16	Imran Khan (Pakistan)	 362
17	{ D. K. Lillee (Australia)	 355
	W. P. U. J. C. Vaas (Sri Lanka)	 355
19	**D. L. Vettori (New Zealand/World)**	. **345**
20	A. A. Donald (South Africa)	 330
21	R. G. D. Willis (England)	 325
22	B. Lee (Australia)	 310
23	L. R. Gibbs (West Indies)	 309
24	F. S. Trueman (England)	 307
25	D. L. Underwood (England)	 297
26	C. J. McDermott (Australia)	 291
27	**Zaheer Khan (India)**	.... **271**
28	**J. H. Kallis (South Africa/World)**	. **270**
29	B. S. Bedi (India)	 266
30	**Danish Kaneria (Pakistan)**	...... **261**

MOST WICKETS FOR EACH COUNTRY

ENGLAND

		T	Balls	R	W	Avge	5W/i	10W/m
1	I. T. Botham	102	21,815	10,878	383	28.40	27	4
2	R. G. D. Willis	90	17,357	8,190	325	25.20	16	–
3	F. S. Trueman	67	15,178	6,625	307	21.57	17	3
4	D. L. Underwood	86	21,862	7,674	297	25.83	17	6
5	J. B. Statham	70	16,056	6,261	252	24.84	9	1
6	M. J. Hoggard	67	13,909	7,564	248	30.50	7	1
7	A. V. Bedser	51	15,918	5,876	236	24.89	15	5
8	A. R. Caddick	62	13,558	6,999	234	29.91	13	1
9	D. Gough	58	11,821	6,503	229	28.39	9	–
10	S. J. Harmison	62†	13,192	7,091	222	31.94	8	1
11	A. Flintoff	78†	14,747	7,303	219	33.34	3	–
12	**J. M. Anderson**	**57**	**12,056**	**6,595**	**212**	**31.10**	**10**	**1**
13	J. A. Snow	49	12,021	5,387	202	26.66	8	1
14	J. C. Laker	46	12,027	4,101	193	21.24	9	3
15	S. F. Barnes	27	7,873	3,106	189	16.43	24	7
16	A. R. C. Fraser	46	10,876	4,836	177	27.32	13	2
17	G. A. R. Lock	49	13,147	4,451	174	25.58	9	3
18	M. W. Tate	39	12,523	4,055	155	26.16	7	1
19	F. J. Titmus	53	15,118	4,931	153	32.22	7	–

† A. Flintoff also took 4-59 and 3-48, and S. J. Harmison also took 1-60 and 3-41, for the ICC World XI v Australia in the Super Series Test of 2005-06.

AUSTRALIA

		T	Balls	R	W	Avge	5W/i	10W/m
1	S. K. Warne	145	40,705	17,995	708	25.41	37	10
2	G. D. McGrath	124	29,248	12,186	563	21.64	29	3
3	D. K. Lillee	70	18,467	8,493	355	23.92	23	7
4	B. Lee	76	16,531	9,554	310	30.81	10	–
5	C. J. McDermott	71	16,586	8,332	291	28.63	14	2
6	J. N. Gillespie	71	14,234	6,770	259	26.13	8	–
7	R. Benaud	63	19,108	6,704	248	27.03	16	1
8	G. D. McKenzie	60	17,681	7,328	246	29.78	16	3

		T	Balls	R	W	Avge	5W/i	10W/m
9	R. R. Lindwall	61	13,650	5,251	228	23.03	12	–
10	C. V. Grimmett...........	37	14,513	5,231	216	24.21	21	7
11	M. G. Hughes	53	12,285	6,017	212	28.38	7	1
12	S. C. G. MacGill........	44	11,237	6,038	208	29.02	12	2
13	J. R. Thomson	51	10,535	5,601	200	28.00	8	–
14	A. K. Davidson..........	44	11,587	3,819	186	20.53	14	2
15	**M. G. Johnson.........**	**42**	**9,689**	**5,378**	**181**	**29.71**	**7**	**2**
16	G. F. Lawson	46	11,118	5,501	180	30.56	11	2
17 {	K. R. Miller	55	10,461	3,906	170	22.97	7	1
	T. M. Alderman.........	41	10,181	4,616	170	27.15	14	1
19	W. A. Johnston..........	40	11,048	3,826	160	23.91	7	–

SOUTH AFRICA

		T	Balls	R	W	Avge	5W/i	10W/m
1	S. M. Pollock	108	24,353	9,733	421	23.11	16	1
2	M. Ntini	101	20,834	11,242	390	28.82	18	4
3	A. A. Donald	72	15,519	7,344	330	22.25	20	3
4	J. H. Kallis............	144†	18,271	8,605	269	31.98	5	–
5	D. W. Steyn............	46	9,515	5,526	238	23.21	16	4
6	H. J. Tayfield	37	13,568	4,405	170	25.91	14	2

† *J. H. Kallis also took 0-35 and 1-3 for the ICC World XI v Australia in the Super Series Test of 2005-06.*

WEST INDIES

		T	Balls	R	W	Avge	5W/i	10W/m
1	C. A. Walsh	132	30,019	12,688	519	24.44	22	3
2	C. E. L. Ambrose........	98	22,103	8,501	405	20.99	22	3
3	M. D. Marshall.........	81	17,584	7,876	376	20.94	22	4
4	L. R. Gibbs.............	79	27,115	8,989	309	29.09	18	2
5	J. Garner	58	13,169	5,433	259	20.97	7	–
6	M. A. Holding	60	12,680	5,898	249	23.68	13	2
7	G. S. Sobers	93	21,599	7,999	235	34.03	6	–
8	A. M. E. Roberts........	47	11,135	5,174	202	25.61	11	2
9	W. W. Hall	48	10,421	5,066	192	26.38	9	1
10	I. R. Bishop	43	8,407	3,909	161	24.27	6	–
11	S. Ramadhin	43	13,939	4,579	158	28.98	10	1

NEW ZEALAND

		T	Balls	R	W	Avge	5W/i	10W/m
1	R. J. Hadlee	86	21,918	9,611	431	22.29	36	9
2	**D. L. Vettori ....**	**104†**	**26,698**	**11,613**	**344**	**33.75**	**19**	**3**
3	C. L. Cairns	62	11,698	6,410	218	29.40	13	1
4	**C. S. Martin ....**	**61**	**12,216**	**6,899**	**199**	**34.66**	**9**	**1**
5	D. K. Morrison..........	48	10,064	5,549	160	34.68	10	–

† *D. L. Vettori also took 1-73 and 0-38 for the ICC World XI v Australia in the Super Series Test of 2005-06.*

INDIA

		T	Balls	R	W	Avge	5W/i	10W/m
1	A. Kumble	132	40,850	18,355	619	29.65	35	8
2	Kapil Dev	131	27,740	12,867	434	29.64	23	2
3	**Harbhajan Singh ......**	**93**	**26,483**	**12,518**	**393**	**31.85**	**25**	**5**
4	**Zaheer Khan...........**	**78**	**15,756**	**8,658**	**271**	**31.94**	**10**	**1**

		T	Balls	R	W	Avge	5W/i	10W/m
5	B. S. Bedi	67	21,364	7,637	266	28.71	14	1
6	B. S. Chandrasekhar	58	15,963	7,199	242	29.74	16	2
7	J. Srinath.	67	15,104	7,196	236	30.49	10	1
8	E. A. S. Prasanna	49	14,353	5,742	189	30.38	10	2
9	V. Mankad	44	14,686	5,236	162	32.32	8	2
10	S. Venkataraghavan	57	14,877	5,634	156	36.11	3	1
11	R. J. Shastri	80	15,751	6,185	151	40.96	2	–

PAKISTAN

		T	Balls	R	W	Avge	5W/i	10W/m
1	Wasim Akram	104	22,627	9,779	414	23.62	25	5
2	Waqar Younis.	87	16,224	8,788	373	23.56	22	5
3	Imran Khan.	88	19,458	8,258	362	22.81	23	6
4	**Danish Kaneria. . . . .**	**61**	**17,697**	**9,082**	**261**	**34.79**	**15**	**2**
5	Abdul Qadir	67	17,126	7,742	236	32.80	15	5
6	Saqlain Mushtaq	49	14,070	6,206	208	29.83	13	3
7	Mushtaq Ahmed	52	12,532	6,100	185	32.97	10	3
8	Shoaib Akhtar.	46	8,143	4,574	178	25.69	12	2
9	Sarfraz Nawaz	55	13,927	5,798	177	32.75	4	1
10	Iqbal Qasim	50	13,019	4,807	171	28.11	8	2

SRI LANKA

		T	Balls	R	W	Avge	5W/i	10W/m
1	**M. Muralitharan. . . . .**	**132†**	**43,715**	**18,023**	**795**	**22.67**	**67**	**22**
2	W. P. U. J. C. Vaas.	111	23,438	10,501	355	29.58	12	2

† *M. Muralitharan also took 2-102 and 3-55 for the ICC World XI v Australia in the Super Series Test of 2005-06.*

ZIMBABWE

		T	Balls	R	W	Avge	5W/i	10W/m
1	H. H. Streak	65	13,559	6,079	216	28.14	7	

BANGLADESH

No player has taken 150 Test wickets for Bangladesh. The highest total is:

	T	Balls	R	W	Avge	5W/i	10W/m
Mohammad Rafique	33	8,744	4,076	100	40.76	7	–

BEST CAREER AVERAGES

(Qualification: 75 wickets)

Avge		T	W	Avge		T	W
10.75	G. A. Lohmann (E)	18	112	18.63	C. Blythe (E)	19	100
16.43	S. F. Barnes (E)	27	189	20.39	J. H. Wardle (E)	28	102
16.53	C. T. B. Turner (A)	17	101	20.53	A. K. Davidson (A)	44	186
16.98	R. Peel (E)	20	101	20.94	M. D. Marshall (WI)	81	376
17.75	J. Briggs (E)	33	118	20.97	J. Garner (WI)	58	259
18.41	F. R. Spofforth (A)	18	94	20.99	C. E. L. Ambrose (WI)	98	405
18.56	F. H. Tyson (E)	17	76				

BEST CAREER STRIKE-RATES

(Balls per wicket. Qualification: 75 wickets)

SR		T	W	SR		T	W
34.19	G. A. Lohmann (E)	18	112	45.42	F. H. Tyson (E)	17	76
38.75	S. E. Bond (NZ)	18	87	45.46	C. Blythe (E)	19	100
39.97	**D. W. Steyn (SA)**	**46**	**238**	45.74	Shoaib Akhtar (P)	46	178
41.65	S. F. Barnes (E)	27	189	46.76	M. D. Marshall (WI)	81	376
43.49	Waqar Younis (P)	87	373	47.02	A. A. Donald (SA)	72	330
44.52	F. R. Spofforth (A)	18	94	**48.78**	**Mohammad Asif (P)**	**23**	**106**
45.12	J. V. Saunders (A)	14	79	49.32	C. E. H. Croft (WI)	27	125
45.18	J. Briggs (E)	33	118	49.43	F. S. Trueman (E)	67	307

BEST CAREER ECONOMY-RATES

(Runs per six balls. Qualification: 75 wickets)

ER		T	W	ER		T	W
1.64	T. L. Goddard (SA)	41	123	1.94	W. J. O'Reilly (A)	27	144
1.67	R. G. Nadkarni (I)	41	88	1.94	H. J. Tayfield (SA)	37	170
1.88	H. Verity (E)	40	144	1.95	A. L. Valentine (WI)	36	139
1.88	G. A. Lohmann (E)	18	112	1.95	F. J. Titmus (E)	53	153
1.89	J. H. Wardle (E)	28	102	1.97	S. Ramadhin (WI)	43	158
1.91	R. Illingworth (E)	61	122	1.97	R. Peel (E)	20	101
1.93	C. T. B. Turner (A)	17	101	1.97	A. K. Davidson (A)	44	186
1.94	M. W. Tate (E)	39	155	1.98	L. R. Gibbs (WI)	79	309

HIGHEST PERCENTAGE OF TEAM'S WICKETS OVER TEST CAREER

(Qualification: 20 Tests)

	Tests	Wkts	Team Wkts	% of Team Wkts
M. Muralitharan (Sri Lanka/World)	**133**	**800**	**2,070**	**38.64**
S. F. Barnes (England)......................	27	189	494	38.25
R. J. Hadlee (New Zealand).................	86	431	1,255	34.34
C. V. Grimmett (Australia)	37	216	636	33.96
Fazal Mahmood (Pakistan)	34	139	410	33.90
W. J. O'Reilly (Australia)	27	144	446	32.28
S. P. Gupte (India)	36	149	470	31.70
D. W. Steyn (South Africa)	**46**	**238**	**772**	**30.82**
Mohammad Rafique (Bangladesh)............	33	100	328	30.48
A. V. Bedser (England)	51	236	777	30.37

Note: Excluding the Super Series Test, Muralitharan took 795 out of 2,050 wickets in his 132 Tests for Sri Lanka, a percentage of 38.78.

The percentage shows the proportion of a team's wickets taken by that player in all Tests in which he played, including team wickets in innings in which he did not bowl.

ALL-ROUND RECORDS

HUNDRED AND FIVE WICKETS IN AN INNINGS

England

A. W. Greig	148	6-164	v West Indies	Bridgetown	1973-74
I. T. Botham	103	5-73	v New Zealand	Christchurch . . .	1977-78
I. T. Botham	108	8-34	v Pakistan	Lord's	1978
I. T. Botham	114	6-58, 7-48	v India	Bombay	1979-80
I. T. Botham	149*	6-95	v Australia	Leeds	1981
I. T. Botham	138	5-59	v New Zealand	Wellington	1983-84

Australia

C. Kelleway	114	5-33	v South Africa	Manchester	1912
J. M. Gregory	100	7-69	v England	Melbourne	1920-21
K. R. Miller	109	6-107	v West Indies	Kingston	1954-55
R. Benaud	100	5-84	v South Africa	Johannesburg . . .	1957-58

South Africa

J. H. Sinclair	106	6-26	v England	Cape Town	1898-99
G. A. Faulkner	123	5-120	v England	Johannesburg . . .	1909-10
J. H. Kallis	110	5-90	v West Indies	Cape Town	1998-99
J. H. Kallis	139*	5-21	v Bangladesh	Potchefstroom . . .	2002-03

West Indies

D. St E. Atkinson	219	5-56	v Australia	Bridgetown	1954-55
O. G. Smith	100	5-90	v India	Delhi	1958-59
G. S. Sobers	104	5-63	v India	Kingston	1961-62
G. S. Sobers	174	5-41	v England	Leeds	1966

New Zealand

B. R. Taylor†	105	5-86	v India	Calcutta	1964-65

India

V. Mankad	184	5-196	v England	Lord's	1952
P. R. Umrigar	172*	5-107	v West Indies	Port-of-Spain	1961-62

Pakistan

Mushtaq Mohammad	201	5-49	v New Zealand	Dunedin	1972-73
Mushtaq Mohammad	121	5-28	v West Indies	Port-of-Spain	1976-77
Imran Khan	117	6-98, 5-82	v India	Faisalabad	1982-83
Wasim Akram	123	5-100	v Australia	Adelaide	1989-90

Zimbabwe

P. A. Strang	106*	5-212	v Pakistan	Sheikhupura	1996-97

† *On debut.*

HUNDRED AND FIVE DISMISSALS IN AN INNINGS

D. T. Lindsay	182	6ct	SA v A	Johannesburg	1966-67
I. D. S. Smith	113*	4ct, 1st	NZ v E	Auckland	1983-84
S. A. R. Silva	111	5ct	SL v I	Colombo (PSS)	1985-86
A. C. Gilchrist	133	4ct, 1st	A v E	Sydney	2002-03
M. J. Prior	**118**	**5ct**	**E v A**	**Sydney**	**2010-11**

100 RUNS AND TEN WICKETS IN A TEST

A. K. Davidson	44 80	5-135 6-87 }	A v WI.........	Brisbane........... }	1960-61
I. T. Botham	114	6-58 7-48 }	E v I...........	Bombay.......... }	1979-80
Imran Khan	117	6-98 5-82 }	P v I...........	Faisalabad......... }	1982-83

2,000 RUNS AND 200 WICKETS

	Tests	Runs	Wkts	Tests for 1,000/100 Double
R. Benaud (Australia)	63	2,201	248	32
†I. T. Botham (England)	102	5,200	383	21
C. L. Cairns (New Zealand)	62	3,320	218	33
A. Flintoff (England/World)	79	3,845	226	43
R. J. Hadlee (New Zealand)............	86	3,124	431	28
Harbhajan Singh (India).............	**93**	**2,008**	**343**	**93**
Imran Khan (Pakistan)	88	3,807	362	30
†**J. H. Kallis (South Africa/World)**.....	**145**	**11,947**	**270**	**53**
Kapil Dev (India).....................	131	5,248	434	25
A. Kumble (India)	132	2,506	619	56
S. M. Pollock (South Africa)	108	3,781	421	26
†G. S. Sobers (West Indies).............	93	8,032	235	48
W. P. U. J. C. Vaas (Sri Lanka)	111	3,089	355	47
D. L. Vettori (New Zealand/World)	**105**	**4,167**	**345**	**47**
S. K. Warne (Australia)	145	3,154	708	58
Wasim Akram (Pakistan)	104	2,898	414	45

Note: H. H. Streak scored 1,990 runs and took 216 wickets in 65 Tests for Zimbabwe.

† *J. H. Kallis has also taken 166 catches, S. K. Warne 125, I. T. Botham 120 and G. S. Sobers 109.*
These four and C. L. Hooper (5,762 runs, 114 wickets and 115 catches for West Indies) are the only
players to have achieved the treble of 1,000 runs, 100 wickets and 100 catches in Test cricket.

WICKETKEEPING RECORDS

MOST DISMISSALS IN AN INNINGS

7 (all ct)	Wasim Bari.........	Pakistan v New Zealand at Auckland	1978-79
7 (all ct)	R. W. Taylor.........	England v India at Bombay...............	1979-80
7 (all ct)	I. D. S. Smith........	New Zealand v Sri Lanka at Hamilton	1990-91
7 (all ct)	R. D. Jacobs.........	West Indies v Australia at Melbourne......	2000-01
6 (all ct)	A. T. W. Grout	Australia v South Africa at Johannesburg ...	1957-58
6 (all ct)	D. T. Lindsay	South Africa v Australia at Johannesburg ...	1966-67
6 (all ct)	J. T. Murray	England v India at Lord's	1967
6 (5ct, 1st)	S. M. H. Kirmani	India v New Zealand at Christchurch	1975-76
6 (all ct)	R. W. Marsh	Australia v England at Brisbane	1982-83
6 (all ct)	S. A. R. Silva	Sri Lanka v India at Colombo (SSC).......	1985-86
6 (all ct)	R. C. Russell.........	England v Australia at Melbourne........	1990-91
6 (all ct)	R. C. Russell.........	England v South Africa at Johannesburg ...	1995-96
6 (all ct)	I. A. Healy	Australia v England at Birmingham	1997
6 (all ct)	A. J. Stewart........	England v Australia at Manchester	1997
6 (all ct)	M. V. Boucher	South Africa v Pakistan at Port Elizabeth ...	1997-98
6 (all ct)	Rashid Latif	Pakistan v Zimbabwe at Bulawayo	1997-98
6 (all ct)	M. V. Boucher	South Africa v Sri Lanka at Cape Town	1997-98
6 (5ct, 1st)	†C. M. W. Read	England v New Zealand at Birmingham	1999
6 (all ct)	M. V. Boucher	South Africa v Zimbabwe at Centurion.....	2004-05

6 (all ct)	G. O. Jones	England v Bangladesh at Chester-le-Street. .	2005
6 (all ct)	C. M. W. Read	England v Australia at Melbourne.	2006-07
6 (5ct, 1st)	C. M. W. Read	England v Australia at Sydney	2006-07
6 (all ct)	M. S. Dhoni	India v New Zealand at Wellington.	2008-09
6 (all ct)	**Adnan Akmal**	**Pakistan v New Zealand at Wellington** . . .	**2010-11**
6 (all ct)	**M. J. Prior**	**England v Australia at Sydney**	**2010-11**

† *On debut.*

MOST STUMPINGS IN AN INNINGS

| 5 | K. S. More . . . . | India v West Indies at Madras . . . . | 1987-88 |

MOST DISMISSALS IN A TEST

11 (all ct)	R. C. Russell.	England v South Africa at Johannesburg . . .	1995-96
10 (all ct)	R. W. Taylor.	England v India at Bombay	1979-80
10 (all ct)	A. C. Gilchrist	Australia v New Zealand at Hamilton	1999-2000
9 (8ct, 1st)	G. R. A. Langley	Australia v England at Lord's	1956
9 (all ct)	D. A. Murray	West Indies v Australia at Melbourne	1981-82
9 (all ct)	R. W. Marsh	Australia v England at Brisbane	1982-83
9 (all ct)	S. A. R. Silva	Sri Lanka v India at Colombo (SSC).	1985-86
9 (8ct, 1st)	S. A. R. Silva	Sri Lanka v India at Colombo (PSS)	1985-86
9 (all ct)	D. J. Richardson	South Africa v India at Port Elizabeth.	1992-93
9 (all ct)	Rashid Latif	Pakistan v New Zealand at Auckland	1993-94
9 (all ct)	I. A. Healy	Australia v England at Brisbane	1994-95
9 (all ct)	C. O. Browne	West Indies v England at Nottingham.	1995
9 (7ct, 2st)	R. C. Russell.	England v South Africa at Port Elizabeth . . .	1995-96
9 (8ct, 1st)	M. V. Boucher	South Africa v Pakistan at Port Elizabeth . . .	1997-98
9 (8ct, 1st)	R. D. Jacobs	West Indies v Australia at Melbourne	2000-01
9 (all ct)	Kamran Akmal	Pakistan v West Indies at Kingston	2004-05
9 (all ct)	G. O. Jones	England v Bangladesh at Chester-le-Street. .	2005
9 (8ct, 1st)	A. C. Gilchrist	Australia v England at Sydney	2006-07
9 (8ct, 1st)	B. B. McCullum	New Zealand v Pakistan at Napier	2009-10
9 (all ct)	**B. J. Haddin**	**Australia v Pakistan at Sydney**	**2009-10**
9 (all ct)	**M. V. Boucher**.	**South Africa v India at Durban**	**2010-11**

Notes: S. A. R. Silva made 18 dismissals in two successive Tests.

The most stumpings in a match is 6 by K. S. More for India v West Indies at Madras in 1987-88.

J. J. Kelly (8ct) for Australia v England in 1901-02 and L. E. G. Ames (6ct, 2st) for England v West Indies in 1933 were the only wicketkeepers to make eight dismissals in a Test before World War II.

MOST DISMISSALS IN A SERIES

(Played in 5 Tests unless otherwise stated)

28 (all ct)	R. W. Marsh	Australia v England	1982-83
27 (25ct, 2st)	R. C. Russell	England v South Africa	1995-96
27 (25ct, 2st)	I. A. Healy	Australia v England (6 Tests)	1997
26 (23ct, 3st)	J. H. B. Waite	South Africa v New Zealand	1961-62
26 (all ct)	R. W. Marsh	Australia v West Indies (6 Tests).	1975-76
26 (21ct, 5st)	I. A. Healy	Australia v England (6 Tests)	1993
26 (25ct, 1st)	M. V. Boucher	South Africa v England	1998
26 (24ct, 2st)	A. C. Gilchrist	Australia v England.	2001
26 (24ct, 2st)	A. C. Gilchrist	Australia v England.	2006-07
25 (23ct, 2st)	I. A. Healy	Australia v England.	1994-95
25 (23ct, 2st)	A. C. Gilchrist	Australia v England.	2002-03
25 (all ct)	A. C. Gilchrist	Australia v India	2007-08

Notes: S. A. R. Silva made 22 dismissals (21ct, 1st) in three Tests for Sri Lanka v India in 1985-86.

H. Strudwick, with 21 (15ct, 6st) for England v South Africa in 1913-14, was the only wicketkeeper to make as many as 20 dismissals in a series before World War II.

150 DISMISSALS

		T	Ct	St
1	**M. V. Boucher (South Africa/World)**	**521**	**139**	**499**	**22**
2	A. C. Gilchrist (Australia).	416	96	379	37
3	I. A. Healy (Australia).	395	119	366	29
4	R. W. Marsh (Australia).	355	96	343	12
5	P. J. L. Dujon (West Indies)	270	79	265	5
6	A. P. E. Knott (England).	269	95	250	19
7	A. J. Stewart (England).	241	82	227	14
8	Wasim Bari (Pakistan)	228	81	201	27
9	R. D. Jacobs (West Indies)	219	65	207	12
	T. G. Evans (England).	219	91	173	46
11	**Kamran Akmal (Pakistan)**.	**206**	**53**	**184**	**22**
12	A. C. Parore (New Zealand)	201	67	194	7
13	S. M. H. Kirmani (India).	198	88	160	38
14	D. L. Murray (West Indies)	189	62	181	8
15	A. T. W. Grout (Australia).	187	51	163	24
16	I. D. S. Smith (New Zealand)	176	63	168	8
17	R. W. Taylor (England).	174	57	167	7
18	**M. S. Dhoni (India)**	**173**	**54**	**148**	**25**
19	**B. B. McCullum (New Zealand)**.	**172**	**51**	**161**	**11**
20	R. C. Russell (England).	165	54	153	12
21	D. J. Richardson (South Africa)	152	42	150	2
22	**K. C. Sangakkara (Sri Lanka)**	**151**	**48**	**131**	**20**
	A. Flower (Zimbabwe)	151	55	142	9

Notes: The record for P. J. L. Dujon excludes two catches taken in two Tests when not keeping wicket; A. J. Stewart's record likewise excludes 36 catches in 51 Tests, A. C. Parore's three in 11 Tests, B. B. McCullum's six in six Tests and A. Flower's nine in eight Tests. K. C. Sangakkara's record excludes 32 catches taken in 46 matches when not keeping wicket but includes two catches taken as wicketkeeper in a match where he took over when the designated keeper was injured.

Excluding the Super Series Test, **M. V. Boucher** has made **519** dismissals (497ct, 22st in 138 Tests) for South Africa, a national record. The most wicketkeeping dismissals for Bangladesh is 87 (Khaled Mashud 78ct, 9st in 44 Tests).

W. A. Oldfield made 52 stumpings, a Test record, in 54 Tests for Australia; he also took 78 catches.

FIELDING RECORDS

(Excluding wicketkeepers)

MOST CATCHES IN AN INNINGS

5	V. Y. Richardson	Australia v South Africa at Durban	1935-36
5	Yajurvindra Singh	India v England at Bangalore.	1976-77
5	M. Azharuddin.	India v Pakistan at Karachi	1989-90
5	K. Srikkanth.	India v Australia at Perth	1991-92
5	S. P. Fleming	New Zealand v Zimbabwe at Harare	1997-98

MOST CATCHES IN A TEST

7	G. S. Chappell	Australia v England at Perth.	1974-75
7	Yajurvindra Singh	India v England at Bangalore.	1976-77
7	H. P. Tillekeratne.	Sri Lanka v New Zealand at Colombo (SSC) .	1992-93
7	S. P. Fleming	New Zealand v Zimbabwe at Harare	1997-98
7	M. L. Hayden.	Australia v Sri Lanka at Galle	2003-04

Note: There have been **25** instances of players taking six catches in a Test, the most recent being A. N. Cook for England v New Zealand at Hamilton, 2007-08.

MOST CATCHES IN A SERIES

(Played in 5 Tests unless otherwise stated)

15	J. M. Gregory	Australia v England	1920-21
14	G. S. Chappell	Australia v England (6 Tests)	1974-75
13	R. B. Simpson	Australia v South Africa	1957-58
13	R. B. Simpson	Australia v West Indies	1960-61
13	B. C. Lara	West Indies v England (6 Tests)	1997-98
13	R. Dravid	India v Australia (4 Tests)	2004-05
13	B. C. Lara	West Indies v India (4 Tests)	2005-06

100 CATCHES

Ct	T		Ct	T	
200	**150†**	**R. Dravid (India/World)**	120	102	I. T. Botham (England)
181	128	M. E. Waugh (Australia)	120	114	M. C. Cowdrey (England)
178	**152**	**R. T. Ponting (Australia)**	**119**	**91†**	**G. C. Smith (SA/World)**
171	111	S. P. Fleming (New Zealand)	115	102	C. L. Hooper (West Indies)
166	**145†**	**J. H. Kallis (SA/World)**	112	168	S. R. Waugh (Australia)
165	**116**	**D. P. M. D. Jayawardene (SL)**	110	62	R. B. Simpson (Australia)
164	131†	B. C. Lara (West Indies/World)	110	85	W. R. Hammond (England)
157	104	M. A. Taylor (Australia)	109	93	G. S. Sobers (West Indies)
156	156	A. R. Border (Australia)	108	125	S. M. Gavaskar (India)
128	103	M. L. Hayden (Australia)	**106**	**177**	**S. R. Tendulkar (India)**
125	145	S. K. Warne (Australia)	105	75	I. M. Chappell (Australia)
122	87	G. S. Chappell (Australia)	105	99	M. Azharuddin (India)
122	**120**	**V. V. S. Laxman (India)**	105	100	G. P. Thorpe (England)
122	121	I. V. A. Richards (West Indies)	103	118	G. A. Gooch (England)

† *Excluding the Super Series Test, Dravid has made 199 catches in 149 Tests for India, Lara 164 in 130 Tests for West Indies, and Kallis 162 in 144 Tests for South Africa, all national records. G. C. Smith has made 116 catches in 90 Tests for South Africa.*

Note: The most catches in the field for other countries are Pakistan 93 in 124 Tests (Javed Miandad); Zimbabwe 60 in 60 Tests (A. D. R. Campbell); Bangladesh **24** in 55 Tests (**Mohammad Ashraful**).

TEAM RECORDS

HIGHEST INNINGS TOTALS

952-6 dec	Sri Lanka v India at Colombo (RPS)	1997-98
903-7 dec	England v Australia at The Oval	1938
849	England v West Indies at Kingston	1929-30
790-3 dec	West Indies v Pakistan at Kingston	1957-58
765-6 dec	Pakistan v Sri Lanka at Karachi	2008-09
760-7 dec	Sri Lanka v India at Ahmedabad	2009-10
758-8 dec	Australia v West Indies at Kingston	1954-55
756-5 dec	Sri Lanka v South Africa at Colombo (SSC)	2006
751-5 dec	West Indies v England at St John's	2003-04
749-9 dec	West Indies v England at Bridgetown	2008-09
747	West Indies v South Africa at St John's	2004-05
735-6 dec	Australia v Zimbabwe at Perth	2003-04
729-6 dec	Australia v England at Lord's	1930
726-9 dec	India v Sri Lanka at Mumbai (BS)	2009-10
713-3 dec	Sri Lanka v Zimbabwe at Bulawayo	2003-04
708	Pakistan v England at The Oval	1987
707	**India v Sri Lanka at Colombo (SSC)**	**2010**
705-7 dec	India v Australia at Sydney	2003-04

701	Australia v England at The Oval..................................	1934
699-5	Pakistan v India at Lahore.....................................	1989-90
695	Australia v England at The Oval..................................	1930
692-8 dec	West Indies v England at The Oval................................	1995
687-8 dec	West Indies v England at The Oval................................	1976
682-6 dec	South Africa v England at Lord's.................................	2003
681-8 dec	West Indies v England at Port-of-Spain............................	1953-54

The highest innings for the countries not mentioned above are:

671-4	New Zealand v Sri Lanka at Wellington............................	1990-91
563-9 dec	Zimbabwe v West Indies at Harare...............................	2001
488	Bangladesh v Zimbabwe at Chittagong............................	2004-05

HIGHEST FOURTH-INNINGS TOTALS

To win

418-7	West Indies (needing 418) v Australia at St John's.................	2002-03
414-4	South Africa (needing 414) v Australia at Perth....................	2008-09
406-4	India (needing 403) v West Indies at Port-of-Spain.................	1975-76
404-3	Australia (needing 404) v England at Leeds.......................	1948
387-4	India (needing 387) v England at Chennai.........................	2008-09
369-6	Australia (needing 369) v Pakistan at Hobart......................	1999-2000
362-7	Australia (needing 359) v West Indies at Georgetown...............	1977-78
352-9	Sri Lanka (needing 352) v South Africa at Colombo (PSS)...........	2006
348-5	West Indies (needing 345) v New Zealand at Auckland..............	1968-69
344-1	West Indies (needing 342) v England at Lord's.....................	1984

To tie

347	India v Australia at Madras....................................	1986-87

To draw

654-5	England (needing 696 to win) v South Africa at Durban..............	1938-39
429-8	India (needing 438 to win) v England at The Oval..................	1979
423-7	South Africa (needing 451 to win) v England at The Oval............	1947
408-5	West Indies (needing 836 to win) v England at Kingston.............	1929-30

To lose

451	New Zealand (lost by 98 runs) v England at Christchurch............	2001-02
445	India (lost by 47 runs) v Australia at Adelaide....................	1977-78
440	New Zealand (lost by 38 runs) v England at Nottingham.............	1973
431	New Zealand (lost by 121 runs) v England at Napier................	2007-08
417	England (lost by 45 runs) v Australia at Melbourne.................	1976-77
413	Bangladesh (lost by 107 runs) v Sri Lanka at Mirpur...............	2008-09
411	England (lost by 193 runs) v Australia at Sydney..................	1924-25
410	Sri Lanka (lost by 96 runs) v Australia at Hobart..................	2007-08
406	Australia (lost by 115 runs) v England at Lord's..................	2009
402	Australia (lost by 103 runs) v England at Manchester..............	1981

MOST RUNS IN A DAY (BOTH SIDES)

588	England (398-6), India (190-0) at Manchester (2nd day).............	1936
522	England (503-2), South Africa (19-0) at Lord's (2nd day)...........	1924
509	Sri Lanka (509-9) v Bangladesh at Colombo (PSS) (2nd day)........	2002
508	England (221-2), South Africa (287-6) at The Oval (3rd day)........	1935

MOST RUNS IN A DAY (ONE SIDE)

509	Sri Lanka (509-9) v Bangladesh at Colombo (PSS) (2nd day)	2002
503	England (503-2) v South Africa at Lord's (2nd day)	1924
494	Australia (494-6) v South Africa at Sydney (1st day)	1910-11
475	Australia (475-2) v England at The Oval (1st day)	1934
471	England (471-8) v India at The Oval (1st day)	1936
458	Australia (458-3) v England at Leeds (1st day)	1930
455	Australia (455-1) v England at Leeds (2nd day)	1934
452	New Zealand (452-9 dec) v Zimbabwe at Harare (1st day)	2005-06
450	Australia (450) v South Africa at Johannesburg (1st day)	1921-22

MOST WICKETS IN A DAY

27	England (18-3 to 53 all out and 62) v Australia (60) at Lord's (2nd day)	1888
25	Australia (112 and 48-5) v England (61) at Melbourne (1st day)	1901-02

HIGHEST AGGREGATES IN A TEST

Runs	Wkts			Days played
1,981	35	South Africa v England at Durban	1938-39	10†
1,815	34	West Indies v England at Kingston	1929-30	9‡
1,764	39	Australia v West Indies at Adelaide	1968-69	5
1,753	40	Australia v England at Adelaide	1920-21	6
1,747	25	Australia v India at Sydney	2003-04	5
1,723	31	England v Australia at Leeds	1948	5
1,702	28	Pakistan v India at Faisalabad	2005-06	5

† *No play on one day.*   ‡ *No play on two days.*

LOWEST INNINGS TOTALS

26	New Zealand v England at Auckland	1954-55
30	South Africa v England at Port Elizabeth	1895-96
30	South Africa v England at Birmingham	1924
35	South Africa v England at Cape Town	1898-99
36	Australia v England at Birmingham	1902
36	South Africa v Australia at Melbourne	1931-32
42	Australia v England at Sydney	1887-88
42	New Zealand v Australia at Wellington	1945-46
42†	India v England at Lord's	1974
43	South Africa v England at Cape Town	1888-89
44	Australia v England at The Oval	1896
45	England v Australia at Sydney	1886-87
45	South Africa v Australia at Melbourne	1931-32
46	England v West Indies at Port-of-Spain	1993-94
47	South Africa v England at Cape Town	1888-89
47	New Zealand v England at Lord's	1958
47	West Indies v England at Kingston	2003-04

The lowest innings for the countries not mentioned above are:

53†	Pakistan v Australia at Sharjah	2002-03
54	Zimbabwe v South Africa at Cape Town	2004-05
62	Bangladesh v Sri Lanka at Colombo (PSS)	2007
71	Sri Lanka v Pakistan at Kandy	1994-95

† *Batted one man short.*

FEWEST RUNS IN A FULL DAY'S PLAY

95	Australia (80), Pakistan (15-2) at Karachi (1st day, 5½ hours)	1956-57
104	Pakistan (0-0 to 104-5) v Australia at Karachi (4th day, 5½ hours)..........	1959-60
106	England (92-2 to 198) v Australia at Brisbane (4th day, 5 hours)............	1958-59
	England were dismissed five minutes before the close of play, leaving no time for Australia to start their second innings.	
111	South Africa (48-2 to 130-6 dec), India (29-1) at Cape Town (5th day, 5½ hours)..	1992-93
112	Australia (138-6 to 187), Pakistan (63-1) at Karachi (4th day, 5½ hours)	1956-57
115	Australia (116-7 to 165 and 66-5 after following on) v Pakistan at Karachi (4th day, 5½ hours)	1988-89
117	India (117-5) v Australia at Madras (1st day, 5½ hours)	1956-57
117	New Zealand (6-0 to 123-4) v Sri Lanka at Colombo (SSC) (5th day, 5¾ hours)..	1983-84

In England

151	England (175-2 to 289), New Zealand (37-7) at Lord's (3rd day, 6 hours)	1978
158	England (211-2 to 369-9) v South Africa at Manchester (5th day, 6 hours)....	1998
159	Pakistan (208-4 to 350), England (17-1) at Leeds (3rd day, 6 hours).........	1971

LOWEST AGGREGATES IN A COMPLETED TEST

Runs	Wkts			Days played
234	29	Australia v South Africa at Melbourne	1931-32	3†
291	40	England v Australia at Lord's	1888	2
295	28	New Zealand v Australia at Wellington	1945-46	2
309	29	West Indies v England at Bridgetown	1934-35	3
323	30	England v Australia at Manchester	1888	2

† *No play on one day.*

LARGEST VICTORIES

Largest Innings Victories

Inns & 579 runs	England (903-7 dec) v Australia (201 & 123‡) at The Oval	1938
Inns & 360 runs	Australia (652-7 dec) v South Africa (159 & 133) at Johannesburg ..	2001-02
Inns & 336 runs	West Indies (614-5 dec) v India (124 & 154) at Calcutta...........	1958-59
Inns & 332 runs	Australia (645) v England (141 & 172) at Brisbane...............	1946-47
Inns & 324 runs	Pakistan (643) v New Zealand (73 & 246) at Lahore.............	2002
Inns & 322 runs	West Indies (660-5 dec) v New Zealand (216 & 122) at Wellington..	1994-95
Inns & 310 runs	West Indies (536) v Bangladesh (139 & 87) at Dhaka.............	2002-03
Inns & 294 runs	New Zealand (452-9 dec) v Zimbabwe (59 & 99) at Harare	2005-06
Inns & 285 runs	England (629) v India (302 & 42†) at Lord's.....................	1974
Inns & 264 runs	Pakistan (546-3 dec) v Bangladesh (134 & 148) at Multan........	2001-02
Inns & 261 runs	England (528-3 dec) v Bangladesh (108 & 159) at Lord's.........	2005
Inns & 259 runs	Australia (549-7 dec) v South Africa (158 & 132) at Port Elizabeth ..	1949-50
Inns & 254 runs	Sri Lanka (713-3 dec) v Zimbabwe (228 & 231) at Bulawayo	2003-04

‡ *Two men absent in both Australian innings.*   † *One man absent in India's second innings.*

Largest Victories by Runs Margin

675 runs	England (521 & 342-8 dec) v Australia (122 & 66†) at Brisbane............	1928-29
562 runs	Australia (701 & 327) v England (321 & 145‡) at The Oval	1934
530 runs	Australia (328 & 578) v South Africa (205 & 171§) at Melbourne	1910-11
491 runs	Australia (381 & 361-5 dec) v Pakistan (179 & 72) at Perth...............	2004-05
465 runs	Sri Lanka (384 and 447-6 dec) v Bangladesh (208 and 158) at Chittagong ...	2008-09
425 runs	West Indies (211 & 411-5 dec) v England (71 & 126) at Manchester	1976
409 runs	Australia (350 & 460-7 dec) v England (215 & 186) at Lord's.............	1948
408 runs	West Indies (328 & 448) v Australia (203 & 165) at Adelaide.............	1979-80
384 runs	Australia (492 & 296-5 dec) v England (325 & 79) at Brisbane...........	2002-03
382 runs	Australia (238 & 411) v England (124 & 143) at Adelaide................	1894-95
382 runs	Australia (619 & 394-8 dec) v West Indies (279 & 352) at Sydney	1968-69
379 runs	Australia (435 & 283-2 dec) v West Indies (210 & 129) at Brisbane	2005-06

† *One man absent in Australia's first innings; two men absent in their second.*
‡ *Two men absent in England's first innings; one man absent in their second.*
§ *One man absent in South Africa's second innings.*

TIED TESTS

West Indies (453 & 284) v Australia (505 & 232) at Brisbane	1960-61
Australia (574-7 dec & 170-5 dec) v India (397 & 347) at Madras...................	1986-87

MOST CONSECUTIVE TEST VICTORIES

16	Australia............	1999-00–2000-01	
16	Australia............	2005-06–2007-08	
11	West Indies.........	1983-84–1984-85	
9	Sri Lanka	2001–2001-02	
9	South Africa........	2001-02–2003	
8	Australia............	1920-21–1921	

8	England	2004–2004-05
7	England	1884-85–1887-88
7	England	1928–1928-29
7	West Indies.........	1984-85–1985-86
7	West Indies.........	1988–1988-89
7	Australia............	2002-03

MOST CONSECUTIVE TESTS WITHOUT VICTORY

44	New Zealand	1929-30–1955-56	
34	Bangladesh.........	2000-01–2004-05	
31	India.............	1981-82–1984-85	
28	South Africa........	1935–1949-50	
24	India	1932–1951-52	
24	Bangladesh.........	2004-05–2008-09	

23	New Zealand	1962-63–1967-68
22	Pakistan	1958-59–1964-65
21	Sri Lanka	1985-86–1992-93
20	West Indies.........	1968-69–1972-73
20	West Indies.........	2004-05–2007

WHITEWASHES

Teams winning every game in a series of four Tests or more:

Five-Test Series

Australia beat England	1920-21	West Indies beat England	1985-86
Australia beat South Africa........	1931-32	South Africa beat West Indies	1998-99
England beat India	1959	Australia beat West Indies	2000-01
West Indies beat India.............	1961-62	Australia beat England	2006-07
West Indies beat England	1984		

Four-Test Series

Australia beat India. 1967-68   England beat West Indies 2004
South Africa beat Australia. 1969-70

Note: The winning team in each instance was at home, except for West Indies in England, 1984.

PLAYERS

YOUNGEST TEST PLAYERS

Years	Days			
15	124	Mushtaq Mohammad	Pakistan v West Indies at Lahore	1958-59
15	128	Mohammad Sharif	Bangladesh v Zimbabwe at Bulawayo	2000-01
16	189	Aqib Javed	Pakistan v New Zealand at Wellington.	1988-89
16	205	S. R. Tendulkar.	India v Pakistan at Karachi	1989-90

The above table should be treated with caution. All birthdates for Bangladesh and Pakistan (after Partition) must be regarded as questionable because of deficiencies in record-keeping. Hasan Raza was claimed to be 14 years 227 days old when he played for Pakistan against Zimbabwe at Faisalabad in 1996-97; this age was rejected by the Pakistan Cricket Board, although no alternative has been offered. Suggestions that Enamul Haque jun. was 16 years 230 days old when he played for Bangladesh against England in Dhaka in 2003-04 have been discounted by well-informed local observers, who believe he was 18.

The youngest Test players for countries not mentioned above are:

Years	Days			
17	122	J. E. D. Sealy.	West Indies v England at Bridgetown	1929-30
17	189	C. D. U. S. Weerasinghe .	Sri Lanka v India at Colombo (PSS).	1985-86
17	239	I. D. Craig.	Australia v South Africa at Melbourne	1952-53
17	352	H. Masakadza	Zimbabwe v West Indies at Harare.	2001
18	10	D. L. Vettori	New Zealand v England at Wellington.	1996-97
18	149	D. B. Close	England v New Zealand at Manchester	1949
18	340	P. R. Adams	South Africa v England at Port Elizabeth	1995-96

OLDEST PLAYERS ON TEST DEBUT

Years	Days			
49	119	J. Southerton.	England v Australia at Melbourne	1876-77
47	284	Miran Bux.	Pakistan v India at Lahore	1954-55
46	253	D. D. Blackie	Australia v England at Sydney	1928-29
46	237	H. Ironmonger.	Australia v England at Brisbane	1928-29
42	242	N. Betancourt	West Indies v England at Port-of-Spain	1929-30
41	337	E. R. Wilson	England v Australia at Sydney	1920-21
41	27	R. J. D. Jamshedji	India v England at Bombay	1933-34
40	345	C. A. Wiles	West Indies v England at Manchester.	1933
40	295	O. Henry	South Africa v India at Durban	1992-93
40	216	S. P. Kinneir	England v Australia at Sydney	1911-12
40	110	H. W. Lee	England v South Africa at Johannesburg	1930-31
40	56	G. W. A. Chubb	South Africa v England at Nottingham.	1951
40	37	C. Ramaswami	India v England at Manchester	1936

Note: The oldest Test player on debut for New Zealand was H. M. McGirr, 38 years 101 days, v England at Auckland, 1929-30; for Sri Lanka, D. S. de Silva, 39 years 251 days, v England at Colombo (PSS), 1981-82; for Zimbabwe, A. C. Waller, 37 years 84 days, v England at Bulawayo, 1996-97; for Bangladesh, Enamul Haque sen. 35 years 58 days, v Zimbabwe at Harare, 2000-01. A. J. Traicos was 45 years 154 days old when he made his debut for Zimbabwe (v India at Harare, 1992-93) having played three Tests for South Africa in 1969-70.

OLDEST TEST PLAYERS

(Age on final day of their last Test match)

Years	Days			
52	165	W. Rhodes	England v West Indies at Kingston	1929-30
50	327	H. Ironmonger	Australia v England at Sydney	1932-33
50	320	W. G. Grace	England v Australia at Nottingham	1899
50	303	G. Gunn	England v West Indies at Kingston	1929-30
49	139	J. Southerton	England v Australia at Melbourne	1876-77
47	302	Miran Bux	Pakistan v India at Peshawar	1954-55
47	249	J. B. Hobbs	England v Australia at The Oval	1930
47	87	F. E. Woolley	England v Australia at The Oval	1934
46	309	D. D. Blackie	Australia v England at Adelaide	1928-29
46	206	A. W. Nourse	South Africa v England at The Oval	1924
46	202	H. Strudwick	England v Australia at The Oval	1926
46	41	E. H. Hendren	England v West Indies at Kingston	1934-35
45	304	A. J. Traicos	Zimbabwe v India at Delhi	1992-93
45	245	G. O. B. Allen	England v West Indies at Kingston	1947-48
45	215	P. Holmes	England v India at Lord's	1932
45	140	D. B. Close	England v West Indies at Manchester	1976

MOST TEST APPEARANCES

177	**S. R. Tendulkar (India)**		132	C. A. Walsh (West Indies)
168	S. R. Waugh (Australia)		131	Kapil Dev (India)
156	A. R. Border (Australia)		131	B. C. Lara (West Indies/World)
152	**R. T. Ponting (Australia)**		**129**	**S. Chanderpaul (West Indies)**
150	**R. Dravid (India/World)**		128	M. E. Waugh (Australia)
145	**J. H. Kallis (South Africa/World)**		125	S. M. Gavaskar (India)
145	S. K. Warne (Australia)		124	Javed Miandad (Pakistan)
139	**M. V. Boucher (South Africa/World)**		124	G. D. McGrath (Australia)
133	**M. Muralitharan (Sri Lanka/World)**		121	I. V. A. Richards (West Indies)
133	A. J. Stewart (England)		120	Inzamam-ul-Haq (Pakistan/World)
132	A. Kumble (India)		**120**	**V. V. S. Laxman (India)**

Note: Excluding the Super Series Test, **J. H. Kallis** has made **144** appearances for South Africa and **M. Muralitharan 132** for Sri Lanka, both national records. The most appearances for New Zealand is 111 by S. P. Fleming; for Zimbabwe, 67 by G. W. Flower; and for Bangladesh **55** by **Mohammad Ashraful**.

MOST CONSECUTIVE TEST APPEARANCES FOR A COUNTRY

153	A. R. Border (Australia)	March 1979 to March 1994
107	M. E. Waugh (Australia)	June 1993 to October 2002
106	S. M. Gavaskar (India)	January 1975 to February 1987
96†	A. C. Gilchrist (Australia)	November 1999 to January 2008
93	R. Dravid (India)	June 1996 to December 2005
87	G. R. Viswanath (India)	March 1971 to February 1983
86	M. L. Hayden (Australia)	March 2000 to January 2008
85	G. S. Sobers (West Indies)	April 1955 to April 1972
84	S. R. Tendulkar (India)	November 1989 to June 2001
75	M. V. Boucher (South Africa)	February 1998 to August 2004
73	**R. T. Ponting (Australia)**	**November 2004 to December 2010**
72	S. P. Fleming (New Zealand)	July 1999 to March 2008
72	D. L. Haynes (West Indies)	December 1979 to June 1988
71	I. M. Chappell (Australia)	January 1966 to February 1976
71	**D. P. M. D. Jayawardene (Sri Lanka)**	**November 2002 to December 2010**
69	M. Azharuddin (India)	April 1989 to February 1999
66	**A. B. de Villiers (South Africa)**	**December 2004 to January 2011**

66	Kapil Dev (India).	October 1978 to December 1984
65	I. T. Botham (England)	February 1978 to March 1984
65	Kapil Dev (India).	January 1985 to March 1994
65	A. P. E. Knott (England)	March 1971 to August 1977

The most consecutive Test appearances for the countries not mentioned above are:

56	A. D. R. Campbell (Zimbabwe).	October 1992 to September 2001
53	Javed Miandad (Pakistan)	December 1977 to January 1984
38	**Mohammad Ashraful (Bangladesh)**	**February 2004 to February 2010**

† *Complete Test career.*

Bold type denotes sequence which was still in progress after January 1, 2010.

MOST TESTS AS CAPTAIN

	P	W	L	D		P	W	L	D
A. R. Border (A)	93	32	22	38*	P. B. H. May (E)	41	20	10	11
G. C. Smith (SA/World)	**83**	**38**	**24†**	**21**	Nawab of Pataudi jun. (I)	40	9	19	12
S. P. Fleming (NZ)	80	28	27	25	R. B. Simpson (A)	39	12	12	15
R. T. Ponting (A)	**77**	**48**	**16**	**13**	G. S. Sobers (WI)	39	9	10	20
C. H. Lloyd (WI)	74	36	12	26	S. T. Jayasuriya (SL)	38	18	12	8
S. R. Waugh (A)	57	41	9	7	Javed Miandad (P)	34	14	6	14
A. Ranatunga (SL)	56	12	19	25	G. A. Gooch (E)	34	10	12	12
M. A. Atherton (E)	54	13	21	20	Kapil Dev (I)	34	4	7	22*
W. J. Cronje (SA)	53	27	11	15	J. R. Reid (NZ)	34	3	18	13
M. P. Vaughan (E)	51	26	11	14	**A. J. Strauss (E)**	**32**	**16**	**5**	**11**
I. V. A. Richards (WI)	50	27	8	15	**D. L. Vettori (NZ)**	**32**	**6**	**16**	**10**
M. A. Taylor (A)	50	26	13	11	D. I. Gower (E)	32	5	18	9
S. C. Ganguly (I)	49	21	13	15	J. M. Brearley (E)	31	18	4	9
G. S. Chappell (A)	48	21	13	14	R. Illingworth (E)	31	12	5	14
Imran Khan (P)	48	14	8	26	Inzamam-ul-Haq (P)	31	11	11	9
M. Azharuddin (I)	47	14	14	19	I. M. Chappell (A)	30	15	5	10
B. C. Lara (WI)	47	10	26	11	G. P. Howarth (NZ)	30	11	7	12
S. M. Gavaskar (I)	47	9	8	30	E. R. Dexter (E)	30	9	7	14
N. Hussain (E)	45	17	15	13					

* *One match tied.*
† *Includes defeat as World XI captain in Super Series Test against Australia.*

Most Tests as captain of other countries:

	P	W	L	D
A. D. R. Campbell (Z)	21	2	12	7
Habibul Bashar (B)	18	1	13	4

Notes: A. R. Border captained Australia in 93 consecutive Tests.

W. W. Armstrong (Australia) captained his country in the most Tests without being defeated: ten matches with eight wins and two draws.

I. T. Botham (England) captained his country in 12 Tests without ever winning: eight draws and four defeats.

UMPIRES

MOST TESTS

		First Test	*Last Test*
128	S. A. Bucknor (West Indies)	1988-89	2008-09
109	**R. E. Koertzen (South Africa)**	**1992-93**	**2010**
94	**D. J. Harper (Australia)**	**1998-99**	**2010-11**
92	D. R. Shepherd (England)	1985	2004-05
78	D. B. Hair (Australia)	1991-92	2008

		First Test	*Last Test*
73	S. Venkataraghavan (India)	1992-93	2003-04
67	**S. J. A. Taufel (Australia)**	**2000-01**	**2010-11**
66	H. D. Bird (England)	1973	1996
65	**B. F. Bowden (New Zealand)**	**1999-2000**	**2010-11**
63	**Aleem Dar (Pakistan)**	**2003-04**	**2010-11**
48	F. Chester (England)	1924	1955
48	**E. A. R. de Silva (Sri Lanka)**	**2000**	**2010-11**
44	D. L. Orchard (South Africa)	1995-96	2003-04
44	R. B. Tiffin (Zimbabwe)	1995-96	2008-09
42	C. S. Elliott (England)	1957	1974
39	R. S. Dunne (New Zealand)	1988-89	2001-02
36	D. J. Constant (England)	1971	1988
36	S. G. Randell (Australia)	1984-85	1997-98
35	**Asad Rauf (Pakistan)**	**2004-05**	**2010-11**
34	Khizar Hayat (Pakistan)	1979-80	1996-97
33	J. S. Buller (England)	1956	1969
33	A. R. Crafter (Australia)	1978-79	1991-92
32	R. W. Crockett (Australia)	1901-02	1924-25
31	**S. J. Davis (Australia)**	**1997-98**	**2010-11**
31	**B. R. Doctrove (West Indies)**	**1999-2000**	**2010-11**
31	D. Sang Hue (West Indies)	1961-62	1980-81

SUMMARY OF TESTS

To January 19, 2011

	Opponents	Tests	E	A	SA	WI	NZ	I	P	SL	Z	B	Wld	Tied	Drawn
England	Australia	326	102	133	–	–	–	–	–	–	–	–	–	–	91
	South Africa	138	56	–	29	–	–	–	–	–	–	–	–	–	53
	West Indies	145	43	–	–	53	–	–	–	–	–	–	–	–	49
	New Zealand	94	45	–	–	–	8	–	–	–	–	–	–	–	41
	India	99	34	–	–	–	–	19	–	–	–	–	–	–	46
	Pakistan	71	22	–	–	–	–	–	13	–	–	–	–	–	36
	Sri Lanka	21	8	–	–	–	–	–	–	6	–	–	–	–	7
	Zimbabwe	6	3	–	–	–	–	–	–	–	0	–	–	–	3
	Bangladesh	8	8	–	–	–	–	–	–	–	–	0	–	–	0
Australia	South Africa	83	–	47	18	–	–	–	–	–	–	–	–	–	18
	West Indies	108	–	52	–	32	–	–	–	–	–	–	–	1	23
	New Zealand	50	–	26	–	–	7	–	–	–	–	–	–	–	17
	India	78	–	34	–	–	–	20	–	–	–	–	–	1	23
	Pakistan	57	–	28	–	–	–	–	12	–	–	–	–	–	17
	Sri Lanka	20	–	13	–	–	–	–	–	1	–	–	–	–	6
	Zimbabwe	3	–	3	–	–	–	–	–	–	0	–	–	–	0
	Bangladesh	4	–	4	–	–	–	–	–	–	–	0	–	–	0
	ICC World XI	1	–	1	–	–	–	–	–	–	–	–	0	–	0
South Africa	West Indies	25	–	–	16	3	–	–	–	–	–	–	–	–	6
	New Zealand	35	–	–	20	–	4	–	–	–	–	–	–	–	11
	India	27	–	–	12	–	–	7	–	–	–	–	–	–	8
	Pakistan	18	–	–	8	–	–	–	3	–	–	–	–	–	7
	Sri Lanka	17	–	–	8	–	–	–	–	4	–	–	–	–	5
	Zimbabwe	7	–	–	6	–	–	–	–	–	0	–	–	–	1
	Bangladesh	8	–	–	8	–	–	–	–	–	–	0	–	–	0
West Indies	New Zealand	37	–	–	–	10	9	–	–	–	–	–	–	–	18
	India	82	–	–	–	30	–	11	–	–	–	–	–	–	41
	Pakistan	44	–	–	–	14	–	–	15	–	–	–	–	–	15
	Sri Lanka	15	–	–	–	3	–	–	–	6	–	–	–	–	6
	Zimbabwe	6	–	–	–	4	–	–	–	–	0	–	–	–	2
	Bangladesh	6	–	–	–	3	–	–	–	–	–	2	–	–	1
New Zealand	India	50	–	–	–	–	9	16	–	–	–	–	–	–	25
	Pakistan	50	–	–	–	–	7	–	23	–	–	–	–	–	20
	Sri Lanka	26	–	–	–	–	9	–	–	7	–	–	–	–	10
	Zimbabwe	13	–	–	–	–	7	–	–	–	0	–	–	–	6
	Bangladesh	9	–	–	–	–	8	–	–	–	–	0	–	–	1
India	Pakistan	59	–	–	–	–	–	9	12	–	–	–	–	–	38
	Sri Lanka	35	–	–	–	–	–	14	–	6	–	–	–	–	15
	Zimbabwe	11	–	–	–	–	–	7	–	–	2	–	–	–	2
	Bangladesh	7	–	–	–	–	–	6	–	–	–	0	–	–	1
Pakistan	Sri Lanka	37	–	–	–	–	–	–	15	9	–	–	–	–	13
	Zimbabwe	14	–	–	–	–	–	–	8	–	2	–	–	–	4
	Bangladesh	6	–	–	–	–	–	–	6	–	–	0	–	–	0
Sri Lanka	Zimbabwe	15	–	–	–	–	–	–	–	10	0	–	–	–	5
	Bangladesh	12	–	–	–	–	–	–	–	12	–	0	–	–	0
Zimbabwe	Bangladesh	8	–	–	–	–	–	–	–	–	4	1	–	–	3
		1,991	321	341	125	152	68	109	107	61	8	3	0	2	694

	Tests	Won	Lost	Drawn	Tied	% Won	Toss Won
England	908	321	261	326	–	35.35	439
Australia	730†	341†	192	195	2	46.71	369
South Africa	358	125	124	109	–	34.91	173
West Indies	468	152	154	161	1	32.47	243
New Zealand	364	68	147	149	–	18.68	184
India	448	109	139	199	1	24.33	226
Pakistan	356	107	99	150	–	30.05	168
Sri Lanka	198	61	70	67	–	30.80	104
Zimbabwe	83	8	49	26	–	9.63	49
Bangladesh	68	3	59	6	–	4.41	36
ICC World XI	1	0	1	0	–	0.00	0

† Includes Super Series Test between Australia and ICC World XI.

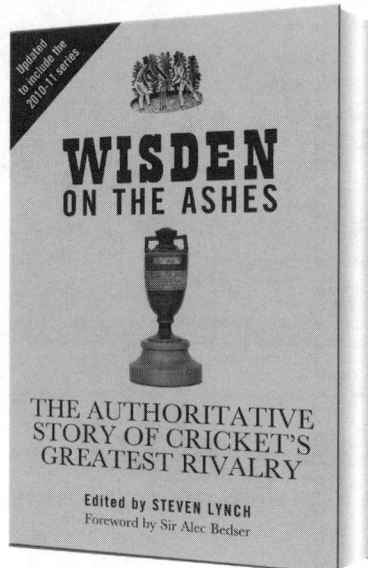

ENGLAND v AUSTRALIA

	Captains					
Season	*England*	*Australia*	*T*	*E*	*A*	*D*
1876-77	James Lillywhite	D. W. Gregory	2	1	1	0
1878-79	Lord Harris	D. W. Gregory	1	0	1	0
1880	Lord Harris	W. L. Murdoch	1	1	0	0
1881-82	A. Shaw	W. L. Murdoch	4	0	2	2
1882	A. N. Hornby	W. L. Murdoch	1	0	1	0

THE ASHES

	Captains						
Season	*England*	*Australia*	*T*	*E*	*A*	*D*	*Held by*
1882-83	Hon. Ivo Bligh	W. L. Murdoch	4*	2	2	0	E
1884	Lord Harris[1]	W. L. Murdoch	3	1	0	2	E
1884-85	A. Shrewsbury	T. P. Horan[2]	5	3	2	0	E
1886	A. G. Steel	H. J. H. Scott	3	3	0	0	E
1886-87	A. Shrewsbury	P. S. McDonnell	2	2	0	0	E
1887-88	W. W. Read	P. S. McDonnell	1	1	0	0	E
1888	W. G. Grace[3]	P. S. McDonnell	3	2	1	0	E
1890†	W. G. Grace	W. L. Murdoch	2	2	0	0	E
1891-92	W. G. Grace	J. McC. Blackham	3	1	2	0	A
1893	W. G. Grace[4]	J. McC. Blackham	3	1	0	2	E
1894-95	A. E. Stoddart	G. Giffen[5]	5	3	2	0	E
1896	W. G. Grace	G. H. S. Trott	3	2	1	0	E
1897-98	A. E. Stoddart[6]	G. H. S. Trott	5	1	4	0	A
1899	A. C. MacLaren[7]	J. Darling	5	0	1	4	A
1901-02	A. C. MacLaren	J. Darling[8]	5	1	4	0	A
1902	A. C. MacLaren	J. Darling	5	1	2	2	A
1903-04	P. F. Warner	M. A. Noble	5	3	2	0	E
1905	Hon. F. S. Jackson	J. Darling	5	2	0	3	E
1907-08	A. O. Jones[9]	M. A. Noble	5	1	4	0	A
1909	A. C. MacLaren	M. A. Noble	5	1	2	2	A
1911-12	J. W. H. T. Douglas	C. Hill	5	4	1	0	E
1912	C. B. Fry	S. E. Gregory	3	1	0	2	E
1920-21	J. W. H. T. Douglas	W. W. Armstrong	5	0	5	0	A
1921	Hon. L. H. Tennyson[10]	W. W. Armstrong	5	0	3	2	A
1924-25	A. E. R. Gilligan	H. L. Collins	5	1	4	0	A
1926	A. W. Carr[11]	H. L. Collins[12]	5	1	0	4	E
1928-29	A. P. F. Chapman[13]	J. Ryder	5	4	1	0	E
1930	A. P. F. Chapman[14]	W. M. Woodfull	5	1	2	2	A
1932-33	D. R. Jardine	W. M. Woodfull	5	4	1	0	E
1934	R. E. S. Wyatt[15]	W. M. Woodfull	5	1	2	2	A
1936-37	G. O. B. Allen	D. G. Bradman	5	2	3	0	A
1938†	W. R. Hammond	D. G. Bradman	4	1	1	2	A
1946-47	W. R. Hammond[16]	D. G. Bradman	5	0	3	2	A
1948	N. W. D. Yardley	D. G. Bradman	5	0	4	1	A
1950-51	F. R. Brown	A. L. Hassett	5	1	4	0	A
1953	L. Hutton	A. L. Hassett	5	1	0	4	E
1954-55	L. Hutton	I. W. Johnson[17]	5	3	1	1	E
1956	P. B. H. May	I. W. Johnson	5	2	1	2	E
1958-59	P. B. H. May	R. Benaud	5	0	4	1	A
1961	P. B. H. May[18]	R. Benaud[19]	5	1	2	2	A
1962-63	E. R. Dexter	R. Benaud	5	1	1	3	A
1964	E. R. Dexter	R. B. Simpson	5	0	1	4	A
1965-66	M. J. K. Smith	R. B. Simpson[20]	5	1	1	3	A
1968	M. C. Cowdrey[21]	W. M. Lawry[22]	5	1	1	3	A
1970-71†	R. Illingworth	W. M. Lawry[23]	6	2	0	4	E
1972	R. Illingworth	I. M. Chappell	5	2	2	1	E

			T	E	A	D	Held by
		Captains					
Season	*England*	*Australia*					
1974-75	M. H. Denness[24]	I. M. Chappell	6	1	4	1	A
1975	A. W. Greig[25]	I. M. Chappell	4	0	1	3	A
1976-77‡	A. W. Greig	G. S. Chappell	1	0	1	0	—
1977	J. M. Brearley	G. S. Chappell	5	3	0	2	E
1978-79	J. M. Brearley	G. N. Yallop	6	5	1	0	E
1979-80‡	J. M. Brearley	G. S. Chappell	3	0	3	0	—
1980‡	I. T. Botham	G. S. Chappell	1	0	0	1	—
1981	J. M. Brearley[26]	K. J. Hughes	6	3	1	2	E
1982-83	R. G. D. Willis	G. S. Chappell	5	1	2	2	A
1985	D. I. Gower	A. R. Border	6	3	1	2	E
1986-87	M. W. Gatting	A. R. Border	5	2	1	2	E
1987-88‡	M. W. Gatting	A. R. Border	1	0	0	1	—
1989	D. I. Gower	A. R. Border	6	0	4	2	A
1990-91	G. A. Gooch[27]	A. R. Border	5	0	3	2	A
1993	G. A. Gooch[28]	A. R. Border	6	1	4	1	A
1994-95	M. A. Atherton	M. A. Taylor	5	1	3	1	A
1997	M. A. Atherton	M. A. Taylor	6	2	3	1	A
1998-99	A. J. Stewart	M. A. Taylor	5	1	3	1	A
2001	N. Hussain[29]	S. R. Waugh[30]	5	1	4	0	A
2002-03	N. Hussain	S. R. Waugh	5	1	4	0	A
2005	M. P. Vaughan	R. T. Ponting	5	2	1	2	E
2006-07	A. Flintoff	R. T. Ponting	5	0	5	0	A
2009	A. J. Strauss	R. T. Ponting	5	2	1	2	E
2010-11	**A. J. Strauss**	**R. T. Ponting[31]**	**5**	**3**	**1**	**1**	**E**
	In Australia		170	57	86	27	
	In England.........................		156	45	47	64	
	Totals		326	102	133	91	

* *The Ashes were awarded in 1882-83 after a series of three matches which England won 2–1.*
A fourth match was played and this was won by Australia.

† *The matches at Manchester in 1890 and 1938 and at Melbourne (Third Test) in 1970-71 were abandoned without a ball being bowled and are excluded.*

‡ *The Ashes were not at stake in these series.*

Notes: The following deputised for the official touring captain or were appointed by the home authority for only a minor proportion of the series:

[1]A. N. Hornby (First). [2]W. L. Murdoch (First), H. H. Massie (Third), J. McC. Blackham (Fourth). [3]A. G. Steel (First). [4]A. E. Stoddart (First). [5]J. McC. Blackham (First). [6]A. C. MacLaren (First, Second and Fifth). [7]W. G. Grace (First). [8]H. Trumble (Fourth and Fifth). [9]F. L. Fane (First, Second and Third). [10]J. W. H. T. Douglas (First and Second). [11]A. P. F. Chapman (Fifth). [12]W. Bardsley (Third and Fourth). [13]J. C. White (Fifth). [14]R. E. S. Wyatt (Fifth). [15]C. F. Walters (First). [16]N. W. D. Yardley (Fifth). [17]A. R. Morris (Second). [18]M. C. Cowdrey (First and Second). [19]R. N. Harvey (Second). [20]B. C. Booth (First and Third). [21]T. W. Graveney (Fourth). [22]B. N. Jarman (Fourth) [23]I. M. Chappell (Seventh). [24]J. H. Edrich (Fourth). [25]M. H. Denness (First). [26]I. T. Botham (First and Second). [27]A. J. Lamb (First). [28]M. A. Atherton (Fifth and Sixth). [29]M. A. Atherton (Second and Third). [30]A. C. Gilchrist (Fourth). [31]M. J. Clarke (Fifth).

HIGHEST INNINGS TOTALS

For England in England: 903-7 dec at The Oval	1938
**in Australia: 644 at Sydney.................................... **	**2010-11**
For Australia in England: 729-6 dec at Lord's....................................	1930
in Australia: 659-8 dec at Sydney	1946-47

LOWEST INNINGS TOTALS

For England in England: 52 at The Oval 1948
            in Australia: 45 at Sydney 1886-87

For Australia in England: 36 at Birmingham 1902
             in Australia: 42 at Sydney 1887-88

DOUBLE-HUNDREDS

For England (13)

364	L. Hutton at The Oval	1938	**227**	**K. P. Pietersen at Adelaide . . . .**	**2010-11**
287	R. E. Foster at Sydney	1903-04	216*	E. Paynter at Nottingham	1938
256	K. F. Barrington at Manchester .	1964	215	D. I. Gower at Birmingham	1985
251	W. R. Hammond at Sydney . . .	1928-29	207	N. Hussain at Birmingham	1997
240	W. R. Hammond at Lord's	1938	206	P. D. Collingwood at Adelaide . .	2006-07
235*	**A. N. Cook at Brisbane . . . .**	**2010-11**	200	W. R. Hammond at Melbourne .	1928-29
231*	W. R. Hammond at Sydney . . .	1936-37			

For Australia (23)

334	D. G. Bradman at Leeds	1930	232	S. J. McCabe at Nottingham	1938
311	R. B. Simpson at Manchester . . .	1964	225	R. B. Simpson at Adelaide	1965-66
307	R. M. Cowper at Melbourne	1965-66	219	M. A. Taylor at Nottingham	1989
304	D. G. Bradman at Leeds	1934	212	D. G. Bradman at Adelaide. . . .	1936-37
270	D. G. Bradman at Melbourne . . .	1936-37	211	W. L. Murdoch at The Oval	1884
266	W. H. Ponsford at The Oval	1934	207	K. R. Stackpole at Brisbane	1970-71
254	D. G. Bradman at Lord's	1930	206*	W. A. Brown at Lord's	1938
250	J. L. Langer at Melbourne.	2002-03	206	A. R. Morris at Adelaide.	1950-51
244	D. G. Bradman at The Oval	1934	201*	J. Ryder at Adelaide	1924-25
234	S. G. Barnes at Sydney	1946-47	201	S. E. Gregory at Sydney	1894-95
234	D. G. Bradman at Sydney	1946-47	200*	A. R. Border at Leeds	1993
232	D. G. Bradman at The Oval	1930			

INDIVIDUAL HUNDREDS

For England (231)

12: J. B. Hobbs.

9: D. I. Gower, W. R. Hammond.

8: H. Sutcliffe.

7: G. Boycott, J. H. Edrich, M. Leyland.

5: K. F. Barrington, D. C. S. Compton, M. C. Cowdrey, L. Hutton, F. S. Jackson, A. C. MacLaren.

4: I. T. Botham, B. C. Broad, **A. N. Cook**, M. W. Gatting, A. C. Gooch, **A. J. Strauss**, M. P. Vaughan.

3: M. A. Butcher, E. H. Hendren, P. B. H. May, **K. P. Pietersen**, D. W. Randall, A. C. Russell, A. Shrewsbury, G. P. Thorpe, **I. J. L. Trott**, J. T. Tyldesley, R. A. Woolmer.

2: C. J. Barnett, L. C. Braund, E. R. Dexter, B. L. D'Oliveira, W. J. Edrich, W. G. Grace, G. Gunn, T. W. Hayward, N. Hussain, A. P. E. Knott, B. W. Luckhurst, K. S. Ranjitsinhji, R. T. Robinson, Rev. D. S. Sheppard, R. A. Smith, A. G. Steel, A. E. Stoddart, R. Subba Row, C. Washbrook, F. E. Woolley.

1: R. Abel, L. E. G. Ames, M. A. Atherton, R. W. Barber, W. Barnes, **I. R. Bell**, J. Briggs, J. T. Brown, A. P. F. Chapman, **P. D. Collingwood**, M. H. Denness, K. S. Duleepsinhji, K. W. R. Fletcher, A. Flintoff, R. E. Foster, C. B. Fry, T. W. Graveney, A. W. Greig, W. Gunn, J. Hardstaff, jun., J. W. Hearne, K. L. Hutchings, G. L. Jessop, A. J. Lamb, J. W. H. Makepeace, C. P. Mead, Nawab of Pataudi, sen., E. Paynter, **M. J. Prior**, M. R. Ramprakash, W. W. Read, W. Rhodes, C. J. Richards, P. E. Richardson, R. C. Russell, J. Sharp, R. T. Simpson, A. J. Stewart, G. Ulyett, A. Ward, W. Watson.

For Australia (287)

19: D. G. Bradman.

10: S. R. Waugh.

9: G. S. Chappell.

8: A. R. Border, A. R. Morris, **R. T. Ponting**.

7: D. C. Boon, W. M. Lawry, M. J. Slater.

6: R. N. Harvey, M. A. Taylor, V. T. Trumper, M. E. Waugh, W. M. Woodfull.

5: M. L. Hayden, J. L. Langer, C. G. Macartney, W. H. Ponsford.

4: W. W. Armstrong, P. J. Burge, I. M. Chappell, **M. J. Clarke**, S. E. Gregory, A. L. Hassett, C. Hill, **M. E. K. Hussey**, S. J. McCabe, K. D. Walters.

3: W. Bardsley, G. S. Blewett, W. A. Brown, H. L. Collins, G. Darling, A. C. Gilchrist, K. J. Hughes, D. M. Jones, P. S. McDonnell, K. R. Miller, K. R. Stackpole, G. M. Wood, G. N. Yallop.

2: S. G. Barnes, B. C. Booth, R. A. Duff, R. Edwards, M. T. G. Elliott, J. H. Fingleton, H. Graham, **B. J. Haddin**, I. A. Healy, F. A. Iredale, R. B. McCosker, C. C. McDonald, G. R. Marsh, D. R. Martyn, W. L. Murdoch, **M. J. North**, N. C. O'Neill, C. E. Pellew, I. R. Redpath, J. Ryder, R. B. Simpson.

1: C. L. Badcock, C. Bannerman, G. J. Bonnor, J. W. Burke, R. M. Cowper, J. Dyson, G. Giffen, J. M. Gregory, R. J. Hartigan, H. L. Hendry, A. M. J. Hilditch, T. P. Horan, A. A. Jackson, **S. M. Katich**, C. Kelleway, A. F. Kippax, R. R. Lindwall, J. J. Lyons, C. L. McCool, C. E. McLeod, R. W. Marsh, G. R. J. Matthews, M. A. Noble, V. S. Ransford, A. J. Richardson, V. Y. Richardson, G. M. Ritchie, H. J. H. Scott, A. Symonds, J. M. Taylor, G. H. S. Trott, D. M. Wellham, K. C. Wessels.

RECORD PARTNERSHIPS FOR EACH WICKET

For England

323 for 1st	J. B. Hobbs and W. Rhodes at Melbourne.	1911-12
382 for 2nd†	L. Hutton and M. Leyland at The Oval	1938
262 for 3rd	W. R. Hammond and D. R. Jardine at Adelaide	1928-29
310 for 4th	P. D. Collingwood and K. P. Pietersen at Adelaide	2006-07
206 for 5th	E. Paynter and D. C. S. Compton at Nottingham	1938
215 for 6th	{ L. Hutton and J. Hardstaff jun. at The Oval	1938
	{ G. Boycott and A. P. E. Knott at Nottingham	1977
143 for 7th	F. E. Woolley and J. Vine at Sydney	1911-12
124 for 8th	E. H. Hendren and H. Larwood at Brisbane	1928-29
151 for 9th	W. H. Scotton and W. W. Read at The Oval	1884
130 for 10th†	R. E. Foster and W. Rhodes at Sydney	1903-04

For Australia

329 for 1st	G. R. Marsh and M. A. Taylor at Nottingham.	1989
451 for 2nd†	W. H. Ponsford and D. G. Bradman at The Oval	1934
276 for 3rd	D. G. Bradman and A. L. Hassett at Brisbane	1946-47
388 for 4th†	W. H. Ponsford and D. G. Bradman at Leeds	1934
405 for 5th†	S. G. Barnes and D. G. Bradman at Sydney	1946-47
346 for 6th†	J. H. Fingleton and D. G. Bradman at Melbourne	1936-37
165 for 7th	C. Hill and H. Trumble at Melbourne	1897-98
243 for 8th†	R. J. Hartigan and C. Hill at Adelaide	1907-08
154 for 9th†	S. E. Gregory and J. McC. Blackham at Sydney	1894-95
127 for 10th†	J. M. Taylor and A. A. Mailey at Sydney	1924-25

† *Record partnership against all countries.*

MOST RUNS IN A SERIES

England in England	732 (average 81.33)	D. I. Gower	1985
England in Australia	905 (average 113.12)	W. R. Hammond	1928-29
Australia in England	974 (average 139.14)	D. G. Bradman	1930
Australia in Australia	810 (average 90.00)	D. G. Bradman	1936-37

TEN WICKETS OR MORE IN A MATCH

For England (38)

13-163 (6-42, 7-121)	S. F. Barnes, Melbourne	1901-02
14-102 (7-28, 7-74)	W. Bates, Melbourne	1882-83
10-105 (5-46, 5-59)	A. V. Bedser, Melbourne	1950-51
14-99 (7-55, 7-44)	A. V. Bedser, Nottingham	1953
11-102 (6-44, 5-58)	C. Blythe, Birmingham	1909
11-176 (6-78, 5-98)	I. T. Botham, Perth	1979-80
10-253 (6-125, 4-128)	I. T. Botham, The Oval	1981
11-74 (5-29, 6-45)	J. Briggs, Lord's	1886
12-136 (6-49, 6-87)	J. Briggs, Adelaide	1891-92
10-148 (5-34, 5-114)	J. Briggs, The Oval	1893
10-215 (3-121, 7-94)	A. R. Caddick, Sydney	2002-03
10-104 (6-77, 4-27)†	R. M. Ellison, Birmingham	1985
10-179 (5-102, 5-77)†	K. Farnes, Nottingham	1934
10-60 (6-41, 4-19)	J. T. Hearne, The Oval	1896
11-113 (5-58, 6-55)	J. C. Laker, Leeds	1956
19-90 (9-37, 10-53)	J. C. Laker, Manchester	1956
10-124 (5-96, 5-28)	H. Larwood, Sydney	1932-33
11-76 (6-48, 5-28)	W. H. Lockwood, Manchester	1902
12-104 (7-36, 5-68)	G. A. Lohmann, The Oval	1886
10-87 (8-35, 2-52)	G. A. Lohmann, Sydney	1886-87
10-142 (8-58, 2-84)	G. A. Lohmann, Sydney	1891-92
12-102 (6-50, 6-52)†	F. Martin, The Oval	1890
11-68 (7-31, 4-37)	R. Peel, Manchester	1888
15-124 (7-56, 8-68)	W. Rhodes, Melbourne	1903-04
10-156 (5-49, 5-107)†	T. Richardson, Manchester	1893
11-173 (6-39, 5-134)	T. Richardson, Lord's	1896
13-244 (7-168, 6-76)	T. Richardson, Manchester	1896
10-204 (8-94, 2-110)	T. Richardson, Sydney	1897-98
11-228 (6-130, 5-98)†	M. W. Tate, Sydney	1924-25
11-88 (5-58, 6-30)	F. S. Trueman, Leeds	1961
11-93 (7-66, 4-27)	P. C. R. Tufnell, The Oval	1997
10-130 (4-45, 6-85)	F. H. Tyson, Sydney	1954-55
10-82 (4-37, 6-45)	D. L. Underwood, Leeds	1972
11-215 (7-113, 4-102)	D. L. Underwood, Adelaide	1974-75
15-104 (7-61, 8-43)	H. Verity, Lord's	1934
10-57 (6-41, 4-16)	W. Voce, Brisbane	1936-37
13-256 (5-130, 8-126)	J. C. White, Adelaide	1928-29
10-49 (5-29, 5-20)	F. E. Woolley, The Oval	1912

For Australia (43)

10-151 (5-107, 5-44)	T. M. Alderman, Leeds	1989
10-239 (4-129, 6-110)	L. O'B. Fleetwood-Smith, Adelaide	1936-37
10-160 (4-88, 6-72)	G. Giffen, Sydney	1891-92
11-82 (5-45, 6-37)†	C. V. Grimmett, Sydney	1924-25
10-201 (5-107, 5-94)	C. V. Grimmett, Nottingham	1930
10-122 (5-65, 5-57)	R. M. Hogg, Perth	1978-79
10-66 (5-30, 5-36)	R. M. Hogg, Melbourne	1978-79
12-175 (5-85, 7-90)†	H. V. Hordern, Sydney	1911-12
10-161 (5-95, 5-66)	H. V. Hordern, Sydney	1911-12
10-164 (7-88, 3-76)	E. Jones, Lord's	1899
11-134 (6-47, 5-87)	G. F. Lawson, Brisbane	1982-83
10-181 (5-58, 5-123)	D. K. Lillee, The Oval	1972
11-165 (6-26, 5-139)	D. K. Lillee, Melbourne	1976-77
11-138 (6-60, 5-78)	D. K. Lillee, Melbourne	1979-80
11-159 (7-89, 4-70)	D. K. Lillee, The Oval	1981
11-85 (7-58, 4-27)	C. G. Macartney, Leeds	1909
11-157 (8-97, 3-60)	C. J. McDermott, Perth	1990-91

12-107 (5-57, 7-50)	S. C. G. MacGill, Sydney	1998-99
10-302 (5-160, 5-142)	A. A. Mailey, Adelaide	1920-21
13-236 (4-115, 9-121)	A. A. Mailey, Melbourne	1920-21
16-137 (8-84, 8-53)†	R. A. L. Massie, Lord's	1972
10-152 (5-72, 5-80)	K. R. Miller, Lord's	1956
13-77 (7-17, 6-60)	M. A. Noble, Melbourne	1901-02
11-103 (5-51, 6-52)	M. A. Noble, Sheffield	1902
10-129 (5-63, 5-66)	W. J. O'Reilly, Melbourne	1932-33
11-129 (4-75, 7-54)	W. J. O'Reilly, Nottingham	1934
10-122 (5-66, 5-56)	W. J. O'Reilly, Leeds	1938
11-165 (7-68, 4-97)	G. E. Palmer, Sydney	1881-82
10-126 (7-65, 3-61)	G. E. Palmer, Melbourne	1882-83
13-148 (6-97, 7-51)	B. A. Reid, Melbourne	1990-91
13-110 (6-48, 7-62)	F. R. Spofforth, Melbourne	1878-79
14-90 (7-46, 7-44)	F. R. Spofforth, The Oval	1882
11-117 (4-73, 7-44)	F. R. Spofforth, Sydney	1882-83
10-144 (4-54, 6-90)	F. R. Spofforth, Sydney	1884-85
12-89 (6-59, 6-30)	H. Trumble, The Oval	1896
10-128 (4-75, 6-53)	H. Trumble, Manchester	1902
12-173 (8-65, 4-108)	H. Trumble, The Oval	1902
12-87 (5-44, 7-43)	C. T. B. Turner, Sydney	1887-88
10-63 (5-27, 5-36)	C. T. B. Turner, Lord's	1888
11-110 (3-39, 8-71)	S. K. Warne, Brisbane	1994-95
11-229 (7-165, 4-64)	S. K. Warne, The Oval	2001
10-162 (4-116, 6-46)	S. K. Warne, Birmingham	2005
12-246 (6-122, 6-124)	S. K. Warne, The Oval	2005

† *On first appearance in England–Australia Tests.*

Note: A. V. Bedser, J. Briggs, J. C. Laker, T. Richardson in 1896, R. M. Hogg, A. A. Mailey, H. Trumble and C. T. B. Turner took ten wickets or more in successive Tests. J. Briggs was omitted, however, from the England team for the first Test match in 1893.

SEVEN WICKETS OR MORE IN AN INNINGS

In addition to those listed above, the following have taken seven wickets or more in an innings:

For England

7-40	R. G. Barlow, Sydney	1882-83	7-40	J. A. Snow, Sydney	1970-71
7-44	R. G. Barlow, Manchester	1886	7-57	J. B. Statham, Melbourne	1958-59
7-60	S. F. Barnes, Sydney	1907-08	7-79	F. J. Titmus, Sydney	1962-63
8-107	B. J. T. Bosanquet, Nottingham	1905	7-27	F. H. Tyson, Melbourne	1954-55
8-81	L. C. Braund, Melbourne	1903-04	7-36	G. Ulyett, Lord's	1884
7-78	J. E. Emburey, Sydney	1986-87	7-50	D. L. Underwood, The Oval	1968
7-68	T. Emmett, Melbourne	1878-79	7-78	R. G. D. Willis, Lord's	1977
7-109	M. J. Hoggard, Adelaide	2006-07	8-43	R. G. D. Willis, Leeds	1981
7-71	W. H. Lockwood, The Oval	1899	7-105	D. V. P. Wright, Sydney	1946-47
7-17	W. Rhodes, Birmingham	1902			

For Australia

7-148	A. Cotter, The Oval	1905	7-63	R. R. Lindwall, Sydney	1946-47
7-117	G. Giffen, Sydney	1884-85	8-141	C. J. McDermott, Manchester	1985
7-128	G. Giffen, The Oval	1893	8-38	G. D. McGrath, Lord's	1997
7-37	J. N. Gillespie, Leeds	1997	7-76	G. D. McGrath, The Oval	1997
7-69	J. M. Gregory, Melbourne	1920-21	7-76	G. D. McGrath, Leeds	2001
7-105	N. J. N. Hawke, Sydney	1965-66	7-153	G. D. McKenzie, Manchester	1964
7-25	G. R. Hazlitt, The Oval	1912	7-60	K. R. Miller, Brisbane	1946-47
7-92	P. M. Hornibrook, The Oval	1930	7-100	M. A. Noble, Sydney	1903-04
7-36	M. S. Kasprowicz, The Oval	1997	7-189	W. J. O'Reilly, Manchester	1934
7-55	T. K. Kendall, Melbourne	1876-77	8-43	A. E. Trott, Adelaide	1894-95
7-64	F. J. Laver, Nottingham	1905	7-28	H. Trumble, Melbourne	1903-04
8-31	F. J. Laver, Manchester	1909	8-143	M. H. N. Walker, Melbourne	1974-75
7-81	G. F. Lawson, Lord's	1981			

MOST WICKETS IN A SERIES

England in England......46 (average 9.60)	J. C. Laker.....................	1956
England in Australia.....38 (average 23.18)	M. W. Tate.....................	1924-25
Australia in England .....42 (average 21.26)	T. M. Alderman (6 Tests).........	1981
Australia in Australia......41 (average 12.85)	R. M. Hogg (6 Tests)	1978-79

WICKETKEEPING – MOST DISMISSALS

	M	Ct	St	Total
†R. W. Marsh (Australia)	42	141	7	148
I. A. Healy (Australia)................	33	123	12	135
A. P. E. Knott (England)	34	97	8	105
A. C. Gilchrist (Australia)	20	89	7	96
†W. A. Oldfield (Australia)	38	59	31	90
A. A. Lilley (England)................	32	65	19	84
A. J. Stewart (England)	26	76	2	78
A. T. W. Grout (Australia)	22	69	7	76
T. G. Evans (England)................	31	64	12	76

† *The number of catches by R. W. Marsh (141) and stumpings by W. A. Oldfield (31) are respective records in England–Australia Tests.*

Note: Stewart held a further 6 catches in 7 matches when not keeping wicket.

SCORERS OF OVER 2,000 RUNS

	T	I	NO	R	HS	100s	Avge
D. G. Bradman..........	37	63	7	5,028	334	19	89.78
J. B. Hobbs	41	71	4	3,636	187	12	54.26
A. R. Border	47	82	19	3,548	200*	8	56.31
D. I. Gower	42	77	4	3,269	215	9	44.78
S. R. Waugh............	46	73	18	3,200	177*	10	58.18
G. Boycott	38	71	9	2,945	191	7	47.50
W. R. Hammond	33	58	3	2,852	251	9	51.85
H. Sutcliffe.............	27	46	5	2,741	194	8	66.85
C. Hill	41	76	1	2,660	188	4	35.46
J. H. Edrich	32	57	3	2,644	175	7	48.96
G. A. Gooch.	42	79	0	2,632	196	4	33.31
G. S. Chappell	35	65	8	2,619	144	9	45.94
M. A. Taylor	33	61	2	2,496	219	6	42.30
R. T. Ponting	**35**	**58**	**2**	**2,476**	**196**	**8**	**44.21**
M. C. Cowdrey	43	75	4	2,433	113	5	34.26
L. Hutton	27	49	6	2,428	364	5	56.46
R. N. Harvey	37	68	5	2,416	167	6	38.34
V. T. Trumper	40	74	5	2,263	185*	6	32.79
D. C. Boon.	31	57	8	2,237	184*	7	45.65
W. M. Lawry...........	29	51	5	2,233	166	7	48.54
M. E. Waugh...........	29	51	7	2,204	140	6	50.09
S. E. Gregory	52	92	7	2,193	201	4	25.80
W. W. Armstrong	42	71	9	2,172	158	4	35.03
I. M. Chappell	30	56	4	2,138	192	4	41.11
K. F. Barrington.	23	39	6	2,111	256	5	63.96
A. R. Morris.	24	43	2	2,080	206	8	50.73

BOWLERS WITH 100 WICKETS

	T	Balls	R	W	5W/i	10W/m	Avge
S. K. Warne	36	10,757	4,535	195	11	4	23.25
D. K. Lillee	29	8,516	3,507	167	11	4	21.00
G. D. McGrath	30	7,280	3,286	157	10	0	20.92
I. T. Botham	36	8,479	4,093	148	9	2	27.65
H. Trumble	31	7,895	2,945	141	9	3	20.88
R. G. D. Willis	35	7,294	3,346	128	7	0	26.14
M. A. Noble	39	6,895	2,860	115	9	2	24.86
R. R. Lindwall	29	6,728	2,559	114	6	0	22.44
W. Rhodes	41	5,790	2,616	109	6	1	24.00
S. F. Barnes	20	5,749	2,288	106	12	1	21.58
C. V. Grimmett	22	9,224	3,439	106	11	2	32.44
D. L. Underwood	29	8,000	2,770	105	4	2	26.38
A. V. Bedser	21	7,065	2,859	104	7	2	27.49
G. Giffen	31	6,391	2,791	103	7	1	27.09
W. J. O'Reilly	19	7,864	2,587	102	8	3	25.36
C. T. B. Turner	17	5,179	1,670	101	11	2	16.53
R. Peel	20	5,216	1,715	101	5	1	16.98
T. M. Alderman	17	4,717	2,117	100	11	1	21.17
J. R. Thomson	21	4,951	2,418	100	5	0	24.18

RESULTS ON EACH GROUND

In England

	Matches	England wins	Australia wins	Drawn
The Oval	35	16	6	13
Manchester	28	7	7	14†
Lord's	34	6‡	14	14
Nottingham	20	4	7	9
Leeds	24	7	9	8
Birmingham	13	5	3	5
Sheffield	1	0	1	0
Cardiff	1	0	0	1

† *Excludes two matches abandoned without a ball bowled.*
‡ *England have won only twice (1934 and 2009) since 1896.*

In Australia

	Matches	England wins	Australia wins	Drawn
Melbourne	54	20	27	7†
Sydney	54	22	25	7
Adelaide	30	9	16	5
Brisbane				
Exhibition Ground	1	1	0	0
Woolloongabba	19	4	10	5
Perth	12	1	8	3

† *Excludes one match abandoned without a ball bowled.*

Bold type denotes performances in the 2010-11 series or, in career figures, players who appeared in that series.

ENGLAND v SOUTH AFRICA

Captains

Season	England	South Africa	T	E	SA	D
1888-89	C. A. Smith[1]	O. R. Dunell[2]	2	2	0	0
1891-92	W. W. Read	W. H. Milton	1	1	0	0
1895-96	Lord Hawke[3]	E. A. Halliwell[4]	3	3	0	0
1898-99	Lord Hawke	M. Bisset	2	2	0	0
1905-06	P. F. Warner	P. W. Sherwell	5	1	4	0
1907	R. E. Foster	P. W. Sherwell	3	1	0	2
1909-10	H. D. G. Leveson Gower[5]	S. J. Snooke	5	2	3	0
1912	C. B. Fry	F. Mitchell[6]	3	3	0	0
1913-14	J. W. H. T. Douglas	H. W. Taylor	5	4	0	1
1922-23	F. T. Mann	H. W. Taylor	5	2	1	2
1924	A. E. R. Gilligan[7]	H. W. Taylor	5	3	0	2
1927-28	R. T. Stanyforth[8]	H. G. Deane	5	2	2	1
1929	J. C. White[9]	H. G. Deane	5	2	0	3
1930-31	A. P. F. Chapman	H. G. Deane[10]	5	0	1	4
1935	R. E. S. Wyatt	H. F. Wade	5	0	1	4
1938-39	W. R. Hammond	A. Melville	5	1	0	4
1947	N. W. D. Yardley	A. Melville	5	3	0	2
1948-49	F. G. Mann	A. D. Nourse	5	2	0	3
1951	F. R. Brown	A. D. Nourse	5	3	1	1
1955	P. B. H. May	J. E. Cheetham[11]	5	3	2	0
1956-57	P. B. H. May	C. B. van Ryneveld[12]	5	2	2	1
1960	M. C. Cowdrey	D. J. McGlew	5	3	0	2
1964-65	M. J. K. Smith	T. L. Goddard	5	1	0	4
1965	M. J. K. Smith	P. L. van der Merwe	3	0	1	2
1994	M. A. Atherton	K. C. Wessels	3	1	1	1
1995-96	M. A. Atherton	W. J. Cronje	5	0	1	4
1998	A. J. Stewart	W. J. Cronje	5	2	1	2
1999-2000	N. Hussain	W. J. Cronje	5	1	2	2
2003	M. P. Vaughan[13]	G. C. Smith	5	2	2	1

THE BASIL D'OLIVEIRA TROPHY

Captains

Season	England	South Africa	T	E	SA	D	Held by
2004-05	M. P. Vaughan	G. C. Smith	5	2	1	2	E
2008	M. P. Vaughan[14]	G. C. Smith	4	1	2	1	SA
2009-10	**A. J. Strauss**	**G. C. Smith**	**4**	**1**	**1**	**2**	**SA**

	T	E	SA	D
In South Africa	**77**	**29**	**18**	**30**
In England	61	27	11	23
Totals	**138**	**56**	**29**	**53**

Notes: *The following deputised for the official touring captain or were appointed by the home authority for only a minor proportion of the series:*
[1]M. P. Bowden (Second). [2]W. H. Milton (Second). [3]Sir T. C. O'Brien (First). [4]A. R. Richards (Third). [5]F. L. Fane (Fourth and Fifth). [6]L. J. Tancred (Second and Third). [7]J. W. H. T. Douglas (Fourth). [8]G. T. S. Stevens (Fifth). [9]A. W. Carr (Fourth and Fifth). [10]E. P. Nupen (First), H. B. Cameron (Fourth and Fifth). [11]D. J. McGlew (Third and Fourth). [12]D. J. McGlew (Second). [13]N. Hussain (First). [14]K. P. Pietersen (Fourth).

HIGHEST INNINGS TOTALS

For England in England: 604-9 dec at The Oval 2003
in South Africa: 654-5 at Durban 1938-39

For South Africa in England: 682-6 dec at Lord's.   2003
         in South Africa: 572-7 at Durban.   1999-2000

LOWEST INNINGS TOTALS

For England in England: 76 at Leeds.   1907
        in South Africa: 92 at Cape Town.   1898-99

For South Africa in England: 30 at Birmingham.   1924
         in South Africa: 30 at Port Elizabeth   1895-96

DOUBLE-HUNDREDS

For England (5)

243	E. Paynter at Durban.	1938-39	211	J. B. Hobbs at Lord's	1924
219	W. J. Edrich at Durban	1938-39	208	D. C. S. Compton at Lord's	1947
219	M. E. Trescothick at The Oval . .	2003			

For South Africa (6)

277	G. C. Smith at Birmingham . . .	2003	236	E. A. B. Rowan at Leeds	1951
275	G. Kirsten at Durban.	1999-2000	210	G. Kirsten at Manchester.	1998
259	G. C. Smith at Lord's	2003	208	A. D. Nourse at Nottingham	1951

INDIVIDUAL HUNDREDS

For England (114)

7: D. C. S. Compton.

6: W. R. Hammond, H. Sutcliffe.

4: L. Hutton.

3: M. A. Atherton, M. C. Cowdrey, W. J. Edrich, N. Hussain, P. B. H. May, C. P. Mead, E. Paynter, **A. J. Strauss**, M. E. Trescothick, F. E. Woolley.

2: L. E. G. Ames, K. F. Barrington, **I. R. Bell**, M. A. Butcher, P. A. Gibb, E. H. Hendren, G. A. Hick, J. B. Hobbs, M. Leyland, **K. P. Pietersen**, A. C. Russell, G. P. Thorpe, E. Tyldesley, R. E. S. Wyatt.

1: R. Abel, G. Boycott, L. C. Braund, **P. D. Collingwood, A. N. Cook**, D. Denton, E. R. Dexter, J. W. H. T. Douglas, F. L. Fane, A. Flintoff, C. B. Fry, T. W. Hayward, A. J. L. Hill, D. J. Insole, F. G. Mann, P. H. Parfitt, J. M. Parks, G. Pullar, W. Rhodes, P. E. Richardson, R. W. V. Robins, R. T. Simpson, M. J. K. Smith, R. H. Spooner, A. J. Stewart, M. W. Tate, J. T. Tyldesley, B. H. Valentine, M. P. Vaughan, P. F. Warner, C. Washbrook, A. J. Watkins, H. Wood.

For South Africa (96)

7: **J. H. Kallis**, B. Mitchell, A. D. Nourse, H. W. Taylor.

6: **G. C. Smith**.

5: G. Kirsten.

4: A. Melville.

3: R. H. Catterall, H. H. Gibbs, R. A. McLean.

2: **H. M. Amla**, K. C. Bland, D. J. Cullinan, E. L. Dalton, **A. B. de Villiers**, D. J. McGlew, R. G. Pollock, **A. G. Prince**, E. A. B. Rowan, G. C. White.

1: E. J. Barlow, **M. V. Boucher**, W. J. Cronje, H. H. Dippenaar, W. R. Endean, G. A. Faulkner, T. L. Goddard, C. M. H. Hathorn, P. N. Kirsten, L. Klusener, N. D. McKenzie, B. M. McMillan, H. G. Owen-Smith, A. J. Pithey, J. N. Rhodes, P. W. Sherwell, I. J. Siedle, J. H. Sinclair, P. G. van der Bijl, K. G. Viljoen, W. W. Wade, J. H. B. Waite, K. C. Wessels, P. L. Winslow.

MOST RUNS IN A SERIES

England in England	753 (average 94.12)	D. C. S. Compton	1947
England in South Africa	656 (average 72.88)	A. J. Strauss	2004-05
South Africa in England	714 (average 79.33)	G. C. Smith	2003
South Africa in South Africa	625 (average 69.44)	J. H. Kallis	2004-05

TEN WICKETS OR MORE IN A MATCH

For England (26)

11-110 (5-25, 6-85)†	S. F. Barnes, Lord's	1912
10-115 (6-52, 4-63)	S. F. Barnes, Leeds	1912
13-57 (5-28, 8-29)	S. F. Barnes, The Oval	1912
10-105 (5-57, 5-48)	S. F. Barnes, Durban	1913-14
17-159 (8-56, 9-103)	S. F. Barnes, Johannesburg	1913-14
14-144 (7-56, 7-88)	S. F. Barnes, Durban	1913-14
12-112 (7-58, 5-54)	A. V. Bedser, Manchester	1951
11-118 (6-68, 5-50)	C. Blythe, Cape Town	1905-06
15-99 (8-59, 7-40)	C. Blythe, Leeds	1907
10-104 (7-46, 3-58)	C. Blythe, Cape Town	1909-10
15-28 (7-17, 8-11)	J. Briggs, Cape Town	1888-89
13-91 (6-54, 7-37)†	J. J. Ferris, Cape Town	1891-92
10-122 (5-60, 5-62)	A. R. C. Fraser, Nottingham	1998
10-207 (7-115, 3-92)	A. P. Freeman, Leeds	1929
12-171 (7-71, 5-100)	A. P. Freeman, Manchester	1929
12-130 (7-70, 5-60)	G. Geary, Johannesburg	1927-28
11-90 (6-7, 5-83)	A. E. R. Gilligan, Birmingham	1924
12-205 (5-144, 7-61)	M. J. Hoggard, Johannesburg	2004-05
10-119 (4-64, 6-55)	J. C. Laker, The Oval	1951
15-45 (7-38, 8-7)†	G. A. Lohmann, Port Elizabeth	1895-96
12-71 (9-28, 3-43)	G. A. Lohmann, Johannesburg	1895-96
10-138 (1-81, 9-57)	D. E. Malcolm, The Oval	1994
11-97 (6-63, 5-34)	J. B. Statham, Lord's	1960
12-101 (7-52, 5-49)	R. Tattersall, Lord's	1951
12-89 (5-53, 7-36)	J. H. Wardle, Cape Town	1956-57
10-175 (5-95, 5-80)	D. V. P. Wright, Lord's	1947

For South Africa (8)

11-127 (6-53, 5-74)	A. A. Donald, Johannesburg	1999-2000
11-112 (4-49, 7-63)†	A. E. Hall, Cape Town	1922-23
10-220 (5-75, 5-145)	M. Ntini, Lord's	2003
11-150 (5-63, 6-87)	E. P. Nupen, Johannesburg	1930-31
10-87 (5-53, 5-34)	P. M. Pollock, Nottingham	1965
12-127 (4-57, 8-70)	S. J. Snooke, Johannesburg	1905-06
13-192 (4-79, 9-113)	H. J. Tayfield, Johannesburg	1956-57
12-181 (5-87, 7-94)	A. E. E. Vogler, Johannesburg	1909-10

† *On first appearance in England–South Africa Tests.*

Notes: S. F. Barnes took ten wickets or more in his first five Tests v South Africa and in six of his seven Tests v South Africa. A. P. Freeman and G. A. Lohmann took ten wickets or more in successive matches.

SEVEN WICKETS OR MORE IN AN INNINGS

In addition to those listed above, the following have taken seven wickets or more in an innings:

For England

7-46 A. R. Caddick, Durban	1999-2000	7-39 J. B. Statham, Lord's	1955
7-42 G. A. Lohmann, Cape Town	1895-96		

For South Africa

7-95	W. H. Ashley, Cape Town	1888-89	7-65	S. J. Pegler, Lord's	1912
7-29	G. F. Bissett, Durban	1927-28	8-69	H. J. Tayfield, Durban	1956-57
7-84	G. A. Faulkner, The Oval	1912	7-128	A. E. E. Vogler, Lord's	1907

MOST WICKETS IN A SERIES

England in England	34 (average 8.29)	S. F. Barnes		1912
England in South Africa	49 (average 10.93)	S. F. Barnes		1913-14
South Africa in England	33 (average 19.78)	A. A. Donald		1998
South Africa in South Africa	37 (average 17.18)	H. J. Tayfield		1956-57

Bold type denotes performances in the 2009-10 series or, in career figures, players who appeared in that series.

ENGLAND v WEST INDIES

		Captains				
Season	England	West Indies	T	E	WI	D
1928	A. P. F. Chapman	R. K. Nunes	3	3	0	0
1929-30	Hon. F. S. G. Calthorpe	E. L. G. Hoad[1]	4	1	1	2
1933	D. R. Jardine[2]	G. C. Grant	3	2	0	1
1934-35	R. E. S. Wyatt	G. C. Grant	4	1	2	1
1939	W. R. Hammond	R. S. Grant	3	1	0	2
1947-48	G. O. B. Allen[3]	J. D. C. Goddard[4]	4	0	2	2
1950	N. W. D. Yardley[5]	J. D. C. Goddard	4	1	3	0
1953-54	L. Hutton	J. B. Stollmeyer	5	2	2	1
1957	P. B. H. May	J. D. C. Goddard	5	3	0	2
1959-60	P. B. H. May[6]	F. C. M. Alexander	5	1	0	4

THE WISDEN TROPHY

		Captains					
Season	England	West Indies	T	E	WI	D	Held by
1963	E. R. Dexter	F. M. M. Worrell	5	1	3	1	WI
1966	M. C. Cowdrey[7]	G. S. Sobers	5	1	3	1	WI
1967-68	M. C. Cowdrey	G. S. Sobers	5	1	0	4	E
1969	R. Illingworth	G. S. Sobers	3	2	0	1	E
1973	R. Illingworth	R. B. Kanhai	3	0	2	1	WI
1973-74	M. H. Denness	R. B. Kanhai	5	1	1	3	WI
1976	A. W. Greig	C. H. Lloyd	5	0	3	2	WI
1980	I. T. Botham	C. H. Lloyd[8]	5	0	1	4	WI
1980-81†	I. T. Botham	C. H. Lloyd	4	0	2	2	WI
1984	D. I. Gower	C. H. Lloyd	5	0	5	0	WI
1985-86	D. I. Gower	I. V. A. Richards	5	0	5	0	WI
1988	J. E. Emburey[9]	I. V. A. Richards	5	0	4	1	WI
1989-90‡	G. A. Gooch[10]	I. V. A. Richards[11]	4	1	2	1	WI
1991	G. A. Gooch	I. V. A. Richards	5	2	2	1	WI
1993-94	M. A. Atherton	R. B. Richardson[12]	5	1	3	1	WI
1995	M. A. Atherton	R. B. Richardson	6	2	2	2	WI
1997-98§	M. A. Atherton	B. C. Lara	6	1	3	2	WI
2000	N. Hussain[13]	J. C. Adams	5	3	1	1	E
2003-04	M. P. Vaughan	B. C. Lara	4	3	0	1	E
2004	M. P. Vaughan	B. C. Lara	4	4	0	0	E
2007	M. P. Vaughan[14]	R. R. Sarwan[15]	4	3	0	1	E
2008-09§	A. J. Strauss	C. H. Gayle	5	0	1	4	WI

Captains

Season	England	West Indies	T	E	WI	D	Held by
2009	A. J. Strauss	C. H. Gayle	2	2	0	0	E

	T	E	WI	D
In England.	80	30	29	21
In West Indies.	65	13	24	28
Totals	145	43	53	49

† The Second Test, at Georgetown, was cancelled owing to political pressure and is excluded.
‡ The Second Test, at Georgetown, was abandoned without a ball being bowled and is excluded.
§ The First Test at Kingston in 1997-98 and the Second Test at North Sound in 2008-09 were called off on their opening days because of unfit pitches and are shown as draws.

Notes: The following deputised for the official touring captain or were appointed by the home authority for only a minor proportion of the series:

[1]N. Betancourt (Second), M. P. Fernandes (Third), R. K. Nunes (Fourth). [2]R. E. S. Wyatt (Third). [3]K. Cranston (Fourth). [4]G. A. Headley (First), G. E. Gomez (Second). [5]F. R. Brown (Fourth). [6]M. C. Cowdrey (Fourth and Fifth). [7]M. J. K. Smith (First), D. B. Close (Fifth). [8]I. V. A. Richards (Fifth). [9]M. W. Gatting (First), C. S. Cowdrey (Fourth), G. A. Gooch (Fifth). [10]A. J. Lamb (Fourth and Fifth). [11]D. L. Haynes (Third). [12]C. A. Walsh (Fifth). [13]A. J. Stewart (Second). [14]A. J. Strauss (First). [15]D. Ganga (Third and Fourth).

HIGHEST INNINGS TOTALS

For England in England: 619-6 dec at Nottingham	1957
in West Indies: 849 at Kingston	1929-30
For West Indies in England: 692-8 dec at The Oval	1995
in West Indies: 751-5 dec at St John's	2003-04

LOWEST INNINGS TOTALS

For England in England: 71 at Manchester	1976
in West Indies: 46 at Port-of-Spain	1993-94
For West Indies in England: 54 at Lord's	2000
in West Indies: 47 at Kingston	2003-04

DOUBLE-HUNDREDS

For England (10)

325	A. Sandham at Kingston	1929-30	221 R. W. T. Key at Lord's	2004
285*	P. B. H. May at Birmingham . . .	1957	205* E. H. Hendren at Port-of-Spain .	1929-30
262*	D. L. Amiss at Bridgetown . . .	1973-74	205 L. Hutton at Kingston	1953-54
258	T. W. Graveney at Nottingham .	1957	203 D. L. Amiss at The Oval	1976
226	K. P. Pietersen at Leeds	2007	202* L. Hutton at The Oval	1950

For West Indies (16)

400*	B. C. Lara at St John's	2003-04	226 G. S. Sobers at Bridgetown	1959-60
375	B. C. Lara at St John's	1993-94	223 C. G. Greenidge at Manchester .	1984
302	L. G. Rowe at Bridgetown . . .	1973-74	223 G. A. Headley at Kingston	1929-30
291	I. V. A. Richards at The Oval . . .	1976	220 C. L. Walcott at Bridgetown	1953-54
291	R. R. Sarwan at Bridgetown . . .	2008-09	214* C. G. Greenidge at Lord's	1984
270*	G. A. Headley at Kingston . . .	1934-35	209* B. F. Butcher at Nottingham	1966
261	F. M. M. Worrell at Nottingham	1950	209 C. A. Roach at Georgetown	1929-30
232	I. V. A. Richards at Nottingham .	1976	206 E. D. Weekes at Port-of-Spain . .	1953-54

INDIVIDUAL HUNDREDS

For England (132)

6: M. C. Cowdrey, A. J. Lamb.

5: G. Boycott, G. A. Gooch, T. W. Graveney, L. Hutton.

4: D. L. Amiss, M. A. Atherton, P. D. Collingwood, A. N. Cook, A. J. Strauss, M. P. Vaughan.

3: L. E. G. Ames, K. F. Barrington, R. S. Bopara, A. W. Greig, P. B. H. May, K. P. Pietersen, R. A. Smith, A. J. Stewart, G. P. Thorpe.

2: D. C. S. Compton, E. R. Dexter, A. Flintoff, E. H. Hendren, M. J. Prior, P. E. Richardson, A. Sandham, M. E. Trescothick, C. Washbrook, P. Willey.

1: A. H. Bakewell, I. R. Bell, J. H. Edrich, T. G. Evans, K. W. R. Fletcher, G. Fowler, D. I. Gower, S. C. Griffith, W. R. Hammond, J. H. Hampshire, F. C. Hayes, G. A. Hick, J. B. Hobbs, N. Hussain, R. Illingworth, D. R. Jardine, R. W. T. Key, A. P. E. Knott, C. Milburn, J. T. Murray, J. M. Parks, W. Place, M. R. Ramprakash, J. D. Robertson, M. J. K. Smith, D. S. Steele, R. Subba Row, E. Tyldesley, W. Watson.

For West Indies (128)

10: G. S. Sobers.

8: G. A. Headley, I. V. A. Richards.

7: C. G. Greenidge, B. C. Lara.

6: F. M. M. Worrell.

5: S. Chanderpaul, D. L. Haynes, R. B. Kanhai, C. H. Lloyd, R. R. Sarwan.

4: R. B. Richardson, C. L. Walcott.

3: R. C. Fredericks, C. H. Gayle, C. L. Hooper, C. C. Hunte, L. G. Rowe, E. D. Weekes.

2: B. F. Butcher, H. A. Gomes, A. I. Kallicharran, S. M. Nurse, A. F. Rae, C. A. Roach, O. G. Smith.

1: J. C. Adams, K. L. T. Arthurton, I. Barrow, C. A. Best, G. M. Carew, C. A. Davis, P. J. L. Dujon, A. G. Ganteaume, D. A. J. Holford, J. K. Holt, R. D. Jacobs, B. D. Julien, C. B. Lambert, B. P. Nash, D. Ramdin, D. S. Smith, K. H. Weekes.

TEN WICKETS OR MORE IN A MATCH

For England (13)

11-98 (7-44, 4-54)	T. E. Bailey, Lord's	1957
11-110 (8-53, 3-57)	A. R. C. Fraser, Port-of-Spain	1997-98
10-93 (5-54, 5-39)	A. P. Freeman, Manchester	1928
13-156 (8-86, 5-70)	A. W. Greig, Port-of-Spain	1973-74
11-48 (5-28, 6-20)	G. A. R. Lock, The Oval	1957
10-137 (4-60, 6-77)	D. E. Malcolm, Port-of-Spain	1989-90
11-96 (5-37, 6-59)†	C. S. Marriott, The Oval	1933
10-187 (4-50, 6-137)	M. S. Panesar, Manchester	2007
10-142 (4-82, 6-60)	J. A. Snow, Georgetown	1967-68
10-195 (5-105, 5-90)†	G. T. S. Stevens, Bridgetown	1929-30
11-152 (6-100, 5-52)	F. S. Trueman, Lord's	1963
12-119 (5-75, 7-44)	F. S. Trueman, Birmingham	1963
11-149 (4-79, 7-70)	W. Voce, Port-of-Spain	1929-30

For West Indies (15)

10-127 (2-82, 8-45)	C. E. L. Ambrose, Bridgetown	1989-90
11-84 (5-60, 6-24)	C. E. L. Ambrose, Port-of-Spain	1993-94
10-174 (5-105, 5-69)	K. C. G. Benjamin, Nottingham	1995
11-147 (5-70, 6-77)†	K. D. Boyce, The Oval	1973
11-229 (5-137, 6-92)	W. Ferguson, Port-of-Spain	1947-48
11-157 (5-59, 6-98)†	L. R. Gibbs, Manchester	1963
10-106 (5-37, 5-69)	L. R. Gibbs, Manchester	1966
14-149 (8-92, 6-57)	M. A. Holding, The Oval	1976
10-96 (5-41, 5-55)†	H. H. H. Johnson, Kingston	1947-48

10-92 (6-32, 4-60)	M. D. Marshall, Lord's	1988
11-152 (5-66, 6-86)	S. Ramadhin, Lord's	1950
11-123 (5-60, 5-63)	A. M. E. Roberts, Lord's	1976
11-204 (8-104, 3-100)†	A. L. Valentine, Manchester	1950
10-160 (4-121, 6-39)	A. L. Valentine, The Oval	1950
10-117 (4-43, 6-74)	C. A. Walsh, Lord's	2000

† *On first appearance in England–West Indies Tests.*

Note: F. S. Trueman took ten wickets or more in successive matches.

SEVEN WICKETS OR MORE IN AN INNINGS

In addition to those listed above, the following have taken seven wickets or more in an innings:

For England

7-34	T. E. Bailey, Kingston	1953-54	7-50 W. E. Hollies, Georgetown.... 1934-35
8-103	I. T. Botham, Lord's	1984	7-103 J. C. Laker, Bridgetown 1947-48
7-43	D. G. Cork, Lord's	1995	7-56 James Langridge, Manchester . 1933
8-75	A. R. C. Fraser, Bridgetown ...	1993-94	7-49 J. A. Snow, Kingston 1967-68
7-12	S. J. Harmison, Kingston	2003-04	

For West Indies

7-69	W. W. Hall, Kingston	1959-60	7-49 S. Ramadhin, Birmingham 1957
7-53	M. D. Marshall, Leeds	1984	7-66 D. J. G. Sammy, Manchester ... 2007
7-22	M. D. Marshall, Manchester....	1988	7-70 F. M. M. Worrell, Leeds....... 1957

ENGLAND v NEW ZEALAND

		Captains				
Season	England	New Zealand	T	E	NZ	D
1929-30	A. H. H. Gilligan	T. C. Lowry	4	1	0	3
1931	D. R. Jardine	T. C. Lowry	3	1	0	2
1932-33	D. R. Jardine[1]	M. L. Page	2	0	0	2
1937	R. W. V. Robins	M. L. Page	3	1	0	2
1946-47	W. R. Hammond	W. A. Hadlee	1	0	0	1
1949	F. G. Mann[2]	W. A. Hadlee	4	0	0	4
1950-51	F. R. Brown	W. A. Hadlee	2	1	0	1
1954-55	L. Hutton	G. O. Rabone	2	2	0	0
1958	P. B. H. May	J. R. Reid	5	4	0	1
1958-59	P. B. H. May	J. R. Reid	2	1	0	1
1962-63	E. R. Dexter	J. R. Reid	3	3	0	0
1965	M. J. K. Smith	J. R. Reid	3	3	0	0
1965-66	M. J. K. Smith	B. W. Sinclair[3]	3	0	0	3
1969	R. Illingworth	G. T. Dowling	3	2	0	1
1970-71	R. Illingworth	G. T. Dowling	2	1	0	1
1973	R. Illingworth	B. E. Congdon	3	2	0	1
1974-75	M. H. Denness	B. E. Congdon	2	1	0	1
1977-78	G. Boycott	M. G. Burgess	3	1	1	1
1978	J. M. Brearley	M. G. Burgess	3	3	0	0
1983	R. G. D. Willis	G. P. Howarth	4	3	1	0
1983-84	R. G. D. Willis	G. P. Howarth	3	0	1	2
1986	M. W. Gatting	J. V. Coney	3	0	1	2
1987-88	M. W. Gatting	J. J. Crowe[4]	3	0	0	3
1990	G. A. Gooch	J. G. Wright	3	1	0	2
1991-92	G. A. Gooch	M. D. Crowe	3	2	0	1
1994	M. A. Atherton	K. R. Rutherford	3	1	0	2
1996-97	M. A. Atherton	L. K. Germon[5]	3	2	0	1
1999	N. Hussain[6]	S. P. Fleming	4	1	2	1
2001-02	N. Hussain	S. P. Fleming	3	1	1	1

Season	England	New Zealand	T	E	NZ	D
2004	M. P. Vaughan[7]	S. P. Fleming	3	3	0	0
2007-08	M. P. Vaughan	D. L. Vettori	3	2	1	0
2008	M. P. Vaughan	D. L. Vettori	3	2	0	1
	In New Zealand		44	18	4	22
	In England		50	27	4	19
	Totals		94	45	8	41

Notes: The following deputised for the official touring captain or were appointed by the home authority for only a minor proportion of the series:

[1]R. E. S. Wyatt (Second). [2]F. R. Brown (Third and Fourth). [3]M. E. Chapple (First). [4]J. G. Wright (Third). [5]S. P. Fleming (Third). [6]M. A. Butcher (Third). [7]M. E. Trescothick (First).

HIGHEST INNINGS TOTALS

For England in England: 567-8 dec at Nottingham	1994
in New Zealand: 593-6 dec at Auckland	1974-75
For New Zealand in England: 551-9 dec at Lord's	1973
in New Zealand: 537 at Wellington	1983-84

LOWEST INNINGS TOTALS

For England in England: 126 at Birmingham	1999
in New Zealand: 64 at Wellington	1977-78
For New Zealand in England: 47 at Lord's	1958
in New Zealand: 26 at Auckland	1954-55

DOUBLE-HUNDREDS

For England (7)

336*	W. R. Hammond at Auckland		1932-33
310*	J. H. Edrich at Leeds		1965
227	W. R. Hammond at Christchurch		1932-33
216	K. W. R. Fletcher at Auckland		1974-75
210	G. A. Gooch at Nottingham		1994
206	L. Hutton at The Oval		1949
200*	G. P. Thorpe at Christchurch		2001-02

For New Zealand (2)

222	N. J. Astle at Christchurch		2001-02
206	M. P. Donnelly at Lord's		1949

INDIVIDUAL HUNDREDS

For England (98)

4: M. A. Atherton, G. A. Gooch, D. I. Gower, W. R. Hammond, A. J. Stewart, G. P. Thorpe.

3: K. F. Barrington, I. T. Botham, J. H. Edrich, L. Hutton, A. J. Lamb, P. B. H. May, A. J. Strauss.

2: L. E. G. Ames, D. L. Amiss, G. Boycott, D. C. S. Compton, M. C. Cowdrey, K. S. Duleepsinhji, K. W. R. Fletcher, J. Hardstaff, jun., N. Hussain, K. P. Pietersen, D. W. Randall, H. Sutcliffe.

1: G. O. B. Allen, T. R. Ambrose, T. E. Bailey, I. R. Bell, E. H. Bowley, B. C. Broad, M. H. Denness, E. R. Dexter, B. L. D'Oliveira, W. J. Edrich, A. Flintoff, G. Fowler, M. W. Gatting, A. W. Greig, G. O. Jones, B. R. Knight, A. P. E. Knott, G. B. Legge, C. A. Milton, P. H. Parfitt, C. T. Radley, P. E. Richardson, J. D. Robertson, P. J. Sharpe, R. T. Simpson, C. J. Tavaré, M. E. Trescothick, M. P. Vaughan, C. Washbrook.

For New Zealand (50)

5: M. D. Crowe.

4: J. G. Wright.

3: N. J. Astle, B. E. Congdon, G. P. Howarth.

2: M. G. Burgess, C. S. Dempster, S. P. Fleming, V. Pollard, B. Sutcliffe, L. R. P. L. Taylor.

1: J. G. Bracewell, J. V. Coney, J. J. Crowe, M. P. Donnelly, T. J. Franklin, M. J. Greatbatch, W. A. Hadlee, M. J. Horne, A. H. Jones, C. D. McMillan, J. E. Mills, J. D. P. Oram, M. L. Page, J. M. Parker, J. R. Reid, M. H. Richardson, K. R. Rutherford, B. W. Sinclair, I. D. S. Smith, S. B. Styris.

TEN WICKETS OR MORE IN A MATCH

For England (9)

11-140 (6-101, 5-39)	I. T. Botham, Lord's	1978
10-149 (5-98, 5-51)	A. W. Greig, Auckland	1974-75
11-65 (4-14, 7-51)	G. A. R. Lock, Leeds	1958
11-84 (5-31, 6-53)	G. A. R. Lock, Christchurch	1958-59
10-139 (4-90, 6-49)†	R. J. Sidebottom, Hamilton	2007-08
11-147 (4-100, 7-47)†	P. C. R. Tufnell, Christchurch	1991-92
11-70 (4-38, 7-32)†	D. L. Underwood, Lord's	1969
12-101 (6-41, 6-60)	D. L. Underwood, The Oval	1969
12-97 (6-12, 6-85)	D. L. Underwood, Christchurch	1970-71

For New Zealand (5)

10-144 (7-74, 3-70)	B. L. Cairns, Leeds	1983
10-140 (4-73, 6-67)	J. Cowie, Manchester	1937
10-100 (4-74, 6-26)	R. J. Hadlee, Wellington	1977-78
10-140 (6-80, 4-60)	R. J. Hadlee, Nottingham	1986
11-169 (6-76, 5-93)	D. J. Nash, Lord's	1994

† *On first appearance in England–New Zealand Tests.*

Note: D. L. Underwood took 12 wickets in successive matches against New Zealand in 1969 and 1970-71.

SEVEN WICKETS OR MORE IN AN INNINGS

In addition to those listed above, the following have taken seven wickets or more in an innings:

For England

7-43	J. M. Anderson, Nottingham. . . .	2008	7-47 R. J. Sidebottom, Napier.	2007-08
7-63	M. J. Hoggard, Christchurch. . . .	2001-02	7-75 F. S. Trueman, Christchurch. . . .	1962-63
7-35	G. A. R. Lock, Manchester.	1958	7-76 F. E. Woolley, Wellington	1929-30

For New Zealand

7-143 B. L. Cairns, Wellington. 1983-84

ENGLAND v INDIA

		Captains				
Season	*England*	*India*	*T*	*E*	*I*	*D*
1932	D. R. Jardine	C. K. Nayudu	1	1	0	0
1933-34	D. R. Jardine	C. K. Nayudu	3	2	0	1
1936	G. O. B. Allen	Maharajkumar of Vizianagram	3	2	0	1
1946	W. R. Hammond	Nawab of Pataudi sen.	3	1	0	2
1951-52	N. D. Howard[1]	V. S. Hazare	5	1	1	3
1952	L. Hutton	V. S. Hazare	4	3	0	1

Captains

Season	England	India	T	E	I	D
1959	P. B. H. May[2]	D. K. Gaekwad[3]	5	5	0	0
1961-62	E. R. Dexter	N. J. Contractor	5	0	2	3
1963-64	M. J. K. Smith	Nawab of Pataudi jun.	5	0	0	5
1967	D. B. Close	Nawab of Pataudi jun.	3	3	0	0
1971	R. Illingworth	A. L. Wadekar	3	0	1	2
1972-73	A. R. Lewis	A. L. Wadekar	5	1	2	2
1974	M. H. Denness	A. L. Wadekar	3	3	0	0
1976-77	A. W. Greig	B. S. Bedi	5	3	1	1
1979	J. M. Brearley	S. Venkataraghavan	4	1	0	3
1979-80	J. M. Brearley	G. R. Viswanath	1	1	0	0
1981-82	K. W. R. Fletcher	S. M. Gavaskar	6	0	1	5
1982	R. G. D. Willis	S. M. Gavaskar	3	1	0	2
1984-85	D. I. Gower	S. M. Gavaskar	5	2	1	2
1986	M. W. Gatting[4]	Kapil Dev	3	0	2	1
1990	G. A. Gooch	M. Azharuddin	3	1	0	2
1992-93	G. A. Gooch[5]	M. Azharuddin	3	0	3	0
1996	M. A. Atherton	M. Azharuddin	3	1	0	2
2001-02	N. Hussain	S. C. Ganguly	3	0	1	2
2002	N. Hussain	S. C. Ganguly	4	1	1	2
2005-06	A. Flintoff	R. Dravid	3	1	1	1

THE PATAUDI TROPHY

Captains

Season	England	India	T	E	I	D	Held by
2007	M. P. Vaughan	R. Dravid	3	0	1	2	I
2008-09	K. P. Pietersen	M. S. Dhoni	2	0	1	1	I
	In England		48	23	5	20	
	In India		51	11	14	26	
	Totals		99	34	19	46	

Notes: The 1932 Indian touring team was captained by the Maharajah of Porbandar but he did not play in the Test match.

The following deputised for the official touring captain or were appointed by the home authority for only a minor proportion of the series:

[1]D. B. Carr (Fifth). [2]M. C. Cowdrey (Fourth and Fifth). [3]Pankaj Roy (Second). [4]D. I. Gower (First). [5]A. J. Stewart (Second).

HIGHEST INNINGS TOTALS

For England in England: 653–4 dec at Lord's	1990
in India: 652–7 dec at Madras	1984–85
For India in England: 664 at The Oval	2007
in India: 591 at Bombay	1992-93

LOWEST INNINGS TOTALS

For England in England: 101 at The Oval	1971
in India: 102 at Bombay	1981-82
For India in England: 42 at Lord's	1974
in India: 83 at Madras	1976-77

DOUBLE-HUNDREDS

For England (9)

333	G. A. Gooch at Lord's	1990
246*	G. Boycott at Leeds	1967
217	W. R. Hammond at The Oval ...	1936
214*	D. Lloyd at Birmingham.	1974
208	I. T. Botham at The Oval	1982

207	M. W. Gatting at Madras	1984-85
205*	J. Hardstaff, jun. at Lord's	1946
201	G. Fowler at Madras	1984-85
200*	D. I. Gower at Birmingham	1979

For India (5)

224	V. G. Kambli at Bombay	1992-93
222	G. R. Viswanath at Madras.....	1981-82
221	S. M. Gavaskar at The Oval	1979

217	R. Dravid at The Oval.........	2002
203*	Nawab of Pataudi, jun. at Delhi .	1963-64

INDIVIDUAL HUNDREDS

For England (93)

5: I. T. Botham, G. A. Gooch.

4: G. Boycott, N. Hussain, M. P. Vaughan.

3: K. F. Barrington, M. C. Cowdrey, M. W. Gatting, A. W. Greig, A. J. Lamb, K. P. Pietersen, A. J. Strauss.

2: D. L. Amiss, M. A. Atherton, P. D. Collingwood, M. H. Denness, K. W. R. Fletcher, D. I. Gower, T. W. Graveney, W. R. Hammond, L. Hutton, G. Pullar, R. A. Smith.

1: A. N. Cook, J. P. Crawley, E. R. Dexter, B. L. D'Oliveira, J. H. Edrich, T. G. Evans, G. Fowler, J. Hardstaff, jun., G. A. Hick, R. Illingworth, B. R. Knight, A. R. Lewis, C. C. Lewis, D. Lloyd, B. W. Luckhurst, P. B. H. May, P. H. Parfitt, D. W. Randall, R. T. Robinson, R. C. Russell, Rev. D. S. Sheppard, M. J. K. Smith, C. J. Tavaré, B. H. Valentine, C. F. Walters, A. J. Watkins, C. White, T. S. Worthington.

For India (78)

7: S. R. Tendulkar.

6: M. Azharuddin.

5: D. B. Vengsarkar.

4: R. Dravid, S. M. Gavaskar, R. J. Shastri, G. R. Viswanath.

3: S. C. Ganguly, V. L. Manjrekar, V. M. Merchant, Nawab of Pataudi, jun., P. R. Umrigar.

2: V. S. Hazare, M. L. Jaisimha, Kapil Dev, B. K. Kunderan, Pankaj Roy.

1: A. B. Agarkar, L. Amarnath, A. A. Baig, D. Dasgupta, F. M. Engineer, G. Gambhir, Hanumant Singh, V. G. Kambli, S. M. H. Kirmani, A. Kumble, V. Mankad, Mushtaq Ali, R. G. Nadkarni, S. M. Patil, D. G. Phadkar, V. Sehwag, N. S. Sidhu, Wasim Jaffer, Yashpal Sharma.

Notes: G. A. Gooch's match aggregate of 456 (333 and 123) for England at Lord's in 1990 is the record in Test matches and the only instance of a batsman scoring a triple-hundred and a hundred in the same first-class match. His 333 is the highest innings in any match at Lord's.

M. Azharuddin scored hundreds in each of his first three Tests.

TEN WICKETS OR MORE IN A MATCH

For England (7)

10-78 (5-35, 5-43)†	G. O. B. Allen, Lord's	1936
11-145 (7-49, 4-96)†	A. V. Bedser, Lord's	1946
11-93 (4-41, 7-52)	A. V. Bedser, Manchester	1946
13-106 (6-58, 7-48)	I. T. Botham, Bombay	1979-80
11-163 (6-104, 5-59)†	N. A. Foster, Madras	1984-85
10-70 (7-46, 3-24)†	J. K. Lever, Delhi	1976-77
11-153 (7-49, 4-104)	H. Verity, Madras	1933-34

For India (5)

10-177 (6-105, 4-72)	S. A. Durani, Madras	1961-62
10-233 (7-115, 3-118)	A. Kumble, Ahmedabad.	2001-02
12-108 (8-55, 4-53)	V. Mankad, Madras	1951-52
10-188 (4-130, 6-58)	Chetan Sharma, Birmingham	1986
12-181 (6-64, 6-117)†	L. Sivaramakrishnan, Bombay.	1984-85

† *On first appearance in England–India Tests.*

Note: A. V. Bedser took 11 wickets in a match in each of the first two Tests of his career.

SEVEN WICKETS OR MORE IN AN INNINGS

In addition to those listed above, the following have taken seven wickets or more in an innings:

For England

7-80 G. O. B. Allen, The Oval . . . . . . 1936 | 8-31 F. S. Trueman, Manchester. 1952

For India

7-86 L. Amar Singh, Madras . . . . 1933-34 | 8-79 B. S. Chandrasekhar, Delhi. 1972-73

ENGLAND v PAKISTAN

		Captains				
Season	*England*	*Pakistan*	*T*	*E*	*P*	*D*
1954	L. Hutton[1]	A. H. Kardar	4	1	1	2
1961-62	E. R. Dexter	Imtiaz Ahmed	3	1	0	2
1962	E. R. Dexter[2]	Javed Burki	5	4	0	1
1967	D. B. Close	Hanif Mohammad	3	2	0	1
1968-69	M. C. Cowdrey	Saeed Ahmed	3	0	0	3
1971	R. Illingworth	Intikhab Alam	3	1	0	2
1972-73	A. R. Lewis	Majid Khan	3	0	0	3
1974	M. H. Denness	Intikhab Alam	3	0	0	3
1977-78	J. M. Brearley[3]	Wasim Bari	3	0	0	3
1978	J. M. Brearley	Wasim Bari	3	2	0	1
1982	R. G. D. Willis[4]	Imran Khan	3	2	1	0
1983-84	R. G. D. Willis[5]	Zaheer Abbas	3	0	1	2
1987	M. W. Gatting	Imran Khan	5	0	1	4
1987-88	M. W. Gatting	Javed Miandad	3	0	1	2
1992	G. A. Gooch	Javed Miandad	5	1	2	2
1996	M. A. Atherton	Wasim Akram	3	0	2	1
2000-01	N. Hussain	Moin Khan	3	1	0	2
2001	N. Hussain[6]	Waqar Younis	2	1	1	0
2005-06	M. P. Vaughan[7]	Inzamam-ul-Haq	3	0	2	1
2006†	A. J. Strauss	Inzamam-ul-Haq	4	3	0	1
2010	**A. J. Strauss**	**Salman Butt**	**4**	**3**	**1**	**0**
	In England		47	20	9	18
	In Pakistan		24	2	4	18
	Totals.		71	22	13	36

† *In 2008, the ICC changed the result of the forfeited Oval Test of 2006 from an England win to a draw, in contravention of the Laws of Cricket, only to rescind their decision in January 2009.*

Notes: The following deputised for the official touring captain or were appointed by the home authority for only a minor proportion of the series:
[1]D. S. Sheppard (Second and Third). [2]M. C. Cowdrey (Third). [3]G. Boycott (Third). [4]D. I. Gower (Second). [5]D. I. Gower (Second and Third). [6]A. J. Stewart (Second). [7]M. E. Trescothick (First).

HIGHEST INNINGS TOTALS

For England in England: 558-6 dec at Nottingham 1954
            in Pakistan: 546-8 dec at Faisalabad 1983-84

For Pakistan in England: 708 at The Oval 1987
            in Pakistan: 636-8 dec at Lahore 2005-06

LOWEST INNINGS TOTALS

For England in England: 130 at The Oval 1954
            in Pakistan: 130 at Lahore 1987-88

For Pakistan in England: **72 at Birmingham** **2010**
            in Pakistan: 158 at Karachi 2000-01

DOUBLE-HUNDREDS

For England (2)

278	D. C. S. Compton at Nottingham	1954	205	E. R. Dexter at Karachi	1961-62

For Pakistan (7)

274	Zaheer Abbas at Birmingham	1971	205	Aamir Sohail at Manchester	1992
260	Javed Miandad at The Oval	1987	200	Mohsin Khan at Lord's	1982
240	Zaheer Abbas at The Oval	1974	202	Mohammad Yousuf at Lord's	2006
223	Mohammad Yousuf at Lahore	2005-06			

INDIVIDUAL HUNDREDS

For England (69)

4: K. F. Barrington, I. R. Bell, P. H. Parfitt.

3: D. L. Amiss, G. Boycott, **A. N. Cook**, M. C. Cowdrey, T. W. Graveney.

2: I. T. Botham, E. R. Dexter, M. W. Gatting, D. I. Gower, **K. P. Pietersen**, A. J. Stewart, **A. J. Strauss**, G. P. Thorpe, M. E. Trescothick.

1: M. A. Atherton, C. W. J. Athey, B. C. Broad, **S. C. J. Broad**, **P. D. Collingwood**, D. C. S. Compton, J. P. Crawley, B. L. D'Oliveira, K. W. R. Fletcher, G. A. Gooch, N. V. Knight, A. P. E. Knott, B. W. Luckhurst, C. Milburn, **E. J. G. Morgan**, **M. J. Prior**, G. Pullar, C. T. Radley, D. W. Randall, R. T. Robinson, R. T. Simpson, R. A. Smith, **I. J. L. Trott**, M. P. Vaughan.

For Pakistan (52)

6: **Mohammad Yousuf**.

5: Inzamam-ul-Haq.

4: Salim Malik.

3: Asif Iqbal, Hanif Mohammad, Javed Burki, Mudassar Nazar, Mushtaq Mohammad.

2: Haroon Rashid, Javed Miandad, Mohsin Khan, Zaheer Abbas.

1: Aamir Sohail, Abdul Razzaq, Alim-ud-Din, Ijaz Ahmed, sen., Imran Khan, Intikhab Alam, **Kamran Akmal**, Moin Khan, Nasim-ul-Ghani, Sadiq Mohammad, Saeed Anwar, **Salman Butt**, Wasim Raja, Younis Khan.

Note: Three batsmen – Majid Khan, Mushtaq Mohammad and D. L. Amiss – were dismissed for 99 at Karachi, 1972-73: the only instance in Test matches.

TEN WICKETS OR MORE IN A MATCH

For England (4)

11-71 (5-54, 6-17)	**J. M. Anderson, Nottingham**	**2010**
11-83 (6-65, 5-18)†	N. G. B. Cook, Karachi	1983-84
11-76 (6-19, 5-57)	S. J. Harmison, Manchester	2006
13-71 (5-20, 8-51)	D. L. Underwood, Lord's	1974

For Pakistan (6)

10-194 (5-84, 5-110)	Abdul Qadir, Lahore	1983-84
10-211 (7-96, 3-115)	Abdul Qadir, The Oval	1987
13-101 (9-56, 4-45)	Abdul Qadir, Lahore	1987-88
10-186 (5-88, 5-98)	Abdul Qadir, Karachi	1987-88
12-99 (6-53, 6-46)	Fazal Mahmood, The Oval	1954
10-77 (3-37, 7-40)	Imran Khan, Leeds	1987

† *On first appearance in England–Pakistan Tests.*

SEVEN WICKETS OR MORE IN AN INNINGS

In addition to those listed above, the following have taken seven wickets or more in an innings:

For England

8-34	I. T. Botham, Lord's	1978	7-50	C. M. Old, Birmingham	1978
7-66	P. H. Edmonds, Karachi	1977-78	7-56	J. H. Wardle, The Oval	1954
8-107	N. A. Foster, Leeds	1987			

For Pakistan

7-52	Imran Khan, Birmingham	1982	8-164	Saqlain Mushtaq, Lahore	2000-01

Bold type denotes performances in the 2010 series or, in career figures, players who appeared in that series.

ENGLAND v SRI LANKA

		Captains				
Season	England	Sri Lanka	T	E	SL	D
1981-82	K. W. R. Fletcher	B. Warnapura	1	1	0	0
1984	D. I. Gower	L. R. D. Mendis	1	0	0	1
1988	G. A. Gooch	R. S. Madugalle	1	1	0	0
1991	G. A. Gooch	P. A. de Silva	1	1	0	0
1992-93	A. J. Stewart	A. Ranatunga	1	0	1	0
1998	A. J. Stewart	A. Ranatunga	1	0	1	0
2000-01	N. Hussain	S. T. Jayasuriya	3	2	1	0
2002	N. Hussain	S. T. Jayasuriya	3	2	0	1
2003-04	M. P. Vaughan	H. P. Tillekeratne	3	0	1	2
2006	A. Flintoff	D. P. M. D. Jayawardene	3	1	1	1
2007-08	M. P. Vaughan	D. P. M. D. Jayawardene	3	0	1	2
	In England		10	5	2	3
	In Sri Lanka		11	3	4	4
	Totals		21	8	6	7

HIGHEST INNINGS TOTALS

For England in England: 551-6 dec at Lord's	2006
in Sri Lanka: 387 at Kandy	2000-01
For Sri Lanka in England: 591 at The Oval	1998
in Sri Lanka: 628-8 dec at Colombo (SSC)	2003-04

LOWEST INNINGS TOTALS

For England in England: 181 at The Oval	1998
in Sri Lanka: 81 at Galle	2007-08
For Sri Lanka in England: 141 at Birmingham	2006
in Sri Lanka: 81 at Colombo (SSC)	2000-01

DOUBLE-HUNDREDS

For Sri Lanka (3)

213* D. P. M. D. Jayawardene at Galle 2007-08 | 201* M. S. Atapattu at Galle 2000-01
213 S. T. Jayasuriya at The Oval .... 1998 |

Highest score for England: 174 by G. A. Gooch at Lord's, 1991.

INDIVIDUAL HUNDREDS

For England (20)

3: M. E. Trescothick.
2: M. A. Butcher, A. J. Stewart, G. P. Thorpe, K. P. Pietersen, M. P. Vaughan.
1: A. N. Cook, J. P. Crawley, G. A. Gooch, G. A. Hick, N. Hussain, A. J. Lamb, R. A. Smith.

For Sri Lanka (20)

6: D. P. M. D. Jayawardene.
2: M. S. Atapattu, P. A. de Silva, M. G. Vandort.
1: R. P. Arnold, T. M. Dilshan, S. T. Jayasuriya, L. R. D. Mendis, T. T. Samaraweera, K. C. Sangakkara, S. A. R. Silva, S. Wettimuny.

TEN WICKETS OR MORE IN A MATCH

For Sri Lanka (4)

16-220 (7-155, 9-65)	M. Muralitharan, The Oval	1998
11-93 (7-46, 4-47)	M. Muralitharan, Galle	2003-04
10-115 (6-86, 4-29)	M. Muralitharan, Birmingham	2006
11-132 (3-62, 8-70)	M. Muralitharan, Nottingham	2006

Note: The best match figures for England are 8-95 (5-28, 3-67) by D. L. Underwood at Colombo (PSS), 1981-82.

SEVEN WICKETS OR MORE IN AN INNINGS

In addition to those listed above, the following has taken seven wickets or more in an innings:

For England

7-70 P. A. J. DeFreitas, Lord's 1991

ENGLAND v ZIMBABWE

		Captains					
Season	*England*		*Zimbabwe*	*T*	*E*	*Z*	*D*
1996-97	M. A. Atherton		A. D. R. Campbell	2	0	0	2
2000	N. Hussain		A. Flower	2	1	0	1
2003	N. Hussain		H. H. Streak	2	2	0	0
	In England			4	3	0	1
	In Zimbabwe			2	0	0	2
	Totals			6	3	0	3

HIGHEST INNINGS TOTALS

For England in England: 472 at Lord's 2003
in Zimbabwe: 406 at Bulawayo 1996-97

For Zimbabwe in England: 285-4 dec at Nottingham 2000
in Zimbabwe: 376 at Bulawayo 1996-97

LOWEST INNINGS TOTALS

For England in England: 147 at Nottingham   2000
    in Zimbabwe: 156 at Harare   1996-97

For Zimbabwe in England: 83 at Lord's   2000
     in Zimbabwe: 215 at Harare   1996-97

HIGHEST INDIVIDUAL INNINGS

For England

137 M. A. Butcher at Lord's 2003

For Zimbabwe

148* M. W. Goodwin at Nottingham . 2000

INDIVIDUAL HUNDREDS

For England (7)

2: A. J. Stewart.
1: M. A. Atherton, M. A. Butcher, J. P. Crawley, G. A. Hick, N. Hussain.

For Zimbabwe (2)

1: A. Flower, M. W. Goodwin.

BEST MATCH BOWLING ANALYSES

For England

7-42 (5-15, 2-27)† E. S. H. Giddins, Lord's 2000

For Zimbabwe

7-186 (5-123, 2-63)† P. A. Strang, Bulawayo 1996-97
† *On first appearance in England–Zimbabwe Tests.*

ENGLAND v BANGLADESH

Season	England	Captains Bangladesh	T	E	B	D
2003-04	M. P. Vaughan	Khaled Mahmud	2	2	0	0
2005	M. P. Vaughan	Habibul Bashar	2	2	0	0
2009-10	**A. N. Cook**	**Shakib Al Hasan**	**2**	**2**	**0**	**0**
2010	**A. J. Strauss**	**Shakib Al Hasan**	**2**	**2**	**0**	**0**
	In England		4	4	0	0
	In Bangladesh		4	4	0	0
	Totals		8	8	0	0

HIGHEST INNINGS TOTALS

For England in England: 528-3 dec at Lord's   2005
    in Bangladesh: 599-6 dec at Mirpur **2009-10**

For Bangladesh in England: 382 at Lord's **2010**
    in Bangladesh: 419 at Mirpur **2009-10**

LOWEST INNINGS TOTALS

		2010
For England in England: **419** at Manchester 2003-04

in Bangladesh: 295 at Dhaka. 2003-04

For Bangladesh in England: 104 at Chester-le-Street 2005

in Bangladesh: 138 at Chittagong 2003-04

DOUBLE-HUNDRED

For England (1)

226 I. J. L. Trott at Lord's **2010**

Highest score for Bangladesh: 108 by Tamim Iqbal at Manchester, 2010.

INDIVIDUAL HUNDREDS

For England (11)

3: **I. R. Bell**, M. E. Trescothick.

2: **A. N. Cook.**

1: **P. D. Collingwood, I. J. L. Trott**, M. P. Vaughan.

For Bangladesh (3)

2: **Tamim Iqbal**.

1: **Junaid Siddique**.

TEN WICKETS OR MORE IN A MATCH

For England (1)

10-217 (5-90, 5-127) G. P. Swann, Chittagong 2009-10

Note: The best match figures for Bangladesh are **5-117 (5-98, 0-19) by Shahadat Hossain** at Lord's, **2010**.

Bold type denotes performances in the 2009-10 or 2010 series or, in career figures, players who appeared in those series.

AUSTRALIA v SOUTH AFRICA

		Captains				
Season	*Australia*	*South Africa*	*T*	*A*	*SA*	*D*
1902-03S	J. Darling	H. M. Taberer[1]	3	2	0	1
1910-11A	C. Hill	P. W. Sherwell	5	4	1	0
1912E	S. E. Gregory	F. Mitchell[2]	3	2	0	1
1921-22S	H. L. Collins	H. W. Taylor	3	1	0	2
1931-32A	W. M. Woodfull	H. B. Cameron	5	5	0	0
1935-36S	V. Y. Richardson	H. F. Wade	5	4	0	1
1949-50S	A. L. Hassett	A. D. Nourse	5	4	0	1
1952-53A	A. L. Hassett	J. E. Cheetham	5	2	2	1
1957-58S	I. D. Craig	C. B. van Ryneveld[3]	5	3	0	2
1963-64A	R. B. Simpson[4]	T. L. Goddard	5	1	1	3
1966-67S	R. B. Simpson	P. L. van der Merwe	5	1	3	1
1969-70S	W. M. Lawry	A. Bacher	4	0	4	0
1993-94A	A. R. Border	K. C. Wessels[5]	3	1	1	1
1993-94S	A. R. Border	K. C. Wessels	3	1	1	1
1996-97S	M. A. Taylor	W. J. Cronje	3	2	1	0
1997-98A	M. A. Taylor	W. J. Cronje	3	1	0	2
2001-02A	S. R. Waugh	S. M. Pollock	3	3	0	0

Captains

Season	Australia	South Africa	T	A	SA	D
2001-02S	S. R. Waugh	M. V. Boucher	3	2	1	0
2005-06A	R. T. Ponting	G. C. Smith	3	2	0	1
2005-06S	R. T. Ponting	G. C. Smith[6]	3	3	0	0
2008-09A	R. T. Ponting	G. C. Smith	3	1	2	0
2008-09S	R. T. Ponting	G. C. Smith[7]	3	2	1	0
	In South Africa........................		45	25	11	9
	In Australia...........................		35	20	7	8
	In England............................		3	2	0	1
	Totals.................................		83	47	18	18

S Played in South Africa. A Played in Australia. E Played in England.

Notes: The following deputised for the official touring captain or were appointed by the home authority for only a minor proportion of the series:
[1]J. H. Anderson (Second), E. A. Halliwell (Third). [2]L. J. Tancred (Third). [3]D. J. McGlew (First). [4]R. Benaud (First). [5]W. J. Cronje (Third). [6]J. H. Kallis (Third). [7]J. H. Kallis (Third).

HIGHEST INNINGS TOTALS

For Australia in Australia: 578 at Melbourne 1910-11
in South Africa: 652-7 dec at Johannesburg 2001-02

For South Africa in Australia: 595 at Adelaide 1963-64
in South Africa: 651 at Cape Town 2008-09

LOWEST INNINGS TOTALS

For Australia in Australia: 111 at Sydney 1993-94
in South Africa: 75 at Durban 1949-50

For South Africa in Australia: 36† at Melbourne............................... 1931-32
in South Africa 85‡ at Johannesburg 1902-03
85‡ at Cape Town............................. 1902-03

† *Scored 45 in the second innings, giving the smallest aggregate of 81 (12 extras) in Test cricket.*
‡ *In successive innings.*

DOUBLE-HUNDREDS

For Australia (8)

299* D. G. Bradman at Adelaide..... 1931-32	205 R. N. Harvey at Melbourne..... 1952-53
226 D. G. Bradman at Brisbane..... 1931-32	204* A. C. Gilchrist at Johannesburg . 2001-02
214* V. T. Trumper at Adelaide 1910-11	203* B. J. Hodge at Perth 2005-06
214 G. S. Blewett at Johannesburg .. 1996-97	203 H. L. Collins at Johannesburg... 1921-22

For South Africa (5)

274 R. G. Pollock at Durban 1969-70	204 G. A. Faulkner at Melbourne ... 1910-11
231 A. D. Nourse at Johannesburg .. 1935-36	201 E. J. Barlow at Adelaide........ 1963-64
209 R. G. Pollock at Cape Town.... 1966-67	

INDIVIDUAL HUNDREDS

For Australia (94)

8: R. N. Harvey, R. T. Ponting.

6: M. L. Hayden.

4: D. G. Bradman, D. R. Martyn, M. E. Waugh.

3: W. Bardsley, J. H. Fingleton, A. L. Hassett, C. Hill.

2: W. W. Armstrong, R. Benaud, B. C. Booth, A. C. Gilchrist, P. J. Hughes, C. Kelleway, J. L. Langer, C. G. Macartney, S. J. McCabe, J. Moroney, A. R. Morris, M. A. Taylor, V. T. Trumper, S. R. Waugh.

1: G. S. Blewett, W. A. Brown, J. W. Burke, A. G. Chipperfield, M. J. Clarke, H. L. Collins, J. M. Gregory, B. J. Hodge, M. E. K. Hussey, M. G. Johnson, S. M. Katich, W. M. Lawry, S. J. E. Loxton, C. C. McDonald, M. J. North, K. E. Rigg, J. Ryder, R. B. Simpson, K. R. Stackpole, W. M. Woodfull.

For South Africa (53)

5: E. J. Barlow, R. G. Pollock.

4: J. H. Kallis.

3: A. B. de Villiers, G. A. Faulkner, D. T. Lindsay.

2: G. Kirsten, D. J. McGlew, A. D. Nourse, A. G. Prince, B. A. Richards, J. H. Sinclair, J. H. B. Waite, J. W. Zulch.

1: K. C. Bland, W. J. Cronje, J-P. Duminy, W. R. Endean, C. N. Frank, H. H. Gibbs, A. C. Hudson, B. L. Irvine, A. W. Nourse, E. A. B. Rowan, J. A. Rudolph, G. C. Smith, S. J. Snooke, K. G. Viljoen.

TEN WICKETS OR MORE IN A MATCH

For Australia (8)

14-199 (7-116, 7-83)	C. V. Grimmett, Adelaide	1931-32
10-88 (5-32, 5-56)	C. V. Grimmett, Cape Town	1935-36
10-110 (3-70, 7-40)	C. V. Grimmett, Johannesburg	1935-36
13-173 (7-100, 6-73)	C. V. Grimmett, Durban	1935-36
11-24 (5-6, 6-18)	H. Ironmonger, Melbourne	1931-32
11-159 (8-61, 3-98)†	M. G. Johnson, Perth	2008-09
12-128 (7-56, 5-72)	S. K. Warne, Sydney	1993-94
11-109 (5-75, 6-34)	S. K. Warne, Sydney	1997-98

For South Africa (5)

10-123 (4-80, 6-43)	P. S. de Villiers, Sydney	1993-94
10-116 (5-43, 5-73)	C. B. Llewellyn, Johannesburg	1902-03
10-178 (6-100, 4-78)	M. Ntini, Johannesburg	2005-06
10-154 (5-87, 5-67)	D. W. Steyn, Melbourne	2008-09
13-165 (6-84, 7-81)	H. J. Tayfield, Melbourne	1952-53

† *On first appearance in Australia–South Africa Tests.*

Note: C. V. Grimmett took ten wickets or more in three consecutive matches in 1935-36, the last three of his career.

SEVEN WICKETS OR MORE IN AN INNINGS

In addition to those listed above, the following have taken seven wickets or more in an innings:

For Australia

7-34 J. V. Saunders, Johannesburg . . . 1902-03

For South Africa

7-91 J. T. Partridge, Sydney . . . . 1963-64 | 7-23 H. J. Tayfield, Durban. 1949-50
7-87 S. M. Pollock, Adelaide . . . . . . 1997-98 |

AUSTRALIA v WEST INDIES

	Captains						
Season	*Australia*	*West Indies*	*T*	*A*	*WI*	*T*	*D*
1930-31A	W. M. Woodfull	G. C. Grant	5	4	1	0	0
1951-52A	A. L. Hassett[1]	J. D. C. Goddard[2]	5	4	1	0	0
1954-55W	I. W. Johnson	D. St E. Atkinson[3]	5	3	0	0	2

THE FRANK WORRELL TROPHY

	Captains							
Season	*Australia*	*West Indies*	*T*	*A*	*WI*	*T*	*D*	*Held by*
1960-61A	R. Benaud	F. M. M. Worrell	5	2	1	1	1	A
1964-65W	R. B. Simpson	G. S. Sobers	5	1	2	0	2	WI
1968-69A	W. M. Lawry	G. S. Sobers	5	3	1	0	1	A
1972-73W	I. M. Chappell	R. B. Kanhai	5	2	0	0	3	A
1975-76A	G. S. Chappell	C. H. Lloyd	6	5	1	0	0	A
1977-78W	R. B. Simpson	A. I. Kallicharran[4]	5	1	3	0	1	WI
1979-80A	G. S. Chappell	C. H. Lloyd[5]	3	0	2	0	1	WI
1981-82A	G. S. Chappell	C. H. Lloyd	3	1	1	0	1	WI
1983-84W	K. J. Hughes	C. H. Lloyd[6]	5	0	3	0	2	WI
1984-85A	A. R. Border[7]	C. H. Lloyd	5	1	3	0	1	WI
1988-89A	A. R. Border	I. V. A. Richards	5	1	3	0	1	WI
1990-91W	A. R. Border	I. V. A. Richards	5	1	2	0	2	WI
1992-93A	A. R. Border	R. B. Richardson	5	1	2	0	2	WI
1994-95W	M. A. Taylor	R. B. Richardson	4	2	1	0	1	A
1996-97A	M. A. Taylor	C. A. Walsh	5	3	2	0	0	A
1998-99W	S. R. Waugh	B. C. Lara	4	2	2	0	0	A
2000-01A	S. R. Waugh[8]	J. C. Adams	5	5	0	0	0	A
2002-03W	S. R. Waugh	B. C. Lara	4	3	1	0	0	A
2005-06A	R. T. Ponting	S. Chanderpaul	3	3	0	0	0	A
2007-08W	R. T. Ponting	R. R. Sarwan[9]	3	2	0	0	1	A
2009-10A	R. T. Ponting	C. H. Gayle	3	2	0	0	1	A
	In Australia		63	35	18	1	9	
	In West Indies		45	17	14	0	14	
	Totals		108	52	32	1	23	

A Played in Australia.   W Played in West Indies.

Notes: The following deputised for the official touring captain or were appointed by the home authority for only a minor proportion of the series:

[1]A. R. Morris (Third). [2]J. B. Stollmeyer (Fifth). [3]J. B. Stollmeyer (Second and Third). [4]C. H. Lloyd (First and Second). [5]D. L. Murray (First). [6]I. V. A. Richards (Second). [7]K. J. Hughes (First and Second). [8]A. C. Gilchrist (Third). [9]C. H. Gayle (Third).

HIGHEST INNINGS TOTALS

For Australia in Australia: 619 at Sydney 1968-69
in West Indies: 758-8 dec at Kingston 1954-55

For West Indies in Australia: 616 at Adelaide 1968-69
in West Indies: 573 at Bridgetown 1964-65

LOWEST INNINGS TOTALS

For Australia in Australia: 76 at Perth   1984-85
in West Indies: 90 at Port-of-Spain   1977-78

For West Indies in Australia: 78 at Sydney   1951-52
in West Indies: 51 at Port-of-Spain   1998-99

DOUBLE-HUNDREDS

For Australia (9)

242	K. D. Walters at Sydney	1968-69	205	W. M. Lawry at Melbourne	1968-69
223	D. G. Bradman at Brisbane	1930-31	204	R. N. Harvey at Kingston	1954-55
216	D. M. Jones at Adelaide	1988-89	201	R. B. Simpson at Bridgetown	1964-65
210	W. M. Lawry at Bridgetown	1964-65	200	S. R. Waugh at Kingston	1994-95
206	R. T. Ponting at Port-of-Spain	2002-03			

For West Indies (7)

277	B. C. Lara at Sydney	1992-93	213	B. C. Lara at Kingston	1998-99
226	C. G. Greenidge at Bridgetown	1990-91	208	I. V. A. Richards at Melbourne	1984-85
226	B. C. Lara at Adelaide	2005-06	201	S. M. Nurse at Bridgetown	1964-65
219	D. St E. Atkinson at Bridgetown	1954-55			

INDIVIDUAL HUNDREDS

For Australia (107)

7: R. T. Ponting, S. R. Waugh.

6: K. D. Walters.

5: G. S. Chappell, I. M. Chappell, M. L. Hayden.

4: W. M. Lawry, K. R. Miller, I. R. Redpath, M. E. Waugh.

3: D. C. Boon, A. R. Border, R. N. Harvey, J. L. Langer.

2: R. M. Cowper, A. L. Hassett, K. J. Hughes, M. E. K. Hussey, S. M. Katich, C. C. McDonald, W. H. Ponsford, G. M. Wood.

1: R. G. Archer, R. Benaud, B. C. Booth, M. J. Clarke, G. J. Cosier, J. Dyson, A. C. Gilchrist, I. A. Healy, A. M. J. Hilditch, P. A. Jaques, D. M. Jones, A. F. Kippax, D. S. Lehmann, R. R. Lindwall, R. B. McCosker, A. R. Morris, N. C. O'Neill, W. B. Phillips, C. S. Serjeant, R. B. Simpson, M. J. Slater, K. R. Stackpole, M. A. Taylor, P. M. Toohey, A. Turner, K. C. Wessels.

For West Indies (102)

9: B. C. Lara, R. B. Richardson.

6: H. A. Gomes, C. H. Lloyd.

5: D. L. Haynes, R. B. Kanhai, I. V. A. Richards, C. L. Walcott.

4: S. Chanderpaul, C. G. Greenidge, A. I. Kallicharran, G. S. Sobers.

3: B. F. Butcher.

2: D. J. Bravo, S. L. Campbell, P. J. L. Dujon, D. Ganga, C. H. Gayle, G. A. Headley, S. M. Nurse, R. R. Sarwan.

1: F. C. M. Alexander, K. L. T. Arthurton, D. St E. Atkinson, A. B. Barath, C. C. Depeiza, M. L. C. Foster, R. C. Fredericks, C. L. Hooper, C. C. Hunte, F. R. Martin, L. G. Rowe, P. V. Simmons, O. G. Smith, J. B. Stollmeyer, E. D. Weekes, A. B. Williams, F. M. M. Worrell.

Note: F. C. M. Alexander and C. C. Depeiza scored the only hundreds of their first-class careers in a Test match.

TEN WICKETS OR MORE IN A MATCH

For Australia (15)

10-113 (4-31, 6-82)	M. G. Bevan, Adelaide	1996-97
11-96 (7-46, 4-50)	A. R. Border, Sydney.	1988-89
11-222 (5-135, 6-87)†	A. K. Davidson, Brisbane	1960-61
11-183 (7-87, 4-96)†	C. V. Grimmett, Adelaide	1930-31
10-115 (6-72, 4-43)	N. J. N. Hawke, Georgetown.	1964-65
10-144 (6-54, 4-90)	R. G. Holland, Sydney	1984-85
13-217 (5-130, 8-87)	M. G. Hughes, Perth	1988-89
11-79 (7-23, 4-56)	H. Ironmonger, Melbourne	1930-31
11-181 (8-112, 3-69)	G. F. Lawson, Adelaide	1984-85
10-127 (7-83, 3-44)	D. K. Lillee, Melbourne.	1981-82
10-78 (5-50, 5-28)	G. D. McGrath, Port-of-Spain	1998-99
10-27 (6-17, 4-10)	G. D. McGrath, Brisbane	2000-01
10-159 (8-71, 2-88)	G. D. McKenzie, Melbourne	1968-69
10-113 (5-81, 5-32)	C. R. Miller, Adelaide	2000-01
10-185 (3-87, 7-98)	B. Yardley, Sydney	1981-82

For West Indies (4)

10-120 (6-74, 4-46)	C. E. L. Ambrose, Adelaide.	1992-93
10-113 (7-55, 3-58)	G. E. Gomez, Sydney.	1951-52
11-107 (5-45, 6-62)	M. A. Holding, Melbourne	1981-82
10-107 (5-45, 6-62)	M. D. Marshall, Adelaide	1984-85

† *On first appearance in Australia–West Indies Tests.*

SEVEN WICKETS OR MORE IN AN INNINGS

In addition to those listed above, the following have taken seven wickets or more in an innings:

For Australia

7-44	I. W. Johnson, Georgetown. . . .	1954-55	7-52	S. K. Warne, Melbourne.	1992-93
7-104	S. C. G. MacGill, Sydney	2000-01	7-89	M. R. Whitney, Adelaide	1988-89

For West Indies

7-25	C. E. L. Ambrose, Perth	1992-93	7-54	A. M. E. Roberts, Perth.	1975-76
7-78	J. J. C. Lawson, St John's	2002-03			

AUSTRALIA v NEW ZEALAND

		Captains				
Season	Australia	New Zealand	T	A	NZ	D
1945-46N	W. A. Brown	W. A. Hadlee	1	1	0	0
1973-74A	I. M. Chappell	B. E. Congdon	3	2	0	1
1973-74N	I. M. Chappell	B. E. Congdon	3	1	1	1
1976-77N	G. S. Chappell	G. M. Turner	2	1	0	1
1980-81A	G. S. Chappell	G. P. Howarth[1]	3	2	0	1
1981-82N	G. S. Chappell	G. P. Howarth	3	1	1	1

TRANS-TASMAN TROPHY

		Captains					
Season	*Australia*	*New Zealand*	*T*	*A*	*NZ*	*D*	*Held by*
1985-86*A*	A. R. Border	J. V. Coney	3	1	2	0	NZ
1985-86*N*	A. R. Border	J. V. Coney	3	0	1	2	NZ
1987-88*A*	A. R. Border	J. J. Crowe	3	1	0	2	A
1989-90*A*	A. R. Border	J. G. Wright	1	0	0	1	A
1989-90*N*	A. R. Border	J. G. Wright	1	0	1	0	NZ
1992-93*N*	A. R. Border	M. D. Crowe	3	1	1	1	NZ
1993-94*A*	A. R. Border	M. D. Crowe[2]	3	2	0	1	A
1997-98*A*	M. A. Taylor	S. P. Fleming	3	2	0	1	A
1999-2000*N*	S. R. Waugh	S. P. Fleming	3	3	0	0	A
2001-02*A*	S. R. Waugh	S. P. Fleming	3	0	0	3	A
2004-05*A*	R. T. Ponting	S. P. Fleming	2	2	0	0	A
2004-05*N*	R. T. Ponting	S. P. Fleming	3	2	0	1	A
2008-09*A*	R. T. Ponting	D. L. Vettori	2	2	0	0	A
2009-10*N*	**R. T. Ponting**	**D. L. Vettori**	**2**	**2**	**0**	**0**	**A**
	In Australia................		26	14	2	10	
	In New Zealand		**24**	**12**	**5**	**7**	
	Totals................		**50**	**26**	**7**	**17**	

A Played in Australia. N Played in New Zealand.

Notes: The following deputised for the official touring captain: [1]M. G. Burgess (Second). [2]K. R. Rutherford (Second and Third).

HIGHEST INNINGS TOTALS

For Australia in Australia: 607-6 dec at Brisbane 1993-94
in New Zealand: 570-8 dec at Wellington 2004-05

For New Zealand in Australia: 553-7 dec at Brisbane........................ 1985-86
in New Zealand: 484 at Wellington 1973-74

LOWEST INNINGS TOTALS

For Australia in Australia: 162 at Sydney 1973-74
in New Zealand: 103 at Auckland 1985-86

For New Zealand in Australia: 76 at Brisbane................................ 2004-05
in New Zealand: 42 at Wellington 1945-46

DOUBLE-HUNDREDS

For Australia (5)

250 K. D. Walters at Christchurch... 1976-77	205 A. R. Border at Adelaide 1987-88
247* G. S. Chappell at Wellington ... 1973-74	200 D. C. Boon at Perth.......... 1989-90
215 J. L. Langer at Adelaide 2004-05	

Highest score for New Zealand: 188 by M. D. Crowe at Brisbane, 1985-86.

INDIVIDUAL HUNDREDS

For Australia (54)

5: A. R. Border.

4: A. C. Gilchrist, J. L. Langer.

3: D. C. Boon, G. S. Chappell, **M. J. Clarke**, **S. M. Katich**, K. D. Walters.

2: I. M. Chappell, G. R. J. Matthews, **R. T. Ponting**, M. J. Slater, M. A. Taylor, S. R. Waugh, G. M. Wood.

1: M. T. G. Elliott, G. J. Gilmour, **B. J. Haddin**, M. L. Hayden, I. A. Healy, G. R. Marsh, R. W. Marsh, D. R. Martyn, **M. J. North**, I. R. Redpath, K. R. Stackpole, M. E. Waugh.

For New Zealand (29)

3: M. D. Crowe.

2: B. E. Congdon, A. H. Jones, G. M. Turner, J. G. Wright.

1: N. J. Astle, C. L. Cairns, J. V. Coney, B. A. Edgar, S. P. Fleming, M. J. Greatbatch, B. F. Hastings, M. J. Horne, **B. B. McCullum**, H. J. H. Marshall, J. F. M. Morrison, J. D. P. Oram, J. M. Parker, A. C. Parore, J. F. Reid, K. R. Rutherford, **L. R. P. L. Taylor**, L. Vincent.

Note: G. S. and I. M. Chappell each hit two hundreds at Wellington in 1973-74, the only instance of two batsmen on the same side scoring twin hundreds in the same Test.

TEN WICKETS OR MORE IN A MATCH

For Australia (3)

10-174 (6-106, 4-68)	R. G. Holland, Sydney	1985-86
10-132 (4-59, 6-73)	**M. G. Johnson, Hamilton**	**2009-10**
11-123 (5-51, 6-72)	D. K. Lillee, Auckland	1976-77

For New Zealand (5)

10-106 (4-74, 6-32)	J. G. Bracewell, Auckland	1985-86
15-123 (9-52, 6-71)	R. J. Hadlee, Brisbane	1985-86
11-155 (5-65, 6-90)	R. J. Hadlee, Perth	1985-86
10-176 (5-109, 5-67)	R. J. Hadlee, Melbourne	1987-88
12-149 (5-62, 7-87)	D. L. Vettori, Auckland	1999-2000

SEVEN WICKETS OR MORE IN AN INNINGS

In addition to those listed above, the following have taken seven wickets or more in an innings:

For New Zealand

7-116 R. J. Hadlee, Christchurch .... 1985-86 | 7-89 D. K. Morrison, Wellington 1992-93

Bold type denotes performances in the 2009-10 series or, in career figures, players who appeared in that series.

AUSTRALIA v INDIA

		Captains					
Season	*Australia*	*India*	*T*	*A*	*I*	*T*	*D*
1947-48*A*	D. G. Bradman	L. Amarnath	5	4	0	0	1
1956-57*I*	I. W. Johnson[1]	P. R. Umrigar	3	2	0	0	1
1959-60*I*	R. Benaud	G. S. Ramchand	5	2	1	0	2
1964-65*I*	R. B. Simpson	Nawab of Pataudi jun.	3	1	1	0	1
1967-68*A*	R. B. Simpson[2]	Nawab of Pataudi jun.[3]	4	4	0	0	0
1969-70*I*	W. M. Lawry	Nawab of Pataudi jun.	5	3	1	0	1
1977-78*A*	R. B. Simpson	B. S. Bedi	5	3	2	0	0
1979-80*I*	K. J. Hughes	S. M. Gavaskar	6	0	2	0	4
1980-81*A*	G. S. Chappell	S. M. Gavaskar	3	1	1	0	1
1985-86*A*	A. R. Border	Kapil Dev	3	0	0	0	3

Season	Australia	Captains India	T	A	I	T	D
1986-87*I*	A. R. Border	Kapil Dev	3	0	0	1	2
1991-92*A*	A. R. Border	M. Azharuddin	5	4	0	0	1

THE BORDER–GAVASKAR TROPHY

Season	Australia	Captains India	T	A	I	T	D	Held by
1996-97*I*	M. A. Taylor	S. R. Tendulkar	1	0	1	0	0	I
1997-98*I*	M. A. Taylor	M. Azharuddin	3	1	2	0	0	I
1999-2000*A*	S. R. Waugh	S. R. Tendulkar	3	3	0	0	0	A
2000-01*I*	S. R. Waugh	S. C. Ganguly	3	1	2	0	0	I
2003-04*A*	S. R. Waugh	S. C. Ganguly	4	1	1	0	2	I
2004-05*I*	R. T. Ponting[4]	S. C. Ganguly[5]	4	2	1	0	1	A
2007-08*A*	R. T. Ponting	A. Kumble	4	2	1	0	1	A
2008-09*I*	R. T. Ponting	A. Kumble[6]	4	0	2	0	2	I
2010-11*I*	**R. T. Ponting**	**M. S. Dhoni**	**2**	**0**	**2**	**0**	**0**	**I**
In Australia			36	22	5	0	9	
In India			**42**	**12**	**15**	**1**	**14**	
Totals			78	34	20	1	23	

A Played in Australia. I Played in India.

Notes: The following deputised for the official touring captain or were appointed by the home authority for only a minor proportion of the series:

[1] R. R. Lindwall (Second). [2] W. M. Lawry (Third and Fourth). [3] C. G. Borde (First). [4] A. C. Gilchrist (First, Second and Third). [5] R. Dravid (Third and Fourth). [6] M. S. Dhoni (Second and Fourth).

HIGHEST INNINGS TOTALS

For Australia in Australia: 674 at Adelaide	1947-48
in India: 577 at Delhi	2008-09
For India in Australia: 705-7 dec at Sydney	2003-04
in India: 657-7 dec at Kolkata	2000-01

LOWEST INNINGS TOTALS

For Australia in Australia: 83 at Melbourne	1980-81
in India: 93 at Mumbai	2004-05
For India in Australia: 58 at Brisbane	1947-48
in India: 104 in Mumbai	2004-05

DOUBLE-HUNDREDS

For Australia (8)

257	R. T. Ponting at Melbourne	2003-04	210	D. M. Jones at Madras	1986-87
242	R. T. Ponting at Adelaide	2003-04	204	G. S. Chappell at Sydney	1980-81
223	J. L. Langer at Sydney	1999-2000	203	M. L. Hayden at Chennai	2000-01
213	K. J. Hughes at Adelaide	1980-81	201	D. G. Bradman at Adelaide	1947-48

For India (5)

281	V. V. S. Laxman at Kolkata	2000-01	**214**	**S. R. Tendulkar at Bangalore**	**2010-11**
241*	S. R. Tendulkar at Sydney	2003-04	206	R. J. Shastri at Sydney	1991-92
233	R. Dravid at Adelaide	2003-04			

INDIVIDUAL HUNDREDS

For Australia (84)

6: D. C. Boon, M. L. Hayden, **R. T. Ponting**.

4: A. R. Border, D. G. Bradman, R. N. Harvey, R. B. Simpson.

3: M. J. Clarke, J. L. Langer.

2: I. M. Chappell, R. M. Cowper, A. C. Gilchrist, K. J. Hughes, **M. E. K. Hussey**, D. M. Jones, **S. M. Katich**, D. R. Martyn, N. C. O'Neill, M. A. Taylor, S. R. Waugh, G. N. Yallop.

1: S. G. Barnes, J. W. Burke, G. S. Chappell, L. E. Favell, A. L. Hassett, W. M. Lawry, A. L. Mann, G. R. Marsh, G. R. J. Matthews, T. M. Moody, A. R. Morris, **M. J. North**, G. M. Ritchie, A. P. Sheahan, K. R. Stackpole, A. Symonds, K. D. Walters, **S. R. Watson**, M. E. Waugh, G. M. Wood.

For India (62)

11: S. R. Tendulkar.

8: S. M. Gavaskar.

6: V. V. S. Laxman.

4: G. R. Viswanath.

3: V. Sehwag.

2: M. Amarnath, M. Azharuddin, **R. Dravid**, **G. Gambhir**, S. C. Ganguly, V. S. Hazare, V. Mankad, R. J. Shastri, D. B. Vengsarkar.

1: N. J. Contractor, M. L. Jaisimha, Kapil Dev, S. M. H. Kirmani, N. R. Mongia, Nawab of Pataudi, jun., S. M. Patil, D. G. Phadkar, G. S. Ramchand, K. Srikkanth, **M. Vijay**, Yashpal Sharma.

TEN WICKETS OR MORE IN A MATCH

For Australia (13)

11-105 (6-52, 5-53)	R. Benaud, Calcutta	1956-57
12-124 (5-31, 7-93)	A. K. Davidson, Kanpur	1959-60
12-166 (5-99, 7-67)	G. Dymock, Kanpur	1979-80
12-358 (8-215, 4-143)†	J. J. Krejza, Nagpur	2008-09
10-168 (5-76, 5-92)	C. J. McDermott, Adelaide	1991-92
10-103 (5-48, 5-55)	G. D. McGrath, Sydney	1999-2000
10-91 (6-58, 4-33)†	G. D. McKenzie, Madras	1964-65
10-151 (7-66, 3-85)	G. D. McKenzie, Melbourne	1967-68
10-144 (5-91, 5-53)	A. A. Mallett, Madras	1969-70
10-249 (5-103, 5-146)	G. R. J. Matthews, Madras	1986-87
12-126 (6-66, 6-60)	B. A. Reid, Melbourne	1991-92
11-31 (5-2, 6-29)†	E. R. H. Toshack, Brisbane	1947-48
11-95 (4-68, 7-27)	M. R. Whitney, Perth	1991-92

For India (11)

10-194 (5-89, 5-105)	B. S. Bedi, Perth	1977-78
12-104 (6-52, 6-52)	B. S. Chandrasekhar, Melbourne	1977-78
10-130 (7-49, 3-81)	Ghulam Ahmed, Calcutta	1956-57
13-196 (7-123, 6-73)	Harbhajan Singh, Kolkata	2000-01
15-217 (7-133, 8-84)	Harbhajan Singh, Chennai	2000-01
11-224 (5-146, 6-78)	Harbhajan Singh, Bangalore	2004-05
12-279 (8-141, 4-138)	A. Kumble, Sydney	2003-04
13-181 (7-48, 6-133)	A. Kumble, Chennai	2004-05
11-122 (5-31, 6-91)	R. G. Nadkarni, Madras	1964-65
14-124 (9-69, 5-55)	J. M. Patel, Kanpur	1959-60
10-174 (4-100, 6-74)	E. A. S. Prasanna, Madras	1969-70

† *On first appearance in Australia–India Tests.*

SEVEN WICKETS OR MORE IN AN INNINGS

In addition to those listed above, the following have taken seven wickets or more in an innings:

For Australia

7-72	R. Benaud, Madras	1956-57	7-38	R. R. Lindwall, Adelaide 1947-48
7-143	J. D. Higgs, Madras	1979-80	7-43	R. R. Lindwall, Madras 1956-57

For India

7-98	B. S. Bedi, Calcutta	1969-70	8-106	Kapil Dev, Adelaide 1985-86

Bold type denotes performances in the 2010-11 series or, in career figures, players who appeared in that series.

AUSTRALIA v PAKISTAN

Season	Australia	*Captains* Pakistan	T	A	P	D
1956-57P	I. W. Johnson	A. H. Kardar	1	0	1	0
1959-60P	R. Benaud	Fazal Mahmood[1]	3	2	0	1
1964-65P	R. B. Simpson	Hanif Mohammad	1	0	0	1
1964-65A	R. B. Simpson	Hanif Mohammad	1	0	0	1
1972-73A	I. M. Chappell	Intikhab Alam	3	3	0	0
1976-77A	G. S. Chappell	Mushtaq Mohammad	3	1	1	1
1978-79A	G. N. Yallop[2]	Mushtaq Mohammad	2	1	1	0
1979-80P	G. S. Chappell	Javed Miandad	3	0	1	2
1981-82A	G. S. Chappell	Javed Miandad	3	2	1	0
1982-83P	K. J. Hughes	Imran Khan	3	0	3	0
1983-84A	K. J. Hughes	Imran Khan[3]	5	2	0	3
1988-89P	A. R. Border	Javed Miandad	3	0	1	2
1989-90A	A. R. Border	Imran Khan	3	1	0	2
1994-95P	M. A. Taylor	Salim Malik	3	0	1	2
1995-96A	M. A. Taylor	Wasim Akram	3	2	1	0
1998-99P	M. A. Taylor	Aamir Sohail	3	1	0	2
1999-2000A	S. R. Waugh	Wasim Akram	3	3	0	0
2002-03S/U	S. R. Waugh	Waqar Younis	3	3	0	0
2004-05A	R. T. Ponting	Inzamam-ul-Haq[4]	3	3	0	0
2009-10A	**R. T. Ponting**	**Mohammad Yousuf**	**3**	**3**	**0**	**0**
2010E	**R. T. Ponting**	**Shahid Afridi[5]**	**2**	**1**	**1**	**0**
	In Pakistan		20	3	7	10
	In Australia		**32**	**21**	**4**	**7**
	In Sri Lanka		1	1	0	0
	In United Arab Emirates		2	2	0	0
	In England		**2**	**1**	**1**	**0**
	Totals		**57**	**28**	**12**	**17**

P Played in Pakistan. A Played in Australia.
S/U First Test played in Sri Lanka, Second and Third Tests in United Arab Emirates. E Played in England.

Notes: The following deputised for the official touring captain or were appointed by the home authority for only a minor proportion of the series:
[1]Imtiaz Ahmed (Second). [2]K. J. Hughes (Second). [3]Zaheer Abbas (First, Second and Third). [4]Yousuf Youhana *later known as Mohammad Yousuf* (Second and Third). [5]Salman Butt (Second).

HIGHEST INNINGS TOTALS

For Australia in Australia: 585 at Adelaide 1972-73
    in Pakistan: 617 at Faisalabad 1979-80
    in Sri Lanka: 467 at Colombo (PSS) 2002-03
    in United Arab Emirates: 444 at Sharjah 2002-03
    in England: 349 at Leeds **2010**

For Pakistan in Australia: 624 at Adelaide 1983-84
    in Pakistan: 580-9 dec at Peshawar 1998-99
    in Sri Lanka: 279 at Colombo (PSS) 2002-03
    in United Arab Emirates: 221 at Sharjah 2002-03
    in England: 289 at Lord's **2010**

LOWEST INNINGS TOTALS

For Australia in Australia: 125 at Melbourne 1981-82
    in Pakistan: 80 at Karachi 1956-57
    in Sri Lanka: 127 at Colombo (PSS) 2002-03
    in United Arab Emirates: 310 at Sharjah 2002-03
    in England: 88 at Leeds **2010**

For Pakistan in Australia: 62 at Perth 1981-82
    in Pakistan: 134 at Dacca 1959-60
    in Sri Lanka: 274 at Colombo (PSS) 2002-03
    in United Arab Emirates: 53 at Sharjah 2002-03
    in England: 148 at Lord's **2010**

DOUBLE-HUNDREDS

For Australia (6)

334*	M. A. Taylor at Peshawar	1998-99	207	R. T. Ponting at Sydney 2004-05
268	G. N. Yallop at Melbourne	1983-84	207	R. T. Ponting at Hobart 2009-10
235	G. S. Chappell at Faisalabad	1979-80	201	G. S. Chappell at Brisbane 1981-82

For Pakistan (3)

237	Salim Malik at Rawalpindi	1994-95	210*	Taslim Arif at Faisalabad 1979-80
211	Javed Miandad at Karachi	1988-89		

INDIVIDUAL HUNDREDS

For Australia (67)

6: A. R. Border, G. S. Chappell.
5: R. T. Ponting.
4: J. L. Langer, M. A. Taylor.
3: M. J. Slater, M. E. Waugh, S. R. Waugh, G. N. Yallop.
2: A. C. Gilchrist, K. J. Hughes, D. M. Jones, D. R. Martyn, R. B. Simpson.
1: J. Benaud, D. C. Boon, I. M. Chappell, **M. J. Clarke**, G. J. Cosier, I. C. Davis, M. L. Hayden, **M. E. K. Hussey, S. M. Katich**, R. B. McCosker, R. W. Marsh, N. C. O'Neill, W. B. Phillips, I. R. Redpath, G. M. Ritchie, A. P. Sheahan, K. D. Walters, **S. R. Watson**, K. C. Wessels, G. M. Wood.

For Pakistan (47)

6: Ijaz Ahmed, sen., Javed Miandad.
3: Asif Iqbal, Majid Khan, Mohsin Khan, Saeed Anwar.
2: Aamir Sohail, Hanif Mohammad, Sadiq Mohammad, Salim Malik, **Salman Butt**, Zaheer Abbas.
1: Imran Khan, Inzamam-ul-Haq, Khalid Ibadulla, Mansoor Akhtar, **Mohammad Yousuf**, Moin Khan, Mushtaq Mohammad, Qasim Omar, Saeed Ahmed, Taslim Arif, Wasim Akram.

TEN WICKETS OR MORE IN A MATCH

For Australia (5)

10-111 (7-87, 3-24)†	R. J. Bright, Karachi.................................	1979-80
10-135 (6-82, 4-53)	D. K. Lillee, Melbourne................................	1976-77
11-118 (5-32, 6-86)†	C. G. Rackemann, Perth...............................	1983-84
11-77 (7-23, 4-54)	S. K. Warne, Brisbane.................................	1995-96
11-188 (7-94, 4-94)	S. K. Warne, Colombo (PSS)............................	2002-03

For Pakistan (6)

11-218 (4-76, 7-142)	Abdul Qadir, Faisalabad..............................	1982-83
13-114 (6-34, 7-80)†	Fazal Mahmood, Karachi..............................	1956-57
12-165 (6-102, 6-63)	Imran Khan, Sydney..................................	1976-77
11-118 (4-69, 7-49)	Iqbal Qasim, Karachi................................	1979-80
11-125 (2-39, 9-86)	Sarfraz Nawaz, Melbourne............................	1978-79
11-160 (6-62, 5-98)†	Wasim Akram, Melbourne.............................	1989-90

† *On first appearance in Australia–Pakistan Tests.*

SEVEN WICKETS OR MORE IN AN INNINGS

In addition to those listed above, the following have taken seven wickets or more in an innings:

For Australia

7-75	L. F. Kline, Lahore...........	1959-60	8-59	A. A. Mallett, Adelaide........	1972-73
8-24	G. D. McGrath, Perth.........	2004-05	7-187	B. Yardley, Melbourne.........	1981-82

For Pakistan

7-188   Danish Kaneria, Sydney 2004-05

Bold type denotes performances in the 2009-10 or 2010 series or, in career figures, players who appeared in those series.

AUSTRALIA v SRI LANKA

		Captains					
Season	*Australia*		*Sri Lanka*	*T*	*A*	*SL*	*D*
1982-83S	G. S. Chappell		L. R. D. Mendis	1	1	0	0
1987-88A	A. R. Border		R. S. Madugalle	1	1	0	0
1989-90A	A. R. Border		A. Ranatunga	2	1	0	1
1992-93S	A. R. Border		A. Ranatunga	3	1	0	2
1995-96A	M. A. Taylor		A. Ranatunga[1]	3	3	0	0
1999-2000S	S. R. Waugh		S. T. Jayasuriya	3	0	1	2
2003-04S	R. T. Ponting		H. P. Tillekeratne	3	3	0	0
2004A	R. T. Ponting[2]		M. S. Atapattu	2	1	0	1

THE WARNE–MURALITHARAN TROPHY

		Captains						
Season	*Australia*		*Sri Lanka*	*T*	*A*	*SL*	*D*	*Held by*
2007-08A	R. T. Ponting		D. P. M. D. Jayawardene	2	2	0	0	A
	In Australia			10	8	0	2	
	In Sri Lanka			10	5	1	4	
	Totals			20	13	1	6	

A Played in Australia.   S Played in Sri Lanka.

Note: The following deputised for the official touring captain:
[1]P. A. de Silva (Third). [2]A. C. Gilchrist (First).

HIGHEST INNINGS TOTALS

For Australia in Australia: 617-5 dec at Perth 1995-96
in Sri Lanka: 514-4 dec at Kandy 1982-83

For Sri Lanka in Australia: 455 at Cairns 2004
in Sri Lanka: 547-8 dec at Colombo (SSC) 1992-93

LOWEST INNINGS TOTALS

For Australia in Australia: 201 at Darwin 2004
in Sri Lanka: 120 at Kandy 2003-04

For Sri Lanka in Australia: 97 at Darwin. 2004
in Sri Lanka: 154 at Galle 2003-04

DOUBLE-HUNDRED

For Australia (1)

219   M. J. Slater at Perth.   1995-96

Highest score for Sri Lanka: 192 by K. C. Sangakkara at Hobart, 2007-08.

INDIVIDUAL HUNDREDS

For Australia (31)

3: M. L. Hayden, D. M. Jones, S. R. Waugh.
2: M. E. K. Hussey, P. A. Jaques, J. L. Langer, D. S. Lehmann, D. R. Martyn, M. A. Taylor.
1: D. C. Boon, A. R. Border, M. J. Clarke, A. C. Gilchrist, D. W. Hookes, T. M. Moody, R. T. Ponting, M. J. Slater, M. E. Waugh, K. C. Wessels.

For Sri Lanka (13)

2: M. S. Atapattu, A. P. Gurusinha, S. T. Jayasuriya.
1: P. A. de Silva, T. M. Dilshan, D. P. M. D. Jayawardene, R. S. Kaluwitharana, A. Ranatunga, K. C. Sangakkara, H. P. Tillekeratne.

TEN WICKETS OR MORE IN A MATCH

For Australia (2)

10-159 (5-116, 5-43)   S. K. Warne, Galle. 2003-04
10-155 (5-65, 5-90)   S. K. Warne, Kandy 2003-04

For Sri Lanka (2)

11-212 (6-59, 5-153)   M. Muralitharan, Galle 2003-04
10-210 (5-109, 5-101)   U. D. U. Chandana, Cairns 2004

SEVEN WICKETS OR MORE IN AN INNINGS

For Australia

7-39   M. S. Kasprowicz, Darwin   2004

AUSTRALIA v ZIMBABWE

	Captains					
Season	*Australia*	*Zimbabwe*	*T*	*A*	*Z*	*D*
1999-2000Z	S. R. Waugh	A. D. R. Campbell	1	1	0	0
2003-04A	S. R. Waugh	H. H. Streak	2	2	0	0
	In Australia......................		2	2	0	0
	In Zimbabwe		1	1	0	0
	Totals		3	3	0	0

A Played in Australia. Z Played in Zimbabwe.

HIGHEST INNINGS TOTALS

For Australia in Australia: 735-6 dec at Perth...............................	2003-04
in Zimbabwe: 422 at Harare	1999-2000
For Zimbabwe in Australia: 321 at Perth	2003-04
in Zimbabwe: 232 at Harare	1999-2000

LOWEST INNINGS TOTALS

For Australia in Australia: 403 at Sydney.....................	2003-04
in Zimbabwe: 422 at Harare	1999-2000
For Zimbabwe in Australia: 239 at Perth	2003-04
in Zimbabwe: 194 at Harare	1999-2000

DOUBLE-HUNDRED

For Australia (1)

380   M. L. Hayden at Perth......... 2003-04

Highest score for Zimbabwe: 118 by S. V. Carlisle at Sydney, 2003-04.

INDIVIDUAL HUNDREDS

For Australia (5)

2: M. L. Hayden.
1: A. C. Gilchrist, R. T. Ponting, S. R. Waugh.

For Zimbabwe (1)

1: S. V. Carlisle.

BEST MATCH BOWLING ANALYSES

For Australia

6-90 (0-25, 6-65)	S. M. Katich, Sydney	2003-04
6-90 (3-44, 3-46)	G. D. McGrath, Harare	1999-2000

For Zimbabwe

6-184 (6-121, 0-63)	R. W. Price, Sydney...................................	2003-04

AUSTRALIA v BANGLADESH

	Captains					
Season	*Australia*	*Bangladesh*	*T*	*A*	*B*	*D*
2003*A*	S. R. Waugh	Khaled Mahmud	2	2	0	0
2005-06*B*	R. T. Ponting	Habibul Bashar	2	2	0	0
	In Australia......................		2	2	0	0
	In Bangladesh....................		2	2	0	0
	Totals		4	4	0	0

A Played in Australia.   B Played in Bangladesh.

HIGHEST INNINGS TOTALS

For Australia in Australia: 556-4 dec at Cairns 2003
     in Bangladesh: 581-4 dec at Chittagong 2005-06

For Bangladesh in Australia: 295 at Cairns 2003
      in Bangladesh: 427 at Fatullah................................. 2005-06

LOWEST INNINGS TOTALS

For Australia in Bangladesh: 269 at Fatullah................................. 2005-06

For Bangladesh in Australia: 97 at Darwin 2003
      in Bangladesh: 148 at Fatullah................................ 2005-06

DOUBLE-HUNDRED

For Australia (1)

201* J. N. Gillespie at Chittagong.... 2005-06

Highest score for Bangladesh: 138 by Shahriar Nafees at Fatullah, 2005-06.

INDIVIDUAL HUNDREDS

For Australia (9)

2: D. S. Lehmann, S. R. Waugh.
1: A. C. Gilchrist, J. N. Gillespie, M. E. K. Hussey, M. L. Love, R. T. Ponting.

For Bangladesh (1)

1: Shahriar Nafees.

TEN WICKETS OR MORE IN A MATCH

For Australia (1)

10-133 (5-77, 5-56)   S. C. G. MacGill, Cairns 2003

Note: The best match figures for Bangladesh are 9-160 (5-62, 4-98) by Mohammad Rafique at Fatullah, 2005-06.

SEVEN WICKETS OR MORE IN AN INNINGS

For Australia

8-108 S. C. G. MacGill, Fatullah 2005-06

AUSTRALIA v ICC WORLD XI

Season	Australia	ICC World XI	T	A	ICC	D
2005-06A	R. T. Ponting	G. C. Smith	1	1	0	0

A Played in Australia.

HIGHEST INNINGS TOTALS

For Australia: 345 at Sydney 2005-06
For ICC World XI: 190 at Sydney 2005-06

LOWEST INNINGS TOTALS

For Australia: 199 at Sydney 2005-06
For ICC World XI: 144 at Sydney 2005-06

HIGHEST INDIVIDUAL INNINGS

For Australia

111 M. L. Hayden at Sydney 2005-06

For ICC World XI

76 V. Sehwag at Sydney 2005-06

BEST MATCH BOWLING ANALYSES

For Australia

9-82 (4-39, 5-43) S. C. G. MacGill at Sydney 2005-06

For ICC World XI

7-107 (4-59, 3-48) A. Flintoff at Sydney 2005-06

SOUTH AFRICA v WEST INDIES

Season	South Africa	Captains West Indies	T	SA	WI	D
1991-92W	K. C. Wessels	R. B. Richardson	1	0	1	0
1998-99S	W. J. Cronje	B. C. Lara	5	5	0	0

SIR VIVIAN RICHARDS TROPHY

Season	South Africa	Captains West Indies	T	SA	WI	D	Held by
2000-01W	S. M. Pollock	C. L. Hooper	5	2	1	2	SA
2003-04S	G. C. Smith	B. C. Lara	4	3	0	1	SA
2004-05W	G. C. Smith	S. Chanderpaul	4	2	0	2	SA
2007-08 S	G. C. Smith	C. H. Gayle[1]	3	2	1	0	SA
2010W	**G. C. Smith**	**C. H. Gayle**	**3**	**2**	**0**	**1**	**SA**
	In South Africa		12	10	1	1	
	In West Indies		**13**	**6**	**2**	**5**	
	Totals		**25**	**16**	**3**	**6**	

S Played in South Africa. W Played in West Indies.

Note: The following deputised for the official touring captain:
[1]D. J. Bravo (Third).

HIGHEST INNINGS TOTALS

For South Africa in South Africa: 658-9 dec at Durban 2003-04
in West Indies: 588-6 dec at St John's 2004-05

For West Indies in South Africa: 427 at Cape Town 2003-04
in West Indies: 747 at St John's 2004-05

LOWEST INNINGS TOTALS

For South Africa in South Africa: 195 at Port Elizabeth 1998-99
in West Indies: 141 at Kingston 2000-01

For West Indies in South Africa: 121 at Port Elizabeth 1998-99
in West Indies: 102 at Port-of-Spain **2010**

DOUBLE-HUNDREDS

For West Indies (4)

317	C. H. Gayle at St John's	2004-05	203*	S. Chanderpaul at Georgetown . .	2004-05
213	W. W. Hinds at Georgetown	2004-05	202	B. C. Lara at Johannesburg	2003-04

Highest score for South Africa: 192 by H. H. Gibbs at Centurion, 2003-04.

INDIVIDUAL HUNDREDS

For South Africa (36)

8: J. H. Kallis.
7: G. C. Smith.
4: A. B. de Villiers.
3: D. J. Cullinan, H. H. Gibbs, G. Kirsten.
2: M. V. Boucher, A. G. Prince.
1: A. C. Hudson, S. M. Pollock, J. N. Rhodes, J. A. Rudolph.

For West Indies (22)

5: S. Chanderpaul.
4: B. C. Lara, R. R. Sarwan.
3: C. H. Gayle.
1: **D. J. Bravo**, W. W. Hinds, R. D. Jacobs, **B. P. Nash**, M. N. Samuels, D. R. Smith.

TEN WICKETS OR MORE IN A MATCH

For South Africa (2)

10-88 (4-56, 6-32) A. Nel, Bridgetown 2004-05
13-132 (6-95, 7-37) M. Ntini, Port-of-Spain 2004-05

Note: The best match figures for West Indies are 8-79 (2-28, 6-51) by C. E. L. Ambrose at Port Elizabeth, 1998-99.

SEVEN WICKETS OR MORE IN AN INNINGS

In addition to those listed above, the following has taken seven wickets or more in an innings.

For West Indies

7-84 F. A. Rose, Durban 1998-99

Bold type denotes performances in the 2010 series or, in career figures, players who appeared in that series.

SOUTH AFRICA v NEW ZEALAND

		Captains				
Season	South Africa	New Zealand	T	SA	NZ	D
1931-32N	H. B. Cameron	M. L. Page	2	2	0	0
1952-53N	J. E. Cheetham	W. M. Wallace	2	1	0	1
1953-54S	J. E. Cheetham	G. O. Rabone[1]	5	4	0	1
1961-62S	D. J. McGlew	J. R. Reid	5	2	2	1
1963-64N	T. L. Goddard	J. R. Reid	3	0	0	3
1994-95S	W. J. Cronje	K. R. Rutherford	3	2	1	0
1994-95N	W. J. Cronje	K. R. Rutherford	1	1	0	0
1998-99N	W. J. Cronje	D. J. Nash	3	1	0	2
2000-01S	S. M. Pollock	S. P. Fleming	3	2	0	1
2003-04N	G. C. Smith	S. P. Fleming	3	1	1	1
2005-06S	G. C. Smith	S. P. Fleming	3	2	0	1
2007-08S	G. C. Smith	D. L. Vettori	2	2	0	0
	In New Zealand		14	6	1	7
	In South Africa..................		21	14	3	4
	Totals		35	20	4	11

N Played in New Zealand. S Played in South Africa.

Note: The following deputised for the official touring captain:
[1]B. Sutcliffe (Fourth and Fifth).

HIGHEST INNINGS TOTALS

For South Africa in South Africa: 512 at Cape Town 2005-06
           in New Zealand: 621-5 dec at Auckland 1998-99

For New Zealand in South Africa: 593-8 dec at Cape Town....................... 2005-06
           in New Zealand: 595 at Auckland.............................. 2003-04

LOWEST INNINGS TOTALS

For South Africa in South Africa: 148 at Johannesburg 1953-54
           in New Zealand: 223 at Dunedin 1963-64

For New Zealand in South Africa: 79 at Johannesburg........................... 1953-54
           in New Zealand: 138 at Dunedin............................... 1963-64

DOUBLE-HUNDREDS

For South Africa (3)

275* D. J. Cullinan at Auckland ..... 1998-99 | 211* H. H. Gibbs at Christchurch 1998-99
255* D. J. McGlew at Wellington.... 1952-53

For New Zealand (1)

262   S. P. Fleming at Cape Town 2005-06

INDIVIDUAL HUNDREDS

For South Africa (33)

5: J. H. Kallis.
3: H. M. Amla, D. J. McGlew.
2: W. J. Cronje, D. J. Cullinan, H. H. Gibbs, G. Kirsten, R. A. McLean.
1: X. C. Balaskas, J. A. J. Christy, H. H. Dippenaar, W. R. Endean, N. D. McKenzie, B. Mitchell, A. R. A. Murray, A. G. Prince, D. J. Richardson, J. A. Rudolph, G. C. Smith, J. H. B. Waite.

For New Zealand (14)

2: J. D. P. Oram, J. R. Reid.

1: P. T. Barton, C. L. Cairns, S. P. Fleming, J. E. C. Franklin, P. G. Z. Harris, G. O. Rabone, B. W. Sinclair, M. S. Sinclair, S. B. Styris, H. G. Vivian.

TEN WICKETS OR MORE IN A MATCH

For South Africa (4)

11-196 (6-128, 5-68)†	S. F. Burke, Cape Town.	1961-62
10-145 (5-94, 5-51)	M. Ntini, Centurion	2005-06
10-93 (5-34, 5-59)	D. W. Steyn, Johannesburg	2007-08
10-91 (4-42, 6-49)	D. W. Steyn, Centurion	2007-08

For New Zealand (1)

11-180 (6-76, 5-104)	C. S. Martin, Auckland	2003-04

† *On first appearance in South Africa–New Zealand Tests.*

SEVEN WICKETS OR MORE IN AN INNINGS

For South Africa

8-53 G. B. Lawrence, Johannesburg . . 1961-62

SOUTH AFRICA v INDIA

	Captains					
Season	*South Africa*	*India*	*T*	*SA*	*I*	*D*
1992-93*S*	K. C. Wessels	M. Azharuddin	4	1	0	3
1996-97*I*	W. J. Cronje	S. R. Tendulkar	3	1	2	0
1996-97*S*	W. J. Cronje	S. R. Tendulkar	3	2	0	1
1999-2000*I*	W. J. Cronje	S. R. Tendulkar	2	2	0	0
2001-02*S*†	S. M. Pollock	S. C. Ganguly	2	1	0	1
2004-05*I*	G. C. Smith	S. C. Ganguly	2	0	1	1
2006-07*S*	G. C. Smith	R. Dravid	3	2	1	0
2007-08*I*	G. C. Smith	A. Kumble[1]	3	1	1	1
2009-10*I*	**G. C. Smith**	**M. S. Dhoni**	**2**	**1**	**1**	**0**
2010-11*S*	**G. C. Smith**	**M. S. Dhoni**	**3**	**1**	**1**	**1**
	In South Africa		15	7	2	6
	In India		12	5	5	2
	Totals		27	12	7	8

S Played in South Africa.   I Played in India.

† *The Third Test at Centurion was stripped of its official status by the ICC after a disciplinary dispute and is excluded.*

Note: The following was appointed by the home authority for only a minor proportion of the series:
  [1]M. S. Dhoni (Third).

HIGHEST INNINGS TOTALS

For South Africa in South Africa: **620-4 dec at Centurion** 2010-11
              in India: **558-6 dec at Nagpur** 2009-10

For India in South Africa: **459 at Centurion** 2010-11
              in India: **643-6 dec at Kolkata** 2009-10

LOWEST INNINGS TOTALS

For South Africa in South Africa: 84 at Johannesburg 2006-07
in India: 105 at Ahmedabad 1996-97

For India in South Africa: 66 at Durban 1996-97
in India: 76 at Ahmedabad 2007-08

DOUBLE-HUNDREDS

For South Africa (3)

253* H. M. Amla at Nagpur .... **2009-10** | 201* **J. H. Kallis at Centurion** **2010-11**
217* A. B. de Villiers at Ahmedabad . 2007-08

For India (1)

319 V. Sehwag at Chennai 2007-08

INDIVIDUAL HUNDREDS

For South Africa (30)

6: J. H. Kallis.
5: H. M. Amla.
3: G. Kirsten.
2: D. J. Cullinan, **A. B. de Villiers,** H. H. Gibbs, L. Klusener.
1: W. J. Cronje, A. J. Hall, A. C. Hudson, N. D. McKenzie, B. M. McMillan, **A. N. Petersen, A. G. Prince,** K. C. Wessels.

For India (23)

7: S. R. Tendulkar.
5: V. Sehwag.
4: M. Azharuddin.
2: R. Dravid.
1: P. K. Amre, **M. S. Dhoni,** Kapil Dev, **V. V. S. Laxman,** Wasim Jaffer.

TEN WICKETS OR MORE IN A MATCH

For South Africa (3)

12-139 (5-55, 7-84)   A. A. Donald, Port Elizabeth 1992-93
10-147 (4-91, 6-56)   S. M. Pollock, Bloemfontein 2001-02
10-108 (7-51, 3-57)   D. W. Steyn, Nagpur **2009-10**

For India (1)

10-153 (5-60, 5-93)   B. K. V. Prasad, Durban 1996-97

SEVEN WICKETS OR MORE IN AN INNINGS

In addition to those listed above, the following have taken seven wickets or more in an innings:

For South Africa

8-64 L. Klusener, Calcutta 1996-97

For India

7-87 Harbhajan Singh, Kolkata. ...... 2004-05 | **7-120 Harbhajan Singh, Cape Town** . **2010-11**

Bold type denotes performances in the 2009-10 or 2010-11 series or, in career figures, players who appeared in those series.

SOUTH AFRICA v PAKISTAN

	Captains					
Season	South Africa	Pakistan	T	SA	P	D
1994-95S	W. J. Cronje	Salim Malik	1	1	0	0
1997-98P	W. J. Cronje	Saeed Anwar	3	1	0	2
1997-98S	W. J. Cronje[1]	Rashid Latif[2]	3	1	1	1
2002-03S	S. M. Pollock	Waqar Younis	2	2	0	0
2003-04P	G. C. Smith	Inzamam-ul-Haq[3]	2	0	1	1
2006-07S	G. C. Smith	Inzamam-ul-Haq	3	2	1	0
2007-08P	G. C. Smith	Shoaib Malik	2	1	0	1
2010-11U	**G. C. Smith**	Misbah-ul-Haq	**2**	**0**	**0**	**2**

In South Africa..................	9	6	2	1
In Pakistan......................	7	2	1	4
In United Arab Emirates..........	**2**	**0**	**0**	**2**
Totals..........................	**18**	**8**	**3**	**7**

S Played in South Africa. P Played in Pakistan. U Played in United Arab Emirates.

Notes: The following deputised for the official touring captain or were appointed by the home authority for only a minor proportion of the series:
[1]G. Kirsten (First). [2]Aamir Sohail (First and Second). [3]Yousuf Youhana *later known as Mohammad Yousuf* (First).

HIGHEST INNINGS TOTALS

For South Africa in South Africa: 620-7 dec at Cape Town 2002-03
in Pakistan: 450 at Karachi 2007-08
in United Arab Emirates: 584-9 dec at Abu Dhabi................ **2010-11**

For Pakistan in South Africa: 329 at Johannesburg....................... 1996-97
in Pakistan: 456 at Rawalpindi 1997-98
in United Arab Emirates: 434 at Abu Dhabi **2010-11**

LOWEST INNINGS TOTALS

For South Africa in South Africa: 124 at Port Elizabeth 2006-07
in Pakistan: 214 at Faisalabad 1997-98
in United Arab Emirates: 380 at Dubai...................... **2010-11**

For Pakistan in South Africa: 106 at Port Elizabeth 1997-98
in Pakistan: 92 at Faisalabad................................. 1997-98
in United Arab Emirates: 248 at Dubai **2010-11**

DOUBLE-HUNDREDS

For South Africa (2)

278* A. B. de Villiers at Abu Dhabi . 2010-11 | 228 H. H. Gibbs at Cape Town 2002-03

Highest score for Pakistan: 136 by Azhar Mahmood at Johannesburg, 1997-98.

INDIVIDUAL HUNDREDS

For South Africa (17)

6: J. H. Kallis.
3: G. C. Smith.
2: G. Kirsten.
1: H. M. Amla, A. B. de Villiers, H. H. Gibbs, B. M. McMillan, **A. G. Prince**, P. L. Symcox.

For Pakistan (11)

3: Azhar Mahmood, **Younis Khan**.
2: Taufeeq Umar.
1: Ali Naqvi, Imran Farhat, Saeed Anwar.

TEN WICKETS OR MORE IN A MATCH

For South Africa (1)

10-108 (6-81, 4-27) † P. S. de Villiers, Johannesburg 1994-95

For Pakistan (1)

10-133 (6-78, 4-55) Waqar Younis, Port Elizabeth 1997-98
† *On first appearance in South Africa–Pakistan Tests.*

SEVEN WICKETS OR MORE IN AN INNINGS

For South Africa

7-128 P. R. Adams, Lahore.......... 2003-04

Bold type denotes performances in the 2010-11 series or, in career figures, players who appeared in that series.

SOUTH AFRICA v SRI LANKA

	Captains					
Season	*South Africa*	*Sri Lanka*	*T*	*SA*	*SL*	*D*
1993-94*SL*	K. C. Wessels	A. Ranatunga	3	1	0	2
1997-98*SA*	W. J. Cronje	A. Ranatunga	2	2	0	0
2000*SL*	S. M. Pollock	S. T. Jayasuriya	3	1	1	1
2000-01*SA*	S. M. Pollock	S. T. Jayasuriya	3	2	0	1
2002-03*SA*	S. M. Pollock	S. T. Jayasuriya[1]	2	2	0	0
2004*SL*	G. C. Smith	M. S. Atapattu	2	0	1	1
2006*SL*	A. G. Prince	D. P. M. D. Jayawardene	2	0	2	0
	In South Africa............................		7	6	0	1
	In Sri Lanka		10	2	4	4
	Totals		17	8	4	5

SA Played in South Africa. SL Played in Sri Lanka.

Note: The following deputised for the official captain:
[1]M. S. Atapattu (Second).

HIGHEST INNINGS TOTALS

For South Africa in South Africa: 504-7 dec at Cape Town 2000-01
       in Sri Lanka: 495 at Colombo (SSC) 1993-94

For Sri Lanka in South Africa: 323 at Centurion............................ 2002-03
       in Sri Lanka: 756-5 dec at Colombo (SSC) 2006

LOWEST INNINGS TOTALS

For South Africa in South Africa: 200 at Centurion 1997-98
       in Sri Lanka: 169 at Colombo (SSC) 2006

For Sri Lanka in South Africa: 95 at Cape Town............................ 2000-01
       in Sri Lanka: 119 at Colombo (SSC) 1993-94

DOUBLE-HUNDREDS

For Sri Lanka (4)

374	D. P. M. D. Jayawardene at Colombo (SSC)............ 2006	237 D. P. M. D. Jayawardene at Galle 2004
287	K. C. Sangakkara at Colombo (SSC) 2006	233 K. C. Sangakkara at Colombo (SSC) 2004

Highest score for South Africa: 180 by G. Kirsten at Durban, 2000-01.

INDIVIDUAL HUNDREDS

For South Africa (12)

5: D. J. Cullinan.
1: W. J. Cronje, G. Kirsten, L. Klusener, N. D. McKenzie, S. M. Pollock, J. N. Rhodes, J. A. Rudolph.

For Sri Lanka (11)

5: D. P. M. D. Jayawardene.
2: K. C. Sangakkara.
1: M. S. Atapattu, S. T. Jayasuriya, A. Ranatunga, H. P. Tillekeratne.

TEN WICKETS OR MORE IN A MATCH

For Sri Lanka (4)

13-171 (6-87, 7-84)	M. Muralitharan, Galle...................................	2000
11-161 (5-122, 6-39)	M. Muralitharan, Durban................................	2000-01
10-172 (4-41, 6-131)	M. Muralitharan, Colombo (SSC)	2006
12-225 (5-128, 7-97)	M. Muralitharan, Colombo (PSS)........................	2006

Note: The best match figures for South Africa are 9-106 (5-48, 4-58) by B. N. Schultz at Colombo (SSC), 1993-94.

SOUTH AFRICA v ZIMBABWE

		Captains				
Season	*South Africa*	*Zimbabwe*	*T*	*SA*	*Z*	*D*
1995-96Z	W. J. Cronje	A. Flower	1	1	0	0
1999-2000S	W. J. Cronje	A. D. R. Campbell	1	1	0	0
1999-2000Z	W. J. Cronje	A. Flower	1	1	0	0
2001-02Z	S. M. Pollock	H. H. Streak	2	1	0	1
2004-05S	G. C. Smith	T. Taibu	2	2	0	0
	In Zimbabwe		4	3	0	1
	In South Africa....................		3	3	0	0
	Totals		7	6	0	1

S Played in South Africa.   Z Played in Zimbabwe.

HIGHEST INNINGS TOTALS

For South Africa in South Africa: 480-7 dec at Centurion	2004-05
in Zimbabwe: 600-3 dec at Harare...............................	2001-02
For Zimbabwe in South Africa: 269 at Centurion	2004-05
in Zimbabwe: 419-9 dec at Bulawayo...............................	2001-02

LOWEST INNINGS TOTALS

For South Africa in South Africa: 417 in Bloemfontein 1999-2000
      in Zimbabwe: 346 at Harare. 1995-96

For Zimbabwe in South Africa: 54 at Cape Town. 2004-05
      in Zimbabwe: 102 at Harare 1999-2000

DOUBLE-HUNDRED

For South Africa (1)

220   G. Kirsten at Harare 2001-02

Highest score for Zimbabwe: 199* by A. Flower at Harare, 2001-02.

INDIVIDUAL HUNDREDS

For South Africa (9)

3: J. H. Kallis.
1: M. V. Boucher, H. H. Gibbs, A. C. Hudson, G. Kirsten, A. G. Prince, G. C. Smith.

For Zimbabwe (2)

2: A. Flower.

TEN WICKETS OR MORE IN A MATCH

For South Africa (1)

11-113 (3-42, 8-71)† A. A. Donald, Harare 1995-96

Note: The best match figures for Zimbabwe are 5-105 (3-68, 2-37) by A. C. I. Lock at Harare, 1995-96.

† *On first appearance in South Africa–Zimbabwe Tests.*

SOUTH AFRICA v BANGLADESH

		Captains				
Season	*South Africa*	*Bangladesh*	*T*	*SA*	*B*	*D*
2002-03*S*	S. M. Pollock[1]	Khaled Mashud	2	2	0	0
2003*B*	G. C. Smith	Khaled Mahmud	2	2	0	0
2007-08*B*	G. C. Smith	Mohammad Ashraful	2	2	0	0
2008-09*S*	G. C. Smith	Mohammad Ashraful	2	2	0	0
	In South Africa.		4	4	0	0
	In Bangladesh.		4	4	0	0
	Totals		8	8	0	0

S Played in South Africa.   *B Played in Bangladesh.*

Note: The following deputised for the official captain:
[1]M. V. Boucher (First).

HIGHEST INNINGS TOTALS

For South Africa in South Africa: 529-4 dec at East London 2002-03
      in Bangladesh: 583-7 dec at Chittagong 2007-08

For Bangladesh in South Africa: 252 at East London 2002-03
      in Bangladesh: 259 at Chittagong 2007-08

LOWEST INNINGS TOTALS

For South Africa in South Africa: 429 at Centurion 2008-09
    in Bangladesh: 170 at Mirpur................................... 2007-08

For Bangladesh in South Africa: 107 at Potchefstroom......................... 2002-03
    in Bangladesh: 102 at Dhaka 2003

DOUBLE-HUNDREDS

For South Africa (4)

232	G. C. Smith at Chittagong......	2007-08	222*	J. A. Rudolph at Chittagong	2003
226	N. D. McKenzie at Chittagong ..	2007-08	200	G. C. Smith at East London	2002-03

Highest score for Bangladesh: 75 by Habibul Bashar at Chittagong, 2003.

INDIVIDUAL HUNDREDS

For South Africa (13)

3: G. C. Smith.
2: G. Kirsten.
1: H. M. Amla, M. V. Boucher, H. H. Dippenaar, H. H. Gibbs, J. H. Kallis, N. D. McKenzie, A. G. Prince, J. A. Rudolph.

TEN WICKETS OR MORE IN A MATCH

For South Africa (1)

10-106 (5-37, 5-69)   P. R. Adams, Chittagong 2003

Note: The best match figures for Bangladesh are 9-97 (6-27, 3-70) by Shahadat Hossain at Mirpur, 2007-08.

WEST INDIES v NEW ZEALAND

	Captains					
Season	*West Indies*	*New Zealand*	*T*	*WI*	*NZ*	*D*
1951-52*N*	J. D. C. Goddard	B. Sutcliffe	2	1	0	1
1955-56*N*	D. St E. Atkinson	J. R. Reid[1]	4	3	1	0
1968-69*N*	G. S. Sobers	G. T. Dowling	3	1	1	1
1971-72*W*	G. S. Sobers	G. T. Dowling[2]	5	0	0	5
1979-80*N*	C. H. Lloyd	G. P. Howarth	3	0	1	2
1984-85*W*	I. V. A. Richards	G. P. Howarth	4	2	0	2
1986-87*N*	I. V. A. Richards	J. V. Coney	3	1	1	1
1994-95*N*	C. A. Walsh	K. R. Rutherford	2	1	0	1
1995-96*W*	C. A. Walsh	L. K. Germon	2	1	0	1
1999-2000*N*	B. C. Lara	S. P. Fleming	2	0	2	0
2002*W*	C. L. Hooper	S. P. Fleming	2	0	1	1
2005-06*N*	S. Chanderpaul	S. P. Fleming	3	0	2	1
2008-09*N*	C. H. Gayle	D. L. Vettori	2	0	0	2
	In New Zealand...................		24	7	8	9
	In West Indies...................		13	3	1	9
	Totals		37	10	9	18

N Played in New Zealand. W Played in West Indies.

Notes: The following deputised for the official touring captain or were appointed by the home authority for only a minor proportion of the series:
[1]H. B. Cave (First). [2]B. E. Congdon (Third, Fourth and Fifth).

HIGHEST INNINGS TOTALS

For West Indies in West Indies: 564-8 at Bridgetown..	1971-72
in New Zealand: 660-5 dec at Wellington.......................................	1994-95

For New Zealand in West Indies: 543-3 dec at Georgetown......................	1971-72
in New Zealand: 518-9 dec at Wellington..........................	1999-2000

LOWEST INNINGS TOTALS

For West Indies in West Indies: 107 at Bridgetown	2002
in New Zealand: 77 at Auckland.................................	1955-56

For New Zealand in West Indies: 94 at Bridgetown	1984-85
in New Zealand: 74 at Dunedin	1955-56

DOUBLE-HUNDREDS

For West Indies (6)

258	S. M. Nurse at Christchurch 1968-69	208* J. C. Adams at St John's.......	1995-96
214	L. G. Rowe at Kingston 1971-72	208 S. L. Campbell at Bridgetown ..	1995-96
213	C. G. Greenidge at Auckland ... 1986-87	204 C. H. Gayle at St George's	2002

For New Zealand (3)

259	G. M. Turner at Georgetown 1971-72	214 M. S. Sinclair at Wellington ...	1999-2000
223*	G. M. Turner at Kingston....... 1971-72		

INDIVIDUAL HUNDREDS

For West Indies (37)

3: D. L. Haynes, L. G. Rowe, E. D. Weekes.

2: J. C. Adams, S. L. Campbell, C. H. Gayle, C. G. Greenidge, A. I. Kallicharran, S. M. Nurse.

1: M. C. Carew, S. Chanderpaul, C. A. Davis, R. C. Fredericks, A. F. G. Griffith, C. L. King, B. C. Lara, J. R. Murray, I. V. A. Richards, R. B. Richardson, R. G. Samuels, G. S. Sobers, J. B. Stollmeyer, J. E. Taylor, C. L. Walcott, F. M. M. Worrell.

For New Zealand (25)

3: M. D. Crowe.

2: N. J. Astle, B. E. Congdon, B. F. Hastings, S. B. Styris, G. M. Turner.

1: M. G. Burgess, J. J. Crowe, B. A. Edgar, S. P. Fleming, R. J. Hadlee, G. P. Howarth, T. W. Jarvis, T. G. McIntosh, A. C. Parore, M. S. Sinclair, B. R. Taylor, J. G. Wright.

Notes: E. D. Weekes in 1955-56 made three hundreds in consecutive innings.

L. G. Rowe and A. I. Kallicharran each scored hundreds in their first two innings in Test cricket. Rowe and Yasir Hameed (for Pakistan v Bangladesh) are the only two batsmen to do so in their first match.

TEN WICKETS OR MORE IN A MATCH

For West Indies (2)

11-120 (4-40, 7-80)	M. D. Marshall, Bridgetown	1984-85
13-55 (7-37, 6-18)	C. A. Walsh, Wellington	1994-95

For New Zealand (4)

10-100 (3-73, 7-27)†	C. L. Cairns, Hamilton	1999-2000
10-124 (4-51, 6-73)†	E. J. Chatfield, Port-of-Spain	1984-85
11-102 (5-34, 6-68)†	R. J. Hadlee, Dunedin	1979-80
10-166 (4-71, 6-95)	G. B. Troup, Auckland	1979-80

† *On first appearance in West Indies–New Zealand Tests.*

SEVEN WICKETS OR MORE IN AN INNINGS

In addition to those listed above, the following have taken seven wickets or more in an innings:

For West Indies

7-53 D. St E. Atkinson, Auckland ... 1955-56 | 7-87 F. H. Edwards, Napier 2008-09

For New Zealand

7-74 B. R. Taylor, Bridgetown 1971-72

WEST INDIES v INDIA

Captains

Season	West Indies	India	T	WI	I	D
1948-49*I*	J. D. C. Goddard	L. Amarnath	5	1	0	4
1952-53*W*	J. B. Stollmeyer	V. S. Hazare	5	1	0	4
1958-59*I*	F. C. M. Alexander	Ghulam Ahmed[1]	5	3	0	2
1961-62*W*	F. M. M. Worrell	N. J. Contractor[2]	5	5	0	0
1966-67*I*	G. S. Sobers	Nawab of Pataudi jun.	3	2	0	1
1970-71*W*	G. S. Sobers	A. L. Wadekar	5	0	1	4
1974-75*I*	C. H. Lloyd	Nawab of Pataudi jun.[3]	5	3	2	0
1975-76*W*	C. H. Lloyd	B. S. Bedi	4	2	1	1
1978-79*I*	A. I. Kallicharran	S. M. Gavaskar	6	0	1	5
1982-83*W*	C. H. Lloyd	Kapil Dev	5	2	0	3
1983-84*I*	C. H. Lloyd	Kapil Dev	6	3	0	3
1987-88*I*	I. V. A. Richards	D. B. Vengsarkar[4]	4	1	1	2
1988-89*W*	I. V. A. Richards	D. B. Vengsarkar	4	3	0	1
1994-95*I*	C. A. Walsh	M. Azharuddin	3	1	1	1
1996-97*W*	C. A. Walsh[5]	S. R. Tendulkar	5	1	0	4
2001-02*W*	C. L. Hooper	S. C. Ganguly	5	2	1	2
2002-03*I*	C. L. Hooper	S. C. Ganguly	3	0	2	1
2005-06*W*	B. C. Lara	R. Dravid	4	0	1	3
	In India		40	14	7	19
	In West Indies		42	16	4	22
	Totals		82	30	11	41

I Played in India. W Played in West Indies.

Notes: The following deputised for the official touring captain or were appointed by the home authority for only a minor proportion of the series:
[1]P. R. Umrigar (First), V. Mankad (Fourth), H. R. Adhikari (Fifth). [2]Nawab of Pataudi jun. (Third, Fourth and Fifth). [3]S. Venkataraghavan (Second). [4]R. J. Shastri (Fourth). [5]B. C. Lara (Third).

HIGHEST INNINGS TOTALS

For West Indies in West Indies: 631-8 dec at Kingston 1961-62
in India: 644-8 dec at Delhi 1958-59

For India in West Indies: 588-8 dec at Gros Islet, St Lucia 2005-06
in India: 644-7 dec at Kanpur 1978-79

LOWEST INNINGS TOTALS

For West Indies in West Indies: 103 at Kingston 2005-06
in India: 127 at Delhi 1987-88

For India in West Indies: 81 at Bridgetown 1996-97
in India: 75 at Delhi 1987-88

DOUBLE-HUNDREDS

For West Indies (6)

256	R. B. Kanhai at Calcutta	1958-59	237	F. M. M. Worrell at Kingston	1952-53
250	S. F. A. F. Bacchus at Kanpur	1978-79	233	C. L. Hooper at Georgetown	2001-02
242*	C. H. Lloyd at Bombay	1974-75	207	E. D. Weekes at Port-of-Spain	1952-53

For India (6)

236*	S. M. Gavaskar at Madras	1983-84	212	Wasim Jaffer at St John's	2005-06
220	S. M. Gavaskar at Port-of-Spain	1970-71	205	S. M. Gavaskar at Bombay	1978-79
212	D. N. Sardesai at Kingston	1970-71	201	N. S. Sidhu at Port-of-Spain	1996-97

INDIVIDUAL HUNDREDS

For West Indies (96)

8: I. V. A. Richards, G. S. Sobers.
7: C. H. Lloyd, E. D. Weekes.
5: S. Chanderpaul, C. G. Greenidge, C. L. Hooper.
4: R. B. Kanhai, C. L. Walcott.
3: A. I. Kallicharran.
2: J. C. Adams, B. F. Butcher, C. A. Davis, R. C. Fredericks, D. L. Haynes, W. W. Hinds, B. C. Lara, A. L. Logie, A. F. Rae, R. B. Richardson, J. B. Stollmeyer.
1: S. F. A. F. Bacchus, R. J. Christiani, P. J. L. Dujon, D. Ganga, H. A. Gomes, G. E. Gomez, J. K. Holt, C. C. Hunte, R. D. Jacobs, E. D. A. McMorris, B. H. Pairaudeau, M. N. Samuels, R. R. Sarwan, O. G. Smith, J. S. Solomon, A. B. Williams, S. C. Williams, F. M. M. Worrell.

For India (72)

13: S. M. Gavaskar.
6: D. B. Vengsarkar.
4: G. R. Viswanath.
3: M. Amarnath, C. G. Borde, R. Dravid, Kapil Dev, V. V. S. Laxman, D. N. Sardesai, N. S. Sidhu, S. R. Tendulkar, P. R. Umrigar.
2: V. S. Hazare, V. Sehwag, R. J. Shastri.
1: H. R. Adhikari, M. L. Apte, S. A. Durani, F. M. Engineer, A. D. Gaekwad, M. Kaif, S. V. Manjrekar, V. L. Manjrekar, R. S. Modi, Mushtaq Ali, B. P. Patel, M. Prabhakar, A. Ratra, Pankaj Roy, E. D. Solkar, Wasim Jaffer.

TEN WICKETS OR MORE IN A MATCH

For West Indies (4)

11-126 (6-50, 5-76)	W. W. Hall, Kanpur	1958-59
11-89 (5-34, 6-55)	M. D. Marshall, Port-of-Spain	1988-89
12-12 (7-64, 5-57)	A. M. E. Roberts, Madras	1974-75
10-101 (6-62, 4-39)	C. A. Walsh, Kingston	1988-89

For India (4)

11-235 (7-157, 4-78)†	B. S. Chandrasekhar, Bombay	1966-67
10-223 (9-102, 1-121)	S. P. Gupte, Kanpur	1958-59
16-136 (8-61, 8-75)†	N. D. Hirwani, Madras	1987-88
10-135 (1-52, 9-83)	Kapil Dev, Ahmedabad	1983-84

† *On first appearance in West Indies–India Tests.*

SEVEN WICKETS OR MORE IN AN INNINGS

In addition to those listed above, the following have taken seven wickets or more in an innings:

For West Indies

8-38	L. R. Gibbs, Bridgetown	1961-62	9-95	J. M. Noreiga, Port-of-Spain	1970-71
7-98	L. R. Gibbs, Bombay	1974-75			

For India

7-162	S. P. Gupte, Port-of-Spain	1952-53	7-159	D. G. Phadkar, Madras	1948-49
7-48	Harbhajan Singh, Mumbai	2002-03			

WEST INDIES v PAKISTAN

		Captains				
Season	*West Indies*	*Pakistan*	*T*	*WI*	*P*	*D*
1957-58W	F. C. M. Alexander	A. H. Kardar	5	3	1	1
1958-59P	F. C. M. Alexander	Fazal Mahmood	3	1	2	0
1974-75P	C. H. Lloyd	Intikhab Alam	2	0	0	2
1976-77W	C. H. Lloyd	Mushtaq Mohammad	5	2	1	2
1980-81P	C. H. Lloyd	Javed Miandad	4	1	0	3
1986-87P	I. V. A. Richards	Imran Khan	3	1	1	1
1987-88W	I. V. A. Richards[1]	Imran Khan	3	1	1	1
1990-91P	D. L. Haynes	Imran Khan	3	1	1	1
1992-93W	R. B. Richardson	Wasim Akram	3	2	0	1
1997-98P	C. A. Walsh	Wasim Akram	3	0	3	0
1999-2000W	J. C. Adams	Moin Khan	3	1	0	2
2001-02U	C. L. Hooper	Waqar Younis	2	0	2	0
2004-05W	S. Chanderpaul	Inzamam-ul-Haq[2]	2	1	1	0
2006-07P	B. C. Lara	Inzamam-ul-Haq	3	0	2	1
	In West Indies		21	10	4	7
	In Pakistan		21	4	9	8
	In United Arab Emirates		2	0	2	0
	Totals		44	14	15	15

P Played in Pakistan.   W Played in West Indies.   U Played in United Arab Emirates.

Note: The following was appointed by the home authority for only a minor proportion of the series:
[1]C. G. Greenidge (First). [2]Younis Khan (First).

HIGHEST INNINGS TOTALS

For West Indies in West Indies: 790-3 dec at Kingston 1957-58
in Pakistan: 591 at Multan 2006-07
in United Arab Emirates: 366 at Sharjah 2001-02

For Pakistan in West Indies: 657-8 dec at Bridgetown 1957-58
in Pakistan: 485 at Lahore 2006-07
in United Arab Emirates: 493 at Sharjah 2001-02

LOWEST INNINGS TOTALS

For West Indies in West Indies: 127 at Port-of-Spain 1992-93
in Pakistan: 53 at Faisalabad 1986-87
in United Arab Emirates: 171 at Sharjah 2001-02

For Pakistan in West Indies: 106 at Bridgetown 1957-58
in Pakistan: 77 at Lahore 1986-87
in United Arab Emirates: 472 at Sharjah 2001-02

DOUBLE-HUNDREDS

For West Indies (4)

365*	G. S. Sobers at Kingston	1957-58	217	R. B. Kanhai at Lahore 1958-59
260	C. C. Hunte at Kingston	1957-58	216	B. C. Lara at Multan 2006-07

For Pakistan (1)

337 Hanif Mohammad at Bridgetown. . 1957-58

INDIVIDUAL HUNDREDS

For West Indies (31)

4: B. C. Lara.
3: D. L. Haynes, C. L. Hooper, C. C. Hunte, G. S. Sobers.
2: I. V. A. Richards.
1: L. Baichan, S. Chanderpaul, P. J. L. Dujon, R. C. Fredericks, C. G. Greenidge, W. W. Hinds, B. D. Julien, A. I. Kallicharran, R. B. Kanhai, C. H. Lloyd, I. T. Shillingford, C. L. Walcott, E. D. Weekes.

For Pakistan (38)

7: Mohammad Yousuf.
4: Inzamam-ul-Haq.
2: Aamir Sohail, Hanif Mohammad, Javed Miandad, Majid Khan, Mushtaq Mohammad, Shahid Afridi, Wasim Raja, Wazir Mohammad, Younis Khan.
1: Asif Iqbal, Ijaz Ahmed, sen., Imran Khan, Imran Nazir, Imtiaz Ahmed, Mohammad Hafeez, Rashid Latif, Saeed Ahmed, Salim Malik.

TEN WICKETS OR MORE IN A MATCH

For Pakistan (4)

12-100 (6-34, 6-66)	Fazal Mahmood, Dacca	1958-59
11-121 (7-80, 4-41)	Imran Khan, Georgetown	1987-88
10-106 (5-35, 5-71)	Mushtaq Ahmed, Peshawar	1997-98
11-110 (6-61, 5-49)	Wasim Akram, St John's	1999-2000

For West Indies (1)

11-134 (7-78, 4-56)	C. D. Collymore at Kingston	2004-05

WEST INDIES v SRI LANKA

		Captains					
Season	*West Indies*		*Sri Lanka*	*T*	*WI*	*SL*	*D*
1993-94*S*	R. B. Richardson		A. Ranatunga	1	0	0	1
1996-97*W*	C. A. Walsh		A. Ranatunga	2	1	0	1
2001-02*S*	C. L. Hooper		S. T. Jayasuriya	3	0	3	0
2003*W*	B. C. Lara		H. P. Tillekeratne	2	1	0	1
2005*S*	S. Chanderpaul		M. S. Atapattu	2	0	2	0
2007-08*W*	C. H. Gayle		D. P. M. D. Jayawardene	2	1	1	0
2010-11*S*	**D. J. G. Sammy**		**K. C. Sangakkara**	**3**	**0**	**0**	**3**
In West Indies	....			6	3	1	2
In Sri Lanka	....			**9**	**0**	**5**	**4**
Totals	....			15	3	6	6

W Played in West Indies.   S Played in Sri Lanka.

HIGHEST INNINGS TOTALS

For West Indies in West Indies: 477-9 dec at Gros Islet, St Lucia. 2003
in Sri Lanka: **580-9 dec at Galle**. **2010-11**

For Sri Lanka in West Indies: 476-8 dec at Providence. 2007-08
in Sri Lanka: 627-9 dec at Colombo (SSC) 2001-02

LOWEST INNINGS TOTALS

For West Indies in West Indies: 147 at St Vincent 1996-97
in Sri Lanka: 113 at Colombo (SSC). 2005

For Sri Lanka in West Indies: 152 at St John's 1996-97
in Sri Lanka: 150 at Kandy. 2005

DOUBLE-HUNDREDS

For West Indies (3)

333 **C. H. Gayle at Galle** .... **2010-11**   209   B. C. Lara at Gros Islet, St Lucia   2003
221   B. C. Lara at Colombo (SSC)... 2001-02

For Sri Lanka (1)

204* H. P. Tillekeratne at Colombo
(SSC) 2001-02

INDIVIDUAL HUNDREDS

For West Indies (8)

5: B. C. Lara.
1: C. H. Gayle, W. W. Hinds, R. R. Sarwan.

For Sri Lanka (9)

3: K. C. Sangakkara.
2: H. P. Tillekeratne.
1: M. S. Atapattu, **D. P. M. D. Jayawardene, T. T. Samaraweera**, B. S. M. Warnapura.

TEN WICKETS OR MORE IN A MATCH

For Sri Lanka (4)

11-170 (6-126, 5-44)	M. Muralitharan, Galle	2001-02
10-135 (4-54, 6-81)	M. Muralitharan, Kandy	2001-02
10-83 (2-37, 8-46)	M. Muralitharan at Kandy	2005
14-191 (7-120, 7-71)	W. P. U. J. C. Vaas, Colombo (SSC)	2001-02

Note: The best match figures for West Indies are 9-85 (2-28, 7-57) by C. D. Collymore at Kingston, 2003.

Bold type denotes performances in the 2010-11 series or, in career figures, players who appeared in that series.

WEST INDIES v ZIMBABWE

	Captains					
Season	West Indies	Zimbabwe	T	WI	Z	D
1999-2000W	J. C. Adams	A. Flower	2	2	0	0
2001Z	C. L. Hooper	H. H. Streak	2	1	0	1
2003-04Z	B. C. Lara	H. H. Streak	2	1	0	1
	In West Indies		2	2	0	0
	In Zimbabwe		4	2	0	2
	Totals		6	4	0	2

W Played in West Indies. Z Played in Zimbabwe.

HIGHEST INNINGS TOTALS

For West Indies in West Indies: 339 at Kingston	1999-2000
in Zimbabwe: 559-6 dec at Bulawayo	2001
For Zimbabwe in West Indies: 308 at Kingston	1999-2000
in Zimbabwe: 563-9 dec at Harare	2001

LOWEST INNINGS TOTALS

For West Indies in West Indies: 147 at Port-of-Spain	1999-2000
in Zimbabwe: 128 at Bulawayo	2003-04
For Zimbabwe in West Indies: 63 at Port-of-Spain	1999-2000
in Zimbabwe: 104 at Bulawayo	2003-04

HIGHEST INDIVIDUAL SCORES

For West Indies

191   B. C. Lara at Bulawayo 2003-04

For Zimbabwe

127* H. H. Streak at Harare. 2003-04

INDIVIDUAL HUNDREDS

For West Indies (4)

1: J. C. Adams, C. H. Gayle, C. L. Hooper, B. C. Lara.

For Zimbabwe (6)

1: A. D. R. Campbell, A. Flower, M. W. Goodwin, H. Masakadza, H. H. Streak, M. A. Vermeulen.

TEN WICKETS OR MORE IN A MATCH

For Zimbabwe

10-161 (6-73, 4-88)   R. W. Price, Harare   2003-04

Note: The best match figures for West Indies are 7-50 (4-42, 3-8) by C. E. L. Ambrose at Port-of-Spain, 1999-2000.

WEST INDIES v BANGLADESH

	Captains					
Season	*West Indies*	*Bangladesh*	*T*	*WI*	*B*	*D*
2002-03*B*	R. D. Jacobs	Khaled Mashud	2	2	0	0
2003-04*W*	B. C. Lara	Habibul Bashar	2	1	0	1
2009*W*	F. L. Reifer	Mashrafe bin Mortaza[1]	2	0	2	0
	In West Indies		4	1	2	1
	In Bangladesh.		2	2	0	0
	Totals		6	3	2	1

B Played in Bangladesh. W Played in West Indies.

Note: The following deputised for the official touring captain for a minor proportion of the series:
[1]Shakib Al Hasan (Second).

HIGHEST INNINGS TOTALS

For West Indies in West Indies: 559-4 dec at Kingston. 2003-04
           in Bangladesh: 536 at Dhaka 2002-03

For Bangladesh in West Indies: 416 at Gros Islet, St Lucia. 2003-04
           in Bangladesh: 212 at Chittagong 2002-03

LOWEST INNINGS TOTALS

For West Indies in West Indies: 181 at St Vincent 2009
           in Bangladesh: 296 at Chittagong 2002-03

For Bangladesh in West Indies: 176 at Kingston. 2003-04
           in Bangladesh: 87 at Dhaka 2002-03

DOUBLE-HUNDRED

For West Indies (1)

261* R. R. Sarwan at Kingston 2003-04

Highest score for Bangladesh: 128 by Tamim Iqbal at St Vincent, 2009.

INDIVIDUAL HUNDREDS

For West Indies (5)

2: R. R. Sarwan.
1: S. Chanderpaul, C. H. Gayle, B. C. Lara.

For Bangladesh (4)

1: Habibul Bashar, Khaled Mashud, Mohammad Rafique, Tamim Iqbal.

BEST BOWLING MATCH ANALYSES

For West Indies

9-117 (3-64, 6-53)   P. T. Collins, Kingston.   2003-04

For Bangladesh

8-110 (3-59, 5-51)   Mahmudullah, St Vincent   2009

NEW ZEALAND v INDIA

	Captains					
Season	New Zealand	India	T	NZ	I	D
1955-56*I*	H. B. Cave	P. R. Umrigar[1]	5	0	2	3
1964-65*I*	J. R. Reid	Nawab of Pataudi jun.	4	0	1	3
1967-68*N*	G. T. Dowling	Nawab of Pataudi jun.	4	1	3	0
1969-70*I*	G. T. Dowling	Nawab of Pataudi jun.	3	1	1	1
1975-76*N*	G. M. Turner	B. S. Bedi[3]	3	1	1	1
1976-77*I*	G. M. Turner	B. S. Bedi	3	0	2	1
1980-81*N*	G. P. Howarth	S. M. Gavaskar	3	1	0	2
1988-89*I*	J. G. Wright	D. B. Vengsarkar	3	1	2	0
1989-90*N*	J. G. Wright	M. Azharuddin	3	1	0	2
1993-94*N*	K. R. Rutherford	M. Azharuddin	1	0	0	1
1995-96*I*	L. K. Germon	M. Azharuddin	3	0	1	2
1998-99*N*†	S. P. Fleming	M. Azharuddin	2	1	0	1
1999-2000*I*	S. P. Fleming	S. R. Tendulkar	3	0	1	2
2002-03*N*	S. P. Fleming	S. C. Ganguly	2	2	0	0
2003-04*I*	S. P. Fleming	S. C. Ganguly[4]	2	0	0	2
2008-09*N*	D. L. Vettori	M. S. Dhoni[5]	3	0	1	2
2010-11*I*	**D. L. Vettori**	**M. S. Dhoni**	**3**	**0**	**1**	**2**
	In India		29	2	11	16
	In New Zealand		21	7	5	9
	Totals.		**50**	**9**	**16**	**25**

I Played in India.   N Played in New Zealand.

† *The First Test at Dunedin was abandoned without a ball being bowled and is excluded.*

Notes: The following deputised for the official touring captain or were appointed by the home authority for a minor proportion of the series:
[1]Ghulam Ahmed (First). [2]B. W. Sinclair (First). [3]S. M. Gavaskar (First). [4]R. Dravid (Second). [5]V. Sehwag (Second).

HIGHEST INNINGS TOTALS

For New Zealand in New Zealand: 619-9 dec at Napier		2008-09
in India: 630-6 dec at Mohali		2003-04
For India in New Zealand: 520 at Hamilton		2008-09
in India: 583-7 dec at Ahmedabad		1999-2000

LOWEST INNINGS TOTALS

For New Zealand in New Zealand: 94 at Hamilton 2002-03
                    in India: 124 at Hyderabad 1988-89

For India in New Zealand: 81 at Wellington 1975-76
                in India: 83 at Mohali 1999-2000

DOUBLE-HUNDREDS

For New Zealand (4)

239 G. T. Dowling at Christchurch .. 1967-68 | **225 B. B. McCullum at Hyderabad 2010-11**
230* B. Sutcliffe at Delhi .... 1955-56 | 201 J. D. Ryder at Napier 2008-09

For India (6)

231 V. Mankad at Madras.......... 1955-56 | 222 R. Dravid at Ahmedabad 2003-04
223 V. Mankad at Bombay......... 1955-56 | 217 S. R. Tendulkar at Ahmedabad 1999-2000
223 P. R. Umrigar at Hyderabad..... 1955-56 | 200* D. N. Sardesai at Bombay..... 1964-65

INDIVIDUAL HUNDREDS

For New Zealand (37)

3: G. T. Dowling, **J. D. Ryder**, B. Sutcliffe, J. G. Wright.
2: **B. B. McCullum**, J. R. Reid, **L. R. P. L. Taylor**, G. M. Turner.
1: N. J. Astle, C. L. Cairns, M. D. Crowe, J. W. Guy, G. P. Howarth, A. H. Jones, **T. G. McIntosh**, C. D. McMillan, J. M. Parker, J. F. Reid, M. H. Richardson, I. D. S. Smith, S. B. Styris, B. R. Taylor, **D. L. Vettori**, L. Vincent, **K. S. Williamson**.

For India (45)

6: **R. Dravid**.
4: **S. R. Tendulkar**.
3: S. C. Ganguly, V. L. Manjrekar.
2: M. Azharuddin, **G. Gambhir**, S. M. Gavaskar, **Harbhajan Singh**, **V. V. S. Laxman**, V. Mankad, Nawab of Pataudi, jun., Pankaj Roy, D. N. Sardesai, **V. Sehwag**.
1: S. Amarnath, C. G. Borde, A. G. Kripal Singh, G. S. Ramchand, S. Ramesh, N. S. Sidhu, P. R. Umrigar, G. R. Viswanath, A. L. Wadekar.

TEN WICKETS OR MORE IN A MATCH

For New Zealand (2)

11-58 (4-35, 7-23) R. J. Hadlee, Wellington 1975-76
10-88 (6-49, 4-39) R. J. Hadlee, Bombay 1988-89

For India (3)

10-134 (4-67, 6-67) A. Kumble, Kanpur....................................... 1999-2000
11-140 (3-64, 8-76) E. A. S. Prasanna, Auckland.............................. 1975-76
12-152 (8-72, 4-80) S. Venkataraghavan, Delhi............................... 1964-65

SEVEN WICKETS OR MORE IN AN INNINGS

In addition to those listed above, the following have taken seven wickets or more in an innings:

For New Zealand

7-65 S. B. Doull, Wellington 1998-99

For India

7-128 S. P. Gupte, Hyderabad. 1955-56

Bold type denotes performances in the 2010-11 series or, in career figures, players who appeared in that series.

NEW ZEALAND v PAKISTAN

	Captains					
Season	*New Zealand*	*Pakistan*	*T*	*NZ*	*P*	*D*
1955-56P	H. B. Cave	A. H. Kardar	3	0	2	1
1964-65N	J. R. Reid	Hanif Mohammad	3	0	0	3
1964-65P	J. R. Reid	Hanif Mohammad	3	0	2	1
1969-70P	G. T. Dowling	Intikhab Alam	3	1	0	2
1972-73N	B. E. Congdon	Intikhab Alam	3	0	1	2
1976-77P	G. M. Turner[1]	Mushtaq Mohammad	3	0	2	1
1978-79N	M. G. Burgess	Mushtaq Mohammad	3	0	1	2
1984-85P	J. V. Coney	Zaheer Abbas	3	0	2	1
1984-85N	G. P. Howarth	Javed Miandad	3	2	0	1
1988-89N†	J. G. Wright	Imran Khan	2	0	0	2
1990-91P	M. D. Crowe	Javed Miandad	3	0	3	0
1992-93N	K. R. Rutherford	Javed Miandad	1	0	1	0
1993-94N	K. R. Rutherford	Salim Malik	3	1	2	0
1995-96N	L. K. Germon	Wasim Akram	1	0	1	0
1996-97P	L. K. Germon	Saeed Anwar	2	1	1	0
2000-01N	S. P. Fleming	Moin Khan[2]	3	1	1	1
2002P‡	S. P. Fleming	Waqar Younis	1	0	1	0
2003-04N	S. P. Fleming	Inzamam-ul-Haq	2	0	1	1
2009-10N	D. L. Vettori	Mohammad Yousuf	3	1	1	1
2010-11N	**D. L. Vettori**	**Misbah-ul-Haq**	**2**	**0**	**1**	**1**
	In Pakistan		21	2	13	6
	In New Zealand		**29**	**5**	**10**	**14**
	Totals.		**50**	**7**	**23**	**20**

N Played in New Zealand. P Played in Pakistan.

† *The First Test at Dunedin was abandoned without a ball being bowled and is excluded.*

‡ *The Second Test at Karachi was cancelled owing to civil disturbances.*

Note: The following were appointed by the home authority for only a minor proportion of the series or deputised for the official touring captain:
[1] J. M. Parker (Third). [2] Inzamam-ul-Haq (Third).

HIGHEST INNINGS TOTALS

For New Zealand in New Zealand: 563 at Hamilton 2003-04
        in Pakistan: 482-6 dec at Lahore 1964-65

For Pakistan in New Zealand: 616-5 dec at Auckland 1988-89
       in Pakistan: 643 at Lahore 2002

LOWEST INNINGS TOTALS

For New Zealand in New Zealand: 93 at Hamilton 1992-93
       in Pakistan: 70 at Dacca 1955-56

For Pakistan in New Zealand: 104 at Hamilton 2000-01
       in Pakistan: 102 at Faisalabad 1990-91

DOUBLE-HUNDREDS

For New Zealand (1)

204* M. S. Sinclair at Christchurch... 2000-01

For Pakistan (8)

329	Inzamam-ul-Haq at Lahore..... 2002	203*	Hanif Mohammad at Lahore.... 1964-65
271	Javed Miandad at Auckland 1988-89	203*	Shoaib Mohammad at Karachi .. 1990-91
209	Imtiaz Ahmed at Lahore....... 1955-56	203	Yousuf Youhana at Christchurch 2000-01
206	Javed Miandad at Karachi 1976-77	201	Mushtaq Mohammad at Dunedin 1972-73

INDIVIDUAL HUNDREDS

For New Zealand (28)

3: J. F. Reid, **D. L. Vettori**.

2: M. G. Burgess, M. D. Crowe.

1: M. D. Bell, J. V. Coney, B. A. Edgar, S. P. Fleming, M. J. Greatbatch, B. F. Hastings, G. P. Howarth, W. K. Lees, S. N. McGregor, R. E. Redmond, J. R. Reid, M. H. Richardson, B. W. Sinclair, M. S. Sinclair, S. A. Thomson, G. M. Turner, J. G. Wright, B. A. Young.

For Pakistan (50)

7: Javed Miandad.

5: Shoaib Mohammad.

3: Asif Iqbal, Hanif Mohammad, Inzamam-ul-Haq, Majid Khan, Mushtaq Mohammad.

2: Ijaz Ahmed, sen., Sadiq Mohammad, Saeed Anwar, Salim Malik.

1: Basit Ali, Imran Farhat, Imran Nazir, Imtiaz Ahmed, Mohammad Ilyas, Mohammad Wasim, Mohammad Yousuf, Moin Khan, Mudassar Nazar, Saeed Ahmed, Saqlain Mushtaq, Umar Akmal, Waqar Hassan, **Younis Khan**, Zaheer Abbas.

Note: Mushtaq and Sadiq Mohammad both hit hundreds at Hyderabad in 1976-77, the fourth time – after the Chappells (thrice) – that brothers had each scored hundreds in the same Test innings.

TEN WICKETS OR MORE IN A MATCH

For New Zealand (1)

11-152 (7-52, 4-100)   C. Pringle, Faisalabad 1990-91

For Pakistan (11)

10-182 (5-91, 5-91)	Intikhab Alam, Dacca....................................	1969-70
11-130 (7-52, 4-78)	Intikhab Alam, Dunedin	1972-73
11-130 (4-64, 7-66)†	Mohammad Zahid, Rawalpindi............................	1996-97
10-171 (3-115, 7-56)	Mushtaq Ahmed, Christchurch	1995-96
10-143 (4-59, 6-84)	Mushtaq Ahmed, Lahore................................	1996-97
11-78 (5-48, 6-30)	Shoaib Akhtar, Christchurch	2003-04
10-106 (3-20, 7-86)	Waqar Younis, Lahore..................................	1990-91
12-130 (7-76, 5-54)	Waqar Younis, Faisalabad..............................	1990-91
10-128 (5-56, 5-72)	Wasim Akram, Dunedin	1984-85
11-179 (4-60, 7-119)	Wasim Akram, Wellington	1993-94
11-79 (5-37, 6-42)†	Zulfiqar Ahmed, Karachi...............................	1955-56

† *On first appearance in New Zealand–Pakistan Tests.*

Note: Waqar Younis's performances were in successive matches.

SEVEN WICKETS OR MORE IN AN INNINGS

In addition to those listed above, the following have taken seven wickets or more in an innings:

For New Zealand

7-87 S. L. Boock, Hyderabad 1984-85

For Pakistan

7-168 Danish Kaneria, Napier . . . . . . **2009-10** | 7-74 Pervez Sajjad, Lahore 1969-70
7-99 Mohammad Nazir, Karachi . . . . . 1969-70 |

Bold type denotes performances in the 2010-11 series or, in career figures, players who appeared in that series.

NEW ZEALAND v SRI LANKA

		Captains					
Season	*New Zealand*	*Sri Lanka*	*T*	*NZ*	*SL*	*D*	
1982-83N	G. P. Howarth	D. S. de Silva	2	2	0	0	
1983-84S	G. P. Howarth	L. R. D. Mendis	3	2	0	1	
1986-87St	J. J. Crowe	L. R. D. Mendis	1	0	0	1	
1990-91N	M. D. Crowe¹	A. Ranatunga	3	0	0	3	
1992-93S	M. D. Crowe	A. Ranatunga	2	0	1	1	
1994-95N	K. R. Rutherford	A. Ranatunga	2	0	1	1	
1996-97N	S. P. Fleming	A. Ranatunga	2	2	0	0	
1997-98S	S. P. Fleming	A. Ranatunga	3	1	2	0	
2003S	S. P. Fleming	H. P. Tillekeratne	2	0	0	2	
2004-05N	S. P. Fleming	M. S. Atapattu	2	1	0	1	
2006-07N	S. P. Fleming	D. P. M. D. Jayawardene	2	1	1	0	
2009S	D. L. Vettori	K. C. Sangakkara	2	0	2	0	
	In New Zealand		13	6	2	5	
	In Sri Lanka		13	3	5	5	
	Totals		26	9	7	10	

N Played in New Zealand. S Played in Sri Lanka.

† *The Second and Third Tests were cancelled owing to civil disturbances.*

Note: The following was appointed by the home authority for only a minor proportion of the series:
¹I. D. S. Smith (Third).

HIGHEST INNINGS TOTALS

For New Zealand in New Zealand: 671-4 at Wellington 1990-91
      in Sri Lanka: 515-7 dec at Colombo (PSS) 2003

For Sri Lanka in New Zealand: 498 at Napier 2004-05
      in Sri Lanka: 483 at Colombo (PSS) 2003

LOWEST INNINGS TOTALS

For New Zealand in New Zealand: 109 at Napier 1994-95
      in Sri Lanka: 102 at Colombo (SSC) 1992-93

For Sri Lanka in New Zealand: 93 at Wellington 1982-83
      in Sri Lanka: 97 at Kandy 1986-87

DOUBLE-HUNDREDS

For New Zealand (4)

299 M. D. Crowe at Wellington . . . . 1990-91 | 267* B. A. Young at Dunedin 1996-97
274* S. P. Fleming at Colombo (PSS) 2003 | 224 L. Vincent at Wellington 2004-05

For Sri Lanka (2)

267 P. A. de Silva at Wellington . . . . 1990-91 | 201* D. S. B. P. Kuruppu at Colombo
                                  (CCC) 1986-87

INDIVIDUAL HUNDREDS

For New Zealand (18)

3: A. H. Jones.

2: M. D. Crowe, S. P. Fleming.

1: N. J. Astle, J. J. Crowe, R. J. Hadlee, C. D. McMillan, H. J. H. Marshall, J. F. Reid, K. R. Rutherford, D. L. Vettori, L. Vincent, J. G. Wright, B. A. Young.

For Sri Lanka (23)

3: A. P. Gurusinha, D. P. M. D. Jayawardene, K. C. Sangakkara.

2: P. A. de Silva, R. S. Mahanama, T. T. Samaraweera, H. P. Tillekeratne.

1: M. S. Atapattu, R. L. Dias, T. M. Dilshan, R. S. Kaluwitharana, D. S. B. P. Kuruppu, L. P. C. Silva.

Note: A. H. Jones and A. P. Gurusinha, on opposing sides, each hit two hundreds at Hamilton in 1990-91, the second time this had happened in Tests, after D. C. S. Compton and A. R. Morris, for England and Australia at Adelaide in 1946-47.

TEN WICKETS OR MORE IN A MATCH

For New Zealand (2)

10-102 (5-73, 5-29)	R. J. Hadlee, Colombo (CCC)	1983-84
10-183 (3-53, 7-130)	D. L. Vettori, Wellington	2006-07

For Sri Lanka (2)

10-118 (4-31, 6-87)	M. Muralitharan, Wellington	2006-07
10-90 (5-47, 5-43)†	W. P. U. J. C. Vaas, Napier	1994-95

† *On first appearance in New Zealand–Sri Lanka Tests.*

NEW ZEALAND v ZIMBABWE

Season	New Zealand	*Captains* Zimbabwe	T	NZ	Z	D
1992-93Z	M. D. Crowe	D. L. Houghton	2	1	0	1
1995-96N	L. K. Germon	A. Flower	2	0	0	2
1997-98Z	S. P. Fleming	A. D. R. Campbell	2	0	0	2
1997-98N	S. P. Fleming	A. D. R. Campbell	2	2	0	0
2000-01Z	S. P. Fleming	H. H. Streak	2	2	0	0
2000-01N	S. P. Fleming	H. H. Streak	1	0	0	1
2005-06Z	S. P. Fleming	T. Taibu	2	2	0	0
	In New Zealand		5	2	0	3
	In Zimbabwe		8	5	0	3
	Totals		13	7	0	6

N Played in New Zealand.   Z Played in Zimbabwe.

HIGHEST INNINGS TOTALS

For New Zealand in New Zealand: 487-7 dec at Wellington	2000-01
in Zimbabwe: 484 at Bulawayo	2005-06
For Zimbabwe in New Zealand: 340-6 dec at Wellington	2000-01
in Zimbabwe: 461 at Bulawayo	1997-98

LOWEST INNINGS TOTALS

For New Zealand in New Zealand: 251 at Auckland 1995-96
        in Zimbabwe: 207 at Harare 1997-98

For Zimbabwe in New Zealand: 170 at Auckland 1997-98
        in Zimbabwe: 59 at Harare 2005-06

DOUBLE-HUNDRED

For Zimbabwe (1)

203* G. J. Whittall at Bulawayo 1997-98
Highest score for New Zealand: 157 by M. J. Horne at Auckland, 1997-98.

INDIVIDUAL HUNDREDS

For New Zealand (14)

3: N. J. Astle.
2: C. L. Cairns, M. J. Horne, C. D. McMillan.
1: M. D. Crowe, R. T. Latham, B. B. McCullum, C. M. Spearman, D. L. Vettori.

For Zimbabwe (6)

2: G. W. Flower, G. J. Whittall.
1: K. J. Arnott, D. L. Houghton.

TEN WICKETS OR MORE IN A MATCH

For New Zealand (1)

10-99 (6-51, 4-48) S. E. Bond, Bulawayo 2005-06

For Zimbabwe (2)

11-255 (6-109, 5-146) A. G. Huckle, Bulawayo 1997-98
10-158 (8-109, 2-49) P. A. Strang, Bulawayo 2000-01

NEW ZEALAND v BANGLADESH

		Captains				
Season	*New Zealand*	*Bangladesh*	*T*	*NZ*	*B*	*D*
2001-02*N*	S. P. Fleming	Khaled Mashud	2	2	0	0
2004-05*B*	S. P. Fleming	Khaled Mashud	2	2	0	0
2007-08*N*	D. L. Vettori	Mohammad Ashraful	2	2	0	0
2008-09*B*	D. L. Vettori	Mohammad Ashraful	2	1	0	1
2009-10*N*	**D. L. Vettori**	**Shakib Al Hasan**	**1**	**1**	**0**	**0**
	In New Zealand		**5**	**5**	**0**	**0**
	In Bangladesh		4	3	0	1
	Totals		**9**	**8**	**0**	**1**

B Played in Bangladesh.   N Played in New Zealand.

HIGHEST INNINGS TOTALS

For New Zealand in New Zealand: **553-7 dec at Hamilton** **2009-10**
        in Bangladesh: 545-6 at Chittagong 2004-05

For Bangladesh in New Zealand: **408 at Hamilton** **2009-10**
        in Bangladesh: 262 at Chittagong 2004-05

LOWEST INNINGS TOTALS

For New Zealand in New Zealand: 357 at Dunedin (Univ)......................... 2007-08
                    in Bangladesh: 171 at Chittagong............................... 2008-09

For Bangladesh in New Zealand: 108 at Hamilton............................... 2001-02
                   in Bangladesh: 126 at Dhaka.................................... 2004-05

DOUBLE-HUNDRED

For New Zealand (1)

202   S. P. Fleming at Chittagong 2004-05

Highest score for Bangladesh: **115 by Mahmudullah at Hamilton, 2009-10**.

INDIVIDUAL HUNDREDS

For New Zealand (8)

2: B. B. McCullum.
1: M. D. Bell, S. P. Fleming, **M. J. Guptill**, C. D. McMillan, J. D. P. Oram, M. H. Richardson.

For Bangladesh (2)

1: Mahmudullah, Shakib Al Hasan.

TEN WICKETS OR MORE IN A MATCH

For New Zealand (1)

12-170 (6-70, 6-100) D. L. Vettori, Chittagong.................................. 2004-05

Note: The best match figures for Bangladesh are 9-115 (7-36, 2-79) by Shakib Al Hasan at Chittagong, 2008-09.

SEVEN WICKETS OR MORE IN AN INNINGS

For New Zealand

7-53 C. L. Cairns, Hamilton 2001-02

For Bangladesh

7-36 Shakib Al Hasan, Chittagong ... 2008-09

Bold type denotes performances in the 2009-10 series or, in career figures, players who appeared in that series.

INDIA v PAKISTAN

		Captains				
Season	India	Pakistan	T	I	P	D
1952-53*I*	L. Amarnath	A. H. Kardar	5	2	1	2
1954-55*P*	V. Mankad	A. H. Kardar	5	0	0	5
1960-61*I*	N. J. Contractor	Fazal Mahmood	5	0	0	5
1978-79*P*	B. S. Bedi	Mushtaq Mohammad	3	0	2	1
1979-80*I*	S. M. Gavaskar[1]	Asif Iqbal	6	2	0	4
1982-83*P*	S. M. Gavaskar	Imran Khan	6	0	3	3
1983-84*I*	Kapil Dev	Zaheer Abbas	3	0	0	3
1984-85*P*	S. M. Gavaskar	Zaheer Abbas	2	0	0	2
1986-87*I*	Kapil Dev	Imran Khan	5	0	1	4

Season	India	Pakistan	T	I	P	D
1989-90*P*	K. Srikkanth	Imran Khan	4	0	0	4
1998-99*I*	M. Azharuddin	Wasim Akram	2	1	1	0
1998-99†*I*	M. Azharuddin	Wasim Akram	1	0	1	0
2003-04*P*	S. C. Ganguly²	Inzamam-ul-Haq	3	2	1	0
2004-05*I*	S. C. Ganguly	Inzamam-ul-Haq	3	1	1	1
2005-06*P*	R. Dravid	Inzamam-ul-Haq³	3	0	1	2
2007-08*I*	A. Kumble	Shoaib Malik⁴	3	1	0	2

Captains

In India	33	7	5	21
In Pakistan.......................	26	2	7	17
Totals............................	59	9	12	38

I Played in India.   P Played in Pakistan.

† *This Test was part of the Asian Test Championship and was not counted as part of the preceding bilateral series.*

Note: The following were appointed by the home authority for only a minor proportion of the series or deputised for the official touring captain:
¹G. R. Viswanath (Sixth). ²R. Dravid (First and Second). ³Younis Khan (Third). ⁴Younis Khan (Second and Third).

HIGHEST INNINGS TOTALS

For India in India: 626 at Bangalore	2007-08
in Pakistan: 675-5 dec at Multan	2003-04

For Pakistan in India: 570 at Bangalore......................................	2004-05
in Pakistan: 699-5 at Lahore..	1989-90

LOWEST INNINGS TOTALS

For India in India: 106 at Lucknow..	1952-53
in Pakistan: 145 at Karachi...................................	1954-55

For Pakistan in India: 116 at Bangalore.......................................	1986-87
in Pakistan: 158 at Dacca	1954-55

DOUBLE-HUNDREDS

For India (8)

309	V. Sehwag at Multan	2003-04	218	S. V. Manjrekar at Lahore	1989-90
270	R. Dravid at Rawalpindi.......	2003-04	202	Wasim Jaffer at Kolkata	2007-08
254	V. Sehwag at Lahore..........	2005-06	201	A. D. Gaekwad at Jullundur	1983-84
239	S. C. Ganguly at Bangalore	2007-08	201	V. Sehwag at Bangalore	2004-05

For Pakistan (7)

280*	Javed Miandad at Hyderabad ...	1982-83	215	Zaheer Abbas at Lahore	1982-83
267	Younis Khan at Bangalore	2004-05	210	Qasim Omar at Faisalabad	1984-85
235*	Zaheer Abbas at Lahore	1978-79	203*	Shoaib Mohammad at Lahore...	1989-90
231	Mudassar Nazar at Hyderabad ..	1982-83			

INDIVIDUAL HUNDREDS

For India (51)

5: R. Dravid, S. M. Gavaskar, P. R. Umrigar.
4: M. Amarnath, V. Sehwag.
3: M. Azharuddin, R. J. Shastri, Yuvraj Singh.
2: S. C. Ganguly, S. V. Manjrekar, S. R. Tendulkar, D. B. Vengsarkar.
1: C. G. Borde, M. S. Dhoni, A. D. Gaekwad, V. S. Hazare, V. V. S. Laxman, I. K. Pathan, S. M. Patil, R. H. Shodhan, K. Srikkanth, G. R. Viswanath, Wasim Jaffer.

For Pakistan (65)

6: Mudassar Nazar, Zaheer Abbas.
5: Javed Miandad, Younis Khan.
4: Kamran Akmal, Mohammad Yousuf.
3: Imran Khan, Inzamam-ul-Haq, Salim Malik, Shahid Afridi.
2: Aamer Malik, Hanif Mohammad, Misbah-ul-Haq, Saeed Ahmed, Shoaib Mohammad.
1: Alim-ud-Din, Asif Iqbal, Faisal Iqbal, Ijaz Faqih, Imran Farhat, Imtiaz Ahmed, Mohsin Khan, Mushtaq Mohammad, Nazar Mohammad, Qasim Omar, Ramiz Raja, Saeed Anwar, Wasim Raja.

TEN WICKETS OR MORE IN A MATCH

For India (6)

11-146 (4-90, 7-56)	Kapil Dev, Madras	1979-80
14-149 (4-75, 10-74)	A. Kumble, Delhi	1998-99
10-161 (3-98, 7-63)	A. Kumble, Kolkata	2004-05
10-126 (7-27, 3-99)	Maninder Singh, Bangalore	1986-87
13-131 (8-52, 5-79)†	V. Mankad, Delhi	1952-53
13-132 (5-46, 8-86)	J. Srinath, Calcutta	1998-99

For Pakistan (7)

12-94 (5-52, 7-42)	Fazal Mahmood, Lucknow	1952-53
11-79 (3-19, 8-60)	Imran Khan, Karachi	1982-83
11-180 (6-98, 5-82)	Imran Khan, Faisalabad	1982-83
10-175 (4-135, 6-40)	Iqbal Qasim, Bombay	1979-80
10-187 (5-94, 5-93)†	Saqlain Mushtaq, Chennai	1998-99
10-216 (5-94, 5-122)	Saqlain Mushtaq, Delhi	1998-99
11-190 (8-69, 3-121)	Sikander Bakht, Delhi	1979-80

† *On first appearance in India–Pakistan Tests.*

SEVEN WICKETS OR MORE IN AN INNINGS

In addition to those listed above, the following have taken seven wickets or more in an innings:

For India

7-220 Kapil Dev, Faisalabad . . . . 1982-83 | 8-85 Kapil Dev, Lahore 1982-83

INDIA v SRI LANKA

		Captains					
Season	*India*		*Sri Lanka*	*T*	*I*	*SL*	*D*
1982-83*I*	S. M. Gavaskar		B. Warnapura	1	0	0	1
1985-86*S*	Kapil Dev		L. R. D. Mendis	3	0	1	2
1986-87*I*	Kapil Dev		L. R. D. Mendis	3	2	0	1
1990-91*I*	M. Azharuddin		A. Ranatunga	1	1	0	0
1993-94*S*	M. Azharuddin		A. Ranatunga	3	1	0	2

Captains

Season	India	Sri Lanka	T	I	SL	D
1993-94*I*	M. Azharuddin	A. Ranatunga	3	3	0	0
1997-98*S*	S. R. Tendulkar	A. Ranatunga	2	0	0	2
1997-98*I*	S. R. Tendulkar	A. Ranatunga	3	0	0	3
1998-99*S*†	M. Azharuddin	A. Ranatunga	1	0	0	1
2001*S*	S. C. Ganguly	S. T. Jayasuriya	3	1	2	0
2005-06*I*	R. Dravid[1]	M. S. Atapattu	3	2	0	1
2008*S*	A. Kumble	D. P. M. D. Jayawardene	3	1	2	0
2009-10*I*	M. S. Dhoni	K. C. Sangakkara	3	2	0	1
2010*S*	**M. S. Dhoni**	**K. C. Sangakkara**	**3**	**1**	**1**	**1**
	In India.		17	10	0	7
	In Sri Lanka		**18**	**4**	**6**	**8**
	Totals.		35	14	6	15

I Played in India.   S Played in Sri Lanka.

† *This Test was part of the Asian Test Championship.*

Note: The following was appointed by the home authority for only a minor proportion of the series:
[1]V. Sehwag (Third).

HIGHEST INNINGS TOTALS

For India in India: 726-9 at Mumbai (BS). 2009-10
    in Sri Lanka: **707 at Colombo (SSC)** **2010**

For Sri Lanka in India: 760-7 dec at Ahmedabad 2009-10
    in Sri Lanka: 952-6 dec at Colombo (RPS) 1997-98

LOWEST INNINGS TOTALS

For India in India: 167 at Chennai. 2005-06
    in Sri Lanka: 138 at Colombo (SSC) 2008

For Sri Lanka in India: 82 at Chandigarh. 1990-91
    in Sri Lanka: 136 at Galle 2008

DOUBLE-HUNDREDS

For India (3)

293 V. Sehwag at Mumbai (BS) 2009-10	201* V. Sehwag at Galle.	2008
203 S. R. Tendulkar at Colombo (SSC) **2010**		

For Sri Lanka (5)

340 S. T. Jayasuriya at Colombo (RPS) 1997-98	225 R. S. Mahanama at Colombo (RPS)	1997-98
275 D. P. M. D. Jayawardene at Ahmedabad. 2009-10	**219 K. C. Sangakkara at Colombo (SSC)**	**2010**
242 D. P. M. D. Jayawardene at Colombo (SSC). 1998-99		

INDIVIDUAL HUNDREDS

For India (47)

9: S. R. Tendulkar.
5: M. Azharuddin, V. Sehwag.
4: N. S. Sidhu.

3: **R. Dravid**, S. C. Ganguly.
2: M. Amarnath, **M. S. Dhoni, G. Gambhir**, S. M. Gavaskar, V. G. Kambli, **V. V. S. Laxman**, D. B. Vengsarkar.
1: Kapil Dev, S. M. Patil, **S. K. Raina**, S. Ramesh.

For Sri Lanka (41)

6: **D. P. M. D. Jayawardene**.
5: P. A. de Silva, **K. C. Sangakkara**.
3: **T. M. Dilshan**, S. T. Jayasuriya, L. R. D. Mendis, **T. T. Samaraweera**.
2: M. S. Atapattu, R. S. Mahanama, **N. T. Paranavitana**.
1: R. L. Dias, **H. A. P. W. Jayawardene**, R. S. Madugalle, A. Ranatunga, S. A. R. Silva, H. P. Tillekeratne, B. S. M. Warnapura.

TEN WICKETS OR MORE IN A MATCH

For India (6)

10-141 (7-62, 3-79)	Harbhajan Singh, Ahmedabad	2005-06
10-153 (6-102, 4-51)	Harbhajan Singh, Galle	2008
11-128 (4-69, 7-59)	A. Kumble, Lucknow	1993-94
10-157 (6-72, 4-85)	A. Kumble, Delhi	2005-06
10-107 (3-56, 7-51)	Maninder Singh, Nagpur	1986-87
11-125 (5-38, 6-87)	S. L. V. Raju, Ahmedabad	1993-94

For Sri Lanka (3)

10-209 (6-117, 4-92)	B. A. W. Mendis, Galle	2008
11-196 (8-87, 3-109)	M. Muralitharan, Colombo (SSC)	2001
11-110 (5-84, 6-26)	M. Muralitharan, Colombo (SSC)	2008

SEVEN WICKETS OR MORE IN AN INNINGS

In addition to those listed above, the following has taken seven wickets or more in an innings:

For Sri Lanka

7-100 M. Muralitharan, Delhi 2005-06

Bold type denotes performances in the 2010 series or, in career figures, players who appeared in that series.

INDIA v ZIMBABWE

Season	India	*Captains* Zimbabwe	T	I	Z	D
1992-93Z	M. Azharuddin	D. L. Houghton	1	0	0	1
1992-93I	M. Azharuddin	D. L. Houghton	1	1	0	0
1998-99Z	M. Azharuddin	A. D. R. Campbell	1	0	1	0
2000-01I	S. C. Ganguly	H. H. Streak	2	1	0	1
2001Z	S. C. Ganguly	H. H. Streak	1	1	1	0
2001-02I	S. C. Ganguly	S. V. Carlisle	2	2	0	0
2005-06Z	S. C. Ganguly	T. Taibu	2	2	0	0
	In India		5	4	0	1
	In Zimbabwe		6	3	2	1
	Totals		11	7	2	2

I Played in India. Z Played in Zimbabwe.

HIGHEST INNINGS TOTALS

For India in India: 609-6 dec at Nagpur 2000-01
        in Zimbabwe: 554 at Bulawayo 2005-06

For Zimbabwe in India: 503-6 at Nagpur 2000-01
              in Zimbabwe: 456 at Harare 1992-93

LOWEST INNINGS TOTALS

For India in India: 354 at Delhi 2001-02
        in Zimbabwe: 173 at Harare 1998-99

For Zimbabwe in India: 146 at Delhi 2001-02
           in Zimbabwe: 161 at Harare 2005-06

DOUBLE-HUNDREDS

For India (3)

227 V. G. Kambli at Delhi 1992-93	200* R. Dravid at Delhi 2000-01
201* S. R. Tendulkar at Nagpur 2000-01	

For Zimbabwe (1)

232*   A. Flower at Nagpur 2000-01

INDIVIDUAL HUNDREDS

For India (14)

3: R. Dravid, S. R. Tendulkar.
2: S. S. Das, S. C. Ganguly.
1: S. B. Bangar, V. G. Kambli, V. V. S. Laxman, S. V. Manjrekar.

For Zimbabwe (6)

3: A. Flower.
1: A. D. R. Campbell, G. W. Flower, D. L. Houghton.

TEN WICKETS OR MORE IN A MATCH

For India (1)

12-126 (7-59, 5-67)   I. K. Pathan at Harare 2005-06

Note: The best match figures for Zimbabwe are 7-115 (3-69, 4-46) by H. H. Streak at Harare, 2001.

INDIA v BANGLADESH

		Captains				
Season	India	Bangladesh	T	I	B	D
2000-01*B*	S. C. Ganguly	Naimur Rahman	1	1	0	0
2004-05*B*	S. C. Ganguly	Habibul Bashar	2	2	0	0
2007*B*	R. Dravid	Habibul Bashar	2	1	0	1
2009-10*B*	**M. S. Dhoni**[1]	**Shakib Al Hasan**	**2**	**2**	**0**	**0**
	In Bangladesh.		7	6	0	1

B Played in Bangladesh.

Note: The following deputised for the official touring captain for a minor proportion of the series:
   [1]V. Sehwag (First).

HIGHEST INNINGS TOTALS

For India: 610-3 dec at Mirpur. 2007

For Bangladesh: 400 at Dhaka. 2000-01

LOWEST INNINGS TOTALS

For India: **243 at Chittagong**. **2009-10**

For Bangladesh: 91 at Dhaka. 2000-01

DOUBLE-HUNDRED

For India (1)

248* S. R. Tendulkar at Dhaka 2004-05

Highest score for Bangladesh: 158* by Mohammad Ashraful at Chittagong, 2004-05.

INDIVIDUAL HUNDREDS

For India (13)

5: **S. R. Tendulkar**.
3: **R. Dravid**.
2: **G. Gambhir**.
1: S. C. Ganguly, **K. D. Karthik**, Wasim Jaffer.

For Bangladesh (4)

1: Aminul Islam, **Mohammad Ashraful, Mushfiqur Rahim, Tamim Iqbal**.

TEN WICKETS OR MORE IN A MATCH

For India (2)

11-96 (5-45, 6-51) I. K. Pathan, Dhaka. 2004-05
10-149 (3-62, 7-87) Zaheer Khan, Mirpur. **2009-10**

Note: The best match figures for Bangladesh are **7-174 (5-62, 2-112)** by Shakib Al Hasan at Chittagong, 2009-10.

Bold type denotes performances in the 2009-10 series or, in career figures, players who appeared in that series.

PAKISTAN v SRI LANKA

			Captains				
Season	*Pakistan*		*Sri Lanka*	*T*	*P*	*SL*	*D*
1981-82P	Javed Miandad		B. Warnapura[1]	3	2	0	1
1985-86P	Javed Miandad		L. R. D. Mendis	3	2	0	1
1985-86S	Imran Khan		L. R. D. Mendis	3	1	1	1
1991-92P	Imran Khan		P. A. de Silva	3	1	0	2

Captains

Season	Pakistan	Sri Lanka	T	P	SL	D
1994-95S†	Salim Malik	A. Ranatunga	2	2	0	0
1995-96P	Ramiz Raja	A. Ranatunga	3	1	2	0
1996-97S	Ramiz Raja	A. Ranatunga	2	0	0	2
1998-99P‡	Wasim Akram	H. P. Tillekeratne	1	0	0	1
1998-99B‡	Wasim Akram	P. A. de Silva	1	1	0	0
1999-2000P	Saeed Anwar ²	S. T. Jayasuriya	3	1	2	0
2000S	Moin Khan	S. T. Jayasuriya	3	2	0	1
2001-02P‡	Waqar Younis	S. T. Jayasuriya	1	0	1	0
2004-05P	Inzamam-ul-Haq	M. S. Atapattu	2	1	1	0
2005-06S	Inzamam-ul-Haq	D. P. M. D. Jayawardene	2	1	0	1
2008-09P§	Younis Khan	D. P. M. D. Jayawardene	2	0	0	2
2009S	Younis Khan	K. C. Sangakkara	3	0	2	1
In Pakistan			21	8	6	7
In Sri Lanka			15	6	3	6
In Bangladesh....................			1	1	0	0
Totals			37	15	9	13

P Played in Pakistan. S Played in Sri Lanka. B Played in Bangladesh.

† *One Test was cancelled owing to the threat of civil disturbances following a general election.*
‡ *These Tests were part of the Asian Test Championship.*
§ *The Second Test ended after a terrorist attack on the Sri Lankan team bus on the third day.*

Note: The following deputised for the official touring captain or were appointed by the home authority for only a minor proportion of the series:
¹L. R. D. Mendis (Second). ²Moin Khan (Third).

HIGHEST INNINGS TOTALS

For Pakistan in Pakistan: 765-6 dec at Karachi	2008-09
in Sri Lanka: 600-8 dec at Galle	2000
in Bangladesh: 594 at Dhaka....................	1998-99
For Sri Lanka in Pakistan: 644-7 dec at Karachi	2008-09
in Sri Lanka: 467-5 at Kandy	2000

LOWEST INNINGS TOTALS

For Pakistan in Pakistan: 182 at Rawalpindi	1999-2000
in Sri Lanka: 90 at Colombo (PSS)...................	2009
For Sri Lanka in Pakistan: 149 at Karachi.....................	1981-82
in Sri Lanka: 71 at Kandy	1994-95

DOUBLE-HUNDREDS

For Pakistan (5)

313 Younis Khan at Karachi 2008-09	203* Javed Miandad at Faisalabad ... 1985-86
211 Ijaz Ahmed, sen. at Dhaka 1998-99	200* Inzamam-ul-Haq at Dhaka 1998-99
206 Qasim Omar at Faisalabad 1985-86	

For Sri Lanka (6)

253 S. T. Jayasuriya at Faisalabad... 2004-05	230 K. C. Sangakkara at Lahore 2001-02
240 D. P. M. D. Jayawardene at	214 T. T. Samaraweera at Lahore ...
Karachi 2008-09	2008-09
231 T. T. Samaraweera at Karachi... 2008-09	207* M. S. Atapattu at Kandy 2000

INDIVIDUAL HUNDREDS
For Pakistan (31)

5: Inzamam-ul-Haq.
4: Younis Khan.
3: Salim Malik.
2: Ijaz Ahmed, sen., Saeed Anwar, Shoaib Malik, Wajahatullah Wasti.
1: Fawad Alam, Haroon Rashid, Javed Miandad, Kamran Akmal, Mohammad Yousuf, Mohsin Khan, Moin Khan, Qasim Omar, Ramiz Raja, Wasim Akram, Zaheer Abbas.

For Sri Lanka (31)

8: P. A. de Silva.
5: K. C. Sangakkara.
4: S. T. Jayasuriya.
3: T. T. Samaraweera.
2: H. P. Tillekeratne.
1: R. P. Arnold, M. S. Atapattu, R. L. Dias, T. M. Dilshan, A. P. Gurusinha, D. P. M. D. Jayawardene, R. S. Kaluwitharana, A. Ranatunga, S. Wettimuny.

TEN WICKETS OR MORE IN A MATCH
For Pakistan (4)

10-190 (3-72, 7-118)	Danish Kaneria, Karachi	2004-05
14-116 (8-58, 6-58)	Imran Khan, Lahore.	1981-82
11-71 (6-44, 5-27)	Mohammad Asif, Kandy	2005-06
11-119 (6-34, 5-85)	Waqar Younis, Kandy	1994-95

For Sri Lanka (1)

10-148 (4-77, 6-71)	M. Muralitharan, Peshawar.	1999-2000

SEVEN WICKETS OR MORE IN AN INNINGS

In addition to those listed above, the following has taken seven wickets or more in an innings:

For Sri Lanka

8-83 J. R. Ratnayeke, Sialkot 1985-86

PAKISTAN v ZIMBABWE

		Captains				
Season	*Pakistan*	*Zimbabwe*	*T*	*P*	*Z*	*D*
1993-94P	Wasim Akram[1]	A. Flower	3	2	0	1
1994-95Z	Salim Malik	A. Flower	3	2	1	0
1996-97P	Wasim Akram	A. D. R. Campbell	2	1	0	1
1997-98Z	Rashid Latif	A. D. R. Campbell	2	1	0	1
1998-99P†	Aamir Sohail[2]	A. D. R. Campbell	2	0	1	1
2002-03Z	Waqar Younis	A. D. R. Campbell	2	2	0	0
	In Pakistan		7	3	1	3
	In Zimbabwe		7	5	1	1
	Totals		14	8	2	4

P Played in Pakistan.   Z Played in Zimbabwe.

† *The Third Test at Faisalabad was abandoned without a ball being bowled and is excluded.*

Notes: The following were appointed by the home authority for only a minor proportion of the series:
[1]Waqar Younis (First). [2]Moin Khan (Second).

HIGHEST INNINGS TOTALS

For Pakistan in Pakistan: 553 at Sheikhupura 1996-97
           in Zimbabwe: 403 at Bulawayo 2002-03

For Zimbabwe in Pakistan: 375 at Sheikhupura 1996-97
          in Zimbabwe: 544-4 dec at Harare 1994-95

LOWEST INNINGS TOTALS

For Pakistan in Pakistan: 103 at Peshawar.................................. 1998-99
          in Zimbabwe: 158 at Harare 1994-95

For Zimbabwe in Pakistan: 133 at Faisalabad 1996-97
          in Zimbabwe: 139 at Harare 1994-95

DOUBLE-HUNDREDS

For Pakistan (1)

257* Wasim Akram at Sheikhupura .. 1996-97

For Zimbabwe (1)

201* G. W. Flower at Harare........ 1994-95

INDIVIDUAL HUNDREDS

For Pakistan (7)

2: Inzamam-ul-Haq, Yousuf Youhana.
1: Mohammad Wasim, Taufeeq Umar, Wasim Akram.

For Zimbabwe (9)

3: G. W. Flower.
2: A. Flower.
1: M. W. Goodwin, N. C. Johnson, P. A. Strang, G. J. Whittall.

TEN WICKETS OR MORE IN A MATCH

For Pakistan (3)

10-155 (7-66, 3-89) Saqlain Mushtaq, Bulawayo................................ 2002-03
13-135 (7-91, 6-44)† Waqar Younis, Karachi (DS)............................. 1993-94
10-106 (6-48, 4-58) Wasim Akram, Faisalabad............................... 1996-97

Note: The best match figures for Zimbabwe are 9-105 (6-90, 3-15) by H. H. Streak at Harare, 1994-95.

† *On first appearance in Pakistan–Zimbabwe Tests.*

PAKISTAN v BANGLADESH

Season	Pakistan		Bangladesh	T	P	B	D
		Captains					
2001-02*P*†	Waqar Younis		Naimur Rahman	1	1	0	0
2001-02*B*	Waqar Younis		Khaled Mashud	2	2	0	0
2003*P*	Rashid Latif		Khaled Mahmud	3	3	0	0
	In Pakistan			4	4	0	0
	In Bangladesh.			2	2	0	0
	Totals			6	6	0	0

P Played in Pakistan.   B Played in Bangladesh.

† *This Test was part of the Asian Test Championship.*

HIGHEST INNINGS TOTALS

For Pakistan in Pakistan: 546-3 dec at Multan. 2001-02
in Bangladesh: 490-9 dec at Dhaka. 2001-02

For Bangladesh in Pakistan: 361 at Peshawar 2003
in Bangladesh: 160 at Dhaka 2001-02

LOWEST INNINGS TOTALS

For Pakistan in Pakistan: 175 at Multan. 2003

For Bangladesh in Pakistan: 96 at Peshawar 2003
in Bangladesh: 148 at Chittagong (in both innings) 2001-02

DOUBLE-HUNDRED

For Pakistan (1)

204* Yousuf Youhana at Chittagong . 2001-02

Highest score for Bangladesh: 119 by Javed Omar at Peshawar, 2003.

INDIVIDUAL HUNDREDS

For Pakistan (12)

2: Abdul Razzaq, Inzamam-ul-Haq, Yasir Hameed, Yousuf Youhana.
1: Mohammad Hafeez, Saeed Anwar, Taufeeq Umar, Younis Khan.

For Bangladesh (2)

1: Habibul Bashar, Javed Omar.

Note: Yasir Hameed and L. G. Rowe (for West Indies v New Zealand) are the only two batsmen to score two hundreds in their first Test.

TEN WICKETS OR MORE IN A MATCH

For Pakistan (2)

12-94 (6-42, 6-52)†　Danish Kaneria, Multan 2001-02
10-80 (6-50, 4-30)　Shoaib Akhtar, Peshawar 2003

Note: The best match figures for Bangladesh are 7-105 (4-37, 3-68) by Khaled Mahmud at Multan, 2003.

† *On first appearance in Pakistan–Bangladesh Tests.*

SEVEN WICKETS OR MORE IN AN INNINGS

For Pakistan

7-77　Danish Kaneria, Dhaka 2001-02

SRI LANKA v ZIMBABWE

		Captains				
Season	*Sri Lanka*	*Zimbabwe*	*T*	*SL*	*Z*	*D*
1994-95Z	A. Ranatunga	A. Flower	3	0	0	3
1996-97S	A. Ranatunga	A. D. R. Campbell	2	2	0	0
1997-98S	A. Ranatunga	A. D. R. Campbell	2	2	0	0
1999-2000Z	S. T. Jayasuriya	A. Flower	3	1	0	2
2001-02S	S. T. Jayasuriya	S. V. Carlisle	3	3	0	0
2003-04Z	M. S. Atapattu	T. Taibu	2	2	0	0
	In Sri Lanka		7	7	0	0
	In Zimbabwe		8	3	0	5
	Totals		15	10	0	5

S Played in Sri Lanka. Z Played in Zimbabwe.

HIGHEST INNINGS TOTALS

For Sri Lanka in Sri Lanka: 586-6 dec at Colombo (SSC) 2001-02
　　　　　　in Zimbabwe: 713-3 dec at Bulawayo 2003-04

For Zimbabwe in Sri Lanka: 338 at Kandy 1997-98
　　　　　　in Zimbabwe: 462-9 dec at Bulawayo. 1994-95

LOWEST INNINGS TOTALS

For Sri Lanka in Sri Lanka: 225 at Colombo (SSC) 1997-98
　　　　　　in Zimbabwe: 218 at Bulawayo 1994-95

For Zimbabwe in Sri Lanka: 79 at Galle 2001-02
　　　　　　in Zimbabwe: 102 at Harare 2003-04

DOUBLE-HUNDREDS

For Sri Lanka (4)

270	K. C. Sangakkara at Bulawayo . . 2003-04	223	M. S. Atapattu at Kandy 1997-98
249	M. S. Atapattu at Bulawayo 2003-04	216*	M. S. Atapattu at Bulawayo . . . 1999-2000

For Zimbabwe (1)

266 D. L. Houghton at Bulawayo ... 1994-95

INDIVIDUAL HUNDREDS

For Sri Lanka (19)

5: M. S. Atapattu.

2: S. T. Jayasuriya, S. Ranatunga, K. C. Sangakkara, H. P. Tillekeratne.

1: R. P. Arnold, P. A. de Silva, T. M. Dilshan, A. P. Gurusinha, D. P. M. D. Jayawardene, T. T. Samaraweera.

For Zimbabwe (4)

2: A. Flower, D. L. Houghton.

TEN WICKETS OR MORE IN A MATCH

For Sri Lanka (2)

12-117 (5-23, 7-94) M. Muralitharan, Kandy.................................... 1997-98
13-115 (9-51, 4-64) M. Muralitharan, Kandy.................................... 2001-02

Note: The best match figures for Zimbabwe are 6-112 (2-28, 4-84) by H. H. Streak at Colombo (SSC), 1997-98.

SEVEN WICKETS OR MORE IN AN INNINGS

In addition to those listed above, the following has taken seven wickets or more in an innings:

For Sri Lanka

7-116 K. R. Pushpakumara, Harare.... 1994-95

SRI LANKA v BANGLADESH

		Captains					
Season	*Sri Lanka*		*Bangladesh*	*T*	*SL*	*B*	*D*
2001-02S†	S. T. Jayasuriya		Naimur Rahman	1	1	0	0
2002S	S. T. Jayasuriya		Khaled Mashud	2	2	0	0
2005-06S	M. S. Atapattu		Habibul Bashar	2	2	0	0
2005-06B	D. P. M. D. Jayawardene		Habibul Bashar	2	2	0	0
2007S	D. P. M. D. Jayawardene		Mohammad Ashraful	3	3	0	0
2008-09B	D. P. M. D. Jayawardene		Mohammad Ashraful	2	2	0	0
	In Sri Lanka..............			8	8	0	0
	In Bangladesh			4	4	0	0
	Totals...................			12	12	0	0

S Played in Sri Lanka. B Played in Bangladesh.

† *This Test was part of the Asian Test Championship.*

HIGHEST INNINGS TOTALS

For Sri Lanka in Sri Lanka: 577-6 dec at Colombo (SSC) 2007
            in Bangladesh: 447-6 dec at Chittagong 2008-09

For Bangladesh in Sri Lanka: 328 at Colombo (SSC)............................ 2001-02
            in Bangladesh: 413 at Mirpur 2008-09

LOWEST INNINGS TOTALS

For Sri Lanka in Sri Lanka: 373 at Colombo (SSC) 2002
            in Bangladesh: 293 at Mirpur 2008-09

For Bangladesh in Sri Lanka: 62 at Colombo (PSS) 2007
            in Bangladesh: 158 at Chittagong 2008-09

DOUBLE-HUNDREDS

For Sri Lanka (4)

222* K. C. Sangakkara at Kandy.....	2007	201 M. S. Atapattu at Colombo (SSC)	2001-02
206 P. A. de Silva at Colombo (PSS)	2002	200* K. C. Sangakkara at Colombo (PSS)..................	2007

Highest score for Bangladesh: 136 by Mohammad Ashraful at Chittagong, 2005-06.

INDIVIDUAL HUNDREDS

For Sri Lanka (18)

4: D. P. M. D. Jayawardene.
3: T. M. Dilshan.
2: K. C. Sangakkara, M. G. Vandort..
1: M. S. Atapattu, P. A. de Silva, S. T. Jayasuriya, H. A. P. W. Jayawardene, T. T. Samaraweera, W. U. Tharanga, W. P. U. J. C. Vaas.

For Bangladesh (4)

4: Mohammad Ashraful.

TEN WICKETS OR MORE IN A MATCH

For Sri Lanka (4)

10-111 (5-13, 5-98)	M. Muralitharan, Colombo (SSC)...........................	2001-02
10-98 (5-39, 5-59)	M. Muralitharan, Colombo (PSS)	2002
12-82 (6-28, 6-54)	M. Muralitharan, Kandy	2007
10-190 (6-49, 4-141)	M. Muralitharan, Mirpur	2008-09

Note: The best match figures for Bangladesh are 6-204 (5-70, 1-134) by Shakib Al Hasan at Mirpur, 2008-09.

ZIMBABWE v BANGLADESH

	Captains					
Season	Zimbabwe	Bangladesh	T	Z	B	D
2000-01Z	H. H. Streak	Naimur Rahman	2	2	0	0
2001-02B	B. A. Murphy[1]	Naimur Rahman	2	1	0	1
2003-04Z	H. H. Streak	Habibul Bashar	2	1	0	1
2004-05B	T. Taibu	Habibul Bashar	2	0	1	1
	In Zimbabwe		4	3	0	1
	In Bangladesh.		4	1	1	2
	Totals		8	4	1	3

Z Played in Zimbabwe.   B Played in Bangladesh.

Note: The following deputised for the official touring captain:

   [1]S. V. Carlisle (Second).

HIGHEST INNINGS TOTALS

For Zimbabwe in Zimbabwe: 457 at Bulawayo................................... 2000-01
                in Bangladesh: 542-7 dec at Chittagong 2001-02

For Bangladesh in Zimbabwe: 331 at Harare 2003-04
                in Bangladesh: 488 at Chittagong 2004-05

LOWEST INNINGS TOTALS

For Zimbabwe in Zimbabwe: 441 at Harare 2003-04
                in Bangladesh: 154 at Chittagong 2004-05

For Bangladesh in Zimbabwe: 168 at Bulawayo.............................. 2000-01
                           168 at Bulawayo.................................... 2003-04
                in Bangladesh: 107 at Dhaka.................................... 2001-02

HIGHEST INDIVIDUAL INNINGS

For Zimbabwe

   153   T. Taibu at Dhaka 2004-05

For Bangladesh

   121   Nafis Iqbal at Dhaka 2004-05

INDIVIDUAL HUNDREDS

For Zimbabwe (6)

1: S. V. Carlisle, A. Flower, T. R. Gripper, T. Taibu, G. J. Whittall, C. B. Wishart.

For Bangladesh (2)

1: Habibul Bashar, Nafis Iqbal.

TEN WICKETS OR MORE IN A MATCH

For Bangladesh (1)

12-200 (7-95, 5-105)   Enamul Haque, jun., Dhaka 2004-05

Note: The best match figures for Zimbabwe are 8-104 (4-41, 4-63) by G. W. Flower at Chittagong, 2001-02.

TEST GROUNDS

in chronological order

	City and Ground	First Test Match		Tests
1	**Melbourne, Melbourne Cricket Ground**	**March 15, 1877**	**A v E**	**103**
2	**London, Kennington Oval**	**September 6, 1880**	**E v A**	**93**
3	**Sydney, Sydney Cricket Ground (No. 1)**	**February 17, 1882**	**A v E**	**99**
4	**Manchester, Old Trafford**	**July 11, 1884**	**E v A**	**74**
5	**London, Lord's**	**July 21, 1884**	**E v A**	**121**
6	**Adelaide, Adelaide Oval**	**December 12, 1884**	**A v E**	**69**
7	Port Elizabeth, St George's Park	March 12, 1889	SA v E	23
8	**Cape Town, Newlands**	**March 25, 1889**	**SA v E**	**46**
9	Johannesburg, Old Wanderers	March 2, 1896	SA v E	22
	Now the site of Johannesburg Railway Station.			
10	**Nottingham, Trent Bridge**	**June 1, 1899**	**E v A**	**56**
11	**Leeds, Headingley**	**June 29, 1899**	**E v A**	**70**
12	**Birmingham, Edgbaston**	**May 29, 1902**	**E v A**	**45**
13	Sheffield, Bramall Lane	July 3, 1902	E v A	1
	Sheffield United Football Club have built a stand over the cricket pitch.			
14	Durban, Lord's	January 21, 1910	SA v E	4
	Ground destroyed and built on.			
15	**Durban, Kingsmead**	**January 18, 1923**	**SA v E**	**38**
16	Brisbane, Exhibition Ground	November 30, 1928	A v E	2
	No longer used for cricket.			
17	Christchurch, Lancaster Park	January 10, 1930	NZ v E	40
	Ground also known under sponsors' names; currently Jade Stadium.			
18	**Bridgetown, Kensington Oval**	**January 11, 1930**	**WI v E**	**46**
19	**Wellington, Basin Reserve**	**January 24, 1930**	**NZ v E**	**52**
20	**Port-of-Spain, Queen's Park Oval**	**February 1, 1930**	**WI v E**	**57**
21	Auckland, Eden Park	February 17, 1930	NZ v E	47
22	Georgetown, Bourda	February 21, 1930	WI v E	30
23	Kingston, Sabina Park	April 3, 1930	WI v E	44
24	**Brisbane, Woolloongabba**	**November 27, 1931**	**A v SA**	**53**
25	Bombay, Gymkhana Ground	December 15, 1933	I v E	1
	No longer used for first-class cricket.			
26	**Calcutta (*now* Kolkata), Eden Gardens**	**January 5, 1934**	**I v E**	**36**
27	Madras (*now* Chennai), Chepauk (Chidambaram Stadium)	February 10, 1934	I v E	30
28	Delhi, Feroz Shah Kotla	November 10, 1948	I v WI	30
29	Bombay (*now* Mumbai), Brabourne Stadium	December 9, 1948	I v WI	18
	Rarely used for first-class cricket.			
30	Johannesburg, Ellis Park	December 27, 1948	SA v E	6
	Mainly a football and rugby stadium, no longer used for cricket.			
31	Kanpur, Green Park (Modi Stadium)	January 12, 1952	I v E	21
32	Lucknow, University Ground	October 25, 1952	I v P	1
	Ground destroyed, now partly under a river bed.			
33	Dacca (*now* Dhaka), Dacca (*now* Bangabandhu) Stadium	January 1, 1955	P v I	17
	Originally in East Pakistan, now Bangladesh, no longer used for cricket.			
34	Bahawalpur, Dring (*now* Bahawal) Stadium	January 15, 1955	P v I	1
	Still used for first-class cricket.			
35	Lahore, Lawrence Gardens (Bagh-e-Jinnah)	January 29, 1955	P v I	3
	Still used for club and occasional first-class matches.			
36	Peshawar, Services Ground	February 13, 1955	P v I	1
	Superseded by new stadium.			
37	Karachi, National Stadium	February 26, 1955	P v I	41
38	Dunedin, Carisbrook	March 11, 1955	NZ v E	10
39	Hyderabad, Fateh Maidan (Lal Bahadur Stadium)	November 19, 1955	I v NZ	3

				Tests
City and Ground	*First Test Match*			
40 Madras, Corporation Stadium	January 6, 1956	I v NZ		9
Superseded by rebuilt Chepauk Stadium.				
41 Johannesburg, Wanderers	**December 24, 1956**	**SA v E**		**32**
42 Lahore, Gaddafi Stadium	November 21, 1959	P v A		40
43 Rawalpindi, Pindi Club Ground	March 27, 1965	P v NZ		1
Superseded by new stadium.				
44 Nagpur, Vidarbha C.A. Ground	October 3, 1969	I v NZ		9
Superseded by new stadium.				
45 Perth, Western Australian C.A. Ground	**December 11, 1970**	**A v E**		**38**
46 Hyderabad, Niaz Stadium	March 16, 1973	P v E		5
47 Bangalore, Karnataka State C.A. Ground	**November 22, 1974**	**I v WI**		**19**
(Chinnaswamy Stadium)				
48 Bombay (*now Mumbai*), Wankhede Stadium	January 23, 1975	I v WI		21
49 Faisalabad, Iqbal Stadium	October 16, 1978	P v I		24
50 Napier, McLean Park	February 16, 1979	NZ v P		9
51 Multan, Ibn-e-Qasim Bagh Stadium	December 30, 1980	P v WI		1
Superseded by new stadium.				
52 St John's (Antigua), Recreation Ground	March 27, 1981	WI v E		22
53 Colombo, P. Saravanamuttu (Sara) Stadium	**February 17, 1982**	**SL v E**		**15**
54 Kandy, Asgiriya Stadium	April 22, 1983	SL v A		21
55 Jullundur, Burlton Park	September 24, 1983	I v P		1
56 Ahmedabad, Sardar Patel (Gujarat) Stadium	**November 12, 1983**	**I v WI**		**11**
57 Colombo, Sinhalese Sports Club Ground	**March 16, 1984**	**SL v NZ**		**34**
58 Colombo, Colombo Cricket Club Ground	March 24, 1984	SL v NZ		3
59 Sialkot, Jinnah Stadium	October 27, 1985	P v SL		4
60 Cuttack, Barabati Stadium	January 4, 1987	I v SL		2
61 Jaipur, Sawai Mansingh Stadium	February 21, 1987	I v P		1
62 Hobart, Bellerive Oval	**December 16, 1989**	**A v SL**		**9**
63 Chandigarh, Sector 16 Stadium	November 23, 1990	I v SL		1
Superseded by Mohali ground.				
64 Hamilton, Seddon Park	**February 22, 1991**	**NZ v SL**		**18**
Ground also known under various sponsors' names.				
65 Gujranwala, Municipal Stadium	December 20, 1991	P v SL		1
66 Colombo, R. Premadasa (Khettarama) Stadium	**August 28, 1992**	**SL v A**		**7**
67 Moratuwa, Tyronne Fernando Stadium	September 8, 1992	SL v A		4
68 Harare, Harare Sports Club	October 18, 1992	Z v I		26
69 Bulawayo, Bulawayo Athletic Club	November 1, 1992	Z v NZ		1
Superseded by Queens Sports Club ground.				
70 Karachi, Defence Stadium	December 1, 1993	P v Z		1
71 Rawalpindi, Rawalpindi Cricket Stadium	December 9, 1993	P v Z		8
72 Lucknow, K. D. "Babu" Singh Stadium	January 18, 1994	I v SL		1
73 Bulawayo, Queens Sports Club	October 20, 1994	Z v SL		17
74 Mohali, Punjab Cricket Association Stadium	**December 10, 1994**	**I v WI**		**10**
75 Peshawar, Arbab Niaz Stadium	September 8, 1995	P v SL		6
76 Centurion (*formerly Verwoerdburg*), Centurion	**November 16, 1995**	**SA v E**		**16**
Park				
77 Sheikhupura, Municipal Stadium	October 17, 1996	P v Z		2
78 St Vincent, Arnos Vale	June 20, 1997	WI v SL		2
79 Galle, International Stadium	**June 3, 1998**	**SL v NZ**		**17**
80 Bloemfontein, Springbok Park	October 29, 1999	SA v Z		4
Ground also known under sponsor's name; currently OUTsurance Oval.				
81 Multan, Multan Cricket Stadium	August 29, 2001	P v B		5
82 Chittagong, Chittagong Stadium	November 15, 2001	B v Z		8
Ground also known as M. A. Aziz Stadium.				
83 Sharjah, Sharjah Cricket Association Stadium	January 31, 2002	P v WI		4
84 St George's, Grenada, Queen's Park New Stadium	June 28, 2002	WI v NZ		2
85 East London, Buffalo Park	October 18, 2002	SA v B		1
86 Potchefstroom, North West Cricket Stadium	October 25, 2002	SA v B		1
Ground now known under sponsor's name as Senwes Park.				
87 Chester-le-Street, Riverside Ground	June 5, 2003	E v Z		4

	City and Ground	*First Test Match*		*Tests*
88	Gros Islet, St Lucia, Beausejour Stadium	June 20, 2003	WI v SL	3
89	Darwin, Marrara Cricket Ground	July 18, 2003	A v B	2
90	Cairns, Cazaly's Football Park	July 25, 2003	A v B	2
	Ground also known under sponsor's name as Bundaberg Rum Stadium.			
91	**Chittagong, Chittagong Divisional Stadium**	**February 28, 2006**	**B v SL**	**8**
	Ground also known as Bir Shrestha Shahid Ruhul Amin Stadium and Zohur Ahmed Chowdhury Stadium.			
92	Bogra, Shaheed Chandu Stadium	March 8, 2006	B v SL	1
93	Fatullah, Narayanganj Osmani Stadium	April 9, 2006	B v A	1
94	**Basseterre (St Kitts), Warner Park**	**June 22, 2006**	**WI v I**	**2**
95	**Mirpur (Dhaka), Shere Bangla National Stadium**	**May 25, 2007**	**B v I**	**6**
96	Dunedin, University Oval	January 4, 2008	NZ v B	3
97	Providence Stadium (Guyana)	March 22, 2008	WI v SL	1
98	North Sound (Antigua), Sir Vivian Richards Stadium	May 30, 2008	WI v A	2
99	**Nagpur, Vidarbha C. A. Stadium, Jamtha**	**November 6, 2008**	**I v A**	**3**
100	Cardiff, Sophia Gardens	July 8, 2009	E v A	1
	Ground now known under sponsor's name as Swalec Stadium.			
101	**Hyderabad, Rajiv Gandhi International Stadium**	**November 12, 2010**	**I v NZ**	**1**
102	**Dubai, Dubai Sports City Stadium**	**November 12, 2010**	**P v SA**	**1**
103	**Abu Dhabi, Sheikh Zayed Stadium**	**November 20, 2010**	**P v SA**	**1**
104	**Pallekele, Muttiah Muralitharan Stadium**	**December 1, 2010**	**SL v WI**	**1**

Bold type denotes grounds used for Test cricket since January 1, 2010.

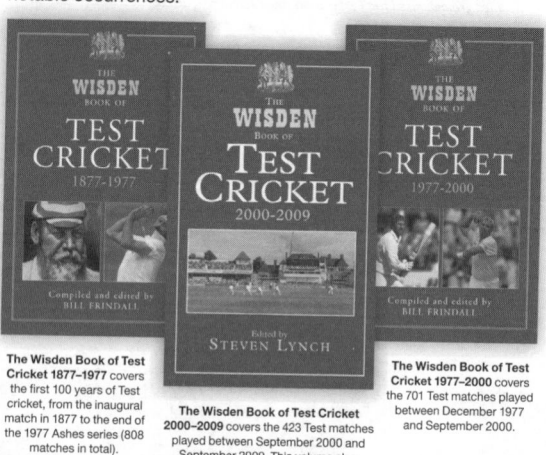

ONE-DAY INTERNATIONAL RECORDS

Matches in this section do not have first-class status.

Note: Throughout this section, bold type denotes performances in the calendar year 2010 or, in career figures, players who appeared in one-day internationals in that year.

SUMMARY OF ONE-DAY INTERNATIONALS

1970-71 to December 31, 2010

Team	Opponents	Matches	Won by														Tied	NR
			E	A	SA	WI	NZ	I	P	SL	Z	B	Ass	Asia	Wld	Afr		
England	Australia	106	41	61	–	–	–	–	–	–	–	–	–	–	–	–	2	2
	South Africa	44	18	–	23	–	–	–	–	–	–	–	–	–	–	–	–	3
	West Indies	82	37	–	–	41	–	–	–	–	–	–	–	–	–	–	2	2
	New Zealand	70	29	–	–	–	35	–	–	–	–	–	–	–	–	–	2	4
	India	70	30	–	–	–	–	38	–	–	–	–	–	–	–	–	–	2
	Pakistan	68	38	–	–	–	–	–	28	–	–	–	–	–	–	–	–	2
	Sri Lanka	44	23	–	–	–	–	–	–	21	–	–	–	–	–	–	–	–
	Zimbabwe	30	21	–	–	–	–	–	–	–	8	–	–	–	–	–	–	1
	Bangladesh	14	13	–	–	–	–	–	–	–	–	1	–	–	–	–	–	–
	Associates	14	13	–	–	–	–	–	–	–	–	–	0	–	–	–	–	1
Australia	South Africa	77	–	39	35	–	–	–	–	–	–	–	–	–	–	–	–	3
	West Indies	125	–	63	–	57	–	–	–	–	–	–	–	–	–	–	2	3
	New Zealand	123	–	84	–	–	34	–	–	–	–	–	–	–	–	–	–	5
	India	104	–	61	–	–	–	35	–	–	–	–	–	–	–	–	–	8
	Pakistan	85	–	52	–	–	–	–	29	–	–	–	–	–	–	–	1	3
	Sri Lanka	71	–	47	–	–	–	–	–	22	–	–	–	–	–	–	–	2
	Zimbabwe	27	–	25	–	–	–	–	–	–	1	–	–	–	–	–	–	1
	Bangladesh	16	–	15	–	–	–	–	–	–	–	1	–	–	–	–	–	–
	Associates	14	–	14	–	–	–	–	–	–	–	–	0	–	–	–	–	–
	ICC World XI	3	–	3	–	–	–	–	–	–	–	–	–	–	0	–	–	–
South Africa	West Indies	50	–	–	37	12	–	–	–	–	–	–	–	–	–	–	–	1
	New Zealand	51	–	–	30	–	17	–	–	–	–	–	–	–	–	–	–	4
	India	60	–	–	36	–	–	22	–	–	–	–	–	–	–	–	–	2
	Pakistan	57	–	–	38	–	–	–	18	–	–	–	–	–	–	–	–	1
	Sri Lanka	46	–	–	22	–	–	–	–	22	–	–	–	–	–	–	1	1
	Zimbabwe	32	–	–	29	–	–	–	–	–	2	–	–	–	–	–	–	1
	Bangladesh	13	–	–	12	–	–	–	–	–	–	1	–	–	–	–	–	–
	Associates	17	–	–	17	–	–	–	–	–	–	–	0	–	–	–	–	7
West Indies	New Zealand	51	–	–	–	24	20	–	–	–	–	–	–	–	–	–	1	2
	India	95	–	–	–	54	–	38	–	–	–	–	–	–	–	–	1	2
	Pakistan	114	–	–	–	64	–	–	48	–	–	–	–	–	–	–	–	2
	Sri Lanka	46	–	–	–	26	–	–	–	18	–	–	–	–	–	–	–	2
	Zimbabwe	41	–	–	–	31	–	–	–	–	9	–	–	–	–	–	–	1
	Bangladesh	16	–	–	–	11	–	–	–	–	–	3	–	–	–	–	–	2
	Associates	17	–	–	–	15	–	–	–	–	–	–	1	–	–	–	–	5
New Zealand	India	88	–	–	–	–	37	46	–	–	–	–	–	–	–	–	1	4
	Pakistan	82	–	–	–	–	32	–	48	–	–	–	–	–	–	–	1	1
	Sri Lanka	72	–	–	–	–	35	–	–	32	–	–	–	–	–	–	1	4
	Zimbabwe	28	–	–	–	–	19	–	–	–	7	–	–	–	–	–	1	1
	Bangladesh	21	–	–	–	–	16	–	–	–	–	5	–	–	–	–	–	–
	Associates	11	–	–	–	–	11	–	–	–	–	–	0	–	–	–	–	–
India	Pakistan	119	–	–	–	–	–	46	69	–	–	–	–	–	–	–	–	4
	Sri Lanka	128	–	–	–	–	–	67	–	50	–	–	–	–	–	–	–	11
	Zimbabwe	51	–	–	–	–	–	39	–	–	10	–	–	–	–	–	2	–
	Bangladesh	22	–	–	–	–	–	20	–	–	–	2	–	–	–	–	–	–
	Associates	22	–	–	–	–	–	20	–	–	–	–	2	–	–	–	–	–
Pakistan	Sri Lanka	120	–	–	–	–	–	–	70	46	–	–	–	–	–	–	1	3
	Zimbabwe	40	–	–	–	–	–	–	36	–	2	–	–	–	–	–	1	1
	Bangladesh	26	–	–	–	–	–	–	25	–	–	1	–	–	–	–	–	–
	Associates	17	–	–	–	–	–	–	16	–	–	–	1	–	–	–	–	–
Sri Lanka	Zimbabwe	46	–	–	–	–	–	–	–	38	7	–	–	–	–	–	–	1
	Bangladesh	29	–	–	–	–	–	–	–	27	–	2	–	–	–	–	–	–
	Associates	13	–	–	–	–	–	–	–	12	–	–	1	–	–	–	–	–
Zimbabwe	Bangladesh	51	–	–	–	–	–	–	–	–	23	28	–	–	–	–	–	–
	Associates	41	–	–	–	–	–	–	–	–	32	–	6	–	–	–	1	2
Bangladesh	Associates	30	–	–	–	–	–	–	–	–	–	20	10	–	–	–	–	–

	Opponents	Matches	E	A	SA	WI	NZ	I	P	SL	Z	B	Ass	Asia	Wld	Afr	Tied	NR
Associates	Associates	121	–	–	–	–	–	–	–	–	–	–	116	–	–	–	–	5
Asian CC XI	ICC World XI	1	–	–	–	–	–	–	–	–	–	–	–	0	1	–	–	–
	African XI	6	–	–	–	–	–	–	–	–	–	–	–	4	–	1	–	1
		3,078	263	464	279	335	256	371	387	288	101	64	137	4	1	1	23	104

Note: Associate Members of ICC who have played one-day internationals are Afghanistan, Bermuda, Canada, East Africa, Hong Kong, Ireland, Kenya, Namibia, Netherlands, Scotland, United Arab Emirates and USA. Sri Lanka, Zimbabwe and Bangladesh also played one-day internationals before being given Test status; these are not included among the Associates' results.

RESULTS SUMMARY OF ONE-DAY INTERNATIONALS

1970-71 to December 31, 2010 (3,078 matches)

	Matches	Won	Lost	Tied	No Result	% Won (excl. NR)
South Africa	447	279	151	5	12	64.71
Australia	751	464	255	8	24	64.37
West Indies	637	335	274	5	23	54.96
Pakistan	728	387	320	6	15	54.69
India	759	371	351	3	34	51.37
England	542	263	256	5	18	50.66
Sri Lanka	615	288	300	3	24	48.98
New Zealand	597	256	305	5	31	45.67
Zimbabwe	387	101	272	5	9	27.38
Bangladesh	238	64	172	–	2	27.11
Asian Cricket Council XI	7	4	2	–	1	66.66
Afghanistan	16	9	7	–	–	56.25
Ireland	58	28	26	1	3	51.81
Netherlands	57	23	32	–	2	41.81
Scotland	50	15	32	–	3	31.91
Kenya	136	38	93	–	5	29.00
Canada	60	16	43	–	1	27.11
ICC World XI	4	1	3	–	–	25.00
Bermuda	35	7	28	–	–	20.00
African XI	6	1	4	–	1	20.00
United Arab Emirates	11	1	10	–	–	9.09
USA	2	–	2	–	–	0.00
East Africa	3	–	3	–	–	0.00
Hong Kong	4	–	4	–	–	0.00
Namibia	6	–	6	–	–	0.00

Note: Matches abandoned without a ball bowled are not included except (from 2004) where the toss took place, in accordance with an ICC ruling. Such matches, like those called off after play began, are now counted as official internationals in their own right, even when replayed on another day. In the percentages of matches won, ties are counted as half a win.

BATTING RECORDS

MOST RUNS

		M	I	NO	R	HS	100s	Avge
1	**S. R. Tendulkar (India)**	**442**	431	41	17,598	200*	46	45.12
2	S. T. Jayasuriya (Sri Lanka/Asia) . . .	444	432	18	13,428	189	28	32.43
3	**R. T. Ponting (Australia/World)**	**352**	343	37	13,082	164	29	42.75
4	Inzamam-ul-Haq (Pakistan/Asia)	378	350	53	11,739	137*	10	39.52
5	S. C. Ganguly (India/Asia)	311	300	23	11,363	183	22	41.02
6	**J. H. Kallis (S. Africa/World/Africa)** . . .	**307**	293	53	11,002	139	17	45.84
7	R. Dravid (India/World/Asia)	339	313	40	10,765	153	12	39.43

		M	I	NO	R	HS	100s	Avge
8	B. C. Lara (West Indies/World)	299	289	32	10,405	169	19	40.48
9	**Mohammad Yousuf (Pakistan/Asia)..**	**288**	**273**	**40**	**9,720**	**141***	**15**	**41.71**
10	A. C. Gilchrist (Australia/World)......	287	279	11	9,619	172	16	35.89
11	M. Azharuddin (India)	334	308	54	9,378	153*	7	36.92
12	P. A. de Silva (Sri Lanka).............	308	296	30	9,284	145	11	34.90
13	**D. P. M. D. Jayawardene (SL/Asia)**	**329**	**310**	**32**	**9,027**	**128**	**12**	**32.47**
14	Saeed Anwar (Pakistan)	247	244	19	8,824	194	20	39.21
15	{ S. Chanderpaul (West Indies)........	261	245	38	8,648	150	11	41.77
	{ D. L. Haynes (West Indies)	238	237	28	8,648	152*	17	41.37
17	**K. C. Sangakkara (SL/Asia/World)**	**279**	**262**	**28**	**8,604**	**138***	**10**	**36.76**
18	M. S. Atapattu (Sri Lanka)	268	259	32	8,529	132*	11	37.57
19	M. E. Waugh (Australia)	244	236	20	8,500	173	18	39.35
20	**H. H. Gibbs (South Africa)**...........	**248**	**240**	**16**	**8,094**	**175**	**21**	**36.13**
21	S. P. Fleming (New Zealand/World)	280	269	21	8,037	134*	8	32.40

Notes: The leading aggregates for players who have appeared for other Test countries are:

	M	I	NO	R	HS	100s	Avge
A. Flower (Zimbabwe)...................	213	208	16	6,786	145	4	35.34
P. D. Collingwood (England).............	**189**	**173**	**35**	**4,978**	**120***	**5**	**36.07**
Mohammad Ashraful (Bangladesh/Asia)....	164	157	13	3,360	109	3	23.33

Excluding runs scored for combined teams, the record aggregate for Sri Lanka is 13,362 in 440 matches by S. T. Jayasuriya; for Australia, **12,967** in 351 matches by **R. T. Ponting**; for Pakistan, 11,701 in 375 matches by Inzamam-ul-Haq; for South Africa, **10,973** in 302 matches by **J. H. Kallis**; for West Indies, 10,348 in 295 matches by B. C. Lara; and for New Zealand, 8,007 in 279 matches by S. P. Fleming. Mohammad Ashraful scored no runs in his two matches for the Asian Cricket Council XI.

BEST CAREER STRIKE-RATES BY BATSMEN

(Runs per 100 balls. Qualification: 700 runs)

SR		Position	M	I	R	Avge
113.30	**Shahid Afridi (P/World/Asia)** ...	**2/7**	**306**	**288**	**6,431**	23.81
105.80	J. M. Davison (Canada)...........	1/2	27	27	766	29.46
104.88	B. L. Cairns (NZ)	9/8	78	65	987	16.72
103.27	**V. Sehwag (I/World/Asia)**.......	**1/2**	**228**	**222**	**7,380**	**34.64**
99.43	I. D. S. Smith (NZ)	8	98	77	1,055	17.29
97.26	**D. R. Smith (WI)**...............	**6/7**	**77**	**61**	**925**	**16.22**
96.94	A. C. Gilchrist (A/World).........	1/2	287	279	9,619	35.89
96.66	R. L. Powell (WI)	6	109	100	2,085	24.82
95.07	Kapil Dev (I)....................	7/6	225	198	3,783	23.79
93.71	**J. R. Hopes (A)**.................	**7**	**84**	**61**	**1,326**	**25.01**
93.53	**H. M. Amla (SA)**	**1/2**	**37**	**36**	**1,906**	**59.56**
92.45	A. Symonds (A)	5	198	161	5,088	39.75
91.92	R. V. Uthappa (I).................	1/7	38	34	786	27.10
91.22	S. T. Jayasuriya (SL/Asia)	1/2	444	432	13,428	32.43
90.20	I. V. A. Richards (WI)............	4	187	167	6,721	47.00
90.18	**S. K. Raina (I)**.................	**5/6**	**106**	**88**	**2,528**	**36.11**

Note: Position means a batsman's most usual position in the batting order.

HIGHEST INDIVIDUAL INNINGS

200*	S. R. Tendulkar	India v South Africa at Gwalior	**2009-10**
194*	C. K. Coventry	Zimbabwe v Kenya at Harare.....................	2009
194	Saeed Anwar	Pakistan v India at Chennai......................	1997-97
189*	I. V. A. Richards	West Indies v England at Manchester	1984
189	S. T. Jayasuriya	Sri Lanka v India at Sharjah	2000-01
188*	G. Kirsten	South Africa v UAE at Rawalpindi	1995-96

186*	S. R. Tendulkar	India v New Zealand at Hyderabad	1999-2000
183*	M. S. Dhoni	India v Sri Lanka at Jaipur	2005-06
183	S. C. Ganguly	India v Sri Lanka at Taunton	1999
181*	M. L. Hayden	Australia v New Zealand at Hamilton	2006-07
181	I. V. A. Richards	West Indies v Sri Lanka at Karachi	1987-88
178*	H. Masakadza	Zimbabwe v Kenya at Harare	2009-10
177	**P. R. Stirling**	**Ireland v Canada at Toronto**	**2010**
175*	Kapil Dev	India v Zimbabwe at Tunbridge Wells	1983
175	H. H. Gibbs	South Africa v Australia at Johannesburg	2005-06
175	S. R. Tendulkar	India v Australia at Hyderabad	2009-10

Note: The highest individual scores for other Test countries are:

172	L. Vincent	New Zealand v Zimbabwe at Bulawayo	2005-06
167*	R. A. Smith	England v Australia at Birmingham	1993
154	Tamim Iqbal	Bangladesh v Zimbabwe at Bulewayo	2009

MOST HUNDREDS

S. R. Tendulkar (I)	46	A. C. Gilchrist (A/World)	16	C. G. Greenidge (WI)	11
R. T. Ponting (A/World)	29	**Mohammad Yousuf (P/As)**	**15**	I. V. A. Richards (WI)	11
S. T. Jayasuriya (SL/Asia)	28	G. Kirsten (SA)	13	M. L. Hayden (A/World)	10
S. C. Ganguly (I/Asia)	22	**V. Sehwag (I/Wld/Asia)**	**13**	Ijaz Ahmed, sen. (P)	10
H. H. Gibbs (SA)	21	R. Dravid (I/World/Asia)	12	Inzamam-ul-Haq (P/Asia)	10
Saeed Anwar (P)	20	**D. P. M. D. Jayawardene**		**K. C. Sangakkara (SL/**	
C. H. Gayle (WI/World)	19	**(SL/Asia)**	**12**	**World/Asia)**	**10**
B. C. Lara (WI/World)	19	M. E. Trescothick (E)	12		
M. E. Waugh (A)	18	**Yuvraj Singh (I/Asia)**	**12**	*Most hundreds for other*	
D. L. Haynes (WI)	17	M. S. Atapattu (SL)	11	*countries:*	
J. H. Kallis (SA/Wld/Af)	**17**	**S. Chanderpaul (WI)**	**11**	A. D. R. Campbell (Z)	7
N. J. Astle (NZ)	16	P. A. de Silva (SL)	11	**Shakib Al Hasan (B)**	**5**

Note: Ponting's hundreds include one for the World XI; no other player reached three figures for a combined team.

FASTEST ONE-DAY INTERNATIONAL FIFTIES

Balls

17	S. T. Jayasuriya	Sri Lanka v Pakistan at Singapore	1995-96
18	S. P. O'Donnell	Australia v Sri Lanka at Sharjah	1989-90
18	Shahid Afridi	Pakistan v Sri Lanka at Nairobi	1996-97
18	Shahid Afridi	Pakistan v Netherlands at Colombo (SSC)	2002
19	M. V. Boucher	South Africa v Kenya at Cape Town	2001-02
19	J. M. Kemp	South Africa v Zimbabwe at Durban	2004-05
19	B. B. McCullum	New Zealand v Bangladesh at Queenstown	2007-08
19	D. J. Hussey	Australia v West Indies at Basseterre	2008
20	Shahid Afridi	Pakistan v India at Kanpur	2004-05
20	Shahid Afridi	Pakistan v South Africa at Durban	2006-07
20	B. B. McCullum	New Zealand v Canada at Gros Islet	2006-07
20	**D. J. G. Sammy**	**West Indies v South Africa at North Sound**	**2010**

FASTEST ONE-DAY INTERNATIONAL HUNDREDS

Balls

37	Shahid Afridi	Pakistan v Sri Lanka at Nairobi	1996-97
44	M. V. Boucher	South Africa v Zimbabwe at Potchefstroom	2006-07
45	B. C. Lara	West Indies v Bangladesh at Dhaka	1999-2000
45	Shahid Afridi	Pakistan v India at Kanpur	2004-05
48	S. T. Jayasuriya	Sri Lanka v Pakistan at Singapore	1995-96

HIGHEST PARTNERSHIP FOR EACH WICKET

286	for 1st	W. U. Tharanga and S. T. Jayasuriya	SL v E	Leeds	2006
331	for 2nd	S. R. Tendulkar and R. Dravid	I v NZ	Hyderabad	1999-2000
237*	for 3rd	R. Dravid and S. R. Tendulkar	I v K	Bristol	1999
275*	for 4th	M. Azharuddin and A. Jadeja	I v Z	Cuttack.	1997-98
223	for 5th	M. Azharuddin and A. Jadeja	I v SL	Colombo (RPS) . .	1997-98
218	for 6th	D. P. M. D. Jayawardene and M. S. Dhoni	As v Af	Chennai	2007
130	for 7th	A. Flower and H. H. Streak	Z v E	Harare.	2001-02
138*	for 8th	J. M. Kemp and A. J. Hall	SA v I	Cape Town.	2006-07
132	**for 9th**	**A. D. Mathews and S. L. Malinga**	**SL v A**	**Melbourne. . . . . .**	**2010-11**
106*	for 10th	I. V. A. Richards and M. A. Holding	WI v E	Manchester.	1984

BOWLING RECORDS

MOST WICKETS

		M	Balls	R	W	BB	4W/i	Avge
1	M. Muralitharan (SL/World/Asia) . . .	339	18,265	11,951	517	7-30	24	23.11
2	Wasim Akram (Pakistan).	356	18,186	11,812	502	5-15	23	23.52
3	Waqar Younis (Pakistan).	262	12,698	9,919	416	7-36	27	23.84
4	W. P. U. J. C. Vaas (SL/Asia)	322	15,775	11,014	400	8-19	13	27.53
5	S. M. Pollock (SA/World/Africa)	303	15,712	9,631	393	6-35	17	24.50
6	G. D. McGrath (Australia/World)	250	12,970	8,391	381	7-15	16	22.02
7	A. Kumble (India/Asia).	271	14,496	10,412	337	6-12	10	30.89
8	B. Lee (Australia).	186	9,478	7,456	324	5-22	20	23.01
9	S. T. Jayasuriya (Sri Lanka/Asia)	444	14,838	11,825	322	6-29	12	36.72
10	J. Srinath (India)	229	11,935	8,847	315	5-23	10	28.08
11	S. K. Warne (Australia/World)	194	10,642	7,541	293	5-33	13	25.73
12	Saqlain Mushtaq (Pakistan).	169	8,770	6,275	288	5-20	17	21.78
	A. B. Agarkar (India).	191	9,484	8,021	288	6-42	12	27.85
	Shahid Afridi (Pakistan/World/Asia) .	306	13,110	10,146	288	6-38	5	35.22
15	D. L. Vettori (New Zealand/World) . . .	263	12,549	8,659	277	5-7	9	31.25
16	A. A. Donald (South Africa)	164	8,561	5,926	272	6-23	13	21.78
17	M. Ntini (South Africa/World)	173	8,687	6,559	266	6-22	12	24.65
18	Abdul Razzaq (Pakistan/Asia)	248	10,461	8,235	259	6-35	11	31.79
	J. H. Kallis (S. Africa/World/Asia) . . .	307	10,270	8,264	259	5-30	4	31.90
20	Kapil Dev (India).	225	11,202	6,945	253	5-43	4	27.45
21	Zaheer Khan (India/Asia).	177	8,850	7,254	243	5-42	8	29.85
22	Shoaib Akhtar (Pakistan/Wld/Asia) .	157	7,506	5,929	242	6-16	10	24.50
	Harbhajan Singh (India/Asia)	212	11,075	7,949	242	5-31	5	32.84
24	H. H. Streak (Zimbabwe)	189	9,468	7,129	239	5-32	9	29.82
25	D. Gough (England/World).	159	8,470	6,209	235	5-44	12	26.42
26	C. A. Walsh (West Indies).	205	10,822	6,918	227	5-1	7	30.47
27	C. E. L. Ambrose (West Indies)	176	9,353	5,429	225	5-17	10	24.12

Notes: The leading aggregates for players who have appeared for other countries are:

Abdur Razzak (Bangladesh)	111	5,885	4,358	162	5-29	8	26.90

Excluding wickets taken for combined teams, the record aggregate for Sri Lanka is **506** in 332 matches by **M. Muralitharan**; for South Africa, 387 in 294 matches by S. M. Pollock; for Australia, 380 in 249 matches by G. D. McGrath; for India, 334 in 269 matches by A. Kumble; for New Zealand, **269** in 259 matches by **D. L. Vettori**; for Zimbabwe, 237 in 187 matches by H. H. Streak; and for England, 234 in 158 matches by D. Gough.

BEST CAREER STRIKE-RATES BY BOWLERS

(Balls per wicket. Qualification: 1,500 balls)

SR		M	W
26.57	**B. A. W. Mendis (SL)**	**44**	**78**
29.21	**S. E. Bond (NZ)**	**82**	**147**
29.25	B. Lee (A)	186	324
29.38	G. I. Allott (NZ)	31	52
29.58	L. S. Pascoe (A)	29	53
29.91	**S. C. J. Broad (E)**	**73**	**124**
30.45	Saqlain Mushtaq (P)	169	288
30.52	Waqar Younis (P)	262	416

BEST CAREER ECONOMY-RATES

(Runs conceded per six balls. Qualification: 50 wickets)

ER		M	W
3.09	J. Garner (WI)	98	146
3.28	R. G. D. Willis (E)	64	80
3.30	R. J. Hadlee (NZ)	115	158
3.32	M. A. Holding (WI)	102	142
3.40	A. M. E. Roberts (WI)	56	87
3.48	C. E. L. Ambrose (WI)	176	225

BEST BOWLING ANALYSES

8-19	W. P. U. J. C. Vaas	Sri Lanka v Zimbabwe at Colombo (SSC)	2001-02
7-15	G. D. McGrath	Australia v Namibia at Potchefstroom	2002-03
7-20	A. J. Bichel	Australia v England at Port Elizabeth	2002-03
7-30	M. Muralitharan	Sri Lanka v India at Sharjah	2000-01
7-36	Waqar Younis	Pakistan v England at Leeds	2001
7-37	Aqib Javed	Pakistan v India at Sharjah	1991-92
7-51	W. W. Davis	West Indies v Australia at Leeds	1983

Note: The best analyses for other countries are:

6-12	A. Kumble	India v West Indies at Calcutta	1993-94
6-19	S. E. Bond	New Zealand v India at Bulawayo	2005-06
6-19	H. K. Olonga	Zimbabwe v England at Cape Town	1999-2000
6-22	M. Ntini	South Africa v Australia at Cape Town	2005-06
6-26	Mashrafe bin Mortaza	Bangladesh v Kenya at Nairobi	2006
6-31	P. D. Collingwood	England v Bangladesh at Nottingham	2005

HAT-TRICKS

Jalal-ud-Din	Pakistan v Australia at Hyderabad	1982-83
B. A. Reid	Australia v New Zealand at Sydney	1985-86
Chetan Sharma	India v New Zealand at Nagpur	1987-88
Wasim Akram	Pakistan v West Indies at Sharjah	1989-90
Wasim Akram	Pakistan v Australia at Sharjah	1989-90
Kapil Dev	India v Sri Lanka at Calcutta	1990-91
Aqib Javed	Pakistan v India at Sharjah	1991-92
D. K. Morrison	New Zealand v India at Napier	1993-94
Waqar Younis	Pakistan v New Zealand at East London	1994-95
Saqlain Mushtaq‡	Pakistan v Zimbabwe at Peshawar	1996-97
E. A. Brandes	Zimbabwe v England at Harare	1996-97
A. M. Stuart	Australia v Pakistan at Melbourne	1996-97
Saqlain Mushtaq	Pakistan v Zimbabwe at The Oval	1999
W. P. U. J. C. Vaas	Sri Lanka v Zimbabwe at Colombo (SSC)	2001-02

Mohammad Sami	Pakistan v West Indies at Sharjah......................	2001-02
W. P. U. J. C. Vaas§	Sri Lanka v Bangladesh at Pietermaritzburg	2002-03
B. Lee	Australia v Kenya at Durban	2002-03
J. M. Anderson	England v Pakistan at The Oval.......................	2003
S. J. Harmison	England v India at Nottingham.........................	2004
C. K. Langeveldt	South Africa v West Indies at Bridgetown.............	2004-05
Shahadat Hossain	Bangladesh v Zimbabwe at Harare.....................	2006
J. E. Taylor	West Indies v Australia at Mumbai	2006-07
S. E. Bond	New Zealand v Australia at Hobart	2006-07
S. L. Malinga†	Sri Lanka v South Africa at Providence................	2006-07
A. Flintoff	England v West Indies at Gros Isle, St Lucia	2008-09
M. F. Maharoof	**Sri Lanka v India at Dambulla**	**2010**

† *Four wickets in four balls.* ‡ *Four wickets in five balls.* § *The first three balls of the match*

WICKETKEEPING AND FIELDING RECORDS

MOST DISMISSALS IN AN INNINGS

6 (all ct)	A. C. Gilchrist.......	Australia v South Africa at Cape Town	1999-2000
6 (all ct)	A. J. Stewart	England v Zimbabwe at Manchester..........	2000
6 (5ct, 1st)	R. D. Jacobs	West Indies v Sri Lanka at Colombo (RPS)	2001-02
6 (5ct, 1st)	A. C. Gilchrist.......	Australia v England at Sydney	2002-03
6 (all ct)	A. C. Gilchrist.......	Australia v Namibia at Potchefstroom........	2002-03
6 (all ct)	A. C. Gilchrist.......	Australia v Sri Lanka at Colombo (RPS)	2003-04
6 (all ct)	M. V. Boucher.......	South Africa v Pakistan at Cape Town	2006-07
6 (5ct, 1st)	M. S. Dhoni	India v England at Leeds....................	2007
6 (all ct)	A. C. Gilchrist.......	Australia v India at Vadodara	2007-08
6 (5ct, 1st)	A. C. Gilchrist.......	Australia v India at Sydney	2007-08
6 (all ct)	M. J. Prior	England v South Africa at Nottingham........	2008

MOST DISMISSALS

			M	Ct	St
1	472	A. C. Gilchrist (Australia/World)......................	282	417	55
2	421	M. V. Boucher (South Africa/Africa)	291	399	22
3	325	K. C. Sangakkara (Sri Lanka/World/Asia)	235	256	69
4	287	Moin Khan (Pakistan)................................	219	214	73
5	234	I. A. Healy (Australia)..............................	168	195	39
6	225	M. S. Dhoni (India/Asia)	172	170	55
7	220	Rashid Latif (Pakistan)..............................	166	182	38
8	206	R. S. Kaluwitharana (Sri Lanka)	186	131	75
9	204	P. J. L. Dujon (West Indies)	169	183	21
10	203	B. B. McCullum (New Zealand)	156	190	13
11	189	R. D. Jacobs (West Indies)..........................	147	160	29
12	165	D. J. Richardson (South Africa)	122	148	17
	165	A. Flower (Zimbabwe)...............................	186	133	32
14	163	A. J. Stewart (England)	138	148	15
15	154	N. R. Mongia (India)................................	140	110	44
16	145	Kamran Akmal (Pakistan)............................	123	124	21
17	136	A. C. Parore (New Zealand)..........................	150	111	25
18	133	T. Taibu (Zimbabwe/Africa)	126	105	28
19	126	Khaled Mashud (Bangladesh)	126	91	35
20	124	R. W. Marsh (Australia)..............................	92	120	4
21	114	D. Ramdin (West Indies)............................	81	109	5
22	103	Salim Yousuf (Pakistan).............................	86	81	22

Notes: Excluding dismissals for combined teams, the most for Australia is 470 (416ct, 54st) in 281 matches by A. C. Gilchrist; for South Africa, **412** (391ct, 21st) in 286 matches by **M. V. Boucher;**

for Sri Lanka, **316** (250ct, 66st) in 228 matches by **K. C. Sangakkara**; and for India, **219** (167ct, 52st) in 169 matches by **M. S. Dhoni**.

M. V. Boucher's list excludes 1 catch taken in 1 one-day international when not keeping wicket; K. C. Sangakkara's record excludes 19 in 44; R. S. Kaluwitharana's excludes 1 in 3; B. B. McCullum's 7 in 22; A. Flower's 8 in 27; A. J. Stewart's 11 in 32; A. C. Parore's 5 in 29; and T. Taibu's 2 in 4. A. C. Gilchrist played five one-day internationals without keeping wicket but made no catches. R. Dravid (India) has made 210 dismissals (196ct, 14st) in 339 one-day internationals but only 86 (72ct, 14st) in 74 as wicketkeeper (including one where he took over during the match).

MOST CATCHES IN AN INNINGS IN THE FIELD

5   J. N. Rhodes . . . .   South Africa v West Indies at Bombay   1993-94

Note: There have been **27** instances of four catches in an innings.

MOST CATCHES

Ct	M		Ct	M	
168	**329**	**D. P. M. D. Jayawardene (SL/Asia)**	108	244	M. E. Waugh (Australia)
156	334	M. Azharuddin (India)	**108**	**248**	**H. H. Gibbs (South Africa)**
152	**352**	**R. T. Ponting (Australia/World)**	108	303	S. M. Pollock (SA/World/Africa)
134	**442**	**S. R. Tendulkar (India)**	**105**	**189**	**P. D. Collingwood (England)**
133	280	S. P. Fleming (New Zealand/World)	105	245	J. N. Rhodes (South Africa)
129	**339**	**M. Muralitharan (SL/World/Asia)**	103	204	Younis Khan (Pakistan)
127	273	A. R. Border (Australia)	**101**	**306**	**Shahid Afridi (Pak/World/Asia)**
124	266	R. Dravid (India/World/Asia)	100	187	I. V. A. Richards (West Indies)
123	444	S. T. Jayasuriya (Sri Lanka/Asia)	100	311	S. C. Ganguly (India/Asia)
120	227	C. L. Hooper (West Indies)			
120	299	B. C. Lara (West Indies/World)			
116	**307**	**J. H. Kallis (SA/World/Africa)**		*Most catches for other countries:*	
113	378	Inzamam-ul-Haq (Pakistan/Asia)	Ct	M	
111	325	S. R. Waugh (Australia)	**86**	**221**	**G. W. Flower (Zimbabwe)**
109	213	R. S. Mahanama (Sri Lanka)	**36**	**116**	**Mashrafe bin Mortaza (Bang)**

Notes: Excluding catches taken for combined teams, the record aggregate for Sri Lanka is **162** in 324 matches by **D. P. M. D. Jayawardene**; for Australia, **151** in 351 by **R. T. Ponting**; for New Zealand, 132 in 279 by S. P. Fleming; for South Africa, **116** in 302 by **J. H. Kallis**; and for Pakistan, 113 in 375 by Inzamam-ul-Haq.

Younis Khan's record excludes 5 catches made in 3 one-day internationals as wicketkeeper.

TEAM RECORDS

HIGHEST INNINGS TOTALS

443-9	(50 overs)	Sri Lanka v Netherlands at Amstelveen	2006
438-9	(49.5 overs)	South Africa v Australia at Johannesburg	2005-06
434-4	(50 overs)	Australia v South Africa at Johannesburg	2005-06
418-5	(50 overs)	South Africa v Zimbabwe at Potchefstroom	2006-07
414-7	(50 overs)	India v Sri Lanka at Rajkot	2009-10
413-5	(50 overs)	India v Bermuda at Port-of-Spain	2006-07
411-8	(50 overs)	Sri Lanka v India at Rajkot	2009-10
402-2	(50 overs)	New Zealand v Ireland at Aberdeen	2008
401-3	**(50 overs)**	**India v South Africa at Gwalior . . . .**	**2009-10**
399-6	**(50 overs)**	**South Africa v Zimbabwe at Benoni . . . .**	**2010-11**
398-5	(50 overs)	Sri Lanka v Kenya at Kandy	1995-96
397-5	(44 overs)	New Zealand v Zimbabwe at Bulawayo	2005-06
392-4	(50 overs)	India v New Zealand at Christchurch	2008-09
392-6	(50 overs)	South Africa v Pakistan at Centurion	2006-07

391-4	(50 overs)	England v Bangladesh at Nottingham	2005
387-5	(50 overs)	India v England at Rajkot	2008-09
385-7	**(50 overs)**	**Pakistan v Bangladesh at Dambulla**	**2010**

Note: The highest totals by other countries are:

360-4	(50 overs)	West Indies v Sri Lanka at Karachi	1987-88
340-2	(50 overs)	Zimbabwe v Namibia at Harare	2002-03
301-7	(50 overs)	Bangladesh v Kenya at Bogra	2005-06

HIGHEST TOTALS BATTING SECOND

438-9	(49.5 overs)	South Africa v Australia at Johannesburg	2005-06
		(Won by 1 wicket)	
411-8	(50 overs)	Sri Lanka v India at Rajkot	2009-10
		(Lost by 3 runs)	
350-9	(49.3 overs)	New Zealand v Australia at Hamilton	2006-07
		(Won by 1 wicket)	
347	(49.4 overs)	India v Australia at Hyderabad	2009-10
		(Lost by 3 runs)	
344-8	(50 overs)	Pakistan v India at Karachi	2003-04
		(Lost by 5 runs)	
340-5	(48.4 overs)	New Zealand v Australia at Auckland	2006-07
		(Won by 5 wickets)	
340-7	(50 overs)	New Zealand v England at Napier	2007-08
		(Tied)	
335-5	(50 overs)	New Zealand v Australia at Perth	2006-07
		(Lost by 8 runs)	

HIGHEST MATCH AGGREGATES

872-13	(99.5 overs)	South Africa v Australia at Johannesburg	2005-06
825-15	(100 overs)	India v Sri Lanka at Rajkot	2009-10
726-14	(95.1 overs)	New Zealand v India at Christchurch	2008-09
697-14	(99.4 overs)	India v Australia at Hyderabad	2009-10
696-14	(99.3 overs)	New Zealand v Australia at Hamilton	2006-07
693-15	(100 overs)	Pakistan v India at Karachi	2003-04
691-19	(98.3 overs)	Netherlands v Sri Lanka at Amstelveen	2006
680-13	(100 overs)	New Zealand v England at Napier	2007-08

LOWEST INNINGS TOTALS

35	(18 overs)	Zimbabwe v Sri Lanka at Harare	2003-04
36	(18.4 overs)	Canada v Sri Lanka at Paarl	2002-03
38	(15.4 overs)	Zimbabwe v Sri Lanka at Colombo (SSC)	2001-02
43	(19.5 overs)	Pakistan v West Indies at Cape Town	1992-93
44	(24.5 overs)	Zimbabwe v Bangladesh at Chittagong	2009-10
45	(40.3 overs)	Canada v England at Manchester	1979
45	(14 overs)	Namibia v Australia at Potchefstroom	2002-03
54	(26.3 overs)	India v Sri Lanka at Sharjah	2000-01
54	(23.2 overs)	West Indies v South Africa at Cape Town	2003-04
55	(28.3 overs)	Sri Lanka v West Indies at Sharjah	1986-87
63	(25.5 overs)	India v Australia at Sydney	1980-81
64	(35.5 overs)	New Zealand v Pakistan at Sharjah	1985-86
65	(24 overs)	USA v Australia at Southampton	2004
65	(24.3 overs)	Zimbabwe v India at Harare	2005-06

The lowest totals by other Test-playing countries are:

69	(28 overs)	South Africa v Australia at Sydney	1993-94
70	(25.2 overs)	Australia v England at Birmingham.	1977
70	(26.3 overs)	Australia v New Zealand at Adelaide.	1985-86
74	(27.4 overs)	Bangladesh v Australia at Darwin	2008
86	(32.4 overs)	England v Australia at Manchester.	2001

LARGEST VICTORIES

290 runs	New Zealand (402-2 in 50 overs) v Ireland (112 in 28.4 ov) at Aberdeen	2008
272 runs	**South Africa (399-6 in 50 overs) v Zimbabwe (127 in 29 overs) at Benoni**	**2010-11**
257 runs	India (413-5 in 50 overs) v Bermuda (156 in 43.1 overs) at Port-of-Spain . . .	2006-07
256 runs	Australia (301-6 in 50 overs) v Namibia (45 in 14 overs) at Potchefstroom . .	2002-03
256 runs	India (374-4 in 50 overs) v Hong Kong (118 in 36.5 overs) at Karachi	2008
245 runs	Sri Lanka (299-5 in 50 overs) v India (54 in 26.3 overs) at Sharjah	2000-01
243 runs	Sri Lanka (321-6 in 50 overs) v Bermuda (78 in 24.4 overs) at P-of-Spain . .	2006-07
234 runs	Sri Lanka (309-5 in 50 overs) v Pakistan (75 in 22.5 overs) at Lahore	2008-09
233 runs	Pakistan (320-3 in 50 overs) v Bangladesh (87 in 34.2 overs) at Dhaka.	1999-2000
232 runs	Australia (323-2 in 50 overs) v Sri Lanka (91 in 35.5 overs) at Adelaide	1984-85

There have been **38** instances of victory by ten wickets.

TIED MATCHES

There have been **23** tied one-day internationals. Australia have tied eight matches; Bangladesh are the only Test-playing country never to have tied. The most recent ties are:

South Africa (259-7 in 50 overs) v Australia (259-9 in 50 overs) at Potchefstroom	2001-02
Sri Lanka (268-9 in 50 overs) v South Africa (229-6 in 45 overs) at Durban (D/L method)	2002-03
England (270-5 in 50 overs) v South Africa (270-8 in 50 overs) at Bloemfontein	2004-05
Australia (196 in 48.5 overs) v England (196-9 in 50 overs) at Lord's.	2005
Ireland (221-9 in 50 overs) v Zimbabwe (221 in 50 overs) at Kingston	2006-07
England (340-6 in 50 overs) v New Zealand (340-7 in 50 overs) at Napier	2007-08

OTHER RECORDS

MOST APPEARANCES

444	S. T. Jayasuriya (SL/Asia)		307	J. H. Kallis (SA/World/Africa)	
442	**S. R. Tendulkar (I)**		**306**	**Shahid Afridi (P/World/Asia)**	
378	Inzamam-ul-Haq (P/Asia)		303	S. M. Pollock (SA/World/Africa)	
356	Wasim Akram (P)		299	B. C. Lara (WI/World)	
352	**R. T. Ponting (A/World)**		**292**	**M. V. Boucher (SA/Africa)**	
339	R. Dravid (I/World/Asia)		288	Mohammad Yousuf (P/Asia)	
339	**M. Muralitharan (SL/World/Asia)**		287	A. C. Gilchrist (A/World)	
334	M. Azharuddin (I)		283	Salim Malik (P)	
329	**D. P. M. D. Jayawardene (SL/Asia)**		280	S. P. Fleming (NZ/World)	
325	S. R. Waugh (A)		**279**	**K. C. Sangakkara (SL/World/Asia)**	
322	W. P. U. J. C. Vaas (SL/Asia)		273	A. R. Border (A)	
311	S. C. Ganguly (I/Asia)		271	A. Kumble (I/Asia)	
308	P. A. de Silva (SL)				

Notes: The most appearances for other countries are **221** by **G. W. Flower** (Z), **191** by **P. D. Collingwood** (E), and **164** by **Mohammad Ashraful** (B). Excluding appearances for combined teams, the record for Sri Lanka is 440 appearances by S. T. Jayasuriya; for Pakistan, 375 by Inzamam-ul-Haq; for Australia, **351** by **R. T. Ponting**; for South Africa, **302** by **J. H. Kallis**; for West Indies, 295 by B. C. Lara; and for New Zealand, 279 by S. P. Fleming.

MOST MATCHES AS CAPTAIN

	P	W	L	T	NR		P	W	L	T	NR
R. T. Ponting (A/World)	**221**	**160**	**48**	**2**	**11**	W. J. Cronje (SA)	138	99	35	1	3
S. P. Fleming (NZ)	218	98	106	1	13	**G. C. Smith (SA/Af)**	**138**	**84**	**47**	**1**	**6**
A. Ranatunga (SL)	193	89	95	1	8	B. C. Lara (WI)	125	59	59	0	7
A. R. Border (A)	178	107	67	1	3	S. T. Jayasuriya (SL)	118	66	47	2	3
M. Azharuddin (I)	174	90	76	2	6	Wasim Akram (P)	109	66	41	2	0
S. C. Ganguly (I/Asia)	147	76	66	0	5	S. R. Waugh (A)	106	67	35	3	1
Imran Khan (P)	139	75	59	1	4	I. V. A. Richards (WI)	105	67	36	0	2

WORLD CUP FINALS

1975	WEST INDIES (291-8) beat Australia (274) by 17 runs	Lord's
1979	WEST INDIES (286-9) beat England (194) by 92 runs	Lord's
1983	INDIA (183) beat West Indies (140) by 43 runs	Lord's
1987	AUSTRALIA (253-5) beat England (246-8) by seven runs	Calcutta
1992	PAKISTAN (249-6) beat England (227) by 22 runs	Melbourne
1996	SRI LANKA (245-3) beat Australia (241-7) by seven wickets	Lahore
1999	AUSTRALIA (133-2) beat Pakistan (132) by eight wickets	Lord's
2003	AUSTRALIA (359-2) beat India (234) by 125 runs	Johannesburg
2007	AUSTRALIA (281-4) beat Sri Lanka (215-8) by 53 runs (D/L method)	Bridgetown

Indrani Mukherjee, AFP/Getty Images

Dutch courage: Ryan ten Doeschate scooped a World Cup hundred for the Netherlands v England, February 2011. Full coverage of the 2011 World Cup will appear in *Wisden 2012*.

TWENTY20 INTERNATIONAL RECORDS

Matches in this section do not have first-class status.

Note: Throughout this section, bold type denotes performances in the calendar year 2010 or, in career figures, players who appeared in Twenty20 internationals in that year.

RESULTS SUMMARY OF TWENTY20 INTERNATIONALS

2004-05 to December 31, 2010 (195 matches)

	Matches	Won	Lost	No Result	% Won (excl. NR)
South Africa	37	25	12	0	67.56
Pakistan	45	27	18	0	60.00
Sri Lanka	34	20	14	0	58.82
India	27	15	11	1	57.69
Australia	39	21	17	1	55.26
England	34	17	15	2	53.12
New Zealand	43	21	22	0	48.83
West Indies	28	12	16	0	42.85
Zimbabwe	14	4	10	0	28.57
Bangladesh	16	3	13	0	18.75
Netherlands	10	6	3	1	66.66
Afghanistan	8	4	4	0	50.00
Ireland	17	7	8	2	46.66
Kenya	12	4	8	0	33.33
Canada	11	3	8	0	27.27
Scotland	12	2	9	1	18.18
Bermuda	3	0	3	0	0.00

* New Zealand, India and Zimbabwe won tied matches with West Indies, Pakistan and Canada respectively in bowling contests. West Indies and New Zealand won tied matches with New Zealand and Australia respectively in one-over eliminators.

BATTING RECORDS

HUNDREDS

117	C. H. Gayle	West Indies v South Africa at Johannesburg	2007-08
116*	**B. B. McCullum**	**New Zealand v Australia at Christchurch**	**2009-10**
101	**S. K. Raina**	**India v South Africa at Gros Islet, St Lucia**	**2010**
100	**D. P. M. D. Jayawardene**	**Sri Lanka v Zimbabwe at Providence**	**2010**

MOST RUNS

		M	I	NO	R	HS	100s	Avge
1	**B. B. McCullum (NZ)**	40	40	7	1,100	116*	1	33.33
2	**G. C. Smith (SA)**	31	31	2	958	89*	0	33.03
3	**K. P. Pietersen (E)**	28	28	4	911	79	0	37.95
4	**D. P. M. D. Jayawardene (SL)**	32	32	4	784	100	1	28.00
5	**K. C. Sangakkara (SL)**	29	28	3	777	78	0	31.08
6	**T. M. Dilshan (SL)**	32	31	5	758	96*	0	29.15
7	**Kamran Akmal (P)**	38	33	3	704	73	0	23.46
8	**Shahid Afridi (P)**	42	40	3	671	54*	0	18.13
9	**L. R. P. L. Taylor (NZ)**	37	34	4	659	63	0	21.96

HIGHEST PARTNERSHIP FOR EACH WICKET

170	for 1st	G. C. Smith and L. L. Bosman...........	SA v E	Centurion	2009-10
166	**for 2nd**	**D. P. M. D. Jayawardene and**			
		K. C. Sangakkara................	**SL v WI**	**Bridgetown**	**2010**
120*	for 3rd	H. H. Gibbs and J. M. Kemp.......	SA v WI	Johannesburg	2005-06
112	**for 4th**	**K. P. Pietersen and E. J. G. Morgan**	**E v P**	**Dubai**	**2009-10**
119*	for 5th	Shoaib Malik and Misbah-ul-Haq.......	P v A	Johannesburg	2007-08
101*	**for 6th**	**M. E. K. Hussey and C. L. White**......	**A v SL**	**Bridgetown**	**2010**
91	for 7th	P. D. Collingwood and M. H. Yardy......	E v WI	The Oval	2007
61	for 8th	S. K. Raina and Harbhajan Singh..........	I v NZ	Christchurch	2008-09
44	for 9th	S. L. Malinga and C. R. D. Fernando......	SL v NZ	Auckland	2006-07
31*	**for 10th**	**Wahab Riaz and Shoaib Akhtar**........	**P v NZ**	**Auckland**	**2010-11**

BOWLING RECORDS

BEST BOWLING ANALYSES

5-6	Umar Gul	Pakistan v New Zealand at The Oval....................	2009
5-18	**T. G. Southee**	**New Zealand v Pakistan at Auckland.................**	**2010-11**
5-19	**R. McLaren**	**South Africa v West Indies at North Sound............**	**2010**
5-20	**N. N. Odhiambo**	**Kenya v Scotland at Nairobi..........................**	**2009-10**
5-26	**D. J. G. Sammy**	**West Indies v Zimbabwe at Port-of-Spain.............**	**2009-10**

HAT-TRICKS

B. Lee	Australia v Bangladesh at Cape Town............................	2007-08
J. D. P. Oram	New Zealand v Sri Lanka at Colombo..........................	2009
T. G. Southee	**New Zealand v Pakistan at Auckland............................**	**2010-11**

MOST WICKETS

		M	B	R	W	BB	4W/i	Avge
1	**Shahid Afridi (P)**..................	42	953	975	53	4-11	3	18.39
2	**Umar Gul (P)**.....................	34	697	752	47	5-6	4	16.00
3	**Saeed Ajmal (P)**..................	29	624	661	41	4-19	2	16.12
4	S. L. Malinga (SL)................	29	588	728	35	3-12	0	20.80
	S. C. J. Broad (E)................	29	611	755	35	3-17	0	21.57
	D. L. Vettori (NZ)................	28	649	580	35	4-20	1	16.57
7	**B. A. W. Mendis (SL)**...........	19	432	409	33	4-15	2	12.39
8	G. P. Swann (E)...................	20	402	435	30	3-14	0	14.50
	M. G. Johnson (A)................	24	512	586	30	3-15	0	19.53

WICKETKEEPING RECORDS

MOST DISMISSALS IN AN INNINGS

4 (all ct)	A. C. Gilchrist	Australia v Zimbabwe at Cape Town.............	2007-08
4 (all ct)	M. J. Prior	England v South Africa at Cape Town............	2007-08
4 (all ct)	A. C. Gilchrist	Australia v New Zealand at Perth................	2007-08
4 (all st)	Kamran Akmal	Pakistan v Netherlands at Lord's.................	2009
4 (3ct, 1st)	N. J. O'Brien	Ireland v Sri Lanka at Lord's....................	2009
4 (2ct, 2st)	**A. B. de Villiers**	**South Africa v West Indies at North Sound......**	**2010**
4 (all ct)	**M. S. Dhoni**	**India v Afghanistan at Gros Islet, St Lucia**	**2010**

MOST DISMISSALS

			M	*Ct*	*St*
1	45	Kamran Akmal (P)......................	37	17	28
2	23	K. C. Sangakkara (SL)	29	14	9
3	21	D. Ramdin (WI)	22	19	2
4	20	B. B. McCullum (NZ)...............	22	16	4

Note: B. B. McCullum's record excludes 9 catches taken in 18 Twenty20 internationals when not keeping wicket. Kamran Akmal played one Twenty20 international in which he did not keep wicket and did not take a catch.

MOST CATCHES IN AN INNINGS IN THE FIELD

4	D. J. G. Sammy............	West Indies v Ireland at Providence	2010

MOST CATCHES

Ct	*M*		*Ct*	*M*	
23	37	L. R. P. L. Taylor (NZ)	22	23	A. B. de Villiers (SA)

Note: A. B. de Villiers's record excludes 14 dismissals (10ct, 4st) in 9 Twenty20 internationals when keeping wicket.

TEAM RECORDS

HIGHEST INNINGS TOTALS

260-6	(20 overs)	Sri Lanka v Kenya at Johannesburg......................	2007-08
241-6	(20 overs)	South Africa v England at Centurion	2009-10
221-5	(20 overs)	Australia v England at Sydney	2006-07
218-4	(20 overs)	India v England at Nagpur	2007-08
215-5	(20 overs)	Sri Lanka v India at Nagpur	2009-10
214-4	**(20 overs)**	**Australia v New Zealand at Christchurch**	**2009-10**
214-5	(20 overs)	Australia v New Zealand at Auckland	2004-05
214-6	**(20 overs)**	**New Zealand v Australia at Christchurch**	**2009-10**

LOWEST INNINGS TOTALS

67	(17.2 overs)	Kenya v Ireland at Belfast	2008
68	**(16.4 overs)**	**Ireland v West Indies at Providence**.....................	**2010**
70	(20 overs)	Bermuda v Canada at Belfast.......................	2008
73	(16.5 overs)	Kenya v New Zealand at Durban.......................	2007-08
74	(17.3 overs)	India v Australia at Melbourne.....................	2007-08
75	(19.2 overs)	Canada v Zimbabwe at King City	2007-08

OTHER RECORDS

MOST APPEARANCES

42	Shahid Afridi (P)		34	M. J. Clarke (A)
40	B. B. McCullum (NZ)		34	Umar Gul (P)
38	Kamran Akmal (P)		33	P. D. Collingwood (E)
37	L. R. P. L. Taylor (NZ)			

WORLD TWENTY20 FINALS

2007-08	INDIA (157-5) beat Pakistan (152) by five runs	Johannesburg
2009	PAKISTAN (139-2) beat Sri Lanka (138-6) by eight wickets...........	Lord's
2010	ENGLAND (148-3) beat Australia (147-6) by seven wickets...........	Bridgetown

MISCELLANEOUS RECORDS

LARGE ATTENDANCES

Test Series

943,000	Australia v England (5 Tests)	1936-37

In England
549,650	England v Australia (5 Tests)	1953

Test Matches

†‡465,000	India v Pakistan, Calcutta	1998-99
350,534	Australia v England, Melbourne (Third Test)	1936-37

Note: Attendance at India v England at Calcutta in 1981-82 may have exceeded 350,000.

In England
158,000+	England v Australia, Leeds	1948
137,915	England v Australia, Lord's	1953

Test Match Day

‡100,000	India v Pakistan, Calcutta (first four days).................	1998-99
90,800	Australia v West Indies, Melbourne (Fifth Test, second day)	1960-61
89,155	Australia v England, Melbourne (Fourth Test, first day).........	2006-07

Other First-Class Matches in England

93,000	England v Australia, Lord's (Fourth Victory Match, 3 days)	1945
80,000+	Surrey v Yorkshire, The Oval (3 days)	1906
78,792	Yorkshire v Lancashire, Leeds (3 days)......................	1904
76,617	Lancashire v Yorkshire, Manchester (3 days)	1926

One-Day Internationals

‡100,000	India v South Africa, Calcutta.............................	1993-94
‡100,000	India v West Indies, Calcutta..............................	1993-94
‡100,000	India v West Indies, Calcutta..............................	1994-95
‡100,000	India v Sri Lanka, Calcutta (World Cup semi-final)	1995-96
‡100,000	India v Australia, Kolkata	2003-04
‡90,000	India v Pakistan, Calcutta	1986-87
‡90,000	India v South Africa, Calcutta	1991-92
87,182	England v Pakistan, Melbourne (World Cup final)	1991-92
86,133	Australia v West Indies, Melbourne	1983-84

Twenty20 International

84,041	Australia v India, Melbourne...............................	2007-08

† *Estimated.*
‡ *No official attendance figures were issued for these games, but capacity at Calcutta (now Kolkata) is believed to have reached 100,000 following rebuilding in 1993.*

LORD'S CRICKET GROUND

Lord's and the Marylebone Cricket Club were founded in London in 1787. The Club has enjoyed an uninterrupted career since that date, but there have been three grounds known as Lord's. The first (1787–1810) was situated where Dorset Square now is; the second (1809–13), at North Bank, had to be abandoned owing to the cutting of the Regent's Canal; and the third, opened in 1814, is the present one at St John's Wood. It was not until 1866 that the freehold of Lord's was secured by MCC. The present pavilion was erected in 1890 at a cost of £21,000.

HIGHEST INDIVIDUAL SCORES MADE AT LORD'S

333	G. A. Gooch	England v India	1990
316*	J. B. Hobbs	Surrey v Middlesex	1926
315*	P. Holmes	Yorkshire v Middlesex	1925
315	M. A. Wagh	Warwickshire v Middlesex	2001
303*	N. V. Knight	Warwickshire v Middlesex	2004

Note: The longest innings in a first-class match at Lord's was N. V. Knight's, which lasted 644 minutes.

HIGHEST TOTALS AT LORD'S

First-Class Matches

729-6 dec	Australia v England	1930
682-6 dec	South Africa v England	2003
665	West Indians v Middlesex	1939
653-4 dec	England v India	1990
652-8 dec	West Indies v England	1973

Minor Matches

735-9 dec	MCC and Ground v Wiltshire	1888

BIGGEST HIT AT LORD'S

The only known instance of a batsman hitting a ball over the present pavilion at Lord's occurred when A. E. Trott, appearing for MCC against Australians on July 31, August 1, 2, 1899, drove M. A. Noble so far and high that the ball struck a chimney pot and fell behind the building.

MINOR CRICKET

HIGHEST INDIVIDUAL SCORES

628*	A. E. J. Collins, Clark's House v North Town at Clifton College. *A junior house match. His innings of 6 hours 50 minutes was spread over four afternoons*	1899
566	C. J. Eady, Break-o'-Day v Wellington at Hobart	1901-02
515	D. R. Havewalla, B. B. and C. I. Railways v St Xavier's at Bombay	1933-34
506*	J. C. Sharp, Melbourne GS v Geelong College at Melbourne	1914-15
502*	Chaman Lal, Mehandra Coll., Patiala v Government Coll., Rupar at Patiala	1956-57
485	A. E. Stoddart, Hampstead v Stoics at Hampstead	1886
475*	Mohammad Iqbal, Muslim Model HS v Islamia HS, Sialkot at Lahore	1958-59
466*	G. T. S. Stevens, Beta v Lambda (University College School house match) at Neasden. *Stevens scored his 466 and took 14 wickets on one day*	1919
459	J. A. Prout, Wesley College v Geelong College at Geelong	1908-09

Note: The highest score in a Minor County match is 323* by F. E. Lacey for Hampshire v Norfolk at Southampton in 1887; the highest in the Minor Counties Championship is 282 by E. Garnett for Berkshire v Wiltshire at Reading in 1908.

HIGHEST PARTNERSHIPS

721* for 1st	B. Manoj Kumar and M. S. Tumbi, St Peter's High School v St Philip's High School at Secunderabad.	2006-07
664* for 3rd	V. G. Kambli and S. R. Tendulkar, Sharadashram Vidyamandir School v St Xavier's High School at Bombay.	1987-88

Notes: Manoj Kumar and Tumbi scored 721 in 40 overs in an Under-13 inter-school match; they hit 103 fours between them, but no sixes. Their opponents were all out for 21 in seven overs.

Kambli was 16 years old, Tendulkar 14. Tendulkar made his Test debut 21 months later.

MOST WICKETS WITH CONSECUTIVE BALLS

There are **two** recorded instances of a bowler taking nine wickets with consecutive balls. Both came in school games: Paul Hugo, for Smithfield School v Aliwal North at Smithfield, South Africa, in 1930-31, and Stephen Fleming (not the future Test captain), for Marlborough College A v Bohally School at Blenheim, New Zealand, in 1967-68. There are five further verified instances of eight wickets in eight balls, the most recent by Mike Walters for the Royal Army Educational Corps v Joint Air Transport Establishment at Beaconsfield in 1979.

TEN WICKETS FOR NO RUNS

There are **24** recorded instances of a bowler taking all ten wickets in an innings for no runs, the most recent by David Morton, for Bayside Muddies v Ranatungas in Brisbane in 1998-99. The previous instance was also in Australia, by the schoolgirl Emma Liddell, for Metropolitan East v West at Penrith (Sydney) in 1995-96. When Jennings Tune did it, for the Yorkshire club Cliffe v Eastrington at Cliffe in 1923, all ten of his victims were bowled.

NOUGHT ALL OUT

In minor matches, this is more common than might be imagined. The historian Peter Wynne-Thomas says the first recorded example was in Norfolk, where an Eleven of Fakenham, Walsingham and Hempton were dismissed for nought by an Eleven of Licham, Dunham and Brisley in July 1815.

MOST DISMISSALS IN AN INNINGS

The only recorded instance of a wicketkeeper being involved in all ten dismissals in an innings was by Welihinda Badalge Bennett, for Mahinda College against Richmond College in Ceylon (now Sri Lanka) in 1952-53. His feat comprised six catches and four stumpings. There are three other known instances of nine dismissals in the same innings, one of which – by H. W. P. Middleton for Priory v Mitre in a Repton School house match in 1930 – included eight stumpings. Young Rangers' innings against Bohran Gymkhana in Karachi in 1969-70 included nine run-outs.

The widespread nature – and differing levels of supervision – of minor cricket matches mean that record claims have to be treated with caution. Additions and corrections to the above records for minor cricket will only be considered for inclusion in Wisden if they are corroborated by independent evidence of the achievement.

Research: Steven Lynch

RECORD HIT

The Rev. W. Fellows, while at practice on the Christ Church ground at Oxford in 1856, drove a ball bowled by Charles Rogers 175 yards from hit to pitch.

THROWING THE CRICKET BALL

140 yards 2 feet, Robert Percival, on the Durham Sands racecourse, Co. Durham......... c1882
140 yards 9 inches, Ross Mackenzie, at Toronto 1872
140 yards, "King Billy" the Aborigine, at Clermont, Queensland 1872

Note: Extensive research by David Rayvern Allen has shown that these traditional records are probably authentic, if not necessarily wholly accurate. Modern competitions have failed to produce similar distances although Ian Pont, the Essex all-rounder who also played baseball, was reported to have thrown 138 yards in Cape Town in 1981. There have been speculative reports attributing throws of 150 yards or more to figures as diverse as the South African Test player Colin Bland, the Latvian javelin thrower Janis Lusis, who won a gold medal for the Soviet Union in the 1968 Olympics, and the British sprinter Charley Ransome. The definitive record is still awaited.

COUNTY CHAMPIONSHIP

MOST APPEARANCES

762	W. Rhodes	Yorkshire..............................	1898–1930
707	F. E. Woolley..............	Kent....................................	1906–1938
668	C. P. Mead	Hampshire	1906–1936
617	N. Gifford................	Worcestershire (484), Warwickshire (133)....	1960–1988
611	W. G. Quaife	Warwickshire............................	1895–1928
601	G. H. Hirst	Yorkshire................................	1891–1921

MOST CONSECUTIVE APPEARANCES

423	K. G. Suttle............	Sussex	1954–1969
412	J. G. Binks............	Yorkshire............................	1955–1969

Notes: J. Vine made 417 consecutive appearances for Sussex in all first-class matches (399 of them in the Championship) between July 1900 and September 1914.

J. G. Binks did not miss a Championship match for Yorkshire between making his debut in June 1955 and retiring at the end of the 1969 season.

UMPIRES

MOST COUNTY CHAMPIONSHIP APPEARANCES

570	T. W. Spencer	1950–1980	517	H. G. Baldwin	1932–1962
531	F. Chester	1922–1955	511	A. G. T. Whitehead	1970–2005
523	D. J. Constant	1969–2006			

MOST SEASONS ON ENGLISH FIRST-CLASS LIST

38	D. J. Constant	1969–2006	27	**B. Dudleston**............	**1984–2010**
36	A. G. T. Whitehead	1970–2005	27	J. W. Holder	1983–2009
31	K. E. Palmer	1972–2002	27	J. Moss.................	1899–1929
31	T. W. Spencer	1950–1980	26	W. A. J. West	1896–1925
30	R. Julian	1972–2001	25	H. G. Baldwin	1932–1962
30	P. B. Wight	1966–1995	25	A. Jepson...............	1960–1984
29	H. D. Bird	1970–1998	25	J. G. Langridge	1956–1980
28	F. Chester	1922–1955	25	B. J. Meyer	1973–1997
28	B. Leadbeater	1981–2008	25	D. R. Shepherd	1981–2005
28	R. Palmer.................	1980–2007			

Bold type denotes umpires who stood in the 2010 season.

WOMEN'S TEST RECORDS

Amended to December 31, 2010

BATTING RECORDS

HIGHEST INDIVIDUAL INNINGS

242	Kiran Baluch	Pakistan v West Indies at Karachi	2003-04
214	M. Raj	India v England at Taunton	2002
209*	K. L. Rolton	Australia v England at Leeds	2001
204	K. E. Flavell	New Zealand v England at Scarborough	1996
204	M. A. J. Goszko	Australia v England at Shenley Park	2001
200	J. Broadbent	Australia v England at Guildford	1998
193	D. A. Annetts	Australia v England at Collingham	1987
190	S. Agarwal	India v England at Worcester	1986
189	E. A. Snowball	England v New Zealand at Christchurch	1934-35
179	R. Heyhoe-Flint	England v Australia at The Oval	1976
177	S. C. Taylor	England v South Africa at Shenley Park	2003
176*	K. L. Rolton	Australia v England at Worcester	1998

1,000 RUNS IN A CAREER

R	T		R	T	
1,935	27	J. A. Brittin (England)	1,110	13	S. Agarwal (India)
1,594	22	R. Heyhoe-Flint (England)	1,078	12	E. Bakewell (England)
1,380	18	C. M. Edwards (England)	1,030	15	S. C. Taylor (England)
1,301	19	D. A. Hockley (New Zealand)	1,007	14	M. E. Maclagan (England)
1,164	18	C. A. Hodges (England)	1,002	14	K. L. Rolton (Australia)

BOWLING RECORDS

BEST BOWLING ANALYSES

8-53	N. David	India v England at Jamshedpur	1995-96
7-6	M. B. Duggan	England v Australia at Melbourne	1957-58
7-7	E. R. Wilson	Australia v England at Melbourne	1957-58
7-10	M. E. Maclagan	England v Australia at Brisbane	1934-35
7-18	A. Palmer	Australia v England at Brisbane	1934-35
7-24	L. Johnston	Australia v New Zealand at Melbourne	1971-72
7-34	G. E. McConway	England v India at Worcester	1986
7-41	J. A. Burley	New Zealand v England at The Oval	1966
7-51	L. C. Pearson	England v Australia at Sydney	2002-03
7-59	Shaiza Khan	Pakistan v West Indies at Karachi	2003-04
7-61	E. Bakewell	England v West Indies at Birmingham	1979

MOST WICKETS IN A MATCH

13-226	Shaiza Khan	Pakistan v West Indies at Karachi	2003-04

50 WICKETS IN A CAREER

W	T		W	T	
77	17	M. B. Duggan (England)	60	19	S. Kulkarni (India)
68	11	E. R. Wilson (Australia)	57	16	R. H. Thompson (Australia)
63	20	D. F. Edulji (India)	55	15	J. Lord (New Zealand)
60	13	C. L. Fitzpatrick (Australia)	50	12	E. Bakewell (England)
60	14	M. E. Maclagan (England)			

WICKETKEEPING RECORDS

SIX DISMISSALS IN AN INNINGS

8 (6ct, 2st) L. Nye.......... England v New Zealand at New Plymouth 1991-92
6 (2ct, 4st) B. A. Brentnall .... New Zealand v South Africa at Johannesburg 1971-72

25 DISMISSALS IN A CAREER

		T	Ct	St
58	C. Matthews (Australia)	20	46	12
43	J. Smit (England).................	21	39	4
36	S. A. Hodges (England).............	11	19	17
28	B. A. Brentnall (New Zealand)	10	16	12

TEAM RECORDS

HIGHEST INNINGS TOTALS

569-6 dec   Australia v England at Guildford.................................... 1998
525   Australia v India at Ahmedabad................................. 1983-84
517-8   New Zealand v England at Scarborough 1996
503-5 dec   England v New Zealand at Christchurch 1934-35

LOWEST INNINGS TOTALS

35   England v Australia at Melbourne 1957-58
38   Australia v England at Melbourne................................... 1957-58
44   New Zealand v England at Christchurch 1934-35
47   Australia v England at Brisbane.................................... 1934-35
50   Netherlands v South Africa at Rotterdam............................ 2007

WOMEN'S ONE-DAY INTERNATIONAL RECORDS

Amended to December 31, 2010

Note: Throughout this section, bold type denotes performances in the calendar year 2010 or, in career figures, players who appeared in women's one-day internationals in that year.

BATTING RECORDS

HIGHEST INDIVIDUAL INNINGS

229*   B. J. Clark .... Australia v Denmark at Mumbai.................... 1997-98
173*   C. M. Edwards....... England v Ireland at Pune 1997-98
168   S. W. Bates .... New Zealand v Pakistan at Sydney 2008-09
156*   L. M. Keightley...... Australia v Pakistan at Melbourne................ 1996-97
156*   S. C. Taylor .... England v India at Lord's 2006
154*   K. L. Rolton........ Australia v Sri Lanka at Christchurch 2000-01
153*   J. Logtenberg........ South Africa v Netherlands at Deventer 2007
151   K. L. Rolton......... Australia v Ireland at Dublin.................... 2005

MOST RUNS IN A CAREER

R	M		R	M	
4,844	118	B. J. Clark (Australia)	4,064	118	D. A. Hockley (New Zealand)
4,814	141	K. L. Rolton (Australia)	**3,963**	**122**	**S. C. Taylor (England)**
4,112	**142**	**C. M. Edwards (England)**	3,836	120	M. Raj (India)

BOWLING RECORDS

BEST BOWLING ANALYSES

7-4	Sajjida Shah	Pakistan v Japan at Amsterdam	2003
7-8	J. M. Chamberlain	England v Denmark at Haarlem	1991
7-24	S. Nitschke	Australia v England at Kidderminster	2005
6-10	J. Lord	New Zealand v India at Auckland	1981-82
6-10	M. Maben	India v Sri Lanka at Kandy	2003-04
6-20	G. L. Page	New Zealand v Trinidad & Tobago at St Albans	1973
6-32	B. H. McNeill	New Zealand v England at Lincoln	2007-08

MOST WICKETS IN A CAREER

W	M		W	M	
180	109	C. L. Fitzpatrick (Australia)	**112**	**100**	**L. C. Sthalekar (Australia)**
141	97	N. David (India)	102	105	C. E. Taylor (England)
120	**105**	**J. Goswami (India)**			

WICKETKEEPING RECORDS

MOST DISMISSALS IN AN INNINGS

6 (4ct, 2st)	S. L. Illingworth	New Zealand v Australia at Beckenham	1993
6 (1ct, 5st)	V. Kalpana	India v Denmark at Slough	1993
6 (2ct, 4st)	Batool Fatima	Pakistan v West Indies at Karachi	2003-04

MOST DISMISSALS IN A CAREER

		M	Ct	St
133	R. J. Rolls (New Zealand)	104	90	43
114	J. Smit (England)	109	69	45
100	J. C. Price (Australia)	84	70	30

TEAM RECORDS

HIGHEST INNINGS TOTALS

455-5	New Zealand v Pakistan at Christchurch	1996-97
412-3	Australia v Denmark at Mumbai	1997-98
397-4	Australia v Pakistan at Melbourne	1996-97
376-2	England v Pakistan at Vijayawada	1997-98
375-5	Netherlands v Japan at Schiedam	2003
373-7	New Zealand v Pakistan at Sydney	2008-09

LOWEST INNINGS TOTALS

22	Netherlands v West Indies at Deventer	2008
23	Pakistan v Australia at Melbourne	1996-97
24	Scotland v England at Reading	2001
26	India v New Zealand as St Saviour	2002
27	Pakistan v Australia at Hyderabad (India)	1997-98
28	Japan v Pakistan at Amsterdam	2003
29	Netherlands v Australia at Perth	1988-89

WOMEN'S WORLD CUP WINNERS

1973	England	1988-89	Australia	2000-01	New Zealand
1977-78	Australia	1993	England	2004-05	Australia
1981-82	Australia	1997-98	Australia	2008-09	England

WOMEN'S TWENTY20 INTERNATIONAL RECORDS

Amended to December 31, 2010

Note: Throughout this section, bold type denotes performances in the calendar year 2010 or, in career figures, players who appeared in women's Twenty20 internationals in that year.

BATTING RECORDS

HIGHEST INDIVIDUAL INNINGS

116*	S. A. Fritz	**South Africa v Netherlands at Potchefstroom**	**2010-11**
112*	D. J. S. Dottin	**West Indies v South Africa at Basseterre**	**2010**
96*	K. L. Rolton	Australia v England at Taunton	2005
90	S. R. Taylor	West Indies v Ireland at Dublin	2008

MOST RUNS IN A CAREER

R	M		R	M	
846	**30**	**C. M. Edwards (England)**	**560**	**18**	**S. R. Taylor (West Indies)**
659	**29**	**A. L. Watkins (New Zealand)**	524	23	S. C. Taylor (England)
610	**27**	**S. W. Bates (New Zealand)**	**504**	**30**	**S. J. McGlashan (New Zealand)**
599	**24**	**S. Nitschke (Australia)**			

BOWLING RECORDS

BEST BOWLING ANALYSES

6-17	A. E. Satterthwaite	New Zealand v England at Taunton	2007
5-10	A. Mohammed	West Indies v South Africa at Cape Town	2009-10
5-16	P. Roy	India v Pakistan at Taunton	2009

MOST WICKETS IN A CAREER

W	M		W	M	
36	**20**	A. Mohammed (West Indies)	**27**	**25**	L. A. Marsh (England)
29	**25**	L. C. Sthalekar (Australia)	**27**	**27**	N. J. Browne (New Zealand)
27	**24**	S. Nitschke (Australia)	**25**	**20**	E. A. Perry (Australia)

WICKETKEEPING RECORDS

MOST DISMISSALS IN AN INNINGS

4 (3ct, 1st)	J. M. Fields	Australia v New Zealand at Brisbane (ABF)......	2009
4 (1ct, 3st)	**S. Naik............**	**India v England at Mumbai (BKC)...........**	**2009-10**
4 (all st)	**S. A. Campbelle .....**	**West Indies v Sri Lanka at Cayon............**	**2010**

MOST DISMISSALS IN A CAREER

			M	Ct	St
26	**R. H. Priest (New Zealand)**		26	13	13
19	**S. Naik (India)**..................		13	5	14
17	**S. J. Taylor (England)**		20	6	11
16	J. M. Fields (Australia).............		12	8	8

TEAM RECORDS

HIGHEST INNINGS TOTALS

205-1	**South Africa v Netherlands at Potchefstroom**	**2010-11**
191-4	**West Indies v Netherlands at Potchefstroom**	**2010-11**
186-7	New Zealand v South Africa at Taunton	2007
184-4	West Indies v Ireland at Dublin	2008
180-5	England v South Africa at Taunton	2007
180-5	**New Zealand v West Indies at Gros Islet, St Lucia**	**2010**

LOWEST INNINGS TOTALS

60	Pakistan v England at Taunton	2009
71	**Sri Lanka v England at Colombo (NCC)**............................	**2010-11**
73	Australia v New Zealand at Wellington................................	2009-10
75	Pakistan v India at Taunton	2009

WOMEN'S WORLD TWENTY20 WINNERS

2009	England	**2010**	**Australia**

BIRTHS AND DEATHS

TEST CRICKETERS

Full list from 1876-77 to January 19, 2011

In the Test career column, dates in italics indicate seasons embracing two different years (i.e. non-English seasons). In these cases, only the first year is given, e.g. *1876* for 1876-77. Some non-English series taking place outside the host country's normal season are dated by a single year.

The Test career figures are complete up to January 19, 2011; the one-day international and Twenty20 international totals are complete up to December 31, 2010. Career figures are for one national team only; those players who have appeared for more than one Test team are listed on page 1560 and for more than one one-day international team on page 1562.

The forename by which a player is known is underlined if it is not his first name.

Family relationships are indicated by superscript numbers; where the relationship is not immediately apparent from a shared name, see the notes at the end of this section. The 5/10 column indicates instances of a player taking five wickets in a Test innings and ten wickets in a match. OT signifies number of one-day and Twenty20 internationals played.

¹ *Father and son(s).*   ² *Brothers.*   ³ *Grandfather, father and son.*   ⁴ *Grandfather and grandson.*   ⁵ *Great-grandfather and great-grandson.*
† *Father and son(s).* ‡ *Excludes matches for another Test team.* ‡ *Excludes matches for another ODI team.*

ENGLAND (650 players)

	Born	Died	Tests	Test Career	Runs	HS	100s	Avge	Wkts	BB	5/10	Avge	Cl/St	OT
Abel Robert	30.11.1857	10.12.1936	13	1888-1902	744	132*	2	37.20	–	–	–/–	–	13	
Absolom Charles Alfred	7.6.1846	30.7.1889	2	*1878*	58	52	0	29.00	–	–	–/–	–	0	
Adams Christopher John	6.5.1970		5	1999	104	31	0	13.00	1	1-42	–/–	59.00	6	5
Afzaal Usman	9.6.1977		3	2001	83	54	0	16.60	1	1-49	0/0	49.00	0	
Agnew Jonathan Philip	4.4.1960		3	1984–1985	10	5	0	10.00	4	2-51	0/0	93.25	0	3
Ali Kabir	24.11.1980		1	2003	10	9	0	5.00	9	3-80	0/0	27.20	0	14
Allen David Arthur	29.10.1935		39	1959–1966	918	88	0	25.50	122	5-30	4/0	30.97	10	
Allen *Sir* George Oswald Browning ("Gubby")	31.7.1902	29.11.1989	25	*1930–1947*	750	122	1	24.19	81	7-80	5/1	29.37	20	
Allom Maurice James Carrick	23.3.1906	8.4.1995	5	*1929–1930*	14	8*	0	14.00	14	5-38	1/0	18.92	4	
Allott Paul John Walter	14.9.1956		13	1981–1985	213	52*	0	14.20	26	6-61	1/0	41.69	4	13
Ambrose Timothy Raymond	1.12.1982		11	2007–2008	447	102	0	29.80	–	–	–/–	–	31	5/1
Ames Leslie Ethelbert George CBE	3.12.1905	27.2.1990	47	*1929–1938*	2,434	149	8	40.56	–	–	–/–	–	74/23	18
Amiss Dennis Leslie MBE	7.4.1943		50	1966–1977	3,612	262*	11	46.30	–	–	–/–	–	24	

Name	Born	Died	Tests	Test Career	Runs	HS	100s	Avge	Wkts	BB	5/10	Avge	Ct/St	O/T
Anderson James Michael	30.7.1982		57	2003–2010	524	34	0	11.64	212	7-43	10/1	31.10	25	133/19
Andrew Keith Vincent	15.12.1929	27.12.2010	2	1954–1963	29	15*	0	9.66	–	–	–/–	–	1	
Appleyard Robert MBE	27.6.1924		9	1954–1956	51	19*	0	17.00	31	5-51	1/0	17.87	4	
Archer Alfred German	6.12.1871	15.7.1935	1	1898	31	24*	0	31.00	0	0-15	0/0	–	0	
Armitage Thomas	25.4.1848	21.9.1922	2	1876	33	21	0	11.00	–	–	–/–	–	0	
Arnold Edward George	7.11.1876	25.10.1942	10	1903–1907	160	40	0	13.33	31	5-37	1/0	25.41	8	
Arnold Geoffrey Graham	3.9.1944		34	1967–1975	421	59	0	12.02	115	6-45	6/0	28.29	9	14
Arnold John	30.11.1907	4.4.1984	1	1931	34	34	0	17.00	–	–	–/–	–		
Astill William Ewart	1.3.1888	10.2.1948	9	1927–1929	190	40	0	12.66	25	4-58	0/0	34.24	7	
Atherton Michael Andrew OBE	23.3.1968		115	1989–2001	7728	185*	16	37.69	2	1-20	0/0	151.00	83	54
Athey Charles William Jeffrey	27.9.1957		23	1980–1988	919	123	1	22.97	–	–	–/–	–	13	31
Attewell William	12.6.1861	11.6.1927	10	1884–1891	150	43*	0	16.66	28	4-42	0/0	22.35	9	
Bailey Robert John	28.10.1963		4	1988–1991	119	43	0	14.87	–	–	–/–	–	0	4
Bailey Trevor Edward CBE	3.12.1923	10.2.2011	61	1949–1958	2290	134*	1	29.74	132	7-34	5/1	29.21	32	
Bairstow David Leslie	1.9.1951	5.1.1998	4	1979–1980	125	59	0	20.83	–	–	–/–	–	12/1	21
Bakewell Alfred Harry	2.11.1908	23.1.1983	6	1931–1935	409	107	1	45.44	0	0-8	0/0	–	3	
Balderstone John Christopher	16.11.1940	6.3.2000	2	1976	39	35	0	9.75	1	1-80	0/0	80.00	1	
Barber Robert William	26.9.1935		28	1960–1968	1495	185	1	35.59	42	4-132	0/0	43.00	21	
Barber Wilfred	18.4.1901	10.9.1968	2	1935	83	44	0	20.75	1	1-0	0/0	0.00	0	
Barlow Graham Derek	26.3.1950		3	1976–1977	17	7*	0	4.25	–	–	–/–	–		6
Barlow Richard Gorton	28.5.1851	31.7.1919	17	1881–1886	591	62	0	22.73	34	7-40	3/0	22.55	14	
Barnes Sydney Francis	19.4.1873	26.12.1967	27	1901–1913	242	38*	0	8.06	189	9-103	24/7	16.43	12	
Barnes William	27.5.1852	24.3.1899	21	1880–1890	725	134	1	23.38	51	6-28	3/0	15.54	19	
Barnett Charles John	3.7.1910	28.5.1993	20	1933–1948	1098	129	2	35.41	0	0-32	0/0	–	14	
Barnett Kim John	17.7.1960		4	1988–1989	207	80	0	29.57	–	–	–/–	–	2	1
Barratt Fred	12.4.1894	29.1.1947	5	1929–1929	28	17	0	9.33	5	1-8	0/0	47.00		
Barrington Kenneth Frank	24.11.1930	14.3.1981	82	1955–1968	6806	256	20	58.67	29	3-4	0/0	44.82	58	
Barton Victor Alexander	6.10.1867	23.3.1906	1	1891	23	23	0	23.00	–	–	–/–	–	0	
Bates Willie	19.11.1855	8.1.1900	15	1881–1886	656	64	0	27.33	50	7-28	4/1	16.42	9	
Batty Gareth Jon	13.10.1977		7	2003–2005	144	38	0	20.57	11	3-55	0/0	66.63	3	10/1
Bean George	7.3.1864	16.3.1923	3	1891	92	50	0	18.40	–	–	–/–	–		
Bedser Sir Alec Victor	4.7.1918	4.4.2010	51	1946–1955	714	79	0	12.75	236	7-44	15/5	24.89	26	
Bell Ian Ronald MBE	11.4.1982		62	2004–2010	4192	199	12	44.12	1	1-33	0/0	76.00	53	83/5
Benjamin Joseph Emmanuel MBE	2.2.1961		1	1994	0	0	0	0.00	4	4-42	0/0	20.00	0	2
Benson Mark Richard	6.7.1958		1	1986	51	30	0	25.50	–	–	–/–	–	0	1
Berry Robert	29.1.1926	2.12.2006	2	1950	6	4*	0	3.00	9	5-63	1/0	25.33	2	

Name	Born	Died	Tests	Test Career	Runs	HS	100s	Avge	Wkts	BB	5/10	Avge	Ct/St	O/T
Bicknell Martin Paul	14.1.1969		4	1993–2003	45	45	0	6.42	14	4-84	0/0	38.78	2	7
Binks James Graham	5.10.1935		2	1963	91	55	0	22.75					8	
Bird Morice Carlos	25.3.1888	9.12.1933	10	1909–1913	280	61	0	18.66	8	3-11	0/0	15.00	5	
Birkenshaw Jack	13.11.1940		5	1972–1973	148	64	0	21.14	13	5-57	1/0	36.07	3	
Blackwell Ian David	10.6.1978		1	2005	4	4	0	4.00	0	0-28	0/0	–	0	34
Blakey Richard John	15.1.1967		2	1992	7	6	0	1.75					2	3
Bligh Hon. Ivo Francis Walter	13.3.1859	10.4.1927	4	1882	62	19	0	10.33					7	
Blythe Colin	30.5.1879	8.11.1917	19	1901–1909	183	27	0	9.63	100	8-59	9/4	18.63	6	
Board John Henry	23.2.1867	15.4.1924	6	1898–1905	108	29	0	10.80					8/3	
Bolus John Brian	31.1.1934		7	1963–1963	496	88	0	41.33	0	0-16	0/0	–	0	
Booth Major William	10.12.1886	1.7.1916	2	1913	46	32	0	23.00	7	4-49	0/0	18.57	5	
Bopara Ravinder Singh	4.5.1985		10	2007–2009	502	143	3	33.46	1	1-39	0/0	199.00	9	54/11
Bosanquet Bernard James Tindal	13.10.1877	12.10.1936	7	1903–1905	147	27	0	13.36	25	8-107	2/0	24.16	9	
Botham Sir Ian Terence OBE	24.11.1955		102	1977–1992	5,200	208	14	33.54	383	8-34	27/4	28.40	120	116
Bowden Montague Parker	1.11.1865	19.2.1892	2	1888	25	25	0	12.50					2	
Bowes William Eric	25.7.1908	4.9.1987	15	1932–1946	28	10*	0	4.66	68	6-33	6/0	22.33	2	
Bowley Edward Henry	6.6.1890	9.7.1974	5	1929–1929	252	109	1	36.00	0	0-7	0/0	–	2	
Boycott Geoffrey OBE	21.10.1940		108	1964–1982	8,114	246*	22	47.72	7	3-47	0/0	54.57	33	36
Bradley Walter Morris	2.1.1875	19.6.1944	2	1899	23	23*	0	23.00	6	5-67	1/0	38.83	0	
Braund Leonard Charles	18.10.1875	23.12.1955	23	1901–1907	987	104	3	25.97	47	8-81	3/0	38.51	39	
Brearley John Michael OBE	28.4.1942		39	1976–1981	1,442	91	0	22.88					52	25
Brearley Walter	11.3.1876	30.1.1937	4	1905–1912	21	11*	0	7.00	17	5-110	1/0	21.11	0	
Brennan Donald Vincent	10.2.1920	9.1.1985	2	1951	16	16	0	8.00					0/1	
Bresnan Timothy Thomas	28.2.1985		3	2009–2010	164	91	0	32.80	25	4-50	0/0	28.28	3	33/14
Briggs John	3.10.1862	11.1.1902	33	1884–1899	815	121	0	18.11	118	8-11	9/4	17.75	12	
Broad Brian Christopher	29.9.1957		25	1984–1989	1,661	162	6	39.54	0	0-4	0/0	–	10	34
Broad Stuart Christopher John	24.6.1986		34	2007–2010	1,096	169	1	27.40	99	6-91	3/0	35.24	9	73/29
Brockwell William	21.1.1865	30.6.1935	7	1893–1899	202	49	0	16.83	5	3-33	0/0	61.80	6	
Bromley-Davenport Hugh Richard	18.8.1870	23.5.1954	4	1895–1898	128	84	0	21.33	4	2-46	0/0	24.50	1	
Brookes Dennis	29.10.1915	9.3.2006	1	1947	17	10	0	8.50						
Brown Alan	17.10.1935		2	1961	3	3*	0		3	3-27	0/0	50.00		
Brown David John	30.1.1942		26	1965–1969	342	44*	0	11.79	79	5-42	2/0	28.31	7	
Brown Frederick Richard MBE	16.12.1910	24.7.1991	22	1931–1953	734	79	0	25.31	45	5-49	2/0	31.06	22	
Brown George	6.10.1887	3.12.1964	7	1921–1922	299	84	0	29.90	0	0-22	0/0	–	9/3	
Brown John Thomas	20.8.1869	4.11.1904	8	1894–1899	470	140	1	36.15					1	
Brown Simon John Emmerson	29.6.1969		1	1996	11	10*	0	11.00	2	1-60	0/0	69.00	1	

	Born	Died	Tests	Test Career	Runs	HS	100s	Avge	Wkts	BB	5/10	Avge	Ct/St	O/T
Buckenham Claude Percival	16.1.1876	23.2.1937	4	1909	43	17	0	6.14	21	5-115	1/0	28.23	2	1
Butcher Alan Raymond	7.1.1954		1	1979	34	20	0	17.00	0	0-9	0/0	—		
Butcher Mark Alan	23.8.1972		71	1997–2004	4,288	173*	8	34.58	15	4-42	0/0	36.06	61	3
Butcher Roland Orlando	14.10.1953		3	1980	71	32	0	14.20	—		—/—		3	
Butler Harold James	12.3.1913	17.7.1991	2	1947–1947	15	15*	0	15.00	12	4-34	0/0	17.91		
Butt Henry Rigden	27.12.1865	21.12.1928	3	1895	22	13	0	7.33	—		—/—		1/1	
Caddick Andrew Richard	21.11.1968		62	1993–2002	861	49*	0	10.37	234	7-46	13/1	29.91	21	54
Calthorpe Hon. Frederick Somerset Gough-	27.5.1892	19.11.1935	4	1929	129	49	0	18.42	1	1-38	0/0	91.00	3	
Capel David John	6.2.1963		15	1987–1989	374	98	0	15.58	21	3-88	0/0	50.66	6	23
Carberry Michael Alexander	29.9.1980		1	2009	64	34	0	32.00	—		—/—			
Carr Arthur William	21.5.1893	7.2.1963	11	1922–1929	237	63	0	19.75	—		—/—		3	
Carr Donald Bryce OBE	28.12.1926		2	1951	135	76	0	33.75	2	2-84	0/0	70.00		
Carr Douglas Ward	17.3.1872	23.3.1950	1	1909	0	0	0	0.00	7	5-146	1/0	40.28		
Cartwright Thomas William MBE	22.7.1935	30.4.2007	5	1964–1965	26	9	0	5.20	15	6-94	1/0	36.26	2	
Chapman Arthur Percy Frank	3.9.1900	16.9.1961	26	1924–1930	925	121	1	28.90	0	0-10	0/0	—	32	20
Charlwood Henry Rupert James	19.12.1846	6.6.1888	2	1876	63	36	0	15.75	—		—/—			
Chatterton William	27.12.1861	19.3.1913	1	1891	48	48	0	48.00	—		—/—			
Childs John Henry	15.8.1951		2	1988	2	2*	0	—	3	1-13	0/0	61.00	1	
Christopherson Stanley	11.11.1861	6.4.1949	1	1884	17	17	0	17.00	1	1-52	0/0	69.00	0	
Clark Edward Winchester	9.8.1902	28.4.1982	8	1929–1934	36	10	0	9.00	32	5-98	1/0	28.09	1	
Clarke Rikki	29.9.1981		2	2003	96	55	0	32.00	4	2-7	0/0	15.00	1	3
Clay John Charles	18.3.1898	11.8.1973	1	1935	0	0	0	—	0	0-30	0/0	—		
Close Dennis Brian CBE	24.2.1931		22	1949–1976	887	70	0	25.34	18	4-35	0/0	29.55	24	3
Coldwell Leonard John	10.1.1933	6.8.1996	7	1962–1964	9	6*	0	4.50	22	6-85	1/0	27.72	1	
Collingwood Paul David MBE	26.5.1976		68	2003–2010	4,259	206	10	40.56	17	3-23	0/0	59.88	96	189/33
Compton Denis Charles Scott CBE	23.5.1918	23.4.1997	78	1937–1956	5,807	278	17	50.06	25	5-70	1/0	56.40	49	
Cook Alastair Nathan	25.12.1984		65	2005–2010	5,130	235*	16	47.50	0	0-1	0/0	—	57	26/4
Cook Cecil ("Sam")	23.8.1921	5.9.1996	1	1947	4	4	0	2.00	0	0-40	0/0	—		
Cook Geoffrey	9.10.1951		7	1981–1982	203	66	0	15.61	0	0-4	0/0	—	9	6
Cook Nicholas Grant Billson	17.6.1956		15	1983–1989	179	31	0	8.52	52	6-65	4/1	32.48	5	3
Cope Geoffrey Alan	23.2.1947		3	1977	40	22	0	13.33	8	3-102	0/0	34.62	1	2
Copson William Henry	27.4.1908	13.9.1971	3	1939–1947	6	6	0	6.00	15	5-85	1/0	19.80	1	
Cork Dominic Gerald	7.8.1971		37	1995–2002	864	59	0	18.00	131	7-43	5/0	29.81	18	32
Cornford Walter Latter	25.12.1900	6.2.1964	4	1929	36	18	0	9.00	—		—/—		5/2	
Cottam Robert Michael Henry	16.10.1944		4	1968–1972	27	13	0	6.75	14	4-50	0/0	23.35	2	
Coventry Hon. Charles John	26.2.1867	2.6.1929	2	1888	13	12	0	13.00	—		—/—		0	

Name	Born	Died	Tests	Test Career	Runs	HS	100s	Avge	Wkts	BB	Avge	5/10	Ct/St	O/T
Cowans Norman George	17.4.1961		19	1982–1985	175	36	0	7.95	51	6-77	39.27	2/0	9	23
[1]Cowdrey Christopher Stuart	20.10.1957		6	1984–1988	101	38	0	14.42	4	2-65	77.25	0/0	5	3
[1]Cowdrey Lord [Michael Colin] CBE	24.12.1932	4.12.2000	114	1954–1974	7,624	182	22	44.06	–	–	–	–	120	
Coxon Alexander	18.1.1916	22.1.2006	1	1948	19	19	0	9.50	3	2-90	57.33	0/0	1	
Cranston James	9.1.1859	10.12.1904	1	1890	31	16	0	15.50	–	–	–	–	0	
Cranston Kenneth	20.10.1917	8.1.2007	8	1947–1948	209	45	0	14.92	18	4-12	25.61	0/0	3	1
Crapp John Frederick	14.10.1912	13.2.1981	7	1948	319	56	0	29.00	–	–	–	–	7	
Crawford John Neville	1.12.1886	2.5.1963	12	1905–1907	469	74	0	22.33	39	5-48	29.48	3/0	13	
Crawley John Paul	21.9.1971		37	1994–2002	1,800	156*	4	34.61	–	–	–	–	29	
Croft Robert Damien Bale	25.5.1970		21	1996–2001	421	37*	0	16.19	49	5-95	37.24	1/0	10	13
Curtis Timothy Stephen	15.1.1960		5	1988–1989	140	41	0	15.55	–	–	–	–	3	
Cuttell Willis Robert	13.9.1863	9.12.1929	2	1898	65	21	0	16.25	6	3-17	12.16	0/0	2	50
Dawson Edward William	13.2.1904	4.6.1979	5	1927–1929	175	55	0	19.44	–	–	–	–	0	
Dawson Richard Kevin James	4.8.1980		7	2001–2002	114	19*	0	11.40	11	4-134	61.54	0/0	3	
Dean Harry	13.8.1884	12.3.1957	3	1912	10	8	0	5.00	11	4-19	13.90	0/0	2	
DeFreitas Phillip Anthony Jason	18.2.1966		44	1986–1995	934	88	0	14.82	140	7-70	33.57	4/0	14	103
Denness Michael Henry	1.12.1940		28	1969–1975	1,667	188	4	39.69	–	–	–	–	28	12
Denton David	4.7.1874	16.2.1950	11	1905–1909	424	104	1	20.19	–	–	–	–	8	
Dewes John Gordon	11.10.1926		5	1948–1950	121	67	0	12.10	–	–	–	–	0	
Dexter Edward Ralph CBE	15.5.1935		62	1958–1968	4,502	205	9	47.89	66	4-10	34.93	0/0	29	36
Dilley Graham Roy	18.5.1959		41	1979–1989	521	56	0	13.35	138	6-38	29.76	6/0	10	
Dipper Alfred Ernest	9.11.1885	7.11.1945	1	1921	51	40	0	25.50	–	–	–	–	0	
Doggart George Hubert Graham OBE	18.7.1925		2	1950	76	29	0	19.00	–	–	–	–	3	
D'Oliveira Basil Lewis OBE	4.10.1931		44	1966–1972	2,484	158	5	40.06	47	3-46	39.55	0/0	29	4
Dollery Horace Edgar ("Tom")	14.10.1914	20.1.1987	4	1947–1950	72	37	0	10.28	–	–	–	–	1	
Dolphin Arthur	24.12.1885	23.10.1942	1	1920	1	1	0	0.50	–	–	–	–	1	
Douglas John William Henry Tyler	3.9.1882	19.12.1930	23	1911–1924	962	119	1	29.15	45	5-46	33.02	1/0	9	
Downton Paul Rupert	4.4.1957		30	1980–1988	785	74	0	19.62	–	–	–	–	70/5	28
Druce Norman Frank	1.1.1875	27.10.1954	5	1897	252	64	0	28.00	–	–	–	–	5	
Ducat Andrew	16.2.1886	23.7.1942	1	1921	5	3	0	2.50	–	–	–	–	0	
Duckworth George	9.5.1901	5.1.1966	24	1924–1936	234	39*	0	14.62	–	–	–	–	45/15	
Duleepsinhji Kumar Shri	13.6.1905	5.12.1959	12	1929–1931	995	173	3	58.52	0	0-7	–	0/0	10	
Durston Frederick John	11.7.1893	8.4.1965	1	1921	8	6*	0	8.00	5	4-21	27.20	0/0	0	
Ealham Mark Alan	27.8.1969		8	1996–1998	210	53*	0	21.00	17	4-102	28.70	0/0	4	64
Edmonds Philippe-Henri	8.3.1951		51	1975–1987	875	64	0	17.50	125	7-66	34.18	2/0	42	29
Edrich John Hugh MBE	21.6.1937		77	1963–1976	5,138	310*	12	43.54	0	0-6	–	0/0	43	7

Name	Born	Died	Test Career	Tests	Runs	HS	100s	Avge	Wkts	BB	5I/10	Avge	Ct/St	O/T
Edrich William John	26.3.1916	24.4.1986	1938–1954	39	2,440	219	6	40.00	41	4-68	0/0	41.29	39	
Elliott Harry	2.11.1891	2.2.1976	1927–1933	4	61	37*	0	15.25					8/3	
Ellison Richard Mark	21.9.1959		1984–1986	11	202	41	0	13.46	35	6-77	3/1	29.94	2	14
Emburey John Ernest	20.8.1952		1978–1995	64	1,713	75	0	22.53	147	7-78	6/0	38.40	34	61
Emmett George Malcolm	2.12.1912	18.12.1976	1948	1	10	10	0	5.00						
Emmett Thomas	3.9.1841	29.6.1904	1876–1881	7	160	48	0	13.33	9	7-68	1/0	31.55	9	
Evans Alfred John	1.5.1889	18.9.1960	1921	1	18	14	0	9.00					0	
Evans Thomas Godfrey CBE.	18.8.1920	3.5.1999	1946–1959	91	2,439	104	2	20.49	0	0-9	-/-	-	173/46	
Fagg Arthur Edward	18.6.1915	13.9.1977	1936–1939	5	150	39	0	18.75					5	
Fairbrother Neil Harvey	9.9.1963		1987–1992	10	219	83	0	15.64					4	75
Fane Frederick Luther	27.4.1875	27.11.1960	1905–1909	14	682	143	1	26.23					6	
Farnes Kenneth	8.7.1911	20.10.1941	1934–1938	15	58	20	0	4.83	60	6-96	2/0	28.65	–	
Farrimond William	23.5.1903	15.11.1979	1930–1935	4	116	35	0	16.57					5/2	
Fender Percy George Herbert.	22.8.1892	15.6.1985	1920–1929	13	380	60	0	19.00	29	5-90	2/0	40.86	14	
Ferris John James.	21.5.1867	17.11.1900	1891	1†	16	16	0	16.00	13	7-37	2/1	7.00	0	
Fielder Arthur	19.7.1877	30.8.1949	1903–1907	6	78	20	0	11.14	26	6-82	1/0	27.34	4	
Finn Steven Thomas	4.4.1989		2009–2010	11	16	9*	0	5.33	46	6-125	1/0	26.23	1	
Fishlock Laurence Barnard.	2.1.1907	25.6.1986	1936–1946	4	31	14	0	11.75					–	
Flavell John Alfred	15.5.1929	25.2.2004	1961–1964	4	31	14	0	7.75	7	2-65	0/0	52.42		
Fletcher Keith William Robert OBE.	20.5.1944		1968–1981	59	3,272	216	7	39.90	7	1-6	0/0	96.50	54	24
Flintoff Andrew MBE.	6.12.1977		1998–2009	79§	3,795	167	5	31.89	219	5-58	3/0	33.34	52	138/7
Flowers Wilfred	7.12.1856	1.11.1926	1884–1893	8	254	56	0	18.14	14	5-46	1/0	21.14	5	
Ford Francis Gilbertson Justice.	14.12.1866	7.2.1940	1894	5	168	48	0	18.66	1	1-47	0/0	129.00	11	
Foster Frank Rowbotham.	31.1.1889	3.5.1958	1911–1912	11	330	71	0	23.57	45	6-91	4/0	20.57		
Foster James Savin	15.4.1980		2001–2002	7	226	48	0	25.11					17/1	11/5
Foster Neil Alan.	6.5.1962		1983–1993	29	446	39	0	11.73	88	8-107	5/1	32.85	7	48
Foster Reginald Erskine ("Tip")	16.4.1878	13.5.1914	1903–1907	8	602	287	1	46.30					13	
Fothergill Arnold James	26.8.1854	1.8.1932	1888	2	33	32	0	16.50	8	4-19	0/0	11.25	0	
Fowler Graeme	20.4.1957		1982–1984	21	1,307	201	3	35.32					10	26
Fraser Angus Robert Charles MBE.	8.8.1965		1989–1998	46	388	50*	0	7.46	177	8-53	13/2	27.32	9	42
Freeman Alfred Percy ("Tich")	17.5.1888	28.1.1965	1924–1929	12	154	50*	0	14.00	66	7-71	5/3	25.86	13	
French Bruce Nicholas	13.8.1959		1986–1987	16	308	59	0	18.11	0	0-3	-/-	-	38/1	13
Fry Charles Burgess	25.4.1872	7.9.1956	1895–1912	26	1,223	144	2	32.18	0	0-6	-/-	-	17	
Gallian Jason Edward Riche.	25.6.1971		1995	3	74	28	0	12.33					–	
Gatting Michael William OBE.	6.6.1957		1977–1994	79	4,409	207	10	35.55	4	1-14	0/0	79.25	59	92

§ Flintoff's figures exclude 50 runs and seven wickets for the ICC World XI v Australia in the Super Series Test in 2005-06.

Name	Born	Died	Tests	Test Career	Runs	HS	100s	Avge	Wkts	BB	5/10	Avge	Ct/St	O/T
Gay Leslie Hewitt	24.3.1871	1.11.1949	1	1894	37	33	0	18.50	–	–	–/–	–	3/1	–
Geary George	9.7.1893	6.3.1981	14	1924–1934	249	66	0	15.56	46	7-70	4/1	29.41	13	–
Gibb Paul Antony	11.7.1913	7.12.1977	8	1938–1946	581	120	2	44.69	–	–	–/–	–	3/1	–
Giddins Edward Simon Hunter	20.7.1971	–	4	1999–2000	10	7	0	2.50	12	5-15	1/0	20.00	0	–
Gifford Norman MBE	30.3.1940	–	15	1964–1973	179	25*	0	16.27	33	5-55	1/0	31.09	8	2
Giles Ashley Fraser MBE	19.3.1973	–	54	1998–2006	1,421	59	0	20.89	143	5-57	5/0	40.60	33	62
[2] Gilligan Alfred Herbert Harold	29.6.1896	5.5.1978	4	1929	71	32	0	17.75	–	–	–/–	–	0	–
[2] Gilligan Arthur Edward Robert	23.12.1894	5.9.1976	11	1922–1924	209	39*	0	16.07	36	6-7	2/1	29.05	3	–
Gimblett Harold	19.10.1914	30.3.1978	3	1936–1939	129	67*	0	32.25	–	–	–/–	–	1	–
Gladwin Clifford	3.4.1916	9.4.1988	8	1947–1949	170	51*	0	28.33	15	3-21	0/0	38.06	1	–
Goddard Thomas William John OBE	1.10.1900	22.5.1966	8	1930–1939	13	8	0	6.50	22	6-29	1/0	26.72	3	–
[2] Gooch Graham Alan OBE	23.7.1953	–	118	1975–1994	8,900	333	20	42.58	23	3-39	0/0	46.47	103	125
Gough Darren	18.9.1970	–	58	1994–2003	855	65	0	12.57	229	6-42	9/0	28.39	13	158‡2
Gover Alfred Richard MBE	29.2.1900	7.10.2001	1	1936–1939	2	2*	0	–	8	3-85	0/0	44.87	1	–
Gower David Ivon OBE	1.4.1957	–	117	1978–1992	8,231	215	18	44.25	1	1-1	0/0	20.00	74	114
Grace Edward Mills	28.11.1841	20.5.1911	1	1880	36	36	0	18.00	–	–	–/–	–	1	–
Grace George Frederick	13.12.1850	22.9.1880	1	1880	0	0	0	0.00	–	–	–/–	–	2	–
Grace William Gilbert (W.G.)	18.7.1848	23.10.1915	22	1880–1899	1,098	170	2	32.29	9	2-12	0/0	26.22	39	–
Graveney Thomas William OBE	16.6.1927	–	79	1951–1969	4,882	258	11	44.38	1	1-34	0/0	167.00	80	–
Greenhough Thomas	9.11.1931	15.9.2009	4	1959–1960	4	2	0	1.33	16	5-35	1/0	22.31	1	–
Greenwood Andrew	20.8.1847	12.2.1889	2	1876	77	49	0	19.25	–	–	–/–	–	2	–
[2] Greig Anthony William	6.10.1946	–	58	1972–1977	3,599	148	8	40.43	141	8-86	6/2	32.20	87	22
[2] Greig Ian Alexander	8.12.1955	–	2	1982	26	14	0	6.50	4	4-53	0/0	28.50	0	–
Grieve Basil Arthur Firebrace	28.5.1864	19.11.1917	2	1888	40	14*	0	40.00	–	–	–/–	–	0	–
Griffith Stewart Cathie CBE ("Billy")	16.6.1914	7.4.1993	3	1947–1948	157	140	1	31.40	–	–	–/–	–	5	–
[2] Gunn George	13.6.1879	29.6.1958	15	1907–1929	1,120	122*	2	40.00	0	0-8	0/0	–	15	–
[2] Gunn John Richmond	19.7.1876	21.8.1963	6	1901–1905	85	24	0	10.62	18	5-76	1/0	21.50	3	–
Gunn William	4.12.1858	29.1.1921	11	1886–1899	392	102*	1	21.77	–	–	–/–	–	5	–
Habib Aftab	7.2.1972	–	2	1999	26	19	0	8.66	–	–	–/–	–	3	–
Haig Nigel Esmé	12.12.1887	27.10.1966	5	1921–1929	126	47	0	14.00	13	3-73	0/0	34.46	4	–
Haigh Schofield	19.3.1871	27.2.1921	11	1898–1912	113	25	0	7.53	24	6-11	1/0	25.91	8	–
Hallows Charles	4.4.1895	10.11.1972	2	1921–1928	42	26	0	42.00	–	–	–/–	–	0	–
Hamilton Gavin Mark	16.9.1974	–	1	1999	0	0	0	0.00	0	0-63	0/0	–	0	0‡
Hammond Walter Reginald	19.6.1903	1.7.1965	85	1927–1946	7,249	336*	22	58.45	83	5-36	2/0	37.80	110	–
Hampshire John Harry	10.2.1941	–	8	1969–1975	403	107	1	26.86	–	–	–/–	–	9	3
[2] Hardinge Harold Thomas William ("Wally")	25.2.1886	8.5.1965	1	1921	30	25	0	15.00	–	–	–/–	–	0	–

	Born	Died	Tests	Test Career	Runs	HS	100s	Avge	Wkts	BB	5/10	Avge	Ct/St	OIT
[1]Hardstaff Joseph, sen	9.11.1882	2.4.1947	5	1907	311	72	0	31.10	–	–	–/–	–	1	–
[1]Hardstaff Joseph, jun	3.7.1911	1.1.1990	23	1935–1948	1,636	205*	4	46.74	–	–	–/–	–	9	–
Harmison Stephen James MBE	23.10.1978	–	63	2002–2009	742	49*	0	12.16	222	7-12	8/1	31.94	7	58/2
Harris Lord [George Robert Canning]	3.2.1851	24.3.1932	4	1878–1884	145	52	0	29.00	0	0-14	0/0	–	2	–
Hartley John Cabourn	15.11.1874	8.3.1963	2	1905	15	9	0	3.75	1	1-62	0/0	115.00	2	–
Hawke Lord [Martin Bladen]	16.8.1860	10.10.1938	5	1895–1898	55	30	0	7.85	–	–	–/–	–	3	–
Hayes Ernest George	6.11.1876	2.12.1953	5	1905–1912	86	35	0	10.75	1	1-28	0/0	52.00	2	6
Hayes Frank Charles	6.12.1946	–	9	1973–1976	244	106*	1	15.25	–	–	–/–	–	7	–
Hayward Thomas Walter	29.3.1871	19.7.1939	35	1895–1909	1,999	137	3	34.46	14	4-22	0/0	36.71	19	13
[2]Headley Dean Warren	27.1.1970	–	15	1997–1999	186	31	0	8.45	60	6-60	1/0	27.85	7	–
[2]Hearne Alec	22.7.1863	16.5.1952	1	1891	9	9	0	9.00	–	–	–/–	–	1	–
[1,2]Hearne Frank	23.11.1858	14.7.1949	2†	1888	47	27	0	23.50	–	–	–/–	–	1	–
[2]Hearne George Gibbons	7.7.1856	13.2.1932	1	1891	0	0	0	0.00	–	–	–/–	–	0	–
Hearne John Thomas	3.5.1867	17.4.1944	12	1891–1899	126	40	0	9.00	49	6-41	4/1	22.08	4	–
Hearne John William	11.2.1891	14.9.1965	24	1911–1926	806	114	1	26.00	30	5-49	1/0	48.73	13	–
Hegg Warren Kevin	23.2.1968	–	2	1998	30	15	0	7.50	–	–	–/–	–	8	–
Hemmings Edward Ernest	20.2.1949	–	16	1982–1990	383	95	0	22.52	43	6-58	1/0	42.44	5	33
Hendren Elias Henry ("Patsy")	5.2.1889	4.10.1962	51	1920–1934	3,525	205*	7	47.63	–	–	–/–	–	33	–
Hendrick Michael	22.10.1948	–	30	1974–1981	128	15	0	6.40	87	4-28	0/0	25.83	25	22
Heseltine Christopher	26.11.1869	13.6.1944	2	1895	18	18	0	9.00	5	5-38	1/0	16.80	3	–
Hick Graeme Ashley MBE	23.5.1966	–	65	1991–2000	3,383	178	6	31.32	23	4-126	1/0	56.78	90	120
Higgs Kenneth	14.1.1937	–	15	1965–1968	185	63	0	11.56	71	6-91	2/0	20.74	4	–
Hill Allen	14.11.1843	28.8.1910	2	1876	101	49	0	50.50	7	4-27	0/0	18.57	0	–
Hill Arthur James Ledger	26.7.1871	6.9.1950	3	1895	251	124	1	62.75	7	4-8	0/0	2.00	0	–
Hilton Malcolm Jameson	2.8.1928	8.7.1990	4	1950–1951	37	15	0	7.40	14	5-61	1/0	34.07	1	–
Hirst George Herbert	7.9.1871	10.5.1954	24	1897–1909	790	85	0	22.57	59	5-48	3/0	30.00	18	–
Hitch John William	7.5.1886	7.7.1965	7	1911–1921	103	51*	0	14.71	7	2-31	0/0	46.42	4	–
Hobbs Sir John Berry	16.12.1882	21.12.1963	61	1907–1930	5,410	211	15	56.94	1	1-19	0/0	165.00	17	–
Hobbs Robin Nicholas Stuart	8.5.1942	–	7	1967–1971	34	15*	0	6.80	12	3-25	0/0	40.08	8	–
Hoggard Matthew James MBE	31.12.1976	–	67	2000–2007	473	38	0	7.27	248	7-61	7/1	30.50	24	26
Hollies William Eric	5.6.1912	16.4.1981	13	1934–1950	37	18*	0	5.28	44	7-50	5/0	30.27	2	–
[2]Hollioake Adam John	5.9.1971	–	4	1997–1997	65	45	0	10.83	2	2-31	0/0	33.50	4	35
Hollioake Benjamin Caine	11.11.1977	23.3.2002	2	1997–1998	45	28	0	11.00	4	2-105	0/0	49.75	2	20
Holmes Errol Reginald Thorold	21.8.1905	16.8.1960	5	1934–1935	114	85*	0	16.28	2	1-10	0/0	38.00	4	–
Holmes Percy	25.11.1886	3.9.1971	7	1921–1932	357	88	0	27.46	–	–	–/–	–	3	–

§ Harmison's figures exclude one run and four wickets for the ICC World XI v Australia in the Super Series Test in 2005-06.

Name	Born	Died	Tests	Test Career	Runs	HS	100s	Avge	Wkts	BB	5/10	Avge	Ct/St	O/T
Hone Leland	30.1.1853	31.12.1896	1	1878	13	7	0	6.50	0	–	–/–	–	2	
Hopwood John Leonard	30.10.1903	15.6.1985	2	1934	12	8	0	6.00	0	0-16	–/–	–	0	
Hornby Albert Neilson ("Monkey")	10.2.1847	17.12.1925	3	1878–1884	21	9	0	3.50	1	1-0	–/–	0.00	0	
Horton Martin John	21.4.1934		2	1959	60	58	0	30.00	2	2-24	0/0	29.50	2	
Howard Nigel David	18.5.1925	31.5.1979	4	1951	86	23	0	17.20	0	–	–/–	–	4	
Howell Henry	29.11.1890	9.7.1932	5	1920–1924	15	5	0	7.50	7	4-115	0/0	79.85	2	
Howorth Richard	26.4.1909	2.4.1980	5	1947–1947	145	45*	0	18.12	19	6-124	1/0	33.42	2	
Humphries Joseph	19.5.1876	7.5.1946	3	1907	44	16	0	8.80	–	–	–/–	–	7	
Hunter Joseph	3.8.1855	4.1.1891	5	1884	93	39*	0	18.60	–	–	–/–	–	8/3	
Hussain Nasser OBE	28.3.1968		96	1989–2004	5,764	207	14	37.18	0	0-15	–/–	–	67	88
Hutchings Kenneth Lotherington	7.12.1882	3.9.1916	7	1907–1909	341	126	1	28.41	1	1-5	0/0	81.00	9	
Hutton Sir Leonard	23.6.1916	6.9.1990	79	1937–1954	6,971	364	19	56.67	3	1-2	0/0	77.33	57	
Hutton Richard Anthony	6.9.1942		5	1971	219	81	0	36.50	9	3-72	0/0	28.55	9	
Iddon John	8.1.1902	17.4.1946	5	1934–1935	170	73	0	28.33	0	0-3	0/0	–	9	
Igglesden Alan Paul	8.10.1964		3	1989–1993	6	3*	0	3.00	6	2-91	0/0	54.83	0	4
Ikin John Thomas	7.3.1918	15.9.1984	18	1946–1955	606	60	0	20.89	3	1-38	0/0	118.00	31	
Illingworth Raymond CBE	8.6.1932		61	1958–1973	1,836	113	2	23.24	122	6-29	3/0	31.20	45	3
Illingworth Richard Keith	23.8.1963		9	1991–1995	128	28	0	18.28	19	4-96	0/0	32.36	5	25
Ilott Mark Christopher	27.8.1970		5	1993–1995	28	15	0	7.00	12	3-48	0/0	45.16	0	
Insole Douglas John CBE	18.4.1926		9	1950–1957	408	110*	1	27.20	–	–	–/–	–	8	
Irani Ronald Charles	26.10.1971		3	1996–1999	86	41	0	17.20	3	1-22	0/0	37.33	2	31
Jackman Robin Charles	13.8.1945		4	1980–1982	42	17	0	7.00	14	4-110	0/0	31.78	0	15
Jackson Sir Francis Stanley	21.11.1870	9.3.1947	20	1893–1905	1,415	144*	5	48.79	24	5-52	1/0	33.29	10	
Jackson Herbert Leslie	5.4.1921	25.4.2007	2	1949–1961	15	8	0	15.00	7	2-26	0/0	22.14	0	
James Stephen Peter	7.9.1967		2	1998	71	36	0	17.75	–	–	–/–	–	0	
Jameson John Alexander	30.6.1941		4	1971–1973	214	82	0	26.75	1	1-17	0/0	17.00	0	3
Jardine Douglas Robert	23.10.1900	18.6.1958	22	1928–1933	1,296	127	1	48.00	0	0-10	0/0	–	26	
Jarvis Paul William	29.6.1965		9	1987–1992	132	29*	0	10.15	21	4-107	1/0	45.95	2	16
Jenkins Roland Oliver	24.11.1918	22.7.1995	9	1948–1952	198	39	0	18.00	32	5-116	1/0	34.31	4	
Jessop Gilbert Laird	19.5.1874	11.5.1955	18	1899–1912	569	104	1	21.88	10	4-68	0/0	35.40	11	
Johnson Richard Leonard	29.12.1974		3	2003–2003	59	26	0	14.75	16	6-33	2/0	17.18	0	10
Jones Arthur Owen	16.8.1872	21.12.1914	12	1899–1909	291	34	0	13.85	3	3-73	0/0	44.33	15	
Jones Geraint Owen MBE	14.7.1976		34	2003–2006	1,172	100	1	23.91	–	–	–/–	–	128/5	49/2
Jones Ivor Jeffrey	10.12.1941		15	1963–1967	38	16	0	4.75	44	6-118	1/0	40.20	4	
Jones Simon Philip MBE	25.12.1978		18	2002–2005	205	44	0	15.76	59	6-53	3/0	28.23	2	8
Jupp Henry	19.11.1841	8.4.1889	2	1876	68	63	0	17.00	–	–	–/–	–		

Name	Born	Died	Tests	Test Career	Runs	HS	100s	Avge	Wkts	BB	5/10	Avge	Ct/St	O/T
Jupp Vallance William Crisp	27.3.1891	9.7.1960	8	1921–1928	208	38	0	17.33	28	4-37	0/0	22.00	5	
Keeton William Walter	30.4.1905	10.10.1980	2	1934–1939	57	25	0	14.25					5	
Kennedy Alexander Stuart	24.1.1891	15.11.1996	5	1922	93	41*	0	15.50	31	5-76	2/0	19.32	5	
Kenyon Donald	15.5.1924	12.11.1996	8	1951–1955	192	87	0	12.80					5	
Key Robert William Trevor	12.5.1979		15	2002–2004	775	221	1	31.00					5	5/1
Khan Amjad	14.10.1980		1	2008		–	–	–	1	1-111	0/0	122.00	0	0/1
Killick Rev. Edgar Thomas	9.5.1907	18.5.1953	2	1929	81	31	0	20.25					2	
Kilner Roy	17.10.1890	5.4.1928	9	1924–1926	233	74	0	33.28	24	4-51	0/0	30.58	6	
King John Herbert	16.4.1871	18.11.1946	1	1909	64	60	0	32.00	1	1-99	0/0	99.00	0	
Kinneir Septimus Paul	13.5.1871	16.10.1928	1	1911	52	30	0	26.00					0	
Kirtley Robert James	10.1.1975		4	2003–2003	32	12	0	5.33	19	6-34	1/0	29.52	3	11/1
Knight Albert Ernest	8.10.1872	25.4.1946	3	1903	81	70*	0	16.20						
Knight Barry Rolfe	18.2.1938		29	1961–1969	812	127	2	26.19	70	4-38	0/0	31.75	14	
Knight Donald John	12.5.1894	5.1.1960	2	1921	54	38	0	13.50					1	
Knight Nicholas Verity	28.11.1969		17	1995–2001	719	113	1	23.96					26	100
Knott Alan Philip Eric	9.4.1946		95	1967–1981	4,389	135	5	32.75					250/19	20
Knox Neville Alexander	10.10.1884	3.3.1935	2	1907	24	8*	0	8.00	3	2-39	0/0	35.00		
Laker James Charles	9.2.1922	23.4.1986	46	1947–1958	676	63	0	14.08	193	10-53	9/3	21.24	12	
Lamb Allan Joseph	20.6.1954		79	1982–1992	4,656	142	14	36.09					75	122
Langridge James	10.7.1906	10.9.1966	8	1933–1946	242	70	0	26.88	19	7-56	2/0	23.00	6	
Larkins Wayne	22.11.1953		13	1979–1990	493	64	0	20.54					8	25
Larter John David Frederick	24.4.1940		10	1962–1965	16	10	0	3.20	37	5-57	2/0	25.43	5	
Larwood Harold MBE	14.11.1904	22.7.1995	21	1926–1932	485	98	0	19.40	78	6-32	4/1	28.35	15	
Lathwell Mark Nicholas	26.12.1971		1	1993	78	33	0	19.50					0	
Lawrence David Valentine ("Syd")	28.11.1964		5	1988–1991	60	34	0	10.00	18	5-106	1/0	37.55	3	1
Leadbeater Edric	15.8.1927	21.4.1981	1	1951	40	38	0	20.00	2	1-38	0/0	109.00	0	
Lee Henry William	26.10.1890	10.9.1924	1	1930	19	19	0	9.50					2	
Lees Walter Scott	25.12.1875	11.11.1940	5	1905	66	25*	0	11.00	26	6-78	2/0	17.96		
Legge Geoffrey Bevington	26.1.1903	21.11.1940	5	1927–1929	299	196	1	49.83					1	
Leslie Charles Frederick Henry	8.12.1861	12.2.1921	4	1882	106	54	0	15.14	4	3-31	0/0	11.00		
Lever John Kenneth MBE	24.2.1949		21	1976–1986	306	53	0	11.76	73	7-46	3/1	26.72	11	22
Lever Peter	17.9.1940		17	1970–1975	350	88*	0	21.87	41	6-38	2/0	36.80	11	10
Leveson Gower Sir Henry Dudley Gresham.	8.5.1873	1.2.1954	3	1909	95	31	0	23.75						
Levett William Howard Vincent ("Hopper")	25.11.1908	1.12.1995	1	1933	7	5	0	7.00					3	
Lewis Anthony Robert CBE	6.7.1938		9	1972–1973	457	125	1	32.64					0	
Lewis Clairmonte Christopher	14.2.1968		32	1990–1996	1,105	117	1	23.02	93	6-111	3/0	37.52	25	53

	Born	Died	Tests	Test Career	Runs	HS	100s	Avge	Wkts	BB	5/10	Avge	Ct/St	O/T
Lewis Jonathan	26.8.1975		1	2006	27	20	0	13.50	3	3-68	0/0	40.66	0	13/2
Leyland Maurice	20.7.1900	1.1.1967	41	1928–1938	2,764	187	9	46.06	6	3-91	0/0	97.50	13	
Lilley Arthur Frederick Augustus ("Dick")	28.11.1866	17.11.1929	35	1896–1909	903	84	0	20.52	1	1-23	0/0	23.00	70/22	
Lillywhite James	23.2.1842	25.10.1929	2	1876	16	10	0	8.00	8	4-70	0/0	15.75	1	
Lloyd David	18.3.1947		9	1974–1974	552	214*	1	42.46	0	0-4	0/0	–	11	8
Lloyd Timothy Andrew	5.11.1956		1	1984	10	10*	0	–	–	–	–/–	–	0	3
Loader Peter James	25.10.1929		13	1954–1958	76	17	0	5.84	39	6-36	1/0	22.51	2	
Lock Graham Anthony Richard	5.7.1929	30.3.1995	49	1952–1967	742	89	0	13.74	174	7-35	9/3	25.58	59	
Lockwood William Henry	25.3.1868	26.4.1932	12	1893–1902	231	52*	0	17.76	43	7-71	5/1	20.53	4	
Lohmann George Alfred	2.6.1865	1.12.1901	18	1886–1896	213	62*	0	8.87	112	9-28	9/5	10.75	28	
Lowson Frank Anderson	1.7.1925	8.9.1984	7	1951–1955	245	68	0	18.84	0	–	–/–	–	5	
Lucas Alfred Perry	20.2.1857	12.10.1923	5	1878–1884	157	55	0	19.62	0	0-23	0/0	–	1	
Luckhurst Brian William	5.2.1939	1.3.2005	21	1970–1974	1,298	131	4	36.05	1	1-9	0/0	32.00	14	3
Lyttelton *Hon.* Alfred	7.2.1857	5.7.1913	4	1880–1884	94	31	0	15.66	4	4-19	0/0	4.75	2	
Macaulay George Gibson	7.12.1897	13.12.1940	8	1922–1933	112	76	0	18.66	24	5-64	1/0	27.58	5	
MacBryan John Crawford William	22.7.1892	14.7.1983	1	1924	–	–	0	–	–	–	–/–	–	0	
McCague Martin John	24.5.1969		3	1993–1994	21	11	0	4.20	6	4-121	0/0	65.00	1	
McConnon James Edward	21.6.1922	26.1.2003	2	1954	18	11	0	9.00	4	3-19	0/0	18.50	4	
McGahey Charles Percy	12.2.1871	10.11.1935	2	1901	38	18	0	9.50	–	–	0/0	–		
McGrath Anthony	6.10.1975		4	2003	201	81	0	40.20	4	3-16	0/0	14.00	3	14
MacGregor Gregor	31.8.1869	20.8.1919	8	1890–1893	96	31	0	12.00	–	–	–/–	–	14/3	
McIntyre Arthur John William	14.5.1918	26.12.2009	3	1950–1955	19	7	0	3.16	–	–	–/–	–	8	
MacKinnon Francis Alexander	9.4.1848	27.2.1947	1	1878	5	5	0	2.50	–	–	–/–	–	0	
MacLaren Archibald Campbell	1.12.1871	17.11.1944	35	1894–1909	1,931	140	5	33.87	–	–	–/–	–	29	
McMaster Joseph Emile Patrick	16.3.1861	7.6.1929	1	1888	0	0	0	0.00	–	–	–/–	–		
Maddy Darren Lee	23.5.1974		3	1999–1999	46	24	0	11.50	0	0-40	0/0	–	0	8/4
Mahmood Sajid Iqbal	21.12.1981		8	2006–2006	81	34	0	8.10	20	4-22	0/0	38.10	4	26/4
Makepeace Joseph William Henry	22.8.1881	19.12.1952	4	1920	279	117	1	34.87	–	–	–/–	–	0	
Malcolm Devon Eugene	22.2.1963		40	1989–1997	236	29	0	6.05	128	9-57	5/2	37.09	7	10
Mallender Neil Alan	13.8.1961		2	1992	8	4	0	2.66	10	5-50	1/0	21.50	0	
[1] Mann Francis George CBE	6.9.1917	8.8.2001	7	1948–1949	376	136*	0	37.60	–	–	–/–	–	3	
[2] Mann Francis Thomas	3.3.1888	6.10.1964	5	1922	281	84	0	35.12	–	–	–/–	–	4	
Marks Victor James	25.6.1955		6	1982–1983	249	83	0	27.66	11	3-78	0/0	44.00	0	34
Marriott Charles Stowell ("Father")	14.9.1895	13.10.1966	1	1933	0	0	0	0.00	11	6-59	2/1	8.72	1	
Martin Frederick	12.10.1861	13.12.1921	2	1890–1891	14	13	0	7.00	14	6-50	2/1	10.07	2	
Martin John William	16.2.1917	4.1.1987	1	1947	26	26	0	13.00	1	1-111	0/0	129.00	0	

Name	Born	Died	Tests	Test Career	Runs	HS	100s	Avge	Wkts	BB	5/10	Avge	Ct/St	O/T
Martin Peter James	15.11.1968			1995–1997	115	29	0	8.84	17	4-60	0/0	34.11	3	20
Mason John Richard	26.3.1874	15.10.1958	5	1897	129	32	0	12.90	2	1-8	0/0	74.50	3	
Matthews Austin David George	3.5.1904	29.7.1977	1	1937	-	2*	-	-	2	1-13	0/0	32.50	1	14
May Peter Barker Howard CBE	31.12.1929	27.12.1994	66	1951–1961	4,537	285*	13	46.77	-	-	-/-	-	42	
Maynard Matthew Peter	21.3.1966		4	1988–1993	87	35	0	10.87	-			-	3	
Mead Charles Philip	9.3.1887	26.3.1958	17	1911–1928	1,185	182*	4	49.37	-	-	-/-	-	4	
Mead Walter	1.4.1868	18.3.1954	1	1899	7	7	0	3.50	1	1-91	0/0	91.00	1	
Midwinter William Evans	19.6.1851	3.12.1890	4†	1881	95	36	0	13.57	10	4-81	0/0	27.20	5	
Milburn Colin	23.10.1941	28.2.1990	9	1966–1968	654	139	2	46.71	-	-	-/-	-	7	
Miller Audley Montague	19.10.1869	26.6.1959	1	1895	24	20*	0	-	-		-/-	-	-	25
Miller Geoffrey	8.9.1952		34	1976–1984	1,213	98*	0	25.80	60	5-44	1/0	30.98	17	
Milligan Frank William	19.3.1870	31.3.1900	2	1898	58	38	0	14.50	0	0-0	-/-	-	1	
Millman Geoffrey	2.10.1934	6.4.2005	6	1961–1962	60	32*	0	12.00	-			-	13/2	
Milton Clement Arthur	10.3.1928	25.4.2007	6	1958–1959	204	104*	1	25.50	0	0-12	0/0	-	5	
Mitchell Arthur	13.9.1902	25.12.1976	6	1933–1936	298	72	0	29.80	0	0-4	0/0	-	9	
Mitchell Frank	13.8.1872	11.10.1935	2†	1898	88	41	0	22.00	-			-	2	
Mitchell Thomas Bignall	4.9.1902	27.11.1996	5	1932–1935	20	9	0	5.00	8	2-49	0/0	62.25	1	
Mitchell-Innes Norman Stewart ("Mandy")	7.9.1914	28.12.2006	1	1935	5	5	0	5.00	-			-	-	
Mold Arthur Webb	27.5.1863	29.4.1921	3	1893	0	0*	0	0.00	7	3-44	0/0	33.42	1	
Moon Leonard James	9.2.1878	23.11.1916	4	1905	182	36	0	22.75	-			-	4/4	
Morgan Eoin Joseph Gerard	10.9.1986		16	2010	256	130	2	32.00	-			-	4	32/14
Morley Frederick	16.12.1850	28.9.1884	4	1880–1882	6	2*	0	1.50	16	5-56	1/0	18.50	4	
Morris Hugh	5.10.1963		3	1991	115	44	0	19.16	-			-	3	8
Morris John Edward	1.4.1964		3	1990	71	32	0	23.66	-			-	3	
Mortimore John Brian	14.5.1933		9	1958–1964	243	73*	0	24.30	13	3-36	0/0	56.38	3	
Moss Alan Edward	14.11.1930		9	1953–1960	61	26	0	10.16	21	4-35	0/0	29.80	1	
Moxon Martyn Douglas	4.5.1960		10	1986–1989	455	99	0	28.43	0	0-3	0/0	-	10	8
Mullally Alan David	12.7.1969		19	1996–2001	127	24	0	5.52	58	5-105	1/0	31.24	6	50
Munton Timothy Alan	30.7.1965		2	1992	25	25*	0	25.00	4	2-22	0/0	50.00		
Murdoch William Lloyd	18.10.1854	18.2.1911	1†	1891	12	12	0	12.00	-			-	0/1	
Murray John Thomas MBE	1.4.1935		21	1961–1967	506	112	1	22.00	-			-	52/3	
Newham William	12.12.1860	26.6.1944	1	1887	26	17	0	13.00	-			-	1	
Newport Philip John	11.10.1962		3	1988–1990	110	40*	0	27.50	10	4-87	0/0	41.70	11	
Nichols Morris Stanley	6.10.1900	26.1.1961	14	1929–1939	355	78*	0	29.58	41	6-35	2/0	28.09	7	
Oakman Alan Stanley Myles	20.4.1930		2	1956	14	10	0	7.00	0	0-21	0/0	-	4	
O'Brien Sir Timothy Carew	5.11.1861	9.12.1948	5	1884–1895	59	20	0	7.37	-			-	4	

Name	Born	Died	Tests	Test Career	Runs	HS	100s	Avge	Wkts	BB	5/10	Avge	Ct/St	O/T
O'Connor Jack	6.11.1897	22.2.1977	4	1929–1930	153	51	0	21.85	1	1-31	0/0	72.00	0	32
Old Christopher Middleton	22.12.1948		46	1972–1981	845	65	0	14.82	143	7-50	4/0	28.11	22	
Oldfield Norman	5.5.1911	19.4.1996	1	1939	99	80	0	49.50					0	4
Onions Graham	9.9.1982		8	2009–2009	30	17*	0	10.00	28	5-38	1/0	31.03	0	
Ormond James	20.8.1977		2	2001–2001	38	18	0	10.00	2	1-70	0/0	92.50	0	
Padgett Douglas Ernest Vernon	20.7.1934		2	1960	51	31	0	12.75	0	0-8	0/0		0	
Paine George Alfred Edward	11.6.1908	30.3.1978	4	1934	97	49	0	16.16	17	5-168	1/0	27.47	5	
Palairet Lionel Charles Hamilton	27.5.1870	27.3.1933	2	1902	49	20	0	12.25					2	
Palmer Charles Henry CBE	15.5.1919	31.3.2005	1	1953	22	22	0	11.00	0	0-15	0/0		0	
Palmer Kenneth Ernest MBE.	22.4.1937		1	1964	10	10	0	10.00	1	1-113	0/0	189.00	0	
Panesar Mudhsuden Singh ("Monty")	25.4.1982		39	2005–2009	187	26	0	5.50	126	6-37	8/1	34.37	9	
Parfitt Peter Howard	8.12.1936		37	1961–1972	1,882	131*	7	40.91	12	2-5	0/0	47.83	42	26/1
Parker Charles Warrington Leonard	14.10.1882	11.7.1959	1	1921	3	3*	0		2	2-32	0/0	16.00	0	
Parker Paul William Giles.	15.1.1956		1	1981	13	13	0	6.50					3	
Parkhouse William Gilbert Anthony	12.10.1925	10.8.2000	7	1950–1959	373	78	0	28.69					3	
Parkin Cecil Harry	18.2.1886	15.6.1943	10	1920–1924	160	36	0	12.30	32	5-38	2/0	35.25	0	
Parks James Horace	12.5.1903	21.11.1980	1	1937	29	22	0	14.50	3	2-26	0/0	12.00	0	
Parks James Michael.	21.10.1931		46	1954–1967	1,962	108*	2	32.16	1	1-43	0/0	51.00	103/11	
Pataudi Iftikhar Ali Khan, Nawab of …	16.3.1910	5.1.1952	3†	1932–1934	144	102	1	28.80					5	
Patel Minal Mahesh	7.7.1970		1	1996	45	27	0	22.50	1	1-101	0/0	180.00	0	
Pattinson Darren John	2.8.1979		1	2008	21	13	0	10.50	2	2-95	0/0	48.00	0	
Paynter Edward	5.11.1901	5.2.1979	20	1931–1939	1,540	243	4	59.23					7	
Peate Edmund	2.3.1855	11.3.1900	9	1881–1886	70	13	0	11.66	31	6-85	2/0	22.03	0	
Peebles Ian Alexander Ross	20.1.1908	27.2.1980	13	1927–1931	98	26	0	10.88	45	6-63	3/0	30.91	3	
Peel Robert.	12.2.1857	12.8.1941	20	1884–1896	427	83	0	14.72	101	7-31	5/1	16.98	17	
Penn Frank.	7.3.1851	26.12.1916	1	1880	50	27*	0	50.00	0	0-2	0/0		2	
Perks Reginald Thomas David	4.10.1911	22.11.1977	2	1938–1939	3	2*	0		11	5-100	2/0	32.27	1	
Philipson Hylton.	8.6.1866	4.12.1935	5	1891–1894	63	30	0	9.00					8/3	
Pietersen Kevin Peter MBE…	27.6.1980		71	2005–2010	5,666	227	17	48.42	5	1-0	0/0	116.80	44	102½/28
Pigott Anthony Charles Shackleton.	4.6.1958		1	1983	12	8*	0	12.00	2	2-75	0/0	37.50	0	
Pilling Richard	11.8.1855	28.3.1891	8	1881–1888	91	23	0	7.58					10/4	
Place Winston	7.12.1914	25.1.2002	3	1947	144	107	1	28.80					0	
Plunkett Liam Edward	6.4.1985		9	2005–2007	126	44*	0	11.45	23	3-17	0/0	39.82	3	
Pocock Patrick Ian	24.9.1946		25	1967–1984	206	33	0	6.24	67	6-79	3/0	44.41	15	
Pollard Richard	19.6.1912	16.12.1985	4	1946–1948	13	10*	0	13.00	15	5-24	1/0	25.20	3	28/1
Poole Cyril John	13.3.1921	11.2.1996	3	1951	161	69*	0	40.25	0	0-9	0/0		1	1

Name	Born	Died	Tests	Test Career	Runs	HS	100s	Avge	Wkts	BB	5/10	Avge	Ct/St	O/T
Pope George Henry	27.1.1911	29.10.1993	1	1947	8	8*	0	–	1	1-49	0/0	85.00	–	–
Pougher Arthur Dick	19.4.1865	20.5.1926	1	1891	17	17	0	17.00	3	3-26	0/0	8.66	–	–
Price John Sidney Ernest	22.7.1937	–	15	1963–1972	66	32	0	7.33	40	5-73	1/0	35.02	7	–
Price Wilfred Frederick Frank	25.4.1902	13.1.1969	1	1938	6	6	0	3.00	–	–	–/–	–	2	–
Prideaux Roger Malcolm	31.7.1939	–	3	1968–1969	102	64	0	20.40	–	–	–/–	–	2	–
Pringle Derek Raymond	18.9.1958	–	30	1982–1992	695	63	0	15.10	70	5-95	3/0	35.97	10	44
Prior Matthew James	26.2.1982	–	40	2007–2010	2,148	131*	4	42.96	–	–	–/–	–	117/4	55/10
Pullar Geoffrey	1.8.1935	–	28	1959–1962	1,974	175	4	43.86	1	1-1	0/0	37.00	2	–
Quaife William George	17.3.1872	13.10.1951	7	1899–1901	228	68	0	19.00	0	0-6	0/0	–	4	–
Radford Neal Victor	7.6.1957	–	3	1986–1987	21	12*	0	7.00	4	2-131	0/0	87.75	–	6
Radley Clive Thornton MBE	13.5.1944	–	8	1977–1978	481	158	2	48.10	–	–	–/–	–	4	4
Ramprakash Mark Ravin	5.9.1969	–	52	1991–2001	2,350	154	2	27.32	4	1-2	0/0	119.25	39	18
Randall Derek William	24.2.1951	–	47	1976–1984	2,470	174	7	33.37	0	0-1	0/0	–	31	49
Ranjitsinhji Kumar Shri	10.9.1872	2.4.1933	15	1896–1902	989	175	2	44.95	1	1-23	0/0	39.00	13	–
Read Christopher Mark Wells	10.8.1978	–	15	1999–2006	360	55	0	18.94	–	–	–/–	–	48/6	36/1
Read Holcombe Douglas ("Hopper")	28.1.1910	5.1.2000	1	1935	–	–	–	–	6	4-136	0/0	33.33	–	–
Read John Maurice	9.2.1859	17.2.1929	17	1882–1893	461	57	0	17.07	–	–	–/–	–	8	–
Read Walter William ("Jack")	23.11.1855	6.11.1907	18	1882–1893	720	117	1	27.69	0	0-27	0/0	–	16	–
Reeve Dermot Alexander OBE	2.4.1963	–	3	1991	124	59	0	24.80	1	1-4	0/0	30.00	–	29
Relf Albert Edward	26.6.1874	26.3.1937	13	1903–1913	416	63	0	23.11	25	5-85	1/0	24.96	14	–
Rhodes Harold James	22.7.1936	–	2	1959	0	0*	0	–	9	4-50	0/0	27.11	–	–
Rhodes Steven John	17.6.1964	–	11	1994	294	65*	0	24.50	–	–	–/–	–	46/3	9
Rhodes Wilfred	29.10.1877	8.7.1973	58	1899–1929	2,325	179	2	30.19	127	8-68	6/1	26.96	60	–
Richards Clifton James ("Jack")	10.8.1958	–	8	1986–1988	285	133	1	21.92	–	–	–/–	–	20/1	22
Richardson Derek William ("Dick")	3.11.1934	–	1	1957	33	33	0	33.00	–	–	–/–	–	3	–
[2]Richardson Peter Edward	4.7.1931	–	34	1956–1963	2,061	126	5	37.47	3	2-10	0/0	16.00	6	–
[2]Richardson Thomas	11.8.1870	2.7.1912	14	1893–1897	177	25*	0	11.06	88	8-94	11/4	25.22	5	–
Richmond Thomas Leonard	23.6.1890	29.12.1957	1	1921	6	4	0	3.00	2	2-69	0/0	43.00	–	–
Ridgway Frederick	10.8.1923	–	5	1951	49	24	0	8.16	7	2-17	0/0	54.14	1	–
Robertson John David Benbow	22.2.1917	12.10.1996	11	1947–1951	881	133	2	46.36	2	2-17	0/0	29.00	6	–
Robins Robert Walter Vivian	3.6.1906	12.12.1968	19	1929–1937	612	108	1	26.60	64	6-32	1/0	27.46	12	–
Robinson Robert Timothy	21.11.1958	–	29	1984–1989	1,601	175	4	36.38	0	0-2	0/0	–	8	26
Roope Graham Richard James	12.7.1946	26.11.2006	21	1972–1978	860	77	0	30.71	0	0-0	0/0	–	35	8
Root Charles Frederick	16.4.1890	20.1.1954	3	1926	–	–	–	–	8	4-84	0/0	24.25	–	–
Rose Brian Charles	4.6.1950	–	9	1977–1980	358	70	0	25.57	–	–	–/–	–	4	2
Royle Vernon Peter Fanshawe Archer	29.1.1854	21.5.1929	1	1878	21	18	0	10.50	0	0-6	0/0	–	2	–

Name	Born	Died	Tests	Test Career	Runs	HS	100s	Avge	Wkts	BB	5/10	Avge	Ct/St	O/T
Rumsey Frederick Edward	4.12.1935	–	5	1964–1965	30	21*	0	15.00	17	4-25	0/0	27.11	5	40
Russell Albert Charles ('Jack')	7.10.1887	23.3.1961	10	1920–1922	910	140	5	56.87	–	–	–	–	8	–
Russell Robert Charles ('Jack')	15.8.1963	–	54	1988–1997	1,897	128*	2	27.10	–	–	–	–	153/12	4
Russell William Eric	3.7.1936	–	10	1961–1967	362	70	0	21.29	0	0-19	–	–	4	–
Saggers Martin John	23.5.1972	–	3	2003–2004	1	1	0	0.33	7	2-29	0/0	–	1	–
Salisbury Ian David Kenneth	21.1.1970	–	15	1992–2000	368	50	0	16.72	20	4-163	0/0	76.95	5	4
Sandham Andrew	6.7.1890	20.4.1982	14	1921–1929	879	325	2	38.21	–	–	–	–	4	0/4
Schofield Christopher Paul	6.10.1978	–	2	2000	67	57	0	22.33	0	0-73	–	–	1	–
Schultz Sandford Spence	29.8.1857	18.12.1937	1	1878	20	20	0	20.00	1	1-16	0/0	26.00	1	–
Scotton William Henry	15.1.1856	9.7.1893	15	1881–1886	510	90	0	22.17	0	0-20	–	–	4	–
Selby John	1.7.1849	11.3.1894	6	1876–1881	256	70	0	23.27	–	–	–	–	1	–
Selvey Michael Walter William	25.4.1948	–	3	1976–1976	15	5*	0	7.50	6	4-41	0/0	57.16	1	–
Shackleton Derek	12.8.1924	28.9.2007	7	1950–1963	113	42	0	18.83	18	4-72	0/0	42.66	1	71/17
Shah Owais Alam	22.10.1978	–	6	2005–2008	269	88	0	26.90	–	–	–	–	2	4/1
Shahzad Ajmal	27.7.1985	–	1	2010	5	5	0	5.00	4	3-45	0/0	15.75	2	–
Sharp John	15.2.1878	28.1.1938	3	1909	188	105	1	47.00	3	3-67	0/0	37.00	2	–
Sharpe John William	9.12.1866	19.6.1936	3	1890–1891	44	26	0	22.00	11	6-84	1/0	27.72	2	–
Sharpe Philip John	27.12.1936	–	12	1963–1969	786	111	1	46.23	–	–	–	–	17	–
Shaw Alfred	29.8.1842	16.1.1907	7	1876–1881	111	40	0	10.09	12	5-38	1/0	23.75	4	–
Sheppard Rt. Rev. Lord [David Stuart]	6.3.1929	5.3.2005	22	1950–1962	1,172	119	3	37.80	–	–	–	–	12	–
Sherwin Mordecai	26.2.1851	3.7.1910	3	1886–1888	30	21*	0	15.00	–	–	–	–	5/2	–
Shrewsbury Arthur	11.4.1856	19.5.1903	23	1881–1893	1,277	164	3	35.47	0	0-2	–	–	29	–
Shuter John	9.2.1855	5.7.1920	1	1888	28	28	0	28.00	–	–	–	–	0	–
Shuttleworth Kenneth	13.11.1944	–	5	1970–1971	46	21	0	7.66	12	5-47	1/0	35.58	1	–
Sidebottom Arnold	1.4.1954	–	1	1985	2	2	0	2.00	1	1-65	0/0	65.00	0	–
Sidebottom Ryan Jay	15.1.1978	–	22	2001–2009	313	31	0	15.65	79	7-47	5/1	28.24	5	25/18
Silverwood Christopher Eric Wilfred	5.3.1975	–	6	1996–2002	29	10	0	7.25	11	5-91	1/0	40.36	2	7
Simpson Reginald Thomas	27.2.1920	–	27	1948–1954	1,401	156*	4	33.35	2	–	0/0	11.00	5	–
Simpson-Hayward George Hayward Thomas	7.6.1875	2.10.1936	5	1909	105	29*	0	15.00	23	6-43	2/0	18.26	1	–
Sims James Morton	13.5.1903	27.4.1973	4	1935–1936	16	12	0	4.00	11	5-73	1/0	43.63	6	–
Sinfield Reginald Albert	24.12.1900	17.3.1988	1	1938	6	6	0	6.00	2	1-51	0/0	61.50	2	–
Slack Wilfred Norris	12.12.1954	15.1.1989	3	1985–1986	81	52	0	13.50	–	–	–	–	3	–
Smailes Thomas Francis	27.3.1910	1.12.1970	1	1946	25	25	0	25.00	3	3-44	0/0	20.66	0	–
Small Gladstone Cleophas	18.10.1961	–	17	1986–1990	263	59	0	15.47	55	5-48	2/0	34.01	9	2
Smith Alan Christopher CBE	25.10.1936	–	6	1962	118	69*	0	29.50	–	–	–	–	20	53
Smith Andrew Michael	1.10.1967	–	1	1997	4	4*	0	4.00	0	0-89	0/0	–	0	–

	Born	Died	Tests	Test Career	Runs	HS	100s	Avge	Wkts	BB	5/10	Avge	Ct/St	O/T
Smith Cedric Ivan James	25.8.1906	8.2.1979	5	1934–1937	102	27	0	10.20	15	5-16	1/0	26.20	7	
Smith Sir Charles Aubrey	21.7.1863	20.12.1948	1	1888	3	3	0	3.00	7	5-19	1/0	8.71	0	
²**Smith** Christopher Lyall	15.10.1958		8	1983–1986	392	91	0	30.15	3	2-31	0/0	13.00	5	4
Smith David Mark	9.1.1956		2	1985	80	47	0	20.00			–/–	–	2	2
Smith David Robert	5.10.1934	17.12.2003	5	1961	38	34	0	9.50	6	2-60	0/0	59.83	4	
Smith Denis	24.1.1907	12.9.1979	2	1935	128	57	0	32.00			–/–	–	1	
Smith Donald Victor	14.6.1923		3	1957	25	16*	0	8.33	1	1-12	0/0	97.00	1	
Smith Edward Thomas	19.7.1977		3	2003	87	64	0	17.40			–/–	–	5	
Smith Ernest James ("Tiger")	6.2.1886	31.8.1979	11	1911–1913	113	22	0	8.69			–/–	–	17/3	
Smith Harry	21.5.1891	12.11.1937	1	1928	7	7	0	7.00			–/–	–	53	
Smith Michael John Knight OBE	30.6.1933		50	1958–1972	2,278	121	3	31.63	1	1-10	0/0	128.00	53	
²**Smith** Robin Arnold	13.9.1963		62	1988–1995	4,236	175	9	43.67	3	0-6	0/0	–	39	71
Smith Thomas Peter Bromley	30.10.1908	4.8.1967	4	1946–1946	33	24	0	6.60	3	2-172	0/0	106.33	1	
Smithson Gerald Arthur	1.11.1926	6.9.1970	2	1947	70	35	0	23.33			–/–	–	1	
Snow John Augustine	13.10.1941		49	1965–1976	772	73	0	13.54	202	7-40	8/1	26.66	16	9
Southerton James	16.11.1827	16.6.1880	2	1876	7	6	0	3.50	7	4-46	0/0	15.28	2	
Spooner Reginald Herbert	21.10.1880	2.10.1961	10	1905–1912	481	119	1	32.06			–/–	–	4	
Spooner Richard Thompson	30.12.1919	20.12.1997	7	1951–1955	354	92	0	27.23			–/–	–	10/2	
Stanyforth Ronald Thomas	30.5.1892	4.6.1964	4	1927	13	6*	0	2.60			–/–	–	7/2	
Staples Samuel James	18.9.1892	4.6.1950	3	1927	65	39	0	13.00	15	3-50	0/0	29.00	7	
Statham John Brian CBE	17.6.1930	10.6.2000	70	1950–1965	675	38	0	11.44	252	7-39	9/1	24.84	28	
Steel Allan Gibson	24.9.1858	15.6.1914	13	1880–1888	600	148	2	35.29	29	3-27	0/0	20.86	5	
Steele David Stanley OBE	29.9.1941		8	1975–1976	673	106	1	42.06	2	1-1	0/0	19.50	7	1
Stephenson John Patrick	14.3.1965		1	1989	36	25	0	18.00			–/–	–	0	
Stevens Greville Thomas Scott	7.1.1901	19.9.1970	10	1922–1929	263	69	0	15.47	20	5-90	2/1	32.40	9	
¹**Stevenson** Graham Barry	16.12.1955		2	1979–1980	28	27*	0	28.00	5	3-111	0/0	36.60	4	4
¹**Stewart** Alec James OBE	8.4.1963		133	1989–2003	8,463	190	15	39.54	0	0-5	0/0	–	263/14	170
¹**Stewart** Michael James OBE	16.9.1932		8	1962–1963	385	87	0	35.00			–/–	–	6	
Stoddart Andrew Ernest	11.3.1863	3.4.1915	16	1887–1897	996	173	2	35.57	2	1-10	0/0	47.00	6	
Storer William	25.1.1867	28.2.1912	6	1897–1899	215	51	0	19.54	2	1-24	0/0	54.00	11	
Strauss Andrew John MBE	2.3.1977		82	2004–2010	6,084	177	19	43.14			–/–	–	94	113/4
Street George Benjamin	6.12.1889	24.4.1924	1	1922	11	7*	0	11.00			–/–	–	0/1	
Strudwick Herbert	28.1.1880	14.2.1970	28	1909–1926	230	24	0	7.93			–/–	–	61/12	
²**Studd** Charles Thomas	2.12.1860	16.7.1931	5	1882–1882	160	48	0	20.00	3	2-35	0/0	32.66	5	
²**Studd** George Brown	20.10.1859	13.2.1945	4	1882	31	9	0	4.42	0	0-2	0/0	–	8	
Subba Row Raman CBE	29.1.1932		13	1958–1961	984	137	3	46.85			–/–	–	5	

Name	Born	Died	Tests	Test Career	Runs	HS	100s	Avge	Wkts	BB	Avge	5/10	Ct/St	O/T
Such Peter Mark	12.6.1964		11	1993–1999	67	14*	0	6.09	37	6-67	33.56	2/0	4	
Sugg Frank Howe	11.1.1862	29.5.1933	2	1888	55	31	0	27.50				–/–	0	
Sutcliffe Herbert	24.11.1894	22.1.1978	54	1924–1935	4,555	194	16	60.73				–/–	23	
Swann Graeme Peter	24.3.1979		29	2008–2010	741	85	0	24.70	128	6-65	28.10	10/1	25	43/20
Swetman Roy	25.10.1933		11	1958–1959	254	65	0	16.93				–/–	24/2	
[1]Tate Frederick William	24.7.1867	24.2.1943	1	1902	9	5*	0	9.00	2	2-7	25.50	0/0	2	
[2]Tate Maurice William	30.5.1895	18.5.1956	39	1924–1935	1,198	100*	1	25.48	155	6-42	26.16	7/1	11	
Tattersall Roy	17.8.1922		16	1950–1954	50	10*	0	5.00	58	7-52	26.08	4/1	8	
Tavaré Christopher James	27.10.1954		31	1980–1989	1,755	149	2	32.50	0	0-0		0/0	20	29
Taylor Jonathan Paul	8.8.1964		3	1992–1994	34	17*	0	17.00	3	1-18	52.00	0/0	0	1
Taylor Kenneth	21.8.1935		3	1959–1964	57	24	0	11.40	0	0-6		0/0	1	
Taylor Leslie Brian	25.10.1953		2	1985	1	1*	0	–	4	2-34	44.50	0/0	0	2
Taylor Robert William MBE	17.7.1941		57	1970–1983	1,156	97	0	16.28	0	0-6		0/0	167/7	27
Tennyson *Lord* Lionel Hallam	7.11.1889	6.6.1951	9	1913–1921	345	74*	0	31.36	0	0-1		0/0	6	
Terry Vivian Paul	14.1.1959		2	1984	16	8	0	5.33				–/–	2	
Thomas John Gregory	12.8.1960		5	1985–1986	83	31*	0	13.83	10	4-70	50.40	0/0	5	3
Thompson George Joseph	27.10.1877	3.3.1943	6	1909–1909	273	63	0	30.33	23	4-50	27.73	0/0	5	
Thomson Norman Ian	23.1.1929		5	1964	69	39	0	23.00	9	2-55	63.11	0/0	1	
Thorpe Graham Paul MBE	1.8.1969		100	1993–2005	6,744	200*	16	44.66	0	0-0		0/0	105	82
Titmus Frederick John MBE	24.11.1932		53	1955–1974	1,449	84*	0	22.29	153	7-79	32.22	7/0	35	2
Tolchard Roger William	15.6.1946		4	1976	129	67	0	25.80				–/–	5	1
Townsend Charles Lucas	7.11.1876	17.10.1958	2	1899	51	38	0	17.00	3	3-50	25.00	0/0	1	
[2]Townsend David Charles Humphery	20.4.1912	27.1.1997	4	1934	77	36	0	12.83	0	0-9		0/0	0	
Townsend Leslie Fletcher	8.6.1903	17.2.1993	4	1929–1933	97	40	0	16.16	6	2-22	34.16	0/0	1	
Tredwell James Cullum	27.2.1982		6	2009	37	37	0	37.00	6	4-82	30.16	0/0	2	2
[4]Tremlett Christopher Timothy	2.9.1981		3	2007–2010	69	25*	0	9.85	30	5-87	26.10	1/0	9	9/1
[4]Tremlett Maurice Fletcher	5.7.1923	30.7.1984	3	1947	20	18*	0	6.66	4	2-98	56.50	0/0	1	
Trescothick Marcus Edward MBE	25.12.1975		76	2000–2006	5,825	219	14	43.79	1	1-34	155.00	0/0	95	123/3
[2]Trott Albert Edwin	6.2.1873	30.7.1914	2	1898	23	16	0	5.75	17	5-49	11.64	1/0	4	
Trott Ian Jonathan Leonard	22.4.1981		18	2009–2010	1,600	226	5	61.53	1	1-16	86.00	0/0	9	11/7
Trueman Frederick Sewards OBE	6.2.1931	1.7.2006	67	1952–1965	981	39*	0	13.81	307	8-31	21.57	17/3	64	
Tudor Alex Jeremy	23.10.1977		10	1998–2002	229	99*	0	19.08	28	5-44	34.39	1/0	3	3
Tufnell Neville Charsley	13.6.1887	3.8.1951	1	1909	14	14	0	14.00				–/–	0/1	
Tufnell Philip Clive Roderick	29.4.1966		42	1990–2001	153	22*	0	5.10	121	7-47	37.68	5/2	12	20
Turnbull Maurice Joseph Lawson	16.3.1906	5.8.1944	9	1929–1936	224	61	0	20.36				–/–	1	
[2]Tyldesley [George] Ernest	5.2.1889	5.5.1962	14	1921–1928	990	122	3	55.00	0	0-2		0/0	2	

	Born	Died	Tests	Test Career	Runs	HS	100s	Avge	Wkts	BB	5/10	Avge	Ct/St	O/T
[2]Tyldesley John Thomas	22.11.1873	27.11.1930	31	1898-1909	1,661	138	4	30.75	–	–	–	–	16	–
Tyldesley Richard Knowles	11.3.1897	17.9.1943	7	1924-1930	47	29	0	9.40	19	3-50	0/0	32.57	1	–
Tylecote Edward Ferdinando Sutton	23.6.1849	15.3.1938	6	1882-1886	152	66	0	19.00	–	–	–	–	5/5	–
Tyler Edwin James	13.10.1864	25.1.1917	1	1895	0	0	0	0.00	4	3-49	0/0	16.25	–	–
Tyson Frank Holmes	6.6.1930	–	17	1954-1958	230	37*	0	10.95	76	7-27	4/1	18.56	4	11
Udal Shaun David	18.3.1969	–	4	2005	109	33*	0	18.16	8	4-14	0/0	43.00	–	–
Ulyett George	21.10.1851	18.6.1898	25	1876-1890	949	149	1	24.33	50	7-36	1/0	20.40	19	26
Underwood Derek Leslie MBE	8.6.1945	–	86	1966-1981	937	45*	0	11.56	297	8-51	17/6	25.83	44	86/2
Valentine Bryan Herbert	17.1.1908	2.2.1983	7	1933-1938	454	136	2	64.85	–	–	–	–	2	–
Vaughan Michael Paul OBE	29.10.1974	–	82	1999-2008	5,719	197	18	41.44	6	2-71	0/0	93.50	44	–
Verity Hedley	18.5.1905	31.7.1943	40	1931-1939	669	66*	0	20.90	144	8-43	5/2	24.37	30	–
Vernon George Frederick	20.6.1856	10.8.1902	1	1882	14	11*	0	14.00	–	–	–	–	0	–
Vine Joseph	15.5.1875	25.4.1946	2	1911	46	36	0	46.00	–	–	–	–	–	–
Voce William	8.8.1909	6.6.1984	27	1929-1946	308	66	0	13.39	98	7-70	3/2	27.88	15	–
Waddington Abraham	4.2.1893	28.10.1959	2	1920	16	7	0	4.00	1	1-35	0/0	119.00	–	–
Wainwright Edward	8.4.1865	28.10.1919	5	1893-1897	132	49	0	14.66	0	0-11	0/0	–	3	–
Walker Peter Michael MBE	17.2.1936	–	3	1960	128	52	0	32.00	0	0-8	0/0	–	5	–
Walters Cyril Frederick	28.8.1905	23.12.1992	11	1933-1934	784	102	1	52.26	–	–	–	–	6	–
Ward Alan	10.8.1947	–	5	1969-1976	40	21	0	8.00	14	4-61	0/0	32.35	3	–
Ward Albert	21.11.1865	6.1.1939	7	1893-1894	487	117	1	37.46	–	–	–	–	12	–
Ward Ian James	30.9.1972	–	5	2001	129	39	0	16.12	–	–	–	–	3	–
Wardle John Henry	8.1.1923	23.7.1985	28	1947-1957	653	66	0	19.78	102	7-36	5/1	20.39	12	–
Warner Sir Pelham Francis	2.10.1873	30.1.1963	15	1898-1912	622	132*	1	23.92	–	–	–	–	3	–
Warr John James	16.7.1927	–	2	1950	4	4	0	1.00	1	1-76	0/0	281.00	0	–
Warren Arnold	2.4.1875	3.9.1951	1	1905	7	7	0	7.00	6	5-57	1/0	18.83	–	–
Washbrook Cyril CBE	6.12.1914	27.4.1999	37	1937-1956	2,569	195	6	42.81	1	1-25	0/0	33.00	12	4
Watkin Steven Llewellyn	15.9.1964	–	3	1991-1993	25	13	0	5.00	11	4-65	0/0	27.72	–	–
Watkins Albert John ("Allan")	21.4.1922	–	15	1948-1952	810	137*	2	40.50	11	3-20	0/0	50.36	17	1
Watkinson Michael MBE	1.8.1961	–	4	1995-1995	167	82*	0	33.40	10	3-64	0/0	34.80	–	–
Watson Willie	7.3.1920	23.4.2004	23	1951-1958	879	116	2	25.85	–	–	–	–	8	–
Webbe Alexander Josiah	16.1.1855	19.2.1941	1	1878	4	4	0	2.00	–	–	–	–	–	1
Wellard Arthur William	8.4.1902	31.12.1980	2	1937-1938	47	38	0	11.75	7	4-81	0/0	33.85	2	–
Wells Alan Peter	2.10.1961	–	1	1995	3	3*	0	3.00	–	–	–	–	2	–
Wharton Alan	30.4.1923	26.8.1993	1	1949	20	13	0	10.00	–	–	–	–	0	–
Whitaker John James	5.5.1962	–	1	1986	11	11	0	11.00	–	–	–	–	–	2
White Craig	16.12.1969	–	30	1994-2002	1,052	121	1	24.46	59	5-32	3/0	37.62	14	51

	Born	Died	Tests	Test Career	Runs	HS	100s	Avge	Wkts	BB	5/10	Avge	Ct/St	O/T
White David William ("Butch")	14.12.1935	1.8.2008	2	1961	0	0	0	0.00	4	3-65	00	29.75	0	
White John Cornish	19.2.1891	2.5.1961	15	1921–1930	239	29	0	18.38	49	8-126	3/1	32.26	6	26
Whysall William Wilfrid	31.10.1887	11.11.1930	4	1924–1930	209	76	0	29.85	0	0-9	00	–	7	
Wilkinson Leonard Litton	5.11.1916	3.9.2002	3	1938	3	2	0	3.00	7	2-12	00	38.71	3	
Willey Peter	6.12.1949		26	1976–1986	1,184	102*	0	26.90	7	2-73	00	65.14	3	26
Williams Neil FitzGerald	2.7.1962		1	1990	38	38	0	38.00	2	2-148	00	74.00	0	
Willis Robert George Dylan MBE	30.5.1949		90	1970–1984	840	28*	0	11.50	325	8-43	16/0	25.20	39	64
² Wilson Clement Eustace Macro	15.5.1875	8.2.1944	2	1898	42	18	0	14.00	–	–	–/–	–	0	
Wilson Donald	7.8.1937		6	1963–1970	75	42	0	12.50	11	2-17	00	42.36	1	
³ Wilson Evelyn Rockley	25.3.1879	21.7.1957	1	1920	10	5	0	5.00	3	2-28	00	12.00	0	
Wood Arthur	25.8.1898	1.4.1973	4	1938–1939	80	53	0	20.00	–	–	–/–	–	10/1	
Wood Barry	26.12.1942		12	1972–1978	454	90	0	21.61	0	0-2	00	–	6	13
Wood George Edward Charles	22.8.1893	18.3.1971	3	1924	7	6	0	3.50	–	–	–/–	–	5/1	
Wood Henry	14.12.1853	30.4.1919	4	1888–1891	204	134*	1	68.00	–	–	–/–	–	2/1	
Wood Reginald	7.3.1860	6.1.1915	1	1886	6	6	0	3.00	–	–	–/–	–	0	
Woods Samuel Moses James	13.4.1867	30.4.1931	3†	1895	122	53	0	30.50	5	3-28	00	25.80	4	
Woolley Frank Edward	27.5.1887	18.10.1978	64	1909–1934	3,283	154	5	36.07	83	7-76	4/1	33.91	64	
Woolmer Robert Andrew	14.5.1948	18.3.2007	19	1975–1981	1,059	149	3	33.09	4	1-8	00	74.75	10	6
Worthington Thomas Stanley	21.8.1905	31.8.1973	9	1929–1936	321	128	1	29.18	8	2-19	00	39.50	8	
Wright Charles William	27.5.1863	10.1.1936	3	1895	125	71	0	31.25	–	–	–/–	–	0	
Wright Douglas Vivian Parson	21.8.1914	13.11.1998	34	1938–1950	289	45	0	11.11	108	7-105	6/1	39.11	10	
Wyatt Robert Elliott Storey	2.5.1901	20.4.1995	40	1927–1936	1,839	149	2	31.70	18	3-4	00	35.66	16	
Wynyard Edward George	1.4.1861	30.10.1936	3	1896–1905	72	30	0	12.00	0	0-2	00	–	0	
Yardley Norman Walter Dransfield	19.3.1915	3.10.1989	20	1938–1950	812	99	0	25.37	21	3-67	00	33.66	14	
Young Harding Isaac ("Sailor")	5.2.1876	12.12.1964	2	1899	43	43	0	21.50	12	4-30	00	21.83	1	
Young John Albert	14.10.1912	5.2.1993	8	1947–1949	28	10*	0	5.60	17	3-65	00	44.52	5	
Young Richard Alfred	16.9.1885	1.7.1968	2	1907	27	13	0	6.75	–	–	–/–	–	6	

AUSTRALIA (419 players)

	Born	Died	Tests	Test Career	Runs	HS	100s	Avge	Wkts	BB	5/10	Avge	Ct/St	O/T
a'Beckett Edward Lambert	11.8.1907	2.6.1989	4	1928–1931	143	41	0	20.42	3	1-41	0/0	105.66	4	65
Alderman Terence Michael	12.6.1956		41	1981–1990	203	26*	0	6.54	170	6-47	14/1	27.15	27	
Alexander George	22.4.1851	6.11.1930	2	1880–1884	52	33	0	13.00	2	2-69	0/0	46.50	2	3
Alexander Harry Houston	9.6.1905	15.4.1993	1	1932	17	17*	0	17.00	1	1-129	0/0	154.00	0	
Allan Francis Erskine	2.12.1849	9.2.1917	1	1878	5	5	0	5.00	4	2-30	0/0	20.00	0	
Allan Peter John	31.12.1935		1	1965	–	–	–	–	2	2-58	0/0	41.50	2	
Allen Reginald Charles	2.7.1858	2.5.1952	1	1886	44	30	0	22.00	–	–	–	–	2	
Andrews Thomas James Edwin	26.8.1890	28.1.1970	16	1921–1926	592	94	0	26.90	1	1-23	0/0	116.00	12	
Angel Jo	22.4.1968		4	1992–1994	35	11	0	5.83	10	3-54	0/0	46.30	1	
²Archer Kenneth Alan	17.1.1928		5	1950–1951	234	48	0	26.00	–	–	–	–	0	
²Archer Ronald Graham	25.10.1933	27.5.2007	19	1952–1956	713	128	0	24.58	48	5-53	1/0	27.45	20	
Armstrong Warwick Windridge	22.5.1879	13.7.1947	50	1901–1921	2,863	159*	6	38.68	87	6-35	3/0	33.59	44	
Badcock Clayvel Lindsay ("Jack")	10.4.1914	13.12.1982	7	1936–1938	160	118	1	14.54	–	–	–	–	3	
²Bannerman Alexander Chalmers	21.3.1854	19.9.1924	28	1878–1893	1,108	94	0	23.08	4	3-111	0/0	40.75	21	
²Bannerman Charles	23.7.1851	20.8.1930	3	1876–1878	239	165*	1	59.75	–	–	–	–	0	
Bardsley Warren	6.12.1882	20.1.1954	41	1909–1926	2,469	193*	6	40.47	–	–	–	–	12	
Barnes Sidney George	5.6.1916	16.12.1973	13	1938–1948	1,072	234	3	63.05	4	2-25	0/0	54.50	14	
Barnett Benjamin Arthur	23.3.1908	29.6.1979	4	1938	195	57	0	27.85	–	–	–	–	3/2	
Barrett John Edward	15.10.1866	6.2.1916	2	1890	80	67*	0	26.66	–	–	–	–	0	
Beard Graeme Robert	19.8.1950		3	1979	114	49	0	22.80	1	1-26	0/0	109.00	0	2
Beer Michael Anthony	9.6.1984		2	2010	4	2*	0	4.00	1	1-112	0/0	112.00	0	
Benaud John	11.5.1944		3	1972	223	142	1	44.60	2	2-12	0/0	6.00	2	
²Benaud Richard OBE	6.10.1930		63	1951–1963	2,201	122	3	24.45	248	7-72	16/1	27.03	65	
Bennett Murray John	6.10.1956		3	1984–1985	71	23	0	23.66	6	3-79	0/0	54.16	5	8
²Bevan Michael Gwyl	8.5.1970		18	1994–1997	785	91	0	29.07	29	6-82	1/1	24.24	8	232
Bichel Andrew John	27.8.1970		19	1996–2003	355	71	0	16.90	58	5-60	1/0	32.24	16	67
Blackham John McCarthy	11.5.1854	28.12.1932	35	1876–1894	800	74	0	15.68	–	–	–	–	37/24	
Blackie Donald Dearness	5.4.1882	18.4.1955	3	1928	24	11*	0	8.00	14	6-94	1/0	31.71	2	
Blewett Gregory Scott	28.10.1971		46	1994–1999	2,552	214	4	34.02	14	2-9	0/0	51.42	45	32
Bollinger Douglas Erwin	24.7.1981		12	2008–2010	54	21	0	7.71	50	5-28	2/0	25.92	2	26
Bonnor George John	25.2.1855	27.6.1912	17	1880–1888	512	128	1	17.06	2	2-84	0/0	42.00	16	
Boon David Clarence	29.12.1960		107	1984–1995	7,422	200	21	43.65	0	0-0	0/0	–	99	181
Booth Brian Charles MBE	19.10.1933		29	1961–1965	1,773	169	5	42.21	3	2-33	0/0	48.66	17	

Name	Born	Died	Test Career	Tests	Runs	HS	100s	Avge	Wkts	BB	5/10	Avge	Ct/St	O/T
Border Allan Robert	27.7.1955		1978–1984	156	11,174	205	27	50.56	39	7-46	2/1	39.10	156	273
Boyle Henry Frederick	10.12.1847	21.11.1907	1878–1884	12	153	36*	0	12.75	32	6-42	1/0	20.03	10	
Bracken Nathan Wade	12.9.1977		2003–2005	5	70	37	0	17.50	12	4-48	0/0	42.08	2	116/19
Bradman Sir Donald George AC	27.8.1908	25.2.2001	1928–1948	52	6,996	334	29	99.94	2	1-8	0/0	36.00	32	
Bright Raymond James	13.7.1954		1977–1986	25	445	33	0	14.35	53	7-87	4/1	41.13	13	11
Bromley Ernest Harvey	2.9.1912	1.2.1967	1932–1934	2	38	26	0	9.50	0	0-19	–/–	–	2	
Brown William Alfred	31.7.1912	16.3.2008	1934–1948	22	1,592	206*	4	46.82	–	–	–/–	–	14	
Bruce William	22.5.1864	3.8.1925	1884–1894	14	702	80	1	29.25	12	3-88	0/0	36.66	12	
Burge Peter John (Parnell)	17.5.1932	5.10.2001	1954–1965	42	2,290	181	4	38.16	–	–	–/–	–	23	5
Burke James Wallace	12.6.1930	2.2.1979	1950–1958	24	1,280	189	3	34.59	8	4-37	0/0	28.75	18	12
Burn Edwin James Kenneth (K.E.)	17.9.1862	20.7.1956	1890	2	41	19	0	10.25	–	–	–	–	0	
Burton Frederick John	2.11.1865	25.8.1929	1886–1887	2	4	2*	0	2.00	–	–	–/–	–	1/1	
Callaway Sydney Thomas	6.2.1868	25.11.1923	1891–1894	3	87	41	0	17.40	6	5-37	1/0	23.66	2	
Callen Ian Wayne	2.5.1955		1977	1	26	22*	0	–	6	3-83	0/0	31.83	1	5
Campbell Gregory Dale	10.3.1964		1989–1989	4	10	6*	0	2.50	13	3-79	0/0	38.69	1	12
Carkeek William ("Barlow")	17.10.1878	20.2.1937	1912	6	16	6*	0	5.33	–	–	–	–	6	
Carlson Phillip Henry	8.8.1951		1978	2	23	21	0	5.75	2	2-41	0/0	49.50	2	4
Carter Hanson	15.3.1878	8.6.1948	1907–1921	28	873	72	0	22.97	–	–	–/–	–	44/21	
Casson Beau	7.12.1982		2007	1	10	10	0	10.00	3	3-86	0/0	43.00	2	
[2,4] **Chappell** Gregory Stephen MBE	7.8.1948		1970–1983	87	7,110	247*	24	53.86	47	5-61	1/0	40.70	122	74
[2,4] **Chappell** Ian Michael	26.9.1943		1964–1979	75	5,345	196	14	42.42	20	2-21	0/0	65.80	105	16
[2,4] **Chappell** Trevor Martin	21.10.1952		1981	3	79	27	0	15.80	–	–	–/–	–	2	20
Charlton Percie Chater	9.4.1867	30.9.1954	1890	2	29	11	0	7.25	3	3-18	0/0	8.00	0	
Chipperfield Arthur Gordon	17.11.1905	29.7.1987	1934–1938	14	552	109	1	32.47	5	3-91	0/0	87.40	15	
Clark Stuart Rupert	28.9.1975		2005–2009	24	248	39	0	13.05	94	5-32	2/0	23.86	4	39/9
Clark Wayne Maxwell	19.9.1953		1977–1978	10	98	33	0	5.76	44	4-46	0/0	28.75	6	2
Clarke Michael John §.	2.4.1981		2004–2010	69§	4,742	168	14	46.49	21	6-9	1/0	39.14	69	182/34
Colley David John	15.3.1947		1972	3	84	54	0	21.00	6	3-83	0/0	52.00	1	1
Collins Herbert Leslie	21.1.1888	28.5.1959	1920–1926	19	1,352	203	4	45.06	4	2-47	0/0	63.00	13	
Coningham Arthur	14.7.1863	13.6.1939	1894	1	13	10	0	6.50	2	2-17	0/0	38.00	0	
Connolly Alan Norman	29.6.1939		1963–1970	29	260	37	0	10.40	102	6-47	4/0	29.22	17	1
Cook Simon Hewitt	29.1.1972		1997	2	3	3*	0	–	7	5-39	1/0	20.28	2	
Cooper Bransby Beauchamp	15.3.1844	7.8.1914	1876	1	18	15	0	9.00	–	–	–/–	–	2	
[5] **Cooper** William Henry	11.9.1849	5.4.1939	1881–1884	2	13	7	0	6.50	9	6-120	1/0	25.11	1	
Corling Grahame Edward	13.7.1941		1964	5	5	3	0	1.66	12	4-60	0/0	37.25	0	

§ *Clarke's figures include 44 runs and one catch for Australia v the ICC World XI in the Super Series Test in 2005-06.*

	Born	Died	Tests	Test Career	Runs	HS	100s	Avge	Wkts	BB	5/10	Avge	Ct/St	O/T
Cosier Gary John	25.4.1953		18	1975–1978	897	168	2	28.93	5	2-26	0/0	68.20	14	9
Cottam John Thomas	5.9.1867	30.1.1897	1	1886	4	3	0	2.00	–	–	–/–	–	1	
Cotter Albert ("Tibby")	3.12.1883	31.10.1917	21	1903–1911	457	45	0	13.05	89	7-148	7/0	28.64	8	
Coulthard George	1.8.1856	22.10.1883	1	1881	6	6*	0	–	–	–	–/–	–	0	
Cowper Robert Maskew	5.10.1940		27	1964–1968	2,061	307	5	46.84	36	4-48	0/0	31.63	21	
Craig Ian David	12.6.1935		11	1952–1957	358	53	0	19.88	–	–	–/–	–	2	
Crawford William Patrick Anthony	3.8.1933	21.1.2009	4	1956–1956	53	34	0	17.66	7	3-28	0/0	15.28	1	5
Cullen Daniel James	10.4.1984		1	2005	–	–	–	–	1	1-25	0/0	54.00	–	30
Dale Adam Craig	30.12.1968		2	1997–1998	5	5	0	2.00	6	3-71	0/0	31.16	1	
Darling Joseph	21.11.1870	2.1.1946	34	1894–1905	1,657	178	3	28.56	–	–	–/–	–	27	
Darling Leonard Stuart	14.8.1909	24.6.1992	12	1932–1936	474	85	0	27.88	0	0-3	0/0	–	8	
Darling Warrick Maxwell	1.5.1957		14	1977–1979	697	91	0	26.80	–	–	–/–	–	5	18
Davidson Alan Keith MBE	14.6.1929		44	1953–1962	1,328	80	0	24.59	186	7-93	14/2	20.53	42	
Davis Ian Charles	25.6.1953		15	1973–1977	692	105	1	26.61	–	–	–/–	–	9	3
Davis Simon Peter	8.11.1959		1	1985	0	0	0	0.00	0	0-70	0/0	–	–	39
De Courcy James Harry	18.4.1927	20.6.2000	3	1953	81	41	0	16.20	–	–	–/–	–	3	
Dell Anthony Ross	6.8.1947		2	1970–1973	6	3*	0	–	6	3-65	0/0	26.66	0	
Dodemaide Anthony Ian Christopher	5.10.1963		10	1987–1992	202	50	0	22.44	34	6-58	1/0	28.02	6	24
Doherty Xavier John	22.12.1982		3	2010	27	16	0	9.00	3	2-41	0/0	102.00	2	2
Donnan Henry	12.11.1864	13.8.1956	5	1891–1896	75	15	0	8.33	0	0-22	0/0	–	2	
Dooland Bruce	1.11.1923	8.9.1980	3	1946–1947	76	29	0	19.00	9	4-69	0/0	46.55	3	
Duff Reginald Alexander	17.8.1878	13.12.1911	22	1901–1905	1,317	146	2	35.59	4	2-43	0/0	21.25	14	
Duncan John Ross Frederick	25.3.1944		1	1970	–	–	–	–	0	0-30	0/0	–	–	
Dyer Gregory Charles	16.3.1959		6	1986–1988	131	60	0	21.83	–	–	–/–	–	22/2	23
Dymock Geoffrey	21.7.1945		21	1973–1979	236	31*	0	9.44	78	7-67	5/1	27.12	15	15
Dyson John	11.6.1954		30	1977–1984	1,359	127*	1	26.64	–	–	–/–	–	10	29
Eady Charles John	29.10.1870	20.12.1945	2	1896–1901	20	10*	0	6.66	7	3-30	0/0	16.00	2	
Eastwood Kenneth Humphrey	23.11.1935		1	1970	5	5	0	2.50	1	1-21	0/0	21.00	0	
Ebeling Hans Irvine	1.1.1905	12.1.1980	1	1934	43	41	0	21.50	3	3-74	0/0	29.66	0	
Edwards John Dunlop	12.6.1860	31.7.1911	3	1888	48	26	0	9.60	–	–	–/–	–	1	
Edwards Ross	1.12.1942		20	1972–1975	1,171	170*	2	40.37	0	0-20	0/0	–	7	9
Edwards Walter John	23.12.1949		3	1974	68	30	0	11.33	–	–	–/–	–	1	
Elliott Matthew Thomas Gray	28.9.1971		21	1996–2004	1,172	199	3	33.48	0	0-0	0/0	–	14	1
Emery Philip Allen	25.6.1964		1	1994	8	8*	0	–	–	–	–/–	–	5/1	1
Emery Sidney Hand	15.10.1885	7.1.1967	4	1912	6	5	0	3.00	5	2-46	0/0	49.80	2	
Evans Edwin	26.3.1849	2.7.1921	6	1881–1886	82	33	0	10.25	7	3-64	0/0	47.42	5	

	Born	Died	Tests	Test Career	Runs	HS	100s	Avge	Wkts	BB	5/10	Avge	Ct/St	O/T
Fairfax Alan George	16.6.1906	17.5.1955	10	1928–1930	410	65	0	51.25	21	4-31	0/0	30.71	15	
Favell Leslie Ernest MBE	6.10.1929	14.6.1987	19	1954–1960	757	101	1	27.03	–	–	–	–	9	
Ferris John James	21.5.1867	17.11.1900	8†	1886–1890	98	20*	0	8.16	48	5-26	4/0	14.25	4	
Fingleton John Henry Webb OBE	28.4.1908	22.11.1981	18	1931–1938	1,189	136	5	42.46	–	–	–	–	13	
Fleetwood-Smith Leslie O'Brien ("Chuck")	30.3.1908	16.3.1971	10	1935–1938	54	16*	0	9.00	42	6-110	2/1	37.38	0	
Fleming Damien William	24.4.1970		20	1994–2000	305	71*	0	19.06	75	5-30	3/0	25.89	9	88
Francis Bruce Colin	18.2.1948		3	1972	52	27	0	10.40	–	–	–	–	1	
Freeman Eric Walter	13.7.1944		11	1967–1969	345	76	0	19.16	34	4-52	0/0	33.17	5	
Freer Frederick Alfred William	4.12.1915	2.11.1998	1	1946	28	28*	0	–	3	2-49	0/0	24.66	0	
Gannon John Bryant ("Sam")	8.2.1947		3	1977	3	3*	0	3.00	11	4-77	0/0	32.81	3	
Garrett Thomas William	26.7.1858	6.8.1943	19	1876–1887	339	51*	0	12.55	36	6-78	2/0	26.94	7	
Gaunt Ronald Arthur	26.2.1934		3	1957–1963	6	3	0	3.00	7	3-53	0/0	44.28	1	
Gehrs Donald Raeburn Algernon	29.11.1880	25.6.1953	6	1903–1910	221	67	0	20.09	–	0-4	0/0	–	6	
George Peter Robert	16.10.1986		1	2010	2	2	0	1.00	0	2-48	0/0	38.50	0	
2 Giffen George	27.3.1859	29.11.1927	31	1881–1896	1,238	161	1	23.35	103	7-117	7/1	27.09	24	
2 Giffen Walter Frank	20.9.1861	28.6.1949	3	1886–1891	11	3	0	1.83	–	–	–	–	0	
Gilbert David Robert	29.12.1960		9	1985–1986	57	15	0	7.12	16	3-48	0/0	52.68	0	14
Gilchrist Adam Craig	14.11.1971		96§	1999–2007	5,570	204*	17	47.60	–	–	–	–	379/37	286§/13
Gillespie Jason Neil	19.4.1975		71	1996–2005	1,218	201*	2	18.73	259	7-37	8/0	26.13	27	97/1
Gilmour Gary John	26.6.1951		15	1973–1976	483	101	1	23.00	54	6-85	3/0	26.03	8	5
Gleeson John William	14.3.1938		29	1967–1972	395	45	0	10.39	93	5-61	3/0	36.20	17	
Graham Henry	22.11.1870	7.2.1911	6	1893–1896	301	107	2	30.10	–	–	–	–	3	
2 Gregory David William	15.4.1845	4.8.1919	3	1876–1878	60	43	0	20.00	0	0-9	0/0	–	0	
1,2 Gregory Edward James	29.5.1839	22.4.1899	1	1876	11	11	0	5.50	–	–	–	–	1	
Gregory Jack Morrison	14.8.1895	7.8.1973	24	1920–1928	1,146	119	2	36.96	85	7-69	4/0	31.15	37	
Gregory Ross Gerald	28.2.1916	10.6.1942	2	1936	153	80	0	51.00	0	0-14	0/0	–	1	
Gregory Sydney Edward	14.4.1870	1.8.1929	58	1890–1912	2,282	201	4	24.53	0	0-4	0/0	–	25	
Grimmett Clarence Victor	25.12.1891	2.5.1980	37	1924–1935	557	50	0	13.92	216	7-40	21/7	24.21	17	
Groube Thomas Underwood	2.9.1857	5.8.1927	1	1880	11	11	0	5.50	–	–	–	–	0	
Grout Arthur Theodore Wallace	30.3.1927	9.11.1968	51	1957–1965	890	74	0	15.08	–	–	–	–	163/24	
Guest Colin Ernest John	7.10.1937		1	1962	11	11	0	11.00	0	0-8	0/0	–	0	
Haddin Bradley James	23.10.1977		32	2007–2010	1,904	169	3	39.66	–	–	–	–	118/3	69/23
Hamence Ronald Arthur	25.11.1915	24.3.2010	3	1946–1947	81	30*	0	27.00	–	–	–	–	1	
Hammond Jeffrey Roy	19.4.1950		5	1972	28	19	0	9.33	15	4-38	0/0	32.53	2	1
Harris Ryan James	11.10.1979		5	2009–2010	42	18*	0	8.40	20	6-47	1/0	24.40	1	17/3

§ Gilchrist's figures include 95 runs, five catches and two stumpings for Australia v the ICC World XI in the Super Series Test in 2005-06.

Name	Born	Died	Tests	Test Career	Runs	HS	100s	Avge	Wks	BB	5/10	Avge	Ct/St	OIT
Harry John	1.8.1857	27.10.1919	1	1894	8	6	0	4.00	0	-	-/-	-	1	1
Hartigan Roger Joseph	12.12.1879	7.6.1958	2	1907	170	116	0	42.50	0	0-7	0/0	-	3	1
Hartkopf Albert Ernst Victor	28.12.1889	20.5.1968	1	1924	80	80	0	40.00	1	1-120	0/0	134.00	1	0
Harvey Mervyn Roye	29.4.1918	18.3.1995	1	1946	43	31	0	21.50	-	-	-/-	-	0	-
[2]Harvey Robert Neil MBE	8.10.1928		79	1947-1962	6,149	205	21	48.41	3	1-8	0/0	40.00	64	
Hassett Arthur Lindsay MBE	28.8.1913	16.6.1993	43	1938-1953	3,073	198*	10	46.56	0	0-1	0/0	-	30	
Hauritz Nathan Michael	18.10.1981		17	2004-2010	426	75	0	25.05	63	5-53	2/0	34.98	9	57/3
Hawke Neil James Napier	27.6.1939	25.12.2000	27	1962-1968	365	45*	0	16.59	91	7-105	6/1	29.41	9	
Hayden Matthew Lawrence	29.10.1971		103§	1993-2008	8,625	380	30	50.73	0	0-7	-/-	-	128	160†/9
Hazlitt Gervys Rignold	4.9.1888	30.10.1915	9	1907-1912	89	34*	0	11.12	23	7-25	1/0	27.08	4	
Healy Ian Andrew	30.4.1964		119	1988-1999	4,356	161*	4	27.39	-	-	-/-	-	366/29	168
Hendry Hunter Scott Thomas Laurie ("Stork")	24.5.1895	16.12.1988	11	1921-1928	335	112	1	20.93	16	3-36	0/0	31.16	10	
Hibbert Paul Anthony	23.7.1952	27.11.2008	1	1977	15	13	0	7.50	-	-	-/-	-	1	
Higgs James Donald	11.7.1950		22	1977-1980	111	16	0	5.55	66	7-143	2/0	31.55	3	
Hilditch Andrew Mark Jefferson	20.5.1956		18	1978-1985	1,073	119	2	31.55	-	-	-/-	-	13	8
Hilfenhaus Benjamin William	15.3.1983		17	2008-2010	242	56*	0	15.12	55	4-57	0/0	34.65	5	15/6
Hill Clement	18.3.1877	5.9.1945	49	1896-1911	3,412	191	7	39.21	-	-	-/-	-	33	
Hill John Charles	25.6.1923	11.8.1974	3	1953-1954	21	8*	0	7.00	8	3-35	0/0	34.12	3	
Hoare Desmond Edward	19.10.1934		1	1960	35	35	0	17.50	2	2-68	0/0	78.00	0	
Hodge Bradley John	29.12.1974		6	2005-2007	503	203*	1	55.88	0	0-8	0/0	-	9	25/8
Hodges John Robart	11.8.1855	d unknown	2	1876	10	8	0	3.33	2	2-7	0/0	14.00	2	
Hogan Tom George	23.9.1956		7	1982-1983	205	42*	0	18.63	15	5-66	1/0	47.06	2	16
Hogg George Bradley	6.2.1971		7	1996-2007	186	79	0	26.57	17	2-40	0/0	54.88	1	123/2
Hogg Rodney Malcolm	5.3.1951		38	1978-1984	439	52	0	9.75	123	6-74	6/2	28.47	3	71
Hohns Trevor Victor	23.11.1954		7	1988-1989	136	40	0	22.66	17	3-59	0/0	34.11	2	
Hole Graeme Blake	6.1.1931	14.2.1990	18	1950-1954	789	66	0	25.45	3	1-9	0/0	42.00	21	
Holland Robert George	19.10.1946		11	1984-1985	35	10	0	3.18	34	6-54	3/2	39.76	5	2
Hookes David William	3.5.1955	19.1.2004	23	1976-1985	1,306	143*	1	34.36	1	1-4	0/0	41.00	12	39
Hopkins Albert Eric Young	3.5.1874	25.4.1931	20	1901-1909	509	43	0	16.41	26	4-81	0/0	26.76	11	
Horan Thomas Patrick	8.3.1854	16.4.1916	15	1876-1884	471	124	1	18.84	11	6-40	1/0	13.00	6	
Hordern Herbert Vivian MBE	10.2.1883	17.6.1938	7	1910-1911	254	50	0	23.09	46	7-90	5/2	23.36	6	
Hornibrook Percival Mitchell	27.7.1899	25.8.1991	6	1928-1930	60	35	0	10.00	17	7-92	1/0	39.05	7	
Howell William Peter	29.12.1869	14.7.1940	18	1897-1903	158	35	0	7.52	49	5-81	1/0	28.71	12	
Hughes Kimberley John	26.11.1954		70	1977-1984	4,415	213	9	37.41	0	0-0	0/0	-	12	97
Hughes Mervyn Gregory	23.11.1961		53	1985-1993	1,032	72*	0	16.64	212	8-87	7/1	28.38	23	33

§ Hayden's figures include 188 runs and three catches for Australia v the ICC World XI in the Super Series Test in 2005-06.

	Born	Died	Tests	Test Career	Runs	HS	100s	Avge	Wkts	BB	5/10	Avge	Ct/St	O/T
Hughes Phillip Joel	30.11.1988		10	2008–2010	712	160	2	39.55	–	–	–/–	–	3	–
Hunt William Alfred	26.8.1908	30.12.1983	1	1931	0	0	0	0.00	–	–	–/–	–	–	–
Hurst Alan George	15.7.1950		12	1973–1979	102	26	0	6.00	43	5-28	2/0	27.90	3	8
Hurwood Alexander	17.6.1902	26.9.1982	2	1930	5	5	0	2.50	11	4-22	0/0	15.45	1	–
Hussey Michael Edward Killeen	27.5.1975		59	2005–2010	4,650	195	13	51.09	2	1-3	0/0	52.50	57	150/27
Inverarity Robert John	31.1.1944		6	1968–1972	174	56	0	17.40	4	3-26	0/0	23.25	4	–
Iredale Francis Adams	19.6.1867	15.4.1926	14	1894–1899	807	140	2	36.68	–	–	–/–	–	16	–
Ironmonger Herbert	7.4.1882	31.5.1971	14	1928–1932	42	12	0	2.62	74	7-23	4/2	17.97	3	–
Iverson John Brian	27.7.1915	24.10.1973	5	1950	3	1*	0	0.75	21	6-27	1/0	15.23	2	–
Jackson Archibald Alexander	5.9.1909	16.2.1933	8	1928–1930	474	164	1	47.40	–	–	–/–	–	7	–
Jaques Phillip Anthony	3.5.1979		11	2005–2007	902	150	3	47.47	–	–	–/–	–	7	6
Jarman Barrington Noel	17.2.1936		19	1959–1968	400	78	0	14.81	–	–	–/–	–	50/4	–
Jarvis Arthur Harwood	19.10.1860	15.11.1933	11	1884–1894	303	82	0	16.83	–	–	–/–	–	9/9	–
Jenner Terrence James	8.9.1944		9	1970–1975	208	74	0	23.11	24	5-90	1/0	31.20	5	1
Jennings Claude Burrows	5.6.1884	20.6.1950	6	1912	107	32	0	17.83	–	–	–/–	–	5	–
Johnson Ian William Geddes CBE	8.12.1917	9.10.1998	45	1945–1956	1,000	77	0	18.51	109	7-44	3/0	29.19	30	–
Johnson Leonard Joseph	18.3.1919	20.4.1977	1	1947	25	25*	0	–	6	3-8	0/0	12.33	2	–
Johnson Mitchell Guy	2.11.1981		42	2007–2010	1,152	123*	1	22.15	181	8-61	7/0	29.71	10	85/24
Johnston William Arras	26.2.1922	25.5.2007	40	1947–1954	273	29	0	11.37	160	6-44	7/0	23.91	16	–
Jones Dean Mervyn	24.3.1961		52	1983–1992	3,631	216	11	46.55	1	1-5	0/0	64.00	34	164
Jones Ernest	30.9.1869	23.11.1943	19	1894–1902	126	20	0	5.04	64	7-88	3/1	29.01	21	–
Jones Samuel Percy	1.8.1861	14.7.1951	12	1881–1887	428	87	0	21.40	6	4-47	0/0	18.66	12	–
Joslin Leslie Ronald	13.12.1947		1	1967	9	7	0	4.50	–	–	–/–	–	0	–
Julian Brendon Paul	10.8.1970		7	1993–1995	128	56*	0	16.00	15	4-36	0/0	39.93	4	25
Kasprowicz Michael Scott	10.2.1972		38	1996–2005	445	25	0	10.59	113	7-36	4/0	32.88	16	43/2
Katich Simon Mathew	21.8.1975		56§	2001–2010	4,188	157	10	45.03	21	6-65	1/0	30.23	39	45/3
Kelleway Charles	25.4.1886	16.11.1944	26	1910–1928	1,422	147	3	37.42	52	5-33	1/0	32.36	24	–
Kelly James Joseph	10.5.1867	14.8.1938	36	1896–1905	664	46*	0	17.02	–	–	–/–	–	43/20	–
Kelly Thomas Joseph Dart	3.5.1844	20.7.1893	2	1876–1878	64	35	0	21.33	–	–	–/–	–	1	–
Kendall Thomas Kingston	24.8.1851	17.8.1924	2	1876	39	17*	0	13.00	14	7-55	1/0	15.35	2	–
Kent Martin Francis	23.11.1953		3	1981	171	54	0	28.50	–	–	–/–	–	6	5
Kerr Robert Byers	16.6.1961		2	1985	31	17	0	7.75	–	–	–/–	–	1	4
Khawaja Usman Tariq	18.12.1986		1	2010	58	37	0	29.00	–	–	–/–	–	0	–
Kippax Alan Falconer	25.5.1897	5.9.1972	22	1924–1934	1,192	146	2	36.12	0	0-2	0/0	–	13	–
Kline Lindsay Francis	29.9.1934		13	1957–1960	58	15*	0	8.28	34	7-75	1/0	22.82	9	–

§ *Katich's figures include two runs and one catch for Australia v the ICC World XI in the Super Series Test in 2005-06.*

	Born	Died	Tests	Test Career	Runs	HS	100s	Avge	Wkts	BB	5/10	Avge	Ct/St	O/T
Krejza Jason John	14.1.1983		2	2008	71	32	0	23.66	13	8-215	1/1	43.23	4	
Laird Bruce Malcolm	21.11.1950		21	1979-1982	1,341	92	0	35.28	0	0-3	0/0	—	16	23
Langer Justin Lee	21.11.1970		105§	1992-2006	7,696	250	23	45.27	0	0-3	0/0	—	73	8
Langley Gilbert Roche Andrews	14.9.1919	14.5.2001	26	1951-1956	374	53	0	14.96					83/15	
Laughlin Trevor John	30.1.1951		3	1977-1978	87	35	0	17.40	6	5-101	1/0	43.66	3	6
Laver Frank Jonas	7.12.1869	24.9.1919	15	1899-1909	196	45	0	11.52	37	8-31	2/0	26.05	8	
Law Stuart Grant	18.10.1968		1	1995	54	54*	0	—	0	0-0	0/0	—		54
Lawry William Morris	11.2.1937		67	1961-1970	5,234	210	13	47.15	0	0-0	0/0	—	30	1
Lawson Geoffrey Francis	7.12.1957		46	1980-1989	894	74	0	15.96	180	8-112	11/2	30.56	10	79
Lee Brett	8.11.1976		76§	1999-2008	1,451	64	0	20.15	310	5-30	10/0	30.81	23	186/17
Lee Philip Keith	15.9.1904	9.8.1980	2	1931-1932	57	42	0	19.00	5	4-111	0/0	42.40	1	
Lehmann Darren Scott	5.2.1970		27	1997-2004	1,798	177	5	44.95	15	3-42	0/0	27.46	11	117
Lillee Dennis Keith MBE	18.7.1949		70	1970-1983	905	73*	0	13.71	355	7-83	23/7	23.92	23	63
Lindwall Raymond Russell MBE	3.10.1921	23.6.1996	61	1945-1959	1,502	118	2	21.15	228	7-38	12/0	23.03	26	
Love Hampden Stanley Bray	10.8.1895	22.7.1969	1	1932	8	5	0	4.00					3	
Love Martin Lloyd	30.3.1974		5	2002-2003	233	100*	1	46.60					7	
Loxton Samuel John Everett	29.3.1921		12	1947-1950	554	101	1	36.93	8	3-55	0/0	43.62	7	
Lyons John James	21.5.1863	21.7.1927	14	1886-1897	731	134	1	27.07	6	5-30	1/0	24.83	3	
McAlister Peter Alexander	11.7.1869	10.5.1938	8	1903-1909	252	41	0	16.80					10	
Macartney Charles George	27.6.1886	9.9.1958	35	1907-1926	2,131	170	7	41.78	45	7-58	2/1	27.55	17	
McCabe Stanley Joseph	16.7.1910	25.8.1968	39	1930-1938	2,748	232	6	48.21	36	4-13	0/0	42.86	41	
McCool Colin Leslie	9.12.1916	5.4.1986	14	1945-1949	459	104*	1	35.30	36	5-41	3/0	26.61	14	
McCormick Ernest Leslie	16.5.1906	28.6.1991	12	1935-1938	54	17*	0	6.00	36	4-101	0/0	29.97	8	
McCosker Richard Bede	11.12.1946		25	1974-1979	1,622	127	4	39.56					21	14
McDermott Craig John	14.4.1965		71	1984-1995	940	42*	0	12.20	291	8-97	14/2	28.63	19	138
McDonald Andrew Barry	15.6.1981		4	2008	107	68	0	21.40	9	3-25	0/0	33.33	2	
McDonald Colin Campbell	17.11.1928		47	1951-1961	3,107	170	5	39.32	0	0-3	0/0	—	14	
McDonald Edgar Arthur	6.1.1891	22.7.1937	11	1920-1921	116	36	0	16.57	43	5-32	2/0	33.27	3	
McDonnell Percy Stanislaus	13.11.1858	24.9.1896	19	1880-1888	955	147	3	28.93	0	0-11	0/0	—	6	
McGain Bryce Edward	25.3.1972		1	2008	2	2	0	1.00	0	0-149	0/0	—		
MacGill Stuart Charles Glyndwr	25.2.1971		44§	1997-2007	349	43	0	9.69	208	8-108	12/2	29.02	16	3
McGrath Glenn Donald	9.2.1970		124§	1993-2006	641	61	0	7.36	563	8-24	29/3	21.64	38	249†2/2
McIlwraith John	7.9.1857	5.7.1938	1	1886	9	7	0	4.50					1	
McIntyre Peter Edward	27.4.1966		2	1994-1996	22	16	0	7.33	5	3-103	0/0	38.80		

§ Langer's figures include 22 runs and one catch, Lee's four runs, two wickets and one catch, MacGill's two runs and three wickets and McGrath's two wickets and nine runs for Australia v the ICC World XI in the Super Series Test in 2005-06.

Name	Born	Died	Tests	Test Career	Runs	HS	100s	Avge	Wkts	BB	5/10	Avge	Ct/St	O/T
McKay Clinton James	22.2.1983		1	2009	1	10	0	10.00	1	1-56	0/0	101.00	1	15/1
Mackay Kenneth Donald MBE	24.10.1925	13.6.1982	37	1956–1962	1,507	89	0	33.48	50	6-42	2/0	34.42	16	
McKenzie Graham Douglas	24.6.1941		60	1961–1970	945	76	0	12.27	246	8-71	16/3	29.78	34	1
McKibbin Thomas Robert	10.12.1870	15.12.1939	5	1894–1897	88	28*	0	14.66	21	3-35	0/0	29.17	4	
McLaren John William	22.12.1886	17.11.1921	1	1911	–	0*	–	–	1	1-23	0/0	70.00	0	
Maclean John Alexander	27.4.1946		4	1978	79	33*	0	11.28	–	–	–	–	18	2
[2]McLeod Charles Edward	24.10.1869	26.11.1918	17	1894–1905	573	112	1	23.87	33	5-65	2/0	40.15	9	
[2]McLeod Robert William	19.1.1868	14.6.1907	6	1891–1893	146	31	0	13.27	12	5-53	1/0	31.83	3	
McShane Patrick George	18.4.1858	11.12.1903	3	1884–1887	26	12*	0	5.20	1	1-39	0/0	48.00	3	
Maddocks Leonard Victor	24.5.1926		7	1954–1956	177	69	0	17.70	–	–	–	–	19/1	
Maguire John Norman	15.9.1956		3	1983	28	15*	0	7.00	10	4-57	–/–	32.30	–	23
Mailey Arthur Alfred	3.1.1886	31.12.1967	21	1920–1926	222	46*	0	11.10	99	9-121	6/2	33.91	14	
Mallett Ashley Alexander	13.7.1945		38	1968–1980	430	43*	0	11.62	132	8-59	6/1	29.84	30	9
Malone Michael Francis	9.10.1950		1	1977	46	46	0	46.00	6	5-63	1/0	12.83	2	10
Mann Anthony Longford	8.11.1945		4	1977	189	105	1	23.62	4	3-12	0/0	79.00	0	
Manou Graham Allan	23.4.1979		1	2009	21	13*	0	21.00	–	–	–	–	2	4
Marr Alfred Percy	28.3.1862	15.3.1940	1	1884	5	5	0	2.50	0	0-3	–/–	–	0	
Marsh Geoffrey Robert	31.12.1958		50	1985–1991	2,854	138	4	33.18	0	–	–	–	38	117
Marsh Rodney William MBE	4.11.1947		96	1970–1984	3,633	132	3	26.51	0	0-3	–/–	–	343/12	92
Martin John Wesley	28.7.1931	16.7.1992	8	1960–1966	214	55	0	17.83	17	3-56	0/0	48.94	5	
Martyn Damien Richard	21.10.1971		67	1992–2006	4,406	165	13	46.37	2	1-0	0/0	84.00	36	208/4
Massie Hugh Hamon	11.4.1854	12.10.1938	9	1881–1884	249	55	0	15.56	0	–	–	–	5	
Massie Robert Arnold Lockyer	14.4.1947		6	1972–1972	78	42	0	11.14	31	8-53	2/1	20.87	1	3
Matthews Christopher Darrell	22.9.1962		3	1986–1988	54	32	0	10.80	6	3-95	0/0	52.16	1	
Matthews Gregory Richard John	15.12.1959		33	1983–1992	1,849	130	4	41.08	61	5-103	2/1	48.22	17	59
Matthews Thomas James	3.4.1884	14.10.1943	8	1911–1912	153	53	0	17.00	16	4-29	3/0	26.18	7	
May Timothy Brian Alexander	26.1.1962		24	1987–1994	225	42*	0	14.06	75	5-9	3/0	34.74	6	47
Mayne Edgar Richard	2.7.1882	26.10.1961	4	1912–1921	64	25*	0	21.33	0	0-1	0/0	–	2	
Mayne Lawrence Charles	23.1.1942		6	1964–1969	76	13	0	9.50	19	4-43	0/0	33.05	3	
Meckiff Ian	6.1.1935		18	1957–1963	154	45*	0	11.84	45	6-38	2/0	31.62	9	
Meuleman Kenneth Douglas	5.9.1923	10.9.2004	1	1945	0	0	0	0.00	–	–	–	–	–	
Midwinter William Evans	19.6.1851	3.12.1890	8†	1876–1886	174	37	0	13.38	14	5-78	1/0	23.78	5	
Miller Colin Reid	6.2.1964		18	1998–2000	174	43	0	8.28	69	5-32	3/1	26.15	5	
Miller Keith Ross MBE	28.11.1919	11.10.2004	55	1946–1956	2,958	147	7	36.97	170	7-60	7/1	22.97	38	
Minnett Roy Baldwin	13.6.1888	21.10.1955	9	1911–1912	391	90	0	26.06	11	4-34	0/0	26.36	0	
Misson Francis Michael	19.11.1938		5	1960–1961	38	25*	0	19.00	16	4-58	0/0	38.50	6	

	Born	Died	Tests	Test Career	Runs	HS	100s	Avge	Wkts	BB	5/10	Avge	Ct/St	O/T
Moody Thomas Masson	2.10.1965		8	1989–1992	456	106	2	32.57	2	1-17	0/0	73.50	9	–
Moroney John	24.7.1917	1.7.1999	7	1949–1951	383	118	2	34.81					0	
Morris Arthur Robert MBE	19.1.1922		46	1946–1954	3,533	206	12	46.48	2	1-5	0/0	25.00	15	
Morris Samuel	22.6.1855	20.9.1931	1	1884	14	10*	0	14.00	2	2-73	0/0	36.50	1	
Moses Henry	13.2.1858	7.12.1938	6	1886–1894	198	33	0	19.80					1	
Moss Jeffrey Kenneth	29.6.1947		1	1978	60	38*	0	60.00			–/–		0	
Moule William Henry	31.1.1858	24.8.1939	1	1880	40	34	0	20.00	3	3-23	0/0	7.66	1	–
Muller Scott Andrew	11.7.1971		2	1999	6	6*	0	–	7	3-68	0/0	36.85	2	
Murdoch William Lloyd	18.10.1854	18.2.1911	18*	1876–1890	896	211	2	32.00			–/–		14	1
Musgrove Henry Alfred	27.11.1858	2.11.1931	1	1884	13	9	0	6.50			–/–		0	
Nagel Lisle Ernest	6.3.1905	23.11.1971	1	1932	21	21*	0	21.00	2	2-110	0/0	55.00	0	
Nash Laurence John	2.5.1910	24.7.1986	2	1931–1936	30	17	0	15.00	10	4-18	0/0	12.60	6	2/1
Nicholson Matthew James	2.10.1974		1	1998	14	9	0	7.00	4	3-56	0/0	28.75	0	
Nitschke Homesdale Carl ("Jack")	14.4.1905	29.9.1982	2	1931	53	47	0	26.50			–/–		3	
Noble Montague Alfred	28.1.1873	22.6.1940	42	1897–1909	1,997	133	1	30.25	121	7-17	9/2	25.00	26	
Noblet Geffery	14.9.1916	16.8.2006	3	1949–1952	22	13*	0	7.33	7	3-21	0/0	26.14	1	
North Marcus James	28.7.1979		21	2008–2010	1,171	128	5	35.48	14	6-55	1/0	42.21	17	–
Nothling Otto Ernest	1.8.1900	26.9.1965	1	1928	52	44	0	26.00	0	0-12	–/–	–	0	
O'Brien Leo Patrick Joseph	2.7.1907	13.3.1981	5	1932–1936	211	61	0	26.37			–/–		3	
O'Connor John Denis Alphonsus	9.9.1875	23.8.1941	4	1907–1909	86	20	0	12.28	13	5-40	1/0	26.15	3	
O'Donnell Simon Patrick	26.1.1963		6	1985–1985	206	48	0	29.42	6	3-37	0/0	84.00	4	87
Ogilvie Alan David	3.6.1951		5	1977	178	47	0	17.80			–/–		5	
O'Keeffe Kerry James	25.11.1949		24	1970–1977	644	85	0	25.76	53	5-101	1/0	38.07	15	2
Oldfield William Albert [Stanley] MBE	9.9.1894	10.8.1976	54	1920–1936	1,427	65*	0	22.65					78/52	
O'Neill Norman Clifford	19.2.1937	3.3.2008	42	1958–1964	2,779	181	6	45.55	17	4-41	0/0	39.23	21	
O'Reilly William Joseph OBE	20.12.1905	6.10.1992	27	1931–1945	410	56*	0	12.81	144	7-54	11/3	22.59	7	
Oxenham Ronald Keven	28.7.1891	16.8.1939	7	1928–1931	151	48	0	15.10	14	4-39	0/0	37.28	4	
Paine Timothy David	8.12.1984		4	2010–2010	287	92	0	35.87					16/1	24/3
Palmer George Eugene	22.2.1859	22.8.1910	17	1880–1886	296	48	0	14.09	78	7-65	6/2	21.51	13	
Park Roy Lindsay	30.7.1892	23.1.1947	1	1920	0	0	0	0.00	0	0-9	0/0	–	0	
Pascoe Leonard Stephen	13.2.1950		14	1977–1981	106	30*	0	10.60	64	5-59	0/0	26.06	2	29
Pellew Clarence Everard ("Nip")	21.9.1893	9.5.1981	10	1920–1921	484	116	2	37.23	0	0-3	0/0	–	4	
Phillips Wayne Bentley	1.3.1958		27	1983–1985	1,485	159	2	32.28			–/–		52	48
Phillips Wayne Norman	7.11.1962		1	1991	22	14	0	11.00			–/–		0	
Philpott Peter Ian	21.11.1934		8	1964–1965	93	22	0	10.33	26	5-90	1/0	38.46	5	
Ponsford William Harold MBE	19.10.1900	6.4.1991	29	1924–1934	2,122	266	7	48.22			–/–		21	

	Born	Died	Tests	Test Career	Runs	HS	100s	Avge	Wkts	BB	5/10	Avge	Ct/St	O/T
Ponting Ricky Thomas	19.12.1974		152§	1995–2010	12,363	257	39	53.51	5	1-0	0/0	48.40	178	351‡/17
Pope Roland James	18.2.1864	27.7.1952	1	1884	3	3	0	1.50	–	–	–	–	–	
Rackemann Carl Gray	3.6.1960		12	1982–1990	53	15*	0	5.30	39	6-86	3/1	29.15	9	52
Ransford Vernon Seymour	20.3.1885	19.3.1958	20	1907–1911	1,211	143*	1	37.84	1	1-9	0/0	28.00	10	
Redpath Ian Ritchie MBE	11.5.1941		66	1963–1975	4,737	171	8	43.45	0	0-0	0/0	–	83	5
Reedman John Cole	9.10.1865	25.3.1924	1	1894	21	17	0	10.50	1	1-12	0/0	24.00	1	
Reid Bruce Anthony	14.3.1963		27	1985–1992	93	13	0	4.65	113	7-51	5/2	24.63	5	61
Reiffel Paul Ronald	19.4.1966		35	1991–1997	955	79*	0	26.52	104	6-71	5/0	26.96	15	92
Renneberg David Alexander	23.9.1942		8	1966–1967	22	9	0	3.66	23	5-39	2/0	36.08	2	
Richardson Arthur John	24.7.1888	23.12.1973	9	1924–1926	403	100	1	31.00	12	2-20	0/0	43.41	1	
⁴Richardson Victor York	7.9.1894	30.10.1969	19	1924–1935	706	138	1	23.53	–	–	–	–	24	
Rigg Keith Edward	21.5.1906	28.2.1995	8	1930–1936	401	127	1	33.41					5	
Ring Douglas Thomas	14.10.1918	23.6.2003	13	1947–1953	426	67	0	22.42	35	6-72	2/0	37.28	5	
Ritchie Gregory Michael	23.1.1960		30	1982–1986	1,690	146	3	35.20	0	0-10	0/0	–	14	44
Rixon Steven John	25.2.1954		13	1977–1984	394	54	0	18.76	–	–	–	–	42/5	6
Robertson Gavin Ron	28.5.1966		4	1997–1998	140	57	0	20.00	13	4-72	0/0	39.61	1	13
Robertson William Roderick	6.10.1861	24.6.1938	1	1884	2	2	0	1.00	0	0-24	0/0	–	–	
Robinson Richard Daryl	8.6.1946		3	1977	100	34	0	16.66	–	–	–	–	4	
Robinson Rayford Harold	26.3.1914	10.8.1965	1	1936	5	3	0	2.50					–	
Rogers Christopher John Llewellyn	31.8.1977		1	2007	19	15	0	9.50	–	–	–	–	1	
Rorke Gordon Frederick	27.6.1938		4	1958–1959	9	7	0	4.50	10	3-23	0/0	20.30	1	
Rutherford John Walter	25.9.1929		1	1956	30	30	0	30.00	1	1-11	0/0	15.00	–	
Ryder John	8.8.1889	3.4.1977	20	1920–1928	1,394	201*	3	51.62	17	2-20	0/0	43.70	17	
Saggers Ronald Arthur	15.5.1917	17.3.1987	6	1948–1949	30	14	0	10.00	–	–	–	–	16/8	
Saunders John Victor	21.3.1876	21.12.1927	14	1901–1907	39	11*	0	2.29	79	7-34	6/0	22.73	5	
Scott Henry James Herbert	26.12.1858	23.9.1910	8	1884–1886	359	102	1	27.61	0	0-9	0/0	–	8	
Sellers Reginald Hugh Durning	20.8.1940		1	1964	0	0	0	0.00	0	0-17	0/0	–	–	
Serjeant Craig Stanton	1.11.1951		12	1977–1977	522	124	1	23.72	–	–	–	–	13	3
⁵Sheahan Andrew Paul	30.9.1946		31	1967–1973	1,594	127	2	33.91	–	–	–	–	17	3
Shepherd Barry Kenneth	23.4.1937	17.9.2001	9	1962–1964	502	96	0	41.83	0	0-3	0/0	–	2	
Siddle Peter Matthew	25.11.1984		22	2008–2010	410	43	0	17.08	74	6-54	4/0	32.10	12	17/2
Sievers Morris William	13.4.1912	10.5.1968	3	1936	67	25*	0	13.40	9	5-21	1/0	17.88	4	
Simpson Robert Baddeley	3.2.1936		62	1957–1977	4,869	311	10	46.81	71	5-57	2/0	42.26	110	2
Sincock David John	1.2.1942		3	1964–1965	80	29	0	26.66	8	3-67	0/0	51.25	2	
Slater Keith Nichol	12.3.1936		1	1958	1	1*	–	–	2	2-40	0/0	50.50	–	

§ *Ponting's figures include 100 runs and one catch for Australia v the ICC World XI in the Super Series Test in 2005-06.*

	Born	Died	Tests	Test Career	Runs	HS	100s	Avge	Wkts	BB	5/10	Avge	Ct/St	O/T
Slater Michael Jonathon	21.2.1970		74	1993–2001	5,312	219	14	42.83	1	1-4	0/0	10.00	33	42
Sleep Peter Raymond	4.5.1957		14	1978–1989	483	90	0	24.15	31	5-72	1/0	45.06	4	
Slight James	20.10.1855	9.12.1930	1	1880	11	11	0	5.50	–	–	–/–	–	0	
Smith David Bertram Miller	14.9.1884	29.7.1963	2	1912	30	24*	0	15.00	–	–	–/–	–	0	
Smith Steven Barry	18.10.1961		3	1983	41	12	0	8.20	–	–	–/–	–	1	28
Smith Steven Peter Devereux	2.6.1989			2010–2010	259	77	0	28.77	3	3-51	0/0	73.33	11	9/14
Spofforth Frederick Robert	9.9.1853	4.6.1926	18	1876–1886	217	50	0	9.43	94	7-44	7/4	18.41	11	
Stackpole Keith Raymond MBE.	10.7.1940		43	1965–1973	2,807	207	7	37.42	15	2-33	0/0	66.73	47	6
Stevens Gavin Byron.	29.2.1932		4	1959	112	28	0	16.00	–	–	–/–	–	2	
Symonds Andrew.	9.6.1975		26	2003–2008	1,462	162*	2	40.61	24	3-50	0/0	37.33	22	198/14
Taber Hedley Brian	29.4.1940		16	1966–1969	353	48	0	16.04	–	–	–/–	–	56/4	
Tait Shaun William	22.2.1983		3	2005–2007	20	8	0	6.66	5	3-97	0/0	60.40	1	25/17
Tallon Donald	17.2.1916	7.9.1984	21	1945–1953	394	92	0	17.13	–	–	–/–	–	50/8	
Taylor John Morris	10.10.1895	12.5.1971	20	1920–1926	997	108	1	35.60	1	1-25	0/0	45.00	11	
Taylor Mark Anthony	27.10.1964		104	1988–1998	7,525	334*	19	43.49	1	1-11	0/0	26.00	157	113
Taylor Peter Laurence	22.8.1956		13	1986–1991	431	87	0	26.93	27	6-78	1/0	39.55	10	83
Thomas Grahame	21.3.1938		8	1964–1965	325	61	0	29.54	–	–	–/–	–	3	
Thoms George Ronald	22.3.1927	29.8.2003	1	1951	44	28	0	22.00	–	–	–/–	–	0	
Thomson Alan Lloyd ("Froggy")	2.12.1945		4	1970	22	12*	0	22.00	12	3-79	0/0	54.50	1	
Thomson Jeffrey Robert	16.8.1950		51	1972–1985	679	49	0	12.81	200	6-46	8/0	28.00	20	50
Thomson Nathaniel Frampton Davis	29.5.1839	2.9.1896	2	1876	67	41	0	16.75	1	1-14	0/0	31.00	3	
Thurlow Hugh Motley ("Pud")	10.1.1903	3.12.1975	1	1931	0	0	0	0.00	0	0-33	0/0	–	0	
Toohey Peter Michael	20.4.1954		15	1977–1979	893	122	1	31.89	0	0-4	0/0	–	9	5
Toshack Ernest Raymond Herbert.	8.12.1914	11.5.2003	12	1945–1948	73	20*	0	14.60	47	6-29	4/1	21.04	4	
Travers Joseph Patrick Francis.	10.1.1871	15.9.1942	1	1901	10	9	0	5.00	1	1-14	0/0	14.00	1	
Tribe George Edward	4.10.1920	5.4.2009	3	1946	35	25*	0	17.50	2	2-48	0/0	165.00	0	
Trott Albert Edwin	6.2.1873	30.7.1914	3†	1894	205	85*	0	102.50	9	8-43	1/0	21.33	4	
Trott George Henry Stevens.	5.8.1866	10.11.1917	24	1888–1897	921	143	1	21.92	29	4-71	0/0	35.13	21	
Trumble Hugh.	12.5.1867	14.8.1938	32	1890–1903	851	70	0	19.79	141	8-65	9/3	21.78	45	
Trumble John William	16.9.1863	17.8.1944	7	1884–1886	243	59	0	20.25	10	3-29	0/0	22.20	3	
Trumper Victor Thomas.	2.11.1877	28.6.1915	48	1899–1911	3,163	214*	8	39.04	8	3-60	0/0	39.62	31	6
Turner Alan.	23.7.1950		14	1975–1976	768	136	1	29.53	–	–	–/–	–	15	
Turner Charles Thomas Biass	16.11.1862	1.1.1944	17	1886–1894	323	29	0	11.53	101	7-43	11/2	16.53	8	
Veivers Thomas Robert.	6.4.1937		21	1963–1966	813	88	0	31.26	33	4-68	0/0	41.66	7	
Veletta Michael Robert John	30.10.1963		8	1987–1989	207	39	0	18.81	–	–	–/–	–	12	20
Waite Mervyn George.	7.1.1911	16.12.1985	2	1938	11	8	0	3.66	1	1-150	0/0	190.00	1	

Name	Born	Died	Tests	Test Career	Runs	HS	100s	Avge	Wkts	BB	5/10	Avge	Ct/St	O/T
Walker Maxwell Henry Norman ("Tim")	12.9.1948		34	1972-1977	586	78*	0	19.53	138	8-143	6/0	27.47	12	17
Wall Thomas Welbourn	13.5.1904	26.3.1981	18	1928-1934	121	20	0	6.36	56	5-14	3/0	35.89	11	
Walters Francis Henry	9.2.1860	1.6.1922	1	1884	12	7	0	6.00						
Walters Kevin Douglas MBE	21.12.1945		74	1965-1980	5,357	250	15	48.26	49	5-66	1/0	29.08	43	28
Ward Francis Anthony	23.2.1906	25.3.1974	4	1936-1938	36	18	0	6.00	11	6-102	1/0	52.18	1	
Warne Shane Keith	13.9.1969		145§	1991-2006	3,154	99	0	17.32	708	8-71	37/10	25.41	125	193‡
Watkins John Russell	16.4.1943		1	1972	39	36	0	39.00	0	0-21				
Watson Graeme Donald	8.3.1945		5	1966-1972	97	50	0	10.77	6	2-67	0/0	42.33	1	
Watson Shane Robert	17.6.1981		27§	2004-2010	1,953	126	2	41.55	43	6-33	2/0	31.41	21	117/20
Waugh William James	31.1.1931		4	1954	106	30	0	17.66	6	0-5	0/0		1	
[2] Waugh Mark Edward	2.6.1965		128	1990-2002	8,029	153*	20	41.81	59	5-40	1/0	41.16	181	244
Waugh Stephen Rodger	2.6.1965		168	1985-2003	10,927	200	32	51.06	92	5-28	3/0	37.44	112	325
Wellham Dirk Macdonald	13.3.1959		6	1981-1986	257	103	1	23.36					2	17
Wessels Kepler Christoffel	14.9.1957		24†	1982-1985	1,761	179	4	42.95	0	0-2	0/0		18	54‡
Whatmore Davenell Frederick	16.3.1954		7	1978-1979	293	77	0	22.53	0	0-11	0/0		13	1
White Cameron Leon	18.8.1983		4	2008	146	46	0	29.20	5	2-71	0/0	68.40	1	72/23
Whitney Michael Roy	24.2.1959		12	1981-1992	68	13	0	6.18	39	7-27	2/1	33.97	2	38
Whitty William James	15.8.1886	30.1.1974	14	1909-1912	161	39*	0	13.41	65	6-17	3/0	21.12	4	
Wiener Julien Mark	1.5.1955		6	1979	281	93	0	25.54	0	0-19	0/0		4	7
Williams Brad Andrew	20.11.1974		4	2003	23	10*	0	7.66	9	4-53	0/0	45.11	4	25
Wilson John William	20.8.1921	13.10.1985	1	1956	–	0*	0	–	1	1-25	0/0	64.00	0	
Wood Graeme Malcolm	6.11.1956		59	1977-1988	3,374	172	9	31.83	0	0-50	0/0		41	83
Woodcock Ashley James	27.2.1947		1	1973	27	27	0	27.00						
Woodfull William Maldon OBE	22.8.1897	11.8.1965	35	1926-1934	2,300	161	7	46.00					7	
Woods Samuel Moses James	13.4.1867	30.4.1931	3†	1888	32	18	0	5.33	5	2-35	0/0		1	
Woolley Roger Douglas	16.9.1954		2	1982-1983	21	13	0	10.50					7	4
Worrall John	20.6.1860	17.11.1937	11	1884-1899	478	76	0	25.15	1	1-97	0/0		13	
Wright Kevin John	27.12.1953		10	1978-1979	219	55*	0	16.84					31/4	5
Yallop Graham Neil	7.10.1952		39	1975-1984	2,756	268	8	41.13	1	1-21	0/0		23	30
Yardley Bruce	5.9.1947		33	1977-1982	978	74	0	19.56	126	7-98	6/1	31.63	31	
Young Shaun	13.6.1970		1	1997	4	4*	0	4.00	0	0-5	0/0		0	
Zoehrer Timothy Joseph	25.9.1961		10	1985-1986	246	52*	0	20.50					18/1	22

§ Warne's figures include 12 runs and six wickets and Watson's 34 runs and no wicket for Australia v the ICC World XI in the Super Series Test in 2005-06.

SOUTH AFRICA (309 players)

	Born	Died	Tests	Test Career	Runs	HS	100s	Avge	Wts	BB	5/10	Avge	Ct/St	O/T
Ackerman Hylton Deon	14.2.1973		4	1997	161	57	0	20.12	–	–	–/–	–	1	
Adams Paul Regan	20.1.1977		45	1995–2003	360	35	0	9.00	134	7-128	4/1	32.87	29	24
Adcock Neil Amwin Treharne	8.3.1931		26	1953–1961	146	24	0	5.40	104	6-43	5/0	21.10	4	
Amla Hashim Mahomed	31.3.1983		51	2004–2010	3,897	253*	12	46.95	0	0-4	0/0	–	46	37/2
Anderson James Henry	26.4.1874	11.3.1926	1	1902	43	32	0	21.50	–	–	–/–	–		
Ashley William Hare	10.2.1862	14.7.1930	1	1888	1	1	0	0.50	7	7-95	1/0	13.57		
Bacher Adam Marc	29.10.1973		19	1996–1999	833	96	0	26.03	–	0-4	0/0	–	11	13
Bacher Aron ("Ali")	24.5.1942		12	1965–1969	679	73	0	32.33	–	–	–/–	–	10	
Balaskas Xenophon Constantine	15.10.1910	12.5.1994	9	1930–1938	174	122*	1	14.50	22	5-49	1/0	36.63	5	
Barlow Edgar John	12.8.1940	30.12.2005	30	1961–1969	2,516	201	6	45.74	40	5-85	1/0	34.05	35	
Baumgartner Harold Vane	17.11.1883	8.4.1938	1	1913	19	16	0	9.50	2	2-99	0/0	49.50	1	
Beaumont Rolland	4.2.1884	25.5.1958	5	1912–1913	70	31	0	7.77	–	–	–/–	–	2	
Begbie Denis Warburton	12.12.1914	10.3.2009	5	1948–1949	138	48	0	19.71	1	1-38	0/0	130.00	1	
Bell Alexander John	15.4.1906	1.8.1985	16	1929–1935	69	26*	0	6.27	48	6-99	4/0	32.64	6	
Bisset Sir Murray	14.4.1876	24.10.1931	3	1898–1909	103	35	0	25.75	–	–	–/–	–	2/1	
Bissett George Finlay	5.11.1905	14.11.1965	4	1927	38	23	0	19.00	25	7-29	2/0	18.76	0	
Blanckenberg James Manuel	31.12.1892	c. 1955	18	1913–1924	455	59	0	19.78	60	6-76	4/0	30.28	9	
Bland Kenneth Colin	5.4.1938		21	1961–1966	1,669	144*	3	49.08	2	2-16	0/0	62.50	10	
Bock Ernest George	17.9.1908	5.9.1961	1	1935	11	9*	0	–	0	0-42	0/0	–	0	
Boje Nico	20.3.1973		43	1999–2006	1,312	85	0	25.23	100	5-62	3/0	42.65	18	113‡/1
Bond Gerald Edward	5.4.1909	27.8.1965	1	1938	0	0	0	0.00	0	0-16	0/0	–	0	
Bosch Tertius	14.3.1966	14.2.2000	1	1991	5	5*	0	–	3	2-61	0/0	34.66	0	2
Botha Johan	2.5.1982		5	2005–2010	83	25	0	20.75	17	4-56	0/0	33.70	3	62‡/25
Botten James Thomas ("Jackie")	21.6.1938	14.5.2006	3	1965	65	33	0	10.83	8	2-56	0/0	42.12	1	
Boucher Mark Verdon	3.12.1976		147	1997–2010	5,295	125	5	30.96	1	1-6	0/0	6.00	497/22	287‡/25
Brann William Henry	4.4.1899	22.9.1953	3	1922	71	50	0	14.20	–	–	–/–	–	2	
Briscoe Arthur Wellesley ("Dooley")	6.2.1911	22.4.1941	2	1935–1938	33	16	0	11.00					0	
Bromfield Harry Dudley	26.6.1932		9	1961–1965	59	21	0	11.80	17	5-88	1/0	35.23	13	
Brown Lennox Sidney	24.11.1910	1.9.1983	2	1931	17	8	0	5.66	3	1-30	0/0	63.00	0	
Burger Christopher George de Villiers	12.7.1935		2	1957	62	37*	0	20.66	–	–	–/–	–	1	
Burke Sydney Frank	11.3.1934		2	1961–1964	42	20	0	14.00	11	6-128	2/1	23.36	0	
Buys Isaac Daniel	4.2.1895	d unknown	1	1922	4	4*	0	4.00	0	0-20	0/0	–	0	

‡ *Boucher's figures exclude 17 runs and two catches for the ICC World XI v Australia in the Super Series Test in 2005-06.*

Name	Born	Died	Tests	Test Career	Runs	HS	100s	Avge	Wkts	BB	5/10	Avge	Ct/St	O/T
Cameron Horace Brakenridge ("Jock")	5.7.1905	2.11.1935	26	1927–1935	1,239	90	0	30.21	–	–	–/–	–	39/12	
Campbell Thomas	9.2.1882	5.10.1924	5	1909–1912	90	48	0	15.00	–	–	–/–	–	7/1	
Carlstein Peter Rudolph	28.10.1938		8	1957–1963	190	42	0	14.61	–	–	–/–	–	3	
Carter Claude Padgett	23.4.1881	8.11.1952	10	1912–1924	181	45	0	18.10	28	6-50	2/0	24.78	2	
Catterall Robert Hector	10.7.1900	3.1.1961	24	1922–1930	1,555	120	3	37.92	7	3-15	0/0	23.14	12	
Chapman Horace William	30.6.1890	1.12.1941	2	1913–1921	39	17	0	13.00	–	–	–/–	–	1	
Cheetham John Erskine	26.5.1920	21.8.1980	24	1948–1955	883	89	0	23.86	1	1-51	0/0	104.00	13	
Chevalier Grahame Anton	9.3.1937		1	1969	0	0*	0	0.00	0	0-2	0/0	–	–	
Christy James Alexander Joseph	12.12.1904	1.2.1971	10	1929–1931	618	103	1	34.33	2	2-13	0/0	20.00	13	
Chubb Geoffrey Walter Ashton	12.4.1911	28.8.1982	5	1951	63	15*	0	10.50	21	6-51	2/0	27.47	3	
Cochran John Alexander Kennedy	15.7.1909	15.6.1987	1	1930	8	4	0	4.00	1	1-46	0/0	46.00	1	
Coen Stanley Keppel ("Shunter")	14.10.1902	29.11.1967	2	1927	101	41*	0	50.50	0	0-47	0/0	–	0	
Commaille John McIllwaine Moore ("Mick")	21.2.1883	28.7.1956	12	1909–1927	355	47	0	16.90	–	–	–/–	–	1	
Commins John Brian	19.2.1965		3	1994	125	45	0	25.00	–	–	–/–	–	–	
Conyngham Dalton Parry	10.5.1897	7.7.1979	1	1922	6	3*	0	3.00	2	1-40	0/0	51.50	2	
Cook Frederick James	1870	30.11.1915	1	1895	7	7	0	3.50	–	–	–/–	–	–	
Cook Stephen James	31.7.1953		3	1992–1993	107	43	0	17.83	–	–	–/–	–	1	4
Cooper Alfred Henry Cecil	2.9.1893	18.7.1963	1	1913	6	6	0	3.00	–	–	–/–	–	0	
Cox Joseph Lovell	28.6.1886	4.7.1971	3	1913	17	12*	0	3.40	–	–	–/–	–	1	
Cripps Godfrey	19.10.1865	27.7.1943	1	1891	21	18	0	10.50	4	4-74	0/0	61.25	–	
Crisp Robert James	28.5.1911	2.3.1994	9	1935–1936	123	35	0	10.25	20	5-99	1/0	37.35	1	
Cronje Wessel Johannes ("Hansie")	25.9.1969	1.6.2002	68	1991–1999	3,714	135	6	36.41	43	3-14	0/0	29.95	33	188
Cullinan Daryll John	4.3.1967		70	1992–2000	4,554	275*	14	44.21	2	1-10	0/0	35.50	67	138
Curnow Sydney Harry	16.12.1907	28.7.1986	7	1930–1931	168	85	0	12.00	–	–	–/–	–	5	
Dalton Eric Londesbrough	2.12.1906	3.6.1981	15	1929–1938	698	117	2	31.72	12	4-59	0/0	40.83	5	
Davies Eric Quail	26.8.1909	11.11.1976	5	1935–1938	9	9	0	1.80	7	4-75	0/0	68.71	5	
Dawson Alan Charles	27.11.1969		2	2003	10	3	0	10.00	5	2-20	0/0	23.40	10	
Dawson Oswald Charles	1.9.1919	22.12.2008	9	1947–1948	293	55	0	20.92	10	2-57	0/0	57.80	8	
Deane Hubert Gouvaine ("Nummy")	21.7.1895	21.10.1939	17	1924–1930	628	93	0	25.12	2	1-6	0/0	30.66	10	
de Bruyn Zander	5.7.1975		3	2004	155	83	0	38.75	3	2-32	0/0	49.50	–	19
de Villiers Abraham Benjamin	17.2.1984		66	2004–2010	4,741	278*	12	47.41	–	–	–/–	–	93/1	104/32
de Villiers Petrus Stephanus ("Fanie")	13.10.1964		18	1993–1997	359	67*	0	18.89	85	6-23	5/2	24.27	11	83
de Wet Friedel	26.6.1980		2	2009	20	3	0	10.00	6	4-55	0/0	31.00	1	
Dippenaar Hendrik Human ("Boeta")	14.6.1977		38	1999–2006	1,718	177*	3	30.14	–	–	–/–	–	27	107/1
Dixon Cecil Donovan	12.2.1891	9.9.1969	1	1913	0	0	0	0.00	3	2-62	0/0	39.33	–	
Donald Allan Anthony	20.10.1966		72	1991–2001	652	37	0	10.68	330	8-71	20/3	22.25	18	164

	Born	Died	Tests	Test Career	Runs	HS	100s	Avge	Wkts	BB	5/10	Avge	Ct/St	O/T
Dower Robert Reid	4.6.1876	15.9.1964	1	1898	9	9	0	4.50	–	–	–/–	–	2	
Draper Ronald George	24.12.1926		2	1949	25	15	0	8.33	–	–	–/–	–	0	
Duckworth Christopher Anthony Russell	22.3.1933		2	1956	28	13	0	7.00	–	–	–/–	–	3	
Dumbrill Richard	19.11.1938		5	1965–1966	153	36	0	15.30	9	4-30	0/0	37.33	3	
Duminy Jacobus Petrus	16.12.1897	31.1.1980	3	1927–1929	30	12	0	5.00	1	1-17	0/0	39.00	2	
Duminy Jean-Paul	14.4.1984		12	2008–2009	518	166	1	28.77	11	3-89	0/0	37.09	12	66/29
Dunell Owen Robert	15.7.1856	21.10.1929	2	1888	42	26*	0	14.00	–	–	–/–	–	1	
Du Preez John Harcourt	14.11.1942		2	1966	0	0	0	0.00	3	2-22	0/0	17.00	1	
Du Toit Jacobus Francois	2.4.1869	10.7.1909	1	1891	2	2*	0	–	1	1-47	0/0	47.00		
Dyer Dennis Victor	2.5.1914	16.6.1990	3	1947	96	62	0	16.00	–	–	–/–	–	2	
Eksteen Clive Edward	2.12.1966		7	1993–1999	91	22	0	10.11	8	3-12	0/0	61.75	5	6
Elgie Michael Kelsey ("Kim")	6.3.1933		3	1961	75	56	0	12.50	0	0-18	0/0	–	4	
Elworthy Steven	23.2.1965		4	1998–2002	72	48	0	18.00	13	4-66	0/0	34.15	1	39
Endean William Russell	31.5.1924	28.6.2003	28	1951–1957	1,630	162*	3	33.95	–	–	–/–	–	41	
Farrer William Stephen ("Buster")	8.12.1936		6	1961–1963	221	40	0	27.62	–	–	–/–	–	6	
Faulkner George Aubrey	17.12.1881	10.9.1930	25	1905–1924	1,754	204	4	40.79	82	7-84	4/0	26.58	20	
Fellows-Smith Jonathan Payn	3.2.1932		4	1960	166	35	0	27.66	0	0-13	0/0	–	2	
Fichardt Charles Gustav	20.3.1870	30.5.1923	2	1891–1895	15	10	0	3.75	–	–	–/–	–	2	
Finlason Charles Edward	19.2.1860	31.7.1917	1	1888	6	6	0	3.00	0	0-7	0/0	–	0	
Floquet Claude Eugene	3.11.1884	22.11.1963	1	1909	12	11*	0	12.00	0	0-24	0/0	–	0	
Francis Howard Henry	26.5.1868	7.1.1936	2	1898	39	29	0	9.75	–	–	–/–	–	1	
Francois Cyril Matthew	20.6.1897	26.5.1944	5	1922	252	72	0	31.50	6	3-23	0/0	37.50	5	
Frank Charles Newton	27.11.1891	25.12.1961	3	1921	236	152	1	39.33	–	–	–/–	–	2	
Frank William Hughes Bowker	23.11.1872	16.2.1945	1	1895	7	5	0	3.50	1	1-52	0/0	52.00	0	
Fuller Edward Russell Henry	2.8.1931	19.7.2008	7	1952–1957	64	17	0	8.00	22	5-66	1/0	30.36	3	
Fullerton George Murray	8.12.1922	19.11.2002	7	1947–1951	325	88	0	25.00	–	–	–/–	–	10/2	
Funston Kenneth James	3.12.1925	15.4.2005	18	1952–1957	824	92	0	25.75	–	–	–/–	–	7	
Gamsy Dennis	17.2.1940		2	1969	39	30*	0	19.50	–	–	–/–	–	5	
Gibbs Herschelle Herman	23.2.1974		90	1996–2007	6,167	228	14	41.95	0	0-4	0/0	–	94	248/23
Gleeson Robert Anthony	6.12.1873	27.9.1919	1	1895	4	3	0	4.00	–	–	–/–	–	2	
Glover George Keyworth	13.5.1870	15.11.1938	1	1895	21	18*	0	21.00	1	1-28	0/0	28.00		
Goddard Trevor Leslie	1.8.1931		41	1955–1969	2,516	112	1	34.46	123	6-53	5/0	26.22	48	
Gordon Norman	6.8.1911		5	1938	8	7*	0	2.00	20	5-103	2/0	40.35	1	
Graham Robert	16.9.1877	21.4.1946	2	1898	6	4	0	1.50	3	2-22	0/0	42.33	2	
Grieveson Ronald Eustace	24.8.1909	24.7.1998	2	1938	114	75	0	57.00	–	–	–/–	–	7/3	
Griffin Geoffrey Merton	12.6.1939	16.11.2006	2	1960	25	14	0	6.25	8	4-87	0/0	24.00	2	

	Born	Died	Tests	Test Career	Runs	HS	100s	Avge	Wkts	BB	5/10	Avge	Ct/St	OIT
Hall Alfred Ewart	23.1.1896	1.1.1964	7	1922–1930	11	5	0	1.83	40	7-63	3/1	22.15	4	88/2
Hall Andrew James	31.7.1975		21	2001–2006	760	163	1	26.20	45	3-1	0/0	35.93	16	
Hall Glen Gordon	24.5.1938	26.6.1987	1	1964	0	0	0	0.00	1	1-94	0/0	94.00	0	
Halliwell Ernest Austin	7.9.1864	2.10.1919	8	1891–1902	188	57	0	12.53			–/–		10/2	
Halse Clive Gray	28.2.1935	28.5.2002	3	1963	30	19*	0		6	3-50	0/0	43.33	1	
²**Hands** Philip Albert Myburgh	18.3.1890	27.4.1951	7	1913–1924	300	83	0	25.00	0	0-1	–/–		3	
²**Hands** Reginald Harry Myburgh	26.7.1888	20.4.1918	1	1913	7	7	0	3.50			–/–			
Hanley Martin Andrew	10.11.1918	2.6.2000	1	1948	0	0	0	0.00	1	1-57	0/0	88.00	0	
Harris Paul Lee	2.11.1978		37	2006–2010	460	46	0	10.69	103	6-127	3/0	37.87	16	3
Harris Terence Anthony	27.8.1916	7.3.1993	3	1947–1948	100	60	0	25.00			–/–		1	
Hartigan Gerald Patrick Desmond	30.12.1884	7.1.1955	5	1912–1913	114	51	0	11.40	1	1-72	0/0	141.00	0	
Harvey Robert Lyon	14.9.1911	20.7.2000	2	1935	51	28	0	12.75			–/–		0	
Hathorn Christopher Maitland Howard	7.4.1878	17.5.1920	12	1902–1910	325	102	1	17.10			–/–		5	
Hayward Mornantau ("Nantie")	6.3.1977		16	1999–2004	66	14	0	7.33	54	5-56	1/0	29.79	4	21
¹·²**Hearne** Frank	23.11.1858	14.7.1949	4†	1891–1895	121	30	0	15.12	2	2-40	0/0	20.00	4	
¹**Hearne** George Alfred Lawrence	27.3.1888	13.11.1978	3	1922–1924	59	28	0	11.80			–/–		2	
Heine Peter Samuel	28.6.1928	4.2.2005	14	1955–1961	209	31	0	9.95	58	6-58	4/0	25.08	8	
Henderson Claude William	14.6.1972		7	2001–2002	65	30	0	9.28	22	4-116	0/0	42.18	2	4
Henry Omar	23.1.1952		3	1992	53	34	0	17.66	3	1-26	0/0	63.00	2	3
Hime Charles Frederick William	24.10.1869	6.12.1940	1	1895	8	8	0	4.00	1	1-20	0/0	31.00	0	
Hudson Andrew Charles	17.3.1965		35	1991–1997	2,007	163	4	33.45			–/–		36	89
Hutchinson Philip	25.1.1862	30.9.1925	2	1888	14	11	0	3.50			–/–		0	
Ironside David Ernest James	2.5.1925	21.8.2005	3	1953	37	13	0	18.50	15	5-51	1/0	18.33	1	
Irvine Brian Lee	9.3.1944		4	1969	353	102	1	50.42			–/–		2	
Jack Steven Douglas	4.8.1970		2	1994	10	7	0	5.00	8	4-69	0/0	24.50	1	2
Johnson Clement Lecky	31.3.1871	31.5.1908	1	1895	10	7	0	5.00	2	0-57	0/0		0	
Kallis Jacques Henry	16.10.1975		144§	1995–2010	11,864	201*	40	57.31	269	6-54	5/0	31.98	162	302‡/16
Keith Headley James	25.10.1927	17.11.1997	8	1952–1956	318	73	0	21.20	9	0-19	0/0		9	
Kemp Justin Miles	2.10.1977		5	2000–2005	80	55	0	13.33	3	3-33	0/0	24.66	3	79‡/8
Kempis Gustav Adolph	4.8.1865	19.5.1890	1	1888	0	0*	0	0.00	4	3-53	0/0	19.00	0	
Khan Imran	27.4.1984		1	2008	20	20	0	20.00			–/–			
²**Kirsten** Gary	23.11.1967		101	1993–2003	7,289	275	21	45.27	2	1-0	0/0	71.00	83	185
²**Kirsten** Peter Noel	14.5.1955		12	1991–1994	626	104	0	31.30	5	0-5	0/0		8	40
Klusener Lance	4.9.1971		49	1996–2004	1,906	174	4	32.86	80	8-64	1/0	37.91	34	171
Kotze Johannes Jacobus ("Kodgee")	7.8.1879	7.7.1931	3	1902–1907	2	2	0	0.40	6	3-64	0/0	40.50	3	

§ *Kallis's figures exclude 83 runs, one wicket and four catches for the ICC World XI v Australia in the Super Series Test in 2005-06.*

	Born	Died	Tests	Test Career	Runs	HS	100s	Avge	Wkts	BB	5/10	Avge	Ct/St	O/T
Kuiper Adrian Paul	24.8.1959	—	1	1991	34	34	0	17.00	—	—	—	—	1	25
Kuys Frederick	21.3.1870	12.9.1953	1	1898	26	26	0	13.00	2	2-31	0/0	15.50	0	
Lance Herbert Roy ("Tiger")	6.6.1940	10.11.2010	13	1961–1969	591	70	0	28.14	12	3-30	0/0	39.91	7	
Langeveldt Charl Kenneth	17.12.1974	—	6	2004–2005	16	10	0	8.00	16	5-46	1/0	37.06	1	72/9
Langton Arthur Chudleigh Beaumont	2.3.1912	27.11.1942	15	1935–1938	298	73*	0	15.68	40	5-58	1/0	45.67	8	
Lawrence Godfrey Bernard	31.3.1932	—	5	1961	141	43	0	17.62	28	8-53	2/0	18.28	2	
le Roux Frederick Louis	5.2.1882	22.9.1963	1	1913	1	1	0	0.50	0	0-5	0/0	—	0	
Lewis Percy Tyson	2.10.1884	30.1.1976	1	1913	0	0	0	0.00	—	—	—	—	0	
Liebenberg Gerhardus Frederick Johannes	7.4.1972	—	5	1997–1998	104	45	0	13.00	—	—	—	—	4	4
Lindsay Denis Thomson	4.9.1939	30.11.2005	19	1963–1969	1,130	182	3	37.66	—	—	—	—	57/2	
Lindsay John Dixon	8.9.1908	31.8.1990	3	1947	21	9*	0	7.00	—	—	—	—	4/1	
Lindsay Nevil Vernon	30.7.1886	2.2.1976	1	1921	35	29	0	17.50	—	—	—	—	1	
Ling William Victor Stone	3.10.1891	26.9.1960	6	1921–1922	168	38	0	16.80	0	0-20	0/0	—	7	
Llewellyn Charles Bennett	26.9.1876	7.6.1964	15	1895–1912	544	90	0	20.14	48	6-92	4/1	29.60	7	
Lundie Eric Balfour	15.3.1888	12.9.1917	1	1913	1	1	0	1.00	4	4-101	0/0	26.75	0	
Macaulay Michael John	19.4.1939	—	1	1964	33	21	0	16.50	2	1-10	0/0	36.50	0	
McCarthy Cuan Neil	24.3.1929	14.8.2000	15	1948–1951	28	5	0	3.11	36	6-43	2/0	41.94	6	
McGlew Derrick John ("Jackie")	11.3.1929	9.6.1998	34	1951–1961	2,440	255*	7	42.06	0	0-7	0/0	—	18	
McKenzie Neil Douglas	24.11.1975	—	58	2000–2008	3,253	226	5	37.39	0	0-1	0/0	—	54	64/2
McKinnon Atholl Henry	20.8.1932	2.12.1983	8	1960–1966	107	27	0	17.83	26	4-128	0/0	35.57	5	
McLaren Ryan	9.2.1983	—	1	2009	33	33*	0	33.00	1	1-30	0/0	43.00	0	10/5
McLean Roy Alastair	9.7.1930	26.8.2007	40	1951–1964	2,120	142	5	30.28	—	—	—	—	23	
McMillan Brian Mervin	22.12.1963	—	38	1992–1998	1,968	113	3	39.36	75	4-65	0/0	33.82	49	78
McMillan Quintin	23.6.1904	3.7.1948	13	1929–1931	306	50*	0	18.00	36	5-66	2/0	34.52	8	
Mann Norman Bertram Fleetwood ("Tufty")	28.12.1920	31.7.1952	19	1947–1951	400	52	0	13.33	28	6-59	1/0	24.78	3	
Mansell Percy Neville Frank MBE	16.3.1920	9.5.1995	13	1951–1955	355	90	0	17.75	11	3-58	0/0	66.90	15	
Markham Lawrence Anderson	12.9.1924	5.8.2000	1	1948	20	20	0	20.00	1	1-34	0/0	72.00	0	
Marx Waldemar Frederick Eric	4.7.1895	2.6.1974	3	1921	125	36	0	20.83	4	3-85	0/0	36.00	0	
Matthews Craig Russell	15.2.1965	—	18	1992–1995	348	62*	0	18.31	62	5-42	2/0	28.88	15	56
Meintjes Douglas James	9.6.1890	17.7.1979	2	1922	43	21	0	14.33	6	3-38	0/0	16.00	4	
Melle Michael George	3.6.1930	28.12.2003	7	1949–1952	68	17	0	8.50	26	6-71	2/0	19.16	3	
Melville Alan	19.5.1910	18.4.1983	11	1938–1948	894	189	4	52.58	—	—	—	—	8	
Middleton James	30.9.1865	23.12.1913	6	1895–1902	52	22	0	7.42	24	5-51	2/0	18.41	1	
Mills Charles Henry	26.11.1867	26.7.1948	1	1891	25	21	0	12.50	2	2-83	0/0	41.50	2	
Milton Sir William Henry	3.12.1854	6.3.1930	3	1888–1891	68	21	0	11.33	2	1-5	0/0	24.00	4	
Mitchell Bruce	8.1.1909	1.7.1995	42	1929–1948	3,471	189*	8	48.88	27	5-87	1/0	51.11	56	

Name	Born	Died	Tests	Test Career	Runs	HS	100s	Avge	Wkts	BB	5/10	Avge	Ct/St	O/T
Mitchell Frank	13.8.1872	11.10.1935	3†	1912	28	12	0	4.66	—	—	—/—	—	0	—
²Morkel Denijs Paul Beck	25.11.1906	6.10.1980	16	1927–1931	663	88	0	24.55	18	4-93	—/—	45.61	13	49½/31
²Morkel Johannes Albertus	10.6.1981			2008	58	58	0	58.00	1	1-44	0/0	132.00	0	30½/17
²Morkel Morne	6.10.1984		31	2006–2010	481	40	0	14.57	113	5-20	4/0	30.22	7	
Murray Anton Ronald Andrew	30.4.1922	17.4.1995	10	1952–1953	289	109	1	22.23	18	4-169	0/0	39.44	3	
Nel Andre	15.7.1977		36	2001–2008	337	34	0	9.91	123	6-32	3/1	31.86	16	79/2
Nel John Desmond	10.7.1928		6	1949–1957	150	38	0	13.63	—	—	—	—	1	
Newberry Claude	1889	1.8.1916	4	1913	62	16	0	7.75	11	4-72	0/0	24.36	3	
Newson Edward Serrurier OBE	2.12.1910	24.4.1988	3	1930–1938	30	16	0	7.50	4	2-58	0/0	66.25	3	
Ngam Mfuneko	29.1.1979		3	2000	0	0*	0	—	11	3-26	0/0	17.18	1	
Nicolson Frank	17.9.1909	30.7.1982	4	1935	76	29	0	10.85	0	0-5	—/—	—	3	
Nicolson John Fairless William	19.7.1899	13.12.1935	3	1927	179	78	0	35.80	0	—	—	—	—	
Norton Norman Ogilvie	11.5.1881	27.6.1968	1	1909	9	7	0	4.50	4	4-47	0/0	11.75	—	
¹Nourse Arthur Dudley	12.11.1910	14.8.1981	34	1935–1951	2,960	231	9	53.81	0	0-0	—/—	—	12	
¹Nourse Arthur William ("Dave")	25.1.1879	8.7.1948	45	1902–1924	2,234	111	1	29.78	41	4-25	0/0	37.87	43	
Nitini Makhaya	6.7.1977		101	1997–2009	699	32*	0	9.84	390	7-37	18/4	28.82	25	172½/9
Nupen Eiulf Peter ("Buster")	1.1.1902	29.1.1977	17	1921–1935	348	69	0	14.50	50	6-46	5/1	35.76	9	
Ochse Arthur Edward	11.3.1870	11.4.1918	2	1888	16	8	0	4.00	—	—	—/—	—	0	
Ochse Arthur Lennox	11.10.1899	5.5.1949	3	1927–1929	11	4*	0	3.66	10	4-79	—/—	36.20	4	
O'Linn Sidney	5.5.1927		7	1960–1961	297	98	0	27.00	1	1-79	0/0	133.00	4	
Ontong Justin Lee	4.1.1980		2	2001–2004	57	32	0	19.00	0	0-3	0/0	—	1	
Owen-Smith Harold Geoffrey ("Tuppy")	18.2.1909	28.2.1990	5	1929	252	129	1	42.00	—	—	—/—	—	4	25½/3
Palm Archibald William	8.6.1901	17.8.1966	1	1927	15	13	0	7.50	—	—	—	—	1	
Parker George Macdonald	27.5.1899	1.5.1969	2	1924	3	2*	0	3.00	8	6-152	1/0	34.12	—	
Parkin Durant Clifford	20.2.1873	20.3.1936	1	1891	6	6	0	6.00	3	3-82	0/0	27.33	1	
Parnell Wayne Dillon	30.7.1989		3	2009	34	22	0	17.00	5	2-17	0/0	45.40	1	
Partridge Joseph Titus	9.12.1932	6.6.1988	11	1963–1964	73	13*	0	10.42	44	7-91	3/0	31.20	6	15/10
Pearse Charles Ormerod Cato	10.10.1884	7.5.1953	1	1910	55	31	0	9.16	3	3-56	0/0	35.33	—	
Pegler Sidney James	28.7.1888	10.9.1972	16	1909–1924	356	35*	0	15.47	47	7-65	1/0	33.44	5	
Petersen Alviro Nathan	25.11.1980		6	2009–2010	572	100	1	33.64	—	—	0/0	36.00	5	
Peterson Robin John	4.8.1979		9	2003–2007	163	61	0	27.16	14	5-33	1/0	35.50	5	
²Pithey Anthony John	17.7.1933	17.11.2006	17	1956–1964	819	154	1	31.50	0	0-5	0/0	—	5	
²Pithey David Bartlett	4.10.1936		8	1963–1966	138	55	0	12.54	12	6-58	1/0	48.08	3	
Plimsoll Jack Bruce	27.10.1917	11.11.1999	1	1947	16	8*	0	16.00	3	3-128	0/0	47.66	6	
¹·²Pollock Peter Maclean	30.6.1941		28	1961–1969	607	75*	0	21.67	116	6-38	9/1	24.18	9	14/2
²Pollock Robert Graeme	27.2.1944		23	1963–1969	2,256	274	7	60.97	4	2-50	0/0	51.00	17	38/6

	Born	Died	Tests	Test Career	Runs	HS	100s	Avge	Wts	BB	5/10	Avge	Ct/St	O/T
[1]Pollock Shaun Maclean	16.7.1973		108	1995–2007	3,781	111	2	32.31	421	7-87	16/1	23.11	72	294¾/12
Poore Robert Montagu	20.3.1866	14.7.1938	3	1895	76	20	0	12.66	1	1-4	0/0	4.00	3	
Pothecary James Edward	6.12.1933		3	1960	26	12	0	6.50	9	4-58	0/0	39.33	2	
Powell Albert William	18.7.1873	11.9.1948	1	1898	16	11	0	8.00	0	1-10	0/0	10.00	2	
Pretorius Dewald	6.12.1977		4	2001–2003	22	9	0	7.33	6	4-115	0/0	71.66	0	
Prince Ashwell Gavin	28.5.1977		62	2001–2010	3,556	162*	11	43.36	1	1-2	0/0	47.00	42	49½/1
Prince Charles Frederick Henry	11.9.1874	2.2.1949	1	1898	6	5	0	3.00	–	–	–/–	–	0	
Pringle Meyrick Wayne	22.6.1966		4	1991–1995	67	33	0	16.75	5	2-62	0/0	54.00	0	17
Procter Michael John	15.9.1946		7	1966–1969	226	48	0	25.11	41	6-73	1/0	15.02	4	
Promnitz Henry Louis Ernest	23.2.1904	7.9.1983	2	1927	14	5	0	3.50	8	5-58	1/0	20.12	1	
Quinn Neville Anthony	21.2.1908	5.8.1934	12	1929–1931	90	28	0	6.00	35	6-92	1/0	32.71	1	
Reid Norman	26.12.1890	6.6.1947	1	1921	17	11	0	8.50	2	2-63	0/0	31.50	0	
Rhodes Jonathan Neil	27.7.1969		52	1992–2000	2,532	117	3	35.66	0	0-0	0/0	–	34	245
[2]Richards Alfred Renfrew	14.12.1867	9.1.1904	1	1895	6	6	0	3.00	–	–	–/–	–	0	
Richards Barry Anderson	21.7.1945		4	1969	508	140	2	72.57	1	1-12	0/0	26.00	3	
[2]Richards William Henry Matthews	26.3.1862	4.1.1903	1	1888	4	4	0	2.00	–	–	–/–	–	0/0	
Richardson David John	16.9.1959		42	1991–1997	1,359	109	0	24.26	–	–	–/–	–	150/2	122
Robertson John Benjamin	5.6.1906		3	1935	51	17	0	10.20	6	3-143	0/0	53.50	2	
Rose-Innes Albert	16.2.1868	22.11.1946	2	1888	14	13	0	3.50	5	5-43	1/0	17.80	2	
Routledge Thomas William	18.4.1867	9.5.1927	4	1891–1895	72	24	0	9.00	–	–	–/–	–	2	
[2]Rowan Athol Matthew Burchell	7.2.1921	22.2.1998	15	1947–1951	290	41	0	17.05	54	5-68	4/0	38.59	7	
[2]Rowan Eric Alfred Burchell	20.7.1909	30.4.1993	26	1935–1951	1,965	236	3	43.66	0	0-0	0/0	–	14	
Rowe George Alexander	15.6.1874	8.1.1950	5	1895–1902	26	13*	0	4.33	15	5-115	1/0	30.40	4	
Rudolph Jacobus Andries	4.5.1981		35	2003–2006	2,028	222*	5	36.21	4	1-1	0/0	108.00	22	43½/1
Rushmere Mark Weir	7.1.1965		1	1991	6	3	0	3.00	–	–	–/–	–	0	
Samuelson Sivert Vause	21.11.1883	18.11.1958	1	1909	22	15	0	11.00	0	0-64	0/0	–	1	
Schultz Brett Nolan	26.8.1970		9	1992–1997	9	6	0	1.50	37	5-48	2/0	20.24	2	
Schwarz Reginald Oscar	4.5.1875	18.11.1918	20	1905–1912	374	61	0	13.85	55	6-47	2/0	25.76	18	
Seccull Arthur William	14.9.1868	20.7.1945	1	1895	23	17*	0	23.00	2	2-37	0/0	18.50	1	
Seymour Michael Arthur ("Kelly")	5.6.1936		7	1963–1969	84	36	0	12.00	9	3-80	0/0	65.33	2	
Shalders William Alfred	12.2.1880	18.3.1917	12	1898–1907	355	42	0	16.13	1	1-6	0/0	6.00	3	
Shepstone George Harold	9.4.1876	3.7.1940	2	1895–1898	38	21	0	9.50	0	0-8	0/0	–	0	
Sherwell Percy William	17.8.1880	17.4.1948	13	1905–1910	427	115	1	23.72	–	–	–/–	–	20/16	
Siedle Ivan Julian ("Jack")	11.11.1903	24.8.1982	18	1927–1935	977	141	1	28.73	1	1-7	0/0	7.00	7	
Sinclair James Hugh	16.10.1876	23.2.1913	25	1895–1910	1,069	106	3	23.23	63	6-26	1/0	31.68	9	
Smith Charles James Edward	25.12.1872	27.3.1947	3	1902	106	45	0	21.20	–	–	–/–	–	2	

	Born	Died	Tests	Test Career	Runs	HS	100s	Avge	Wkts	BB	5/10	Avge	Ct/St	O/T
Smith Frederick William	31.3.1861	17.4.1914	3	1888-1895	45	12	0	9.00	—	—	—/—	—	2	
Smith Graeme Craig	1.2.1981		90§	2001-2010	7,445	277	22	50.30	8	2-145	0/0	104.00	116	159½/31
Smith Vivian Ian	23.2.1925		9	1947-1957	39	11*	0	3.90	12	4-143	0/0	64.08	3	
Snell Richard Peter	12.9.1968		5	1991-1994	95	48	0	13.57	19	4-74	0/0	28.31	1	42
[2]Snooke Sibley John ("Tip")	1.2.1881	14.8.1966	26	1905-1922	1,008	103	1	22.40	35	8-70	1/1	20.05	24	
[2]Snooke Stanley de la Courtte	11.11.1878	6.4.1959	1	1907	4	2	0	2.00	—	—	—/—	—	2	
Solomon William Rodger Thomson	23.4.1872	13.7.1964	1	1898	13	9	0	6.50	—	—	—/—	—		
Stewart Robert Burnard	3.9.1856	12.9.1913	1	1888	13	9	0	6.50	—	—	—/—	—		
Steyn Dale Willem	27.6.1983		46	2004-2010	620	76	0	13.77	238	7-51	16/4	23.21	13	41¼/21
Steyn Philippus Jeremia Rudolf	30.6.1967		3	1994	127	46	0	21.16	—	—	—/—	—	1	1
Stricker Louis Anthony	26.5.1884	5.2.1960	13	1909-1912	344	48	0	14.33	1	1-36	0/0	105.00	2	
Strydom Pieter Coenraad	10.6.1969		2	1999	35	30	0	11.66	0	0-27	0/0	—	0	10
Susskind Manfred John	8.6.1891	9.7.1957	5	1924	268	65	0	33.50	—	—	—/—	—	3	
Symcox Patrick Leonard	14.4.1960		20	1993-1998	741	108	1	28.50	37	4-69	0/0	43.32	5	80
[2]Taberer Henry Melville	7.10.1870	5.6.1932	1	1902	2	2	0	2.00	1	1-25	0/0	48.00	1	
[2]Tancred Augustus Bernard	20.8.1865	23.11.1911	2	1888	87	29	0	29.00	—	—	—/—	—	0	
[2]Tancred Louis Joseph	7.10.1876	28.7.1934	14	1902-1913	530	97	0	21.20	—	—	—/—	—	2	
[2]Tancred Vincent Maximillian	7.7.1875	3.6.1904	1	1898	25	18	0	12.50	—	—	—/—	—	3	
[2]Tapscott George Lancelot ("Dusty")	7.11.1889	13.12.1940	1	1913	5	4	0	2.50	—	—	—/—	—	0	
[2]Tapscott Lionel Eric ("Doodles")	18.3.1894	7.7.1934	2	1922	58	50*	0	29.00	0	0-2	0/0	—	2	
Tayfield Hugh Joseph	30.1.1929	24.2.1994	37	1949-1960	862	75	0	16.90	170	9-113	14/2	25.91	26	
[2]Taylor Alistair Innes ("Scotch")	25.7.1925	7.2.2004	2	1956	18	12	0	9.00	—	—	—/—	—	0	
[2]Taylor Daniel	9.1.1887	24.1.1957	2	1913	85	36	0	21.25	—	—	—/—	—	0	
[2]Taylor Herbert Wilfred	5.5.1889	8.2.1973	42	1912-1931	2,936	176	7	40.77	5	3-15	0/0	31.20	19	
Terbrugge David John	31.1.1977		7	1998-2003	16	4*	0	5.33	20	5-46	1/0	25.85	4	4
Theunissen Nicolaas Hendrik Christiaan de Jong	4.5.1867	9.11.1929	1	1888	2	2*	0	2.00	0	0-51	0/0	—	0	
Thornton George	24.12.1867	31.1.1939	1	1902	1	1*	0	—	1	1-20	0/0	20.00	1	
Tomlinson Denis Stanley	4.9.1910	11.7.1993	1	1935	9	9	0	9.00	0	0-38	0/0	—		
Traicos Athanasios John	17.5.1947		3†	1969	8	5*	0	4.00	4	2-70	0/0	51.75	4	0‡
Trimborn Patrick Henry Joseph	18.5.1940		4	1966-1969	13	11*	0	6.50	11	3-12	0/0	23.36	7	
Tsolekile Thami Lungisa	9.10.1980		3	2004	47	22	0	9.40	—	—	—/—	—	6	
Tsotsobe Lonwabo Lennox	7.3.1984		5	2010-2010	19	8*	0	6.33	9	3-43	0/0	51.57	1	14/5
[2]Tuckett Lindsay	6.2.1919		9	1947-1948	131	40*	0	11.90	19	5-68	2/0	49.77	9	
[2]Tuckett Lindsay Richard ("Len")	19.4.1885	8.4.1963	1	1913	0	0*	0	0.00	—	—	—/—	—	2	
Twentyman-Jones Percy Sydney	13.9.1884	8.3.1954	1	1902	0	0	0	0.00	0	0-24	0/0	—	0	

§ G. C. Smith's figures exclude 12 runs and three catches for the ICC World XI v Australia in the Super Series Test in 2005-06.

Name	Born	Died	Tests	Test Career	Runs	HS	100s	Avge	Wkts	BB	5/10	Avge	Ct/St	O/T
van der Bijl Pieter Gerhard Vincent	21.10.1907	16.2.1973	5	1938	460	125	1	51.11	–		–/–	–	–	
van der Merwe Edward Alexander	9.11.1903	26.2.1971	2	1929–1935	27	19	0	9.00	–		–/–	–	3	
van der Merwe Peter Laurence	14.3.1937		15	1963–1966	533	76	0	25.38	1	1-6	0/0	22.00	11	11
van Jaarsveld Martin	18.6.1974		9	2002–2004	397	73	0	30.53	0	0-28	0/0	–	11	
van Ryneveld Clive Berrange	19.3.1928		19	1951–1957	724	83	0	26.81	17	4-67	0/0	39.47	14	
Varnals George Derek	24.7.1935		3	1964	97	23	0	16.16	0	0-2	0/0	–	0	
[2] Viljoen Kenneth George	14.5.1910	21.1.1974	27	1930–1948	1,365	124	2	28.43	0	0-10	0/0	–	5	
Vincent Cyril Leverton	16.2.1902	24.8.1968	25	1927–1935	526	60	0	20.23	84	6-51	3/0	31.32	27	
Vintcent Charles Henry	2.9.1866	28.9.1943	3	1888–1891	26	9	0	4.33	4	3-88	0/0	48.25	1	
Vogler Albert Edward Ernest	28.11.1876	9.8.1946	15	1905–1910	340	65	0	17.00	64	7-94	5/1	22.73	20	
[2] Wade Herbert Frederick	14.9.1905	23.11.1980	10	1935–1935	327	40*	0	20.43	–		–/–	–	4	
[2] Wade Walter Wareham ("Billy")	18.6.1914	31.5.2003	11	1938–1949	511	125	1	28.38	–		–/–	–	15/2	
Waite John Henry Bickford	19.1.1930		50	1951–1964	2,405	134	4	30.44	–		–/–	–	124/17	
Walter Kenneth Alexander	5.11.1939	13.9.2003	2	1961	11	10	0	3.66	6	4-63	0/0	32.83	3	
Ward Thomas Alfred	2.8.1887	16.2.1936	23	1912–1924	459	64	0	13.90	–		–/–	–	19/13	
Watkins John Cecil	10.4.1923		15	1949–1956	612	92	0	23.53	29	4-22	0/0	28.13	12	
Wesley Colin	5.9.1937		3	1960	49	35	0	9.80	–		–/–	–	–	
Wessels Kepler Christoffel	14.9.1957		16†	1991–1994	1,027	118	2	38.03	–		–/–	–	12	55‡
Westcott Richard John	19.9.1927		5	1953–1957	166	62	0	18.44	0	0-22	0/0	–	0	
White Gordon Charles	5.2.1882	17.10.1918	17	1905–1912	872	147	2	30.06	9	4-47	0/0	33.44	10	3
Willoughby Charl Myles	3.12.1974		2	2003	–	–	–	–	1	1-47	0/0	125.00	0	
Willoughby Joseph Thomas	7.11.1874	11.3.1952	2	1895	8	5	0	2.00	6	2-37	0/0	26.50	0	
Wimble Clarence Skelton	22.4.1861	28.1.1930	1	1891	0	0	0	0.00	–		–/–	–	–	
Winslow Paul Lyndhurst	21.5.1929		5	1949–1955	186	108	1	20.66	–		–/–	–	1	
Wynne Owen Edgar	1.6.1919	13.7.1975	6	1948–1949	219	50	0	18.25	–		–/–	–	3	
Zondeki Monde	25.7.1982		6	2003–2008	82	59	0	16.40	19	6-39	1/0	25.26	1	
Zulch Johan Wilhelm	2.1.1886	19.5.1924	16	1909–1921	983	150	2	32.76	0	0-2	0/0	–	4	11½/1

WEST INDIES (288 players)

	Born	Died	Tests	Test Career	Runs	HS	100s	Avge	Wkts	BB	5/10	Avge	Ct/St	O/T
Achong Ellis Edgar	16.2.1904	30.8.1986	6	1929–1934	81	22	–	8.10	8	2-64	0/0	47.25	6	–
Adams James Clive	9.1.1968		54	1991–2000	3,012	208*	6	41.26	27	5-17	1/0	49.48	48	127
Alexander Franz Copeland Murray ("Gerry")	2.11.1928		25	1957–1960	961	108	1	30.03	–	–	–/–	–	85/5	–
Ali Imtiaz	28.7.1954		1	*1975*	–	1*	0	–	2	2-37	0/0	44.50	0	–
Ali Inshan	25.9.1949	24.6.1995	12	1970–1976	172	25	0	10.75	34	5-59	1/0	47.67	7	–
Allan David Walter	5.11.1927		5	1961–1966	75	40*	0	12.50	–	–	–/–	–	15/3	–
Allen Ian Basil Alston	6.10.1965		2	*1991*	5	4*	0	–	5	2-69	0/0	36.00	0	–
Ambrose Curtly Elconn Lynwall	21.9.1963		98	1987–2000	1,439	53	0	12.40	405	8-45	22/3	20.99	18	176
Arthurton Keith Lloyd Thomas	21.2.1965		33	1988–1995	1,382	157*	2	30.71	1	1-17	0/0	183.00	22	105
Asgarali Nyron Sultan	28.12.1920		2	*1957*	62	29	0	15.50	–	–	–/–	–	0	–
² Atkinson Denis St Eval	9.8.1926	9.11.2001	22	1948–1957	922	219	1	31.79	47	7-53	3/0	35.04	11	–
² Atkinson Eric St Eval	6.11.1927	29.5.1998	8	1957–1958	126	37	0	15.75	25	5-42	1/0	23.56	2	–
Austin Richard Arkwright	5.9.1954		2	*1977*	22	20	0	11.00	–	–	–/–	–	2	–
Austin Ryan Anthony	15.11.1981		2	*2009*	39	19	0	9.75	3	1-29	0/0	51.66	3	1
Bacchus Sheik Faoud Ahamul Fasiel	31.11.1954		19	1977–1981	782	250	1	26.06	0	0-3	–/–	–	17	29
Baichan Leonard	12.5.1946		3	1974–1975	184	105*	1	46.00	–	–	–/–	–	2	–
Baker Lionel Sionne	6.9.1984		4	2008–2009	23	17	0	11.50	5	2-39	0/0	79.00	1	10/3
Banks Omari Ahmed Clemente	17.7.1982		10	2002–2005	318	50*	0	26.50	28	4-87	0/0	48.82	6	5
Baptiste Eldine Ashworth Elderfield	12.3.1960		10	1983–1989	233	87*	0	23.30	16	3-31	0/0	35.18	2	43
Barath Adrian Boris	14.4.1990		4	2009–2010	200	104	1	28.57	–	–	–/–	–	2	5/1
Barrett Arthur George	4.4.1944		6	1970–1974	40	19	0	6.66	13	3-43	0/0	46.38	2	–
Barrow Ivanhoe Mordecai	16.1.1911	2.4.1979	11	1929–1939	276	105	1	16.23	–	–	–/–	–	17/5	–
Bartlett Edward Lawson	10.3.1906	21.12.1976	5	1928–1930	131	84	0	18.71	–	–	–/–	–	2	–
Baugh Carlton Seymour	23.6.1982		8	2002–2010	256	68	0	21.33	–	–	–/–	–	7/1	30/1
Benjamin Kenneth Charlie Griffith	8.4.1967		26	1991–1997	222	43*	0	7.92	92	6-66	4/1	30.27	2	26
Benjamin Winston Keithroy Matthew	31.12.1964		21	1987–1994	470	85	0	18.80	61	4-46	0/0	27.01	12	85
Benn Sulieman Jamaal	22.7.1981		17	2007–2010	381	42	0	15.87	51	6-81	3/0	41.41	7	18/17
Bernard David Eddison	19.7.1981		3	2002–2009	202	69	0	40.40	4	2-30	0/0	46.25	0	20/1
Bess Brandon Jeremy	13.12.1987		1	*2010*	11	11*	0	11.00	1	1-65	0/0	92.00	0	–
Best Carlisle Alonza	14.5.1959		8	1985–1990	342	164	1	28.50	0	0-2	–/–	–	8	24
Best Tino la Bertram	26.8.1981		14	2002–2009	196	27	0	9.80	28	4-46	0/0	48.67	1	12
Betancourt Nelson	4.6.1887	12.10.1947	1	*1929*	52	39	0	26.00	–	–	–/–	–	0	–
Binns Alfred Phillip	24.7.1929		5	1952–1955	64	27	0	9.14	–	–	–/–	–	14/3	–

	Born	Died	Tests	Test Career	Runs	HS	Avge	100s	Wkts	BB	5/10	Avge	Ct/St	O/T
Birkett Lionel Sydney	14.4.1905	16.1.1998	4	1930	136	64	17.00	0	1	1-16	0/0	71.00	4	84
Bishop Ian Raphael	24.10.1967		43	1988–1997	632	48	12.15	0	161	6-40	6/0	24.27	8	84
Black Marlon Ian	7.6.1975		6	2000–2001	21	6	2.62	0	12	4-83	0/0	49.75	8	8
Boyce Keith David	11.10.1943	11.10.1996	21	1970–1975	657	95*	24.33	0	60	6-77	2/1	30.01	5	8
Bradshaw Ian David Russell	9.7.1974		5	2005	96	33	13.71	0	2	3-73	0/0	60.00	3	62/1
[2] Bravo Dwayne John	7.10.1983		40	2004–2010	2,200	113	31.42	3	86	6-55	2/0	39.83	41	107/22
[2] Bravo Darren Michael	6.2.1989		3	2010	206	80	68.66	0			–/–		1	10/1
Breese Gareth Rohan	9.1.1976		1	2002	5	5	2.50	0	2	2-108	0/0	67.50		
Browne Courtney Oswald	7.12.1970		20	1994–2004	387	68	16.12	0			–/–		79/2	46
Browne Cyril Rutherford	8.10.1890	12.1.1964	4	1928–1929	176	70*	25.14	0	6	2-72	0/0	48.00	1	
Butcher Basil Fitzherbert	3.9.1933		44	1958–1969	3,104	209*	43.11	7	5	5-34	1/0	18.00	15	
Butler Lennox Stephen	9.2.1929		1	1954	16	16	16.00	0	2	2-151	0/0	75.50	0	
Butts Clyde Godfrey	8.7.1957		7	1984–1987	108	38	15.42	0	10	4-73	0/0	59.50	2	90
Bynoe Michael Robin	23.2.1941		4	1958–1966	111	48	18.50	0	1	1-5	0/0	5.00	4	
Camacho George Stephen	15.10.1945		11	1967–1970	640	87	29.09	0	0	0-12	0/0	–	4	
Cameron Francis James	22.6.1923	10.6.1994	5	1948	151	75*	25.16	0	3	2-74	0/0	92.66	0	
[2] Cameron John Hemsley	8.4.1914	13.2.2000	2	1939	6	5	2.00	0	3	3-66	0/0	29.33	2	
Campbell Sherwin Legay	1.11.1970		52	1994–2001	2,882	208	32.38	4			–/–		47	90
Carew George McDonald	4.6.1910	9.12.1974	4	1934–1948	170	107	28.33	1	0	0-2	0/0	–	13	
Carew Michael Conrad ("Joey")	15.9.1937	8.1.2011	19	1963–1971	1,127	109	34.15	1	8	1-11	0/0	54.62	13	
Challenor George	28.6.1888	30.7.1947	3	1928	101	46	16.83	0			–/–			
Chanderpaul Shivnarine	16.8.1974		129	1993–2010	9,063	203*	48.98	22	8	1-2	0/0	105.62	52	261/22
Chang Herbert Samuel	22.7.1952		1	1978	127	46	18.14	0			–/–			
Chattergoon Sewnarine	3.4.1981		4	2007–2008	98	32*	19.60	0			–/–		4	18
[2] Christiani Cyril Marcel	28.10.1913	4.4.1938	4	1934	98	32*	19.60	0			–/–		6/1	
[2] Christiani Robert Julian	19.7.1920	4.1.2005	22	1947–1953	896	107	26.35	1			–/–		19/2	
Clarke Carlos Bertram OBE	7.4.1918	14.10.1993	3	1939	3	2	1.00	0	6	3-59	0/0	36.00	0	
Clarke Carlos Sylvester Theophilus	11.12.1954	4.12.1999	11	1977–1981	172	24	15.63	0	42	5-126	1/0	43.50	2	10
[2] Collins Pedro Tyrone	12.8.1976		32	1998–2005	235	24	5.87	0	106	6-53	3/0	27.85	7	30
Collymore Corey Dalanelo	21.12.1977		30	1998–2007	197	16*	7.88	0	93	7-57	4/1	34.63	6	84
Constantine *Lord* [Learie Nicholas]	21.9.1901	1.7.1971	18	1928–1939	635	90	19.24	2	58	5-75	3/0	32.30	28	
Croft Colin Everton Hunte	15.3.1953		27	1976–1981	158	33	10.53	0	125	8-29	5/1	23.30	8	19
Cuffy Cameron Eustace	8.2.1970		15	1994–2002	58	15	4.14	0	43	4-82	0/0	33.83	1	41
Cummins Anderson Cleophas	7.5.1966		5	1992–1994	98	50	19.60	0	8	4-54	0/0	42.75	5	63
[2] Da Costa Oscar Constantine	11.9.1907	1.10.1936	5	1929–1934	153	39	19.12	0	3	1-14	0/0	58.33	5	
Daniel Wayne Wendell	16.1.1956		10	1975–1983	46	11	6.57	0	36	5-39	1/0	25.27	4	18

Name	Born	Died	Tests	Test Career	Runs	HS	100s	Avge	Wkts	BB	5/10	Avge	Ct/St	O/T
[2]Davis Bryan Allan	2.5.1940		4	1964	245	68	0	30.62	—	—	—/—	—	4	
[2]Davis Charles Allan	1.1.1944		15	1968–1972	1,301	183	4	54.20	2	1-27	0/0	165.00	4	35
Davis Winston Walter	18.9.1958		15	1982–1987	202	77	0	15.53	45	4-19	0/0	32.71	10	35
De Caires Francis Ignatius	12.5.1909	2.2.1959	3	1929	232	80	0	38.66	0	0-9	0/0	—	1	
Deonarine Narsingh	16.8.1983		8	2004–2010	370	82	0	30.83	4	2-74	0/0	61.50	5	20/7
Depeiza Cyril Clairmonte	10.10.1928	10.11.1995	5	1954–1955	187	122	1	31.16	0	0-3	0/0	—	7/4	
Dewdney Charles Thomas	23.10.1933		9	1954–1957	17	5*	0	2.42	21	5-21	1/0	38.42	0	
Dhanraj Rajindra	6.2.1969		4	1994–1995	17	9	0	4.25	8	2-49	0/0	74.37	1	6
Dillon Mervyn	5.6.1974		38	1996–2003	549	43	0	8.44	131	5-71	2/0	33.57	16	108
Dowe Uton George	29.3.1949		4	1970–1972	8	5*	0	8.00	12	4-69	2/0	44.50	3	
Dowin Travis Montague	24.2.1977		6	2009–2010	343	95	0	31.18	0	0-3	0/0	—	5	11/2
Drakes Vasbert Conniel	5.8.1969		12	2002–2003	386	67	0	21.44	33	5-93	1/0	41.27	2	34
Dujon Peter Jeffrey Leroy	28.5.1956		81	1981–1991	3,322	139	5	31.94	—	—	—/—	—	267/5	169
[2]Edwards Fidel Henderson	6.2.1982		43	2003–2009	248	21	0	5.16	122	7-87	8/0	39.43	7	50/10
Edwards Richard Martin	3.6.1940		5	1968	65	22	0	9.28	18	5-84	1/0	34.77	0	
Ferguson Wilfred	14.12.1917	23.2.1961	8	1947–1953	200	75	0	28.57	34	6-92	3/1	34.26	11	
Fernandes Maurius Pacheco	12.8.1897	8.5.1981	2	1928–1929	49	22	0	12.25	—	—	—/—	—	0	
Findlay Thaddeus Michael MBE	19.10.1943		10	1969–1972	212	44*	0	16.30	—	—	—/—	—	19/2	
Foster Maurice Linton Churchill	9.5.1943		14	1969–1977	580	125	1	30.52	9	2-41	0/0	66.66	3	2
Francis George Nathaniel	11.12.1897	12.1.1942	10	1928–1933	81	19*	0	5.78	23	4-40	0/0	33.17	7	
Frederick Michael Campbell	6.5.1927		1	1953	30	30	0	15.00	—	—	—/—	—	0	
Fredericks Roy Clifton	11.11.1942	5.9.2000	59	1968–1976	4,334	169	8	42.49	7	1-12	0/0	78.28	62	12
Fuller Richard Livingston	30.1.1913	3.5.1987	1	1934	1	1	0	1.00	0	0-2	0/0	—	0	
Furlonge Hammond Allan	19.6.1934		3	1954–1955	99	64	0	19.80	—	—	—/—	—	0	
Ganga Daren	14.1.1979		48	1998–2007	2,160	135	3	25.71	1	1-20	0/0	106.00	30	35/1
Ganteaume Andrew Gordon	22.1.1921		1	1947	112	112	0	112.00	—	—	—/—	—	0	
Garner Joel MBE	16.12.1952		58	1976–1986	672	60	0	12.44	259	6-56	7/0	20.97	42	98
Garrick Leon Vivian	11.11.1976		1	2000	27	27	0	13.50	—	—	—/—	—	0	3
Gaskin Berkeley Bertram McGarrell	21.3.1908	2.5.1979	2	1947	17	10	0	5.66	2	1-15	0/0	79.00	1	
Gayle Christopher Henry	21.9.1979		91	1999–2010	6,373	333	13	41.65	72	5-34	2/0	41.59	85	217±20
Gibbs Glendon Lionel	27.12.1925	21.2.1979	1	1954	12	12	0	6.00	0	0-2	0/0	—	1	
Gibbs Lancelot Richard	29.9.1934		79	1957–1975	488	25	0	6.97	309	8-38	18/2	29.09	52	3
Gibson Ottis Delroy	16.3.1969		13	1995–1998	93	37	0	23.25	3	2-81	0/0	91.66	0	15
Gilchrist Roy	28.6.1934	18.7.2001	13	1957–1958	60	12	0	5.45	57	6-55	1/0	26.68	4	
Gladstone Morais George	14.1.1901	19.5.1978	1	1929	12	12*	0	—	1	1-139	0/0	189.00	0	
Goddard John Douglas Claude OBE	21.4.1919	26.8.1987	27	1947–1957	859	83*	0	30.67	33	5-31	1/0	31.81	22	

Name	Born	Died	Tests	Test Career	Runs	HS	100s	Avge	Wkts	BB	5/10	Avge	Ct/St	O/T
Gomes Hilary Angelo ("Larry")	13.7.1953		60	1976–1986	3,171	143	9	39.63	15	2-20	0/0	62.00	18	83
Gomez Gerald Ethridge	10.10.1919	6.8.1996	29	1939–1953	1,243	101	1	30.31	58	7-55	1/1	27.41	18	
[2] Grant George Copeland ("Jackie")	9.5.1907	26.10.1978	12	1930–1934	413	71*	0	25.81	0	0-1	0/0	–	10	
[2] Grant Rolph Stewart	15.12.1909	18.10.1977	7	1934–1939	220	77	0	22.00	11	3-68	0/0	32.09	13	
Gray Anthony Hollis	23.5.1963		5	1986	48	12*	0	8.00	22	4-39	–/–	17.13	6	25
Greenidge Alvin Ethelbert	20.8.1956		6	1977–1978	222	69	0	22.20					5	1
Greenidge Cuthbert Gordon MBE	1.5.1951		108	1974–1990	7,558	226	19	44.72	0	0-0	0/0	–	96	128
Greenidge Geoffrey Alan	26.5.1948		5	1971–1972	209	50	0	29.85	0	0-2	0/0	–	3	
Grell Mervyn George	18.12.1899	11.1.1976	1	1929	34	21	0	17.00	0	0-7	0/0	–	1	
Griffith Adrian Frank Gordon	19.11.1971		14	1996–2000	638	114	1	24.53					5	9
Griffith Charles Christopher	14.12.1938		28	1959–1968	530	54	0	16.56	94	6-36	5/0	28.54	16	
Griffith Herman Clarence	1.12.1893	18.3.1980	13	1928–1933	91	18	0	5.05	44	6-103	2/0	28.25	4	
Guillen Simpson Clairmonte ("Sammy")	24.9.1924		5†	1951	104	54	0	26.00					9/2	
Hall Wesley Winfield	12.9.1937		48	1958–1968	818	50*	0	15.73	192	7-69	9/1	26.38	11	
Harper Roger Andrew	17.3.1963		25	1983–1993	535	74	0	18.44	46	6-57	1/0	28.06	36	105
Haynes Desmond Leo	15.2.1956		116	1977–1993	7,487	184	18	42.29					65	238
[3] Headley George Alphonso MBE	30.5.1909	30.11.1983	22	1929–1953	2,190	270*	10	60.83				8.00	14	
Headley Ronald George Alphonso	29.6.1939		2	1973	62	42	0	15.50					2	1
Hendriks John Leslie	21.12.1933		20	1961–1969	447	64	0	18.62					42/5	
Hinds Ryan O'Neal	17.2.1981		15	2001–2009	505	84	0	21.04	13	2-45	0/0	66.92	7	14
Hinds Wavell Wayne	7.9.1976		45	1999–2005	2,608	213	5	33.01	16	3-79	0/0	36.87	32	119/5
Hoad Edward Lisle Goldsworthy	29.1.1896	5.3.1986	4	1928–1933	98	36	0	12.25					1	
Holder Roland Irvine Christopher	22.12.1967		11	1996–1998	380	91	0	25.33					9	37
Holder Vanburn Alonzo MBE	10.10.1945		40	1969–1978	682	42	0	14.20	109	6-28	3/0	33.27	22	12
Holding Michael Anthony	16.2.1954		60	1975–1986	910	73	0	13.78	249	8-92	13/2	23.68	22	102
Holford David Anthony Jerome	16.4.1940		24	1966–1976	768	105*	1	22.58	51	5-23	1/0	39.39	18	
Holt John Kenneth Constantine	12.8.1923	3.6.1997	17	1953–1958	1,066	166	2	36.75	1	1-20	0/0	20.00	8	
Hooper Carl Llewellyn	15.12.1966		102	1987–2002	5,762	233	13	36.46	114	5-26	4/0	49.42	115	227
Howard Anthony Bourne	27.8.1946		1	1971	–	–	–	–	2	2-140	0/0	70.00	0	
Hunte Sir Conrad Cleophas	9.5.1932	3.12.1999	44	1957–1966	3,245	260	8	45.06	2	1-17	0/0	55.00	16	
Hunte Errol Ashton Clairmonte	3.10.1905	26.6.1967	3	1929	166	58	0	33.20					5	
Hylton Leslie George	29.3.1905	17.5.1955	6	1934–1939	70	19	0	11.66	16	4-27	0/0	26.12	1	
Jacobs Ridley Detamore	26.11.1967		65	1998–2004	2,577	118	3	28.31					207/12	147
Jaggernauth Amit Sheldon	16.11.1983		3	2007	0	0*	0	0.00	1	1-74	0/0	96.00	0	
Johnson Hophnie Hobah Hines	13.7.1910	24.6.1987	3	1947–1950	38	22	0	9.50	13	5-41	2/1	18.30	0	
Johnson Tyrell Fabian	10.1.1917	5.4.1985	1	1939	9	9*	0	–	3	2-53	0/0	43.00	1	

Name	Born	Died	Tests	Test Career	Runs	HS	100s	Avge	Wkts	BB	Avge	5/10	Ct/St	O/T
Jones Charles Ernest Llewellyn	3.11.1902	10.12.1959		1929–1934	63	19	0	9.00	0	0-2	–	0/0	3	–
Jones Prior Erskine Waverlyn	6.6.1917	21.11.1991	9	1947–1951	47	10*	0	5.22	25	5-85	30.04	1/0	4	–
Joseph David Rolston Emmanuel	15.11.1969		4	1998	141	50	0	20.14	0	0-8	–	0/0	10	13
Joseph Sylvester Cleofoster	5.9.1978		4	2004–2007	147	45	0	14.70	0	0-57	–	0/0	3	12
Julien Bernard Denis	13.3.1950		24	1973–1976	866	121	2	30.92	50	5-57	37.36	1/0	14	–
Jumadeen Raphick Rasif	12.4.1948		12	1971–1978	84	56	0	21.00	29	4-72	39.34	0/0	4	–
Kallicharran Alvin Isaac	21.3.1949		66	1971–1980	4,399	187	12	44.43	4	2-16	39.50	0/0	51	31
Kanhai Rohan Bholalall	26.12.1935		79	1957–1973	6,227	256	15	47.53	0	0-1	–	0/0	50	7
Kentish Esmond Seymour Maurice	21.11.1916		2	1947–1953	1	1*	0	1.00	8	5-49	22.25	1/0	1	–
King Collis Llewellyn	11.6.1951		9	1976–1980	418	100*	1	32.15	3	1-30	94.00	0/0	5	18
King Frank McDonald	14.12.1926	23.12.1990	14	1952–1955	116	21	0	8.28	29	5-74	39.96	1/0	5	–
King Lester Anthony	27.2.1939	9.7.1998	2	1961–1967	41	20	0	10.25	9	5-46	17.11	1/0	5	–
King Reon Dane	6.10.1975		19	1998–2004	66	12*	0	3.47	53	5-51	32.69	1/0	2	50
Lambert Clayton Benjamin	10.2.1962		5	1991–1998	284	104	1	31.55	1	1-4	5.00	0/0	8	11
Lara Brian Charles	2.5.1969		130§	1990–2006	11,912	400*	34	53.17	0	0-0	–	0/0	164	295‡
Lashley Patrick Douglas ("Peter")	11.2.1937		4	1960–1966	159	49	0	22.71	1	1-1	1.00	0/0	4	–
Lawson Jermaine Jay Charles	13.11.1982		13	2002–2005	52	14	0	3.46	51	7-78	29.64	2/0	3	13
Legall Ralph Archibald	1.12.1925	2003	4	1952	50	23	0	10.00	–		–	–/–	8/1	–
Lewis Desmond Michael	21.2.1946		3	1970	259	88	0	86.33	–		–	–/–	8	–
Lewis Rawl Nicholas	5.9.1974		5	1997–2007	89	40	0	8.90	4	2-42	114.00	0/0	8	28/1
Lloyd Clive Hubert CBE	31.8.1944		110	1966–1984	7,515	242*	19	46.67	10	2-13	62.20	0/0	90	87
Logie Augustine Lawrence	28.9.1960		52	1982–1991	2,470	130	2	35.79	0	0-0	–	0/0	57	158
McGarrell Neil Christopher	12.7.1972		4	2000–2001	61	33	0	15.25	17	4-23	26.64	0/0	2	17
McLean Nixon Alexei McNamara	20.7.1973		19	1997–2000	368	46	0	12.26	44	3-53	42.56	0/0	5	45
McMorris Easton Dudley Ashton St John	4.4.1935		13	1957–1966	564	125	1	26.85	–		–	–/–	5	–
McWatt Clifford Aubrey	1.2.1922	20.7.1997	6	1953–1954	202	54	0	28.85	1	1-16	16.00	0/0	9/1	–
Madray Ivan Samuel	2.7.1934	23.4.2009	2	1957	3	2	0	1.00	0	0-12	–	0/0		–
Marshall Malcolm Denzil	18.4.1958	4.11.1999	81	1978–1991	1,810	92	0	18.85	376	7-22	20.94	22/4	25	136
[2] Marshall Norman Edgar	27.2.1924	11.8.2007	1	1954	8	8	0	4.00	2	1-22	31.00	0/0		–
[2] Marshall Roy Edwin	25.4.1930	27.10.1992	4	1951	143	30	0	20.42	0	0-3	–	0/0	1	–
Marshall Xavier Melbourne	27.3.1986		7	2005–2008	243	85	0	20.25	0	0-0	–	0/0	7	24/6
[2] Martin Frank Reginald	12.10.1893	23.11.1967	9	1928–1930	486	123*	1	28.58	8	3-91	77.37	0/0	7	–
Martindale Emmanuel Alfred	25.11.1909	17.3.1972	10	1933–1939	58	22	0	5.27	37	5-22	21.72	3/0	5	–
Mattis Everton Hugh	11.4.1957		4	1980	145	71	0	29.00	0	0-4	–	0/0	3	–
Mendonca Ivor Leon	13.7.1934		2	1961	81	78	0	40.50	–		–	–/–	8/2	2

§ *Lara's figures exclude 41 runs for the ICC World XI v Australia in the Super Series Test in 2005-06.*

	Born	Died	Tests	Test Career	Runs	HS	100s	Avge	Wkts	BB	5/10	Avge	Ct/St	O/T
Merry Cyril Arthur	20.1.1911	19.4.1964	2	1933	34	13	0	8.50	0	–	–/–	–	1	33/7
Miller Nikita O'Neil	16.5.1982			2009	5	5	0	2.50	0	0-27	0/0	–	0	
Miller Roy	24.12.1924		1	1952	23	23	0	23.00	0	0-28	0/0	–	0	7
Mohammed Dave	8.10.1979		5	2003-2006	225	52	0	32.14	13	3-98	0/0	51.38	0	
Moodie George Horatio	26.11.1915	8.6.2002	1	1934	5	5	0	5.00	3	2-23	0/0	13.33	0	
Morton Runako Shakur	22.7.1978		15	2005-2007	573	70*	0	22.03	0	0-4	0/0	–	20	56/7
Moseley Ezra Alphonsa	5.1.1958		2	1989	35	26	0	8.75	6	2-70	0/0	43.50	1	9
Murray David Anthony	29.5.1950		19	1977-1981	601	84	0	21.46	–	–	–/–	–	57/5	10
Murray Deryck Lance	20.5.1943		62	1963-1980	1,993	91	0	22.90	–	–	–/–	–	181/8	26
Murray Junior Randolph	20.1.1968		33	1992-2001	918	101*	1	22.39	–	–	–/–	–	99/3	55
Nagamootoo Mahendra Veeren	9.10.1975		5	2000-2002	185	68	0	26.42	12	3-119	0/0	53.08	2	24
Nanan Rangy	29.5.1953		1	1980	16	8	0	8.00	4	2-37	0/0	22.75	2	
Nash Brendan Paul	14.12.1977		18	2008-2010	1,049	114	2	38.85	2	1-21	0/0	108.50	6	9
Neblett James Montague	13.11.1901	28.3.1959	1	1934	16	11*	0	16.00	1	1-44	0/0	75.00	0	
Noreiga Jack Mollinson	15.4.1936	8.8.2003	4	1970	11	9	0	3.66	17	9-95	2/0	29.00	2	
Nunes Robert Karl	7.6.1894	23.7.1958	4	1928-1929	245	92	0	30.62	–	–	–/–	–	2	
Nurse Seymour MacDonald	10.11.1933		29	1959-1968	2,523	258	6	47.60	0	0-0	0/0	–	21	
Padmore Albert Leroy	17.12.1946		2	1975-1976	8	8*	0	8.00	1	1-36	0/0	135.00	0	
Pagon Donovan Jomo	13.9.1982		2	2004	37	35	0	12.33	0	0-3	0/0	–	0	
Pairaudeau Bruce Hamilton	14.4.1931		13	1952-1957	454	115	1	21.61	–	–	–/–	–	6	
Parchment Brenton Anthony	24.6.1982		2	2007	55	20	0	13.75	0	0-3	0/0	–	4	
Parry Derick Recaldo	22.12.1954		12	1977-1979	381	65	0	22.41	23	5-15	1/0	40.69		7/1
Pascal Nelon Troy	25.4.1987		2	2010-2010	12	10	0	6.00	0	0-27	0/0	–		6
Passailaigue Charles Clarence	4.8.1901	7.1.1972	1	1929	46	44	0	46.00	0	0-15	0/0	–		1
Patterson Balfour Patrick	15.9.1961		28	1985-1992	145	21*	0	6.59	93	5-24	5/0	30.90	5	59
Payne Thelston Rodney O'Neale	13.2.1957		1	1985	5	5	0	5.00	–	–	–/–	–	5/1	7
Perry Nehemiah Odolphus	16.6.1968		4	1998-1999	74	26	0	12.33	10	5-70	1/0	44.60	5	21
Phillip Norbert	12.6.1948		9	1977-1978	297	47	0	29.70	28	4-48	1/0	37.17		1
Phillips Omar Jamel	12.10.1986		2	2009	160	94	0	40.00	0	0-9	0/0	–		
Pierre Lancelot Richard	5.6.1921	14.4.1989	1	1947	13	9	0	–	–	–	–/–	–	0	
Powell Daren Brentlyle	15.4.1978		37	2002-2008	407	36*	0	7.82	85	5-25	1/0	47.85	8	55/5
Powell Ricardo Lloyd	16.12.1978		2	1999-2003	53	30	0	17.66	0	0-13	0/0	–		109
Rae Allan Fitzroy	30.9.1922	27.2.2005	15	1948-1952	1,016	109	4	46.18	–	–	–/–	–	10	
Ragoonath Suruj	22.3.1968		2	1998	13	9	0	4.33	–	–	–/–	–	0	
Ramadhin Sonny	1.5.1929		43	1950-1960	361	44	0	8.20	158	7-49	10/1	28.98	9	
Ramdass Ryan Rakesh	3.7.1983		1	2005	26	23	0	13.00	–	–	–/–	–	0	1

Name	Born	Died	Test Career	Tests	Runs	HS	100s	Avge	Wkts	BB	5/10	Avge	Ct/St	OIT
Ramdin Denesh	13.3.1985		2005–2010	42	1,482	166	1	22.80	–	–	–	–	119/3	81/22
Ramnarine Dinanath	4.6.1975		1997–2001	12	106	35*	0	6.23	45	5-78	1/0	30.73	8	4
Rampaul Ravindranath	15.10.1984		2009–2010	5	114	40*	0	19.00	4	1-21	0/0	109.75	–	508
Reifer Floyd Lamonte	23.7.1972		1996–2009	5	111	29	0	9.25	–	–	–	–	1	8/1
Richards Dale Maurice	16.7.1976		2009–2010	3	125	69	0	20.83	–	–	–	–	6	8/1
Richards Sir Isaac Vivian Alexander	7.3.1952		1974–1991	121	8,540	291	24	50.23	32	2-17	0/0	61.37	122	187
Richardson Richard Benjamin	12.1.1962		1983–1995	86	5,949	194	16	44.39	0	0-0	0/0	–	90	224
Rickards Kenneth Roy	22.8.1923	21.8.1995	1947–1951	2	104	67	0	34.66	–	–	–	–	0	
Roach Clifford Archibald	13.3.1904	16.4.1988	1928–1934	16	952	209	2	30.70	2	1-18	0/0	51.50	5	
Roach Kemar Andre Jamal	30.6.1988		2009–2010	10	72	17	0	7.20	36	6-48	2/0	28.25	5	13/10
Roberts Alphonso Theodore	18.9.1937	24.7.1996	1955	1	28	28	0	14.00	–	–	–	–	0	
Roberts Anderson Montgomery Everton CBE	29.1.1951		1973–1983	47	762	68	0	14.94	202	7-54	11/2	25.61	9	56
Roberts Lincoln Abraham	4.9.1974		1998	1	0	0	0	0.00	–	–	–	–	0	
Rodriguez William Vicente	25.6.1934		1961–1967	5	96	50	0	13.71	7	3-51	0/0	53.42	3	
Rose Franklyn Albert	1.2.1972		1996–2000	19	344	69	0	13.23	53	7-84	2/0	30.88	4	27
Rowe Lawrence George	8.1.1949		1971–1979	30	2,047	302	7	43.55	0	0-1	0/0	–	17	11
Russell Andre Dwayne	29.4.1988		2010	1	2	2	0	2.00	2	1-73	0/0	104.00	–	
[2]St Hill Edwin Lloyd	9.3.1904	21.5.1957	1929	2	18	12	0	4.50	2	2-110	0/0	73.66	0	
[2]St Hill Wilton H.	6.7.1893	c. 1957	1928–1929	3	117	38	0	19.50	0	0-9	0/0	–	11	
Sammy Darren Julius Garvey	20.12.1983		2007–2010	11	301	48	0	16.72	29	7-66	3/0	31.03	13	43/19
Samuels Marlon Nathaniel	5.1.1981		2000–2007	29	1,408	105	2	28.73	7	2-49	0/0	127.00	8	107/6
[2]Samuels Robert George	13.3.1971		1995–1996	6	372	125	1	37.20	–	–	–	–	4	
Sanford Adam	12.7.1975		2001–2003	11	72	18*	0	4.80	30	4-132	0/0	43.86	4	
Sarwan Ramnaresh Ronnie	23.6.1980		1999–2009	83	5,759	291	15	41.73	23	4-37	0/0	50.56	50	156/18
Scarlett Reginald Osmond	15.8.1934		1959	3	54	29*	0	18.00	2	1-46	0/0	104.50	0	
[1]Scott Alfred Homer Patrick	29.7.1934	15.6.1961	1952	1	5	5	0	5.00	0	0-52	0/0	–	0	
[1]Scott Oscar Charles ("Tommy")	14.8.1892	12.9.1963	1928–1930	8	171	35	0	17.10	22	5-266	1/0	42.04	2	2
Sealey Benjamin James	12.8.1899		1933	1	41	29	0	20.50	–	–	–	–	4	
Sealy James Edward Derrick	11.9.1912	3.1.1982	1929–1939	11	478	92	0	28.11	3	2-7	0/0	31.33	6/1	
Shepherd John Neil	9.11.1943		1969–1970	5	77	32	0	9.62	19	5-104	1/0	25.21	2	
Shillingford Grayson Cleophas	25.9.1944	23.12.2009	1969–1971	7	57	25	0	8.14	15	3-63	0/0	35.80	3	
Shillingford Irvine Theodore	18.4.1944		1976–1977	4	218	120	1	31.14	–	–	–	–	6	
Shillingford Shane	22.2.1983		2010–2010	5	65	27	0	10.83	14	4-123	0/0	56.78	3	
Shivnarine Sewdatt	13.5.1952		1977–1978	8	379	63	0	29.15	1	1-63	0/0	167.00	3	1
Simmons Lendl Mark Platter	25.1.1985		2008–2009	2	87	24	0	14.50	1	1-60	0/0	139.00	3	19/8
Simmons Philip Verant	18.4.1963		1987–1997	26	1,002	110	1	22.26	4	2-34	0/0	64.25	26	143

Name	Born	Died	Tests	Test Career	Runs	HS	100s	Avge	Wkts	BB	5/10	Avge	Ct/St	O/T
Singh Charran Kamkaran	27.11.1935		2	1959	11	11	0	3.66	5	2-28	0/0	33.20	2	–
Small Joseph A.	3.11.1892	26.4.1958	3	1928–1929	79	52	0	13.16	4	2-67	0/0	61.33	3	–
Small Milton Aster	12.2.1964		2	1983–1984	3	3*	0	–	4	3-40	0/0	38.25	0	–
Smith Cameron Wilberforce	29.7.1933		5	1960–1961	222	55	0	24.66	0	0-3	0/0	–	4/1	–
Smith Devon Sheldon	21.10.1981		32	2002–2010	1,370	108	1	25.37	–	–	–	–	27	32/6
Smith Dwayne Romel	12.4.1983		10	2003–2005	320	105*	1	24.61	7	3-71	0/0	49.14	9	7/8
Smith O'Neil Gordon ("Collie")	5.5.1933	9.9.1959	26	1954–1958	1,331	168	4	31.69	48	5-90	1/0	33.85	9	–
Sobers Sir Garfield St Aubrun	28.7.1936		93	1953–1974	8,032	365*	26	57.78	235	6-73	6/0	34.03	109	1
Solomon Joseph Stanislaus	26.8.1930		27	1958–1964	1,326	100*	1	34.00	4	1-20	0/0	67.00	13	–
Stayers Sven Conrad ("Charlie")	9.6.1937	6.1.2005	4	1961	58	35*	0	19.33	9	3-65	0/0	40.44	0	–
[2]Stollmeyer Jeffrey Baxter	11.3.1921	10.9.1989	32	1939–1954	2,159	160	4	42.33	13	3-32	0/0	39.00	20	–
[2]Stollmeyer Victor Humphrey	24.1.1916	21.9.1999	1	1939	96	96	0	96.00	–	–	–	–	0	–
Stuart Colin Ellsworth Laurie	28.9.1973		6	2000–2001	24	12*	0	3.42	20	3-33	0/0	31.40	2	5
Taylor Jaswick Ossie	3.1.1932	13.11.1999	3	1957–1958	4	4*	0	2.00	10	5-109	1/0	27.30	2	–
Taylor Jerome Everton	22.6.1984		29	2003–2009	629	106	1	15.72	82	5-11	3/0	35.64	5	66/17
Thompson Patterson Ian Chesterfield	26.9.1971		2	1995–1996	17	10*	0	8.50	5	2-58	0/0	43.00	0	–
Tonge Gavin Courtney	13.2.1983		1	2009	25	23*	0	25.00	1	1-28	0/0	113.00	2	2/5
Trim John	25.1.1915	12.11.1960	4	1947–1951	21	12	0	5.25	18	5-34	1/0	16.16	0	–
Valentine Alfred Louis	28.4.1930	11.5.2004	36	1950–1961	141	14	0	4.70	139	8-104	8/2	30.32	13	–
Valentine Vincent Adolphus	4.4.1908	6.7.1972	2	1933	35	19*	0	11.66	1	1-55	0/0	104.00	2	–
Walcott Sir Clyde Leopold	17.1.1926	26.8.2006	44	1947–1959	3,798	220	15	56.68	11	3-50	0/0	37.09	53/11	–
Walcott Leslie Arthur	18.1.1894	27.2.1984	1	1929	40	24	0	40.00	1	1-17	0/0	32.00	0	–
Wallace Philo Alphonso	2.8.1970		7	1997–1998	279	92	0	21.46	–	–	–	–	9	33
Walsh Courtney Andrew	30.10.1962		132	1984–2000	936	30*	0	7.54	519	7-37	22/3	24.44	29	205
Walton Chadwick Antonio Kirkpatrick	3.7.1985		2	2009	13	10	0	3.25	–	–	–	–	10	2
Washington Dwight Marlon	5.3.1983		1	2004	7	7*	0	–	0	0-20	0/0	–	3	–
Watson Chester Donald	1.7.1938		7	1959–1961	12	5	0	2.40	19	4-62	0/0	38.10	1	–
Weekes Sir Everton de Courcy	26.2.1925		48	1947–1957	4,455	207	15	58.61	1	1-8	0/0	77.00	49	–
Weekes Kenneth Hunnell	24.1.1912	9.2.1998	2	1939	173	137	1	57.66	–	–	–	–	0	–
White Anthony Wilbur	20.11.1938		2	1964	71	57*	0	23.66	3	2-34	0/0	50.66	0	–
Wight Claude Vibart	28.7.1902	4.10.1969	2	1928–1929	67	23	0	22.33	–	–	–	–	0	–
Wight George Leslie	28.5.1929	4.1.2004	1	1952	21	21	0	21.00	0	0-6	0/0	–	0	–
Wiles Charles Archibald	11.8.1892	4.11.1957	1	1933	2	2	0	1.00	–	–	–	–	0	–
Willett Elquemedo Tonito	1.5.1953		5	1972–1974	74	26	0	14.80	11	3-33	0/0	43.81	0	–
Williams Alvadon Basil	21.11.1949		7	1977–1978	469	111	2	39.08	–	–	–	–	5	–
Williams David	4.11.1963		11	1991–1997	242	65	0	13.44	–	–	–	–	40/2	36

	Born	Died	Tests	Test Career	Runs	HS	100s	Avge	Wkts	BB	5/10	Avge	Ct/St	O/T
Williams Ernest Albert Vivian ("Foffie")	10.4.1914	13.4.1997	4	1939–1947	113	72	0	18.83	9	3-51	0/0	26.77	2	
Williams Stuart Clayton	12.8.1969		31	1993–2001	1,183	128	1	24.14	0	0-19	0/0	–	27	57
Wishart Kenneth Leslie	28.11.1908	18.10.1972	1	1934	52	52	0	26.00	–	–	–/–	–	0	
Worrell Sir Frank Mortimer Maglinne	1.8.1924	13.3.1967	51	1947–1963	3,860	261	9	49.48	69	7-70	2/0	38.72	43	

NEW ZEALAND (250 players)

	Born	Died	Tests	Test Career	Runs	HS	100s	Avge	Wkts	BB	5/10	Avge	Ct/St	O/T
Adams Andre Ryan	17.7.1975		1	2001	18	11	0	9.00	6	3-44	0/0	17.50	1	42/4
Alabaster John Chaloner	11.7.1930		21	1955–1971	272	34	0	9.71	49	4-46	0/0	38.02	7	
Allcott Cyril Francis Walter	7.10.1896	19.11.1973	6	1929–1931	113	33	0	22.60	6	2-102	0/0	90.16	5	
Anderson Geoffrey Ian	24.12.1971		4	1995–1999	27	8*	0	3.37	19	4-74	0/0	58.47	2	31
[1] Anderson Robert Wickham	2.10.1948		9	1976–1978	423	92	0	23.50	–	–	–/–	–	1	2
[1] Anderson William McDougall	8.10.1919	21.12.1979	1	1945	5	4	0	2.50	–	–	–/–	–	–	
Andrews Bryan	4.4.1945		2	1973	22	17	0	22.00	2	2-40	0/0	77.00	1	
Arnel Brent John	3.1.1979		4	2009–2010	34	8*	0	4.85	9	4-95	0/0	55.77	3	
Astle Nathan John	15.9.1971		81	1995–2006	4,702	222	11	37.02	51	3-27	0/0	42.01	70	223/4
Badcock Frederick Theodore ("Ted")	9.8.1897	9.9.1982	7	1929–1932	137	64	0	19.57	16	4-80	0/0	38.12	1	
Barber Richard Trevor	3.6.1925		1	1955	17	12	0	8.50	–	–	–/–	–	–	
Bartlett Gary Alex	3.2.1941		10	1961–1967	263	40	0	15.47	24	6-38	1/0	33.00	8	
Barton Paul Thomas	9.10.1935		7	1961–1962	285	109	1	20.35	–	–	–/–	–	4	
Beard Donald Derek	14.11.1920	15.7.1982	4	1951–1955	101	31	0	20.20	9	3-22	0/0	33.55	2	
Beck John Edward Francis	1.8.1934	23.4.2000	8	1953–1955	394	99	0	26.26	–	–	–/–	–	2	
Bell Matthew David	25.2.1977		18	1998–2007	729	107	2	24.30	–	–	–/–	–	19	7
Bell William	5.9.1931	23.7.2002	2	1953	21	21*	0	–	2	1-54	0/0	117.50	1	
Bennett Hamish Kyle	22.2.1987		1	2010	4	4	0	4.00	0	0-47	0/0	–	–	2
Bilby Grahame Paul	7.5.1941		2	1965	55	28	0	13.75	–	–	–/–	–	3	
Blain Tony Elston	17.2.1962		11	1986–1993	456	78	0	26.82	–	–	–/–	–	19/2	38
Blair Robert William	23.6.1932		19	1952–1963	189	64*	0	6.75	43	4-85	0/0	35.23	5	
Blunt Roger Charles	3.11.1900	22.6.1966	9	1929–1931	330	96	0	27.50	12	3-17	0/0	39.33	5	
Bolton Bruce Alfred	31.5.1935		2	1958	59	33	0	19.66	–	–	–/–	–	3	
Bond Shane Edward	7.6.1975		18	2001–2009	168	41*	0	12.92	87	6-51	5/1	22.09	8	82/20
Boock Stephen Lewis	20.9.1951		30	1977–1988	207	37	0	6.27	74	7-87	4/0	34.64	14	14
[2] Bracewell Brendon Paul	14.9.1959		6	1978–1984	24	8	0	2.40	14	3-110	0/0	41.78	1	1

Name	Born	Died	Tests	Test Career	Runs	HS	100s	Avge	Wkts	BB	5/10	Avge	Ct/St	O/T
[2]Bracewell John Garry	15.4.1958		41	1980–1990	1,001	110	0	20.42	102	6-32	4/1	35.81	31	53
Bradburn Grant Eric	26.5.1966		7	1990–2000	105	30*	0	13.12	6	3-134	0/0	76.66	6	11
[1]Bradburn Wynne Pennell	24.11.1938	25.9.2008	2	1963	62	32	0	15.50	–	–	–	–	2	
Brown Vaughan Raymond	3.11.1959		2	1985	51	36*	0	25.50	1	1-17	0/0	176.00	3	
Burgess Mark Gordon	17.7.1944		50	1967–1980	2,684	119*	5	31.20	6	3-23	0/0	35.33	34	3
Burke Cecil	27.3.1914	4.8.1997	1	1945	4	3	0	2.00	2	2-30	0/0	15.00	0	26
Burtt Thomas Browning	22.1.1915	24.5.1988	10	1946–1952	252	42	0	21.00	33	6-162	3/0	35.45	2	
Butler Ian Gareth	24.11.1981		8	2001–2004	76	26	0	9.50	24	6-46	1/0	36.83	4	26/15
Butterfield Leonard Arthur	29.8.1913	5.7.1999	1	1945	0	0	0	0.00	0	0-24	0/0	–	0	
[1]Cairns Bernard Lance	10.10.1949		43	1973–1985	928	64	0	16.28	130	7-74	6/1	32.91	30	78
[1]Cairns Christopher Lance	13.6.1970		62	1989–2004	3,320	158	5	33.53	218	7-27	13/1	29.40	14	214/2
Cameron Francis James MBE	1.6.1932		19	1961–1965	116	27*	0	11.60	62	5-34	3/0	29.82	1	
Cave Henry Butler	10.10.1922	15.9.1989	19	1949–1958	229	22*	0	8.80	34	4-21	0/0	43.14	8	
Chapple Murray Ernest	25.7.1930	31.7.1985	14	1952–1965	497	76	0	19.11	1	1-24	0/0	84.00	10	
Chatfield Ewen John MBE	3.7.1950		43	1974–1988	180	21*	0	8.57	123	6-73	3/1	32.17	7	114
Cleverley Donald Charles	23.12.1909	16.2.2004	2	1931–1945	19	10*	0	19.00	0	0-51	0/0	–	0	
Collinge Richard Owen	2.4.1946		35	1964–1978	533	68*	0	14.40	116	6-63	3/0	29.25	10	15
Colquhoun Ian Alexander	8.6.1924	26.2.2005	2	1954	1	1*	0	0.50	–	–	–	–	4	
Coney Jeremy Vernon MBE	21.6.1952		52	1973–1986	2,668	174*	3	37.57	27	3-28	0/0	35.77	64	88
Congdon Bevan Ernest OBE	11.2.1938		61	1964–1978	3,448	176	7	32.22	59	5-65	1/0	36.50	44	11
Cowie John OBE	30.3.1912	3.6.1994	9	1937–1949	90	45	0	10.00	45	6-40	4/1	21.53	3	
Cresswell George Fenwick	22.3.1915	10.1.1966	3	1949–1950	14	12*	0	7.00	13	6-168	1/0	22.46	0	
Cromb Ian Burns	25.6.1905	6.3.1984	5	1931–1931	123	51*	0	20.50	8	3-113	0/0	55.25	1	
Crowe Jeffrey John	14.9.1958		39	1982–1989	1,601	128	3	26.24	0	0-0	0/0	–	41	75
[2]Crowe Martin David MBE	22.9.1962		77	1981–1995	5,444	299	17	45.36	14	2-25	0/0	48.28	71	143
Cumming Craig Derek	31.8.1975		11	2004–2007	441	74	0	25.94	–	–	–	–	3	13
Cunis Robert Smith	5.1.1941	9.8.2008	20	1963–1971	295	51	0	12.82	51	6-76	1/0	37.00	1	
D'Arcy John William	23.4.1936		5	1958	136	33	0	13.60	–	–	–	–	0	
Davis Heath Te-Ihi-O-Te-Rangi	30.11.1971		5	1994–1997	20	8*	0	6.66	17	5-63	1/0	29.35	4	11
de Groen Richard Paul	5.8.1962		5	1993–1994	45	26	0	7.50	11	3-40	0/0	45.90	0	12
Dempster Charles Stewart	15.11.1903	14.2.1974	10	1929–1932	723	136	2	65.72	0	0-10	0/0	–	2	
Dempster Eric William	25.1.1925		5	1952–1953	106	47	0	17.66	2	1-24	0/0	109.50	1	
Dick Arthur Edward	10.10.1936		17	1961–1965	370	50*	0	14.23	–	–	–	–	47/4	
Dickinson George Ritchie	11.3.1903	17.3.1978	3	1929–1931	31	11	0	6.20	8	3-66	0/0	30.62	3	
Donnelly Martin Paterson	17.10.1917	22.10.1999	7	1937–1949	582	206	1	52.90	0	0-20	0/0	–	7	
Doull Simon Blair	6.8.1969		32	1992–1999	570	46	0	14.61	98	7-65	6/0	29.30	16	42

Name	Born	Died	Tests	Test Career	Runs	HS	100s	Avge	Wkts	BB	5I/10	Avge	Ct/St	O/T
Dowling Graham Thorne OBE	4.3.1937		39	1961–1971	2,306	239	3	31.16	1	1-19	0/0	19.00	23	5
Drum Christopher James	10.7.1974		5	2000–2001	10	10	0	3.33	16	3-36	0/0	30.12	4	
Dunning John Angus	6.2.1903	24.6.1971	4	1932–1937	38	19	0	7.60	5	2-35	0/0	98.60	2	
Edgar Bruce Adrian	23.11.1956		39	1978–1986	1,958	161	3	30.59	0	0-3	—/—	—	14	64
Edwards Graham Neil ("Jock")	27.5.1955		8	1976–1980	377	55	0	25.13	—	—	—	—	7	6
Elliott Grant David	21.3.1979		5	2007–2009	86	25	0	10.75	4	2-8	0/0	35.00	2	37/1
Emery Raymond William George	28.3.1915	18.12.1982	2	1951	46	28	0	11.50	2	2-52	0/0	26.00	0	
Fisher Frederick Eric	28.7.1924	19.6.1996	1	1952	23	14	0	11.50	1	1-78	0/0	78.00	0	
Fleming Stephen Paul	1.4.1973		111	1993–2007	7,172	274*	9	40.06	—	—	—	—	171	279‡/5
Flynn Daniel Raymond	16.4.1985		16	2008–2009	689	95	0	28.70	—	—	—	—	7	16/4
Foley Henry	28.1.1906	16.10.1948	1	1929	4	2	0	2.00	—	—	—	—	0	
Franklin James Edward Charles	7.11.1980		27	2000–2010	683	122*	1	21.34	80	6-119	3/0	33.10	11	78/16
Franklin Trevor John	15.3.1962		21	1983–1990	828	101	0	23.00	—	—	—	—	8	3
Freeman Douglas Linford	8.9.1914	31.5.1994	2	1932	2	1	0	1.00	1	1-91	0/0	169.00	0	
Fulton Peter Gordon	1.2.1979		10	2005–2009	314	75	0	20.93	—	—	—	—	12	49/11
Gallichan Norman	3.6.1906	25.3.1969	1	1937	32	30	0	16.00	3	3-99	0/0	37.66	0	
Gedye Sidney Graham	2.5.1929		4	1963–1964	193	55	0	24.12	—	—	—	—	2	
Germon Lee Kenneth	4.11.1968		12	1995–1996	382	55	0	21.22	—	—	—	—	27/2	37
Gillespie Mark Raymond	17.10.1979		3	2007–2008	25	16*	0	6.25	11	5-136	1/0	34.54	0	32/11
Gillespie Stuart Ross	2.3.1957		1	1985	28	28	0	28.00	1	1-79	0/0	79.00	0	10
Gray Evan John	18.11.1954		10	1983–1988	248	50	0	15.50	17	3-73	0/0	52.11	6	19
Greatbatch Mark John	11.12.1963		41	1987–1996	2,021	146*	3	30.62	0	0-0	—/—	—	27	84
[2] Guillen Simpson Clairmonte ("Sammy")	24.9.1924		3†	1955	98	41	0	16.33	—	—	—	—	4/1	
Guptill Martin James	30.9.1986		15	2008–2010	944	189	1	34.96	3	3-37	0/0	45.33	11	38/23
Guy John William	29.8.1934		12	1955–1967	440	102	0	20.95	—	—	—	—	2	
[1,2] Hadlee Dayle Robert	6.1.1948		26	1969–1977	530	56	0	14.32	71	4-30	0/0	33.64	8	11
[1] Hadlee Sir Richard John	3.7.1951		86	1972–1990	3,124	151*	2	27.16	431	9-52	36/9	22.29	39	115
[1] Hadlee Walter Arnold CBE	4.6.1915	29.9.2006	11	1937–1950	543	116	0	30.16	—	—	—	—	6	
Harford Noel Sherwin	30.8.1930	30.3.1981	8	1955–1958	229	93	0	15.26	—	—	—	—	0	
Harford Roy Ivan	30.5.1936		3	1967	7	6	0	2.33	—	—	—	—	11	
[1] Harris Chris Zinzan	20.11.1969		23	1992–2002	777	71	0	20.44	16	2-16	0/0	73.12	14	250
[1] Harris Parke Gerald Zinzan	18.7.1927	1.12.1991	9	1955–1964	378	101	1	22.23	0	0-14	—/—	—	6	
Harris Roger Meredith	27.7.1933		2	1958	31	13	0	10.33	—	—	—	—	0	
[2] Hart Matthew Norman	16.5.1972		14	1993–1995	353	45	0	17.65	29	5-77	1/0	49.58	14	13
[2] Hart Robert Garry	2.12.1974		11	2002–2003	260	57*	0	16.25	—	—	—	—	29/1	2
Hartland Blair Robert	22.10.1966		9	1991–1994	303	52	0	16.83	—	—	—	—	5	16

	Born	Died	Tests	Test Career	Runs	HS	100s	Avge	Wkts	BB	5/10	Avge	Ct/St	O/T
Haslam Mark James	26.9.1972		4	1992–1995	4	3	0	4.00	2	1-33	0/0	122.50	2	1
Hastings Brian Frederick	23.3.1940		31	1968–1975	1,510	117*	4	30.20	–	0-3	0/0	–	23	1
Hayes John Arthur	11.1.1927	25.12.2007	15	1950–1958	73	19	0	4.86	30	4-36	0/0	40.56	3	11
Henderson Matthew	2.8.1895	17.6.1970	1	1929	8	6	0	8.00	2	2-38	0/0	32.00	1	–
Hopkins Gareth James	24.11.1976		4	2008–2010	71	15	0	11.83	–	–	–/–	–	9	25/10
² Horne Matthew Jeffery	5.12.1970		35	1996–2003	1,788	157	4	28.38	0	0-4	0/0	–	17	50
Horne Philip Andrew	21.1.1960		4	1986–1990	71	27	0	10.14					3	4
Hough Kenneth William	24.10.1928	20.9.2009	2	1958	62	31*	0	62.00	6	3-79	0/0	29.16	3	
How Jamie Michael	19.5.1981		19	2005–2008	772	92	0	22.70	0	0-0	0/0	–	18	35/5
² Howarth Geoffrey Philip OBE.	29.3.1951		47	1974–1984	2,531	147	6	32.44	3	1-13	0/0	90.33	29	70
² Howarth Hedley John	25.12.1943	7.11.2008	30	1969–1976	291	61	0	12.12	86	5-34	2/0	36.95	33	9
Ingram Peter John	25.10.1978		2	2009	61	42	0	15.25					0	8/3
James Kenneth Cecil	12.3.1904	21.8.1976	11	1929–1932	52	14	0	4.72	–	–	–/–	–	11/5	–
Jarvis Terrence Wayne	29.7.1944		13	1964–1972	625	182	1	29.76	–	0-0	0/0	–	3	–
Jones Andrew Howard	9.5.1959		39	1986–1994	2,922	186	7	44.27	1	1-40	0/0	194.00	25	87
Jones Richard Andrew	22.10.1973		1	2003	23	16	0	11.50	0	0-6	0/0	–	0	5
Kennedy Robert John	3.6.1972		4	1995	28	22	0	7.00	6	3-28	0/0	63.33	2	7
Kerr John Lambert	28.12.1910	27.5.2007	7	1931–1937	212	59	0	19.27	–	–	–/–	–	4	7
Kuggeleijn Christopher Mary	10.5.1956		2	1988	7	7	0	1.75	1	1-50	0/0	67.00	0	16
Larsen Gavin Rolf	27.9.1962		8	1994–1995	127	26*	0	14.11	24	3-57	0/0	28.70	5	121
Latham Rodney Terry	12.6.1961		4	1991–1992	219	119	1	31.28	0	0-6	0/0	–	5	33
Lees Warren Kenneth MBE	19.3.1952		21	1976–1983	778	152	1	23.57	0	0-4	0/0	–	52/7	31
Leggat Ian Bruce	7.6.1930		1	1953	0	0	0	0.00	0	0-6	0/0	–	2	–
Leggat John Gordon	27.5.1926	9.3.1973	9	1951–1955	351	61	0	21.93					0	–
Lissette Allen Fisher	6.11.1919	24.1.1973	2	1955	2	1*	0	1.00	3	2-73	0/0	41.33	0	–
Loveridge Greg Riaka	15.1.1975		1	1995	4	4*	0	–	–	–	–/–	–	0	–
Lowry Thomas Coleman	17.2.1898	20.7.1976	7	1929–1931	223	80	0	27.87	0	0-0	0/0	–	8	–
McCullum Brendon Barrie	27.9.1981		57	2003–2010	3,389	225	6	37.24	0	0-18	0/0	–	167/11	178/40
McEwan Paul Ernest	19.12.1953		4	1979–1984	96	40*	0	16.00	0	0-6	0/0	–	5	17
MacGibbon Anthony Roy	28.8.1924	6.4.2010	26	1950–1958	814	66	0	19.85	70	5-64	1/0	30.85	13	–
McGirr Herbert Mendelson	5.11.1891	14.4.1964	2	1929	51	51	0	51.00	1	1-65	0/0	115.00	0	–
McGregor Spencer Noel	18.12.1931	21.11.2007	25	1954–1964	892	111	1	19.82					9	–
McIntosh Timothy Gavin	4.12.1979		17	2008–2010	854	136	2	27.54					10	–
McKay Andrew John	17.4.1980		1	2010	25	20*	0	25.00	1	1-120	0/0	120.00	0	13/2
McLeod Edwin George	14.10.1900	14.9.1989	1	1929	18	16	0	18.00	0	0-5	0/0	–	0	–
McMahon Trevor George	8.11.1929		5	1955	7	4*	0	2.33					7/1	–

	Born	Died	Tests	Test Career	Runs	HS	100s	Avge	Wkts	BB	5/10	Avge	Ct/St	O/T
McMillan Craig Douglas	13.9.1976		55	1997–2004	3,116	142	6	38.46	28	3-48	0/0	44.89	22	197/8
McRae Donald Alexander Noel	25.12.1912	10.8.1986		*1945*			0	4.00	0	0-44	0/0	–	0	
²Marshall Hamish John Hamilton	15.2.1979		13	*2000–2005*	652	160	2	38.35	0	0-4	0/0	–	1	66/3
²Marshall James Andrew Hamilton	15.2.1979		1	2004–2008	218	52	0	19.81	0	0-4	0/0	–		10/3
Martin Christopher Stewart	10.12.1974		61	2000–2010	109	12*	0	2.53	199	6-54	9/1	34.66	5	206
Mason Michael James	27.8.1974		1	*2003*	3	3	0	1.50	0	0-32	0/0	–		26/3
Matheson Alexander Malcolm	27.2.1906	31.12.1985	2	*1929–1931*	7	7	0	7.00	2	2-7	0/0	68.00	0	
Meale Trevor	11.11.1928		1	1958	21	10	0	5.25			–/–	–	0	
Merritt William Edward	18.8.1908	9.6.1977	6	*1929–1931*	73	19	0	10.42	12	4-104	–/–	51.41	0	
Meuli Edgar Milton	20.2.1926	15.4.2007	1	1952	38	23	0	19.00			–/–	–	0	
Milburn Barry Douglas	24.11.1943		3	1968	8	4*	0	8.00			–/–	–	6/2	
Miller Lawrence Somerville Martin	31.3.1923	17.12.1996	13	1952–1958	346	47	0	13.84	0	0-1	0/0	–	0	
Mills John Ernest	3.9.1905	11.12.1972	7	*1929–1932*	241	117	1	26.77			–/–	–	4	
Mills Kyle David	15.3.1979		19	2004–2008	289	57	0	11.56	44	4-16	2/0	33.02	2	123/22
Moir Alexander McKenzie	17.7.1919	17.6.2000	17	1950–1958	327	41*	0	14.86	28	6-155	2/0	50.64	3	
Moloney Denis Andrew Robert ("Sonny")	11.8.1910	15.7.1942	3	1937	156	64	0	26.00	0	0-9	0/0	–	2	
Mooney Francis Leonard Hugh	26.5.1921	8.3.2004	14	1949–1953	343	46	0	17.15	0	0-0	0/0	–	22/8	
Morgan Ross Winston	12.2.1941		20	1964–1971	734	97	0	22.24	5	1-16	0/0	121.80	12	
Morrison Bruce Donald	17.12.1933		1	1962	10	10	0	5.00	2	2-129	0/0	64.50		
Morrison Daniel Kyle	3.2.1966		48	1987–1996	379	42	0	8.42	160	7-89	9/1	34.68	14	96
Morrison John Francis MacLean	27.8.1947		17	1973–1981	656	117	1	22.62	2	2-52	0/0	35.50	9	18
Motz Richard Charles	12.1.1940	29.4.2007	32	1961–1969	612	60	0	11.54	100	6-63	5/0	31.48	9	
Murray Bruce Alexander Grenfell	18.9.1940		13	1967–1970	598	90	1	23.92	1	1-0	0/0	0.00	21	
Murray Darrin James	4.9.1967		8	1994	303	52	0	20.20			–/–	–	6	1
Nash Dion Joseph	20.11.1971		32	1992–2001	729	89*	0	23.51	93	6-27	3/1	28.48	13	81
Newman Sir Jack	3.7.1902	23.9.1996		*1931–1933*	33	19	0	8.25	2	2-76	0/0	127.00	2	
O'Brien Iain Edward	10.7.1976		22	2004–2009	219	31	0	7.55	73	6-75	1/0	33.27	7	10/4
O'Connor Shayne Barry	15.11.1973		19	1997–2001	103	20	0	5.72	53	5-51	1/0	32.52	6	38
Oram Jacob David Philip	28.7.1978		33	2002–2009	1,780	133	5	36.32	60	4-41	0/0	33.05	15	141/27
O'Sullivan David Robert	16.11.1944		11	1972–1976	158	23*	0	9.29	18	5-148	1/0	67.83	2	3
Overton Guy William Fitzroy	8.6.1919	7.9.1993	3	1953	8	3*	0	1.60			–/–	–	1	
Owens Michael Barry	11.11.1969		8	1992–1994	16	8*	0	2.66	17	4-99	0/0	28.66	3	1
Page Milford Laurenson ("Curly")	8.5.1902	13.2.1987	14	1929–1937	492	104	0	24.60	5	2-21	0/0	34.41	6	
Papps Michael Hugh William	2.7.1979		8	2003–2007	246	86	0	16.40			–/–	–	11	6
Parker John Morton	21.2.1951		36	1972–1980	1,498	121	3	24.55	1	1-24	0/0	46.20	30	24
²Parker Norman Murray	28.8.1948		3	1976	89	40	0	14.83	1	1-24	0/0	24.00	2	1

	Born	Died	Tests	Test Career	Runs	HS	100s	Avge	Wkts	BB	5/10	Avge	Ct/St 197/7	O/T
Parore Adam Craig	23.1.1971		78	1990–2001	2,865	110	2	26.28	–		–/–			179
Patel Dipak Narshibhai	25.10.1958		37	1986–1996	1,200	99	0	20.68	75	6-50	3/0	42.05	15	75
Patel Jeetan Shashi	7.5.1980		12	2005–2010	167	27*	0	12.84	40	5-110	1/0	44.85	7	39/11
Petherick Peter James	25.9.1942		6	1976	34	13	0	4.85	16	3-90	0/0	42.81	4	
Petrie Eric Charlton	22.5.1927	14.8.2004	14	1955–1965	258	55	0	12.90	–		–/–		25	
Playle William Rodger	1.12.1938		8	1958–1962	151	65	0	10.06	–				4	
Pocock Blair Andrew	18.6.1971		15	1993–1997	665	85	0	22.93	0	0-10	0/0		5	
Pollard Victor	7.9.1945		32	1964–1973	1,266	116	2	24.34	40	3-3	0/0	46.32	19	3
Poore Matt Beresford	1.6.1930		14	1952–1955	355	45	0	15.43	9	2-28	0/0	40.77	1	
Priest Mark Wellings	12.8.1961		3	1990–1997	56	26	0	14.00	3	2-42	0/0	52.66	0	18
Pringle Christopher	26.1.1968		14	1990–1994	175	30	0	10.29	30	7-52	1/1	46.30	3	64
Puna Narotam	28.10.1929	7.6.1996	3	1965	31	18*	0	15.50	4	2-40	0/0	60.00	1	
Rabone Geoffrey Osborne	6.11.1921	19.1.2006	12	1949–1954	562	107	1	31.22	16	6-68	1/0	39.68	5	
Redmond Aaron James	23.9.1979		7	2008–2008	299	83	1	23.00	3	2-47	0/0	20.66	5	6/7
Redmond Rodney Ernest	29.12.1944		1	1972	163	107	1	81.50	0	0-0	–/–		0	2
Reid John Fulton	3.3.1956		19	1978–1985	1,296	180	6	46.28	0	0-0	0/0		9	25
Reid John Richard OBE	3.6.1928		58	1949–1965	3,428	142	6	33.28	85	6-60	1/0	33.35	43/1	
Richardson Mark Hunter	11.6.1971		38	2000–2004	2,776	145	4	44.77	1	1-16	0/0	21.00	26	4
Roberts Albert William	20.8.1909	13.5.1978	5	1929–1937	248	66*	0	27.55	7	4-101	0/0	29.85	4	
Roberts Andrew Duncan Glenn	6.5.1947	26.10.1989	7	1975–1976	254	84*	0	23.09	4	1-12	0/0	45.50	4	1
Robertson Gary Keith	15.7.1960		1	1985	12	12	0	12.00	1	1-91	0/0	91.00	0	10
Rowe Charles Gordon	30.6.1915	9.6.1995	1	1945	0	0	0	0.00	–		–/–		1	
Rutherford Kenneth Robert	26.10.1965		56	1984–1994	2,465	107*	3	27.08	1	1-38	0/0	161.00	32	121
Ryder Jesse Daniel	6.8.1984		16	2008–2010	1,211	201	3	44.85	5	2-7	0/0	56.00	10	24/17
Scott Roy Hamilton	6.3.1917	5.8.2005	1	1946	18	18	0	18.00	1	1-74	0/0	74.00	0	
Scott Verdun John	31.7.1916	2.8.1980	10	1945–1951	458	84	0	28.62	–	0-5	0/0		7	
Sewell David Graham	20.10.1977		1	1997	1	1*	0	–	1	0-9	0/0	–	0	
Shrimpton Michael John Froud	23.6.1940		10	1962–1973	265	46	0	13.94	5	3-35	0/0	31.60	2	
Sinclair Barry Whitley	23.10.1936		21	1962–1967	1,148	138	3	29.43	2	2-32	0/0	16.00	8	
Sinclair Ian McKay	1.6.1933		2	1955	25	18*	0	8.33	1	1-79	0/0	120.00	1	
Sinclair Mathew Stuart	9.11.1975		33	1999–2009	1,635	214	3	32.05	0	0-1	–/–		31	54/2
Smith Frank Brunton	13.3.1922	6.7.1997	4	1946–1951	237	96	0	47.40	–				0	
Smith Horace Dennis	8.1.1913	25.1.1986	1	1932	4	4	0	4.00	1	1-113	0/0	113.00	0	
Smith Ian David Stockley MBE	28.2.1957		63	1980–1991	1,815	173	2	25.56	0	0-5	0/0	–	168/8	98
Snedden Colin Alexander	7.1.1918		1	1946					0	0-46	0/0		0	
Snedden Martin Colin	23.11.1958		25	1980–1990	327	33*	0	14.86	58	5-68	1/0	37.91	7	93

Name	Born	Died	Tests	Test Career	Runs	HS	Avge	100s	Wkts	Avge	BB	5/10	Ct/St	O/T
Southee Timothy Grant	11.12.1988		13	2007–2010	385	77*	21.38	0	35	42.54	5-55	1/0	4	38/19
Sparling John Trevor	24.7.1938		11	1958–1963	229	50	12.72	0	5	65.40	1-9	–/–	4	
Spearman Craig Murray	4.7.1972		19	1995–2000	922	112	26.34	1					21	51
Stead Gary Raymond	9.1.1972		5	1998–1999	278	78	34.75	0					2	
Stirling Derek Alexander	5.10.1961		6	1984–1986	108	26	15.42	0	13	46.23	4-88	0/0	2	6
Styris Scott Bernard	10.7.1975		29	2002–2007	1,586	170	36.04	5	20	50.75	3-28	0/0	23	174/31
Su'a Murphy Logo	7.11.1966		13	1991–1994	165	44	12.69	0	36	38.25	5-73	2/0	8	12
Sutcliffe Bert MBE	17.11.1923	20.4.2001	42	1946–1965	2,727	230*	40.10	5	4	86.00	2-38	–/–	20	
Taylor Bruce Richard	12.7.1943		30	1964–1973	898	124	20.40	2	111	26.60	7-74	4/0	10	2
Taylor Donald Dougald	2.3.1923	5.12.1980	3	1946–1955	159	77	31.80	0					2	
Taylor Luteru Ross Poutoa Lote	8.3.1984		30	2007–2010	2,221	154*	41.12	5	2	21.50	2-4	–/–	52	93/37
Thomson Keith	26.2.1941		2	1967	94	69	31.33	0	1	9.00	1-9	–/–	0	
Thomson Shane Alexander	27.1.1969		19	1989–1995	958	120*	30.90	1	19	50.15	3-63	–/–	7	56
Tindill Eric William Thomas	18.12.1910	1.8.2010	5	1937–1946	73	37*	9.12	0					6/1	
Troup Gary Bertram	3.10.1952		15	1976–1985	55	13*	4.58	0	39	37.28	6-95	1/1	2	22
Truscott Peter Bennetts	14.8.1941		1	1964	29	26	14.50	0					1	
Tuffey Daryl Raymond	11.6.1978		26	1999–2009	427	80*	16.42	0	77	31.75	6-54	2/0	15	94/3
Turner Glenn Maitland	26.5.1947		41	1968–1982	2,991	259	44.64	7			0-5	–/–	42	41
Twose Roger Graham	17.4.1968		16	1995–1999	628	94	25.12	0	3	43.33	2-36	–/–	4	87
Vance Robert Howard	31.3.1955		4	1987–1989	207	68	29.57	0					0	8
Vaughan Justin Thomas Caldwell	30.8.1967		6	1992–1996	201	44	18.27	0	11	40.90	4-27	–/–	4	18
Vettori Daniel Luca	27.1.1979		104§	1996–2010	4,159	140	30.35	6	344	33.75	7-87	19/3	57	259½/28
Vincent Lou	11.11.1978		23	2001–2007	1,332	224	34.15	3					19	102/9
Vivian Graham Ellery	28.2.1946		5	1964–1971	110	43	18.33	0			0-2	–/–	3	1
Vivian Henry Gifford	4.11.1912	12.8.1983	7	1931–1937	421	100	42.10	1	17	107.00	4-58	–/–	4	
Wadsworth Kenneth John	30.11.1946	19.8.1976	33	1969–1975	1,010	80	21.48	0					92/4	13
Walker Brooke Graeme Keith	25.3.1977		5	2000–2002	118	27*	19.66	0	5	37.23	2-92	0/0	5	11
Wallace Walter Mervyn	19.12.1916	21.3.2008	13	1937–1952	439	66	20.90	0					5	
Walmsley Kerry Peter	23.8.1973		3	1994–2000	13	5	2.60	0	6	79.80	3-70	–/–	0	2
Ward John Thomas	11.3.1937		8	1963–1967	75	35*	12.50	0					16/1	
Watling Bradley-John	9.7.1985		9	2009–2010	203	60*	25.37	0					7/2	
Watson William	31.8.1965		15	1986–1993	60	11	5.00	0	40	43.44	6-78	1/0	7	61
Watt Leslie	17.9.1924	15.11.1996	1	1954	2	2	1.00	0					4	
Webb Murray George	22.6.1947		3	1970–1973	12	12	6.00	0	4	34.67			0	
Webb Peter Neil	14.7.1957		2	1979	11	5	3.66	0	2	117.75	2-114	–/–	2	5

§ Vettori's figures exclude eight runs and one wicket for the ICC World XI v Australia in the Super Series Test in 2005-06.

Name	Born	Died	Tests	Test Career	Runs	HS	100s	Avge	Wkts	BB	5/10	Avge	Ct/St	O/T
Weir Gordon Lindsay	2.6.1908	31.10.2003	11	1929-1937	416	74*	0	29.71	7	3-38	0/0	29.85		3
White David John	26.6.1961		2	1990	31	18	0	7.75	0	0-5	0/0	–	0	
Whitelaw Paul Erskine	10.2.1910	28.8.1988	2	1932	64	30	0	32.00					0	
Williamson Kane Stuart	8.8.1990		5	2010	299	131	1	33.22	2	1-45	–/–	88.00	1	9
Wiseman Paul John	4.5.1970		25	1997-2004	366	36	0	14.07	61	5-82	2/0	47.59	11	15
Wright John Geoffrey MBE	5.7.1954		82	1977-1992	5,334	185	12	37.82	0	0-1	0/0	–	38	149
Young Bryan Andrew	3.11.1964		35	1993-1998	2,034	267*	7	31.78					54	74
Young Reece Alan	15.9.1979		2	2010	103	57	0	25.75					3	
Yuile Bryan William	29.10.1941		17	1962-1969	481	64	0	17.81	34	4-43	–/–	35.67	12	

INDIA (267 players)

Name	Born	Died	Tests	Test Career	Runs	HS	100s	Avge	Wkts	BB	5/10	Avge	Ct/St	O/T
Abid Ali Syed	9.9.1941		29	1967-1974	1,018	81	0	20.36	47	6-55	1/0	42.12	32	5
Adhikari Hemchandra Ramachandra	31.7.1919	25.10.2003	21	1947-1958	872	114*	1	31.14	3	3-68	0/0	27.33	8	
Agarkar Ajit Bhalchandra	4.12.1977		26	1998-2005	571	109*	1	16.79	58	6-41	1/0	47.32	6	191/4
Amar Singh Ladha	4.12.1910	21.5.1940	7	1932-1936	292	51	0	22.46	28	7-86	2/0	30.64	3	
[1,2] Amarnath Mohinder	24.9.1950		69	1969-1987	4,378	138	11	42.50	32	4-63	0/0	55.68	47	85
[1] Amarnath Nanik ("Lala")	11.9.1911	5.8.2000	24	1933-1952	878	118	1	24.38	45	5-96	2/0	32.91	13	
[1,2] Amarnath Surinder	30.12.1948		10	1975-1978	550	124	1	30.55	1	1-5	0/0	5.00	13	3
Amir Elahi	1.9.1908	28.12.1980	1†	1947	17	13	0	8.50						
Amre Pravin Kalyan	14.8.1968		11	1992-1993	425	103	1	42.50					9	37
Ankola Salil Ashok	1.3.1968		1	1989	6	6	0	6.00	2	1-35	0/0	64.00	0	20
[2] Apte Arvindrao Laxmanrao	24.10.1934		1	1959	15	8	0	7.50					0	
[2] Apte Madhavrao Laxmanrao	5.10.1932		7	1952	542	163*	1	49.27		0-3	0/0	–	2	
Arshad Ayub	2.8.1958		13	1987-1989	257	57	0	17.13	41	5-50	3/0	35.07	2	32
Arun Bharathi	14.12.1962		2	1986	4	2*	0	4.00	4	3-76	0/0	29.00	2	4
Arun Lal	1.8.1955		16	1982-1988	729	93	0	26.03	0	0-0	0/0	–	13	13
Azad Kirtivardhan	2.1.1959		7	1980-1983	135	24	0	11.25	3	2-84	0/0	124.33	3	25
Azharuddin Mohammad	8.2.1963		99	1984-1999	6,215	199	22	45.03	0	0-4	0/0	–	105	334
Badani Hemang Kamal	14.11.1976		4	2001	94	38	0	15.66	0	0-17	0/0	–	6	40
Badrinath Subramaniam	30.8.1980		2	2009	63	56	0	21.00					2	3
Bahutule Sairaj Viasant	6.1.1973		2	2000-2001	39	21*	0	13.00	3	1-32	0/0	67.66	1	8
Baig Abbas Ali	19.3.1939		10	1959-1966	428	112	1	23.77	0	0-2	0/0	–	6	

	Born	Died	Test Career	Tests	Runs	HS	100s	Avge	Wkts	BB	5/10	Avge	Ct/St	O/T
Balaji Lakshmipathy	27.9.1981		2003-2004	8	51	31	0	5.66	27	5-76	1/0	37.18	1	30
Banerjee Sarobindu Nath ("Shute")	3.10.1911	14.10.1980	1948	1	13	8	0	6.50	5	4-54	0/0	25.40	0	
Banerjee Subroto Tara	13.2.1969		1991	1	3	3	0	3.00	3	3-47	0/0	15.66	0	6
Banerjee Sudangsu Abinash	1.11.1917	14.9.1992	1948	1	0	0	0	0.00	5	4-120	0/0	36.20	3	
Bangar Sanjay Bapusaheb	11.10.1972		2001-2002	12	470	100*	1	29.37	7	2-23	0/0	49.00	4	15
Baqa Jilani Mohammad	20.7.1911	2.7.1941	1936	1	16	12	0	16.00	0	0-55	0/0	–	0	
Bedi Bishan Singh	25.9.1946		1966-1979	67	656	50*	0	8.98	266	7-98	14/1	28.71	26	10
Bhandari Prakash	27.11.1935		1954-1956	3	77	39	0	19.25	1	0-12	0/0	–	1	
Bharadwaj Raghvendrarao Vijay	15.8.1975		1999	3	28	22	0	9.33	1	1-26	0/0	107.00	3	10
Bhat Adwai Raghuram	16.4.1958		1983	2	6	6	0	3.00	4	2-65	0/0	37.75	0	
Binny Roger Michael Humphrey	19.7.1955		1979-1986	27	830	83*	0	23.05	47	6-56	2/0	32.63	11	72
Borde Chandrakant Gulabrao	21.7.1934		1958-1969	55	3,061	177*	5	35.59	52	5-88	1/0	46.48	37	
Chandrasekhar Bhagwat Subramanya	17.5.1945		1963-1979	58	167	22	0	4.07	242	8-79	16/2	29.74	25	1
Chauhan Chetandra Pratap Singh	21.7.1947		1969-1981	40	2,084	97	0	31.57	2	1-4	0/0	53.00	38	7
Chauhan Rajesh Kumar	19.12.1966		1992-1997	21	98	23	0	7.00	47	4-48	0/0	39.51	12	35
Chawla Piyush Pramod	24.12.1988		2005-2007	3	5	4	0	2.50	7	2-66	0/0	45.66	0	21/3
Chopra Aakash	19.9.1977		2003-2004	10	437	60	0	23.00	0	–	–/–	–	15	
Chopra Nikhil	26.12.1973		1999	1	7	2*	0	3.50	1	0-78	0/0	205.00	0	39
Chowdhury Nirode Ranjan	23.5.1923	14.12.1979	1948-1951	2	3	4	0	3.00	1	1-130	0/0	–	0	
Colah Sorabji Hormasji Munchersha	22.9.1902	11.9.1950	1932-1933	2	69	31	0	17.25					2	
Contractor Nariman Jamshedji	7.3.1934		1955-1961	31	1,611	108	1	31.58	1	1-9	0/0	80.00	18	
Dahiya Vijay	10.5.1973		2000	2			0	–						
Dani Hemchandra Tukaram	24.5.1933	19.12.1999	1952	1			0		1	1-9	0/0	19.00	1	
Das Shiv Sunder	5.11.1977		2000-2001	23	1,326	110	2	34.89	0	0-7	–/–	–	6	19
Dasgupta Deep	7.6.1977		2001	8	344	100	1	28.66					13	4
Desai Ramakant Bhikaji	20.6.1939	27.4.1998	1958-1967	28	418	85	0	13.48	74	6-56	2/0	37.31	13	
Dhoni Mahendra Singh	7.7.1981		2005-2010	54	2,925	148	4	40.06	0	0-1	–/–	–	148/25	169/25
Dighe Sameer Sudhakar	8.10.1968		2000-2001	6	141	47	0	15.66					12/2	23
Dilawar Hussain	19.3.1907	26.8.1967	1933-1936	3	254	59	0	42.33					6/1	
Divecha Ramesh Vithaldas	18.10.1927	11.2.2003	1951-1952	5	60	26	0	12.00	11	3-102	0/0		5	
Doshi Dilip Rasiklal	22.12.1947		1979-1983	33	129	20	0	4.60	114	6-102	6/0	30.71	6	15
Dravid Rahul	11.1.1973		1996-2010	149§	12,040	270	31	52.80	1	1-18	0/0	39.00	199	335‡
Durani Salim Aziz	11.12.1934		1959-1972	29	1,202	104	1	25.04	75	6-73	3/1	35.42	14	
Engineer Farokh Maneksha	25.2.1938		1961-1974	46	2,611	121	2	31.08	0			–	66/16	5
Gadkari Chandrasekhar Vaman	3.2.1928	11.1.1998	1952-1954	6	129	50*	0	21.50	0	0-8	0/0	–	6	

§ Dravid's figures exclude 23 runs and one catch for the ICC World XI v Australia in the Super Series Test in 2005-06.

	Born	Died	Tests	Test Career	Runs	HS	100s	Avge	Wks	BB	5/10	Avge	Ct/St	O/T
1 Gaekwad Anshuman Dattajirao	23.9.1952		40	1974–1984	1,985	201	2	30.07	2	1-4	0/0	93.50	15	15
1 Gaekwad Dattajirao Krishnarao	27.10.1928		11	1952–1960	350	52	0	18.42	0	0-4	0/0	–	5	
Gaekwad Hiralal Ghasulal	29.8.1923	2.1.2003	1	1952	22	14	0	11.00	0	0-47	0/0	–	0	
Gambhir Gautam	14.10.1981		38	2004–2010	3,234	206	9	51.33				–	29	105/23
Gandhi Devang Jayant	6.9.1971		4	1999	204	88	0	34.00				–	3	3
Gandotra Ashok	24.11.1948		2	1969	54	18	0	13.50				–	3	
Ganesh Doddanarasiah	30.6.1973		4	1996	25	8	0	6.25	5	2-28	0/0	57.40	0	1
Ganguly Sourav Chandidas	8.7.1972		113	1996–2008	7,212	239	16	42.17	32	3-28	0/0	52.53	71	308‡
Gavaskar Sunil Manohar	10.7.1949		125	1970–1986	10,122	236*	34	51.12	1	1-34	0/0	206.00	108	108
Ghavri Karsan Devjibhai	28.2.1951		39	1974–1980	913	86	0	21.23	109	5-33	4/0	33.54	16	19
Ghorpade Jayasinghrao Mansinghrao	2.10.1930	29.3.1978	8	1952–1959	229	41	0	15.26	0	0-17	0/0	–	4	
Ghulam Ahmed	4.7.1922	28.10.1998	22	1948–1958	192	50	0	8.72	68	7-49	4/1	30.17	11	
Gopalan Morappakam Joysam	6.6.1909	21.12.2003	1	1933	18	11*	0	18.00	1	1-39	0/0	39.00	3	
Gopinath Coimbatarao Doraikannu	1.3.1930		8	1951–1959	242	50*	0	22.00	1	1-11	0/0	11.00	2	
Guard Ghulam Mustafa	12.12.1925	13.3.1978	2	1958–1959	11	7	0	5.50	3	2-69	0/0	60.66	2	
Guha Subrata	31.1.1946		4	1967–1969	17	6	0	3.40	3	2-55	0/0	103.66	2	
Gul Mahomed	15.10.1921	8.5.1992	8†	1946–1952	166	34	0	11.06	2	2-21	0/0	12.00	3	
2 Gupte Balkrishna Pandharinath	30.8.1934	5.7.2005	3	1960–1964	28	17*	0	28.00	3	1-54	0/0	116.33	1	
2 Gupte Subhashchandra Pandharinath	11.12.1929	31.5.2002	36	1951–1961	183	21	0	6.31	149	9-102	12/1	29.55	14	
Gursharan Singh	8.3.1963		1	1989	18	18	0	18.00				–	2	1
Hafeez Abdul (see Kardar)														
Hanumant Singh	29.3.1939	29.11.2006	14	1963–1969	686	105	1	31.18	0	0-5	0/0	–	11	
Harbhajan Singh	3.7.1980		93	1997–2010	2,008	115	2	18.59	393	8-84	25/5	31.85	42	210‡/22
Hardikar Manohar Shankar	8.2.1936	4.2.1995	2	1958	56	32*	0	18.66	1	1-9	0/0	55.00	3	
Harvinder Singh	23.12.1977		3	1997–2001	6	6	0	2.00	4	2-62	0/0	46.25	0	16
Hazare Vijay Samuel	11.3.1915	18.12.2004	30	1946–1952	2,192	164*	7	47.65	20	4-29	0/0	61.00	11	
Hindlekar Dattaram Dharmaji	1.1.1909	30.3.1949	4	1936–1946	71	26	0	14.20				–	3	
Hirwani Narendra Deepchand	18.10.1968		17	1987–1996	54	17	0	5.40	66	8-61	4/1	30.10	5	18
Ibrahim Khanmohammad Cassumbhoy	26.1.1919	12.11.2007	4	1948	169	85	0	21.12				–	5	
Indrajitsinhji Kumar Shri	15.6.1937		4	1964–1969	51	23	0	8.50				–	6/3	
Irani Jamshed Khudadad	18.8.1923	25.2.1982	2	1947	3	2*	0	3.00	0	–		–	2/1	
Jadeja Ajaysinhji	1.2.1971		15	1992–1999	576	96	0	26.18	1	–	–/–	–	5	196
3 Jahangir Khan Mohammad	1.2.1910	23.7.1988	4	1932–1936	39	13	0	5.57	4	4-60	0/0	63.75	4	
Jai Laxmidas Purshottamdas	1.4.1902	29.11.1968	1	1933	19	19	0	9.50				–	0	
Jaisimha Moganhalli Laxmanarsu	3.3.1939	6.7.1999	39	1959–1970	2,056	129	3	30.68	9	2-54	0/0	92.11	17	
Jamshedji Rustomji Jamshedji Dorabji	18.11.1892	5.4.1976	1	1933	5	4*	0	–	3	3-137	0/0	45.66	2	

	Born	Died	Tests	Test Career	Runs	HS	100s	Avge	Wkts	BB	5/10	Avge	Ct/St	O/T
Jayantilal Kenia	13.1.1948		1	1970	5	5	0	5.00					0	
Johnson David Jude	16.10.1971		2	1996	8	5	0	4.00	3	2-52	0/0	47.66	0	
Joshi Padmanabh Govind	27.10.1926	8.1.1987	12	1951-1960	207	52*	0	10.89					18/9	
Joshi Sunil Bandacharya	6.6.1969		15	1996-2000	352	92	0	20.70	41	5-142	1/0	35.85	7	69
Kaif Mohammad	1.12.1980		13	1999-2005	624	148*	1	32.84	0	0-4	0/0		14	125
Kambli Vinod Ganpat	18.1.1972		17	1992-1995	1,084	227	4	54.20					7	104
[1]Kanitkar Hrishikesh Hemant	14.11.1974		2	1999	74	45	0	18.50	0	0-2	0/0		0	34
[1]Kanitkar Hemant Shamsunder	8.12.1942		2	1974	111	65	0	27.75					0	
Kapil Dev	6.1.1959		131	1978-1993	5,248	163	8	31.05	434	9-83	23/2	29.64	64	225
[1]Kapoor Aashish Rakesh	25.3.1971		4	1994-1996	97	42	0	19.40	6	2-19	0/0	42.50	1	17
Kardar Abdul Hafeez	17.1.1925	21.4.1996	3†	1946	80	43	0	16.00					1	
Karim Syed Saba	14.11.1967		1	2000	15	15	0	15.00					1	34
Karthik Krishankumar Dinesh	1.6.1985		23	2004-2009	1,000	129	1	27.77					51/5	52.9
Kartik Murali	11.9.1976		8	1999-2004	88	43	0	9.77	24	4-44	0/0	34.16	2	37.1
Kenny Ramnath Baburao	29.9.1930	21.11.1985	5	1958-1959	245	62	0	27.22					1	
Kirmani Syed Mujtaba Hussein	29.12.1949		88	1975-1985	2,759	102	2	27.04					160/38	49
Kishenchand Gogumal	14.4.1925	16.4.1997	5	1947-1952	89	44	0	8.90					4	
[1]Kripal Singh Amritsar Govindsingh	6.8.1933	22.7.1987	14	1955-1964	422	100*	1	28.13	10	3-43	0/0	58.40	4	
Krishnamurthy Pochiah	12.7.1947	28.11.1999	5	1970	33	20	0	5.50					7/1	
Kulkarni Nilesh Moreshwar	3.4.1973		3	1997-2000	5	2	0	5.00	2	1-70	0/0	166.00	1	1
Kulkarni Rajiv Ramesh	25.9.1962		3	1986	5	2	0	1.00					0	10
Kulkarni Umesh Narayan	7.3.1942		4	1967	13	7	0	4.33	5	3-85	0/0	45.40	1	10
Kumar Vaman Viswanath	22.6.1935		2	1960-1961	6	6	0	3.00	7	5-64	1/0	28.85	1	
Kumble Anil	17.10.1970		132	1990-2008	2,506	110*	1	17.77	619	10-74	35/8	29.65	60	269‡
Kunderan Budhisagar Krishnappa	2.10.1939	23.6.2006	18	1959-1967	981	192	2	32.70	0	0-13	0/0		23/7	
Kuruvilla Abey	8.8.1968		10	1996-1997	66	35*	0	6.60	25	5-68	1/0	35.68	2	25
Lall Singh	16.12.1909	19.11.1985	1	1932	44	29	0	22.00					1	
Lamba Raman	2.1.1960	22.2.1998	4	1986-1987	102	53	0	20.40					5	32
Laxman Vangipurappu Venkata Sai	1.11.1974		120	1996-2010	7,903	281	16	47.32	2	1-2	0/0	63.00	122	86
Madan Lal	20.3.1951		39	1974-1986	1,042	74	0	22.65	71	5-23	4/0	40.08	15	67
Maka Ebrahim Suleman	5.3.1922	d unknown	2	1952	2	2*	0	2.00					2/1	
Malhotra Ashok Omprakash	26.1.1957		7	1981-1984	226	72*	0	25.11	0		0/0		2	20
Maninder Singh	13.6.1965		35	1982-1992	99	15	0	3.80	88	7-27	3/2	37.36	9	59
[1]Manjrekar Sanjay Vijay	12.7.1965		37	1987-1996	2,043	218	4	37.14	1	1-4	0/0	47.60	25/1	74
[1]Manjrekar Vijay Laxman	26.9.1931	18.10.1983	55	1951-1964	3,208	189*	7	39.12	1	1-16	0/0	44.00	19/2	
[1]Mankad Ashok Vinoo	12.10.1946	1.8.2008	22	1969-1977	991	97	0	25.41	0	0-0	0/0		12	1

	Born	Died	Tests	Test Career	Runs	HS	100s	Avge	Wkts	BB	5/10	Avge	Ct/St	O/T
[1]Mankad Mulvantrai Himmatlal ("Vinoo")	12.4.1917	21.8.1978	44	1946–1958	2,109	231	5	31.47	162	8-52	8/2	32.32	33	—
Mantri Madhav Krishnaji	1.9.1921		4	1951–1954	67	39	0	9.57	0	—	—/—	—	8/1	
Meherhomji Khershedji Rustomji	9.8.1911	10.2.1982	1	1936	0	0*	0	—					1	
Mehra Vijay Laxman	12.3.1938	25.8.2006	8	1955–1963	329	62	0	25.30	0	0-1	0/0	—	1	
Merchant Vijay Madhavji	12.10.1911	27.10.1987	10	1933–1951	859	154	3	47.72	0	0-17	0/0	—	7	
Mhambrey Paras Laxmikant	20.6.1972		2	1996	58	28	0	29.00	2	1-43	0/0	74.00	1	3
[2]Milkha Singh Amritsar Govindsingh	31.12.1941		4	1959–1961	92	35	0	15.33	0	0-2	0/0	—	2	
Mishra Amit	24.11.1982		10	2008–2010	205	50	0	18.63	36	5-71	1/0	39.69	6	10/1
Mithun Abhimanyu	25.10.1989		3	2010	120	46	0	30.00	6	4-105	0/0	62.00	0	2
Modi Rustomji Sheryar	11.11.1924	17.5.1996	10	1946–1952	736	112	1	46.00	0	0-14	0/0	—	3	
Mohanty Debasis Sarbeswar	20.7.1976		2	1997	0	0*	0	—	4	4-78	0/0	59.75	0	45
Mongia Nayan Ramlal	19.12.1969		44	1993–2000	1,442	152	1	24.03	0			—	99/8	140
More Kiran Shankar	4.9.1962		49	1986–1993	1,285	73	0	25.70	0	0-12	0/0	—	110/20	94
Muddiah Venatappa Musandra	8.6.1929	1.10.2009	2	1959–1960	11	11	0	5.50	3	2-40	0/0	44.66	0	
Mushtaq Ali Syed	17.12.1914	18.6.2005	11	1933–1951	612	112	2	32.21	3	1-45	0/0	67.33	7	
Nadkarni Rameshchandra Gangaram ("Bapu")	4.4.1933		41	1955–1967	1,414	122*	1	25.70	88	6-43	4/1	29.07	22	
Naik Sudhir Sakharam	21.2.1945		3	1974–1974	141	77	0	23.50	0			—	2	2
Naoomal Jeoomal	17.4.1904	28.7.1980	3	1932–1933	108	43	0	27.00	2	1-4	0/0	34.00	0	
Narasimha Rao Modireddy Venkateshwar	11.8.1954		4	1978–1979	46	20*	0	9.20	3	2-46	0/0	75.66	8	
Navle Janaradan Gyanoba	7.12.1902	7.9.1979	2	1932–1933	42	13	0	10.50	0			—	1	
Nayak Surendra Vithal	20.10.1954		2	1982	19	11	0	9.50	1	1-16	0/0	132.00	1	4
[2]Nayudu Cottari Kanakaiya	31.10.1895	14.11.1967	7	1932–1936	350	81	0	25.00	9	3-40	0/0	42.88	4	
Nayudu Cottari Subbanna	18.4.1914	22.11.2002	11	1933–1951	147	36	0	9.18	2	1-19	0/0	179.50	3	
[2]Nazir Ali Syed	8.6.1906	18.2.1975	2	1932–1933	30	13	0	7.50	4	4-83	0/0	20.75	0	
Nehra Ashish	29.4.1979		17	1999–2003	77	19	0	5.50	44	4-72	3/0	42.40	5	110/7
Nissar Mohammad	1.8.1910	11.3.1963	6	1932–1936	55	14	0	6.87	25	5-90	3/0	28.28	1	
Nyalchand Shah	14.9.1919	4.1.1997	1	1952	7	6*	0	7.00	3	3-97	0/0	32.33	0	
Ojha Pragyan Prayish	5.9.1986		11	2009–2010	67	18*	0	16.75	42	4-107	0/0	40.40	3	16/6
Pai Ajit Manohar	28.4.1945		1	1969	10	9	0	5.00	2	2-29	0/0	15.50	0	
Palia Phiroze Edulji	5.9.1910	9.9.1981	2	1932–1936	29	16	0	9.66	0	0-2	0/0	—	0	
Pandit Chandrakant Sitaram	30.9.1961		5	1986–1991	171	39	0	24.42				—	14/2	36
Parkar Ghulam Ahmed	25.10.1955		1	1982	7	6	0	3.50				—	1	10
Parkar Ramnath Dhondu	31.10.1946	11.8.1999	2	1972	80	35	0	20.00	0			—	1	
Parsana Dhiraj Devshibhai	2.12.1947		2	1978	1	1	0	0.50	1	1-32	0/0	50.00	0	
Patankar Chandrakant Trimbak	24.11.1930		1	1955	14	13	0	14.00	0			—	3/1	
[1]Pataudi Iftikhar Ali Khan, Nawab of	16.3.1910	5.1.1952	3†	1946	55	22	0	11.00	0			—	0	

	Born	Died	Tests	Test Career	Runs	HS	100s	Avge	Wkts	BB	5/10	Avge	Ct/St	O/T
[1] Pataudi Mansur Ali Khan, Nawab of.	5.1.1941		46	1961–1974	2,793	203*	6	34.91	1	1-10	0/0	88.00	27	10
Patel Brijesh Pursuram	24.11.1952		21	1974–1977	972	115*	1	29.45			–/–		17	
Patel Jasubhai Motibhai	26.11.1924	12.12.1992	7	1954–1959	25	12	0	2.77	29	9-69	2/1	21.96	2	
Patel Munaf Musa	12.7.1983		12	2005–2008	56	15*	0	7.00	34	4-25	0/0	36.17	6	49
Patel Parthiv Ajay	9.3.1985		20	2002–2008	683	69	0	29.69			–/–		41/8	16
Patel Rashid	1.6.1964		1	1988	0	0	0	0.00	0	0-14	0/0		1	1
Pathan Irfan Khan	27.10.1984		29	2003–2007	1,105	102	1	31.57	100	7-59	7/2	32.26	8	107/16
Patiala Maharajah of (Yadavendra Singh)	17.1.1913	17.6.1974	1	1933	84	60	0	42.00			–/–		2	
Patil Sadashiv Raoji	10.10.1933		1	1955	14	14*	0		2	1-15	0/0	25.50	1	
Patil Sandeep Madhusudan	18.8.1956		29	1979–1984	1,588	174	4	36.93	9	2-28	0/0	26.66	12	45
Phadkar Dattatraya Gajanan	12.12.1925	17.3.1985	31	1947–1958	1,229	123	2	32.34	62	7-159	3/0	36.85	21	
Powar Ramesh Rajaram	20.5.1978		2	2007	13	7	0	6.50	6	3-33	0/0	19.66	0	31
Prabhakar Manoj	15.4.1963		39	1984–1995	1,600	120	1	32.65	96	6-132	3/0	37.30	20	130
Prasad Bapu Krishnarao Venkatesh	5.8.1969		33	1996–2001	203	30*	0	7.51	96	6-33	7/1	35.00	6	161
Prasad Mannava Sri Kanth	24.4.1975		6	1999	106	19	0	11.77			–/–		15	17
Prasanna Erapalli Anatharao Srinivas	22.5.1940		49	1961–1978	735	37	0	11.48	189	8-76	10/2	30.38	18	
Pujara Cheteshwar Arvind	25.1.1988		3	2010	107	72	0	21.40			–/–		6	4
Punjabi Pananmal Hotchand	20.9.1921		5	1954	164	33	0	16.40			–/–		5	53
Rai Singh Kanwar	24.2.1922		1	1947	26	24	0	13.00			–/–		0	27
Raina Suresh Kumar	27.11.1986		8	2010–2010	373	120	1	33.90	6	2-1	0/0	35.66	9	106/18
Rajinder Pal	18.11.1937		1	1963	6	3*	0	6.00	0	0-3	0/0		0	
Rajindernath Vijay	7.1.1928	22.11.1989	1	1952							–/–		0/4	
Rajput Lalchand Sitaram	18.12.1961		2	1985	105	61	0	26.25			–/–		1	4
Raju Sagi Lakshmi Venkatapathy	9.7.1969		28	1989–2000	240	31	0	10.00	93	6-12	5/1	30.72	6	53
Raman Woorkeri Venkat	23.5.1965		11	1987–1996	448	96	0	24.88	2	1-7	0/0	64.50	6	27
Ramaswami Cotar	16.6.1896	1.1990	2	1936	170	60	0	56.66			–/–		6	
Ramchand Gulabrai Sipahimalani	26.7.1927	8.9.2003	33	1952–1959	1,180	109	2	24.58	41	6-49	1/0	46.31	20	
Ramesh Sadagoppan	16.10.1975		19	1998–2001	1,367	143	2	37.97	0	0-5	0/0		18	24
[2] Ranji Ladha	10.2.1900	20.12.1948	4	1933	8	8*	0	0.50	0	0-64	0/0		0	
Rangachari Commandur Rajagopalachari	14.4.1916	9.10.1993	4	1947–1948	8	8*	0	2.66	9	5-107	1/0	54.77	0	
Rangnekar Khanderao Moreshwar	27.6.1917	11.10.1984	3	1947	33	18	0	5.50			–/–		1	
Ranjane Vasant Baburao	22.7.1937		7	1958–1964	40	16	0	6.66	19	4-72	0/0	34.15	1	12
Rathore Vikram	26.3.1969		6	1996–1996	131	44	0	13.10			–/–		12	7
Ratra Ajay	13.12.1981		6	2001–2002	163	115*	1	18.11	0	0-1	0/0		11/2	12
Razdan Vivek	25.8.1969		2	1989	6	6*	0	6.00	5	5-79	1/0	28.20	0	3
Reddy Bharath	12.11.1954		4	1979	38	21	0	9.50			–/–		9/2	3

	Born	Died	Tests	Test Career	Runs	HS	100s	Avge	Wkts	BB	5/10	Avge	Ct/St	O/T
Rege Madhusudan Ramachandra	18.3.1924	–	1	1948	15	15	0	7.50	–	–	–/–	–	0	–
Roy Ambar	5.6.1945	19.9.1997	4	1969	91	48	0	13.00	–	–	–/–	–	–	–
Roy Pankaj	31.5.1928	4.2.2001	43	1951–1960	2,442	173	5	32.56	1	1-6	–/–	66.00	16	3
Roy Pranab	10.2.1957	–	2	1981	71	60*	0	35.50	–	–	–/–	–	1	–
Saha Wriddhaman Prasanta	24.10.1984	–	2	2009	36	36	0	18.00	–	–	–/–	–	1	3
Sandhu Balwinder Singh	3.8.1956	–	8	1982–1983	214	71	0	30.57	10	3-87	0/0	55.70	0	22
Sanghvi Rahul Laxman	3.9.1974	–	1	2000	2	2	0	1.00	2	2-67	0/0	39.00	0	10
Sarandeep Singh	21.10.1979	–	3	2000–2001	43	39*	0	43.00	10	4-136	0/0	34.00	4	5
Sardesai Dilip Narayan	8.8.1940	2.7.2007	30	1961–1972	2,001	212	5	39.23	0	0-3	0/0	–	1	–
Sarwate Chandrasekhar Trimbak	22.7.1920	23.12.2003	9	1946–1951	208	37	0	13.00	3	1-16	0/0	124.66	–	–
Saxena Ramesh Chandra	20.9.1944	–	1	1967	25	16	0	12.50	0	0-11	0/0	–	1	–
Sehwag Virender	20.10.1978	–	86	2001–2010	7,611	319	22	53.59	39	5-104	1/0	42.12	66	218§/14
Sekhar Thirumalai Ananthanpillai	28.3.1956	–	2	1982	0	0*	0	–	0	0-43	0/0	–	0	4
Sen Probir Kumar ("Khokhan")	31.5.1926	27.1.1970	14	1947–1952	165	25	0	11.78	–	–	–/–	–	20/11	–
Sen Gupta Apoorva Kumar	3.8.1939	–	1	1958	9	8	0	4.50	–	–	–/–	–	1	–
Sharma Ajay Kumar	3.4.1964	–	1	1987	53	30	0	26.50	0	0-9	0/0	–	1	31
Sharma Chetan	3.1.1966	–	23	1984–1988	396	54	0	22.00	61	6-58	4/1	35.45	7	65
Sharma Gopal	3.8.1960	–	5	1984–1990	11	10*	0	3.66	10	4-88	0/0	41.80	2	11
Sharma Ishant	2.9.1988	–	31	2007–2010	319	31*	0	13.29	90	5-118	1/0	35.97	10	45/11
Sharma Parthasarathy Harishchandra	5.1.1948	20.10.2010	5	1974–1976	187	54	0	18.70	0	0-2	0/0	–	1	2
Sharma Sanjeev Kumar	25.8.1965	–	2	1988–1990	56	38	0	28.00	6	3-37	0/0	41.16	1	23
Shastri Ravishankar Jayadritha	27.5.1962	–	80	1980–1992	3,830	206	11	35.79	151	5-75	2/0	40.96	36	150
Shinde Sadashiv Ganpatrao	18.8.1923	22.6.1955	7	1946–1952	85	14	0	14.16	12	6-91	1/0	59.75	1	–
Shodhan Roshan Harshadlal ("Deepak")	18.10.1920	–	3	1952	181	110	1	60.33	0	0-1	0/0	–	–	–
Shukla Rakesh Chandra	4.2.1948	–	1	1982	29	29	0	29.00	2	2-82	0/0	76.00	1	–
Siddiqui Iqbal Rashid	26.12.1974	–	1	2001	24	15	0	–	1	1-32	0/0	48.00	–	–
Sidhu Navjot Singh	20.10.1963	–	51	1983–1998	3,202	201	9	42.13	0	0-9	0/0	–	9	136
Singh Rabindra Ramanarayan ("Robin")	14.9.1963	–	1	1998	27	15	0	13.50	0	0-16	0/0	–	5	136
Singh Robin	1.1.1970	–	1	1998	0	0	0	0.00	3	2-74	0/0	58.66	–	–
Singh Rudra Pratap	6.12.1985	–	13	2005–2007	91	30	0	6.50	40	5-59	1/0	39.10	6	55/10
Singh Vikram Rajvir	17.9.1984	–	5	2005–2007	47	29	0	11.75	8	3-48	0/0	53.37	2	2
Sivaramakrishnan Laxman	31.12.1965	–	9	1982–1985	130	25	0	16.25	26	6-64	3/1	44.03	9	16
Sohoni Sriranga Wasudev	5.3.1918	19.5.1993	4	1946–1951	83	29*	0	16.60	2	1-16	0/0	101.00	2	–
Solkar Eknath Dhondu	18.3.1940	26.6.2005	27	1969–1976	1,068	102	1	25.42	18	3-28	0/0	59.44	53	7
Sood Man Mohan	6.7.1939	–	1	1959	3	3	0	1.50	–	–	–/–	–	0	–

§ Sehwag's figures exclude 83 runs and one catch for the ICC World XI v Australia in the Super Series Test in 2005-06.

Name	Born	Died	Tests	Test Career	Runs	HS	100s	Avge	Wkts	BB	5/10	Avge	Ct/St	O/T
Sreesanth Shanthakumaran	6.2.1983		24	2005–2010	263	35	0	11.43	79	5-40	3/0	35.16	5	51/10
Srikkanth Krishnamachari	21.12.1959		43	1981–1991	2,062	123	2	29.88	0	0-1	–	–	40	146
Srinath Javagal	31.8.1969		67	1991–2002	1,009	76	0	14.21	236	8-86	10/1	30.49	22	229
Srinivasan Thirumalai Echambadi	26.10.1950		1	1980	48	29	0	24.00	–	–	–/–	–	0	2
Subramanya Venkataraman	16.7.1936	6.12.2010	9	1964–1967	263	75	0	18.78	3	2-32	0/0	67.00	9	2
Sunderam Gundibali Rama	29.3.1930	20.6.2010	2	1955	3	3*	0	–	3	2-46	0/0	55.33	0	
Surendranath	4.1.1937		11	1958–1960	136	27	0	10.46	26	5-75	2/0	40.50	4	
Surti Rusi Framroze	25.5.1936	1.5.1983	26	1960–1969	1,263	99	0	28.70	42	5-74	1/0	46.71	26	
Swamy Venkatraman Narayan	23.5.1924		1	1955	–	–	0	–	0	0-15	0/0	–	0	
Tamhane Narendra Shankar	4.8.1931	19.3.2002	21	1954–1960	225	54*	0	10.22	0	–	–	–	35/16	
Tarapore Keki Khurshedji	17.12.1910	15.6.1986	1	1948	2	2	0	2.00	0	0-72	0/0	–	0	
Tendulkar Sachin Ramesh	24.4.1973		177	1989–2010	14,692	248*	51	56.94	45	3-10	2/0	53.06	106	442/1
Umrigar Pahlanji Ratanji ("Polly")	28.3.1926	7.11.2006	59	1948–1961	3,631	223	12	42.22	35	6-74	2/0	42.08	33	
Unadkat Jaydev Dipakbhai	18.10.1991		1	2010	–	1*	0	2.00	2	0-101	0/0	–	0	
Vengsarkar Dilip Balwant	6.4.1956		116	1975–1991	6,868	166	17	42.13	0	0-3	0/0	–	78	129
Venkataraghavan Srinivasaraghavan	21.4.1945		57	1964–1983	748	64	0	11.68	156	8-72	3/1	36.11	44	15
Venkataramana Margashayam	24.4.1966		1	1988	–	0*	0	–	0	0-3	0/0	58.00	1	1
Vijay Murali	1.4.1984		9	2008–2010	537	139	0	38.35	1	1-10	0/0	–	7	8/6
Viswanath Gundappa Rangnath	12.2.1949		91	1969–1982	6,080	222	14	41.93	1	1-11	–/–	46.00	63	25
Viswanath Sadanand	29.11.1962		3	1985	31	20	0	6.20	–	–	–/–	–	11	22
Vizianagram, Maharajkumar of (Sir Vijaya Anand)	28.12.1905	2.12.1965	3	1936	33	19*	0	8.25	–	–	–	–	–	
Wadekar Ajit Laxman	1.4.1941		37	1966–1974	2,113	143	1	31.07	0	0-0	–/–	–	46	2
Wasim Jaffer	16.2.1978		31	1999–2007	1,944	212	5	34.10	2	2-18	0/0	–	27	2
Wassan Atul Satish	23.3.1968		4	1989–1990	94	53	0	23.50	10	4-108	0/0	50.40	1	9
Wazir Ali Syed	15.9.1903	17.6.1950	7	1932–1936	237	42	0	16.92	0	0-0	0/0	–	10	
[1,2] Yadav Nandlal Shivlal	26.1.1957		35	1979–1986	403	43	0	14.39	102	5-76	3/0	35.09	10	7
Yadav Vijay	14.3.1967		1	1992	30	30	0	30.00	0	–	–	–	1/2	19
Yajurvindra Singh	1.8.1952		4	1976–1979	109	43*	0	18.16	0	0-2	0/0	–	11	
Yashpal Sharma	11.8.1954		37	1979–1983	1,606	140	2	33.45	1	1-6	0/0	17.00	16	42
[1] Yograj Singh	25.3.1958		1	1980	10	6	0	5.00	1	1-63	0/0	63.00	–	6
Yohannan Tinu	18.2.1979		3	2001–2002	13	8*	0	–	5	2-56	0/0	51.20	0	
[1] Yuvraj Singh	12.12.1981		34	2003–2010	1,639	169	3	35.63	9	2-9	0/0	53.87	30	257±22
Zaheer Khan	7.10.1978		78	2000–2010	1,045	75	0	12.90	271	7-87	10/1	31.94	18	171±12

PAKISTAN (206 players)

Player	Born	Died	Tests	Test Career	Runs	HS	100s	Avge	Wkts	BB	5/10	Avge	Ct/St	O/T
Aamer Malik	3.1.1963		14	1987–1994	565	117	2	35.31	1	1-0	0/0	89.00	15/1	24
Aamir Nazir	2.1.1971		6	1992–1995	31	11	0	6.20	20	4-54	0/0	29.85	2	9
Aamir Sohail	14.9.1966		47	1992–1999	2,823	205	5	35.28	25	5-54	0/0	41.96	36	156
Abdul Kadir	10.5.1944	12.3.2002	4	1964	272	95	0	34.00	–	–	–/–	–	0/1	
Abdul Qadir	15.9.1955		67	1977–1990	1,029	61	0	15.59	236	9-56	15/5	32.80	15	104
Abdul Razzaq	2.12.1979		46	1999–2006	1,946	134	3	28.61	100	5-35	1/0	36.94	15	244‡/26
Abdur Rauf	9.12.1978		3	2009–2009	52	31	0	8.66	6	4-105	0/0	46.33	1	4/1
Abdur Rehman	1.3.1980		6	2007–2010	128	60	0	21.33	31	4-86	0/0	34.80	0	14/6
[2]Adnan Akmal	13.3.1985		3	2010	95	44	0	23.75	–	–	–/–	–	16/1	
Afaq Hussain	31.12.1939	25.2.2002	2	1961–1964	66	35*	0	–	1	1-40	0/0	106.00	0	
Aftab Baloch	1.4.1953		2	1969–1974	97	60*	0	48.50	0	0-2	0/0	–	3	
Aftab Gul	31.3.1946		6	1968–1971	182	33	0	22.75	0	0-4	0/0	–	3	
Aftab Gul														
Agha Saadat Ali	21.6.1929	25.10.1995	1	1955	8	8*	0	–	–	–	–/–	–	0	
Agha Zahid	7.1.1953		1	1974	15	14	0	7.50	–	–	–/–	–	1	
Akram Raza	22.11.1964		9	1989–1994	153	24	0	15.30	13	3-46	0/0	56.30	8	49
Ali Hussain Rizvi	6.1.1974		1	1997	2	2*	0	–	2	2-72	0/0	36.00	0	
Ali Naqvi	19.3.1977		5	1997	242	115	1	30.25	0	0-11	0/0	–	1	
Alim-ud-Din	15.12.1930		25	1954–1962	1,091	109	2	25.37	1	1-17	0/0	75.00	8	
Amir Elahi	1.9.1908	28.12.1980	5†	1952	65	47	0	10.83	7	4-134	0/0	35.42	0	
Anil Dalpat	20.9.1963		9	1983–1984	167	52	0	15.18	–	–	–/–	–	22/3	15
Anwar Hussain	16.7.1920	9.10.2002	4	1952	42	17	0	7.00	1	1-25	0/0	29.00	1	
Anwar Khan	24.12.1955		1	1978	15	15	0	15.00	0	0-12	0/0	–	0	
Aqib Javed	5.8.1972		22	1988–1998	101	28*	0	5.05	54	5-84	1/0	34.70	2	163
Arif Butt	17.5.1944	10.7.2007	3	1964	59	20	0	11.80	14	6-89	1/0	20.57	0	
Arshad Khan	22.3.1971		9	1997–2004	31	9*	0	5.16	32	5-38	1/0	30.00	1	58
Asad Shafiq	28.1.1986		3	2010	168	83	0	42.00	–	–	–/–	–	0	10/2
Ashfaq Ahmed	6.6.1973		1	1993	1	1*	0	1.00	2	2-31	0/0	26.50	0	3
Ashraf Ali	22.4.1958		8	1981–1987	229	65*	0	45.80	0	0-2	0/0	–	17/5	16
Asif Iqbal	6.6.1943		58	1964–1979	3,575	175	11	38.85	53	5-48	2/0	28.33	36	10
Asif Masood	23.11.1946		16	1968–1976	93	30*	0	10.33	38	5-111	1/0	41.26	5	7
Asif Mujtaba	4.11.1967		25	1986–1996	928	65*	0	24.42	4	1-0	0/0	75.75	19	66
Asim Kamal	31.5.1976		12	2003–2005	717	99	0	37.73	–	–	–/–	–	10	
Ata-ur-Rehman	28.3.1975		13	1992–1996	76	19	0	8.44	31	4-50	0/0	34.54	2	30

Name	Born	Died	Tests	Test Career	Runs	HS	100s	Avge	Wkts	BB	5/10	Avge	Ct/St	O/T
Atif Rauf	3.3.1964		1	1993	25	16	0	12.50	–	–	–/–	–	5	3
Atiq-uz-Zaman	20.7.1975		1	1999	26	25	0	13.00	–	–	–/–	–	0/5	6
Azam Khan	1.3.1969		1	1996	14	14	0	14.00	–	–	–/–	–	1	15
Azeem Hafeez	29.7.1963		18	1983–1984	134	24	0	8.37	63	6-46	4/0	34.98	1	
Azhar Ali	19.2.1985		10	2010–	629	92*	0	37.00	0	0-9	0/0	–	7	
Azhar Khan	7.9.1955		1	1979	14	14	0	14.00	1	1-1	0/0	2.00	–	
Azhar Mahmood	28.2.1975		21	1997–2001	900	136	3	30.00	39	4-50	0/0	35.94	14	143
[2] Azmat Rana	3.11.1951		1	1979	49	49	0	49.00	0		–/–	–	–	2
Basit Ali	13.12.1970		19	1992–1995	858	103	1	26.81	0	0-6	0/0	–	6	50
[3] Bazid Khan	25.3.1981		1	2004	32	23	0	16.00	–	–	–/–	–	0	
Danish Kaneria	16.12.1980		61	2000–2010	360	29	0	7.05	261	7-77	15/2	34.79	18	18
D'Souza Antao	17.1.1939		6	1958–1962	76	23*	0	38.00	17	5-112	1/0	43.82	3	
Ehtesham-ud-Din	4.9.1950		5	1979–1982	2	–	0	1.00	16	5-47	1/0	23.43	–	
Faisal Iqbal	30.12.1981		26	2000–2009	1,124	139	1	26.76	0	0-7	0/0	–	22	18
Farhan Adil	25.9.1977		1	2003	33	25	0	16.50	–	–	–/–	–	0	
Farooq Hamid	3.3.1945		1	1964	3	3	0	1.50	1	1-82	0/0	107.00	0	
Farrukh Zaman	2.4.1956		1	1976	–	–	–	–	0	0-7	0/0	–	0	
Fawad Alam	8.10.1985		3	2009–	250	168	1	41.66	1	1-82	0/0	–	3	27/24
Fazal Mahmood	18.2.1927	30.5.2005	34	1952–1962	620	60	0	14.09	139	7-42	13/4	24.70	11	
Fazl-e-Akbar	20.10.1980		5	1997–2003	52	25	0	13.00	11	3-85	0/0	46.45	2	2
Ghazali Mohammad Ebrahim Zainuddin	15.6.1924	26.4.2003	2	1954	32	18	0	8.00	0	0-18	0/0	–	0	
Ghulam Abbas	1.5.1947		1	1967	12	12	0	6.00	–	–	–/–	–	0	
Gul Mahomed	15.10.1921	8.5.1992	1†	1956	39	27*	0	39.00	2		0/0	95.00	0	
[1,2] Hanif Mohammad	21.12.1934		55	1952–1969	3,915	337	12	43.98	1	1-1	0/0	–	40	
Haroon Rashid	25.3.1953		23	1976–1982	1,217	153	3	34.77	0	0-3	0/0	–	16	12
Hasan Raza	11.3.1982		7	1996–2005	235	68	0	26.11	0	0-1	0/0	–	5	16
Haseeb Ahsan	15.7.1939		12	1957–1961	61	14	0	6.77	27	6-202	2/0	49.25	1	
[2] Humayun Farhat	24.1.1981		1	2000	54	28	0	27.00	0		0/0	–	3	
Ibadulla Khalid ("Billy")	20.12.1935		4	1964–1967	253	166	1	31.62	1	1-42	0/0	99.00	3	5
Iftikhar Anjum	1.12.1980		1	2005	9	9*	0	–	0	0-8	0/0	–	0	62/2
Ijaz Ahmed sen.	20.9.1968		60	1986–2000	3,315	211	12	37.67	2	1-9	0/0	38.50	45	250
Ijaz Ahmed jun.	2.2.1969		2	1995	29	16	0	9.66	0	0-1	0/0	–	3	2
Ijaz Butt	10.3.1938		8	1958–1962	279	58	0	19.92	–	–	–/–	–	5	
[2] Ijaz Faqih	24.3.1956		5	1980–1987	183	105	1	26.14	4	1-38	0/0	74.75	5	27
[2] Imran Farhat	20.5.1982		39	2000–2010	2,327	128	3	31.87	3	2-69	0/0	94.66	40	375
Imran Khan	25.11.1952		88	1971–1991	3,807	136	6	37.69	362	8-58	23/6	22.81	28	175

Name	Born	Died	Tests	Test Career	Runs	HS	100s	Avge	Wkts	BB	5/10	Avge	Ct/St	O/T
Imran Nazir	16.12.1981		8	1998–2010	427	131	2	32.84		–	–/–	–	4	79/16
Imtiaz Ahmed	5.1.1928		41	1952–1962	2,079	209	3	29.28	0	0-0	0/0	–	77/16	
Intikhab Alam	28.12.1941		47	1959–1976	1,493	138	1	22.28	125	7-52	5/2	35.95	20	4
Inzamam-ul-Haq	3.3.1970		119§	1992–2007	8,829	329	25	50.16	0	0-8	0/0	–	81	375½/1
Iqbal Qasim	6.8.1953		50	1976–1988	549	56	0	13.07	171	7-49	8/2	28.11	42	15
Irfan Fazal	2.11.1981		1	1999	56	3	0	4.00	2	1-30	0/0	32.50		
Israr Ali	1.5.1927		4	1952–1959	33	10	0	4.71	6	2-29	0/0	27.50	1	
Jalal-ud-Din	12.6.1959		6	1982–1985	3	2	0	3.00	11	3-77	0/0	48.81	0	8
Javed Akhtar	21.11.1940		1	1962	4	2*	0	4.00	0	0-52	0/0	–	0	
Javed Burki	8.5.1938		25	1960–1969	1,341	140	3	30.47	0	0-2	0/0	–	7	
Javed Miandad	12.6.1957		124	1976–1993	8,832	280*	23	52.57	17	3-74	0/0	40.11	93/1	233
Kabir Khan	12.4.1974		4	1994	24	10	0	8.00	9	3-26	0/0	41.11	0	10
[2] Kamran Akmal	13.1.1982		53	2002–2010	2,648	158*	6	30.79		–	–/–	–	184/22	123/38
Kardar Abdul Hafeez	17.1.1925	21.4.1996	23†	1952–1957	847	93	0	24.91	21	3-35	0/0	45.42	15	
Khalid Hassan	14.7.1937		1	1954	17	10	0	17.00	2	2-116	0/0	58.00	0	
[1] Khalid Wazir	27.4.1936		2	1954	14	9*	0	7.00	0	–	–/–	–	0	
Khan Mohammad	1.1.1928	4.7.2009	13	1952–1957	100	26*	0	10.00	54	6-21	4/0	23.92	4	7
Khurram Manzoor	10.6.1986		7	2008–2010	326	93	0	29.63		–	–/–	–	3	
Liaqat Ali Khan	21.5.1955		5	1974–1978	28	12	0	7.00	6	3-80	0/0	59.83	0	3
Mahmood Hussain	2.4.1932	25.12.1991	27	1952–1962	336	35	0	10.18	68	6-67	2/0	38.64	5	
[3] Majid [Jahangir] Khan	28.9.1946		63	1964–1982	3,931	167	8	38.92	27	4-45	0/0	53.92	70	23
Mansoor Akhtar	25.12.1957		19	1980–1989	655	111	1	25.19		–	–/–	–	9	41
[1] Manzoor Elahi	15.4.1963		6	1984–1994	123	52	0	15.37	7	2-38	0/0	27.71	7	54
Maqsood Ahmed	26.3.1925	4.1.1999	16	1952–1955	507	99	0	19.50	3	2-12	0/0	63.66	13	
Masood Anwar	12.12.1967		1	1990	39	37	0	19.50	3	2-59	0/0	34.00	0	
Mathias Wallis	4.2.1935	1.9.1994	21	1955–1962	783	77	0	23.72		0-20	0/0	–	22	
Miran Bux	20.4.1907	8.2.1991	2	1954	1	1*	0	1.00	2	2-82	0/0	57.50	0	
Misbah-ul-Haq	28.5.1974		23	2000–2010	1,459	161*	2	42.91		–	–/–	–	28	58/31
Mohammad Aamer	13.4.1992		14	2009–2010	278	30*	0	12.63	51	6-84	3/0	29.09	4	15/18
Mohammad Akram	10.9.1974		9	1995–2000	24	10*	0	2.66	17	5-138	1/0	50.52	4	23
Mohammad Asif	20.12.1982		23	2004–2010	141	29	0	5.64	106	6-41	7/1	24.36	3	35½/11
Mohammad Aslam Khokhar	5.1.1920	22.1.2011	1	1954	34	18	0	17.00		–	–/–	–	1	
Mohammad Farooq	8.4.1938		7	1960–1964	85	47	0	17.00	21	4-70	1/0	32.47	1	
Mohammad Hafeez	17.10.1980		15	2003–2010	849	104	2	31.44	8	2-31	0/0	60.25	5	58/21
Mohammad Hussain	8.10.1976		2	1996–1998	18	17	0	6.00	3	2-66	0/0	29.00	1	14

§ *Inzamam-ul-Haq's figures exclude one run for the ICC World XI v Australia in the Super Series Test in 2005-06.*

Name	Born	Died	Tests	Test Career	Runs	HS	100s	Avge	Wkts	BB	5/10	Avge	Ct/St	O/T
Mohammad Ilyas	19.3.1946		10	1964–1968	441	126	1	23.21	0	0-1		–	6	–
Mohammad Khalil	11.11.1982		2	2004	9	5	0	3.00	0	0-38		–	0	3
Mohammad Munaf	2.11.1935		4	1959–1961	63	19	0	12.60	11	4-42	0/0	31.00	0	–
Mohammad Nazir	8.3.1946		14	1969–1983	144	29*	0	18.00	34	7-99	3/0	33.05	4	4
Mohammad Ramzan	25.12.1970		1	1997	36	29	0	18.00				–	1	–
Mohammad Sami	24.2.1981		35	2000–2010	475	49	0	11.87	84	5-36	2/0	52.27	7	87/13
Mohammad Talha	15.10.1988		1	2008	–	–	–	–	1	1-88	0/0	88.00	0	–
Mohammad Wasim	8.8.1977		18	1996–2000	783	192	2	30.11				–	7	25
Mohammad Yousuf (formerly Yousuf Youhana)	27.8.1974		90	1998–2010	7,530	223	24	52.29	0	0-3	0/0	–	65	288/3
Mohammad Zahid	2.8.1976		5	1996–2002	7	6*	0	1.40	15	7-66	1/1	33.46	0	11
Mohsin Kamal	16.6.1963		9	1983–1994	37	13*	0	9.25	24	4-116	0/0	34.25	4	19
Mohsin Khan	15.3.1955		48	1977–1986	2,709	200	7	37.10	0	0-0		–	34	75
[2] Moin Khan	23.9.1971		69	1990–2004	2,741	137	4	28.55				–	128/20	219
[1] Mudassar Nazar	6.4.1956		76	1976–1988	4,114	231	10	38.09	66	6-32	1/0	38.36	48	122
Mufasir-ul-Haq	16.8.1944	27.7.1983	1	1964	8	8*	0	–	3	2-50	0/0	28.00	1	–
Munir Malik	10.7.1934		3	1959–1962	7	4	0	2.33	9	5-128	1/0	39.77	1	–
Mushtaq Ahmed	28.6.1970		52	1989–2003	656	59	0	11.71	185	7-56	10/3	32.97	23	144
[2] Mushtaq Mohammad	22.11.1943		57	1958–1978	3,643	201	10	39.17	79	5-28	3/0	29.22	42	10
Nadeem Abbasi	15.4.1964		3	1989	46	36	0	23.00				–	6	–
Nadeem Ghauri	12.10.1962		1	1989	0	0	0	0.00	0	0-20		–	0	6
Nadeem Khan	10.12.1969		2	1992–1998	34	25	0	17.00	2	2-147	0/0	115.00	0	2
Nasim-ul-Ghani	14.5.1941		29	1957–1972	747	101	1	16.60	52	6-67	2/0	37.67	11	1
Naushad Ali	1.10.1943		6	1964	156	39	0	14.18				–	7	–
Naved Anjum	27.7.1963		2	1989–1990	44	22	0	14.66	4	2-57	0/0	40.50	1	13
Naved Ashraf	4.9.1974		2	1998–1999	64	32	0	21.33				–	3	–
Naved Latif	21.2.1976		1	2001	20	20	0	10.00				–	0	11
Naved-ul-Hasan	28.2.1978		9	2004–2006	239	42*	0	19.91	18	3-30	0/0	58.00	3	74/4
[1] Nazar Mohammad	5.3.1921	12.7.1996	5	1952	277	124*	1	39.57	0	0-4		–	7	–
Niaz Ahmed	11.11.1945	12.4.2000	2	1967–1968	17	16*	0	–	3	2-72	0/0	31.33	0	–
[2] Pervez Sajjad	30.8.1942		19	1964–1972	123	24	0	13.66	59	7-74	3/0	23.89	9	–
Qaiser Abbas	7.5.1982		1	2000	2	2	0	2.00				–	0	–
Qasim Omar	9.2.1957		26	1983–1986	1,502	210	3	36.63	0	0-35		–	15	31
Ramiz Raja	14.8.1962		57	1983–1996	2,833	122	2	31.83	0	0-0		–	34	198
Rashid Khan	15.12.1959		4	1981–1984	155	59	0	51.66	8	3-129	0/0	45.00	2	29
Rashid Latif	14.10.1968		37	1992–2003	1,381	150	1	28.77	0	0-10		–	119/11	166

Name	Born	Died	Tests	Test Career	Runs	HS	100s	Avge	Wkts	BB	5/10	Avge	Ct/St	O/T
Rehman Sheikh Fazalur	11.6.1935		1	1957	10	8	0	5.00	1	1-43	0/0	99.00	1	
Riaz Afridi	21.1.1985		1	2004	9	9	0	9.00	2	2-42	0/0	43.50		3
Rizwan-uz-Zaman	4.9.1961		11	1981–1988	345	60	0	19.16	4	3-26	0/0	11.50	4	19
Sadiq Mohammad	3.5.1945		41	1969–1980	2,579	166	5	35.81	0	0-0	0/0	–	28	
[2] Saeed Ahmed	1.10.1937		41	1957–1972	2,991	172	5	40.41	22	4-64	0/0	36.45	13	
Saeed Ajmal	14.10.1977		9	2009–2010	98	50	0	10.88	33	5-82	1/0	39.72		35/29
Saeed Anwar	6.9.1968		55	1990–2001	4,052	188*	11	45.52				–	18	247
Salah-ud-Din	14.2.1947		5	1964–1969	117	34*	0	19.50	7	2-36	0/0	26.71	3	
Saleem Jaffer	19.11.1962		14	1986–1991	42	10*	0	5.25	36	5-40	1/0	31.63	2	39
Salim Altaf	19.4.1944		21	1967–1978	276	53*	0	14.52	46	4-11	0/0	37.17	3	6
[2] Salim Elahi	21.11.1976		13	1995–2002	436	72	0	18.95				–	10/1	48
Salim Malik	16.4.1963		103	1981–1998	5,768	237	15	43.69	5	1-3	0/0	82.80	65	283
Salim Yousuf	7.12.1959		32	1981–1990	1,055	91*	0	27.05				–	91/13	86
Salman Butt	7.10.1984		33	2003–2010	1,889	122	3	30.46	1	1-36	0/0	106.00	12	78/24
Saqlain Mushtaq	29.12.1976		49	1995–2003	927	101*	1	14.48	208	8-164	13/3	29.83	15	169
Sarfraz Ahmed	22.5.1987		1	2009	6	6	0	3.00	0	0-1	0/0	–		9/2
Sarfraz Nawaz Malik	1.12.1948		55	1968–1983	1,045	90	0	17.71	177	9-86	4/1	32.75	26	45
Shabbir Ahmed	21.4.1976		10	2003–2005	88	24*	0	8.80	51	5-48	2/0	23.03	3	32/1
Shadab Kabir	12.11.1977		5	1996–2001	148	55	0	21.14	0	0-9	0/0	–	11	
Shafiq Ahmed	28.3.1949		6	1974–1980	99	27*	0	11.00	0	0-1	0/0	–		
[2] Shafqat Rana	10.8.1943		5	1964–1969	221	95	0	31.57	1	1-2	0/0	9.00	5	
Shahid Afridi	1.3.1980		27	1998–2010	1,716	156	5	36.51	48	5-52	1/0	35.60	10	301†/42
Shahid Israr	1.3.1950		1	1976	7	7*	0	–				–	3/1	
Shahid Mahboob	25.8.1962		1	1989	25	16	0	12.50	2	2-131	0/0	65.50		
Shahid Mahmood	17.3.1939		1	1962	12	12	0	12.00	0	0-23	0/0	–		
Shahid Nazir	4.12.1977		15	1996–2006	194	40	0	14.80	36	5-53	1/0	35.33	5	17
Shahid Saeed	6.1.1966		1	1989	1	1	0	1.00	0	0-7	0/0	–		10
Shakeel Ahmed, sen.	12.2.1966		1	1998				–				–	5	
Shakeel Ahmed, jun.	12.11.1971		3	1992–1994				–				–	4	2
Sharpe Duncan Albert	3.8.1937		3	1959	134	56	0	22.33	4	4-91	0/0	34.75	2	
Shoaib Akhtar	13.8.1975		46	1997–2007	544	47	0	10.07	178	6-11	12/2	25.69	12	152†/15
Shoaib Malik	1.2.1982		32	2001–2010	1,606	148*	2	33.45	21	4-42	0/0	61.47	16	192/32
Shoaib Mohammad	8.1.1961		45	1983–1995	2,705	203*	7	44.34	5	2-8	0/0	34.00	22	63
Shuja-ud-Din Butt	10.4.1930	7.2.2006	19	1954–1961	395	47	0	15.19	20	3-18	0/0	40.05	8	
Sikander Bakht	25.8.1957		26	1976–1982	146	22*	0	6.34	67	8-69	3/1	36.00	7	27
Sohail Khan	6.3.1984		1	2008	–	–	–	–	0	0-33	0/0	–	0	4/1

	Born	Died	Tests	Test Career	Runs	HS	100s	Avge	Wkts	BB	5/10	Avge	Ct/St	O/T
Sohail Tanvir	12.12.1984		2	2007	17	13	0	5.66	5	3-83	0/0	63.20	2	31/15
Tahir Naqqash	6.6.1959		15	1981–1984	300	57	0	21.42	34	5-40	2/0	41.11		40
Talat Ali Malik	29.5.1950		10	1972–1978	370	61	0	23.12	–	0-1	0/0	–	4	–
Tanvir Ahmed	20.12.1978		5	2010	55	30	0	18.33	14	6-120	1/0	25.78	1	0/1
Taslim Arif	15.1.1954		6	1979–1980	501	210*	1	62.62	1	1-28	0/0	28.00	6/3	2
Taufeeq Umar	20.6.1981		29	2001–2010	2,002	135	4	39.25	0	0-0	0/0	–	36	19
²Tauseef Ahmed	10.5.1958	13.3.2008	34	1979–1993	318	35*	0	17.66	93	6-45	3/0	31.72	9	70
Umar Akmal	26.5.1990		13	2009–2010	822	129	2	35.73	–	–	–/–	–	7	24/21
Umar Amin	16.10.1989		4	2010	99	33	0	12.37	3	1-7	0/0	21.00	1	3
Umar Gul	14.4.1984		34	2003–2010	490	65*	0	11.95	125	6-135	4/0	33.92	7	75/34
Wahab Riaz	28.6.1985		5	2010–2010	41	27	0	10.25	13	5-63	1/0	32.69	1	9/5
Wajahatullah Wasti	11.11.1974		6	1998–1999	329	133	2	36.55	–	–	–/–	–	7	15
²Waqar Hassan	12.9.1932		21	1952–1959	1,071	189	0	31.50	–	0-0	0/0	–	10	–
Waqar Younis	16.11.1971		87	1989–2002	1,010	45	0	10.20	373	7-76	22/5	23.56	18	262
Wasim Akram	3.6.1966		104	1984–2001	2,898	257*	0	22.64	414	7-119	25/5	23.62	44	356
Wasim Bari	23.3.1948		81	1967–1983	1,366	85	0	15.88	–	–	–/–	–	201/27	51
²Wasim Raja	3.7.1952	23.8.2006	57	1972–1984	2,821	125	3	36.16	51	4-50	0/0	35.80	5	54
²Wazir Mohammad	22.12.1929		20	1952–1959	801	189	2	27.62	–	–	–/–	–	26	–
Yasir Ali	15.10.1985		1	2003	1*	1*	0	–	2	1-2	0/0	27.50		–
Yasir Arafat	12.3.1982		3	2007–2008	94	50*	0	47.00	9	5-161	1/0	48.66	5	117
Yasir Hameed	28.2.1978		25	2003–2010	1,491	170	2	32.41	0	0-0	0/0	–	20	56
²Younis Ahmed	20.10.1947		4	1969–1986	177	62	0	29.50	0	0-6	0/0	–	0	2
Younis Khan	29.11.1977		67	1999–2010	5,617	313	17	50.60	7	2-23	0/0	58.14	74	207/25
Yousuf Youhana (see Mohammad Yousuf)														
Zaheer Abbas	24.7.1947		78	1969–1985	5,062	274	12	44.79	3	2-21	0/0	44.00	34	62
Zahid Fazal	10.11.1973		9	1990–1995	288	78	0	18.00	–	–	–/–	–	5	19
²Zahoor Elahi	1.3.1971		2	1996	30	22	0	10.00	–	–	–/–	–	1	14
Zakir Khan	3.4.1963		2	1985–1989	9*	9*	0	–	5	3-80	0/0	51.80	1	17
Zulfiqar Ahmed	22.11.1926	3.10.2008	9	1952–1956	200	63*	0	33.33	20	6-42	2/1	18.30	5	–
Zulqarnain	25.5.1962		3	1985	24	13	0	6.00	–	–	–/–	–	8/2	16
Zulqarnain Haider	23.4.1986		1	2010	88	88	0	44.00	–	–	–/–	–	2	4/3

SRI LANKA (114 players)

Name	Born	Died	Tests	Test Career	Runs	HS	100s	Avge	Wkts	BB	5/10	Avge	Ct/St	O/T
Abangama Franklyn Saliya	14.9.1959		3	1985	11	11	0	5.50	18	5-52	1/0	19.33	1	1
Amalean Kaushik Naginda	7.4.1965		2	1985–1987	9	7*	0	9.00	7	4-97	0/0	22.28	1	8
Ameerasinghe Ameresinghe Mudalige Jayantha Gamini	2.2.1954		2	1983	54	34	0	18.00	3	2-73	0/0	105.00	3	8
Anurasiri Sangarange Don	25.2.1966		18	1985–1997	91	24	0	5.35	41	4-71	0/0	37.75	4	45
Arnold Russel Premakumaran	25.10.1973		44	1996–2004	1,821	123	3	28.01	11	3-76	0/0	54.36	51	180/1
Atapattu Marvan Samson	22.11.1970		90	1990–2007	5,502	249	16	39.02	1	1-9	0/0	24.00	58	268/2
Bandara Herath Mudiyanselage Charitha Malinga	31.12.1979		8	1997–2005	124	43	0	15.50	16	3-84	0/0	39.56	4	31/4
Bandaratilleke Mapa Rallage Chandima Niroshan	16.5.1975		7	1997–2001	93	25	0	11.62	23	5-36	1/0	30.34	–	3
Chandana Umagiliya Durage Upul	7.5.1972		16	1998–2004	616	92	0	26.78	37	6-179	3/1	41.48	7	147
Dassanayake Pubudu Bathiya	11.7.1970		11	1993–1994	196	36	0	13.06	–	–	–/–	–	19/5	16
de Alwis Ronald Guy	15.2.1959		11	1982–1987	152	28	0	8.00	–	–	–/–	–	21/2	31
de Mel Ashantha Lakdasa Francis	9.5.1959		17	1981–1986	326	34	0	14.17	59	6-109	3/1	36.94	9	57
de Saram Samantha Indika	2.9.1973		4	1999	117	39	0	23.40	–	–	–/–	–	4	15/1
de Silva Ashley Matthew	3.12.1963		10	1992–1993	10	9	0	3.33	–	–	–/–	–	4/1	4
de Silva Dandeniyage Somachandra	11.6.1942		12	1981–1984	406	61	0	21.36	37	5-59	1/0	36.40	5	41
de Silva Ellawalakankanamge Asoka Ranjit	28.3.1956		10	1985–1990	185	50	0	15.41	8	2-67	0/0	129.00	4	28
de Silva Gingalgodage Ramba Ajit	12.12.1952		4	1981–1982	41	14	0	8.20	7	2-38	0/0	55.00	6	6
de Silva Karunakalage Sajeewa Chanaka	11.1.1971		8	1996–1998	65	27	0	9.28	16	5-85	1/0	55.56	5	38
de Silva Pinmaduwage Aravinda	17.10.1965		93	1984–2002	6,361	267	20	42.97	29	3-30	0/0	41.65	43	308
de Silva Sanjeewa Kumara Lanka	29.7.1975		3	1997	36	20*	0	18.00	–	–	–/–	–	–	11
de Silva Weddikkara Ruwan Sujeewa	7.10.1979		3	2002–2007	10	5*	0	10.00	11	4-35	0/0	19.00	–	
Dharmasena Handumettige Deepthi Priyantha Kumar	24.4.1971		31	1993–2003	868	62*	0	19.72	69	6-72	3/0	42.31	14	141
Dias Roy Luke	18.10.1952		20	1981–1986	1,285	109	3	36.71	0	0-17	0/0	–	6	58
Dilshan Tillekeratne Mudiyanselage	14.10.1976		66	1999–2010	3,990	168	11	42.44	19	4-10	0/0	33.31	73	191/32
Dunusinghe Chamara Iroshan	19.10.1970		5	1994–1995	160	91	0	16.00	–	–	–/–	–	13/2	1
Fernando Congenige Randhi Dilhara	19.7.1979		35	2000–2010	198	36*	0	7.33	90	5-42	3/0	36.22	–	139/16
Fernando Ellekunge Rufus Nemesion Susil	19.12.1955		5	1982–1983	112	46	0	11.20	4	3-63	0/0	27.00	0	7
Fernando Hasantha Ruwan Kumara	14.10.1970		5	2002	38	24	0	9.50	1	1-29	0/0	107.00	1	7
Fernando Kandana Arachchige Dinusha Manoj	10.8.1979		2	2003	56	51*	0	28.00	–	–	–/–	–	0	1

	Born	Died	Tests	Test Career	Runs	HS	100s	Avge	Wkts	BB	5/10	Avge	Ct/St	O/T
Fernando Thudellage Charitha Buddhika	22.8.1980		9	2001–2002	132	45	0	26.40	18	4-27	0/0	44.00	4	17
Gallage Indika Sanjeewa	22.11.1975		1	1999	3	3	0	3.00	0	0-24	0/0	–	–	1
Goonatillake Hettiarachige Mahes	16.8.1952		1	1981–1982	177	56	0	22.12	–	–	–	–	10/3	3
Gunasekera Yohan	8.11.1957		5	1982	48	23	0	12.00	–	–	–	–	6	6
Gunawardene Dhan Avishka	26.5.1977		2	1998–2005	181	43	0	16.45	–	–	–	–	2	3
Guneratne Roshan Punyajith Wijesinghe	26.1.1962	21.7.2005	6	1982	0*	0*	0	–	0	0-84	0/0	–	0	61
Gurusinha Asanka Pradeep	16.9.1966		41	1985–1996	2,452	143	7	38.92	20	2-7	0/0	34.05	33	147
Hathurusinghe Upul Chandika	13.9.1968		26	1990–1998	1,274	83	0	29.62	17	4-66	0/0	46.41	7	35
Herath Herath Mudiyanselage Rangana Keerthi Bandara	19.3.1978		24	1999–2010	311	80*	0	13.52	78	5-99	4/0	36.15	5	9
Hettiarachchi Dinuka	15.7.1976		1	2000	0	0*	0	0.00	2	2-36	0/0	20.50	0	–
Jayasekera Rohan Stanley Amarasiriwardene	7.12.1957		1	1981	2	2	0	1.00	–	–	–	–	0	2
Jayasuriya Sanath Teran	30.6.1969		110	1990–2007	6,973	340	14	40.07	98	5-34	2/0	34.34	78	440±/30
Jayawardene Denagamage Proboth Mahela de Silva	27.5.1977		116	1997–2010	9,527	374	28	53.82	6	2-32	0/0	48.66	165	324±/32
Jayawardene Hewasandactchige Asiri Prasanna Wishwanath	9.10.1979		36	2000–2010	1,172	154*	2	30.05	0	–	–	–	67/25	6
Jeganathan Sridharan	11.7.1951	14.5.1996	1	1982	19	8	0	4.75	0	0-12	0/0	–	2	5
John Vinothen Bede	27.5.1960		6	1982–1984	53	27*	0	10.60	28	5-60	2/0	21.92	2	45
Jurangpathy Baba Roshan	25.6.1967		2	1985–1986	1	1	0	0.25	2	1-69	0/0	93.00	2	–
Kalavitigoda Shantha	23.12.1977		1	2004	8	7	0	4.00	–	–	–	–	2	–
Kalpage Ruwan Senani	19.2.1970		11	1993–1998	294	63	0	18.37	12	2-27	0/0	64.50	10	86
Kaluhalamulla Hewa Kaluhalamullage Suraj Randiv (see Randiv, Suraj)														
[2] Kaluperuma Lalith Wasantha Silva	25.6.1949		2	1981	12	11*	0	4.00	0	0-24	0/0	–	2	4
[2] Kaluperuma Sanath Mohan Silva	22.10.1961		4	1983–1987	88	23	0	11.00	2	2-17	0/0	62.00	6	2
Kaluwitharana Romesh Shantha	24.11.1969		49	1992–2004	1,933	132*	3	26.12	0	0-9	0/0	–	93/26	189
Kapugedera Chamara Kantha	24.2.1987		8	2006–2009	418	96	0	34.83	–	–	–	–	6	82/20
Kulasekara Kulasekara Mudiyanselage Dinesh Nuwan	22.7.1982		12	2004–2010	262	64	0	16.37	26	4-21	0/0	33.80	4	81/12
Kuruppu Don Sardha Brendon Priyantha	5.1.1962		4	1986–1991	320	201*	1	53.33	–	–	–	–	8/1	54
Kuruppuarachchi Ajith Kosala	1.11.1964		2	1985–1986	0	0*	0	–	8	5-44	1/0	18.62	0	6
Labrooy Graeme Fredrick	7.6.1964		9	1986–1990	158	70*	0	14.36	27	5-133	1/0	44.22	1	44
Lakmal Ransinghe Arachchige Suranga	10.3.1987		2	2010	–	–	–	–	3	2-85	0/0	44.33	0	–
Lakshitha Materha Kanatha Gamage Chamila Premanath	4.1.1979		2	2002–2002	42	40	0	14.00	5	2-33	0/0	31.60	1	7

	Born	Died	Tests	Test Career	Runs	HS	100s	Avge	Wkts	BB	5/10	Avge	Ct/St	O/T
Liyanage Dulip Kapila	6.6.1972		9	1992-2001	69	23	0	7.66	17	4-56	0/0	39.17	0	16
Lokuarachchi Kaushal Samaraweera	20.5.1982		4	2003-2003	94	28*	0	23.50	5	2-47	0/0	59.00	1	21
Madugalle Ranjan Senerath	22.4.1959		21	1981-1988	1,029	103	1	29.40	0	0-0	0/0	–	9	63
Madurasinghe Madurasinghe Arachchige														
Wijayasiri Ranjith	30.1.1961		3	1988-1992	24	11	0	4.80	3	3-60	0/0	57.33	0	12
Mahanama Roshan Siriwardene	31.5.1966		52	1985-1997	2,576	225	4	29.27	0	0-3	0/0	–	56	213
Maharoof Mohamed Farveez	7.9.1984		20	2003-2007	538	72	0	19.92	24	4-52	0/0	60.75	6	94/7
Malinga Separamadu Lasith	28.8.1983		30	2004-2010	275	64	0	11.45	101	5-50	3/0	33.15	7	75/29
Mathews Angelo Davis	2.6.1987		13	2009-2010	527	99	0	35.13	6	1-13	0/0	70.16	4	32/21
Mendis Balapuwaduge Ajantha Winslo	11.3.1985		15	2008-2010	151	78	0	13.72	61	6-117	3/1	31.93	2	44/19
Mendis Louis Rohan Duleep	25.8.1952		24	1981-1988	1,329	124	4	31.64	–	–	–/–	–	3	79
Mirando Magina Thilan Thushara	1.3.1981		10	2003-2010	94	15*	0	8.54	28	5-83	1/0	37.14	3	38/6
Mubarak Jehan	10.1.1981		10	2002-2007	254	48	0	15.87	0	0-1	–/–	–	13	38/16
Muralitharan Muttiah	17.4.1972		133§	1992-2010	1,259	67	0	11.87	795	9-51	67/22	22.67	70	332‡/12
Nawaz Mohamed Naveed	20.9.1973		1	2002	99	78*	0	99.00	0	–	–/–	–	0	3
Nissanka Ratnayake Arachchige Prabath	25.10.1980		4	2003	18	12*	0	6.00	10	5-64	1/0	36.60	0	23
Paranavitana Nishad Tharanga	15.4.1982		16	2008-2010	963	111	2	37.03	1	1-26	0/0	76.00	7	–
Perera Anhettige Suresh Asanka	16.2.1978		3	1998-2001	77	43*	0	25.66	1	1-104	0/0	180.00	1	20
Perera Panagodage Don Ruchira Laksiri	6.4.1977		8	1998-2002	33	11*	0	11.00	17	3-40	0/0	38.88	2	19/2
Prasad Kuriyawasam Tirana Gamage Dammika	30.5.1983		6	2008-2010	113	47	0	22.60	13	3-82	0/0	60.30	0	5
Pushpakumara Karuppiahvage Ravindra	21.7.1975		23	1994-2001	166	44	0	8.73	58	7-116	4/0	38.65	10	31
Ramanayake Champaka Priyadarshana Hewage	8.1.1965		18	1987-1993	143	34*	0	9.53	44	5-82	1/0	42.72	6	62
Ramyakumara Wijekoon Mudiyanselage														
Gayan	21.12.1976		2	2005	38	14	0	12.66	2	2-49	0/0	33.00	0	0/3
Ranasinghe Anura Nandana	13.10.1956	9.11.1998	2	1981-1982	88	77	0	22.00	1	1-23	0/0	69.00	0	9
Ranatunga Arjuna	1.12.1963		93	1981-2000	5,105	135*	4	35.69	16	2-17	0/0	65.00	47	269
²**Ranatunga Dammika**	12.10.1962		2	1989	87	45	0	29.00	–	–	–/–	–	0	4
²**Ranatunga Sanjeeva**	25.4.1969		9	1994-1996	531	118	2	33.18	–	–	–/–	–	2	13
Randiv Suraj (also known as Hewa Kaluhalamullage Suraj Randiv Kaluhalamulla; formerly M. M. M. Suraj)	30.1.1985		3	2010-2010	26	12	0	8.66	14	5-82	1/0	40.50	0	21/6
²Ratnayake Rumesh Joseph	2.1.1964		23	1982-1991	433	56	0	14.43	73	6-66	5/0	35.10	9	70
²Ratnayeke Joseph Ravindran	2.5.1960		22	1981-1989	807	93	0	25.21	56	8-83	4/0	35.21	3	78
Samarasekera Maitipage Athula Rohitha	5.8.1961		4	1988-1991	118	57	0	16.85	3	2-38	0/0	34.66	3	39
²Samaraweera Dulip Prasanna	12.2.1972		7	1993-1994	211	42	0	15.07	0	–	–/–	–	5	5

§ *Muralitharan's figures exclude two runs, five wickets and two catches for the ICC World XI v Australia in the Super Series Test in 2005–06.*

	Born	Died	Tests	Test Career	Runs	HS	100s	Avge	Wkts	BB	Avge	5/10	Avge	Ct/St	O/T
[2]Samaraweera Thilan Thusara	22.9.1976		63	2001–2010	4,395	231	12	54.25	14	4-49	–	0/0	48.50	37	41
Sangakkara Kumar Chokshanada	27.10.1977		94	2000–2010	8,244	287	24	57.25	0	0-4	–	–/–	–	163/20	272±/29
Senanayake Charith Panduka	19.12.1962		3	1990	97	64	0	19.40					–	2	7
Silva Kelaniyage Jayantha	2.6.1973		7	1995–1997	6	6*	0	2.00	20	4-16		0/0	32.35	1	7
Silva Lindamullage Prageeth Chamara	14.12.1979		11	2006–2007	537	152*	1	33.56	1	1-57		0/0	65.00	7	64/15
Silva Sampathwaduge Amal Rohitha	12.12.1960		9	1982–1988	353	111	2	25.21				–/–	–	33/1	20
Tharanga Warushavithana Upul	2.2.1985		15	2005–2007	713	165	1	28.52					–	11	108±/8
Tillekeratne Hashan Prasantha	14.7.1967		83	1989–2003	4,545	204*	11	42.87	0	0-0	–	0/0	–	122/2	200
Upashantha Kalutarage Eric Amila	10.6.1972		2	1998–2002	10	6	0	3.33	4	2-41		0/0	50.00	0	12
Vaas Warnakulasurya Patabendige Ushantha Joseph Chaminda	27.1.1974		111	1994–2009	3,089	100*	1	24.32	355	7-71		12/2	29.58	31	321±/6
Vandort Michael Graydon	19.1.1980		20	2001–2008	1,144	140	4	36.90	0	0-4		–/–	–	6	1
Warnapura Bandula	1.3.1953		4	1981–1982	96	38	0	12.00	0	0-1		0/0	–	2	12
Warnapura Basnayake Shalith Malinda	26.5.1979		14	2007–2009	821	120	2	35.69	0	0-40		0/0	–	14	3
Warnaweera Kahakatchchi Patabandige Jayananda	23.11.1960		10	1985–1994	39	20	0	4.33	32	4-25		0/0	31.90	0	6
Weerasinghe Colombage Don Udesh Sanjeewa	1.3.1968		1	1985	3	3	0	3.00	0	0-8		0/0	–	0	
Welagedara Uda Walawwe Mahim Bandaralage Chanaka Asanka	20.3.1981		6	2007–2010	27	8	0	6.75	12	4-87		0/0	58.91	2	10/2
[2]Wettimuny Mithra de Silva	11.6.1951		2	1982	28	17	0	7.00	0				–	2	1
[2]Wettimuny Sidath	12.8.1956		23	1981–1986	1,221	190	2	29.07	0	0-16		0/0	–	10	35
Wickremasinghe Angupulige Gamini Dayantha	27.12.1965		3	1989–1992	17	13*	0	8.50	0			–/–	–	0	4
Wickremasinghe Gallage Pramodya	14.8.1971		40	1991–2000	555	51	0	9.40	85	6-60		3/0	41.87	9/1	134
Wijegunawardene Kapila Indaka Weerakkody	23.11.1964		2	1991–1991	14	6*	0	4.66	7	4-51		0/0	21.00	18	26
Wijesuriya Roger Gerard Christopher Ediriweera	18.2.1960		4	1981–1985	22	8	0	4.40	1	1-68		0/0	294.00	1	8
Wijetunge Piyal Kashyapa	6.8.1971		1	1993	10	10	0	5.00	2	1-58		0/0	59.00	0	
Zoysa Demuni Nuwan Tharanga	13.5.1978		30	1996–2004	288	28*	0	8.47	64	5-20		1/0	33.70	4	9

ZIMBABWE (74 players)

	Born	Died	Tests	Test Career	Runs	HS	100s	Avge	Wkts	BB	5/10	Avge	Ct/St	OIT
Arnott Kevin John	8.3.1961		4	1992	302	101*	1	43.14	–	–	–	–	4	13
Blignaut Arnoldus Mauritius ("Andy")	1.8.1978		19	2000–2005	886	92	0	26.84	53	5-73	3/0	37.05	13	54/1
Brain David Hayden	4.10.1964		9	1992–1994	115	28	0	10.45	30	5-42	1/0	30.50	1	23
Brandes Eddo André	5.3.1963		10	1992–1999	121	39	0	10.08	26	3-45	0/0	36.57	4	59
Brent Gary Bazil	13.1.1976		4	1999–2001	35	25	0	5.83	7	3-21	0/0	44.85	1	70/3
Briant Gavin Aubrey	11.4.1969		1	1992	17	16	0	8.50	–	–	–	–	0	5
Bruk-Jackson Glen Keith	25.4.1969		2	1993	39	31	0	9.75	–	–	–	–	0	–
Burmester Mark Greville	24.1.1968		3	1992	54	30*	0	27.00	3	3-78	0/0	75.66	1	8
Butchart Iain Peter	9.5.1960		1	1994	23	15	0	11.50	0	0-11	0/0	–	1	20
Campbell Alistair Douglas Ross	23.9.1972		60	1992–2002	2,858	103	2	27.21	0	0-1	0/0	–	60	188
Carlisle Stuart Vance	10.5.1972		37	1994–2005	1,615	118	2	26.91	–	–	–	–	34	111
Chigumbura Elton	14.3.1986		6	2003–2004	187	71	0	15.58	9	5-54	1/0	55.33	2	119/14
Coventry Charles Kevin	8.3.1983		2	2005	88	37	0	22.00	–	–	–	–	3	345
Cremer Alexander Graeme	19.9.1986		6	2004–2005	29	12	0	2.63	13	3-86	0/0	45.76	3	377
Crocker Gary John	16.5.1962		3	1992	69	33	0	23.00	3	2-65	0/0	72.33	1	6
Dabengwa Keith Mbusi	17.8.1980		3	2005	90	35	0	15.00	5	3-127	0/0	49.80	0	37/8
Dekker Mark Hamilton	5.12.1969		14	1993–1996	333	68*	0	15.85	0	0-5	0/0	–	12	23
Duffin Terrence	20.3.1982		2	2005	80	56	0	20.00	–	–	–	–	2	23
Ebrahim Dion Digby	7.8.1980		29	2000–2005	1,226	94	0	22.70	–	–	–	–	16	82
Ervine Sean Michael	6.12.1982		5	2003–2003	261	86	0	32.62	9	4-146	0/0	43.11	7	42
Evans Craig Neil	29.11.1969		3	1996–2003	52	22	0	8.66	0	0-8	0/0	–	1	53
Ewing Gavin Mackie	21.11.1981		3	2003–2005	108	71	0	18.00	2	1-27	0/0	130.00	0	7
Ferreira Neil Robert	3.6.1979		1	2005	21	16	0	10.50	0	0-0	0/0	–	0	–
[2] Flower Andrew	28.4.1968		63	1992–2002	4,794	232*	12	51.54	0	0-0	0/0	–	151/9	213
[2] Flower Grant William	20.12.1970		67	1992–2003	3,457	201*	6	29.54	25	4-41	1/0	61.48	43	221
Friend Travis John	7.1.1981		13	2001–2003	447	81	0	29.80	25	5-31	1/0	43.60	2	51
Goodwin Murray William	11.12.1972		19	1997–2000	1,414	166*	3	42.84	0	0-3	0/0	–	10	71
Gripper Trevor Raymond	28.12.1975		20	1999–2003	809	112	1	21.86	6	2-91	0/0	84.83	14	8
Hondo Douglas Tafadzwa	7.7.1979		8	2001–2004	83	19	0	9.22	21	6-59	1/0	36.85	5	56
Houghton David Laud	23.6.1957		22	1992–1997	1,464	266	4	43.05	0	0-0	0/0	–	17	63
Huckle Adam George	21.9.1971		8	1997–1998	74	28*	0	6.72	25	6-109	2/1	34.88	3	19
James Wayne Robert	27.8.1963		4	1993–1994	61	33	0	15.25	–	–	–	–	16/2	11
Jarvis Malcolm Peter	6.12.1955		5	1992–1994	4	2*	0	2.00	11	3-30	0/0	35.72	2	12

	Born	Died	Tests	Test Career	Runs	HS	100s	Avge	Wkts	BB	Avge	5/10	Ct/St	O/T
Johnson Neil Clarkson	24.1.1970		13	1998–2000	532	107	1	24.18	15	4-77	39.60	0/0	12	48
Lock Alan Charles Ingram	10.9.1962		1	1995	8	8*	0	8.00	5	3-68	21.00	0/0	1	8
Madondo Trevor Nyasha	22.11.1976	11.6.2001	3	1997–2000	90	74*	0	30.00					1	8
Mahwire Ngonidzashe Blessing	31.7.1982		10	2002–2005	147	50*	0	13.36	18	4-92	50.83	0/0	1	13
Maregwede Alester	5.8.1981		2	2003	74	28	0	18.50					1	23
Marillier Douglas Anthony	24.4.1978		5	2000–2001	185	73	0	30.83	2	1-9	19.50	0/0	1	11
Masakadza Hamilton	9.8.1983		15	2001–2005	785	119	1	27.06	2	1-9	62.50	0/0	8	48
Matambanadzo Everton Zvikomborero	13.4.1976		8	1996–1999	17	7	0	4.25	2	1-58	172.50	0/0	0	102/14
Matsikenyeri Stuart	3.5.1983		15	2003–2004	351	57	0	23.40	4	3-23	31.43	0/0	7	7
Mbangwa Mpumelelo ("Pommie")	26.6.1976		15	1996–2000	34	8	0	2.00	32	4-109	69.50	0/0	2	109/8
Mpofu Christopher Bobby	27.11.1985		6	2004–2005	17	7	0	2.83	8	3-82	66.09	0/0	2	29
Mupariwa Tawanda	16.4.1985		1	2003	15	14	0	15.00	0	0-136		0/0	0	49/8
Murphy Brian Andrew	1.12.1976		11	1999–2001	123	30	0	10.25	18	3-32	61.83	0/0	11	35/4
Mutendera David Travolta	25.1.1979		1	2000	10	10	0	5.00	0	0-29		0/0	0	31
Mwayenga Waddington	20.6.1984		1	2005	15	14*	0	15.00	1	1-79	79.00	0/0	0	9
Nkala Mluleki Luke	1.4.1981		10	2000–2004	187	47	0	14.38	11	3-82	66.09	0/0	3	3
Olonga Henry Khaaba	3.7.1976		30	1994–2002	184	24	0	5.41	68	5-70	38.52	2/0	0	50/1
Panyangara Tinashe	21.10.1985		4	2003–2004	128	40*	0	32.00	8	3-28	75.75	0/0	4	50
Peall Stephen Guy	2.9.1969		18	1993–1994	60	30	0	15.00	4	2-89	35.86	0/0	3	23
Price Raymond William	12.6.1976		18	1999–2003	224	36	0	9.73	69	6-73	29.27	5/1	2	21
Pycroft Andrew John	6.6.1956		3	1992	152	60	0	30.40					3	83/9
Ranchod Ujesh	17.5.1969		1	1992	8	7	0	4.00	1	1-45	45.00	0/0	2	20
²Rennie Gavin James	12.11.1976		23	1997–2001	1,023	93	0	22.73	1	1-40	84.00	0/0	13	3
²Rennie John Alexander	29.7.1970		4	1993–1997	62	22	0	12.40	3	2-22	125.00	0/0	2	40
Rogers Barney Guy	20.8.1982		4	2004	90	29	0	11.25	0	0-17		0/0	3	44
Shah Ali Hassimshah	7.8.1959		3	1992–1996	122	62	0	24.40	3	1-46	97.66	0/0	4	15
Sibanda Vusimuzi	10.10.1983		3	2003–2004	48	18	0	8.00					0	28
²Strang Bryan Colin	9.6.1972		26	1994–2001	465	53	0	12.91	56	5-101	39.33	1/0	4	83⅓/3
²Strang Paul Andrew	28.7.1970		24	1994–2001	839	106*	1	27.06	70	8-109	36.02	5/1	15	49
Streak Heath Hilton	16.3.1974		65	1993–2005	1,990	127*	1	22.35	216	6-73	28.14	7/0	17	95
Taibu Tatenda	14.5.1983		24	2001–2005	1,273	153	1	29.60					48/4	187⅛
Taylor Brendan Ross Murray	6.2.1986		10	2003–2005	422	78	0	21.10	1	1-27	27.00	0/0	4	129⅔/13
Traicos Athanasios John	17.5.1947		4†	1992	11	5	0	2.75	14	5-86	40.14	1/0	4	112/9
Utseya Prosper	26.3.1985		1	2003	45	45	0	22.50	0	0-55		0/0	2	27
Vermeulen Mark Andrew	2.3.1979		8	2002–2003	414	118	1	25.87	0	0-5		0/0	6	121/13
Viljoen Dirk Peter	11.3.1977		2	1997–2000	57	38	0	14.25	1	1-14	65.00	0/0	1	43

	Born	Died	Tests	Test Career	Runs	HS	100s	Avge	Wkts	BB	5/10	Avge	Ct/St	O/T
Waller Andrew Christopher	25.9.1959		2	1996	69	50	0	23.00	–	–	–/–	–	1	39
Watambwa Brighton Tonderai	9.6.1977		6	2000-2001	11	4*	0	3.66	14	4-64	0/0	35.00	0	–
Whittall Andrew Richard	28.3.1973		10	1996-1999	114	17	0	7.60	7	3-73	0/0	105.14	8	63
Whittall Guy James	5.9.1972		46	1993-2002	2,207	203*	4	29.42	51	4-18	0/0	40.94	19	147
Wishart Craig Brian	9.1.1974		27	1995-2005	1,098	114	1	22.40	–	–	–/–	–	15	90

BANGLADESH (59 players)

	Born	Died	Tests	Test Career	Runs	HS	100s	Avge	Wkts	BB	5/10	Avge	Ct/St	O/T
Abdur Razzak	15.6.1982		8	2005-2010	160	33	0	16.00	16	3-93	0/0	67.43	3	111/13
Aftab Ahmed	10.11.1985		16	2004-2009	582	82*	0	20.78	5	2-31	0/0	47.40	7	85/11
Akram Khan	1.11.1968		8	2000-2003	259	44	0	16.18	–	–	–/–	–	3	44
Al Sahariar	23.4.1978		15	2000-2003	683	71	0	22.76	–	–	–/–	–	10	29
Alamgir Kabir	10.1.1981		3	2002-2003	8	4	0	2.00	0	0-39	0/0	–	0	–
Alok Kapali	1.1.1984		17	2002-2005	584	85	0	17.69	6	3-3	0/0	118.16	5	65/6
Aminul Islam	2.2.1968		13	2000-2002	530	145	1	21.20	1	1-66	0/0	149.00	5	39
Anwar Hossain Monir	31.12.1981		3	2003-2005	22	13	0	7.33	1	1-95	0/0	–	0	1
Anwar Hossain Piju	10.12.1983		1	2002	14	12	0	7.00	–	–	–/–	–	1	1
Bikash Ranjan Das	14.7.1982		1	2000	2	2	0	1.00	1	1-64	0/0	72.00	0	–
Ehsanul Haque	1.12.1979		1	2002	7	5	0	3.50	0	0-18	0/0	–	0	6
Enamul Haque, sen.	27.2.1966		10	2000-2003	180	24*	0	12.00	18	4-136	0/0	57.05	1	29
Enamul Haque, jun.	5.12.1986		14	2003-2009	53	13	0	5.88	41	7-95	3/1	39.24	3	10
Fahim Muntasir	1.11.1980		3	2001-2002	53	33	0	8.66	5	3-131	0/0	68.40	1	3
Faisal Hossain	26.10.1978		1	2003	7	5	0	3.50	–	–	–/–	–	–	6
Habibul Bashar	17.8.1972		50	2000-2007	3,026	113	3	30.87	0	0-1	0/0	–	22	111
Hannan Sarkar	1.12.1982		17	2002-2004	662	76	1	20.06	–	–	–/–	–	7	20
Hasibul Hossain	3.6.1977		5	2000-2001	97	31	0	10.77	6	2-125	0/0	95.16	2	32
Imrul Kayes	2.2.1987		13	2008-2010	453	75	0	17.42	–	–	–/–	–	12	30/2
Jahurul Islam	12.12.1986		3	2009-2010	114	46	0	19.00	–	–	–/–	–	3	6/1
Javed Omar Belim	25.11.1976		40	2000-2007	1,720	119	1	22.05	0	0-12	0/0	–	10	59
Junaid Siddique	30.10.1987		18	2007-2010	942	106	1	26.91	0	0-2	0/0	–	11	46/5
Khaled Mahmud	26.7.1971		12	2001-2003	266	45	0	12.09	13	4-37	0/0	64.00	2	77
Khaled Mashud	8.2.1976		44	2000-2007	1,409	103*	1	19.04	–	–	–/–	–	78/9	126
Mahbubul Alam	1.12.1983		4	2008	5	2	0	1.25	5	2-62	0/0	62.80	0	5
Mahmudullah	4.2.1986		9	2009-2010	590	115	1	36.87	22	5-51	1/0	36.31	7	61/11

Name	Born	Died	Test Career	Tests	Runs	HS	100s	Avge	Wkts	BB	5/10	Avge	Ct/St	O/T
Manjural Islam	7.11.1979		2000-2003	17	81	21	0	3.68	28	6-81	1/0	57.32	3	34
Manjural Islam Rana	4.5.1984	16.3.2007	2003-2004	6	257	69	0	25.70	5	3-84	0/0	80.20	3	25
Masrafe bin Mortaza	5.10.1983		2001-2009	36	797	79	0	12.85	78	4-60	0/0	41.52	9	116/13
Mehrab Hossain, sen.	22.9.1978		2000-2003	9	241	71	0	13.38	0	0-5	0/0	–	6	18
Mehrab Hossain, jun.	8.7.1987		2007-2008	7	243	83	0	20.25	4	2-29	0/0	70.25	2	18/2
Mohammad Ashraful	9.9.1984		2001-2010	55	2,306	158*	5	22.38	20	2-42	0/0	59.40	24	162/15
Mohammad Rafique	5.9.1970		2000-2007	33	1,059	111	1	18.57	100	6-77	7/0	40.76	3	123/1
Mohammad Salim	15.10.1981		2003	2	49	26	0	16.33	–	–	–/–	–	3/1	1
Mohammad Sharif	12.12.1985		2000-2007	10	122	24*	0	7.17	14	4-98	0/0	79.00	5	9
Mushfiqur Rahim	1.9.1988		2005-2010	23	1,140	101	1	27.14	–	–	–/–	–	32/7	84/15
Mushfiqur Rahman	1.1.1980		2000-2004	10	232	46*	0	13.64	13	4-65	0/0	63.30	6	28
Naeem Islam	31.12.1986		2008-2009	4	180	59*	0	25.71	1	1-11	0/0	150.00	2	40/7
[2]Nafis Iqbal	31.1.1985		2004-2005	11	518	121	1	23.54	–	–	–/–	–	4	16
Naimur Rahman	19.9.1974		2000-2002	8	210	48	0	15.00	12	6-132	1/0	59.83	7	29
Nazmul Hossain	5.10.1987		2004	1	8	8*	0	8.00	2	2-114	0/0	57.00	0	34/2
Rafiqul Islam	7.11.1977		2002	1	7	6	0	3.50	–	–	–/–	–	0	1
Rajin Saleh	20.11.1983		2003-2008	24	1,141	89	0	25.93	2	1-9	0/0	134.00	15	43
Raqibul Hasan	8.10.1987		2008-2009	7	268	65	0	19.14	1	1-5	0/0	5.00	7	49/5
Rohail Islam	20.10.1986		2010	1	9	9*	0	–	0	0-12	–/–	–	0	21/3
Rubel Hossain	1.1.1990		2009-2010	8	43	17	0	4.77	12	5-166	1/0	83.08	1	27
Sajidul Islam	18.1.1988		2007	2	14	6	0	3.50	5	2-71	0/0	58.33	0	23/3
Sanwar Hossain	5.8.1973		2001-2003	9	345	49	0	19.16	5	2-128	0/0	62.00	7	46/5
Shafiul Islam	6.10.1989		2009-2010	5	137	53	0	15.22	7	3-86	0/0	71.71	0	20
Shahadat Hossain	7.8.1986		2005-2010	29	394	40	0	9.85	66	6-27	4/0	45.33	12	64/1
Shahriar Hossain	1.6.1976		2000-2003	3	99	48	0	19.80	–	–	–/–	–	1	
Shahriar Nafees	25.1.1986		2005-2009	16	835	138	1	26.09	–	–	–/–	–	8	
Shakib Al Hasan	24.3.1987		2007-2010	21	1,179	100	0	31.02	75	7-36	7/0	32.13	20	102/14
Syed Rasel	3.7.1984		2005-2007	6	37	19	0	4.62	12	4-129	0/0	47.75	1	52/8
Talha Jubair	10.12.1985		2002-2004	6	52	31	0	6.50	14	3-135	0/0	55.07	1	6
[2]Tamim Iqbal	20.3.1989		2007-2010	19	1,445	151	4	40.13	–	–	–/–	–	12	89/14
Tapash Baisya	25.12.1982		2002-2005	21	384	66	0	11.29	36	4-72	0/0	59.36	6	56
Tareq Aziz	4.9.1983		2003-2004	3	22	10*	0	11.00	1	1-76	0/0	261.00	1	10
Tushar Imran	10.12.1983		2002-2007	5	89	28	0	8.90	0	0-48	0/0	–	1	41

Notes

In one Test, A. and G. G. Hearne played for England; their brother, F. Hearne, for South Africa.

The Waughs and New Zealand's Marshalls are the only instance of Test-playing twins.

Adnan Akmal: brother of Kamran and Umar Akmal.

Amarsingh, L.: brother of L. Ramji.

Azmat Rana: brother of Shafqat Rana.

Bazid Khan: son of Majid Khan and grandson of M. Jahangir Khan.

Bravo, D. J. and D. M.: half-brothers.

Chappell, G. S., I. M. and T. M.: grandsons of V. Y. Richardson.

Collins, P. T.: half-brother of F. H. Edwards.

Cooper, W. H.: great-grandfather of A. P. Sheahan.

Edwards, F. H.: half-brother of P. T. Collins.

Hanif Mohammad: brother of Mushtaq, Sadiq and Wazir Mohammad, and father of Shoaib Mohammad.

Hearne, F.: father of G. A. L. Hearne (South Africa).

Jahangir Khan, M.: father of Majid Khan and grandfather of Bazid Khan.

Kamran Akmal: brother of Adnan nd Umar Akmal.

Khalid Wazir: son of S. Wazir Ali.

Kirsten, P. N. and G.: half-brothers.

Majid Khan: son of M. Jahangir Khan and father of Bazid Khan.

Manzoor Elahi: brother of Salim and Zahoor Elahi.

Moin Khan: brother of Nadeem Khan.

Mudassar Nazar: son of Nazar Mohammad.

Mushtaq Mohammad: brother of Hanif, Sadiq and Wazir Mohammad.

Nadeem Khan: brother of Moin Khan.

Nafis Iqbal: brother of Tamim Iqbal.

Nazar Mohammad: father of Mudassar Nazar.

Nazir Ali, S.: brother of S. Wazir Ali.

Pervez Sajjad: brother of Waqar Hassan.

Ramiz Raja: brother of Wasim Raja.

Ramji, L.: brother of L. Amarsingh.

Richardson, V. Y.: grandfather of G. S., I. M. and T. M. Chappell.

Sadiq Mohammad: brother of Hanif, Mushtaq and Wazir Mohammad.

Saeed Ahmed: brother of Younis Ahmed.

Salim Elahi: brother of Manzoor and Zahoor Elahi.

Shafqat Rana: brother of Azmat Rana.

Sheahan, A. P.: great-grandson of W. H. Cooper.

Shoaib Mohammad: son of Hanif Mohammad.

Tamim Iqbal: brother of Nafis Iqbal.

Umar Akmal: brother of Adnan and Kamran Akmal.

Waqar Hassan: brother of Pervez Sajjad.

Wasim Raja: brother of Ramiz Raja.

Wazir Ali, S.: brother of S. Nazir Ali and father of Khalid Wazir.

Wazir Mohammad: brother of Hanif, Mushtaq and Sadiq Mohammad.

Yograj Singh: father of Yuvraj Singh.

Younis Ahmed: brother of Saeed Ahmed.

Yuvraj Singh: son of Yograj Singh.

Zahoor Elahi: brother of Manzoor and Salim Elahi.

PLAYERS APPEARING FOR MORE THAN ONE TEST TEAM

Fourteen cricketers have appeared for two countries in Test matches, namely:

Amir Elahi (India 1, Pakistan 5)
J. J. Ferris (Australia 8, England 1)
S. C. Guillen (West Indies 5, New Zealand 3)
Gul Mahomed (India 8, Pakistan 1)
F. Hearne (England 2, South Africa 4)
A. H. Kardar (India 3, Pakistan 23)
W. E. Midwinter (England 4, Australia 8)

F. Mitchell (England 2, South Africa 3)
W. L. Murdoch (Australia 18, England 1)
Nawab of Pataudi, sen. (England 3, India 3)
A. J. Traicos (South Africa 3, Zimbabwe 4)
A. E. Trott (Australia 3, England 2)
K. C. Wessels (Australia 24, South Africa 16)
S. M. J. Woods (Australia 3, England 3)

Wessels also played 54 one-day internationals for Australia and 55 for South Africa.

The following players appeared for the ICC World XI against Australia in the Super Series Test in 2005-06: M. V. Boucher, R. Dravid, A. Flintoff, S. J. Harmison, Inzamam-ul-Haq, J. H. Kallis, B. C. Lara, M. Muralitharan, V. Sehwag, G. C. Smith, D. L. Vettori.

Note: In 1970, England played five first-class matches against the Rest of the World after the cancellation of South Africa's tour. Players were awarded England caps, but the matches are no longer considered to have Test status. Alan Jones (born 4.11.1938) made his only appearance for England in this series, scoring 5 and 0; he did not bowl and took no catches.

ONE-DAY INTERNATIONAL CRICKETERS

The following players have appeared for Test-playing countries in one-day internationals but had not represented their countries in Test matches by December 31, 2010. (Numbers in brackets signify number of one-day internationals for each player: where a second number appears, e.g. (5/1), it signifies the number of Twenty20 internationals for that player.)

England

M. W. Alleyne (10), I. D. Austin (9), A. D. Brown (16), D. R. Brown (9), G. Chapple (1), J. W. M. Dalrymple (27/3), S. M. Davies (6/3), J. L. Denly (9/5), M. V. Fleming (11), P. J. Franks (1), I. J. Gould (18), A. P. Grayson (2), G. W. Humpage (3), T. E. Jesty (10), E. C. Joyce (17/2), C. Kieswetter (12/9), G. D. Lloyd (6), A. G. R. Loudon (1), J. D. Love (3), M. B. Loye (7), M. A. Lynch (3), A. D. Mascarenhas (20/14), P. Mustard (10/2), P. A. Nixon (19/1), S. R. Patel (11), A. U. Rashid (5/5), M. J. Smith (5), N. M. K. Smith (7), J. N. Snape (10/1), V. S. Solanki (51/3), J. O. Troughton (6), C. M. Wells (2), V. J. Wells (9), A. G. Wharf (13), L. J. Wright (42/27), M. H. Yardy (19/12).
   Note: D. R. Brown also played 16 one-day internationals for Scotland.

Australia

G. A. Bishop (2), R. J. Campbell (2), M. J. Cosgrove (3), M. J. Di Venuto (9), B. R. Dorey (4), C. J. Ferguson (26/3), B. Geeves (2/1), S. F. Graf (11), S. M. Harwood (1/3), I. J. Harvey (73), J. W. Hastings (2/1), J. R. Hazlewood (1), M. C. Henriques (2/1), J. R. Hopes (84/12), D. J. Hussey (23/26), B. Laughlin (5/1), S. Lee (45), M. L. Lewis (7/2), R. J. McCurdy (11), K. H. MacLeay (16), J. P. Maher (26), S. E. Marsh (29/3), D. P. Nannes (1/15), A. A. Noffke (1/2), G. D. Porter (2), L. Ronchi (4/3), D. J. Siddons (1), M. A. Starc (2), A. M. Stuart (3), G. S. Trimble (2), A. C. Voges (14/4), D. A. Warner (7/23), B. E. Young (6), A. K. Zesers (2).
   Notes: At the end of December 2010, J. R. Hopes was the most experienced international player never to have appeared in Test cricket, with 84 one-day internationals and 12 Twenty20 internationals. D. P. Nannes also played two Twenty20 internationals for the Netherlands.

South Africa

S. Abrahams (1), D. M. Benkenstein (23), G. H. Bodi (2/1), L. E. Bosman (13/14), R. E. Bryson (7), D. J. Callaghan (29), D. N. Crookes (32), C. A. Ingram (8/4), J. C. Kent (2), L. J. Koen (5), G. J. P. Kruger (3/1), J. Louw (3/2), D. A. Miller (11/5), P. V. Mpitsang (1), S. J. Palframan (7), V. D. Philander (7/7), N. Pothas (3), A. G. Puttick (1), C. E. B. Rice (3), M. J. R. Rindel (22), D. B. Rundle (2), T. G. Shaw (9), E. O. Simons (23), E. L. R. Stewart (6), R. Telemachus (37/3), J. Theron (4/4), T. Tshabalala (4), R. E. van der Merwe (13/13), J. van der Wath (10/8), V. B. van Jaarsveld (2/3), M. N. van Wyk (6/2), C. J. P. G. van Zyl (3), H. S. Williams (7), M. Yachad (1).

West Indies

H. A. G. Anthony (3), D. Brown (3), B. St A. Browne (4), P. A. Browne (5), H. R. Bryan (15), D. C. Butler (5/1), R. T. Crandon (1), R. R. Emrit (2), S. E. Findlay (9/2), A. D. S. Fletcher (15/14), R. S. Gabriel (11), R. C. Haynes (8), R. O. Hurley (9), K. C. B. Jeremy (6), L. R. Johnson (3), K. A. Pollard (30/20), K. O. A. Powell (2), M. R. Pydanna (3), A. C. L. Richards (1/1), K. F. Semple (7), D. C. Thomas (2/1), C. M. Tuckett (1), L. R. Williams (15).

New Zealand

M. D. Bailey (1), B. R. Blair (14), N. T. Broom (22/9), C. E. Bulfin (4), T. K. Canning (4), P. G. Coman (3), B. J. Diamanti (1/1), M. W. Douglas (6), B. G. Hadlee (2), L. J. Hamilton (2), R. T. Hart (1), R. L. Hayes (1), P. A. Hitchcock (14/1), L. G. Howell (12), N. L. McCullum (15/25), P. D. McGlashan (4/11), B. J. McKechnie (14), E. B. McSweeney (16), J. P. Millmow (5), C. J. Nevin (37), A. J. Penn (5), R. G. Petrie (14), R. B. Reid (9), S. J. Roberts (2), S. L. Stewart (4), L. W. Stott (1), G. P. Sulzberger (3), A. R. Tait (5), E. P. Thompson (1/1), M. D. J. Walker (3), R. J. Webb (3), J. W. Wilson (6), W. A. Wisneski (3).

India

R. Ashwin (7/2), A. C. Bedade (13), A. Bhandari (2), Bhupinder Singh, sen. (2), G. Bose (1), V. B. Chandrasekhar (7), U. Chatterjee (3), N. A. David (4), P. Dharmani (1), S. Dhawan (1), A. B. Dinda (5/3), S. V. Gavaskar (11), R. S. Ghai (6), M. S. Gony (2), R. A. Jadeja (35/9), Joginder Sharma (4/4), A. V. Kale (1), S. C. Khanna (10), G. K. Khoda (2), A. R. Khurasiya (12), V. Kohli (40/2), A. M. P. Kumar (48/3), T. Kumaran (8), J. J. Martin (10), D. Mongia (57/1), S. P. Mukherjee (3), A. M. Nayar (3), N. V. Ojha (1/2), A. K. Pandey (2), Pankaj Singh (1), J. V. Paranjpe (1), A. K. Patel (8), Y. K. Pathan (42/18), Randhir Singh (2), S. S. Raul (2), A. M. Salvi (4), R. G. Sharma (16/9), L. R. Shukla (3), R. P. Singh (2), R. S. Sodhi (18), S. Somasunder (2), S. Sriram (8), R. Sudhakar Rao (1), M. K. Tiwary (1), S. S. Tiwary (3), S. Tyagi (4/1), R. V. Uthappa (38/9), P. S. Vaidya (4), Y. Venugopal Rao (16), R. Vinay Kumar (2/3), Jai P. Yadav (12), U. T. Yadav (3).

Note: S. K. Raina appeared for India in 98 one-day internationals before making his Test debut.

Pakistan

Aamer Hameed (2), Aamer Hanif (5), Ahmed Shehzad (4/5), Akhtar Sarfraz (4), Arshad Pervez (2), Asif Mahmood (2), Faisal Athar (1), Ghulam Ali (3), Haafiz Shahid (3), Hasan Jamil (6), Imran Abbas (2), Iqbal Sikander (4), Irfan Bhatti (1), Javed Qadir (1), Junaid Zia (4), Kamran Hussain (2), Kashif Raza (1), Khalid Latif (5/5), Mahmood Hamid (1), Mansoor Amjad (1/1), Mansoor Rana (2), Manzoor Akhtar (7), Maqsood Rana (1), Masood Iqbal (1), Mohammad Irfan (2), Moin-ul-Atiq (5), Mujahid Jamshed (1), Naeem Ahmed (1), Naeem Ashraf (2), Najaf Shah (1), Naseer Malik (3), Nasir Jamshed (12), Naumanullah (1), Parvez Mir (3), Rizwan Ahmed (1), Saadat Ali (8), Saeed Azad (4), Sajid Ali (13), Sajjad Akbar (2), Salim Pervez (1), Samiullah Khan (2), Shahid Anwar (1), Shahzaib Hasan (3/10), Shakil Khan (1), Sohail Fazal (1), Tanvir Mehdi (1), Wasim Haider (3), Zafar Iqbal (8), Zahid Ahmed (2).

Sri Lanka

J. W. H. D. Boteju (2), L. D. Chandimal (4/5), D. L. S. de Silva (2), G. N. de Silva (4), L. H. D. Dilhara (8/2), E. R. Fernando (3), T. L. Fernando (1), U. N. K. Fernando (2), J. C. Gamage (4), W. C. A. Ganegama (4), F. R. M. Goonatilleke (1), P. W. Gunaratne (23), A. A. W. Gunawardene (1), P. D. Heyn (2), W. S. Jayantha (17), P. S. Jayaprakashdaran (1), S. A. Jayasinghe (2), S. H. T. Kandamby (33/4), S. H. U. Karnain (19), B. M. A. J. Mendis (5), C. Mendis (1), A. M. N. Munasinghe (5), H. G. D. Nayanakantha (3), A. R. M. Opatha (5), S. P. Pasqual (2), K. G. Perera (1), M. D. K. Perera (4), N. L. T. C. Perera (15/7), H. S. M. Pieris (3), H. S. M. Pushpakumara (3/1), S. K. Ranasinghe (4), N. Ranatunga (2), N. L. K. Ratnayake (2), A. P. B. Tennekoon (4), H. D. R. L. Thirimanne (3), M. H. Tissera (3), M. L. Udawatte (9/5), D. M. Vonhagt (1), A. P. Weerakkody (1), K. Weeraratne (15/5), S. R. de S. Wettimuny (3), R. P. A. H. Wickremaratne (3).

Zimbabwe

R. D. Brown (7), R. W. Chakabva (5/1), C. J. Chibhabha (56/11), K. M. Curran (11), S. G. Davies (4), K. G. Duers (6), C. R. Ervine (14/3), E. A. Essop-Adam (1), D. A. G. Fletcher (6), T. N. Garwe (1), J. G. Heron (6), R. S. Higgins (11), V. R. Hogg (2), S. A. J. Ireland (26/1), K. M. Jarvis (3), T. Kamungozi (1), F. Kasteni (3), G. A. Lamb (9/5), A. J. Mackay (3), G. C. Martin (5), T. Maruma (8/4), S. W. Masakadza (6/2), T. M. K. Mawoyo (2), M. A. Meman (1), K. O. Meth (7), T. V. Mufambisi (6), F. Mutizwa (9), I. A. Nicolson (2), G. A. Paterson (10), G. E. Peckover (3), E. C.

Rainsford (39/2), P. W. E. Rawson (10), H. P. Rinke (18), R. W. Sims (3), G. M. Strydom (12), M. N. Waller (14), S. C. Williams (45/1), C. Zhuwao (1/3).

Bangladesh

Ahmed Kamal (1), Alam Talukdar (2), Aminul Islam, jun. (1), Anisur Rahman (2), Ather Ali Khan (19), Azhar Hussain (3), Dhiman Ghosh (14/1), Dolar Mahmud (7), Farhad Reza (32/7), Faruq Ahmed (2), Gazi Ashraf (7), Ghulam Faruq (5), Ghulam Nausher (9), Hafizur Rahman (2), Harunur Rashid (2), Jahangir Alam (3), Jahangir Badshah (5), Jamaluddin Ahmed (1), Mafizur Rahman (4), Mahbubur Rahman (1), Mazharul Haque (1), Minhazul Abedin (27), Moniruzzaman (2), Morshed Ali Khan (3), Mosharraf Hossain (1), Nasir Ahmed (7), Nazimuddin (7/7), Neeyamur Rashid (2), Nurul Abedin (4), Rafiqul Alam (2), Raqibul Hasan, sen. (2), Saiful Islam (7), Sajjad Ahmed (2), Samiur Rahman (2), Shafiuddin Ahmed (11), Shahidur Rahman (2), Shariful Haq (1), Sheikh Salahuddin (6), Suhrawadi Shuvo (11/1), Wahidul Gani (1), Zahid Razzak (3), Zakir Hassan (2).

PLAYERS APPEARING FOR MORE THAN ONE ONE-DAY INTERNATIONAL TEAM

The following players have played one-day internationals for the **African XI** in addition to their national side:

N. Boje (2), L. E. Bosman (1), J. Botha (2), M. V. Boucher (5), E. Chigumbura (3), A. B. de Villiers (5), H. H. Dippenaar (6), J. H. Kallis (3), J. M. Kemp (6), J. A. Morkel (2), M. Morkel (3), T. M. Odoyo (5), P. J. Ongondo (1), J. L. Ontong (3), S. M. Pollock (6), A. G. Prince (3), J. A. Rudolph (2), V. Sibanda (2), G. C. Smith (1), D. W. Steyn (2), H. H. Streak (2), T. Taibu (1), S. O. Tikolo (4), M. Zondeki (2). (Odoyo, Ongondo and Tikolo play for Kenya, which does not have Test status.)

The following players have played one-day internationals for the **Asian Cricket Council XI** in addition to their national side:

Abdul Razzaq (4), M. S. Dhoni (3), R. Dravid (1), C. R. D. Fernando (1), S. C. Ganguly (3), Harbhajan Singh (2), Inzamam-ul-Haq (3), S. T. Jayasuriya (3), S. C. Ganguly (3), A. Kumble (2), Mashrafe bin Mortaza (2), Mohammad Ashraful (2), Mohammad Asif (3), Mohammad Rafique (2), Mohammad Yousuf (7), M. Muralitharan (4), A. Nehra (3), K. C. Sangakkara (4), V. Sehwag (3), Shahid Afridi (3), Shoaib Akhtar (3), W. U. Tharanga (1), W. P. U. J. C. Vaas (1), Yuvraj Singh (3), Zaheer Khan (6).

The following players have played one-day internationals for the **ICC World XI** in addition to their national side:

C. L. Cairns (1), R. Dravid (3), S. P. Fleming (3), A. Flintoff (3), C. H. Gayle (3), A. C. Gilchrist (1), D. Gough (1), M. L. Hayden (1), J. H. Kallis (3), B. C. Lara (4), G. D. McGrath (1), M. Muralitharan (3), M. Ntini (1), K. P. Pietersen (2), S. M. Pollock (3), R. T. Ponting (1), K. C. Sangakkara (3), V. Sehwag (3), Shahid Afridi (2), Shoaib Akhtar (3), D. L. Vettori (3), S. K. Warne (1).

K. C. Wessels has appeared for both Australia and South Africa. D. R. Brown has appeared for both England and Scotland. E. J. G. Morgan has appeared for both Ireland and England.

G. M. Hamilton has played Test cricket for England and one-day internationals for Scotland. D. P. Nannes has played one-day and Twenty20 internationals for Australia and Twenty20 internationals for the Netherlands.

TWENTY20 INTERNATIONAL CRICKETERS

The following players have appeared for Test-playing countries in Twenty20 internationals but had not represented their countries in Test matches or one-day internationals by December 31, 2010:

England M. J. Lumb (7); **Australia** T. R. Birt (3), D. T. Christian (3), S. N. J. O'Keefe (1), L. A. Pomersbach (1); **South Africa** Y. A. Abdulla (2), T. Henderson (1), R. K. Kleinveldt (2), H. G. Kuhn (3), A. C. Thomas (1); **West Indies** W. K. D. Perkins (1); **New Zealand** D. G. Brownlie (2), A. F. Milne (2), R. J. Nicol (3), L. J. Woodcock (1); **Pakistan** Anwar Ali (1), Shoaib Khan (1); **Sri Lanka** C. U. Jayasinghe (5), H. G. J. M. Kulatunga (2), R. J. M. G. M. Rupasinghe (1), I. Udana (5); **Zimbabwe** T. L. Chatara (1); **Bangladesh** Nadif Chowdhury (3), Nazmus Sadat (1).

ELITE TEST UMPIRES

The following umpires were on the ICC's elite panel in January 2011. The figures for Tests, one-day internationals and Twenty20 internationals and the Test Career dates refer to matches in which they have officiated as umpires (excluding abandoned games). The totals of Tests are complete up to January 19, 2011, the totals of one-day and Twenty20 internationals up to December 31, 2010.

	Country	Born	Tests	Test Career	ODIs	T20Is
Aleem Dar	P	6.6.1968	63	*2003–2010*	138	18
Asad Rauf	P	12.5.1956	35	*2004–2010*	81	17
Bowden Brent Fraser ("Billy")..........	NZ	11.4.1963	65	*1999–2010*	149	19
Davis Stephen James	A	9.4.1952	31	*1997–2010*	94	14
de Silva Ellawalakankanamge Asoka Ranjit..	SL	28.3.1956	48	*2000–2010*	108	9
Doctrove Billy Raymond	WI	3.7.1955	31	*1999–2010*	101	17
Erasmus Marais	SA	27.2.1964	5	*2009–2010*	23	11
Gould Ian James.....................	E	19.8.1957	18	*2008–2010*	48	15
Harper Daryl John	A	23.10.1951	94	*1998–2010*	168	10
Hill Anthony Lloyd..................	NZ	26.6.1951	22	*2001–2010*	76	16
Taufel Simon James Arthur	A	21.1.1971	67	*2000–2010*	154	22
Tucker Rodney James	A	28.8.1964	8	*2009–2010*	17	8

Note: R. E. Koertzen left the panel in 2010; his final figures were as follows:

	Country	Born	Tests	Test Career	ODIs	T20Is
Koertzen Rudolf Eric.................	SA	26.3.1949	108	*1992–2010*	209	14

BIRTHS AND DEATHS

OTHER CRICKETING NOTABLES

The following list shows the births and deaths of cricketers, and people associated with cricket, who have *not* played in Test matches.

Criteria for inclusion The following are included: all non-Test players who have either (1) scored 20,000 runs in first-class cricket, or (2) taken 1,500 first-class wickets, or (3) achieved 750 dismissals, or (4) reached *both* 15,000 runs *and* 750 wickets. It also includes (5) the leading players who flourished before the start of Test cricket and (6) all others deemed of sufficient merit or interest for inclusion, either because of their playing skill, their present position, their contribution to the game in whatever capacity or their fame in other walks of life.

Names Where players were normally known by a name other than their first, this is underlined.

Teams Where only one team is listed, this is normally the one for which the player made most first-class appearances. Additional teams are listed only if the player appeared for them in more than 20 first-class matches or if they are especially relevant to their career. School and university teams are not given unless especially relevant (e.g. for the schoolboys chosen as wartime Cricketers of the Year in the 1918 and 1919 *Wisdens*).

	Teams	Born	Died
Aird Ronald MC	Hampshire	4.5.1902	16.8.1986
Secretary of MCC 1953–62; president of MCC 1968–69.			
Aislabie Benjamin	Surrey, Secretary of MCC 1822–42	14.1.1774	2.6.1842
Alcock Charles William	Secretary of Surrey 1872–1907	2.12.1842	26.2.1907
Editor, Cricket magazine, 1882–1907. Captain of Wanderers and England football teams.			
Alley William Edward	NSW, Somerset; Test umpire	3.2.1919	26.11.2004
Altham Harry Surtees CBE	Surrey, Hampshire; historian	30.11.1888	11.3.1965
Coach at Winchester for 30 years; president of MCC 1959–60.			
Arlott Leslie Thomas <u>John</u> OBE	Broadcaster and writer	25.2.1914	14.12.1991
Arthur John <u>Michael</u>	Griq. W., OFS, South Africa coach 2005–10	17.5.1968	
Ashdown William Henry	Kent	27.12.1898	15.9.1979
The only cricketer to appear in English first-class cricket before and after the two wars.			
Ashley-Cooper Frederick Samuel	Historian	22.3.1877	31.1.1932
Austin *Sir* Harold Bruce Gardiner	Barbados	15.7.1877	27.7.1943
Bailey Jack Arthur	Essex; secretary of MCC 1974–87	22.6.1930	
Bannister John David	Warwickshire; writer and broadcaster	23.8.1930	
Barker Gordon	Essex	6.7.1931	10.2.2006
Bayliss Trevor Harley	NSW, Sri Lanka coach 2007–11	21.12.1962	
Beauclerk *Rev. Lord* Frederick	Middlesex, Surrey, MCC	8.5.1773	22.4.1850
Beldam William ("Silver Billy")	Hambledon, Surrey	5.2.1766	26.2.1862
Beldham George William	Middlesex; photographer	1.5.1868	23.11.1937
Beloff Michael Jacob QC	Head of ICC Code of Conduct Commission	18.4.1942	
Berry Leslie George	Leicestershire	28.4.1906	5.2.1985
Bird Harold Dennis MBE	Yorkshire, Leicestershire; Test umpire	19.4.1933	
Blofeld Henry Calthorpe OBE	Cambridge Univ; broadcaster	23.9.1939	
Booth Roy	Yorkshire, Worcestershire	1.10.1926	
Bowley Frederick Lloyd	Worcestershire	9.11.1873	31.5.1943
Bradshaw Keith	Tasmania, Secretary/chief executive MCC 2006–	2.10.1963	
Buchanan John Marshall	Queensland; Australia coach 1999–2007	5.4.1953	
Bucknor Stephen Anthony	ICC umpire	31.5.1946	
Umpire of 128 Tests, a record.			
Buller John Sydney MBE	Worcestershire; Test umpire	23.8.1909	7.8.1970
Cardus *Sir* Neville	Writer	3.4.1888	27.2.1975
Chester Frank	Worcestershire; Test umpire	20.1.1895	8.4.1957
Stood in 48 Tests between 1924 and 1955, a record that lasted until 1992.			
Clark David Graham	Kent; president of MCC 1977–78	27.1.1919	
Clarke Charles <u>Giles</u>	Chairman of ECB, 2007–	9.5.1953	
Clarke William	Nottinghamshire	24.12.1798	25.8.1856
Founded the All-England XI, Trent Bridge ground.			

	Teams	Born	Died
Collier David Gordon	Chief executive of ECB 2005–	22.4.1955	
Collins Arthur Edward Jeune	Clifton College	18.8.1885	11.11.1914
Made the highest score in any cricket, 628* in a house match in 1899.			
Conan Doyle *Dr Sir* Arthur Ignatius	MCC	22.5.1859	7.7.1930
Creator of Sherlock Holmes; his only victim in first-class cricket was W. G. Grace.			
Cook Thomas Edwin Reed	Sussex	5.1.1901	15.1.1950
Cox George, jun.	Sussex	23.8.1911	30.3.1985
Cox George, sen.	Sussex	29.11.1873	24.3.1949
Cozier Tony	Broadcaster and writer	10.7.1940	
Dalmiya Jagmohan	President of ICC 1997–2000	30.5.1940	
Davies Emrys	Glamorgan; Test umpire	27.6.1904	10.11.1975
Davison Brian Fettes	Rhodesia, Leics, Tasmania, Gloucestershire	21.12.1946	
Dawkes George Owen	Leicestershire, Derbyshire	19.7.1920	10.8.2006
de Lisle Timothy John March Phillipps	Editor of *Wisden* 2003	25.6.1962	
Dennett George	Gloucestershire	27.4.1880	14.9.1937
Di Venuto Michael James	Tasmania, Derbys, Durham	12.12.1973	
Eagar Edward Patrick	Photographer	9.3.1944	
Edwards Charlotte Marie MBE	England Women	17.12.1979	
Ehsan Mani	President of ICC 2003–06	23.3.1945	
Engel Matthew Lewis	Editor of *Wisden* 1993–2000, 2004–07	11.6.1951	
"Felix" (Nicholas Wanostrocht)	Kent, Surrey, All-England	4.10.1804	3.9.1876
Batsman, artist, author (Felix on the Bat) and inventor of the Catapulta bowling machine.			
Ferguson William Henry BEM	Scorer	6.6.1880	22.9.1957
Scorer and baggage-master for five Test teams on 43 tours over 52 years and "never lost a bag".			
Fletcher Duncan Andrew Gwynne	Zimbabwe, England coach 1999–2007	27.9.1948	
Frindall William Howard MBE	Statistician	3.3.1939	30.1.2009
Gibbons Harold Harry Haywood	Worcestershire	8.10.1904	16.2.1973
Grace *Mrs* Martha	Mother and cricketing mentor of W.G.	18.7.1812	25.7.1884
Grace William Gilbert, jun.	Gloucestershire; son of W.G.	6.7.1874	2.3.1905
Graveney David Anthony	Gloucestershire, Somerset, Durham	2.1.1953	
Chairman of England selectors 1997–2008			
Gray James Roy	Hampshire	19.5.1926	
Gray Malcolm Alexander	President of ICC 2000–03	30.5.1940	
Grieves Kenneth James	New South Wales, Lancashire	27.8.1925	3.1.1992
Hair Darrell Bruce	ICC umpire	30.9.1952	
Hallam Maurice Raymond	Leicestershire	10.9.1931	1.1.2000
Heyhoe-Flint Lady [Rachael] OBE	England Women	11.6.1939	
Horton Henry	Hampshire	18.4.1923	2.11.1998
Howard Cecil Geoffrey	Middlesex; administrator	14.2.1909	8.11.2002
Huish Frederick Henry	Kent	15.11.1869	16.3.1957
Hunter David	Yorkshire	23.2.1860	11.1.1927
Hutchinson James Metcalf	Derbyshire	29.11.1896	7.11.2000
Believed to be the longest-lived first-class cricketer at 103 years 344 days.			
Ingleby-Mackenzie Alexander Colin David OBE	Hampshire	15.9.1933	9.3.2006
President of MCC 1996–98.			
Isaac Alan Raymond	Vice-president of ICC 2010–12; President-elect	20.1.1952	
Jackson Victor Edward	NSW, Leicestershire	25.10.1916	30.1.1965
James Cyril Lionel Robert	Writer	4.1.1901	31.5.1989
Jesty Trevor Edward	Hants, Griqualand W, Surrey, Lancs; umpire	2.6.1948	
Johnson Paul	Nottinghamshire	24.4.1965	
Johnston Brian Alexander CBE, MC	Broadcaster	24.6.1912	5.1.1994
Jones Alan MBE	Glamorgan	4.11.1938	
Played once for England v Rest of the World, 1970, regarded at the time as a Test match.			
King John Barton	Philadelphia	19.10.1873	17.10.1965
"Beyond question the greatest all-round cricketer produced by America" – Wisden.			
Knight Roger David Verdon CBE	Surrey, Gloucestershire, Sussex	6.9.1946	
Secretary of MCC 1994–2005			
Lacey *Sir* Francis Eden	Hants; Secretary of MCC 1898–1926	19.10.1859	26.5.1946
Lamb Timothy Michael	Middlesex, Northants	24.3.1953	
Chief executive of ECB 1997–2004.			

	Teams	Born	Died
Langridge John George MBE	Sussex; Test umpire	10.2.1910	27.6.1999
Lillywhite Frederick William	Sussex	13.6.1792	21.8.1854
Long Arnold	Surrey, Sussex	18.12.1940	
Lord Thomas	Middlesex; founder of Lord's Cricket Ground	23.11.1755	13.1.1832
Lorgat Haroon	Chief executive of ICC 2008–	26.5.1960	
McEwan Kenneth Scott	Eastern Province, Essex	16.7.1952	
McGilvray Alan David MBE	NSW; broadcaster	6.12.1909	17.7.1996
MacLaurin of Knebworth, Lord	Chairman of ECB 1997–2002	30.3.1937	
Majola Mongezi Gerald	Chief executive, Cricket South Africa	20.11.1959	
Marlar Robin Geoffrey	Sussex; writer	2.1.1931	
Martin-Jenkins Christopher Dennis Alexander MBE	Writer; broadcaster	20.1.1945	
President of MCC 2010-11.			
Mendis Gehan Dixon	Sussex, Lancashire	20.4.1955	
Mercer John	Sussex, Glamorgan; coach and scorer	22.4.1893	31.8.1987
Meyer Rollo John Oliver OBE	Somerset	15.3.1905	9.3.1991
Modi Lalit Kumar	Chairman, Indian Premier League 2008–10	29.11.1963	
Moles Andrew James	Warwickshire, NZ coach 2008–09	12.2.1961	
Moores Peter	Sussex; England coach 2007–09	18.12.1962	
Morgan Derek Clifton	Derbyshire	26.2.1929	
Morgan Frederick David OBE	Chairman of ECB 2003–07, President of ICC 2008–10	6.10.1937	
Mynn Alfred	Kent, All-England	19.1.1807	1.11.1861
Neale Phillip Anthony	Worcestershire; England manager	5.6.1954	
Newman John Alfred	Hampshire	12.11.1884	21.12.1973
Nicholas Mark Charles Jefford	Hampshire; broadcaster	29.9.1957	
Nicholls Ronald Bernard	Gloucestershire	4.12.1933	21.7.1994
Nielsen Timothy John	South Australia, Australia coach 2007–	5.5.1968	
Nyren John	Hampshire	15.12.1764	28.6.1837
Author of The Young Cricketer's Tutor, *1833.*			
Nyren Richard	Hampshire	1734	25.4.1797
Proprietor of the Bat & Ball Inn, Broadhalfpenny Down.			
Ontong Rodney Craig	Border, Glamorgan, N. Transvaal	9.9.1955	
Ormrod Joseph Alan	Worcestershire, Lancashire	22.12.1942	
Pardon Sydney Herbert	Editor of *Wisden* 1891–1925	23.9.1855	20.11.1925
Parks Henry William	Sussex	18.7.1906	7.5.1984
Parr George	Nottinghamshire, All-England	22.5.1826	23.6.1891
Captain and manager of the All-England XI.			
Pawar Sharadchandra Govindrao	Pres. BCCI 2005–08, ICC 2010–12	12.12.1940	
Payton Wilfred Richard Daniel	Nottinghamshire	13.2.1882	2.5.1943
Pearce Thomas Neill	Essex; administrator	3.11.1905	10.4.1994
Pearson Frederick	Worcestershire	23.9.1880	10.11.1963
Perrin Percival Albert	Essex	26.5.1876	20.11.1945
Pilch Fuller	Norfolk, Kent	17.3.1804	1.5.1870
"The best batsman that has ever yet appeared" – Arthur Haygarth, 1862.			
Preston Norman MBE	Editor of *Wisden* 1952–80	18.3.1903	6.3.1980
Rait-Kerr Col. Rowan Scrope	Europeans; Secretary MCC 1936–52	13.4.1891	2.4.1961
Reeves William	Essex; Test umpire	22.1.1875	22.3.1944
Rice Clive Edward Butler	Transvaal, Nottinghamshire	23.7.1949	
Robertson-Glasgow Raymond Charles	Somerset; writer	15.7.1901	4.3.1965
Robins Derrick Harold	Warwickshire; tour promoter	27.6.1914	3.5.2004
Robinson Mark Andrew	Northants, Yorkshire, Sussex, coach	23.11.1966	
Roebuck Peter Michael	Somerset; writer	6.3.1956	
Sainsbury Peter James	Hampshire	13.6.1934	
Sellers Arthur Brian MBE	Yorkshire	5.3.1907	20.2.1981
Seymour James	Kent	25.10.1879	30.9.1930
Shepherd David Robert MBE	Gloucestershire; ICC umpire	27.12.1940	27.10.2009
Shepherd Donald John	Glamorgan	12.8.1927	
Siddons James Darren	Victoria, S. Australia, Bangladesh coach 2007–	25.4.1964	

	Teams	Born	Died
Silk Dennis Raoul Whitehall CBE	Somerset	8.10.1931	
President of MCC 1992–94; chairman of TCCB 1994–96.			
Simmons Jack MBE	Lancashire, Tasmania	28.3.1941	
Skelding Alexander	Leicestershire; umpire	5.9.1886	17.4.1960
First-class umpire 1931–1958, when he was 72.			
Smith William Charles	Surrey	4.10.1877	15.7.1946
Speed Malcolm Walter	Chief executive of ICC 2001–08	14.9.1948	
Spencer Thomas William OBE	Kent; Test umpire	22.3.1914	1.11.1995
Stephenson Harold William	Somerset	18.7.1920	23.4.2008
Stephenson Heathfield Harman	Surrey, All-England	3.5.1832	17.12.1896
Captained first English team to Australia, 1861-62; umpired first Test in England, 1880.			
Stephenson Lt.-Col. John Robin CBE	Secretary MCC 1987–93	25.2.1931	2.6.2003
Studd Sir John Edward Kynaston	Middlesex	26.7.1858	14.1.1944
Lord Mayor of London 1928–29; President of MCC 1930.			
Surridge Walter Stuart	Surrey	3.9.1917	13.4.1992
Sutherland James Alexander	Victoria; CEO Cricket Australia 2001–	14.7.1965	
Suttle Kenneth George	Sussex	25.8.1928	25.3.2005
Swanton Ernest William CBE	Middlesex; writer	11.2.1907	22.1.2000
Tarrant Francis Alfred	Victoria, Middlesex	11.12.1880	29.1.1951
Taylor Brian	Essex	19.6.1932	
Taylor Samantha Claire MBE	England Women	25.9.1975	
Thornton Charles Inglis	Middlesex	20.3.1850	10.12.1929
Timms John Edward	Northamptonshire	3.11.1906	18.5.1980
Todd Leslie John	Kent	19.6.1907	20.8.1967
Tunnicliffe John	Yorkshire	26.8.1866	11.7.1948
Turner Francis Michael MBE	Leicestershire; administrator	8.8.1934	
Turner Robert Julian	Somerset	25.11.1967	
Ufton Derek Gilbert	Kent	31.5.1928	
van der Bijl Vintcent Adriaan Pieter	Natal, Middx, Transvaal	19.3.1948	
van Zyl Cornelius Johannes Petrus Gerthardus	OFS, Glam, South Africa coach 2010–	1.10.1961	
Virgin Roy Thomas	Somerset, Northamptonshire	26.8.1939	
Ward William	Hampshire	24.7.1787	30.6.1849
Scorer of the first double-century: 278 for MCC v Norfolk, 1820.			
Wass Thomas George	Nottinghamshire	26.12.1873	27.10.1953
Watson Frank	Lancashire	17.9.1898	1.2.1976
Webber Roy	Statistician	23.7.1914	14.11.1962
Weigall Gerald John Villiers	Kent; coach	19.10.1870	17.5.1944
Wheatley Oswald Stephen CBE	Warwickshire, Glamorgan	28.5.1935	
Wight Peter Bernard	Somerset; umpire	25.6.1930	
Wilson John Victor	Yorkshire	17.1.1921	5.6.2008
Wisden John	Sussex	5.9.1826	5.4.1884
"The Little Wonder"; founder of Wisden Cricketers' Almanack, 1864.			
Wood Cecil John Burditt	Leicestershire	21.11.1875	5.6.1960
Woodcock John Charles OBE	Writer; editor of *Wisden* 1981–86	7.8.1926	
Wooller Wilfred	Glamorgan	20.11.1912	10.3.1997
Wright Graeme Alexander	Editor of *Wisden* 1987–92, 2001–02	23.4.1943	
Young Douglas Martin	Worcestershire, Gloucestershire	15.4.1924	18.6.1993

REGISTER OF CURRENT PLAYERS

The qualifications for inclusion are as follows:
1. All players who appeared in Tests, one-day internationals or Twenty20 internationals for a Test-playing country in the calendar year 2010.
2. All players who appeared in the County Championship, the Sheffield Shield, the SuperSport Series, the West Indian four-day regional competition for the WICB President's Trophy, or the Duleep Trophy in the calendar year 2010.
3. All players who appeared in a first-class match in a Test-playing country in the calendar year 2010 who have previously played Tests, one-day international cricket or Twenty20 international cricket for a Test-playing country.
4. All players who appeared in a first-class match for a Test-playing country on tour or the A-team of a Test-playing country in the calendar year 2010.

Notes: The forename by which the player is known is underlined if it is not his first name.
Teams are those played for in the calendar year 2010, or the last domestic team for which that player appeared.
Countries are those for which players are qualified.
The country of birth is given if it is not the one for which a player is qualified. It is also given to differentiate between West Indian nations, and where it is essential for clarity.

* *Denotes Test player.*

	Team	Country	Born	Birthplace
Aamer Sajjad	WAPDA	P	5.2.1981	*Lahore*
Abbott Kyle John	KwaZulu-Natal/Dolphins	SA	18.6.1987	*Empangeni*
***Abdul Razzaq**	ZTBL	P	2.12.1979	*Lahore*
Abdulla Yusuf Adam	KwaZulu-Natal	SA	17.1.1983	*Johannesburg*
***Abdur Rauf**	Multan	P	9.12.1978	*Renala Khurd*
***Abdur Razzak**	Khulna	B	15.6.1982	*Khulna*
***Abdur Rehman**	Habib Bank	P	1.3.1980	*Sialkot*
Abid Ali	Lahore Ravi	P	16.10.1987	*Lahore*
Absolem Alfred	Hyderabad	I	23.1.1986	*Hyderabad*
***Adams** Andre Ryan	Nottinghamshire/Auckland	NZ	17.7.1975	*Auckland*
Adams James Henry Kenneth	Hampshire	E	23.9.1980	*Winchester*
Adkin William Anthony	Sussex	E	9.4.1990	*Redhill*
***Adnan Akmal**	Sui Northern	P	13.3.1985	*Lahore*
Adshead Stephen John	Derbyshire	E	29.1.1980	*Redditch*
***Aftab Ahmed**	Chittagong	B	10.11.1985	*Chittagong*
***Afzaal** Usman	Surrey	E	9.6.1977	*Rawalpindi, Pakistan*
Aga Ragheb Gul	Sussex/Kenya	K	10.7.1984	*Nairobi*
***Agarkar** Ajit Bhalchandra	Mumbai	I	4.12.1977	*Bombay*
Ahmed Abu Nachim	Assam	I	5.11.1988	*Guwahati*
Ahmed Shehzad	Habib Bank	P	23.11.1991	*Lahore*
Aldridge Graeme William	Northern Districts	NZ	15.11.1977	*Christchurch*
Alexander Craig John	Lions/North West	SA	5.1.1987	*Cape Town*
***Ali** Kabir	Hampshire	E	24.11.1980	*Moseley*
Ali Kadeer	Gloucestershire	E	7.3.1983	*Moseley*
Ali Moeen Munir	Worcestershire	E	18.6.1987	*Birmingham*
***Ali Naqvi**	KRL	P	19.3.1977	*Lahore*
Allenby James	Glamorgan	E	12.9.1982	*Perth, Australia*
***Alok Kapali**	Sylhet	B	1.1.1984	*Sylhet*
***Ambrose** Timothy Raymond	Warwickshire	E	1.12.1982	*Newcastle, Australia*
Amla Ahmed Mahomed	Dolphins	SA	15.9.1979	*Durban*
***Amla** Hashim Mahomed	Dolphins/Notts	SA	31.3.1983	*Durban*
***Anderson** James Michael	Lancashire	E	30.7.1982	*Burnley*
Andrew Gareth Mark	Worcestershire	E	27.12.1983	*Yeovil*
Anwar Ali	PIA	P	25.11.1987	*Karachi*
Anyon James Edward	Sussex	E	5.5.1983	*Lancaster*
Aravind Sreesanth	Karnataka	I	8.4.1984	*Bangalore*
***Arnel** Brent John	Northern Districts	NZ	3.1.1979	*Te Awamutu*

	Team	Country	Born	Birthplace
Arun Karthik Konda Bhaskar	Tamil Nadu	I	15.2.1986	*Walajapet*
*****Asad Shafiq**	Karachi Blues/PIA	P	28.1.1986	*Karachi*
Ashling Christopher Paul	Glamorgan	E	26.11.1988	*Manchester*
Ashraf Moin Aqeeb	Yorkshire	E	5.1.1992	*Bradford*
Ashwin Ravichandran	Tamil Nadu	I	17.9.1986	*Madras*
*****Asim Kamal**	Karachi Blues/Kar. Whites	P	31.5.1976	*Karachi*
Athanaze Justin Jason	Leeward Islands	WI	29.1.1988	*Antigua*
August Clayton John	Boland /Titans/Northerns	SA	16.2.1990	*Vredenburg*
Aushik Srinivas Raju	Tamil Nadu	I	16.3.1993	*Coimbatore*
*****Austin** Ryan Anthony	Com. Campuses & Colls.	WI	15.11.1981	*Arima, Trinidad*
Awana Parvinder	Delhi	I	19.7.1986	*Noida*
Azeem Ghumman	Hyderabad	P	24.1.1991	*Hyderabad*
Azeem Rafiq	Yorkshire	E	27.2.1991	*Karachi, Pakistan*
*****Azhar Ali**	KRL	P	19.2.1985	*Lahore*
*****Azhar Mahmood**	Kent/Habib Bank	P	28.2.1975	*Rawalpindi*
*****Badani** Hemang Kamal	Haryana	I	14.11.1976	*Madras*
*****Badrinath** Subramaniam	Tamil Nadu	I	30.8.1980	*Madras*
*****Bahutule** Sairaj Vasant	Andhra	I	6.1.1973	*Bombay*
Bailey Cullen Benjamin	South Australia	A	26.2.1985	*Bedford Park*
Bailey George John	Tasmania	A	7.9.1982	*Launceston*
Bailey Ryan Tyrone	Eagles/Knights	SA	8.9.1982	*Cape Town*
Bairstow Jonathan Marc	Yorkshire	E	26.9.1989	*Bradford*
Baker Gavin Charles	Lough MCCU/Northants	E	3.10.1988	*Edgware*
*****Baker** Lionel Sionne	Leeward Islands	WI	6.9.1984	*Montserrat*
Balaji Lakshmipathy	Tamil Nadu	I	27.9.1981	*Madras*
Balcombe David John	Hampshire	E	24.12.1984	*London*
Ballance Gary Simon	Yorks/Mid West Rhinos	Z	22.11.1989	*Harare*
*****Bandara** Herath Mudiyanselage				
Charitha <u>Malinga</u>	Basnahira South/Kent	SL	31.12.1979	*Kalutara*
Bandy David Charles	Western Australia	A	19.7.1978	*Subiaco*
Banerjee Vikram	Gloucestershire	E	20.3.1984	*Bradford*
*****Bangar** Sanjay Bapusaheb	Railways	I	11.10.1972	*Bid*
*****Banks** Omari Ahmed Clemente	Leeward Islands	WI	17.7.1982	*Road Bay, Antigua*
*****Barath** Adrian Boris	Trinidad & Tobago	WI	14.4.1990	*Chaguanas, Trinidad*
Barker Keith Hubert Douglas	Warwickshire	E	21.10.1986	*Manchester*
Barnes Bradley Graeme	KwaZulu-Natal/Dolphins	SA	20.10.1988	*Johannesburg*
Barnwell Christopher Dion	Guyana	WI	6.1.1987	*McKenzie, Guyana*
Bascombe Miles Cameron	Windward Islands	WI	12.1.1986	*St Vincent*
Bates Alexander <u>Michael</u>	Hampshire	E	10.10.1990	*Portsmouth*
Batticciotto Glen Charles	Queensland	A	18.8.1981	*Redcliffe*
*****Batty** Gareth Jon	Surrey	E	13.10.1977	*Bradford*
Batty Jonathan Neil	Gloucestershire	E	18.4.1974	*Chesterfield*
*****Baugh** Carlton Seymour	Jamaica	WI	23.6.1982	*Kingston, Jamaica*
*****Bazid Khan**	KRL	P	25.3.1981	*Lahore*
Beard Nicholas Brendan	Otago	NZ	16.9.1989	*Dunedin*
*****Beer** Michael Anthony	Western Australia	A	9.6.1984	*Malvern*
Beer William Andrew Thomas	Sussex	E	8.10.1988	*Crawley*
Behardien Farhaan	Titans	SA	9.10.1983	*Johannesburg*
Bell Ian Ronald	Warwickshire	E	11.4.1982	*Walsgrave*
*****Bell** Matthew David	Wellington	NZ	25.2.1977	*Dunedin*
Benham Christopher Charles	Hampshire	E	24.3.1983	*Frimley*
Benkenstein Dale Martin	Durham	SA	9.6.1974	*Salisbury, Zimbabwe*
*****Benn** Sulieman Jamaal	Barbados	WI	22.7.1981	*Haynesville, Barbados*
Bennett Bevan Leon	Border/Warriors	SA	9.9.1981	*East London*
*****Bennett** Hamish Kyle	Canterbury	NZ	22.2.1987	*Timaru*
Bennett Jason Peterson	Com. Campuses & Colls.	WI	3.6.1983	*Mount Standfast, Barb.*
Benning James Graham Edward	Leicestershire	E	4.5.1983	*Mill Hill*
Berg Gareth Kyle	Middlesex	SA	18.1.1981	*Cape Town*
*****Bernard** David Eddison	Jamaica	WI	19.7.1981	*Kingston, Jamaica*

	Team	Country	Born	Birthplace
***Bess** Brandon Jeremy	Guyana	WI	13.12.1987	Rosignol, Guyana
***Best** Tino la Bertram	Barbados/Yorkshire	WI	26.8.1981	3rd Avenue, Barbados
Bhatia Rajat	Delhi	I	22.10.1979	Delhi
Bhupinder Singh	Auckland	NZ	31.10.1986	Kurputala, India
Birch Andrew Charles Ross	E. Province/Warriors	SA	7.6.1985	East London
Birt Travis Rodney	Tasmania	A	9.12.1981	Sale
Bishoo Devendra	Guyana	WI	6.11.1985	New Amsterdam, Guy.
***Blackwell** Ian David	Durham	E	10.6.1978	Chesterfield
Blake Alexander James	Kent	E	25.11.1989	Farnborough
***Blignaut** Arnoldus Mauritius (Andy)	Zimbabwe	Z	1.8.1978	Salisbury (now Harare)
Blizzard Aiden Craig	South Australia	A	27.6.1984	Shepparton
Bodi Goolam Hussain	Titans/Easterns	SA	4.1.1979	Hathuran, India
***Boje** Nico	Northants/Warriors	SA	20.3.1973	Bloemfontein
***Bollinger** Douglas Erwin	New South Wales	A	24.7.1981	Baulkham Hills
Bond Shane Edward	Canterbury	NZ	7.6.1975	Christchurch
Bonner Nkruma Eljego	Jamaica	WI	23.1.1989	St Catherine, Jamaica
***Bopara** Ravinder Singh	Essex/Dolphins	E	4.5.1985	Forest Gate
Borgas Cameron James	South Australia	A	1.9.1983	Melrose Park
Borrington Paul Michael	Derbyshire	E	24.5.1988	Nottingham
Borthwick Scott George	Durham	E	19.4.1990	Sunderland
Bose Ranadeb Ranjit	Bengal	I	27.2.1979	Calcutta
Bosman Lungile Edgar (Loots)	Dolphins	SA	14.4.1977	Kimberley
Botha Anthony Greyvensteyn	Warwickshire	SA	17.11.1976	Pretoria
***Botha** Johan	Warriors	SA	2.5.1982	Johannesburg
***Boucher** Mark Verdon	Warriors	SA	3.12.1976	East London
Boyce Cameron John	Queensland	A	27.7.1989	Charleville
Boyce Matthew Andrew Golding	Leicestershire	E	13.8.1985	Cheltenham
Bragg William David	Glamorgan	E	24.10.1986	Newport
Brathwaite Kraigg Clairmonte	Barbados	WI	1.12.1992	Belfield, Barbados
Brathwaite Ruel Marlon Ricardo	Durham	WI	6.9.1985	Bridgetown
***Bravo** Darren Michael	Trinidad & Tobago	WI	6.2.1989	Santa Cruz, Trinidad
***Bravo** Dwayne John	Trinidad & Tobago	WI	7.10.1983	Santa Cruz, Trinidad
***Breese** Gareth Rohan	Durham	WI	9.1.1976	Montego Bay, Jamaica
***Bresnan** Timothy Thomas	Yorkshire	E	28.2.1985	Pontefract
Briggs Danny Richard	Hampshire	E	30.4.1991	Newport
Broad Ryan Andrew	Queensland	A	9.3.1982	Herston
***Broad** Stuart Christopher John	Nottinghamshire	E	24.6.1986	Nottingham
Brooks Jack Alexander	Northamptonshire	E	4.6.1984	Oxford
Brooks Sharmarh Shaqad Joshua	Barbados	WI	1.10.1988	St John's Land, Barb.
Broom Neil Trevor	Otago	NZ	20.11.1983	Christchurch
Brophy Gerard Louis	Yorkshire	E	26.11.1975	Welkom, SA
Brown Alistair Duncan	Nottinghamshire	E	11.2.1970	Beckenham
Brown Ben Christopher	Sussex	E	23.11.1988	Crawley
Brown Bevon Mark	Jamaica	WI	2.9.1979	Kingston, Jamaica
Brown Karl Robert	Lancashire	E	17.5.1988	Bolton
Brown Odean Vernon	Jamaica	WI	8.2.1982	Westmoreland, Jam.
Browne Daynason Junior	Leeward Islands	WI	6.5.1986	Nevis
Browne Patrick Anderson	Barbados	WI	26.1.1982	Bayfield, Barbados
Brownlie Dean Graham	Canterbury	NZ	30.7.1984	Perth, Australia
Buck Nathan Liam	Leicestershire	E	26.4.1991	Leicester
Burton David Alexander	Northamptonshire	E	23.8.1985	Dulwich
Butler Deighton Kelvin	Windward Islands	WI	17.7.1974	South Rivers, St Vinc.
***Butler** Ian Gareth	Otago	NZ	24.11.1981	Middlemore
Butterworth Luke Rex	Tasmania	A	28.10.1983	Hobart
Buttler Joseph Charles	Somerset	E	8.9.1990	Taunton
Cameron James Gair	Worcestershire	Z	31.1.1986	Harare
Cameron Mark Alan	New South Wales	A	31.1.1981	Waratah
Campbell Jon-Ross Charles	Jamaica	WI	9.7.1990	Kingston
Canning Ryan Clement Cavanagh	W. Province/Cape Cobras	SA	22.2.1984	Cape Town

	Team	Country	Born	Birthplace
***Carberry** Michael Alexander	Hampshire	E	29.9.1980	*Croydon*
Carseldine Lee Andrew	Queensland	A	17.11.1975	*Nambour*
Carter Andrew	Essex	E	27.8.1988	*Lincoln*
Carter Jonathan Lyndon	Barbados	WI	16.11.1987	*Belleplaine, Barbados*
Carter Neil Miller	Warwickshire	SA	29.1.1975	*Cape Town*
Cassell Robert James	South Australia	A	28.4.1983	*Melbourne*
Catlin Khismar	Com. Campuses & Colls.	WI	16.4.1987	*Shop Hill, Barbados*
Cazzulino Steven John	Tasmania	A	1.2.1987	*Riverwood*
Chakabva Regis Wiriranai	Mashonaland Eagles	Z	20.9.1987	*Harare*
Chambers Maurice Anthony	Essex	E	14.9.1987	*Port Antonio, Jamaica*
***Chanderpaul** Shivnarine	Guyana/Lancashire	WI	16.8.1974	*Unity Village, Guyana*
Chandimal Lokuge Dinesh	Ruhuna	SL	18.11.1989	*Balapitiya*
Chandrika Rajindra	Guyana	WI	8.8.1989	*Enterprise*
Chapple Glen	Lancashire	E	23.1.1974	*Skipton*
Charles Nikolai Gabriel Ramon	Barbados	WI	1.10.1986	*Wildey, Barbados*
Chatara Tendai Larry	Mountaineers	Z	28.2.1991	*Chimaniamani*
***Chattergoon** Sewnarine	Guyana	WI	3.4.1981	*Fyrish, Guyana*
***Chawla** Piyush Pramod	Uttar Pradesh	I	24.12.1988	*Aligarh*
Cheetham Steven Philip	Surrey	E	5.9.1987	*Oldham*
Chetty Kemeshin	KZN Inland/Dolphins	SA	9.1.1988	*Durban*
Chibhabha Chamunorwa Justice	Southern Rocks	Z	6.9.1986	*Masvingo*
***Chigumbura** Elton	Mash. Eagles/Northants	Z	14.3.1986	*Kwekwe*
Chilton Mark James	Lancashire	E	2.10.1976	*Sheffield*
Chinouya Michael Tawanda	MW Rhinos/Southern Rocks	Z	9.6.1986	*Kwekwe*
***Chopra** Aakash	Rajasthan	I	19.9.1977	*Agra*
Chopra Varun	Warwickshire	E	21.6.1987	*Barking*
Choudhry Shaaiq Hussain	Worcestershire	E	3.11.1985	*Rotherham*
Christian Daniel Trevor	South Australia/Hampshire	A	4.5.1983	*Camperdown*
Christian Derwin O'Neil	Guyana	WI	9.5.1983	*Kilen, Guyana*
Clare Jonathan Luke	Derbyshire	E	14.6.1986	*Burnley*
Clark Stuart Rupert	New South Wales	A	28.9.1975	*Sutherland*
***Clarke** Michael John	New South Wales	A	2.4.1981	*Liverpool*
***Clarke** Rikki	Warwickshire	E	29.9.1981	*Orsett*
Claydon Mitchell Eric	Durham/Canterbury	E	25.11.1982	*Fairfield, Australia*
Cleary Mark Francis	South Australia/Victoria	A	19.7.1980	*Moorabbin*
Cobb Joshua James	Leicestershire	E	17.8.1990	*Leicester*
Coetsee Werner Loubser	North West/Lions	SA	16.3.1983	*Bethlehem*
Coetzer Kyle James	Scotland/Durham	Scotland	14.4.1984	*Aberdeen*
Coles Matthew Thomas	Kent	E	26.5.1990	*Maidstone*
***Collingwood** Paul David	Durham	E	26.5.1976	*Shotley Bridge*
***Collins** Pedro Tyrone	Barbados/Middlesex	WI	12.8.1976	*Boscobelle, Barbados*
***Collymore** Corey Dalanelo	Sussex	WI	21.12.1977	*Boscobelle, Barbados*
Comber Michael Andrew	Essex	E	26.10.1989	*Colchester*
Compton Nicholas Richard Denis	Somerset/Mash. Eagles	E	26.6.1983	*Durban, SA*
Conway Devon Philip	Gauteng/KZN Inland/Dolphins	SA	8.7.1991	*Johannesburg*
***Cook** Alastair Nathan	Essex	E	25.12.1984	*Gloucester*
Cook Simon James	Kent	E	15.1.1977	*Oxford*
Cook Stephen Craig	Gauteng/Lions	SA	29.11.1982	*Johannesburg*
Cooper Tom Lexley William	South Australia	A	26.11.1986	*Wollongong*
Copeland Trent Aaron	New South Wales	A	14.3.1986	*Gosford*
Corbin Kyle Anthony McDonald	Com. Campuses & Colls.	WI	15.5.1990	*Newbury, Barbados*
***Cork** Dominic Gerald	Hampshire	E	7.8.1971	*Newcastle-under-Lyme*
Cornwall Wilden Winston	Leeward Islands	WI	29.4.1973	*Liberta, Antigua*
Cosgrove Mark James	S. Australia/Glam/Tasmania	A	14.6.1984	*Elizabeth*
Cosker Dean Andrew	Glamorgan	E	7.1.1978	*Weymouth*
Coulter-Nile Nathan Mitchell	Western Australia	A	11.10.1987	*Perth*
***Coventry** Charles Kevin	Matabeleland Tuskers	Z	8.3.1983	*Kwekwe*
Cowan Edward James McKenzie	Tasmania	A	16.6.1982	*Paddington*
Cox Oliver Benjamin	Worcestershire	E	2.2.1992	*Wordsley*
Coyte Scott James	New South Wales	A	7.3.1985	*Liverpool, Australia*

	Team	Country	Born	Birthplace
Crandon Esuan Asqui	Guyana	WI	17.12.1981	*Rose Hall, Guyana*
Crandon Royston Tycho	Guyana	WI	31.5.1983	*Courtland, Guyana*
*****Cremer** Alexander <u>Graeme</u>	Mid West Rhinos	Z	19.9.1986	*Harare*
*****Croft** Robert Damien Bale	Glamorgan	E	25.5.1970	*Morriston*
Croft Steven John	Lancashire	E	11.10.1984	*Blackpool*
Cross Gareth David	Lancashire	E	20.6.1984	*Bury*
Cruickshank Daron Alfred	Trinidad & Tobago	WI	17.6.1988	*Port-of-Spain, Trinidad*
*****Cumming** Craig Derek	Otago	NZ	31.8.1975	*Timaru*
Currency Romel Kwesi	Com. Campuses & Colls.	WI	7.5.1982	*Mesopotamia, St Vinc.*
Cutting Benjamin Colin James	Queensland	A	30.1.1987	*Sunnybank*
*****Dabengwa** Keith Mbusi	Matabeleland Tuskers	Z	17.8.1980	*Bulawayo*
Daggett Lee Martin	Northamptonshire	E	1.10.1982	*Bury*
Dalrymple James William Murray	Glamorgan	E	21.1.1981	*Nairobi, Kenya*
*****Danish Kaneria**	Essex/Habib Bank	P	16.12.1980	*Karachi*
Das Arindam Shibendranarayan	Bengal	I	16.10.1981	*Calcutta*
*****Das** Shiv Sunder	Orissa	I	5.11.1977	*Bhubaneswar*
Davey Joshua Henry	Middlesex	Scotland	3.8.1990	*Aberdeen*
Davids Henry	Boland/Cape Cobras/ Northerns/Titans	SA	19.1.1980	*Stellenbosch*
Davies Mark	Durham	E	4.10.1980	*Stockton-on-Tees*
Davies Steven Michael	Surrey	E	17.6.1986	*Bromsgrove*
Davis Liam Murray	Western Australia	A	2.8.1984	*Perth*
Dawes Jason O'Brian	Jamaica	WI	27.12.1988	*Westmoreland, Jam.*
Dawson Liam Andrew	Hampshire	E	1.3.1990	*Swindon*
Deacon Wycliffe Andrew	North West/Lions	SA	23.6.1980	*Kroonstad*
*****de Bruyn** Zander	Lions/Somerset	SA	5.7.1975	*Johannesburg*
Deeb Dale Robin	North West/Lions	SA	8.9.1990	*Johannesburg*
DeFreitas Bront Arson	Leeward Islands	WI	12.11.1978	*St Vincent*
de Lange Con de Wet	Free State/Eagles/Knights	SA	11.2.1981	*Bellville*
Denly Joseph Liam	Kent	E	16.3.1986	*Canterbury*
Dent Christopher David James	Gloucestershire	E	20.1.1991	*Bristol*
*****Deonarine** Narsingh	Guyana	WI	16.8.1983	*Chesney Estate, Guy.*
Dernbach Jade Winston	Surrey	E	3.3.1986	*Johannesburg, SA*
*****de Saram** Samantha <u>Indika</u>	Ruhuna	SL	2.9.1973	*Matara*
*****de Silva** Weddikkara Ruwan Sujeewa	Ruhuna	SL	7.10.1979	*Beruwala*
*****de Villiers** Abraham Benjamin	Titans	SA	17.2.1984	*Pretoria*
de Villiers Cornelius Johannes du Preez	Free State/Eagles/Titans	SA	16.3.1986	*Kroonstad*
Dewan Rahul	Haryana	I	15.7.1986	*Delhi*
*****de Wet** Friedel	North West/Lions	SA	26.6.1980	*Durban*
Dexter Neil John	Middlesex	E	21.8.1984	*Johannesburg, SA*
Dharmani Pankaj	Punjab	I	27.9.1974	*Delhi*
Dhawan Shikhar	Delhi	I	5.12.1985	*Delhi*
Dhiman Ghosh	Rajshahi	B	23.11.1987	*Dinajpur*
*****Dhoni** Mahendra Singh	Jharkhand	I	7.7.1981	*Ranchi*
Diamanti Brendon John	Central Districts	NZ	30.4.1981	*Blenheim*
*****Dilshan** Tillekeratne Mudiyanselage	Bloomfield	SL	14.10.1976	*Kalutara*
Dinda Ashok Bhimchandra	Bengal	I	25.3.1984	*Medinipur*
*****Dippenaar** Hendrik Human (<u>Boeta</u>)	Eagles/Knights	SA	14.6.1977	*Kimberley*
Di Venuto Michael James	Durham	A	12.12.1973	*Hobart*
*****Doherty** Xavier John	Tasmania	A	22.11.1982	*Scottsdale*
Dolar Mahmud	Khulna	B	30.12.1988	*Narail*
Dolley Corbyn Richard	Eastern Province/Warriors	SA	26.11.1987	*Port Elizabeth*
Doolan Alexander James	Tasmania	A	29.11.1985	*Launceston*
Dorey Brett Raymond	Western Australia	A	3.10.1977	*East Fremantle*
*****Dowlin** Travis Montague	Guyana	WI	24.2.1977	*Guyhock Gardens, Guy.*
Dowrich Shane Omari	Barbados	WI	30.10.1991	*West Terrace*
*****Dravid** Rahul	Karnataka	I	11.1.1973	*Indore*

	Team	Country	Born	Birthplace
Drew Brendan Gerard	Tasmania	A	16.12.1983	*Lismore*
Duffield Ryan	Western Australia	A	20.6.1988	*Darkan*
*****Duffin** Terrence	Matabeleland Tuskers	Z	20.3.1982	*Kwekwe*
*****Duminy** Jean-Paul	Cape Cobras	SA	14.4.1984	*Strandfontein*
Dunk Ben Robert	Queensland	A	11.3.1987	*Innisfail*
du Plessis Francois (Faf)	Titans	SA	13.7.1984	*Pretoria*
du Preez Dillon	Free State/Knights	SA	8.1.1981	*Queenstown*
Durston Wesley John	Derbyshire	E	6.10.1980	*Taunton*
du Toit Jacques	Leicestershire	SA	2.1.1980	*Port Elizabeth*
Duval Chris John	South Australia	A	3.8.1983	*Elizabethvale*
*****Ebrahim** Dion Digby	Matabeleland Tuskers	Z	7.8.1980	*Bulawayo*
Edmondson Ben Matthew	W. Australia/S. Australia	A	28.9.1978	*Southport*
Edwards Corey Raymond	Barbados	WI	2.9.1983	*Bridgetown*
Edwards Kirk Anton	Barbados	WI	3.11.1984	*Mile and a Quarter, Barbados*
Edwards Neil James	Nottinghamshire	E	14.10.1983	*Treliske*
Edwards Philip Duncan	Kent	E	16.4.1984	*Minster*
Elgar Dean	Free State/Eagles/Knights	SA	11.6.1987	*Welkom*
*****Elliott** Grant David	Wellington	NZ	21.3.1979	*Johannesburg, SA*
Emmanuel Craig Walt	Windward Islands	WI	5.5.1986	*Mon Repos, St Lucia*
Emrit Rayad Ryan	Trinidad & Tobago	WI	8.3.1981	*Mount Hope, Trinidad*
*****Enamul Haque, jun.**	Sylhet	B	5.12.1986	*Sylhet*
Ervine Craig Richard	Southern Rocks	Z	19.8.1985	*Harare*
*****Ervine** Sean Michael	Southern Rocks/Hampshire	Z	6.12.1982	*Harare*
Evans Daniel	Middlesex	E	24.7.1987	*Hartlepool*
Evans Laurie John	Surrey/Warwickshire	E	12.10.1987	*Lambeth*
Evans Luke	Durham/Northamptonshire	E	26.4.1987	*Sunderland*
*****Ewing** Gavin Mackie	Matabeleland Tuskers	Z	21.1.1981	*Harare*
Faisal Athar	State Bank of Pakistan	P	15.10.1975	*Hyderabad*
*****Faisal Hossain**	Chittagong	B	26.10.1978	*Chittagong*
*****Faisal Iqbal**	PIA	P	30.12.1981	*Karachi*
Farhad Hossain	Rajshahi	B	10.2.1987	*Rajshahi*
Farhad Reza	Rajshahi	B	16.6.1986	*Rajshahi*
Faulkner James Peter	Tasmania	A	29.4.1990	*Launceston*
*****Fawad Alam**	National Bank	P	8.10.1985	*Karachi*
Feldman Luke William	Queensland	A	1.8.1984	*Sunnybank*
Ferguson Callum James	South Australia	A	21.11.1984	*North Adelaide*
Ferley Robert Steven	Kent	E	4.2.1982	*Norwich*
Fernando Aththachchi Nuwan Pradeep Roshan	Basnahira North	SL	19.10.1986	*Negombo*
*****Fernando** Congenige Randhi Dilhara	Sinhalese	SL	19.7.1979	*Colombo*
*****Fernando** Kandage Hasantha Ruwan Kumara	Basnahira South	SL	14.10.1979	*Panadura*
Finch Aaron James	Victoria	A	17.11.1986	*Colac*
Findlay Shawn Eli	Jamaica	WI	3.3.1984	*Mandeville, Jamaica*
*****Finn** Steven Thomas	Middlesex	E	4.4.1989	*Watford*
Fletcher Andre David Stephon	Windward Islands	WI	28.11.1987	*La Tante, Grenada*
Fletcher Luke Jack	Nottinghamshire	E	18.9.1988	*Nottingham*
*****Flower** Grant William	Essex	Z	20.12.1970	*Salisbury*
*****Flynn** Daniel Raymond	Northern Districts	NZ	16.4.1985	*Rotorua*
Footitt Mark Harold Alan	Derbyshire	E	25.11.1985	*Nottingham*
Forrest Peter James	New South Wales	A	15.11.1985	*Windsor, Australia*
*****Foster** James Savin	Essex	E	15.4.1980	*Whipps Cross*
*****Franklin** James Edward Charles	Wellington/Gloucestershire	NZ	7.11.1980	*Wellington*
Franks Paul John	Notts/Mid West Rhinos	E	3.2.1979	*Mansfield*
Friend Quinton	KwaZulu-Natal/Dolphins	SA	16.2.1982	*Bellville*
Frylinck Robert	Lions	SA	27.9.1984	*Durban*

	Team	Country	Born	Birthplace
Fudadin Assad Badyr	Guyana	WI	1.8.1985	*Rose Hall, Guyana*
*****Fulton** Peter Gordon	Canterbury	NZ	1.2.1979	*Christchurch*
Gabriel Shannon Terry	Trinidad & Tobago	WI	28.4.1988	*Trinidad*
Gale Andrew William	Yorkshire	E	28.11.1983	*Dewsbury*
*****Gambhir** Gautam	Delhi	I	14.10.1981	*Delhi*
Ganapathy Chandrasekharan	Tamil Nadu	I	10.6.1981	*Madras*
Ganegama Withanaarchchige Chamara Akalanka	Kandurata	SL	29.3.1981	*Colombo*
*****Ganga** Daren	Trinidad & Tobago	WI	14.1.1979	*Barrackpore, Trinidad*
Ganga Sherwin	Trinidad & Tobago	WI	13.2.1982	*Barrackpore, Trinidad*
Ganguly Sourav Chandidas	Bengal	I	8.7.1972	*Calcutta*
Gannon Cameron John	Queensland	A	23.1.1989	*Baulkham Hills*
Garwe Trevor Nyasha	Mashonaland Eagles	Z	7.1.1982	*Harare*
Gatting Joe Stephen	Sussex	E	25.11.1987	*Brighton*
Gautam Chidambaram Muralidharan	Karnataka	I	8.3.1986	*Bangalore*
*****Gayle** Christopher Henry	Jamaica	WI	21.9.1979	*Kingston, Jamaica*
Geeves Brett	Tasmania	A	13.6.1982	*Claremont*
*****George** Peter Robert	South Australia	A	16.10.1986	*Woodville*
*****Gibbs** Herschelle Herman	Cape Cobras	SA	23.2.1974	*Green Point*
Gidman Alexander Peter Richard	Gloucestershire	E	22.6.1981	*High Wycombe*
*****Gillespie** Mark Raymond	Wellington	NZ	17.10.1979	*Wanganui*
Goddard Lee James	Derbyshire	E	22.10.1982	*Dewsbury*
Godleman Billy Ashley	Essex	E	11.2.1989	*Camden*
Gony Manpreet Singh	Punjab	I	4.1.1984	*Roopnagar*
*****Goodwin** Murray William	Sussex	Z	11.12.1972	*Salisbury*
Goswami Dhiraj Satyen	Assam	I	1.5.1985	*Nagaon*
Gray Alistair John Alec	W. Province/Cape Cobras	SA	8.7.1982	*Johannesburg*
Griffith Adam Richard	Tasmania	A	11.2.1978	*Launceston*
Griffiths David Andrew	Hampshire	E	10.9.1985	*Newport, Isle of Wight*
Groenewald Timothy Duncan	Derbyshire	SA	10.1.1984	*Pietermaritzburg*
Guillen Justin Christopher	Trinidad & Tobago	WI	2.1.1986	*Port-of-Spain, Trinidad*
Gunaratne Liyanabadlge Janaka Prabath	Basnahira South	SL	14.3.1981	*Panadura*
*****Guptill** Martin James	Auckland	NZ	30.9.1986	*Auckland*
Gurney Harry Frederick	Leicestershire	E	25.10.1986	*Nottingham*
Haberfield Jake Andy	South Australia	A	18.6.1986	*Townsville*
*****Habibul Bashar**	Khulna	B	17.8.1972	*Nagakanda*
Haddin Bradley James	New South Wales	A	23.10.1977	*Cowra*
Hales Alexander Daniel	Nottinghamshire	E	3.1.1989	*Hillingdon*
*****Hall** Andrew James	Northants/Mash. Eagles	SA	31.7.1975	*Johannesburg*
Hamilton Jahmar Neville	Leeward Islands	WI	22.9.1990	*St Thomas, Anguilla*
Hamilton-Brown Rory James	Surrey	E	3.9.1987	*St John's Wood*
Hammad Azam	National Bank	P	16.3.1991	*Attock*
*****Hannan Sarkar**	Barisal	B	1.12.1982	*Dhaka*
Hannon-Dalby Oliver James	Yorkshire	E	20.6.1989	*Halifax*
*****Harbhajan Singh**	Punjab	I	3.7.1980	*Jullundur*
Harinath Arun	Surrey	E	26.3.1987	*Sutton*
Harmison Ben William	Durham	E	9.1.1986	*Ashington*
*****Harmison** Stephen James	Durham	E	23.10.1978	*Ashington*
Harris Andrew James	Leicestershire	E	26.6.1973	*Ashton-under-Lyne*
Harris Daniel Joseph	South Australia	A	31.12.1979	*North Adelaide*
Harris James Alexander Russell	Glamorgan	E	16.5.1990	*Morriston*
*****Harris** Paul Lee	Lions	SA	2.11.1978	*Salisbury, Zimbabwe*
*****Harris** Ryan James	Queensland	A	11.10.1979	*Nowra*
Harrison David Stuart	Glamorgan	E	30.7.1981	*Newport*
Harrison Paul William	Northamptonshire	E	22.5.1984	*Cuckfield*
Hartley Christopher Desmond	Queensland	A	24.5.1982	*Nambour*

	Team	Country	Born	Birthplace
*Hasan Raza	Habib Bank	P	11.3.1982	*Karachi*
Hastings John Wayne	Victoria	A	4.11.1985	*Nepean*
Hatchett Lewis James	Sussex	E	21.1.1990	*Shoreham-by-Sea*
*Hauritz Nathan Michael	New South Wales	A	18.10.1981	*Wondai*
Haynes Jason Adrian McCarthy	Barbados	WI	3.7.1981	*Jackman Main Road, Barbados*
Hazlewood Josh Reginald	New South Wales	A	8.1.1991	*Tamworth*
Heal Aaron Keith	Western Australia	A	13.3.1983	*Armadale*
Hector Donwell Banister	Windward Islands	WI	31.10.1988	*St Vincent*
Henderson Claude William	Leics/Cape Cobras	SA	14.6.1972	*Worcester*
Hendricks Reeza Raphael	Griq. W./Eagles/ Knights	SA	14.8.1989	*Kimberley*
Henriques Moises Constantino	New South Wales	A	1.2.1987	*Funchal, Portugal*
*Herath Herath Mudiyanselage Rangana Keerthi Bandara	Wayamba/Hampshire	SL	19.3.1978	*Kurunegala*
*Hettiarachchi Dinuka	Basnahira South	SL	15.7.1976	*Colombo*
Hildreth James Charles	Somerset	E	9.9.1984	*Milton Keynes*
*Hilfenhaus Benjamin William	Tasmania	A	15.3.1983	*Ulverstone*
Hill Michael William	Victoria	A	29.9.1988	*Melbourne*
*Hinds Ryan O'Neal	Barbados	WI	17.2.1981	*Holders Hill, Barb.*
*Hinds Wavell Wayne	Jamaica	WI	7.9.1976	*Kingston, Jamaica*
Hockley James Bernard	Kent	E	16.4.1979	*Beckenham*
Hodd Andrew John	Sussex	E	12.1.1984	*Chichester*
Hodge Montcin Verniel	Leeward Islands	WI	29.9.1987	*Anguilla*
Hogan Michael Garry	Western Australia	A	31.5.1981	*Newcastle*
Hogg Kyle William	Lancashire	E	2.7.1983	*Birmingham*
*Hoggard Matthew James	Leicestershire	E	31.12.1976	*Leeds*
Holder Jason Omar	Barbados	WI	5.11.1991	*Rouens Village, Barb.*
Holland Jonathan Mark	Victoria	A	29.5.1987	*Sandringham*
*Hondo Douglas Tafadzwa	Mashonaland Eagles	Z	7.7.1979	*Bulawayo*
Hope Kyle Antonio	Barbados	WI	20.11.1988	*Field Place*
Hopes James Redfern	Queensland	A	24.10.1978	*Townsville*
*Hopkins Gareth James	Auckland	NZ	24.11.1976	*Lower Hutt*
Horton Paul James	Lancs/Matabeleland Tuskers	E	20.9.1982	*Sydney, Australia*
Housego Daniel Mark	Middlesex	E	12.10.1988	*Windsor*
*How Jamie Michael	Central Districts	NZ	19.5.1981	*New Plymouth*
Howgego Benjamin Harry Nicholas	Northamptonshire	E	3.3.1988	*Kings Lynn*
Hughes Chesney Francis	Derbyshire	WI	20.1.1991	*Anguilla*
*Hughes Phillip Joel	New South Wales/Hants	A	30.11.1988	*Macksville*
*Humayun Farhat	Habib Bank	P	24.1.1981	*Lahore*
Hussain Gemaal Maqsood	Gloucestershire	E	10.10.1983	*Waltham Forest*
Hussey David John	Victoria/Notts	A	15.7.1977	*Morley*
*Hussey Michael Edward Killeen	Western Australia	A	27.5.1975	*Morley*
Hyatt Danza Pacino	Jamaica	WI	17.3.1983	*St Catherine, Jamaica*
*Iftikhar Anjum	Surrey/ZTBL	P	1.12.1980	*Khanewal*
*Ijaz Ahmed, jun.	Faisalabad	P	2.2.1969	*Lyallpur*
Imran Arif	Worcestershire	P	15.11.1984	*Kotli*
*Imran Farhat	Habib Bank	P	20.5.1982	*Lahore*
*Imran Nazir	ZTBL	P	16.12.1981	*Gujranwala*
Imran Tahir	Easterns/Warwicks/Dolphins	SA	27.3.1979	*Lahore, Pakistan*
*Imrul Kayes	Khulna	B	2.2.1987	*Meherpur*
Inder Singh Ravi	Punjab	I	4.11.1987	*Patiala*
Ingram Colin Alexander	Warriors	SA	3.7.1985	*Port Elizabeth*
*Ingram Peter John	Central Districts	NZ	25.10.1978	*Hawera*
Iqbal Abdulla	Mumbai	I	2.12.1989	*Bombay*
Ireland Anthony John	Gloucestershire	Z	30.8.1984	*Masvingo*
*Irfan Fazil	Habib Bank	P	2.11.1981	*Lahore*
Jackson Simon	Com. Campuses & Colls.	WI	18.5.1985	*Jamaica*
Jacobs Arno	Warriors	SA	13.3.1977	*Potchefstroom*

	Team	Country	Born	Birthplace
Jacobs David Johan	Warriors	SA	4.11.1982	Klerksdorp
Jadeja Ravindrasinh Anirudhsinh	Saurashtra	I	6.12.1988	Navagam-Khed
Jadhav Dheeraj Subash	Assam	I	16.9.1979	Malegaon
*****Jaggernauth** Amit Sheldon	Trinidad & Tobago	WI	16.11.1983	Lennard St, Trinidad
Jaggi Ishank Rajiv	Jharkhand	I	27.1.1989	Bacheli
*****Jahurul Islam**	Rajshahi	B	12.12.1986	Rajshahi
Jakati Shadab Bashir	Goa	I	27.11.1980	Vasco da Gama
James Lindon Omrick Dinsley	Windward Islands	WI	30.12.1984	South Rivers, St Vinc.
*****Jaques** Philip Anthony	New South Wales/Worcs	A	3.5.1979	Wollongong
Jarvis Kyle Malcolm	Mashonaland Eagles	Z	16.2.1989	Harare
Jaskaran Singh	Punjab	I	4.9.1989	Mohali
Javid Ateeq	Warwickshire	E	15.10.1991	Birmingham
Jayasinghe Chinthaka Umesh	Kandurata	SL	19.5.1978	Kalutara
*****Jayasuriya** Sanath Teran	Bloomfield	SL	30.6.1969	Matara
*****Jayawardene** Denagamage Proboth Mahela de Silva	Sinhalese	SL	27.5.1977	Colombo
*****Jayawardene** Hewasandatchige Asiri Prasanna Wishvanath	Basnahira South	SL	9.10.1979	Colombo
Jefferson William Ingleby	Leicestershire	E	25.10.1979	Derby
Jewell Nicholas	Victoria	A	27.8.1977	Melbourne
Jewell Thomas Melvin	Surrey	E	13.1.1991	Reading
Johnson Delorn Edison	Windward Islands	WI	15.9.1988	St Vincent
*****Johnson** Mitchell Guy	Western Australia	A	2.11.1981	Townsville
Johnson Richard Matthew	Warwickshire	E	1.9.1988	Solihull
Johnston Matt James	Western Australia	A	15.10.1985	South Perth
Jones Brady	Tasmania	A	16.9.1988	Franklin
Jones Christopher Robert	Somerset	E	5.11.1990	Harold Wood
*****Jones** Geraint Owen	Kent	E	14.7.1976	Kundiawa, Papua N. G.
Jones Philip Steffan	Derbyshire	E	9.2.1974	Llanelli
Jones Richard Alan	Worcestershire	E	6.11.1986	Stourbridge
*****Jones** Richard Andrew	Auckland	NZ	22.10.1973	Auckland
*****Jones** Simon Philip	Hampshire	E	25.12.1978	Morriston
Joseph Keon	Guyana	WI	25.11.1991	Guyana
Joseph Robert Hartman	Kent	E	20.1.1982	St John's, Antigua
*****Joshi** Sunil Bandacharya	Karnataka	I	6.6.1969	Gadag
Joubert Pierre	Titans	SA	2.5.1978	Pretoria
Joyce Edmund Christopher	Sussex	E	22.9.1978	Dublin, Ireland
Junaid Khan	Abbottabad	P	24.12.1989	Matra
*****Junaid Siddique**	Rajshahi	B	30.10.1987	Rajshahi
Junaid Zia	ZTBL	P	11.12.1983	Lahore
*****Kaif** Mohammad	Uttar Pradesh	I	1.12.1980	Allahabad
*****Kallis** Jacques Henry	Warriors	SA	16.10.1975	Pinelands
*****Kamran Akmal**	National Bank	P	13.1.1982	Lahore
Kamran Hussain	Habib Bank	P	9.5.1977	Bahawalpur
Kamungozi Tafadzwa	Southern Rocks	Z	8.6.1987	Harare
Kandamby Sahan Hewa Thilina	Basnahira North	SL	4.6.1982	Colombo
Kanitkar Hrishikesh Hemant	Rajasthan	I	14.11.1974	Pune
Kantasingh Kavesh	Com. Campuses & Colls.	WI	30.9.1986	Trinidad
*****Kapugedera** Chamara Kantha	Kandurata	SL	24.2.1987	Kandy
*****Karthik** Krishankumar Dinesh	Tamil Nadu	I	1.6.1985	Madras
*****Kartik** Murali	Somerset/Railways	I	11.9.1976	Madras
Karunaratne Frank Dimuth Madushanka	Basnahira North	SL	28.4.1988	Colombo
Kashif Raza	WAPDA	P	29.12.1979	Sheikhupura
Kasteni Friday	Mid West Rhinos	Z	25.3.1988	Kadoma
*****Katich** Simon Mathew	New South Wales/Lancs	A	21.8.1975	Middle Swan
Kaul Uday	Punjab	I	2.12.1987	Kangra
Keedy Gary	Lancashire	E	27.11.1974	Sandal
Kelly Richard Alexander	Trinidad & Tobago	WI	19.2.1984	Trinidad

	Team	Country	Born	Birthplace
*Kemp Justin Miles	Cape Cobras	SA	2.10.1977	Queenstown
Kent Jon Carter	KwaZulu-Natal/Dolphins	SA	7.5.1979	Cape Town
Kerrigan Simon Christopher	Lancashire	E	10.5.1989	Preston
Kervezee Alexei Nicolaas	Netherlands/Worcs	NL	11.9.1989	Walvis Bay, Namibia
*Key Robert William Trevor	Kent	E	12.5.1979	East Dulwich
Khadiwale Harshad Hemantkumar	Maharashtra	I	21.10.1988	Pune
*Khaled Mashud	Rajshahi	B	8.2.1976	Rajshahi
Khalid Latif	Karachi Blues/Karachi Whites	P	4.11.1985	Karachi
*Khan Amjad	Kent	E	14.10.1980	Copenhagen, Denmark
*Khan Imraan	Dolphins	SA	27.4.1984	Durban
Khan Imran	Trinidad & Tobago	WI	6.12.1984	Port-of-Spain, Trinidad
*Khawaja Usman Tariq	New South Wales	A	18.12.1986	Islamabad, Pakistan
*Khurram Manzoor	PIA	P	10.6.1986	Karachi
Kieswetter Craig	Somerset	E	28.11.1987	Johannesburg
Kirby Steven Paul	Gloucestershire	E	4.10.1977	Ainsworth
Kleinveldt Rory Keith	Cape Cobras	SA	15.3.1983	Cape Town
Klinger Michael	South Australia	A	4.7.1980	Kew
Knowles Bradley Aaron	Western Australia	A	29.10.1981	Moe
Kohli Virat	Delhi	I	5.11.1988	Delhi
*Krejza Jason John	Tasmania	A	14.1.1983	Newtown
Kreusch Justin Peter	Warriors	SA	27.9.1979	East London
Kruger Garnett John-Peter	Warriors	SA	5.1.1977	Port Elizabeth
Kruger Nicholas James	Queensland	A	14.8.1983	Paddington, Australia
Kuhn Heino Gunther	Titans	SA	1.4.1984	Piet Retief
Kulasekara Chamith Kosala Bandara	Ruhuna	SL	15.7.1985	Mavanalle
*Kulasekara Kulasekara Mudiyanselage Dinesh Nuwan	Basnahira North	SL	22.7.1982	Nittambuwa
Kulatunga Hettiarachchi Gamage Jeevantha Mahesh	Wayamba	SL	2.11.1973	Kurunegala
Kulkarni Dhawal Sunil	Mumbai	I	10.12.1988	Bombay
Kumar Praveenkumar	Uttar Pradesh	I	2.10.1986	Meerut
Lahiri Saurasish Sukanta	Bengal	I	9.9.1981	Howrah
*Lakmal Ranasinghe Arachchige Suranga	Basnahira South	SL	10.3.1987	Matara
Lakshitha Ahangama Baduge Tharanga	Ruhuna	SL	30.4.1982	Matara
Lamb Gregory Arthur	Mashonaland Eagles	Z	4.3.1980	Harare
Lambert Grant Michael	New South Wales	A	5.8.1977	Parramatta
Lambert Tamar Lansford	Jamaica	WI	15.7.1981	St Catherine, Jamaica
Lancefield Thomas John	Surrey	E	8.10.1990	Epsom
Lang Timothy Elwyn	South Australia	A	26.3.1981	Mudgee
*Langeveldt Charl Kenneth	Cape Cobras	SA	17.12.1974	Stellenbosch
Laughlin Ben	Queensland	A	3.10.1982	Box Hill
*Laxman Vangipurappu Venkata Sai	Hyderabad	I	1.11.1974	Hyderabad
Lesporis Keddy	Windward Islands	WI	27.12.1988	St Lucia
Levi Richard Ernst	W. Province/Cape Cobras	SA	14.1.1988	Johannesburg
*Lewis Jonathan	Gloucestershire	E	26.8.1975	Aylesbury
*Lewis Rawl Nicholas	Windward Islands	WI	5.9.1974	Union Village, Grenada
Liburd Steve Stuart Wayne	Leeward Islands	WI	26.2.1985	Basseterre, St Kitts
Linley Timothy Edward	Surrey	E	23.3.1982	Leeds
Lockyear Rhett John Gaven	Tasmania	A	28.2.1983	Mudgee
*Lokuarachchi Kaushal Samaraweera	Wayamba	SL	20.5.1982	Colombo
London Adam Brian	Middlesex	E	12.10.1988	Ashford
Louw Johann	Cape Cobras	SA	12.4.1979	Cape Town
Loye Malachy Bernard	Northamptonshire	E	27.9.1972	Northampton

	Team	Country	Born	Birthplace
Lucas David Scott	Northamptonshire	E	19.8.1978	Nottingham
Ludeman Timothy Paul	South Australia	A	23.6.1987	Warrnambool
Lumb Michael John	Hampshire	E	12.2.1980	Johannesburg, SA
Lungley Tom	Derbyshire	E	25.7.1979	Derby
Lynn Christopher Austin	Queensland	A	10.4.1990	Herston
Lyth Adam	Yorkshire	E	25.9.1987	Whitby
McClean Kevin Ramon	Com. Campuses & Colls.	WI	24.1.1988	Castle, Barbados
***McCullum** Brendon Barrie	Otago	NZ	27.9.1981	Dunedin
McCullum Nathan Leslie	Otago	NZ	1.9.1980	Dunedin
***McDonald** Andrew Barry	Victoria/Leics	A	15.6.1981	Wodonga
Macdonald Timothy Peter	Tasmania	A	7.9.1980	Subiaco
***McGain** Bryce Edward	Victoria/Essex	A	25.3.1972	Mornington
McGlashan Peter Donald	Northern Districts	NZ	22.6.1979	Napier
***McGrath** Anthony	Yorkshire	E	6.10.1975	Bradford
***McIntosh** Timothy Gavin	Auckland	NZ	4.12.1979	Auckland
***McKay** Andrew John	Wellington	NZ	17.4.1980	Auckland
***McKay** Clinton James	Victoria	A	22.2.1983	Melbourne
McKenzie Neil Douglas	Lions/Hampshire	SA	24.11.1975	Johannesburg
McLaren Adrian Peter	Griqualand West/Knights	SA	21.4.1980	Kimberley
***McLaren** Ryan	Knights	SA	9.2.1983	Kimberley
Maddinson Nicolas James	New South Wales	A	21.12.1991	Shoalhaven
***Maddy** Darren Lee	Warwickshire	E	23.5.1974	Leicester
Madsen Wayne Lee	Derbyshire	SA	2.1.1984	Durban
Magoffin Steven James	Western Australia	A	17.12.1979	Corinda
Maharaj Keshav Athmanand	KwaZulu-Natal/Dolphins	SA	7.2.1990	Durban
***Maharoof** Mohamed Farveez	Wayamba	SL	7.9.1984	Colombo
***Mahbubul Alam**	Dhaka	B	1.12.1983	Faridpur
Maher Adam John	Tasmania	A	14.11.1981	Newcastle
***Mahmood** Sajid Iqbal	Lancashire	E	21.12.1981	Bolton
Mahmudul Hasan	Chittagong	B	10.12.1990	Bangladesh
***Mahmudullah**	Dhaka	B	4.2.1986	Mymensingh
***Mahwire** Ngonidzashe Blessing	Southern Rocks	Z	31.7.1982	Bikita
Malan Dawid Johannes	Middlesex	E	3.9.1987	Roehampton
Malan Pieter Jacobus	Northerns/Titans	SA	13.8.1989	Nelspruit
Malik Muhammad Nadeem	Leicestershire	E	6.10.1982	Nottingham
Malik Vikramjeet	Himachal Pradesh	I	9.5.1983	Solan
***Malinga** Separamadu Lasith	Nondescripts	SL	4.9.1983	Galle
Manhas Mithun	Delhi	I	12.9.1977	Jammu
***Manou** Graham Allan	South Australia	A	23.4.1979	Modbury
Mansoor Amjad	Sialkot	P	25.12.1986	Sialkot
***Maregwede** Alester	Southern Rocks	Z	5.8.1981	Harare
Marillier Stephan James	Southern Rocks	Z	25.9.1984	Harare
Marsh Daniel James	Tasmania	A	14.6.1973	Subiaco
Marsh Mitchell Ross	Western Australia	A	20.10.1991	Armadale
Marsh Shaun Edward	Western Australia	A	9.7.1983	Narrogin
***Marshall** Hamish John Hamilton	Northern Districts/Glos	NZ	15.2.1979	Warkworth
***Marshall** James Andrew Hamilton	Northern Districts	NZ	15.2.1979	Warkworth
***Marshall** Xavier Melbourne	Jamaica	WI	27.3.1986	St Ann, Jamaica
Marshall Ayub	Dhaka	B	5.12.1988	Dhaka
Martin Anthony	Leeward Islands	WI	18.11.1982	Bethesda, Antigua
***Martin** Christopher Stewart	Canterbury/Essex	NZ	10.12.1974	Christchurch
Martin-Jenkins Robin Simon Christopher	Sussex	E	28.10.1975	Guildford
Maruma Timycen	Mountaineers	Z	19.4.1988	Harare
***Masakadza** Hamilton	Mountaineers	Z	9.8.1983	Harare
Masakadza Shingirai Winston	Mountaineers	Z	4.9.1986	Harare
Mash Lloyd Ryan	Victoria	A	1.12.1981	Melbourne
Mashimbyi Mandla Abednigo	Northerns/Titans	SA	10.11.1980	Phalaborwa
***Mashrafe bin Mortaza**	Khulna	B	5.10.1983	Narail

	Team	Country	Born	Birthplace
Mason Matthew Sean	Worcestershire	A	20.3.1974	Claremont
***Mason** Michael James	Central Districts	NZ	27.8.1974	Carterton
Masters David Daniel	Essex	E	22.4.1978	Chatham
Masvaure Prince Spencer	Mashonaland Eagles	Z	7.10.1988	Bulawayo
***Mathews** Angelo Davis	Colts/Basnahira North	SL	2.6.1987	Colombo
Mathurin Garey Earl	Windward Islands	WI	23.9.1983	St Lucia
Matshikwe Pumelela	Gauteng/Lions	SA	19.6.1984	Johannesburg
***Matsikenyeri** Stuart	Mountaineers/S. Rocks	Z	3.5.1983	Harare
Maunders John Kenneth	Essex	E	4.4.1981	Ashford
Mawoyo Tinotenda Mbiri Kanayi	Mountaineers	Z	8.1.1986	Umtali
Maynard Thomas Lloyd	Glamorgan	E	25.3.1989	Cardiff
Mbhalati Nkateko Ethy	Titans	SA	18.11.1981	Tzaneen
Meaker Stuart Christopher	Surrey	E	21.1.1989	Durban, SA
***Mehrab Hossain, jun.**	Dhaka	B	8.7.1987	Rajshahi
***Mendis** Balapuwaduge Ajantha Winslo	Army	SL	11.3.1985	Moratuwa
Mendis Balapuwaduge Manukulasuriya Amith Jeewan	Kandurata	SL	15.1.1983	Colombo
Meth Keagan Orry	Matabeleland Tuskers	Z	8.2.1988	Bulawayo
Meyer Lyall	Eastern Province/Warriors	SA	23.3.1982	Port Elizabeth
Mickleburgh Jaik Charles	Essex	E	30.3.1990	Norwich
Middlebrook James Daniel	Northamptonshire	E	13.5.1977	Leeds
Miller Andrew Stephen	Warwickshire	E	27.9.1987	Preston
Miller David Andrew	Dolphins	SA	10.6.1989	Pietermaritzburg
Miller Horace	Jamaica	WI	26.10.1989	Jamaica
***Miller** Nikita O'Neil	Jamaica	WI	16.5.1982	St Elizabeth, Jamaica
***Mills** Kyle David	Auckland	NZ	15.3.1979	Auckland
Milne Adam Fraser	Central Districts	NZ	13.4.1992	Palmerston North
***Mirando** Magina Thilan Thushara *Also known as Thilan Thushara*	Sinhalese	SL	1.3.1981	Balapitiya
***Misbah-ul-Haq**	Sui Northern	P	28.5.1974	Mianwali
***Mishra** Amit	Haryana	I	24.11.1982	Delhi
Mishra Vikas	Delhi	I	27.12.1992	Delhi
Mitchell Daryl Keith Henry	Worcestershire	E	25.11.1983	Badsey
***Mithun** Abhimanyu	Karnataka	I	25.10.1989	Dasarahalli
Moffat Thomas Lincoln	South Australia	A	2.8.1987	Adelaide
Mohamed Zaheer	Guyana	WI	10.10.1985	Georgetown, Guyana
***Mohammad Aamer**	National Bank	P	13.4.1992	Gujjar Khan
***Mohammad Ashraful**	Dhaka	B	9.9.1984	Dhaka
***Mohammad Asif**	National Bank	P	20.12.1982	Sheikhupura
***Mohammad Hafeez**	Sui Northern	P	17.10.1980	Sargodha
Mohammad Irfan	KRL	P	6.6.1982	Gaggu Mandi
***Mohammad Khalil**	ZTBL	P	11.11.1982	Lahore
Mohammad Rameez	State Bank of Pakistan	P	19.2.1990	Rawalpindi
***Mohammad Sami**	Karachi Blues/Kar. Whites	P	24.2.1981	Karachi
***Mohammad Sharif**	Dhaka	B	12.12.1985	Narayanganj
***Mohammad Talha**	National Bank	P	15.10.1988	Faisalabad
***Mohammad Wasim**	KRL	P	8.8.1977	Rawalpindi
***Mohammad Yousuf** *Formerly known as Yousuf Youhana*	Lahore Shalimar	P	27.8.1974	Lahore
***Mohammed** Dave	Trinidad & Tobago	WI	8.10.1979	Knolly St, Trinidad
Mohammed Gibran	Trinidad & Tobago	WI	31.7.1983	Barrackpore, Trinidad
Mohammed Jason Nazimuddin	Trinidad & Tobago	WI	23.9.1986	Barrackpore, Trinidad
***Mohanty** Debasis Sarbeswar	Orissa	I	20.7.1976	Bhubaneswar
Moore Gilford	Com. Campuses & Colls.	WI	26.2.1982	Henrietta, Guyana
Moore Stephen Colin	Lancashire	E	4.11.1980	Johannesburg, SA
Morgan Eoin Joseph Gerard	Middlesex	E	10.9.1986	Dublin, Ireland
***Morkel** Johannes Albertus	Titans	SA	10.6.1981	Vereeniging
***Morkel** Morne	Titans	SA	6.10.1984	Vereeniging
***Morton** Runako Shakur	Leeward Islands	WI	22.7.1978	Rawlins, Nevis

	Team	Country	Born	Birthplace
Mosehle Mangaliso	Easterns/Titans	SA	24.4.1990	Duduza
Moses Bradley	KZN Inland/Dolphins	SA	3.4.1983	Durban
Mosharraf Hossain	Dhaka	B	20.11.1981	Dhaka
Mpitsang Phenyo Victor	Free State/Eagles/Knights	SA	28.3.1980	Kimberley
*Mpofu Christopher Bobby	Matabeleland Tuskers	Z	27.11.1985	Plumtree
*Mubarak Jehan	Wayamba	SL	10.1.1981	Washington, USA
Muchall Gordon James	Durham	E	2.11.1982	Newcastle-upon-Tyne
Mukund Abhinav	Tamil Nadu	I	6.1.1990	Madras
Mullaney Steven John	Nottinghamshire	E	19.11.1986	Warrington
Munday Michael Kenneth	Somerset	E	22.10.1984	Nottingham
*Mupariwa Tawanda	Matabeleland Tuskers	Z	16.4.1985	Bulawayo
*Muralitharan Muttiah	Tamil Union	SL	17.4.1972	Kandy
Murphy David	Lough MCCU/Northants	E	24.7.1989	Welwyn Garden City
Murtagh Timothy James	Middlesex	E	2.8.1981	Lambeth
Mushangwe Natsai	Mountaineers	Z	9.2.1991	Mhangura
*Mushfiqur Rahim	Sylhet	B	1.9.1988	Bogra
Mustard Philip	Durham	E	8.10.1982	Sunderland
Mutizwa Forster	Mashonaland Eagles	Z	24.8.1985	Harare
Muzarabani Taurai	Mid West Rhinos	Z	27.3.1987	Chitungwiza
Nabil Samad	Sylhet	B	9.10.1986	Dhaka
Nadif Chowdhury	Dhaka	B	21.4.1987	Manikganj
Naeem Anjum	Islamabad	P	15.9.1987	Mandi Bahauddin
*Naeem Islam	Rajshahi	B	31.12.1986	Gaibandha
*Nafis Iqbal	Chittagong	B	31.1.1985	Chittagong
Naik Jigar Kumar Hakumatrai	Leicestershire	E	10.8.1984	Leicester
Najaf Shah	PIA	P	17.12.1984	Gujarkhan
Nannes Dirk Peter	Victoria	A	16.5.1976	Mount Waverly
Napier Graham Richard	Essex	E	6.1.1980	Colchester
Narine Sunil Philip	Trinidad & Tobago	WI	26.5.1988	Trinidad
*Nash Brendan Paul	Jamaica	WI	14.12.1977	Attadale, Australia
Nash Christopher David	Sussex	E	19.5.1983	Cuckfield
Nasir Jamshed	National Bank	P	6.12.1989	Lahore
Naumanullah	National Bank	P	20.5.1975	Karachi
*Naved Ashraf	Pakistan Television	P	4.9.1974	Rawalpindi
*Naved Latif	Faisalabad	P	21.2.1976	Sargodha
Naved Yasin	State Bank of Pakistan	P	15.7.1987	Gaggu Mandi
*Naved-ul-Hasan				
Also known as Rana Naved	Sussex/WAPDA	P	28.2.1978	Sheikhupura
Nawela Nawela Mahagamaralalage				
Nadeera Prabath	Kandurata	SL	4.10.1984	Maharagama
Nayar Abhishek Mohan	Mumbai	I	26.10.1983	Secunderabad
Nazimuddin	Chittagong	B	1.10.1985	Chittagong
*Nazmul Hossain	Sylhet	B	5.10.1987	Hobiganj
Nazmus Sadat	Khulna	B	18.10.1986	Khulna
Ncube Njabulo	Mountaineers/Mat. Tuskers	Z	14.10.1989	Bulawayo
*Nehra Ashish	Delhi	I	29.4.1979	Delhi
*Nel Andre	Lions/Surrey	SA	15.7.1977	Germiston
Nel Johann Dewald	Scotland/Kent	Scotland	6.6.1980	Klerksdorp, SA
Neser Michael Gertges	Queensland	A	29.3.1990	Pretoria
Nevill Peter Michael	New South Wales	A	13.10.1985	Hawthorne
Nevin Christopher John	Wellington	NZ	3.8.1975	Dunedin
New Thomas James	Leicestershire	E	18.1.1985	Sutton-in-Ashfield
Newman Scott Alexander	Middlesex	E	3.11.1979	Epsom
Newton Robert Irving	Northamptonshire	E	18.1.1990	Taunton
Nicol Robert James	Canterbury	NZ	28.5.1983	Auckland
Nicolson Ian Alan	Mid West Rhinos	Z	9.10.1986	Harare
Nixon Paul Andrew	Leicestershire	E	21.10.1970	Carlisle
*Nkala Mluleki Luke	Mid West Rhinos	Z	1.4.1981	Bulawayo
Noffke Ashley Allan	Western Australia	A	30.4.1977	Nambour

	Team	Country	Born	Birthplace
Noor Hossain	Dhaka	B	12.3.1992	*Bangladesh*
*****North** Marcus James	Western Australia	A	28.7.1979	*Pakenham*
Northeast Sam Alexander	Kent	E	16.10.1989	*Ashford*
*****Ntini** Makhaya	Kent/Warriors	SA	6.7.1977	*Mdingi*
O'Brien Aaron Warren	South Australia	A	2.10.1981	*St Leonards*
*****O'Brien** Iain Edward	Middlesex	NZ	10.7.1976	*Lower Hutt*
O'Brien Niall John	Ireland/Northants	Ireland	8.11.1981	*Dublin*
Ojha Naman Vijaykumar	Madhya Pradesh	I	20.7.1983	*Ujjain*
*****Ojha** Pragyan Prayish	Hyderabad	I	5.9.1986	*Khurda*
O'Keefe Stephen Norman John	New South Wales	A	9.12.1984	*Malaysia*
Olivier Mario Wicus	W. Prov./Northerns/Titans	SA	3.11.1982	*Pretoria*
Onions Graham	Durham	E	9.9.1982	*Gateshead*
*****Ontong** Justin Lee	Boland/Cape Cobras	SA	4.1.1980	*Paarl*
Oram Jacob David Philip	Central Districts	NZ	28.7.1978	*Palmerston North*
Ord James Edward	Warwickshire	E	9.11.1987	*Birmingham*
Osborne Max	Essex	E	21.11.1990	*Orsett*
Ottley Kjorn Yohance	Com. Campuses & Colls.	WI	9.12.1989	*Trinidad*
Owen William Thomas	Glamorgan	E	2.9.1988	*St Asaph*
*****Pagon** Donovan Jomo	Jamaica	WI	13.9.1982	*Kingston, Jamaica*
*****Paine** Timothy David	Tasmania	A	8.12.1984	*Hobart*
Palladino Antonio Paul	Namibia/Essex	E	29.6.1983	*Tower Hamlets*
Pandey Manish Krishnanand	Karnataka	I	10.9.1989	*Nainital*
*****Panesar** Mudhsuden Singh (<u>Monty</u>)	Sussex	E	25.4.1982	*Luton*
Pankaj Singh	Rajasthan	I	6.5.1985	*Sultanpur*
*****Panyangara** Tinashe	Mountaineers	Z	21.10.1985	*Marondera*
*****Papps** Michael Hugh William	Canterbury	NZ	2.7.1979	*Christchurch*
*****Paranavitana** Nishad <u>Tharanga</u>	Kandurata	SL	15.4.1982	*Kegalle*
*****Parchment** Brenton Anthony	Jamaica	WI	24.6.1982	*St Elizabeth, Jamaica*
Park Garry Terence	Derbyshire	E	19.4.1983	*Empangeni, SA*
*****Parnell** Wayne Dillon	E. Province/Warriors	SA	30.7.1989	*Port Elizabeth*
Parris Nekoli	Com. Campuses & Colls.	WI	6.6.1987	*Lowland Park, Barb.*
Parvinder Singh	Uttar Pradesh	I	8.12.1981	*Meerut*
*****Pascal** Nelon Troy	Windward Islands	WI	25.4.1987	*St David's, Grenada*
*****Patel** Jeetan Shashi	Wellington	NZ	7.5.1980	*Wellington*
*****Patel** Munaf Musa	Baroda	I	12.7.1983	*Ikhar*
*****Patel** Parthiv Ajay	Gujarat	I	9.3.1985	*Ahmedabad*
Patel Samit Rohit	Nottinghamshire	E	30.11.1984	*Leicester*
Pathak Chirag Rajeshbhai	Saurashtra	I	2.2.1987	*Keshod*
*****Pathan** Irfan Khan	Baroda	I	27.10.1984	*Baroda*
Pathan Yusuf Khan	Baroda	I	27.11.1984	*Baroda*
Patterson Steven Andrew	Yorkshire	E	3.10.1983	*Hull*
*****Pattinson** Darren John	Victoria/Nottinghamshire	E	2.8.1979	*Grimsby*
Pattinson James Lee	Victoria	A	3.5.1990	*Melbourne*
Pawan Kolar Balasubramanya	Karnataka	I	19.12.1987	*Bangalore*
Perera Aganpodi <u>Madura Lakmal</u>	Wayamba	SL	21.7.1985	*Kalutara*
Perera Mahawaduge <u>Dilruwan</u> Kamalaneth	Basnahira South	SL	22.7.1982	*Panadura*
Perera Narangoda Liyanaarachchilage <u>Tissara</u> Chirantha	Colts/Wayamba	SL	3.4.1989	*Colombo*
*****Perera** Panagodage Don <u>Ruchira</u> Laksiri	Basnahira South	SL	6.4.1977	*Colombo*
Perkins William Keith Donald	Trinidad & Tobago	WI	8.10.1986	*Barbados*
Permaul Veerasammy	Guyana	WI	11.8.1989	*Belvedere, Guyana*
Peters Keon <u>Kenroy</u>	Windward Islands	WI	24.2.1982	*Mesopotamia, St Vinc.*
Peters Stephen David	Northamptonshire	E	10.12.1978	*Harold Wood*
*****Petersen** Alviro Nathan	Lions	SA	25.11.1980	*Port Elizabeth*
*****Peterson** Robin John	Cape Cobras/Derbyshire	SA	4.8.1979	*Port Elizabeth*

	Team	Country	Born	Birthplace
Pettini Mark Lewis	Essex	E	7.8.1983	Brighton
Philander Vernon Darryl	Cape Cobras	SA	24.6.1985	Bellville
Philipson Craig Andrew	Queensland	A	18.11.1982	Herston
Phillips Ben James	Somerset	E	30.9.1974	Lewisham
*****Phillips** Omar Jamel	Com. Campuses & Colls.	WI	12.10.1986	Boscobel, Barbados
Phillips Timothy James	Essex	E	13.3.1981	Cambridge
Pienaar Abraham Jacobus	Free State/Knights	SA	12.12.1989	Bloemfontein
Pienaar Jacobus Johannes	Easterns/Titans	SA	23.10.1985	Klerksdorp
Pietersen Charl	Griqualand West/Knights	SA	6.1.1983	Kimberley
*****Pietersen** Kevin Peter	Surrey/Dolphins	E	27.6.1980	Pietermaritzburg, SA
Piolet Steffan Andreas	Warwickshire	E	8.8.1988	Redhill
Plunkett Liam Edward	Durham	E	6.4.1985	Middlesbrough
Pollard Kieron Adrian	Trinidad & Tobago	WI	12.5.1987	Cacariqua, Trinidad
Pomersbach Luke Anthony	Western Australia	A	28.9.1984	Bentley
Ponting Ricky Thomas	Tasmania	A	19.12.1974	Launceston
Porter Drew Nathan	Western Australia	A	7.9.1985	Attadale
Porterfield William Thomas Stuart	Ireland/Gloucestershire	Ireland	6.9.1984	Londonderry
Pothas Nic	Hampshire	SA	18.11.1973	Johannesburg
*****Powar** Ramesh Rajaram	Mumbai	I	20.5.1978	Bombay
*****Powell** Daren Brentlyle	Jamaica/Lancashire	WI	15.4.1978	Malvern, Jamaica
Powell Elsroy Junior	Leeward Islands	WI	9.11.1981	St Kitts
Powell Kieran Omar Akeem	Leeward Islands	WI	6.3.1990	Government Rd, Nevis
Powell Michael John	Glamorgan	E	3.2.1977	Abergavenny
Poynton Thomas	Derbyshire	E	25.11.1989	Burton-on-Trent
*****Prasad** Kariyawasam Tirana Gamage Dammika	Basnahira North	SL	30.5.1983	Ragama
Prasanna Seekkuge	Kandurata	SL	27.6.1985	Balapitiya
*****Price** Raymond William	Mashonaland Eagles	Z	12.6.1976	Salisbury
*****Prince** Ashwell Gavin	Lancashire/Warriors	SA	28.5.1977	Port Elizabeth
*****Prior** Matthew James	Sussex	E	26.2.1982	Johannesburg, SA
Procter Luke Anthony	Lancashire	E	24.6.1988	Oldham
*****Pujara** Cheteshwar Arvind	Saurashtra	I	25.1.1988	Rajkot
Pushpakumara Muthumudalige	Basnahira North	SL	26.9.1981	Colombo
Putland Gary David	South Australia	A	10.2.1986	Flinders
Puttick Andrew George	Cape Cobras	SA	11.12.1980	Cape Town
Pyrah Richard Michael	Yorkshire	E	1.11.1982	Dewsbury
*****Qaiser Abbas**	National Bank	P	7.5.1982	Muridke
Quiney Robert John	Victoria	A	20.8.1982	Brighton, Australia
Rahane Ajinkya Madhukar	Mumbai	I	6.6.1988	Ashwi Kurd
*****Raina** Suresh Kumar	Uttar Pradesh	I	27.11.1986	Ghaziabad
Rainsford Edward Charles	Mid West Rhinos	Z	14.12.1984	Kadoma
*****Rajin** Saleh	Sylhet	B	20.11.1983	Sylhet
*****Ramdin** Denesh	Trinidad & Tobago	WI	13.3.1985	Mission Rd, Trinidad
Ramela Omphile Abel	Boland/Cape Cobras	SA	14.3.1988	Soweto
*****Rampaul** Ravindranath	Trinidad & Tobago	WI	15.10.1984	Preysal, Trinidad
*****Ramprakash** Mark Ravin	Surrey	E	5.9.1969	Bushey
*****Ramyakumara** Wijekoon Mudiyanselage Gayan *Also known as Gayan Wijekoon*	Basnahira North	SL	21.12.1976	Gampaha
*****Randiv** Suraj *Also known as Hewa Kaluhalamullage Suraj Randiv Kaluhalamulla; formerly known as M. M. M. Suraj*	Kandurata	SL	30.1.1985	Matara
Rankin William Boyd	Warwickshire	Ireland	5.7.1984	Londonderry
*****Raqibul Hasan**	Barisal	B	8.10.1987	Jamalpur
Rashid Adil Usman	Yorkshire	E	17.2.1988	Bradford
*****Ratra** Ajay	Goa	I	13.12.1981	Faridabad

	Team	Country	Born	Birthplace
Rayner Oliver Philip	Sussex	E	1.11.1985	*Fallingbostel, Germany*
*****Read** Christopher Mark Wells	Nottinghamshire	E	10.8.1978	*Paignton*
Reardon Nathan Jon	Queensland	A	8.11.1984	*Chinchilla*
Redfern Daniel James	Derbyshire	E	18.4.1990	*Shrewsbury*
*****Redmond** Aaron James	Otago	NZ	23.9.1979	*Auckland*
Rees Gareth Peter	Glamorgan	E	8.4.1985	*Swansea*
*****Reifer** Floyd Lamonte	Com. Campuses & Colls.	WI	23.7.1972	*Parish Land, Barbados*
*****Riaz Afridi**	Peshawar	P	21.1.1985	*Peshawar*
*****Richards** Dale Maurice	Barbados	WI	16.7.1976	*Isolation Rd, Barbados*
Richards Mali Alexander	Leeward Islands	WI	2.9.1983	*Taunton*
Richardson Alan	Worcestershire	E	6.5.1975	*Newcastle-under-Lyme*
Richardson Andrew Peter	Jamaica	WI	6.9.1981	*Kingston, Jamaica*
Rimmington Nathan John	Queensland	A	11.11.1982	*Redcliffe*
Rizwan Ahmed	Hyderabad	P	1.10.1978	*Hyderabad*
*****Roach** Kemar Andre Jamal	Barbados	WI	30.6.1988	*Checker Hall, Barb.*
Robinson Andrew William	Queensland	A	10.6.1981	*Devonport*
Robinson Wesley Michael	Western Australia	A	26.12.1980	*Duncraig*
*****Robiul Islam**	Khulna	B	20.10.1986	*Satkhira*
Robson Samuel David	Middlesex	A	1.7.1989	*Paddington*
*****Rogers** Christopher John Llewellyn	Victoria/Derbyshire	A	31.8.1977	*St George*
Rogers Codville Leon	Leeward Islands	WI	4.7.1976	*Sinletts, Nevis*
Rogers John William	Tasmania	A	11.4.1987	*Canberra*
Rohan Prem Preambhasan	Kerala	I	13.9.1986	*Trivandrum*
Rohrer Ben James	New South Wales	A	26.3.1981	*Bankstown*
Roland-Jones Tobias Skelton	Middlesex	E	29.1.1988	*Ashford, Middlesex*
Ronchi Luke	Western Australia	A	23.4.1981	*Dannevirke, NZ*
Rossouw Riley Roscoe	Free State/Eagles/Knights	SA	9.10.1989	*Bloemfontein*
Roy Jason Jonathan	Surrey	E	21.7.1990	*Durban*
*****Rubel Hossain**	Chittagong	B	1.1.1990	*Bagerhat*
*****Rudolph** Jacobus Andries	Titans/Yorkshire	SA	4.5.1981	*Springs*
Rupasinghe Rupasinghe Jayawardene Mudiyanselage Gihan Madushanka	Basnahira South	SL	5.3.1986	*Watupitiwala*
Rushworth Christopher	Durham	E	11.7.1986	*Sunderland*
*****Russell** Andre Dwayne	Jamaica	WI	29.4.1988	*Jamaica*
*****Ryder** Jesse Daniel	Wellington	NZ	6.8.1984	*Masterton*
Sadler John Leonard	Derbyshire	E	19.11.1981	*Dewsbury*
*****Saeed Ajmal**	ZTBL	P	14.10.1977	*Faisalabad*
Saghir Hossain	Khulna	B	14.8.1986	*Khulna*
*****Saha** Wriddhaman Prasanta	Bengal	I	24.10.1984	*Siliguri*
*****Sajidul Islam**	Barisal	B	18.1.1988	*Rangpur*
Sales David John	Northamptonshire	E	3.12.1977	*Carshalton*
Salim Elahi	Habib Bank	P	21.11.1976	*Sahiwal*
*****Salman Butt**	National Bank	P	7.10.1984	*Lahore*
Salvi Aavishkar Madhav	Mumbai	I	20.10.1981	*Bombay*
*****Samaraweera** Thilan Thusara	Kandurata	SL	22.9.1976	*Colombo*
Samiullah Khan	Sui Northern	P	4.8.1982	*Mianwali*
*****Sammy** Darren Julius Garvey	Windward Islands	WI	20.12.1983	*Micoud, St Lucia*
*****Sangakkara** Kumar Chokshanada	Nondescripts	SL	27.10.1977	*Matale*
*****Sarfraz Ahmed**	PIA	P	22.5.1987	*Karachi*
*****Sarwan** Ramnaresh Ronnie	Guyana	WI	23.6.1980	*Wakenaam Island, Guy.*
Satish Ganesh	Karnataka	I	15.3.1988	*Davanagere*
Saxena Jalaj Sahai	Madhya Pradesh	I	15.12.1986	*Indore*
Sayers Joseph John	Yorkshire	E	5.11.1983	*Leeds*
*****Schofield** Christopher Paul	Surrey	E	6.10.1978	*Wardle*
Scott Ben James Matthew	Worcestershire	E	4.8.1981	*Isleworth*
Sebastien Liam Andrew Shannon	Windward Islands	WI	9.9.1984	*Roseau, Dominica*
*****Sehwag** Virender	Delhi	I	20.10.1978	*Delhi*

	Team	Country	Born	Birthplace
Senanayake Senanayake Mudiyanselage <u>Sachithra</u> Madhushanka	Ruhuna	SL	9.2.1985	*Colombo*
***Shabbir Ahmed**	Lahore Ravi	P	21.4.1976	*Khanewal*
Shafayat Bilal Mustapha	Nottinghamshire/Habib Bank	E	10.7.1984	*Nottingham*
***Shafiul Islam**	Rajshahi	B	6.10.1989	*Bogra*
***Shah** Owais Alam	Middlesex/Cape Cobras	E	22.10.1978	*Karachi, Pakistan*
Shah Pinal Rohitbhai	Baroda	I	3.11.1987	*Baroda*
***Shahadat Hossain**	Dhaka	B	7.8.1986	*Narayanganj*
***Shahid Afridi**	Habib Bank	P	1.3.1980	*Khyber Agency*
***Shahid Nazir**	Habib Bank	P	4.12.1977	*Faisalabad*
***Shahriar Nafees**	Barisal	B	25.1.1986	*Dhaka*
***Shahzad Ajmal**	Yorkshire	E	27.7.1985	*Huddersfield*
Shahzaib Hasan	Karachi Blues/Kar. Whites	P	25.12.1989	*Karachi*
***Shakib Al Hasan**	Worcestershire	B	24.3.1987	*Magura*
Shamsi Tabraiz	Gauteng/Lions/Dolphins/ KZN	SA	18.2.1990	*Johannesburg*
Shamsur Rahman	Dhaka	B	5.6.1988	*Comilla*
Shan Masood	Habib Bank	P	14.10.1989	*Kuwait*
Shantry Jack David	Worcestershire	E	29.1.1988	*Shrewsbury*
***Sharma** Ishant	Delhi	I	2.9.1988	*Delhi*
Sharma Joginder	Haryana	I	23.10.1983	*Rohtak*
Sharma Rohit Gurunath	Mumbai	I	30.4.1987	*Bansod*
Sheharyar Ghani	Karachi Blues/PIA	P	9.9.1985	*Karachi*
Sheikh Atif	Derbyshire	E	18.2.1991	*Nottingham*
Sheridan William David	Victoria	A	5.7.1987	*Chertsey, England*
Shezi Mthokozisi	KwaZulu-Natal/Dolphins	SA	9.9.1987	*Imbali*
***Shillingford** Shane	Windward Islands	WI	22.2.1983	*Dominica*
***Shoaib Akhtar**	KRL	P	13.8.1975	*Rawalpindi*
Shoaib Khan	State Bank of Pakistan	P	13.4.1985	*Bostan*
***Shoaib Malik**	PIA	P	1.2.1982	*Sialkot*
Shreck Charles Edward	Nottinghamshire	E	6.1.1978	*Truro*
Shukla Laxmi Ratan	Bengal	I	6.5.1981	*Howrah*
***Sibanda** Vusimuzi	Mid West Rhinos	Z	10.10.1983	*Highfields*
***Siddle** Peter Matthew	Victoria	A	25.11.1984	*Traralgon*
***Sidebottom** Ryan Jay	Nottinghamshire	E	15.1.1978	*Huddersfield*
Silva Jayan <u>Kaushal</u>	Basnahira North	SL	27.5.1986	*Colombo*
***Silva** Lindamillage Prageeth <u>Chamara</u>	Basnahira South	SL	14.12.1979	*Panadura*
***Simmons** Lendl Mark Platter	Trinidad & Tobago	WI	25.1.1985	*Port-of-Spain, Trinidad*
Simpson Christopher Patrick	Queensland	A	9.1.1982	*Brisbane*
Simpson John Andrew	Middlesex	E	13.7.1988	*Bury*
***Sinclair** Mathew Stuart	Central Districts	NZ	9.11.1975	*Katherine, Australia*
Singh Gajanand	Guyana	WI	3.10.1987	*Cumberland, Guyana*
***Singh** Rudra Pratap	Uttar Pradesh	I	6.12.1985	*Rae Bareli*
Singh Vishan Anthony	Guyana	WI	12.1.1989	*Georgetown, Guyana*
Smit Darren	Dolphins	SA	28.1.1984	*Durban*
Smith Benjamin Francis	Worcestershire	E	3.4.1972	*Corby*
Smith Daniel Lindsay Richard	New South Wales	A	17.3.1982	*Westmead*
***Smith** Devon Sheldon	Windward Islands	WI	21.10.1981	*Hermitage, Grenada*
***Smith** Dwayne Romel	Barbados	WI	12.4.1983	*Storey Gap, Barbados*
***Smith** Graeme Craig	Cape Cobras	SA	1.2.1981	*Johannesburg*
Smith Greg Phillip	Durham MCCU/Leics	E	16.11.1988	*Leicester*
Smith Gregory Marc	Derbyshire/Mountaineers	SA	20.4.1983	*Johannesburg*
Smith Jamal	Com. Campuses & Colls.	WI	16.10.1984	*Deacon Rd, Barbados*
Smith James David	South Australia	A	11.10.1988	*Murray Bridge*
Smith Michael Bruce Argo	Eastern Province/Warriors	SA	5.5.1980	*King William's Town*
***Smith** Steven Peter Devereux	New South Wales	A	2.6.1989	*Sydney*
Smith Thomas Christopher	Lancashire	E	26.12.1985	*Liverpool*
Smith Thomas Michael John	Middlesex	E	22.8.1987	*Eastbourne*

	Team	Country	Born	Birthplace
Smith William Rew	Durham	E	28.9.1982	*Luton*
Smuts Jon-Jon Trevor	Eastern Province/Warriors	SA	21.8.1988	*Grahamstown*
Smuts Kelly Royce	Eastern Province/Warriors	SA	22.11.1990	*Grahamstown*
Snell Stephen David	Gloucestershire	E	27.2.1983	*Winchester*
Snijman Blake Douglas	Titans	SA	28.10.1985	*Krugersdorp*
*****Sohail Khan**	Karachi Whites	P	6.3.1984	*Malakand*
*****Sohail Tanvir**	ZTBL	P	12.12.1984	*Rawalpindi*
Solanki Vikram Singh	Worcestershire	E	1.4.1976	*Udaipur, India*
*****Southee** Timothy Grant	Northern Districts	NZ	11.12.1988	*Whangarei*
Spriegel Matthew Neil William	Surrey	E	4.3.1987	*Epsom*
*****Sreesanth** Shanthakumaran	Kerala	I	6.2.1983	*Kothamangalam*
Srikkanth Anirudh	Tamil Nadu	I	14.4.1987	*Madras*
Sriram Sridharan	Assam	I	21.2.1976	*Madras*
Srivastava Tanmay Manoj	Uttar Pradesh	I	7.11.1989	*Lucknow*
Starc Mitchell Aaron	New South Wales	A	13.1.1990	*Baulkham Hills*
Stevens Darren Ian	Kent	E	30.4.1976	*Leicester*
Stewart Navin Derrick	Trinidad & Tobago	WI	13.6.1983	*Roxborough, Tobago*
Stewart Shanan Luke	Canterbury	NZ	21.6.1982	*Christchurch*
*****Steyn** Dale Willem	Titans	SA	27.6.1983	*Phalaborwa*
Stiff David Alexander	Somerset	E	20.10.1984	*Dewsbury*
Stokes Benjamin Andrew	Durham	E	4.6.1991	*Christchurch*
Stoneman Mark Daniel	Durham	E	26.6.1987	*Newcastle-upon-Tyne*
Stoute Kevin Andre	Barbados	WI	12.11.1985	*Black Rock, Barbados*
*****Strauss** Andrew John	Middlesex	E	2.3.1977	*Johannesburg, SA*
Strydom Gregory Mark	Matabeleland Tuskers	Z	26.3.1984	*Pretoria, SA*
*****Styris** Scott Bernard	Northern Districts	NZ	10.7.1975	*Brisbane, Australia*
Suhrawadi Shuvo	Rajshahi	B	21.11.1988	*Rajshahi*
Suppiah Arul Vivasvan	Somerset	E	30.8.1983	*Kuala Lumpur, Malay.*
Sutton Luke David	Lancashire	E	4.10.1976	*Keynsham*
Swan Christopher Richard	Queensland	A	10.8.1978	*Southport*
*****Swann** Graeme Peter	Nottinghamshire	E	24.3.1979	*Northampton*
Swart Michael Richard	Western Australia	A	1.10.1982	*Subiaco*
*****Syed Rasel**	Khulna	B	3.7.1984	*Jessore*
Symes Jean	Gauteng/Lions	SA	13.11.1986	*Johannesburg*
Tabish Khan	Karachi Blues	P	12.12.1984	*Karachi*
Tahir Naqaash Sarosh	Warwickshire	E	14.11.1983	*Birmingham*
*****Taibu** Tatenda	Mountaineers/S. Rocks	Z	14.5.1983	*Harare*
*****Tait** Shaun William	South Australia	A	22.2.1983	*Bedford Park*
*****Talha** Jubair	Dhaka	B	10.12.1985	*Faridpur*
*****Tamim** Iqbal	Chittagong	B	20.3.1989	*Chittagong*
*****Tanvir** Ahmed	Karachi Blues/Kar. Whites	P	20.12.1978	*Kuwait City*
*****Tapash** Baisya	Sylhet	B	25.12.1982	*Sylhet*
*****Tareq** Aziz	Chittagong	B	4.9.1983	*Chittagong*
*****Taufeeq** Umar	Habib Bank	P	20.6.1981	*Lahore*
*****Taylor** Brendan Ross Murray	Mid West Rhinos	Z	6.2.1986	*Harare*
Taylor Christopher Glyn	Gloucestershire	E	27.9.1976	*Bristol*
Taylor Jack Martin Robert	Gloucestershire	E	12.11.1991	*Banbury*
Taylor James William Arthur	Leicestershire	E	6.1.1990	*Nottingham*
*****Taylor** Jerome Everton	Jamaica	WI	22.6.1984	*St Elizabeth, Jamaica*
*****Taylor** Luteru <u>Ross</u> Poutoa Lote	Central Districts	NZ	8.3.1984	*Lower Hutt*
ten Doeschate Ryan Neil	Netherlands/Essex	NL	30.6.1980	*Port Elizabeth, SA*
*****Tendulkar** Sachin Ramesh	Mumbai	I	24.4.1973	*Bombay*
Terblanche Roman Kelvin	Free State/Knights	SA	10.6.1986	*Bloemfontein*
Thaker Bhavik Dinbandhubhai	Gujarat	I	23.10.1982	*Ahmedabad*
*****Tharanga** Warushavithana <u>Upul</u>	Ruhuna	SL	2.2.1985	*Balapitiya*
Theophile Tyrone	Windward Islands	WI	12.8.1989	*Dominica*
Theron Juan (<u>Rusty</u>)	Warriors	SA	24.7.1985	*Vereeniging*
Thirimanne Hettige Don Rumesh <u>Lahiru</u>	Basnahira South	SL	8.9.1989	*Moratuwa*

	Team	Country	Born	Birthplace
Thomas Alfonso Clive	Somerset	SA	9.2.1977	Cape Town
Thomas Devon Cuthbert	Leeward Islands	WI	12.11.1989	Bethesda, Antigua
Thompson Ewen Paul	Central Districts	NZ	17.12.1979	Warkworth
Thornely Dominic John	New South Wales	A	1.10.1978	Albury
Thornely Michael Alistair	Sussex	E	19.10.1987	Camden
Thorp Callum David	Durham	A	11.2.1975	Mount Lawley
Thyssen Craig Andre	Warriors	SA	25.3.1984	Port Elizabeth
Tiwary Manoj Kumar	Bengal	I	14.11.1985	Howrah
Tiwary Saurabh Sunil	Jharkhand	I	30.12.1989	Jamshedpur
Tomlinson James Andrew	Hampshire	E	12.6.1982	Winchester
*****Tonge** Gavin Courtney	Leeward Islands	WI	13.2.1983	St John's, Antigua
Townsend Wade James	Queensland	A	29.1.1986	Herston
*****Tredwell** James Cullum	Kent	E	27.2.1982	Ashford
Trego Peter David	Somerset	E	12.6.1981	Weston-super-Mare
Tremlett Christopher Timothy	Surrey	E	2.9.1981	Southampton
*****Trescothick** Marcus Edward	Somerset	E	25.12.1975	Keynsham
Tripathi Vishal	Northamptonshire	E	3.3.1988	Burnley
*****Trott** Ian Jonathan Leonard	Warwickshire	E	22.4.1981	Cape Town, SA
Troughton Jamie Oliver	Warwickshire	E	2.3.1979	Camden
Tshabalala Mthandeki Samson (Thandi)	Free State/Knights	SA	19.11.1984	Welkom
*****Tsolekile** Thami Lungisa	Lions	SA	9.10.1980	Cape Town
*****Tsotsobe** Lonwabo Lennox	Warriors	SA	7.3.1984	Port Elizabeth
*****Tuffey** Daryl Raymond	Auckland	NZ	11.6.1978	Milton
*****Tushar** Imran	Khulna	B	10.12.1983	Kharki
Tyagi Sudeep	Uttar Pradesh	I	19.9.1987	Ghaziabad
*****Udal** Shaun David	Middlesex	E	18.3.1969	Cove
Udana Isuru	Wayamba	SL	17.2.1988	Balangoda
Udawatte Mahela Lakmal	Wayamba	SL	19.7.1986	Colombo
Umair Khan	Islamabad	P	31.7.1985	Kohat
*****Umar Akmal**	Sui Northern	P	26.5.1990	Lahore
*****Umar Amin**	National Bank	P	16.10.1989	Rawalpindi
*****Umar Gul**	Habib Bank	P	14.4.1984	Peshawar
*****Unadkat** Jaydev Dipakbhai	Saurashtra	I	18.10.1991	Porbandar
Uthappa Robin Venu	Karnataka	I	11.11.1985	Coorg
*****Utseya** Prosper	Mountaineers	Z	26.3.1985	Harare
*****Vaas** Warnakulasuriya Patabendige Ushantha Joseph Chaminda	Northamptonshire	SL	27.1.1974	Mattumagala
van der Merwe Roelof Erasmus	Titans	SA	31.12.1984	Johannesburg
van der Wath Johannes Jacobus	Eagles	SA	10.1.1978	Newcastle
Vandiar Jonathan David	Lions	SA	25.4.1990	Paarl
*****Vandort** Michael Graydon	Wayamba	SL	19.1.1980	Colombo
*****van Jaarsveld** Martin	Kent	SA	18.6.1974	Klerksdorp
van Jaarsveld Vaughn Bernard	Lions/Dolphins	SA	2.2.1985	Johannesburg
van Wyk Divan Jaco	Free State/Dolphins/KZN	SA	25.2.1985	Bloemfontein
van Wyk Jandre	Eagles/Free State	SA	20.3.1989	Pretoria
van Wyk Morne Nico	Eagles/Knights	SA	20.3.1979	Bloemfontein
van Zyl Stiaan	Cape Cobras/Boland	SA	19.9.1987	Cape Town
van Zyl Willem Johannes	Free State/Knights	SA	14.4.1988	Bloemfontein
Venugopal Rao Yalaka	Andhra	I	26.2.1982	Visakhapatnam
*****Vermeulen** Mark Andrew	Mountaineers	Z	2.3.1979	Salisbury
*****Vettori** Daniel Luca	Northern Districts	NZ	27.1.1979	Auckland
Vidanapathirana Chaminda Wijayakumara	Kandurata	SL	25.1.1983	Morawake
*****Vijay** Murali	Tamil Nadu	I	1.4.1984	Madras
Viljoen Gerhardus C. (Hardus)	Easterns/Titans	SA	6.3.1989	Witbank
Vinay Kumar Ranganath	Karnataka	I	12.2.1984	Davanagere
Vince James Michael	Hampshire	E	14.3.1991	Cuckfield

	Team	Country	Born	Birthplace
Voges Adam Charles	W. Australia/Notts	A	4.10.1979	Perth
von Berg Shaun	Northerns/Titans	SA	16.9.1986	Pretoria
Vries Gino Angelo	Free State/Eagles/Knights	SA	14.11.1987	Bloemfontein
Wade Matthew Scott	Victoria	A	26.12.1987	Hobart
Wagg Graham Grant	Derbyshire	E	28.4.1983	Rugby
Wagh Mark Anant	Nottinghamshire	E	20.10.1976	Birmingham
***Wahab Riaz**	National Bank	P	28.6.1985	Lahore
Wainwright David John	Yorkshire	E	21.3.1985	Pontefract
Wakely Alexander George	Northamptonshire	E	3.11.1988	Hammersmith
Walker Matthew Jonathan	Essex	E	2.1.1974	Gravesend
Wallace Gavin	Com. Campuses & Colls.	WI	22.12.1984	Jamaica
Wallace Mark Alexander	Glamorgan	E	19.11.1981	Abergavenny
Waller Malcolm Noel	Mid West Rhinos	Z	28.9.1984	Harare
Waller Nathan	Zimbabwe XI	Z	19.11.1991	Harare
Walter Scott Hugh	Queensland	A	2.5.1989	South Brisbane
Walters Basheeru-Deen	Easterns/Titans/Eastern Province/Warriors	SA	16.9.1986	Port Elizabeth
Walters Stewart Jonathan	Surrey	E	25.6.1983	Mornington, Australia
***Walton** Chadwick Antonio Kirkpatrick	Com. Campuses & Colls.	WI	3.7.1985	Jamaica
***Warnapura** Basnayake Shalith Malinda	Basnahira South	SL	26.5.1979	Colombo
Warner David Andrew	New South Wales	A	27.10.1986	Paddington
***Wasim Jaffer**	Mumbai	I	16.2.1978	Bombay
Waters Huw Thomas	Glamorgan	E	26.9.1986	Cardiff
***Watling** Bradley-John	Northern Districts	NZ	9.7.1985	Durban, SA
***Watson** Shane Robert	New South Wales	A	17.6.1981	Ipswich
Weeraratne Kaushalya	Kandurata	SL	29.1.1981	Gampola
***Welagedara** Uda Walawwe Mahim Bandaralage Chanaka Asanka	Wayamba	SL	20.3.1981	Matale
Wells Jonathan Wayne	Tasmania	A	13.8.1988	Hobart
Wells Luke William Peter	Sussex	E	29.12.1990	Eastbourne
Westley Thomas	Essex/Durham MCCU	E	13.3.1989	Cambridge
Westwood Ian James	Warwickshire	E	13.7.1982	Birmingham
Wheeldon David Antony	Worcestershire	E	12.4.1989	Staffordshire
Whelan Christopher David	Worcestershire	E	8.5.1986	Liverpool
***White** Cameron Leon	Victoria	A	18.8.1983	Bairnsdale
White Graeme Geoffrey	Nottinghamshire	E	18.4.1987	Milton Keynes
White Robert Allan	Northamptonshire	E	15.10.1979	Chelmsford
White Wayne Andrew	Leicestershire	E	22.4.1985	Derby
Wiese David	Easterns/Titans	SA	18.5.1985	Roodepoort
Willett Tonito Akanni	Leeward Islands	WI	6.2.1983	Government Rd, Nevis
Willey David Jonathan	Northamptonshire	E	28.2.1990	Northampton
Williams Gavin Anjez	Leeward Islands	WI	18.11.1984	Bolans
Williams Reece Chesray	Eastern Province/Warriors	SA	12.1.1990	Kimberley
Williams Sean Colin	Matabeleland Tuskers	Z	26.9.1986	Bulawayo
***Williamson** Kane Stuart	Northern Districts	NZ	8.8.1990	Tauranga
***Willoughby** Charl Myles	Somerset	SA	3.12.1974	Cape Town
Wilson Gary Craig	Ireland/Surrey	Ireland	5.2.1986	Dundonald
Woakes Christopher Roger	Warwickshire	E	2.3.1989	Birmingham
Wood Christopher Philip	Hampshire	E	27.6.1990	Basingstoke
Wood Matthew James	Nottinghamshire	E	30.9.1980	Exeter
Woodcock Luke James	Wellington	NZ	19.3.1982	Wellington
Wright Ben James	Glamorgan	E	5.12.1987	Preston
Wright Christopher Julian Clement	Essex	E	14.7.1985	Chipping Norton
Wright Damien Geoffrey	Victoria/Somerset	A	25.7.1975	Casino
Wright Luke James	Sussex	E	7.3.1985	Grantham
Yadav Jai Prakash	Railways	I	7.8.1974	Bhopal

	Team	Country	Born	Birthplace
Yadav Umeshkumar Tilak	Vidarbha	I	25.10.1987	Nagpur
Yardy Michael Howard	Sussex	E	27.11.1980	Pembury
***Yasir Ali**	KRL	P	15.10.1985	Hazro
***Yasir Arafat**	Sussex/KRL	P	12.3.1982	Rawalpindi
***Yasir Hameed**	ZTBL	P	28.2.1978	Peshawar
Yasir Shah	Sui Northern	P	2.5.1986	Swabi
Young Edward George Christopher	Oxford MCCU/Glos	E	21.5.1989	Chertsey
***Young** Reece Alan	Auckland/Canterbury	NZ	15.9.1979	Auckland
***Younis Khan**	Habib Bank/Surrey	P	29.11.1977	Mardan
***Yuvraj Singh**	Punjab	I	12.12.1981	Chandigarh
***Zaheer Khan**	Mumbai	I	7.10.1978	Shrirampur
***Zahoor Elahi**	KRL	P	1.3.1971	Sahiwal
Zhuwao Cephas	Mashonaland Eagles	Z	15.12.1984	Harare
***Zondeki** Monde	W. Province/Cape Cobras	SA	25.7.1982	King William's Town
Zondo Khayelihle	KwaZulu-Natal/Dolphins	SA	7.3.1990	Durban
Zulfiqar Babar	WAPDA	P	10.12.1978	Okara
***Zulqarnain Haider**	ZTBL	P	3.4.1986	Lahore

REGISTER OF WOMEN PLAYERS

The qualifications for inclusion are as follows:

All players who appeared in an international match, or in the County Championship in England, the Women's National Cricket League in Australia, or the Action Cricket Cup in New Zealand, in the calendar year 2010

AND have scored 1,000 runs/taken 50 wickets in one-day internationals, or scored a hundred/taken five in an innings in a Test, one-day international or Twenty20 international since 2008.

* *Denotes Test player.*

	Team	Country	Born	Birthplace
***Al Khader** Nooshin	Railways	I	13.2.1981	Tehran, Iran
***Andrews** Sarah Joy	New South Wales	A	26.12.1981	Moruya
***Atkins** Caroline Mary Ghislaine	Sussex	E	13.1.1981	Brighton
Bates Suzannah Wilson	Otago	NZ	16.9.1987	Dunedin
***Blackwell** Alexandra Joy	New South Wales	A	31.8.1983	Wagga Wagga
***Brindle** Arran (*née Thompson*)	Lancashire	E	23.11.1981	Steeton
Brits Cri-Zelda	Gauteng	SA	20.11.1983	Rustenburg
***Browne** Nicola Jane	Northern Districts	NZ	14.9.1983	Matamata
***Brunt** Katherine Helen	Yorkshire	E	2.7.1985	Barnsley
***Chopra** Anjum	Delhi	I	20.5.1977	Delhi
***Colvin** Holly Louise	Sussex	E	7.9.1989	Chichester
***David** Neetu	Railways	I	1.9.1977	Kanpur
***Dhar** Rumeli	Railways	I	9.12.1983	Calcutta
Dottin Deandra Jalisa Shakira	Barbados	WI	21.6.1991	Barbados
***Drumm** Emily Cecilia	Kent	NZ	15.9.1974	Avondale
***Edwards** Charlotte Marie	Kent	E	17.12.1979	Huntingdon
***Fahey** Maria Frances	Canterbury	NZ	5.3.1984	Timaru
***Farrell** Rene Michelle	Western Australia	A	13.1.1987	Kogarah
Fernando Wannakawattawadune Hiruka Dilani	Colts	SL	30.9.1976	Moratuwa
***Fields** Jodie Maree (*née Purves*)	Queensland	A	19.6.1984	Toowoomba
***Fritz** Shandre Alvida	Western Province	SA	21.7.1985	Cape Town
***Goswami** Jhulan	Bengal	I	25.11.1982	Kalyani
***Greenway** Lydia Sophie	Kent	E	6.8.1985	Farnborough, Kent
***Guha** Isa Tara	Berkshire	E	21.5.1985	High Wycombe
***Gunn** Jennifer Louise	Nottinghamshire	E	9.5.1986	Nottingham
***Jones** Melanie	Tasmania	A	11.8.1972	Barnstaple, England
***Kala** Hemlata	Railways	I	15.8.1975	Agra
***Keightley** Lisa Maree	Wiltshire	E	26.8.1971	Mudgee
Lanning Meghann Moira	Victoria	A	25.5.1992	Singapore

	Team	Country	Born	Birthplace
McGlashan Sara Jade	Central Districts	NZ	28.3.1982	*Napier*
Marsh Laura Alexandra	Sussex	E	5.12.1986	*Pembury*
Mohammed Anisa	Trinidad & Tobago	WI	7.8.1988	*Trinidad*
***Nitschke** Shelley	South Australia	A	3.12.1976	*Adelaide*
***Perry** Ellyse Alexandra	New South Wales	A	3.11.1990	*Wahroonga*
***Poulton** Leah Joy	New South Wales	A	27.2.1984	*Newcastle*
***Raj** Mithali	Railways	I	3.12.1982	*Jodhpur*
***Richardson** Eimear Ann Jermyn	Ireland A/C. Districts	Ireland	14.9.1986	*Dublin*
***Rolton** Karen Louise	South Australia	A	21.11.1974	*Adelaide*
Roy Priyanka	Railways	I	2.3.1988	*Calcutta*
***Sajjida Shah**	ZTBL	P	3.2.1988	*Hyderabad*
Sana Mir	ZTBL	P	5.1.1986	*Abbottabad*
***Sharma** Amita	Railways	I	12.9.1982	*Delhi*
***Sharma** Jaya	Delhi	I	17.9.1980	*Ghaziabad*
Siriwardene Hettimulla Appuhamilage <u>Shashikala</u> Dedunu	Marians	SL	14.2.1985	*Colombo*
***Smit** Jane	Nottinghamshire	E	24.12.1972	*Ilkeston*
***Smith** Alicia Esther	Boland	SA	13.3.1984	*Cape Town*
***Sthalekar** Lisa Caprini	New South Wales	A	13.8.1979	*Poona, India*
***Taylor** Clare Elizabeth	Otago	E	22.5.1965	*Huddersfield*
***Taylor** Samantha <u>Claire</u>	Berkshire	E	25.9.1975	*Amersham*
***Taylor** Sarah Jane	Sussex	E	20.5.1989	*Whitechapel*
Taylor Stafanie Roxann	Jamaica	WI	11.6.1991	*Jamaica*
***Watkins** Aimee Louise (*née Mason*)	Central Districts/Devon	NZ	11.10.1982	*New Plymouth*

CRICKETERS OF THE YEAR, 1889–2011

1889	*Six Great Bowlers of the Year:* J. Briggs, J. J. Ferris, G. A. Lohmann, R. Peel, C. T. B. Turner, S. M. J. Woods.
1890	*Nine Great Batsmen of the Year:* R. Abel, W. Barnes, W. Gunn, L. Hall, R. Henderson, J. M. Read, A. Shrewsbury, F. H. Sugg, A. Ward.
1891	*Five Great Wicketkeepers:* J. McC. Blackham, G. MacGregor, R. Pilling, M. Sherwin, H. Wood.
1892	*Five Great Bowlers:* W. Attewell, J. T. Hearne, F. Martin, A. W. Mold, J. W. Sharpe.
1893	*Five Batsmen of the Year:* H. T. Hewett, L. C. H. Palairet, W. W. Read, S. W. Scott, A. E. Stoddart.
1894	*Five All-Round Cricketers:* G. Giffen, A. Hearne, F. S. Jackson, G. H. S. Trott, E. Wainwright.
1895	*Five Young Batsmen of the Season:* W. Brockwell, J. T. Brown, C. B. Fry, T. W. Hayward, A. C. MacLaren.
1896	W. G. Grace.
1897	*Five Cricketers of the Season:* S. E. Gregory, A. A. Lilley, K. S. Ranjitsinhji, T. Richardson, H. Trumble.
1898	*Five Cricketers of the Year:* F. G. Bull, W. R. Cuttell, N. F. Druce, G. L. Jessop, J. R. Mason.
1899	*Five Great Players of the Season:* W. H. Lockwood, W. Rhodes, W. Storer, C. L. Townsend, A. E. Trott.
1900	*Five Cricketers of the Season:* J. Darling, C. Hill, A. O. Jones, M. A. Noble, Major R. M. Poore.
1901	*Mr R. E. Foster and Four Yorkshiremen:* R. E. Foster, S. Haigh, G. H. Hirst, T. L. Taylor, J. Tunnicliffe.
1902	L. C. Braund, C. P. McGahey, F. Mitchell, W. G. Quaife, J. T. Tyldesley.
1903	W. W. Armstrong, C. J. Burnup, J. Iremonger, J. J. Kelly, V. T. Trumper.
1904	C. Blythe, J. Gunn, A. E. Knight, W. Mead, P. F. Warner.
1905	B. J. T. Bosanquet, E. A. Halliwell, J. Hallows, P. A. Perrin, R. H. Spooner.
1906	D. Denton, W. S. Lees, G. J. Thompson, J. Vine, L. G. Wright.
1907	J. N. Crawford, A. Fielder, E. G. Hayes, K. L. Hutchings, N. A. Knox.
1908	A. W. Hallam, R. O. Schwarz, F. A. Tarrant, A. E. E. Vogler, T. G. Wass.
1909	*Lord Hawke and Four Cricketers of the Year:* W. Brearley, Lord Hawke, J. B. Hobbs, A. Marshal, J. T. Newstead.
1910	W. Bardsley, S. F. Barnes, D. W. Carr, A. P. Day, V. S. Ransford.
1911	H. K. Foster, A. Hartley, C. B. Llewellyn, W. C. Smith, F. E. Woolley.
1912	*Five Members of the MCC's Team in Australia:* F. R. Foster, J. W. Hearne, S. P. Kinneir, C. P. Mead, H. Strudwick.
1913	*Special Portrait:* John Wisden.
1914	M. W. Booth, G. Gunn, J. W. Hitch, A. E. Relf, Hon. L. H. Tennyson.
1915	J. W. H. T. Douglas, P. G. H. Fender, H. T. W. Hardinge, D. J. Knight, S. G. Smith.
1916–17	No portraits appeared.
1918	*School Bowlers of the Year:* H. L. Calder, J. E. D'E. Firth, C. H. Gibson, G. A. Rotherham, G. T. S. Stevens.
1919	*Five Public School Cricketers of the Year:* P. W. Adams, A. P. F. Chapman, A. C. Gore, L. P. Hedges, N. E. Partridge.
1920	*Five Batsmen of the Year:* A. Ducat, E. H. Hendren, P. Holmes, H. Sutcliffe, E. Tyldesley.
1921	*Special Portrait:* P. F. Warner.
1922	H. Ashton, J. L. Bryan, J. M. Gregory, C. G. Macartney, E. A. McDonald.
1923	A. W. Carr, A. P. Freeman, C. W. L. Parker, A. C. Russell, A. Sandham.
1924	*Five Bowlers of the Year:* A. E. R. Gilligan, R. Kilner, G. G. Macaulay, C. H. Parkin, M. W. Tate.
1925	R. H. Catterall, J. C. W. MacBryan, H. W. Taylor, R. K. Tyldesley, W. W. Whysall.
1926	*Special Portrait:* J. B. Hobbs.
1927	G. Geary, H. Larwood, J. Mercer, W. A. Oldfield, W. M. Woodfull.
1928	R. C. Blunt, C. Hallows, W. R. Hammond, D. R. Jardine, V. W. C. Jupp.
1929	L. E. G. Ames, C. Duckworth, M. Leyland, S. J. Staples, J. C. White.
1930	E. H. Bowley, K. S. Duleepsinhji, H. G. Owen-Smith, R. W. V. Robins, R. E. S. Wyatt.
1931	D. G. Bradman, C. V. Grimmett, B. H. Lyon, I. A. R. Peebles, M. J. Turnbull.

1932	W. E. Bowes, C. S. Dempster, James Langridge, Nawab of Pataudi sen., H. Verity.
1933	W. E. Astill, F. R. Brown, A. S. Kennedy, C. K. Nayudu, W. Voce.
1934	A. H. Bakewell, G. A. Headley, M. S. Nichols, L. F. Townsend, C. F. Walters.
1935	S. J. McCabe, W. J. O'Reilly, A. A. E. Paine, W. H. Ponsford, C. I. J. Smith.
1936	H. B. Cameron, E. R. T. Holmes, B. Mitchell, D. Smith, A. W. Wellard.
1937	C. J. Barnett, W. H. Copson, A. R. Gover, V. M. Merchant, T. S. Worthington.
1938	T. W. J. Goddard, J. Hardstaff jun., L. Hutton, J. H. Parks, E. Paynter.
1939	H. T. Bartlett, W. A. Brown, D. C. S. Compton, K. Farnes, A. Wood.
1940	L. N. Constantine, W. J. Edrich, W. W. Keeton, A. B. Sellers, D. V. P. Wright.
1941– 46	No portraits appeared.
1947	A. V. Bedser, L. B. Fishlock, V. (M. H.) Mankad, T. P. B. Smith, C. Washbrook.
1948	M. P. Donnelly, A. Melville, A. D. Nourse, J. D. Robertson, N. W. D. Yardley.
1949	A. L. Hassett, W. A. Johnston, R. R. Lindwall, A. R. Morris, D. Tallon.
1950	T. E. Bailey, R. O. Jenkins, John Langridge, R. T. Simpson, B. Sutcliffe.
1951	T. G. Evans, S. Ramadhin, A. L. Valentine, E. D. Weekes, F. M. M. Worrell.
1952	R. Appleyard, H. E. Dollery, J. C. Laker, P. B. H. May, E. A. B. Rowan.
1953	H. Gimblett, T. W. Graveney, D. S. Sheppard, W. S. Surridge, F. S. Trueman.
1954	R. N. Harvey, G. A. R. Lock, K. R. Miller, J. H. Wardle, W. Watson.
1955	B. Dooland, Fazal Mahmood, W. E. Hollies, J. B. Statham, G. E. Tribe.
1956	M. C. Cowdrey, D. J. Insole, D. J. McGlew, H. J. Tayfield, F. H. Tyson.
1957	D. Brookes, J. W. Burke, M. J. Hilton, G. R. A. Langley, P. E. Richardson.
1958	P. J. Loader, A. J. McIntyre, O. G. Smith, M. J. Stewart, C. L. Walcott.
1959	H. L. Jackson, R. E. Marshall, C. A. Milton, J. R. Reid, D. Shackleton.
1960	K. F. Barrington, D. B. Carr, R. Illingworth, G. Pullar, M. J. K. Smith.
1961	N. A. T. Adcock, E. R. Dexter, R. A. McLean, R. Subba Row, J. V. Wilson.
1962	W. E. Alley, R. Benaud, A. K. Davidson, W. M. Lawry, N. C. O'Neill.
1963	D. Kenyon, Mushtaq Mohammad, P. H. Parfitt, P. J. Sharpe, F. J. Titmus.
1964	D. B. Close, C. C. Griffith, C. C. Hunte, R. B. Kanhai, G. S. Sobers.
1965	G. Boycott, P. J. Burge, J. A. Flavell, G. D. McKenzie, R. B. Simpson.
1966	K. C. Bland, J. H. Edrich, R. C. Motz, P. M. Pollock, R. G. Pollock.
1967	R. W. Barber, B. L. D'Oliveira, C. Milburn, J. T. Murray, S. M. Nurse.
1968	Asif Iqbal, Hanif Mohammad, K. Higgs, J. M. Parks, Nawab of Pataudi jun.
1969	J. G. Binks, D. M. Green, B. A. Richards, D. L. Underwood, O. S. Wheatley.
1970	B. F. Butcher, A. P. E. Knott, Majid Khan, M. J. Procter, D. J. Shepherd.
1971	J. D. Bond, C. H. Lloyd, B. W. Luckhurst, G. M. Turner, R. T. Virgin.
1972	G. G. Arnold, B. S. Chandrasekhar, L. R. Gibbs, B. Taylor, Zaheer Abbas.
1973	G. S. Chappell, D. K. Lillee, R. A. L. Massie, J. A. Snow, K. R. Stackpole.
1974	K. D. Boyce, B. E. Congdon, K. W. R. Fletcher, R. C. Fredericks, P. J. Sainsbury.
1975	D. L. Amiss, M. H. Denness, N. Gifford, A. W. Greig, A. M. E. Roberts.
1976	I. M. Chappell, P. G. Lee, R. B. McCosker, D. S. Steele, R. A. Woolmer.
1977	J. M. Brearley, C. G. Greenidge, M. A. Holding, I. V. A. Richards, R. W. Taylor.
1978	I. T. Botham, M. Hendrick, A. Jones, K. S. McEwan, R. G. D. Willis.
1979	D. I. Gower, J. K. Lever, C. M. Old, C. T. Radley, J. N. Shepherd.
1980	J. Garner, S. M. Gavaskar, G. A. Gooch, D. W. Randall, B. C. Rose.
1981	K. J. Hughes, R. D. Jackman, A. J. Lamb, C. E. B. Rice, V. A. P. van der Bijl.
1982	T. M. Alderman, A. R. Border, R. J. Hadlee, Javed Miandad, R. W. Marsh.
1983	Imran Khan, T. E. Jesty, A. I. Kallicharran, Kapil Dev, M. D. Marshall.
1984	M. Amarnath, J. V. Coney, J. E. Emburey, M. W. Gatting, C. L. Smith.
1985	M. D. Crowe, H. A. Gomes, G. W. Humpage, J. Simmons, S. Wettimuny.
1986	P. Bainbridge, R. M. Ellison, C. J. McDermott, N. V. Radford, R. T. Robinson.
1987	J. H. Childs, G. A. Hick, D. B. Vengsarkar, C. A. Walsh, J. J. Whitaker.
1988	J. P. Agnew, N. A. Foster, D. P. Hughes, P. M. Roebuck, Salim Malik.
1989	K. J. Barnett, P. J. L. Dujon, P. A. Neale, F. D. Stephenson, S. R. Waugh.
1990	S. J. Cook, D. M. Jones, R. C. Russell, R. A. Smith, M. A. Taylor.
1991	M. A. Atherton, M. Azharuddin, A. R. Butcher, D. L. Haynes, M. E. Waugh.
1992	C. E. L. Ambrose, P. A. J. DeFreitas, A. A. Donald, R. B. Richardson, Waqar Younis.
1993	N. E. Briers, M. D. Moxon, I. D. K. Salisbury, A. J. Stewart, Wasim Akram.
1994	D. C. Boon, I. A. Healy, M. G. Hughes, S. K. Warne, S. L. Watkin.
1995	B. C. Lara, D. E. Malcolm, T. A. Munton, S. J. Rhodes, K. C. Wessels.
1996	D. G. Cork, P. A. de Silva, A. R. C. Fraser, A. Kumble, D. A. Reeve.
1997	S. T. Jayasuriya, Mushtaq Ahmed, Saeed Anwar, P. V. Simmons, S. R. Tendulkar.

1998	M. T. G. Elliott, S. G. Law, G. D. McGrath, M. P. Maynard, G. P. Thorpe.
1999	I. D. Austin, D. Gough, M. Muralitharan, A. Ranatunga, J. N. Rhodes.
2000	C. L. Cairns, R. Dravid, L. Klusener, T. M. Moody, Saqlain Mushtaq.
Cricketers of the Century	D. G. Bradman, G. S. Sobers, J. B. Hobbs, S. K. Warne, I. V. A. Richards.
2001	M. W. Alleyne, M. P. Bicknell, A. R. Caddick, J. L. Langer, D. S. Lehmann.
2002	A. Flower, A. C. Gilchrist, J. N. Gillespie, V. V. S. Laxman, D. R. Martyn.
2003	M. L. Hayden, A. J. Hollioake, N. Hussain, S. M. Pollock, M. P. Vaughan.
2004	C. J. Adams, A. Flintoff, I. J. Harvey, G. Kirsten, G. C. Smith.
2005	A. F. Giles, S. J. Harmison, R. W. T. Key, A. J. Strauss, M. E. Trescothick.
2006	M. J. Hoggard, S. P. Jones, B. Lee, K. P. Pietersen, R. T. Ponting.
2007	P. D. Collingwood, D. P. M. D. Jayawardene, Mohammad Yousuf, M. S. Panesar, M. R. Ramprakash.
2008	I. R. Bell, S. Chanderpaul, O. D. Gibson, R. J. Sidebottom, Zaheer Khan.
2009	J. M. Anderson, D. M. Benkenstein, M. V. Boucher, N. D. McKenzie, S. C. Taylor.
2010	S. C. J. Broad, M. J. Clarke, G. Onions, M. J. Prior, G. P. Swann.
2011	E. J. G. Morgan, C. M. W. Read, Tamim Iqbal, I. J. L. Trott.

Note: From 2000 to 2003 the award was made on the basis of all cricket round the world, not just the English season. This ended in 2004 with the start of *Wisden's* Leading Cricketer in the World award. Jayasuriya in 1997 was chosen for his "influence" on the English season, stemming from the 1996 World Cup.

CRICKETERS OF THE YEAR: AN ANALYSIS

The special portrait of John Wisden in 1913 marked the 50th anniversary of his retirement as a player – and the 50th edition of the Almanack. Wisden died in 1884. The special portraits of P. F. Warner in 1921 and J. B. Hobbs in 1926 were in addition to their earlier selection as a Cricketer of the Year in 1904 and 1909 respectively. These three special portraits and the Cricketers of the Century in 2000 are excluded from the following analysis.

The four players selected to be Cricketers of the Year for 2011 bring the number chosen since selection began in 1889 to 561. They have been chosen from 40 different teams as follows:

Derbyshire	13	Northants	14	Australians	71	Cheltenham College	1
Durham	5	Nottinghamshire	29	South Africans	26	Cranleigh School	1
Essex	23	Somerset	18	West Indians	24	Eton College	2
Glamorgan	11	Surrey	49	New Zealanders	8	Malvern College	1
Gloucestershire	17	Sussex	22	Indians	14	Rugby School	1
Hampshire	15	Warwickshire	22	Pakistanis	12	Tonbridge School	1
Kent	26	Worcestershire	15	Sri Lankans	5	Univ. Coll. School	1
Lancashire	33	Yorkshire	42	Zimbabweans	1	Uppingham School	1
Leicestershire	8	Oxford Univ.	6	Bangladeshis	1	Winchester College	1
Middlesex	28	Cambridge Univ.	10	Staffordshire	1	England Women	1

Notes: Schoolboys were chosen in 1918 and 1919 when first-class cricket was suspended due to war. The total of sides comes to 580 because 19 players played regularly for two teams (England excluded) in the year for which they were chosen.

Types of Players

Of the 561 Cricketers of the Year, 284 are best classified as batsmen, 161 as bowlers, 79 as all-rounders and 37 as wicketkeepers or wicketkeeper-batsmen.

Research: Robert Brooke

DATES IN CRICKET HISTORY

c. 1550   Evidence of cricket being played in Guildford, Surrey.

1610   Reference to "cricketing" between Weald and Upland and North Downs near Chevening, Kent.

1611   Randle Cotgrave's French–English dictionary translates the French word "crosse" as a cricket staff.
Two youths fined for playing cricket at Sidlesham, Sussex.

1624   Jasper Vinall becomes first man known to be killed playing cricket: hit by a bat while trying to catch the ball – at Horsted Green, Sussex.

1676   First reference to cricket being played abroad, by British residents in Aleppo, Syria.

1694   Two shillings and sixpence paid for a "wagger" (wager) about a cricket match at Lewes.

1697   First reference to "a great match" with 11 players a side for fifty guineas, in Sussex.

1700   Cricket match announced on Clapham Common.

1709   First recorded inter-county match: Kent v Surrey.

1710   First reference to cricket at Cambridge University.

1727   Articles of Agreement written governing the conduct of matches between the teams of the Duke of Richmond and Mr Brodrick of Peperharow, Surrey.

1729   Date of earliest surviving bat, belonging to John Chitty, now in the pavilion at The Oval.

1730   First recorded match at the Artillery Ground, off City Road, central London, still the cricketing home of the Honourable Artillery Company.

1744   Kent beat All England by one wicket at the Artillery Ground.
First known version of the Laws of Cricket, issued by the London Club, formalising the pitch as 22 yards long.

c. 1767   Foundation of the Hambledon Club in Hampshire, the leading club in England for the next 30 years.

1769   First recorded century, by John Minshull for Duke of Dorset's XI v Wrotham.

1771   Width of bat limited to $4\frac{1}{4}$ inches, where it has remained ever since.

1774   LBW law devised.

1776   Earliest known scorecards, at the Vine Club, Sevenoaks, Kent.

1780   The first six-seamed cricket ball, manufactured by Dukes of Penshurst, Kent.

1787   First match at Thomas Lord's first ground, Dorset Square, Marylebone – White Conduit Club v Middlesex.
Formation of Marylebone Cricket Club by members of the White Conduit Club.

1788   First revision of the Laws of Cricket by MCC.

1794   First recorded inter-schools match: Charterhouse v Westminster.

1795   First recorded case of a dismissal "leg before wicket".

1806   First Gentlemen v Players match at Lord's.

1807   First mention of "straight-armed" (i.e. round-arm) bowling: by John Willes of Kent.

1809   Thomas Lord's second ground opened at North Bank, St John's Wood.

1811   First recorded women's county match: Surrey v Hampshire at Ball's Pond, London.

1814   Lord's third ground opened on its present site, also in St John's Wood.

1827   First Oxford v Cambridge match, at Lord's. A draw.

1828   MCC authorise the bowler to raise his hand level with the elbow.

1833   John Nyren publishes his classic *Young Cricketer's Tutor* and *The Cricketers of My Time*.

1836   First North v South match, for many years regarded as the principal fixture of the season.

c. **1836**   Batting pads invented.

1841   General Lord Hill, commander-in-chief of the British Army, orders that a cricket ground be made an adjunct of every military barracks.

1844   First official international match: Canada v United States.

1845   First match played at The Oval.

1846   The All-England XI, organised by William Clarke, begins playing matches, often against odds, throughout the country.

1849   First Yorkshire v Lancashire match.

c. **1850**   Wicketkeeping gloves first used.

1850   John Wisden bowls all ten batsmen in an innings for North v South.

1853   First mention of a champion county: Nottinghamshire.

1858   First recorded instance of a hat being awarded to a bowler taking three wickets with consecutive balls.

1859   First touring team to leave England, captained by George Parr, draws enthusiastic crowds in the US and Canada.

1864   "Overhand bowling" authorised by MCC.
                John Wisden's *The Cricketer's Almanack* first published.

1868   Team of Australian aborigines tour England.

1873   W. G. Grace becomes the first player to record 1,000 runs and 100 wickets in a season.
                First regulations restricting county qualifications, often regarded as the official start of the County Championship.

1877   First Test match: Australia beat England by 45 runs in Melbourne.

1880   First Test in England: a five-wicket win against Australia at The Oval.

1882   Following England's first defeat by Australia in England, an "obituary notice" to English cricket in the *Sporting Times* leads to the tradition of The Ashes.

1889   Present Lord's pavilion begun.
                  South Africa's first Test match.
                  Declarations first authorised, but only on the third day, or in a one-day match.

1890   County Championship officially constituted.

1895   W. G. Grace scores 1,000 runs in May, and reaches his 100th hundred.

1899   A. E. J. Collins scores 628 not out in a junior house match at Clifton College, the highest individual score in any match.
                  Selectors choose England team for home Tests, instead of host club issuing invitations.

1900   Six-ball over becomes the norm, instead of five.

1909   Imperial Cricket Conference (ICC – now the International Cricket Council) set up, with England, Australia and South Africa the original members.

1910   Six runs given for any hit over the boundary, instead of only for a hit out of the ground.

1912   First and only triangular Test series played in England, involving England, Australia and South Africa.

1915   W. G. Grace dies, aged 67.

1926   Victoria score 1,107 v New South Wales at Melbourne, the record total for a first-class innings.

1928   West Indies' first Test match.
                  A. P. Freeman of Kent and England becomes the only player to take more than 300 first-class wickets in a season: 304.

1930   New Zealand's first Test match.
                  Donald Bradman's first tour of England: he scores 974 runs in the five Ashes Tests, still a record for any Test series.

1931   Stumps made higher (28 inches not 27) and wider (nine inches not eight – this was optional until 1947).

1932   India's first Test match.
                  Hedley Verity of Yorkshire takes ten wickets for ten runs v Nottinghamshire, the best innings analysis in first-class cricket.

1932-33   The Bodyline tour of Australia in which England bowl at batsmen's bodies with a packed leg-side field to neutralise Bradman's scoring.

1934   Jack Hobbs retires, with 197 centuries and 61,237 runs, both records.
                  First women's Test: Australia v England at Brisbane.

1935   MCC condemn and outlaw Bodyline.

1947   Denis Compton of Middlesex and England scores a record 3,816 runs in an English season.

1948   First five-day Tests in England.
Bradman concludes Test career with a second-ball duck at The Oval and a batting average of 99.94 – four runs short of 100.

1952   Pakistan's first Test match.

1953   England regain the Ashes after a 19-year gap, the longest ever.

1956   Jim Laker of England takes 19 wickets for 90 v Australia at Manchester, the best match analysis in first-class cricket.

1960   First tied Test, Australia v West Indies at Brisbane.

1963   Distinction between amateurs and professionals abolished in English cricket.
The first major one-day tournament begins in England: the Gillette Cup.

1969   Limited-over Sunday league inaugurated for first-class counties.

1970   Proposed South African tour of England cancelled: South Africa excluded from international cricket because of their government's apartheid policies.

1971   First one-day international: Australia v England at Melbourne.

1975   First World Cup: West Indies beat Australia in final at Lord's.

1976   First women's match at Lord's, England v Australia.

1977   Centenary Test at Melbourne, with identical result to the first match: Australia beat England by 45 runs.
Australian media tycoon Kerry Packer signs 51 of the world's leading players in defiance of the cricketing authorities.

1978   Graham Yallop of Australia wears a protective helmet to bat in a Test match, the first player to do so.

1979   Packer and official cricket agree peace deal.

1981   England beat Australia in Leeds Test, after following on with bookmakers offering odds of 500–1 against them winning.

1982   Sri Lanka's first Test match.

1991   South Africa return, with a one-day international in India.

1992   Zimbabwe's first Test Match.
Durham become first county since Glamorgan in 1921 to attain first-class status.

1993   The ICC ceases to be administered by MCC, becoming an independent organisation with its own chief executive.

1994   Brian Lara becomes the first player to pass 500 in a first-class innings: 501 not out for Warwickshire v Durham.

2000   South Africa's captain Hansie Cronje banned from cricket for life after admitting receiving bribes from bookmakers in match-fixing scandal.
Bangladesh's first Test match.
County Championship split into two divisions, with promotion and relegation.
The Laws of Cricket revised and rewritten.

2001   Sir Donald Bradman dies, aged 92.

2003   Twenty20 Cup, a 20-over-per-side evening tournament, inaugurated in England.

2004 Lara becomes the first man to score 400 in a Test innings, against England.

2005 England regain the Ashes after 16 years.

2006 Pakistan become first team to forfeit a Test, for refusing to resume at The Oval.
England lose the Ashes after 462 days, the shortest tenure in history.
Shane Warne becomes the first man to take 700 Test wickets.

2007 Australia complete 5–0 Ashes whitewash for the first time since 1920-21.
Australia win the World Cup for the third time running.
India beat Pakistan in the final of the inaugural World Twenty20 tournament.

2008 Indian Premier League of 20-over matches launched, featuring many international
  players on lucrative contracts.
Durham win the County Championship for the first time.
Sachin Tendulkar becomes the leading scorer in Tests, passing Brian Lara.
England lose a $US20m winner-takes-all Twenty20 match in Antigua.

2009 Terrorists attack Sri Lankan team bus in Lahore.
Umpire Decision Review System implemented by the ICC.

2010 Tendulkar scores the first double-century in a one-day international, against South
  Africa; later in the year, he scores his 50th Test century.
Muttiah Muralitharan retires from Test cricket, after taking his 800th wicket.
Pakistan bowl three no-balls in Lord's Test against England, which an ICC independent
  tribunal later find to have been deliberate, resulting in bans for the three players
  concerned.

2011 England complete 3–1 Ashes win in Australia, with their third innings victory of the
  series.

ANNIVERSARIES IN 2011-12

COMPILED BY STEVEN LYNCH

2011

April 1   Major E. G. "Teddy" Wynyard (England) born, 1861.
Hampshire amateur batsman who played five Tests for England in the "Golden Age".

May 5   Norman "Buddy" Oldfield (England) born, 1911.
Lancashire batsman who made 80 in his only Test, in 1939, and later umpired Tests as well.

May 20   E. M. Grace (England) dies, 1911.
The older brother of W. G., Edward Mills Grace was a fine player himself.

May 20   Ted Alletson (Nottinghamshire) scores 189 in 90 minutes, 1911.
One of cricket's most famous innings: the last 142 runs came in just 40 minutes, with the No. 11 at the other end, against Sussex at Hove.

May 28   Bob Crisp (South Africa) born, 1911.
Fast bowler and decorated war hero who twice took four wickets in four balls in first-class matches.

July 3   Joe Hardstaff, jun. (England) born, 1911.
Stylish batsman who made four Test centuries, including 169* v Australia at The Oval in 1938.

July 8   First recorded match at Lord's "Middle" Ground, 1811.
This ground was used for only three years before the Regent's Canal was run through it and MCC moved to the current site.

July 8   Ken Farnes (England) born, 1911.
Tall Essex fast bowler who took 60 wickets in 15 Tests: killed in action in 1941.

August 6   Norman Gordon (South Africa) born, 1911.
Fast bowler who, at the end of 2010, was the oldest surviving Test cricketer.

August 29   Warwickshire win the County Championship for the first time, 1911.
Warwickshire finished with a points percentage of 74.00 from 20 matches, just ahead of Kent's 73.46% from 26.

September 6   W. E. "Bill" Alley (Somerset) reaches 3,000 runs in the season, 1961.
Alley, who was 42, is the last to reach this landmark in an English first-class summer.

September 11   Lala Amarnath (India) born, 1911.
Competitive all-rounder – and future captain – who scored India's first Test century in 1933-34.

September 16   Percy Chapman (England) dies, 1961.
Flamboyant Kent amateur who captained England to Ashes success in Australia in 1928-29.

October 4   Reg Perks (England) born, 1911.
Stalwart fast bowler who took over 2,000 wickets for Worcestershire.

October 12   Frederick "Nutty" Martin (England) born, 1861.
Kent fast bowler who took 12 wickets in his only Ashes Test, at The Oval in 1890.

October 12   Vijay Merchant (India) born, 1911.
Stylish batsman whose first-class average of 71.64 has been bettered only by Don Bradman.

November 5   Sir Timothy O'Brien (England) born, 1861.
Irish-born baronet who captained England in South Africa in 1895-96.

November 23   Merv Hughes (Australia) born, 1961.
Combative and charismatic fast bowler who finished with 212 Test wickets.

December 13   Reggie Duff (Australia) dies, 1911.
Made a century – batting at No. 10 – on Test debut v England at Melbourne in 1903-04.

2012

January 1   First English team plays in Australia, 1862.
The team captained by Surrey's H. H. Stephenson played several matches, mostly against sides of 22 players.

January 12   Richie Richardson (West Indies) born, 1962.
Mild-mannered murderer of bowling attacks who scored 5,949 runs in 86 Tests.

March 1   England complete 4–1 Ashes victory at Sydney, 1912.
Jack Hobbs scored 662 runs; S. F. Barnes took 34 wickets and Frank Foster 32 as England won the last four Tests.

March 30   Jack Cowie (New Zealand) born, 1912.
Fast bowler of whom Wisden *said in 1938: "Had he been an Australian, he might have been termed a wonder of the age."*

April 15   J. B. Thayer (Philadelphia) dies on the *Titanic*, 1912.
Thayer, from a prominent American cricketing family, was the only known first-class cricketer lost in the disaster.

ONE HUNDRED YEARS AGO

from Wisden Cricketers' Almanack 1912

THE MARYLEBONE CLUB IN 1911   The 124th Annual General Meeting of the Marylebone CC was held in the pavilion at Lord's on Wednesday afternoon, May 3rd [1911]. The Earl of Londesborough (the retiring president) took the chair.

- The annual report, which was unanimously adopted, stated that in 1910 the Club consisted of 5,219 members – a decrease of 29 from the previous year – of whom 4,657 paid, 353 were life members, and 386 were abroad.
- During the season 124,275 people passed through the turnstiles at Lord's, as against 199,318 in 1909.
- The drainage of the ground has been thoroughly overhauled, and it is hoped that the effect of the works will be to encourage a more rapid run off of storm water. Close attention has been given to the removal of the plantain roots.
- In consequence of the wet season there was a loss on the working of the refreshment department in 1910 of £140 0s. 4d.
- Owing to complaints, the sale of daily and evening papers in the pavilion will be discontinued.

GLOUCESTERSHIRE v NORTHAMPTONSHIRE, AT CHELTENHAM, AUGUST 21, 22, 23 [1911]   In the third game of the Cheltenham Festival, Gloucestershire proved successful by 79 runs. As a matter of record it should be stated that owing to the railway strike the Northampton cricketers journeyed to Cheltenham by motor cars.

YORKSHIRE v NORTHAMPTONSHIRE, AT DEWSBURY, JUNE 23, 24, 25 [1911]   Rain stopping play soon after lunch on Friday and preventing any cricket at all on Saturday, so little progress was made with this match that, with less than an innings completed on each side, the game furnished the solitary instance during the whole summer of a Championship contest yielding no points to either side… During the interval on Thursday – Coronation Day – the large company present joined in singing the National Anthem.

SUSSEX v NOTTINGHAMSHIRE, AT BRIGHTON, MAY 18, 19, 20 [1911]   A phenomenal display of driving on the part of Edward Alletson rendered this match memorable. Alletson went in when Notts in their second innings, with seven men out, were only nine runs ahead. Before lunch, he took fifty minutes to make 47, but on resuming hit away with such extraordinary power and freedom that he added 142 out of 152 for the last wicket in forty minutes, actually scoring his last 89 runs in fifteen minutes. Twice he sent the ball over the stand, and on six other occasions cleared the ring, while in one over from Killick that included two no-balls he hit three 6's and four 4's – 34 runs in all. His glorious innings was made up by eight 6's, twenty-three 4's, four 3's, ten 2's and seventeen singles.

CRICKETER OF THE YEAR, HERBERT STRUDWICK   In one respect he is unique. I cannot remember any wicket-keeper who was so marvellously quick on his feet. One catch that he made last season in the Leicestershire match at the Oval, flinging himself down full length in front of the wicket, was the most remarkable thing of its kind I have ever seen. Strudwick bubbles over with an energy that sometimes carries him over too far. I can see no advantage in his habit of leaving his post and chasing the ball to the boundary. The practice is simply the result of over-keenness, but as it does no good it ought to be checked, and I would suggest to the Surrey captain a system of modest fines, the amount being increased by each offence.

FIFTY YEARS AGO

from Wisden Cricketers' Almanack 1962

NOTES BY THE EDITOR [Norman Preston]   The automatic disappearance of South Africa from the Imperial Cricket Conference when the country ceased to be a member of the British Commonwealth has left a complex problem. South Africa's matches against other countries can no longer be classified as Tests… Efforts are being made to find a means of restoring South Africa to membership of the Conference. This move may receive support from England, Australia and New Zealand, whom South Africa meet on the field, but it is likely to be vehemently opposed by the West Indies, India and Pakistan, who because of the colour question, have never met the Springboks at cricket… Pakistan, I understand, are putting forward a novel suggestion to form a kind of "second division" to incorporate all the cricket-playing countries which are not Conference members, such as Ceylon, Malaya, Kenya, East and West Africa, Hong Kong, Singapore, Canada, the United States of America, Denmark and Holland. In the end, everything may depend upon whether or not South Africa will agree to change their ideas and consent to play against the "coloured" countries.

HAMPSHIRE IN 1961   Hampshire carried off the County Championship crown for the first time in their history after a long and exciting battle with Yorkshire and Middlesex. Sixty-six years of fruitless striving for the honour terminated at Bournemouth on September 1… Ingleby-Mackenzie, who has always been known for his views on "brighter" cricket, revealed a hitherto unknown talent for master strategy… He balanced perfectly the ability of his batsmen – especially Marshall – to score quickly with his bowling strength. It was on this that Hampshire's success was almost entirely based… Of Hampshire's nineteen victories in the Championship, ten were the direct result of declarations in their third innings and only two counties, Northamptonshire and Middlesex, managed to escape defeat – both drew – after being set a task.

LEAGUE CRICKET IN 1961   Test cricketers of the West Indies dominated the Lancashire Leagues in 1961 and Garfield Sobers proved himself the most deadly all-rounder the Central Lancashire League has seen in years. Ensuring that his club, Radcliffe, won both the championship and the Wood Cup, Sobers hit 1,008 runs… and captured 144 wickets… In the Lancashire League Seymour Nurse came direct from the West Indies tour of Australia and scored 1,129 runs… and Conrad Hunte was close behind with 933 runs… The championship went to Accrington, for whom Wesley Hall claimed 106 wickets at 11.28 each.

AUSTRALIANS IN ENGLAND, 1961   The tour was a personal triumph for Richie Benaud, possibly the most popular captain of any overseas team to come to Great Britain. As soon as he arrived Benaud emphasised that he and his men wanted to play attractive cricket wherever they went and that they desired to keep the game moving by bowling as many overs as possible when they were in the field… The whole series was virtually decided during the twenty minutes which preceded the tea interval on the last day at Old Trafford. England began the fourth innings wanting 256 to win in three hours fifty minutes. They lost Pullar at 40 and then while Subba Row remained steady, Dexter gave such a wonderful display of driving that he kept England well up with the clock. At five minutes to four England's total stood at 150 for one wicket. Then Dexter, having hit 76 out of 110 in eighty-four minutes, fell to Benaud and by a quarter-past four England had slumped to 165 for five wickets. The rest was plain sailing for Australia and the man of the moment was Benaud who claimed six wickets.

CRICKETER OF THE YEAR, W. E. ALLEY   Most players think of retiring at the age that "Bill" Alley entered county cricket. He was 38 when he joined Somerset in 1957 and... boasts that he never had a single coaching lesson in his life... At one time, he was a boxer of renown in Australia. As a professional pugilist he won all his 28 contests and had set his sights on the World Welterweight title when, of all things, a mishap at cricket compelled him to hang up his gloves. His jaw was broken by a cricket ball. Twenty stitches were necessary and he never boxed again... His ideal life would be a cricket professional on Saturday and a chicken-farmer the rest of the week... At one time, Alley thought that 1961 would be his last cricket season, but after his phenomenal success and the generous Testimonial he received, he is convinced that he should endeavour to continue for at least two more summers.

NORTH v SOUTH, AT BLACKPOOL, SEPTEMBER 6, 7, 8 [1961]   The highlight of the match was a century in fifty-two minutes in the South's first innings by Prideaux – the fastest in first-class cricket since 1937... On the second day, 685 runs were scored for the loss of twenty-three wickets.

Only once have more runs been scored in a day in a first-class match, when the Australians made 721 on the first day against Essex at Southend in 1948.

from Wisden Cricketers' Almanack 1963

MCC TEAM IN INDIA, PAKISTAN AND CEYLON, 1961-62 [by Leslie Smith]   Between October 8, 1961 and February 20, 1962, the MCC cricketers took part in one of the most strenuous tours undertaken by any side. They played 24 matches in India, Pakistan and Ceylon, including eight five-day Tests, three in Pakistan and five in India. The original tour plans had to be changed because India subsequently arranged a trip to West Indies in the February. This meant a strange programme, with three games, including one Test, being played in Pakistan, followed by the complete Indian part of the tour and then a return to Pakistan to finish the programme. Winning the fourth and fifth Test Matches, the first three having been drawn, India defeated England in a series for the only time in history. England gained partial compensation by winning the rubber against Pakistan, being victorious in the first Test, and three months later, drawing the next two.

A solitary success in eight Tests could scarcely be regarded as satisfactory from England's point of view, even though there were extenuating circumstances. In the first place England were not represented by their full-scale side. Players like Cowdrey, Statham and Trueman would almost certainly have made a big difference and, perhaps, tipped the balance in England's favour, for there was never much between the Test teams.

This business of leading players declining certain tours needs consideration by the authorities. India rightly point out that they have never seen a full-strength MCC side and resent the fact that the star players make a habit of turning down the trip. Admittedly English players find the tour harder and less comfortable than any other, but this scarcely justifies players, once they are established, picking and choosing which tour they want to make. It is no secret that in general the men who go to India, Pakistan and Ceylon regard themselves as a second eleven, often play like it and are caustic about the stars who stay at home. India and Pakistan, for their parts, deserve the best, for the enthusiasm there has grown remarkably in a few years.

Close on two million people watched the MCC, with approximately 1,200,000 at the eight Tests... The English players never did accustom themselves to the different type of food, the all-too-many functions and the unusual living conditions, but in the main they were a cheerful set of players.

Compiled by Christopher Lane

HONOURS AND AWARDS 2010-11

In 2010-11, the following were decorated for their services to cricket:

Queen's Birthday Honours, 2010: F. C. Duckworth (D/L method; services to mathematics and cricket) MBE; D. S. English (services to cricket and to charity) CBE; A. J. Lewis (D/L method; services to mathematics and cricket) MBE; W. K. McCallan (former Irish captain; services to cricket in Northern Ireland) MBE.

Queen's Birthday Honours (Australia), 2010: A. C. Gilchrist (Western Australia and Australia; services to cricket and the community) AM; A. T. Lantry (services to education and the NSW Cricket Association) OAM; R. J. Webster (services to cricket in Shoalhaven) OAM.

House of Lords: Former England Women's captain Rachael Heyhoe-Flint was appointed a working peer on November 19, 2010.

New Year's Honours, 2011: S. D. Hill (player, umpire and MCC Laws subcommittee; services to women's cricket) MBE; R. Jackson (president of Northumberland & Tyneside Senior Cricket League; services to cricket in the North-East) MBE; P. M. Walker (Glamorgan and England, broadcaster; services to cricket) MBE.

New Year's Honours (New Zealand), 2011: D. O. Neely (Wellington and Auckland, administrator and writer; services to cricket) MNZM; H. M. Tiffen (Canterbury and New Zealand Women; services to women's cricket) MNZM.

Australia Day Honours, 2011: L. D. Cooper (Queensland; services to cricket in Queensland) OAM; B. S. Fry (Grange CC, Adelaide; services to cricket) OAM; J. C. Kilborn (regional coaching co-ordinator; services to cricket in New South Wales) OAM; B. D. Phelan (deputy chairman of Queensland Cricket and director of Cricket Australia; services to cricket) OAM; C. G. Rackemann (Queensland and Australia; services to cricket as player, coach and administrator) OAM; M. J. Silver (director of Cricket Australia; services to cricket as administrator) OAM; E. O. Thorburn (Cootamundra CC; services to cricket) OAM; M. J. Walters (Queensland, former administrator, services to cricket) OAM.

ICC AWARDS

The International Cricket Council's seventh annual award ceremony, presented in association with the Federation of International Cricketers' Associations, was held in Bangalore in October 2010.

Sir Garfield Sobers Trophy (Cricketer of the Year)	**Sachin Tendulkar**
Test Player of the Year	**Virender Sehwag**
One-day International Player of the Year	**A. B. de Villiers**
Women's Cricketer of the Year	**Shelley Nitschke**
Emerging Player of the Year	**Steve Finn**
Associate/Affiliate Player of the Year	**Ryan ten Doeschate**
Twenty20 International Performance of the Year	**Brendon McCullum**
Umpire of the Year	**Aleem Dar**
Team Best Exemplifying the Spirit of Cricket	**New Zealand**

ICC DEVELOPMENT PROGRAMME AWARDS

The International Cricket Council announced the global winners of its 2009 Development Programme Awards in March 2010. Each award secured $2,000 of equipment for the winning national cricket body.

Best Overall Cricket Development Programme	**Namibia Cricket Board**
Best Women's Cricket Initiative	**Deutsche Cricket Bund**
Best Junior Cricket Initiative	**Cricket Association of Nepal**
Best Cricket Promotion and Marketing Programme	**Cricket Papua New Guinea**
Best "Spirit of Cricket" Initiative in partnership with UNAIDS/UNICEF	**Israel Cricket Association**
Lifetime Service Award	**Binaya Raj Pandey (Nepal)**
Volunteers of the Year	**James Bennett (Ireland) and S. Gopalkrishnan (Indonesia)**
Photo of the Year	**Rob O'Connor (Cricket Ireland)**

ALLAN BORDER MEDAL

Shane Watson won the Allan Border Medal, for the best Australian international player of the past 12 months, at a ceremony in February 2010. Previous winners were Glenn McGrath, Steve Waugh, Matthew Hayden, Adam Gilchrist, Ricky Ponting (four times), Michael Clarke (twice) and Brett Lee. Watson received 125 votes from team-mates, umpires and journalists, well ahead of Clarke (90) and Mitchell Johnson (87). Watson was also named One-Day International Player of the Year, while **Simon Katich** was Test Cricketer of the Year. **Michael Klinger** of South Australia was State Player of the Year for the second time running; **John Hastings**, who helped Victoria to the Sheffield Shield title a month later, was Bradman Young Player of the Year. **Shelley Nitschke** won her second successive award as Women's International Cricketer of the Year.

BRIT INSURANCE ENGLAND PLAYERS OF THE YEAR AWARDS

England spinner **Graeme Swann** won the men's Brit Insurance England Cricketer of the Year Award in May 2010. Since his Test debut in December 2008, he had taken 85 wickets in 18 Tests, rising to second place in the ICC Test bowler rankings in March 2010, and also played some forceful innings. The women's award went to **Katherine Brunt**, who had figures of 4–2–6–3 in England's victory in the Women's World Twenty20 final against New Zealand in June 2009. She previously won in 2006. **Chris Edwards**, a 17-year-old all-rounder in the England Learning Disability Team, which reached the final of a triangular tournament with Australia and South Africa in December 2009, won the ECB Disability Cricketer of the Year Award.

PROFESSIONAL CRICKETERS' ASSOCIATION AWARDS

The following awards were announced at the PCA's annual dinner in September 2010.

Reg Hayter Cup (NatWest PCA Player of the Year)	**Neil Carter**
John Arlott Cup (NatWest PCA Young Player of the Year)	**Adam Lyth**
ECB Special Award	**Johnny Dennis**
PCA Special Merit Award	**Peter Walker**
Sky Sports Sixes League	**Ryan ten Doeschate**
Impossible is Nothing Award	**Josh Mierkalns**
FTI England Player of the Summer	**Graeme Swann**
NatWest One-Day International Player of the Year	**Eoin Morgan**

Tournament Players of the Year: **Adil Rashid** (County Championship), **Chaminda Vaas** (Friends Provident T20), **Jacques Rudolph** (Clydesdale Bank 40).

FTI Team of the Year **Jimmy Adams, *Marcus Trescothick, Jonathan Trott, James Hildreth, Darren Stevens, †Steve Davies, Stuart Broad, Adil Rashid, Graeme Swann, Neil Carter, Alfonso Thomas.**

WALTER LAWRENCE TROPHY

The Walter Lawrence Trophy for the fastest century in 2010 was won by **Adam Gilchrist**, playing for Middlesex, who reached three figures in 47 balls, including nine fours and seven sixes, against Kent at Canterbury on June 11. The 38-year-old Gilchrist had taken over the captaincy on the same day after Shaun Udal stepped down. Gilchrist received £5,000 along with the trophy. This was the third time in the Trophy's 75-year history that the competition was extended to cover all senior cricket in England; traditionally, it was reserved for the fastest first-class hundred against authentic bowling (in 2010, this was for the second year running scored for Somerset to beat Yorkshire at Taunton in a fourth-innings run-chase; following Peter Trego's 54-ball hundred in 2009, James Hildreth did it in 68 balls to help Somerset score 364 inside 66 overs on May 20). Cardiff's left-handed opener **Rory Burns** won the Walter Lawrence award for the highest score by a batsman from the University/MCCU teams against a first-class county or another university side; he made 230*, with 23 fours and four sixes in 345 balls, away to Oxford in an MCC Universities Championship match in April, and received a silver medallion and £1,000.

CRICKET WRITERS' CLUB AWARDS

The Young Cricketer of the Year was **Steve Finn** of Middlesex, who had made his Test debut in March. The Peter Smith Memorial Award "for services to the presentation of cricket to the public" went to **Vanburn Holder**, for his role as a cricketer for Barbados, Worcestershire and West Indies and then as an umpire. The Cricket Book of the Year award, sponsored by npower, was given to *Golden Boy: Kim Hughes and the bad old days of Australian cricket* by Christian Ryan.

A list of Young Cricketers from 1950 to 2004 appears in Wisden 2005, page 995. *A list of Peter Smith Award winners from 1992 to 2004 appears in* Wisden 2005, page 745.

DENIS COMPTON SCHOLAR

The Compton Scholar is the overall winner of an award given to the most promising player at each county, organised by NBC Sports Management since 1997. The winner in 2010 was 21-year-old batsman **Alex Hales**, who helped Nottinghamshire to win the County Championship.

SECOND ELEVEN PLAYER OF THE YEAR

The Association of Cricket Statisticians and Historians named **Michael Richardson** of Durham the Les Hatton Second Eleven Player of the Year for 2010. A wicketkeeper-batsman like his father, the former South African Test player Dave Richardson, he scored 562 runs at 70.25 in nine Second Eleven Championship matches, including 133* against MCC Young Cricketers and 159* against Derbyshire, and made 30 catches and two stumpings.

GROUNDSMEN OF THE YEAR

Mick Hunt of Lord's was named the ECB's Groundsman of the Year for his four-day pitches, with Bill Gordon of The Oval – which had won for seven years running from 2002 to 2008 – as runner-up and Paul Marshall at Northampton winning a commendation. The one-day title went to **Andy Mackay** from Hove, ahead of Andy Fogarty at Headingley, with Steve Rouse commended for Edgbaston. **Robbie Thackray** at Scarborough won the outgrounds prize, with Adam Shoesmith of Whitgift School runner-up; Ross Spry (Cheltenham), Vic Demain (Uxbridge) and Tim Nicholls (Chesterfield) were all commended. **John Moden** at Fenner's in Cambridge retained the award for the best MCC Universities pitch, and Will Relf at Loughborough was second.

CRICKET SOCIETY AWARDS

Wetherell Award for Leading First-class All-rounder	**Neil Carter** (Warwickshire)
Wetherell Award for Leading Schools All-rounder	**Zafar Ansari** (Hampton School)
Most Promising Young Cricketer	**Chris Woakes** (Warwickshire)
Most Promising Young Woman Cricketer	**Heather Knight** (Berkshire)
Sir John Hobbs Silver Jubilee Memorial Prize	**Kilshen Velani** (Brentwood School)
(for outstanding Under-16 schoolboy)	
A. A. Thomson Fielding Prize (for best schoolboy fielder)	**Jonathan Tattersall** (Yorkshire)
Christopher Box-Grainger Memorial Trophy	**Woodfield School** (Kingsbury)
(for schools promoting cricket to underprivileged children)	
Don Rowan Memorial Trophy	**Bensham Manor School** (Croydon)
(for primary schools promoting cricket)	
Ian Jackson Award (for services to cricket)	**David English**
The Perry-Lewis/Kershaw Trophy (for contribution to the Cricket Society XI)	**Adrian Gale**

WOMBWELL CRICKET LOVERS' SOCIETY AWARDS

George Spofforth Cricketer of the Year	**Marcus Trescothick**
Brian Sellers County Captain of the Year	**Andrew Gale**
C. B. Fry Young Cricketer of the Year	**Adam Lyth**
Arthur Wood Wicketkeeper of the Year	**Chris Read**
Learie Constantine Fielder of the Year	**Martin van Jaarsveld**

Denis Compton Memorial Award for Flair	**Neil Carter**
Dr Taylor Award (best performance in Yorks–Lancs matches)	**Adil Rashid**
Les Bailey Most Promising Young Yorkshire Player	**Jonathan Bairstow**
Ted Umbers Services to Yorkshire Cricket	**Stuart Anderson***
J. M. Kilburn Cricket Writer of the Year	**Andrew Collomosse**
Jack Fingleton Cricket Commentator of the Year	**Kevin Howells**

* *Stuart Anderson is a long-serving Yorkshire coach working with youngsters and YCB/ECB Regional representative.*

NPOWER PHOTO COMPETITION

Patrick Eagar won first prize in the npower Photo Competition in November 2010 for a photograph of Umar Akmal being run out during the Oval Test between England and Pakistan in August.

ECB OSCAs

The ECB presented the 2010 NatWest Outstanding Service to Cricket Awards to volunteers from recreational cricket in October. The winners were:

Young Volunteer Award (for under-25s)   **Tom Mills** (Lancashire)
   Raised funds for Formby CC and took over the management of the club ground following the sudden departure of the groundsman; umpires voted his pitch best in the league.

Building Partnerships Award   **Michael Prentice** (Sussex)
   Raised over £120,000 for St Andrew's CC and worked with local council and community groups to create the Burgess Hill Street20 project, introducing cricket to young people in a disused car park.

Behind the Scenes Award   **Kevin Malone** (Derbyshire)
   Treasurer and assistant groundsman at Killamarsh Juniors CC; assists with the organisation of all junior teams and plays a major role in fundraising and seeking sponsorship for the club.

Leagues and Boards Award   **Sheila Hill** (Middlesex)
   Has developed the junior women's game and been involved with the Women's Southern Cricket League since its inception; an influential figure on the MCC Laws subcommittee.

Officiating and scoring   **Peter Marshall** (Hampshire)
   Spearheaded the creation of the Blind Cricket England & Wales Umpires Panel, recruiting 25 umpires from across the country to stand in league and cup matches.

NatWest CricketForce Award   **Lisa Phillimore** (Sussex)
   Attained significant sponsorship and recruited 130 volunteers for Bexhill Cricket Club NatWest CricketForce events.

Outstanding contribution to disability cricket   **Martin Haselock** (Leicestershire)
   Tournament organiser for the County Championship for cricketers with disabilities.

Lifetime Achiever   **Bob Cherry** (Staffordshire)
   Seventy years in Staffordshire cricket as a player, umpire, and administrator and in the development of boys' and girls' cricket.

ACS STATISTICIAN OF THE YEAR

In March 2011, the Association of Cricket Statisticians and Historians awarded the Statistician of the Year trophy to **Martin Wilson** for his research into 18th-century scorecards published in *Great Cricket Matches 1772–1800*.

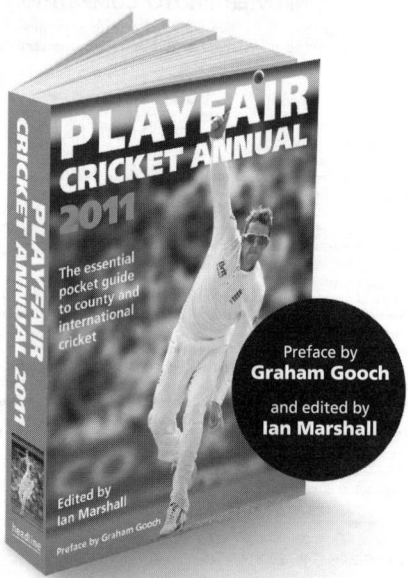

2011 FIXTURES

np Test	npower Test match
LV=CC D1/D2	LV= County Championship Division 1/Division 2
CB40	Clydesdale Bank 40-over one-day league
FP T20	Friends Provident Twenty20 Cup
NW T20I	NatWest Twenty20 International
Univs	University matches
♀	Day/night or floodlit game

Note: All matches of three days or more are first-class, except those involving England Women, England Under-19 or Leeds/Bradford or Cardiff MCCUs.

Sun Mar 27–Wed 30	**Friendly**	MCC	v Nottinghamshire	Abu Dhabi ♀
Sat Apr 2–Mon 4	**Univs**	Cambridge MCCU	v Essex	Cambridge
		Glamorgan	v Cardiff MCCU	Cardiff
		Loughboro MCCU	v Northamptonshire	Loughborough
		Oxford MCCU	v Lancashire	Oxford
		Worcestershire	v Leeds/Brad MCCU	Worcester
Sun Apr 3–Tue 5	**Univs**	Durham MCCU	v Durham	Durham
Fri Apr 8–Mon 11	**LV=CC D1**	Hampshire	v Durham	Southampton
		Lancashire	v Sussex	Liverpool
		Worcestershire	v Yorkshire	Worcester
	LV=CC D2	Essex	v Kent	Chelmsford
		Gloucestershire	v Derbyshire	Bristol
		Leicestershire	v Glamorgan	Leicester
		Surrey	v Northamptonshire	The Oval
Sat Apr 9–Mon 11	**Univs**	Cambridge MCCU	v Middlesex	Cambridge
		Durham MCCU	v Warwickshire	Durham
		Oxford MCCU	v Nottinghamshire	Oxford
		Somerset	v Cardiff MCCU	Taunton Vale
Thu Apr 14–Sun 17	**LV=CC D1**	Nottinghamshire	v Hampshire	Nottingham
		Somerset	v Warwickshire	Taunton
		Yorkshire	v Durham	Leeds
	LV=CC D2	Derbyshire	v Leicestershire	Derby
		Glamorgan	v Gloucestershire	Cardiff
		Middlesex	v Essex	Lord's
		Northamptonshire	v Kent	Northampton
Wed Apr 20–Sat 23	**LV=CC D1**	Durham	v Sussex	Chester-le-St
		Lancashire	v Somerset	Liverpool
		Worcestershire	v Warwickshire	Worcester
		Yorkshire	v Nottinghamshire	Leeds
	LV=CC D2	Derbyshire	v Middlesex	Derby
		Glamorgan	v Surrey	Cardiff
		Northamptonshire	v Essex	Northampton
Wed Apr 20–Fri 22	**Univs**	Gloucestershire	v Cardiff MCCU	Bristol
		Hampshire	v Leeds/Brad MCCU	Southampton
		Leicestershire	v Loughboro MCCU	Leicester
Sun Apr 24	**CB40**	Durham	v Scotland	Chester-le-St
		Gloucestershire	v Glamorgan	Bristol
		Hampshire	v Warwickshire	Southampton
		Lancashire	v Unicorns	Manchester
		Northamptonshire	v Leicestershire	Northampton
		Nottinghamshire	v Somerset	Nottingham
		Worcestershire	v Middlesex	Worcester
		Yorkshire	v Netherlands	Leeds

Mon Apr 25	CB40	Derbyshire	v Netherlands	Derby
		Leicestershire	v Scotland	Leicester
Tue Apr 26–Fri 29	LV=CC D1	Durham	v Warwickshire	Chester-le-St
		Nottinghamshire	v Worcestershire	Nottingham
		Sussex	v Lancashire	Hove
	LV=CC D2	Essex	v Glamorgan	Chelmsford
		Kent	v Gloucestershire	Canterbury
Wed Apr 27–Sat 30	LV=CC D1	Hampshire	v Somerset	Southampton
	LV=CC D2	Leicestershire	v Derbyshire	Leicester
		Middlesex	v Surrey	Lord's
Wed Apr 27–Fri 29	Univs	Durham MCCU	v Yorkshire	Durham
Sun May 1	CB40	Derbyshire	v Sussex	Derby
		Durham	v Northamptonshire	Chester-le-St
		Essex	v Nottinghamshire	Chelmsford
		Kent	v Worcestershire	Canterbury
		Middlesex	v Netherlands	Lord's
		Surrey	v Scotland	The Oval
		Unicorns	v Somerset	Wormsley
		Warwickshire	v Leicestershire	Birmingham
Mon May 2	CB40	Essex	v Lancashire	Chelmsford
		Gloucestershire	v Unicorns	Bristol
		Hampshire	v Surrey	Southampton
		Leicestershire	v Durham	Leicester
		Middlesex	v Kent	Lord's
		Somerset	v Glamorgan	Taunton
		Sussex	v Netherlands	Hove
		Warwickshire	v Scotland	Birmingham
		Yorkshire	v Derbyshire	Leeds
Wed May 4–Sat 7	LV=CC D1	Hampshire	v Sussex	Southampton
		Nottinghamshire	v Yorkshire	Nottingham
		Somerset	v Worcestershire	Taunton
		Warwickshire	v Lancashire	Birmingham
	LV=CC D2	Gloucestershire	v Middlesex	Bristol
		Kent	v Northamptonshire	Canterbury
		Surrey	v Leicestershire	The Oval
Wed May 4–Fri 6	Univs	Derbyshire	v Leeds/Brad MCCU	Derby
Fri May 6	CB40	Glamorgan	v Essex	Cardiff ⚲
Sun May 8	CB40	Kent	v Yorkshire	Canterbury
		Lancashire	v Glamorgan	Manchester
		Northamptonshire	v Warwickshire	Northampton
		Somerset	v Gloucestershire	Taunton
		Surrey	v Leicestershire	The Oval
		Sussex	v Middlesex	Hove
		Unicorns	v Essex	Bury St Edmunds
		Worcestershire	v Derbyshire	Worcester
Tue May 10–Fri 13	LV=CC D1	Durham	v Somerset	Chester-le-St
		Sussex	v Nottinghamshire	Hove
	LV=CC D2	Derbyshire	v Essex	Derby
		Glamorgan	v Kent	Cardiff
Wed May 11–Sat 14	LV=CC D1	Warwickshire	v Worcestershire	Birmingham
		Yorkshire	v Hampshire	Leeds
	LV=CC D2	Gloucestershire	v Northamptonshire	Bristol
Wed May 11–Fri 13	Univs	Cambridge MCCU	v Surrey	Cambridge
Thu May 12	CB40	Netherlands	v Middlesex	Deventer

Sat May 14–Mon 16	Tour Match	Middlesex	v Sri Lanka	Uxbridge
Sun May 15	CB40	Durham	v Hampshire	Chester-le-St
		Glamorgan	v Gloucestershire	Cardiff
		Leicestershire	v Warwickshire	Leicester
		Scotland	v Surrey	Edinburgh
		Somerset	v Lancashire	Taunton
		Sussex	v Derbyshire	Hove
		Unicorns	v Nottinghamshire	Wormsley
		Yorkshire	v Kent	Leeds
Mon May 16	CB40	Scotland	v Durham	Edinburgh
Tue May 17	CB40	Middlesex	v Worcestershire	Lord's ♥
		Netherlands	v Derbyshire	Deventer
Wed May 18–Sat 21	LV=CC D1	Lancashire	v Yorkshire	Liverpool
		Nottinghamshire	v Warwickshire	Nottingham
		Sussex	v Somerset	Hove
		Worcestershire	v Durham	Worcester
	LV=CC D2	Leicestershire	v Gloucestershire	Leicester
		Surrey	v Essex	Whitgift School
Wed May 18–Fri 20	Univs	Kent	v Loughboro MCCU	Canterbury
Thu May 19–Sun 22	LV=CC D2	Middlesex	v Glamorgan	Lord's
	Tour Match	England Lions	v Sri Lanka	Derby
Fri May 20	CB40	Hampshire	v Northamptonshire	Southampton ♥
Sun May 22	CB40	Essex	v Unicorns	Chelmsford
		Kent	v Sussex	Canterbury
		Lancashire	v Nottinghamshire	Manchester
		Northamptonshire	v Scotland	Northampton
		Surrey	v Hampshire	Whitgift School
		Warwickshire	v Durham	Birmingham
		Worcestershire	v Yorkshire	Worcester
Tue May 24–Fri 27	LV=CC D1	Hampshire	v Lancashire	Southampton
		Somerset	v Yorkshire	Taunton
		Warwickshire	v Durham	Birmingham
	LV=CC D2	Essex	v Middlesex	Chelmsford
		Kent	v Derbyshire	Canterbury
		Northamptonshire	v Leicestershire	Northampton
		Surrey	v Glamorgan	The Oval
Wed May 25	CB40	Nottinghamshire	v Gloucestershire	Nottingham ♥
Wed May 25–Fri 27	Univs	Oxford MCCU	v Sussex	Oxford
Thu May 26–Mon 30	1st np Test	**ENGLAND**	**v SRI LANKA**	**Cardiff**
Sun May 29–Wed Jun 1	LV=CC D1	Durham	v Lancashire	Chester-le-St
		Sussex	v Yorkshire	Hove
		Worcestershire	v Nottinghamshire	Worcester
	LV=CC D2	Derbyshire	v Surrey	Derby
		Gloucestershire	v Essex	Bristol
		Kent	v Leicestershire	Tunbridge Wells
		Northamptonshire	v Glamorgan	Northampton
Wed Jun 1	FP T20	Hampshire	v Somerset	Southampton ♥
Thu Jun 2	FP T20	Derbyshire	v Lancashire	Derby ♥
		Durham	v Warwickshire	Chester-le-St
		Surrey	v Gloucestershire	The Oval ♥
		Sussex	v Essex	Hove ♥

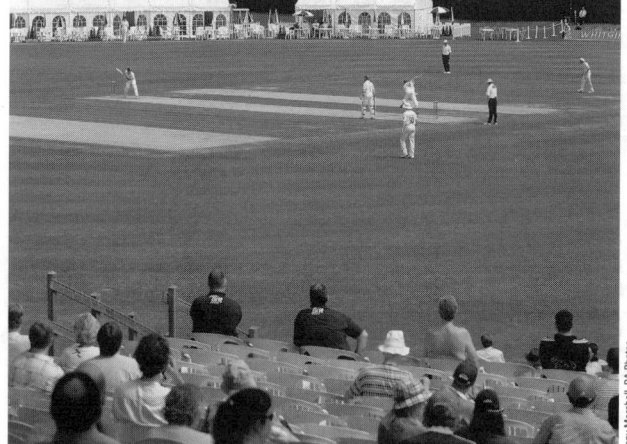

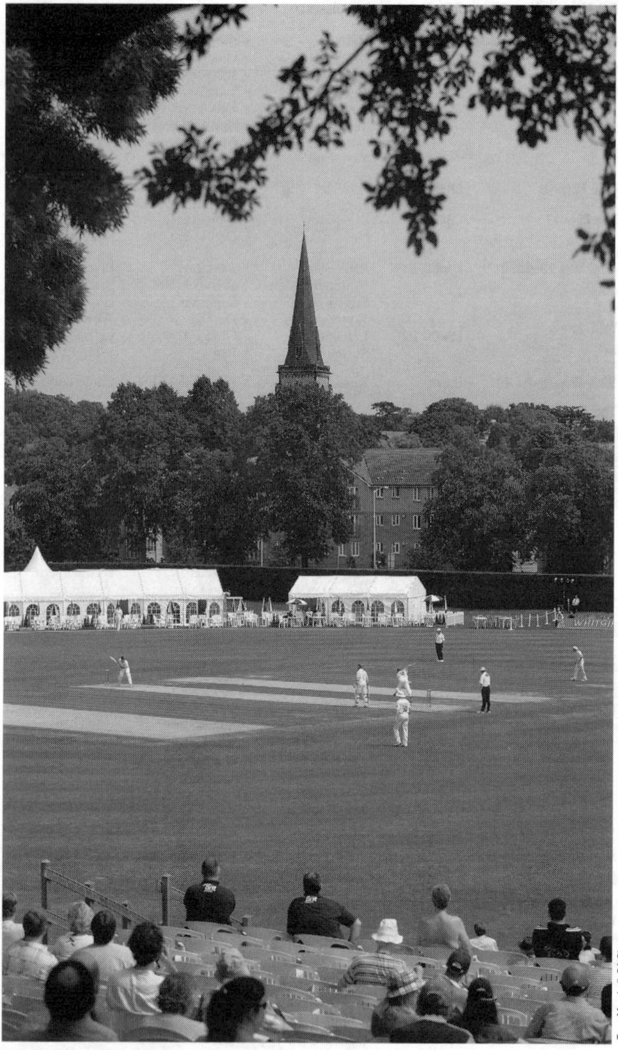

Tony Marshall, PA Photos

Whitgift School, Croydon.

Fri Jun 3–Tue 7	2nd np Test	**ENGLAND**	**v SRI LANKA**	**Lord's**
Fri Jun 3	FP T20	Essex	v Gloucestershire	Chelmsford ♥
		Glamorgan	v Middlesex	Cardiff ♥
		Hampshire	v Surrey	Southampton ♥
		Kent	v Somerset	Tunbridge Wells
		Lancashire	v Worcestershire	Manchester
		Northamptonshire	v Leicestershire	Northampton ♥
		Nottinghamshire	v Derbyshire	Nottingham
		Yorkshire	v Warwickshire	Leeds
Sun Jun 5	FP T20	Gloucestershire	v Sussex	Bristol
		Kent	v Hampshire	Tunbridge Wells
		Leicestershire	v Lancashire	Leicester
		Nottinghamshire	v Yorkshire	Nottingham
		Somerset	v Middlesex	Taunton
		Warwickshire	v Northamptonshire	Birmingham
		Worcestershire	v Durham	Worcester
Wed Jun 8	FP T20	Essex	v Sussex	Chelmsford ♥
		Hampshire	v Glamorgan	Southampton ♥
		Lancashire	v Leicestershire	Manchester
		Warwickshire	v Nottinghamshire	Birmingham
Thu Jun 9	FP T20	Middlesex	v Essex	Lord's ♥
		Northamptonshire	v Durham	Northampton
		Yorkshire	v Worcestershire	Leeds
Fri Jun 10	FP T20	Derbyshire	v Durham	Derby ♥
		Gloucestershire	v Hampshire	Gloucester
		Lancashire	v Yorkshire	Manchester
		Leicestershire	v Nottinghamshire	Leicester
		Somerset	v Kent	Taunton
		Surrey	v Glamorgan	The Oval ♥
		Sussex	v Middlesex	Hove ♥
		Worcestershire	v Northamptonshire	Worcester
Fri Jun 10–Sun 12	Tour Match	Essex	v Sri Lanka	Chelmsford
Sat Jun 11	FP T20	Glamorgan	v Kent	Cardiff ♥
		Nottinghamshire	v Warwickshire	Nottingham
Sun Jun 12	FP T20	Durham	v Derbyshire	Chester-le-St
		Gloucestershire	v Surrey	Gloucester
		Leicestershire	v Warwickshire	Leicester
		Somerset	v Hampshire	Taunton
		Worcestershire	v Lancashire	Worcester
		Yorkshire	v Northamptonshire	Leeds
Mon Jun 13	FP T20	Surrey	v Essex	The Oval ♥
Tue Jun 14	FP T20	Durham	v Nottinghamshire	Chester-le-St
		Middlesex	v Glamorgan	Richmond
		Sussex	v Somerset	Hove ♥
Wed Jun 15	FP T20	Derbyshire	v Worcestershire	Derby ♥
		Essex	v Somerset	Chelmsford ♥
		Kent	v Gloucestershire	Beckenham
		Northamptonshire	v Warwickshire	Northampton
Thu Jun 16–Mon 20	3rd np Test	**ENGLAND**	**v SRI LANKA**	**Southampton**
Thu Jun 16	FP T20	Middlesex	v Sussex	Lord's ♥
	FP T20	Nottinghamshire	v Durham	Nottingham ♥

Fri Jun 17	FP T20	Glamorgan	v Hampshire	Cardiff ⚲
		Gloucestershire	v Essex	Bristol
		Leicestershire	v Durham	Leicester
		Northamptonshire	v Derbyshire	Northampton ⚲
		Somerset	v Surrey	Taunton
		Sussex	v Kent	Hove ⚲
		Warwickshire	v Worcestershire	Birmingham
		Yorkshire	v Lancashire	Leeds
Sat Jun 18–Tue 21	LV=CC D1	Durham	v Yorkshire	Chester-le-St
		Worcestershire	v Hampshire	Worcester
Sat Jun 18	FP T20	Derbyshire	v Leicestershire	Derby
		Kent	v Middlesex	Canterbury ⚲
		Nottinghamshire	v Northamptonshire	Nottingham
Sun Jun 19–Wed 22	LV=CC D2	Leicestershire	v Northamptonshire	Leicester
	LV=CC D2	Middlesex	v Kent	Lord's
		Surrey	v Gloucestershire	The Oval
Sun Jun 19	FP T20	Warwickshire	v Lancashire	Birmingham
Mon Jun 20–Thu 23	LV=CC D1	Nottinghamshire	v Lancashire	Nottingham
		Warwickshire	v Somerset	Birmingham
Tue Jun 21	FP T20	Glamorgan	v Essex	Cardiff ⚲
Wed Jun 22	FP T20	Yorkshire	v Derbyshire	Leeds
	Tour Match	Worcestershire	v Sri Lanka	Worcester
Thu Jun 23	Women's T20I	**England Women**	**v NZ Women**	**Chelmsford**
		Australia Women	**v India Women**	**Billericay**
	FP T20	Essex	v Hampshire	Chelmsford ⚲
		Glamorgan	v Sussex	Cardiff ⚲
		Surrey	v Middlesex	The Oval ⚲
Fri Jun 24	FP T20	Durham	v Lancashire	Chester-le-St
		Essex	v Surrey	Chelmsford ⚲
		Hampshire	v Gloucestershire	Southampton ⚲
		Middlesex	v Kent	Uxbridge
		Nottinghamshire	v Leicestershire	Nottingham
		Somerset	v Sussex	Taunton
		Warwickshire	v Yorkshire	Birmingham
		Worcestershire	v Derbyshire	Worcester
Sat Jun 25	NW T20I	**ENGLAND**	**v SRI LANKA**	**Bristol**
	Women's T20I	**England Women**	**v Australia Women**	**Bristol**
		India Women	**v NZ Women**	**Clifton College**
Sat Jun 25–Tue 28	LV=CC D2	Essex	v Northamptonshire	Chelmsford
Sat Jun 25	FP T20	Leicestershire	v Worcestershire	Leicester
Sun Jun 26	Women's T20I	**England Women**	**v India Women**	**Taunton**
		Australia Women	**v NZ Women**	**Taunton Vale**
	FP T20	Derbyshire	v Warwickshire	Leek
		Durham	v Leicestershire	Chester-le-St
		Kent	v Surrey	Beckenham
		Middlesex	v Gloucestershire	Uxbridge
		Nottinghamshire	v Lancashire	Nottingham
		Somerset	v Glamorgan	Taunton
		Worcestershire	v Yorkshire	Worcester
	Varsity	Oxford U	v Cambridge U	Lord's
Mon Jun 27	Women's T20I	**Quadrangular Tournament Final**		**Southampton**
	Women's T20I	**Third-Place Playoff**		**Aldershot**

Mon Jun 27–Thu 30	LV=CC D1	Lancashire	v Durham	Liverpool
	LV=CC D2	Glamorgan	v Derbyshire	Cardiff
		Middlesex	v Gloucestershire	Uxbridge
Mon Jun 27	FP T20	Hampshire	v Sussex	Southampton ♥
	Univs	MCCU Challenge Final		Lord's
Tue Jun 28	ODI	**ENGLAND**	**v SRI LANKA**	**The Oval** ♥
Wed Jun 29–Sat Jul 2	LV=CC D1	Sussex	v Warwickshire	Arundel
Wed Jun 29	FP T20	Leicestershire	v Yorkshire	Leicester
		Northamptonshire	v Worcestershire	Milton Keynes
Thu Jun 30	Women's ODI	**England Women**	**v India Women**	**Derby** ♥
		Australia Women	**v NZ Women**	**Chesterfield**
	FP T20	Hampshire	v Kent	Southampton ♥
		Surrey	v Somerset	The Oval ♥
Fri Jul 1	ODI	**ENGLAND**	**v SRI LANKA**	**Leeds**
	FP T20	Derbyshire	v Nottinghamshire	Derby ♥
		Glamorgan	v Surrey	Cardiff ♥
		Gloucestershire	v Somerset	Bristol
		Kent	v Essex	Canterbury ♥
		Lancashire	v Durham	Manchester
		Middlesex	v Hampshire	Uxbridge
		Northamptonshire	v Yorkshire	Northampton ♥
		Worcestershire	v Leicestershire	Worcester
Sat Jul 2	Women's ODI	**England Women**	**v NZ Women**	**Derby**
		Australia Women	**v India Women**	**Chesterfield**
	FP T20	Essex	v Middlesex	Chelmsford
Sun Jul 3	ODI	**ENGLAND**	**v SRI LANKA**	**Lord's**
	FP T20	Durham	v Worcestershire	Chester-le-St
		Kent	v Glamorgan	Canterbury
		Lancashire	v Derbyshire	Manchester
		Leicestershire	v Northamptonshire	Leicester
		Sussex	v Gloucestershire	Arundel
		Yorkshire	v Nottinghamshire	Leeds
Mon Jul 4	FP T20	Somerset	v Essex	Bath
		Surrey	v Sussex	Whitgift School
Tue Jul 5–Fri Jul 8	Varsity	Cambridge U	v Oxford U	Fenner's
Tue Jul 5	Women's ODI	**England Women**	**v Australia Women**	**Lord's**
		India Women	**v NZ Women**	**Southgate**
	FP T20	Glamorgan	v Somerset	Cardiff ♥
		Worcestershire	v Nottinghamshire	Worcester
Wed Jul 6	ODI	**ENGLAND**	**v SRI LANKA**	**Nottingham** ♥
	FP T20	Gloucestershire	v Kent	Bristol
		Hampshire	v Essex	Southampton ♥
		Warwickshire	v Derbyshire	Birmingham
		Yorkshire	v Leicestershire	Leeds
Thu Jul 7	Women's ODI	**Quadrangular Tournament Final**		**Wormsley**
	Women's ODI	**Third-Place Playoff**		**Aston Rowant**
	FP T20	Middlesex	v Surrey	Lord's ♥
		Sussex	v Glamorgan	Hove ♥
Fri Jul 8	FP T20	Durham	v Yorkshire	Chester-le-St
		Essex	v Glamorgan	Chelmsford ♥
		Kent	v Sussex	Canterbury ♥
		Leicestershire	v Derbyshire	Leicester

Fri Jul 8	FP T20	Northamptonshire	v Nottinghamshire	Northampton ♀
		Somerset	v Gloucestershire	Taunton
		Surrey	v Hampshire	The Oval ♀
		Worcestershire	v Warwickshire	Worcester
Sat Jul 9	ODI	**ENGLAND**	**v SRI LANKA**	**Manchester**
	FP T20	Derbyshire	v Northamptonshire	Derby
Sun Jul 10–Wed 13	LV=CC D2	Leicestershire	v Essex	Leicester
		Surrey	v Kent	The Oval
Sun Jul 10	FP T20	Gloucestershire	v Glamorgan	Bristol
		Lancashire	v Nottinghamshire	Manchester
		Middlesex	v Somerset	Southgate
		Sussex	v Hampshire	Hove
		Yorkshire	v Durham	Scarborough
Mon Jul 11–Thu 14	LV=CC D1	Nottinghamshire	v Somerset	Nottingham
		Sussex	v Hampshire	Hove
		Yorkshire	v Worcestershire	Scarborough
	LV=CC D2	Derbyshire	v Glamorgan	Derby
Mon Jul 11	FP T20	Warwickshire	v Durham	Birmingham
Tue Jul 12	FP T20	Northamptonshire	v Lancashire	Northampton
Wed Jul 13	FP T20	Gloucestershire	v Middlesex	Bristol
		Lancashire	v Warwickshire	Manchester ♀
Thu Jul 14	FP T20	Durham	v Northamptonshire	Chester-le-St
		Surrey	v Kent	The Oval ♀
Fri Jul 15	FP T20	Derbyshire	v Yorkshire	Derby ♀
		Essex	v Kent	Chelmsford ♀
		Glamorgan	v Gloucestershire	Cardiff ♀
		Hampshire	v Middlesex	Southampton ♀
		Lancashire	v Northamptonshire	Manchester ♀
		Nottinghamshire	v Worcestershire	Nottingham ♀
		Sussex	v Surrey	Hove ♀
		Warwickshire	v Leicestershire	Birmingham ♀
Fri Jul 15–Sun 17	Tour Match	Somerset	v India	Taunton
Sat Jul 16	U19 ODI	England U19	v South Africa U19	Birmingham
Sun Jul 17	CB40	Durham	v Surrey	Chester-le-St
		Glamorgan	v Unicorns	Cardiff
		Leicestershire	v Hampshire	Leicester
		Netherlands	v Kent	Rotterdam
		Nottinghamshire	v Essex	Nottingham
		Scotland	v Northamptonshire	Edinburgh
		Yorkshire	v Middlesex	Leeds
Mon Jul 18	CB40	Lancashire	v Somerset	Manchester ♀
		Netherlands	v Worcestershire	Rotterdam
		Nottinghamshire	v Unicorns	Nottingham
		Scotland	v Warwickshire	Edinburgh
	U19 ODI	England U19	v South Africa U19	Northampton
Tue Jul 19	CB40	Hampshire	v Durham	Southampton ♀
Wed Jul 20–Sat 23	LV=CC D1	Hampshire	v Nottinghamshire	Southampton
		Warwickshire	v Sussex	Birmingham
		Yorkshire	v Lancashire	Leeds
	LV=CC D2	Gloucestershire	v Kent	Cheltenham
		Northamptonshire	v Derbyshire	Northampton
		Surrey	v Middlesex	Guildford

Wed Jul 20	CB40	Essex	v Glamorgan	Chelmsford ☂
Wed Jul 20–Sat 23	Tour Match	Leicestershire	v Sri Lanka A	Leicester
Thu Jul 21–Mon 25	1st np Test	**ENGLAND**	**v INDIA**	**Lord's**
Thu Jul 21–Sun 24	LV=CC D1	Somerset	v Durham	Taunton
Thu Jul 21	U19 ODI	England U19	v South Africa U19	Arundel
Sat Jul 23	U19 ODI	England U19	v South Africa U19	Arundel
Sun Jul 24	CB40	Derbyshire	v Kent	Derby
		Gloucestershire	v Nottinghamshire	Cheltenham
		Leicestershire	v Northamptonshire	Leicester
		Surrey	v Warwickshire	Guildford
		Unicorns	v Lancashire	Colwyn Bay
		Worcestershire	v Sussex	Worcester
Mon Jul 25	CB40	Northamptonshire	v Hampshire	Northampton ☂
Tue Jul 26–Fri 29	LV=CC D1	Lancashire	v Nottinghamshire	Southport
		Worcestershire	v Somerset	Worcester
Tue Jul 26	CB40	Gloucestershire	v Essex	Cheltenham
		Warwickshire	v Hampshire	Birmingham ☂
	U19 ODI	England U19	v South Africa U19	Taunton
Wed Jul 27–Sat 30	LV=CC D2	Essex	v Leicestershire	Southend
		Glamorgan	v Northamptonshire	Swansea
		Gloucestershire	v Surrey	Cheltenham
Wed Jul 27	CB40	Sussex	v Yorkshire	Hove ☂
Wed Jul 27–Sat 30	Tour Match	Durham	v Sri Lanka A	Chester-le-St
Thu Jul 28	CB40	Middlesex	v Derbyshire	Lord's ☂
	U19 ODI	England U19	v South Africa U19	Canterbury
Fri Jul 29–Tue Aug 2	2nd np Test	**ENGLAND**	**v INDIA**	**Nottingham**
Fri Jul 29–Mon Aug 1	LV=CC D2	Middlesex	v Derbyshire	Lord's
Sat Jul 30	CB40	Netherlands	v Sussex	Amstelveen
	U19 ODI	England U19	v South Africa U19	Canterbury
Sun Jul 31	CB40	Durham	v Warwickshire	Chester-le-St
		Essex	v Somerset	Southend
		Glamorgan	v Nottinghamshire	Swansea
		Gloucestershire	v Lancashire	Cheltenham
		Hampshire	v Leicestershire	Southampton
		Netherlands	v Yorkshire	Amstelveen
		Worcestershire	v Kent	Worcester
Mon Aug 1–Thu 4	LV=CC D1	Lancashire	v Warwickshire	Liverpool
Tue Aug 2–Fri 5	LV=CC D1	Durham	v Nottinghamshire	Chester-le-St
		Hampshire	v Yorkshire	Southampton
		Somerset	v Sussex	Taunton
	LV=CC D2	Glamorgan	v Essex	Cardiff
		Leicestershire	v Kent	Leicester
	Tour Match	England Lions	v Sri Lanka A	Leeds
Wed Aug 3	CB40	Surrey	v Northamptonshire	The Oval ☂
Thu Aug 4	CB40	Derbyshire	v Worcestershire	Derby ☂
Fri Aug 5	CB40	Lancashire	v Gloucestershire	Manchester ☂
Fri Aug 5–Sat 6	Tour Match	Northamptonshire	v India	Northampton

Sat Aug 6	FP T20 Quarter-Finals			
Sun Aug 7	FP T20 Quarter-Finals			
Mon Aug 8	FP T20 Quarter-Finals			
	Tour Match	Lancashire	v Sri Lanka A	Manchester
Wed Aug 10–Sun 14	3rd np Test	**ENGLAND**	**v INDIA**	**Birmingham**
Wed Aug 10–Sat 13	LV=CC D1	Durham	v Hampshire	Chester-le-St
		Sussex	v Worcestershire	Horsham
	LV=CC D2	Derbyshire	v Gloucestershire	Derby
		Kent	v Surrey	Canterbury
Wed Aug 10	CB40	Middlesex	v Yorkshire	Lord's ☂
	Tour Match	Nottinghamshire	v Sri Lanka A	Nottingham
Thu Aug 11–Sun 14	LV=CC D2	Middlesex	v Northamptonshire	Lord's
Fri Aug 12	CB40	Nottinghamshire	v Glamorgan	Nottingham ☂
	Tour Match	England Lions	v Sri Lanka A	Worcester
Sat Aug 13	CB40	Scotland	v Leicestershire	Aberdeen
Sun Aug 14	CB40	Derbyshire	v Yorkshire	Chesterfield
		Durham	v Leicestershire	Chester-le-St
		Glamorgan	v Somerset	Cardiff
		Kent	v Netherlands	Canterbury
		Lancashire	v Essex	Manchester
		Scotland	v Hampshire	Aberdeen
		Sussex	v Worcestershire	Horsham
		Unicorns	v Gloucestershire	Exmouth
	Tour Match	England Lions	v Sri Lanka A	Worcester
Mon Aug 15	CB40	Northamptonshire	v Surrey	Northampton ☂
		Somerset	v Nottinghamshire	Taunton ☂
Tue Aug 16	CB40	Kent	v Middlesex	Canterbury ☂
	Tour Match	England Lions	v Sri Lanka A	Northampton
Wed Aug 17–Sat 20	LV=CC D1	Lancashire	v Worcestershire	Blackpool
		Somerset	v Nottinghamshire	Taunton
		Yorkshire	v Sussex	Scarborough
	LV=CC D2	Derbyshire	v Northamptonshire	Chesterfield
		Essex	v Gloucestershire	Colchester
		Glamorgan	v Leicestershire	Colwyn Bay
		Kent	v Middlesex	Canterbury
Wed Aug 17	CB40	Warwickshire	v Surrey	Birmingham ☂
Thu Aug 18–Mon 22	4th np Test	**ENGLAND**	**v INDIA**	**The Oval**
Thu Aug 18–Sun 21	LV=CC D1	Warwickshire	v Hampshire	Birmingham
Sun Aug 21	CB40	Derbyshire	v Middlesex	Chesterfield
		Essex	v Gloucestershire	Colchester
		Glamorgan	v Lancashire	Colwyn Bay
		Leicestershire	v Surrey	Leicester
		Northamptonshire	v Durham	Northampton
		Somerset	v Unicorns	Taunton
		Worcestershire	v Netherlands	Worcester
		Yorkshire	v Sussex	Scarborough
Mon Aug 22–Thu 25	LV=CC D1	Nottinghamshire	v Durham	Nottingham
Tue Aug 23–Fri 26	LV=CC D1	Hampshire	v Worcestershire	Southampton
		Yorkshire	v Warwickshire	Leeds
	LV=CC D2	Essex	v Derbyshire	Chelmsford
		Leicestershire	v Surrey	Leicester
		Northamptonshire	v Middlesex	Northampton

Tue Aug 23	CB40	Sussex	v Kent	Hove ♀
Wed Aug 24	CB40	Gloucestershire	v Somerset	Bristol ♀
Thu Aug 25	ODI	**IRELAND**	**v ENGLAND**	**Dublin**
	Tour Match	Sussex	v India	Hove
Fri Aug 26	**Tour Match**	Kent	v India	Canterbury ♀
Sat Aug 27	**FP T20 Semi-finals and Final**			Birmingham ♀
Mon Aug 29	CB40	Hampshire	v Scotland	Southampton
		Kent	v Derbyshire	Canterbury
		Middlesex	v Sussex	Lord's
		Nottinghamshire	v Lancashire	Nottingham
		Somerset	v Essex	Taunton
		Surrey	v Durham	The Oval
		Unicorns	v Glamorgan	Wormsley
		Warwickshire	v Northamptonshire	Birmingham
		Yorkshire	v Worcestershire	Leeds
	Tour (T20)	Leicestershire	v India	Leicester
Tue Aug 30–Fri Sep 2	LV=CC D2	Middlesex	v Leicestershire	Lord's
Wed Aug 31	NW T20I	**ENGLAND**	**v INDIA**	**Manchester** ♀
Wed Aug 31–Sat Sep 3	LV=CC D1	Sussex	v Durham	Hove
		Somerset	v Hampshire	Taunton
		Warwickshire	v Yorkshire	Birmingham
		Worcestershire	v Lancashire	Worcester
	LV=CC D2	Gloucestershire	v Glamorgan	Bristol
		Kent	v Essex	Canterbury
		Northamptonshire	v Surrey	Northampton
Sat Sep 3	ODI	**ENGLAND**	**v INDIA**	**Chester-le-St**
Sun Sep 4	**CB40 Semi-Finals**			
Tue Sep 6	ODI	**ENGLAND**	**v INDIA**	**Southampton** ♀
Wed Sep 7–Sat 10	LV=CC D1	Lancashire	v Hampshire	Manchester
		Warwickshire	v Nottinghamshire	Birmingham
		Worcestershire	v Sussex	Worcester
		Yorkshire	v Somerset	Leeds
	LV=CC D2	Derbyshire	v Kent	Derby
		Essex	v Surrey	Chelmsford
		Glamorgan	v Middlesex	Cardiff
		Gloucestershire	v Leicestershire	Bristol
Fri Sep 9	ODI	**ENGLAND**	**v INDIA**	**The Oval** ♀
Sun Sep 11	ODI	**ENGLAND**	**v INDIA**	**Lord's**
Mon Sep 12–Thu 15	LV=CC D1	Durham	v Worcestershire	Chester-le-St
		Hampshire	v Warwickshire	Southampton
		Nottinghamshire	v Sussex	Nottingham
		Somerset	v Lancashire	Taunton
	LV=CC D2	Kent	v Glamorgan	Canterbury
		Leicestershire	v Middlesex	Leicester
		Northamptonshire	v Gloucestershire	Northampton
		Surrey	v Derbyshire	The Oval
Fri Sep 16	ODI	**ENGLAND**	**v INDIA**	**Cardiff** ♀
Sat Sep 17	**CB40 Final**			Lord's

ERRATA

WISDEN, 1973

Page 703   Surrey's John Player League match v Worcestershire was not their first visit to St John's School, Leatherhead; they played Northants there in 1969 (*Wisden 1970* page 694).

WISDEN, 1978

Page 974   Mushtaq Mohammad was out hit wicket, not bowled, in the second innings of the Kingston Test.

WISDEN, 1986

Page 650   Kent's openers put on 188, not 88, against Surrey in their NatWest Bank Trophy match at Canterbury on July 3.

WISDEN, 1988

Page 975   It is believed that the 177 overs bowled with the same ball in New Zealand's second innings v West Indies at Wellington in 1986-87 were exceeded by 185.3 overs in India's second innings against West Indies at Bridgetown in 1961-62 (*Wisden 1963*, page 921).

WISDEN, 1991

Page 276   G. A. Gooch and J. P. Stephenson shared first-wicket partnerships of 135 and 100* for Essex v Nottinghamshire at Southend.

WISDEN, 2003

Page 1540   Kandy v Moratuwa (February 15–17) was played at Moors SC, Braybrooke Place, Colombo (not Reid Avenue).

WISDEN, 2009

Page 527   Bangladesh A's opening match in Dublin was at College Park.
Page 922   The Haileybury bowler's correct name is W. J. D. Hughes-D'Aeth.
Page 1243   Karachi Blues v PIA (December 26–29) was played at National Stadium, Karachi (not Gaddafi Stadium, Lahore).

WISDEN, 2010

Page 101   Under First-Wicket Partnership of 100 in Each Innings, Nondescripts' second-innings opening pair was C. G. Wijesinghe and C. K. B. Kulasekara, while for Eastern Province M. L. Price was joined in the second innings by M. B. A. Smith.

Page 104   Hat-tricks should include Anwar Ali for PIA v National Bank at Faisalabad, Kamran Hussain for Habib Bank v Lahore Shalimar at Lahore, and Tabish Khan for Karachi Whites v ZTBL at Karachi, all in 2009-10. Kamran and Tabish both took four wickets in four balls.

Page 577   The total number of wickets in the 2009 County Championship was 4,022.

Page 1035   J. M. Gregory (Australia) scored 765 runs at 54.64 and took 51 wickets at 24.82 in 12 Tests in the calendar year 1921; the first Test he played started in December 1920 but he played no part until January 1. V. Mankad (India) scored 558 runs at 42.92 and took 53 wickets at 22.07 in ten Tests in 1952, excluding 20 runs and four wickets in the first two days of a Test which began on December 30, 1951. Botham's figures for 1978 should read 587 runs at 41.92 and 63 wickets at 18.41, excluding ten runs and three wickets in a Test which ran into 1979.

Page 1052   In the final innings of the Adelaide Test, Haddin scored 20* and there were 11 extras (B 2), with Barath conceding three runs.

Page 1288   South Africa's extras in the Centurion Test (first innings) should be B 1, l-b 16, w 5.

Page 1298   South Africa's extras in the Johannesburg Test should be B 7, l-b 10, w 5, n-b 1.

CHARITIES IN 2010

ARUNDEL CASTLE CRICKET FOUNDATION: nearly 300,000 youngsters, mainly from the inner cities areas and London's boroughs, and many with special needs, have received instruction and encouragement at Arundel since 1986. In 2010, more than 90 days were devoted to activities and over 5,000 young people benefited. Director of cricket: John Barclay, Arundel Park, Sussex BN18 9LH. Tel: 01903 882602; website: www.arundelcastlecricketfoundation.co.uk

THE BRIAN JOHNSTON MEMORIAL TRUST supports cricket for the blind, and aims to ease the financial worries of talented young cricketers through scholarships. At the Johnners Dinner at Lord's in October 2010, the new BJMT elite spin-bowling programme in support of the ECB was launched; this aims to provide expert coaching to all the first-class county academies and the MCCUs. Trust administrator: Richard Anstey, 178 Manor Drive North, Worcester Park, Surrey KT4 7RU. Website: www.lordstaverners.org

BRITISH ASSOCIATION FOR CRICKETERS WITH DISABILITIES was formed in 1991 to promote cricket to people with disabilities. It administers the national county championship for cricketers with physical and learning disabilities on behalf of the ECB. Hon. secretary: Richard Hill, 25 Nutfield, Welwyn Garden City, Hertfordshire AL7 1UL. Tel: 01707 882236; website: www.bacd.hitssports.com

BUNBURY CRICKET CLUB has raised more than £13m for national charities and local good causes over 24 years, although it is not a registered charity. In 2010, the Bunbury-sponsored ESCA Under-15 festival – which has produced many England players – was held at the University of Chester. The annual Bunbury ball in May saluted Sir Ian Botham's 25 years of walks in aid of Leukaemia Research. Founder: Dr David English CBE, 1 Highwood Cottages, Nan Clark's Lane, London NW7 4HJ. Website: www.bunburycricket.com

CAPITAL KIDS CRICKET, formed in 1990, delivers cricket tuition to state schools throughout the 16 inner London boroughs, assists emerging clubs and organises competitions and festivals in local centres and parks, including its base in Regent's Park. Its British Land Kids Cricket League involves 2,500 primary school children. William Greaves, 13 Canonbury Grove, London N1 2HR. Tel: 020 7226 2705; website: www.capitalkidscricket.co.uk

CRICKET FOR CHANGE uses cricket to change the lives of disadvantaged young people, running its "Street 20" version of the game with the Lord's Taverners across the UK and with *Chance to shine* and the Metropolitan Police in London. Its disability programme "Hit the Top" is partnered with the Taverners and the county boards. Overseas work in 2010 included setting up programmes (many with UNICEF and the ICC) in Afghanistan, Israel and the West Bank, Jamaica, Sri Lanka, India, Bangladesh and New York. Chief executive: Andy Sellins, The Cricket Centre, Plough Lane, Wallington, Surrey SM6 8JQ. Tel: 020 8669 2177; website: www.cricketforchange.org.uk

THE CRICKET FOUNDATION: *Chance to shine*, the foundation's campaign to regenerate competitive cricket in state schools, is the single biggest sport for development programme in the UK. In 2010, the campaign celebrated its fifth year, and one million children across 3,700 schools have participated. The charity has so far raised £20.3m of its £25m private funding target, which the Government has pledged to match. Chief executive: Wasim Khan, Lord's Cricket Ground, London NW8 8QZ. Tel: 020 7432 1259; website: www.chancetoshine.org

THE CRICKET SOCIETY TRUST's principal aim is to support schools and organisations to encourage enjoyment of the game and to develop skills. Particular effort and concentration is given to children with special needs through a programme arranged with Arundel Castle Cricket Foundation. Hon. secretary: Ken Merchant, 16 Louise Road, Rayleigh, Essex SS6 8LW. Tel: 01268 747414; website: www.cricketsocietytrust.org.uk

THE DICKIE BIRD FOUNDATION, set up by the former umpire in 2004, helps financially disadvantaged young people under the age of 18 to participate in the sport of their choice. Grants are made towards the cost of equipment, clothing and travel. Chairman of the trustees: Les Smith, 47 Ripon Road, Earlsheaton, Dewsbury, West Yorkshire WF12 7LG. Tel: 01924 430593 or 07904 440367; website: www.thedickiebirdfoundation.co.uk

ENGLAND AND WALES CRICKET TRUST was established in 2005 to aid community participation in cricket, with a fund from which to make interest-free loans to amateur cricket clubs. In its latest financial year it incurred costs on charitable activities of £12.6m – primarily grants to county cricket boards to support their programmes. Trustee: Brian Havill, Lord's Cricket Ground, London NW8 8QZ. Tel: 020 7432 1201; email: brian.havill@ecb.co.uk

FIELDS IN TRUST is dedicated to protecting and improving outdoor space for sport, play and recreation. The Queen Elizabeth II Fields Challenge, headed by Prince William, aims to permanently protect 2,012 fields to mark the Queen's Diamond Jubilee in 2012, creating a grassroots legacy to benefit communities across the UK. Chief executive: Alison Moore-Gwyn, 15 Crinan Street, London N1 9SQ. Tel: 020 7427 2110; website: www.fieldsintrust.org

THE HORNSBY PROFESSIONAL CRICKETERS' FUND, established in 1928 from a bequest from the estate of J. H. J. Hornsby (Middlesex, MCC and the Gentlemen), supports former professionals and their families, both through regular financial help or one-off grants towards healthcare or similar essential needs. Secretary of trust: The Rev. Prebendary Mike Vockins OBE, Birchwood Lodge, Birchwood, Storridge, Malvern, Worcestershire WR13 5EZ. Tel: 01886 884366.

THE LORD'S TAVERNERS is the official charity of recreational cricket and the UK's leading youth cricket and disability sports charity, whose mission is "to give young people, particularly those with special needs, a sporting chance". In their diamond jubilee year of 2010, the Taverners donated nearly £3m to help young people of all abilities and backgrounds to participate in cricket and other sporting activities. The Lord's Taverners, 10 Buckingham Place, London SW1E 6HX. Tel: 020 7821 2828; website: www.lordstaverners.org

THE OVAL CRICKET RELIEF TRUST assists in areas affected by natural disasters. In 2010, it assisted with educational projects in Barbados, contributed to the Haiti earthquake appeal, and supported Magic Bus, a charity that works with children living in poverty in India. Chairman of trustees: Paul Sheldon, The Oval, Kennington, London SE11 5SS. Tel: 020 7582 6660; website: www.britoval.com/about/csr/charity

PCA BENEVOLENT FUND is part of the commitment of the Professional Cricketers' Association to aid current and former players and their dependants in times of hardship and upheaval, or to help them readjust to the world beyond the game. Assistant CEO: Jason Ratcliffe, 3 Utopia Village, 7 Chalcot Road, Primrose Hill, London NW1 8LH. Tel: 07768 558050; website: www.thepca.co.uk

THE PRIMARY CLUB provides sporting and recreational facilities for the blind and partially sighted. Membership is nominally restricted to those dismissed first ball in any form of cricket; almost 10,000 belong. In total, the club has raised £3m, helped by sales of its tie, popularised by *Test Match Special*. Andrew Strauss is president of the Primary Club Juniors. Hon. Secretary: Chris Larlham, PO Box 12121, Saffron Walden, Essex CB10 2ZF. Tel: 01799 586507; website: www.primaryclub.org

THE PRINCE'S TRUST CRICKET INITIATIVE harnesses the power of the game to support the engagement and positive development of young people aged 14 to 25 who are unemployed or struggling with education. Through partnerships with the county boards and clubs, they gain cricket qualifications, complete work placements and attend coaching sessions, motivational talks, competitions and workshops on healthy lifestyles. Programme executive, sport: Rebecca Pike, The Prince's Trust, 18 Park Square East, London NW1 4LH. Tel: 020 7543 7315; website: www.princes-trust.org.uk/cricket

THE PROFESSIONAL CRICKETERS' ASSOCIATION CHARITY: there are many worthy and needy cases among cricketers (and their dependants) who played in the era before professionalism; working with the PCA, the trustees visit beneficiaries of the charity to do all they can where necessary. Chairman of trustees: David Graveney, PCA, 3 Utopia Village, 7 Chalcot Road, Primrose Hill, London NW1 8LH. Website: www.thepca.co.uk

YOUTH TRUSTS Most of the first-class counties operate youth trusts through which donations, legacies and the proceeds of fundraising are channelled for the development of youth cricket and cricket in the community. Information may be obtained from the county chief executives.

CRICKET TRADE DIRECTORY

BOOKSELLERS

AARDVARK BOOKS, 19 Vanwall Drive, Waddington, Lincoln, Lincolnshire LN5 9LT. Tel: 01522 722671; email: pete@aardvarkcricketbooks.co.uk. Peter Taylor specialises in *Wisdens*, including rare hardbacks and early editions. Catalogues sent on request. *Wisdens* purchased. Cleaning, gilding and restoration undertaken.

ACUMEN BOOKS, Nantwich Road, Audley, Staffordshire ST7 8DL. Tel: 01782 720753; email: wca@acumenbooks.co.uk; website: www.acumenbooks.co.uk. Everything for umpires, scorers, officials, etc. MCC Lawbooks, open-learning manuals, Tom Smith and other textbooks, Duckworth/Lewis, scorebooks, equipment, over & run counters, gauges, heavy and Hi-Vis bails, etc; import/export.

BOUNDARY BOOKS, The Haven, West Street, Childrey OX12 9UL. Tel: 01235 751021; email: boundarybooks@btinternet.com. Rare and second-hand books, autographs and memorabilia bought and sold. Catalogues issued. Limited-editions published. Unusual and scarce items always available.

CHRISTOPHER SAUNDERS, Kingston House, High Street, Newnham-on-Severn, Gloucestershire GL14 1BB. Tel: 01594 516030; fax: 01594 517273; email: chrisbooks@cricket-books.com; website: www.cricket-books.com. Office/bookroom open by appointment. Second-hand/antiquarian cricket books and memorabilia bought and sold. Regular catalogues issued containing selections from over 12,000 items in stock.

GRACE BOOKS AND CARDS (TED KIRWAN), 3 Pine Tree Garden, Oadby, Leicester LE2 5UT. Tel: 0116 271 6363 (weekdays) and 0116 271 4267 (evenings and weekends); email: edward.kirwan@btinternet.com. Second-hand and antiquarian cricket books, *Wisdens*, autographed material and cricket ephemera of all kinds. Now also modern postcards.

IAN DYER CRICKET BOOKS, 29 High Street, Gilling West, Richmond, North Yorkshire DL10 5JG. Tel: 01748 822786; website: www.cricketbooks.co.uk (keyword search & postage calculator); **email: iandyer@cricketbooks.co.uk.** *Wisdens*, annuals (English/overseas), new/used/ antiquarian books, programmes/scorecards, tour guides, benefit brochures, videos/DVDs, memorabilia. Payment by Paypal or CC with SagePay security. Visit by appointment.

JOHN JEFFERS, The Old Mill, Aylesbury Road, Wing, Leighton Buzzard LU7 0PG. Tel: (044) (0)1296 688543 Mobile: 07846 537 692; e-mail: edgwarerover@live.co.uk. *Wisden* specialist. Immediate decision and top settlement for purchase of *Wisden* collections. Why wait for the next auction? Why pay the auctioneer's commission anyway?

J. W. McKENZIE, 12 Stoneleigh Park Road, Ewell, Epsom, Surrey KT19 0QT. Tel: 020 8393 7700; email: mckenziecricket@btconnect.com; website: www.mckenziecricket.co.uk. Specialist since 1971 in antiquarian and second-hand books, particularly *Wisdens*. Cricket memorabilia, including autographs and prints. Regular catalogues issued. Cricket book publisher. Large shop premises open regular business hours, 30 minutes from London.

KEN FAULKNER, 65 Brookside, Wokingham, Berkshire RG41 2ST. Tel: 0118 978 5255. Email: kfaulkner@bowmore.demon.co.uk; website: www.bowmore.demon.co.uk. My stall, with a strong *Wisden* stock, will be operating at the Cheltenham Cricket Festival in July/August 2011. Collections which include pre-1946 *Wisdens* wanted.

MARTIN WOOD CRICKET BOOKS, 1c Wickenden Road, Sevenoaks, Kent TN13 3PJ. Tel: 01732 457205; email: martin@martinwoodcricketbooks.co.uk; website: www.martinwoodcricketbooks.co.uk. Established 1970.

PARKER'S CRICKET BOOKS. Tel: 01689 835426; email: kpark499@aol.com; website: www.parkerscricketbooks.co.uk. *Wisden Cricketers' Almanacks* and *Lillywhite's* purchased.

ROGER HEAVENS, 125 Keddington Road, Louth, Lincolnshire LN11 0BL. Tel: 01507 606102; mobile: 07967 096924; email: roger.heavens@btinternet.com; website: www.booksoncricket.net. Cricket publisher specialising in the works of Arthur Haygarth and early history of cricket. Send for free catalogue. Order direct – all major credit cards accepted.

ROGER PAGE, 10 Ekari Court, Yallambie, Victoria 3085, Australia. Tel: (+61) 3 9435 6332; fax: (+61) 3 9432 2050; email: rpcricketbooks@unite.com.au. Dealer in new and second-hand cricket books. Distributor of overseas cricket annuals and magazines. Agent for Association of Cricket Statisticians and Cricket Memorabilia Society.

ST MARY'S BOOKS & PRINTS, 9 St Mary's Hill, Stamford, Lincolnshire PE9 2DP. Tel: 01780 763033; email: info@stmarysbooks.com; website: www.stmarysbooks.com. Dealers in *Wisdens* 1864–2009, second-hand, rare cricket books and *Vanity Fair* prints. Book-search service offered.

SPORTSPAGES, The Oast House, Park Row, Farnham, Surrey GU9 7JH. Tel: 01252 727222; email: info@sportspages.com; website: www.sportspages.com. Large stock of *Wisdens*, fine cricket books, scorecards, autograph material, tour brochures. Books and memorabilia also purchased, please offer.

STUART TOPPS, 25 Ramsker Drive, Armthorpe, Doncaster DN3 3SE. Tel: 01302 300906. Our 120-page-plus catalogue of cricket books, *Wisdens*, booklets, brochures and county yearbooks is always available.

TIM BEDDOW, 66 Oak Road, Oldbury, West Midlands B68 0BD. Tel: 0121 421 7117; mobile: 07956 456112; email: wisden1864@hotmail.com. Wanted: cash paid for football, cricket, speedway and rugby union memorabilia, badges, books, programmes (amateur and professional), autographed items, match tickets, yearbooks and photographs – anything considered.

WILLIAM H. ROBERTS, The Crease, 113 Hill Grove, Salendine Nook, Huddersfield, West Yorkshire HD3 3TL. Tel/fax: 01484 654463; email: william.roberts2@virgin.net; website: www.williamroberts-cricket.com. Second-hand/antiquarian cricket books, *Wisdens*, autographs and memorabilia bought and sold.

WILLOWS PUBLISHING, 17 The Willows, Stone, Staffordshire ST15 0DE. Tel: 01785 814700; email: jenkins.willows@ntlworld.com. *Wisden* reprints 1880–1938 and 1940–1945. Send SAE for prices.

WISDEN DIRECT, website: www.wisden.com. Various editions of *Wisden Cricketers' Almanack* since 1998 and other Wisden publications, all at discounted prices.

WWW.WISDENS.ORG, Tel: 07793 060706; email: wisdens@cridler.com. The unofficial *Wisden* collectors' website. Valuations, guide, discussion forum, all free to use. We also buy and sell *Wisdens* for our members. Email us for free advice about absolutely anything to do with collecting *Wisdens*.

WWW.WISDENWORLD.COM, Tel: 01480 819272; email: info@wisdenworld.com; website: www.wisdenworld.com. A unique and friendly service; quality *Wisdens* bought and sold at fair prices, along with free advice on the value of your collection. Other cricket memorabilia available.

AUCTIONEERS

ANTHEMION AUCTIONS, 15 Norwich Road, Cardiff CF23 9AB. Tel: 029 2047 2444; email: anthemions@aol.com; website: www.anthemionauctions.com. Sporting memorabilia specialists with an international clientele and extensive dedicated database of buyers.

BONHAMS AUCTIONEERS, New House, 150 Christleton Road, Chester CH3 5TD. Tel: 01244 353117; email: sport@bonhams.com; website: www.bonhams.com. Valuations can be arranged at our offices throughout the UK; please visit our website for further information. *Bonhams, the world's leading auctioneer of sporting memorabilia.*

CHRISTIE'S, 85 Old Brompton Road, London SW7 3LD. Tel: 020 7389 2674; email: rneelands@christies.com. Beginning with the MCC Bicentenary auction in 1987, Christie's have held many important sales, including the Peter MacKinnon collection, the E. D. R. Eagar and Guy Curry libraries, and duplicates from the MCC library in 2010. For free valuations and other enquiries, contact Rupert Neelands.

DOMINIC WINTER BOOK AUCTIONS, Specialist Auctioneers & Valuers, Mallard House, Broadway Lane, South Cerney, Gloucestershire GL7 5UQ. Tel: 01285 860006; website: www.dominicwinter.co.uk. Check our website for forthcoming specialist sales.

GRAHAM BUDD AUCTIONS in association with Sotheby's, PO Box 47519, London N14 6XD. Tel: 020 8366 2525; website: www.grahambuddauctions.co.uk. Specialist auctioneer of sporting memorabilia.

KNIGHTS WISDEN, Norfolk. Tel: 01263 768488; email: tim@knights.co.uk; website: www.knightswisden.co.uk. Established and respected auctioneers; two specialist *Wisden* auctions and three major cricket/sporting memorabilia auctions per year. World-record *Wisden* prices achieved in 2007. *Wisden* auctions: April and September. Entries invited.

MULLOCK'S SPECIALIST AUCTIONEERS & VALUERS, The Old Shippon, Wall under Heywood, Church Stretton, Shropshire SY6 7DS. Tel: 01694 771771; email: info@mullocksauctions.co.uk; website: www.mullocksauctions.co.uk. For worldwide exposure, contact Europe's No. 1 sporting auction specialists. Regular cricket sales are held throughout the year and are fully illustrated on our website.

T. VENNETT-SMITH, 11 Nottingham Road, Gotham, Nottinghamshire NG11 0HE. Tel: 0115 983 0541; email: info@vennett-smith.com; website: www.vennett-smith.com. Auctioneers and valuers. Regular sales of cricket and sports memorabilia. The cricket auction is run by cricketers for cricket-lovers worldwide.

WWW.WISDENAUCTION.COM. Tel: 07793 060706; email: wisdenauction@cridler.com. A specially designed auction website for buying and selling *Wisdens*. List your spares today and bid live for that missing year. No sale, no fee. Many books ending daily. Built by collectors for collectors, with the best descriptions on the internet. See advert on page 143.

CRICKET ART

DD DESIGNS, 62 St Catherine's Grove, Lincoln, Lincolnshire LN5 8NA. Tel: 01522 800298; email: denise@dd-designs.co.uk; website: www.dd-designs.co.uk. Official producers of *Wisden's* "Five Cricketers of the Year" limited edition postcards and prints (many signed by cricketers) and other signed cricket portfolios.

CRICKET DATABASES

CSW DATABASE FOR PCs. Contact Ric Finlay, email: ric@tastats.com.au; website: www.tastats.com.au. Men's and Women's International, IPL, Australian and English domestic. Full scorecards and over 2,000 records. Suitable for professionals and hobbyists alike.

CRICKET EQUIPMENT

CRAZY CATCH, Walltree House Farm, Steane, Brackley, Northamptonshire NN13 5NS. Tel: 01295 816765; fax: 01295 810298; email: flicxuk@flicx.com; websites: www.crazycatch.com/ uk, www.flicx.co.uk. Crazy Catch, distributed in the UK and Europe by Flicx UK Ltd.

CRICKET DIRECT, 5 Metro Centre, Ronsons Way, St Albans Road, Sandridge, St Albans, Hertfordshire AL4 9QT. Tel: 08452 303052; Fax: 01727 736969; email: info@cricketdirect.com; website: www.cricketdirect.com. Cricket Direct is the world's finest online cricket store, offering the very best and latest cricket equipment to cricketers of all levels. Worldwide delivery. Visit our website for the most up-to-date prices.

DUKE SPORTSWEAR, Unit 4, Magdalene Road, Torquay, Devon TQ1 4AF. Tel/fax: 01803 292012. Test-standard sweaters to order in your club colours, using the finest yarns.

EXITO SPORTS COMPANY, Unit C1, Burley Heyes, Arley Road, Appleton Thorn, Warrington, Cheshire WA4 4RS. Tel: 01565 777300; email: info@exitosports.com; website: www.exitosports.com. Manufacturers and suppliers of quality cricket clothing and leisurewear to first-class and minor counties, amateur clubs, schools and colleges.

FORDHAM SPORTS, 81/85 Robin Hood Way, Kingston Vale, London SW15 3PW. Tel: 020 8974 5654; email: fordham@fordhamsports.co.uk; website: fordhamsports.co.uk. Cricket, hockey and rugby equipment specialist with largest range of branded stock in London at discounted prices. Mail order available. Free catalogue.

SOMERSET COUNTY SPORTS, The County Ground, St James Street, Taunton, Somerset TA1 1JT. Tel/fax: 01823 337597; email: sales@somerset-countysports.com; website: www. somerset-countysports.com. Somerset County Sports is the leading cricket specialist in the south-west of England, stocking an even more extensive range for the 2011 season.

STUART & WILLIAMS (BOLA), 6 Brookfield Road, Cotham, Bristol BS6 5PQ. Tel: 0117 924 3569; email: info@bola.co.uk; website: www.bola.co.uk. Manufacturer of bowling machines and ball-throwing machines for all sports. Machines for recreational and commercial application for sale to the UK and overseas.

CRICKET TEAM MANAGEMENT SOFTWARE

WWW.TEAMER.NET, International House, 6th Floor, 223 Regent Street, London W1B 2QD. Tel: 020 3468 7040; email: help@teamer.net; website: www.teamer.net. *Taking the hassle out of team organisation*. Teamer is a FREE to use online team management system which includes FREE text messaging to notify team events to players.

CRICKET TOURS

GULLIVERS SPORTS TRAVEL, Fiddington Manor, Tewkesbury, Gloucestershire GL20 7BJ. Tel: 01684 293175; email: gullivers@gulliverstravel.co.uk; website: www.gulliverstravel.co.uk. The UK's longest established and leading cricket tour operator – supporters' tours and playing tours for schools, clubs and universities. Official travel and tour provider for the International Cricket Council.

INSPIRE TRAVELS, 122 Waterside Drive, Chichester, West Sussex, PO19 8PJ. Tel: 0784 600 8174; email: info@inspirecricket.com; website: www.inspiretravels.co.uk. *Using Cricket to Change Lives*. Specialists in cricket playing tours for schools and clubs to Sri Lanka and South Africa. A family-run company, dedicated to personalised, affordable tours.

ITC SPORTS, Concorde House, Canal Street, Chester CH1 4EJ. Tel: 01244 355390; email: sports@itc-uk.com; website: www.itcsports.co.uk. ITC Sports is the UK's leading provider of luxury overseas sports tours and tailor-made holidays. Celebrity-escorted tours and tailor-made holidays to all England's tours. Packages also available for Horse Racing, Rugby, Formula One, Tennis and Golf.

SPORT ABROAD, TUI Travel Sport, 4th Floor, Tuition House, 27-37 St George's Road, Wimbledon SW19 4EU. Tel: 08456 803 086; email: cricket@sportabroad.co.uk; website: www.sportabroad.co.uk. Established 1984 – one of the UK's leading cricket and sport tour operators.

SPORTING GETAWAYS. Tel: 0208 966 7124; email: sgreservations@sportinggetaways.co.uk; website: www.sportinggetaways.co.uk. Specialist tour operators to the Caribbean, Abu Dhabi, Dubai, Thailand, Sri Lanka, South Africa and Australia. Schools, club sides, benefit tours, testimonials, intensive coaching academy – founders of Sir Garry Sobers Seniors and School Tournament in Barbados.

PITCHES AND GROUND EQUIPMENT

CRICKET CARPETS DIRECT, Standards House, Meridian East, Meridian Business Park, Leicester LE19 1WZ. Tel: 08702 400 700; email: sales@cricketcarpetsdirect.co.uk; website: www.cricketcarpetsdirect.co.uk. Installation and refurbishment of artificial cricket pitches. Save money. Top quality carpets supplied and installed direct from the manufacturer. Over 20 years' experience. Nationwide service.

FLICX UK, Walltree House Farm, Steane, Brackley, Northants NN13 5NS. Tel: 01295 816765; fax: 01295 810298; email: flicxuk@flicx.com; websites: www.flicx.co.uk, www.crazycatch.com/uk. Manufacturers and suppliers of portable cricketing equipment, including Flicx pitches, Bola bowling machines, portable nets and coaching equipment. Brochure and video available. UK distributors of Crazy Catch.

HUCK NETS (UK) LTD, Gore Cross Business Park, Corbin Way, Bradpole, Bridport, Dorset DT6 3UX. Tel: 01308 425100; email: sales@huckcricket.co.uk; websites: www.huckcricket.co.uk. Alongside manufacturing our unique knotless high quality polypropylene cricket netting, we offer the complete portfolio of ground and club equipment necessary for cricket clubs of all levels.

NOTTS SPORT, Innovation House, Magna Park, Lutterworth, LE17 4XH. Tel: 01455 883730; fax: 01455 883755; email: info@nottssport.com; website: www.nottssport.com. With over 25 years' experience, Notts Sport is the world's leading supplier of non-turf cricket pitch systems for coaching, practice and matchplay.

PLUVIUS, King Henry VIII Farm, Myton Road, Warwick CV34 6SB Tel: 01926 311324; email: pluviusltd@aol.com; website: www.pluvius.uk.com. Manufacturers of value-for-money pitch covers and sightscreens, currently used on Test, county, school and club grounds throughout the UK.

POWER PRECISION & FABRICATION, Gunnislake, Cornwall PL18 9AS. Tel: 01822 832608; fax: 01822 834796; email: sales@poweroll.com; website: www.poweroll.com. Poweroll wicket rollers. The largest range of purpose-built ride-on grass-rolling machines available, to suit most budgets.

STADIA SPORTS INTERNATIONAL AT BROXAP, 19/20 Lancaster Way Business Park, Ely, Cambridgeshire CB6 3NW. Tel: 01353 668686; fax: 01353 669444; email: sales@stadia-sports.co.uk; website: www.stadia-sports.co.uk. Stadia Sports supplies sightscreens, cages, netting, scoreboards, stumps, balls, bowling-machines, matting and grounds equipment for indoor and outdoor matchplay and practice. Buy online.

SCOREBOARDS AND SCOREBOOKS

FSL ELECTRONICS LTD. Tel: 0288 676 6131; website: www.electronicscoreboards.com. UK-designed and manufactured. FSL offer complete range of electronic scoreboards in portable and self-install kits. The range of scoreboards includes one suitable for every club and budget.

WISDEN SCOREBOOKS, Specials Ltd, Nyewood House, Main Road, East Boldre, Brockenhurst, Hampshire SO42 7WL. Tel: 01590 612778; email: info@specialsgifts.com; website: www.specialsgifts.com. Official producers of *Wisden* Scorebooks.

SPEAKERS AND SOCIETIES

CRICKET MEMORABILIA SOCIETY. Honorary Secretary: Steve Cashmore, 4 Stoke Park Court, Stoke Road, Bishops Cleeve, Cheltenham, Gloucestershire GL52 8US. Email: cms87@btinternet.com; website: www.cricketmemorabilia.org. For collectors worldwide: magazines, meetings, auctions, speakers, and – most of all – friendship.

LOOK WHO'S TALKING (Ian Holroyd), PO Box 3257, Ufton, Leamington Spa CV33 9YZ. Tel: 01926 614443; email: ian@look-whos-talking.co.uk; website: www.look-whos-talking.co.uk. A company specialising in providing first-class public speakers for cricket and other sporting events. Contact us to discuss the event and type of speaker. All budgets catered for.

THE CRICKET SOCIETY, c/o David Wood, Hon Secretary, PO Box 6024, Leighton Buzzard, LU7 2ZS. Email: davidwood@cricketsociety.com; website: www.cricketsociety.com. A society that promotes a love of cricket in all its spheres for all ages and interests – playing, watching, reading and listening.

CHRONICLE OF 2010

JANUARY

6 Australia overcome 206-run first-innings deficit to beat Pakistan in Second Test at Sydney. **7** England maintain 1–0 lead by drawing the Third Test at Cape Town; last man Graham Onions survives the final over, as he had done in the First Test. **17** South Africa beat England by an innings in final Test at Johannesburg to square the series. **22 Betty Wilson, "the Bradman of Australian women's cricket", dies aged 88. 30** Australia win Under-19 World Cup, defeating Pakistan by 25 runs in the final in New Zealand. Mark Greatbatch appointed New Zealand's head coach.

FEBRUARY

2 Ottis Gibson confirmed as West Indies head coach, replacing John Dyson who was sacked late in 2009. **6** India's West Zone score a world-record 541 for seven in the fourth innings to beat South Zone in the Duleep Trophy final. **9** South Africa beat India by an innings in First Test at Nagpur; Hashim Amla scores 253 not out and Dale Steyn takes ten wickets. **13** Afghanistan win World Twenty20 qualifying competition, beating fellow-qualifiers Ireland in the final. **18** At Kolkata, India beat South Africa by an innings to end series 1–1. **20** Former Surrey and England batsman Alan Butcher appointed coach of Zimbabwe. **23** Australia complete unbeaten home season, beating West Indies 4–0 in one-day series after whitewashing Pakistan. Brett Lee retires from Test cricket. **24 Sachin Tendulkar hits first double-century in men's one-day internationals, v South Africa at Gwalior.**

MARCH

2 Former Australian prime minister John Howard nominated for ICC presidency. **3** Waqar Younis appointed Pakistan coach. **10** Pakistan board ban Mohammad Yousuf and Younis Khan "indefinitely", and Naved-ul-Hasan and Shoaib Malik for a year, after a disastrous tour of Australia (the bans were later lifted). **21** IPL announces two new teams for 2011, based in Kochi and Pune. **24** England complete 2–0 Test series win in Bangladesh. Ron Hamence, one of Don Bradman's 1948 "Invincibles", dies aged 94. **29 English first-class season begins… in Abu Dhabi, where MCC take on county champions Durham under floodlights and with pink balls. 31** Australia win Second Test in New Zealand – Daniel Vettori's 100th – to take series 2–0.

APRIL

4 Former England fast bowler Alec Bedser dies, aged 91. 8 Former Victoria medium-pacer David Saker named as England bowling coach. **9** Police investigating "match irregularities" in county cricket question two Essex players, Danish Kaneria and Mervyn Westfield. **21** Lalit Modi, self-appointed "commissioner" of the IPL, is suspended by the Indian board for "alleged acts of individual misdemeanours". **25** Chennai Super Kings, led by M. S. Dhoni, win the third IPL, defeating Mumbai Indians in the final.

MAY

5 West Indies' Deandra Dottin hits the first century in women's Twenty20 internationals – from 38 balls – against South Africa in the opening match of the women's World Twenty20 in St Kitts. **11** Prosper Utseya resigns captaincy of Zimbabwe, to be replaced by Elton Chigumbura. **14** New Zealand fast bowler Shane Bond announces his retirement. **16 England win the World Twenty20 – their first victory in a global event – beating Australia in the final at Bridgetown; Australia beat New Zealand to take the women's title. 23** Amateur side Unicorns score 327 for four to beat Sussex in a CB40 match at Arundel. **24** Victorious England World Twenty20 team given reception at 10 Downing Street. **25** Three days after rescinding his retirement from Test cricket, Shahid Afridi is named Pakistan Test captain against Australia and England. **31** England defeat Bangladesh in First Test at Lord's. Chris Gayle orders Sulieman Benn off the pitch after he refuses to change his bowling style in a one-day international against South Africa in Dominica.

JUNE

6 England beat Bangladesh at Old Trafford in three days to win two-Test series 2–0. **11** Shaun Udal resigns as Middlesex captain. **12** Frank Duckworth and Tony Lewis, of D/L Method fame, awarded MBEs. **17 Kevin Pietersen announces he will leave Hampshire at the end of the season. 27** England clinch one-day series v Australia by winning third match, by one wicket (Australia win the last two games but lose 2–3). **28** Fit-again Mashrafe bin Mortaza restored as Bangladesh captain for one-day series in England. **29** South Africa win Third Test in Barbados to take series against West Indies 2–0. **30** John Howard's bid to become ICC's president-elect fails after opposition by several national boards.

JULY

1 Bangladesh announced as host of World Twenty20 in 2014. **2** MCC's World Cricket Committee call for day/night Tests. Mark Pettini resigns as Essex captain. **6** Muttiah Muralitharan says the forthcoming First Test against India at Galle will be his last. **10** Bangladesh beat England for the first time, by five runs in a one-day international at Bristol. **16** Australia beat Pakistan in the first "neutral" Test staged at Lord's since 1912: Shahid Afridi resigns as Pakistan's Test captain after one match in charge. The ICC announce a profit of $US84.7m in 2009 (after a $3m deficit in 2008). **21** Pakistan, now led by Salman Butt, bowl Australia out for 88 on first day of Second Test at Headingley, and go on to square the short series. **22 Muttiah Muralitharan seals victory over India at Galle with his 800th Test wicket, and retires.** Robert Croft becomes the first player to take 1,000 wickets as well as score 10,000 runs for Glamorgan. **29** Suresh Raina, making his Test debut after 98 one-day internationals for

India, scores a century in drawn Second Test against Sri Lanka. Azeem Rafiq suspended by Yorkshire after foul-mouthed Twitter tirade on being dropped from England's Under-19 side.

AUGUST

1 England win First Test at Trent Bridge by 354 runs, bowling Pakistan out for 80 in their second innings. Eric Tindill, the longest-lived Test cricketer of all, dies in New Zealand aged 99. **2** New Zealander Alan Isaac is nominated in place of John Howard as ICC vice-president. **7** V. V. S. Laxman's century helps India win the Third Test and square their series in Sri Lanka. **14** Hampshire win Friends Provident T20 final, beating Somerset by virtue of losing fewer wickets in a tied match. **16** Sri Lankan off-spinner Suraj Randiv bowls a deliberate no-ball to end a one-day international against India with Virender Sehwag stranded on 99 not out – and is suspended from the next match. **23** Greg Chappell appointed Australia's first full-time selector. Matthew Hoggard, Leicestershire's captain, calls for the resignation of county chairman Neil Davidson, saying he interfered in cricket matters. **28 The *News of the World* alleges three Pakistan players – captain Salman Butt and bowlers Mohammad Aamer and Mohammad Asif – agreed to bowl deliberate no-balls at predetermined moments during ongoing Lord's Test. 29** England complete victory at Lord's to take series against Pakistan 3–1. **31** Kevin Pietersen dropped from England's one-day side; he joins Surrey in an attempt to recapture form before the Ashes tour. Derbyshire bowled out for 44 by Gloucestershire in the Championship at Bristol – but go on to win.

SEPTEMBER

3 The ICC suspend Salman Butt, Mohammad Aamer and Mohammad Asif from international cricket pending an inquiry. **8** Sussex clinch promotion in County Championship. **14** An ICC committee suggest a format for a Test championship, slimmed-down World Cup and enlarged World Twenty20 competitions. **16 Unable to overcome injury problems, Andrew Flintoff announces his retirement from all cricket.** After rain-affected match, Nottinghamshire clinch the County Championship on final day of the competition. Essex fast bowler Mervyn Westfield charged with fraud over claims he bowled wides at pre-arranged times in county match in 2009. **18** Warwickshire win the CB40 final at Lord's; Somerset are runners-up in all three county tournaments. **19** PCB chairman Ijaz Butt accuses England players of taking money to lose the third one-day international of their series against Pakistan; after a retraction the players agree to complete the series, which England eventually win 3–2. **20** Ryan Sidebottom announces his retirement from international cricket. **26** Chennai Super Kings win Champions League Twenty20, beating South Africa's Warriors in the Johannesburg final. **29** Chris Gayle follows Dwayne Bravo and Kieron Pollard in turning down central contract from the West Indian board.

OCTOBER

5 India beat Australia by one wicket in First Test at Mohali. **8** Misbah-ul-Haq named Pakistan Test captain. **10** Kings XI Punjab and Rajasthan Royals (Shane Warne's team) are expelled from the IPL for administrative irregularities: court proceedings ensue. **13** Boosted by Sachin Tendulkar's 214, India beat Australia at Bangalore to take short series 2–0. **The ICC board approves a four-year programme for Test cricket, leading to a Championship play-off final in April 2014.** **17** Bangladesh complete 4–0 victory over New Zealand in one-day series (one match was abandoned). Darren Sammy named West Indies captain in place of Chris Gayle.

NOVEMBER

1 Rajasthan bowl out Hyderabad for 21, the lowest total in Ranji Trophy history. **2** Makhaya Ntini announces his retirement from international cricket, after taking 390 Test wickets. **3** A ninth-wicket stand of 132 spirits Sri Lanka to an improbable victory over Australia at the MCG in the first match of a one-day series they ultimately win 2–1. **7** Kane Williamson scores 131 on Test debut for New Zealand v India at Ahmedabad; the first two Tests are drawn before India take the series with an innings victory in the last. **8 Pakistan wicketkeeper Zulqarnain Haider flees to London, claiming he received threats from match-fixers after hitting the winning run in a one-day international against South Africa in Dubai three days previously.** **9** Former England batsman Ed Joyce cleared to play for his native Ireland in 2011 World Cup. **10** Owais Shah, released by Middlesex, signs for Essex. **16** Glamorgan name South African Test batsman Alviro Petersen as captain for 2011. Chris Gayle scores 333 for West Indies in drawn First Test against Sri Lanka at Galle (a rain-affected series is eventually drawn 0–0). **17** England captain Charlotte Edwards plays a record 142nd one-day international. **22** Jim Troughton appointed Warwickshire captain after resignation of Ian Westwood. **25** Peter Siddle takes a hat-trick on the first day of the Ashes, in Brisbane. **29** England save First Test, scoring 517 for one in their second innings, with Alastair Cook making 235 not out.

DECEMBER

7 England, with Kevin Pietersen scoring 227, win Second Test at Adelaide by an innings. **19** Australia draw level by winning the Third Test at Perth by 267 runs. **20** South Africa beat India in First Test at Centurion, despite Sachin Tendulkar's 50th Test century. **21** West Indies off-spinner Shane Shillingford is banned from bowling in international cricket after tests show anomalies in his action. **29 England retain the Ashes after winning the Fourth Test at Melbourne by an innings.** India level their series in South Africa with 87-run victory in Second Test at Durban (the series was drawn early in 2011).

The following items were also reported in the media during 2010:

COURIER-MAIL, BRISBANE   January 1

Holly Ferling, 13, an emergency selection for the Kingaroy Services senior men's team playing South Burnett Warriors, took a hat-trick with her first three balls, and a fourth wicket with her fifth ball. Warriors captain Paul Clegg described her bowling as "brilliant".

DAILY EXPRESS   January 5

Geoffrey Boycott has written to the struggling football star Michael Owen advising him to try the ancient Chinese belief in feng shui to restore his ambitions for playing in the 2010 World Cup. Boycott credited feng shui with helping his recovery from throat cancer. "I slept in different rooms, facing different ways. They believe that as you sleep you heal. People who don't know anything about it say it is rubbish but it worked for me – I'm alive," said Boycott. Owen had not replied. [He was not selected by England either.]

SYDNEY MORNING HERALD   January 7

The fast food chain KFC (formerly Kentucky Fried Chicken), a major sponsor of Australian cricket, pulled an advert being shown during broadcasts of Tests after accusations of racism appeared in the US media. The ad depicted a white Australian fan offering fried chicken to ingratiate himself with West Indian supporters around him. Website complainants said it perpetuated racist stereotypes.

HALESOWEN NEWS   January 30

The grave of Ted Arnold, a Worcestershire and England stalwart before the First World War, is to be restored after enthusiasts noticed it had fallen into disrepair. They tracked down a grandson who said he was "somewhat embarrassed" to be told that the headstone had been knocked down. Arnold was the first player to do the double for the county and played in ten Tests.

HERALD SUN, MELBOURNE January 30
Mark O'Brien of Broadmeadows Third XI had figures of 13–11–3–8, bowling Sunshine out for 71 in a Victorian sub-district match. O'Brien then hit 112 not out on the way to an innings victory.

SUNDAY TELEGRAPH, SYDNEY January 31
After 43 years and an estimated 785,300 cigarettes, former Australian batting hero Doug Walters, 64, says he has given up smoking after undergoing laser treatment in a Sydney clinic. Walters, a former 70–80-a-day man, said he would continue to drink beer and bet.

SUN-HERALD, SYDNEY January 31
The Australian Cricketers' Association says it has helped several leading players remove fake profiles from social networking sites. Ricky Ponting's manager, James Henderson, said he had closed down "three or four" bogus pages. Ponting's "I Laugh Hysterically Whenever Shane Watson Gets Dismissed in the 90s" page was among the fakes.

ASSOCIATED PRESS February 10
Hindu nationalists rampaged through Mumbai, tearing up film posters and stoning a cinema, to protest against remarks by Bollywood star Shahrukh Khan, who had expressed regret that no Pakistanis were playing in the 2010 Indian Premier League.

ACCRINGTON OBSERVER   February 12

Stanley Johnson, a cricket fan who watched more than 200 overseas Tests, is to have his ashes scattered round his 12 favourite grounds, from Accrington to Sydney. Johnson died in New Zealand, aged 72, during a Test against Pakistan. An Oxford-educated accountant who spoke eight languages, he had retired aged 44 and devoted himself to watching cricket. In his will he told his friends to drink beer at each ground wearing a special T-shirt with the words "The Stan Johnson Ashes Tour".

THE SPIN   February 16

In New Zealand, Central Districts left-arm seamer Ewen Thompson was given emergency surgery after he complained of feeling ill during the team's one-day semi-final against Canterbury. An undigested chunk of doner kebab meat was removed from his oesophagus.

SUNDAY ISLAND, COLOMBO   February 21

The second day of a Sri Lankan school match between St Sylvester's College and Kalutara Vidyalaya in Kandy had to be abandoned after an air force helicopter carrying a politician landed on the ground before the start and remained there all day. Players waited in vain for the return of Faizer Mustapha, former minister for tourism promotion.

TIMES & STAR, WORKINGTON   February 25

Only one item remained untouched in Workington CC's pavilion, devastated when the town was flooded last November – a bottle of whisky donated by the town's MP, Tony Cunningham.

GEELONG ADVERTISER   March 16/19

Two cricketers from the Thomson club were banned for sledging by the Geelong Cricket Association in Victoria, but were cleared of racial abuse after a nine-hour hearing. This followed a bust-up at a match between Thomson and the largely Indian club Waurn Ponds.

DAILY TELEGRAPH   March 21

BBC broadcaster John Simpson has unearthed claims that Hitler wanted to use cricket to prepare German soldiers for war. In his new book, *Unreliable Sources*, Simpson cites a 1930 article in the *Daily Mirror* claiming that Hitler was taught the game by British PoWs during the First World War but declared it "insufficiently violent" for his purposes. In particular, he wanted to abolish pads, which he considered "unmanly and unGerman".

March 21

ANKA   April 2010

All 15 players (plus the manager) in the Twirupa Brai High School Under-16 squad at the Polly Umrigar national schools competition had the same surname: Jamatia. They all belong to the same tribe in Tripura. The Tripura state senior women's team also fielded a team of Jamatias in a tournament.

ANA DERANA   April 9

Sanath Jayasuriya has been elected to the Sri Lankan parliament after topping the poll in the Matara district on behalf of the ruling UPFA party.

THE ARGUS, BRIGHTON   April 13

Residents living near the County Ground at Hove called police after hearing gunshots after midnight. Sussex CCC later admitted that they had brought in a pest control company to shoot a fox. Chief executive Dave Brooks said it had been causing problems by "scratching around on covers and acting oddly". He insisted: "We really didn't want to do it, but it was a last resort."

ALL INDIAN/PAKISTANI PAPERS   April

Two of the subcontinent's most controversial sporting personalities, Pakistani cricketer Shoaib Malik and Indian tennis player Sania Mirza, became even more controversial when they were married in Hyderabad, India, amid general frenzy. Some commentators expressed hope that their romance would help bring the two countries closer together; extreme political groups condemned the match. Both bride and groom are Muslim, but Mirza had been much criticised for her short tennis skirts; Shoaib had been involved in a complex dispute over an alleged previous marriage, and had just been banned from cricket for a year following Pakistan's disastrous tour of Australia. They appeared to be very happy.

BBC.CO.UK April 23

Renovations at a cricket pavilion in Musselburgh, Scotland had to be postponed after the discovery of Roman altar stones. The pavilion, in Lewisvale Park, is on the site of an old fort.

THE CITIZEN, GLOUCESTER April 24

Guy Berryman from the rock group Coldplay has offered to sponsor Gloucestershire village club Slaughters United. Lead singer Chris Martin used to play for nearby Great Rissington.

ASIAN TRIBUNE May 2

A new variety of mango, developed by a horticulturist in Uttar Pradesh, has been named "Sachin" in honour of Sachin Tendulkar. However, the grower claimed he would not be selling the fruit. "Our Sachin is a world hero and he is priceless," said Hajj Kalimullah. "My attempt will be to send all the mangoes on this tree to Sachin so he can enjoy them with his friends."

JERSEY EVENING POST May 5

James Vallois, 17, of Aztec Springfield took six wickets, all bowled, in an eight-ball over in an Evening League match against Optimus Colts (WW.W.WWW). Colts went from 30 for two to 30 for eight before recovering to 64 all out; Aztec won by ten wickets.

YORKSHIRE EVENING POST May 5

Schoolboy Oliver Hardaker, 18, scored 329 not out from 144 balls in a 40-over fixture for Sunday league team Horsforth against Upper Wharfedale. "It was the best day of my life," said Hardaker after hitting 27 sixes and 28 fours.

CHARLIERANDALL.ORG May 7

Umpire John Whittaker was recovering in hospital and "significantly better", after suffering a fractured skull during a league match in Yorkshire. Whittaker was standing at square leg in the Illingworth v Harden match in the Airedale and Wharfedale League when he was hit by a throw from the boundary. The incident came less than a year after umpire Alcwyn Jenkins was killed by a throw in Swansea.

LANCASHIRE TELEGRAPH May 19

Jason Rawson, 39, who plays for Salesbury, claimed a record for the longest run-up in history after running a pre-season marathon concluding with a formal 1.6-mile run-in to bowl to a batsman waiting in position on the club ground. Ian Riley scrambled a leg-bye. The stunt raised £3,250 for club funds.

May 19

WEST SUSSEX COUNTY TIMES   May 20
Marc Livesley hit nine successive sixes for Kings Arms, Billingshurst, against Cherry Tree in a Gullick Cup match, and reached a century off 32 balls.

HERALD EXPRESS, TORQUAY   May 25
Matt Quartley of Ipplepen scored 102 not out off 28 balls against Whitchurch in the Devon League D Division. He hit 13 sixes and four fours.

DAILY MAIL   May 26
Britain's new prime minister David Cameron talked enthusiastically about his love of cricket at a reception for the victorious England squad from the Twenty20 World Cup. However, his credibility was somewhat dented when he called captain Paul Collingwood "Colin" and gave the impression that he thought the final had been at Kennington Oval rather than Kensington Oval.

MIRROR.CO.UK/CHARLIERANDALL.ORG May 26/29

Three police cars arrived at the third XI match in Shropshire between Oswestry and Whitchurch after a player acting as umpire allegedly head-butted an opposing fielder. An argument had broken out when a catch claimed by Whitchurch was ruled as a bump ball; Oswestry said the umpire was acting in self-defence. Whitchurch refused to continue the match. The incident occurred with the score on 128 for nought with the reprieved batsman, New Zealander Rhys McCarthy, on 84.

DAILY TELEGRAPH June 11

Probably the only medal awarded for bravery on the cricket field was sold at auction for £21,600 yesterday. The George Cross was awarded to Major Douglas Brett of the Indian Army when Hindu protesters attacked a match in Chittagong in 1934. Major Brett saved spectators and fellow players from a rebel brandishing a revolver. He died in 1963.

DAILY MAIL June 18

England goalkeeper Robert Green, blamed for the United States' equaliser in his team's opening 2010 World Cup match, said his ambition was to become a cricket correspondent when he retired from football.

THE ISLAND June 21

A woman employed by Sri Lanka Cricket was slightly hurt when the car in which she was travelling was attacked by an elephant near Dambulla. She and a colleague had been attending an Asian Cricket Council function.

LIVERPOOL ECHO June 21

Members of Sefton Park CC played a 20-over match starting at 4.43 a.m. (sunrise on the longest day of the year) and finishing in time for the players to go to work. The Long Shadows beat the Early Risers by nine runs, but Chris Brereton failed in his bid to score a fifty before breakfast. The club hope to make the Solstice Cup an annual event.

THE GUARDIAN   June 21

Oxfam stand to benefit by £62,750 if Ramnaresh Sarwan passes 9,000 Test runs by the end of 2019. Nicholas Newlife from Oxfordshire, who died in 2009, left his entire estate to Oxfam, including a series of sports betting slips. One was a bespoke £250 bet at 66-1 on Sarwan. [Sarwan, 30, ended 2010 with 5,759 Test runs.] Another bet will net more than £100,000 if Roger Federer wins a seventh Wimbledon men's singles title.

AFP   June 29

Oxfam also benefited when the first four *Wisdens*, the 1864 to 1867 editions, were sold by auctioneers Bonhams for £8,520 after they were dropped off at the charity's shop in Hertford. Manager Pauline Wilby spotted the books in a pile of donations and had them rebound.

SUNDAY INDEPENDENT, PLYMOUTH   July 4

Andrew Barrett of Wadebridge hit six sixes in the final over against Werrington in Division Three East of the Cornwall League.

DERBY TELEGRAPH   July 13

Derby Congs scored 37 off the last over of their Butterley Cup semi-final against Swarkestone Second XI. Amar Nawaz hit four sixes and two fours; there was also a wide that reached the boundary.

GUARDIAN.CO.UK   July 19

A de luxe edition of Sachin Tendulkar's autobiography is to be published in 2011, in which the signature page will be tinted with a sample of the author's blood. The 852-page "blood edition" of the *Official Sachin Tendulkar Opus* will weigh 37kg and cost about £50,000. Only ten copies are being printed and all have been pre-ordered. Publisher Karl Fowler admitted: "It's not to everyone's taste and some may think it's a bit weird. But the key thing here is that Sachin Tendulkar to millions of people is a religious icon. And we thought how, in a publishing form, can you get as close to your god as possible?" Tendulkar later denied the blood-letting.

CRICINFO   July 19

Former Australian Test batsman Dean Jones has been stripped of his 2007
Father of the Year award by the Father's Day Council of Victoria after he
admitted fathering a son with an air hostess. Jones had won the award for his
work with the Bone Marrow Council and for being a good father. "From now
on, 2007 will simply show as blank – that's our attitude," council president
Don Parsons said. "To take off and have a love child, and that he hasn't even
seen the child… We are somewhat rocked by it. What sort of fathering is
that?"

ESSEX CHRONICLE   July 22

Essex players Billy Godleman and Tom Westley have been fined by the club
for damaging the dressing-room during a Second Eleven match against Sussex
at Coggeshall. Both were reacting furiously to umpiring decisions: Godleman
wrecked a vacuum cleaner with a bat; Westley kicked in two doors. Coggeshall
Town chairman Roger Stubbings said the incident soured the club's festival.
"It seems as though a football attitude is starting to infiltrate cricket," he said.

BUCKINGHAMSHIRE ADVERTISER   July 22

The Mid-Bucks League match between Knotty Green and Ibstone was
abandoned after a player was allegedly head-butted and hit.

DAILY MIRROR, COLOMBO   July 22

Eheliyaoda Central Under-15 scored 500 for eight in a 50-over match for a
313-run win against Seevali MMV Ratnapura. Avishka Umayanga scored 188.

THE AGE   July 26

The ashes of Pooran Singh, a hawker who plied his trade in western Victoria
more than 60 years ago, have been handed over to former Indian captain Kapil
Dev in a ceremony at Warnambool. Pooran, a much-loved figure in the area,

wanted his ashes scattered on the Ganges but he died in 1947, when India was in the throes of partition, and no one came to collect his remains. Kapil heard the story from a journalist and agreed to fly to Australia specially to collect the urn from the local undertaking firm, which had looked after it since Pooran's death.

WEST BRITON — July 29

Chris Pearn, 38, scored the first double-century in Redruth CC's 180-year history, playing for the Fourth XI against Constantine Second XI in Division Seven West of the Cornwall League. His 201 came in 25 overs and included 20 sixes, 14 fours and 13 lost balls – fortunately a team-mate had brought a bag of spares. Pearn, who had been out of the game for 13 years because of "children and football", had made 190 in his previous innings.

DAILY TELEGRAPH — July 30

The Lord Chancellor, Kenneth Clarke, admitted losing the key to the red box containing his official papers while watching the Trent Bridge Test against Pakistan. Interviewed on *Test Match Special*, he denied that he had lost it deliberately so he could watch the game without having to work. "Honestly, if they send the key, I will do the papers tonight," he said. Officials denied suggestions that there had been a breach of security.

JOURNAL OF QUANTITATIVE ANALYSIS IN SPORTS — August

Researchers Vani Borooah and John Mangan have invented a new mathematical formula to replace batting averages, which takes account of the value of a player's runs. This uses the Gini coefficient to identify consistency and value to the team of a player's numbers. Bradman remains No. 1.

BBC.CO.UK — August 2

Retired teachers Carole and Mike Russell, both in their seventies, were denied admission to the Lancashire–Glamorgan CB40 match in Colwyn Bay because they were carrying metal spoons to eat strawberries. The steward also objected to their jars containing tea and coffee. The club blamed "overenthusiastic" stewarding, but said their ban on metal cutlery would continue. "What do you think two pensioners are going to do with a couple of dessert spoons?" asked Carole.

BBC.CO.UK — August 2

After four years, cricket returned to Skate Bank, the sandspit in the Moray Firth which appears only every few years during exceptionally low tides. The previous match in 2006 led to a helicopter and lifeboat being scrambled after a walker thought the players were drowning (see pages 65–7 of *Wisden 2007*). This time the players, from Chanonry Sailing Club, warned the coastguard in advance. Crew from eight boats stayed for about half an hour before the waters closed in and also took part in "extreme ironing" which involves ironing clothes in improbable places.

NZPA   August 12

The urn containing the ashes of New Zealand Test batsman Bert Sutcliffe has been lost under the turf at Carisbrook in Dunedin. The old stadium, the traditional home of Otago cricket and rugby, is being replaced, and cricket has already moved to the University Oval, where officials wanted to rebury the urn. But, despite the use of sonar and metal detectors, it has proved impossible to locate. Bert's son Gary was relaxed about the situation: "Dad's ashes are proving as elusive as bowlers found taking his wicket," he said.

BURY FREE PRESS   August 13

Tom Huggins of Bury St Edmunds took five wickets in five balls in the final over of the East Anglian Premier League Twenty20 competition. "I had no idea until I walked off," said Huggins. "We were more concerned with winning the game." Huggins played 11 first-class matches for Northamptonshire – but never bowled.

EVENING STANDARD   August 24

Former England batsman turned musician Mark Butcher, 38, has released his first album, "Songs from the Sun House".

BBC.CO.UK   August 31

Blunham CC, Bedfordshire, have reclaimed the currently much sought-after record for the world's longest cricket match. Blunham's first and second teams played through 105 consecutive hours, many of them windy and rainy, to recapture the record from Cornwall CC in New Zealand. Blunham set a mark of 59 hours in 2008, which was then beaten twice. The latest marathon raised £17,000 for the club and charities.

TIMES OF INDIA   September 4

Sachin Tendulkar was made an honorary Group Captain in the Indian Air Force, complete with uniform and epaulettes, at a ceremony in New Delhi.

THE COURIER, DUNDEE   September 6

Kirriemuir, birthplace of J. M. Barrie, helped celebrate the 150th anniversary of the town's most famous son by re-enacting a match played when Barrie opened the sports pavilion in 1930. Among those present to watch Kirriemuir play the Wayward Gentlemen was Leslie Kettles, 85, who watched his father open the batting in the original 1930 match. "I could hardly see Barrie for dignitaries," he recalled.

NEWS & STAR, CARLISLE   September 16

Tony Pietersen, brother of the more famous Kevin, is the new minister of Emmanuel Church, Workington.

September 16

METRO   September 20
England fast bowler Jimmy Anderson has posed naked (though not full-
frontally) for gay magazine *Attitude*. Anderson, who is married, said he did not
believe there was homophobia in cricket. Asked how he would respond if a
cricketer came out, he said: "I'd throw them a special gay cricket tea."

METRO   September 28
Ethan Peel, 15, from Oxfordshire has qualified as an umpire after passing a
BTEC intermediate certificate.

THE SPIN   September 28
Lancashire wicketkeeper Gareth Cross, expected to become the county's first-
choice keeper in 2011, was awarded a cut-glass trophy for the champagne
moment of the season at the club awards night. He promptly dropped and
smashed it.

TIMES OF INDIA   October 2
Yet another epic scoring record from an Indian teenager came when Ali Zorain
Khan, 15, scored 461 not out for the Nagpur Cricket Academy against
Reshimbag CC, 22 more than Sarfaraz Khan's score in Mumbai in 2009. "I
could have scored 500, but we needed enough time to bowl them out twice,"
he said. The academy declared on 1,025 for five.

AFTERNOON DESPATCH & COURIER, MUMBAI/PTI   October 7/14
Researchers have concluded that an Indian defeat in a one-day international
seriously affects the Indian stock market. Russell Smyth, head of the economics
department at Monash University in Australia, said a win had no noticeable
effect but "a loss generates a significant downward movement". However,
India's Test win in Bangalore over Australia on October 13 was greeted by a
484-point surge in the exchange's main index.

MACCLESFIELD EXPRESS   November 9

Macclesfield CC's bonfire night display raised £10,000 for club funds. After it finished, two cars were driven on to the square to perform "donuts" and did £3,000 worth of damage. Later that night intruders smashed up the sightscreen and threw it on the bonfire (cost: another £2,000). "It's absolutely gutting," said committee member Andrew Towle.

THE NATION, COLOMBO   November 14

An Under-13 match at Bandarawela produced one of the most one-sided cricket matches in history. Bandarawela Central scored 553 for three in 46 overs, with 222 from Damitha Prabatha; their opponents, Pussellakanda Vidyalaya, were then bowled out for three. Following on, they improved, reaching 31 to lose by an innings and 519.

HERALD SUN, MELBOURNE   November 19

Wearing a pink rose named in honour of his late wife Jane, Glenn McGrath yesterday married Sara Leonardi in a private ceremony at their home in Sydney. Only family members were invited, and the terrace of the house was covered by thick plastic to maintain privacy. The former Test bowler, 40, now runs the McGrath Foundation, which aims to provide specialist nurses for all breast cancer patients in Australia. Jane McGrath died of breast cancer in 2008.

SYDNEY MORNING HERALD   December 15

Aboriginal cricket, which reached its apogee when a team of indigenous Australians toured England in 1868, is to be revived at the Sydney Cricket Ground next month when a team of rugby league players will take on a side drawn from Cricket Australia's youth indigenous squad in a Twenty20 match. They will compete for the Jack Marsh Cup, named after the Aboriginal fast bowler who played for New South Wales early in the 20th century before being driven out of the game because of controversy over his arm action and/ or racism.

INDEX OF UNUSUAL OCCURRENCES

INDEX OF ADVERTISEMENTS

THE WISDEN 2010 QUIZ

The *Wisden 2010* quiz appeared on page 1727. The winner, Andrew Brown of Banchory, won a selection of reference books, plus a limited-edition leatherbound copy of *The Wisden Anthology 1978–2006.*

The five runners-up were Beryl Pickering of Otley, Philip Greenwood of Banstead, Tim Walker of West Bridgford, John Whelan of Crowborough and Sharon Buchalter of Altrincham.

The answers were: 1. Umar Akmal (*page 1182*). 2. Croatia (*page 1483*). 3. Gubby Allen (*page 53*). 4. Rudi Koertzen's hat (*page 549*). 5. An Oxfam shop in Hertford (*page 1633*). 6. Romel Currency (*page 407*) or Kenroy Peters (*page 416*) (both born in Mesopotamia, St Vincent). 7. Lord Moore (*page 1676*). 8. Kirkham GS (*page 956*). 9. Geoff Holmes (*page 1667*). 10. Prior Park College (*page 941*). 11. David Willey (*page 691*). 12. Nabil Samad (*page 1100*).

PART TITLES

Advertisement